England

written and researched by

**Robert Andrews, Jules Brown,
Phil Lee and Rob Humphreys**

www.roughguides.com

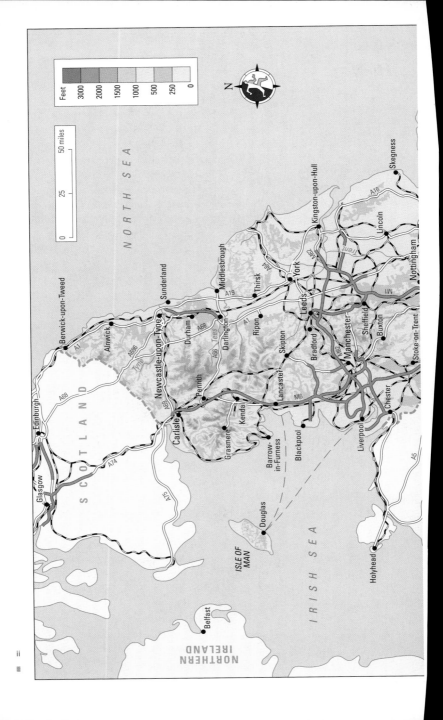

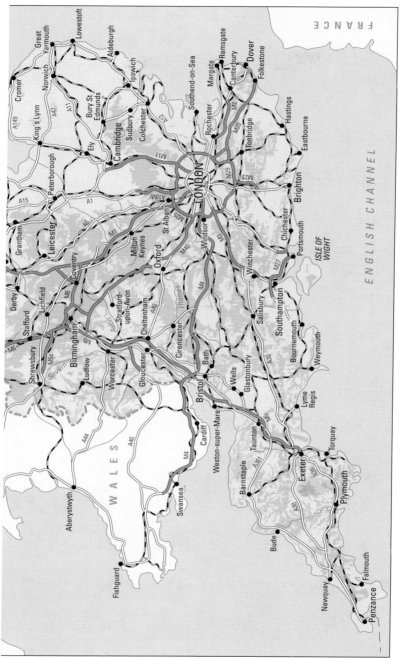

WALES

ENGLISH CHANNEL

FRANCE

ISLE OF WIGHT

▲ The Isles of Scilly

Introduction to
England

Like an ageing cabaret star shuffling onto the stage, England really needs no introduction. When even the world's most remote communities are on first-name terms with its footballers, princes, pop stars and prime ministers, it's clear that everyone knows something about this crowded island nation, perched on the western fringe of Europe. Visitors can pick their favourite slice of "Englishness" and indulge themselves in a country with a notorious taste for nostalgia. The tales of King Arthur; the works of Shakespeare; the exploits of Drake; the intellect of Johnson; the invention of Brunel; the leadership of Churchill; the cult of Diana – all are endlessly recycled in England, providing a cultural backdrop to an unparalleled range of historic buildings, sites and monuments.

Of course, this isn't the whole story of England, or anything like it. For every tourist who wants to stand outside the gates of Buckingham Palace or visit Stratford-upon-Avon, there's another who makes a beeline for the latest Tracey Emin show or the contemporary cityscape of downtown Manchester. The difficulty is in saying which is the truer image of a country which flaunts proudly its many contradictions. Contemporary England is at the same time a deeply conservative place with a richly multi-ethnic culture. Famously, fish and chips has given way to chicken tikka masala as the country's favourite dish, and while the nation tends to distrust all things European, the English also increasingly embrace a continental lifestyle. Enjoy a fried English breakfast or a Devonshire cream tea by all means, but notice the locals at the next-door café-bar tucking into a croissant and a cappuccino.

v

Fact file

• As part of the United Kingdom of Great Britain and Northern Ireland, England is a parliamentary democracy, with Queen Elizabeth II as its head of state. Its traditional industries – fishing, farming, mining, engineering, shipbuilding – are all in decline, some terminal, and major contemporary income sources are banking and finance, communications technology, the production of steel, transport equipment, oil and gas, and tourism.

• Bordered by Scotland to the north and Wales to the west, England is the largest country in Great Britain, occupying an area of 50,085 sq miles (129,720 sq km). There's a diverse terrain, from plains to peaks, cliffs to beaches, though its superlatives are all modest on a world scale – the largest lake, Windermere, is 10 milies (16km) long, the highest mountain, Scafell, 3205ft (just 978m) above sea level.

• A population of approximately 50 million is dense for a country of its size, but settlement is concentrated in the southeast conurbations around the capital, London, and in the large industrial cities of the Midlands and the North.

• This is one of the world's most multi-ethnic countries, made up largely of people of Anglo-Saxon, Scots, Welsh and Irish descent, but with sizeable communities from the Caribbean, Africa, Bangladesh, Pakistan, India and Eastern Europe.

• The famous face of England has changed, not always for the best – red telephone boxes are hard to find and the police increasingly carry guns, but it's easier to get a drink after 11pm and shops are open on Sundays.

Ask an English person to define their country in terms of what's worth seeing and you're most likely to have your attention drawn to the country's golden rural past. The classic images are found in every brochure – the village green, the duckpond, the country lane and the farmyard. And it's true that it's impossible to overstate the bucolic attractions of various English regions, from Cornwall to the Lake District, or the delights they provide – from walkers' trails and prehistoric stone circles to traditional pubs and obscure festivals. But despite celebrating their rural heritage, the modern-day English have an ambivalent attitude towards "the country". Farming today forms only a tiny proportion of the national income and

Contemporary England is at the same time a deeply conservative place with a richly multi-ethnic culture

there's a real dislocation between the urban population and the small rural communities badly hit by the current crisis in English farming.

So perhaps the heart of England is found in its towns and cities instead? The shift towards urban living and working has not been reversed since the Industrial Revolution, and industry – and the Empire it inspired – has provided a framework for much of what's on show. Virtually every English town bears a mark of former wealth and power, whether it be a magnificent Gothic cathedral financed from a monarch's treasury, a parish church funded by the tycoons of the medieval wool trade, or a triumphalist civic building raised on the back of the slave and sugar trade. In the south of England you'll find old dockyards from which the navy patrolled the

The national game

Football, soccer, call it what you will – the English invented it and subsequently appropriated it as an expression of (often misguided) national pride. The country has the oldest league and cup competitions in the world, the best-known club on the planet in Manchester United and players who are more famous than pop stars (or, like the incomparable David Beckham, who are married to pop stars). For outsiders, though, the nuances of supporting a team can be difficult to unravel. The city of Manchester, like Liverpool or Sheffield, has two teams; London has thirteen (none of them called London). Supporters of geographically adjacent teams (Burnley and Blackburn, say, or Southampton and Portsmouth) despise the other; while everyone despises Manchester United. And once you've got to the bottom of this, you still might never get to see a live game as tickets for the famous teams sell out a year in advance. You could watch it on TV (there's a game most nights between August and May), but for the real football experience you have to visit the unfashionable provincial clubs inhabiting the lower divisions. Huddersfield Town against Wycombe Wanderers on a wet Tuesday night in February – that's a proper football match, everything else is entertainment.

England isn't a simple destination, but rather a deeply engrained series of influences which ripple out into the world.

oceans, while in the north there are mills that employed entire town populations. England's museums and galleries – several of them ranking among the world's finest – are full of treasures trawled from its imperial conquests. And in their grandiose stuccoed terraces and wide esplanades the old resorts bear testimony to the heyday of the English holiday towns, as fashionable once as any European spa.

In short, England isn't a simple destination, but rather a deeply engrained series of influences which ripple out into the world. Much of western history and culture is contained within its very fabric. Its inventions and creative momentum, from the Industrial Revolution to Cool Britannia, continue to inspire; while its idiosyncrasies and prejudices leave their mark across the English-speaking world. And the only certainty for visitors is that, however long you spend in the country and however much you see, it still won't be enough to understand England. After all, the English have lived here all their lives and they still can't agree whether the milk goes in before or after the tea.

Where to go

To begin to get to grips with England, **London** is the place to start. Nowhere else in the country can match the scope and innovation of the metropolis, a colossal, frenetic city, perhaps not as immediately attractive as its European counterparts, but with so much variety that lack of cash is the only obstacle to a great time. It's here that you'll find England's best spread of nightlife, cultural events, museums, galleries, pubs and restaurants. However, each of the other large cities, such as **Birmingham**, **Newcastle**, **Leeds**, **Sheffield**, **Manchester** and **Liverpool**, makes its own claim for historic and cultural diversity, and you certainly won't have a representative urban view of the country if you venture no further than the capital. It's in these regional centres that, arguably, the most exciting architectural and social developments are taking place, though for many visitors they come a long way behind ancient cities such as **Lincoln**, **York**, **Salisbury**, **Durham** and **Winchester** – to name just those with the most celebrated of England's cathedrals. Most beguiling of all, though, are the long-established **villages** of England, hundreds of which amount to nothing more than a pub, a shop, a gaggle of cottages and a farmhouse offering bed and breakfast. Devon, Cornwall, the Cotswolds and the Yorkshire Dales harbour some especially picturesque specimens, but every county can boast a decent showing of photogenic hamlets.

Standing Stones

Why the prehistoric peoples of England built dramatic circles of standing stones may never be fully known. The theories are as diverse as the sites themselves: perhaps they were places of sacrifice and celebration, or erected for an astronomical function. But two things remain obvious, even at a distance of five thousand years. Firstly, each series of standing stones represents a highly organized effort by ancient peoples once thought of as unsophisticated. And secondly, whatever their

function, there's a powerful presence at work even today, recognized by the disparate bands of druids and New Age travellers who still seek solace in the stones. Mass tourism has dragged famous sites like Stonehenge into the embrace of the heritage industry, but there are other stone circles which retain their sense of mystery and isolation. At Castlerigg, near Keswick in the Lake District; or the site known as Long Meg and Her Daughters near Penrith; or the circles on Bodmin Moor in the west country – here you can still wander alone, forming your own theories as the early morning mist rises above the stones.

Evidence of England's pedigree is scattered between its settlements as well. Wherever you're based, you're never more than a few miles from a **ruined castle**, a majestic **country house** or a **monastery**, and in some parts of the country you'll come across the sites of civilizations that thrived here before England existed as a nation. In the southwest there are remnants of a **Celtic** culture that elsewhere was all but eradicated by the Romans, and from the south coast to the northern border you can find traces of **prehistoric** settlers, the most famous being the megalithic circles of Stonehenge and Avebury.

Then of course there's the English **countryside**, an extraordinarily diverse terrain from which Constable, Turner, Wordsworth, Emily Brontë and a host of other native luminaries took inspiration. Most dramatic and best known are the moors and uplands – **Exmoor, Dartmoor, Bodmin Moor**, the **North York Moors** and the **Lake District** – each of which has its over-visited spots, though a brisk walk will usually take you out of the throng. Quieter areas are tucked away in every corner of England, from the lush vales of **Shropshire** near the border with Wales, to the flat waterlands of the eastern **Fens** and the chalk downland of **Sussex**. It's a similar story on the **coast**, where the finest sands and most rugged cliffs have long

been discovered, and sizeable resorts have grown to exploit many of the choicest locations. But again, if it's peace you're after, you can find it by heading for the exposed strands of **Northumberland**, the pebbly flat horizons of **East Anglia** or the crumbling headlands of **Dorset**.

When to go

onsidering the temperateness of the English **climate**, it's amazing how much mileage the locals get out of the subject – a two-day cold snap is discussed as if it were the onset of a new Ice Age, and a week in the upper 70s Fahrenheit starts rumours of drought. The fact is that English summers rarely get hot and the winters don't get very cold, and there's not a great deal of regional variation, as the chart shows. The average **summer temperature** in the landlocked Midlands is much the same as down on the southwest beaches, and within a degree or two of the average in the north. Summer rainfall is fairly even over all of England as well, though in general the south gets more **hours of sunshine** than the north. Differences between the regions are slightly more marked in **winter**, when the south tends to be appreciably milder and wetter than the north.

The bottom line is that it's impossible to say with any degree of certainty that the weather will be pleasant in any given month. May might be wet and grey one year and gloriously sunny the next, and the same goes for the autumnal months. November stands an equal chance of being crisp and clear or foggy and grim. Obviously, if you're planning to lie on a beach, or camp in the dry, you'll want to go between June and September – a period when you shouldn't go anywhere without booking your accommodation well in advance. Elsewhere, if you're balancing the likely fairness of the weather against the density of the crowds, the best time to get into the countryside or the towns would be between **April and early June** or in **September** or **October**.

Considering the temperateness of the English climate, it's amazing how much mileage the locals get out of the subject.

Average temperatures and rainfall

	Jan	Feb	Mar	Apr	May	June	July	Aug	Sept	Oct	Nov	Dec
Birmingham												
(°F)	42	43	48	54	60	66	68	68	63	55	48	44
(°C)	5	6	9	12	16	19	20	20	17	13	9	7
(inches)	3	2.1	2	2.1	2.5	2	2.7	2.7	2.4	2.7	3.3	2.6
(mm)	74	54	50	53	64	50	69	69	61	69	84	67
London												
(°F)	43	44	50	56	62	69	71	71	65	58	50	45
(°C)	6	7	10	13	17	20	22	21	19	15	10	7
(inches)	2.1	1.6	1.5	1.5	1.8	1.8	2.2	2.3	1.9	2.2	2.5	1.9
(mm)	54	40	37	37	46	45	57	59	49	57	64	48
Plymouth												
(°F)	47	47	50	54	59	64	66	67	64	58	52	49
(°C)	8	8	10	12	15	18	19	19	18	15	11	10
(inches)	3.9	2.9	2.7	2.1	2.5	2.1	2.8	3	3.1	3.6	4.5	4.3
(mm)	99	74	69	53	63	53	70	77	78	91	113	110
York												
(°F)	43	44	49	55	61	67	70	69	64	57	49	45
(°C)	6	7	10	13	16	19	21	20	18	14	10	7
(inches)	2.3	1.8	1.5	1.6	2	2	2.4	2.7	2.2	2.2	2.6	2
(mm)	59	46	37	41	50	50	62	68	55	55	65	50

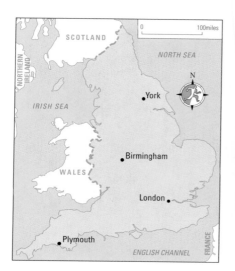

40

things not to miss

It's not possible to see everything England has to offer in one trip — and we don't suggest you try. What follows is a selective taste of the country's highlights — architecture, dramatic landscapes and even good things to eat and drink. Arranged in five colour-coded categories, you can browse through to find the very best things to see, do and experience. All highlights have a page reference to take you straight into the guide, where you can find out more.

01 **A pint down the pub** Page **36** • From trendy micro-breweries to ancient coaching inns, England's pubs are an essential part of any visit to the country. The best brews to sample, and the best places to try them, are listed in the Guide.

02 North York Moors Page 975
• The North York Moors Railway steams along a dramatic course across the moors, providing access to some of the best hikes in this part of the country.

03 St Ives Tate, Cornwall Page
497 • The southwest's best arts collection occupies a superb site overlooking Porthmeor Beach, with a wonderful rooftop café.

04 Scafell and Scafell Pike Page 844
• The two highest peaks in England are on every serious hiker's hitlist though any reasonably fit person could tackle them, too.

05 Royal Crescent, Bath Page 407
• After visiting the baths, mellow out on England's most elegant Georgian terrace, perfectly sited for views across the golden stone of Bath to the green hills beyond.

06 Surfing, Newquay Page **509** • The beaches strung along the northern coast of Devon and Cornwall offer some great breaks. Newquay is still the place to go to see and be seen.

07 The Royal Pavilion, Brighton Page **227** • George IV's pleasure dome, designed by Nash, is the supreme (and only) example of Oriental-Gothic architecture.

08 Chiltern hills Page **323** • Within easy striking distance of London, the Chiltern hills offer delightful wooded countryside studded with top-notch country pubs. Ideal for hiking and cycling.

09 Notting Hill Carnival Page **123** • One of Europe's biggest and loudest street carnivals takes place every August Bank Holiday weekend in the streets of this west London district.

10 **The Proms, London** Page **161** • Running from July to September, this massive classical music festival is centred on the Royal Albert Hall. World-class performances and rock-bottom ticket prices (from £3) mean long queues for those that haven't booked ahead.

11 **Avebury stone circle**
Page **313** • Stonehenge might get all the publicity, but the stones at nearby Avebury have a raw appeal and are far more accessible than the fenced-off site of Stonehenge.

12 **Westonbirt Arboretum, Gloucestershire** Page **375** • Autumn is the best time to appreciate the majestic beauty of this amazing collection of trees and plants set in beautiful peaceful countryside.

13 Afternoon tea Page 65 • The rooms may be out of most people's league, but London's top hotels serve up wickedly calorific afternoon teas to all and sundry.

14 Tate Modern, London
Page 000 • Housed in a spectacular disused power station, London's new modern-art gallery is simply awesome.

15 Hiking on Dartmoor Page 454 • Southern England's greatest expanse of wilderness offers solitude for experienced hikers and riders.

16 Books, Hay-on-Wye Page 631 • An outpost on the English-Welsh border, Hay-on-Wye may be remote, but it does cut a dash with the size and the variety of its second-hand bookshops.

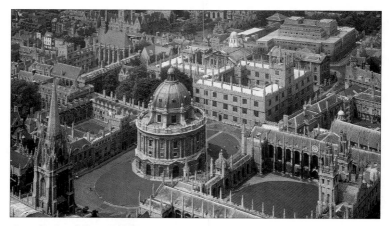

17 **Oxford** Page **330** • The famous old university town boasts many beautiful old buildings, but perhaps the most imposing is the Italianate rotunda, Radcliffe Camera.

18 **The Beatles in Liverpool** Page **780** • The Sixties never stopped in Liverpool, where every August The Beatles Festival fills the city with bands and music honouring the world's most famous pop group.

19 **Blackpool Tower** Page **789** • The British seaside's best-known landmark provides a touch of grace to the Blackpool skyline.

20 **Glastonbury** Page **417** • One of the oldest and biggest rock festivals still retains its authentic aura, less commercialized than most of the ilk, and still drawing the alternative crowd.

21 **Eden Project, Cornwall** Page **482** • With its strong ecological thrust, the West Country's most spectacular new attraction presents a refreshing alternative to the hard-sell, commercial edge of most of the region's crowd-pullers.

22 **York Minster** Page **942** • Britain's biggest Gothic church has a thousand-year history and treasures to match, including the world's largest medieval stained-glass window.

23 **Camden Market, London** Page **125** • England's largest, most diverse flea market sprawls across the old warehouses beside the Regent's Canal in Camden.

24 **Newcastle Nightlife** Page **1033** • Lock up your inhibitions, leave your coat at home and hit the Toon...

25 Canterbury Cathedral

Page **189** • Mother Church of the Church of England, this cathedral is famous for its shrine to the murdered Archbishop, Thomas à Becket, and the tales that Chaucer weaved round a fictitious pilgrimage to the martyr's tomb.

26 Punting on the Cam

Page **591** • With every justification, Cambridge is an immensely popular tourist destination, famous for its university, whose handsome old stone buildings dot its compact centre. De rigueur is punting on the River Cam, even if you do get stuck in the mud.

27 Bonfire Night (Nov 5)

Page **43** • Most famous of the Gunpowder Plot conspirators, Guy Fawkes, was a native of York where they throw the country's most exuberant Bonfire Night celebrations.

28 Lizard Point, Cornwall

Page **489** • This headland has none of the razzmatazz of Land's End, which is all to its favour, yet still has the views; there are some great beaches within a short coastal hike, too.

29 Fish and chips Page 34 •
There's nothing better than fish and chips, nor any better way to eat them than wrapped in paper and eaten on the bracing North Yorkshire seafront in the little port of Whitby.

30 Ely Page 578 • An isolated Cambridgeshire town in the heart of the eerie fenland landscape, Ely is noted for its magnificent cathedral.

31 Football at Old Trafford Page 757 • The self-styled "Theatre of Dreams" is home to Manchester United, arguably the world's most famous football club. Unless you have friends in powerful places, you won't get a ticket to a home match, but there's plenty to see at the club's museum and plenty of other English clubs at which you can view the beautiful game.

32 Appleby Horse Fair Page 864 • Britain's most important gathering of caravans, horse-drawn and otherwise, plus horse-trading, racing, daredevil stunts and festivities in the usually quiet Eden Valley.

33 Cowes Week, Isle of Wight Page **271** • Held in the first week of August, the spirited atmosphere and sense of occasion at this yachting jamboree draw thousands, infecting even the staunchest landlubbers.

34 WOMAD Page **328** • This event, a celebration of World Music, Arts and Dance, is now held all over the world; but the first and best is held at Reading's Rivermead Leisure Complex each July.

35 The Peak District Page **665** • The Peak District offers great walking countryside and some of England's most appealing landscapes. Aim for the spa town of Buxton and head on out from there.

36 Windermere Page **824** • England's largest lake is also the gateway to the Lake District National Park. An easy day-trip from the conurbations of the northwest, Windermere is great for a waterside picnic, a gentle stroll or a slow cruise by steamer.

xxiii

37 **Wimbledon** Page **42** • The only one of tennis's Grand Slam events to be staged on grass courts is a quintessentially English and (if you're prepared to queue up) democratic event.

38 **Cumberland sausage** Page **34** • An essential ingredient of the Full English Breakfast, the coiled, spicy, herb-and-pork Cumberland sausage sets you up for the day.

39 **Chester's city walls** Page **765** • The most complete set of Roman and medieval walls in Britain encircle the historic city of Chester, providing fine views of the tightly knit kernel of Tudor and Victorian buildings.

40 **Durdle Door** Page **293** • One of the highlights of the Dorset coast, this spectacular limestone arch has an immediate appeal, and is close to the marine wildlife reserve of Kimmeridge Bay as well as some choice beaches.

contents

Using the Rough Guide

We've tried to make this Rough Guide a good read and easy to use. The book is divided into four main sections, and you should be able to find whatever you want in one of them.

colour section

The front colour section offers a quick tour of England. The **introduction** aims to give you a feel for the place, with suggestions on where to go. We also tell you what the weather is like and include a basic country fact file. Next, our authors round up their favourite aspects of England in the **things not to miss** section – whether it's great food, amazing sights or a special hotel. Right after this comes a full **contents** list.

basics

The Basics section covers all the **pre-departure** nitty-gritty to help you plan your trip. This is where to find out which airlines fly to your destination, what paperwork you'll need, what to do about money and insurance, about internet access, food, security, public transport, car rental – in fact just about every piece of **general practical information** you might need.

guide

This is the heart of the Rough Guide, divided into user-friendly chapters, each of which covers a specific region. Every chapter starts with a list of **highlights** and an **introduction** that helps you to decide where to go, depending on your time and budget. Likewise, introductions to the various towns and smaller regions within each chapter should help you plan your itinerary. We start most town accounts with information on arrival and accommodation, followed by a tour of the sights, and finally reviews of places to eat and drink, and details of nightlife. Longer accounts also have a directory of practical listings. Each chapter concludes with **public transport** details for that region.

contexts

Read Contexts to get a deeper understanding of what makes England tick. We include a brief **history**, articles about **architecture**, **wildlife and movies** and a detailed further reading section that reviews dozens of **books** relating to the country.

index + small print

Apart from a **full index**, which includes maps as well as places, this section covers publishing information, credits and acknowledgements, and also has our contact details in case you want to send in updates and corrections to the book – or suggestions as to how we might improve it.

contents ▶

basics ▶

guide ▶

① London ② Surrey, Kent and Sussex ③ Hampshire, Dorset and Wiltshire
④ Oxford and around ⑤ The Cotswolds and Somerset ⑥ Devon and Cornwall
⑦ East Anglia ⑧ The West Midlands ⑨ The East Midlands ⑩ The Northwest
⑪ Cumbria and the Lakes ⑫ Yorkshire ⑬ The Northeast

contexts ▶

index ▶

chapter map of **England**

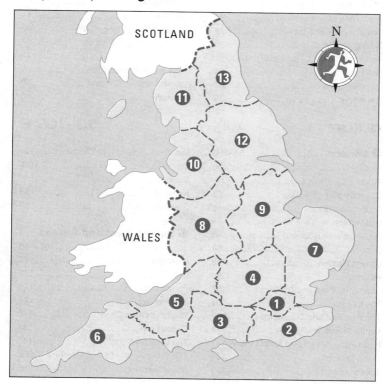

contents

colour section

i–xxiv

Colour map of the country ....ii–iii
Where to go ix
When to go xi
Things not to miss xiv

basics

9–51

Getting there 11
Red tape and visas 19
Information, maps and websites..........20
Health and insurance 22
Costs, money and banks 24
Getting around 26
Accommodation 31
Food and drink 34
Communications...................................37
The media 38
Opening hours and public holidays 40
Admission to museums and
monuments 40
Festivals 41
Sports and outdoor pursuits................43
Crime and personal safety 47
Work 48
Travellers with disabilities 49
Gay and lesbian England 50
Directory 51

guide

53–1076

❶ **London**..................................55–166
Highlights 56
Arrival 61
City transport 63
Accommodation 64
Westminster and Whitehall 75
St James's, Mayfair and Marylebone ..83
Soho 88
Covent Garden 92
Bloomsbury...94
Strand, Holborn and Clerkenwell 97
The City...101
The East End and Docklands 107
Lambeth and Southwark.....................111
Hyde Park, Kensington and Chelsea 117
North London 124
South London 129
Out West: Chiswick to Windsor 134
Eating 141
Drinking...149
Nightlife...153
Travel details 165

❷ **Surrey, Kent and Sussex**
....167–246
Highlights 168
Guildford 172
Farnham 175
Dorking 177
The North Kent Coast 178
Canterbury 189
The Channel Ports 196
The Romney and Denge Marshes 203
Royal Tunbridge Wells.......................206

Hastings	214
Eastbourne	220
Lewes	223
Brighton	227
Arundel	238
Chichester	241
Travel details	245

❸ Hampshire, Dorset and Wiltshire 247–318
Highlights	248
Portsmouth	252
Southampton	257
The Isle of Wight	260
Winchester	273
The New Forest	281
Bournemouth	284
Christchurch	286
Poole	286
Dorchester	293
Lyme Regis	301
Salisbury Plain	311
Marlborough	313
Travel details	317

❹ Oxford and around 319–358
Highlights	320
The Chiltern Hills	323
Reading	327
The Vale of White Horse	328
Oxford	331
Woodstock	347
Blenheim Palace	348
Buckingham	349
Woburn	351
St Albans	353
Travel details	357

❺ The Cotswolds and Somerset 359–424
Highlights	360
Lechlade	364
Burford	365
Stow-on-the-Wold	366
Moreton-in-Marsh	366
Northleach	367
Chipping Norton	369
Chipping Campden	370

Winchcombe	371
Cirencester	372
Cheltenham	376
Stroud	380
Gloucester	383
Tewkesbury	387
Bristol	390
Bath	403
Wells	411
The Mendips	413
Glastonbury	416
Bridgwater	419
Taunton	420
The Quantock Hills	421
Travel details	423

❻ Devon and Cornwall ..425–522
Highlights	426
Exeter	431
Torquay	441
Dartmouth	446
Plymouth	449
Dartmoor	454
Ilfracombe	464
Bideford Bay	465
Lundy Island	468
Exmoor	469
Looe and Polperro	479
Truro	484
The Lizard	488
Penzance	492
Land's End	495
St Ives	497
The Isles of Scilly	499
Redruth	506
Newquay	507
Padstow	509
Tintagel	513
Bodmin Moor	517
Travel details	522

❼ East Anglia 523–600
Highlights	524
Southend-on-Sea	527
Colchester	529
Harwich	535
The Stour Valley	536
Bury St Edmunds	542

Ipswich 544
The Suffolk Coast 546
Norwich.....................................554
The Norfolk Broads...........................562
Great Yarmouth................................564
King's Lynn 572
Ely 578
Cambridge 581
Newmarket 599
Travel details 600

❽ The West Midlands 601–682
Highlights 602
Stratford-upon-Avon..........................605
Warwick 614
Coventry 616
Worcester 620
The Malvern Hills 622
Hereford 625
The Wye River Valley.........................629
Shrewsbury...................................640
Birmingham..................................647
The Black Country 659
Lichfield.......................................662
The Peak District...............................665
Derby 668
Travel details 681

❾ The East Midlands 683–736
Highlights 684
Nottingham 687
Leicester 699
Northampton..................................710
Lincoln 720
The Wolds and the coast 725
The Fens 728
Boston.......................................729
Travel details 736

❿ The Northwest..............737–814
Highlights 738
Manchester...................................741
Chester 765
Northwich 771
Knutsford 772
Macclesfield 773
Nantwich.....................................774
Liverpool 774

Blackpool 789
Preston 794
Lancaster 797
Morecambe....................................800
Isle of Man 802
Travel details 814

⓫ Cumbria and the Lakes
   815–870
Highlights 816
Kendal.......................................821
Windermere and Bowness 824
Troutbeck 827
Ambleside 828
Langdale 830
Grasmere 831
Coniston Water 834
Hawkshead 837
Keswick and Derwent Water.............839
Borrowdale and Scafell.....................843
Buttermere and Crummock Water 845
Wast Water and Eskdale...................846
Cockermouth 847
Ullswater.....................................848
The Cumbrian Coast........................852
The Eden Valley and Penrith 863
Carlisle 866
Travel details 869

⓬ Yorkshire 871–992
Highlights 872
Sheffield 877
Leeds 882
Bradford 890
Haworth 894
Wharfedale 903
Malhamdale 908
Ribblesdale 910
The Western Dales 913
Wensleydale 917
Swaledale 922
Richmond 924
Harrogate 927
Ripon..932
York 935
Hull 955
The North York Moors......................961
Helmsley 968

Pickering 973
Scarborough 979
Whitby 985
Travel details 990

⑬ **The Northeast** 993–1076
Highlights 994
Durham 999
Teesdale 1013
Weardale 1014
The Allen Valley 1015
Darlington 1018

Hartlepool 1021
Saltburn 1022
Newcastle upon Tyne 1023
Hadrian's Wall 1043
Northumberland National Park 1053
Warkworth..1063
Alnmouth...1064
Alnwick 1065
Bamburgh 1069
Holy Island 1070
Berwick-upon-Tweed 1073
Travel details 1074

contexts

1077–1136

The historical framework..................1079
The monuments and buildings of England
....1098
Wildlife 1110

Books 1117
Film 1126
Glossaries 1135

index and small print

1137–1159

Full index...1138
Twenty years of Rough Guides 1156
Rough Guide credits 1157
Publishing information 1157

Help us update 1157
Acknowledgements 1158
Readers' letters................................1158
Photo credits....................................1159

map symbols

maps are listed in the full index using coloured text

Motorway	🏛 Stately home/historic house
Major road	⚘ Public gardens
Minor road	✕ Battlefield
Pedestrianized street	⌂ Abbey (regional maps)
Road with steep incline	♜ Castle
Tunnel	✝ Church (regional maps)
Path	⊠-⊠ Gate
Steps	⊐⊏ Bridge
Wall	🅿 Parking
Railway	⊖ London Underground station
Ferry route	Ⓜ Metro station
River	⛭ Motor racing circuit
National boundary	✈ Airport
County boundary	ⓘ Tourist information
Chapter boundary	✉ Post office
▲ Mountain peak	◉ Hotel
Gorge	▣ Restaurant
Waterfall	Building
Cliffs	▢ Market
⌂ Caves	✚ Church/cathedral
Point of interest	Park/national park
∴ Ruin	Forest
Museum	Marshland

basics

basics

Getting there 11

Red tape and visas 19

Information, maps and websites 20

Health and insurance 22

Costs, money and banks 24

Getting around 26

Accommodation 31

Food and drink 34

Communications 37

The media 38

Opening hours and public holidays 40

Admission to museums and monuments 40

Festivals and events 41

Sports and outdoor pursuits 43

Crime and personal safety 47

Work 48

Travellers with disabilities 49

Gay and lesbian England 50

Directory 51

Getting there

London is one of the busiest transport hubs of the world, and stiff competition between the airlines ensures a plethora of choice and good deals on flights. The city's Heathrow and Gatwick airports take the bulk of transatlantic and long-haul flights, but several companies fly into Manchester, useful if you're heading for the north of the country. It's also possible to connect from London to many other regional airports, such as Birmingham, Newcastle or the Isle of Man, on one of Britain's domestic carriers. London's other three airports – Stansted, Luton and City Airport – are well served by low-cost flights from mainland Europe, as are Manchester and the country's other regional airports. Travelling from the Continent, drivers, foot and rail passengers can either cross the Channel by ferry or go under it via Eurotunnel (car) or the Eurostar (passenger train). If you really want to – or are on a very tight budget – you might consider picking up a bus from any of the major European cities. From Ireland, it's quickest to fly, but there are plenty of ferry crossings if you prefer not to.

Airfares always depend on the season, with the highest being around early June to mid-September, when the weather is best; fares drop during the "shoulder" seasons – mid-September to early November and mid-April to early June – and you'll get the best prices during the low season, November through to April (excluding Christmas and New Year when prices are hiked up and seats are at a premium; it's wise to book at least two or three months ahead for this period). Note also that flying at weekends is generally more expensive; price ranges quoted below assume mid-week travel.

You can often cut costs by going through a specialist flight agent – either a **consolidator**, who buys up blocks of tickets from the airlines and sells them at a discount, or a **discount agent**, who in addition to dealing with discounted flights may also offer special student and youth fares and a range of other travel-related services such as travel insurance, rail passes, car rentals, tours and the like. Some agents specialize in **charter flights**, which may be cheaper than anything available on a scheduled flight, but departure dates are fixed and withdrawal penalties are high. Don't automatically assume that tickets purchased through a travel specialist will be cheapest, however – once you get a quote, check with the airlines and you may turn up an even better deal. A further possibility is to see if you can arrange a **courier flight**, although you'll need a flexible schedule, and preferably be travelling alone with very little luggage. In return for shepherding a parcel through customs, you can expect to get a deeply discounted ticket. You'll probably also be restricted in the duration of your stay.

If England is only one stop on a longer journey, you might want to consider buying a **Round-the-World** (RTW) ticket. Some travel agents can sell you an "off-the-shelf" RTW ticket that will have you touching down in about half a dozen cities (London is usually on the itinerary); others will have to assemble one for you, which can be tailored to your needs but is apt to be more expensive. Prices start from $1850 from Australia, $1295 from the US; for tailor-made itineraries and more flexible options such as Qantas/British Airways "Global Explorer", you'll be paying a lot more.

Booking flights online

Many airlines and discount travel websites offer you the opportunity to book your tickets on-line, cutting out the costs of agents and middle-men. Good deals can often be found through discount or auction sites, as well as through the airlines' own websites.

Useful websites

ⓦ**www.cheapflights.com** Flight deals, travel agents, plus links to other travel sites.

ⓦ**www.cheaptickets.com** Discount flight specialists.

ⓦ**www.expedia.com** Discount airfares, all-airline search engine and daily deals.

ⓦ**www.gaytravel.com** Gay online travel agent, concentrating mostly on accommodation.

ⓦ**www.hotwire.com** Bookings from the US only. Last-minute savings of up to 40 percent on regular published fares. Travellers must be at least 18 and there are no refunds, transfers or changes allowed. Log-in required.

ⓦ**www.lastminute.com** Offers good last-minute holiday package and flight-only deals.

ⓦ**www.priceline.com** Name-your-own-price website that has deals at around 40 percent off standard fares. You cannot specify flight times (although you do specify dates) and the tickets are non-refundable, non-transferable and non-changeable.

ⓦ**www.skyauction.com** Bookings from the US only. Auctions tickets and travel packages using a "second bid" scheme. The best strategy is to bid the maximum you're willing to pay, since if you win you'll pay just enough to beat the runner-up regardless of your maximum bid.

ⓦ**www.travelocity.com** Destination guides, hot web fares and best deals for car rental, accommodation and lodging as well as fares. Provides access to the travel-agent system SABRE, the most comprehensive central reservations system in the US.

ⓦ**www.travelshop.com.au** Australian website offering discounted flights, packages, insurance and online bookings.

ⓦ**www.uniquetravel.com.au** Australian site with a good range of packages and good-value flights.

ⓦ**travel.yahoo.com** Incorporates a lot of Rough Guide material in its coverage of destination countries and cities across the world, with information about places to eat and sleep.

Flights from the US and Canada

Figure on six and a half hours' **flying time** from New York to any of the British airports (it's an hour extra coming the other way, due to headwinds). Most eastbound flights cross the Atlantic overnight, depositing you at your destination the next morning without much sleep, but if you can manage to stay awake until after dinner that night, you should be over the worst of the jet lag by the next morning. Some flights from the East Coast depart early in the morning, arriving late the same evening, but this lands you in London just as the city is shutting down – a recipe for a disorienting and expensive first night.

Dozens of airlines fly from New York to London, and a few fly direct from other East Coast and Midwestern hubs. The best low-season **fares** from New York to London hover around $360 return with a similar price from Boston. In the same period you'll pay in the region of $390 from Washington DC, $430 from Chicago and $440 from Houston. You can pick up flights from Los Angeles for under $400, but for the west coast in general you're looking at paying $500 or more. For high-season fares, add $150–250 and bear in mind that travelling late on a Saturday can considerably reduce the fare.

Several **airlines** fly to Manchester from some of the above cities, and American, Aer Lingus and BA fly to Birmingham. Manchester and Birmingham are common rated with London, which means that the Apex fare should be the same. If you fly to London on a discounted ticket, expect to pay about $100 each way for an onward connection within England.

In **Canada**, you'll get the best deal flying to London from the big gateway cities of Toronto and Montréal, where low-season deals start from around CDN$510 return; direct flights from Ottawa and Halifax will probably cost only slightly more. From Edmonton, Calgary and Vancouver to London the equivalent fare is CDN$710. If you're travelling in high-season, fares are likely to be about $200 higher.

Only Air Canada flies nonstop to Manchester (from Ottawa and Toronto), but you can pick up direct flights from many Canadian cities to Manchester, Birmingham and Newcastle (usually via London) and often at no extra cost over the fare to London.

Airlines in the US and Canada

Aer Lingus ☏1-800/223-6537, ⓦ**www.aerlingus.ie**. Boston, Chicago, Los Angeles and New York to Dublin or Shannon with connections to many major British airports.

Air Canada ☏1-888/247-2262, ⓦ**www.aircanada.ca**. Calgary, Halifax, Montreal, Ottawa, Toronto and Vancouver to London; Ottawa and Toronto to Manchester.

American Airlines ☏1-800/433-7300, ⓦ**www.aa.com**. Chicago, Dallas/Fort Worth, Los Angeles, Miami, New York and Raleigh to London;

Chicago to Birmingham and Manchester; Dallas/Forth Worth to Manchester.

bmi/British Midland ☎1-800/788-0555, ⊛www.flybmi.com. Washington and Chicago to Manchester.

British Airways ☎1-800/247-9297, ⊛www.british-airways.com. Atlanta, Baltimore, Boston, Charlotte, Chicago, Dallas/Fort Worth, Denver, Detroit, Houston, Los Angeles, Miami, Montreal, New York, Orlando, Philadelphia, Phoenix, Pittsburgh, San Diego, San Francisco, Seattle, Tampa, Toronto, Vancouver and Washington DC to London (with extensive connections on to other UK destinations); also Chicago, New York and Toronto to Birmingham and Manchester.

Continental Airlines ☎1-800/231-0856, ⊛www.continental.com. Cleveland, Houston and Newark to London; Newark to Manchester.

Delta Air Lines ☎1-800/241-4141, ⊛www.delta.com. Atlanta and Cincinnati to London; Atlanta and New York to Manchester.

Northwest/KLM Airlines ☎1-800/447-4747, ⊛www.nwa.com. Detroit and Minneapolis to London.

United Airlines ☎1-800/538-2929, ⊛www.ual.com. Chicago, Los Angeles, Newark, New York, San Francisco and Washington DC to London.

Virgin Atlantic Airways ☎1-800/862-8621, ⊛www.virgin-atlantic.com. Boston, Chicago, Los Angeles, Miami, Newark, New York, Orlando, San Francisco and Washington DC to London.

Courier flights from the US and Canada

Air Courier Association ☎1-800/282-1202, ⊛www.aircourier.org.
Now Voyager ☎212/431-1616, ⊛www.nowvoyagertravel.com.

Discount travel companies from the US and Canada

Air Brokers International ☎1-800/883-3273 or 415/397-1383, ⊛www.airbrokers.com. Consolidator and specialist in RTW packages.
Airtech ☎212/219-7000, ⊛www.airtech.com. Standby seat broker. Also deals in consolidator fares and courier flights, mainly from northeastern US cities.
Council Travel ☎1-800/226-8624 or 617/528-2091, ⊛www.counciltravel.com. Nationwide organization that mostly, but by no means exclusively, specializes in student/budget travel.
Educational Travel Center ☎1-800/747-5551 or 608/256-5551, ⊛www.edtrav.com.

Student/youth discount agent.
New Frontiers/Nouvelles Frontières ☎1-800/677-0720 or 212/986-6006, ⊛www.NewFrontiers.com. French discount-travel firm. Other branches in LA, San Francisco and Québec City.
STA Travel ☎1-800/777-0112 or 1-800/781-4040, ⊛www.sta-travel.com. Worldwide specialists in independent travel; also student IDs, travel insurance, car rental and rail passes.
TFI Tours International ☎1-800/745-8000 or 212/736-1140. Consolidator.
Travac ☎1-800/872-8800, ⊛www.thetravelsite.com. Consolidator and charter broker.
Travel Avenue ☎1-800/333 3335, ⊛www.travelavenue.com. Full-service travel agent that offers discounts in the form of rebates.
Travel Cuts Canada ☎1-800/667-2887, US ☎416/979-2406. Canadian student-travel organization.
Worldtek Travel ☎1-800/243-1723, ⊛www.worldtek.com. Discount travel agency for worldwide travel.

Package holidays and organized tours

Although you'll want to see England at your own speed, you shouldn't dismiss the idea of a **package deal** out of hand. Many agents and airlines put together very flexible deals, sometimes amounting to nothing more restrictive than a flight plus accommodation and car or rail pass, and these can actually work out cheaper than the same arrangements made on arrival – especially car rental, which is fairly expensive in England. A package can also be great for your peace of mind, if only to ensure a worry-free first week while you're finding your feet for a longer tour. It's worth checking, too, for last-minute deals, especially out of season.

There's no shortage of **tour operators** specializing in travel to the British Isles. Most can do packages of the standard highlights, but of greater interest are the outfits that help you explore England's unique points: many organize walking or cycling trips through the countryside, boat trips along canals and any number of theme tours based around the country's literary heritage, history, pubs, gardens, theatre, golf – you name it. A few of the possibilities are listed on p.14, and a travel agent will be able to point out others. For a full listing, contact the

British Tourist Authority (see p.21).

Be sure to examine the fine print of any deal, and bear in mind that everything in brochures always sounds great. Choose only an operator that is a member of the United States Tour Operator Association (USTOA) or has been approved by the American Society of Travel Agents (ASTA).

US and Canadian tour operators

All these companies' tours can be booked through a travel agent at no extra cost.

BCT Scenic Walking ☏1-800/473-1210, ⓦwww.bctwalk.com. Extensive line-up of walking trips of eight to sixteen days in the Cotswolds, Cornwall, the Lake District, the Yorkshire Dales and from coast-to-coast.
British Airways Holidays ☏1-877/428-2228, ⓦwww.british-airways.com. Flight-inclusive vacations and customized itineraries.
British Travel International ☏1-800/327-6097, ⓦwww.britishtravel.com. Agent for all independent arrangements: rail and bus passes, hotels and a comprehensive B&B and vacation-homes reservation service.
English Experience ☏1-800/892-9317, ⓦwww.english-experience.com. Small-group guided tours in homestays or hotels, covering Sussex, Bath, the Cotswolds, the Lake District and Shropshire.
English Lakeland Ramblers ☏1-800/724-8801, ⓦwww.ramblers.com. Walking tours (usually seven or eight days) in the Lake District and the Cotswolds.
International Gay & Lesbian Travel Association ☏ -800/448-8550, ⓦwww.iglta.org. General.
Le Boat ☏1-800/922-0291, ⓦwww.leboat.com. Specializes in canal trips in Cambridgeshire, Gloucestershire and on the River Thames.
Lynott Tours ☏1-800/221-2474, ⓦwww.lynotttours.com. Escorted tours, hotel and castle stays, self-drives and cottage rental.
Select Travel Service ☏1-800/752-6787, ⓦwww.selecttravel.com. Customized history, literature, theatre and horticulture tours.
Sterling Tours ☏1-800/727-4359, ⓦwww.sterlingtours.com. Variety of independent itineraries, packages, country-house hotels and activity holidays.
Virgin Atlantic Vacations ☏1-800/862-8621, ⓦwww.virgin-atlantic.com. Custom-made packages for independent travellers, including hotel, theatre and airfare deals.
Wilderness Travel ☏1-800/368-2794, ⓦwww.wildernesstravel.com. Inn-to-inn hiking

packages in the Cotswolds, through the Lake District and from coast to coast.

Flights from Australia and New Zealand

Travel time from Australia and New Zealand to England is over twenty hours and as long-haul flights can be very taxing you might want to consider taking advantage of a stopover and good night's sleep en route.

The route to London is a highly competitive one, with flights via Southeast Asia generally being the cheapest option; the lowest **fares** start from A$1500/NZ$2000 with such airlines as Britannia Airways and Garuda Air. More expensive, but worth it for the extras, such as fly-drive, accommodation packages and onward travel to other European destinations, are airlines such as Singapore Airlines, Qantas, British Airways and Air New Zealand, whose fares start at around A$1800/NZ$2275.

Fares **from Australia**'s eastern cities are common rated while flights from Perth via Asia and Africa are $200–400 less, and via the Americas about $400 more. The most direct route **from New Zealand** is via North America, with United Airlines offering the best value, stopping in Los Angeles and Chicago for $2150 low season and $3340 in high season, while Air New Zealand have a similar deal for around $2370/$3500. British Airways are a bit more expensive starting at $2410/$3700, but this does include onward connections to other destinations in Britain. Garuda, Korean Air and Thai Airways fly to London via Asia with either a transfer or stopover in their home city for around $2120; for a little more money and comfort Qantas fly via Sydney and Bangkok from $2350.

Airlines in Australia and New Zealand

Air New Zealand ☏0800/737 000 or 09/357 3000, Australia ☏13/2476. Daily flights to London from Brisbane, Melbourne and Sydney via Asia and from New Zealand via Los Angeles.
Britannia Airways Australia ☏02/9251 1299, New Zealand ☏0800/887 997, ⓦ www.britanniaairways.com. Several flights a month (Nov–March only) from Auckland, Brisbane, Cairns and Sydney to London and once a week to Manchester via Bangkok and Abu Dhabi.

British Airways Australia ☎ 02/8904 8800,
New Zealand ☎ 09/356 8690, ⊛ www.british-airways.com. Daily direct flights from Brisbane,
Melbourne, Perth and Sydney. Code share with
Qantas (part owners of the company) from other
major cities to London via Los Angeles and
Singapore and twice weekly via Harare or
Johannesburg from Sydney; daily from Auckland via
Los Angeles. Onward connections to other
destinations in Britain.

Canadian Airlines Australia ☎ 1300/655 767,
New Zealand ☎ 09/309 9159, ⊛ www.cddnair.ca.
Several flights a week from Auckland, Melbourne and
Sydney to London via Toronto or Vancouver.

Cathay Pacific Australia ☎ 13/1747 or 02/9931
5500, New Zealand ☎ 09/379 0861, ⊛ www
.cathaypacific.com. Several flights a week from
Auckland, Brisbane, Cairns, Melbourne, Perth and
Sydney to London and Manchester via Hong Kong.

Garuda Australia ☎ 13/1223 or 02/9334 9900,
New Zealand ☎ 09/366 1862 or 1800/128 510,
⊛ www.garuda-indonesia.com. Several flights
weekly from Adelaide, Auckland, Brisbane, Cairns,
Darwin, Melbourne, Perth and Sydney to London via
Denpasar or Jakarta.

KLM Australia ☎ 1300/303 747, New Zealand
☎ 09/309 1782, ⊛ www.klm.com. Twice weekly
flights from Sydney to London via Singapore and
Amsterdam.

Malaysia Airlines Australia ☎ 13/2627, New
Zealand ☎ 09/373 2741 or 0800/657 472,
⊛ www.malaysiaair.com. Several flights a week
from Auckland, Melbourne, Perth and Sydney to
London via Kuala Lumpur. With onward connections
to the northwest.

Qantas Australia ☎ 13/13 13, New Zealand
☎ 09/357 8900 or 0800/808 767,
⊛ www.qantas.com.au. Daily flights from Adelaide,
Auckland, Brisbane, Christchurch, Darwin,
Melbourne, Perth, Sydney and Wellington to London
via Bangkok or Singapore.

Singapore Airlines Australia ☎ 13/10 11 or
02/9350 0262, New Zealand ☎ 09/303 2129 or
0800/808 909, ⊛ www.singaporeair.com. Daily
flights from Auckland, Brisbane, Christchurch,
Melbourne, Perth and Sydney and several weekly
from Adelaide and Cairns to London and Manchester
via Singapore.

Thai Airways Australia ☎ 1300/651 960, New
Zealand ☎ 09/377 3886, ⊛ www.thaiair.com.
Several flights a week from Auckland, Brisbane,
Melbourne, Perth and Sydney to London via
Bangkok.

United Airlines Australia ☎ 13/1777, New
Zealand ☎ 09/379 3800, ⊛ www.ual.com. Daily
flights from Auckland to Melbourne, Sydney and
London and Manchester via Los Angeles and
Chicago, New York or Washington.

Virgin Atlantic Airways Australia ☎ 02/9244
2747, New Zealand ☎ 09/308 3377,
⊛ www.virgin-atlantic.com. Daily flights from
Sydney and several weekly from Melbourne to
London via Kuala Lumpur. Code-share with Malaysia
Airlines for the first leg.

Travel Agents in Australia and New Zealand

Budget Travel New Zealand ☎ 09/366 0061 or
0800/808 040. Long-established agent with budget
airfares and accommodation packages.

Destinations Unlimited New Zealand ☎ 09/373
4033. Discount fares with a good selection of tours
and holiday packages.

Flight Centres Australia ☎ 02/9235 3522,
nearest branch on 13/1600; New Zealand
☎ 09/358 4310; ⊛ www.flightcentre.com.au.
Concentrates on discounted air fares.

STA Travel Australia ☎ 13/1776 or 1300/360 960,
New Zealand ☎ 09/309 0458 or 09/366 6673,
⊛ www.statravel.com.au. Fare discounts for
students and under 25s as well as student cards, rail
passes and accommodation.

Student Uni Travel Australia ☎ 02/9232 8444,
⊛ wwww.sut.com.au. Discounted air fares and
student/youth travel specialists

Thomas Cook Australia ☎ 13/1771 or 1800/801
002, New Zealand ☎ 09/379 3920,
⊛ www.thomascook.com.au. Low cost flights, tours
and accommodation; also issues travellers' cheques.

Trailfinders Australia ☎ 02/9247 7666.
⊛ www.trailfinders.com.au. Discounted flights, car
rental, tailor-made tours, rail passes and RTW tours.

Usit Beyond New Zealand ☎ 09/379 4224 or
0800/788 336, ⊛ www.usitbeyond.co.nz.
Student/youth travel specialists.

Tour operators in Australia and New Zealand

Adventures Abroad Australia ☎ 1/800/147 827,
New Zealand ☎ 0800/800 434,
⊛ www.adventures-abroad.com. Arranges trips of
eight to fifteen days in the South of England.

Adventure World Australia ☎ 02/8913 0755,
⊛ www.adventureworld.com.au; New Zealand
☎ 09/524 5118, ⊛ www. adventureworld.co.nz.
Offers a wide variety of independent, customized and
escorted tours round England.

Best of Britain Australia ☎ 02/9909 1055. Can
organize flights, accommodation, car rental, tours,
canal boats and B&Bs in the UK.

Explore Holidays Australia ☎02/9857 6200 or 1300/731 000, ⓦwww.exploreholidays.com.au. Accommodation and package tours to Britain and Ireland.

YHA Travel Centre Australia ☎02/9261 1111 or 03/9670 9611, ⓦwww.yha.com.au; New Zealand ☎09/379 4224, ⓦwww.yha.co.nz. Organizes budget accommodation throughout Britain for YHA members.

Flights from Ireland

Stiff competition on routes between Ireland and England has kept the **cost of flights** relatively low, with airlines offering return tickets from Dublin as little as €60 in off-peak seasons, though these will need to be booked well in advance. Ryanair fly to eleven destinations in England from Cork, Kerry, Knock and Shannon as well as Dublin and are generally the cheapest carrier. If there are no special deals available, expect to pay around €125 for a return ticket to Stansted. Aer Lingus offer deals from Galway and Sligo in addition to the departure points above, with fares around €115 for journeys including a Saturday night, and British Airways often give good discounts on their published fares from Dublin. Flying from Belfast, however, your best bet is with either Easyjet, whose one-way flight to Luton Airport costs from £17.50 (excluding tax), or Go, who fly into Stansted and offer a mid-week single for £37.50. Flights into Heathrow with bmi/British Midland cost from £73; BA are generally more expensive but have special deals from around £80.

Airlines in Ireland

Aer Lingus Northern Ireland ☎0845/973 7747, Republic of Ireland ☎01/866 3333/844 4777, ⓦwww.aerlingus.ie.
British Airways Northern Ireland ☎0845/773 3377, Republic of Ireland ☎0141/222 2345, ⓦwww.britishairways.com.
bmi/British Midland Northern Ireland ☎0345/554 554, Republic of Ireland ☎01/283 8833, ⓦwww.flybmi.com.
easyJet Northern Ireland ☎0870/600 0000, ⓦwww.easyjet.com.
Go Northern Ireland ☎0870/607 6543, ⓦwww.go-fly.com).
Ryanair Northern Ireland ☎0870/156 9569, Republic of Ireland ☎01/609 7800, ⓦwww.ryanair.com.

By rail

There are frequent through trains for passengers from Paris, Brussels and Lille to London run by **Eurostar**, which travel through the Channel Tunnel to Waterloo International in London via Ashford in Kent. The least expensive return fare (which must be booked 14 days in advance, include any two nights away or just a Sat night) is £79 from Paris and Brussels and £69 from Lille. Full **fares** with no restrictions are £298 from Paris and Brussels and £230 from Lille. Youth tickets (for under-26s) are fully flexible and cost £75 from Paris and Brussels and £65 from Lille. Eurail and Britrail pass holders qualify for a Passholder return which allows unrestricted journeys for £75 from Paris and Brussels and £65 from Lille.

Drivers from Europe have the option of using **Eurotunnel**, crossing underneath the Channel on freight trains which carry coaches, cars and motorbikes. The service runs every fifteen minutes at peak periods and takes thirty-five minutes to get between the loading terminals at Folkestone and Calais. You can just turn up, but booking is advised, especially at weekends; you should arrive at least thirty minutes before departure. A five-day fully flexible return for a car and passengers travelling off-peak costs £180, £215 in high season. Travelling between 10pm and 6am brings the price down to £145.

From the Republic of Ireland, you can get **rail/ferry deals**, but if you're starting from the south or west the best ferry crossings are the more expensive Cork–Swansea or Rosslare–Fishguard/Rosslare–Pembroke routes, which can bring the fare to around the same as a flight. If you're willing to travel overnight, the return fare from Dublin to London works out at £43; it rises to £73 during the day. For more information, contact British and European Rail.

Useful rail contacts

British and European Rail ☎01/703 4095.
Eurostar UK ☎0870/160 6600, France ☎08.36.35.33.39, ⓦwww.eurostar.com.
Eurotunnel UK ☎0870/535 3535, France ☎03.21.00.61.00, ⓦwww.eurotunnel.com.

Ferry connections

	Company	Frequency	Duration
From Belgium			
Ostend–Dover	Hoverspeed (SeaCat)	3 daily	2hr
Zeebrugge–Hull	P & O North Sea Ferries	1 daily	14hr 45min
From Denmark			
Esbjerg–Harwich	DFDS	3–4 weekly	20hr
From France			
Caen–Portsmouth	Brittany	2–3 daily	6hr
Calais–Dover	Hoverspeed (SeaCat)	6–10 daily	40min
Calais–Dover	P&O Stena	30 daily	1hr 15min
Calais–Dover	SeaFrance	15 daily	90min
Cherbourg–Poole	Brittany	1–3 daily	2hr 15min–4hr 15min
Cherbourg–Portsmouth	P&O	1–4 daily	4hr–8hr
Dieppe–Newhaven	Hoverspeed (SeaCat/Super SeaCat)	3–5 daily	2 hr
St Malo–Poole (via Jersey or Guernsey)	Condor	late May–Sept 1 daily	4hr
St Malo–Portsmouth	Brittany	1–7 weekly	8hr 45min
Le Havre–Portsmouth	P&O	2–3 daily	4hr 30min–8hr 30min
Roscoff–Plymouth	Brittany	1–12 weekly	6hr
From Germany			
Hamburg–Harwich	DFDS	3–4 weekly mid Jan to Dec	19hr
From Holland			
Amsterdam–Newcastle	DFDS	daily mid-Feb to Dec	16hr
Hook of Holland–Harwich	Stena	3 daily	3hr 40min–6hr 15min
Rotterdam–Hull	P&O North Sea	1 daily	15hr
From Ireland			
Cork–Swansea	Swansea–Cork Ferries	4–6 weekly mid-March to Nov	10hr
Dun Laoghaire–Holyhead	Stena (Catamaran)	3–4 daily	1hr 40min
Dublin–Holyhead	Stena/Irish Ferries	7 daily	1hr 50min/3hr 50 min
Dublin–Liverpool	Isle of Man Steam Packet (SeaCat)	April to early Nov 1 daily	4hr
Dublin–Liverpool	Irish Sea	6 weekly	6hr 30min
Rosslare–Fishguard	Stena	2 daily May–Sept	3hr 30min
Rosslare–Fishguard	Stena Lynx	2–4 daily May–Sept	1hr 50min
Rosslare–Pembroke	Irish Ferries	2 daily	3hr 45min
From Norway			
Stavanger/Bergen–Newcastle	Fjord Line	2–3 weekly	20–27hr
Kristiansand–Newcastle	DFDS	Jan to mid-Nov 2 weekly	18hr
From Spain			
Bilbao–Portsmouth	P&O	Feb–Dec 1–2 weekly	29hr
Santander–Plymouth	Brittany	March to mid-Nov 1–2 weekly	24hr
From Sweden			
Gothenburg–Newcastle	DFDS	Jan to mid-Nov 2 weekly	26hr

By ferry

Tariffs on the ferries **from mainland Europe** are bewilderingly complex: prices vary with the month, day or even hour at certain times of the year, not to mention how long you're staying and the size of your car. Another thing to bear in mind is that some kind of sleeping accommodation is often obligatory on the longer crossings if made at night, pushing the price way above the basic rate. As an indication of cost, two people driving in a small car from Calais, Dieppe or Ostend to one of the English Channel ports by fast ferry or catamaran could expect to pay from £130 (the return fares are usually just twice the price); for a foot passenger the single fare is £24. On the Bergen–Newcastle route, one of the longest crossings, the one-way fare for four people and a car runs from £150 at off-peak periods to as much as £350 in high season, with foot passengers paying from £38 to £108. For a cabin supplement you can pay between £14 and £114. All current crossings, including foot-passenger, hovercraft and catamaran services, are listed on p.17.

Bringing your car **from Ireland** can make this an expensive alternative if you're travelling alone and can't split the fare. A full run-down of the ferry routes between Ireland and England appears on p.17; fares fluctuate wildly depending on the time of year and the day of the week you travel, and also the length of your car, but expect to pay around €180 for a small vehicle and up to five adults on the ferry route between Dublin and Holyhead (€25–35 for a foot passenger), or €140–240 on the Cork–Swansea route (€30–45 foot passenger).

Ferry companies

Brittany Ferries UK ☎0870/536 0360, France ☎0800.38.28.61, Spain ☎942.36.06.11, ⊛www.brittanyferries.com.
Condor UK ☎0845/345 2001, France ☎02.99.20.03.00, ⊛www.condorferries.co.uk.
Fjord Line UK ☎0191/296 1313, Norway ☎55/548800, ⊛www.fjordline.com.
DFDS Seaways UK ☎0875/333000, Holland ☎0255/534546, Sweden ☎031/650650, Germany ☎040/389 0371, Denmark ☎79.17.79.17, ⊛www.dfdsseaways.co.uk.
Hoverspeed UK ☎0870/524 0241, France ☎0820.00.35.55,

Belgium ☎059.53.99.55, ⊛www.hoverspeed.com.
Irish Ferries UK ☎0870/517 1717, Ireland ☎01/661 0511, ⊛www.irishferries.com.
Isle of Man Steam Packet UK ☎0870/552 3523, ⊛www.sea-cat.co.uk.
P&O Irish Sea ☎0870/242 4777, Ireland ☎1/800 409409, ⊛www.poirishsea.com.
P&O North Sea Ferries UK ☎0870/129 6002, Belgium ☎050.54.34.30, Holland ☎0181/255555, ⊛www.ponsf.com or mycruiseferries.co.uk.
P&O Portsmouth UK ☎0870/242 4999, France ☎0803.01.30.13,
Spain ☎944.23.44.77, ⊛www.poportsmouth.com.
P&O Stena Line UK ☎0870/600 0600, France ☎08.20.01.00.20, ⊛www.posl.com.
Sea France UK ☎0870/571 1711, France ☎08.25.04.40.45, ⊛www.seafrance.com.
Stena Line UK ☎0870/570 7070, Ireland ☎01/204 7777, Holland ☎017/438 9333, ⊛www.stenaline.co.uk.
Swansea Cork Ferries UK ☎01792/456116, Ireland ☎021/427 1166, ⊛www.swansea-cork.ie.

By bus

You can, of course, catch **buses** from a long list of **European** countries to England. Given the low cost of air fares from many cities, however, you'd have to be a masochist to want to travel by bus from, say, Athens – a journey of two nights and three days that actually costs more than the price of a three-and-a-half-hour flight to London. Eurolines (⊛www.eurolines.com) is Britain's largest international coach company, with departures to London from 48 European cities, including Amsterdam, Brussels, Frankfurt, Hamburg, Madrid, Paris and Rome.

If you're coming **from Ireland** and want to keep costs to a minimum, then take the coach. Eurolines (Northern Ireland ☎0870/514 3219 or 01232/33702, Republic of Ireland ☎01/836 6111, ⊛www.eurolines.com) runs a service from Belfast (from £52 return) and Dublin (from IR£36) – with connections throughout Ireland – via Birmingham to London. You can also travel from Cork, Killarney, Limerick and Tralee to London via Fishguard and Bristol. Considering the distances involved, these fares are great value; the downside is that the trip, which can involve an overnight ferry crossing to Holyhead, takes around ten hours from Belfast, twelve hours from Dublin and up to fourteen hours from elsewhere.

Red tape and visas

Citizens of all the countries of Europe – other than Albania, Romania, Bulgaria, Slovakia, the republics of the former Soviet Union (with the exception of the Baltic States) and the former Federal Republic of Yugoslavia (with the exception of Slovenia) – can enter Britain with just a passport, generally for up to three months. US, Canadian, Australian and New Zealand citizens can enter the country for up to six months with just a passport. All other nationalities require a visa, obtainable from the British Consular office in the country of application.

If you want to extend your visa, you should write, before the expiry date given on the endorsement in your passport, to: The Under Secretary of State, Home Office, Immigration and Nationality Dept, Lunar House, Wellesley Rd, Croydon CR9 2BY (☎0870/606 7766, ☜www.ind.homeoffice.gov.uk), enclosing your passport or National Identity Card and form IS120 (if these were your entry documents).

British embassies and high commissions abroad

Australia British High Commission, Commonwealth Ave, Yarralumla, Canberra, ACT 2600 ☎02/6270 6666, ☜www.uk.emb.gov.au.
Canada British High Commission, 80 Elgin St, Ottawa, ON K1P 5K7 ☎613/237-1530, ☜www.britain-in-canada.org.
Ireland 29 Merrion Rd, Dublin 4 ☎01/205 3700, ☜www.britishembassy.ie.
New Zealand British High Commission, 44 Hill St, Wellington ☎04/924 2888, ☜www.britain.org.nz.
USA 3100 Massachusetts Ave, NW, Washington, DC 20008 ☎202/588-6500, ☜www.britainusa.com.

Overseas embassies and high commissions in England

American Embassy 24 Grosvenor Sq, London W1A 1AE ☎020/7499 9000, ☜www.usembassy.org.uk.
Australian High Commission Australia House, The Strand, London WC2B 4LA ☎020/7379 4334, ☜www.australia.org.au.
Canadian High Commission 1 Grosvenor Square, London W1X 0AB ☎020/7258-6600, ☜www.canada.org.uk.
Irish Embassy 17 Grosvenor Place, London SW1X

7HR ☎020/7235 2171, ☜www.irlgov.ie.
New Zealand High Commission New Zealand House, 80 Haymarket, London SW1Y 4TQ ☎020/7930 8422, ☜www.nzembassy.com.

Customs

Since the inauguration of the EU Single Market, travellers coming into Britain directly from another EU country do not have to make a declaration to Customs at their place of entry. In other words, you can bring almost as many cigarettes and as much French wine or German beer into the country as you can carry. The guidance levels are 10 litres of spirits, 90 litres of wine and 110 litres of beer, which should suffice for anyone's requirements – any more than this and you'll have to provide proof that it's for personal use only. The guidelines for tobacco are 800 cigarettes, 400 cigarillos, 200 cigars or 1kg of loose tobacco. If you're travelling to or from a non-EU country, you can still buy duty-free goods, but within the EU, this perk no longer exists. The duty-free allowances are:

❑ **Tobacco:** 200 cigarettes; or 100 cigarillos; or 50 cigars; or 250 grammes of loose tobacco.
❑ **Alcohol:** 2 litres of still wine plus 1 litre of drink over 22 percent alcohol, or 2 litres of alcoholic drinks not over 22 percent.
❑ **Perfumes:** 60ml of perfume plus 250ml of toilet water.
❑ Plus **other goods** to the value of £145.

There are **import restrictions** on a variety of articles and substances, from firearms to furs derived from endangered species, none of which should bother the average tourist. However, if you need any clarification on British import regulations, contact the Excise Contact Centre on ☎0845/010 9000, ☜www.hmce.gov.uk.

Most goods in Britain, with the chief exceptions of books and food, are subject to **Value Added Tax** (VAT), which increases the cost of an item by 17.5 percent (included in the marked price of goods). Visitors from non-EU countries can save a lot of money through the **Retail Export Scheme** (tax-free shopping), which allows a refund of VAT on goods to be taken out of the country. (Savings will usually be minimal for EU nationals because of the rates at which the goods will be taxed upon import to the home country.) Note that not all shops participate in this scheme (those doing so will display a sign to this effect) and that you cannot reclaim VAT charged on hotel bills or other services.

Pets

Since England abandoned its strict **quarantine** rules in 2000, it is now possible to bring cats and dogs from most countries in Europe. However, there are still some restrictions: your pet must not have been out of any of the accepted countries in the six months before entering England, must be microchipped, at least three months old and be vaccinated against rabies. For a list of participating countries and more detailed information call ☎0870/241 1710 or check at ⊛www.defra.gov.uk.

Information, maps and websites

If you want to do a bit of research before arriving in Engand, you could contact the British Tourist Authority (BTA) in your country – the addresses are given below. The BTA will send you a wealth of free literature, some of it just rose-tinted advertising copy, but much of it extremely useful; you'll find their website very comprehensive with plenty of good links. If you want more information on a particular area, you should contact the regional tourist offices in England, which are also listed below.

In England, **tourist offices** (usually called Tourist Information Centres, or "TICs" for short) exist in virtually every town – you'll find their phone numbers and opening hours in the relevant sections of the *Guide*. The average opening hours are much the same as standard shop hours – though hours are extended during the summer months and often curtailed in the depths of winter, especially in more remote areas. All centres offer information on accommodation, local public transport, attractions and restaurants as well as town and regional maps. In many cases this is free, but a growing number of offices make a small charge for an accommodation list or a town guide with an accompanying street plan. Areas designated as **national parks** (such as the Lake District, the North York Moors and Dartmoor) also have a fair sprinkling of information centres, which are generally more expert in giving guidance on local walks and outdoor pursuits. For information on accommodation-booking services, see p.31.

Regional tourist boards in England

British Tourist Authority Thames Tower, Black's Rd, London W6 9EL ☎0208/846 9000, ⊛www.visitbritain.com.
Britain Visitor Centre 1 Regent St, London SW1Y 4XT ⊛www.visitbritain.com. No telephone enquiries.
Cumbria Tourist Board Ashleigh, Holly Rd, Windermere, Cumbria LA23 2AQ ☎01539/444444, ⊛www.golakes.co.uk.
East of England Tourist Board Toppesfield Hall, Hadleigh, Suffolk IP7 5DN ☎01473/822922, ⊛www.eastofenglandtouristboard.com.
Heart of England Tourist Board Larkhill Rd, Worcester WR5 2EZ ☎1905/763436; Apex Court, City Link, Nottingham NG2 4LA ☎0115/959 8383. ⊛www. visittheartofengland.com.
London Tourist Board Glen House, Stag Place, London SW1E 5LT ☎0207/932 2000, ⊛www.londontouristboard.com.
North West Tourist Board Swan House, Swan

Meadow Road, Wigan Pier, Wigan WN3 5BB
℡ 01942/821222, ⓦ www.visitnorthwest.com.
Northumbria Tourist Board Aykley Heads,
Durham DH1 5UX ℡ 0191/375 3000,
ⓦ www.visitnorthumbria.com.
South East England Tourist Board The Old
Brew House, Warwick Park, Tunbridge Wells, Kent
TN2 5TU ℡ 01892/540766,
ⓦ www.southeastengland.uk.com.
Southern Tourist Board 40 Chamberlayne Rd,
Eastleigh, Hampshire SO50 5JH ℡ 02380/625400,
ⓦ www.gosouth.co.uk.
South West Tourism Woodwater Park, Exeter,
Devon EX2 5WT ℡ 0870/442 0830,
ⓦ www.westcountrynow.com.
Yorkshire Tourist Board 312 Tadcaster Rd, York
YO24 1GS ℡ 01904/707161,
ⓦ www.yorkshirevisitor.com.

British tourist offices overseas

Australia Level 16, The Gateway, 1 Macquarie
Place, Circular Quay, Sydney NSW 2000
℡ 02/9377 4400, ⓦ www.visitbritain.com/au.
Canada 5915 Airport Rd, Suite 120, Mississanga,
ON 1T1 3J8 ℡ 1-888/ VISIT UK or 905/405-1720,
ⓦ www.visitbritain.com/ca.
Ireland BTA, 18–19 College Green, Dublin 2
℡ 1/670 8000, ⓦ www.visitbritain.com/ie.
New Zealand Floor 17, NZI House, 151 Queen St,
Auckland ℡ 09/303 1446, ⓦ www.visitbritain.
com/nz.
US 551 5th Ave, 7th Floor, New York, NY 10176
℡ 1-800/ GO-2-BRITAIN or 212-986-2266,
ⓦ www.travelbritain.org.

Websites

Weaving your way in and out of the numerous **websites** before leaving for England is a
good way to familiarize yourself with the
country, book up accommodation and arm
yourself with tips and information. We've
indicated relevant websites throughout this
chapter, but listed here are some useful general sites.
ⓦ **www.backpackers.co.uk** Gives the low-down
on the independent hostels and budget
accommodation.
ⓦ **www.goodguides.com** A combination of
information from *Good Britain Guide* and *Good Pub
Guide*.
ⓦ **www.information-britain.co.uk**
Comprehensive site with a county by county guide.
ⓦ **www.knowhere.co.uk** A self-styled user's

guide to Britain. Up-to-date info, with readers
comments, including best-of and worst-of
sections.
ⓦ **www.multimap.com** Town plans and area
maps with scales up to 1:10,000.
ⓦ **www.ngs.org.uk** Details gardens, many of
them private, open throughout the year for charity.
ⓦ **www.tiac.net/users/namarie** The site is
named Anglophilia and provides a host of links to
other sites – from shops to bands.
ⓦ **www.ordsvy.gov.uk** Information on the full
range of Ordnance Survey maps, including digital
maps.

Maps

The most comprehensive range of maps is
produced by the **Ordnance Survey**, a series
renowned for its accuracy and clarity. The
204 maps in their 1:50,000 (a little over one-
inch-to-one-mile) Landranger series cover
the whole of Britain and show enough detail
to be useful for most walkers. More detailed,
and invaluable for serious hiking, are the
1:25,000 Outdoor Leisure maps, which deal
with national parks and areas of outstanding
beauty, and the Explorer set of maps, which
is gradually replacing the Pathfinder series;
between them they cover the entire country.
Less well known than the Ordnance Survey
publications is the Goldeneye series, a range
of fairly ordinary road maps for various
English counties, but made interesting with
the addition of historical and recreational
details on the back. The best **road atlases**
are the large-format ones produced by the
AA, RAC, Collins and Ordnance Survey,
which cover all of Britain at around three-
miles-to-one-inch and include larger-scale
plans of major towns. Virtually every motorway service station in England stocks one or
more of the big road atlases.

The full range of Ordnance Survey maps is
only available at a few big-city stores, but in
any walking district of England you'll find the
relevant maps in local shops or information
offices. Check their website (see above) for
information on the full range of maps.

Map outlets

In the US and Canada

The Complete Traveler Bookstore 199 Madison
Ave, New York, NY 10016 ℡ 212/685-9007.
Elliot Bay Book Company 101 S Main St,

Seattle, WA 98104 ☏206/624-6600 or 1-800/962-5311, ⊛www.elliotbaybook.com.
Map Link Inc. 30 S La Patera Lane, Unit 5, Santa Barbara, CA 93117 ☏805/692-6777, ⊛www.maplink.com.
Open Air Books and Maps 25 Toronto St, Toronto M5R 2C1 ☏416/363-0719 or 1-800/748-9171.
Phileas Fogg's Travel Center #87 Stanford Shopping Center, Palo Alto, CA 94304 ☏1-800/533-3644, ⊛www.foggs.com.
Rand McNally Mail order on ☏1-800/333-0136 ext 2111, ⊛www.randmcnally.com. Branches at 444 N Michigan Ave, Chicago, IL 60611 ☏312/321-1751; 150 E 52nd St, New York, NY 10022 ☏212/758-7488; and 595 Market St, San Francisco, CA 94105 ☏415/777-3131.
Ulysses Travel Bookshop 4176 St-Denis, Montréal H2W 2M5 ☏514/843-9882, ⊛www.ulysses.ca.
World Wide Books and Maps 1247 Granville St, Vancouver V6Z 1G3 ☏604/687-3320, ⊛www.worldofmaps.com.

In Australia and New Zealand

The Map Shop 6 Peel St, Adelaide ☏08/8231 2033, ⊛www.mapshop.net.au.
Mapland 372 Little Bourke St, Melbourne ☏03/9670 4383, ⊛www.mapland.com.au.
Mapworld 173 Gloucester St, Christchurch ☏03/374 5399, ⊛www.mapworld.co.nz.
Perth Map Centre 1/884 Hay St, Perth ☏08/9322 5733, ⊛www.perthmap.com.au.
Specialty Maps 46 Albert St, Auckland ☏09/307 2217, ⊛www.ubd-online.co.nz/maps.
Travel Bookshop Shop 3, 175 Liverpool St,

Sydney ☏02/9261 8200.
Worldwide Maps and Guides 187 George St, Brisbane ☏07/3221 4330.

In the UK and Ireland

Blackwell's Map and Travel Shop 53 Broad St, Oxford OX1 3BQ ☏01865/333604, ⊛www.bookshop.blackwell.co.uk.
Daunt Books 83 Marylebone High St, London W1M 3DE ☏020/7224 2295; 193 Haverstock Hill London NW3 4QL ☏020/7794 4006.
Easons Bookshop 40 O'Connell St, Dublin 1 ☏01/873 3811, ⊛www.eason.ie.
Heffers Map and Travel 20 Trinity St, Cambridge CB2 1TJ ☏01223/568568, ⊛www.heffers.co.uk. Mail order available.
The Map Shop 30a Belvoir St, Leicester, LE1 6QH ☏0116/247 1400. Mail order available.
National Map Centre 22–24 Caxton St, London SW1H 0QU ☏020/7222 2466, ⊛www.mapsnmc.co.uk.
Newcastle Map Centre 55 Grey St, Newcastle upon Tyne NE1 6EF ☏0191/261 5622, ⊛www.traveller.ltd.uk.
Stanfords 12–14 Long Acre, London WC2E 9LP ☏020/7836 1321, ⊛www.stanfords.co.uk. Maps for mail order available from this store and at ✉sales@stanfords.co.uk. Other branches within British Airways offices at 156 Regent St, London W1B 5SN ☏020/7434 4744; and 29 Corn St, Bristol BS1 1HT ☏0117/929 9966.
The Travel Bookshop 13–15 Blenheim Crescent, London W11 2EE ☏020/7229 5260, ⊛www.thetravelbookshop.co.uk.

Health and insurance

No vaccinations are required for entry into Britain. Citizens of all EU countries and those with a reciprocal health care agreement with this country are entitled to free medical treatment at National Health Service hospitals. If you don't fall into either of these categories, you will be charged for all medical services, in which case health insurance is strongly advised. Even though EU health care privileges apply in England, visitors from elsewhere in the EU would do well to take out an insurance policy before travelling to cover against theft, loss and illness or injury.

Pharmacies and medical emergencies

Pharmacists (known as chemists in

England) can dispense only a limited range of drugs without a doctor's prescription. Most pharmacies are open standard shop hours, though in large towns some may stay open as late as 10pm – local newspapers carry lists of late-opening pharmacies. **Doctor**'s surgeries tend to be open from about 9am to noon and then for a couple of hours in the evenings; outside surgery hours, you can turn up at the casualty department of the local hospital for complaints that require immediate attention.

For medical advice by phone you can call **NHS Direct** (☎0845/4647, ⊛www.nhsdirect .nhs.uk), who also run an increasing number of drop-in centres (usually 7.30am–9pm) in the bigger towns and cities. In an **emergency**, call for an ambulance on ☎999.

Insurance policies

Before spending out on a new policy, it's worth checking whether you are already covered: some all-risks home **insurance policies**, for example, may cover your possessions against loss or theft when overseas, and many private medical schemes include cover when abroad, including baggage loss, cancellation or curtailment and cash replacement as well as sickness or accident. **Canadians** will find that they are usually covered by their provincial health plans, while holders of official student /teacher/youth cards in Canada and the US are entitled to be reimbursed for accident coverage and hospital in-patient benefits. **Students** will often find that their student health coverage extends during the vaca-

tions and for one term beyond the date of last enrolment. Some bank and credit cards include certain levels of medical or other insurance and you may automatically get travel insurance if you use a major credit card to pay for your trip.

After exhausting the possibilities above, you might want to contact a specialist **travel insurance company**, or consider the travel insurance deal we offer (see below). A typical travel insurance policy usually provides cover for the loss of baggage, tickets and – up to a certain limit – cash or cheques, as well as cancellation or curtailment of your journey. Most of them exclude so-called dangerous sports unless an extra premium is paid: in England this can mean cliff-diving, rock-climbing and mountaineering. Many policies can be chopped and changed to exclude coverage you don't need – for example, sickness and accident benefits can often be excluded or included at will. If you do take medical coverage, ascertain whether benefits will be paid as treatment proceeds or only after return home, and whether there is a 24-hour medical emergency number. When securing baggage cover, make sure that the per-article limit – typically under £500 – will cover your most valuable possession. If you need to make a claim, you should keep receipts for medicines and medical treatment, and in the event you have anything stolen, you must obtain an official statement from the police.

Rough Guide travel insurance

Rough Guides offers its own travel insurance, customized for our readers by a leading UK broker and backed by a Lloyds underwriter. It's available for anyone, of any nationality, travelling anywhere in the world.

There are two main Rough Guide insurance plans: **Essential**, for basic, no-frills cover; and **Premier** – with more generous and extensive benefits. Alternatively, you can take out **annual multi-trip insurance**, which covers you for any number of trips throughout the year (with a maximum of 60 days for any one trip). Unlike many policies, the Rough Guides schemes are calculated by the day, so if you're travelling for 27 days rather than a month, that's all you pay for. If you intend to be away for the whole year, the Adventurer policy will cover you for 365 days. Each plan can be supplemented with a "Hazardous Activities Premium" if you plan to indulge in sports considered dangerous, such as skiing, scuba-diving or trekking. Rough Guides also does good deals for older travellers, and will insure you up to any age, at prices comparable to SAGA's.

For a policy quote, call the Rough Guide Insurance Line on UK freefone ☎0800/015 09 06; US freefone ☎1-866/220 5588, or, if you're calling from elsewhere, ☎+44 1243/621 046. Alternatively, get an online quote at ⊛www.roughguides.com/insurance.

Costs, money and banks

England is an expensive place to visit. The minimum expenditure, if you're camping, or hostelling, using public transport, buying picnic food and eating in pubs and cafes, would be in the region of £30–40 a day. Couples staying at budget B&Bs, eating at unpretentious restaurants and visiting a fair number of tourist attractions are looking at around £50–60 each per day, and if you're renting a car, staying in comfortable B&Bs or hotels and eating well, budget on at least £80 each per day. Single travellers should budget on spending around 60 percent of what a couple would spend (single rooms cost more than half a double), and on any visit to London, work on the basis that you'll need an extra £15 per day to get much pleasure out of the place. For more detail on the cost of accommodation, transport and eating, see below.

Currency

Britain has so far declined to adopt the euro, preferring instead its pound sterling (£), divided into 100 pence (p). Coins come in denominations of 1p, 2p, 5p, 10p, 20p, 50p and £1 and £2. Notes are in denominations of £5, £10, £20 and £50. Very occasionally you may receive Scottish banknotes: they're legal tender throughout Britain, but you may want to get rid of them sooner rather than later as some traders may be unwilling to accept them.

Currency exchange

Banks or the larger post offices are the best places to **change money**. Every sizeable town in England has a branch of at least one of the big four high-street **banks**: Barclays, Lloyds TSB, HSBC and NatWest. **Opening hours** are generally Mon–Fri 9.30am–4.30pm, though many branches in larger towns open at 9am, close at 5.30pm and also remain open until 3 or 4pm on Saturdays. Outside banking and office hours you're best advised to go to a **bureau de change**; these are to be found in most city centres, often at train stations or airports. Try to avoid changing money or cheques in hotels, where the rates are normally the poorest on offer.

There are no exchange controls in Britain, so you can bring in as much cash as you like and change travellers' cheques up to any amount.

Travellers' cheques

The easiest and safest way to carry your money is in **travellers' cheques**, available for a small commission (normally 1 percent) from any major bank. The most commonly accepted are issued by American Express, followed by Visa and Thomas Cook. Neither American Express nor Thomas Cook will charge commission if you exchange cheques at their own offices, but banks charge around 1.5 percent commission. Keep a record of the cheques as you cash them, and you can get the value of all uncashed cheques refunded immediately if they are lost.

It pays to get a selection of denominations. Make sure to keep the purchase agreement and a record of cheque serial numbers safe and separate from the cheques themselves. In the event that cheques are lost or stolen, the issuing company will expect you to report the loss immediately; most companies claim to replace lost or stolen cheques within 24 hours.

Credit and debit cards

Credit cards can be very handy as a backup source of funds, and can be used either in ATMs or over the counter. Mastercard, Visa, American Express and Diners Club are accepted in most hotels, shops and restaurants in England, although they're less useful in the most rural areas, and smaller establishments all over the country, such as B&Bs, will often accept cash only. You may also be able to make withdrawals using your **debit card** –

your bank's international banking department should be able to advise on this.

Make sure you have a **personal identification number (PIN)** that's designed to work overseas. You'll find ATMs at most large supermarkets, train stations, motorway service areas, some petrol stations and even in some pubs and shops.

Wiring money

Having **money wired** from home through a money-wiring company (see below for contacts) is never convenient or cheap and should be considered a last resort. **Fees** depend on the country, method of payment and amount being transferred, but as an example, wiring £500 to England from the US will cost £20–35, Moneygram and Travelex (Thomas Cook) being the cheaper options.

It's also possible to have money wired directly from a bank in your home country to a bank in England, although this is somewhat less reliable because it involves two separate institutions. If you go down this route, your home bank will need the address of the branch bank where you want to pick up the money and the address and telex number of the London head office, which will act as the clearing house; money wired this way normally takes at least two working days to arrive and costs around £25 per transaction.

Money-wiring companies

Moneygram ☎0800/018 0104,
ⓦwww.moneygram.com. Money can be wired in twenty minutes from post offices in the UK; a brochure is available at post offices detailing countries where money can be sent and received.
Travelex (Thomas Cook) ☎01733/318922. The cheapest company to approach if you don't need the money on the spot as it takes up to two days to

arrive. They can also credit foreign bank accounts for the same fee (up to three days).
Western Union Money Transfer ☎0800/833 833, ⓦwww.westernunion.com. Money can be transferred in minutes, either by phone or in person from an agency; call for the nearest location.

Youth and student discounts

Various official and quasi-official youth and student ID cards soon pay for themselves in savings. Full-time students are eligible for the **International Student ID Card (ISIC)**, which entitles the bearer to special air, rail and bus fares and discounts at museums, theatres and other attractions. For Americans there's also a health benefit, providing up to $3000 in emergency medical coverage and $100 a day for 60 days in the hospital, plus a 24-hour hotline to call in the event of a medical, legal or financial emergency. The card costs $22 for Americans; CDN$16 for Canadians; A$16.50 for Australians; NZ$21 for New Zealanders; and £6 for UK residents. A university photo ID might open some doors, but is not as easily recognizable as the ISIC, although the latter is often not accepted as valid proof of age in bars and pubs.

You only have to be 26 or younger to qualify for the **International Youth Travel Card**, which costs around the same as the ISIC and carries the same benefits. Teachers qualify for the **International Teacher Card**, for the same rates and deal. All these cards are available in the US from Council Travel, STA, Travel CUTS and, in Canada, Hostelling International (see pp.13 and 33 for addresses); in Australia and New Zealand they are available from STA or Campus Travel; and in the UK from Usit Campus and STA.

Several other travel organizations and accommodation groups also sell their own cards, good for various discounts.

Getting around

As you'd expect of such a small and densely populated country, just about every place in England is accessible by train or bus. However, costs are among the highest in Europe – London's commuters spend more on getting to work than any of their European counterparts – while cross-country travel can eat up a large part of your budget. It pays to plan ahead and make sure you're aware of all the passes and special deals on offer – note that some are only available outside England and must be purchased before you arrive. It's often cheaper to drive yourself around the country, though fuel and car rental costs again are among the highest in Europe and will seem prohibitive to North Americans. Congestion around the main cities can be bad, and even the motorways (notoriously the M25, London's orbital road) are liable to sporadic gridlocks, especially on public holidays when what seems like half the population takes to the roads

By train

In the recent past the **rail network** has suffered a foolhardy privatization process and a chronic under-investment, resulting in a severe decline in services. With the track and stations owned by Railtrack and the trains and services run by a tangle of private companies, there's no little confusion when it comes to trying to figure out routes and prices. The train disasters at Paddington in 1999 and Hatfield in 2000 did nothing to bolster public confidence and caused passengers to run for their cars, but have at least resulted in a major overhaul of the tracks.

After a disastrous few months, most trains once more run more-or-less to schedule (except on Sundays when maintenance work takes place) and it's fair to say that there are but a few major towns that cannot be reached by rail. Travelling across the country, however, can be a bit of a lengthy business, involving connections with several different services, but main-line routes out of London are fast – York and Exeter for instance can be reached in two hours.

You can buy **tickets** at the train station on the day of travel, but it should hardly come as a surprise to find that booking as far ahead as possible ensures the cheapest fares – or that travelling most places on a Friday, or just turning up at the station to buy a ticket, are the most expensive ways to go. In all instances, an essential first call is National Rail Enquiries (see rail contacts, below), which can advise on booking, routes

and services throughout the country. Credit-card **bookings** are made through the privatized rail companies; if you're booking three or more days in advance, you can do this through any of the companies, otherwise you will need to contact the network which covers the station you depart from. National Rail Enquiries will supply the necessary contact name and number.

At the time of going to press, there were four types of **reduced-fare ticket** – Saver, SuperSaver, SuperAdvanced and Apex – all with byzantine restrictions which are often different from route to route and company to company (for instance, it's often cheaper to travel return from the north to London, rather than from London to the north). **Apex** tickets are issued in limited numbers on certain intercity journeys of 150 miles or more, and have to be booked at least 7 days before travelling; a seat reservation is included with the ticket. To give you an idea of the differing fares, using the London–Manchester service as an example, an open return fare costs £164, a Saver £49, a SuperSaver £47 and an Apex £30, with special deals bringing the fare as low as £10 at certain times of the year. For all special-offer tickets you should book as far in advance as you possibly can – many Apex tickets are sold out weeks before the travel date.

Children aged 5–15 inclusive pay half the adult fare on most journeys – but there are no discounts on Apex tickets. Under-5s travel free, although they are not entitled to a seat.

At weekends and on public holidays, many long-distance services have a special deal whereby you can convert your second-class ticket to a first-class one by buying a **first-class supplement**, which costs between £5 and £15 and is well worth paying if you're facing a five-hour journey on a popular route – every Brit has a horror story about having to stand all the way from London to Newcastle in a smelly second-class carriage.

If the station's ticket office is closed – which is likely at rural stations at weekends – or does not have a vending machine, you may buy your ticket on the train. Otherwise, boarding without a ticket will render you liable to paying the full fare to your destination.

Rail passes

For foreign visitors who anticipate covering a lot of ground around Britain, a rail pass is a wise investment. The **BritRail Classic Pass**, which must be bought before you enter the country, is available from the companies listed below and many specialist tour operators outside Britain (see pp.14 & 15). It gives unlimited travel in England, Scotland and Wales for eight days ($265), fifteen days ($400), twenty-two days ($505) or one month ($600). The **BritRail Flexipass** is good for travel on four days out of one month ($235), eight days out of two months ($340), or fifteen days out of two months ($515). Note that with both these passes there are discounts for those under 25 (BritRail Youth passes) or over 60 (BritRail Senior passes). The **BritRail Pass'n'Drive** allows unlimited train travel for three days plus two days car rental within a two-month period and costs from $257.50 for two adults, depending on the type of car. Up to five additional car days can be added.

Other passes include the **BritRail Family Pass** – buy one of the special passes listed above (such as the Flexipass) and one accompanying child gets a pass of the same type free, other children getting the appropriate pass at half price. There's also a **BritRail SouthEast Pass**, which works like the standard Flexipass, but coverage is limited to the southeast counties. The SouthEast Pass comes in three sizes – valid for three days out of eight ($74), five days out of eight ($105) and seven days out of fifteen ($142). For unlimited bus and Tube travel in the capital, there's the **London Visitor Travelcard**

($32 for three days, $42 for four days, $63 for a week).

Some passes are available only in Britain itself. The **Young Person's Railcard** costs £18 and is available to full-time students and those aged between 16 and 25 and gives a third off all standard, Saver, Supersaver and day-return fares. A **Senior Citizens' Rail Card**, also £18 and offering the same discounts, is available to those aged 60 or over. Families would do well to make use of the **Family Railcard**, which costs £20 and covers up to four adults who are entitled to a 33 percent discount, and up to four children who travel on a 60 percent reduction of the child's full fare. Up to four adults and four children can travel on a **Network Card** which costs £20 and applies to off-peak services throughout London and the south (including Oxford, Cambridge and all the Home Counties). Adults travel at a 34 percent discount and children for a flat fare of £1.

If you are planning to travel widely around Europe by train, then it may be worth while buying a **Eurail Pass**, though this is unlikely to pay for itself if you stick to England alone. The pass, which must be purchased before arrival in Europe, allows unlimited free train travel in the UK and sixteen other countries. The **Eurail Youthpass** (for under-26s) costs $388 for fifteen days, $499 for twenty-one days, or $623 for one month; if you're 26 or over you'll have to buy a first-class pass, available in fifteen-day ($554), twenty-one-day ($718), and one-month ($890) versions. You stand a better chance of getting your money's worth out of a **Eurail Flexipass**, which is valid for a certain number of travel days in a two-month period. This, too, comes in under-26/first-class versions: ten days, costing $458/$654, and $599/$862 for fifteen days.

Rail information and enquiries

In the US and Canada

BritRail Travel International ☎ 1-888/BRITRAIL or 212/490-6688, ⊛ www.raileurope.com. All rail passes, rail-drive and multi-country passes and tickets for Eurotunnel. Also sells ferry tickets across the Channel.
Europrail International Inc. ☎ 1/888-667-9734, ⊛ www.europrail.net. Specializes in Eurail and other rail passes.

Online Travel ☎1-800/660-5300 or 847/318-8890, ⊛www.eurorail.com. Eurail and Britrail passes.
Rail Europe US ☎1-800/438-7245, Canada ☎1-800/361-7245, ⊛www.raileurope.com/us. Official Eurail Pass agent in North America.

In Australia and New Zealand

Rail Plus Australia ☎1300/555 003 or 03/9642 8644, ⊕ info@railplus.com.au; New Zealand ☎09/303 2484. Sells Eurail and Britrail passes.
Trailfinders Australia ☎02/9247 7666. Sells Eurail passes.

In the UK

National Rail Enquiries ☎08457/48 49 50, ⊛www.rail.co.uk. For all timetable and fare information in the UK. Calls are charged at local rates and are usually answered very promptly.

By bus and coach

Inter-town bus services (known as **coaches** in England) duplicate many rail routes, very often at half the price of the train or less. The frequency of service is often comparable to rail, and in some instances the difference in journey time isn't great enough to be a deciding factor; buses are comfortable, and the ones on longer routes often have drinks and sandwiches available on board. There's a plethora of regional companies operating buses and coaches, but by far the biggest national operator is **National Express**, whose network extends to every corner of the country. With rail prices becoming exorbitant, National Express services are so popular that for busy routes, and on any route at weekends and during holidays, it's advisable to book ahead, rather than just turn up.

Local bus services are run by a bewildering array of companies, most private, a few not. In many cases, timetables and routes are well integrated, but it's increasingly the case that private companies duplicate the busiest routes in an attempt to undercut the commercial opposition, leaving the farther-flung spots neglected. Thus, if you want to get from one end of a big English city to another, you'll probably have a choice of buses all offering cut-price fares, but to get out into the suburbs or to a satellite village, you may have to wait several hours. As a rule, the further away from urban areas you get, the less frequent and more expensive bus services become, but there are very few rural areas which aren't served by at least the occasional privately owned minibus.

National and local bus enquiries

Local bus information and hotline numbers are listed throughout the *Guide*, but for the latest details contact one of the following:
Traveline ☎0870/608 2 608,
⊛www.traveline.org.uk. Phone enquries daily 7am–9pm. A new, and very useful service, that can give you the latest details on all national and local services throughout the country.
National Express ☎0870/580 8080,
⊛www.gobycoach.com. For inter-town and city connections.

Bus passes

UK residents in full-time education, under 25 or over 50 can buy a **National Express Discount Coach Card**, which costs £9, is valid for a year and entitles the holder to a 30 percent discount. Foreign travellers of any age can purchase a **Tourist Trail Pass**, which offers unlimited travel on the National Express network for two days within three (£39 for students and under-23s, otherwise £49), five days within thirty (£69/£85), eight days within thirty (£99/£135) or fifteen days within thirty (£145/£190). In England you can obtain both passes from major travel agents, at Gatwick and Heathrow airports, at the Britain Visitor Centre (see p.20), and at the main National Express at Victoria Coach Station, London. In North America these passes are available for the dollar equivalent through specialist tour operators or direct from British Travel Associates, PO Box 299, Elkton, VA 22827 ☎1-800/327-6097.

Post Bus Network

Many rural areas not covered by other forms of public transport are served by the **Post Bus Network**, which operates minibuses carrying mail and about eight fare-paying passengers. They set off in the morning – usually around 8am from the main post office – and collect mail from (or deliver it to) the outlying regions. It's a cheap way to travel (£2–4/journey), and can be a convenient way of getting to hidden-away B&Bs, and even round the M25, although it is often excruciatingly slow. You can get a free booklet of routes and timetables from the Royal

Mail, Road Transport Consultancy, Room BT 20/3rd Floor, Rowland Hill House, Boythorpe Road, Chesterfield S49 1HQ (☎0845/774 0740 or 01246/546329, ⊛www.royalmail .com/postbus).

"Jump-On-Jump-Off" minibus and guided tours

A popular service pitched at budget travellers and backpackers is the "**Jump-On-Jump-Off**" **minibus** run by the Stray company. Starting in London, it travels three days each week in a clockwise direction around England, Wales and Scotland via Windsor, Bath, Snowdonia, Liverpool, The Lakes, Edinburgh, York, Stratford and Oxford before heading back to the capital. Tickets cost £139, and are valid for for up to 4 months. There is also a shorter trip from London to Liverpool (£99). You can use this bus as a "Jump-On-Jump-Off" option or as a six-day **guided tour**, either arranging accommodation (average price £10/night) along the way yourself or letting the company do the hard work for you. Contact Stray, 171 Earls Court Rd, Earls Court, London SW5 9RF (☎020/7373 7737, ⊛www .straytravel.com).

In addition to the "Jump-On-Jump-Off" buses, several companies offer **organized bus tours** of the country

Bus tour operators

Road Trip 501 International House, 223 Regent St, London W1B 2EB ☎0800/056 0505, ⊛www .roadtrip.co.uk. Runs weekend and five-day tours from April to mid-November, with accommodation, meals and entrance fees thrown in. Weekend trips (£99) cover Cornwall, Dartmoor, the Lake District, York and Sherwood Forest; and the five-day tours (£199) explore either York, Liverpool, Snowdonia and the Cotswolds or the southwest, from Wiltshire to Cornwall.
Trafalgar 22 Craven Terrace, London W2 3QH ☎020/7574 7444, ⊛www.trafalgar.com. Offers round coach trips from London; four-day trips covering York, Edinburgh and Chester run all year and cost from £240. From late April to mid-September their five-day tours (from £295) also pack in Cornwall.
Gareloch House 6 Gareloch Rd, Port Glasgow, PA14 5XH ☎0870/514 3433, ⊛www .insightvacations.com. Put on four-day tours as far as Edinburgh (year round), with seven-day tours from London of the south of England, taking in Dartmoor, North Devon and the Cotswolds (April–Oct); and up to Glasgow via Bristol, the Cotswolds and the Lake District (March–Dec). Both tours cost from £499.

By car

In order to **drive** in England you need a current full **driving licence**. If you're bringing your own vehicle into the country you should also carry your **vehicle registration** or **ownership document** at all times. Furthermore, you must be **adequately insured**: check your existing insurance policy.

In England you **drive on the left**, a situation which can lead to a few tense days of acclimatization for overseas drivers. Speed limits are 30–40mph (50–65kph) in built-up areas, 70mph (110kph) on motorways and dual carriageways (freeways) and 50mph (80kph) on most other roads. As a rule, assume that in any area with street lighting the speed limit is 30mph (50kph) unless otherwise stated.

Fuel is expensive compared to North American prices – unleaded petrol (gasoline) and diesel cost in the region of 77p per litre, leaded 4-star 80p. The lowest prices of all are charged at out-of-town supermarkets; suburban service stations are usually fairly reasonable; and the highest prices are charged by motorway stations.

The AA (Automobile Association), RAC (Royal Automobile Club) and Green Flag all operate **24-hour emergency breakdown**. The first two also provide many other motoring services, including a reciprocal arrangement for free assistance through many overseas motoring organizations – check the situation with your own association before setting out. For emergency help the AA and RAC can be called from roadside booths on motorways; elsewhere ring ☎0800/887766 for the AA, ☎0800/828282 for the RAC and ☎0800/400600 for Green Flag. You can make use of these emergency services if you are not a member of the organizations, but you will be required to join at the roadside and you will incur a hefty surcharge as well.

Car **parking** in cities and in popular tourist spots can be a nightmare and will also cost you a small fortune. If you're in a tourist city for a day, look out for the **Park-and-Ride schemes** where you can park your car a short way out and take a cheap or free bus to the centre. Parking in the long- or short-stay car parks will be cheaper than using meters, which restrict parking time to two or three hours at the most. As a rule, the smaller the town, the cheaper the parking. A yellow line along the edge of the road indicates **parking restrictions**; check the nearest sign to see exactly what they are. A double-yellow line means no parking at any time, though you can stop briefly to unload or pick up people or goods (maximum stop two minutes), but if the lines are red, that means absolutely no stopping at all.

Compared to rates in North America, **car rental** in England is expensive, and you'll probably find it cheaper to arrange things in advance through one of the multinational chains, or by opting for a fly/drive deal. If you do rent a car from a company in England, the least you can expect to pay is around £110 a week, which is the rate for a small hatchback from Thrifty; reckon on paying around £40 per day for something direct from one of the multinationals, £10 or so less at a local firm. Rental agencies prefer you to pay by credit card and you may have to leave a deposit of £100 or more on top of the rental charge. There are very few automatics at the lower end of the price scale – if you want one, you should book well ahead. To rent a car you need to show your driving licence; few companies will rent to drivers with less than one year's experience and most will only rent to people between 21 and 75 years of age.

Car rental agencies

In the US and Canada

Alamo ⓣ1-800/522-9696, ⓦwww.goalamo.com.
Avis US ⓣ1-800/331-1084, Canada ⓣ1-800/272-5871, ⓦwww.avis.com.
Budget ⓣ1-800/527-0700, ⓦwww.budgetrentacar.com.
Europe by Car ⓣ1-800/576-1590, ⓦwww.europebycar.com.
Hertz US ⓣ1-800/654–3001, Canada ⓣ1-800/263 0600, ⓦwww.hertz.com.
Kemwel Holiday Autos ⓣ1-800/422-7737, ⓦwww.kemwel.com.
National ⓣ1-800/227-7368, ⓦwww.nationalcar.com.
Thrifty ⓣ1-800/847-4389, ⓦwww.thrifty.com.

In Australia

Avis ⓣ13/6333, ⓦwww.avis.com.
Budget ⓣ1300/362 848, ⓦwww.budget.com.
Hertz ⓣ1 800/550 067, ⓦwww.hertz.com.
Thrifty ⓣ1300/367 227, ⓦwww.thrifty.com.au.

In New Zealand

Avis ⓣ09/526 5231 or 0800 655 111, ⓦwww.avis.com.
Budget ⓣ0800/ 652 227 or 09/375 2270, ⓦwww.budget.com.
Hertz ⓣ09/309 0989 or 0800 655 955, ⓦwww.hertz.com.
Thrifty ⓣ09/309 0111, ⓦwww.thrifty.com.nz.

In England

Avis ⓣ0870/606 0100, ⓦwww.avisworld.com.
Budget ⓣ0800/181181, ⓦwww.go-budget.co.uk.
Europcar ⓣ0845/722 2525, ⓦwww.europcar.co.uk.
National ⓣ0870/536 5365, ⓦwww.nationalcar.com.
Hertz ⓣ0870/844 8844, ⓦwww.hertz.co.uk.
Holiday Autos ⓣ0870/400 0000, ⓦwww.holidayautos.co.uk.
Thrifty ⓣ01494/751600, ⓦwww.thrifty.co.uk.

In Ireland

Avis Northern Ireland ⓣ0870/606 0100 or 028/9442 3333, ⓦwww.avis.co.uk; Republic of Ireland ⓣ01/605 7555, ⓦwww.avis.ie.
Budget Northern Ireland ⓣ028/9442 3332, ⓦwww.go-budget.co.uk; Republic of Ireland ⓣ01/878 7814, ⓦwww.budgetcarrental.ie.
Europcar Northern Ireland ⓣ0870/607 5000 or 028/9442 3444, ⓦwww.europcar.co.uk; Republic of Ireland ⓣ01/614 2800, ⓦwww.europcar.ie.
Hertz Northern Ireland ⓣ028/9442 2533 Republic of Ireland ⓣ0903/27711, ⓦwww.hertz.co.uk.
Holiday Autos Northern Ireland ⓣ0870/400 000, ⓦwww.holidayautos.co.uk; Republic of Ireland ⓣ01/872 9366, ⓦwww.holidayautos.ie.
Thrifty Northern Ireland ⓣ0800/973 163 or 028/9445 2565, ⓦwww.thrifty.co.uk; Republic of Ireland ⓣ1/800 575 163, ⓦwww.thrifty.ie.

Motoring organizations

In North America

American Automobile Association (AAA). ⓦwww.aa.com. Each state has its own club – check the web or the phone book for local address and phone number.
Canadian Automobile Association ⓦwww.caa.com. Each region has its own club –

check the web or the phone book for local address and phone number.

In Australia and New Zealand

Australian Automobile Association ☏ 02/6247 7311, ⓦ www.aaa.asn.au.
New Zealand Automobile Association ☏ 09/377 4660, ⓦ www.nzaa.co.nz.

In the UK and Ireland

RAC ☏ 0800/550550, ⓦ www.rac.co.uk.
AA ☏ 0800/444500, ⓦ www.theaa.com.
AA Travel ☏ 01/617 9988, ⓦ www.aaireland.ie.
Green Flag ☏ 0800/000111,
ⓦ www.directline.co.uk.

Taxis

Taxis are a useful option for finding that hostel or sight that's off the beaten track or when time is limited. Also, if you're with a group hiring a taxi can work out as cheap as taking a bus. Reckon on paying around £3 for the first mile and £1 for subsequent miles in cities, and £1.40 a mile in country districts. Black cabs are generally a little more expensive than minicabs, but are usually more reliable. You can hail a black cab on the street, but you must book minicabs by phone – we have given numbers for reliable minicab services throughout the book.

Accommodation

England has scores of upmarket hotels, ranging from bland business-oriented places to plush country mansions, as well as budget accommodation in B&Bs, guest houses and youth hostels. Nearly all tourist offices will book rooms for you, although the fee for this service can vary. In some areas you will pay a deposit that's deducted from your first night's bill (usually 10 percent), in others the office will take a percentage or flat-rate commission – on average around £3. Another useful service operated by the majority of tourist offices is the "Book-a-bed-ahead" service, which locates accommodation in your next port of call – again for a charge of about £3, though the service is sometimes free. For a full explanation of the price-coding system used in this book see the box below.

Hotels and B&Bs

To help you in your choice of accommodation, a nationwide system for grading **hotels** and **B&Bs** has been adopted in England by the tourist authorities and the various private organizations which classify accommodation. Hotels are graded by stars, with five stars being the top rank, and B&Bs by diamonds with additional gold and silver awards for those that achieve distinction.

Though there's not a hard and fast correlation between standards and price, you'll probably be paying in the region of £50–60 per night for a double room at a one-star **hotel** (breakfast included), rising to around £100 in a three-star and from around £200 for a five-star – in London you pay twice that. In some larger towns and cities you'll find that the larger hotels often offer **cut-price deals** on Saturdays and Sundays to fill the rooms vacated by the week's busi-

---

Accommodation price codes

Throughout this guide, hotel and B&B accommodation is priced on a scale of ❶ to ❾, the number indicating the lowest price you could expect to pay per night in that establishment for a double room in high season. The prices indicated by the codes are as follows:

❶ under £40	❹ £60–70	❼ £110–150
❷ £40–50	❺ £70–90	❽ £150–200
❸ £50–60	❻ £90–110	❾ over £200

ness trade, but these places tend to be soulless multinational chain operations. If you have money to throw around, stay in a nicely refurbished old building – the historic towns of England are chock-full of top-quality old coaching inns and similar ancient hostelries, while out in the countryside there are numerous converted mansions and manor houses, often with brilliant restaurants attached.

At the lower end of the scale, it's sometimes difficult to differentiate between a hotel and a **B&B**. At their most basic, these typically English places – often known also as **guest houses** in resorts and other tourist towns – are ordinary private houses with a couple of bedrooms set aside for paying guests and a dining room for the consumption of a rudimentary breakfast. At their best, however, B&Bs offer rooms as well furnished as those in hotels costing twice as much, delicious home-prepared breakfasts and an informal hospitality that a larger place couldn't match. As a guideline on costs, you should be able to find a one-diamond place for under £40 per night for a double room and, though the sky is the limit at the top end of the scale, it is possible to stay in some four-diamond places for as little as £70 – farmhouse B&Bs are especially good value. As many B&Bs, even the pricier ones, have a very small number of rooms, you should certainly book a place as far in advance as possible, especially if you're travelling on your own. Finally, don't assume that a B&B is no good if it's ungraded. There are so many B&Bs in England that the grading inspectors can't possibly keep track of them all, and in the rural backwaters some of the most enjoyable accommodation is to be found in welcoming and beautifully set houses whose facilities may technically fall short of official standards.

Hostels, student halls and camping barns

The **Youth Hostels Association** (**YHA**), affiliated to Hosteling International (HI), has over 230 properties in England and Wales, offering bunk-bed accommodation in single-sex dormitories or smaller rooms of four to six beds. A few new hostels and many refurbished older ones also now have double and family rooms available, and in cities the facilities are often every bit as good as some

hotels. Indeed, although a few places are spartan establishments of the sort traditionally associated with the wholesome, fresh-air ethic of the first hostels, most have moved well away from the old-fashioned, institutional ambience, and boast cafés, laundry facilities, internet access, entertainment and bike rental.

Visitors who belong to any HI association have automatic membership of the YHA; if you aren't a member of such an organization, you can join through the YHA by writing to their head office (address below) or in person at any YHA-affiliated hostel. **Membership** costs £6.25 per year for under-18s, £12.50 for others.

Prices at most English youth hostels are around £7 per night for under-18s and £10 for the over-18s. Students aged 18–25 can get a £1 reduction on production of a valid student card. Length of stay is normally unlimited and the hostel warden will provide a linen sleeping bag for a small charge. The cost of hostel **meals** is low: breakfast is £3.30, a packed lunch £2.90 or £3.80, and evening meals start at £4.90. Nearly all hostels have kitchen facilities for those who prefer self-catering.

At any time of year it's best to **book your place** well in advance, and it's essential at Easter, from May to August and at Christmas. Most hostels accept payment by Mastercard or Visa; with those that don't, you should confirm your booking in writing, with payment, at least seven days before arrival. Bookings made less than seven days in advance will be held only until 6pm on the day of arrival. If you're tempted to turn up on the spur of the moment, bear in mind that very few are open year-round, many are closed at least one day a week, even in high season, and several have periods during which they take bookings from groups only. We have indicated the months during which individual hostels are closed, but to give the full details of opening times within this guide would be impossibly unwieldy, so always phone to check – we've given the number for every hostel mentioned. Most hostels are closed from 10am to 5pm, with an 11.30pm curfew, although all seven of the London hostels offer 24-hour access.

At best, **independent hostels**, which are more likely to be found in town centres than in the backwoods, offer facilities commensurate with those of YHA places, and at a lower price. However, many of these hostels make their money by over-cramming their rooms with beds, kitchens are often inadequate or non-existent and washing facilities can be similarly poor. That said, a lot of people find the lack of curfews and lockouts ample compensation. A useful publication to have is the annually updated *Independent Hostel Guide* (£4.95), published by The Backpackers Press.

Some cities also have **YMCA** and **YWCA** hostels, though these are only worth considering if you're staying for at least a week, in which case you can get discounts on rates that otherwise are no better than budget B&Bs.

In England's university towns you should be able to find out-of-term accommodation in the **student halls**, usually one-bedded rooms either with their own or shared bathrooms. In some instances, this may be the only budget accommodation on offer in the centre of town. All the useful university addresses are given in the *Guide*, but if you want a list of everything that's on offer, contact Venuemasters (The Work Station, Paternoster Row, Sheffield, S1 2BX ☎0114/249 3090, ⓦwww.venuemasters. co.uk).

In the wilder parts of England, such as the north Pennines, North Yorkshire, Dartmoor and Exmoor, the YHA also administers some basic accommodation for walkers in **camping barns**. Holding up to twenty people, these agricultural outbuildings are often unheated and are very sparsely furnished, with wooden sleeping platforms – or bunks if you're lucky – a couple of tables, a toilet and a cold-water supply, but they are weatherproof, extremely good value (from £4/night) and perfectly situated for walking tours. You do not have to be a YHA member to stay in any of these. Similar barns, often called **bunkhouses**, are run by private individuals in these areas – the useful ones are mentioned in the *Guide*.

Youth Hostel Associations

USA

Hostelling International–American Youth Hostels (HI-AYH) 733 15th St NW, Suite 840, Washington, DC 20005 ☎202/783 6161, ⓦwww.hiayh.org.

Canada

Hostelling International–Canadian Hostelling Association Suite 400, 205 Catherine St, Ottawa, ON K2P 1C3 ☎613/237-7884 or 800/663-5777, ⓦwww.hostellingti.ca.

Australia

Australian Youth Hostels Association Level 3, 10 Mallet St, Camperdown, NSW 2050 ☎02/9565 1699, ⓦwww.yha.org.au.

New Zealand

Youth Hostels Association of New Zealand PO Box 436, Christchurch 1 ☎03/379 9970, ⓦwww.yha.co.nz.

England and Wales

Youth Hostels Association (YHA) Trevelyan House, 8 St Stephen's Hill, St Albans, Herts AL1 2DY ☎0870/870 8808, ⓦwww.yha.org.uk.

Scotland

Scottish Youth Hostel Association 7 Glebe Crescent, Stirling FK8 2JA ☎0870/155 3255, ⓦwww.syha.org.uk.

Ireland

An Oige 61 Mountjoy St, Dublin 7 ☎01/830 4555, ⓦwww.irelandyha.org.
Youth Hostel Association of Northern Ireland 22 Donegal Rd, Belfast BT12 5JN ☎01232/324733, ⓦwww.hini.org.

Camping and caravanning

There are hundreds of **campsites** in England, charging from £5 per tent per night to around £12 for the plushest sites, with amenities such as laundries, shops and sports facilities. Some YHA hostels have small campsites on their property, charging half the indoor overnight fee. In addition to these official sites, farmers may offer pitches for as little as £3 per night, but don't expect tiled bathrooms and hair dryers for that kind of money. Even farmers without a reserved camping area may let you pitch in a field if you ask first, possibly for free; setting up a tent without asking is an act of trespass, which will not be well received. Free camping is illegal in national parks and nature reserves.

The problem with many campsites in the most popular parts of rural England – especially the West Country coast – is that tents have to share the space with **caravans**.

Every summer the country's byways are clogged by migrations of these cumbersome trailers, which are still far more numerous than camper vans in England. The great majority of caravans, however, are permanently moored at their sites, where they are rented out to families for self-catering holidays, and the ranks of nose-to-tail trailers in the vicinity of most of England's best beaches might make you think that half the population of Britain shacks up in a caravan for the midsummer break.

Detailed, annually revised guides to England's camping and caravan sites include the British Tourist Authority's *Caravan and Camping Parks in Britain* (£5.99), which lists graded sites, and Cade's *Camping, Touring and Motor Caravan Site Guide* (£4.99), published by Marwain.

Self-catering accommodation

There are thousands of BTA-approved properties for rent by the week, ranging from city penthouses to secluded cottages. The least you can expect to pay for four-berth self-catering accommodation in low season would be around £120 per week, but in summer for something attractive – such as a small house near the West Country moors – you should budget for around £400 upwards.

Every regional tourist board has details of cottage rentals in its area; alternatively get hold of a copy of *Self Catering Holiday Homes: Where to Stay in England* (£7.99) published by the English Tourist Board.

Alternative sources of information on all types of self-catering accommodation, from canal boats to lighthouses, are *Dalton's Weekly* (available from most newsagents) and the Sunday newspapers; and of course most English travel agents can offer a range of self-catering holiday packages.

Self-catering accommodation firms

Country Holidays ☎ 0870/072 3723, ⊛ www.country-holidays.co.uk. More than three thousand properties all over England.

English Country Cottages ☎ 0870/585 1100, ⊛ www.english-country-cottages.co.uk. Around two thousand cottages in various parts of rural England.

Hoseasons Country Cottages ☎ 01502/501515, ⊛ www.hoseasons.co.uk. Wide range of cottages throughout the country.

Landmark Trust ☎ 01628/825925, ⊛ www.landmarktrust.co.uk. Their brochure (£9.50) lists around one hundred and sixty converted historic properties, ranging from restored forts and Martello towers to a tiny radio shack used in the last war.

National Trust (Enterprises) Ltd
☎ 01225/791199. Around 250 NT-owned cottages and farmhouses, most set in their own gardens or grounds.

Rural Retreats ☎ 01386/701177, ⊛ www.ruralretreats.co.uk. Upmarket accommodation in restored old buildings, many of them listed.

Vivat Trust ☎ 0207/930 8030, ⊛ www.vivat.org.uk. Small, select range of historic properties in Shropshire, Dorset, Cumbria and Derbyshire – including North Lees Hall, Charlotte Brontë's inspiration for Mr Rochester's Thornfield Hall in *Jane Eyre*.

Food and drink

Though the English still tend to regard eating as a functional necessity rather than a focal point of the day, great advances towards a more sophisticated appreciation of the culinary arts have been made in recent years; new restaurants offering Modern British cuisine – in effect anything inventive – proliferate. Every major town has its top-class restaurant, while it's also possible to eat well and inexpensively thanks chiefly to the influence of England's various immigrant communities. However, the pub will long remain the centre of social life in England, a drink in a traditional "local" often making the best introduction to the life of a town.

Restaurant price codes

Restaurants listed in this guide have been assigned one of four price categories:

Inexpensive under £10   Expensive £20–30
Moderate £10–20   Very Expensive over £30

This is the price you can expect to pay per person for a three-course meal or equivalent, excluding
drinks and service. Listed restaurants take credit cards unless otherwise stated.

Eating

In many hotels and B&Bs you'll be offered
what's termed an **"English breakfast"**,
which is basically sausage, bacon and eggs
plus tea and toast. This used to be the typical working-class start to the day, but these
days the English have adopted the healthier
cereal alternative, and most places will give
you this option as well. In any town you
won't have to walk far to find a so-called
"greasy spoon" or **"caff"**, where the early-
day menu will include cholesterol-rich variations on the theme of sausage, beans, fried
egg and chips.

For most overseas visitors the quintessential English meal is **fish and chips**, a dish
that can vary from the succulently fresh to
the indigestibly oily – in many fish-and-chip
joints it's little wonder that lashings of salt,
vinegar and tomato ketchup or the fruitier
brown sauce are common additions. The
classier places have tables, but more often
they serve **takeaway** (takeout) food only,
supplying a wooden fork so that you can
guzzle your roadside meal with a modicum
of decorum. Fish-and-chip shops can be
found on most high streets and main suburban thoroughfares, although in larger towns
they're beginning to be outnumbered by
pizza places, **curry houses** and **burger**
outlets.

Other sources of straightforward food at
lunchtime and early evening are the "greasy
spoon" places mentioned above (which tend
to close at around 6–7pm), and **pubs** (which
often stop serving food at 9pm), where you'll
find plain "meat-and-two-veg" dishes: steak-
and-kidney pie, chops or steaks, accompanied by boiled potatoes, carrots or some
such vegetable. However, a lot of English
pubs now take their food very seriously
indeed, having separate dining areas and
menus that can compete with some of the
better mid-range restaurants. Another recent
development is the growing number of specialist **vegetarian** restaurants, especially in
the larger towns, and the increasing awareness of vegetarian preferences in other eating places. Also on the rise in the major
towns are vaguely French **brasseries**, informal bar/restaurants offering simple meals
from around £10–12 per head and often with
a set lunchtime menu for around half that.

England has its diverse immigrant communities to thank for the range of foods in the
mid-range category. Of the innumerable
types of ethnic restaurants offering the
good-value high-quality meals you'll find
Chinese, **Indian** and **Bangladeshi** specialities in every town of any size (with take-away
options usually available), the widest choice
being in London and the industrial cities of
the Midlands and the north. If you're looking
for a meal late at night, these are your most
likely options. **Thai, Indonesian** and **North
African** are now becoming more widespread, but are generally a shade more
expensive, while farther up the economic
scale there's no shortage of **French** and
Italian places – by far the most popular
European cuisines, though most cities have
their share of more-or-less **Spanish** tapas
bars. **Japanese** food has been one of the
success stories of recent years, with diners
and sushi places joining the expense-
account restaurants that have been established for some time in the business centres
of England.

The ranks of England's **gastronomic
restaurants** grow with each passing year,
with cordon-bleu chefs producing high-class
French-style dishes, California-influenced
menus, internationalist hybrid creations and
traditional English meat- and fish-dishes that
are as delicious as the more arty creations of
their cross-Channel counterparts.

London of course has the highest concentration of top-flight places, but wherever
you are in England you're never more than
half an hour's drive from a really good meal
– some of the very best dining rooms are to

be found in the countryside hotels. The problem is that fine food costs more in England than it does anywhere else in Europe. If a place has any sort of reputation in foodie circles you're unlikely to be spending less than £30 per head, and for the services of the country's glamour chefs you could be paying a preposterous £120.

Our restaurant listings include a mix of high-quality and good-value establishments, but if you're intent on a culinary pilgrimage, you would do well to arm yourself with a copy of the *Which Good Food Guide* (£15.99), which is updated annually and includes nearly 1300 detailed recommendations. Throughout this book, we've supplied the phone number for all restaurants where you may need to book a table. We've also coded restaurants from "Inexpensive" to "Very Expensive"; for details of what this means, see the box on p.35.

Drinking

The combination of an inclement climate and an English temperamental aversion to casual chat makes the simple **café** a rare phenomenon outside the biggest cities – there are probably more in London's Soho and surrounding area than in the rest of the country combined. **Coffee shops**, however, have made inroads into the high streets and a growing number of pubs are happy to serve tea and coffee during the day. All tourist towns sport an abundance of **tea shops**, unlicensed establishments where the normal procedure is to order a slice of cake or some other pastry with your tea or coffee – the former is far more popular. Increasingly common in the big cities are **brasseries** or equivalent establishments (see p.35), where the majority of customers are there for a bite to eat, but where you're generally welcome to spend half an hour nursing a cappuccino or a glass of wine.

Nothing is likely to dislodge the **pub** from its status as the great English social institution, however. Originating as wayfarers' hostelries and coaching inns, pubs have outlived the church and marketplace as the focal points of English communities, and at their best they can be as welcoming as the full name – "public house" – suggests. Pubs are as varied as the country's townscapes: in larger market towns you'll find huge oak-beamed inns with open fires and polished

brass fittings; in the remoter upland villages there are stone-built pubs no larger than a two-bedroomed cottage; and in the more inward-looking parts of industrial England you'll come across no-nonsense pubs where something of the old division of the sexes and classes still holds sway – the "spit and sawdust" public bar is where working men can bond over a pint or two; the plusher saloon bar, with a separate entrance, is the preferred haunt of mutually preoccupied couples, the middle classes and unaccompanied women. Whatever the species of pub, its **opening hours** are daily 11am–11pm (but in quieter spots, pubs tend to close between about 3 and 5.30pm).

Most pubs are owned by large breweries who favour their own **beers** and **lagers**, as well as some "guest beers", all dispensed by the pint or half-pint. (A pint costs anything from around £1.50 to £2.70, depending on the brew and the locale of the pub.) The most widespread type of English beer is **bitter**, an uncarbonated and dark beverage that should be pumped by hand from the cellar and served at room temperature. (The sweeter, darker "mild" beer is now virtually extinct.) In recent years, boosted by aggressive advertising, **lager** has overtaken beer in popularity, and every pub will have at least two brands on offer, but the major breweries are now capitalizing on a backlash against foreign-sounding, pale, chilly and often tasteless drinks, a reaction in large part due to the work of **CAMRA** (Campaign for Real Ale; Ⓦwww.camra.org.uk). Some of the beer touted as good English ale is nothing of the sort (if the stuff comes out of an electric pump, it isn't the real thing), and some of the genuine beers have been adulterated since being taken over by the big companies, but the big breweries do widely distribute some very good beers – for example, Directors, produced by the giant Courage group, is a very classy strong bitter. Guinness, a very dark, creamy Irish stout, is also on sale virtually everywhere, and is an exception to the high-minded objection to electrically pumped beers – though purists will tell you that the stuff the English drink does not compare with the home variety.

Smaller operations whose fine ales are available over a wide area include Young's, Fuller's, Wadworth's, Adnams, Greene King, Hook Norton and Marston's. However, if you want to find out how good English beer can be, sample the products of the innumerable small breweries producing real ales to traditional recipes – every region has its distinctive brew. These regional concoctions are frequently available at free houses, independently run establishments that sell what they please and are generally more characterful than so-called "tied pubs". If you see a CAMRA sticker on the window, the beer inside is certainly worth a try, but for serious research the *Good Beer Guide* (£11.99), published annually by CAMRA, is essential. Also useful is the annual *Good Pub Guide* (Ebury Press; £14.99), a thousand-page handbook that rates each pub's ambience and food as well as its beer.

Cider, the fermented produce of apples, is a sweet, alcoholic beverage produced in the West Country, where it's often preferred to

beer. The cider sold in pubs all over England is a fizzy drink that only approximates to the far more potent and less refined **scrumpy**, the type of cider consumed by aficionados of the apple. As with beer, the best scrumpy is available within a short radius of the factory, but the drink has nothing like the variety of beer.

Wines sold in pubs are generally appalling, a strange situation in view of the excellent range of wine available in off-licences and supermarkets. The wine lists in brasseries and **wine bars** are nearly always better, but the mark-ups are often outrageous, and any members of the party who prefer beer will have to be content with the bottled variety. Nonetheless, many people are prepared to pay the extra in return for a less boozy, less male-dominated atmosphere.

Communications

You should experience no problems with communications either within the country or from abroad; the only difficulty being queues at the post office. The mail service is quick and generally efficient, public payphones are numerous, and the outlets offering internet access are ever increasing.

Phones

Most public **payphones** are operated by BT and, at least in the towns, are widespread. Many payphones take all coins from 10p upwards (minimum payment 20p), although an increasing proportion only accept **phonecards**, available from post offices and newsagents which display BT's green logo. These cards come in denominations of £3, £5, £10 and £20; many phones also accept **credit cards**.

Inland calls are cheapest at weekends and between 6pm and 8am on weekdays. Reduced rate periods for most **international calls** are 6pm–8am from Monday to Friday and all day Saturday and Sunday. A cheaper way to call is from one of the number of **independent telecom centres**, though you're likely to find these only in the major cities.

Throughout the *Guide*, every English telephone number is prefixed by the area code, separated from the subscriber number by an

oblique slash, which can be omitted if dialling from within the area covered by that prefix. However, some prefixes relate to the cost of calls rather than the location of the subscriber, and should never be omitted: numbers with ☎0800, ☎0808 and ☎0500 prefixes are free of charge to the caller; ☎0845 numbers are charged at local rates and ☎0870 up to the national rate, irrespective of where in the country you are calling from in both cases. Beware of premium-rate numbers, which are common for pre-recorded information services – and usually have the prefix ☎0897 or ☎0909; these are charged at anything up to £1.50 a minute.

Mobile phones

More and more people are taking their **mobile phones** with them when they travel, but it is always worth checking with your phone provider to see if your phone will work abroad, and what the call charges will be. Unless you have a tri-band phone, it is unlikely that a mobile bought for use in the US will work outside the States and vice versa, with many only working within the region designated by the area code in the phone number i.e. 212, 415 etc. Most mobiles in Australia and New Zealand use GSM, so should work well in England, where most mobile phones use GSM, too – though it's still advisable to check with your provider before travelling.

Operator services

Domestic operator ☎100
International operator ☎155
Domestic directory assistance ☎192 (20p from payphones, otherwise 36–42p)
International directory assistance ☎153 (minimum 20p from payphones, otherwise £1.50; charged according to length of call)

International calls

To call England from overseas dial the international access code (☎011 from the US and Canada, ☎0011 from Australia and ☎00 from New Zealand) followed by 44, the area code minus its initial zero, and then the number. To dial out of England it's ☎00 followed by the country code, area code (usually without the zero if there is one) and subscriber number. Country codes are as follows:
Australia ☎61
Republic of Ireland ☎353
New Zealand ☎64
US and Canada ☎1

Email

A useful way of keeping in touch while travelling is using one of the **free internet email sites** that can be accessed from anywhere, for example YahooMail and Hotmail – accessible through ⊛www.yahoo.com and ⊛www.hotmail.com. Once you've set up an account, you can use these sites to pick up and send mail from anywhere that provides internet access – cafés, hotels, libraries, etc. You'll find **internet cafés** (£3–5/hour) in the major towns and cities; some public libraries now offer free access, but you'll need to book this in advance.

Mail

Virtually all **post offices** are open Mon–Fri 9am–5.30pm, Sat 9am–12.30 or 1pm; in small communities you'll find sub-post offices operating out of general stores, open the same hours, even if the shop itself is open for longer. **Stamps** can be bought at supermarkets and newsagents, as well as from post office counters, in books of six or twelve. A first-class stamp for **letters** and **postcards** to anywhere in the British Isles currently costs 27p and should – in theory, at least – arrive the next day; second-class costs 19p and take from two to four days. **Airmail** weighing less than 20g (0.7oz) to European countries costs 37p and elsewhere overseas from 45p for 10g, and 65p for 20g. Pre-stamped airletters conforming to overseas airmail weight limits of under 10g can be bought for 40p from post offices only. For more information about Royal Mail postal services, call ☎08457/740740.

The media

England is well served with newspapers catering to all tastes; each city produces a local journal and newsagents' shelves are stacked floor to ceiling with magazines of every description. Although the proliferation of channels has caused eyebrows to be raised, and accusations of "dumbing–down" to be hurled, British television and radio programmes still remain among the most highly regarded in the world.

Newspapers and magazines

English **daily newspapers** are predominantly right wing, with the Murdoch-owned *Times* and the staunchly Conservative *Daily Telegraph* occupying the "quality" end of the market, trailed by the *Independent*, which strives worthily to live up to its self-righteous name, and the *Guardian*, which inhabits a niche marginally to the left of centre. At the opposite end of the scale in terms of intellectual weight and volume of sales is the pernicious *Sun*, the sleaziest occupant of the Murdoch stable; its chief rivals in the sex and scandal stakes are the *Daily Star* and self-consciously ridiculous *Daily Sport*, but the only tabloid that manages anything approximating to a thought-out response to the *Sun*'s reactionary politics is the *Daily Mirror*. The middle-brow daily tabloids – the *Daily Mail* and the *Daily Express* – are heavily Tory-biased and show a depressing preoccupation with the Royal Family and TV celebrities. The scene is a little more varied on a Sunday, when the *Guardian*-owned *Observer*, England's oldest **Sunday newspaper**, supplements the Sunday editions of the dailies, whose ranks are also swelled by the amazingly popular *News of the World*, a smutty rag commonly known as "The News of the Screws".

When it comes to **specialist periodicals**, English newsagents can offer a range covering just about every subject, with motoring, music, sport, computers, gardening and home improvements leading the way. One noticeably poor area is current events – the best-selling commentary magazine is the *Economist*, which is essential reading in the boardrooms of England. The socialist alternative, the weekly *New Statesman*, is subsidized by a few socialist millionaires and is complemented by the glossy monthly *Red Pepper*. The satirical bi-weekly *Private Eye* is a much-loved institution that prides itself on printing the stories the rest of the press won't touch, and on riding the consequent stream of libel suits.

Australians and New Zealanders in London will be gratified by the weekly free magazine, *TNT*, which provides a résumé of the news from home as well as jobs, accommodation and events in the capital. *USA Today* and the *International Herald Tribune* are widely distributed, as are the magazines *Time* and *Newsweek*.

Television and radio

In England, there are five television stations received by all sets. These are divided between the state-owned BBC, with two public service channels, and three independent commercial channels, ITV1, Channel 4 and Channel 5. Though assailed by critics in the Conservative party, who think that it maintains a definite left-wing bias, the **BBC** is just about maintaining its worldwide reputation for in-house quality productions, ranging from expensive costume dramas to intelligent documentaries. BBC 2 is the more offbeat and heavyweight BBC channel; BBC 1 is avowedly mainstream. Various regional companies together form the **ITV1** network, but they are united by a more tabloid approach to programme making – necessarily so, because if they don't get the advertising they don't survive. **Channel 4**, a partly subsidized institution, is the most progressive of the bunch, with a reputation for broadcasting an eclectic spread of "arty" and minority-pleasing programmes, and for supporting small-budget motion pictures. **Channel 5** is a self-consciously "young 'n' fun" alternative distinguished by its lurid colour schemes, breathless presenters and mediocre programming.

As the government plans to switch off the analogue system somewhere between 2006 and 2010, **satellite** and **cable** TV companies are increasingly adopting the **digital** system, through which hundreds of channels are on offer, including interactive shopping, games and internet access; Rupert Murdoch's dominant Sky network (now digital) is receiving serious challenge from the latest player in this field, ITV's Ondigital. Although a large proportion of viewers remain content with their core five analogue channels, the ITV network presents ITV2 and ITV Sport and the BBC its News 24, Knowledge, Parliament and Choice channels solely through the digital system.

Market forces are eating away rather more quickly at the BBC's **radio** network, which has five stations: Radio 1 is almost exclusively pop music, with a chart-biased view of the rock world; Radio 2 is a combination of easy listening and sassier jazz, rock and arts programmes; Radio 3 is predominantly classical music; Radio 4, a blend of current affairs, arts and drama; and Radio 5, a sports and news channel. Radio 1 has rivals on all fronts, with Virgin running a youth-oriented nationwide commercial network, and a plethora of local commercial stations – notably London's Capital Radio – also attracting large sections of Radio 1's target audience. Melody Radio has whittled away at the Radio 2 easy listening market, as has Jazz FM, while Classic FM has lured people away from Radio 3 by offering a less earnest approach to its subject, though it sometimes degenerates into a "Greatest Hits" view of the greats. The BBC also operates several regional stations, but they are usually rather like listening to a broadcast of the local newspaper interspersed with the "Top 20"; the commercial stations, some of them real fly-by-wire operations, tend to be much livelier.

One BBC institution that has stayed in front despite the arrival of downmarket pretenders is the *Radio Times*, a weekly **listings magazine** that gives full details on all national TV and radio programmes, not just the ones broadcast by the BBC.

Opening hours and public holidays

Most attractions are open daily in summer, with one or two closed days in the winter, though the major state museums are open daily all year. We've given full details of opening hours in the *Guide*.

General **shop hours** are Mon–Sat 9am–5.30 or 6pm, although you'll find Sunday and late-night shopping in the larger towns, with Thursday and Friday the favoured evenings. The big supermarkets also tend to stay open until 8 or 9pm from Monday to Saturday, some staying open through the night. On Sundays, supermarkets and high-street stores can legally open for just six hours – though in the case of the latter, this tends only to happen in larger centres and out of town shopping complexes; supermarkets tend to open from 10am to 4pm, while most stores choose to open from 11am or noon to 5pm or 6pm. By contrast, many provincial towns still retain an **early-closing day**, when shops close at 1pm; Wednesday is the favourite.

Note that not all **service stations** on motorways are open for 24 hours, although you can usually get fuel around the clock in larger towns and cities.

Public holidays

Most fee-charging sites are open on **public holidays** (known as **bank holidays** in England), when Sunday hours usually apply. These are:
January 1
Good Friday (late March or early April)
Easter Monday (late March or early April)
First Monday in May
Last Monday in May
Last Monday in August
December 25
December 26
Note that if January 1, December 25 or December 26 falls on a Saturday or Sunday, the next week day becomes a public holiday.

Admission to museums and monuments

Many of England's most treasured sites – from castles, abbeys and great houses to tracts of protected landscape – come under the control of the private National Trust or the state-run English Heritage, whose properties are denoted in the guide with "NT" or "EH" after the opening hours. Both these organizations charge an entry fee for the majority of their sites, and these can be quite high, especially for the more grandiose National Trust estates.

If you think you'll be visiting more than half a dozen places owned by the National Trust or more than a dozen owned by English Heritage, it's worth taking out **annual membership** (around £30/person), which allows free entry to the organization's respective properties. A lot of **stately homes**, however, remain in the hands of the landed gentry, who tend to charge in the region of £5 for admission to edited highlights of their domain – even more if, as at Longleat, they've added some theme-park attractions to the historic pile.

Many other old buildings, albeit rarely the most momentous structures, are owned by the local authorities, which are generally more lenient with their admission charges, sometimes allowing free access. You may find that a history museum or a similar collection has been installed in the local castle or half-rebuilt ruin, and in these cases there's usually a modest entry charge. However, **municipal art galleries and museums** are often free, a situation that holds with many of the great **state museums** – both the British Museum and the National Gallery are free to all visitors, for example. On the other hand, these cash-starved institutions are nowadays obliged to request voluntary donations, as are several of the country's **cathedrals**. Most cathedrals charge a pound or two for admission to the most beautiful parts of the structure – usually the chapter house or cloister – or for a climb up the tower.

You will certainly have to pay to visit any of England's burgeoning **heritage museums**, which in some instances are large multi-building sites staffed by people in period costume, but more often consist of interactive displays, speaking dummies and atmospheric background noises or smells. Tickets for these can cost anywhere between £5 and £10, and

expense is not necessarily an indication of quality. However, the most expensive attractions in England are those aimed squarely at tourists with cash to spend – Madame Tussaud's and the London Planetarium, one of the country's top earners of foreign cash, now charges £13.95 for admission.

The majority of fee-charging attractions in England have **reductions** for senior citizens, the unemployed, full-time students and children under 16, with under-5s being admitted free almost everywhere. Proof of eligibility will be required in most cases, though even the flintiest desk clerk will probably take on trust the age of a babe-in-arms. The entry charges given in the *Guide* are the full adult charges – as a rule, adult reductions are in the range of 25–35 percent, while reductions for children are around 50 percent.

Finally, foreign visitors planning on seeing more than a dozen stately homes, monuments or gardens might find it worthwhile to buy a **Great British Heritage Pass**, which gives free admission to over six hundred sites, many of which are not run by the National Trust or English Heritage. Costing £30 for seven days, £45 for fifteen days and £60 for a month, the pass can be purchased through most travel agents at home, on arrival at any large UK airport, from most major tourist offices and the Britain Visitor Centre at 1 Regent St, London W1 (walk-in service only).

Useful contacts

English Heritage PO Box 39, Bromley, Kent BR1 3XL ☎0870/458 4000, ⊛www.english-heritage.org.uk.
National Trust 23 Savile Row, London W1X 1AB ☎0207/973 3000, ⊛www.nationaltrust.org.uk.

Festivals and events

In terms of the number of tourists they attract, the biggest occasions in the English calendar are the rituals that have associations with the ruling classes – from the courtly pageant of the Trooping of the Colour to the annual rowing race between Oxford and Cambridge universities. Such anachronisms certainly reflect the endemic English taste for nostalgia, but to gauge the spirit of the country you should sample a wider range of events. London's large-scale festivals range from the riotous street party of the Notting Hill Carnival to the Promenade concerts, Europe's most egalitarian high-class music season, while practically every town has its local arts festival, some of which have attained international status.

To see England at its most idiosyncratic, take a look at one of the numerous regional celebrations that perpetuate **ancient customs**, the origins and meanings of which have often been lost or conveniently forgotten. The sight of the entire population of a village scrambling around a field after a barrel, or chasing a cheese downhill, is not easily forgotten. The best of these festivals, along with various other local fairs and commemorative shows, are mentioned in the main part of the *Guide*, but a good selection is listed below. Also included in the list are the main **sports** finals, which may often be difficult to get tickets for, but are invariably televised. In addition to these, there are football matches every Saturday (plus some Sundays and mid-week as well) from late August to mid-May, and cricket matches every day throughout the summer – interesting social phenomena even for those unenthralled by team sports.

Events calendar

Mid-Feb Chinese New Year. Festivities in London's and Manchester's Chinatown districts.

Mid-March Cheltenham Gold Cup meeting. The country's premier national hunt horseracing event.

End of March or early April University Boat Race. Hugely popular rowing contest on the Thames, between the teams of Oxford and Cambridge.

Shrove Tues Purbeck Marblers and Stonecutters Day, Corfe Castle, Dorset. Ritual football game through the streets of the village.

Maundy Thurs The Queen dispenses the Royal Maundy Money (at a different cathedral annually).

Good Fri British and World Marbles Championship, Tinsley Green, near Crawley, Sussex.

Easter Mon Hare Pie Scramble and Bottle-Kicking, Hallaton, Leicestershire.

Sat in late March or early April Grand National meeting, Aintree, Liverpool. Cruelly testing steeplechase that entices most of Britain's population into the betting shops.

May 1 Padstow Hobby Horse, Padstow, Cornwall. Processions, music and dancing through the streets.

May 8 Helston Furry Dance, Helston, Cornwall.

Early May FA Cup Final. The deciding contest in the premier football tournament is currently without a home of its own. For the time being, the English

national game's most important fixture will be held in the Welsh capital, Cardiff.

Spring Bank Hol Mon Cheese Rolling, Brockworth, Gloucestershire. Pursuit of a cheese wheel down a murderous incline – one of the weirdest customs in England.

May–July Glyndebourne Opera Festival, East Sussex. The classiest and most snobbish arts festival in the country.

Late May and early June Bath International Festival. International arts jamboree.

Last week of May Chelsea Flower Show, Royal Hospital, Chelsea, London. Essential event for England's green-fingered legions.

June Aldeburgh Festival. Jamboree of classical music held on the Suffolk Coast. Established by Benjamin Britten.

First Fri in June Cotswold Olimpicks, Chipping Campden, Gloucestershire. Rustic sports festival and torchlight procession.

First week in June Derby week, Epsom racecourse, Surrey. The world's most expensive horseflesh competing in the Derby, the Coronation Cup and the Oaks.

First or second Sat in June Trooping the Colour, Horse Guards Parade, London. Equestrian pageantry for the Queen's Official Birthday.

Mid-June Appleby Horse Fair, Appleby-in-Westmorland, Cumbria.

Mid-June Royal Ascot, Berkshire. High-class horseracing attended by high-class people; the best seats go to royalty and their satellites, while the proles mill around in the outfield.

End of June World Worm-Charming Championships, Willaston, Cheshire.

Last week of June Glastonbury Festival, Somerset. Hugely popular festival, with international bands, indie music and loads of hippies.

Last week of June and first week of July Lawn Tennis Championships, Wimbledon, London. Queues are phenomenal even for the early rounds, and you need to know a freemason or ex-champion to get in to the big games.

First week in July Henley Royal Regatta, Oxfordshire. Rowing event attended by much the same crew as populates the grandstands at Ascot.

First week of July Tynwald Ceremony, St John's, Isle of Man.

Second week in July York Early Music Festival. The country's premier early music festival, lasting for ten days.

Second or Third Sat in July Durham Miners' Gala, Durham.

Mid-July British Open Golf Championship, variable venue. The season's last Grand Slam golf tournament.

Third week in July Swan Upping, River Thames from Sunbury to Pangbourne. Ceremonial registering of the Thames cygnets.

Last week of July Royal Tournament, Earl's Court Exhibition Centre, London. Precision military displays.

Last week of July Cambridge Folk Festival. Biggest event of its kind in England.

Late July WOMAD, Reading. Three-day world music festival.

July to early Sept The Promenade Concerts ("The Proms"), Royal Albert Hall, London. Classical music concerts ending in the fervently patriotic Last Night of the Proms.

Early Aug Sidmouth Folk Festival. Folk and roots performers from around the world, plus theatre and dance.

Aug Bank Hol Notting Hill Carnival, around Notting Hill, West London. Vivacious celebration by London's Caribbean community – plenty of music, food and floats.

Aug Bank Hol Reading Festival, Berkshire. Three-day hard rock jamboree.

Weekend in mid-Aug Bristol Balloon Fiesta. Hundreds of balloons take to the skies early morning and evening.

Last Sun in Aug Plague Memorial, Eyam, Derbyshire.

Early Sept to early Nov Blackpool Illuminations, Lancashire. Five miles of extravagant light displays.

First Mon after Sept 4 Abbots Bromley Horn Dance, Abbots Bromley, Staffordshire. Vaguely pagan mass dance in mock-medieval costume – one of the most famous ancient customs.

Late Oct to early Nov Huddersfield Contemporary Music Festival. One of Europe's premier showcases for up-to-the-minute highbrow music.

First Sun in Nov London to Brighton Veteran Car Rally. Ancient machines lumbering the 57 miles down the A23 to the seafront.

Nov 5 Guy Fawkes Night. Nationwide fireworks and bonfires commemorating the foiling of the Gunpowder Plot in 1605 – especially raucous celebrations at York (Fawkes' birthplace), Ottery St Mary in Devon and at Lewes, East Sussex.

Mid-Nov Lord Mayor's Procession and Show, the City of London. Cavalcade to mark the inauguration of the new mayor.

Dec 31 Tar Barrels Parade, Allendale Town, Northumberland.

Sports and outdoor pursuits

No matter where you are in England, you're never far from a stretch of country-side in which you can lose the crowds on a brief walk or cycle ride. For more hardy types, there are numerous long-distance footpaths, as well as opportunities for the more extreme disciplines of rock climbing and potholing (caving). On the coast and many of the country's inland lakes you can follow the more urbane pursuits of sailing and windsurfing, and there are plenty of fine beaches for less structured fresh-air activities or just slobbing around.

Walking

England's finest **walking** areas are the granite moorlands and spectacular coastlines of **Devon and Cornwall** in the southwest, and the highlands of the north – the low limestone and millstone crags of the **Peak District**, between Sheffield and Manchester; the **Yorkshire Dales**, the stretch of the Pennines to the north of the Peak District; the **North York Moors**, a bleak, treeless upland to the east of the Pennines; and the glaciated Cumbrian Mountains, better known as the **Lake District**. On summer weekends the more accessible reaches of these regions can get very crowded with day-trippers, but at any time of the year you'll find yourself in relative isolation if you head out on one of the **Long Distance Footpaths** (LDPs). Defined as any route over twenty miles long, LDPs exist all over the country and are marked at frequent intervals with an acorn waymarker. Youth hostels are littered along most routes, though you may need a tent for some of the more heroic hikes – stretches of the Pennine Way, Britain's longest, at over 250 miles, for example. It goes without saying that for any kind of serious walking, and even for day hikes on high ground, you need to be properly equipped and prepared, follow local advice and listen out for the local weather reports. England's climate may be benign on the whole, but the weather is changeable in any given season and people die on the moors and mountains every year.

At the time of writing, some footpaths were closed as a precaution against the further spreading of the Foot and Mouth epidemic. For the latest on this situation, contact any local tourist office or one of the companies listed below.

Walking-holiday specialists

Adventureline ☎ 01209/820847, ⊛ www.chyycor .co.uk/adventureline. Small group tours with local guides around the Celtic landscapes of Cornwall.
Explore Britain ☎ 01740/650900. Guided or independent walking holidays countrywide with luggage transfer.
Footpath Holidays ☎ 01985/840049, ⊛ www.footpath-holidays.com. Packages to various hill and coastal districts in England, with experienced group leaders.
Instep Walking Holidays ☎ 01903/766475, ⊛ www.instephols.co.uk. Self-guided holidays with accommodation in small country hotels and guest houses, mainly in the south of England.
HF Walking Holidays ☎ 020/8905 9556 or 905 9388, ⊛ www.hfholidays.co.uk. A wide choice of locations and lodging in comfortable country houses.
Sherpa Expeditions ☎ 0181/577 2717, ⊛ www.sherpa-walking-holidays.co.uk. At-your-own-pace, self-guided walks between country pubs all over England.

Cycling

Although there has been a boom in the sale of mountain bikes and a rise in the number of towns and cities that have incorporated designated cycle routes into their traffic schemes, **cyclists** tend to be treated with disrespect by many motorists. British cyclists are estimated to be twelve times more likely to be killed or injured on the road (per miles cycled) than their counterparts in Denmark, where a network of safe cycle paths and traffic-calming schemes has been created, although the organization **SUSTRANS** (see p.45) is attempting to go some way towards addressing this problem.

Surprisingly, cycle **helmets** are not compulsory in Britain – but if you're hellbent on tackling the congestion, pollution and aggression of city traffic, you're well advised to get one. You do have to have a **rear reflector** and front and back **lights** when riding at night, and are not allowed to carry children without a special child seat. It is also illegal to cycle on pavements (sidewalks), and in most public parks. A secure **lock** (preferably some kind of "D" lock) is also indispensable and it's always a good idea to make a note of your frame number in case you have to report a theft to the police.

Bike rental is available at cycle shops in most large towns, and at villages within national parks and other scenic areas; the addresses and telephone numbers of these appear in the relevant sections of the *Guide*. Expect to pay in the region of £10–20 per day for something sturdy, with discounts for longer periods.

Carrying your bike on public transport

The majority of **airlines** will carry bicycles as part of your luggage allowance on plane journeys, although protruding parts, such as pedals and handlebars, have to be removed, and the tyres deflated; some carriers also require you to stash the machine in a bike bag or cardboard cover. Check with your airline well in advance to find out exactly what their terms and conditions are, and bear in mind that you may have to pay excess baggage. Transporting cycles by **ferry** is also free, but a lot more straightforward; you just wheel them on and off, and reservations are not normally required.

Carrying your bike by **train** is a good way of getting to the interesting parts of England without a lot of stressful or boring pedalling. For some reason, however, rail companies seem hellbent on making life difficult for cyclists by slapping on hefty surcharges. Most suburban trains will carry cycles outside of morning and evening rush hours (7.30–9.30am & 4–7pm), but they are not allowed at all on some express trains (or Eurostar), while those that do accept cycles charge between £1 and £3; this usually has to be paid at least 24 hours in advance, and for each separate leg of the trip, which can work out to be ridiculously expensive if your journey involves a couple of changes. If you reserve 14 days in advance, Eurotunnel will carry you and your bike on the 12.30pm or 6pm train from Calais and the 9.30am or 3.30pm train from Folkestone. A day trip costs £15, a five-day return £31 and an open return £59. For information and to book, call ☎01303/288933 or 288680.

Cycle routes

There are currently around 6000 miles of official **cycle tracks** in England. Funded by a £43,500,000 grant by the Millennium Commission, in partnership with local authorities and organizations such as the National Trust and Countryside Agency, the charity **SUSTRANS** hopes by 2005 to expand this to a 10,000-mile National Cycle Network, passing within two miles of some twenty million people. A large proportion of the network is made up of quiet backroads, dubbed "Cycleways", but more than half runs along disused railways and canal towpaths, including the showpiece section connecting the cities of Bath and Bristol.

Aside from these, the backroads of rural England (those labelled with the prefix "B") make infinitely more enjoyable routes than trunk routes (or "A" roads), with generally amiable gradients and a sufficient density of pubs and B&Bs to keep the days manageable. Your main problem out in the countryside will be getting hold of any spare parts – only inner tubes and tyres are easy to find.

Off-road cycling is popular in the highland walking areas, but cyclists should remember to keep to rights of way designated on maps as Bridleways, BOATs ("Byways Open To All Traffic") or RUPFs ("Roads Used As Public Footpaths") and to pass walkers at considerate speeds. Footpaths, unless otherwise marked, are for pedestrian use only. Other rules of the road to bear in mind are that cycles are not permitted on motorways (labelled with the prefix "M").

Armed with a detailed OS **map** of any area, you can improvise scenic routes of your own that avoid the main roads – better still, most good bookshops stock a range of **cycling guides**, featuring suggestions for rides of varying length, with coloured maps and detailed route descriptions. Also useful

are SUSTRANS' maps of the official cycle network network (£5.99) and their *Official Guide to the National Network* (£9.99).

With more time, you may want to take on one of England's challenging **long-distance routes**. The Cycle Touring Club, or CTC, publishes special maps for some of these, and supplies members with touring and technical advice as well as insurance. The classic cross-Britain route is Land's End, in the far southwest of England, to John O'Groats, on the northeast tip of Scotland – roughly a thousand miles that can be covered in two to three weeks, depending on which of the three CTC-recommended routes you choose. Another favourite coast-to-coast option is the journey from Lowestoft, in the southeast county of Suffolk, to the Ardnamurchan peninsula in northwest Scotland. The CTC suggests a ten-day itinerary, but you could easily spend twice that long scaling the English watershed. The same applies to the wonderful 130-mile Wye Valley route, which winds from the Severn Estuary through forests and moorlands of the Welsh borders to the rough mountains of mid-Wales. Other tempting long-distance tours could take you around the Yorkshire Dales, Pennines, and Peak district, around Dartmoor and the Cornish coast, or across the austere North Yorkshire Moors. Visitors from abroad can get copies of their leaflets (costing £2–4) which detail tour routes in these and other regions.

Useful cycling contacts

The Cycle Touring Club (CTC) ☎ 01483/417217, ⊛ www.CTC.org.uk. **SUSTRANS** ☎ 0117/929 0888, ⊛ www.sustrans.org.uk.

Cycling holidays

For those who want a guaranteed hassle-free **cycling holiday**, there are various companies offering easy-going packages. These can take all sorts of forms, but generally include transport of your gear to each night's halt, pre-booked accommodation, detailed route instructions, a packed lunch and back-up support. Most companies offer some budget cycling holidays, with hostels or B&Bs instead of hotels.

Cycling holiday specialists

Activities ☎0870/740 5055, ⊛www
.acornactivities.co.uk. Weekend and one-week
tours, with bikes, accommodation, luggage
transportation and maps provided.

Rough Tracks ☎0700/0560 749, ⊛www.rough-
tracks.co.uk. Mountain bike and road weekend tours
across the country. Also bike maintenance
weekends.

Bike Breaks ☎0151/722 8050, ⊛www.byways-
breaks.com. Tours of varying length in the Cheshire
and Shropshire countryside.

Compass Holidays ☎01242/250642, ⊛www
.compass-holidays.com. Guided or independent
tours in the Cotswolds, the Lake District, Cornwall
and Warwickshire.

Country Lanes ☎01425/655022, ⊛www
.countrylanes.co.uk. Tours in the New Forest, the
Cotswolds and the Lake District starting from train
stations.

Holiday Lakeland ☎01697/371871, ⊛www
.holiday-lakeland.co.uk. Tours of three and five
nights in the Lake District (May–Sept only).

Beaches

England is ringed by fine **beaches** and
bays, many of the best of which are readily
accessible by public transport – though of
course that means they tend to get very
busy in high summer. For a combination of
decent climate and good sand, the southwest is the best area, especially the coasts
of north Cornwall and Devon. The beaches
of England's southern coast become more
pebbly as you approach the southeastern
corner of the country – resorts round here
are more garish than their southwestern
counterparts. Moving up the east coast, the
East Anglian shore is predominantly pebbly
and very exposed – making it ideal for those
who want to escape the crowds rather than
bask in the sun – while right up in the northeast there are some wonderful sandy
strands and old-fashioned seaside resorts,
though the North Sea breezes often require
a degree of stoicism. Over in the northwest,
the inland hills of Cumbria are a greater
attraction than anything on the coast,
though Blackpool has a certain appeal as
the apotheosis of the "kiss-me-quick" holiday town.

It has to be said that English beaches are
not the cleanest in Europe, and many of
those that the British authorities declare to
be acceptable actually fall below **EU stan-**
dards. Although the situation is improving
year by year, far too many stretches of the
English coastline are contaminated by seaborne effluent or other rubbish. For annually
updated, detailed information on the condition of Britain's beaches, the definitive
source is the *Good Beach Guide* (£3.50),
compiled by the Marine Conservation
Society (☎01989/566017, ⊛www.good
beachguide.co.uk).

Surfing

For most people, **surfing** in England means
surfing in Newquay. And while it's true that
the southwest is the heartland of the English
surf scene, it would be a mistake to think
that there aren't decent waves elsewhere.
The **northeast** coast, from Yorkshire to
Northumberland, has a growing population
of hardy surfers willing to endure temperatures as low as 5°C in winter (and no higher
than 14–15°C in summer) to surf clean
northerly ground swells breaking over a
selection of quality reef and beach breaks.
The coastline here is often spectacular,
especially in Northumberland, and although
the more popular breaks, such as Cayton
Bay and Saltburn, are now crowded, you
can find relative isolation off the beaten
track.

Nevertheless, the **southwest**, or more
specifically **Newquay** in Cornwall, remains
England's undisputed surf centre. Visiting
surfers are often amazed to see the hype
surrounding this self-styled "surf city". In
summer, every other male seems to be a
surfer, sporting regulation bleached hair and
surf gear, some only turning up to cruise surf
babes. It can still be hectic out in the water,
though, especially at the main break, Fistral,
which regularly hosts international contests.
Head out of town and things quieten down
noticeably. Try spots such as **Perranporth**
or **Polzeath**, or head up to Devon, which
also gets decent waves, despite the overcrowding of its main break, **Croyde**.

The southwest has relatively mild waters
(up to 18°C in summer). Even so, you'll still
need a **wetsuit** year round, with a thicker
suit from October to May, plus boots and
gloves, and maybe a hood (winter water
temperatures get down to 9–10°C). There
are plenty of places where you can **rent or**
buy equipment, which means gear tends
to be cheaper in southwest England than

elsewhere in the UK. Even if you can escape no further than the Channel coast, you may still be lucky enough to find a wave, especially in winter. It's unlikely to be of good quality, but for the desperate surf traveller places such as **Brighton** and **Bournemouth** may have something worth getting wet for.

Top ten English breaks

An asterisk (*) Indicates that the breaks are for experienced surfers only.

Fistral, Newquay. Hype, crowds, but still a good wave if you can get one to yourself.

Staithes*, Yorkshire. Excellent reef breaks, crowded and jealously guarded by locals.

Croyde Bay, Devon. Good beach breaks, but again, crowds can be a problem.

Sennen Cove, Cornwall. Picks up any swell going.

Woolacombe, Devon. Two miles of fun beach breaks.

Kimmeridge*, Dorset. A popular reef break that doesn't work that often, but is great when it does.

Saltburn, Cleveland. Another good beach break, with atmosphere to match.

Bamburgh, Northumberland. A wonderfully scenic quiet beach, with seals in the water and a spectacular castle as a backdrop.

Porthleven*, Cornwall. A heavy reef break, and heavy locals.

Constantine, Cornwall. Another southwest hot spot that picks up a lot of swell.

Crime and personal safety

Although the traditional image of the friendly British "Bobby" has become increasingly tarnished by stories of corruption, racism and crooked dealings, the police continue to be approachable and helpful. If you're lost in a major town, asking a police officer is generally the quickest way to pinpoint your destination – alternatively, you could ask a traffic warden, a species of law-enforcer much maligned in car-loving England. Most traffic wardens are distinguishable by their flat caps with a yellow band (though uniforms do vary), and by the fact that they are generally armed with a hand-set for dispensing parking-fine tickets; police officers on street duty wear a distinctive domed hat with a silver tip, and are generally armed with just a truncheon.

As with any country, the major towns of England have their dangerous spots, but these tend to be inner-city housing estates where no tourist has any reason to be. The chief risk on England's streets is **pickpock-**

Emergencies

For Police, Fire Brigade, Ambulance and, in certain areas, Mountain Rescue or Coastguard, dial ☏999.

eting, and there are some virtuoso villains at work in London, especially on the big shopping streets and on the Underground. Carry only as much money as you need, and keep all bags and pockets fastened. Should you have anything stolen or be involved in some incident that requires reporting, go to the local police station – we've given address and contact numbers throughout the *Guide* for those in the bigger towns and cities; the ☏999 number in the box below should only be used in real emergencies.

Work

The kind of work you can expect to find in England as a visitor is generally unskilled employment in hotels, bars and restaurants, cleaning companies and on farms. As a casual employee you can expect poor pay of around £4–5 per hour and you may be fired at short notice. If you want to come to grips with the country a little more, you could also consider voluntary work, which can range from work camps, archeological digs and placements with service organizations, or even working holidays, whereby you may be required to contribute a small amount for food and lodging.

The British Tourist Authority's **websites** can provide some information on working in England (see p.20), as can ⓦ www.hotre-ruit.co.uk, an excellent resource for temporary and seasonal work throughout the country. There are also several useful **publications**. *Working Holidays*, by the Central Bureau for Educational Visits and Exchanges (CBEVE; £9.99), can provide you with scores of ideas; *Summer Jobs in Britain* by David Woodworth (£9.99) gives comprehensive information on paid seasonal work in the UK; and *Work Your Way Around the World* by Susan Griffith (£12.95) is also worth a try.

For **conservation work**, BTCV can fix you up with schemes for improving footpaths or building dry-stone walls (around £70) and so on, as can the National Trust.

If you're between 17 and 27, you might also consider **working as an au pair**. This enables you to live for a maximum of two years with an English-speaking family. In return for your accommodation, food and a small amount of pocket money (say £50 per week), you'll be expected to help around the house and to look after the children for a maximum of five hours each day. The easiest way to find au pair work is through a licensed agency. The Recruitment and Employment Confederation (REC) has a list of reputable agents (ie those which are vetted annually by the government). Alternatively, look in the listings section of *The Lady* magazine.

Work permits

Unless you're a resident of an EU country, you need a **permit** to work legally in the UK,

although without the backing of an established employer or company this can be very difficult to obtain. Persons aged between 17 and 27 may, however, apply for a **Working Holiday-Maker Entry Certificate**, which entitles you to a two-year stay in the UK, during which time you are permitted to undertake work of a casual nature – in other words, not in a profession, or as a sportsperson or entertainer. The certificates are only available abroad, from British embassies and consulates, and when you apply you must be able to convince the officer you have a valid return or onward ticket, and the means to support yourself while you're in Britain without having to claim state benefits of any kind. Note, too, that the certificates are valid from the date of entry into Britain – you won't be able to recoup time spent out of the country in the two-year period of validity.

In **North America**, full-time college students can get temporary work or study permits through BUNAC. Permits are valid for up to six months and cost $250; allow two to three weeks for processing of your application.

Other visitors entitled to work in Britain are **Commonwealth citizens**. Those whose parent was born in the UK can apply for a Certificate of Entitlement to the Right of Abode; if you have a grandparent who was born in the UK or Ireland before 1922, you may be entitled to a UK Ancestry Employment Certificate, allowing you to work for up to four years in the UK. For further information contact your nearest British Mission (embassy or consulate) or the Foreign and Commonwealth Office in London (☎020/7270 1500, ⓦ www.fco. gov.uk).

Useful addresses

BUNAC PO Box 430, Southbury, CT 06488 ☎1-800-GO-BUNAC, ⊛ www.bunac.org.
BTCV 36 St Mary's St, Wallingford, Oxfordshire OX10 0EU ☎01491/839 766, ⊛ www.btcv.org.uk.

National Trust (Enterprises) The Stable Block, Heywood House, Westbury, Wiltshire BA13 4NA ☎01225/7911199, ⊛ www.nationaltrust.org.uk.
The Recruitment and Employment Confederation (REC) 36–38 Mortimer St, London W1W 7RG ☎020/7462 3260, ⊛ www.rec.uk.com.

Travellers with disabilities

Should you go it alone, you'll find that English attitudes towards **travellers with disabilities** are often begrudging and guilt ridden, and are still way behind advances towards independence made in North America and Australia. However, there is movement in the right direction, in no small measure due to Part 3 of the Disability Discrimination Act of 1995, which states that all barriers to access must be removed by 2004. As a consequence all new tourist attractions and hotels make full provision for wheelchair users, and **access** to museums, theatres, cinemas and other public places has greatly improved. Most towns offer free parking for wheelchair orange/blue badge holders and you'll find reserved parking bays at the majority of tourist attractions.

England has numerous specialist **tour operators** catering for travellers with disabilities, and the number of non-specialist operators who welcome clients with disabilities is increasing. For more information on these operators and on facilities for the disabled traveller, you should get in touch with the organizations listed below. RADAR produces an annual holiday guide *Holidays in Britain and Ireland* (£8) and both the National Trust and English Heritage (see p.41) can send you free **guides** for visitors with disabilites.

As for **accommodation** needs, disabled travellers will find that modified suites are available only at higher-priced establishments and perhaps at the odd B&B, where a ground-floor room has been adapted. **Public transport** companies rarely make any effort to help disabled people, though some rail services now accommodate wheelchair users in comfort and some new buses (including the post buses, see p.28) have accessible doors and steps. Wheelchair users and blind or partially sighted people are automatically given a third off the price of train fares, and people with other disabilities are eligible for the **Disabled Persons Railcard** (£14/year), which also gives a third off most tickets, but can take up to two weeks to process. Applications for

this card must be made in writing to the Disabled Persons Railcard Office, PO Box 1YT, Newcastle upon Tyne NE99 1YT. There are no bus discounts for the disabled, while of the major **car rental** firms only Hertz offer models with hand controls at the same rate as conventional vehicles, and even these are in the more expensive categories.

Contacts for travellers with disabilities

In North America

⊛ **www.access-able.com.** An online resource for travellers with disabilities.
Mobility International USA 451 Broadway, Eugene, OR 97401 ☎541/343-1284 (voice and TDD), ⊛ www.miusa.org. For an annual membership fee of $35, they will provide support and advice; membership includes a quarterly newsletter.
Society for the Advancement of Travelers with Handicaps (SATH) 347 5th Ave, New York NY 10016 ☎212/447-7284, ⊛ www.sath.org. Non-profit educational organization that has actively represented travellers with disabilities since 1976.
Travel Information Service ☎215/456-9600. Telephone-only information and referral service.
Wheels Up! ☎1-888/389-4335, ⊛ www .wheelsup.com. Telephone and website information,

including discounted airfare, tour and cruise prices for disabled travellers; also publishes a free monthly newsletter.

In Australia and New Zealand

ACROD (Australian Council for Rehabilitation of the Disabled) PO Box 60, Curtin ACT 2605 ☎02/6282 4333, ⓦwww.acrod.org.au. Regional offices provide lists of travel agencies, tour operators and accommodation.

Disabled Persons Assembly 173–75 Victoria St, Wellington, New Zealand ☎04/801 9100. Resource centre with lists of travel agencies and tour operators for people with disabilities.

In the UK and Ireland

ⓦ **www.allgohere.co.uk** Useful website providing information on accommodation suitable for disabled travellers throughout the UK.

Holiday Care 2nd floor, Imperial Building, Victoria Rd, Horley, Surrey RH6 7PZ ☎01293/774535, Minicom ☎01293/776943,
ⓦ **www.holidaycare.org.uk.** Gives out a free list of accessible attractions in the UK. Also has information on financial help for holidays.

RADAR (Royal Association for Disability and Rehabilitation) 12 City Forum, 250 City Rd, London EC1V 8AF ☎020/7250 3222, Minicom ☎020t/7250 4119,
ⓦwww.radar.org.uk. Has a wide range of information and advice for travellers.

Tripscope Vassall Centre, Gill Avenue, Bristol BS16 2QQ ☎08457/585641.
ⓦ **www.justmobility.co.uk/tripscope.** Provides a national telephone information service offering free advice on travel and access in England.

Gay and lesbian England

Homosexual acts between consenting males were legalized in Britain in 1967, but it wasn't until as recently as 1994 that the age of consent was finally reduced from 21 to 18 (still two years older than that for heterosexuals). Lesbianism has never specifically been outlawed, apocryphally owing to the fact that Queen Victoria refused to believe that such a thing existed.

As in so many other aspects of English life, attitudes towards homosexuality are riven with contradictions. Despite its draconian laws and the sensationalist trash in the tabloid press, England offers one of the most diverse and accessible **lesbian and gay scenes** to be found anywhere in Europe. Nearly every town of any size has some kind of organized gay life – pubs, clubs, community groups, campaigning organizations, shops and phone lines – with the major scenes being found in **London, Manchester** and **Brighton.** Many venues are listed in this book, and you'll find a free gay listings sheet in virtually any one of these.

Of the nationwide **publications**, the weekly *Pink Paper* is newsy and contains limited listings; also worth checking are the frothy weekly *Boyz*, and its monthly women's sibling, *Diva*. The best bet for a comprehensive **national directory** of pubs, clubs, groups, gay accommodation and local lesbian and gay switchboards is the glossy monthly *Gay Times*, available from many newsagents and alternative bookstores. Useful **books** include *Gay Times: Great Britain and Ireland* (£12.99) by John Szponarski, which gives the low-down on pubs, clubs, cafés and accommodation in the UK; *Gay London* by Will McLoughlin (£7.99), which takes a look at London from an arts and cultural perspective; and *Dyke London* (£10), by Rose Ainsley.

Useful contacts for Gay and Lesbian travellers in the UK

ⓦ **www.gaytravel.co.uk** Online gay and lesbian travel agent, offering good deals on all types of holidays. Also lists gay- and lesbian-friendly hotels.

ⓦ **www.gayguide.co.uk** Lists gay venues by location.

ⓦ **www.gaybritain.co.uk** Information on events, restaurants and travel, with good links.

Directory

CIGARETTES The last decade has seen a dramatic change in attitudes towards smoking and a significant reduction in the consumption of cigarettes. Smoking is now outlawed from just about all public buildings and on public transport, and many restaurants and hotels have become non-smoking establishments. Smokers are advised, when booking a table or a room, to check that their vice is tolerated there.

DRUGS Likely-looking visitors coming to England from Holland or Spain can expect scrutiny from customs officers on the lookout for hashish (marijuana resin). Being caught in possession of a small amount of hashish or grass may lead to a fine, but possession of larger quantities or of "harder" narcotics could lead to imprisonment or deportation.

ELECTRICITY In England the current is 240V AC. North American appliances will need a transformer and adaptor; those from Australia and New Zealand will only need an adaptor.

LAUNDRY Coin-operated laundries (launderettes) are to be found in nearly all English towns and are open about twelve hours a day from Monday to Friday, less on weekends. A wash followed by a spin or tumble dry costs about £3.50, with "service washes" (your laundry done for you in a few hours) about £1 more.

PUBLIC TOILETS These are found at all train and bus stations and are signposted on town high streets. In urban locations a fee of 10p or 20p is usually charged.

TIME Greenwich Mean Time (GMT) is used from late October to late March, when the clocks go forward an hour for British Summer Time (BST). GMT is five hours ahead of the US Eastern Standard Time and ten hours behind Australian Eastern Standard Time.

TIPPING There are no fixed rules for tipping in England. If you think you've received good service, particularly in restaurants or cafés, you may want to leave a tip of 10 percent of the total bill (unless service has already been included). It is not normal, however, to leave tips in pubs, although bar staff are sometimes offered drinks, which they may accept in the form of money (the assumption is they'll spend this on a drink after closing time). Taxi drivers, on the other hand, will expect tips on longer journeys – expect to add about 10 percent to the fare. The only other occasions when you'll be expected to tip are in hairdressers, and upmarket hotels where, in common with most other countries, porters, bell boys and table waiters rely on being tipped to bump up their often dismal wages.

VIDEOS Visitors from North America should note that there is a different format for videotapes in Britain than there is in the US and Canada – so even though they look the same, VHS tapes recorded in Britain (in what's called the PAL format) will not work when you get them home and try to play them back on your VCR (which is NTSC format). If you are shooting with your own camera, however, you can use a blank tape purchased in Britain to record your trip's highlights, since your camera will format the tape while it records.

guide

guide

1 London 55–166

2 Surrey, Kent and Sussex 167–246

3 Hampshire, Dorset and Wiltshire.............................247–318

4 Surrey, Kent and Sussex 319–358

5 The Cotswolds and Somerset...................................359–424

6 Devon and Cornwall...425–522

7 East Anglia...523–600

8 The West Midlands and the Peak District...............601–682

9 The East Midlands..683–736

10 The Northwest...737–814

11 Cumbria and the lakes 815–870

12 Yorkshire...871–992

13 The Northeast...993–1076

London

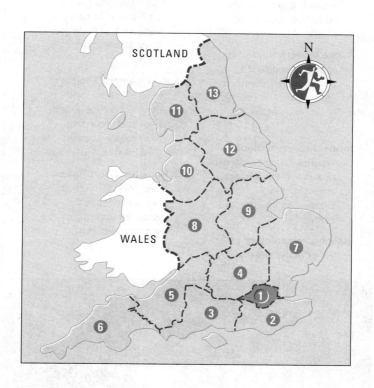

CHAPTER 1 # Highlights

* **British Museum** The BM has reinvented itself with a wonderful new glass-covered courtyard, surrounding the old library. See p.94

* **London Eye** The universally loved observation wheel is a graceful new addition to London's skyline. See p.112

* **Tate Modern** Housed in a spectacular disused power station, London's new modern-art gallery is simply awesome. See p.114

* **Shakespeare's Globe Theatre** Catch an open-air show in this amazing reconstructed Elizabethan theatre. See p.114

* **Highgate cemetery** Take a tour of the steeply sloping terraces of the West Cemetery, whose overgrown graves are the last word in Victorian Gothic gloom. See p.128

* **Greenwich** The most picturesque riverside spot in London, boasting a busy weekend market, the National Maritime Museum and the old Royal Observatory. See p.130

* **Kew Gardens** London's superb botanic gardens. Stroll amidst the exotic trees and shrubs; or head for the steamy glasshouses. See p.137

* **Hampton Court Palace** Exceptional Tudor interiors, architecture by Wren, a hedge maze and vast gardens and grounds. See p.139

London

What strikes visitors more than anything about **LONDON** is the sheer size of the place. With a population of just under eight million, it's Europe's largest city by far, spreading across an area of more than 620 square miles from its core on the **River Thames**. Londoners tend to cope with this by compartmentalizing the city, identifying with the neighbourhoods in which they work or live, and making the occasional forays into the "centre of town". Ethnically it's also Europe's most diverse metropolis: around two hundred languages are spoken within its confines, and more than thirty percent of the population is made up of first, second- and third-generation immigrants.

Despite Scottish, Welsh and Northern Irish devolution, London still dominates the national horizon, too: this is where the country's news and money are made, it's where the central government resides and, as far as its inhabitants are concerned, provincial life begins beyond the circuit of the city's orbital motorway. Londoners' sense of superiority causes enormous resentment in the regions, yet it's undeniable that the capital has a unique aura of excitement and success – in most walks of British life, if you want to get on you've got to do it in London.

For the visitor, too, London is a thrilling place. And since the beginning of the new millennium, the city has also been in exceptionally buoyant mood. Thanks to the frenzy of lottery- and millennium-funding of the last few years, virtually every one of London's **world-class museums and galleries** and institutions has been reinvented, from the Royal Opera House to the British Museum. With the Tate Modern, the city can now boast the largest modern art gallery in the world, not to mention the world's largest observation wheel; a new tube extension and the first new bridges to cross the Thames for over a hundred years. And after sixteen years of being the only major city in the world *not* to have its own governing body, London finally has its own elected mayor, and assembly.

In the meantime, London's **traditional sights** – Big Ben, Westminster Abbey, Buckingham Palace, St Paul's Cathedral and the Tower of London – continue to draw in millions of tourists every year. Monuments from the capital's more glorious past are everywhere to be seen, from medieval banqueting halls and the great churches of Sir Christopher Wren to the eclectic Victorian architecture of the triumphalist British Empire. There is also much enjoyment to be had from the city's quiet Georgian squares, the narrow alleyways of the City of London, the riverside walks, and the quirks of what is still identifiably a collection of villages. And even London's traffic pollution – one of its worst problems – is offset by surprisingly large **expanses of greenery**: Hyde Park,

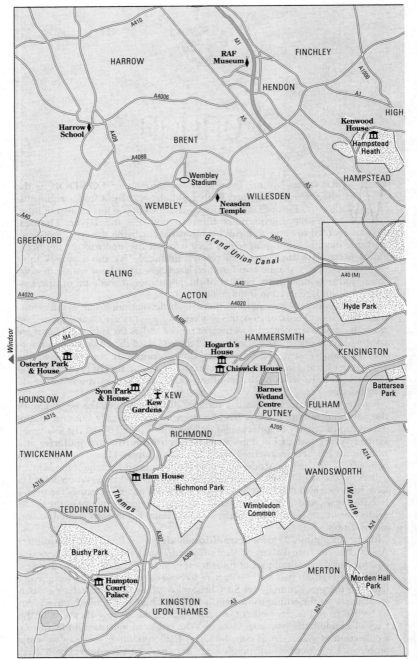

© Crown copyright

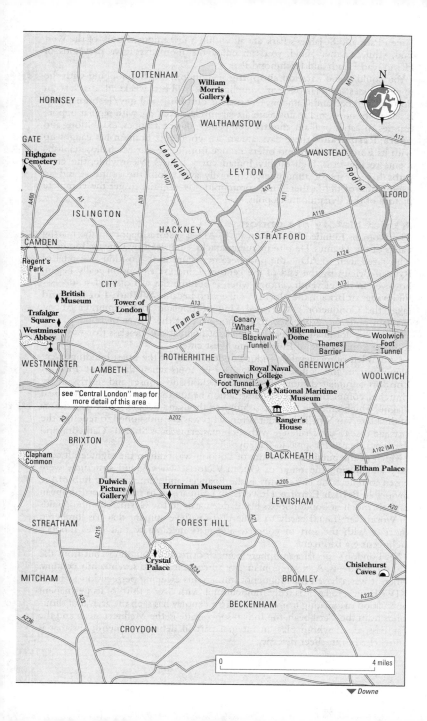

N

TOTTENHAM

HORNSEY

William
Morris
Gallery

WALTHAMSTOW

GATE

Highgate
Cemetery

Lea Valley

WANSTEAD

LEYTON

A12

ILFORD

Roding

ISLINGTON

A10

A118

A13

HACKNEY

STRATFORD

A124

CAMDEN

A13

Regent's
Park

CITY

British
Museum

Tower of
London

A13

Thames

Canary
Wharf

Millennium
Dome

Woolwich
Foot
Tunnel

Trafalgar
Square

Blackwall
Tunnel

Thames
Barrier

Westminster
Abbey

ROTHERHITHE

GREENWICH

WOOLWICH

WESTMINSTER

LAMBETH

Royal Naval
Greenwich College
Foot Tunnel
Cutty Sark

National Maritime
Museum

see "Central London" map for
more detail of this area

A202

Ranger's
House

BRIXTON

A102 (M)

Clapham
Common

BLACKHEATH

Eltham Palace

Dulwich
Picture
Gallery

Horniman Museum

A205

LEWISHAM

A20

STREATHAM

A215

FOREST HILL

A21

MITCHAM

Crystal
Palace

A234

Chislehurst
Caves

BROMLEY

A23

A222

BECKENHAM

A236

CROYDON

| 0 | | 4 miles |

▼ Downe

Green Park and St James's Park are all within a few minutes' walk of the West End, while, further afield, you can enjoy the more expansive parklands of Hampstead Heath and Richmond Park.

You could spend days just **shopping** in London, too, hobnobbing with the upper classes in Harrods, or sampling the offbeat weekend markets of Portobello Road and Camden. The **music**, **clubbing** and **gay/lesbian scene** is second to none, and mainstream arts are no less exciting, with regular opportunities to catch brilliant **theatre** companies, **dance** troupes, exhibitions and **opera**. **Restaurants**, these days, are an attraction, too. London has caught up with its European rivals, and offers a range from three-star Michelin establishments to low-cost, high-quality Indian curry houses. Meanwhile, the city's **pubs** have heaps of atmosphere, especially away from the centre – and an exploration of the farther-flung communities is essential to get the complete picture of this dynamic metropolis.

A brief history of London

The Romans founded Londinium in 43 AD as a stores depot on the marshy banks of the Thames. Despite frequent attacks – not least by Queen Boudicca, who razed it in 61 AD – the port became secure in its position as capital of Roman Britain by the end of the century. London's expansion really began, however, in the eleventh century, when it became the seat of the last successful invader of Britain, the Norman duke who became **William I of England** (aka "the Conqueror"). Crowned king of England in Westminster Abbey, William built the White Tower – centrepiece of the Tower of London – to establish his dominance over the merchant population, the class that was soon to make London one of Europe's mightiest cities.

Little is left of medieval or Tudor London. Many of the finest buildings were wiped out in the course of a few days in 1666 when the **Great Fire of London** annihilated more than thirteen thousand houses and nearly ninety churches, completing a cycle of destruction begun the year before by the Great Plague, which killed as many as a hundred thousand people. Chief beneficiary of the blaze was Sir Christopher Wren, who was commissioned to redesign the city and rose to the challenge with such masterpieces as St Paul's Cathedral and the Royal Naval Hospital in Greenwich.

Much of the public architecture of London was built in the eighteenth century and during the reign of Queen Victoria, when grand structures were raised to reflect the city's status as the financial and administrative hub of the invincible **British Empire**. However, in comparison to many other European capitals, much of London looks bland, due partly to the German bombing raids in World War II, and partly to some postwar development that has lumbered the city with the sort of concrete-and-glass mediocrity that gives modern architecture a bad name.

Yet London's special atmosphere comes not from its buildings, but from the life on its streets. A cosmopolitan city since at least the seventeenth century, when it was a haven for Huguenot immigrants escaping persecution in Louis XIV's France, today it is truly multicultural, with over a third of its permanent population originating from overseas. This century has seen the arrival of thousands from the Caribbean, the Indian subcontinent, the Mediterranean and the Far East, all of whom play an integral part in defining a metropolis that is unmatched in its sheer diversity.

Arrival

Flying into London, you'll arrive at one of the capital's five **international airports**: Heathrow, Gatwick, Stansted, Luton or City Airport, all of which are less than an hour from the city centre.

Heathrow (☎0870/000 0123, ⌨www.baa.co.uk), twelve miles west of the city, has four terminals, and two train/tube stations: one for terminals 1, 2 and 3, and a separate one for terminal 4. The high-speed **Heathrow Express** (every 15min; 15–20min; ☎0845/600 1515, ⌨www.heathrowexpress.co.uk) trains travel nonstop to Paddington Station for £12 each way or £22 return (£2 extra if you purchase your ticket on board the train). A much cheaper alternative is to take the slow Piccadilly **Underground** line into central London (every 2–5min; 50min) for £3.60. If you plan to make several sightseeing journeys on your arrival day, buy a multi-zone One-Day Travelcard for £4.90 (see p.63). There is also a **National Express** service from Heathrow, direct to Victoria Coach Station (every 30min; 35min–1hr depending on the traffic; ☎08705/808080, ⌨www.nationalexpress.co.uk), which costs £7 single, £10 return, as well as **Airbus #2** (☎08705/747777, ⌨www.go-by-coach .com), which runs from outside all four Heathrow terminals to several destinations in the city (every 30min; 1hr) and cost £7 single, £10 return. From midnight, you'll have to take **night bus** #N97 to Trafalgar Square (every 30min; 1hr 10min) for a bargain £1.50. **Taxis** are plentiful, but cost at least £35 to central London, and take around an hour (longer in the rush hour).

Gatwick (☎01293/535353, ⌨www.baa.co.uk), thirty miles to the south, has two terminals, North and South, connected by a monorail. The nonstop **Gatwick-Express** (every 15–30min; 30min; ☎0990/301530, ⌨www.gatwick express.co.uk) train runs day and night between the South Terminal and Victoria Station for £10.50 each way. Other options include the 24-hour **Connex** service to Victoria (every 15min–1hr; 40min) for £8.20 single, or the **Thameslink** to King's Cross (Mon–Sat every 15–30min; 50min) for £9.50 single. **Airbus #5** runs from both terminals to Victoria Coach Station (hourly; 1hr 30min) and costs £7 single, £10 return. A **taxi** ride into central London will set you back £50 or more, and take at least an hour.

Stansted (☎01279/680500, ⌨www.baa.co.uk), London's swankiest international airport, lies 34 miles northeast of the capital and is served by the **Stansted Express** to Liverpool Street (every 15min–30min; 45min), which costs £13 single, £21 return. **Airbus #6 or #7** also run to Victoria Coach Station (every 30min; 1hr 15min) and cost £7 single, £10 return. A **taxi** ride will set you back £50 or more, and take at least an hour.

Luton airport (☎01582/405100, ⌨www.london-luton.com) is roughly thirty miles north of the city centre, and mostly handles charter flights. Luton Airport Parkway station is connected by **rail** to King's Cross (or St Pancras), via **Thameslink** (every 15min; 30–40min); tickets cost £9.50 single. **Bus #757** connects Luton to Victoria Station, taking just over an hour, and costing £6.50 single, £9 return. A **taxi** will cost in the region of £70 and take at least an hour from central London

London's smallest airport, **City Airport** (☎020/7646 0000, ⌨www.london cityairport.com), is situated in Docklands, nine miles east of central London, and handles European flights only. **Shuttle buses** connect City Airport with Canning Town DLR station (every 10min; 5min; £2), with Canary Wharf DLR and tube (every 10min; 10min; £3), and Liverpool Street station (every 10min; 30min; £6). Another option is to take the North London Line run by Silverlink from Silvertown, which is ten minutes' walk from the airport.

Arriving by **train** from elsewhere in Britain, you'll come into one of London's numerous main line stations, all of which have adjacent Underground stations linking into the city centre's tube network. **Eurostar** trains arrive at **Waterloo International**, south of the river. Trains from Harwich arrive at Liverpool Street, while trains from Dover arrive at Charing Cross; **coaches** terminate at **Victoria Coach Station**, a couple of hundred yards south of Victoria train station, down Buckingham Palace Road.

Information

The **London Tourist Board** (LTB; ⓦwww.londontown.com) has a desk in the Underground station concourse for Heathrow Terminals 1, 2 and 3 (daily 8am–6pm), but the main central office can be found near Piccadilly Circus in the **British Visitor Centre**, 1 Regent St (Mon 9.30am–6.30pm, Tues–Fri 9am–6.30pm, Sat & Sun 10am–4pm; June–Oct same times except Sat 9am–5pm). There are also offices in the forecourt of Victoria Station (Jan & Feb Mon–Sat 8am–7pm, Sun 8am–6.15pm; March–May & Oct–Dec Mon–Sat closes 8pm; June–Sept Mon–Sat closes 9pm), in the arrivals hall of Waterloo International (daily 8.30am–10.30pm) and in Liverpool Street Underground station (Mon–Fri 8am–6pm, Sat 8am-5.30pm & Sun 9am-5.30pm).

Individual boroughs also run tourist offices at various prime locations. The most useful are in the **City of London** to the south of St Paul's Cathedral (April–Sept daily 9.30am–5pm; Oct–March Mon–Fri 9.30am–5pm, Sat 9.30am–12.30pm; ☎020/7332 1456, ⓦwww.cityoflondon.gov.uk) in **Southwark**, at the south end of London Bridge (April–Sept Mon–Sat 10am–6pm, Sun 11am–6pm; Nov–March closes 4pm; ☎020/7403 8299, ⓦwww.southwark .gov.uk); and in **Greenwich** at 46 Greenwich Church St, SE10 (daily: April–Oct 10am–5pm; Nov–March 11am–4pm; ☎020/8858 6376, ⓦwww .greenwich.gov.uk). These offices will answer enquiries by phone; the best that the LTB can offer is **Visitorcall** (☎0839/123456), a spread of prerecorded phone announcements – you're far better off visiting their website ⓦwww .londontown.com.

Most information offices hand out a useful reference **map** of central London, plus plans of the public transport systems, but to find your way around every cranny of the city you need to invest in either an *A–Z Atlas* or a *Nicholson Streetfinder*, both of which have a street index covering every street in the capital; you can get them at most bookshops and newsagents for around £5. The only comprehensive and critical weekly **listings** magazine is *Time Out*, which costs £2.20 and comes out every Tuesday afternoon. In it you'll find details of all the latest exhibitions, shows, films, music, sport, guided walks and events in and around the capital.

The London Pass

If you're thinking of hitting quite a few of the major sights in a short space of time, it might be worth considering investing in a **London Pass**, which not only gives you entry to a whole range of attractions from the London Aquarium and Buckingham Palace to St Paul's Cathedral and Windsor Castle, but also throws in an all-zone Travelcard, £5 worth of free phone calls and various other perks and incentives. The pass costs from £22 for one day to £79 for six days. The London Pass can be bought over the phone (☎0870/242 9988) or on the internet (ⓦwww.londonpass .com).

City transport

London's transport network is among the most complex and expensive in the world. The **London Transport information office**, at Piccadilly Circus tube station (daily 9am–6pm), will provide free transport maps; there are other desks at Euston Station, Heathrow (terminals 1, 2, & 3), King's Cross, Liverpool Street, Paddington and Victoria stations. There's also a 24-hour phone line for transport information (☎020/7222 1234, ⓦwww.londontransport.co.uk). If you can, avoid travelling during the **rush hour** (Mon–Fri 8–9.30am & 5–7pm) when tubes become unbearably crowded and some buses get so full, you literally won't be allowed on.

The fastest way of moving around the city is by Underground or **Tube** (ⓦwww.thetube.com), as it's known to all Londoners. The eleven different tube lines cross much of the metropolis, although London south of the river is not very well covered. Each line has its own colour and name – all you need to know is which direction you're travelling in: northbound, eastbound, southbound or westbound. Services operate from around 5.30am Monday to Saturday, and from 7.30am on Sundays, and end around midnight every day; you rarely have to wait more than five minutes for a train from central stations. **Tickets** must be bought in advance from the machines or booths in the station entrance hall; ticket inspectors operate throughout the system and if you cannot produce a valid ticket you will be charged an on-the-spot Penalty Fare of £10. A single journey in the central zone costs an unbelievable £1.50; a **Carnet** of ten tickets costs £11.50. If you're intending to travel about a lot, a Travelcard is by far your best bet (see box below).

The network of **buses** is very dense, but much slower going than the Tube. **Tickets** for all bus journeys within, to or from the Central Zone costs a flat fare of £1; journeys outside the central zone cost 70p. Normally you pay the driver on entering, but some routes are covered by older Routemaster buses, staffed by a conductor and with an open rear platform. Note that at request stops (easily recognizable by their red sign) you must stick your arm out to hail the bus you want. In addition to the Travelcards mentioned below, a **One-Day Bus Pass** is also available and can be used before 9.30am; it costs £3 for zones 1 to 4. Regular buses run between about 6am and midnight; **night buses** (prefixed with the letter "N") operate outside this period. Night bus routes radiate out from Trafalgar Square at hourly intervals, more frequently on some routes and on Friday and Saturday nights. Travelcards are valid on night buses; otherwise journeys within, to or from the Central Zone costs a flat fare of £1.50; journeys outside the central zone cost £1.

Travelcards

To get the best value out of the transport system, buy a **Travelcard**. Available from machines and booths at all tube and train stations and at some newsagents as well (look for the sticker), they are valid for the bus, tube, Docklands Light Railway (DLR) and suburban rail networks. **One-Day Travelcards**, valid on weekdays from 9.30am and all day at weekends, cost £4 (central Zones 1 & 2), rising to £4.90 for All Zones (1–6, including Heathrow); the respective **Weekend Travelcards**, for unlimited travel on Saturdays and Sundays, cost £6 and £7.30. If you need to travel before 9.30am on a weekday, but don't need to use suburban trains, you can buy a **One-Day LT Card**, which costs from £5.10 (Zones 1 & 2) to £7.70 (All Zones). **Weekly Travelcards** begin at £15.90 for Zone 1; for these cards you need a **Photocard**, available free of charge from tube and train stations on presentation of a passport photo.

Large areas of London's suburbs are best reached by the **suburban train** network (Travelcards valid). Wherever a sight can only be reached by overground train, we've indicated the nearest train station and the central terminus from which you must depart. If you're planning to use the railway network a lot, you might want to purchase a **Network Card**, which is valid for a year, costs £20, and gives you up to 33 percent discount on fares to destinations in and around the southeast. To find out about a particular service, phone **National Rail Enquiries** on ☎08457/484950 or visit ⓦwww.britrail.co.uk.

If you're in a group of three or more, London's metered **black cabs** can be an economical way of getting around the centre – a ride from Euston to Victoria, for example, should cost around £10. A yellow light over the windscreen tells you if the cab is available – just stick your arm out to hail it. If you want to book one in advance, call ☎020/7272 0272.

Minicabs are less reliable than black cabs, but considerably cheaper, so you might want to take one back from a late-night club. Most minicabs are not metered, so always establish the fare beforehand. If you want to be certain of a woman driver, call Ladycabs (☎020/7254 3501), or a gay/lesbian driver, call Freedom Cars (☎020/7734 1313).

Accommodation

There's no getting away from the fact that **accommodation** in London is expensive. Compared with most European cities, you pay over the odds in every category. The city's hostels are among the most expensive in the world, while venerable institutions such as the *Ritz*, the *Dorchester* and the *Savoy* charge guests the very top international prices – up to £300 and more per luxurious night.

The cheapest places to stay are the dorm beds of the city's numerous independent **hostels**, followed closely by the official YHA hostels. Even the most basic **B&Bs** struggle to bring their tariffs below £40 for a double with shared facilities, and you're more likely to find yourself paying £50 or more.

We've given phone numbers and websites or email addresses where available for all our listed accommodation, but if you fail to find a bed in any of the places we've recommended, you could turn to one of the various **accommodation agencies**. The British Hotel Reservation Centre (BHRC) desks at Heathrow, Gatwick and City airports, at Victoria train and coach stations, and Waterloo International and Paddington train stations, don't charge a fee for booking rooms, and most of their offices are open daily from 6am till midnight. You can also book for free via the 24-hour phone line (☎020/7828 0601) or the internet (ⓦwww.bhrc.co.uk).

In addition, all London tourist offices (listed on p.62) operate a room-booking service, which costs £5; with a credit card you can book over the

Accommodation price codes

Throughout this guide, hotel and B&B accommodation is priced on a scale of ❶ to ❾, the number indicating the **lowest price** you could expect to pay per night in that establishment for a **double room** in high season. The prices indicated by the codes are as follows:

❶ under £40	❹ £60–70	❼ £110–150
❷ £40–50	❺ £70–90	❽ £150–200
❸ £50–60	❻ £90–110	❾ over £200

phone (☎020/7932 2020) or via the internet (🌐www.londontown.com). **Thomas Cook** (☎0800/371321) also has accommodation desks at Charing Cross, Euston, Gatwick Airport, King's Cross, Paddington and Victoria train stations, plus Earl's Court and South Kensington tubes, at the British Visitor Centre on Lower Regent Street (see p.62). Most (though not all) of these are open daily from 7am till 11pm, and will book anything from youth hostels (£2 fee) through to five-star hotels (£5 fee).

Hotels and B&Bs

With **hotels** you get less for your money in London than elsewhere in the country – generally breakfasts are more meagre and rooms more spartan than in similarly priced places in the provinces. In high season you should phone as far in advance as you can if you want to stay within a couple of tube stops of the West End, and expect to pay around £50 for an unexceptional double room without a private bathroom. If travelling with two or more companions, it's always worth asking the price of the family rooms, which generally sleep four and can save you a few pounds.

When choosing your **area**, bear in mind that the West End – Soho, Covent Garden, St James's, Mayfair and Marylebone – the City or financial district and the western districts of Knightsbridge and Kensington are dominated by expensive, upmarket hotels. For cheaper rooms, the widest choice (and some of the most dubious B&Bs) are close to the main train stations of Victoria and Paddington, and around Earl's Court. Those close to King's Cross tend to cater for people on welfare, or charge by the hour, although neighbouring Bloomsbury is both inexpensive and very central.

St James's, Mayfair and Marylebone

Edward Lear Hotel 28–30 Seymour St, W1 ☎020/7402 5401, 🌐www.edlear.com. A great location close to Oxford Street and Hyde Park, lovely flower boxes and a plush foyer. The rooms themselves need a bit of a makeover, but the low prices reflect this and the fact that most only have shared facilities or shower only. Marble Arch tube. ➎

Durrants Hotel George St, W1 ☎020/7935 8131, 🌐www.durrantshotel.co.uk. Just round the corner from the Wallace Collection and Oxford Street, this Georgian terrace hotel first opened in 1790, and has been run by the same family since 1921. Inside, it's a great exercise in period-piece nostalgia, with lots of wood-panelling, old prints and doormen. Bond Street tube. ➐

The Metropolitan Old Park Lane, W1 ☎020/7447 1000, 🌐www.metropolitan.co.uk. Run by Christina Ong, this terrifyingly trendy hotel adheres to the 1990s fad for pared-down minimalism. The staff are kitted out in designer labels, the Japanese restaurant is outstanding, and the *Met* bar is members and residents only in the evenings. Double rooms from £300. Green Park or Hyde Park Corner tube. ➒

Wigmore Court Hotel 23 Gloucester Place, W1 ☎020/7935 0928, 🌐www.wigmore-court-hotel .co.uk. The relentlessly pink decor may not be to everyone's taste, but this Georgian town house is a better than average B&B, boasting a high tally of returning clients. Comfortable rooms with en-suite facilities, plus a couple of cheaper rooms for just £80. Unusually, there's also a laundry and basic kitchen for guests' use. Marble Arch or Baker Street tube. ➎

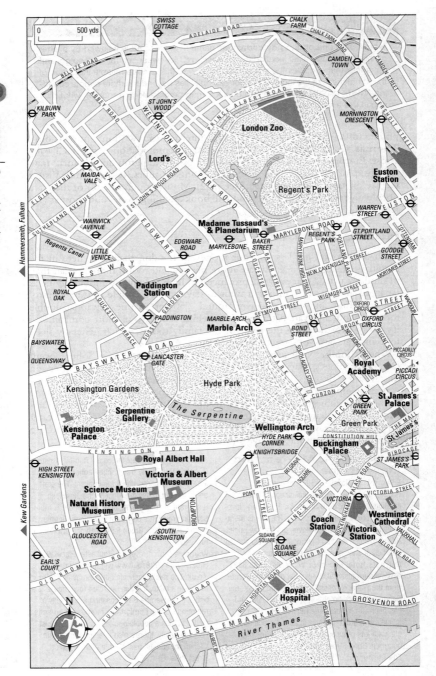

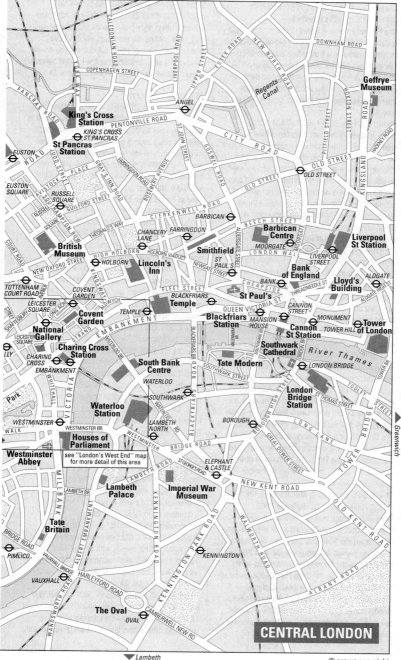

CENTRAL LONDON

67

© crown copyright

▼ Lambeth

▶ Greenwich

Soho, Covent Garden and The Strand

The Fielding Hotel 4 Broad Court, Bow St, WC2 ☏020/7836 8305, ⊛www.the-fielding-hotel.co.uk. Quietly situated on a traffic-free and gas-lit court, this excellent hotel is one of Covent Garden's hidden gems. A firm favourite with visiting performers, since it's just a few yards from the Royal Opera House. Breakfast is extra. Covent Garden tube. ❻

Hazlitt's 6 Frith St, W1 ☏020/7434 1771, ⊛www.hazlittshotel.com. Located off the south side of Soho Square, this early-eighteenth-century building is a hotel of real character and charm, offering en-suite rooms decorated and furnished as close to period style as convenience and comfort allow. There is no dining room, but some of London's best restaurants are a stone's throw away; continental breakfast isn't included in the rates, unless you go for one of their weekend deals. Tottenham Court Road tube. ❾

Manzi's 1–2 Leicester St, W1 ☏020/7734 0224, ⊛www.manzis.co.uk. Set over the Italian and seafood restaurant of the same name, *Manzi's* is one of very few downtown hotels in this price range. It's certainly right in the thick of the West End, just off Leicester Square, although noise might prove to be a nuisance. Continental breakfast is included in the price. Leicester Square tube. ❻

One Aldwych 1 Aldwych, WC2 ☏020/7300 1000, ⊛www.onealdwych.co.uk. On the outside, this is one of London's few vaguely Art Nouveau buildings, built in 1907 for the *Morning Post* newspaper. However, little survives from those days, as the interior of this desperately fashionable luxury hotel firmly follows the 1990s minimalist trend. The draws now are the underwater music in the hotel's vast pool, the oodles of modern art about the place, and the TVs in the bathrooms of the £300-plus rooms. Covent Garden or Temple (Mon–Sat) tube. ❾

St Martin's Lane 45 St Martin's Lane, WC2 ☏020/7300 5500 or ☏0800/634 5500, ⊛www.hotelbook.com. So cool you wouldn't know it was a hotel, this self-consciously chic "boutique hotel" from the New York-based Ian Schrager chain has proved an immediate hit with the media crowd. From the fluorescent yellow-and-white minimalist lobby to the large Portuguese limestone bathrooms, the interior has been designed throughout by the mischievous Philippe Starck. Rooms currently start at around £300 a double, but rates come down at the weekend. Leicester Square tube. ❾

Strand Continental Hotel 143 Strand, WC2 ☏020/7836 4880. This tiny Indian-run hotel near Aldwych offers very basic rooms with shared facilities, plus continental breakfast. Rooms have recently had a lick of paint, but nothing too drastic, making this an unbeatable central London bargain. Covent Garden or Temple (Mon–Sat) tube. ❷

Bloomsbury

Hotel Cavendish 75 Gower St, WC1 ☏020/7636 9079, ⊛www.hotelcavendish.com. Gower Street is very busy with traffic, but get a room at the back here and you'll have a peaceful night, and a real bargain, too, with lovely owners, two beautiful overrun gardens and some quite well-preserved original features. All rooms have shared facilities, and there are some good-value family rooms, too. Goodge Street tube. ❷

Crescent Hotel 49–50 Cartwright Gardens, WC1 ☏020/7387 1515, ⊛www.crescenthoteloflondon .com. Very comfortable and tastefully decorated Regency B&B – definitely a cut above the rest, with a lovely blacked-up range in the breakfast room. All doubles are en suite and have TVs, but there are a few bargain singles with shared facilities; guests also have use of tennis courts in the nearby gardens. Euston or Russell Square tube. ❺

Jenkins Hotel 45 Cartwright Gardens, WC1 ☏020/7387 2067, ⊛www.jenkinshotel.demon. co.uk. Smartly kept, family-run place in this fine Regency crescent, with fourteen fairly small but well-equipped and very clean rooms, some en-suite. The lovely in-house black labrador is a big hit with visitors, and a full English breakfast is included in the price. Euston or Russell Square tube. ❺

myhotel 11–13 Bayley St, WC1 ☏020/7667 6000, ⊛www.myhotels.co.uk. The aquarium in the lobby is the tell-tale sign that this is a feng shui hotel. Despite the positive vibes, and Conran-designed look, the double-glazed, air-conditioned rooms are on the small side for the price. Still, there's a gym, a very pleasant library and a restaurant, and it's well located for the West End. Tottenham Court Road tube. ❾

Ridgemount Hotel 65–67 Gower St, WC1 ☏020/7636 1141. Old fashioned, family-run place, with small rooms, mostly with shared facilities, a garden, free hot-drinks machine and a laundry service. A reliable, basic bargain for Bloomsbury. Goodge Street tube. ❸

Hotel Russell Russell Square, WC1 ☏020/7837 6470, ⊛www.principalhotels.co.uk. From its grand 1898 exterior to its opulent interiors of marble, wood and crystal, this late-Victorian landmark fully retains its period atmosphere. The rooms have less character but all are well appointed and decorated in a homely manner. Expensive, but various deals are available subject to availability. Russell Square tube. **❼**

Clerkwenwell and the City

City Hotel 12 Osborn St, E1 ☎020/7247 3313, ⍵www.cityhotellondon.co.uk. Spacious, clean and modern inside, this hotel stands on the eastern edge of the City, and in the heart of the Bengali East End at the bottom of Brick Lane. The plainly decorated rooms are all en suite, and many have kitchens, too; four-person rooms are a bargain for small groups. Aldgate East tube. **❻**

Great Eastern Hotel Liverpool St, EC2, ☎020/7618 5000, ⍵www.great-eastern-hotel .co.uk. Without doubt, *the* place to stay if you need or wish to be near the City. This venerable late-nineteenth-century station hotel has had a complete Conran makeover, yet manages to retain much of its clubby flavour. The rooms themselves are impeccably well-appointed and tastefully furnished – to maximize your natural light, get a room facing out. Doubles start from around £250, but rates are cut at the weekend. Liverpool Street tube. **❾**

Jurys Inn 60 Pentonville Rd, N1 ☎020/7282 5500, ⍵www.jurys.com. This modern Irish chain hotel is not a pretty sight on the busy Pentonville Road, but it's close to the tube, and equally convenient for the City and for Islington and Clerkenwell's trendy bars and restaurants. Service is very friendly, and the fixed room-rate is a bargain for three adults sharing or for those with kids. Breakfast is extra. Angel tube. **❺**

The Rookery Peter's Lane, Cowcross St EC1 ☎020/7336 0931, ⍵www.rookeryhotel.com. Rambling Georgian town house on the edge of the City in trendy Clerkenwell that makes a fantastically discreet little hideaway. The rooms start at around £225 a double (ask about weekend rates); each one has been individually designed in a sort of modern, camp take on the Baroque period, and all have super bathrooms with lots of character. Farringdon tube. **❽**

The South Bank

Holiday Inn Express 103–109 Southwark St, SE1 ☎020/7401 2525, ⍵www.hiexpress.com/lon-southwark. Unbeatable location just a stone's throw from the Tate Modern, and a relative bargain if you can stomach the motorway service station feel of the place. Southwark or Blackfriars tube. **❺**

London Bridge Hotel 8–18 London Bridge St, SE1 ☎020/7855 2200, ⍵www.london-bridge-hotel.co.uk. Perfectly placed for Southwark and Bankside or the City, this is a tastefully smart new hotel right by the station. As it attracts a mainly business clientele, rates do go down considerably at the weekend. London Bridge tube. **❽**

London County Hall Travel Inn Belvedere Rd, SE1 ☎020/7902 1600, ⍵www.travelinn.co.uk. Don't expect river views at these prices, but the location in County Hall itself is pretty good if you're up for a bit of sightseeing. Decor and ambience are functional, but for those with kids, the flat-rate rooms are a bargain. Waterloo or Westminster tube. **❺**

London Marriott Hotel, County Hall The County Hall, SE1 ☎020/7928 5200, ⍵www.marriotthotel .com. If you want river views from County Hall, you'll need to book in here. Over three quarters of the rooms overlook the Thames, and many have little balconies, too, with prices hovering around £300 (weekend rates are lower). It's all suitably pompous inside, and there's a full-size indoor pool. Waterloo or Westminster tube. **❾**

Mad Hatter 3–7 Stamford St, SE1 ☎020/7401 9222, ⍵www.fullers.co.uk. Situated above a Fuller's pub on the corner of Blackfriars Road, and run by the Fuller's brewery. Breakfast is extra, and is served in the pub, but this is a great location, a short walk from the Tate Modern and the South Bank. Ask about the weekend rates. Southwark or Blackfriars tube. **❺**

Victoria

Dover Hotel 42–44 Belgrave Rd, SW1 ☎020/7821 9085, ⍵www.dover-hotel.co.uk. One of the best B&Bs in this area. All rooms are tastefully decorated, and have a shower, toilet, phone and TV. Victoria tube. **❹**

The Goring 15 Beeston Place, SW1 ☎020/7396 9000, ⍵www.goringhotel.co.uk. This Edwardian hotel, owned and run by the Goring family for three generations, succeeds in creating an atmosphere of elegance and tranquillity. Afternoon tea is served on the delightful private garden-terrace in fine weather; rooms are a pricey £250 and upwards (breakfast not included). Victoria tube. **❾**

Noël Coward Hotel 111 Ebury St SW1 ☎020/7730 2094, ⍵www.noelcowardhotel.com. Elegant-fronted gay-friendly hotel in the heart of Belgravia, and former home of Coward between 1917 and 1930. Rooms are either en suite or with shared toilet, there's an attractive patio garden, and theatre or club package deals are available. Sloane Square. **❺**

Melbourne House Hotel 79 Belgrave Rd, SW1 ⊕020/7828 3516, ⊛www.melbournehousehotel. co.uk. One of the best B&Bs along Belgrave Road: family run, well furnished, offering clean and bright rooms, excellent communal areas and friendly service. All doubles have en-suite facilities, but there are a couple of very cheap singles without. Victoria or Pimlico tube. ❺

Oxford House Hotel 92–94 Cambridge St, SW1 ⊕020/7834 6467. Probably the best value rooms you can get in the vicinity of Victoria station. Showers and toilets are shared, but kept pristine. Full English breakfast is included in the price. Victoria tube. ❸

Sanctuary House Hotel 33 Tothill St, SW1 ⊕020/7799 4044, ⊛www.fullers.co.uk. Run by Fuller's Brewery, situated above a Fuller's pub, and decked out like one, too, in smart, pseudo-Victoriana. Breakfast is extra, but the location right by St James's Park is very central. Ask about the weekend deals. St James's Park tube. ❻

Topham's Hotel 26 Ebury St, SW1 ⊕020/7730 8147, ⊛www.tophams.co.uk. Charming family-owned hotel in the English country-house style, just a couple of minutes' walk from the Victoria stations. Sumptuously furnished en-suite twins and doubles, with full English breakfast. Victoria tube. ❼

Windermere Hotel 142–144 Warwick Way, SW1 ⊕020/7834 5163, ⊛www.windermere-hotel.co.uk. Situated at the western end of Warwick Way, this is a tastefully decorated and quietly stylish place, with a few good-value doubles with shared facilities and en-suite doubles for considerably more. There's a good restaurant downstairs, too. Sloane Square, Pimlico or Victoria tube. ❺

Woodville House & Morgan House 107 & 120 Ebury St, SW1 ⊕020/7730 1048, ⊛www .woodvillehouse.co.uk. Two above-average B&Bs, run by the same vivacious couple, with great breakfasts, patio gardens, and an iron and fridge for guests to use. All rooms at *Woodville* are with shared facilities; some at *Morgan* are en suite. Victoria tube. ❹

Paddington, Bayswater and Notting Hill

The Columbia 95–99 Lancaster Gate, W2 ⊕020/7402 0021, ⊛www.columbiahotel.co.uk. The spacious public lounge, well-worn decor and useful late bar make this large white-stucco hotel a rock-band favourite. The en-suite rooms themselves are actually very sober, and retain some original Victorian fittings. Lancaster Gate tube. ❺

Garden Court Hotel 30–31 Kensington Garden Square, W2 ⊕020/7229 2553, ⊛www.gardencourt

hotel.co.uk. Presentable, family-run B&B on a quiet square close to Portobello market; half the rooms are with shared facilities, half are en-suite. Full English breakfast included. Queensway or Bayswater tube. ❸

The Gresham Hotel 116 Sussex Gardens, W2 ⊕020/7402 2920, ⊛www.the-gresham-hotel .co.uk. B&B with a touch more class than many in the area. Rooms are small but tastefully kitted out, and all have TV. Continental breakfast included. Paddington tube. ❺

Inverness Court Hotel 1 Inverness Terrace, W2 ⊕020/7229 1444, ⊛www.cjhotels.com. Late-Victorian facade, reception area, bar and lounges lend a charming ambience, even if most of the en-suite rooms are in an undistinguished modern style. Continental breakfast included. Bayswater or Queensway tube. ❼

Pavilion Hotel 34–36 Sussex Gardens, W2 ⊕020/7262 0905, ⊛www.msi.com.mt/pavilion. The successful rock star's home-from-home, with outrageously over-the-top decor and every room individually themed. Paddington tube. ❻

Pembridge Court Hotel 34 Pembridge Gardens, W11 ⊕020/7229 9977, ⊛www.pemct.co.uk. Attractively converted town house close to Portobello Market, with spacious, fully equipped rooms. Two cats add to the homely feel, as does the lively *Caps Restaurant and Bar*. Notting Hill Gate or Holland Park tube. ❽

Prince William Hotel 42–44 Gloucester Terrace, W2 ⊕020/7724 7414, ⊛www.princewilliamhotel. co.uk. Cheap, gay-friendly place close to the West End. Most rooms are en suite, and the *Pearl of India* restaurant is on site. Paddington or Lancaster Gate. ❺

Knightsbridge, Kensington and Chelsea

Abbey House 11 Vicarage Gate, W8 ⊕020/7727 2594, ⊛www.abbeyhousekensington.com. Inexpensive Victorian B&B in a quiet street just north of Kensington High Street, maintained to a very high standard by its attentive owners. Rooms are large and bright – prices are kept down by sharing facilities rather than fitting the usual cramped bathroom unit. Full English breakfast, with free tea and coffee available all day. Cash only. High Street Kensington tube. ❺

Aster House 3 Sumner Place, SW7 ⊕020/7581 5888, ⊛www.asterhouse.com. Pleasant, non-smoking B&B in a luxurious white-stuccoed South Ken street; there's a lovely garden at the back and a large conservatory, where breakfast is served. Singles with shared facilities start at a bargain £75 a night. South Kensington. ❼

Blakes 33 Roland Gardens, SW7 ⑦ 020/7370 6701, ⓦ www.blakeshotels.com. Blakes' dramatic interior (designed by Anouska Hempel) and glamorous suites have long attracted visiting celebs. A faintly Rafflesesque flavour pervades, with bamboo furniture and old travelling trunks mixing with unusual *objets d'art*, tapestries and prints. Doubles from £250 are smart but small; fully equipped suites are spectacular. The restaurant and bar are excellent, and service is of a very high standard. Gloucester Road tube. ❾

Five Sumner Place 5 Sumner Place, SW7 ⑦ 020/7584 7586, ⓦ www.sumnerplace.com. Discreetly luxurious B&B in one of South Ken's prettiest white-stucco terraces. All rooms are en suite and breakfast is served in the house's lovely conservatory. South Kensington tube. ❼

The Gore 189 Queen's Gate, SW7 ⑦ 020/7584 6601, ⓦ www.gorehotel.co.uk. Popular, privately owned century-old hotel, only a step away from Hyde Park, and awash with oriental rugs, rich mahogany, walnut panelling and other Victoriana. Ask about weekend rates. South Kensington, Gloucester Road or High Street Kensington tube. ❽

The Hempel 31–35 Craven Hill Gardens, W2 ⑦ 020/7298 9000, ⓦ www.thehempelhotel.com. Deeply fashionable minimalist hotel, designed by the actress Anouska Hempel, with a huge and very empty atrium entrance. White-on-white rooms start around £300 a double, and there's an excellent postmodern Italian/Thai restaurant called *I-Thai*. Lancaster Gate or Queensway tube. ❾

Hotel 167 167 Old Brompton Rd, SW5 ⑦ 020 /7373 0672, ⓦ www.hotel167.com. Small, stylishly furnished B&B with en-suite facilities, double glazing and a fridge in all rooms. Continental buffet-style breakfast is served in the attractive morning room/reception. Gloucester Road tube. ❻

Vicarage Hotel 10 Vicarage Gate, W8 ⑦ 020/7229 4030, ⓦ www.londonvicaragehotel.com. Ideally located B&B a step away from Hyde Park. Clean rooms with shared facilities and a full English breakfast. Cash/travellers' cheques only. High Street Kensington or Notting Hill tube. ❺

Earl's Court

Philbeach Hotel 30–31 Philbeach Gardens, SW5 ⑦ 020/7373 1244, ⓦ www.philbeachhotel. freeserve.co.uk. London's busiest gay hotel, large and friendly, with room-only and en-suite options, internet and pleasant TV lounge area, *Appleby's Bar* and the popular *Wilde About Oscar* conservatory restaurant. Earl's Court tube. ❸

Rushmore Hotel 11 Trebovir Rd, SW5 ⑦ 020/7370 3839, ⓦ www.rushmore.activehotels.com. A cut above the average, with its colourful murals and imaginative room decor, in this often dreary area. The attic rooms are especially spacious and comfortable. Full continental breakfast. Earl's Court tube. ❺

Hampstead

La Gaffe 107–111 Heath St, NW3 ⑦ 020/7435 4941, ⓦ www.lagaffe.co.uk. Small and warren-like but characterful hotel, situated over an Italian restaurant and bar in the heart of Hampstead village. All rooms are en suite and there's a roof terrace for use in fine weather. Hampstead tube. ❻

Hampstead Village Guest House 2 Kemplay Rd, NW3 ⑦ 020/7435 8679, ⓔ hvguesthouse@dial. pipex.com. Lovely B&B in an old house set in a quiet backstreet between Hampstead village and the Heath. Rooms (some en suite, all non-smoking) have "lived-in" clutter, which makes a pleasant change from anodyne hotels and spartan B&Bs. Hampstead tube. ❺

Hostels, student halls and camping

London's seven **YHA hostels** are generally the cleanest, most efficiently run hostels in the capital. However, at around £20 a night, they charge around fifty percent more than most private hostels, and tend to get booked up several months in advance. Members of any association affiliated to Hostelling International have automatic membership of the YHA; non-members can join at any of the hostels. Note that you can book a bed in advance with a credit card either by ringing individual hostels or via ⓦ www.yha.org.uk. At peak periods, or to get an immediate overview of the availability of beds, and make an immediate booking, contact the **YHA central reservations** (⑦ 020/7373 3400). In addition to the official hostels, there's a wide range of **independent hostels** which charge less and tend to be more laid-back; unlike YHA hostels, however, there's no quality control, so standards can vary wildly. Some accommodation in **student halls of residence** is available outside term time, but the prices aren't all that attractive and the rooms get booked up quickly.

London's **campsites** are all out on the perimeters of the city, offering pitches for around £2–4, plus a fee of around £3–4 per person per night (reductions for children and out of season).

Hostels
YHA hostels

City of London 36 Carter Lane, EC4 ☎020/7236 4965, ℮city@yha.org.uk. Two-hundred-bed hostel in a great situation opposite St Paul's Cathedral; some twins, but mostly four- and five-bed dorms or triple bunks in larger dorms. No groups. St Paul's tube.

Earl's Court 38 Bolton Gardens, SW5 ☎020/7373 7083, ℮earlscourt@yha.org.uk. Better than a lot of accommodation in Earl's Court, but only offering dorms of mostly ten beds – the triple-bunks take some getting used to. Kitchen, café and patio garden. No groups. Earl's Court tube.

Hampstead Heath 4 Wellgarth Rd, NW11 ☎020/8458 9054, ℮hampstead@yha.org.uk. One of London's biggest and best-appointed YHA hostels, with its own garden and the wilds of Hampstead Heath nearby. Rooms with three to six beds and family rooms with two to five beds. Golders Green tube.

Holland House Holland Walk, W8 ☎020/7937 0748, ℮hollandhouse@yha.org.uk. Idyllically situated in the wooded expanse of Holland Park and fairly convenient for the centre of town, this extensive dorm-only hostel offers a decent kitchen and an inexpensive café. Popular with school groups. Holland Park or High Street Kensington tube.

Oxford Street 14 Noel St, W1 ☎020/7734 1618, ℮oxfordst@yha.org.uk. Its unbeatable West End location and modest size (seventy five beds in rooms of one, two, three and four beds) mean that this hostel tends to be full even out of high season. No children under 6, no groups, no café, but a large kitchen. Oxford Circus or Tottenham Court Road tube.

Rotherhithe Island Yard, Salter Rd, SE16 ☎020/7232 2114, ℮rotherhithe@yha.org.uk. London's largest purpose-built hostel is located in a Docklands area that has little going for it compared to the location of other London YHAs, but it's only a twenty-minute tube ride from the West End and often has space. Rooms have two, four, five or ten beds. Rotherhithe or Canada Water tube.

St Pancras 79–81 Euston Road, NW1 ☎020/7388 9998, ℮stpancras@yha.org.uk. Big hostel situated opposite the new British Library, on the busy Euston Road. Rooms are very clean, bright, triple-glazed and air-conditioned – some even have en-suite facilities. There are a few en-suite doubles and family rooms available with TVs. King's Cross or Euston tube.

Private hostels

Boka Hotel 33 Eardley Crescent SW5 ☎020/7370 1388, ⓦwww.bokahotel.activehotels.com. Famously popular with Aussies and South Africans, this is a laid-back and friendly hotel-cum-hostel with bargain singles and doubles as well as dorm beds. Communal kitchen available. Earl's Court tube.

Generator Compton Place, off Tavistock Place, WC1 ☎020/7388 7666, ⓦwww.the-generator.co.uk. The neon- and UV-lighting and post-industrial decor may not be to everyone's taste, but the youthful clientele certainly enjoy the cheap bar that's open daily until 2am. You don't share with strangers, so prices get progressively cheaper the more there are in your posse. Russell Square or Euston tube.

Leinster Inn 7–12 Leinster Square, W2 ☎020/7229 9641, ⓦwww.astorhostels.com. The biggest and liveliest of the Astor hostels, with a party atmosphere, and two bars open until the small hours. Singles, doubles and dorm beds available. Under 30s only. Queensway or Notting Hill Gate tube.

Museum Hostel 27 Montague St, WC1 ☎020/7580 5360, ⓦwww.astorhostels.com. In a lovely Georgian house in Bloomsbury, this is the quietest of the Astor hostels. There's no bar, though it's still a sociable, laid-back place, and well situated. Small kitchen, TV lounge and baths as well as showers. Under 30s only. Russell Square tube.

St Christopher's Village 161–165 Borough High St, SE1 ☎020/7407 1856, ⓦwww.st-christophers.co.uk. A new chain of independent hostels, with no fewer than three properties on Borough High Street (and more branches in Camden, Greenwich and Shepherd's Bush). The decor is upbeat and cheerful, the place is efficiently run and there's a party-animal ambience, fuelled by the neighbouring bar and the rooftop sauna and pool. London Bridge tube.

Student halls

Imperial College ☎020/7594 9507, ⓦwww.ad.ic.ac.uk/conferences. Singles and twins available (with breakfast) in three halls of residence in South Kensington and Notting Hill. You can book online. Open Easter & July to late-Sept.

International Student House 229 Great Portland

St, NW1 ☎020/7631 8300, ⊛www.ish.org.uk.
Hundreds of singles, twins, quads and dorm beds
in a vast complex at the southern end of Regent's
Park. Open year round. Great Portland Street or
Regent's Park tube.

John Adams Hall 15–23 Endsleigh St, WC1
☎020/7387 4086. A hall of residence belonging to
the Institute of Education, set in a Georgian terrace
in Bloomsbury. Singles and doubles, with breakfast; discounts for students and longer stays. Open
Easter & July–Sept. Euston Square tube.

King's College ☎020/7928 3777, ⊛www.kcl.ac
.uk. King's College has a wide range of accommo-

dation available on the South Bank, in Victoria and
Hampstead from July to September. You can either
contact the Vacation Bureau by phone or book
online. All rates including breakfast.

London School of Economics (LSE)
☎020/7955 7370, ⊛www.lse.ac.uk/vacations.
The LSE offers singles, twins, triples and quads in
various halls across London, en suite or with
shared facilities, and on either a bed-and-breakfast or self-catering basis. To find out about availability, you can ring the central office, or visit the
website and book online.

Campsites

Abbey Wood Federation Rd, Abbey Wood, SE2
☎020/8311 7708. Enormous, and well equipped
Caravan Club site east of Greenwich, ten miles
from central London. Train from Charing Cross to
Abbey Wood.

Crystal Palace Crystal Palace Parade, SE19
☎020/8778 7155. Caravan Club site, with maximum stays of two weeks in summer, three weeks

in winter. Train from Victoria or London Bridge to
Crystal Palace.

Lea Valley Leisure Centre Caravan Park
Meridian Way, N9 ☎020/8803 6900. Well-
equipped site, situated behind the leisure centre at
Pickett's Lock, backing on to a vast reservoir.
Ponders End train station from Liverpool Street.

The City

Stretching for more than thirty miles at its broadest point, **London** is by far
the largest city in Europe. The majority of its sights are situated to the north of
the River Thames, which loops through the city from west to east. However,

London tours

Standard **sightseeing bus tours** are run by several rival companies, their open-top
double-deckers setting off every thirty minutes from Victoria station, Trafalgar
Square, Piccadilly, and other conspicuous tourist spots. The Original Tour
(☎020/8877 1722, ⊛www.theoriginaltour.com) run several buses on several routes;
24-hour tickets cost around £14, and you can hop on and off as often as you like.
Alternatively, you can hop aboard one of the bright yellow World War II amphibious
vehicles used by Frog Tours (☎020/7928 3132, ⊛www.frogtours.com) for a combined **bus and boat tour**. After fifty minutes driving round the usual sights, you
plunge into the river and go on a half-hour cruise. Tours set off every hour or so from
behind County Hall, from 10am to dusk; tickets cost £15. Another money-saving
option is to skip the commentary by hopping on a real London bus – the #11 from
Victoria will take you past Westminster Abbey, the Houses of Parliament,
up Whitehall, round Trafalgar Square, along the Strand and on to St Paul's Cathedral.

   Walking tours are infinitely more appealing, mixing solid historical facts with juicy
anecdotes in the company of a local specialist. Walks on offer range from a literary
pub crawl round Bloomsbury to a tour of places associated with The Beatles. Tours
cost around £5 and usually take two hours. To find out what's on offer, check in the
"Around Town" section of *Time Out*. The widest range of walks on offer are run by
Original London Walks (☎020/7624 3978, ⊛www.walks.com).

△ Outside the Opera House, Bow Street

there is no single predominant focus of interest, for London has grown not through centralized planning but by a process of agglomeration – villages and urban developments that once surrounded the core are now lost within the amorphous mass of Greater London.

One of the few areas which is manageable on foot is **Westminster** and **Whitehall**, the city's royal, political and ecclesiastical power base, where you'll find the **National Gallery** and a host of other London landmarks from **Buckingham Palace** to **Westminster Abbey**. The grand streets and squares of **St James's**, **Mayfair** and **Marylebone**, to the north of Westminster, have been the playground of the rich since the Restoration, and now contain the city's busiest shopping zones.

East of Piccadilly Circus, **Soho** and **Covent Garden** are also easy to walk around and form the heart of the West End entertainment district, containing the largest concentration of theatres, cinemas, clubs, flashy shops, cafés and restaurants. To the north lie the university quarter of **Bloomsbury**, home to the ever-popular British Museum, and the secluded quadrangles of **Holborn**'s Inns of Court, London's legal heartland.

The City – the City of London, to give it its full title – is at one and the same time the most ancient and the most modern part of London. Settled since Roman times, it is now one of the world's great financial centres, yet retains its share of historic sights, notably the **Tower of London** and a fine cache of Wren churches that includes **St Paul's Cathedral**. Despite creeping trendification, the **East End**, to the east of the City, is not conventional tourist territory, but to ignore it entirely is to miss out a crucial element of contemporary London. **Docklands** is the converse of the down-at-heel East End, with the Canary Wharf tower, still the country's tallest building, epitomizing the pretensions of the Thatcherite dream.

Lambeth and **Southwark** comprise the small slice of central London that lies south of the Thames. The **South Bank Centre**, London's little-loved concrete culture bunker, is enjoying a new lease of life thanks to its proximity to the new **Tate Modern** in Bankside, which is linked to the City by the famous bouncing **Millennium Bridge**.

The largest segment of greenery in central London is Hyde Park, which separates wealthy **Kensington** and **Chelsea** from the city centre. The **museums** of South Kensington – the Victoria and Albert Museum, the Science Museum and the Natural History Museum – are a must; and if you have shopping on your agenda, you'll want to check out the hive of plush stores in the vicinity of **Harrods**.

The capital's most hectic weekend market takes place around Camden Lock in **North London**. Further out, in the literary suburbs of Hampstead and Highgate, there are unbeatable views across the city from half-wild Hampstead Heath, the favourite parkland of thousands of Londoners. The glory of **South London** is Greenwich, with its nautical associations, royal park and observatory (not to mention its Dome). Finally, there are plenty of rewarding day-trips along the Thames from **Chiswick** to **Windsor**, most notably to Hampton Court Palace and Windsor Castle.

Westminster and Whitehall

Political, religious and regal power has emanated from **Westminster** and **Whitehall** for almost a millennium. It was Edward the Confessor who first established Westminster as London's royal and ecclesiastical power base, some three miles west of the City of London. The embryonic English parliament met in the abbey in the fourteenth century and eventually took over the old royal palace of Westminster. In the nineteenth century, Whitehall became the "heart of the Empire", its ministries ruling over a quarter of the world's population. Even now, though the UK's world status has diminished, the institutions that run the country inhabit roughly the same geographical area: Westminster for the politicians, Whitehall for the civil servants.

The monuments and buildings in and around Whitehall and Westminster also span the millennium, and include some of London's most famous landmarks – **Nelson's Column**, **Big Ben** and the **Houses of Parliament**, **Westminster Abbey** and **Buckingham Palace**, plus two of the city's finest permanent art collections, the **National Gallery** and **Tate Britain**. This is a well-trodden tourist circuit since it's also one of the easiest parts of London to walk round, with all the major sights within a mere half-mile of each other, linked by two of London's most triumphant avenues, **Whitehall** and **The Mall**.

Trafalgar Square

Despite being little more than a glorified, sunken traffic island, infested with scruffy urban pigeons, **Trafalgar Square** is still one of London's grandest architectural set-pieces. John Nash designed the basic layout in the 1820s, but died long before the square took its present form. The Neoclassical National Gallery (see below) filled up the northern side of the square in 1838, followed five years later by the central focal point, **Nelson's Column**; the famous bronze lions didn't arrive until 1868, and the fountains – a rarity in a London square – didn't take their present shape until the eve of World War II.

As one of the few large public squares in London, Trafalgar Square has been both a tourist attraction and a focus for **political demonstrations** since the Chartists assembled here in 1848 before marching to Kennington Common. On a more festive note, the square is graced each December with a giant Christmas tree, donated by Norway in thanks for liberation from the Nazis, and on **New Year's Eve**, thousands of inebriates sing in the New Year.

Stranded on a traffic island to the south of the column, and predating the entire square, is the **equestrian statue of Charles I**, erected shortly after the Restoration on the very spot where eight of those who had signed the king's death warrant were disembowelled. Charles's statue also marks the original site of the thirteenth-century **Charing Cross**, from where all distances from the capital are measured – a Victorian imitation now stands outside Charing Cross train station.

The northeastern corner of the square is occupied by James Gibbs's church of **St Martin–in–the–Fields** (ⓦ www.stmartin-in-the-fields.org), fronted by a magnificent Corinthian portico and topped by an elaborate and distinctly unclassical tower and steeple. Completed in 1726, the interior is purposefully simple, though the Italian plasterwork on the barrel vaulting is exceptionally rich; it's best appreciated while listening to one of the church's free lunchtime concerts. There's a licensed café in the roomy **crypt**, not to mention a shop, gallery and brass-rubbing centre (Mon–Sat 10am–6pm, Sun noon–6pm).

The National Gallery

Unlike the Louvre or the Hermitage, the **National Gallery**, on the north side of Trafalgar Square (Mon–Sat 10am–6pm, Wed until 8pm, Sun noon–6pm; free; ⓦ www.nationalgallery.org.uk; Leicester Square or Charing Cross tube), is not based on a royal collection, but was begun as late as 1824 when the government bought 38 paintings belonging to a Russian emigré banker, John Julius Angerstein. The gallery's canny acquisition policy has resulted in a collection of more than 2200 paintings, but the collection's virtue is not so much its size, but the range, depth and sheer quality of its contents.

To view the collection chronologically, begin with the **Sainsbury Wing**, the softly-softly, Postmodern 1980s adjunct which playfully imitates elements of the original gallery's Neoclassicism. However, with more than a thousand paintings on permanent display in the main galleries, you'll need real stamina to see everything in one day, so if time is tight your best bet is to home in on your areas of special interest, having picked up a gallery plan at one of the information desks. A welcome innovation is the **Gallery Guide Soundtrack**, with a brief audio commentary on each of the paintings on display. The Soundtrack is available free of charge, though you're asked for a "voluntary contribution". Another possibility is to join up with one of the gallery's **free guided tours** (daily 11.30am & 2.30pm, plus Wed 6.30pm), which set off from the Sainsbury Wing foyer.

Among the National's **Italian** masterpieces are Leonardo's melancholic *Virgin of the Rocks*, Uccello's *Battle of San Romano*, Botticelli's *Venus and Mars* (inspired by a Dante sonnet) and Piero della Francesca's beautifully composed *Baptism of Christ*, one of his earliest works. The fine collection of Venetian works includes Titian's colourful early masterpiece *Bacchus and Ariadne*, his very late, much gloomier *Death of Acteon*, and Veronese's lustrous *Family of Darius before Alexander*. Elsewhere, Bronzino's erotic *Venus, Cupid, Folly and Time* and Raphael's trenchant *Pope Julius II* keep company with Michelangelo's unfinished *Entombment*. Later Italian works to look out for include a couple by Caravaggio, a few splendid examples of Tiepolo's airy draughtsmanship and glittering vistas of Venice by Canaletto and Guardi.

From **Spain** there are dazzling pieces by El Greco, Goya, Murillo and Velázquez, among them the provocative *Rokeby Venus*. From the **Low Countries**, standouts include van Eyck's *Arnolfini Marriage*, Memlinc's perfectly poised *Donne Triptych*, and a couple of typically serene Vermeers. There are numerous genre paintings, such as Frans Hals' *Family Group in a Landscape*, and some superlative landscapes, most notably Hobbema's *Avenue, Middleharnis*. An array of Rembrandt paintings that features some of his most searching portraits – two of them self-portraits – is followed by abundant examples of Rubens' expansive, fleshy canvases.

Holbein's masterful *Ambassadors* and several of van Dyck's portraits were painted for the English court, and there's home-grown **British** art, too, represented by important works such as Hogarth's satirical *Marriage à la Mode*, Gainsborough's translucent *Morning Walk*, Constable's ever popular *Hay Wain*, and Turner's *Fighting Téméraire*. Highlights of the **French** contingent include superb works by Poussin, Claude, Fragonard, Boucher and Watteau, and the only two paintings in the country by David.

Finally, there's a particularly strong showing of **Impressionists** and **Post-Impressionists** in rooms 43–46 of the East Wing. Among the most famous works are Manet's unfinished *Execution of Maximilian*, Renoir's *Umbrellas*, Monet's *Thames below Westminster*, Van Gogh's *Sunflowers*, Seurat's pointillist *Bathers at Asnières*, a Rousseau junglescape, Cézanne's proto-Cubist *Bathers* and Picasso's Blue Period *Child with a Dove*.

The National Portrait Gallery

Around the east side of the National Gallery lurks the **National Portrait Gallery** (Mon–Sat 10am–6pm, Sun noon–6pm; free; Ⓦ www.npg.org.uk;

Leicester Square or Charing Cross tube), founded in 1856 to house uplifting depictions of the good and the great. Though it has some fine works in its collection, many of the studies are of less interest than their subjects, and the overall impression is of an overstuffed shrine to famous Brits rather than a museum offering any insight into the history of portraiture. However, it is fascinating to trace who has been deemed worthy of admiration at any moment: aristocrats and artists in previous centuries, warmongers and imperialists in the early decades of this century, writers and poets in the 1930s and 1940s, and, latterly, retired footballers, and film and pop stars.

The NPG's **new extension** opened in 2000, with a bigger Tudor gallery, and a new contemporary gallery to expand the section that's by far the most popular. There's also a new computer gallery, a lecture theatre and rooftop café/restaurant with a view over the cityscape. The NPG's **Sound Guide**, which gives useful biographical background information to some of the pictures, is provided free of charge, though you're strongly invited to give a "voluntary contribution".

The Mall and St James's Park

The tree-lined sweep of **The Mall** – London's nearest equivalent to a leafy Parisian boulevard – was laid out in the first decade of the twentieth century as a memorial to Queen Victoria, and runs from Trafalgar Square to Buckingham Palace. The bombastic **Admiralty Arch** was erected to mark the entrance at the Trafalgar Square end of The Mall, while at the other end stands the ludicrous Victoria Memorial, Edward VII's overblown tribute to his mother.

Flanking nearly the whole length of the Mall, **St James's Park** is the oldest of the royal parks, having been drained and enclosed for hunting purposes by

The Royal Family

Tourists may still flock to see London's royal palaces, but the British public have become less and less happy about footing the huge tax bill that keeps the **Royal Family** (@ www.royal.gov.uk) in the style to which they are accustomed. This creeping republicanism can be traced back to 1992, which the Queen herself, in one of her few memorable Christmas Day speeches, accurately described as her *annus horribilis*. This was the year that saw the marriage break-ups of Charles and Di, and Andrew and Fergie, and the second marriage of divorcee Princess Anne.

Matters came to a head, though, over who should pay the estimated £50 million costs of repairs after the fire at Windsor Castle (p.139). Misjudging the public mood, the Conservative government offered taxpayers' money to foot the entire bill. After a furore, it was agreed that some of the cost would be raised from astronomical admission charges to Windsor Castle and Buckingham Palace. In addition, under pressure from the media, the Queen also reduced the number of royals paid out of the Civil List, and, for the first time in her life, agreed to pay taxes on her enormous personal fortune.

Given the mounting public resentment against the Royal Family, it was hardly surprising that public opinion tended to side with Princess Diana rather than Prince Charles during their various disputes. Diana's subsequent death, and the huge outpouring of grief that accompanied her funeral, further damaged the reputation of the royals, though her demise has also meant the loss of one of the Royal Family's most vociferous critics. Despite the Royal Family's low poll ratings, none of the political parties currently advocates abolishing the monarchy, and public appetite for stories about the adolescent princes (and their potential girlfriends), or the private life of Charles and Camilla, shows no signs of abating.

Henry VIII. It was landscaped by Nash in the 1820s, and today its tree-lined lake is a favourite picnic spot for the civil servants of Whitehall. Pelicans can still be seen at the eastern end of the lake, and there are ducks, swans and geese aplenty. From the bridge across the lake there's also a fine view over to Westminster and the jumble of domes and pinnacles along Whitehall.

Buckingham Palace

The graceless colossus of **Buckingham Palace** (Aug & Sept daily 9.30am–4.15pm; £11; Ⓦwww.royal.gov.uk; Green Park tube), popularly known as "Buck House", has served as the monarch's permanent London residence only since the accession of Victoria. It began its days in 1702 as the Duke of Buckingham's city residence, built on the site of a notorious brothel, and was sold by the duke's son to George III in 1762. The building was overhauled in the late 1820s by Nash and again in 1913, producing a palace that's as bland as it's possible to be.

For two months of the year, the hallowed portals are grudgingly nudged open; timed tickets are sold from the marquee-like box office in Green Park at the western end of The Mall – to avoid queuing, you must book in advance on ☏020/7321 2233. The interior, however, is a bit of an anticlimax: of the palace's 660 rooms you're permitted to see around twenty, and there's little sign of life, as the Queen decamps to Scotland every summer. For the other ten months of the year there's little to do here – not that this deters the crowds who mill around the railings, and gather in some force to watch the **Changing of the Guard** (see p.80), in which a detachment of the Queen's Foot Guards marches to appropriate martial music from St James's Palace (unless it rains, that is).

From spring 2002, the public will also be able to view the best of the Royal Collection at the rebuilt, greatly expanded **Queen's Gallery**, on the south side of the palace. Among the highlights will be works by Michelangelo, Reynolds, Gainsborough, Vermeer, van Dyck, Rubens, Rembrandt and Canaletto, as well as the odd Fabergé egg and heaps of Sèvres china.

There's more pageantry on show at the Nash-built **Royal Mews** (Mon–Thurs: Aug & Sept 10.30am–4.30pm; rest of year noon–4pm; £4; Victoria tube), further along Buckingham Palace Road. The royal carriages, lined up under a glass canopy in the courtyard, are the main attraction, in particular the Gold Carriage, made for George III in 1762, smothered in 22-carat gilding and weighing four tons, its axles supporting four life-size figures.

Whitehall

Whitehall, the broad avenue connecting Trafalgar Square to Parliament Square, is synonymous with the faceless, pin-striped bureaucracy charged with the day-to-day running of the country. Since the sixteenth century, nearly all the key governmental ministries and offices have migrated here, rehousing themselves on an ever-increasing scale. The statues dotted about Whitehall recall the days when this street stood at the centre of an empire on which the sun never set. Nowadays, with Scotland, Wales and Northern Ireland each having their own assemblies, Whitehall's remit is ever-decreasing.

During the sixteenth and seventeenth centuries Whitehall was the permanent residence of the kings and queens of England, and was synonymous with royalty. The original **Whitehall Palace** was the London seat of the Archbishop of York, confiscated and greatly extended by Henry VIII after a fire at Westminster forced him to find alternative accommodation; it was here that Henry celebrated his marriage to Anne Boleyn in 1533, and here that he died fourteen years later.

The Changing of the Guard

The Queen is colonel-in-chief of the seven **Household Regiments**: the Life Guards (who dress in red and white) and the Blues and Royals (who dress in blue and red) are the two Household Cavalry regiments; while the Grenadier, Coldstream, Scots, Irish and Welsh Guards make up the Foot Guards.

The Foot Guards can only be told apart by the plumes (or lack of them) in their busbies, and by the arrangement of their tunic buttons. The first three date back to the seventeenth century, and all these regiments still form part of the modern army as well as performing ceremonial functions such as the Changing of the Guard. If you're keen to find out more about the Foot Guards, pay a visit to the **Guards' Museum** (daily 10am–4pm; £2), in the Wellington Barracks on the south side of St James's Park.

The **Changing of the Guard** takes place at two separate locations in London: the two Household Cavalry regiments take it in turns to stand guard at Horse Guards on Whitehall (Mon–Sat 11am, Sun 10am, with inspection daily at 4pm), while the Foot Guards take care of Buckingham Palace (May–Aug daily 11.30am; Sept–April alternate days; no ceremony if it rains). A ceremony also takes place regularly in Windsor Castle (see p.139).

The chief section of the old palace to survive the fire of 1698 was the **Banqueting House** (Mon–Sat 10am–5pm; £3.90; ⓦwww.hrp.org.uk; Westminster tube), begun by Inigo Jones in 1619 and the first Palladian building to be built in England. The one room now open to the public has no original furnishings, but is well worth seeing for the superlative Rubens ceiling paintings glorifying the Stuart dynasty, commissioned by Charles I in the 1630s. Charles himself walked through the room for the last time in 1649 when he stepped onto the executioner's scaffold from one of its windows.

Across the road, two mounted sentries of the Queen's Household Cavalry and two horseless colleagues, all in ceremonial uniform, are posted daily from 10am to 4pm. Ostensibly they are protecting the **Horse Guards** building, originally built as the old palace guard house, but now guarding nothing in particular. The mounted guards are changed hourly; those standing every two hours. Try to coincide your visit with the Changing of the Guard (see box above), when a squad of twelve mounted troops arrive in full livery. The main action takes place in the parade ground at the rear of the building overlooking Horse Guards' Parade.

Further down this west side of Whitehall is London's most famous address, **Number 10 Downing Street** (ⓦwww.number-10.gov.uk; Westminster tube), the seventeenth-century terraced house that has been the residence of the prime minister since it was presented to Sir Robert Walpole, Britain's first PM, by George II in 1732. Just beyond the Downing Street gates, in the middle of the road, stands Edwin Lutyens' **Cenotaph**, eschewing any kind of Christian imagery, and inscribed simply with the words "The Glorious Dead". The memorial remains the focus of the Remembrance Sunday ceremony in November.

In 1938, in anticipation of Nazi air raids, the basements of the civil service buildings on the south side of King Charles Street were converted into the **Cabinet War Rooms**, now open to the public (daily: April–Sept 9.30am–6pm; Oct–March 10am–6pm; £5; ⓦwww.iwm.org.uk; Westminster tube). It was here that Winston Churchill directed operations and held Cabinet meetings for the duration of World War II. The rooms have been left pretty much as they were when they were finally abandoned on VJ Day 1945, and make for an atmospheric underground trot through wartime London. The museum's free acoustophone commentary helps bring the place to life and includes various eyewitness accounts by folk who worked there.

The Houses of Parliament

Clearly visible at the south end of Whitehall is one of London's best-known monuments, the Palace of Westminster, better known as the **Houses of Parliament**. The city's finest Victorian Gothic Revival building and symbol of a nation once confident of its place at the centre of the world, it is distinguished above all by the ornate, gilded clock tower popularly known as **Big Ben**, after the thirteen-ton main bell that strikes the hour (and is broadcast across the world by the BBC).

The original Westminster Palace was built by **Edward the Confessor** in the first half of the eleventh century, so that he could watch over the building of his abbey. It then served as the seat of all the English monarchs until a fire forced Henry VIII to decamp to Whitehall. The Lords have always convened at the palace, but it was only following Henry's death that the House of Commons moved from the abbey's Chapter House into the palace's St Stephen's Chapel, thus beginning the building's associations with parliament.

In 1834 the old palace burned down. Virtually the only relic of the medieval palace is the bare expanse of **Westminster Hall** (guided tours only, see below), on the north side of the complex. Built by William Rufus in 1099, it's one of the most magnificent secular medieval halls in Europe— you get a glimpse of the hall en route to the public galleries. The **Jewel Tower** (daily: April–Sept 10am–6pm; Oct 10am–5pm; Nov–March 10am–4pm; £1.50; EH; Westminster tube), across the road from parliament, is another remnant of the medieval palace, now housing an excellent exhibition on the history of parliament.

To watch the proceedings in either the House of Commons or the Lords, simply join the queue for the **public galleries** (known as Strangers' Galleries) outside St Stephen's Gate. The public are let in slowly from about 4.30pm onwards from Monday to Thursday and from 10am on Fridays; the security checks are very tight, and the whole procedure can take an hour or more. If you want to avoid the queues, turn up an hour or more later, when the crowds have usually thinned. Recesses (holiday closures) of both Houses occur at Christmas, Easter, and from August to the middle of October; phone ☎020 /7219 4272 for more information or visit the parliamentary websites (ⓦwww .parliament.uk and ⓦwww.explore.parliament.uk).

To see **Question Time** (Mon–Thurs 2.30–3.30pm) you need to book a ticket several weeks in advance from your local MP (if you're a UK citizen) or your embassy in London (if you're not). To contact your MP, simply phone ☎020/7219 3000 and ask to be put through. In recent years, it's also been possible to join a **guided tour** of the whole of parliament (excluding Big Ben) during the summer recess (Aug & Sept Mon–Sat only; £3.50), lasting an hour and fifteen minutes. Visitors are required to book in advance by phoning ☎020 /7344 9966.

Westminster Abbey

The Houses of Parliament dwarf their much older neighbour, **Westminster Abbey** (Mon, Tues, Thurs & Fri 9.30am–4.45pm, Wed 9.30am–4.45pm & 6–8pm, Sat 9.30am–2.45pm; £6; ⓦwww.westminster-abbey.org; Westminster or St James's Park tube), yet this single building embodies much of the histo-

Henry Purcell

Henry Purcell (1659–95) is the undisputed father of English classical music and was, until Elgar rose to international prominence in the 1930s, the country's only world-renowned composer. He had a short and fairly remarkable life. His father was a musician in the court of James II, while Henry himself was a chorister at the Chapel Royal. The year after his voice broke in 1673, he became organ tuner at Westminster Abbey and was abbey organist by the tender age of 20. He wrote the music for the coronations of James II and William and Mary. The music he wrote for Queen Mary's funeral was also performed when Purcell, a notorious alcoholic, died just a few months later at the age of 36 and was laid to rest in the abbey. Legend has it that, following a particularly heavy bout of drinking, his wife locked him out and he caught a cold and died.

ry of England: it has been the venue for all but two coronations since the time of William the Conqueror, and the site of more or less every royal burial for some five hundred years between the reigns of Henry III and George II. Scores of the nation's most famous citizens are honoured here, too (though many of the stones commemorate people buried elsewhere), and the interior is cluttered with hundreds of monuments, reliefs and statues.

Entry is currently via the **north door**, where you can pick up an audioguide for £2, or join a guided tour with one of the vergers for £3 (Mon–Sat only). The north transept is cluttered with monuments to politicians and traditionally known as **Statesmen's Aisle**, shortly after which you come to the abbey's most dazzling architectural set-piece, the **Lady Chapel**, added by Henry VII in 1503 as his future resting place. With its intricately carved vaulting and fan-shaped gilded pendants, the chapel represents the final spectacular gasp of the English Perpendicular style. Unfortunately, the public are no longer admitted to the **Shrine of Edward the Confessor**, the sacred heart of the building, though you do get to inspect Edward I's **Coronation Chair**, a decrepit oak throne dating from around 1300 and still used for coronations.

Nowadays, the abbey's royal tombs are upstaged by **Poets' Corner**, in the south transept, though the first occupant, Geoffrey Chaucer, was in fact buried here not because he was a poet, but because he lived nearby. By the eighteenth century this zone had become an artistic pantheon, and since then, the transept has been filled with tributes to all shades of talent. From the south transept, you can view the central sanctuary, site of the coronations, and the wonderful **Cosmati floor mosaic**, constructed in the thirteenth century by Italian craftsmen, and often covered by a carpet to protect it.

Doors in the south choir aisle lead to the **Great Cloisters** (daily 8am–6pm), rebuilt after a fire in 1298 and now home to a café. At the eastern end of the cloisters lies the octagonal **Chapter House** (daily: April–Oct 10am–5.30pm or dusk; Nov–March 10am–4pm; £2.50 or £1 with an abbey ticket; EH), where the House of Commons met from 1257. The thirteenth-century decorative paving-tiles and wall-paintings have survived intact. Chapter House tickets include entry to some of the few surviving Norman sections of the abbey: the neighbouring **Pyx Chamber** (daily 10.30am–4pm), which displays the abbey's plate, and the **Undercroft Museum** (daily 10.30am–4pm), filled with generations of bald royal death masks and wax effigies.

It's only after exploring the cloisters that you get to see the **nave** itself: narrow, light and, at over a hundred feet in height, by far the tallest in the country. Close by the west door is a doleful fourteenth-century portrait of Richard II, the oldest-known image of an English monarch painted from life. The most famous monument is the **Tomb of the Unknown Soldier**; it stands right in front of the west door, which now serves as the main exit.

Westminster Cathedral

Halfway down Victoria Street, which runs east from Westminster Abbey, you'll find one of London's most surprising churches, the stripey neo-Byzantine concoction of the Roman Catholic **Westminster Cathedral** (Mon–Fri & Sun 7am–7pm, Sat 8am–7pm; free; ⓦwww.westminsterdiocese. org.uk; Victoria tube). Begun in 1895, it is one of the last and wildest monuments to the Victorian era: constructed from more than twelve million terracotta-coloured bricks, decorated with hoops of Portland stone, it culminates in a magnificent tapered campanile which rises to 274 feet, served by a lift (daily 9am–5pm; £2). The **interior** is only half finished, so to get an idea of what the place will look like when it's finally completed, explore the series of **side chapels** whose rich, multicoloured decor makes use of over one hundred different marbles from around the world.

Tate Britain

From Parliament Square the unprepossessing Millbank runs south along the river to the **Tate Britain** (daily 10am–5.50pm; free; ⓦwww.tate.org.uk; Pimlico tube). Founded in 1897 with money from Sir Henry Tate, inventor of the sugar cube, the purpose-built Tate Gallery, half a mile south of parliament, is now devoted exclusively to British art. With the new Tate Modern now established in the disused Bankside Power Station (see p.114), the original building on Millbank has now been rechristened **Tate Britain**. As well as displaying British art from 1500 to 2000, plus a whole wing devoted to Turner, Tate Britain also showcases contemporary British artists, puts on large-scale exhibitions of British art, and continues to sponsor the Turner Prize, the country's most prestigious modern-art prize.

The galleries are rehung more or less annually, but always include a fair selection of **British art** by the likes of Hogarth, Constable, Gainsborough, Reynolds and Blake, plus foreign artists such as van Dyck who spent much of their career over here. The ever-popular **Pre-Raphaelites** are always well represented, as are established twentieth-century greats such as Stanley Spencer and Francis Bacon alongside living artists such as David Hockney and Lucien Freud. Lastly, don't miss the Tate's outstanding **Turner collection**, displayed in the Clore Gallery. The gallery offers audioguides to the collections for £3 each.

St James's, Mayfair and Marylebone

St James's, **Mayfair** and **Marylebone** emerged in the late seventeenth century as London's first real suburbs, characterized by grid-plan streets feeding into grand, formal squares. This expansion set the westward trend for middle-class migration, and as London's wealthier consumers moved west, so too did the city's more upmarket shops and luxury hotels, which are still a feature of the area.

Aristocratic **St James's**, the rectangle of land to the north of St James's Park, was one of the first areas to be developed and remains the preserve of the seriously rich. **Piccadilly**, which forms the border between St James's and Mayfair, is no longer the fashionable promenade it once was, but a whiff of exclusivity still pervades **Bond Street** and its tributaries. **Regent Street** was created as a new "Royal Mile", a tangible borderline to shore up these new fashionable suburbs against the chaotic maze of Soho and the City, where the working population still lived. Now, along with **Oxford Street**, it has become London's busiest shopping district – it's here that Londoners mean when they talk of "going shopping up the West End".

Marylebone, which lies to the north of Oxford Street, is another grid-plan Georgian development, a couple of social and real-estate leagues below Mayfair, but a wealthy area nevertheless. It boasts a very fine art gallery, the **Wallace Collection**, and, in its northern fringes, one of London's biggest tourist attractions, **Madame Tussaud's**, the oldest and largest wax museum in the world.

St James's

St James's, the exclusive little enclave sandwiched between The Mall and Piccadilly, was laid out in the 1670s close to St James's Palace. Royal and aristocratic residences predominate along its southern border, gentlemen's clubs cluster along Pall Mall and St James's Street, while jacket-and-tie restaurants and expense-account gentlemen's outfitters line Jermyn Street. Hardly surprising, then, that most Londoners rarely stray into this area.

St James's does, however, contain some interesting architectural set pieces, such as **Lower Regent Street**, which was the first stage in John Nash's ambitious plan to link George IV's magnificent Carlton House with Regent's Park. Like so many of Nash's grandiose schemes, it never quite came to fruition, as George IV, soon after ascending the throne, decided that Carlton House – the most expensive palace ever to have been built in London – wasn't quite luxurious enough, and had it pulled down. Instead, Lower Regent Street now opens up into **Waterloo Place**, at the centre of which stands the Guards' Crimean Memorial, fashioned from captured Russian cannon and featuring a statue of Florence Nightingale. Clearly visible, beyond, is the "Grand Old" **Duke of York's Column**, erected in 1833, ten years before Nelson's more famous one in Trafalgar Square.

Cutting across Waterloo Place, **Pall Mall** – named after the croquet-like game of *paglio a maglio* (literally "ball and mallet") that was popular at the time – leads west to **St James's Palace**, whose main red-brick gate-tower is pretty much all that remains of the Tudor palace erected here by Henry VIII. When Whitehall Palace burned down in 1698, St James's became the principal royal residence and, in keeping with tradition, an ambassador to the UK is still known as "Ambassador to the Court of St James", even though the court moved down the road to Buckingham Palace when Queen Victoria ascended the throne. The rambling, crenellated complex now provides a bachelor pad for Prince Charles (ⓦwww.princeofwales.gov.uk) and is off limits to the public, with the exception of the **Chapel Royal** (Oct to Good Friday Sun 8.30am & 11.15am; Green Park tube), situated within the palace, and the **Queen's Chapel** (Easter–July Sun 8.30am & 11.15am; Green Park tube), on the other side of Marlborough Road; both are open for services only.

One palatial St James's residence you can visit, however, is Princess Diana's ancestral home, **Spencer House** (Feb–July & Sept–Dec Sun 11.30am–4.45pm; £6), a superb Palladian mansion erected in the 1750s. Inside, tour guides take you through nine of the state rooms, the most outrageous of which is Lord Spencer's Room, with its astonishing gilded palm-tree columns. Note that children under 10 are not admitted.

Piccadilly Circus and around

Anonymous and congested it may be, but **Piccadilly Circus** is, for many Londoners, the nearest their city comes to having a centre. A much-altered product of Nash's grand 1812 Regent Street plan and now a major traffic bottleneck, it may not be a picturesque place, but thanks to its celebrated aluminium statue, popularly known as **Eros**, it's prime tourist territory. The fountain's archer is one of the city's top attractions, a status that baffles all who live here. Despite the bow and arrow, it's not the god of love at all but the *Angel of Christian Charity*, erected to commemorate the Earl of Shaftesbury, a bible-thumping social reformer who campaigned against child labour. If Eros's fame remains a mystery, that anyone bothers to wander into the tacky **Trocadero** (daily 10am–1am; ⓦwww.troc.co.uk), is a good deal more perplexing. For all the hype – it's quick to tout its position as Europe's largest indoor virtual-reality theme park – this is really just a glorified amusement arcade with a few virtual-reality rides thrown in.

Regent Street

Drawn up by John Nash in 1812 as both a luxury shopping street and a triumphal way between George IV's Carlton House and Regent's Park, **Regent Street** was the city's first attempt at dealing with traffic congestion, and its first stab at slum clearance and planned social segregation, which would later be perfected by the Victorians.

Despite the subsequent destruction of much of Nash's work in the 1920s, it's still possible to admire the stately intentions of his original Regent Street plan. The increase in the purchasing power of the city's middle classes in the last century brought the tone of the street "down" and heavyweight stores catering for the masses now predominate. Among the best known are **Hamley's**, reputedly the world's largest toy shop, and **Liberty**, the department store that popularized Arts and Crafts designs at the beginning of the last century.

Piccadilly

Piccadilly apparently got its name from the ruffs or "pickadills" worn by the dandies who used to promenade here in the late seventeenth century. Despite its fashionable pedigree, it's no place for promenading in its current state, with traffic careering down it nose to tail most of the day and night. Infinitely more pleasant places to window-shop are the **nineteenth-century arcades**, originally built to protect shoppers from the mud and horse-dung on the streets, but now equally useful for escaping exhaust fumes.

Piccadilly may not be the shopping heaven it once was, but there are still several old firms here that proudly display their royal warrants. One of the oldest institutions is the food emporium of **Fortnum & Mason** (ⓦwww .fortnumandmason.com) at no. 181, established in the 1770s by one of George III's footmen, Charles Fortnum, and his partner, Hugh Mason. In a kitsch addition dating from 1964, the figures of Fortnum and Mason bow to each other on the hour every day as the clock over the main entrance clanks out the Eton school anthem.

Further along Piccadilly, with its best rooms overlooking Green Park, stands the **Ritz Hotel** (ⓦwww.theritzhotel.co.uk), a byword for decadence since it first wowed Edwardian society in 1906; the hotel's design, with its two-storey French-style mansard roof and long arcade, was based on the buildings of Paris's Rue de Rivoli. For a prolonged look inside, you'll need to be in good appetite, dress appropriately, and book in advance, for the famous afternoon tea in the hotel's Palm Court.

Across the road from Fortnum & Mason, the **Royal Academy of Arts** (daily 10am–6pm, Fri until 10pm; £6–8; guided tours of the permanent collection Tues–Fri 1pm; free; ⊛www.royalacademy.org.uk; Green Park or Piccadilly Circus tube) occupies the enormous Burlington House, one of the few survivors from the ranks of aristocratic mansions that once lined the north side of Piccadilly. The Academy itself was the country's first-ever formal art school, founded in 1768 by a group of English painters including Thomas Gainsborough and Joshua Reynolds. Reynolds went on to become the academy's first president, and his statue now stands in the courtyard, palette in hand.

The Academy has always had a conservative reputation for its teaching and, until recently, most of its shows. The **Summer Exhibition**, which opens in June each year, remains a stop on the social calendar of upper middle-class England. Anyone can enter paintings in any style, and the lucky winners get hung, in rather close proximity, and sold. Supposed gravitas is added by the RA "Academicians", who are allowed to display six of their own works – no matter how awful. The result is a bewildering display, which gets panned annually by highbrow critics.

Along the west side of the Royal Academy runs the **Burlington Arcade**, built in 1819 for Lord Cavendish, then owner of Burlington House, to prevent commoners throwing rubbish into his garden. It's Piccadilly's longest and most expensive nineteenth-century arcade, lined with mahogany-fronted jewellers, gentlemen's outfitters and the like. Upholding Regency decorum, it is still illegal to whistle, sing, hum, hurry or carry large packages or open umbrellas on this small stretch, and the arcade's beadles (known as Burlington Berties), in their Edwardian frock-coats and gold-braided top hats, take the prevention of such criminality very seriously.

Bond Street

While Oxford Street, Regent Street and Piccadilly have all gone downmarket, **Bond Street**, which runs parallel with Regent Street, has carefully maintained its exclusivity. It is, in fact, two streets rolled into one: the southern half, laid out in the 1680s, is known as Old Bond Street; its northern extension, which followed less than fifty years later, is known as New Bond Street. They are both pretty unassuming streets architecturally, being a mixture of modest Victorian and Georgian town houses. However, the shops that line them, and those of neighbouring Conduit Street and South Molton Street, are among the flashiest in London, dominated by perfumeries, **jewellers** and designer clothing stores, including Versace, Gucci, Nicole Farhi and Yves St-Laurent.

In addition to fashion, Bond Street is also renowned for its **auction houses** and for its fine art galleries. Sotheby's, 34–35 New Bond St (⊛www.sothebys .com), is the oldest of the auction houses, and its viewing galleries are open free of charge. Bond Street's **art galleries** – exclusive mainstays of the street – are actually outnumbered by those on nearby Cork Street. The main difference between the two locations is that the Bond Street dealers are basically heirloom offloaders, whereas Cork Street galleries sell largely contemporary art. Both have impeccably presented and somewhat intimidating staff, but if you're interested, walk in and look around. They're only shops, after all.

Two famous musicians lived in Brook Street, just off Bond Street. The most recent one was **Jimi Hendrix**, who lived at no. 23 and is commemorated by a blue plaque; some two hundred years earlier, Georg Friedrich Handel lived next door at no. 25. Both houses are now part of the **Handel House Museum**, which should be open by the time you read this. It was here that Handel composed most of his music including the *Messiah* and *Music for the Royal Fireworks*. Highlights of the exhibition include the Byrne Collection which consists of several hundred objects including Mozart's handwritten arrangement of a Handel fugue and early editions of operas and oratorios.

Oxford Street

As wealthy Londoners began to move out of the City in the eighteenth century in favour of the newly developed West End, so **Oxford Street** (@www .oxfordstreet.co.uk) – the old Roman road to Oxford – gradually became London's main shopping street. Today, despite successive recessions and sky-high rents, this scruffy, two-mile hotchpotch of shops is still one of the world's busiest streets.

East of Oxford Circus, the street forms the border between Soho and Fitzrovia, and features two of the city's main record stores, HMV and Virgin Megastore. West of Oxford Circus, the street is dominated by more upmarket stores, including one great landmark, **Selfridge's** (@www.selfridges.co.uk), a huge Edwardian pile fronted by giant Ionic columns, with the Queen of Time, riding the ship of commerce and supporting an Art Deco clock, above the main entrance. The store was opened in 1909 by Chicago millionaire Gordon Selfridge, who flaunted its 130 departments under the slogan, "Why not spend a day at Selfridge's?", but was later pensioned off after running into trouble with the Inland Revenue.

The Wallace Collection

Immediately north of Oxford Street, on Manchester Square, stands Hertford House, a miniature eighteenth-century French chateau which holds the splendid **Wallace Collection** (Mon–Sat 10am–5pm, Sun noon–5pm; free; @www .wallace-collection.org.uk; Bond Street tube), a museum-gallery best known for its eighteenth-century French paintings and decorative art. There's a restaurant in the newly glassed-over courtyard, and a hands-on section downstairs, but at heart, the Wallace Collection remains an old-fashioned place, with exhibits piled high in glass cabinets, and paintings covering every inch of wall space. The fact that these exhibits are set amidst period fittings – and a bloody great armoury – makes the place even more remarkable.

If you're here for the paintings, head for the first floor which has the most famous works, the tone of which is set by **Boucher**'s sumptuous mythological scenes over the staircase. Among the Rococo delights in the West Gallery are **Fragonard**'s coquettes, one of whom flaunts herself to a smitten beau in *The Swing*. In addition to all this French finery there's a good collection of Dutch paintings in the East Galleries: **de Hooch**'s *Women Peeling Apples*, oil sketches by Rubens and landscapes by Ruisdael.

The Great Gallery, the largest room in the house, holds the best paintings, however, including several vast **van Dyck** portraits, **Titian**'s *Perseus and Andromeda*, **Rembrandt**'s affectionate portrait of his teenage son, Titus, and **Hals**'s arrogant *Laughing Cavalier*. Also here are **Velázquez**'s typically searching *Lady with a Fan*, and **Gainsborough**'s deceptively innocent portrait of the actress Mary Robinson, in which she insouciantly holds a miniature of the Prince of Wales, her lover (later George IV).

Baker Street, Madame Tussaud's and the Planetarium

A small percentage of tourists emerging from **Baker Street** tube station are on the trail of English literature's languid super-sleuth, Sherlock Holmes, whose statue now stands outside the main exit. The man himself is celebrated in two museums round the corner in Baker Street itself, though neither place has any real connection with the fictional character (no. 221b doesn't actually exist), nor his creator, Arthur Conan Doyle. The **Sherlock Holmes Museum** (daily 9.30am–6pm; £6; ⓦ www.sherlockholmes.co.uk; Baker Street tube) at no. 239 (in deference to the character, the sign on the door now says 221b) is a competent exercise in period reconstruction, but there's little attempt to impart any insights (or even basic facts) about Holmes or Doyle. Much better value for money is the **Sherlock Holmes Experience** (Mon–Sat 10am–5pm, Sun 11am–4pm; £1.50; ⓣ 020/7486 1426; ⓦ www.sh-memorabilia .co.uk; Baker Street tube), situated on the opposite side of the street above a memorabilia shop at no. 230. The curator is a real enthusiast, and has re-created the study from the 1980s British TV series, starring Jeremy Brett, and filled it with artefacts from the show, plus an impressive collection of first editions.

Just round the corner on Marylebone Road, **Madame Tussaud's** (daily: June to mid-Sept 9am–5.30pm; mid-Sept to May Mon–Fri 10am–5.30pm, Sat & Sun 9.30am–5.30pm; £11.50; combined ticket with the Planetarium £13.95; ⓦ www.madame-tussauds.com; Baker Street tube) has been pulling in the crowds ever since the good lady arrived in London from Paris in 1802 bearing the sculpted heads of guillotined aristocrats (she herself only just managed to escape the same fate – her uncle, who started the family business, was less fortunate). The entrance fee might be extortionate, the likenesses occasionally dubious and the automated dummies hardly state-of-the-art, but you can still rely on finding London's biggest queues here – to avoid queuing, book your ticket in advance over the phone or on the internet.

As well as the usual parade of wax figures, the tour of Tussaud's ends with a manic five-minute "ride" through the history of London in a miniaturized taxi cab. The adjoining and equally crowded London **Planetarium** (Mon–Fri 11.30am–5pm, Sat, Sun & school holidays 10am–5pm; £6.50; combined ticket with Madame Tussaud's £13.95) features a thirty-minute high-tech presentation, projected onto a giant dome; a standard romp through the basics of astronomy accompanied by a cosmic astro-babble commentary.

Soho

Soho gives you the best and worst of London. It's here you'll find the city's street fashion on display, its theatres, mega-cinemas and the widest variety of restaurants and cafés – where, whatever hour you wander through, there's always something going on. Uniquely, though, Soho retains an unorthodox and slightly raffish air born of an immigrant history as rich as that of the East End. The porn joints that made the district notorious in the 1970s are still in evidence, especially to the west of Wardour Street, as are the media types who pushed up the rents in the 1980s.

In the 1990s, Soho transformed itself again, this time into one of Europe's leading gay centres, with bars and cafés bursting out from the Old Compton Street area. Nevertheless, the area continues to boast a lively fruit and vegetable market on **Berwick Street** and a nightlife that has attracted writers and ravers to the place since the eighteenth century. The big movie houses on **Leicester Square** always attract crowds of punters, and the tiny enclave of **Chinatown** continues to double as a focus for the Chinese community and a popular place for inexpensive Chinese restaurants.

Leicester Square and Chinatown

By night, when the big cinemas and discos are doing good business, and the buskers are entertaining the crowds, **Leicester Square** is one of the most crowded places in London, particularly on a Friday or Saturday when huge numbers of tourists and half the youth of the suburbs seem to congregate here. By day, queues form for half-price deals at the Society of West End Theatres booth at the south end of the square, while touts haggle over the price of dodgy tickets for the top shows, and clubbers hand out flyers to likely looking punters.

It wasn't until the mid-nineteenth century that the square actually began to emerge as an entertainment zone, with accommodation houses (for prostitutes and their clients) and music halls such as the grandiose Empire and the Hippodrome (just off the square), edifices which survive today as cinemas and discos. Cinema moved in during the 1930s, a golden age evoked by the sleek black lines of the Odeon on the east side, and maintains its grip on the area. The Empire, at the top end of the square, is the favourite for the big royal premieres and, in a rather half-hearted imitation of the Hollywood (and Cannes) tradition, there are hand prints visible in the pavement by the southwestern corner of the square.

Chinatown, hemmed in between Leicester Square and Shaftesbury Avenue, is a self-contained jumble of shops, cafés and restaurants that makes up one of London's most distinct and popular ethnic enclaves. **Gerrard Street**, Chinatown's main drag, has been endowed with ersatz touches – telephone kiosks rigged out as pagodas and fake oriental gates – and few of London's 60,000 Chinese actually live in the three small blocks of Chinatown. Nonetheless, it remains a focus for the community, a place to do business or the weekly shopping, celebrate a wedding, or just meet up for meals, particularly on Sundays, when the restaurants overflow with Chinese families tucking into *dim sum*.

Old Compton Street and around

If Soho has a main drag, it has to be **Old Compton Street**, which runs parallel with Shaftesbury Avenue. The corner shops, peep shows, boutiques and trendy cafés here are typical of the area and a good barometer of the latest Soho fads. Soho has been a permanent fixture on the **gay scene** for the better part of a century, but the approach is much more upfront nowadays, with gay bars, clubs and cafés jostling for position on Old Compton Street and round the

---

London bookshops

Charing Cross Road, Soho's eastern border and a thoroughfare from Trafalgar Square to Oxford Street, boasts the highest concentration of **bookshops** anywhere in London. One of the first to open here was the chaotic, antiquated Foyles at no. 119, which now struggles to compete with the nearby heavyweight chain bookshops such as Books Etc, Borders, Blackwell's and Waterstones. The street retains more of its original character south of Cambridge Circus, where you'll find the capital's main feminist bookshop, Silver Moon, along with a cluster of ramshackle second-hand bookshops, such as Quinto.

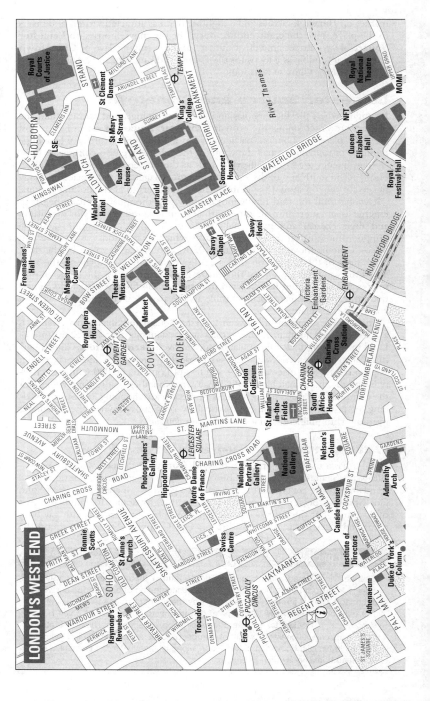

LONDON'S WEST END

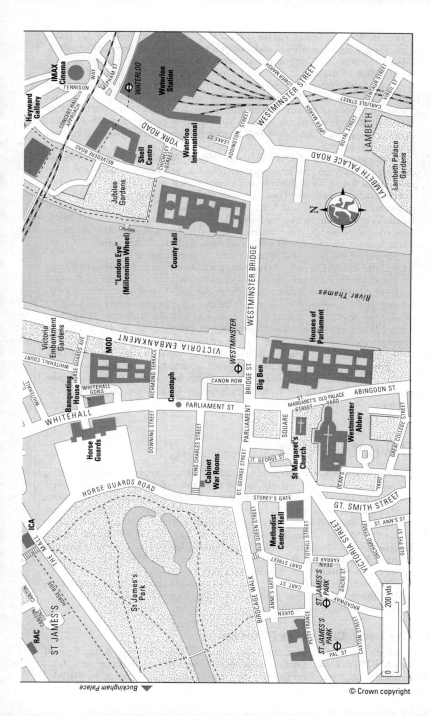

IMAX Cinema
Hayward Gallery
Shell Centre
Waterloo International
Waterloo Station
WESTMINSTER STREET
LAMBETH
Lambeth Palace Gardens
CARLISLE STREET
CENTAUR STREET
VIRGIL ST
ROYAL STREET
UPPER MARSH
LOWER MARSH
ADDINGTON STREET
LEAKE CT
CHICHELEY STREET
YORK ROAD
BELVEDERE ROAD
CONCERT HALL APPROACH
TENNISON WAY
MEPHAM ST
WATERLOO
Jubilee Gardens
"London Eye" (Millennium Wheel)
County Hall
WESTMINSTER BRIDGE
River Thames
Houses of Parliament
Big Ben
LAMBETH PALACE ROAD
N
Victoria Embankment Gardens
Banqueting House
MOD
VICTORIA EMBANKMENT
WESTMINSTER
Cenotaph
Horse Guards
WHITEHALL
WHITEHALL COURT
HORSE GUARDS AVE
WHITEHALL GDNS
RICHMOND TERRACE
PARLIAMENT ST
DOWNING STREET
KING CHARLES STREET
Cabinet War Rooms
GT. GEORGE STREET
BRIDGE ST
CANON ROW
PARLIAMENT SQUARE
LIT. GEORGE ST.
ST MARGARET'S STREET
OLD PALACE YARD
ABINGDON ST
St Margaret's Church
Westminster Abbey
GREAT COLLEGE STREET
DEAN'S YARD
HORSE GUARDS ROAD
St James's Park
THE MALL
ICA
RAC
ST JAMES'S
HORSE GUARDS
CARLTON HO TERRACE
STABLE YARD
Buckingham Palace
BIRDCAGE WALK
STOREY'S GATE
OLD QUEEN STREET
Methodist Central Hall
TOTHILL STREET
GT. SMITH STREET
VICTORIA STREET
ORCHARD STREET
ST. ANN'S ST
OLD PYE ST
DEAN FARRAR ST
DART STREET
ANNE'S GATE
QUEEN ANNE'S GATE
CART. ST.
PETTY FRANCE
BROADWAY
DACRE STREET
CAXTON STREET
PAL ST
ST JAMES'S PARK
200 yds
0
91

© Crown copyright

corner in Wardour Street. And it doesn't stop there: there's now a gay travel agency, a gay financial adviser and, even more convenient, a gay taxi service.

The streets off Old Compton Street are lined with Soho institutions past and present. One of the best known is London's longest-running jazz club, *Ronnie Scott's*, on Frith Street, founded in 1958 and still capable of pulling in the big names. Opposite is the *Bar Italia*, an Italian café with a big screen for satellite TV transmissions of Italian football games, and late-night hours popular with Soho's clubbers. It was in this building, appropriately enough for such a media-saturated area, that John Logie Baird made the world's first public television transmission in 1926.

At the western end of Old Compton Street is **Wardour Street**, a kind of dividing line between the trendier, eastern half of Soho and the seedier western zone. Immediately west of Wardour Street, the **vice and prostitution** rackets still have the area well staked out. However, straight prostitution makes up a small proportion of what gets sold here, and has been since Paul Raymond – one of Britain's richest men – set up his Folies-Bergère style *Revue Bar* in the late 1950s, now complemented by the transvestite floor show next door at *Madame Jo-Jo's*. These last two are paragons of virtue compared with the dodgy videos, short con outfits and rip-off joints that operate in the neighbouring streets.

Until the 1950s, **Carnaby Street** was a backstreet on Soho's western fringe, occupied, for the most part, by sweatshop tailors who used to make up the suits for nearby Savile Row. Then, sometime in the mid-1950s, several trendy boutiques opened catering for the new market in flamboyant men's clothing. In 1964 – the year of the official birth of the Carnaby Street myth – Mods, West Indian Rude Boys and other "switched-on people", as the *Daily Telegraph* noted, began to hangout here. The area quickly became the epicentre of Swinging Sixties' London, and its street sign London's most popular postcard. A victim of its own hype, Carnaby Street declined equally quickly into an avenue of overpriced tack. More recently, things have started to pick up again, especially in neighbouring Newburgh Street, and the whole area is currently enjoying a new lease of life.

Covent Garden

Covent Garden's transformation from a fruit and vegetable market into a fashion-conscious quarter is one of the most miraculous and enduring developments of the 1980s. More sanitized and brazenly commercial than Soho, Covent Garden today is a far cry from its heyday when the piazza was the great playground (and red-light district) of eighteenth-century London. The buskers in front of St Paul's Church, the theatres round about, and the **Royal Opera House** are survivors in this tradition, and on a balmy summer evening, **Covent Garden Piazza** is still an undeniably lively place to be. Another positive side-effect of the market development has been the renovation of the run-down warehouses to the north of the piazza, especially around the **Neal Street** area, which now boasts some of the trendiest shops in the West End, selling everything from shoes to skateboards.

Covent Garden Piazza

London's oldest planned square, laid out in the 1630s by Inigo Jones, **Covent Garden Piazza** was initially a great success, its novelty value alone attracting a rich and aristocratic clientele, but over the next century the tone of the place fell as the fruit and vegetable market expanded, and theatres and coffee houses began to take over the peripheral buildings. When the market closed in 1974, the piazza narrowly survived being turned into an office development. Instead, the elegant Victorian market hall and its environs were restored to house shops, restaurants and arts-and-crafts stalls. Boosted by buskers and street entertainers, the piazza has now become one of London's major tourist attractions, its success prompting a wholesale gentrification of the streets to the north of the market.

Of Jones's original piazza, the only remaining parts are the two rebuilt sections of north-side arcading, and **St Paul's Church**, facing the west side of the market building. The proximity of so many theatres has earned it the nickname of the "Actors' Church", and it's filled with memorials to international thespians from Boris Karloff to Gracie Fields. The space in front of the church's Tuscan portico – where Eliza Doolittle was discovered selling violets by Henry Higgins in George Bernard Shaw's *Pygmalion* – is now a legalized venue for buskers and street performers, who must audition for a slot months in advance.

The piazza's history of entertainment goes back to May 1662, when the first recorded performance of Punch and Judy in England was staged by Italian puppeteer Pietro Gimonde, and witnessed by Samuel Pepys. This historic event is commemorated every second Sunday in May by a **Punch and Judy Festival**, held in the gardens behind the church; for the rest of the year, the churchyard provides a tranquil respite from the activity outside (access is from King, Henrietta and Bedford streets).

The piazza's museums

An original flower-market shed on the piazza's east side is occupied by the **London Transport Museum** (daily 10am–6pm, Fri from 11am; £4.95; Ⓦ www.ltmuseum.co.uk; Covent Garden tube). A herd of old buses, trains and trams make up the bulk of the exhibits, though there's enough interactive fun – touch-screen computers and the odd costumed conductor and vehicles to climb on – to keep most children amused. There's usually a good smattering of London Transport's stylish maps and posters on display, too, and you can buy reproductions, plus countless other LT paraphernalia, at the shop on the way out.

The rest of the old flower market now houses the **Theatre Museum** (Tues–Sun 10am–6pm; £4.50; Ⓦ www.theatremuseum.org), displaying three centuries of memorabilia from every conceivable area of the performing arts in the West (the entrance is on Russell St). The corridors of glass cases cluttered with props, programmes and costumes are not especially exciting, but the various temporary exhibitions are usually much more interactive and fun. There are guides on hand to bring the displays to life, and various workshops and performances to take advantage of. The museum also runs a **booking service** for West End shows and has an unusually good selection of cards and posters.

The Royal Opera House

The Corinthian portico opposite Bow Street magistrates' court belongs to the **Royal Opera House** (backstage tours Mon–Sat 10.30am, 12.30 & 2.30pm; £6; Ⓦ www.royaloperahouse.org; Covent Garden tube), whose main building dates from 1811, but which has recently undergone a £220 million redevelopment. Part and parcel of the rebuilding has been the construction of arcading in the northeast side of the piazza, from which there's now a passageway through to Bow Street. The public can also gain access to the spectacular wrought-iron **Floral Hall** (daily 10am–3pm), on the first floor, which now serves as the opera house's main foyer, and the *Amphitheatre* bar/restaurant, which has a glorious terrace overlooking the piazza.

North of the piazza

The area to the north of Covent Garden Piazza is, on the whole, more interesting in terms of its shops, pubs and eating places than is the piazza itself. Floral Street, Long Acre, Shelton Street and especially Neal Street are all good shopping locales.

Looking east down the gentle curve of Long Acre, it's difficult to miss the austere, Pharaonic mass of the **Freemasons' Hall** (Mon–Fri 10am–5pm; free; Ⓦ www.grand-lodge.org; Covent Garden tube), built as a memorial to all the masons who died in World War I. Whatever you may think of this reactionary, male-only, secretive organization, the interior is worth a peek for the Grand Temple alone, whose pompous, bombastic decor is laden with heavy symbolism. To see the Grand Temple, turn up for one of the free hourly **guided tours** (Mon–Fri 11am–4pm).

North from Long Acre runs **Neal Street**, one of the most sought-after commercial addresses in Covent Garden, which features some fine Victorian warehouses, complete with stair towers for loading and shifting goods between floors. Neal Street is now dominated by trendy fashion stores such as Mango, Diesel and, on nearby Shorts Gardens, About Time. A decade or so ago, the feel of the street was a lot less monied and more alternative, but that ambience only really survives in **Neal's Yard**, a wholefood haven set in a tiny little courtyard off Shorts Gardens, prettily festooned with flower boxes and ivy.

Bloomsbury

Bloomsbury gets its name from its medieval landowners, the Blemunds, though nothing was built here until the 1660s. Through marriage, the Russell family, the earls and later dukes of Bedford, acquired much of the area and established the many formal, bourgeois squares which are the main distinguishing feature of the area. The Russells named the grid-plan streets after their various titles and estates, and kept the pubs and shops to a minimum to maintain the tone of the neighbourhood.

This century, Bloomsbury acquired a reputation as the city's most learned quarter, dominated by the dual institutions of the **British Museum** and **London University** and home to many of London's chief book publishers, but perhaps best known for its literary inhabitants (for more on the Bloomsbury Group, see p.227). Today, the British Museum is clearly the star attraction, but there are other sights, such as the **Dickens House Museum**, that are high on many people's itineraries. In its northern fringes, the character of the area changes dramatically, becoming steadily more seedy as you near the two big main-line train stations of **Euston** and **King's Cross**, where cheap B&Bs and run-down council estates provide fertile territory for prostitutes and drug dealers, and an unlikely location for the new **British Library**.

The British Museum

One of the great museums of the world, the **British Museum** (daily 10am–5.30pm, Thurs & Fri until 8.30pm; free; Ⓦ www.british-museum.ac.uk; Russell Square, Tottenham Court Road or Holborn tube) is Britain's most popular tourist attraction after Blackpool, drawing more than six million visitors a year. With over four million exhibits ranged over two and a half miles of galleries, the BM contains one of the most comprehensive collections of antiquities, prints, drawings and books to be housed under one roof.

The building itself, begun in 1823, is the grandest of London's Greek Revival edifices, dominated by the giant Ionian colonnade and portico that forms the main entrance. The British Library's departure to St Pancras (see p.96) has allowed the museum to open up and re-develop the building's **Great Court** (Mon–Wed 9am–9pm, Thurs–Sat 9am–11pm, Sun 9am–6pm), which now features a remarkable, curving glass-and-steel roof, designed by Norman Foster. At the centre stands the copper-domed former **Round Reading Room**, built in the 1850s to house the British Library. It was here, at desk O7, beneath one of the largest domes in the world, that Karl Marx penned *Das Kapital*. The building continues to function as a public study area, and features a multimedia guide to the museum's collections.

The BM's collection of **Roman and Greek antiquities** is unparalleled, and is perhaps most famous for the Parthenon sculptures, better known as the **Elgin Marbles**, a series of exquisite friezes, metopes and pedimental sculptures, carved between 447 and 432 BC for the **Parthenon**. Removed from Athens in 1801 by Lord Elgin, British ambassador to Constantinople, ostensibly in order to protect them from damage, the sculptures have caused more controversy than any other of the museum's trophies, with the Greek government repeatedly requesting that they be returned. A CD audioguide (£3) is available to rent, but it's by no means essential as the explanatory panels and video are good enough. Amidst the plethora of Greek and Roman statuary and vases, the only other single item with a similarly high profile is the **Portland Vase**, made from cobalt-blue blown glass around the beginning of the first century, and decorated with opaque white cameos.

The museum's **Egyptian collection** is easily the most significant outside Egypt, and ranges from monumental sculptures, such as the colossal granite head of Amenophis III, to the ever-popular **mummies** and their ornate outer caskets. Also on display is the **Rosetta Stone**, which finally unlocked the secret of Egyptian hieroglyphs. Close by the Egyptian Hall, you'll find a splendid series of **Assyrian reliefs** from Nineveh, depicting events such as the royal lion hunts of Ashurbanipal, in which the king slaughters one of the cats with his bare hands. Among the most extraordinary artefacts from **Mesopotamia** are the enigmatic Ram in the Thicket (a lapis lazuli and shell statuette of a goat), an equally mysterious box known as the Standard of Ur, and the remarkable hoard of goldwork known as the Oxus Treasure.

The leathery half-corpse of the 2000-year-old **Lindow Man**, discovered in a Cheshire bog, and the Anglo-Saxon treasure from the **Sutton Hoo** ship burial, are among one of the highlights of the Prehistoric and Romano-British collection. The medieval and modern collections, meanwhile, range from the twelfth-century **Lewis Chessmen**, carved from walrus ivory, to twentieth-century exhibits such as a copper vase by Frank Lloyd Wright. It's also worth seeking out the museum's **Money Gallery**, which begins with the use of grain in Mesopotamia around 2000 BC, ends with a 1990s five hundred thousand million Yugoslav dinar note, and includes coins from all over the world.

The dramatically lit Mexican Gallery, and the North American Gallery, mark the beginning of the return of the museum's **ethnographic collection**, but lack of space means that only a fraction of the BM's enormous collection of prints and drawings can be displayed at any one time. In addition, there are fabulous **Oriental treasures** in the north wing of the museum, closest to the back entrance on Montague Place. The displays include ancient Chinese porcelain, ornate snuffboxes, miniature landscapes, a bewildering array of Buddhist and Hindu gods, and – the showpiece of the collection – dazzling limestone reliefs from the second-century stupa of Amaravati in south India.

Dickens House

A couple of Bloomsbury's lesser museums, although dwarfed by the British Museum, are worth dipping into. The **Dickens House**, 48 Doughty St (Mon–Sat 10am–5pm; £4; ⓦ www.dickensmuseum.com; Russell Square tube), is the area's only house museum – surprisingly, given the plethora of blue plaques marking the residences of local luminaries. Dickens moved here in 1837 shortly before his marriage to Catherine Hogarth, and they lived here for two years, during which time he wrote *Nicholas Nickleby* and *Oliver Twist*. This is the only one of Dickens' fifteen London addresses to survive intact, but only the drawing room has been restored to its original Regency style. Letters, manuscripts and lots of memorabilia, including first editions, the earliest known portrait and the annotated books he used during extensive lecture tours, are the rewards for those with more than a passing interest in the novelist.

The University

London has more students than any other city in the world (over half a million at the last count), which isn't bad going for a city that only organized its own **University** in 1826 (ⓦ www.lon.ac.uk; Russell Square or Goodge Street tube), more than six hundred years after the likes of Oxford and Cambridge. The university started life in Bloomsbury, but it wasn't until after World War I that the institution really began to take over the area.

However, the university's piecemeal development has left the place with no real focus other than a couple of landmarks in the form of the 1930s **Senate House** skyscraper, behind the British Museum, and the Neoclassical **University College** (UCL; ⓦ www.ucl.ac.uk), near the top of Gower Street. UCL is home to London's most famous art school, the **Slade**, which puts on temporary exhibitions in the **Strang Print Room**, in the south cloister of the main quadrangle (term time: Wed–Fri 1–5pm; free). Also on display in the south cloisters is the fully clothed skeleton of philosopher **Jeremy Bentham** (1748–1832), one of the university's founders, topped by a wax head and wide-brimmed hat.

The university also runs a couple of specialist museums. On the first floor of the Watson building, down Malet Place, the **Petrie Museum of Egyptian Archeology** (Tues–Fri 1–5pm, Sat 10am–1pm; free) has a couple of rooms jam-packed with antiquities, including the world's oldest dress. Tucked away in the southeast corner of Gordon Square, at no. 53, the **Percival David Foundation of Chinese Art** (Mon–Fri 10.30am–5pm; free) houses two floors of top-notch Chinese ceramics.

The British Library

After fifteen years of hassle and £500 million of public money, the new **British Library** (Mon & Wed–Fri 9.30am–6pm, Tues 9.30am–8pm, Sat 9.30am–5pm, Sun 11am–5pm; free; ⓦ www.bl.uk; King's Cross or Euston tube), located on the busy Euston Road on the northern fringes of Bloomsbury, finally opened to the public in 1998. As the country's most expensive public building, it's hardly surprising that the place has come under fierce criticism from all sides. Architecturally the charge has been led, predictably enough, by Prince Charles, who compared it to an academy for secret policemen. Yet while it's true that the architect, Colin St John Wilson, has a penchant for red-brick brutalism that's horribly out of fashion, and compares unfavourably with its cathedralesque Victorian neighbour, the former Midland

Grand Hotel, the interior of the library has met with general approval and the new high-tech exhibition galleries are superb.

With the exception of the reading rooms, the library is open to the general public. The three exhibition galleries are to the left as you enter; straight ahead is the spiritual heart of the BL, a multistorey glass-walled tower housing the vast **King's Library**, collected by George III and donated to the museum by George IV in 1823; to the side of the King's Library is the **philatelic collection**. If you want to explore the parts of the building not normally open to the public, you must sign up for a **guided tour** (Mon, Wed & Fri 3pm, Sat 10.30am & 3pm; £5; Tues 6.30pm & Sun 11.30am & 3pm; to include the reading rooms; £6).

The first of the three exhibition galleries to head for is the dimly lit **John Ritblat Gallery**, where a superlative selection of the BL's ancient manuscripts, maps, documents and precious books, including the richly illustrated Lindisfarne Gospels, are displayed. One of the most appealing innovations is "**Turning the Pages**", a small room off the main gallery, where you can turn the pages of selected texts "virtually" on a computer terminal. The **Workshop of Words, Sounds and Images** is a hands-on exhibition of more universal appeal, where you can design your own literary publication, while the **Pearson Gallery of Living Words** puts on excellent temporary exhibitions, for which there is sometimes an admission charge.

Strand, Holborn and Clerkenwell

This area lies on the periphery of the entertainment zone of the West End and the financial district of the City. The **Strand**, as its name suggests, once lay along the riverbank: it achieved its present-day form when the Victorians shored up the banks of the Thames to create the Embankment. **Holborn** (pronounced "Ho-burn"), to the northeast, has long been associated with the law, and its **Inns of Court** make for an interesting stroll, their archaic, cobbled precincts exuding the rarefied atmosphere of an Oxbridge college, and sheltering one of the city's oldest churches, the twelfth-century **Temple Church**. Close by the Inns, in Lincoln's Inn Fields, is the **Sir John Soane's Museum**, one of the most memorable and enjoyable of London's small museums, packed with architectural illusions and an eclectic array of curios. **Clerkenwell**, further to the northeast, is off the tourist trail, but harbours the vestiges of two pre-Fire-of-London priories, and a whole host of trendy new bars and restaurants.

Strand and Embankment

Once famous for its riverside mansions, and later its music halls, the **Strand** – the main road connecting Westminster to the City – is a shadow of its former self. Nowadays, it's best known for the young homeless who shelter in the shop doorways at night. The **Victoria Embankment**, which runs parallel with the Strand, was built between 1868 and 1874 by the French engineer Joseph Bazalgette, whose project simultaneously relieved congestion along the Strand, provided an extension to the underground railway and sewage systems, and created a new stretch of parkland with a riverside walk – no longer much fun due to the volume of traffic.

London's oldest monument, **Cleopatra's Needle**, languishes little-noticed on the Thames side of the busy Victoria Embankment, guarded by two

Victorian sphinxes. The 60-foot-high, 180-ton stick of granite in fact has nothing to do with Cleopatra – it's one of a pair erected in Heliopolis in 1475 BC (the other one is in New York's Central Park) and taken to Alexandria by the Emperor Augustus fifteen years after Cleopatra's suicide. This obelisk was presented to Britain in 1819 by the Turkish viceroy of Egypt, but nearly sixty years passed before it finally made its way to London.

The **Benjamin Franklin House** (℡020/7930 9121, ⓦwww.rsa.org.uk/franklin; Charing Cross or Embankment tube), on the other side of Charing Cross Station at 36 Craven St, will probably attract more visitors than Cleopatra's Needle. Restored with the help of, among others, the nearby Royal Society of Arts, the museum should be open early in 2002. The tenth son of a candlemaker, Franklin (1706–1790) had "genteel lodgings" here more or less continuously from 1757 to 1775. Whilst Franklin was espousing the cause of the British colonies (as the US then was), the house served as the first de facto American Embassy; eventually, he returned to America to help draft the Declaration of Independence, negotiate the peace treaty with Britain and frame the Constitution.

Aldwych

The wide crescent of **Aldwych**, forming a neat "D" with the eastern part of the Strand, was driven through the slums of this zone in the last throes of the Victorian era. A confident ensemble occupies the centre, with the enormous **Australia House** and **India House** sandwiching **Bush House**, home of the BBC's World Service (ⓦwww.bbc.co.uk/worldservice; Holborn tube) since 1940. Despite its thoroughly British associations, Bush House was actually built by the American speculator Irving T. Bush, whose planned trade-centre flopped in the 1930s. The giant figures on the north facade and the inscription, "To the Eternal Friendship of English-speaking Nations", thus refer to the friendship between the US and Britain, and are not, as many people assume, the declaratory manifesto of the current occupants.

Somerset House

South of Aldwych and the Strand stands **Somerset House** (ⓦwww.somerset house.org.uk; Temple – Mon–Sat only – or Covent Garden tube), sole survivor of the grandiose edifices which once lined this stretch of the riverfront, its four wings enclosing a large courtyard rather like a Parisian hôtel. The present building was begun in 1776 by William Chambers as a purpose-built governmental office development. There are now three entrances – off the Strand, via a terrace off Waterloo Bridge, and straight from the Victoria Embankment – all of which will bring you eventually to the main courtyard (daily 7.30am–11pm), which is centred on a startling 55-jet fountain that spouts straight from the cobbles from spring to autumn.

The south wing, overlooking the Thames, now houses the magnificent **Gilbert Collection** (Mon–Sat 10am–6pm, Sun noon–6pm; £4, free Mon 10am–2pm; £7 joint ticket with the Courtauld; ⓦwww.gilbert-collection .org.uk), a new museum of decorative arts displaying European silver and gold, micro-mosaics, clocks, portrait miniatures and snuffboxes. While there's no denying the outstanding craftsmanship of the pieces that attracted the magpie-like attention of the Beverley Hills-based collector Arthur Gilbert, the sheer opulence and gaudiness of many of the exhibits may prove too much for some. Also housed in the south wing are the **Hermitage Rooms** (Mon–Sat 10am–6pm, Sun noon–6pm; £6; ⓦwww.hermitagerooms.com), five galleries featuring changing exhibitions of similarly over-the-top objets d'art – drawn from St Petersburg's Hermitage Museum (housed in the Winter Palace).

Part of the north wing has, for some time now, been home to the galleries of the **Courtauld** (Mon–Sat 10am–6pm, Sun noon–6pm; £4, free Mon 10am–2pm; £7 joint ticket with the Gilbert Collection; ⓦ www.courtauld.ac.uk; Temple – Mon–Sat only – or Covent Garden tube), chiefly known for its dazzling collection of Impressionist and Post-Impressionist paintings, whose virtue is quality rather than quantity. Among works by Gauguin, Toulouse-Lautrec, Seurat, Van Gogh and Modigliani are one or two highly prized paintings: a small-scale version of Manet's *Déjeuner sur l'herbe*, Renoir's *La Loge* and Degas' *Two Dancers*, plus a whole heap of Cézanne's canvases, including one of his series of *Card Players*. The Courtauld also boasts earlier works by the likes of Rubens, van Dyck, Tiepolo and Cranach the Elder. During the course of 2002, the Courtauld plan to move their permanent collection into the south wing, leaving the north wing for large temporary exhibitions.

Temple and the Royal Courts of Justice

Temple is the largest and most complex of the Inns of Court, where every barrister in England must study before being called to the Bar. Temple itself is comprised of two Inns – **Middle Temple** (ⓦ www.middletemple.org.uk) and **Inner Temple** (ⓦ www.innertemple.org.uk) – both of which lie to the south of the Strand, and, strictly speaking, just within the boundaries of the City of London. A few very old buildings survive here, but the overall scene is dominated by the soulless neo-Georgian reconstructions that followed the devastation of the Blitz. Still, the maze of courtyards and passageways is fun to explore – especially after dark, when Temple is gas-lit.

There are several points of access, simplest of which is Devereux Court. Medieval students ate, attended lectures and slept in the **Middle Temple Hall** (Mon–Fri 10am–noon & 3–4pm; Temple tube – Mon–Sat only – or Blackfriars), across the courtyard, still the Inn's main dining room. The present building was constructed in the 1560s and provided the setting for many great Elizabethan masques and plays – probably including Shakespeare's *Twelfth Night*, which is believed to have been premiered here in 1602. The hall is worth a visit for its fine hammerbeam roof, wooden panelling and decorative Elizabethan screen.

The two Temple Inns share use of the complex's oldest building, **Temple Church** (Wed–Sun 11am–4pm Temple tube – Mon–Sat only – or Blackfriars), built in 1185 by the Knights Templar. An oblong chancel was added in the thirteenth century, and the whole building was damaged in the Blitz, but the original round church – modelled on the Church of the Holy Sepulchre in Jerusalem – still stands, with its striking Purbeck marble piers, recumbent marble effigies of knights and tortured grotesques grimacing in the spandrels of the blind arcading.

Across the Strand from Temple, the **Royal Courts of Justice** (Mon–Fri 8.30am–4.30pm; Temple tube – Mon–Sat only – or Blackfriars), home to the Court of Appeal and the High Court, where the most important civil cases are tried. Appeals and libel suits are heard here – it was from here that the likes of the Guildford Four and Birmingham Six walked to freedom, and it is where countless pop and soap stars have battled it out with the tabloids. The fifty-odd courtrooms are open to the public, though you have to go through stringent security checks first (strictly no cameras allowed).

Lincoln's Inn Fields

North of the Law Courts lies **Lincoln's Inn Fields**, London's largest square, laid out in the early 1640s with **Lincoln's Inn** (Mon–Fri 9am–6pm; ⊛www .lincolnsinn.org.uk; Holborn tube), the first – and in many ways the prettiest – of the Inns of Court on its east side. The Inn's fifteenth-century **Old Hall** is open by appointment only (☎020/7405 1393), but you can view the early seventeenth-century **chapel** (Mon–Fri noon–2pm), with its unusual fan-vaulted open undercroft and, on the first floor, its late Gothic nave, hit by a Zeppelin in World War I and much restored since.

The south side of Lincoln's Inn Fields is occupied by the gigantic **Royal College of Surgeons** (⊛www.rcseng.ac.uk), home to the **Hunterian Museum** (Mon–Fri 9am–5pm; free; Holborn tube), a fascinating collection of pickled bits and bobs. Also on view are the skeletons of the Irish giant, O'Brien (1761–83), who was seven feet ten inches tall, and the Sicilian midget Caroline Crachami (1815–24), who was just one foot ten and a half inches when she died at the age of 9.

A group of buildings on the north side of Lincoln's Inn Fields house **Sir John Soane's Museum** (Tues–Sat 10am–5pm; first Tues of the month also 6–9pm; free; ⊛www.soane.org; Holborn tube), one of London's best-kept secrets. The chief architect of the Bank of England, Soane (1753–1837) was an avid collector who designed this house not only as a home and office, but also as a place to stash his large collection of art and antiquities. Arranged much as it was in his lifetime, the ingeniously planned house has an informal, treasure-hunt atmosphere, with surprises in every alcove. At 2.30pm every Saturday, a fascinating, hour-long **free guided tour** takes you round the museum and the enormous research library, next door, containing architectural drawings, books and exquisitely detailed cork and wood models.

Gray's Inn and Staple Inn

North of Lincoln's Inn, **Gray's Inn** (Mon–Fri 10am–4pm; ⊛www. graysinn.org.uk; Chancery Lane tube – Mon–Sat only – or Holborn), entered from High Holborn, is named for the de Grey family, who owned the original mansion. The entrance is through an anonymous cream-coloured building next door to the venerable *Cittie of Yorke* pub. Established in the fourteenth century, most of what you see today was rebuilt after the Blitz, with the exception of the **hall** (by appointment only; ☎020/7458 7800), with its fabulous Tudor screen and stained glass, where the premiere of Shakespeare's *Comedy of Errors* is thought to have taken place in 1594.

Heading east along High Holborn, it's worth pausing to admire **Staple Inn** on the right, not one of the Inns of Court, but one of the now defunct Inns of Chancery, which used to provide a sort of foundation course for those aspiring to the Bar. Its overhanging half-timbered facade and gables date from the sixteenth century and are the most extensive in the whole of London; they survived the Great Fire, which stopped just short of Holborn Circus, but had to be extensively rebuilt after the Blitz.

Clerkenwell

Poverty and overcrowding were the main features of nineteenth-century Clerkenwell, and **Clerkenwell Green** became known in the press as "the headquarters of republicanism, revolution and ultra-non-conformity". The Green's connections with **radical politics** have continued into this century, and its oldest building, built as a Welsh Charity School in 1737, is now home to the **Marx Memorial Library** (Mon 1–6pm, Tues–Thurs 1–8pm, Sat 10am–1pm; free; ⓦwww.marxmemoriallibrary.sageweb.co.uk; Farringdon tube), at no. 37a. One-time headquarters of the Social Democratic Federation press, this is where **Lenin** edited seventeen editions of the Bolshevik paper *Iskra* in 1902–03. Visitors are welcome to visit the poky little back room where he worked, which is maintained as it was then, as a kind of shrine.

Of Clerkenwell's three medieval religious establishments, remnants of two survive, hidden away to the southeast of Clerkenwell Green. The oldest is the priory of the Order of St John of Jerusalem; the sixteenth-century **St John's Gate** (Mon–Fri 10am–5pm, Sat 10am–4pm; free; ⓦwww.sja.org.uk/history; Farringdon tube), on the south side of Clerkenwell Road, is the most visible survivor of the foundation. Today, the gatehouse forms part of a **museum**, which traces the development of the order before its dissolution in this country by Henry VIII, and its re-establishment in the nineteenth century. In 1877, the St John Ambulance was founded to provide a voluntary first-aid service to the public. It's in this field that the order is now best known in Britain, and a splendid new interactive gallery is now devoted to the history of the service. To get to see the rest of the gatehouse, and to visit the Norman crypt of the Grand Priory Church over the road, you must take a **guided tour** (Tues, Fri & Sat 11am & 2.30pm; £4).

A little to the southeast of St John's, on the edge of Smithfield, lies **Charterhouse** (guided tours only: April–July Wed 2.15pm; £3; Barbican tube), founded in 1371 as a Carthusian monastery. The public school, with which the foundation is now most closely associated, moved out to Surrey in 1872, but forty-odd pensioners – known, in the monastic tradition, as "brothers" – continue to be cared for here. The only way to visit the site is to join one of the exhaustive two-hour **guided tours**, which start at the gatehouse on Charterhouse Square. Very little remains of the original monastic buildings, but there's plenty of Tudor architecture to admire, dating from after the Dissolution when Charterhouse was rebuilt as a private residence.

The City

The City is where London began. Long established as the financial district, it stretches from Temple Bar in the west to the Tower of London in the east – administrative boundaries that are only slightly larger than those marked by the

The Corporation of London

The one unchanging aspect of the City is its special status, conferred on it by William the Conqueror and extended and reaffirmed by successive monarchs and governments ever since. Nowadays, with its Lord Mayor, its Beadles, Sheriffs and Aldermen, its separate police force and its select electorate of freemen and liverymen, the City is an anachronism of the worst kind. **The Corporation** (ⓦwww.corpoflondon.gov.uk), which runs the City like a one-party mini-state, is an unreconstructed old boys' network whose medievalist pageantry camouflages the very real power and wealth which it holds – the Corporation owns nearly a third of the Square Mile (and several tracts of land elsewhere in and around London). Its anomalous status is all the more baffling when you consider that the City was once the cradle of British democracy: it was the City that traditionally stood up to bullying sovereigns.

Roman walls and their medieval successors. However, in this Square Mile (as the City is sometimes referred to), you'll find few leftovers of London's early days, since four-fifths of the area burnt down in the Great Fire of 1666. Rebuilt in brick and stone, the City gradually lost its centrality as London swelled westwards, though it has maintained its position as Britain's financial heartland. What you see on the ground is mostly the product of three fairly recent building phases: the Victorian construction boom of the late nineteenth century; the overzealous postwar reconstruction following the Blitz and the money-grabbing frenzy of the Thatcherite 1980s, in which nearly fifty percent of the City's office space was rebuilt.

When you consider what has happened here, it's amazing that so much has survived to pay witness to the City's two-thousand-year history. Wren's spires still punctuate the skyline here and there and his masterpiece, **St Paul's Cathedral**, remains one of London's geographical pivots. At the eastern edge of the City, the **Tower of London** still stands protected by some of the best-preserved medieval fortifications in Europe. Other relics, such as the City's few surviving medieval alleyways, Wren's **Monument** to the Great Fire and London's oldest synagogue and church, are less conspicuous, and even locals have problems finding the more modern attractions of the **Museum of London** and the **Barbican** arts complex.

Perhaps the biggest change of all, though, has been in the City's population. Up until the eighteenth century the majority of Londoners lived and worked in or around the City; nowadays 300,000 commuters spend the best part of Monday to Friday here, but only 5000 people remain at night and at weekends. The result of this demographic shift is that the City is fully alive only during office hours. This means that weekdays are by far the best time to visit; many pubs, restaurants and even some tube stations and tourist sights close down at the weekend.

Fleet Street

In 1500 a certain Wynkyn de Worde, a pupil of William Caxton, moved the Caxton presses from Westminster to **Fleet Street**, to be close to the lawyers of the Inns of Court and to the clergy of St Paul's. However, the street really boomed two hundred years later when, in 1702, the now-defunct *Daily Courant*, Britain's first daily newspaper, was published here. By the nineteenth century all the major national and provincial dailies had their offices and printing presses in the Fleet Street district, a situation that prevailed until the 1980s, when the press barons relocated their operations elsewhere.

The best source of information about the old-style Fleet Street is the so-called "journalists' and printers' cathedral", the church of **St Bride's** (Mon–Sat 8am–5pm; Blackfriars tube), which boasts Wren's tallest and most exquisite spire (said to be the inspiration for the tiered wedding cake). The crypt contains a little museum of Fleet Street history, with information on the *Daily Courant* and the *Universal Daily Register*, which later became *The Times*, claiming to be "the faithful recorder of every species of intelligence...circulated for a particular set of readers only."

The western section of Fleet Street was spared the Great Fire, which stopped just short of **Prince Henry's Room** (Mon–Sat 11am–2pm; free), a fine Jacobean house with timber-framed bay windows. The first-floor room now contains material relating to the diarist **Samuel Pepys**, who was born nearby in Salisbury Court in 1633 and baptized in St Bride's. Even if you've no interest in Pepys, the wooden-panelled room is worth a look – it contains one of the finest Jacobean plasterwork ceilings in London, and a lot of original stained glass.

Numerous narrow alleyways lead off the north side of Fleet Street, two of which – Bolt Court and Hind Court – eventually open out into Gough Square, on which stands **Dr Johnson's House** (May–Sept Mon–Sat 11am–5.30pm; Oct–April Mon–Sat 11am–5pm; £3; ⓦ www.drjh.dircon.co.uk). The great savant, writer and lexicographer lived here from 1747 to 1759, whilst compiling the 41,000 entries for the first dictionary of the English language, two first editions of which can be seen in the grey-panelled rooms of the house. You can also view the open-plan attic, in which Johnson and his six helpers put together the dictionary.

St Paul's Cathedral

St Paul's Cathedral (Mon–Sat 8.30am–4pm; £5; ⓦ stpauls.co.uk; St Paul's tube), topped by an enormous lead-covered dome that's second in size only to St Peter's in Rome, has been a London icon since the Blitz, when it stood defiantly unscathed amid the carnage (or so it appeared on wartime propaganda photos). It remains a dominating presence in the City, despite the encroaching tower blocks – its showpiece west facade is particularly magnificent, and is at its most impressive at night when bathed in sea-green arc lights. Westminster Abbey has the edge, however, when it comes to celebrity corpses, pre-Reformation sculpture, royal connections and sheer atmosphere. St Paul's, by contrast, is a soulless but perfectly calculated architectural set piece, a burial place for captains rather than kings, though it does contain more artists than Westminster Abbey. The cathedral's services, featuring the renowned St Paul's choir, are held from Monday to Saturday at 5pm and on Sunday at 10.15am, 11.30am and 3.15pm.

The best place from which to appreciate the glory of St Paul's is beneath the **dome**, decorated (against Wren's wishes) by Thornhill's trompe l'oeil frescoes. By far the most richly decorated section of the cathedral, however, is the **chan-**

The City churches

The City of London boasts over forty churches (ⓦ www.london-city-churches.org), the majority of them built or rebuilt by Wren after the Great Fire. As a general rule, weekday lunchtimes are the best time to visit these churches, many of which put on free lunchtime concerts for the local wage slaves.

On the surface, many of the City churches appear quite similar: plain, light-filled interiors, in white, gold and dark wood furnishings. Below is a list of six of the most varied and interesting churches within the Square Mile:

St Bartholomew-the-Great Cloth Fair; Barbican tube. The oldest surviving church in the City and by far the most atmospheric; a fascinating building. St Paul's aside, if you visit just one church in the City, it should be this one.

St Mary Abchurch Abchurch Lane, Cannon Street; Cannon Street or Bank tube. Uniquely for Wren's City churches, the interior features a huge painted domed ceiling, plus the only authenticated Gibbons reredos.

St Mary Aldermary Queen Victoria Street; Mansion House tube. Wren's most successful stab at Gothic, with fan vaulting in the aisles

and a panelled ceiling in the nave.

St Mary Woolnoth Lombard Street; Bank tube. Hawksmoor's only City church, sporting an unusually broad, bulky tower and a Baroque clerestory that floods the church with light from its semicircular windows.

St Olave Hart Street; Tower Hill tube. Built in the fifteenth century, and one of the few pre-Fire Gothic churches in the City.

St Stephen Walbrook Walbrook; Bank tube. Wren's dress rehearsal for St Paul's, with a wonderful central dome and plenty of wood-carving by Gibbons.

cel, in particular the spectacular, swirling, gilded mosaics of birds, fish, animals and greenery, dating from the 1890s. The intricately carved oak and limewood **choir stalls**, and the imposing organ case, are the work of Wren's master carver, Grinling Gibbons. Meanwhile, in the south-choir aisle, is the only complete effigy to have survived from Old St Paul's, the upstanding shroud of **John Donne**, poet, preacher and one-time Dean of St Paul's.

A series of stairs, beginning in the south aisle, lead to the dome's three **galleries**, the first of which is the internal **Whispering Gallery**, so called because of its acoustic properties – words whispered to the wall on one side are distinctly audible over one hundred feet away on the other, though the place is usually so busy you can't hear very much above the hubbub except a ghostly murmur. The other two galleries are exterior: the **Stone Gallery**, around the balustrade at the base of the dome, and ultimately the **Golden Gallery**, below the golden ball and cross which top the cathedral.

Although the nave is crammed full of overblown monuments to military types, burials in St Paul's are confined to the **crypt**, reputedly the largest in Europe. The whitewashed walls and bright lighting, however, make this one of the least atmospheric mausoleums you could imagine. Immediately to your right you'll find **Artists' Corner**, which boasts as many painters and architects as Westminster Abbey has poets, including Christopher Wren himself, who was commissioned to build the cathedral after its Gothic predecessor was destroyed in the Great Fire. The crypt's two other star tombs are those of **Nelson** and **Wellington**, both occupying centre stage and both with more fanciful monuments upstairs.

Museum of London and the Barbican

Despite London's long pedigree, very few of its ancient structures are now standing. However, numerous Roman, Saxon and Elizabethan remains have been discovered during the City's various rebuildings and many of these finds are now displayed at the **Museum of London** (Mon–Sat 10am–5.50pm, Sun noon–5.50pm; free; St Paul's or Barbican tube), hidden above the western end of London Wall, in the southwestern corner of the Barbican complex. The museum's permanent exhibition is basically an educational trot through London's history from prehistory to the present day. This is interesting enough (and attracts a lot of school groups), but the real strength of the museum lies in the excellent temporary exhibitions, lectures, walks and videos it organizes throughout the year.

The City's only large residential complex is the **Barbican**, a phenomenally ugly and expensive concrete ghetto built on the heavily bombed Cripplegate area. The zone's solitary prewar building is the heavily restored sixteenth-century church of **St Giles Cripplegate** (Mon–Fri 9.30am–5.15pm, Sat 9am–noon); it is situated across from the famously user-repellent **Barbican Arts Centre**, the "City's gift to the nation", which was formally opened in 1982. The complex does, however, serve as home to the London Symphony Orchestra and the London chapter of the Royal Shakespeare Company, and holds various free gigs in the foyer.

Guildhall

Situated at the geographical centre of the City, **Guildhall** (May–Sept daily 10am–5pm; Oct–April Mon–Sat 10am–5pm; free; ⓦ www.corpoflondon. gov.uk; St Paul's or Bank tube) has been the ancient seat of the City administration for over eight hundred years. It remains the headquarters of the

Corporation of London, and is still used for many of the City's formal civic occasions. Architecturally, however, it is not quite the beauty it once was, having been badly damaged in both the Great Fire and the Blitz, and scarred by the addition of a grotesque 1970s concrete cloister and wing.

Nonetheless, the **Great Hall**, basically a postwar reconstruction of the fifteenth-century original, is worth a brief look, as is the **Guildhall Clock Museum** (Mon–Fri 9.30am–4.30pm; free), a collection of over six hundred timepieces, including one of the clocks that won John Harrison the Longitude prize (see p.132). Also worth a visit is the new, purpose-built **Guildhall Art Gallery** (Mon–Sat 10am–5pm, Sun noon–4pm; £2.50, free on Fri and daily after 3.30pm; Ⓦ www.guildhall-art-gallery.org.uk), which contains one or two exceptional works, such as Rossetti's *La Ghirlandata*, and Holman Hunt's *The Eve of St Agnes*, plus a massive painting depicting the 1782 Siege of Gibraltar, commissioned by the Corporation.

The financial centre

Bank is the finest architectural arena in the City. Heart of the finance sector and the busy meeting point of eight streets, it's overlooked by a handsome collection of Neoclassical buildings – among them, the Bank of England, the Royal Exchange and Mansion House (the Lord Mayor's official residence) – each one faced in Portland Stone.

Sadly, only the **Bank of England** (Ⓦ www.bankofengland.co.uk), which stores the nation's vast gold reserves in its vaults, actually encourages visitors. Established in 1694 by William III to raise funds for the war against France, the so-called "Grand Old Lady of Threadneedle Street" wasn't erected on its present site until 1734. All that remains of the building on which Sir John Soane spent the best part of his career from 1788 onwards is the windowless, outer curtain wall, which wraps itself round the three-and-a-half-acre island site. However, you can view a reconstruction of Soane's Bank Stock Office, with its characteristic domed skylight, in the **museum** (Mon–Fri 10am–5pm; free; Bank tube), which has its entrance on Bartholomew Lane.

East of Bank, beyond Bishopsgate, stands Richard Rogers' glitzy **Lloyd's Building**, completed in 1984. A startling array of glass and blue steel pipes – a vertical version of Rogers' own Pompidou Centre – this is easily the most popular of the modern City buildings, at least with the general public. However, it's due to be upstaged by Norman Foster's "upside-down ice-cream cone" building for **Swiss Re** currently being built on the site of the Old Baltic Exchange.

Just south of the Lloyd's building you'll find the picturesque **Leadenhall Market**, whose richly painted, graceful Victorian cast-ironwork dates from 1881. Inside, the traders cater mostly for the lunchtime City crowd, their barrows laden with exotic seafood and game, fine wines, champagne and caviar.

If you walk down Gracechurch Street from Leadenhall Market, you should be able to make out Wren's **Monument** (daily 10am–5.40pm; £1.50; Monument tube), which was designed by Wren to commemorate the Great Fire of 1666. Crowned with spiky gilded flames, this plain Doric column stands 202 feet high, making it the tallest isolated stone column in the world; if it were laid out flat it would touch the bakery where the Fire started, east of Monument. The bas-relief on the base, now in very bad shape, depicts Charles II and the Duke of York in Roman garb conducting the emergency relief operation. The 311 steps to the viewing gallery once guaranteed an incredible view; nowadays it is dwarfed by the buildings around it.

The Tower of London

The **Tower of London** (March–Oct Mon–Sat 9am–5pm, Sun 10am–5pm; Nov–Feb Mon & Sun 10am–4pm, Tues–Sat 9am–4pm; £11.30; ⓦ www.hrp .org.uk; Tower Hill tube), one of London's main tourist attractions, overlooks the river at the eastern boundary of the old city walls. Despite all the hype and heritage claptrap, it remains one of London's most remarkable buildings, site of some of the goriest events in the nation's history and somewhere all visitors and Londoners should explore at least once. Chiefly famous as a place of imprisonment and death, it has variously been used as a royal residence, armoury, mint, menagerie, observatory and – a function it still serves – a safe-deposit box for the Crown Jewels.

Amidst the crush of tourists and the weight of history surrounding the place, it's easy to forget that the Tower is, above all, the most perfectly preserved (albeit heavily restored) medieval fortress in the country. Begun by William the Conqueror as a simple watchtower, much of what's visible today was already in place by the end of the thirteenth century. Before you set off to explore the Tower complex, it's a good idea to get your bearings by taking one of the free **guided tours**, given every thirty minutes by one of the forty-odd **Beefeaters** (officially known as Yeoman Warders), ex-servicemen in Tudor costume, who can get you into areas otherwise inaccessible.

Visitors today enter the Tower along Water Lane, but in times gone by most prisoners were delivered through **Traitors' Gate**, on the waterfront. The near-by **Bloody Tower**, which forms the main entrance to the Inner Ward, is where the 12-year-old Edward V and his 10-year-old brother were accommodated "for their own safety" in 1483 by their uncle, the future Richard III, and later murdered. It's also where **Sir Walter Raleigh** was imprisoned on three separate occasions, including a thirteen-year stretch.

The **White Tower**, at the centre of the Inner Ward, is the original "Tower", begun in 1076, and now home to displays from the **Royal Armouries**, the majority of which now reside in Leeds (see p.885). Even if you've no interest in military paraphernalia, you should at least pay a visit to the **Chapel of St John**, a beautiful Norman structure on the second floor that was completed in 1080 – making it the oldest intact church building in London. To the west of the White Tower is the execution spot on **Tower Green** where seven highly placed but unlucky individuals were beheaded, among them Anne Boleyn and her cousin Catherine Howard (Henry VIII's second and fifth wives).

The Waterloo Barracks, to the north of the White Tower, hold the **Crown Jewels**, perhaps the major reason so many people flock to the Tower; however, the moving walkways are disappointingly swift, allowing you just 28 seconds' viewing during peak periods. The oldest piece of regalia is the twelfth-century **Anointing Spoon**, but the vast majority of exhibits postdate the Commonwealth (1649–60), when many of the royal riches were melted down for coinage or sold off. Among the jewels are the three largest cut diamonds in the world, including the legendary **Koh-i-Noor**, set into the Queen Mother's Crown in 1937.

The Tower is also home to eight **ravens**, their wings clipped so they can't fly away – legend says that the Tower and the kingdom will fall if they do. The birds are descendants of early scavengers attracted by the waste from palace kitchens, and are the latest in a long line protected by royal decree since the reign of Charles II. They even have their own graveyard, in the moat near the ticket barrier.

Tower Bridge

Tower Bridge (April–Oct 10am–6.30pm; Nov–March 9.30am–6pm; guided tour £6.25; ⊛ www.towerbridge.org.uk; Tower Hill tube) is less than 110 years old, yet it ranks with Big Ben as the most famous of all London landmarks. Completed in 1894, its neo-Gothic towers are clad in Cornish granite and Portland stone, but conceal a steel frame, which, at the time, represented a considerable engineering achievement, allowing a road crossing that could be raised to give tall ships access to the upper reaches of the Thames. The raising of the bascules (from the French for "see-saw") remains an impressive sight (ring ahead to find out when the next opening is). The elevated walkways linking the summits of the towers (intended for public use) were closed from 1909 to 1982 due to their popularity with prostitutes and the suicidal. You can only visit them now on an overpriced **guided tour**, dubbed the "Tower Bridge Experience", that employs videos and an animatronic chirpy Cockney to describe the history of the bridge.

The East End and Docklands

Few places in London have engendered so many myths as the **East End** (a catch-all title which covers just about everywhere east of the City, but has its heart closest to the latter). Its name is synonymous with slums, sweatshops and crime, as epitomized by antiheroes such as Jack the Ripper and the Kray Twins, but also with the rags-to-riches careers of the likes of Harold Pinter and Vidal Sassoon, and whole generations of Jews who were born in the most notorious of London's cholera-ridden quarters and have now moved to wealthier pastures. Old East Enders will tell you that the area's not what it was – and it's true, as it always has been. The East End is constantly changing as newly arrived immigrants assimilate and move out.

The East End's first immigrants were French Protestant Huguenots, fleeing religious persecution in the late seventeenth century. Within three generations the Huguenots were entirely assimilated, and the Irish became the new immigrant population, but it was the influx of Jews escaping pogroms in eastern Europe and Russia that defined the character of the East End in the second half of the nineteenth century. The area's Jewish population has now dispersed throughout London, though the East End remains at the bottom of the pile; even the millions poured into the **Docklands** development have failed to make much impression on local unemployment and housing problems. Unfortunately, racism is still rife, and is directed, for the most part, against the extensive Bengali community, who came here from the poor rural area of Sylhet in Bangladesh in the 1960s and 1970s.

Most visitors to the East End come for its famous Sunday **markets** since the area is not an obvious place for sightseeing, and certainly no beauty spot – Victorian slum clearances, Hitler's bombs and postwar tower blocks have all left their mark. However, there's plenty more to get out of a visit, including several **Hawksmoor churches**, and the vast **Canary Wharf** redevelopment, which has to be seen to be believed.

Whitechapel and Spitalfields

The districts of **Whitechapel** and, in particular, **Spitalfields**, within sight of the sleek tower blocks of the financial sector, represent the old heart of the East

East End Sunday markets

Most visitors to the East End come here for the **Sunday markets**. Approaching from Liverpool Street, the first one you come to is **Petticoat Lane** (Sun 9am–2pm; Liverpool Street or Aldgate East tube), not one of London's prettiest streets, but one of its longest-running Sunday markets, specializing in cheap (and often pretty tacky) clothing. The authorities renamed the street Middlesex Street in 1830 to avoid the mention of ladies' underwear, but the original name has stuck.

To the north lies **Spitalfields Market** (organic market Fri & Sun 10am–5pm; general market Mon–Fri 11am–3pm & Sun 10am–5pm; Liverpool Street tube), once the capital's premier wholesale fruit and vegetable market, now specializing in organic food, plus clothes, crafts and jewellery. Further east lies **Brick Lane** (Sun 8am–1pm; Aldgate East, Shoreditch or Liverpool Street tube), heart of the Bengali community, famous for its bric-a-brac Sunday market, wonderful curry houses and nonstop bagel bakery, and now also something of a magnet for young designers. From Brick Lane's northernmost end, it's a short walk to **Columbia Road** (Sun 8am–1pm; bus #26 from Aldwych or Liverpool Street tube), the city's best market for flowers and plants.

End, where the French Huguenots settled in the seventeenth century, where the Jewish community was at its strongest in the late nineteenth century, and where today's Bengali community eats, sleeps, works and prays. If you visit just one area in the East End, it should be this zone, which preserves mementoes from each wave of immigration.

The easiest approach is from Liverpool Street Station, a short stroll west of **Spitalfields Market**, the strange-looking red-brick and green-gabled market hall that forms the centrepiece of the area. Originally built in 1893, the market was extended in the 1920s, and it is this extension which is now under threat of demolition to make way for more office blocks. The dominant architectural presence in Spitalfields is **Christ Church** (Mon–Fri 12.30–2.30pm), built between 1714 and 1729 to a characteristically bold design by Nicholas Hawksmoor and now facing the market hall. Best viewed from Brushfield Street, the church's main features are its huge 225-foot-high broach spire and a giant Tuscan portico, raised on steps and shaped like a Venetian window (a central arched opening flanked by two smaller rectangles), a motif repeated in the tower and doors.

Whitechapel Road – as Whitechapel High Street and the Mile End Road are collectively known – is still the East End's main street, shared by all the many races who live in the borough of Tower Hamlets. The East End institution that draws in more outsiders than any other is the **Whitechapel Art Gallery** (Tues & Thurs–Sun 11am–5pm, Wed 11am–8pm; free; ⓦwww .whitechapel.org), a little further up the High Street in a beautiful crenellated 1899 Arts and Crafts building by Charles Harrison Townsend, architect of the similarly audacious Horniman Museum (see p.129). The gallery stages some of London's most innovative exhibitions of contemporary art, as well as hosting the biennial Whitechapel Open, a chance for local artists to get their work shown to a wider audience.

Just before the point where Whitechapel Road turns into Mile End Road stands the gabled entrance to the former Albion Brewery, where the first bottled brown ale was produced in 1899. Next door lies the **Blind Beggar**, the East End's most famous pub since March 8, 1966, when Ronnie Kray walked into the crowded pub and shot gangland rival George Cornell for calling him a "fat poof". This murder spelled the end of the infamous Kray Twins, Ronnie and Reggie, both of whom were sentenced to life imprisonment, though their well-publicized gifts to local charities created a Robin Hood image that still persists in these parts of town.

East End museums

The East End boasts two fascinating museums, both of them open to the public free of charge. The easiest one to get to is the **Bethnal Green Museum of Childhood** (daily except Fri 10am–5.50pm; free; ⓦ www.vam.ac.uk), situated opposite Bethnal Green tube station. The open-plan, wrought-iron hall, originally part of (and still a branch of) the V&A museum (see p.119), was transported here in the 1860s to bring art to the East End. The variety of exhibits means that there's something here for everyone from 3 to 93, but the museum's most frequent visitors are children – that said, the displays are not very hands-on. The ground floor is best known for its unique collection of antique dolls' houses dating back to 1673. You'll need a pile of 20p pieces with you to work the automata – Wallace the Lion gobbling up Albert is always a favourite. Elsewhere, there are puppets, a jumble of toys, a vast doll collection and excellent temporary exhibitions.

The **Geffrye Museum** (Tues–Sat 10am–5pm, Sun noon–5pm; free; ⓦ www. geffrye-museum.org.uk; bus #67, #149 or #242 from Liverpool Street tube), housed in a peaceful little enclave of eighteenth-century ironmongers' almshouses, set back from Kingsland Road, is essentially a furniture museum. A series of period living rooms, ranging from the oak-panelled seventeenth century through refined Georgian and cluttered Victorian, leads to the state-of-the-art New Gallery Extension, housing the new café and the excellent twentieth-century section, with a room devoted to virtually every decade, and temporary exhibitions in the basement.

Docklands

The architectural embodiment of Thatcherism – a symbol of 1980s smash-and-grab culture according to its critics, a blueprint for inner-city regeneration to its free-market supporters – the **Docklands** redevelopment provokes extreme reactions. Despite its catch-all name, however, Docklands is far from homogeneous. Canary Wharf, with its Manhattan-style skyscraper, is only its most visible landmark; industrial-estate sheds and huge swathes of dereliction are more indicative. Wapping, the westernmost district, has retained much of its old Victorian warehouse architecture, while the Royal Docks, further east, are only just beginning to be transformed from an industrial wasteland.

Docklands transport

Although Canary Wharf is now on the Jubilee line, the best way to view Docklands is either from one of the boats that course up and down the Thames (see p.73.), or from the driverless, overhead **Docklands Light Railway** (DLR; ⓦ www.dlr.co.uk), which sets off from Bank and from Tower Gateway, close to Tower Hill tube. Travelcards are valid on the DLR, or you can get a City Flyer South ticket for £2.90, giving you unlimited travel between Tower Gateway or Bank and Lewisham for a whole day. Tour guides give a free running commentary on certain DLR trains that set off from Tower Gateway (Mon–Fri hourly 10am–2pm, Sat & Sun every 30min 11am–4pm; ⓣ020/7363 9511), but phone ahead to make sure. If you're heading for Greenwich, and fancy taking a boat back into town, it might be worth considering a Sail & Rail ticket (£8.30), which gives you unlimited travel on the DLR, plus a boat trip between Greenwich and Westminster piers.

The docks were originally built from 1802 onwards to relieve congestion on the Thames quays, and eventually became the largest enclosed cargo-dock system in the world. However, competition from the railways, and later, the development of container ships, signalled the closure of the docks in the 1960s. Then, at the height of the recession in the 1980s, regeneration began in earnest. No one thought the old docks could ever be rejuvenated, and twenty years on, more has been achieved than many thought possible (and less than some had hoped). Travelling through on the DLR overhead railway, Docklands comes over as an intriguing open-air design museum, not a place one would choose to live or work – most people stationed here still see it as a bleak business-oriented outpost – but a spectacular sight nevertheless.

Wapping to Limehouse

From the DLR, you get a good view of Hawksmoor's two other landmark East End churches; the first one is **St George-in-the-East**, built in 1726 and visible to the south just before you reach Shadwell station. It's easy to spot thanks to its four domed corner towers and distinctive west-end tower topped by an octagonal lantern. You're missing nothing by staying on the train, though, as the interior was devastated in the Blitz. As the DLR leaves Limehouse station and skirts Limehouse Basin marina, Hawksmoor's **St Anne's Church** is visible to the north. Begun in 1714 and dominated again by a gargantuan west tower, the church is topped by an octagonal lantern and adorned with the highest church clock in London. Again, the interior isn't worth the effort as it was badly damaged by fire in 1850.

An alternative to the DLR is to walk from Wapping to Limehouse, along the Thames Path, which sticks to, or close to, the riverbank. You begin at **St Katharine's Dock**, immediately east of the Tower of London, and the first of the old docks to be renovated way back in the 1970s. St Katharine's redeeming qualities are the old swing bridges and the boats themselves, many of which are beautiful old sailing ships. Continue along desolate **Wapping High Street**, lined with tall brick-built warehouses, most now tastefully converted into yuppie flats, and you will eventually find yourself in Limehouse, beyond which lies the Isle of Dogs. The fairly well-signposted walk is about two miles in length, and will bring you eventually to Westferry DLR station.

The Isle of Dogs

The Thames begins a dramatic horseshoe bend at Limehouse, thus creating the **Isle of Dogs**, currently the geographical and ideological heart of the new Docklands. The area reaches its apotheosis in **Canary Wharf** (@ www.canarywharf .com), the strip of land in the middle of the former West India Docks, previously a destination for rum and mahogany, later tomatoes and bananas (from the Canary Islands – hence the name). The only really busy bit of the new Docklands, Canary Wharf is best known as the home of Britain's tallest building. Cesar Pelli's landmark tower is officially known as **One Canada Square**, and at 800ft, it's the highest building in Europe after Frankfurt's Messerturm. The world's first skyscraper to be clad in stainless steel, it's an undeniably impressive sight, both from a distance (its flashing pinnacle is a feature of the horizon at numerous points in London) and close up. Unless you work here, however, there is no access except to the ground-floor marble atrium.

The warehouses to the north of Canary Wharf are currently being converted into flats, bars, restaurants and a **Museum in Docklands** (for more information call @ 020/7515 1162 or visit the website @ www.museumindocklands .org; West India Quay DLR), and will include a thirty-storey tower block and a multiplex cinema. Unless you're keen to visit the museum, there's little point in getting off the DLR as it cuts right through the middle of the Canary Wharf office buildings under a parabolic steel and glass canopy.

The rest of the Isle of Dogs remains surreally lifeless, an uneasy mix of drab high-rises, council estates, warehouses converted into expensive apartments, and a lot of new architecture – some of it startling, some of it crass, much of it empty. If you're heading for Greenwich (see p.130), you have a choice: either get off at **Island Gardens**, Christopher Wren's favourite spot from which to contemplate his masterpieces across the river (the Royal Naval College and Royal Observatory), and walk through the 1902 foot-tunnel to Greenwich; alternatively, you can stay on the DLR, which now tunnels underneath the Thames, and alight at Cutty Sark station.

Lambeth and Southwark

Until well into the seventeenth century, the only reason for north-bank residents to cross the Thames, to what is now **Lambeth** and **Southwark**, was to visit the disreputable Bankside entertainment district around the south end of London Bridge, which lay outside the jurisdiction of the City. South London (a catch-all term for everything south of the river) still has a reputation, among north Londoners at least, as a boring, sprawling, residential district devoid of any local culture or life.

As it turns out, this is not too far from the truth: both boroughs are, for the most part, residential. However, along **Lambeth**'s riverbank harbours several important cultural institutions, collectively known as the **South Bank Centre**. Although a mess architecturally, these galleries, theatres and concert halls, plus the nearby **Imperial War Museum**, draw large numbers across the river.

There are even more sights further east along **Southwark**'s riverfront, most notably a reconstruction of Shakespeare's **Globe Theatre**, and the spectacular new **Tate Modern**, housed in a converted power station. Another rash of popular museums can be found along Clink Street and Tooley Street, while further east still, **Butler's Wharf** is a thriving little warehouse development centred on the excellent **Design Museum**.

The South Bank

In 1951, the South Bank Exhibition, held on derelict land south of the Thames, formed the centrepiece of the **Festival of Britain**, an attempt to revive postwar morale by celebrating the centenary of the Great Exhibition (when Britain really did rule over half the world). The most striking features of the site were the Royal Festival Hall (which still stands), the ferris wheel (which returned to the South Bank for the millennium), the saucer-shaped Dome of Discovery (inspiration for the current Millennium Dome), and the cigar-shaped Skylon tower.

The festival's success provided the impetus for the eventual creation of the **South Bank Centre** (Ⓦwww.sbc.org.uk), home to institutions such as the National Theatre, the National Film Theatre, the British Film Institute's new IMAX cinema, and the Museum of the Moving Image or MOMI (due to re-open in 2002). Sadly, the South Bank has become London's much unloved culture bunker, a mess of "weather-stained concrete, rain-swept walkways and urine-soaked stairs", as one critic aptly put it. On the plus side, the South Bank is currently under inspired artistic direction and stands at the heart of the capital's arts scene. Its unprepossessing appearance is softened, too, by its riverside location, its avenue of trees, its fluttering banners, excellent signposting, and its occasional buskers and skateboarders.

London Eye (Millennium Wheel) and County Hall

South of the South Bank Centre proper, beside County Hall, is London's most prominent new landmark, the Millennium Wheel or **London Eye** (daily: April–Sept 10am–8pm or later; Oct–March 10.30am–7pm; £9; ☎0870 /500 0600, ⓦwww.ba-londoneye.com; Waterloo or Westminster tube), British Airways' magnificently graceful observation wheel which spins slowly and silently over the Thames. Standing 450ft high, the wheel is the largest ever built, and it's constantly in slow motion – a full-circle "flight" in one of its 32 pods takes around thirty minutes, and lifts you high above the city. It's one of the few places (apart from a plane window) from which London looks a manageable size, as you can see right out to the very edge of the city where the suburbs slip into the countryside. Queues can be bad at the weekend, and tickets are often completely sold out, so get there early or book in advance over the phone.

The colonnaded crescent of **County Hall** is the only truly monumental building in this part of town. Designed to house the London County Council, it was completed in 1933 and enjoyed its greatest moment of fame as the headquarters of the GLC (Greater London Council), abolished by Margaret Thatcher in 1986, leaving London as the only European city without an elected authority. Since May 2000, London has had its own elected mayor, the former GLC leader Ken Livingstone, as well as a GLA (Greater London Authority), which will eventually be housed in a new building near Tower Bridge. County Hall, meanwhile, is now in the hands of a Japanese property company, and currently houses two hotels, several restaurants, an amusement arcade, the London Aquarium and the Dalí Universe.

So far, the most popular attraction in County Hall is the **London Aquarium** (daily 10am–6pm or later; £8.75; ⓦwww.londonaquarium.co.uk; Waterloo or Westminster tube), laid out across three floors of the basement. With some super-large tanks, and everything from dog-face puffers to piranhas, this is somewhere that's pretty much guaranteed to please younger kids. The "**Beach**", where children can actually stroke the (non-sting) rays, is particularly popular. Though impressive in scale, the aquarium is fairly conservative in design, however, with no walk-through tanks and only the very briefest of information on any of the fish.

Three giant surrealist sculptures on the riverside walkway in front of County Hall advertise the building's latest attraction, **Dalí Universe** (daily 10am–6pm; £8.50; ⓦwww.daliuniverse.com). There's no denying Salvador Dalí was an accomplished and prolific artist, but you'll be disappointed if you're expecting to see his "greatest hits" – those are scattered across the globe. Most of the works here are little-known bronze and glass sculptures, and various drawings from the many illustrated books which he published, ranging from works by Ovid to the Marquis de Sade. Aside from these, there's one of the numerous Lobster Telephones, which Edward James commissioned for his London home, a copy of his famous Mae West lips sofa, and the oil painting from the dream sequence in Hitchcock's movie *Spellbound*.

South of County Hall

On the south side of Westminster Bridge, in the midst of **St Thomas's Hospital**, on Lambeth Palace Road, is the **Florence Nightingale Museum** (Mon–Fri 10am–5pm, Sat & Sun 11.30am–4.30pm; £4.80; ⓦwww.florence

nightingale.co.uk; Westminster tube), celebrating the woman who revolutionized the nursing profession by establishing the first school of nursing at St Thomas's in 1859. The exhibition hits just the right note, putting the two years she spent in the Crimea in the context of a lifetime of tireless social campaigning. Exhibits include the white lantern that earned her the nickname "The Lady with the Lamp", and a reconstruction of a Crimean military hospital ward.

A short walk south of St Thomas's is the Kentish ragstone church of St Mary-at-Lambeth, which now contains a café and an unpretentious little **Museum of Garden History** (Feb to mid-Dec daily 10.30am–5pm; free). The graveyard has been transformed into a small seventeenth-century garden, where two interesting sarcophagi lurk among the foliage: one belongs to Captain Bligh, the commander of the *Bounty* in 1787; the other is a memorial to John Tradescant, gardener to James I and Charles I.

The domed building at the east end of Lambeth Road, formerly the infamous lunatic asylum of Bethlehem Royal Hospital (better known as Bedlam), is now the **Imperial War Museum** (daily 10am–6pm free; Ⓦwww.iwm .org.uk; Lambeth North or Elephant & Castle tube), by far the best military museum in the capital. The treatment of the subject is impressively wide-ranging and fairly sober, with the main hall's militaristic display of guns, tanks and planes offset by the lower-ground-floor array of documents and images attesting to the human damage of war. The museum also has a harrowing new **Holocaust Exhibition** (not recommended for children under 14), which pulls few punches, and has made a valiant attempt to avoid depicting the victims of the Holocaust as nameless masses by focusing on individual cases, and interspersing the archive footage with eyewitness accounts from contemporary survivors.

Southwark

Southwark – originally the name of the area around the southern end of London Bridge, but now a vast borough reaching as far south as Dulwich – was a lively Roman red-light district whose brothels continued to do a thriving illegal trade until 1161 when they were licensed by royal decree. This measure imposed various restrictions on the prostitutes, who could now be fined three shillings for "grimacing to passers-by", and brought in a lot of revenue for the bishops of Winchester, who owned the area for the four centuries after the Norman Conquest. Under the bishops' rule, bull- and bear-baiting, drinking, cockfighting and gambling were also rife, especially on **Bankside**, to the west. After 1556, Southwark came under the jurisdiction of the City, it was still not subject to its regulations on entertainment, and the area remained the pleasure quarter of Tudor and Stuart London, where brothels and other disreputable institutions banned in the City – notably theatres – continued to flourish until the Puritan purges of the 1640s.

Four hundred years on, and Bankside is once more a magnet for visitors and Londoners alike, thanks to the newly rebuilt **Globe Theatre** (where most of Shakespeare's plays had their first performances), and the **Tate Modern** art gallery housed in the old Bankside power station. In addition, the area will eventually be linked to St Paul's and the City by the notorious Norman Foster-designed **Millennium Bridge**, London's famous bouncing bridge, which wobbled so worryingly when it first opened in 2000 that it was closed indefinitely while the engineers tried to work out how to fix it. By the time you read this, London's first pedestrian-only Thames bridge and the first one to cross the river for over a century should finally be open for business.

Tate Modern

Bankside is dominated by the austere power station of the same name, which has been transformed by the Swiss duo Herzog & de Meuron into the **Tate Modern** (daily 10am–6pm; Fri & Sat till 10pm; free; ⊛ www.tate.org.uk; Southwark or Blackfriars tube). The conversion, completed in May 2000, has been masterfully executed, leaving plenty of the original feel of an industrial giant, while providing wonderfully light and spacious galleries in which to show off the Tate's vast international twentieth-century art collection. The best way to enter is down the ramp from the west, so you get the full effect of the stupendously large turbine hall. It's easy enough to find your way around the galleries, with levels 3 and 5 displaying the permanent collection, level 4 used for fee-paying temporary exhibitions, and level 7 home to a rooftop café with a great view over the Thames – eventually visitors are to be given access to a viewing platform at the top of the central chimney.

Given that Tate Modern is the largest modern art gallery in the world, you really need to spend the best part of a day here to do justice to the place. Pick up a plan (and, for an extra £1, an audioguide), and take the escalator to level 3. As at Tate Britain, the curators have eschewed the usual chronological approach through the "isms", and instead plumped for grouping works together thematically: Landscape/Matter/Environment, Still Life/Object/Real Life, History/Memory/Society and Nude/Action/Body. On the whole this works very well, though the early twentieth-century canvases, in their gilded frames, do struggle when made to compete with contemporary installations.

Although the displays change every six months or so, you're still pretty much guaranteed to see at least some works by **Monet** and Bonnard, Cubist pioneers **Picasso** and Braque, Surrealists such as **Dalí**, abstract artists such as **Mondrian**, Bridget Riley and Pollock, and Pop supremos **Warhol** and Lichtenstein. There are seminal works, including a replica of **Duchamp's** urinal, entitled *Fountain* and signed "R. Mutt", Yves Klein's totally blue paintings and Carl André's trademark piles of bricks. And such is the space here that several artists get whole rooms to themselves, among them the painter Francis Bacon, Joseph Beuys and his shamanistic wax and furs, and **Mark Rothko**, whose abstract "Seagram Murals", originally destined for a posh restaurant in New York, have their own shrine-like room in the heart of the collection.

From the Globe to the Cathedral

Seriously dwarfed by the Tate Modern is the equally spectacular **Shakespeare's Globe Theatre** (⊛ www.shakespeares-globe.org; Southwark or Blackfriars tube), a reconstruction of the polygonal playhouse where most of the Bard's later works were first performed, and which was originally erected on nearby Park Street in 1598. To find out more about Shakespeare and the history of Bankside, the Globe's pricey but stylish new **exhibition** (daily 9am–5pm; £7.50) is well worth a visit. It begins by detailing the long campaign by American actor Sam Wanamaker to have the Globe rebuilt, but it's the imaginative hands-on exhibits that really hit the spot. You can have a virtual play on medieval instruments such as the crumhorn or sackbut, prepare your own edition of Shakespeare, and feel the thatch, hazelnut-shell and daub used to build the theatre. Visitors also get taken on an informative **guided tour** round the theatre itself, except in the afternoons during the summer season, when you can only visit the exhibition (for a reduced entrance fee). You can also view the archeological remains of another Elizabethan playhouse, the **Rose Theatre**, nearby at 56 Park St (daily 10am–5pm; £3; ⊛ www.rdg.ac.uk /rose).

East of Bankside, beyond Southwark Bridge, is **Vinopolis** (daily 11am–6pm or later; £11.50; www.evinopolis.com), a big-money venture discreetly housed in former wine vaults under the railway arches on Clink Street. The focus of the complex is the "**Wine Odyssey**", a light-hearted trot through the world's wine regions, equipped with a CD audioguide. There are plenty of visual gags – you get to tour round the Italian vineyards on a Vespa – but the most appealing and educative aspect of the tour is the **wine-tasting**. Visitors get five generous samples – from champagne to vintage port – with the option of buying another five for a mere £2.50 extra.

Further down the suitably gloomy confines of dark and narrow Clink Street is the **Clink Prison Museum** (daily 10am–6pm; £4; www.clink.co.uk; London Bridge tube), built on the site of the former Clink Prison, origin of the expression "in the clink". The prison began as a dungeon for disobedient clerics, built under the Bishop of Winchester's Palace – the rose window of the palace's Great Hall survives just east of the museum – and later became a dumping ground for heretics, prostitutes and a motley assortment of Bankside lowlife. Today's exhibition features a handful of prison life tableaux, and dwells on the torture and grim conditions within, but, given the rich history of the place, this is a disappointingly lacklustre museum.

An exact replica of the **Golden Hinde** (daily 10am to dusk; £3; www .goldenhinde.co.uk), the galleon in which Sir Francis Drake sailed around the world from 1577 to 1580, nestles in St Mary Overie Dock, at the eastern end of Clink Street. The ship is surprisingly small, and its original crew of eighty-plus must have been cramped to say the least. There's a refreshing lack of inter-pretive panels, so it's worth paying the little bit extra and getting a guided tour from one of the folk in period garb – ring ahead to check a group hasn't booked the place up (☎0870/011 8700).

Close by the *Golden Hinde* stands **Southwark Cathedral**, built as the medieval Augustinian priory church of St Mary Overie, and given cathedral status only in 1905. Of the original thirteenth-century church, only the choir and retrochoir now remain, separated by a tall and beautiful stone Tudor screen, making them probably the oldest Gothic structures left in London. The nave was entirely rebuilt in the nineteenth century, but the cathedral contains numerous interesting monuments, from a thirteenth-century oak effigy of a knight to an early twentieth-century memorial to Shakespeare, whose brother is buried here.

The London Bridge area

The most educative and strangest of Southwark's museums is the **Old Operating Theatre Museum and Herb Garret** on St Thomas Street (daily 10am–4pm; £3.25; www.thegarret.co.uk; London Bridge tube). Built in 1821 at the top of a church tower, where the hospital apothecary's herbs were stored, this women's operating theatre dates from the pre-anaesthetic era. Despite being entirely gore-free, the museum is as stomach-churning as the London Dungeon (see p.115). The surgeons who used this room would have concentrated on speed and accuracy (most amputations took less than a minute), but there was still a thirty percent mortality rate, with many patients simply dying of shock, and many more from bacterial infection, about which very little was known.

A walk under the railway bridges and down Tooley Street brings you to the vaults beneath the railway arches of London Bridge train station, which are now occupied by two museums. Young teenagers and the credulous probably get the most out of the ever-popular **London Dungeon** (daily: April–Sept

10am–5.30pm; Oct–March 10am–5pm; £10.95; ⓦwww.thedungeons.com;
London Bridge tube) – to avoid the inevitable queue, buy your ticket from the
nearby Southwark tourist office at 6 Tooley St. The life-sized waxwork tableaux
inside include a man being hung, drawn and quartered and one being boiled
alive, the general hysteria being boosted by actors, dressed as top-hatted Victorian
vampires, pouncing out of the darkness. Visitors are then herded into a court
room, condemned to the "River of Death" boat ride, and forced to endure the
"Jack the Ripper Experience", an exploitative trawl through post-mortem photos and wax mock-ups of the victims, followed by the "Great Fire of London",
in which visitors get to experience the heat and the smell of the plague-ridden
city, before being forced to walk through a revolving tunnel of flames.

A little further east on Tooley Street is **Winston Churchill's Britain at War**
(daily: April–Sept 10am–5.30pm; Oct–March 10am–4.30pm; £5.95;
ⓦwww.britainatwar.co.uk; London Bridge tube), an illuminating insight into the
stiff-upper-lip London mentality during the Blitz. The museum contains hundreds of wartime artefacts, including an Anderson shelter, where you can hear the
chilling sound of the V1 "doodlebugs" and tune in to contemporary radio broadcasts. The grand finale is a walk through the chaos of a just-bombed street.

There's more World War II history, from a more aggressive angle, at **HMS
Belfast** (daily: March–Oct 10am–6pm; Nov–Feb 10am–5pm; £5.40;
ⓦwww.iwm.org.uk; London Bridge tube), a huge cruiser permanently moored
between London Bridge and Tower Bridge. Armed with six torpedoes and six-
inch guns with a range of over fourteen miles, the *Belfast* spent over two years
of the war in the Royal Naval shipyards, after being hit by a mine in the Firth
of Forth at the beginning of hostilities. It later saw action in the Barents Sea and
again during the Korean War, before being decommissioned. To find out more
about the *Belfast*, head for the exhibition on level 5; otherwise the ship is a bit
short on information, but the maze of cabins is fun to explore.

Butler's Wharf

In contrast to the brash offices on Tooley Street, **Butler's Wharf**, east of Tower
Bridge, has retained its historical character. **Shad Thames**, the narrow street at
the back of Butler's Wharf, has kept the wrought-iron overhead gangways by
which the porters used to transport goods from the wharves to the warehouses further back from the river, and is one of the most atmospheric alleyways in
the whole of Bermondsey. The eight-storey Butler's Wharf warehouse itself,
with its shops and restaurants, forms part of Terence Conran's commercial
empire and caters for a moneyed clientele, but the wide promenade on the
riverfront is open to the public.

The chief attraction of Butler's Wharf is Conran's superb riverside **Design
Museum** (Mon–Fri 11.30am–6pm, Sat & Sun 10.30am–6pm; £5.50;
ⓦwww.designmuseum.org; Bermondsey or Tower Hill tube), a stylish, white,
Bauhaus-like conversion of a 1950s warehouse at the eastern end of Shad
Thames. The museum's excellent temporary **exhibitions** on important
designers, movements or single products are staged on the first floor, while the
Collection and Review **galleries**, on the top floor, offer a brief overview of
mass-produced industrial design from TVs to Tupperware. The small coffee bar
in the foyer is a great place to relax, and there's a pricey Conran restaurant on
the top floor.

The **Bramah Tea and Coffee Museum** (daily 10am–6pm; £4; ⓦwww
.bramahmuseum.co.uk; Tower Hill or Bermondsey tube), housed in an old tea
warehouse, Tamarind House, on Maguire Street behind the Design Museum,
is not quite in the same league as its neighbour. Still, it's a fun museum, and

well worth a visit. Founded in 1992 by Edward Bramah, who began his career on an African tea garden in 1950, the museum's emphasis is firmly on tea. There's an impressive array of teapots from Wedgwood to novelty, and coffee machines spanning the twentieth century, from huge percolator siphons to espresso machines.

Hyde Park, Kensington and Chelsea

Hyde Park, together with its westerly extension, Kensington Gardens, covers a distance of two miles from Speakers' Corner in the northeast to **Kensington Palace** in the southwest. At the end of your journey, you've made it to one of London's most exclusive districts, the Royal Borough of Kensington and Chelsea. Other districts go in and out of fashion, but this area has been in vogue ever since royalty moved into Kensington Palace in the late seventeenth century.

Aside from the shops around Harrods in Knightsbridge, however, the popular tourist attractions lie in **South Kensington**, where three of London's top museums – the **Victoria and Albert**, **Natural History** and **Science museums** – stand on land bought with the proceeds of the Great Exhibition of 1851. **Chelsea**'s character is slightly more bohemian. In the 1960s, the **King's Road** carved out its reputation as London's catwalk, while in the late 1970s it was the epicentre of the punk explosion. Nothing so risqué goes on in Chelsea now, though its residents like to think of themselves as rather more artistic and intellectual than the purely moneyed types of Kensington.

Once slummy, now swanky, Bayswater and **Notting Hill**, to the north of Hyde Park, were the bad boys of the borough for many years, dens of vice and crime comparable to Soho. Despite gentrification over the last twenty-five years, they remain the borough's most cosmopolitan districts, with a strong Arab presence and vestiges of the black community who initiated and still run the city's (and Europe's) largest street **carnival**, which takes place every August Bank Holiday.

Hyde Park and Kensington Gardens

Seized from the Church by Henry VIII to satisfy his desire for yet more hunting grounds, **Hyde Park** (⊛www.royalparks.co.uk) was first opened to the public by James I, and soon became a fashionable gathering place for the beau monde, who rode round the circular drive known as the Ring, pausing to gossip and admire each other's *equipage*. Hangings, muggings and duels, the Great Exhibition of 1851 and numerous public events have all taken place in Hyde Park – and it's still a popular gathering point or destination for political demonstrations. For most of the time, however, the park is simply a leisure ground – a wonderful open space which allows you to lose all sight of the city beyond a few persistent tower blocks.

Located at the treeless northeastern corner of the park, **Marble Arch** was originally erected in 1828 as a triumphal entry to Buckingham Palace, but is now stranded on a ferociously busy traffic island at the west end of Oxford Street. This is the most historically charged spot in Hyde Park, as it marks the site of **Tyburn gallows**, the city's main public execution spot until 1783. It's also the location of **Speakers' Corner**, once an entertaining and peculiarly English Sunday tradition, featuring an assembly of characterful speakers and hecklers – now, sadly, a forum for soap-box religious extremists.

A better place to enter the park is at **Hyde Park Corner**, the southeast corner, where **Wellington Arch** (April–Sept daily 10am–6pm; Oct daily 10am–5pm; Nov–March Wed–Sun 10am–4pm; £2.50; EH; Hyde Park Corner tube) stands in the midst of another of London's busiest traffic interchanges. Erected in 1828 to commemorate Wellington's victories in the Napoleonic Wars, the arch originally served as the northern gate into Buckingham Palace grounds. Now it houses a small exhibition on the history of the arch and on the city's numerous outdoor memorials.

Close by stands **Apsley House** (Tues–Sun 11am–5pm; £4.50; ⓦwww.vam .ac.uk; Hyde Park Corner tube), Wellington's London residence and now a museum to the "Iron Duke". Unless you're a keen fan of the Duke (or Louis XV interiors), the highlight of the museum is the **art collection**, much of which used to belong to the King of Spain. Among the best pieces, displayed in the Waterloo Gallery on the first floor, are works by de Hooch, van Dyck, Velázquez, Goya, Rubens and Murillo. The famous, more than twice life-size nude statue of Napoleon by Antonio Canova stands at the foot of the main staircase.

Hyde Park is divided in two by the **Serpentine Lake**, which has a popular **Lido** (June–Sept daily 10am–6pm; £2.50; Lancaster Gate or Knightsbridge tube) on its south bank. By far the prettiest section of the lake, though, is the upper section known as the **Long Water**, which narrows until it reaches a group of four fountains, laid out symmetrically in front of an Italianate summerhouse designed by Wren.

The western half of the park is officially known as **Kensington Gardens**, and is, strictly speaking, a separate entity, though you hardly notice the change. Its two most popular attractions are the **Serpentine Gallery** (daily 10am–6pm; free; ⓦwww.serpentinegallery.org; South Kensington tube), which has a reputation for lively, and often controversial, contemporary art exhibitions, and the richly decorated, High Gothic **Albert Memorial** (guided tours Sun 2 & 3pm; £3.50), clearly visible to the west. Erected in 1876, the monument is as much a hymn to the glorious achievements of Britain as to its subject, Queen Victoria's husband (who died of typhoid in 1861). Recently restored to his former gilded glory, Albert occupies the central canopy, clutching a catalogue for the 1851 Great Exhibition that he helped to organize.

The Exhibition's most famous feature, the gargantuan glasshouse of the Crystal Palace, no longer exists, but the profits were used to buy a large tract of land south of the park, now home to South Kensington's remarkable cluster of museums and colleges, plus the vast **Royal Albert Hall**, a splendid iron-and-glass-domed concert hall, with an exterior of red brick, terracotta and marble that became the hallmark of South Ken architecture. The hall is venue for Europe's most democratic music festival, the Henry Wood Promenade Concerts, better known as the **Proms** (ⓦwww.bbc.co.uk/proms), which take place from July to September, with standing-room tickets for as little as £3.

Kensington Palace

On the western edge of Kensington Gardens stands **Kensington Palace** (daily: March–Oct 10am–5pm; Nov–Feb 10am–4pm; £8.80; ⓦwww.hrp .org.uk; High Street Kensington tube), a modestly proportioned Jacobean brick mansion bought by William and Mary in 1689, and the chief royal residence for the next fifty years. KP, as it's fondly known in royal circles, is, of course, best known today as the place where Princess Diana lived up until her death in 1997. It was, in fact, the official London residence of both Charles and Di until the couple formally separated. In the weeks following Diana's death, literally millions of flowers, mementoes, poems and gifts were deposited at the gates to the south of the palace.

Visitors don't get to see Diana's apartments, which were on the west side of the palace, where various minor royals still live. Instead, they are given an audio-guide which takes them round the **Royal Ceremonial Dress Collection**, where they get to view some of the Queen's frocks, and then the sparsely furnished state apartments. The highlights are the trompe l'oeil ceiling paintings by William Kent, in particular the Cupola Room, and the oil paintings in the King's Gallery. En route, you also get to see the tastelessly decorated rooms in which the future Queen Victoria spent her unhappy childhood. To recover from the above, take tea in the exquisite **Orangery** (daily: Easter–Sept 10am–6pm; Oct–Easter 10am–4pm), to the north of the palace.

The Victoria and Albert Museum (V&A)

In terms of sheer variety and scale, the **Victoria and Albert Museum**, on Cromwell Road (daily 10am–5.45pm, Wed also 6.30–9.30pm; free; ⓦwww .vam.ac.uk; South Kensington tube), popularly known as the V&A, is the greatest museum of applied arts in the world. The range of exhibits on display here means that, whatever your taste, there is almost bound to be something to grab your attention.

Beautifully but haphazardly displayed across a seven-mile, four-storey maze of halls and corridors, the V&A's treasures are impossible to survey in a single visit. Floor plans from the information desks can help you decide on which areas to concentrate. If you're flagging, there's *Millburns* restaurant in the basement of the Henry Cole Wing, or a more edifying café in the museum's period-piece **Poynter, Morris and Gamble** refreshment rooms.

The most celebrated of the V&A's numerous exhibits are the **Raphael Cartoons**, seven vast biblical paintings that served as templates for a set of tapestries destined for the Sistine Chapel. Close by, you can view highlights from the country's largest dress collection, and the world's largest collection of **Indian art** outside India. In addition, there are galleries devoted to Chinese, Islamic, Japanese and Korean art, as well as costume jewellery, glassware, metalwork and photography. Wading through the huge collection of European sculpture, you come to the surreal **Plaster Casts** gallery, filled with copies of European art's greatest hits, from Michelangelo's David to Trajan's Column (sawn in half to make it fit). There's even a gallery of **twentieth-century objets d'art** – everything from Bauhaus furniture to Swatch watches – to rival that of the Design Museum.

Over in the **Henry Cole Wing**, meanwhile, you'll find an entire office interior by Frank Lloyd Wright, a collection of sixteenth-century portrait miniatures, more **Constable** paintings than the Tate, and a goodly collection of sculptures by **Rodin**. As if all this were not enough, the V&A's temporary shows are among the best in Britain, ranging over vast areas of art, craft and technology.

Like all London's major museums, the V&A has big plans for the future, with a £75 million multifaceted extension, known as the "**Spiral**" and designed by controversial Polish-born architect Daniel Libeskind, due to open in 2004.

The Science Museum

Established as a technological counterpart to the V&A, the **Science Museum**, on Exhibition Road (daily 10am–6pm; free; ⓦwww.nmsi.ac.uk; South Kensington tube), is undeniably impressive, filling seven floors with items drawn from every conceivable area of science, including space travel, telecommunications, time measurement, chemistry, computing, photography and medicine. Keen to dispel the enduring image of museums devoted to its subject as boring and full of dusty glass cabinets, the Science Museum has been busy updating its galleries with more interactive displays, and puts on daily demonstrations to show that not all science teaching has to be deathly dry.

Once you've paid your entrance fee, head for the **information desk** in the Power hall and find out what events and demonstrations are taking place; you can also sign up for a guided tour on a specific subject. Beyond the Power hall and the **Space** exhibition, which follows the history of rockets, lies the old Transport hall, now the **Making of the Modern World**, a display of iconic inventions such as *Puffing Billy*, the world's oldest surviving steam train, and Robert Stephenson's *Rocket* of 1829, as well as a Ford Model T, the world's first mass-produced car.

From here, the darkened, ultra-purple **Wellcome Wing** beckons you on, its ground floor dominated by the floating, sloping underbelly of the museum's state-of-the-art **IMAX cinema** (£6.75). The four floors of the Wellcome Wing are filled with high-tech hands-on computer gadgetry that's great fun to play with: you can morph yourself into the opposite sex or test the gender of your brain, learn about digital technology, and ponder moral questions such as: "should you be able to choose the gender of your child?" There's also plenty of interactive stuff aimed at **younger kids**, from Pattern Pod and the ever-popular Launch Pad, in the Wellcome Wing, to the Garden and Things galleries in the basement.

The rest of the museum – and there's a more than enough to keep you occupied for a whole day – covers such diverse topics as flight and shipping to gas exploration and nuclear physics. Some galleries, such as the one devoted to **Materials**, are admirably stylish; others, such as the sections on **Computing** and **Mathematics**, are rather more old fashioned, though the museum's piecemeal revamping continues apace.

The Natural History Museum

Alfred Waterhouse's purpose-built mock-Romanesque colossus ensures the **Natural History Museum** (Mon–Sat 10am–5.50pm, Sun 11am–5.50pm; free; ⓦwww.nhm.ac.uk; South Kensington tube) its status as London's most handsome museum. The museum underwent massive redevelopment in the 1990s, and is now, by and large, imaginatively designed, though there are still one or two sections that have changed little since the museum's opening in 1881. To be fair, the museum is caught in a real conundrum, for while its dinosaur collection is a real hit with the kids, its collections are also an important resource for serious zoologists.

The main entrance brings you straight into the Central Hall of the **Life Galleries**, dominated by a plaster-cast skeleton of a Diplodocus. The "side chapels" are filled with wonders of the natural world – the largest egg, a sabretooth tiger – but it's the **Dinosaur gallery** that pulls in the crowds, a show of massive-jawed skeletons and models much enlivened by a grisly life-size animatronic Tyrannosaurus Rex, accompanied by much roaring, slurping and oozing blood. Other popular sections include the Creepy-Crawlies Room and the Ecology Gallery, plus the somewhat ancient displays of stuffed creatures.

If the queues for the museum are long (as they can be at weekends and during school holidays), you're better off heading for the side entrance on Exhibition Road, which leads into the former Geology Museum, now known as the **Earth Galleries**, an expensively revamped and visually exciting romp through the earth's evolution. The most popular sections are the slightly taste-less Kobe earthquake simulator, and the spectacular display of gems and crys-tals in the Earth's Treasury.

Kensington High Street

Shopper-thronged **Kensington High Street** is dominated architecturally by the twin presences of Sir George Gilbert Scott's neo-Gothic church of St Mary Abbots, whose 250-foot spire makes it London's tallest parish church, and the Art Deco colossus of Barkers department store, remodelled in the 1930s.

Kensington's sights are mostly hidden away in the backstreets, the one excep-tion being the **Commonwealth Institute** (☎020/7603 4535; ⓦwww .commonwealth.org.uk; High Street Kensington tube), housed in a bold 1960s building set back from the High Street. The whole place has recently under-gone a massive restoration and refurbishment programme. Gone is the perma-nent collection with a section on each of the member states; instead, the Institute aims to put on more up-to-date, interactive temporary exhibitions focusing on a particular Commonwealth country.

Two paths along the side of the Commonwealth Institute lead to densely wooded **Holland Park** (daily 7.30am–dusk; High Street Kensington tube), the former grounds of a Jacobean mansion (only the east wing still stands). Theatrical and musical performances are staged here throughout the summer, and several **formal gardens** surround the house, most notably the Japanese-style Kyoto Gardens, while the rest of the park is dotted with a newly installed series of abstract sculptures.

A number of wealthy Victorian artists rather self-consciously founded an artists' colony in the streets that lie between the High Street and Holland Park. It's possible to visit one of the most remarkable of these artist pads, **Leighton House** at 12 Holland Park Rd (daily except Tues 11am–5.30pm; free; ⓦwww .rbkc.cgov.uk). "It will be opulence, it will be sincerity," Lord Leighton opined before starting work on the house in the 1860s – he later became President of the Royal Academy and was ennobled on his deathbed. The big attraction is the domed Arab Hall, decorated with Saracen tiles, gilded mosaics and wood-work drawn from all over the Islamic world. The other rooms are less spectac-ular but, in compensation, are hung with paintings by Lord Leighton and his Pre-Raphaelite chums.

Knightsbridge and Harrods

Knightsbridge is irredeemably snobbish, revelling in its reputation as the swankiest shopping area in London, a status epitomized by **Harrods** on Brompton Road (Mon, Tues & Sat 10am–6pm, Wed–Fri 10am–7pm; ⓦwww .harrods.com; Knightsbridge tube). London's most famous department store started out as a family-run grocery store in 1849, with a staff of two. The cur-rent 1905 terracotta building is owned by the Egyptian Mohammed Al Fayed and employs in excess of 3000 staff. Tourists flock to Harrods – it's thought to be one of the city's top-ranking tourist attractions – though if you can do without the Harrods' carrier bag, you can buy most of what the shop stocks more cheaply elsewhere.

The store does, however, have a few sections that are architectural sights in their own right: the Food Hall, with its exquisite Arts and Crafts tiling, and the Egyptian Hall, with its pseudo-hieroglyphs and sphinxes, are particularly strik-ing. Now that a fountain dedicated to Di and Dodi is in place, the Egyptian-style escalators are an added attraction, but don't bother taking them to the first floor "washrooms", unless you want to pay £1 for the privilege of relieving yourself. Note, too, that the store has a draconian dress code: no shorts, no ripped jeans, no vest T-shirts and no backpacks.

Chelsea

It wasn't until the latter part of the nineteenth century that **Chelsea** began to earn its reputation as London's very own Left Bank. Its household fame, however, came through King's Road's role as the unofficial catwalk of the "Swinging Sixties". The road remained a fashion parade for hippies, too, and in the Jubilee Year of 1977 it witnessed the birth of punk, masterminded from a shop called Sex, run by Vivienne Westwood and Malcolm McLaren. The posey cafés and boutiques still persist, but these days, the area has a more subdued feel, with high rents and house prices keeping things pretty staid, and chain stores and interior design shops rather than avant-garde fashion the order of the day.

The area's other aspect, oddly enough considering its boho reputation, is a military one. For among the most nattily attired of all those parading down the King's Road are the scarlet or navy-blue clad Chelsea Pensioners, army veterans from the nearby **Royal Hospital** (Mon–Fri 9am–noon & 2–4.30pm, Sat & Sun closes 3pm; free; Sloane Square tube), founded by Charles II in 1681. The hospital's majestic red-brick wings and grassy courtyards became a blueprint for institutional and collegiate architecture all over the English-speaking world. The public are allowed to view the austere hospital chapel, and the equally grand, wood-panelled dining hall, opposite, which has a vast allegorical mural of Charles II.

The concrete bunker next door to the Royal Hospital, on Royal Hospital Road, houses the **National Army Museum** (daily 10am–5.30pm; free; ⓦwww .national-army-museum.ac.uk; Sloane Square tube). The militarily obsessed are unlikely to be disappointed by the succession of uniforms and medals, but there is very little here for non-enthusiasts. The temporary exhibitions staged on the ground floor are the museum's strong point, but it's rather disappointing overall – you're better off visiting the infinitely superior Imperial War Museum (see p.113).

Cheyne Walk and Cheyne Row

The quiet riverside locale of **Cheyne Walk** (pronounced "chainy") drew artists and writers in great numbers during the nineteenth century. Since the building of the Embankment and the increase in the volume of traffic, however, the character of this peaceful haven has been lost. Novelist Henry James, who lived at no. 21, used to take "beguiling drives" in his wheelchair along the Embankment; today, he'd be hospitalized in the process.

The chief reason to come here nowadays is to visit the **Chelsea Physic Garden** (April–Oct Wed noon–5pm & Sun 2–6pm; £4; ⓦwww.cpgarden. demon.co.uk; Sloane Square tube), which marks the beginning of Cheyne Walk. Founded in 1673, this small walled garden is the second oldest botanical garden in the country. At the entrance (on Swan Walk) you can pick up a map of the garden with a list of the month's most interesting flowers and shrubs, whose labels are slightly more forthcoming than the usual terse Latinate tags. The garden also has an excellent teahouse, where you can get delicious home-made cakes.

It's also worth popping into the nearby **Chelsea Old Church** (daily 9.30am–1pm & 2–4.30pm; Sloane Square tube), halfway down Cheyne Walk, where Thomas More built his own private chapel in the south aisle. The church was badly bombed in the last war, but an impressive number of monuments were retrieved from the rubble and continue to adorn the church's interior.

A short distance inland from Cheyne Walk, at 24 Cheyne Row, is **Carlyle's House** (April–Oct Wed–Sun 11am–5pm; £3.50; NT; Sloane Square tube), where the historian Thomas Carlyle set up home, having moved down from his native Scotland in 1834. The house became a museum just fifteen years after Carlyle's death and is a typically dour Victorian abode, kept much as the Carlyles would have had it: the historian's hat still hanging in the hall, his socks in the chest of drawers. The top floor contains the garret study where Carlyle tried in vain to escape the din of the neighbours' noisy roosters in order to complete his final magnum opus on Frederick the Great.

Notting Hill

Epicentre of the country's first race riots, when bus-loads of whites attacked West Indian homes in the area, **Notting Hill** is now more famous for the eponymous 1998 film, and for its annual Carnival (see box below), which began life in direct

Notting Hill Carnival

When it emerged in the 1960s, **Notting Hill Carnival** (Ⓦ www.nottinghillcarnival. net.uk) was little more than a few church hall events and a Carnival parade, inspired by that of Trinidad – home of many of the area's immigrants. Today the Carnival, held over the August Bank Holiday weekend at the end of the month, still belongs to West Indians (from all parts of the city), but there are participants, too, from London's Latin American and Asian communities, and, of course, Londoners of all descriptions turn out to watch the bands and parades, and just hangout.

The main sights of Carnival are the **costume parades**, which take place on the Sunday (for kids) and Monday (for adults) from around 10am until just before midnight. The parade makes its way around a three-mile route, starting at the top end of Ladbroke Grove, heading south under the Westway, then turning into Westbourne Grove, before looping north again via Chepstow Road, Great Western Road and Kensal Road. The procession consists of "big trucks", which carry the sound systems and *mas* (masquerade) bands, behind which the masqueraders dance in outrageous costumes.

Most of the *mas* bands play a variety of soca music, while others feature steel bands – the "pans" of the steel bands are one of the chief sounds of the Carnival and have their own contest on the Saturday at Horniman's Pleasance. In addition to those playing *mas*, there are three or four **stages for live music** – Portobello Green and Powis Square are regular venues – where you can catch reggae, ragga, drum 'n' bass, jungle, garage, house and much more. A lot of people just mill around the sound systems, dancing as the day progresses, fuelled by cans of Red Stripe, curried goat and Jamaican patties, which are sold by a multitude of weekend entrepreneurs.

Over the last few years, the Carnival has been fairly relaxed, considering the huge numbers of people it attracts. However, this is not an event for those at all bothered by crowds – you can be wedged stationary during the parades – and very loud music. It is worth taking more than usual care about crime, too: leave expensive cameras and jewellery at home, and bring only enough money for the day, as pickpockets turn up from all over. As far as safety goes, don't worry unduly about the media's horror stories as you're in plentiful company. However, the static sound systems are switched off at 7pm every day, and if there's going to be any trouble, it tends to come after that point. If you feel at all uneasy, head home early.

Getting to and from Carnival is quite an event in itself. Ladbroke Grove tube station is closed for the duration, while Notting Hill Gate and Westbourne Park are open only for incoming visitors. The nearest fully operative tube stations are Latimer Road and Royal Oak. Alternatively, there's a whole network of buses running between most points of London and Notting Hill Gate.

response to the riots. The rest of the year, Notting Hill is a lot quieter, though its cafés and restaurants are cool enough places to pull in folk from all over. On Saturdays, big crowds of Londoners and tourists alike descend on the mile-long **Portobello Road Market**, which is lined with stalls selling everything from antiques to cheap second-hand clothes and fruit and vegetables.

Within easy walking distance of Portobello Road, on the other side of the railway tracks, gasworks and canal, is **Kensal Green Cemetery** (daily: April–Sept 8am–6pm; Oct–March 9am–5pm; Kensal Rise tube), opened in 1833 and still a functioning burial ground. Graves of the more famous incumbents – Thackeray, Trollope and Brunel – are less interesting architecturally than those arranged on either side of the Centre Avenue, which leads from the easternmost entrance on Harrow Road.

North London

Just a handful of the capital's satellite villages in **North London**, now subsumed into the general mass of the city, are worth bothering with. However, all are easily accessible by tube from the centre; in fact, it was the expansion of the Tube which encouraged the forward march of bricks and mortar into many of these suburbs. **Regent's Park**, framed by Nash-designed architecture and home of **London Zoo**, is one of London's finest parks. Within easy walking distance, to the northeast, is **Camden Town**, where the weekend market is now one of the city's big attractions – a warren of stalls selling street fashion, books, records and ethnic goods. The real highlights of north London, though, for visitors and residents alike, are **Hampstead** and **Highgate**, elegant, largely eighteenth-century developments which still reflect their village origins. They have the added advantage of proximity to one of London's wildest patches of greenery, **Hampstead Heath**, where you can enjoy stupendous views, kite-flying and nude bathing, as well as outdoor concerts and high art in the setting of **Kenwood House**.

Regent's Park

As with almost all of London's royal parks, we have Henry VIII to thank for **Regent's Park** (daily 5am–dusk; ⊛ www.royalparks.co.uk; Regent's Park, Baker Street or Great Portland Street tube), which he confiscated from the Church for yet more hunting grounds. However, it wasn't until the reign of the Prince Regent (later George IV) that the park began to take its current form. According to the masterplan, devised by John Nash in 1811, the park was to be girded by a continuous belt of terraces, and sprinkled with a total of 56 villas, including a magnificent pleasure palace for the Prince himself, which would be linked by Regent Street to Carlton House in St James's. The plan was never fully realized, due to lack of funds, but enough was built to create something of the idealized garden city that Nash and the Prince Regent envisaged.

To appreciate the special quality of Regent's Park, take a closer look at the architecture, starting with the Nash terraces, which form a near-unbroken horseshoe of cream-coloured stucco around the Outer Circle. Within the Inner Circle is the **Open Air Theatre**, which puts on summer performances of Shakespeare, opera and ballet, and **Queen Mary's Gardens**, by far the prettiest section of the park. A large slice of the gardens is taken up with a glorious rose garden, featuring some four hundred varieties, surrounded by a ring of ramblers.

Regent's canal by boat

Three companies run **boat services** on the Regent's Canal between Camden (Camden Town tube) and Little Venice (Warwick Avenue tube), stopping off at London Zoo on the way and passing through the Maida Hill tunnel en route. The narrowboat *Jenny Wren* (☎020/7485 4433) starts off at Camden, while Jason's narrowboats (☎020/7286 3428) start off at Little Venice; the London Waterbus Company (☎020/7482 2660) – the only one to run all year round – sets off from both places. Whichever you choose, you can board at either end; **tickets** cost around £5–6 return and journey time is 35–45 minutes one-way.

Those interested in the history of the canal should head off to the **London Canal Museum** (Tues–Sun 10am–4.30pm; £2.50; ⊛www.canalmuseum.org.uk; King's Cross tube), on the other side of York Way, down New Wharf Road, ten minutes' walk from King's Cross Station.

Clearly visible on the western edge of the park is the shiny copper dome and minaret of the **London Central Mosque**, an entirely appropriate addition given the Prince Regent's taste for the Orient. Non-Muslim visitors are welcome to look in at the information centre, and glimpse inside the hall of worship, which is packed out with a diversity of communities for the lunchtime Friday prayers.

The northeastern corner of the park is occupied by **London Zoo** (daily: March–Oct 10am–5.30pm; Nov–Feb 10am–4pm; £10; ⊛www.zsl.org; Camden tube), founded in 1826. It may not be the most uplifting place for animal lovers, but kids will love the place, especially the children's enclosure, where they can actually handle the animals, and the regular "Animals in Action" displays in the Lifewatch House. The zoo boasts some striking architectural features, too, most notably the 1930s modernist, spiral-ramped, concrete penguin pool (where Penguin Books' original colophon was sketched), designed by the Tecton partnership, led by Russian emigré Berthold Lubetkin. Other zoo landmarks include the colossal tetrahedral aluminium-framed tent of the Snowdon Aviary, and the excellent, eco-conscious invertebrate-filled Web of Life.

Camden Town

For all the gentrification of the last twenty years, **Camden Town** retains a seedy air, compounded by the various railway lines that plough through the area, the canal, and Europe's largest dosshouse. The market, however, gives the area a positive lift on the weekends, and is now the district's best-known attribute.

Having started out as a tiny crafts market in the cobbled courtyard by the lock, **Camden Market** has since mushroomed out of all proportion. More than 100,000 shoppers turn up here each weekend, and parts of the market now stay open week-long, alongside a similarly oriented crop of shops, cafés and bistros. The market's overabundance of cheap leather, DM shoes and naff jewellery is compensated for by the sheer variety of what's on offer: from bootleg tapes to furniture, along with a mass of street fashion that may or may not make the transition to mainstream stores. To avoid the crowds, which can be overpowering on a summer weekend afternoon, get here by 10am.

Despite having no significant Jewish associations, Camden is home to London's **Jewish Museum** (Mon–Thurs 10am–4pm, Sun 10am–5pm; £3.50; ⊛www.jewmusm.ort.org; Camden Town tube), at 129 Albert St, just off Parkway. The purpose-built premises are smartly designed, but the conventional style and contents of the museum are disappointing: apart from the usual displays of Judaica, there's a video and exhibition explaining Jewish religious practices and the history of the Jewish community in Britain. More challenging temporary exhibitions are held in the museum's Finchley branch on East End Road, N3 (☎020/8349 1143).

Hampstead

Perched on a hill above Camden Town, **Hampstead** village developed into a fashionable spa in the eighteenth century, after a celebrated physician declared the waters of its spring as being of great medicinal value. Its sloping site, which deterred Victorian property speculators and put off the railway companies, saved much of the Georgian village from destruction, and it's little altered to this day. Later, it became one of the city's most celebrated literary quarters and even now it retains its reputation as a bolt hole of the high-profile intelligentsia. You can get some idea of its tone from the fact that the local Labour MP is currently the actress-turned-politician Glenda Jackson.

The steeply inclined High Street, lined with trendy clothes shops and arty cafés, flaunts the area's ever-increasing wealth without completely losing its picturesqueness. There are several small house museums to explore, but proximity to the Heath is the real joy of Hampstead, for this mixture of woodland, smooth pasture and landscaped garden is quite simply the most exhilarating patch of greenery in London.

Whichever route you take north of Hampstead tube, you'll probably end up at the small triangular green on Holly Bush Hill, on the north side of which stands the late seventeenth-century **Fenton House** (April–Oct Wed–Fri 2–5pm, Sat & Sun 11am–5pm; NT; £4.30; Hampstead tube). As well as housing a collection of European and Oriental ceramics, this National Trust house contains the superb Benton-Fletcher collection of early musical instruments, chiefly displayed on the top floor. Among the many spinets, virginals and clavichords are the earliest extant English grand piano, and an Unverdorben lute from 1580 (one of only three in the world).

The Queen Anne mansion of **Burgh House** (Wed–Sun noon–5pm; free; Hampstead tube), on New End Square, dates from the halcyon spa days of Hampstead Wells – as Hampstead was briefly known – and was at one time occupied by Dr Gibbons, the physician who discovered the spring's medicinal qualities. Surrounded by council housing, it now serves as the **Hampstead Museum**, an exhibition space and a modest local museum, with special emphasis on such notable locals as Constable and Keats; there's also a nice tea room in the basement.

Hampstead's most modern attraction is **2 Willow Road** (guided tours April–Oct Thurs–Sat 12.15–4pm every 45min; £4.30; NT; Hampstead tube), a modernist red-brick terraced house, built in the 1930s by the Hungarian-born architect Ernö Goldfinger. When Goldfinger moved in, this was a state-of-the-art house, but Goldfinger changed little of it in the following sixty years, so what you see is a 1930s avant-garde dwelling preserved in aspic, a house at once both modern and old-fashioned. An added bonus is that the rooms are packed with works of art by the likes of Max Ernst, Duchamp, Henry Moore and Man Ray. There are a limited number of tickets for the **guided tours**, so it's worth booking ahead. Incidentally, James Bond's adversary is indeed named after Ernö, as Ian Fleming lived close by and had a deep personal dislike of both Goldfinger and his modernist abode.

Hampstead's most lustrous figure is celebrated at **Keats' House** (May–Oct Tues–Sun noon–5pm; £3; ⓦwww.keatshouse.org.uk; Hampstead tube), an elegant, whitewashed Regency double villa on Keats Grove, a short walk south of Willow Road. Inspired by the peacefulness of Hampstead and by his passion for girl-next-door Fanny Brawne (whose house is also part of the museum), Keats wrote some of his most famous works here, before leaving for Rome, where he died from consumption in 1821. The neat, rather staid interior contains books and letters, Fanny's engagement ring and the four-poster bed in which the poet first coughed up blood, confiding to his companion, Charles Brown, "that drop of blood is my death warrant".

One of the most poignant of London's house museums is the **Freud Museum**, hidden away in the leafy streets of south Hampstead at 20 Maresfield Gardens (Wed–Sun noon–5pm; £4; Ⓦwww.freud.org.uk; Finchley Road tube). Having lived in Vienna for his entire adult life, Freud, by now a semi-invalid with only a year to live, was forced to flee the Nazis, arriving in London in the summer of 1938. The ground-floor study and library look exactly as they did when Freud lived here; the collection of erotic antiquities and the famous couch, sumptuously draped in Persian carpets, were all brought here from Vienna. Upstairs, home movies of family life in Vienna are shown continually and a small room is dedicated to his daughter, Anna, herself an influential child analyst, who lived in the house until her death in 1982.

Hampstead Heath and Kenwood

North London's "green lung", **Hampstead Heath** is the city's most enjoyable public park. It may not have much of its original heathland left, but it packs a wonderful variety of bucolic scenery into its 800 acres. At its southern end are the rolling green pastures of **Parliament Hill**, north London's premier spot for kite-flying. On either side are numerous ponds, three of which – one for men, one for women and one mixed – you can swim in. The thickest woodland is to be found in the **West Heath**, beyond Whitestone Pond, also the site of the most formal section, **Hill Garden**, a secretive and romantic little gem with eccentric balustraded terraces and a ruined pergola. Beyond lies **Golders Hill Park**, where you can gaze at pygmy goats and fallow deer, and inspect the impeccably maintained aviaries, home to flamingos, cranes and other exotic birds.

Finally, don't miss the landscaped grounds of Kenwood, in the north of the Heath, which are focused on the whitewashed, Neoclassical mansion of **Kenwood House** (daily: April–Sept 10am–6pm; Oct 10am–5pm; Nov–March 10am–4pm; free; Hampstead tube or EH bus #210 from Highgate tube). The house is now home to the **Iveagh Bequest**, a collection of seventeenth- and eighteenth-century art, including a handful of real masterpieces by the likes of Vermeer, Rembrandt, Boucher, Gainsborough and Reynolds. Of the house's period interiors, the most spectacular is Robert Adam's sky-blue and gold **library**, its book-filled apses separated from the central entertaining area by paired columns. To the south of the house, a grassy amphitheatre slopes down to a lake where outdoor classical concerts are held on summer evenings.

Highgate

Northeast of the Heath, and fractionally lower than Hampstead (appearances notwithstanding), **Highgate** lacks the literary cachet of its neighbour, but makes up for it with London's most famous cemetery, resting place of Karl Marx. It also retains more of its village origins, especially around **The Grove**, Highgate's finest row of houses, the oldest dating as far back as 1685.

To reach Highgate High Street from the tube, you must walk up Southwood

Lane; to reach the cemetery, head south down Highgate High Street and **Highgate Hill**, with its amazing views towards the City. When you get to the copper dome of "Holy Joe", the Roman Catholic Church which stands on Highgate Hill, pop into the pleasantly landscaped **Waterlow Park**, next door, with its fine café and restaurant.

The park provides a through route to **Highgate Cemetery**, which is ranged on both sides of Swain's Lane. Highgate's most famous corpse, that of **Karl Marx**, lies in the **East Cemetery** (daily: April–Sept 10am–5pm; Oct–March 10am–4pm; £2). Marx himself asked for a simple grave topped by a headstone, but by 1954 the Communist movement decided to move his grave to a more prominent position and erect the vulgar bronze bust that now surmounts a granite plinth. Close by lies the much simpler grave of the author George Eliot.

What the East Cemetery lacks in atmosphere is in part compensated for by the fact that you can wander at will through its maze of circuitous paths, whereas to visit the more atmospheric and overgrown **West Cemetery**, with its spooky Egyptian Avenue and terraced catacombs, you must go round with a guided tour (Mon–Fri noon, 2pm & 4pm, Sat & Sun hourly 11am–4pm; £3). Among the prominent graves usually visited are those of artist Dante Gabriel Rossetti and lesbian novelist Radclyffe Hall. No children under 8 admitted.

Hendon: The RAF Museum

A world-class assembly of historic military aircraft can be seen at the **RAF Museum** (daily 10am–6pm; ⓦ www.rafmuseum.org.uk; Colindale tube), located in a godforsaken part of north London beside the M1 motorway. Enthusiasts won't be disappointed, but those looking for a balanced account of modern aerial warfare will – the overall tone is unashamedly militaristic, not to say jingoistic. Those with children should head for the hands-on Fun 'n' Flight gallery; those without might prefer to explore the often overlooked display galleries, ranged around the edge of the Main Aircraft Hall, which contain an art gallery and an exhibition on the history of flight, accompanied by replicas of some of the death-traps of early aviation.

Neasden: the Shri Swaminarayan temple

Perhaps the most remarkable building in the whole of London lies just off the North Circular, in the glum suburb of **Neasden**. Here, rising majestically above the surrounding semi-detached houses like a mirage, is the **Shri Swaminarayan Mandir** (daily 9am–7.30pm; free; ⓦ www.swaminarayan-babs .org; Stonebridge Park or Neasden tube), a traditional Hindu temple topped with domes and shikharas, erected in 1995 in a style and scale unseen outside of India for more than a millennium. To reach the temple, you must enter through the adjacent Haveli, or cultural complex, with its carved wooden portico and balcony. After taking off your shoes, you can proceed to the **Mandir** (temple) itself, carved entirely out of Carrara marble, with every possible surface transformed into a honeycomb of arabesques, flowers and seated gods. Beneath the Mandir, an **exhibition** (Mon–Fri 9am–6pm, Sat & Sun 7am–7pm; £2) explains the basic tenets of Hinduism and details the life of Lord Swaminarayan, and includes a video about the history of the building.

South London

Now largely built-up into a patchwork of Victorian terraces, one area of **South London** stands head and shoulders above all the others in terms of sightseeing, and that is **Greenwich**. At its heart is the outstanding ensemble of the Royal Naval College and the Queen's House, courtesy of Christopher Wren and Inigo Jones respectively. Most visitors, however, come to see the Cutty Sark, the National Maritime Museum and the Royal Observatory, though Greenwich also pulls in an ever-increasing volume of Londoners in search of bargains at its Sunday **market**.

Greenwich is, of course, also famous as the "home of time", thanks to its status as the **Prime Meridian of the World**, from where time all over the globe is measured. It's partly for this reason that Greenwich was chosen as the centrepiece of the country's millennium celebrations, though the **Dome** is, in fact, situated in the reclaimed industrial wasteland of North Greenwich, a mile or so northeast of Greenwich town centre, and is currently closed to the public.

The only other suburban sights that stand out are the **Dulwich Picture Gallery**, a public art gallery even older than the National Gallery, and the eclectic **Horniman Museum**, in neighbouring Forest Hill.

Dulwich and Forest Hill

Dulwich Village, one of south London's prettier patches, is built on land owned in the seventeenth century by the actor Edward Alleyn, who founded **Dulwich College** in 1619 as almshouses and a school for poor boys on the profits of his whorehouses and bear-baiting pits on Bankside (see p.113). The college has long since outgrown its original buildings, which still stand to the north of the Picture Gallery (see below), and is now housed in a fanciful Italianate complex designed by Charles Barry (son of the architect of the Houses of Parliament), south of Dulwich Common; Alleyn is buried in the college chapel. The college is now a fee-paying public school, with an impressive roll call of old boys, including Raymond Chandler, P.G. Wodehouse and World War II traitor Lord Haw-Haw, though they tend to keep quiet about the last of the trio.

Recently refurbished, **Dulwich Picture Gallery** (Tues–Fri 10am–5pm, Sat & Sun 11am–5pm; £4, free on Fri; ⓦ www.dulwichpicturegallery.org.uk; West Dulwich train station, from Victoria), on College Road, is the nation's oldest public art gallery, designed by Sir John Soane and opened in 1817. Soane created a beautifully spacious building, awash with natural light and crammed with superb paintings – elegiac landscapes by Cuyp, one of the world's finest Poussin series, and splendid works by Hogarth, Gainsborough, van Dyck, Canaletto and Rubens. Rembrandt's *Portrait of a Young Man* is probably the most valuable picture in the gallery, and has been stolen no fewer than four times. At the centre of the museum is a tiny mausoleum designed by Soane for the sarcophagi of the gallery's founders.

To the southeast of Dulwich Park, on the busy South Circular road, is the wacky **Horniman Museum** (Mon–Sat 10.30am–5.30pm, Sun 2–5.30pm; free; ⓦ www.horniman.ac.uk; Forest Hill train station, from Victoria or London Bridge), purpose-built in 1901 by Frederick Horniman, a tea trader with a passion for collecting. The museum is principally a monument to its creator's free-wheeling eclecticism: in addition to its small aquarium and its large collection of stuffed creatures, there's a wide-ranging anthropology section, and a musical department with more than 1500 instruments from Chinese gongs to electric guitars. However, the museum, including its new "centre for understanding the environment", is undergoing a massive rebuilding programme, which should be completed during the course of 2002.

Greenwich

Greenwich is one of London's most beguiling spots, and the one place in southeast London that draws large numbers of visitors. At its heart stands one of the capital's finest architectural set pieces, the former Royal Naval College overlooking the Thames. To the west lies Greenwich town centre, while to the south, you'll find Greenwich's two prime tourist sights, the National Maritime Museum and the Royal Observatory.

If you're heading straight for National Maritime Museum from central London, the quickest way to get there is to take the **train** from Charing Cross (every 30min) to Maze Hill, on the eastern edge of Greenwich Park. Those wanting to start with the town or the *Cutty Sark* should alight at Greenwich station. A more scenic way of getting to Greenwich is to take a **boat** from one of the piers in central London (see p.73). A third possible option is to take the **Docklands Light Railway** (DLR) to the Cutty Sark station. For the best view of the Wren buildings, though, get out at Island Gardens, and then take the Greenwich Foot Tunnel under the Thames.

The town centre

Greenwich town centre, laid out in the 1820s with Nash-style terraces, is nowadays plagued with heavy traffic. To escape the busy streets, head for the old covered market, now at the centre of the weekend **Greenwich Market** (Sat & Sun 9am–5pm), a lively place full of antiques, crafts and clothes stalls that have spilled out up the High Road, Stockwell Road and Royal Hill. The best sections are the indoor second-hand book markets, flanking the Central Market on Stockwell Road; the antiques hall, further down on Greenwich High Road; and the flea market on Thames Street.

A short distance in from the old covered market, on the opposite side of Greenwich Church Street, rises the Doric portico and broken pediment of Nicholas Hawksmoor's **St Alfege's Church** (Mon–Sat 10am–4pm, Sun

The Millennium Dome

London's controversial **Millennium Dome** is clearly visible from the riverside at Greenwich and from the upper parts of Greenwich Park. Built at a cost of over £800 million, and designed by Richard Rogers (of Lloyd's Building and Pompidou Centre fame), it is by far the world's largest dome – over half a mile in circumference and 160ft in height – held up by a dozen, 300ft-tall yellow steel masts. In 2000, for one year only, it housed the nation's chief millennium extravaganza: an array of high-tech themed zones set around a stage, on which a circus-style performance took place twice a day.

Like most grand projects, the Dome had a rough ride from the press right from the beginning. The hiccups and headaches continued into the year 2000, with bad reviews and over-optimistic estimates of visitor numbers costing the first Dome chief her job. Nevertheless, millions paid up £20 each to visit the Dome, and millions went away happy. Nobody quite knows what the future holds for the Dome, which has its very own, very large, very fancy Jubilee line tube station, designed by Norman Foster. Various organizations, including Charlton Athletic football club, have put in bids to take over the site, but as the book went to print, there were still no takers lined up.

1–4pm; ⓦwww.longitude0.co.uk/st-alfege). Built in 1712–18, the church was flattened in the Blitz, but it has been magnificently restored to its former glory.

Wedged in a dry dock by the Greenwich Foot Tunnel is the majestic **Cutty Sark** (daily 10am–5pm; £3.50; ⓦwww.cuttysark.org.uk), the world's last surviving tea clipper, built in 1869. The *Cutty Sark* lasted just eight years in the China tea trade, and it was as a wool clipper that it actually made its name, making a return journey to Australia in just 72 days. Inside, there's little to see beyond the exhibition in the main hold which tells the ship's story from its inception to its arrival in Greenwich in 1954.

It's entirely appropriate that the one London building that makes the most of its riverbank location should be the **Old Royal Naval College** (Mon–Sat 10am–5pm, Sun 12.30–5pm; £3, free after 3.30pm & all day Sun; ⓦwww.greenwichfoundation.org.uk), Wren's beautifully symmetrical Baroque ensemble, initially built as a royal palace, but eventually converted into a hospital for disabled seamen. From 1873 until 1998 it was home to the Royal Naval College, but now houses the University of Greenwich and the Trinity College of Music.

The two grandest rooms, situated underneath Wren's twin domes, are open to the public and well worth visiting. The entrance to the college is on King William Walk, and visitors are ushered first into the **RNC Chapel** in the east wing. The exquisite pastel-shaded plasterwork and spectacular, decorative detailing on the ceiling were designed by James "Athenian" Stuart after a fire in 1799 destroyed the original interior. From the chapel, you can take the underground Chalk Walk to gain access to the magnificent **Painted Hall** in the west wing, which is dominated by James Thornhill's gargantuan allegorical ceiling painting and his trompe l'oeil fluted pilasters.

National Maritime Museum

The **National Maritime Museum** (daily 10am–5pm; free; ⓦwww.nmm. ac.uk), which occupies the old Naval Asylum, has recently undergone a lengthy £20 million redevelopment programme. The main entrance is now on Romney Road, and brings you out into the spectacular glass roofed central courtyard, which houses the museum's largest artefacts, among them the splendid 63ft-long gilded **Royal Barge**, designed in Rococo style by William Kent for Prince Frederick, the much unloved eldest son of George II.

The various themed galleries are superbly designed to appeal to visitors of all ages. In "Explorers", on Level 1, you get to view some of the museum's most highly prized relics, such as **Captain Cook**'s sextant and K1 marine clock, Shackleton's compass, and **Captain Scott**'s furry sleeping bag and sledging goggles. Sponsors P&O get to display their wares in "Passengers", which traces the history of modern passenger liners, and "Cargoes", which concentrates on containerization. On Level 2, there's a large maritime **art gallery**, an eco-conscious section on the future of the sea and biodiversity, and a gallery devoted to the legacy of the British Empire, warts and all.

Greenwich Passport

If you're planning to visit the National Maritime Museum, the Royal Observatory and the *Cutty Sark*, it's worth buying a **Greenwich Passport**, which costs £12 and is valid for two days, and includes a repeat visit to each sight within a year. Alternatively, you can buy a simple combined ticket for the National Maritime Museum and the Royal Observatory for £10.50.

Level 3 boasts two **hands-on galleries**: "The Bridge", where you can attempt to navigate a catamaran, a paddle steamer and a rowing boat to shore; and "All Hands", where children can have a go at radio transmission, loading miniature cargo, firing a cannon and so forth. Finally, you reach the **Nelson Gallery**, which contains the museum's vast collection of Nelson-related memorabilia, including Turner's *Battle of Trafalgar, 21st October, 1805*, his largest work and only royal commission.

Inigo Jones's **Queen's House**, originally built amidst a rambling Tudor royal palace, is now the focal point of the Greenwich ensemble, and is an integral part of the Maritime Museum. As royal residences go, it's an unassuming country house, but as the first Neoclassical building in the country, it has enormous architectural significance. An audioguide is available from the desk in the Great Hall; off which lies the beautiful Tulip Staircase, Britain's earliest cantilevered spiral staircase – its name derives from the floral patterning in the wrought-iron balustrade. The ground floor is given over to temporary exhibitions from the Maritime Museum, while the Royal Apartments on the first floor have been decked out with skilful repro furniture, rush matting and damask silk wall hangings.

Royal Observatory

Crowning the hill in Greenwich Park, behind the National Maritime Museum, the **Royal Observatory** (daily 10am–5pm; £5; combined ticket with the National Maritime Museum £10.50; ⓦ www.rog.nmm.ac.uk) was established in 1675 by Charles II to house the first Astronomer Royal, John Flamsteed. Flamsteed's chief task was to study the night sky in order to discover an astronomical method of finding the longitude of a ship at sea, the lack of which was causing enormous problems for the emerging British Empire. Astrologers continued to work here at Greenwich until the postwar smog forced them to decamp to Herstmonceux Castle and the clearer skies of Sussex (they've since moved to the Pacific); the old observatory, meanwhile, is now a very popular museum.

The oldest part of the observatory is the Wren-built **Flamsteed House**, whose northeastern turret sports a bright red time-ball that climbs the mast at 12.58pm and drops at 1pm GMT precisely; it was added in 1833 to allow

Greenwich Mean Time

Greenwich's other great claim to fame is of course as the home of **GMT** and the **Prime Meridian** – a meridian being any north–south line used as a basis for astronomical observations, and therefore also for the calculation of longitude and time. In 1852, Britain adopted "London time", which meant, in effect, Greenwich Mean Time (GMT), though, in fact, this wasn't formally acknowledged until 1880. Three years later the USA adopted Greenwich as the Prime Meridian, and in 1884 persuaded an international convention in Washington DC to agree to make Greenwich the Prime Meridian of the World – in other words, zero longitude. As a result, the entire world sets its clocks in relation to GMT.

The red strip in the main courtyard lies along the Greenwich Prime Meridian, which is still used as an absolute today. However, what the Royal Observatory don't tell you is that, as a result of communications problems encountered during the Vietnam War, the Americans starting using satellites to work out longitude in the 1980s. The global standard for air navigation, and used widely by the military, is now the **Global Positioning System** or GPS, which bases its calculations on the centre of the earth not the surface, and places the meridian approximately 336ft to the east of the red strip.

△ The London Eye

ships on the Thames to set their clocks. Passing quickly through Flamsteed's restored apartments and the Octagon Room, where the king used to show off to his guests, you reach the Chronometer Gallery, which focuses on the search for the precise measurement of longitude, and displays four of the clocks designed by **John Harrison**, including "H4", which helped win the Longitude Prize in 1763.

Flamsteed's own meridian line is a brass strip in the floor of the Meridian Building. Edmond Halley, Flamsteed's successor, who charted the comings and goings of the famous comet, worked out his own meridian, and the Bradley Meridian Room reveals yet another, standard from 1750 to 1850 and still used for Ordnance Survey maps. Finally, you reach a room that's spliced in two by the present-day Greenwich Meridian, fixed by the cross-hairs in Airy's "Transit Circle", the astrological instrument that dominates the room.

The exhibition ends on a soothing note in the Telescope Dome of the octagonal **Great Equatorial Building**, home to Britain's largest telescope. In addition, there are half-hourly presentations in the **Planetarium** (Mon–Fri 2.30pm; £2), housed in the adjoining South Building.

The Ranger's House and the Fan Museum

Southwest of the observatory, and backing onto Greenwich park's rose garden, is the **Ranger's House** (April–Oct daily 10am–6pm; Oct–March Wed–Sun 10am–4pm; £2.50; EH), a red-brick Georgian villa that has been undergoing a programme of refurbishment which should have finished by spring 2002. If you do visit the house, be sure to check out the Architectural Study Centre across the stable yard, filled with all manner of bits and bobs salvaged from London's buildings.

Croom's Hill boasts some of Greenwich's finest Georgian buildings, one of which houses the **Fan Museum** at no. 12 (Tues–Sat 11am–5pm, Sun noon–5pm; £3.50; Ⓦ www.fan-museum.org). It's a fascinating little place (and an extremely beautiful house), revealing the importance of the fan as a social and political document. The permanent exhibition on the ground floor traces the history of the materials employed, from peacock feathers to straw, while temporary exhibitions on the first floor explore such subjects as techniques of production and changing fashion.

Out west: Chiswick to Windsor

Most people experience west London en route to or from Heathrow airport, either from the confines of the train or tube (which runs overground at this point), or the motorway. The city and its satellites seem to continue unabated, with only fleeting glimpses of the countryside. However, in the five-mile stretch from Chiswick to Osterley there are several former country retreats, now surrounded by suburbia, which are definitely worth digging out.

The Palladian villa of **Chiswick House** is perhaps the best known of these attractions. However, it draws nothing like as many visitors as **Syon House**, most of whom come for the gardening centre rather than for the **house** itself, a showcase for the talents of Robert Adam, who also worked at **Osterley House**, another Elizabethan conversion, now owned by the National Trust.

Running through much of the area is the **River Thames**, once known as the "Great Highway of London" and still the most pleasant way to travel in these parts during the summer. Boats plough up the Thames all the way from central London via the **Royal Botanic Gardens** at **Kew** and the picturesque riverside at **Richmond**, as far as **Hampton Court**, home of the country's largest royal residence and the famous maze. To reach the heavily touristed royal outpost of **Windsor Castle**, however, you really need to take the train.

Chiswick

Chiswick House (April to mid-Oct daily 10am–6pm; mid-Oct to March Wed–Sun 10am–4pm; £3.30; EH; Chiswick train station, from Waterloo), is a perfect little Neoclassical villa, designed in the 1720s by Richard Boyle, Earl of Burlington, and set in one of the most beautifully landscaped gardens in London. Like its prototype, Palladio's Villa Rotonda near Vicenza, the house was purpose-built as a "temple to the arts" – here, amid his fine-art collection, Burlington could entertain artistic friends such as Swift, Handel and Pope. Visitors enter via the **lower floor**, where you can pick up an audio guide, before heading up to the **upper floor**, a series of cleverly interconnecting rooms, each enjoying a wonderful view out onto the gardens – all, that is, except the Tribunal, the central octagonal hall, where the earl's finest paintings and sculptures would have been displayed.

To do a quick circuit of the **gardens**, head across the smooth carpet of grass, punctuated by urns and sphinxes that sit under the shadow of two giant cedars of Lebanon. A great place from which to admire the northwest side of the house is from the stone benches of the exedra, the set of yew-hedge niches harbouring lions and copies of Roman statuary, situated beyond the cedars. Elsewhere, there's an Italian garden, a maze of high-hedge alleyways, a lake and a grassy amphitheatre, centred on an obelisk in a pond and overlooked by an Ionic temple.

If you leave Chiswick House gardens by the northernmost exit, beyond the Italian garden, it's just a short walk along the thunderous A4 road to **Hogarth's House** (April–Oct Tues–Fri 1–5pm, Sat & Sun 1–6pm; Nov–March closes 1hr earlier; closed Jan; free), where the artist spent each summer with his wife, sister and mother-in-law from 1749 until his death in 1764. Nowadays it's difficult to believe Hogarth came here for "peace and quiet", but in the eighteenth century the house was almost entirely surrounded by countryside. In addition to scores of Hogarth's engravings, you can see copies of his satirical series *An Election*, *Marriage à la Mode* and *A Harlot's Progress*, and compare the modern view from the parlour with the more idyllic scene in *Mr Ranby's House*.

Barnes: the Wetland Centre

For anyone even remotely interested in wildlife, the new **Wetland Centre** (daily: summer 9.30am–6pm; rest of year 9.30am–5pm; £6.75; ⓦ www.wetlandcentre.org.uk; bus #283 from Hammersmith tube, or walk from Barnes train station) in well-to-do Barnes, across the river from Chiswick, is something of an unexpected boon. On the site of four disused reservoirs, the Wildfowl & Wetland Trust (WWT) have created a high-tech 105-acre mosaic of wetland habitats. Heading north from the visitor centre, you enter **World Wetlands**, where a variety of extremely rare wildfowl – from White-faced Whistling Ducks to Blue Ducks – are breeding in captivity in miniature versions of their own endangered wetland habitats. Beyond, in the **Wildside**, are the reedbeds and pools that attract native species, such as lapwing, tufted ducks, grebes and swans. **Waterlife**, east of the visitor centre, includes a chance for younger children to get near some domesticated wildfowl, and, best of all, do some pond-dipping. At the far end is the mother of all hides: a triple-decker octagonal one with a lift, allowing views over the whole of the reserve.

Kew Bridge

Difficult to miss thanks to its stylish Italianate standpipe tower, **Kew Bridge Steam Museum** (daily 11am–5pm; weekdays £3, weekends £4; ⓦwww.kbsm.org.uk; Kew Bridge train station, from Waterloo; or bus #237 or #267 from Gunnersbury tube) occupies a former pumping station, on the corner of Kew Bridge Road and Green Dragon Lane, 100m west of the bridge itself. At the heart of the museum is the Steam Hall, which contains a triple expansion steam engine and four gigantic nineteenth-century Cornish beam engines, while two adjoining rooms house the pumping station's original beam engines, one of which is the largest in the world. The steam engines may be things of great beauty, but they are primarily of interest to enthusiasts. Not so the museum's hands-on "Water for Life" gallery in the basement, devoted to the history of the capital's water supply. The best time to visit is at weekends, when each of the museum's industrial dinosaurs is put through its paces, and the small narrow-gauge steam railway runs back and forth round the yard (March–Nov).

Five minutes' walk west of the Steam Museum along Kew Bridge Road and Brentford High Street is the superb **Musical Museum** (April–Oct Sat & Sun 2–5pm; July & Aug also Wed 2–4pm; £3.50), a converted church packed with musical automata and run by wildly enthusiastic and engaging volunteers. During the noisy ninety-minute demonstrations, you get to hear every kind of mechanical music-making machine, from cleverly crafted music boxes to the huge orchestrions that were once a feature of London's swish cafés. The museum also boasts one of the world's finest collections of player-pianos, and an enormous Art Deco Wurlitzer cinema organ.

Syon House

Across the water from Kew stands **Syon Park** (ⓦwww.syonpark.co.uk), seat of the Duke of Northumberland since Elizabethan times, now as much a working commercial concern as a family home, embracing a garden centre, a wholefood shop, an aquatic centre stocked with tropical fish, a mini-zoo and a butterfly house, as well as the old aristocratic mansion and its gardens.

From its rather plain castellated exterior, you'd never guess that **Syon House** (mid-March to Oct Wed, Thurs & Sun 11am–5pm; £6.25, including entry to the gardens; bus #237 or #267, from Gunnersbury tube or Kew Bridge train station) contains the most opulent eighteenth-century interiors in the whole of London. The splendour of Robert Adam's refurbishment is immediately revealed, however, in the pristine **Great Hall**, an apsed double cube with a screen of Doric columns at one end and classical statuary dotted around the edges. There are several more Adam-designed rooms to admire in the house, plus a smattering of works by van Dyck, Lely, Gainsborough and Reynolds.

While Adam beautified Syon House, Capability Brown laid out its **gardens** (daily 10am–5.30pm; £3) around an artificial lake, surrounding it with oaks, beeches, limes and cedars. The gardens' chief focus now, however, is the crescent-shaped **Great Conservatory**, an early nineteenth-century addition which is said to have inspired Joseph Paxton, architect of the Crystal Palace. Those with young children will be compelled to make use of the **miniature steam train**, which runs through the park at weekends from April to October.

Another plus point for kids is Syon's **Butterfly House** (daily: May–Sept 10am–5pm; Oct–April 10am–3pm; £3.50; ⓦwww.butterflies.org.uk), a small, mesh-covered hothouse, where you can walk amid hundreds of exotic butterflies from all over the world, as they flit about the foliage. An adjoining room houses a collection of iguanas, millipedes, tarantulas and giant hissing Tanzanian cockroaches. If your kids show more enthusiasm for life-threatening reptiles than delicate insects, then you could skip the butterflies and go instead for the adjacent **London Aquatic Experience** (daily 10am–5pm; £3.50; ⓦwww .aquatic-experience.org), a purpose-built centre with a mixed range of aquatic creatures from the mysterious basilisk, which can walk on water, to the perennially popular piranhas.

Osterley Park and House

Robert Adam redesigned another colossal Elizabethan mansion three miles northwest of Syon at **Osterley Park** (daily 9am–7.30pm or dusk; free), which maintains the impression of being in the middle of the countryside, despite the presence of the M4 to the north of the house. The park itself is well worth exploring, and there's a great café in the Tudor stables, but anyone with a passing interest in Adam's work should pay a visit to **Osterley House** (April–Oct Wed–Sun 1–4.30pm; £4.30; NT; Osterley tube).

From the outside, Osterley bears some similarity to Syon, the big difference being Adam's grand entrance portico, with its tall, Ionic colonnade. From here, you enter a characteristically cool **Entrance Hall**, followed by the so-called State Rooms of the south wing. Highlights include the **Drawing Room**, with Reynolds portraits on the damask walls and a coffered ceiling centred on a giant marigold, and the **Etruscan Dressing Room**, in which every surface is covered in delicate painted trelliswork, sphinxes and urns, a style that Adam (and Wedgwood) dubbed "Etruscan", though it is in fact derived from Greek vases found at Pompeii.

Kew Gardens

Established in 1759, the **Royal Botanic Gardens** (daily 9.30am to 7.30pm or dusk; £6.50; ⓦwww.kew.org; Kew Gardens tube) have grown from their original eight acres into a three-hundred-acre site in which more than 33,000 species are grown in plantations and glasshouses, a display that attracts over a million visitors every year, most of them with no specialist interest at all. There's always something to see, whatever the season, but to get the most out of the place, come sometime between spring and autumn, bring a picnic and stay for the day. The only drawbacks to Kew are the high entry fee, and the fact that it lies on a frequently used (and very noisy) flight path to Heathrow.

There are four entry points to the gardens, but the majority of people arrive at Kew Gardens tube and train station, a few minutes' walk east of the **Victoria Gate**. Of all the glasshouses, by far the most celebrated is the **Palm House**, a curvaceous mound of glass and wrought-iron, designed by Decimus Burton in the 1840s. Its drippingly humid atmosphere nurtures most of the known palm species, while in the basement there's a small but excellent tropical aquarium. The largest of the glasshouses, however, is the **Temperate House**, to the south, which contains plants from every continent, including one of the largest indoor palms in the world, the sixty-foot Chilean Wine Palm.

Kew's origins as an eighteenth-century royal pleasure garden are evident in the numerous follies dotted about Kew, the most conspicuous of which is the ten-storey 163-foot-high **Pagoda**. The original royal pad, **Kew Palace**, a three-storey red-brick mansion bought by George II as a nursery for his umpteen children, is tentatively scheduled to re-open after a lengthy period of renovation during the course of 2002. Alternatively, you could explore **Queen Charlotte's Cottage** (April–Sept Sat & Sun 10.30am–4pm; free), a tiny thatched summerhouse built in the 1770s as a royal picnic spot for George III's wife in the thickly wooded, southwestern section of the park – a sure way to lose the crowds.

Richmond

On emerging from the station at **Richmond**, you'd be forgiven for wondering why you're here, but the procession of chain stores spread out along the one-way system is only half the story. To see Richmond's more interesting side, take one of the narrow pedestrianized alleyways off busy George Street, which bring you to the wide open space of **Richmond Green**, one of the finest village greens in London, and no doubt one of the most peaceful before it found itself on the main flight path into Heathrow. Handsome seventeenth- and eighteenth-century houses line the south side of the green, where the medieval royal palace of **Richmond** once stood, though only its unspectacular **Tudor Gateway** survives.

The other place to head for in Richmond is the **Riverside**, pedestrianized, terraced and redeveloped by Quinlan Terry, Prince Charles's favourite purveyor of ersatz classicism, in the late 1980s. The real joy of the waterfront, however, is **Richmond Bridge**, London's oldest extant bridge, an elegant span of five arches made from Purbeck stone in 1777. The old town hall, set back from the new development, houses the **tourist office** (Mon–Sat 10am–5pm; May–Sept also Sun 10.30am–1.30pm; ☏020/8940 9125, ⓦwww.guidetorichmond.co.uk) and, on the second floor, the **Richmond Museum** (April–Oct Tues–Sat 11am–5pm, Sun 2–5pm; Nov–March Tues–Sat 11am–5pm; £2), but most folk prefer to ensconce themselves in the riverside pubs, or head for the numerous boat- and bike-rental outlets.

Richmond's greatest attraction, though, is the enormous **Richmond Park** (daily: March–Sept 7am–dusk; Oct–Feb 7.30am–dusk; free; ⓦwww.royalparks.co.uk), at the top of Richmond Hill – 2500 acres of undulating grassland and bracken, dotted with coppiced woodland and as wild as anything in London. Eight miles across at its widest point, this is Europe's largest city park, famed for its red and fallow deer, which roam freely, and for its ancient oaks. For the most part untamed, the park does have a couple of deliberately landscaped plantations which feature splendid springtime azaleas and rhododendrons, in particular the Isabella Plantation.

If you continue along the towpath beyond Richmond Bridge, after a mile or so, you will eventually leave the rest of London far behind and arrive at **Ham House** (April–Oct Mon–Wed, Sat & Sun 1–5pm; £6, including gardens; NT; bus #371 or walk from Richmond tube), home to the Earls of Dysart for nearly three hundred years. Expensively furnished in the seventeenth century, but little altered since then, the house boasts one of the finest Stuart interiors in the country, from the stupendously ornate Great Staircase to the Long Gallery, featuring six "Court Beauties" by Peter Lely. Elsewhere, there are several fine Verrio ceiling paintings, some exquisite parquet flooring and works by van Dyck and Reynolds. Another bonus are the formal seventeenth-century **gardens** (open all year: Mon–Wed, Sat & Sun 11am–6pm; £2), especially the Cherry Garden, laid out with a pungent lavender parterre, surrounded by yew hedges and pleached hornbeam arbours. The Orangery, overlooking the original kitchen garden, currently serves as a tea room.

Hampton Court

Hampton Court Palace (April–Oct Mon 10.15am–6pm, Tues–Sun 9.30am–6pm; rest of year closes 4.30pm; £10.80; ⓦ www.hrp.org.uk; Hampton Court train station, from Waterloo), a sprawling red-brick ensemble on the banks of the Thames, thirteen miles southwest of London, is the finest of England's royal abodes. Built in 1516 by the upwardly mobile **Cardinal Wolsey**, Henry VIII's Lord Chancellor, it was purloined by Henry himself after Wolsey fell from favour. Charles II laid out the gardens, inspired by what he had seen at Versailles, while William and Mary had large sections of the palace remodelled by Wren.

The **Royal Apartments** are divided into six thematic walking tours. There's not a lot of information in any of the rooms, but guided tours, each lasting 45 minutes, are available at no extra charge for Henry VIII's and the King's apartments; all are led by period-costumed historians, who do a fine job of bringing the place to life. If your energy is lacking – and Hampton Court is huge – the most rewarding sections are: **Henry VIII's State Apartments**, which feature the glorious double hammerbeamed Great Hall; the **King's Apartments** (remodelled by William III); and the vast **Tudor Kitchens**. The last two are also served by audio tours. The royal art collection is housed in the **Renaissance Picture Gallery** and is chock-full of treasures, among them paintings by Tintoretto, Lotto, Titian, Cranach, Bruegel and Holbein.

Tickets to the Royal Apartments cover entry to the rest of the sites in the grounds. Those who don't wish to visit the apartments are free to wander around the gardens, but will have to pay extra to visit the curious **Royal Tennis Courts** (50p), the palace's famously tricky hedge **Maze** (£2.50), laid out in 1714 north of the palace, and the **South Gardens** (£2.50), where you can view Andrea Mantegna's colourful, heroic canvases, *The Triumphs of Caesar*, housed in the Lower Orangery, and the celebrated **Great Vine**, grown from a cutting in 1768 and now producing about seven hundred pounds of black grapes per year, which are sold at the palace each September. Further afield, across Hampton Court Road, Wren's royal road, Chestnut Avenue, cuts through the semi-wild **Bushy Park**, which sustains a few fallow deer.

Windsor and Eton

Every weekend trains from Waterloo and Paddington are packed with people heading for **WINDSOR**, the royal enclave 21 miles west of London, where they join the human conveyor belt round **Windsor Castle** (April–Sept 9.45am–5.15pm; Oct–March 9.45am–4.15pm; £11; ⓦ www.royal.gov.uk; Paddington to Windsor & Eton Central via Slough, or Waterloo to Windsor & Eton Riverside). Towering above the town on a steep chalk bluff, the castle is an undeniably awesome sight, its chilly grey walls, punctuated by mighty medieval bastions, continuing as far as the eye can see. The small selection of state rooms open to the public is unexciting, though the magnificent St George's Chapel and the chance to see another small selection of the Queen's private art collection make the trip worthwhile. On a fine day, it pays to put aside some time for exploring Windsor Great Park, which stretches for several miles to the south of the castle.

Windsor has two **train stations**, both very close to the centre. Direct trains from Waterloo (Mon–Sat every 30min, Sun hourly; journey time 50min) arrive at **Windsor & Eton Riverside**, five minutes' walk from the centre; trains from Paddington require a change at Slough (Mon–Fri every 20min, Sat & Sun every 30min; journey time 30–40min), and arrive at **Windsor & Eton Central**, directly opposite the castle. Note that you must arrive and depart from the same station, as tickets are not interchangeable. The **tourist office** is at 24 High St (daily 10am–4pm; longer hours in summer; ☎01753/743900).

Once inside the castle, it's best to head straight for **St George's Chapel** (Mon–Sat 10am–4pm), a glorious Perpendicular structure ranking with Henry VII's chapel in Westminster Abbey, and the second most important resting place for royal corpses after the Abbey. Entry is via the south door and a one-way system operates, which brings you out by the **Albert Memorial Chapel**, built by Henry VII as a burial place for Henry VI, completed by Cardinal Wolsey for his own burial, but eventually converted for Queen Victoria into a High Victorian memorial to her husband, Prince Albert.

Before entering the State Apartments, pay a quick visit to **Queen Mary's Dolls' House**, a palatial micro-residence designed for the wife of George V, and the **Gallery**, where special exhibitions culled from the Royal Art Collection are staged. Most visitors just gape in awe at the monotonous, gilded grandeur of the **State Apartments**, while the real highlights – the paintings from the Royal Collection that line the walls – are rarely given a second glance. The **King's Dressing Room**, for example, despite its small size, contains a feast of art treasures, including a dapper Rubens self-portrait, van Dyck's famous triple portrait of Charles I, and *The Artist's Mother*, a perfectly observed portrait of old age by Rembrandt.

You'd hardly know that Windsor suffered the most devastating **fire** in its history in 1992, so thorough (and uninspired) has the restoration been in rooms such as **St George's Hall**. By contrast, the octagonal **Lantern Lobby**, beyond, is clearly an entirely new room, a safe neo-Gothic design replacing the old chapel. At this point, those visiting during the winter season (Oct–March) are given the privilege of seeing four **Semi-State Rooms**, created in the 1820s by George IV, and still used in the summer months by the Royal Family.

Crossing the bridge at the end of Thames Avenue in Windsor town brings you to **ETON**, a one-street village lined with bookshops and antique dealers, but famous all over the world for **Eton College** (college and chapel: Easter, July & Aug daily 10.30am–4.30pm; after Easter to June & Sept daily 2–4.30pm; £3; guided tours daily 2.15pm & 3.15pm; £4; ⊛www.etoncollege.com), a ten-minute walk from the river. When the school was founded in 1440, its aim was to give free education to seventy poor scholars and choristers; how times have changed. The original fifteenth-century **schoolroom**, gnarled with centuries of graffiti, survives, but the real highlight is the **College Chapel**, completed in 1482, a wonderful example of English Perpendicular architecture. The self-congratulatory **Museum of Eton Life**, where you're deposited at the end of the tour, is well worth missing unless you have a fascination with flogging, fagging and bragging about the school's facilities and alumni – Percy Bysshe Shelley is a rare rebellious figure in the roll call of Establishment greats. If you're thinking of going on a guided tour, phone ahead to make sure the school isn't closed for some special reason.

Among younger kids, the attractions of Windsor Castle are overshadowed by the town's **Legoland** (March–Oct daily 10am–5pm or later; adults £18.50, under-15s £15.50, under 3s free; ⊛www.legoland.co.uk) theme park aimed at pre-teenage children (the perfect age is around 5 to 8). The entrance charges are enough to put off most people, but if you've got the money, and several small kids in tow, it's one way of keeping them happy for a day. Whatever you do, though, try not to go at the weekend or during the school holidays, when the queues for the various rides become grievously long. On arrival, a funicular railway takes visitors down into the park, disgorging them close to Miniland, with its miniature lego depictions of various European landmarks. The rest of the park is really just a series of rides, most of them very gentle. There are numerous places to eat, though it makes sense to take a picnic and save yourself some money

Eating, drinking and nightlife

No matter what your taste in food, drink or entertainment, you'll find what you're looking for in London, a city that in many ways becomes a more appealing place after dark. The capital's rich ethnic mix and concentration of creative talent give it a diversity and energy that no other town in England comes close to matching – Birmingham might have a better concert hall, Manchester might have a couple of top clubs, but nowhere can match the capital's consistent quality and choice. The weekly calendar of gigs, movies, plays and other events is charted most completely in *Time Out*, the main listings magazine, and there are any number of specialist publications for those who want to make sure they are not missing a thing – from solemn books on the foodie shrines of London to esoteric little mags for the dance crowd. However, the listings that follow should be more than enough for any visitor who's planning on spending less than a couple of months in the city.

Eating

London is a great place in which to **eat out**. You can sample more or less any kind of cuisine here, and, wherever you come from, you should find something new and quite possibly unique. Home to some of the best **Cantonese** restaurants in the whole of Europe, London is also a noted centre for **Indian** and **Bangladeshi** food, and has numerous **French**, **Greek**, **Italian**, **Japanese**, **Spanish** and **Thai** restaurants; and within all these cuisines, you can choose anything from simple meals to gourmet spreads. Traditional and **Modern British** food is available all over town, and some of the best venues are reviewed below.

Cafés and fast food

There are plenty of **cafés** and small, basic restaurants all over London that can fill you up for under £10, including tea or coffee. A huge number of them are run by Anglo-Italians, which means you're guaranteed proper coffee and ciabatta sandwiches. Several of the places listed are also open in the evening, but

Cheap eats

As well as the places we've listed below, there are several **London-wide chains** that are well worth checking out. **EAT** (⊕www.eatcafe.co.uk) is a promising newcomer, and makes up excellent sandwiches on their own-baked bread; **Prêt à Manger** also does ready-made sandwiches (though it helps if you like mayo), as well as hot stuffed croissants and sushi selections. **Caffè Nero** serves terrific coffee, a range of Italian cakes, and pasta, calzone and pizza. As far as other coffee chains go; there's **Costa Coffee**, the train-station favourite, which serves some of the best coffee in town, as does **Starbucks** (⊕www.starbucks.com), the infamous clean-cut Seattle coffee company – **Coffee Republic** is a slightly less memorable replica.

For more substantial fare, the white and blue, Art Deco-ish **Café Flo** does decent French brasserie fare, as does the red-clad **Café Rouge**; **Ed's Easy Diner** (whose main branch is at 12 Moor St in Soho) is a 1950s-theme fast-food joint dishing up some of the city's best burgers and fries; and **Stockpot** (the main branch is on Soho's Old Compton St) serves big portions of stew and suchlike at rock-bottom prices.

the turnover is fast, so don't expect to linger; they're best seen as fuel stops before – or in a few cases, after – a night out. It's worth bearing in mind that most **pubs** (which are covered in the following section) serve food, and some have restaurants attached.

Mayfair and Marylebone

La Madeleine 5 Vigo St, W1. An authentic French patisserie and café, with mountains of tempting pastries from which to indulge yourself; tables at the back are for punters who want more substantial bistro fare. Green Park or Piccadilly Circus tube.

Mô 25 Heddon St, W1. The ultimate Arabic pastiche, but a successful one at that. The adjacent restaurant is pricey, but the tearoom serves delicious snacks and is a great place to hangout, with tables and hookahs spilling out onto the pavement of this little alleyway off Regent Street. Piccadilly Circus tube.

Patisserie Valerie at Sagne 105 Marylebone High St, W1. Founded as *Maison Sagne* in the 1920s, and preserving its wonderful decor from those days, the café is now run by Soho's fab patisserie makers, and is Marylebone's finest without doubt. Bond Street tube.

Soho

Bar Italia 22 Frith St, W1. A tiny café that's a Soho institution, serving coffee, croissants and sandwiches more or less around the clock – as it has been since 1949. Popular with late-night clubbers and those here to watch the Italian-league soccer on the giant screen. Leicester Square tube.

Bar du Marché 19 Berwick St, W1. A weird find in the middle of raucous Berwick Street market: a licensed French café serving quick snacks, brasserie staples, fried breakfasts and set meals

for under £10. Closed Sun. Tottenham Court Road, Piccadilly Circus or Leicester Square tube.

Centrale 16 Moor St, W1. Tiny, friendly Italian café that serves up huge plates of steaming, garlicky pasta, as well as omelettes, chicken and chops for around £5. You'll almost certainly have to wait for – or share – a formica-topped table. Bring your own booze; there's a 50p–£1 corkage charge. Closed Sun. Leicester Square tube.

Lee Ho Fook 4 Macclesfield St, W1. A genuine Chinese barbecue house – small, spartan and cheap – that is very difficult to find. Macclesfield Street runs from Shaftesbury Avenue to Gerrard Street; on the west side is Dansey Place, and on the corner with a red and gold sign in Chinese and a host of ducks hanging on a rack is this place. Leicester Square tube.

Maison Bertaux 28 Greek St, W1. Long-standing, old-fashioned and downbeat Soho patisserie, with tables on two floors (and one or two outside) and a loyal clientele that keeps things busy. You'll be tempted in by the window full of elaborate cakes, but be warned: the service can be brusque and when it comes to coffee, they only do *café au lait*. Leicester Square tube.

Patisserie Valerie 44 Old Compton St, W1. Popular 1920s coffee, croissant and cake emporium attracting a loud-talking, arty Soho crowd. The same outfit now have a branch at 8 Russell St, WC2, and also run *Patisserie Valerie at Sagne* in Marylebone (see above). Leicester Square or Piccadilly Circus tube.

Internet cafés

If you just need to send a quick email to someone, or go online, head for a branch of *easyEverything* (@www.easyeverything.com), the no-frills internet café chain – there's a 24-hour branch just up the Strand, off Trafalgar Square: Net access starts at £1. Alternatively, the internet cafés listed below are worth a visit in their own right and offer free or very nearly free internet access.

Cyberia, 39 Whitfield St, W1, @www. cyberia.co.uk. The city's first internet café, with trip-hop in the background, chilled beers, coffee and cakes for refuelling, and fourteen computers lined up for their netizens. Internet access 50p for 15min, occasionally free. Goodge Street tube.

The Vibe Bar, Truman Brewery, 91 Brick Lane, E1, @www.vibe-bar.co. uk. Head for "Room Service", a row of terminals in the corner of this trendy bar in a former East End brewery; internet access is free, if you buy a drink. Aldgate East tube.

Tokyo Diner 2 Newport Place, WC2. Providing conclusive proof that you don't need to take out a second mortgage to enjoy Japanese food in London, this friendly eatery on the edge of Chinatown shuns elaboration for fast food, Tokyo style. Minimalist decor lets the sushi and sumo do the talking, which – if the number of Japanese who frequent the place is anything to go by – it does fluently. Leicester Square tube.

Covent Garden and Bloomsbury

Coffee Gallery 23 Museum St, WC1. Excellent, if small, café close by the British Museum, serving mouthwatering Italian sandwiches and more substantial dishes at lunchtime. Get there early to grab a seat. Tottenham Court Road tube.
Café in the Crypt St Martin-in-the-Fields, Duncannon St, WC2. The self-service buffet food is nothing special, but there are regular veggie dishes, and the handy location – below the church in the crypt – makes this an ideal spot to fill up before hitting the West End. Charing Cross tube.
Food for Thought 31 Neal St, WC2. Long-established but minuscule bargain veggie restaurant and takeaway counter – the food is good, with the

menu changing twice daily, plus regular vegan and wheat-free options. Expect to queue and don't expect to linger at peak times. Closed Sun. Covent Garden tube.
Frank's Cafe 52 Neal St, WC2. Classic Anglo-Italian café/sandwich bar with easy-going service. All-day breakfasts, plus plates of pasta and omelettes; come either side of lunch to make sure of a table. Closed Sun. Covent Garden tube.
Gaby's 30 Charing Cross Rd, WC2. Busy café and takeaway joint serving a wide range of home-cooked veggie and Middle Eastern specialities. Hard to beat for value, choice, location or long hours – it's licensed, too, and the takeaway felafel are a central London bargain. Leicester Square tube.
India Club 143 Strand, WC2. There's a faded period charm to this long established, inexpensive Anglo-Indian eatery, sandwiched between floors of the cheap *Strand Continental Hotel* (see p.68). The "chillie bhajais" are to be taken very seriously. Closed Sun. Covent Garden or Temple (Mon–Sat) tube.
Mode 57 Endell St, WC2. The best things about this stylish Covent Garden café are the Italian sandwiches, the cheeses from nearby Neal's Yard

Liquid refuelling

Over the last few years, lunchtime catering in London has gone liquid, with an explosion of diminutive **soup and juice bars**. The trio below are a mere soupçon:

Crussh 48 Cornhill, EC3. Tiny, unusually funky, City juice bar selling wraps, salads, sushi and, of course, fresh juices. Bank tube. Closed Sat & Sun.
Soup Works 9 D'Arblay St. Noodles served here as well as every type of soup from chicken to chilled borscht. Branches in Monmouth St, WC1, and

Moor St, W1. Mon–Fri 8am–5pm, Sat noon–5pm. Oxford Circus tube.
Squeeze 27 Kensington High St, W8. Fruit smoothies, wraps, salads, sushi and muffins as well as fresh juices at this healthy pitstop. High Street Kensington tube.

Dairy, and the laid-back, funky atmosphere. Closed Sun. Covent Garden tube.

Monmouth Coffee Company 27 Monmouth St, WC2. The marvellous aroma is the first thing you notice here, while the cramped wooden booths and daily newspapers on hand evoke an eighteenth-century coffee-house atmosphere – pick and mix your coffee from a fine selection (or buy the beans to take home). No smoking. Closed Sun. Covent Garden or Leicester Square tube.

Wagamama 4 Streatham St, WC1. Austere, minimalist canteen-style place where the waiters take your orders on hand-held computers. Diners share long benches and slurp huge bowls of noodle soup or stir-fried plates. You may have to queue, however, and the rapid turnover means it's not a place to consider for a long, romantic dinner. Tottenham Court Road tube.

Clerkenwell, the City and the East End

Arkansas Café Unit 12, Old Spitalfields Market, E1. American barbecue fuel stop, using only the very best ingredients. Try chef Bubb's own smoked beef brisket and ribs, and be sure to taste his home-made barbie sauce (made to a secret formula). Liverpool Street tube.

Brick Lane Beigel Bake 159 Brick Lane, E1. The bagels at this no-frills 24-hour takeaway in the heart of the East End are freshly made and unbelievably cheap, even when stuffed with smoked salmon and cream cheese. Shoreditch or Aldgate East tube.

Clark & Sons 46 Exmouth Market, EC1. Exmouth Market is currently undergoing something of a transformation, so it's all the more surprising to find this genuine eel and pie shop still going strong. Closed Sun. Angel or Farringdon tube.

Feast 86 St John St, 7 EC1. Delicious tortilla-wrapped sandwiches made to order; takeaway or eat in this small, trendy, designer Clerkenwell café. Closed Sat & Sun. Farringdon or Barbican tube.

The Place Below St Mary-le-Bow, Cheapside, EC2. Something of a find in the midst of the City – a café serving imaginative (albeit slightly pricey) vegetarian dishes. Added to that, the wonderful Norman crypt makes for a very pleasant place in which to dine. Closed Sat & Sun. St Paul's or Bank tube.

The South Bank

Konditor & Cook Young Vic Theatre, 66 The Cut, E1. Cut above your average theatre café, this place gets its cakes and so forth made by the fabulous Konditor & Cook bakery, round the corner in Cornwall Road. You can also get snacks, organic ice creams and sorbets, and, of course, drinks at the bar. Closed Sun. Waterloo tube.

Kensington, Chelsea and Notting Hill

Jenny Lo's Teahouse 14 Ecclestone St, SW1 ☎020/7259 0399. Bright, bare and utilitarian yet somehow stylish and fashionable, too, *Jenny Lo's* serves good Chinese food at low prices. Be sure to check out the therapeutic teas. Closed Sun. Victoria tube.

Lisboa Patisserie 57 Golborne Rd, W10. Authentic and friendly Portuguese pastelaria, with coffee and cakes including the best custard tarts this side of Lisbon. The *Oporto*, at 62a Golborne Rd, is a good fallback if this place is full. Ladbroke Grove tube.

Maison Blanc 102 Holland Park Ave, W11. French patisserie (with other branches in St John's Wood, Hampstead, Chelsea and Richmond), where you can guarantee you'll get the real thing when it comes to croissants and the like. Holland Park tube.

New Culture Revolution 305 King's Rd, SW3. Great name, great concept – big bowls of freshly cooked noodles in sauce or soup or dumplings and rice dishes, all offering a one-stop meal at bargain prices in simple, minimalist surroundings. Not a place to linger. Sloane Square tube.

Raison d'Etre 18 Bute St, SW7. Smack in the middle of South Kensington's French quarter, this is a top-notch patisserie/boulangerie, serving excellent coffee. Closed Sun. South Kensington tube.

Camden and Hampstead

Brew House Kenwood, Hampstead Lane, NW3. Everything from full English breakfast to lunches, cakes and teas, all served in the old laundry at Kenwood, or enjoyed on the terrace overlooking the lake. Bus #210 from Highgate tube or a walk across the Heath.

Café Mozart 17 Swains Lane, N6. Viennese café that's usefully close to the southeast side of Hampstead Heath, and also serves a few hearty Austrian dishes. Gospel Oak train station, or bus #C2.

Louis Patisserie 32 Heath St, NW3. Popular central-European tea room in Hampstead village serving sticky cakes to a mix of Heath-bound hordes and elderly locals. Hampstead tube.

Marine Ices 8 Haverstock Hill, NW3. Situated halfway between Camden and Hampstead, this is a splendid and justly famous old-fashioned Italian ice-cream parlour; pizza and pasta are served in the adjacent restaurant. Chalk Farm tube.

Greenwich

Pistachio's Café 15 Nelson Rd, SE10. Just about the only decent sandwich café in the centre of Greenwich, serving excellent coffee, and with a small garden out back. Cutty Sark DLR, or Greenwich DLR and train station.

Tai Won Mein 49 Greenwich Church St, SE10. Good quality fast-food noodle bar that gets very busy at weekends. Decor is functional and minimalist; choose between rice, fried or soup noodles and *ho fun* (a flatter, softer, ribbon-like noodle). Cutty Sark DLR or Greenwich DLR and train station.

Restaurants

Many of the restaurants we've listed will be busy on most nights of the week, particularly on Thursday, Friday and Saturday, and you're best advised to **reserve a table** wherever you're headed. As for **prices**, you can pay an awful lot for a meal in London, and if you're used to North American portions, you're not going to be particularly impressed by the volume in most places. For cheaper eats, see the section above.

St James's, Mayfair and Marylebone

Abu Ali 136–138 George St, W1 ☎020/7724 6338. Spartan place that's the Lebanese equivalent to a northern working men's club, serving honest fare that's terrific value for money, from the *tabbouleh* to the kebabs – wash it all down with fresh mint tea. Cash or cheque only. Inexpensive. Marble Arch tube.

The Criterion 224 Piccadilly, W1 ☎020/7930 0488. One of the city's most beautiful restaurants, behind Eros on Piccadilly Circus. The high vaulted gold mosaic ceiling sparkles, and the menu is courtesy of scourge of the faint-hearted, Marco Pierre White. The set menu lunch (under £20 a head) is the best value and allows you to keep your table all afternoon. Closed Sun lunch. Expensive. Piccadilly Circus tube.

Mandalay 444 Edgware Rd, W2 ☎020/7258 3696, ⊛www.bcity.com/mandalay. Small non-smoking restaurant that serves pure, freshly cooked and unexpurgated Burmese cuisine – a *melange* of Thai, Malaysian, a lot of Indian and a few things that are unique. The portions are huge, flavours hit the mark, the service friendly and the prices low. Closed Sun. Inexpensive. Edgware Road tube.

Quaglino's 16 Bury St, SW1 ☎020/7930 6767, ⊛www.conran.com. Huge 1930s ballroom revived by Terence Conran as one of the capital's busiest and most glamorous eating spots, so you'll need to book well in advance. There's an unmistakable buzz about the place, the surroundings are splendid, and the fish and seafood dishes are excellent – it's also open late. Closed Sun lunch. Expensive. Green Park tube.

La Spighetta 43 Blandford St, W1 ☎020/7486 7340. Not a spaghetti house – *spighetta* actually means wheat – but a large basement buzzing with activity and serving pizza, pasta and standard Italian main courses. The pizzas and pasta dishes are very good, as are the classic puddings. Closed Sun lunch. Moderate. Bond Street tube.

Soho and Chinatown

Aroma II 118 Shaftesbury Ave, W1 ☎020/7437 0370, ⊛www.aromares.co.uk. Bright, modernist Chinese restaurant with an exhausting and exhaustive menu ranging from traditional hand-pulled noodles to braised sea slug or shark fin. This is one of the more serious but accessible gastronomic Chinatown places, so if you're stuck for what to choose, ask for advice. Inexpensive. Leicester Square tube.

China City White Bear Yard, 25a Lisle St, WC2 ☎020/7734 3388. Large restaurant tucked into a little courtyard off Lisle Street; fresh and bright, with *dim sum* that's up there with the best, service that is "Chinatown brusque", and a menu with eminently reasonable prices. Closed Sun. Inexpensive to Moderate. Leicester Square tube.

Fung Shing 15 Lisle St, WC2 ☎020/7437 1539, ⊛www.fungshing.com. Bigger and brassier than ever, this is a classy Chinatown restaurant that takes its cooking and its service seriously. Prices are above average, but the portions are large, and the food has an earthy, robust quality redolent of a chef who is absolutely confident of his flavours and textures. Moderate. Leicester Square tube.

Kettner's 29 Romilly St, W1 ☎020/7734 6112. Despite the very handsome *belle époque* Baroque decor and the pianist, this place is by no means exclusive. In fact, it's one of the reliable *Pizza Express* restaurants, serving thin-based pizzas and the like. You can't book and might be forced to hangout a while in the noisy *Champagne Bar* – no great hardship. Closed Sun. Moderate. Leicester Square tube.

Kulu Kulu 76 Brewer St, W1 ☎020/7734 7316. Small, friendly *kaiten* (or conveyor belt) sushi restaurant which pulls off the unlikely trick of serving really good sushi without being impersonal or intimidating. Open your box containing a pair of disposable chopsticks, pickled ginger and soy sauce, grab one or two plates (they're priced/coded by design not colour here) and tuck in. Closed Sun. Inexpensive. Piccadilly Circus tube.

Mezzo 100 Wardour St, W1 ☎ 020/7314 4000, ⓦ www.conran.com. Mezzo has remained popular ever since Terence Conran opened this six-hundred-seater in 1995. There's a bar, an informal *Mezzonine* restaurant upstairs and, down the sweeping staircase, the full-on *Mezzo* with a space for performers. The tables are packed close, and there's a fashionable mayhem of noise, but considering the numbers served here, the French/Med food is pretty good. There's a £5 "live music cover charge" after 8pm. Closed Sat lunch. Moderate to Very Expensive. Piccadilly Circus or Tottenham Court Road tube.

Mr Kong 21 Lisle St, WC2 ☎ 020/7437 7923. One of Chinatown's finest, with a chef/owner who pioneered many of the modern Cantonese dishes now on menus all over town. To sample the restaurant's more unusual dishes – order from the "Today's" and "Chef's Specials" menu, and don't miss the mussels in black-bean sauce or the fresh razor clam with garlic. Moderate. Leicester Square tube.

New World 1 Gerrard Place, W1 ☎ 020/7734 0396. Very probably the largest single restaurant in London, with four to six hundred seats. The menu is twenty pages long, but luckily you don't need it in order to enjoy the authentic *dim sum*, which is served daily (11am–6pm) from circulating "themed" trolleys. Moderate. Leicester Square tube.

Randall & Aubin 16 Brewer St, W1 ☎ 020/7287 4447. Converted butcher's, now a champagne-oyster bar, rotisserie, sandwich shop and charcuterie, to boot – in the summer, this is a wonderfully airy place to eat. Closed Sun lunch. Moderate. Piccadilly Circus tube.

Covent Garden

Belgo Centraal 50 Earlham St, WC2 ☎ 020/7813 2233, ⓦ www.belgo-restaurants.com. Massive metal-minimalist cavern off Neal Street, serving excellent kilo-buckets of moules marinière, with frites and mayonnaise, a bewildering array of Belgian beers to choose from, and waffles for dessert. The £5 lunchtime specials are a bargain for central London. Inexpensive to Moderate. Covent Garden tube.

Café Pacifico 5 Langley St, WC2 ☎ 020/7379 7728, ⓦ www.cafepacifico-laperla.com. The salsa is hot here – both types – and the menu includes all the favourites, such as fajitas, flautas and

tacos. Portions are generous and spicy, and there are nine varieties of Mexican beer and more than sixty types of tequila. The place is very popular and lively in the evening – in fact, you're advised to book. Moderate. Covent Garden tube.

Livebait 21 Wellington St, WC2 ☎ 020/7836 7161, ⓦ www.sante-gcg.com. Innovative, irrepressible restaurant with a large, bustling, black-and-white-tiled dining room. The emphasis is on fish so fresh you expect to see it flapping on the slab, and superb crustacea. The breads are still a feature and service is friendly. Closed Sun. Expensive. Covent Garden tube.

J. Sheekey 28–32 St Martin's Court, WC2 ☎ 020/7240 2565. *J. Sheekey*'s pedigree goes back to WWI, but the place has recently been totally redesigned and refurbished. The menu is still focused on fish, but in addition to traditional fare such as grilled Dover sole, you're just as likely to find Modernist dishes such as grilled cuttlefish with creamed brandade. The weekend lunches at between £10–15 are great value. Expensive. Leicester Square tube.

Fitzrovia and Bloomsbury

Great Nepalese 48 Eversholt St, NW1 ☎ 020 /7388 6737. Friendly, homely Nepalese restaurant round the back of Euston Station. Delve into the authentic Nepalese dishes, whose names you won't be familiar with, but only try the Coronation rum from Kathmandu if you know what you're doing. Inexpensive. Euston or Euston Square tube.

Ikkyu 67a Tottenham Court Rd, W1 ☎ 020/7636 9280. Busy, basic basement Japanese restaurant, good enough for a quick lunch or a more elaborate dinner. Either way, prices are infinitely more reasonable than elsewhere in the capital, and the food is tasty and authentic. Be warned, however: it's hard to find, and when you do, shockingly popular. Closed all Sat & Sun lunch. Moderate. Goodge Street tube.

Malabar Junction 107a Great Russell St, WC1 ☎ 020/7580 5230. Inexpensive yet fully licensed, top quality Keralan restaurant with two entirely (and religiously) separate kitchens: one serving mouthwatering, spicy and nutty veggie dishes, the other dishing out equally tasty meat and fish fare. Inexpensive to Moderate. Tottenham Court Road tube.

Rasa Samudra 5 Charlotte St, W1 ☎ 020/7637 0222, ⓦ www.rasarestaurants.com. Above average prices for exceptional South Indian fish dishes, which are freshly prepared using top quality ingredients, and come complete with accompaniments. The cooking is well-judged and the spices well-balanced, but if you're still nervous of the bill, go for the fixed-price three-course lunch at £10 (vegetarian) or £15 (seafood). Closed Sun. Moderate to Expensive. Goodge Street tube.

Clerkenwell and the City

Cicada 132 St John St, EC1 ☎ 020/7608 1550. Part bar, part restaurant, *Cicada* is set back from the street and, when the weather's fine, it's a great place for eating alfresco. The unusual Thai-based menu allows you to mix and match from small, large and side dishes ranging from hot, lemony, fishy tom yum soup, to sweet ginger noodles, fresh clams, white miso or kinome leaves. Closed Sat lunch & Sun. Moderate. Farringdon tube.

St John 26 St John St, EC1 ☎ 020/7272 1587, ⓦ www.stjohnrestaurant.co.uk. A genuinely English restaurant, only a stone's throw from Smithfield meat market and specializing in offal. All those strange and unfashionable cuts of meat that were once commonplace in rural England – brains, bone marrow, meat from a cow's sternum – are on offer at this white-painted former smokehouse. Closed Mon lunch. Expensive. Farringdon tube.

Singapura 1–2 Limeburner Lane, EC4 ☎ 020/7329 1133, ⓦ www.singapura.co.uk. Beautiful, large, modern restaurant off Ludgate Hill that is one of the few places outside Singapore where you can sample *Nonya* cuisine – a fusion of Malayan and Chinese traditions and ingredients. The food is generally (but not always) spicy, and is characterized by a good deal of garlic, galangal, sweetness and lime leaves. Closed Sat & Sun. Moderate. Blackfriars or St Paul's tube.

East End

Café Spice Namaste 16 Prescott St, E1 ☎ 020/7488 9242, ⓦ www.book2eat.com. Very popular Indian on the fringe of the City that is definitely not your average curry house. Parsee delicacies rub shoulders with dishes from Goa, Hyderabad and Kashmir, and the tandoori specialities are awesome. Be sure to check out the speciality menu, which changes weekly. Closed Sat lunch & Sun. Moderate. Tower Hill tube.

Café Naz 46–48 Brick Lane, E1 ☎ 020/7247 0234, ⓦ www.cafenaz.com. Self-proclaimed contemporary Bangladeshi restaurant that cuts an imposing modern figure on Brick Lane. The menu has all the standard Indian dishes plus a load of "baltis", the kitchen is open-plan, and the prices keen – as you'd expect in a street replete with rival curry houses. Inexpensive. Aldgate East tube.

Real Greek 15 Hoxton Market, N1 ☎ 020/7739 8212, ⓦ www.therealgreek.co.uk. Yes, it's run by a real Greek, but this is nothing like your average London Greek-Cypriot joint. Small, modern and comfortable, the menu shows off the authentic dishes of Greece, and the service is excellent. Set lunch and early doors dinner are a bargain. Closed Sun. Moderate. Old Street or Shoreditch tube.

Viet Hoa Café 72 Kingsland Rd, E2 ☎ 020/7729 8293. Large, light and airy Vietnamese café with a golden parquet floor, situated not far from the Geffrye Museum in Hoxton/Shoreditch, and serving splendid "meals in a bowl" – soups and noodle dishes with everything from spring rolls to tofu. Be sure to try the *Pho* soup, a Vietnamese staple that's eaten at any and every meal. Bus #67, #149 or #242 from Inexpensive to Moderate. Liverpool Street Station.

Lambeth and Southwark

Butlers Wharf Chop House 36e Shad Thames, SE1 ☎ 020/7403 3403, ⓦ www.conran.com. Conran-owned restaurant showcasing British meat, fish and cheeses. Prices are high, but the *Chop House* tries to cater for all: you could enjoy a simple dish at the bar, a well-priced set lunch, or an extravagant dinner. You can't reserve the terrace tables but try and book ahead for a window seat. Restaurant closed Sat lunch, bar closed Sun eve. Moderate (bar) to Expensive (restaurant). Tower Hill, London Bridge or Bermondsey tube.

Fish! Cathedral St, SE1 ☎ 020/7234 3333, ⓦ www.fishdiner.co.uk. Busy, buzzy, tank-like restaurant, with huge windows and a glass ceiling, right in the middle of Borough Market. Choose your fish, decide how you want it cooked, and with what sauce, and then sit back and wait. Portions are huge, and the fish is as good and fresh as you'd expect. Closed Sun eve. Moderate. London Bridge tube.

Fina Estampa 150 Tooley St, SE1 ☎ 020/7403 1342. This may be London's only Peruvian restaurant, but it also happens to be the very best, bringing a little of downtown Lima to London Bridge. The menu is traditional Peruvian, with a big emphasis on seafood. Closed Sat lunch & all Sun. Moderate. London Bridge tube.

Little Saigon 139 Westminster Bridge Rd, SE1 ☎ 020/7207 9747. Great Vietnamese spring rolls, grilled squid-cake and crystal pancakes, all served with a wonderful array of sauces, plus great crispy fried noodles. Closed Sat & Sun lunch. Moderate. Waterloo tube.

RSJ 13a Coin St, SE1 ☎ 020/7928 4554, ⓦ www.rsj.uk.com. Regularly high standards of Anglo-French cooking make this a good spot for a meal after or before an evening at a South Bank theatre or concert hall. The set meals for around £15 are particularly popular. Closed Sat lunch & Sun. Expensive. Waterloo tube.

Kensington and Chelsea

Bibendum Oyster House Michelin House, 81 Fulham Rd, SW3 ☎020/7589 1480, ⓦwww.bibendum.co.uk. A glorious tiled affair built in 1911, this former garage is the best place to eat shellfish in London. There are three types of rock oysters, but if you're really hungry, try the *plateau de fruits de mer*, which also has crab, clams, langoustine, prawns, shrimps, whelks and winkles. Moderate. South Kensington tube.

Boisdale 15 Ecclestone St, SW1 ☎020/7730 6922, ⓦwww.boisdale.co.uk. Owned by Ranald MacDonald, son of the Chief of Clanranald, this is a very Scottish place, strong on hospitality, and with a befuddlingly large range of rare malt whiskies. Fresh Scottish produce rules wherever possible, including MacSween's haggis (sheep's innards and oatmeal), venison and salmon. Closed Sun. Moderate to Expensive. Victoria tube.

Hunan 51 Pimlico Rd, SW1 ☎020/7730 5712. Probably England's only restaurant serving Hunan food, a relative of Sichuan cuisine, with the same spicy kick to most dishes and a fair wallop of pepper in those that aren't actively riddled with chiles. Most people opt for the £25 "Hunan's special leave-it-to-us feast", a multi-course extravaganza which lets the maître d', Mr Peng, show what he can do. Closed Sun. Expensive. Sloane Square tube.

Wódka 12 St Alban's Grove, W8 ☎020/7937 6513. The food is cooked with imagination, which makes the smart *Wódka* the place to go if you want to experience the best that Polish cuisine has to offer. It's not an expensive place to eat (especially if you go for the daily set-menu lunch), unless you start working your way through the large selection of flavoured vodkas. Moderate. High Street Kensington or Gloucester Road tube.

Bayswater and Notting Hill

Alounak 44 Westbourne Grove, W2 ☎020/7229 0416. Don't be put off by the dated sign outside – this place turns out really good, really cheap Iranian grub. The mixed starter is a fine sampler of all the usual dips, served with freshly baked flat bread; lamb dishes feature heavily, but look out for the daily specials, and wash it all down with a pot of Iranian black tea. Inexpensive. Queensway or Bayswater tube.

The Mandola 139–141 Westbourne Grove, W11 ☎020/7229 4734. Small, seriously informal, supremely popular, unlicensed neighbourhood restaurant serving strikingly delicious "urban Sudanese" food at sensible prices. Be sure to check out the Sudanese spiced coffee at the end. Closed Mon lunch. Moderate. Notting Hill Gate tube.

Rodizio Rico 111 Westbourne Grove, W11 ☎020/7792 4035. No menu, no prices, but no problem either as this Brazilian eatery specializes in smoky, grilled meat. Carvers come round and lop off chunks of freshly grilled meats, while you help yourself from the salad bar and hot buffet to prime your plate. Closed Mon–Fri lunch. Moderate. Notting Hill Gate or Bayswater tube.

Rôtisserie Jules 133a Notting Hill Gate, W11 ☎020/7221 3331, ⓦwww.rotisseriejules.com. One of three consistently sound restaurants – the other two are at 6 Bute St, SW7, and 338 King's Rd, SW3 – which excels in freshly roasted chicken hot off the spit at very reasonable prices. You can have a leg and thigh, a breast and wing, the whole chicken or even an entire leg of lamb, which will feed three or four people. Inexpensive to Moderate. Notting Hill Gate tube.

Camden and Hampstead

Cucina 45a South End Rd, NW3 ☎020/7435 7814. Brightly painted, wooden-floored, roof-lit first-floor restaurant that's very contemporary, very fashionable and very Hampstead. The Modern British menu changes every two weeks or so and darts about a bit from cuisine to cuisine, but wherever you alight, each dish is well-presented, and the set lunch is a bargain at under £15. Expensive. Belsize Park tube.

Gresslin's 13 Heath St, NW3 ☎020/7794 8386. Small, Modern European restaurant in the heart of Hampstead, with dishes ranging from Mediterranean French to Thai served up by efficient French waiters. Closed Mon lunch & Sun eve. Moderate. Hampstead tube.

Sauce barorganicdiner 214 Camden High St, NW1 ☎020/7482 0777. *Sauce* offers food free of chemicals, pesticides and preservatives in a bright, colourful diner, with a juice and cocktail bar attached. Burgers, sandwiches and wraps are on the menu, and it's also fine to go just for a coffee or a beer. Inexpensive. Camden Town tube.

Greenwich

Time 7a College Approach, SE10 ☎020/8305 9767, ⓦwww.timerestaurant.com. *Time* is a small, appealing restaurant, with roomy tables and an elegant clientele. The menu is not long, but it offers plenty of choice, celebrating flavours borrowed from around the world. Closed all Mon & Tues–Sat lunch. Expensive. Cutty Sark DLR.

Chiswick to Richmond

Chez Lindsay 11 Hill Rise, Richmond, Surrey ☎020/8948 7473. Small, bright, authentic Breton creperie, with a loyal local following, and fixed-price lunchtime menus for under £10. Choose between galettes, crepes or more formal French main courses, including lots of fresh fish and shellfish, and wash it all down with Breton cider in traditional earthenware *bolées*. Moderate. Richmond tube.

The Glasshouse 14 Station Parade, Kew, Surrey ☎020/8940 6777. Clean-cut, modern restaurant on the very doorstep of Kew Gardens tube, with blissfully comfortable chairs. The menu changes on a daily basis, with five or six choices for each course, and set-menu prices hovering around the

£20 mark. The cooking is imaginative and straight-forward, and owes much to genuine French food. Closed Sun eve. Expensive. Kew Gardens tube.

Springbok Café 42 Devonshire Rd, W4 ☎020/8742 3149, ⓦ www.springbokcafecuisine. com. Small, informal and ambitious South African restaurant, with an open-plan barbie-oriented kitchen. Many of the ingredients are imported, so there's plenty of biltong, game and fish from SA, plus smoked English ostrich to please expats. Closed Mon–Sat lunch & all Sun. Expensive. Turnham Green tube.

Drinking

Older-style inns, with oak beams, open fires and polished-brass fittings survive here and there, but they're not a great feature of the capital. London's great period of **pub** building took place in the Victorian era, to which many pubs still pay homage; genuine Victorian interiors, however, are increasingly difficult to find, as indeed are genuinely individual pubs. Chain pubs can now be found all over the capital: branches of All Bar One, Pitcher & Piano and the Slug & Lettuce are the most obvious, as they all share the chain name, whereas J.D. Wetherspoon and Fuller's pubs do at least vary theirs. The traditional image of London **pub food** is dire but the last couple of decades have seen plenty of improvements. You can get a palatable lunchtime meal at many of the pubs listed below, and at a few of them, you're looking at cooking worthy of high, restaurant-standard praise.

Standard pub **opening hours** are Mon–Sat 11am–11pm, Sun noon–10.30pm (the listings below only specify the exceptions). However, with England's licensing likely to change in the near future, many of the pubs listed will probably stay open later. Until then, in order to drink beyond 11pm, you're probably best off heading for one of the city's bars, which go in and out of fashion with incredible speed. These are very different places to your average pub, catering to a somewhat cliquey, often youngish crowd, with designer interiors and drinks; they also tend to be more expensive (and will charge entry after 11pm). We've listed a fair few – while covering those tied to, or more like, clubs and dance venues on p.59.

Whitehall and Westminster

Albert 52 Victoria St, SW1. Roomy High-Victorian pub, situated halfway between Parliament Square and Victoria, with big bay windows and glass partitions; good bar food, too, and an excellent carvery upstairs. St James's Park or Victoria tube.

ICA Bar 94 The Mall, SW1 ☎020/7930 2402, ⓦ www.ica.org.uk. You have to be a member (or be visiting an exhibition or cinema/theatre/talk event) to drink at the late-opening *ICA Bar* – but anyone can join on the door (Mon–Fri £1.50; Sat & Sun £2.50). It's a cool drinking venue, with a noir dress code observed by the arty crowd and staff. Piccadilly Circus or Charing Cross tube.

Paviour's Arms Page St, SW1. A unique survivor, this large, stylish 1930s Art Deco pub, in the back-

streets close to the Tate Gallery, has much of its original decor intact; you can also get decent Thai food with your beer. Be warned, though: the place is heaving with civil servants and locals at lunchtime. Closed Sat & Sun. Pimlico tube.

St James's, Mayfair and Marylebone

Dover Castle 43 Weymouth Mews, W1. A really nice, traditional boozer down a quiet Marylebone mews. Restful, racing-green upholstery, dark wood, a nicotine-stained lincrusta ceiling and cheap Sam Smith's beer on tap. Regent's Park or Oxford Circus tube. Closed Sun.

Mulligans 13–14 Cork St, W1. A fine and very smart Irish pub with an odd mix of clientele – Cork Street gallery staff and Irish lads – and some of the best Guinness in London. Also has a high-class restaurant downstairs, with fine Modern British/Irish cooking. Closed Sun. Green Park or Piccadilly tube.

O'Conor Don 88 Marylebone Lane, W1. A stripped bare, anti-theme Irish pub that's a cut above the average, with excellent Guinness, a pleasantly measured pace and Irish food on offer. Closed Sat & Sun. Bond Street tube.

Red Lion 23 Crown Passage, SW1. Not to be confused with the nearby pub of the same name, this is a small, local, wood-panelled pub hidden away in a passageway off Pall Mall. Green Park tube.

Soho and Fitzrovia

Coach & Horses 29 Greek St, W1. Long-standing – and, for once, little-changed – haunt of the ghosts of old Soho, *Private Eye*, nightclubbers, and art students from nearby St Martin's College. 1950s red plastic stools and black formica tables make up the spartan, unchanging decor. Leicester Square tube.

Dog & Duck 18 Bateman St, W1. Tiny Soho pub that retains much of its old character, beautiful Victorian tiling and mosaics, and a loyal clientele that often includes jazz musicians from nearby *Ronnie Scott's* club. Closed Sat & Sun lunch. Leicester Square or Tottenham Court Road tube.

French House 49 Dean St, W1. The tiny French pub has been a Soho institution since before World War I. Free French and literary associations galore, half pints only at the bar (no real ale) and a fine little restaurant upstairs (book ahead). Leicester Square tube.

The Hope 15 Tottenham St, W1. Chiefly remarkable for its sausage (veggie ones included), beans and mash lunches, and its real ales. Lunchtime only. Goodge Street tube.

Newman Arms 23 Rathbone St, W1. What the *Hope* is to sausages, the *Newman Arms* is to pies, with every sort from gammon to steak-and-kidney. Closed Sat & Sun. Tottenham Court Road tube.

The Toucan 19 Carlisle St ☎020/7437 4123, ⓦwww.thetoucan.co.uk. Small bar serving excellent Guinness and a wide range of Irish whiskeys, plus cheap, wholesome and filling food. So popular it can get mobbed. Closed Sun. Tottenham Court Road tube.

Two Floors 3 Kingly St, W1. Relaxed, modernist Soho bar, laid out, unsurprisingly on two floors, attracting a mixed gay/straight crowd, and pumping out drum'n'bass in the evenings – quite a find in an area short of decent drinking holes. Closed Sun. Oxford Circus or Piccadilly Circus tube.

Covent Garden

Freedom Brewing Company 41 Earlham St, WC2, ⓦwww.freedombrew.com. Busy, brick-vaulted basement brewery bar with wrought-iron pillars, lots of brushed steel and pricey, strong brews, made on the premises – in particular, there's a very fine organic honey wheat beer. Covent Garden tube.

Lamb & Flag 33 Rose St, WC2. Busy, tiny and highly atmospheric pub, tucked away down an alley between Garrick Street and Floral Street, where John Dryden was attacked in 1679 for writing scurrilous verses about one of Charles II's mistresses. Leicester Square tube.

Punch & Judy 40 The Market, WC2. Horribly mobbed and loud, but this Covent Garden Market pub does boast an unbeatable location with a very popular balcony overlooking the Piazza – and a stone-flagged cellar. Covent Garden tube.

Salisbury 90 St Martin's Lane, WC2. Easily one of the most beautifully preserved Victorian pubs in the capital – and certainly the most central – with cut, etched and engraved windows, bronze figures, red velvet seating and a fine lincrusta ceiling. Leicester Square tube.

Bloomsbury

Lamb 94 Lamb's Conduit St, WC1. Pleasant pub with a marvellously well-preserved Victorian interior of mirrors, old wood and "snob" screens. Russell Square tube.

Museum Tavern 49 Great Russell St, WC1. Large and characterful old pub, right opposite the main entrance to the British Museum, erstwhile drinking hole of Karl Marx. Tottenham Court Road or Russell Square tube.

Strand, Holborn and Clerkenwell

Café Kick 43 Exmouth Market, EC1. Stylish take on a local French-style café-bar in the heart of newly fashionable Exmouth Market, with table football to complete the retro theme. Farringdon or Angel tube.

Clerkenwell House 23–27 Hatton Wall, EC1. One of a whole host of new bars to open on and off the Clerkenwell Road. The retro 1970s furniture includes some wickedly comfy semi-circular sofas. The Med food is good, and there are four American pool tables in the basement bar. Farringdon tube.

Eagle 159 Farringdon Rd, EC1. The first of London's pubs to go foody, this place is heaving at lunch and dinnertimes, as *Guardian* workers tuck into Med dishes, but you should be able to find a seat at other times. Closed Sun eve. Farringdon tube.

Fox & Anchor 115 Charterhouse St, EC1. Handsome Smithfield market pub famous for its early opening hours (from 7am) and huge break-fasts. Closed Sat & Sun. Farringdon or Barbican tube.

Jerusalem Tavern 55 Britton St, EC1. Cosy little converted Georgian parlour, stripped bare and slightly "distressed", serving tasty food along with an excellent range of draught beers from St Peter's Brewery in Suffolk. Closed Sat & Sun. Farringdon tube.

Na Zdrowie 11 Little Turnstile, WC1. Great Polish bar hidden in an alleyway behind Holborn tube, with a wicked selection of flavoured vodkas, and cheap Polish food. Holborn tube.

Princess Louise 208 High Holborn, WC1. Old-fashioned place, with highly decorated ceilings, lots of glass, brass and mahogany, and a good range of real ales. Closed Sun. Holborn tube.

The City: Fleet Street to St Paul's

Blackfriar 174 Queen Victoria St, EC4. A gorgeous, utterly original pub, with Art Nouveau marble friezes of boozy monks and a wonderful highly decorated alcove – all original, dating from 1905. Closed Sat & Sun. Blackfriars tube.

Old Bank of England 194 Fleet St, EC4. Not the actual Bank of England, but the former Law Courts' branch, this imposing High Victorian banking hall is now a magnificently opulent ale and pie pub. Closed Sat & Sun. Temple (Mon–Sat) or Chancery Lane tube.

Old Cheshire Cheese Wine Office Court, 145 Fleet St, EC4. A famous seventeenth-century watering hole, with several snug, dark panelled bars and real fires. Popular with tourists, but by no means exclusively so. Closed Sun eve. Temple (Mon–Sat) or Blackfriars tube.

The City: Bank to Bishopsgate

The Counting House 50 Cornhill, EC2. Another City bank conversion, with fantastic high ceilings a glass dome, chandeliers and a central oval bar. Naturally enough, given the location, it's wall-to-wall suits. Closed Sat & Sun. Bank tube.

The George Bishopsgate, EC2. *The George* – the pub on the corner of Liverpool Street – is part of Conran's smoothly-run refurbished *Great Eastern Hotel*, and retains its wonderful original mock-Tudor decor. Liverpool Street tube

Hamilton Hall Liverpool Street Station, EC2. Cavernous, gilded, former ballroom of the *Great Eastern* hotel, adorned with nudes and chande-liers. Packed out with City commuters tanking up before the train home, but a great place nonethe-less. Liverpool Street tube.

Jamaica Wine House St Michael's Alley, EC3. An old City institution tucked away down a narrow alleyway. Despite the name, this is really just a pub, divided into four large "snugs" by high wooden-panelled partitions. Closed Sat & Sun. Bank tube.

East End and Docklands

Dickens Inn St Katharine's Way, E1. Eighteenth-century timber-framed warehouse transported on wheels from its original site, and then much altered. Still, it's a remarkable building, with a great view, but very firmly on the tourist trail. Tower Hill tube or Tower Gateway DLR.

The Gun 27 Cold Harbour, E14. An old dockers' pub with lots of maritime memorabilia, and – the main attraction – an unrivalled view of the Millennium Dome. South Quay or Blackwall DLR, or Canary Wharf tube.

The Pool 104–108 Curtain Rd, EC2. The three pool tables looking out onto busy, busy Curtain Road give this bar its name; the big bean bags in the basement add a retro touch. Old Street tube.

Prospect of Whitby 57 Wapping Wall, E1. London's most famous riverside pub with a flag-stone floor, a cobbled courtyard and great views over the Thames. Wapping tube.

Town of Ramsgate 62 Wapping High St, E1. Dark, narrow medieval pub located by Wapping Old Stairs, which once led down to Execution Dock. Captain Blood was discovered here with the crown jewels under his cloak, and Admiral Bligh and Fletcher Christian were regular drinking part-ners in pre-mutiny days. Wapping tube.

Via Fossa West India Quay, E14, ☎020/7515 8549. Housed in a nineteenth-century warehouse, and accessible from Canary Wharf via a footbridge. If the weather's warm, the south-facing terrace is great to sit out on. Mon–Sat noon–11pm, Sun noon–7pm. West India Quay DLR.

Lambeth and Southwark

Anchor Bankside 34 Park St, SE1. While the rest of Bankside has changed almost beyond all recog-nition, this pub still looks much as it did when first built in 1770 (on the inside, at least). Good for alfresco drinking by the river. London Bridge, Southwark or Blackfriars tube.

Fire Station 150 Waterloo Rd, SE1. This gloriously red former fire station is a step away from Waterloo, and therefore a popular place for an after-work pint. The restaurant at the back is good, too. Waterloo tube.

George Inn 77 Borough High St, SE1. London's only surviving coaching inn, dating from the sev-enteenth century and now owned by the National Trust; it also serves a good range of real ales. Borough or London Bridge tube.

Kensington, Chelsea & Notting Hill

Bunch of Grapes 207 Brompton Rd, SW3. This popular High-Victorian pub, complete with "snob" screens, is the perfect place for a post-V&A (or post-Harrods) pint, pie and chips. South Kensington tube.

The Cow 89 Westbourne Park Rd, W2. Sort of vaguely Irish-themed pub owned by Tom Conran, son of gastro-magnate Terence, which pulls in the beautiful W11 types thanks to its spectacular food, including a daily supply of fresh oysters, and excellent Guinness. Westbourne Park or Royal Oak tube.

Front Page 35 Old Church St, SW3, ⓦ www.front-pagepubs.com. Tucked away in the centre of villagey, boho Chelsea and infinitely preferable to anything on offer on the King's Road, the *Front Page* is small and snug, and serves very good Mediterranean food. Sloane Square tube.

Market Bar 240a Portobello Rd, W11. Self-consciously bohemian pub divided by gilded mirrors and ruched curtains and scattered with weird *objets* – all very Portobello Road. Occasional live music and DJs. Ladbroke Grove tube.

Orange Brewery 37 Pimlico Rd, SW1. The area may be posh, but this is a fairly down-to-earth boozer with its very own micro-brewery. Sloane Square tube.

Prince Bonaparte 80 Chepstow Rd, W2. Pared-down, minimalist pub, with acres of space for sitting and supping or enjoying the excellent Mediterranean food. Closed Tues lunch. Notting Hill Gate or Royal Oak tube.

St John's Wood and Maida Vale

Prince Alfred 9 Formosa St, W9. A fantastic period-piece Victorian pub with all its original 1862 fittings intact, right down to the glazed "snob" screens. The beer and food don't quite live up to the surroundings. Warwick Avenue tube.

Warrington Hotel 93 Warrington Crescent, W9. Yet another architectural gem – this time flamboyant Art Nouveau – in an area replete with them. The interior is rich and satisfying, as are the draught beers and the Thai restaurant upstairs. It is, however, incredibly, spilling-out-onto-the-street, popular. Warwick Avenue or Maida Vale tube.

Camden Town

Bartok 78–79 Chalk Farm Rd, NW1. Mean Fiddler-run bar where punters can sink into one of the sofas and sup beer or wine while listening to classical music and live jazz instead of the usual muzak. Closed Mon–Fri lunch. Chalk Farm or Camden Town tube.

The Engineer 65 Gloucester Ave, NW1. One of a number of gastropubs in the much sought-after residential area of Primrose Hill, the *Engineer* is a smart, grandiose place which serves exceptional Modern Brit/Med food; it's pricey, though, and you're best off booking if you intend to nosh. Chalk Farm tube.

Hampstead and Highgate

The Flask 14 Flask Walk, NW3. Convivial Hampstead local, hidden away along the pedestrianized Flask Walk, which retains its original Victorian snob screen. Serves above-average food and Young's ale. Hampstead tube.

The Flask 77 Highgate West Hill, N6. Ideally situated at the heart of Highgate village green, with a rambling low-ceilinged interior and a summer terrace. The range of beers is good, but the food is nothing special. Highgate tube.

Freemason's Arms 32 Downshire Hill, NW3. Big, smart pub close to the Heath, popular on sunny days primarily for its large beer garden; also does comfort pub food, has a basement skittle alley, and an outdoor pell mell pitch. Hampstead tube.

Holly Bush 22 Holly Mount, NW3. A lovely old wood-panelled, gas-lit pub, tucked away in the steep backstreets of Hampstead village. Mobbed on the weekend. Hampstead tube.

Dulwich and Greenwich

Crown & Greyhound 73 Dulwich Village, SE21. Grand, spacious Victorian pub with an ornate plasterwork ceiling and a nice summer beer garden. Convenient for the Picture Gallery, but be prepared for the Sunday lunchtime crowds. West Dulwich train station from Victoria.

Cutty Sark Ballast Quay, off Lassell St, SE10. The nicest riverside pub in Greenwich, spacious, more of a local and much less touristy than the more famous *Trafalgar Tavern* (it's a couple of minutes walk further east, following the river). The views are great, as is the draught beer, and the bar food is a cut above the norm. Cutty Sark DLR or Maze Hill train station.

Trafalgar Tavern 5 Park Row, SE10. A great riverside position and a mention in Dickens' *Our Mutual Friend* have made this Regency-style inn a firm tourist favourite, which is fair enough really, as it's a convivial period piece, and serves good food. Cutty Sark DLR or Maze Hill train station.

Chiswick to Richmond

Dove 19 Upper Mall, W6. Old, old riverside pub with literary associations, a short walk from Hammersmith Bridge – has the smallest back bar in the UK (4ft by 7ft). Ravenscourt Park tube.

White Cross Hotel Water Lane, Richmond. With a longer pedigree and more character than its clinical chain rivals nearby, the *White Cross* is also much closer to the river (its front garden regularly gets flooded), and serves Young's beer and standard pub food. Richmond tube.

White Swan Riverside, Twickenham. Filling pub food, draught beer and a quiet riverside location – with a beer pontoon overlooking Eel Pie Island if you want to get even closer to the water – make this a good halt on any towpath ramble. Twickenham train station.

Nightlife

On any night of the week London offers a bewilderingly range of things to do after dark, ranging from top-flight opera and theatre to clubs with a life span of a couple of nights. The **listings magazine** *Time Out*, which comes out every Tuesday afternoon, is essential if you want to get the most out of this city, giving full details of prices and access, plus previews and reviews.

The **live music** scene remains extremely diverse, encompassing all variations of **rock, blues, roots**, and **world music**; and although London's **jazz** clubs aren't on a par with those in the big American cities, there's a highly individual scene of home-based artists, supplemented by top-name visiting players.

If you're looking for **dance music**, then welcome to Europe's party capital. After dark, London is thriving, with diverse scenes championing everything from hip-hop to house, techno to trance, samba to soca and drum 'n' bass to R&B on virtually any night of the week. Venues once used exclusively by performing bands now pepper the week with club nights, and you often find dance sessions starting as soon as a band has stopped playing. Bear in mind that there's sometimes an overlap between "live music venues" and "clubs" in the listings below; we've indicated which places serve a double function.

As for **theatre**, London has enjoyed a reputation for quality since the time of Shakespeare, and despite the continuing prevalence of fail-safe blockbuster musicals and revenue-spinning star vehicles, the city still provides a platform for innovation. **Cinema** is rather less healthy, for London's repertory film theatres are a dying breed, edged out by the multiscreen complexes, which show mainstream Hollywood fare some months behind America. There are a few excellent independent cinemas, though, including the National Film Theatre, which is the focus of the richly varied **London International Film Festival**, in November.

Live music venues

London is hard to beat for its musical mix: whether you're into **jazz, indie rock, R&B, blues** or **world music** you'll find something worth hearing on almost any night of the week. Entry prices for gigs run from a couple of pounds for an unknown band thrashing it out in a pub to around £30 for the likes of U2, but £10–15 is the average price for a good night out – not counting expenses at the bar. If you have a credit card, it's often cheaper to book tickets in advance via the internet at ⓦ www.ticketweb.co.uk, ⓦ www.ticketsonline.co.uk or ⓦ www.gigsandtours.com.

Rock and blues clubs and pubs

12 Bar Club 22–23 Denmark Place, WC2, ⓦ www.12bar.com. A combination of live blues and contemporary country seven nights a week. Tottenham Court Road tube.

Astoria 157 Charing Cross Rd, WC2,

ⓦ www.meanfiddler.com. One of London's best and most central medium-sized venues, this large, balconied one-time theatre tends to host slightly alternative bands, with club nights on Fri & Sat. More adventurous than most other big venues. Tottenham Court Road tube.

Borderline Orange Yard, off Manette St, W1,

Ⓦwww.borderline.co.uk. Intimate basement joint with diverse musical policy; a good place to catch new bands. Also has club nights. Tottenham Court Road tube.

Brixton Academy 211 Stockwell Rd, SW9. This refurbished Victorian hall, complete with Roman decorations, can hold 4000, and usually does, but still manages to seem small and friendly, probably because no one is forced to sit down. Hosts mainly mid-league bands. Brixton tube.

Forum 9–17 Highgate Rd, NW5, Ⓦwww.meanfiddler.com. The *Forum* is perhaps the capital's best medium-sized venue – large enough to attract established bands, and with great views and good bars. Pretty safe music policy. Kentish Town tube.

Mean Fiddler 24–28a Harlesden High St, NW10, Ⓦwww.meanfiddler.com. An excellent, if unfortunately located, small venue with a main hall and smaller acoustic room. The music veers from rock to world to folk to soul (and even, occasionally, gospel). Willesden Junction tube.

Ocean 270 Mare St E8, Ⓦwww.ocean.org.uk. Brand new medium-sized venue (plus two smaller halls) in deepest Hackney, with a very varied music policy, everything from reggae to the latest muzak, plus club nights. Hackney Central train station.

Orange 3 North End Crescent, North End Rd W14. Pub-like venue for serious-minded jazz-funkers. There are also club nights (nights vary). West Kensington tube.

Roadhouse Jubilee Hall, 35 The Piazza, WC2, Ⓦwww.roadhouse.co.uk. American food, 1950s US-style decor and a lineup of mainly blues and rock 'n' roll bands performing to a mature, nostalgic crowd. Covent Garden tube.

Rock Garden 35 The Piazza, WC2. Central, loud joint where you can get in free if you dine at the attached burger place first. Live music tends toward conventional rock, but the venue hosts a garage and R&B club night on Saturdays. Covent Garden tube.

Station Tavern 41 Bramley Rd, W10. Arguably London's best blues venue, with free – and occasionally great – blues six nights a week. Latimer Road tube.

Subterania 12 Acklam Rd, W10, Ⓦwww.meanfiddler.com. One of the original live music/club

crossover venues in an arch under a bridge. The crowd is as trendy as the music, which is often dance-oriented. Ladbroke Grove tube.

Underworld 174 Camden High St, NW1. This labyrinthine venue is good for new bands and has sporadic club nights. Camden Town tube.

Jazz, world music and roots

100 Club 100 Oxford St, W1. After a brief spell as a stage for punk bands, the *100 Club* is once again an unpretentious and inexpensive jazz venue – in a very central location. Tottenham Court Road tube.

606 Club 90 Lots Rd, SW10. A rare all-jazz venue, located just off the less trendy end of King's Road. You can book a table, and the licensing laws dictate that you must eat if you want to drink, but there's no cover charge. Fulham Broadway tube.

Africa Centre 38 King St, WC2, Ⓦwww.africacentre.org.uk. The packed old hall was the venue that launched Soul II Soul; these days, it hosts African bands and nights like Saturday's P-funk-heavy *Funkin Pussy*, but still draws a vibrantly enthusiastic crowd. Covent Garden tube.

Jazz Café 5 Parkway, NW1, Ⓦwww.jazzcafe.co.uk. Futuristic, white-walled venue with an adventurous booking policy exploring Latin, rap, funk, hip-hop and musical fusions. Diehard trad-jazz fans won't be happy, despite the fact that there's a rather good restaurant upstairs with a few prime view tables overlooking the stage. Camden Town tube.

Pizza Express 10 Dean St, W1. Enjoy a good pizza, then listen to the resident band or highly skilled guest players in this long-running basement venue. There's also a late-night session on Saturdays which starts at 9pm and finishes in the early hours of Sunday. Oxford Street tube.

Ronnie Scott's 47 Frith St, W1, Ⓦwww.ronniescotts.co.uk. The most famous jazz club in London: small, smoky and still going strong, even though the great man himself has passed away. The place for top-line names, who play two sets – one at around 10pm, the other after midnight. Book a table, or you'll have to stand. Leicester Square tube.

Clubs

More than a decade after the explosion of acid-house, London remains *the* place to come if you want to party after dark. The sheer diversity of dance music has enabled the city to maintain its status as **Europe's dance capital** – and it's still a port of call for DJs from around the globe. The relaxation of late-night licensing has encouraged many venues to keep serving alcohol until 6am or even later, and the resurgence of alcohol in clubland (much to the relief of the breweries) has been echoed by the meteoric rise of the club-bar (see p.156).

Nearly all of London's **dance clubs** open their doors between 10pm and midnight. Some are open six or seven nights a week, some keep irregular days, others just open at the weekend – and very often a venue will host a different club on each night of the week. Many of the best nights take place during the week, especially Wednesdays and Thursdays; for up-to-the-minute details of these, and of all the nights listed below, pop into one of Soho's many record shops to pick up flyers or check magazines such as *7*, *DJ* and *Time Out* for details.

Admission charges vary enormously, with small midweek sessions starting at around £3 and large weekend events charging as much as £25; around £10 is the average for a Friday or Saturday night, but bear in mind that profit margins at the bar are often more outrageous than at live-music venues.

The most notable event in the clubbing world in the past few years has been the rapid growth of **club-bars**: essentially bars with modern decor, a club clientele, and usually a DJ (unknown and otherwise). Perhaps most importantly, though, the club-bar is a more social environment than a club – there's no denying it gets tedious when you have to yell.

Clubs

333 333 Old St, EC1. Three floors of drum 'n' bass, twisted disco and breakbeat madness. Old Street tube.

Aquarium 256 Old St, EC1. The place with the pool – when all the beautiful young things get hot and sweaty they can dive in and cool off. Popular for speed garage nights. Old Street tube.

Bagley's Studios King's Cross Goods Yard, off York Way, N1. Vast warehouse-style venue. The perfect place for enormous raves, with a different DJ in each of the three rooms, and a chill-out bar complete with sofas. King's Cross tube.

Bar Rumba 36 Shaftesbury Ave, W1. Small West End venue with a programme of Latin, jazz-based and funk dance. Many of the punters are regulars. An unpretentious place frequented by happy people and well noted in clubbing circles for its amazing diversity. Piccadilly Circus tube.

Café de Paris 3 Coventry St, W1. Elegantly restored ballroom that plays house, garage and disco to a smartly dressed, trendy crowd – no jeans or trainers. Leicester Square tube.

Camden Palace 1 Camden High St, NW1. Most often home to Balearic beats; great lights, great sound, heaving crowds. Camden Town tube.

The Cross Goods Way Depot, off York Way, N1. Hidden underneath the arches the favourite flavours of this renowned club are hard-house, house and garage. It's bigger than you imagine, but always crammed with chic clubby types, and there's a fabulous garden – perfect for those chill-out moments. King's Cross tube.

Cuba 11–13 Kensington High St, W8. Grab a cocktail upstairs in the sociable bar before heading below for club nights that focus around Latin, salsa and Brazilian bossa-nova. Kensington High Street tube.

Electric Ballroom 184 Camden High St, NW1. Attracts a mixed crowd with a wide range of sounds: from rock to hip-hop, jazz to house. Camden Town tube.

The End 18 West Central St, WC1. A club designed for clubbers, by clubbers – large and spacious with chrome minimalist decor. Well known for all music styles, and especially noted for monthly nights hosted by other clubs or record labels. Holborn tube.

Fabric 77a Charterhouse St, EC1, ⓦ www.fabric-london.com. If you're a serious dance music fan then there really isn't a better weekend venue in London than *Fabric*, a cavernous, underground brewery-like space. Fridays alternate between hard house and hip-hop/drum 'n' bass, while Saturdays concentrate on the most cutting-edge house sounds around, played by the best of the big-name DJs from around the globe. Get there early. Farringdon tube.

Fridge Town Hall Parade, Brixton Hill, SW2. South London's big night out, with a musical policy running from funk to garage. Great gay nights and top techno tunes. Occasional home to *Escape from Samsara*, the night with the psychedelic, trancy vibe and hippie market. Brixton tube.

Gardening Club 4 The Piazza, WC2. Unusually for a central London club, the *Gardening Club* is surprisingly good. A popular choice for house and garage, but be warned, early on you'll be sharing the dance floor with beer-boys and bemused tourists. Covent Garden tube.

Gossips 69 Dean St, W1, ⊛ www.gossips.co.uk. Cave-like basement club that seems to have been around forever. Located deep in the heart of Soho, it's a popular stop for reggae and hip-hop fans. Tottenham Court Road tube.

Hanover Grand 6 Hanover St, W1, ⊛ www .hanovergrand.co.uk. A former Masonic hall, that's now a cool and extravagant club, with a great lights-and-sound system, a fine dance floor, lots of alcoves – and air conditioning. Popular with the glammed up, glittery and beautiful crew. Oxford Circus tube.

Home 1 Leicester Square, WC2, ⊛ www.homecorp .com. Central London rival to *Fabric*, this multi-floored superclub may often feel like a leisure complex, but with some of the best resident DJs in Britain and one of the finest sound systems around, it's hard to feel too depressed. Piccadilly Circus or Leicester Square tube.

HQs West Yard, Camden Lock, NW1. Smallish venue by the canal with a range of nights, although the emphasis is on uplifting house through to salsa. Friendly vibe. Camden Town tube.

The Leisure Lounge 121 Holborn, EC1. This place has had its share of the big-name nights, and is always a good place to check out the latest grooves. Two dance floors – one a full-on dance zone, the other a more relaxed bar area. Chancery Lane or Farringdon tube.

Ministry of Sound 103 Gaunt St, SE1. A vast, state-of-the-art club based on New York's legendary *Paradise Garage*, with an exceptional sound system. Corporate clubbing and full of tourists, but it still draws the top talent. Elephant & Castle tube.

Notting Hill Arts Club 21 Notting Hill Gate, W11. Basement club that's popular for everything from Latin inspired funk, jazz and disco through to soul, house and garage, and famed for its Sunday night deep disco house sessions. Notting Hill Gate tube.

The Office 3–5 Rathbone Place W1. Various music styles, but noted as home to the original mid-week session where you can play silly board games such as Ker-Plunk. Booking a table in advance is advised. Tottenham Court Road tube.

Salsa! 96 Charing Cross Rd, WC2. Funky salsa-based club where you can book a table to eat as you jive. Leicester Square tube.

The Scala 278 Pentonville Rd, N1, ⊛ www.scala -london.co.uk. Once a cinema, *The Scala* is now one of London's best clubs, holding unusual and multi-faceted nights that take in film, live bands and music ranging from quirky hip-hop to drum 'n' bass and deep house. King's Cross tube.

Turnmills 63 Clerkenwell Rd, EC1, ⊛ www.turnmills .com. Swanky coffee bar upstairs, fantastic alien-invasion-style bar and funky split-level dance floor in the main room. Saturday night sessions are followed at 4am by the awesomely glorious gay extravaganza, *Trade*. Farringdon tube.

Velvet Room 143 Charing Cross Rd, WC2. Very cool velvet-dripping interior, with house, techno and drum 'n' bass nights. Tottenham Court Road tube.

Club-bars

A.K.A. West Central St, WC1, ⊛ www.the-end.co.uk. Minimalist, twenty-first century-style bar next door to *The End*. A chrome balcony overlooks the main floor, which includes a well stocked bar and restaurant where you can partake of such delights as chive and butternut squash soup. Tottenham Court Road tube.

Alphabet 61–63 Beak St, W1. Upstairs is light and spacious, with decadent leather sofas, a great choice of European beers and mouthwatering food; downstairs, the dimmed coloured lights and car seats make for an altogether seedier atmosphere. Oxford Circus tube.

Bar Vinyl 6 Inverness St, NW1. Funky glass-bricked place with a record shop downstairs and a break-beat and trip-hop vibe. Camden Town tube.

Bug Bar St Matthew's Church, Brixton Hill, SW2, ⊛ www.bugbar.co.uk. Set in a church crypt, this place certainly has character. A popular stop-off before the *Fridge*, playing reggae, drum 'n' bass and house. Closed Mon & Tues. Brixton tube.

Detroit 35 Earlham St, WC2. Cavernous underground venue with an open-plan bar area, secluded, Gaudiesque booths and a huge range of spirits. DJs take over at the weekends, with underground house on Saturdays. Closed Sun. Covent Garden tube.

Dog House 187 Wardour St, W1, ⊛ www. doghouse.co.uk. Colourful basement bar, popular for hip-hop, funk and acid-jazz, that draws a friendly mix of office types, students and film runners. Closed Sun. Leicester Square tube.

Fridge Bar 1 Town Hall Parade, Brixton Hill, SW2, ⊛ www.fridge.co.uk. The two-floored *Fridge Bar* is a real melting pot, with a multi-tribal clientele grooving to R&B, house and drum 'n' bass in the intimate, pitch-black downstairs club, or slamming shots in the bright upstairs bar. Free entry during the week, and until 9pm on the weekend (when it gets packed). Brixton tube.

Hoxton Square Bar and Kitchen 2–4 Hoxton Square, N1. Next door to the Lux cinema, this concrete bar attracts the area's artists, writers and wannabees with its mix of modern European food, kitsch-to-club soundtracks, leather sofas and temporary painting and photography exhibitions. Best in the summer, though, when the drinking spills into the square in a carnival-like spirit. Old Street tube.

Jerusalem 33–34 Rathbone Place, W1. Decor is all chandeliers and velvet drapes; especially good music on Thursday nights, though it does attract a large proportion of office workers. Closed Sun. Tottenham Court Road tube.

Lab 12 Old Compton St, W1, ⓦwww.lab-bar.co.uk. Chic, multi-coloured former strip joint that stirs up some of the best cocktails in town to its style-con-scious crowd of beautiful Soho-ites. Tottenham Court Road tube.

The Social 5 Little Portland St, W1, ⓦwww.social.com. Bacchanalian, industrial club-bar, with great DJs playing everything from rock to rap, a truly hedonistic-cum-alcoholic crowd and the ultimate snacks – beans on toast and cosy soup in a mug – for when you get an attack of the munchies. Fab music on the upstairs jukebox, too. Closed Sun. Oxford Circus tube.

Gay and lesbian bars and clubs

London's **lesbian and gay scene** is so huge, diverse and well-established that it's easy to forget just how much – and how fast – it has grown over the last few years. **Soho** is the obvious place to start exploring, with a mix of traditional gay pubs, trendy café-bars and a range of gay-run services. Details of most events appear in *Time Out* and in *The Pink Paper* and *Axiom News*, which carry news and arts coverage as well as listings. Another excellent source of information is the London **Lesbian and Gay Switchboard** (☎020/7837 7324), which operates around the clock. The biggest annual queer party in the country is **Mardi Gras** (ⓦwww.londonmardigras.com), a colourful, whistle-blowing march through the city streets followed by a huge, ticketed party in Finsbury Park.

Bars

There are loads of lesbian and gay **eating and watering holes** in London, many of them operating as cafés by day and transforming into drinking dens at night. Lots have **cabaret or disco nights** and are open until the early hours, making them a fine alternative to the more expensive clubs. The places listed here are merely a small selection of the most central, although almost every corner of London has its own gay local. Bear in mind that, as ever, "mixed" tends to mean mostly men.

Mixed bars

Bar Aquda 13–14 Maiden Lane, Covent Garden WC2. Bright, modern and fashionable café-bar with good food. Mixed, but mostly boys. Leicester Square or Covent Garden tube.

The Black Cap 171 Camden High St, NW1. North London institution, offering drag and cabaret of wildly varying quality almost every night. *Mrs Shufflewick's Bar* upstairs is quieter, and opens onto a lush and lovely roof garden in the summer. Camden Town tube.

The Box 32–34 Monmouth St, WC2. Popular café-bar serving good food for a mixed gay/straight crowd during the day, and becoming queerer as the night draws on. Covent Garden or Leicester Square tube.

The Edge 11 Soho Square, W1. Busy, style-con-scious and pricey Soho café-bar spread over several floors, although this doesn't seem to stop everyone ending up on the pavement, especially in summer. Tottenham Court Road tube.

First Out 52 St Giles High St, WC2. The West End's original gay café-bar, and still permanently packed, serving good veggie food at reasonable prices. Upstairs is airy and non-smoking, down-stairs dark and foggy. *Girl Friday* is a busy Friday night pre-club session for girls; gay men are wel-come as guests. Tottenham Court Road tube.

Freedom 60–66 Wardour St, W1. Hip, busy café-bar, popular with a mixed straight/gay Soho crowd. Great juices and healthy food in the daytime, cock-tails and overpriced beer in the evening. Piccadilly Circus tube.

Liquid Lounge 275 Pentonville Rd, N1. Happy-go-lucky weekend dance bar popular with a young, indie-minded crowd. DJs and reliably cheap beer. Thurs–Sat only. King's Cross tube.

Old Compton Café 34 Old Compton St, W1. This enduringly busy Soho institution never closes. Strong coffee and a cosmopolitan range of cakes and snacks make it the obvious solution to sudden mid- or post-party wooziness. Tottenham Court Road or Leicester Square tube.

The Yard 57 Rupert St, W1. Attractive café-bar with courtyard and loft areas. Good food, weekly cabaret and regular fortune tellers. Closed Sun. Piccadilly Circus tube.

Lesbian bars

Candy Bar 23–24 Bateman St, W1. Right in the heart of boys-land, the UK's first seven-day all-girl bar offers a retro-style cocktail bar-cum-pool room upstairs; a noisy, beery, long and narrow ground level cruising bar, and a range of club nights. Gay men welcome as guests. Tottenham Court Road tube.

The Glass Bar West Lodge, Euston Square Gardens, 190 Euston Rd, NW1, ⊛ www.glassbar. ndo.co.uk. This friendly and intimate women-only members bar (you become a member once you've found it) is housed in a listed building and features a wrought iron spiral staircase which becomes increasingly perilous as the night goes on. Knock on the door to get in. Closed Sun. Euston tube.

Vespa Lounge Under Centrepoint House, St. Giles High Street, WC1, ⊛ www.vespalounge.com. London's newest girl bar sets up shop in this prime location at weekends, and it gets busy. Pool

table, video screen, cute bar staff and a mostly young crowd. Gay men welcome as guests. Tottenham Court Road tube.

Gay men's pubs

79CXR 79 Charing Cross Rd, WC2. Busy, cruisey men's den on two floors, with industrial decor, late licence and a no-messing atmosphere. Leicester Square tube.

Brief Encounter 41–43 St Martin's Lane, WC2. One of the longest-running men's bars in London. A popular pre-*Heaven* or post-opera hangout (it's next door to the *Coliseum*); the front bar is light, the back bar dark, and both are busy. Leicester Square tube.

Compton's of Soho 53 Old Compton St, W1. This large, traditional-style pub is a Soho institution, always busy with a youngish crowd, but still a relaxed place to cruise or just hangout. Leicester Square or Piccadilly tube.

Substation Soundshaft Hungerford Lane (behind *Heaven*), WC2. The original late-night cruising pit. Steamy, cruisey and sleazy, offering a diverse seven day menu of sartorial and musical preferences. Charing Cross tube.

Clubs

Clubs move, change and close down fast, so we've listed only the longest-running and most popular nights here – it's always a good idea to check the gay press, listings magazines and websites for up-to-date times and prices before you plan your night out.

Crash 66, Goding St, SE11. Four bars, two dancefloors, chillout areas and plenty of hard bodies make this weekly Saturday-nighter busy, buzzy, sexy and mostly boysy. Vauxhall tube.

DTPM at *Fabric*, 77a Charterhouse St, EC1. This long-running Sunday-nighter can now be found in *Fabric's* chic surroundings, with three dancefloors offering soul, jazz, funk, R&B, hip hop, Latino house and progressive to hard house. Farringdon Road tube.

Duckie at *The Royal Vauxhall Tavern*, 372 Kennington Lane, SE11, ⊛ www.duckie.co.uk. Modern rock-based hurdy gurdy for "homosexualists", their friends and fans. Regular live art performances, occasional bouncy castles, and fabulously-titled theme nights. Vauxhall tube.

Exilio Latino 229 Great Portland St, W1. Every other Saturday night, *Exilio* erupts in a fabulous Latin frenzy, spinning salsa, cumbia and merengue, and featuring live acts. Great Portland Street tube.

G.A.Y. at *The Astoria*, 157 Charing Cross Rd, WC2. *The Astoria* hosts huge, unpretentious and fun-loving dance nights for a young crowd on Fridays and Saturdays, which are always packed and often

feature big-name PAs. Tottenham Court Road tube.

Heaven under The Arches Villiers St, WC2. Widely regarded as the UK's most popular gay club, this legendary, 2000-capacity club continues to reign supreme. Big nights are Wednesdays (*Fruit Machine*) and Saturdays (just *Heaven*), all with big-name DJs, PAs and shows. More Muscle Mary than Diesel Doris. Charing Cross or Embankment tube.

Love Muscle at *The Fridge*, Town Hall Parade, Brixton Hill, SW2, ⊛ www.fridge.co.uk. A regular Saturday night workout for oiled torsos, disco dykes and fag-hag friends, this sweaty, eight-year-old all-nighter offers everything from fluffy techno to hard house via Europop. Big stage shows, stunning lights, go-go dancers and a chill-out zone top off the party madness. Brixton tube.

Popstarz at the S*cala, 27* Pentonville Rd, N1. Groundbreaking Friday night indie club, now in its fifth year and its sixth venue, and with a consistently winning formula of indie and alternative tunes, 70s and 80s trash, cheap beer and no attitude. King's Cross tube.

Queer Nation at *Substation South*, 9 Brighton Terrace, SW9. Long-running and popular New

York-style house and garage night for funksters. Brixton tube.

Trade at *Turnmills*, 63b Clerkenwell Rd, EC1, ⓦ www.turnmills.com. This legendary Saturday all-nighter (business kicks off at 4am and will see you well through to Sunday lunchtime) is still going

strong. Expect techno and hard house from some of the best DJs in the country, lots of lasers and special effects, and some very sweaty hard bodies – of all genders and flavours, but mostly boys. Farringdon tube.

Theatre, comedy and cinema

London has enjoyed a reputation for quality **theatre** since the time of Shakespeare, and despite the continuing prevalence of fail-safe blockbuster musicals and revenue-spinning star vehicles, the city still provides a platform for innovation. The **comedy** scene in London goes from strength to strength, so much so that the capital now boasts more comedy venues than any other city in the world, while comedians who have made the transition to television also stage shows in major theatres. **Cinema** is rather less healthy, for London's repertory film theatres are a dying breed, edged out by the multiscreen complexes which show mainstream Hollywood fare some months behind America. There are a few excellent independent cinemas, though, including the National Film Theatre, which is the focus of the richly varied **London Film Festival** in November.

Theatre

At first glance, it might seem as though London's **theatreland** has become a province of the Andrew Lloyd Webber empire; however, few cities in the world can match the variety of the London scene. The state-funded **Royal Shakespeare Company** and the **National Theatre** often put on extremely original productions of mainstream masterpieces, while some of the most exciting work is performed in what have become known as the **Off West End** theatres, which consistently stage interesting and often challenging productions. Further still down the financial ladder are the **fringe theatres**, more often than not pub venues, where ticket prices are low, and quality variable.

Unfortunately, most theatre-going doesn't come particularly cheap. **Tickets** under £10 are very thin on the ground; the box-office average is closer to £15, with £30 the usual top whack. Tickets for the durable musicals and well-reviewed plays are like gold dust. The Society of London Theatre (SOLT) **half-price ticket booth** in Leicester Square (Mon–Sat 10am–7pm, Sun noon–3pm) sells tickets for that day's performances of all the West End shows, but they tend to be in the top end of the price range, and carry a service charge of £2.50 per ticket. If the SOLT booth has sold out, you could turn to reputable agencies such as Ticketmaster (☎020/7344 4444; ⓦ www.ticketmaster.co.uk) or First Call (☎020/7497 9977; ⓦ www.firstcalltickets.com), which can get seats for all West End shows, but add a ten percent mark-up on the ticket price.

What follows is a highly selective list. For the most consistent Off West End and fringe venues, check out *Time Out* for what's on at the Almeida, Donmar Warehouse, Royal Court, Young Vic, ICA and Tricycle theatres.

Barbican Centre Silk St, EC2, ☎020/7638 8891, ⓦ www.barbican.org.uk. After a season in the company's HQ at Stratford, Royal Shakespeare Company productions move to one of the Barbican's two venues: the excellently designed Barbican Theatre and the much smaller Pit. A wide range of work is produced, though the writings of the Bard predominate. Barbican or Moorgate tube.

National Theatre South Bank Centre, South Bank, SE1, ☎020/7452 3000, ⓦ www.nt-online.org. The Royal National Theatre, as it's now officially known, consists of three separate theatres: the 1100-seater Olivier, the proscenium-arched Lyttelton and the experimental Cottesloe. Standards set by the late Laurence Olivier, founding artistic director, are maintained by the country's top actors and directors in a programme ranging from *Wind in the Willows* to the work of Arthur Miller. Some productions sell out months in advance, but a few discounted tickets go on sale on the morning of each performance – get there by 8am for the popular shows. Waterloo tube.

Open Air Theatre Regent's Park, Inner Circle, NW1, ☎020/7486 2431. If the weather's good, there's nothing quite like a dose of alfresco drama. This beautiful space in Regent's Park hosts a tourist-friendly summer programme of Shakespeare, musicals, plays and concerts.

Regent's Park or Baker Street tube.

Shakespeare's Globe New Globe Walk, SE1, ☎020/7902 1500, ☝www.shakespeares-globe.org. This thatch-roofed replica Elizabethan theatre uses only natural light and the minimum of scenery, and currently puts on solid, fun shows from mid-May to mid-September, with "groundling" tickets (standing-room only) for a mere £5. The new indoor Inigo Jones Theatre is set to continue the season throughout the winter months. London Bridge, Blackfriars or Southwark tube.

Comedy and cabaret

London's **comedy scene** continues to live up to its media-coined status as the new rock 'n' roll with the leading comics catapulted to unlikely stardom on both stage and screen. Note that many venues operate only on Friday and Saturday nights, and that August is a lean month, as much of London's talent then heads north for the Edinburgh Festival.

Banana Cabaret *The Bedford*, 77 Bedford Hill, SW12, ☎020/8673 8904. This double-stage pub has become one of London's finest comedy venues – well worth the trip out from the centre of town. Fri & Sat from 9pm. Balham tube.

Comedy Store Haymarket House, 1a Oxendon St, SW1, ☎020/7344 0234, ☝www.thecomedystore.co.uk. Widely regarded as the birthplace of alternative comedy, though no longer in its original venue, the Comedy Store has catapulted many a stand-up onto prime-time TV. Improvisation by in-house comics on Wednesdays and Sundays, in addition to a stand-up bill; Thursday night offers try-out spots for those brave enough to handle the hecklers, while Friday and Saturday are the busiest

nights, with two shows, at 8pm and midnight – book ahead. Piccadilly Circus tube.

Jongleurs Camden Lock Dingwalls Building, 36 Camden Lock Place, Chalk Farm Rd, NW1, ☎020/7564 2500, ☝www.jongleurs.com. Camden link in a top-ranking chain of venues, with a spot of post-revelry disco-dancing included in the ticket price on Fridays, and two shows on a Saturday. Book well in advance. Fri & Sat. Camden Town tube.

Lee Hurst's Backyard Comedy Club 231 Cambridge Heath Rd, E2, ☎020/7739 3122, ☝www.leehurst.com. Purpose-built club in Bethnal Green established by comedian Lee Hurst, who has successfully managed to attract a consistently strong line-up. Fri & Sat. Bethnal Green tube.

Cinema

There are an awful lot of **cinemas** in the West End, but only a very few places committed to non-mainstream movies, and even fewer repertory cinemas programming serious films from the back catalogue. November's **London Film Festival**, which occupies half a dozen West End cinemas, is now a huge event, and so popular that most of the films sell out a couple of days after publication of the festival's programme. Below are the city's main arthouse cinemas.

ICA Cinema Nash House, The Mall, SW1, ☎020/7930 3647, ☝www.ica.org.uk. Vintage and underground movies shown on one of two tiny screens in the avant-garde HQ of the Institute of Contemporary Arts. Piccadilly Circus or Charing Cross tube.

BFI London Imax Centre South Bank, SE1, ☎020/79021234, ☝www.bfi.org.uk. The British Film Institute's remarkable glazed drum sits in the middle of the roundabout at the end of Waterloo Bridge. It's stunning, state-of-the-art stuff alright, showing 2D and 3D films on a massive screen, but

like all IMAX cinemas, it suffers from the paucity of good material that's been shot on the format. Waterloo tube.

Lux Cinema 2–4 Hoxton Square, N1, ☎020/7684 0201, ☝www.lux.org.uk. Relatively new arts cinema in trendy Hoxton, showing an eclectic mix of films, and with an art gallery on the first floor. Old Street tube.

National Film Theatre South Bank, SE1, ☎020/7928 3232, ☝www.bfi.org.uk/nft. Known for its attentive audiences and an exhaustive, eclectic programme that includes directors' seasons and thematic series. Around six films daily are shown in the vast NFT1 and the smaller NFT2. Waterloo tube. **Prince Charles** 2–7 Leicester Place, WC2, ☎020/7734 9127. The bargain basement of London's cinemas (entry for most shows is just £3.50/£2.50), with a programme of new movies, classics and cult favourites –*Sing-Along-A-Sound-of-Music* is a regular. Leicester Square tube.

Classical music, opera and dance

London is spoilt for choice when it comes to **orchestras**. On most days you'll be able to catch a concert by either the London Symphony Orchestra, the London Philharmonic, the Royal Philharmonic, the Philharmonia or the BBC Symphony Orchestra, or a smaller-scale performance from the English Chamber Orchestra, London Sinfonietta or the Academy of St Martin-in-the-Fields. During the week, there are also **free lunchtime concerts** by students or professionals in many of London's churches, particularly in the City; performances in the Royal College of Music and Royal Academy of Music are of an amazingly high standard, and the choice of work a lot riskier than the commercial venues can manage.

The principal **large-scale venue** is the South Bank Centre (☎020/7960 4242, ⓦwww.sbc.org.uk), where the biggest names appear at the Royal Festival Hall, with more specialized programmes staged in the Queen Elizabeth Hall and Purcell. Programming at the Barbican, Silk St, EC2 (☎020/7638 8891, ⓦwww.barbican.org.uk), has become much more adventurous recently, and the free music in the foyer is often very good. For **chamber music**, the intimate and elegant Wigmore Hall, 36 Wigmore St, W1 (☎020/7935 2141, ⓦwww.wigmore-hall.org.uk), is many a Londoner's favourite.

From July to September each year, **the Proms** at the Royal Albert Hall (☎020/7589 8212, ⓦwww.royalalberthall.com) feature at least one concert daily, with hundreds of standing tickets sold for just £3 on the night. The acoustics aren't the world's best, but the calibre of the performers is unbeatable and the programme is a fascinating mix of standards and new or obscure works. The hall is so vast that if you turn up half an hour before the show starts there should be little risk of being turned away.

Despite enjoying an increase in popularity, opera remains an elitist genre and has had a bad press in London, largely owing to the travails of Covent Garden's **Royal Opera House** (☎020/7304 4000, ⓦwww.royaloperahouse.org), which is attempting to make itself more accessible following its multi-million pound refurbishment. The **English National Opera** at the Coliseum, St Martin's Lane (☎020/7632 8300, ⓦwww.eno.org), has more radical producers and is a more democratic institution, with all works sung in English.

From the time-honoured showpieces of the **Royal Ballet** (☎020/7304 4000, ⓦwww.royaloperahouse.org) to the diverse and exciting range of British and international dance that goes on at the newly rebuilt Sadler's Wells (☎020/7863 8000, ⓦwww.sadlers-wells.com), there's always a **dance performance** of some kind afoot in London, and the city also has a good reputation for international dance festivals showcasing the work of a spread of ensembles. The biggest of the annual events is the **Dance Umbrella** (☎020/8741 5881), a six-week season (Oct–Nov) of new work from bright young choreographers and performance artists at venues across the city.

Shopping

Whether it's time or money you've got to burn, London is one big shoppers' playground. And although chains and superstores predominate along the high streets, you're still never too far from the kind of oddball, one-off establishment that makes shopping an adventure rather than a chore. From the *folie de grandeur* that is Harrods to the frantic street markets of the East End, there's nothing you can't find in some corner of the capital.

In the centre of town, **Oxford Street** is the city's most frantic chain store mecca, and together with **Regent Street**, which crosses it halfway, offers pretty much every mainstream clothing label you could wish for. Just off Oxford Street, high-end designer outlets line **St Christopher's Place** and **South Molton Street**, and you'll find even pricier designers and jewellers along the very chic **Bond Street**.

Tottenham Court Road, which heads north from the east end of Oxford Street, is the place to go for electrical goods and furniture and design shops. **Charing Cross Road**, heading south, is the centre of London's book trade, both new and second-hand. At its north end, and particularly on **Denmark Street**, you can find music shops selling everything from instruments to sound equipment and sheet music. **Soho** offers an offbeat mix of sex boutiques, records and silks, while the streets surrounding **Covent Garden** yield art and design shops, mainstream fashion stores and designer wear.

Just off Piccadilly, **St James's** is the natural habitat of the quintessential English gentleman, with **Jermyn Street** in particular harbouring shops dedicated to his grooming. **Knightsbridge**, further west, is home to Harrods, and the big name fashion stores of **Sloane Street** and **Brompton Road** are adjacent.

Books

The biggest bookstore in the capital is Waterstones' Piccadilly branch (Piccadilly Circus), but the largest choice of bookshops is still on **Charing Cross Road**, where you'll not only find all the **chain stores** – Borders at no. 120, and Blackwell's at no. 100 – but also Foyles at no. 113–119, and other smaller **independent shops** such as the feminist outlet Silver Moon at no. 64–68, art specialists Zwemmer at no. 80, crime specialists Murder One at 71–73 and numerous **second-hand stores**, including Any Amount of Books at nos. 56 & 62.

Department stores

Fortnum & Mason, 181 Piccadilly (Green Park or Piccadilly Circus tube), is the place to go for fabulous, gorgeously presented and pricey food, plus upmarket clothes, furniture and stationery. **Harrods**, Knightsbridge (Knightsbridge tube), is famous for its fantastic Art Nouveau tiled food hall, obscenely huge toy department and supremely tasteless memorial to Diana and Dodi; beware the draconian dress code – no backpacks allowed, for example. Nearby, **Harvey Nichols**, 109–125 Knightsbridge (Knightsbridge tube), offers all the latest designer collections and famously frivolous and pricey luxury foods. Over at Oxford Circus, several major stores are close at hand, among them: **John Lewis**, 278–306 Oxford St (Oxford Circus tube), which offers everything from buttons to stockings to furniture and household goods; **Liberty**, 210–220 Regent St (Oxford Circus tube), founded as a retail outlet for the Victorian Arts and Crafts Movement, and still the place to go for regal fabrics and decorative household goods; and **Selfridge's**, 400 Oxford St (Bond Street tube), London's first great department store, which has a wide range of clothing, food and furnishings.

Markets

Camden, running from Camden High Street to Chalk Farm Road (mainly Thurs–Sun 9.30am–5.30pm; Camden Town tube), is top of the list for market shopping on most tourist itineraries; the atmosphere is grungy studenty and the stuff on sale is mainly cheap clothes and jewellery, though the stalls around Camden Lock are generally more interesting; weekends are the best – and busiest – times to visit. **Spitalfields**, Commercial Street (Mon–Fri 11am–3pm, Sun 10am–5pm; Liverpool Street tube), is an arty-crafty market similar to Camden, but on a much smaller scale; it also offers organic fruit and veg on Fridays and Sundays. Nearby, **Brick Lane** (Sun 8am–1pm; Aldgate East, Shoreditch or Liverpool Street tube) has everything from sofas to antique cameo brooches; and **Petticoat Lane**, Middlesex Street and Goulston Street (Sun 9am–2pm; Aldgate East or Liverpool Street tube), offers cheap and cheerful clothes. **Bermondsey** (New Caledonian) Market, Bermondsey Square (Fri 5am–2pm; Borough, London Bridge or Bermondsey tube), is a huge, unglamorous but highly regarded antique market; while **Portobello**, Portobello Rd (Sat 9am–5pm; Notting Hill or Ladbroke Grove tube), is mostly boho-chic clothes and portable antiques. South of the river, **Greenwich**, Market Square (mainly Thurs–Sun, 9.30am–5pm; Greenwich DLR or train station), is a small arty-crafty market, with second-hand clothing and antiques on sale, too.

Music

The **megastores** are: HMV, 150 Oxford St (Oxford Circus tube); Tower Records, 1 Piccadilly Circus (Piccadilly Circus tube); Virgin Megastore, 14–16 Oxford St (Tottenham Court Road tube). For **jazz**, try Ray's Jazz Shop, 180 Shaftesbury Ave (Leicester Square or Tottenham Court Road tube). For **indie music**, there's Sister Ray, 94 Berwick St (Oxford Circus or Piccadilly Circus tube). For **reggae**, **ragga** and **drum 'n' bass**, head to Daddy Kool, 12 Berwick St (Oxford Circus or Tottenham Court Road tube). **Hip-hop** is available at Deal Real Records, Noel St (Oxford Circus tube). For **house**, **techno** and **trance** go to Eukatech, 49 Endell St (Covent Garden tube).

Listings

Airport enquiries Gatwick ☎01293/535353,
☻www.baa.co.uk; Heathrow ☎0870/000 0123,
☻www.baa.co.uk; London City Airport ☎020/7646
0000, ☻www.londoncityairport.com; Luton
☎01582/405100, ☻www.london-luton.com;
Stansted ☎0870/000 0303, ☻www.baa.co.uk.
American Express 30–31 Haymarket, SW1
☎020/7484 9600, ☻www.americanexpress.com.
Mon–Fri 9am–7pm, Sat 9am–6pm, Sun
10am–5pm. Piccadilly Circus tube.
Bike rental Bikepark, 14 Stukeley St, WC2
☎020/7430 0083, ☻www.bikepark.co.uk.
Mon–Fri 8.30am–7pm, Sat 10am–6pm. Covent
Garden tube.
Bus information Long-distance coach services
depart from Victoria Coach Station, Buckingham
Palace Rd (Victoria tube). National Express have
ticket offices here (☎0990/808080) and can tell

you about European services operated by
Eurolines.
Cricket Two Test matches are played in London
each summer: one at Lord's (☎020/7289 1611,
☻www.lords.org), the home of English cricket, in
St John's Wood, the other at The Oval (☎020/7582
6660, ☻www.surreyccc.co.uk), in Kennington. In
tandem with the full-blown five-day Tests, there's
also a series of one-day internationals, two of
which are usually held in London.
Consulates and Embassies Australia, Australia
House, Strand, WC2 ☎020/7379 4334,
☻www.australia.org.uk; Canada, MacDonald
House, 1 Grosvenor Square, W1 ☎020/7258 6600,
☻www.canada.org.uk; Ireland, 17 Grosvenor
Place, SW1 ☎020/7235 2171,
☻www.iolgov.ie/iveagh; New Zealand, New
Zealand House, 80 Haymarket, SW1 ☎020/7930

8422, ⊛www.newzealandhc.org.uk; South Africa, South Africa House, Trafalgar Square, WC2 ☏020/7451 7299, ⊛www.southafricahouse.com; USA, 24 Grosvenor Square, W1 ☏020/7499 9000, ⊛www.usembassy.org.uk.

Dentist Emergency treatment: Guy's Hospital, St Thomas St, SE1 ☏020/7955 4317. Mon–Fri 8.45am–3.30pm.

Football London's top club at the moment is Arsenal (☏020/7704 4000, ⊛www.arsenal.co.uk), who won the double (league and FA Cup) in the 1997–98 season; their closest rivals (geographically) are Tottenham Hotspur (☏020/8365 5000, ⊛www.spurs.co.uk). Meanwhile, in west London, Chelsea (☏020/7386 7799, ⊛www.chelseafc.co.uk) waltzed away with the last-ever European Cup Winners' Cup in 1999.

Hospitals For 24-hour accident and emergency: Charing Cross Hospital, Fulham Palace Rd, W6 ☏020/8846 1234; Chelsea & Westminster Hospital, 369 Fulham Rd, SW10 ☏020/8746 8000; Royal Free Hospital, Pond St, NW3 ☏020/7794 0500; Royal London Hospital, Whitechapel Rd, E1 ☏020/7377 7000; St Mary's Hospital, Praed St, W2 ☏020/7886 6666; University College Hospital, Grafton Way, WC1 ☏020/7387 9300; Whittington Hospital, Highgate Hill, N19 ☏020/7272 3070.

Left luggage AIRPORTS Gatwick: North Terminal ☏01293/502013 (daily 6am–10pm); South Terminal ☏01293/502014 (24hr). Heathrow: Terminal 1 ☏020/8745 5301 (daily 6am–11pm); Terminal 2 ☏020/8745 4599 (daily 6am–10.30pm); Terminal 3 ☏020/8759 3344 (daily 5.30am–10.30pm); Terminal 4 ☏020/8745 7460 (daily 5.30am–11pm). London City Airport ☏020/7646 0000 (daily 6.30am–10pm). Stansted Airport ☏01279/680500 (24hr). TRAIN STATIONS Charing Cross ☏020/7839 4282 (daily 7am–11pm); Euston ☏020/7320 0528 (Mon–Sat 6.45am–11.15pm, Sun 7.15am–11pm); Victoria ☏020/7928 5151 ext 27523 (daily 7am–10.15pm, plus lockers); Waterloo International ☏020/7928 5151 (Mon–Fri 4am–11pm, Sat & Sun 6am–11pm).

London Transport enquiries 24-hour information on ☏020/7222 1234, ⊛www.londontransport.co.uk.

Lost property AIRPORTS Gatwick ☏01293/503162 (daily 7.30am–5.30pm); Heathrow ☏020/8745 7727 (Mon–Fri 8am–5pm, Sat & Sun 8am–4pm); London City Airport ☏020/7646 0000 (Mon–Fri 6am–9.30pm, Sat 6am–1am, Sun 10.30am–9.30pm); Stansted

☏01279/680500 (daily 5.30am–11pm). BUSES ☏020/7222 1234. HEATHROW EXPRESS ☏020/8745 7727. TAXIS (black cabs only) ☏020/7833 0996. TRAIN STATIONS Euston ☏020/7922 6477 (Mon–Sat 6.45am–11pm, Sun 7.15am–11pm); King's Cross ☏020/7922 9081 (daily 8am–7.45pm); Liverpool Street ☏020/7928 9158 (Mon–Fri 7am–7pm, Sat & Sun 7am–2pm); Paddington ☏020/7313 1514 (Mon–Fri 9am–5.30pm); Victoria ☏020/7922 9887 (Mon–Fri 7.30am–10pm); Waterloo ☏020/7401 7861 (Mon–Fri 7.30am–8pm). TUBE TRAINS London Regional Transport ☏020/7486 2496.

Police Central police stations include: Charing Cross, Agar St, WC2 ☏020/7240 1212; Holborn, 70 Theobalds Rd, WC1 ☏020/7404 1212; King's Cross, 76 King's Cross Rd, WC1 ☏020/7704 1212; Tottenham Court Road, 56 Tottenham Court Rd, W1 ☏020/7637 1212; West End Central, 10 Vine St, W1 ☏020/7437 1212. City of London Police, Bishopsgate, EC2 ☏020/7601 2222.

Post offices The only late-opening post office is the Trafalgar Square branch at 24–28 William IV St, WC2 4DL (Mon–Fri 8am–8pm, Sat 9am–8pm; ☏020/7484 9304); it's also the city's poste restante collection point. For general postal enquiries phone ☏08457/740740, or visit the website ⊛www.royalmail.co.uk.

Tennis Tennis in England is synonymous with Wimbledon (☏020/8946 2244, ⊛www.wimbledon.org), the only Grand Slam tournament in the world to be played on grass, and for many players the ultimate goal of their careers. To buy tickets on the day, you must arrive by around 7am for tickets on Centre and No. 1 courts, or around 9am for the outside courts.

Train stations and information As a rough guide, Euston handles services to northwest England and Glasgow; King's Cross northeast England and Edinburgh; Liverpool Street eastern England; Paddington western England; Victoria and Waterloo southeast England. For information, call national rail enquiries on ☏08457/484950.

Travel agents Campus Travel, 52 Grosvenor Gardens, SW1 ☏0870/240 1010, ⊛www.usitcampus.co.uk; Council Travel, 28a Poland St, W1 ☏020/7437 7767, ⊛www.destination-group.com; STA Travel, 86 Old Brompton Rd, SW7 ☏020/7361 6161, ⊛www.statravel.co.uk; Trailfinders, 42–50 Earl's Court Rd, SW5 ☏020/7938 3366, ⊛www.trailfinders.co.uk.

Travel details

Buses

For information on all local and national bus services, contact Traveline: ☏ 0870/608 2 608 (daily 7am–9pm), ⓦ www.traveline.org.uk.

Victoria Coach Station to: Bath (11 daily; 3hr 15min); Birmingham (hourly; 2hr); Brighton (hourly; 1hr 45min); Bristol (hourly; 2hr 20min); Cambridge (hourly; 2hr); Canterbury (hourly; 1hr 50min); Carlisle (3–4 daily; 6hr); Chester (5–6 daily; 5hr 30min); Dover (hourly; 2hr 45min); Exeter (8 daily; 4hr); Gloucester (10 daily; 3hr) Liverpool (5–6 daily; 4hr 30min); Manchester (9 daily; 4hr 15min); Oxford (frequently; 1hr 30min); Plymouth (7 daily; 4hr 40min); York (3 daily; 4hr 20min).

Trains

For information on all local and national rail services, contact National Rail Enquiries: t08457/48 49 50, ⓦ www.rail.co.uk.

London Charing Cross to: Dover Priory (every 30min; 1hr 45min–2hr).

London Euston to: Birmingham New St (every 30min; 1hr 40min); Carlisle (every 1–2hr; 3hr 50min); Chester (3 daily; 2hr 40min); Crewe (hourly; 2hr); Lancaster (8 daily; 3hr); Liverpool Lime St (hourly; 2hr 45min); Manchester Piccadilly (hourly; 2hr 30min).

London King's Cross to: Brighton (every 10–40min; 1hr 15min); Cambridge (every 30min; 50min); Durham (every 1–2hr; 2hr 50min); Leeds (hourly; 2hr 20min); Newcastle (every 30min; 2hr 40min–3hr); York (every 30min; 1hr 40min–2hr).

London Liverpool Street to: Cambridge (hourly; 1hr 20min); Harwich (every 2hr; 1hr 10min); Norwich (hourly; 2hr); Stansted (every 30min; 45min).

London Paddington to: Bath (every 30min–hourly; 1hr 25min); Bristol Parkway (every 30min–1hr; 1hr 20min); Exeter St Davids (hourly; 2hr 10min); Oxford (every 30min–hourly; 50min–1hr); Penzance (7 daily; 5hr); Plymouth (every 1–2hr; 3hr–3hr 40min); Worcester (11 daily; 2hr–2hr 15min).

London St Pancras to: Leicester (every 30min; 1hr 15min); Nottingham (hourly; 1hr 50min); Sheffield (hourly; 2hr 20min).

London Victoria to: Brighton (every 30min; 1hr–1hr 20min); Canterbury East (every 30min; 1hr 30min); Canterbury West (hourly; 1hr 50min); Dover Priory (hourly; 1hr 50min); Gatwick (frequently; 30min) ; Ramsgate (hourly; 1hr 50min);.

London Waterloo to: Portsmouth Harbour (every 30min; 1hr 35min); Southampton Central (every 20min; 1hr 15min); Winchester (every 20min; 55min–1hr 5min)

Surrey, Kent and Sussex

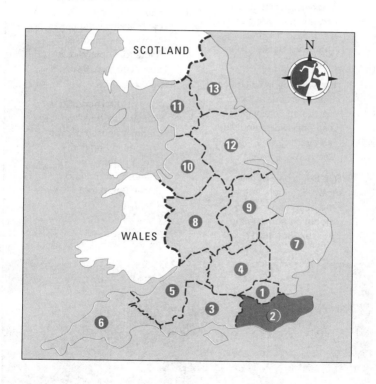

CHAPTER 2 # Highlights

* **Canterbury Cathedral** An essential stop on many a tourist itinerary, this place lives up to the hype. The cathedral was the destination of pilgrims in Chaucer's *Canterbury Tales* and the magnificent sixteenth-century interior includes a shrine to the murdered Thomas à Becket. **See p.189**

* **The white cliffs of Dover** Best seen from a boat, the famed chalky cliffs also offer walks and vistas over the Channel. **See p.198**

* **Rye** Superbly set hilltop town offering some of the best meals, accommodation and pubs in Sussex. **See p.217**

* **The Royal Pavilion, Brighton** George IV's pleasure dome, designed by Nash, is the supreme (and only) example of Oriental-Gothic architecture. **See p.227**

* **Petworth House** Not just one of the country's most attractive stately homes, this place is home to a splendid art collection, too. **See p.240**

* **A day at the races** Surrey and Sussex have the greatest density of racecourses in England, offering plenty of chances for fun and a flutter. **See p.242**

Surrey, Kent and Sussex

The southeast corner of England was traditionally where London went on holiday. In the past, trainloads of Eastenders were shuttled to the hop fields and orchards of **Kent** for a working break from the city; boats ferried people down the Thames to the beach at Margate; and everyone from royalty to cuckolding couples enjoyed the seaside at Brighton, a blot of decadence in the otherwise sedate county of **Sussex**. **Surrey** is the least pastoral and historically significant of the three counties – the home of wealthy metropolitan professionals prepared to commute from what has become known as the "stockbroker belt".

The late twentieth century brought big changes to the southeast region. In purely administrative terms the three counties have become four, since local government reorganization split Sussex into East and West. More significantly, many of the coastal towns have faced an uphill struggle to keep their tourist custom in the face of evermore accessible foreign destinations. For the old seaside resorts are still at the mercy of the English weather – in winter, or bad weather, the prom is not a fun place to be. To make matters worse, **Brighton**, long known as "London beside the sea", now matches the capital with one of the highest proportions of homeless people in the country.

The proximity of Kent and Sussex to the continent has dictated the history of this region, which has served as a gateway for an array of invaders, both rapacious and benign. **Roman** remains dot the coastal area – most spectacularly at **Bignor** in Sussex and **Lullingworth** in Kent – and many roads, including the main A2 London to Dover road, follow the arrow-straight tracks laid by the legionaries. When **Christianity** spread through Europe, it arrived in Britain

Accommodation price codes

Throughout this guide, hotel and B&B accommodation is priced on a scale of ❶ to ❾, the number indicating the **lowest price** you could expect to pay per night in that establishment for a **double room** in high season. The prices indicated by the codes are as follows:

❶ under £40	❹ £60–70	❼ £110–150
❷ £40–50	❺ £70–90	❽ £150–200
❸ £50–60	❻ £90–110	❾ over £200

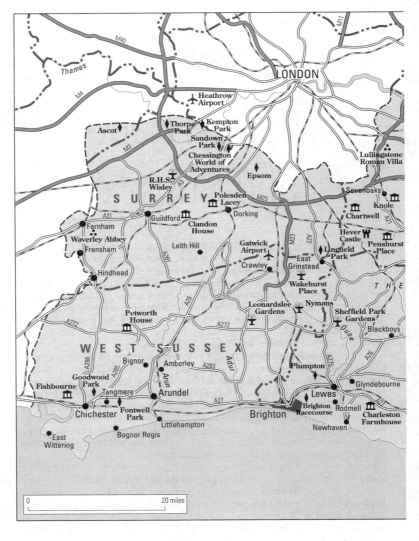

on the **Isle of Thanet** – the northeast tip of Kent, since rejoined to the mainland by silting and subsiding sea levels. In 597 AD Augustine moved inland and established a monastery at **Canterbury**, still the home of the Church of England and the county's prime historic attraction. (Surprisingly, Sussex was among the last counties to accept the Cross – due more to the region's then impenetrable forest than to its innate ungodliness.)

The last successful invasion of England took place in 1066, when the **Normans** overran King Harold's army near **Hastings**, on a site now marked by **Battle Abbey**. The Normans left their mark all over this corner of England, and Kent remains unmatched in its profusion of medieval castles, among them

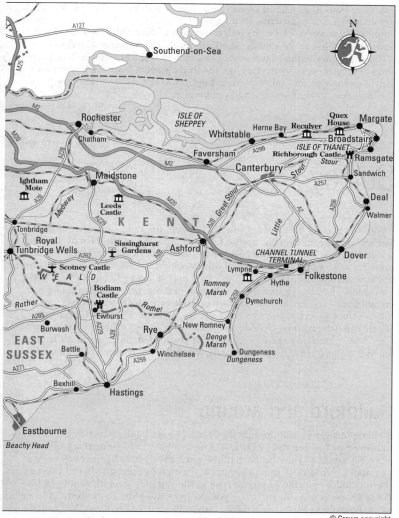

© Crown copyright

Dover's sprawling cliff-top fortress guarding against continental invasion and **Rochester**'s huge, box-like citadel, close to the old dockyards of **Chatham**, power-base of the formerly invincible British navy.

Away from the great historic sites, you can spend unhurried days in elegant old towns such as **Royal Tunbridge Wells**, **Rye** and **Lewes**, or enjoy the less-elevated charms of the traditional resorts, of which **Brighton** is far and away the best, combining the buzz of a university town with a blowsy good-time atmosphere and an excellent range of eating options. Dramatic scenery may be in short supply, but in places the **South Downs Way** offers an expanse of rolling chalk uplands that, as much as anywhere in the crowded southeast, gets you away from it all. And of course Kent, Sussex and Surrey harbour some of the country's finest **gardens**, ranging from Kew Botanical Gardens' country home at **Wakehurst Place**, the lush flowerbeds of **Sissinghurst** and the great landscaped estates of **Petworth**, **Sheffield Park** and **Scotney Castle**.

The commuter traffic in this corner of England is the heaviest in Europe, so almost everywhere of interest is close to a **train** station. National Express services from London and other parts of England to the region are pretty good, but local **bus** services are much less impressive.

Surrey

Effectively a rural suburb of southern London, for those who can afford it, **Surrey** is bisected laterally by the chalk escarpment of the **North Downs** which rise west of Guildford, peak around Box Hill near **Dorking**, and continue east into Kent. The portion of Surrey within the M25 orbital motorway has little natural and virtually no historical appeal, being a collection of satellite towns and light industrial installations serving the capital, although an enjoyable day can be spent at **Sandown Park** or **Epsom** racecourses, or trying the rides at one of Surrey's theme parks, **Thorpe Park** or **Chessington World of Adventures**. Outside the M25's ring, Surrey takes on a more pastoral demeanour, with the county town of **Guildford**, the open heath land of Surrey's western borders and **Farnham**, which has the county's only intact castle.

Guildford and around

Nestling in a gap carved through the North Downs by the River Wey, 35 miles southwest of London, **GUILDFORD** has a reputation as something of a dull place. Yet, while it's true that parts of the town are blighted by the one-way system and a surfeit of shopping precincts, the town centre does have a certain charm. Guildford came to prominence in the early seventeenth century, when the town became a major staging post halfway along the route from London to the flourishing Portsmouth docks; the canalization of the River Wey in 1648 reinforced its position on the trade map, with the High Street's Guildhall being the most significant landmark from this era. Within easy reach of the city are two National Trust properties, **Clandon Park** and **Hatchlands Park**, as well as the Royal Horticultural Society's gardens at **Wisley**.

Arrival, information and accommodation

Guildford's main **train station**, with regular trains from London Waterloo and Portsmouth, lies just over the river to the west of the town centre. Between the town centre and the train station, at the western end of North Street, the **bus station** has regular connections to London, Dorking, Portsmouth and

Winchester. The county's main **tourist office** is at 14 Tunsgate (May–Sept Mon–Sat 9am–5.30pm, Sun 10am–4.30pm; Oct–April Mon–Sat 9.30am –5.30pm; ☎01483/444333, ⓦwww.guildfordborough.co.uk), just off the High Street near the Guildhall. Free guided **tours** of the town leave from Tunsgate Arch, just below the tourist office (May–Aug Mon, Wed & Sun 2.30pm, Thurs 7.30pm; Sept Mon, Wed & Sun 2.30pm).

Guildford's less expensive **accommodation** options are all some distance from the town centre and include the homely *Atkinsons Guest House*, 129 Stoke Rd (☎01483/538260; ❷), with en-suite rooms, ten minutes' walk up the A320 Woking road. Plusher lodgings can be found at the *Jarvis Guildford Hotel*, 253 High St (☎01483/564511; ❻) and at the timber-beamed, 500-year-old *Angel Posthouse and Livery*, 91 High St (☎01483/564555; ❽). The nearest **youth hostel** is in the village of Holmbury St Mary, eight miles southeast of Guildford (see p.178). *Loseley Farm* (☎01483/304440), famous for its delicious dairy produce, three miles southwest of the town, also offers basic **camping** facilities.

The Town

Guildford's sloping **High Street** retains a great deal of architectural interest and several picturesque narrow lanes and courts lead off it to the adjoining North Street, and south towards the castle. As you look up the cobbled High Street, however, you can't fail to spot the wonderful gilded clock projecting over the street that has marked the town's time for more than three hundred years. The clock belongs to the **Guildhall** (guided tours Tues & Thurs 2pm & 3pm; free; ⓦwww.guildfordborough.co.uk) with its elaborate Restoration facade disguising Tudor foundations. A little further up the High Street is the **Archbishop Abbot's Hospital**, a hospice built for the elderly in 1619 fronted by a palatial red-brick Tudor gateway. You can take a peek at the pretty courtyard, but if you want to inspect the Flemish stained glass and oak beams that characterize the interior you must sign up for a guided tour (by appointment; contact the tourist office for details). Back down towards the river on the left, at no. 72, is the **Undercroft** (May–Sept Tues–Thurs 2–4pm, Sat noon–4pm; free), a well-preserved thirteenth-century basement of vaulted arches.

Guildford **Castle**'s Norman keep (due to reopen in 2003 after extensive renovation; for the latest information, ask at the tourist office or check ⓦwww.guildfordborough.co.uk) sits on its motte behind the High Street, surrounded by flower-filled gardens. Frequently used as a palace by King John, who may have departed from here to Runnymede to sign the Magna Carta in 1215, the castle was enlarged and improved during Henry III's reign, after which it was left to crumble into its present state. Beneath the castle, **Guildford Museum**, in Castle Arch on Quarry Street (Mon–Sat 11am–5pm; free), gives an account of the region's pre-Christian culture and displays cases of ceramic relics as well as some exquisite Saxon jewellery. Upstairs are mementoes to the writer Lewis Carroll (aka the Reverend Charles Dodgson), author of the children's classics, *Alice's Adventures in Wonderland* and *Alice through the Looking Glass*. An imaginative sculpture of Alice passing through the looking glass is a recent addition to the Castle Gardens, and Dodgson's grave can be visited in the cemetery off the Mount, on the other side of the river.

At the bottom of the High Street runs the **River Wey**, a rather neglected feature of the town, although the once-crucial River Wey and Godalming Navigation Canal has been restored into a picturesque waterway. From Easter to October, you can **rent canoes** (swimmers only) and **rowing boats** (Mon–Sat 9am–5.30pm, Sun 10am–6pm; canoes £4/hour; rowing boats £6/hour; £20 deposit) from Guildford Boat House, based in the Millbrook car park, and take the same company's **pleasure cruises** up the river from the town wharf, at the bottom of the High Street (mid-April to mid-July & last 2 weeks Sept Wed & Sun 1.45pm & 3.30pm; mid-July to mid-Sept Tues–Thurs, Sat & Sun noon, 1.45pm & 3.30pm; £4.25; ⓦwww.guildfordboats.co.uk). Half a mile further north up the river is **Dapdune Wharf** (April–Oct Thurs–Sun 11am–5pm; £2.50; NT), whose buildings house an interactive museum recounting the story of what is claimed to be Britain's oldest working water-way, while outside you can visit the restored barge *Reliance*.

Ostentatiously perched on Stag Hill by the university, a mile northwest of the centre, is Guildford's monumentally unremarkable red-brick **Cathedral** (daily 8am–5.30pm; ⓦwww.guildford-cathedral.org), one of only four Anglican cathedrals built in England in the twentieth century, topped by a gaudy gilded angel. Resembling an outsized crematorium and consecrated in 1961 follow-ing wartime delays, the cathedral's plain, bright interior, with its concrete vault-ing, has all the spirituality of a concert hall, but without the acoustics. Its most notable claim to fame is having been a location in the film *The Omen*.

Eating and drinking

For **eating** options, it's best to head off the High Street down Chapel Street, where the stylish Italian-run *Cambio* at no. 10 (☎01483/577702; closed Mon lunch & Sun) offers a set two-course lunch for £10, and the tiny *Café Austria*, at no. 20 (☎01483/537979; closed Sun), serves up everything from free-range Schnitzel to authentic *Gugelhupf*. Just around the corner, the *Café de Paris* at 35 Castle St (☎01483/564555; closed Sun) is a busy French-style brasserie in a listed building, offering three-course meals from around £15, while *Olivo*, at 53 Quarry St (☎01483/564555; closed Sun), serves delicious regional Italian dishes, housed in the town's sixteenth-century dispensary. This place is a food-ie's delight: check out their roof-terrace for an alfresco evening meal, but be sure to reserve as they can get very busy, especially at weekends. Virtually next door is one of Guildford's better **pubs**, the *King's Head*, also with a terrace, serving real ales and inexpensive meals. Guildford's oldest hostelry, *Ye Olde Ship Inn,* is on Portsmouth Road and boasts open fires; alternatively, try the *Jolly Farmer,* a pleasant riverside pub on Millbrook, which offers reasonably priced bar meals and welcomes kids. Also on Millbrook is one of the most well-known **theatres** outside London, the Yvonne Arnaud Theatre, which often stages plays before they reach the West End. Alternatively, in more ways than one, The Electric Theatre, based in the former electric works on Onslow Street, is an innovative riverside venue for both music and theatre and houses an excellent café.

Clandon Park, Hatchlands Park and Wisley

Five miles east of Guildford, the Palladian **Clandon Park** (April–Oct Tues–Thurs & Sun 11am–5pm; £5; NT) was built in the 1730s by Venetian architect Giacomo Leoni, for the second Lord Onslow. The two-storey Marble Hall is particularly impressive as is the Gubbay collection of porce-lain, furniture and needlework and the Ivo Forde collection of Meissenware Italian comedy figures, also housed here. Within the extensive grounds, landscaped by Capability Brown, there's an outsized souvenir in the form of a Maori meeting house brought back from New Zealand by the fourth Lord Onslow, who had been governor there.

If you're up for another National Trust stately home, buy a combined ticket to get you into **Hatchlands Park** (house April–July, Sept & Oct Tues–Thurs & Sun 2–5.30pm; Aug also Fri 2–5.30pm; grounds April–Oct daily 11am–6pm; house £5, park & gardens £2; NT), a mile or two further along the A246. The grounds are reason enough to come here, with woodland walks and a small Gertrude Jekyll garden, while the **house** itself is a splendid red-brick Palladian pile with richly ornate Robert Adam interiors, a stunning collection of eighteenth- and nineteenth-century keyboard instruments played by the likes of Mozart, Chopin and Mahler, and an exhibition on Admiral Edward Boscowen, who built the house in 1758. Outside, an additional dummy set of windows on the south side of the house adds grandeur, making it look as if there's a third floor, though in fact there are only two.

Five miles northeast of Guildford, signposted off the A3, the Royal Horticultural Society's gardens at **Wisley** (June & July Mon–Fri 10am–9pm, Sat 9am–9pm; rest of year Mon–Fri 10am–6pm or dusk if earlier, Sat 9am–6pm or dusk if earlier; £5; ⓦwww.rhs.org.uk) are a research establishment and a gardeners' garden, with staff on hand to offer advice and solve horticultural queries. The greenhouses contain a vast array of fragile specimens, including orchids and fuchsias; late spring is the best time to visit. The best way to get there by public transport is to catch a train to Woking, from where there is a special bus to Wisley (May–Sept Mon–Fri 11am, returning at 3.30pm; £3).

Farnham and around

Tucked into Surrey's southwestern corner, ten miles west of Guildford along the exposed ridge-top of the Hog's Back, lies **FARNHAM**. Smaller and, in parts, more charming than Guildford, the town moves at a slower pace – though, despite its bypass, the town centre is often clogged by traffic. Notwithstanding its thousand-year history, the majority of Farnham's architecture dates from the eighteenth century, when it enjoyed a boom period based on hop farming.

Yet Farnham is also home to Surrey's only intact **Castle**, built around 1138 by Henry de Blois, Bishop of Winchester, as a convenient residence halfway between his diocese and London. The castle was continuously occupied until 1927, but now houses a conference venue. The **keep** (April–Sept daily 10am–6pm; Oct daily 10am–5pm; £2.10; EH), from where there are good views over the rooftops to the Downs beyond, is the only part of the castle that is open to the public.

Farnham's refined Georgian dwellings are at their best along the broad **Castle Street**, which links the town centre with the castle, but you can actually step inside one of the smart Georgian houses at 38 West St. Once home to one of Farnham's wealthy hop merchants and now containing the **Museum of Farnham** (Tues–Sat 11am–5pm; free) the house on West Street contains a refreshingly succinct rundown on the town's history, its local hero, the eighteenth-century journalist and social reformer William Cobbett, and the highly regarded local art school. On the same street, the town's library is housed in **Vernon House**, where Charles I spent the night in 1648 en route to his trial and eventual execution in London.

Farnham **train station**, with frequent connections to London Waterloo, is five minutes from the centre, over the river on the south edge of town, down South Street and over the bypass. The **tourist office** is housed in the council offices on South Street, midway between the station and the centre (Mon–Thurs 9.30am–5.15pm, Fri 9.30am–4.45pm, Sat 9am–noon; ☎01252/715109, ⍟www.waverley.gov.uk). For **accommodation**, *The Bush Hotel*, a former seventeenth century coaching inn, is slap bang in the centre of town on The Borough (☎01252/715237; ❽) and has a number of rooms with four-poster beds, while vying for lavishness and age is *The Bishop's Table Hotel*, West St (☎01252/710222, ⍟www.bishopstable.com; ❼); both offer much-reduced weekend deals. Alternatively, there's comfortable townhouse accommodation at *Meads Guest House*, 48 West St (☎01252/715298; ❷), or try the excellent *Stafford House Hotel*, 22 Firgrove Hill (☎01252/724336; ❷), close to the station. Out of town, the best of the **B&B** options is *High Wray*, 73 Lodge Hill Rd (☎01252/715589, ✉highwray73@freenetname.co.uk; ❷), which lies about a mile south of Farnham Station off the Tilford Road; it's a little off the beaten track, so be sure to ask for clear directions if you're making your own way there, or get a cab there from the station. Once you find it, you'll be rewarded with a peaceful, semi-rural setting, which is conveniently close to the start of the North Downs Way for those that are hiking. Back in town, the French-style brasserie *Café Rouge* on the Borough (☎01252/733688; closed Sun) does decent **food**, while the oak-beamed *Nelson Arms*, Castle St, offers reasonable bar meals. Alternatively, if you prefer to eat Italian, the best bet is the friendly *Caffè Piccolo*, 84 West St (☎01252/723277), and there are also branches of both *Pizza Express* (☎01252/733220) and *Caffè Uno* (☎01252/721193) on Castle Street.

Waverley Abbey, Frensham and Hindhead

From Farnham station, the B3001 leads two miles southeast to the evocative riverside ruins of **Waverley Abbey**, the first of many Cistercian bases on British soil. Much of the stone was removed from the abbey after the Dissolution to construct Tudor houses in the area, a common fate of many such monastic establishments.

Three miles south of Farnham, **FRENSHAM** is set among the heather-covered heath lands that typify the Surrey/Hampshire borders. **Frensham Ponds**, established in medieval times as fish repositories and now popular with anglers, lies just south of town; the land hereabouts is as wild as Surrey gets. Five miles south of here on the A287 lies the village of **HINDHEAD**, whose most famous former resident was Arthur Conan Doyle, creator of the opium-puffing detective Sherlock Holmes. Fans of Conan Doyle might be interested in staying in his Edwardian home, now the *Undershaw Hotel* (☎01428/604039; ❶), which overlooks Hindhead's main junction. On the northeast edge of town, the curious depression known as the **Devil's Punchbowl** is crisscrossed with walking trails and bridle-paths. Local legends tell of witches, abductions and satanic rituals in the Punchbowl area, but perpetrators of these stories were most likely cattle thieves and highwaymen preying on the Portsmouth-bound stages. Yak-like Highland cattle graze in the area and the nearby Gibbet Hill, a mile east of the village, a former site of executions, gives the best views of the vicinity.

There is a tiny **youth hostel** (☎01428/604285), on the rim of the Punchbowl, one mile north of Hindhead, signposted off the A3. This secluded hostel, converted from National Trust cottages, makes an idyllic base from which to explore the Punchbowl's trails.

Dorking and around

Set at the mouth of a gap carved by the River Mole through the North Downs, **DORKING**, 25 miles from London (frequent trains from Victoria), lies at the intersection of the former Roman Stane Street and the medieval byway known as the **Pilgrim's Way**, which linked Winchester with Canterbury. There's nothing much to see in Dorking itself, but it makes a convenient base for exploring the surrounding countryside. If you want to **stay**, try *The White Horse Hotel* (☎0870/400 8282, ⓦwww.heritage-hotels.com; ❹) on the High Street, an oak-beamed former coaching inn dating from the seventeenth century which is also the town's best **food** option.

Box Hill, on the northern edge of town, is a popular draw for suburban weekenders and a staple of school trips during the week, when the intricacies of the River Mole's contrary flow through the chalk downs are explained. It's a three-hour climb to the top, but the snack-bar (daily 11am–4pm) and the view south over the town and the Weald's sandstone ridges reward the effort. You'll also find the grave of the eccentric local resident Major Peter Labilliere here; the major was famously buried head first, so that, in a topsy-turvy world, he would be the only one to "face his Maker the right way up". The nearest **train station** to Box Hill is at Westhumble on the Dorking–London line. Box Hill is situated on the 135-mile **North Downs Way**, a tame long-distance footpath stretching from Farnham to Dover and at its best around here with two **youth hostels** nearby.

North Surrey Theme Parks

Less than an hour's drive southwest of central London lie two popular **theme parks** – **Chessington** and **Thorpe Park**. Both primarily appeal to the 8–14 age group, and can become extremely crowded during school holidays; an early arrival on summer weekends will avoid long queues for the more popular rides. If it's action you're after, Chessington has the edge, but both easily return their seemingly pricey entrance fees with activities that fill the best part of a day.

Thorpe Park

Purpose-built and water-oriented **Thorpe Park** (times vary, call to check on ☎08704/444466; £19, less by advanced online booking; ⓦwww.thorpepark.co.uk) is well signposted off the A320 south of Staines and easily reached by train from London's Waterloo to Staines or Chertsey stations, with buses taking you on to the park itself. Set in an old gravel pit, the park continues to develop new attractions, such as the gravity-defying *Vortex*, but is still fairly low-key. It's advisable to bring swimwear for small children, who are excluded from the more exhilarating rides for safety reasons, but are well catered for elsewhere.

Chessington World of Adventures

Smaller and more animated, but marginally tackier than Thorpe Park, is **Chessington World of Adventures** (April to mid-July, Sept & Oct daily 10am–5pm; mid-July & Aug daily 10am–9pm; last admission 2hr before closing; £19.95, £17 by advanced online booking; ⓦwww.chessington.co.uk). The park is signposted off the A243, twelve miles southwest of London, and reached from London's Waterloo train station (to Chessington South) or bus #777 from Victoria. Located in a former zoo, the park's yellow *Safari Skyway* monorail introduces you to the few remaining animals while the *Chessington Railroad* circulates around the rest of the park. The better rides tend to be fun rather than frightening. *Seastorm* is a watery favourite, as is *Rameses' Revenge*, though it's slightly scarier.

From the purpose-built **youth hostel** in the village of **HOLMBURY ST MARY** (℡01306/730777, ✉holmbury@yha.org.uk; Gomshall train station), six miles southwest of Dorking, it's about an hour's walk to **Leith Hill**, southeastern England's highest point, offering views south to the Channel and north across London. Former local resident Richard Hull built a tower at the hill's summit in 1764, bringing its height up to 1029ft, and is now buried beneath it. You can look through a telescope from the top of the **tower** (April–Sept Wed, Sat & Sun 10am–5pm; Oct–March Sat & Sun 10am–3.30pm; £1.50; NT). There's a kiosk nearby, selling light refreshments and open the same times as the tower, or you could head for the *Plough* in neighbouring Coldharbour, for real ales and bar meals.

Tanners Hatch **youth hostel**, a basic cottage at the end of a muddy track, two and a half miles northwest of Dorking (℡01306/877964, ✉tanners@ yha.org.uk), lies just a mile away from **Polesden Lacey** (April–Oct Wed–Sun 1–5pm; grounds daily 11am–6pm or dusk; £7, grounds only £4; NT), a Regency-era villa built by Thomas Cubitt in 1824. Renovated in Edwardian times, it houses an assortment of silver, Chinese porcelain, French furniture and paintings, including works by Reynolds.

Kent

Not so long ago Kent's tourist industry was focused chiefly on the resorts of its northern coast and the **Isle of Thanet**. Nowadays these seaside towns have lost much of their gloss, but the county still boasts one of the most popular destinations in the entire country – the county town of **Canterbury**, site of one of the great English cathedrals. Furthermore, Kent can also boast its fair share of alluring castles and gardens, the best known of which are the estate of **Knole**, on the edge of Sevenoaks, **Leeds Castle**, to the west of Maidstone, and **Sissinghurst Gardens**, in the heart of the Weald and an inspiration to thousands of amateur horticulturalists. Exploration of the county's other scattered attractions – such as **Scotney Castle**, Winston Churchill's home at **Chartwell**, **Penshurst Place**, **Hever Castle** or the remnants of the Roman villa at Lullingstone – could fill a long and pleasurable weekend.

Transport links from London are good: the A2, M2 and M20 link the Channel ports of Ramsgate, Dover and Folkestone with the capital and rail connections to the county's key towns from London's Charing Cross, Waterloo East and Victoria stations are reliable. Sevenoaks, Maidstone, Tunbridge Wells and Canterbury are well served by daily National Express bus services, but local rail and bus links are slow.

The North Kent coast

It's a commonly held view that the northern part of Kent is a scenic and cultural wasteland, a prejudice that stems partly from the fact that most visitors only glimpse the area as they race to or from the Channel ports. However, the region has its fair share of attractions, all of which are easily accessible from the capital. The knot of historic sites at **Rochester** and **Chatham** is followed by the seaside towns of **Whitstable**, **Margate** and **Broadstairs**, once popular resorts that make an interesting mix of the stuffy and the purely frivolous.

Rochester and around

ROCHESTER, the most pleasant of the Medway towns, was first settled by the Romans, who built a fortress on the site of the present **Castle** (daily: April–Sept 10am–6pm; Oct 10am–5pm; Nov–March 10am–4pm; £3.60; Ⓦwww.medway.gov.uk), at the northwest end of the High Street; some kind of fortification has remained here ever since. In 1077, William I gave Gundulf, architect of the White Tower at the Tower of London, the See of Rochester and the job of improving the defences on the River Medway's northernmost bridge on Watling Street. The castle remains one of the best-preserved examples of a Norman fortress in England. The stark hundred-foot-high keep glowers over the town, while its interior is all the better for having lost its floors, allowing clear views up and down the dank interior. It has three square towers and a cylindrical one, the southwest tower, which was rebuilt following its collapse during the siege of the castle in 1215, when the bankrupt King John eventually wrested the castle from its archbishop. The outer walls and two of the towers retain their corridors and spiral stairwells, allowing access to the uppermost battlements.

The foundations of the adjacent **Cathedral** (daily 7.30am–6pm; free; Ⓔchapterclerk@rochester.anglican.org) were also Gandulf's work, but the building has been much modified over the past nine hundred years. Plenty of Norman touches have endured, particularly in the cathedral's west front, with its pencil-shaped towers, blind arcading and richly carved portal and tympanum above the doorway. Norman round arches, decorated with zigzags and made from lovely honey-coloured Caen stone, also line the nave. Some fine paintings survived the Dissolution of the Monasteries, most notably the thirteenth-century depiction of the Wheel of Fortune on the walls of the choir (only half of which survives); shown as a treadmill, it is a trenchant image of medieval life's relentless slog. The cathedral once enshrined the remains of St William of Perth, a pious baker from Scotland, who in 1201 embarked on a pilgrimage to the Holy Land, but got only as far as Rochester, where he was robbed and murdered. The monks of Rochester, envying the popular appeal of St Thomas à Becket's shrine at nearby Canterbury, used William's demise as an opportunity to establish a rival shrine – indeed substantial additions to the cathedral were financed by donations from pilgrims paying their respects to the canonized baker's tomb, which has long since disappeared.

Rochester's long, semi-pedestrianized **High Street** is a handsome affair, lined with antique shops, cafés and pubs, many of which are housed within appealingly old half-timbered and weatherboarded buildings. With an *Oliver Twist* bakery and a restaurant called *A Taste of Two Cities*, it's not difficult to guess the identity of Rochester's most famous son. **Charles Dickens** spent his youth here, but would seem to have been less than impressed by the place – it appears as "Mudfog" in *The Mudfog Papers*, and "Dullborough" in *The Uncommercial Traveller*. Many of the buildings feature in his novels: the *Royal Victoria and Bull Hotel*, at the top of the High Street, became the *Bull* in *Pickwick Papers* and the *Blue Boar* in *Great Expectations*, while most of his last book, the unfinished *Mystery of Edwin Drood*, was set in the town.

A gritty picture of Victorian life is conjured up by the tableaux at the **Charles Dickens Centre** in the distinctive red-brick and timber-framed

Eastgate House at the southeast end of the High Street (daily: April–Sept 10am–6pm; Oct–March 10am–4pm; £3.70; ⑩www.medway.gov.uk). Key scenes from his well-known books are enacted at the push of a button and the whole place is entertaining and informative, whether you're a Dickens enthusiast or not. Even if you've no intention of visiting the centre, it's worth taking a look round the back of the building where **Dickens' Chalet** now stands, having been removed from his house at Gad Hill Place. A pretty little two-storey wooden structure with sky-blue gables, balcony and shutters, this Swiss-style chalet was used by Dickens as his summer study and it was here that he was working on *The Mystery of Edwin Drood* just before he died in 1870.

Back up the High Street, past the French Huguenot Hospital, **La Providence**, which moved into this peaceful early Victorian cul-de-sac in 1960, stands **Watts' Charity** (March–Oct Tues–Sat 2–5pm; free), a sixteenth-century almshouse founded by the philanthropist, Richard Watts, for passing travellers and immortalized in Dickens' short story *The Seven Poor Travellers*. The building was used for its original purpose until as late as 1940, and, behind the eighteenth-century stone facade, with its trio of triangular gables, it still boasts a series of galleried Elizabethan bedrooms.

Lastly, it's worth giving Rochester's excellent **Guildhall Museum** at the northwest end of the High Street (daily 10am–4.30pm; free; ⑩www.medway .gov.uk) the once-over. Inside this splendid building, built in 1687, you'll find a vivid model of King John's siege of the castle and a chilling exhibition on the prison ships or hulks. Following American Independence in 1776, England was stuck for a place to transport her growing numbers of convicts – an increase caused as much by desperate poverty and draconian sentencing as any wave of criminality. Until the penal colony of Botany Bay was established a decade or so later, criminals were housed in appalling and overcrowded conditions inside decommissioned naval vessels moored in the Thames. With the clever use of mirrors, the exhibit replicates the grim conditions inside these floating prisons.

Practicalities

Rochester **train station**, served by regular trains from London's Charing Cross and Victoria, is at the southeastern end of the High Street. The **tourist office** is halfway along the High Street, opposite the cathedral at no. 95 (Mon–Sat 10am–5pm, Sun 10.30am–5pm; ☎01634/843666, ⑩www.medway.gov.uk). The Charles Dickens centre, near the train station, provides free guided tours of the town (Easter–Sept Wed, Sat & Sun 2.15pm).

As for **accommodation**, you can spend the night with some Dickensian ghosts at the ancient *Royal Victoria and Bull Hotel*, 16–18 High St (☎01634 /846266, ⑩www.rvandb.co.uk; ❺), or at the plush *Gordon House Hotel* at no. 91 (☎01634/83100, ⑩www.smoothhound.co.uk/hotels/gordon1; ❹). Decent B&Bs include the *Grayling House*, 54 St Margaret's St (☎01634/826593; ❷), further up the hill behind the castle. The nearest **youth hostel** (☎01634/400788, ✉medway@yha.org.uk) is at Capstone Farm, Gillingham, two miles southeast of Chatham; to get there by bus, take the #114 from Chatham bus station and get off at the *Waggon at Hale* pub.

Rochester has an unremarkable selection of greasy-spoon cafés and indifferent **restaurants**. Your best bet is to go Italian, either at the modest, family-run *Casa Lina,* 146 High St (☎01634/844993), or at *Giannino's* in the *Royal Victoria and Bull Hotel* (☎01634/828555). Alternatively, *The Singapora*, 51 High St (☎01634/842178), offers a broad range of Southeast Asian food. As for **pubs** *The Coopers Arms* on St Margaret's Street, which runs uphill between the castle and cathedral, serves good lunches in its small beer garden. A couple of newer **bars** worth checking out are the *City Wall*, 122 High St, with a spicy Tex-Mex-Med menu, and the stylish media hangout *Expressions*, 188 High St, while traditionalists might prefer *The Golden Lion* at 149 High St. *Amadeus* (☎01634/723370), one of the biggest **nightclubs** in the southeast, is part of the Medway Valley Park, a big entertainment complex a couple of miles west of the centre with a multiplex cinema.

Chatham

CHATHAM, less than two miles east of Rochester, has none of the charms of its neighbour and is, in truth, rather a grim place. Its chief attraction is its dockyards, originally founded by Henry VIII and once the major base of the Royal Navy, many of whose vessels were built, stationed and victualled here, commanding worldwide supremacy from the Tudor era until the end of the Victorian age. Well sheltered, yet close to London and the sea, and lined with tidal mud flats which helped support ships' keels during construction, the port expanded quickly and by the time of Charles II it had become England's largest naval base. This era of shipbuilding came to an ignominious end when the dockyards were closed in 1984, re-opening soon afterwards as a tourist attraction.

The **Historic Dockyard** (April–Oct daily 10am–5pm; Feb, March & Nov Wed, Sat & Sun 10am–4pm; £8.50; ⓦwww.worldnavalbase.org.uk) occupies a vast eighty-acre site about one mile north of the town centre along the Dock Road; it's a not very pleasant fifteen-minute walk from Chatham town centre, or a short bus ride (ask at the tourist office in Rochester for latest timetable). Behind the stern brick wall you'll find an array of historically and architecturally fascinating buildings dating back to the early eighteenth century. In addition to an impressive display of fifteen historic RNLI lifeboats, there's the "Wooden Walls" gallery, where you can experience life as an apprentice in the eighteenth-century dockyards. Here too lies the Ocelot Submarine, the last warship built at Chatham, whose crew endured unbelievably cramped conditions, a major deterrent to visiting claustrophobes. The main part of the exhibition, however, consists of the Ropery complex including the former rope-making room – at a quarter of a mile long, it's the longest room in the country.

Signposted to the east of the dockyards, up Wood Street, the **Royal Engineers Museum** (Mon–Thurs 10am–5pm, Sat, Sun & public holidays 11.30am–5pm; £3.50; ⓦwww.royalengineers.org.uk) is devoted to the army's all-purpose construction corps, nicknamed the "sappers", who were responsible for building London's Royal Albert Hall as well as numerous temporary wartime structures. Over the years the museum has acquired several artefacts from the sappers' campaigns, including Wellington's map of Waterloo and General Gordon's silk robes.

Less interesting by far is **Fort Amherst**, back towards the town centre at the bottom of Dock Road (April–Sept daily 10.30am–5pm; Oct–April Wed–Sun 10.30am–4pm; £4; ⓦwww.fortamherst.org.uk). Built to defend the dockyard in the mid-eighteenth century, the fort was extended by prisoners-of-war during the Napoleonic era. The fort's honeycomb of tunnels has been restored, but the one-and-a-half-hour guided tour is overlong and fails to impress – though an amusingly acted World War II Civil Defence "sketch" offers some light relief. The best time to come is on Sundays during the summer, when there's usually some costumed military re-enactment to help bring the place alive.

Boat trips run throughout the summer from Chatham along the River Medway on Britain's last working coal-fired paddle steamer, the *Kingswear Castle*, built in 1924 (ⓦwww.pskc.freeserve.co.uk). The trips set off from

Rochester Pier and the Historic Dockyard, and a **cruise to Upnor Castle** (April–Sept daily 10am–6pm; Oct daily 10am–4pm; £3.60; EH), an atmospheric sixteenth-century gun fort built on the river to protect Elizabeth I's fleet, costs £9.

Whitstable

Peculiarities of silt and salinity have made **WHITSTABLE** an oyster-friendly environment since classical times, when the Romans feasted on the region's marine delicacies. Indeed, production grew to such levels during the Middle Ages that **oysters** were exported all over Europe, and they were so cheap and plentiful that they became regarded as poor people's food – as Dickens observed, "where there are oysters, there's poverty". However, the whole industry collapsed during the twentieth century, the result of pollution and, in particular, a destructive storm in the 1950s which wrecked all the farms. Though oysters are once more farmed in the area – mostly the faster-growing Pacific Oysters, which have displaced the original Native Oysters – Whitstable is now more dependent on its commercial port, fishing and seaside tourism, while small-scale boat-building and a mildly bohemian ambience make this one of the few pleasant spots along the north Kent coast and a popular day-trip destination for Londoners.

Walking along Whitstable's busy High Street, you'd never guess that you're just a stone's throw from the sea. There's no promenade or bandstand – for that you have to go to Tankerton, Whitstable's easternmost suburb, or Herne Bay, six miles further east. Follow the signs at the top of the High Street to reach the seafront, a very pleasant, quiet shingle beach, backed onto by some pretty weatherboard cottages. Most folk come to Whitstable to eat the local oysters, and a brand new **Oyster and Fishery Exhibition** is due to open in late 2001 on the harbour, just off Harbour Street. One of Whitstable's last surviving wooden oyster yawls – built in 1890 when there were around one hundred and fifty working out of the harbour – can be seen along Island Wall, a ten-minute walk west at the end of Harbour Street. If your fascination with Whitstable's maritime history is still not sated, head for the more staid **Whitstable Museum and Gallery** (July & Aug Mon–Sat 10am–4pm, Sun 1–4pm; rest of year closed Sun; free), housed in the former Foresters' Hall, heralded by its eye-catching entrance on Oxford Street, with displays on diving and some good photographs and old film footage of the town's heyday. Back in 1830, Whitstable became the northern terminus for one of Britain's first steam-powered passenger railway services – the so-called "Crab & Winkle Line" which linked the town via a half-mile tunnel (the world's longest at that time) with Canterbury, ten miles to the south. Relics of this line still survive today.

Whitstable's **train station** is a five minutes' walk along Cromwell Road, east of Oxford St, the southern continuation of the High Street, while the **tourist office** is next to the museum at 7 Oxford St (July & Aug Mon–Sat 10am–5pm; rest of year Mon–Sat 10am–4pm; ☎01227/275482, ⓦwww.visit whitstable.co.uk). For **accommodation** along the seafront, try *Copeland House*, 4 Island Wall (☎01227/266207; ❸), west of the High Street, with a garden which backs onto the beach; the plush *Hotel Continental*, 29 Beach Walk (☎01227/280280, ⓦwww.oysterfishery.co.uk; ❼), off the northern tip of Harbour Street; or *The Cherry Garden*, 62 Joy Lane (☎01227/266497; ❷), a homely B&B with a delightful garden ten minutes' stroll along the Seasalter road. For **campsites**, you're best off heading to *Seaview Caravan Park* (☎01227/792246; closed Nov–March), which backs onto the beach towards Herne Bay.

Whitstable's fishing background is reflected in its **eating** places, from any number of fish-and-chip outlets along the High Street and Harbour Street to the very popular *Royal Native Oyster Stores,* The Horsebridge (℡01227/276856; closed Sun eve & Mon), one of the town's best restaurants, with main fish dishes starting at £10, and half a dozen oysters costing £12.50. A good alternative is *Pearson's Crab and Oyster House*, opposite (℡01227/272005), which offers bar meals downstairs and has a pricier restaurant upstairs. On the way into town *Giovanni's*, 49–55 Canterbury Rd (℡01227/273034: closed Sun eve & all Mon), is deservedly reckoned to be one of the best Italian restaurants in the county. *Tea and Times*, 36 High St, caters for the town's arty fringe, providing free newspapers and serving a decent English breakfast with real coffee. For a **drink** and excellent atmosphere check out the *Old Neptune*, standing alone in its white weatherboards on the shore, while another excellent locals' pub is the *Wall Tavern*, Middle Wall. Whitstable is at its most lively during its **Oyster Festival**, held annually in the last two weeks of July, featuring not only lots of crustacean crunching, but also jazz and parades.

Herne Bay and Reculver

Six miles east of Whitstable is the drab seaside resort of **HERNE BAY** which, like its storm-severed pier, is something of a relic from a bygone age when holiday-makers believed that sitting on a wind-blasted patch of shingle and sand was something to look forward to. Certain temperaments may find something stirring in moribund resorts like this, but overall Herne Bay has neither the energetic tackiness nor the discreet refinement of the larger resorts further east. Indeed, thanks to its large numbers of retired senior citizens, the town is often disparagingly referred to as Hernia Bay. The handsome Neoclassical clock tower on the seafront, and the King's Hall, further east, with its slender wrought-iron colonnade, hint at Herne Bay's halcyon days, but even the prom's new modern Sculpture Trail can't really hide the fact that the resort's glory days are over.

For a brief rundown of the attractions that once drew thousands of tourists here each summer, there's a small exhibition in the back of the **tourist office** at 12 William St (July & Aug Mon–Sat 10am–5pm, Sun 1–4pm; rest of year Mon–Sat 10am–4pm; ℡01227/361911, ⓦwww.visithernebay.co.uk). Herne Bay's decline as a holiday resort has left just a few **B&Bs**, clustered together on the seafront. A better alternative is *Foxden*, 5 Landen Rd (℡01227/363514; ❷), offering en-suite accommodation and a pretty garden, fifteen minutes from the centre off Beltinge Road. Greasy-spoon cafés are plentiful in Herne Bay, but for superior fish and chips head for *Andrews Fish Bar*, 76–77 Central Parade, by the clock tower. *The Ship*, at the junction of East Street and Central Parade, has more character than most Herne Bay **pubs**, and serves a good range of real ales.

One good reason to come to Herne Bay is to go on a **boat trip** (℡01227 /366712) to an offshore sandbank, home to a large herd of seals; the trip, in a lovely open yacht, takes four to five hours and costs around £10 per person, depending on the size of the group. Other cruises are also available. For most visitors, though, Herne Bay's main value lies in its proximity to the ruins of England's oldest-known **Roman Fort**, situated inside Reculver Country Park, which occupies an isolated headland two miles east of Herne Bay; to get there, either walk along the coast or catch one of the local buses from the train station. The original fort, built around 280 AD by Carausis, self-styled Emperor of Britain, was used to guard the Wantsum Channel which separated the Isle of Thanet from the mainland and made an easily defended harbour for the

Roman fleet. In the seventh century the Saxon **Church of St Mary** was built within the fort's walls, surviving until 1809, when coastal erosion brought about its collapse. Trinity House – the government's maritime navigation authority – bought the ruins the following year, rebuilding the twin twelfth-century **Reculver Towers** in order to render them "sufficiently conspicuous to be useful to navigation". An **interpretation centre** (April–June & Sept Sun 11am–5pm; July & Aug daily 11am–5pm; Oct–March Sun 11am–3pm; free) near the car park tells the full story and provides details on ecological aspects of this part of the coast. The *King Ethelbert* **pub**, close to the towers, provides an important refuelling function for passing tourists.

The Thanet resorts

The **Isle of Thanet**, a featureless plain fringed by low chalk cliffs and the odd sandy bay, became part of the mainland when the navigable Wantsum Channel began silting up around the time of the first Roman invasion. This northeastern corner of Kent has witnessed successive waves of incursions. In 43 AD, nearly a century after Julius Caesar's exploratory visit, the Romans got into their stride when they landed near Pegwell Bay and established Richborough port in preparation for the march inland. The Saxons followed them four hundred years later – the island is named after the "tenets", or fire beacons, which used to warn local residents of the Saxons' raids – and Augustine arrived here in 597 on a divine mission to end Anglo-Saxon paganism. The evangelist is supposed to have met King Ethelbert of Kent and preached his first sermon at a spot three miles west of Ramsgate – a cross marks the location at Ebbsfleet, next to St Augustine's Golf Club.

Over the next thousand years or so, civilization advanced to the point at which, in 1751, a resident of Margate, one Mr Benjamin Beale, invented the bathing machine, a wheeled cubicle that enabled people to slip into the sea without undue exhibitionism. It heralded the birth of sea bathing as a recreational and recuperative activity, and led to the growth of **seaside resorts**. By the mid-twentieth century the Isle's intermittent expanses of sand had become fully colonized as the "bucket and spade" resorts of the capital's leisure-seeking proletariat. That heyday has passed, but these earliest of resorts still cling to their traditional attractions to varying degrees.

Getting to the Thanet resorts is straightforward: **trains** and **buses** make the two-hour journey from London Victoria to Margate, Ramsgate and Broadstairs several times a day, and there are local rail and bus services from Canterbury and Dover. Once there, one easy way to visit Thanet is to take the **open top bus service** which plies a clockwise circuit from Ramsgate and allows for time to visit both Margate and Broadstairs (day ticket £5.50; ⓦ www.guidefriday.com).

Margate

MARGATE – memorably summarized by Oscar Wilde as "the nom-de-plume of Ramsgate" – is a ragged assortment of cafés, shops and amusement arcades wrapped around a broad bay, a rather less elegant place than the one with which it's been twinned, the Black Sea resort of Yalta. Yet more than two centuries of tourism are embodied in Margate: at its peak thousands of Londoners were ferried down the Thames every summer's day, to be disgorged at the pier – the functional precursor of all such seaside structures. Even today, on a fine summer weekend, the place is heaving with day-trippers enjoying the traditional fish and chips, candyfloss and donkey rides.

Other than the agreeable, if small, sandy beach, Margate's main attraction along its unashamedly tacky seafront is **Dreamland** on Marine Terrace (Easter–June & Sept daily 11am–5.30pm; July & Aug 11am–10pm), an amusement park heralded by a streamline 1930s' portal, with a rollercoaster dating back to 1863. If this doesn't appeal you could always visit the **Shell Grotto** on Grotto Hill, off Northdown Road (Easter to mid-Oct Mon–Fri 10am–5pm, Sat & Sun 10am–4pm; £1.50), which claims to be the world's only underground shell temple and has been open to the public since it was discovered by some schoolkids in 1835. Its passages are intricately decorated with shell mosaics and its caverns were once linked to the less interesting **Margate Caves** further down Northdown Road (daily: July & Aug 10am–5pm; April–June, Sept & Oct daily 10am–4pm; £1.80) – if nothing else, a good place to cool off on a hot day. The narrow streets of Margate's old town, centred on the Market Place, have potential, but many of the shopfronts are now boarded up, having been superseded by the town's ugly out-of-town shopping centres. Still, you can take a trip down memory lane in the **Margate Museum** on the Market Place (April–Sept daily 10am–5pm; Oct–March Mon–Fri 9.30am–4.30pm; £1; ⓔmargatemuseum@bonkers16.freeserve.co.uk); the building also served as the town's police station from 1858 to 1959 – you can see several surviving police cells on the ground floor.

The **tourist office** is at 12–13 The Parade (Easter–Sept Mon–Fri 9am–5pm, Sat 9am–4pm, Sun 10am–4pm; Oct–Easter Mon–Sat 9am–4pm; ⓣ01843/230203, ⓦwww.tourism.thanet.gov.uk) and the **train station** is on All Saints' Ave, just a couple of minutes' walk from Dreamland. Margate has plenty of **B&Bs**, the better ones lining the Regency crescents of the Cliftonville area – try the family-run *Ocean View Hotel*, 8–10 Ethelbert Terrace (ⓣ01843/220641, ⓦwww.oceanviewhotel.co.uk; ❷), or the nearby and welcoming *Hotel Marina*, 8 Dalby Square (ⓣ01843/230120; ❶). Alternatively, there's the grand 1920s-style *Walpole Bay Hotel*, Fifth Avenue (ⓣ01843/221703, ⓦwww.walpolebayhotel.co.uk; ❻). Margate's YHA hostel (ⓣ01843/221616, ⓔmargate@yha.org.uk) is situated in the former Beachcomber Hotel, 3–4 Royal Esplanade, by Westbrook Bay to the west of the train station. Prosaic **seaside food** is on offer at all of the seafront greasy spoons and fish-and-chip outlets, but you can get very fine **pastries** and snacks from *Batchelor's Patisserie*, at 246 Northdown Rd in Cliftonville. Most of Margate's **pubs** are a bit rough at the edges, so it's worth steering away from the seafront: try the tiny Victorian *Rose in June*, on peaceful Trinity Square, the larger *Wig and Pen*, 10 Market Place, or for real ales (and pizzas), the *Spread Eagle*, at the top of Victoria Road.

Broadstairs and around

Said to have been established on the profits of shipbuilding and smuggling, today **BROADSTAIRS** is the smallest, quietest, predominantly middle class and, undoubtedly, the most pleasant of Thanet's resort towns, overlooking the pretty little Viking Bay from its cliff-top setting. The town's charm lies in its quiet self-sufficiency: there are no big hotels to dominate and tourism seems to have endured without spoiling the place. Viking Bay is just one of several **sandy coves** which punctuate Thanet's eastern shore; between Broadstairs and Margate you'll find Stone, Joss, Kingsgate and Botany bays with Louisa Bay to the south – all quiet and undeveloped gems that make a good antidote to the busier resort areas.

However, Broadstairs' main claim to fame is as Dickens' holiday retreat – he described it as "one of the freest and freshest little places in the world". Throughout his most productive years he stayed in various hostelries here, and

△ The White Cliffs of Dover

eventually rented an "airy nest" overlooking Viking Bay from Fort Road, since renamed **Bleak House** (daily: July & Aug 10am–7.30pm; Sept–Dec & mid-Feb to June 10am–6pm; £3) and opened to the public. It was here that he planned the eponymous novel as well as finishing *David Copperfield*, and three rooms in the house have been preserved as the author would have known them. There's more of the same on the main cliff-top seafront at the **Dickens House Museum**, 2 Victoria Parade (April to mid-Oct daily 2–5pm; £2), in the house Dickens used as a model for Betsy Trotwood's House. The town's **Dickens Festival**, held annually since 1937, takes place during the third week in June and features lectures, dramatizations of the author's works and a nightly Victorian music hall.

If you're in search of further diversions, pay a visit to the **Crampton Tower Museum** (Easter to mid-Oct Mon, Tues, Thurs & Fri, plus Sun 2.30–5pm on bank-holiday weekends; £1.50), on the other side of the road and railway tracks from the train station. Named after local-born Victorian engineer, Thomas Crampton, who built the town's first water system, it's the museum's buildings rather than its contents that are intriguing: the flint-studded tower, the pumping-engine shed and the nearby "beehive" building are all relics of Crampton's sophisticated water system.

It's a ten-minute walk from the **train station** to Broadstairs' seafront along the High Street, where you'll find the **tourist office** at no. 6b (April–Sept daily 9am–5pm; Oct–March Mon–Sat 9am–4.30pm; ☎01843/862242, ⓦwww.tourism.thanet.gov.uk). Many **hotels**, restaurants and other establishments cash in on the Dickens angle; he wrote part of *Nicholas Nickleby* at the family-run *Royal Albion Hotel*, 6–12 Albion St (☎01843/868071, ⓦwww .albion-bstairs.demon.co.uk; ❺), a comfortable treat for Dickens fans – ask about the B&B deal, which includes a meal in the *Marchesi Brothers* restaurant, two doors down. Alternatively, try the *East Horndon Hotel*, 4 Eastern Esplanade (☎01843/868306; ❷), or the *Devonhurst Hotel*, also on the Eastern Esplanade (☎01843/863010; ⓦwww.devonhurst.co.uk; ❸). There are several ivy-covered Georgian establishments in Belvedere Road, behind the High Street: the *Admiral Dundonald Hotel* at no. 43 (☎01843/862236; ❷) and the *Hanson Hotel* next door (☎01843/868936, ⓔhotelhanson@aol.com; ❷) may lack sea views, but both are good value. There is also a **youth hostel** at 3 Osborne Rd just two minutes' walk from the train station (☎01843/604121, ⓔbroadstairs@ yha.org.uk); it's housed in a Victorian villa and has a pleasant family atmosphere.

For **food**, there are plenty of fish-and-chip outlets and cafés along Albion Street and down Harbour Street. If you're looking for a more congenial setting, *Harpers Wine Bar*, also on Harbour Street (☎01843/602494; eve only), serves moderately priced fish and seafood dishes. Broadstairs' top restaurant is the aforementioned Swiss-run *Marchesi Brothers* restaurant, 18 Albion St (☎01843/862481), where a main course will set you back at least £10, though it also offers set lunches from £11.50 and dinners from £16.50; alternatively, the inexpensive *Osteria Pizzeria Posillipo*, next door (☎01843/601133), does excellent pizzas, pasta and other Italian standards, and has a balcony overlooking the bay. As for **pubs**, *Ballard's Lounge* at the *Royal Albion Hotel* also has bay views from its garden, while the popular and friendly *Neptune's Hall*, at the top of Harbour St, serves great beer and has regular live folk-music evenings. The *Tartar Frigate,* also on Harbour St, with it own seafood restaurant upstairs, and the *Lord Nelson*, round the corner in Nelson Place, are solid sociable English pubs. The Broadstairs **Folk Week**, held usually in the middle of August, is one of England's longest-standing folk music events and features singers, bands and dancing in locations around the town, both indoor and alfresco (Ⓦwww.broad stairsfolkweek.com).

If you have time to explore the surrounding area, you could spend a reward-ing afternoon at **Quex House**, a rambling Regency stately home set in its own gardens in the village of Birchington, four miles from Margate. The build-ing houses the **Powell-Cotton Museum** (April–Oct daily 11am–5pm; Nov, Dec & March Sun 11am–4pm; £4; Ⓦwww.powell-cottonmuseum.co.uk), a collection of trophies and artefacts amassed by Major Powell-Cotton, a nine-teenth-century big-game hunter, from his 28 expeditions to the African bush. The major built special galleries to house the dioramas in which over five hun-dred stuffed animals have been arranged, and there's also a wonderful collec-tion of early photographs documenting the expeditions, along with displays of ethnographic material. In the nearby village of Birchington, the graveyard holds the tomb of Dante Gabriel Rossetti, the Victorian painter and poet, and the village also has a memorial garden to him at Sandles Road, right by the train station.

Ramsgate

If Thanet had a capital, it would be **RAMSGATE**, a handsome resort, rich in robust Victorian red-brick, but whose centre's boarded-up shops reveal its eco-nomic decline. Most of the town is set high on a cliff linked to the seafront and harbour by broad, sweeping ramps, with the villas on the seaward side display-ing wrought-iron verandas and bricked-in windows – a legacy of the tax on glazed windows. Overall the port has avoided Margate's vulgarity while retain-ing some of Broadstairs' class, and the large-scale regeneration project in the harbour and along the seafront by the Maritime Museum is likely to breathe new life into the area.

Currently, the most entertaining sight in Ramsgate is the subterranean **Motor Museum** at West Cliff Hall, on The Paragon just by the ferry termi-nal (April–Oct daily 10.30am–5.30pm; Nov–Easter Sun 10am–5pm; £2.50), which spices up its eclectic collection of cars and motorbikes by placing each vehicle in historical context. A 1905 Rex pushbike is on show alongside a newspaper proclaiming the increase of third-class steamer fares to the USA to £6, and a 1904 De Dion Bouton is displayed along with details of events from the same year – the founding of Rolls-Royce and the arrest of a New York woman for the heinous crime of smoking in public.

A predictable chronicle of municipal life from Roman times onwards is pre-sented at the **Ramsgate Maritime Museum**, in the harbour's nineteenth century Clock House (Easter–Sept daily 10am–5pm; Oct–Easter Tues–Fri 10am–4.30pm; £1.50; Ⓦwww.ekmt.fsnet.co.uk); the display is brightened by an illuminating section on the Goodwin Sands sandbanks – six miles southeast of Ramsgate – the occasional playing field of the eccentric Goodwin Sands Cricket Club.

Ramsgate's **train station** is about a mile northwest of the centre, at the end of Wilfred Road, at the top of the High Street, and the **tourist office** is at 17 Albert Court, York St (daily 9.30am–4.30pm; ⓉOl843/583333, Ⓦwww .tourism.thanet.gov.uk). For an overnight **stay**, the *Spencer Court Hotel*, 37 Spencer Square (ⓉOl843/594582; ❶), offers comfortable accommodation in a listed Regency building, directly above the ferry terminal; while, in Eastcliff, the Victorian *Eastwood Guest House*, 28 Augusta Rd (ⓉOl843/591505; ❸), has some rooms with balconies. *The Crescent*, 19 Wellington Crescent (ⓉOl843 /591419; ❶), is an attractive seafront option in a Georgian terrace originally built to house the duke's officers. The nearest **campsite** is *Nethercourt Touring*

Park, just two miles southwest of the town centre (☎01843/595485; closed Nov–March). For **food**, you could go oriental at *Thai Style*, a cosy Thai restaurant overlooking the harbour at 1–2 Westcliff Arcade (☎01843/585505), with some outside tables and very reasonable prices. *Seadrive Internet Café* is at 62 Harbour Parade and serves coffee and snacks. Many of Ramsgate's **pubs** also offer good food – try the *Falstaff*, halfway up Addington Street from the seafront, which does a decent ploughman's lunch, or the *Camden Arms* in nearby La Belle Alliance Square, for good-value fish and chips; for cliff-top views, real ales and live music (Wed & Sat), head for the *Churchill Tavern* on The Paragon, overlooking the harbour.

Canterbury

One of England's most venerable cities, **CANTERBURY** offers a rich slice through two thousand years of history, with Roman and early Christian ruins, a Norman castle and a famous cathedral that dominates a medieval warren of time-skewed Tudor dwellings. The city began as a Belgic settlement that was overrun by the Romans and renamed **Durovernum**, which they established as a garrison and supply base and from where they went on to build a system of roads that was to reach as far as the Scottish borders. With the empire's collapse came the Saxons, who renamed the town **Cantwarabyrig**; it was a Saxon king, Ethelbert, who in 597 welcomed Augustine, despatched by the pope to convert the British Isles to Christianity. By the time of his death, Augustine had founded two Benedictine monasteries, one of which – Christ Church, raised on the site of the Roman basilica – was to become the first cathedral in England.

At the turn of the first millennium Canterbury suffered repeated sackings by the Danes until Canute, a recent Christian convert, restored the ruined Christ Church, only for it to be destroyed by fire a year before the Norman invasion. As the new religion became a tool of control, a struggle for power developed between the archbishops, the abbots from the nearby Benedictine abbey and King Henry II, culminating in the assassination of Archbishop Thomas à Becket in 1170, a martyrdom that effectively established the autonomy of the archbishops and made this one of Christendom's greatest shrines. Geoffrey Chaucer's *Canterbury Tales*, written towards the end of the fourteenth century, portrays the unexpectedly festive nature of pilgrimages to Becket's tomb, which was later plundered and destroyed on the orders of Henry VIII.

In 1830 a pioneering passenger railway service linked Canterbury to the sea and prosperity grew until the city suffered extensive German bombing on June 1, 1942, in one of the notorious **Baedeker Raids** – the Nazi plan to destroy the most treasured historic sites as described in the eponymous German travel guides. Today the cathedral and compact town centre, enclosed on three sides by medieval walls, remain the focus for leisure-motivated pilgrims from across the globe.

Arrival and information

Canterbury has two **train stations**, Canterbury East for services from London Victoria and Dover Priory, and Canterbury West for services from London Charing Cross and the Isle of Thanet – the stations are northwest and south of the centre respectively, each a ten-minute walk from the cathedral. National Express services and local **buses** use the bus station just inside the city walls on

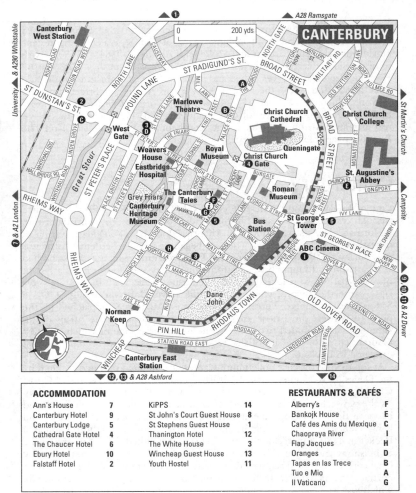

© Crown copyright

ACCOMMODATION

Ann's House	7
Canterbury Hotel	9
Canterbury Lodge	5
Cathedral Gate Hotel	4
The Chaucer Hotel	6
Ebury Hotel	10
Falstaff Hotel	2
KiPPS	14
St John's Court Guest House	8
St Stephens Guest House	1
Thanington Hotel	12
The White House	3
Wincheap Guest House	13
Youth Hostel	11

RESTAURANTS & CAFÉS

Alberry's	F
Bankojk House	E
Café des Amis du Mexique	C
Chaopraya River	I
Flap Jacques	H
Oranges	D
Tapas en las Trece	B
Tuo e Mio	A
Il Vaticano	G

St George's Lane. Car drivers should note that finding a **parking** space can be problematic and are best advised to use the signposted Park-and-Ride services available on Wincheap, Sturry Road and New Dover Road. The busy **tourist office** is at 34 St Margaret's St (May–Sept Mon–Sat 9.30am–6pm, Sun 9.30am–5pm; rest of year closed Sun; ☎01227/766567, ⊛www.canterbury. co.uk), right in the middle of the city centre, just south of the High Street. The Canterbury Environment Centre (Tues–Fri 10am–5pm, Sun 10am–4pm), a converted church and vegetarian café near the Cathedral on St Alphege's Lane, publishes a number of detailed **historical walks**, available for a small charge. If you're planning on visiting any of the local museums, it might be worth getting hold of the **museum passport** (£4.50), which gives entry to the Canterbury Heritage Museum, the Roman Museum and the West Gate

Museum and is available from the ticket offices of each. **Bike rental** is available from Downland Cycle Hire (☎01227/479643) at Canterbury West railway station.

Accommodation

Accommodation consists mostly of B&Bs and small hotels and can be difficult to secure in July and August. In the town centre, some old hotels offer all the creaking, authentic antiquity you could ask for, while there's a host of B&Bs to be found just outside the city walls. The tourist office can help you find a place to stay, though they charge £2.50 for the service. Alternatively, both the University of Kent (☎01227/828000, ⓦ www.ukc.ac.uk/hospitality), a mile or so north of town, and Christ Church University College, North Holmes Rd (☎01227/782225; ⓦ www.canterbury.ac.uk), behind St. Augustine's Abbey, offer bed and breakfast in student accommodation (single and double) during the Easter and Summer vacations (from £17–26 per person).

Hotels and B&Bs

Ann's House 63 London Rd ☎01227/768767. Traditional Victorian villa offering comfortable rooms, most of which are en suite. **②**

The Canterbury Hotel 71 New Dover Rd ☎01227/450551, ⓔ canterbury.hotel@ btinternet.com. Fifteen minutes' walk from the town centre with a French restaurant and friendly service. **⑥**

Canterbury Lodge St Margaret's St ☎01227 /463271, ⓔ slatters@netcomuk.com. Luxury, lodge-style hotel with an elegant designer bar and restaurant and great central location. **④**

Cathedral Gate Hotel 36 Burgate ☎01227 /464381, ⓔ cgate@cgate.demon.co.uk. Built in 1438 and set in the city's medieval heart, this venerable pilgrims' hostelry features crooked floors and exposed timber beams alongside more modern amenities. **⑤**

The Chaucer Hotel 63 Ivy Lane ☎01227/464427, ⓦ www.thechaucerhotel.co.uk. Large hotel just beyond the city walls, fully refurbished with modern comforts but retaining some of its early Georgian charm. **⑦**

Ebury Hotel 65–67 New Dover Rd ☎01227 /768433, ⓦ www.ebury-hotel.co.uk. Very comfortable and spacious family-owned Victorian hotel, fifteen minutes' walk from the centre; indoor pool and well-appointed rooms. **⑤**

The Falstaff Hotel 8–10 St Dunstan's St ☎01227 /462138, ⓦ www.corushotels.com/thefalstaff. Popular fifteenth-century coaching inn by the West Gate, with four-poster beds and an award-winning restaurant. **⑦**

St John's Court Guest House St John's Lane ☎01227/456425, ⓔ nrow5@netscapeonline.co.uk.

Good-value guest house, offering B&B in a quiet but central location, just south of the old town. **①**

St Stephen's Guest House 100 St Stephen's Rd, ☎01227/767644. On the northern side of the city, ten minutes' walk along the Stour and handily placed for the university, offering excellent value en-suite accommodation. **②**

Thanington Hotel 140 Wincheap ☎01227 /453227, ⓔ thanington-hotel.co.uk. Comfortably converted Georgian building, ten minutes' walk from the centre with an indoor pool, games room and friendly, attentive service. **⑤**

The White House 6 St Peter's Lane ☎01227/ 761836, ⓔ whwelcom@aol.com. Small and friendly guest house offering en-suite accommodation in a fine Regency building, midway between the cathedral and Canterbury West station. **③**

Wincheap Guest House 94 Wincheap ☎01227/ 762309. Good-value Victorian B&B, with shared facilities, close to Canterbury East station. **①**

Hostels and campsites

The Caravan and Camping Club Site Bekesbourne Lane ☎01227/463216. Large year-round caravan park, one and a half miles east of the city off the A257 road to Sandwich.

KiPPS 40 Nunnery Fields ☎01227/786121, ⓦ www.kipps-hostel.com. Self-catering hostel offering single, double and dormitory accommodation a few minutes' walk from Canterbury East station. £11–16 per person.

Youth Hostel 54 New Dover Rd ☎01227/462 911, ⓔ canterbury@yha.org.uk. Half a mile out of town, and 15min on foot from Canterbury East station, this friendly hostel is set in a Victorian villa. Closed Jan.

The City

Despite the presence of a university and art and teacher-training college, England's second most visited city is a surprisingly small place with a population of just 35,000. The town centre, ringed by ancient walls, is virtually car free, but this doesn't stop the High Street seizing up all too frequently with tourists, two million of whom visit the city each year. Having said that, the very reason for the city's popularity is its rich tapestry of historical sites, combined with a good selection of places to stay, eat and drink, and no visit to southeast England would be complete without, at the very least, a quick stop here.

Canterbury is compact enough to find your own way around, but there are various **tours** available. The *Guild of Guides Walking Tours* (April–June, Sept & Oct daily 2pm; July & Aug also 11.30am; 1hr 30min; £3.50) leave from the tourist office to take you on an informative walking tour of the city, while *The Ghostly Tour of Old Canterbury* (Fri & Sat 8pm; 1hr; £5) is a spicy mix of the supernatural and local folklore, leaving from the *Billabong Bar*, St Margaret's St. A more leisurely alternative is to take a guided **boat trip** along the Stour on a *Historic River Tour* (April–Oct Mon–Sat 10am–5pm, Sun 11am–4pm; £4.50), or you could cock a snook at pedestrians by riding in one of the **horse-drawn carriages** from Canterbury Carriage (April–Sept daily 10am-8pm; minimum charge £12/ carriage), which depart from outside the County Hotel on Stour Street.

The cathedral

Mother Church of the Church of England, seat of the Primate of All England, **Canterbury Cathedral** (Mon–Sat 9am–7pm, Sun 12.30–2.30pm & 4.30 –5.30pm; closes Mon–Sat 5pm in winter; also closed on some days in mid-July for university graduation ceremonies; £3.50, free on Sun; Ⓦwww.canterbury cathedral.org) is ecclesiastically supreme and fills the northeast quadrant of the city with a befitting sense of authority, even if architecturally it's perhaps not among the country's most impressive. A cathedral has stood here since 602, but in 1070 the first Norman archbishop, Lanfranc, levelled the original Saxon structure to build a new cathedral. Over successive centuries the masterpiece was heavily modified, and with the puritanical lines of the Perpendicular style gaining ascendancy in late medieval times, the cathedral now derives its distinctiveness from the thrust of the 235-foot-high Bell Harry Tower, completed in 1505. The precincts (daily 7am–9pm) are entered through the superbly ornate early-sixteenth-century **Christ Church Gate**, where Burgate and St Margaret's Street meet. This junction, the city's medieval core, is known as the Buttermarket, where religious relics were once sold to pilgrims hoping to prevent an eternity in damnation. Having paid your entrance fee, you pass through the gatehouse and get one of the finest views of the cathedral, foreshortened and crowned with soaring towers and pinnacles.

Once in the magnificent **interior**, look for the tomb of Henry IV and his wife, Joan of Navarre, and for the gilded effigy of Edward III's son, the Black Prince, all of them to be found in the Trinity Chapel, behind the main altar. The **shrine of Thomas à Becket**, in the northwest transept, is marked by the Altar of Sword's Point, where a crude sculpture of the assassins' weapons is suspended above the spot where Becket died and was later enshrined – until Henry VIII's act of ecclesiastical vandalism in 1538. Steps from here descend to the low, Romanesque arches of the **crypt**, one of the few remaining relics of the Norman cathedral and considered the finest such structure in the country, with some amazingly well-preserved carvings on the capitals of the columns.

On the cathedral's north flank are the fan-vaulted colonnades of the **Great Cloister**, from where you enter the **Chapter House**, with its intricate web of fourteenth-century tracery supporting the roof and a wall of stained glass, which illustrates scenes from St Thomas's life and death. In 1935 it was a fitting venue for the inaugural performance of T.S. Eliot's *Murder in the Cathedral*.

St Augustine's Abbey and St Martin's Church

Passing through the cathedral grounds and out through the city walls at the (exit-only) Queningate, you come to the vestigial remains of **St Augustine's Abbey** (daily: April–Sept 10am–6pm; Oct 10am–5pm; Nov–March 10am–4pm; £2.60; EH), occupying the site of the church founded by Augustine in 598. It was built outside the city because of a Christian tradition which forbade burials within the walls, and became the final resting place of Augustine, Ethelbert and successive archbishops and kings of Kent, although no trace remains either of them or of the original Saxon church. Shortly after the Normans arrived, the church was demolished in the same building frenzy which saw the creation of the cathedral. It was replaced by a much larger abbey, most of which was destroyed in the Dissolution so that today only the ruins and foundations remain. To help bring the site to life, pick up an audio tour from the abbey's excellent interpretive centre.

Nearby, on the corner of North Holmes Road and St Martin's Lane is **St Martin's Church** (daily 9am–5pm excluding services; free), one of England's oldest churches, built on the site of a Roman villa or temple and used by the earliest Christians. Although medieval additions obscure the original Saxon structure, this is perhaps the earliest Christian site in Canterbury – it was here that Queen Bertha welcomed St Augustine in 597, and her husband King Ethelbert was baptized.

Along the High Street

For the most part, the **High Street** is lined with picturesque and ancient buildings – the view up Mercery Lane towards Christ Church Gate is one of the most photographed views in the city: a narrow, medieval street of crooked, overhanging houses behind which loom the turreted gatehouse and the cathedral's towers.

Just before High Street becomes St Peter's Street, you come to the **Royal Museum and Art Gallery** (Mon–Sat 10am–5pm; free), housed on the first floor of an awesome mock-Tudor building, with big wooden gables and a mosaic infilling between its timbers. There's lots of military memorabilia in the Buffs regimental gallery, which traces the history of the local regiment raised in Tudor times and merged in 1967. The art gallery is worth a quick perusal, with the odd Henry Moore and Gainsborough hidden among the local artists, and interesting temporary exhibitions in the Slater Gallery.

Where the street passes over a branch of the River Stour, stands **Eastbridge Hospital** (Mon–Sat 10am–4.45pm; £1), founded in the twelfth century to provide poor pilgrims with shelter. Downstairs is an exhibition on Chaucer's life, while storytellers in feudal garb recite parts of his book. Over the road is the wonky, half-timbered **Weavers' House**, built around 1500 and now a café, this was once inhabited by Huguenot textile workers who had been offered religious asylum in post-Reformation England.

St Peter's Street terminates at the two massive crenellated towers of the medieval **West Gate**, between which local buses just manage to squeeze. The only one of the town's seven city gates to have survived intact, its prison cells and guard chambers house a small **museum** (Mon–Sat 11am–12.30pm &

1.30–3.30pm; £1; @www.canterbury-museums.co.uk), which displays contemporary armaments and weaponry used by the medieval city guard, as well as giving access to the battlements. In fine weather, you can take a forty-minute trip on a **chauffeured punt** (£6/person; minimum charge £15/boat) along the gentle River Stour from the nearby bridge.

The Roman Museum, The Canterbury Tales and the Heritage Museum

The redevelopment of the Longmarket area (situated between Burgate and the High St) in the early 1990s exposed Roman foundations and mosaics that are now part of the **Roman Museum** (summer Mon–Sat 10am–5pm, Sun 1.30–5pm; rest of year closed Sun; £2.50; @www.canterbury-museum.co.uk). The extant remnants of the larger building are pretty dull, and better mosaics can be seen at Lullingstone (see p.211), but the display of recovered artefacts and general scenes of the museum are tasteful, with Roman domestic scenes re-created, as well as a computer-generated view of Durovernum.

Turning in the other direction down St Margaret's Street leads to the former church that's now **The Canterbury Tales** (daily: mid-Feb to June, Sept & Oct 10am–5pm; July & Aug 9.30am–5.30pm; Nov to mid-Feb 10am–4.30pm; £5.90; @www.canterburytales.org.uk), a quasi-educational show based on Geoffrey Chaucer's book, which lays claim to being the first original work of English literature ever to be printed. Equipped with a headset, visitors set off on a wander through mildly odour-enhanced galleries in which mannequins occupy idealized fourteenth-century tableaux and recount five of Chaucer's tales.

Genuinely educational and better value is **Canterbury Heritage Museum**, round the corner in Stour Street (June–Oct Mon–Sat 10.30am–5pm, Sun 1.30–5pm; Nov–May Mon–Sat 10.30am–5pm; £1.90; @www.canterbury-museums.co.uk), an interactive exhibition spanning local history from the splendour of Durovernum through to the more recent literary figures of Joseph Conrad (buried in the cemetery on London Road) and local-born Mary Tourtel, creator of the check-trousered philanthropist Rupert Bear. An excellent thirty-minute video on the Becket story details the intriguing personalities and events that led up to his assassination, presenting Becket as an overbearing and unpopular figure whose genuine piety was only recognized after his death.

Eating and drinking

The combination of a large student population and the tourist trade means Canterbury has a good selection of places to eat and drink, with many **restaurants** and **pubs** in genuinely old settings. However, the Church, which owns much of the city within the walls, keeps a tight rein on any wanton revelry and, bar the odd, agonized yelp of an over-intoxicated student, at night all is as quiet as Becket's tomb.

Snacks

Café St Pierre 41 St Peter's St. Excellent French patisserie and bakery with tables inside and out on the pavement and garden when the weather's fine.

Caffe Venezia 60–61 Palace St. Spacious self-service Italian café with decent sandwiches, pasta dishes, pizza slices and good coffee.

Whittard St Peter's St. Specialist tea and coffee vendor opposite the Eastbridge Hospital with plenty of pavement tables for watching Canterbury's world go by.

Restaurants

Alberry's St Margaret's St ☎01227/452378. Just up from the tourist office, this lively wine bar has good snacks and a range of more substantial meals, including various pastas, fish and meat dishes. Moderate.

Bankokj House 13 Church St ☎01227/471141. Excellent, well-presented Thai fare with spices adjusted to suit every palate in this small restaurant near St Augustine's Abbey. Closed Mon. Inexpensive.

Café des Amis du Mexique 95 St Dunstan's St ☎01227/464390. Very popular authentic Mexican eatery close to Westgate; try the sizzling chicken *fajitas* or the delicious paella followed by a bubbling chocolate *fondido*. "Phenomenally hot" habanero chiles are only for the brave. Moderate.

Chaopraya River 2 Dover St ☎01227/462876. The refined delights of Thai cuisine at a reasonable price – the *Nua pud naman hoy*, beef marinated in oyster sauce and served sizzling with mushrooms, baby corn and spring onions, is delicious. Closed Mon. Inexpensive.

Flap Jacques 71 Castle St ☎01227/781000. Homely little French bistro offering *moules*, *frites* and Breton pancakes. Live music Sun lunch and most evenings. Inexpensive to moderate.

Oranges 18 St Peter's St ☎01227/464227. Converted pub given a breath of fresh Mediterranean air, polished pine and sunny colours, and offering imaginative Med cooking, too. Inexpensive to moderate.

Tapas en las Trece 13 Palace St ☎01227 /762637. Tasty Spanish tapas at around £4–5 a dish and a special lunch menu at £4.95. Occasional live music. Inexpensive.

Tuo e Mio 16 The Borough ☎01227/761471. Long-established restaurant offering classy Italian dishes, a range of pizzas and some delicious, home-made desserts. Moderate.

Il Vaticano 35 St Margaret's St ☎01227/765333. A pleasant pasta bar, with a few other basic Italian dishes. Moderate.

Pubs and bars

Bell & Crown 10 Palace St. Authentic and cramped medieval hostelry.

The Bishop's Finger 13 St Dunstan's St. Popular wood-panelled bar just through the West Gate with a fine range of ales and a patio suntrap.

Canterbury Tales 12 The Friars. Marble-top bar and lots of polished wood in this tidy little pub opposite the Marlowe Theatre. Nachos and BLTs on the bar menu.

Casey's 5 Butchery Lane. Cosy, low-ceilinged Irish pub serving oysters and soda bread and other pub grub, with occasional live Irish music.

Miller's Arms Mill Lane. A pleasant waterside spot for a summertime pint whose splendid bar snacks and meals ensure its continued popularity.

New Inn on the corner of Havelock St, off Broad St ring road. One of Canterbury's tiniest pubs, this converted terraced house is popular with students and locals and offers a decent selection of real ale.

Simple Simon's Radigund's Hall, 3 Church Lane. Old hostelry that's popular with the university and King's School crowd; occasional live music.

Nightlife

Nightlife in Canterbury keeps a low profile – check out what's happening in the free *The Sticks* **listings magazine** available at the tourist office. Opposite Canterbury East station there are two **nightclubs** in the same building: the *Works*, which is a bit of a meat market, and the more civilized *Bizz*, appealing to the over-30s. On the other side of town, the university puts on a good range of arty **films** (Wed–Fri during term-time) – for details of what's on, call in at Forwood's Music, 35–37 Palace St, where you can also buy a ticket in advance – and has the best **live music**. There are more commercial celluloid offerings at the ABC, a two-screen cinema on St George's Place by the ring road. The university also houses the **Gulbenkian Theatre**, a venue which shares the city's more edifying cultural events with the **Marlowe Theatre** – named after the sixteenth century Canterbury-born playwright – in The Friars. In Northgate, the Penny Theatre presents local and global **live music**. Finally, there's the **Canterbury Festival**, an international potpourri of music, theatre and arts worth catching if you're in the area in the middle two weeks of October.

The Channel Ports: Sandwich to Folkestone

Dover, just 21 miles from mainland Europe (Calais' low cliffs are visible on a clear day), is the southeast's principal cross-Channel port. As a town it is not immensely appealing, even though its key position has left it with a clutch of historic attractions. To the north lie **Sandwich**, once the most important of the Cinque Ports but now no longer even on the coast, and the pleasant resort towns of **Deal** and **Walmer**, each with its own set of distinctive fortifications as well as a smattering of traditional seaside B&Bs. Sadly, **Folkestone**, Kent's second major port, seven miles southwest of Dover, is even more forlorn than its neighbour.

There are frequent **train** and **bus** connections to both the main Channel ports during the day – trains leave from London Victoria and Charing Cross, buses from London Victoria. A useful branch-line offers train connections from Dover up the coast to Walmer, Deal and Sandwich and on to Ramsgate. However, if you arrive by ferry at Dover late in the evening you'll be stuck in town whether you like it or not – the last direct train service leaves for London at 10pm.

Sandwich and around

SANDWICH, situated on the River Stour four miles north of Deal, is best known nowadays for giving rise to England's favourite culinary contribution when, in 1762, the Fourth Earl of Sandwich, passionately absorbed in a game of cards, ate his meat between two bits of bread for a quick snack. Aside from this incident, the town's main interest lies in its maritime connections – it was chief among the Cinque Ports (see box below) until the Stour silted up. Unlike other former harbour inlets, however, the Stour hasn't silted up completely and still flows through town, its grassy willow-lined banks adding to the once great medieval port's present charm.

By the bridge over the Stour stands Sandwich's best-known feature, the six-teenth-century **Barbican**, a stone gateway decorated with chequerwork,

---

The Cinque Ports

In 1278 Dover, Hythe, Sandwich, New Romney and Hastings – already part of a long-established but unofficial confederation of defensive coastal settlements – were formalized under Edward I's charter as the **Cinque Ports** (pronounced "sink", despite its French origin). In return for providing England with maritime support when necessary, chiefly in the transportation of troops and supplies to the Continent during times of war, the five ports were given trading privileges and other liberties, which enabled them to prosper while neighbouring ports struggled to survive. Some took advantage of this during peacetime, boosting their wealth by various nefarious activities such as piracy and the smuggling of tax-free contraband.

Later, Rye and Winchelsea were added to the confederation along with several other "limb" ports on the southeast coast which joined up at various times. The confederation continued until 1685, when the ports' privileges were revoked. Their maritime services were no longer necessary as Henry VIII had founded a professional navy and, due to a shifting coastline, several of the ports' harbours had silted up anyway. Nowadays, only Dover is still a major working port, though the post of Lord Warden of the Cinque Ports still exists. This honorary title, bestowed by the presiding monarch, is currently held by the Queen Mother.

where tolls were once collected. Running parallel to the river is **Strand Street**, whose crooked half-timbered facades front antique shops and private homes while, back in the town centre, another fine sixteenth century edifice, the **Guildhall**, houses both the tourist office (see below) and a small **museum** recounting the town's history (April–Sept Tues, Wed & Fri 10.30am–12.30pm & 2–4pm, Thurs & Sat 10.30am–4pm, Sun 2–4pm; Oct to mid-Dec & March Tues, Wed, Fri & Sun 2–4pm, Thurs & Sat 10.30am–4pm; £1). The genteel town is separated from the sandy beaches of Sandwich Bay by the **Royal St George Golf Course** – frequent venue of the British Open tournament – and a mile of nature reserves. The reserve that most ornithologists make for is the **Gazen Salts Nature Reserve** – renowned for its diversity of seabirds – three miles north of town, across the Stour.

Overlooking the doleful expanse of Pegwell Bay, two miles northwest of Sandwich, is **Richborough Fort** (April–Sept daily 10am–6pm; Oct daily 10am–5pm; Nov–Feb Sat & Sun 10am–4pm; March Wed–Sun 10am–4pm; £2.70; EH; ⓦwww.english-heritage.org.uk), one of the earliest coastal strongholds built by the Romans along what later became known as the Saxon Shore on account of the frequent raids by the Germanic tribe. Like Reculver (see p.183), it guarded the southern entrance to the Wantsum Channel, which then isolated the Isle of Thanet from the mainland. Rumour has it that Emperor Claudius, on his way to London, once rode on an elephant through a triumphal arch erected inside the castle, but all that remains within the well-preserved Roman walls are the relics of an early Saxon church. Richborough's historical significance far outshines its present appearance, especially as Pegwell Bay is now blighted by an ugly chemical works. The nicest way of reaching the fort is to take a **boat trip** up the Stour from Sandwich Quay (ⓣ01304 /820171; £4).

Finding **accommodation** in Sandwich shouldn't be much of a problem – the local **tourist office**, housed in the Guildhall (May–Sept daily 10am–4pm; ⓣ01304/613565, ⓦwww.whitecliffscountry.org.uk), will provide you with a list of local **hotels** and **guest houses**. The golfers' choice, the *Bell Hotel* on The Quay by the Barbican (ⓣ01304/613388, ⓦwww.hotelworld.com; ❻), is out of most people's range – though its weekend deals are good value; the en-suite rooms at the old coaching inn, the *Fleur de Lis*, near the Guildhall at 6–8 Delf St (ⓣ01304/611131, ⓦwww.verinitaverns.co.uk/fleurdelis/hotel.htm; ❹), are more affordable; or try the modest *Le Trayas* bungalow, Poulders Rd (ⓣ01304 /611056, ⓔfreespace.virgin.net/le.trayas; ❶), a ten-minute walk from The Quay. If you don't mind being a bit further out of town, try the *St Crispin Inn*, an attractive fifteenth-century pub in the village of Worth, a couple of miles south of Sandwich (ⓣ01304/612081; ❹). Your best choice for top-class **food** is the pricey *Fishermans Wharf* on the quayside (ⓣ01304/613636), which serves excellent seafood; for something less expensive try one of the pubs by the Barbican or *The Haven*, 20a King St, for good coffee, snacks and light meals. For the definitive Sandwich sandwich, head for the twee *Little Cottage Tearooms*, on The Quay.

Deal and around

One of the most unusual of Henry VIII's forts is the diminutive castle at **DEAL**, six miles southeast of Sandwich and site of Julius Caesar's first successful landfall in Britain in 55 BC. The **castle** (April–Sept daily 10am–6pm; Oct daily 10am–5pm; Nov–March Wed–Sun 10am–4pm; £3.10; EH) is situated off the Strand at the south end of town. Its unusual shape – viewed from the air it looks like a Tudor rose – is as much an affectation as a defensive design, though the premise was that the rounded walls would be better at deflecting missiles; inside, the comprehensive display on the other similar forts built during Henry VIII's reign is well worth a visit. Much more recently, the town was the focal point of Kent's small-scale coal industry, until the pits were closed during the bitterly fought downsizing of the 1980s.

Another aspect of Deal's history is reflected by the **Maritime Museum** (April–Sept Mon–Sat 2–5pm; £1.50) in St George's Road, just around the corner from the tourist office, a mildly interesting look at the town's seafaring past, containing both real and model boats, relics from ships and tales of the destructive powers of the Goodwin Sands. Out on the seafront, at the corner with Sondes Road, stands a real oddity, the **Timeball Tower** (July & Aug Tues–Sun 10am–5pm; £1.25), a four-storey pink-faced building which began life as a shutter telegraph during the Napoleonic Wars. Following the Wars' end in 1815 it was reconstructed as a semaphore tower aimed at catching smugglers. Yet again, in 1853, the tower was converted to house a giant timeball surmounted by a cross, large enough to be visible from ships at sea, which drops from the roof at exactly 1pm in summer, so providing an accurate time check in the days before radio. The ball still drops regularly and the building also houses a small museum of horology and telegraphy.

Deal's **tourist office** is situated in the town hall on High Street near the sea (mid-May to mid-Sept Mon–Fri 9am–5pm, Sat 10am–4pm; rest of year Mon–Fri 9am–12.30pm & 1.30–5pm; ☎01304/369576, ⓦwhitecliffs country.org.uk). There's a whole host of places offering **accommodation** on Beach Street: try the winsome *King's Head* pub at no. 9 (☎01304/368194; ❸), or the nearby town house of *Channel View* at no. 17 (☎01304/368194; ❸), run by the same proprietor. Another option is *Dunkerley's*, next door at no. 19 (☎01304/375016, ⓦwww.dunkerleys.co.uk; ❻), whose **restaurant** is possibly Deal's finest (and priciest). For more reasonably priced seafood try the *Lobster Pot* (☎01304/374713) on Beach Road, opposite the pier.

Walmer Castle

A mile south of Deal **Walmer Castle** (April–Sept daily 10am–6pm; Oct daily 10am–5pm; Nov, Dec & March Wed–Sun 10am–4pm; Feb Sat & Sun 10am–4pm; £4.80; EH) is another rotund Tudor-rose-shaped affair, commissioned when the castle became the official residence of the Lord Warden of the Cinque Ports in 1730. Now it resembles a heavily fortified stately home more than a military stronghold. The best-known resident was the Duke of Wellington, who died here in 1842, and not surprisingly, the house is devoted primarily to his life and times. Busts and portraits of the Iron Duke crowd the rooms and corridors, where you'll also find the armchair in which he expired and the original Wellington boots in which he triumphed at Waterloo. The castle's terraced gardens, overlooking the channel, are a good spot for a picnic, or you can have afternoon tea in The Lord Warden's Tearooms (April–Oct daily; Nov–March Sun).

To get to Walmer Castle from Deal, you can either catch one of the hourly buses or, if the weather's good, make the pleasant walk along the seafront (45min).

Dover

Badly bombed during the war **DOVER**'s town centre and seafront just don't have what it takes to induce many travellers to linger before speeding onwards to Europe, or inland to London or Canterbury. That said, the town authorities have put a lot of effort and money into sprucing the place up, particularly the

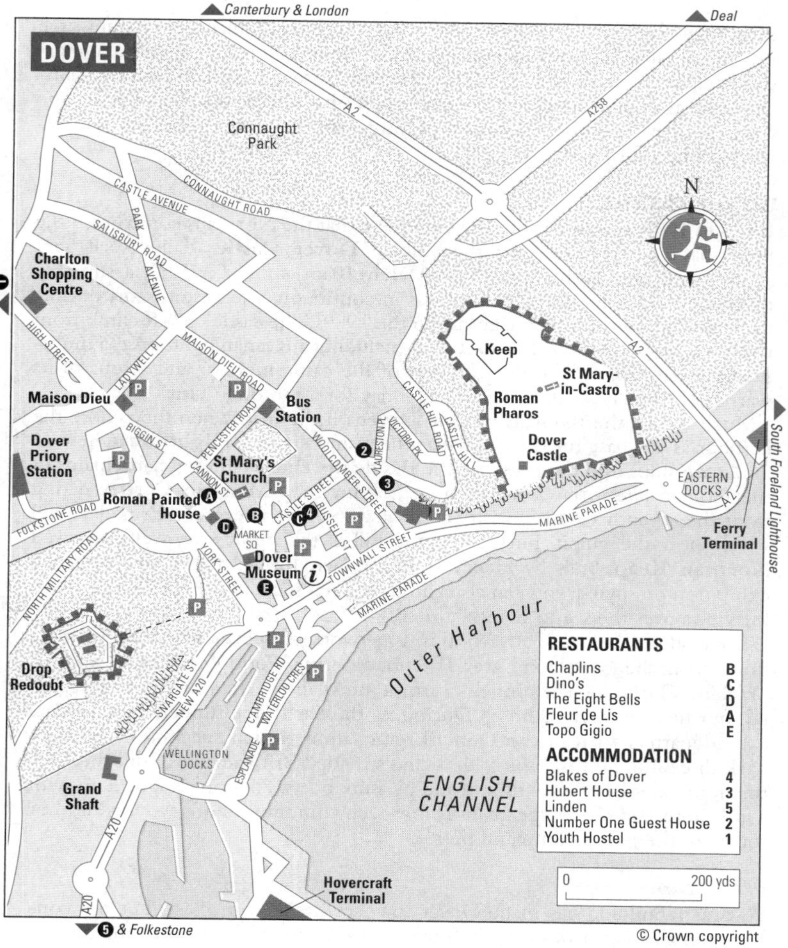
DOVER
Canterbury & London
Deal
Connaught Park
A2
A258
CASTLE AVENUE
CONNAUGHT ROAD
SALISBURY ROAD
PARK AVENUE
Charlton Shopping Centre
1
HIGH STREET
MAISON DIEU ROAD
LADYWELL PL
Maison Dieu
Bus Station
Keep
St Mary-in-Castro
Roman Pharos
Dover Castle
CASTLE HILL ROAD
CASTLE HILL
VICTORIA PK
LAURESTON PL
WOOLCOMBER STREET
Dover Priory Station
BIGGIN ST
PENCESTER ROAD
CANNON ST
St Mary's Church
Roman Painted House
CASTLE STREET
RUSSELL ST
MARKET SQ
Dover Museum
FOLKSTONE ROAD
YORK STREET
TOWNWALL STREET
MARINE PARADE
EASTERN DOCKS
Ferry Terminal
South Foreland Lighthouse
NORTH MILITARY ROAD
Drop Redoubt
SNARGATE ST
NEW A20
CAMBRIDGE RD
WATERLOO CRES
ESPLANADE
WELLINGTON DOCKS
Outer Harbour
ENGLISH CHANNEL
Grand Shaft
A20
Hovercraft Terminal
5 & Folkestone
N
RESTAURANTS
Chaplins B
Dino's C
The Eight Bells D
Fleur de Lis A
Topo Gigio E
ACCOMMODATION
Blakes of Dover 4
Hubert House 3
Linden 5
Number One Guest House 2
Youth Hostel 1
0 200 yds

© Crown copyright

Cross-channel transport services from Dover and Folkestone

Dover Eastern Docks to Calais: P&O Stena Line (30 daily; journey time 1hr 15min); Seafrance (15 daily, journey time 1hr 30min).
Dover Eastern Docks to Zeebrugge: P&O Stena Line (3–4 daily; journey time 4hr).
Dover Western Docks to Calais: Hoverspeed (10 daily; journey time 40min).
Dover Western Docks to Ostend: Hoverspeed (July–Sept 3 daily; journey time 2hr).
Folkestone to Calais: Eurotunnel (up to 4 hourly; journey time 35min).

Reservations: Eurotunnel ⓣ08705/353535, ⓦwww.eurotunnel.co.uk; Hoverspeed ⓣ08705/240241, ⓦwww.hoverspeed.com; P&O Stena Line ⓣ08706/000600, ⓦwww.posl.com; SeaFrance ⓣ08705/711711, ⓦwww.seafrance.com.

early Victorian New Bridge development along the Esplanade. Despite such valiant attempts, **Dover Castle** is still by far the most interesting of the numerous attractions which plug the port's defensive history. Entertainment of a saltier nature is offered by Dover's legendary **White Cliffs**, which dominate the town and have long been a source of inspiration for lovers, travellers and soldiers sailing off to war.

Dover Castle

It was in 1168, a century after the Conquest, that the Normans constructed the keep that now presides over the bulk of **Dover Castle** (daily: April–Sept 10am–6pm; Oct 10am–5pm; Nov–March 10am–4pm; £7; EH), a superbly positioned defensive complex that was in continuous use as some sort of military installation from then right up to the 1980s. The castle's stiff climb from the town centre, and there's a lot to see, including a Roman lighthouse, a multimedia re-creation of the French siege of the castle in 1216 and a tour of its warren of tunnels, so allow up to half a day for a thorough visit.

Much earlier, the Romans had put Dover on the map when they chose the harbour as the base for their northern fleet, and erected a **lighthouse** here to guide the ships into the river mouth. Beside the chunky hexagonal remains of the Roman *pharos* stands a Saxon-built church, **St Mary-in-Castro**, dating from the seventh century, with motifs graffitied by irreverent Crusaders still visible near the pulpit. Further up the hill is the impressive, well-preserved **Norman Keep**, built by Henry II as a palace. Inside, there's an interactive exhibition on spying; you can also climb its spiral stairs to the lofty battlements for views over the sea to France.

The castle's other main attraction is its network of **Secret Wartime Tunnels** dug during the Napoleonic war. Extended during World War II, you can tour "Hellfire Corner" – the tunnels' wartime nickname – on a fifty-minute guided tour (leaving every 20min). During World War II, the tunnels were used as a headquarters to plan the Dunkirk evacuation, which successfully brought back three hundred and thirty thousand stranded British troops from the continent in a flotilla of local fishing and pleasure boats. The tour is spiced up with a little gore, and reveals the quaintly low-tech communications systems and war rooms of the navy's command post.

The Town

Postwar rebuilding has made Dover town centre a grim place, but the construction of a car park on New Street in 1970 did at least lead to the discovery of an ancient guest house. The **Roman Painted House** (April–Sept Tues–Sun 10am–5pm; £2), once a hotel for official guests, possesses some reasonable Roman wall paintings, the remains of an underground Roman heating system and some mosaics – it's worth a look if you've some time to kill. The nearby **Dover Museum** on the Market Square (daily: April–Oct 10am–6pm; Nov–March 10am–5.30pm; £1.75; ⊛ www.dovermuseum.co.uk) has three floors packed with informative displays on Dover's past, including a restored Bronze Age boat discovered in the town in 1992 – and a stuffed polar bear.

As you walk along pedestrianized Cannon Street, the main shopping street, you pass **St Mary's Church**, Victorian for the most part, but of Norman origin as the tower makes clear. Further up the road in Biggin Street, there's another very ancient building, the **Maison Dieu**, founded in the thirteenth century as a place for pilgrims en route to Canterbury. After the Reformation, it was turned into a naval storehouse, and in the last century became part of the town hall. The Stone Hall, with its fine timber roof, dates from 1253; the neighbouring neo-Gothic Connaught Hall and the Council Chamber upstairs are the work of the great Victorian architects Poynter and Burges.

The high ground to the west of town, originally the site of a Napoleonic-era fortress, retains one interesting oddity, the **Grand Shaft** (July & Aug Tues–Sun 2–5pm; £1.25), a 140-foot triple staircase, entered on Snargate Street (opposite the Hoverport access road) by which troops could go down at speed to defend the port in case of attack.

Dover's cliffs

As the first and last sight of England for travellers throughout the centuries, the **white cliffs of Dover** hold a complex role in the English psyche. Matthew Arnold invoked their massive grandeur in his famous elegy for a lost time, *Dover Beach*, written in the 1860s. Today, the beach has little of the romance invested in the spot by Arnold, but the cliffs flanking the town retain their majesty, even if pollution has taken some of the edge off their whiteness. The best views, of course, are to be had from several miles out to sea and **boats** leave hourly from De Bradelei Wharf in Dover Marina (hourly; £5; ⓦwww .whitecliffsboattours.co.uk), but an alternative vantage point on land is the Prince of Wales pier in the harbour.

There are some great **walks** to be had along the cliffs themselves. To reach **Shakespeare Cliff**, catch bus #D2A from Worthington Street towards Aycliff. Alternatively, there's a steep two-and-a-half-mile climb to Shakespeare Cliff from North Military Road, off York Street, taking you by the **Western Heights**, a series of defensive battlements built into the cliff in the nineteenth century. From here there is a sweeping panorama of the Straits of Dover – the world's busiest shipping lanes – and a bird's-eye view of the harbour and the surrounding cliffs. It's even possible to catch a glimpse of France on a clear day.

At Langdon Cliffs is the recently constructed **Gateway to the White Cliffs** (daily: March–Oct 10am–5pm; Nov–Feb 11am–4pm; free; NT), a purpose-built centre whose excellent displays explain the ecology and history of the local coast and countryside. There's a coffee shop here too and regular countryside events and guided walks (ⓣ01304/202756). An exhilarating two-mile walk from here takes you above the Eastern Docks towards St Margaret's Bay and the **South Foreland Lighthouse** (March–Oct Mon & Thurs–Sun 11am–5.30pm; £1.80; NT). This Victorian construction, that looks somewhat like a minaret, was built to warn shipping off the dangerous Goodwin Sands; it was also where Marconi conducted his first ship-to-shore radio experiments in 1898.

Practicalities

There are frequent train services from both Charing Cross and Victoria stations in London to Dover Priory **train station**, situated off Folkestone Road, a ten-minute walk west of the centre; there are regular shuttle buses to the Eastern Docks, but none to the Western Docks. Buses from London (hourly; 2hr 30min) run to the Eastern Docks and the town-centre **bus station** on Pencester Road.

The **tourist office**, in the town centre underneath the high-rise *County Hotel* on Townwall Street (daily: July & Aug 8am–7.30pm; rest of year 9am–6pm; ⓣ01304/205108, ⓦwww.whitecliffscountry.org.uk), can advise about accommodation, which is plentiful. It also has a free *White Cliffs Trails* pamphlet that outlines many good walks near Dover, both coastal and inland. **Bikes** can be rented from Andy's Shop, 156 London Rd (ⓣ01304/204401).

The biggest concentration of small **hotels and B&Bs** is to be found on the Folkestone Road, close to Priory station, but the ones around the base of Castle Hill Road on the other side of town are generally nicer. *Hubert House*, 9 Castle Hill Rd (℡01304/202253; ❷), is a friendly B&B, convenient for the Eastern Dock, as is the good-value *Number One Guesthouse*, opposite, at 1 Castle St (℡01304/202007, ⓦwww.number1guesthouse.co.uk; ❷). *Blakes of Dover*, further up at no. 52 (℡01304/202194, ⓔblakes-of-dover@activebooking.com; ❸), is a lovely wood-panelled wine bar, restaurant and hotel with a genial owner; *Linden*, at no. 231 (℡01304/205449, ⓔlindenrog@aol.com;❷), is one of the better B&Bs along the Folkestone Road. There's a very busy **youth hostel** in a listed Georgian house at 306 London Rd (℡01304/201314, ⓔdover @yha.org.uk), a mile up the High Street from Dover Priory station. The most convenient **campsite** is *Hawthorn Farm* (℡01304/852658; closed Dec–Feb) close to Martin Mill train station, one stop up the line towards Ramsgate.

Given the town's uninspiring appearance, Dover's **pubs** are surprisingly characterful, although the town gets a rather rough reputation from its shift-workers servicing the docks and ferries. There are two decent pubs near the town hall: *Park Inn*, a big old place on Park Street with plenty of real ales, and the *Prince Albert*, on the corner of Biggin Street and Priory Road. *The White Horse* is a nice old eighteenth-century pub at the foot of the castle. Dover's culinary offerings are poor, though *Chaplins*, 2 Church St, serves excellent value **lunches** and probably the town's best coffee. Alternatively, there's **pub food** at *The Eight Bells*, a big Wetherspoon's pub on Cannon St. Despite its garish exterior, *Topo Gigio*, 1–2 King St (℡01304/201048), offers acceptable and inexpensive Italian food, as does *Dino's*, 58 Castle St (℡01304/204678). The French restaurant, *Fleur-de-Lis*, at 10 Effingham Crescent (℡01304/240224; eve only, closed Sun), is the best place in town, though it is quite pricey. For more on the local **nightlife**, pick up the free monthly *What's On* leaflet from the tourist office.

Folkestone

Seven miles down the coast from Dover, **FOLKESTONE** started life as a fishing village and rose to prominence as a resort in the nineteenth century, when the grandiose terraces which still dominate the town were built. In theory, Folkestone, with its narrow cobbled streets and cliff-top marine promenade, should be a more appealing place than, say, Dover, but the truth is that, rather like the Channel Tunnel itself, the good times seem to have passed Folkestone by.

Aside from the **Folkestone Museum and Art Gallery** on Grace Hill (Mon, Tues & Thurs 9.30am–6pm; Wed & Sat 9.30am–5pm, Fri 9.30am–7pm; free; ⓦwww.kent-museums.org.uk/folkston.html), whose main virtue is that it's free, Folkestone's only major tourist attraction is the **Russian Submarine**, *U-475 Foxtrot* (daily 10am–dusk; £3.95), docked at the South Quay, beside the former Hoverspeed terminal. This Soviet sub carried nuclear weapons and could operate at a depth of 250 yards, making it almost impossible to detect. Very little has been altered inside which means that visitors must be prepared to squeeze through numerous awkward hatches and claustrophobes should stay away.

The Victorian **Leas Lift**, to the west along the run-down Marine Parade (Easter–Sept daily 9am–6pm; Oct–Easter Sun 9am–5pm; 50p), will transport you to **The Leas**, the town's justly famous marine promenade. It's worth persevering to the far end of the Leas to admire the fantastically ornate red-brick and terracotta Metropole Hotel, and its architectural cousin and neighbour, the Grand – sadly neither function as hotels any more, though the Metropole now houses an **arts centre and gallery** (April–Oct Mon–Sat 10am–5pm, Sun 2.30–5pm; Nov–March Tues–Sat 10am–4pm, Sun 2.30–5pm).

Up on Folkestone's East Cliff is **Martello Tower No. 3** (Easter–Sept daily 10.30am–5pm; £1), one of 74 similar towers along this stretch of coast, about which you can learn more from the tower's small exhibition (see also p.204). Further east along the cliffs, at Capel-le-Ferne on the B2011, you should be able to spot the new **Battle of Britain Memorial**, a giant seated figure of an RAF pilot gazing out to sea, with the various squadron badges carved onto the sandstone base. Those with a further interest in the subject should head three miles inland on the A260 to the **Kent Battle of Britain Museum** (Easter–Sept daily 10am–5pm; Oct daily 11am–4pm; £3; ⓦ www.kbobm.org), at Hawkinge airfield, where several hangars house World War II memorabilia, including a crashed Messerschmitt and replica Spitfires and Hurricanes.

Practicalities

Thanks to competition from the Channel Tunnel, passenger **ferries** are no longer running from Folkestone harbour. **Eurostar passengers** for Paris and Brussels can climb aboard at the pompously named Ashford International train station, just up the line from Folkestone Central **train station**, fifteen minutes' walk northwest of Folkstone town centre, off Cheriton Road. National Express **coaches** to London leave from the **bus station** on Bouverie Square, a short distance west of the pedestrianized shopping streets.

The **tourist office** is in a public car park at the junction of Tontine Street and The Tram Road, near the quayside (daily: July & Aug 9am–7pm; rest of year Mon–Sat 9am–5.30pm, Sun 9am–1pm & 2–4pm; ☎01303/258594, ⓦ www.kents-garden-coast.co.uk). For **overnight** stays, the nicest part of town is to the west along the Leas, which were once patrolled by the local Lord Radnor's own police force. The red-brick and terracotta *Burlington Hotel*, Earls Ave (☎01303/255301; ❺), and the *Chilton House Hotel*, 14–15 Marine Parade (☎01303/249786, ⓔchiltonhousehotel@freenetname.co.uk; ❶), with very reasonably priced en-suite rooms, are the best among the scores of hotels and B&Bs. If you fancy proximity to the sea, then try the *Sandgate Hotel*, The Esplanade (☎01303/220444; ❷), slap bang on the front in Sandgate, a couple of miles towards Hythe; it also has its own excellent French restaurant, *La Terrasse*. The *Guildhall*, in the old town on The Bayle, is a pleasant **pub** to relax in; for **food**, head to the excellent and reasonably priced Italian, *Osteria Posillipo*, 18 Rendezvous St, at the top of the Old High Street (☎01303 /246666; closed Tues), or the expensive but exquisite *Paul's*, 2a Bouverie Road West (☎01303/259697) for Modern-British cuisine.

Hythe to Dungeness: the Romney and Denge marshes

In Roman times, the **Romney and Denge marshes** – now the southern-most part of Kent – were submerged beneath the English Channel. Then the lowering of the sea levels in the Middle Ages and later reclamation created a forty-square-mile area of shingle and marshland which, until the nineteenth century, was afflicted by malaria and various other malaises. Contrasting strong-ly with the wooded pastures of Kent's interior, the sheep-speckled marshes have an eerie, forlorn appearance, as if still unassimilated with the mainland and haunted by their maritime origins. The ancient town of **Hythe** is on the eastern edge of the reclaimed marshes and is linked with Rye in East Sussex (see p.217), on the marsh's western edge, by the arc of the twenty-three-mile Napoleonic-era **Royal Military Canal**.

Hythe and Lympne

Separated from Folkestone by the massive earthworks of the Channel Tunnel, **HYTHE** is a sedate seaside resort bisected by the disused waterway of the Royal Military Canal, which was built as a defensive obstacle during the perceived threat of Napoleonic invasion. Hythe's receding shoreline reduced its usefulness as a port and the nearby coast is now just a sweep of beach punctuated by **Martello Towers**, part of the chain of 74 such towers built along the south and east coasts in the early nineteenth century as a defence against potential French invasion.

The nicest part of Hythe is not the seafront, but the old town, and in particular the quiet back alleys to the north of the High Street. To give purpose to your wandering, follow the signs to the macabre collection of various ancient bones and skulls in the **crypt** (May–Sept Mon–Sat 10.30am–noon & 2.30–4pm; 50p) of the eleventh-century St Leonard's Church. A ride on the world's largest toy train – or smallest public railway – the **Romney, Hythe and Dymchurch Railway** (R, H & DR), a fifteen-inch-gauge line which runs the fourteen miles from Hythe to Dungeness (Easter–Sept daily; March & Oct Sat & Sun; plus school holidays throughout the year; ☎01797/362353, ⓦwww.rhdr.demon.co.uk), is also a must. Built in the 1920s as a tourist attraction linking the resorts along the shore, its fleet of steam locomotives – mainly one-third scale models from the Twenties and Thirties – are now maintained by volunteers. The station is to the west of the town centre, on the south bank of the canal by Station Bridge. The price of a return ticket from Hythe to Dungeness is £9.20.

LYMPNE (pronounced "lim"), set on top of a rise that was once lapped by the sea, three and a half miles inland from Hythe, was the site of the Roman **Portus Lemanis**, which continued to be an important harbour until the Channel receded and stranded the settlement at its present location. Little remains of the Roman port, bar some stonework scattered at the foot of the hill, but on top of the hill, offering fine views over the marshes, is a small Norman church and the much modified **Lympne Castle** (June to mid-Sept Mon–Thurs 10.30am–5.30pm; £2.50; ⓦwww.lympnecastle.co.uk), both built by Archbishop Lanfranc, the Norman architect of Canterbury's cathedral. The castle served as a residence for later archbishops, and retains its fourteenth-century Grand Hall. Two miles west of the castle, the overpriced **Howletts and Port Lympne Wild Animal Park** (daily: May–Sept 10am–7pm; Oct–April 10am–4pm, last admission 2hr before closing; £9.80; ⓦwww.howletts.co.uk) houses more than five hundred beasts, including gorillas, elephants, wolves, lions, tigers and rhinos.

Practicalities

Hythe's **tourist office** is, bizarrely, situated in the old public toilets in Red Lion Square (April–June & Sept daily 9am–5.30pm; July & Aug daily 9am–7pm; Oct–March Mon–Sat 9am–5.30pm, Sun 10am–4pm; ☎01303 /267799, ⓦwww.kents-garden-coast.co.uk). For **accommodation** check out the secluded *White House*, 27 Napier Gardens (☎01303/266252; ❸), overlooking the cricket green just a couple of minutes from the sea, the *Swan Hotel*, a friendly pub on the High Street (☎01303/266311; **①**), the Edwardian *Fern Lodge*, a mile east of the town centre at 87 Seabrook Rd (☎01303/267315; **②**), or if you've got more money to spend, the very superior *Hythe Imperial*, Prince's Parade (☎01303/267441, ⓦwww.marstonhotels. com; **③**). For high-class **fish and chips**, eat-in or takeaway, drop into *Torbay of Hythe*, 81 High St (closed Sun & Mon); alternatively, there's the *Capri*, 32–34 High St (☎01303/269898), which serves good pizzas and other **Italian dishes**.

Along the coast to Dungeness

The Romney, Hythe and Dymchurch Railway stops at five stations along the bleak stretch of coastline en route to Dungeness, the first of which is Dymchurch, a tacky seaside resort worth passing over in favour of the sandy strand of **St Mary's Bay**, an easy walk from the next station, **St Mary-in-the-Marsh**; if you need to stop for lunch, head for the excellent *Star* pub opposite the village church, not far from the station.

Next stop on the railway is one of the original Cinque Ports, **NEW ROM-NEY**, nine miles southwest of Hythe. It's now really only of interest to con-noisseurs of miniature railways, who will be enthralled by the R, H & DR's **Toy and Model Train Museum** (same days as the railway; 10am–5pm; £1) at New Romney station, halfway between the town and the seafront. There's a **tourist office** on Church Approach, just off the High Street (April–June & Sept daily 9am–5.30pm; July & Aug daily 9am–7pm; Oct–March Mon–Sat 9am–5.30pm, Sun 10am–4pm; ☎01797/364044, ⓦwww.kents-garden-coast.co.uk), where you'll also find the sixteenth-century *Cinque Ports Arms* (☎01797/361894; **③**), a nice-looking pub with inexpensive rooms; for some-thing a bit more special, head for *Romney Bay House* (☎01797/364747, ⓦwww.uk-travelguide.co.uk/rombayho.htm; **④**), a wonderfully secluded place to stay by the beach in neighbouring **LITTLESTONE-ON-SEA**.

Dungeness

DUNGENESS, six miles south of Romney and the southern terminus for the R, H & DR, is set in the sort of wasteland normally used as an army firing range, but in this case the former Atomic Energy Authority grabbed the tip of the Denge Marsh site and built a nuclear power station here in the 1960s. Ten minutes' walk from the station a **British Nuclear Fuels Visitor Centre** (guided tours only: April–Sept daily 10am, 11.30am, 1pm & 2.45pm; Oct–March Mon–Fri same times; free; ⓦwww.bnfl.com), with an upbeat "harness-ing nature's forces" message, even offers free reactor tours, which will probably only appeal to children (no under-5s), who'll enjoy wearing the yellow hard hats with retractable ear defenders. Another landmark you can visit, right by the station, is the **Old Lighthouse** (May–Sept daily 10.30am–5pm; March–April & Oct Sat & Sun 10.30am–5pm; £2.20), built in 1904 and the fourth one on the site since 1615 – the fifth and present one is visible half a mile away.

The spooky, shingle-swathed expanse of Dungeness has become the abode of eccentric and reclusive characters living in basic fishermen's cabins or disused railway carriages, apparently relishing the area's bleak austerity and carcino-genic threat. The barren environment of the Denge Marsh also supports a unique floral ecology and all around you'll see tiny communities of wildflow-ers struggling against the unrelenting breeze. If you follow the road back towards Lydd, past the two lighthouses, you will eventually come to **Prospect Cottage**, where the avant-garde film director, writer and artist, Derek Jarman, spent much of his time until his death in 1995 from AIDS. The cottage is still privately owned and not a tourist attraction as such, but a steady stream of pilgrims come here to pay their respects. The flotsam sculptures and unusual flora in the shingle garden make an eye-catching sight – as does the poem "The Sunne Rising" by John Donne, which adorns the southern wall – and were the subject of one of Jarman's last books, *The Garden* (1995).

A few houses up the road from Prospect Cottage, there's a traditional oak-fired smokery where you can buy delicious picnic fodder; alternatively, you can refuel at the unprepossessing but welcoming *Britannia* **pub**, which lies between the two lighthouses. The Dungeness shingle bank also attracts huge colonies of gulls and terns, as well as smews and gadwalls – if you're interested in finding out more, pop into the **RSPB visitor centre** (daily: March–Oct 10am–5pm; Nov–Feb 10am–4pm; £2.50), off the road from Dungeness to Lydd.

The Kent Weald

The Weald is usually taken to refer to the region around the spa town of **Royal Tunbridge Wells**, but in fact it stretches across a much larger area between the North and South Downs and includes parts of both Kent and Sussex, though the majority of its attractions are just inside Kent. We've taken the wider definition to include the medieval manor at **Penshurst** and nearby **Hever Castle**, just northeast of Tunbridge Wells, as well as the towns of **Sevenoaks** and **Maidstone**, on the edge of the North Downs.

During Saxon times, much of the Weald was covered in thick forest – the word itself derives from the Germanic word *Wald*, meaning forest, and the suffixes -hurst (meaning wood) and -den (meaning clearing) are commonly found in Wealden village names. Now, however, the region is epitomized by gentle hills, sunken country lanes and somnolent villages as well as some of England's most beautiful gardens – **Sissinghurst**, fifteen miles east of Tunbridge Wells, being the best known.

Public transport to the area is good, but in order to explore the Wealden countryside in any depth, you'll need your own vehicle. If you are driving or on a bicycle, you may want to follow the signs indicating the **High Weald Country Tour**, a seventy-mile back-country loop stretching through the best of the Kentish Weald, from Penshurst in the west to Tenterden in the east. Ask for the leaflet and map at tourist offices in the area.

Regular **trains** from London's Victoria, Waterloo East and Charing Cross stations run to Sevenoaks, Maidstone and Tunbridge Wells, and take under an hour. National Express operates several **bus** services daily to the above towns from Victoria Coach Station. Regional bus companies also run regular services from Victoria to the major Wealden towns as well as providing an adequate service between the major towns in Kent.

Royal Tunbridge Wells and around

ROYAL TUNBRIDGE WELLS – not to be confused with the more mundane Tonbridge, a few miles to the north – is the home of the mythical whingeing right-wing letter-writer known as "Disgusted of Tunbridge Wells". Most British people, therefore, view it with derision, but don't be misled – this prosperous spa town, surrounded by gorgeous countryside, is an elegant and diverting place, meriting a few hours' visit.

In 1606 Lord North discovered a bubbling spring while riding through the Waterdown Forest, which covered the area at that time. From the claim that this spring had curative properties a spa resort evolved: Charles I's wife camped out here for several weeks after giving birth to the future Charles II, whose own wife later came here in an attempt to cure her infertility. The spa reached its height of popularity during the Regency period when such restorative cures were in vogue. The distinctively well-mannered architecture of that period, generously surrounded by parklands in which the rejuvenated gentry exercised, gives the southern and western part of town its special character. The architecture also has an effect on the locals. If you turn up around the beginning of August, you'll find that many of the townsfolk have taken to the streets in eighteenth-century garb for the five-day **Georgian Festivities**.

The spa and the town

The icon of those genteel times, and the best place to start your wanderings, is the **Pantiles**, an elegant colonnaded parade of shops, ten minutes' walk south of the train station, where the fashionable once gathered to promenade and take the waters. The name stems from the chunky Kent tiles made of baked clay, which were put down as paving during Queen Anne's reign. Hub of the Pantiles is the original **Chalybeate Spring**, in the Bath House (Easter–Sept daily 10am–5pm), where a "Dipper" has been employed since the late eighteenth century to serve the ferrous waters. A period-dressed incumbent will fetch you a glass from the cool spring for 25p – or, if you bring your own cup, you can help yourself for free from the adjacent source. The Bath House itself was built in 1804, but failed as an enterprise as the water turns a nasty colour when heated; it closed in 1847 and now houses a pharmacy.

You can view one of the original Pantiles in the exhibition, **A Day at the Wells** (daily: April–Oct 10am–5pm; Nov–March 10am–4pm; £5.50; ⓦwww.heritageattractions.co.uk), situated in the basement of the nearby Corn Exchange. An audio tour, narrated as if by Richard "Beau" Nash – self-appointed arbiter of good taste (see box on p.406) – attempts to re-create, with the help of various historical tableaux, spa life in the eighteenth century. In bad weather, a stroll along the museum's reconstruction of the Pantiles might seem preferable to the real thing.

Apart from tiles, Tunbridge also produced domestic ceramics, on view with other local relics and historical artefacts in the **Museum and Art Gallery** built in the 1950s at the top of Mount Pleasant Road (Mon–Sat 9.30am–5pm; free; ⓦwww.tunbridgewells.gov.uk/museum), a fifteen-minute walk up the old-fashioned High Street, from the Pantiles. The museum's main attraction is a superb collection of locally made wooden boxes, known as "Tunbridge Ware", introduced in the 1830s, whose "mosaic-style" inlaid lids are decorated with rural scenes and ornamental borders. The gallery also puts on excellent temporary exhibitions in its one-room art gallery.

On the east side of the High Street, the Grove and, to the north, Calverley Grounds are havens of urban tranquillity, while **The Common**, spreading out on the west side of town, is laced with pathways carved by the original visitors to the spa. You can trace the course of the old horse-racing track, or simply sit among the strange sandstone formations of Wellington Rocks. If you fancy a more energetic scramble, head three miles west of Tunbridge Wells to **High Rocks** (daily 9am–6pm or dusk; £1), another fissured outcrop of towering rocks linked by stairways and bridges and bursting with rhododendrons; traces of a Neolithic settlement are also visible here.

Practicalities

The Tunbridge Wells **tourist office** is housed in the Old Fish Market, in the Pantiles (Mon–Sat 9am–6pm, Sun 10am–5pm; ℡01892/515675, Ⓦwww .heartofkent.org.uk) and will hand out a map of the town. The **train station**, on the London Charing Cross to Hastings line, is south of the town centre, where High Street becomes Mount Pleasant Road.

Tunbridge Wells has a fair number of very plush **hotels**, relics of the good old days, such as the exemplary *Royal Wells Inn*, overlooking the Common from Mount Ephraim (℡01892/511188, Ⓦwww.royalwells.co.uk;❺), and *The Swan Hotel*, a worthwhile splurge in the Pantiles itself (℡01892/543319, Ⓦwww .the-swan-hotel.com;❺). For **B&B** the elegant *Ephraim Lodge* on The Common (℡01892/523053; ❹), and the nearby *Clarken Guest House*, a large Victorian house with gardens at 61 Frant Rd (℡01892/533397, Ⓔbarry.kench@virgin .net; ❸), are both good value.

The town has a good selection of **restaurants**, one of the best (and most expensive) being *Thackeray's House*, one-time home of the writer, at 85 London Rd (℡01892/511921; closed Sun eve & Mon). At the other end of the cultural spectrum, there's *Gracelands Palace*, a Chinese restaurant on Cumberland Walk (℡01892/540754; closed Sun & Mon), with a live Chinese Elvis show. For top-notch seafood try *Sankey's* at 39 Mount Ephraim (℡01892/511422; main restaurant closed Sun) which also has a great selection of specialist beers in its cosy cellar wine bar. Apart from *Zapata's*, a Tex-Mex specialist on Union Square, at the far end of the Pantiles, the cheaper end of the market is dominated by the chains such as the reliable *Pizza Express*, with a branch at 81 High St. *Flippers*, 9 High St (closed Sun), fry superior fish and chips, while there are great veggie options both at the *Trinity Arts Centre Café* in a converted church on Church Road (lunch & pre-theatre deals only; closed Sun) and at *Continental Flavour*, 14 Mount Pleasant, a wholefood restaurant and shop (open daytime only).

One **pub** you're unlikely to miss is the popular *Opera House*, a Wetherspoon's conversion in the town's former 1902 theatre on Mount Pleasant Road – you can sit in the foyer, the stalls or even on stage and gaze up at the balconies. *Chaplins*, in the Pantiles, is much smaller and snug, as is the pleasant *Grape Vine* wine bar at 8 Chapel Place. For a cocktail or beer, check out the curiously named *Orson Welles* on Grove Hill Road or *Bar Zia* at the bottom of High St.

Penshurst and Hever Castle

Tudor timber-framed houses and shops line the high street of the attractive village of **PENSHURST**, five miles northwest of Tunbridge Wells (bus #231 or #233; not Sun). Its village church, **St John the Baptist**, is capped by an unusual four-spired tower and is entered under a beamed archway which conceals a rustic post office. However, the main reason for coming here is to visit **Penshurst Place** (March Sat & Sun noon–5.30pm; April–Oct daily noon–5.30pm; grounds same days 10.30am–6pm; £6, grounds only £4.50; Ⓦwww.penshurstplace.com), home to the Sidney family since 1552 and birthplace of the Elizabethan soldier and poet, Sir Philip Sidney. The fourteenth-century Barons Hall, built for Sir John de Pulteney, four times Mayor of London, is the chief glory of the interior, with its sixty-foot-high chestnut roof still in place. The ten acres of grounds include a formal Italian garden with clipped box hedges, and double herbaceous borders mixed with an abundance of yew hedges.

The moated and much-altered **Hever Castle**, three miles further west (daily: March–Nov noon–5pm; £7.80; Ⓦwww.hevercastle.co.uk), is where Anne

Boleyn, second wife of Henry VIII, grew up, and where Anne of Cleves, Henry's fourth wife, lived after their divorce. In 1903, having fallen into disrepair, the castle was bought by William Waldorf-Astor, American millionaire owner of *The Times*, who had the house assiduously restored, panelling the rooms with fine reproductions of Tudor woodcarvings. In the Inner Hall hangs a fine portrait of Henry VIII by Holbein; a further Holbein painting of Elizabeth I has recently been restored and is hanging on the middle floor. Upstairs, in Anne Boleyn's room, you can see her book of prayers which she carried with her to the executioner's block, but more impressive is the Anne of Cleves room, which houses an unusually well-preserved tapestry, illustrating the marriage of Henry's sister to King Louis XII of France, with Anne Boleyn as one of the ladies-in-waiting.

Outside in the grounds, next to the gift shop, is the absorbing **Guthrie Miniature Model Houses Collection**, showing the development of aristocratic seats from feudal times on. However, the best feature of the grounds is Waldorf-Astor's beautiful **Italian Garden**, built on reclaimed marshland and decorated with Roman statuary. For kids (and adults) there's a traditional **yew hedge maze** to figure out, an adventure playground and a **water maze**. Also in the grounds is a twenty-bedroom mock-Tudor annexe, built by Waldorf-Astor, who decided that the castle didn't have enough rooms to accommodate the guests of a thrusting newspaper magnate in style; it's now used solely as a conference venue.

Scotney Castle and Sissinghurst

Picturesque **Scotney Castle**, eight miles southeast of Tunbridge Wells (April–Oct Wed–Fri 11am–6pm, Sat & Sun 2–6pm; March Sat & Sun noon–4pm; £4.40; NT), sits half-ruined within romantically landscaped gardens on the edge of a small lake (bus #256 then a mile's walk southeast; not Sun). The only part of the small castle still intact is the Jacobean wing (open May to mid-Sept only), which houses artefacts from the sixteenth century, but the real reason to visit is to admire the castle's delightful setting and its superb grounds.

Sissinghurst, twelve miles east of Tunbridge Wells (April to mid-Oct Tues–Fri 1–6.30pm, Sat & Sun 10am–5.30pm; £6.50; NT), was described by Vita Sackville-West as "a garden crying out for rescue" when she and her husband took it over in the 1920s. Over the following years they transformed the five-acre plot into one of England's greatest and most popular modern gardens.

Spread over the site of a medieval moated manor (which was rebuilt into an Elizabethan mansion of which only one wing remains today), the gardens were designed around the linear pattern of the former buildings' walls. A major part of Sissinghurst's appeal derives from the way that the flowers are allowed to spill over onto the narrow walkways, defying the classical formality of the great gardens that preceded it. The brick tower that Vita had restored and used as her study acts as a focal point and offers the best views of the walled gardens. Most impressive are the **White Garden**, composed solely of white flowers and silvery-grey foliage, and the **Cottage Garden**, featuring flora in shades of orange, yellow and red.

The reputation of the gardens, as well as its limited capacity for visitors, is such that Sissinghurst gets extremely busy in summer when timed tickets for half-hourly visits are issued. Food options in the gardens are limited and overpriced – your best bet is to bring a picnic. **Bus #297** from Royal Tunbridge Wells (not Sun) takes you within two miles of the gardens, and buses #4 and #5 run between Maidstone and Hastings (not Sun), stopping in Sissinghurst en route.

Sevenoaks and around

Set among the green sand ridges of west Kent, 25 miles from London, **SEVENOAKS** was once a small Kent village – it is now a very popular commuter town, with trains reaching London in under an hour. Sadly, the place lost all but one of the ageing oaks from which it derives its name in a freakish storm that struck southern England in October 1987. With mere saplings having taken their place, the only real reason to come to the town is to visit the immense baronial estate of Knole.

Knole (April–Oct Wed–Sat noon–4pm, Sun 11am–5pm; garden May–Sept first Wed of month 11am–4pm; £5, garden £1; NT) is entered from the south end of the Sevenoaks High Street, making it very nearly half an hour's walk from the train station. The house was created in 1456 by Archbishop Thomas Bourchier, who transformed the existing dwelling into a palace for himself and succeeding archbishops of Canterbury. The palace, numerically designed to match the calendar with 7 courtyards, 52 staircases and 365 rooms, was appropriated by Henry VIII, who lavished further expense on it and hunted in the thousand acres of **parkland** (free access throughout the year), still home to several hundred deer. Henry's daughter, Elizabeth I, passed the estate on to her cousin, Thomas Sackville, who remodelled the house in 1605. Part of Knole's allure is that it has preserved its Jacobean exterior and remained in the family's hands ever since. Vita Sackville-West, who in 1923 penned a definitive history of her family entitled *Knole and the Sackvilles*, was brought up here, and her one-time lover Virginia Woolf derived inspiration for her novel *Orlando* from her frequent visits to the house. Only thirteen rooms are open to the public, featuring an array of fine, if well-worn, furnishings and tapestries. Paintings by Gainsborough and Van Dyck are on display, as are Reynolds's depictions of George III and of Queen Charlotte – between them hangs a painting of their strutting, dandified progeny, George IV, one of the fifteen children she bore the king.

Sevenoaks' **tourist office** is in the library building (April–Sept Mon–Sat 9.30am–5pm; Oct–March Mon–Fri 9.30am–5pm, Sat 9.30am–4.30pm; ☎01732/450305, ⓦwww.heartofkent.org.uk), just beyond the **bus station** in Buckhurst Lane; the **train station** is fifteen minutes' walk north of the town centre on the London Road. The town's priciest and smartest **accommodation** is at the excellent *Royal Oak Hotel*, a seventeenth-century coaching inn at the south end of the High Street (☎01732/451109, ⓦwww.brookhotels.co.uk/royaloak.html; ❼), beyond the entrance to Knole. In most people's range is the spacious family room at *Burley Lodge*, Rockdale Road (☎01732/455761; ❶), close to the entrance to Knole, or you can have a timber-clad cottage to yourself at *4 Old Timber Top Cottages*, Bethel Road (☎01732/460506, ⓔanthony@ruddassociates.ndo.co.uk; ❸); breakfast is included in the nightly rate, though the cottage also has basic self-catering facilities. The nearest **youth hostel** (☎01732/761341) is an imposing Victorian vicarage set in its own grounds in Kemsing, four miles northeast of Sevenoaks; it's a two-mile hike from Kemsing station or you can take bus #425/6 or #433 from Sevenoaks to Kemsing post office, which is close by – note that no public transport runs to Kemsing on Sundays.

For inexpensive filling **food**, you can't fault *Pizza Express*, 146 High St, but for something more snackish (and a really good coffee), pop into *Coffee Call*, on Dorset St. The menu at the nearby *Dorset Arms* is better than your average **pub**, as is also *The Black Boy*, Bank St, but for some truly delicious food, you need to go to *No. 5* (☎01732/455555), the restaurant at the *Royal Oak Hotel*, which offers a two-course lunch for just over £10, though in the evening one main dish will cost you more than that; for an inexpensive evening meal, head for the hotel's bistro (in other words the bar), which is also good – and half the price.

Lullingstone Roman Villa

Lullingstone Roman Villa, seven miles north of Sevenoaks and half a mile along the river west of the village of Eynsford (daily: April–Sept 10am–6pm; Oct 10am–5pm; Nov–March 10am–4pm; £2.60; EH), has some of the best-preserved Roman mosaics in southeast England on show, in a pleasant location alongside the trickle of the River Darent. Believed to have been the first-century residence of a farmer, the site has yielded some fine marble busts – these are now on display in the British Museum in London, but a superb floor remains depicting the killing of the Chimera, a mythical fire-breathing beast with a lion's head, goat's body and a serpent's tail. Excavation in a nearby chamber has revealed early Christian iconography, which suggests that the villa may have become a Romano-Christian chapel in the third century, pre-empting the official arrival of that religion by three hundred years and making Lullingstone one of the earliest sites of clandestine Christian worship in England.

Chartwell

The residence of Winston Churchill from 1924 until his death in 1965, **Chartwell**, six miles west of Sevenoaks (April–June, Sept & Oct Wed–Sun 11am–5pm; July & Aug Tues–Sun 11am–5pm; £5.60; NT), is one of the most visited of the National Trust's properties. It's an unremarkable, heavily restored Tudor building whose main appeal is the wartime premier's memorabilia, including his paintings, which show an unexpectedly contemplative side to the famously gruff statesman. Entry to the house is by timed ticket at peak times – expect long queues. A direct bus service runs to Chartwell from Sevenoaks bus station five times daily on weekends and public holidays from late May until the beginning of September with further services on Thursdays and Fridays in July and August.

Ightham Mote

The secluded, moated manor house of **Ightham Mote** (pronounced "I-tam"), six miles southeast of Sevenoaks just off the A227 (April–Oct Mon, Wed–Fri, Sun & public holidays 11am–5.30pm; £5; NT), originates from the fourteenth century and is one of the southeast's most picturesque National Trust properties, though the original defensive appearance of this half-timbered ragstone building has been muted by Tudor alterations. A tour of the interior reveals a mixture of architectural styles ranging from the fourteenth-century Old Chapel and crypt, through a barrel-vaulted Tudor chapel with a painted ceiling to an eighteenth-century Palladian window. This idyllically situated medieval dwelling is being restored by the National Trust, whose efforts are described in a small exhibition on the ground floor. Ightham is tricky to get to by bus, with only the infrequent #404 from Sevenoaks (not Sat or Sun) making the trip.

Maidstone and around

If you missed out **MAIDSTONE**, you wouldn't be missing much. A minor Roman and later a Saxon settlement, Maidstone is Kent's principal commercial, industrial and agricultural centre, but the only bit of town that holds any interest at all to the visitor is the cluster of ancient buildings south of the High Street down Mill Street, by the banks of the River Medway, a spot whose charm is somewhat tempered by the fact that it lies right by a six-lane highway.

Of most interest is the **Archbishop's Palace** (daily 10.30am–4pm; free), built around 1348 and formerly used as a stopping-off point for the Archbishop of Canterbury on journeys to London. Although the building is now used as a registry office, with a café upstairs, it's worth checking out the impressive oak-panelled function rooms. Close by is **All Saints' Church**, a good example of late-fourteenth-century Perpendicular architecture. Standing on its very own traffic island, opposite the Archbishop's Palace, is a wonderful old red-brick, ragstone and timber building, originally the archbishop's stables, and now appropriately enough the **Tyrwhitt-Drake Museum of Carriages** (daily 10.30am–5pm; £2), housing every type of carriage from infant perambulators to royal wagons. If you've time to spare, it's worth paying a visit to **Maidstone Museum and Bentlif Art Gallery** (Mon–Sat 10am–5.15pm, Sun 11am–4pm; free; @www.museum.maidstone.gov.uk), which occupies a grandiose red-brick Elizabethan mansion built by a former local MP on St Faith's Street, two blocks north of High St. The highlights of the museum's vast collection are a half-unravelled Egyptian mummy, a statue of Lady Godiva and a whole cabinet of curiosities brought back from around the Pacific Ocean by the local-born Victorian explorer, Julius Brenchley.

Maidstone's **tourist office** is situated in the gatehouse of the Archbishop's Palace (April–Oct Mon–Sat 9.30am–5pm, Sun 10am–4pm; Nov–March Mon–Fri 9.30am–5pm, Sat 9.30am–4pm; ☎01622/602169, @www.heartofkent .org.uk). Maidstone has no fewer than three **train stations**: Maidstone East, served by trains from London Victoria, is ten minutes' walk north of the High Street up pedestrianized Week Street; while Maidstone Barracks and Maidstone West, both on the west bank of the Medway and less than ten minutes' walk from the High Street, are served by local trains from Tonbridge and Strood.

Thanks to its proximity to the motorways, Maidstone's **accommodation** has seen much recent development, especially at the top end of the scale. Options include the large new *Hilton Hotel* on Bearsted Road (☎01622 /734322; ❺), close to the M20 access point; the elegant *Best Western-Russell Hotel*, 136 Boxley Rd (☎01622/69221; ❻), northeast of the town centre. For something more affordable, try the *Rock House Hotel*, 102 Tonbridge Rd (☎01622/751616, @www.smoothhound.co.uk/hotels/rockh.html; ❷), west of the centre, or, if you have your own transport, head for the characterful converted oast houses on Barn Hill in Hunton (☎01622/820206; ❶), seven miles southwest of Maidstone. **Food** options in town include the *Paramount*, Middle Row (☎01622/606941), which has a tasty and moderately priced menu, and the more exotic *Frobisher and Friends*, 57 High St (☎01622/678628; closed Sunday), which specializes in an unusual mixture of Portuguese and vegetarian food. Otherwise, there's reliable **pub grub** and real ales at the *Muggleton Inn*, a big Wetherspoon's pub on High St, and a branch of *Pizza Express* in the old Conservative Club on Earl St. If you're in the mood for a pricey gastronomic treat, head for *Le Soufflé*, on The Green in Bearsted (☎01622/737065; closed Sun eve & Mon), two miles east of Maidstone on the A20, which specializes in classic French dishes.

Cobtree Museum of Kent Life

Though too close to the M20 to re-create any rural idyll, the **Cobtree Museum of Kent Life** two miles north (mid-Feb to Oct daily 10am–5.30pm; £4.70) offers a fascinating account of rural life in the county over the last hundred years or so. The farm was bought in 1904 by local big-wigs, the Tyrwhitt-Drakes, and was at one time a zoo – today, the animals are purely livestock. The section on hop-picking in the traditional oast house is particularly fascinating. Nearby, you can view a series of hopper huts, in which East Enders from London used to spend their hop-picking "holidays". To get to the museum, you need to take **bus** #155 (not Sun) from Maidstone; or instead you can catch a **boat** (daily 11.30am–4.30pm; £3 return).

Leeds Castle

Leeds Castle, five miles east of Maidstone, off the A20 (daily: March–Oct 10am–5pm; Nov–Feb 10am–3pm; grounds close 2hr later; castle, park & gardens £10; park & gardens £7.50; ⓦwww.leeds-castle.co.uk), more closely resembles a fairytale palace than a defensively efficient fortress. Named after the local village, work on the castle began around 1120. The present stone castle dates from Norman times and is set half on an island in the middle of a lake and half on the mainland surrounded by landscaped parkland. Following centuries of regal and noble ownership (and, less glamorously, service as a prison) the castle is now run as a commercial concern, hosting conferences as well as sporting and cultural events. Its interior fails to match the castle's stunning, much-photographed external appearance and, in places, twentieth-century renovations have quashed any of its historical charm; possibly the most unusual feature inside is the dog collar museum in the gatehouse. In the grounds, there's a fine aviary with some superb and colourful exotic specimens, as well as manicured gardens and a mildly challenging maze. The easiest way to get to Leeds Castle by public transport is to buy an all-inclusive rail ticket to Bearsted station, which pays for a shuttle service and entry to the castle; services run from London Victoria via Maidstone East.

Sussex

Although now separated into two counties, East and West, **Sussex** (deriving from "land of the south Saxons") retains a unified identity. Most of the region was covered in dense forest until the Tudor era, when the huge demand for timber and charcoal began its deforestation. However, large areas of woodland still exist in inland parts of the counties and contribute to Sussex's bucolic character. Nowhere is this rural atmosphere more evident than on the southeast's main long-distance footpath, the **South Downs Way**, which runs along the grassy ridge of the South Downs, giving dramatic views over some fine countryside as well as over the coast, where the Downs meet the sea at the chalk cliffs of **Beachy Head** and **Seven Sisters**.

However, Sussex also has its fair share of urban centres, many of which are populated by London commuters. The best known is the traditional seaside resort of **Brighton**, the counties' biggest and brashest town, while a few miles inland more sedate **Lewes**, the county town of East Sussex, is famed for its bonfire night celebrations. **Hastings**, farther east, is renowned for its historical connections, although the eponymous fight actually took place six miles away at **Battle**. Farther east still, on the edge of the Romney marshes, the former Cinque Port of **Rye** exemplifies rustic English tweeness. In West Sussex, the main centres of interest are the attractive hilltop town of **Arundel**, surrounded by unspoilt countryside, and the county town of **Chichester**.

Hastings and around

During the twelfth and thirteenth centuries, **Hastings** flourished as an influential Cinque Port (see p.196). In 1287 its harbour creek was silted up by the same storm which washed away nearby **Winchelsea**, forcing the settlement to be temporarily abandoned. These days, Hastings is a curious mixture of unpretentious fishing port, traditional seaside resort and arty retreat popular with painters (there's even a street and quarter named Bohemia). In 1066, William, Duke of Normandy, landed at Pevensey Bay, a few miles west of town, and made Hastings his base, but his forces met Harold's army – exhausted after quelling a Nordic invasion near York – at **Battle**, six miles northwest of Hastings. Battle today boasts a magnificent abbey built by William in thanks for his victory, which makes a good afternoon's excursion from Hastings. Farther north, **Batemans**, once the home of Rudyard Kipling, and the classic **Bodiam Castle** are both easily reached from Hastings in a day-trip.

Hastings

Hastings **old town**, east of the pier, holds most of the appeal of this part tacky, part pretty seaside resort. With the exception of the oddly neglected Regency architecture of **Pelham Crescent**, directly beneath the castle ruins, **All Saints Street** is by far the most evocative thoroughfare, punctuated with the odd, rickety, timber-framed dwelling from the fifteenth century. The thirteenth-century **St Clement's Church** stands in the High Street, which runs parallel to All Saints Street, on the other side of The Bourne. By a louvred window at the top of the church's tower rests a cannonball that was lodged there by a Dutch galleon in the 1600s – its poignancy rather dispelled by a companion fitted in the eighteenth century for the sake of symmetry. On the right as you walk up the High Street, you'll see **Starr's Cottages**, one of which is wedge-shaped and painted to resemble a piece of cheese, while the **Old Town Hall Museum** on High Street (daily: April–Sept 10am–5pm; Oct–March 11am–4pm; free) offers the customary spread on local history.

Down by the seafront, the area known as **The Stade** is characterized by its tall, black weatherboard **net shops**, most dating from the mid-nineteenth century (and still in use), but which first appeared here in Tudor times. To raise Hastings' tone, the town council attempted to shift the fishermen and their malodorously drying nets from the beach by increasing rents per square foot, and these sinister-looking towers were their response. Somewhat remarkably, Hastings still boasts a working fishing fleet, the boats being dragged up onto the shingle, and you can still buy fresh fish from several of the net shops.

There's a trio of nautical attractions on nearby Rock-a-Nore Road. The **Fisherman's Museum** (daily: April–Oct 10am–5pm; Nov–March 11am–4pm; free), a converted seaman's chapel, offers an account of the port's commercial activities and displays one of Hastings' last clinker-built luggers – exceptionally stout trawlers able to withstand being winched up and down the shingle beach. The neighbouring **Shipwreck Heritage Centre** (Feb–Easter daily 11am–4pm; Easter–Oct daily 10am–5pm; £1) details the dramas of unfortunate mariners, focusing on the wreck of the *Amsterdam*, beached in 1749 and now embedded in the sand three miles west of town awaiting excavation. Opposite is **Underwater World** (daily: Easter–Sept 10am–5pm; Oct–Easter; £5.25; ⓦwww.underwaterworld-hastings.co.uk), a series of aquariums with walk-through tunnels, magnified tanks housing marine creatures and an excellent and sympathetic film on sharks.

Castle Hill, separating the old town from the visually less-interesting modern quarter, can be ascended by the **West Hill Cliff Railway**, from George St, off Marine Parade, one of two Victorian funicular railways in Hastings (daily: April–Oct 10.30am–5.30pm; Nov–March 11am–4pm; 80p), the other being the **East Cliff Railway**, on Rock-a-Nore Road (same times and price). This hilltop is where William the Conqueror erected his first **Castle** in 1066, one of several prefabricated wooden structures brought over from Normandy in sections. Built on the site of an existing fort, probably of Saxon origins, it was soon replaced by a more permanent stone structure, but in the thirteenth century storms caused the cliffs to subside, tipping most of the castle into the sea; the surviving ruins, however, offer an excellent prospect of the town. The castle is home to **The 1066 Story** (daily: April–Sept 10am–5pm; Oct–March 11am–3.30pm; £3.20), in which the events of the last successful invasion of the British mainland are described inside a mock-up of a siege tent. The twenty-minute audiovisual details the history of the castle and corrects a few myths about the famous battle.

More fun is the **Smugglers' Adventure**, over the hill (daily: Easter–Sept 10am–5.30pm; Oct–Easter 11am–3.30pm; £5.25; combined ticket with The 1066 Story £7; ⓦwww.smugglersadventure.callnetuk.com). Here the labyrinthine St Clement's caves, named after a carving resembling St Clement but probably predating Christianity, have been converted to house a number of amusing and educational dioramas depicting the town's long history of duty dodging. During the eighteenth century, smuggling – especially of alcohol and tobacco – was the region's biggest source of income after agriculture and a farm worker could earn more than a week's wages with one night's contraband. Large-scale smuggling waned in the 1830s when a more efficient coastguard and diminishing taxes reduced its viability.

Hastings also has its fair share of traditional English seaside activities – mini-golf, boating, go-karts and **Hastings Pier**, west of the old town, where bingo and palm-reading are on offer, along with the usual video games and slot machines.

Arrival, information and accommodation

The **train station**, served by regular trains from both London's Charing Cross (via Ashford International) and Victoria (via Lewes) stations, is a ten-minute walk from the seafront along Havelock Road; National Express **bus** services operate from the station at the junction of Havelock and Queen's roads. The **tourist office** is located within the Town Hall on Queen's Road (April–Oct Mon–Fri 8.30am–6.15pm, Sat 9am–5pm, Sun 10am–4.30pm; Nov–March Mon & Fri 8.30am–6.15pm, Tues–Thurs 8.30am–5pm, Sat 9am–5pm, Sun 10am–4pm; ☏01424/781111, ⓦwww.hastings.gov.uk); there's also a smaller seafront office (April–Sept Mon–Sat 10am–5pm, Sun 10am–4.30pm; Oct–March Sat & Sun 11am–4pm; ☏01424/781120) near the Boating Lake on East Parade by the old town. **Bikes** and even rickshaws can be rented from the appropriately named *Palm Court Rickshaws and Bicycle Hire* (☏01424 /431878) at Hastings Pier.

Hotels, guest houses and B&Bs

Argyle Guest House 32 Cambridge Gardens ⌾01424/421294, ⓔargyle.1066country@ talk21.com. Good value rooms in a street near the station which has several other options. ❶

Jenny Lind Hotel 69 High St ⌾01424/421392. ⓦwww.the-entertainer-online.co.uk/pubs/jenny-lind.html. An old town location featuring pleasantly uncluttered, clean rooms above its own pub/restaurant. ❷

Lavender and Lace 106 All Saints St ⌾01424/716290. Popular, cosy, timber-framed guest house right in the middle of the old town. ❷

West Hill Cottage Exmouth Place, near the bottom of West Hill ⌾01424/716021. An attractive listed cottage with friendly hosts and generous breakfasts. ❷

Hostels and campsites

Youth Hostel Guestling Hall ⌾01424/812373. Set in a large manor house with its own grounds, three miles east of Hastings on the road to Rye. Camping possible in the grounds. Take bus #711 from the main tourist office.

Shear Barn Holiday Park Barley Lane ⌾01424/423583. The nearest campsite is situated next to the seafront Hastings Country Park, a mile east of the town centre off All Saints Street.

Restaurants

Bella Napoli 9 George St ⌾01424/429211. The waft of garlic emanating from this excellent Italian restaurant is a positive enticement to enter. Moderate.

The Cinnamon Tree above the Jenny Lind Hotel, 69 High St ⌾01424/437075. Tasty and filling vegetarian and meat curries. Closed Mon, Tues & Sun. Inexpensive.

Gannets Bistro 45 High St. Offers everything from breakfast to a wide choice of evening meals. Inexpensive.

Harris 58 High St ⌾01424/437221. Wood-panelled walls and potted plants enhance the ambi-

ence of this specialist in tapas. Closed Sun. Moderate.

The Hastings Arms 3 George St. A fine pub, noted for its imaginative fish and meat dishes. Inexpensive.

Mermaid 2 Rock-a-Nore. The best fish and chips in town are at the eat-in restaurant, right by the beach; jellied eels can be sampled from the adjacent net shop.

Rösers 64 Eversfield Place, St. Leonard's-on-Sea ⌾01424/712 218. A classy option specializing in fish. On the seafront in St Leonards-on-Sea, a short walk west of central Hastings. Expensive.

Drinking and nightlife

There are more than thirty **pubs** to choose from in Hastings: the local fishermen's favourite is the *Lord Nelson* right by the front on The Bourne; others to check out are the ever-popular *First In Last Out,* 15 High St in the old town, the creaky-beamed hostelry, *Ye Olde Pump House,* George St, or the trendy clubby bar, *The Street,* Robertson St, accessible via a tiny entrance on Cambridge Road in the new town centre.

For **entertainment**, *The Hastings Arms* has a longstanding blues night every Monday, with jazz at *The Anchor* further up George Street on Tuesdays. *The Stag Inn,* 14 All Saints St, has a folk session on Wednesdays and bluegrass the following night. *The* town's one and only decent **club** is *The Crypt,* on Havelock Road (closed Mon, Tues & Sun), popular with students from the town's thirty-odd language schools. Look out too for events at the innovative arts venue, *St. Mary-in-the Castle* on Pelham Crescent. For comprehensive **listings** of what's on, get the free *Ultimate Alternative,* available in pubs, clubs and record shops and at ⓦwww.ua1066.co.uk.

Battle

The town of **BATTLE** – a ten-minute train ride inland from Hastings – occupies the site of the most famous land battle in British history. Here, on October 14, 1066, the invading Normans swarmed up the hillside from Senlac Moor and overcame the Anglo-Saxon army of King Harold, who was killed not by an arrow through the eye – a myth resulting from the misinterpretation of the

Bayeux Tapestry – but by a workaday clubbing about the head. Before the battle took place, William vowed that, should he win the engagement, he would build a religious foundation on the very spot of Harold's slaying to atone for the bloodshed, and, true to his word, **Battle Abbey** (daily: April–Sept 10am–6pm; Oct 10am–5pm; Nov–March 10am–4pm; £4.30; EH) was built four years later and subsequently occupied by a fraternity of Benedictines. The magnificent structure, though partially destroyed in the Dissolution and much rebuilt and revised over the centuries, still dominates the town, with the huge gatehouse, added in 1338, now containing a good audiovisual exhibition on the battle. You can also wander through the ruins of the abbey to the spot where Harold was clubbed – the site of the high altar of William's abbey, now marked by a memorial stone.

Though nothing can match the resonance of the abbey, the rest of the town is worth a stroll. **St Mary's Church**, on High St, has a fine Norman font and nave and the churchyard contains the grave of one Isaac Ingall who, according to the inscription on his tomb, was 120 years old when he died in 1798. At the far end of High Street is the fourteenth-century **Almonry** (Mon–Sat 10am–4.30pm; £1) – the present town hall – which contains a miniature model of Battle and the oldest Guy Fawkes in the country. Every year, on the Saturday nearest to November 5, this 300-year-old effigy is paraded along High Street at the head of a torch-lit procession culminating at a huge bonfire in front of the abbey gates – similar celebrations occur in Lewes (see p.223).

Wealden Hall House, just past the tourist office, houses a more modern diversion, though one still firmly rooted in the past. **Buckleys Yesterday's World** (daily 9.30am–6pm, last entry 4.45pm; £4.50; @www.yesterdaysworld.co.uk) is a must for nostalgia buffs consisting of thirty re-created rooms and shop settings stocked with original materials and goods. Highlights include a Bakelite-crammed 1930s wireless shop and a Victorian kitchen replete with authentic accessories. The grounds outside include a country garage and railway station, a café and play areas for children and toddlers.

The **tourist office** is at 88 High St (June–Sept Mon–Sat 9.30am–5.30pm, Sun 9.30am–5.30pm; rest of year closed Sun; ☎01424/773721, @www.battle town.co.uk). Battle's **accommodation** tends to be agreeable but expensive, as at the *George Hotel*, an old coaching inn with fully en-suite rooms at 23 High St (☎01424/774466; ❺), and at the luxurious country house, *Powdermills Hotel*, Powdermill Lane (☎01424/775511, @www.powdermill.co.uk; ❽). For less pricey B&B deals try the elegant *Abbey View*, Caldbec Hill (☎01424/775513; ❹), only two minutes' walk from town down Mount Street, or the en-suite rooms above the *Gateway Café*, 78 High St (☎01424/772856; ❷). For town-centre **pubs** in Battle, all serving decent food, try the fifteenth-century *Old King's Head* on Mount St, the *1066* at 12 High St, or the *Chequers Inn* at Lower Lake, on High St.

Rye and Winchelsea

Perched on a hill overlooking the Romney Marshes, ten miles east of Hastings, sits the ancient town of **RYE**. Added as a "limb" to the original Cinque Ports (see p.196), the town then became marooned two miles inland with the retreat of the sea and the silting-up of the River Rother. It is now one of the most popular places in East Sussex – half-timbered, skew-roofed and quintessentially English, but also very commercialized.

From Strand Quay, head up The Deals to Rye's most picturesque street, the sloping cobbled lane of **Mermaid Street**, which will bring you eventually to the peaceful oasis of Church Square. Henry James, who strangely suggested that "Rye would … remind you of Granada", lived from 1898 until his death in 1916 in **Lamb House** at the east end of Mermaid Street (April–Oct Wed & Sat 2pm–6pm; £2.60; NT). The house's three rooms and garden are of interest chiefly to fans of James's novels, or to admirers of E.F. Benson, who lived here after James. A blue plaque in High Street also testifies that Radclyffe Hall, author of the seminal lesbian novel, *The Well of Loneliness*, was also once a resident of the town. At the centre of Church Square stands **St Mary's Church**, boasting the oldest functioning pendulum clock in the country; the ascent of the church tower – whose bells were looted by French raiders in 1377 and then retrieved with similar audacity – offers fine views over the clay-tiled roofs and grid of narrow lanes. In the far corner of the square stands the **Ypres Tower** (April–Oct Mon, Thurs & Fri 10am–1pm & 2–5pm, Sat & Sun 10.30am–1pm & 2–5pm; Nov–March Sat & Sun 10.30am–3.30pm; £1.90), formerly used to keep watch for cross-Channel invaders, and now a part of the **Rye Castle Museum** on nearby East Street (April–Oct Mon, Thurs & Fri 2–5pm, Sat & Sun 10.30am–1pm & 2–5pm; £1.90; combined ticket for both sites £2.90). Both sites house a number of relics from Rye's past, including an eighteenth-century fire-engine. Also worth seeking out are the **Rye Art Galleries** (daily 10.30am–5pm; free), located in two lovely houses: the Easton Rooms, 107 High St, stage exhibitions by local contemporary artists, while the Stormont Studio, around the corner in Ockman Lane, off East St, has a small permanent collection, including works by artists associated with Rye, such as Burra and Nash. One unusual sonic treat is the **Rye Treasury of Mechanical Music** (daily 10am–5pm; £3) at 20 Cinque Ports St (near the railway station) which houses a fascinating collection of antique barrel organs, music boxes, player pianos and other musical curiosities. Rye's **festival**, one of the best-known literary festivals in the country, takes place over the first two weeks in September and also features a wide range of musical and visual arts events.

  WINCHELSEA, perched on a hill two miles southwest of Rye and easily reached by train, bus, foot or bike, shares Rye's indignity of having become detached from the sea, but has a very different character. Rye gets all the visitors, whereas Winchelsea feels positively deserted, an impression augmented as you pass through the medieval Strand Gate and see the ghostly ruined **Church of St Thomas à Becket**. The original settlement was washed away in the great storm in 1287, after which Edward I planned a new port with a che-querboard pattern of streets. Even at the height of Winchelsea's economic activity, however, not all the plots on the grid were used. The town also suffered from incursions by the French in the fourteenth and fifteenth centuries, at which time the church was pillaged; the remains of the church constitute Sussex's finest example of the Decorated style. Head south for a mile and a half and you get to **Winchelsea beach**, a long expanse of pebbly sand.

Practicalities

Hourly **trains** run to Rye and Winchelsea from Hastings; Rye's station is a the bottom of Station Approach, off Cinque Ports St, while Winchelsea's is a mile north of the town. **Bus** #711 runs into the centre of both towns from Hastings. Rye's **tourist office**, on Strand Quay (April–Oct Mon–Sat 9am–5.30pm, Sun 10am–5pm; Nov–March Mon–Sat 10am–4pm; ☎01797 /226696, ⓦwww.rye.org.uk/heritage), has masses of information on local attractions. The same building houses Rye's **museum** (same hours; £2) with an interesting twenty-minute audiovisual about the town and a scaled-down model of Rye on show – they also rent out audio tours to take you round the town itself (£2).

The town's popularity with weekending Londoners gives it an excellent choice of **accommodation**. The most luxurious option is *The Mermaid* (☎01797/223065; ❼), a fifteenth-century inn on Mermaid St; and there's also the handsomely furnished rooms in *Jeake's House*, also on Mermaid Street (☎01797/222828, ✉jeakeshouse@btinternet.com; ❸). Both are deservedly popular. Alternatively, there's *Old Vicarage*, 66 Church Square (☎01797/222119, ⓦhomepages.tesco.net/~oldvicaragerye; ❷), a lovely pink Georgian house next to the church; the *Durrant House Hotel*, 2 Market St (☎01797/223182, ⓦwww.durranthouse.com; ❷), is another friendly and well-equipped Georgian House with a garden looking out towards Dungeness and the marshes; and finally, the best option out of town is *Playden Cottage Guest House*, Military Road (☎01797/222234; ❸), a listed family house in a semi-rural setting off the A268 and about a mile from the centre. The fourteenth-century *Strand House* (☎01797/226276, ⓦwww.tuckedup.com/thestrandhouse.html; ❷), at the foot of the cliff below Strand Gate, is the best accommodation option in Winchelsea. The *Mermaid* is by far the most atmospheric **pub**, with heavy exposed timbers throughout, though an excellent alternative is the *Ypres Castle* in Gun Gardens (down the steps behind the Ypres Tower), an unspoiled pub often used for film locations; a younger crowd frequents the more laid-back *Strand Quay*, at the bottom of Mermaid St.

The best **restaurant** in town is the pricey *Landgate Bistro* at 5–6 Landgate (☎01797/222829; Tues–Sat eve only), which serves good steaks, but if you want something a touch less expensive try the seafood at the *Old Forge*, 24 Wish St (☎01797/223227; closed all Sun & Mon, plus Tues & Wed lunch), or the small and intimate *Gatehouse Restaurant*, 1 Tower St (☎01797/222 327; closed Mon lunch). For more excellent seafood dishes, head for the *Flushing Inn* on Market Street (☎01797/223292; closed Mon eve & all Tues). *The Peacock*, 8 Lion St (☎01797/226702), serves up everything from beans on toast to moderately priced fresh Rye Bay plaice in a suitably ancient setting – it's also a good place for delicious cream teas.

Bodiam Castle

Ask a child to draw a castle and the outline of **Bodiam Castle**, nine miles north of Hastings (Feb–Oct daily 10am–6pm or dusk; Nov–Feb Sat & Sun 10am–4pm or dusk; £3.70; NT), would be the result: a classically stout square block with rounded corner turrets, battlements and a moat. When it was built in 1385 to guard what were the lower reaches of the River Rother, Bodiam was state-of-the-art military architecture, but during the Civil War a company of Roundheads breached the fortress and removed its roof to reduce its effectiveness as a possible stronghold for the king. Over the next 250 years Bodiam fell into neglect until restoration earlier this century by Lord Curzon. Nowadays, the castle particularly appeals to children who enjoy clambering up the narrow spiral staircases which lead to crenellated battlements, and watching the absorbing fifteen-minute video portraying medieval life in a castle.

If you've got money to burn and/or children to entertain, it's worth knowing about the **Kent and East Sussex Railway** (May–Sept 6 daily 11.25am–5.40pm; March, April & Oct Sat & Sun only; Nov–Feb Sun only; plus school holidays throughout the year; ☎01580/765155; £7.50, ⓦwww.kesr.org.uk), which runs full-scale steam trains from Bodiam to Tenterden, ten miles to the northeast.

The best **accommodation** and **food** options are a couple of miles southeast, in the lovely village of Ewhurst, which houses a quaint country pub, the

White Dog Inn (☎01580/830264, ⓦwww.hey-presto.co.uk/sussex/04bodiam
/whitedog/whitedog.htm; ➋).

Burwash and Bateman's

Fifteen miles northwest of Hastings on the A265, halfway to Tunbridge Wells,
BURWASH, with its red brick and weatherboarded cottages and Norman
church tower, exemplifies the pastoral idyll of inland Sussex. Half a mile south
of the village lies the main attraction, **Bateman's** (April–Oct Mon–Wed, Sat,
Sun & public holidays 11am–5pm; March Sat & Sun only; £5; NT), home of
the Nobel Prize-winning writer and journalist Rudyard Kipling from 1902
until his death in 1936. Built by a local ironmaster in the seventeenth century
and set amid attractive gardens, the house features a working watermill converted by Kipling to generate electricity, and which now grinds corn every
Saturday at 2pm. Inside, the house is laid out as Kipling left it, with letters, early
editions of his work and mementoes from his travels on display. Next to the
house, a garage houses the last of Kipling's Rolls-Royces, one of the many that
he owned during his lifetime, although he never actually drove them himself,
preferring the services of a chauffeur.

Eastbourne and around

Like so many of the southeast's seaside resorts, **EASTBOURNE** was kick-
started into life in the 1840s, when the Brighton, Lewes and Hastings Rail
Company built a branch line from Lewes to the sea. The Seventh Duke of
Devonshire, William Cavendish, promptly developed the resort, an achievement
zealously commemorated in the town's Devonshire Park, Devonshire swimming
baths and Devonshire Place, where a self-satisfied statue of the duke stands. Past
holiday-makers include George Orwell, the composer Claude Debussy, who
finished writing *La Mer* here, as well as Marx and Engels. Nowadays Eastbourne
has a solid reputation as a retirement town – albeit one that's a touch livelier

---

The South Downs Way

Following the undulating crest of the South Downs, from the village of Buriton on the
Sussex–Hampshire border, two miles southwest of Petersfield train station, to their
spectacular end at Beachy Head, the **South Downs Way** rises and dips over eighty
miles along the chalk uplands, offering the southeast's finest walks. If undertaken in
its entirety, the bridle-path is best traversed from west to east, taking advantage of
the prevailing wind, Eastbourne's better transport services and accommodation,
and the psychological appeal of ending at the sea. **Steyning**, the halfway-point,
marks a transition between predominantly wooded sections and more exposed
chalk uplands – to the east of here you'll pass the modern **youth hostel** at Truleigh
Hill (☎01903/813419). Other hostels along the way are at Telscombe and at Alfriston,
where a southern loop can be taken which brings you to Eastbourne along the cliffs
of the Seven Sisters, and an old bothy at Gumber Farm (☎01243/814484; closed
Nov–Easter), near Bignor Hill.

The OS Landranger **maps** #198 and #199 cover the eastern end of the route; you'll
need #185 and #197 as well to cover the lot. Half a dozen guides are available, the
best being *South Downs Way* by Miles Jebb (Cicerone Press), or the more detailed
South Downs Way by Paul Millmore (Aurum Press).

than the nearby custom-built Peacehaven. Eastbourne's elegant three-mile seafront consists of houses and hotels and is tainted by barely a shop, but the greatest draw around is the South Downs, which the sea has ground into a series of dramatic chalk cliffs around **Beachy Head**, just west of town.

Conforming to tradition, the **Pier** is the focal point of the seafront: opened in 1872, it was intended to match the best on the south coast, which it certainly does. To the west, along the Grand Parade, is the ever-popular sunken **Bandstand**, with its regular (frequently military) band concerts (April–Sept daily 11am–12.30pm & 3–4.30pm). Further west along the promenade, the **Wish Tower**, the first of the prom's two prominent red-brick Martello Towers – whose name derives from an old Sussex word meaning "marsh" – has been transformed into a **puppet museum** (mid-July to Sept daily 11am–5pm; April to mid-July, Oct & Nov Sat & Sun 11am–5pm; £1.80; ⓦwww.puppets.co.uk), while the **Redoubt Fortress**, half a mile east of the pier, now houses a military museum (April–Nov daily 9.45am–5.30pm; £1.50; ⓦwww.eastbourne-museums.co.uk) and is the venue for evening classical music concerts (mid-June to Sept Wed & Fri) – often the *1812 Overture* – with accompanying firework displays.

One bright spark in sedate Eastbourne is the **Towner Art Gallery and Museum** (April–Oct Tues–Sat noon–5pm, Sun 2–5pm; Nov–March Tues–Sat noon–4pm, Sun 2–5pm; free; ⓦwww.eastbourne.org/entertainment), a ten-minute walk northwest of the train station; it shows a refreshingly contemporary and ever-changing range of work. Another place of distraction is the **"How We Lived Then" Museum of Shops** at 20 Cornfield Terrace (daily 10am–5.30pm; £3), just down from the tourist office. The amount of artefacts – old packages, coronation cups, toys – from the last hundred years of consumerism is just staggering, all crammed into mock-up shops spread over several floors. Finally, a more serious attempt to tackle the history of the town is made at the **Eastbourne Heritage Centre** (May–Sept daily 2–5pm; £1; ⓔowenboydell@tinyworld.co.uk), in a distinctive corner house opposite the Winter Gardens.

Practicalities

Eastbourne is served by hourly trains from London Victoria (via Lewes), with the **train station**, a splendid Italianate terminus, ten minutes' walk from the seafront up Terminus Road; there are also frequent services between here and Hastings (see p.214) and Brighton (see p.227). The **bus station**, on Cavendish Place right by the pier, receives daily services from London and has hourly services to Brighton via Newhaven. The **tourist office** is at 3 Cornfield Rd, just off Terminus Road (June–Sept Mon–Sat 9.30am–5.30pm, Sun 10am–1pm; Oct–May closed Sun; ☎01323/411400, ⓦwww.eastbourne.org), with a smaller seasonal office on the pier itself (May–Sept daily 11am–5pm). The town's trackless **Dotto trains** ply up and down the sea front and into the centre from around 10am to 6pm and a day ticket (£5.25) allows visitors to hop on or off at a series of designated stops.

There are hundreds of places to **stay** here: a couple of good choices are *Sea Breeze Guest House*, 6 Marine Rd (☎01323/725440; ❷), a cheap and cheerful place just a hundred yards from the sea, and *Sea Beach House Hotel*, 39–40 Marine Parade (☎01323/410458, ⓦwww.seabeachhousehotel.com; ❸), on the seafront. A mile and a half west along the A259 to East Dean there's a **youth hostel** (☎01323/721081) with spectacular views across Eastbourne; take bus #712 from the train station. You can camp right by a sandy beach at the secluded *Bay View* **campsite** (☎01323/768688; closed Nov–March), off the A259 east to Pevensey.

The Terminus Road area, between the train station and the sea, has the highest concentration of **restaurants**, with *Tequila Sunset*, 71 Seaside Rd (☎01323/732832), offering new Mexican food, including a wide range of fajitas, and the town's best Italian, *Luigi's*, nearby at no. 72 (☎01323/736994; closed Sun); both are moderately priced. If you're in need of a large ice-cream sundae, go to *Fusciardi's* opposite the Winter Gardens on Carlyle Road.

The best **pubs** are some distance from the seafront: *Cornfield Garage*, a capacious Wetherspoon's bar at 21–27 Cornfield Rd; the *Hurst Arms* at 76 Willingdon Rd, a ten-minute walk inland from the station up Upperton Road, has Harvey's locally brewed beers on tap, with the same brew also available at the *Lamb*, a slightly over-enthusiastic but very pleasant version of a traditional English inn situated in nearby High St. Slightly out of the centre at 220 Seaside is the ornate Victorian *Black Horse* pub (along the A259 to Bexhill), one of Eastbourne's least touristy places, offering wholesome food.

Beachy Head, Seven Sisters and the Cuckmere

A short walk west from Eastbourne takes you out along the most dramatic stretch of coastline in Sussex, where the chalk uplands of the Sussex Downs are cut by the sea into a sequence of splendid cliffs. The most spectacular of all, **Beachy Head**, is 575ft high, with a diminutive-looking lighthouse, but no beach – the headland's name derives from the French *beau chef* meaning "beautiful head". The beauty certainly went to Friedrich Engels' head; he insisted his ashes be scattered here, and depressed individuals regularly try to join him by leaping to their doom from this well-known suicide spot. An open top bus runs half-hourly (Easter & May–Sept; £6) from Eastbourne Pier to the top of Beachy Head.

West of the headland the scenery softens into a diminishing series of cliffs, a landmark known as the **Seven Sisters**. The country park after which they are named provides some of the most impressive walks in the county, taking in the cliff-top walk and the lower valley of the meandering River Cuckmere, into which the Seven Sisters subside. At **LITLINGTON**, five miles up the Cuckmere, the idyllic *Litlington Tea Gardens* provide a beautiful refreshment halt. On the opposite bank of the river in **ALFRISTON** is the wonderfully ancient timber-framed and thatched **Clergy House** (April–Oct Mon, Wed, Thurs, Sat & Sun 10am–5pm; March Sat & Sun 10am–5pm; £2.60; NT), built in the fourteenth century and the first property to be acquired by the National Trust in 1896. Less edifying, but potentially more fun for kids, a mile or so up the valley, is **Drusillas Park** (daily: April–Sept 10am–5pm; Oct–March 10am–4pm; £7.99; ⊛www.drusillas.co.uk), where visitors can get to look at penguins and meerkats, milk a cow, touch snakes, and lark about on the adventure playground and miniature railway.

If you'd rather stay round this neck of the woods than in Eastbourne, check in at the *Birling Gap Hotel* (☎01323/423197; ❸), overlooking the dramatic cliffs between Seven Sisters and Beachy Head, or bed down at the Frog Firle **youth hostel** (☎01323/870423, ⒺQalfriston@yha.org.uk) in a traditional Sussex flint building a couple of miles south of Alfriston, wonderfully set in the Cuckmere Valley.

Herstmonceux

Twelve miles northeast of Eastbourne is the huge partially moated, castellated castle of **Herstmonceux** (tours only; call ahead to confirm times ☎01323/834444; gardens April–Oct daily 10am–6pm; tours £2.50, gardens £4; ⊛www.seetb.org.uk/herstmonceux), whose Elizabethan grounds, featuring a formal walled garden and extensive woodland, make an ideal picnic spot. Tours are of a restricted area of the house only, as most of it forms part of Queen's University of Canada. Highlights include the Ballroom, Medieval Room and a stunning staircase – claimed to be one of the finest in the country – from the Elizabethan era, though most of the building has been extensively renovated and is very plain. Also in the grounds is the **Science Centre** (April–Sept daily 10am–6pm; Oct daily 10am–5pm; £4.75; combined ticket with castle grounds £7.75; ⊛www.science-project.org), former home of the Royal Observatory, which moved here from Greenwich in the 1950s to escape the postwar smog, only to be forced to leave for the clearer skies over the Pacific Ocean in the 1980s. The observatory's domes and telescopes are now open to the public and make an enjoyable day's outing for budding astronomers.

Lewes and around

East Sussex's county town, **LEWES** straddles the River Ouse as it carves a gap through the South Downs on its final stretch to the sea. Though there's been some rebuilding in the riverside Cliffe area (the place where Lewes started), and new housing estates are spreading from the town's fringes, the core of Lewes remains remarkably good-looking: Georgian and crooked older dwellings still line the High Street and the narrow lanes – or "Twittens" – lead off this main street and its continuations, with views onto the downs. With

---

The Bonfire Societies

Each November 5, while the rest of Britain lights small domestic bonfires or attends municipal firework displays to commemorate the foiling of a Catholic plot to blow up the Houses of Parliament, Lewes puts on a more dramatic show, whose origins lie in the deaths of the town's Protestant martyrs. By the end of the eighteenth century, Lewes' **Bonfire Boys** had become notorious for the boisterousness of their anti-Catholic demonstrations, in which they set off fireworks indiscriminately and dragged rolling tar barrels through the streets – a tradition still practised today, although with a little more caution. In 1845 events came to a head when the incorrigible pyromaniacs of Lewes had to be read the Riot Act, instigating a night of violence between the police and Bonfire Boys. Lewes' first **bonfire societies** were established soon afterwards, to try to get a bit more discipline into the proceedings, and in the early part of the last century they were persuaded to move their street fires to the town's perimeters.

Today's tightly knit bonfire societies, each with its quasi-militaristic motto ("Death or Glory", "True to Each Other", etc), spend much of the year organizing the Bonfire Night shenanigans, when their members dress up in traditional costumes and parade through the town carrying flaming torches, before marching off onto the downs for their society's big fire. At each of the fires effigies of Guy Fawkes and the pope are burned alongside contemporary, but equally reviled, figures – Chancellors of the Exchequer and Prime Ministers are popular choices.

some of England's most appealing chalkland right on its doorstep, and numerous traces of a history that stretches back to the Saxons, Lewes is a worthwhile stopover on any tour of the southeast – and an easy one, with good rail connections with London and along the coast.

Following the Norman Conquest, William's son-in-law, William de Warenne, built a priory and castle here, the latter still dominating the High Street. In 1264 Henry III's incompetence caused a baronial revolt led by Simon de Montfort which culminated in the king's surrender at the Battle of Lewes, although de Montfort and his reduced force were annihilated within a year at the Battle of Evesham. De Montfort's name crops up all over the town, as do references to the Lewes Martyrs, the seventeen Protestants burned here in 1556, at the height of Mary Tudor's militant revival of Catholicism – an event commemorated in spectacular fashion every November 5 (see box below). Intellectual non-conformity is something of a Lewes trademark, its roll call of free-thinkers featuring pioneer paleontologist Gideon Mantell and the radical humanist Tom Paine, whose *Common Sense* and *The Rights of Man* inspired or supported the revolutions in France and America. The conservative spirit triumphed in 1914, however, after a pair of local enthusiasts commissioned a version of Rodin's majestic sculpture *The Kiss*, depicting Paolo and Francesca – lovers from Dante's *Inferno* – clinched in a full-on embrace. Local sentiment was outraged when the piece was unveiled in Lewes town hall, leading to its rapid removal amid a flurry of controversy (the sculpture was re-exhibited in the town hall in June 1999, 85 years after the scandal).

The Town

The best way to begin a tour of the town from the train station is to walk up Station Road, then left down the High Street. Lewes's **Castle** (Mon–Sat 10am–5.30pm, Sun 11am–5.30pm; winter closes at dusk; £4; ⓦwww.sussexpast .co.uk) is hidden from view behind the houses on your right. Inside the castle complex – unusual for being built on two mottes, or mounds – the shell of the eleventh-century keep remains, and both the towers can be climbed for excellent views over the town to the surrounding downs. Tickets for the castle include admission to the **museum** (same hours as castle), by the castle entrance, which is much better than the usual stuffy town museum.

A few minutes' walk further west along the High Street past St Michael's Church, with its unusual twin towers – one wooden and the other flint – brings you to the steep cobbled and much photographed **Keere Street**, down which the reckless Prince Regent is alleged to have driven his carriage. Keere Street leads to **Southover Grange** (Mon–Sat 8am–dusk, Sun 9am–dusk; free), with its lovely gardens. Built in 1572 from the priory's remains, the Grange was also the childhood home of the diarist John Evelyn and now houses the local Registry Office. Past the gardens, a right turn down Southover High Street leads to the Tudor-built **Anne of Cleves House** (mid-Feb to Oct Mon–Sat 10am–5pm, Sun noon–5pm; Nov & Dec Tues–Sat 10am–5pm, Sun noon–5pm; Jan to mid-Feb Tues, Thurs & Sat 10am–5pm; £2.60; combined ticket with the castle £5.50; ⓦwww.sussexpast.co.uk), given to her in settlement after her divorce from Henry VIII – though she never actually lived there. The magnificent oak-beamed Tudor bedroom is impressive, with its cumbersome "bed wagon", a bed-warming brazier which would fail the slackest of fire regulations and which the 400-year-old Flemish four-poster has managed to survive. The house's decor dates from the sixteenth century when the Wealden iron industry was flourishing and Sussex produced most of England's iron, with Lewes being a centre of cannon manufacture.

On the opposite side of the road and closer to the train station is the church of **St John the Baptist**, with its squat, brick tower capped by a six-foot shark for a weather vane; inside there's some superb stained glass and a tiny chapel with the lead coffins of William de Warenne and his wife Gundrada, William I's daughter. De Warenne was one of the six barons presiding over the new administrative provinces – known as the **Rapes of Sussex** – created by the Normans soon after the Conquest. Behind the church are the ruins of de Warenne's **St Pancras Priory**, once one of Europe's principal Cluniac institutions, with a church the size of Westminster Abbey. Sadly it was dismantled to build town houses following the Dissolution and is now an evocative ruin surrounded by playing fields.

Back in the town centre, the **Star Brewery Studio** off Fisher St, north of the High Street, displays the creative talents of a collective of artists, bookbinders, carpenters and other artisans; the attached **Star Gallery** (Mon–Sat 10.30am–5.30pm; free) presents a changing series of exhibitions. At the east end of the High Street, School Hill descends towards **Cliffe Bridge**, built in 1727 and entrance to the commercial centre of the medieval settlement. For the energetic, a path leads up onto the Downs from the end of Cliffe High Street – site of England's worst avalanche disaster in 1836, when a bank of snow slid onto Cliffe village, killing eight people. The path passes close to an obelisk, commemorating the town's seventeen Protestant martyrs.

Practicalities

The **train station**, south of High Street down Station Road, has regular services from London Victoria and along the coast to Brighton, Eastbourne, Hastings and the **ferry port** at Newhaven, from where Hoverspeed runs to Dieppe (℡08705/240241). Buses leave from the **bus station** on Eastgate Street near the foot of School Hill. The **tourist office** is at the junction of the High Street and Fisher Street (Easter–Sept Mon–Fri 9am–5pm, Sat 10am–5pm, Sun 10am–2pm; Oct–Easter Mon–Fri 9am–5pm, Sat 10am–2pm; ℡01273/483448, ⓦwww.lewes.gov.uk).While there, pick up a copy of the free monthly **listings magazine**, *Lewes News*, for details of events in the town.

For **accommodation** try *Castle Banks Cottage*, 4 Castle Banks (℡01273 /476291, ⓔa1tourism.com/uk/castlebanks.html; ❷), a beamed period house with great views, tucked away off West St. The *Crown Inn*, 191 High St, close to the tourist office (℡01273/480670, ⓦwww.crowninn-lewes.co.uk; ❸), is a reasonable fallback. The nearest **youth hostel** is in the village of Telscombe, six miles south of Lewes (see p.223); there's another – a rustic wooden cabin with basic facilities – eleven miles northeast of town at Blackboys, near Uckfield (℡01825/890607).

Lewes is home of the excellent Harvey's brewery and most of the **pubs** serve its wares – try the *Brewers' Arms*, opposite St John the Baptist, the *Lewes Arms* tucked behind the Star Brewery Studios, or the *King's Head*, down on Southover High St; the last also specializes in game and fish dishes. Other **food** alternatives include the inexpensive Indian *Dilraj*, 12 Fisher St (℡01273 /479279), *La Cucina*, a moderately priced Italian joint at 13 Station St (℡01273 /476707), and the inexpensive *Pailin Thai* restaurant, opposite at no. 20 (℡01273/473906). Pricier options include *Thackery's* at 3 Malling St (℡01273/474634; Tues–Sat eve only), over the river at the east end of Cliffe High St, which serves traditional English and French-style food at moderate prices.

Glyndebourne

Glyndebourne, Britain's only unsubsidized opera house, is situated near the village of Glynde, three miles east of Lewes. Founded in 1934, the Glyndebourne season is an indispensable part of the high-society calendar, with ticket prices and a distribution system that excludes all but the most devoted opera-lovers. On one level, Glyndebourne is a repellent spectacle, its lawns thronged with gentry and corporate bigwigs ingesting champagne and smoked salmon – the productions have massive intervals to allow an unhurried repast. On the other hand, the musical values are the highest in the country, using young talent rather than expensive star names, and taking the sort of risks Covent Garden wouldn't dream of taking – for example, *Porgy and Bess* is now taken seriously as an opera largely as a result of a great Glyndebourne production. The recent arrival of a new, award-winning theatre (seating 1200) has broadened the appeal of this exclusive venue to a wider audience. There are tickets available at reduced prices for dress rehearsals or for standing-room-only tickets; call ☎01273/813813 for details or check the website at ⓦwww.glyndebourne.com.

Rodmell and around

Three miles south of Lewes lies the village of **RODMELL**, whose main source of interest is the **Monk's House** (April–Oct Wed & Sat 2–5.30pm; £2.60; NT), former home of Virginia Woolf, a leading figure of the Bloomsbury Group (see box opposite). She and her husband, Leonard, moved to the weatherboarded cottage in 1919 and Leonard stayed there until his death in 1969; both Virginia's and Leonard's remains are interred in the gardens. Nearby, you can see the River Ouse where Virginia killed herself in 1941 by walking into the water with her pockets full of stones. The house's interior is nothing special and will only really be of interest to ardent Bloomsbury fans; admirers can look round the study where Virginia wrote several of her novels, and her bedroom which is laid out with period editions of her work. To get there, catch a train to Southease, from where it's a mile northwest to Rodmell village, across the river.

Three miles south of Rodmell, in the village of **TELSCOMBE**, is a quiet **youth hostel** (☎01273/301357), whose simple accommodation is in 200-year-old cottages; take bus #123 from Lewes.

Charleston Farmhouse

Six miles east of Lewes, off the A27, is another Bloomsbury Group shrine, **Charleston Farmhouse** (March–June, Sept & Oct Wed–Sun 2–6pm; July & Aug Wed–Sun 11am–6pm; £5.50; ⓦwww.charleston.org.uk), home to Virginia Woolf's sister Vanessa Bell, Vanessa's husband, Clive Bell, and her lover, Duncan Grant. As conscientious objectors, the trio moved here during World War I so that the men could work on local farms (farm labourers were exempted from military service). The farmhouse became a gathering point for other members of the Bloomsbury Group, including the biographer Lytton Strachey, the economist Maynard Keynes and the novelist E.M. Forster. Duncan Grant continued to live in the house until his death in 1978. Unless it's a Sunday, you have to join a fifty-minute guided tour in order to view the interior of the farmhouse, where almost every surface is painted and the walls are hung with paintings by Picasso, Renoir and Augustus John, alongside the work of the markedly less talented residents. Many of the fabrics, lampshades and other artefacts bear the unmistakable mark of the Omega Workshop, the Bloomsbury equivalent of William Morris's artistic movement.

The Bloomsbury Group

The **Bloomsbury Group** were essentially a bevy of upper-middle-class friends, who took their name from the Bloomsbury area of London, where most of them lived before acquiring houses in the Sussex countryside. The Group revolved around Virginia, Vanessa, Thoby and Adrian Stephen, who lived at 46 Gordon Square, the London base of the Bloomsbury Group. Thoby's Thursday evening gatherings and Vanessa's Friday Club for painters attracted a whole host of Cambridge-educated snobs who subscribed to Oscar Wilde's theory that "aesthetics are higher than ethics". Their diet of "human intercourse and the enjoyment of beautiful things" was hardly revolutionary, but their behaviour, particularly that of the two sisters (unmarried, unchaperoned, intellectual and artistic), succeeded in shocking London society, especially through their louche sexual practices (most of the group swung both ways).

All this, though interesting, would be forgotten were it not for their individual work. In 1922 Virginia declared, without too much exaggeration, "Everyone in Gordon Square has become famous": Lytton Strachey had been the first to make his name with *Eminent Victorians*, a series of unprecedentedly frank biographies; Vanessa, now married to the art critic Clive Bell, had become involved in Roger Fry's prolific design firm, Omega Workshop; and the economist John Maynard Keynes had become an adviser to the Treasury (he later went on to become the leading economic theorist of his day). The Group's most celebrated figure, Virginia, married Leonard Woolf and became an established novelist; she and Leonard also founded the Hogarth Press, which published T.S. Eliot's *Waste Land* in 1922.

Eliot was just one of a number of writers, such as Aldous Huxley, Bertrand Russell and E.M. Forster, who were drawn to the interwar Bloomsbury set, but others, notably D.H. Lawrence, were repelled by the clan's narcissism and snobbish narrow-mindedness. Whatever their limitations, the Bloomsbury Group were Britain's most influential intellectual coterie of the interwar years, and their appeal shows little sign of waning – even now, scarcely a year goes by without the publication of the biography or memoirs of some Bloomsbury peripheral.

Brighton

Recorded as the tiny fishing village of Brithelmeston in the Domesday Book, **BRIGHTON** seems to have slipped unnoticed through history until the mid-eighteenth-century sea-bathing trend established a resort that has never looked back. The fad received royal approval in the 1770s when the decadent Prince Regent, later George IV, began patronizing the town in the company of his mistress, thus setting a precedent for the "dirty weekend", Brighton's major contribution to the English collective consciousness. Trying to shake off this blowsy reputation, Brighton now highlights its Georgian charm, its upmarket shops and classy restaurants, and its thriving conference industry. Yet, however much it tries to present itself as a comfortable middle-class town, the essence of Brighton's appeal is its faintly bohemian vitality, a buzz that comes from a mix of English holiday-makers, thousands of young foreign students from the town's innumerable language schools, a thriving gay community and an energetic local student population from the art college and two universities.

Arrival, information and accommodation

Brighton is served by numerous trains from London's Victoria, London Bridge and King's Cross stations. There are also regular services along the coast from

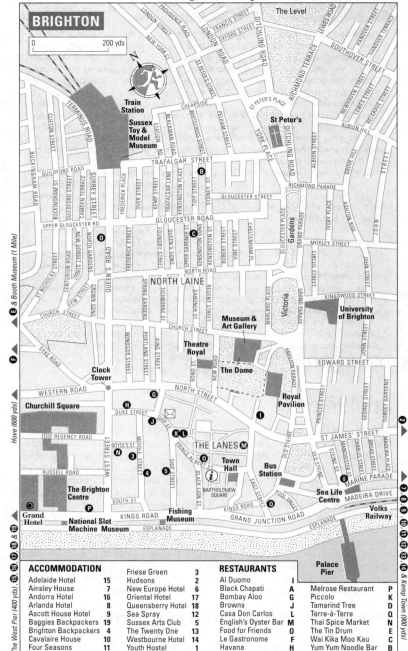

BRIGHTON

▲ **A**, Preston Manor, **1** & A23 London   ▲ A27 Lewes

0 — 200 yds

◀ & Booth Museum (1 Mile)   Hove (600 yds) ◀   The West Pier (400 yds), ◀

SURREY, KENT AND SUSSEX | Brighton

228

ACCOMMODATION

Adelaide Hotel	15
Ainsley House	7
Andorra Hotel	16
Arlanda Hotel	8
Ascott House Hotel	9
Baggies Backpackers	19
Brighton Backpackers	4
Cavalaire House	10
Four Seasons	11
Friese Green	3
Hudsons	2
New Europe Hotel	6
Oriental Hotel	17
Queensberry Hotel	18
Sea Spray	12
Sussex Arts Club	5
The Twenty One	13
Westbourne Hotel	14
Youth Hostel	1

RESTAURANTS

Al Duomo	I
Black Chapati	A
Bombay Aloo	G
Browns	J
Casa Don Carlos	L
English's Oyster Bar	M
Food for Friends	O
Le Gastronome	F
Havana	H
Melrose Restaurant	P
Piccolo	K
Tamarind Tree	D
Terre-à-Terre	Q
Thai Spice Market	N
The Tin Drum	E
Wai Kika Moo Kau	C
Yum Yum Noodle Bar	B

Hastings, Eastbourne via Lewes, and from Portsmouth via Chichester. The **train station** is at the head of Queen's Road, which descends to the Clock Tower and then becomes West Street which eventually leads to the seafront – a distance of about half a mile. National Express and Southdown **bus services** arrive at Pool Valley **bus station**, tucked just in from the seafront on the south side of the Old Steine. Open-top **bus tours** (April–Oct; £6.50) operate on a circular route around the town and up and down the sea front, passing both the train station and tourist office – tickets are valid all day.

The **tourist office** is at 10 Bartholomew Square (June–Sept Mon–Fri 9am–6pm, Sat 10am–5pm, Sun 10am–4pm; rest of year Mon–Sat 9am–5pm, Sun 10am–4pm; ℡0906/7112255), behind the town hall on the southern side of the Lanes – the maze of narrow alleyways marking Brighton's old town. You'll find most budget **accommodation** clustered around the **Kemp Town** district, to the east of the Palace Pier, with the more elegant and expensive hotels west of the town centre around Regency Square, opposite the West Pier; many places offer reductions for stays of two nights or more so it's always worth enquiring. Brighton's official **campsite** is the *Sheepcote Valley* site (℡01273/626546), just north of Brighton Marina; take bus #1 or #1A to Wilson Ave, or take the Volks railway and walk up Arundel Road to Wilson Avenue.

Hotels, B&Bs and guest houses

Adelaide Hotel 51 Regency Square ℡01273 /205286, ⓦwww.smoothhound.co.uk/hotels /adelaide.html. Top-notch guest house in the fancier part of town. One room has a four-poster bed. ❺

Ainsley House 28 New Steine ℡01273/605310, ⓦwww.ainsleyhotel.com. Friendly, upmarket guest house in an attractive Regency terrace. ❸

Andorra Hotel 15–16 Oriental Place ℡01273/321787. At the west end of town, this hotel has comfortable rooms with good facilities. ❷

Arlanda Hotel 20 New Steine ℡01273/699300, ⓦwww.arlandahotel.co.uk. Plusher than average choice in the New Steine square, with wide price range depending on the room; the cheapest are on the top floor and quite poky. ❷

Ascott House Hotel 21 New Steine ℡01273/ 688085, ⓦwww.ascotthousehotel.com. Very comfortable guest house near the sea front. ❸

Cavalaire House 34 Upper Rock Gardens ℡01273/696899, ⓦwww.cavalaire.co.uk. Average B&B, just off Marine Parade, which has triples and offers the seventh night free. ❷

Four Seasons 3 Upper Rock Gardens ℡01273 /673574, ⓔjoehalpenny@compuserve. com. Cosy B&B in the Kemp Town area, with good vegetarian breakfast options. ❹

Hudsons 22 Devonshire Place ℡01273/683642. Relaxed and exclusively gay guest house east of the centre off St James's St. ❹

New Europe Hotel 31–32 Marine Parade ℡01273/624462, ⓦwww.new europehotel.co.uk. Large, buzzing, gay hotel on the seafront, with late bar and regular cabaret nights. ❹

Oriental Hotel 9 Oriental Place ℡01273/205050, ⓔinfo@orientalhotel.co.uk. Friendly, laid-back staff and very funky decor throughout; full veggie breakfasts are served in the hotel's mellow café. ❸

Queensbury Hotel 58 Regency Square ℡01273 /325558. Comfortable guest house in Brighton's definitive Georgian district. ❸

Sea Spray 25 New Steine ℡01273/680332, ⓔseaspray@brighton.co.uk. Good-value B&B with showers in all rooms. ❷

Sussex Arts Club 7 Ship St ℡01273/727371, ⓦwww.sussexarts.com. Laid-back and lively hotel, though with just seven rooms, in a Regency house right in the centre of town, with a pub on the ground floor and a club in the basement. ❺

The Twenty One 21 Charlotte St, off Marine Parade ℡01273/686450, ⓔrooms@the21.co.uk. Classy Kemp Town B&B with very comfortable rooms in an ornate, early Victorian house. ❸

Westbourne Hotel 46 Upper Rock Gardens ℡01273/686920, ⓔmail@westbournehotel.net. Well-appointed B&B close to the seafront and all amenities. ❸

Hostels

Baggies Backpackers 33 Oriental Place ℡01273/733740. Spacious house a little west of the West Pier with large bright dorms, starting at £9 a night, decent showers and plenty of room to spread out.

Brighton Backpackers 75 Middle St ℡01273 /777717, ⓦwww.brightonbackpackers. com. Brighton's established independent hostel with a lively, easy-going atmosphere and vivid murals. A new annexe just round the corner overlooks the seafront and offers a quieter alternative; dorm beds £9, twin rooms £25.

Friese Green 20 Middle St ☎ 01273/747551, ⓦ www.friese-green.demon.co.uk. The folk here are friendly enough, and it's very central, but lacks the atmosphere and comforts of its competitors. Dorm beds £9; small rooms £12.50 per person.

Youth Hostel Patcham Place, London Rd ☎ 01273/556196, ⓔ brighton@yha.org.uk. Brighton's YHA hostel is housed in a splendid Queen Anne mansion, in parkland four miles north of the sea, close to the junction of the roads to Lewes and London. Take bus #5A from the town centre.

The Town

Any visit to Brighton inevitably begins with a visit to its two most famous landmarks – the exuberant **Royal Pavilion** and the wonderfully tacky **Palace Pier**, a few minutes away – followed by a stroll along the seafront promenade or the pebbly beach. Just as interesting, though, is an exploration of Brighton's car-free **Lanes**, where some of the town's diverse restaurants, bars and tiny bric-a-brac, jewellery and antique shops can be found, or an idle meander through the quaint, but more bohemian streets of **North Laine**.

The Royal Pavilion and the Brighton Museum

In any survey to find England's most loved building, there's always a bucketful of votes for Brighton's exotic extravaganza, the **Royal Pavilion** (daily: June–Sept 10am–6pm; Oct–May 10am–5pm; £5.20; ⓦ www.royalpavilion. brighton.co.uk), which flaunts itself in the middle of the Old Steine, a main thoroughfare along which most of the seafront-bound road traffic gets funnelled. Until 1787, the building that stood here was a well-appointed but conventional farmhouse, which was first rented by the fun-loving Prince of Wales in the previous year. He then commissioned its conversion into something more regal, and for a couple of decades the prince's south-coast pied-à-terre was a Palladian villa, with mildly oriental embellishments.

Upon becoming Prince Regent, however, George was fully able to indulge his taste for excess, and in 1815 his patronage fell upon John Nash, architect of London's Regent Street. What Nash came up with was an extraordinary confection of slender minarets, twirling domes, pagodas, balconies and miscellaneous motifs imported from India and China and supported on an innovative cast-iron frame, creating an exterior profile that defines a genre of its own – Oriental-Gothic. George had the time of his life here, frolicking with his mistress, Mrs Fitzherbert, whom he installed in a house on the west side of the Old Steine.

On ascending the throne in 1837 the dour Queen Victoria was not amused by George's taste in architecture, and she shifted the royal seaside residence to the Isle of Wight. All the Pavilion's valuable fittings were carted off to Buckingham and Kensington palaces and Victoria sold the gutted building to the town. The Pavilion was then pressed into a series of humdrum roles – tea room, hospital, concert hall, radar station, ration office – but has now been brilliantly restored, completely eradicating damage caused by an arson attack in 1975, and by the storm in October 1987, which hurled a dislodged minaret through the roof and floor of the nearly completed Music Room.

Inside the Pavilion the exuberant compendium of Regency exotica has been enhanced by the return of many of the objects which Victoria had taken away. One of the highlights – approached via the restrained Long Gallery – is the **Banqueting Room**, which erupts with ornate splendour and is dominated by a one-ton chandelier hung from the jaws of a massive dragon cowering in a plantain tree. Next door, the huge, high-ceilinged kitchen, fitted with the most modern appliances of its time, has iron columns disguised as palm trees.

△ Funfair, Brighton

Nearby, the stunning **Music Room**, the first sight of which reduced George to tears of joy, has a huge dome lined with more than twenty-six thousand individually gilded scales and hung with exquisite umbrella-like glass lamps. After climbing the famous cast-iron staircase with its bamboo-look banisters, you can go into Victoria's sober and seldom-used bedroom and the North Gallery where the king's portrait hangs, along with a selection of satirical cartoons. More notable, though, is the **South Gallery**, decorated in sky blue with trompe l'oeil bamboo trellises and a carpet which appears to be strewn with flowers.

Across the gardens from the Pavilion stands the **Dome**, once the royal stables and now the town's main concert hall; it adjoins the **Brighton Museum and Art Gallery** (Mon, Tues & Thurs–Sat 10am–5pm, Sun 2–5pm; free), which is entered just around the corner on Church Street. It houses an eclectic mix including modern fashion and design, archeology, painting and local history, including a large collection of pottery, from basic Neolithic earthenware to delicate porcelain figurines popular in the eighteenth century. The collection of classic Art Deco and Art Nouveau furniture stands out, the highlight being Dalí's famous sofa based on Mae West's lips. The *Balcony Café* is the perfect setting for a coffee or tea, perched above a sea of exhibits from which you can enjoy the lines of this lovingly restored Victorian building.

The Lanes and North Laine

Tucked between the Pavilion and the seafront is a warren of narrow, pedestrianized thoroughfares known as **the Lanes** – the core of the old fishing village from which Brighton evolved. Long-established antiques shops, designer outlets and several bars, pubs and restaurants generate a lively and intimate atmosphere in this part of town. **North Laine** – "laine" was the local term for a strip of land – which spreads north of North Street along Kensington, Sydney, Gardner and Bond streets, is more bohemian with its hub along pedestrianized Kensington Gardens. Here the shops are more eclectic, selling second-hand records, clothes, bric-a-brac and New Age objects, and mingle with earthy coffee shops and downbeat cafés. Slightly to the north of here is the **Sussex Toy and Model Museum** (Mon–Fri 10am–1pm & 2–5pm, Sat 11am–1pm & 2–5pm; £3), housed in an old stables underneath the train station. The collection is impressive, ranging from an entire cabinet full of Smurfs to a set of Pelham puppets, but it's the working model railways that are likely to be the focus of most children's attention.

The seafront

Most of the seafront is an ugly mix of shops, entertainment complexes and hotels, ranging from the impressively pompous plasterwork of the *Grand Hotel* – scene of the IRA's attempted assassination of the Conservative Cabinet in October 1984 – to the green-glass monstrosity on the seaward side of the Lanes. To appreciate fully the tackier side of Brighton, you must take a stroll along the **Palace Pier** whose every inch is devoted to fun and money-making, from the cacophonous *Palace of Fun* to the *Pleasure Dome*, from the state-of-the-art video games to the fairground rides and karaoke sessions at the end of the pier. Brighton's architecturally superior West Pier, built in 1866 half a mile west along the seafront, was damaged in World War II and then fell into disrepair, but looks set to be restored to its former glory by 2002.

Underneath the arches between the Palace and West piers, there are two small museums: the **National Museum of Penny Slot Machines** (April–Oct Sat & Sun 11am–6pm; also during school holidays daily 11am–6pm; free), which houses decrepit antique slot machines which struggle to function; and the **Brighton Fishing Museum** (May–Oct daily 9am–5pm; free), which has old photos and video footage of the golden days of the local fishing industry and shelters a large Sussex clinker, once a common boat on Brighton beach.

Across the road from the Palace Pier, on Marine Parade, is the **Sea-Life Centre** (daily 10am–5pm; £5.50; ✆ www.sealife.co.uk), one of the best marine life displays of its kind, with a transparent tunnel passing through a huge aquarium – a walk along the bottom of the sea with sharks and rays gliding overhead. Nearby, the antiquated locomotives of **Volks Electric Railway** (April to mid-Sept; £1.60 return) – the first electric train in the country – run eastward towards the Marina and the nudist beach, usually the preserve of just a few thick-skinned souls. En route, you pass the **Madeira Lift** (Easter to mid-Sept 9.45am–7.15pm; free), a pagoda-like Victorian tower built in 1890 from which you can enjoy a great view over Brighton and out to sea.

Booth Museum and Preston Manor

In the north of Brighton's suburbs there are two museums worth a look. The big municipal museum, the **Booth Museum of Natural History** (Mon–Wed, Fri & Sat 10am–5pm, Sun 2–5pm; free), is a mile up Dukes Road from the centre of town (bus #10 or #10A). Purpose-built to house Mr E.T. Booth's prodigious collection of stuffed birds, this is a wonderfully fusty old Victorian museum with beetles, butterflies and animal skeletons galore, but which also displays very imaginative temporary shows.

The delightful **Preston Manor** (Mon 1–5pm, Tues–Sat 10am–5pm, Sun 2–5pm; £3) was originally built in 1250, though the present building dates from 1738 and 1905. Inside a series of period interiors evokes the life of the Edwardian gentry, from the servants' quarters downstairs to the luxury nursery upstairs. The house is two miles north of Brighton on the A23, but only a short walk from Preston Park train station.

Eating, drinking and nightlife

Brighton has the greatest concentration of **restaurants** anywhere in the southeast, outside London. Around North Laine are some great, inexpensive cafés, while for classier establishments head to the Lanes and out towards neighbouring Hove. Many of the cheaper places fight hard to attract the large student market with discounted deals of around ten percent, so if you have a student ID, use it.

Nightlife is hectic and compulsively pursued throughout the year, making Brighton unique in the sedate southeast. There are a couple of outstanding **clubs**, lots of **live music** and more cinema screens per head than anywhere else in Britain. Midweek entry into the clubs can cost just a couple of pounds and cinema seats are similarly priced before 6pm.

Every May the three-week-long **Brighton Festival** (✆01273/700747) takes place in various venues around town. This arty celebration includes funfairs, exhibitions, street theatre and concerts from classical to jazz. Running at the same time is the **Brighton and Hove Fringe Festival** (✆01273 /295590), which also stages live music and drama, literature readings and tons of club nights.

Brighton has one of the longest established and most thriving gay communities in Britain, with a variety of lively clubs and bars drawing people from all over the southeast. It also hosts a number of gay events including the annual **Gay Pride Festival**, held over two weeks at the beginning of July. It's a great excuse for a party with loads going on from the performing arts to exhibitions, not to mention the **Brighton Parade**, a day-and-night-long jamboree. For details on all events, call ☎0906/683642.

For up-to-date details of **what's on**, pick up a copy of the monthly *Insight* (£1) from newsagents or the free monthly listing magazines *What's On* or *Source* from the tourist office while the similarly free *Gscene*, covering gay events, can be found in gay bars, clubs and shops. If you've access to the internet check out the the highly praised **website** ⓦ www.brighton.co.uk. See "Listings" (p.236) for details of Brighton's internet cafés.

Restaurants

Al Duomo 7 Pavilion Buildings ☎01273/326741. Brilliant pizzeria, with a genuine wood-burning oven. Has a more intimate sister restaurant, *Al Forno*, at 36 East St ☎01273/324905. Inexpensive.

Black Chapati 12 Circus Parade ☎01273 /699011. Innovative Asian cooking with Japanese and Thai influences as well as more conventional Indian dishes, which are brilliantly executed. Something of a Brighton landmark despite its out-of-the-way location, more than a mile inland, at the point where the London road enters town. Moderate.

Bombay Aloo 39 Ship St ☎01273/776038. No flock wallpaper and an all-you-can-eat veggie buffet for a fiver – what more could you ask for? Inexpensive.

Browns 3–4 Duke St ☎01273/323501. A mixture of steak, seafood and pasta dishes as well as traditional favourites such as Guinness-marinated steak-and-mushroom pie, served in a sophisticated continental setting with wooden floors, palms and background jazz. Moderate.

Casa Don Carlos 5 Union St ☎01273/327177. Small, long-established tapas bar in the Lanes with outdoor seating and daily specials. Also serves more substantial Spanish dishes and drinks. Inexpensive.

English's Oyster Bar 29–31 East St ☎01273 /327980. Three fishermen's cottages knocked together to house a marble and brass oyster bar and a red velvet dining room. Seafood's the speciality with a mouth-watering menu and better value than you might expect, especially the set menus. Brighton institution famed for its atmosphere as much as its food. Expensive.

Food for Friends 17 Prince Albert St ☎01273 /202310. Brighton's ever-popular wholefood veggie eatery is imaginative enough to please die-hard meat-eaters. It's usually busy, but well worth the squeeze and offers discounts for students and music on Sun evenings. Inexpensive.

Le Gastronome 3 Hampton Place ☎01273 /777399. Well known for its good-value classic French cuisine, friendly service and outstanding selection of wines; choose the dish of the day for

£8 or a five-course blow-out for £22.50. Closed Sun & Mon. Moderate.

Havana 33 Duke St ☎01273/773388. Very stylish continental brasserie with just a hint of colonial ambience – palms and rattan chairs – to evoke tropical luxury and a feeling of being pampered. The menu is eclectic, ranging from Med to Thai – the lunchtime menu is particularly good value. Moderate.

Melrose Restaurant 132 King's Rd ☎01273 /326520. Traditional and decent seafront establishment which has been serving seafood, roasts and custard-covered puddings for over forty years. The *Regency Restaurant* next door is a similar and smaller option. Inexpensive.

Piccolo 56 Ship St ☎01273/380380. Informal Italian restaurant with pizza and pasta dishes from around £5 and special deals for students. Inexpensive.

Tamarind Tree 48 Queen's Rd ☎01273/298816. Mellow Caribbean café decked in turquoise and wickerwork, with a surprisingly large range of veggie dishes. Main dishes around £9, or you could just have a filling starter. Moderate.

Terre-à-Terre 71 East St ☎01273/729051. Imaginative, global, veggie cuisine in a modern arty setting. Closed Mon lunch & Sun. Moderate.

Thai Spice Market 13 Boyces St ☎01273 /325195. Classical Thai interior and cuisine, serving meat, seafood and vegetarian varieties. Inexpensive to moderate.

The Tin Drum 95–97 Dyke Rd ☎01273/777575. Buzzing new continental-style café-bar and restaurant with a taste for Baltic-rim cooking and a blend of Eastern European influences; fresh seasonal ingredients and speciality vodkas are distilled on the premises. Moderate.

Wai Kika Moo Kau 11 Kensington Gardens ☎01273/671117. Slightly distressed decor at this funky global veggie café/restaurant with everything from Thai curry to aubergine bake – all for under £5. Inexpensive.

Yum Yum Noodle Bar 22–23 Sydney St ☎01273 /606777. Serves anything Southeast Asian – Chinese, Thai, Indonesian and Malaysian noodle dishes at good-value prices – situated above a Chinese supermarket. Lunch only. Inexpensive.

Cafés and bars

Bar Centro 6 Ship St. Brighton's biggest, most spacious pre-club bar with occasional in-house DJs spinning tunes.

Bar Latino 62, Middle St. Tapas bar with regular live screenings of Spanish and Portuguese football matches and a healthy dose of salsa too.

Dorset Street Bar corner of Gardner St and North Rd. Bar, café and restaurant rolled into one, with delicious international vegetarian and vegan dishes to tempt you and vegan beers too. They also do real cream teas.

The Fish Bowl East St. A popular pre-club choice for its range of music – sometimes better than the clubs themselves.

Good Bean 16 Prince Albert St and 41 Trafalgar St. Great tasting coffee in uncluttered surroundings.

Grinders, 10 Kensington Gardens. Upstairs trip-happy café serving tasty cheap snacks and great soups, with a balcony for watching life in North Laine go by, and lots of club fliers to hand.

Innocent Bystander 54 Preston St, off King's Rd, near the West Pier. Hungry clubbers' favourite greasy spoon with all the usuals plus vegan breakfasts and the infamous "Gut Buster" breakfast, served to a background of MTV; open till 3am.

Kai 52 Gardner St. Fully organic café offering both wheat- and gluten-free options; non-smoking.

Mock Turtle, 4 Pool Valley. Old-fashioned tea shop crammed with bric-a-brac and cheap, home-made cakes. Closed Sun & Mon.

The Sanctuary 51–55 Brunswick St East, Hove ☎01273/770012. Cool and arty vegetarian café with soft furnishings and a cosy, relaxed ambience. Deservedly popular, despite its not-very-central location.

The Squid 78 Middle St. A self-styled pre-club bar in those ever popular primary colours, with drinks at £2.50 a shot to fire you up for the night.

Sumo 8–12 Middle St. Designer-cool Pacific-rim bar with DJs spinning R&B and hip-hop plus internet access too.

Zanzibar 129 St James's St. Premier pre-club gay bar out towards Kemp Town.

Pubs

The Aquarium 6 Steine St. A gay pub that's simply a pub and extremely popular too with occasional cabaret.

The Cricketers 15 Black Lion St. Just west of the Lanes, this is Brighton's oldest pub and it looks it too; very popular with good pub grub served in the pleasant setting of its Courtyard Bar.

Dr Brighton's 16 King's Rd. Popular gay venue.

Druid's Head, 9 Brighton Place. Great, old pub in the heart of the Lanes with a flagstone floor and a raucous jukebox.

Fiddler's Elbow Boyces St. Irish pub with traditional music on Wed nights.

Font & Firkin Union St. Spacious converted chapel with a bar in place of the altar and occasional live music.

Free Butt Inn Albion St. Busy pub with a full calendar of live music.

The Full Moon Boyces St. A garish yellow and blue facade hides an airy interior where you can pick from a menu consisting of almost entirely organic food.

The Great Eastern 103 Trafalgar St. Relaxing pub with bare boards and bookshelves, lots of real ales, and no fruit machines or TV.

The Greys 105 Southover St. Old-fashioned pub with an open fire, stone floors and wooden benches – with some great food available courtesy of the Belgian chef. Frequent live bands.

The Hand in Hand 33 Upper St James St. An agreeable pub with its own brewery out the back.

Hector's House Grand Parade. Big bare-boards-and-sofa student pub that has nightly pre-club music (except Mon) with in-house DJs.

The Market Inn Market St. Old-fashioned real ale pub offering reasonably priced lunches and evening meals.

The Marlborough Prince's St. Friendly pub just off Old Steine, popular with a gay and mixed crowd.

O'Neill's 27 Ship St. Big Irish-themed pub, but popular and with occasional live music.

The Prince Albert 48 Trafalgar St. A listed building, right by the train station, popular with students. Live rock upstairs, real ale downstairs; free pool in the afternoon.

The Smugglers 10 Ship St. A young crowd packs out this place, with a good jazz club upstairs, dance club downstairs, and free pool during the day.

Arts centres and comedy clubs

Akademia 14–17 Manchester St ☎01273/622633. Stand-up comedy and late bar.

Brighton Media Centre/Cinematheque 9–12 Middle St ☎01273/384300. Art-house cinema and exhibition space, with internet facilities available.

Gardner Arts Centre University of Sussex, Falmer ☎01273/685861, ⊛www.gardnerarts.co.uk. Performing and visual arts; theatre, cinema, workshops, exhibition space and café.

Komedia Gardner St, North Laine ☎01273/647100, ⊛www.komedia.co.uk. Lively alternative theatre-café notable for its regular roll call of stand-up comedy and live music. Late bar.

Sussex Arts Club Ship St ☎01273/727371. Live bands, theatre and performance, plus exhibition space. The building includes a late bar and hotel.

Clubs and live music venues

The Beach King's Road Arches ☎01273/722222. R'n'b, classic grooves and occasional stand-up comedy nights.

Casablanca 3 Middle St ☎01273/321817. Basement venue featuring live bands and all types of funk, including latin and jazz.

Club New York 11 Dyke Rd ☎01273/208678. Salsa seven nights a week upstairs and a mixture of everything from 60s nights to highlife downstairs.

Concorde 2 Madeira Shelter, Madeira Drive ☎01273/207241. Live music venue, with an admirable booking policy featuring everyone from Bert Jansch to Sparklehorse; also has club nights at the weekend and a Tues night comedy club.

Cuba 160 King's Rd Arches ☎01273/770505. Disco, salsa, techno and hip-hop nights at this lofty bar/club by the beach opposite West St.

Escape 10 Marine Parade ☎01273/606906. Brighton's trendiest nightclub packs them in night after night, specializing in funk and techno.

Honey Club 214 King's Rd Arches ☎01273/202807. Garage, house and hip-hop – and a lively crowd.

The Jazz Rooms, *Smugglers Inn*, 10 Ship St ☎01273/328439. Popular jazz venue in the basement, with the livelier *Enigma* upstairs catering for active ravers and fronting the occasional abstract dance troupe.

The Joint 37 West St ☎01273/321692. Indie and disco sounds.

Paradox 78 West St ☎01273/321628. The best option after the *Zap Club*. Its *Wild Fruits* gay nights on the first Mon of the month are particularly popular.

Revenge 32 Old Steine ☎01273/606064. The south's largest gay club with Mon night cabarets plus upfront dance and retro boogie on two floors.

The Tavern Castle Square ☎01273/827641. Classic soul, funk and disco go down a treat at this central club, off Old Steine.

Volks Tavern 3 The Colonnade, Madeira Drive ☎01273/682828. Under the arches on Marine Parade, you'll find a groovy crowd with live bands, reggae revival nights and some break beats. There's even a fetish night if you're up for it.

Zap Club 188–193 Kings Rd Arches ☎01273/821588. Brighton's most durable club, right on the seafront opposite Ship Street.

Listings

Banks and Exchanges There are branches of all the major high-street banks in the main shopping streets leading away from the Clock Tower. Exchanges include: American Express, 82 North St ☎01273/712901; Streetwise, Castle Square ☎01273/729948; and Thomas Cook, 58 North St ☎01273/367700.

Bike Rental Freedom Bikes, 96 St James's St ☎01273/681698; Rayment's Cycles, 13–14 Circus Parade, New England Rd ☎01273/697217; Sunrise Cycle Hire, West Pier, King's Rd Arches ☎01273/748881. Rental from £12/day, £30/week. Deposit £20.

Books Borders, Churchill Square ☎01273/731122; Bredon's, 56 East St ☎01273/328032; Waterstone's, 55 North St ☎01273/327867.

Buses One Stop Travel, 16 Old Steine ☎01273/886200; Brighton and Hove Buses, kiosk in the Gardens, Old Steine ☎01273/606141; Stagecoach/Coastline South Coast Buses ☎01903/237661; National Express ☎0990/808080.

Car rental Affordable Car Hire, 1–2 Victoria Terrace, Kingsway, Hove ☎01273/724464; Hertz, 47 Trafalgar St ☎01273/738227.

Cinemas Duke of York's Picturehouse, Preston Circus ☎01273/602503; Odeon, West St ☎08705/505000; UCG Multiplex, Brighton Marina ☎0541/555145.

Dentist ☎01273/777790.

Hospitals For emergencies Royal Sussex County, Eastern Rd ☎01273/696955.

Internet Sumo restaurant, 8–12 Middle St ☎01273/823344; Brighton Reference Library, Church St ☎01273/296968; Brighton Internet Café, 37 Preston St ☎01273/227185; Internet Junction, 109 Western Rd ☎01273/772272 & 101 St George St ☎01273/607650.

Laundry Wash-a-Rama, 12 Elm Grove; Bubbles 1, 75 Preston St; KG Launderette, 116 St George's Rd.

Left Luggage At the train station (24-hour service).

Lesbian and Gay Switchboard Daily 6–11pm ☎01273/204050.

Pharmacies Ashton's, 98 Dyke Rd ☎01273/325020. Daily till 10pm.

Police John St, off Edward St, near the Pavilion ☎01273/606744.

Post offices 51 Ship St (Mon–Sat 9am–5.30pm).

Taxis ☎01273/205205, 414141 or 747474.

Travel agents Going Places, 125 Queens Rd ☎01273/202676; STA Travel, 38 North St ☎01273/728282; Thomas Cook, 58 North St ☎01273/367700.

Mid-Sussex

The principal attraction of **Mid-Sussex** is its wealth of fine gardens, ranging from the majestic **Sheffield Park** to the tree plantations of **Wakehurst**, the luscious flowerbeds of **Nymans** to the landscaped lakes of **Leonardslee**. Exploring this region by public transport isn't really feasible unless you take your bike on the train; tourist information is thin on the ground too – it's best to get clued up at Brighton's tourist office beforehand, if you're interested in doing a thorough tour.

Sheffield Park and the Bluebell Railway

Around twenty miles northeast of Brighton lies the country estate of **Sheffield Park**, its centrepiece a Gothic mansion built for Lord Sheffield by James Wyatt. The house is closed to the public, but you can roam around the hundred-acre **gardens** (Jan & Feb Sat & Sun 10.30am–4pm; March–Oct Tues–Sun & public holidays 10.30am–6pm; Nov & Dec Tues–Sun 10.30am–4pm; £4.60; combined ticket with Bluebell Railway £10.50; NT), which were laid out by Capability Brown, the Christopher Wren of the grassy knoll. The gardens and pathways are based around a series of five landscaped ponds – vestiges of Sussex's industrial iron-smelting days. At their best in spring and autumn, the gardens feature a wide range of exotic plants and trees, with the taller conifers mimicking the house's spires.

A mile southwest of the gardens lies the southern terminus of the **Bluebell Railway** (May–Sept daily; Oct–April Sat, Sun & school holidays; day ticket £8; ☎01825/720800, ⓦwww.bluebell-railway.co.uk), whose vintage steam locomotives chuff nine miles north via Horsted Keynes to Kingscote. Although the service gets extremely crowded at weekends – especially in May, when the bluebells blossom in the woods through which the line passes – it's an entertaining and nostalgic way of travelling through the Sussex countryside and your day ticket lets you go to and fro as often as you like. A vintage bus service connects the northern terminus of Kingscote (no car access) with East Grinstead train station (hourly trains from London Victoria), though plans are afoot to re-lay the remaining two miles of track and link the Bluebell directly with East Grinstead.

Wakehurst Place and Nymans

Wakehurst Place, eighteen miles north of Brighton (daily: Feb & Oct 10am–5pm; March 10am–6pm; April–Sept 10am–7pm; Nov–Jan 10am–4pm; £5; NT), is the country home of Kew Royal Botanic Gardens (ⓦwww .kew.org/traveltrade). The 25-acre site is given over mainly to trees and shrubs but, like many gardens in the area, was badly hit by the a major storm in 1987 when it lost more than fifteen thousand trees. However, the collection has been gradually replenished and now features a variety of horticultural environments, including a Himalayan Glade and an Asian Heath Garden. The gardens spread down from the Jacobean mansion to beyond Westwood lake, from where paths then lead back to the house, making a pleasant hour-and-a-half's round walk. Wakehurst's newest development is the part-Lottery funded Millennium Seed Bank whose aim is to safeguard some 24,000 plant species by cleaning and then freezing the seeds in underground vaults. The nearest station is Haywards Heath, on the London–Brighton line, from where you can catch bus #772 – a limited daily service, which actually starts its journey from Old Steine in Brighton.

For one of the southeast's greatest gardens, head five miles southwest of Wakehurst Place to **Nymans** (March to early Nov Wed–Sun 11am–6pm; £6; NT), near the village of Handcross; bus #773 from Brighton to Crawley can drop you off on the A23 beside the village. Created by Ludwig Messel, an inspired gardener and plant collector, the gardens contain a valuable collection of exotic trees and shrubs as well as more everyday plants, of which the colourful rhododendrons are particularly prolific. Nymans consists of a series of different enclosures and gardens, the highlight of which is the large, romantic walled garden, almost hidden from sight by an abundance of climbing plants and housing a collection of rare Himalayan magnolia trees. The gardens are centred on the picturesque ruins of a mock-Tudor manor house, now covered in wisteria, roses and honeysuckle, and are laced with gently sloping paths linking the huge beds of rhododendrons, azaleas and roses.

Leonardslee Gardens

The most picturesque of all the mid-Sussex gardens are those at **Leonardslee** (daily: April–Oct 9.30am–6pm; £5, £7 in May; ⓦ www.leonardslee.com), four miles southwest of Nymans, near the village of Crabtree; bus #107 from Brighton to Horsham passes by the garden gates. Set in a wooded valley, the seventy-acre gardens are crisscrossed by steep paths, which link six lakes created – like those at Sheffield Park – in the sixteenth century to power water-wheels for iron foundries. The range of flora is especially impressive here, featuring many hybrid species of rhododendron that were created specifically for this garden and are at their best in May. Wallabies, sika and fallow deer roam freely, adding to the Edenic atmosphere.

Arundel and around

The hilltop town of **ARUNDEL**, eighteen miles west of Brighton, has for seven centuries been the seat of the dukes of Norfolk, whose fine castle looks over the valley of the River Arun. The medieval town's well-preserved appearance and picturesque setting draws in the crowds on summer weekends, but at any other time a visit reveals one of West Sussex's least-spoilt old towns. Arundel also has a unique place in English cricket: traditionally, the first match of every touring side is played against the Duke of Norfolk's XI on the ground beneath the castle and other matches are played regularly throughout the summer.

The Town

Arundel Castle, towering over the High Street (April–Oct Mon–Fri & Sun noon–5pm; castle, grounds & chapel £7.50; grounds & chapel £2.50; ⓦ www.arundelcastle.org), is what first catches the eye and, despite its medieval appearance, most of what you see is only a century old. The structure dated from Norman times, but was ruined during the Civil War, then lavishly reconstructed during the nineteenth century by the eighth, eleventh and fifteenth dukes. From the top of the keep, you can see the current duke's spacious residence and the pristine castle grounds. Inside the castle, the renovated quarters include the impressive **Barons Hall** and the **library**, which boasts paintings by Gainsborough, Holbein and Van Dyck. On the edge of the castle grounds, the fourteenth-century **Fitzalan Chapel** houses tombs of past dukes of

Norfolk including twin effigies of the seventh duke – one as he looked when he died and, underneath, one of his emaciated corpse. The Catholic chapel belongs to the Norfolk estate, but is actually physically joined to the **Church of St Nicholas**, the parish church, whose entrance is in London Road. It is separated from the altar of the main Anglican church by an iron grille and a glass screen. Although traditionally Catholics, the dukes of Norfolk have shrewdly played down their papal allegiance in sensitive times – such as during the Tudor era when two of the third duke's nieces, Anne Boleyn and Catherine Howard, became Henry VIII's wives.

West of the parish church, further along London Road, is Arundel's other major landmark, the towering Gothic bulk of **Arundel Cathedral**. Constructed in the 1870s by the fifteenth duke of Norfolk over the town's former Catholic church, the cathedral's spire was designed by John Hansom, inventor of the hansom cab, the earliest taxi. Inside are the enshrined remains of St Philip Howard, the fourth duke's son, exhumed from the Fitzalan Chapel after his canonization in 1970. Following his wayward youth, Howard returned to the Catholic fold at a time when the Armada's defeat saw anti-Catholic feelings soar. Caught fleeing overseas and sentenced to death for praying for Spanish victory, he spent the next decade in the Tower of London, where he died. The cathedral's impressive outline is more appealing than the interior, but it fits in well with the townscape of the medieval seaport.

The rest of Arundel is pleasant to wander round, with the antique shop-lined Maltravers and Arun streets being the most attractive thoroughfares. Halfway up the High Street, in the same building as the tourist office, is the **Arundel Heritage Museum** (April–Sept Mon–Sat 10.30am–5pm, Sun 2–5pm; £1), a surprisingly interesting local museum with a history of medicine on the ground floor and lots of information on Arundel's days as a busy port, once connected by canal to Weybridge on the Thames.

Practicalities

Arundel is served by regular trains from London Victoria, Portsmouth, Brighton and Chichester. The **train station** is half a mile south of the town centre over the river on the A27, with **buses** arriving either on High Street or River Road. The **tourist office** is at 61 High St (June–Aug Mon–Fri 9am–5pm, Sat & Sun 10am–5pm; rest of year Mon–Fri 9am–5pm, Sat & Sun 10am–3pm; ☎01903/882268, ⓦwww.sussexbythesea.com). **Boat rental** and riverboat **cruises** upstream to the village of Amberley are available from *Skylark Cruises* (☎07957/866815) by the bridge.

For **accommodation**, try *Portreeves Acre*, The Causeway (☎01903/883277; ❷), a welcoming place with en-suite rooms south of Queen's Bridge, or the venerable *Swan Hotel* at the bottom of High Street (☎01903/882314, ⓦwww .swan-hotel.co.uk; ❹), a fine old house with a cosy adjoining restaurant. *Castle View* (☎01903/883029; ❷), next door to the tourist office above the tea rooms of the same name, is reasonable, and neighbouring *Dukes Restaurant*, 65 High St, with its spectacular gilded ceiling, also has a few rooms available (☎01903 /883847, ⓦwww.dukesofarundel.com; ❷). For a real splurge, head for Amberley, four miles north, where you can get a luxury double room at the 600-year-old *Amberley Castle* (☎01798/831992, ⓦwww.amberleycastle.co.uk; ❽). Arundel's **youth hostel** (☎01903/882204) is in a large Georgian house by the river at Warningcamp, a mile and a half northeast of town. You can **camp** at the hostel, or try the *Maynards* site (☎01903/882075) at the top of the hill on the A27 two miles southeast of town.

First choice for reasonably priced, good-quality food is the **restaurant** attached to the *White Hart* pub over the river at 3 Queen St (℡01903 /882374); alternatively try the *Red Lion*, on High St, for solid pub grub and real ales. *Butlers Wine Bar*, 25 Tarrant St (℡01903/882222), is a popular choice for steak-lovers while further down the same road at number 41 is the best real-ale **pub** in town, *The Eagle*, which dispenses King and Barnes beer from nearby Horsham and Fuller's London Pride. A ten minute stroll from the bridge along Mill Road takes you to *The Black Rabbit* set right beside the River Arun.

Arundel's **festival** takes place throughout the last week in August in a variety of locations, indoor and outdoor, around the town and features everything from open air theatre to salsa bands. For details see ⓦwww.arundelfestival. co.uk.

Bignor and Petworth

Six miles north of Arundel, the excavated second-century ruins of the **Bignor Roman Villa** (March & April Tues–Sun 10am–5pm; May & Oct daily 10am–5pm; June–Sept daily 10am–6pm; £3.50) include some well-preserved mosaics, of which the Ganymede is the most outstanding. The site, first excavated between 1811 and 1819, is superbly situated at the base of the South Downs and features the longest extant section of mosaic in England, as well as the remains of a hypocaust, the underfloor heating system developed by the Romans.

Adjoining the pretty little village of **PETWORTH**, replete with antiques shops, eleven miles north of Arundel, is **Petworth House** (April–June, Sept & Oct Mon–Wed, Sat & Sun 1–5.30pm; July & Aug Mon–Wed & Fri–Sun 1–5.30pm; park daily 8am–dusk; £6, park free; NT), one of the southeast's most impressive stately homes. Built in the late seventeenth century, the house contains an outstanding art collection, including paintings by Van Dyck, Titian, Gainsborough, Bosch, Reynolds, Blake and Turner – the last a frequent guest here. Highlights of the interior decor are Louis Laguerre's murals around the **Grand Staircase** and the **Carved Room**, where carvings by Grinling Gibbons and Holbein's full-length portrait of Henry VIII can be seen. The seven-hundred-acre grounds were landscaped by Capability Brown and are considered one of his finest achievements. For an alternative and intriguing view of the life of one of the house's former employees, **Petworth Cottage Museum**, 346 High St (April–Oct Wed–Sun 2–4.30pm; £2), is well worth a call. This gaslit abode was the home of Mary Cummings, erstwhile seamstress, and re-creates her home, using her own possessions, as it must have looked in 1910.

Petworth's **tourist office** is on the Market Square (April–Sept Mon–Sat 10am–5pm, Sun 11am–4pm; March & Oct Mon–Sat 10am–4pm; Nov–Feb Fri–Sat 11am–3pm; ℡01798/343523, ⓦwww.chichester.gov.uk). For a memorable night's **stay**, book in at the converted *Old Railway Station* (℡01798 /342346, ⓦwww.old-station.co.uk; ⑤), two miles south of Petworth on the A285 Chichester road.

Chichester and around

The county town of West Sussex and its only city, **CHICHESTER** is an attractive, if stuffy, market town, which began life as a Roman settlement – the Roman cruciform street plan is still evident in the four-quadrant symmetry of the town centre, spread around the Market Cross. The city has built itself up as one of southern England's cultural centres, hosting the **Chichester Festival** (Ⓦ www.chifest.org.uk) in early July; its focus is a fairly safe programme of middlebrow plays, though the studio theatre is a bit more adventurous; for the latest details check their website. The racecourse at **Goodwood Park**, north of the city, hosts one of England's most fashionable racing events at the same time (see box below). The Gothic cathedral is the chief permanent attraction in the city, but two miles west of the town are the restored Roman ruins of **Fishbourne**, one of the most visited ancient sites in the county. To the south is the flat headland of Selsey Bill, a dull section of coast, fringed with retirement estates for the well-to-do; if you want some fresh sea air, your best bet is to make for the inlets of **Chichester Harbour** or the Witterings, east of the harbour mouth, though there's little here of interest other than the sandy expanses of beach.

The City

The main streets lead off to the compass's cardinal points from the Gothic **Market Cross**, a bulky octagonal rotunda topped by ornate finials and a crown lantern spire, and built in 1501 to provide shelter for the market traders, although it appears far too small for its function.

A short stroll down West Street brings you to the neat form of the **Cathedral** (daily: Easter to mid-Sept 7.30am–7pm; mid-Sept to Easter 7.30am–5pm; Ⓔ vo@chicath.freeserve.co.uk), whose slender spire – a nineteenth-century addition – is visible out at sea. Building began in the 1070s, but the church was extensively rebuilt following a fire a century later and has been only minimally modified since about 1300, except for the spire and the unique, freestanding fifteenth-century bell tower, which now houses the cathedral shop. The **interior** is renowned for its contemporary devotional art, which includes a stained glass window by Marc Chagall and an enormous altar-screen tapestry by John Piper. Other points of interest are the sixteenth-century painting in the north transept of the past bishops of Chichester, and the fourteenth-century Fitzalan tomb which inspired a poem by Philip Larkin. However, the highlight is a pair of reliefs in the south aisle, close to the tapestry – created around 1140, they show the raising of Lazarus and Christ at the gate of Bethany. Originally highly coloured, the reliefs once featured semi-precious stones set in the figures' eyes and are among the finest Romanesque stone carvings in England.

There are several fine buildings up **North Street**, including a dinky little Market House, built by Nash in 1807 and fronted by a Doric colonnade and a tiny flint Saxon church – now an ecclesiastical bookshop – with a diminutive wooden shingled spire. Finally, you come to the appealingly dumpy red-brick **Council House**, built in 1731, with Ionic columns and delightful intersecting tracery on its street facade, and crowned by a wonderful stone lion. East off South Street, in the well-preserved Georgian quadrant of the city known as the Pallants, you'll find **Pallant House Gallery**, 9 North Pallant (Tues–Sat 10am–5pm; Sun & public holidays 12.30–5pm; £4; Ⓦ www.pallanthouse-gallery.com). Stone dodos stand guard over the gates of this fine mansion, which houses artefacts and furniture from the early eighteenth century.

Horse racing in the southeast

A popular way to spend a day out in southeast England is to go to the races at one of the many tracks in the region. **Glorious Goodwood** and the **Derby week** are the fashionable meetings to attend, as is **Royal Ascot**, in Berkshire, but the less well-known courses, such as Brighton, Fontwell Park and Kempton Park, offer equally entertaining meetings throughout the year. For course locations, see the map on pp.170–171. Generally it'll cost you around £8–10 to get into a "basic" enclosure, but you can pay much higher prices for admission into the grandstand and more exclusive enclosures, where the social event often takes precedence over the racing.

Ascot ☎01344/622211, ⊕www.ascot.co.uk. Ten minutes' walk from Ascot train station. No account of racing in southeast England would be complete without Ascot, the jewel in the crown of English racecourses. Admission is rather expensive, but the facilities and atmosphere make it worth the price. The week-long Royal Meeting in mid-June is the one to attend, and to dress up for, with a selection of outrageous hats, outfits and royals on display, especially on Ladies' Day. The racecourse hosts less glamorous meetings throughout the rest of the year.

Brighton ☎01273/603580, ⊕www.brighton racecourse.co.uk. Brighton train station with free connecting buses on race days; or local services #2, #21 or #22. Overlooking Brighton Marina at the east end of town, Brighton's racecourse has a U-shaped track and is one of the few courses in England that doesn't form a complete circuit; binoculars are useful and can be rented. The racecourse's situation, on top of the South Downs overlooking the English Channel, makes it particularly appealing for a day out. Up to twenty meetings take place from April to early November every year with the three-day meeting in early August providing the best action.

Epsom Downs ☎01372/726311, ⊕www.epsomderby.co.uk. Epsom Downs or Tattenham Corner train station with connecting buses on race days. Home of two of England's most famous races, the Derby and the Oaks, both of which take place during Derby week, the first week in June. The Derby has been run for nearly two hundred years and is the time when Epsom really comes alive – a fun day out for all classes of persons. There are very few meetings at other times: evening meetings at the end of June and July and a two-day event at the end of August.

Fontwell Park ☎01243/543335, ⊕www.fontwellpark.co.uk. Barnham train station with connecting buses on race days. Midway

Modern works of art are also included, among them pieces by Henry Moore and Barbara Hepworth and Graham Sutherland's portrait of Walter Hussey, the former Dean of Chichester, who commissioned much of the cathedral's contemporary art.

Continuing in an anticlockwise direction around the town and crossing East Street to head north up Little London brings you to the **Chichester District Museum** (Tues–Sat 10am–5.30pm; free), housed in an old white weatherboarded corn store. Inside, the modest but entertaining display on local life includes a portable oven carried by Joe Faro, the city pieman, as well as the portable stocks used for the ritual humiliation of petty criminals. The **Guildhall** (June–Aug Sat noon–4pm; free), a branch museum within a thirteenth-century Franciscan church in the middle of Priory Park, at the north end of Little London, has some well-preserved medieval frescoes. It was formerly a town hall and court of law, and the poet, painter and visionary William Blake was tried here for sedition in 1804.

Practicalities

A regular service runs from London Victoria to Chichester's **train station** on Stockbridge Road, with the **bus station** across the road at South Street. From either station it's a ten-minute walk north to the Market Cross, passing the between Arundel and Chichester, Fontwell Park, which held its first meeting in the 1920s, is a lesser-known racecourse which makes it a friendly and welcoming venue for first-time race-goers. It's one of only two figure-of-eight racecourses in Britain. One-day meetings take place once or twice a month in May and from August to December, with around a dozen fixtures a year.

Goodwood Park ☏ 01243/774107, ⓦ www.goodwood.co.uk. Four miles from Chichester train station, with connecting buses on race days. Goodwood boasts a wonderful location, on a lush green hill overlooking Chichester with the South Downs as a backdrop. Even if you have only the mildest interest in the sport, and no interest in betting, it's worth a visit for the main meeting, Goodwood Week – or "Glorious Goodwood" to its fans; held in late July, it's second only to Ascot in its social cachet. There are plenty of other meetings from May to late September.

Kempton Park ☏ 01932/782292, ⓦ www.kempton.co.uk. Five minutes' walk from Kempton Park train station. Just fifteen miles from London, this popular course has excellent facilities, including covered enclosures for inclement meetings; the majority of the fixtures are run on the flat. Racing takes place all year with evening meetings in April and from June to August. A highlight is the very popular two-day Christmas Festival which starts on Boxing Day.

Lingfield Park ☏ 01342/834800, ⓦ www .arenaleisureplc.com/lingfieldpark/home.htm. Ten minutes' walk from Lingfield train station. Has an all-weather synthetic track so races can be run here when they would have to be abandoned elsewhere, but unfortunately this hasn't really caught on with the public, and crowds are poor. If you want a lively atmosphere, stick to the turf (grass) events – especially the Turf National Hunt at the beginning of December and the Turf Flat in early May.

Plumpton ☏ 01273/890383. A short walk from Plumpton train station. Eight miles out of Brighton, this course has one of the sharpest tracks in the country (leading to its being nicknamed the "Wall of Death"), with extremely tight bends and a downhill back straight. Facilities here are good and races take place all year except in June and July.

Sandown Park ☏ 01372/470047, ⓦ www.sandown.co.uk. Ten minutes' walk from Esher train station. Only fourteen miles from Central London, this hugely popular venue near Esher has been frequently voted "Racecourse of the Year". Atmosphere, an excellent location and superb facilities all add up to a great day's racing, with the Whitbread Gold Cup towards the end of April and the Coral-Eclipse Stakes in early June bringing out the crowds and being well worth attending.

tourist office at 29a South St (April–Sept Mon–Sat 9.15am–5.15pm, Sun 10am–4pm; Oct–March closed Sun; ☏ 01243/775888, ⓦ www.chichester. gov.uk).

Every other house on the main roads out of Chichester seems to offer B&B **accommodation**, so there's no problem finding a place to stay other than during the festival. If you want to splash out, try *The Ship Hotel*, North St (☏ 01243/778000, ⓦ www.shiphotel.com; ❽), a comfortable and characterful inn in the centre of town. Less expensive central B&B options include the brick and flint *Riverside Lodge*, 7 Market Ave, outside the Pallants quarter (☏ 01243/783164, ⓔ tregeardavid@aol.com; ❷), or the 200-year-old *Friary Close*, Friary Lane (☏ 01243/527294, ⓔ friaryclose@argonet.co.uk; ❹), just inside the city wall. You can **camp** at the *Red House Farm*, Brookers Lane, Earnley (☏ 01243/512959; closed Nov–Easter), six miles southwest of town, a mile or so from the beach.

As well as offering excellent accommodation, *The Ship* is a good place for a **drink**, or you could try *The Park Tavern*, a convivial pub, serving excellent Gale's ales on Priory Lane, overlooking Priory Park. *The Fountain Inn*, a fourteenth century pub at the top of Southgate, makes an excellent alternative. For something to **eat**, the intimate *Café Coco*, 13 South St (☏ 01243/786989), specializes in French cuisine and serves splendid set dinners from £11.95; and further down the street there's a branch of *Pizza Express*. Chichester's best Indian is the aptly named *Little London Indian Restaurant*, 38 Little London, off East Street (℡01243/537550), and on East Street itself there's the popular *Ask* at no. 38, serving wholesome pasta and pizza, and, a little further east, *Sadlers Bistro and Bar* (℡01243/774765), offering innovative modern English cooking. There's also the *Internet Junction*, internet café at 2 Southgate Parade next to the bus station.

Fishbourne Roman Palace

Fishbourne, two miles west of Chichester (March–July, Sept & Oct daily 10am–5pm; Aug daily 10am–6pm; Nov to mid-Dec daily 10am–4pm; mid-Dec to Feb Sat & Sun 10am–4pm; £4.50; ◍www.sussexpast.co.uk), is the largest and best-preserved Roman palace in the country. Roman relics have long been turning up in Fishbourne and in 1960 a workman unearthed their source – the site of a depot used by the invading Romans in 43 AD which is thought later to have become the vast, hundred-room palace of the Romanized Celtic aristocrat, Cogidubnus. A pavilion has been built over the north wing of the excavated remains, where floor mosaics depict Fishbourne's famous dolphin-riding cupid as well as the more usual geometric patterns.

Like the more evocative remains at Bignor (see p.240), only the residential wing of the former quadrangle has been excavated – other parts of the dwelling fulfilled mundane service roles and probably lacked the mosaics which give both sites their singular appeal. The underfloor heating system has also been well restored and an audiovisual programme gives a fuller picture of the palace as it was in Roman times. The extensive gardens attempt to re-create the appearance of the palace grounds as they would have been then.

To get to Fishbourne take the train to Fishbourne station, turn right as you leave the station and the palace is a few minutes' walk away.

Tangmere Military Aviation Museum

Three miles east of Chichester, signposted off the A27, is **Tangmere Military Aviation Museum** (Feb & Nov daily 10am–4.30pm; March–Oct daily 10am–5.30pm; £4; ◍www.tangmere-museum.org.uk), sited at one of England's earliest airfields, which was established in 1917 and closed in 1970. On display are a number of aircraft including replicas of the legendary Hurricane and Spitfire fighters which took off from Tangmere airfield during the Battle of Britain. Early supersonic jets are also housed, with a display about Neville Duke whose Hawker Hunter reached 727mph along the nearby coast in the early 1950s. Up the road the *Bader Arms* is a reasonable **pub**, which commemorates the famous Battle of Britain pilot Douglas Bader who lost both his legs in a 1931 stunt accident, yet fought in the war, survived being shot down, and continued flying afterwards. To get to Tangmere, take bus #58 from Chichester.

Goodwood House and Sculpture at Goodwood

Three miles north of Chichester lies **Goodwood House** (April–July, Sept & Oct Sun & Mon 1–5pm; Aug Mon–Thurs & Sun 1–5pm; closed on racing days; £6.50; ◍www.goodwood.co.uk), an imposing Regency mansion set in the heart of a 12,000 acre estate and home to the Dukes of Richmond for three hundred years. In addition to collections of furniture and porcelain, the house's highlights include Canaletto's views from the family's London home and paintings of the family's horses by Stubbs. Just to the east of Goodwood House, **Sculpture at Goodwood** (April–Oct Thurs–Sat 10.30am–4.30pm; £10; ⓦ www.sculpture.org.uk) is an absolute must for anyone interested in contemporary art – the entry fee appears deliberately designed to put off casual punters. Since 1994 Wilfred and Jeanette Cass, long-time collectors of sculpture, have created a unique woodland environment for more than forty large-scale works, some of which have been specially commissioned and each of which is sited to allow you to appreciate it in isolation. The selection of pieces on display changes from year to year, but has been known to include Turner Prize winners.

Weald and Downland Open-Air Museum

Five miles north of Chichester, the **Weald and Downland Open-Air Museum** (March–Oct daily 10.30am–6pm; rest of year Wed, Sat & Sun 10.30am–4pm; £7; ⓦ www.wealddown.co.uk), just outside the village of Singleton, is one the best rural museums in the southeast. More than forty old buildings – from a Tudor market hall to a medieval farmstead – have been saved from destruction and reconstructed at the forty-acre museum site. A substantial lottery award in the late 1990s has gone towards the construction of a new visitors' centre, due to open in late 2001, though still incomplete at the time of writing. Besides a whole range of livestock as permanent residents there are also numerous special events and activities to visit, particularly in July and August, so it's worthwhile calling ahead for details of the current season's programme; ⓣ 01243/811348. There's a half-hourly bus from Chichester (#60), which will drop you off in Singleton.

Travel details

Buses

For information on all local and national bus services, contact Traveline: ⓣ 0870/608 2 608 (daily 7am–9pm), ⓦ www.traveline.org.uk.

Trains

For information on all local and national rail services, contact National Rail Enquiries: ⓣ 08457/48 49 50, ⓦ www.rail.co.uk.

Arundel to: London Victoria (Mon–Sat 2 hourly, Sun hourly; 1hr 20min).

Battle to: Hastings (Mon–Sat 2 hourly, Sun hourly; 15min); London Charing Cross (2 hourly; 1hr 15min); Sevenoaks (Mon–Sat 2 hourly, Sun hourly; 45min); Tunbridge Wells (Mon–Sat 2 hourly, Sun hourly; 30min).

Brighton to: Chichester (Mon–Sat 2 hourly, Sun hourly; 1hr); Gatwick Airport (every 10–20min; 25–40min); Hastings (Mon–Sat 2 hourly, Sun hourly; 1hr 10min); Lewes (Mon–Sat every 10–20min, Sun 2 hourly; 15min); London Victoria (2 hourly; 1hr–1hr 20min); London King's Cross (Mon–Sat 4 hourly, Sun 2 hourly; 1hr–1hr 15min); London Bridge (Mon–Sat 4 hourly, Sun 2 hourly; 1hr–1hr 5min); Oxford (Mon–Sat 2 daily, Sun 1 daily; 2hr 50min); Portsmouth Harbour (hourly; 1hr 25min).

Broadstairs to: London Victoria (Mon–Sat 2 hourly, Sun hourly; 2hr); Ramsgate (2–3 hourly; 5min).

Canterbury East to: Dover Priory (Mon–Sat 2 hourly, Sun hourly; 30min); London Victoria (Mon–Sat 2 hourly, Sun hourly; 1hr 30min).

Canterbury West to: London Charing Cross (hourly; 1hr 40min); Ramsgate (hourly; 20min).

Chatham to: Dover Priory (Mon–Sat 2 hourly, Sun hourly; 1hr 10min); London Victoria (Mon–Sat every 10–30min, Sun 2 hourly; 50min–1hr).

Chichester to: London Victoria (Mon–Sat 2 hourly, Sun hourly; 1hr 45min); Portsmouth Harbour (Mon–Sat 2 hourly, Sun hourly; 40min).

Dorking to: Farnham (hourly; 1hr); London Waterloo (2 hourly; 40min).

Dover Priory to: Folkestone Central (Mon–Sat 2 hourly, Sun hourly; 15min); London Charing Cross

(Mon–Sat 2 hourly, Sun hourly; 1hr 40min); London Victoria (Mon–Sat 2 hourly, Sun hourly; 1hr 50min).

Eastbourne to: Gatwick Airport (2 hourly; 1hr); Hastings (Mon–Sat 3 hourly, Sun hourly; 40min); Lewes (Mon–Sat every 10–25min, Sun hourly; 20–30min); London Victoria (Mon–Sat 2 hourly, Sun hourly; 1hr 40min).

Farnham to: Aldershot (for connections to London Waterloo; Mon–Sat 1–2 hourly, Sun hourly; 10min); Guildford (Mon–Sat 1–2 hourly, Sun hourly; 45min).

Folkestone Central to: London Charing Cross (Mon–Sat 2 hourly, Sun hourly; 1hr 40min).

Folkestone West to: London Charing Cross (Mon–Sat 2 hourly; Sun hourly; 1hr 40min).

Gatwick Airport to: London Victoria (very frequent; 30min).

Guildford to: Farnham (Mon–Sat 1–2 hourly, Sun hourly; 45min); London Waterloo (Mon–Sat 3–4 hourly, Sun hourly; 40min).

Hastings to: Gatwick Airport (hourly; 1hr 40min); London Victoria (hourly; 2hr); Rye (1 hourly; 20min).

Herne Bay to: London Victoria (Mon–Sat 2 hourly, Sun hourly; 1hr 30min); Ramsgate (Mon–Sat 2 hourly, Sun hourly; 30min).

Lewes to: Brighton (Mon–Sat 4 hourly, Sun 2 hourly; 15min); London Victoria (Mon–Sat 2 hourly, Sun hourly; 1hr 15min).

Maidstone East to: London Victoria (Mon–Sat 2 hourly, Sun hourly; 1hr); London Charing Cross (hourly; 1hr).

Margate to: Canterbury West (hourly; 30–45min); London Victoria (Mon–Sat 2 hourly, Sun hourly; 1hr 40min).

Ramsgate to: London Victoria (Mon–Sat 2 hourly, Sun hourly; 2hr).

Rochester to: Dover Priory (Mon–Sat 2 hourly, Sun hourly; 1hr 10min); Herne Bay (Mon–Sat 2 hourly; Sun hourly; 45min); London Victoria (Mon–Sat 3–4 hourly, Sun 2 hourly; 40min).

Rye to: Hastings (1 hourly; 20min).

Sandwich to: Dover Priory (hourly; 30min); Ramsgate (hourly; 15min).

Sevenoaks to: London Blackfriars (Mon–Sat 2 hourly; 1hr); London Victoria (Mon–Sat 1 hourly, Sun 2 hourly; 1hr).

Tunbridge Wells to: London Charing Cross (Mon–Sat 2 hourly, Sun hourly; 50min).

Whitstable to: London Victoria (hourly; 1hr 20min); Ramsgate (Mon–Sat 2 hourly, Sun hourly; 30min).

Woking to: London Waterloo (every 10–40min; 40min).

Hampshire, Dorset and Wiltshire

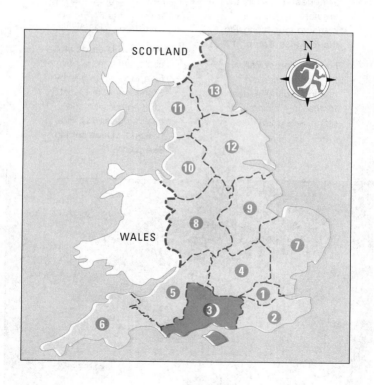

CHAPTER 3 # Highlights

* **Cowes Week, Isle of Wight** This yachting jamboree draw thousands, infecting even the staunchest landlubbers. See p.271

* **Wykeham Arms, Winchester** Ancient tavern serving gourmet-standard food alongside the real ales. See p.277

* **The New Forest** William the Conqueror's old hunting ground is ideal for walking, biking and riding. See p.281

* **Corfe Castle** Picturesque ruins with a weathered, romantic charm. See p.291

* **Durdle Door** This crumbly natural arch stands at the end of a splendid beach – a great place for walkers and swimmers alike. See p.293

* **Avebury** This crude stone circle has a more powerful appeal, than nearby Stonehenge, not least for its great size and easy accessibility, in a peaceful village setting. See p.313

Hampshire, Dorset and Wiltshire

The distant past is perhaps more tangible in **Hampshire**, **Dorset** and **Wiltshire** than in any other part of England. Predominantly rural, these three counties overlap substantially with the ancient kingdom of **Wessex**, whose most famous ruler, Alfred, repulsed the Danes in the ninth century and came close to establishing the first unified state in England. Before Wessex came into being, however, many earlier civilizations had left their stamp on the region. The chalky uplands of Wiltshire boast several of Europe's greatest Neolithic sites, including **Stonehenge** and **Avebury**, while in Dorset you'll find **Maiden Castle**, the most striking Iron Age hill fort in the country, and the **Cerne Abbas Giant**, source of many a legend. The Romans tramped all over these southern counties, leaving the most conspicuous signs of their occupation at the amphitheatre of **Dorchester** – though that town is more closely associated with the novels of Thomas Hardy and his distinctively gloomy vision of Wessex.

None of the landscapes of this region could be described as grand or wild, but the countryside is consistently seductive, its appeal exemplified by the crumbling fossil-bearing cliffs around **Lyme Regis**, the managed woodlands of the **New Forest** and the gentle, open curves of **Salisbury Plain**. Its towns are also generally modest and slow-paced, with the notable exceptions of the two great maritime bases of **Portsmouth** and, to a lesser extent, **Southampton**, a fair proportion of whose visitors are simply passing through on their way to the more genteel pleasures of the **Isle of Wight**. This is something of an injustice, though neither place can compete with the two most interesting cities in this part of England – **Salisbury** and **Winchester**, each of

---

Accommodation price codes

Throughout this guide, hotel and B&B accommodation is priced on a scale of ❶ to ❾, the number indicating the **lowest price** you could expect to pay per night in that establishment for a **double room** in high season. The prices indicated by the codes are as follows:

❶ under £40	❹ £60–70	❼ £110–150
❷ £40–50	❺ £70–90	❽ £150–200
❸ £50–60	❻ £90–110	❾ over £200

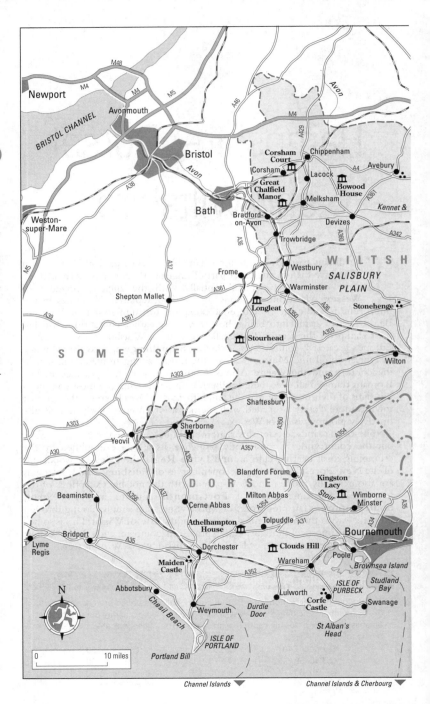

Channel Islands ▼   Channel Islands & Cherbourg ▼

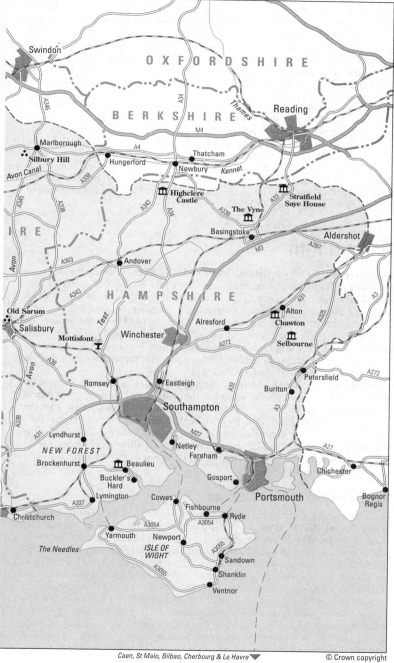

Swindon

OXFORDSHIRE

BERKSHIRE

Reading

Thames

Marlborough

Silbury Hill

Hungerford

A4

Thatcham

Newbury

Kennet

Avon Canal

Highclere Castle

The Vyne

Stratfield Saye House

Basingstoke

Aldershot

M3

Andover

A303

HAMPSHIRE

Old Sarum

Salisbury

Test

Mottisfont

Winchester

Alresford

Alton

Chawton

Selbourne

A272

Petersfield

A272

Avon

Romsey

Eastleigh

Buriton

Southampton

Lyndhurst

NEW FOREST

Netley

Fareham

Brockenhurst

Beaulieu

Buckler's Hard

Lymington

Cowes

Gosport

Portsmouth

Chichester

Bognor Regis

Christchurch

Fishbourne

Ryde

Yarmouth

Newport

The Needles

ISLE OF WIGHT

Sandown

Shanklin

Ventnor

Caen, St Malo, Bilbao, Cherbourg & Le Havre ▼

© Crown copyright

which possesses a stupendous cathedral amid an array of other historic sights. Of the region's great houses, **Wilton**, **Stourhead**, **Longleat** and **Kingston Lacy** are the ones that attract the crowds, but every cranny has its medieval church, manor house or unspoilt country inn – there are few parts of England in which an aimless meander can be so rewarding. If it's straightforward seaside fun you're after, **Bournemouth** leads the way, with Weymouth and Lyme Regis heading the ranks of the minor resorts, along with the yachties' havens over on the Isle of Wight.

The **roads** in this area get choked in summer, the bulk of the traffic heading either for the more celebrated holiday centres of the West Country or for the ferry ports of Poole, Portsmouth and Southampton. If you're heading for one particular spot, it's often easier to reach it by **rail**, on the fast direct services from London's Waterloo station. To tour the area extensively and conveniently, though, you definitely need your own transport, as the hinterland is not well served by public transport. Keen **walkers** can avoid the hordes by taking to the New Forest's quieter spots or to the **Dorset Coast Path**, which stretches all the way from Lyme Regis to Poole.

Portsmouth

Britain's foremost naval station, **PORTSMOUTH** occupies the bulbous peninsula of Portsea Island, on the eastern flank of a huge, easily defended harbour. The ancient Romans raised a fortress on the northernmost edge of this inlet, and a small port developed during the Norman era, but this strategic location wasn't fully exploited until Tudor times, when Henry VII established the world's first dry dock here and made Portsmouth a royal dockyard. It has flourished ever since and nowadays Portsmouth is a large industrialized city, its harbour clogged with naval frigates, ferries bound for the continent or the Isle of Wight, and swarms of dredgers and tugs.

Portsmouth was heavily bombed during the last war due to its military importance and, although the Victorian slums got what they deserved, bland tower blocks from the nadir of British architectural endeavour now give the city an ugly profile. Only **Old Portsmouth**, based around the original harbour, preserves some Georgian and a little Tudor character. East of here is **Southsea**, a residential suburb of terraces with a half-hearted resort strewn along its shingle beach, where a mass of B&Bs face stoic naval monuments and tawdry seaside amusements.

The Royal Naval Base

For most visitors, a trip to Portsmouth begins and ends at the **Historic Ships**, in the **Royal Naval Base** at the end of Queen Street (daily: March–Oct 10am–5.30pm; Nov–Feb 10am–5pm; last entry 1hr before closing). The complex comprises three ships and as many museums, with each ship visitable separately, though most people opt for a "3 for 2" ticket (£12.50), with which you can choose any three of the main four attractions – the Mary Rose Museum, *HMS Victory* (including the Royal Naval Museum), *HMS Warrior* and Action Stations (an interactive simulation of life aboard a modern naval frigate) – or a passport ticket, taking in various exhibitions and a harbour-tour (£17.50), which will easily take half a day. Note that visits to the *Victory* are guided, with limited numbers at set times, so it's worth booking early to ensure a place, and even then you may have to wait up to two hours for your turn. Also, visitors

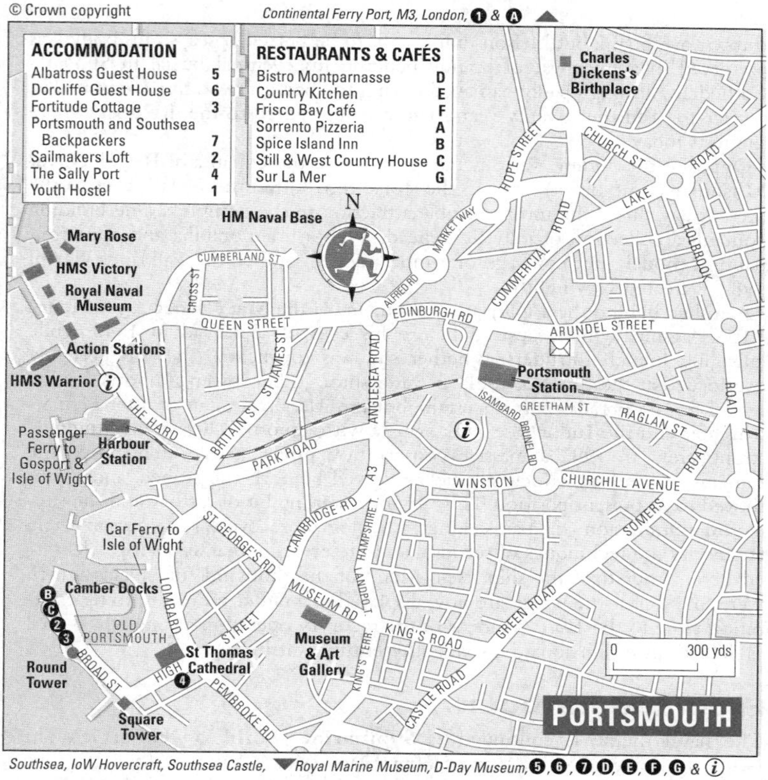
© Crown copyright
Continental Ferry Port, M3, London, 1 & A
ACCOMMODATION
Albatross Guest House 5
Dorcliffe Guest House 6
Fortitude Cottage 3
Portsmouth and Southsea Backpackers 7
Sailmakers Loft 2
The Sally Port 4
Youth Hostel 1
RESTAURANTS & CAFÉS
Bistro Montparnasse D
Country Kitchen E
Frisco Bay Café F
Sorrento Pizzeria A
Spice Island Inn B
Still & West Country House C
Sur La Mer G
N
HM Naval Base
Mary Rose
HMS Victory
Royal Naval Museum
Action Stations
HMS Warrior
Passenger Ferry to Gosport & Isle of Wight
Harbour Station
Car Ferry to Isle of Wight
Camber Docks
OLD PORTSMOUTH
Round Tower
Square Tower
St Thomas Cathedral
Museum & Art Gallery
Charles Dickens's Birthplace
Portsmouth Station
CUMBERLAND ST
CROSS ST
QUEEN STREET
ST JAMES ST
BRITAIN ST
THE HARD
PARK ROAD
ANGLESEA ROAD
A3
EDINBURGH RD
ALFRED RD
MARKET WAY
HOPE STREET
CHURCH ST
COMMERCIAL ROAD
LAKE ROAD
HOLBROOK ROAD
ARUNDEL STREET
ISAMBARD BRUNEL RD
GREETHAM ST
RAGLAN ST
WINSTON CHURCHILL AVENUE
SOMERS ROAD
CAMBRIDGE RD
ST GEORGE'S RD
HAMPSHIRE T.
LANDPO. T.
MUSEUM RD
KING'S ROAD
KING'S TERR.
GREEN ROAD
CASTLE ROAD
LOMBARD
STREET
HIGH
BROAD ST
PEMBROKE RD
0 300 yds
PORTSMOUTH
Southsea, IoW Hovercraft, Southsea Castle, Royal Marine Museum, D-Day Museum, 5, 6, 7, D, E, F, G & i

with disabilities will have a hard time moving between decks on the two complete ships; a virtual tour by video (call ☎023/9272 2562 for details) is a good alternative.

Nearest the entrance to the complex is the youngest ship, **HMS Warrior** (£6), dating from 1860. It was Britain's first armoured, or "iron-clad" battleship, complete with sails and steam engines, and was the pride of the fleet in its day. Longer and faster than any previous naval vessel, and the first to be fitted with washing machines, the *Warrior* was described by Napoleon III as a "black snake amongst the rabbits". You can wander around its main deck and see where eighteen seamen ate, slept and relaxed in the tiny spaces between each of the ship's thirty-six cannons. Not surprisingly, the captain's cabin, at the stern of the ship, resembles a sumptuous four-star suite, while the navigator also had a cabin to himself, although he shared it with a massive cannon. Other weaponry, including rifles, pistols and sabres, is all neatly stowed, but the *Warrior* was never challenged nor even fired a cannon in her twenty-two years at sea.

HMS Victory (£6.50) was already forty years old when she set sail from Portsmouth for Trafalgar on September 14, 1805, returning victorious three months later, but bearing the corpse of Admiral Nelson. Shot by a sniper from a French ship at the height of the battle, Nelson expired below decks three hours later, having been assured that victory was in sight. The usual fate of casualties at sea was to be sewn into their hammocks with a cannon ball and thrown overboard, but Nelson didn't wish to be buried at sea, so his body was preserved in a huge vat of brandy pending his eventual burial in St Paul's Cathedral. Although badly damaged during the battle, the *Victory* continued in service for a further twenty years, before being retired to the dry dock where she rests today.

Opposite the *Victory*, various buildings house the exhaustive **Royal Naval Museum** (same ticket). Tracing the story from Alfred the Great's fleet to the present day, this is the most resistible attraction in the complex. One building contains a collection of jolly figureheads, Nelson memorabilia and numerous nautical models, but coverage of a more recent conflict, the Falklands War of 1982, is treated very lightly.

In a shed behind the *Victory* are the remains of the **Mary Rose** (£6), Henry VIII's flagship, which capsized before his eyes off Spithead in 1545 while engaging French intruders. Whether she was top-heavy (she was certainly overloaded at the time) or took in water through her lower gunports, having reeled from a broadside, is uncertain, but the *Mary Rose*, named after Henry's daughter and the Tudor rose, sank swiftly with almost all her seven-hundred-strong crew. In 1982 a massive conservation project successfully raised the remains of the hull, which silt had preserved beneath the seabed, and it was moved to its present position. This may be a sterling bit of history and the successful culmination of a painstaking archeological recovery, but you can't help feeling it's the techniques of retrieval and preservation that are being celebrated here, rather than the ship itself. Many of the thousands of objects which were found near the wreck are now displayed in a rather more absorbing exhibition close to the *Warrior*. Videos of the recovery operation are shown, as well as depictions of life aboard a sixteenth-century warship.

From the harbour

The naval theme is continued at **Submarine World** on Haslar Jetty in Gosport (daily: April–Oct 10am–5.30pm; Nov–March 10am–4.30pm; last tour 1hr before closing; £4), reached by taking the passenger ferry from Harbour train station jetty (daily 5.30am–midnight; £1.60 return), just south of the entrance to the Royal Naval Base, or, from the same place, the water-bus, which gives you a half-hour tour of the harbour before dropping you in Gosport (Easter–Oct 10.30am–5pm; £3.50). Allow yourself a couple of hours to explore these slightly creepy vessels – a guided tour inside *HMS Alliance* gives you an insight into life on board and the museum elaborates evocatively on the long history of submersible craft.

From the pontoon beside *HMS Warrior*, regular ferries depart (Wed & Sun 2.45pm; £6.95, including entry to the fort) for the mile-long ride to **Spitbank Fort**, an offshore bastion of granite, iron and brick little altered since its construction in the 1860s. With over fifty rooms linked by passages and steps on two floors, the complex includes a 400-foot deep well, which still draws fresh water from below the seafloor, and an inner courtyard complete with a café and sheltered terrace. The artificial island hosts pub nights, supper nights (both currently Wed) and parties (Fri & Sat) – call ☏01329/664286 or ask at the tourist office for details – and you can also stay here (see p.256).

The rest of the city

Back at the Harbour train station in Portsmouth, it's a well-signposted twenty-minute walk south to what remains of **Old Portsmouth**. Along the way, you pass the simple **Cathedral of St Thomas** on the High Street, whose original twelfth-century features have been obscured by rebuilding after the Civil War and again in the twentieth century. The High Street ends at a maze of cobbled Georgian streets huddling behind a fifteenth-century wall protecting the **Camber**, or old port, where Walter Raleigh landed the first potatoes and tobacco from the New World. Nearby, the Round and Square Towers, which punctuate the Tudor fortifications, are popular vantage points for observing nautical activities. There's also a couple of lively shoreside pubs, the *Still & West Country House* and *Spice Island* (see p.257), with seats outside for viewing the comings and goings in the Solent.

Southsea's main attraction is the **D-Day Museum** on Clarence Esplanade (daily: April–Oct 10am–5.30pm; Nov–March 10am–5pm; last entry 1hr before closing; £5), relating how Portsmouth had a chance to avenge its wartime bombing by being the main assembly point for the D-Day invasion, code-named "Operation Overlord". The museum's most striking exhibit is the 270-feet long *Overlord Embroidery*, which tells the tale of the Normandy landings. Next door to the museum, the squat profile of **Southsea Castle** (April–Oct daily 10am–5.30pm; £2.50), built from the remains of Beaulieu Abbey (see p.283), may have been the spot from where Henry VIII watched the *Mary Rose* sink in 1545. A mile further along the shoreside South Parade, just past South Parade pier, the **Royal Marines Museum** (daily: June–Sept 10am–5pm; Oct–May 10am–4.30pm; last entry 1hr before closing; £4) describes the origins and greatest campaigns of the navy's elite fighting force. Outside, a junior assault course gives aspirant young commandos a chance to get in shape.

The remainder of Portsmouth has little else of interest apart from **Charles Dickens' Birthplace** at 393 Commercial Rd (daily: April–Sept 10am–5.30pm; £2.50), half a mile north of the town centre, where the writer was born in

Naval vernacular

Many phrases in today's English language owe their origins to the country's seafaring heritage. Below are some of the more familiar expressions whose daily use has blurred their naval ancestry:

❑ "Three square meals a day". Sailors aboard the Victory were served a meagre trio of daily meals on square wooden plates.

❑ "Let the cat out of the bag" and "Not enough room to swing a cat". Both refer to the cat-o'-nine-tails, a nine-thonged whip with knots at the end of each thong. Taking the "cat" out of its baize bag made subsequent intentions obvious, and floggings were carried out on the upper deck where the bosun could get a good swing at the wrongdoer.

❑ "Limeys". This nickname for Brits derives from the casks of lime juice ships carried to prevent scurvy.

❑ "Grog". Slang for alcohol still current in Australia. In Nelson's time sailors were allocated a gallon of beer or a pint of rum per day; in the early 1700s, Admiral Vernon, noted for his coat made of grogram and so nicknamed "Old Grog", became notorious for diluting the daily servings with water, producing an insipid brew akin to some Australian beers.

❑ "Turn a blind eye". Part of Nelson's early reputation was made on his irreverent attitude to authority. At the Battle of Copenhagen, the arrogant second-in-command thought he knew best and "ignored" unnecessary signals from other ships by holding the telescope to his blind eye.

❑ "Son of a gun". A scoundrel. Women unfortunate enough to give birth on ship did so between the cannons to keep the gangways clear.

1812. A couple of rooms have been fitted out as they were during his lifetime, but for true fans there's far more of interest in Rochester (see p.179) and, to a lesser extent, Broadstairs (see p.185), where Dickens wrote many of his greatest books.

The city's outstanding monument is six miles out of the centre – just past the burgeoning marina development at Port Solent. **Portchester Castle** (daily: April–Sept 10am–6pm; Oct 10am–5pm; Nov–March 10am–4pm; £3; EH) was built by the Romans in the third century and is the finest surviving example in northern Europe. Its walls are over twenty-feet high and incorporate some twenty bastions, making it so robust that the Normans felt no need to alter it when they moved in. Later, a castle was built within Portchester's precincts by Henry II, which Richard II extended and Henry V used as his garrison when assembling the army that was to fight the Battle of Agincourt. Today its grassy enclosure makes a sheltered spot for a congenial game of cricket or a kickabout with a football.

Practicalities

Portsmouth's main **train station** is in the city centre, but the line continues to **Harbour Station**, the most convenient stop for the main sights and old town. There are regular fast services from London Waterloo, and a frequent bus and train service between Portsmouth and Winchester, 25 miles to the northwest. Passenger **ferries** leave from the jetty at the Harbour station for Ryde, on the Isle of Wight (see p.261), and Gosport, on the other side of Portsmouth Harbour. Wightlink car ferries depart from the ferry port off Gunwharf Road for Fishbourne on the Isle of Wight (see p.261). There are three **tourist offices** (all ☎023/9282 6722, ⊛www.portsmouthharbour.co.uk) in Portsmouth, one on the Hard, by the entrance to the dockyards (daily: Easter–Sept 9.30am–5.45pm; Oct–Easter 9.30am–5.15pm); another in the library at Guildhall Square, near the main train station (Mon–Sat 10am–5pm); and a third on Southsea's seafront, next to the Sea Life Centre (daily 9.30am–5.45pm).

Accommodation
Hotels and guest houses

Albatross Guest House 51 Waverley Rd, Southsea ☎023/9282 8325. One of many good-value B&Bs in this part of Southsea, this one with nautically themed rooms and some parking space. No smoking. No credit cards. ❷

Dorcliffe Guest House 42 Waverley Rd, Southsea ☎023/9282 8283, ⊜dorcliffe@supanet.com. Family-run guest house overlooking a small park, close to restaurants and seafront. En-suite rooms are available. No credit cards. ❶

Fortitude Cottage 51 Broad St, Old Portsmouth ☎023/9282 3748, ⊜fortcott@aol.com. Harbourside cottage with three comfortable en-suite rooms, and a beamed breakfast room overlooking the boats. ❷

Sailmakers Loft 5 Bath Square, Old Portsmouth ☎023/9282 3045. Spithead views from this small B&B in a quiet location next to the *Spice Island Inn*. Most rooms are en suite. ❷

The Sally Port 57–58 High St, Old Portsmouth

☎023/9282 1860. Opposite the cathedral, this old pub with sloping floors serves good bar food and has fully equipped, extremely comfortable bedrooms, most of which are en suite. ❹

Spitbank Fort ☎01329/664286 or 07771/666 6289, ⊛www.spitbankfort.co.uk. One mile from Portsmouth Harbour and accessible by ferry, this man-made island in the middle of the Solent has two very basic rooms – the Sergeants' Room and the Officers' Room – available when the weather permits between April and September. No credit cards. ❷

Hostels and campsites

Portsmouth and Southsea Backpackers 4 Florence Rd, Southsea ☎023/9283 2495 or 9282 2963, ⊛www.portsmouthbackpackers.co.uk. Fifty-bed hostel with full facilities, including a large kitchen, at the east end of Clarence Esplanade. Dorm beds go for £10, doubles and twins for £22 (en suite for £25), and there are discounts for

longer stays. A forty-minute walk from the city centre, or catch bus #5, #6, #7 from the Harbour station, or any bus to South Parade Pier.
Southsea Leisure Park Melville Rd, Southsea ☎ 023/9273 5070. Well-appointed campsite right at the east end of Southsea Esplanade (bus #15 from the Harbour station to Ferry Road, from where it's a short walk).

Youth Hostel Wymering Manor, Old Wymering Lane, Cosham ☎ 023/9237 5661, ⓔ portsmouth @yha.org.uk. Housed in an attractive Tudor manor, ten minutes west of Cosham train station. Alternatively, take bus #5 or #12 from the Harbour station as far as Cosham Health Centre (from where it's the first left). Dorm beds £10.

Eating and drinking

Bistro Montparnasse 103 Palmerston Rd, Southsea ☎ 023/9281 6754. Stands out from the many restaurants in this part of Southsea for its good-quality French and seafood dishes. Closed Sun & Mon. Moderate.
Country Kitchen 59 Marmion Rd, Southsea ☎ 023/9281 1425. Vegetarian and vegan restaurant with newspapers on hand and free coffee refills. Closed Mon–Sat eve & all Sun. Inexpensive.
Frisco Bay Café 40 South Parade, Southsea. American-themed diner with an adjacent bar and nightclub. Inexpensive.
Sorrento Pizzeria Port Solent ☎ 023/9220 1473. Swish Italian restaurant in Portsmouth's prestigious marina development, six miles north of the city

centre, near Porchester Castle. Moderate.
Spice Island Inn Bath Square, Old Portsmouth. Old hostelry in a quiet location in the oldest part of town, boasting a handsome front and cosy interior; serves a great range of hot and cold dishes. Inexpensive.
Still & West Country House Bath Square, Old Portsmouth. Adjacent pub to the *Spice Island*, and of similar age, with an innovative seafood menu and a range of Gale's beers, as well as tables outside overlooking the Solent. Inexpensive.
Sur La Mer 69 Palmerston Rd, Southsea. A good-value French and seafood restaurant with set-price three-course meals for around £7 and £12. Closed Sun. Inexpensive.

Southampton and around

A glance at the map gives some idea of the strategic maritime importance of **SOUTHAMPTON**, which stands on a triangular peninsula formed at the place where the rivers Itchen and Test flow into Southampton Water, an eight-mile inlet from the Solent. Sure enough, Southampton has figured in numerous stirring events: it witnessed the exodus of Henry V's Agincourt-bound army, the Pilgrim Fathers' departure in the *Mayflower* in 1620 and the maiden voyages of such ships as the *Queen Mary* and the *Titanic*. Unfortunately, since its pummelling by the Luftwaffe and some disastrous postwar planning, the thousand-year-old city has changed beyond recognition. Now a sprawling conurbation easily bypassed by motorways, it'll be pretty low on your list of places to visit in southern England, but you may pass through on your way to the Isle of Wight, and it has enough of interest to occupy a couple of hours while you wait for the ferry.

King Canute is alleged to have commanded the waves to retreat at Southampton – not, as legend has it, from a misguided sense of his kingly powers, but to rebuke his obsequious courtiers. Whatever his motive, the task would have been especially difficult here, for Southampton, like other Solent ports, enjoys the phenomenon of "double tides" – a prolonged period of high water as the Channel first swirls up the westerly side of the Solent, then, two hours later, backs up round Spithead. This means that exceptionally large vessels can berth here and, even though ocean-going liners are pretty much a rarity nowadays, there'll certainly be some sort of large-scale vessels floating by, either to the **Eastern Docks** at the tip of the promontory, or in the **Western Docks**, which has the largest commercial dry dock in England.

Core of the modern town is the **Civic Centre**, a short walk east of the train station. Its clock tower is the most distinctive feature of the skyline, and it houses an excellent **art gallery** that's particularly strong on twentieth-century British artists such as Sutherland, Piper and Spencer (Tues–Sat 10am–5pm, Sun 1–4pm; free). The **Western Esplanade**, curving southward from the station, runs alongside the best remaining bits of the old city **walls**. Rebuilt after a French attack in 1338, they feature towers with evocatively chilly names – Windwhistle, Catchcold and **God's House Tower** – the last of these, at the southern end of the old town in Winkle Street, houses a **Museum of Archeology**, though lack of funding has meant that this is currently indefinitely closed except to groups by prior arrangement (☏023/8063 5904). Best preserved of the city's seven gates is **Bargate**, at the opposite end of the old town, at the head of the High Street; an elaborate structure, cluttered with lions, classical figures and machicolations (defensive apertures through which missiles could be dropped), it was formerly the guildhall and court house.

Other ancient buildings survive amid the piecemeal redevelopment of the High Street area. The oldest church is **St Michael's**, to the west of the High Street, with a twelfth-century font of black Tournai marble. The nearby **Tudor House Museum**, in Bugle Street (Tues–Fri 10am–noon & 1–5pm, Sat 10am–noon & 1–4pm, Sun 2–5pm; free), is an impressive fifteenth-century timber-framed building, its grand banqueting hall and reconstructed Tudor garden outshining the sundry exhibits of Georgian, Victorian and early twentieth-century social history, which include a 680cc Ackland motor-bike from 1923. On the opposite side of the High Street, the ruined **Holy Rood** church, bomb-damaged in World War II, stands as a monument to the merchant navy men killed in that war; it also has a memorial fountain to the crew of the *Titanic*, many of whom came from Southampton. Down at the southwest corner of the old town, by the seafront, the **Wool House** is a fine fourteenth-century stone warehouse; formerly used as a jail for Napoleonic prisoners, it now houses a **Maritime Museum** (same times as Tudor House Museum; free) with accounts of the heyday of ocean liners, and includes a huge model of the *Queen Mary* and various mementoes from the *Titanic*. The museum also offers the opportunity to listen to the recorded voices of various survivors of the *Titanic* tragedy relating their experiences, while *Titanic* obsessives can follow a "*Titanic* Trail" walking tour around Southampton – ask for the free pamphlet at the tourist office.

If you're an aviation enthusiast you should visit the **Hall of Aviation** in Albert Road South, by the car ferry terminal (Tues–Sat 10am–5pm, Sun noon–5pm; also Mon 10am–5pm during school holidays; last entry 1hr before closing; £3). Dedicated to local aviation designer R.J. Mitchell, it has sixteen of his aircraft on display, including the Spitfire, the Sandringham Flying Boat and the Supermarine seaplane, which in 1931 won the Schneider Trophy by whizzing round the Isle of Wight at an average speed of 340mph. Check first with the tourist office if you're planning to visit, as plans are afoot to transfer the exhibits to new premises in Marchwood, on the western side of Southampton Water off the A326.

Practicalities

Services from London Waterloo arrive twice-hourly at the central **train station** in Blechynden Terrace, west of the Civic Centre; the **bus** and **coach stations** are immediately south and north of the Civic Centre. The **tourist office** is at 9 Civic Centre Rd (Mon, Tues & Thurs–Sat 8.30am–5.30pm, Wed 10am–5.30pm; ☏023/8083 3333, ⊛www.southampton.gov.uk). Southampton isn't a wildly attractive **place to stay**, but there are plenty of business hotels and commercial guest houses in the centre, including the large and solid *Elizabeth House* 43–44 The Avenue (☏023/8022 4327, ⓦwww .elizabethhousehotel.com; ❸), and *Linden*, just north of the train station on the Polygon (☏023/8022 5653; no credit cards; ❶), which has more modest but still bright, good-value rooms. For a grander atmosphere, try the four-hundred-year-old *Star* (☏023/8033 9939; ❺) or the slightly younger *Dolphin* (☏023/8033 9955; ❹); both hotels are halfway down the High Street and provide accommodation with all the antique trimmings.

There's not a great choice of original **eating** places in town either. Near the art gallery, you could try *Buon Gusto*, 1 Commercial Rd, an attractive and inexpensive Italian restaurant (☏023/8033 1543; closed Sun), but you'll find more choice and character among the eateries clustered on Oxford Street, off Bernard Steet from the High Street. Here, you'll find the non-smoking *Town House* at no. 59 for vegetarian specialities alongside meat and fish dishes (closed Sat lunch & all Sun); *Kuti's Brasserie* at no. 39, a moderately priced top-class Bengali restaurant with live jazz on Tuesdays and magic shows on Wednesdays (☏023/8022 1585), and the *Oxford Brasserie* at no. 35, a relaxed place for baguettes, salads, pastas and fuller evening meals. As for **pubs**, the tiny old *Platform Tavern* in Winkle Street, at the south end of the High Street, and the ancient *Red Lion*, complete with minstrels' gallery at 55 High St, are more charismatic alternatives to the bars at the *Star* and *Dolphin* hotels.

Around Southampton

There are a few places in the immediate vicinity of Southampton which are well worth a visit, and all are easily accessible by bus. **NETLEY**, three miles southeast on Southampton Water, has a picturesquely ruined Cistercian abbey (open during daylight; free; EH), a Solent fortress and the Royal Victoria Country Park, which makes a good picnic spot overlooking the water. **ROMSEY**, ten miles northwest (bus #15 from Southampton), offers a largely original Norman **abbey church** (daily 8.30am–5.30pm), completed in 1150 and bought by the townsfolk a few years after the Dissolution. Just south of the town is the stately home of **Broadlands**, a Palladian mansion on the River Test which was the birthplace and country residence of Lord Palmerston (his statue adorns Romsey's main square) and former home of Lord Mountbatten (mid-June to early-Sept daily noon–5.30pm, last admission 4pm; £5.95), who lies buried in the abbey and whose family still live in the house. Five miles north of Romsey, **Mottisfont Abbey House and Garden** (mid-March to early June & late June to Oct Mon–Wed, Sat & Sun 11am–6pm or dusk; middle two weeks June daily 11am–8.30pm; last entry 1hr before closing; £6; NT) enjoy a lovely location right by the Test. The house of this former twelfth-century Augustinian priory (daily 1–5pm) is noted for the drawing room decorated by Whistler and the medieval cellarium, but it's the gardens that are the real draw, particularly for their old-fashioned rose collection, at its best in June. Mottisfont is accessible by train from Southampton – get off at Dunbridge, from where it's a fifteen-minute walk – or by bus from Romsey.

Another horticultural attraction, **Houghton Lodge Gardens**, lies another five miles north of Mottisfont (March–Sept Mon, Tues, Thurs & Fri 2–5pm, Sat & Sun 10am–5pm; £5), one and a half miles south of Stockbridge. Surrounded by gardens which sweep down to the River Test – and a choice trout-fishing spot – the Lodge is a rare example of an eighteenth-century cottage *orné*, or rural retreat for rich townsfolk. Admission also includes a tour of the hydroponicum and a talk on the art of hydroponics (a system of growing plants in water).

The Isle of Wight

Having achieved county status after years of being lumped in with Hampshire, the **ISLE OF WIGHT** still has difficulty in shaking off its image as a mere adjunct of rural southern England – comfortably off, scrupulously tidy and desperately unadventurous. However, in recent years expensive ferry prices and unimaginative marketing have seen the Isle of Wight's holiday-making hordes diminish and related services sell up. Surviving hotels are converting into retirement homes, a dependable, year-round enterprise for which the island's mild climate is well suited.

Measuring less than 23 miles at its widest point and divided fairly neatly by a chalk spine that runs east to west across its centre, the Isle of Wight packs a surprising variety of landscapes and coastal scenery within its bounds. North of the ridge is a terrain of low-lying woodland and pasture, deeply cut by meandering rivers; southwards is open chalky downland fringed by high cliffs. Two **Heritage Coast** paths follow the best of the shoreline, one running from Totland to St Lawrence on the south coast, the other from east of Yarmouth to west of Cowes along the north coast. What's more, the island harbours several historic buildings and a splendid array of well-preserved Victoriana clad in fretted bargeboards and pseudo-Gothic gables. The Victorian character of the Isle of Wight is scarcely surprising, for the founding Victorian herself felt most at home here – **Osborne House**, near Cowes, originally designed as a summer retreat for the royal family, became Queen Victoria's permanent home after Albert died. Several other great Victorians also had close associations with the island: Tennyson lived at Freshwater in a frowsty old mausoleum that is now a hotel, Dickens stayed and wrote in Winterbourne House (now also a hotel) in Bonchurch, the town where Swinburne grew up and is now buried.

Information and getting around

If you're dependent upon **public transport**, pick up the Southern Vectis bus route map and timetable (50p) from the tourist office, ferry office or bus station at your point of arrival. The company's hourly Island Explorer buses

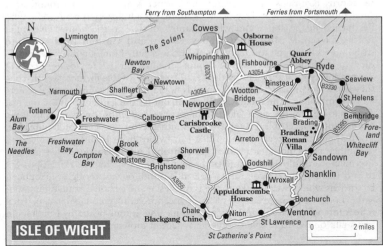

© Crown copyright

Hovertravel ☏ 023/9281 1000 or 01983 /811000, ⊛ www.hovertravel.co.uk. Year-round hovercraft service from Southsea to Ryde Mon–Fri 7.10am– 8.10pm, Sat & Sun 8.15am– 8.10pm (early Oct to early April last sailing at 7.35pm); every 30min; 10min; £9.10 for foot passengers only.

Red Funnel ☏ 023/8033 4010, ⊛ www .redfunnel.co.uk. Year-round ferries on two routes, one of them a high-speed service: **Southampton–East Cowes** daily 6am–1am; hourly; 55min; £9 for foot passengers; £65 for car and driver plus £9 per passenger. **Southampton –West Cowes** high-speed service daily 5.50am–10.35pm (Mon–Wed & Sun) or 11.40pm (Thurs–Sat); hourly; 22min;

£13 for foot passengers only.

Wightlink Ferries ☏ 0870/582 7744, ⊛ www.wightlink.co.uk. Three year-round ferry routes, including a faster but more expensive catamaran service to Ryde: **Portsmouth–Ryde** catamaran 4.30am–12.40am; 1–2 hourly; 15min; £11.70 for foot passengers only. **Portsmouth–Fishbourne** ferry 3am– 1.30am; 1–2 hourly; 35min; £9.50 for foot passengers; £65.50–£81.90 according to season and day for car and driver plus £9.50 per passenger. **Lymington–Yarmouth** ferry (June–Dec) 4am–1am; 1–2 hourly; 30min; £9.50 for foot passengers; £65.50–£81.90 according to season and day for car and driver plus £9.50 per passenger.

All the prices quoted are for a ninety-day (Wightlink and Red Funnel) or one-year (Hovertravel) standard return ticket. Wightlink and Red Funnel offer day and half-day returns as well as a range of other short-break deals for cars, with discounts of around 35 percent.

(routes #7 and #7A) run all round the island in about four hours. A Rover Ticket allows you unlimited travel on the bus network, costing £6.70 for a Day Rover, £10.90 for a Two-Day Rover and £27.50 for a Weekly Rover; tickets are available from any train station or tourist office. The **rail line** is a short east-coast stretch linking Ryde, Sandown and Shanklin.

Cycling is a very popular way of getting around the Isle of Wight, especially as bikes are carried free on all ferry services, but beware that in summer the narrow lanes can get very busy. For **bike rental**, you can expect to pay around £10 a day; ask at any tourist office for the four trail leaflets with recommended off-road cycling routes (90p) – best used in conjunction with a good map – and the free leaflet giving the best on-road routes round the island, which are all clearly signposted. If you're planning to do a lot of cycling, it may be worth getting hold of Ron Crick's detailed *Cyclist's Guide to the Isle of Wight* (£2.95), and off-road cyclists should check out the routes described in *Cycling Wight 1* and *2* (£2.95 each) by John Goodwin and Ian Williams, sold by Offshore Sports, Orchardleigh Rd, Shanklin (☏ 01983/866269), and 2–4 Birmingham Rd, Cowes (☏ 01983/290514); both outlets rent out mountain bikes (deposit and ID required). Tourist offices can supply a full list of bike rental shops.

For **information about the whole island**, call ☏ 01983/813818, consult ⊛ www.islandbreaks.co.uk, or call the individual tourist offices detailed below.

Ryde and around

As a major ferry terminal, **RYDE** is the first landfall many visitors make on the island, but one where few choose to linger. A working town which came to prominence as a resort in the Victorian era, Ryde offers some grand nineteenth-century architecture and decent beach amusements, but is unexceptional by island standards.

Reaching out over the shallows of Ryde Sands, the functional half-mile-long **pier** is where the ferries dock and former London Underground rolling stock carries the seasonal throngs inland. Union Street rises steeply from the pier's base to the town centre and at its crest sits All Saints' church whose spire acts as a landmark from vantage points all across the east of the island and even from parts of the mainland. The **Esplanade** extends eastwards from the pier, and along it are found traditional diversions: Ryde Arena and Ice Rink, the Eastern Pavilion (mimicking Brighton's original) and boating lake, all backed by sandy beaches. At the Esplanade's far end is the small Gothic Revival folly of Appley Tower, celebrating the sailing of the First Fleet to Botany Bay from Mother Bank, off Ryde, in 1787. It was once part of Appley House (now an expensive country hotel) built in the 1720s on the vast ill-gotten gains of arch-smuggler Daniel Boyce. Successful in bribing witnesses, sheriffs and juries at his many trials, he was finally convicted in 1733 when the law introduced the random appointment of jurors.

Practicalities

The **tourist office** (March–Oct Mon–Sat 9am–5.30pm, Sun 9am–5pm; Nov–Feb daily 9am–4.30pm; ☎01983/562905), **bus station**, **Hovercraft terminal** and **Esplanade train station** (the northern terminus of the Island Line train line, which runs south to Shanklin) are all located near the base of the pier; there's also a **taxi** rank nearby. **Boat trips** to the Solent forts leave from Ryde jetty; for details contact Solent & Wight Line Cruises (☎01983/564602).

Accommodation is available just over the road from the jetty in St Thomas Street, where the *Biskra House Hotel and Restaurant* at no. 17 (☎01983/567913; ❺) offers balconied rooms and a terrace looking out to sea as well as a fine restaurant. *Yelf's Hotel* on Union Street (☎01983/564062; ❸) is one of Ryde's oldest hotels, right in the town centre, but is mainly geared up for business travellers. Inexpensive **B&Bs** don't exactly jump out at you in Ryde, but the *Trentham Guest House*, 38 The Strand (☎01983/563418; no credit cards; ❶), offers great value, as does the similar *Vine Guest House*, 16 Castle St (☎01983 /566633; ❶; closed Nov & Dec) – both are just south of the Esplanade. The nearest **campsites** are the *Pondwell Caravan Park* two miles east of town on the way to Seaview (☎01983/612330), and *Beaper Farm*, three miles south on the Sandown road (☎01983/615210).

The area around Union Street offers the best **eating** opportunities. *Joe Daflo's Café Bar* at no. 24 has an appealing continental air, while just off it, on Castle Street, the *Blue Moon* has a cool sophistication and good fish and meat dishes (closed lunch, plus all Sun & Mon). On the Esplanade, the *Seafood Cabin* has seafood and sandwiches in plainer surroundings (closed Nov–Easter). The *Redan* at no. 76–7 is a traditional **pub** with bar meals and live bands on Thursday and Saturday nights.

Around Ryde

As elsewhere on the island, just a couple of miles can remove you from an undistinguished urban setting into one of idyllic rusticity. Just outside the village of Binstead, two miles west of Ryde's centre, lies one of the island's earliest Christian relics. In 1132 **Quarr Abbey** was founded by Richard de Redvers for Savigny monks; its name was derived from the quarries nearby, where stone was mined for use in the construction of Winchester and Chichester cathedrals. Subsequently the abbey was occupied by Benedictine and, later, Cistercian monks. Only stunted ruins survived the Dissolution and ensuing plunder of ready-cut stone, although an ivy-clad archway still hangs picturesquely over a farm track. In 1907 a new abbey was founded just west of the ruins – it's a striking rose-brick building with Byzantine overtones, and is open to the public (daily 9am–9pm; Vespers 5pm).

Two miles south of Binstead, the village of **HAVENSTREET** houses the **Brickfields Horse Country** (daily 10am–5pm; £4.95), a centre for all things equine. Its attractions include a horse museum with a carriage collection, saddlery and blacksmith and wagon rides pulled by huge, docile Shires.

Three miles west of Havenstreet, **Wootton Bridge** is the end-stop of the **Isle of Wight Steam Railway** (late March to Oct 10.30am–4.15pm; £7, valid all day; ☎01983/882204), which starts its delightful ten-mile round trip at Smallbrook on the main Ryde–Shanklin line to the east. Though it doesn't stop anywhere of interest along the way, the impeccably restored carriages in traditional green livery pass through lovely unspoilt countryside, and the ride makes a nostalgic way of spending an afternoon.

Two miles east of Ryde's centre, the quiet village of **SEAVIEW** used to be dominated by maritime industries, before the popularity of sea bathing elevated it to a select resort in the middle of the nineteenth century. And so it remains today, a discreet hideaway of holiday homes and quiet pubs, looking across to the rotund naval forts sitting in the Solent. For an **overnight stay** in Seaview try the *Spring Vale Hotel* (☎01983/612533; ❸), along the seafront west of town, a grand late-Georgian building with a lovely terrace overlooking the garden. More expensive, the *Seaview Hotel* on High Street (☎01983/612711, ⓦwww.seaviewhotel.co.uk; ❺) is a charming, privately owned hotel with a superb and moderately priced restaurant, serving traditional English dishes.

Bembridge and around

BEMBRIDGE, a residential area set around its own harbour in the east of the island, has little to attract visitors, save for its **Shipwreck Centre and Maritime Museum**, Sherbourne St (late March to Oct daily 10am–5pm; £2.75), stuffed with nautical odds and ends salvaged from the seabed by the museum's deep-sea-diving owner. A couple of old **pubs** make for a good refreshment break: the *Pilots' Boat Inn* by the mouth of Bembridge harbour and the *Crab & Lobster*, tucked away at the very eastern tip of the Foreland and renowned for its locally caught seafood.

In summer a ferry runs from Bembridge across the mouth of the harbour to the spit of land and adjacent beach known as the **Duver**, where you'll find the seasonal *Baywatch Café*. At the Duver's northern edge are the buttressed remains of St Helens Church, built by the Normans on the site where Hildila, an early Saxon missionary, set about converting the islanders to Christianity. From the church, follow the path southwest, which curls round the harbour past an old mill and returns to Bembridge along the boat-lined Embankment, built to reclaim from the sea the former inlet which once extended all the way to Brading (see p.264).

The island's easternmost tip, the **Foreland**, is a rather dreary corner, although the tidal beach at **Whitecliff Bay**, to the south, lightens the pallid air. From Whitecliff Bay a path gradually ascends towards the chalk cliffs of Culver and then onto **Bembridge Down**. A monument to Lord Yarborough, first commodore of the Royal Yacht Squadron at Cowes, caps the down, with refreshments available at the adjacent *Culver Haven Inn*. If you're not up to walking up the steep two-mile path, you can drive to the top of the down (there's no bus service) and then stroll around up there; leave Bembridge on the Sandown road, the B3395, and soon after the airport a sharp left turn leads steeply upwards past a mid-nineteenth-century fort (currently occupied by an electronics company). The road ends in a warren of World War II emplacements – now colonized by rabbits – with island-wide views.

Brading

On the busy Ryde to Sandown road (A3055), the ancient village of **Brading** boasts a surprisingly disparate collection of ancient and modern sites. Just south of the village are the remains of **Brading Roman Villa** (April–Oct daily 9.30am–5pm; £2.75), one of two such villas on the island (the other is in Newport; see p.272), both of which were probably sites of bacchanalian worship. The Brading site is renowned for its superbly preserved mosaics, including intact images of Medusa and depictions of Orpheus – associated with the cult of Bacchus – as well as the mysterious and unique man with a cockerel's head.

In the centre of Brading, what is believed to be the island's oldest intact dwelling – dating from 1228 – now houses the **Isle of Wight Wax Museum** (daily: mid-May to mid-Sept 10am–10pm; rest of year 10am–5pm; last entry 1hr before closing; £4.95; ⊛www.iwwaxworks.co.uk). Inside, various dioramas portray island celebrities from Vespasian, the conqueror of Vectis (the Roman name of the island), to Tennyson. The Chamber of Horrors is as gruesome as you'd expect, with Animal World offering a little relief until you get to the "freaks of nature" section. Next door is the **Old Town Hall**, which still has the original stocks and whipping post once used to immobilize miscreants. Across the road, *Penny Plain* is a good place for snacks and teas in its walled garden (closed Nov–Easter), or try the *Bugle Inn*, formerly a smugglers' rendezvous. From behind the pub, a path leads to Brading Haven, once an inlet connected to the sea, where the smugglers used to land their contraband. Note that the museum has a free car park to the rear, more convenient than the pay-to-park one on the High Street.

Nunwell House (July to early Sept Mon–Wed 1–5pm; £4), signposted off the A3055 less than a mile northwest of Brading, was where, in 1647, Charles I spent his last night of freedom before being taken to Carisbrooke Castle (see p.272) and thence to his eventual execution in Whitehall. The house has been in the Oglander family for nearly nine hundred years, with the present building being a mix of Jacobean and Georgian styles with Victorian additions. It sits in five acres of lovely gardens and remains very much the family home of the present owners, whose military legacy is reflected inside in a small exhibition commemorating the Home Guard, the voluntary defence force recruited during the early years of World War II when the island prepared to resist Nazi occupation. Guided tours of the house take place at 1.30pm, 2.30pm and 3.30pm, and the entry ticket includes a free guide booklet.

Sandown and Shanklin

The two eastern resorts of Sandown and Shanklin merge into each other across the sandy reach of Sandown Bay, representing the island's holiday-making epicentre. Frequently recorded as among Britain's sunniest spots, Sandown is a relic of a traditional Sixties bucket-and-spade resort, while Shanklin, with its auburn cliffs, Old Village and scenic Chine, has a marginally more sophisticated aura.

Appropriately, **SANDOWN** possesses the island's only surviving pleasure **Pier**, bedecked with amusement arcades, cafeterias, dodgems and a large theatre with nightly entertainment in season – but out of season the town becomes rather desolate. The main distractions here lie next to each other at the northern end of the Esplanade. **Dinosaur Isle** on Culver Parade (daily

10am–6pm; £4.60) is a lively exhibition of locally excavated dinosaur bones, with an animatronic model and working laboratory, and incorporating an illuminating **geological collection**, displaying some massive ammonites recovered locally. The adjacent **Tiger and Big Cat Sanctuary and Isle of Wight Zoological Gardens** (Easter–Oct daily 10am–5pm; rest of year may also open Sun & school half-term holidays; check on ☎01983/403883; £5.75) contains several species of tigers, panthers and other big cats, some of which are heading for extinction in the wild, as well as some frisky lemurs and monkeys. The zoo's reptile house has an exhaustive selection of spiders and snakes, and in summer there are snake-handling displays and talks.

Possibly being separated from the shore by hundred-foot cliffs has preserved **SHANKLIN** from the tawdry excesses of its northern neighbour – though it hasn't stopped the promotion of the **Old Village**'s rose-clad, thatched charm with the same zeal as Sandown's pier. The real thing can be found in any number of inland villages, but with the adjacent **Shanklin Chine** (daily: Easter–May & Oct 10am–5pm; June–Sept 10am–10pm; £2.50), a twisting pathway descending a mossy ravine and decorated on summer nights with fairy lights, it all adds up to a picturesque spot, popular since early Victorian times when local resident John Keats drew his Romantic imagery from the environs.

Arrival and information

Sandown's **tourist office** is located at 8 High St (Easter–Oct Mon–Sat 9am–5.30pm, Sun 9am–5pm; Nov–Easter irregular hours, alternating with Shanklin tourist office; ☎01983/403886); Shanklin's is at 67 High St (same hours; ☎01983/862942). Both towns have Island Line train stations about half a mile inland from their beachfront centres.

Accommodation

Hotels and B&Bs

Grange Hall Hotel Grange Rd, Sandown ☎01983/403531, ✉grangehall@C4.com. Good-value cliff-top hotel in its own grounds, with all rooms en suite. **④**

Holliers Hotel 3 Church Rd, Shanklin Old Village ☎01983/862764, ⊛www.holliers-hotel.com. Well-appointed old hotel in the Old Village with indoor and outdoor swimming pools and a good restaurant. **⑤**

Luccombe Hall Luccombe Rd, Shanklin ☎01983/862719, ⊛www.luccombehall.co.uk. Originally built as the summer palace for the Bishop of Portsmouth, this is now a secluded and finely situated hotel with two pools, a mile from the Old Village. **⑤**

Mount Brocas 15 Beachfield Rd, Sandown ☎01983/406276. Good-value B&B at the west end of High Street, very close to the beach. **②**

Ocean Hotel Esplanade, Sandown ☎01983/402351, ⊛www.ocean-hotel.co.uk. Grand seafront hotel right in town with good deals and facilities for children. Closed Jan & Feb. **⑤**

Pink Beach Hotel 20 Esplanade, Shanklin ☎01983/862501. Shocking pink Victorian hotel, fronted by lawns, a stone's throw from the beach.

All rooms are en suite with TV and tea/coffee-making facilities. **③**

St Catherine's Hotel 1 Winchester Park Rd, Sandown, ☎01983/402392. Comfortable B&B with rooms all en suite, just five minutes' walk from the beach. **③**

Hostels and campsites

Cheverton Copse Holiday Park Sandown ☎01983/403161. Spacious park set among woodland, two miles from the beach, mainly for caravans but with some tent pitches. Signposted off the A3056 road. Closed Nov–March.

Fairway Holiday Park Sandown ☎01983/ 403462. Inexpensive and well-equipped campsite, ten-minutes' walk northeast of the train station. Closed Nov–Feb.

Landguard Camping Park Landguard Manor Rd, Shanklin ☎01983/867028. Similar to the above and just ten minutes' walk north of the train station. Closed Oct–Easter.

Sandown Youth Hostel Fitzroy St, Sandown ☎01983/402651. Converted house right in the town centre, but only a few minutes' walk from the beach. Dorm beds £11 per night.

Restaurants and cafés

Barnaby's Restaurant4 Pier St, Sandown. Good-looking eatery, close to the pier with meals and snacks under £5. Inexpensive.

Cottage Restaurant8 Eastcliff Rd, Shanklin Old Village ☎01983/862504. Olde-worlde restaurant serving traditional English dishes. Closed lunchtime, Sun & Mon. Moderate.

Fisherman's Cottage Free House Esplanade, Shanklin. Atmospheric seafaring pub at the southern end of the Esplanade, on Appley Beach, serving wholesome food. Closed Nov–Feb. No credit cards. Moderate.

Francine's Restaurant16 High St, Sandown ☎01983/403289. Licensed restaurant with a good variety of English and seafood dishes. No smoking. Closed Dec–Easter. Inexpensive to Moderate.

King's Bar Café High St, Sandown. Continental-style licensed café with great views over the sea; snacks plus a dish of the day available from noon to 2pm. No credit cards. Moderate.

Ocean Deck Inn Esplanade, Sandown. Free house with an outdoor patio. Hot and cold meals are served as well as teas and coffees. Inexpensive to Moderate.

Ventnor and around

The attractive seaside resort of **VENTNOR** and its two village suburbs of **Bonchurch** and **St Lawrence** sit at the foot of St Boniface Down, the island's highest point at 787ft. The Down periodically disintegrates into landslides, creating the jumbled terraces known locally as the **Undercliff**, whose sheltered, south-facing aspect, mild winter temperatures and thick carpet of undergrowth have contributed to the former fishing village becoming a fashionable health spa. Thanks to these unique factors, the town possesses rather more character than the island's other resorts, its Gothic Revival buildings clinging dizzily to zigzagging bends.

The floral terraces of the **Cascade** curve down to the slender Esplanade and narrow beach, where former boat builders' cottages now provide more recreational services. Among them the **Longshoreman's Museum** (Easter–Christmas daily 9.30am–5pm; £1) offers a peep into Ventnor's bygone days with a collection of nautical objects, models and old photographs. From the shoreside *Spyglass Inn* (see below) on the Esplanade, it's a pleasant mile-long stroll to Ventnor's famous **Botanical Gardens**, where 22 landscaped acres of subtropical vegetation flourish. Displays are divided thematically, including the South African and Australian banks, the Culinary Herb and the Medicinal gardens. There's also a **Smuggling Museum** inside the gardens (April–Sept daily 10am–5pm; £2.40), which capitalizes on Ventnor's long history of "owling", as the nefarious nocturnal activity was once known.

To the east of Ventnor, the ancient village of **BONCHURCH** exudes an alluring rustic charm with its duck pond and rows of quaint cottages set on the Undercliff's wooded slopes. Behind high stone walls loom grand Victorian country houses where writers such as Dickens, Thackeray and Swinburne once stayed. At Bonchurch's east end is the spartan, towerless edifice of the eleventh-century **Old Church of St Boniface** with its wreath of skewed gravestones and mature trees further enhancing the village. Above the village the **Landslip Footpath** descends the Undercliff. It's recently been restored and reopened to the public, but remains prone to subsidence, so it's still worth checking with the tourist office that it's open before you set off on an exploration.

Heading west from Ventnor, the road, still prone to subsidence, winds its way along the wooded hillside where the village of **St Lawrence** appears lost in the tumbling Undercliff. The studios of **Isle of Wight Glass** in the Old Park (April–Sept Mon–Fri 9am–5pm, Sat & Sun 10am–4.30pm; Oct–March Mon–Fri 9am–5pm; 70p; ⓦwww.isleofwightstudioglass.co.uk) give a rare chance to observe the process of glassblowing.

Practicalities

Ventnor's **tourist office** is at 34 High St (Easter–Oct Mon–Sat 9.30am–5.30pm, Sun 10am–3pm; ☎01983/853625). For **accommodation**, try the *Spyglass Inn* on Ventnor's Esplanade (☎01983/855338; ❸), which has a few self-contained rooms and balconies, and offers a small discount for week-long stays. A few doors down is *St Martin's* (☎01983/852345; no credit cards; ❷), with comfortable rooms and sea views, right next to the little wooden cottage where, in 1860, Turgenev started his novel *Fathers and Sons*. Alternatively, the *Horseshoe Bay House Café* in Horseshoe Bay, Bonchurch, offers B&B accommodation right on the beach (☎01983/856800; ❷). Also in Bonchurch, on Shore Road, is the *Under Rock Hotel* (☎01983/855274; no credit cards; ❷), a small Georgian country house in a subtropical rock garden, while the *Bonchurch Inn* (☎01983/852611), a quieter pub than the *Spyglass*, has a self-catering flat available, located off the Shute (£350/week). On the main A3055, at Undercliff Drive, *Lisle Combe* (☎01983/852582; no credit cards; ❷), former home of poet Alfred Noyes, offers B&B accommodation in a beautifully preserved early Victorian villa. Apart from *St Martin's* – which does do cream teas and snacks – and *Lisle Combe*, all the above have dining facilities, and the excellent *Horseshoe Bay House Café* is worth exploring in any case, boasting 180-degree views from its outdoor tables, and crab salad, sea-bass and lobster on the menu, as well as baguettes (closed eve & weekdays in winter; no credit cards). The best of the many restaurants in Ventnor town centre is the *Thistle Café*, 30 Pier St, offering inexpensive seafood and vegetarian meals as well as an all-day breakfast (closed all Jan, plus all Mon & Tues–Sun eve Oct–March).

Appuldurcombe House and Godshill

Follow the B3327 for a couple of miles inland, over St Boniface Down, through arable farmland and past market gardens, to Wroxall, where a track leads left for half a mile to the ruins of **Appuldurcombe House** (daily: May–Sept 10am–6pm; Oct to mid-Dec & Jan–April 10am–4pm; £2; EH), the island's grandest pre-Victorian house. The present mansion was built in the late eighteenth century in the Palladian style on the site of an eleventh-century priory and an Elizabethan manor. Its gardens landscaped by Capability Brown (which included the erection of a "scenic" castle ruin – since dismantled – across the valley), the house was the home of Lord Yarborough before impecuniousness and neglect led to its semi-abandonment in the early twentieth century. What makes Appuldurcombe unusual is that it has been preserved in this state of decay, a partially roofed but intact shell where the evidence of a former owner's extravagant raising of all floor levels and doorways can clearly be seen. The house's stately eastern facade, spring-fed fountain and impressive situation, overlooking a fold in the downs, make for an illuminating visit. Back down the track, *Appuldurcombe Holiday Park* (☎01983/852597; closed Nov–March) offers facilities for **campers**.

Pass through Freemantle Gate, an Ionic triumphal arch reputedly designed by James Wyatt and formerly the entrance to Appuldurcombe House, then follow the old carriage drive across the fields for a couple of miles and you'll come out opposite the village car park in **GODSHILL**. By road it's twice the distance to this "tourist village", jammed with summertime day-trippers come to appreciate the fairy-tale cuteness of its old core where the square-towered **Church of the Lily Cross** overlooks a cluster of thatched cottages and high-walled lanes. The church contains a very rare fifteenth-century painting, rediscovered in 1857, depicting Christ crucified on a triple-branched lily, as well as effigies of past owners of Appuldurcombe House, the Leighs and the Worsleys.

Other attractions have sprung up to capitalize on Godshill's enduring popularity. **Godshill Model Village** (April to late July & Sept daily 10am–5pm; late July to Aug 10am–6pm; March & Oct daily 10.30am–4pm; £2.75) is just what it says; and there's an Old Smithy, antique shops and a brace of quaint tea- and scone-shops on site, too.

St Catherine's Point to the Needles

The western Undercliff begins to recede at the village of Niton, where a footpath continues to the most southerly tip of the island, **St Catherine's Point**, marked by a modern lighthouse. A prominent landmark on the downs behind is **St Catherine's Oratory**, known locally as the "Pepper Pot". In fact it's a medieval lighthouse, reputedly built in 1325 as an act of expiation by Walter de Goditon who had attempted to pilfer a cargo of wine owned by a monastic community whose ship was wrecked off Atherfield Point in 1313. An adjacent oratory was also constructed but demolished during the Dissolution, although the crude lighthouse remained in use for over three hundred years.

A short distance west, there's **accommodation** at the very popular *Clarendon Hotel and Wight Mouse Inn*, Chale (☎01983/730431; ⓦwww.wightmouseinns.co.uk; ❺), a cluttered, family-run combination of pub, restaurant and hotel which welcomes children and puts on nightly live entertainment. The inn is only half a mile from **Blackgang Chine** (daily: end March to June & early Sept to Oct 10am–5.30pm; July to early Sept 10am–10pm; £6.50), which, having opened as a landscaped garden in 1843, gradually evolved into a theme park – possibly the world's first – and now offers a half-dozen exhibits from Cowboy Town to Jungleland, a giant maze, a rendition of a Victorian Quay and a high-speed water ride.

From Chale, Military Road continues west along the coast, a flat windswept drive with occasional turn-offs to small bays and chines of which **Hanover Point** is the most impressive. Along this coastline, the narrow beaches backed by low cliffs are too exposed for safe swimming. Several old buildings in the area – including the *Wight Mouse Inn* – were once extended using timber salvaged from wrecks which foundered here.

Inland to Shorwell, Brighstone and Calbourne

A leisurely and rewarding inland detour westwards can fill a half-day or more and passes through many of the island's prettiest villages, containing nothing more than picturesque, typically English village greens, ancient churches and country pubs. **SHORWELL**, for example, has its terrace of thatched cottages, the *Crown Inn*'s delectable ales and a fine walk through the woodlands up onto Chillerton Downs, signposted near the wooden footbridge on the village's northern exit. For an overnight stay in the village, try *North Court* (☎01983/740415; no credit cards; ❸), an impressive mansion with six bedrooms, all en suite, a music room, lovely gardens, a tennis court and a croquet lawn.

The pretty village of **BRIGHSTONE**, a couple of miles west of Shorwell, has a fine pub, the *Three Bishops,* while three miles north of Brighstone, **CALBOURNE**'s quaint Winkle Street makes a much photographed rural, thatched scene. *Swainston Manor Hotel*, a mile and a half east of Calbourne (☎01983/521121, ⓔhotel@swainstonmanor.freeserve.co.uk; ❼), can provide a memorably grand overnight stay, and for those on a smaller budget, there are **campsites** at *Chine Farm*, Atherfield Bay (☎01983/740228; closed Oct–April),

Grange Farm, Brighstone Bay (℡01983/740296; closed Nov–Feb), and at *Compton Farm*, Brook (℡01983/740215; closed Oct–April). At the village of Brook, the inland route rejoins Military Road – look back up the valley at the impressive Brook House – which then ascends the flank of Compton Down before descending into Freshwater Bay.

Dimbola Lodge, Alum Bay and the Needles

The western tip of the Isle of Wight holds sundry traces of some of the venerable Victorians who were drawn to the area. On the coastal road at Freshwater Bay, on the corner with Terrace Lane, **Dimbola Lodge** (Tues–Sun 10am–5pm; £3; ⒲www.dimbola.co.uk) was the home of pioneer photographer Julia Margaret Cameron. After visiting local resident Tennyson in 1860, Cameron immediately bought adjacent land on the nearby coast, joining two cottages to make a substantial home for herself and her family, where she practised her art until moving to Ceylon in 1875. The building now houses a gallery of her work, including an impressive range of her portraits of some of the foremost society figures of her day, and also features changing exhibitions. There's also a bookshop and a tea room and vegetarian restaurant on the premises. If you want **accommodation** around here and are prepared to fork out, book into *Farringford Hotel*, on Bedbury Lane (℡01983/752500, ⒲www.farringford.co.uk; ❻), Tennyson's former home, where the facilities now include an outdoor pool, putting green and tennis courts as well as several cottage suites. On the way, you'll pass Freshwater's unusual ninety-year-old thatched Church of St Agnes; Tennyson's wife is buried in the churchyard. Inside, there are memorials to Tennyson as well as Thackeray's daughter, Lady Ritchie.

Between Freshwater Bay and the Needles, the breezy four-mile ridge of **Tennyson Down** is one of the island's most satisfying walks, with yet another monument to the poet at its 485-feet summit and vistas onto rolling downs and vales. There's a **youth hostel** a short walk northeast from the Needles, at Totland Bay (℡01983/752165; closed Sun in winter), where beds are available for £11 a night; take bus #7A, #11, #12 or #42, alighting at Totland War Memorial, and walk a quarter-mile up Weston Road and Hurst Hill.

The focal points of the isle's western tip are **Alum Bay**'s multichrome cliffs and the chalk stacks of the Needles where Tennyson Down slips into the Channel. The road ends at **The Needles Pleasure Park** (April to early Nov daily 10am–5pm), a collection of fairground amusements, a glass studio and companies running boat trips out around the Needles. There's a plinth commemorating Marconi's first telegraph messages to a tug moored in the bay, a little less than a century ago. A chair lift (£3 return) runs down to the foot of the cliffs of Alum Bay whose ochre-hued sands, used as pigments for painting local landscapes in the Victorian era, contrast brightly with the chalk face of the Needles headland.

It's a twenty-minute walk to the lookout on top of the three tall chalk stacks known as **The Needles**, best seen from a boat trip leaving from Alum Bay (Needles Pleasure Cruises; ℡01983/754477; 25min; £3), or from the tunnel by the **Old Battery**, a fort dating from 1862 (April to June, Sept & Oct Mon–Thurs & Sun 10.30am–5pm; July & Aug daily 10.30am–5pm; last entry 1hr before closing; £3; NT). During the 1950s the fort was a military establishment where rockets were strapped down and their engines tested. You can see the original gun tunnels, one of which, 250ft long, holds an exhibition. The fort is sometimes closed in bad weather; call to check on ℡01983/754772.

Yarmouth and around

Situated at the mouth of the River Yar, the pleasant town of **YARMOUTH** was the island's first purpose-built port. Although razed by the French in 1377 on their way to Newtown and Carisbrooke, the port began to prosper again after **Yarmouth Castle** (April–Sept daily 10am–6pm; Oct 10am–5pm; £2.20; EH), tucked between the quay and the pier, was built on the command of Henry VIII. The castle today holds exhibitions of paintings and photography relating to the Isle of Wight. Although there is little more to see in town, Yarmouth, linked to Lymington in the New Forest by car ferry, makes an appealing arrival or departure point; for details of ferry departures, see p.261.

The **tourist office** is on Yarmouth Quay (Easter–Oct Mon–Sat 9am–5.30pm, Sun 9am–5pm; Nov–Easter daily 10am–4pm; ☎01983/760015). There's a decent range of affordable **accommodation** in town. *Jireh House* in St James's Square (☎01983/760513; ❸) is a pretty seventeenth-century stone guest house and tea room, which serves evening meals in summer; while *Wavell's*, a grocer's shop also on the square (☎01983/760738; ❷), has bright, contemporary-style rooms; and opposite is the cosy *Bugle Hotel* (☎01983 /760272; ❸), which has a range of rooms (all non-smoking) and also holds one of the town's many good **pubs**. There are bar meals in the *Bugle's* pub and more sophisticated fare at its moderately priced *Poacher's Restaurant*. Alternatively, try the less expensive *Fender's Bistro* – its ceiling plastered with board games – in Bridge Road.

Two miles west of town **Fort Victoria Country Park** (free access) is a Palmerston-era fort looking out to Hurst Castle on the mainland, less than a mile away. Besides footpaths through the woodlands and along the coast, there's an **aquarium** (April–Oct daily 10am–6pm; £1.90), a **planetarium** (during school holidays daily 10am–5pm; last ticket 1hr before closing; at other times, call to check; £2.50; ☎0800/195 8295), a **Sunken History Exhibition** (April–Oct daily 10am–5pm; £1.50), focusing on the work of marine archeologists, and a **model railway**, claimed to be the largest in England (April–Sept daily 10am–5pm; Oct Sat & Sun 10am–5pm; £3.50).

Newtown and Shalfleet

At the time of the fourteenth-century raids on the island, **NEWTOWN**, sitting on an inlet of the eponymous estuary on the northwest coast, had been the Isle of Wight's capital for 150 years. This purpose-built medieval settlement never fully recovered from the French sacking in 1377 and nothing remains of the ancient town, bar a trace of its gridded street pattern and an incongruously stranded Jacobean **town hall** (April–June, Sept & Oct Mon, Wed & Sun 2–5pm; July & Aug Mon–Thurs & Sun 2–5pm; £1.50; NT). North of the town, a jetty leads out around a nature reserve, past the disintegrating quays of Newtown's former harbour, where curlews, geese and other waterfowl nest.

Just a mile's walk away, at the head of one of the estuary's inlets, **SHALFLEET**'s position on the Newport road makes it more lively than Newtown. The *New Inn*, just opposite the largely unrestored Norman church, serves delicious seafood dishes, and over the road the *Old Malthouse* (☎01983 /531329; no credit cards; ❷) is a quiet and comfortable **B&B**. Heading north up Mill Road, you'll pass the old watermill and the stunted remains of the quays which once lined the inlet. At the end of Mill Road a boatyard looks out onto the tidal creeks, another popular spot for birdwatchers.

Cowes and around

COWES, at the island's northern tip, is inextricably associated with sailing craft and boat building: Henry VIII built a castle here to defend the Solent's expanding naval dockyards from the French and Spanish, and in the 1950s the world's first hovercraft made its test runs here. In 1820 the Prince Regent's patronage of the yacht club gave the port its cachet with the *Royal Yacht Squadron*, now one of the world's most exclusive sailing clubs, permitted to fly the St George's Ensign guaranteeing free entry to all foreign ports. Only its three hundred members and their guests are permitted within the hallowed precincts of the club house in the remains of Henry VIII's castle, and the club's landing stage is sacrosanct. The first week of August sees the international yachting festival known as **Cowes Week**, which visiting royalty turns into a high-society gala, although most summer weekends see some form of yachting or powerboat racing off Cowes.

The town is bisected by the River Medina, with West Cowes being the older and more interesting half, its High Street meandering up from the waterfront Parade. Along the High Street you'll find shops reflecting the town's gentrified heritage, with boatyards, chandlers and Beken's famous yachting gallery – a photo by Beken of your yacht is considered as prestigious as a family portrait by Lord Snowdon.

Practicalities

The Cowes **tourist office** is at the Arcade, Fountain Quay (April–Oct Mon–Sat 9am–5pm, Sun 10am–4pm, with extended hours during Cowes Week; Nov–March Mon–Sat 10am–4pm; ☎01983/291914). **Boat trips** upriver and around the harbour leave from the Parade; for details contact Solent & Wight Line Cruises (☎01983/564602).

The more affordable **accommodation** options include the *Union Inn* in Watch House Lane, off High Street (☎01983/293163; ②), and *Halcyone Villa*, Grove Road, up Mill Hill Road from the east end of the High Street (☎01983/291334, ⓦwww.halcyonevilla.freeuk.com; ①), and in East Cowes, there's the *Doghouse* (☎01983/293677; ③), Crossways Rd, opposite Osborne House, and, nearby, the *Crossways House Hotel* (☎01983/298282; ③). Prices rise steeply during Cowes Week, and most places are booked up well in advance. The town has a decent selection of places to **eat**: *Baan Thai*, 10 Bath Rd (at the west end of the High Street), offers good-quality oriental food at moderate prices, while the *Octopus's Garden*, 63 High St, is a café and bistro serving baguettes and pies and filled with Beatles memorabilia. Along the High Street, there are numerous other wholesome snack and sandwich shops, as well as traditional **pub** meals served at the *Fountain*, *Anchor* and *Harbour Lights*. The *Fountain* (☎01983/292397; ⑤) and *Anchor* (☎01983/292823; ②) also have rooms, and the *Anchor* has a garden and live music Wednesday to Saturday.

Osborne House and Whippingham

A "floating bridge", or chain ferry (Mon–Sat 5am–midnight, Sun 6.35am–midnight; pedestrians free, cars £1.30) connects West Cowes to the more industrial East Cowes, where the only place of interest is Queen Victoria's family home, **Osborne House** (April–Oct daily 10am–5pm; grounds April–Sept daily 10am–6pm; Oct 10am–5pm; last admission 1hr before closing; £7.20, including carriage ride to the Swiss Cottage; EH), signposted one mile southeast of town (bus #4 from Ryde or #5 from Newport). The house was built in the late 1840s by Prince Albert and Thomas Cubitt, with extensions such as the Household Wing, the Swiss Cottage – where Victoria's children played and studied – and the exotic Durbar Room with its elaborate Indian plasterwork, which were all added over the next half-century. Albert designed the private family home as an Italianate villa, with balconies and large terraces overlooking the landscaped gardens towards the Solent. The state rooms, used for entertaining visiting dignitaries, exude an expected formality, while the private apartments feel more homely, like the affluent family holiday residence that Osborne was – far removed from the pomp and ceremony of state affairs in London. Following Albert's death, the desolate Victoria spent much of her time here, where she eventually died in 1901. Since then, according to her wishes, the house has remained virtually unaltered, allowing an unexpectedly intimate glimpse into Victoria's family life.

At **WHIPPINGHAM**, a mile south of Osborne, there's another of Albert's architectural extravaganzas, the Gothic Revival **Royal Church of St Mildred** (Easter–Sept Mon–Fri 10am–5pm; Oct closes 4pm). Its exterior evokes the many-pinnacled Rhine castles of Albert's homeland, while the interior boasts huge rose windows, a finely carved altarpiece of the Last Supper and a large octagonal lantern. The German Battenberg family, who later adopted the anglicized name Mountbatten, have a chapel here and the parents of the present Queen's late uncle, Earl Mountbatten, the island's last governor, are buried in the churchyard.

Newport and Carisbrooke Castle

NEWPORT, the capital of the Isle of Wight, sits at the centre of the island at a point where the River Medina's commercial navigability ends. Apart from a few pleasant old quays dating from its days as an inland port, the town isn't particularly engaging, content to fulfil its role as the island's municipal and commercial centre, where familiar chain stores draw in the shoppers. Newport offers little of cultural interest apart from a cinema, the Medina and Apollo theatres and the remains of the **Roman villa** in Cypress Road (March–Oct Mon–Sat 10am–4.15pm; £2). A well-signposted ten minutes' walk southeast of the town centre, a few rudimentary foundations of the third-century villa are on show, as well as some excavated artefacts in the museum, but frankly you'd be better off visiting its sister villa in Brading (see p.264).

The town's main attraction, however, lies in the hilltop fortress of **Carisbrooke Castle** (daily: April–Sept 10am–6pm; Oct 10am–5pm; Nov–March 10am–4pm; £4.50; EH), on the southwest outskirts (bus #9 from Newport). The austere Norman keep was greatly extended over the years, first in the thirteenth century by the imperious Countess Isabella who inherited much of the island and ruled it as a petty kingdom. Having tolerated her excesses, the Crown bought her estates as she lay dying in 1293 and appointed governors to defend the island, rather than risking its security to the vagaries of birthright. This precaution proved timely as the following century saw repeated French raids right across the island.

Carisbrooke's most famous visitor was Charles I, detained here (and caught one night ignominiously jammed between his room's bars while attempting escape) prior to his execution in London. The **museum** in the centre of the castle features many relics from his incarceration, as well as those of the last royal resident, Princess Beatrice, Queen Victoria's youngest daughter. The castle's other notable curiosity is the sixteenth-century well-house, where donkeys still trudge inside a huge treadmill to raise a barrel 160ft up the well shaft.

A stroll around the battlements provides several lofty perspectives on the castle's interior as well as sweeping views across the centre of the island.

Newport's **tourist office** is in the centre of town at the Guildhall, High Street (Mon–Sat 9am–5.30pm, Sun 10am–4pm; ☎01983/823366). Your best option for a meal or a drink is to stick around Carisbrooke: try the *Eight Bells* **pub**, near the castle, or the ever-popular, moderately priced *Valentino's* Italian **restaurant** (closed Sun), both on Carisbrooke High Street, at the top of the hill.

Winchester

Nowadays a tranquil, handsome market town, set amid docile hay-meadows and watercress beds, **WINCHESTER** was once one of the mightiest settlements in England. Under the Romans it was Venta Belgarum, the fifth largest town in Britain, but it was **Alfred the Great** who really put Winchester on the map when he made it the capital of his Wessex kingdom in the ninth century. For the next couple of centuries Winchester ranked alongside London, its status affirmed by William the Conqueror's coronation in both cities and by his commissioning of the local monks to prepare the **Domesday Book**. As the shrine of St Swithun, King Alfred's tutor, Winchester attracted innumerable pilgrims, and throughout the medieval era the city continued to command enormous ecclesiastical and political influence – Bishop **William of Wykeham**, founder of Winchester College and Oxford's New College, was twice chancellor of England. It wasn't until after the Battle of Naseby in 1645, when Cromwell took the city, that Winchester began its decline into provinciality.

Hampshire's county town now has a scholarly and slightly anachronistic air, embodied by the ancient almshouses that still provide shelter for senior citizens of "noble poverty" – the pensioners can be seen wandering round the town in medieval black or mulberry-coloured gowns with silver badges. A trip to this secluded old city is a must – not only for the magnificent **cathedral**, chief relic of Winchester's medieval glory, but for the all-round well-preserved ambience of England's one-time capital.

The City

The first minster to be built in Winchester was raised by Cenwalh, the Saxon king of Wessex in the mid-seventh century and traces of this building have been unearthed near the present **Cathedral** (daily 7.30am–6.30pm; £3.50 donation requested), which was begun in 1079 and completed some three hundred years later, producing a church whose elements range from early Norman to Perpendicular styles. The exterior is not its best feature – squat and massive, the cathedral crouches stumpily over the tidy lawns of the Cathedral Close. The interior is rich and complex, however, and its 556-foot nave makes this Europe's longest medieval church. Outstanding features include its carved Norman font of black Tournai marble, the fourteenth-century misericords (the choir stalls are the oldest complete set in the country) and some amazing monuments – **William of Wykeham's Chantry**, halfway down the nave on the right, is one of the best. Jane Austen, who died in Winchester, is commemorated close to the font by a memorial brass and slab beneath which she's interred, though she's recorded simply as the daughter of a local clergyman. Above the high altar lie the mortuary chests of pre-Conquest kings, including Canute; William Rufus, killed while hunting in the New Forest in 1100, lies in the presbytery. The statuary on the impressive screen at the end of the presby-

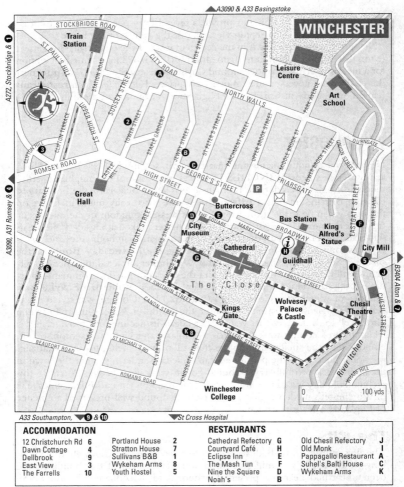

ACCOMMODATION

12 Christchurch Rd	6	Portland House	2
Dawn Cottage	4	Stratton House	7
Dellbrook	9	Sullivans B&B	1
East View	3	Wykeham Arms	8
The Farrells	10	Youth Hostel	5

RESTAURANTS

Cathedral Refectory	G	Old Chesil Refectory	J
Courtyard Café	H	Old Monk	I
Eclipse Inn	E	Pappagallo Restaurant	A
The Mash Tun	F	Suhel's Balti House	C
Nine the Square	D	Wykeham Arms	K
Noah's	B		

tery, showing Queen Victoria and Alfred the Great among many others, was added in the Victorian era, to replace the original images destroyed during the Reformation. Beyond the screen, near Cardinal Beaufort's Chantry Chapel, look out too for the memorial shrine to St Swithun. Originally buried outside in the churchyard, his remains were later interred inside the cathedral where the "rain of heaven" could no longer fall on him, whereupon he took revenge and the heavens opened for forty days – hence the legend that if it rains on St Swithun's Day (July 15) it will continue for another forty. His exact burial place is unknown. Accessible from the north transept, the Norman **crypt** is only rarely open, since it's flooded for much of the time – the cathedral's original foundations were dug in marshy ground, and at the beginning of last century a steadfast diver, William Walker, spent five years replacing the rotten timber foundations with concrete (Deep Sea Adventure in Weymouth gives you the full story; see p.297). If you catch it open, though, have a look inside at the two fourteenth-century statues of William of Wykeham as well as Antony Gormley's standing figure, "Sound II", one of the country's most adventurous ecclesiastical commissions in recent years. To appreciate the Cathedral at its most atmospheric, try to be here for Evensong, currently 5.30pm most days, 3.30pm on Sundays.

Outside the cathedral, the **City Museum**, a basic local history display, sits on the Square (April–Sept Mon–Sat 10am–5pm; Oct–March closed Mon; free). The nearby High Street is a standard municipal mishmash of ancient and modern facades. Walk west along here and you'll eventually arrive at **Great Hall** on Castle Street (April–Oct daily 10am–5pm; Nov–March Mon–Fri 10am–5pm, Sat & Sun 10am–4pm; free), the vestigial remains of a thirteenth-century castle destroyed by Cromwell. Sir Walter Raleigh heard his death sentence here in 1603, though he wasn't finally dispatched until 1618, and Judge Jeffreys held one of his Bloody Assizes in the castle after Monmouth's rebellion in 1685. The main interest now, however, is a large, brightly painted disc slung on one wall like some curious antique dartboard. This is alleged to be King Arthur's Round Table, but the woodwork is probably fourteenth-century, later repainted as a PR exercise for the Tudor dynasty – the portrait of Arthur at the top of the table bears an uncanny resemblance to Henry VIII. Below the table, the floor of the Great Hall is dominated by a huge and gaudy sculpture of Queen Victoria, carved by Sir Alfred Gilbert (responsible for *Eros* in London's Piccadilly Circus) to mark her Golden Jubilee in 1887, and deposited here for lack of anywhere else in town large enough to hold it. Adjoining the Great Hall, an illuminating exhibition relates the history of the Norman castle and Great Hall, and you can also take a brief wander in Queen Eleanor's Medieval Garden – a re-creation of a noblewoman's shady retreat.

Head east along the High Street, past the Guildhall and the august bronze statue of King Alfred on the Broadway, to reach the River Itchen and the **City Mill** (March Sat & Sun 11am–4.45pm; April–June, Sept & Oct Wed–Sun 11am–4.45pm; July & Aug daily 11am–4.45pm; £2; NT), where you can see restored mill machinery; the building is now part-occupied by a youth hostel. Turning right before the bridge you pass what remains of the Saxon walls, which bracket the ruins of the twelfth-century **Wolvesey Castle** (April–Sept daily 10am–6pm; Oct daily 10am–5pm; £1.90; EH) and the Bishop's Palace, built by Christopher Wren. Immediately west up College Street stand the buildings of **Winchester College**, the oldest public school in England – established in 1382 by William of Wykeham for "poor scholars", it now educates few but the wealthy and privileged. The cloisters and chantry are open during term time and the chapel is open all year. Jane Austen moved to the house at 8 College St from Chawton in 1817, when she was already ill with Addison's Disease, dying there later the same year. The thirteenth-century **Kings Gate**, at the top of College Street, is one of the city's original medieval gateways, housing the tiny St Swithun's Church.

About a mile south of College Walk, reached by a pleasant stroll across the watermeadows of the Itchen, lies **St Cross Hospital** (Easter–Sept Mon–Sat 9.30am–5pm; Oct–Easter 10.30am–3.30pm; £2). Founded in 1136 as a hostel for poor brethren, it boasts a fine church, begun in that year and completed a century or so later. Needy wayfarers may still apply for the "dole" at the Porter's Lodge – a tiny portion of bread and beer.

Practicalities

Winchester **train station** is about a mile northwest of the cathedral on Stockbridge Road. If you arrive by **bus**, you'll find yourself on the Broadway, conveniently opposite the **tourist office** in the imposing Guildhall (June–Sept Mon–Sat 10am–6pm, Sun 11am–2pm; Oct–May Mon–Sat 10am–5pm; ☎01962/840500, ⓦwww.winchester.gov.uk). The tourist office has plenty of information about the city and its environs, including an excellent visitor's guide (£1). Ask here about the daily, **guided walks** of the city (1hr 30min; £3), or pick up the free "Winchester Walk" leaflet which allows you to take in all the sights at your own pace.

Accommodation

Hotels and guest houses

12 Christchurch Rd ☎01962/854272. There are just two rooms at this neat and homely B&B with a conservatory and garden. No credit cards. ❶

Dawn Cottage Romsey Rd ☎01962/869956. Classy non-smoking B&B about a mile west of the centre and connected by frequent bus services. The comfortable rooms – one with a spa bath at a slightly higher rate – have great views over the Itchen Valley. ❸

Dellbrook Hubert Rd ☎01962/865093. Pleasant Edwardian-era, family-run B&B by the watermeadows near St Cross Hospital, a mile south of the city centre, with rooms with en-suite or shared bathrooms. ❷

East View 16 Clifton Hill ☎01962/862986. Small Victorian town house overlooking the city and surrounding countryside. ❷

The Farrells 5 Ranelagh Rd ☎01962/869555. Small, inexpensive B&B in a Victorian house off St Cross Road. No smoking. ❷

Portland House 63 Tower St ☎01962/865195, ⓔtony@knightworld.com. Georgian house in a quiet mews between the cathedral and train station. All rooms are en suite and fully equipped, and there's a guests' lounge. No credit cards. ❸

Stratton House Stratton Rd, St Giles Hill ☎01962/863919, ⓔStrattongroup@btinternet. com. Hundred-year-old house in its own grounds with good views of the city. Large grounds and car park. Free collection from bus or train stations. ❹

Sullivans 29 Stockbridge Rd ☎01962/862027. Terrace house a few minutes' walk from the train station, with shared bathrooms, low rates and multilingual owners. No credit cards. ❶

Wykeham Arms 75 Kingsgate St ☎01962/ 853834. Fine old hostelry where the art of classy inn-keeping has not yet vanished. Quirkily shaped rooms with beams and assorted antiques enhance the flavour. ❺

Hostels and campsites

Folly Farm Touring Caravan Park Crawley ☎01962/776486. Flat site with full facilities, four miles west of town towards Stockridge off the B3049. Take any bus towards Salisbury (#7, #25, #26 and #28 are most frequent) – there's a stop right outside the back gate. Closed Nov–Feb.

Youth Hostel City Mill, 1 Water Lane ☎01962/853723. Lovely eighteenth-century mill, which is one of the original YHA hostels and very popular, so book ahead. Beds cost £9.25.

Eating and drinking

Cathedral Refectory The Close. Good-value lunch-spot run by the Friends of Winchester Cathedral. Inexpensive.

Courtyard Café The Guildhall, Broadway. Casual café with gallery attached and outdoor eating; more substantial food and ales are served at the indoor bistro. Also accessed from tourist office. Closed evenings. Inexpensive.

Eclipse Inn The Square. Picturesque old inn specializing in pies and casseroles, with pavement seating. Inexpensive.

The Mash Tun 60 Eastgate St. Riverside alehouse with a terrace. Food available all day, and there are discounts for students. Inexpensive.

Nine The Square 9 Great Minster St. Light meals at the downstairs wine bar, opposite Cathedral. Closed Sun. Inexpensive to moderate.

Noah's Jewry St. Good-value café/restaurant, serving home-cooked dishes with Thai, Caribbean and Mediterranean influences. Closed Mon–Thurs eve & all Sun. Inexpensive.

Old Chesil Rectory 1 Chesil St ☎01962/851555. Fifteenth-century oak-beamed restaurant serving traditional English cooking. Moderate.

The Old Monk Bridge Street. Deep comfy sofas and armchairs enhance this large bar and eaterie with a riverside terrace. Grills, curries and salads are on the menu. Inexpensive.

Pappagallo Restaurant 1 City Rd ☎01962
/841107. The better of the city's two Italian restaurants. Closed Sun. Moderate.
Suhel's Balti House 8 St George's St. Excellent-
value, well-presented Indian and Bengali dishes.
Inexpensive.

Wykeham Arms 75 Kingsgate St ☎01962
/853838. Winchester's best pub is somewhat
unprepossessing from the outside, but inside it's a
maze of characterful, intimate spaces where gourmet-standard food is served daily. Moderate.

Central and northern Hampshire

Aside from a few centres of population of little interest to the visitor, such as
Petersfield and Basingstoke, central and northern Hampshire is a relatively rural
region. It holds a few points of interest, such as the village of **Chawton**, where
Jane Austen wrote most of her books, and **Alton**, the jumping-off point for the
Mid-Hants Watercress Railway Line. Hampshire's northern reaches are most
notable for their stately homes: **Stratfield Saye**, Wellington's reward for winning at Waterloo; the superbly preserved Tudor manor house, **the Vyne**; and
the outstanding excess of **Highclere Castle** in the county's northwest corner.
Although Alton, Petersfield and Basingstoke are all easily accessible by train
from Waterloo, getting to the sites described below is far more easily accomplished with your own transport.

Queen Elizabeth Country Park

Petersfield, situated on the Portsmouth to London road, originally grew up as
a staging post on the old coach road and today is an unassuming provincial
town with little appeal for tourists. Its main attraction lies three miles south of
town where the A3 cuts through the South Downs. The **Queen Elizabeth
Country Park** (free access; information centre April–Oct daily 10am–
5.30pm; Nov & Dec Mon–Fri 10am–dusk; Jan–March Sat & Sun 10am–dusk;
☎023/9259 5040) marks the official western end of the eighty-mile South
Downs Way (see p.220), although the path actually continues another quarter
of a mile to Buriton. A mixture of chalk downland and managed forest, the
park is crisscrossed with marked trails which you can explore on foot, horse or
mountain bike; the more adventurous can try hang- and para-gliding from
Butser Hill on the other side of the A3.

Local information is available from Petersfield's **tourist office,** housed in the
library on Petersfield Square and keeping the same hours (April–Sept Mon &
Tues 9.30am–5pm, Wed & Fri 9.30am–7pm, Sat 9.30am–5pm; Oct–March
Mon–Wed & Fri 9.30am–5pm, Sat 9.30am–1pm; ☎01730/268829), and
mountain bikes can be rented from Owen Cycles, Lavant St, Petersfield
(£10/day; ☎01730/260446) – phone first to make sure of availability. Bed and
breakfast **accommodation** is available at the nearby village of Buriton, on the
north side of the park; try the secluded fifteenth-century cottages comprising
Toad's Alley in South Lane (☎01730/263880; no credit cards; **❶**), or the eighteenth-century farmhouse *Nursted Farm* (☎01730/264278; no credit cards; **❶**)
a few minutes' drive northeast of the village off the B2146. Alternatively, in the
pretty village of East Meon, three miles west of Buriton, *South Farm* (☎01730
/823261; no credit cards; **❸**) offers B&B rooms in a lovely, five-hundred-year-
old building.

Alton, Chawton and Selborne

Thirteen miles north of Petersfield and accessible hourly by train from
London Waterloo or bus from Winchester, **ALTON** is an attractive town,

whose major point of interest is the fifteenth-century **Church of St Lawrence** (daily 9am–6pm). The church is notable for its austere Perpendicular style; its south door still bears the marks of the shot which killed Royalist commander Colonel Boles, who had been chased by Roundheads through the streets of Alton and into the church during the Civil War. Buried in the church's cemetery is Fanny Adams, a little girl brutally hacked to death in 1867, whose name gave rise to the expression "sweet Fanny Adams" – meaning something negligible or without value; sailors at that time used the murder victim's name to describe the recent issue of tinned mutton, whose nutritional value they doubted.

Alton is the terminus for the **Mid-Hants Watercress Line** (March, April & Oct Sat & Sun; May–Sept & school holidays daily; ℡01962/733810, www .watercressline.co.uk; £9), a jolly, steam-powered train, so named because it passes through the former watercress beds which once flourished here. The train chuffs ten miles to Alresford, east of Winchester, with gourmet dinners served on board on Saturday evenings and traditional Sunday lunches too.

A mile southwest of Alton lies the village of **CHAWTON**, where Jane Austen lived from 1809 to 1817, during the last and most prolific years of her life, and where she wrote or revised almost all her six books, including *Sense and Sensibility* and *Pride and Prejudice*. **Jane Austen's House** (Jan & Feb Sat & Sun 11am–4.30pm; rest of year daily 11am–4.30pm; £3), in the centre of the village, is a plain red-brick building, containing first editions of some of her greatest works.

Four miles south of Chawton is the little village of **SELBORNE** where the eighteenth-century naturalist Gilbert White wrote his ecological treatise, *The Natural History and Antiquities of Selborne*. In the High Street his house, **The Wakes** (daily 11am–5pm; £4), is preserved as a memorial to his work and contains the original manuscript. White constructed the Zig Zag Path with his brother and made many of his observations on Selborne Hill, just southwest of the village. The house also contains a museum commemorating Captain Oates, a member of Scott's ill-fated Antarctic expedition in 1912. It's a pleasant hour's walk up to the top of the hill from here.

The Vyne

A couple of miles north of Basingstoke, just outside the village of Sherborne St John, **the Vyne** is a distinguished country house dating from several different periods (April–Oct Mon–Wed, Sat & Sun 1.30–5.30pm; grounds Feb–March Sat & Sun 11am–4.30pm; April–Oct Mon–Wed, Sat & Sun 11am–6pm; £5.50; NT). The original Tudor building was started in 1520, and the classical portico, supposedly the oldest in England, was added in 1645. Inside the superbly preserved rooms, some featuring their original oak panelling, are many unusual antiques, among them two late-seventeenth-century maps of London and England, a camera obscura and a portrait of a dashing young Isaac Newton. The Chute family owned the house for two hundred years (ancestral portraits decorate many walls) until an heirless Charles Chute bequeathed the house to the National Trust in the 1950s.

Outside the sombre Tudor chapel, which features its original Flemish glass and tiles, a row of truncheons inscribed with the letter "P" line one wall. These are a relic from the civil unrest which took place in protest at the Corn Laws. The weapons were securely stored here at the Vyne in order to arm local officers in the event of trouble. The "P" refers to Robert Peel, founder of the Metropolitan Police, whose officers were commissioned to suppress any popular discontent. Ironically, as prime minister, Peel repealed the Corn Laws in 1846.

Stratfield Saye

Stratfield Saye House, five miles northeast of the Vyne (June–Aug Wed–Sun 11.30am–5pm; last entry at 3pm; £5.50), was given to the Duke of Wellington as a reward for victory at Waterloo in 1815. The house, still home of the current duke, contains a plethora of "Wellingtonia" as well as copious Regency ornaments, many originating from dispossessed French aristocrats. The mosaics in the entrance hall were taken from the Roman ruins at nearby Silchester. In the former stables is an absorbing exhibition of Wellington's life and times, ending in the Gothic monstrosity of his funeral carriage which bore him to his final resting place at St Paul's, where his nautical counterpart Admiral Nelson already lay. Note that the house will be closed until 2003 for major renovation work: call ☏01256/882882 for the latest details.

Highclere Castle

The "Gothic" profile of **Highclere Castle**, four miles south of Newbury off the A34 Winchester road (July to early Sept Mon–Fri & Sun 11am–5pm, Sat 11am–3.30pm; last admission 1hr before closing; £6.50), results from its lavish remodelling by Sir Charles Barry, co-architect of the Houses of Parliament. Formerly a Georgian mansion set in parkland designed by Capability Brown, this ancestral home of the earls of Carnarvon was completely refurbished inside and out by Barry and others in the 1840s. Inside the house, the ostentatious style continues unbridled, from the Gothic "Saloon" or entrance hall to the adjacent state rooms, one of them in the Rococo style – all examples of the excessive opulence so beloved of the Victorian aristocracy. The house also contains a collection of personal mementoes of the Fifth Earl of Carnarvon who, along with Howard Carter, unearthed Tutankhamun's tomb near Luxor in 1922. There are artefacts from that excavation as well as his earlier Egyptian treasures, which were discovered after the Earl's death in Egypt in 1923. His tomb is situated atop Beacon Hill, a mile southeast of the house. Also on view here is Napoleon's desk and chair and a collection of old master paintings, including works by Reynolds and Van Dyck.

Sandham Memorial Chapel

Four miles east of Highclere on the A34, the **Sandham Memorial Chapel** at Burghclere (April–Oct Wed–Sun 11.30am–5pm; March & Nov Sat & Sun 11.30am–4pm; £2.50; NT) houses murals by the artist Stanley Spencer, inspired by his experiences as a medical orderly in Macedonia during World War I. Working for over four years here *in situ*, on what he described as "a mixture of real and spiritual fact", Spencer abandoned his initial decision to paint in fresco in imitation of Giotto – whose Scrovegni chapel in Padua was the model for this one – in favour of his usual medium of oils on canvas. Above the altar, the dominating central *Resurrection of the Soldiers*, with its jumble of white crosses, is flanked by scenes of a soldier's daily routine – scrubbing floors, making sandwiches, shaving under mosquito nets and scraping the dead skin off frost-bitten feet. It's best to come here on a sunny day if you can, as only natural light illuminates Spencer's subdued tones.

△ Cowes Week, Isle of Wight

The New Forest

The name of the **NEW FOREST** is misleading, for much of this region's woodland was cleared for agriculture and settlement long before the Normans arrived, and its poor sandy soils support only a meagre covering of heather and gorse in many areas. The forest was requisitioned by William the Conqueror in 1079 as a game reserve, and the rights of its inhabitants soon became subservient to those of his precious deer. Fences to impede their progress were forbidden and terrible punishments were meted out to those who disturbed the animals – hands were lopped off, eyes put out. Later monarchs less passionate about hunting than the Normans gradually restored the forest-dwellers' rights, and today the New Forest enjoys a unique patchwork of ancient laws and privileges, enveloped in an arcane vocabulary dating from feudal times. The forest boundary is the "perambulation", and owner-occupiers of forest land have common rights to obscure practices such as "turbary" (peat-cutting), "estover" (firewood collecting) and "mast" (letting pigs forage for acorns and beech mast), as well as the more readily comprehensible right of pasture, permitting domestic animals to graze freely.

The **trees** of the New Forest are now much more varied than they were in pre-Norman times, with birch, holly, yew, Scots pine and other conifers interspersed with the ancient oaks and beeches. The main wooded areas are around **Lyndhurst**, the "capital" of the New Forest, and one of the most venerable trees is the much-visited **Knightwood Oak**, just a few hundred yards north of the A35 three miles southwest of Lyndhurst, which measures about 22ft in circumference at shoulder height. The most obvious species of New Forest **fauna** are the New Forest **ponies** (reputedly descendants of the Armada's small Spanish horses which survived the battle), now thoroughly domesticated – you'll see them grazing nonchalantly by the roadsides and ambling through some villages. The local deer are less likely to be seen now that some of the faster roads are fenced, although several species still roam the woods, including the tiny **sika deer**, descendants of a pair which escaped from nearby Beaulieu in 1904.

Covering about 144 square miles – a third now in private ownership, the rest administered by the Forestry Commission – the New Forest is one of southern England's main rural playgrounds, and about eight million visitors annually flock here to enjoy a breath of fresh air, often after spending hours in traffic jams. To get the best from the region, you need to **walk** or **ride** through it, avoiding the places cars can reach. There are 150 miles of car-free gravel roads in the forest, making cycling an appealing prospect – pick up a book of route maps from tourist offices or **bike rental** shops (£3.50). The Ordnance Survey Leisure Map 22 of the New Forest is worth getting if you want to explore in any detail, and in Lyndhurst you can pick up numerous specialist walking books and natural history guides. **Trains** from London Waterloo serve Brockenhurst once or twice hourly; for Lyndhurst you have to alight at Lyndhurst Road station, a couple of miles east of the town proper. Lyndhurst and nearby Brockenhurst are centres of County Bus routes to most parts of the forest, and both have plenty of reasonably priced accommodation, though there are also several expensive country house hotels and restaurants scattered in isolated settings. The forest has ten **campsites** run by the Forestry Commission, most closed between October and Easter – to get the full list, write to 231 Corstorphine Rd, Edinburgh EH12 7AT (☎0131/334 0066) – and there's a **youth hostel** in Cottesmore House, Cott Lane, Burley, in the west of the Forest (☎01425/403233; closed early Oct–March, limited opening April & Sept to early Oct), which offers beds for £10 a night.

Lyndhurst and Brockenhurst

LYNDHURST, its town centre skewered by an agonizing one-way system, isn't a particularly interesting place, though the brick **parish church** is worth a glance for its William Morris glass, a fresco by Lord Leighton and the grave of one Mrs Reginald Hargreaves, better known as Alice Liddell, Lewis Carroll's model for Alice. The town is of most interest to visitors for the **New Forest Museum and Visitor Centre** in the central car park off the High Street (daily: mid-July to mid-Sept 10am–6pm; rest of year 10am–5pm; ☎023/8028 2269, ⊛www.thenewforest.co.uk), where you can buy Explorer bus passes and maps for cycling and riding. There's also a small **museum** here focusing on the forest, its history, wildlife and industries (same times as tourist office; £2.75). Nearby in Gosport Lane, AA Bike Hire (☎023/8028.3349) rents **bikes** for £10 a day. For **accommodation** try the clean and airy *Clarendon Villa*, also in Gosport Lane (☎02380/282803; ❷); *Forest Cottage*, at the west end of the High Street (☎02380/283461; no credit cards; ❷), where you can consult a natural history library; or *Burwood Lodge*, 27 Romsey Rd (☎023/8028 2445; ❸), a large old house a few minutes from the High Street. *Le Café Parisien* at 64 High St sells **snacks** which you can eat in its small garden in summer; for larger **meals**, head for the nearby *Crown Hotel*.

The forest's most visited site, the **Rufus Stone**, stands a few hundred yards from the M27 motorway, three miles northwest of Lyndhurst. Erected in 1745, the monument marks the putative spot where the Conqueror's ghastly son and heir, **William II** – aka William Rufus after his ruddy complexion – was killed in 1100. The official version is that a crossbow bolt fired by a member of the royal hunting party glanced off a stag and struck the king in the heart. Sir William Tyrrell took the rap for the "accident" and fled incriminatingly to France, though he later swore on his deathbed that he had not fired the fatal arrow. As William II was a tyrant with many enemies, his death probably was a political assassination – a strong suspect was William's brother Henry, also in the shooting party, who promptly raced to Winchester to claim the crown, leaving Rufus to be carted ignominiously to the cathedral by a passing charcoal burner. The stone is remarkably unimpressive for such a landmark: the Victorians encased it in a protective layer of metal to deter vandals, and now it can't be seen at all clearly.

Three miles southwest of Lyndhurst you'll find the popular **Ornamental Drives** of Bolderwood and Rhinefield, Victorian plantations of exotic trees, which are suggestive of overgrown ancient woodland. If you fancy a guided woodland hike, ask at the visitor centre in Lyndhurst about the ranger-led walks organized by the Forestry Commission, or call ☎023/8028 3141.

BROCKENHURST, four miles to the south of Lyndhurst, is a useful centre for visitors without their own transport. There's a train station right in town and **bikes for rent** right by the level-crossing at New Forest Cycle Experience (☎01590/624204; £9.50/day). The town also has some decent places to **stay**; try the *Cottage Hotel* on Sway Road (☎01590/622296; ❺ closed Dec–Feb) or *Cater's Cottage*, Latchmoor (☎01590/623225; no credit cards; ❸), an above-average B&B on the southern outskirts of Brockenhurst. A short distance farther south in Sway, there's a quiet B&B at *Little Purley Farm* in Chapel Lane (☎01590/682707; no credit cards; ❶), with views over to the Isle of Wight. The *Snakecatcher* on Lyndhurst Road is a good **pub** that also serves terrific bar food.

Beaulieu and Buckler's Hard

The village of **BEAULIEU** (whose name originates from the French meaning "Beautiful Place", but is pronounced "Bewley"), in the southeast corner of the New Forest, was the site of one of England's most influential monasteries, a Cistercian house founded in 1204 by King John – in remorse, it is said, for ordering a group of supplicating Cistercian monks to be trampled to death. Built using stone ferried from Caen and Quarr on the Isle of Wight, the **abbey** managed a self-sufficient estate of ten thousand acres and became a famous sanctuary, offering shelter to Queen Margaret of Anjou among many others. The abbey was dismantled soon after the Dissolution, and its refectory now forms the parish church, which, like everything else in Beaulieu, has been subsumed by the Montagu family who have owned a large chunk of the New Forest since one of Charles II's illegitimate progeny was created duke of the estate.

The estate has been transformed with a prodigious commercial vigour into **Beaulieu** (daily: May–Sept 10am–6pm; Oct–April 10am–5pm; £9.95), a tourist complex comprising **Palace House**, the attractive if unexceptional family home, the abbey and the main attraction, Lord Montagu's **National Motor Museum**. An undersized monorail and an old London bus ease the ten-minute walk between the entry point and Palace House. The house, formerly the abbey's gatehouse, contains masses of Montagu-related memorabilia while the undercroft of the adjacent abbey houses an exhibition depicting medieval monastic life. Inside the celebrated Motor Museum, a collection of 250 cars and motorcycles includes a £650,000 McLaren F1, spindly antiques and recent classics, as well as a couple of svelte land-speed racers, including the record-breaking *Bluebird*. The entertaining "Wheels", a dizzying ride-through display, takes you on a trip through the history of motoring.

If Beaulieu amply deserves its name, **Buckler's Hard**, a couple of miles downstream on the River Beaulieu (daily: Easter–Sept 10am–6pm; Oct–Easter 11am–4pm; £3.50), has an even more wonderful setting. It doesn't look much like a shipyard now, but from Elizabethan times onwards dozens of men o' war were assembled here from giant New Forest oaks. Several of Nelson's ships, including *HMS Agamemnon*, were launched here, to be towed carefully by rowing boats past the sandbanks and across the Solent to Portsmouth. The largest house in this hamlet of shipwrights' cottages, which forms part of the Montagu estate, belonged to Henry Adams, the master builder responsible for most of the Trafalgar fleet; it's now an upmarket **hotel** and **restaurant**, the *Master Builder's House Hotel* (☎01590/616253; ❽). At the top of the village, the **Maritime Museum** traces the history of the great ships and incorporates a labourer's cottage as it was in the 1790s, as well as the *New Inn*, shipwright's cottage and chapel – all preserved in their eighteenth-century form.

Lymington

The most pleasant point of access for the Isle of Wight (for ferry details, see p.261) is **LYMINGTON**, a sheltered haven that's linked by ferry to Yarmouth and has become one of the busiest leisure harbours on the south coast. Rising from the quay area, the old town is full of cobbled streets and Georgian houses and has one unusual building – the partly thirteenth-century church of **St Thomas the Apostle**, with a cupola-topped tower built in 1670.

Information is available in summer from the local **visitor centre** in New Street, off the High Street (May–Sept Mon–Sat 10am–5pm, Sun 2–5pm;

Oct–April Mon–Sat 10am–4pm; ☎01590/689000). Places to **stay** in town include *Jack in the Basket*, 7 St Thomas St (☎01590/673447; ❷), an old building off the High Street with a café/restaurant attached; *Dolphins*, 6 Emsworth Rd (☎01590/676108; ❷), which rents out bikes and offers use of a chalet by the beach, and *Wheatsheaf House*, Gosport Lane (☎01590/679208; no credit cards; ❹), a quaint listed building offering two rooms, "Paris" and "Venice", themed accordingly. For **snacks**, try the *Jack in the Basket* (see above), or the cheap and cheerful *Coffee Mill*, opposite the visitor centre on New Street. Lymington's best **pubs** are the *Chequers* on Ridgeway Lane, on the west side of town, the *Bosun's Chair*, on Station Road, and the harbourfront *Ship Inn*, on the quayside, with seats outside looking over the water.

Signposted two miles east of Lymington, the **Sammy Miller Museum**, in New Milton (daily 10am–4.30pm; £3.50), gives classic motorcycles the "Beaulieu" treatment. Many of the once-eminent British marques from Ariel to Vincent are displayed, as well as exotica from MV, NSU and several acclaimed trials bikes ridden by Sammy Miller himself, one of Britain's most successful trials riders.

Bournemouth and around

Renowned for its clean sandy beaches, the resort of **Bournemouth** is the nucleus of Europe's largest non-industrial conurbation stretching between Lymington and Poole harbour. The resort has a single-minded holiday-making atmosphere, though neighbouring **Poole** and **Christchurch** are more interesting historically. North of this coastal sprawl, the pleasant old market town of **Wimborne** has one of the area's most striking churches, while the stately home of **Kingston Lacy** contains an outstanding collection of old masters and other paintings.

Arrival, information and accommodation

Trains from London Waterloo stop just under a mile east of the centre, but frequent **buses** run into town from the bus station opposite. The **tourist office**, right in the centre of town on Westover Road (mid-July to mid-Sept Mon–Sat 9.30am–7pm, Sun 10.30am–5pm; rest of year Mon–Sat 9.30am–5.30pm; ☎0906/8020234, ⊛www.bournemouth.co.uk), exchanges money and books National Express tickets.

There's no shortage of **accommodation** in the Bournemouth area – the town has more than four hundred hotels and guest houses covering all budget ranges. There are no **campsites** in central Bournemouth; the nearest is just north of Christchurch (see p.287). The small, friendly **hostel**, *Bournemouth Backpackers*, is at 3 Frances Rd (☎01202/299491, ⊛www.bournemouthbackpackers.co.uk), three minutes from train and bus stations; dorm beds cost up to £16 (doubles £42) for peak season, less at other periods or for two nights or more.

Connaught Hotel West Hill Rd, West Cliff ☎01202/298020, ⊛www.theconnaught.co.uk. Well-equipped three-star hotel, five minutes' walk from the town centre and beach, with excellent leisure facilities and restaurant, and discounts on longer stays. ❼

Grove Hotel 2 Grove Rd, East Cliff ☎01202/552233, ⊛www.grovehotel.net. Well-positioned

family-run hotel set in its own grounds. ❺

Langtry Manor 26 Derby Rd, East Cliff ☎01202/553887, ⊛www.langtrymanor.com. Former hideaway of Edward VII and his mistress, Lillie Langtry, this comfortable, well-equipped hotel has Edwardian furnishings. It also hosts period-style banquets on Saturday evenings. ❼

The City

BOURNEMOUTH dates only from 1811, when a local squire, Louis
Tregonwell, built a summer house on the wild, unpopulated heathland that
once occupied this stretch of coast, and planted the first of the pine trees that
now characterize the area. By the end of the century Bournemouth's mild climate, sheltered site and glorious sandy beach had attracted nearly sixty thousand inhabitants. Today the resort has twice that number of residents, and an
unshakably genteel, elderly image, though its geriatric nursing homes are
counterbalanced by burgeoning numbers of language schools and a nightclub
scene fuelled by a transient youthful population.

The blandly modern town that you see today has little to remind you of
Bournemouth's Victorian heyday, though the River Bourne still runs down
through a park to the town's centre, which consists of a network of one-way
streets running around the Square and down to **Bournemouth Pier**. Other
than sunbathing along the pristine sandy beach – one of southern England's
cleanest – the town's greatest attraction is its unusually high proportion of
green space, set aside during the boom years at the end of the last century. As
well as having more than three million pine trees, a sixth of the town – around
two thousand acres – is given over to horticultural displays, and exploring
Bournemouth's **public gardens** can easily fill a day.

The most enthralling experience in Bournemouth, however, is one of the
region's best collections of Victoriana, the excellent **Russell-Cotes Art
Gallery and Museum** on East Cliff Promenade (Tues–Sun 10am–5pm; free)
which houses a motley assortment of artworks and oriental souvenirs gathered
from around the world by the Russell-Cotes family, hoteliers who grew
wealthy during Bournemouth's late-Victorian tourist boom. The benefactors'
lavishly decorated former home, featuring unusual stained glass and ornate
painted ceilings, is jam-packed with their eclectic collections, of which the
Japanese artefacts are especially interesting. There are some good examples of
Pre-Raphaelite and other British art downstairs, period decor throughout and
a cliff-top landscaped garden.

In the centre of town, you might visit the graveyard of **St Peter's** church, just
east of the Square, where Mary Shelley, author of the Gothic horror tale
Frankenstein, is buried, together with the heart belonging to her husband, the
Romantic poet Percy Bysshe Shelley, former resident of Boscombe. The tombs
of Mary's parents – radical thinker William Godwin and early feminist Mary
Wollstonecraft – are also here.

Eating and drinking

sels with a variety of sauces, and with a good fish selection. Closed Sun & Mon. Moderate.

Chez Fred 10 Seamoor Rd, Westbourne. Well-known fish-and-chips outlet offering deals such as a bread roll, mushy peas and a glass of wine to accompany your meal. Inexpensive.

Goat and Tricycle 27–29 West Hill Rd. Worth a trek up the hill for the real ales and home-made

food in this quiet and unpretentious pub. Inexpensive to Moderate.

Mr Pang's 234 Holdenhurst Rd. Better than average Chinese situated just east of the train station. Closed lunchtime & Sun. Moderate.

Salathai 1066 Christchurch Rd, Boscombe. Authentically spicy Thai dishes, including chile-laced chicken and fried noodles. Closed Sun. Moderate.

Nightlife and entertainment

The university, foreign-language students and young holiday-makers have helped liven up Bournemouth's **nightlife** – though the traditional entertainment scene continues to throw up a steady stream of dire pier-end comedians well past their prime. Chief among the established venues all lie just north of the pier – the Pavilion Theatre, with its own ballroom; the Winter Gardens, home of Bournemouth's symphony orchestra; a multiplex cinema; and an ice-skating rink. Pick up a copy of the free monthly listings magazine *Live Wire* for news of live gigs in the town.

Of the **nightclubs**, the biggest and best known is *Elements*, right in the centre of town on Firvale Road (nightly). Mainstream club and house sounds predominate, along with R&B and revival evenings, and there's an adjoining pub/club, *Circo*, which takes in the overflow and also stays open until 2am. Next door on Firvale Road, you can sample Art Deco style at the *Slam Bar*, which plays everything from garage to Eurotrash, has a brasserie menu and shows sport on a big screen TV. On Terrace Road, the *K-Bar*, also a bar and restaurant, offers a nightly diet of R&B, garage, funk and house, alternating with films on Monday and live jazz on Thursday, while the *Triangle Club* is Bournemouth's biggest **gay** club, located at the top of Commercial Road from The Square. In Boscombe, the flamboyant *Opera House*, 570 Christchurch Rd, has student nights on Thursday, guest DJs on Friday and more commercial sounds on Saturday. *Bumbles* on Poole Hill (Wed, Fri & Sat) reverberates to dance and Seventies and Eighties music.

On a more sedate note, the fortnight at the end of June and the beginning of July sees the **Bournemouth International Festival** draw performers of every musical genre. There's also a buskers' festival that takes place around the second weekend of May – check at the tourist office for further details.

Christchurch

CHRISTCHURCH, five miles east of Bournemouth, is best known for its colossal parish church, **Christchurch Priory** (Mon–Sat 9.30am–5pm, Sun 2.15–5.30pm; £1 donation requested), bigger than most cathedrals. Built on the site of a Saxon minster dating from 650 AD, but exhibiting chiefly Norman and Perpendicular features, the church is the longest in England, at 311ft, and its fan-vaulted North Porch is the country's biggest. Legend tells of how the building materials were moved overnight to the present location and of the hand of a mysterious carpenter who assisted in the work, hence the priory's name. The choir, beautifully lit by huge, clear-glass windows and separated from the nave by a finely carved Jesse Screen, contains what is probably the oldest misericord in England, dating from 1210, and complemented by a 1960s mural by Hans Feibusch above the stone reredos. Fine views can be gained from the top of the 120-foot tower (ask at desk; £1).

The area round the old town quay has a carefully preserved charm. The **Red House Museum and Gardens** on Quay Road (Tues–Sat 10am–5pm, Sun 2–5pm; £1.50) contain an affectionate collection of local memorabilia, and **boat trips** (Easter to mid-Oct daily; ☎01202/429119) can be taken from the grassy banks of the riverside quay east to Mudeford (30min; £4.50 return) or up the river to the *Tuckton Tea Rooms* outside Bournemouth (15 min; £2 return).

The **tourist office**, 23 High St (June–Sept Mon–Fri 9.30am–5.30pm, Sat 9.30am–5pm; July & Aug also Sun 10am–2pm; Oct–May Mon–Fri 9.30am–5pm, Sat 9.30am–4.30pm; ☎01202/471780, ✆www.resort-guide.co .uk/christchurch), can supply you with a town map and a Visitor's Guide. Good **accommodation** options in or around town can be fairly pricey, though a few minutes northwest of the centre, Barrack and Stour roads are lined with a selection of unexciting but reliable guest houses, such as *Grosvenor Lodge*, 53 Stour Rd (☎01202/499008, ✆www.grosvenorlodge.co.uk; ❸). In the centre, try the *King's Arms Toby Hotel*, 18 Castle St (☎01202/484117; ❺); eastwards lie more exclusive choices, such as the *Avonmouth Hotel*, 95 Mudeford (☎0870 /4008120, ✆www.avonmouth-hotel.co.uk; ❼), and *Waterford Lodge*, Bure Lane, Friars Cliff, Highcliffe (☎01425/278801; ❻), two miles east of the town cen-tre. **Campers** should head out to *Mount Pleasant Touring Park*, Matchams Lane, Hurn, Christchurch (☎01202/475474; closed Nov–Feb), five miles northeast of town on the road to Ringwood. For something **to eat**, try *La Mamma*, 51 Bridge St (☎01202/471608; closed Sun lunch & Mon in winter), where you can enjoy candle-lit Italian classics (including pizzas) at moderate prices, with alfresco eating in summer, or the *Bistro on the Bridge*, 3 Bridge St (☎01202/482522; closed Mon & Tues), where you can have inexpensive Bistro Express lunches, afternoon tea, or pricier evening meals, and there's riverside seating on a veranda. Recommended **pubs** include the *King's Arms Hotel*, right by the priory, with a nice garden area; or check out Christchurch's oldest pub, *Ye Olde George Inn*, 2a Castle St, which has a beer garden and serves meals at lunchtime.

Poole

POOLE, west of Bournemouth, is an ancient seaport on a huge, almost land-locked harbour. The town developed in the thirteenth century and was suc-cessively colonized by pirates, fishermen and timber traders, more recently replaced by companies prospecting for oil in the shallow waters – the harbour's environmental significance ensures that the extraction process is carefully dis-guised. The old quarter by the quayside is worth exploring: the old Custom House, Scaplen's Court and Guildhall are the most striking of over a hundred historic buildings within a fifteen-acre site.

At the bottom of Old High Street, near the Poole Pottery showroom and crafts centre, is **Scaplen's Court** (Aug Mon–Sat 10am–5pm, Sun noon–5pm; £4, including entry to the Waterfront Museum), a late medieval building where Cromwell's troops were once billeted (you can see their graffiti around the fireplace). It has now been restored as an educational centre, with recon-structions of a Victorian kitchen, pharmacy and school room and displays of old-time toys and games. Over the road, local history is more accessibly elab-orated at the **Waterfront Museum** (April–Oct Mon–Sat 10am–5pm, Sun noon–5pm; Nov–March Mon–Sat 10am–3pm, Sun noon–3pm; £2; combined ticket with Scaplen's Court £4), tracing Poole's development over the cen-turies and featuring well-displayed local ceramics and tiles and a rare Iron Age log boat, as well as changing exhibitions.

In the middle of the harbour between Poole and the Isle of Purbeck, **Brownsea Island** (April–June & Sept to early Oct daily 10am–5pm; July & Aug daily 10am–6pm; £3.50; NT) is linked by regular boats ferrying visitors over from Poole's quayside (25min; £5 return). Now a National Trust property, this five-hundred-acre island is famed for its red squirrels, wading birds and other wildlife, which you can spot along themed trails that reveal a surprisingly diverse landscape – including heath, woodland and fine beaches – and good views. One shore holds a grand pile of a castle, rebuilt after the original was gutted by fire in 1896; it's now leased to a large retail group for staff holidays. But the most regular visitors to Brownsea are scouts and guides: the Boy Scout movement was formed in the wake of a camping expedition to the island led by Lord Baden-Powell in 1907, and scouts are now the only people allowed to camp here.

From Poole Quay, you can also join a **cruise** to the Isle of Wight (Mon, Tues & Thurs–Sat 9am; £15 return), allowing excellent views over Poole Bay to Bournemouth and Christchurch, and a four-hour stop in Yarmouth (see p.270). From Poole Harbour, reached across the bridge at the end of Poole Quay, **ferries** leave for France and the Channel Islands. Brittany Ferries (℡08705/360360, ⓦwww.brittanyferries.com) leave for Cherbourg and Caen several times daily all year, while Condor Ferries (℡0845/345 2000, ⓦwww .condorferries.co.uk) operate a catamaran service to Jersey and Guernsey daily between April and October, with connections to St Malo in Brittany between May and September.

One of the area's most famous gardens lies on the outskirts of Poole, **Compton Acres** (March–Oct daily 10am–6pm; £5.75; ⓦwww.comptonacres .co.uk), signposted off the A35 Poole Road, towards Bournemouth. Here you'll find seven gardens, each with a different international theme, the best of which, the elegantly understated Japanese Garden, contrasts with the more familiar classical symmetry of the Italian Garden. Buses #150 and #151 between Poole and Bournemouth, and in summer the open-top coastal #12 service stop outside.

Poole's **tourist office** is in the Waterfront Museum (April, May & Oct Mon–Sat 10am–5pm, Sun noon–5pm; June, July & Sept Mon–Fri 10am–5.30pm, Sat & Sun 10am–5pm; Aug daily 10am–6pm; Nov–March Mon–Fri 10am–5pm, Sat 10am–3pm, Sun noon–3pm; ℡01202/253253, ⓦwww.poole.gov.uk/tourism). Best choice for **accommodation** is the *Antelope Hotel* at the quay end of the High Street (℡01202/672029; ➍), a handsome old hostelry in the old town centre; if you fancy a stay in a former mayoral residence, try the eighteenth-century *Mansion House*, Thames Street (℡01202/685666, ⓦthemansionhouse.co.uk; ➏). Cheaper rooms can be had at the *Crown Hotel* (℡01202/672137; ➌), an inn on the parallel Market Street. Further out, at Canford Cliffs, smaller hotels worth trying include the *Sea Witch*, 47 Haven Rd (℡01202/707697; ➍), and *Norfolk Lodge*, 1 Flaghead Rd (℡01202/708614; ➍), both of which are convenient for the Sandbanks beaches. Less central, but great value, is the *Harbour Lights Hotel*, 121 North Rd, Parkstone (℡01202/748417; no credit cards; ➋), a mile or so north of the centre; it has basic but comfortable rooms with shared bathrooms. There's a collection of good **restaurants** at the southern end of the High Street; look out for *Storm* seafood restaurant at no. 16 (℡01202/674970; closed lunchtime) – it's flanked by *Hardy's* (closed Mon) and *Café Cadini*, which are both good for light lunches and sandwiches. At the top end of the High Street, *Alcatraz* is a trendy Italian brasserie with outdoor tables, while, at the other end, on the Quayside, *Corkers* has a café and bar downstairs and a restaurant above, serving traditional English dishes and seafood; it also has five en-suite rooms available (℡01202/681393; no smoking in bedrooms; ❸). For **pubs** try the medieval hall in the *King Charles* on Thames Street, with its leather armchairs and big screen, or, on the quayside, the green tile-fronted *Poole Arms* which serves inexpensive pub grub.

Wimborne Minster and Kingston Lacy

An ancient town on the banks of the Stour, just a few minutes' drive north from the suburbs of Bournemouth, **WIMBORNE MINSTER**, as the name suggests, is mainly of interest for its great church, the **Minster of St Cuthberga** (daily: Jan & Feb 9.30am–4pm; rest of year 9.30am–5.30pm). Built on the site of an eighth-century monastery, its massive twin towers of mottled grey and tawny stone dwarf the rest of the town, and at one time the church was even more imposing – its spire crashed down during morning service in 1602, though amazingly no one was injured, and since then Wimborne has not risked heavenly ire by replacing it. What remains today is basically Norman with later features added – such as the Perpendicular west tower, which bears a figure dressed as a grenadier of the Napoleonic era, who strikes every quarter-hour with a hammer. Inside, the church is crowded with memorials and eye-catching details – look out for the orrery clock inside the west tower, with the sun marking the hours and the moon marking the days of the month, and for the organ with trumpets pointing out towards the congregation instead of pipes. The **Chained Library** above the choir vestry (Easter–Oct Mon–Thurs 10.30am–12.30pm & 2–4pm, Fri 10.30am–12.30pm), dating from 1686, is Wimborne's most prized possession and one of the oldest public libraries in the country.

Wimborne's older buildings stand around the main square near the minster, and are mostly from the late eighteenth or early nineteenth century. The **Priest's House** on the High Street started life as lodgings for the clergy, then became a stationer's shop. Now it is an award-winning **museum** (April, May & June Mon–Sat 10.30am–5pm; June–Sept Mon–Sat 10.30am–5pm, Sun 2–5pm; £2.40), each room furnished in the style of a different period. A working Victorian kitchen, a Georgian parlour and an ironmonger's shop are among its exhibits, and there's a display of items relating to local archeology and history; a walled garden at the rear provides an excellent place for summer teas.

Kingston Lacy (house: April–Oct Wed–Sun noon–5.30pm; grounds: Feb–March Sat & Sun 11am–4pm; April–Oct daily 11am–6pm or dusk if earlier; Nov–Dec Fri–Sun 11am–4pm; house & grounds £6.50, grounds only £3; NT), one of the country's finest seventeenth-century country houses, lies two miles northwest of Wimborne Minster, in 250 acres of parkland grazed by a herd of Red Devon cattle. Designed for the Bankes family, who were exiled from Corfe Castle (see p.291) after the Roundheads reduced it to rubble, the Queen Anne brick building was clad in grey stone during the nineteenth century by Sir Charles Barry, co-architect of the Houses of Parliament. William Bankes, then owner of the house, was a great traveller and collector, and the **Spanish Room** is a superb scrapbook of his Grand Tour souvenirs, lined with gilded leather and surmounted by a Venetian ceiling. Kingston Lacy's **picture collection** is also outstanding, featuring Titian, Rubens, Velázquez and many other old masters. Be warned, though, that this place gets so swamped with visitors that the National Trust has to issue timed tickets on busy weekends.

You'll find Wimborne's **tourist office** at 29 High St (April–Sept Mon–Sat 9.30am–5.30pm; Oct–March 9.30am–4.30pm; ℡01202/886116). This is a place that is unlikely to hold your attention for longer than half a day, but if

you want to **stay**, try *Homestay* at 22 West Borough (☎01202/849015; no credit cards; ②), a friendly place with en-suite facilities. Otherwise, there's the *King's
Head* on The Square, which offers comfortable if pricey rooms
(☎01202/880101; ⑤), or the three-hundred-year-old *Henbury Farmhouse*
(☎01258/857306; closed Nov–Feb; no credit cards; ②), four miles west of
Wimborne in Sturminster Marshall. For bistro **lunches** or suppers try *Primizia*
(closed Sun & Mon) on West Borough, or *Cloisters* on East Street, which also
serves teas, coffees and snacks (closed eve & Sun afternoon).

The Isle of Purbeck

Though not actually an island, the **ISLE OF PURBECK** – a promontory of
low hills and heathland jutting out beyond Poole Harbour – does have an insu-
lar and distinctive feel. Reached from the east by the **ferry from Sandbanks**,
at the narrow mouth of Poole harbour, or by a long and congested landward
journey via the bottleneck of **Wareham**, Purbeck can be a difficult destination
to reach, but its villages are immensely pretty, none more so than **Corfe
Castle**, with its majestic ruins. **Swanage**, a low-key seaside resort, is flanked by
more exciting coastlines, all accessible on the Dorset Coast Path: to one side
the chalk stacks and soft dunes of Studland Bay, to the other the cliffs of
Durlston Head and Dancing Ledge, leading to the oily shales of Kimmeridge
Bay and the spectacular cove at Lulworth. Like Portland, further west, the area
is pockmarked with stone quarries – Purbeck marble is the finest grade of the
local oolitic limestone.

Wareham and around

The grid pattern of its streets indicates the Saxon origins of **WAREHAM**, and
the town is surrounded by even older earth ramparts known as the Walls. A
riverside setting adds greatly to its charms, though the major road junction at
its heart causes horrible traffic queues in summer, and the scenic stretch along
the Quay also gets fairly overrun. Nearby lies an oasis of quaint houses around
Lady St Mary's Church, which contains the marble coffin of Edward the
Martyr, murdered at Corfe Castle in 978 by his stepmother, to make way for
her unready son Ethelred. **St Martin's Church**, at the north end of town,
dates from Saxon times and the chancel contains a faded twelfth-century mural
of St Martin offering his cloak to a beggar, but the church's most striking feature is a romantic effigy of T.E. Lawrence in Arab dress, which was originally
destined for Salisbury Cathedral, but was rejected by the dean there who dis-
approved of Lawrence's sexual proclivities. Lawrence was killed in 1935 in a
motorbike accident on the road from Bovington, after returning to Dorset
from his Middle Eastern adventures. His simply furnished cottage is at **Clouds
Hill**, seven miles northwest of Wareham (April–Oct Wed–Fri & Sun
noon–5pm or dusk; £2.60; NT). In Wareham the small **museum** next to the
town hall in East Street (Easter–Oct Mon–Sat 11am–1pm & 2–4pm; free) displays some of Lawrence's memorabilia, as does the absorbing but over-priced
Tank Museum in Bovington Camp, five miles west of Wareham (daily
10am–5pm; £7; ⦿www.tankmuseum.co.uk). You can walk through a replica
trench of the Somme, and catch the first tanks that went into battle in action
(July & Sept Thurs at noon; Aug Thurs & Fri at noon).
    A much-advertised local tourist honeypot is the **Blue Pool**, an intensely

coloured clay-pit lake near Furzebrook, some three miles south of Wareham. A small museum (Easter to early Oct daily 9.30am–6pm; £3) gives the background to the local clay industry, and there are cream teas, nature trails and other amenities for less studious customers.

Holy Trinity Church, on South Street, contains Wareham's **tourist office** (June to mid-Sept Mon–Sat 9.30am–5pm, Sun 10am–1pm; mid-Sept to May Mon–Sat 9.30am–1pm & 1.45–5pm; ☏01929/552740). From the nearby Quay, row- and motor-boats are available to rent (£8–12 an hour). The best **accommodation** options are *Anglebury House*, 15 North St (☏01929/552988; ❸), whose previous guests have included Thomas Hardy and T.E. Lawrence, and the pleasant *Belle Vue*, West Street (☏01929/552056; no credit cards; ❷), with all rooms en suite. The *Old Granary* **restaurant** on the Quay (☏01929 /552010; ❷) also has rooms, with views over the river and the meadows beyond. *Kemps*, one and a half miles west of town in East Stoke (☏01929 /462563), serves imaginative but unpretentious food and is particularly good value at lunchtime – rooms are also available here (❺).

Corfe Castle

The romantic ruins crowning the hill behind the village of **CORFE CASTLE** (daily: March 10am–5pm; April–Oct 10am–6pm; Nov–Feb 10am–4pm; £4.20; NT) are perhaps the most evocative in England. The family seat of Sir John Bankes, Attorney General to Charles I, this Royalist stronghold withstood a Cromwellian siege for six weeks, gallantly defended by Lady Bankes. One of her own men, Colonel Pitman, eventually betrayed the castle to the Roundheads, after which it was reduced to its present gap-toothed state by gunpowder. Apparently the victorious Roundheads were so impressed by Lady Bankes's courage that they allowed her to take the keys to the castle with her – they can still be seen in the library at the Bankes's subsequent home, Kingston Lacy (see p.289).

The village is well stocked with tearooms and gift shops and has a couple of good **pubs** too: the *Fox* on West Street, where you can drink or have lunch in a large garden with views to the castle, and, below the castle ramparts, the *Greyhound*. If you can't afford the high **room** rates and expensive dinners at the Elizabethan *Mortons House Hotel* on East Street (☏01929/480988, ⓦwww .mortonshouse.co.uk; ❻), you can still enjoy a reasonably priced bar meal or tea. For more moderately priced accommodation, head for *The Old Curatage*, 30 East St (☏01929/481441; no smoking; no credit cards; ❶), or the *Bankes Arms Hotel* (☏01929/480206; ❷), an old inn outside the castle entrance.

Shell Bay to St Alban's Head

Purbeck's most northerly coastal stretch, **Shell Bay**, is a magnificent beach of icing-sugar sand backed by a remarkable heathland ecosystem that's home to all six British species of reptile – adders are quite common, so be careful. At the top end of the beach a chain **ferry** (daily 7am–11pm every 20min; pedestrians £1, bikes 90p, cars £2.50) crosses the mouth of Poole harbour connecting the Isle of Purbeck with Sandbanks in Poole.

To the south, beyond the broad sweep of Studland Bay, is **SWANAGE**, a traditional seaside resort with a pleasant sandy beach and an ornate town hall, the facade of which once adorned the Mercers' Hall in the City of London and was brought back here as ballast on a cargo ship. The town's station is the southern terminus of the **Swanage Steam Railway** (April–Oct daily; Nov, Dec & late Feb to March Sat & Sun; £6 return), which is slowly being restored to run as far as Wareham, but has currently only reached Norden (on the A351). For timetables, call ☎01929/435800, check at ⊛swanagerailway.co.uk or pick up a leaflet from the tourist office.

Swanage's **tourist office** is by the beach on Shore Road (Easter–Oct daily 10am–5pm; Nov–Easter Mon–Thurs 10am–5pm, Fri 10am–4pm; ☎01929 /422885, ⊛www.swanage.gov.uk), and there's a **youth hostel**, with good views across the bay, on Cluny Crescent (☎01929/422113, ⓔswanage@yha .org.uk; closed Nov to mid-Feb). There are scores of **B&Bs** in Swanage; you'll find a handy trio on King's Road near the train station or try the *Purbeck Hotel,* 19 High St (☎01929/425160; ❷), which also has a decent pub. Swanage has a wide variety of places **to eat**, ranging from fish-and-chip shops to upmarket restaurants, the best of which is the excellent *Galley,* 9 High St (☎01929 /427299; closed Mon except July & Aug), which specializes in well-prepared local fish dishes served at moderate prices. If you're interested in exploring on the Purbeck Cycleway (map available from the tourist office), **rent bikes** from Bikeabout, 71 High St (☎01929/425050), opposite the town hall, open daily (£10 a day, £35 a week).

Highlights of the coast beyond Swanage are the cliffs of **Durlstone Head**, topped by a lighthouse. Nearby stands a vast stone globe weighing forty tonnes, installed by George Burt, an eccentric Victorian building contractor from Swanage, who also erected the local folly castle. The cliffs continue to **St Alban's Head**, their ledges crowded with seabirds and rare wildflowers in spring. Paths lead inland to the attractive villages of **Langton Matravers**, where the **Coach House Museum** interprets the local stone-quarrying industry (April–Sept Mon–Sat 10am–noon & 2–4pm; 60p), and **Worth Matravers**, where there's a fine Norman church and a great **pub**, the *Square & Compass*, which produces filling, unfancy bar **snacks** at reasonable prices.

Kimmeridge Bay to Durdle Door

Beyond St Alban's Head the coastal geology suddenly changes as the grey-white chalk and limestone give way to darker beds of shale. **Kimmeridge Bay** may not have a sandy beach but it does have a remarkable marine wildlife reserve much appreciated by divers – there's a Dorset Wildlife Trust **information centre** by the slipway (daily 10am–5pm; ☎01929/481044). The amazing range of species is all the more surprising because the bay has been the site of small-scale industry for centuries. The Saxons crafted amulets from the shale and the extraction of alum (for glassmaking) and coal followed. Today a low-tech "nodding donkey" oil well fits unobtrusively into the landscape. In the village, the sixteenth-century *Kimmeridge Farmhouse* (☎01929/480990; no credit cards; ❷) is a quiet and scenic spot for an overnight **stay**.

The Lulworth artillery ranges west of Kimmeridge are inaccessible during weekdays but generally open at weekends and in school holidays – watch out for the red warning flags and notices and always stick to the path. Roads in this area have similar restrictions, but generally open before 9am and after 5pm to allow commuters through. The coastal path passes close to the deserted village of **Tyneham**, whose residents were summarily evicted by the army in 1943; the abandoned stone cottages have an eerie fascination, and an exhibition in the church explains the history of the village. Ironically, the army's presence has actually helped to preserve the local habitat which plays host to many species of flora and fauna long since vanished from farmed or otherwise developed areas.

The quaint thatch-and-stone villages of East and West Lulworth form a prelude to **Lulworth Cove**, a perfect shell-shaped bite formed when the sea broke through a weakness in the cliffs and then gnawed away at them from behind, forming a circular cave which eventually collapsed to leave a bay enclosed by sandstone cliffs. Lulworth's scenic charms are well known, and as you descend the hill through West Lulworth in summer the sun glints off the metal of a thousand car roofs in the parking lot behind the cove. At the **Lulworth Heritage Centre** the mysteries of the local geology are explained (March–Oct daily; 10am–6pm, Nov–Feb 10am–4pm; free; parking £2.50/2hr, £5/day).

Immediately west of the cove you come to **Stair Hole**, a roofless sea cave riddled with arches that will eventually collapse to form another Lulworth, and a couple of miles west is **Durdle Door**, a famous limestone arch that appeals to serious geologist and casual sightseer alike. Most people take the uphill route to the arch which starts from the car park but, if you want to avoid the steep climb, you can drive a mile from the village towards East Chaldon and park at the *Durdle Door Holiday Park* for a small fee. An alternative, if tide-dependent, route goes up the private drive from the Heritage Centre and down into the secluded St Oswald's Bay which separates Lulworth from Durdle Door. If you've timed it right you can slip round the headland and climb up to the arch although you may prefer to stay on the more agreeable St Oswald's beach.

WEST LULWORTH is the obvious **place to stay** or eat on this section of coast. The *Castle Inn* (℡01929/400311; **➋**), *Cromwell House Hotel* (℡0929/400253; **➍**), right on the coast path and sporting a heated pool, and *Ivy Cottage* (℡01929/400509; no credit cards; **➊**), a seventeenth-century cottage with inglenook fireplace, all make for good stop-offs. You'll find a **youth hostel** at the end of School Lane West (℡01929/400564; closed mid-Nov to Feb); a plain chalet with small rooms, it's a stone's throw away from the Dorset Coast Path. **Campers** can find a pitch at the above-mentioned *Durdle Door Holiday Park* (℡01929/400200; closed Nov–Feb). In **EAST LULWORTH**, the *Weld Arms* also has rooms (℡01929/400211; **➋**) and the easily overlooked *Sailor's Return* in East Chaldon, four miles northwest of Lulworth Cove, is unsurpassed locally for its mouthwatering **pub food**.

Dorchester and around

The county town of Dorset, **DORCHESTER** still functions as the main agricultural centre for the region, and if you catch it on a Wednesday when the market is in full swing you'll find it livelier than usual. For the local tourist authorities, however, this is essentially **Thomas Hardy**'s town; he was born at Higher Bockhampton, three miles east of here, his heart is buried in Stinsford, a couple of miles northeast (the rest of him is in Westminster Abbey), and he spent much of his life in Dorchester itself, where his statue now stands on High West Street. Even without the Hardy connection, Dorchester makes an attractive stop, with its pleasant central core of mostly seventeenth-century and Georgian buildings, and the prehistoric Maumbury Rings on the outskirts. To the southwest of town looms the massive hill fort of **Maiden Castle**, the most impressive of Dorset's many pre-Roman antiquities, and the Tudor **Athelhampton House**, near the village of Puddletown, six miles east of Dorchester, stands out because of its decorative gardens.

The Town

Dorchester was Durnovaria to the Romans, who founded the town in about 70 AD. The original Roman walls were replaced in the eighteenth century by tree-lined avenues called "Walks" (Bowling Alley Walk, West Walk and Colliton

Thomas Hardy (1840–1928) resurrected the old name of **Wessex** to describe the region in which he set most of his fiction. In his books, the area stretched from Devon and Somerset ("Lower" and "Outer Wessex") to Berkshire and Oxfordshire ("North Wessex"), though its central core was Dorset ("South Wessex"), the county where Hardy spent most of his life. His books richly depict the life and appearance of the towns and countryside of the area, often thinly disguised under fictional names. Thus Salisbury makes an appearance as "Melchester", Weymouth (where he briefly lived) as "Budmouth Regis", and Bournemouth as "Sandbourne" – described as "a fairy palace suddenly created by the stroke of a wand, and allowed to get a little dusty" in *Tess of the d'Urbervilles*. But it is **Dorchester**, the "Casterbridge" of his novels, which is portrayed in most detail, to the extent that many of the town's buildings and landmarks that still remain can be identified in the books (especially *The Mayor of Casterbridge* and *Far From the Madding Crowd*). Hardy knew the town well; he attended school here (walking daily from the family home at Higher Bockhampton) and set up as an architect (his father and grandfather were both stonemasons), a profession which he later practised in Cornwall and London. He returned to Dorchester in 1885, spending the rest of his life in a house built to his own designs at Max Gate, on the Wareham Road.

Today, the Hardy industry takes two forms; the bookish and low-profile activities of the Thomas Hardy Society, whose diehard zealots help to preserve the relics and places with which the author is associated, and the high-profile overkill of the tourist mandarins who have made sure that some reminder of Hardy and his works greets the visitor to Dorchester at every turn. The Thomas Hardy Society (Box 1438, Dorchester, Dorset DT1 1YH ☎01305/251501) can provide plenty of material for enthusiasts to pore over, and organizes walks and tours, including a fifteen-mile hike which follows in the steps of Tess on her Sunday mission to her father-in-law, Parson Clare of Beaminster, in an attempt to rescue her failed marriage. If this sounds ambitious, content yourself with one of the walking itineraries outlined in the leaflets sold by the Society (and also available in the museum and tourist office) at 30p each.

Alternatively, you could read the books. Recommended reading includes *Under the Greenwood Tree* (1872) for an evocation of Hardy's childhood in and around Higher Bockhampton; *Tess of the d'Urbervilles* (1891), for elegiac descriptions of the Frome Valley; *The Return of the Native* (1878), for wild Egdon Heath and the eerie yew forest of Cranborne Chase; and *The Mayor of Casterbridge* (1886) for Dorchester and Maumbury Rings.

Walk), but some traces of the Roman period have survived. At the back of County Hall excavations have uncovered a fine Roman villa with a well-preserved mosaic floor, and on the southeast edge of town you'll find **Maumbury Rings**, where the Romans held vast gladiatorial combats in an amphitheatre adapted from a Stone Age site. The gruesome traditions continued into the Middle Ages, when gladiators were replaced by bear-baiting and public executions or "hanging fairs".

Continuing the sanguinary theme, after the ill-fated rebellion of the Duke of Monmouth (another of Charles II's illegitimate offspring) against James II, Judge Jeffreys was appointed to punish the rebels. His "Bloody Assizes" of 1685, held in the Oak Room of the **Antelope Hotel** on Cornhill, sentenced 292 men to death. In the event, 74 were hung, drawn and quartered, and their heads then stuck on pikes throughout Dorset and Somerset; the luckier suspects were merely flogged and transported to the West Indies. Judge Jeffreys lodged just round the corner from the *Antelope* in High West Street, where a half-timbered restaurant now capitalizes on the lurid association.

In 1834 the **Shire Hall**, further down High West Street, witnessed another *cause célèbre*, when six men from the nearby village of Tolpuddle were sentenced to transportation for banding together to form the Friendly Society of Agricultural Labourers, in order to present a request for a small wage increase on the grounds that their families were starving. After a public outcry the men were pardoned, and the **Tolpuddle Martyrs** passed into history as founders of the trade union movement. The room in which they were tried is preserved as a memorial to the martyrs, and you can find out more about them in Tolpuddle itself, eight miles east on the A35, where there's a fine little **museum** (April–Oct Tues–Sat 10am–5.30pm, Sun 11am–5.30pm; Nov–March closes at 4pm; free).

The best place to find out about Dorchester's history is in the engrossing **Dorset County Museum** on High West Street (May–Oct daily 10am–5pm; Nov–April Mon–Sat 10am–5pm; £3.50), where archeological and geological displays trace Celtic and Roman history, including a section on Maiden Castle. Pride of place goes to the re-creation of Thomas Hardy's study, where his pens are inscribed with the names of the books he wrote with them. Other museums in town include the formidably turreted **Keep Military Museum** (July & Aug Mon–Sat 9.30am–5pm, Sun 10am–4pm; rest of year closed Sun; £3; ⓦwww.keepmilitarymuseum.org), just west of Hardy's Monument, which traces the fortunes of the Dorset and Devonshire regiments over three hundred years and offers sweeping views over the town; and a small **Dinosaur Museum** off High East Street on Icen Way (daily: April–Sept 9.30am–5.30pm; Oct–March 10am–4.30pm; £4.75; ⓦwww.dinosaur-museum.org.uk), that appeals chiefly to children. Best of all is **Tutankhamun: The Exhibition** on the High Street (daily 9.30am–5.30pm; £4.75; ⓦwww.tutankhamun-exhibition.co.uk), a fascinating and thorough exploration of the young pharaoh's life and afterlife through to the eventual discovery of his tomb in 1922. Everything from the mummified remains, complete burial chamber and the celebrated golden mask has been carefully and atmospherically re-created with painstaking detail.

If you're on the Hardy trail, you'll want to visit **Thomas Hardy's Cottage** (April–Oct Mon–Thurs & Sun 11am–5pm or dusk; £2.60; NT), where the writer lived from 1840 to 1862 and from 1867 to 1870, and his last and longest abode, **Max Gate** (April–Sept Mon, Wed & Sun 2–5pm; £2.30; NT), though you may be disappointed by the paucity of what there is to see. The nearer of the two, Max Gate, where the writer completed *Tess of the D'Urbervilles*, *Jude the Obscure* and much of his poetry, is a twenty-minute walk east from the centre on the Wareham road (A352), but only the garden and dining and drawing rooms are open to the public. Hardy's birthplace in Higher Bockhampton, about three miles northeast of Dorchester, has even less on offer: bits of period furniture and some original manuscripts. Infrequent buses (#184–189) all pass within half a mile – otherwise you can walk (on the A35 and Bockhampton Road) or take a taxi.

Practicalities

Dorchester has two **train stations**, both of them to the south of the centre: trains from Weymouth and London arrive at Dorchester South, while Bristol trains use the Dorchester West station. Most **buses** stop around the car park on Acland Road, to the east of South Street; there are about four services daily from Poole and Salisbury, and several times hourly from Weymouth. There are also two daily bus connections with London, operated by National Express and First Southern National (☎01305/783645) – the latter is one of two main bus operators in the region, the other being Wilts & Dorset (☎01202/673555). The **tourist office** is in Antelope Walk (April–Sept Mon–Sat 9am–5pm, Sun

10am–3pm; Oct Mon–Sat 9am–5pm; Nov–March Mon–Sat 9am–4pm; ☎01305/267992, ⊛www.westdorset.com). **Bikes for rent** are available at Dorchester Cycles, 31 Great Western Rd (☎01305/268787), for £10 per day or £50 per week, including helmet, panniers and lock (deposit or ID required).

Dorchester has a good selection of **accommodation**, including top of the range *Casterbridge Hotel*, 49 High East St (☎01305/264043, ⊛www.caster-bridgehotel.co.uk; ❺), a superior Georgian guest house; and the best budget option, *Maumbury Cottage*, 9 Maumbury Rd (☎01305/266726; no credit cards; ❶), a small, friendly and central B&B. The *King's Arms*, High East St (☎01305/265353; ❷), a historic local landmark, also serves good food, including vegetarian dishes. Out of town, try the *Old Rectory* in Winterbourne Steepleton three miles to the west (☎01305/889468; no smoking; no credit cards; ❸), surrounded by lawns, or, two miles north of town in Charminster, *Slades Farm*, North Street (☎01305/265614; no credit cards; ❷), a converted barn with en-suite rooms. The nearest **youth hostel** is at Litton Cheney (☎01308/482340; closed Sept–March), halfway between Dorchester and Bridport, and the closest **campsite** is the *Giant's Head Caravan and Camping Park*, Old Sherborne Rd (☎01300/341242; closed Nov–Easter), about five miles north of town, above the Cerne Abbas giant (see p.304).

When it comes to **food**, your best bet is a pub meal; try the *Royal Oak* or the *Old Ship Inn*, both on High West Street and both highly recommended. Near the tourist office at 19 Durngate St, the *Potter In* has wholesome snacks and a range of cakes (closed Sun), while the famous *Judge Jeffreys Restaurant*, at 6 High West St, is inevitably touristy, but offers fair value – both places have courtyard gardens. Further up at 34 High West St, the *Mock Turtle* (☎01305/889468, ⊛www.themockturtle.com; closed Mon lunch & Sun) offers quality English cuisine at moderate prices, right across the road from the seventeenth-century *Old Tea House*, good for teas and snacks. Dorchester's **nightlife** is limited, but *Paul's Nightclub* at 33 Trinity St and *Liberty's* at the top of High West Street lay on comedy and live-music nights as well as club sounds.

Maiden Castle and Athelhampton House

One of southern England's finest prehistoric sites, **Maiden Castle** (free access) stands on a hill two miles or so south of Dorchester. Covering about 115 acres, it was first developed around 3000 BC by a Stone Age farming community and then used during the Bronze Age as a funeral mound. Iron Age dwellers expanded it into a populous settlement and fortified it with a daunting series of ramparts and ditches, just in time for the arrival of Vespasian's Second Legion. The ancient Britons' slingstones were no match for the more sophisticated weapons of the Roman invaders, and Maiden Castle was stormed in a bloody massacre in 43 AD.

What you see today is a massive series of grassy concentric ridges about sixty feet high, creasing the surface of the hill. The site is best visited early or late in the day, when the low-angled sun casts the earthworks in shadow, showing them up more clearly. The main finds from the site are displayed in the Dorset County Museum (see above).

Five miles east of Dorchester on the A35, just past the village of Puddletown, lies **Athelhampton House** (March–Oct Mon–Fri & Sun 10.30am–5pm; Nov–Feb Sun 10.30am–5pm; £5.50), a fine fifteenth-century house surrounded by walled gardens resplendent with fountains and unusual topiary pyramids of yew. Inside, the oak-panelled Great Hall is Athelhampton's most outstanding feature, with its hammer-beam ceiling, original fireplace and oriel window.

3

Other rooms don't quite live up to the Hall's Tudor grandeur, but feature an interesting collection of antiques which the house was bought to display.

Weymouth to Bridport

Whether George III's passion for sea bathing was a symptom of his eventual madness is uncertain, but it was at the bay of **Weymouth** that in 1789 he became the first reigning monarch to follow the craze. Sycophantic gentry rushed into the waves behind him, and soon the town, formerly a workaday harbour, took on the elegant Georgian stamp which it bears today. A likeness of the monarch on horseback is even carved into the chalk downs northwest of the town, like some guardian spirit. Weymouth nowadays plays second fiddle to the vast resort of Bournemouth to the east, but it's still a lively family holiday destination, with several costly new attractions to augment its more sedate charms.

Just south of the town stretch the giant arms of Portland Harbour, and a long causeway links Weymouth to the strange five-mile-long excrescence of the **Isle of Portland**. West of the causeway, the eighteen-mile bank of pebbles known as **Chesil Beach** runs northwest in the direction of **Bridport**.

Weymouth

WEYMOUTH had long been a port before the Georgians popularized it as a resort. It's possible that a ship unloading a cargo here in 1348 first brought the Black Death to English shores – and on a happier note it was from Weymouth that John Endicott sailed in 1628 to found Salem in Massachusetts. A few buildings survive from these pre-Georgian times: the restored **Tudor House** on Trinity Street (June–Sept Tues–Fri 11am–3.45pm; Oct–May first Sun of month 2–4pm; £1.50) and the ruins of **Sandsfoot Castle** (free access), built by Henry VIII, overlooking Portland Harbour. But Weymouth's most imposing architectural heritage stands along the Esplanade, a dignified range of bow-fronted and porticoed buildings gazing out across the graceful bay, an ensemble rather disrupted by the garish **Clock Tower** commemorating Victoria's jubilee. The more intimate quayside of the Old Harbour, linked to the Esplanade by the main pedestrianized throroughfare St Mary's Street, is lined with waterfront pubs from where you can view the passing yachts, trawlers and ferries.

Like most British seaside resorts, Weymouth has had to supply more than sand and saucy postcards to its clientele in recent years. Its slightly faded gentility is now counterbalanced by a number of "all-weather" attractions, the most high-profile of which is the **Sea Life Park** in Lodmoor Country Park east of the Esplanade (daily: 10am–5pm; winter weekdays closes at 4pm; last admission 1hr before closing; £6.50, £4.95 from tourist office; ☎01305/761070), where you can get close to sharks and rays and wander among multichrome birds in the tropical house. Other attractions include the **Deep Sea Adventure** at the Old Harbour (late July to early Sept 9.30am–8pm; rest of year 9.30am–7pm; last entry 1hr 30min before closing; £3.75), which describes the origins of modern diving and the sobering story of the *Titanic* disaster. Over the river on Hope Square, **The Timewalk**, housed in Brewer's Quay (Mon–Sat 10am–5.30pm, Sun 11am–4.30pm; public & school holidays open until 9pm; £4.25), contains an entertaining and educational walk-through exhibition of Weymouth's maritime and brewing past. A fifteen-minute walk southwards leads to the Palmerston-era **Nothe Fort** (May to mid-Sept daily 10.30am–5.30pm; rest of year hours are variable; ☎01305/787243; £3) which has a number of displays on military themes, as well as a museum detailing the centuries-old practice of coastal defence, made obsolete in 1956 by advancing technology. If you're interested in exploring the bay, check out the glass-bottomed *Fleet Observer*, which sails from the Ferrybridge pub near Abbotsbury Oysters on the A354 Portland Rd (June–Sept 5 daily; 1hr 30min; £4; ☎01305 /773396).

Practicalities

Weymouth is easily reached by public transport: there is a regular **train** service from London, Bournemouth and Poole, and less frequent services from Bristol and Bath. There are also good **bus** services between Weymouth and Dorchester, eight miles north, a hub for many other routes. Condor Ferries (☎0845/345 2000, ⓦwww.condorferries.co.uk) operates a daily **catamaran** service to the Channel Islands between April and Oct, leaving at 7.30am from Weymouth's harbour. The town's **tourist office** is at King's Statue, the Esplanade (daily: April–Sept 9.30am–5pm; Oct–March 10.30am–3pm; ☎01305/785747, ⓦwww.weymouth.gov.uk).

A cluster of the town's **accommodation** options lies at the south end of the Esplanade, between the bay and harbour, for instance *Chatsworth*, 14 The Esplanade (☎01305/785012, ⓦwww.thechatsworth.co.uk; ❺), which has a garden terrace, and the good-value *Cavendish House*, 5 The Esplanade (☎01305 /782039; no credit cards; ❷), in a detached Georgian terrace overlooking the bay with harbour views at the back. Just a few steps from the seafront, the *Globe Hotel* is a pub on the corner of East and Mitchell streets with plain, inexpensive rooms (☎01305/785849; no credit cards; ❶). At the quieter northern end of the Esplanade, *Bay Lodge*, at 27 Greenhill (☎01305/782419, ⓦwww.baylodge .co.uk; ❹), is a better-than-average B&B with good sea views and a car park. There are some excellent choices a little further from the centre, such as the *Streamside Hotel*, two miles northeast at 29 Preston Rd, close to the beach on Weymouth Bay (☎01305/833121; ❺); the restaurant here serves well-prepared traditional British dishes with added French flair.

Weymouth is also well served by its refreshment outlets and **restaurants**. If it's seafood you're after, you can't do better than *Perry's*, a moderately priced place overlooking the quayside at 4 Trinity Rd (☎01305/785799, ⓦwww.perrysrestaurant.co.uk; closed Sat lunch & Mon lunch, also Sun eve in winter). Other cheaper places include *Criterion* at 63 The Esplanade (behind the statue of George III), a useful self-service restaurant near the beach with all-day breakfasts, and the *Seagull Café*, 10 Trinity Rd, a family-run chippie with fresh fish and lashings of chips (closed Sun & Mon). On pedestrianized St Mary's St, *Bon Appetit* and, two doors along, *Crusty's* both make good lunchspots with a range of hot baguettes and sandwiches and some outdoor seating, while the cheerful *Café 21* at 21 East St is Weymouth's only vegetarian restaurant, where you can just have a toasted sandwich or something more substantial, with courtyard seating and also offering **internet access** (open lunch, plus Fri & Sat eve; no credit cards). On the corner of St Nicholas St and Commercial Rd, the *Sailor's Return* is one of a number of amenable **pubs** in town, a harbourside tavern with in-your-face angling paraphernalia and fresh fish on the menu; others include the *Old Rooms Inn* on Trinity Rd, an inexpensive lunch venue, again with a strong maritime theme, and the *Nothe Tavern*, buried among Nothe Gardens (south of the harbour on Barrack Road), which offers bar meals and Eldridge Pope beer and has views from the garden. For a rowdier time, head for the *Rendezvous*, by the Town Bridge, a bar/restaurant/nightclub open until 2am, and located above the *Anchor*, which itself has **live bands**.

Portland

Stark, wind-battered and treeless, the **Isle of Portland** is famed above all for its hard white limestone, which has been quarried here for centuries – Wren used it for St Paul's Cathedral, and it clads the UN headquarters in New York. It was also used for the six-thousand-foot breakwater that protects Portland Harbour – the largest artificial harbour in Britain, which was built by convicts in the mid-nineteenth century. Poorer grades of Portland stone are pulverized for cement – the industrial stone-crushing plant is a prominent and unlovely feature of the island.

The causeway road by which the Isle of Portland is approached stands on the easternmost section of the Chesil shingle. To the east you get a good view of the harbour, a naval base since 1872, but now jeopardized by the post-Cold War rundown of Britain's defences. The first settlement you come to, **FOR-TUNESWELL**, overlooks the huge harbour and is itself surveyed by a 450-year-old Tudor fortress, **Portland Castle** (April–Sept daily 10am–6pm; Oct daily 10am–5pm; Nov–March Fri–Sun 10am–4pm; £3; EH), commissioned by Henry VIII. South of **EASTON**, the main village on the island, Wakeham Road holds **Pennsylvania Castle** (now a private house), built in 1800 for John Penn, governor of the island and a grandson of the founder of Pennsylvania. A couple of hundred yards beyond the house, the seventeenth-century **Avice's Cottage**, a gift of Marie Stopes, the pioneer of birth control, is home to a small **museum** (Easter–July, Sept & Oct Mon, Tues & Fri–Sun 10.30am–1pm & 1.30–5pm; Aug & school holidays daily 10.30am–1pm & 1.30–5pm; £2), with exhibitions on local shipwrecks, smuggling and quarrying. The cottage owes its name to Thomas Hardy, who described it in his novel, *The Well-Beloved*. Nearby, in **Church Ope Cove**, you can see the ruins of St Andrew's Church and eleventh-century Rufus Castle.

The craggy limestone of the island rises to 496 feet at **Portland Bill**, where a lighthouse has guarded the promontory since the eighteenth century. You can climb the 153 steps of the present one, dating from 1906, for the views (Easter–Sept Mon–Fri & Sun 11am–5pm; tours £2), and it also houses Portland's **tourist office** (Easter–Sept Mon, Tues & Thurs–Sun 10am–4pm, Wed 11am–4pm; ☎01305/861233), which can supply leaflets on the area's special features, including geology and wildlife. **Accommodation** options in the area include *Sturt Corner* (☎01305/822846; no credit cards; ❶) and the *Pulpit Inn* (☎01305/821237; ❷), both nearby on Portland Bill, and there's a **youth hostel** in Portland itself, on Castle Road, Castletown (☎01305/861368; closed Oct–March); it's left off Victory Square onto Victory Road, then left again. If you want to stay in a lighthouse, the *Old Higher Lighthouse* (☎01305/822300; no smoking) offers **self-catering** facilities by the week, as do the *Old Coastguard Cottages* (☎01903/785052) and *Church Ope Cove Cottage* in Church Ope Cove (☎01580/240700). Expect to pay £125–480 per week, depending on season, and book well in advance.

Chesil Beach to Bridport

Chesil Beach is the strangest feature of the Dorset coast, a two-hundred-yard-wide, fifty-foot-high bank of pebbles that extends for eighteen miles, its component stones gradually decreasing in size from fist-like pebbles at Portland to "pea gravel" at Burton Bradstock in the west. This sorting is an effect of the powerful coastal currents, which make this one of the most dangerous beaches in Europe – churchyards in the local villages display plenty of evidence of wrecks and drownings. Though not a swimming beach, Chesil is popular with sea anglers, and its wild, uncommercialized atmosphere makes an appealing antidote to the south coast resorts. To explore it, you need your own transport or plenty of time – infrequent bus services connect the main villages, and the Dorset Coast Path runs close to the shore for most of the way.

Chesil Beach encloses a brackish lagoon called The Fleet for much of its length – it was the setting for J. Meade Faulkner's classic smuggling tale, *Moonfleet*. Overlooking the lagoon, *Moonfleet Manor* (☎01305/786948; ❼), a **hotel** and large sports resort three miles west of Weymouth, capitalizes on the Faulkner connection. At the point where the shingle beach attaches itself to the shore is the pretty village of **ABBOTSBURY**, all tawny ironstone and thatch. Its Tithe Barn is a fifteenth-century building, the last remnant of the village's Benedictine abbey, and today, as the **Smuggler's Barn** (daily: Easter–Oct 10am–6pm; Nov–Easter Sat & Sun 11am–dusk; last admissions 1hr before closing; £4.20), features the ins and outs of contrabanding and is the venue for occasional exhibitions. The village **Swannery** (mid-March to Oct daily 10am–6pm; last admissions 1hr before closing; £5.20), a wetland reserve for mute swans, dates back to medieval times, when presumably it formed part of the abbot's larder. The eel-grass reeds through which the swans paddle were once harvested to thatch roofs throughout the region. Other attractions are the hilltop **Chapel of St Catherine**, also dating from the fifteenth century, and the **Subtropical Gardens** (daily: April–Oct 10am–6pm; Nov–March 10am–dusk; last admission 1hr before closing; £4.70), where delicate species thrive in the micro-climate created by Chesil's stones, which act as a giant radiator to keep out all but the worst frosts. Up on the downs a couple of miles inland from Abbotsbury is a monument to Thomas Hardy, not the usual one associated with Dorset, but the flag captain in whose arms Admiral Nelson expired.

If you want to **stay** in Abbotsbury try *Swan Lodge*, 1 Rodden Row, for good B&B accommodation (☎01305/871249; ❷), which has fully-equipped rooms, some en suite, or the *Ilchester Arms* in the village centre, a handsome stone inn with comfortable facilities and fine food (☎01305/871243; ❷). West of the village three miles along the coast at **West Bexington**, the *Manor Hotel* is an excellent unpretentious hostelry offering accommodation and a sumptuous range of food (☎01305/897616, ⓦwww.manorhotel/dorset; ❻); while inland and further west, in the lovely village of **Shipton Gorge**, *Innsacre Farmhouse* (☎01308/456137; ❹; closed Nov) provides similar services.

BRIDPORT, just beyond the far end of Chesil Beach, is a pleasant old town of brick rather than stone, with unusually wide streets, a hangover from its rope-making days when cords made of locally grown hemp and flax were stretched between the houses. Bridport has several fine buildings: a medieval church, a Georgian town hall, a fourteenth-century chantry and a Tudor building housing the local **museum** (April–Oct Mon–Sat 10am–5pm; £2). If you want to know about the rope and net industry head for the fishing resort of **West Bay**, Bridport's access to the sea, where majestic red cliffs rear up above the sea. The **Harbour Life Exhibition** (April–Oct daily 10am–5pm; £1) will fill you in about "Bridport daggers" (hangmen's nooses) and more besides. West Bay also has the area's best place to **eat**, the *Riverside Restaurant*, a renowned but informal fish place with good views out to sea and worth booking ahead (☎01308/422011). Across the harbour, the *Bridport Arms Hotel* (☎01308 /422994; ❹) offers good **accommodation** near the beach; also worth trying is the *Britmead House*, 154 West Bay Rd (☎01308/422941; ❸), on the road back to Bridport. In the centre of town, try *Cranston Cottage*, 27 Church St (☎01308 /456240; no credit cards; ❶), which has three rooms with and without bathroom. The Bridport **tourist office** is at 32 South St (April–Oct Mon–Sat 9am–5pm; Nov–March Mon–Sat 10am–3pm; ☎01308/424901), and there's a seasonal office at West Bay sharing the same premises with the Harbour Life Exhibition (April–Oct daily 10am–5pm; ☎01308/422807).

Lyme Regis and around

From the end of Chesil Beach an ever more dramatic sequence of cliffs runs westward, followed as closely as possible by the **Dorset Coast Path**, which has to deviate inland in a few places to avoid areas of landslip. The most prominent feature along this coast is **Golden Cap**, an outcrop of sandstone close to west Dorset's main resort, **Lyme Regis**. On summer days it can seem that tourism is threatening to choke the life out of Lyme – but you can quickly find refuge inland, where **Beaminster** makes a good base for exploring scenic little Dorset villages of golden stone and thatched cottages.

Lyme Regis

LYME REGIS, Dorset's most westerly town, shelters snugly between steep hills, just before the grey, fossil-filled cliffs lurch into Devon. Its intimate size and undeniable photogenic qualities make Lyme so popular that in high summer car-borne crowds jostle with pedestrians for the limited space along its narrow streets. For all that, the town lives up to the classy impression created by its regal name, which it owes to a royal charter granted by Edward I in 1284. It has some upmarket literary associations to further bolster its self-esteem – Jane Austen penned *Persuasion* in a seafront cottage here, while novelist John Fowles is the town's most famous current resident; but it was the film adaptation of his book, *The French Lieutenant's Woman*, shot on location here, that did more than any tourist board production ever could to place the resort firmly on the map.

Though Lyme Regis now relies mostly on holiday-makers for its keep, it was for centuries a port for the wool traders of Somerset, and shipbuilding thrived here until Victorian times. Colourwashed cottages and elegant Regency and Victorian villas line its seafront and flanking streets, but Lyme's best-known feature is a briskly practical reminder of its commercial origins. **The Cobb**, the curving harbour wall, was first constructed in the thirteenth century but has suffered many alterations since, most notably in the nineteenth century, when its massive boulders were clad in neater blocks of Portland stone.

As you walk along the seafront and out towards The Cobb, look for the outlines of ammonites in the walls and paving stones. The cliffs around Lyme are made up of a complex layer of limestone, greensand and unstable clay, a perfect medium for preserving fossils, which are exposed by landslips of the waterlogged clays. One of the most famous landslides occurred in 1839, when a large block of land, complete with a crop of turnips, was severed from its neighbouring fields by a chasm so dramatic that Queen Victoria came to inspect the scene from her yacht. In 1811, after a fierce storm caused parts of the cliffs to collapse, 12-year-old Mary Anning, a keen fossil-hunter, discovered an almost complete dinosaur skeleton, a 30-foot ichthyosaurus now displayed in London's Natural History Museum (see p.120).

Hammering fossils out of the cliffs is frowned on by today's conservationists, and in any case is rather hazardous. Hands-off inspection of the area's complex geology can be enjoyed on both sides of town: to the west lies the **Undercliff**, a fascinating jumble of overgrown landslips, now a nature reserve. East of Lyme, the Dorset Coast Path is closed as far as jaded **Charmouth** (Jane Austen's favourite resort), but at low tide you can walk for two miles along the beach, then, just past Charmouth, rejoin the coastal path to the headland of **Golden Cap**, whose brilliant outcrop of auburn sandstone is crowned with gorse.

Lyme's excellent **Philpot Museum** on Bridge Street (April–Oct Mon–Sat 10am–5pm, Sun 11am–5pm; Nov–March Sat 10am–5pm, Sun 11am–5pm, also open Christmas & school half-terms at same times; £1.50) provides a crash course in local history and geology, while **Dinosaurland** on Coombe Street (daily: Aug 10am–6pm; rest of year 10am–5pm; £3.50) fills out the story on ammonites and other local fossils. Also worth seeing is the small **marine aquarium** on The Cobb (Easter–Oct 10am–5pm, with later closing in July & Aug; £2), where local fishermen bring unusual catches, and the fifteenth-century **parish church** of St Michael the Archangel, up Church Street, which contains a seventeenth-century pulpit and a massive chained Bible.

Practicalities

Lyme's nearest **train station** is in Axminster, five miles north; the #31 **bus** runs from here to Lyme Regis; a **taxi** will cost around £9. National Express runs a daily service from Exeter. The **tourist office** is on Church Street (May–Oct Mon–Sat 10am–5am, Sun 10am–4pm; Nov–April Mon–Sat 10am–2pm; ☎01297/442138, ⓦwww.lymeregistourism.co.uk).

Lyme's sole seafront hotel is the pricey *Bay Hotel* on Marine Parade (☎01297/442059; ➎), but you don't have to walk far for more moderately priced accommodation. The *Old Monmouth Hotel* is centrally located at 12 Church St (☎01297/442456; ➋), while *Cliff Cottage* on Cobb Road (☎01297/443334; no credit cards;➊) has harbour views, a garden chalet and a fish restaurant; the *Red House*, a ten-minute walk out of town on Sidmouth Road (☎01297/442055; ➋; closed mid-Nov to mid-March), offers an especially warm welcome as well as fabulous views. Other good choices include the *White House,* 47 Silver St (☎01297/443420; no credit cards; ➋; closed Oct–Easter), the *New Haven*, 1 Pound St (☎01297/442499;➊), which has one standard room on the ground floor, more expensive rooms upstairs, and the *Cobb Arms*, Marine Parade (☎01297/443242; ➋). For inexpensive daytime meals, try the *Bell Cliff Restaurant* at 5–6 Broad St. Reasonably priced choices in the evening include the *Millside Restaurant and Wine Bar*, 1 Mill Lane (☎01297/445999; closed Mon), serving good pasta and fish dishes. The best **pubs** are the *Royal Standard* on Ozone Parade, and the *Pilot Boat* on Bridge Street, which also does smashing seafood and vegetarian meals.

Inland Dorset and southern Wiltshire

The main pleasures of inland Dorset come from unscheduled meandering through its ancient landscapes and tiny rural settlements, many of which boast preposterously winsome names such as Ryme Intrinseca, Piddletrenthide, Up Sydling and Plush. Two of the most interesting of these villages are **Milton Abbas** and **Cerne Abbas**, the former attractive on account of its curious artificiality, the latter for its rumbustious chalk-carved giant. The major tourist honeypots, though, are the towns of **Blandford Forum**, **Shaftesbury** and **Sherborne**, the landscaped garden at **Stourhead** across the county boundary in Wiltshire, and the brasher stately home at **Longleat**, an unlikely hybrid of safari park and historic monument.

Blandford Forum

BLANDFORD FORUM, the gateway into mid-Dorset from Bournemouth, owes its latinate name not to the Romans but to medieval pedantry – the original Saxon name Cheping, meaning "market", was translated as Forum by Latin-speaking tax officials in the thirteenth century. The Romans weren't far away, however – their main route from Old Sarum to Dorchester ran through the Iron Age fortification of Badbury Rings, just east of the town, where it made an uncharacteristic bend.

In 1731 Blandford was all but destroyed by fire, the fourth such conflagration since the end of the sixteenth century. The phoenix that rose from these ashes – as the Fire Monument near the church puts it – was designed by the unfortunately named Bastard brothers, John and William, whose "Blandford School" produced buildings characterized by mellow dapplings of brick and stone. Sleepy Blandford still boasts one of the most harmonious and complete Georgian townscapes in England, with its centrepieces being the **Town Hall** and the **Church of St Peter and St Paul**, built in 1739. Outside, the church's distinguishing feature is the cupola perched on its handsome square tower; inside, it has fine box pews and huge Ionic columns. It doesn't quite look as John Bastard intended, though: the church was daringly altered at the end of the nineteenth century, when the chancel was sawn off the nave, stuck on wheels, rolled out of the way so that a new section could be built in the gap, and then stuck back onto the extension. The town **museum** in Bere's Yard, opposite the church (Easter–Sept daily 11am–4pm; £1.50), offers a pithy account of local history, while **Mrs Penny's Cavalcade of Costume** at Lime Tree House, The Plocks (Easter–Sept Mon & Thurs–Sun 11am–5pm; Oct–Easter same days 11am–4pm; £3), presents over five hundred items of costume and accoutrements from 1730 to the 1950s, collected throughout the lifetime of a local woman, Mrs Penny.

Blandford's **tourist office** is in the car park on West Street (Mon–Sat: April–Oct 10am–5pm; Nov–March 10am–1pm; ☎01258/454770, ⊛www .ruraldorset.com). There are numerous **B&Bs** along Whitecliff Mill Street to choose from, or try *Gone Walkabout*, at 3 Alexandra St (☎01258/455699, ⓔ101454.1674@compuserve.com; no smoking; no credit cards; ❶), a Georgian house close to the town centre and welcoming walkers and cyclists. The local Hall & Woodhouse brewery supplies many local **hostelries** – the *Greyhound*, in quiet Greyhound Place (off Market Place), is a good-looking pub with outdoor seating and great food. Other eating options include the moderately priced *Ottoman* Turkish restaurant, at 65 East St.

Milton Abbas and Cerne Abbas

The village of **MILTON ABBAS**, six miles southwest of Blandford, is an unusual English rural idyll. It owes its model-like neatness to the First Earl of Dorchester who, in the eighteenth century, found the medieval squalor of former "Middleton" a blot on the landscape of his estate. Although some see the earl as an enlightened advocate of modern town planning, the more likely truth is that he simply wanted to beautify his land, so he had the village razed and rebuilt in its present location as thirty semi-detached, whitewashed and thatched cottages on wide grassy verges. No trace remains of the old village which once surrounded the fourteenth-century **abbey church** (dawn–dusk; small charge during school holidays), a mile's walk away near the lake at the bottom of the village. Delayed by the Black Death and cut short by the Dissolution, the abbey church lacks much internal decoration, and instead retains a spacious, uncluttered feel.

Not far from the village, the brick and flint cottage *Dunbury Heights* (☎01258 /880445; no smoking; no credit cards; ❷), about a mile towards Blandford, and the eighteenth-century thatched farmhouse *Park Farm* (☎01258/880828; no smoking; no credit cards; ❷), near Milton Abbey, both offer B&B **accommodation**. The *Dorset Tea Rooms* provides light lunches and the *Hambro Arms* **pub** at the top of the hill is the best bet for more substantial evening meals.

The most visited site in Dorset lies a further ten miles west, just off the A352, on the regular bus route between Dorchester and Sherborne (#216). **CERNE ABBAS** has bags of charm in its own right, with gorgeous Tudor cottages and abbey ruins, not to mention a clutch of decent pubs. Its main attraction, however, is the enormously priapic **giant** carved in the chalk hillside, standing 180-feet high and flourishing a club over his disproportionately small head. The age of the monument is disputed, some authorities believing it to be pre-Roman, others thinking it might be a Romano-British figure of Hercules, but in view of his prominent feature it's probable that the giant originated as some primeval fertility symbol. Folklore has it that lying on the outsize member will induce conception, but the National Trust, who now own the site, do their best to stop people wandering over it and eroding the two-foot trenches that form the outlines.

Shaftesbury

Ten miles north of Blandford, **SHAFTESBURY** perches on a spur of lumpy green-gold hills, with severe gradients on three sides of the town. On a clear day, views from the town are terrific – one of the best vantage points is **Gold Hill**, quaint, cobbled and very steep. The local history **museum** at the top of Gold Hill (Easter–Sept daily 10.30am–4.30pm; also some weekends in winter, call ☎01747/854146 to check; £1) is worth a glance – its contents include a collection of locally made buttons, for which the area was once renowned.

Pilgrims used to flock to Shaftesbury to pay homage to the bones of Edward the Martyr, which were brought to the **Abbey** in 978, though now only the footings of the abbey church survive, just off the main street (April–Oct daily 10am–5pm; £1.50). **St Peter's Church** on the market place is one of the few reminders of Shaftesbury's medieval grandeur, when it boasted a castle, twelve churches and four market crosses.

The helpful **tourist office** on Bell Street (mid-March to Nov daily 10am–5pm; Dec to mid-March Mon–Wed 10am–1pm, Thurs–Sat 10am–5pm; ☎01747/853514, ⓦwww.ruraldorset.com) can provide a full list of available **accommodation**. *Maple Lodge* on Christy's Lane has rooms with or without attached bathroom (☎01747/853945; no credit cards; ❷), while the *Knoll* in Bleke Street (☎01747/855243; no credit cards; ❸) boasts views over three counties. Three miles south of town in the village of **Compton Abbas**, on the scenic A350 to Blandford, the *Old Forge*, on Chapel Hill (☎01747/811881, ⓔtheoldforge@hotmail.com; no credit cards; ❷), offers B&B in an eighteenth-century cottage with log fires. For a **snack** or main **meal** in Shaftesbury, the *Salt Cellar* at the top of Gold Hill makes a great place to sit, without suffering from over-quaintness.

Stourhead

Landscape gardening – the creation of an artificially improved version of nature – was a favoured mode of display among the grandest eighteenth-century landowners, and **Stourhead**, ten miles northwest of Shaftesbury, is one of the most accomplished survivors of the genre (April–Oct Mon–Wed, Sat & Sun noon–5.30pm or dusk; garden: daily 9am–7pm or dusk; house & garden £8.50; house £4.80; garden £4.80 or £3.70 in winter; NT). The Stourton estate was bought in 1717 by Henry Hoare, who commissioned Colen Campbell to build a new villa in the Palladian style. Hoare's heir, another Henry, returned from his Grand Tour in 1741 with his head full of the paintings of Claude and Poussin, and determined to translate their images of well-ordered, wistful classicism into real life. He dammed the Stour to create a lake, then planted the terrain with blocks of trees, domed temples, stone bridges, grottoes and statues, all mirrored vividly in the water. In 1772 the folly of **King Alfred's Tower** (April–Oct Tues–Fri 2–5.30pm or dusk, Sat & Sun 11.30am–5.30pm or dusk; £1.60) was added and today affords fine views across the estate and into neighbouring counties. The rhododendrons and azaleas that now make such a splash in early summer are a later addition to this dream landscape. The house, in contrast, is fairly run-of-the-mill, though it has some good Chippendale furniture.

A mile to the southeast, in the showpiece village of **STOURTON**, also now owned by the National Trust, the *Spread Eagle Inn* has five en-suite **rooms** available (☎01747/840587; ❺) with prices halving in winter – it's also a good place to have **lunch**. However, Stourton is difficult to reach without your own transport – the nearest train station is at Gillingham, over six miles away.

Longleat

If Stourhead is an unexpected outcrop of Italy in Wiltshire, the African savannah intrudes even more bizarrely at **Longleat** (Easter–Sept daily 10am–5.30pm; Oct–Easter guided tours at set times 10am–3pm, call ☎01985/844400; safari park Easter–Oct Mon–Fri 10am–4pm, Sat, Sun & school holidays 10am–5pm; house £7; safari park £7; combined ticket £14), two and a half miles south of the road from Warminster to Frome. In 1946 the sixth marquess of Bath raised eyebrows among his peers as the first stately-home owner to open his house to the paying public on a regular basis to help make ends meet. In 1966 he caused even more amazement when Longleat's Capability Brown landscapes were turned into a drive-through **safari park** – the first in the country. (The car-less visitor can survey the lions, tigers, giraffes, elephants, zebras and hippos from a safari bus for an extra £3.) Once committed to such commercial enterprise, the bosses of Longleat knew no limits: other attractions now include the world's largest hedge maze, a Doctor Who exhibition, a hi-tech simulation of the world's most dangerous modes of travel and the seventh marquess's steamy murals encapsulating his interpretation of life and the universe (children may not be admitted). Beyond the brazen razzmatazz, though, there's an exquisitely furnished Elizabethan house, built for Sir John Thynne, Elizabeth's High Treasurer, with the largest private library in Britain and a fine collection of pictures, including Titian's *Holy Family*.

Longleat is about four miles from the train stations of Frome and Warminster and is currently served by a Lion-Link bus (Easter–Oct only) that leaves Warminster train station at 11.10am and returns from the Information Centre at Longleat at 5.15pm – the service is provided free to coach- and rail-ticket holders, and otherwise costs £1.50. Alternatively, there's the #53 bus (Mon–Sat) which shuttles roughly every hour between Warminster and Frome train stations – though be prepared to walk the two and a half miles from the entrance of the house to its grounds.

Sherborne

Tucked away in the northwest corner of Dorset, the pretty town of **SHERBORNE** was once the capital of Wessex, its church having cathedral status until Old Sarum (see p.310) usurped the bishopric in 1075. This former glory is embodied by the magnificent **Abbey Church** (daily: April–Oct 8.30am–6pm; Nov–March 8.30am–4pm), which was founded in 705, later becoming a Benedictine abbey. Most of its extant parts date from a rebuilding in the fifteenth century, and it is one of the best examples of Perpendicular architecture in Britain, particularly noted for its outstanding **fan vaulting**. The church also has a famously weighty peal of bells, led by "Great Tom", a tenor bell presented to the abbey by Cardinal Wolsey. Among the abbey church's many tombs are those of Alfred the Great's two brothers, Ethelred and Ethelbert, and the Elizabethan poet Thomas Wyatt, all located in the northeast corner. The **almshouse** on the opposite side of the Abbey Close was built in 1437 and is a rare example of a medieval hospital; another wing provides accommodation for Sherborne's well-known public school.

Sherborne also has two "castles", both associated with Sir Walter Raleigh. Queen Elizabeth I first leased, then gave, Raleigh the twelfth-century **Old Castle** (April–Sept daily 10am–6pm; Oct daily 10am–1pm & 2–5pm; Nov–March Wed–Sun 10am–1pm & 2–4pm; £1.80; EH), but it seems that he despaired of feudal accommodation and built himself a more comfortably domesticated house, **Sherborne Castle**, in adjacent parkland (April–Oct Tues, Thurs & Sun 12.30–5pm, Sat 2.30–5pm; gardens: April–Oct daily except Wed 10am–5pm; castle & gardens £5.50, gardens only £2.75). When Sir Walter fell from the queen's favour by seducing her maid of honour, the Digby family acquired the house and have lived there ever since; portraits, furniture and books are displayed in a whimsically Gothic interior, remodelled in the nineteenth century. The Old Castle fared less happily, and was pulverized by Cromwellian cannonfire for the obstinately Royalist leanings of its occupants. The **museum** near the abbey on Church Lane (Easter–Oct Tues–Sat 10.30am–4.30pm, Sun 2.30–4.30pm; £1) includes a model of the Old Castle and photographs of parts of the fifteenth-century Sherborne Missal, a richly illuminated tome weighing nearly fifty pounds, now housed in the British Library.

The **tourist office** is at 3 Tilton Court, Digby Rd (Mon–Sat: April–Oct 9am–5pm; Nov–Easter 10am–3pm; ☎01935/815341). For an **overnight stay** try the *Half Moon Hotel*, Half Moon St (☎01935/812017; ❹), the *Britannia Inn*, on Westbury, just down from the abbey (☎01935/813300; ❷), or the *Cross Keys Hotel*, 88 Cheap St (☎01935/812492; ❷), which has a few tables out front for drinks and meals. *Oliver's* on Cheap Street and the *Church House Gallery* close to the abbey on Half Moon Street are both good for teas and light lunches.

Salisbury

SALISBURY, huddled below Wiltshire's chalky plain in the converging valleys of the Avon and Nadder, looks from a distance very much as it did when Constable painted his celebrated view of it from across the water meadows,

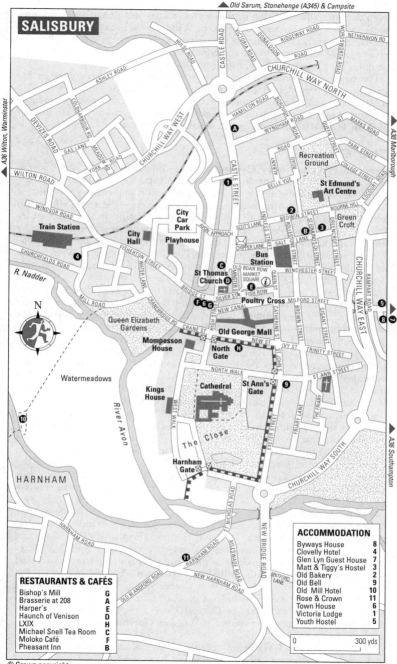

SALISBURY

Old Sarum, Stonehenge (A345) & Campsite

A36 Wilton, Warminster

A30 Marlborough

A30 Marlborough

A36 Southampton

CASTLE ROAD
VICTORIA ROAD
DONALDSON ROAD
RIDGEWAY ROAD
NETHERAVON RD
WORDSWORTH ROAD
CHURCHILL WAY NORTH
HULSE ROAD
ASHLEY ROAD
CHURCHILL WAY WEST
HAMILTON ROAD
RUNFOLD ROAD
WYNDHAM ROAD
ST MARKS ROAD
PARK STREET
QUEEN STREET
COLLEGE STREET
ESCOURT ROAD
Recreation Ground
St Edmund's Art Centre
COLDHARBOUR LANE
MEADOW ROAD
GAS LANE
YORK RD
DEVIZES ROAD
WILTON ROAD
WINDSOR ROAD
ALBANY ROAD
BELLE VUE
BEDWIN STREET
Green Croft
BOURNE HILL
GREENCROFT STREET
RAMPART ROAD
CHURCHILL WAY EAST
Train Station
City Hall
City Car Park
Playhouse
AVON APPROACH
SCOT'S LANE
ENDLESS STREET
ST EDMUND'S CH STREET
CHIPPER LANE
SALT LANE
WINCHESTER STREET
Bus Station
CHURCHFIELDS ROAD
FISHERTON STREET
WATER LANE
BRIDGE ST
St Thomas Church
Old George Mall
Poultry Cross
BOAR ROW
MARKET SQUARE
FISH ROW
MILFORD STREET
CATHERINE ST
BROWN STREET
GIGANT STREET
R. Nadder
MILL ROAD
Queen Elizabeth Gardens
CRANE ST
HIGH STREET
NEW CANAL
NEW ST
Mompesson House
North Gate
NORTH WALK
St Ann's Gate
IVY ST
TRINITY STREET
ST JOHN'S
Watermeadows
Kings House
WEST WALK
Cathedral
The Close
ST ANN STREET
FRIARY LANE
THE FRIARY
River Avon
Harnham Gate
EXETER STREET
CHURCHILL WAY SOUTH
HARNHAM
ST NICHOLAS ROAD
NEW BRIDGE ROAD
HARNHAM ROAD
AYLESWADE ROAD
OLD BLANDFORD ROAD
NEW HARNHAM ROAD
BRITFORD LANE

N

ACCOMMODATION

Byways House	8
Clovelly Hotel	4
Glen Lyn Guest House	7
Matt & Tiggy's Hostel	3
Old Bakery	2
Old Bell	9
Old Mill Hotel	10
Rose & Crown	11
Town House	6
Victoria Lodge	1
Youth Hostel	5

RESTAURANTS & CAFÉS

Bishop's Mill	G
Brasserie at 208	A
Harper's	E
Haunch of Venison	D
LXIX	H
Michael Snell Tea Room	C
Moloko Café	F
Pheasant Inn	B

0   300 yds

© Crown copyright

A338 Bournemouth

even though traffic may clog its centre and military jets scream overhead from local air bases. Prosperous and well-kept, Wiltshire's only city is designed on a pleasantly human scale, with no sprawling suburbs or high-rise buildings to challenge the supremacy of the cathedral's immense spire – unusually, the local planners have imposed a height limit on new construction.

The town sprang into existence in the early thirteenth century, when the bishopric was moved from **Old Sarum**, an ancient Iron Age hillfort settled by the Romans and their successors. The deserted remnant of Salisbury's precursor now stands on the northern fringe of the town, just a bit closer in than **Wilton House** to the west, one of Wiltshire's great houses.

The City

Begun in 1220, **Salisbury Cathedral** (June–Aug Mon–Sat 7.15am–8.15pm, Sun 7.15am–6.15pm; Sept–May daily 7am–6.15pm; £3.50 suggested donation) was mostly completed within forty years and is thus unusually consistent in its style, with one extremely prominent exception – the **spire**, which was added a century later and at 404ft is the highest in England. Its survival is something of a miracle, for the foundations penetrate only about six feet into marshy ground, and when Christopher Wren surveyed it he found the spire to be leaning almost two and a half feet out of true. The tie-rods inserted by Wren arrested the problem, but didn't cure it, and this remains a long-term problem that is yet to be resolved.

The interior is over-austere after James Wyatt's brisk eighteenth-century tidying, but there's an amazing sense of space and light in its high nave, despite the sombre pillars of grey Purbeck marble, which are visibly bowing beneath the weight they bear. Monuments and carved tombs line the walls, where they were neatly placed by Wyatt, and in the north aisle there's a fascinating clock dating from 1386, one of the oldest functioning clock mechanisms in Europe. Other features not to miss are the vaulted colonnades of the **cloisters**, and the octagonal **chapter house** (June–Aug Mon–Sat 9.30am–7.45pm, Sun noon–5.30pm; rest of year Mon–Sat 9.30am–5.30pm, Sun noon–5.30pm), which displays a rare original copy of the Magna Carta, and whose walls are decorated with a frieze of scenes from the Old Testament. On most days, you can join a free 45-minute tour of the church leaving two or more times a day, and there are also tours to the roof and spires (variable times; £3).

Surrounding the cathedral is the **Close**, the largest and most impressive in the country, a peaceful precinct of lawns and mellow old buildings. Most of the houses have seemly Georgian facades, though some, like the Bishop's Palace and the deanery, date from the thirteenth century. **Mompesson House** (April–Oct Mon–Wed, Sat & Sun noon–5.30pm; £3.90, garden only 80p; NT), built by a wealthy merchant in 1701, is a fine example of a Queen Anne house and contains some beautifully furnished eighteenth-century rooms and a superbly carved staircase, as displayed to great effect in the film *Sense and Sensibility*; the entry price includes a thirty-minute guided tour. The other building to head for in the Close is the **King's House**, in which you'll find the **Salisbury and South Wiltshire Museum** (July & Aug Mon–Sat 10am–5pm, Sun 2–5pm; rest of year closed Sun; £3.50) – an absorbing account of local history. It includes a good section on Stonehenge and also focuses on the life and times of General Pitt-Rivers, the father of modern archeology, who excavated many of Wiltshire's prehistoric sites, including Avebury (see p.313).

The Close's **North Gate** opens onto the centre's older streets, where narrow pedestrianized alleyways bear names like Fish Row and Salt Lane, indicative of their trading origin. Many half-timbered houses and inns have survived all over the centre, and the last of four market crosses, **Poultry Cross**, stands on stilts in Silver Street, near the Market Square. The market, held on Tuesdays and Saturdays, still serves a large agricultural area, as it did in earlier times when the city grew wealthy on wool. Nearby, the church of **St Thomas** – named after Thomas à Becket – is worth a look inside for its carved timber roof and "Doom painting" over the chancel arch, depicting Christ presiding over the Last Judgment. Dating from 1475, it's the largest of its kind in England. Opposite the church, *Snell's* sells memorable chocolates and cakes.

Lastly, to best appreciate the city's inspiring silhouette – the view made famous by Constable – take a twenty-minute walk through the water meadows southwest of the centre to **HARNHAM**; the *Old Mill* here serves drinks and modestly priced meals.

Practicalities

Salisbury is a major transport hub, with regular **trains** from London, Exeter, Bristol, Southampton and Portsmouth; National Express **bus** services from London; and local buses to such sights as Stonehenge and Avebury. Trains arrive half a mile west of the centre, on South Western Road; the bus station is a short way north of the Market Place, on Endless Street, with an adjacent office (Mon–Fri 8.15am–5.15pm, Sat 8.45am–4.45pm; ☎01722/336855) providing details of services throughout the region, including tours to Stonehenge and around. For details on all Wiltshire bus routes, ring ☎08457/090899. For a **taxi**, call ☎01722/505050.

The **tourist office** is on Fish Row, just off the Market Place (May, June & Sept Mon–Sat 9.30am–6pm, Sun 10.30am–4.30pm; July & Aug Mon–Sat 9.30am–7pm, Sun 10.30am–5pm; Oct–April Mon–Sat 9.30am–5pm; ☎01722/334956) and is the starting point for informative and inexpensive **guided walks** of the city (May–Sept daily 11am, also Mon & Thurs–Sun 8pm; 1hr 30min; £2.50); the tourist office also has details of the Cathedral Walk and Ghost Walk, costing about the same. A.S. Tours (☎01980/862931) runs frequent minibus **tours** to Stonehenge and Old Sarum (£12); to Stonehenge and Avebury (£20); and to Wells, Glastonbury and "King Arthur Country" (£25). If you want to **rent a bike**, go to Hayball's Cycle Shop, 30 Winchester St (☎01722/411378), which charges £9 per day, £55 for a week (with £25 cash deposit). There's a dedicated Cycling and Walking Hotline which provides information on itineraries around Salisbury (Mon–Fri 9am–5pm; ☎01980 /623255).

Accommodation
Hotels and B&Bs

Byways House 31 Fowlers Rd ☎01722/328364. Victorian house in a quiet location, offering rooms with or without bath. Two rooms have a view of the cathedral. **❷**

Clovelly Hotel 17 Mill Rd ☎01722/322055, ✉clovelly.hotel@virgin.net. Good-value hotel close to the train station. No smoking. **❹**

Glen Lyn Guest House 6 Bellamy Lane, Milford Hill ☎01722/327880, ✉glen.lyn@btinternet.com. Elegant Victorian house in quiet lane a ten-minute walk east of the centre. **❷**

Town House 1 Bridge St ☎01722/415386. Very central pub with bland but clean, modern and good-value rooms upstairs, all en suite; rates come down a bracket on weekdays. **❷**

Old Bakery 35 Bedwin St ☎01722/320100. Oak-beamed city-centre B&B in a 500-year-old building. There's no breakfast, hence the low rates. No credit cards. **❶**

Old Bell 2 St Ann St ☎01722/327958. Attractive inn right opposite St Ann's Gate, near the cathedral. **❸**

Old Mill Hotel, Town Path, Harnham ☎01722/327517. Great views across the meadows to the cathedral from this riverside pub with real ales and an adjoining 800-year-old restaurant; about a mile from the centre. ❺

Rose & Crown Harnham Rd ☏01722/399955. Upmarket riverside hostelry dating from the thirteenth century. ❼

Victoria Lodge 61 Castle Rd ☏01722/320586, ⍟www.viclodge.co.uk. One of several good-value B&Bs along this main road to Stonehenge. All rooms with bath, and there's a good restaurant (meals by pre-arrangement). ❸

Hostels and campsites

Matt and Tiggy's Hostel 51 Salt Lane

☏01722/327443. Eighteen beds available in three properties (one a 450-year-old cottage) run by a young couple; expect to pay around £10 for a dorm bed (sheets included), and breakfast is available in a separate café at £2.95. Close to the bus station.

Salisbury Camping and Caravanning Club Site Hudson's Field ☏01722/320713. Well-appointed campsite a mile and a half north of Salisbury close to Old Sarum. Closed Oct to mid-March.

Youth Hostel Milford Hill ☏01722/327572, ⍟salisbury@yha.org.uk. A 220-year-old building in its own spacious grounds, ten-minutes' walk east of the cathedral. Beds cost £10.15.

Eating and drinking

Bishop's Mill Bridge St. Popular pub with outdoor seating, right in the city centre. Ruddles and Greene King IPA on tap, and food, tea and coffee available until 7pm.

Harper's Market Square ☏01722/333118. Serves good-value, traditional English lunches and evening meals. Closed Sun eve in winter. Inexpensive.

Haunch of Venison Minster St. One of the city's most atmospheric pubs which also serves good food. Look out for the mummified hand of a nineteenth-century card player still clutching his cards.

LXIX 69 New St ☏01722/340000. Very close to the cathedral, this has an elegant, modern style and upmarket local cooking, such as smoked river eel. Closed Sat lunch, all Sun, last week Dec & first

week Jan. Expensive.

Michael Snell Tea Room 8 St Thomas's Square. Established and popular patisserie in the city centre, with outdoor tables. Closed Sun.

Brasserie at 208 206 Castle St ☏01722/417411. Part of the Milford Hall Hotel, this smart restaurant offers such dishes as wild boar sausages, or you can have morning coffees and afternoon teas in the hotel's lounge or garden. No smoking. Moderate.

Moloko Café 5 Bridge St. Cool café and cocktail bar with croissants, panini and salads also available.

Pheasant Inn Salt Lane. This atmospheric fifteenth-century inn serves sandwiches as well as traditional pub food and decent vegetarian dishes. Inexpensive.

Old Sarum and Wilton

The ruins of **Old Sarum** (daily: April–June & Sept 10am–6pm; July & Aug 9am–6pm; Oct 10am–5pm; Nov–March 10am–4pm; £2; EH) occupy a bleak hilltop site two miles north of the city centre – an easy walk, but there are plenty of buses: #5, #6, #8 and #9 running every fifteen minutes or so (less frequent on Sun). Possibly occupied up to five thousand years ago, then developed as an Iron Age fort whose double protective ditches remain, it was settled by Romans and Saxons before the Norman bishopric of Sherborne was moved here in the 1070s. Within a couple of decades a new cathedral had been consecrated at Old Sarum, and a large religious community was living alongside the soldiers in the central castle. Old Sarum was an uncomfortable place, parched and windswept, and in 1220 the dissatisfied clergy – additionally at loggerheads with the castle's occupants – appealed to the pope for permission to decamp to Salisbury (still known officially as New Sarum). When permission was granted, the stone from the cathedral was commandeered for Salisbury's gateways, and once the church had gone the population waned. By the nineteenth century Old Sarum was deserted, but it continued to exist as a political constituency – William Pitt was one of its representatives. The most notorious of the "rotten boroughs", it returned two MPs at a time to Westminster up until the 1832 Reform Act put a stop to it.

WILTON, five miles west of Salisbury, is renowned for its carpet industry and the splendid **Wilton House** (mid-April to Oct daily 10.30am–5.30pm; last entry 1hr before closing; £7.25, grounds only £3.75; ⓦ www.wiltonhouse.com), of which Daniel Defoe wrote: "One cannot be said to have seen any thing that a man of curiosity would think worth seeing in this county, and not have been at Wilton House." The Tudor house, built for the First Earl of Pembroke on the site of a dissolved Benedictine abbey, was ruined by fire in 1647 and rebuilt by Inigo Jones, whose classic hallmarks can be seen in the sumptuous Single Cube and Double Cube rooms, so called because of their precise dimensions. Sir Philip Sidney, illustrious Elizabethan courtier and poet, wrote part of his magnum opus *Arcadia* here – the dado round the Single Cube Room illustrates scenes from the book – and the Double Cube room was the setting for the ballroom scene in Ang Lee's film, *Sense and Sensibility*. The easel **paintings** are what makes Wilton really special, however – the collection includes paintings by Van Dyck, Rembrandt, two of the Brueghel family, Poussin, Andrea del Sarto and Tintoretto. In the grounds, the famous **Palladian Bridge** has been joined by ancillary attractions including an adventure playground, garden centre and an audiovisual show on the colourful earls of Pembroke, all designed to subsidize a massive programme of structural renovation.

Salisbury Plain and northwards

The Ministry of Defence is the landlord of much of **Salisbury Plain**, the hundred thousand acres of chalky upland to the north of Salisbury. Flags warn casual trespassers away from MoD firing ranges and tank training grounds, while rather stricter security cordons off such secretive establishments as the research centre at Porton Down, Britain's centre for chemical and biological warfare. As elsewhere, the army's presence has ironically saved much of the plain from modern agricultural chemicals, thereby inadvertently nurturing species that are all but extinct in more trampled landscapes.

Though now largely deserted except by forces families living in ugly, temporary-looking barracks quarters, Salisbury Plain once positively throbbed with communities. Stone Age, Bronze Age and Iron Age settlements left hundreds of burial mounds scattered over the chalklands, as well as major complexes at Danebury, Badbury, Figsbury, Old Sarum, and, of course, the great circle of **Stonehenge**. North of Salisbury Plain, beyond the A342 Andover–Devizes road, lies the softer Vale of Pewsey, traversed by the Kennet canal. **Marlborough**, to the north of the Vale, is the centre for another cluster of ancient sites, including the huge stone circle of **Avebury**, the mysterious grassy mound of **Silbury Hill** and the chamber graves of **West Kennet**. Malmesbury, though in Wiltshire, is covered in chapter five (see p.359), as it feels more closely allied to the Cotswolds area than to the rest of its county, from which it's cut off by the M4 and the rail line.

Stonehenge

No ancient structure in England arouses more controversy than **Stonehenge** (daily: mid-March to May & Sept to mid-Oct 9.30am–6pm; June–Aug 9am–7pm; mid-Oct to end Oct 9.30am–5pm; end Oct to mid-March 9.30am–4pm; £4.20; NT & EH; ⓦ www.stonehengematerplan.org), a mysterious ring of monoliths nine miles north of Salisbury. While archeologists argue over whether it was a place of ritual sacrifice and sun-worship, an astronomical calculator or a royal palace, the guardians of the site struggle to accommodate its year-round crowds who are resentful at no longer being able to walk among the stones; it is, however, possible to make a supervised tour of the stones by calling ahead on ☏ 01980/626267. Annual battles between the police and gatherings of druids and New Age travellers trying to celebrate the summer solstice are a thing of the past since the passage of the draconian Criminal Justice Act in 1994 – though low-key solstice celebrations are now permitted.

Conservation of Stonehenge, one of UNESCO's 380 designated World Heritage Sites, is obviously an urgent priority, and the current custodians are trying to address the dissatisfaction that many feel on visiting this landmark. A new visitors' centre is planned two miles east of the stones at the Amesbury roundabout (scheduled to open 2005), and a re-routing of the nearby roads is projected. In the meantime, visitors are issued with handsets programmed to dispense a range of information on the site – some of the soundtrack is interesting, but much is misleading and patronizing.

What exists today is only a small part of the original prehistoric complex, as many of the outlying stones were probably plundered by medieval and later farmers for building materials. The construction of Stonehenge is thought to have taken place in several stages. In about 3000 BC the outer circular bank and ditch were constructed, and the massive Heel Stone placed outside the entrance to the central enclosure; just inside the ditch was dug a ring of 56 pits, which at a later date were filled with a mixture of earth and human ash. Around 2500 BC the first stones were raised within the earthworks, comprising approximately forty great blocks of dolerite (bluestone), whose ultimate source was Preseli in Wales. Some archeologists have suggested that these monoliths were found lying on Salisbury Plain, having been borne down from the Welsh mountains by a glacier in the last Ice Age, but the lack of any other glacial debris on the plain would seem to disprove this theory. It really does seem to be the case that the stones were cut from quarries in Preseli and dragged or floated here on rafts, a prodigious task which has defeated recent attempts to emulate it.

The crucial phase in the creation of the site came in during the next six hundred years, when the incomplete bluestone circle was transformed by the construction of a circle of twenty-five **trilithons** (two uprights crossed by a lintel) and an inner horseshoe formation of five trilithons. Hewn from Marlborough Downs sandstone, these colossal stones (called sarsens), ranging from 13ft to 21ft in height and weighing up to 30tons, were carefully dressed and worked – for example, to compensate for perspective distortion the uprights have a slight swelling in the middle, the same trick as the builders of the Parthenon were to employ several hundred years later. More bluestones were arranged within the outer circle in various patterns, but the purpose of all this work remains baffling. The symmetry and location of the site (a slight rise in a flat valley with even views of the horizon in all directions) as well as its alignment towards the points of sunrise and sunset on the summer and winter solstices tend to support the supposition that it was some sort of observatory or time-measuring device. The site ceased to be used at around 1600 BC, and by the Middle Ages it had already become a "landmark".

There's a lot less charisma about the reputedly significant Bronze Age site of **Woodhenge** (dawn–dusk; free), two miles northwest of Stonehenge. The site consists of a circular bank about 220ft in diameter enclosing a ditch and six concentric rings of post holes, which would originally have held timber uprights, possibly supporting a roofed building of some kind. The holes are now marked more durably if less romantically by concrete pillars. A child's grave was found at the centre of the rings, suggesting that it may have been a place of ritual sacrifice.

Marlborough

An obvious base from which to explore Salisbury Plain is **MARLBOROUGH**, a peaceful spot now that the M4 deflects traffic from the old stagecoach route passing through the town. It's a handsome town too: the wide High Street, a dignified assembly of Georgian buildings, has a fine Perpendicular church standing at each end and half-timbered cottages rambling up the alleyways behind. The famous public school is not especially old – it was established in 1843 – but incorporates an ancient coaching inn among its red-brick buildings.

Marlborough **tourist office** is in the car park on George Lane, accessible from the High Street via Hilliers Yard (Easter–Oct Mon–Sat 10am–5pm; Nov–Easter Mon–Sat 10am–4.30pm; ☎01672/513989, ⓦwww.kennet.gov.uk) and there are several inns and guest houses offering **accommodation** along the High Street. Top of the range are *Ivy House* at no. 43 (☎01672/515333, ⓦwww.ivyhousemarlborough.co.uk; ❺), the antique *Castle and Ball* (☎01672 /515201; ❺) and the *Merlin* pub at no. 36–39(☎01672/512151;❹). Less expensive central options include the B&B at 63 George Lane (☎01672/512771; no credit cards;❶), which overlooks water meadows, while with your own transport you could try one of a couple of excellent B&Bs outside town: *Clench Farmhouse* (☎01672/810264; no credit cards;❸), an eighteenth-century farmhouse equipped with a tennis court and pool four miles south near Wootton Rivers, or *Rosegarth* in West Grafton (☎01672/810288; no credit cards; ❶), seven miles to the southeast. **Eating** options in central Marlborough include the reasonable bistro food at *Ivy House*, while *Polly Tea Rooms* serves good snacks and ice cream.

If you fancy a woodland walk or picnic, head out southeast of town into **Savernake Forest**, an ancient royal forest of oak and beech, crossed by eight long avenues that converge at its centre. You can walk there in less than thirty minutes, or else take a bus to Great Bedwyn from Marlborough (roughly hourly), asking the driver to let you off en route.

Silbury Hill, West Kennet and Avebury

The neat green mound of **Silbury Hill**, five miles west of Marlborough, is probably overlooked by the majority of drivers whizzing by on the A4. At 130ft it's no great height, but when you realize it's the largest prehistoric artificial mound in Europe, and was made by a people using nothing more than primitive spades, it commands more respect. It was probably constructed around 2600 BC, but like so many of the sites of Salisbury Plain, no one knows quite what it was for, though the likelihood is that it was a burial mound. You can't actually walk on the hill – so having admired it briefly from the car park, cross the road to the footpath that leads half a mile to the **West Kennet Long Barrow**. Dating from about 3250 BC, this was definitely a chamber tomb – nearly fifty burials have been discovered at West Kennet.

Immediately to the west, the village of **AVEBURY** stands in the midst of a **stone circle** (free access; NT & EH) that rivals Stonehenge – the individual stones are generally smaller, but the circle itself is much wider and more complex. A massive earthwork 20ft high and 1400ft across encloses the main circle, which is approached by four causeways across the inner ditch, two of them leading into wide avenues stretching over a mile beyond the circle. The best guess is that it was built soon after 2500 BC, and presumably had a similar ritual or religious function to Stonehenge's. The structure of Avebury's diffuse circle is quite difficult to grasp, but there are plans on the site, and you can get an excellent overview at the **Alexander Keiller Museum**, at the western entrance to the site (daily: April–Oct 10am–6pm or dusk if earlier; Nov–March 10am–4pm; £3.50 also for Barn Gallery; NT & EH), which displays excavated material and explanatory information. Nearby, the **Barn Gallery** (same times and prices) holds a permanent exhibition of Avebury and the surrounding country, and shows clips from recently discovered home-movies of Keiller excavating the stones aided by a bevy of nubile assistants. Having absorbed the contents of the various collections, you can wander round the peaceful circle, accompanied by sheep and cattle grazing unconcernedly among the stones. To the southeast, an avenue of standing stones leads half a mile beyond West Kennet towards a spot known as the Sanctuary, though there is little left to see here.

Back in the placid **village** of Avebury, you might drop in on **Avebury Manor** (April–Oct Tues, Wed & Sun 2–5.30pm; gardens April–Oct Tues, Wed & Fri–Sun 11am–5.30pm; £3.50, garden only £2.50; NT), behind the Alexander Keiller Museum. This sixteenth-century house – incorporating later alterations – has four or five panelled and plastered rooms, for which you are issued with over-shoes to protect the wooden floors from the chalk dust, and a **garden** with topiary and medieval walls. House and garden are distinctly low-key attractions, however, and little to do with the spirit of Avebury; you might find it more satisfying poking around the small village, half inside the circle, having a **snack** or cream tea at *The Circles* vegetarian restaurant, or a drink in the *Red Lion* **pub** which also serves reasonable **meals** as well as providing a few en-suite rooms should you wish to **stay** over (☎01672/539266; ❸). There's a **tourist office** (daily: summer 10am–5.30pm; rest of year 10am–4.30pm; ☎01672/539425) in the Avebury Chapel Centre on Green Street. Good bus routes connect Avebury with Salisbury, Marlborough and Devizes, and A.S. Tours runs regular guided trips here from Salisbury (see p.306).

Devizes

DEVIZES, seven miles down the A361 from Avebury at the mouth of the Vale of Pewsey, is a pleasant place, with some attractive eighteenth-century houses, a stately semicircular market place and a couple of fine churches, St Mary's and St John's. It's chiefly worth a stop, however, for the excellent **Museum** at 41 Long St (Mon–Sat 10am–5pm, Sun noon–4pm; £3, free Sun & Mon), housing an exceptional collection of prehistoric finds from barrows and henges throughout the county. Star exhibit is the so-called Marlborough Bucket, decorated with bronze reliefs from the first century BC.

The town offers some appealing nooks to explore: seek out the timbered and jettied row of Elizabethan-era houses on the cobbled St John's Alley, tucked away behind St John's Street. Out of town, you can enjoy a pleasant canalside stroll along the **Kennet and Avon Canal** which boasts 29 locks at Caen Hill, roughly an hour-and-a-half's walk westwards, but easily cyclable too.

Devizes has a very helpful **tourist office** at Cromwell House, Market Place (Mon–Sat 9.30am–5pm; ☎01380/729408). The best place **to stay** is the *Castle Hotel*, on New Park Street, a former coaching inn with a bar and restaurant (☎01380/729300; ❹); less expensive are the *Craven* B&B, Station Rd (☎01380 /723514; no credit cards; ❶), with bathrooms en suite or shared; and the *White Bear Inn*, Monday Market St (☎01380/722583; no credit cards; ❷). For **eating**, try the *Wiltshire Kitchen*, St John's St, which serves good lunches and snacks, as does the *The Cheesecake* in Market Place. Also in Market Place, you'll find *Seafoods Restaurant,* a fish-and-chip takeaway which also provides more substantial sit-down meals at cheap prices.

Lacock and around

LACOCK, ten miles northwest of Devizes, is the perfect English feudal village, albeit one gentrified by the National Trust to within a hair's breadth of natural life, and besieged by tourists all summer. Appropriately for so photogenic a spot, it has a fascinating museum dedicated to the founding father of photography, Henry Fox Talbot, a member of the dynasty which has lived in the local **Abbey** since it passed to Sir William Sharington on the Dissolution of the Monasteries in 1539. Ten years later Sharington was arrested for colluding with Thomas Seymour, Treasurer of the Mint, in a plot to subvert the coinage: he narrowly escaped with his life by shopping his partner in crime – who was beheaded – and after a period of disgrace managed to buy back his estates. His descendant, William Henry Fox Talbot, was the first to produce a photographic negative, and the **Fox Talbot Museum**, in a sixteenth-century barn by the abbey gates (March–Oct daily 11am–5.30pm; Nov–Feb Sat & Sun 11am–4pm; £3.80; NT), captures something of the excitement he must have experienced as the dim outline of an oriel window in the abbey steadily imprinted itself on a piece of silver nitrate paper. The postage-stamp-sized result is on display in the museum. The **abbey** itself (April–Oct Mon & Wed–Sun 1–5.30pm; £4.80; £6 including museum; NT) preserves a few monastic fragments amid the eighteenth-century Gothic, while the church of **St Cyriac** (free access) contains the opulent tomb of the nefarious Sir William Sharington, buried beneath a splendid barrel-vaulted roof.

The village's delightfully Chaucerian-sounding hostelry, *At the Sign of the Angel*, is a good, if expensive, **hotel** and **restaurant** (☎01249/730230; ⊙).

Corsham Court and Bowood House

The main sight within a short drive of Lacock is **Corsham Court** (mid-March to Oct Tues–Sun 2–5.30pm; Oct, Nov & Jan to mid-March Sat & Sun 2–4.30pm; £5, garden only £2), three miles west. It dates from Elizabethan times, though what you see now bears the Georgian stamp of Nash and Capability Brown, and the house, furnished by Robert Adam and Thomas Chippendale among others, contains a fine collection of art, including pieces by Caravaggio, Rubens, Reynolds and Michelangelo. The village of **CORSHAM** is another dignified little cloth-making town of Bath stone, riddled with underground limestone quarries and a long railway tunnel engineered by Brunel.

Ten miles east of Corsham, off the A342 Chippenham–Devizes road and just outside the village of Calne, **Bowood House** (April–Oct daily 11am–6pm; £5.90; ⓦwww.bowood-estate.co.uk) was designed in the eighteenth century by the likes of Henry Keene, Charles Barry and – again – Robert Adam. Adam was primarily responsible for the great south front and the Orangery, and, inside the house, the library – though the present appearance of this owes more to Charles Robert Cockerell, architect of Oxford's Ashmolean Museum, who also built the Neoclassical chapel. But it is the magnificent grounds of Bowood that are the real draw, with rhododendron gardens, a Doric temple on the banks of its placid lake and a waterfall in the woods; there's also an adventure playground for kids, and a restaurant.

Bradford on Avon and around

With its buildings of mellow auburn stone, reminiscent of the townscapes just over the county border in Bath and the Cotswolds, **BRADFORD ON AVON** is the most appealing town in the northwest corner of Wiltshire, offering far more than the dull county town of Trowbridge, or the slightly more distant Chippenham and Warminster. Sheltering against a steep wooded slope, it takes its name from its "broad ford" across the Avon, though the original fording place was replaced in the thirteenth century by a **bridge** that was in turn largely rebuilt in the seventeenth century. The domed structure at one end is a quaint old jail converted from a chapel.

The local industry, based on textiles like that of its Yorkshire namesake, was revolutionized with the arrival of Flemish weavers in 1659, and many of the town's handsome buildings reflect the prosperity of this period. Yet Bradford's most significant building is the tiny **St Lawrence Church** on Church Street, an outstanding example of Saxon architecture dating from about 700 AD. Wrecked by Viking invaders, and later used as a school and a simple dwelling, it was rehabilitated by a local vicar in 1856. Its distinctive features are the carved angels over the chancel arch.

Trains call regularly at Bradford from Weymouth, Dorchester, Bath and Bristol; the **train station** is on St Margaret's Street close to the town centre, while regular **bus** services from Bath, Trowbridge and Frome arrive at town bridge. **Bike rental** is available at *Lock Inn Cottage*, 48 Frome Rd (☎01225/868068; £12/day). The well-equipped **tourist office** is near the bridge at 34 Silver St (daily: April–Dec 10am–5pm; Jan–March 10am–4pm; ☎01225/865797, ⑩www.bradfordonavontown.com). Bradford has a good range of **accommodation**, none more characterful than *Bradford Old Windmill*, a B&B up the hill at 4 Mason's Lane (☎01225/866842; ❸, ❺), where an imaginative vegetarian menu is served house-party style (evening meals currently on Mon, Thurs & Sat). The lowest rates are given for anyone arriving after 6pm (assuming there's space); winter opening is irregular. *Priory Steps*, closer to the centre on Newtown (☎01225/862230; ❺), is a family home with bags of personality, well-prepared dinners and excellent views over a roofscape of weavers' cottages. The *Riverside Inn,* 49 St Margaret's St (☎01225/863526; ❷), lives up to its name, with private facilities in all rooms. For light lunches or cakes, try the *Bridge Tea Rooms* on Bridge Street, or *Scribbling Horse* at 34 Silver St. For alcohol or more substantial food, head for the *Bunch of Grapes* **pub** on Silver Street, also a venue for jazz, folk and blues every other Tuesday.

Great Chalfield

Great Chalfield Manor (guided tours: April–Oct Tues–Thurs 12.15pm, 2.15pm, 3pm, 3.45pm & 4.30pm; £3.80; NT), two and a half miles northeast of Bradford, is a splendid moated complex of house, church and outbuildings dating from about 1470, sensitively restored at the beginning of the twentieth century as a family home. The exterior looks like a typical Cotswold manor, all gables and mullions; inside, the Great Hall is overlooked by a minstrels' gallery from which three gargoyle-like masks gaze down into the hall, the eyes cut away so that the womenfolk could inspect the proceedings below without jeopardizing their modesty. The interior of the church features some fifteenth-century wall paintings.

Travel details

Buses

For information on all local and national bus services, contact Traveline: ☎0870/608 2 608 (daily 7am–9pm), ⊛www.traveline.org.uk.

Trains

For information on all local and national rail services, contact National Rail Enquiries: ☎08457/48 49 50, ⊛www.rail.co.uk.

Bournemouth to: Brockenhurst (3 hourly; 15–25min); Dorchester (hourly; 45min); London (2 hourly; 1hr 45min–2hr); Poole (1–3 hourly; 10–15min); Southampton (3 hourly; 30–45min); Weymouth (hourly; 1hr); Winchester (1–3 hourly; 1hr).

Dorchester to: Bournemouth (hourly; 45min); Brockenhurst (hourly; 1hr); London (hourly; 2hr 30min); Weymouth (hourly; 12min).

Portsmouth to: London (3 hourly; 1hr 30min–2hr); Salisbury (hourly; 1hr 30min); Southampton (2 hourly; 40–50min); Winchester (hourly; 1hr).

Ryde (Isle of Wight) to: Shanklin (2 hourly; 25min).

Salisbury to: Exeter (every 2hr; 2hr); London (2–3 hourly; 1hr 20min); Portsmouth (hourly; 1hr 30min); Southampton (2 hourly; 30–40min).

Southampton to: Bournemouth (3 hourly; 30–45min); Bristol (hourly; 1hr 50min); Brockenhurst (3 hourly; 15min); London (2 hourly; 1hr 15min–1hr 30min); Portsmouth (2 hourly; 40–50min); Salisbury (2 hourly; 30–40min); Weymouth (hourly; 1hr 30min); Winchester (3–4 hourly; 20min).

Winchester to: Bournemouth (2 hourly; 1hr); London (2 hourly; 1hr); Portsmouth (hourly; 1hr); Southampton (3–4 hourly; 20min).

Ferries and Hovercraft

Lymington to: Yarmouth, Isle of Wight (1–2 hourly; 30min).

Poole to: Cherbourg (1–3 daily; 2hr 15min–7hr); Jersey (April to mid-May & Oct 4–6 weekly; mid-May to Sept 1–2 daily; 3hr–3hr 45min); Guernsey (April to mid-May & Oct 4–6 weekly; mid-May to Sept 1–2 daily; 2hr 30min); St Malo (mid-May to Sept 1 daily; 4hr 35min).

Portsmouth to: Bilbao (1–2 weekly; 35hr); Caen (Jan to mid-Nov 2–3 daily; 6hr–7hr 15min); Cherbourg (6–8 7 daily; 2hr 45min–7hr 15min); Fishbourne, Isle of Wight (1–2 hourly; 35min);

Guernsey (Mon–Sat 1 daily; 6hr 30min); Jersey (Mon–Sat 1 daily; 10hr); Le Havre (2–3 daily; 5hr 30min–7hr 45min); Ryde, Isle of Wight (1–2 hourly; 15min); St Malo (1 daily Jan to mid-Nov; 8hr 45min).

Southampton to: East Cowes, Isle of Wight (hourly; 55min); West Cowes, Isle of Wight (hourly; 22min).

Southsea to: Ryde, Isle Of Wight (2 hourly;10min).

Weymouth to: Guernsey (April–Oct 1 daily; Nov–March irregular service; 2hr); Jersey (April–Oct 1 daily; Nov–March irregular service; 3hr 15min–3hr 35min).

Oxford and around

* **Chiltern Hills** Stretching
  southwest from Luton to
  the River Thames near
  Reading, the Chiltern
  Hills offer lovely wooded
  scenery. Henley-on-
  Thames, site of the
  famous Henley Regatta,
  is the best base for further explorations. See
  p.323

* **The Vale of White Horse**
  Takes its name from the
  huge, prehistoric horse
  cut into the chalk of the
  Berkshire Downs. See
  p.329

* **Radcliffe Camera,
  Oxford** Oxford boasts
  many beautiful old buildings, but the most
  imposing is the Italianate
  rotunda, Radcliffe
  Camera. See p.340

* **Le Petit Blanc restaurant, Oxford** Oxford has
  several excellent restaurants, but the pick is *Le
  Petit Blanc*, creation of
  the French chef,
  Raymond Blanc. See
  p.345

* **St Albans** This appealing
  city on the northern
  periphery of London has
  a splendid cathedral and
  some wonderful Roman
  remains, including several fine mosaics. See
  p.353

Oxford and around

Arching around the peripheries of London, beyond the orbital M25, the "Home Counties" of England form London's commuter-belt. Beyond the suburban sprawl, however, there is plenty to entice the visitor. The northwestern Home Counties – **Berkshire**, **Buckinghamshire** and **Hertfordshire** – are at their most enticing amidst the **Chiltern Hills**, a picturesque band of chalk uplands whose wooded ridges rise near Luton, beside the M1, and stretch southwest, petering out beside the River Thames near Reading. The hills provide an exclusive setting for many of the capital's wealthiest commuters, but for the casual visitor the obvious target is **Henley-on-Thames**, a good-looking old town famous for its Regatta and with a good supply of accommodation. Henley is also a handy base for further explorations, with the village of **Cookham** – and its Stanley Spencer gallery - leading the way, though **Reading** is also of interest as the host of two of Europe's most prestigious music festivals.

The Chilterns are traversed by the **Ridgeway**, a prehistoric track – and now a national trail – that offers excellent hiking. However, the finest portion of the trail is further to the west, across the Thames, on the downs straddling the Berkshire-Oxfordshire border. Here, the Ridgeway visits a string of prehistoric sites, the most extraordinary being the gigantic chalk horse that gives the **Vale of White Horse** its name. The Vale is dotted with pleasant little villages, and both **Woolstone** and plainer **Uffington** have places to stay; but neither is it far to the university city of **Oxford**, which, with its superb architecture, museums and lively student population, can keep you busy for days. Oxford is this region's star turn and it's also close to **Woodstock**, the handsome little town abutting one of England's most imposing country homes, **Blenheim Palace**.

To the northeast of Oxford, beyond the Chilterns, the plain landscapes of north Buckinghamshire hardly fire the soul, though modest **Buckingham** is pleasant enough and it is also within easy striking distance of **Stowe Gardens**, which hold a remarkable collection of outdoor sculptures, monuments and

Accommodation price codes

Throughout this guide, hotel and B&B accommodation is priced on a scale of ❶ to ❾, the number indicating the **lowest price** you could expect to pay per night in that establishment for a **double room** in high season. The prices indicated by the codes are as follows:

❶	under £40	❹	£60–70	❼	£110–150
❷	£40–50	❺	£70–90	❽	£150–200
❸	£50–60	❻	£90–110	❾	over £200

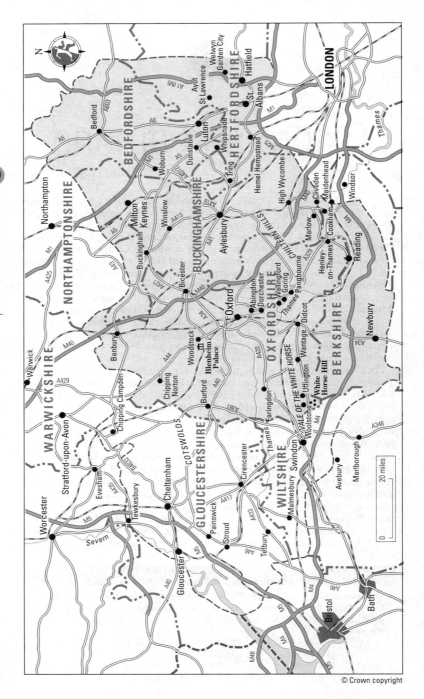

© Crown copyright

Thames passenger boat services

Salter Brothers run **passenger boats** along the River Thames from late May to early September. There are services between Oxford and Abingdon, Reading and Henley, Henley and Marlow, and between Marlow, Cookham and Windsor. Prices are reasonable – Oxford to Abingdon costs £7, Henley to Marlow £6.90 – and there are one or two boats daily on the more popular routes, three weekly on others. Further details from local tourist office or direct from Salter Brothers on ☎01865/243421, ⊛www.salterbros.co.uk.

decorative buildings. Travel east from Buckingham and you soon reach **Woburn**, home to another whopping stately home, **Woburn Abbey**, as well as **Woburn Safari Park**, and it's another short hop over into Bedfordshire, mostly flat agricultural land with a hint of industrial Midlands. It is not a county you'd cross England to visit, but **Bedford** is interesting for its John Bunyan connection and possibly useful for its hotels and restaurants.

Hit Bedfordshire and you're on the edge of the East Midlands (see chapter 000), but travel back towards London and you'll cross Hertfordshire. The prime target here is **St Albans**, an ancient and dignified town with Roman remains and a superb cathedral – but marooned amidst a knot of motorways and new towns on the fringes of London. These new towns – among them Welwyn Garden City and Hemel Hempstead – have little obvious appeal, but there are a few surprises hereabouts, principally **Hatfield House**, one of the country's finest ancestral homes.

The area covered in this chapter is threaded by five **motorways**, the M25, M4, M40, M1 and A1(M). These give swift access from all directions, though drivers will need a detailed map to successfully explore the rural nooks and crannies. Long-distance **buses** mostly stick to the motorways, too, providing an efficient service to all the larger towns, but local services between the villages are patchy, sometimes non-existent. There are mainline **train** services from London's Paddington station to Oxford, Henley-on-Thames and Reading, and from London's St Pancras to St Albans and Bedford. These main routes are supplemented by a number of branch lines, the most useful of which links Henley-on-Thames with Cookham.

The Chiltern Hills and the Vale of White Horse

The **Chiltern Hills** extend southwest from the workaday town of Luton, beside the M1, bumping across Buckinghamshire and Oxfordshire as far as the River Thames, just to the west of Reading. At their best, the hills offer handsome countryside, comprising a band of forested chalk hills with steep ridges and deep valleys interrupted by easy, rolling farmland. The Chilterns are also one of the country's wealthiest areas, liberally sprinkled with exclusive commuter hideaways-cum-country homes – though there are unappetising suburban blotches too. For non-residents, the obvious target is **Henley-on-Thames**, a pleasant riverside town within easy striking distance of the area's key attractions and with a reasonable range of accommodation. Nearby highlights include the sumptuous Victorian mansion of **Cliveden** and the village of **Cookham**, home to the fascinating Stanley Spencer gallery. Spare a thought

The Ridgeway

The Iron Age inhabitants of Britain developed the **Ridgeway** as a major thorough-fare, a fast route that beetled across the chalky downs of modern-day Berkshire and Oxfordshire, negotiated the Thames and then traversed the Chiltern Hills. It was probably part of a longer route extending from the Dorset coast to the Wash in Norfolk, but this is conjecture. Today, the Ridgeway is one of England's fourteen national trails, running from **Overton Hill**, near Avebury in Wiltshire, to **Ivinghoe Beacon**, 85 miles to the northeast near Tring, which is itself just a few miles south-west of Luton. Crossing five counties, the trail avoids densely populated areas, keeping to the hills, except where the Thames slices through the trail at **Goring Gap** and marks the transition from the wooded valleys of the Chilterns to the more open Berkshire–Oxfordshire downs. By and large, the Ridgeway is fairly easy hiking and over half of it is accessible to cyclists and RVs. The prevailing winds mean that it is best walked in a northeasterly direction. The Ridgeway is strewn with prehistoric monuments of one description or another, though easily the finest archeological remains are on the downs edging the **Vale of White Horse** and around **Avebury**. There are several youth hostels within reach of the Ridgeway – most notably the *Ridgeway Centre Youth Hostel* near Wantage – and numerous B&Bs. The *Ridgeway National Trail Companion*, available from the National Trails Office (Cultural Services, Holton, Oxford OX33 1QQ, ☎01865/810224), gives the low-down and also includes details of local accommodation. There's also a useful website: ⓦ www.nationaltrails .gov.uk.

also for **Reading**, beside the Thames at the southern tip of the Chilterns, not so much for itself (it's brusquely modern), but for its two big music festivals, Reading Rock Festival and the World Music extravaganza, WOMAD.

Crossing the Chilterns to the north and west of Henley, the **Ridgeway National Trail** (see box below) offers splendid hiking, though the most diverting part of the trail is further to the west, beyond the Chilterns and the Thames, amongst the more open scenery of the Berkshire and Oxfordshire downs. Here, on the edge of the **Vale of White Horse**, the trail sticks to a chalky ridge that provides magnificent views of the surrounding countryside and skirts the giant prehistoric figure after which the Vale is named. Here, you might opt to stay locally in the superb YHA hostel on the ridge above **Wantage**, in the humdrum town itself or in one of the Vale's quaint villages – tiny **Woolstone** is perhaps the most appealing.

With regards to public transport, Henley and Reading are easy to reach by **train** and **bus**, but for the smaller towns and the Vale of White Horse you will, for the most part, have to cope with intermittent local bus services.

Henley-on-Thames and around

Three counties – Oxfordshire, Berkshire and Buckinghamshire – meet at **HENLEY-ON-THAMES**, a long-established stopping place for travellers between London and Oxford. Henley is a good-looking, affluent commuter town that is at its prettiest among the old brick and stone buildings that flank the short main drag, **Hart Street**. At one end of Hart Street is the Market Place and its large and fetching **Town Hall**, at the other stands the easy Georgian curves of **Henley Bridge**. Overlooking the bridge is the **parish church of St Mary**, whose sturdy square tower sports a set of little turrets worked in chequerboard flint and stone, a popular decorative motif in the fif-teenth and sixteenth centuries. Several operators run boat trips out along the Thames from near the bridge and there is also an imaginative **River and**

Rowing Museum (daily: May–Aug 10am–5.30pm; rest of year closes 5pm; £4.95), a ten-minute walk south along the river bank from the foot of Hart Street via Thames Side. This focuses on three main themes – the history of the town, the development of rowing from the Greeks onwards, and the Thames both as a wildlife habitat and as a trading link.

Henley is, however, best known for its **Royal Regatta**, the world's most important amateur rowing tournament, when the town gets all puffed up and arrogant. Established in 1839, the Regatta is the boating equivalent of the Ascot races (see p.242), a quintessentially English parade ground for the rich, aristocratic and aspiring, whose champagne-swilling antics are inexplicably found thrilling by larger numbers of the hoi polloi. The Regatta, featuring past and potential Olympic rowers, begins on the Wednesday before the first weekend in July and runs for five days. Further information is available from the Regatta Headquarters on the east side of the Hart Street bridge (℡01491/572153).

Practicalities

Two or three times daily a direct train runs from London's Paddington station to Henley, but mostly you have to change at Twyford. From Henley **train station**, it's a five-minute walk north to Hart Street, using Station Road and its continuation Thames Side. Henley is easy to reach by bus, too, with regular services from Oxford, Reading and London. **Buses** from Reading and points south and west mostly pull in on Hart Street, while those the north and east – including Marlow and Cookham – stop on Bell Street, immediately to the north of Hart Street. The **tourist office** (April–Sept Mon–Sat 9.30am–6pm, Sun 11am–5pm; Oct–March daily 10am–4pm; ℡01491/578034) is located in a refurbished old barn, in a courtyard across from the Town Hall – it's clearly signed.

Henley has several first-rate **B&Bs**. One especially good option is the smart and tastefully furnished *Alftrudis*, 8 Norman Ave (℡01491/573099, ⓔb&b @alftrudis.fsnet.co.uk; no credit cards; ❷), which occupies a handsome Victorian town house in a quiet, leafy residential street. There are three guest rooms here, all en suite. Another excellent choice is *Lenwade*, 3 Western Rd (℡01491/573468, ⓔlenwadeuk@compuserve.com; no credit cards; ❸), an attractive Edwardian house with three en-suite guest rooms, comfortable furnishings and fittings and an unusual stained glass window in the hallway. **Hotels** are thin on the ground here, but pick of the bunch is the delightful, wisteria-clad old coaching inn, the *Red Lion*, beside Henley Bridge, with over twenty well-appointed bedrooms, individually decorated in period style (℡01491/572161, ⓦwww.redlionhenley.co.uk; ❼).

The *Red Lion* has the best **restaurant** in town, but there are other more informal and less expensive places on Hart Street, including the *Thai Orchard* at no. 8 (℡ 01491/412227). **Pubs** line up on Hart Street, but the *Angel*, by the bridge, has the advantage of an outside deck overlooking the river. Within easy striking distance of Henley are several outstanding **country pubs**. *Horns* (℡01189/401416), some three miles to the southeast off the A321, in the hamlet of Crazies Hill, is an ancient place with open fires and low-beamed ceilings; Brakspear beers – product of the local brewery – and excellent, moderately priced food are on offer (not Sun eve). The *Stag & Huntsman* (℡01491 /571227), in Hambleden, some three miles to the northeast off the Marlow Road, the A4155, has a short but delicious menu – and the village itself is a pretty spot on the edge of the Chilterns. And finally, there's the *Crooked Billet* (℡01491/681048), in Stoke Row, five miles west of Henley off the B481, which is more a restaurant than a pub – a much lauded place dating from the 1640s and offering exquisite food from a creative menu.

Stonor House

Nestling in a fold of the Chiltern Hills five miles north of Henley, the tranquillity of **Stonor House** (July & Aug Wed & Sun 2–5.30pm; April–June & Sept Sun only; £4.50), a Tudor mansion, on the edge of the eponymous village, belies its turbulent history. After the Reformation, the Stonor family remained steadfastly Catholic, refusing to take the oath acknowledging the monarch as head of the Church of England. As a result, Stonor became a haven for refugee Catholics, notably the Jesuit scholar and evangelist Edmund Campion, who was eventually hunted down and executed for high treason in 1581. Though punished for their Catholicism and deprived of their land, the Stonors were later reinstated, and their descendants (the Camoys) still live here today.

The **house**, with its Tudor facade superimposed onto the original medieval building, presents an harmonious exterior, the rich ochre brickwork punctuated by towers and backdropped by a lightly forested hill. However, the interior lacks cohesion and contains little old furniture, its mediocrity only redeemed by Campion memorabilia and the occasional surprise, such as the chapel frieze carved from tea chests by a Polish artist during World War II. The frieze was given by Graham Greene, a family friend who was staying here when he wrote *Our Man in Havana* – a book of far greater renown than poor old Campion's *Ten Reasons for Being a Catholic*.

Marlow

Heading north and then east out of Henley along the A4155, it's eight leafy miles to bustling **MARLOW**, another pleasant Thames-side town, its centre dotted with comely Georgian buildings. Here, you can while away an hour or two watching boats go through the lock or tracing Marlow's literary connections. In 1817 Shelley and his wife Mary moved to a house on West Street (between Hayes Place and the school) and stayed for a year – just long enough for him to compose the *Revolt of Islam* and for her to write *Frankenstein*. T.S. Eliot lived down the road at no. 31 for a time in 1918, and Jerome K. Jerome wrote parts of *Three Men in a Boat* in the *Two Brewers* on St Peter's St, Marlow's best pub.

There are regular **buses** from Henley to Marlow and the two are also linked by **train** – though you have to change twice and it takes about an hour. Buses drop passengers close to Marlow High Street, a couple of minutes walk from the **tourist office**, at no. 31 (Mon–Fri 9am–5pm, Sat 9.30am–5pm; winter closes 4pm; ☏01628/483597). From the train station, it's a short walk west along Station Road to the tourist office.

Cookham

Tiny **COOKHAM**, on the other side of the Thames just three miles southeast of Marlow – and not to be confused with neighbouring Cookham Dean and Cookham Rise – is noteworthy as the former home of **Stanley Spencer** (1891–1959), one of Britain's greatest – and most eccentric – artists. The Bible fired Spencer's imagination and many of his paintings depict biblical tales transposed into his Cookham surroundings – remarkable, visionary works in which the village is turned into a sort of earthly paradise. Spencer made his artistic name in the 1920s, firstly as an official war artist and then for his *Resurrection: Cookham*, which attracted rave reviews when it was exhibited in London in 1927. No-one minded much that his brand of Christianity was extremely unorthodox – he called his religious system the "Church of Me" – but in the 1930s his reputation temporarily dipped and he took endless critical flak when

his work took an erotic turn. In part, this reflected his own changing circumstances; in 1937, he divorced his first wife, Hilda, in order to marry his mistress,
Patricia Preece, but the latter exploited him financially and, so most contemporaries thought, regularly humiliated him. Perhaps surprisingly, Spencer continued writing to Hilda throughout his troubled second marriage, a passionate
correspondence that – bizarrely – continued after her death in 1950. Much of
Spencer's most acclaimed work is displayed at the Tate Britain, in London (see
p.83), but there's a fine sample here at the **Stanley Spencer Gallery**
(Easter–Oct daily 10.30am–5.30pm; Nov–Easter Sat & Sun 11am–5pm; £1),
which occupies the old Wesleyan Chapel on the High Street. Three prime
exhibits are *Listening from Punts*, *Conversation between Punts* and the wonderful
(but unfinished) *Christ Preaching at Cookham Regatta*. The permanent collection
is enhanced by regular exhibitions of Spencer paintings and the gallery also
contains incidental Spencer letters, documents and memorabilia, including the
pram in which he used to wheel his artist's clobber around the village. As a boy,
Spencer worshipped in the chapel, and his home, *Fernlea* (no access), is on the
High street. The gallery has a leaflet detailing an hour-long walk round
Cookham, visiting all those places with which he is associated.

There's an hourly **train** service from Marlow to Cookham and from the station it's a pleasant ten-minute walk east across the common to the Spencer
Gallery. Cookham's *Bel & Dragon* **pub**, with ancient beams and ample leather
chairs, pulls a good pint and serves decent home-made food.

Cliveden

Perched on a ridge across the Thames just to the east of Cookham, **Cliveden**
is a grand Victorian mansion, whose sweeping Neoclassical lines were designed
by Sir Charles Barry, architect of the Houses of Parliament. Its most famous
occupant was Nancy Astor, the first woman to sit in the House of Commons
and, together with her husband, Lord Astor, a leading light of the "Cliveden
set" – a weekly gathering of influential politicians who came here at weekends
in the run up to World War II. Reactionary to the core, their ability to appreciate the difficulties faced by Hitler was not readily understood by many of
their compatriots, but this didn't stop Churchill appointing Lord Astor a minister in his wartime cabinet. The National Trust owns the property and leases
the house as a luxury **hotel** (☎01628/668561; ⓞ) – doubles cost from £380-
a-night – which boasts an extraordinarily lavish interior. Acres of wood panelling, portraits of past owners and fancy chimneypieces culminate in the
French Dining Room, containing the complete fittings and furnishings of
Madame de Pompadour's eighteenth-century dining room, bought as a job lot
in Paris by one of the Astors. Most of the hotel is only open to guests, but visitors are permitted into the west wing to gawp at all the luxury (April–Oct
Thurs & Sun 3–5.30pm; £6, including the grounds). More satisfying are the
grounds (mid-March to Oct daily 11am–6pm; Nov & Dec daily 11am–4pm;
£5), which comprise a series of themed gardens – roses, topiary, water gardens
and so forth – and offer fine views of the Thames. The gardens teem with
tourists at the weekend, but you can find peace and quiet in the woods along
the river.

Reading

READING is a modern, prosperous town on the south bank of the River
Thames, ten miles south of Henley. Guarding the western approaches to the
capital, it has always been important, long a stopping-off point for kings and
queens and once home to one of the country's richest abbeys. Henry VIII took

care of the abbey, seizing its lands and hanging the abbot from the main gate, and today almost nothing remains of the old town except the shattered remains of the aforementioned abbey, a short walk to the east of the pedestrianized shopping centre.

There is a flourishing **arts scene** in the town, with both the Reading Film Theatre (☎0118/9868497) and the Hexagon Theatre (☎0118/9606060) offering a good programme of shows, but you wouldn't make a beeline for the place were it not for its two big summertime **music festivals**. The first, the three-day **WOMAD** festival (ⓦwww.womad.org; tickets ☎0118/9390930), held each July, is a celebration of World Music, Arts and Dance, originally inspired by Peter Gabriel. Since the first WOMAD in 1982, there have been about a hundred spin-off events in twenty countries, but the Reading festival remains the focus, held at the Rivermead Leisure Complex, Richfield Avenue, just to the north of the town centre. Also held at the Rivermead Leisure Complex, but a little later in the summer, the **Reading Festival** (ⓦwww.readingfestival.com) is a three-day event featuring many of the big names of contemporary music. Details of who is performing are published in the music press at least a couple of months in advance and tickets are available from record shops across the country. The vast majority of festival-goers **camp** on site and special buses run there in their hundreds, or you can walk from Reading train station – it only takes fifteen minutes.

Reading can be reached by train from London Paddington and Waterloo. The **tourist office**, in the town hall, in the town centre on Blagrave St (Mon–Fri 10am–5pm, Sat 10am–4pm; ☎0118/9566226), runs an accommodation-booking service; be sure to reserve a room months in advance if you're planning on being here for either festival.

The Vale of White Horse

The **Vale of White Horse**, situated between Wantage, a modest market town about thirty miles west of Henley, and Faringdon, seventeen miles southwest of Oxford, is a shallow valley, whose fertile farmland is studded with tiny villages. It takes its name from the prehistoric figure carved into the chalk downs above two of its smaller hamlets – **Uffington** and **Woolstone**. Carved in the first century BC, the horse is the most conspicuous of a string of prehistoric remains that dots the downs and includes burial mounds and Iron Age forts. The **Ridgeway National Trail** (see box on p.324), running along – or near – the top of the downs, links several of these sites and offers wonderful, breezy views over the Vale. Originally a prehistoric footpath, the Ridgeway was long used as a drove road, with sheep taken over the downs to market. Nowadays, horses are more common, the well-drained turf providing an ideal training ground for racehorses.

Wantage

Workaday **WANTAGE** is an unassuming, somewhat care-worn market town, whose crowded Market Place is overseen by a statue of its most famous son, Alfred the Great (849–99), the most distinguished of England's Saxon kings. Unveiled in 1877, the statue doesn't do Alfred any favours – though he must have been very strong to stand any chance of lifting his over-large axe. From the south side of the Market Place, a couple of alleys lead through to Church Street, where the tourist office shares its premises with the **Vale and Downland Museum** (Mon–Sat 10am–4.30pm, Sun 2.30–5pm; £1.50), which is good on local history.

Wantage is handy for the finest portion of the **Ridgeway** and the museum is also the place to pick up local hiking maps and bus timetables. The quickest way to reach the Ridgeway direct from Wantage is to take bus #38 (Mon–Sat only, hourly; 10min) from the Market Place to **Letcombe Bassett**, less than a mile from the path – and the model for Cresscombe village in Hardy's *Jude the Obscure*. The best walks along the Ridgeway take you westwards from Letcombe Bassett to the White Horse (see below), a distance of about seven miles.

Long distance **buses** drop passengers in Wantage's Market Place, footsteps from the **tourist office**, on Church Street (☎01235/760176). One of the better **B&Bs** is the well-kept *Alfred's Lodge*, 23 Ormond Rd (☎01235/762409; ❶), in a detached Victorian house about five minutes' walk southeast of the centre: from the east end of the Market Place, take Newbury Street and watch for Ormond on the left. Alternatively, the **Ridgeway youth hostel** (☎01235/760253; limited opening Oct to mid-March), just off the A338 a couple of miles south of Wantage and a short walk from the Ridgeway, occupies five converted barns. To get there, take bus #38 from Wantage to Letcombe Regis, and walk a mile or so uphill to the hostel from there. Wantage has one excellent **restaurant**, *Foxes* (☎01235/760568), at the foot of Newbury Street near the east end of the Market Place. This serves a changing menu of imaginatively prepared contemporary dishes featuring local ingredients, but it's expensive, with a two-course set meal costing around £20. For a less pricey deal, try either the *Cellar Bar*, a café serving tasty snacks and lunches at the east end of the Market Place on Newbury Street, or *The Lamb* (☎01235/766768), a revamped seventeenth-century building inn at the bottom of Mill Street – head northwest from the Market Place.

White Horse Hill

White Horse Hill, six miles west of Wantage along the B4507, follows close behind Stonehenge (see p.311) and Avebury (see p.313) in the hierarchy of Britain's ancient sites, though it attracts nothing like the same number of visitors. Carved into the north-facing slope of the downs above the villages of Uffington and Woolstone, the 374-foot-long **horse** looks like something created with a few swift strokes of an immense brush, and there's been no lack of weird and wonderful theories as to its origins. Some have suggested it was a glorified signpost, created to show travellers where to join the Ridgeway; others that it represented the horse (or even the dragon) of St George; and in Victorian times, the best-loved legend – popularized in a ballad by G.K. Chesterton – claimed that it was cut by King Alfred to celebrate his victory over the Danes at the battle of Ashdown, fought around here in 871 AD. In fact, burial sites excavated in the surrounding area point to the horse having some kind of sacred function, though frankly no-one knows quite what. The first written record of the horse's existence dates from the time of Henry II, but it was cut much earlier, probably in the first century BC, making it one of the oldest chalk figures in Britain. A detailed 1994 study showed that its creators dug out the soil to a depth of a metre and then filled the hollow with clear white chalk taken from a nearby hilltop. Just below the horse is **Dragon Hill**, a small flat-topped hillock that has its own legend. Locals long asserted that this was where St George killed and buried the dragon, a theory proved, so they argued, by the bare patch at the top and the channel down the side, where blood trickled from the creature's wounds. Here also, at the top of the hill, is the Iron Age earthwork of **Uffington Castle**, which provides wonderful views over the Vale.

The Ridgeway runs alongside the horse and continues west to reach, after one-and-a-half miles, **Wayland's Smithy**, a 5000-year-old burial mound encircled by trees. It is one of the best Neolithic remains along the Ridgeway, though heavy restoration has rather detracted from its mystery. In ignorance of its original function, the invading Saxons named it after Wayland Smith, an invisible smith who, according to their legends, made invincible armour and shoed horses without ever being seen.

Travelling west from Wantage, the **B4507** passes the narrow lane that leads after 500 yards up to the car park just below the White Horse. Getting here by public transport is difficult: the only **bus**, the Ridgeway Explorer, linking Wantage and Swindon via the B4507, runs only on Sundays and Bank Holidays between June and October (timetable details on ☎0870/608 2608).

Woolstone and Uffington

About three quarters of a mile below the White Horse car park, on the north side of the B4057, is the minuscule hamlet of **WOOLSTONE**. Here, the attractive *White Horse Inn* (☎01367/820726; ❸) occupies a rickety, half-timbered, partly thatched old building and offers both good quality pub food and **accommodation**, mostly in a modern annexe. A second option is the *Hickory House* (☎01367/820303; no credit cards; ❷), offering two en-suite guest rooms in a spick-and-span modern house close to the pub. A mile or two to the north of Woolstone, the much larger (and plainer) village of **UFFINGTON** has a couple of **B&Bs**, notably the well-kept and unassuming *Norton House*, next to the post office on the main street (☎01367/820230; no credit cards; ❷). Uffington's most famous son was Thomas Hughes (1823–96), the author of *Tom Brown's School Days* – hence the pocket-sized Tom Brown's School Museum.

Oxford

Think of **OXFORD** and inevitably you think of its university, revered as one of the world's great academic institutions, inhabiting honey-coloured stone buildings set around ivy-clad quadrangles. Much of this is accurate enough, but although the university dominates central Oxford both physically and mentally, the wider city has an entirely different character, its economy built on the car plants of Cowley to the south of the centre. It was here that Britain's first mass-produced cars were produced in the 1920s and, despite the fact that there have been more downs than ups in recent years, the plants are still vitally important to the area.

Oxford started late, in Anglo-Saxon times, and blossomed even later, under the Normans, when the cathedral was constructed and Oxford was chosen as a royal residence. The origins of the university are obscure, but it seems that the reputation of **Henry I**, the so-called "Scholar King", helped attract students in the early twelfth century, their numbers increasing with the expulsion of English students from the Sorbonne in 1167. The first colleges, founded mostly by rich bishops, were essentially ecclesiastical institutions and this was reflected in collegiate rules and regulations – until 1877 lecturers were not allowed to marry and women were not granted degrees until 1920. There are common architectural features, too, with the private rooms of the students arranged around quadrangles (quads) as are most of the communal rooms – the chapels, halls (dining rooms) and libraries.

Though they share a similar history, each of the thirty five colleges has its own character and often a particular label, whether it's the richest (St John's), most left-wing (Wadham and Balliol) or most public-school-dominated (Christ Church). Collegiate rivalries are long established, usually revolving around sports, and tension between the university and the city – "Town" and "Gown" – has existed as long as the university itself. Relations became especially fractious during the **Civil War**, when the colleges sided with Charles I (who turned Oxford into a Royalist stronghold) while the city backed the Parliamentarians. The privileges enjoyed by the colleges – until 1950 the university had two MPs of its own, for example – have also stoked resentment and this still flares into the occasional confrontation, but a non-communicative coexistence is more typical. Given that thousands of tourists and foreign-language students also invade the city throughout the year, it is no surprise that Oxford's 120,000 permanent inhabitants tend to keep themselves to themselves.

Despite – indeed, partly because of – its idiosyncrasies, Oxford should be high on anyone's itinerary, and can keep you occupied for several days. The university buildings include some of England's finest architecture, and the city can also boast some excellent museums and numerous bars and restaurants. Getting there is easy, too: from London the journey takes just an hour by train, and around two hours by bus.

Arrival, information and guided tours

From Oxford **train station**, it's a five- to ten-minute walk east to the centre along Park End Street and its continuation, Hythe Bridge Street. Long-distance and many county-wide buses terminate at the Gloucester Green **bus station**, in the centre adjoining George Street. Many of these buses make other city stops prior to arriving at the bus station – ask the respective company for details. Most city services – including Park and Ride – are operated by the Oxford Bus Company (℡01865/785400) and many of their buses pull in on the High Street and St Giles. Oxford's (municipally engineered) lack of convenient downtown **parking** makes the city's Park-and-Ride scheme very attractive, except on Sundays when the scheme pretty much closes down and you should be able to park in the centre without much problem. There are Park-and-Ride car parks on all the main access routes into the city.

The Gloucester Green bus station is yards from the **tourist office** (April–Sept Mon–Sat 9.30am–5pm, Sun 10am–3.30pm; Oct–March closed Sun; ℡01865/726871, @www.visitoxford.org). They have a wealth of information about the city's sights, though precious little is issued free. One of their better booklets is the *Oxford Visitors' Guide* (£1), which provides a general overview of the city and has a wide range of more specific information on everything from shopping and pubs to self-guided city walks and college opening hours. There are also two free **listings magazines**, the plodding *This Month in Oxford* and the livelier *WOW*.

The tourist office also operates an accommodation-booking service (see below) and offers excellent **guided tours** – a two-hour stroll round the city centre costs £5.85. There are several tours daily, but it's still a good idea to book in advance. More specialized tours are available, too, with one following in the footsteps of Lewis Carroll, others devoted to Tolkien and to British TV's Inspector Morse; these need to be arranged ahead of time – ring the tourist office for details.

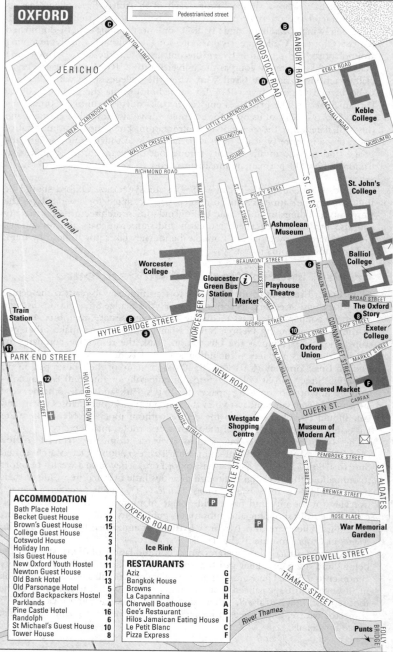

OXFORD

Pedestrianized street

JERICHO

Keble College

St. John's College

Ashmolean Museum

Balliol College

Worcester College

Gloucester Green Bus Station

Playhouse Theatre

Market

The Oxford Story

Exeter College

Train Station

HYTHE BRIDGE STREET

PARK END STREET

Oxford Union

Covered Market

Westgate Shopping Centre

Museum of Modern Art

Ice Rink

War Memorial Garden

Punts

ACCOMMODATION

Bath Place Hotel	7
Becket Guest House	12
Brown's Guest House	15
College Guest House	2
Cotswold House	3
Holiday Inn	1
Isis Guest House	14
New Oxford Youth Hostel	11
Newton Guest House	17
Old Bank Hotel	13
Old Parsonage Hotel	5
Oxford Backpackers Hostel	9
Parklands	4
Pine Castle Hotel	16
Randolph	6
St Michael's Guest House	10
Tower House	8

RESTAURANTS

Aziz	G
Bangkok House	E
Browns	D
La Capannina	H
Cherwell Boathouse	A
Gee's Restaurant	B
Hilos Jamaican Eating House	I
Le Petit Blanc	C
Pizza Express	F

1, 2, Stratford, Woodstock & Blenheim ▲ 3, 4, A, ▲ A34 & (M40) Birmingham

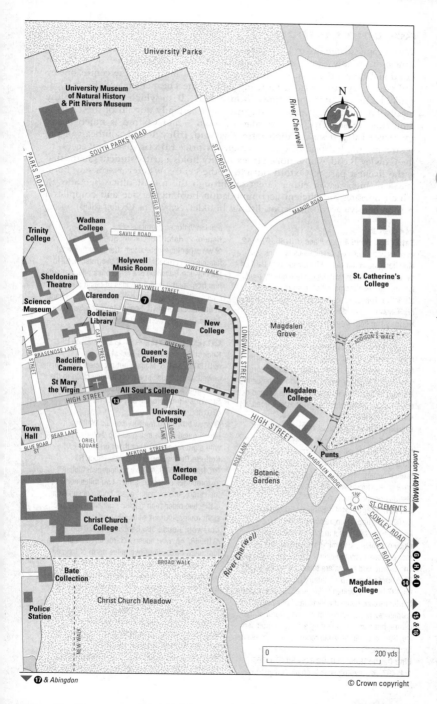

University Parks

University Museum
of Natural History
& Pitt Rivers Museum

River Cherwell

N

SOUTH PARKS ROAD

ST CROSS ROAD

MANSFIELD ROAD

MANOR ROAD

PARKS ROAD

Trinity
College

Wadham
College

SAVILE ROAD

JOWETT WALK

St. Catherine's
College

Sheldonian
Theatre

Holywell
Music Room

Science
Museum

Clarendon

HOLYWELL STREET

7

Bodleian
Library

New
College

Magdalen
Grove

CATTE STREET

QUEENS LANE

ADDISON'S WALK

BRASENOSE LANE

Radcliffe
Camera

Queen's
College

LONGWALL STREET

TURL STREET

St Mary
the Virgin

All Soul's College

Magdalen
College

HIGH STREET

13

University
College

HIGH STREET

Town
Hall

BEAR LANE

LOGIC LANE

ROSE LANE

MAGDALEN BRIDGE

Punts

BLUE BOAR ST

ORIEL
SQUARE

MERTON STREET

Botanic
Gardens

London (A40/M40)

Merton
College

THE PLAIN

ST. CLEMENT'S

Cathedral

COWLEY ROAD

Christ Church
College

IFFLEY ROAD

G, H & I

BROAD WALK

River Cherwell

14

Bate
Collection

Magdalen
College

15 & 16

Police
Station

Christ Church Meadow

NEW WALK

0   200 yds

17 & Abingdon

© Crown copyright

Accommodation

With supply struggling to keep pace with demand, Oxford's central **hotels** are almost invariably expensive, though nowhere near as pricey as those in London. There are one or two inexpensive hotels in or near the centre, but by and large they are far from inspiring and, at the cheaper end of the market, you're better off choosing a **guest house** or **B&B**, of which there is a healthy supply. The problem is that the majority (but certainly not all) of these establishments are scattered on the edge of town – and Oxford is much better appreciated if you stay in the centre. That said, **Iffley Road**, southeast of the centre and the location of several reasonably priced B&Bs, gives easy access to the Cowley Road, whose northern extremity holds a gritty student ghetto that is the liveliest part of Oxford outside of the centre. Wherever you stay, book ahead in high season either direct or through the tourist office (see above), which operates an efficient accommodation-booking service and compiles a comprehensive accommodation listings booklet, *Staying in Oxford* (80p).

Hotels

Bath Place Hotel 4 Bath Place ☎01865/791812, ⒲www.bathplace.co.uk. This unusual, pink and blue hotel, down an old cobbled courtyard flanked by ancient buildings with higgledy-piggledy roofs, has just thirteen rooms, all of them reasonably attractive. The location is excellent – in the centre, off Holywell Street. ❺

Holiday Inn Pear Tree Roundabout ☎0870 /4009086, ⒲www.holiday-inn.com/oxford. Well-designed chain hotel with smart, comfortable rooms furnished in a crisp modern style. Sports facilities, a pool and an excellent restaurant are all provided. Just under four miles north of the centre beside the Pear Tree Roundabout – the second one out from the centre along the Woodstock Road. ❼, ❻ at weekends.

Old Bank Hotel 92 High St ☎01865/799599, ⒺInfo@oldbank-hotel.co.uk. Great location for a first-rate hotel, a slick, glistening conversion of an old bank. Over forty immaculate bedrooms decorated in smart, modern style. Some of the rooms have great views over All Souls college. The *Quod* bistro is on the ground floor. ❽

Old Parsonage Hotel 1 Banbury Rd ☎01865 /310210, ⒺInfo@oldparsonage-hotel.co.uk. Arguably the best hotel in town, this lovely little place occupies a charming, wisteria-clad stone former-parsonage by the church at the top of St Giles. The twenty-odd rooms are tastefully furnished. ❽

Parklands Hotel 100 Banbury Rd ☎01865 /554374, Ⓔtheparklands@freenet.co.uk. Pleasant fourteen-room hotel in a Victorian house with a garden, licensed restaurant and bar. North of the centre, but connected to it by a frequent bus service. Standard and en-suite rooms offer good-value for the rate. ❺

Pine Castle Hotel 290–92 Iffley Rd ☎01865 /241497, ⒺStay@pinecastle.co.uk. Small, trim hotel in Victorian premises. ❸

Randolph Hotel 1 Beaumont St ☎0870/4008200, ⒲www.heritage-hotels.com. Certainly the most famous and probably the most overrated hotel in the city, the *Randolph* is a large brick pile that suffers from all the disadvantages of being part of a chain – its main recommendation is that it is bang in the middle of town. Scenes from the *Inspector Morse* TV series were shot here. ❽

Guest houses and B&Bs

Becket Guest House 5 Becket St ☎01865/724675. Modest but proficient bay-windowed guest house in a plain terrace close to the train station. Most rooms en suite. ❷

Brown's Guest House 281 Iffley Rd ☎01865/246822, ⒲www.brownsgh.freeserve.co.uk. Well-maintained guest house in a pleasing Victorian property with eight rooms, most of them en suite. ❸

College Guest House 103 Woodstock Rd ☎01865/552579, ⒲www.collegeguesthouse .oxfordpages.co.uk. Less than two miles north of the centre, this pleasant guest house occupies a distinctive older, high-gabled building. There are eight rooms, four en suite. ❸

Cotswold House 363 Banbury Rd ☎01865 /310558, ⒲www.house363.freeserve.co.uk. This top-notch B&B, about two miles north of the centre, occupies a bright and breezy modern brick house on the busy Banbury Road. Excellent breakfasts and comfortable, well-appointed en-suite rooms. ❹

Isis Guest House 45–53 Iffley Rd ☎01865 /248894. Large college house, just across Magdalen Bridge, open from July to September only. Good value, but spartan. ❶

Newton Guest House 82–84 Abingdon Rd ☎01865/240561, ⒺNewton.house@btinternet.com.

The most central of the south Oxford guest houses, well placed for evening strolls along the Thames. Ten rooms, none single. ❷

St Michael's Guest House 26 St Michael's St ☎01865/242101. Often full, this friendly, well-kept B&B, in a cosy three-storey terrace house, has unsurprising furnishings and fittings, but a charming, central location. A real snip at the top of this price range. ❷

Tower House 15 Ship St ☎01865/246828, Ⓦ www.scoot.co.uk/towerhouse. There's been a bit of a hatchet job on an old house here, but the central location is a plus and the eight rooms – most en suite – are comfortable enough. ❹, ❻ for en suites.

Hostels

New Oxford Youth Hostel 2A Botley Rd ☎01865/727275, Ⓔ oxford@yha.org.uk. Next door to the train station, this popular hostel has 184 beds divided up into two-, four- and six-bedded rooms. There's 24-hour access, good self-catering facilities and inexpensive prepared meals available, too. £18.

Oxford Backpackers Hostel 9A Hythe Bridge St ☎01865/721761, Ⓔ oxford@hostels.co.uk. Independent hostel with ten bunkrooms holding up to ten people each. Fully equipped kitchen, laundry, bar and internet facilities. Handy location between the train station and the centre; 24-hour access. £11.

The City

The compact centre of Oxford lies in between the Thames and the Cherwell rivers, just to the north of the point where they join. In theory, and on most maps, the Thames is known within the city as the "Isis", but few locals actually use the term. Central Oxford's principal point of reference is **Carfax**, a busy junction from where three of the city's main thoroughfares begin: the **High Street** runs east to Magdalen Bridge and the Cherwell; **St Aldate's** south to

---

On the river

Punting is a favourite summer pastime among both students and visitors, but handling a punt – a flat-bottomed boat ideal for the shallow waters of the Thames and Cherwell rivers – requires some practice. The punt is propelled and steered with a long pole, which beginners inevitably get stuck in riverbed mud: if this happens, let go and paddle back, otherwise you're likely to be pulled overboard. The Cherwell, though much narrower than the Thames and therefore trickier to navigate, provides more opportunities for pulling to the side for a picnic, an essential part of the punting experience. As regards **boat rental**, Magdalen Bridge boat house (☎01865/202643), beside the Cherwell at the east end of the High Street, is the most central spot, but in summer the queues soon build up, so either get there early in the morning – at around 10am – or head off to the Cherwell Boat House (☎01865 /515978), by Wolfson College off Banbury Road, a mile or so north of the centre. Alternatively, there's the Thames boat station at Folly Bridge (☎01993/868190), at the south end of St Aldate's, but from here you'll have to punt a fair way along a broad stretch of river before being able to turn off into the Cherwell. Expect to pay about £10 per hour for a boat plus a £30 deposit, and sometimes ID is required. Five people make an ideal group – four sitting and one punting. If you're determined not to do any actual punting, you might consider hiring a **chauffeured punt** (£25 for 30min, plus free booze). Other types of craft are also available for rent. Call the boathouses for more information or if there are any doubts about the weather.

The other boats most commonly seen on the Thames belong to the university's **rowing clubs**, which started up in the early nineteenth century, when top hats were *de rigueur*: the first Oxford versus Cambridge boat race (now staged in Putney, London) took place in 1829. Rowers mostly practise along the wide stretch of river to the south of Folly Bridge, which is also used for college races. The so-called **Torpids** are held in March and the **Eights** at the end of May – the latter are the more important and therefore attract the larger crowds.

the Thames; and **Cornmarket** north to the broad avenue of St Giles. Many of the oldest **colleges** face onto the High Street or the sidestreets adjoining it, their mellow stonework combining to create one of the most beautiful parts of Oxford. Here, as elsewhere in the city, all of the more visited colleges have restricted opening hours to enable them to control the flow of tourists, and some impose an admission charge, too, while others permit no regular public access at all. Of those that do open their doors, **opening times** are fairly consistent throughout the year, but there are sporadic term-time variations, especially at weekends. It's also worth noting that during the exam season, which stretches from late April to early June, all the colleges have periods when they are closed to the public. For more specific information, call the relevant college – the **phone numbers** are given in the text below.

From the Carfax to University College

Too busy to be comfortable and too modern to be pretty, the **Carfax** is not a place to hang around, but it is overlooked by an interesting remnant of the medieval town, a chunky fourteenth-century **tower**, adorned by a pair of clock-tower jacks dressed in vaguely Roman gear. The tower is all that remains of St Martin's church, where legend has it that William Shakespeare stood sponsor at the baptism of one of his friend's children. You can climb the **tower** (daily: April–Oct 10am–5.30pm; Nov–March 10am–3.30pm; £1.20) for wide views over the centre, though other vantage points have the edge.

As you stroll east along the High Street from Carfax, the first building to demand your attention is **St Mary the Virgin** – on the left just after Brasenose College. The church is a hotchpotch of architectural styles, mostly fifteenth century, but with an elaborate, thirteenth-century pinnacled spire and a distinctive Baroque porch, flanked by chunky corkscrewed pillars – and paid for by one of Archbishop Laud's friends in 1637. Curiously, the House of Commons cited the porch when they tried Laud, the Archbishop of Canterbury and religious adviser to Charles I, for high treason in 1640, the objection being that the porch was idolatrous or at least too "Catholic". The real beef was Laud's sustained persecution of the Puritans and, although the trial dragged on and on, he was finally executed at the height of the Civil War in 1644. The church's interior is disappointingly mundane, but the **tower** (daily: July & Aug 9am–7pm; rest of year closes 5pm; £1.60) – entered round the back opposite the Radcliffe Camera (see p.340) – provides exquisite views over the centre.

Further along the High Street, beyond the south entrance to All Souls (see p.340), lies **Queen's College** (no set opening times; ☎01865/279120), whose handsome Baroque buildings cut an impressive dash. The only Oxford college to have been built in one period (1682–1765), Queen's benefited from the skills of several talented architects, most notably Nicholas Hawksmoor and Christopher Wren. Wren designed (or at least influenced the design of) the college's most diverting building, the **Chapel**, whose ceiling is filled with cherubs amidst dense foliage.

Across the High Street from Queen's is **University College** (no set opening times; ☎01865/276602), where the long curved facade and twin gateway towers date from the seventeenth century. Known as "Univ", the college claims Alfred the Great as its founder, but things really got going with a formal endowment in 1249, making it Oxford's oldest college – though nothing of that period survives. A year Univ may prefer to forget is 1811, when it expelled **Percy Bysshe Shelley** for distributing a paper called *The Necessity of Atheism*. Guilt later induced Univ to accept a memorial to the poet, who drowned in

Italy in 1822: the white marble monument, showing the limp body of the poet borne by winged lions and mourned by the Muse of Poetry, occupies a shrine-like domed chamber in the northeast corner of the Front Quad. The college's most famous recent alumnus was Bill Clinton, the non-inhaling Rhodes Scholar; former Australian premier Bob Hawke also studied here.

Merton College

At the east end of the University College, narrow Logic Lane threads through to **Merton College** (Mon–Fri 2–4pm, Sat & Sun 10am–4pm; free; ☎01865/276310), historically the city's most important college. Balliol and University colleges may have been founded earlier, but it was Merton – opened in 1264 – which set the model for colleges in both Oxford and Cambridge, being the first to gather its students and tutors together in one place. Furthermore, unlike the other two, Merton retains some of its original medieval buildings with the best of the thirteenth-century architecture clustering around **Mob Quad**, a charming courtyard with mullioned windows and Gothic doorways. The quad's **Library** is of interest too, built in the 1370s and the first library in England to store books upright on shelves as distinct from in piles. Much of the woodwork, including the panelling, screens and bookcases, dates from the Tudor period, but some fittings are original and there's a small display on one of the college's most distinguished alumni, Max Beerbohm. The adjacent **Chapel** is earlier, dating from 1290, and has never had a nave, leaving the transepts as ante-chapels in which a curious monument shows Thomas Bodley (founder of Oxford's most important library) surrounded by masculine-looking women in classical garb. The windows of the choir were donated by Henry de Mamesfeld, an egocentric who appears as a kneeling figure no less than 24 times.

Other famous Merton alumni include T.S. Eliot, Angus Wilson, Louis MacNeice and Kris Kristofferson.

Magdalen College and around

Doubling back to the High Street, it's a short walk east to **Magdalen College** (pronounced "Maudlin"; Mon–Fri noon–6pm, Sat & Sun 2–6pm; £2; ☎01865/276000), dominated by its chunky medieval bell tower. The college is entered via a grand Victorian gateway, just beyond which is the **Chapel**, which has a handsome reredos – though you have to admire it from a distance, from behind a stone screen. The adjacent **cloisters**, arguably the finest in Oxford, are adorned by standing figures, some of which are biblical and others folkloric – most notably the cacophony of bizarre grotesques. Magdalen also boasts better **grounds** than most other colleges, with a bridge – at the back of the cloisters – spanning the River Cherwell to join **Addison's Walk**, which you can follow along the river and around a water meadow; rare wild fritillaries flower there in spring. Magdalen has a fine choir, whose annual duties include singing madrigals from the top of the bell tower at 6am on May 1. Pubs open especially for this May Day event and the din made by drunken students often drowns out the singing. Magdalen's alumni include Oscar Wilde, C.S. Lewis, John Betjeman, Julian Barnes, A.J.P. Taylor and Dudley Moore.

Just beyond the college, you can rent punts at **Magdalen Bridge** (see box, p.335); opposite, on the other side of High Street, are the **Botanic Gardens** (daily: April–Sept 9am–5pm; Oct–March 9am–4.30pm; glasshouses April–Sept 10am–4.30pm; Oct–March 2–4pm; £2), bounded by a graceful curve of the Cherwell. First planted in 1621, the gardens are on the site of a medieval Jewish cemetery and predate all others in the country.

New College

Retracing your steps back along the High Street to Queen's, cut up **Queen's Lane** and you'll dog-leg your way north to **New College** (daily: April–Oct 11am–5pm; Nov–March 2–4pm; £2, free in winter; ✆01865/279555). Founded in 1379, the college has splendid Perpendicular Gothic architecture in its **Front Quad**, even if the addition of an extra storey in 1674 spoiled the overall effect. The **Chapel** has been mucked about, too, yet it can still lay claim to being the finest in Oxford, not so much for its design as its contents. The ante-chapel contains some superb fourteenth-century stained glass and the west window – of 1778 – holds an intriguing (if somewhat unsuccessful) Nativity scene based on a design by Sir Joshua Reynolds. Beneath it, shoved up against the wall, stands the wonderful *Lazarus* by Jacob Epstein – Khrushchev, after a visit to the college, claimed that the memory of this haunting sculpture kept him awake at night. The entire east wall of the main chapel is occupied by a magnificent nineteenth-century stone reredos, consisting of about fifty canopied figures, mostly saints and apostles, with Christ for a centrepiece. Notable New College alumni include the Labour Party leader Hugh Gaitskell, Tony Benn and the author John Fowles.

An archway on the east side of the Front Quad leads through to the grounds, a pleasant lawn skirted by the best-preserved part of the thirteenth-century **city walls**. You can leave the college either through the north entrance into Holywell Street, or back the way you came and into New College Lane. Both are close to the east end of Broad Street.

The Sheldonian Theatre and the Bodleian Library

The east end of Broad Street abuts some of Oxford's most monumental architecture, beginning with the **Sheldonian Theatre** (Mon–Sat 10am–12.30pm & 2–4.30pm; winter closes 3.30pm; ✆01865/277299; £1.50), ringed by a series of glum-looking, pop-eyed classical heads. The Sheldonian was Christopher Wren's first major work, a reworking of the Theatre of Marcellus in Rome, semi-circular at the back and rectangular at the front. It was conceived in 1663, when the 31-year-old Wren's main job was as professor of astronomy. Designed as a stage for university ceremonies, nowadays it also functions as a concert hall, but the interior, painted in gold and a dull brown, lacks any sense of drama, and even the views from the cupola are disappointing.

Wren's colleague, Nicholas Hawksmoor, designed the **Clarendon Building**, a domineering, solidly symmetrical edifice topped by allegorical figures that is set at right angles to – and lies immediately east of – the Sheldonian. The Clarendon was built to house the University Press, but is now part of the **Bodleian Library** – the UK's largest after the British Library in London – which has an estimated eighty miles of shelves distributed among various buildings. The heart of the Bodleian is located straight across from the Clarendon in the **Old Library**, which inhabits the beautifully proportioned **Old Schools Quadrangle**, built in the early seventeenth-century in the ornate Jacobean-Gothic style that distinguishes many of the city's finest buildings. On the quad's east side is the handsome **Tower of the Five Orders**, which gives a lesson in architectural design, with tiers of columns built according to the five classical styles – Tuscan, Doric, Ionic, Corinthian and Composite. On the west side is the library's main entrance and, although most of the complex is out of bounds to the general public, you can pop into the **Divinity School** (Mon–Fri 9am–5pm, Sat 9am–12.30pm; free), one large room where, until the nineteenth century, degree candidates were questioned in detail about their subject by two interlocutors, with a professor acting as

△ Radcliffe Camera, Oxford

umpire. Begun in 1424, and sixty years in the making, the Divinity School boasts an extravagant vaulted ceiling, a riot of pendants and decorative bosses that comprises an exquisite example of late Gothic architecture. However, this elaborate design was never carried right through – funding was a constant problem – and parts of the school were finished off in a much plainer style with the change being especially pronounced on the south wall.

You can also sign up for an hour-long **guided tour** (March–Oct Mon–Fri 10.30am, 11.30am, 2pm & 3pm, Sat 10.30am & 11.30am; £3.50) of **Convocation House**, adjacent to the Divinity School, and **Duke Humfrey's Library**, immediately above. The former is a sombre wood-panelled chamber graced by a fancy fan-vaulted ceiling, completed in 1759 but designed to look much older, while the latter is distinguished by its painted beams and carved corbels, dating from the fifteenth century, but restored and remodelled by Thomas Bodley at the turn of the seventeenth century.

Behind the Old Schools Quadrangle rises Oxford's most imposing – or vainglorious – building, the Bodleian's **Radcliffe Camera** (formerly the Radcliffe Library; no public access), a mighty rotunda, built between 1737 and 1748 by James Gibbs, architect of London's St Martin-in-the-Fields church. There's no false modesty here. Dr John Radcliffe was, according to a contemporary diarist, "very ambitious of glory" and when he died in 1714 he bequeathed a whopping chunk of money for the construction of a library – the "Radcliffe Mausoleum" as one wag termed it. Gibbs was one of the few British architects of the period to have been trained in Rome and his rotunda was thoroughly Italian in style, its limestone columns ascending to a delicate balustrade, decorated with pin-prick urns and encircling a lead-sheathed dome. For a less overpowering perspective, climb the tower of the church of **St Mary the Virgin** (daily: July & Aug 9am–7pm; rest of year 9am–5pm; £1.60) to the rear of the rotunda. The views can't be bettered, both across to the rotunda and east over **All Souls College** (Mon–Fri 2–4.30pm; free; ☏01865/279379), with its twin mock-Gothic towers (the work of Hawksmoor) and a coloured sundial designed by Wren.

Trinity, Balliol and Exeter colleges

Back on Broad Street, the classical heads that shield the Sheldonian continue along the front of the modest **History of Science Museum** (Tues–Sat noon–4pm; free), where microscopes and early calculators are immaculately displayed alongside Islamic and European astrolabes. Across the street, **Trinity College** (daily 10.30am–noon & 2–4pm; £2; ☏01865/279900) sits back from the road behind trim gardens, its attractive ensemble of old stone buildings begun at the end of the seventeenth century. The expansive **Front Quad** holds the college's architectural pride and joy, its **Chapel**, where Grinling Gibbons did some of his finest carving – a distinctive performance, with cherubs' heads peering out from delicate foliage. Recent alumni include Richard Burton, Terence Rattigan and the Labour Party politician, Anthony Crosland.

Next door, **Balliol College** (term-time daily 2–5pm; free; ☏01865/277777) is Trinity's arch rival, the collegiate antipathy ritualized in the tradition of Gordouli, when Balliol students chant abuse at their adversaries across the wall, usually at unsociable hours of the night. It's historically appropriate: the college was founded in the 1260s by the Balliol family of Scotland as a penance after one of the clan had insulted the Bishop of Durham. Nevertheless, despite its antiquity, Balliol has little to offer: remodelled and rebuilt in the nineteenth century, it now presents an unexceptional assembly of buildings, haphazardly gathered around two quads. Amongst many notable alumni are Adam Smith,

Hilaire Belloc, Graham Greene and Aldous Huxley, plus a raft of politicians, including Harold Macmillan, Edward Heath, Denis Healey and Roy Jenkins.

From the south side of Broad Street, take Turl Street and you'll soon reach the entrance to **Exeter College** (daily: term-time 2–5pm; otherwise 10am–5pm; free; ☎01865/279600), another medieval foundation whose original buildings were chopped about in the nineteenth century. On this occasion, however, the Victorians did create something of interest in the elaborate, neo-Gothic **Chapel**, whose intricate, almost fussy detail was conceived by Sir Gilbert Scott in the 1850s. The chapel contains a superb Pre-Raphaelite tapestry, the *Adoration of the Magi*, a fine collaboration between William Morris and Edward Burne-Jones. Morris and Burne-Jones were both students here, as were J.R.R. Tolkien, Alan Bennett and Imogen Stubbs.

Near the west end of Broad Street, the **Oxford Story** (daily: April–June, Sept & Oct 9.30am–5pm; July & Aug 9.30am–5.30pm; Nov–March Mon–Fri 10am–4.30pm, Sat & Sun 10am–5pm; £6) is a purpose-built tourist attraction devoted to the history of the city and its university. It begins with an audio-visual display on university life and thereafter you hop on a "time-car", which moves through a series of historical dioramas; the same people designed the Jorvik Viking Centre in York (see p.947).

Cornmarket and the Oxford Union

Broad Street leads into the pedestrianized **Cornmarket**, a busy shopping strip lined by major stores. There's precious little here to fire the imagination, but **St Michael's Street** – the first turning on the right – is a pleasant residential street and the location of the **Oxford Union** (no public access), which occupies an inconsequential Victorian pile that belies its political importance. The Union is home to the university debating society, where scores of budding British politicians have flexed their oratorical muscles. The Union has also hosted a mixed bag of internationally famous celebrity speakers in recent years, among them Yasser Arafat, Archbishop Desmond Tutu, Ronald Reagan, Mother Theresa and Diego Maradona. The original debating hall, shaped rather like an upturned boat and now the union library, is decorated with Pre-Raphaelite murals illustrating the Arthurian legend, created (but never completed) in the 1850s by William Morris, Rossetti, Burne-Jones and a few like-minded friends. The position of the windows between the badly faded panels makes a full appreciation of the murals difficult, but they remain a fascinating oddity.

South from Carfax and Christ Church College

Spreading down St Aldates from the Carfax, Oxford's **Town Hall** is an ostentatious Victorian confection that reflects a municipal determination not to be overwhelmed by the university. A staircase on its south side gives access to the **Museum of Oxford** (Tues–Fri 10am–4pm, Sat 10am–5pm, Sun noon–4pm; £1.50), which makes good use of photographs to tell the history of the city. In the face of tough competition this museum often gets ignored, but you'll discover far more here than at the "Oxford Story" in Broad Street.

Just down from the museum, the Tom Tower, added by Christopher Wren to house the weighty "Great Tom" bell in 1681, marks the main entrance to **Christ Church College** (Mon–Sat 9.30am–5.30pm, Sun 11.30am–5.30pm; £4; ☎01865/276492), Oxford's largest, most prestigious and – some would say – most pretentious college. Albert Einstein, William Gladstone and no fewer than twelve other British prime ministers were educated here, and it claims the distinction of having been founded three times, firstly by Cardinal Wolsey in

1525, then by Henry VIII after the cardinal's fall from favour and finally, after the Reformation – when the second college was suppressed – in 1545, when it assumed its present name. Beyond the main entrance is the striking **Tom Quad**, the largest quad in Oxford, so large in fact that the Royalists penned up their mobile larder of cattle here during the Civil War. The Quad's soft, honey-coloured stone makes a harmonious whole, but it was built in two main phases with the southern side dating back to Wolsey, the north finally finished in the 1660s. A staircase in the southeast corner of the quad reaches the **dining hall**, the grandest refectory in Oxford with a fanciful hammer-beam roof and a set of stern portraits of past scholars by a roll-call of well-known artists, including Reynolds, Gainsborough and Millais. Charles I held court here when the Parliamentarians were in control of London and, in one of those snippets of information beloved of academics, Lewis Carroll, former student and author of *Alice's Adventures in Wonderland*, ate eight thousand meals here. A passage at the northeast corner of the Tom Quad leads through to the **Peckwater Quad**, the site of the library, and from here you can pass through to the **Canterbury Quad**, where the **Picture Gallery** provides a pokey home for works by many of Italy's finest artists, from the fifteenth to eighteenth centuries, including Leonardo da Vinci and Michelangelo.

To the rear of the Tom Quad stands the **Cathedral**, which is also – in a most unusual arrangement – the college chapel. The site was originally occupied by the Anglo-Saxon church of St Frideswide Priory, but this disappeared long ago and the present structure is essentially Norman, though it has been hacked at – Wolsey destroyed part of the west end to make space for the Tom Quad and Sir Gilbert Scott made further alterations in 1870. The Norman legacy is most apparent in the choir, where massive Norman columns rise to delicate fif-teenth-century stone vaulting. Much fine medieval carving and several impres-sive tombs have also survived here. The shrine of St Frideswide, by the Lady Chapel, had to be rebuilt following its destruction during the Dissolution, but it retains the first known example of natural foliage in English sculpture, a splendid confection of leaves dating from around 1290. A window in the adja-cent Latin Chapel depicts the life of the saint, an early work by Pre-Raphaelite luminary Edward Burne-Jones – and one of several windows he completed in the choir.

Leaving Christ Church by the south entrance, you emerge at the top of **Christ Church Meadow**, which fills in the tapering gap between the rivers Cherwell and Thames. Head east along Broad Walk for the Cherwell or keep straight down tree-lined (and more appealing) New Walk for the Thames. Alternatively, if you stroll west, past the tiny War Memorial Garden, you quick-ly return to St Aldates and the **Bate Collection** (Mon–Fri 2–5pm; free), which contains England's most comprehensive collection of European wood-wind instruments. Though only music buffs will make sense of some of the explanatory notes, you don't have to be an expert to enjoy the collection. In addition to rows of flutes and clarinets, there are all sorts of other instruments on show, from medieval crumhorns, looking like rejected walking sticks, to the country's finest example of a gamelan.

Finally, back towards the Carfax and off to the left along Pembroke Street, the **Museum of Modern Art** or MOMA (Tues–Sun 11am–6pm, till 9pm on Thurs; sometimes closed between exhibitions, call ☎01865/722733; £2.50, free till 1pm on Wed & from 6pm on Thurs) is always worth checking out. The gallery has an excellent programme of temporary exhibitions, featuring inter-national contemporary art in a wide variety of media; the basement café serves good vegetarian food, too.

The Ashmolean

The university's principal museums grew up around the collections of the magpie-like **John Tradescant**, gardener to Charles I and an energetic traveller. During his wanderings, Tradescant built up a huge collection of artefacts and natural specimens, which became known as Tradescant's Ark. He bequeathed his collection to his friend and sponsor, the lawyer Elias Ashmole, who in turn gave it to the university – and they eventually split it up between the Ashmolean and the Pitt-Rivers museums. Tradescant's Ark has been added to ever since.

The **Ashmolean** (June–Aug Tues, Wed, Fri & Sat 10am–5pm, Thurs 10am–7pm, Sun noon–5pm; rest of year Tues–Sat 10am–5pm, Sun 2–5pm; free), the oldest museum in the country, occupies a mammoth Neoclassical building to the north of the centre on the corner of Beaumont Street and St Giles. The building is enormous and so is the collection – far too much to absorb in one visit, so either allow for several or stick to the highlights. Plans are available at reception and the museum shop sells a useful introductory guide for £3.95. Beginning on the ground floor, the **Egyptian** rooms should not be missed: in addition to well-preserved mummies and sarcophagi, there are unusual frescoes, rare textiles from the Roman and Byzantine periods and several fine examples of relief carving, such as on the shrine of Taharqa. Nearby, the **Islamic Art** room includes superb Islamic ceramics, while the five **Chinese Art** rooms contain some remarkable early Chinese pottery with the simple monochrome pots of the Sung dynasty (960–1279) looking surprisingly modern.

On the First Floor, a selection from Tradescant's Ark is gathered together in **Room 27**. Amongst the assorted curiosities, highlights include Guy Fawkes' lantern, Oliver Cromwell's death mask and Powhatan's mantle, a hanging made of deerskin and decorated with shells. Powhatan was the father of Pocahontas, and this mantle dates back to the earliest contacts between English colonists and the Native Americans of modern-day Virginia. Moving on, the archeologist Arthur Evans had close ties with the museum and he gifted it a stunning collection of Minoan finds from his years working at Knossos in Crete (1900–06). These artefacts are displayed in the **Crete & Aegean Room** and pride of place goes to the storage jars, sumptuously decorated with sea creatures and marine plants. Close by, in **Room 35**, is the extraordinary Alfred Jewel, a delicate gold, enamel and rock crystal piece of uncertain purpose. The inscription reads "Alfred ordered me to be made" – almost certainly a reference to King Alfred the Great.

Most of the rest of the first floor is devoted to European painting from the Italian Renaissance to the twentieth century with a series of clearly labelled galleries arranged in roughly chronological order. Amongst the **Italian** works, look out for Piero di Cosimo's *Forest Fire* and Paolo Uccello's *Hunt in the Forest*, though Tintoretto, Veronese and Bellini are all well represented too. There's also a strong showing of **French paintings**, with Pissarro, Monet, Manet and Renoir featuring alongside Cézanne and Bonnard. Part of the Ashmolean's hoard of prints is on display in the **Prints & Drawings Room** with Michelangelo and Raphael taking the lead.

Up on the second floor, one room each is devoted to eighteenth- and nineteenth-century **British art**: Samuel Palmer's visionary paintings run rings around the rest, though there's lashings of Pre-Raphaelite stuff from Rossetti and Holman Hunt to assorted cohorts.

St John's College and onto the University and Pitt-Rivers museums

Across St Giles from the Ashmolean, the sturdy stone walls of **St John's College** (daily 1–5pm; ☎01865/277300; free) shield four immaculate quads. The first – the Front Quad – is the oldest, but the second – the **Canterbury Quad** – is the most enjoyable, decorated with Baroque gargoyles and dainty statues of Charles I and his wife, Henrietta Maria.

Back outside, it's a brief walk up St Giles to the *Lamb & Flag* pub, beside which an alley cuts through to Parks Road and the **University Museum of Natural History** (Mon–Sat noon–5pm; free), opposite the mottled brick facade of Keble College. The building, constructed under the guidance of John Ruskin, looks more like a cross between a railway station and a church than a museum and the same applies inside, where a high Victorian–Gothic fusion of cast iron and glass features soaring columns and capitals decorated with animal and plant motifs.

Exhibits include a working beehive and some impressive fossil dinosaurs, though the museum's natural history displays are outdone by the **Pitt-Rivers Museum** (Mon–Sat 1–4.30pm; free), reached through a door at the far end. Founded in 1884 from the bequest of grenadier guard turned archeologist Augustus Henry Lane Fox Pitt-Rivers, this is one of the world's finest ethnographic museums and an extraordinary relic of the Victorian age, arranged like an exotic junk shop with each bulging cabinet labelled meticulously by hand. The exhibits, brought to England by several explorers, Captain Cook among them, range from totem poles and mummified crocodiles to African fetishes and gruesome shrunken heads from Ecuador.

Eating and drinking

With so many students and tourists to cater for, Oxford has developed a wide choice of places to eat and drink. For a midday bite, the numerous **sandwich bars** are ideal – some of the best are listed below and you'll find several others in the Covered Market, between the High and Cornmarket, an Oxford institution as essential to local shoppers as the Bodleian is to academics. There's also a sprinkling of first-rate (and pricey) **restaurants**, but the majority cater for the less expensive end of the market with varying degrees of success – again some of the better options are listed below. Reasonable food is served at most **pubs**, but those listed have been singled out for their ambience or selection of beers rather than for their menus.

Snacks and cafés

Beat Café Little Clarendon St. Hippified café with fancy decor and stained-glass windows. Sells a good line in inexpensive sandwiches, salads and smoothies.

Café Coco 23 Cowley Rd. American-style brasserie offering a wide selection of aperitifs and shorts plus delicious coffee. The food is mainly Mediterranean and a tad pricey, but the service is slick and the atmosphere lively.

Café Rico Gloucester Green. Footsteps from the bus station, this modern, chrome-decorated place doesn't look especially enticing, but the sandwiches and soups are tasty and fresh. Pavement terrace too.

Convocation Coffee House Radcliffe Square. Attached to the church of St Mary the Virgin, this inexpensive café occupies an atmospheric stone-vaulted room and serves up good quality coffee and cake and quiche-and-salad lunches. There's a small outside area, but it's more than a little glum. Daily 10am–5pm. No smoking.

Felson's 32 Little Clarendon St. Another hot contender for Oxford's best sandwich bar, this tiny, friendly place has a huge range of fillings for its baguettes and rolls.

George & Davies Little Clarendon St. An established ice-cream parlour that stays open well after the pubs and cinemas. The cow mural is good fun too.

Heroes 8 Ship St. Sandwich bar with some of the best (and most adventurous) fillings in town.

News Café 1 Ship St. Breakfasts, bagels and daily specials offered here, plus beers and wines and, as the name suggests, newspapers and TVs tuned to news broadcasts. Open daily 9am–9pm.

Nosebag 6 St Michael's St. A civilized but unassuming place, with chintzy decor and classical background music. The hot and cold food attracts queues at lunchtime; not so in the evening, when it is a good place for a quick but wholesome meal. Good selection of veggie food. Open till 9pm.

St Giles' Café 52 St Giles. Oxford's favourite greasy spoon. The huge fry-ups and strong coffee pull an interesting mix of people, including the poet Elizabeth Jennings, who is said to be a regular here.

Restaurants

Aziz 228–230 Cowley Rd ☎01865/798033. Spacious and brightly decorated Bangladeshi restaurant, with bamboo furniture and rugs. The food's delicious and they do an exceptional range of vegetarian dishes. Reservations recommended at weekends. Inexpensive.

Bangkok House 42a Hythe Bridge St ☎01865/200705. Best Oriental restaurant in town, with superb Thai food and excellent service. The mixed starter and the coconut-milk curries are particularly good. Closed Sun & Mon lunch. Moderate.

Browns 5–11 Woodstock Rd ☎01865/319600. Buzzing and stylish brasserie-restaurant with abundant foliage. Main courses from hamburgers to fresh salmon, in addition to legendary Guinness pies. Open for breakfast. Moderate.

La Capannina 247 Cowley Rd ☎01865/248200. Oxford's most authentic Italian is cosy and unpretentious. A mile or so up the Cowley Road, it's easy to find thanks to the extravagant mock-log-cabin facade. Inexpensive.

Cherwell Boathouse Bardwell Rd, off Banbury Rd ☎01865/552746. A deservedly popular spot for an unhurried meal at a riverside setting, about a mile north of town. Closed Mon & Tues, plus Sun eve. Reservations essential. Moderate.

Gee's Restaurant 61A Banbury Rd ☎01865/553540. Chic conservatory setting, but not as expensive as it looks. The inventive menu includes such items as chargrilled vegetables with polenta, roasted beetroot, a variety of steaks and a wide choice of breads. Strong on fish, too, with seafood main courses for around £14. Open daily for lunch and dinner plus brunch at weekends. Moderate.

Hilos Jamaican Eating House 68 Cowley Rd ☎01865/725984. Legendary West Indian restaurant with oodles of atmosphere and imported Jamaican beer; the menu's meat-oriented (curried goat often features), the lighting low and the background music heavy reggae. Moderate.

Le Petit Blanc 71–72 Walton St ☎01865/510999. Renowned French chef Raymond Blanc's affordable, and much hyped, alternative to his famous *Manoir aux Quat' Saisons* in Great Milton, some seven miles east of Oxford (☎01844/278881). The food is a refreshing mix of French gourmet (corn-fed quail with lime leaf and ginger) and traditional English (pan-fried Gloucester old spot pork). If you want to splash out, this is the place to do it – main courses are a very reasonable £12–15. Expensive.

Pizza Express, 8 Golden Cross, Cornmarket ☎01865/790442. In an imaginatively renovated Tudor building, this reliable chain offers the best-value pizzas in central Oxford. Expect a long wait at weekends. Inexpensive.

Pubs and bars

Eagle & Child 49 St Giles. Known variously as the "Bird & Baby", "Bird & Brat" or "Bird & Bastard", this pub was once the haunt of J.R.R. Tolkien and C.S. Lewis, and still attracts a comparatively genteel mix of professionals and academics.

Isis by Iffley Lock ☎01865/242466. Lovely spot amid the flood meadows, just under two miles' walk southeast along the Thames from Folly Bridge; definitely a summer pub. Take any bus running along the Abingdon Road to Donnington Bridge, from where it's a ten-minute walk south along the river.

King's Arms 40 Holywell St. Prone to student overkill on term-time weekends, but otherwise very pleasant, with snug rooms at the back and a good choice of beers.

Lamb & Flag St Giles. Generations of university students have hung out in this old pub, which comes complete with low-beamed ceilings and a series of cramped but cosy rooms. Good range of ales.

The Turf Bath Place, off Holywell St. Small, extraordinarily atmospheric seventeenth-century pub with a fine range of beers, and mulled wine in winter. Abundant seating outside.

White Horse 52 Broad St. A tiny, old pub with snug rooms, pictures of old university sports teams on the walls and Real Ales. It was used as a set for the *Inspector Morse* TV series.

Entertainment and nightlife

Having spawned both Supergrass and Radiohead, you'd think Oxford would be hot on popular music, but the star quality of its local heroes is not reflected in either the **live-music** or **club scene** which, aside from a couple of noteworthy venues, is comparatively lame. Part of the reason for this is that the city's students tend to fall back on college discos, an option closed to the rest. By comparison, devotees of **classical music** are well catered for, with the city's main concert halls and certain college chapels – primarily Christ Church, Merton and New College – offering a wide-ranging programme of concerts and recitals. As regards **theatre**, student productions dominate the city repertoire, but the quality of acting varies, particularly when they tackle Shakespeare, the favourite for the open-air college productions put on for tourists during the summer.

For **listings** of upcoming gigs and concerts, consult either *This Month in Oxford* or *WOW*, a glossy listings magazine. Both are available free at the tourist office. The Friday edition of the *Oxford Times* has a listings section too. **Tickets** to most musical events are on sale at the Oxford Playhouse (see below).

Live music and clubs

The Coven Oxpens Rd ☎01865/242770. Formerly a gay disco, but now gone more or less straight. Tacky grottoes for tête-à-têtes, but generally a good atmosphere and decent music with techno/acid/hard house featuring prominently. Open Tues–Sat 9pm–2am.

Freud Walton St ☎01865/311171. Occupying a grand building in the style of a Roman temple, this new and fashionable café-bar-cum-club serves food till 8pm. Frequent live music. About five minutes' walk north of Worcester College – opposite Great Clarendon St. Open Mon & Tues 11am–midnight, Wed–Sat 11am–2am.

Old Fire Station (OFS) 40 George St ☎01865 /794494. Multi-purpose venue with musicals and theatre, plus DJ club nights Fri & Sat 9pm–3am.
Park End Club Cantay House, 37 Park End St ☎01865/250181. A slick outfit, currently the most popular mainstream club in Oxford, with heavies on the door and a cattle-market atmosphere at weekends. Open Mon, Wed & Thurs–Sat 9.30pm–2am.
Zodiac 190 Cowley Rd ☎01865/420042. Far and away Oxford's most respected indie and dance venue, with live bands throughout the week. Open Mon–Sat 9pm–2am.

Classical music and theatre

Apollo George St ☎0870/6063500, ⊛www .oxford-apollo.co.uk. Known locally as the "Appalling", but the UK's top opera and ballet companies occasionally break up the monotonous programme of ageing pop acts and pantomimes.
Holywell Music Room 32 Holywell St ☎01865 /276125, outside term tim, call ☎01865/277579. This small, plain, Georgian building was opened in 1748 as the first public music hall in England. Haydn once conducted here. It has a varied programme, from straight classical to experimental, with occasional jazz.

Oxford Playhouse Beaumont St ☎01865/798600, ⊛www.oxfordplayhouse.co.uk. The city's best theatre. Professional touring companies perform a mixture of plays, opera and concerts, with the odd production by Oxford University Dramatic Society (OUDS), the top student group.
Pegasus Theatre Magdalen Rd ☎01865/722851, ⊛www.pegasustheatre.org.uk. Low-budget, avant-garde productions dominate the programme of this east Oxford theatre.
Sheldonian Theatre Broad St ☎01865/277299. Hard seats and less-than-perfect acoustics, but still Oxford's top concert hall.

Listings

Banks and exchanges All the major banks have branches on or near Cornmarket.
Bike rental Bikezone, 6 Lincoln House, Market St, off Cornmarket ☎01865/728877.

Books Blackwells Map & Travel Shop, Broad St ☎01865/792792; Borders, Magdalen St ☎01865 /203901; Waterstones, Broad St ☎01865 /790212.

Buses Fast and frequent buses to London are operated by Oxford Tube, a subsidiary of Stagecoach (☎01865/772250), who also run most medium-range services across Oxfordshire. Most urban routes – including Park-and-Ride schemes – are operated by the Oxford Bus Company (☎01865/785400), who also offer a frequent service to London. Most other long-distance services are in the hands of National Express (☎08705/808080).

Car rental Avis, 1 Abbey Rd ☎01865/249000; Hertz, at Hartwells, Wolvercote Roundabout, Woodstock Rd ☎01865/319972; National Car Rental, 2 Dawson St, bottom of Cowley Rd ☎01865/240471.

Cinema The ABC cinemas on Magdalen Street and George Street (both ☎01865/251998) show the latest blockbusters, while the best arts cinema is the Ultimate Picture Palace (UPP) on Jeune St, off Cowley Rd (☎01865/245288). The Phoenix on Walton Street (☎01865/512526) shows mainstream and arts films, and regularly screens foreign-language films.

Hospital John Radcliffe Hospital, Headley Way, Headington ☎01865/741166. It's a couple of miles east of the centre – take St Clements Street from the roundabout just east of the Magdalen Bridge and keep going.

Internet Internet Exchange Café, Costa Coffee, 8–12 George St ☎01865/241601; Wired to, 138 Magdalen St ☎01865/727770.

Pharmacies Boots, 6 Cornmarket ☎01865/247461.

Police St Aldate's ☎01865/266000.

Post Office 102 St Aldate's ☎0345/223344.

Taxis Ranks are liberally distributed across the city centre, including at the train station, Broad St, High St and St Giles. Alternatively, call City Taxis ☎01865/201201 or 001 Taxis ☎01865/240000.

Around Oxford

As a base for exploring some of the most delightful parts of central England, Oxford is hard to beat. It's a short drive west to the Cotswolds (see pp.363–383) and near at hand also are the Vale of White Horse (see p.328) and the Chiltern Hills (see pp.323–327). If, on the other hand, you're using public transport, the options are much more limited, the best choice being the short and easy bus ride north to the charming little town of **Woodstock** and its imperious neighbour, **Blenheim Palace**.

Woodstock

WOODSTOCK, eight miles north of Oxford, has royal associations going back to Saxon times, with a string of kings attracted by its excellent hunting. Henry I built a royal lodge here and his successor, Henry II, enlarged it to create a grand manor house-cum-palace, where, incidentally, the Black Prince was born in 1330. The Royalists used Woodstock as a base during the Civil War, but, after their defeat, Cromwell never got round to destroying either the town or the palace, but the latter was ultimately given to (and flattened by) the Duke of Marlborough, in 1704. Long dependent on royal and then ducal patronage, Woodstock is now both a well-heeled commuter town for Oxford and a provider of food, drink and beds for visitors to Blenheim. It is also an extremely pretty little place, its handsome stone buildings gathered around the main square, at the junction of Market and High streets. It is here that you'll find the town's one specific sight, the **Oxfordshire Museum** (Tues–Sat 10am–5pm, Sun 2–5pm; £1), a well-composed review of the archeology, social history and industry of the county.

The museum shares its premises with the town's **tourist office** (Mon–Sat 9.30am–5.30pm, Sun 1–5pm; ☎01993/813276), which has a useful range of information on the nearby Cotswolds. Woodstock has several good **pubs**, the best being the *Bear*, a delightful old coaching inn with low-beamed ceilings and antique furnishings across from the museum; it offers a varied menu and serves a good range of beers. **Buses** from Oxford run every thirty minutes or so (reduced service on Sun), with some continuing on to Stratford-upon-Avon.

Blenheim Palace

Nowadays, successful British commanders get medals and titles, but in 1704, as a thank-you for his victory over the French at the battle of Blenheim, Queen Anne gave **John Churchill, Duke of Marlborough** (1650–1722), the royal estate of Woodstock, along with the promise of enough cash to build himself a gargantuan palace. Marlborough was an exceptionally brilliant general – undoubtedly, one of Britain's all-time military greats – and this was just one of his victories. Nonetheless, the largesse shown him had more to do with the queen's fear of Louis XIV – and the relief she felt after the battle – than it did to a recognition of his genius, as events were to prove.

Work started promptly on **Blenheim Palace** (mid-March to Oct daily 10.30am–5.30pm; £9.50) with the principal architect being Sir John Vanbrugh, who was also responsible for Castle Howard in Yorkshire. All seemed set fair, but things went downhill fast. The duke's formidable wife, Sarah Jennings, who had wanted Christopher Wren as architect, was soon at logger-heads with Vanbrugh, while Queen Anne had second thoughts, stifling the flow of money. Construction work was halted and the house was only finished after the duke's death at the instigation of his widow, who ended up paying most of the bills and designing much of the interior herself. The end result is the country's grandest example of Baroque civic architecture, an Italianate palace that is more a monument than a house – which was Vanbrugh's intention.

The **interior** is stuffed with paintings and tapestries, plus all manner of *objets d'art*, including furniture from Versailles, and stone and marble carvings by Grinling Gibbons. The ceiling of the Great Hall sports painted allegories cele-brating Marlborough's martial skills and the Dining Saloon holds murals by Louis Laguerre, but frankly it's hard to warm to all this conspicuous consump-tion. Horace Walpole, the eighteenth-century wit and social commentator, had it about right when he wrote that Blenheim resembled "the palace of an auc-tioneer who had been chosen King of Poland". Neither is the guided tour conducive to much idle rumination, with guides whisking visitors through the palace in about an hour. As for the Marlboroughs, John Churchill was one of the few members of the clan to have made anything but a poor impression, the spectacular exception being **Sir Winston Churchill**, born here in 1874. Several rooms are dedicated to the wartime prime minister, who is buried with his wife in the graveyard of **Bladon Church**, visible from the palace.

Formal **gardens** (mid-March to Oct daily 10.30am–5.30pm; entry covered by ticket to palace) flank the house, but the open **parkland** (daily 9am–4.45pm; £2, £6 for cars, including passengers) is more enticing, especial-ly just north of the house, where the ground falls away dramatically to an exquisite artificial lake, Queen Pool. It's said that Capability Brown, who land-scaped the grounds, laid out the trees and avenues to represent the battle of Blenheim. Whatever the truth of the tale, fine vistas fan out in every direction, including one from Vanbrugh's Grand Bridge, over the main lake, up to the Column of Victory, erected by Sarah Jennings and topped by a statue of her husband posing heroically in a toga.

There are two entrances to Blenheim, one just south of Woodstock on the Oxford road and another through the Triumphal Arch at the end of Park Street in Woodstock itself.

There are fast train, bus and road routes between Oxford and London, but with more time it's worth considering a slower route, following the rambling course of the **River Thames**. The first port of call is **ABINGDON**, an old market town five miles south of Oxford, which has a scattering of medieval buildings plus the splendid church of St Helen, with its expansive, four-aisle nave and fourteenth-century painted ceiling. From here, it's on to pocket-sized **DORCHESTER**, whose past importance is recalled by the medieval abbey church of St Peter and St Paul. The church's chancel is an outstanding example of the Decorated style with three soaring windows, one of which sports a splendid Jesse Tree.

Moving on, **WALLINGFORD** retains its medieval street plan and the remains of the earth ramparts that once encircled it; **GORING** marks the spot where The Ridgeway National Trail (see p.324) crosses the Thames; and **PANGBOURNE** was where Kenneth Grahame wrote *The Wind in the Willows*. Pangbourne is six miles from Reading (see p.327) and the M4, fourteen miles from Henley-on-Thames (see p.324).

North Buckinghamshire and Bedfordshire

The untidy landscapes of **north Buckinghamshire** and **Bedfordshire** herald a transition between the satellite towns of London and the Midlands. Since the war, the character of the region has been transformed by the attempt to solve London's overcrowding. Sprawling suburbs now festoon many of the small country towns of yesteryear and, in the 1960s, Milton Keynes swallowed thirteen existing villages to become the country's largest new town. Nonetheless, there are several interesting targets. North Buckinghamshire weighs in with three National Trust properties – two country houses and, pick of the bunch, **Stowe Gardens**, dotted with a remarkable assortment of outdoor sculptures and follies. Over in Bedfordshire, the county's most distinctive feature is the wriggling River Ouse, whose banks were once lined with dozens of watermills, though these were not nearly as important as the brickworks that long underpinned the local economy. For the casual visitor, the county might not warrant a major detour, but **Woburn Abbey**, a whopping country mansion, and neighbouring **Woburn Safari Park** together comprise one of the country's premier tourist attractions. In addition, **Bedford** itself deserves more than just a sideward glance, if for no other reason than for its links with John Bunyan.

As regards public transport, local **buses** link all the larger towns and there is a fast and frequent **train** service from London to Bedford and Milton Keynes.

Buckingham and around

Unassuming **BUCKINGHAM** is tucked into a sharp bend in the River Ouse about twenty-five miles northeast of Oxford. It became the county town of Buckinghamshire in the tenth century and flourished during medieval times, but it was bypassed by the Industrial Revolution and remained a forgotten backwater until a recent wave of incomers created the modern suburbs that surround it today. The town centre is at its prettiest along the wide, sloping Market Hill, standing in the middle of which is the **Old Gaol**, a chunky, stone structure that is home to the **tourist office** and a modest, local history **museum** (Mon–Sat 10am–4pm; £1.50). Otherwise, Buckingham is short on sights, though you might take a peek inside the sombre **Church of St Peter and St**

Paul, which perches on the hill where the castle once stood – take Castle Street from the west end of Market Hill and you can't miss it.

There's no train service to Buckingham, but there are **bus** links from neighbouring towns, principally Milton Keynes. Buses stop on the High Street a few yards from the **tourist office** in the Old Gaol (July & Aug Mon–Sat 10am–4pm, Sun noon–4pm; rest of year closed Sun; ℡01280/823020). They have a small supply of **B&Bs**, which they will book on your behalf, or you can target Buckingham's best **hotel**, the *Villiers*, which occupies an imaginatively modernized old inn bang in the centre of town at 3 Castle St (℡01280/822444;❼). Most of the rooms flank the courtyard to the rear of the main building and each is decorated in smart modern style. The best spot for **food** is the *Dipalee Indian Restaurant* (℡01280/813151), just along Castle Street from the hotel and with a good range of dishes; main courses average about £7.

Stowe Gardens

Just three miles northwest of Buckingham off the A422, **Stowe Gardens** (March–Oct Wed–Sun 10am–5.30pm; Dec Wed–Sun 10am–4pm; but call ahead to confirm times, ℡01280/822850; £4.60; NT) contain an extraordinary collection of outdoor sculptures, monuments and decorative buildings by some of the greatest designers and architects of the eighteenth century. They worked at the behest of the prodigiously wealthy Temple and Grenville families and later the dukes of Buckingham and Chandos. This ornamental miscellany has a partly naturalistic setting, representing one of the first breaks with the strictly formal garden tradition that had dominated Europe for decades. On display is work by Sir John Vanbrugh, James Gibbs and William Kent, and the grounds incorporate one of only three Palladian bridges in the country, as well as the "Grecian valley" that was Capability Brown's first large-scale design. The curious obelisk surmounted by a monkey that stands on an island in the middle of the Octagonal Lake is a monument to the dramatist William Congreve, erected in 1736 by William Kent.

At the heart of the gardens, the main **house** (£3) is also open to the public, but much less frequently as it is occupied by Stowe school.

Claydon House and Waddesdon Manor

The plain Neoclassical facade of **Claydon House** (April–Oct Mon–Wed, Sat & Sun 1–5pm; £4.30; NT), five miles south of Buckingham in tiny Middle Claydon, conceals an exuberant, stunningly persuasive Rococo interior, commissioned in the middle of the eighteenth century by the second earl Verney. The intricacy of the woodcarving peaks in the Chinese rooms, probably the finest example of chinoiserie in Britain with the delicate ornamentation dripping like icing.

Heading south from Claydon House, a network of obscure country lanes eventually reaches the A41 at Waddesdon, on the southern edge of which is the extraordinarily flashy **Waddesdon Manor** (April–Oct Wed–Sun 11am–4pm; house £7 timed ticket, grounds £3; NT). From 1874 to 1889, minions of Baron Ferdinand de Rothschild laboured to transform this dreary slice of Buckinghamshire into a palatial country estate, with the main house built in the style of a French chateau. The end result is too pompous for many tastes, but there's no denying the magnificence of the contents. The interior holds a vast collection of French eighteenth-century decorative arts including Savonnerie carpets, some of the finest examples of Sèvres porcelain in England, Beauvais tapestries and furniture once owned by the French royal family. There are also paintings by early Dutch and Flemish masters and portraits by major English artists including Gainsborough and Reynolds. The extravagance is overwhelming – even the cast-iron aviary in the **grounds** (March–Dec Wed–Sun 10am–5pm; £3) is a work of art.

Woburn and Woburn Abbey and Safari Park

About sixteen miles east of Buckingham, on the peripheries of Milton Keynes, the little village of **WOBURN** makes a healthy living from its location beside Woburn Abbey and Safari Park. Little more than one main street lined with some sterling Georgian buildings, the village's most interesting feature is **St Mary's Church**, whose cumbersome stonework is guarded by a couple of peculiar – and peculiarly large – gargoyles, one of which looks like a prototype Tolkien hobgoblin. The interior is less distinctive but certainly impressive, refitted in fancy Gothic style by the Duke of Bedford in the 1860s and supplemented with an elaborate reredos a few years later. Woburn has several good **restaurants**, where you can prime up for – or unwind after – an excursion into the Abbey and the Safari Park. Amongst several options, the *Nicholls Brasserie* (℡01525/290896) is a chic establishment with an imaginative menu that ranges from guinea fowl to fish cakes, with main courses averaging £10. Alternatively, try the *Black Horse*, which sells top-notch pub food.

Woburn Abbey and Safari Park

The grandiloquent Georgian facade of **Woburn Abbey** (April–Sept Mon–Sat 11am–5pm, Sun 11am–6pm; Oct & Jan–March Sat & Sun 11am–5pm; £7.50, half price with a ticket for the Safari Park) overlooks a huge area of parkland just to the east of the eponymous village. Called an "abbey" since it was built on the site of a Cistercian foundation, the house is the ancestral pile of the dukes of Bedford, whom Queen Victoria once dismissed as a dull lot. Judging from the family's penchant for canine portraits, she may have had a point, but the lavish state rooms also contain some fine paintings, including an exquisite set of **Tudor portraits** hanging in the Long Gallery, most notably the famous *Armada Portrait* of Elizabeth I by George Gower. Elsewhere are works by Van Dyck, Velázquez, Gainsborough and Rembrandt, whilst Reynolds and Canaletto each have a room to themselves. The surrounding parkland, with its rolling hills and trees, was landscaped by Humphry Repton and supports nine species of deer.

Another part of the duke's enormous estate is given over to **Woburn Safari Park** (early March to Oct daily 10am–5pm or dusk; Nov to early March Sat & Sun 11am–3pm; £12.50, with discounts outside high season; ⓦwww.woburnsafari.co.uk), the largest drive-through wildlife reserve in Britain – which means that you have to have your own car to enter. The animals include endangered species such as the African white rhino and bongo antelope, and appear to be in excellent health. A posse of guards tours around on the lookout for drivers in distress, but the main danger is an overheated engine rather than an attack by an enraged animal – the Safari Park is extraordinarily popular and in high season the traffic can achieve rush-hour congestion, so turn up as early as possible for a quieter experience.

Bedford

BEDFORD, some fourteen miles northeast of Woburn, has struggled to retain a modicum of character in the face of redevelopment, but the end result is pleasant enough, the town's neat and tidy centre hugging the north bank of the

River Ouse. Bedford also makes the most of its connections with **John Bunyan** (1628–88), a blaspheming tinker turned Nonconformist preacher, who lived most of his life in and around the town. Bunyan fought for Parliament in the Civil War and became a well-known public speaker during Cromwell's Protectorate, but the Restoration proved disastrous for him. In 1660, he was arrested for breaking Charles II's new religious legislation, which restricted the activities of Nonconformist preachers, and he spent most of the next seventeen years in Bedford prison. During his incarceration, he wrote *The Pilgrim's Progress*, a seminal text whose simple language and powerful allegories were to have a profound influence on generations of Nonconformists – and it was they who championed a raft of progressive causes, most notably the campaign for the abolition of slavery.

Built in 1850 on the spot where Bunyan founded his first Independent Congregation, the **Bunyan Meeting Free Church** (Tues–Sat 10am–4pm), just east of the High Street on Mill Street, is still a Nonconformist church. It bears several memorials to Bunyan, beginning with the splendid bronze doors, decorated with ten finely worked panels depicting scenes from *The Pilgrim's Progress*. Inside, the stained glass windows develop the theme, again depicting scenes from the book, plus one showing Bunyan scribbling away in prison. Next door, the homely **Bunyan Museum** (March–Oct Tues–Sat 11am–4pm; free) features extracts from his book and tracks through the author's life and times – including his notably insignificant military exploits. Bunyan spent the war on garrison duty at nearby Newport Pagnell, where he never saw a shot fired in anger, though he did suffer the indignities of being poorly supplied – at one point, the garrison only had one pair of breeches for every two men.

Bedford's other noteworthy attraction is the **Cecil Higgins Art Gallery**, just to the south of Mill Street on Castle Lane (Tues–Sat 11am–5pm & Sun 2–5pm; £2.10, free on Fri). The gallery holds strong collections of ceramics, glass and local lace as well as a competent range of watercolours and prints, though these are not always on display due to their sensitivity to light. There are also several period rooms, done out in high Victorian style, and it's here you'll find the eccentric Burges Room, a colourful fantasy of ersatz classical and medieval decoration created by William Burges (1827–81), one of the leading figures in the Gothic Revival movement. Burges's main interest was French Gothic, but he was a playful soul – witness the bookcase painted with the signs of the zodiac in a vaguely Assyrian manner and the wardrobe featuring Adam trying on different clothes after his ejection from the Garden of Eden. The gallery's admission charge covers the adjacent **Bedford Museum** (same hours), an extremely dull trawl through the city's history.

Practicalities

Bedford is on the London St Pancras–Sheffield rail line with **trains** arriving at Midland Station, from where it's a ten-minute walk east to the centre – just follow the signs. The **bus station** is on All Hallows and from here it's a couple of minutes' walk east to the short High Street, which runs north–south and spans the River Ouse. The **tourist office** (Mon–Sat 9.30am–5pm; ☎01234/215226) is just off the High Street near the river at 10 St Paul's Square.

The town's best **hotel** is *The Swan* (☎01234/346565, ⓦ www.bedfordswan hotel.co.uk; ❺), whose Georgian stonework conceals a lavish and tastefully modernized interior; it's down by the river at the foot of the High Street. As a second choice, the *Moat House Hotel* (☎01234/799988; ❼) occupies a blotchy high-rise across the river from *The Swan*, but its upper rooms have great views and there's a good range of fitness facilities. The tourist office has a small cachet of **B&Bs**.

Bedford's large Italian community adds a bit of zip to the local **restaurant** scene. Pick of the bunch, serving the tastiest pizzas and pastas in town, is *Pizzeria Santaniello*, 9 Newnham St, immediately to the east of Mill Street's Bunyan Meeting Free Church. Further down Newnham Street, at no. 36, *Bar Cappuccino* chips in with authentic coffee, ice cream, pizzas and snacks. In between the two, *The Castle* has bar food and Real Ales, and occupies ancient (but heavily modernized) premises.

St Albans

ST ALBANS is one of the most appealing towns on the peripheries of London, its well-blended medley of medieval and modern features grafted onto the site of Verulamium, the town founded by the Romans soon after their successful invasion of 43 AD. Boudicca and her followers burned this settlement to the ground eighteen years later, but reconstruction was swift and the town grew into a major administrative base. It was here, in 209 AD, that a Roman soldier by the name of Alban became the country's first Christian martyr, when he was beheaded for giving shelter to a priest. Pilgrims later flocked to the town that had come to bear his name, with the place of execution marked by a hilltop cathedral that was once one of the largest churches in the Christian world.

Not just a religious centre, St Albans also flourished as a trading town and a staging post on the route to London from the north, its economy further buttressed by two local industries, brewing and straw-hat-making. In the nineteenth century, the coaching trade faded away with the coming of the railways, but when St Albans was connected to London by train in 1868, it rapidly reinvented itself as a prosperous and pleasant commuter town, a description that fits it well today.

St Albans' best-known attraction is its **cathedral**, but the town also possesses the outstanding **Verulamium Museum**, home to several breathtaking Roman mosaics, as well as a likeable riverside park and a number of charming old streets. All the town's main sights are within easy walking distance of each other, making St Albans an ideal day out, but if you do decide to stay the night be sure to try out some of the excellent pubs.

The City

One good way to start a tour of the city is by climbing to the top of the fifteenth-century **Clock Tower**, plumb in the centre of town where the High Street and Market Place meet (Easter–Oct Sat & Sun 10.30am–4.30pm; 35p). The climb is a tight squeeze, but worth it for the view over the **Cathedral** (daily 8.30am–5.45pm; donation requested), a vast brick and flint edifice close by and reached down a narrow passageway across from the foot of the tower. An abbey was constructed here in 1077, on the site of a Saxon abbey founded by King Offa of Mercia, and despite subsequent alterations – including the ugly nineteenth-century west front – the legacy of the Normans remains the most impressive aspect. The sheer scale of their design is breathtaking: the **nave**, almost 300-foot long, is the longest medieval nave in Britain, even if it isn't the most harmonious – the massive Norman **pillars** on the north side stand out from those in the later Early English style opposite. Some of the Norman pillars retain thirteenth- and fourteenth-century paintings, the detail clear though the ochre colours are much faded. Two- and three-tone geometric designs decorate the Norman **arches** in the nave and at the central crossing, where the impact of the original design reaches its peak with the mighty Norman tower. Behind the high altar an elaborate stone reredos (a clumsy construction compared with the splendid Gothic rood screen) hides the fourteenth-century shrine of St Alban. The tomb was smashed up during the Dissolution, but the Victorians discovered the pieces and gamely put them all together again. Some of the carving on the Purbeck marble is now remarkably clear – look out for the scene on the west end depicting the saint's martyrdom.

A few yards to the west of the cathedral's main entrance, the **abbey gateway** is the only other part of the original complex to have survived the Dissolution. From here, Abbey Mill Lane leads down past the *Fighting Cocks* (one of the oldest pubs in the country) and across the trickle of the River Ver to **Verulamium Park**, whose sloping lawns and duck-happy ponds occupy the site of the Roman city. The park holds a scattering of Roman remains – primarily fragments of the old Roman wall and the remains of a town house with its underfloor heating system (hypocaust) – but these are hardly riveting. Instead, follow the signs to the **Verulamium Museum** (Mon–Sat 10am–5.30pm, Sun 2–5.30pm; £3), which occupies an attractive circular building on the northern edge of the park. Inside, a series of well-conceived displays illustrate and explain life in Roman Britain, but these are eclipsed by the **mosaic** room, containing five wonderful floor mosaics unearthed hereabouts in the 1930s and 1950s. Dated to about 200 AD, the Sea God Mosaic has created its share of academic debate, with some arguing it depicts a god of nature with stag antler horns rather than a sea god with lobster claws, but there's no disputing the subject of the Lion Mosaic, in which a lion carries the bloodied head of a stag in its jaws. The most beautiful of the five is the Shell Mosaic, a gorgeous work of art whose semicircular design depicts a beautifully crafted scallop shell within a border made up of rolling waves.

Close by, the **Roman Theatre of Verulamium** (daily: April–Sept 10am–5pm; Oct–March 10am–4pm; £1.50), across a busy road from the museum, and signposted from there, was built around 140 AD, but reduced to the status of municipal rubbish dump by the fifth century. Little more than a small hollow now, the site is still impressive enough and gives a real sense of how these theatres would once have looked. Further excavation is underway nearby, revealing a house and several workshops. From the theatre, you can walk back to the centre along **St Michael's Street**, over one of the prettier stretches of the Ver, past a sixteenth-century **watermill**, now a museum and café (Easter–Oct Mon–Sat 10am–6pm, Sun 11am–6pm; Nov–Easter closes 5pm; £1.10), and up the gently curving **Fishpool Street**, a quiet road lined with medieval inns and handsome Georgian houses.

On the other side of the city centre, about fifteen minutes' walk away, off the northern end of St Peter's Street, Hatfield Road is home to the **Museum of St Albans** (Mon–Sat 10am–5pm, Sun 2–5pm; free), which provides a thorough history of the city, from Boudicca to the building of the M25. You can also learn about Matthew Paris, the most famous occupant of St Albans abbey – his chronicles, covering events before and during his own lifetime in the thirteenth century, are some of the wittiest and most detailed written in medieval Europe. The museum uses reproductions of some of his manuscripts to tell the city's early history, including an illustration of the martyrdom of Alban.

Practicalities

Trains on the Bedford to London King's Cross line call at St Albans station, from where it's a ten-minute walk west up the hill along Victoria street to the centre – and the Clock Tower. Trains from Watford Junction (for London Euston and the North) serve the small St Albans Abbey Station, a similar distance from the centre, but this time to the south at the bottom of Holywell Hill. Most **buses** terminate at St Albans station, but virtually all services stop along the main commercial drag, St Peter's Street, too. St Peter's Street extends north from the Market Place. The **tourist office** is in the Town Hall, on the Market Place (Easter–Oct Mon–Sat 9.30am–5.30pm; Nov–Easter Mon–Sat 10am–4pm; ☏01727/864511, ⓦwww.stalbans.gov.uk).

St Albans has a good supply of **B&Bs** with several clustered near St Albans station, including the first-rate *Wren Lodge* (☏01727/855540; no credit cards; ❷), a well-maintained Edwardian house with four comfortable and attractively furnished bedrooms – two en suite. Fishpool Street is, however, a much prettier spot to head for and it's here you'll find the pleasant *Black Lion Inn*, at no. 198 (☏01727/851786, ⒺInfo@blacklioninn.abelartis.com; ❹), an ancient pub with sixteen agreeable rooms, fourteen en suite.

When it comes to **food**, St Albans' restaurant scene is a tad humdrum, but the **pubs** serve up some interesting fare. *The Goat*, on Sopwell Lane off Holywell Hill (☏01727/833934), serves some of the best food and beer in town, while the *Blue Anchor*, on Fishpool Street, is a more solidly local pub with an open fire in winter and garden seating in summer. The antique *Fighting Cocks*, on Abbey Mill Lane, has been chopped around a bit and does get mightily crowded on sunny summer days, but still has lots of enjoyable nooks and crannies in which to nurse a pint.

Around St Albans

St Albans lies just five minutes' drive outside the M25 and midway between the two main routes to the Midlands and the North – the M1 and A1. The best day-trips take you north away from the traffic into (what's left of) rural Hertfordshire, with the obvious target being the hamlet of **Ayot St Lawrence**, site of George Bernard Shaw's old home, Shaw's Corner. There's no avoiding the congestion if you travel east, but neighbouring **Hatfield** is home to Hatfield House, a splendid Jacobean manor house; while to the northwest of the city is one of the country's best zoos, **Whipsnade Wild Animal Park**.

Ayot St Lawrence and Shaw's Corner

The tiny village of **AYOT ST LAWRENCE**, hiding among gentle hills in one of the prettiest corners of Hertfordshire, was the home of **George Bernard Shaw** from 1906 until his death in 1950. He lived in a trim Edwardian Villa known as **Shaw's Corner** (April–Oct Wed–Sun 1–5pm; £3.50; NT), which has been left pretty much as it was at the time of his demise, packed with literary bits and pieces and his personal effects. There's also the shed at the bottom of the garden where Shaw used to write, but this is little more than a cell, the only luxuries being a telephone and the hut's ability to revolve in order to maximize the available sunlight. The village's other point of interest is the Greek Revival **Church of St Lawrence**, built in the 1770s on the instructions of the local bigwig, Lyonel Lyde, who simultaneously turned the existing medieval church into a picturesque ruin to make the village more "romantic". When the bishop heard of these antics, he threw a fit, but it was too late. The ruined church is hidden among the trees opposite the village's excellent **pub**, the *Brocket Arms* (☎01438/820250; 5), a cosy, half-timbered old place with low-beamed ceilings and a walled garden. The food here is excellent – daily specials cover the full range of meat and seafood dishes – they serve Real Ales and there are six bedrooms decorated in a crisp modern style.

Ayot St Lawrence is eight miles north of St Albans, accessible along narrow country lanes. There's no direct public transport, but the nearest train station is Welwyn Garden City, from where it's a four-mile taxi ride.

Hatfield House and Hatfield town

Hatfield House (April–Sept daily 12–4pm; £7), six miles east of St Albans, is an impressive Jacobean house that was built for the powerful royal adviser Sir Robert Cecil at the beginning of the seventeenth century. Cecil's mansion replaced a much earlier manor house that Henry VIII had used as a country retreat – though for his daughter, Elizabeth, kept here by her half-sister Mary, it was more a prison than a home. James I, on succeeding to the throne in 1603, took a dislike to Hatfield and did a house-swap with Cecil, who promptly had the place remodelled by the architect Robert Lyminge. The commission made Lyminge's name and he went on to design Norfolk's Blickling Hall (see p.567).

E-shaped, Hatfield House boasts an imposing red-brick and stone-trimmed exterior, its south facade equipped with a dainty clock tower and loggia. Inside, amidst oodles of dark wood panelling, there are some magnificent Tudor and Jacobean portraits, a roll call of the great, the good and the not-so-good. Elizabeth I provides a central theme, her memorabilia including a hat, gloves and a pair of silk stockings, as well as an extraordinary genealogical tree tracing her descent from Adam and Eve via Noah and King Lear. The banqueting hall is the main survivor from the earlier building, but it is rarely open, being used for "Elizabethan banquets" and so forth. The splendid oak staircase bears a relief of John Tradescant, the royal gardener and collector who kick-started Oxford's Ashmolean Museum (see p.343). Tradescant planned Hatfield's original garden, the flavour of which is provided by today's knot garden.

Hatfield House is easy to reach by **train** – its entrance is opposite Hatfield town train station, on the King's Cross–Cambridge line. As for **HATFIELD** town, it's mostly a suburban sprawl, but the old centre is worth exploring. To get there from the station, take North Street south to the roundabout, turn left along Broadway and steep Fore Street is on the right – a five- to ten-minute walk in total. Climb the steep Fore Street to the **Church**, which has a window by the Pre-Raphaelite artist Edward Burne-Jones and the tomb of Sir Robert Cecil, a macabre affair with Cecil's effigy resting over a skeleton. The *Eight Bells* pub at the bottom of Fore Street serves a good pint and a reasonable lunch.

Whipsnade Wild Animal Park

Whipsnade Wild Animal Park (Mon–Sat 10am–6pm or dusk, Sun 10am–6pm or dusk; £10.70), the free-range menagerie of the Zoological Society of London, perches high up on the downs about eleven miles northwest of St Albans – and six miles southwest of Luton. Whipsnade takes its educational role seriously and runs a number of major breeding programmes – there's a flourishing cheetah population, and the rare Burmese elephant has also been bred here successfully. Most animals, from tigers to wallabies, are kept in large enclosures, separated from the public by a fence or a ditch. You can drive around the zoo (£8.50/car), but it's possible to see everything perfectly well on foot. Alternatively, you could hop on the free Safari bus that stops at the main enclosures, or take a ride in the little steam train (£2), which offers an "Asian Railway Safari" as it pulls past herds of elephants and one-horned rhinos.

To reach Whipsnade by **car**, leave the M1 at Junction #9 (approaching from the south) or #12 (from the north) and follow the signs. The nearest **train station** is at Luton, from where there are regular **buses** to the zoo; call ☏01582/872171 for details.

Travel Details

Buses

For information on all local and national bus services, contact Traveline: ☏ 0870/608 2 608 (daily 7am–9pm), ⓦ www.traveline.org.uk.

Trains

For information on all local and national rail services, contact National Rail Enquiries: ☏ 08457/48 49 50, ⓦ www.rail.co.uk.

Bedford to: London (1–2 hourly; 30min–1hr); St Albans (1–2 hourly; 40min).
Hatfield to: London (1–2 hourly; 20min).
Henley to: London (3 daily; 1hr).

Oxford to: Birmingham (hourly; 1hr 30min); London (1–2 hourly; 1hr); Worcester (hourly; 1hr 10min).
St Albans to: Bedford (1–2 hourly; 40min); London (14 daily; 20–40min).

The Cotswolds
and Somerset

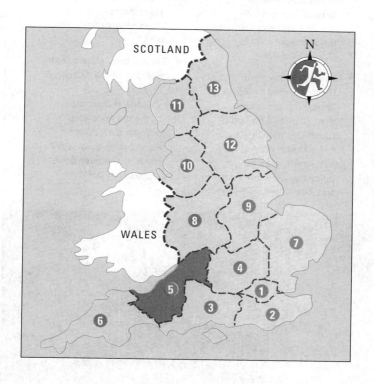

CHAPTER 5

Highlights

✳ **Westonbirt Arboretum, Gloucestershire** Long boulevards of elegant trees distinguish this tranquil park, an excellent spot for a picnic on a fine autumn day. See p.375

✳ **Clifton Suspension Bridge** Brunel's lofty construction rears above the impressive Avon Gorge. See p.400

✳ **Harvey's restaurant, Bristol** Linked to the famous sherry house, this place lays on sumptuous banquets in its converted medieval cellars, and there's an adjoining wine museum, too. See p.399

✳ **Bath** The beautifully preserved old baths complex at the heart of the town is one of the country's most fascinating Roman remains. See p.403

✳ **Wells Cathedral** A gem of medieval masonry, not least for its richly ornamented west front. See p.411

✳ **Glastonbury music festival** One of the oldest and biggest rock festivals still retains its authentic aura, less commercialized than most of the ilk, and still drawing the alternative crowd. See p.417

5

The Cotswolds
and Somerset

T he rolling green swards of **Gloucestershire** and **Somerset**, a wedge of land linking the Midlands with the West Country, encapsulate a vision of rural England which has very largely survived the inroads of modern urban culture. The relatively remote settlements may not, for the most part, be peopled by shepherds and farmers, but the landscape has preserved its slumberous charm, and wears a mellow tranquillity which has even seeped into the towns which grew rich on its wealth. Occupying the eastern side of Gloucestershire, the **Cotswolds**, in particular, show plenty of evidence of past prosperity, not least in the beautiful old mansions and churches endowed from the fortunes made through the medieval wool trade. Moreover, the remarkable continuity of Cotswold architecture has created villages as picturesque as any in England, though the resulting tourist deluge makes some spots nightmarish in summer. Tourism is less of a nuisance in the south of this region, around the busy market town of **Cirencester**, once an important Roman stronghold and still an important transport hub.

To the west, the land drops sharply from the Cotswold escarpment down to **Cheltenham**, an elegant Regency spa town most famous these days for its horse racing. The town's reputation as a bastion of blue-stockinged conservatism is fairly passé now, and it has developed a more sophisticated veneer in recent years, boasting some of the best restaurants and nightlife in the region. Cheltenham would also make a good base for visits to **Gloucester**, with its superb cathedral and rejuvenated harbour area, and **Stroud**, where the much praised Museum in the Park has recently opened. The Vale of Gloucester follows the route of the **River Severn** northeast towards Worcestershire, the

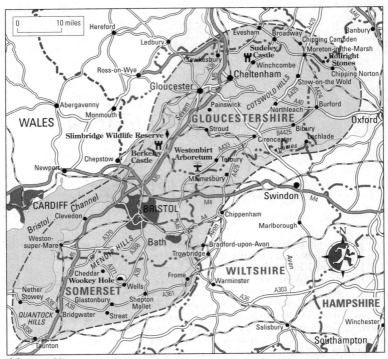

© Crown copyright

stone cottages of the Cotswolds giving way to the thatched, half-timbered and red-brick houses which are characteristic of **Tewkesbury**, a solidly provincial town with a magnificent abbey.

South down the M5, **Bristol** is the biggest city in these parts, and one of the most go-ahead, cosmopolitan places outside London. Its dynamism and flare have saddled it with dense traffic and some pretty hideous postwar architecture, but all is compensated for by its surviving traces of every phase in its long maritime history. Bristol is within reach of old-fashioned seaside resorts – more alluring for their nostalgic atmosphere than for their swimming possibilities – and only a few miles from Georgian **Bath**, whose symmetrical honey-toned terraces contribute to its operatic setting. The proximity of urban grace to panoramic splendour is characteristic of much of **Somerset**, as in the exquisite cathedral city of **Wells**, lying on the edge of the Mendip Hills. The landscape assumes more dramatic lines west of here, where the hills are pocked by cave systems, as at **Wookey Hole**, and sliced through by the **Cheddar Gorge**. The ancient town of **Glastonbury** lies close at hand, a site steeped in Christian lore and Arthurian legend, and popular with New Age mystics. To the west, **Bridgwater** and **Taunton** lie at the southern end of the **Quantock Hills**, where Coleridge and Wordsworth roamed, a time recalled in Coleridge's old house at **Nether Stowey**.

The line between London's Paddington station and Bristol provides the backbone of the **rail network** through this region, though you could also make use of the London–Oxford–Worcester line which runs through

Moreton-in-Marsh, in the middle of the Cotswolds. There are also direct lines to Cheltenham and Gloucester, and these towns form the hubs of **bus routes** which connect nearly all the places covered here – though beware that services in the Cotswolds can be extremely sketchy, with little running at all on a Sunday. Your own transport would be ideal for exploring this area, while the M4 and M5 motorways are useful through-routes for longer-distance jaunts.

The Cotswolds

The limestone hills of the **Cotswolds** are preposterously photogenic, strewn with countless picture-book villages built by wealthy cloth merchants. Wool was important here as far back as the Roman era, but the greatest fortunes were made between the fourteenth and sixteenth centuries, during which period many of the region's fine manors and churches were built. Largely bypassed by the Industrial Revolution, which heralded the area's commercial decline, much of the Cotswolds is a relic, its architecture preserved in often immaculate condition. Numerous churches are decorated with beautiful Norman carving,

William Morris and the Pre-Raphaelites

William Morris, the nineteenth-century socialist, writer and craftsman, had a profound influence on his contemporaries and on subsequent generations. In some respects he was an ally of Karl Marx, railing against the iniquities of private property and the squalor of industrialized society. Where he differed from Marx, however, was in his belief that machines necessarily enslave the individual, and in his vision of a world in which each person would be liberated through a sort of communistic, crafts-based economy. His prose/poem story *News from Nowhere* vaguely described his Utopian society, but his main legacy was the **Arts and Crafts Movement**, a direct offshoot of his work and a lasting influence on British crafts.

His career as an artist began at Oxford, where he met Edward Burne-Jones, who shared his admiration for the arts of the Middle Ages. After graduating they both ended up in London, painting under the direction of Dante Gabriel Rossetti, the leading light of the **Pre-Raphaelites** – a loose grouping of artists intent on regaining the spiritual purity characteristic of art before Raphael and the Renaissance tainted the world with humanism. In 1861 Morris founded **Morris & Co** ("The Firm"), whose designs came to embody the ideas of the Arts and Crafts Movement, one of whose basic tenets was formulated by its founder: "Have nothing in your houses that you do not know to be useful or believe to be beautiful." Rossetti and Burne-Jones were among the designers, though the former remains better known for his paintings of Jane Morris, his friend's wife and his own mistress, whom he turned into the archetypal Pre-Raphaelite woman. Morris's own designs for fabrics, wallpapers and numerous other products were to prove a massive – some would say negative – influence in Britain, as evidenced by the success of the Laura Ashley aesthetic, a lineal descendant of Morris's rustic nostalgia.

Morris's energy was not exhausted by his work for The Firm. In 1890 he set up the **Kelmscott Press**, named after but not located at his summer home, whose masterpiece was the so-called *Kelmscott Chaucer*, the collected poems of one of the Pre-Raphaelites' great heroes, with woodcuts by Burne-Jones. Morris also pioneered interest in the architecture of the Cotswolds – it was in response to hideous restoration work in this region that Morris instigated the **Society for the Protection of Ancient Buildings**, still an active force in preserving the country's architectural heritage.

for which the local limestone was ideal: soft and easy to carve when first quarried, but hardening after long exposure to the sunlight. The use of this local stone is a strong unifying characteristic, though its colour modulates as subtly as the shape of the hills, ranging from a deep golden tone in **Chipping Campden** to a silvery grey in **Painswick**.

The consequence of all this is that the Cotswolds have become one of the country's main tourist attractions, with many towns afflicted by plagues of tea and souvenir and antiques shops – this is Morris Dancing country. To see the Cotswolds at their best, you should visit in winter or avoid the most popular towns and instead escape into the hills themselves. This might be a tamed landscape, but there is good scope for walks, either in the gentler valleys that are most typical of the Cotswolds or along the dramatic escarpment which marks the boundary with the Severn Valley. A long-distance path called the **Cotswold Way** runs along the top of the ridge, stretching about one hundred miles from Chipping Campden past Cheltenham, Gloucester and Stroud as far as Bath. A number of prehistoric sites provide added interest along the route, with some – such as **Belas Knap** near Winchcombe – being well worth a diversion.

There are a few large settlements in this region, the biggest true Cotswold town being **Cirencester**, a buzzing community dating back to the Romans.

Lechlade and around

Marking the westernmost navigable point of the Thames, **LECHLADE** teems with pleasure boats, but for most people it's handy as a springboard for exploring the southern fringe of the Cotswolds. For **overnight stops** the best place is the modern and stylish *Cambrai Lodge* (℡01367/253173; no credit cards; ❷) in Oak Street, or failing that, the *New Inn* (℡01367/252296, ⓦwww.newinnhotel .com; ❸). You can pitch a tent either at the St John's Priory **campsite** (℡01367 /252360), a mile southeast along the A417 (follow the signs for Faringdon), or in the field by the *Trout* pub (℡01367/252313) next door. The boating fraternity congregates at the *Trout*, reachable by footpath across the meadow from by the church. It's a real anglers' pub, with stuffed fish on the wall, and a meeting point for the boating fraternity; on Tuesday and Sunday there's live jazz, too. From Easter to October the *Trout* rents out **boats** (£6/hour).

There's lots to see around Lechlade, the nearest sight being the tiny, disused church at **INGLESHAM**, by a farm about a mile south. Its oldest parts are late Saxon, from which period is the carved Madonna and Child on the south wall; the colourful fragments of wall paintings date from the fourteenth century. You can walk to the church along the east bank of the Thames, though you must rejoin the A361 for a short distance at the end. There are two other churches well worth visiting nearby, and in a far better state of repair, the first at **FAIRFORD**, four miles west, renowned for its complete set of narrative medieval stained-glass windows. The choir stalls reveal an entertaining set of secular scenes on their polished misericords, including various incidents and altercations such as a dog stealing food from a cooking pot. The second at the edge of the village at **QUENINGTON**, two miles north of Fairford, is renowned for both porches, decorated with vigorous Romanesque carvings.

Isolated among fields just three miles east of Lechlade, **KELMSCOTT** has become a place of pilgrimage for devotees of **William Morris** (see box on p.363), who used the Tudor manor as a summer home from 1871 to his death in 1896. The simple beauty of the **house** (April–Sept Wed & first Sat of month 11am–1pm & 2–5pm; July & Aug also third Sat of month 11am–1pm & 2–5pm; £7; ℡01367/252486, ⓦwww.kelmscottmanor.co.uk) is enhanced by the furniture, fabrics, wallpapers and tapestries – some rescued from dog baskets – that were created by Morris and his Pre-Raphaelite friends, including Burne-Jones and Rossetti. The attics contain more basic green workmen's furniture. Morris and his wife Jane are buried in the southeast corner of the churchyard, in the shadow of the tiny church. Entry is by timed ticket and it's wise to call first to confirm the opening hours, which are erratic. You can't reach Kelmscott on public transport, but it's a pleasant stroll along the north bank of the Thames from Lechlade, and, should you need one, there's a **bed** for the night in the nearby *Plough Inn* (☎01367/253543; ❸) which also serves **meals**.

Burford and the Windrush Valley

Nine miles north of Lechlade you get your first real taste of the Cotswolds at **BURFORD**, where the magnificent High Street, which slopes down to the bridge over the **River Windrush**, holds every variety of golden Cotswold stone. Try to avoid visiting the town in summer, when cars battle for space while tourists fight it out on the pavements and in the antique shops, though the huge **parish church**, originally Norman but remodelled in the fifteenth century, is a delight at any time. An unusual monument to Henry VIII's barber, Edmund Harman, shows four Amazonian Indians, said to be the first representation of native Americans in Britain.

Spare a morning to follow the footpath along the Windrush through **WIDBROOK**, a hamlet with an idyllic medieval chapel built in the middle of a field on the site of a Roman villa, and on to **SWINBROOK**, just under three miles east of Burford. The church in this immaculate village contains a monument showing six members of the Fettiplace family reclining comically on their elbows: the Tudor effigies rigid and stony-faced, their Stuart counterparts stylish and rather camp. The best place for lunch or a drink in Swinbrook is the *Swan Inn*.

Burford straddles several main Cotswold routes. **Buses** along the A40 between Oxford and Cheltenham stop several times a day; buses along other routes are mostly once-a-week market-day services. The **tourist office** is situated in Sheep Street (April–Sept Mon–Sat 9.30am–5.30pm, Sun 10am–3pm; Oct–March Mon–Sat 10am–4.30pm; ☎01993/823558, ⓦwww.oxfordshire cotswolds.com). Many of Burford's old inns have metamorphosed into expensive **hotels**, but the *Highway Hotel* at 117 High St (☎01993/822136, ⓦwww.oxlink.co.uk/burford; ❷) is good value. There are several **B&Bs**, including the discreetly signed *Tudor Cottage* at 40 Witney St, off the main High Street, beautifully furnished with antiques (☎01993/823251, ⓔbunkered @compuserve.com; no credit cards; ❸). A good fallback is *Langley Farm* (☎01367/878686, ⓔGwenGreves@ Farmline.com; ❶; closed Nov–April), a former hunting lodge three and a half miles northeast near the village of Leafield: head north along the A361, turn right at the crossroads onto the B4437, then first right and first left – the farm is one mile on the left. For good **food** *The Angel Brasserie* (☎01993/822714, ⓦwww.theangel-uk.com; closed Sun & Mon eve, plus late Jan to early Feb) at 14 Witney St should satisfy; there are three themed bedrooms as well (❺).

Motorists heading to Cirencester, ten miles southwest (see p.372), should take the B4425 via **BIBURY**: this village is completely overrun with visitors, but anyone interested in the early industrial age should make a point of going to the seventeenth-century **Arlington Mill**, for a close-up demonstration of the workings of water power (daily: Easter–Oct 10am–6pm; Nov–Easter 10am–5pm; £2).

Stow-on-the-Wold

Straddling eight roads, including the Roman Fosse Way (now the A429), windswept **STOW-ON-THE-WOLD** sucks in a disproportionate number of visitors for its size and attractions, which essentially comprise an old marketplace surrounded by brassy pubs, antiques shops and souvenir boutiques. The narrow walled alleyways, or "tunes", running into the square were designed for funnelling sheep into the market, dominated by an imposing Victorian hall and, just to the south, a medieval cross allegedly raised to instil honesty among the traders.

Stow is the logical springboard for trips deeper into the region with its good bus connections from Moreton-in-Marsh and Cheltenham, and its abundant selection of accommodation options. The **tourist office** on the Market Square (April–Oct Mon–Sat 9.30am–5.30pm, Sun 10.30am–4pm; Nov–March Mon–Sat 9.30am–4.30pm; ☎01451/831082, ⓦwww.cotswold.gov.uk), sells National Express bus tickets and keeps a list of local **B&Bs**, among them the conveniently central and relaxed *Pear Tree Cottage*, on the High Street (☎01451/831210; no credit cards; ❷). Tucked away on Union St (take the short cut passage through the *King's Arms* pub from the square) is the secluded and pretty *Honeysuckle Cottage* (☎01451/830973; no credit cards; closed Nov & Jan; ❷), or you could try *Tall Trees* (☎01451/831296; no credit cards; ❸), on the edge of town off the Oddington road (A436), which has sweeping views and a cosy wood burner in its modern sitting room annexe. Close to the tourist office stands the popular **youth hostel** (☎01451/830497; £12.50), but if you're camping you'll have to press on a mile or so east along the Oddington road (A436) to the Stow Rugby Club (☎01451/830887), the nearest **campsite**. For **food**, you've a choice of several old coaching inns on the square, including the *Queen's Head*, where main courses are around the £7 mark. Nearby, the *Royalist* (☎01451/830670, ⓦwww.theroyalisthotel.co.uk), now an up-market hotel (❻), on the corner of Park and Digbeth streets, is yet another inn billing itself the oldest in Britain, a claim in part substantiated by wooden beams carbon-dated at around one thousand years old. You can eat pub food here or sit down to dinner (£30) in the *947AD* restaurant.

Moreton-in-Marsh and around

MORETON-IN-MARSH, on the Roman Fosse Way, five miles north of Stow and fifteen miles northwest of Burford, has more of a buzz than most Cotswold towns, particularly on Tuesdays, when the High Street disappears beneath a huge market. But the thing not to miss in Moreton is the **Batsford Arboretum** (March to mid-Nov daily 10am–5pm; mid-Nov to Feb Sat & Sun 10am–4pm; £4), a fifteen-minute walk from the High Street. The largest private collection of rare trees in the country, it was planted in the 1880s by Lord Redesdale following his return from a posting in Tokyo. The hilly gardens have a distinctly Japanese flavour, and you can sit here amid magnolias and Chinese pocket-handkerchief trees enjoying wonderful views. Beside the entrance to the arboretum is the **Cotswold Falconry Centre** (March–Nov daily 10.30am–5pm; £4) which, in addition to a collection of beautiful birds of prey, gives flying displays (at 11.30am, 1.30pm, 3pm & 4.30pm; no 4.30pm flight in Nov) against a backdrop of the sweeping Evenlode Valley.

Moreton has better **public transport** services than most other towns in the region, with daily **buses** (except Sun) to Stow-on-the-Wold, Chipping Campden, Evesham, Malvern, Stratford and Cheltenham. In addition, Moreton is on the London–Oxford–Worcester **train** line. There's a useful **tourist office** in the High Street (Mon 8.45am–5pm, Tues–Thurs 8.45am–5.15pm, Fri 8.45am–4.45pm, Sat 9.30am–1pm; ☎01608/650881, ⓦwww.cotswold.gov.uk). Best value of the **hotels** is the lively *Bell Inn* (☎01608/652195, ⓦwww .bellinncotswold.com; ❸), also on the High Street. For **B&B**, try *Acacia*, at 2 New Rd, on the way to the station (☎01608/650130; no credit cards; ❶), or *Townend Coach House* on the High Street (☎01608/650846; no credit cards; ❷). **Places to eat** line the High Street, where blackboards advertise any number of inexpensive pub lunches. For a splash-out gourmet meal, head for the *Marsh Goose* **restaurant** (☎01608/653500; closed Mon & Tues lunch & Sun eve), on the east side of the thoroughfare, which serves superb fresh seafood and game dishes, with an à la carte menu in the evening or a set lunch for around £18.50 a head. You can also snack at the daytime café. **Bike rental** is available from Brian Jeffrey's toyshop on the High Street (☎01608/650756; £14/day).

Two miles southwest along the A44, just before you reach Bourton-on-the-Hill, are the blue onion domes and miniature minarets of **Sezincote** (May–July & Sept Thurs & Fri 2.30–5.30pm; garden Jan–Nov Thurs & Fri 2pm–dusk; £5, garden only £3.50), tucked gracefully if incongruously among the Cotswold hills. This extraordinary house, built in the early nineteenth century, was the result of a collaboration between architect Samuel Pepys Cockerell (a distant relative of the diarist), and artist Thomas Daniell, both of whom had spent some time in India and been inspired by Moghul architecture. The end result so impressed the Prince Regent on a visit in 1806 that he ordered the designs for Brighton Pavilion to be changed along these exotic lines. Inside, a curious classical-cum-Chinese style takes precedence; outside, temples, statues and unusual trees and shrubs are scattered about the small but exquisite garden – and in the early months of the year the snowdrops and aconites make a glorious display.

The other stately home in this area worth a visit is **Chastleton House**, three miles southeast of Moreton off the A44 (April–Oct Wed–Sat 1–4pm; £5.20; NT; bookings Tues–Fri 10am–4pm ☎01494/755585); entry is by timed ticket, which it's always wise to pre-book. Built between 1605 and 1612 by Walter Jones, the wealthy Welsh wool merchant and member of parliament for Worcester, this ranks among the most splendid Jacobean properties in the country, set amid ornamental gardens that include England's first-ever croquet lawn (the rules of this eccentric and most English of games were codified here in 1865). Inside, the house looks as if it's been in a time warp for four hundred years, with unwashed upholstery, unpolished wood panelling and clutter and cobwebs clogging some corners. The air of general shabbiness derives in part from the fact that the Jones family lost their fortune after the Civil War (they supported the losing side), and could not subsequently afford to clutter their home with fancy Renaissance fittings; and in part because the National Trust, who took on the property in 1991, wisely decided the beguiling "lived-in look" should be retained. Three million pounds later, the house and its treasures – which include the huge barrel-vaulted long gallery, elaborate plasterwork and panelling, tapestries and exquisite glassware, geraniums and, in the beer cellar, the longest ladder (dated 1805) you're ever likely to come across – are safely preserved, minus the rope barriers and surface sheen that can sometimes mar NT properties. There's also a topiary garden, where the hedges are clipped into bulbous shapes reminiscent of squirrels and tortoises.

Northleach

Secluded in a shallow depression just off the Fosse Way, **NORTHLEACH**, seven miles southwest of Stow-on-the-Wold, is one of the most attractive, and least spoilt, villages in the Cotswolds. This fact, together with its location at the heart of the plateau, within easy reach of Oxford, Stratford and the picturesque Windrush Valley, makes it a perfect base from which to explore the region. Rows of immaculate late-medieval cottages cluster around a spacious central square, many of them with traditional stone-tiled roofs, but the village's most outstanding feature is its handsome Perpendicular **church**, erected in the fifteenth-century at the height of the wool boom, when the surrounding fields of rich limestone grasses supported a vast population of sheep. The local breed, known as the Cotswold Lion, was a descendant of flocks introduced by the Romans, and by the thirteenth century had become the largest in the country, producing heavy fleeces that were exported to the Flemish weaving towns. The income from this lucrative trade, initially controlled by the clergy but later by a handful of wealthy merchants, financed the construction of three major churches in the region, of which the one at Northleach is arguably the most impressive (the others are in Cirencester and Chipping Campden). Inside, the floor of the beautifully proportioned nave, lit by wide clerestory windows, is inlaid with an exceptional collection of **memorial brasses** marking the tombs of the merchants whose endowments paid for the church. On several, you can make out the woolsacks laid out beneath the corpse's feet – a symbol of wealth and power that features to this day in the House of Lords, where a woolsack is placed on the Lord Chancellor's seat.

Two minutes' walk up the main street from the village square, **Keith Harding's World of Mechanical Music** (daily 10am–6pm; £5) is Northleach's other main attraction, comprising a bewildering collection of antique musical boxes, automata, barrel organs and mechanical instruments all stuffed into one room. For your money you get an hour-long demonstration tour of the collection, of which the highlight is hearing the likes of Rachmaninov, Gershwin or Paderewski playing their own masterpieces on piano rolls.

The former eighteenth-century prison, at the turn-off for the village on the main road, now houses the **tourist office** (April–Oct Mon–Sat 10am–5pm & Sun noon–5pm; ℡01451/860715, ⓦwww.cotswold.gov.uk) and **Cotswold Heritage Centre** (same hours; £2.50), outside which stands a grand circle of carts, wagons and old shepherds' vans, and inside there are colour films from the 1930s on video. Excellent **accommodation** can be had right in the centre of the village: *Cotteswold House* on the Market Place (℡01451/860493, ⓔwww.cotteswoldhouse.com; ❹), a wonderfully well-preserved Tudor cottage, has exposed stone arches and thirteenth-century oak panelling on the walls, while the *Wheatsheaf Hotel* (℡01451/860244, ⓔwheatsheaf@ establishment.ltd.uk; ❸), just from the square on West End, is elegantly modern and does great breakfasts. The *Red Lion Inn* on the square (℡01451/860251; ❷) makes a less luxurious option. For **food**, your best bets are full meals at the *Wheatsheaf* or less expensive bar meals at the *Sherborne Arms*, both on the Market Place. In addition, the relaxed *Country Wine Merchant* on the square doubles as a wine bar and shop (closed Sun & Mon) and offers its clients the use of a barbecue in their back garden, where you can grill your own food provided you buy a bottle of wine from them first. Those for whom money is no object, however, may prefer to splurge on a meal at the famous *Old Woolhouse* restaurant on the Market Place (℡01451/860366; reservations essential), where you can expect to spend around £40 per head for top-notch French cuisine; the food is superb, and so is the wine list, where half-bottles run from £13 upwards.

Chipping Norton and around

The bustling market town of **CHIPPING NORTON**, 22 miles northwest of Oxford, presides over one of the least explored, but most scenic, corners of the Cotswolds – a region of rambling limestone uplands latticed by long dry-stone walls and dotted with picturesque villages. The western approach to the town, via the A44 from Moreton-in-Marsh, is dominated by the extraordinary chimney stack of the **Bliss Tweed Mill**, mounted on a domed tower and the quirkiest of a crop of monuments dating from the boom of the textile trade. Granted a charter in the twelfth century by King John to hold a wool fair, Chipping Norton reached its peak three hundred years later, when it acquired most of the stalwart stone houses and half-timber-framed coaching inns lining the market square. Also paid for by wealthy wool merchants, **St Mary's Parish Church**, just below the square in Church Street, harbours a fine fifteenth-century Perpendicular nave, in addition to some well-preserved brasses and tombs. More remnants of the town's former prominence are housed in the small **museum** at the top of the square above the Westgate Centre (Easter–Oct Tues–Sun 2–4pm; Nov–Easter Tues–Sat 2–4pm; £1), among them a carved head of a Roman river god unearthed by a local farmer, equipment salvaged from the Victorian wool mill and brewery, and a display on Fred Lewis, who founded the English Baseball Club in 1920.

Buses to Chipping Norton drop passengers in front of the town hall, at the opposite end of the square to the **tourist office** (March–Oct Mon–Sat 9.30am–5.30pm; Nov–Feb Mon–Sat 10am–3pm; ☎01608/644379), where you can book **accommodation**. Most central is *The Old Vicarage* (☎01608/641562, ✉anthony.ross@virgin.net; no credit cards; ❸), close to the church, while further out lie *Kingsmoor Cottage* (☎01608/643276; no credit cards; ❸), two miles west along the A44 in the sleepy village of Salford, and *Southcombe Lodge* (☎01608/643068, ⊛www.smoothhound.co.uk/hotels/southcombe; ❷), a modern bungalow one mile east in the hamlet of Southcombe. The best **pubs** are both in Goddards Lane, on the square: the stone-tiled *Blue Boar* serves imaginative bar food and real ales, as does the *Chequers* a little further down, which has regular guest beers. If you prefer the **café-bar** atmosphere, try *Whistlers* (☎01608/643363; closed Sun eve) just along from the tourist office at 9 Middle Row, where a set lunch will cost £10.95.

A labyrinth of lanes spreads east of Chipping Norton through a string of well-manicured villages and valleys to tiny **GREAT TEW**, the perfect target for a pub walk. Hidden deep amid woodland, this hamlet of honey-coloured, thatched houses contains one of England's most idyllic pubs, the **Falkland Arms**, which rotates a dozen or so guest beers (including the legendary local bitter, Hook Norton), and sells a fine selection of single malts, herbal wines, snuff, and clay pipes you can fill with tobacco for a smoke in the flower-filled garden. Little has changed in the flagstone-floored bar since the sixteenth century, although the adjacent snug was recently converted into a small restaurant serving snacks and evening meals. It's also a popular place to stay (☎01608/683653;❹), and at weekends is booked up months ahead.

Another local expedition takes in the **Rollright Stones**, high up on the wolds about five miles northwest of Chipping Norton, and the third most important stone circle in Britain after Stonehenge and Avebury. Legend recounts that these gnarled Bronze Age rocks are a king and his army (of unknown identity), petrified by a witch while on a campaign to conquer England.

Chipping Campden and around

CHIPPING CAMPDEN, six miles northwest of Moreton-in-Marsh, gives a better idea than anywhere else in the Cotswolds as to what a prosperous wool town might have looked like in the Middle Ages. The houses have undulating, weather-beaten roofs and many retain their original mullioned windows, while the fine Perpendicular **church** dates from the fifteenth century, the zenith of the town's wool-trading days. Inside, an ostentatious monument commemorates the family of Sir Baptist Hicks, a local benefactor who built the nearby almshouses and the market hall in the High Street. His own home was burnt down during the Civil War, but you can glimpse the ruins over the wall beside the church.

A fine panoramic view rewards those who make the short but severe hike up the Cotswold Way northwest to **Dover's Hill** (follow Hoo Lane north off the High Street). Since 1610 this natural amphitheatre has been the stage for an Olympics of rural sports, though the event was suspended last century when games such as shin-kicking became little more than licensed thuggery. A more civilized version, the **Cotswold Olimpick Games**, has been staged each June since 1951: no shin-kicking, but still the odd bit of hammer-throwing and tug-of-war pulling.

Such a museum-piece as Chipping Campden must inevitably cope with a bevy of visitors in summer. Try to stay overnight and explore in the evening or at dawn, when the streets are empty and the golden hues of the stone at their richest. **Public transport** to the area is good, with frequent bus services to Moreton, Evesham and Stratford. You can't move for **guest houses** along the High Street, most of which can be booked through the **tourist office** (daily 10am–5.30pm; ☎01386/841206, ⓦ www.chippingcampden.co.uk). Distinguished by its blue door, *Mrs Benfield's* on Lower High St (☎01386/840163; no credit cards; ❷) has fewer lacy trimmings than most (with correspondingly low prices), as does the *Volunteer Inn* on Park Rd, a few doors up on the opposite side of the road (☎01386/840688; no credit cards; ❸). Most other **pubs** have rooms but are in a different price bracket, such as the *Noel Arms* (☎01386/840317, ⓦ www.cotswold-inns-hotels.co.uk; ❼). The standard of **pubs** is good, but the *Eight Bells Inn*, around the corner from the church, is particularly cosy, and it serves top food. There's a window in the floor showing the passage once used by Catholic priests escaping from the church.

Winchcombe and around

The journey to **WINCHCOMBE**, twelve miles southwest of Chipping Campden, is stunning, whether you take the dramatic descent over the escarpment or the exhilarating ride down the B4632, which weaves along the lower folds of the cliff. Under the Saxons, Winchcombe became the provincial capital of the kingdom of **Mercia**, and it was the most important town in the Cotswolds until the early Middle Ages. The Saxon abbey didn't survive the Dissolution, and the town's main place of worship is the rather plain fifteenth-century church, most notable for its gargoyles. Apart from that, Winchcombe has an attractive blend of stone and half-timbered buildings and a museum, but the real attractions are **Sudeley Castle**, **Belas Knap** and **Hailes Abbey**, all located just outside the town. These, together with some of the finest scenery in the region and Tewkesbury only a short hop away, make Winchcombe a quieter place to base yourself than Cheltenham, and an appealing alternative to the more touristy towns and villages in the Cotswolds.

Bus #606 runs about once an hour through the day from Cheltenham to Winchcombe (less on Sun) bound for Broadway. Winchcombe's efficient

Drained by the sinuous River Isbourne, the scenic valley around Winchcombe is rid-dled with rewarding and well-marked trails, among them the **Cotswold Way** (see p.364), which cuts through the town before climbing to Belas Knap and the plateau of Cleve Common and West Down. From the edge of the escarpment, reached after a stiff one- to two-hour hike, the views over Cheltenham and the Severn Valley to the distant Malverns are superb.

A less strenuous, but equally inspiring, option is the three-and-a-half-hour round route to **Spoonley Farm**, just over two miles southeast of town, which takes in a ruined Roman villa where you can see a beautifully preserved **Roman mosaic** *in situ*. The existence of this antiquity was one of the area's best kept secrets until the American travel writer Bill Bryson featured it in his chart topping *Notes From A Small Island*, since when the tourist office has been inundated with requests for its *Country Walks Around Winchcombe* booklet (£1.25), which describes the route in detail. If you can't get hold of one of these, check OS Outdoor Leisure Map 45. The footpath to Spoonley Farm starts in the same place as the Cotswold Way, opposite the church at the south end of the main street, but shortly after peels left towards Sudeley Castle. After crossing the castle grounds, it follows the contour of the hill to Waterhatch Woods, site of the old villa; the mosaic is covered in sheets of plastic held down with stones, which you have to remove yourself (be sure to replace them afterwards). From the ruin, strike uphill as far as a farm track, which you can follow southwest, turning right at Cole's Hill towards Waterhatch Farm. The path then drops gently down to river level and eventually back to Winchcombe.

---

tourist office (April–Oct Mon–Sat 10am–1pm & 2–5pm, Sun 10am–1pm & 1.30–4pm; Nov–March Sat & Sun 10am–1pm & 1.30–4pm; ☎01242/602925, Ⓦwww.winchcombe.co.uk/sites) in the Town Hall is right next to the small **Police and Folk Museum** (April–Oct 10am–5pm; 80p), which has exam-ples of 1829 Peeler, Japanese and Nazi uniforms on display. Of the many **B&Bs** in Winchcombe, among the best is the Jacobean *Great House* on Castle St (☎01242/602490; no credit cards;❷), full of old family furniture and one love-ly four-poster room; the *Gower House* at 16 North St (☎01242/602616; no credit cards;❷) offers a more modern alternative on a main road, while *Clevely*, three miles out of the village on Corndean Lane (☎01242/602059; no credit cards; ❷), is the least expensive option in the area. The nearest **campsite** is *Winchcombe Caravan Club Site* at Alderton (☎01242/620259), three miles north along the Stow road (B4077).

There's little to choose between the town's two main **pubs**, the *White Hart* and the *Plaisterers Arms*, which are both on the main street and serve food, though the latter always has Scandinavian fare on offer (specials on Wed eve).

Sudeley Castle

A short walk west of Winchcombe, **Sudeley Castle** (April–Oct daily 11am–5pm; gardens March–Oct daily 10.30am–5.30pm; £6.20, gardens only £4.70) was once a favourite country retreat of Tudor and Stuart monarchs, though it never belonged to the royal family. It has a particularly strong con-nection with Catherine Parr, the sixth wife of Henry VIII, who came to live here after her marriage to Thomas Seymour, Lord of Sudeley, following the king's death. During the Civil War the house became a base for the Royalists (Charles I sought refuge here several times), then was later all but destroyed by the Parliamentarians. What remained stood empty until 1830, when the ruins were bought by the Dent family, whose work re-created an extremely hand-some exterior but not the atmosphere of a fifteenth-century home. The motley collection inside includes paintings by Turner and Constable, a bed Charles I once slept in and one of Catherine Parr's teeth – her tomb is in the chapel. The real joy of Sudeley lies outside: in the **Queen's Garden**, with its huge yew hedges cut like masonry; in the creeper-covered ruins of the banqueting hall; and, above all, in the setting, with the green slopes of the escarpment behind.

Belas Knap

Up on the ridge overlooking Winchcombe, the Neolithic long barrow of **Belas Knap** occupies one of the most breathtaking spots in the Cotswolds. Dating from around 3000 BC, this is the best-preserved burial chamber in England, stretching out like a strange sleeping beast cloaked in green velvet. The two-mile climb up the Cotswold Way from Winchcombe contributes to the fun, giving good views back over Sudeley Castle. The path strikes off to the right near the entrance to Sudeley; when you reach the road at the top, turn right and then left up into the woods, from where it's a ten-minute hike to Belas Knap.

Hailes Abbey

Hailes Abbey (April–Sept daily 10am–6pm; Oct daily 10am–5pm; Nov–March Sat & Sun 10am–4pm; £2.60), a two-mile stroll northeast of Winchcombe, was once one of England's great Cistercian monasteries. Pilgrims came here from all over the country to pray before the abbey's phial of Christ's blood, a relic shown to be a fake at the time of the Dissolution, when the thirteenth-century monastery was demolished. Not much of the original complex remains beyond the foundations, but some cloister arches survive, worn by wind and rain. The ruin is undramatic, but Hailes is still worth visiting for the attached museum, where you can get a close-up look at thirteenth-century bosses, for the tranquillity of the spot and for the nearby **church**, which is older than the abbey and contains beautiful wall paintings dating from around 1300. The cartoon-like hunting scene was probably a warning to Sabbath-breakers.

Snowshill Manor

Three miles northeast of Hailes Abbey, the traditional Cotswold manor house of **Snowshill Manor** (April–June & Sept to early Nov Wed–Sun noon–5pm; July & Aug Mon & Wed–Sun noon–5pm; garden same months & days 11am–5.30pm; £6, gardens only £3; NT) invites a detour. Inspired as a boy by his grandmother's "wonderful" Chinese cabinet (now in the Zenith room of the house), the architect, craftsman and poet Charles Paget Wade (1883–1956) spent fifty years of his life in the pursuit of objects which were not "rare or valuable" but "of interest as records of various vanished handicrafts". The results of his forays – model carts, boneshaker bicycles, children's prams, wooden toys, beds, beetles, all kinds of musical instruments – were crammed into the house, while he himself lived in a cottage in the garden. It's an endlessly diverting collection, a veritable trove of exotic curiosities. Most dramatic is the arrangement of 26 Samurai warriors dating from the seventeeth to the nineteenth centuries in the Green Room. Note that entry is by timed ticket and there is a ten-minute walk to the house from the entrance to the grounds.

Cirencester and around

On the southern fringes of the Cotswolds, **CIRENCESTER** makes a refreshing change from its more gentrified neighbours. The "olde-worlde" image that many Cotswold towns indulge in has been exchanged for an endearingly old-fashioned atmosphere, generated partly by shops that haven't changed for decades.

Under the Romans, the town was called Corinium and ranked second only to Londinium in size and importance. A provincial capital and a centre of trade, it flourished for three centuries and had one of the largest forums north of the Alps. Few Roman remains are visible in Cirencester itself thanks to the destruction meted out by the Saxons in the sixth century. The new occupiers built an abbey (the longest in England at the time), but the town's prosperity was restored only with the wool boom of the Middle Ages, when the wealth of local merchants financed the construction of one of the finest Perpendicular churches in England. Cirencester has survived as one of the most affluent towns in the area, hence the much-vaunted title "Capital of the Cotswolds".

Cirencester's heart is the delightful swirling **Market Place**, on Mondays and Fridays packed by traders' stalls. An irregular line of eighteenth-century facades along the north side contrasts with the heavier Victorian structures opposite, but the parish church of **St John the Baptist**, built in stages during the fifteenth century, dominates. The extraordinary flying buttresses which support the tower had to be added when it transpired that the church had been constructed upon a filled-in ditch. Its grand three-tiered south porch, the largest in England – big enough to function as the town hall at one stage – leads to the nave, where slender piers and soaring arches create a superb sense of space, enhanced by clerestory windows that bathe the nave in a warm light. The church contains much of interest, including a colourful wineglass **pulpit**, carved in stone in around 1450 and one of the few pre-Reformation pulpits to have survived in Britain. North of the chancel, superb fan vaulting hangs overhead in the **chapel of St Catherine**, who appears in a still vivid fragment of a fifteenth-century wall painting. In the adjacent **Lady Chapel** are two good seventeenth-century monuments, to Humphrey Bridges and his family and to the dandified Sir William Master. Outside, one of the best views of the church is from the **Abbey Grounds**; site of the Saxon abbey, it's now a small park skirted by the modest river Churn and a fragment of the Roman city wall.

Few medieval buildings other than the church have survived in Cirencester. The houses along the town's most handsome streets – Park, Thomas and Coxwell – date mostly from the seventeenth and eighteenth centuries. One of those on Park Street houses the **Corinium Museum** (Mon–Sat 10am–5pm, Sun 2–5pm; £2.50), which devotes itself mainly to the Roman era. Given that the museum has one of the largest Roman collections in Britain, the number of exhibits on display is disappointing, but a lot of space is taken up by **mosaic pavements**, which are among the finest in the country, and the reconstructed triclinium (dining room with couches), kitchen, peristyle and butcher's shop.

A yew hedge the height of telegraph poles runs along Park Street, concealing **Cirencester House**, the home of the Earl of Bathurst. At no point can you see the building (it is plain anyway), but the attached three-thousand-acre park is open to the public: you enter it from Cecily Hill, a lovely street except for the eccentric Victorian barracks. Although the avenues in the park restrict the scope for walks, you can still enjoy a pleasant stroll. The polo pitches here attract some of the country's top players, with games held almost daily between May and September.

The **Brewery Arts Centre**, off Cricklade Street, is occupied by more than a dozen resident artists, whose studios you can visit and whose work you can buy in the shop. The centre's theatre hosts high-calibre plays and concerts (from jazz to classical), and there is a buzzing café on the first floor, open Monday to Saturday.

Practicalities

Nine roads radiate from Cirencester, five of them Roman, and **bus** services to the town could be better given its position, but there are daily connections from Swindon, fourteen miles southeast, and Cheltenham, fifteen miles north. All services stop in the Market Place. The **tourist office** (April–Dec Mon–Sat 9.30am–5.30pm; Jan–March Mon–Sat 9.30am–5pm; ℡01285/654180, ⓦwww.cotswold.gov.uk), in the Corn Hall on the Market Place, covers the whole of the Cotswolds and has a list of local **accommodation** pinned outside. A string of **B&Bs** lines Victoria Road, a short walk east: choose the house you fancy, since facilities and prices barely differ, though *The Ivy House* at no. 2 (℡01285/656626, ⓦwww.ivyhousecotswolds.com; no credit cards; ❷), *Abbeymead*, at no. 39a (℡01285/653740; no credit cards; ❷), and *The Leauses*, at no. 101 (℡01285/653643, Ⓔthe.leauses@virgin.net; no credit cards; ❷), are cheaper than most; all are non-smoking. For a little more luxury, stay at the *Crown of Crucis Hotel* in Ampney Crucis (℡01285/851806, ⓦwww.thecrown ofcrucis.co.uk; ❺), a sixteenth-century former coaching inn with riverside gardens, a good restaurant and a no-smoking rule; to reach it, head two-and-a-half miles east on the A417. There's a **youth hostel** in Duntisbourne Abbots (℡01285/821682; dorm beds £8.50), a lovely rural spot five miles west reachable on the infrequent bus #52 between Cirencester and Gloucester (weekdays only). The most accessible **campsite** is at the *Mayfield Touring Park* at Perrotts Brook (℡01285/831301, Ⓔjhutson@btclick.com), two miles north on the A435; any Cheltenham-bound bus will drop you there.

For **snacks** you can't do much better than *Keith's Coffee Shop* on Blackjack Street, which also serves the best coffee in town. The *Café Bar* **restaurant**, next to the Brewery Centre, is inexpensive and goes out of its way to make its vegetarian dishes interesting (no credit cards; closed Sun). The best choice for a relaxing evening meal, however, is *Harry Hare's* at 3 Gosditch St (℡01285 /652375), just behind the church, which specializes in classy renditions of down-to-earth English dishes for under £20. If you're splashing out and have transport, the *Crown of Crucis* in Ampney Crucis (see accommodation, above) is another option also worth considering.

Cirencester has plenty of **pubs**, their clientele swollen by tweedy students from the nearby Royal Agricultural College. Try the *Kings Head* on the Market Place or, for **bar meals**, the *Waggon & Horses* on London Road, and the *Butcher's Arms* in Ampney Crucis.

The Dunt Valley and Elkstone

The area northwest of Cirencester has a number of delightful churches well worth seeing, particularly in the **Dunt Valley**, one of the quietest corners of the Cotswolds yet just a stone's throw from the A417. Barn conversions and new houses attest to the number of cityfolk who've come here to escape the rat race, but few villages are large enough even to have a pub. Those without a car or a bike should not be discouraged from exploring: to visit the two best churches in the valley, at Daglingworth and Duntisbourne Rouse, will involve just a seven-mile walk. An excellent Ramblers' Association pamphlet, available from the tourist office, describes the route, or else use OS Landranger Map 163.

The hilltop **church** at **DAGLINGWORTH**, just two miles from Cirencester, has an unremarkable exterior, but inside there are four small stone panels – of Christ in Majesty, St Peter and two of the Crucifixion – that are among the best preserved Anglo-Saxon carving in the country. The simplicity and eccentric proportions of the figures, carved in deep relief, appear disconcertingly modern. Less than a mile beyond (you can walk along the Dunt for most of the way), the Saxon **church** of **DUNTISBOURNE ROUSE** perches on a steep bank beneath the road: a minute church for a minute valley, the Dunt being more a stream than a river. If you're driving, it's easy to miss; look for the small wooden sign in the hedge. The interior of the church can't quite live up to the setting, but it has a finely carved Norman chancel arch and a delightful thirteenth-century wall painting of daisies. The road follows the valley north past Duntisbourne Leer, gathered around a ford, and **DUNTIS-BOURNE ABBOTS** (two miles beyond Duntisbourne Rouse), where the houses tumble prettily down the hillside but the church is a disappointment by local standards.

On the other side of the A417, eight miles north of Cirencester and out of the Dunt Valley, **ELKSTONE** boasts the most beautiful **Norman church** in the Cotswolds. The fifteenth-century tower aside, the church retains its original Norman structure and carving, the latter at its best in the south porch. Inside, the simple harmony of the vaulted chancel outshines even the exquisite carving around the arches and east window, the whole bathed in golden light from the side windows. A tiny spiral staircase on the left of the altar leads to a rare priest's dovecote above the chancel.

Westonbirt Arboretum

About twelve miles southwest of Cirencester, **Westonbirt Arboretum** (daily 10am–8pm or sunset; £4.25; @www.westonbirtarboretum.com) claims one of the largest collections of temperate trees and shrubs in the world: the maple trees, which set the place ablaze in autumn, and the blankets of bluebells and anemones in spring draw the biggest crowds. Azaleas, rhododendrons and camellias provide other great splashes of colour. Numerous paths crisscross the six-hundred-acre garden: an average circular walk takes about an hour and a half, but you can easily stroll about for much longer than that. The arboretum flanks the A433, just west of Westonbirt village and three miles southwest of Tetbury, a handsome but untouristy Cotswold town. (Keen royalists should keep an eye open for the Prince of Wales and Princess Anne, who live nearby, at Highgrove and Gatcombe Park respectively.) The most useful public transport is the #620 Stroud–Bath **bus**, which runs past the arboretum every two hours or so (not Sun).

Malmesbury

The striking half-ruin of a Norman abbey presides over the small hilltown of **MALMESBURY**, one of the oldest boroughs in England. Lying eleven miles south of Cirencester (and only five miles north off the M4 motorway), it's not part of the Cotswolds geologically, though the town's early wealth was based on wool. Malmesbury certainly lacks the tweeness of the Cotswold towns to the north, with new housing estates encircling the centre, and modern developments marring views over the Avon. But none of this can detract from the splendour of the abbey, a majestic structure with some of the finest Romanesque sculpture in the country. The #92 bus service connects Cirencester and Malmesbury every one or two hours Monday to Saturday. Coming from Bath, it's best to catch a train to Chippenham and pick up a bus from there.

The High Street, which begins at the bottom of the hill by the old silk mills (converted into flats) and heads north across the river and up past a jagged row of ancient cottages, ends up at the octagonal **Market Cross**. Built in around 1490 to provide shelter from the rain, nowadays it is a favourite haunt of the local youth, whatever the weather. Nearby, the eighteenth-century **Tolsey Gate** leads through to the **Abbey** (daily: April–Oct 10am–5pm; Nov–March 10am–4pm). Founded in the seventh century and once a powerful Benedictine foundation, the abbey burnt down in about 1050; the twelfth-century building which replaced it was damaged during the Dissolution, and other parts collapsed at a later date. The **nave** is the only substantial Norman part to have survived, which it has done beautifully. Taking pride of place is the south porch, a multitude of sadly worn figures in three tiers surround the doorway, depicting scenes from the Creation, the Old Testament and the life of Christ, while inside the porch the apostles and Christ are carved in a fine deep relief: stately figures in flowing folds are topped by a flying angel. The tympanum shows Christ on a rainbow, supported by gracefully gymnastic angels. Within the main body of the church, the pale stone brings a dramatic freshness, particularly to the carving of the nave arches (look out for the Norman beak-heads) and of the clerestory. To the left of the high altar, the pulpit virtually hides the **tomb of King Athelstan**, grandson of Alfred the Great and the first Saxon to be recognized as king of England; the tomb, however, is empty, the location of the king's remains unknown. The abbey's greatest surviving treasures are housed in the parvise (room above the porch), reached via a narrow spiral staircase right of the main doorway, where pride of place is given to four Flemish **medieval Bibles**, written on parchment and sumptuously illuminated with gilt ink and exquisite miniature paintings.

As well as harbouring the tomb of a former king of England, Malmesbury was the birthplace of **Thomas Hobbes**, the moral and political philosopher who suggested in his book *Leviathan* that the only way to avoid social chaos was for people to surrender their rights to an all-powerful authority, an ideology that has led to his being claimed as a precursor by the Left and Right alike. Another local celebrity is **Elmer the Monk**, who in 1005 attempted to fly from the abbey tower with the aid of wings: he limped for the rest of his life, but won immortal fame as the "flying monk".

The **tourist office** in the town hall off Cross Hayes car park (Mon–Thurs 9am–noon & 1–4.50pm, Fri closes 4.20pm, Sat 10am–noon & 1–4pm; ☏01666/823748, ⊛www.wiltshiretourism.co.uk) has an **accommodation** list outside. There are a number of choices right in the centre of town: *The Old Manor House* on Oxford St, above the material shop, has nicely old-fashioned rooms (☏01666/823494; no credit cards; ❶), and on High St, the pricier *Kings Arms* (☏01666/823383, ⊛www.malmesburywilts.freeserve.co.uk; ❸) has more standard facilities. The *Old Bell* (☏01666/822344, ⊛www.oldbellhotel.com; ❻), in Abbey Row, originally built as a guest house for the abbey, sports Japanese-themed bedrooms in its coach house. For **food** the *Whole Hog*, a stone-walled tearoom-cum-pub overlooking the Market Place, is inexpensive, and *Summer Café* on the High St, is better for teas and coffees and also does good sandwiches. The *Guild Hall Bar* on Oxford St, opposite the tourist office, is a free house with good ale and pool.

Cheltenham

Until the eighteenth century **CHELTENHAM** was like any other Cotswold town, but then the discovery of a spring in 1716 transformed it into Britain's most popular **spa**. During Cheltenham's prime, a century or so later, the royal, the rich and the famous descended in hordes to take the waters, which were said to cure anything from constipation to worms. These days, while a fair

Cheltenham racecourse, a ten-minute walk north of Pittville Park at the foot of Cleeve Hill, is Britain's main steeplechasing venue. The principal event of the season, the three-day **National Hunt Festival** in March, attracts forty thousand people each day. A fair proportion of them come from Ireland, the birthplace of some of the greatest horses to have raced here, including the supreme steeplechaser, **Arkle**. Other meetings take place in January, April, October, November and December: a list of fixtures is posted up at the tourist office. For the cheapest but arguably the best view, pay £5 (rising to £15 during the Festival) for entry to the Courage Enclosure, as the pen in the middle is known. For schedules and other information, call ☎01242/513014 or access the website at ⓦwww.cheltenham.co.uk. For the National Hunt Festival it's essential to buy tickets in advance.

A popular pre-meet watering hole is the *King's Arms*, a short walk east of the racecourse in **Prestbury**, an old Cotswold village with a reputation for being the most haunted village in England, and which has now been subsumed into the town. **Fred Archer**, considered by many to have been the finest Flat jockey of all time, was brought up here, and he features prominently among the pub's racing memorabilia. The pub has sadly lost much of its character since becoming part of a chain, and you might find the nearby *Royal Oak* more congenial.

proportion of Cheltenham's hundred thousand-odd inhabitants are undoubtedly well-heeled, of Conservative persuasion (true of the Cotswolds in general) and above retirement age, the town saves itself from too smug an image by a lively and increasingly cosmopolitan atmosphere. It's by far the best spot around for nightlife and makes a convenient base for touring the area.

Cheltenham is a natural stopping-off place en route to the Severn Valley, and the haughty elegance of the Regency architecture, characterized by fancy ironwork and Greek columns, can be a pleasant change after the folksy Cotswolds. The town is also a thriving arts centre, famous for its festivals of **jazz** (April), **classical music** (July) and **literature** (October) – and then, of course, there are the races (see box below). In addition, Coopers' Hill, six miles southwest on the A46, is the venue for the region's most bizarre, and established, competition. On the second bank holiday in May, a steep section of the Cotswold escarpment hosts the village's annual **Cheese Rolling Festival**, when a large Double Gloucester cheese is rolled down the one-in-two incline and chased by dozens of drunken folk; the first to grab the cheese is the winner. The damage to life and limb has resulted in the race being banned in recent years, but it has been reinstated by popular demand, and now there are four races run, three for men and one for women.

Arrival, information and accommodation

All long-distance **buses** arrive at the station in Royal Well Road, just west off the Promenade. The **train station** is on Queen's Road, southwest of the centre; buses G and F run into town every fifteen minutes, otherwise it's a twenty-minute walk. Among the many leaflets and brochures handed out at the **tourist office**, at 77 Promenade (Mon–Sat 9.30am–5.15pm; ☎01242/ 522878, ⓦwww.visitcheltenham.gov.uk), is one giving a rundown of bus services to and from most destinations in the area. They also sell tickets for walking **tours** of the town (Mon–Fri at 11am; £2.50), and for guided bus tours stopping at several destinations in the Cotswolds that are otherwise difficult to reach on public transport (late June to mid-Sept Tues & Wed; £16); they're popular, so book in advance.

© Crown copyright

CHELTENHAM

Pedestrianized street

RESTAURANTS
The Belgian Monk   B
Boogaloos   C
The Daffodil   F
Le Petit Blanc   D
Orange Tree   A
Upstairs at the Beehive E
ACCOMMODATION
Abbey Hotel   2
Brennan   6
Crossways   4
Kandinsky Hotel   3
Lawn Hotel   1
Lypiatt House   8
Willoughby Hotel   7
YMCA   5

Racecourse

PITTVILLE   Pitville Pump Room

Campsite

Art Gallery & Museum

Bus Station

LANSDOWN

Railway Station

Montpellier Gardens

Sandford Park

0   400 yds

Cheltenham makes an excellent base for exploring the Cotswolds by **bike** if you can face the hills: they're available to rent from Compass Holidays, who operate from a portakabin at the train station (book on ☎01242/250642, ⓦwww.compass-holidays.com; £11/day). They also arrange cycling holidays. **Hotels** and **guest houses** abound, many of them in fine Regency houses, and rooms are easy to come by – except during the races and festivals, when you should book weeks in advance. There are several B&Bs on or near Bath Road, east of the promenade.

Hotels & B&Bs

Abbey Hotel 14–16 Bath Parade ☎01242 /516053, ⓦwww.abbeyhotel-cheltenham.com. Rooms here are attractively and individually furnished and breakfast is taken overlooking the garden. Friendly service. ❹

Brennan 21 St Luke's Rd ☎01242/525904. This is a good value option in a small Regency building, on a quiet square. Non-smoking dining room. ❷

Crossways 57 Bath Rd ☎01242/527683, ⓦwww.cross.ways.btinternet.co.uk. This comfortable, non-smoking Regency house makes a good base, only two minutes' walk from the centre. ❷

Kandinsky Hotel Bayshill Rd ☎01242/527788,

ⓦwww.hotelkandinsky.com. Recently opened hotel with colourful and stylish bedrooms, Chinese and Indonesian decoration, and 1950s style disco (residents and members only) – not at all bad value for the price. ❺

Lawn Hotel 5 Pittville Lawn ☎01242/526638. Near the park, this is quiet and excellent value. Themed rooms are artistically decorated and vegetarians and vegans are welcomed. No credit cards. ❷

Lypiatt House Lypiatt Rd ☎01242/224994, ⓦwww.travel-uk.net/lypiatthouse. Set in its own grounds, this place rates highly for comfort and personal attention. Open fires and a conservatory with a small bar set the tone. ❹

Willoughby Hotel 1 Suffolk Square ☎01242 /522798, ⓦ www.wlloughbyhouse.com. South of the centre, this smart place has high-class home comforts at fairly steep prices. Self-catering available.➏

Hostels and camping

YMCA 6 Victoria Walk ☎01242/524024. Cheltenham's cheapest central option is a short walk from the town hall. There are also extremely good-value lunches on offer. Private room £15.
Woodmancote Park Woodmancote ☎01242 /674372. The nearest campsite, three miles north and accessible on Stagecoach bus #51 from Pittville Street. If you're driving, follow the signs for Prestbury/Winchcombe/B4362 and continue until you see a sign pointing left to Woodmancote village.

The Town

The focus of Cheltenham, the broad **Promenade**, sweeps majestically south from the High Street, lined with the town's grandest houses, smartest shops and most genteel public gardens. A short walk north of the High Street brings you to **Pittville**, which, planned as a spa town to rival Cheltenham, was never completed and is now mostly parkland. Here you can stroll along a few solitary Regency avenues and visit the grandest spa building, the domed **Pump Room** (Mon & Wed–Sun 11am–4pm), whose chief function nowadays is as a concert hall – though you can sample England's only naturally alkaline water for free here. On your return route, the **Holst Birthplace Museum** is worth a glance, at 4 Clarence Rd (Tues–Sat 10am–4pm; £2.50). Once the home of the composer of *The Planets*, the intimate rooms hold plenty of Holst memorabilia, including his piano, and also give a good insight into Victorian family life. Back in the centre, the well-set out **Art Gallery and Museum** on Clarence St (Mon–Sat 10am–5.20pm, Sun 2–4.20pm; free; ⓦwww.cheltenhammuseum.org.uk) marks the high point of Cheltenham. It's very good on social history, with different eras represented by table displays of personal belongings and a typical dinner of the time. There's also a fine room dedicated to the Arts and Crafts Movement, containing several pieces by Charles Voysey and Ernest Gimson, two of the period's most graceful designers. Also on display is an array of rare Chinese ceramics, works by Cotswold artists such as Stanley Spencer and Vanessa Bell, and a section devoted to Edward Wilson, a local man who died on Scott's ill-fated expedition to the Antarctic.

For a matchless view over the town, catch bus #606 out to Southam, one mile north of Prestbury village on the B4632, and follow the public footpath east up the sheer face of the Cotswold escarpment to the top of **Cleeve Common**. The summit, known as Cleeve Cloud and topped by a cluster of radio masts, is the highest point along the Cotswold escarpment (1083ft). To round off the walk, head north along the ridge to Cleeve Hill, from where you can pick up buses back into town via the main road.

Eating, drinking and nightlife

Cheltenham has experienced a **restaurant** renaissance in the last few years and caters for all tastes and pockets. It's also got the best style bars and **pubs** in the area, and its **clubs** draw in the punters from nearby Gloucester as well as the Cotswolds.

Restaurants

The Belgian Monk 45 Clarence St. Just down from the museum, Belgian beers, buckets of mussels and a hearty atmosphere are the order of the day. Inexpensive to moderate.
Boogaloos 16 Regent St. Good for salads and sandwiches. Chill out in the relaxed sofa basement or the buzzing, brightly coloured upstairs rooms. Closed Mon–Sat eve & all Sun. Inexpensive to moderate.
The Daffodil 18–20 Suffolk Parade. Eat in the circle bar or auditorium of this former cinema, where the screen has been replaced with a hubbub of chefs. Three-course set menu £12.50. Moderate to expensive.

Orange Tree 317 High St ☏01242/234232. Vegetarians, vegans and allergy sufferers will appreciate the wide range of dishes on offer here. There's a pleasant courtyard, and breakfasts, organic wines and beers are all available. Closed Mon eve & all Sun. Moderate.

Le Petit Blanc next to Queen's Hotel, The Promenade ☏01242/266800, ⊛www.petit-blanc.com. An outpost of Raymond Blanc's famed *Manoir Aux Quat' Saisons* where you can eat contemporary French cuisine at prices which become distinctly affordable at lunchtime – the three-course set lunch menu is £15 per head. Moderate to expensive.

Upstairs at the Beehive 1–3 Montpellier Villas ☏01242/702270. Friendly ambience and great French food in a lofty, blue-draped room above the pub make this newly opened restaurant a popular spot. Closed Sun eve, Mon & Tues. Moderate.

Pubs and clubs

The Beehive 1–3 Montpellier Villas. Easygoing Cheltenham institution. Games shed, courtyard garden and cosy snug.

Kemble Brewery 27 Fairview St. A little way out from the centre, this is more like a front room than a pub; serving local beer it is full of welcoming locals.

Montpellier Wine Bar Bayshill Lodge, Montpellier St. Stylish wine bar with restaurant, with lovely bow-fronted windows for people-watching or being seen.

The Retreat 10–11 Suffolk Parade. Lively venue which caters to the business fraternity at lunchtime and Cheltenham Ladies College set in the evening. Good lunches served. Closed Sun.

Subtone 115–117 The Promenade ⊛www.subtone.co.uk. Cheltenham's most popular club, playing 70s and 80s to funk.

Tailor's Wine Bar 4 Cambray Place. Just off the High Street, here you can relax in old leather armchairs, watch sport on a big screen or sit in the pavement courtyard.

Time 33–35 Albion St ☏01242/570583. The county's largest dance club, playing mainstream sounds.

Vodka Bar 6 Regent St. Killer drinks from a range of 24 vodkas, served to the accompaniment of DJs playing house and funk.

Stroud and around

Five heavily populated valleys converge at **STROUD**, twelve miles west of Cirencester, creating an exhausting jumble of hills and a sense of high activity atypical of the Cotswolds. The bustle is not a new phenomenon. During the heyday of the wool trade the Frome River powered 150 mills, turning Stroud into the centre of the local cloth industry. Even now, Stroud is very much a working town, and one which doesn't need to peddle its heritage to the tourists in order to survive. While some of the old mills have been converted into flats, others contain factories, but only two continue to make cloth – no longer the so-called Stroudwater Scarlet used for military uniforms, but high-quality felt for tennis balls and snooker tables. In recent years, Stroud has become a thriving alternative centre, its town council Green since 1990, and is on line for implementing one of the country's first eco-housing projects. You'll see mountains of organic food and sustainable goods for sale in the centre, while the nearby valleys are home to a growing community of artists and New Agers. Sadly, however, in spite of its scenic setting, the town remains the dowdiest of the region.

For visitors, the main point of interest is the excellent and family-friendly **Museum in the Park**, housed in an eighteenth-century mansion in Stratford Park, half a mile from the centre of town on the Gloucester road (April–Sept Tues–Fri noon–5pm, Sat & Sun 11am–5pm; Oct–March Tues–Fri 1–5pm, Sat & Sun 11am–4pm; £2.50). Opened in 2001, and beautifully decorated and laid out, the collection demonstrates the history of the town through imaginatively themed rooms such as "Clean, Fit and Tidy" and "Industry and Invention", which are complemented by numerous questions and quotations. You can hear the voice of local author Laurie Lee and see the world's first lawnmower invented in 1830 by another local, Edward Budding, who took his inspiration from the machines which cut the nap on cloth. Look out for the lovely eighteenth-century paintings showing the tentering (hanging out) of the scarlet cloth on the hillsides.

Industrial archeology is strewn the length of the Frome Valley – the so-called Golden Valley. Council offices occupy one of the valley's finest mills, **Ebley Mill**, a twenty-minute walk west of the centre along the old Stroudwater Canal – for the best view you should then walk south across the field to the village of **Selsley**.

The unused **Severn and Thames Canal** east of Stroud cuts a more picturesque route, particularly beyond Chalford, three miles east, where houses perch precariously on the hillside. Walk thirty minutes along the towpath from here and you'll end up at the mouth of the **Sapperton tunnel**, more than two miles long and a great feat of eighteenth-century engineering. It is unsafe to go inside, so seek sustenance at the nearby *Daneway Inn* instead, or head for the hilltop village of Sapperton, a world away from the hurly-burly of the Frome Valley.

Trains on the London–Gloucester rail line stop at Stroud, which is also well served by **buses** from Cirencester. These and other bus services arrive at the station on Merrywalks. The **tourist office** is in the Subscription Rooms on Kendrick St (Mon–Sat 10am–5pm; ☎01453/760960, ⊛www.visitthecotswolds.org.uk). The most central place to **stay** is the *London Hotel* (☎01453/759992, ⊛www.the-london-hotel.co.uk; ❸), otherwise head for the (non-smoking) townhouse, the *Lay-Bye*, at 7 Castlemead Rd (☎01453/751514; no credit cards; ❷), fifteen minutes' walk south of the centre, or the *Downfield Hotel* at 134 Cainscross Rd (☎01453/764496, ⊛www.downfieldotel.demon.co.uk; ❸), in a Georgian building five minutes from the High Street. You'll find the nearest **youth hostel** and **campsite** at Slimbridge (see below).

For **food** in the daytime go straight to *Mills Café* in Withey's Yard off High Street, which sells scrumptious cakes, home-made soups and other wholesome concoctions. In the evenings, the choice narrows down to Indian or Chinese as Stroud's nightlife gives over to laddish pub culture. Its saving grace, however, is the *Retreat* wine bar in Church St, which is smartish but not overpriced.

Uley

The B4066 cuts a glorious route along the valley ridge southwest of Stroud, passing through **ULEY**, six miles from town. Boasting one of the best settings in the region, the village **church** lords it over the small green and the *Old Crowne* pub, where the local brews include one called Pigor Mortis. **Uley Bury**, among the largest hill forts in Britain, extends along the ridge above the village. The path from the church takes you up the shortest and steepest route, though motorists can opt to drive up to the car park right by the fort. Fences prevent you from clambering on top of the bury, but you can walk around the edge – a distance of about two miles altogether – and take in some staggering views. The atmosphere peaks on a winter's day, when bracing winds blow across the ridge while mist gathers in the valley below.

Slimbridge

Eight miles southwest of Stroud, out of the Cotswolds, **SLIMBRIDGE** sits in a narrow corridor between the M5 and the Severn – a surprising location for the **Slimbridge Wildfowl and Wetlands Centre** (daily: April–Oct 9.30am–6pm; Nov–March 9.30am–5pm; last entry 1hr before closing; £6), covering 120 acres between Sharpness Canal and the river. Since ornithologist Sir Peter Scott created it in 1946, the centre has become Britain's largest **wildfowl sanctuary**, and a breeding ground with an important conservation role.

Geese, swans, ducks and a huge gathering of flamingos make up the bulk of the birdlife. While some birds are resident all year round, many are migratory: the greatest numbers congregate in the winter months, when Bewick swans, for example, migrate from Russia. There is an extensive network of trails around the sanctuary, with hides for observation.

Slimbridge has a comfortable, purpose-built **youth hostel** (℡01453/ 890275), with beds for £10, accessible from a lane opposite the *Tudor Arms* pub in the village, and a **campsite**, the *Tudor Caravan Park* (℡01453/890483), midway between the village and the wildfowl centre, about half a mile from each. The only **buses** to go anywhere near Slimbridge are those between Gloucester and Bristol or Dursley, which stop by the turn-off on the A38, just over a mile east of the village.

Berkeley

Though quite secluded within a swathe of meadows and neat gardens, **Berkeley Castle** (April & May Tues–Sun 2–5pm; June & Sept Tues–Sat 11am–5pm, Sun 2–5pm; July & Aug Mon–Sat 11am–5pm, Sun 2–5pm; Oct Sun 2–5pm; £5.70, grounds only £2) dominates the little village of **BERKE-LEY**, five miles southwest of Slimbridge on the A38. The fortress has an agreeably turreted medieval look, the robust twelfth-century walls softened by later accretions acquired in its gradual transformation into a family home. The interior is packed with mementoes of its long history, including its grisliest moment in 1327, when Edward II was murdered here – apparently by a red-hot iron thrust into his bowels. You can view the cell where the event took place, along with dungeons, dining room, kitchen, picture gallery and the Great Hall. Outside, the grounds include an Elizabethan terraced garden and a Butterfly Farm (£2), and within easy walking distance, in the village itself, is the **Jenner Museum** (April–Sept Tues–Sat 12.30–5.30pm, Sun 1–5.30pm; Oct Sun 1–5.30pm; £2.80), dedicated to Edward Jenner, discoverer of the principle of vaccination.

Berkeley is fiendishly difficult to reach by public transport, connected only by coaches from Gloucester operated by Beaumont Travel (Mon–Sat 5 daily, none on Sun; ℡01452/309770). For a lunchtime stop near Berkeley, follow the narrow High Street out of the centre of the village for about a mile to reach the *Salutation*, an unpretentious country **pub** with a garden; it serves up bacon sandwiches and the like at lunchtimes.

Painswick

The A46 and the B4070 are equally attractive routes linking Stroud and Cheltenham, but the former has the edge because after four miles you reach the old wool town of **PAINSWICK**, where ancient buildings jostle for space on narrow streets running downhill off the busy main street. The fame of Painswick's **church** stems not so much from the building itself as from the surrounding **graveyard**, where 99 yew trees, cut into bizarre bulbous shapes resembling lollipops, surround a collection of eighteenth-century table-tombs unrivalled in the Cotswolds. However, it's the **Rococo Garden** (mid-Jan to April, Oct & Nov Wed–Sun 11am–5pm; May–Sept daily 11am–5pm; £3.30; ⊛www.rococogarden.co.uk), about half a mile north up the Gloucester road and attached to Painswick House (not open to the public), that ranks as the town's main attraction. Created in the early eighteenth century and later abandoned, the garden is being restored to its original form with the aid of a painting dated 1748. Although there's usually some restoration in progress, it's a beautiful example – and the country's only one – of Rococo garden design, a short-lived fashion typified by a mix of formal geometrical shapes and more naturalistic, curving lines. With a vegetable patch as an unusual centrepiece, the Painswick garden spreads across a sheltered gully – for the best vistas, walk around anticlockwise. In February and March people flock to see the snow-drops that smother the slopes beneath the pond, during which time the garden is open daily (call to check exact dates: ☎01452/813204).

The best **bus** service to Painswick is the #46 between Stroud and Cheltenham, which runs hourly during the week and four times on Sundays. The number of **guest houses** and **hotels** attests to the amount of people who find Painswick a more congenial place than Stroud, and the **tourist office**, housed in an old school at the bottom of the main street (April–Oct Tues–Sun 10am–4pm; ☎01452/813552), can help you find somewhere at the right price if the following places are booked: *Thorne Guest House* on Friday St (☎01452/812476; no credit cards; closed Dec & Jan; ❸), one of the oldest houses in the village, or *Cardynham House* on St Mary's St (☎01452/814006, Ⓦwww.cardynham.co.uk; ❹), where all rooms have four-posters or half-testers, and one has a lounge and private pool (£120 a night). In the evenings, there's a set meal on offer in the attached Thai **restaurant** for £21.20 (closed Sun & Mon), which is almost the only place to eat in the village – not counting the nearby *Royal Oak*, reckoned to be the best **pub** hereabouts. Alternatively, you might consider heading out of Painswick, to the village of Edge, half a mile west, where *Upper Dorey's Mill* (☎01452/812459, Ⓦwww.doreys.co.uk;❸) offers plenty of rural atmosphere in a converted eighteenth-century cloth mill by the riverside (non-smokers only).

Gloucester

For centuries life was good for **GLOUCESTER**. The Romans chose the spot for a garrison to guard the Severn and spy on Wales, and later for a *colonia* or home for retired soldiers – the highest status a provincial Roman town could dream of. Commercial prestige came with trade up the River Severn, which developed into one of the busiest trade routes in Europe. The city's political importance hit its peak under the Normans, when William the Conqueror met here frequently with his council of nobles. The Middle Ages saw Gloucester's rise as a religious centre, and the construction of what is now the cathedral, but also saw its political and economic decline: navigating the Severn as far up as Gloucester was so difficult that most trade gradually shifted south to Bristol. In a brave attempt to reverse the city's decline, a canal was opened in 1827 to link Gloucester to Sharpness, on a broader stretch of the Severn further south. Trade picked up for a time, but it was only a temporary stay of execution.

Today, the canal is busy once again, though this time with pleasure boats. The Victorian dockyards too have undergone a facelift and are touted as the city's great new tourist attraction (and at the time of writing a development scheme to include restaurants, offices, housing and a hotel is due for completion in 2002). Gloucester's most magnificent possession, however, is the **cathedral**, its tower visible for miles around. Few other buildings in the city have survived the ravages of history and the twentieth century, with the centre a mish-mash of medieval ruins swallowed up by ugly new buildings. Gloucester is solidly downmarket, discount stores taking the place of the boutiques which characterize nearby Cheltenham. Yet this comes almost as a relief: Gloucester is without airs, and as variegated culturally as it is architecturally; you can mingle with farmers at the livestock market on Priory Road (Mon & Thurs) and then head

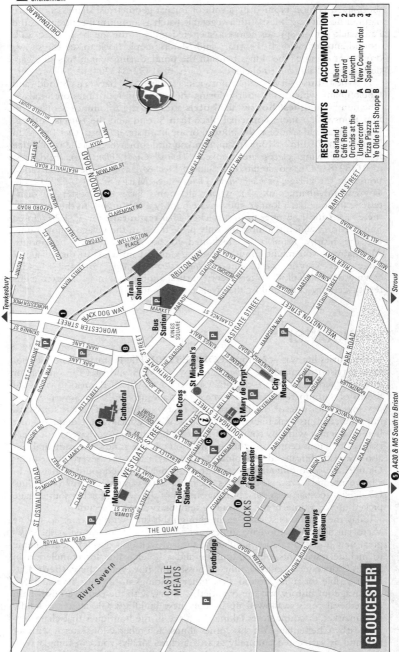

GLOUCESTER

Cheltenham

Tewkesbury

Ross & Ledbury

Stroud

, A430 & M5 South to Bristol

ACCOMMODATION

Albert	C	1
Edward	E	2
Lulworth		5
New County Hotel	A	3
Spalite	D	4

RESTAURANTS

Bearland
Café René
Orchids at the
Undercroft
Pizza Piazza
Ye Olde Fish Shoppe B

Train Station

Bus Station

Kings Square

Market Parade

St Michael's Tower

The Cross

Cathedral

Folk Museum

Police Station

Regiments of Gloucester Museum

St Mary de Crypt

City Museum

DOCKS

National Waterways Museum

CASTLE MEADS

River Severn

Footbridge

THE QUAY

© Crown copyright

along to the Guildhall on Eastgate Street, a buzzing arts centre with a cinema, regular exhibitions and a full and varied programme of concerts.

A web of roads engulfs Gloucester, surrounding the city like the tentacles of an octopus. If you're **driving**, head for the docks (well signposted) and park there. National Express runs **buses** from all neighbouring cities and beyond, and there are frequent local services from Cheltenham. **Trains** arrive every one or two hours from London, Cheltenham, Cardiff, Worcester and Bristol.

The City

Gloucester lies on the east bank of the Severn, its centre spread around a curve in the river. **The Cross**, once the entrance to the Roman forum, marks the heart of the city and the meeting-point of Northgate, Southgate, Eastgate and Westgate streets, all Roman roads. **St Michael's Tower**, the remains of an old church, overlooks it. The main shopping area lies east of the Northgate–Southgate axis, with the **cathedral** and the **docks**, the focus of interest, to the west of it.

Southgate and Westgate streets

The most interesting parish church in Gloucester is **St Mary de Crypt** on Southgate Street, mostly late medieval but with some of its original Norman features. A soft, soothing light filters through the stained-glass windows, and fragments of a sixteenth-century wall painting of the Adoration of the Magi in the chancel shows unusual detail for work of that period. The church is kept locked, but you can get the key from the tourist office across the road. Greyfriars runs alongside St Mary's, past the ruins of a Franciscan church and the Eastgate Market to the **City Museum** on Brunswick Rd (July–Sept Mon–Sat 10am–5pm, Sun 10am–4pm; rest of year Mon–Sat 10am–5pm; £2; combined ticket with Folk Museum £3; ⓦwww.mylife.gloucester.gov.uk), with a good archeological collection including the decorative bronze Birdlip mirror and what's claimed to be the world's oldest complete backgammon set (1100 AD), carved from bone and amber. A fragment of the Roman city wall, preserved *in situ* below ground level, can be viewed from the museum on summer Saturdays only, or at any time from Eastgate Street. Westgate Street, quieter and many times more pleasant than its three Roman counterparts, retains several medieval buildings. One of them, a creaking timber-framed house at the bottom of the street, contains the **Folk Museum** (July–Sept Mon–Sat 10am–5pm, Sun 10am–4pm; rest of year Mon–Sat 10am–5pm; £2; combined ticket with City Museum £3; ⓦwww.mylife.gloucester.gov.uk), which illustrates the social history of the Gloucester area using an impressive collection of objects, from huge wrought-iron cheese presses to salt-filled rolling pins used to scare off witches. College Court alley leads from Westgate Street to the haven of the cathedral, passing the Beatrix Potter shop and museum – the house sketched by the children's artist and author while she was on holiday here in 1897 and subsequently appearing in every copy of *The Tailor of Gloucester*.

The Cathedral

The superb condition of Gloucester **Cathedral** (daily 7.30am–6pm; ⓦwww.gloucestercathedral.uk.com) is striking in a city that has lost so much of its past. An abbey was founded on this spot by the Saxons, but four centuries later Benedictine monks came and built their own church, begun in 1069. As a place of worship it shot to importance after the murder at Berkeley Castle of Edward II in 1327: Bristol and Malmesbury wouldn't take his body, but

Gloucester did, and the king's shrine became a major place of pilgrimage. The money generated helped to finance the conversion of the church into the country's first and greatest example of the **Perpendicular style**: the magnificent 225-foot tower crowns the achievement. Henry VIII recognized the church's prestige by conferring on it the status of cathedral.

Beneath the reconstructions of the fourteenth and fifteenth centuries, some Norman aspects remain, best seen in the **nave**, flanked by sturdy pillars and arches adorned with immaculate zigzag mouldings. Only when you reach the choir and transepts can you see how skilfully the new church was built inside the old, the Norman masonry hidden beneath the finer lines of the Perpendicular panelling and tracery. The **choir** has extraordinary fourteenth-century misericords, and also provides the best vantage point for admiring the east window (at present scaffolded over), completed in around 1350 and – at almost 80 feet tall – the **largest medieval window** in Britain. Beneath it, to the left (as you're facing the east window) is the **tomb of Edward II**, immortalized in alabaster and marble and in good fettle apart from some graffiti. In the nearby **Lady Chapel**, delicate carved tracery holds a staggering patchwork of windows, virtually creating walls of stained glass. There are well-preserved monuments here, too, but the tomb of Robert II, in the **south ambulatory**, is far more unusual. Robert, eldest son of William the Conqueror, died in 1134, but the painted wooden effigy dates from around 1290. Dressed as a crusader, he lies in a curious pose, with his arms and legs crossed, his right hand gripping his sword ready to do battle with the infidel. The modern, vibrantly blue glass installed in the south ambulatory chapel works surprisingly well in the context.

The innovative nature of the cathedral's design can perhaps be best appreciated in the beautiful **cloisters**, completed in 1367 and featuring the first fan vaulting in the country. The fine quality of the work is outdone perhaps only by Henry VII's Chapel in Westminster Abbey, which it inspired. Back inside, an **exhibition** in the upstairs galleries, reached from the north transept (April–Oct Mon–Fri 10.30am–4pm, Sat 10.30am–3pm; £1.50), traces the history of the cathedral, putting it into context with that of the city as a whole. Here, you can try out the **Whispering Gallery**, where you can pick up the tiniest sounds from across the vaulting. Admission to the exhibition includes access to the **treasury**, the usual assortment of ecclesiastical bric-a-brac, including flagons and chalices. You can also climb the **tower** for the best views of Gloucester (April–Oct Wed, Thurs, Fri 2.30pm, Sat 2pm & 3pm; £2.50).

The Docks

The **Docks** complex was developed during the fifty years following the opening of the Sharpness canal in 1827. The import of corn represented the bulk of the port's business at that time, and huge **warehouses** were built for storing the grain. Fourteen of them have survived, mostly now converted into municipal offices, shops and museums, a redevelopment at its most crudely commercial in the **Merchants' Quay** shopping centre, an oversized greenhouse full of forlorn shoppers.

The **National Waterways Museum** (daily 10am–5pm, last admission 4pm; £4.95; ⓦ www.nwm.org.uk), in the southernmost Llanthony Warehouse, completely immerses you in the canal mania which swept Britain in the eighteenth and nineteenth centuries, touching on everything from the engineering of the locks to the lives of the horses that trod the towpaths. The three floors contain plenty of atmospheric noises off, videos, accessible information and interactive displays. Out from the main building you can practise "walking the wall" in the time honoured manner of boatmen, who propelled their narrowboats through the tunnels by their feet, and explore the boats themselves along the quayside. In the old customs house, the **Regiments of Gloucestershire Museum** (June–Sept daily 10am–5pm; Oct–May Tues–Sun 10am–5pm; ⓦwww .glosters.org.uk; £4) does an award-winning job of making a potentially dull or alienating subject fascinating. It doesn't rely on the displays of uniforms and miscellaneous memorabilia used in most military museums, but concentrates on all aspects of life as a soldier, both in war and during peacetime.

Practicalities

The bus and train stations are opposite one another across Bruton Way, five minutes' walk east of the Cross. The **tourist office** is at 28 Southgate St (Mon–Sat 10am–5pm; ☏01452/396572, ⓦwww.visit-glos.org.uk). Judging from the amount of **accommodation** in the city centre, Gloucester doesn't expect many visitors to stay overnight. Of the few **hotels** within easy walking distance of the train station and centre, the *Albert* at 56–58 Worcester St (☏01452/502081, ⓦwww.alberthotel.com; ❷), a listed red-brick building from the 1830s, and the Victorian *Edward* at 88 London Rd (☏01452/525865; ❸) offer the best value. Also very central, and with more comforts but fairly bland, is the *New County Hotel* at 44 Southgate St (☏01452/307000, ⓦwww.meridianleisure.com; ❹). Among the central, inexpensive B&Bs is *Spalite* (☏01452/380828; ❷), at the bottom of Southgate Street near the docks, although it's right on the main road and a bit prone to traffic noise, and the four-storey *Lulworth* at 12 Midland Rd (☏01452/521881; ❶), in a quiet location behind the park.

The selection of **restaurants** is only slightly more remarkable than the hotels, and many places are open only during the day. You'll find reliable if rather unimaginative fare in the *Orchids at the Undercroft* restaurant in the cathedral, open until 5pm, and at the café-bar in the Guildhall on Eastgate Street – open until 11pm and always lively. *Ye Olde Fish Shoppe* on Hare Lane, even more of a Gloucester institution, occupies a sixteenth-century building and is the fanciest take-away for miles; it serves excellent crispy fish until 6.30pm, though the attached restaurant stays open later (☏01452/255502; no credit cards; closed all Sun & Mon eve). In the evenings, choice extends to the vaulted *Bearland Restaurant* in Longsmith Street, with a set-price menu at £11.95, or the atmospherically French *Café René*, Greyfriars, Southgate Street, where walls and ceilings are smothered with bottles (closed Mon & Tues). For pizzas go to *Pizza Piazza* at Merchants' Quay – the only reason to venture to the docks in the evening.

There isn't a huge choice of **pubs**, the best are all within spitting distance of the Cross. The rambling fifteenth-century *New Inn* in Northgate Street has a good atmosphere, a splendid galleried courtyard and cheap meals, but for really tasty hot food at rock bottom prices go to the *Fountain Inn*, down a narrow alley off Westgate Street; this pub pulls a sublime pint of Abbot ale and has tables in an olde-worlde adjacent courtyard – ideal for a sunny day.

Tewkesbury and around

The small market town of **TEWKESBURY**, ten miles north of Gloucester, stands hemmed in by the Avon and Severn rivers, which converge nearby, and the threat of floods has curbed expansion more efficiently than any conservation-conscious planning office could. Pressure of space accounts for the narrow alleys and courts leading off from the main streets, of which thirty of the original ninety still survive. The comparatively unchanging face of Tewkesbury is also due to the fact that it almost completely missed out on the Industrial Revolution. Elegant Georgian houses and medieval timber-framed buildings still line several of the town's main streets – especially Church Street – and the Norman **abbey** has survived as one of the greatest in England. Some old buildings inevitably fell to postwar bulldozers, however, particularly along the High Street, and recent years haven't been kind to the town's economy. Tewkesbury is still recovering from the recession which hit local aerospace and electronics industries particularly badly – its title "The Silicon Valley of the West Country" rings rather hollow these days.

The constant rumble of traffic through Tewkesbury can be troublesome, but the fact that four main roads meet here (Gloucester, Worcester, Evesham and Ledbury are all within fifteen miles) means that getting to the town is fairly easy. Stagecoach, Swanbrook and Midland Red operate most **buses** to Tewkesbury, running from Gloucester, Cheltenham, Worcester and Evesham; for current timetable information, call the tourist office (see opposite).

Tewkesbury Abbey

The site of **Tewkesbury Abbey** (daily 7.30am–6pm, closes 5pm in winter) was first selected for a Benedictine monastery in the eighth century, but virtually nothing of the Saxon complex survived a sacking by the Danes, and a new abbey was founded by a Norman nobleman in 1092. The work took about sixty years to complete, with some additions made in the fourteenth century. Two hundred years later the Dissolution brought about the destruction of most of the monastic buildings, but the abbey itself survived thanks to a buy-out in which the local people paid Henry VIII £453 for the property.

The sheer scale of the abbey's exterior makes a lasting impact: its colossal **tower** is the largest Norman tower in the world, while the west front's soaring recessed arch – 65 feet high – is the only exterior arch in the country to boast such impressive proportions. In the nave, fourteen stout Norman pillars steal the show, graceful despite their size, and topped by a fourteenth-century ribbed and vaulted ceiling, studded with gilded bosses (look for the musical angels). On the blue and scarlet **choir** roof the bosses include a ring of shining suns (emblem of the Yorkist cause), said to have been put there by Edward IV after the defeat of the Lancastrians at Tewkesbury in 1471, the last important battle of the Wars of the Roses. (The battlefield, known as Bloody Meadow, is off Lincoln Green Lane, southwest of the abbey.) The best way to appreciate the bosses is to look in the mirror trolley from the west door. South of the choir is the **Milton Organ**, played by the poet when he was secretary to Oliver Cromwell at Hampton Court and bought by the townspeople in 1727. The abbey's medieval tombs celebrate Tewkesbury's greatest patrons, the Fitzhamons, De Clares, Beauchamps and Despensers, who turned the building into something of a mausoleum for themselves. The Despensers have the best monuments, particularly Sir Edward, standard-bearer to the Black Prince, who died in 1375 and is shown as a kneeling figure on the roof of the **Trinity Chapel** to the right of the high altar: you can see it best from beside the Warwick Chantry Chapel in the north aisle. Nearby, in the ambulatory, the macabre so-called **Wakeman Cenotaph**, carved in the fifteenth century but of otherwise uncertain origin, represents a decaying corpse being consumed by snakes and other creatures.

Practicalities

The **tourist office** at 64 Barton St (April–Oct Mon–Sat 9am–5pm, Sun 10am–4pm; rest of year closed Sun; ☎01684/295027, ⊛www.tewkesburybc. gov.uk) has inexpensive town and walking maps, plus a small museum (£1) upstairs, which includes two good models, one of the Battle of Tewkesbury of 1471 and the other a delightful, miniature fairground completed in 1958 by Mr Salt, a local resident. You won't have to look far to find a **room**, though noise can be a problem. There are several guest houses and B&Bs on Barton Road, including *Barton House* at no. 5 (☎01684/292049 or 07946/460601; no credit cards; ❶) which has an eclectic mix of old furniture. More genteel are the *Two Back of Avon*, a beautiful period building on Riverside Walk, left off Quay Street (☎01684/298935; non-smoking; no credit cards; ❷), and the quiet *Carrant Brook House* on Rope Walk (☎01684/290355; no credit cards; ❸). The *Malvern View Guest House* at 1 St Mary's Lane (☎01684/292776; no credit cards; ❶) has good views but little character. Most of Tewkesbury's old **hotels** are run by chains; best are the *Royal Hop Pole*, Church St (☎01684/293236, ⊛www.regalhotels.co.uk; ❺), whose annexe has a loggia facing the garden, and the *Tudor House*, High St (☎01684/297755; ❺), where you can take coffee in the panelled Mayor's Parlour. There are no fewer than five **campsites** within striking distance of the city, the most easily accessible being the *Abbey Caravan Club* in the park at the bottom of Gander Lane (☎01684/294035).

For daytime **snacks** or **lunches**, choose between the chrome of the *Aubergine* café-bar for good salads and sandwiches or the ancient *Berkeley Arms* **pub** on Church Street, which is popular with pensioners and serves astoundingly cheap but fairly basic food, or *Ye Olde Black Bear* at the top of the High Street, which also pulls some of the best pints in town. In the evenings, the blue and oak-furnished *Rendezvous* at 78 Church St (☎01684/290357; closed Sun eve & Mon) concentrates on moderately priced Mediterranean-style fish and meat dishes, but also caters to vegetarians.

Deerhurst

Before the construction of Tewkesbury's Norman abbey, **Deerhurst**, just south of the town, was the most prestigious religious centre in the area. As the chief monastery in the Saxon kingdom of Hwicce, it was considered a suitable venue for the meeting in 1016 between the English king Edmund Ironside and Cnut (Canute) the Dane, at which the partition of England was agreed. Deerhurst's importance declined after 1100, but two outstanding buildings date back to the village's heyday.

The monastery church of **St Mary's** is a chronological jumble: some masonry dates back to the eighth century, but the Saxon work was done mainly in the tenth. The Normans then chopped the insides about a bit (they had the nerve to knock arches into the nave walls, which somehow didn't collapse), and other additions came later. The interior remains remarkably simple considering, and contains several very rare features, none more so than the series of curious **windows and holes** which puncture the nave walls: these small triangular piercings, cut by the Saxons, are said to represent the eyes of God. In the north aisle, a ninth-century **font** of golden Cotswold stone has intricate spiral decoration unique for that period. Outside, a sign directs you to a stylized carved angel high up on the wall of the ruined apse; though also Saxon, the relief looks more Celtic in inspiration. The adjoining house once formed part of the monastery's cloister.

The nearby **Odda's Chapel**, which also clings to another building (in this case a half-timbered cottage), lay neglected until last century, its Saxon masonry smothered underneath plaster. It is only slightly younger than St Mary's, having been built in 1056 by Odda in honour of his brother Aelfric, both relatives of the king. The small chapel, just forty feet long, has survived in good condition apart from a few damp patches. The original dedicatory inscription is in the Ashmolean Museum in Oxford, but a copy has been put in its original place.

Deerhurst is four miles south of Tewkesbury by road, but only two miles on foot across the fields or along the Severn. Alternatively, you can catch the #372 **bus** (not Sun) from Tewkesbury to Gloucester, which stops within a mile of Deerhurst.

Bredon Hill

The most important Iron Age fort in the area once crowned **Bredon Hill**, six miles northeast of Tewkesbury and visible for miles around in the flat Severn Vale. Excavation of the site revealed more than fifty bodies, all hacked to pieces, seemingly the victims of a final assault by unknown attackers in the first century AD. Inside the rampart, a huge expanse covering eleven acres, an eighteenth-century tower called Parson's Folly is an incongruous centrepiece, but the views are supreme, with deer often grazing on the slopes.

Bredon Hill can be approached from various places around the southern foot of the hill. From **Overbury**, one of the prettier villages, the climb takes less than an hour. If you're relying on public transport, buses bound for Evesham from Tewkesbury pass through the village of **Bredon** (except Sun), from where you should allow about three hours to walk to the hill and back.

Bristol and around

South and west of Gloucester, the distinctive burr that is typical of West Country speech is immediately audible in **BRISTOL**. Alongside it, however, you will also hear the more strident tones of fast money and big business which in recent years have combined to re-energize the city's old commercial traditions. New technology, the arts and a vibrant youth culture have also helped to make this one of Britain's most cutting-edge cities, in the process generating some of the best nightlife in the southwest.

Weaving through its centre, the River Avon forms part of a system of waterways that made Bristol a great inland port, in later years booming on the transatlantic trafficking of such goods as rum, tobacco and slaves. In the nineteenth century the illustrious **Isambard Kingdom Brunel** laid the foundations of a tradition of engineering, creating two of Bristol's greatest monuments – the SS *Great Britain* and the lofty Clifton Suspension Bridge. More recently, spin-offs from the aerospace industry have placed the city at the cutting edge in the fields of communications, computing, design and finance. Though the ports have long since fallen into decline, the old docks area has been the beneficiary of a massive renewal programme, and now forms the heart of an extensive leisure and entertainment scheme which includes a pedestrian- and cycle-way linking the redeveloped train station at Temple Meads with the docks as far as the SS *Great Britain*, taking in St Mary Redcliffe and Queen Square.

Beneath the prosperous surface, Bristol has its negative aspects – one of England's highest populations of homeless people, some of the most notorious housing estates and the highest proportion of cars to inhabitants. Nonetheless, it remains an attractive city, predominantly hilly, and surrounded by rolling countryside. It's also just a short ride from the sea, where you might spend a day at the Victorian resorts of **Clevedon** and the much grander **Weston–super–Mare**, though be warned that the Bristol Channel is not the most inspiring place to swim, the sea reduced to a distant ribbon on the horizon at low tide.

Arrival, information and accommodation

Bristol is an easy place to get to. Twice-hourly **trains** from London Paddington arrive at either Bristol Parkway or Bristol Temple Meads. The latter, a twenty-minute walk from the centre, is used by services to and from the west, and served by frequent buses #8, #9, #508 and #509, which pass through the centre on their way to Cotham and Clifton. Parkway is too far out of town to walk from: take bus #73 (on Sundays, #73, #82 or #584). The **bus station**, where National Express coaches from London arrive hourly, is in Marlborough Street, right next to Broadmead, the modern shopping centre. Cheaper Bakers Dolphin Coaches (℡01934/413000) also connect Bristol with London's Marble Arch, leaving from the bus station. For all bus timetables and routes in the Bristol and Bath area, call ℡0870/608 2608 (8am–8pm).

The **tourist office** is in the at-Bristol complex, on Wildscreen Walk, Harbourside (March–Oct daily 10am–6pm; Nov–Feb Mon–Sat 10am–5pm, Sun 11am–4pm; ℡0117/926 0767, ⓦwww.visitbristol.co.uk); they offer a free booking service for rooms in hotels and B&Bs – though you'll have to leave a ten percent deposit. Most of Bristol's **accommodation** is in the leafy Georgian areas of Cotham and Clifton, which are also the districts where the majority of the city's students live.

Hotels and B&Bs

Arches Hotel 132 Cotham Brow ℡0117/924 7398, ⓦwww.arches-hotel.co.uk. In an attractive area of town, though a good bus ride from the centre. Small but comfortable rooms with or without bath. Non-smoking. ❷

Clifton Hotel St Paul's Rd ℡0117/973 6882. In Lower Clifton, near the centre of town, this is one of a row of smart, Georgian-style hotels, all with similar prices. This one, sporting comfortable rooms with period furnishings, is enlivened by Rack's, a popular pavement café and nightspot. A two-night stay at weekends brings the price down to ❸, otherwise ❺.

Downs View 38 Upper Belgrave Rd ℡0117/973 7046. As the name implies, this B&B enjoys a good view over Clifton Downs, though the view from the back is even better. Rooms are plain, but adequate. ❷.

Glenroy Hotel Victoria Square ℡0117/973 9058, ⓔadmin@glenroyhotel.demon.co.uk. The choice location near Clifton Village and the attractive exterior promise more than the diminutive rooms deliver, though it's adequate for an overnight stay. ❺, ❸ for a two-night stay at weekends.

Naseby House Hotel 105 Pembroke Rd ℡0117 /973 7859, ⓦwww.nasebyhousehotel.co.uk. This plush Victorian building is comfortable and beautifully furnished, located in Clifton but within walking distance of the centre. ❹

Oakfield Hotel 52 Oakfield Rd ℡0117/973 5556. In Clifton, about a mile from the city centre; the public rooms are gloomy, though the bedrooms are fine, with shared bathrooms. No credit cards. ❶

St Michael's Guest House 145 St Michael's Hill ℡0117/907 7820. Simple accommodation situated near one of Cotham's most popular cafés, near the university. Tea- and coffee-making facilities, plus cable-linked TVs in all rooms, but no en-suite bathrooms. ❶

Hostels, student halls and campsites

Baltic Wharf Cumberland Rd ℡0117/926 8030. The prime riverside location of this campsite in the centre of town compensates for the cramped space, which is dominated by caravans. Unless you bag one of the nine grass pitches, you'll have to cope with unforgiving stone chippings. There is no space for campers' cars on-site.

Bristol Backpackers 17 St Stephen's St ℡0117/925 7900, ⓦwww.bristolbackpackers. co.uk. Very central, this friendly independent hostel housed in a lovely old building has a late-drinking bar, washing facilities and first-class showers. Kitchen and cheap internet access. Can be noisy. Dorm beds cost £13.

Bristol YHA Hayman House, 14 Narrow Quay ☎0117/922 1659, ✆bristol@yha.org.uk. Modern and central, located in a refurbished warehouse on

the quayside; most dorms have four or six beds at £12.50 each, though there are also some twin rooms (£25, or £12.50/person). Kitchen, laundry, games room and bike storage available.

Brook Lodge Farm Cowslip Green, Redhill ☎01934 /862311. Nine miles southwest of Bristol, this is the

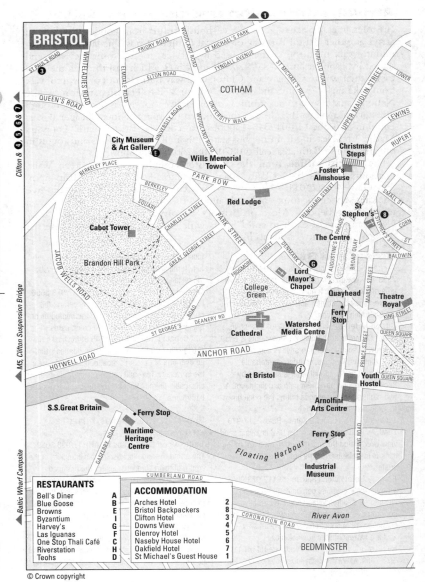

BRISTOL

Clifton & ①②③ & ⑦

▲ M5, Clifton Suspension Bridge

▲ Baltic Wharf Campsite

PRIORY ROAD
ST PAUL'S ROAD
WHITELADIES ROAD
ST MICHAEL'S PARK
WOODLAND ROAD
ELMDALE ROAD
ELTON ROAD
TYNDALL AVENUE
ST MICHAEL'S HILL
HORFIELD ROAD
TOWER
QUEEN'S ROAD
COTHAM
UNIVERSITY WALK
UPPER MAUDLIN STREET
LEWINS
RUPERT

City Museum & Art Gallery Ⓔ
Wills Memorial Tower
Christmas Steps
Foster's Almshouse
BERKELEY PLACE
PARK ROW
TRENCHARD STREET
SMALL ST
BERKELEY
SQUARE
Red Lodge
St Stephen's ⑧
Cabot Tower
CHARLOTTE STREET
PARK STREET
DENMARK ST
The Centre
ST STEPHEN'S STREET
CORN ST
BALDWIN
JACOB'S WELLS ROAD
GREAT GEORGE STREET
FROGMORE
Brandon Hill Park
College Green
Lord Mayor's Chapel Ⓖ
ST AUGUSTINE'S PARADE
BROAD QUAY
MARSH STREET
Quayhead
Theatre Royal
ST GEORGE'S ROAD
DEANERY RD
Cathedral
Watershed Media Centre
Ferry Stop
KING STREET
QUEEN SQUARE
HOTWELL ROAD
ANCHOR ROAD
PRINCE STREET
QUEEN SQUARE
at Bristol ⓘ
Youth Hostel
GASFERRY ROAD
S.S.Great Britain
Ferry Stop
Maritime Heritage Centre
Arnolfini Arts Centre
WAPPING ROAD
Ferry Stop
Floating Harbour
Industrial Museum
CUMBERLAND ROAD
River Avon
CORONATION ROAD
BEDMINSTER

RESTAURANTS

Bell's Diner	A
Blue Goose	B
Browns	E
Byzantium	I
Harvey's	G
Las Iguanas	F
One Stop Thali Café	C
Riverstation	H
Teohs	D

ACCOMMODATION

Arches Hotel	2
Bristol Backpackers	8
Clifton Hotel	3
Downs View	4
Glenroy Hotel	5
Naseby House Hotel	6
Oakfield Hotel	7
St Michael's Guest House	1

© Crown copyright

nearest rural campsite to town, a mile southwest of the village of Redhill off the A38. Closed Nov–Feb.

University of Bristol The Hawthorns Woodland Road, Clifton, ☎0117/954 5555, ⊛www.bris.ac. uk/depts/conferences. The university's main hall of residence opens its doors to non-students during the Easter and summer vacations (usually July–Sept), renting out singles (£23.50, £26 en suite) and twins (£35.50, £45 en suite); a limited number of hotel-style rooms are available all year, currently £63.45 for a double. All prices include breakfast. Rooms must be prior booked.

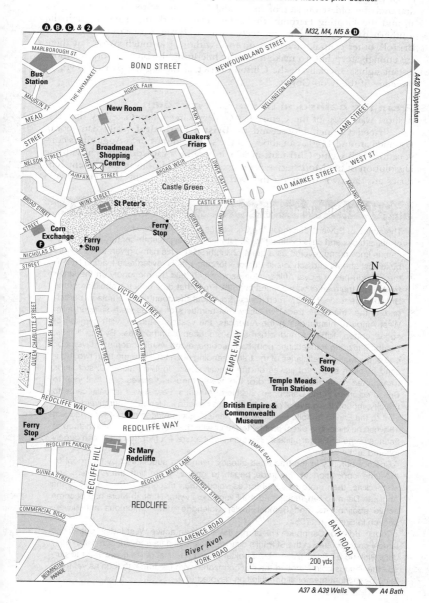

The City

A good place to start exploring, **the Centre** was once an extension of the port but is now the traffic-ridden nucleus of the city, with cars swirling round the statues of Edmund Burke, MP for Bristol from 1774 to 1780, and local bene-factor Edward Colston. The Centre is only a few minutes' walk from the cathe-dral and the oldest quarter of town, and linked by water-taxi to the sights around the Floating Harbour, the waterway network that runs through the southern part of town and connects with the River Avon. You could cover Bristol's other central attractions on foot without too much sweat, but there are enough steep hills to make it worthwhile using the bus network for more distant sights, especially in the Clifton district, at the highest part of town, on the edge of the Avon Gorge.

From the cathedral to the city museum

A short walk west of the Centre lies College Green, dominated by the cres-cent-shaped Council House and by **Bristol Cathedral** (daily 8am–6pm). Founded around 1140 as an abbey on the supposed spot of St Augustine's con-vocation with Celtic Christians in 603, it became a cathedral church with the Dissolution of the Monasteries. Among the many additions in subsequent cen-turies are the two towers on the west front, erected in the last century in a

---

The slave trade in Bristol

The statue of Edward Colston in the Centre has more than once been the subject of graffiti attacks and calls for its removal. Although the eighteenth-century sugar mag-nate is known and revered as a great philanthropist – his name given to numerous buildings, streets and schools in Bristol – for many he is reviled as a leading light in the London-based Royal African Company, which held the monopoly on the **slave trade** until the market was opened in 1698. From that date until the abolition of the British slave trade in 1807, merchants throughout the country were able to partici-pate in the "triangular trade" whereby vast numbers of slaves were shipped from West Africa to plantations in the Americas, the vessels returning with cargoes of sugar, cotton, tobacco and other slave-produced commodities. By the 1730s, Bristol, a leading transatlantic port, had become, along with London and Liverpool, one of the main beneficiaries of the trade, sending out a total of more than two thou-sand ships in search of slaves on the African coast; in 1750 alone, Bristol ships transported some eight thousand of the twenty thousand slaves sent that year to British colonies in the Caribbean and North America. Few slaves actually came to the city, though the grave of one who did can be seen in Henbury churchyard: a ser-vant to the Earl of Suffolk, the slave was named Scipio Africanus and was aged just 18 when he died. The direct profits, together with the numerous spin-offs, helped to finance some of Bristol's finest Georgian architecture – a fact that has been largely ignored in the past.

Bristol's primacy in the trade had already been long supplanted by Liverpool by the time opposition to the trade began to gather force: first the Quakers and Methodists, then more powerful forces voiced their discontent. By the 1780s the Anglican Dean Josiah Tucker and the Evangelical writer Hannah More had become active abolitionists, and Samuel Taylor Coleridge made a famous anti-slavery speech in Bristol in 1795.

Today, Bristol's Caribbean link is maintained by an active West Indian population largely concentrated in the St Paul's district – scene of a flamboyant carnival in early July. Pick up a "Slave Trade Trail" booklet from the tourist office if you want to pur-sue the various points around the city connected with the trade, though as yet there is no permanent memorial or exhibition devoted to it.

faithful act of homage to Edmund Knowle, architect and abbot at the start of the fourteenth century. Inside the cathedral, Abbot Knowle's **choir** offers one of the country's most exquisite examples of the early Decorated style of Gothic, while the adjoining **Elder Lady Chapel**, dating from the early thirteenth century, contains some fine tombs and some eccentric carvings of animals, including a monkey playing the bagpipes accompanied by a ram on the violin. The ornate **Eastern Lady Chapel** has some of England's finest examples of heraldic glass. From the south transept, a door leads through to the **Chapter House**, a strongly carved piece of late Norman architecture.

Opposite the cathedral's west front, take a look at the Norman **Abbey Gateway**, which blends harmoniously with the cathedral on one side and the city library – constructed at the beginning of this century – on the other, though nothing on this side of College Green can completely efface the brutal effect of the Council House opposite. There is one more vestige from the Middle Ages, however, on the northeast side of the green, where the **Lord Mayor's Chapel** (Tues–Sat 10am–noon & 1–4pm) has some lovely French and Flemish stained glass, and striking effigies of the thirteenth-century founders of the hospital of which this church once formed a part.

Climbing steeply up from the green, the shop-lined **Park Street** has some elegant Georgian streets leading off it – for instance Great George Street and Berkeley Square, from either of which you can enter **Brandon Hill Park**, site of the landmark **Cabot Tower**, built at the end of the last century to commemorate the 400th anniversary of John Cabot's voyage to America. You can climb up the 105-foot tower for the city's best panorama.

At the top of Park Street stands central Bristol's other chief landmark, the **Wills Memorial Tower**, erected in the 1920s to lend some stature to the newly opened university. One of the last great neo-Gothic buildings in England, the tower was the gift of the local Wills tobacco dynasty, the university's main benefactors.

Next to the tower, on Queen's Road, the **City Museum and Art Gallery** (daily 10am–5pm; free) occupies another building donated by the Wills clan. The sections on local archeology, geology and natural history are pretty well what you'd expect, but the scope of the museum is occasionally surprising – it has the largest collection of Chinese glass on show outside China itself, and some magnificent Assyrian reliefs, carved in the eighth century BC. The second-floor gallery of paintings and sculptures includes work by English Pre-Raphaelites and French Impressionists, as well as a few choice older pieces, among them a portrait of Martin Luther by Cranach and Giovanni Bellini's *Descent into Limbo*.

Opposite the tower, on Park Row, you can visit the **Red Lodge** (April–Oct Mon–Wed, Sat & Sun 10am–5pm; free), a sixteenth-century building that was originally a merchant's home and later a finishing school for young ladies, then England's first girls' reform school. Highlight is the Great Oak Room, featuring a splendid carved stone fireplace and sumptuous oak panelling.

From the Centre to Broadmead

There are some niches of older architecture off the northern end of the Centre. Hidden behind offices, leading steeply up from Rupert Street on the west side of the Centre, **Christmas Steps** is a stepped shop-lined alley with a cramped, timeworn flavour, though none of the present buildings dates further back than the eighteenth century. At the top stands **Foster's Almshouse**, a red brick, gabled and turreted affair built in 1481 but remodelled in the last century on a Burgundian Gothic pattern. Founder of the almshouse was Bristol merchant and mayor John Foster, also responsible for the adjacent **Chapel of the Three Kings of Cologne**, a tiny church named after a chapel in Cologne Cathedral, which was no doubt admired on Foster's Rhineland journeys. The three kings carved on the facade were added in the 1960s.

One of Bristol's oldest churches, **St Stephen's**, stands on the opposite side of the Centre. Established in the thirteenth century, rebuilt in the fifteenth and thoroughly restored with plenty of neo-Gothic trimmings in 1875, the parish church has some flamboyant tombs inside, mainly of various members of the merchant class who were the church's main patrons. Especially good are those of Justice Snygge and Edmund Blanket, a fourteenth-century cloth merchant.

On nearby **Corn Street**, the city's financial centre, you'll find the Georgian Corn Exchange, designed by John Wood of Bath, and now holding the covered St Nicholas markets, good for all kinds of bric-a-brac as well as record shops, bookshops and cafés. Outside the entrance stand four engraved bronze pillars, dating from the sixteenth and seventeenth centuries and transferred from a nearby arcade where they served as trading tables – thought to be the "nails" from which the expression "pay on the nail" is derived.

Beyond the market, Wine Street runs along the site of the old **Bristol Castle**, an eleventh-century structure that was completely dismantled at the end of the Civil War. The site is now a park, with the hollow shell of the four-teenth-century **St Peter's Church** – gutted during World War II – the only thing still standing, though the castle's moat is still visible. The park, which runs alongside a stretch of Bristol waterways, attracts lunchers from the surrounding shops and offices, and is the occasional venue for summer concerts and fairs.

North of Castle Green extends Bristol's **Broadmead** shopping centre, an uninspiring development laid out on the ruins left by wartime bombing. A couple of relics from before that period survive. Accessible from both the central strip of Broadmead and the Horsefair, **the New Room** (Jan & Feb Mon–Sat 11am–2.30pm; rest of year Mon–Sat 10am–4pm) was the country's first Methodist chapel, established by John Wesley in 1739. Lying very much as Wesley left it, the chapel has a double-deck pulpit beneath a hidden upstairs window, from which the evangelist could observe the progress of his trainee preachers. Tours of the chapel and some of the rooms used by Wesley and his acolytes are available for £2. Outside the chapel is an equestrian statue of Wesley, and, in the main courtyard, another one representing John's brother Charles, also a leading Methodist and hymn-writer. Nearby, another testimony to Bristol's close links with nonconformist sects has also survived: **Quakers' Friars**, a thirteenth-century construction whose name derives from the Dominican friars who first used the building, and the Quakers who took it over from the sixteenth century. William Penn, founder of Pennsylvania, was married here, as was the Quaker founder George Fox.

King Street to St Mary Redcliffe

King Street, a short walk east from the Centre, was laid out in 1633 and still holds some fine seventeenth-century buildings, among them the **Merchant Venturers' Almshouses** for retired seamen, founded in the fifteenth century but restored in 1699 by Edward Colston. Further down is the **Theatre Royal**, the oldest working theatre in the country, opened in 1766 and preserving many of its original Georgian features. The theatre hosted most of the famous names of its time, including Sarah Siddons, whose ghost is said to stalk the building.

In a different architectural style, one of King Street's most prominent buildings is the timber-framed **Llandoger Trow** pub, its name taken from the flat-bottomed boats that traded between Bristol and the Welsh coast. Traditionally the haunt of seafarers, it is reputed to have been the meeting place of Daniel Defoe and Alexander Selkirk, the model for Robinson Crusoe. The area around here and the *Old Duke* jazz pub opposite has Bristol's thickest profusion of pubs, restaurants and nightclubs, and brims with life at weekends and summer evenings.

Behind King Street spreads **Queen Square**, an elegant grassy area focused on a statue of William III by Rysbrack, reckoned to be the best equestrian statue in the country. The square was the site of some of the worst civil disturbances ever seen in England when the Bristolians rioted in support of the Reform Bill of 1832, burning houses on two sides of the square; among the survivors was no. 37, where the first American consulate was established in 1792. The square has a decent pub at its southeastern corner, the *Hole in the Wall*, so-called after the narrow window at the back of the building used to keep watch for press gangs – it was reputedly the model for the *Spyglass Inn* in Robert Louis Stevenson's *Treasure Island*.

The southeast corner of the square leads to Redcliffe Bridge and on to the area of Redcliffe, where the spire of **St Mary Redcliffe** (daily 8.30am–5pm) provides one of the distinctive features of the city's skyline. Described by Elizabeth I as "the goodliest, fairest, and most famous parish church in England", the church was largely paid for and used by merchants and mariners who prayed here for a safe voyage. The present building was begun at the end of the thirteenth century, though it was added to in subsequent centuries and the spire was constructed in 1872. Inside, memorials and tombs recall some of the figures associated with the building, including the arms and armour of Sir William Penn, admiral and father of the founder of Pennsylvania, on the north wall of the nave, and the Handel Window in the North Choir aisle, installed in 1859 on the centenary of the death of Handel, who composed on the organ here. The whale bone above the entrance to the Chapel of St John the Baptist is thought to have been brought back from Newfoundland by John Cabot. The poets Samuel Taylor Coleridge and Robert Southey were both married in St Mary, within six weeks of each other in 1795.

Above the church's north porch is the muniment room, where **Thomas Chatterton** claimed to have found a trove of medieval manuscripts; the poems, distributed as the work of a fifteenth-century monk named Thomas Rowley, were in fact dazzling fakes. The young poet committed suicide when his forgery was exposed, thereby supplying English literature with one of its most glamorous stories of self-destructive genius. The "Marvellous Boy" is remembered by a memorial stone in the south transept, and there is another one to his family, who were long associated with the church, in the churchyard. Chatterton's birthplace is just across the busy Redcliffe Way, administered by the city museum and viewable only on application there – though there is precious little to see inside.

A few minutes' walk away, Bristol's **Old Station** stands outside Temple Meads station, the original terminus of the Great Western Railway linking London and Bristol. The terminus, like the line itself, was designed by Brunel in 1840, and was the first great piece of railway architecture. Part of the original building now houses the **British Empire and Commonwealth Museum** (Tues–Sun 9am–5pm; ⓦ www.empiremuseum.co.uk), which focuses on the history of the empire and Commonwealth, including trade, slavery, and the various cultures which it has encompassed. Film, photographs and sound recordings help to fill out the picture, though it is probably most interesting for the exhibitions which take place here throughout the year, on such themes as aboriginal art.

Around Bristol's waterways

At the southern end of the Centre, the River Frome disappears underground at the **Quayhead**, a spot marked by a statue of Neptune and a memorial plaque to Samuel Plimsoll, inventor of the eponymous line that's painted on the hulls of merchant ships. **St Augustine's Reach**, the central part of the Floating Harbour, is flanked by the **Arnolfini** and **Watershed** arts centres, bastions of Bristol's cultural scene and both housed in refurbished Victorian warehouses. Outside the Arnolfini is a statue of **John Cabot**, the Genoan-born explorer licensed by Henry VII to sail from Bristol in 1497; his landing at Newfoundland formed the basis of England's later claims on the New World (he disappeared on his second expedition the following year). Moored onto the adjacent quays are several boats converted into pubs, restaurants and music venues.

Beyond the Watershed, Bristol's newly developed Harbourside is the home of Bristol's highest-profile attraction, **at-Bristol** (daily 10am–6pm; £6.50 for one attraction, £11 for two, £15.50 for all, valid for a week; ⓦ www.at-bristol .org.uk), a large-scale entertainment complex which pivots on three principal sites: Explore-at-Bristol, an interactive science centre; Wildwalk-at-Bristol, a multimedia wildlife complex, including an indoor "tropical forest"; and an IMAX cinema (film screenings need to be booked in advance). Although chiefly aimed at families and schoolkids, there's enough here for anyone to occupy a whole day or more. The wildlife displays and scientific wizardry are most impressive, and subsidiary attractions include the Imaginarium (£2), a metal-clad spherical planetarium.

To explore further afield, take advantage of the **ferry service**, which connects the various parts of the Floating Harbour, and which leaves every forty minutes from near Neptune's statue at the Quayhead (April–Sept Mon–Fri 10.50am–5.45pm, Sat & Sun 10.50am–4.50pm; Oct–March Sat & Sun only; £1 single fare; £3 forty-minute round trip; £3.50 one-hour round trip; ⓦ www.bristolferryboat.co.uk). The first stop is the **Industrial Museum**, featuring a diverse collection of vehicles, mostly with Bristol connections, and a display of maritime models and reconstructions (April–Oct Mon–Wed, Sat & Sun 10am–5pm; Nov–March Sat & Sun 10am–5pm; free). On weekends between March and October, you can take a thirty-minute **harbour cruise** from here (£3), on either a motor tug, a fireboat or what is claimed to be the oldest steam tug in the world (built in 1861), and when one of these isn't operating, there's the **Bristol Harbour Railway** (Sat & Sun noon–5pm; every 15min; £1 return; ☎ 0117/9251470), a steam train which runs along the quayside. Call to find out which of these is operating on a particular weekend.

From the Industrial Museum, you could use the Bristol Harbour Railway, catch the ferry or walk the 500 yards along the quayside to visit the **SS Great Britain**. Built in 1843 by Brunel, the *SS Great Britain* was the first propeller-driven, ocean-going iron ship, used initially between Liverpool and New York, then between Liverpool and Melbourne, circumnavigating the globe 32 times over a period of 26 years. Her ocean-going days ended in 1886 when she was caught in a storm off Cape Horn, and abandoned in the Falkland Islands; she was recovered from there and returned to Bristol in 1968. Now berthed in the same dry dock where she was constructed, the *Great Britain* is still undergoing restoration work, but is **open to visitors** (daily: April–Oct 10am–5.30pm; Nov–March 10am–4.30pm; ⓦ www.ss-great-britain.com; £6.25). Some cabins have been restored, the bunks occupied by eerily breathing mannequins, and you can peer into the immense engine room. Alongside is docked a much smaller affair: a replica of the **Matthew** (same times as the *Great Britain*; entry covered by that ticket), the vessel in which John Cabot sailed to America in 1497, rebuilt in time for the voyage to be re-enacted on the 500th anniversary. The adjoining **Maritime Heritage Centre** (same times as the *Great Britain*; entry covered by that ticket) gives the full history of both the *Great Britain* and the *Matthew*, and the few facts which are known about Cabot and his exploits. The museum also illustrates the port's long shipbuilding history from the eighteenth century, when it was second only to London, to its decline in the last century, when Bristol's inability to berth the increasingly large vessels led to its decline.

Clifton

North and west of the Wills Tower (see p.395) extends **Clifton**, once an aloof spa resort, now Bristol's most elegant quarter. Clifton Village, its select enclave, is centred on the Mall, close to **Royal York Crescent**, the longest Georgian crescent in the country, offering splendid views over the steep drop to the River Avon below.

A few minutes' walk behind the Crescent is Bristol's most famous symbol, **Clifton Suspension Bridge**, 702ft long and poised 245ft above high water. Money was first put forward for a bridge to span the Avon Gorge by a Bristol wine merchant in 1753, though it was not until 1829 that a competition was held for a design, won by Isambard Brunel on a second round, and not until 1864 that the bridge was completed, five years after Brunel's death. Hampered by financial difficulties, the bridge never quite matched the engineer's original ambitious design, which included Egyptian-style towers topped by sphinxes on each end. The original drawings of Brunel's designs are in the university's Brunel Collection and can be viewed on application, but you can see copies in the **Visitor Centre** on Sion Place (daily: Easter–Sept 10am–5pm; Oct–Easter Mon–Fri 11am–4pm, Sat & Sun 11am–5pm; £1.90), alongside the other designs proposed by Brunel's rivals, some of them frankly bizarre. Display boards in the three rooms here give the full background on the various competitions and the vicissitudes which accompanied the bridge's construction, and there are models and photographs.

Just above the bridge in Clifton, a small **Observatory** sits on an arm of Clifton Downs overlooking the gorge, and contains a working camera obscura (daily: summer 11am–5.30pm; rest of year 11am–4pm; £1). You can also buy a ticket (£1) for the 190-foot tunnel leading from here to the "Giant's Cave" set in the cliffs overlooking the gorge; it housed a Roman Catholic chapel in the fifteenth century. Both attractions may be closed in bad weather, however. Adjoining the Downs is **Bristol Zoo** (daily: June–Aug 9am–5.30pm; Sept–May 9am–4.30pm; Ⓦwww.bristolzoo.org.uk; £8.40), renowned for its animal conservation work, and also featuring a collection of rare trees and shrubs.

Cross the bridge for the view, and continue over to reach the thick Leigh Woods, and Bristol's widest expanse of parkland, **Ashton Court**, scene of a free music festival held each July.

Eating, drinking and nightlife

Bristol's numerous **pubs** and **restaurants** are nearly always buzzing – especially those around King Street. Nightlife is equally lively; if you want to check out the **clubs**, look for the music that suits your tastes rather than simply turning up at a venue – and be prepared to queue. You can usually find something happening every night until late – pick up a copy of *Venue*, the Bristol and Bath fortnightly listings magazine (£1.90), for details of what's on where.

Restaurants

Bell's Diner 1 York Rd ⓣ0117/924 0357. In the fashionable Montpelier quarter (ten minutes from the bus station up Stokes Croft), this corner bistro offers an inventive menu with good-value, award-winning food. No smoking in dining area. Closed Sat & Mon lunch, plus all day Sun. Moderate.

Blue Goose 344 Gloucester Rd ⓣ0117/942 0940. It's worth the ten-minute bus ride north of the Centre to this popular place serving English and Mediterranean cuisine with Pacific elements. Closed lunchtimes, plus all Sun. Moderate.

Browns 38 Queen's Rd ⓣ0117/930 4777. Spacious and relaxed place for a cocktail, hamburger or delicious fisherman's pie; it's housed in the former university refectory, a Venetian-style structure next to the City Museum. Moderate.

Byzantium 2 Portwall Lane ⓣ0117/922 1883, ⓦwww.byzantium.co.uk. Opposite St Mary Redcliffe, a warehouse that's been transformed into a highly theatrical dining area, themed along the lines of a Beirut hotel circa 1930. The food is superb, with a good-value set-price menu, and there's an equally exotic bar downstairs that stays open late, with magicians and belly-dancers adding to the ambience. Closed Sun. Expensive.

Harvey's 12 Denmark St ⓣ0117/927 5034. Owned by a famous name in the world of wines and sherries, this is a showcase restaurant in a medieval cellar complex adjoining a museum of wine that's an attraction in itself, and can be visited while waiting for food. The atmosphere is formal, the food French and the wine list both encyclopedic and outstanding. Closed Sat lunch & all Sun. Very Expensive.

Las Iguanas 10 St Nicholas St ⓣ0117/927 6233. Boisterous Latin American restaurant where the fajitas are highly recommended; there's also a swinging basement bar with DJs Thurs, Fri & Sat. Closed Sun. Moderate.

One Stop Thali Café 12 York Rd ⓣ0117/942 6687. Dhaba-style Asian food in soothing surroundings in the heart of Montpelier. There's no menu, but a combination of dishes are served on a steel plate. Closed Mon. Inexpensive.

Riverstation The Grove ⓣ0117/914 4424. A former river-police station that has been artfully transformed into two great restaurants: downstairs you can chew on deli-type snacks or just have a drink, while the upstairs restaurant offers a bigger range of international dishes. Inexpensive to Moderate.

Teohs 28–34 Lower Ashley Rd. On the edge of the St Paul's area, this oriental bistro is well worth tracking down for its relaxed atmosphere and extremely low prices, offering thirty-odd dishes from Thailand, Malaysia and Japan. Bottled beers and house wine at £11 a carafe. Closed Mon. Inexpensive.

Pubs, bars and cafés

Arnolfini Narrow Quay. This art centre serves excellent vegetarian and meat dishes, plus drinks at the bar. There are communal wooden benches, and the crowd spills onto the the cobbled quayside.

Avon Gorge Hotel Sion Hill. On the edge of the Gorge in Clifton Village, this mediocre bar has a broad terrace with tables from which to contemplate the magnificent views. Snacks available.

Belgo The Old Granary, Queen Charlotte St. Like its London cousins, this branch of the tiny Belgian-food chain offers a fantastic range of Belgian draught and bottled beers in part of a restored warehouse near King Street, and there's also a good deal for early-evening eating where you pay according to the time you come in, e.g. £6.45 if you come at 6.45pm (until 7.30pm).

Boston Tea Party 75 Park St. Cosy place in the centre of town for teas and coffees as well as soups and pies, with seating on two floors and a heated terrace garden.

The Farm Hopetoun Rd, St Werburgh's. A country pub in the city, off Ashley Hill to the northeast of the centre; vegetarian cooking, baguettes and DJs at weekends make this a popular spot, especially in summer when the beer garden is usually buzzing.

Mud Dock Café 40 The Grove. A winning if unlikely combination of bike shop and café-bar/restaurant by the river. There's good food, a barbecue on the balcony in summer, and DJs most nights.

Nova Scotia Cumberland Basin. Traditional dock-side pub with seats by the nineteenth-century lock. Inexpensive food available.

Old England Bath Buildings (bottom of Picton St). Pool tables inside, benches outside, good beer and often packed, in an area of Montpelier rich with drinking-holes.

Star & Garter 33 Brook Rd, Montpelier. Smoky, loud and cramped – an excellent reggae pub, with a coffin to sit around in the back room.

Tantric Jazz Café 39–41 St Nicholas St ⓦwww.tantric-jazz.co.uk. Relaxed coffee stop near the Old Markets; there's food too, and live jazz and world music nightly.

Taverna dell'Artista King St. A haunt of theatrical folk as well as a rowdy bunch of regulars, this is a successful Anglo-Italian dive with a late licence.

The pizzas, pastas and salads are nothing special, though.
Watershed 1 Canons Rd, St Augustine's Reach

ⓦ www.watershed.co.uk. A good bar and café in the arts complex overlooking the boats, with food available until 9pm.

Clubs and venues

The Academy Frogmore St ☎0117/927 9227. Near the Centre, this big and popular place is open Thurs, Fri and Sat for mainstream and hard-house parties.
Bierkeller All Saints St, off Broadmead ☎0117/926 8514, ⓦ www.bristolbierkeller.co.uk. Steamy venue for live music from thrash metal to 60s and 80s revival bands.
Colston Hall Colston Ave ☎0117/922 3686. Major names appear in this stalwart of mainstream venues. Most of the events in the classical Proms Festival, at the end of May, take place here.
Fiddlers Willway St, Bedminster ☎0117/987 3403. Mainly live folk and world music at this relaxed and well-run club on the south side of the river, off Bedminster Parade.
Fleece and Firkin 12 St Thomas St ☎0117/929 9008. Stone-flagged ex-wool warehouse, this loud

and sweaty pub puts on live rock and comedy six nights a week.
Lakota 6 Upper York St ☎0117/942 6208. Bristol's most celebrated club, attracting the biggest DJs as well as live bands, and often generating queues to get in. There's also a bistro open day and night.
Po Na Na 67 Queen Rd ☎0117/904 4445. Underground club with Moroccan decor; it's near the university and popular with students. Mainly garage and house sounds. Closes at 2am.
Thekla Phoenix Wharf, off Queen Square ☎0117/929 3301. A youthful riverboat venue staging regular club nights Thurs–Sat, and open until 2am or 4am.
Winn's 23–25 West St, Old Market ☎0117/941 4024, ⓦ www.winnsclub.com. Cheerful gay club near the centre with student night on Thurs and themed party night on Sun.

Listings

Airport Lulsgate Airport ☎01275/474444. Eight miles southwest of the centre on the A38. National and international flights.
Banks and Exchanges Barclays, 40 Corn St; Lloyds, 55 Corn St; HSBC, 24 College Green; National Westminster, 32 Corn St; American Express 74 Queen's Rd ☎0117/906 5101 & 31 Union St, Broadmead ☎0117/927 7788.
Bike rental Mud Dock Cycleworks, 40 The Grove ☎0117/929 2151. Mountain bikes £12 a day; £50 deposit and ID required. Advance booking advised.
Buses Local services ☎0870/608 2608; National Express ☎0870/580 8080.
Car rental Avis, Rupert St ☎0117/929 2123; Speedway, 654 Fishponds Rd ☎0117/965 5555; Victoria Car Hire, 155 Victoria St ☎0117/927 6909.
Hospital Bristol Royal Infirmary, 2 Marlborough St ☎0117/923 0000.
Internet Netgates Café, 51 Broad St ☎0117/907

4040; Bristol Life, 27 Baldwin St ☎0117/945 9926.
Laundry 78 Alma Rd, Clifton; 34 Princess Victoria St, Clifton.
Left luggage Temple Meads station, in the subway (Mon–Fri 6.15am–9.30pm, Sat 8.30am–4pm, Sun noon–8pm).
Pharmacy Boots, 19 St Augustine's Parade, the Centre (Mon–Fri 8am–5.30pm, Sat 8.30am–7.30pm).
Police Broad St ☎0117/927 7777.
Post office The Galleries, Wine St (Mon–Sat 9am–5.30pm).
Taxis AA Taxis ☎0117/955 5000; Ace Taxis ☎0117/977 7477.
Trains ☎08457/484950.
Travel agents STA Travel, 43 Queen's Rd, Clifton ☎0117/929 4399; Usit CAMPUS, 39 Queen's Rd, Clifton ☎0117/929 2494.

Clevedon

Fifteen miles south of Bristol, **CLEVEDON** is centred on hills inland from the sea, but its handsome beach promenade invites a stroll, with wind-bent trees and views across to Wales. Focal point is the **pier** (April–Oct daily 9am–4.30pm; Nov–March closed Wed; 75p), from where you can take cruises to Bristol, Gloucester, along the coast to Devon, and over to Wales; tickets can be obtained from the pier's Tollhouse, which also houses a small **tourist office** (same hours as pier; ☎01275/878846). Here, you can pick up a leaflet on the **Poet's Walk**, an easy stroll you can make round the headland. The path, which was supposed to have provided inspiration for Tennyson and Coleridge, winds round Church Hill, passing St Andrew's churchyard and climbing Wain's Hill, taking in some bracing views en route – about a mile in all. Two hundred yards down from the pier on the seafront, you might also drop in to the **Clevedon Heritage Centre** (April–Oct daily 10.30am–4pm; Nov–March closed Wed; 75p), which offers some historical background on the locality, including the local picture house, claimed to be the oldest continuously used cinema in Europe – it's located close by on Old Church Road if you want to see it.

Clevedon is also the site of **Clevedon Court** (April–Sept Wed, Thurs & Sun 2–5pm; £4.50; NT), a fourteenth- and fifteenth-century manor house a couple of miles inland. Since 1709 it has been the property of the Elton family, among whose offspring were Sir Arthur Hallam Elton – inspiration for Tennyson's elegy *In Memoriam* – and his son Edmund, whose internationally known pottery is displayed here. You'll also find a fascinating collection of glassware, some fine specimens of furniture spanning three hundred years and portraits of and drawings by William Makepeace Thackeray, who wrote much of *Vanity Fair* here, as well as making it the setting of *Henry Esmond*. The chapel is worth a look for its fine tracery, and the terraced gardens give good views seaward.

It's easy to get here from Bristol – **buses** run at least hourly, and as well as services exclusively for Clevedon, you can take many of the buses bound for Weston-super-Mare. There are a few **pubs and restaurants** on or around Clevedon's seafront, including *Il Giardino* (℡01275/878832; closed Sun & Mon). For **accommodation**, *Fairview* is a comfortable B&B with some rooms overlooking the sea at 20 Lea Grove Rd (℡01275/872176; no credit cards; ❶); bathrooms are shared.

Weston-super-Mare

Buses and trains from Bristol – and a regular bus service from Clevedon – run frequently to the major resort on this coast, **WESTON-SUPER-MARE**, eight miles south of Clevedon. A tiny fishing village at the beginning of the nineteenth century, Weston boomed to become one of the chief West Country seaside towns of the Edwardian era. It is rather moth-eaten today, though its sandy beaches and seafront amusements still attract busloads of trippers. If the crowds get you down, you can always climb up into Weston Woods, rising to the north of the main beach and reachable just around the point on Kewstoke Road. Beyond the point lies **Sand Bay**, a less-developed beach zone bounded to the north by Sand Point, a headland maintained by the National Trust. More adventurously, you can cross to the southern end of Weston – walk or bus to Uphill (#5a to Links Rd) – to join the **West Mendip Way** footpath, following the Mendip hills for thirty miles to Wells and beyond (see p.415).

Trains arrive at Neva Road, a ten-minute walk from the seafront; the **bus station** is nearer, on Beach Road, though some buses stop in the streets around. The **tourist office** is on Beach Lawns, a traffic island between Beach Road and Marine Parade (April–Sept daily 9.30am–5.30pm; Oct–March Mon–Fri 9.30am–5pm, Sat 9.30am–1pm & 1.45–4pm; ℡01934/888800, Ⓦwww.somersetcoast.com). If you want to stay in Weston, you can take your pick from a good selection of **B&Bs**: try *Jamesfield*, very near to the seafront at 1a Ellenborough Park North (℡01934/642898; no credit cards; ❷), or else the non-smoking *Edelweiss* at 24 Clevedon Rd (℡01934/624705; no credit cards; ❷); all rooms are en suite in both. There are a couple of **campsites** in the area: *Country View* in Sand Bay (℡01934/627595; closed Nov–Feb) north of town and, some way inland and south of town, *Slimbridge Farm* on Links Road (℡01934/641641; closed Nov–Feb) – very close to the Mendip Way.

Bath and around

Though only twelve miles from Bristol, **BATH** has a very different feel from its neighbour – more harmonious, compact, leisurely and complacent. Jane Austen wrote *Persuasion* and *Northanger Abbey* here, it is where Gainsborough established himself as a portraitist and landscape painter, and the city's elegant crescents and Georgian buildings are studded with plaques naming Bath's eminent inhabitants from its heyday as a spa resort. Nowadays Bath ranks as one of Britain's top ten tourist cities – the Roman Baths are the busiest fee-charging historic site outside London – yet the place has never lost the exclusive air those names evoke.

Bath owes its name and fame to its **hot springs** – the only ones in the country – which made it a place of reverence for the local Celtic population, though it had to wait for Roman technology to create a fully fledged bathing establishment. The baths fell into decline with the departure of the Romans, but the town later regained its importance under the Saxons, its abbey seeing the coronation of the **first king of all England**, Edgar, in 973. A new bathing complex was built in the sixteenth century, popularized by the visit of Elizabeth I in 1574, and the city reached its fashionable zenith in the eighteenth century, when **Beau Nash** ruled the town's social scene. It was at this time that Bath acquired its ranks of Palladian mansions and town houses, all of them built in the local **Bath stone** which is now enshrined in building regulations as an obligatory element in any new constructions in the city.

The swathes of parkland between the Regency developments lend the city a spacious feel, but the sheer weight of traffic pouring through the central streets can often counteract the pleasures of these open spaces. Drivers are advised to use one of the **Park-and-Ride** car parks around the periphery – and if you're coming from Bristol, note that you can **cycle** all the way along a cycle-path that follows the route of a disused railway line and the course of the Avon.

Arrival, information and accommodation

Bath Spa **train station** and the city's **bus station** are both on Manvers Street, a short walk from the centre. The **tourist office** is right next to the abbey on Abbey Churchyard (May–Sept Mon–Sat 9.30am–6pm, Sun 10am–4pm; Oct–May Mon–Sat 9.30am–5pm, Sun 10am–4pm; ☎01225/477101, ⓦwww.visitbath.co.uk). Here you can find a detailed list of **accommodation**; most establishments are small, so always phone first.

Hotels and B&Bs

Belmont 7 Belmont, Lansdown Rd ☎01225/423082. Huge rooms – though the single's a bit poky – some with en-suite shower in a house designed by John Wood, very near to the Assembly Rooms, Circus and Royal Crescent. No credit cards. ❷

Cranleigh 159 Newbridge Hill ☎01225/310197, ⓔcranleigh@btinternet.com. Above the city, with fine views from some of the back rooms. *Objets d'art* abound, and period fittings include original fireplaces. No smoking. ❺

Henry Guest House 6 Henry St ☎01225/424052. Just round the corner from the abbey, with more rooms than most (none en suite), but its location

means that availability is limited. No credit cards. ❷

Holly Villa 14 Pulteney Gardens ☎01225/310331, ⓔhollyvilla.bb@ukgateway.net. High-class B&B, close to the Kennet and Avon Canal, with friendly management, a nice garden and six rooms (all en suite or with private facilities), one very large. No smoking and no credit cards. Closed Jan & Feb. ❷

Koryu 7 Pulteney Gardens ☎01225/337642. The name means "Sunshine" in Japanese – the mother-tongue of the landlady, who has made cleanliness and simplicity the keynotes. No shoes inside and no smoking. No credit cards. ❸

Paradise House 88 Holloway ☎01225/317723, ⓦwww.paradise-house.co.uk. The wonderful view justifies the ten-minute uphill trudge from the cen-

BATH

⬆ 1 & A36 Warminster

◀ A4 Chippenham

◀ 4 & A4 Bristol

◀ 10 & A38 Tiverton

⬆ 5 (1 mile) & American ▲ Museum (3 miles)

▶ Bus & train stations

ACCOMMODATION

Bath Backpackers Hostel	6
Belmont	2
Cranleigh	4
Henry Guest House	7
Holly Villa	8
Koryu	9
Newton Mill Camping	10
Paradise House	11
Tasburgh House Hotel	1
White Hart	12
YMCA	3
Bath YHA	5

RESTAURANTS

Bathtub Bistro	E
Circus Restaurant	B
Demuth's	J
Café Retro	K
Eastern Eye	C
The Hole in the Wall	D
No. 5 Bistro	F
Pimpernel's	A
Popjoy's Restaurant	H
Pump Room	I
Tilley's Bistro	L
Walrus and Carpenter	G

Pedestrianized street

© Crown copyright

0 — 200 yds

Sydney Gardens

Holburne Museum

Henrietta Park

Royal Victoria Park

Royal Crescent

Building of Bath Museum

Assembly Rooms

Jane Austen Centre

Theatre Royal

Herschel Museum

Green Park

Pulteney Bridge

Rugby Ground

Recreation Ground

Cricket Ground

Abbey

Roman Baths

Pump Room

River Avon

Kennet & Avon Canal

tre. Croquet or boules in the lush garden and open fires in the winter are other attractions, and all rooms are en suite. ⑤

Tasburgh House Hotel Warminster Rd ☏01225 /425096, ✉www. bathtasburgh.co.uk. This Victorian mansion about one mile east of the centre is decidedly posh, but the views and location are excellent, with access to the Kennet and Avon Canal at the bottom of six acres of gardens and meadows. Gourmet meals and picnics are provided. ⑥

Hostels and campsite

Bath Backpackers Hostel 13 Pierrepoint St ☏01225/446787, ✉stayinbath@backpackers-uk.demon.co.uk. Cheap stop right in the centre of things. There's no curfew, no lockout, a kitchen, bar and pool room, but no breakfast. Dorm beds are £12, doubles with bath £30.

Newton Mill Touring Centre ☏01225/333909. The nearest campsite, three miles west of the centre at Newton St Loe (bus #5 to Newton Mill). The

site holds a laundry, restaurant and shop, and the price includes use of showers.

Bath YHA Bathwick Hill ☏01225/465674, ✉bath@yha.org.uk. An Italianate mansion a mile from the centre, with gardens and panoramic views. Dorm beds (£11 each) and double rooms with evening meals also available. Take buses #18 or #418 from the station.

White Hart Widcombe Hill ☏01225/313985, ✉www.whitehartbath.co.uk. The comfiest of Bath's hostels has basic facilities, though these are due to be expanded. There is a kitchen and a café, however, dorms with six to twelve beds with duvets (at £12.50 each), and doubles available (£30).

YMCA International House, Broad St ☏01225/460471, ✉info@ymcabath.u-net.com. Clean, central, with lots of room and convenient prices, this place offers good central accommodation, charging £11 for dorm beds, £16 for singles, £28 for doubles, and with reductions for weekly stays; all prices include breakfast.

The City

Although Bath could easily be seen on a day-trip from Bristol, it really deserves a couple of days on the spot, particularly to explore some of the out-of-town attractions. The city itself is chock-full of museums, but some of the greatest enjoyment comes simply from the streets, with their pale gold architecture and sweeping vistas. With limited time you might consider viewing these on an open-top bus tour leaving from Grand Parade, or one of the free walking tours from outside the Pump Room in the Abbey Church Yard. Otherwise you could see much under your own steam by renting a bike (see "Listings", p.410).

The Baths and the Abbey

Bath's centrepiece is, naturally enough, the **Roman Baths** located in front of the abbey in the pedestrianized Abbey Church Yard (daily: March–June, Sept & Oct 9am–6pm; July & Aug 9am–10pm; Nov–Feb 9.30am–5.30pm; £7.50, £9.50 combined ticket with Museum of Costume). Although the tickets are pricey, there's two or three hours' worth of well-balanced, informative entertainment here, with a taped commentary provided on handsets allowing you to wander at your own pace around the temple and bathing complex, where a spring still issues water at a constant 46.5°C. Highlights of the remains are the open-air (but originally covered) Great Bath, its vaporous waters surrounded by nineteenth-century pillars, terraces and statues of famous Romans; the Circular Bath, where bathers cooled off; the Norman King's Bath; and part of the temple of Minerva. Among a quantity of coins, jewellery and sculpture exhibited are the gilt bronze head of Sulis Minerva, the local deity, and a grand, Celtic-inspired gorgon's head from the temple's pediment. Models of the complex at its greatest extent give some idea of the awe which it must have inspired, while the graffiti salvaged from the Roman era – mainly curses and boasts – give a nice personal slant on this antique leisure centre. You can get a free glimpse into the baths from the next-door **Pump Room**, the social hub of the Georgian spa community and still redolent of that era, housing an excellent tearoom and restaurant.

Richard **"Beau" Nash** was an ex-army officer, ex-lawyer, dandy and gambler, who became Bath's Master of Ceremonies in 1704, conducting public balls of an unprecedented splendour. Wielding dictatorial powers over dress and behaviour, Nash orchestrated the social manners of the city and even extended his influence to cover road improvements and the design of buildings. In an early example of health awareness, he banned smoking in Bath's public rooms at a time when pipe-smoking was a general pastime among men, women and children. Less philanthropically, he also encouraged gambling and even took a percentage of the bank's takings. Nonetheless, he was generally held in high esteem and succeeded in establishing rules such as the setting of specific hours and procedure for all social functions. Balls were to begin at six and end at eleven and every ball had to open with a minuet "danced by two persons of the highest distinction present". White aprons were banned, gossipers and scandalmongers were shunned, and, most radical of all, the wearing of swords in public places was forbidden, a ruling referred to in Sheridan's play *The Rivals*, in which Captain Absolute declares, "A sword seen in the streets of Bath would raise as great an alarm as a mad dog." By such measures, Nash presided over the city's greatest period, during the first four decades of the eighteenth century. He lived in Bath until his death at the age of 87, by which time he had been reduced to comparative poverty.

Next to the innovations of Nash and the architectural creations of the two John Woods, the name of **William Oliver** should not be forgotten in the story of Regency Bath. A physician and philanthropist, Oliver did more than anyone to boost the city's profile as a therapeutic centre, thanks to publications such as his *Practical Essay on the Use and Abuse of Warm Bathing in Gouty Cases* (1751), and by founding the Bath General Hospital to enable the poor to make use of the waters. He is remembered today by the Bath Oliver biscuit, which he invented, and by the use of Olivers as the exchange currency in a local community bartering scheme.

Although there has been a church on the site since the seventh century, **Bath Abbey** (daily 9am–5pm; closes 4pm in winter; requested donation £2) did not take its present form until the end of the fifteenth century, when Bishop Oliver King began work on the ruins of the previous Norman building, some of which were incorporated into the new church. The bishop was said to have been inspired by a vision of angels ascending and descending a ladder to heaven, which the present facade recalls on the turrets flanking the central window. The west front also features the founder's signature in the form of carvings of olive trees surmounted by crowns, a play on his name.

Much of the building underwent restoration following the destruction that took place under Henry VIII; his daughter, Queen Elizabeth, played a large part in the repairs. The interior is in a restrained Perpendicular style, and boasts splendid fan vaulting on the ceiling, which was not properly completed until the nineteenth century. The floor and walls are crammed with elaborate monuments and memorials, and traces of the grander Norman building are visible in the Norman Chapel.

To the Circus and the Royal Crescent

From Abbey Church Yard, the elegantly colonnaded Bath Street leads onto Westgate Street and Sawclose, where you can take a glance at the **Theatre Royal**, opened in 1805 and one of the country's finest surviving Georgian theatres. Next door is the house where Beau Nash spent his last years, now a restaurant. Up from the Theatre Royal, off Barton Street, the gracious **Queen Square** was the first Bath venture of the architect **John Wood**, who with his son (also John) was chiefly responsible for the Roman-inspired developments of the areas outside the confines of the medieval city. Wood himself lived at no. 24, giving him a vista of the northern terrace's palatial facade.

Just north of the square, at 40 Gay St, the **Jane Austen Centre** (Mon–Sat 10am–5.30pm, Sun 10.30am–5.30pm; £4; @www.janeausten.co.uk) shows various scenes from the Bath that the author might have known, but it's all rather a pointless exercise, and doesn't enlighten or inform. Austen herself lived just down the road at 25 Gay St – one of a number of places the author inhabited while in Bath. West of Queen Square, at 19 New King St, another typical Bath townhouse was where the musician and astronomer Sir William Herschel, in collaboration with his sister Caroline, discovered the planet Uranus in 1781. You can take a brisk whirl around the small **Herschel Museum** here (March–Oct daily 2–5pm; Nov–Feb Sat & Sun 2–5pm; £3.50), showing contemporary furnishings, musical instruments, a replica of the telescope with which Uranus was identified and various knick-knacks from the Herschels' life. There's also the Star Vault, a sort of mini planetarium which allows you to go on a virtual trip through the solar system.

Up from Queen Square, at the end of Gay Street, is the elder John Wood's masterpiece, **The Circus**, consisting of three crescents arranged in a tight circle of three-storey houses, with a carved frieze running round the entire circle. Wood died soon after laying the foundation stone for this enterprise, and the job was finished by his son. The painter Thomas Gainsborough lived at no. 17 from 1760 to 1774.

The Circus is connected by Brock Street to the **Royal Crescent**, grandest of Bath's crescents, begun by the younger John Wood in 1767. The stately arc of thirty houses is set off by a spacious sloping lawn from which a magnificent vista extends to green hills and distant ribbons of honey-coloured stone. The interior of **No. 1 Royal Crescent**, on the corner with Brock Street, has been restored to reflect as nearly as possible its original Georgian appearance (mid-Feb to Oct Tues–Sun 10.30am–5pm; Nov Tues–Sun 10.30am–4pm; £4; @www.bath-preservation-trust.org.uk).

At the bottom of the Crescent, Royal Avenue leads onto **Royal Victoria Park**, the city's largest open space, containing an aviary and botanical gardens.

The Assembly Rooms, the Paragon and Milsom Street

The younger John Wood's **Assembly Rooms**, east of the Circus on Bennett Street, were, with the Pump Room, the centre of Bath's social scene. A fire virtually destroyed the building in 1942, but it has now been perfectly restored and houses a **Museum of Costume** (daily 10am–5pm; £4.20, or £9.50 with Baths), an entertaining collection of clothing from the Stuart era to the latest Japanese designs.

From the Assembly Rooms, Alfred Street leads to the area known as the **Paragon**, at the top of Milsom Street. Here, an old Methodist chapel houses the **Building of Bath Museum** (mid-Feb to Nov Tues–Sun 10.30am–5pm; £4), an educational explanation of the construction and architecture of Bath. At the bottom of the Paragon, off George Street, lies **Milsom Street**, a wide shopping strand designed by the elder Wood as the main thoroughfare of Georgian Bath.

The river and Great Pulteney Street

The flow of the River Avon – a crucial ingredient in the city's charm – is interrupted by a graceful V-shaped weir just below the shop-lined **Pulteney Bridge**, an Italianate structure designed by the eighteenth-century Scottish architect Robert Adam. The bridge was intended to link the city centre with **Great Pulteney Street**, a handsome avenue originally planned as the nucleus of a large residential quarter on the eastern bank. The work ran into financial difficulties, however, so the roads running off it now stop short after a few yards, though there is a lengthy vista to the imposing classical facade of the **Holburne Museum** at the end of the street (mid-Feb to mid-Dec Tues–Sat 11am–5pm, Sun 2.30–5.30pm; £3.50; Ⓦwww.bath.ac.uk/holburne). The three-storey building contains an impressive range of decorative and fine art, mostly furniture, silverware, porcelain and paintings (including the newly acquired *Byam Family* portrait by Gainsborough) from the eighteenth century, plus a good collection of twentieth-century craftwork. Behind Holburne House, **Sydney Gardens** make a delightful place to take a breather. When Holburne House was a bustling hotel, the pleasure gardens were the venue for concerts and fireworks, as witnessed by Jane Austen, a frequent visitor here – the family had lodgings across the street at 4 Sydney Place in the autumn of 1801. Today, the bosky slopes are cut through by the railway and the Kennet and Avon Canal. From here, it's a pleasant one-and-a-half mile saunter along the canal to the *George* pub (see below).

If you want to explore the river itself, rent a skiff, punt or canoe in summer from the **Victorian Bath Boating Station** at the end of Forester Road, behind the Holburne Museum (about £6 per person per hour). Organized river trips can be made from Pulteney Bridge and weir, and there are cruises on the Kennet and Avon Canal from Sydney Wharf, near Bathwick Bridge. A two-mile **nature trail** winds along the banks of the restored canal, which itself extends east as far as Reading.

Eating and drinking

Bath has a reputation for gourmet cuisine, even if too many of the town's **restaurants** do over-exploit the period trappings. In the less exalted regions of the price scale, there are several decent, inexpensive places to eat, and coffee shops and snack bars are ubiquitous in the centre, as are pubs offering lunchtime fare. Try and be in Bath for the **Bath International Music Festival** (two weeks in May or June; see "Listings", p.410), which features big names in classical music, jazz, folk and blues, with a plethora of fringe events accompanying the official programme, plus fireworks, literary and art events and lots of busking. For concerts, gigs and other events during the rest of the year, refer to *Venue*, the fortnightly listings magazine (£1.90).

Restaurants

Bathtub Bistro 2 Grove St ☎01225/460593, Ⓦwww.bathtubbistro.co.uk. Round the corner from Argyle Street, off Pulteney Bridge, this place looks tiny from the outside but reveals several eating areas on different levels. The menu is international, and includes one hundred percent-beef hamburgers, innovative vegetarian dishes and spiced ice cream. Inexpensive to moderate. BYOB Mon & Tues.

Circus Restaurant 34 Brock St ☎01225/318918. Homely but elegant, just around the corner from the Circus, serving mainly French cuisine. Set-price dinners available Mon–Thurs. Non-smoking. Moderate to expensive.

Demuth's 2 North Parade Passage ☎01225/446059. Bath's favourite eating place for veggies and vegans, offering original and delicious dishes, as well as organic beers, wines and coffees. Decor is bright and modern. No smoking. Booking advisable on Fri, Sat & Sun. Moderate to expensive.

Café Retro 18 York St. A laid-back place near the Abbey offering an inventive international menu, all to mellow sounds. Also a good spot for a cappuccino break during the day. BYOB. Moderate.

Eastern Eye 8 Quiet St ☎01225/422323, Ⓦwww.easterneye.co.uk. Just off Milsom Street in the centre of Bath, this designer curry house occupies a Georgian bank, with a spectacular vaulted ceiling. The food's good too, impeccably presented and served. Moderate.

The Hole in the Wall 16 George St ☎01225/425242. Smart and select basement retreat offering Modern-British cuisine and variations of traditional dishes. Closed Sun. Expensive.

No. 5 Bistro 5 Argyle St ☎01225/444499. Candles, posters on the walls and a jazzy soundtrack set the tone here, just up from the *Bathtub Bistro*. BYOB Mon & Tues; Wed is fish night, and the desserts are always good. It also operates a good takeway shop for sandwiches and breakfast baps open until 2.30pm. No smoking. Closed all Sun & Mon lunch. Expensive.

Pimpernel's *Royal Crescent Hotel*, 16 Royal Crescent ☎01225/823333. English-based classics with Mediterranean influences make this the best restaurant in Bath, all in sumptuous surroundings. Non-smoking. Very Expensive.

Popjoy's Restaurant Sawclose ☎01225/460494. Though somewhat touristy and twee, this restaurant is still worth sampling for its prime location next to the Theatre Royal, and for the curiosity value of being Beau Nash's house (it's named after his mistress). The food is high-quality Modern British, with great desserts, and there's a good-value pre-theatre menu. Closed Sun. Expensive.

Pump Room Abbey Church Yard ☎01225/444477. If you don't want to splash out on an Eggs Benedict brunch, you might succumb to a Bath bun here in the morning, or a bewildering range of cream teas in the afternoon, or the excellent lunch-time menu, all to the accompaniment of a classical trio. You get a good view of the baths, and a chance to sample the waters, though be prepared to queue. Open daytime only, plus evenings during the Bath Festival. Inexpensive to moderate.

Tilley's Bistro 3 North Parade Passage ☎01225/484200. Informal, rather cramped French restaurant with starter-sized and -priced portions to allow more samplings, good set-price lunchtime menus and a separate vegetarian menu. Closed Sun. Moderate.

Walrus and Carpenter 25 Barton St. Popular spot near the Theatre Royal, serving steaks, burgers, poultry dishes and a full vegetarian menu. Moderate.

Pubs and cafés

Bar Karanga 8–10 Manvers St. Cool pre-club bar with lots of rooms, ultra-violet lighting and comfy chairs.

The Bath Tap 19–20 St James's Parade. Home of Bath's gay and lesbian scene, though without so much of the "scene". It's lively but relaxed, with a mixed crowd enjoying the regular cabaret (strippers currently monthly on Fri) as well as *Club Eros* in the cellar (see below). For news and events, see their website ⊛ www.bathtaponline.co.uk.

The Bell 103 Walcot St. Excellent pub with a grungy atmosphere, a garden, live music three times a week (Mon & Wed eve, plus Sun lunchtime) and bar billiards.

Coeur de Lion Northumberland Place, off High St. Centrally located tavern on a flagstoned shopping alley; this is Bath's smallest boozer and is invariably packed, but it makes for a good lunchtime stop, with some bench seating outside.

The George Mill Lane, Bathampton. Popular canal-side pub twenty minutes' walk from the centre. Better than average bar food.

Grapes Westgate St. Again, popular, sometimes touristy, but usefully located old pub. Fruit machines and jukebox are present.

Hat & Feather London St. Further up from Walcot Street, this drinking hole continues the quarter's alternative theme, with table football, DJs and live music on some nights.

Pig & Fiddle corner of Saracen and Walcot streets. Real ales and outside terraces, north of Pulteney Bridge. Table football and food helps to pull in the crowds.

The Porter Miles Buildings, George St. Part of *Moles* club (see below), this is the only vegetarian pub in Bath – serving only veggie food and some organic ales – though it feels more like a café. Live music twice weekly & DJs other nights in the cosy cellar bar.

St James' Wine Vaults St James' St. A varied clientele is attracted to this dive north of the Circus, which has music in the basement.

Nightlife, entertainment and festivals

Town-centre **clubs** include *T's* (under Pulteney Bridge), popular with students and younger clubbers; *Moles* on George Street, a Bath institution which has live music for half the week and DJs playing club sounds the other half; the *Porter Butt* pub on London Road, with live music most weekends embracing roots and Irish music; the *Fez Club*, The Paragon, plays funk, trance and old skool, and *Po Na Na*, 8 North Parade, basement dive playing club sounds to a largely student crowd. The best gay and lesbian venue is *Club Eros*, situated under the *Bath Tap* pub (see above) at 19 St James's Parade, open on Fridays and Saturdays until 2am. There are three floors in all, including a chill-out zone.

Theatre and ballet fans should check out what's showing at the Theatre Royal on Sawclose (℡01225/448844), which stages more experimental productions in the Ustinov Studio.

Bath has a great range of festivals throughout the year, offering talks, gigs and other events in often sumptuous surroundings. Best of the bunch are: the **Bath International Music Festival** (ⓦwww.bathmusicfest.org.uk), held between mid-May and June and featuring jazz, classical and World Music; the **Bath Fringe Festival** (ⓦwww.bathfringe.co.uk), running from the end of May to mid-June, with the accent on art, theatre and music; and **Bath Literature Festival** (ⓦwww.bathlitfest.org.uk), taking place over ten days in Feb/March. For further information on each, check out the individual websites, or call ℡01225/463362.

Listings

Banks and Exchanges National Westminster, bottom of High Street; American Express, 5 Bridge St ℡01225/444747. There is also a bureau de change in Bath's tourist office.

Bike rental Avon Valley Cyclery, at the back of the train station ℡01225/442442. Open daily. Bikes £14 a day, £9 for half a day. Deposit and ID required.

Buses Local services ℡0870/608 2608; National Express ℡0870/580 8080.

Car rental Avis, Unit 4b, Riverside Business Park, Riverside Road ℡01225/446680.

Internet Click Internet Café, 19 Broad St & 13 Manvers St. Open daily until 10pm. ℡01275/474444, ⓦwww.clickcafe.co.uk.

Post office New Bond Street (Mon–Sat 9am–5.30pm).

Trains ℡08457/484950.

Claverton, Frome and Dyrham Park

For a quick sample of the lovely countryside around Bath you could make an easy excursion to **CLAVERTON**, on the eastern edge of Bath, where the **American Museum** (late March to July & Sept–Nov Tues–Sun 2–5pm; Aug daily 2–5pm; grounds Tues–Fri 1–6pm, Sat & Sun noon–6pm; £5.50, grounds only £3) merits at least half a day. Occupying the early nineteenth-century Claverton Manor, where Winston Churchill made his maiden political speech in 1897, this was the first museum of Americana to be established outside the US, and consists of a series of reconstructed rooms illustrating life in the New World from the seventeenth to the nineteenth centuries, as well as special sections devoted to textiles, whaling, the opening of the West, Native Americans and Hispano-American culture. The glorious **grounds** contain a replica of George Washington's garden, an arboretum and assorted relics resembling items from a movie set. University buses #18 and #418 run throughout the year to the Avenue (the stop before the campus), from where it's a ten-minute walk to the museum.

Fifteen miles south of Bath, at the eastern end of the Mendip Hills, the town of **FROME** (pronounced "Froom") is a picturesque ensemble of steep cobbled streets, yellow-stone weavers' cottages, Georgian rows and some dusty old shops. You could spend a pleasant hour or two roaming Frome's nooks and crannies, such as Gentle Street, or perusing the old gravestones in the churchyard of St John's. Buses #184 and #267 connect Bath with Frome at least hourly (fewer on Sun). From here, it's only five miles across the Wiltshire border to Longleat (see p.305).

A visit to **Dyrham Park**, seven miles north of Bath (daily noon–5.30pm or dusk; house April–Oct Mon, Tues & Fri–Sun noon–5.30pm; grounds & house

£7.80, grounds £3, park only £1.90; NT), is almost worth it for the journey alone, which takes in a far-reaching panorama at the top of Tog Hill, where the A420 intersects with the A46. Standing on the site of a calamitous defeat of the Britons by the Saxons in 677, the house is a late seventeenth-century Baroque mansion, finely decorated and panelled in oak, cedar and walnut. Alongside furniture used by the diarists Pepys and Evelyn, many of the contents reflect the career of the first owner William Blathwayt, a diplomat who collected pieces from Holland and North America. The name Dyrham means "deer enclosure", and the surrounding 268 acres of parkland are still grazed by fallow deer – the deer park gives views as far as the Welsh hills.

Bus connections are limited to two daily from Bath, currently leaving the bus station at 10.40am and 1.40pm, returning at 2.40pm and 5.30pm (25-minute journey): the route passes through Dyrham village, half a mile from the park.

Wells, the Mendips and Glastonbury

Wells, twenty miles south of Bristol across the Somerset border and the same distance southwest from Bath, is a miniature cathedral city that has not significantly altered in eight hundred years. You could spend a good half-day kicking around here, and you might decide to make it an accommodation stop for visiting nearby attractions in the **Mendip Hills**, such as the **Wookey Hole** caves and the **Cheddar Gorge**. On the southern edge of the range, and just a jump away from Wells, the town of **Glastonbury** has for centuries been one of the main Arthurian sites of the West Country, and is now the country's most enthusiastic centre of New Age cults.

Wells

Technically the smallest city in the country, **WELLS** owes its celebrity entirely to its Cathedral (daily: May, June & Sept 7am–7pm; July & Aug 7am–8.30pm; Oct–April 7am–6pm; suggested donation £4). Hidden from sight until you pass into its spacious close from the central Market Place, the building presents a majestic spectacle, the broad lawn of the former graveyard providing a perfect foreground. The west front teems with some three hundred thirteenth-century figures of saints and kings, once brightly painted and gilded, though their present honey tint has a subtle splendour of its own. Close up, the impact is slightly lessened, as most of the statuary is badly eroded and many figures were damaged by Puritans in the seventeenth century. You might expect some disruption too, as major renovation work in the cathedral's entrance and Undercroft is carried out in the next couple of years. The facade was constructed about fifty years after work on the main building was begun in 1180. The **interior** is a supreme example of early English Gothic, the long nave punctuated by a dramatic "scissor arch", one of three that were constructed in 1338 to take the extra weight of the newly built tower. Though some wax enthusiastic about the ingenuity of these so-called "strainer" arches, others argue that they're "grotesque intrusions" from an artistic point of view.

Other features worth scrutinizing are the narrative carvings on the **capitals and corbels** in the transepts – including men with toothache and an old man caught pilfering an orchard. In the north transept, don't miss the 24-hour astronomical clock, dating from 1390, whose jousting knights charge each other every quarter-hour, as announced by a figure known as Jack Blandiver, who kicks a couple of bells from his seat high up on the right – on the hour he strikes the bell in front of him. Opposite the clock, a doorway leads to a graceful, much-worn flight of steps rising to the **Chapter House** (closes 4.30pm), an octagonal room elaborately ribbed in the Decorated style. There are some gnarled old tombs to be seen in the aisles of the **choir**, at the end of which is the richly coloured stained glass of the fourteenth-century **Lady Chapel**. The best way to see it all is on one of the **free guided tours**, which take place up to five times daily (two on Sun), but twice daily in winter (none on Sun). If you want to take pictures, you have to buy a photographic permit.

The row of clerical houses on the north side of the cathedral green are mainly seventeenth- and eighteenth-century, though one, the **Old Deanery**, shows traces of its fifteenth-century origins. The chancellor's house is now a **museum** (Easter–July, Sept & Oct daily 10am–5.30pm; Aug daily 10am–8pm; Nov–Easter Mon & Wed–Sun 11am–4pm; £2.50), displaying, among other items, some of the cathedral's original statuary, placed here for conservation reasons (and replaced by replicas), as well as a good geological section with fossils from the surrounding area, including Wookey Hole.

A little further along the street, the cobbled medieval **Vicars' Close** holds more clerical dwellings, linked to the cathedral by the Chain Gate and fronted by small gardens. The cottages were built in the mid-fourteenth century – though only no. 22 has not undergone outward alterations – and have been continuously occupied by members of the cathedral clergy ever since.

On the other side of the cathedral – and accessible through the cathedral shop – are the cloisters, from which you can enter the tranquil grounds of the **Bishop's Palace** (April–July, Sept & Oct Tues–Fri 10.30am–5pm, Sun 2–5pm; Aug daily 10.30am–5pm, though may close on first or second Sat of month for wedding receptions; £3.50), also reachable from Market Place through the Bishop's Eye archway. The residence of the Bishop of Bath and Wells, the palace was walled and moated as a result of a rift with the borough in the fourteenth century, and the imposing gatehouse still displays the grooves of the portcullis and a chute for pouring oil and molten lead on would-be assailants. Its tranquil gardens contain the springs from which the city takes its name – and which still feed the moat as well as the streams flowing along the gutters of Wells's High Street – and the ruined **Great Hall**, built at the end of the thirteenth century and despoiled during the Reformation.

Practicalities

Wells is not connected to the rail network, but its **bus station**, off Market Street, receives hourly buses from Bristol and Bath (less frequent on Sun). The **tourist office** is on Market Place (daily: April–Oct 9.30am–5.30pm; Nov–March 10am–4pm; ☎01749/672552).

There are several central choices of **accommodation**: of the B&Bs, try *Canon Grange*, right on the Cathedral Green, its spacious rooms facing the west front (☎01749/671800, ✉canongrange@email.com; ②), or *Bekynton House*, a little farther out at 7 St Thomas St (☎01749/672222, ⓦwww.bekyntonhouse +.freeserve.co.uk; ②), with four rooms available; en-suite rooms just nudge up into the next category. There are some nice old coaching inns in the centre of town, including the *Crown Hotel*, Market Place, near the tourist office (☎01749/673457; ⑤), where William Penn was arrested in 1695 for illegal preaching, and the *Swan*, further down the High Street and completely renovated within (☎01749/836300; ⑥).

For a coffee or **snack**, *Crofter's* tea rooms on Market Place is the best bet close to the cathedral. If you need something more substantial, head for *Chapel's* in Union St (off High St), a modern café-bar offering dishes such as prawn volau-vents and fisherman's pie. Good Continental and traditional English dishes are available from the Italian-run *Ancient Gate House*, Sadler St (℡01749/672029); at no. 5 on the same street, *Ritcher's* (℡01749/679085) combines a downstairs bar/patisserie with a restaurant in a plant-filled loft serving top-notch dishes on set-price menus. Excellent wholefood is served at the *Good Earth* on Priory Rd, near the bus station (℡01749/678600; closed Sun), with pizzas, flans and "real" ice cream, and there are inexpensive three-course meals on offer at lunchtime and also good stuff to take away. You can eat decent, inexpensive meals in the upstairs restaurant as well as **pub** fare at the *City Arms* on Cuthbert St, formerly the city jail, with an overcrowded, flower-filled courtyard.

The area around Wells makes good cycling country: you can **rent bikes** at *Bike City*, 31 Broad St, at the bottom of the High St (℡01749/671711; £6.95/half day; £8.95/day), though, with few available, it's a good idea to reserve one as far ahead as possible.

The Mendips

The **Mendip Hills**, rising to the north of Wells, are chiefly famous for Wookey Hole – the most impressive of many caves in this narrow limestone chain – and for the **Cheddar Gorge**, where a walk through the narrow cleft might make a starting point for more adventurous trips across the Mendips. From Monday to Saturday there's an hourly bus to Wookey Hole from Wells (#172), from where there's also an hourly bus to the gorge (#126 or #826) – every two hours on Sunday.

Wookey Hole

Hollowed out by the River Axe a couple of miles outside Wells, **Wookey Hole** is an impressive cave complex of deep pools and intricate rock formations, but it's folklore rather than geology that takes precedence on the guided tours (daily: April–Oct 10am–5pm; Nov–March 10.30am–4.30pm; closed Dec 17–25; £7.30). Highlight of the tour is the alleged petrified remains of the Witch of Wookey, a "blear-eyed hag" who was said to turn her evil eye on crops, young lovers and local farmers until the Abbot of Glastonbury inter-vened; he despatched a monk who drove the witch into the inner cave, sprin-kled her with holy water and turned her into stone. Some substance was lent to the legend when an ancient skeleton – in fact Romano-British – was unearthed here in 1912, together with a dagger, sacrificial knife and a big rounded ball of pure stalagmite, the so-called witch's ball. Beside her were found two skeletons, the remains of goats tied to a stake. The guides point out several other fancied resemblances to people and things during the hour-long tour, at the end of which you can use your ticket to visit a functioning Victorian paper mill by the river, and rooms containing speleological exhibits. On a less earnest note is the range of amusements laid on by Madame Tussauds, owners of the complex – notably a collection of gaudy, sometimes ghoulish, Edwardian fairground pieces.

A walkable couple of miles uphill west of Wookey Hole, **Ebbor Gorge** offers a wilder alternative to the more famous Cheddar Gorge, with tranquillity guar-anteed on the wooded trails that follow the ravine up to the Mendip plateau.

Cheddar Gorge

Six miles west of Wookey on the A371, Cheddar has given its name to Britain's best-known cheese – most of it now mass-produced far from here – and is also renowned as a centre for strawberry growing. However, the biggest selling

△ Royal Crescent, Bath

point of this rather plain village is the **Cheddar Gorge**, lying beyond the neighbourhood of Tweentown about a mile to the north.

Cutting a jagged gash across the Mendip Hills, the limestone gorge is an impressive geological phenomenon, though its natural beauty is undermined by the minor road running through it and by the Lower Gorge's mile of shops, coach park and **tourist office** (mid-March to mid-Nov daily 10am–5pm; mid-Nov to mid-March Sun 11am–4pm; ☎01934/744071, ⓦwww.sedgemoor .gov.uk/tourism). Few trippers venture further than the first few curves of the gorge, beyond the shops, which admittedly holds its most dramatic scenery, though each turn of the two-mile length presents new, sometimes startling vistas. At its narrowest the path squeezes between cliffs towering almost five hundred feet above, and if you don't want to follow the road as far as **Priddy**, the highest village in the Mendips, you can reach more dramatic destinations by branching off onto marked paths to such secluded spots as **Black Rock**, just two miles from Cheddar, or **Black Down**, at 1067ft the Mendips' highest peak. Cliff-top paths winding along the rim of the gorge provide an alternative to walking next to the road. The tourist office can give you details of a two-and-a-half-hour circular walk and of the **West Mendip Way**, a forty-mile route extending from Uphill, near Weston-super-Mare, to Wells and Shepton Mallet.

Beneath the gorge, the **Cheddar Caves** (daily: May to mid-Sept 10am–5pm; mid-Sept to April 10am–4.30pm; £7.90) were scooped out by underground rivers in the wake of the Ice Age, and subsequently occupied by primitive communities. The bigger of the two main groups, **Gough's Caves**, is a sequence of chambers with names such as Solomon's Temple, Aladdin's Cave and the Swiss Village, all arrayed with tortuous rock formations that resemble organ pipes, waterfalls and giant birds. **Cox's Caves** (same ticket), entered lower down the main drag, have floodlighting that picks out subtle pinks, greys, greens and whites in the rock, and a set of lime blocks known as "the Bells", which produce a range of tones when struck. The Crystal Quest, attached to Cox's Caves, is the kids' favourite, with high-tech light and laser effects playing on its gushing waterfall.

Outside again, close to Cox's Caves, the 274 steps of **Jacob's Ladder** (same ticket as caves) lead to a cliff-top viewpoint towards Glastonbury Tor, Exmoor and the sea. It's a muscle-wrenching climb – anyone not in a state of honed fitness can reach the same spot with a great deal more ease via the narrow lane winding up behind the cliffs. You can also survey the panorama from **Pavey's Lookout Tower** nearby, and there's a circular three-mile clifftop Gorge Walk accessible from here.

Practicalities

Among Cheddar's handful of **B&Bs**, there's *Chedwell Cottage*, Redcliffe St (☎01934/743268; no credit cards; ❷), which has two en-suite rooms; and *Wossells House*, Upper New Rd (☎01934/744317; no credit cards; ❷), where huge breakfasts are served; booking ahead is recommended for both of these. Other options include the **youth hostel**, opposite the fire station, off the Hayes (☎01934/742494; closed Jan & very limited opening mid-Nov to Dec & Feb; beds £11); and three **campsites**, two near the centre of Cheddar – *Froglands* (☎01934/742058; closed mid-Oct to Easter), a hundred yards past the church, and *Cheddar Bridge Park,* a five-star camping and caravan complex opposite (☎01934/743048) – and the fully equipped *Broadway House* on the northwestern outskirts of the village off the A371 to Axbridge (☎01934/742610; closed Dec–Feb). If you want to stay in the heart of the

Mendips, there's a fourth site to consider: *Mendip Heights* (☎01934/870241, ⓦ www.mendipheights.co.uk; closed mid-Nov to Feb), outside the village of Priddy lies east along the B3135 road through the Gorge to Priddy, from which it's a signposted five hundred yards.

Glastonbury

Six miles south of Wells, and reachable from there in twenty minutes on frequent buses, **GLASTONBURY** lies at the centre of the so-called **Isle of Avalon**, a region rich with mystical associations. At the heart of it all is the early Christian legend that the young Christ once visited this site, a story that is not as far-fetched as it sounds. The Romans had a heavy presence in the area, mining lead in the Mendips, and one of these mines was owned by **Joseph of Arimathea**, a well-to-do merchant said to have been related to Mary. It's not completely impossible that the merchant took his kinsman on one of his many visits to his property, in a period of Christ's life of which nothing is recorded. It was this possibility to which William Blake referred in his *Glastonbury Hymn*, better known as *Jerusalem*: – "And did those feet in ancient times/Walk upon England's mountains green?"

Another legend relates how Joseph was imprisoned for twelve years after the Crucifixion, miraculously kept alive by the **Holy Grail**, the chalice of the Last Supper, in which the blood was gathered from the wound in Christ's side. The Grail, along with the spear which had caused the wound, were later taken by Joseph to Glastonbury, where he founded the abbey and commenced the conversion of Britain.

According to the official version, however, **Glastonbury Abbey** (daily: Feb 10am–5pm; March 9.30am–5.30pm; April–Sept 9.30am–6pm; Oct 9.30am–5pm; Nov 9.30am–4.30pm; Dec & Jan 10am–4.30pm; £3; ⓦ www.glastonbury abbey.com) was a Celtic monastery founded in the fourth or fifth century – making this the oldest Christian foundation in England and enlarged by St Dunstan, under whom it became the richest Benedictine abbey in the country. Three Anglo-Saxon kings (Edmund, Edgar and Edmund Ironside) were buried here, the library had a far-reaching fame, and the church had the longest known nave of any monastic church at the time of the Dissolution (580ft – Wells Cathedral's nave reaches 415ft). The original building was destroyed by fire in 1184 and the ruins are the rather scanty remains of what took its place, reduced to their present state at the Dissolution. Hidden behind walls at the centre of town, surrounded by grassy parkland and shaded by trees, the ruins only hint at the extent of the building, which was financed largely by a constant procession of medieval pilgrims. Most prominent and photogenic remains are the transept piers and the shell of the Lady Chapel, with its carved figures of the Annunciation, the Magi and Herod.

The abbey's **choir** introduces another strand to the Glastonbury story, for it holds what is alleged to be the tomb of **Arthur and Guinevere**. As told by William of Malmesbury and Thomas Malory, the story relates how, after being mortally wounded in battle, King Arthur sailed to Avalon where he was buried alongside his queen. The discovery of two bodies in an ancient cemetery outside the abbey in 1191 – from which they were transferred here in 1278 – was taken to confirm the popular identification of Glastonbury with Avalon. In the grounds, the fourteenth-century abbot's kitchen is the only monastic building to survive intact, with four huge corner fireplaces and a great central lantern above. Behind the main entrance to the grounds, look out for the thorn-tree that is supposedly from the original **Glastonbury Thorn** said to have sprouted from the staff of Joseph of Arimathea when he landed here to convert the country. The plant grew for centuries on a nearby hill known as Wyrral, or Weary-All, and despite being hacked down by Puritans, lived long enough to provide numerous cuttings whose descendants still bloom twice a year (Easter & Dec). Only at Glastonbury do they flourish, it is claimed – anywhere else they die after a couple of years.

On the edge of the abbey grounds, the medieval abbey barn forms the centrepiece of the engaging **Somerset Rural Life Museum** (April–Oct Tues–Fri 10am–5pm, Sat & Sun 2–6pm; Nov–March Tues–Sat 10am–3pm; £2.50, valid for multiple entry for one year), illustrating a range of local rural occupations, from cheese- and cider-making to peat-digging, thatching and farming.

From the ruins it's a mile-long hike to **Glastonbury Tor**, at 521ft a landmark for miles around. The conical hill is topped by the dilapidated **St Michael's Tower**, sole remnant of a fourteenth-century church; it commands stupendous views encompassing Wells, the Quantocks, the Mendips, the once-marshy peat moors rolling out to the sea, and sometimes the Welsh mountains. Pilgrims once embarked on the stiff climb here with hard peas in their shoes as penance – nowadays people come to feel the vibrations of crossing ley-lines. If you don't fancy the steep ascent, take the easier path farther up Wellhouse Lane, the road that leads to the Tor Park from the centre of town. You can also save some legwork by taking advantage of the **Glastonbury Tor Bus**, a summer service (July to mid-Sept) which ferries people from the High Street to the base of the Tor every thirty minutes; your £1 ticket can be used all day.

At the bottom of Wellhouse Lane, in the middle of a lush garden intended for quiet contemplation, the **Chalice Well** (daily: Feb, March & Nov 11am–5pm; April–Oct 10am–6pm; Dec & Jan noon–4pm; £2.20; ⓦwww .chalicewell.org.uk) is alleged to be the hiding-place of the Holy Grail. The iron-red waters were considered to have curative properties, making the town a spa for a brief period in the eighteenth century, and they are still prized – there's a tap in Wellhouse Lane.

Back in town, you might take a glance at the fifteenth-century church of **St John the Baptist**, halfway along the High Street. The tower is reckoned to be one of Somerset's finest, and the **interior** has a fine oak roof and stained glass illustrating the legend of St Joseph of Arimathea, both from the period of the church's construction. The Glastonbury thorn in the churchyard is the biggest in town.

Further down the street, the fourteenth-century **Tribunal** was where the abbots presided over legal cases; it later became a hotel for pilgrims, and now holds a small museum of finds from the Iron Age lake villages that once fringed the marshland below the Tor (April–Sept Mon–Thurs & Sun 10am–5pm, Fri & Sat 10am–5.30pm; Oct–March closes 1hr earlier; £2).

Glastonbury is of course best known for its **music festival** which takes place most years over three days at the end of June outside the nearby village of Pilton. Having started in the 1970s, the festival has become one of the biggest and best organized in the country, without shedding too much of its alternative feel. Bands range from huge acts such as REM and Pulp to up-and-coming indie groups and such old hands as Tom Jones. Ticket prices are steep (around £90) and are snapped up early: for general information, contact the promoters on ☎01749/890470, or Glastonbury's tourist office (see below), which is also licensed to sell tickets.

Practicalities

Bus #376 runs once or twice an hour from Wells. Glastonbury's **tourist office** is housed in the Tribunal on the High St (April–Sept Mon–Thurs & Sun

10am–5pm, Fri & Sat 10am–5.30pm; Oct–March closes 1hr earlier; ☎01458 /832954 or ☎832020 for information on tickets for the festival, ⓦwww .glastonburytic.co.uk).

There is a rich assortment of good-value **accommodation** in town; among the budget B&Bs, the seventeenth-century *Waterfall Cottage*, 20 Old Wells Rd (☎01458/831707; no credit cards; ❶), boasts a garden and views, while close to the Chalice Well and Rural Life Museum at 32 Chilkwell St, the *Bolthole* (☎01458/832800; no credit cards; ❶) caters for vegetarians. Far grander is the *Ramala Centre* on nearby Dod Lane (☎01458/832459; ❸). This old manor house is the headquarters of a meditation group and offers accommodation without strings, including use of a library of esoteric philosophy – smokers and carnivores are not welcome. Another retreat, the *Shambhala Healing Centre* on Coursing Batch, abutting the Tor (☎01458/831797, ⓔisisandargon@shambha-la.co.uk; ❺), has Tibetan, Egyptian and Chinese guestrooms, offers four types of massage and a water garden, and specializes in short breaks to replenish your spiritual batteries. If you prefer a more medieval mood, head straight for the *George & Pilgrims*, an old oak-panelled inn on the High Street (☎01458/831146; ❺). Beautifully furnished bedrooms make for a stylish stay at 3 Magdalene St (☎01458/832129; ❺), a listed Georgian house with a large walled garden, right next to the abbey. Just as centrally located, *Glastonbury Backpackers*, 4 Market Place (☎01458/833353, ⓔglastonbury@backpackers-online.com), offers a livelier atmosphere, with clean pastel-coloured doubles costing £26 with shared bath, or £30 with private facilities, while dorm beds go for £10. There's a café, first-floor restaurant, pool room and no curfew, plus occasional bands playing in the bar. The nearest YHA **hostel**, at the Chalet, Ivythorn Hill (☎01458/442961; closed Oct–March; £9.25), lies a couple of miles outside the nearby village of **Street**, an easy bus ride on the #376 between Wells and Glastonbury. There's also a decent **campsite** within sight of the Tor, the *Isle of Avalon* (☎01458/833618), ten minutes' walk up Northload Street on Godney Road.

Wedged between the esoteric shops of Glastonbury's High Street are several decent **cafés** serving inexpensive homemade meals, including the *Blue Note Café* at no. 4, a good place to hang out over coffees and cakes with live or recorded music, and *Rainbow's End* at no. 17, which has vegetarian and vegan food and a small garden, and stays open for evening meals on Fridays and Saturdays, for which booking is strongly recommended (☎01458/833896). On Market Place, almost opposite the abbey entrance, *Grafton's* has a buzzy feel and serves omelettes, wraps and a range of real ales and organic ciders. Halfway up the High Street, the Assembly Rooms has a funky wholefood café, but is better known as the venue for talks and musical and theatrical **performances**, including an international **dance festival** which takes place over a week between July and August. You can also buy tickets for concerts and miracle plays staged within the abbey grounds between mid-June and mid-September – call ☎01458/832267 for details, or view the Abbey's website (see p.416).

If you're spending a few days in the area, think about renting a **bike**; cycling is an ideal way of getting around the Somerset Levels – the area of reclaimed marshes between Glastonbury and the sea. Bikes can be rented for about £7 a day at Pedalers, in Wirral Park, a small trading estate a few minutes from the centre towards Street, near B&Q (☎01458/834562).

Bridgwater, Taunton and the Quantocks

Travelling west through the Somerset Levels, your route could take you through both **Bridgwater** and **Taunton**, each of which would make a handy starting point for excursions into the gently undulating **Quantock Hills**, a mellow landscape of snug villages set in scenic wooded valleys or "combes". Public transport is fairly minimal round here, but you can see quite a lot on the **West Somerset Railway** between Bishops Lydeard and the coastal resort of Minehead, with stops at some of the thatched, typically English villages along the west flank of the Quantocks; and there are **horse-riding** facilities at many local farms.

Bridgwater

Sedate **BRIDGWATER** has seen little excitement since it was embroiled in the Civil War and its aftermath, in particular the events surrounding the **Monmouth Rebellion** of 1685. Having landed from his base in Holland, the Protestant Duke of Monmouth, an illegitimate son of Charles II, was enthusiastically proclaimed king at Taunton, and was only prevented from taking Bristol by the encampment of the Catholic James II's army there. Monmouth turned round and attempted to surprise the king's forces on **Sedgemoor**, three miles outside Bridgwater. The disorganized rebel army was mown down by the royal artillery, Monmouth himself was captured and later beheaded, and a period of repression was unleashed under the infamous Judge Jeffreys, whose Bloody Assizes created a folk-memory in Somerset of gibbets and gutted carcasses displayed around the county.

The town was once one of Somerset's major ports and, despite some ugly outskirts, still has some handsome red-brick buildings around its centre. Northgate leads to the River Parrett and King's Square, which occupies the site of the keep of Bridgwater Castle, built in the thirteenth century but fallen into decay after the Civil War. A few traces remain above ground: part of the main wall is visible on West Quay, and a lesser wall on Queen Street – much of the original material was recycled for the construction of other houses in town. The thirteenth- to fourteenth-century **St Mary's** church (Mon–Wed & Sat 10.30am–noon, Thurs 10.30am–noon & 2–3.30pm), immediately identifiable by its polygonal, acutely angled steeple that soars over the town centre, has an oak pulpit and a seventeenth-century Italian altarpiece. The church is starkly contrasted by the Neoclassical Baptist church opposite, dating from 1600 but rebuilt in 1837. Just round the corner from the red-brick Christ Church, where Coleridge preached in 1797 and 1798, Bridgwater's **Blake Museum**, by the River Parrett on Blake Street (Tues–Sat 10am–4pm; free) shows relics, models and a video-documentary relating to the Battle of Sedgemoor. The sixteenth-century building is reputedly the birthplace of local hero Robert Blake, admiral under Oliver Cromwell, whose swashbuckling career against Royalists, Dutch and Spanish is chronicled and illustrated here.

You can spend a rewarding hour or two here and the surrounding area: equip yourself with the Bridgwater Castle Trail pamphlet from the **tourist office**, beyond the tall white Town Hall on High St (March–Oct Mon–Fri 10am–5pm Sat 10am–4.30pm; Nov–Feb Mon, Wed & Fri 10am–1pm & 1.45–4pm; ☎01278/427652), which can also tell you about available **accommodation** hereabouts. An atmospheric and central choice would be the elegant green and white *Old Vicarage* right opposite St Mary's Church (☎01278/458891, ⓔoldvicaragehotel@aol.com; ❹), which calls itself one of Bridgwater's oldest buildings – and you can still see some of the wattle and daub of the original walls on the left of the gateway into the courtyard. One of the best local **B&Bs** is *Chinar*, 17 Oakfield Rd (☎01278/458639; no credit cards; ❷), a modern house in a quiet neighbourhood offering two double rooms; or try the *Acorns*, 61 Taunton Rd (☎01278/445577; no credit cards; ❶), on the banks of the Bridgwater–Taunton Canal, which has fourteen rooms, mostly en suite. For **snacks** head for the *Nutmeg House* in Angel Crescent, behind the shopping centre off the High Street, offering good pastas, soups, salads and a breakfast menu (closed Sun); alternatively, pick up a bag of fish and chips at the *West Quay Fish Bar*, by the river at the bottom of Castle Street. You can also eat well at the *Old Vicarage*, or just have a **drink** here, while the *Holts Arms*, on the other side of St Mary's (but with another entrance on High St), has tables outside facing the church. At the far end of St Mary Street, Bridgwater has a cluster of places where you can while away an evening in more boisterous style: *TDF*, a mainstream club; the *Rock Garden*, a café-bar/brasserie; and the *Three Crowns* pub, which often has live bands.

A good time to be in Bridgwater would be for the **carnival** celebrations, which usually take place on the nearest Thursday or Friday to Guy Fawkes Day (one of the Catholic conspirators of the Gunpowder Plot hailed from nearby Nether Stowey; see p.421). Grandly festooned floats of the local Carnival Clubs roll through town, before heading off to do the same in various other Somerset towns and villages, including North Petherton, Glastonbury, Wells and Shepton Mallet.

Taunton

Twelve miles from Bridgwater, Somerset's county town of **TAUNTON** lies in the fertile Vale of Taunton, wedged between the Quantock, Brendon and Blackdown hills. The region is famed for its production of cider and scrumpy (cider's less refined cousin), while Taunton itself is host to one of the country's biggest cattle markets.

Taunton's **Castle**, started in the twelfth century, staged the trial of royal claimant Perkin Warbeck, who in 1490 declared himself to be the Duke of York, the younger of the "Princes in the Tower" – the sons of Edward IV, who had been murdered seven years earlier. Most of the castle was pulled down in 1662, but a part of it now houses the **County Museum** (Tues–Sat: April–Oct 10am–5pm; Nov–March 10am–3pm; £2.50), which includes a portrait of Judge Jeffreys among other memorabilia of local interest. Overlooking the county cricket ground are the pinnacled and battlemented towers of the town's two most important churches: **St James** and **St Mary Magdalene**, both fifteenth-century though remodelled by the Victorians. St Mary's is worth a look inside for its roof-bosses carved with medieval masks.

Otherwise Taunton should only detain you as a base to visit the Quantock villages or Exmoor. Information is on hand at the **tourist office** on Paul St (April–Sept Mon–Thurs 9.30am–5.30pm, Fri 9.30am–7pm, Sat 9.30am–5pm; Oct–March Mon–Fri 9.30am–5.30pm, Sat 9.30am–5pm; ☎01823/336344), in the library building. If you want to stay here, head for Wellington Road at the centre of town, where there are three **B&Bs** within a few steps of each other: *Brookfield* at no. 16 (☎01823/272786; no credit cards; ❷), *Beaufort Lodge* at no. 18 (☎01823/326420; no credit cards; ❷) – both with all rooms en suite – and *Acorn Lodge* at no. 22 (☎01823/337613; no credit cards; ❶) with shared bathrooms for its two single and three twin rooms, all of which have TVs. The most atmospheric place in town is next to the museum: the *Castle*, Castle Green

(☎01823/272671, ⓦwww.the-castle-hotel.com; ❼), a wisteria-clad, three-hundred-year-old hotel exuding old-fashioned good taste – the place to stop for a cup of tea if nothing else. On a more down-to-earth note, *Prockters Farm*, a couple of miles outside town, near the village of West Monkton (☎01823 /412269; no credit cards; ❷), is a comfortable old country retreat with brass beds and antiques plus a large garden, offering rooms with or without private bathroom. For a snack or **meal**, head down East Street from Fore Street to *Brettons*, a congenial and inexpensive wine bar at 49 East Reach (closed lunchtime Sat & Mon, and all day Sun). Vegetarian dishes are served at the *Brewhouse Theatre and Arts Centre* on Coal Orchard, by the cricket ground, a good place to come in the evening, when there's usually something going on.

The Quantock Hills

Geologically closer to Devon than Somerset, the **Quantock Hills** are a cultivated outpost of Exmoor, similarly crossed by clear streams and grazed by red deer. Just twelve miles in length and mostly between 800 and 900 feet high, the range is enclosed by a triangle of roads leading up from Bridgwater and Taunton, within which snake a tangle of narrow lanes connecting secluded hamlets, reached by local buses from Taunton and Bridgwater. Along the western edge of the range, a restored steam railway is also a useful transport link, originally built to serve the harbour of Watchet, now used by tourists, bird-watchers and trekkers.

Bishops Lydeard and Combe Florey

North of Taunton, the first villages you pass through on the A358 give you an immediate introduction to the flavour of the Quantocks. **BISHOPS LYDEARD**, four miles up, has a splendid church tower in the Perpendicular style; the church's interior is also worth a look for its carved bench-ends, one of them illustrating the allegory of a pelican feeding its young with blood from its own breast – a symbol of the redemptive power of Christ's blood. The village is the terminus of the **West Somerset Railway**, linked by buses #28A and, on Sunday, #928 from Taunton's train station (from which you can save money by buying a combined bus-and-rail ticket to Minehead). From mid-March to the first week of November (plus some dates in December) steam and diesel trains depart up to eight times daily, stopping at renovated stations on the way to Minehead, some twenty miles away (see p.472). For a talking timetable call ☎01643/707650, for other enquiries call ☎01643/704996, or log on at ⓦwww.west-somerset-railway.co.uk.

A couple of miles north, **COMBE FLOREY** is almost exclusively built of the pink-red sandstone characteristic of Quantock villages. For over fifteen years (1829–45), the local rector was the unconventional cleric Sydney Smith, called "the greatest master of ridicule since Swift" by Macaulay; more recently it's been home to Evelyn Waugh.

Nether Stowey and around

Eight miles west of Bridgwater on the A39, on the edge of the hills, the pretty village of **NETHER STOWEY** is best known for its association with **Samuel Taylor Coleridge**, who walked here from Bristol at the end of 1796, to join his wife and child at their new home. This "miserable cottage", as Sara Coleridge called it, was visited six months later by William Wordsworth and his sister Dorothy, who soon afterwards moved into Alfoxton House, near Holford, a couple of miles down the road. The year that Coleridge and Wordsworth spent as neighbours was extraordinarily productive – Coleridge composed some of his best poetry at this time, including *The Rime of the Ancient Mariner* and *Kubla Khan*, and the two poets in collaboration produced the *Lyrical Ballads*, the poetic manifesto of early English Romanticism. Many of the greatest figures of the age made the trek down to visit the pair, among them Charles Lamb, Thomas De Quincey, Robert Southey, Humphry Davy and William Hazlitt, and it was the coming and going of these intellectuals that stirred the suspicions of the local authorities in a period when England was at war with France. Spies were sent to track them and Wordsworth was finally given notice to leave in June 1798, shortly before *Lyrical Ballads* rolled off the press. In **Coleridge Cottage** (April–Sept Tues–Thurs & Sun 2–5pm; £3; NT), not such an "old hovel" now, you can see the man's parlour and reading room, and, upstairs, his bedroom and an exhibition room containing various letters and first editions.

The village library in nearby Castle Street has a **Quantock Information Centre** (Mon 2.30–5pm, Wed 10am–12.30pm & 2–5pm, Fri 10am–12.30pm, 2–5pm & 5.30–7pm; ☎01278/732845), which can provide walking itineraries and local information. As for **accommodation**, the only choice in the village is the *Rose & Crown Inn*, St Mary St (☎01278/732265; ●); this and the tile-fronted *George* next door also provide the only sustenance to be had in the village, including bar meals – and the *George* has a pool table and occasional live bands. **Campers** should head for *Mill Farm* (☎01278/732286), a couple of miles east of Nether Stowey on the A39, outside the village of Fiddington. There's also a stables here, and a heated pool is laid on for campers and riders.

The nearby village of **HOLFORD** makes for a good place to stop. There's *Quantock House* (☎01278/741439; no credit cards; ●), a beautiful Elizabethan thatched cottage, and a signposted two-mile walk from the village centre is a **youth hostel** (☎01278/741224; closed Sept to mid-April), where you can also **camp** in the grounds. Beds cost £9.25 each. Holford's *Plough Inn*, where Virginia and Leonard Woolf spent their honeymoon, serves simple **snacks**, and is also a stop on the #15 Bridgwater–Minehead bus route.

From Nether Stowey, a minor road winds south off the A39 to the highest point on the Quantocks at **Wills Neck** (1260ft); park at Triscombe Stone, on the edge of Quantock Forest, from where a footpath leads to the summit about a mile distant. Stretching between the Wills Neck and the village of Aisholt, the bracken- and heather-grown moorland plateau of **Aisholt Common** is the heart of the Quantocks – the best place to begin exploring this central tract is near **West Bagborough**, where a five-mile path starts at Birches Corner. Lower down the slopes, outside the village of Aisholt, the banks of **Hawkridge Reservoir** make a lovely picnic stop.

The Quantocks make wonderful riding country, and the hills are notorious for confrontations between hunting parties and anti-hunt activists. If you want to do some horse-back trekking, contact Mill Farm at Fiddington, near Nether Stowey (see above). **Mountain bikes** can be rented for £9 per day from the Quantock Orchard Caravan Park (☎01984/618618), between Crowcombe – a stop on the West Somerset Railway – and Triscombe.

Kilve, Watchet and Cleeve Abbey

The Quantock seaboard can be seen at its best at **Kilve Beach**, signposted off the A39 below Holford. Not so much a beach as a grand shale-studded foreshore, it's perfect for messing about in the rock pools and roaming the sea-weedy shore.

Six miles to the west, **WATCHET** is Somerset's only port of any conse-quence, and the place from which Coleridge's Ancient Mariner set sail. Having made a halt at the harbour, the quiet heart of the village, you can get a good all-round view from **St Decuman's** church above it, built on the site of the saint's martyrdom. Decuman, who floated over the sea from Wales, was decap-itated by a Danish invader who was instantly converted when the saint picked up his bleeding head, washed it in a stream, and gently placed it next to him as he lay down to die. Watchet is only a stop away on the West Somerset Railway from **Washford**, from where it's a ten-minute walk to **Cleeve Abbey** (daily: April–Sept 10am–6pm; Oct 10am–5pm; Nov–March 10am–1pm & 2–4pm; £2.60; EH), a Cistercian house founded in 1198. Although the church itself has been mostly destroyed, the convent buildings are in excellent condition, pro-viding the country's most complete collection of domestic buildings belong-ing to this austere order. An exhibition on the premises illustrates how the monks lived and how the local population unsuccessfully pleaded with Henry VIII for the abbey's survival.

Travel details

Buses

For information on all local and national bus services, contact Traveline: ☎ 0870/608 2 608 (daily 7am–9pm), ⓦ www.traveline.org.uk.

Trains

For information on all local and national rail services, contact National Rail Enquiries: ☎ 08457/48 49 50, ⓦ www.rail.co.uk.

Bath to: Bristol (every 20min; 20min); Dorchester (Mon–Sat 6–8 daily, Sun 2 daily; 2hr 10min); London (1–2 hourly; 1hr 30min); Salisbury (hourly; 1hr); Southampton (1–2 hourly; 1hr 30min).
Bristol to: Bath (every 20min; 20min); Birmingham (hourly; 1hr 30min); Cheltenham (hourly; 1hr); Exeter (1–2 hourly; 1hr 20min–1hr 40min); Gloucester (hourly; 1hr); London (2 hourly; 1hr 40min); Penzance (7 daily; 4hr–4hr 45min); Plymouth (1–2 hourly; 2hr–2hr 50min); Truro (7 daily; 3hr 20min–4hr).
Cheltenham to: Bristol (hourly; 1hr); Gloucester (1–2 hourly; 15min); London (1–2 hourly; 1hr 40min–2hr); Worcester (hourly; 20–30min).
Gloucester to: Bristol (hourly; 1hr); Cheltenham (1–2 hourly; 15min); London (1–2 hourly; 1hr 50min–2hr 10min); Stroud (hourly; 15–20min).

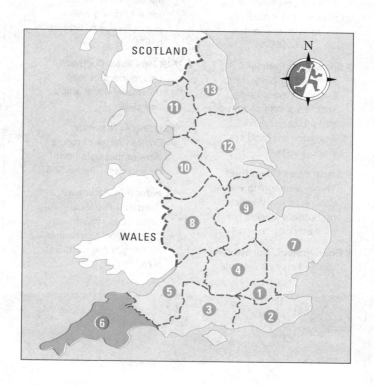

Devon and Cornwall

SCOTLAND

N

WALES

CHAPTER 6   # Highlights

* **Sidmouth International Festival** Folk and world music predominate at this annual festival, held at the beginning of August. See p.439

* **Wistman's Wood, Devon** This tangled forest in the middle of Dartmoor has an ancient, enchanted air. See p.456

* **Barnstaple Pannier Market** The biggest of Devon's covered markets has a long pedigree, and offers bargains alongside the local craftwork. See p.462

* **South West Coast Path** The ever-changing vistas ensure constant variety on Britain's longest way-marked path. See p.473

* **Eden Project, Cornwall** A disused clay pit is home to a panoply of exotic plants and crops, many reared in vast geodesic domes. See p.482

* **Lizard Point, Cornwall** Battered by waves, this unspoiled headland is the starting point for some inspiring walks along the coast. See p.489

* **St Ives Tate, Cornwall** This modern gallery showcases local artists. See p.497

* **Surfing in Newquay** Endless ranks of rollers draw enthusiasts from far and wide. See p.509

* **Seafood in Padstow, Cornwall** The local catch goes straight into the excellent restaurants of this bustling port. See p.511

6

Devon and Cornwall

At the western extremity of England, the counties of **Devon and Cornwall** encompass everything from genteel, cosy villages to vast Atlantic-facing strands of golden sand and wild expanses of granite moorland. The combination of rural peace and first-class beaches has made the peninsula perennially popular with tourists, so much so that tourism has replaced the traditional occupations of fishing and farming as the main source of employment and income. Enough remains of these beleaguered communities to preserve the region's authentic character, however – even if this can be occasionally obscured during the summer season. Avoid the peak periods and you'll be seduced by the genuine appeal of this region, which beckons ever westwards into rural backwaters where increasingly exotic place-names and idiosyncratic pronunciations recall that this was once England's last bastion of Celtic culture.

Although the human history of the region has left its stamp, it is the natural landscape which exerts the strongest pull, and not just in the beauty of the long, deeply indented seaboard. Straddling the border between Devon and Somerset, **Exmoor** is one of the peninsula's three great moors, its heathery slopes much favoured by hunting parties as well as by hikers. For wilderness, however, nothing can beat the remoter tracts of **Dartmoor**, which takes up much of the southern half of inland Devon. The greatest of the West Country's granite massifs, most of Dartmoor retains its solitude in spite of its proximity to the only major cities at this end of the country, either of which would make a good touring base. Of the two, **Exeter** is by far the more interesting, dominated by the twin towers of its medieval cathedral and offering a rich selection of restaurants and nightlife. Much of the city was destroyed by bombing during World War II, though the largest city of Devon and Cornwall, **Plymouth**, suffered far worse, the consequence of its historic role as a great naval port. Bland postwar development inflicted almost as much damage as the Luftwaffe, although enough of Plymouth's Elizabethan core has survived to merit a visit, and the city, by capitalizing on its maritime associations, has succeeded in reviving its port area.

Accommodation price codes

Throughout this guide, hotel and B&B accommodation is priced on a scale of ❶ to ❾, the number indicating the **lowest price** you could expect to pay per night in that establishment for a **double room** in high season. The prices indicated by the codes are as follows:

❶ under £40	❹ £60–70	❼ £110–150
❷ £40–50	❺ £70–90	❽ £150–200
❸ £50–60	❻ £90–110	❾ over £200

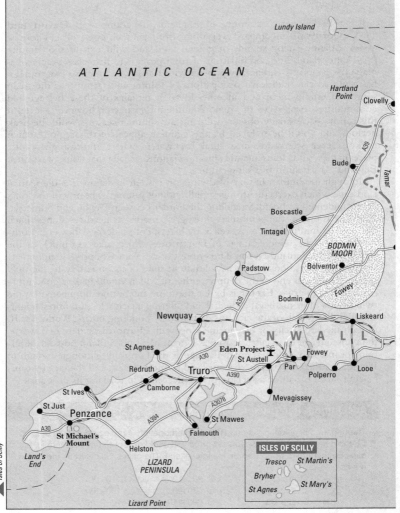

N

Lundy Island

ATLANTIC OCEAN

Hartland Point
Clovelly

A39

Tamar

Bude

Boscastle

Tintagel

BODMIN MOOR

Padstow

Bolventor

A39

Fowey

Bodmin

Newquay

Liskeard

C O R N W A L L

St Agnes

Eden Project

Fowey

A30

St Austell

Redruth

Truro

Par

Looe

Camborne

A390

Polperro

St Ives

A3078

St Just

Mevagissey

Penzance

A394

St Mawes

St Michael's Mount

Falmouth

Land's End

A30

Helston

LIZARD PENINSULA

ISLES OF SCILLY

Tresco   *St Martin's*

Bryher

St Agnes   *St Mary's*

Lizard Point

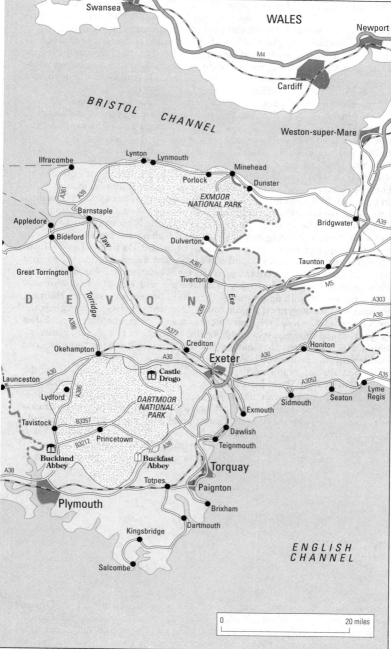

© Crown copyright

The coastline on either side of Exeter and Plymouth is within easy reach. Warmed by the Gulf Stream, and enjoying more hours of sunshine than virtually anywhere else in England, this part of the country can sometimes come fairly close to the atmosphere of the Mediterranean, and indeed Devon's principal resort, **Torquay**, styles itself the capital of the "English Riviera". St Tropez it ain't, but there's no denying a certain glamour, far removed from the old-fashioned charm of the seaside towns of **East Devon**, or the cliff-backed resorts of the county's northern littoral.

Cornwall too has its pockets of concentrated tourist development – chiefly at **Falmouth** and **Newquay**, the first of these a sailing centre, the second a mecca for surfers drawn to its choice of west-facing beaches. **St Ives**, too, has long attracted the crowds, though the town has a separate identity as a magnet for the arts. Despite the tourist incursions, this county is essentially less domesticated than its agricultural neighbour, in part due to the overbearing presence of the turbulent Atlantic, which is never more than half an hour's drive away. The restless waves give Cornwall's old fishing ports an almost embattled character, especially on the north coast, where the fortified headland of **Tintagel** – the most famous of the many places hereabouts to boast a connection with King Arthur and his knights – and the clenched little harbour of **Boscastle** are typical of the county's craggy appeal, but the full elemental power of the ocean can best be appreciated on the twin pincers of **Lizard Point** and **Land's End**, where the splintered cliffs resound to the constant thunder of the waves. And there's another factor contributing to Cornwall's starker feel – unlike Devon, this county was once considerably industrialized, and is dotted with remnants of its now defunct mining industries, their ruins presenting a salutary counterpoint to the tourist-centred seaside towns. One disused clay-pit, though, is the site of one of Cornwall's biggest success stories of recent times, the **Eden Project**, which imaginatively highlights the diversity of the planet's plant-systems, with the help of science-fiction "biomes" where tropical and Mediterranean climates and conditions have been re-created.

The best way of exploring the coast of Devon and Cornwall is along the **South West Coast Path**, Britain's longest waymarked footpath, which allows the dauntless hiker to cover almost six hundred miles from the Somerset border to the edge of Bournemouth in Dorset. Getting around by **public transport** in the West Country can be a convoluted and lengthy process, especially if you're relying on the often skimpy bus network. By train, you can reach Bristol, Exeter, Plymouth and Penzance, with a handful of branch lines wandering off to the major coastal resorts – though there's nothing like the extensive network the Victorians once enjoyed.

Devon

With its rolling meadows, narrow lanes and remote thatched cottages, **Devon** has long been the urbanite's ideal vision of a pre-industrial, "authentic" England, and a quick tour of the county might suggest that this is largely a region of cosy, gentrified villages inhabited mainly by retired folk and urban refugees. Certainly parts of Devon suffer from an excess of cloying nostalgia and an abundance of commercialism, but its popularity has a positive side to it as well – chiefly that zealous care is taken to preserve the undeveloped stretches of countryside and coast in the condition that has made them so popular. Pockets of genuine tranquillity are still to be found all over the county, from moorland villages with an appeal that goes deeper than mere picturesqueness, to quiet coves on the spectacular coastline.

Devon has played a leading part in England's **maritime history**, and you can't go far without meeting some reminder of the great names of Tudor and Stuart seafaring, particularly at the two cities of **Exeter** and **Plymouth**. These days the nautical tradition is perpetuated on a domesticated scale by yachtspeople taking advantage of Devon's numerous creeks and bays, especially on its southern coast, where ports such as Dartmouth and Salcombe are awash with amateur sailors. Land-bound tourists flock to the sandy beaches and seaside resorts, of which **Torquay**, on the south coast, and **Ilfracombe**, on the north, are the busiest – though the most attractive are those which have retained something of their nineteenth-century elegance, such as Sidmouth, in East Devon. Other seaside villages retain a low level of fishing activity but otherwise live on a stilted Old World image, of which **Clovelly** is the supreme example. **Inland**, Devon is characterized by swards of lush pasture and a scattering of sheltered villages, the county's low population density dropping to almost zero on **Dartmoor**, the wildest and bleakest of the West's moors, and **Exmoor**, whose seaboard constitutes one of the West Country's most scenic littorals.

Exeter and Plymouth are on the main **rail** lines from London and the Midlands, with branch lines from Exeter linking the north coast at Barnstaple and the south-coast towns of Exmouth and Torquay. **Buses** from the chief stations fan out along the coasts and into the interior, though the service can be extremely rudimentary for the smaller villages.

Exeter

EXETER's sights are richer than those of any other town in Devon or Cornwall, the legacy of an eventful history since its Celtic foundation and the establishment here of the most westerly Roman outpost. After the Roman withdrawal, Exeter was refounded by Alfred the Great and by the time of the Norman Conquest had become one of the largest towns in England, profiting from its position on the banks of the River Exe. The expansion of the wool trade in the Tudor period sustained the city until the eighteenth century, and Exeter has maintained its status as commercial centre and county town, despite having much of its ancient centre gutted by World War II bombing.

You are likely to pass through this transport hub for Devon at least once on your West Country travels, and Exeter's sturdy cathedral and the remnants of its compact old quarter would repay an overnight stay.

Arrival, information and accommodation

Exeter has two **train stations**, Exeter Central and St David's, the latter a little further out from the centre of town, though connected by frequent city buses. South West trains on the London Waterloo–Salisbury line stop at both, as do trains on the Tarka Line to Barnstaple (see p.462) and those to Exmouth, though Exeter Central is not served by most other long-distance trains. **Buses**

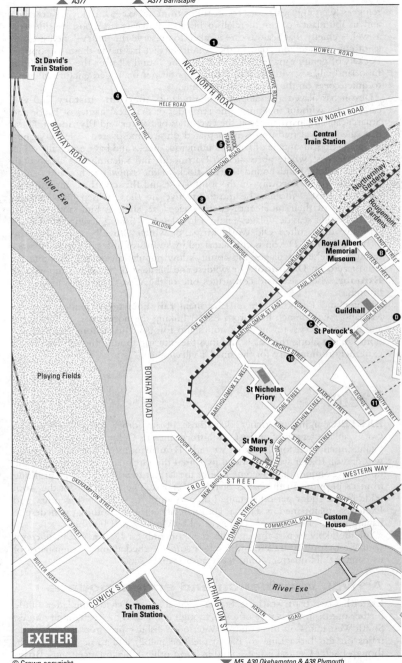

EXETER

© Crown copyright

▼ M5, A30 Okehampton & A38 Plymouth

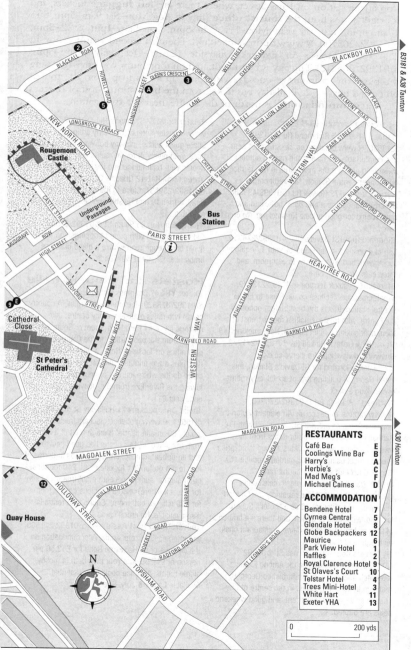

RESTAURANTS

Café Bar	E
Coolings Wine Bar	B
Harry's	A
Herbie's	C
Mad Meg's	F
Michael Caines	D

ACCOMMODATION

Bendene Hotel	7
Cyrnea Central	5
Glendale Hotel	8
Globe Backpackers	12
Maurice	6
Park View Hotel	1
Raffles	2
Royal Clarence Hotel	9
St Olaves's Court	10
Telstar Hotel	4
Trees Mini-Hotel	3
White Hart	11
Exeter YHA	13

0   200 yds

stop at the station on Paris Street, where there are **left luggage** lockers, and it's right across from the **tourist office** (July & Aug Mon–Sat 9am–5pm, Sun 10am–4pm; rest of year Mon–Fri 9am–5pm, Sat 9am–1pm & 2–5pm; ☎01392/265700, ⊛www.thisisexeter.co.uk). There's a second visitor centre in The Quay House on Exeter's Quayside (Easter–Oct daily 10am–5pm; ☎01392/265213). The city is best negotiated on foot, but if you envisage using the buses on an intensive one-day visit, pick up a bus map from the tourist office and buy a £2.90 all-day bus ticket from the bus station. Most of Exeter's B&B **accommodation** lies north of the centre, near the two stations.

Hotels and B&Bs

Bendene Hotel 15 Richmond Rd ☎01392 /213526, ⊛www.bendene.co.uk. Small but neat and comfortable rooms and the heated outdoor swimming pool are the main lures in this terrace house near Central Station. No credit cards. **❶**

Cyrnea Central 73 Howell Rd ☎01392/438386. Cheerful management and basic but clean and quiet rooms for good prices. No smoking. No credit cards. **❶**

Glendale Hotel St David's Hill ☎01392/274350. Useful if unspectacular stand-by with TV-equipped rooms with and without private bathroom, and three cats. No credit cards. **❷**

Maurice 5 Bystock Terrace ☎01392/213079, ⓔhotel.maurice@eclipse.co.uk. Close to Exeter Central station, this is the best budget option in the centre, with bright, smallish rooms, most of them overlooking a quiet square. Non-smoking. **❶**

Park View Hotel 8 Howell Rd ☎01392/271772, ⊛www.parkviewhotel.freeserve.co.uk. Conveniently located for St David's Station, this listed Georgian building has peaceful, airy rooms overlooking a park. **❷**

Raffles 11 Blackall Rd ☎01392/270200, ⊛www.raffffles-exeter.co.uk. An elegant Victorian house with rooms individually furnished with Pre-Raphaelite etchings and other items from the owner's antique business. Does a good fixed-price evening meal using organic garden produce. **❸**

Royal Clarence Hotel Cathedral Yard ☎01392/319955, ⊛www.regalhotels.co.uk/ clarence. Built in 1769 and reputedly the first inn in England to be described as a "hotel". Superb location, with rates to match, and there's a branch of the celebrated *Michael Caine's* restaurant chain on the ground floor. **❻**

St Olave's Court Mary Arches St ☎01392 /217736, ⊛www.olaves.co.uk. Among Exeter's top-notch hotels, this is a refurbished Georgian mansion in its own grounds in the centre of town. There's an excellent restaurant, and good weekend deals are offered. **❻**

Telstar Hotel 77 St David's Hill ☎01392/272466, ⊛www.telstar-hotel.co.uk. Fairly ordinary but adequate guest house, midway between the train stations, with plenty of rooms, some non-smoking. Rooms with bath nudge into the next category. **❶**

Trees Mini-Hotel 2 Queen's Crescent ☎01392/259531. Close to the bus station off York Road, a friendly and reliable choice. Evening meals available. **❶**

The White Hart 65 South St ☎01392/279897. Old coaching inn with period trappings and a lovely old bar, though rooms have a bland business ambience. **❻**, **❹** at weekends.

Hostels and student halls

Exeter YHA 47 Countess Wear Rd ☎01392/873329, ⓔexeter@yha.org.uk. A country house two miles outside the city centre; take minibus #K or #T from High Street or South Street, or #57 from the bus station, to the Countess Wear post office on Topsham Road, a fifteen-minute ride, plus a ten-minute walk. Alternatively, you could do the whole journey on foot on a path following the River Exe from the Quayside. Dorm beds cost £11.

Globe Backpackers 71 Holloway St ☎01392 /215521, ⊛www.globebackpackers.freeserve .co.uk. Clean and central (though a bit of a hike from the stations), this hostel has good showers and an upbeat atmosphere. Bunk-beds in dorms of four to ten go for £11 for one night, £10 for subsequent nights, and the seventh night free if you stay for a week. There's also a spacious double room for £30 (shared bathroom). Cheap bike rental is also available. No credit cards.

University Halls of Residence ☎01392/211500, ⓔconferences@exeter.ac.uk. Accommodation on the campus or on Heavitree Road for £12.50 per person or £17.50 with your own bath in mostly single rooms. Advance booking is essential. Available Easter & July–Sept.

The City

The most distinctive feature of Exeter's skyline, **St Peter's Cathedral** (Mon–Sat 8am–6.30pm, Sun 8am–7.30pm; £3 suggested donation; ⓦwww .exeter-cathedral.org.uk), is a stately monument made conspicuous by the two great Norman towers flanking the nave. Close up, it is the facade's ornate Gothic screen that commands attention: its three tiers of sculpted (and very weathered) figures – including Alfred, Athelstan, Canute, William the Conqueror and Richard II – were begun around 1360, part of a rebuilding programme which left only the Norman towers from the original construction.

Entering the cathedral, you're confronted by the longest unbroken **Gothic ceiling** in the world, its **bosses** vividly painted – one, towards the west front, shows the murder of Thomas à Becket. The **Lady Chapel** and **Chapter House** – respectively at the far end of the building and off the right transept – are thirteenth-century, but the main part of the nave, including the lavish rib-vaulting, dates from the full flowering of the English Decorated style, a century later. There are many fine examples of sculpture from this period, including, in the minstrels' gallery high up on the left side, angels playing musical instruments, and, below them, figures of Edward III and Queen Philippa.

Dominating the cathedral's central space are the organ pipes installed in the seventeenth century and harmonizing perfectly with the linear patterns of the roof and arches. In the **Choir** don't miss the sixty-foot **bishop's throne** or the **misericords** – decorated with mythological figures around 1260, they are thought to be the oldest in the country. Near the entrance stands a comparatively recent addition to the many medieval tombs and memorials lining the cathedral's walls: a monument to R.D. Blackmore, author of *Lorna Doone*. If you want to make sure you don't miss a thing, take one of the **tours** (April–Oct daily 11am & 2.30pm; Nov–March Thurs 11am; £2.50 suggested donation).

Outside, a graceful statue of the theologian Richard Hooker surveys the **Cathedral Close**, a motley mixture of architectural styles from Tudor to Regency, though most display Exeter's trademark red-brick work. One of the finest buildings is the Elizabethan **Mol's Coffee House**, impressively timbered and gabled, now a map-shop.

Some older buildings are still standing amid the banal concrete of the modern town centre, including Exeter's finest civic building, the fourteenth-century **Guildhall** – claimed to be England's oldest municipal building in regular use. Standing not far from the cathedral on the pedestrianized **High Street**, it's fronted by an elegant Renaissance portico, and the main chamber merits a glance for its arched roof timbers, which rest on carved bears holding staves, symbols of the Yorkist cause during the Wars of the Roses. The Guildhall is usually **open to visitors** on weekdays from 10.30am to 1pm and 2pm to 4pm, and on Saturdays from 10am to noon, and when things are quiet the doorman will give you a brief tour. Just down from here, opposite **St Petrock's** – one of Exeter's six surviving medieval churches in the central area – you'll find the impossibly narrow Parliament Street, just 25 inches wide at this end.

On the west side of Fore Street, the continuation of the High Street, a turning leads to **St Nicholas Priory** (Easter–Oct Mon, Wed & Sat 3–4.30pm; free), part of a small Benedictine foundation that became a merchant's home after the Dissolution; the interior has been restored to what it might have looked like in the Tudor era. On the other side of Fore Street, trailing down towards the river, cobbled **Stepcote Hill** was once the main road into Exeter from the west, though it is difficult to imagine this steep and narrow lane as a main thoroughfare. Another of central Exeter's ancient churches, **St Mary**

Steps, stands surrounded by mainly Tudor houses at the bottom, with a fine seventeenth-century clock on its tower and a late Gothic nave inside.

Exeter's centre is bounded to the southwest by the River Exe, where the port area is now mostly devoted to leisure activities, particularly around the old **Quayside**. Pubs, shops and cafés share the space with handsomely restored nineteenth-century warehouses and the smart **Custom House**, built in 1681, its opulence reflecting the former importance of the cloth trade. Next door, the Quay House from the same period has an information desk and, upstairs, a video on Exeter's history (Easter–Oct). The area comes into its own at night, but is worth a wander at any time, and you can **rent bikes** (£12/day) and **canoes** (from £14/day) at Saddles & Paddles on the quayside (☎01392/424241, ⊛www.saddlepaddle.co.uk) to explore the **Exeter Canal**, which runs five miles to Topsham and beyond.

Back at the north end of the High Street, Romansgate Passage (next to Boots) holds the entrance to a network of **underground passages** first excavated in the thirteenth century to bring water to the cathedral precincts. The passages can be visited as part of a fascinating 35-minute guided **tour** (July–Sept & school holidays Mon–Sat 10am–5.30pm; rest of year Tues–Fri noon–5pm, Sat 10am–5pm; £2.75, July & Aug £3.75) – not recommended to claustrophobes, however. Nearby, Castle Street leads to what remains of **Rougemont Castle**, now little more than a perimeter of red-stone walls that are best appreciated from the surrounding Rougemont and Northernhay Gardens. Following the path through this park, exit at Queen Street to drop in at the excellent **Royal Albert Memorial Museum** (Mon–Sat 10am–5pm; free), the closest thing in Devon to a county museum. Exuding the Victorian spirit of wide-ranging curiosity, this motley assortment includes everything from a menagerie of stuffed animals to mock-ups of the various building styles used at different periods in the city. The collections of silverware, watches and clocks contrast nicely with the colourful ethnography section, and the picture gallery has some good specimens of West Country art alongside work by other artists associated with Devon.

Eating and drinking

The cafés inside the Royal Albert Memorial Museum and the Exeter Arts Centre, behind the museum off Gandy Street, would be reason enough to come here, with wholesome **snacks** served in a convivial atmosphere. Round the corner from the museum, in medieval Gandy Street, *Coolings Wine Bar* is a popular and stylish lunch stop that's also open until late evening with DJs on Fridays and Saturdays. Opposite the cathedral, the *Café Bar* is a casually modish spot for a coffee or lunch, serving toasties, salads, burgers and pastas in small or large sizes until 10pm daily. It's part of the next-door *Michael Caine's* (☎01392/310031, ⊛www.michaelcaines.com), one of Exeter's classiest **restaurants** where you'll find sophisticated modern European cuisine in sleek surroundings; prices are fairly high, though there are reasonable fixed-price menus at lunchtime. In total contrast, the Olde Worlde atmosphere is laid on thickly at *Mad Meg's* (closed Mon & Tues lunch) – once a nunnery, now staffed by waitresses in wench costume – but there are some good-value traditional dishes here; it's tucked away near the top of Fore Street, below a bike shop. Nearby *Herbie's*, 15 North St (☎01392/258473; closed all day Sun & Mon eve), is the only wholefood restaurant in town, and has organic ice cream on the menu, while good-value Mexican and Italian staples are on the menu at *Harry's*, in a converted church at 86 Longbrook St (☎01392/202 234).

Among the **pubs** the *Ship Inn*, in St Martin's Lane (between the High Street and the cathedral), serves reasonably priced lunches and prides itself on the claim that it was once Francis Drake's local. The pubs and clubs on Exeter's Quay make this a lively spot to while away an evening. You can eat and drink sitting outside at the seventeenth-century *Prospect Inn* and the more contemporary *On the Waterside*.

Nightlife and entertainment

You'll find Exeter's two biggest **club complexes** facing each other on the Quay: the *Warehouse*, *Boxes* and *Boogies*, and *Volts* and *Hothouse*, all open in various combinations and playing mainstream dance and retro sounds. Some of the best dance and live-music venues are in the centre, including the *Cavern Club*, with entrances in Queen and Gandy streets (also open 10.30am–4pm for snacks) and the *Timepiece*, Little Castle St, formerly a prison that now also has a good daytime bar with a garden. For live music, you could also try the university's *Lemon Grove* (term-time only) and the *Fizgig*, a pub below the iron bridge on Lower North Street, which attracts occasional big names. Try also *Bar Bomba*, a cool pre-club lounge beneath Fruta Bomba on Queen Street.

The **Phoenix Exeter Arts Centre** (℡01392/667080) is the focus of a medley of cultural pursuits, including regular non-mainstream films, exhibitions, gigs and various workshops. Of the town's theatres, the **Northcott**, near the university on Stocker Road (℡01392/493493), and the **Barnfield**, on Barnfield Road (℡01392/271808), have the best productions, with the former also staging ballet and opera performances. The **Exeter Festival** takes place during the first three weeks of July, and features jazz and blues concerts as well as classical performances and cabaret, at various venues around town.

Around Exeter

The coast south and east of Exeter holds an architectural oddity, **A La Ronde**, and a string of old-fashioned seaside resorts, none of them over-commercialized, though still best seen outside the summer peak. **Sidmouth** would be a good choice for an overnight stop, as would the neighbouring villages of **Beer** and **Seaton**.

A La Ronde, Exmouth and Budleigh Salterton are all served by **bus** #57 running every twenty minutes from Exeter's bus station, while #52, #52A and #52B are best for Sidmouth (some #57 buses also connect Exmouth with Sidmouth). The #899 minibus service connects Sidmouth with Beer and Seaton; it runs seven times daily on weekdays, three times on Saturday and not at all on Sunday. You can also get to Exmouth by **train**, and from the train station at **Honiton**, eight miles inland, #340 runs every couple of hours to Sidmouth (3 on Sun).

A La Ronde

The Gothic folly of **A La Ronde** (April–Oct Mon–Thurs & Sun 11am–5.30pm; £3.40), a couple of miles outside Exmouth off the A376, was the creation of two cousins, Jane and Mary Parminter, who in the 1790s were inspired by their European Grand Tour to construct a sixteen-sided house possibly based on the Byzantine basilica of San Vitale in Ravenna. The end product, sketchily related to its alleged source, is filled with mementoes of the Parminters' tour as well as a number of their more offbeat creations, such as a frieze made of feathers culled from game birds and chickens. In the upper rooms are a gallery and staircase completely covered in shells, too fragile to be visited, though part can be glimpsed from the completely enclosed octagonal room on the first floor – a closed-circuit TV system enables visitors to home in on details.

The women intended that the house should be inherited only by female descendants, though the conditions of Mary Parminter's will (she died in 1849) were broken at the end of the nineteenth century when the building was inherited by the Reverend Oswald Reichel, the only male owner of the house in its history. Reichel gave it a refurbishment that in some ways improved the building, for instance by the addition of dormer windows on the second floor, which had previously not enjoyed any natural light, let alone the superb views over the Exe Estuary to Haldon Hill and Dawlish Warren.

Exmouth and Budleigh Salterton

EXMOUTH started as a Roman port and went on to become the first of the county's resorts to be popularized by holiday-makers in the late eighteenth century. Overlooking lawns, rock pools and a respectable two miles of beach, Exmouth's Georgian terraces once accommodated such folk as the wives of Nelson and Byron – installed at no. 6 and 19 The Beacon respectively (on a rise overlooking the seafront, above the public gardens). The town's still unhurried air contrasts sharply with the cranes and warehouses of the docks beyond the Esplanade. From April to October, Exmouth is linked by **ferry** to Starcross, on the other side of the Exe estuary (hourly service; £2.50 single fare), where you can pick up a bus route to Dawlish and Teignmouth (see p.440). **Staying** here is a good option, with plenty of choice: near the tourist office and the beach, try the non-smoking *Blenheim Guest House*, 39 Morton Rd (☎01395 /223123, ⊛www.come.to/freesunshine; no credit cards; ❷), which offers spacious rooms in an easy-going atmosphere, though there's a two-night minimum stay in summer. Spending a bit more, you can enjoy wonderful panoramic views from the rooms at the *Manor Hotel*, The Beacon (☎01395 /274477; ❸). The **tourist office** is on Alexandra Terrace (Easter–June, Sept & Oct Mon–Sat 9.30am–5pm; July & Aug Mon–Sat 9.30am–5pm, Sun 10am–3pm; Nov–Easter Mon–Sat 9.30am–1.30pm; ☎01395/222299, ⊛www.exmouth -guide.co.uk).

Four miles east of Exmouth, bounded on each side by red sandstone cliffs, **BUDLEIGH SALTERTON** continues the genteel theme – its thatched and whitewashed cottages attracted such figures as Noël Coward and P.G. Wodehouse, and John Millais painted his famous *Boyhood of Raleigh* on the shingle beach here. (Sir Walter Raleigh was born in the pretty East Budleigh, a couple of miles inland.) Three miles east, **Ladram Bay** is a popular pebbly beach sheltered by woods and beautiful eroded cliffs. If you want to stay in the area, contact the **tourist office** on Fore Street (Easter–June, Sept & Oct Mon–Sat 10am–5pm; July & Aug Mon–Sat 10am–5pm, Sun 11am–5pm; Nov–Easter Mon–Thurs & Sat 10am–1pm, Fri 10am–3pm; ☎01395/445275).

Sidmouth

Set amidst a shelf of crumbling red sandstone, cream-and-white **SIDMOUTH** is the chief resort on this stretch of coast and boasts nearly five hundred buildings listed as having special historic or architectural interest, among them the stately Georgian homes of **York Terrace** behind the Esplanade. Moreover, the **beaches** are better tended than many along this coast, not only the mile-long main town beach but also Jacob's Ladder, a cliff-backed shingle and sand strip beyond Connaught Gardens to the west of town. To the east, the South Devon Coast Path (part of the South West Coast Path) climbs steep Salcombe Hill to follow cliffs that give sanctuary to a range of birdlife including yellowhammers and green woodpeckers, as well as the rarer grasshopper warbler. Farther on, the path descends to meet one of the most isolated and attractive beaches in the area, **Weston Mouth**.

The **tourist office** is on Ham Lane, off the eastern end of the Esplanade (March & April Mon–Thurs 10am–4pm, Fri & Sat 10am–5pm, Sun 10am–1pm; May–July & Sept Mon–Sat 10am–5pm, Sun 10am–1pm; Aug & Oct Mon–Sat 10am–6pm, Sun 10am–4pm; Nov–Feb Mon–Sat 10am–1.30pm; ☎01395/516441). Of the **B&Bs**, *Cranmere*, close to the Esplanade at 2 Fortfield Place (☎01395/513933; no credit cards; ❶), is one of the cheapest, with a homely atmosphere and most rooms en suite. A little further from the seafront, the *Old Farmhouse*, on Hillside Road (☎01395/512284; no credit cards; ❸; closed Nov–Jan), offers attractive rooms with plenty of atmosphere, and delicious meals on request. There's more choice in the string of decent guest houses along Salcombe Road, including *Berwick Guest House* at 4 Albert Terrace (☎01395/513621; no smoking; no credit cards; ❸). For **meals** in town, try the seafood and vegetarian salads at *Brown's Bistro* on Fore Street (closed Sun), while *Osborne's* further down Fore Street serves teas and light **snacks**. On Old Fore Street, two hundred yards from the seafront, the *Old Ship* and *Anchor* **pubs** provide excellent bar meals and suppers as well as a good range of ales.

Sidmouth hosts what many consider to be the country's best **folk festival** over eight days at the beginning of August. Folk and roots artists from around the world as well as dance and theatre companies take over various venues including the *Arena Theatre* and various pubs and parks. A campsite is laid on outside Sidmouth with shuttle buses to the centre, and tickets can be bought for specific days, for the weekend or the entire week. For detailed information, call the tourist office, call ☎01296/433669 or check out the website at ⓦwww .mrscasey.co.uk/sidmouth. Book early for the main acts.

Beer and Seaton

Eight miles east along the coast, the fishing village of **BEER** lies huddled within a small sheltered cove between gleaming white headlands. A stream rushes along a deep channel dug into Beer's main street, and if you can ignore the crowds in high summer much of the village looks unchanged since the time when it was a smugglers' eyrie, its inlets used by such characters as Jack Rattenbury, who published his *Memoirs of a Smuggler* in 1837. The village is best known for its quarries, which were worked from Roman times until the last century: **Beer Stone** was used in many of Devon's churches and houses, and also went into the construction of some London buildings. You can visit the complex of **underground quarries** (Easter–Sept 10am–5pm; Oct 11am–4pm; last entry 1hr before closing; £4.25) a mile or so west of the village on a guided tour, along with a small exhibition of pieces carved by medieval masons, among others. Take something warm to wear. *Bay View* (☎01297/20489; no credit cards; ❶; closed Nov–Easter), overlooking the sea on Fore Street, is easily the best of the **B&Bs**, and Beer's **youth hostel** is half a mile northwest, at Bovey Combe, Townsend (☎01297/20296; closed Nov–March). For **food**, head straight to the *Barrel* pub, on the main street, where the superb menu includes local delicacies such as Devon oysters and home-smoked fish; there are imaginative vegetarian options, too.

SEATON, a smooth stroll less than a mile eastwards, has a steep, pebbly beach like Beer's, but this is a much more developed resort, mutating from a placid, slow-moving haven at its western end to a much gaudier affair to the east. One of the main attractions is the open-top **tramway** which follows the path of the old railway line to the inland village of Colyton. Seaton's **tourist office** is on the Underfleet, in the main car park on Harbour Road (April–June & Sept Mon–Sat 10am–5pm, Sun 1.30–5.30pm; July & Aug Mon–Sat 10am–5pm, Sun 10am–2pm; Oct Mon–Sat 10am–5pm; Nov–March Mon–Sat 10am–2pm; ☎01297/21660). On Trevelyan Road, at the far end of the Esplanade on the eastern edge of town, you'll find *Beach End* (☎01297/23388; no credit cards; ❷; closed Nov–March), a bright and roomy Edwardian **B&B**, or, just across from the tourist office, the friendly *Beaumont* on Castle Hill (☎01297/20832, ✉tony@lymebay.demon.co.uk; no credit cards; ❸), on the west side – both have sea views.

The "English Riviera" region

The wedge of land between Dartmoor and the sea contains some of Devon's most fertile pastures, backing onto some of the West's most popular coastal resorts. Chief of these is **Torbay**, an amalgam of **Torquay**, **Paignton** and **Brixham**, together forming the nucleus of an area optimistically known as "The English Riviera". To the north of the Torbay conurbation lie small-scale **Teignmouth** and **Dawlish**, while to the south the port of **Dartmouth** offers another calmer alternative, linked by riverboat to historic and almost unspoiled **Totnes**. West of the River Dart, the rich agricultural district of **South Hams** extends as far as Plymouth, cleft by a web of rivers flowing off Dartmoor. The main town here is **Kingsbridge**, at the head of an estuary down which you can ferry to the sailing resort of **Salcombe**.

Trains from Exeter to Plymouth run down the coast as far as Teignmouth before striking inland for Totnes – to get to Torbay, change at Newton Abbot. The hourly #X46 **bus** connects Exeter and Torquay in an hour, while the #85 and #85A serve Teignmouth and Dawlish. For the hinterland and points south and west along the coast, you can rely on a network of buses from Torquay, and travellers to Totnes and Dartmouth could make use of the **South Devon Railway** and **boats** along the River Dart.

Teignmouth and Dawlish

The estuary town of **TEIGNMOUTH** (pronounced "Tinmouth"), once a terminus for shipments of Dartmoor granite, still has a thriving harbour along the banks of the Teign, and fishing boats are still hauled up onto the pebble beach from which juts a pier that formerly segregated male and female bathers. The town began to attract holiday-makers at the end of the eighteenth century – Fanny Burney and John Keats both stayed – and some dainty Georgian and Victorian villas adorn Powderham Terrace and the Den. Behind the town centre, the lanes hold some interesting old pubs, while the estuary crossing to **Shaldon**, either by road bridge or by passenger ferry (last one at around 8.45pm), deposits you in a smaller version of Teignmouth, relatively unscathed by the seasonal crowds.

Teignmouth's **tourist office** is near the pier (May–Sept daily 9am–5pm; Oct–April Mon–Sat 9am–1pm & 2–5pm; ☎01626/215666). The *Hill Rise Hotel* (☎01626/773108; no credit cards; ❶) provides great-value **accommodation** on Winterbourne Road, a quiet cul-de-sac away from the sea but handy for the station; rooms come with and without private bath. Nearer the seafront and just a few steps from the river, *Seaway Guest House*, 27 Northumberland Place (☎01626/879024, ⬥www.seawayteignmouth.com; ❶), has spacious, well-equipped rooms. For **food and drink**, Teignmouth's back-streets and alleys unearth some choice pubs, notably the *Ship Inn* on Queen Street, overlooking the water and opposite the reasonable *Harbour Lights* snack bar, which offers seafood salads.

North of Teignmouth, **DAWLISH** is a smaller, more sedate resort, known to Jane Austen and Charles Dickens, whose character Nicholas Nickleby was born here. The seafront, a mile from the older inland centre, is spanned by a granite railway viaduct built by Brunel, under which you pass to reach a beach of sand and shingle. A better beach lies a little further south, at Coryton Cove, though most people head a couple of miles north to **Dawlish Warren**, a sandy area backed by dunes and caravan parks and also holding a nature reserve. If you want to **stay**, make for the *Walton Guest House*, a Georgian building five minutes from the seafront on Plantation Terrace (☎01626/862760; no credit cards; ❷).

Torquay

Five miles south of Teignmouth, the coast is heavily urbanized around **Torbay**, a tourist conglomeration entirely dedicated to the exploitation of the bay's sheltered climate and exuberant vegetation. **TORQUAY**, the largest component of the super-resort, comes closest to living up to the self-penned "English Riviera" sobriquet, sporting a mini-corniche and promenades landscaped with flowerbeds. The much-vaunted palm trees (actually New Zealand cabbage trees) and the coloured lights that festoon the harbour by night contribute to the town's unique flavour, a slightly frayed combination of the exotic and the classically English. Torquay's transformation from a fishing village began with its establishment as a fashionable haven for invalids, among them the consumptive Elizabeth Barrett Browning, who spent three years here. In recent years the most famous figures previously associated with Torquay – crimewriter Agatha Christie and traveller Freya Stark – have given way to the fictional TV hotelier Basil Fawlty, whose jingoism and injured pride perfectly encapsulate the town's adaptation to the demands of mass tourism.

Arrival, information and accommodation

The **train station** is off Rathmore Road, next to the Torre Abbey gardens; most **buses** leave from outside the Pavilion, including the #X80 to Totnes and Plymouth, and the frequent #12 and #12B service linking Torquay with Paignton and Brixham. Torquay's **tourist office** is on Vaughan Parade, near the Pavilion (late May to Sept Mon–Sat 9.30am–6pm, Sun 10am–6pm; Oct to late May Mon–Sat 9am–5.15pm; ☎0906/680 1268, ⓦwww.TheEnglishRiviera.co.uk).

Torquay has plenty of **accommodation**, but you'll need to book in advance during peak season. Most of the budget choices lie along Belgrave Road and, slightly further out, Avenue Road, though you'll do better at the *Charnwood Guest House*, 8 Bampfylde Rd, off Belgrave Road and a ten-minute walk from the train station (☎01803/293879; ❶), which has bright, small rooms and a peaceful location. Non-smokers with a yen for antique pine furnishings and crisp bed-linen should head for *Mulberry House*, 1 Scarborough Rd (☎01803/213639; ❸), with showers in the attached bathrooms and a rated wholefood restaurant on the premises (see below). For views and statelier surroundings, try the *Allerdale Hotel* on Croft Road (☎01803/292667; ❸), which has a long, lawned garden sloping below it. Outside the centre, the touristy village of Cockington, a couple of miles west, makes a pleasant rural retreat connected by frequent buses – head for the elegant *Lanscombe House* (☎01803

/606938; ❸), or *Morningside Hotel* on Babbacombe Downs (☎01803/327025; ❸), ideally placed for Babbacombe Beach, with views over the bay. The village is linked to Torquay's centre by buses #32, #33, #85 and the summer-only #120. If you're looking for cheap and friendly **hostel** accommodation, make a beeline for *Torquay Backpackers*, 119 Abbey Rd (☎01803/299924; no credit cards). It's very central for the town, and just a ten-minute walk from the station; there's a free pick-up service offered – phone ahead to arrange this.

The Town

Torquay is focused on the small **harbour** and marina, where the mingling crowds can seem almost Mediterranean, especially at night. To one side stands the copper-domed **Pavilion**, an Edwardian building that originally housed a ballroom and assembly hall and is now refurbished with shops. Behind the Pavilion, limestone cliffs sprouting white high-rise hotels and apartment blocks separate the harbour area from Torquay's main beach, **Abbey Sands**. Good for chucking a frisbee about but too busy for serious relaxation, it takes its name from **Torre Abbey**, sited in ornamental gardens behind the beachside road. The Norman church that once stood here was razed by Henry VIII, though a gatehouse, tithe barn, chapter house and tower escaped demolition. The present **Abbey Mansion** (Easter–Oct daily 9.30am–6pm; £3) is a seventeenth- and eighteenth-century construction, now containing the mayor's office, a suite of period rooms with collections of paintings, silver and glass, and one devoted to Agatha Christie. There's more material relating to the Mistress of Murder at the main **Torquay Museum**, 529 Babbacombe Rd (Easter–Oct Mon–Sat 10am–5pm, Sun 1.30–5pm; Nov–Easter Mon–Fri 10am–5pm; £3), but most of the space is given over to the local history and natural history collections. Bus #32 stops outside.

You'll probably find the walk round the promontory at Torbay's north end more stimulating, as it leads to some good sand beaches. To reach the nearest, follow the pretty half-mile coastal walk that takes you through Daddyhole Plain, a large chasm in the cliff caused by a landslide locally attributed to the devil ("Daddy"). The path descends to meet the seawall at **Meadfoot Beach**, where boats and pedalos can be rented. If you're searching for something a little more low-key, continue round the point to where a string of beaches extends along the coast as far as the cliff-backed coves of **Watcombe** and **Maidencombe**.

Eating, drinking and nightlife

There is a surprisingly high standard of cuisine in Torquay's restaurants, one of the best being the *Mulberry House Restaurant*, 1 Scarborough Rd (☎01803 /213639; closed Fri–Sun eve, plus Mon & Tues to non-residents), where the moderately priced English and Continental menu is colour-coded according to its cholesterol content. Nearby, the inexpensive *Bombay Express* at 98 Belgrave Rd claims to be the southwest's "first and only original Balti House"; you can bring your own bottle and it's also good for takeaways. Alternatively, you can sample French provincial cuisine at moderate prices at *Flynn's Bistro*, 14 Parkhill Rd, where there's a small garden for dining out in summer (☎01803/213936; eve only; closed Sun). For simple steaks and fish, however, you can eat more cheaply at the *Torwood Grill* at 10 Torwood St, just up from the marina, while the cobbled *Hole in the Wall* **pub** on nearby Park Lane serves some vegetarian dishes and has sing-songs round the piano – it was the Irish playwright Sean O'Casey's boozer when he lived in Torquay.

Torquay's main **clubs** are the *The Venue* on Torwood Street and *Claire's* at

41 Torwood Ave, while *Valbonne's* on Higher Union Street caters to a slightly older and smarter crowd. The alcohol-free *Monastery*, on Torwood Gardens Road, has more character, and has all-night sessions on Saturdays. *Rocky's*, near the Pavilion on Rock Road (off Abbey Road), is a long-established gay club.

Paignton

Not so much a rival to Torquay as its complement, **PAIGNTON** lacks the gloss of its neighbour, but also its pretensions. Activity is concentrated at the southern end of the wide town beach, around the small harbour that nestles in the lee of the appropriately named Redcliffe headland. Otherwise, diversion-seekers could wander over to **Paignton Zoo** (daily 10am–6pm or dusk if earlier; £7.70; ⓦwww.paigntonzoo.org.uk), a mile out on Totnes Road, or board the **Paignton & Dartmouth Steam Railway** at Paignton's Queen's Park train station near the harbour. Running daily from June to September, with a patchy service in April, May, October and December, the line connects with Paignton's other main beach – **Goodrington Sands** – before trundling alongside the Dart estuary to Kingswear, seven miles away. The accent is on Victorian nostalgia, with railway personnel in period uniforms, but it's a pleasant way to view the scenic countryside, and you could make a day of it by taking the ferry connection from Kingswear to Dartmouth (see p.446), then taking a river boat up the Dart to Totnes, from where you can take any bus back to Paignton – a "Round Robin" ticket (£10.50) lets you do this.

Paignton's bus and train stations are next to each other off Sands Road. Five minutes away, on the seafront, is a **tourist office** (late May to Sept Mon–Sat 9.30am–6pm, Sun 10am–6pm; Oct to late May Mon–Sat 9.30am–5.15pm; ℡0906/680 1268). Torquay has a far better selection of **accommodation**, though if you'd like to stay in Paignton, you could do worse than *St Weonard's Hotel*, 12 Kernou Rd (℡01803/558842; ❶), a couple of minutes' walk from the seafront; en-suite rooms are in the next price category, and there's a small surcharge for payment by credit card. The harbour area has a few pubs and restaurants, including the inexpensive *Harbour Light*, and the nearby *Pier Inn*.

Brixham

From Paignton, it's a fifteen-minute bus ride down to **BRIXHAM**, the prettiest of the Torbay towns. Fishing was for centuries Brixham's life-blood, its harbour extending some way farther inland than it does now to afford a safe anchorage – a function performed today by an extensive breakwater. Indeed, at the beginning of the nineteenth century, this was the major fish-market in the West Country, and it still supplies fish to restaurants as far away as London. Among the trawlers on Brixham's quayside is moored a full-size reconstruction of the **Golden Hind**, the surprisingly small vessel in which Francis Drake circumnavigated the world – it has no real connection with the port, however. The harbour is overlooked by an unflattering statue of William III, a reminder of his landing in Brixham to claim the crown of England in 1688. From here, steep lanes and stairways thread up to the older centre around Fore Street, where the bus from Torquay pulls in.

From the harbour, you can reach the promontory of **Berry Head** along a path winding up from the *Berry Head House Hotel*. Fortifications built during the Napoleonic wars are still standing on this southern limit of Torbay, which is now a conservation area, attracting colonies of nesting seabirds and affording fabulous views.

The town's **tourist office** (June to Sept daily 9.30am–6pm, Sun 10am–6pm; Oct Mon–Sat 9.30am–5.15pm; Nov–May Mon–Fri 9.30am–5.15pm; ☎0906 /680 1268) is on the quayside, next to William's statue. **Accommodation** is listed on the door when the office is closed. The places on King Street, overlooking the harbour, have the best views – for example the *Harbour View Hotel*, at no. 65 (☎01803/853052; ❷), with all rooms en suite, and two doors down the classier *Quayside Hotel* (☎01803/855751, ⓦwww. quaysidehotel.co.uk; ❺), which has two bars and a restaurant. Away from the harbour, the reputedly ghost-ridden *Smugglers' Haunt* on Church Hill (☎01803/853050, ⓦwww .smugglershaunt-hotel-devon.co.uk; ❸) is creaky and cramped, but useful if everywhere else is full. The nearest YHA **hostel** is four miles away outside the village of Galmpton, on the banks of the Dart (☎01803/842444; closed Nov to mid-Feb), a one-and-a-half-mile walk from Churston Bridge, accessible on bus #12 or #12A (every 15min) – you can also get there on the Paignton & Dartmouth Steam Railway (see above). There is a landscaped **campsite** at Hillhead (☎01803/853204; closed Oct–Easter), two and a half miles south of Brixham on the Kingswear road.

When it comes to **eating options**, Brixham offers fish and more fish – from the stalls selling cockles, whelks and mussels on the harbourside to the moderately expensive *Yardarms* (☎01803/858266; closed lunch & all Mon, plus all Tues in winter), on Beach Approach off the quayside, one of Brixham's top choices for seafood. By the harbour, the *Sprat & Mackerel* offers staple **pub** snacks. For a more relaxed pint, try out the *Blue Anchor* on Fore Street, with coal fires and low beams.

Totnes

Most of the Plymouth buses from Paignton and Torquay make a stop at **TOTNES**, on the west bank of the River Dart. The town has an ancient pedigree, its period of greatest prosperity occurring in the sixteenth century when this inland port exported cloth to France and brought back wine. Some handsome structures from that era remain, and there is still a working port down on the river, but these days Totnes has mellowed into a residential market town, enjoying an esoteric fame as a centre of the New Age arts-and-crafts crowd. With its arcaded High Street and secretive flowery lanes, Totnes has its syrupy side, partly the result of its proximity to the Torbay tourist hive, but so far its allure has survived more or less intact.

Totnes centres on the long main street that starts off as Fore Street, site of the town's **museum** (April–Oct Mon–Fri 10.30am–5pm; £1.75), which occupies a four-storey Elizabethan house at no. 70. Showing how wealthy clothiers lived at the peak of Totnes's success, it is packed with domestic objects and furniture, and also has a room devoted to local mathematician Charles Babbage, whose "analytical engine" was the forerunner of the computer. There are a number of other houses along Fore and High streets in an equally good state of preservation: the late eighteenth-century, mustard-yellow "Gothic House", a hundred yards up Fore Street on the left; 28 High St, overhung by some curious grotesque masks; and 16 High St, a house built by pilchard merchant Nicholas Ball, whose initials are carved outside. His wealth, inherited by his widow, was eventually bequeathed by her second husband, Thomas Bodley, to found Oxford's Bodleian Library.

Fore Street becomes the **High Street** at the East Gate, a much retouched medieval arch. Beneath it, Rampart Walk trails off along the old city walls, curling round the fifteenth-century church of **St Mary**. Inside, an exquisitely carved roodscreen stretches across the full width of the red sandstone building. Behind the church, the eleventh-century **Guildhall** (April–Sept Mon–Fri 10.30am–1pm & 2–4.30pm; £1) was originally the refectory and kitchen of a Benedictine priory. Granted to the city corporation in 1553, the building still houses the town's Council Chamber, which you can see together with the former jail cells, used until the end of the last century, and the courtroom, which ceased its function only in 1974.

Totnes **Castle** (April–Sept daily 10am–6pm; Oct daily 10am–5pm; Nov–March Wed–Sun 10am–1pm & 2–4pm; £1.60; EH) on Castle Street – leading off the High Street – is a classic Norman structure of the motte and bailey design, its simple crenellated keep atop a grassy mound offering wide views of the town and Dart valley. Totnes assumes a much livelier air at the bottom of Fore Street, at river level. This is the highest navigable point on the **River Dart** for seagoing vessels, and there is constant activity around the craft arriving from and leaving for European destinations. More locally, there are also cruises to Dartmouth between Easter and October, leaving from Steamer Quay, on the other side of the Dart. Riverside walks in either direction pass some congenial pubs, and near the railway bridge you can board a steam train of the **South Devon Railway** on its run along the course of the Dart to Buckfastleigh, adjacent to Buckfast Abbey (see p.458).

A walkable couple of miles out of Totnes, both rail and river pass near the estate of **Dartington Hall**, the arts and education centre set up in 1925 by US millionairess Dorothy Elmhirst and her husband. A constant programme of films, plays, concerts, dance and workshops is run here, but you can walk through the sculpture-strewn gardens and – when it's not in use – visit the fourteenth-century Great Hall, rescued from dereliction by the Elmhirsts.

Practicalities

Totnes's **tourist office** is in the Town Mill, signposted off the Plains near the Safeway car park (Aug Mon–Sat 9.30am–5pm, Sun 9.30am–1pm; rest of year Mon–Sat 9.30am–5pm; ☎01803/863168). You'll find a good **B&B** a stone's throw from the station: *Number Four*, Queen's Terrace, Station Rd (☎01803/867365, ✉tobsjq@aol.com; no credit cards; ❷), where vegetarian breakfasts include eggs from the hens in the garden, figs and waffles. Opposite the castle car park on North Street, the *Elbow Room* (☎01803/863480; no smoking; no credit cards; ❸) occupies a 200-year-old converted cottage and cider press. For a bit extra, pamper yourself at the atmospheric *Royal Seven Stars Hotel* on The Plains (☎01803/862125; ❹), or, just over the river in Seymour Place, at the *Old Forge* (☎01803/862174; non-smoking; ❸) – a working medieval forge with comfortably modernized rooms and a secluded walled garden. If you want to stay nearer to Dartington, try the *Cott*, Shinner's Bridge, (☎01803/863777; ❺) – two miles west of Totnes on the A385 – outwardly almost unchanged since its construction in 1320. The local **youth hostel** (☎01803/862303; closed Oct to mid-April), in a sixteenth-century cottage, lies next to the River Bidwell two miles from Totnes and half a mile from Shinner's Bridge, a stop on the #X80 Torquay–Plymouth bus route.

You don't need to stray off the Fore Street/High Street axis to find a good place to **eat** in Totnes. *Willow*, 87 High St (☎01803/862605), has inexpensive vegetarian wholefood snacks and evening meals (Wed–Sat) when there is occasional live music (closed Sun). Indonesian food is on offer at *Rickshaws*, 98 High St (☎01803/866171; closed eve, plus all Sun & Mon), while *Rumour*, 30 High St, serves coffees, snacks and good-value full meals including home-made pizzas. There are also several decent **pubs**: the lively *Castle*

Inn on Fore Street, the *Bull Inn* at the top of the High Street and the *Kingsbridge Inn* on Leechwell Street (off Kingsbridge Hill) – all have a warm atmosphere, bar snacks and good ale. By the riverside, try the *Steampacket*, on St Peter's Quay. **Bike rental** is available from *Hot Pursuit*, 4 Fore St (℡01803 /865174; £10/day).

Dartmouth

South of Torbay, and eight miles downstream from Totnes, **DARTMOUTH** has thrived since the Normans recognized the potential of this deepwater port for trading with their home country, and today its activities embrace fishing, freight and a booming leisure industry – as well as the education of the senior service's officer class at the Royal Naval College, built at the start of this century on a hill overlooking the port. Coming from Torbay, visitors to Dartmouth can save time and a long detour through Totnes by using the frequent ferries crossing over the Dart's estuary from Kingswear (50p, £2 for cars), the last one at around 10.45pm.

Behind the enclosed boat basin at the heart of town stands Dartmouth's most photographed building, the four-storey **Butterwalk**, built in the seventeenth century for a local merchant. Richly decorated with wood carvings, the timber-framed construction was restored after bombing in World War II, though still looks precarious as it overhangs the street on eleven granite columns. This arcade now holds shops and Dartmouth's small **museum** (Mon–Sat: April–Sept 11am–4.30pm; Oct–March noon–3pm; £1.50), mainly devoted to maritime curios, including old maps, prints and models of ships. Nearby **St Saviour's**, rebuilt in the 1630s from a fourteenth-century church, has long been a landmark for boats sailing upriver. The building stands at the head of Higher Street, the old town's central thoroughfare and the site of another tottering medieval structure, the *Cherub* inn. More impressive is **Agincourt House** on the parallel Lower Street, built by a merchant after the battle for which it is named, then restored in the seventeenth century and again in the twentieth.

Lower Street leads down to **Bayard's Cove**, a short cobbled quay lined with well-restored eighteenth-century houses, where the Pilgrim Fathers touched en route to the New World. A twenty-minute walk from here along the river takes you to **Dartmouth Castle** (April–Sept daily 10am–6pm; Oct daily 10am–5pm; Nov–March Wed–Sun 10am–1pm & 2–4pm; £3.20; EH), one of two fortifications on opposite sides of the estuary. The site includes coastal defence works from the last century and from World War II, though the main interest is in the fifteenth-century castle, the first in England to be constructed specifically to withstand artillery. The castle was never actually tested in action, and consequently is excellently preserved. If you don't relish the return walk, you can take advantage of a ferry back to town, leaving roughly every fifteen minutes from Easter to October (£1).

Continuing south along the coastal path brings you through the pretty hilltop village of **Stoke Fleming** to **Blackpool Sands** (45min from the castle), the best and most popular beach in the area. The unspoilt cove, flanked by steep, wooded cliffs, was the site of a battle in 1404 in which Devon archers repulsed a Breton invasion force sent to punish the privateers of Dartmouth for their raiding across the Channel.

From Dartmouth there are regular ferries across the river to **Kingswear**, terminus of the **Paignton & Dartmouth Steam Railway** (see p.443). There are also various summer cruises from Dartmouth's quay up the River Dart to

Totnes (1hr 15min; £7 return); this is the best way to see the river's deep creeks and the various houses overlooking the river, among them the **Royal Naval College** and **Greenway House**, birthplace of Walter Raleigh's three seafaring half-brothers, the Gilberts, and later rebuilt for Agatha Christie.

Practicalities

Dartmouth's **tourist office** is opposite the car park at Mayor's Avenue (Easter–Oct Mon–Sat 9.30am–5.30pm, Sun 10am–4pm; Nov–Easter Mon–Sat 10am–4pm; ☎01803/834224, ✆www.dartmouth-tourism.org.uk). The less **accommodation** is either at the top of steep hills or strung along Victoria Road, a continuation of Duke Street. The hill-top choices are preferable for their views, such as the spacious and elegant *Avondale* at 5 Vicarage Hill (☎01803/835831, ✉avondaleco@aol.com; no credit cards; ➋), though the choices on Victoria Road are also enticing – not least *The Middle House*, offering two large and colourful en-suite rooms at no. 16 (☎01803/833935; no credit cards; ➋) – as is the nearby *Sunnybanks* at 1 Vicarage Hill (☎01803 /832766, ✆www.sunnybanks.com; no credit cards; ➋). Alternatively, splurge on the *Royal Castle Hotel* (☎01803/833033, ✆www.royalcastle.co.uk; ➏), right on the central quay, converted from two seventeenth-century merchants' houses. For something a little different, book a berth on the *Res Nova Inn* (☎0777/062 8967; may close in winter), a barge moored in mid-river run by a friendly couple who will ferry guests to and from town. Comfy cabins – one en suite – can sleep up to three, costing £25 for a single berth, £45 for a double (£55 en suite), £60 for three (no credit cards).

As for eating, the *Café Alf Resco* on Lower Street is good for breakfasts and coffees and has outdoor tables (closed Mon & Tues). Dartmouth has a good range of **restaurants**; *Bayard's*, 28 Lower St (☎01803/833523), serves moderately priced fish and vegetarian dishes, or you could try *Cutter's Bunch*, a French bistro a few doors down at no. 33 (☎01803/832882; eve only, closed Mon). The expensive *Carved Angel*, at 2 South Embankment (☎01803/832465, ✆www.thecarvedangel.com; closed Sun eve, Mon lunch & Jan to mid-Feb), is a high-class fish restaurant with views over the riverfront; it also excels in game in winter. If you're put off by the prices and ambience, drop into its inexpensive offshoot at 7 Foss St, the *Carved Angel Café* (☎01803/834842; no smoking; closed Sun eve & Mon lunch). The menu may lack the sparkle of its parent, but it offers some great soups and puddings. The *Res Nova Inn* (see above) also offers fish suppers as well as late-night drinks: call to be picked up.

The South Hams

The area between the Dart and Plym estuaries, the **South Hams**, holds some of Devon's comeliest villages and most striking coastline. The "capital" of the region, **KINGSBRIDGE**, is easily accessible by hourly buses from Dartmouth or Totnes, and is the hub of local services to the South Hams villages. Fine Tudor and Georgian buildings distinguish this busy market town, especially along the steep Fore Street, where the colonnaded Shambles is largely Elizabethan on the ground floor, its granite pillars supporting an upper floor added at the end of the eighteenth century. The town hall hosts a craft **market** on Tuesdays and Fridays (Tues only in winter), and there are also regular markets on the Quay, right by the **tourist office**, where you can pick up information on the whole region (Easter–Sept Mon–Sat 9am–5.30pm, Sun 10am–4pm; Oct–Easter Mon–Sat 9am–5pm; ☎01548/853195).

Salcombe

A summer ferry runs from Kingsbridge to Devon's southernmost resort of **SALCOMBE**, almost at the mouth of the Kingsbridge estuary. Once a non-descript fishing village, Salcombe is now a full-blown sailing and holiday resort, its calm waters strewn with small craft and the steep streets overflowing with leisurewear. There is still some fishing activity here, and a few working boat-yards, but a certain serenity prevails, with the ruined Fort Charles at the entrance to the harbour injecting a touch of romance amid the villas and hotels. You can bone up on boating and local history at **Salcombe Maritime Museum** on Market Street, off the north end of the central Fore Street (April to late Sept 10.30am–12.30pm & 2.30–4.30pm; £1). The same building also houses a **tourist office** (April–June, Sept & Oct Mon–Sat 10am–5pm; July & Aug Mon–Sat 10am–5.30pm, Sun 10am–4pm; Nov–March Mon–Sat 10am–1pm & 2–4pm; ☎01548/844673, ⓦwww.salcombeinformation.co.uk). Most of the **hotels** are above Fore Street, enjoying excellent estuary views, for example *Rocarno* on Grenville Road (☎01548/842732; no credit cards; ❷). Lower down, there are rooms but no breakfast round the corner from Fore Street at 7 Courtenay St (☎01548/842276; no credit cards; ❶); ask for the bal-cony room.   Near the car park on Shadycombe Road, *The Old Porch House* (☎01548/842157; ❸) dates back to 1660, making it the oldest house in Salcombe – though it has full modern facilities amid the brass ornaments and hanging tankards. **Campers** have a good choice in the area, the nearest sites being *Ilton Farm* (☎01548/842858) and *Alston Farm* (☎01548/561260), both signposted off the A381 Malborough road, while *Sun Park* at Soar Mill Cove (☎01548/561378) and *Higher Rew* at Rew Cross, south of Salcombe (☎01548/842681), are both within good walks of two of the area's finest beaches. Back in town, fish is top of the menu at *Spinnaker's Restaurant*, a moderately priced place that shares a building with the *Salcombe Hotel* on Fore Street, looking out over the river.

From a quay off Fore Street, a regular ferry crosses the narrow channel from here to **East Portlemouth**, from where you can follow the coastal path past the craggily photogenic Gammon Point to Devon's most southerly tip at **Prawle Point**, where a broken-backed freighter is a reminder of the hazards of this stretch of coast. A couple of miles inland from Lannacombe Bay, which links Prawle Point with Start Point, the headland at the top of Start Bay, you can find a quiet nook to stay at *South Allington House* (☎01548/511272; non-smoking; no credit cards; ❷).

Sharpitor

At **SHARPITOR**, a couple of miles south of Salcombe, the National Trust runs **Overbecks Museum** (April–July & Sept Mon–Fri & Sun 11am–5.30pm; Aug daily 11am–5.30pm; Oct Mon–Thurs & Sun 11am–5pm; £4.10; NT), which is mainly given over to natural history and houses a capacious **youth hostel** (☎01548/842856; closed Nov–March) in its grounds. South of here, the six-mile hike from Bolt Head to Bolt Tail takes you along a ragged coast where shags, cormorants and other marine birds swoop over the rocks, and wild thyme and sea thrift grow underfoot.

Seven miles east of Kingsbridge, the lagoon of the **Slapton Ley nature reserve** supports heron, terns, widgeon and – rarest of all – great crested grebes. A bus links Torcross with Kingsbridge, though of course you could walk from Prawle Point (see above) round the dramatic headland at Start Point, or from Dartmouth, five miles along the coast from the lagoon's northern tip.

West of Kingsbridge, **THURLESTONE** is a chocolate-box village of pink-washed thatched cottages, with a splendid undeveloped sandy beach backed by rolling farmland. Surfers prefer the extensive sands to the opposite side of the Avon estuary at **BIGBURY-ON-SEA**, reachable in summer by a ferry between the hamlets of Bantham and Cockleridge – or by wading the river at low tide. A special tractor-like vehicle ferries visitors the short distance from Bigbury's beach to Burgh Island, where a grand Art Deco hotel and the atmospheric *Pilchard Inn* are the main attractions. For an **overnight stay** in the area, Bantham's *Sloop Inn* (☏01548/560489; no credit cards; ❹) has several low-slung rooms overlooking the sea and estuary, and a restaurant serving good seafood.

Plymouth

PLYMOUTH's predominantly bland and modern face belies its great historic role as a naval base, a role assured in the sixteenth century by the patronage of such national heroes as John Hawkins and Francis Drake. It was from here that the latter sailed to defeat the Spanish Armada in 1588, and 32 years later the port was the last embarkation point for the Pilgrim Fathers, whose New Plymouth colony became the nucleus for the English settlement of North America. The sustained prominence of the city's Devonport dockyards as a shipbuilding and military base made it a target in World War II, when the Luftwaffe reduced the old centre to rubble, apart from the compact area around the Barbican. Subsequent reconstruction, spurred on by growth that has made Plymouth by far Devon's biggest town, has done nothing to enhance the place. That said, it would be difficult to spoil the glorious vista over **Plymouth Sound**, the basin of calm water at the mouth of the combined Plym, Tavy and Tamar estuaries, which has remained largely unchanged since Drake played his famous game of bowls on the Hoe before joining battle with the Armada. This alone makes a visit to Plymouth a memorable one, and you could also spend a couple of hours wandering around the Elizabethan warehouses and inns of the **Barbican**. The latter is the focus of occasionally raucous nightlife, and a gamut of excellent restaurants specializing in freshly caught seafood. Although this area is easy to stroll around, you could also make use of the regular and frequent circular **bus** service (#25) for getting around the town, which stops at the train station, Sutton Harbour, the Hoe and the Citadel. Plymouth makes a good starting point for forays onto Dartmoor, and a base for visiting a trio of elegant country houses with both aesthetic appeal and historical resonance, though transport connections are not always easy.

Arrival, information and accommodation

Plymouth's **train station** is off Saltash Road, from where bus #25 leaves every fifteen minutes for the central Royal Parade. The **bus station** is just over St Andrew's Cross from Royal Parade, at Bretonside, and holds **left-luggage lockers** (maximum stay 24hr). The **tourist office** is off Sutton Harbour at 9 The Barbican (April–Oct Mon–Sat 9am–5pm, Sun 10am–4pm; Nov–March Mon–Fri 9am–5pm, Sat 10am–4pm; ☏01752/304849, ⓦwww.plymouth.gov.uk). Ask here about guided tours, a useful way to get an informed view of the city and surrounding areas.

Plymouth has plenty of choice when it comes to **accommodation**: try first the row of B&Bs edging the Hoe on Citadel Road if you want to be near the sights, though you won't be more than a twenty-minute walk from the Hoe and Barbican areas if you prefer to stay close to the train station. Ferry passengers might want to be nearer the docks in the Millbay district, on the western side of town.

Hotels and B&Bs

Acorns and Lawns 171 Citadel Rd ⊕01752/229474. One of the terrace of competitively priced B&Bs off the eastern side of Plymouth Hoe, this one offering superb-value accommodation and a choice of rooms with shared bathrooms, en-suite shower or full private facilities. No credit cards. ❶

The Beeches 175 Citadel Rd ⊕01752/266475. A good choice on this row close to the Barbican, with access at all times. No credit cards. ❶

Bowling Green Hotel 9–10 Osborne Place, Lockyer St ⊕01752/209090, ⊛www.bowling-greenhotel.co.uk. Smart establishment overlooking Francis Drake's fabled haunt on the west side of the Hoe. ❷

Brittany Guest House 28 Athenaeum St ⊕01752/262247. More stylish than the similar establishments in the area, this easy going place offers kippers for breakfast and use of a private car park (a bonus around here). ❷

Georgian House, 51 Citadel Rd ⊕01752/663237. Small hotel with all rooms en suite, and facilities for bike storage. ❶

Grosvenor Park Hotel 114 North Road East ⊕01752/229312. Convenient stop for the train station, off the North Cross roundabout. Excellent value, and evening meals available on request. ❷

Oliver's Hotel, 33 Sutherland Rd ⊕01752/663923. A few minutes from the train station, with a good restaurant. ❷

Osmond Guest House 42 Pier St ⊕01752/229705. Comfortable choice close to the Great Western Docks, with bright red walls and offering a pick-up service from the bus and train stations. ❶

Phantele 176 Devonport Rd ⊕01752/561506. Unpretentious budget place towards the Torpoint ferry on the west side of town, near the youth hostel; useful if everywhere central is booked up. No credit cards. ❶

Hostels

Plymouth Backpackers Hotel 172 Citadel Rd ⊕01752/225158, ⊛www.backpackers.co.uk/plymouth. Relaxed place in a convenient location on the hotel strip near the Hoe and Royal Parade. Call ahead, as beds fill up quickly. Dorm beds £10, double rooms £25.

Plymouth YHA Belmont House, Devonport Rd ⊕01752/562189, ⊕plymouth@yha.org.uk. Walk a quarter-mile from Devonport train station, or catch a bus from the centre (Citybus #18a, #33 or #34, or First Western National #15A or #81). Dorm beds cost £11.

The City

A good place to start a tour of the city is **Plymouth Hoe**, an immense esplanade studded with reminders of the great events in the city's history. Resplendent in fair weather, with glorious views over the sea, the Hoe can also attract some pretty ferocious winds, making it well-nigh impossible to explore in wintry conditions. Approaching from the Civic Centre – the hub of the town centre – the most distinctive landmark is a tall white naval war memorial, standing alongside smaller monuments to the defeat of the Spanish Armada and to the airmen who defended the city during the wartime blitz, and a rather portly statue of Sir Francis Drake, gazing grandly out to the sea. Appropriately, there's a bowling green back from the brow.

In front of the memorials the red-and-white striped **Smeaton's Tower** (Easter–Sept 10.30am–4.30pm; 90p, free for Plymouth Dome visitors) was erected in 1759 by John Smeaton on the treacherous Eddystone Rocks, fourteen miles out to sea. When replaced by a larger lighthouse in 1882, it was reassembled here, where it gives the loftiest view over Plymouth Sound. Below Smeaton's Tower is the **Plymouth Dome** leisure complex (April–Oct daily 9am–6pm; last entry 1hr before closing; £4.10), which includes tricksy audio-visual exhibitions of Plymouth's history and the lives of local heroes such as Drake, the Mayflower Pilgrims and Captain Cook. On the seafront, Plymouth's **Royal Citadel** (May–Sept tours at 2.30pm lasting 1hr 15min; £3; EH) is an

Francis Drake

Born around 1540 near Tavistock, **Francis Drake** worked in the domestic coastal trade from the age of 13, but was soon taking part in the first English slaving expeditions between Africa and the West Indies, led by his Plymouth kinsman John Hawkins. Later, Drake was active in the secret war against Spain, raiding and looting merchant ships in actions unofficially sanctioned by Elizabeth I. In 1572 he became the first Englishman to sight the Pacific, and soon afterwards, on board the *Golden Hind*, became the first one to **circumnavigate the world**, for which he received a knighthood on his return in 1580. The following year Drake was made mayor of Plymouth, settling in Buckland Abbey (see p.453), but was back in action before long – in 1587 he "singed the king of Spain's beard" by entering Cadiz harbour and destroying 33 vessels that were to have formed part of Philip II's **armada**. When the replacement invasion fleet appeared in the English Channel in 1588, Drake – along with Raleigh, Hawkins and Frobisher – played a leading role in wrecking it. The following year he set off on an unsuccessful expedition to help the Portuguese against Spain, but otherwise most of the next decade was spent in relative inactivity in Plymouth, Exeter and London. Finally, in 1596 Drake left with Hawkins for a raid on Panama, a venture that cost the lives of both captains.

Drake has come to personify the Elizabethan Age's swashbuckling expansionism and patriotism, but England's naval triumphs were as much the result of John Hawkins' humbler work in building and maintaining a new generation of warships as they were of the skill and bravery of their captains. Drake was simply the most flamboyant of a generation of reckless and brilliant mariners who broke the Spanish hegemony on the high seas, laying the foundations for England's later imperialist pursuits.

uncompromising fortress constructed in 1666 to intimidate the populace of the only town in the southwest to be held by the Parliamentarians in the Civil War. The stronghold is still used by the military, though there are guided tours through some of its older parts, including the seventeenth-century Governor's House and the Royal Chapel of St Katherine; tickets for tours are available from the Plymouth Dome and the tourist office.

Round the corner, the old town's quay at **Sutton Harbour** is still used by the trawler fleet and is the scene of a boisterous early-morning fish market. The **Mayflower Steps** here commemorate the sailing of the Pilgrim Fathers and a nearby plaque lists the names and professions of the 102 Puritans on board. All three of Captain Cook's voyages to the South Seas, Australia and the Antarctic also started from here, as did the nineteenth-century transport ships to Australia, carrying thousands of convicts and colonists. Nowadays, the harbour is the starting point for cruises, ranging from one-hour tours around the Sound and the Devonport naval dockyard, to longer sea trips and the four-hour cruise up the Tamar to the Cornish village of Calstock.

The **Barbican** district, which edges the harbour, is the heart of old Plymouth. Most of the buildings are now shops and restaurants, but off the quayside, New Street holds most of the oldest buildings, among them the **Elizabethan House** (April–Sept Wed–Sun 10am–5.30pm; £1), a captain's dwelling retaining most of the original architectural features, including a lovely old pole staircase. The Pilgrim Fathers are thought to have spent their last night in England in Island House, at the end of the parallel Southside Street, now home to the tourist office.

Cross the bridge over Sutton Harbour to reach Plymouth's newest exhibit, the grand **National Marine Aquarium** (daily: April–Oct 10am–6pm; Nov–March 10am–4pm; £6.50). On three levels, the complex represents a range of marine environments from moorland stream to coral reef and deep-sea ocean, including sharks and Europe's largest collection of seahorse species. Talks and presentations take place throughout the day, and the feeding-times – carried out by divers – are among the highlights. Back in the centre of town, the handsome timber-framed, mainly seventeenth-century **Merchant's House Museum**, 33 St Andrew St (April–Sept Tues–Fri 10am–1pm & 2–5.30pm, Sat 10am–1pm & 2–5pm; £1) goes into various aspects of Plymouth's history. Behind it, off Royal Parade, stands the city's chief place of worship, **St Andrew's**, a reconstruction of a fifteenth-century building that was almost completely gutted by a bomb in 1941. The entrails of the navigator Martin Frobisher are buried here, as are those of Admiral Blake, the Parliamentarian who died as his ship entered Plymouth after destroying a Spanish treasure fleet off Tenerife. Local boy William Bligh, of *Mutiny on the Bounty* fame, was baptized here.

Eating and drinking

You'll find a wildly eclectic range of **restaurants** in and around Plymouth's Barbican area. One of the best fish restaurants is *Piermaster's*, at 3 Southside St (℡01752/229345; closed Sun), whose kitchen is supplied straight from the nearby harbour; it's plain but elegant, with a good fixed-price menu offered for lunch. Across the road, the *Barbican Pasta Bar* attracts the crowds, while Notte Street, at the top of Southside, has the inexpensive *Revival*, a Mexican/Italian/American diner with lots of jazzy ambience. If you hanker for simple English cuisine, head for the cramped *Queen Anne Eating House* in the Barbican's White Lane, which serves budget meals (closed Sun eve & Mon), or the similarly priced, but unlicensed, *Tudor Rose*, 36 New St, which is good for cottage pies and teas and opens its garden in summer. *Plymouth Arts Centre*, 38 Looe St, has a self-service vegetarian restaurant open until around 8pm, though the major reason for coming here is to see its films and live performances.

The *Dolphin* **pub** on Southside Street is a landmark in the Barbican, and is crowded with fishermen in the morning and locals and boisterous boozers at night; it also serves simple lunchtime snacks. In the Mount Batten area, reachable by water taxi from the Mayflower Steps, the *Mount Batten Bar*, Lawrence Rd, has wrought iron pillars and a good choice of snacks and meals, with **live bands** at weekends, and there's a more formal restaurant upstairs.

Around Plymouth

One of the best local day excursions from Plymouth is to **Mount Edgcumbe**, where woods and meadows provide a welcome antidote to the urban bustle, and are within easy reach of some fabulous sand. East of Plymouth, the aristocratic opulence of **Saltram House** includes some fine art and furniture, while to the north of town you can visit Drake's old residence at **Buckland Abbey**.

Mount Edgcumbe

Lying on the Cornish side of Plymouth Sound and visible from the Hoe, **Mount Edgcumbe** features a Tudor house, landscaped gardens and acres of rolling parkland and coastal paths. The **house** (April to Sept Wed–Sun 11am–4.30pm; £4.50) is a reconstruction of the bomb-damaged Tudor original, though inside the predominant note is eighteenth-century, the rooms elegantly restored with authentic Regency furniture. The house alone, however, would not merit the expedition here: far more enticing are the **grounds**, which include impeccable gardens divided into French, Italian and English sections – the first two a blaze of flowerbeds adorned with classical statuary, the last an acre of sweeping lawn shaded by exotic trees. The **park**, which is free and open all year, covers the whole of the peninsula facing the estuary and the sea, including a part of the Cornish Coastal Path. From the peninsula's two headlands, Rame Head and Penlee Point, extensive views show Plymouth in its best light.

You can reach the house by the passenger **ferry** to Cremyll, leaving at least hourly from Admiral's Hard, a small mooring in the Stonehouse district of town, reachable on bus #33 or #34 from outside the Guildhall; in summer there's also a direct motor launch (4 daily) between the Mayflower Steps and the village of **Cawsand**, an old smugglers' haunt two hours' walk from the house. Cawsand itself is just a mile from the southern tip of the huge **Whitsand Bay**, the best bathing beach for miles around.

Saltram House

The remodelled Tudor mansion **Saltram House** (April–Sept Mon–Thurs & Sun noon–5pm: Oct closes 4pm; garden April–Oct Mon–Thurs & Sun 10.30am–5.30pm; Feb & March Sat & Sun 11am–4pm; £6, garden only £3; NT), two miles east of Plymouth off the A38, is Devon's largest country house, featuring work by the great architect Robert Adam and fourteen portraits by **Joshua Reynolds**, who was born nearby in Plympton. Showpiece is the Saloon, a fussy but exquisitely furnished room dripping with gilt and plaster, and set off by a huge Axminster carpet especially woven for it in 1770. Saltram's landscaped park provides a breather from this riot of interior design, though it is marred by the proximity of the road. You can get here on the hourly #22 bus (#19b on Sun) from Royal Parade to Cot Hill, from where it's a ten-minute signposted walk. Keep your bus ticket – it'll get you a small reduction on the admission fee.

Buckland Abbey

Six miles north of Plymouth, close to the River Tavy and on the edge of Dartmoor, stands **Buckland Abbey** (April–Oct Mon–Wed & Fri–Sun 10.30am–5.30pm; Nov–March Sat & Sun 2–5pm; £4.60, grounds only £2.40; NT), once the most westerly of England's Cistercian abbeys. After its dissolution Buckland was converted to a family home by the privateer Richard Grenville (cousin of Walter Raleigh), from whom the estate was acquired by Sir Francis Drake in 1582, the year he became mayor of Plymouth. It remained his home until his death, but the house reveals few traces of Drake's residence, as he spent most of his retirement years plundering on the Spanish main. There are, however, numerous maps, portraits and mementoes of his buccaneering exploits on show, most famous of which is Drake's Drum, which was said to beat a supernatural warning of impending danger to the country. Apart from Drake's knick-knacks, the collection includes some stirring relics of the Elizabethan era of seafaring, as well as a gallery filled with model ships. The house stands in majestic grounds which contain a fine fourteenth-century **Great Barn**, buttressed and gabled and larger than the abbey itself. To get here, take bus #83, #84 or #86 from Plymouth to Tavistock, changing at Yelverton to the hourly #55 minibus (not Sun).

Dartmoor

The longer one stays here the more does the spirit of the moor sink into one's soul, its vastness, and also its grim charm. When you are once out upon its bosom you have left all traces of modern England behind you, but on the other hand you are conscious everywhere of the homes and the work of the prehistoric people... . If you were to see a skin-clad, hairy man crawl out from the low door, fitting a flint-tipped arrow on to the string of his bow, you would feel that his presence there was more natural than your own.

Arthur Conan Doyle, *The Hound of the Baskervilles*

Occupying the main part of the county between Exeter and Plymouth, **DARTMOOR** is southern England's greatest expanse of wilderness, some 365 square miles of raw granite, barren bogland, sparse grass and heather-grown moor. It was not always so desolate, as testified by the remnants of scattered Stone Age settlements and the ruined relics of the area's nineteenth-century tin-mining industry. Today desultory flocks of sheep and groups of ponies are virtually the only living creatures to be seen wandering over the central fastnesses of the National Park, with solitary birds – buzzards, kestrels, pipits, stonechats and wagtails – wheeling and hovering high above.

The core of Dartmoor, characterized by tumbling streams and high tors chiselled by the elements, is **Dartmoor Forest**, which has belonged to the Duchy of Cornwall since 1307, though there is almost unlimited public access as long as certain guidelines are followed – for instance, you are not allowed to park overnight in unauthorized places, and no vehicles are allowed farther than fifteen yards from the road. Camping is permitted out of sight of houses and roads, but fires are strictly forbidden. Though networks of signposts or painted stones do exist to guide **walkers**, map-reading abilities are a prerequisite for any but the shortest walks, and a good deal of experience is essential for longer distances – it is not uncommon for search parties to have to be rounded up to look for hikers gone astray. Two- to six-hour guided walks are listed in the *Dartmoor Visitor* newspaper, available free from National Park Visitor Centres in Dartmoor's major towns and villages, and from information points in smaller villages. The *Dartmoor Visitor* also has info on camping and other accommodation, events, facilities for the disabled, and military firing-range schedules (see below); ask at visitor centres about **riding** facilities on the moor.

Princetown, at the heart of the moor, has the Dartmoor National Park's main information centre and a selection of stores, pubs and places to stay. A few other villages, such as **Postbridge** and **Widecombe**, have B&Bs and shops, though for the widest choice of accommodation you have to go to the towns and villages circling the moor – chief of them **Tavistock**, **Lydford** and **Okehampton**. It would not be impossible to base yourself in Exeter or Plymouth, neither more than an hour's ride from the central **Two Bridges**, at the intersection of the B3212 and B3357, which gives access to some of the wildest tracts of Dartmoor. Always plan ahead and book places to stay – availability can be extremely restricted in high season.

Much to the irritation of locals and visitors alike, the **Ministry of Defence** has appropriated a significant portion of northern Dartmoor, an area that contains Dartmoor's highest tors and some of its most famous beauty spots. The MoD firing ranges are marked by red and white posts; when firing is in progress, red flags or red lights signify that entry is prohibited. As a general rule, you can assume that if no warning flags are flying by 9am between April

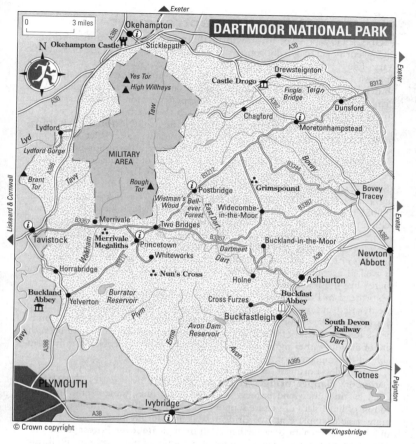

© Crown copyright

Kingsbridge

and September, or by 10am from October to March, there is to be no firing on that day.

In summer, a Transmoor **bus** service (#82) operates between Exeter and Plymouth, with stops at Two Bridges and Princetown – for most of the year it runs on weekends only, but there are at least three daily services from late May to late September. Also from Exeter, the regular #173 runs to Castle Drogo and Chagford (not Sun), on the northeast side of the moor. Okehampton is served by National Express coaches between Cornwall and Exeter, as well as #X9 and #X10 between Bude, Boscastle and Exeter; #86, connecting Plymouth and Barnstaple and taking in Tavistock and Lydford; and #118 (a classic red double-decker operating on Sundays in summer only), running between Plymouth, Tavistock, Lydford and Okehampton. Bus #98 connects Princetown with Tavistock five or six times daily from Monday to Friday, and buses run from Tavistock to Plymouth roughly every twenty minutes. Apart from these, there's little except once-weekly runs to remote villages. The *Dartmoor Discovery Guide* (free from bus stations and some tourist offices) gives all timetables for transport on the moor, and has helpful advice on combining walks with bus routes.

Princetown and the central moor

PRINCETOWN owes its growth to the proximity of Dartmoor Prison, a high-security jail originally constructed for POWs captured in the Napoleonic wars. The grim presence seeps into the village, which has a somewhat oppressed air and functional grey stone houses, some of them – like the parish church of St Michael – built by French and American prisoners. What Princetown lacks in beauty is amply compensated for by the surrounding country, the best of which lies immediately to the north.

Information on all of Dartmoor is given by the main **National Park information centre**, on the village's central green (daily: Easter–Oct 10am–5pm; Nov–March 10am–4pm; ☎01822/890414, ⓦwww.dartmoor-npa.gov.uk). One of the best places to stay is right in the centre of the village at *Lamorna*, a friendly **B&B** with a view of the prison on Two Bridges Road (☎01822 /890360; no credit cards; ❶). Alternatively, you might head for the non-smoking *Duchy House*, 200 yards from the centre, on Tavistock Road (☎01822 /890552, ⓔduchyhouse@aol.com; ❶; closed Nov), which has rooms with and without private bath, and also runs a **café**. Two pubs in Princetown's central square also offer accommodation, the *Railway Inn* (☎01822/890232; ❶) and the *Plume of Feathers* (☎01822/890240; ❶); the latter claims to be the oldest building in town, and also has dormitory accommodation in two bunkhouses as well as a convenient **campsite** – staple bar-food is always available, and there's live music on Sundays.

Northeast of Princetown, two miles north of the crossroads at Two Bridges, the dwarfed and misshapen oaks of **Wistman's Wood** are an evocative relic of the original Dartmoor Forest, cluttered with lichen-covered boulders and a dense undergrowth of ferns. The gnarled old trees are alleged to have been the site of druidic gatherings, a story unsupported by any evidence but quite plausible in this solitary spot.

Three miles northeast of Two Bridges, the largest and best preserved of Dartmoor's **clapper bridges** crosses the East Dart river at **POSTBRIDGE**. Used by tin-miners and farmers since medieval times, these simple structures consist of huge slabs of granite supported by piers of the same material; another more basic example is at Two Bridges. Walkers from Postbridge can explore up and down the river, or press further south through **Bellever Forest** to the open moor beyond. On the edge of the forest, a couple of miles south of Postbridge on the banks of the East Dart river, lies one of Dartmoor's three **youth hostels** (☎01822/880227; closed Nov–March) – it's on a minor road from Postbridge, but there's no public transport. There's also a **camping barn** close to Bellever Forest at Runnage Farm with a bunkhouse and outdoor camping facilities alongside – for this and any of Dartmoor's other camping barns, it's wise to book ahead, particularly at weekends: ☎01200/420102. You'll find more luxury in the riverside *Lydgate House Hotel*, signposted off the main road half a mile southwest of Postbridge and offering easy access to Bellever Forest and the moor (☎01822/880209; ❺); they have a no kids and no smoking policy. Two miles northeast of Postbridge, the solitary *Warren House Inn* offers warm, firelit comfort and **meals** in an unutterably bleak tract of moorland.

To the east of the B3212, reachable on a right turn towards Widecombe-in-the-Moor, the Bronze Age village of **Grimspound** lies below Hameldown Tor, about a mile off the road. Inhabited some three thousand years ago, when Dartmoor was fully forested and enjoyed a considerably warmer climate than it does today, this is the most complete example of Dartmoor's prehistoric settlements, consisting of twenty-four circular huts scattered within a four-acre enclosure. A stone wall nine-feet thick surrounds the huts, several of which have raised bed-places, and you can see how the villagers ensured a constant water supply by enclosing part of a stream with a wall. Grimspound itself is thought to have been the model for the Stone Age settlement in which Sherlock Holmes camped in *The Hound of the Baskervilles*, while **Hound Tor**, an outcrop three miles to the southwest, was the inspiration for Conan Doyle's tale – according to local legend, phantom hounds were sighted racing across the moor to hurl themselves on the tomb of a hated squire following his death in 1677.

Buckland-in-the-Moor and the southeastern moor

Four miles east of the crossroads at Two Bridges, **Dartmeet** marks the place where the East and West Dart rivers merge after tortuous journeys from their remote sources. Crowds home in on this beauty spot, but the valley is memorably lush and you don't need to walk far to leave the car park and ice-cream vans behind. From here the Dart pursues a more leisurely course, joined by the River Webburn near the pretty moorland village of **BUCKLAND-IN-THE-MOOR**, one of a cluster of moorstone-and-thatched hamlets on this southeastern side of the moor.

Four miles north is another candidate for most popular Dartmoor village, **WIDECOMBE-IN-THE-MOOR**, set in a hollow amid high granite-strewn ridges. Its church of **St Pancras** provides a famous local landmark, its pinnacled tower dwarfing the fourteenth-century main building, whose interior boasts a beautiful painted rood screen. Look out here too for the carved one-eared rabbits above the communion rail. The nearby **Church House** was built in the fifteenth century for weary churchgoers from outlying districts, and was later converted into almshouses. Widecombe's other claim to fame is the traditional song, *Widdicombe Fair*: the **fair** is still held annually on the second Tuesday of September, but is now primarily a tourist attraction. You could **stay** in Widecombe in the elegant *Old Rectory* (☏01364/621231, ✉rachel.belgrave@care4free.net; no credit cards; ❶), opposite the post office and set in a lovely garden; or try *Manor Cottage* (☏01364/621218; no credit cards; ❶), next to the post office, which has an inglenook fireplace in the dining room and a garden where breakfast can be taken; meals and packed lunches are also available. Half a mile out, *Higher Venton Farm* (☏01364/621235; no credit cards; ❷) is a peaceful thatched longhouse close to a couple of good pubs. You can **camp** at *Cockingford Farm*, one and a half miles south of Widecombe (☏01364 /621258; closed mid-Nov to mid-March). There is also a **pony-trekking** centre near the village at Shilstone Rocks Riding and Trekking Centre (☏01364 /621281).

South of Buckland, the village of **HOLNE** is another rustic idyll surrounded on three sides by wooded valleys. The vicarage here was the birthplace of Charles Kingsley, author of *The Water Babies* and such Devon-based tales as *Westward Ho!*. A window commemorates him in the village church, which also has a whimsical epitaph on the grave of Edward Collins, landlord of the next-door *Church House* inn until 1780. The pub itself was built three hundred years before that, and offers excellent **meals** and some **accommodation** (☏01364/631208; ❷). Oliver Cromwell is said to have stayed here. On the edge of Holne, on the route of the Two Moors Way, there is a **camping** barn with good facilities (☏01364/631544), backing onto a small camping field.

A couple of miles east, the Dart weaves through a wooded green valley to enter the grounds of **Buckfast Abbey** (daily: May–Oct 9am–5.30pm; Nov–April 10am–4pm; free), a modern monastic complex occupying the site of an abbey founded in the eleventh century by Canute, abandoned two hundred years later, refounded, and finally dissolved by Henry VIII. The present buildings were the work of a handful of French Benedictine monks who consecrated their new abbey in 1932, though work on the other monastic buildings has continued until recently. The church itself is in a traditional Anglo-Norman style, following the design of the Cistercian building razed in 1535, and shows examples of the monks' dexterity in making stained glass windows – which, along with honey, handicrafts and tonic wine, help to keep the community funded. An exhibition covers the abbey's history and displays its treasures.

The northeastern moor

The essentially unspoilt market town of **MORETONHAMPSTEAD**, lying on the northeastern edge of the moor, makes an attractive entry point from Exeter – and, incidentally, shares with Woolfardisworthy (near Bideford) the honour of having the longest single-word place-name in England. Local **information** is handled by a Visitor Information Point at 10 The Square (Easter–Oct daily 10am–5pm; Nov–Easter Fri–Sun 10am–1pm & 2–5pm; ☎01647/440043). There is classy **accommodation** on the western edge of the village, the *Old Post House* in Court Street (☎01647/440900, ⊛ www.the-oldposthouse.com; no credit cards; non-smoking; ❶), a friendly B&B which welcomes walkers and will set you up with a packed lunch if required, and at

---

Dartmoor's northern tors

A seven-mile, three-hour walk from Okehampton skirts the east of the MoD's Okehampton Range, brings you within view of the highest points on the moor, then plunges you into the recesses of the East Okement River, before rounding Belstone Common and returning north to Okehampton via the village of Belstone. From Okehampton, follow signs for Ball Hill and the East Okement Valley from the Mill Street car park near the centre, passing under the graceful arches of the **Fatherford Viaduct**, which carries the Exeter–Okehampton railway. Follow a well-defined path for about a mile through Halstock Wood, sloping down diagonally until meeting the East Okement River, which you can cross at **Chapel Ford** – a good spot for a pause. Walk up the eastern bank of the East Okement for five hundred yards before passing through an opening in the hedge, leaving the valley to head towards **Winter Tor**, a little more than a mile due south of the ford. At the tor, carry on up to the top of the ridge, from which a splendid panorama unfolds, with Dartmoor's highest peaks of **Yes Tor** (2028ft) and **Willhays Tor** (2039ft) about three miles southwest. To the east the great bowl of Taw Marsh can be seen.

Follow the rock-strewn ridge northwards, to the rocky pinnacles of **Belstone Common**. Between **Higher Tor** and **Belstone Tor** you'll pass **Irishman's Wall**, the vestige of an attempt to enclose part of the moor against the wishes of the locals, who waited until the wall was nearly complete before gathering to push the structure down. Carry on heading north, descending sharply towards the **Nine Stones** cairn circle, seven hundred yards below Belstone Tor. This Bronze Age burial ground was popularly held to be the petrified remains of nine maidens turned to stone for dancing on Sunday (there are in fact twelve stones). A little way north, a track brings you northeast to the village of Belstone, half a mile away.

From Belstone, follow the road signed "Okehampton Indirect" for about half a mile northwest; you can then either turn left to Cleave House, descend to the river and return northwards up the East Okement to Okehampton, or continue along the road.

Cookshayes, a little further out at 33 Court St (☎01647/440374; ❷; closed Nov–Feb), offering good home cooking. The village also has a first-rate new **hostel**, the *Sparrowhawks Backpackers Hostel*, at 45 Ford St (☎01647/440318). There's another hostel nearby: the *Steps Bridge* youth hostel (☎01647/252435; closed Sept–March) is on the outskirts of **Dunsford**, three miles northeast of Moretonhampstead and right on the boundary of the National Park – buses #359 (not Sun) and #82 stop nearby. Its woodland setting overlooking the Teign Gorge makes it a popular overnight stop for hikers.

Moretonhampstead has a historic rivalry with neighbouring **CHAGFORD**, a Stannary town (a chartered centre of the tin trade) that also enjoyed prosperity as a centre of the wool industry. It stands on a hillside overlooking the River Teign, with a fine fifteenth-century church on its edge and enough attractions within and around to keep its pubs and hotels in business. The ancient *Globe* (☎01647/433485, ⓦwww.the-globe.org.uk; no young children; ❷), facing the church, is one of a number of decent pubs in the village, and offers spacious rooms, though subject to noise from the church clock. A quieter alternative is the thatched, seventeenth-century *Lawn House* (☎01647 /433329; closed Nov–Feb; no credit cards; no smoking; ❷), on the other side of the main square on Mill Street, and next to a famed local **restaurant**, the non-smoking *22 Mill Street* (☎01647/432244; closed Sun and lunchtime Mon & Tues), which offers pricey, but top quality modern cuisine.

There are numerous **walks** to be made in the immediate vicinity, for instance to Fernworthy Reservoir, four miles to the southwest along signposted narrow lanes, or downstream along the Teign to the twentieth-century extravaganza of **Castle Drogo** (April–Oct Mon–Thurs, Sat & Sun 11am–5.30pm; grounds daily 10.30am–dusk; £5.60, grounds only £2.80; NT), which occupies a stupendous site overlooking the Teign gorge. Having retired at the age of 33, grocery magnate Julius Drewe unearthed a link that suggested his descent from a Norman baron, and set about creating a castle befitting his pedigree. Begun in 1910, to a design by **Sir Edwin Lutyens**, it was not completed until 1930, but the result was an unsurpassed synthesis of medieval and modern elements. The croquet lawn is available for use, with mallets for rent.

Paths lead from Drogo east to **Fingle Bridge**, one of Dartmoor's most noted beauty spots, where shaded green pools hold trout and the occasional salmon. The *Angler's Rest* pub has an adjoining **restaurant**.

The north and northwestern moor

The main centre on the northern fringes of Dartmoor, **OKEHAMPTON** grew prosperous as a market town for the medieval wool trade, and some fine old buildings survive between the two branches of the River Okement that meet here, among them the prominent fifteenth-century tower of the **Chapel of St James**. Across the road from the seventeenth-century town hall, a granite archway leads into the **Museum of Dartmoor Life** (Easter–Sept Mon–Sat 10am–5pm, Sun 10am–4.30pm; Oct–Easter Mon–Sat 10am–5pm; £2; ⓦwww.museumofdartmoorlife.eclipse.co.uk), an excellent overview of habitation on the moor since earliest times. Four miles east of Okehampton at Sticklepath (bus #X9 or #X10), **Finch Foundry** (April–Oct Mon & Wed–Sun 11am–5.30pm; £2.90; NT) is a Victorian forge with working machinery and demonstrations. Loftily perched above the West Okement on the other side of town, **Okehampton Castle** (April–Sept daily 10am–6pm; Oct daily 10am–5pm; £2.50; EH) is the shattered hulk of a stronghold laid waste by Henry VIII; its ruins include a gatehouse, Norman keep and the remains of the Great Hall, buttery and kitchens.

Between late May and late September, an old goods line provides Okehampton with a useful Sunday **rail** connection, linking the town with Exeter via Crediton in about forty minutes: ask about the Sunday Rover ticket (£6) which also covers the Plymouth-Gunnislake rail link and bus travel on Dartmoor (℡01392/382800). The station is a fifteen-minute walk up Station Road from Fore Street in Okehampton's centre, where the **tourist office** (April, May & mid-Sept to Oct Mon–Sat 10am–5pm; June to mid-Sept daily 10am–5pm; Nov–March Mon, Fri & Sat 10am–5pm; ℡01837 /53020) sits next to the museum. Alongside them lies the expensive *White Hart* (℡01837/52730; ❹), though cheaper **accommodation** can be found a short walk north of the centre around the station. Here, the traffic noise from the A30 is compensated by views towards Exmoor and the outdoor heated pool at *Heathfield House*, the old station-master's home above the station on Klondyke Road (℡01837/54211, ❂www.tgibbins.freeserve.co.uk; no smoking; ❷); alternatively, opt for the more economical *Meadowlea* lower down at 65 Station Rd (℡01837/53200; no credit cards; ❶). If you prefer rural surroundings, you'll find the comfortable and spacious *Upcott House* on Upcott Hill, half a mile north of the centre (℡01837/53743; no credit cards; ❷), while six miles north of Okehampton on the Hatherleigh Road, *Higher Cadham Farm* (℡01837/851647, ❂www.internetsouthwest.co.uk/highercadham; closed Dec; ❶) is located right on the Tarka Trail, and offers oak-beamed ambience with some rooms in a refurbished cowshed; it's signposted past the church at **Jacobstowe**. Okehampton's **youth hostel** (℡01837/53916, ❂www.okehampton-yha.co.uk; closed Dec & Jan) provides four- and six-bed bunkrooms in a converted goods shed at the station, and offers a range of outdoor activities including rock climbing and pony-trekking. The nicest **campsites** in the vicinity are the small *Yertiz* (℡01837/52281, ✉yertiz@dial .pipex.com), three-quarters of a mile east of Okehampton on the B3260, and *Olditch Caravan and Camping Park*, Sticklepath (℡01837/840734, ❂www .olditch.co.uk; closed Dec–Feb), which has walking access to the moor. Okehampton has no great choice when it comes to **eating**, though the *Coffee Pot*, tucked away behind the museum in Fairplace Terrace, can be relied upon for breakfasts, coffees and meals (closed eve Oct–May); *Le Café Noir* (closed Sun), across West Street in Red Lion Yard, is good for inexpensive lunches, and *Cellars Bistro*, a candlelit basement off West Street (closed Sun), offers moderately priced evening meals. For **riding** on the moor, contact Skaigh Riding Stables (℡01837/840917) or Eastlake (℡01837/52513), both east of town in the Belstone/Sticklepath area.

Lydford

Five miles southwest of Okehampton, the village of **LYDFORD** boasts the sturdy but small-scale Lydford Castle, a Saxon outpost, then a Norman keep and later used as a prison. The chief attraction here, though, is **Lydford Gorge** (April–Sept 10am–5.30pm; Oct 10am–4pm; Nov–March 10.30am–3pm; £3.60; NT), whose main entrance is a five-minute walk downhill. Two routes – one above, one along the banks – follow the ravine burrowed through by the River Lyd as far as the hundred-foot White Lady Waterfall, coming back on the opposite bank. Overgrown with thick woods, the one-and-a-half-mile gorge is alive with butterflies, spotted woodpeckers, dippers, herons and clouds of insects. The full course would take you roughly two hours at a leisurely pace, though there is a separate entrance at the south end of the gorge if you only want to visit the waterfall. In winter months, when the river can flood, the waterfall is the only part of the gorge open.

Back in the village, the picturesque *Castle Inn* sits right next to the castle, and provides a fire-lit sixteenth-century bar where you can drink and snack. The inn also offers en-suite **accommodation** in low-ceilinged oak-beamed rooms (℡01822/820242, ℯcastleinnlyd@aol.com; ➍), and there is a rather pricey but first-rate **restaurant** too, in a back room cluttered with curios and memorabilia; cheaper rooms are available at the family-run *Moorlands* (℡01822/820229; no credit cards; ➊; closed Nov–Easter), 300yds from the A386 on the Lydford turning. **Horse-riding** in the area is on offer at the *Lydford House Hotel* (℡01822/820321).

The western moor

Southwest from Princetown, walkers can trace the grassy path of the defunct rail line to **Burrator Reservoir**, four miles away; flooded in the 1890s to provide water for Plymouth, this is the biggest stretch of water on Dartmoor. The wooded lakeside teems with wildlife, and the boulder-strewn slopes are overlooked by the craggy peaks of **Sharpitor** (1312ft) and **Sheep's Tor** (1150ft). From here, the best walk is to strike northwest to meet the valley of the **River Walkham**, which rises in a peat bog at Walkham Head, five miles north of Princetown, then scurries through moorland and woods to join the River Tavy at Double Waters, two miles south of Tavistock. The fast-flowing water attracts herons, kingfishers and other colourful birdlife, to be seen darting in and out of dense woods of alder, ash and sycamore.

The river crosses the B3357 Tavistock road at **MERRIVALE**, a tiny village with a decent **pub** (the *Dartmoor Arms*), four miles west of Princetown. Merrivale makes another good starting point for moorland walks – there's a decent **campsite** at *Higher Longford Farm*, Moorshop, less than a mile out of Merrivale on the Tavistock Road (℡01822/613360) – and it's only half a mile west of the most spectacular of Dartmoor's stone rows, the **Merrivale Megaliths**. Just a few yards from the B3357, the upright stones form a stately procession, stretching 850ft across the bare landscape. Dating from between 2500 BC and 750 BC, and probably connected with burial rites, the rows are known locally as "Potato Market" or "Plague Market" in memory of the time when provisions for plague-stricken Tavistock were deposited here. A mile to the southwest, on the western slopes of the Walkham valley, the sphinx-like pinnacle of **Vixen Tor** looms over the barren moor.

Tavistock

The main town of the western moor, **TAVISTOCK** owes its distinctive Victorian appearance to the building boom that followed the discovery of copper deposits here in 1844. Originally, however, this market and Stannary town on the River Tavy grew around what was once the West Country's most important Benedictine abbey, established in the eleventh century and, at the time of its dissolution, owning land as distant as the Isles of Scilly. Some scanty remnants survive in the churchyard of **St Eustace**, a mainly fifteenth-century building with stained glass from William Morris's studio in the south aisle.

Half a mile south of Tavistock, on the Plymouth Road, stands a statue of Francis Drake, who was born and raised on Crowndale Farm, a mile south of town; the statue on Plymouth Hoe is a replica of this one.

Tavistock's **tourist office**, in the town hall on Bedford Square (Easter to late July & early Sept to Oct Mon–Sat 10am–5pm; late July to early Sept daily 9.30am–5pm; Nov–Easter Mon, Tues, Fri & Sat 10am–4pm; ℡01822/612938), can supply you with information on the western moor, for which the town would make an ideal base. There's a good range of **accommodation** choices, including the Georgian *Eko Brae* at 4 Bedford Villas, in the Springhill quarter of town (☎01822/614028, ⓔekobrae@aol.com; no credit cards; ❶), and, about half a mile east of Tavistock off the B3357 Princetown Road, *Mount Tavy Cottage* (☎01822/614253, ⓦwww.mounttavy.freeserve.co.uk; ❷), set in a lush garden and offering organic breakfasts. There's a decent **campsite** at *Higher Longford Farm*, Moorshop, two miles out of Tavistock on the B3357 Princetown Road (☎01822/613360). **Bikes** can be rented from Tavistock Cycles, Paddons Row, Brook St (☎01822/617630), and from Dartmoor Cycle Hire, signposted off the Plymouth Road next to Safeway (☎01822/617630, ⓦwww.dartmoor-cyclehire.co.uk).

North of Tavistock, a four-mile lane wanders up to **Brent Tor**, 1130-foot high and dominating Dartmoor's western fringes. Access to its conical summit is easiest along a path gently ascending through gorse on its southwestern side, leading to the small church of St Michael at the top. Bleak, treeless moorland extends in every direction, wrapped in silence that's occasionally pierced by the shrill cries of stonechats and wheatears. A couple of miles eastwards, **Gibbet Hill** looms over Black Down and the ruined stack of the abandoned Wheal Betsy silver and lead mine.

North Devon

From Exeter the A377 runs alongside the scenic Tarka Line railway to **North Devon**'s major town, **Barnstaple**. Within easy reach of here, the resorts of **Ilfracombe** and **Woolacombe** draw the crowds, though the fine sandy beaches surrounding the latter give ample opportunity to find your own space. The river port of **Bideford** gives its name to a long bay that holds another beach resort, **Westward Ho!**, as well as the precipitous village of **Clovelly**, perhaps Devon's most famous beauty spot. Inspiring coastal walks follow the bay, particularly to the stormy **Hartland Point** and beyond. Away from the coast, there is plenty of scope for walking and cycling along the Tarka Trail long-distance path, passing through some of the region's loveliest countryside, while for a complete break, the tiny island of **Lundy** provides further opportunities for stretching the legs and clearing the lungs.

Barnstaple

BARNSTAPLE, at the head of the Taw estuary, makes an excellent springboard, being well connected to the resorts of Bideford Bay, Ilfracombe and Woolacombe, as well as to the western fringes of Exmoor. The town's centuries-old role as a marketplace is perpetuated in the daily bustle around the huge timber-framed **Pannier Market** off the High Street, alongside which runs **Butchers Row**, its 33 archways now converted to a variety of uses. Also off the High Street, in the pedestrianized area between that and Boutport Street, lies Barnstaple's **parish church**, itself worth a look, and the fourteenth-century **St Anne's Chapel**, converted into a grammar school in 1549 and later numbering among its pupils John Gay, author of *The Beggar's Opera*; it's now closed to the public (though you can apply at the tourist office for the key). At the end of Boutport Street, make time to visit the **Museum of North Devon** (Tues–Sat 10am–4.30pm; £1, free on Sat till noon), a lively miscellany including wildlife displays and a collection of eighteenth-century pottery for which the region was famous. The museum lies alongside the Taw, where footpaths

The Tarka Line and the Tarka Trail

Henry Williamson's *Tarka the Otter* (1927), rated by some as one of the finest pieces of nature writing in the English language, has been appropriated as a promotional device by the Devon tourist industry. As parts of the book are set in the Taw valley, it was inevitable that the Exeter to Barnstaple rail route – which follows the Taw for half of its length – should be dubbed the **Tarka Line**. Leaving almost hourly from Exeter St David's station, trains on this branch line cut through the sparsely popu-lated heart of Devon, the biggest town en route being **Crediton**, ancient birthplace of St Boniface (patron saint of Germany and the Netherlands) and site of the bish-opric before its transfer to Exeter in the eleventh century.

Barnstaple forms the centre of the figure-of-eight traced by the **Tarka Trail**, which tracks the otter's wanderings for a distance of over 180 miles. To the north, the trail penetrates Exmoor then follows the coast back, passing through Williamson's home village of **Georgeham** on its return to Barnstaple. South, the path takes in Bideford (see p.465), following a disused rail line to Meeth, and continuing as far as Okehampton (see p.459), before swooping up via Eggesford, the point at which the Tarka Line joins the Taw valley.

Twenty-three miles of the trail follow a former rail line that's ideally suited to **bicy-cles**, and there are rental shops at Barnstaple (near the train station), and Bideford (see p.465). Sculptures have been placed along the route to mark its inclusion in the National Cycle Network. A good ride from Barnstaple is to **Torrington** (fifteen miles south), where you can eat at the *Puffing Billy* pub, formerly the train station.

Tourist offices give out leaflets on individual sections of the trail, but the best over-all book is *The Tarka Trail: A Walker's Guide* (Devon Books; £4.95), available from tourist offices or bookshops.

make for a pleasant riverside stroll, with the colonnaded eighteenth-century **Queen Anne's Walk** – built as a merchants' exchange – providing some archi-tectural interest.

Barnstaple's well-equipped **tourist office** lies opposite Butchers Row on Boutport Street (May–Sept Mon–Sat 9.30am–5.30pm; Oct–April Mon–Sat 9.30am–5pm; ☎01271/375000, ⍟www.northdevon.com). There are plenty of **places to stay** in town, two of them five hundred yards south of Long Bridge, at the bottom of the High Street: the Georgian *Nelson House*, 99 Newport Rd (☎01271/345929; no credit cards; ❶), backing onto Rock Park and the river, has shared bathrooms but private showers, while, around the corner on Victoria Road, *Ivy House* (☎01271/371198; no credit cards; ❶) has rooms with or with-out private bathrooms. A little further out, on Landkey Road – a continuation of Newport Road – is the first-rate *Mount Sandford* (☎01271/342354; no cred-it cards; ❷), which has a beautiful garden. Convenient for the station, *Herton* (☎01271/323302; no credit cards; ❶) is a semi-rural B&B out on Lake Road (left onto Sticklepath Terrace, then left again) that boasts its own tennis court, a twenty-minute walk from the centre. On a plusher note, the Victorian *Royal and Fortescue Hotel* off the square on Boutport Street (☎01271/342289, ⍟www.roy-alfortescue.co.uk; ❹) is a rather formal place with a decent restaurant.

You can pick up coffees and **snacks** at the *Old School Coffee House*, a building dating from 1659 on Church Lane, near St Anne's Chapel, and the coolly mod-ern *PV*, 70 Boutport St (closed Sun), has a moderately priced upstairs **restau-rant** and the ground floor becomes a wine bar in the evening. On Butchers Row, *Marshford Organic Produce* sells pies, breads and other wholefoods to take away, while for gourmet dining, head a mile south of the centre to Bishops Tawton Road, where the non-smoking *Lynwood House* (closed Sun) serves a moderate set lunch, though in the evenings you'll have to splash out on the expensive, but choice, seafood dishes; **accommodation** is also available here (℡01271/343695, ⊛www.lynwoodhouse.co.uk; ❹). Cyclists on the Tarka Trail can **rent bikes** from Tarka Trail Cycle Hire at the train station (℡01271 /324202; £8/day) or Rolle Quay Cycle Hire on Rolle Street (℡01271 /325361; £12/day), at the top end of the High Street, conveniently placed for the northern section of the Trail towards Braunton. The *Rolle Quay Inn* here can provide lunches to eat in or take as a picnic, and also has accommodation (❷).

Ilfracombe and around

The most popular resort on Devon's northern coast, **ILFRACOMBE** is essentially little changed since its evolution into a Victorian and Edwardian tourist centre, large-scale development having been restricted by the surrounding cliffs. Nonetheless, the relentless pressure to have fun and the ubiquitous smell of chips can become oppressive, though in summer you can always pop down to the small harbour and escape on a coastal tour, a cruise to Lundy Island (see p.468) or a fishing trip. An attractive stretch of coast runs east out of Ilfracombe, beyond the grassy cliffs of Hillsborough, where a succession of undeveloped coves and inlets is surrounded by jagged slanting rocks and heather-covered hills. Three miles to the east, above the almost enclosed Watermouth Bay, lies **Watermouth Castle** (April–Oct Mon–Fri & Sun 10am–4pm; £7), an imposing nineteenth-century mansion, best admired from the outside unless you have kids, who will appreciate the water shows, dungeons and carousel.

The pick of the **beaches** in the area – indeed the best on Devon's northern coast – are round **Morte Point**, five miles west of Ilfracombe, from which the view takes in the island of Lundy, fifteen miles out to sea. Below the promontory stretches a rocky shore whose menacing sunken reef inspired the Normans to give it the name Morte Stone. A break in the rocks makes space for the pocket-sized **Barricane Beach**, famous for the tropical shells washed here from the Caribbean by the Atlantic currents, and a popular swimming spot. Luckily there's room for everyone on the two miles of **Woolacombe Sands**, a broad, west-facing expanse much favoured by surfers and families alike. The beach can get crowded towards its northern end, where a cluster of hotels, villas and retirement homes makes up the summer resort of **WOOLACOMBE**. At the quieter southern end, **Putsborough Sands** is a choice swimming spot bracketed by **Baggy Point**, where from September to November the air is a swirl of gannets, shags, cormorants and shearwaters. South of this promontory, **Croyde Bay** is another surfers' delight, more compact than Woolacombe, with stalls on the sand renting surfboards and wet-suits, while **Saunton Sands** is a magnificent long stretch of coast pummelled by endless ranks of classic breakers.

Practicalities

From Barnstaple, First Red Bus #1, #2 and #30 run daily several times an hour to Ilfracombe, and the frequent #303 runs to Woolacombe. From Minehead and Lynton, take the three-times-daily "Transmoor Link" #300. You can reach Woolacombe from Ilfracombe on First Red Bus #31 and #31a, while DevonBus #308 travels from Barnstaple to Croyde, via Saunton. There's no service between Woolacombe and Croyde. The Ilfracombe **tourist office** is at the Landmark on the Seafront (daily: Easter–Oct 10am–5.30pm; Nov–Easter 10am–5.30pm; ℡01271/863001, ⊛www.ilfracombe-guide.org.uk).

Ilfracombe has a good range of **accommodation**, including inexpensive **B&Bs** such as *Kinvara*, very central at 6 Avenue Rd (℡01271/863013; no credit cards; ❶; closed Nov–Easter), and the *Cavendish* at 9 Larkstone Terrace (℡01271/863994; no credit cards; ❸), which offers harbour views. There's also an excellent independent **hostel**, *Ocean Backpackers*, near the bus station and harbour at 29 St James Place (℡01271/867835), and the YHA hostel, *Ashmour House* (℡01271/865337; closed Nov to mid-Feb), occupies a Georgian building above the harbour on Hillsborough Terrace. The area's best **campsites** are around Morte Point – good choices are *North Morte Farm* (℡01271/870381; closed Oct–Easter), 500yds from the beach and also offering caravans for rent, or try the *Little Meadow* site at Lydford Farm (℡01271/862222; closed Oct–Easter), connected by footpath to Watermouth Castle and the beach – bus #30 goes there. Ilfracombe's best **place to eat** is the *Atlantis*, below *Ocean Backpackers* (see above), specializing in international dishes, with ambient, world and jazz musical background; *Swivel*, 155 High St, is a modern **bar** with cocktails and a laid-back atmosphere.

In **Woolacombe**, *Baggy Leap* has mostly spacious rooms with or without bathrooms, and views of the whole bay (℡01271/870222; no credit cards; ❷), while surfers and others gather at the *Red Barn*, a popular **bar** and **restaurant** just behind the beach. In **Croyde**, *Parminter*, at 16 St Mary's Rd (℡01271 /890030; ❶), is a flagstoned cottage with large loft rooms and friendly owners; the *Thatch* pub is the local hangout. Woolacombe's **tourist office** is on the Esplanade (Easter–Oct Mon–Sat 10am–5pm, Sun 10am–3pm; Nov–Easter Mon–Sat 10am–1pm; ℡01271/870553).

Bideford Bay

BIDEFORD BAY (sometimes called Barnstaple Bay) encapsulates the variety of Devon, encompassing the downmarket beach resort of **Westward Ho!**, the savage windlashed rocks of **Hartland Point** and the photogenic village of **Clovelly**. **Instow** and **Appledore**, sheltered towns in the mouth of the Torridge estuary, have a lower-key attraction, while **Bideford** itself is mainly a transit centre, with some decent accommodation and bus connections to all the towns on the bay, and regular boats for Lundy.

Bideford

Like Barnstaple, nine miles to the east, the estuary town of **BIDEFORD** formed an important link in the north Devon trade network, mainly due to its **bridge**, which still straddles the River Torridge. First built in 1300, the bridge was reconstructed in stone in the following century, and subsequently reinforced and widened, hence the irregularity of its twenty-four arches, no two of which have the same span. Bideford's greatest prosperity arose in the seventeenth and eighteenth centuries, when it enjoyed a flourishing trade with the New World, and today the tree-lined quay along the west riverbank is still the focal point for the knot of narrow shop-lined streets.

From the Norman era until the eighteenth century, the port was the property of the Grenville family, whose most celebrated scion was **Richard Grenville**, commander of the ships that carried the first settlers to Virginia, and later a major player in the defeat of the Spanish Armada. Grenville also featured in *Westward Ho!*, the historical romance by **Charles Kingsley** who wrote part of the book in Bideford and is thus commemorated by a statue at the quay's northern end. Behind, **Victoria Park** extends up the riverbank, containing guns captured from the Spanish in 1588.

Alongside the park is the **tourist office** (Easter–June & Sept Mon–Sat 10am–5pm, Sun 10am–1pm; July & Aug Mon–Sat 10am–5pm, Sun 10am–1pm; Oct–Easter Mon, Tues, Thurs & Fri 10am–4.30pm, Wed & Sat 10am–1pm; ☎01237/477676), from which you can pick up an accommodation list as well as information on coastal cruises and the boat to Lundy (see p.468) – tickets from here or the booths along the quayside. A useful **B&B** nearby is the *Cornerhouse*, 14 The Strand, two minutes from Victoria Park (☎01237/473722; no credit cards; ❶), or opt for the attractive *Mount* (☎01237/473748, ⓦwww .themount1.cjb.net; ❸), further out on Northdown Road, but linked to the centre by a footpath, and set in its own walled garden; both are non-smoking. The swanky *Royal Hotel* (☎01237/472005, ⓦwww.royalbideford.co.uk; ❷), just over the old bridge on Barnstaple Street, offers comfortable, good-value rooms but no views. For a **meal** or a drink, head up Bridge Street from Bideford's bridge to Market Place, where the porticoed *Old Coach Inn* provides ales and hearty snacks, while the more up-to-date *Praxis II* across the square has French sticks and vegan pasties during the day (closed Wed pm & all Sun; no credit cards).

For exploring the Tarka Trail by **bike**, there's Bideford Bicycle Hire, Torrington St (☎01237/424123), 200yds south of the bridge on the far river-bank (£9.50/day).

Appledore and Instow

The old shipbuilding port of **APPLEDORE**, near the confluence of the Taw and Torridge rivers, still has several operating boatyards and a small sailing fleet moored in the river, but the peaceful pastel-coloured Georgian houses give lit-tle hint of the extent of the industry in earlier times. Take time to explore West Appledore and walk along Irsha Street where you can stop for a pint and enjoy the view at the *Royal George* or *Beaver Inn*. There are a few **B&Bs** overlooking the estuary on Marine Parade, including *Regency House* at no. 2 (☎01237 /473689; ❶); further along the Quay, there's the plain *Seagate Hotel* (☎01237/472589; ❷), where rooms with a view fall into the next price cate-gory up. Pub **meals** are also available here.

In summer, foot passengers can take the five-minute **ferry** journey (April–Oct; every 15min during high tide; £1.80, plus £1 for bikes) across to **INSTOW**, whose sandy beach stretches in a long line, broadening to a muddy flat at low tide. There's little more than a couple of pubs serving snacks here, and a good **B&B** 60yds from the beach: *The Rectory* on Quay Lane (☎01271/860605; no credit cards; no smoking; ❶), formerly a girls' boarding school dating from 1820, and now offering basic rooms with shared bathroom.

Westward Ho!

WESTWARD HO!, three miles northwest of Bideford, is the only English town to be named after a book. After the publication of Kingsley's historical romance in 1855, speculators recognized the tourist potential of what was then an empty expanse of sand and mud pounded by Atlantic rollers, and the town's first villa was built within a decade. Rudyard Kipling spent four years of his youth here, as described by him in *Stalky and Co*, and his presence is recalled in Kipling Terrace – the site of his school – and **Kipling Tors**, the heights at the west end of the three-mile sand and pebble beach, affording excellent views.

Kingsley didn't think much of the new resort when he paid a visit, and he certainly wouldn't care for it now, with its spawning amusement arcades, cara-van sites and holiday chalets, and its substandard sea water. You might content yourself with the **walk** along the magnificent beach, however, or else across

Northam Burrows extending behind it – a flat, marshy expanse of dunes and meadows rich in flora and attracting plenty of migratory birds.

Clovelly

The impossibly picturesque village of **CLOVELLY**, which must have featured on more calendars, biscuit boxes and tourist posters than anywhere else in the West Country, was put on the map in the second half of the nineteenth century by two books: Charles Dickens' *A Message From the Sea* and, inevitably, *Westward Ho!* – Charles Kingsley's father was rector here for six years. To an extent, the tone of the village has been preserved since then by limiting hotel accommodation and precluding holiday homes, but on summer days it's impossible to see past the artifice. Although the strict commercial control has meant that the presence of coach parties has been contained, there's still a fairly regular stream of visitors.

The first hurdle to surmount is the **visitor centre** (daily: April–Oct 9am–5pm; Nov–March 10am–4pm; ⓦ www.clovelly.co.uk), where you are charged £3.50 for access to shops, snack bars and an audiovisual show, and also for use of the car park (it's well-nigh impossible to leave your motor anywhere else). Walkers, cyclists and users of public transport have right of way to the village (there's a separate entrance to the right of the visitor centre). Below the centre, the cobbled, traffic-free main street plunges past neat, flower-smothered cottages where sledges are tethered for transporting goods – the only way to carry supplies since the use of donkeys ceased.

At the bottom lies Clovelly's stony beach and tiny harbour, snuggled under a cleft in the cliff wall. A lifeboat operates from here, and a handful of fishing boats are the only remnants of a fleet that provided the village's main business before the herring stocks became depleted. The jetty was built in the fourteenth century to shelter the coast's only safe harbour between Appledore and Boscastle in Cornwall. If you can't face the return climb, take the Land Rover, which leaves about every fifteen minutes from behind the *Red Lion* (Easter–Oct 9am–5.30pm; £1.60) back to the top of the village. It is here, immediately below the visitors centre, that Hobby Drive begins, a three-mile **walk** you can make along the cliffs through woods of sycamore, oak, beech, rowan and the occasional holly, with grand views over the village.

You can reach Clovelly by Western National **bus** #319, which traces a route from Barnstaple to Hartland, also passing through Bideford. There are just two **hotels** in the village, both pricey: the *New Inn* halfway down the High Street (ⓣ01237/431303; ❺), and, enjoying a superb position, the *Red Lion* at the harbour (ⓣ01237/431237, ⓔredlion@clovelly.demon.co.uk; ❻). Below the *New Inn* is a small **B&B**, *Donkey Hill Cottage* (ⓣ01237/431601; no credit cards; ❶), which you should book a long way in advance. There's a greater selection of guest houses a twenty-minute walk up from the visitor centre in Higher Clovelly: try the *Old Smithy*, on the main road (ⓣ01237/431202; no credit cards; ❶) or, farther out – but just ten minutes' walk from lower Clovelly along a track through fields – *Fuchsia Cottage* on Burscott Lane (ⓣ01237/431398; no smoking; no credit cards; ❶), a modern house with views from its first-floor rooms. Clovelly's best **eating** option is the *Red Lion*, which offers a two-course dinner for £20.

Hartland Point and around

You could drive along minor roads to **Hartland Point**, ten miles west of Clovelly, but the best approach is on foot along the coastal path. Shortly before arriving, the path touches at the only sandy beach between Westward Ho! and the Cornish border, **Shipload Bay**.The headland presents one of Devon's most dramatic sights, its jagged black rocks battered by the sea and overlooked by a solitary lighthouse 350ft up. South of Hartland Point, the saw-toothed rocks and near-vertical escarpments defiantly confront the waves, with spectacular waterfalls tumbling over the cliffs.This sheer stretch of coast has seen dozens of shipwrecks over the centuries, though many must have been prevented by the sight of the tower of fourteenth-century **St Nectan's** – a couple of miles south of the point in the village of **STOKE** – which acted as a landmark to sailors before the construction of the lighthouse.At 128ft, it is the tallest church tower in north Devon, and overlooks a weathered old graveyard containing memorials to various members of the Lane family – of the Bodley Head and Penguin publishing empire – who were associated with the area; inside, the church boasts a finely carved rood screen and a Norman font, all covered by a repainted wagon-type roof. Tea and home-made scones are served in summer on Wednesdays, Thursdays and at weekends at *Stoke Barton Farm*, just opposite.

Half a mile east of the church, gardens and lush woodland surround **Hartland Abbey** (May, June & Sept Wed, Thurs & Sun 2–5.30pm; July & Aug also Tues 2–5.30pm; £4.25), an eighteenth-century country house incorporating the ruins of an abbey dissolved in 1539, and displaying fine furniture, old photographs and recently uncovered frescoes.There's a nice walk through grounds to the beach here. **HARTLAND** itself, further inland, holds little appeal beyond its three pubs and café, but on the coast, **Hartland Quay** deserves a linger: once a busy port, financed in part by the mariners Raleigh, Drake and Hawkins, it was mostly destroyed by storms in the nineteenth century, and now holds a solitary pub and hotel, surrounded by beautiful slate cliffs.About one mile south of here, **Speke's Mill Mouth** is a select surfers' beach.

Accommodation options in the area are scattered, and you'll need your own transport unless you stay in Hartland itself, where you'll find a friendly B&B, at 2 Harton Manor, North St, off Fore St (☎01237/441670; no credit cards; ❶). For isolated atmosphere, the *Hartland Quay Hotel* (in Hartland Quay) can't be beaten (☎01237/441218; ❷; closed Nov to mid-Feb), but if you want to be nearer Shipload Bay and Hartland Point, try *West Titchberry Farm* (☎01237/441287; no credit cards; ❶), for which you should follow signs for Hartland Lighthouse. In nearby Stoke, *Stoke Barton Farm* (see above) also provides **B&B** (☎01237/441238; no credit cards; ❶) and basic camping facilities, while further south, at Elmscott, at the end of a three-and-a-half-mile signposted footpath from Hartland, and about half a mile inland, there's a **youth hostel** in a converted Victorian schoolhouse (☎01237/441367; closed mid-Sept to mid-March). The only public transport is bus #319 from Barnstaple, and buses #119 and #128 from Bude; alight at Hartland.

Lundy Island

There are fewer than twenty full-time residents on **Lundy**, a tiny windswept island twelve miles north of Hartland Point. Now a refuge for thousands of marine birds, Lundy has no cars, just one pub and one shop – indeed little has changed since the Marisco family established itself here in the twelfth century, making use of the shingle beaches and coves to terrorize shipping along the Bristol Channel. The family's fortunes only fell in 1242 when one of their number, William de Marisco, was found to be plotting against the king, whereupon he was hung, drawn and quartered at Tower Hill in London.

After the Mariscos, Lundy's most famous inhabitants were Thomas Benson, MP for Barnstaple in the eighteenth century – who was discovered using slave labour to work the granite quarries, and later found guilty of a massive insurance fraud – and **William Hudson Heaven**, who bought the island in 1834 and established what became known as the "Kingdom of Heaven". His home, **Millcombe House**, an incongruous piece of Georgian architecture in the desolate surroundings, is one of many relics of former habitation scattered around the island, though a recent addition compared with the castle standing on Lundy's southern end, which was erected by Henry III following the downfall of the Mariscos.

Tracks and footpaths interweave all over the island, and **walking** is really the only thing to do here. Inland, the grass, heather and bog is crossed by dry-stone walls and grazed by ponies, goats, deer and the rare soay sheep. The shores – mainly cliffy on the west, softer and undulating on the east – shelter a rich variety of **birdlife**, including kittiwakes, fulmars, shags and Manx shearwaters, which often nest in rabbit burrows. The most famous birds, though, are the **puffins** after which Lundy is named – from the Norse *Lunde* (puffin) and *ey* (island). They can only be sighted in April and May, when they come ashore to mate. Offshore, **grey seals** can be seen all the year round.

Practicalities

The Oldenburg crosses to Lundy from Bideford throughout the year apart from a few weeks in January and February, with additional sailings from Ilfracombe and from Clovelly from April to September (1–4 weekly). From Bideford, sailings increase in frequency from twice a week in winter to four times in midsummer, taking around two hours; day return tickets cost around £25, period returns £40 (to reserve a place, call ☎01237/423233 or 01271 /863636).

Accommodation on the island can be booked up months in advance, and B&B is only available in houses that have not already been taken for weekly rentals. Since B&B bookings can only be made within two weeks of the proposed visit, this limits the options, though outside the holiday season it is still eminently possible to find a double room for under £45 per night. **Bookings** must be made through the Landmark Trust's Shore Office in Bideford (☎01237/423233). Options range from the remote *Admiralty Lookout* (lacking electricity and with only hand-pumped water), through the two-storey granite *Barn*, a hostel sleeping fourteen, to the comfortable *Old House*, where Charles Kingsley stayed in 1849, and the *Old Light*, a lighthouse built in 1820 by the architect of Dartmoor Prison. A single person might find the *Radio Room* cosy; it once housed the radio transmitter that was the island's only link with the outside world. There's also a **campsite** on the island open throughout the year, though it can get pretty rainy and windswept in winter.

Exmoor

A high bare plateau sliced by wooded combes and splashing rivers, **EXMOOR** can be one of the most forbidding landscapes in England, especially when its sea-mists fall. When it's clear, though, the moorland of this National Park reveals rich swathes of colour and an amazing diversity of wildlife, from buzzards to the unique **Exmoor ponies**, a species closely related to prehistoric horses. In the treeless heartland of the moor around **Simonsbath**, in particular, it is not difficult to spot these short and stocky animals, though fewer than twelve hundred are registered, and of these only about two hundred are free-living on the moor. Much more elusive are the **red deer**, England's largest native wild animal, of which Exmoor supports England's only wild population.

The effect of hunting through the centuries has accounted for a drastic depletion in numbers, though they have a strong recovery rate, and about two and half thousand are thought to inhabit the moor today, their annual culling by stalking as well as hunting is a regular point of issue among conservationists and nature-lovers.

Endless permutations of **walking routes** are possible along a network of some six hundred miles of footpaths and bridleways. In addition, the National Park Authority and other local organizations have put together a programme of guided walks, graded according to distance, speed and duration and costing from £2–3.50 per person. Contact any of the Visitor Centres or else contact the National Park base at Dulverton (℡01398/323665, ⓦwww.exmoor-nationalpark.gov.uk) for details. **Horseback** is another option for getting the most out of Exmoor's desolate beauty, and stables are dotted throughout the area – the most convenient are mentioned below; expect to pay around £10 an hour. Whether walking or riding, bear in mind that over seventy percent of the National Park is privately owned and that access is theoretically restricted to public rights of way; special permission should certainly be sought before camping, canoeing, fishing or similar.

There are four obvious bases for inland walks: **Dulverton** in the southeast, site of the main information facilities and useful also for excursions into the neighbouring Brendon Hills; **Simonsbath** in the centre; **Exford**, near Exmoor's highest point of Dunkery Beacon; and the attractive village of **Winsford**, close to the A396 on the east of the moor. Exmoor's coastline offers an alluring alternative to the open moorland, all of it accessible via the **South West Coast Path**, which embarks on its long coastal journey at **Minehead**, though there is more charm to be found farther west at the sister-villages of **Lynmouth** and **Lynton**, just over the Devon border.

Minehead stands at the end of the **West Somerset Railway**, but otherwise you have to rely on infrequent local **buses** for public transport. The main lines are run in the summer only; for the winter you'll have to rely on once- or twice-weekly community buses connecting Dulverton, Minehead and Lynton. From late May until the end of September, the most useful lines are the #285, looping between Minehead, Dunster, Wheddon Cross, Exford and Porlock (not Sat); and the #295 connecting Dulverton with Lynton via Tarr Steps, Exford and Simonsbath (not Sat or Sun); while the #398 runs throughout the year (not Sun) between Minehead, Dulverton and Tiverton. On the coast, the most useful route is the #300 (summer daily; winter Sat & Sun only) connecting Minehead with Lynton and Ilfracombe three times daily, extending as far as Taunton on one of its journeys; while the #38 runs four times daily between Minehead and Porlock (not Sun). If you're planning to make good use of the buses, purchase a money-saving "Red Day Rider" (£5) or "Explorer" (£6) ticket, valid for one day's travel, or a "3-Day" (£9.50) ticket – both available from the bus driver.

Dulverton

The village of **DULVERTON**, on the southern edge of the National Park, is the Park Authority's headquarters and so makes a good introduction to Exmoor. Information on the whole moor is available at the **visitor centre**, 7 Fore St (daily: Easter–Oct 10am–1.15pm & 1.45–5pm; Nov–Easter 10.30am–2.30pm; ℡01398/323841). Dulverton's best **accommodation** choice is *Town Mills* (℡01398/323124; no credit cards; ❶), an old mill house in the centre of the village. If the handful of other options are full, or you hanker after beams

Walks from Dulverton and Tarr Steps

The most popular short walk from Dulverton goes along the east bank of the Barle to the seventeen-span medieval bridge at **Tarr Steps**, five miles to the northwest. You could combine this walk with a hike up **Winsford Hill**, a circular walk of less than four hours from Tarr Steps. Follow the riverside path upstream from Tarr Steps, turning right after about half a mile along Watery Lane, a rocky track that deteriorates into a muddy lane near Knaplock Farm. Stay on the track until you reach a cattle-grid, on open moorland. Turn left here, cross a small stream and climb up Winsford Hill, a heather moor whose 1400-foot summit is invisible until you are almost there. At the top, from where there are views as far as Dartmoor, you can see the **Wambarrows**, three Bronze Age burial mounds. If you want a refreshment stop, descend the hill on the other side to the village of Winsford.

A quarter-mile due east of the barrows, the ground drops sharply by more than two hundred feet to the Punchbowl, a bracken-grown depression resembling an amphitheatre. Keep on the east side of the B3223 which runs up Winsford Hill, following it south for a mile, until you come across the **Caractacus Stone**, an inscribed stone just by Spire Cross. The stone is thought to date from between 450 and 650, the damaged inscription reading "Carataci Nepos" – that is, "kinsman of Caractacus", the first-century British king.

Continue south on the east side of the road, cross it after about a mile, and pass over the cattle grid on the Tarr Steps road, from which a footpath takes you west another one and a half miles back to Tarr Steps. The *Tarr Farm* café here provides food and refreshment.

and four-posters, try the equally central but slightly more expensive *Lion Hotel* in Bank Square (℡01398/323444; **❸**), or the plainer *Crispin's*, in a nook off 26 High St (℡01398/323397; **❶**); the latter also serves moderately priced snacks and full evening **meals**, while further down the High Street, *Lewis's Tea Rooms* serves teas and snacks. Moorland **horse riding** and tuition at all levels is offered at West Anstey Farm (℡01398/341354), a couple of miles west of Dulverton; there's also a **camping barn** here.

Winsford

Just west of the A396 five miles north of Dulverton, **WINSFORD** – birthplace of the renowned Labour politician Ernest Bevin – lays good claim to being the moor's prettiest village. A scattering of thatched cottages ranged around a sleepy green, it is watered by a confluence of streams and rivers – one of them the Exe – giving it no fewer than seven bridges. *Larcombe Foot* (℡01643/851306; no credit cards; **❷**; closed Dec–Feb), one mile to the north, offers excellent **B&B** overlooking the Exe, and there's a well-equipped **campsite** nearby at *Halse Farm* (℡01643/851259, ⒲www.halsefarm.co.uk; closed Nov to mid-March). The *Royal Oak*, a thatched and rambling old inn on the village green, can offer you drinks, snacks and full restaurant **meals**, though the rooms are pricey (℡01643/851455, ⒲www.royaloak-somerset.co.uk; **❺**).

Exford and Dunkery Beacon

The hamlet of **EXFORD**, an ancient crossing-point on the River Exe, is popular with hunting folk as well as with walkers here for the four-mile hike to **Dunkery Beacon**, Exmoor's highest point at 1700ft. There's a good range of **accommodation**, including *Exmoor Lodge*, a friendly vegetarian and vegan B&B (℡01643/831694, ⒲www.exmoorlodge.co.uk; no smoking; **❶**), and the village also holds Exmoor's main **youth hostel**, a rambling Victorian house in the centre (℡01643/831288; closed Nov to mid-Feb). Two and a half miles northwest of Exford off the Porlock Road, *Westermill Farm* (℡01643/831238, ⓦwww.exmoorcamping.co.uk) provides a tranquil **campsite** on the banks of the Exe.

Exmoor Forest and Simonsbath

At the centre of the National Park stands **Exmoor Forest**, the barest part of the moor, scarcely populated except by roaming sheep and a few red deer – the word "forest" denotes simply that it was a hunting reserve. In the middle of it stands the village of **SIMONSBATH** (pronounced "Simmonsbath"), at a crossroads between Lynton, Barnstaple and Minehead on the River Barle. The village was home to the Knight family, who bought the forest in 1818 and, by introducing tenant farmers, building roads and importing sheep, brought systematic agriculture to an area that had never before produced any income. The Knights also built a wall round their land – parts of which can still be seen – as well as the intriguing Pinkworthy (pronounced "Pinkery") Pond, four miles to the northwest, whose exact function remains unexplained.

Simonsbath would make a useful base for hikes in the heart of the moor, but there are only two **accommodation** possibilities: the *Exmoor Forest Hotel* (℡01643/831341; ❸), which has numerous hunting trophies, old-fashioned rooms, and also space for free **camping**; and the *Simonsbath House Hotel* (℡01643/831259; ❺), former home of the Knights and now a cosy bolt-hole offering seven agreeably gnarled rooms, all en suite, and a good, if fairly expensive **restaurant**. In a converted barn next to the hotel, *Boevey's* offers coffees and snack lunches, while a couple of miles outside the village on the Brayford Road is the *Poltimore Arms* at **Yarde Down,** a classic country **pub** serving excellent **food**, including vegetarian dishes.

The Brendon Hills

Sandwiched between the Quantocks and Exmoor, the **Brendon Hills** are effectively an extension of the moor, separated from it by the rivers Avill and Exe. The A396, which runs alongside the rivers, offers opportunities to take woodland paths rising to such scenic spots as **Wimbleball Lake**, accessible from the village of **Brompton Regis**. Exmoor's major reservoir, the lake is the habitat of herons and kingfishers, and footpaths lead from its southern shores up **Haddon Hill**, enjoying sweeping panoramas from its 1164ft summit.

Overlooking Wimbleball Lake, *Holworthy Farm* offers comfortable en-suite **accommodation** and traditional farmhouse food to its guests (℡01398/ 371244, ⓔholworthy7@netscapeonline.co.uk; no credit cards; ❸). Further north, **Wheddon Cross** has the excellent *Rest and Be Thankful* inn, with a beer garden, good food and several rooms (℡01643/841222, ⓔrbtinn@btconnect. com; ❹). There's also a **riding stables** nearby at Huntscott House Stables (℡01643/841272), which caters for experienced riders.

Minehead and around

A chief port on the Somerset coast, **MINEHEAD** quickly became a favourite Victorian watering-hole with the arrival of the railway, and it has preserved an upbeat holiday-town atmosphere ever since. Steep lanes link the two quarters of **Higher Town**, on North Hill, containing some of the oldest houses, and **Quay Town**, the harbour area. It is in Quay Town that the **Hobby Horse** per-

The South West Coast Path

The South West Coast Path, the longest footpath in Britain, starts at Minehead and tracks the coastline as closely as it possibly can along Devon's northern seaboard, round Cornwall, back into Devon, and on to Dorset, where it finishes close to the entrance to Poole Harbour. The path was conceived in the 1940s, but it is only in the last twenty years that – barring a few significant gaps – the full **six-hundred-mile route** has been open, much of it on land owned by the National Trust, and all of it well signposted with the acorn symbol of the Countryside Agency.

Some degree of **planning** is essential for any long walk along the South West Coast Path, in particular on the south Devon stretch, where there are six ferries to negotiate and one ford to cross between Plymouth and Exmouth. **Accommodation** needs to be considered too: don't expect to arrive late in the day at a holiday town in season and immediately find a bed. Even campsites can fill to capacity, though campers have the flexibility of asking farmers for permission to pitch in a corner of a field.

The relevant Ordnance Survey **maps** can be found at most village shops on the route, while many newsagents, bookshops and tourist offices will stock books or pamphlets containing route plans and details of local flora and fauna. Aurum Press (ⓦwww.aurumpress.co.uk) produces a series of four books using Ordnance Survey maps and describing different parts of the path, while the **South West Coast Path Association** publishes an annual guide (£7) to the whole path, including accommodation lists, ferry timetables and transport details; contact them at Windlestraw, Penquit, Ermington, Devon PL21 0LU (ⓣ01752/896237, ⓦwww.swcp.org.uk).

forms its dance in the town's three-day May Day celebrations, snaring maidens under its prancing skirt and tail in a fertility ritual resembling the more famous festivities at the Cornish port of Padstow (see p.509).

The **tourist office** is midway between Higher Town and Quay Town at 17 Friday St, off the Parade (April–June, Sept & Oct Mon–Sat 9.30am–5pm; July & Aug Mon–Sat 9.30am–5.30pm, Sun 10am–1pm; Nov–March Mon–Sat 10am–4pm; ⓣ01643/702624). If you want to **stay** in Minehead, try the budget *Avill House* on Townsend Road (ⓣ01643/704370; no credit cards; ❶), a short walk from the seafront past the tourist office; or 100 yards further up on the same road, the more comfortable *Kildare Lodge* (ⓣ01643/702009; no credit cards; ❸), a reconstructed Tudor inn designed by a pupil of Lutyens. There's a **youth hostel** a couple of miles southeast, outside the village of Alcombe (ⓣ01643/702595; closed Sept–March), in a secluded combe on the edge of Exmoor.

Dunster

As well as being the start of the South West Coast Path (see box above), Minehead is a terminus for the **West Somerset Railway**, which curves eastwards into the Quantocks as far as Bishops Lydeard (see p.421). The Minehead area's major attraction, the old village of **DUNSTER**, is about a mile from the line's first stop, three miles inland. Dunster's main street is dominated by the towers and turrets of its **Castle** (April–Sept Mon–Wed, Sat & Sun 11am–5pm; Oct Mon–Wed, Sat & Sun 11am–4pm; grounds daily: April–Sept 10am–5pm; Oct–March 11am–4pm; £6, grounds only £3; NT). Most of its fortifications were demolished after the Civil War, after which time the castle became something of an architectural showpiece, and Victorian restoration has made it more like a Rhineland Schloss than a Norman stronghold.

On a tour of the castle you can see various portraits of the Luttrells, owners of the house for six hundred years before the National Trust took over in the

1970s; a bedroom once occupied by Charles I; a fine seventeenth-century carved staircase; and a richly decorated banqueting hall. The grounds include terraced gardens and riverside walks – and drama productions are periodically staged here in the summer (call ☎01985/843601 for details). The nearby hill-top tower is a folly, **Conygar Tower**, dating from 1776.

Despite the influx of seasonal visitors, Dunster village preserves relics of its wool-making heyday; the octagonal **Yarn Market**, in the High Street below the castle, dates from 1609, while the three-hundred-year-old **water mill** at the end of Mill Lane is still used commercially for milling the various grains which go to make the flour and muesli sold in the shop (April–Oct daily 10.30am–5pm; £2.20; NT) – the café, overlooking its riverside garden, is a good spot for lunch. For somewhere to **stay**, try *The Gables*, 33 High St (☎01643/821496; no smoking; ❸), which has rooms under the eaves overlooking the Yarn Market. There's a **visitor centre** at the top of Dunster Steep by the main car park (Easter–Oct daily 10am–5pm; Nov–Easter Sat & Sun 11am–3pm; ☎01643/821835).

Porlock

The real enticement of **PORLOCK**, six miles west of Minehead, is its extraordinary position in a deep hollow, cupped on three sides by the hog-backed hills of Exmoor. The thatch-and-cob houses and dripping charm of the village's long main street have led to invasions of tourists, some of whom are also drawn by the place's literary links. According to Coleridge's own less than reliable testimony, it was a "man from Porlock" who broke the opium trance in which he was composing *Kubla Khan*, while the High Street's beamed *Ship Inn* prides itself on featuring prominently in the Exmoor romance *Lorna Doone* and, in real life, having sheltered the poet Robert Southey, who staggered in rain-soaked after an Exmoor ramble.

Porlock's **tourist office** is at West End, High St (Easter–Oct Mon–Sat 10am–5pm, Sun 10am–1pm; Nov–Easter Mon–Fri & Sun 10am–1pm; ☎01643/863150, ◉www.porlock.co.uk). The best **accommodation** in town is on the High Street, where the Victorian *Lorna Doone Hotel* (☎01643/862404; ❷) offers three sizes of rooms, all with private bath and TV. Further down, *The Cottage* is smaller and quainter, but a little pricier (☎01643/862687; ❸). Both *The Cottage* and the *Lorna Doone* serve snacks, meals and teas – as does *Lowerbourne House*, a tearoom and bookshop with useful local information, and the yellow-walled *Whortleberry*, both also on the High Street. Porlock has a central **campsite**, *Sparkhayes Farm* (☎01643/862470; closed Nov–March), signposted off the main road near the *Lorna Doone*.

If you walk two miles west over the reclaimed marshland, you'll come to the tiny harbour of **PORLOCK WEIR**, which gives little inkling of its former role as a hard-working port trafficking with Wales. It's a peaceful spot, giving onto a bay that enjoys the mildest climate on Exmoor. An easy two-mile stroll west from here along the South West Coast Path brings you to **St Culbone**, a tiny church – claimed to be the country's smallest – sheltered within woods once inhabited by a leper colony.

Lynton and Lynmouth

West from Porlock, the road climbs 1350ft in less than three miles, though cyclists and drivers might prefer the gentler and more scenic toll-road alternative to the direct uphill trawl (cars £2, bikes 50p). Nine miles along the coast, on the Devon side of the county line, the Victorian resort of **LYNTON** perches above a lofty gorge with splendid views over the sea. Almost com-

Walks from Lynton and Lynmouth

As well as the draws of the coastal path, there are several popular walks inland in this region. The one-and-a-half-mile tramp to **Watersmeet**, for example, follows the East Lyn River to where it is joined by Hoar Oak Water, a tranquil spot transformed into a roaring torrent after a bout of rain. From the fishing lodge here – now owned by the National Trust and open as a café and shop in summer – you can branch off on a range of less-trodden paths, such as the three-quarters-of-a-mile route south to **Hillsford Bridge**, the confluence of Hoar Oak and Farley Water.

North of Watersmeet, a path climbs up **Countisbury Hill** and the higher **Butter Hill** (nearly 1000ft) giving riveting views of Lynton, Lynmouth and the north Devon coast, and there is also a track leading to the lighthouse at **Foreland Point**, close to the coastal path. East from Lynmouth you can reach the point via a fine sheltered shingle beach at the foot of Countisbury Hill – one of a number of tiny coves that are easily accessible on either side of the estuary.

From Lynton, an undemanding expedition takes you west along the North Walk, a mile-long path leading to the **Valley of the Rocks**, a steeply curved heathland dominated by rugged rock formations. At the far end of the valley, herds of wild goats range free, as they have done here for centuries.

pletely cut off from the rest of the country for most of its history, the village struck lucky during the Napoleonic wars, when frustrated Grand Tourists – unable to visit their usual continental haunts – discovered in Lynton a domestic piece of Swiss landscape. Coleridge and Hazlitt trudged over to Lynton from the Quantocks, but the greatest spur to the village's popularity came with the publication in 1869 of R.D. Blackmore's Exmoor melodrama *Lorna Doone*, a book based on the outlaw clans who inhabited these parts in the seventeenth century. Since then the area has become indelibly associated with the swash-buckling romance.

Lynton's imposing **town hall** on Lee Road epitomizes the Victorian –Edwardian accent of the village. It was the gift of publisher George Newnes, who also donated the nearby **cliff railway** connecting Lynton with Lynmouth (March to mid-July & mid-Sept to Nov daily 9am–7pm; mid-July to mid-Sept daily 9am–10pm; £1). The device is an ingenious hydraulic system, its two carriages counterbalanced by water tanks, which fill up at the top, descend, and empty their load at the bottom.

Five hundred feet below, **LYNMOUTH** lies at the junction and estuary of the East and West Lyn rivers, in a spot described by Gainsborough as "the most delightful place for a landscape painter this country can boast". The picturesque scene was shattered in August 1952 when Lynmouth was almost washed away by floodwaters coming off Exmoor, a disaster of which there are many reminders around the village. Having recovered its calm, Lynmouth is only ruffled now by the summer crowds, though nothing could compromise the village's unique location. Shelley spent his honeymoon here with his 16-year-old bride Harriet Westbrook, making time in his nine-week sojourn to write his polemical *Queen Mab* – two different houses claim to have been the Shelleys' love-nest. R.D. Blackmore, author of *Lorna Doone*, stayed in **Mars Hill**, the oldest part of the town, its creeper-covered cottages framing the cliffs behind the Esplanade. In summer, the harbour offers boat trips and fishing expeditions, and you can explore the **Glen Lyn Gorge** up the wooded valley with its walks and waterfalls and displays of the uses and dangers of water power (daily 9am–dusk; exhibition Easter–Oct 10am–dusk; £3) – this was the course taken by the destructive floods of 1952.

Practicalities

Lynton's **tourist office** is in the town hall (Easter–Oct Mon–Sat 9.30am–5.30pm, Sun 9.30am–5pm; Nov–Easter Mon–Sat 10am–4pm; ☎01598/752225 or 0845/458 3775), while Lynmouth has a **National Park Visitor Centre** on the seafront (Easter–Oct daily 10am–5pm; Nov, Dec & Feb–Easter Sat & Sun 11am–3pm; ☎01598/752509).

Lynton has the better choice of **B&Bs** at the cheaper end of the market, among them the Victorian *The Turret*, 33 Lee Rd (☎01598/753284; ❶), one of the least expensive options of the row of accommodation lining this street, built by the same engineer who built the cliff railway. It's run by a friendly Scot and has six spacious rooms, four of them en suite including the turreted room at the top. Also cheap, but more central, is *St Vincent* (☎01598/752244, ⓔkeen-stvincent@lineone.net; ❶), a whitewashed, Georgian house on Castle Hill with spacious bedrooms and a garden. The *Lynhurst*, Lyn Way (☎01598/752241, ⓔlynhurst@demon.co.uk; ❸), is farther out from the centre, but has striking views over the valley. There is a **youth hostel** (☎01598/753237; closed Nov–Easter) in a homely Victorian house about one mile inland from Lynton's centre, and signposted off Lynbridge Road. Intimate **evening meals** are served at *Lily May's*, 1 Castle Hill, and you can pick up wholefoods and quality picnic fare from *Gourmet Organix* at 4 Queen St.

In **Lynmouth**, the most inspiring place to stay is *Harbour Point*, a **B&B** right on the harbour at 1 The Esplanade, (☎01598/752321; no credit cards; ❷; closed Oct–April) – the slightly pricier Turret Room and the Balcony Room are the best choices here. Other good options include the posh *Shelley's Hotel*, right next to the Glen Lyn Gorge (☎01598/753219; ❹), where you can sleep in the room supposed to have been occupied by the poet – he apparently left without paying his bill – and the *Rock House Hotel*, Harbourside (☎01598/753508, ⓔdave@rockh.freeserve.co.uk; ❸), which also serves scones in the garden, snacks at the bar and meals in its **restaurant**. The *Village Inn*, Lynmouth St, does inexpensive lunches and dinners, including vegetarian options, though you'll find better food at the traditional and fairly expensive *Rising Sun*, on the Harbourside, and at the nearby *Bath Hotel*, which charges £16 for a four-course dinner in its no-smoking restaurant.

From April to October you can take a **boat trip** with Exmoor Coast Boat Cruises (☎01598/753207) from Lynmouth harbour, an excellent way to view the bird-life on the cliffs; excursions range from a one hour trip west along the coast (£5) to a four-hour sail to Porlock Weir and back (£7.50). **Bikes** can be rented from Biketrail at 19 Queen St (☎01598/753987, ⓦwww.biketrail.co.uk).

Cornwall

When D.H. Lawrence wrote that being in **Cornwall** was "like being at a window and looking out of England", he wasn't just thinking of its geographical extremity. Virtually unaffected by the Roman conquest, Cornwall was for centuries the last haven for a **Celtic culture** elsewhere eradicated by the Saxons –

a land where princes communed with Breton troubadours, where chroniclers and scribes composed the epic tales of Arthurian heroism, and where itinerant monks from Welsh and Irish monasteries disseminated an elemental and visionary Christianity. Primitive granite crosses and a crop of Celtic saints remain as traces of this formative period, and though the Cornish language had ebbed away by the eighteenth century, it is recalled in Celtic place names that in many cases have grown more exotic as they have become corrupted over time.

Another strand of Cornwall's folkloric character comes from the **smugglers** who thrived here right up until the last century, exploiting the sheltered creeks and hidden anchorages of the southern coasts. For many fishing villages, such as Polperro and Mousehole, contraband provided an important secondary income, as did the looting of the ships that regularly came to grief on the reefs and rocks. Further distinguishing it from its neighbour, Cornwall has also had a strong **industrial economy**, based mainly on the mining of **copper** and **tin** in the north, centred on the towns of Redruth and St Agnes, and in the south on the deposits of **china clay**, which are still being mined in the area around St Austell.

Nowadays, of course, Cornwall's most flourishing industry is tourism. The repercussions of the holiday business on Cornwall have been uneven, for instance shamefully defacing **Land's End** with a clutter of pseudo-historical twaddle but leaving Cornwall's other great promontory, **Lizard Point**, untainted. All the stops are pulled out in the thronged resorts of **Falmouth** and **Newquay**, the West's chief surfing centre, though the effects of mass tourism have been more destructive in smaller, quainter places, such as **Mevagissey**, **Polperro** and **Padstow**, whose genuine charms are hard to make out in full season. Other villages, such as **Charlestown, Port Isaac** and **Boscastle**, are hardly touched, however, and you couldn't wish for anything more remote than **Bodmin Moor**, a tract of wilderness in the heart of Cornwall – and even **Tintagel**, site of what is fondly known as King Arthur's castle, has preserved its sense of desolation. Near **St Austell**, the spectacular and high-profile **Eden Project**, located in an abandoned clay pit, has pointed the way to a less destructive and exploitative form of crowd-pulling, while other places – such as **St Ives**, **Fowey** and **Bude** – have reached a happy compromise with the seasonal influx, or else are saved from saturation by sheer distance, as is the case with the **Isles of Scilly**. Throughout the county, though, it only requires a shift of a few miles to escape the crowds, and there are enough good beaches around for everyone to find a space.

The best way to reach the quietest spots is along the **South West Coast Path** (see box on p.473), but a car is almost indispensable for anyone wanting to see a lot in a short time, as the system of public transport is limited to a couple of **rail** branch lines off the main line to Penzance and a thin network of local bus services.

From Looe to Veryan Bay

The southeast strip of the Cornish coast from Looe to Veryan Bay holds a string of medieval harbour towns tarnished by various degrees of commercialization, but there are also a few spots where you can experience the best of Cornwall, including some wonderful coastline. The main rail stop is **St Austell**, the capital of Cornwall's china clay industry, though there is a branch line connecting nearby **Par** with the north coast at Newquay. To the east of St

△ Surfers, Bude Beach

Austell Bay, the touristy **Polperro** and **Looe** are easily accessible by bus from Plymouth, and there's a rail link to Looe from Liskeard. The estuary town of **Fowey**, in a niche of Cornwall closely associated with the author Daphne Du Maurier, is most easily reached by bus from St Austell and Par, as is **Mevagissey**, to the west.

Looe and Polperro

LOOE was drawing crowds as early as 1800, when the first "bathing-machines" were wheeled out, but the arrival of the railway in 1879 was what really packed its beaches. Though Looe now touts itself as something of a shark-fishing centre, most people come here for the sand, the handiest stretch being the beach in front of East Looe – the busier half of the river-divided town. Away from the river mouth, you'll find a cleaner spot to swim a mile eastwards at **Millendreath**. Most of Looe's attractions are in boating and bathing, and in summer, you'll find a range of **boating and fishing trips** advertised on the long quayside, spread along the river parallel to the main Fore Street. If the weather's bad, you could always shelter in the **Old Guildhall Museum** (May–Sept Mon–Fri & Sun 11.30am–4.30pm; £1), a diverse collection of maritime models and exhibits, though none so interesting as the building itself, a fifteenth-century construction preserving its prisoners' cells and raised magistrates' benches.

East Looe's **tourist office** is at the Guildhall on Fore Street (Easter & May to mid-Sept daily 10am–5pm; April & mid-Sept to Oct daily 10am–2pm; ☎01503/262072). There's plenty of **accommodation** here: for estuary views, try the *Dolphin Hotel* (☎01503/262578; no credit cards; ❷), but for more character, head for *Osborne House*, a converted cottage in Lower Chapel Street (☎01503/262970; ❷; closed Nov & Jan), or the chintzier *Sea Breeze*, a three-storey B&B further up the same street (☎01503/263131, ✉johnjenkin@ sbgh.freeserve.co.uk; ❶); both are close to the beach and harbour. *Osborne House* also has a moderately priced **restaurant;** other places to eat include the *Cellar Wine Bar* for inexpensive lunches on the harbourside, and, opposite on Buller Quay, the posher *Trawlers* (☎01503/263593; closed Sun), whose French-inspired menu concentrates mainly on lobster and other seafood, at moderately expensive prices. For plainer food, try the inexpensive *Golden Guinea* on Fore Street, a seventeenth-century building that does a brisk trade in staple seaside meals as well as cream teas.

Looe is linked by hourly buses (less frequent on Sun & in winter) with neighbouring **POLPERRO**, a smaller and quainter place, but with a similar feel. From the bus stop and car park at the top of the village, it's a five- or ten-minute walk alongside the River Pol to the pretty harbour. The surrounding cliffs and the tightly packed houses rising on each side of the stream have an undeniable charm, and the tangle of lanes is little changed since the village's heyday of smuggling and pilchard fishing, but the "discovery" of Polperro has almost ruined it, and its straggling main street – the Coombes – is now an unbroken row of tourist shops and fast-food outlets.

Polperro's best places to **stay** include *The House on Props*, Talland St (☎01503 /272310; no credit cards; ❷), which, as the name suggests, is propped up over the river; the next-door *Talland House*, which has two simple en-suite cottage-style rooms (☎01503/273176; no credit cards; ❶); and the relatively secluded *Old Mill House*, an agreeable old pub on Mill Hill offering eight comfortable rooms (☎01503/272362, ⓦwww.oldmillhouse.i12.com; ❸). There's a separate **restaurant** at the *Old Mill*, though you'll find better quality fare at the non-

smoking *Kitchen* on the Coombes (℡01503/272780), especially if you're a vegetarian or seafood fan. Also on the main road, the *Plantation Café* provides
cream teas and snacks and has some outdoor seating (closed Sat).

Fowey and around

The ten miles west from Polperro to Polruan are among the best stretches of
the coastal path in south Cornwall, giving access to some beautiful secluded
sand beaches. There are frequent ferries across the River Fowey from Polruan,
giving a fine view of the quintessential Cornish port of **FOWEY** (pronounced
"Foy"), a cascade of neat, pale terraces at the mouth of one of the peninsula's
greatest rivers. The major port on the county's south coast in the fourteenth
century, Fowey finally became so ambitious that it provoked Edward IV to strip
the town of its military capability, though it continued to thrive commercially, coming into its own as the leading port for china clay shipments in the last
century. In addition to the bulkier freighters sailing from wharves north of the
town, the harbour today is crowded with trawlers and yachts, giving the town
a brisk, purposeful character lacking in many of Cornwall's south-coast ports.

Fowey's steep layout centres on the church of **St Fimbarrus**, a distinctive fifteenth-century construction replacing a church that was sacked by the French.
The church marks the traditional end of the ancient **Saints' Way footpath**
from Padstow, linking the north and south Cornish coasts (see p.510). Beside
St Fimbarrus, the **Literary Centre** on South Street is a small exhibition
including a twelve-minute video of Daphne Du Maurier's life and work (daily
10am–5pm; free), while behind the church stands **Place House**, an extravagance belonging to the local Treffry family, with a Victorian Gothic tower
grafted onto the fifteenth- and sixteenth-century fortified building. Below the
church, the **Ship Inn**, sporting some fine Elizabethan panelling and plaster
ceilings, was originally home to the Rashleighs – a recurring name in the
annals of this region – and held the local Roundhead HQ during the Civil
War. From here, Fore Street, Lostwithiel Street and the Esplanade fan out, the
Esplanade leading to a footpath that gives access to some splendid walks
around the coast. Past the remains of a blockhouse that once supported a
defensive chain hung across the river's mouth, the small beach of
Readymoney Cove is soon reached – so-called either because it was where
smugglers buried their ill-gotten gains, or because it was where the flotsam of
shipwrecks came ashore. Close by stand the ruins of **St Catherine's Castle**,
built by Thomas Treffry on the orders of Henry VIII, and offering fine views
across the estuary.

You don't have to take on the entire thirty miles of the Saints' Way to get the
flavour of this trail, though if you prefer a circular route you can try the **Hall
Walk**, a scenic four-mile hike north of Fowey. More details are available from
the tourist office, though it's simple enough: cross the river on the car ferry (at
the car park north of town) to **Bodinnick**, walk downstream on the other
side, crossing the footbridge over the narrow creek of Pont Pill, then take the
passenger ferry back from Polruan. The route passes a memorial to "Q", alias
Sir Arthur Quiller-Couch, who lived on Fowey's Esplanade between 1892 and
1944, and whose writings helped popularize the place he called "Troy Town".
Fans of Daphne Du Maurier can join a guided walk (summer only) around
scenes described in her books – contact the tourist office for details.

Beyond the west bank ferry stage you come to **Golant**, a riverside hamlet a
little more than a mile from the Iron Age fort of **Castle Dore**, which features
in Arthurian romance as the residence of King Mark of Cornwall, husband of

Iseult.You can also get to the fort from Fowey on bus #24, though there is still a ten-minute walk from the stop on the crossroads.

LOSTWITHIEL, three miles further upriver (train from Par, or bus or train from St Austell), is an old market town on the lowest bridging point of the Fowey. It's an appealing mixture of Georgian houses and medieval passageways, with a peculiar, Breton-inspired octagonal spire on St Bartholomew's church. The town lies below the watchful eye of **Restormel Castle** (April–Sept daily 10am–6pm; Oct daily 10am–5pm; £1.80; EH), a shale-built shell of a circular keep that crowns a hill a mile or so north. It's a peaceful, panoramic spot, which last saw service when Royalist forces prised it out of the hands of the Earl of Essex's Parliamentarian army in 1644.

Practicalities

Separated from eastern routes by its river, Fowey is most accessible by twice-hourly #24 **buses** from St Austell (hourly on Sun). Travellers to or from the west might make use of the **ferry** linking Fowey with Mevagissey (see p.483), which operates several times daily between May and October, (35min; £7.50 return). There is a small **tourist office** in the town's post office on Custom House Hill (May–Sept Mon–Fri 9am–5.30pm, Sat 9am–5pm, Sun 10am–5pm; Oct–April Mon–Sat 9am–5.30pm; ☎01726/833616). All of the central pubs offer **B&B**; on Lostwithiel Street, try the *Ship* (☎01726/833230; ②) or the *Safe Harbour* (☎01726/833379; no credit cards; ②), both offering en-suite rooms and parking. At 6 Fore St is the *Dwelling House* (☎01726/833662; ①), with three en-suite rooms, the best of them in the attic. From The Esplanade, climb up Daglands Road to *Seahorses* at 14 St Fimbarrus Rd (☎01726/833148, ✉jandh@globalnet.co.uk; no smoking; no credit cards; ①; closed Oct–April), which provides stylish rooms, bathrobes and offers Dutch pancakes for breakfast, and has a banjo-playing owner. Outside Fowey, *Coombe Farm* (☎01726/833123; no credit cards; ②) provides perfect rural isolation just twenty minutes' walk from town, at the end of a lane off the B3269 – and there's a bathing area just 300yds away. There is a **youth hostel** outside Golant at *Penquite House*, a Georgian mansion with views over the valley (☎01726 /833507, ✉golant@yha.org.uk; closed Nov–Jan). The nearest **campsite** is at *Yeate Farm* (☎01726/870256; closed Nov–Feb), on the eastern bank of the river, three-quarters of a mile up from the Bodinnick ferry crossing.

Fowey has some good seafood **restaurants**; among the best is *Ellis's* at 3 the Esplanade (☎01726/832359), specializing in lobster, and *Food For Thought* on the quay, which offers a two-course fixed-price menu for £12.95 on weekdays (☎01726/832221) – both are quite formal, expensive places. The area is also well provided with good **pubs**, some of which can be sampled on walkabouts, such as Golant's *Fisherman's Arms*, the *Old Ferry Inn* at Bodinnick and Polruan's excellent *Lugger Inn*. The *Old Ferry* also has comfortable rooms (☎01726 /870237; ②, ④ for a room with a view).

St Austell and the Eden Project

It was the discovery of china clay, or kaolin, in the downs to the north of **ST AUSTELL** that spurred the town's growth in the eighteenth century. An essential ingredient in the production of porcelain, kaolin had until then only been produced in northern China, where a high ridge, or *kao-lin*, was the sole known source of the raw material. Still a vital part of Cornwall's economy, the clay is now mostly exported for use in the manufacture of paper, as well as paint and medicines. The conical spoil heaps left by the mines are a feature of the local landscape, especially on Hensbarrow Downs to the north, the great green and white mounds making an eerie sight.

A disused clay pit four miles northeast of St Austell holds the newest and highest-profile of Cornwall's attractions, the **Eden Project** (daily: March–Oct 10am–6pm; Nov–Feb 10am–4.30pm; £9.50; ⓦ www.edenproject.com), reachable on bus #T9 from St Austell station and #T10 (summer only) from Newquay, and signposted on most roads in the area. Occupying a 160-foot-deep crater whose awesome scale only reveals itself once you have passed the entrance at its lip, the project showcases the diversity of the planet's plant-life in an imaginative, sometimes wacky, but refreshingly ungimmicky style. The whole site is stunningly landscaped with an array of various crops and flower beds, but at centre stage are the vast geodesic "biomes", or conservatories made up of eco-friendly Teflon-coated, hexagonal panels. One cluster holds groves of olive and citrus trees, cacti and other plants more usually found in the warm, temperate zones of the Mediterranean, southern Africa and southwestern USA, while the larger group contains plants from the tropics, including teak and mahogany trees (which have yet to reach a respectable height), and there's a waterfall and river gushing through – things can get pretty steamy here, and you can take cool refuge in an air-conditioned bunker halfway along the course. Equally impressive are the external grounds (described as "Picasso meeting the Aztecs"), where plantations of bamboo, tea, hops, hemp and tobacco are interspersed with brilliant swathes of flowers. The whole "living theatre" presents a constantly changing spectacle, and should ideally be visited in different seasons. Allow at least half a day for a full exploration, but arrive early to avoid congestion. There are timed "story-telling" sessions, a lawn-carpeted arena where Celtic and other music is played, and good food on hand.

Charletown

St Austell's nearest link to the sea is at **CHARLESTOWN**, an easy downhill walk from the centre of town. This unassuming and unspoilt port is named after the entrepreneur Charles Rashleigh, who in 1791 began work on the harbour in what was then a small fishing community two miles south of St Austell, widening its streets to accommodate the clay wagons daily passing through. The wharves are still used, loading clay onto vessels that appear oversized beside the tiny jetties. Behind the harbour, the **Shipwreck Museum** (March–Oct daily 10am–6pm; £4.45) is entered through tunnels once used to convey the clay to the docks, and shows a good collection of photos and relics as well as tableaux of historical scenes.

On each side of the dock the coarse sand and stone **beaches** have small rock pools, above which cliff walks lead around St Austell Bay. Eastwards, you soon arrive at overdeveloped **Carlyon Bay**, whose main resort is **Par**. The beaches here get clogged with clay – the best swimming is to be found by pressing on to the sheltered crescent of **Polkerris**. The easternmost limit of St Austell Bay is marked by **Gribbin Head**, near which stands Menabilly House, where Daphne Du Maurier lived for 24 years – it was the model for the "Manderley" of *Rebecca*. The house is not open to the public, but you can walk down to Polridmouth Cove, where Rebecca met her watery end.

Practicalities

Trains on the main London–Penzance line serve St Austell, with most services also stopping at Par, which is also connected to Newquay on the north coast. Western National run the half-hourly to hourly **bus** service #24 linking St Austell, Charlestown, Par and Polkerris.

Charlestown has two really attractive places **to stay**: *T'Gallants* (☎01726
/70203; ❷), a smart Georgian B&B at the back of the harbour where cream
teas are served in the garden, and *Broad Meadow House*, behind the Shipwreck
Centre on Quay Road (☎01726/76636, ✉BestTribe@ tinyworld.co.uk; no
credit cards; ❶), which has one beautifully furnished bedroom, a large sitting
room and choice breakfasts. Behind *T'Gallants*, the *Rashleigh Arms* offers real
ale and a range of **food**, though the most highly commended **pub** in the area
is the *Rashleigh Inn* at Polkerris. The best **campsite** in St Austell Bay is *Carlyon
Bay* (☎01726/812735, ✉jeffst@globalnet.co.uk; closed Nov–March), at
Bethesda, near the beach at Carlyon Bay.

Mevagissey to Veryan Bay

MEVAGISSEY was once known for the construction of fast vessels, used for
carrying contraband as well as pilchards. Today the tiny port might display a
few stacks of lobster pots, but the real business is tourism, and in summer the
maze of back streets is saturated with day-trippers, converging on the inner
harbour and overflowing onto the large sand beach at **Pentewan** a mile to the
north, despite the poor water quality.

A couple of miles north of Mevagissey lie the **Lost Gardens of Heligan**
(daily: late March to late Oct 10am–6pm, last entry 4.30pm; late Oct to late
March 10am–5pm, last entry 3.30pm; £5.50; ⓦwww.heligan.com), a fascinating resurrection of a Victorian garden which had fallen into neglect and was
rescued from a ten-foot covering of brambles by Tim Smit, the visionary instigator of the Eden Project (see opposite). The abundant palm trees, giant
Himalayan rhododendrons, immaculate vinery and glasshouses scattered about
all look as if they've been transplanted from warmer climes; a boardwalk takes
you past interconnecting ponds, through a jungle and under a canopy of bamboo and ferns down to the Lost Valley, where there are lakes, wild flower meadows and leafy oak, beech and chestnut rides. You can get here on #26 and #26a
buses from St Austell and Mevagissey.

Past the headland to the south of Mevagissey, the small sandy cove of
Portmellon retains little of its boat-building activities but is freer of tourists.
Further still, **GORRAN HAVEN** was formerly a crab-fishing village but now
looks merely suburban, though it has a neat rock-and-sand beach, and a footpath that winds round to the even more attractive **Vault Beach**, half a mile
south. South of here juts the most striking headland on Cornwall's southern
coast, **Dodman Point**, cause of many a wreck and topped by a stark granite
cross built by a local parson as a seamark in 1896. The promontory holds the
substantial remains of an Iron Age fort, with an earthwork bulwark cutting
right across the point.

Curving away to the west, the elegant parabola of **Veryan Bay** is barely
touched by commercialism. Just west of Dodman Point lies one of Cornwall's
most beautiful coves, **Hemmick Beach**, an excellent swimming spot with
rocky outcrops affording a measure of privacy. Visually even more impressive is
Porthluney Cove, a crescent of sand whose centrepiece is the battlemented
Caerhays Castle (mid-March to mid-April Mon–Fri 2–4pm; gardens mid-
March to mid-May Mon–Fri 10am–4pm; house £3.50, garden £3.50, combined ticket £6), built in 1808 by John Nash and surrounded by beautiful gardens which are open in spring and on occasional charity days only.

A little farther on, the minuscule and whitewashed **Portloe** is fronted by
jagged black rocks that throw up fountains of seaspray, giving it a good, end-
of-the-road kind of atmosphere. Sequestered inland, **VERYAN** has a pretty
village green and pond, but is best known for its curious circular white houses

built in the 19th century by one Reverend Jeremiah Trist. A lane from Veryan leads down to one of the cleanest swimming spots on Cornwall's southern coast, **Pendower Beach**. Two-thirds of a mile long and backed by dunes, Pendower joins with the neighbouring **Carne Beach** at low tide to create a long sandy continuum.

Practicalities

From St Austell's train station, **buses** #26 and #26A leave hourly for Mevagissey, sometimes continuing to Gorran Haven. Veryan and Portloe are reachable on #51 from Truro. Right in the heart of Mevagissey, the best **accommodation** option is the fifteenth-century *Fountain Inn* (☎01726 /842320, ℮fountain_meva@hotmail.com; ❷), on Cliff Street, off East Quay; alternatively try *Lawn House*, 1 Church Lane (☎01726/842754; no credit cards; ❷; phone ahead Nov–Easter), a lovely, spacious Queen Anne construction with candelabra and brass beds. You might appreciate the coast better by staying in Portmellon, where the weathered old *Rising Sun Inn* (☎01726/843235; ❸; closed Oct to mid-March) confronts the sea. In Gorran Haven, the well-situated *Llawnroc Inn* (☎01726/843461; ❶) is the only budget option; all rooms are en suite. The nearest **youth hostel** (☎01726/843234; closed Nov–March) is in a former farmhouse at **Boswinger**, a remote spot half a mile from Hemmick Beach. Difficult to reach without your own transport, it's about a mile from the bus stop at Gorran Church Town, served infrequently by some #26 buses. Boswinger also has a **campsite**, *Seaview* (☎01726/843425, ⓦwww.seaviewinter national.com; closed Oct–Easter), with, as the name implies, a panoramic position overlooking Veryan Bay; it's popular, and not very big, so you'd be advised to book ahead in July and August. If you want to stay in **Veryan**, head for the *Elerkey Guest House* (☎01872/501261, ⓦwww.elerkey-guest-house.co.uk; ❷), an ex-farmhouse with a spacious garden and adjoining art gallery and coffee shop; it's the first on the left after the church. The *New Inn* serves pub meals and also provides B&B (☎01872/501362; ❷).

There's no shortage of **restaurants** in Mevagissey, most specializing in fish – for location you might try the large harbour-front *Shark's Fin Hotel*. The dainty *Alvorada* (closed Feb–Easter & Oct, plus weekdays Nov–Jan; ☎01726 /842254), one street back from West Quay at 2 Polkirt Hill, has seafood with a Portuguese slant, while the *Fountain Inn* and the *Ship Inn* on Fore Street both offer pub grub.

Truro, Falmouth and St Mawes

Lush tranquillity collides with frantic tourist activity around **Carrick Roads**, the complex estuary basin to the south of **Truro**, a stop on the main line to Penzance and the region's main centre for transport and accommodation. At the end of a branch line from Truro and at the mouth of the Carrick Roads, **Falmouth** is the major resort around here, and the site of one of Cornwall's mightiest castles, Pendennis. Its sister fort lies across the Carrick Roads in **St Mawes**, the main settlement on the **Roseland** peninsula, a luxuriant backwater of woods and sheltered creeks between the River Fal and the sea.

Truro

TRURO, seat of Cornwall's law courts and other county bureaucracies, has a distinctly small-scale provincial feel, even if its Georgian houses do reflect the prosperity that came with the tin-mining boom of the 1800s. Blurring the town's overall identity, its modern shopping centre stands alongside the powerful but chronologically confused **Cathedral**. Completed in 1910, this was the first Anglican cathedral to be built in England since St Paul's in London, but it incorporates part of the fabric of the old parish church that previously occupied the site. The airy interior's best feature is its neo-Gothic baptistry, complete with emphatically pointed arches and elaborate roof vaulting. To the right of the choir, St Mary's aisle is a relic of the original Perpendicular building, other fragments of which adorn the walls, including – in the north transept – a colourful Jacobean memorial to local Parliamentarian John Robartes and his wife.

Truro's other unmissable attraction is the **Royal Cornwall Museum** (Mon–Sat 10am–5pm; £3), housed in an elegant Georgian building on River Street. The exhibits include minerals, Celtic inscriptions and paintings by Cornish artists. In summer, passenger **ferries** depart four times daily from the quayside on a scenic river cruise to Falmouth (about £5.50 return).

Practicalities

Truro's **tourist office** is on Boscawen Street (Easter–May & Sept Mon–Fri 9am–5.30pm, Sat 9.30am–1pm; June–Aug Mon–Fri 9am–5.30pm, Sat 9.30am–5.30pm; Oct–Easter Mon–Fri 9am–5pm, Sat 9.30am–1pm; ☎01872/274555). Buses stop nearby at Lemon Quay, or near the train station on Richmond Hill. Best **accommodation** near the train station is the *Gables*, at the bottom of Station Road at 49 Treyew Rd (☎01872/242318; no credit cards; ➊), where all rooms have showers and shared WC; near the centre of town, the *Bay Tree* is a restored Georgian house halfway between the station and the centre at 28 Ferris Town (☎01872/240274; ➊). Much of Truro's inexpensive accommodation is on or around the pleasant Lemon Street: try *Patmos*, 8 Burley Close, off Barrack Lane, where Lemon Street meets Falmouth Road, with views over the river (☎01872/278018; no-smoking; no credit cards; ➊); or the B&B at 4 Upper Lemon Villas (☎01872/278018; no-smoking; no credit cards; ➊), one of a row of Georgian houses at the top of Lemon Street. On the other side of the river, to the northwest of town, there are several more guest houses on Tregolls Road, including the elegant *Conifers* at no. 36 (☎01872/279925; ➋). The nearest **campsite** is *Carnon Downs*, three miles outside Truro on the A39 Falmouth Road (☎01872/862283, ⓦ www.carnon-downs .co.uk; closed Nov–March).

A good selection of Truro's **restaurants** lie on or around Kenwyn Street, including *Number Ten* at no. 10, where you can choose wholesome dishes from around the world at inexpensive prices (☎01872/272363); teas, coffees and healthy fruit drinks are on the menu, or bring your own booze. There's an outdoor eating area round the back, as there is at the *Feast*, 15 Kenwyn St, which cooks up excellent wholefoods to eat in or take away, and offers a choice of Belgian beers (daytime only; closed Sun). Elsewhere in town, *Saffron* at 5 Quay St offers inexpensive brunches and an especially good-value pre-theatre menu (☎01872/263771; closed Mon eve & all Sun), while *Pizza Express* on Boscawen Street is housed in the imposing old Coinage Hall, which sports carpets on the walls alongside portraits of George II and other notables. On the corner of Frances and Castle streets, *Oliver's* is an award-winning restaurant with moderately expensive fixed-price menus (☎01872 /273028; closed Sun). The adjoining *Wig and Pen* is a decent **pub** with bar food, real ale and jazz on Wednesdays and Fridays; next door, the *Globe Inn* also serves hot snacks.

Falmouth

The construction of Pendennis Castle on the southern point of Carrick Roads in the sixteenth century prepared the ground for the growth of **FAL-MOUTH**, then no more than a fishing village. The building of its deepwater harbour was proposed a century later by Sir John Killigrew, and Falmouth's prosperity was assured when in 1689 it became chief base of the fast Falmouth Packets, which sped mail to the Americas. The port has maintained its allure for sailors but its character has become submerged beneath the waves of tourist traffic, attracted to the lush beaches to the south of town. Recent years have seen the growth of a local arts scene, however, and the castle alone is reason enough to brave the hard sell.

The long **High Street** and its continuations Market and Church streets are crammed with humdrum bars and cafés, though at the southern end, Arwenack Street does have the Tudor remains of the Killigrews' **Arwenack House** (closed to the public). The peculiar granite pyramid standing opposite the house, built in 1737, is probably intended to commemorate the local family, though its exact significance has never been clear. The dynasty's most eminent member was Thomas Killigrew, an indifferent Restoration dramatist who was also manager of the king's company of actors. The founder of London's Theatre Royal in Drury Lane, Charles II's former companion-in-exile obtained permission to use female actors for the first time on stage – thereby introducing Nell Gwyn to the king's notice. Apart from this, the centre of town only offers a clamber up the precipitous 111 steps of **Jacob's Ladder** from the Moor, the old town's main square, to give a bird's-eye view of the harbour. From the Prince of Wales Pier, below the Moor, frequent **ferries** leave for St Mawes, accompanied in summer by boats touring the local estuaries.

Falmouth's links with the sea are explored at the **Maritime Museum** at Bell's Court, at the Moor end of the High Street (Easter–Oct daily 10am–5pm; Oct–Easter Mon–Sat 10am–3pm; £2.20), which tracks the evolution of boat design with a focus on traditional local boat-building and repairing skills. It's a rather lacklustre collection at present, but will be revitalized when it transfers in 2002 to a purpose-built exhibition centre in a waterfront setting on Arwenack Street, with exhibits from all over the country alongside an education centre and a restaurant.

Standing sentinel at the tip of the promontory that separates Carrick Roads from Falmouth Bay, **Pendennis Castle** (daily: April–June & Sept 10am–6pm; July & Aug 9am–6pm; Oct 10am–5pm; Nov–March 10am–4pm; £3.80; EH) shows little evidence of its five-month siege by the Parliamentarians during the Civil War, which ended only when half its defenders had died and the rest had been starved into submission. Though this is a less-refined contemporary of the castle at St Mawes, its site wins hands down, facing right out to sea on its own pointed peninsula, the stout ramparts offering the best all-round views of Carrick Roads and Falmouth Bay. In August, the castle grounds stay open late for concerts and other events.

Round Pendennis Point, south of the centre, stretches a long sandy bay with various **beaches** backed by expensive hotels. If you wanted to swim, the best spot is from **Swanpool Beach**, accessible by cliff path from the more popular **Gyllyngvase Beach** – or walk a couple of miles farther on to **Maenporth**, from where there are some fine cliff-top walks.

Practicalities

Falmouth's **tourist office** is off the Moor, on Killigrew Street (Easter–June & Sept Mon–Thurs & Sat 9.30am–5.30pm, Fri 9am–4.45pm; July & Aug also

Sun 10am–2pm; Oct–Easter Mon–Thurs 9am–1pm & 2–5pm, Fri 9am–1pm & 2–4.45pm; ☎01326/312300, ⓦwww.falmouth-sw-cornwall.co.uk). Most of the town's **accommodation** is south, near the train station and beach area: *Brandywine Lodge*, 3 Bay View Crescent (☎01326/318709; no credit cards; ❶), a cosy cottage just off Castle Drive, represents excellent value, or try the *Melvill House Hotel*, 52 Melvill Rd (☎01326/316645; no credit cards; ❷), run by a Franco-Scottish couple who also provide dinners by prior arrangement. If you prefer to be near the centre, you can't do better than the *Anvenack Hotel* at 27 Arwenack St (☎01326/311185; no credit cards; ❶). Expect to pay more for places nearer the beaches: *Gyllyngvase House Hotel* is a staid but comfortable choice on Gyllyngvase Road (☎01326/312956; ❸), two minutes from the sea, with a restaurant and views from two of its rooms, and *Chellowdene* (☎01326 /314950; no credit cards; ❸; closed Oct–April) on the parallel Gyllyngvase Hill has very similar rates, its well-equipped, non-smoking rooms just 50yds from the sea. Among the overdeveloped caravan parks on the coast south of Falmouth, the nearest **campsite** is *Tremorvah Tent Park* (☎01326/318311), about a mile outside town behind Swanpool Beach and on the coast path.

Pasties, pizzas and chips are available everywhere in Falmouth, but if you prefer to eat in congenial surroundings try *No. 33*, 33 High St (☎01326/211944; closed Sun), an easy-going **café/restaurant** offering well-cooked dishes including seafood and vegetarian; there's an excellent deli next-door for take-away lunches. The best fish in town is to be found off the main drag at the *Seafood Bar*, Lower Quay Hill (☎01326/315129; closed lunch, plus all Sun & Mon), where thick crab soup is a speciality. Plainer fare is on offer at the unlicensed *Simply Sugar*, Upton Slip, off 48 Church St (closed Sun & Mon eve), and the *Quayside Inn*, further up on Arwenack Street, is the pick of the **pubs**. Drivers or boaters might like to head out of town to the *Pandora Inn* at Restronguet, four miles north of Falmouth, where you can drink by the waterside; superior bar food is available at lunchtime, or you can eat in the formal restaurant – good for fresh seafood (☎01326/372678).

St Mawes and the Roseland peninsula

Stuck at the very end of a prong of land at the bottom of Carrick Roads, the secluded, unhurried town of **ST MAWES** has an attractive walled seafront lying below a hillside of villas and abundant gardens. Just out of sight at the end of the seafront stands the small and pristine **St Mawes Castle** (April–Sept daily 10am–6pm; Oct daily 10am–5pm; Nov–March Wed–Sun 10am–1pm & 2–4pm; £2.70; EH). Built during the reign of Henry VIII, the castle owes its excellent condition to its early surrender during the Civil War when it was placed under siege by Parliamentary forces in 1646, a move which hastened the bloody occupation of Pendennis Castle over in Falmouth. Both castles adhere to the same cloverleaf design, with a round central keep surrounded by robust gun-emplacements, but this is the more attractive of the pair. The dungeons and gun installations contain various artillery exhibits as well as some background on local social history.

Moving away from St Mawes, you could spend a pleasant afternoon poking around the Roseland peninsula between the Percuil River and the eastern shore of Carrick Roads. It's only two and a half miles north to the scattered hamlet of **ST JUST-IN-ROSELAND**, where the strikingly picturesque church of St Just stands right next to the creek, surrounded by palms and sub-tropical shrubbery, its gravestones tumbling down to the water's edge.

A couple of miles farther north, the chain-driven King Harry **ferry** (May & Sept Mon–Sat 8am–8pm, Sun 10am–8pm; June–Aug Mon & Tues 8am–9pm,

Wed–Sat 8am–10.20pm, Sun 10am–10.20pm; Oct–April Mon–Sat 8am–7pm, Sun 10am–5pm; £2.50/car; foot-passengers 20p) crosses the River Fal every twenty minutes, docking close to **Trelissick Garden** (April–Sept Mon–Sat 10.30am–5.30pm, Sun 12.30–5.30pm; March & Oct closes at 5pm; £4.40; NT), which is celebrated for its hydrangeas and other Mediterranean species, and has a splendid woodland walk along the Fal (free access). Take bus #T7 (not Sun) or #51B (Sun) from Truro to get here.

In summer, there's a **ferry** from St Mawes to the southern arm of the Roseland Peninsula, which holds the twelfth- to thirteenth-century church of **St Anthony-in-Roseland** and the **lighthouse** on St Anthony's Head, marking the entry into Carrick Roads. There's also a ferry crossing from St Mawes to Falmouth (every 30min in summer, less frequent in winter).

Practicalities

St Mawes makes an attractive – though fairly pricey – place **to stay**. The best budget choices are a ten-minute walk up from the seafront on Newton Road: *Little Newton* (℡01326/270664; **❷**) and *Newton Farm*, next door (℡01326/270427; **❷**), both have spacious en-suite rooms and friendly hosts. Otherwise, you'll have to dig deep for the upmarket *St Mawes Hotel*, located right on the seafront with glorious views over the estuary (℡01326/270266; **❽**; closed Nov to mid-Feb) – or else cross over to Falmouth, where there's plenty more choice. There's a decent **campsite** at Trethem Mill, three miles north, outside St-Just-in-Roseland (℡01872/580504; closed Nov–March). Back in St Mawes, the *Victory Inn* is a fine old oak-beamed **pub** just off the seafront, which also serves seafood meals.

The Lizard peninsula

The **Lizard peninsula** – from the Celtic *lys ardh*, or "high point" – preserves a thankfully undeveloped appearance in contrast to many other areas of Cornwall. If this flat and treeless expanse can be said to have a centre, it is **Helston**, a junction for buses running from Falmouth and Truro to the spartan villages of the peninsula's interior and the tiny fishing ports on its coast. From Truro, Truronian's **bus** #T1 takes about an hour to reach Helston – which is linked to Penzance by the frequent First Western National #2 – and goes on via **Mullion** to the village of **The Lizard**. Truronian's #T2 connects Helston with the east-coast villages of **St Keverne** and **Coverack**, and #T3 "Lizard Rambler" links all the villages two or three times daily (neither service runs on Sun in winter).

The east coast to Lizard Point

To the north of the peninsula, the snug hamlets sprinkled in the valley of the **River Helford** are a complete contrast to the rugged character of most of the Lizard. At the river's mouth stands **MAWNAN**, whose granite church of St Mawnan-in-Meneage is dedicated to the sixth-century Welsh missionary St Maunanus – Meneage (rhyming with "vague"), means "land of monks". Upstream on the south side, **Frenchman's Creek** is one of a splay of creeks and arcane inlets running off the river, and was the inspiration for Daphne Du Maurier's novel of the same name – her evocation of it holds true: "still and soundless, surrounded by the trees, hidden from the eyes of men".

You can get over to the south bank by the seasonal ferry from Helford

Passage to Helford, an agreeable old smugglers' haunt worth a snack-stop – *Rose Cottage* provides teas and light meals, or you can eat pub lunches in the garden of the *Shipwright's Arms*, overlooking the river. South of here, on the B3293, the broad windswept plateau of Goonhilly Downs is interrupted by the futuristic saucers of Goonhilly Satellite Station, and the nearby ranks of wind turbines. East, the road splits: left to **ST KEVERNE**, an inland village whose tidy square is flanked by two pubs and a church, right to meet the sea at COVERACK, a fishing port at one end of a sheltered bay. Three miles offshore lurk the dreaded Manacles rocks, the cause of numerous shipwrecks over the centuries, many of which were gleefully claimed by the local wreckers. Coverack has a few decent places to stay, including the pleasant and friendly *Fernleigh* (☎01326/280626; no credit cards; ❶), on Chymbloth Way, a turn-off from Harbour Road, which has three rooms – including one spacious one at the front with en-suite bathroom and wonderful bay views – and amiable proprietors who can cook up a good three-course meal for £10. Alternatively, try the smaller *Bakery Cottage* (☎01326/280474; no credit cards; ❶), where two rooms share a bathroom; at the seafront, ask in the *Harbour Lights* restaurant about vacancies in a neighbouring cottage that sleeps four, usually available for three-day minimum stays, though occasionally available for one or two nights only (☎01326/280507; ❷). There's a youth hostel just west of Coverack's centre overlooking the bay (☎01326/280687; closed Nov–March), and a campsite outside the village, *Little Trevothan* (☎01326/280260; closed Oct–Easter). For eating, the *Old Lifeboat House Seafood Restaurant* (☎01326/280899; closed Mon & Oct–Easter) is pricey and often fully booked, but the fish is superb, and you can pick up first-class fish and chips from the attached takeaway. Ask at the Coverack Windsurfing Centre, below the post office, about windsurfing courses (☎01326/280939).

Beyond the safe and clean swimming spot of **Kennack Sands**, the south tip of the promontory, **Lizard Point**, is marked by a plain lighthouse and a couple of low-key cafés and gift shops. Sheltered from the ceaselessly churning sea, a tiny cove holds a disused lifeboat station. Behind the point, a road and footpath leads a mile inland to the nondescript village called simply **THE LIZARD**, holding a handful of places to sleep and eat: the non-smoking *Caerthillian* is a comfortable Victorian **B&B** in the centre of the village (☎01326/290019, ⓦwww.connexions.co.uk/caerthillian; ❷), while Penmenner Road has several possibilities, including *Parc Brawse House* (☎01326/290466; ❷) and the non-smoking *Penmenner House Hotel* (☎01326/290370; ❷), both a twenty-minute walk from Lizard Point and forty minutes from Kynance Cove. The *Witchball Restaurant* in the village provides evening **meals**, and you can pick up snacks and pub grub at the *Top House* in the village centre.

A mile westward lies the peninsula's best-known beach, **Kynance Cove**. With its sheer hundred-foot cliffs, its stacks and arches of serpentine rock and its offshore islands, the beach has a wild grandeur, and the water quality is excellent – but take care not to be stranded on the islands by the tide, which submerges the entire beach at its flood.

The west coast

Four miles north of Kynance Cove, the inland village of **MULLION** has a fifteenth- to sixteenth-century church dedicated to the Breton **St Mellane** (or Malo), with a dog-door for canine churchgoers. In the centre of the village, behind an enclosed garden at the top of Nansmellyon Road, *The Old Vicarage* (☎01326/240509; ❸) provides elegant **accommodation** in four spacious en-suite rooms; a brief distance outside Mullion, try *Campden House*, a friendly

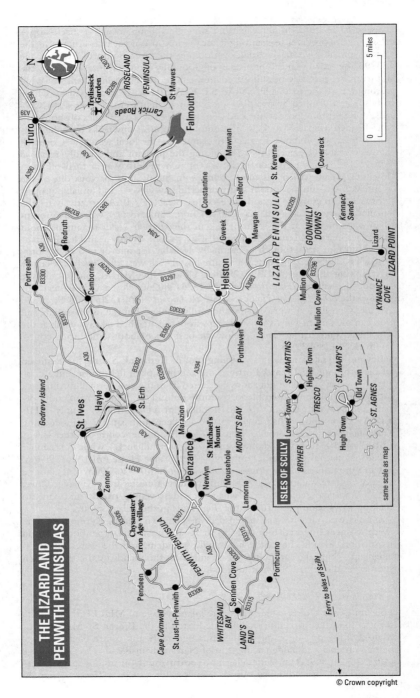

THE LIZARD AND PENWITH PENINSULAS

© Crown copyright

B&B with a fuchsia-filled garden (℡01326/240365; no credit cards; ❶), less than ten minutes' walk from the sea; evening meals are also available. A mile south of Mullion on the coast, next to the car park above Mullion Cove, *Criggan Mill* (℡01326/240496; ❷) provides accommodation in timber lodges in a peaceful narrow field 200 yards up from the sea, including self-catering. In the village, *Stock's* is a decent **restaurant**, and the shop across the road offers sandwiches and a glorious range of dairy ice cream.

There's a small beach at tiny **Mullion Cove**, sheltered behind a lovely harbour and more rock stacks, though the neighbouring sands at **Polurrian** and **Poldhu**, to the north, are better and attract surfers. At the cliff-edge, the Marconi Monument marks the spot from which the first transatlantic radio transmission was made in 1901. Three miles further north, strong currents make it unsafe to swim at the beautiful beach at **Loe Bar**, a strip of shingle which separates the freshwater **Loe Pool** from the sea. The elongated Pool is one of two places claiming to be where the sword Excalibur was restored to its watery source (the other is on Bodmin Moor), and there's a path running along its western shore as far as Helston, five miles north, making a nice **walk**.

Another three or four miles up the coast, **PORTHLEVEN** is a sizeable port that once served to export tin ore from the inland Stannary town of **HELSTON**, the main transport junction and centre for the Lizard peninsula. The town is best known for its **Furry Dance** (or Flora Dance), which dates from the seventeenth century. Held on May 8 (unless this falls on a Sun or Mon, when the procession takes place on the nearest Sat), it's a stately procession of top-hatted men and summer-frocked women performing a solemn dance through the town's streets and gardens. You can learn something about it and absorb plenty of other local history and lore in the eclectic **Helston Folk Museum** (Mon–Sat 10am–5pm; £2), housed in former market buildings behind the Guildhall on Church Street. The town's most conspicuous attraction, however, is the garish **Flambards Theme Park**, to the west of town (mid-April to mid-July, Sept & Oct daily 10.30am–5pm; mid-July to Aug daily 10am–6pm; outside summer sometimes closes Mon & Fri, call to check ℡01326/564093; £9.50), which combines a costumed nostalgia theme park with white-knuckle rides. Helston has the peninsula's only **tourist office** at 79 Meneage St (Aug Mon–Fri 10am–1pm & 2–4.30pm, Sat 10am–4.30pm; rest of year closes 1pm on Sat; ℡01326/565431). Just along from the tourist office at 95 Meneage Rd is *Hutchinson's*, an award-winning fish-and-chip shop. For a drink or a **pub** snack, check out the *Blue Anchor*, 50 Coinagehall St, a fifteenth-century monastery rest house, now a cramped pub with flagstone floors and mellow Spingo beer brewed on the premises in three strengths. Next door to the pub, the **B&B** at 52 Coinagehall St makes a smart night-stop, with solid old furnishings (℡01326/569334; ❷). For those wanting to explore the Lizard peninsula **by bike** – a great way to get the best out of the network of tiny lanes connecting the villages and coastal tracts – apply to Helston's Bike Services on Meneage Road (℡01326/564564), which rents out mountain bikes (£8/day), provides a repair service and supplies accessories.

The Penwith peninsula

Though more densely populated than the Lizard, the **Penwith peninsula** is a more rugged landscape, with a raw appeal that is still encapsulated by **Land's End**, despite the commercial paraphernalia superimposed on that headland.

The seascapes, the quality of the light and the slow tempo of the local fishing communities made this area a hotbed of artistic activity towards the end of the nineteenth century, when the painters of **Newlyn**, near **Penzance**, established a distinctive school of painting. More innovative figures – among them Ben Nicholson, Barbara Hepworth and Naum Gabo – were soon afterwards to make **St Ives** one of England's liveliest cultural communities, and their enduring influence is illustrated in the St Ives branch of the Tate Gallery, showcasing the Modern artists associated with the locality.

Penwith is far more easily toured than the Lizard, with a road circling its coastline and a better network of public transport from the two main towns, St Ives and Penzance, which have most of the accommodation. From Penzance – the terminus for **rail** services from London and Birmingham – **buses** #1 and (Sun only) #10A go straight to Land's End, whereas the #5A, #5B, #6A, #6B and #6C take in Newlyn and Mousehole (#6C also goes to Lamorna). North of Land's End, the comparatively neglected headland of Cape Cornwall is served by the #10C and #10D buses from Penzance to St Just, while Zennor, St Just, Sennen Cove and Land's End are linked by #15 from St Ives (not Sun in winter) – one of Cornwall's most scenic bus routes. St Ives can be reached by branch rail line or numerous buses from Penzance and Truro. **Hikers** might consider walking the eight miles separating Penzance from St Ives along the old St Michael's Way, a waymarked pilgrim's route for which the tourist office in both these towns can provide a free route-map.

Penzance and around

Occupying a sheltered position at the northwest corner of Mount's Bay, **PENZANCE** has always been a major port, but most traces of the medieval town were obliterated at the end of the sixteenth century by a Spanish raiding party. Today the dominant style of Penzance is Georgian, particularly at the top of **Market Jew Street** (from *Marghas Jew*, meaning "Thursday Market"), which climbs from the harbour and the train and bus stations. At the top of the street stands the green-domed Victorian **Market House** before which stands a statue of **Humphry Davy** (1778–1829), the local woodcarver's son who pioneered the science of electrochemistry and invented the life-saving miners' safety-lamp, which his statue holds.

Turn left here into **Chapel Street**, which has some of the town's finest buildings, including the flamboyant **Egyptian House**, built in 1835 to contain a geological museum but subsequently abandoned until its restoration twenty-odd years ago. Across the street, the **Union Hotel** dates from the seventeenth century, and originally housed the town's assembly rooms: the news of Admiral Nelson's victory at Trafalgar and the death of Nelson himself were first announced from the minstrels' gallery here in 1805. At no. 19, the **Maritime Museum** (Easter–Oct Mon–Sat 10.30am–4.30pm; £2) holds a good collection of seafaring articles, including an array of items salvaged from local wrecks and a full-size section of an eighteenth-century man o' war.

Bulging out of the Promenade into Mount's Bay, the Art Deco **Jubilee Pool** (mid-May to mid-Sept daily 10.30am–6pm; £1.70) is a tidal, salt-water (though chlorinated) open-air swimming pool, built to mark the Silver Jubilee of George V in 1935. It's a classic example of the style, and non-swimmers can stroll around (60p) to get a closer view of the pool and bay.

If your interest is roused by the art scene that flourished hereabouts at the turn of the nineteenth century, head up Morrab Road from the Promenade (you can also reach it from Alverton Street, a continuation of Market Jew Street), where the **Penlee House Gallery and Museum** (Mon–Sat: May–Sept 10am–5pm;

Oct–April 10.30am–4.30pm; £2, free on Sat) holds the biggest collection of the works of the Newlyn School – impressionistic harbour scenes, frequently sentimentalized but often bathed in an evocatively luminous light. There are frequent exhibitions, and also displays on local history.

Newlyn itself, Cornwall's biggest fishing port, lies immediately south of Penzance, protected behind two long piers. The colony of artists who gathered here around the Irish painter Stanhope Forbes is represented in the collection in Penzance, but Newlyn's **art gallery**, near the harbour at 24 New Rd (Mon–Sat 10am–5pm; free), which concentrates on contemporary art, gives an often stimulating insight into how that tradition has evolved.

Practicalities

Penzance's **tourist office** (May–Sept Mon–Fri 9am–5pm, Sat 9am–4pm, Sun 10am–1pm; Oct–April Mon–Fri 9am–5pm, Sat 10am–1pm; ☎01736/362207, ⓦwww.west-cornwall-tourism.co.uk) is right next to the train and bus stations on the seafront. Drivers can deposit their vehicles during excursions to the Isles of Scilly at Avalon **car park** near the harbour at South Place (☎01736 /364622), for £2.50 per day. For **bike rental** head for Pedals on the seafront in the Wharfside shopping centre (☎01736/360600).

Guest houses nearest the bus and train stations include *Honeydew* at 3 Leskinnick St (☎01736/364206; no credit cards; ❶), at the bottom of Market Jew Street, though you should venture further afield for a bit more character. On Chapel Street, there's the seventeenth-century *Trevelyan Hotel* (☎01736 /362494; no credit cards; ❶) – ask for a top-floor room for the view – or you could soak up the atmosphere in the *Union Hotel* (☎01736/362319; ❸) or at the *Penzance Arts Club*, at the bottom of Chapel Street (☎01736/363761; ❹), where four tasteful rooms are available in what was once the Portuguese embassy; there's a good café in the basement too. For a top-of-the-league treat, the seventeenth-century *Abbey Hotel*, owned by former model Jean Shrimpton and her husband, has lashings of old-fashioned comfort, superb views and an excellent restaurant, off Chapel Street on Abbey Street (☎01736/366906, ⓦwww.abbey-hotel.co.uk; ❻). Most cheaper B&Bs are along Morrab and Alexandra roads to the west of the centre: on Morrab Road, try *Kimberley House* at no. 10 (☎01736/362727; no credit cards; ❶); on Alexandra Road, *Holbein House* (☎01736/332625; no credit cards; ❶) is a cheerful and spacious B&B, with breakfast served in the bright-painted rooms. On the seafront, the non-smoking *Camilla House Hotel* is useful for the harbour at Regent Terrace, on a parallel road to the Promenade (☎01736/363771, ⓦwww.camilla house-hotel.co.uk; ❸); most rooms have sea views, and the top room is cosiest. Alexandra Road is also the location of the tidy and friendly *Blue Dolphin* **hostel** (☎01736/363836). The YHA hostel is out of town, housed in a Georgian mansion at Castle Horneck, Alverton (☎01736/326666, Ⓔpenzance@yha .org.uk; closed late Dec to Jan), a two-mile hike from the station up Market Jew Street into Alverton Road, then turn right at the *Pirate Inn*, or take bus #5B, #6B, #6C or #10B from Penzance station as far as the *Pirate Inn*.

Penzance does not have a great choice of **restaurants**, though *Co-Co's Tapas Bar* on Chapel Street is good for coffees and cakes as well as beers and tapas. Quality cuisine can be had at the formal *Harris's* nearby at 46 New St (☎01736/364408; closed Mon, plus Sun in winter), and the contrastingly ultra-modern *Abbey Restaurant* in Abbey Street (☎01736/330680; closed Sun & Mon), both expensive. Vegetarians can choose between the tiny *Dandelions*, at the top of the pedestrianized Causeway Head, or the spacious and relaxed *Brown's*, above a health shop in nearby Bread Street; the latter is currently open on Friday evenings, otherwise both are open daytime only and closed all day Sunday. There are also a couple of congenial café-bars serving ciabattas, salads and wraps: the *Blue Snappa*, 18 Market Place (at the top of Chapel Street), and the *Boatshed*, opposite the harbour on the Promenade. *The Olive Farm* in the Wharfside shopping centre on the Promenade is the place for delicious take-away rolls.

Chapel Street has a couple of characterful **pubs**, the *Admiral Benbow*, crammed with gaudy ships' figureheads and other nautical items, and the *Turk's Head*, the town's oldest inn, reputed to date back to the thirteenth century, with a garden and the remains of a contrabanders' tunnel to the harbour.

St Michael's Mount

Buses from Penzance bus station leave every thirty minutes for Marazion, five miles east, from where the medieval chimneys and towers of **St Michael's Mount** (April–Oct Mon–Fri 10.30am–5.30pm, plus most weekends; Nov–March phone for opening times ☎01736/710507; £4.50; NT) can be seen a couple of hundred yards offshore. A vision of the archangel Michael led to the building of a church on this granite pile around the fifth century, and within three centuries a Celtic monastery had been founded here. The present building derives from a chapel raised in the eleventh century by Edward the Confessor, who handed over the abbey to the Benedictine monks of Brittany's Mont St Michel, whose island abbey – also founded after a vision of St Michael – was the model for this one. The complex was appropriated by Henry V during the Hundred Years War, and it became a fortress after its dissolution a century later. After the Civil War, when it was used to store arms for the Royalist forces, it became the residence of the St Aubyn family, who still inhabit the castle.

The fortress-isle has a milder, more pedestrian feel than its prototype off the Breton coast, but there's no doubting its eye-catching site, which demands a first-hand inspection from anyone travelling along this part of the Cornish littoral. A good number of its buildings date from the twelfth century, but the later additions are more interesting, such as the battlemented **chapel** and the seventeenth-century decorations of the Chevy Chase Room, the former refectory. Other rooms are crowded with paintings of the castle, portraits of various St Aubyns and general memorabilia.

At low tide the promontory can be approached via a cobbled causeway; at high tide there are boats from Marazion (£1).

Mousehole to Land's End

Accounts vary as to the derivation of the name of **MOUSEHOLE** (pronounced "Mowzle"), though it may be from a smugglers' cave just south of town. In any case, the name evokes perfectly this minuscule harbour, cradled in the arms of a granite breakwater three miles south of Penzance. The village attracts more visitors than it can handle, so hang around until the crowds have departed before you walk through its tight tangle of lanes to take in Mousehole's oldest house, the fourteenth-century Keigwin House (a survival of the 1595 attack when the village was burned by the Spaniards), and/or a drink at the *Ship Inn*, which also has **rooms** (☎01736/731234; no credit cards; ❸) – those with a view are slightly more expensive. Half a mile inland, the churchyard wall at **Paul** holds a monument to Dolly Pentreath, a resident of Mousehole who died in 1777 and was reputed to have been the last person to speak the Cornish language. The inscription includes a Cornish translation of a verse from the Bible.

Three miles south round the coast, **Lamorna Cove** is squeezed between granite headlands, linked by a flower-bordered lane to the tiny village of **LAMORNA**, where you can see an old flour mill and drink at the comfortable old *Lamorna Wink* pub – as the sign shows, it was the wink that signified that contraband spirits were available. The spot makes a nice starting point for exploring the coastpath: following it westwards brings you round Boscawen Point to **St Loy's Cove**, a hike of a couple of miles, where *Cove Cottage* serves up teas, delicious cakes or savoury snacks, and also offers **B&B** in a huge double room with a fabulous panorama (℡01736/810010; ④).

Five miles west of Lamorna lies one of the best beaches on Penwith, at **PORTHCURNO**. The name means "Port Cornwall", but its beach of tiny white shells suggests privacy and isolation rather than the movement of ships. Steep steps lead up from here to the cliff-hewn **Minack Theatre**, created in the 1930s and since enlarged to hold 750 seats, though the basic Greek-inspired design has remained intact. The spectacular backdrop of Porthcurno Bay makes this one of the country's most inspiring theatres – providing the weather holds. The summer season lasts seventeen weeks from May to September, presenting a gamut of plays, opera and musicals, with tickets costing just £5.50 for afternoon performances, £6.50 for evening ones (box office Mon–Fri from 9.30am; ℡01736/810181, ⓦwww.minack.com). Bring a cushion and a rug. You can also visit the **Exhibition Centre** (daily: April–Sept 9.30am–5.30pm; Oct–March 10am–4pm; closed during performances; £2.50), which allows you to see the theatre and follow the story of its creation through photographs and audiovisual displays.

The peculiar white pyramid on the shore to the east of Porthcurno marks the spot where the first transatlantic cables were laid in 1880. On the headland beyond lies an Iron Age fort, **Treryn Dinas**, close to the famous rocking stone called **Logan's Rock**, a seventy-ton monster that was knocked off its perch by a nephew of playwright Oliver Goldsmith and a gang of sailors in 1824. Somehow they replaced the stone, but it never rocked again.

The best way to approach **Land's End** is unarguably on foot along the coastal path. Although nothing can completely destroy the potency of this extreme western tip of England, the colossal theme park built behind this majestic headland in 1987 comes close to violating irreparably the spirit of the place. The trivializing **Land's End Experience** (daily: Easter–Oct 10am–6pm; Oct–Easter 10am–5pm, or earlier at quiet times; ℡0870/4580099) substitutes a tawdry panoply of lasers and unconvincing sound effects for the real open-air experience, but the location is still a public right of way (though you'll have to pay to use the car park; £3), and once past the paraphernalia, nature takes over. Turf-covered cliffs sixty feet high provide a platform to view the Irish Lady, the Armed Knight, Dr Syntax Head and the rest of the Land's End outcrops, beyond which you can spot the Longships lighthouse, a mile and a half out to sea, and sometimes the Wolf Rock lighthouse, nine miles south-west, or even the Isles of Scilly, twenty five miles away.

Whitesand Bay to Zennor

To the north of Land's End the rounded granite cliffs fall away at **Whitesand Bay** to reveal a glistening mile-long shelf of beach that offers the best swimming on the Penwith peninsula. The rollers make for good surfing and boards can be rented at **Sennen Cove**, the more popular southern end of the beach. There are a few places to **stay** around the southern end of the strand, including *Myrtle Cottage* (℡01736/871698; no credit cards; ②), which also has a cosy café open to non-residents, and the nearby *Polwyn Cottage*, tucked away on Old Coastguard Row (☎01736/871349; no credit cards; **❶**). If you don't mind being a few minutes' walk inland, *Whitesands Lodge*, a backpackers' **hostel**, would make a good base for the whole area, offering dormitory accommodation and single, twin or family rooms (☎01736/871776; **❶**). As well as the self-catering facilities, there's a relaxed café-restaurant (also open to non-residents), a library, studio workspace, and access to bike rental and land and sea tours. When all else fails, try the *Sennen Cove Hotel*, visible from the strand, which has low rates and great views (☎01736/871275; **❸**).

Cape Cornwall, three miles northward, shelters another superb beach, overlooked by the chimney of the Cape Cornwall Mine, which closed in 1870. Half a mile inland the grimly grey village of **ST JUST-IN-PENWITH** was a centre of the tin and copper industry, and the rows of trim cottages radiating out from Bank Square are redolent of the close-knit community that once existed here. The tone is somewhat lightened by the grassy open-air theatre where the old Cornish miracle plays were staged; it was later used by Methodist preachers as well as Cornish wrestlers. Three out of the four pubs in and off Bank Square have **accommodation**, the best of them is the traditional *Star Inn* (☎01736/788767; no credit cards; **❷**). The village has a **youth hostel** on its outskirts (☎01736/788437; closed Nov–Feb) – take the left fork past the post office – and there's an excellent secluded **campsite**, *Kelynack Caravan and Camping Park* (☎01736/787633), just outside the hamlet of Kelynack a couple of miles south of St Just, one of the few sheltered sites on Penwith, which also has bunks in small dorms. For **lunches** and inexpensive **dinners**, step into *Kegen Teg*, 12 Market Square (closed Sun eve), which offers fish pie, rich chocolate cake and wonderful Kelly's ice creams, or *St Just Tea Rooms*, 3 Cape Cornwall Rd (closed Sun eve & all Nov–March; no credit cards).

A couple of miles north of St Just, outside **PENDEEN**, you can get a close-up view of the Cornish mining industry at **Geevor Tin Mine** (April–Oct Mon–Fri & Sun 10am–5pm; Nov–March Mon–Fri 10am–4pm; £5.50), where you can tour the surface machinery and explore the innards of an underground mine and visit the museum, which is the only part of the site open for visits in winter (£2). East of here, the landscape is all rolling moorland and an abundance of granite, the chief building material of **ZENNOR**. D.H. Lawrence and Frieda came to live here in 1916: "It is a most beautiful place," Lawrence wrote, "lovelier even than the Mediterranean". The Lawrences were soon joined by John Middleton Murry and Katherine Mansfield, with the hope of forming a writers' community, but the new arrivals soon left for a more sheltered haven near Falmouth. Lawrence stayed on to write *Women in Love*, spending in all a year and a half in Zennor before being given notice to quit by the local constabulary, who suspected Lawrence and his German wife of unpatriotic sympathies. His Cornish experiences were later described in *Kangaroo*.

At the bottom of the village, the **Wayside Museum** is dedicated to Cornish life from prehistoric times (April to late July, Sept & Oct Mon–Fri & Sun 11am–5pm; late July to Aug daily 10.30am–5.30pm; £2.20). Note the "plague stone" on the road outside the building, where a hole containing vinegar was used to disinfect visiting merchants' money during cholera outbreaks in the nineteenth century. At the top of the lane, the church of **St Sennen** displays a sixteenth-century bench-carving of a mermaid who, according to local legend, was so entranced by the singing of a chorister that she lured him down to the sea, from where he never returned – though his singing can still occasionally be heard. Nearby, the *Tinners Arms*, where Lawrence stayed before moving into Higher Tregerthen, is a homely place to **drink** and **eat**. If you don't mind sleeping up to six to a room, the *Old Chapel Backpackers Hostel* makes a fun place **to stay**, right next to the Wayside Museum (☎01736 /798307).

The Iron Age village of **Chysauster** (April–Sept daily 10am–6pm; Oct daily 10am–5pm; £1.70; EH), located on a windy hillside a couple of miles inland from Zennor, off the minor road to Penzance, is the best-preserved ancient settlement in the southwest. Dating from about the first century BC, it contains two rows of four buildings, each consisting of a courtyard with small chambers leading off it, and a garden that was presumably used for growing vegetables.

St Ives

East of Zennor, the road runs four hilly miles on to the steeply built town of **ST IVES**, a place that has smoothly undergone the transition to holiday haunt from its previous role as a centre of the fishing industry. So productive were the offshore waters that a record sixteen and a half million fish were caught in one net on a single day in 1868, and the diarist Francis Kilvert was told by the local vicar that the smell was sometimes so great as to stop the church clock. Virginia Woolf, who spent every summer here to the age of 12, described St Ives as "a windy, noisy, fishy, vociferous, narrow-streeted town; the colour of a mussel or a limpet; like a bunch of rough shell fish clustered on a grey wall together." By the time the pilchard reserves dried up around the early years of the last century, the town was beginning to attract a vibrant **artists' colony**, precursors of the wave later headed by Ben Nicholson, Barbara Hepworth (second of Nicholson's three wives), Naum Gabo and the potter Bernard Leach, who in the 1960s were followed by a third wave including Terry Frost, Peter Lanyon, Patrick Heron, Bryan Wynter and Roger Hilton.

Sunday painters dominate the dozens of galleries sandwiched between the town's restaurants and bars; the place to view the best work created in St Ives is the **St Ives Tate Gallery**, overlooking Porthmeor Beach on the north side of town (March to mid-June daily 10am–5:30pm; mid-June to Aug daily 10am–6:30pm; Nov–Feb Tues–Sun 10am–4:30pm; £3.95; combined ticket with Barbara Hepworth Museum £6.50; ⊛www.tate.org.uk). The sights and sounds of the beachfront are a constant presence inside the airy, gleaming-white building, creating a dialogue with the gallery's paintings, sculptures and ceramics, most of which date from the period 1925 to 1975. Apart from these, the Tate has some specially commissioned contemporary works on view. The museum's rooftop **café** is one the best places in town for tea and cake.

A short distance away on Barnoon Hill, the **Barbara Hepworth Museum** (March–October daily 10am–5.30pm; Nov–Feb Tues–Sun 10am–4.30pm; £3.75; combined ticket with the Tate £6.50) gives another insight into the local arts scene. One of the foremost non-figurative sculptors of her time, Hepworth lived in the building from 1949 until her death in a studio fire in 1975. Apart from the sculptures, which are arranged in positions chosen by Hepworth in the house and garden, the museum has masses of background on her art, from photos and letters to catalogues and reviews. A few Hepworths are scattered around the town, including a tender *Madonna* in the harbourside church of **St Ia** – a fifteenth-century building dedicated to the female missionary who was said to have floated over from Ireland on an ivy leaf.

Devotees of Bernard Leach's Japanese-inspired ceramics can visit his studio, the **Leach Pottery** (Mon–Sat 10am–5pm; £2.50), in the Higher Stennack neighbourhood, three-quarters of a mile outside St Ives on the Zennor road (bus #16, #17 or #17A). Some examples of Leach's work are on display here, alongside that of his wife, Janet Leach, as well as pieces by Shoji Hamada, Michael Cardew and other more contemporary artworks. Products of the Leach pottery can also be found in the New Craftsman shop at 24 Fore St.

The wide expanse of **Porthmeor Beach** dominates the northern side of St Ives, the stone houses tumbling almost onto the yellow sands. Unusually for a town beach, the water quality is excellent, and the rollers make it popular with surfers (boards available for rent below the Tate); there's also a good open-air café here. South of the station, **Porthminster Beach** is another favourite spot for sunbathing and swimming, but if you hanker for a quieter stretch you need to head east out of town to the string of magnificent golden beaches lining **St Ives Bay** – the strand is especially fine on the far side of the port of Hayle, at the mouth of the eponymous river.

Arrival and information

To reach St Ives by **train**, change at St Erth on the main line to Penzance or there are direct services from Penzance. **Buses** #16, #17 and #17A, B or C connect Penzance with St Ives, but the only service from here to Truro is run by National Express. The train station is off Porthminster Beach, just north of the bus station on Station Hill. The **tourist office** is in the Guildhall, in the narrow Street-an-Pol, two minutes' walk away (July & Aug Mon–Sat 9.30am–6pm, Sun 10am–1pm; Sept Mon–Sat 9.30am–5.30pm; Oct to mid-May Mon–Thurs 9.30am–5.30pm, Fri 9.30am–5pm; mid-May to June Mon–Sat 9.30am–5.30pm, Sun 10am–1pm; ☎01736/796297). Among the places where you can rent **surfing equipment** are Porthmeor Beach and the surf specialists on Fore Street and by the harbour. The St Ives **Festival** of folk, jazz and blues, also taking in classical music and theatre, takes place over two weeks in mid-September.

Accommodation

Hotels and B&Bs

Allamanda 83 Back Road East ☎01736/793548, ⓦwww.allamanda.co.uk. Superior Georgian conversion in the cobbled heart of St Ives, with two small but elegant en-suite rooms. No smoking, no under-12s and no credit cards. **❹**

Bowden's 4 Trepolpen, Street-an-Pol ☎01736 796281. Opposite the tourist office, this will appeal to anyone tired of the "fisherman's cottage" style of B&B that rules in these parts, with bold minimalist designs and modern art on the walls. No credit cards. **❷**

Chy-Roma 2 Seaview Terrace ☎01736/797539, ⓦconnexions.co.uk/chyroma. Convenient for the bus and train stations, among a cluster of similar lodgings, this one offers home-made muesli, breads and jams for breakfast and boasts great panoramic views. No credit cards. **❷**

Garrack Hotel Burthallan Lane ☎01736/796199, ⓦwww.garrack.com. One of the best hotels in the area, outside the town's bustle, but within walking distance of Porthmeor Beach. Family-run, the hotel has an indoor pool and sauna, and an excellent

restaurant (see below); the atmosphere is polite but friendly. **❼**

The Grey Mullet 2 Bunkers Hill ☎01736/796635. Oak-beamed and bedecked with flowers and prints, this eighteenth-century house – said to be the oldest in town – is 20yds from the harbour on a cobbled lane. No credit cards. **❷**

Kandahar 11 The Warren ☎01736/796183. Best choice among the B&Bs edging the seafront below the bus station; four rooms have a view. No smoking. Closed Nov to Easter. **❸**

Kynance 24 The Warren ☎01736/796636. Another good choice in this area of town near Porthminster Beach, with some parking space. The top-floor rooms have good views but get booked up early. No smoking. Closed mid-Nov to early March. **❷**

Campsites and hostels

Ayr Higher Ayr ☎01736/795855, ⓦwww.ayrholidaypark.demon.co.uk. St Ives has no campsites right on the seafront, but this one has a good sea prospect, half a mile west of the centre, above Porthmeor Beach. It's close to the coast path, and

buses #6B and #15 to Land's End pass close by.
Higher Chellew Nancledra ☎01736/364532.
Good out-of-town alternative to the *Ayr*, and much
cheaper. Facilities are basic but clean and include
washing machines. Located on the B3311 road,
equidistant between St Ives and Penzance.
St Ives Backpackers The Stennack ☎01736
/799444, ⊛www.backpackers.co.uk/st-ives.

Restored Wesleyan chapel school from 1845, usefully located in the centre of St Ives opposite the
cinema. Comfortable and clean, with barbecues
and free tours around the area. Dorms have four,
six or eight beds for £12 per night and there are
double and twin rooms for £28 according to season. Rates drop in winter.

Restaurants, bars and cafés

The Café Island Square ☎01736/793621.
Vegetarian snacks and full evening meals in this
tiny place, reasonably priced and served with a
smile. Moderate.
Cobblestones 5 St Andrews St. Basic English
seaside nosh, or just tea and cakes, with few frills
and late opening till 10pm in summer, 5pm for the
rest of the year. Inexpensive.
Garrack Hotel Burthallan Lane ☎01736/796199.
A bit out of the way, but worth the detour. The
kitchen excels at fish, but meat dishes are also
excellent, and there are some astounding desserts.
Expensive.
The Grapevine 7 High St ☎01736/794030. Bistro
serving breakfasts and lunches and fresh local fish
at night, all in a pleasant woody decor. Moderate.
Isobar Tregenna Place ☎01736/799199,
⊛www.theisobar.com. Cool bar at the top of

Street-an-Pol. serving coffees, chunky ciabattas,
salads and seafood. DJs play most evenings
downstairs and there's a club upstairs (July & Aug
Mon–Sat; rest of year Wed–Sat) playing dance
music from 1970s to the latest.
Peppers 22 Fore St ☎01736/794014. Up-to-date
pizza and pasta parlour, also serving fish and
steaks. Inexpensive.
Saltwater Café Fish Street ☎01736/794928.
Bright, beachy fishy paintings on the walls and a
good choice of seafood, from swordfish to pan-
fried scallops wrapped in pancetta. The seafood
risotto is especially good. Closed Sun (except
July–Sept) & daytime. Moderate.
Wilbur's Café St Andrew's St ☎01736/796661.
Movie stars on the walls and a lively atmosphere
with pastas and fish prominent on the menu, and a
vegetarian option. Moderate.

The Isles of Scilly

The **Isles of Scilly** are a compact archipelago of about a hundred islands 28
miles southwest of Land's End, none of them bigger than three miles across, and
only five of them inhabited – **St Mary's**, **Tresco**, **Bryher**, **St Martin's** and **St
Agnes**. In the annals of folklore, the Scillies are the peaks of the submerged land
of Lyonesse, a fertile plain that extended west from Penwith before the ocean
broke in, drowning the land and leaving only one survivor to tell the tale. In fact
they form part of the same granite mass as Land's End, Bodmin Moor and
Dartmoor, and despite rarely rising above a hundred feet, they possess a remarkable variety of landscape. All are swept by an energizing briny air filled with the
cries of seabirds, and though the water is cold the beaches are well-nigh irresistible, ranging from small coves to vast untrammelled strands. Other points of
interest include Cornwall's greatest concentration of prehistoric remains, some
fabulous rock formations, and masses of **flowers**. Along with tourism, the main
source of income here is flower-growing, for which the equable climate and the
long hours of sunshine – their name means "Sun Isles" – make the islands ideal.
The profusion of wild flowers is even more noticeable than the fields of narcis-
si and daffodils, and the heaths and pathways are often dense with marigolds,
gorse, sea thrift, trefoil and poppies, not to mention a host of more exotic varieties introduced by visiting foreign vessels.

Free of traffic, theme parks and amusement arcades, the Scillies are a welcome
respite from the tourist trail, the main drawbacks being the high cost of reaching the islands and the shortage of accommodation – making advance book-

ing essential at any time. Note that most places offer – and often insist on – a dinner, bed and breakfast package, and this option should not be automatically rejected, considering the tiny choice of places to eat (Hugh Town in St Mary's is better supplied), though basic groceries are always available. If you're coming between May and September, try to time your visit to be here on a Wednesday or Friday evening to witness the **gig races**, the most popular sport on the Scillies, performed by six-oared vessels some thirty feet in length. Some of the boats used are over a hundred years old, built originally to carry pilots to passing ships.

Getting to the islands

The islands are accessible by sea or air. **Boats from Penzance to St Mary's** are operated by the Isles of Scilly Steamship Company on the South Pier (℡0845/710 5555, ⓦwww.islesofscilly-travel.co.uk). Sailings, which can be nauseatingly rough, take place daily and last about two-and-three-quarter hours; single tickets cost £38, day returns £32–35, short-break returns (one to three nights) £45–55, and period returns £65–74, with discounts for students, families and children. There are ferries between each of the inhabited islands (about £5 return fare), though these are sporadic in winter.

The main departure points for **flights** (also operated by the Isles of Scilly Steamship Company) are **Land's End**, near St Just (Mon–Sat; 15min; £50–98 return), **Newquay** (Mon–Sat; 30min; £67–104 return), **Plymouth** (Mon, Wed & Fri; 45min; £110–150 return), **Exeter** (Mon–Sat; 50min; £142–196 return) and **Bristol** (Mon–Sat; 1hr 10min; £148–199 return). In winter, there are departures only from Land's End and Newquay. British International also runs **helicopter** flights (℡01736/363871, ⓦwww.scillyhelicopter.co.uk) from the heliport a mile east of Penzance to St Mary's (not Sun) and Tresco (not Sun) taking about twenty minutes, with return fares costing about £98 – though you can get discounted day returns, advance returns and short break returns.

St Mary's

The island of **ST MARY'S** holds the overwhelming majority of the archipelago's population and most of its tourist accommodation. From the airport there are buses to shuttle passengers the mile to **HUGH TOWN**, straddling a neck of land at the southwestern end of the island. Ferries from Penzance dock on the north side of town, under a knob of land still known as the Garrison, where the eight-pointed **Star Castle**, built in Elizabeth I's reign after the scare of the Spanish Armada, has been converted into a hotel. The rampart walk hereabout is a good place to gain your bearings, affording views over all the islands and the myriad rocky fragments around them.

Hugh Town itself has a limited appeal, and once you've exhausted the pubs and shops there's little to occupy your time apart from the engaging **Isles of Scilly Museum** on Church Street, well worth an hour or two's wander (April–Oct daily 10am–noon, 1.30–4.30pm & 7.30–9pm; Nov–March Wed 1.30–4.30pm; £1). Most of the exhibits are relics salvaged from the many ships foundered on or around the islands, including the happy miscellany of finds recovered from the most recent wreck, the *Cita*, which sank off St Mary's Porth Hellick in March 1997 en route from Southampton to Belfast, much of its cargo, ranging from trainers to tobacco, finding its way into the islanders' homes. Hugh Town's best bathing **beach** is in the sheltered bay of Porthcressa, where you can also find Buccabu Bike Hire (℡01720/422289), which offers a good way to get around the island if you don't want to take advantage of the circular **bus** service leaving from The Parade, at the end of the main street (summer 6 daily, reduced service rest of year) – though neither bike nor bus is ideal for exploring the remoter coastal sections.

From Porthcressa a path wanders south to skirt the **Peninnis Headland**, passing some impressive sea-sculpted granite rocks. Other weathered boulders stand behind the Peninnis Lighthouse, notably the formation known as the **Kettle and Pans**, where a rock said to resemble a kettle stands close to some massive rounded basins. The path follows the coast to **Old Town Bay**, around which the modern houses of **OLD TOWN** give little hint of its former role as the island's chief port. The town has cafés and a sheltered south-facing beach, where there's a **diving** school, where equipment cant be rented (℡01720/422732).

Three-quarters of a mile east, **Porth Hellick** is the next major inlet on the island's southern coast, marked by a rugged quartz monument to the fantastically named Sir Cloudesley Shovell, who in 1707 was washed up here from a shipwreck which claimed four ships and nearly 1700 lives. On one side of the bay is another rock shape, the **Loaded Camel**; near it a gate leads to a 4000-year-old **barrow**, probably used by Bronze Age people from the Iberian peninsula who were the Scillies' first colonists.

Pelistry Bay, on the northeastern side of St Mary's, less than two miles from Hugh Town, is one of the most secluded spots on the island, its sandy beach and crystal-clear waters sheltered by the outlying **Toll's Island**. The latter, joined to St Mary's at low tide by a slender strand, holds the remains of an old battery known as Pellow's Redoubt as well as several pits in which kelp was burned to produce a substance used for the manufacture of soap and glass. Grey seals are a common sight here.

The best remnants of early human settlement on the Scillies are to be found at **Halangy Down**, a mile or so north of Hugh Town, overlooking the sea. Dating from around 200 BC, it's an extensive complex of stone huts, chief of them a structure built around a courtyard with interconnecting buildings. Most complete is **Bant's Carn**, part of a much earlier site, probably contemporaneous with the one at Porth Hellick, comprising a long rectangular roofed chamber where cremations were carried out.

Practicalities

Hugh Town's **tourist office**, in the Old Wesleyan Chapel on Garrison Lane (Jan–March Mon–Thurs 8.30am–5pm, Fri 8.30am–4.30pm, Sat 10am–1pm; April to mid-June & Oct Mon–Sat 8.30am–5.30pm; mid-June to Sept Mon–Sat 8.30am–5.30pm, Sun 10am–noon; Nov & Dec Mon–Thurs 8.30am–5pm, Fri 8.30am–4.30pm; ℡01720/422536, ⓦwww.simplyscilly.co.uk), has information on available accommodation for all the Scillies. Though rooms can be fairly scarce in peak season, the town is relatively well supplied with **B&Bs**: The Strand has the friendly, non-smoking *Lyonesse Guest House* (℡01720/422458; no credit cards; ❸; closed Nov–Feb), right on the harbourfront, while *The Boathouse*, on the Thoroughfare, also enjoys a good view over the harbour and has a restaurant (℡01720/422688; ❸; closed Nov–March). If you can afford it, you might consider the island's most atmospheric hotel, the *Star Castle* (℡01720/422317, ⓦwww.starcastlescilly.demon.co.uk; ❼; closed mid-Oct to mid-March), high up on the Garrison. In the same area is the more modest *Veronica Lodge*, The Garrison (℡01720/422585; no credit cards; ❷), a comfortably solid house with a spacious garden and excellent views. There is much to be said for staying outside Hugh Town, for example at *Atlantic View* (℡01720/422684; no credit cards; ❷; closed Nov–Feb), in the centre of the island on High Lanes (right off Telegraph Road heading north), which also offers **riding** excursions and **bike**

rental. The island's **campsite** is *Garrison Campsite*, near the playing field at the top of the eponymous promontory in Hugh Town (☎01720/422670). Camping elsewhere is not allowed.

There are plenty of **places to eat** in Hugh Town. The *Pilot's Gig* is a basement restaurant below the Garrison Gate at the end of Hugh Street, specializing in fish but also offering simple snacks at lunchtime. In the middle of the main street, the *Kavorna Bakery* is a handy spot for daytime refreshment, while the *Star Castle Hotel* in the Garrison has two quality restaurants – the seafood-based *Conservatory* is the most amenable – and the informal *Dungeon Bar*, where you can eat salads and jacket potatoes. Out of town, *Juliet's* (☎01720/423611) serves light meals and moderately priced early dinners in its garden between Porthmellon and Porthloo beaches.

Tresco

After St Mary's, **TRESCO** is the most visited island of the Scillies, yet the boatloads of visitors somehow manage to lose themselves on the two-miles-by-one island, the second largest in the group. Once the private estate of Devon's Tavistock Abbey, Tresco still retains a cloistered, slightly privileged air, and it has none of St Mary's short-term budget accommodation.

According to the tide, boats pull in at **New Grimsby**, halfway up the west coast, or the smaller quay at Old Grimsby, on the east coast, or the southernmost point of Carn Near. Whichever the case, it is only a few minutes' walk to the entrance to **Abbey Gardens** (daily 10am–4pm; £6.50), featuring a few ruins from the priory amid subtropical gardens first laid out in 1834. Many of the plants were grown from seeds taken from London's Kew Gardens, others were brought here from Africa, South America and the Antipodes. The entry ticket also admits you to a collection of figureheads and name plates taken from the numerous vessels that have come to grief around here.

You don't need to walk far to find alluring sandy beaches: one of the best – **Appletree Bay** – is only a few steps from the southern ferry landing at Carn Near. **Old Grimsby**, on the island's eastern side, has another couple of sand beaches, looking out to a submarine-shaped rock offshore, though the wide strands south of here are the island's best, and good for shell-hunting.

There is another gorgeous sandy bay around the cluster of cottages that make up **New Grimsby**, on the island's eastern shore. North of here, Tresco's tidy fields give way to an untended heathland of heather and gorse, while a narrow path traces the coast to **Charles' Castle**, built in the 1550s. Strategically positioned on a height to cover the lagoon-like channel separating Tresco from Bryher, the castle was in fact badly designed, its guns unable to depress far enough to be effective, and it was superseded in 1651 by the much better-preserved **Cromwell's Castle**, actually no more than a gun-tower, built at sea level next to a pretty sandy cove.

The shore path winds northwest from here, round to **Piper's Hole**, a deep underground cave accessible from the cliff-edge on the northern coast. The entrance can be a little difficult to negotiate but it's worth pressing ahead to its freshwater pool. A torch is essential.

Practicalities

Apart from the exclusive *Island Hotel* at the centre of the island (☎01720/422883; ❾; closed Nov to mid-March), and the *New Inn* at New Grimsby (☎01720/422844; ❼), the only **accommodation** on the island comprises self-catering homes, usually available for weekly rent only, though it's worth asking if you want a place for less time. Prices run from £200 to

£430 a week: contact *Boro Farm* (☎01720/422843; closed Nov–Feb); *Borough Farm* (☎01720/422840; closed Dec–Feb) or Tresco's Estate Office (☎01720/422849, ⊛www.tresco.co.uk) for bookings and further details. The *New Inn* has a **restaurant** with a three-course set menu, and you can eat pub snacks in its garden. For gourmet cuisine, head for the restaurant at the *Island Hotel*, where fresh fish is the speciality.

Bryher and Samson

Covered with a thick carpet of bracken, heather and bramble, **BRYHER** is the wildest of the inhabited islands, but the seventy-odd inhabitants have introduced some pockets of order in the form of flower plantations, mostly confined to the small settlement around the quay and climbing up the slopes of **Watch Hill** on Bryher's eastern side, from which you can enjoy a grand panorama of the whole group of islands.

It is the exposed western seaboard that takes the full brunt of the Atlantic, and nowhere more spectacularly so than at the aptly named **Hell Bay**, cupped by a limb of land on the northwestern shore, and worth catching when the wind's up. In contrast to this sound and fury, peace reigns in the southern cove of **Rushy Bay**, one of the best beaches on the island.

From the quay, there is a daily boat service to the other islands, and frequent tours to seal and bird colonies as well as fishing expeditions. You could make a quick hop to the small isle of **SAMSON**, deserted since 1855 when the last impoverished inhabitants were ordered off by the island's proprietor. Most of the abandoned cottages are on the **South Hill**, site of several primitive burial chambers dating from the second millennium BC. The North Hill has a stone coffin from the same period, thought to be the sepulchre of a tribal chief. Most of the famous **gig races** start off from Nut Rock, to the east of Samson, finishing at St Mary's quay.

Practicalities

Bryher has a tiny choice of **B&Bs**, the best of which are *Soleil D'Or*, on the eastern side of the island with views over to Tresco (☎01720/422003; ❷; closed Nov–Feb), and *Bank Cottage*, on the western side near Gweal Pool (☎01720/422612; ❷; closed Nov–Feb) – both of which offer meals. There is a **campsite** at Jenford Farm on Watch Hill (☎01720/422886; closed Nov–Feb). For refreshment, the island's one hotel, the *Hell Bay* (☎01720/422947; ❽; closed Nov–Feb) – actually a safe distance away from Hell Bay, near the pool below Gweal Hill – has a **bar** and **restaurant**. You can also eat inexpensively at the *Vine Café*, below Watch Hill, and the *Fraggle Rock Café*, near the post office, which has an upstairs restaurant – Friday is fish-and-chips night.

St Martin's

The main landing stage at **ST MARTIN'S** is on the southern promontory, at the head of the majestic sweep of **Par Beach** – a fitting entry to the island that boasts the best of the Scillies' beaches. From the quay, a road leads up past a public tennis court (rackets and balls for rent) to **HIGHER TOWN**, the main concentration of houses and location of the only shop. Here you can also find St Martin's Diving Centre (☎01720/422848), giving tuition at all levels. The water here is among the clearest in Britain, and is much favoured by scuba enthusiasts.

Beyond the church, follow the road westwards along the island's long, narrow ridge to **LOWER TOWN**, little more than a cluster of cottages on the western extremity, where there's a second quay for coming and going. The town overlooks the uninhabited isles of **Teän** and **St Helen's**, the latter holding the remains of a tenth-century oratory, monks' dwellings and a chapel, as well as a pest house, erected in 1756 to house plague-carriers entering British waters.

Along the southern shore, the gentler side of the island, you'll find the long strand of **Lawrence's Bay** and large areas of flowerbeds. On the northern side, the coast is rougher, with the exception of **Great Bay**, a beautiful half-mile recess of sand, utterly secluded and ideal for swimming. From its western end, you can climb across boulders at low tide to the hilly and wild **White Island**, on the northeastern side of which is a vast cave, **Underland Girt**, accessible at low tide.

At **St Martin's Head** on the northeastern tip of the main island lies the red and white Daymark erected in 1683 (not 1637 as inscribed) as a warning to shipping. On a clear day you can see the foam breaking against the Seven Stones Reef seven miles distant, where the tanker *Torrey Canyon* was wrecked in 1967, causing one of the world's worst oil spills. Below St Martin's Head, on the southeastern shore, lies another fine beach, **Perpitch**, looking out to the scattered Eastern Isles, slivers of rock to which boats take trippers to view puffins and grey seals.

Practicalities

St Martin's has just one **B&B** listed: *Polreath* (℡ 01720/422046, ℮ polreathscilly @virginnet.co.uk; ❹), in Higher Town, where the six comfortable rooms have all-round views. You can find out about other possibilities by looking at the notice board in the post office in Higher Town. There's also a choice **hotel**, *St Martin's on the Isle* in Lower Town (℡ 01720/422090; closed Nov–March; ❾), consisting of a cluster of cottages with modern rooms looking onto a sandy beach. In Middletown, between Higher Town and Lower Town, you'll find a **campsite** (℡ 01720/422888, ℮ chris@stmartinscampsite.freeserve.co.uk; closed Nov–Feb), just off the road near Lawrence's Bay – the only Scillies' campsite enjoying some degree of shelter. *Polreath* also has a simple **café** serving light meals, or you could venture down the valley south of Higher Town to the wholefood café and restaurant at *Little Arthur Farm* for a range of delicious home-baked cakes, organic salads and hot meals (April–Sept). The only **pub** on the island is the *Sevenstones Inn* in Lower Town, where snacks are available.

St Agnes

Visitors to the southernmost inhabited island of the Scillies, **ST AGNES**, disembark at **Porth Conger**, from where a road leads to the western side of the island, on the way passing the disused **Old Lighthouse**, one of the oldest in the country – dating from 1680 – and the most significant landmark on St Agnes. From here the right-hand fork leads to **Periglis Cove**, a mooring for boats on the western side of the island, while the left-hand fork goes to **St Warna's Cove**, where the patron saint of shipwrecks is reputed to have landed from Ireland, the exact spot being marked by a holy well. Between the two coves is a fine coastal path which passes the miniature **Troy Town Maze**, thought to have been created a couple of centuries ago, but possibly much older. Beyond St Warna's Cove, the path continues down over Wingletang Down to the southern headland of **Horse Point**, where there are some tortuous wind-eroded rocks. **Beady Pool**, an inlet on the eastern side of the headland, gained its name from the trove of beads washed ashore from the wreck of a seventeenth-century Dutch trader; some of the reddish-brown stones still occasionally turn up. The eastern side of St Agnes has one of the best beaches, the small, sheltered **Covean** (accessible from the path opposite *Covean Cottage*). Between here and Porth Conger a sand bar appears at low tide to connect the smaller isle of **Gugh**, the strand creating another lovely sheltered beach. You can walk across the bar to see a scattering of untended Bronze Age remains, and there is a good panorama of the islands from the hill at Gugh's northern end; take care not to be marooned by the incoming tide, which is extremely fierce.

St Agnes's western side looks out onto the **Western Rocks**, a horseshoe of islets that can be explored on boat tours. Biggest of them is Annet, a nesting-place for a variety of birds such as the stormy petrel and Manx shearwater, as well as colonies of puffins and shags, though many have been chased out or slaughtered in recent years by the predatory great black-beaked gull – largest of the gull family. The islands forming the western arm of the group are the best place to see grey seals. The island of **Rosevean** has the remains of houses used by the builders of the Bishop Rock Lighthouse, five miles out – at 175ft the tallest in Britain and the westernmost one on this side of the Atlantic.

Practicalities

Best of the **B&B**s on St Agnes is the *Coastguards*, one of a smart row of cottages past the Old Lighthouse and post office on the island's western side (℡01720/422373; ❸; closed Nov–March). Others include *Covean Cottage*, above Porth Conger (℡01720/422620; ❸), and the *Parsonage* (℡01720 /422370; no credit cards; ❸), nestled below the lighthouse behind a copse of Cornish elms. There's a good **campsite** at *Troy Town Farm* above Periglis Cove (℡01720/422360; closed Nov–Feb), enjoying first-rate views over to the Western Rocks. Just above the jetty at Porth Conger, the *Turk's Head* serves superb St Agnes pasties to go with its beer.

Redruth to Bude

Though generally harsher than the county's southern seaboard, the north Cornish coast is punctuated by some of the finest beaches in England, the most popular of which are to be found around **Newquay**, the surfers' capital. Other major holiday centres are to be found down the coast at the ex-mining town of **St Agnes** and north around the Camel estuary, where the port of **Padstow** makes a good base for some remarkable beaches as well as a fine inland walk. North of the Camel, the coast is an almost unbroken line of cliffs as far as the Devon border, the gaunt, exposed terrain making a melodramatic setting for **Tintagel**, though the wide strand at **Bude** attracts legions of surfers and family holiday-makers.

Offsetting the beaches and caravan parks, parts of the more westerly stretches are littered with the derelict stacks and castle-like ruins of the engine-houses that once powered the region's **copper** and **tin mines**, industries that at one time led the world. Also prominent are the grey nonconformist chapels that reflect the impact of John Wesley on Cornwall's mining communities. His open-air meetings attracted thousands of listeners in such places as Gwennap Pit outside **Redruth**, the centre of the industry.

North Cornwall's network of public transport leaves a lot to be desired. Newquay is the terminus for the cross-peninsula **train** route from Par, while the main line to Penzance stops at Redruth and Camborne, which are connected to St Agnes on the #43 and #57 **bus** routes, and to Falmouth on #41. Truronian runs a regular #T1 service from Perranporth and St Agnes to Truro,

Helston and The Lizard, while Western National's #57, which starts in Penzance, also takes in St Ives and continues on to Perranporth and Newquay. Bus #56 runs between Newquay and Padstow, the latter also served by the regular #55 from Bodmin (not Sun in winter). Services #X4, #122 and #125 link Boscastle and Tintagel (the last two going on to Bude) and #124 runs between Port Isaac, Polzeath and Wadebridge (not Sun in winter). Finally, Okehampton and Exeter are linked to Bude by #X9, and to Tintagel and Boscastle by #X10 (not Sun).

Redruth and around

In the 1850s **REDRUTH** and neighbouring **CAMBORNE**, with which it is now amalgamated, accounted for two-thirds of the world's copper production, the 350 pits employing some fifty thousand workers, many of whom were forced to emigrate when cheaper deposits of tin and copper were discovered overseas at the turn of the century. The simple granite mine buildings bear a family resemblance to the numerous Methodist chapels in the area – testimony to the success enjoyed by the nonconformist sects in Cornwall. Between 1762 and 1786 the grassy hollow of Gwennap Pit, outside **St Day**, a mile southeast of Redruth, was the scene of huge gatherings of miners and their families to hear John Wesley preach. The first visits to Cornwall by the founder of Methodism were met with derision and violence, but he later won over the tough mining communities who could find little comfort in the gentrified established church. At one time Wesley estimated that the congregation at Gwennap Pit exceeded thirty thousand, noting in his diary, "I shall scarce see a larger congregation till we meet in the air." The present tiered amphitheatre was created in 1805, and is today the venue of Methodist meetings for the annual Whit Monday service.

The town's former harbour lies two and a half miles away at **PORTREATH**, a surfing beach that enjoys the cleanest water on this stretch. The village is within walking distance of the awe-inspiring **Hell's Mouth**, a cauldron of waves and black rocks at the base of two-hundred-foot cliffs five miles down the coast at the top of St Ives Bay; it's also just three miles south of **Porthtowan**, another popular surfing beach.

You can find a good selection of **B&Bs** in Redruth, among them the attractive *Lansdowne House*, five minutes from the bus and train stations at 42 Clinton Rd (℡01209/216002; no credit cards; ❶), which has rooms with and without private facilities. Portreath has the light and airy *Cliff House*, just off the harbourside on The Square (℡01209/842008; no credit cards; ❷), or venture a little further out to the charmingly old-fashioned restored Georgian mansion *Fountain Springs*, Glenfeadon House, Glenfeadon Terrace (℡01209/842650; no credit cards; ❷), about a quarter-mile from the sea – take the second left turning after the school on the B3300.

St Agnes and around

Though the village is surrounded by ruined engine houses, **ST AGNES** today gives little hint of the conditions in which its population once lived, the straggling streets of uniform grey cottages now housing retired people, whose immaculate flower-filled gardens are admired by the troops of holiday-makers striding up and down the steep terrace called Stippy-Stappy.

Well connected by bus to Truro, St Ives, Redruth and Newquay, St Agnes makes a useful stopover for exploring the coast in the area. At the end of a steep valley below St Agnes, **Trevaunance Cove** is the site of several failed attempts to create a harbour for the town. Its fine sandy beach is a favourite with surfers and other bathing enthusiasts, despite the poor water quality. West of St Agnes lies one of Cornwall's most famous vantage points, **St Agnes Beacon**, 630ft high, from which views extend inland to Bodmin Moor and even across the peninsula to St Michael's Mount. A short distance away, the headland of **St Agnes Head** has the area's largest colony of breeding kittiwakes, and the nearby cliffs also shelter fulmars and guillemots, while grey seals are a common sight offshore. Past the old World War II airfield three miles north of St Agnes, the resort of **Perranporth** lies at the southern end of Perran Beach, a three-mile expanse of sand enhanced by caves and natural rock arches, very popular with surfers – boards and equipment are available to rent from Surf Shack, Beach Rd.

There's a good choice of **accommodation** in and around the town, including the eighteenth-century *Malthouse*, Peterville, the lower part of the village, a former brewing-house where you'll find a relaxed and bohemian atmosphere (℡01872/553318; no credit cards; ❶). Near the centre on Penwinnick Road, *Penkerris* (℡01872/552262; ❶) is a spacious creeper-clad house, with log fires in winter, a big garden, and good home-cooked dinners. If you want to be near the beach, head down to Trevaunance Cove, where the whitewashed *Driftwood Spars* (℡01872/552428; ❹) occupies a seventeenth-century tin miners' warehouse. In Perranporth, the *Cellar Cove Hotel* enjoys bird's-eye views over the beach but requires a two-night minimum stay in season (℡01872/572110; ❹), while, right next to the beach, the *Seiners' Arms* is a huge pub and restaurant where you can sit outside and also sleep (℡01872/573118, ⓦwww.connexions.co.uk/seiners; ❹). On the cliff-top outside Perranporth, the **youth hostel** (℡01872/573812; closed Sept–March), in a former coastguard station, enjoys great views towards Ligger Point at the north end of the beach. Back in St Agnes, the most interesting **pub** is the *Railway Inn* on Vicarage Road; decorated with an idiosyncratic collection of shoes, horsebrasses and naval memorabilia, it also has a good selection of ales and snacks.

Newquay

It is difficult to imagine a lineage for **NEWQUAY** that extends more than a few decades, but the "new quay" was built in the fifteenth century in what was already a long-established fishing port. Up to then it had been more colourfully known as Towan Blistra, and was concentrated in the sheltered west end of the bay. The town was given a boost in the nineteenth century when its harbour was expanded for coal import and a railway was constructed across the peninsula for china clay shipments. With the trains came a swelling stream of seasonal visitors, drawn to the town's superb position on a knuckle of cliffs overlooking fine golden sands and Atlantic rollers, natural advantages which have made Newquay the premier resort of north Cornwall.

The centre of town is a somewhat tacky parade of shops and restaurants, partly pedestrianized, from which lanes lead to ornamental gardens and sloping lawns on the cliff-tops. Below, adjacent to the small harbour in the crook of the massive Towan Head, **Towan Beach** is the most central of the seven miles of firm sandy beaches that follow in an almost unbroken succession. You can reach all of them on foot, though for some of the farther ones, such as **Porth Beach**, with its grassy headland, or the extensive **Watergate Bay**, you might prefer to make use of local buses #53 and #56. The beaches can all be unbearably crowded in full season, and all are popular with surfers, particularly Watergate and – west of Towan Head – **Fistral Bay**, the largest of the town beaches. On the other side of East Pentire Head from Fistral, **Crantock Beach** – reachable over the Gannel River by ferry or upstream footbridge – is usually less crowded, and has a lovely backdrop of dunes and undulating grassland. Try to coincide your visit to Newquay with one of the **surfing competitions** and events that run right through the summer – contact the tourist office for details.

Arrival, information and accommodation

Newquay's **train station** is off Cliff Road, a couple of hundred yards from the **bus station** on East Street. All buses for the beaches stop on Cliff Road and its extension Narrowcliff. The **tourist office** lies opposite the bus station at Marcus Hill (May–Sept Mon–Sat 9.30am–5.30pm, Sun 9.30am–3.30pm; Oct–April Mon–Fri 9.30am–4.30pm, Sat 9.30am–12.30pm; ⓣ01637/854020, ⓦwww.newquay.co.uk).

There's loads of **accommodation** in Newquay, though rooms can still be at a premium in July and August. In the centre of town, the *Bay View House Hotel* offers good value and superb views (ⓣ01637/871214; ❸; closed Nov–Easter), while fans of Fistral Beach will appreciate the proximity of *Links Hotel* on Headland Rd (ⓣ01637/873211; no credit cards; ❷). Newquay has a handful of independent **hostels** offering beds in dorms and some double rooms, including the grand-daddy of them all, *Newquay International Backpackers*, 69 Tower Rd (ⓣ01637/879366, ⓦwww.backpackers.co.uk/newquay); day trips and discounts on surf rental are offered. Other hostels operate to varying standards, including the nearby *Home Surf Lodge*, 18 Tower Rd (ⓣ01637/873387, ⓦwww.newquay-online.com/homesurf), the newest and tidiest of the town's hostels, and *Matt's Surf Lodge*, 110 Mount Wise Rd (ⓣ01637/874651, ⓦwww.matts-surf-lodge.co.uk), set slightly further out than the others, but with friendly staff and a licensed bar. All hostels have TVs, kitchens, and places to store your surfboard. The **campsites** in the area are all mega-complexes, but many of them are unwilling to take same-sex groups or even couples. The most convenient site, *Porth Beach* (ⓣ01637/876531, ⓦwww.porthbeach.co.uk; closed Nov to mid-March), behind the beach of the same name to the east of town, falls into this category, and a little further back, on Trevelgue Road, *Trevelgue* (ⓣ01637/851851, ⓦwww.trevelgue.co.uk) separates families from groups. The next-door *Smugglers Haven* (ⓣ01637/852000, ⓦwww.surfshack.co.uk), however, run by the same management, has a more relaxed attitude, while the *Sunnyside* on Quintrell Downs (ⓣ01637/873338, ⓦwww.sunnyside.co.uk) goes out of its way to attract the 18 to 30 singles crowd – it's a couple of miles inland, close to a stop on the train line.

Eating, drinking and nightlife

Newquay is filled with places to eat, but most are pretty bland. There are a few casual **cafés** just up from the beach on Tower Road, including the *Lifebuoy Café*, which serves all-day breakfasts (also vegetarian). At 38 Fore St, the lattice-windowed *Cottage* serves snacks and teas by day, Tex-Mex, steaks and salads in the upstairs **restaurant** in the evenings, to musical accompaniment (closed Sat lunch & all Sun). The *Bay View House Hotel* (see above) has a terrace café open during the day and good-value set-price evening meals.

Newquay has become Cornwall's biggest centre for **nightclubbing**: the town's current hot spots are *Berties* on East Street, *Sailors* and *The Beach* on Fore Street, and *Tall Trees* on Tolcarne Road, though these places tend to be fairly glittery and overwhelmed in summer. You can sometimes hear more underground sounds at *Foster's* pub in Narrowcliff and the *Koola Bar* on Beach Road; otherwise ask around and watch the posters for the current venues. The *Sandridge Hotel* on Headland Road has gay dance parties on Fridays and Saturdays.

Surfing and other outdoor activities

You can rent or buy **surfing** equipment from beach stalls, or else try Tunnel Vision, 6 Alma Place, off Fore Street (℡01637/879033, ✉andy@tunnel-vision .demon.co.uk), or Fistral Surf Shop, 1 Beacon Rd, on the harbour side of the headland (℡01637/850520). Boards cost around £5 a day. For kite-surfing, land yachting, surf canoeing and paragliding, head for The Extreme Academy on Watergate Bay (℡01637/860840; ⓦwww.watergatebay.co.uk); a day's kite-surfing will cost £45. The British Surfing Association (℡01736/360250, ⓦwww.britsurf.co.uk) puts on courses of up to ten lessons from May to October at both Fistral and Tolcarne Beaches. Dolphin Surf School (℡01637/873707, ⓦwww.surfschool.co.uk) runs courses from March to November and also offers accommodation. Reef Surf School (℡0707/123 4455) is open all year round and arranges three-day surfing holidays including B&B. If you're more interested in **biking**, head for the rental place on Towan Beach (℡01637/874668) or try Newquay Bike Hire at Unit 1, Wesley Yard (℡01637/874040), which will deliver a bike free.

Padstow and around

The small fishing port of **PADSTOW** is nearly as popular as Newquay, but has a very different feel. Enclosed within the estuary of the Camel – the only river of any size that empties on Cornwall's north coast – the town long retained its position as the principal fishing port on this coast, and still has something of the atmosphere of a medieval town. Its chief annual festival is also a hangover from times past, the **Obby Oss**, a May Day romp when one of the locals garbs himself as a horse and prances through the town preceded by a masked and club-wielding "teaser" – a spirited if rather institutionalized re-enactment of old fertility rites.

On the hill overlooking Padstow, the church of **St Petroc** is dedicated to Cornwall's most important saint, a Welsh or Irish monk who landed here in the sixth century, died in the area and gave his name to the town – "Petrock's Stow". The building has a fine fifteenth-century font, an Elizabethan pulpit and some amusing carved bench-ends. The walls are lined with monuments to the local Prideaux family, who still occupy nearby **Prideaux Place**, an Elizabethan manor house with grand staircases, richly furnished rooms full of portraits, fantastically ornate ceilings and formal gardens (Easter & June–Sept Mon–Thurs & Sun 1.30–5pm; £5, grounds only £2), all of which have been used as settings for a plethora of films, such as *Twelfth Night* and *Oscar and Lucinda*. The grounds contain an ancient deer park, and give good views over the Camel estuary.

The harbour is jammed with launches and boats offering cruises in Padstow Bay, while a regular **ferry** (daily: Easter–Oct 8am–7.30pm; Nov–Easter Mon–Sat 8am–5pm; £2 return) carries people across the river to **ROCK** – close to the sand-engulfed church of **St Enodoc** (John Betjeman's burial place) and to the good beaches around Polzeath. The ferry leaves from the harbour's North Pier except at low water when it goes from near the war memorial downstream.

The coast on the **south side** of the estuary also offers some good **beach** country, which you can reach in summer on bus #556, though walking would enable you to view some terrific coastline. Out of Padstow, the rivermouth is clogged by **Doom Bar**, a sand bar that was allegedly the curse of a mermaid who had been mortally wounded by a fisherman who mistook her for a seal. Apart from thwarting the growth of Padstow as a busy commercial port, the bar has scuppered some three hundred vessels, with great loss of life. Round

The Saints' Way

Padstow's St Petroc church is the traditional starting point for one of Cornwall's oldest walking routes, the **Saints' Way**. Extending for some thirty miles between Cornwall's north and south coasts, and connecting the principal ports of Padstow and Fowey, the path originates from the Bronze Age when traders preferred the cross-country hike to making the perilous sea journey round Land's End. The route was later travelled by Irish and Welsh missionaries crossing the peninsula between the fifth and eighth centuries, on pilgrimage to the principal shrines of Cornwall's Celtic culture.

Skirting Bodmin Moor, the reconstructed Saints' Way is rarely dramatic, though it passes a variety of scenery and several points of interest along the way, from Neolithic burial chambers to medieval churches and the more austere lines of Wesleyan chapels. The route is well marked and can be walked in stages, the country paths that constitute it stretching for two to six miles each; although it crosses several trunk roads, these do not impinge too much. You can pick up **guides and leaflets** giving detailed directions in Padstow, Bodmin and Fowey tourist offices.

From St Petroc's, follow Hill Street, crossing New Street, and continue along Dennis Lane to the lake at Dennis Cove, from where the path climbs through fields to the monument to Queen Victoria, the point at which most people stop. If you choose to continue, you'll find that seven or eight miles out of Padstow, the route crosses the **St Breock Downs** with views stretching from the Camel estuary to the white clay mountains around St Austell. From here the path veers southeast to pass through **Lanivet**, the halfway point of the Way lying a couple of miles outside Bodmin. For **B&Bs** around here, see accommodation for Bodmin p.517. The *Lanivet Inn* provides welcome refreshment, or you can eat good fish meals at the village's *Welcome Stranger* **restaurant**.

South of here, **Helman Tor** (674ft) holds the trail's most impressive scenery, studded with bare boulders and wind-eroded rocks and flanked by acres of gorse. At Helman Tor Gate, the path divides, giving you the choice of reaching Fowey via **Lanlivery** – home of St Brevita's church with one of Cornwall's landmark towers – or **Luxulyan**, which boasts a lush gorge crossed by a viaduct and aqueduct built in 1842 and a holy well below the fifteenth-century church. The eastern route through Lanlivery takes you through the wooded estuary of the River Fowey – legendary meeting place of Tristan and Iseult – to the port. The longer western route follows an old cobbled causeway for part of the way, and passes through **Tywardreath**, which once marked the inland extent of the sea before the port of Par was built by industrialist Joseph Treffry (builder of the viaduct at Luxulyan). Tywardreath means "house on the strand", and was described by Daphne Du Maurier in her novel of that name. Fowey is four miles southeast of here. The end of the route is the church of St Fimbarrus in Fowey; see p.480 for accommodation hereabouts.

Stepper Point you can reach the sandy and secluded Harlyn Bay and, turning the corner southwards, **Constantine Bay**, the area's best surfing beach. The dunes backing the beach and the rock pools skirting it make this one of the most appealing bays on this coast; moreover it boasts the best water quality, though the tides can be treacherous and bathing hazardous near the rocks. Surfers are attracted to other beaches in the neighbourhood, too, but the surrounding caravan-sites can make these claustrophobic in summer – the sands around **Porthcothan** are worth exploring.

Three or four miles further south lies one of Cornwall's most dramatic beaches, **Bedruthan Steps**. Traditionally held to be the stepping-stones of a giant called Bedruthan (a legendary figure conjured into existence in the nineteenth century), these slate outcrops can be readily viewed from the cliff-top path, at a point which drivers can reach on the B3276. Steps lead down to the broad beach below (closed in winter), which has dangerous tides and thunderous waves and is not advised for swimming.

Padstow is also the start of an excellent **cycle-track** converted from the old railway line between Wadebridge and Padstow, forming part of the **Camel Trail**, a fifteen-mile traffic-free path that follows the river up as far as Wenfordbridge, on the edge of Bodmin Moor, with a turn-off for Bodmin. The five-mile Padstow–Wadebridge stretch offers glimpses of a variety of birdlife, especially around the small **Pinkson Creek**, habitat of terns, herons, curlews and egrets. You can **rent bikes** from Brinham's (℡01841/532594) and Padstow Cycle Hire (℡01841/533533), both on South Quay, by the Camel Trail. Further up the Trail, at the top of the estuary outside Wadebridge, Bridge Bike Hire has a greater stock, though it's still advisable to book (℡01208/813050). **Walkers** can set out from Padstow on the thirty-mile **Saints' Way** across the peninsula to Fowey (see box opposite).

Practicalities

Padstow's **tourist office** is on the harbour (Mon–Sat 9.30am–5pm, Sun 9.30am–2pm; winter closed Sun; ℡01841/533449, ⓦwww.padstow.uk.com). Central **accommodation** includes the B&B at 4 Riverside (℡01841/532383; no credit cards; ❷), a three-storey building right on the harbour; the top bedroom has a French window leading onto a balcony. A few minutes away, *Armside*, 10 Cross St (℡01841/532271; no credit cards; ❸), is an elegant eighteenth-century town house with parking space, while the posher *Old Ship* on Mill Square (℡01841/532357; ❺) has plenty of character, strewn with antique furnishings and stacked with paintings, and all rooms are equipped with double showers. The nearest **youth hostel** has stunning views and is excellently sited almost on the beach at Treyarnon Bay (℡01841/520322; closed Nov–March); to get there, take a bus to Constantine (#556, also from Newquay) then walk for half a mile. The nearest congenial **campsites** to Padstow are *Trerethern Tourist Park* (℡01841/532061; closed Nov–March), a mile southwest, and *Dennis Cove* (℡01841/532349; closed Oct–Easter), alongside the estuary about a ten-minute walk south of town.

Padstow's quayside is lined with snack bars and pasty shops as well as pubs where you can sit outside, such as the *Shipwright's* on the harbour's north side. But foodies know the town best for its high-class **restaurants**, particularly those associated with star chef Rick Stein, whose *Seafood Restaurant*, at Riverside (℡01841/532700, ⓦwww.rickstein.com), is one of England's top fish restaurants – and expensive, with most main courses around £25 (though cod, chips and mushy peas cost a very reasonable £16.50). Nevertheless, the waiting list for a table here can be months long, though a reservation on a weekday out of season can mean booking only a day or two ahead, and there's always the chance of a cancellation if you turn up on spec. The TV chef has responded to the demand by opening up another couple of places in town, *St Petroc's Bistro* at 4 New St (℡01841/532700; closed Mon), which has a lighter, slightly cheaper but more restricted version of the *Seafood Restaurant's* menu, and the casual *Rick Stein's Café* nearby at 10 Middle St, whose small tables lend it the style of a Milanese bar (except that you can't smoke), and which serves snacks at lunch and moderate meals at night (closed Sun). All three establishments also offer accommodation (❻, ❺ at the *Café*).

Rick Stein doesn't have a monopoly of classy restaurants in Padstow; *No. 6*, at 6 Middle St (℡01841/532359; closed lunchtime & Nov–Dec), is an excellent but quite pricey Mediterranean-style restaurant which uses organic produce whenever possible (no smoking except in the courtyard). For cheaper eats, the *Old Custom House* on the harbourside serves pub snacks (and also has an adjoining fine restaurant, *Pescadou*: ☎01841/532359), while *Rojano's* on Mill Square dishes up pizza and pasta (closed Mon & Nov–Feb). Otherwise, the *London Inn* on Lanadwell Street, adorned with hanging baskets outside and wood panelling within, does sandwiches, pasties and more substantial meals, as does the *Old Ship*, where you can eat outside. And if you really can't leave Padstow without sampling some of Rick Stein's creations, you could always feast on a gourmet picnic, supplied by the master's **delicatessen** next to his café on Middle Street.

Polzeath to Port Isaac

Facing west into Padstow Bay, the beaches of and around **POLZEATH** are the finest in the vicinity, pelted by rollers which make this one of the best surfing sites in the West Country; Daymer Bay is more popular with the windsurfing crowd. *Pentire View* is a pleasant **B&B** a few yards up the hill from Polzeath's beach (☎01208/862484; no credit cards; ❶), and the popular *Tristram* **campsite** (☎01208/862215; closed Nov–Feb) sits on a cliff overlooking the beach. In recent years, Polzeath campsites, like those in Newquay, have barred same-sex groups of young people owing to past fracas, though *Trenant Steading* (☎01208/862407; closed Nov–Easter) between Polzeath and New Polzeath is currently still admitting them, but check first. On the beach, the *Galleon* does various snacks and takeaways, and *Finn's* does full meals as well as cream teas. *Mother's Kitchen*, just off the beach next to the Spar supermarket, offers a range of ice cream, pasta and takeaway pizzas (not chips), and the *Oyster Catcher* bar is a lively evening hangout just up the hill. *Surf's Up* at 21 Trenant Close (☎01208/862003, ⒲www.surfsupsurfchool.com) and on the beach offers **surfing** tuition; the gear can be rented from shops.

Heading east, the coastal path brings you through cliff-top growths of feathery tamarisk, which flower spectacularly in July and August. From the headland of **Pentire Point**, views unfold for miles over the offshore islets of **The Mouls** and **Newland**, with their populations of grey seals and puffins. Half a mile east, the scanty remains of an Iron Age fort stand on the humpy back of **Rump's Point**, from where the path descends a mile or so to **Lundy Bay**, a pleasant sandy cove surrounded by green fields. Climbing again, you pass the shafts of an old antimony mine on the way to **Doyden Point**, which is picturesquely ornamented with a nineteenth-century castle folly once used for gambling parties.

The inlet of **Port Quin** has a few cottages but no shops – the next settlement of any size is **PORT ISAAC**, wedged in a gap in the precipitous cliffwall and dedicated to the crab and lobster trade. Only seasonal trippers ruffle the surface of life in this cramped harbour town, whose narrow lanes focus on a couple of pubs at the seafront, where a pebble beach and rock pools are exposed by the low tide. The village offers a range of **accommodation**, best of all the *Slipway Hotel* (☎01208/880264, ⒲www.portisaac.com; ❺), a sixteenth-century building right opposite the harbour; the management is youthful and friendly, and there's a bar and excellent restaurant too. Cheaper choices are outside the centre and away from the sea, among them the Victorian *Bay Hotel*, 1 The Terrace (☎01208/880380, ⒠jacki.burns@talk21.com; ❷), with views from the light, bright rooms and a wood-burning stove in winter, and, overlooking the neighbouring Port Gaverne Bay, *Anchorage Guest House*, 12 The Terrace (☎01208/880629; non-smoking; ❶), where rooms with a shared bathroom get the best views. The *Old School* also has wonderful views and a seafood restaurant (☎01208/880721, ⓦwww.cornwall-online.co.uk/old-school-hotel; ❸). The *Golden Lion* is Port Isaac's most cheerful **pub** and has an adjoining bistro and balcony seating overlooking the harbour. Crab is what Port Isaac does best; try it here or to take away on the harbourfront; other places to sample crab or lobster include the *Slipway Hotel*. The *Old School* is a good place for snacks, teas and full fish meals, or you might be tempted by the fresh fish and chips across the road at the *Old Drugstore*.

At the main car park at the top of the village, a kiosk which alternates between Port Isaac and Tintagel provides information on **walking along the heritage coast** on either side of the town. **Port Gaverne**, the next cove to the east, is a serene cluster of houses, with a snug bar at the *Port Gaverne Inn* (☎01208/880244, ⓦwww.chycor.co.uk/hotels/port-gaverne; ❺), where you can pick up a "surfer's lunch" or eat in the expensive restaurant – quaint rooms are also available here.

Tintagel

East of Port Isaac, the coast is wild and unspoiled, making for some steep and strenuous walking, and interspersed with some stupendous strands of sandy beaches such as that at **Trebarwith**. A few miles further north, the rocky littoral provides an appropriate backdrop for the black, forsaken ruins of **Tintagel Castle** (daily: April to mid-July & late Aug to Sept 10am–6pm; mid-July to late Aug 10am–7pm; Oct 10am–5pm; Nov–March 10am–4pm; £3; EH). It was the twelfth-century chronicler Geoffrey of Monmouth who first popularized the notion that this was the **birthplace of King Arthur**, son of Uther Pendragon and Ygrayne, but by that time local folklore was already saturated with tales of King Mark of Cornwall, Tristan and Iseult, Arthur and the knights of Camelot. Twin influences were at work in Geoffrey's story, which merges the historic figure of Arthur with a separate body of legend centring on the missionary activity of the Celtic monastery that occupied this site in the sixth century. Tintagel is certainly a plausibly resonant candidate for the abode of the Once and Future King, but the **castle** ruins in fact belong to a Norman stronghold occupied by the earls of Cornwall, who after sporadic spurts of rebuilding allowed it to decay, most of it having been washed into the sea by the sixteenth century. The remains of the **Celtic monastery** are still visible on the headland and are an important source of knowledge of how the country's earliest monastic houses were organized. Recent digs on the eastern side of the island have also revealed glass fragments dating from the sixth or seventh centuries believed to originate in Malaga, as well as a 1500-year-old section of slate bearing two Latin inscriptions, one of them attributing authorship to one "Artognou, father of Coll's descendant". You can find out more at the story-telling events held at the castle in summer (currently Wed at 6pm & some weekends at noon); there are occasionally musical evenings as well – call ☎01840/770328 for information.

The best approach to the site is from **Glebe Cliff** to the west, where the parish church of **St Materiana** sits in isolation; the South West Coast Path passes the church, and for drivers it's a good place to park before descending to the castle. From the village of **TINTAGEL** the shortest access is from the signposted path, a well-trodden route. The only item of note in this dreary collection of cafés and B&Bs is the **Old Post Office** (April–Sept daily 11am–5.30pm; Oct daily 11am–5pm; £2.20; NT), a rickety-roofed slate-built construction dating from the fourteenth century, now restored to its appearance in the Victorian era when it was used as a post office.

Buses stop on the main Fore Street close to the octagonal **tourist office** (daily: March–Oct 10am–5pm; Nov–Feb 10.30am–4pm; ℡01840/779084), sited in the council car park on the road from Camelford. The village has plen-

King Arthur in Cornwall

Did **King Arthur** really exist? If he did, it is likely that he was an amalgam of two peo-ple; a sixth-century Celtic warlord who united the local tribes in a series of suc-cessful battles against the invading Anglo-Saxons, and a local Cornish saint. Whatever his origins, his role was recounted and inflated by poets and troubadours in later centuries (particularly in Welsh poems, the earliest of which is *Gododdin*). Though there is no mention of him in the ninth- to twelfth-century *Anglo-Saxon Chronicle*, his exploits were elaborated later by the unreliable medieval chronicler Geoffrey of Monmouth, who made Arthur the conqueror of western Europe, and was the first to record the belief that **Tintagel** was his birthplace. Twelfth-century chron-icler William of Malmesbury narrated the story of Glastonbury, including the popular legend that, after being mortally wounded in battle, Arthur sailed to Avalon (Glastonbury), where he was buried alongside Guinevere. The Arthurian legends were crystallized in Thomas Malory's epic, *Morte d'Arthur* (1485), further romanti-cized in Tennyson's *Idylls of the King* (1859–85) and resurrected in T.H. White's saga, *The Once and Future King* (1937–58).

Although there are places throughout Britain and Europe which claim some asso-ciation with Arthur, it is England's West Country, and **Cornwall** in particular, that has the greatest concentration of places boasting a link. Relatively untouched by the Saxon invasions, Cornwall has practically appropriated the hero as its own, a far more authentic bond than the efforts of the county's tourist industry might suggest. Here, the legends (fertilized by fellow Celts from Brittany and Wales) have estab-lished deep roots, so that, for example, the spirit of Arthur is said to be embodied in the Cornish chough – a bird now almost extinct. Cornwall's most famous Arthurian site is **Tintagel**, which is said to be the birthplace of Arthur. Meanwhile, Merlin is thought to have lived in a cave under the castle – and also on a rock near Mousehole, south of Penzance. Nearby Bodmin Moor is full of places with associ-ated names such as "King Arthur's Bed" and "King Arthur's Downs", while Camlan, the battlefield where Arthur was mortally wounded fighting against his nephew Mordred, is thought to lie on the northern reaches of the moor at Slaughterbridge, near Camelford (which is also sometimes identified as Camelot itself). Nearby, at Dozmary Pool, the knight Bedivere was dispatched by the dying Arthur to return the sword Excalibur to the mysterious hand emerging from the water – though Loe Pool in Mount's Bay also claims this honour. According to some, Arthur's body was trans-ported after the battle to Boscastle, on Cornwall's northern coast, from where a funeral barge transported the body to Avalon. Cornwall is also the presumed home of King Mark, at the centre of a separate cycle of myths which later became inter-woven with the Arthurian one. It was Mark who sent the knight Tristan to Ireland to fetch his betrothed, Iseult; his headquarters is supposed to have been at Castle Dore, north of Fowey. Out beyond Land's End, the fabled, vanished country of Lyonesse is also said to be the original home of Arthur, as well as being (according to Spenser's Faerie Queene) the birthplace of Tristan.

Much of the Cornish tourist office's celebration of the Arthurian sagas has the same cynical basis as the more ancient desire to claim Arthur by the various villages and sites throughout England and Wales: the cachet and hence profit to be had from the veneration of a secular saint. Witness the "discovery" of the tomb of Arthur and Guinevere by the Benedictine monks of Glastonbury in the twelfth century, which helped to boost the profile of this powerful abbey. Today in Tintagel you will find Arthurian tack galore, including every kind of Merlin-esque hogwash (crystal balls, sugar-coated wands, etc), and even Excaliburgers.

ty of **accommodation**, most of it fairly basic, though the *Old Malt House* (℡01840/770461; ❷; closed Jan), which has two restaurants, and the *Tintagel Arms Hotel* (℡01840/770780; ❷), both on Fore Street, have more character and are conveniently located for the castle. Further up the same street, the *Wharncliffe Arms* (℡01840/770393; ❷) has more ordinary rooms, including ones for three, four and five people (£65–75). Alternatively, head a mile or so inland of Tintagel to Trenale, where *Trebrea Lodge* (℡01840/770410; ❺; closed Jan), a Cornish manor house, lies in a lush rural location with all bedrooms facing the sea, and with an elegant first-floor guests' sitting room. Three-quarters of a mile outside the village at Dunderhole Point, past St Materiana, the offices of a former slate quarry now house a **youth hostel** with great views of the coastline (℡01840/770334; closed Oct to mid-April). At the end of Atlantic Road, the *Headland* site offers scenic **camping** (℡01840/770239, ⓦwww .headlandcp-tintagel.co.uk; closed Nov–March).

Boscastle

Three miles east of Tintagel, the port of **BOSCASTLE** lies compressed within a narrow ravine drilled by the rivers Jordan and Valency, its tidy riverfront bordered by thatched and lime-washed houses giving on to the twisty harbour. Above and behind, a collection of seventeenth- and eighteenth-century cottages can be seen on a circular walk, starting either from Fore Street or the main car park, where there is a local map. The walk traces the valley of the Valency for about a mile to reach Boscastle's graceful **parish church**, tucked away in a peaceful glen. A mile and a half further up the valley lies another church, **St Juliot's**, restored by Thomas Hardy when he was plying his trade as a young architect. It was while he was working here that he met Emma Gifford, whom he married in 1874, a year after the publication of *A Pair of Blue Eyes*, the book that kicked off Hardy's literary career. It opens with an architect arriving in a Cornish village to restore its church, and is full of descriptions of the country around Boscastle.

Boscastle's **tourist office** is situated in the car park at the bottom of the main road into the village (daily: March–Oct 10am–5pm; Nov–Feb 10.30am–4pm; ℡01840/250010). One of the most appealing **places to stay** is *St Christopher's Hotel* (℡01840/250412, ⓦwww.stchristophershotel.co.uk; ❷; closed Dec–Feb), a restored Georgian manor house at the top of the High Street, but for a real Hardy experience, head for the non-smoking *Old Rectory*, on the road to St Juliot (℡01840/250225, ⓦwww.stjuliot.com; ❷; closed Dec–Feb), where you can stay in either Hardy's or Emma's bedroom, and roam the extensive grounds. The harbour has a lovely old **youth hostel** (℡01840/250287; closed Oct–March) which is right by the sea. Nearby, you can eat at the *Harbour Restaurant* (℡01840 /250380; closed mid-Nov to Easter), which serves moderately priced organic, Asian-influenced food at wooden kitchen tables, as well as sandwiches and teas; it's worth booking ahead at weekends. By the youth hostel, pick up an ice cream from the *Harbour Light*, whose splendidly saggy roof marks it out as one of Boscastle's oldest buildings. The village has three good **pubs**: in the upper part of town, the *Napoleon* has the advantage of a good seafood bistro and a spacious lawned garden, while the *Cobweb* down near the harbour rates highly on atmosphere and has bar food; both have live music evenings.

Bude and around

There is little distinctively Cornish in Cornwall's northernmost town of **BUDE**, four miles west of the Devon border. Built around an estuary surrounded by a fine expanse of sands, the town has sprouted a crop of holiday homes and hotels, though these have not unduly spoiled the place nor the magnificent cliffy coast surrounding it.

Of the excellent beaches hereabouts, the central **Summerleaze** is clean and wide, growing to such immense proportions when the tide is out that a sea water swimming pool has been provided near the cliffs. The mile-long **Widemouth Bay**, two and a half miles **south** of Bude, is the main focus of the holiday hordes – it has the cleanest water monitored between Bude and Polzeath, though bathing can be dangerous near the rocks at low tide. Surfers also congregate five miles down the coast at **Crackington Haven**, wonderfully situated between 430-foot crags at the mouth of a lush valley, though the water quality is poor. The cliffs on this stretch are characterized by remarkable zigzagging strata of shale, limestone and sandstone, a mixture which erodes into vividly contorted detached formations.

To the **north** of Bude, acres-wide **Crooklets** is the scene of **surfing** and life-saving demonstrations and competitions. A couple of miles farther on, **Sandy Mouth** holds a pristine expanse of sand with rock pools beneath the encircling cliffs. The water quality is up to EU standards despite the seaborne litter, and myriad wildflowers dot the country around. It is a short walk from here to another surfers' delight, **Duckpool**, a tiny sandy cove flanked by jagged reefs at low tide. The beach is dominated by the three-hundred-foot **Steeple Point**, at the mouth of a stream that flows through the **Coombe Valley**. Once the estate of the master Elizabethan mariner Sir Richard Grenville, the valley is now managed by the National Trust, who have laid out a one-and-a-half-mile nature trail alongside the wooded stream, half a mile inland.

Between Duckpool and the Devon border stretch five miles of strenuous but exhilarating coast. The only village along here is **Morwenstow**, just south of **Henna Cliff**, at 450ft the highest sheer drop of any sea-cliff in England after Beachy Head, affording magnificent views along the coast and beyond Lundy to the Welsh coast.

Practicalities

Bude's **tourist office** is in the centre of town at the Crescent (April–Sept Mon–Sat 9.30am–5pm, Sun 10am–4pm; Oct–March Mon–Fri 10am–4pm, Sat 10am–2pm; ⓣ01288/354240, ⓦwww.bude.co.uk). Among the town's **accommodation**, *Tee Side* (ⓣ01288/352351, ⓔtee_side@hotmail.com; no credit cards; ❶) and *Sea Jade* (ⓣ01288/353404; no credit cards; ❶) at no. 2 and no. 15 Burn View respectively are among a cluster of very similar B&Bs near the golf course. The *Falcon Hotel* on Breakwater Road is a much fancier affair (ⓣ01288/352005; ❺), supposed to be the oldest coaching house in north Cornwall. If you don't mind being further from the beaches, head a mile inland to Cot Hill, Stratton, where the *Stratton Gardens Hotel* (ⓣ01288/352500, ⓦwww.cornwall-online.co.uk/accommodation; no smoking; ❹; closed Nov) provides all the comforts in a small, white-washed, sixteenth-century building; there's a great restaurant, too. There are numerous campsites around Bude, the nearest of them being *Upper Lynstone Caravan and Camping Park* (ⓣ01288/352017; closed Nov–March), three quarters of a mile south of the centre on the coastal road to Widemouth Bay, and *Wooda Park* (ⓣ01288/352069; closed Nov–March) away from the sea at Poughill (pronounced "Poffil"), two miles north of Bude.

The *Falcon Hotel* offers abundant portions at its bar and has a more formal and expensive **restaurant**, which specializes in seafood. For snacks and salads, try the central *Carriers Inn* on the Strand, which has seating outside. A mile inland from

Bude, the village of **Stratton** offers two good possibilities: the *Stratton Gardens Hotel* (see above) and the *Tree Inn*, which was used as the Royalist headquarters during the battle of Stamford Hill – an engagement re-enacted annually on the nearest weekend to May 16. The pub was the home of the "Cornish Giant" Anthony Paine, manservant of Lord Grenville, who commanded the king's forces at their victory. There's a choice of **surfing equipment rental** outlets, including Zuma Jay on Belle Vue Lane and, visible at the end of the street, XTC on Princes Street. On a different note, the **Bude Jazz Festival** attracts a range of stomping sounds from around the world for a week at the end of August (Ⓦwww.tony-davis.demon.co.uk/budejazzfestival).

Bodmin and Bodmin Moor

Bodmin Moor, the smallest, mildest and most accessible of the West Country's great moors, has some beautiful tors, torrents and rock formations, but much of its fascination lies in the strong human imprint, particularly the wealth of relics left behind by its **Bronze Age** population, including such important sites as Trethevy Quoit and the stone circles of the Hurlers. Separated from these by some three millennia, the churches in the villages of St Neot's, Blisland and Altarnun are among the region's finest examples of fifteenth-century art and architecture.

The biggest centre in the area, **Bodmin**, stands outside the moor but can provide information on walking routes and on the Camel Trail, which touches here. With the north moor village of **Camelford**, Bodmin has the area's widest choice of accommodation, and is the most accessible town, sitting on the main A30 and within reach of the main rail line. Thanks to its central position, Bodmin is also well connected on bus routes, but the only services onto the moor are the sporadic #X3, #X7 and #X8 from Bodmin to Launceston via Bolventor, Tilley's Coaches #225, running four times daily on weekdays between Launceston and Altarnun, the more frequent #77 and #X77 from Liskeard (also a train stop) to St Neot (not Sun), and the hourly #73, which runs between Liskeard and Pensilva via St Cleer and Darite (not Sun).

Bodmin

The town of **BODMIN** lies on the western edge of Bodmin Moor, equidistant from the north and south Cornish coasts and the Fowey and Camel rivers, a position that encouraged its growth as a trading town. It was also an important ecclesiastical centre after the establishment of a priory by St Petroc, who moved here from Padstow in the sixth century. The priory disappeared but Bodmin retained its prestige through its church of St Petroc, built in the fifteenth century and still the largest in Cornwall. Though officially the county town, Bodmin sacrificed much of its administrative role by refusing access to the Great Western Railway in the 1870s, as a result of which much local business transferred down the road to Truro. **Bodmin Parkway** station lies three miles outside town, with a regular bus connection to the centre. By **bus** you can reach the town from Padstow or Wadebridge on Western National #55 (not Sun) and from St Austell on any of the #29s (not Sun); in summer the #55 connects St Austell, Bodmin and Wadebridge four times daily. From Penzance, Plymouth or Newquay it is easiest to take the twice-daily National Express coaches.

Bodmin's most prominent landmark is the **Gilbert Memorial**, a 144-foot obelisk honouring a descendant of Walter Raleigh and occupying a commanding location on Bodmin Beacon, a high area of moorland near the centre of town. Below, at the end of Fore Steet, stands **St Petroc's Church**; inside, there's an extravagantly carved twelfth-century font and an ivory casket that once held the bones of the saint, while the southwest corner of the churchyard holds a sacred well. Close by, the notorious **Bodmin Jail** (Mon–Fri & Sun 10am–5pm, Sat 11am–6pm; £3.50) glowers darkly on Berrycombe Road, redolent of the public executions that were guaranteed crowd-pullers until 1862, from which time the hangings continued behind closed doors until the jail's closure in the early years of the twentieth century. You can visit part of the original eighteenth-century structure, including the condemned cell and some grisly exhibits chronicling the lives of the inmates.

Further up Berrycombe Road begins a section of the **Camel Trail** (see p.511), linking the town by cycle- and footpath to the main route along the Camel river at Boscarne Junction a mile up, which is itself connected by steam locomotives of the **Bodmin & Wenford Railway** to the restored station on St Nicholas Street and beyond to Bodmin Parkway (April–Sept 2–4 daily). The trains make a stop at Colesloggett, a good place to get off to explore **Cardinham Woods**, an excellent place for a day's rambling (see below for bike rental).

From Parkway it's less than two miles' walk to one of Cornwall's most celebrated country houses, **Lanhydrock** (April–Sept Tues–Sun 11am–5.30pm; Oct Tues–Sun 11am–5pm; £6.80, grounds only £3.70; NT), originally seventeenth-century but totally rebuilt after a fire in 1881. The granite exterior remains true to its original form, but the 42 rooms show a very different style, including a long picture gallery with a plaster ceiling depicting scenes from the Old Testament, and – most illuminating of all – servants' quarters that reveal the daily workings of a Victorian manor house. The grounds have magnificent beds of magnolias, azaleas and rhododendrons, and a huge area of wooded parkland bordering onto the River Fowey.

Practicalities

Bodmin's **tourist office** (May–Sept Mon–Sat 10am–5pm; Oct–April Mon–Fri 10am–5pm, Sat 10am–1pm; ☎01208/76616) is near the main car park at the bottom of St Nicholas Street. Comfortable **B&B** is available at *Higher Windsor Cottage*, 18 Castle St (☎01208/76474, ⓦwww.ji77.dial.pipex.com; no credit cards; ❶), and the beflowered and lattice-windowed *Priory Cottage*, near St Petroc's church at 34 Rhind St (☎01208/73064, ⓦwww.priorycottage1.co.uk; no smoking; no credit cards; ❶), which dates from the seventeenth century. There are a couple of good **B&Bs** three miles south of town near Lanivet and so well-located for the Saints' Way (see p.510): *Tremorvah* (☎01208/831379, ⓔwendy@tremorvah.fsnet.co.uk; no credit cards; ❶), a fifteen-minute walk from the village located on Rosehill (the Bodmin Road), and *Bokiddick Farm*, two miles east of Lanivet, towards the Lanhydrock estate (☎01208/831481; no credit cards; ❸); both boast magnificent views and are non-smoking. There's a decent **campsite** on Old Callywith Road, a fifteen-minute walk from Castle Street in the centre (☎01208/73834; closed Nov–March).

Off Fore Street, the *Hole in the Wall* **pub** in Crockwell Street has a pleasant backroom bar in what used to be the debtors' prison, with exposed fourteenth-century walls enclosing a collection of antiquities and bric-a-brac. There are bar lunches available, and in summer you can drink in the courtyard; for fuller meals there's an upstairs **restaurant**. Wholesome snacks are also served at the *Maple Leaf*, a tiny café just across from St Petroc's at 14 Honey St (closed Sun). If you want to **rent a bike**, head for Glynn Valley Cycle Hire in Cardinham

Woods (℡01208/74244), which has off-roaders, suitable for the cycle route here and beyond to the moor.

Bodmin Moor

Just ten miles in diameter, **BODMIN MOOR** is a wilderness on a small scale, its highest tor rising to just 1375ft from a platform of 1000ft. Yet the moor conveys a sense of loneliness quite out of proportion to its size, with scattered ancient remains providing in places the only distraction from an empty horizon. Aside from its tors, the main attractions of the landscape are the small Dozmary Pool, a site steeped in myth, and a quartet of rivers – the Fowey, Lynher, Camel and De Lank – that rise from remote moorland springs and effectively bound the moor to the north, east and south.

Blisland and the western moor

BLISLAND stands in the Camel valley on the western slopes of Bodmin Moor, three miles northeast of Bodmin. Georgian and Victorian houses cluster around a village green and a church whose well-restored interior has an Italianate altar and a startlingly painted screen. On **Pendrift Common** above the village, the gigantic **Jubilee Rock** is inscribed with various patriotic insignia commemorating the jubilee of George III's coronation in 1809. From this seven-hundred-foot vantage point you look eastward over the De Lank gorge and the boulder-crowned knoll of **Hawk's Tor**, three miles away. On the shoulder of the tor stand the Neolithic **Stripple Stones**, a circular platform once holding 28 standing stones, of which just four are still upright.

Blisland lies just a couple of miles east of the **Merry Meeting** crossroads, a point near the end of the Camel Trail. There's a really nice **place to stay** in the area, *Lavethan* (℡01208/850487, ⓦwww.cornwall-online.co.uk/lavethan; no credit cards; ❹), a beautiful sixteenth-century manor house set in thirty acres of park-like fields and gardens sloping to a small river; it's ten minutes' walk from the village towards St Mabyn. One and half miles north of Blisland on the St Breward Road, the small *South Penquite* **campsite** (℡01208 850296; closed Nov–March) is a good option and has mountain **bikes** available for rent.

Bolventor and Dozmary Pool

The village of **BOLVENTOR**, lying at the centre of the moor midway between Bodmin and Launceston, is an uninspiring place close to one of the moor's chief focuses for walkers and sightseers alike – **Jamaica Inn** (℡01566/86250, ⓦwww.jamaicainn.co.uk; ❸). A staging-post even before the precursor of the A30 road was laid here in 1769, the inn was described by Daphne Du Maurier as being "alone in glory, four square to the winds", and the combination of its convenient position and its association with her has led to its growth into a hotel and restaurant complex. One corner exhibits the room where the author stayed in 1930, soaking up inspiration for her smugglers' yarn. At the other end of the building is the silly but highly entertaining **Mr Potter's Museum of Curiosities** (daily: Easter–Oct 10am–6pm, until 8pm during school holidays; Nov–Easter 11am–4pm; £2.50; combined ticket with Smuggler's Museum £4), a zany fairground miscellany of Victorian toys, mummified and stuffed animals, a collection of pipes and a guinea pigs' cricket match. The **Smuggler's Museum** across the road (same hours; £2.50), while not in the same league as its neighbour, still provides some amusement, showing the diverse ruses used for concealing contraband.

The inn's car park is a useful place to leave your vehicle and venture forth on foot. Just a mile away, along what must be the most travelled path on the moor, **Dozmary Pool** is another link in the West Country's Arthurian mythologies – after Arthur's death Sir Bedevere hurled Excalibur, the king's sword, into the pool, where it was seized by an arm raised from the depths. Loe Pool, near Porthleven on the Lizard, also claims the honour. Despite its proximity to the A30, the diamond-shaped lake usually preserves an ethereal air, though it's been known to run dry in summer, dealing a bit of a blow to the legend that the pool is bottomless.

The lake is also the source of another, more obviously Cornish legend, that of John Tregeagle, a steward at Lanhydrock, whose unjust dealings with the local tenant farmers in the seventeenth century brought upon his spirit the curse of endlessly baling out the pool with a perforated limpet shell. As if this were not enough, his ghost is further tormented by a swarm of devils pursuing him as he flies across the moor in search of sanctuary; their infernal howling is sometimes audible on windy nights.

Liskeard and St Neot

LISKEARD, a bus and rail junction just off the southern limits of the moor, makes a decent overnight stop, with **accommodation** at two decent B&Bs: *Elnor*, 1 Russell St (℡01579/342472; no credit cards; ❶), located on the way to the train station, and the immaculately kept *Hyvue* just north of the centre at Barras Cross (℡01579/348175; non-smoking; no credit cards; ❶). From here, buses go on to **ST NEOT**, one of Bodmin Moor's prettiest villages, approached through a lush wooded valley. Its fifteenth-century **church** contains some of the most impressive stained-glass windows of any parish church in the country, the oldest glass being the fifteenth-century **Creation Window**, at the east end of the south aisle. Next along, **Noah's Window** continues the sequence, but the narration soon dissolves into windows portraying patrons and local bigwigs, while others present cameos of the ordinary men and women of the village. Among the best of St Neot's **accommodation** options is the seventeenth-century *Dye Cottage* (℡01579/321394, ⊛www.cornwall-info.co.uk/dye-cottage; no credit cards; ❶), which has a suite sleeping up to four, a guests' lounge, and a garden that slopes down to a stream; breakfast includes homegrown produce and home-made bread.

This southern edge of the moor is far greener and more thickly wooded than the northern reaches, due to the confluence of a web of rivers into the Fowey. One of the moor's best-known beauty spots is a couple of miles east, below Draynes Bridge, where the Fowey tumbles through the **Golitha Falls**, less a waterfall than a series of rapids. Dippers and wagtails flit through the trees, and there's a pleasant woodland walk you can take to the dam at the Siblyback Lake reservoir just over a mile away: follow the river up to Draynes Bridge, then walk north up a minor road until a path branches off on the right after a half-mile, leading down to the water's edge.

Camelford and the northern tors

The northern half of Bodmin Moor is dominated by its two highest tors, both of them easily accessible from **CAMELFORD**, a town once associated with King Arthur's Camelot, while Slaughterbridge, which crosses the River Camel north of town, is one of the contenders for his last battleground. The town has resisted trading on the Arthurian myths, but does have a couple of museums providing some diversion: the **British Cycling Museum** (daily: Mon–Thurs & Sun 10am–5pm, phone ahead for Fri & Sat ℡01840/212811; £2.50), housed in the old station one mile north of town on the Boscastle Road, is a cyclophile's dream, containing some four hundred examples of bikes through the ages and a library of books and manuals. The collection may be of special interest to bikers on Route 3 on the National Cycle Way, which runs through Camelford. Meanwhile, the more conventional **North Cornwall Museum** (April–Sept Mon–Sat 10am–5pm; £1.50) in Camelford's centre contains domestic items and exhibits showing the development of the local slate industry, and also has a **tourist office** (same hours; ☏01840/212954).

Although it lacks excitement, Camelford makes a useful touring base. Among its **accommodation** is the central *Countryman Hotel*, at 7 Victoria Rd (☏01840/212250, ⓦwww.cornwall-online.co.uk/countryman; ❷), which welcomes cyclists, and the thirteenth-century, slate-hung *Darlington Inn* on Fore St (☏01840/213314; ❶). The *Mason's Arms* on Market Place (☏01840 /213309; no credit cards; ❶) has rooms, a beer garden and **food**, and the *Darlington Inn* also makes a good refreshment pit-stop. There are two **campsites** in the area, at *King's Acre* (☏01840/213561; closed Nov–Easter) and *Lakefield Caravan Park*, Lower Pendavey Farm (☏01840/213279; closed Nov–March), the latter much larger with more facilities and also providing **horse-riding**.

Rough Tor, the second highest peak on Bodmin Moor at 1311ft, is four miles' walk southeast from Camelford. The hill presents a different aspect from every angle: from the south an ungainly mass, from the west a nobly proportioned mountain. A short distance to the east stand the Little Rough Tor, where there are the remains of an Iron Age camp, and Showery Tor, capped by a prominent formation of piled rocks.

Easily visible to the southeast, **Brown Willy** is, at 1375ft, the highest peak in Cornwall, as its original name signified – Bronewhella, or "highest hill". Like Rough Tor, Brown Willy shows various faces, its sugarloaf appearance from the north sharpening into a long multi-peaked crest as you approach. The tor is accessible by continuing from the summit of Rough Tor across the valley of the De Lank, or, from the south, by footpath from Bolventor. The easiest ascent is by the worn path which climbs steeply up from the northern end of the hill.

Altarnun and the eastern moor

ALTARNUN is a pleasant, granite-grey village snugly sheltered beneath the eastern heights of the moor. Its prominent **church**, dedicated to St Nonna, mother of David, patron saint of Wales, contains a fine Norman font and 79 bench-ends carved at the beginning of the sixteenth century, depicting saints, musicians and clowns. The village also has a Methodist chapel, over the door of which there is an effigy of John Wesley – a regular visitor to the neighbourhood – by Nevill Northey Burnard (1818–78), a local sculptor who, despite the praise of his contemporaries, ended his days in a Redruth poorhouse. Accessed by a private gate from St Nonna's (and also from the road), *Penhallow Manor* (☏01566/86206, ⓦwww.penhallow-manor.co.uk; ❻), originally the vicarage, now offers tasteful **accommodation** and a set three-course dinner at £20 (book ahead if you're not staying); morning coffees and afternoon teas are also available. Cheaper rooms can be found 500yds towards the A30, where the *King's Head* (☏01566/86241; no credit cards; ❶) has beams, saggy ceilings and **meals** for under a fiver.

South of Altarnun, **Withey Brook** tumbles four hundred feet in less than a mile of gushing cascades before meeting up with the River Lynher, which bounds Bodmin Moor to the east. Beyond the brook, on **Twelve Men's Moor**, lie some of Bodmin Moor's grandest landscapes. The quite modest elevations of Hawk's Tor (1079ft) and the lower Trewartha Tor appear enormous from the north, though they are overtopped by **Kilmar**, highest of the hills on the moor's eastern flank at 1280ft.

Withey Brook starts life about six miles from Altarnun on **Stowe's Hill**, site of the moor's most famous stone pile, **The Cheesewring**, a precarious pillar of balancing granite slabs, marvellously eroded by the wind. Gouged out of the hillside nearby, the disused Cheesewring Quarry is a centre of rockclimbing. A mile or so south down Stowe's Hill stands an artificial rock phenomenon, **The Hurlers**, a wide complex of three circles dating from about 1500 BC. The purpose of these stark upright stones is not known, though they owe their name to the legend that they were men turned to stone for playing the Celtic game of hurling on the Sabbath.

The Hurlers are easily accessible just outside **MINIONS**, Cornwall's highest village, three miles south of which stands another Stone Age survival, **Trethevy Quoit**, a chamber tomb nearly nine feet high, surmounted by a massive capstone. Originally enclosed in earth, the stones have been stripped by centuries of weathering to create Cornwall's most impressive megalithic monument. Bus #73 from Liskeard calls at St Cleer and Darite, both of which are close to Trethevy Quoit; alternatively, it's a three-mile walk from Liskeard.

Travel details

Buses

For information on all local and national bus services, contact Traveline: ☏0870/608 2 608 (daily 7am–9pm), ⊛www.traveline.org.uk.

Trains

For information on all local and national rail services, contact National Rail Enquiries: ☏08457/48 49 50, ⊛www.rail.co.uk.

Barnstaple to: Exeter (Mon–Sat 9–11 daily, Sun 5 daily; 1hr).

Bodmin to: Exeter (1–2 hourly; 1hr 30min–2hr); London (8–10 daily; 4hr 15min); Penzance (hourly; 1hr 20min); Plymouth (1–2 hourly; 40min).

Exeter to: Barnstaple (Mon–Sat 9–11 daily, Sun 5 daily; 1hr); Birmingham (hourly; 2hr 20min–2hr 40min); Bodmin (1–2 hourly; 1hr 45min); Bristol (1–2 hourly; 1hr 20min); Exmouth (Mon–Sat 2 hourly, Sun hourly; 30min); Honiton (every 1–2hr; 30min); Liskeard (1–2 hourly; 1hr 30min); London (1–2 hourly; 2hr 30min–3hr 20min); Par (hourly; 2hr); Penzance (hourly; 3hr); Plymouth (2 hourly; 1hr); Salisbury (every 2hr; 2hr); Torquay (hourly; 45min); Totnes (2 hourly; 35min); Truro (1–2 hourly; 2hr 15min).

Falmouth to: Truro (10–12 daily; 25min).

Honiton to: Exeter (hourly; 30min); Salisbury (every 1–2hr; 1hr 20min).

Liskeard to: Exeter (1–2 hourly; 1hr 30min); London (8 daily; 4hr); Looe (8–10 daily, not Sun in winter; 30min); Penzance (hourly; 1hr 30min); Plymouth (1–2 hourly; 30min); Truro (hourly; 50min).

Newquay to: Par (4–7 daily, not Sun in winter; 50min).

Par to: Newquay (4–7 daily, not Sun in winter; 50min); Penzance (hourly; 1hr 10min); Plymouth (hourly; 1hr).

Penzance to: Bodmin (hourly; 1hr 20min); Bristol (11 daily; 4hr); Exeter (hourly; 3hr); Liskeard (hourly; 1hr 30min); London (8 daily; 5–6hr); Par (hourly; 1hr 10min); Plymouth (hourly; 2hr); St Ives (3–5 daily; 20min); Truro (1–2 hourly; 40min).

Plymouth to: Birmingham (10 daily; 3hr 45min); Bodmin (1–2 hourly; 40min); Bristol (1–2 hourly; 2hr–2hr 50min); Exeter (2 hourly; 1hr); Liskeard (1–2 hourly; 30min); London (8 daily; 3hr–4hr); Par (hourly; 1hr); Penzance (hourly; 2hr); St Erth (hourly; 1hr 50min); Truro (hourly; 1hr 20min).

St Ives to: Penzance (3–5 daily; 20min); St Erth (2 hourly; 15min).

Torquay to: Exeter (hourly; 45min).

Truro to: Bristol (11 daily; 3hr 20min); Exeter (1–2 hourly; 2hr 15min); Falmouth (10–12 daily; 25min); Liskeard (hourly; 50min); London (8 daily; 4hr 40min); Penzance (1–2 hourly; 40min); Plymouth (hourly; 1hr 20min).

East Anglia

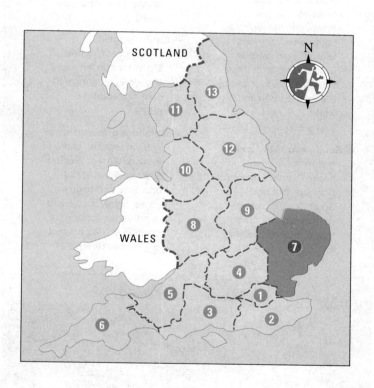

CHAPTER 7

Highlights

✳ **Orford** Remote and peaceful, this hamlet is hidden away on the Suffolk coast and makes for a wonderful weekend away. See p.548

✳ **The Aldeburgh Festival** Held in the Snape Maltings, outside Aldeburgh, the region's prime classical music festival takes place in June and lasts for three weeks; it was founded by Benjamin Britten and his works features heavily. See p.550

✳ **Southwold** Many English resorts have been hacked around by the planners, but not Southwold, a picture-perfect seaside town that is ideal for walking and bathing. See p.552

✳ **Norwich Market** Huddled under brightly-striped awnings, this open-air market, held in the Market Place every day except Sunday, is the region's biggest and best for everything from whelks to wellies. See p.554

✳ **Ely** An isolated Cambridgeshire town, Ely has a true fenland flavour – and a magnificent cathedral. See p.578

✳ **Cambridge** This university town features some of England's finest architecture, its dignified old churches and handsome, tightly manicured quadrangles jostling for position in the compact city centre. See p.581

East Anglia

Strictly speaking, **East Anglia** is made up of just three counties – Suffolk, Norfolk and Cambridgeshire – which were settled by Angles from Holstein in the fifth century, though in more recent times it's come to be loosely applied to parts of Essex too. As a region it's renowned for its wide skies and flat landscapes, and of course such generalizations always contain more than a grain of truth – if you're looking for mountains, you've come to the wrong place. That said, East Anglia often fails to conform to its stereotype: parts of Suffolk are positively hilly, and its coastline can induce vertigo; the north Norfolk coast holds steep cliffs as well as wide sandy beaches; and even the pancake-flat fenlands are broken by wide, muddy rivers and hilly mounds, on one of which perches Ely's magnificent cathedral. Indeed, the whole region is sprinkled with fine medieval churches, the legacy of the days when this was England's most progressive and prosperous region.

Of all the region's counties, **Suffolk** is the most varied. Its undulating southern reaches, straddling the River Stour, are home to a string of picturesque, well-preserved little towns – **Lavenham** and **Kersey** are two excellent examples – which enjoyed immense prosperity during the thirteenth to sixteenth centuries, the heyday of the wool trade. Elsewhere, **Bury St Edmunds** can boast not just the ruins of its once-prestigious abbey, but also some fine Georgian architecture on its grid-plan streets. Even the much maligned county town of **Ipswich** has more to offer than it's generally given credit for. Nevertheless, for many visitors it's the north Suffolk coast that steals the local show. In **Southwold**, with its comely Georgian high street, Suffolk possesses a delightful seaside resort, elegant and relaxing in equal measure, while neighbouring **Aldeburgh** hosts one of the best music festivals in the country. **Norfolk**, as everyone knows thanks to Noël Coward, is very flat. It's also one of the most sparsely populated and tranquil counties in England, a remarkable turnaround from the days when it was an economic and political powerhouse

Accommodation price codes

Throughout this guide, hotel and B&B accommodation is priced on a scale of ❶ to ❾, the number indicating the **lowest price** you could expect to pay per night in that establishment for a **double room** in high season. The prices indicated by the codes are as follows:

❶ under £40	❹ £60–70	❼ £110–150
❷ £40–50	❺ £70–90	❽ £150–200
❸ £50–60	❻ £90–110	❾ over £200

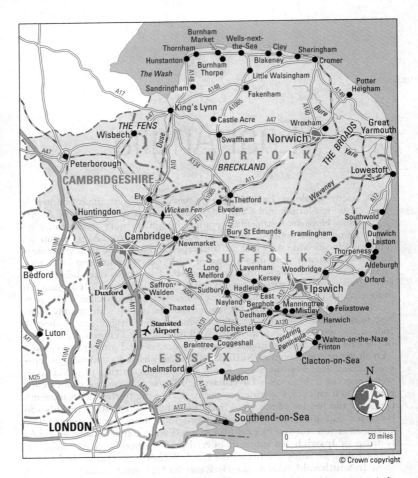

© Crown copyright

– until, that is, the Industrial Revolution simply passed it by. Its capital, **Norwich**, is still East Anglia's largest city, renowned for its Norman cathedral and castle, and for its high-tech Sainsbury Centre, a provocative collection of twentieth-century art. The one part of Norfolk which has been well and truly discovered is the **Broads**, a unique landscape of reed-ridden waterways that has been over-exploited by farmers and boat-rental companies for the last twenty years. Too far from London to attract day-trippers, the Norfolk coast – with the exception of touristy **Great Yarmouth** and, to a lesser extent, the Victorian resort of **Cromer** – remains one of the most unspoilt in England, with **Blakeney Point** and the surrounding marshes among the country's top nature reserves. Meanwhile, sheltering inland, are two outstanding stately homes – **Blickling Hall** and **Holkham** – with several more within easy striking distance of **King's Lynn**, a strange, almost disconcerting mixture of fenland town and ancient seaport.

Cambridge is, however, the one place in East Anglia everyone visits, large-ly on account of its world-renowned university, whose ancient colleges boast some of the finest medieval and early modern architecture in the country. The rest of Cambridgeshire is dominated by the landscape of the **Fens**, for centuries an inhospitable marshland, which was eventually drained to provide rich alluvial farming land. The one great highlight here is the cathedral town of **Ely**, settled on one of the few areas of raised ground in this region and an easy and popular day-trip from Cambridge – as is burgeoning **Peterborough**'s magnificent cathedral.

Heading into the region from the south almost inevitably takes you through **Essex**, though there's little here to divert you. Not properly part of East Anglia, but generally lumped together with the region, Essex's proximity to London has turned many places into soulless commuter towns, while its inhabitants – "Essex man and woman" – are typically dubbed brash, conservative and uncultured by the rest of the English. The county capital, Chelmsford, is no great shakes and instead it's best to aim for the historic town of **Colchester** and, at a pinch, the popular seaside resort of **Southend-on-Sea**.

Getting around

The **train** network is at its best to and from London, with quick and frequent services from the capital to all of East Anglia's major towns. One main line service links Colchester, Ipswich and Norwich, another Cambridge, Ely and Peterborough, which means it is relatively easy to move from one major town to another. However, once you get away from the major towns, you're going to have to rely on local **buses**, whose services, run by a multitude of companies, are very patchy – especially on Sundays and in winter. Indeed, in parts of north Norfolk and inland Suffolk, you may find the only way to get about is by your own transport. The largest regional bus operator is First Eastern Counties, who sell Ranger tickets providing unlimited travel for one day or more on their buses. These are available either in advance or from their drivers. Most tourist offices carry details of local buses and some of the more useful services are detailed in the text. For bus information lines, see the box below.

Hiking, naturally enough, is less strenuous here than in most English regions, and there are several **long-distance footpaths** worth considering. The main routes run through Norfolk, starting with the **Peddars Way**, from Knettishall near Thetford and heading north to the coast at Hunstanton. The route then continues east as the **Norfolk Coast Path** as far as Cromer, from where the **Weaver's Way** then wends through the Broads to Great Yarmouth. Most local tourist offices can provide trail guides.

Southend-on-Sea

SOUTHEND-ON-SEA owes its existence to the Prince Regent, who in 1809 decided that the village of Prittlewell – now a suburb of Southend – would provide a healthier atmosphere for his wife, Princess Caroline, than London, forty miles to the west. Caroline lodged at Prittlewell's "south end", which henceforth became the town's official name. As the nearest sandy beach to London, Southend has doggedly maintained the popularity that followed from its royal patronage, though nowadays it has come to epitomize the downmarket English seaside resort of fish and chips, candyfloss and slot machines.

With a population of over a hundred and fifty thousand, Southend today incorporates many of the neighbouring towns along a seven-mile stretch of sand, which faces south onto the muddy Thames estuary. It's a rather dull geographical backdrop, with little in the town itself to raise the spirits and nothing on the promenade that isn't repeated up and down the English coast in dozens of comparable resorts. Nothing, that is, save for Southend's **pier** (April–Sept daily 8am–10pm; Oct–March Mon–Fri 8am–5pm, Sat & Sun till 7pm), which, at one and a third miles, is reputedly the longest in the world. Paul Theroux finished his grumpy circuit of Britain here, recounted in *The Kingdom By The Sea*, and to emulate him you can either walk or take the special pier shuttle train. Gazing out over the Thames estuary is not perhaps the most enduring of scenic experiences, but it's pleasant enough and afterwards you can wander the seafront, with its amusement arcades, brash pubs and fast-food joints. Just west of the pier, the resort's early days are recalled by the Georgian **Royal Terrace**, with its distinctive wrought-iron verandas, on the embankment above the seafront; Princess Caroline stayed here, at nos. 7 and 9.

Two other seafront attractions are worth pointing out, beginning with **Sea Life Adventure** (℡01702/601834, ⊕www.sealifeadventure.co.uk; £4.95), about half a mile east of the pier, where, if there's nothing hanging about the estuary, you can gawp through the glass at the usual suspects from sharks and starfish to spiky spider crabs. A short walk beyond is the **Marine Activity Centre** (℡01702/612770), which offers sailing, windsurfing and canoeing. Needless to say, Southend has its share of **amusement parks**, the two major ones being Adventure Island (℡01702/468023) and the tiny tots' Never Never Land (℡01702/460618), both of which are near the pier on the Western Esplanade. And then there's the **beach** – crowded near the arcades and amusement parks, but more secluded to the east towards Shoeburyness.

Practicalities

Trains from London's Fenchurch Street station take just under an hour to reach Southend Central Station, which lies at the top of the pedestrianized High Street, a good ten minutes' walk from the pier: head down the High Street onto Pier Hill and you can't miss it. Services from Liverpool Street arrive a little further out of the centre at Southend Victoria. The **bus station** is at the junction of High Street and Heygate Avenue, opposite the Royals Shopping Centre – the best place for drivers to aim for, since it has a large multistorey **car park**. The **tourist office** is located about five minutes' walk from the pier at 19 High St (July & Aug Mon–Sat 9.30am–5pm, Sun 11am–4pm; rest of year closed Sun; ℡01702/215120).

The bulk of Southend's visitors are day-trippers and it's difficult to conceive of a reason to buck the trend. Nevertheless, if you're determined to find **accommodation**, you should have no problems as Southend abounds in inexpensive B&Bs, many along the Eastern Esplanade, though by far the nicest places to stay are the few Georgian properties on Royal Terrace, off the High Street. Here, both the flower-decked *Mayflower Hotel*, at nos. 5–6 (℡01702/340489; ❷), and the *Terrace Hotel*, at no. 8 (℡01702/348143; ❶), are neat and well-kept. The nearest **campsite** is the *East Beach Caravan and Camping Park* (℡01702/292466; closed Nov–Feb), which overlooks an undeveloped slice of the coast in Shoeburyness, the easternmost suburb of Southend.

Southend's proximity to London has had a beneficial effect on the quality of its **restaurants**. One of the best places to eat is the *Fleur de Provence*, just west of the High Street at 52 Alexandra St (℡01702/352987; closed Sun), where the Provençal food is delicious. Alternatively, for a cheap fill-up, there's *Bailey's Fry-Inn*, a traditional Southend chippy on the Eastern Esplanade. Various **festivals**

Boudicca

Boudicca – aka Boadicea – was the wife of Prasutagus, chief of the Iceni tribe of Norfolk, who allied himself to the Romans during the conquest of Britain in 43 AD. Five years later, when the Iceni were no longer useful, the Romans attempted to disarm them and, although the Iceni rebelled, they were soon brought to heel. On Prasutagus's death, the Romans ignored his will and confiscated his property – and when Boudicca protested, the Romans flogged her and raped her daughters. Enraged, Boudicca determined to take her revenge, quickly rallying the Iceni and their allies before setting off on a rampage across southern Britain in 60 AD.

As the ultimate symbol of Roman oppression, the Temple of the Deified Claudius in Colchester was the initial focus of hatred, but once Colchester had been demolished Boudicca turned her sights elsewhere. She laid waste to London and St Albans, massacring over seventy thousand citizens and inflicting crushing defeats on the Roman units stationed there. She was far from squeamish, ripping traitors' arms out of their sockets and torturing every Roman and Roman collaborator in sight. The Roman governor Suetonius Paulinus eventually defeated her in a pitched battle, which cost the Romans just four hundred lives and the Britons untold thousands. Boudicca knew what to expect from the Romans, so she opted for suicide, thereby ensuring her later reputation as a patriotic Englishwoman, who died fighting for liberty and freedom – claims which Boudicca would have found incomprehensible.

throughout the year add more focus to a visit. One of the best is the annual summer jazz festival (dates vary, check with the tourist office), followed by carnival week in August, complete with processions and a fireworks display. The biggest event each year, though, is the **Air Show** held over the May bank holiday weekend, with aerial displays and fly-overs along the Thames estuary.

Colchester and around

If you visit anywhere in Essex, it should be **COLCHESTER**, an agreeable town with a castle, a university and a large army base, fifty miles or so northeast of London. More than anything else, Colchester prides itself on being England's oldest town and there is documentary evidence of a settlement here as early as the fifth century BC. By the first century AD, the town was the region's capital under King Cunobelin – better known as Shakespeare's Cymbeline – and when the Romans invaded Britain in 43 AD they chose Colchester (Camulodunum) as their new capital, though it was soon eclipsed by London, becoming a retirement colony for legionaries instead. The first Roman temple in the country was erected here, and in 60 AD the colony was the target of Boudicca's abortive revolt (see box above). A millennium later, the conquering Normans built one of their mightiest strongholds in Colchester, but the conflict that most marked the town was the Civil War. In 1648, Colchester was subjected to a gruelling siege by the Parliamentarian army led by Lord Fairfax; after three months, during which the population ate every living creature within the walls, the town finally surrendered and the Royalist leaders were promptly executed for their pains.

Today, Colchester makes a good base for further explorations of the surrounding countryside – particularly the Stour valley towns of Constable country (see pp.536–542), within easy reach to the north, and the handsome little village of **Coggeshall** a few miles to the west.

Arrival, information and accommodation

Colchester has two **train stations**. Services from London, Ipswich and Harwich arrive at the mainline Colchester North Station, from where it's a fifteen-minute walk south into town – follow North Station Road and its continuation North Hill until you reach the west end of the High Street. Trains from Frinton, Walton and Clacton-on-Sea arrive at Colchester Town Station, to the south of the centre at the bottom of St Botolph's Street. The **bus station** is off Queen Street, the northerly continuation of St Botolph's Street, and a couple of minutes' walk from the east end of High Street. You can get bus timetables here from the First Eastern National office (Mon–Fri 8.45am–5pm, Sat 9am–1pm; ☎01206/572478), which also sells Bus Ranger tickets (£6) valid for a day's travel throughout much of East Anglia.

The **tourist office** is at 1 Queen St (April–Oct Mon–Sat 9.30am–6pm, Sun 10am–5pm; Nov–March Mon–Sat 10am–5pm; ☎01206/282920), at the east end of High Street, just behind the castle. As well as helping with accommodation, they sell leaflets detailing local walks and co-ordinate daily **guided walks** around town (June–Sept; £2.50). You can rent a **bike** from Action Bikes, beside the Odeon Cinema on Crouch St (☎01206/541744; £12/day) – a good way of getting out to see the nearby "Constable Country" (see pp.536–542).

For **accommodation**, Colchester has more than its fair share of old hotels as well as a scattering of pleasant, well-located B&Bs. The *Rose & Crown Hotel*, East St (☎01206/866677, ⊛www.rose-and-crown.com; ❹), occupies an old, tastefully refurbished Tudor inn – the oldest inn in town, while the *George Hotel*, 116 High St (☎01206/578494; ❺), is an attractive old coaching inn, whose recently revamped rooms come with all mod cons. The *Red Lion*, 43 High St (☎01206/577986; ❸), is another old-timer, a fifteenth century timber building containing 24 modernized en-suite rooms. The *Old Manse*, 15 Roman Rd (☎01206/545154, ⊛www.doveuk.com/oldmanse; ❷), is the best of the many B&B options along Roman Road, with three pleasant guestrooms; Roman Road is on the east side of the Castle.

The Town

Most visitors start off at the town's rugged, honey-coloured **Castle**, the perfect introduction to Colchester's long history, set in attractive parkland, which stretches down to the River Colne. Begun less than ten years after the Battle of Hastings, it boasts a phenomenally large keep – the largest in Europe at the time – built on the site of the defunct Roman temple. The castle's **museum** (Mon–Sat 10am–5pm, Sun 11–5pm; £3.90) contains the best of the region's Romano-British archeological finds, although, apart from a fine bronze of Mercury, the messenger of the gods, this amounts to little more than a smattering of coins, tombstones, statues and mosaics. Perhaps the most impressive mosaic – depicting sea beasts pursuing dolphins – is on display at the castle entrance, next to the castle well. The museum also covers the Boudicca revolt and the 1648 siege, and you can sign up for a **guided tour** of the underground tunnels (45min; £1.20), which give access to the foundations of the Roman temple and the Norman chapel and walls – parts not otherwise accessible to regular visitors. Outside, down towards the river in Castle Park is a section of the old **Roman walls**, whose battered remains are still visible around much of the town centre. They were erected after Boudicca had sacked the city in 60 AD and, as such, are a case of too little too late.

The castle stands at the eastern end of the wide, and largely pedestrianized,

High Street, which lies pretty much along the same route as it did in Roman times. The most arresting building here is the flamboyant **Town Hall**, built in 1902 and topped by a statue of St Helena, mother of Constantine the Great and daughter of "Old King Cole" of nursery-rhyme fame – after whom, some say, the town was named. Immediately north of the High Street is the so-called **Dutch Quarter**, where Flemish refugees settled in the sixteenth century giving a boost to the town's ailing cloth trade. The area's lofty buildings still make this a pleasant place to stroll, particularly along West and East Stockwell streets. South of the High Street, much of the medieval street plan has been subsumed within a vast shopping precinct and an open-air **market** held every Friday and Saturday in Vineyard Street. Nearby, narrow Trinity Street is home to the **Tymperleys Clock Museum** (April–Oct Tues–Sat 10am–1pm & 2–5pm; free), featuring locally made clocks and housed in a wonderful fifteenth-century timber-framed building with its own little garden with scented lavender and rosemary.

Looming above the western end of the High Street is the town landmark, "**Jumbo**", a disused nineteenth-century water tower, considerably more imposing than the nearby **Balkerne Gate**, which marked the western entrance to Roman Colchester. Built in 50 AD, this is the largest surviving Roman gateway in the country, though with the remains at only a touch over six feet in height, it's far from spectacular. The gate is joined to another section of the town's **Roman Walls**, though here the effect is spoiled by the adjacent ring road.

With a little time to spare, it's worth strolling down **East Hill**, a continuation of the High Street east of the castle. Splendid Georgian houses line the top end of the hill, one of which – opposite the tourist office – is now the **Hollytrees Museum** (Mon–Sat 10am–5pm, Sun 11am–5pm; free), containing a modest collection of costumes, toys, domestic items, trade implements and decorative arts from the eighteenth to the twentieth century. Over the road at the **Minories** (April–Sept Mon–Sat 10am–5pm, Sun 11am–5pm; rest of year closed Sun; free) another Georgian exterior conceals a contemporary arts centre, with a changing exhibition programme, a garden and a great café. Just along the street, **Priory Galleries** sells the work of local artists, and is well worth a look.

Doubling back, Queen Street heads south, becoming St Botolph's Street before it reaches Colchester Town Station. Just before the station are the ruins of **St Botolph's Priory**, beside the squat, quasi-fortified church of the same name. As the first Augustinian priory built in England, St Botolph's became head of the black-clad order until the Dissolution. It was reduced to rubble, like so much of the town, in 1648, though the twelfth-century western doorway and the thick piers of the nave give some idea of its Romanesque glories.

Eating, drinking and nightlife

Colchester's oysters have been highly prized since Roman times and the local vineyards have an equally long heritage, so it's no surprise to find the town has a good choice of first-rate **restaurants**. Pickings are slim on Sundays, however, when most places are closed. Probably the best place in town is the *Red Onion Bistro*, 19 Head St (℡01206/366379), which offers tasty dishes at moderate prices from a wide-ranging, contemporary menu. Alternatively, try *Ruan Thai*, 82a East Hill (℡01206/870770), an excellent and moderately priced Thai restaurant near the top of East Hill; *Tilly's*, 22 Trinity St (closed Sun), a Victorian tearoom that serves snacks and full English meals; or the garden café at the Minories (closed Sun in winter), where the lunches are delicious. *The Lemon Tree*, 48 St John's St (℡01206/767337; closed Sun), is a moderately priced option, popular for its lunch specials and sunny courtyard seating. For pizza, try *Pizza Express*, 1 St Runwald's St, off West Stockwell St (℡01206 /760680), or *Toto's*, 5–7 Museum St (℡01206/573235).

Colchester's town centre is crowded with **pubs**, with three of the best being the *Red Lion*, 43 High St, the *Foresters Arms*, a nice backstreet local on Castle Rd, and the *Goat & Boot*, just one of several lively spots down East Hill. And, as you'd expect in a university town, the town rates reasonably well when it comes to the **arts and nightlife**. The Colchester Arts Centre, on Church St next to the Balkerne Gate (℡01206/500900), puts on a good programme of rock, folk, jazz, theatre and dance, plus some club nights – all in a converted Victorian church. Nearby is the Mercury Theatre (℡01206/573948), the town's main drama venue. In term time it's also worth checking what's on at the university's Lakeside Theatre (℡01206/873261), a mile or so east of the centre, where they provide a varied programme of theatre and music.

Coggeshall

COGGESHALL, eight miles west of Colchester, boasts a wealth of sixteenth- and seventeenth-century timber-framed housing, the legacy of its days as a prosperous lace town. The most interesting buildings sport fine decorative pargeting, a once-fashionable style in which the faults of any building could be concealed by plasterwork with incised patterns – the more ornate the pattern, the wealthier the householder. This makes for some enjoyable viewing, as does the Victorian **clock tower**, faced with deep-blue weatherboarding and surmounted by a dinky white belfry, which lords it over the main square.

The village also contains two National Trust properties. The first, **Paycocke's House** on West St (April to early Oct Tues, Thurs & Sun 2–5pm; £2.20; combined ticket for Grange Barn £3), is a rambling, cloth merchant's house dating from around 1500. The half-timbered facade, with its oriel windows and woodcarvings, is charming, but the interior is even more appealing, containing a wide variety of decorative carving – look for the detail in the linenfold panelling of the dining room and over the main fireplace. A small sample of locally made lace is on display here too. The second property, **Grange Barn** (same details), a twelfth-century timber-framed barn, the oldest in Europe, lies half a mile south of the village centre across the River Blackwater.

For **lunch**, head for any one of Coggeshall's antique pubs, the oldest of which is the medieval *Woolpack Inn* at the far end of Church Street.

The Tendring Peninsula

East of Colchester a nub of land juts out into the North Sea to form the **Tendring Peninsula**. The clean sandy beaches strung along the peninsula's southeast shore, the so-called "Essex Sunshine Coast," have been thoroughly developed over the last hundred years, resulting in a series of brash resorts, the most famous of which is **Clacton-on-Sea**. All are accessible by train from Colchester (or London's Liverpool Street), but in truth, none stands out, with the flat hinterland providing little visual relief from the dull seascape. By contrast, the attractive old quarter of **Harwich**, the international ferry terminal at the northeastern tip of the peninsula, is worth at least an hour or two of anyone's time.

△Flatford Mill, Suffolk

It's disappointing that Tendring's most alluring historical sight, the privately owned medieval remains and gardens of **St Osyth Priory**, just west of Clacton, are closed to the public. The priory is associated with the gruesome legend of Osyth, daughter of Frithwald, the first king of East Anglia, who, as the story goes, refused to renounce her Christianity when asked to do so by Viking raiders. In response they lopped off her head, which she then carried to the church (that then stood here) before collapsing.

Clacton-on-Sea

CLACTON-ON-SEA, the Tendring's chief town, is a tad more polished than Southend and immediately more attractive, with its floral promenade gardens and broad sands. Attempts to lure you onto its pier with precisely phrased promises – the "largest" (as opposed to Southend's "longest") pleasure pier in the UK – and to "the new shopping experience at Clacton Common" are a tad desperate, but actually it has little need of such boosterism. Clacton is a pleasant, unassuming family resort – it's as straightforward as that.

The **train station** is a couple of blocks east of the resort's main drag, Pier Avenue. **Buses** mostly stop near the seafront promenade. The **tourist office** at 23 Pier Ave (June to mid-Sept daily 9.30am–4.30pm; mid-Sept to May closed Sun; ☎01255/423400) can dish out details on local attractions, accommodation and campsites. As you might expect, there's plenty of **places to stay** with two good options being the bright and breezy, green and white seafront *Grand Hotel*, on Marine Parade East (☎01255/222020; ❸), and the well-kept *Dingle Dolphin Guest House*, 46 Wellesley Rd (☎01255/474312; ❶), painted pink and bedecked with hanging baskets.

Frinton and Walton

FRINTON-ON-SEA, five miles further up the coast from Clacton, is a smaller, slightly snootier resort, sporting manicured lawns, sea views and a clutch of sedate-looking hotels and B&Bs. There's nothing so downmarket as an amusement arcade here, though fortunately you can still buy plastic buckets and spades to shovel in the sand. The main street, Connaught Avenue, was once pronounced the "Bond Street of East Anglia" – though this claim seems more than a little far-fetched today.

Nearby **WALTON-ON-THE-NAZE** is a quiet place with a garish pier and a rather forlorn air. Its most appealing aspect is **The Naze** itself, a spatulate promontory which pokes north of the resort to form the eastern perimeter of **Hamford Water**, a large area of muddy creeks and salt marshes that produces the tastiest of oysters. It is also a major wintering area for wildfowl and thousands of migrating birds pause here during spring and autumn. A few footpaths nudge into the area from the nearest minor roads – the B1034 to the south, the B1414 in the west – enabling visitors to get a closer look at the birdlife.

To reach Frinton and Walton-on-The-Naze by **train**, change at Thorpe-le-Soken on the Colchester–Clacton line – both resorts are on a tiny branch line. Neither resort has a tourist office, but finding your way around is hardly problematic and there are lots of reasonably priced **B&Bs** to choose from. In Frinton, an especially good choice is the *Uplands Guest House*, 41 Hadleigh Rd (☎01255/674889; ❷), a pleasant 1920s dwelling with eight attractively furnished bedrooms; it's located in a quiet residential area, just a couple of hundred yards from the beach. Walton's best hotel – not perhaps a zealously fought-for title – is the seafront *Regency Hotel*, 45 The Parade (℡01255/676300; ❸), an amiable seaside guest house with its own bar – ask for a room with sea views.

Harwich

HARWICH, at the northeastern tip of the Tendring Peninsula, has a long history as a sea and river port. It equipped Elizabethan mariners such as Drake and Hawkins and provided the dockyards that built the *Mayflower*, the ship that took the Pilgrim Fathers to America. Sitting beside the estuary of the rivers Stour and Orwell, it also prospered from the proceeds of the Essex wool trade, slipping into prolonged decline when the focus of English trade moved from Europe to the Americas in the eighteenth century. Today, it's Britain's main North Sea ferry terminal, though since ferry traffic goes no further than Parkeston Quay, this has left the old town, a mile or so to the east, relatively undisturbed – and all the more appealing for it.

The most interesting sites of old Harwich are conveniently clustered on the east side of a stumpy little headland. Start on **King's Quay Street**, a short walk from the town train station – take Main Road up along the headland, turn right down Wellington Road and then make the second turning on the left. Here you'll find the brightly painted **Electric Palace**, a purpose-built cinema fashioned in Edwardian Baroque in 1911 – and still going strong. Doubling back, it's a short stroll south to **Harwich Green**, abutting the esplanade, and the only surviving **Treadwheel Crane** in the world, a seventeenth-century wooden structure from the local shipyards, with two giant wheels operated by men walking inside them. Just to the west stands the imposing **High Lighthouse** and then it's a few yards south across the green to the **Low Lighthouse**, home to the local maritime museum (June–Sept daily 10am–5pm; 50p). From here, head southwest to Main Road for the entrance into the **Harwich Redoubt** (June–Sept daily 10am–5pm; £1), a well-preserved circular fort constructed in 1808 as part of the coastal defences against Napoleon's expected invasion.

Practicalities

Harwich has three **train stations**: Harwich International Port Station by the Parkeston Quay ferry terminal; Dovercourt Bay Station on the edge of Harwich; and Harwich Town Station just off Main Rd, near Harwich Green. The **bus** service from Colchester to Parkeston Quay and Harwich old town is fast and frequent. Harwich **tourist office** is at the Safeway supermarket store, off the A120 between Parkeston Quay and Harwich old town (April–Sept daily 8.30am–7.30pm; Oct–March Mon–Fri 8.30am–5.30pm & Sat 9am–4pm; ℡01255/506139). For **accommodation**, Harwich has about a dozen hotels and B&Bs, but only one in the old town – which is where you'll probably want to stay. This is *The Pier*, down on The Quay (℡01255/241212; ❺), a hotel with just six en-suite rooms, each decorated in a broadly nautical style. Downstairs, the eponymous **restaurant** is an outstanding but moderately priced place specializing in the freshest of seafood.

The ferry agents at Parkeston Quay can provide up-to-date details of **continental ferry services** to the Hook of Holland (Stena Lines; local number ℡01255/243333), and Hamburg and Esbjerg in Denmark (Scandinavian Seaways; local number ℡01255/240240).

The Stour Valley and the old wool towns of south Suffolk

Five miles or so north of Colchester, the **Stour River Valley** forms the border between Essex and Suffolk, and signals the beginning of East Anglia proper. Compared with much of the region it is positively hilly, a handsome landscape of farms and woodland latticed by dense, well-kept hedges and thick grassy banks that once kept the Stour in check. The valley is dotted with lovely little villages, where rickety, half-timbered Tudor houses and elegant Georgian dwellings cluster around medieval churches, proud buildings with square, self-confident towers. The Stour's prettiest villages are concentrated along its lower reaches – to the east of the A134 – in Dedham Vale, with **Stoke-by-Nayland** and **Dedham** arguably the most appealing of them all. The vale is also known as "**Constable Country**", as it was the home of John Constable, one of England's greatest artists, and the subject of his most famous works. Inevitably, there's a Constable shrine – the much-visited complex of old buildings down by the river at **Flatford Mill**.

The villages along the River Stour and its tributaries were once busy little places at the heart of East Anglia's weaving trade, which boomed from the thirteenth to the fifteenth century. By the 1490s, the region produced more cloth than any other part of the country, but in Tudor times production shifted to Colchester, Ipswich and Norwich and, although most of the smaller settlements continued spinning cloth for the next three hundred years, their importance slowly dwindled. Bypassed by the Industrial Revolution, south Suffolk had, by the late nineteenth century, become a remote rural backwater, an impoverished area whose decline had one unforeseen consequence. With few exceptions, the towns and villages were never well enough off to modernize, and the architectural legacy of medieval and Tudor times survived. The two best-preserved villages are **Lavenham** and **Kersey**, both of which heave with sightseers on summer weekends, but there are other attractive spots too, notably **Long Melford** and **Sudbury**. The latter boasts an excellent museum devoted to the work of Thomas Gainsborough, another great English artist and a native of the town who spent much of his time painting the local landscape.

Seeing the region by **public transport** is problematic – distances are small (Dedham Vale is only about ten miles long), but buses between the villages are infrequent and you'll find it difficult to get away from the towns. Several rail lines cross south Suffolk, the most useful being the London–Colchester–Sudbury route. The area is crisscrossed by **footpaths**, some of the most enjoyable of which are in the vicinity of Dedham village.

Manningtree and Mistley

At the turn of the eighteenth century work was undertaken to make the **River Stour** navigable between Manningtree, where the river suddenly narrows, and Sudbury about fifteen miles inland. All manner of goods were to be transported into the Essex and Suffolk hinterland by this route over the next two centuries, including regular supplies of grindstones supplied to the mills which lined the river. One of the beneficiaries of the scheme was **MANNINGTREE**, around seven miles northeast of Colchester (and connected by a regular train service), whose largely Georgian High Street is evidence of its heyday as a river port. Only a small quay has survived, but a much larger working dockyard exists a mile or so to the east at **MISTLEY**, where the air is pungent with malt from the local maltings. The B1352 between the two forms a pleasant riverside promenade, passing by the incongruous Neoclassical **Mistley Towers**, Robert Adam's only foray into church architecture. Built as embell-ishments to the local church, which was later demolished, the towers were paid for by a local bigwig, a certain Richard Rigby. Rigby's pet idea was to turn Mistley into a fashionable spa resort, but his grandiose plans never got off the ground – all that's left is an unusual swan basin with an oval basin just beyond the towers on the main road. More peculiar still, and signposted off the B1352, is Mistley's **Secret Bunker** (March to Oct daily 10.30am–4pm; rest of year Sat & Sun 10.30am–4.30pm; £4.95), formerly Essex's nuclear battle-plan-ning centre, only decommissioned in 1993. Archive film and tours of the underground system let you into all the awful secrets of a place designed to withstand megaton bomb damage and be self-supporting for months follow-ing an attack.

With much prettier places close at hand, there's really no need to stay here-abouts, but *The Crown* pub, 51 High St (☎01206/396333; ❸), offers simple, en-suite accommodation as well as a pleasant spot for a drink.

East Bergholt, Flatford Mill and John Constable

"I associate my careless boyhood to all that lies on the banks of the Stour" wrote **John Constable**, who was born the son of a miller in **EAST BERGHOLT**, nine miles northeast of Colchester in 1776. The house in which he was born has long since disappeared, so it has been left to **Flatford Mill**, a mile or so to the south, to take up the painter's cause. The mill was owned by his father and was where Constable painted his most famous canvas, *The Hay Wain* (now in the National Gallery, London), which created a sensa-tion when it was exhibited in 1824. To the chagrin of many of his contempo-raries, Constable turned away from the landscape-painting conventions of the day, rendering his scenery with a realistic directness that harked back to the Dutch landscape painters of the seventeenth century. Typically, he justified this approach in unpretentious terms, observing that, after all "no two days are alike, nor even two hours; neither were there ever two leaves of a tree alike since the creation of the world." The mill itself – not the one he painted, but a Victorian replacement – is not open to the public, but the sixteenth-century thatched **Bridge Cottage** (March & April Wed–Sun 11am–5.30pm; May–Sept daily 10am–5.30pm; Oct daily 11am–5.30pm; Nov & Dec Wed–Sun 11am–3.30pm; Jan & Feb Sat & Sun 11am–3.30pm; free, but park-ing £1.90; NT), which overlooks the scene, has been painstakingly restored and stuffed full of Constabilia. Unfortunately, none of Constable's paintings are displayed here, though the adjacent granary contains mezzotints of the artist's works and there's a pleasant riverside tearoom to take in the view. Beyond stands **Willy Lott's Cottage** (also closed to the public), which does actually feature in *The Hay Wain*.

In summer, the National Trust organizes **guided walks** around the sites of Constable's paintings (call ☎01206/298260 for details), but there are many other pleasant walks to be had along this deeply rural bend in the Stour. One footpath connects the mill to the **train station** at Manningtree, two miles to the east, and another runs over to the village of Dedham, a mile and a half to the west.

Dedham

Constable went to school in **DEDHAM**, just upriver from Flatford Mill. It's one of the region's most attractive villages, with a scattering of ancient timber-framed houses strung along the wide main street. The only sights as such are **St Mary's Church**, an early sixteenth-century structure which Constable painted on several occasions, and the **Sir Alfred Munnings Art Museum**, in Castle House (Easter–July & Sept Wed & Sun 2–5pm; Aug Wed, Thurs, Sat & Sun 2–5pm; £3), just south of the village on the road to Ardleigh. A locally born academician, Munnings is barely remembered today, but in his time he was well-known for his portraits of horses. In the 1940s, Munnings became a controversial figure when, as President of the Royal Academy, he savaged almost every form of modern art there was. Few would say his paintings were inspiring, but seeing them is a pleasant way to fill a rainy afternoon. It is, however, the general flavour of Dedham which appeals most.

There is a limited **bus** service from Colchester to Dedham, but this only runs in the early evening. To get there in the morning, catch the more regular bus from Colchester to Stratford St Mary, from where it's a mile and a half walk east to Dedham. Dedham has one of the smartest **hotels** in the area, *Maison Talbooth* (☎01206/322367, @www.talbooth.com; ❽), which occupies a good-looking Victorian country house about fifteen minutes' walk southwest of the village on the road to Stratford St Mary. All of the hotel's ten large bedrooms are individually decorated in sumptuous style and dinner can be had close by at *Le Talbooth* (☎01206/323150), an expensive, but top-notch **restaurant** in an ancient timber-framed house down by the River Stour. Alternatively, there's *Dedham Hall* (☎01206/323027; ❻), an old manor house set in its own grounds on the east side of the village off Brook Street – be sure to ask for a room in the house itself. The restaurant here is very good too (closed Mon). You can also stay in the heart of Dedham itself at the *Marlborough Head* pub (☎01206 /323250; ❸), where a handful of very pleasant rooms are available above the bar, and excellent, moderately priced **food** can be had from an inventive and wide-ranging menu.

Stoke-by-Nayland and Nayland

Heading northwest from Dedham, the B1029 dips beneath the A12 to reach the byroad to Higham, an unremarkable hamlet where you pick up the road to **STOKE-BY-NAYLAND**, four miles to the west. This is the most pictur-esque of villages, where a knot of half-timbered, pastel-painted cottages snug-gle up to **St Mary's Church**. With its pretty brick and stone-trimmed tower, the church was one of Constable's favourite subjects. The doors of the south porch are sumptuously covered by the carved figures of a medieval Jesse Tree. The village also boasts a great old **pub**, the *Angel Inn* (☎01206/263245; ❹), known for its adventurous food (eat in the bar or book for the restaurant) and cosy **rooms**. There are several other good places to stay in and near the village, including *Thorington Hall* (☎01206/337329; ❷), which offers four bedrooms in a seventeenth-century house.

Southwest from here, it's two miles back to the River Stour at **NAYLAND**, a workaday little place that is chiefly remarkable for its church's altar painting, *Christ Blessing the Bread and Wine*. It's one of only two attempts by Constable at a religious theme – and, dated to 1809, it was completed long before he found his artistic rhythm. There's also a fine, largely Norman church a mile or so to the west at tiny **Wissington**, where the nave is decorated with a rare series of thirteenth-century frescoes. Back in Nayland, you can wet your whistle and sample quality bar food at the venerable *White Hart*, 11 High St. Local **accommodation** is available at *Hill House*, Gravel Hill (℡01206/262782, ✉heigham.hillhouse@rdplus.net; ❷), on the edge of the village, and at *Gladwins Farm*, Harper's Hill (℡01206/262261, ⓦwww.gladwinsfarm.co.uk; ❹), a secluded timber-framed farmhouse with its own indoor pool.

Sudbury

SUDBURY – the fictional "Eatanswill" of Dickens' *Pickwick Papers* – has doubled in size in the last thirty years, to become easily the most important town in this part of the Stour Valley. A handful of timber-framed houses hark back to its days of wool-trade prosperity, but its three Perpendicular churches were underwritten by another local industry, silk weaving, which survives on a small scale to this day. Sudbury's most famous export, however, is **Thomas Gainsborough**, the leading English portraitist of the eighteenth century, whose statue, with brush and palette, stands on Market Hill, the town's predominantly Victorian market place. A superb collection of the artist's work is on display a few yards away in the house where he was born – **Gainsborough's House**, at 46 Gainsborough St (April–Oct Tues–Sat 10am–5pm, Sun 2–5pm; Nov–March Tues–Sat 10am–4pm, Sun 2–4pm; £3). Gainsborough left Sudbury when he was just 13, moving to London where he was apprenticed to an engraver, but it seems he was soon moonlighting and the earliest of his surviving portrait paintings – his *Boy and Girl*, a remarkably self-assured work dated to 1744 – is displayed here. In 1752, Gainsborough moved on to Ipswich, where he quickly established himself as a portrait painter to the Suffolk gentry with one of his specialities being wonderful "conversation pieces", so-called because the sitters engage in polite chitchat – or genteel activity – with a landscape as the backdrop. Seven years in Ipswich was followed by a move up-market to Bath, where he painted high society figures, as he did when he moved on to London in 1774. During his years in Bath, Gainsborough developed a fluid, flatteringly easy style that was ideal for his aristocratic subjects, who posed in becoming postures painted in soft, evanescent colours. Examples of Gainsborough's later work exhibited here include the *Portrait of Harriet, Viscountess Tracy* (1763) and the particularly striking *Portrait of Abel Moysey, MP* (1771). In his later years, Gainsborough also dabbled with romantic paintings of country scenes – as in *A Wooded Landscape with Cattle by a Pool* – a playful variation of the serious landscaping painting he loved to do best; the rest, he often said, just earned him money. Gainsborough never bothered with assistants, with one exception, his nephew Gainsborough Dupont, and there's a room devoted to his work on the top floor.

Sudbury is just seven miles northwest of Nayland – and twice that from Colchester – along the A134. It's accessible by **train** from Colchester (for some services, change at Marks Tey) and is the hub of **bus** services to and from neighbouring towns and villages including Colchester and Ipswich. Once you've seen Gainsborough's house, though, there's little reason to hang around. If you do decide to stay, the **tourist office** in the town hall on Market Hill (April–Sept Mon–Fri 9am–5pm & Sat 10am–4.45pm; Oct–March Mon–Fri 9am–5pm & Sat 10am–2.45pm; ℡01787/881320, ✉sudburytic@babergh.gov.uk) can provide **accommodation** details.

Long Melford

True to its name, **LONG MELFORD**, just three miles north of Sudbury, has possibly the longest main street in the country. That in itself is not much of a recommendation, but more to the point, for much of its two miles the street is lined with handsome timber-framed houses. At its northern end, it opens up into a wide sloping green, beyond which stands a collection of sixteenth-century almshouses presided over by the mighty stone and flint **Holy Trinity Church**. Built in the fifteenth century, around the same time as Lavenham's (see p.540), it's one of the most majestic of the so-called wool churches, with huge windows which flood the nave with light. For centuries, rich benefactors have left their legacy here in the form of brightly coloured stained glass, including one window decorated with three rabbits representing the Holy Trinity. A guide is usually on hand during the day.

To the east of the green, behind a high brick wall, is **Melford Hall** (April & Oct Sat & Sun 2–5.30pm; May–Sept Wed–Sun 2–5.30pm; £4.40; NT), a turreted red-brick Tudor mansion that was once a country retreat for the abbots of nearby Bury St Edmunds. The exterior has changed little since its construction in the 1570s, but the interior has been remodelled on several occasions – witness the Regency library and the Victorian bedrooms. Half a mile north of the green, a mile-long lime-tree drive leads to **Kentwell Hall** (April–June & Oct specified days noon–5pm; July to late Sept most days noon–5pm; £5.70; gardens & farm only £3.60; ☎01787/310207), a moated Tudor mansion that's still in private hands. From April to September, the grounds are frequently given over to touristy "historical re-creations", with admission prices rising to match the event. The house holds a string of period rooms and the grounds are dotted with antique bits and pieces – an ice house, a dovecote, an Elizabethan cottage and so forth – as well as several gardens, including the Walled Garden and the Sunken Garden.

If you want to **stay** in Long Melford, the *George & Dragon* (☎01787/371285; ❹), on Hall St, a continuation of High Street, is the best option. *The Bull* (☎01787/378494) on the same stretch of road is a real heavyweight among old inns, shouting its Elizabethan credentials throughout and serving decent, reasonably priced food in its public bar. There is a reasonably frequent bus service from Sudbury to Long Melford (not Sun).

Lavenham

Four miles northeast of Long Melford, off the A134, lies **LAVENHAM**, formerly a centre of the region's wool trade and today one of the most visited villages in Suffolk, thanks to its unrivalled ensemble of perfectly preserved half-timbered houses. The whole place has changed little since the demise of the wool industry in the seventeenth century, owing in part to a zealous local preservation society, which has carefully maintained the village's antique appearance by banning from view such excrescences of twentieth-century life as TV aerials.

The village is at its most beguiling in the triangular **Market Place**, an airy spot flanked by pastel-painted, medieval dwellings whose beams have been bent into all sorts of wonky angles by the passing of the years. It's here you'll find Lavenham's most celebrated building, the pale-white, timber-framed **Corpus Christi Guildhall** (April–Oct daily 11am–5pm; £3; NT), erected in the sixteenth century as the headquarters of one of Lavenham's four guilds. In the much-altered interior (used successively as a prison and workhouse), there's an exhibition on the woollen industry, but most visitors quickly reach the walled garden and the teashop. Just to the east across the plaza is the mostly fifteenth-century **Little Hall** (April–Oct Wed, Thurs, Sat & Sun 2–5.30pm; £1.50), which contains a modest collection of furniture and *objets d'art*; close by – from beside the *Angel Hotel* – there's a stunning view down Prentice Street with a line of antique, timber-framed dwellings dipping into the deep green countryside beyond. The other building worthy of special notice is the Perpendicular **church of St Peter and St Paul** (daily: summer 8.30am–5.30pm; winter 8.30am–3.30pm), though it's sited a short walk south-west of the centre, at the top of Church Street. Local merchants endowed the church with a nave of majestic proportions and a mighty flint tower, at 141ft the highest for miles around, partly to celebrate the Tudor victory at the Battle of Bosworth in 1485 (see p.704), but mainly to show off their wealth.

There are fairly frequent **buses** to Lavenham from Colchester via Sudbury and Long Melford, with the service continuing on to Bury St Edmunds. The **tourist office** is located on Lady St (April–Oct daily 10am–4.45pm; Nov–March Sat & Sun 11am–3pm; ☎01787/248207, ✉lavenhamtic@babergh .gov.uk), just south off Market Place. They can help with **accommodation** and sell a detailed, street-by-street walking guide. Rooms at the *Swan Hotel* (☎01787/247477, ⓦwww.heritage-hotels.com; ❻), a splendid old inn on High Street, are some of the most comfortable in town; the building incorporates part of the Elizabethan Wool Hall and has a whole host of cosy lounges and courtyard gardens. There's more luxurious accommodation at *Lavenham Priory*, on Water St (t01787/247404, ⓦwww.lavenhampriory.co.uk; ❺), where four immaculate rooms are contained within the old Benedictine priory. Less expensive options on the Market Place include the ancient *Angel Hotel* (☎01787/247388, ⓦwww.lavenham.co.uk/angel; ❺), which has eight pleasant rooms above its bar, and the dinky *Angel Gallery* (☎01787/248417, ❸), where the three guest rooms are situated above a pocket-sized art shop. For cheaper B&B options, you'll probably end up staying outside Lavenham itself; the tourist office will provide you with details. For **food**, the *Angel Hotel* serves up excellent, moderately priced bar meals, as does the *Swan*. The other choice in Market Place is the *Great House* (☎01787/247431; closed Sun & Mon), whose outstanding restaurant serves moderately priced food on both its à la carte and set menus.

Kersey and Hadleigh

Eight miles southeast off the A1141, **KERSEY** vies with Lavenham as the most photographed village in Suffolk. Another old wool town, Kersey has been bypassed by history and is now little more than one exquisite street of timber-framed houses, which dips in the middle to cross a ford that's inhabited by a family of fearless ducks. Prime real estate today, Kersey's more populous past is recalled by its large and austere parish church, visible for miles around, perched on high ground above the village. There's nowhere to stay, but there are two good **pubs**, the *White Horse* and the *Bell*, both of which serve good, reasonably priced bar food.

Another two miles southeast, the market town of **HADLEIGH** is a positive metropolis compared to Kersey, but everything of interest is within a stone's throw of the **Parish Church of St Mary's**. The church, one block west of the elongated High Street, is mainly fifteenth century, a good-looking replacement for several earlier versions. Legend asserts that Guthrum, the Danish chieftain and arch-rival of **Alfred the Great**, was buried underneath the south aisle in 889, but his remains have never been definitively identified. Opposite the church, across the graveyard, is the half-timbered **Guildhall** (guided tours June–Sept Thurs & Sun 2–5pm; £1.50), every bit as immaculate as Lavenham's, with the earliest sections dating from 1438 – and offering very-English cream teas in the garden from June to September (Mon–Fri & Sun 2.30–5pm). At the back of the church is the extravagantly ornate **Deanery Tower**, a fifteenth-century gatehouse whose palace was never completed. In the garret room at the top of the tower, the Oxford Movement, which opposed liberal tendencies within the Anglican Church and sought to promote Anglo-Catholicism, was founded in 1833 by local rector Hugh Rose.

Hadleigh is easy to reach by bus with regular services from Sudbury, Lavenham, Ipswich and Colchester, though Sundays can be a bit tricky. Several Hadleigh-bound buses pass through Kersey too. Tourist information on Hadleigh is available at the library on the High Street and the town is also home to the **East of England Tourist Board**, just off the High Street at Toppesfield Hall (Mon–Fri 9am–5pm; ☏01473/822922). Both can help with local **accommodation**, though there's no real reason to tarry once you've seen the sights. For a bite to eat, Ferguson's Delicatessen, 48 High St (closed Sun), sells delicious sandwiches.

Bury St Edmunds

Appealing **BURY ST EDMUNDS** started out as a Benedictine monastery, founded to house the remains of Edmund, the last Saxon king of East Anglia, who was tortured and beheaded by the marauding Danes in 869. Almost two centuries later, England was briefly ruled by the kings of Denmark and the shrewdest of them, King Canute, made a gesture of reconciliation to his Saxon subjects by conferring on the monastery the status of abbey. It was a popular move and the abbey prospered, so much so that before its dissolution in 1539, it had become the richest religious house in the country. Most of the abbey disappeared long ago, and nowadays Bury is better known for its graceful Georgian streets, its flower gardens and its sugar-beet plant than for its ancient monuments. Nonetheless, it's an amiable, eminently likeable place, one of the prettiest towns in Suffolk, and, with good transport connections on to Cambridge, Colchester, Ipswich and Norwich, it demands at least half a day of anyone's time.

The Town

The town centre has preserved its Norman street plan, a gridiron in which Churchgate was aligned with – and sloped up from – the abbey's high altar. It was the first planned town of Norman Britain and, for that matter, the first example of urban planning in England since the departure of the Romans. Beside the abbey grounds is **Angel Hill**, a broad, spacious square partly framed by Georgian buildings, the most distinguished being the ivy-covered **Angel Hotel**, which features in Dickens' *Pickwick Papers*. Dickens also gave readings of his work in the **Athenaeum**, the Georgian assembly rooms at the far end of the square. A twelfth-century wall runs along the east side of Angel Hill, with the bulky fourteenth-century **Abbey Gate** forming the entrance to the abbey gardens and ruins.

The **abbey ruins** themselves are like nothing so much as petrified porridge, with little to remind you of the grandiose Norman complex that dominated the town. Thousands of medieval pilgrims once sought solace at St Edmund's altar and the cult was of such significance that the barons of England gathered here to swear that they would make King John sign their petition – the Magna Carta of 1215. The only significant remnants of the abbey are behind the more modern cathedral (see below) on the far side of the public **gardens** – where the suntrap rose garden, hemmed in by giant yew hedges, is a particular delight – with the rubbled remains of a small part of the old **abbey church** integrated into a set of unusual Georgian houses. In front, across the green, is the imposing **Norman Tower**, once the main gateway into the abbey and now a solitary monument with dragon gargoyles and fancily decorated capitals.

Incongruously, the tower is next to the front part of Bury's Anglican **Cathedral of St James** (daily: 8.30am–6pm; £2 donation requested), with chancel and transepts added as recently as the 1960s. That its thousand-odd kneelers are often cited as one of its major highlights gives an idea of the paucity of the interior – notwithstanding the hammer-beam roof and a couple of quality stained glass windows. In fact, it was a toss-up between this place and **St Mary's Church** (Mon–Sat 10am–4pm, 3pm in winter), further down Crown Street, as to which would be given cathedral status in 1914. The presence of the tomb of the resolutely Catholic Mary Tudor in the latter was probably the clinching factor.

Round the corner from St Mary's, just off Crown Street on Honey Hill, the **Manor House Museum** (Tues, Wed, Sat & Sun noon–5pm; £3) occupies a grand Georgian mansion built by the wife of the First Earl of Bristol as a pied-à-terre party house. An enjoyable assortment of clocks and watches forms the core of the museum's collection, which is supplemented by a modest sample of portrait and landscape paintings. The museum also mounts extremely popular temporary exhibitions on art and textiles, often based on TV and film costume dramas. At the far end of Crown Street stands Bury's most important industrial concern, the pungent **Greene King Brewery** (June–Aug Mon–Fri 1–4pm, Sat 11am–4pm, Sun 11am–4pm; rest of year closed Sun), whose powerful Abbot Ale is an intense bittersweet beer to be quaffed with caution. The brewery and the National Trust are joint owners of the neighbouring Regency **Theatre Royal**, at the junction of Crown and Westgate streets, built in 1819 by William Wilkins and still staging plays.

The town's main commercial area is on the west side of the centre, a five-minute walk up Abbeygate Street from Angel Hill. There's been some intrusive modern planning here, but dignified Victorian buildings flank both **Cornhill** and **Buttermarket**, the two short main streets, as well as the narrower streets in between. Older still is the Cornhill's flint-walled **Moyse's Hall**, one of the few surviving Norman houses in England, while the streets to the south are lined by an attractive medley of architectural styles, from elegant Georgian town houses to Victorian brick terraces. You'll see the best by strolling along Guildhall Street and turning left down Churchgate, which brings you back to Angel Hill.

Practicalities

From Bury St Edmunds' **train station**, it's ten minutes' walk south to Angel Hill, along Northgate Street. The **bus station** is on St Andrew Street North, near Cornhill. The town's **tourist office**, at 6 Angel Hill (Easter–Sept Mon–Sat 9.30am–5.30pm, Sun 10am–3pm; Oct–Easter Mon–Fri 10am–4pm, Sat 10am–1pm; ☎01284/764667, ✉tic@stedsbc.gov.uk), provides free town maps and has a useful range of leaflets.

The pick of the town's **hotels** is the *Angel*, on Angel Hill (☎01284/714000; ⑤), an immaculately maintained, county-set hotel with thick carpets, oodles of wood panelling and suitably luxurious rooms. A good alternative is the *Chantry Hotel*, 8 Sparhawk St (☎01284/767427; ④), which has sixteen comfortable rooms in a converted Georgian building near the Manor House Museum. The town has a good supply of **B&Bs**, including the excellent *South Hill House*, 43 Southgate St (℡01284/755650, Ⓦwww.southill.cwc.net; ❷), a handsome old town house with many Georgian features and three large en-suite bedrooms.

For **restaurants**, *Maison Bleue*, 31 Churchgate St (℡01284/760623; closed Sun), serves wonderfully fresh seafood at moderate prices. *The Vaults*, inside the medieval undercroft at the *Angel Hotel*, is also first-rate, with tasty main dishes from £7.50. Otherwise, aim for coffee, cakes and **snacks** in either the Cathedral *Refectory* (closed Sun) or the *Scandinavia Coffee House*, 30 Abbeygate St.

Of the **pubs**, one you shouldn't miss is the *Nutshell* (closed Sun), on The Traverse at the top of Abbeygate, which, at sixteen feet by seven and a half, claims to be Britain's smallest. Greene King's brewery tap is the ancient-looking *Dog & Partridge*, 29 Crown St. For entertainment, there's a year-round programme of cultural events held at the **Theatre Royal**, on Westgate St (℡01284/769505).

Ipswich

Situated at the head of the Orwell estuary, **IPSWICH** was a rich trading port in the Middle Ages, but its appearance today is mainly the result of a revival of fortunes in the Victorian era – give or take some clumsy postwar development. The two surviving reminders of old Ipswich – **Christchurch Mansion** and the splendid **Ancient House** – plus the recently renovated quayside are all reason enough to spend at least an afternoon here. Ipswich also boasts a wealth of medieval flint churches, some now locked and slowly rusting away, but others sympathetically restored. One now houses the tourist office, from where **guided walks** depart a couple of times a week during the season (May–Sept Tues & Thurs 2.15pm; £1.75) – perhaps the best way to see the town on a short visit.

The Town

The ancient Saxon market place, **Cornhill**, is still the town's focal point, a likeable urban space flanked by a bevy of imposing Victorian edifices – the Italianate town hall, the old Neoclassical Post Office and the pseudo-Jacobean Lloyds building. From here, it's just a couple of minutes' walk to the Buttermarket and Ipswich's most famous building, the **Ancient House**, whose exterior was decorated around 1670 in extravagant style, a riot of pargeting and stuccowork that together make one of the finest examples of Restoration artistry in the country. There are plasterwork reliefs of pelicans and nymphs as well as representations of the four continents known at the time. Europe is symbolized by a Gothic church, America a tobacco pipe, Asia an Oriental dome and Africa, eccentrically enough, by an African astride a crocodile. Since the house is now a shop, you're free to take a peek inside to view yet more of the decor, including the hammer-beam roof on the first floor.

From the Ancient House, head up Dial Lane past the fifteenth-century church of **St Lawrence** and you are soon on Tavern Street, where two wonderful mock-Tudor shops, built in the 1930s, face the **Great White Horse Hotel**, the "overgrown tavern" which appears in Dickens' *Pickwick Papers*. Heading north from here up Northgate Street takes you past the much-restored sixteenth-century, half-timbered **Oak House**, once an inn and now housing office space, to busy St Margaret's Plain and the gates of **Christchurch**

Mansion (Tues–Sat 10am–5pm, Sun 2.30–4.30pm; free). This handsome, if much-restored Tudor building, sporting seventeenth-century Dutch gables, is set in 65 acres of parkland, an area larger than the town centre itself. The mansion's labyrinthine interior is well worth exploring, with period furnishings and a good collection of paintings by Constable and Gainsborough, as well as more contemporary art exhibitions.

Back in the town centre, the western half of old Ipswich has been transformed by some fairly hideous, postwar development along **Civic Drive**, but there is one modern building which puts the rest to shame. It's the **Willis Corroon Building**, designed by Norman Foster in the 1970s, whose smoked glass exterior snakes its way along Princes Street at Franciscan Way, reflecting the older buildings around it by day but allowing a startling X-ray vision of the illuminated interior after dusk. From here, it's a short stroll east to College Street, named after the college that Cardinal Wolsey, a native of Ipswich, established here in 1528, but failed to complete before his fall from grace. All that remains of Cardinal College now is the solitary **Wolsey's Gateway**, next to the fourteenth-century St Peter's Church.

Pressing on, head east along College Street and, after rounding St-Mary-at-Quay, another medieval church, follow Key Street and you'll soon reach the Neptune Quay marking the northern edge of the **Wet Dock**, the largest in Europe when it opened in 1845 and looking much as it did then, apart from the rash of yachts in the marina. The smell of malt and barley still wafts across the quayside, and several of the granaries continue to function, though other warehouses have been turned into pubs, restaurants and offices. Halfway along the Neptune Quay stands the proud Neoclassical **Customs House**, built for the opening of the dock.

Fifteen minutes' walk south of Neptune Quay via Orwell Quay is the **Tolly Cobbold Brewery** (guided tours £4.50; for latest times & details call ☎01473/261112), which rewards visitors with a sample of its brew after the tour of its Victorian premises. Tours begin in the *Brewery Tap* **pub** (closed Sun) next door.

Practicalities

Ipswich **train station** is on the south bank of the Orwell, ten minutes' walk from Cornhill along Princes Street. The **bus station** is more central, occupying part of the old cattle market, a short walk south of Cornhill and close to the **tourist office** (Mon–Sat 9am–5pm; ☎01473/258070, ✉tourist@ipswich .gov.uk), in the converted St Stephen's Church in St Stephen's Lane. The town is compact enough to walk around, though a special summer **bus** (late July to Aug Mon–Fri & Sun 11am–3pm hourly; ☎01473/232600) runs a circular route connecting the bus station to all the main sights, including the Wet Dock and the brewery.

There's no real need **to stay**, especially with the Suffolk coast so close, but a full list of B&Bs is available from the tourist office. One of the best is *Burlington Lodge*, 30 Burlington Rd (☎01473/251868, ✉burlingtonlodge@bigfoot.com; ❷), an attractive Victorian detached house with five comfortable bedrooms, ten minutes' walk west of the Cornhill. Alternatively, try the ultra-modern *Novotel Hotel*, in the centre near Wolsey's Gateway, on Grey Friars Rd (☎01473 /232400; ❹).

There are several good **restaurants** down by the Wet Dock. *Il Punto*, on Neptune Quay (☎01473/289748), which offers good quality French cuisine at moderate prices, has the most distinctive premises – on board a Dutch pleasure boat – while the more expensive *Mortimer's On The Quay Restaurant*

(☎01473/230225), in one of the old red-brick warehouses down on Wherry Quay, specializes in seafood. Meals here cost £20–30 a head, though it's cheaper at lunch. **Cafés** in town include *Jacey's* at 1 St Stephen's Lane and *Pickwick's*, 1 Dial Lane, with courtyard seating next to St Lawrence's Church.

For a **drink**, try either the *Black Horse* on Black Horse Lane, near the Civic Centre, or the *Glasshouse* on the Buttermarket. For **entertainment**, head for the Ipswich Film Theatre, in the Corn Exchange complex (☎01473/433100), behind the town hall on King Street, which shows mainstream and art movies.

Woodbridge, Sutton Hoo and Framlingham

Beyond Ipswich, the obvious destination is the Suffolk coast, but on the way it's worth considering a short stop at the breezy little town of **Woodbridge** along with neighbouring **Sutton Hoo**, where a brand new National Trust visitor centre has been built beside an Anglo-Saxon burial site unearthed in 1939. Near here also, a short detour to the north, is the tranquil village of **Framlingham**, a delightful place with a gaunt, ruined castle.

Woodbridge

Stringing along the banks of the River Deben eight miles northeast of Ipswich, **WOODBRIDGE** is a pleasant if somewhat unremarkable town whose easy access to the sea – along the river's long and sheltered estuary – once nourished a thriving seaport and shipbuilding industry. These heady nautical days are recalled by the yachts in the marina and the adjacent **Tide Mill** (May–Sept daily 11am–5pm; April & Oct Sat & Sun 11am–5pm; £1.50), which comes complete with its antique milling machinery. From the waterfront, it's an easy five-minute walk up Quay and Church streets to **Market Hill**, the heart of the town since the Middle Ages. Here you'll find two moderately diverting museums; the **Woodbridge Museum** (Easter–Oct Thurs–Sat 10am–4.30pm, Sun 2.30–4.30pm; £1), tracing the town's history and the discovery of the Sutton Hoo treasure; and the **Suffolk Horse Museum** (Easter–Sept Wed, Fri & Sun noon–4pm, Thurs & Sat 10am–4pm; £1.80), housed in the eye-catching, sixteenth-century Shire Hall and featuring paintings, photographs and exhibits celebrating the Suffolk Punch breed, heavy working horses bred in the town since the fifteenth century.

Woodbridge **train station** is handily located at the foot of Quay Street, beside the waterfront. **Buses** pull in here too. The **tourist office** is at the train station (Easter–Sept Mon–Sat 9am–5.30pm, Sun 9.30am–5pm; Oct–Easter Mon–Sat 9am–5.30pm, Sun 10am–1pm; ☎01394/382240) and can help with accommodation as well as providing sketch maps of the town. Among several **hotels** and **B&Bs**, two of the more appealing are the *Station Hotel*, at the station (☎01394/384831; ❸), which has pleasant en-suite rooms and river views, and the *Bull Hotel* on Market Hill (☎01394/382089, ⓦwww.bullhotel.co.uk; ❹), a well-run seventeenth-century coaching inn opposite Shire Hall. There are several first-rate **restaurants**, but the best is *Spice*, 17 The Thoroughfare (☎01394/382557; closed Sun), which serves delicious Malaysian and Mediterranean-influenced dishes at moderate prices; it also has a **bar** with a buzz. Alternatively, there's the *Bull Hotel*, on Market Hill, which offers tasty bar meals and prides itself on its puddings, while the *King's Head*, 17 Market Hill

(☎01394/387750), has good beer and bar meals which make full use of the products of nearby Orford's fine smokehouses (see p.548).

Sutton Hoo

In the summer of 1939, at **SUTTON HOO**, a couple of miles east of Woodbridge on the opposite side of the River Deben, a local landowner stumbled across the richest single archeological find in Britain, an Anglo-Saxon royal burial site belonging to Raedwald, king of East Anglia, who died around 625 AD. A forty-oar open ship was discovered, containing a wooden tomb stuffed with gold and jewelled ornaments. Further archeological research was conducted on the site in the 1980s, and in November 1991 a second undisturbed grave was uncovered. Most of the artefacts are displayed in London's British Museum (see p.94), but some (along with replicas of others) have been returned to Sutton Hoo, where the National Trust have recently opened an immaculate visitor centre and **exhibition hall** (mid-March to May & Oct Wed–Sun 10am–5pm; June–Sept daily 10am–5pm; Nov–Feb most Sat & Sun 11am–4pm; £3.50). The latter explains the history and significance of the finds and afterwards you can wander out onto the burial site itself. To get to Sutton Hoo, take the Melton Road – the B1438 – out of Woodbridge, turn right onto the A1152 and right again onto the B1083, the Bawdsey road, at the roundabout.

Framlingham and around

FRAMLINGHAM, ten miles north of Woodbridge, boasts a magnificent **Castle** (daily: April–Oct 10am–6pm; Nov–March 10am–4pm; £3.70; EH), whose severe, turreted walls date from the twelfth century. The original seat of the Dukes of Norfolk, the fortress is little more than a shell inside, but the curtain-wall, with its thirteen towers, has survived almost intact, a splendid example of medieval military architecture topped by ornamental Tudor chimney stacks. Footpaths crisscross the earthen banks encircling the castle, and from the internal wall walkways there are sweeping views across town to the imposing red-brick mass of Framlingham College, but nothing remains of the Great Hall where Mary Tudor was proclaimed Queen of England in 1553.

The sleepy little village next to the castle is a real pleasure to visit, its elongated main street, **Market Hill**, flanked by a harmonious ensemble of sedate old buildings, including the *Crown Hotel* (☎01728/723521; ❺), a traditional seventeenth-century inn with roaring fires, wood panelling and snug bedrooms. The parish **Church of St Michael** is also intriguing, its finely crafted hammer-beam roof sheltering several wonderful, sixteenth-century tombs belonging to the Howard family, who owned the castle at the time. They were a turbulent clan. During the reign of Henry VIII, both Thomas Howard, the Duke of Norfolk and his son Henry Howard, the Earl of Surrey, schemed away, determined to be the leading nobles of their day. They brought down the powerful Chancellor of the Exchequer, Thomas Cromwell, in 1540 and their position seemed secure when the king married one of their kin, Catherine, later the same year. But the Howards had over-reached themselves. In 1542, the king had Catherine beheaded for adultery and, from his deathbed in 1547, he ordered that Henry Howard should be executed. The same fate would have befallen Howard's father had the king lived a few days longer.

In the hamlet of **DENNINGTON**, a couple of miles to the north of Framlingham along the B1116, stands another interesting church. This is **St Mary's**, a sturdy, medieval edifice, whose benches and pews sport a fantastical series of carvings – wild and folkloric figures and beasts. In particular, there is a rare representation of a sciapod, a mythical creature that avoided sunlight by shading itself with its one, large foot. The sciapod died if it smelt contaminated air, so it carried sniffable fresh fruit everywhere it went. Equally unusual is a rare pyx canopy over the altar. The pyx was the vessel in which the Holy Sacrament was kept and there are only two such surviving canopies in Europe.

The district is also a centre of East Anglia's developing wine industry and several local vineyards offer tours and tastings. The well-established **Shawsgate Vineyard** (March–Nov 10.30am–5pm; ☏01728/724060) is situated one mile north of Framlingham along the B1120.

The Suffolk coast

The **Suffolk coast** feels detached from the rest of the county: the road and rail lines from Ipswich to Lowestoft funnel traffic five miles inland for most of the way, and patches of marsh and woodland make the separation still more complete. The coast has long been plagued by erosion and this has contributed to the virtual extinction of the local fishing industry, and, in the case of **Dunwich**, destroyed virtually the entire town. What is left, however, is undoubtedly one of the most unspoilt shorelines in the country – if, that is, you set aside the **Sizewell** nuclear power station. Highlights include the sleepy isolation of minuscule **Orford** and several genteel resorts, most notably **Southwold**, which has evaded the lurid fate of so many English seaside towns. There are scores of delightful **walks** hereabouts, easy routes along the coast that are best followed with either OS map #156 or #0169, or the simplified *Footpath Maps* available at most tourist offices. The Suffolk coast is also host to East Anglia's most compelling cultural gathering, the three-week-long **Aldeburgh Festival**, which takes place each June.

Orford

Twelve miles east of Woodbridge, on the far side of the Forest of Rendlesham, the tiny village of **ORFORD** is dominated by two buildings, both of them medieval. The more impressive is the twelfth-century **Castle** (April–Oct daily 10am–6pm; Nov–March Wed–Sun 10am–1pm & 2–4pm; £3.10; EH), built on high ground to the southwest of the village by Henry II, and under siege within months of its completion from Henry's rebellious sons. Most of the castle disappeared centuries ago, but the lofty keep remains, its impressive stature hinting at the scale of the original fortifications. Orford's other medieval edifice, on the far side of the main square, is **St Bartholomew's Church**, where Benjamin Britten premiered his most successful children's work, *Noye's Fludde*, as part of the 1958 Aldeburgh Festival (see box on p.550).

From the top of the castle keep, there's a great view across **Orford Ness**, a six-mile-long shingle spit that has all but blocked off Orford from the sea since Tudor times. Its mud flats and marshes harbour sea lavender beds, which act as feeding and roosting areas for wildfowl and waders. The National Trust offers **boat trips** (July–Sept Tues–Sat outward boats between 10am–2pm, last ferry back 5pm; mid-April to June & Oct Sat only; £5.60; NT members £3.60; ☏01394/450057) across to the Ness from Orford Quay, four hundred yards down the road from the church, and a five-mile hiking trail threads its way along the spit. En route, the trail passes the occasional, abandoned military building. Some of the pioneer research on radar was carried out here, but the radar station was closed at the beginning of World War II because of the threat of German bombing – though the military stayed on until the 1980s. There are also plenty of walks to be had around Orford itself. One of the best is the five-mile hike north along the river wall that guards the west bank of the River Alde, returning via Ferry Road, a narrow country lane.

Orford's gentle, unhurried air is best experienced on a night's stay. **Rooms** are available at the *Crown & Castle* (T01394/450205, Wwww.crownandcastle-hotel.co.uk; ➎), an attractive inn across from the castle with comfortable bed-rooms kitted out with all mod cons, and at the marginally less enticing *King's Head* (T01394/450271; ➌), on Market Hill, the main square. For **meals**, don't miss the *Butley Orford Oysterage* (T01394/450277; closed Nov–March) also on Market Hill. This has a very reasonably priced café/restaurant, whose menu focuses on fresh oysters and oak-wood smoked fish. Finally, down near the quay, the *Jolly Sailor Inn* serves bar meals, teas and coffee.

Aldeburgh and around

ALDEBURGH is best known for its annual arts festival, the brainchild of composer **Benjamin Britten**, who is buried in the village churchyard along-side the tenor Peter Pears, his lover and musical collaborator. They lived by the seafront in Crag House on Crabbe Street – the street named for the poet who provided Britten with his greatest inspiration (see box below). Outside of June, when the festival takes place, and November, when the three-day internation-al poetry festival fills the town, Aldeburgh is the quietest of places, with just a small fishing fleet selling its daily catch from wooden shacks along the pebbled shore.

The wide **High Street** and its narrow sidestreets run close to the beach, but this was not always the case – hence their garbled appearance. The ocean swal-lowed most of what was once an extensive medieval town long ago and today Aldeburgh's oldest remaining building, the sixteenth-century **Moot Hall** (Easter–May & Oct Sat & Sun 2.30–5pm; June & Sept daily 2.30–5pm; July & Aug daily 10.30am–12.30pm & 2.30–5pm; 50p), which began its days in the centre of town, finds itself on the seashore. It's a handsome building made out of a mixture of red brick, flint and timber and the interior accommodates a modest museum of local finds and history. One of Aldeburgh's newest build-ings, the **RNLI Lifeboat Station**, is situated bang in the middle of the seafront opposite the Jubilee Hall. From the public viewing deck you can look at the town's lifeboat and the tractor used to drag it out to sea.

Several **footpaths** radiate out from Aldeburgh, with the most obvious trail leading along the seashore north to Thorpeness (see p.551), with others lead-ing southwest to the winding estuary of the River Alde, an area rich in wild-fowl.

Practicalities

Aldeburgh's festival box office shares its High Street premises with the local **tourist office** (daily 9am–5.30pm, till 5.15pm in winter; T01728/453637), who have a useful range of local leaflets. They will also book **accommoda-tion** on your behalf, though things get very tight during the main festival and leading events when you should book months in advance. The town boasts sev-eral splendidly sited **hotels**, including the comfortable *Wentworth* (T01728/452312, Wwww.wentworth-aldeburgh.com; ➏), a family-owned hotel along the seafront from the Moot Hall. Of the **B&Bs**, the *Ocean House*, 25 Crag Path (T01728/452094; ➍), is probably the best. An immaculately maintained Victorian dwelling right on the seafront in the centre of town, it's decorated in

Benjamin Britten and the Aldeburgh Festival

Benjamin Britten was born in Lowestoft in 1913, and was closely associated with Suffolk for most of his life. However, it was during his self-imposed exile in the USA during World War II – he was a conscientious objector – that Britten first read the work of the nineteenth-century Suffolk poet, George Crabbe. Crabbe's *The Borough*, a grisly portrait of the life of the fishermen of Aldeburgh, was the basis of the libretto of Britten's best-known opera, *Peter Grimes* which was premiered in London in 1945 to great acclaim.

In 1947 Britten founded the English Opera Group and the following year launched the **Aldeburgh Festival** as a showpiece for his own works and those of his contemporaries. He lived in the town for the next ten years and it was during this period that he completed much of his best work as a conductor and pianist. For the rest of his life he composed many works specifically for the festival, including his masterpiece for children, *Noye's Fludde* and the last of his fifteen operas, *Death in Venice*.

By the mid-1960s, the festival had outgrown the parish churches in which it began, and moved into a collection of disused malthouses, five miles west of Aldeburgh on the River Alde, just south of the small village of **SNAPE** along the B1069. **Snape Maltings** were subsequently converted into one of the finest concert venues in the country. In addition to the concert hall, there is now a recording studio, a music school, various craft shops and galleries, a tearoom, and a nice pub, the *Plough & Sail*. Even if there's nothing specific on, it's worth calling into the complex to browse in the shops or perhaps take one of the daily summer **river trips** (April–Sept 1hr; £5) along the Alde estuary to see the birdlife.

For more information on the Aldeburgh Festival, contact the **festival box office**, 152 Aldeburgh High Street (℡01728/687110, ⊛www.aldeburgh.co.uk). Tickets for the concerts, talks, exhibitions and other special events go on sale to the public towards the end of March, and usually sell out fast for the big-name recitals; prices range from £9 to £50. There are all sorts of concerts and performances at other times of the year too – again details are available from the booking office – with showcase events including the Proms season in August and the three-day Britten Festival in late October.

period style, with two of its three guest rooms overlooking the beach; dinner is available by prior arrangement. Also in the town centre is *East Cottage*, 55 King St (℡01728/453010; ❷; closed Sept–May), a brightly painted Victorian cottage a block back from the sea. Another option is *Wateringfield*, on Golf Lane (℡01728/453163; ❷), a spacious 1930s house overlooking the golf course on the edge of town. There's also a **youth hostel** on Heath Walk in the hamlet of Blaxhall (℡01728/688206; closed Nov–March), a couple of miles west of the concert facilities at Snape Maltings. The hostel has forty beds and is housed in a former village school ⊛www.yha.org.uk.

There are tearooms and takeaway fish-and-chip shops on the High Street, but Aldeburgh does much better than that with the town's highbrow leanings sustaining a glut of terrific **restaurants**. *Café 152*, 152 High St (℡01728/454152), is the most moderately priced, a simple painted wooden café where stylishly cooked fresh fish is served at lunch and dinner. There are more Mediterranean flavours and adventurous use of local ingredients at both the *Lighthouse*, 77 High St (℡01728/453377), and the *Regatta*, 171–173 High St (℡01728 /452011; closed Mon & Tues in winter), each moderately priced and the latter open to the pavement in summer. For **drinks**, head for the *White Lion Hotel*, just along the seafront from the Moot Hall.

Thorpeness

THORPENESS, two miles up the coast from Aldeburgh, is a strange little resort, planned as a "fantasy" holiday village in 1910 by local landowner Stuart Ogilvie "for people who want to experience life as it was in Merrie England". This eccentricity explains the mock-Tudor style of much of the architecture – eye-catching follies such as the watertower-shaped *House in the Clouds* – and, less tangibly, the sense of keep-out privacy that pervades the place. The large pleasure lake at the centre of the village, the "Meare", has its islets named after characters from *Peter Pan*, whose author, J.M. Barrie, was an Ogilvie family friend. For further details on the history of Thorpeness, head for the **windmill** (July & Aug Mon–Fri 2–5pm, Sat & Sun 11am–1pm; May, June & Sept Sat & Sun only; free), a few hundred yards back from the sea and signposted down a lane from the main street, The Whinlands.

Sizewell and Leiston

It's impossible to wander along the seashore around Aldeburgh without noticing the ominous presence of the **Sizewell nuclear power station**, whose superstructure, topped by what looks like a giant golf ball, is located two miles beyond Thorpeness. The gas-cooled reactor, Sizewell A, has been producing electricity since 1966, and will continue to do so for the foreseeable future. It was the plan to build a second pressurized-water reactor (PWR), **Sizewell B** – the first of its kind in the UK – that provoked one of the longest public enquiries in the country's history, lasting 340 days. Work began shortly after the disaster at Chernobyl, and the reactor was completed in the early part of 1995. In an attempt to assuage public unease, Sizewell B offers free guided tours, beginning at the **visitor centre**, which cheerfully explains how unbelievably safe nuclear power is. Tours need to be booked in advance – call ☎0800/3760676. Sizewell A is about to get into the act too – as soon as its visitor centre is completed.

A couple of miles inland from Sizewell, the small town of **LEISTON** was synonymous with the agricultural engineering firm Garretts for over two centuries, until the company closed in 1980. Much of the original plant has been removed, but the main iron- and timber-framed factory building, built in 1852 and nicknamed "the cathedral", now forms part of the **Long Shop Museum** on Main St (April–Oct Mon–Sat 10am–5pm, Sun 11am–5pm; £3). Here, you can view a selection of Garretts finest products from steamrollers and trolley-buses to bakers' ovens and dry-cleaning machines.

Dunwich

Seat of the kings of East Anglia, a bishopric and once the largest port on the Suffolk coast, the ancient city of **DUNWICH**, about twelve miles up the coast from Aldeburgh, reached its peak of prosperity in the twelfth century. Over the last millennium, however, something like a mile of land has been lost to the sea, a process that continues at the rate of about a yard a year. As a result, the whole of the medieval city now lies under the ocean, including all twelve churches, the last of which toppled over the cliffs in 1919. All that survives are fragments of the Greyfriars monastery, which originally lay to the west of the city and now dangles at the sea's edge. For a potted history of the lost city, head for the **museum** (April–Sept daily 11.30am–4.30pm; Oct daily noon–4pm; free) in what's left of Dunwich – little more than one small street of terraced houses built by the local landowner in the nineteenth century.

A sprawling, coastline car park gives ready access to this part of the seashore and is also where fishing boats still sell their daily catch off the shingle beach.

From the car park, it's a short stroll west to the village and south to Greyfriars. Or you can hike further south, out along the beach to **Dunwich Heath**, where the coastguard cottages have been turned into a National Trust information centre (April–Oct daily; rest of year Wed–Sun) with displays on the heath and local wildlife. The heath is itself next to the **Minsmere RSPB Nature Reserve**, whose star turn is a colony of avocets. You can rent binoculars from the RSPB **visitor centre** (for times, call ☎01728/648281) and strike out on the trails to the birdwatching hides; there's a café on site, too.

The coastline and its heaths have an eerie quality – P.D. James distils this perfectly in her *Unnatural Causes*, portraying the coast as the "battlefield where for nearly nine centuries the land had waged its losing fight against the sea." This atmosphere is best appreciated by **staying** at Dunwich's one and only pub, the *Ship Inn* (☎01728/648219; ❸). With its low wooden beams and open fire, the bar here is a great place for a drink and the **food** is both moderately priced and very tasty with seafood the main event.

Southwold and around

Perched on robust cliffs just to the north of the River Blyth, **SOUTHWOLD** gained what Dunwich lost, and by the sixteenth century it had overtaken all its local rivals. Its days as a busy fishing port are, however, long gone – though a small fleet still brings in herring, sprats and cod – and today it's a genteel seaside resort, an eminently appealing little town with none of the crassness of many of its competitors. There are fine old buildings, a long sandy beach, open heathland, a dinky harbour and even a little industry – in the shape of the Adnams brewery – but no burger bars and certainly no amusement arcades. This gentility was not to the liking of George Orwell, who lived for a time at his parents' house at 36 High St (a plaque marks the house). Orwell heartily disliked the town's airs and graces, and has left no trace of his time here – apart from disguised slights in a couple of early novels.

Southwold's breezy **High Street** is framed by attractive, mainly Georgian buildings, which culminate in the pocket-sized Market Place. From here, it's a brief stroll along East Street to the curious **Sailors' Reading Room** (daily 9am–5pm; free), decked out with model ships and nautical texts, and the bluff above the **beach**, where row upon row of candy-coloured huts march across the sands. Queen Street begins at the Market Place too, quickly leading to **South Green**, the prettiest of several greens dotted across town. In 1659, a calamitous fire razed much of Southwold and when the town was rebuilt the greens were left to act as firebreaks. Beyond, both Ferry Road and the Ferry footpath lead down to the **harbour**, at the mouth of the River Blyth, an idyllic spot, where fishing smacks rest against old wooden jetties and nets are spread out along the banks to dry. There's a footpath along the harbourside that leads to a tiny **ferry** (Easter–May Sat & Sun 10am–12.30pm & 2–4.30pm; June–Aug daily 10am–12.30pm & 2–4.30pm; 40p), which pops across the river to Walberswick (see below). Turn right after the Harbour Inn and right again to walk back into town across **Southwold Common**. The whole circular walk takes about thirty minutes.

Back on the Market Place, it's a couple of hundred yards north along Church Street to East Green, with Adnams Brewery on one side, the stumpy lighthouse on another. Close by is Southwold's architectural pride and joy, the **Church of St Edmund** (daily: June–Aug 9am–6pm; Sept–May 9am–4pm), a handsome fifteenth-century structure whose solid symmetries are balanced by its long and elegantly carved windows. Inside, the slender, beautifully proportioned nave is distinguished by its panelled roof, embellished with praying angels, and its intricate rood screen. The latter carries paintings of the apostles and the prophets, though the Protestants defaced them during the Reformation. Beyond the screen, the choir stalls carry finely carved human and animal heads as well as grotesques – look out for the man in the throes of toothache. Look out also for "**Southwold Jack**", a brightly painted, medieval effigy of a man in armour nailed to the wall beside the font. No one knows when or why this very military carving was moved into the church – it certainly doesn't fit in – but the betting is that he was once part of a clock, nodding belligerently as he struck the hours. From the church, it's a short walk north to the **pier**, the latest incarnation of a structure that dates from 1899. Built as a landing stage for passenger ferries, the pier has had a troubled history: it has been repeatedly damaged by storms, was hit by a sea-mine and then partly chopped up by the army as a protection against German invasion in World War II. Work started on rebuilding the pier in 1999 and will take several years to complete.

Practicalities

With frequent services from other towns along the coast, Southwold is easy to reach by **bus**. These stop on the Market Place, yards from the **tourist office**, at 69 High St (April–Sept Mon–Fri 10am–5pm, Sat 10am–5.30pm, Sun 11am–4pm; Oct–March Mon–Fri 10.30am–3.30pm, Sat 10am–4.30pm; ☎01502/724729, ⊛www.visit-southwold.co.uk), which has details of local attractions and sells walking maps. The town has two well-known **hotels** beside the Market Place, both owned and operated by Adnams. The smarter of the two is the *Swan* (☎01502/722186; ❺), which occupies a splendid Georgian building with lovely period rooms, though the bedrooms – in the main house and in a garden annexe behind – are a little on the small side. The *Crown,* just along the High Street (☎01502/722275; ❺), has just twelve simple bedrooms, all of which are en suite. The best **B&B** in town is the delightful *Acton Lodge*, 18 South Green (☎01502/723217; no credit cards; ❹), which occupies a grand Victorian house complete with its own neo-Gothic tower. The interior is decorated in period style and the three comfortable bedrooms are all en suite. Breakfasts are delicious, too. Alternatively, there's a string of **guest houses** down along the seafront on North Parade: try the *North Parade*, at no. 21 (☎01502/722573; ❷), a well-tended Victorian house with sprucely decorated bedrooms; or the attractive *Dunburgh*, at no. 28 (☎01502/723253; ❸), housed in a rambling building with its own mini-tower.

Southwold has two outstanding **places to eat**. The *Crown*'s front bar provides superb informal meals, encompassing daily fish and meat specials combined with an enlightened wine list where all the choices are available by the glass. Turn up, wait for a table and expect to pay just £12 or so for two courses; you'll have to make a booking if you want to eat in the adjacent restaurant, which is pricier, slightly more adventurous and just as terrific. The *Swan*'s more formal dining room is the place for a gourmet blow-out, offering a choice of set dinners at £20–30 a head. For a **drink**, sample Adnams' brews in the *Crown*'s wood-panelled back-bar or stroll along to the *Red Lion* on South Green.

Walberswick and Blythburgh

Just across the River Blyth from Southwold lies the leafy little village of **WALBERSWICK**, another once-prosperous port, now fallen into peaceful decline. For many years, it was the home of the English Impressionist painter, Philip Wilson Steer, and is now a seaside escape popular with well-heeled holidaymakers, who consider its larger neighbour too boisterous. As such, there's not much to see and most visitors make a bee-line for the *Bell*, an old village pub close to the riverfront which offers tasty bar food and Adnams beer. There are two ways for walkers to get here from Southwold – either via the ferry (see above) or over the Bailey bridge about a mile further inland. The footpath to the bridge begins on Station Road, a continuation of Southwold's High Street.

Up until the sixteenth century, **BLYTHBURGH**, five miles west of Southwold, was a thriving port at the head of a wide estuary, but the silting up of the River Blyth slowly strangled the town, reducing it to an inconsequential hamlet. The **Church of the Holy Trinity**, a handsome flint and stone structure dating from the 1440s, recalls the village's previous prosperity – its sheer bulk earning it the moniker, "Cathedral of the Marshes". Inside, the light and airy nave is decorated with carved angels and brightly painted flower patterns similar to St Edmund's in Southwold. The bench-ends depict the Seven Deadly Sins with gusto and, in another echo of Southwold, there's a "Jack-o'-the-Clock" here, too.

Lowestoft

LOWESTOFT, the easternmost point in the British Isles, is a world apart from the likes of Southwold and Aldeburgh. It's a fishing port and has been so since the railway arrived here in 1847, when Lowestoft began seriously to challenge its Norfolk neighbour, Great Yarmouth (see p.564). The town is bisected by its Inner Harbour with the older part to the north. Here, the narrow alleyways, known locally as "scores", once lined with fishermen's huts and smokehouses, run east off the High Street towards the giant Bird's Eye factory, destination of much of the trawlers' haul. If you've an interest in Lowestoft's history, visit the **Maritime Museum** on Whapload Road (May–Oct daily 10am–5pm; 75p), near the lighthouse on the north side of town. Alternatively, you could take a **guided harbour tour** in a trawler, details of which can be found at the **tourist office**, East Point Pavilion (April–Sept daily 9.30am–5.30pm; Oct–March Mon–Fri 10.30am–5pm, Sat & Sun 10am–5pm; ☎01502 /533600), on the south side of the harbour.

Norwich

One of the five largest cities in Norman England, **NORWICH** once served a vast hinterland of cloth producers in the eastern counties, whose work was brought here by river and exported to the continent. Its isolated position beyond the Fens meant that it enjoyed closer links with the Low Countries than with the rest of England – it was, after all, quicker to cross the North Sea than to go cross-country to London. The local textile industry, based on worsted cloth (named after the nearby village of Worstead), was further enhanced by an influx of Flemish and Huguenot weavers, who made up more than a third of the population in Tudor times. By 1700, Norwich was the second richest city in the country after London.

With the onset of the Industrial Revolution, Norwich lost ground to the northern manufacturing towns – the city's famous mustard company, Colman's, is one of its few industrial success stories. This, and its continuing geographical isolation, has helped preserve much of the ancient street plan as well as many of the city's older buildings. Pride of place goes to the beautiful cathedral and the castle, but the city's hallmark is its medieval **churches**, thirty or so squat flintstone structures with sturdy towers and sinuous stone tracery round the windows. Isolation has also meant that the population has never

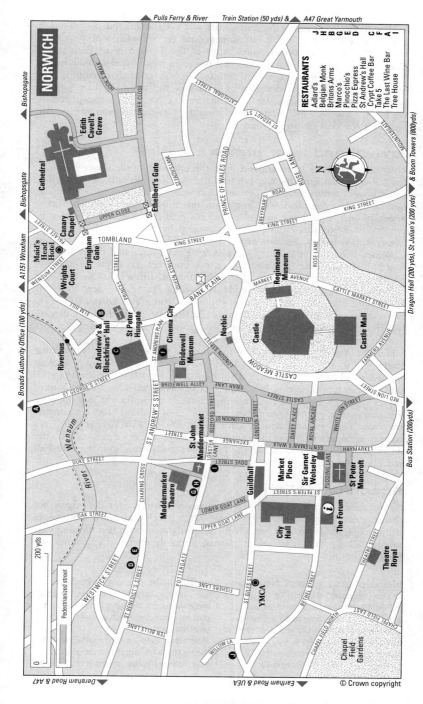

NORWICH

EAST ANGLIA | Norwich

7

RESTAURANTS

Adlard's	J
Belgian Monk	H
Britons Arms	B
Marco's	G
Pinocchio's	E
Pizza Express	D
St Andrew's Hall	C
Crypt Coffee Bar	F
Take 5	A
The Last Wine Bar	I
Tree House	

Pulls Ferry & River   Train Station (50 yds) &   A47 Great Yarmouth

Bishopsgate

Bishopsgate

A1151 Wroxham

Broads Authority Office (100 yds)

Dereham Road & A47

Earlham Road & UEA

© Crown copyright

Dragon Hall (200 yds), St Julian's (200 yds)   & Boom Towers (800yds)

Bus Station (200yds)

Cathedral

Edith Cavell's Grave

Canary Chapel

Maid's Head Hotel

Wrights Court

Erpingham Gate

Ethelbert's Gate

TOMBLAND

Regimental Museum

Castle

Castle Mall

Norvic

St Peter Hungate

St Andrew's & Blackfriars' Hall

Cinema City

Bridewell Museum

Riverbus

St John Maddermarket

Maddermarket Theatre

Guildhall

Market Place

Sir Garnet Wolseley

St Peter Mancroft

The Forum

City Hall

Theatre Royal

YMCA

Chapel Field Gardens

PALACE STREET

WENSUM STREET

ELM HILL

ST GEORGE'S STREET

DUKE STREET

CHARING CROSS

OAK STREET

WESTWICK STREET

ST BENEDICT'S STREET

POTTERGATE

TEN BELLS LANE

FISHERS LANE

ST GILES STREET

WILLOW LA

CHAPEL FIELD NORTH

BETHEL STREET

THEATRE STREET

CHAPEL FIELD EAST

ST PETER'S STREET

LOWER GOAT LANE

UPPER GOAT LANE

DOVE STREET

LOBSTER LANE

EXCHANGE STREET

BEDFORD STREET

LITTLE LONDON ST

LONDON STREET

BRIDEWELL ALLEY

SWAN LANE

CASTLE STREET

DAVEY PLACE

ROYAL ARCADE

WHITE LION STREET

GENTLEMAN'S WALK

HAYMARKET

PUDDING LANE

RED LION STREET

FARMERS AVENUE

CATTLE MARKET STREET

CASTLE MEADOW

MARKET AVENUE

ROSE LANE

KING STREET

KING STREET

KING STREET

ROSE LANE

GREYFRIAR'S ROAD

PRINCE OF WALES ROAD

ST FAITH'S LANE

CATHEDRAL STREET

ST VEDAST ST

MOUNTERGATE

UPPER CLOSE

LOWER CLOSE

HOOK'S WALK

BANK PLAIN

QUEEN STREET

PRINCES STREET

WENSUM STREET

ST ANDREW'S STREET

ST ANDREWS PLAIN

River Wensum

N

200 yds

Pedestrianized street

555

swelled to any great extent and today, with just 170,000 inhabitants, Norwich remains an easy and enjoyable city to negotiate. Yet Norwich is no provincial backwater. In the 1960s, the foundation of the University of East Anglia (UEA) made it more cosmopolitan and bolstered its arts scene, while in the 1980s it attracted new high-tech companies, who created something of a mini-boom, making the city one of England's wealthiest. As East Anglia's unofficial capital, Norwich also lies at the hub of the region's transport network and serves as a useful base for visiting the Broads, and even as a springboard for the north Norfolk coast.

Arrival and information

Norwich's grandiose **train station** is on the east bank of the River Wensum, ten minutes' walk from the city centre along Prince of Wales Road. Long distance **buses** terminate at the Surrey Street station, also little more than ten minutes' walk from the town centre, but this time to the south off Surrey Street, though some pause in the centre on Castle Meadow too. Information on local and regional bus services is provided by NORBIC, 17–19 Castle Meadow (Mon–Sat 8.30am–5pm; ☎0845/6020121). The First Eastern Counties' Bus Ranger ticket (£7), valid for a day's unlimited travel on most East Anglian bus routes, is available here, as is the three-day ticket for unlimited travel on three days in seven (£16). The **tourist office** is in The Forum, a gleamingly new, glassy building beside the Market Place (June–Sept Mon–Sat 10am–5pm; Oct–May Mon–Fri 10am–4pm, Sat 10am–2pm; ☎01603/666071, ⓦwww.norwich.gov.uk). The **Broads Authority Office**, 18 Colegate (☎01603/610734, ⓦwww.broads-authority.gov.uk), is a useful source of information for those heading for the Broads.

The best way to see the city is on foot and the tourist office's **city walking tours** (April, May & Oct Sat 1 daily; June & Sept 4 weekly; July & Aug Mon–Sat 1–2 daily; 1hr 30min; £2.50) are a good way of getting the lie of the land. It's also worth bearing in mind the **riverbus** (April–Oct 5 daily; 15min; 75p), which runs from the Elm Hill Quay to the Thorpe Road Quay, opposite the train station, providing an inexpensive means of cruising Norwich's central waterway. They are operated by City Boats (☎01603/701701, ⓦwww.city-boats.fsnet.co.uk), who also offer a limited range of longer cruises out into the surrounding countryside and to the Norfolk Broads from both the Elm Hill and Thorpe Road quays.

Accommodation

As you might expect, Norwich has **accommodation** to suit all budgets, but there's precious little in the town centre. Most **B&Bs** and **guest houses** are strung along the Earlham Road, a tedious, mostly Victorian street running west towards UEA, which itself offers **rooms**, primarily during the summer and Easter vacations.

Hotels and guest houses

The Beeches Hotel 2–6 Earlham Rd ☎01603/621167, ⓦwww.beeches.co.uk. Just across the ring road from the centre, this medium-sized hotel occupies three fully modernized Victorian townhouses. All 36 rooms are en suite and the place is popular with visiting business folk. ❺
Earlham Guest House 147 Earlham Rd ☎01603/454169, ✉earlhamgh@hotmail.com. Spick-and-span lodgings at this family-run guest house, located in a two-storey Victorian house a good ten minutes' walk from the centre. Seven bedrooms, each with a TV. ❷
Maid's Head Hotel Tombland ☎01603/209955. Bang in the centre, opposite the cathedral, this smart hotel incorporates all sorts of architectural

bits and pieces from Art Deco flourishes through to heavy Victorian-style wood panelling. The end result is quite pleasing and the bedrooms come complete with modern furnishings and fittings. ❻
Rosedale Guest House 145 Earlham Rd ☎01603/453743, ✉drcbac@aol.com. Typical Victorian guest house containing six frugal but perfectly adequate bedrooms, each with a TV. A good ten-minute walk from the town centre. ❷
Swallow Nelson Hotel Prince of Wales Rd ☎01603/760260. This modern, riverside hotel, directly opposite the train station, caters to a mainly business clientele. It offers spick-and-span rooms, some of which overlook the water, an indoor pool and a health club. ❼

Hostels and student halls

Norwich youth hostel 112 Turner Rd ☎01603 /627647, ⊛www.yha.org.uk. This straightforward, sixty-bed hostel is located in the suburbs two miles west of the centre. Closed Nov–March.
University of East Anglia ☎01603/593297. There are sixty en-suite rooms available year-round in Nelson Court (£49 per double), and also single student rooms with shared bathrooms (£23) and en suite (£32) available during Easter and summer vacations. The campus is four miles west of the centre along the Earlham Road; of the many buses running here from the centre – #25, #26 and #27 from Castle Meadow are the most frequent.

The City

Tucked into a sweeping bend of the River Wensum, Norwich's irregular street plan, a Saxon legacy, can make orientation difficult. There are, however, three obvious landmarks to help you find your way – the cathedral with its giant spire, the Norman castle on its commanding mound and the distinctive clock-tower of City Hall. The **cathedral** and the **castle** are the town's premier attractions and the latter also holds one of the region's most satisfying collections of fine art. Finally, note that **Sunday** can be a disastrous day to visit if you want to see anything other than the cathedral: most museums and attractions are closed, not to mention most restaurants.

The Cathedral

Norwich **Cathedral** (daily: May–Sept 7.30am–7pm; Oct–April 7.30am–6pm; free tours May–Oct Mon–Sat; £3 donation requested) is distinguished by its prickly octagonal spire which rises to a height of 315ft, second only to Salisbury. It's best viewed from the Lower Close (see below) to the west, where the thick curves of the flying buttresses, the rounded excrescences of the ambulatory chapels – unusual in an English cathedral – and the straight symmetries of the main body can all be seen to perfection.

The **interior** is pleasantly light thanks to a creamy tint in the stone and the clear glass windows of much of the nave, where the thick pillars are a powerful legacy of the Norman builders who began the cathedral in 1096. Look up to spy the nave's fan vaulting, delicate and geometrically precise carving adorned by several hundred roof **bosses** recounting – from east to west – the story of the Old and New Testaments from the Creation to the Last Judgement. Moving on, wander down the south side of the ambulatory to reach **St Luke's Chapel**, where the cathedral's finest work of art, the *Despenser Reredos*, is a superb painted panel commissioned to celebrate the crushing of the Peasants' Revolt of 1381. Across the aisle, encased by the choir, is the **bishop's throne**, a sturdy stone structure placed directly behind the high altar. Norman bishops were barons as much as religious leaders, and to emphasize their direct relationship with Almighty God they usually put their thrones behind the high altar. Most were later relocated, but this one occupies its original position. Here in Norwich, the bishop also had a spiritual prop: a flue runs down from the back of the throne to a reliquary recess behind in the ambulatory, the idea being that divine essences would be transported up to him. Accessible from the south aisle of the nave are the cathedral's unique **cloisters**.

Built between 1297 and 1450, and the only two-storey cloisters left standing in England, they contain a remarkable set of sculpted **bosses**, similar to the ones in the main nave, but close enough to be scrutinized without binoculars. The carving is fabulously intricate and the dominant theme is the Apocalypse, but look out also for the bosses depicting green men, pagan fertility symbols. A computer screen by the main entrance gives the low-down on all of the bosses.

Outside, beside the main entrance, stands the medieval **Canary Chapel**. This is the original building of Norwich School, whose blue-blazered pupils are often visible during term time – the rambling school buildings are adjacent. A statue of the school's most famous boy, Horatio Nelson, faces the chapel, standing on the green of the **Upper Close**, which is guarded by two ornate and imposing medieval gates, **Erpingham** and, a few yards to the south, **Ethelbert**. Beside the Erpingham gate is a memorial to Edith Cavell, a local woman who was a nurse in occupied Brussels during World War I. She was shot by the Germans in 1915 for helping allied prisoners to escape, a fate that made her an instant folk hero; her grave is beside the cathedral ambulatory. Both gates lead onto the old Saxon market place, **Tombland**, a wide and busy thoroughfare whose name derives from the Saxon word for an open space.

Tombland is a convenient place to start an exploration of the rest of the city centre (see below), but instead you might prefer to wander pedestrianized **Cathedral Close**, which extends east to the river from – and including – the Upper Close. Just beyond the Upper Close is the **Lower Close**, where a scattering of silver birches is flanked by attractive Georgian and Victorian houses. Keeping straight, the footpath continues east to **Pull's Ferry**, a landing stage at the city's medieval watergate, named after the last ferryman to work this stretch of the river. It's a picturesque spot and from here you can wander along the riverbank either south to the railway station or north to Bishopgate, by means of which you can regain Tombland.

From Tombland to Elm Hill and Pottergate

At the north end of Tombland, fork left at the Maid's Head Hotel and cobbled **Elm Hill**, more a gentle slope than a hill, soon appears on the left. Priestley, in his *English Journey* of 1933, thought this part of Norwich to be overbearingly Dickensian, proclaiming "it difficult to believe that behind those bowed and twisted fronts there did not live an assortment of misers, mad spinsters, saintly clergymen, eccentric comic clerks, and lunatic sextons." Since then, the tourist crowds have sucked the atmosphere, but the quirky half-timbered houses still appeal and while you're here take a look at **Wright's Court**, down a passageway at no. 43, one of the few remaining enclosed courtyards which were once a feature of the city. Elm Hill quickly opens out into a triangular square centred on a plane tree, planted on the spot where the eponymous elm tree from Henry VIII's time once stood. It then veers left up to **St Peter Hungate**, a good-looking, fifteenth-century flint church equipped with a solid square tower and gentle stone tracery round its windows.

Turn right at the church and it's just a few yards to **St Andrew's Hall** and **Blackfriars Hall**, two adjoining buildings that were originally the nave and chancel, respectively, of a Dominican monastery church. Imaginatively recycled, the two halls are now used for a variety of public events, including concerts, weddings and antique fairs; the crypt of the former now serves as a café (Mon–Sat 9am–4.30pm). South of here, off St Andrews Street and along Bridewell Alley, stands the **Bridewell Museum** (April–Sept Mon–Sat 10am–5pm; £2), one of the city's more enjoyable museums. Formerly the city jail, the Bridewell holds a pot-pourri of old machines, adverts, signs, and reconstructed shops celebrating Norwich's old trades and industry. Inevitably, there's much on the all-important mustard industry, which did much to keep the city's economy afloat in its more troubled times.

From the top of Bridewell Alley, Bedford Street and then Lobster Lane lead west to Pottergate's **St John Maddermarket** (June–Sept Tues–Sat 10.30am–5pm; free), one of thirty medieval churches standing within the boundaries of the old city walls. Most are redundant and are rarely open to the public, but this is one of the more accessible, courtesy of dedicated volunteers. Apart from the stone trimmings, the church is almost entirely composed of flint rubble, the traditional building material of east Norfolk, an area chronically short of decent stone. It is a good example of the Perpendicular style, a sub-division of English Gothic which flourished from the middle of the fourteenth to the early sixteenth century and is characterized by straight vertical lines – as you might expect from the name – and large windows framed by flowing, but plain, tracery. By comparison, the interior is something of a disappointment, its furnishings and fittings thoroughly remodelled at the start of the twentieth century. It's from this period that the heavy–duty oak altar canopy and the extensive wood panelling date. The church also has a good selection of **brasses** and the volunteers will kit you out so you can rub away to your heart's content. Back outside, the arch under the church tower leads through to the **Maddermarket Theatre**, built in 1921 in the style of an Elizabethan playhouse. Incidentally, Maddermarket is named after the yellow flower that the weavers used to make red vegetable dye, or madder.

The Market Place

From Pottergate, several narrow alleys lead through to the city's **Market Place**, site of one of the country's largest open-air markets (closed Sun), with stalls selling everything from bargain-basement clothes to local mussels and whelks. Four very different but equally distinctive buildings oversee the market's stripy awnings, the oldest of them being the fifteenth-century **Guildhall**, an attractive flint and stone structure begun in 1407. Opposite, commanding the heights of the market place, are the austere **City Hall**, a lumbering brick pile with a landmark clock tower built in the 1930s in a Scandinavian style – it bears a striking resemblance to Oslo's city hall – and the **The Forum**, a flashy, glassy structure completed in 2001. On the south side of the Market Place is the finest of the four buildings, **St Peter Mancroft** (Mon–Fri 9.30am–4.30pm, Sat 10am–12.30pm; free), whose long and graceful nave leads to a mighty stone tower, an intricately carved affair surmounted by a spiky little spire. The church once delighted John Wesley, who declared "I scarcely ever remember to have seen a more beautiful parish church," a fair description of what remains an exquisite example of the Perpendicular style with the slender columns of the nave reaching up towards the delicate groining of the roof. Completed in 1455, the open design of the nave was meant to express the mystery of the Christian faith with light filtering in through the stained-glass windows in a kaleidoscope of colours. Some of the original glass has survived, most notably in the east window which boasts a cartoon strip of biblical scenes from the Virgin nursing the baby Jesus, through to the Crucifixion and Resurrection.

Back outside and just below the church is the bubble-gum-orange **Sir Garnet Wolseley** pub, sole survivor of the 44 ale houses that once crowded the Market Place and stirred the local bourgeoisie into endless discussions about the drunken fecklessness of the working class. Opposite the pub, across **Gentlemen's Walk**, the town's main promenade, which runs along the bottom of the market place, is the **Royal Arcade**, an Art Nouveau extravagance from 1899. The arcade has been beautifully restored to reveal the swirl and blob of the tiling, ironwork and stained glass, though it's actually the eastern entrance, further from Gentlemen's Walk, which is the most appealing section.

The Castle

Perched high on a grassy mound in the centre of town, and imaginatively tailored into a brand new shopping mall down below, the stern walls of **Norwich Castle**, replete with blind arcading and dating from the twelfth century, were built to intimidate the local population. To begin with they were a reminder of Norman power and then, when the castle was turned into a prison, they served as a grim warning to potential law-breakers. Recently refurbished in lavish style, the castle now holds an excellent **Museum and Art Gallery** (July & Aug 10.30am–7pm, Sun 2–5pm; rest of year Mon–Sat 10.30am–5pm; £4.90 all zones), which is divided into three colour-coded zones – yellow for Art and Exhibitions, green for Natural History, and pink for the Castle Keep. The **Natural History** section holds a fairly routine collection of stuffed and mounted wildlife, but **Art and Exhibitions** scores well with its temporary displays and boasts an outstanding selection of work by the **Norwich School**. Founded in 1803, and in existence for just thirty years, this school of landscape painters produced – for the most part at least – richly coloured, formally composed land- and seascapes in oil and watercolour, paintings whose realism harked back to the Dutch landscape painters of the seventeenth century. The leading figures were John Crome – aka "Old Crome" – and more particularly John Sell Cotman, who is generally acknowledged as one of England's finest watercolourists. Both have a gallery to themselves and, helpfully, there's also a gallery given over to those Dutch painters who influenced them.

Moving on, the **Castle Keep** is no more than a shell, its gloomy walls towering above a scattering of local archeological finds and exhibits that illustrate traditional forms of punishment. The gibbet and its instruments of torture attract most attention, but more unusual is a bloated model dragon, known as Snap, which was paraded round town on the annual guilds' day procession – a folkloric hand-me-down from the dragon St George had so much trouble polishing off. To see more of the Keep, join one of the regular **guided tours** (an extra £2.50) that explore the battlements and – at some time in the near future – the dungeons.

Finally, a long and dark (and one-way) tunnel leads down from the Castle Museum to the **Royal Norfolk Regimental Museum** (Mon–Sat 10am–5pm), which tracks through the history of the regiment with remarkable candour – including an even-handed account of the Norfolks' police-keeping role in Northern Ireland. The exit leaves you below the castle on Market Avenue.

King Street and the river

Behind the castle, **King Street** possesses one or two surprises, beginning with the **Dragon Hall**, at no. 115–123 (April–Oct Mon–Sat 10am–4pm; Nov–March Mon–Fri 10am–4pm; £2), an extraordinarily long, half-timbered showroom built for the cloth merchant Robert Toppes in the fifteenth century. Bowed and bent by age, you get a good impression of the building from the outside, but enthusiasts can pop in to have a closer look at the roof – there's nothing else to see. A right turn opposite the hall up St Julian's Alley leads to **St Julian's Church** (daily 7am–6pm; free) and an adjoining monastic cell, thatched and standing in open countryside as late as the mid-nineteenth century. One of the smallest of the city's religious foundations, this was the retreat of St Julian, a Norwich woman who took to living here after experiencing visions of Christ in 1373. Her mystical *Revelations of Divine Love* – written after twenty years' meditation on her visions – was the first widely distributed book written by a woman in the English language, and has been in print ever since.

Still further down King Street, at Carrow Bridge near the football ground, are the ruins of two medieval **boom towers**, which formed part of the city's defences. From here, a **riverside walk** – initially on the east bank – follows the Wensum around the city centre to Bishopgate, switching to the inner (west) bank at Foundry Bridge, beside the train station. The walk is at its most appealing between Pull's Ferry and **Cow Tower**, a 50-foot-high watchtower where the bishop's retainers collected river tolls. This is one of the few survivors of Norwich's **fortified walls**, which once stretched for over two miles, surrounding the city and incorporating thirty such circular towers and ten defensive gates. Up until the 1790s, the gates were closed at dusk and all day on Sundays.

The University

The **University of East Anglia** (UEA) occupies a sprawling campus on the western outskirts of the city beside the B1108. Its buildings are resolutely modern concrete-and-glass blocks of varying designs – some quite ordinary, others like the prize-winning "ziggurat" halls of residence, designed by Denys Lasdun, eminently memorable. The main reason to visit is the flashy, high-tech **Sainsbury Centre for Visual Arts** (Tues–Sun 11am–5pm; £2; ⓦwww .uea.ac.uk/scva), built by Norman Foster in the 1970s. The interior houses one of the most varied collections of sculpture and painting in the country, donated by the family which founded the Sainsbury supermarket chain, in which the likes of Degas, Seurat, Picasso, Giacometti, Bacon and Henry Moore rub shoulders with Mayan and Egyptian antiquities. The centre also runs a first-rate programme of temporary exhibitions (call ☎01603/593199 for further details). **Buses** #25, #26 and #27 run frequently to UEA from Castle Meadow.

Eating and drinking

There are plenty of **cafés and restaurants** in the city centre – most of them very good value. Decent **pubs**, though, are harder to find – maybe because previously serviceable places have been turned into ersatz "traditional" drinking dens for students.

Cafés and restaurants

Adlard's 79 Upper Giles St ☎01603/633522. Engaging Modern-British restaurant with accomplished seasonal cooking from a brief but enticing menu. Closed all Sun & Mon lunch. Expensive.

Belgian Monk 7 Pottergate ☎01603/767222. Perhaps too theme-ish for some tastes, this new bar and restaurant specializes in all-things Flemish – from beers through to soup and, of course, mussels and chips. Moderate.

Britons Arms 9 Elm Hill. Home-made quiches, tarts, cakes and scones plus pies and salads in a quaint Elm Hill house with a terraced garden. Open Mon–Sat 9.30am–5pm. Inexpensive.

The Last Wine Bar, 70–76 St George's St ☎01603/626626. Converted factory building hold-ing a smart wine bar, which serves up tasty bistro-style dishes. A couple of minutes' walk north of the river. Closed Sun. Moderate.

Marco's 17 Pottergate ☎01603/624044. The city's oldest and finest Italian restaurant, serving all the classics with panache. Smart and formal. Closed Sun & Mon. Expensive.

Pinocchio's 11 St Benedict's St ☎01603/613318. Relaxed Italian restaurant with inventive food combinations and featuring live music a couple of times a week. Occupies a pleasantly converted old general store. Closed Sun. Moderate.

Pizza Express 15 St Benedict's St. No surprises, of course, on the menu, but you get the city centre's best pizzas. Inexpensive.

St Andrew's Hall Crypt Coffee Bar St Andrew's

Plain at St George's St. Bargain spot for budget meals or just a coffee and cake. Open Mon–Sat 9am–4.30pm. Inexpensive.

Take 5 at Cinema City, St Andrew's Plain. Imaginative, budget bistro food served in amenable surroundings. A student favourite. Mon–Sat 11am–11pm. Inexpensive.

Tree House 14 Dove St, above the Rainbow wholefood shop. Vegetarian wholefood café-restaurant offering a daily changing menu of soups, salads and main courses, plus organic wines and beers. Closed Sun. Inexpensive.

Pubs, bars and clubs

Adam & Eve Bishopgate. There's been a pub on this site for seven hundred years and it's still the top spot in town for the discerning drinker – with a changing range of real ales and an eclectic wine list supplied by Adnams.

Coach & Horses Bethel St. Pleasant city-centre pub – across the street from City Hall – with lived-in furnishings and fittings. Good for a quiet drink.

Ribs of Beef Wensum St. Boisterous riverside drinking haunt popular with students and townies alike. Well-kept ales and inexpensive bar food.

Waterfront 139–41 King's St ☎01603/632717. Norwich's principal club and alternative music venue, with gigs and DJs most nights. Sponsored by UEA.

Wild Man Bedford St. Long-established, popular city-centre watering hole that has greased many a student wheel.

Entertainment

Predictably, Norwich has its fair share of multi-screen **cinemas** showing Hollywood blockbusters, but it also has the excellent art-house Cinema City, in Suckling House on St Andrew's Plain (☎01603/622047, ⊛www.cinemacity .co.uk). The **arts scene** here is a tad self-conscious, but the city does possess several first-rate **theatres**. The Theatre Royal, on Theatre Street (☎01603 /630000, ⊛www.theatreroyalnorwich.co.uk), has a wide-ranging programme of mainstream and more adventurous plays and dance, while the amateur Maddermarket, St John's Alley, off Pottergate (☎01603/620917), offers an interesting range of modern theatre. Predictably enough, **UEA** is a major source of entertainment for students and locals alike, with gigs at the Union and classical concerts at the Music Centre. The annual **Norfolk and Norwich Festival** each October (☎01603/766400) features music, film, theatre, comedy, dance, walks and talks at venues all over the city.

The Norfolk Broads

Three rivers – the Yare, Waveney and Bure – meander across the flatlands to the east of Norwich, converging on Breydon Water before flowing into the sea at Great Yarmouth. In places these rivers swell into wide expanses of water known as "broads", which for years were thought to be natural lakes. In fact they're the result of extensive peat cutting, several centuries of accumulated diggings made in a region where wood was scarce and peat a valuable source of energy. The pits flooded when sea levels rose in the thirteenth and fourteenth centuries to create the **Norfolk Broads**, now one of the most important wetlands in Europe – a haven for many birds such as kingfishers, grebes and warblers – and the county's major tourist attraction.

The Broads' delicate ecological balance suffered badly during the 1970s and 1980s. The careless use of fertilizers poisoned the water with phosphates and nitrates, encouraging the spread of algae; the decline in reed cutting – previously in great demand for thatching – made the broads partly unnavigable; and the enormous increase in pleasure-boat traffic began to erode the banks. National Park status was, however, accorded to the area in 1988, and efforts are now under way to clear the waters and protect the ecosystem. Co-ordinating the clean up is the **Broads Authority** (☎01603/610734, ⊛www.broads-authority

.gov.uk), which maintains a series of information centres throughout the region – as well as a **Broads Information Line** (℡01603/782281). At any of these locations, you can pick up a free copy of the *Broadcaster*, a useful newspaper guide to the Broads as a whole.

The region is crossed by several **train** lines, with connections from Norwich to Wroxham, Acle and Reedham, as well as Berney Arms, near Breydon Water, one of the few places in England that can be reached by rail but not road. However, the best – really the only – way to see the Broads themselves is **by boat**, and you could happily spend a week or so exploring the 125 miles of lock-free navigable waterways, visiting the various churches, pubs and windmills en route. Among many **boat rental** companies, two of the more established are Blakes Holiday Boating (℡01603/739400, ⓦwww.blakes.co.uk) and Broads Tours Ltd (℡01603/782207, ⓦwww.broads.co.uk), both of whom operate out of Wroxham (see below). Prices for cruisers start at around £700 a week for four people in peak season, but less expensive, short-term rentals are widely available too. Houseboats are much cheaper than cruisers, but they are, of course, static.

Trying to explore the Broads by car is – as you might imagine – pretty much a waste of time, but cyclists and walkers have a much better time, taking advantage of the region's network of footpaths and cycling trails. There are eight Broads Authority **bike rental** points dotted round the Broads (£8 per day; ℡01603/782281). **Walkers** might consider the 56-mile Weavers' Way, a long-distance footpath that winds through the best parts of the Broads on its way from Cromer to Great Yarmouth, though there are many shorter options too.

The easiest boating centre to reach from Norwich is **WROXHAM**, seven miles to the northeast and accessible by train, bus and car. Wroxham is itself short on charm, but it has a useful **information centre**, on Station Road (Easter–Oct daily 9am–1pm & 2–5pm; ℡01603/782281), and plenty of places where you can stock up with food before heading out on a cruise.

Some six miles east of Wroxham, the village of **LUDHAM** straggles along the roadside at the tip of the Womack Water, an offshoot of the River Thurne. Just north of the village is How Hill, where the Broads Authority maintain **Toad Hole Cottage** (June–Sept daily 10am–6pm; April, May & Oct Mon–Fri 11am–1pm & 1.30-5pm; free), an old eel catcher's cottage housing a small exhibit on the history of the trade, which was common hereabouts until the 1940s. Behind the cottage is the narrow River Ant, where there are hour-long, wildlife-viewing boat trips in the *Electric Eel* from Easter to October – call ℡01692/678763 for schedule and reservations; trips cost £3.

A couple of miles east of Ludham, **POTTER HEIGHAM** is the nominal capital of the Broads, taking its name from the pottery which once stood here on the River Thurne and from the Saxon lord of Heacham who founded the first settlement. Again, there's not much to keep your attention, though you can watch boaters struggling with the village's fourteenth-century bridge, regarded as one of the most difficult passages in the Broads. All the major boat rental companies have outlets here and there's also an **information centre** (Easter–Oct daily 9am–1pm & 2–5pm; ℡01692/670779). The only public transport to Potter Heigham is by bus from Great Yarmouth.

Tiny **RANWORTH**, around twelve miles east of Norwich via the B1140, is a quieter spot altogether. There's no point in coming here if you're after a boat, but the village does have its own **information office** (Easter–Oct daily 9am–1pm & 2–5pm; ℡01603/270453), with stacks of stuff on local walking and wildlife. Ranworth also possesses a good-looking **church**, which is graced by a much-admired fifteenth-century rood screen, and from here it's just a couple of miles downstream along the River Bure to the isolated ruins of **St Benet's Abbey** – but note you can't get there by car.

Great Yarmouth

First and foremost, **GREAT YARMOUTH** is a seaside resort, its promenade a parade of amusement arcades and rainy-day attractions, deserted in winter, heaving in summer. But it's also a port with a long history and, despite extensive wartime bomb damage, it retains a handful of sights that give some idea of the place Daniel Defoe thought "far superior to Norwich".

Yarmouth was a major trading port by the fourteenth century, its economy underpinned by its control of the waterways leading inland to Norwich. It also benefited from fishing, especially during the nineteenth century when there was a spectacular boom in the herring industry. The fishing finally fizzled out in the 1960s, but the timely discovery of gas and oil deposits off the Norfolk coast helped mitigate the effects and have since made the town a major base for the offshore gas industry, second only to Aberdeen for North Sea oil.

The Town

Arriving by train or car from Norwich, initial impressions are favourable thanks to the appealing silhouette of the church of **St Nicholas**, which boasts one of the widest naves in the country and, consequently, an impressive west front. The church stands at the northern end of the broad Market Place, which served as the centre of medieval Yarmouth, but is now mostly undistinguished. The one exception, at the square's northeast corner, is the **Hospital for Decayed Fishermen**, almshouses built in 1702 and opening out into a lovely little courtyard flanked by Dutch gables, the central cupola topped by a chilly looking statue of the fishermen's friend himself, St Peter. Just beyond, in Prior Plain and now a tea shop, is Sewell House, the childhood home of Anna Sewell, author of *Black Beauty*.

Despite considerable wartime damage, sections of the **medieval walls** remain, with one of the best-preserved portions located along Ferrier Road, just north of St Nicholas. Another interesting feature of the old town is the narrow parallel alleys, known locally as rows, which were built to connect South Quay, running beside the River Yare just to the southwest of the Market Place, with the town. Sixty-nine rows have survived, and English Heritage maintain two seventeenth-century row houses – the **Old Merchant's House** in Row 117 and a **Row 111 House**, each with furnishings and fittings illustrating the life of local folk between the 1870s and the 1940s (April–Oct daily 10am–1pm & 2–5pm; combined entry £2.40; EH). For more on Yarmouth's past, head for the **Elizabethan House Museum**, at 4 South Quay (April-Oct Mon–Fri 10am–5pm, Sat & Sun 1–5pm; £2; NT), whose period rooms concentrate on domestic life and include a Tudor bedroom and dining room. Here also is the Conspiracy Room where legend has it that Cromwell and his Puritan colleagues plotted the trial and execution of Charles I.

The vast majority of tourists simply head for the Victorian-built seafront, **Marine Parade**, whose wide sandy beach was the unlikely setting for many of the most dramatic events in Dickens' *David Copperfield*. There are the usual promenade gardens and seafront attractions here, bolstered by the presence of the town's **Maritime Museum** (June–Sept Mon–Fri 10am-5pm, Sat & Sun 13.15pm–5pm; £1.10), which traces the history of the herring industry and the inland waterways.

Practicalities

It's a good ten-minute walk east from Great Yarmouth's **train station** to the central Market Place – cross the river by the footbridge and you'll find yourself on North Quay, from where The Conge leads straight there. **Buses** terminate one block from the sea on Wellesley Road and about 600 yards to the northeast of Market Place. There are two **tourist offices**: one in the town hall, on South Quay (Mon–Fri 9am–5pm; ☎01493/846345, ⓦwww.great-yarmouth .co.uk), and a seasonal office on Marine Parade (June–Sept Mon–Sat 9.30am–5.30pm, Sun 10am–5pm; April, May & Oct daily 10am–1pm & 2–5pm; ☎01493/842195). There's also a useful **Broads Information Centre** in the North West Tower, at the foot of North Quay (July–Sept daily 10am– 3.45pm; ☎01493/332095).

B&Bs line every street, with price a fair indication of quality, but if you don't have much luck, call in at the tourist office, which operates an accommodation booking service. Among many options, the *Willow Guest House*, 26 Trafalgar Rd (☎01493/332355; ❶), offers sea views from some of its nine bedrooms, while *Senglea Lodge*, 7 Euston Rd (☎01493/859632; ❶), is a cosy, well-maintained terraced house with seven pleasant bedrooms a short walk from Marine Parade. For a **hotel**, try the *Royal*, 4 Marine Parade (☎01493/844215; ❸), arguably Yarmouth's grandest – and where Dickens stayed. Yarmouth's **youth hostel**, with self-catering facilities but no café, is in a large Victorian house near the bus station at 2 Sandown Rd (☎01493/843991; ⓦwww.yha.org.uk.

Far and away the best **restaurant** in town is the reasonably priced *Seafood Restaurant*, 85 North Quay (☎01493/856009; closed Sun), which does a superb fish soup and Mediterranean-influenced seafood dishes.

The north Norfolk coast

Beyond Yarmouth, the first thirty miles of the **north Norfolk coast** is preoccupied by its beach, with barely a village, never mind an estuary or a harbour, in sight. The first place of any note is **Cromer**, a workaday seaside town whose bleak and blustery cliffs have drawn tourists for over a century. A few miles to the west is another well-established resort, **Sheringham**, but thereafter the shoreline becomes a ragged patchwork of salt marshes, dunes and shingle spits which form an almost unbroken series of nature reserves, supporting a fascinating range of flora and fauna. It's a lovely stretch of coast and the villages bordering it, principally **Cley-next-the-Sea**, **Blakeney** and **Wells**, are prime targets for an overnight stay. The other major attractions hereabouts are the string of stately homes that lie a short distance inland – some, such as **Felbrigg** and **Holkham Hall**, are among the finest in the region.

Cromer and Sheringham are the only places reachable by **train**, with an hourly service from Norwich on the Bittern Line. Local **bus** services fill in (most of) the gaps, connecting all of the towns and many of the villages. There's also the **Coasthopper bus** (June–Sept Mon–Sat hourly, Sun 4 daily; ☎0845/3006116), which provides regular services along the whole length of the coast from Cromer to Hunstanton, with some buses continuing to Great

Yarmouth and King's Lynn. The Coasthopper Rover ticket (£4) gives a day's unlimited travel on the route. For **walkers**, there's the **Norfolk Coast Path**, which runs from Hunstanton to Cromer (where it joins the Weavers' Way), an exhilarating route through the dunes and salt marshes; a National Trail Guide covers the route in detail, otherwise you'll need OS Landranger maps 132 and 133.

Cromer and around

Dramatically poised on a high bluff, **CROMER** should be the most memorable of the Norfolk coastal resorts, but its fine aspect is undermined by a dispiriting shabbiness in the streets and shopfronts – an "atrophied charm" as Paul Theroux called it. The tower of **St Peter and St Paul**, at 160ft the tallest in Norfolk, attests to the port's medieval wealth, but it was the advent of the railway in the 1880s that heralded the most frenetic flurry of building activity. A bevy of grand Edwardian hotels was constructed along the seafront and for a moment Cromer became the most fashionable of resorts, but the gloss soon wore off and only the seen-better-days **Hotel de Paris** has survived. While you're here, be sure to take a stroll out onto the **pier**, which was badly damaged in a storm in November 1993, but has since been repaired and struggles gamely on.

Somewhat miraculously Cromer has managed to retain its rail link with Norwich; the **train station** is a five-minute walk west of the centre. **Buses** terminate on Cadogan Road, next to the **tourist office** (April–June, Sept & Oct Mon–Sat 10am–5pm, Sun 10am–4pm; July & Aug Mon–Sat 9.30am–6pm, Sun 9.30am–5pm; Nov–March 10am–1pm & 1.45–4pm; ☏01263/512497), which is just 200 yards from the cliff-top promenade. An hour or two in Cromer is probably enough, though the beach is first-rate and the cliff-top walk exhilarating. There's no shortage of inexpensive **accommodation** – the tourist office has all the details.

Felbrigg Hall

Just a couple of miles southwest of Cromer off the A148, **Felbrigg Hall** (April–Oct Mon–Wed, Sat & Sun 1–5pm; £5.80; NT) is a charming Jacobean mansion. The main facade is particularly appealing, the soft hues of the ageing limestone and brick intercepted by three bay windows which together sport a large, cleverly carved inscription – Gloria Deo in Excelsis – in celebration of the reviving fortunes of the family who then owned the place, the Windhams. The interior is splendid too, with the studied informality of both the dining room and the drawing room enlivened by some magnificent seventeenth-century plasterwork ceilings and sundry *objets d'art*. Many of the paintings in the hall were purchased by William Windham II, who did his Grand Tour in the 1740s. In the drawing room are several marine scenes, notably two paintings of the Battle of the Texel by Willem van de Velde the Elder, hung just as William had them, with pride of place going to the six oils and twenty-odd gouaches of Rome and southern Italy by Giovanni Battista Busiri.

The surrounding **parkland** (daily dawn to dusk) divides into two, with woods to the north and open pasture to the south. Footpaths crisscross the park and a popular spot to head for is the medieval church of **St Margaret's** in the southeastern corner, which contains a fine set of brasses and a fancy memorial to William Windham I and his wife by Grinling Gibbons. Nearer the house, there's the extensive **walled garden**, which features flowering borders and an octagonal dove house, and the stables, which have been converted into very pleasant **tearooms**.

Blickling Hall

Blickling Hall (April–Sept Wed–Sun 1–4.30pm; Oct 1–3.30pm; house & gardens £6.70, gardens only £3.80; NT), set in a sheltered, wooded valley ten miles south of Cromer via the A140, is another grand Jacobean pile. Built for Sir Henry Hobart, a Lord Chief Justice, the hall dates from the 1620s and although it was extensively remodelled over a century later, the modifications respected the integrity of the earlier design. Consequently, the long facade, with its slender chimneys, high gables and towers, is the apotheosis of Jacobean design. Inside, highlights include a superb plasterwork ceiling in the Long Gallery and an extraordinarily grand main staircase. There's also a gargantuan tapestry depicting Peter the Great defeating the Swedes, given to one of the family by Catherine the Great.

The surrounding **parkland** (daily dawn to dusk) incorporates a mile-long lake and a weird pyramidal mausoleum holding the earthly remains of the last of the male Hobarts.

Sheringham

SHERINGHAM, a popular seaside town four miles west of Cromer, has an amiable, easy-going air and makes a reasonable overnight stop, though frankly you're still only marking time until you hit the more appealing places further west. One of the distinctive features of the town is the smooth local beach pebbles that face and decorate the houses, a flinting technique used frequently in this part of Norfolk – the best examples here are off the High Street. The downside is that the power of the waves which makes the pebbles smooth has also forced the local council to spend thousands rebuilding the sea defences. The resultant mass of reinforced concrete makes for a less than pleasing seafront – all the more reason to head, instead, for **Sheringham Park**, the 770-acre woodland park a couple of miles southwest of the town, laid out by Humphry Repton in the early 1800s. The park boasts a wonderful array of rhododendrons and azaleas, at their best in late May to early June, and a series of lookout posts from which you can admire the view down to the coast. The other out-of-town jaunt is on the **North Norfolk Railway**, whose steam trains operate along the five miles of track southwest from Sheringham to the modest market town of Holt (June–Sept daily; all-day ticket £7.50; ☎01263 /820800).

Sheringham's two **train stations** are opposite each other on either side of Station Road. The main station, the terminus of the Bittern Line from Norwich, is just to the east, the North Norfolk Railway station to the west. The **tourist office** (April–Oct Mon–Sat 10am–5pm, Sun 10am–4pm; ☎01263/824329) is in between them on Railway Approach. From the tourist office, it's a five-minute walk north to the seafront, straight down Station Road and its continuation, the High Street. You can rent **bikes** from Bike Riders, 7 St Peter's Rd (☎01263/821906), adjacent to the North Norfolk Railway station.

There are plenty of **B&B** options, with one of the best being *Oak Lodge* at 2 Morris St (☎01263/823158, ⊛www.oak-lodge.co.uk; ❸), a smart Edwardian house with four attractive bedrooms right in the centre of town. A good alternative is the *Two Lifeboats*, 2 High St (☎01263/822401; ❹), a small hotel on the promenade offering sea views from most of its bedrooms. The **youth hostel** is a short walk south of the main train station at 1 Cremer's Drift (☎01263/823215; £11), set in its own grounds just off Cromer Road. The *Two Lifeboats* serves inexpensive **bar meals** and more formal dinners in its **restaurant**, and prides itself on its fresh fish.

Cley-next-the-Sea and Blakeney

Travelling west from Sheringham, the A149 meanders through a pretty rural landscape offering occasional glimpses of the sea and a shoreline protected by a giant shingle barrier erected after the catastrophic flood of 1953, a disaster which claimed over one thousand lives. After seven miles you reach **CLEY-NEXT-THE-SEA**, once a busy wool port but now little more than a row of flint cottages and Georgian mansions set beside a narrow, marshy inlet that (just) gives access to the sea. The original village was destroyed in a fire in 1612, which explains why Cley's fine medieval **Church of St Margaret** is located half a mile inland at the very southern edge of the current village, overlooking the green. The Black Death brought church construction to a sudden halt, hence the contrast between the stunted, unfinished chancel and the splendid nave, which boasts several fine medieval brasses and some folksy fifteenth-century bench ends depicting animals and grotesques. Cley's other great draw – housed in an old forge on the main street – is the excellent **Cley Smoke House**, selling local smoked fish and other delicacies, while nearby Picnic Fayre has long been one of the finest delis in East Anglia.

It's about 400 yards east from the village to the mile-long byroad that leads to the shingle mounds of **Cley beach**. This is the starting point for the four-mile hike west out along the spit to **Blakeney Point**, a nature reserve famed for its colonies of terns and seals. The seal colony is made up of several hundred common and grey seals, and the old lifeboat house, at the end of the spit, is now a summer-only National Trust information centre. The shifting shingle can, however, make the going difficult, so keep to the low-water mark – which also means that you won't accidentally trample any nests. The easier alternative is to take one of the boat trips to the point from Blakeney or Morston. The Norfolk Coast Path passes close to the beach too, continuing south along the edge of the **Cley Marshes**, which attract a bewildering variety of waders – and, of course, "twitchers".

Cley has several great places **to stay**, beginning with the *Cley Mill B&B* (℡01263/740209; ❹) housed in a converted windmill complete with sails and a balcony offering wonderful views over the surrounding salt marshes and seashore. Other options in the village include the attractive *Whalebone House*, on the main street (℡01263/740336; ❸), and the *Three Swallows* pub (℡01263/740526; ❷) on the green by the church, which has several pleasant en-suite rooms and serves good **food**.

Blakeney

BLAKENEY is delightful. Once a bustling port exporting fish, corn and salt, it's now a dreamy little place of pebble-covered cottages sloping up from a narrow harbour just a mile west of Cley. Crab sandwiches are sold from stalls at the quayside, the meandering high street is flanked by family-run shops, and footpaths stretch out along the sea wall to east and west, allowing long, lingering looks over the salt marshes. The only sight as such is the **Church of St Nicholas**, beside the A149 at the south end of the village, whose sturdy tower and nave are made of flint rubble with stone trimmings, the traditional building materials of north Norfolk. Curiously, the church has a second, much smaller tower at the back. In the nineteenth century this was used as a lighthouse to guide ships into harbour, but its original function is unknown. Inside, the oak and chestnut hammer-beam roof and the delicate rood screen are the most enjoyable features of the nave, which is attached to a late thirteenth-

568

century chancel, the only survivor from the original Carmelite friary church. With its seven stepped lancet windows, the east window is a rare example of Early English design, though the stained glass is much later.

Blakeney **harbour** is linked to the sea by a narrow channel, which wriggles its way through the salt marshes. The channel is, however, only navigable for a few hours at high tide – at low tide the harbour is no more than a muddy creek. Depending on the tides, there are **boat trips** from Blakeney or Morston quay, a mile or two to the west, to Blakeney Point (see above); as well as the two-hour round trips which land passengers at the National Trust information centre on Blakeney Point there are also hour-long seal-watching trips. The main operators advertise departure times on blackboards by the quayside.

For **accommodation**, the quayside *Blakeney Hotel* (℡01263/740797, Ⓦwww.blakeney-hotel.co.uk; ❼) is one of the most charming hotels in Norfolk, a rambling building with high-pitched gables and pebble-covered walls. The hotel has a heated indoor swimming pool, a secluded garden, cosy lounges decorated in soft pastel colours and sea views, and serves outstanding food. The cheaper rooms can be poky and somewhat airless, but pay a little more and you'll be rewarded with splendid views across the harbour and the marshes. There are discounts for longer stays with full board. A very good alternative is the *Manor Hotel* (℡01263/740376, Ⓦwww.blakeneymanor.co.uk; ❻), which occupies a low-lying courtyard complex a few yards to the east of the harbour; or you might try the excellent *King's Arms*, just back from the quay on Westgate (℡01263/740341; ❸), a traditional pub, with low, beamed ceilings and seven en-suite bedrooms. The latter also serves up delicious, reasonably priced **bar food**. For longer stays, contact *Blakeney Cottage Holidays* (℡01692/405188), who rent some super local cottages – there's an office halfway up the High Street.

Wells-next-the-Sea and around

Despite its name, **WELLS-NEXT-THE-SEA**, some eight miles west of Blakeney, is situated a good mile or so from open water. In Tudor times, when it enjoyed much easier access to the ocean, it was one of the great ports of eastern England, a major player in the trade with the Netherlands. It's still one of the more attractive towns on the north Norfolk coast, and the only one to remain a commercially viable port. There's nothing specific to see among its narrow lanes, but it does make a very good base for exploring the surrounding coastline.

The town divides into three distinct areas, starting with the broad rectangular green to the south, lined with oak and beech trees and some very fine Georgian houses, and known as **The Buttlands** since the days when it was used for archery practice. North from here, across Station Road, are the narrow lanes of the town centre with **Staithe Street**, the tiny main drag, flanked by quaint old-fashioned shops. At the north end of Staithe Street stands the **quay**, a slightly forlorn affair inhabited by a couple of amusement arcades and fish-and-chip shops. A few yards away is the mile-long road to the **beach**, a handsome sandy tract backed by pine-clad dunes. The road is shadowed by a high flood defence and a tiny narrow-gauge railway, which scoots down to the beach every forty minutes or so during the season.

Buses to Wells stop on the Buttlands, a short stroll from the **tourist office** at the foot of Staithe Street (March to mid-July & Oct Mon–Sat 10am–5pm, Sun 10am–4pm; mid-July to Sept Mon–Sat 9.30am–7pm, Sun 9.30am–6pm; ℡01328/710885). Several of the best **guest houses** are along Standard Road, which runs up from the eastern end of the quayside. First choice should be the elegant *Normans* (℡01328/710657; ❸), whose six spacious and tastefully decorated rooms are all en suite; the TV lounge has a log fire and racks of games and the first-floor look-out window provides a wide view over the marshes – binoculars are provided. Other options include *Mill House*, a dignified old mill-owner's home on Northfield Lane (℡01328/710739; ❷), and *Ilex House* on Bases Lane (℡01328/710556; ❷); the latter is a good-looking Georgian villa with three guest rooms that sits in its own grounds, just to the west of the centre. There's also a **campsite**, the sprawling *Pinewoods Caravan and Camping Park*, by the beach (℡01328/710439; closed Nov to mid-March).

For **pub** food, head straight for the *Crown* on the Buttlands, the best pub in town. *Nelson's*, 21 Staithe St, is a pleasant tea and coffee shop that serves inexpensive meals.

Holkham Hall

One of the most popular outings from Wells is to **Holkham Hall** (June–Sept Mon–Thurs & Sun 1–5pm; £5), three miles to the west and a stop on the Coasthopper bus (see opposite). This grand and self-assured stately home was designed by the eighteenth-century architect William Kent for the first earl of Leicester and is still owned by the family. The severe sandy-coloured Palladian exterior belies the warmth and richness of the interior, which retains much of its original decoration, notably the much-admired marble hall, with its fluted columns and intricate reliefs. The rich colours of the state rooms are an appropriate backdrop for a fabulous selection of **paintings**, including canvases by Van Dyck, Rubens, Gainsborough and Gaspar Poussin. One real treat is the Landscape Room where around twenty landscape paintings are displayed in the cabinet style of the eighteenth century. Most depict classical stories or landscapes, a poetic view of the past that enthralled the English aristocracy for decades.

The **grounds** (free) are laid out on sandy, saline land, much of it originally salt marsh. The focal point is an 80-foot-high obelisk, atop a grassy knoll, from where you can view both the hall to the north and the triumphal arch to the south. In common with the rest of the north Norfolk coast, there's plenty of **birdlife** to observe in and around the park – Holkham's lake attracts Canada geese, heron and grebes and several hundred deer graze the open pastures.

A footpath leads north from the estate across the marshes to **Holkham Bay**, where one of the finest sandy beaches on this stretch of coast is fringed by pine-studded sand dunes. Waders inhabit the mud and salt flats, while farther inland you can see warblers, flycatchers and redstarts.

Little Walsingham

For centuries **LITTLE WALSINGHAM**, five miles south of Wells, rivalled Canterbury as the foremost pilgrimage site in England. In 1061 the Lady of the Manor, Richeldis de Faverches, was prompted to build a replica of the **Santa Casa** (Mary's home in Nazareth) here – inspired, it is said, by visions of the Virgin Mary. Whatever the reason for her actions, it brought instant fame and fortune to this little Norfolk village. By the fourteenth century, both the Augustinians and the Franciscans had established themselves here and every English king since Henry III had visited the place, walking barefoot for the last mile. Henry VIII followed in his predecessors' footsteps in 1511, though he subsequently destroyed the shrine during the Dissolution and brought the village's principal trade to an abrupt halt. Pilgrimages resumed in earnest after

1922, when the local vicar, Alfred Hope Patten, organized an Anglo-Catholic pilgrimage, the prelude to the building of an Anglican shrine in the 1930s. Today the village does good business out of its holy connections and the narrow-gauge **steam railway** from Wells (Easter–Sept daily; ☎01328/710631).

Little Walsingham now has a number of shrines catering to a variety of denominations – there are even two Russian Orthodox shrines – though the main one is the **Anglican shrine** inside the heavily restored parish church, a few yards from the main square beside the road to Holt. It's a strange-looking building – a cross between an English village hall and a Greek Orthodox church – and inside the candle-lit Santa Casa contains the statue of Our Lady of Walsingham.

Shrines apart, Little Walsingham has an attractive **High Street**, overlooked by handsome Georgian and half-timbered houses, several of which are given over to shrine shops and religious bookstores. At its southern end is **Friday Market**, a pretty little square which backs onto the grounds and ruins of the old Franciscan Friary. Along the High Street itself are yet more ecclesiastical ruins, those of **The Abbey** – more accurately the Augustinian Priory – whose landscaped grounds stretch east to the River Stiffkey. The abbey ruins are not much to look at, but the fifteenth-century **gatehouse**, on the High Street, is an impressive affair – look up and you'll spy Christ peering out from a window. At the north end of the High Street is the main square, the **Common Place**, whose half-timbered buildings surround a quaint octagonal structure built to protect the village **pump** in the sixteenth century.

The Coasthopper **bus** – as well as the fairly frequent Fakenham (for Norwich) to Wells bus – stops outside the Anglican shrine. The **train station** (for the steam train from Wells) is a five-minute walk from the north end of the village. To get to the village from the station, turn left along Egmere Road and take the second major right down Bridewell Street. The **tourist office** is on Common Place (April–Oct daily 10am–4.30pm; ☎01328/820510). It's difficult to find accommodation during major **pilgrimages** – the main ones are the national pilgrimage on May 31 and the pilgrimage for the sick and disabled on August 30. That said, the *Black Lion* pub on Friday Market (☎01328/820235; ❸) has comfortable en-suite rooms and a restaurant, as does the *Bull Inn* on Common Place (☎01328/820333; ❸).

Burnham Market and Burnham Thorpe

A quick diversion off the A149 five miles west of Wells puts you in the picturesque village of **BURNHAM MARKET**, whose Georgian houses are ranged around an appealing green. The target here is the *Hoste Arms* (☎01328/738777, ⓦ www.hostearms.co.uk; ❺), an old coaching inn which offers some of the best restaurant and bar food on the coast – and attracts a well-heeled crew to match.

A mile or so to the east, **BURNHAM THORPE** was the birthplace of **Horatio Nelson**, who was born in the parsonage on September 29, 1758. Nelson joined the navy at the tender age of 12, and was sent to the West Indies, where he met and married Frances Nisbet, retiring to Burnham Thorpe in 1787. Back in action by 1793, his bravery cost him first the sight of his right eye, and shortly afterwards his right arm. His personal life was equally eventful – famously, his infatuation with Emma Hamilton, wife of the ambassador to Naples, caused the eventual break-up of his marriage. His finest hour was during the Battle of Trafalgar in 1805, when he led the British navy to victory against the combined French and Spanish fleets, a crucial engagement that set the scene for Britain's century-long domination of the high seas. The victory, as everyone knows, didn't do Nelson much good – he was shot in the chest during the battle and even the kisses of Hardy failed to revive him.

The parsonage was demolished years ago, but Nelson is celebrated in the **All Saints Parish Church**, where the lectern is made out of timbers taken from the *Victory*, the chancel sports a Nelson bust, and the south aisle has a small exhibition on his life. It was actually Nelson's express wish that he should be buried here, but instead he was laid in state at Greenwich and then buried at St Paul's. The other place to head for here is the **village pub** (no prizes for guessing the name) where Nelson held a farewell party for the locals in 1793.

Titchwell Marsh and Thornham

Beyond Burnham Market there's more rich marshland filled with wildfowl, especially at **Titchwell Marsh** where the RSPB maintains a reserve based around reed beds and fresh and saltwater lagoons. **TITCHWELL** itself has the excellent *Titchwell Manor Hotel* (☎01485/210221; ❺), beside the A149, where the bar offers great seafood – from grilled oysters and mussels to monkfish and plaice. Lunch can easily be had for under a tenner and there are good value dinner, bed and breakfast deals too. **THORNHAM**, a mile further west, has three more likely looking pubs, including the splendid *Lifeboat Inn* on Ship Lane (☎01485/512236; ❹), again with great food and good all-in deals.

Hunstanton

The Norfolk coast pretty much ends at **HUNSTANTON**, a Victorian seaside resort that grew up to the southwest of the original fishing village – now Old Hunstanton. Like Yarmouth, it has its fair share of amusement arcades, crazy golf, and entertainment complexes, but it has also hung on to its genteel origins – and its sandy beaches, backed by stripy gateau-like cliffs, are among the cleanest in Norfolk. Incidentally, in "The World of Fun" on Greevegate, Hunstanton possesses the self-proclaimed largest joke shop in Britain with more whoopee cushions and Dracula fangs than even the most unpleasant 10-year-old could want.

The **tourist office** is in the town hall (daily: April–Sept 9.30am–5pm; Oct–March 10.30am–4pm; ☎01485/532610) on the wide sloping green, which serves as the focal point of the town. They can help out with **accommodation**, though it's easy enough to find. The nicest and priciest places are among the cottages of Old Hunstanton. One particular recommendation is *Le Strange Arms*, Golf Course Rd (☎01485/534411; ❺), an expansive mansion dating from the nineteenth century and with gardens running down to the beach. At the other end of the market, the **youth hostel** occupies a Victorian town house at 15 Avenue Rd (☎01485/532061, ⓦwww.yha.org.uk; closed Nov–March), south of Hunstanton green.

King's Lynn and around

An ancient port, **KING'S LYNN** straddles the mouth of the Great Ouse, a mile or so before it flows into The Wash. It occupies an improbably marshy location, but was strategically placed for easy access to seven English counties. Consequently, the town's merchants grew rich, importing fish from Scandinavia, timber from the Baltic and wine from France, while exporting wool, salt and corn to the Hanseatic ports. The town stagnated when the focus of maritime trade moved to the Atlantic seaboard, but its port facilities have been reinvigorated since the UK joined the EU. Much of the old centre was demolished during the 1950s and 1960s to make way for commercial development and, as a result, Lynn lacks the concentrated historic charm of towns such as Bury St Edmunds. That said, it does have a number of well-preserved buildings, including the oldest guildhall in the country, that taken together are well worth an hour or two of anyone's time. In addition, a handful of stately homes and medieval castle ruins are within easy reach.

Arrival, information and accommodation

From the **train station**, it's a short walk west along Waterloo Street to Railway Road, the principal thoroughfare, which borders the eastern edge of the town centre. The **bus station** is nearer the centre, a few yards to the west of Railway Road. The **tourist office** is by the river, bang in the centre in the Custom House on Purfleet Quay (April–Oct Mon–Sat 9.15am–5pm, Sun 10am–5pm; Nov–March daily 10.30am–4pm; ☎01553/763044).

Accommodation presents few problems. Most of the budget **B&Bs** lie southeast of the train station on Tennyson Road and Goodwins Road, its continuation to the south. To get to Tennyson Road on foot from the station, take St John's Walk across the park. Options on Goodwins Road include the *Old Rectory*, at no. 33 (☎01553/768544; ❷), with two, smart en-suite guest rooms in a good-looking nineteenth-century villa; and *Fairlight Lodge*, no. 79 (☎01533 /762234; ❶), a trim Victorian brick house holding seven guest rooms, most en suite. Of Lynn's **hotels**, try the *Russet House*, 53 Goodwins Rd (☎01553 /773098; ❸), a family-run establishment offering a dozen comfortable rooms in a rambling Victorian house. The town's **youth hostel** enjoys a central location in the converted Thoreseby College on College Lane (☎01533/772461; closed Sept to mid-April; £9.25).

The Town

Lynn's historic core lies in the two blocks between the High Street and the quayside. A good place to begin is the **Saturday Market Place**, the older and smaller of the town's two marketplaces, presided over by the hybrid **Church of St Margaret**, which contains two of the most fanciful medieval brasses in East Anglia. These are the Walsoken brass, adorned with country scenes, and the Braunche brass, named after a certain Robert Braunche and depicting the lavish feast he laid on for Edward III. Across the square is Lynn's prettiest building, the **Trinity Guildhall**, its wonderful chequered flint and stone facade dating to 1421 and repeated in the Elizabethan addition to the left and in the adjoining Victorian Town Hall. Next door to the Guildhall is the entrance to the **Tales of the Old Gaol House** (April–Oct daily 10am–5pm; Nov–March Mon, Tues & Fri–Sun 10am–4pm; £2.40), which incorporates a series of eighteenth-century cells within a small museum on local baddies. There's also access to the Guildhall undercroft, which displays an exhibition of the town's rich collection of civic regalia. This is actually more stimulating than you might think, since the treasures include King John's Cup and Sword, the latter a gift to the town prior to the king's ill-fated and ill-timed dash across The Wash, during which he was caught by the incoming waters and saved himself, but lost the crown jewels.

Of the medieval warehouses which survive along the quayside, the most evocative is the former **Hanseatic Warehouse**, built around 1475, whose half-timbered upper floor juts unevenly over the cobbles of St Margaret's Lane. The other architectural highlight is a short stroll north, at the end of the gentle Georgian curve of Queen Street. It's here you'll find the splendid **Custom House**, erected in 1683 in a style clearly influenced by the Dutch. There are classical pilasters, petite dormer windows and a roof-top balustrade, but it's the dinky little cupola that catches the eye. The Custom House holds the tourist office (see below) and overlooks **Purfleet Quay**, a short and stumpy harbour once packed with merchant ships.

Beyond the Custom House, King Street, with its much wider berth, continues where Queen Street left off. On the left, just after Ferry Lane, stands Lynn's most precious building, **St George's Guildhall** (Mon–Sat 10am–5pm; free), dating from 1410 and the oldest surviving guildhall in England. It was a theatre in Elizabethan times and is now part of the King's Lynn Arts Centre. Beyond the Guildhall is the later and much larger **Tuesday Market Place**, with the pastel-pink Duke's Head Hotel, dating from 1689, and the Neoclassical **Corn Exchange** – imaginatively converted into a second arts centre for the town – standing out against an otherwise unspectacular assemblage.

Eating, drinking and entertainment

There's a good **café**, *Crofter's* (closed Sun), in the undercroft of the Guildhall arts centre, and *Pizza Express* have got to Lynn too – they are at 1 Saturday Market Place and, unlike most of their rivals here, they are open on Sundays. In addition, the town has one highly recommendable, if comparatively expensive, **restaurant** – the *Riverside*, 27 King St (☎01553/773134; closed Sun), in an old fifteenth-century warehouse round the back of the arts centre. The food – light lunches and dinner – is excellent and you get river views and tables outside in decent weather too. Alternatively, tasty **pub meals** are available at the *Tudor Rose* on St Nicholas Street, off Tuesday Market Place, and this is also the best place for a **drink**.

Entertainment in Lynn revolves around the King's Lynn Arts Centre, housed in St George's Guildhall on King Street (☎01553/764864). Its galleries, cinema and theatre stage much of the town's annual festival, held in July. The Corn Exchange, on the Tuesday Market Place (same number as Guildhall), offers a wide-ranging programme from theatre and music to comedy and dance. As for **markets**, which still attract large fenland crowds, there's one on the Saturday Market Place every Saturday and two others on the Tuesday Market Place – on Tuesdays and Fridays.

Around King's Lynn

Within a ten-mile radius of King's Lynn are several notable attractions. The architectural highlight is **Houghton Hall**, a splendid Palladian mansion with baroque flourishes, but it's **Sandringham**, one of the Queen's country residences, that pulls in the crowds. The area also holds some fine Norman ruins at **Castle Rising** and **Castle Acre**.

Castle Rising

Situated at the centre of extensive earthworks five miles north of Lynn, the shell of the twelfth-century keep of **Castle Rising** (April–Oct daily 10am–6pm; Nov–March Wed–Sun 10am–4pm; £3.25; EH) is in remarkably good condition. Towering over the surrounding flatlands, it's a powerful, imposing structure and some of its finer architectural details have survived as well – from the blind arcading and ox-eye windows on the outside to the vaulted ceilings and ornamented fireplaces within. The nearby village is laid out on a grid plan and contains a quadrangle of beautiful seventeenth-century **almshouses**, whose elderly inhabitants still go to church in red cloaks and pointed black hats, the colours of the original benefactor, the Earl of Northampton. First Eastern Counties **buses** #410 and #411 (hourly) from King's Lynn to Hunstanton stop off at the *Black Horse* pub in the village.

Sandringham House

Another four miles on from Castle Rising looms the seven-thousand-acre estate of **Sandringham House** (mid-April to Oct daily 11am–4.45pm; closed for two weeks late-July or early Aug; £6), bought in 1861 by Queen Victoria for her son, the future Edward VII. The house is billed as a private home, but few families have a drawing room crammed with Russian silver and Chinese jade. The **museum**, housed in the old coach and stable block, contains an exhibition of royal memorabilia from dolls to cars, but much more arresting are the beautifully maintained **grounds** (10.30am–5pm), a mass of rhododendrons and azaleas in spring and early summer. The estate's sandy soil is also ideal for game birds, which was the attraction of the place for the terminally bored Edward, whose tradition of posh shooting parties is still followed by the royals. Local **buses** #410 and #411 make the journey from King's Lynn, as does the summer Coasthopper service (see p.571).

Houghton Hall

Located five miles due east of Sandringham, along narrow country lanes, **Houghton Hall** (Easter–Sept Thurs & Sun 2–5pm; £6) is an early Palladian extravagance dating from the 1720s. It was built for Sir Robert Walpole, a leading Whig politician whose roller-coaster career included a couple of terms as prime minister and a period of imprisonment for corruption. As at Holkham Hall (see p.570), the exterior, with its classical portico, is formal and severe, though the four corner domes do add a touch of frivolity. Inside, the lavishness of the state rooms is at its most overpowering in the stone hall and saloon, the ceilings dripping with fancy plasterwork. Look out also for the overmantels in the parlour, the work of Grinling Gibbons. The original Walpole art collection was flogged to Catherine the Great of Russia in 1779 to pay off family debts, but there are still plenty of *objets d'art* on display, notably Sèvres porcelain and Mortlake tapestries.

There's no bus service to the hall – the nearest you'll get is the village of **Harpley**, a mile or so to the south.

Castle Acre

The remote hamlet of **CASTLE ACRE** stands in the shadow of one of the few hilltops in Norfolk, nineteen miles east of King's Lynn. Taking advantage of the terrain, one of William I's most trusted lieutenants, William Warenne, built a fortified manor house here shortly after the Conquest. The site was refortified as a stone **castle** (free access; EH) in the 1140s, but little remains from either period – except, that is, for the Norman earthworks. These are some of the most complete in the whole of England, with the mound of the keep and the circular bailey easy to discern. To the west, on the banks of the River Nar, there are more medieval ruins, those of the Cluniac **priory** (April–Sept daily 10am–6pm; Oct daily 10am–5pm; Nov–March Wed–Sun 10am–4pm; £3.50; EH) founded by Warenne's son in 1090. The most significant remains are at the west front of the priory church, an excellent illustration of the way different medieval styles were blended together, with the Norman doorway and delicate blind arcading set beneath an arching Early English window.

The *Ostrich* **pub** on the village green makes a great target for lunch, not so much for the food as for its ancient atmosphere and good location. There is a **bus** service linking Castle Acre with King's Lynn, but it runs infrequently.

Breckland

Until the late eighteenth century **Breckland**, a chunky slab of land running south from Fakenham to Thetford, was a sparsely populated district characterized by open heaths and pastureland grazed by thousands of sheep. The animals had to contend with frequent sandstorms as the wind whipped the dry, sandy soils and travellers had the added problem of the highwaymen who plagued the area. The next century saw some hard-won agricultural gains, but it was the work of the Forestry Commission that changed the character of the area in the 1920s when they launched a vast tree-planting programme, covering much of the heathland with the assorted conifers of **Thetford Forest**. Further dramatic change came during World War II when the establishment of a mock "battle area" destroyed five villages and thousands of acres of farmland. The end result was the largest concentration of military bases in the country. All of this hardly makes the area seem alluring, but in **Thetford** the district has a pleasant market town with one or two historical curiosities and there are lots of woodland walks to be enjoyed nearby. In addition, Thetford is within easy striking distance of a diverting medieval manor house, **Oxburgh Hall**, and the tomb of the last Sikh Maharajah in **Elveden**.

Thetford

The Breckland's most interesting town is **THETFORD**, birthplace of the radical eighteenth-century ideologue **Thomas Paine**, and, way back in the eleventh century, seat of the kings and bishops of East Anglia. It's a pleasant place, with riverside walks and gardens, though the remains of the Cluniac priory and the giant earthworks of Castle Hill – at opposite ends of the town centre – are the only reminders of the town's former importance. On King Street, the partly pedestrianized main drag, there's a striking gilt **statue** of Paine, paid for by the Thomas Paine Foundation of America. For years disowned by his native town, Paine was the chief British apologist for the French Revolution, and a prominent theorist for the American one, publishing his most famous tract, *The Rights of Man*, in 1791. In this, he advocated, among other things, the abolition of the monarchy and the establishment of a social welfare system to succour the poor. His books were subsequently banned and his effigy burned in many towns, and then, accused of sedition, he was forced to flee the country, going first to France and then to America. Paine's birthplace, on White Hart Street, was pulled down long ago – the Thomas Paine Hotel now stands on the site – but the timber-framed **Ancient House Museum**, close by at 21 White Hart St (June–Aug Mon–Sat 10am–12.30pm & 1–5pm, Sun 2–5pm; rest of year Mon–Sat 10am–12.30pm & 1–5pm; £1 in July & Aug, free rest of year), has an interesting display on the man. It also possesses replicas of the Thetford treasure of Roman gold and silverwork (the originals are in the British Museum) and a herb garden.

From Thetford **train station**, it's about half a mile south to King Street – follow Station Road and veer right at the end over Thomas Paine Avenue and onto White Hart Street. The **bus station** is closer to King Street – it's just south of the river and from here it's a short walk over the bridge and up Bridge

Street. There's no **tourist office** as such, but information is available from the Ancient House Museum (℡01842/752599). Thetford has a good range of **accommodation**, including *The Bell*, a smartly updated fifteenth-century inn on King St (℡01842/754455; ❺). There's also the *Thomas Paine Hotel* on White Hart St (℡01842/755631; ❹) and, opposite, the *Wereham House Hotel* (℡01842 /761956; ❸).

Elveden

The tiny village of **ELVEDEN**, strung out along the A11 three miles south-west of Thetford, is – strange though it may seem – a place of pilgrimage for Britain's 250,000-strong Sikh community. The pilgrims come to pay homage to the last Sikh Maharajah, **Prince Duleep Singh**, who is buried beside his wife and son in the local churchyard. Having been forced to sign away his Punjab kingdom and the famous Koh-i-Noor diamond to the British, he was sent to England and handed the 17,000-acre estate at Elveden in 1863. He became a favourite of Queen Victoria, who thought him "extremely hand-some", and with his state pension he transformed Elveden Hall (no public access) into an oriental extravaganza.

Thetford Forest and Oxburgh Hall

The biggest change affecting the Breckland has been the creation of **Thetford Forest**, eighty thousand acres planted with unerring regularity in the 1920s immediately to the west of Thetford town. Realizing the error of their ways, the Forestry Commission (FC) is currently engaged in more imaginative

---

The Fens – and Wicken Fen

One of the strangest of all English landscapes, the **Fens** cover a vast area from just north of Cambridge right up to Boston in Lincolnshire. For centuries, they were an inhospitable wilderness of quaking bogs and marshland, punctuated by clay islands on which small communities eked out a livelihood cutting peat for fuel, using reeds for thatching and living on a diet of fish and wildfowl. Piecemeal land reclamation took place throughout the Middle Ages, but it wasn't until the seventeenth century that the systematic draining of the fens was undertaken – amid fierce local opposition – by the Dutch engineer **Cornelius Vermuyden**. The transformation of the fens had unforeseen consequences: as it dried out, the peaty soil shrank to below the level of the rivers, causing further flooding, a situation only exacerbated by the numerous windmills, erected to help drain the fens, but which actually resulted in further shrinkage. The problem of shrinkage was only resolved in the 1820s with the introduction of steam-driven pumps, as these leviathans could control water levels with much greater precision, enabling the fens to be turned into the valuable agri-cultural land of today.

At **Wicken Fen** (daily dawn to dusk; visitor centre Tues–Sun 10am–5pm; ℡01353 /720274; £3.70; NT), nine miles south of Ely via the A142, you can visit one of the few remaining areas of undrained fenland. Its survival is thanks to a group of Victorian entomologists who donated the land to the National Trust in 1899, making it the oldest nature reserve in the UK. The seven hundred acres are undrained but not uncultivated – sedge and reed cutting are still carried out to preserve the land-scape as it is – and the reserve also features one of the last surviving fenland wind pumps. Traditional "droves" (wide footpaths) enable visitors to explore the fen and a boardwalk nature trail gives access to several hides. The NT also organizes a vari-ety of events and guided walks – call ahead for details.

replanting, and has laid out several **forest walks**, wildlife hides and other recreational facilities to try and entice people to come here. Call in at **High Lodge Forest Centre**, five miles west of Thetford on the B1107 (Easter–Oct daily 10am–5pm; Nov–Easter Sat & Sun 11am–4pm; ☎01842/810271), for trail maps or to rent a bike to get you around the forest.

A mile or so to the west of High Lodge, the B1107 leaves the forest as it approaches the outskirts of Brandon. From here, it's about twelve miles northwest to **Oxburgh Hall** (April–Oct Mon–Wed, Sat & Sun 1–5pm; gardens open 11am; £5.30, gardens only £2.60; NT), a medieval manor house of postcard prettiness, whose dappled brickwork overlooks a reed-choked moat. The hall was built in 1482 for the Bedingfeld family, staunch Catholics whose religious sympathies gave them all sorts of trouble from the Reformation onwards. The approach to the hall is via an eighty-foot-high ceremonial gateway, matched by the main gate tower of the house itself, but the interior is something of a disappointment. Aside from the tapestries executed by the imprisoned Mary Queen of Scots, the rooms are routinely Victorian, the product of extensive renovations in the middle of the nineteenth century. The most exquisite Bedingfeld legacy – a set of terracotta tombs – is just outside the grounds of the hall in the partly ruined parish church.

Ely and around

Perched on a mound of clay above the River Ouse, **ELY** – literally "eel island" – was to all intents and purposes a true island until the draining of the fens in the seventeenth century. Up until then, the town was encircled by treacherous marshland, which could only be crossed with the help of the locals, "fen-slodgers" who knew the firm tussock paths. In 1070, **Hereward the Wake** turned this inaccessibility to military advantage, holding out against the Normans and forcing William the Conqueror to undertake a prolonged siege – and finally to build an improvised road floated on bundles of sticks. Centuries later, the Victorian writer Charles Kingsley resurrected this obscure conflict in his novel *Hereward the Wake*. He presented the protagonist as the Last of the English who "never really bent their necks to the Norman yoke and...kept alive those free institutions which were the germs of our British liberty" – a heady mixture of nationalism and historical poppycock that went down a storm.

Since then, Ely has always been associated with Hereward, which is really rather ridiculous as Ely is, above all else, an ecclesiastical town and a Norman one to boot. The Normans built the **cathedral**, a towering structure visible for miles across the flat landscape and Ely's only significant sight. It's easy to see the town on a day-trip from Cambridge, but Ely does make a pleasant night's stop in its own right. It's also close to a couple of Cambridgeshire's other historic sights – namely the cathedral at **Peterborough** and the small town of **Wisbech** – not to mention the undrained and unmolested **Wicken Fen** (see box on p.577).

The Town

Ely **Cathedral** (June–Sept daily 7am–7pm; Oct–May Mon–Sat 7.30am–6pm, Sun 7.30am–5pm; £4) is seen to best advantage from the south, the crenellated towers of the west side perfectly balanced by the prickly finials to the east with the distinctive timber lantern rising above them both. To approach from this direction, follow the footpath leading up the hill into the cathedral precincts from **Broad Street** – also the second turning on the right as you walk up Station Road from the train station. At the top of the footpath, pass through the medieval **Porta**, once the principal entrance to the monastery complex, and turn right to reach the main entrance on the lopsided **west front** – one of the transepts collapsed in a storm in 1701.

The first things to strike you as you enter the **nave** are the sheer length of the building and the lively nineteenth-century painted ceiling, largely the work of amateurs. The procession of plain late-Norman arches, built around the same time as Peterborough, leads to the architectural feature that makes Ely so special, the **octagon** – the only one of its kind in England – built in 1322 to replace the collapsed central tower. Its construction, employing the largest oaks available in England to support some four hundred tons, is one of the wonders of the medieval world, and the effect, as you look up into this Gothic dome, is simply breathtaking. **Octagon tours** depart several times a day from the desk at the entrance and venture up into the octagon itself.

When the central tower collapsed, it fell eastwards, onto the **choir**, which was subsequently rebuilt in a fussier decorative style. The thirteenth-century presbytery, beyond, houses the relics of **St Ethelreda**, founder of the abbey in 673, who, despite being twice married, is honoured liturgically as a virgin. At the east end are three **chantry chapels**, the most charming of which (on the left) is an elaborate Renaissance affair dated to 1533. The other marvel at Ely is the **Lady Chapel**, in actual fact a separate building accessible via the north transept. It lost its sculpture and its stained glass during the Reformation, but its fan vaulting remains, an exquisite example of English Gothic. Retracing your steps, the south triforium near the main entrance holds the **Stained Glass Museum** (Easter–Sept Mon–Sat 10.30am–5pm, Sun noon–6pm; Oct–March Mon–Sat 10.30am–5pm, Sun noon–4.15pm; £3.50), another Anglican money-spinner exhibiting examples of this applied art from 1240 to the present day.

The **precincts** of the cathedral boast a fine ensemble of medieval domestic architecture, a higgledy-piggledy assortment of old stone, brick and half-timbered buildings that runs south from the Infirmary complex, abutting the presbytery, to the Prior's buildings near the Porta gate. Many of the buildings are used by the King's boarding school – where the cathedral's choristers are trained – others by the clergy, but although you can't go in any of them, it's still a pleasant area to stroll; a free map and brochure are available from the cathedral.

The rest of Ely is pretty enough, but hardly compelling after the wonders of the cathedral. To the north, the **High Street**, with its Georgian buildings and old-fashioned shops, makes for an enjoyable browse and, if you push on past the Market Place down Forehill and then Waterside, you'll soon reach the **Babylon Gallery** (Tues–Sat 10am–4pm, Sun 11am–5pm; free), where an imaginative programme of temporary exhibitions featuring contemporary art and craft is displayed in an attractively renovated old brewery warehouse. Alternatively, head west from the cathedral entrance across the triangular Palace Green, to **Oliver Cromwell's House** at 29 St Mary's St (April–Sept daily 10am–5.30pm; Oct–March Mon–Sat 10am–5pm, Sun 11am–4pm; £3.50), a timber-framed former vicarage, which holds a small exhibition on the Protector's ten-year sojourn in Ely, when he was employed as a tithe collector.

Practicalities

Ely lies on a major rail intersection, with direct **trains** from as far afield as Liverpool, Norwich and London, as well as from Cambridge, just twenty minutes to the south. The **train station** is a ten-minute walk from the cathedral straight up Station Road and its continuation Back Hill. **Buses** (from King's Lynn and Cambridge) stop on Market Street immediately to the north of the cathedral. The **tourist office** is in Oliver Cromwell's House (April–Sept daily 10am–5.30pm; Oct–March Mon–Sat 10am–5pm, Sun 11am–4pm; ☏01353/662062) and they issue free town maps and will help with accommodation.

Ely has several appealing **B&Bs**, the best being the handy *Cathedral House*, 17 St Mary's St (☏01353/662124; ❸), an attractive Georgian town house with three comfortable, en-suite bedrooms. Several other good options are concentrated along Egremont Street, about five minutes' walk north from the cathedral via the Lynn Road. Possibilities here include the spacious *Old Egremont House* at no. 31 (☏01353/663118; ❷), with cathedral views and a walled garden, and the more modern, spick and span *Posthouse* at no. 12a (☏01353 /667184; ❶).

Of the numerous **tearooms** in town, *The Almonry* (daily 10am–5pm), in the grounds to the north of the cathedral, is by far the best sited, with garden seats granting great views of the cathedral. Two other good choices are the *Steeplegate Tea Rooms* at 16–18 High St (closed Sun), backing onto the cathedral grounds, and *Dominique's*, 8 St Mary's St (closed Sun). The pick of the town's **restaurants** is the *Old Fire Engine House*, 25 St Mary's St (☏01353 /662582; closes 9pm, 5pm on Sun), a gourmet English restaurant of some local repute. Ely's friendliest **pub** is the *Prince Albert*, 62 Silver St. For **entertainment**, the riverside *Maltings*, on Ship Lane, has a cinema (☏01353/666388) as well as a waterfront brasserie and bar.

Wisbech

The small town of **WISBECH** sits in the middle of an agricultural area some twenty-five miles north of Ely. The town first developed as Peterborough's seaport, but the silting up of the Wash has slowly pushed it back from the coast, which is now ten miles away along the navigable River Nene. The Nene slices through the heart of old Wisbech with the town's most interesting buildings to either side on the "brink". The North Brink has the edge architecturally, thanks partly to **Peckover House** (April–Sept Wed, Sat & Sun 12.30–5.30pm; Oct same days but closes 4pm; £3.80, gardens only £2.50; NT), a substantial early Georgian property which was bought by a wealthy local banker named Jonathan Peckover towards the end of the eighteenth century. The exterior of the house is typically plain, and the interior is only sparsely furnished – it's the Rococo woodwork and plaster decorations that make the trip worthwhile, as well as the Victorian garden with its orangery, summer-houses, reed barn and herbaceous borders. It's an easy drive to Wisbech from Ely, though rather more complicated by **public transport**: take the train to March (20min) and catch a local bus on to Wisbech, but note that services are infrequent so check out times before you depart. Wisbech is only twelve miles west of King's Lynn and daily buses make the onward journey from there.

Peterborough

In the northwest corner of Cambridgeshire, booming **PETERBOROUGH** has shaken off its dusty history as a brick-making town, attracting a raft of high-tech industries, whose employees now occupy the sprawling, leafy suburbs that surround its compact centre. But, whatever the merits of Peterborough as a place to live and work, for the casual visitor it has but one distinct – and unmissable – attraction, its superb Norman **Cathedral** (Mon–Sat 8.30am–5.15pm, Sun noon–5.15pm; £3.50 suggested donation). A site of Christian worship since the seventh century, the first two churches here were destroyed – the original Saxon monastery by the Danes in 870, its replacement by fire in 1116. Work on the present structure began a year after the fire and was pretty much completed within the century. The one significant later addition is the thirteenth-century **west facade**, one of the most magnificent in England, made up of three grandiloquent, deeply recessed arches, though the purity of the design is marred slightly by an incongruous central porch added in 1370.

The **interior** is a wonderful example of Norman architecture – round-arched rib vaults and shallow blind arcades line the nave, while up above the painted wooden ceiling, dating from 1220, is an exquisite example of medieval art, one of the most important in Europe. There are several notable tombs here, too, beginning with that of **Catherine of Aragon**, who is buried in the north aisle of the presbytery under a slab of black Irish marble. Catherine was Henry VIII's first wife and the king's determination to divorce her in favour of Anne Boleyn precipitated the English Reformation. The marriage was finally declared void in 1533, but much to the king's chagrin, Catherine insisted till her death (in 1536) that she remained Henry's lawful wife. Mary Queen of Scots was also interred here, in the south aisle, after her execution in 1587, but twenty-five years later she was transferred to Westminster Abbey.

With frequent connections in all directions – including Ely about thirty miles to the southeast – Peterborough is easy to reach by rail. The **train station** is a short, signposted walk across the pedestrianized town centre from the Cathedral. The **tourist office** is in the lovely little close that surrounds the Cathedral at no. 3–5 (June–Sept Mon–Fri 9am–5pm, Sat 10am–4pm, Sun 11.30am–4pm; rest of year Mon–Fri 9am–5pm, Sat 10am–4pm; ☏01733/452336). Predictably, there are lots of cafés and bars in the town centre. For a quick bite to **eat**, *Caffe Nero*, footsteps from the tourist office on Cathedral Square, is as good as anywhere.

Cambridge

On the whole, **CAMBRIDGE** is a much quieter and more secluded place than Oxford, though for the visitor what really sets it apart from its scholarly rival is "the Backs" – the green swathe of land that straddles the languid River Cam, providing exquisite views over the backs of the old colleges. At the front, the handsome facades of these same colleges dominate the layout of the town centre, lining up along the main streets. Most of the older colleges date back to the late thirteenth and early fourteenth centuries and are designed to a similar plan with the main gate leading through to a series of "courts," typically a carefully manicured slab of lawn surrounded on all four sides by college residences or offices. Many of the buildings are extraordinarily beautiful, but the most famous is **King's College**, whose magnificent **King's College Chapel** is one of the great statements of late Gothic architecture. There are thirty-one university colleges in total, each an independent, self-governing body, proud of its achievements and attracting – for the most part at least – a close loyalty from its students, amongst whom privately educated boys remain hopelessly over-represented despite decades of perfectly adequate state education. This intrinsic elitism is amplified by all sorts of eccentric (some say charming) rules and regulations and by an arcane vocabulary unfamiliar to ordinary mortals. "Heads

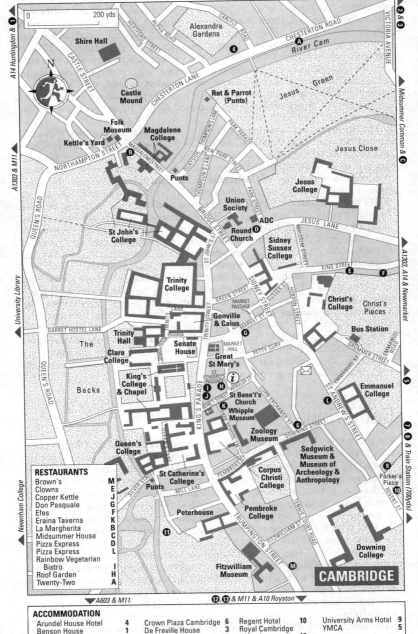

RESTAURANTS

Brown's	M
Clowns	E
Copper Kettle	J
Don Pasquale	G
Efes	F
Eraina Taverna	K
La Margherita	B
Midsummer House	C
Pizza Express	D
Pizza Express	L
Rainbow Vegetarian Bistro	I
Roof Garden	H
Twenty-Two	A

CAMBRIDGE

ACCOMMODATION

Arundel House Hotel	4	Crown Plaza Cambridge	6	Regent Hotel	10
Benson House	1	De Freville House	3	Royal Cambridge	
Cambridge Garden House	11	Lensfield Hotel	12	Hotel	13
Cambridge YHA	7	Netley Lodge	2	Sleeperz Hotel	8
				University Arms Hotel	9
				YMCA	5

© Crown copyright

of house" are heads of college – whether they be "Masters", "Provosts", "Principals", "Presidents" or "Wardens" – and most of them are elected by the "Fellows", graduates or senior members with teaching responsibilities. "The Other Place" is Oxford, "bedders" are college domestics and "porters" wear bowler hats and keep good order. There are three terms – Michaelmas (Oct–Dec), Lent (Jan–March) and Easter (April–June) – and the students' biggest annual knees-up, the "May balls", are held in June.

Tradition has it that Cambridge was founded in the late 1220s by scholastic refugees from Oxford, who fled the town after one of their number was lynched by hostile townsfolk – though the first proper college wasn't founded until 1271. Rivalry has existed between the two institutions ever since – epitomized by the annual Boat Race on the River Thames – while internal tensions between **"town and gown"** have inevitably plagued a place where, from the late fourteenth century onwards, the university has tended to control local life. The first (but by no means the last) rebellion against the scholars occurred during the Peasants' Revolt of 1381, and had to be put down with armed troops by the Bishop of Norwich.

In the sixteenth century, Cambridge became a centre of **church reformism**, educating some of the most famous Protestant preachers in the country, including Cranmer, Latimer and Ridley, all of whom were martyred in Oxford by Mary Tudor. Later, during the Civil War, Cambridge once again found itself at the centre of events: Cromwell himself was both a graduate of Sidney Sussex and the local MP, while the university was largely Royalist. After the Restoration, the university regained most of its privileges, though by the eighteenth century it was in the doldrums, better known, as Byron put it, for its "din and drunkenness" than for its academic record.

During the nineteenth century, the university finally lost its ancient privileges over the town, which was expanding rapidly thanks to the arrival of the railway – the population quadrupled between 1800 and 1900. The university expanded too, with the number of students increasing dramatically following the broadening of the curriculum to include new subjects such as natural science and history. More recently, change has been much slower in coming to the university, particularly when it comes to **equality of the sexes**. The first two women's colleges were founded in the 1870s, but it was only in 1947 that women were actually awarded degrees and one or two colleges held out against accepting women students until the 1980s. In the meantime, the city and university had been acquiring a reputation as a **high-tech centre** of excellence, what locals refer to half-seriously as "Silicon Fen". Cambridge has always been in the vanguard of scientific research – its alumni have garnered no less than ninety Nobel prizes – and it has now become a major international player in the lucrative electronic communications industry.

Cambridge is an extremely compact place, and you can **walk** round the centre, visiting the most interesting colleges, in an afternoon. A more thorough exploration, covering more of the colleges, a visit to the fine art of the Fitzwilliam Museum and a leisurely afternoon on a **punt**, will however take at least a couple of days – maybe more. If possible you should avoid coming in high summer, when the students are replaced by hordes of sightseers and posses of foreign-language students, though you can still miss the crowds by getting up early – the tourists only start to appear in numbers from around 10.30am. Faced with such crowds, the more popular colleges have restricted their opening times and several have introduced admission charges. Bear in mind, too, that during the exam period (late April to early June), most colleges close their doors to the public at least some of the time.

Arrival, information and getting around

The **train station** is a mile or so southeast of the city centre, off Hills Road. It's an easy but tedious twenty-minute walk into the centre, or take shuttle bus #3, which runs to downtown Emmanuel Road every ten minutes or so (less frequently on Sun). The **bus station** is centrally located on Drummer Street, right by Christ's Pieces – and Emmanuel Road. **Stansted**, London's third airport, with its striking terminal building designed by Norman Foster, is just thirty miles south of Cambridge on the M11; there are hourly trains from the airport to the city, and regular bus services too. Arriving by **car**, you'll find much of the city centre closed to traffic and on-street parking well-nigh impossible – for a day trip, at least, the best option is a **Park-and-Ride** car park; they are signposted on all major approaches.

The city centre is small enough to walk round comfortably, so apart from getting to and from the train station, you shouldn't have to use the city's buses. On the other hand, cycling is an enjoyable way of getting around and has long been extremely popular with locals and students alike. **Bike rental** outlets are dotted all over town (see p.596), including a couple of places handy for the train station. When and wherever you leave your bike, padlock it to something immovable – bike theft is commonplace.

Cambridge **tourist office** is conveniently situated in the ornate, domed former public library on Wheeler Street, off King's Parade (April–Oct Mon–Fri 10am–6pm, Sat 10am–5pm, Sun 11am–4pm; Nov–March Mon–Fri 10am–5.30pm, Sat 10am–5pm; ☎01223/322640, ⊛www.tourismcambridge.com). They issue city maps, have lots of leaflets on local attractions and sell an in-depth guide to the city (£4). They can also help with accommodation, which is a useful service especially in the summer when vacant rooms can be hard to find. The best source of **information** on eating out and entertainment is *Adhoc's What's On?*, a free monthly brochure available at the tourist office and larger bookshops.

The tourist office runs very popular **walking tours** of the centre (1–4 daily; 2hr; £7), which are expensive but include entrance to at least one college that normally charges for the privilege. Book well in advance in summer. The other high-profile tour is Guide Friday's open-top **bus tour** (daily; £8.50; ☎01223/362444), which runs in a continuous loop around the city centre – tickets allow you to get on and off at will and are on sale from the driver, at the tourist office and from the Guide Friday Tourism Centre in the train station. Their principal competitor, CitySightseeing (☎01708/866000), operates a similar service.

Accommodation

Cambridge is short of central accommodation and those few **hotels** that do occupy prime locations are expensive. That said, Chesterton Road, the busy street running east from the top of Magdalene Street, has several reasonably priced hotels and guest houses. There are lots of **B&Bs** on the outskirts of town, with several in the vicinity of the train station, and it's here you'll find the **youth hostel** too. In high season, when rooms are often difficult to find, the tourist office's efficient **accommodation booking service** can be very useful (Mon–Fri 9.30am–4pm; ☎01223/457581).

Hotels, guest houses and B&Bs

Arundel House Hotel 53 Chesterton Rd ☎01223 /367701, ⊛www.arundelhousehotels.co.uk. A con-
verted row of late-Victorian houses overlooking Jesus Green makes for one of the better mid-range B&B choices. Neat and tidy rooms with mundanely modern furnishings. Breakfasts are good. ❺

Benson House 24 Huntingdon Rd ☎01223 /311594. Pleasant, well-kept guest house in a demure brick house about five minutes' walk north from the Magdalene Bridge near New Hall College. Five rooms, three en suite. ❷

Cambridge Garden House Moat House Granta Place, Mill Lane ☎01223/259988. Disregard the clumsy name, for this is arguably Cambridge's best central hotel, set in its own gardens with a fine riverside location, rooms with balconies, indoor pool and health club. ❽

Crowne Plaza Cambridge Downing St ☎01223 /464466. Immaculately tailored behind a dignified facade, this sleek and slick hotel is first-rate. The foyer is adventurously designed and the rooms are resolutely modern in efficient chain-hotel style. Great central location. ❼

De Freville House 166 Chesterton Rd ☎01223 /354993. Six large and tastefully furnished en-suite rooms in an attractive, high-gabled Victorian guest house. A little bit too far out from the centre for comfort, but otherwise a very good choice. No credit cards. ❸

Lensfield Hotel 53 Lensfield Rd ☎01223/355017, ⓦwww.lensfieldhotel.co.uk. Small, well-kept family-ly-owned hotel on the ring road, just round the corner from the Fitzwilliam Museum. ❺

Netley Lodge 112 Chesterton Rd ☎01223 /363845. Cosy B&B in a Victorian town house, a manageable one-mile walk from the centre. Three attractively furnished bedrooms, two en suite. No credit cards. ❷

Regent Hotel 41 Regent St ☎01223/351470, ⓦwww.regenthotel.co.uk. Small-scale, family-owned hotel in an old brick town house within easy walking distance of the centre, beside Parker's Piece. The thirty-odd rooms are decorated in an efficient modern style. ❺

Royal Cambridge Hotel Trumpington St ☎01223 /351631. One of the city's more polished hotels, occupying a rehashed Georgian terrace. The conversion is rather heavy handed, and the furniture and fittings look too chain-like to be at ease, but no quibbles about the location, just down from the Fitzwilliam. ❼

Sleeperz Hotel Station Rd ☎01223/304050, ⓦwww.sleeperz.com. This popular hotel is in an imaginatively converted granary warehouse, right outside the train station. Most of the rooms are bunk-style affairs done out in the manner of a ship's cabin, and there are a few doubles too. All are en suite, with shower and TV. ❷

University Arms Hotel Regent St ☎01223 /351241. This chain hotel – it's a De Vere – is a bit of a mixed bag with a brutal modern wing glued onto an older, grander brick mansion of Victorian provenance. Standard issue chain-hotel-at-the-expensive-end-of-the-market furnishings and fittings. Handy location, though, overlooking Parker's Piece, on the south side of the city centre. ❽

Hostels and campsites

Cambridge YHA 97 Tenison Rd ☎01223/354601, ⓦwww.yha.org.uk. This well-equipped hostel has laundry and self-catering facilities, a cycle store, a games room and a small courtyard garden. It's close to the train station – Tenison Road is a right turn a couple of hundred yards down Station Road.

Cherry Hinton Caravan Club Site Lime Kiln Road, Cherry Hinton ☎01223/244088. Three miles east of the city centre in the village of Cherry Hinton, this pleasantly landscaped camping and caravan site spreads over five acres. Closed Jan & Feb.

YMCA Queen Anne House, Gonville Place ☎01223 /356998. Central location on the south side of Parker's Piece. Offers singles (£23) and doubles (£37), with breakfast included in the price, but very busy during summer – book well in advance. ❶

The City

Cambridge's main shopping street is Bridge Street, which becomes Sidney Street, St Andrew's Street and finally Regent Street; the other main thoroughfare is the procession of St John's Street, Trinity Street, King's Parade and Trumpington Street. The university developed on the land west of this latter route along the banks of the Cam, and now forms a continuous half-mile parade of **colleges** from Magdalene to Peterhouse, with sundry others scattered about the periphery. The **Fitzwilliam Museum**, with easily the city's finest art collection, is just along Trumpington Street south of Peterhouse. The account below starts with **King's College**, whose chapel is the university's most celebrated attraction, and covers the rest of the town in a broadly clockwise direction.

College admission charges and opening times

All of the more visited colleges now impose an **admission charge**, partly to control the number of tourists and partly to raise cash. It is, however, a creeping trend, so don't be surprised if other, lesser-known colleges follow suit. **Opening times** are fairly consistent throughout the year, though there are sporadic term-time variations especially at the weekend. It's also worth noting that during the exam season, which stretches from late April to early June, all the colleges have periods when they are closed to the public. Where no opening hours are given, you're usually free to tour the grounds at any time during the day. For more specific information, call the relevant college; **phone numbers** are given in the text.

King's College

Henry VI founded **King's College** (☎01223/331100) in 1441, but he was disappointed with his initial efforts, so four years later he cleared away half of medieval Cambridge to make room for a much grander foundation. His plans were ambitious, but the Wars of the Roses – and bouts of royal insanity – intervened and by the time of his death in 1471 very little had been finished. Indeed, work on Henry's **Great Court** hadn't even started and the site remained empty for three hundred years. The present complex – facing King's Parade from behind a long stone screen – is largely neo-Gothic, built in the 1820s to a design by William Wilkins. However, Henry's workmen did start on the college's finest building, the much celebrated **King's College Chapel** (term time Mon–Fri 9.30am–3.30pm, Sat 9.30am–3.15pm, Sun 1.15–2.15pm; rest of year Mon–Sat 9.30am–4.30pm, Sun 10am–5pm; £3.50), on the north side of today's Great Court. Committed to canvas by Turner and Canaletto, and eulogized in three sonnets by Wordsworth, it's now best known for its **boys' choir**, whose members process across the college grounds during term time in their antiquated garb to sing evensong (Tues–Sat at 5.30pm) and carols on Christmas Eve. Begun in 1446 and over sixty years in the making, the chapel is an extraordinary building. From the outside, it seems impossibly slender, its streamlined buttresses channelling up to a dainty balustrade and four spiky turrets, but the exterior was, in a sense at least, a happy accident – its design predicated by the carefully composed interior. Here, in the final flowering of the Gothic style, the mystery of the Christian faith was expressed by a long, uninterrupted **nave** flooded with kaleidoscopic patterns of light filtering in through copious stained-glass windows. Paid for by Henry VIII, the **stained glass** was largely the work of Flemish glaziers, with the lower windows portraying scenes from the New Testament and the Apocrypha, and the upper windows displaying the Old Testament. Henry VIII also paid for the intricately carved wooden choir screen, one of the earliest examples of Italian Renaissance woodcarving in England, but the choir stalls beyond date from the 1670s. Above the altar hangs Rubens' *Adoration of the Magi*. Finally, an exhibition in the chantries puts more historical flesh on Henry's grand plans.

Like Oxford's New College, King's enjoyed an exclusive supply of students from one of the country's public schools – in this case, Eton – and until 1851 claimed the right to award its students degrees without taking any examinations. The first non-Etonians were only accepted in 1873. Times have changed since those days, and, if anything, King's is now one of the more progressive colleges, having been one of the first to admit women in 1972. Among its most famous alumni are E.M. Forster, who described his experiences in *Maurice*, film director Derek Jarman, poet Rupert Brooke and John Maynard Keynes, whose

△ Windmill, Norfolk

economic theories did much to improve the college's finances when he became the college bursar.

From King's Parade to Clare College

King's Parade, originally the medieval High Street, is inevitably dominated by King's College and Chapel, but the higgledy-piggledy shops opposite are an attractive foil to William Wilkins's architectural screen. At the northern end of King's Parade is **St Mary's the Great** (daily 8am–6pm; free), the university's pet church, a sturdy Gothic structure dating from the fifteenth century. Its tower (Mon–Sat 9.30am–5.30pm, Sun 12.30–5.30pm; £1.85) offers a good overall view of the colleges and a bird's-eye view of **Market Hill**, east of the church, where food and bric-a-brac stalls are set out daily. Opposite the church stands **Senate House**, an exercise in Palladian classicism by James Gibbs, and the scene of graduation ceremonies on the last Saturday in June, when champagne corks fly around the rabbit-fur collars and black gowns. It's not usually open to the public, though you can wander around the quad if the gate is open.

The northern continuation of King's Parade is Trinity Street, a short way along which, on the left, is the main entrance to **Gonville and Caius College** (℡01223/332400), known simply as Caius (pronounced "keys"), after the co-founder John Keys, who latinized his name, as was then the custom with men of learning. The design of the college owes much to Keys, who placed a gate on three sides of two adjoining courts, each representing a different stage on the path to academic enlightenment: the Gate of Humility, through which the student entered the college, now stands in the Fellows' Garden; the Gate of Virtue, sporting the female figures of Fame and Wealth, marks the entrance to Caius Court; while the Gate of Honour, capped with sundials and decorated with classical motifs, leads to Senate House Passage and on to Senate House.

Senate House Passage continues west beyond the Gate of Honour to Trinity Lane and **Trinity Hall** (℡01223/332500) – not to be confused with Trinity College – where the Elizabethan library retains several of its original chains, designed to prevent students from purloining the texts. A few metres to the south is the much more diverting **Clare College** (daily 10am–5pm; £2; ℡01223/333200). One of seven colleges founded, rather surprisingly, by women, its plain period-piece courtyards, completed in the early eighteenth century, lead to one of the most picturesque of all the bridges over the Cam, **Clare Bridge**. Beyond lies the Fellows' Garden, one of the loveliest college gardens open to the public (times as college). Back at the entrance to Clare, it's a few metres more to the North Gate of King's College, beside the chapel.

Trinity

Trinity College, on Trinity Street (daily 10am–5pm; £1; ℡01223/338400), is the largest of the Cambridge colleges and to ram home the point it also has the largest courtyard. It comes as little surprise then that its list of famous alumni is longer than any other college: literary greats, including Dryden, Byron, Tennyson and Vladimir Nabokov; the Cambridge spies Blunt, Burgess and Philby; two prime ministers, Balfour and Baldwin; William Thackeray, Isaac Newton, Lord Rutherford, Vaughan Williams, Pandit Nehru, Bertrand Russell and Ludwig Wittgenstein, not to mention a trio of (much less talented) royals, Edward VII, George VI and Prince Charles.

A statue of Henry VIII, who founded the college in 1546, sits in majesty over Trinity's **Great Gate**, his sceptre replaced with a chair leg by a student wit. Beyond lies the vast asymmetrical expanse of **Great Court**, which displays a fine range of Tudor buildings, the oldest of which is the fifteenth-century clock tower – the annual race against its midnight chimes is now common currency thanks to the film *Chariots of Fire*. The centrepiece of the court is the delicate fountain, in which, legend has it, Lord Byron used to bathe naked with his pet bear – the college forbade students from keeping dogs.

To get through to **Nevile's Court** – where Newton first calculated the speed of sound – you must pass through "the screens", a passage separating the Hall from the kitchens, a common feature of Oxbridge colleges. The west end of Nevile's Court is enclosed by the university's most famous building after King's College Chapel, the **Wren Library** (term time Mon–Fri noon–2pm, Sat 10.30am–12.30pm; rest of year Mon–Fri noon–2pm; free). Viewed from the outside, it's impossible to appreciate the scale of the interior thanks to Wren's clever device of concealing the internal floor level. In contrast to many modern libraries, natural light pours into the white stuccoed interior, which contrasts wonderfully with the dark lime-wood bookcases, also Wren-designed and housing numerous valuable manuscripts including Milton's *Lycidas*, Wittgenstein's journals and A.A. Milne's *Winnie the Pooh*.

St John's

Next door, **St John's College**, on St John's St (daily 10am–5pm; £2; ☎01223 /338600), sports a grandiloquent Tudor gatehouse, distinguished by the coat of arms of the founder, Lady Margaret Beaufort, the mother of Henry VII, held aloft by two spotted, mythical beasts. Beyond, three successive courts lead to the river, but there's an excess of dull reddish brickwork here – enough for Wordsworth, who lived above the kitchens on F staircase, to describe the place as "gloomy". The arcade on the far side of Third Court leads through to the **Bridge of Sighs**, a chunky, covered bridge built in 1831 but in most other respects very unlike its Venetian namesake. The bridge is closed to the public, and in any case is best viewed either from a punt or from the much older, more stylish Wren-designed bridge a few metres to the south. The Bridge of Sighs links the old college with the fanciful nineteenth-century **New Court**, a crenellated neo-Gothic extravaganza topped by a feast of pinnacles and a central cupola – and known as "the wedding cake".

From the Round Church to Magdalene

Back on St John's Street, it's a few seconds' walk to Bridge Street and the **Round Church** (daily: June–Sept 10am–5pm; Oct–May 1–4pm; free), built in the twelfth century on the model of the Holy Sepulchre in Jerusalem. It's a curious-looking structure, squat with an ill-considered late medieval extension to the rear, but the Norman pillars of the original church remain, overseen by sturdy arcading and a ring of finely carved faces. The church is also geared up for **brass rubbing**. It holds a varied selection of brasses and sells all the necessary tackle. Staff will help you get started. In addition, the church is the starting point for Christian heritage walks around the city (Feb–Nov Wed 11am, Sun 2.30pm; £3 recommended donation; ☎01223/311602).

Set back from the road, down a footpath beside the church, is the **Union Society**, a bastion of male-dominated debating culture, founded in 1815 and finally opened to women in the 1960s. The society likes to think of itself as a miniature House of Commons – its debating chamber is designed as such – and its debates continue to attract many of the leading politicians and speakers of the day. These are presided over by the Union's officers, who tend to be made up of the university's more ambitious, conservative elements. In the normal scheme of things, election to the Union presidency leads about twenty years later to a place in Cabinet – the last Tory administration barely contained a Minister who hadn't been Union president.

Saving nearby Jesus College till later (see below), it only takes a minute or two to stroll up from the Round Church to **Magdalene Bridge**, the site of the old Roman ford. Just beyond is **Magdalene College** (℡01223/332100) – pronounced "maudlin" – which was founded as a hostel by the Benedictines and became a university college in 1542. Magdalene was the last of the colleges to admit women, finally succumbing in 1988. Here, the main focus of attention is the **Pepys Building** (Nov & mid-Jan to mid-March Mon–Sat 2.30–3.30pm; late April to Aug Mon–Sat 11.30am–12.30pm & 2.30–3.30pm; free), in the second of the college's ancient courtyards. Samuel Pepys, a Magdalene student, bequeathed his entire library to the college, where it has been displayed ever since in its original red-oak bookshelves – though his famous diary, which also now resides here, was only discovered in the nineteenth century.

Castle Street

Cross busy Chesterton Lane at the top of Magdalene Street and you'll reach two of the city's less visited attractions, sandwiched together at the foot of **Castle Street**. These are the **Folk Museum**, 2–3 Castle St (April–Sept Mon–Sat 10.30am–5pm, Sun 2–5pm; Oct–March closed Mon; £2.50), with a collection of domestic items from the seventeenth century onwards, and **Kettle's Yard** (gallery Tues–Sun 11.30–5pm; house Tues–Sun 2–4pm; free), a deceptively spacious open-plan conversion of some old slum dwellings, originally owned by the art critic Jim Ede. The gallery here holds an enjoyable collection of paintings, including many by the St Ives primitivist Alfred Wallis, and has an imaginative programme of exhibitions featuring contemporary artists.

A little further up Castle Street, a short, signposted footpath leads to the grassy mound which is all that remains of **Cambridge Castle**. Climb it for the view over the city centre.

Jesus

Back down Magdalene Street then Bridge Street, take the first left after the Round Church to reach **Jesus College** (℡01223/339339), whose intimate cloisters are reminiscent of a monastic institution. This is not too surprising as the Bishop of Ely founded the college on the grounds of a suppressed Benedictine nunnery in 1496. The main red-brick gateway is approached via a distinctive walled walkway strewn with bicycles and known as "the Chimney". Beyond, much of the ground plan of the nunnery has been preserved, especially around **Cloister Court**, the prettiest of the college's courtyards, dripping with ivy and overflowing hanging baskets. Entered from the court, the college **chapel** occupies the former priory chancel and looks like a medieval parish church; it was imaginatively restored in the nineteenth century, using ceiling designs by William Morris and Pre-Raphaelite stained glass. The poet Samuel Taylor Coleridge was the college's most famously bad student, absconding in his first year to join the Light Dragoons, and returning only to be kicked out for a combination of bad debts and unconventional opinions.

Sidney Sussex and Christ's College

Near Jesus, Malcolm Street cuts off Jesus Lane to reach King Street, from where it's a short stroll through to **Sidney Sussex College** (℡01223/338800), whose sombre, mostly mock-Gothic facade glowers over Sidney Street. Oliver

On the river

Punting is the quintessential Cambridge activity, though it's a good deal harder than it looks. First-timers find themselves zigzagging across the water and "punt jams" are very common on the stretch of the Cam beside the Backs in summer. **Punt rental** is available at several points, including the boatyard at Mill Lane (beside the Silver Street bridge), at Magdalene Bridge, and at the *Rat & Parrot* pub on Jesus Green. It costs around £12 an hour (and most places charge a deposit), with up to six people in each punt. If you find it all too daunting you can always hire a **chauffeur punt** from any of the rental places; this works out at about a fiver a head. Cambridge is also famous for its **rowing clubs**, which are clustered along the north bank of the river across from Midsummer Common. For their convenience, this stretch of water is punt-free. The most important inter-college races are the **May Bumps**, which, confusingly, take place in June.

Cromwell studied here and, in 1960, his skull was brought to the college and buried in a secret location in the ante-chapel.

Just to the south of Sidney Sussex, on St Andrew's Street, you hit the hustle and bustle of the town's central shopping area, dominated by the **Lion Yard** shopping centre. This was one of the few town-planning mistakes in the centre of Cambridge, a brutally modern structure that rumbles along **Petty Cury**, formerly a cobbled curve of leaning half-timbered houses. Aesthetic relief is, however, close at hand, just opposite Lion Yard, in the turreted gateway of **Christ's College** (℡01223/334900), which features the coat of arms of the founder, Lady Margaret Beaufort, who also founded St John's. Passing through First Court you come to the Fellows' Building, attributed to Inigo Jones, whose central arch gives access to the **Fellows' Garden** (Mon–Fri 10am–12pm; free). The poet John Milton is said to have either painted or composed beneath the garden's elderly mulberry tree, though there's no definite proof that he did either; Christ's other famous undergraduate was Charles Darwin, who showed little academic promise and spent most of his time hunting and shooting. If you continue walking through the college, you come to its modern adjunct, Denys Lasdun's concrete pyramidal accommodation block, dubbed "the typewriter".

Emmanuel College

A little further along St Andrew's Street is **Emmanuel College** (℡01223 /334200), whose stolid Neoclassical facade hides a neat and trim Front Court, where the college **chapel** was designed by Wren in a simple Classical style, its wood-panelled nave set beneath a fancy stucco ceiling. The college was founded in 1584 to train a new generation of Protestant clergy following the Reformation. Emmanuel men were numbered among the Pilgrims who settled New England, which not only explains the derivation of the place name Cambridge in Massachusetts but also accounts for Harvard University – **John Harvard**, another alumnus, is remembered by a memorial window in the chapel.

Downing Street and the museums

Opposite Emmanuel, **Downing Street** and its continuation **Pembroke Street** link St Andrew's and Trumpington streets. To either side is a rambling assortment of large, mostly Victorian buildings, in parts of which are a group of scientific and specialist museums. Each museum is connected to one of the university faculties and forms an important resource for students, but is also open to the public. First up, on the left, is the **Sedgwick Geology Museum** (Mon–Fri 9am–1pm & 2–5pm, Sat 10am–1pm; free), which displays fossils and skeletons of dinosaurs, reptiles and mammals, plus the oldest geological collection in the world. In the same complex is the **Museum of Archeology and Anthropology** (Tues–Sat 2–4.30pm; free), which is probably the pick of the bunch for the non-specialist, covering the development of the city from prehistoric times to the nineteenth century and, better still, holding a superb ethnographical gallery. This is centred on a soaring fifty-foot native totem pole and many of the exhibits derive from the "cabinets of curiosities" collected by eighteenth-century explorers. Several pieces on show were gathered on Captain Cook's first voyage to the South Pacific between 1768 and 1771.

A little further down – and on the opposite side of – Downing Street is the **Museum of Zoology** (Mon–Fri 2.15–4.45pm; free), some of whose exhibits were donated by Darwin. Next up, with its entrance round the corner on Free School Lane, is the **Whipple Museum of the History of Science** (Mon–Fri 1.30–4.30pm; free), crammed with hundreds of scientific instruments from the fourteenth century onwards.

St Catherine's and Corpus Christi

There are four more town-centre colleges clustered at the west end of Pembroke Street, around the foot of King's Parade and the top of Trumpington Street. On the west side of King's Parade is **St Catherine's College** (☏01223 /338300) – popularly known as "Catz" – which was founded by the provost of King's in 1473. In contrast to King's, its glamorous neighbour, the Principal Court here is a cheerless affair, whose dour, heavy-duty brick buildings mirror the college's relative impecuniousness – in 1880 St Catherine's was so broke that it was nearly forced to close. Much more enticing is **Corpus Christi College** (☏01223/338000), just across King's Parade, founded by two of the town's guilds in 1352. Ignore the first court and instead head north into **Old Court**, which dates from the foundation of the college and is where Christopher Marlowe wrote *Tamburlaine* before graduating in 1587. The college library, on the south side, contains a priceless collection of Anglo-Saxon manuscripts, while the north side is linked by a gallery to **St Bene't's Church**, which served as the college chapel, but is of much earlier Saxon origin. Inside, Thomas Hobson's Bible is exhibited in a glass case; Hobson was the owner of a Cambridge livery stable, where he would only allow customers to take the horse nearest the door – hence "Hobson's choice".

Nearby **Queens' College** (daily 10am–4.30pm; £1.20; ☏01223/335511), accessed through the gate on Queens' Lane, just off Silver Street, is the most popular college with university applicants, and it's not difficult to see why. In the **Old Court** and the **Cloister Court**, Queens' possesses two fairy-tale Tudor courtyards, with the first of the two the perfect illustration of the original collegiate ideal with kitchens, library, chapel, hall and rooms all set around a tiny green. Cloister Court is flanked by the Long Gallery of the President's Lodge, the last remaining half-timbered building in the university, and, in its southeast corner, by the tower where Erasmus is thought to have beavered away during his four years here, probably from 1510 to 1514. Be sure to pay a visit to the college **Hall**, off the screens passage between the two courts, which holds mantel tiles by William Morris, and portraits of Erasmus and one of the college's cofounders, Elizabeth Woodville, wife of Edward IV. Equally eye-catching is the wooden **Mathematical Bridge** over the Cam (visible for free from the Silver Street Bridge), a copy of the mid-eighteenth-century original which, it was claimed, would stay in place even if the nuts and bolts were removed.

Pembroke and Peterhouse

Doubling back to Trumpington Street, **Pembroke College** (℡01223 /338100) contains Wren's first ever commission, the college **chapel**, paid for by his Royalist uncle, erstwhile Bishop of Ely and a college fellow, in thanks for his deliverance from the Tower of London after seventeen years' imprisonment. It holds a particularly fine, though modern, stained-glass east window and a delicate fifteenth-century marble relief of St Michael and the Virgin, the product of an unusually skilled early English workshop. Outside the library there's a statue of William Pitt the Younger, clad here in a toga, who entered the college at 15 and was prime minister at 25, and is just one of a long list of college alumni, which includes poets Edmund Spenser, Thomas Gray and Ted Hughes.

Across the street and just along from Pembroke is the oldest and smallest of the colleges, **Peterhouse** (℡01223/338200), founded in 1284. Few of the original buildings have survived, the principal exception being the thirteenth-century **Hall**, entered from the main court, whose interior was remodelled by William Morris. As at Corpus Christi, Peterhouse used the church next door – in this case Little St Mary's – as the college chapel, until the present one, a sterling, somewhat overblown structure, was plonked in the main court in 1632.

The Fitzwilliam Museum

Of all the museums in Cambridge, the **Fitzwilliam Museum**, on Trumpington Street (Tues–Sat 10am–5pm, Sun 2.15–5pm; £3 donation suggested), stands head and shoulders above the rest. The building itself is a splendidly grandiloquent interpretation of Neoclassicism, built in the mid-nineteenth century to house the vast collection bequeathed by Viscount Fitzwilliam in 1816. Since then, the museum has been bequeathed a string of private collections, most of which are focused on a particular specialism. Consequently, the Fitzwilliam says much about the changing tastes of the British upper class. The **Lower Galleries** contain a wealth of antiquities including Egyptian sarcophagi and mummies, fifth-century BC black- and red-figure Greek vases, plus a bewildering display of European ceramics. Further on, there are sections dedicated to armour, glass and pewterware, medals, portrait miniatures and illuminated manuscripts, and – right at the far end – galleries devoted to Far Eastern applied arts and Korean ceramics.

The **Upper Galleries** concentrate on painting and sculpture with three of the first five rooms containing an eclectic assortment of mostly nineteenth- and early twentieth-century European paintings. Among many, there are works by Picasso, Matisse, Monet, Renoir, Delacroix, Cézanne and Degas. The other two rooms feature British painting, with works by William Blake, Constable and Turner, Hogarth, Reynolds, Gainsborough and Stubbs. Moving on, the Italian section displays paintings by Fra Filippo Lippi and Simone Martini, Titian and Veronese, while Frans Hals and Ruisdael feature in the Flemish section. The post-1945 gallery is packed with a fascinating selection including pieces by the likes of Lucian Freud, David Hockney, Henry Moore, Ivon Hitchens, Ben Nicholson and Barbara Hepworth.

To the University Botanic Gardens

Past the Fitzwilliam Museum, turn left along busy Lensfield Road for the **Scott Polar Research Institute** (Mon–Fri 2.30–4pm; free), founded in 1920 in memory of the explorer, Captain Scott, with displays from the expeditions of various polar adventurers, plus exhibitions on native cultures of the Arctic.

There's more general interest near at hand in the shape of the **University Botanic Gardens** (daily 10am–6pm, 4pm in winter; glasshouses till 3.30pm; £2), whose entrance is on Bateman Street, about 500 yards to the south of Lensfield Road via Panton Street. Founded in 1760 and covering forty acres, the gardens are second only to Kew with glasshouses as well as bountiful outdoor displays. The outdoor beds are mostly arranged by natural order, but there is also a particularly unusual series of chronological beds, showing when different plants were introduced into Britain.

Eating and drinking

Even at Cambridge, students are not the world's greatest customers for restaurateurs, so although the downtown **takeaway** and **café** scene is fine, decent **restaurants** are a little thin on the ground. On any kind of budget, the myriad Italian places – courtesy of Cambridge's large Italian population – will stand you in good stead; otherwise, choose carefully, particularly in the more touristy areas, where quality isn't always all it should be. Happily, Cambridge abounds in excellent **pubs**, and our list rounds up some of the best traditional student and local drinking haunts.

Cafés and restaurants

Brown's 23 Trumpington St. Breezy brasserie with a competent, fairly wide-ranging menu housed in a former hospital outpatients department (the rest of the hospital has become a Management Institute). The grand setting – all plants and fans – sets the meal off a treat. Inordinately popular, but no reservations – wait in line or at the bar. Moderate.

Clowns 54 King St. Italian-style cappuccino and cakes, sandwiches and snacks, plus newspapers to browse. Off the tourist route and not part of a chain – bonuses in anyone's books.

Copper Kettle 4 King's Parade. Generations of students have whiled away time in this resolutely old-fashioned café opposite King's College, sipping coffee, eating pastries and putting the world to rights.

Don Pasquale 12 Market Hill. Great, marketside location, with seats on the square for lunchtime diners. Tasty food and an especially good place for a quick pick-me-up espresso and slice of pizza.

Efes 80 King St ℡01223/350491. Intimate Turkish restaurant, with chargrilled meats prepared under your nose and a decent meze selection. Moderate.

Eraina Taverna 2 Free School Lane ℡01223/368786. Packed Greek taverna which satisfies the hungry hordes with huge platefuls of stews and grills, as well as pizzas, curries and a whole host of other menu madness. Try to avoid getting stuck in the basement, though at weekends (when you'll probably have to queue) you'll be lucky to get a seat anywhere. Inexpensive.

La Margherita 15 Magdalene St ℡01223/315232. Cheapish and cheerful Italian outfit offering pizzas and pastas as well as standard meat and fish dishes. Inexpensive to moderate.

Midsummer House Midsummer Common ℡01223/369299. Lovely riverside restaurant with conservatory, specializing in top-notch French-Mediterranean cuisine. Reservations essential. On the south side of the river, beside the footbridge just to the east of Victoria Avenue. Expensive.

Nadia's Patisserie 11 St John's St. Good sandwich and cake takeaway in the centre, opposite St John's. One of several outlets – there's another at 20 King's Parade.

Pizza Express 7a Jesus Lane. Superior pizza chain outlet located in the grand, marbled hall of the former Pitt Club. Also, smart premises in an uninspiring modern block at 28 St Andrew's St. Inexpensive.

Prêt-à-Manger 19 Petty Cury. Designer coffee and tasty, additive-free sandwiches from this London-based chain.

Rainbow Vegetarian Bistro 9a King's Parade ℡01223/321551. Vegetarian restaurant with main courses – ranging from couscous to lasagne and Indonesian *gado-gado* – all under £7. Good-value breakfasts, and organic wines served with meals. Great location, opposite King's College. Closed Sun. Inexpensive.

Roof Garden Cambridge Arts Theatre, 6 St Edward's Passage. Conservatory-style rooftop café serving home-made snacks, salads and sandwiches, as well as main meals (three courses for £17) and pre-theatre dinners. Closed Sun.

Starbucks 2 Quay Side. No points for originality, but this outlet of the worldwide coffee house chain does what it does competently enough. Handy location for the punt rental point at Magdalene Bridge.

Twenty-Two 22 Chesterton Rd ℡01223/351880. Consistently the best restaurant in Cambridge, a candlelit townhouse in which the good-value, fixed-price menu (at around £25) touches all the modern bases. Closed Sun & Mon. Expensive.

Pubs and bars

Anchor Silver St. Very popular riverside tourist haunt with views of the Backs, adjacent punt rental and an outdoor deck.

Champion of the Thames 68 King St. Gratifyingly old-fashioned central pub with decent beer and a student/academic clientele.

Blackwood's Cambridge Arts Theatre, 6 St Edward's Passage. The first-floor bar at the theatre makes a civilized meeting spot. Closed Sun.

Eagle Bene't St. An ancient inn with a cobbled courtyard where Crick and Watson sought inspiration in the 1950s, at the time of their discovery of DNA. It's been tarted up since and gets horribly crowded, but is still worth a pint of anyone's time.

Elm Tree 42 Orchard St. Cosy local with frequent live music, mainly jazz. Just to the north of Parker's Piece and full of furiously smoking refugees from the nearby *Free Press* (see below). Well worth seeking out: to get there, follow Emmanuel Road north off Drummer Street, near the bus station, and take the third turning on the right – it's on the corner with Eden Street.

Free Press 7 Prospect Row. Classic, superbly maintained backstreet local with an admirable no-smoking policy, good beer and fine food. It's located a few yards along the street from the *Elm Tree* – for directions, see above.

Fort St George Midsummer Common. Boisterous pub with a pleasant riverside location, overlooking the boathouses from the south side of the river, beside the footbridge just to the east of Victoria Avenue.

Maypole 20a Park St. Small, well-kept pub with an invigorating atmosphere. In the centre near the Round Church.

Rat & Parrot Thompson's Lane, Jesus Green. The latest incarnation of this riverside pub sees it reinvented as a themed café-bar, with courtyard seating and heavy-duty bouncers.

Entertainment

The **performing arts** scene is at its best during term time, with numerous student **drama** productions, **classical concerts** and **gigs** culminating in the traditional orgy of excess following the exam season, though the more firmly town-based venues, such as the Corn Exchange, do put on events throughout the year. Apart from the places highlighted below, each college and several churches contribute to the performing arts scene too, with the **King's College choir** being, of course, the most famous attraction (see p.586), though the choral scholars who perform at the chapels of St John's and Trinity are also exceptionally good. For all upcoming events, check the **listings** section of *Adhoc's What's On?* (Ⓦ www.adhoc.co.uk), a free weekly magazine that is widely available in downtown bookshops and newsagents as well as from the tourist office. For advance tickets for most events, pop into the Corn Exchange (see below).

June and July are the busiest times in Cambridge's calendar of **events**. The fortnight of post-exam celebrations, which take place in the first two weeks of June – and are confusingly known as **May Week** – herald the ball and garden-party season, and include boat races, known as the "May Bumps", on the Cam by Midsummer Common. The vaguely hippified **Midsummer Fair**, descendant of the town's famous medieval Stourbridge Fair, discontinued in 1934, takes place in mid-June on Midsummer Common, with bands, theatre and much more besides – all for free. By contrast, you'll have to pay out around £50 for a tent pitch and entry into the three-day **Cambridge Folk Festival**, held annually at the end of July at Cherry Hinton, and attracting a wide variety of loosely folk-based acts.

Arts Picture House 38–39 St Andrew's St ☎01223/504444. Art house cinema with an excellent, wide-ranging programme.

Boat Race 170 East Rd ☎01223/508533. Lively pub venue for all kinds of music, with gigs every night.

Cambridge Arts Theatre 6 St Edward's Passage, off King's Parade ☎01223/503333. The city's main repertory theatre, founded by John Maynard Keynes, and launching pad of a thousand-and-one famous careers, offers a top-notch range of cutting-edge and classic productions.

Cambridge Corn Exchange Wheeler St ℡01223/357851. Revamped nineteenth-century trading hall, now the main city-centre venue for opera, ballet, musicals and comedy as well as regular rock and folk gigs.

Cambridge Modern Jazz Club at Sophbeck Sessions, 14 Tredgold Lane, Napier St ℡01223 /722811. Attracts top-ranking artists from around the world. East of the city centre, near the Grafton Centre shopping mall, off Newmarket Road.

Junction Clifton Rd ℡01223/511511. Rock, Indie, jazz, reggae or soul gigs, plus occasional comedy acts and dance groups at this popular arts and entertainments venue.

Listings

Airport London Stansted Airport ℡0870/0000303.

Banks and exchanges There are banks all over the city centre, and you can also exchange traveller's cheques at the main post office (see below); at American Express, 25 Sidney St ℡01223/345201; and Thomas Cook, in the Grafton Centre ℡01223/543000, and at 23 St Andrew's St ℡01223/543100.

Bike rental Geoff's Bike Hire, near the train station at 65 Devonshire Rd ℡01223/365629; Mikes Bikes, 28 Mill Rd ℡01223/312591; and H. Drake, near the train station at 56–60 Hills Rd ℡01223/363468. Rates start at around £7 a day.

Bookshops Heffers has several outlets with its main branch at 20 Trinity St; Cambridge University Press has a shop at 1 Trinity St; Borders are at 12–13 Market St; and Waterstones at 22 Sidney St. For second-hand books try the shops down St Edward's Passage off King's Parade: G. David, at no.3, is an antiquarian's and hard-back hunter's paradise; the Haunted Bookshop, at no. 9, is better for first editions, travel and illustrated books.

Buses Most city buses pull in to – and depart from – the stops along Emmanuel Street. Close by, at the top of Emmanuel Street, the Drummer Street bus station is for long distance services. For information on Cambridgeshire bus services, call the information line (℡0870/608 2608), or drop by the Premier Travel Agency, beside the Drummer Street station (℡01223/572300). In addition, Airlinks (℡0870/574 7777) operates direct services to the London airports; and National Express (℡0870/5808080) runs services to London and other major cities.

Car rental Avis, 245 Mill Rd ℡01223/212551; Budget, 303–305 Newmarket Rd ℡01223/323838; Europcar, 22 Cambridge Rd ℡01223/233644; National, 264 Newmarket Rd ℡01223/365438.

Hospitals Addenbrooke's Hospital, Hills Road ℡01223/245151.

Left luggage 24-hour lockers at the train station.

Pharmacies Boots, 28 Petty Cury ℡01223/350213; Lloyds, 30 Trumpington St ℡01223/359449.

Police Parkside at East Road ℡01223/358966.

Post office The main office is at 9–11 St Andrew's St (Mon–Sat 9am–5.30pm).

Taxis There are ranks at the train and bus stations. To book, call Diamond ℡01223/523523; or Panther ℡01223/715715.

Travel agent STA, 38 Sidney St ℡01223/366966.

Around Cambridge

Within easy reach of Cambridge, across the flat fen landscape, are several absorbing, day-trip destinations. South of the city is **Grantchester**, a smart little place that's typical of the villages hereabouts – though the real draw is that you can cycle or punt there through open countryside. To the southwest is **Wimpole Hall**, a rambling eighteenth-century country house, and to the northeast is **Anglesey Abbey**, a handsome old mansion that holds an outstanding collection of fine and applied art. A little further afield, south along the M11, is **Duxford Imperial War Museum** and beyond, among the rolling hills of northwest Essex, the straggling market town of **Saffron Walden**. Horse-racing aficionados will, however, have little truck with all of this, heading straight for **Newmarket**, just thirteen miles to the east of Cambridge.

Grantchester

The pretty little village of **GRANTCHESTER**, replete with thatched cottages and chestnut trees, is just a couple of miles up the River Cam from Cambridge. It's a popular destination on sunny days since it's an easy bike or punt ride away through **Grantchester Meadows** – the signposted route starts at the southern end of Newnham Road. The poet Rupert Brooke, who died in World War I, lodged in the old vicarage here as an undergraduate, penning the much-quoted lines "Stands the Church clock at ten to three? And is there honey still for tea?" The clock in the pub named after Brooke stands permanently at ten to three, though of the three village **pubs**, you're better off heading for the *Red Lion* or the *Green Man*, both sited where the path from Cambridge emerges on the village's main street.

Wimpole Hall

Wimpole Hall (mid-March to July, Sept & Oct Tues–Thurs, Sat & Sun 1–5pm; Aug Tues–Sun 1–5pm; £5.90, garden only £2.50; NT), once the home of Rudyard Kipling's daughter, is a huge eighteenth-century pile ten miles southwest of Cambridge. The interior contains a library by James Gibbs, stunning trompe l'oeil decor by James Thornhill in the chapel, and several rooms by the celebrated Neoclassical architect, Sir John Soane. The 360-acre grounds were landscaped by Capability Brown and Humphry Repton, and contain several follies including a Chinese bridge. Soane also designed **Wimpole Home Farm** (mid-March to June, Sept & Oct Tues–Thurs, Sat & Sun 10.30am–5pm; July & Aug Tues–Sun 10.30am–5pm; Nov to mid-March Sat & Sun 11am–4pm; £2.50, combined ticket with the hall £8.50; NT), now a rare breeds farm with Suffolk Punch horses in the stables and an exhibition of agricultural tools in the great barn.

The Cambridge-Biggleswade **bus** #175 (not Sun) comes out this way, but the nearest you'll get is the village of Arrington, a mile or so to the west.

Anglesey Abbey

Anglesey Abbey (April to mid-Oct Wed–Sun 1–5pm; £6.25, garden & mill £3.85; NT), six miles northeast of Cambridge near the village of Lode, was actually never an abbey at all, but a priory (of which only the chapter house and monks' parlour now survive). For once, the house, dating from 1600, is of less interest than its contents, which feature the Fairhaven collection of paintings and furniture. There's everything here from an Egyptian bronze cat to Ming vases, works by Lorrain, Constable, Cuyp and Gainsborough, all gathered together by the house's last, very wealthy owner, Lord Fairhaven. Fairhaven also transformed the surrounding fenland into a glorious hundred-acre **garden** (April–June & mid-Sept to mid-Oct Wed–Sun 10.30am–5.30pm; July to mid-Sept daily 10.30am–5.30pm; mid-Oct, Dec, Jan & Feb Wed–Sun 10.30am–4.30pm), dotted with sculptures and urns from his collection. At the far end of the gardens, an old **watermill** (April to June & mid-Sept to mid-Oct Wed–Sun 1–4.30pm; July to mid-Sept daily 1–4.30pm; mid-Oct to Dec, Jan & Feb Sat & Sun 11am–4pm) has been restored and now grinds grain and sells the flour.

To get to the abbey from Cambridge, take Stagecoach **bus** #111 or #122.

Duxford: Imperial War Museum

Eight miles south of Cambridge, and visible from the M11 – it's next to junction 10 – are the giant hangars of the **Imperial War Museum** (daily mid-

March to mid-Oct 10am–6pm; mid-Oct to mid-March 10am–4pm; £7.70; Ⓦ www.iwm.org.uk/duxford), based at Duxford airfield. Throughout World War II, East Anglia was a centre of operations for the RAF and the USAF, with the flat, unobstructed landscape dotted by dozens of airfields. Duxford itself was a Battle of Britain station, equipped with Spitfires, and there's a reconstructed Operations Room in one of the control towers. In total, Duxford holds over 150 historic aircraft, a wide-ranging collection of civil and military planes from the Sunderland flying boat to Concorde and the Vulcan B2 bombers, which were used for the first and last time in the Falklands; the Spitfires remain the most enduringly popular. Most of the planes are kept in full working order and are taken out for a spin several times a year at **Duxford Air Shows**, which attract thousands of visitors. There are usually three Air Shows a year and tickets cost from £12.50 to £15.50; advance bookings are strongly recommended (Ⓣ01223/499353). For details of the free courtesy bus service linking Duxford with Cambridge, call Ⓣ01223/835000.

Saffron Walden

Some twelve miles south of Cambridge, the fenlands are left behind for the hillier landscapes of Uttlesford, the district council's euphemism for the northwest corner of Essex. The main event here is **SAFFRON WALDEN**, a goodlooking town that possesses dozens of antique timber-framed houses. There are several particularly fine examples on the main road, but the nicest areas of town to explore are away from the thundering traffic, in the network of alleyways around the **Market Place** and the book and antique shops of **Church Street**. Many of these old houses sport fancy decorative plasterwork, known as pargeting – the last word on which is provided by the stepped gables of the **Old Sun Inn**, on Church Street, which Cromwell once used as his headquarters. The town's prefix was coined in medieval times when saffron crocuses were cultivated here for their dye and medicinal qualities. You can learn more about this and other aspects of the town's history at the **museum** on Museum Street, off Church Street (March–Oct Mon–Sat 10am–5pm, Sun 2–5pm; Nov–Feb Mon–Sat 10am–4.30pm, Sun 2–4.30pm; £1). Behind the museum are the scant ruins of the twelfth-century **castle**.

The nearest **train station** is Audley End, a couple of miles to the southwest of town off the B1383 (and a good mile from Audley End village). **Buses** are much more convenient, stopping close to the Market Place, where the **tourist office** (April–Oct Mon–Sat 9.30am–5.30pm; Nov–March Mon–Sat 10am–5pm; Ⓣ01799/510 444) issues free maps and has plenty of leaflets on local attractions. Just to the north of Market Place are Castle and Church streets, and to the west are High Street and its continuation Bridge Street. Saffron Walden is best enjoyed as a day-trip, but there are several **B&Bs**, with one of the best being the *Archway Guest House*, Church St (Ⓣ A01799/501500; ❷), which – oddly enough – has a working 1960s' Juke Box in the breakfast room. The forty-bed **youth hostel**, 1 Myddylton Place (Ⓣ01799/523117; closed Nov–March; £9.25), occupies a converted, half-timbered medieval maltings, footsteps from the junction of Bridge and Castle streets. The best **pub** in town is the ancient *Eight Bells*, on Bridge Street.

Audley End House

A mile or so to the west of Saffron Walden – and beyond the village that bears its name – the palatial Jacobean mansion of **Audley End House** (April–Sept Wed–Sun noon–5pm; Oct Wed–Sun 11am–3pm; house & grounds £6.75, grounds only £4; EH) was built for the Earl of Suffolk at the start of the seventeenth century. A spectacularly lavish building, it was soon the talk of the aristocracy, so much so that Charles II purchased it in 1668, staying here whenever he went to the races at Newmarket. Returned to the Suffolks after the king's death, Audley End was modified on several later occasions, most notably when one of the Suffolks demolished the east wing in 1735 to reduce his overheads. Highlights include the striking wood panelling and plasterwork of the Great Hall and, less ostentatiously, the subtle elegance of Robert Adam's two Drawing Rooms. English Heritage has worked hard on renovating the **grounds**, which were first laid out by Capability Brown and contain a river, a lake and a splendid flower garden.

To get to Audley End House from Saffron Walden, take the signed byroad that leads west through Audley End village. Confusingly, Audley End train station is about a mile southwest of the village, off the B1383.

Thaxted

THAXTED, eight miles southeast of Saffron Walden, enjoyed its heyday in the fourteenth and fifteenth centuries, when it prospered on the profits of the local cutlery industry. It was during this period that the town's splendid three-tiered, half-timbered **Guildhall** was erected on the marketplace, its beams now twisted with age and leaning at an alarming angle. There are more half-timbered buildings on nearby Stony Lane, which leads to the town's gargantuan **parish church of St John the Baptist**, completed in 1500, its landmark spire reaching 181ft. Gustav Holst (1874–1934) was organist here during his twelve-year stay in Thaxted and it was then that he wrote much of *The Planets* as well as initiating the town's annual music festival, held from mid-June to mid-July (call ☎01371/831421 for details). Head down Mill Lane from the church's west door, past a neat little row of almshouses, to Thaxted's other principal sight, its **windmill** (May–Sept Sat & Sun 2–6pm; £1), which has been restored to full working order, though it hasn't ground flour since 1907.

There's a reasonably regular **bus** service from Saffron Walden to Thaxted (not Sun).

Newmarket

NEWMARKET, thirteen miles east of Cambridge, on springy heathland just over the county border in Suffolk, is famous for just one thing – **horse-racing**. According to legend, Boudicca's Iceni were keen on Ben-Hur style chariot-racing, but history gives James I the honour of founding modern horse-racing here. James may have started it off, but Charles II brought the sport to prominence, visiting twice a year and bringing the entire royal court – and Nell Gwyn – with him. Two of the country's five flat-racing classics are held at Newmarket, the One Thousand Guineas and the Two Thousand Guineas, both held early in the season, which runs from the middle of April to October.

Coming in from Cambridge, you'll pass the Rowley Mile Racecourse, named after one of Charles's own steeds. This, as well as the other approach roads, are flanked by bridleways, and in the morning dozens of racehorses exercise along them. Newmarket itself is a one-horse town, with the Georgian Jockey Club, founded in 1752, occupying pride of place on the High Street. Next door is the **National Horse Racing Museum** (April–June, Sept & Oct Tues–Sun 10am–5pm; July & Aug daily 10am–5pm; £4.50), telling you more than you'll ever want to know about the sport. It also offers a variety of guided tours, including trips to the equine pool, a stud and a couple of horse-training yards (for further details, call ☎01638/667333, ⊛www.nhrm.co.uk). There are also tours of the prestigious National Stud, a couple of miles southwest of town at the junction of the A1304 and A1303 (March–Sept 1–2 daily; £4.50; reservations on ☎01638/666789).

Several **buses** make the half-hour journey to town from Cambridge and there's also a regular **train** service.

Travel details

Buses

For information on all local and national bus services, contact Traveline: ☎ 0870/608 2 608 (daily 7am–9pm), ⊛www.traveline.org.uk.

Trains

For information on all local and national rail services, contact National Rail Enquiries: ☎ 08457/48 49 50, ⊛www.rail.co.uk.

Cambridge to: Audley End (2 hourly; 15min); Birmingham (hourly; 2hr 50min); Bury St Edmunds (8 daily; 40min); Ely (hourly; 15min); Ipswich (6 daily; 1hr 20min); King's Lynn (hourly; 45min); Leicester (hourly; 1hr 50min); London (2 hourly; 1hr); Newmarket (8 daily; 20min); Norwich (hourly; 1hr); Peterborough (hourly; 50min); Stansted (10 daily; 40min); Thetford (hourly; 20–30min).

Colchester to: Clacton-on-Sea (hourly; 40min); Ipswich (2 hourly; 25min); London (2 hourly; 50min); Norwich (hourly; 1hr).

Ely to: King's Lynn (hourly; 30min); Liverpool (hourly 4hr 30min); Manchester (hourly; 3hr 30min); Nottingham (hourly 1hr 45min); Peterborough (hourly; 30min); Thetford (hourly; 30min).

Ipswich to: Bury St Edmunds (10 daily; 30min); Ely (7 daily; 1hr); Felixstowe (every 1–2hr; 25min);

London (2 hourly; 1hr 10min); Lowestoft (every 1–2hr; 1hr 30min); Norwich (hourly; 45min); Peterborough (7 daily; 1hr 50min); Woodbridge (every 1–2hr; 15min).

Norwich to: Ely (hourly; 50min); Cromer (every 1–2hr; 50min); Great Yarmouth (hourly; 30min); Liverpool (hourly; 5hr 30min); London (hourly; 2hr); Lowestoft (hourly; 30–45min); Manchester (hourly; 4hr 30min); Nottingham (hourly; 2hr 30min); Peterborough (hourly; 1hr 30min); Sheringham (every 1–2hr; 1hr); Thetford (hourly; 30min).

Peterborough to: Bury St Edmunds (6 daily; 1hr); Cambridge (hourly; 50min); Liverpool (hourly; 4hr); London (2 hourly; 1hr); Manchester (hourly; 3hr); Norwich (hourly; 1hr 30min); Nottingham (hourly; 1hr 10min).

The West Midlands and the Peak District

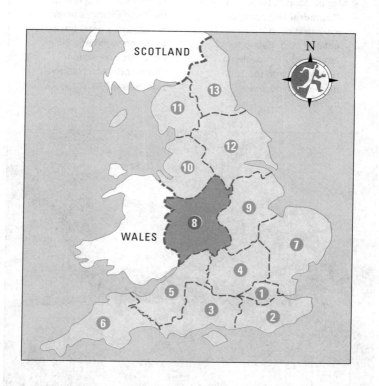

* **The theatres, Stratford-upon-Avon** *The* place to see Shakespeare's plays, performed by the world-renowned Royal Shakespeare Company. See p.611

* **Mappa Mundi, Hereford Cathedral** The complex iconography of this antique map, dating to around 1300, provides a real insight into the medieval mind. See p.625

* **Ironbridge Gorge** The first iron bridge ever to be constructed is the showpiece here: arching high above the River Severn. See p.635

* **Fischer's Hotel, Baslow** *Fischer's Hotel* is one of the Peak District's finest hotels and a great base for some wonderful hiking as well as visits to Chatsworth and Haddon Hall. See p.678

The West Midlands and the Peak District

T he factories of the **West Midlands** were the powerhouses of the Industrial Revolution and **Birmingham**, Britain's second city, was once the world's greatest industrial metropolis. Long saddled with a reputation as a culture-hating, car-loving backwater, Birmingham has redefined its image in recent years, initiating some ambitious architectural and environmental schemes, jazzing up its museums and industrial heritage sites and giving itself a higher profile on the nation's cultural map than it's ever had before. It's not an especially good-looking city, it must be admitted, but it does hold several excellent attractions and it's certainly lively, with nightlife encompassing everything from Royal Ballet productions to all-night raves, and a great spread of restaurants and pubs in between. To some extent change was forced on Birmingham by the decline in its manufacturing base – it lost over a third of its manufacturing jobs between 1974 and 1983 – but things were even worse in the **Black Country**, that knot of industrial towns clinging to the western side of the city. This area has found it difficult to re-route itself through the maze of post-industrialization and more amply fulfils the negative stereotypes once attached to Birmingham. Nonetheless, even here you'll find a few pleasant surprises, in the shape of several excellent museums and galleries.

The counties to the south and west of Birmingham and beyond the Black Country – Warwickshire, Worcestershire, Herefordshire and Shropshire – comprise a rural stronghold that maintains an emotional and political distance from the conurbation. The left-wing politics of the big city seem remote indeed when you're in Shrewsbury, but in fact it's only seventy miles from the big city.

Accommodation price codes

Throughout this guide, hotel and B&B accommodation is priced on a scale of ❶ to ❾, the number indicating the **lowest price** you could expect to pay per night in that establishment for a **double room** in high season. The prices indicated by the codes are as follows:

❶ under £40	❹ £60–70	❼ £110–150
❷ £40–50	❺ £70–90	❽ £150–200
❸ £50–60	❻ £90–110	❾ over £200

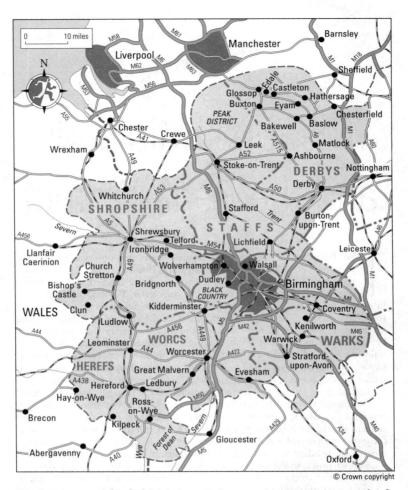

© Crown copyright

For the most part, the four counties constitute a quiet, unassuming stretch of pastoral England whose beauty is rarely dramatic, but whose charms become more evident the longer you stay. Of the four counties, **Warwickshire** is the least obviously scenic, but draws by far the largest number of visitors, for – as the road-signs declare at every entry point – this is "Shakespeare Country". The prime target is, of course, **Stratford-upon-Avon**, with its handful of Shakespeare-related sites and world-class theatre, but spare time also for the diverting town of **Warwick**, which has a superb church and a whopping castle, and the magnificent modernity of **Coventry cathedral**.

Neighbouring **Worcestershire**, which stretches southwest from the urban fringes of the West Midlands, holds two principal places of interest, **Worcester**, which is graced by a mighty cathedral, and **Great Malvern**, a mannered inland resort spread along the rolling contours of the **Malvern Hills** – prime walking territory. From here, it's west again for **Herefordshire**, a large and sparsely populated county that's home to several charming market towns, most notably picture-postcard **Ledbury** and **Hay-on-Wye**; the latter has the largest concentration of second-hand bookshops in the world. There's also **Hereford**, where the remarkable medieval Mappa Mundi map is displayed, and pocket-sized **Ross-on-Wye**, which is within easy striking distance of an especially scenic stretch of the **Wye River Valley**. Next door, to the north, rural **Shropshire** weighs in with **Ludlow**, one of the region's prettiest towns, awash with antique half-timbered buildings, and the amiable county town of **Shrewsbury**, which is also close to the hiking trails of the **Long Mynd**. Shropshire has a fascinating industrial history, too, for it was here in the **Ironbridge Gorge** that British industrialists built the world's first iron bridge and pioneered the use of coal as a smelting fuel. These were two key events in the Industrial Revolution and, appropriately, the Gorge's industrial heyday is recalled by a phalanx of first-rate museums.

To the east of Shropshire, sprawling north of the Birmingham conurbation, is **Staffordshire**, where **Lichfield** makes a good hand of its links with **Samuel Johnson**, while **Stoke-on-Trent** remembers the good times, when its potteries dominated the world market, in an excellent museum and several heritage sites – and factory shops. Beyond lies **Derbyshire**, whose northern reaches incorporate the region's finest scenery in the rough landscapes of the **Peak District National Park**. The latter offers great opportunities for moderately strenuous walks, as well as the diversions of the former spa town of **Buxton**, the limestone caverns of **Castleton** and the so-called "Plague Village" of **Eyam**. In addition, there's the grandiose stately pile of **Chatsworth House** and **Haddon Hall**, an exceptionally fascinating old manor house.

Birmingham, the region's public transport hub, is easily accessible by **train** from London Euston, Liverpool, Manchester, Leeds, York and a score of other towns. It is also well served by the National Express **bus** network, with dozens of buses leaving every hour for destinations all over Britain. Local **bus** services are excellent around the West Midlands conurbation and very good in the Peak District, but fade away badly in amongst the villages of Herefordshire and Shropshire.

Stratford-upon-Avon and around

Despite its worldwide fame, **STRATFORD-UPON-AVON** is, at heart, an unassuming market town with an unexceptional pedigree. Its first settlers forded, and later bridged, the River Avon, and developed commercial links with the farmers who tilled the surrounding flatlands. A charter for Stratford's weekly market was granted in the twelfth century, a tradition continued to this day, and the town later became an important stopping-off point for stagecoaches between London, Oxford and the north. Like all such places, Stratford had its clearly defined class system and within this typical milieu John and Mary **Shakespeare** occupied the middle rank, and would have been forgotten long ago had their first son, **William**, not turned out one of the greatest writers ever to use the English language. A consequence of their good fortune is that this ordinary little place is nowadays all but smothered by package-tourist hype and its central streets groan under the weight of thousands of tourists. Don't let that deter you: dodging the multitudes is possible by avoiding the busiest attractions – principally the Birthplace Museum – and the **Royal Shakespeare Company** offers superb theatre. Moreover, Stratford still has the ability to surprise and delight, whether in the excellence of some of its restaurants or by the gentle river views beside the lovely **Holy Trinity Church**. It is also within easy striking distance of two country houses dating back to Tudor times – **Charlecote Park** and **Coughton Court**.

Arrival and information

Stratford's **train station** is on the northwestern edge of town, ten minutes' walk from the centre. Now the end of the line, it receives hourly services from Birmingham (Moor Street and Snow Hill stations) and frequent trains from Warwick (for connections to London Paddington and London Marylebone) except on Sundays, when there are only a couple of services all day. Local **bus services** arrive and depart from the central Bridge Street; National Express services and most other long-distance and regional buses pull into the Riverside station on the east side of the town centre, off Bridgeway.

The **tourist office** (April–Oct Mon–Sat 9am–6pm, Sun 11am–5pm; Nov–March Mon–Sat 9am–5pm, Sun 11am–4pm; ☎01789/293127, ⓦwww.shakespeare-country.co.uk) is located a couple of minutes' walk from the bus station by the bridge at the junction of Bridgeway and Bridgefoot. They have oodles of information on local attractions and operate an accommodation-booking service (see below), which is very useful during the height of the summer when rooms can be in very short supply. It also issues bus timetables and sells bus tickets. General tourist information is available from the Guide Friday office in the centre at 14 Rother St (☎01789/299866), but they basically exist to flog tickets for their bus tours of the town and environs (£8.50, excluding admission to properties). The tourist office will sell you an all-in ticket for all five **Shakespeare Birthplace Trust** properties (£12), or a

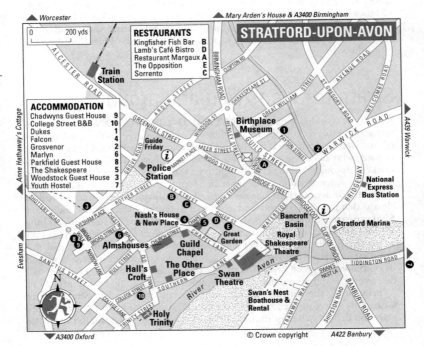

RESTAURANTS
Kingfisher Fish Bar   B
Lamb's Café Bistro   D
Restaurant Margaux   A
The Opposition   E
Sorrento   C

STRATFORD-UPON-AVON

ACCOMMODATION
Chadwyns Guest House   9
College Street B&B   10
Dukes   1
Falcon   4
Grosvenor   2
Marlyn   6
Parkfield Guest House   8
The Shakespeare   5
Woodstock Guest House   3
Youth Hostel   7

© Crown copyright

Three In-Town Shakespeare Property Ticket (£8.50) for the three Trust properties in Stratford – both tickets are also available from each of the sites themselves.

Accommodation

As one of the most popular tourist destinations in England, Stratford's **accommodation** is a tad pricey and gets booked up well in advance. In peak months, and during the Shakespeare birthday celebrations around April 23, it's essential to book ahead. The town has a couple of dozen **hotels**, the pick of which occupy old half-timbered buildings right in the centre of town, but most visitors choose to stay in a **B&B**. These have sprung up in every part of Stratford, but there's a particular concentration to the southwest of the centre around Grove Road, Evesham Place and Broad Walk. The tourist office operates an efficient and extremely useful **Accommodation Booking Hotline** (Mon–Fri 9.30am–4.30pm; ☎01789/415061; £3).

Hotels

Dukes Payton St ☎01789/269300, ⊛www .dukeshotel.co.uk. On the north side of the town centre, a couple of minutes' walk from the Birthplace Museum, this comfortable, privately owned hotel has a pleasant interior dotted with antiques. ❹

Falcon Chapel St ☎01789/279953. Handily situated in the middle of town, this place has a half-timbered facade dating from the sixteenth century, though the rest is an unremarkable modern rebuild. ❺

Grosvenor Warwick Rd ☎01789/269213. Close to the canal, just a couple of minutes' walk from the town centre, the Grosvenor occupies a row of pleasant, two-storey Georgian houses. The interior is crisp and modern and there's ample parking at the back. Discounted short break deals available. ❻

Marlyn 3 Chestnut Walk ☎01789/293752. In a pleasant two-storey brick house with sash windows, this small hotel is good value and has comfortable rooms. Convenient for the town centre, too. ❸

The Shakespeare Chapel St ☎0870/4008182. Right in the centre of town. Now part of a chain, this old hotel, with its mullion windows and half-timbered facade, is one of Stratford's best known. The interior has low beams and open fires and represents a fairly successful amalgamation of the old and new. ❼

Guest Houses and B&Bs

Chadwyns Guest House 6 Broad Walk ☎01789 /269077, ⊛www.chadwyns.freeserve.co.uk. Just off Evesham Place, this well-maintained, most agreeable guest house occupies pleasant Victorian premises and offers seven en-suite rooms. Great breakfasts with vegetarian options. ❷

College Street B&B 32 College St ☎01789 /266784. Handy location, just west of the centre, for this friendly B&B, which has two bright and cheerful, en-suite guest rooms. No cards. ❷

Parkfield Guest House 3 Broad Walk ☎01789/293313, ✉parkfiel@btinternet.com. Very pleasant B&B in a rambling Victorian house in a residential street off Evesham Place. There's a private car park – a useful facility in crowded Stratford – and most rooms are en suite. Under ten minutes' walk from the centre. ❷

Woodstock Guest House 30 Grove Rd ☎01789/299881, ✉woodstockhouse@compuserve.com. A smart and neatly kept B&B ten minutes' walk from the centre, by the start of the path to Anne Hathaway's Cottage. It has five extremely comfortable bedrooms, all en suite. No credit cards. ❷

Hostels and camping

Stratford-upon-Avon Youth Hostel Hemmingford House, Alveston ☎01789/297093, ✉stratford@yha.org.uk. This hostel occupies a rambling Georgian mansion on the edge of the pretty village of Alveston. There are dormitories and family rooms, some of which are en suite. Laundry, internet-access, self-catering facilities and evening meals, too. It's located two miles east of the town centre on the B4086 and served by regular bus from Stratford's Riverside bus station. Open all year. £15.50.

Stratford Racecourse Camp Site Luddington Rd ☎01789/267949. Well-equipped camping and caravan site one mile southwest of the town centre. Regular buses into town (not Sun). Closed Oct–March. Tent pitches from £4, caravans from £6.

The Town

Spreading back from the River Avon, Stratford's **town centre** is fairly flat and compact, its mostly modern buildings filling out a simple gridiron just two blocks deep and four blocks long. Running along the northern edge of the centre is **Bridge Street**, the main thoroughfare lined with shops and chock-a-block with local buses. At its west end, Bridge Street divides into Henley Street, home of the **Birthplace Museum**, and Wood Street, which leads up to the market place. It also intersects with High Street. This, and its continuation Chapel and Church streets, cuts south to pass most of the old buildings that the town still possesses, most notably **Nash's House** and, on neighbouring Old Town Street, **Hall's Croft**. From here, it's a short hop to the charming **Holy Trinity Church**, where Shakespeare lies buried, and then only a few minutes back along the river past the **theatres** to the foot of Bridge Street. In itself, this circular walk only takes about fifteen minutes, but it takes all day if you potter around the attractions. In addition, there are two outlying Shakespearean properties, **Anne Hathaway's Cottage** in Shottery and **Mary Arden's House** in

Shakespeare: What's in a name?

Over the past hundred years or so, the deification of **William Shakespeare** (1564–1616) has been dogged by a loony backlash among a fringe of revisionist scholars and literary figures known as **"Anti-Stratfordians"**. According to these heretics, the famous plays and sonnets were not written by a wool merchant's son from Stratford at all, but by someone else, and William Shakespeare was merely a *nom de plume*. The American novelist Henry James, among the most notorious arch-sceptics, once claimed that he was "haunted by the conviction that the divine William is the biggest and most successful fraud ever practised on a patient world."

A variety of candidates have been proposed for the authorship of Shakespeare's works, and they range from the faintly plausible (Christopher Marlowe, Ben Jonson, and the Earls of Rutland, Southampton and Oxford) to the manifestly whacko (Queen Elizabeth I, King James I and Daniel Defoe, author of *Robinson Crusoe*, who was born six years after publication of the first Folio). The wildest theories, however, have been reserved for **Francis Bacon**. In his book *The Great Cryptogram*, American congressman Ignatius Donnelly postulates that the word "honorificabilitudinitatibus", which crops up in *Love's Labours Lost*, was actually an anagram for the Latin "Hi ludi F Baconis nati tuiti orbi" ("These plays, F. Bacon's offspring, are preserved for the world"). Others have rallied around the Earl of Oxford's banner; Sigmund Freud maintained that Oxford wrote the plays, and Orson Welles agreed, saying that otherwise there were "... some awfully funny coincidences to explain away".

Lying at the root of the authorship debate are several **unresolved questions** that have puzzled scholars for years. How could a man of modest background from the provinces have such an intimate knowledge of royal protocol? How could he know so much about Italy without ever having travelled there? Why was he allowed to write potentially embarrassing love poems to one of England's most powerful aristocrats? Why did he not leave a library in his will, when the author of the plays clearly possessed an intimate knowledge of classical literature? And why, given that Shakespeare was supposedly a well-known dramatist, did no death notice or obituary appear in publications of the day?

The speculation surrounding Shakespeare's work stems from the lack of definite information about his life. The few details that have been preserved come mostly from official archives – birth, marriage and death certificates and court records. From these we know that on April 22 or 23, 1564, a certain John Shakespeare, var-

Wilmcote – though you have to be a really serious sightseer to want to see them all.

The Birthplace Museum

Top of everyone's Bardic itinerary is the **Birthplace Museum** (late March to mid-Oct Mon–Sat 9am–5pm, Sun 9.30am–5pm; mid-Oct to late March Mon–Sat 9.30am–4pm, Sun 10am–4pm; £6), comprising an ugly modern visitor centre attached to the heavily restored half-timbered building on Henley Street where the great man was born. The visitor centre pokes into every corner of Shakespeare's life and times, making the most of what little hard evidence there is. His will is interesting in so far as he passed all sorts of goodies to his daughter, but precious little to his wife – the museum commentary tries to gainsay this apparent meanness, but fails to convince. Next door, the half-timbered dwelling is actually two buildings knocked into one. The northern half, now fitted out in the style of a sixteenth-century domestic interior, was the business premises of the poet's father, who is thought to have worked as a glover, though some argue that he was a wool merchant or a butcher. Neither

iously described as a glove-maker, butcher, wool merchant and corn trader, and his wife, Mary, had their first son, William. We also know that the boy attended a local grammar school until financial problems forced him into his father's business, and that, at the age of 18, he married a local woman, **Anne Hathaway**, seven years his senior, who five months later bore a daughter, Susanna, the first of three children. Several years later, probably around 1587, the young Shakespeare was forced to flee Stratford after being caught poaching on the estate of Sir Thomas Lucy at nearby Charlecote (see p.613). Five companies of players passed through the town on tour that year, and it is believed he **absconded** with one of them to London, where a theatre boom was in full swing. *Henry VI*, Shakespeare's first play, appeared soon after, followed by the hugely successful *Richard III*. Over the next decade, Shakespeare's output was prodigious. Thirty-eight plays appeared, most of them performed by his own theatre troupes based in the **Globe**, a large timber-framed theatre overlooking the south bank of the River Thames, in which he had a one-tenth share.

Success secured Shakespeare the patronage of London's fashionable set, among them the dashing young courtier, Henry Wriothesley, Earl of Southampton, with whom the playwright is believed to have had a passionate affair (Southampton is thought to have been the "golden youth" of the Sonnets). The ageing Queen Elizabeth I, bewigged and decked in opulent jewellery, regularly attended the Globe, as did her successor, James I, whose Scottish ancestry and fascination with the occult partly explain the subject matter of *Macbeth* – Shakespeare knew the commercial value of appealing to the rich and powerful. This, as much as his extraordinary talent, ensured his plays were the most acclaimed of the day, earning him enough money to **retire** comfortably to Stratford, where he largely abandoned literature in the last years of his life to concentrate on business and family affairs.

Ultimately, the sketchy details of Shakespeare's life are of far less importance than the plays, sonnets and songs he left behind. Whoever wrote them – and despite all the conjecture, William Shakespeare almost certainly did – the body of work attributed to this shadowy historical figure comprises some of the most inspired and exquisite English ever written. The greatest irony is not that *King Lear* and *The Tempest* were penned by a provincial middle-class merchant's son, but that of all the millions of visitors who pass through Stratford each year, the majority appear to be more interested in the writer himself than in what he wrote.

is it certain that Shakespeare was born in this building nor that he was born on April 23, 1564 – it's just known that he was baptized on April 26, and it's an irresistible temptation to place the birth of the national poet three days earlier, on St George's Day. However, both suppositions are now treated as fact at this shrine, where the south half of the building – bought by John Shakespeare in 1556 – displays a modest range of period artefacts designed to illuminate a life which remains distinctly enigmatic.

Nash's House and New Place

Follow the High Street south from the junction of Bridge and Henley streets, and you'll soon come to another Birthplace Trust property, **Nash's House** on Chapel Street (late March to mid-Oct Mon–Sat 9.30am–5pm, Sun 10am–5pm; mid-Oct to late March Mon–Sat 10am–4pm, Sun 10.30am–4pm; £3.50, includes entry to New Place). The house was the property of Thomas Nash, first husband of Shakespeare's granddaughter, Elizabeth Hall. The ground floor is kitted out with a pleasant assortment of period furnishings and upstairs has more of the same, plus a competent potted biography of Shakespeare. The adjacent gardens contain the bare foundations of **New Place** (same hours), Shakespeare's last residence, which was demolished in 1759 by its owner, the Reverend Francis Gastrell, during a bitter dispute with the town council over taxation. Gastrell also chopped down the mulberry tree that Shakespeare was reputed to have planted in the garden, but for different reasons – he was fed up with all the pilgrims. An enterprising woodcarver bought the wood and carved Shakespearean mementoes from it and there's a cabinet of these upstairs in the house. A replacement mulberry tree has been planted beside the house and there are others in the adjacent **Great Garden** (March–Oct Mon–Sat 9am–dusk, Sun 10am–dusk; Nov–Feb Mon–Fri 9am–4pm, Sun noon–4pm; free), a formal affair of topiary, lawns and flowerbeds. A path leads into the Great Garden from New Place, but the main entrance is on Chapel Lane. One of the mulberries – it's got a plaque – was planted by Peggy Ashcroft.

On the other side of Chapel Lane stands the **Guild Chapel**, whose chunky tower and sturdy stonework shelter a plain interior enlivened by some rather crude stained-glass windows and a faded mural above the triumphal arch. The adjoining King Edward VI **Grammar School**, where it's assumed Shakespeare was educated, incorporates a creaky line of fifteenth-century almshouses running along Church Street.

Hall's Croft

Chapel Street continues south as Church Street. At the end, turn left along Old Town Street for Stratford's most impressive medieval house, the Birthplace Trust's **Hall's Croft** (late March to mid-Oct Mon–Sat 9.30am–5pm, Sun 10am–5pm; mid-Oct to late March Mon–Sat 10am–4pm, Sun 10.30am–4pm; £3.50). The former home of Shakespeare's elder daughter, Susanna, and her doctor husband, John Hall, the immaculately maintained Croft, with its creaking wooden floors, beamed ceilings and fine kitchen range, holds a scattering of period furniture and a fascinating display on Elizabethan medicine. Hall established something of a reputation for his medical know-how and after his death some of his case notes were published in a volume entitled *Select Observations on English Bodies*. You can peruse extracts from Hall's book – noting that Joan Chidkin of Southam "gave two vomits and two stools" after being "troubled with trembling of the arms and thighs" – and then suffer vicariously at the displays of eye-watering forceps and other implements. The best view of the building itself is at the back, in the neat walled garden.

Holy Trinity Church

Beyond Hall's Croft, Old Town Street steers right to reach the handsome **Holy Trinity Church** (March–Oct Mon–Sat 8.30am–6pm, Sun 2–5pm; Nov–Feb Mon–Sat 9am–4pm, Sun 2–5pm; free), whose mellow, honey-coloured stonework dates from the thirteenth century. Enhanced by its riverside setting and flanked by the yews and weeping willows of its graveyard, the dignified proportions of this quintessentially English church are the result of several centuries of chopping and changing, culminating in the replacement of the original wooden spire with today's stone version in 1763. At the entrance, on the second set of doors, the **Sanctuary Knocker** is a reminder of medieval times when local criminals could seek refuge from the law here, but only for thirty-seven days. This, so local custom dictated, was long enough for them to negotiate a deal with their persecutors. Inside, the nave is bathed in light from the **stained glass windows,** some of which (predominantly along the south aisle) date from the fourteenth century. Quite unusually, you'll see that the nave is built on a slight skew from the line of the chancel – supposedly to represent Christ's inclined head on the cross. In the north aisle, beside the transept, is the **Clopton Chapel**, where the tomb of George Carew is a superbly carved Renaissance extravagance decorated with military insignia appropriate to George's job as master in ordnance to James I. But poor old George is long forgotten, unlike William Shakespeare, who lies buried in the **chancel** (£1), his remains overseen by a sedate and studious memorial plaque and effigy added just seven years after his death.

The theatres and the Gower Memorial

Doubling back from the church, turn right along Southern Lane and its continuation, Waterside, home to the town's three Royal Shakespeare Company **theatres** – The Other Place, the Swan Theatre and the Royal Shakespeare Theatre. There was no theatre in Stratford in Shakespeare's day and indeed the first home-town festival in his honour was only held in 1769 at the behest of London-based David Garrick. Thereafter, the idea of building a permanent home in which to perform Shakespeare's works slowly gained momentum, and finally, in 1879, the first Memorial Theatre was opened on land donated by local beer baron Charles Flower. A fire in 1926 necessitated the construction of a new theatre, and the ensuing architectural competition was won by Elisabeth

Tickets for the RSC

As the Royal Shakespeare Company works on a repertory system, you could stay in Stratford for a few days and see four or five different plays. Tickets for the **Royal Shakespeare Theatre** start at around £5 for standing room and a restricted view, rising to £40 for the best seats in the house. However, very popular shows get booked up months in advance. **Swan** tickets are generally between £5 and £36, with tickets for **The Other Place** hovering between £10 and £20.

The RSC's **box office** (Mon–Sat from 9am; ☎01789/403403) serves as the central booking agent for all three houses, although you collect your tickets from the theatre in question. At the Royal Shakespeare Theatre, twenty tickets are kept back for that evening's performance and sold at between £10 and £20 each; for a real blockbuster, arriving to queue at 5am will not be too early. Stand-by tickets (for unsold seats) are also available on the day of performance, but only concessionary groups (OAPs, students, etc) are eligible. If all else fails, turn up about an hour before the performance and try your luck – though last-minute **returns** are quite rare. For more **information**, call ☎01789/403404 or check ⊛www.rsc.org.uk.

Scott. Her theatre is today's **Royal Shakespeare Theatre**. In the 1980s, the burnt-out original theatre round the back was turned into a replica "in-the-round" Elizabethan stage – the **Swan**; it's used for works by Shakespeare's contemporaries, classics from all eras and one annual piece by the man himself. The third auditorium, **The Other Place**, showcases modern and experimental pieces. The RSC also organizes a number of behind-the-scenes tours – ask at the box office for details.

Next to the Royal Shakespeare Theatre, the manicured lawns of a small riverside park stretch north as far as **Bancroft Basin**, where the Stratford canal meets the river. The basin is usually packed with narrowboats and in the parklet on the far side, over the little hump-backed pedestrian bridge, is the finely sculpted **Gower Memorial** of 1888 in which a seated Shakespeare is surrounded by figures from his plays.

Anne Hathaway's Cottage and Mary Arden's House

Anne Hathaway's Cottage (late March to mid-Oct Mon–Sat 9am–5pm, Sun 9.30am–5pm; late Oct to mid-March Mon–Sat 9.30am–4pm, Sun 10am–4pm; £4.50), also operated by the Birthplace Trust, is located just over a mile west of the town centre in Shottery. The most agreeable way to get there is on the signposted footpath from Evesham Place, at the south end of Rother Street. The cottage, complete with its dinky wooden beams and thatching, was the home of Anne Hathaway before she married Shakespeare in 1582. A few yards away, the **Shakespeare Tree Garden** has a patch that is planted with species mentioned in the plays.

The Birthplace Trust also keeps **Mary Arden's House**, three miles northwest of the town centre in **Wilmcote** (late March to mid-Oct Mon–Sat 9.30am–5pm, Sun 10am–5pm; late Oct to mid-March Mon–Sat 10am–4pm, Sun 10.30am–4pm; £5.50). Mary Arden was Shakespeare's mother, the only unmarried daughter when her father, Robert, died in 1556. Unusually for the time, she inherited the house and land, thus becoming one of the neighbourhood's most eligible women – John Shakespeare, eager for self-improvement, married her within a year. The house is a well-furnished example of an Elizabethan farmhouse and, though the labelling is rather scant, a platoon of guides fills in the details of family life and traditions.

Eating and drinking

Stratford is used to feeding and watering thousands of visitors, so finding refreshment is never difficult. The problem is that many places are geared to serving the day-tripper as rapidly as possible – not a recipe for much gastronomic delight. That said, there is a scattering of very good **restaurants**, several of which have been catering to theatre-goers for many years, and a handful of **pubs** and **cafés** offering good food, too. The best restaurants are concentrated along Sheep Street, running up from Waterside near the theatres.

Restaurants and cafés

Kingfisher Fish Bar 13 Ely St. The best fish-and-chip shop in town. A five-minute walk from the theatres. Take out only. Closed Sun.

Lamb's Café Bistro 12 Sheep St ☎01789 /292554. Smart restaurant serving a mouth-watering range of stylish English and continental dishes.

A good option for pasta lovers. Moderate.

Restaurant Margaux 6 Union St ☎01789/269106. Smart and intimate restaurant serving top-quality seafood and meat dishes with a Mediterranean slant. Expensive.

The Opposition 13 Sheep St ☎01789/269980. Top-quality, imaginative international cuisine in a busy but amiable atmosphere. The dishes of the day, chalked up on a board inside, are excellent value. Moderate.

Sorrento 8 Ely St ☎01789/297999. Classy Italian restaurant offering great pizzas, pastas along with meat and seafood. Closed Sun. Moderate.

Pubs

Dirty Duck 53 Waterside. The archetypal actors' pub, stuffed to the gunwales every night with a vocal entourage of RSC employees and hangers-on. Essential viewing.

The Garrick Inn 25 High St. Arguably the town's most photogenic and best-preserved old ale house: exposed beams, real ales and good food.

Windmill Inn Church St. Popular pub of cosy little rooms with low-beamed ceilings. A good range of beers, too.

Listings

Banks and exchanges There are lots of banks in the town centre and all of them will change foreign currency and travellers' cheques. Lloyds are at 22 Bridge St; HSBC at 13 Chapel St.
Bike rental Pashley Cycles, 3 Guild St ☎01789/205057.
Boat rental and cruises Avon Boating, Swan's Nest Boathouse, Swan's Nest Lane ☎01789/267073, ⊛www.avon-boating.co.uk (Easter–Oct 10am to dusk; cruises £3/person).
Books Waterstones, 18 High Street ☎01789/414418.
Buses Stagecoach Midland Red ☎0870/6082608; Stratford Blue Buses ☎01789/292085; West Midlands Centro Hotline ☎024/76559559.

Car rental Hertz, at the train station ☎01789/298827; Marbella, 1 Central Chambers, Henley St ☎01789/268002.
Hospital Stratford-upon-Avon Hospital, Arden St ☎01789/205831.
Laundry Sparklean, 74 Bull St, off Old Town ☎01789/269075.
Pharmacy Boots, 11 Bridge St ☎01789/292173 (Mon–Sat 9am–5.30pm; late opening rosta posted on the door).
Police Rother Street near the junction with Ely Street ☎01789/414111.
Post office Henley Street (Mon–Fri 9am–5.30pm, Sat 9am–6pm)
Taxis Stratford Taxis ☎01789/415888.

Around Stratford: Charlecote Park and Coughton Court

Some five miles east of Stratford off the B4086, **Charlecote Park house** (late March to June, Sept & Oct Mon, Tues & Fri–Sun noon–5pm; July & Aug also Wed noon–5pm; £5.60; NT) is an ornate Elizabethan mansion at the heart of an expansive country estate. The house, refurbished in a rather heavy Victorian interpretation of Elizabethan style, is awash with souvenirs of the British empire, paintings of the estate and portraits of the Lucy family, who have lived here since 1247. An exploration takes a good hour and afterwards you can stroll the formal **gardens**, which feature borders of plants and flowers from Shakespeare's plays as well as a croquet lawn – you can rent equipment at the house. The gardens are a preamble to the surrounding deer **park** (late March to June, Sept & Oct Mon, Tues & Fri–Sun 11am–6pm; July & Aug also Wed 11am–6pm; Feb to mid-March Sat & Sun 11am–6pm; £3) watered by the rivers Avon and Dene and providing wide views over the Warwickshire countryside. Grazing the estate are herds of fallow deer, whose ancestors are supposed to have been poached by the young William Shakespeare. Stagecoach Midland Red **buses** #18 and #X18 run to Charlecote village on the edge of the park (not Sun).

Coughton Court (late March & Oct Sat & Sun 11.30am–5pm; April–July & Sept Wed–Sun 11.30am–5pm; Aug Tues–Sun 11.30am–5pm; hours may vary, call to check ☎01789/762435; £6.95, grounds only £5.10; NT), one of the region's finest Tudor houses, is located about nine miles west of Stratford via the A46 and the A435. It boasts a particularly impressive central gatehouse, equipped with dinky turrets and a multitude of mullioned windows, and a courtyard framed by charming half-timbered houses. The Throckmortons have lived here since the beginning of the fifteenth century and now manage the property in conjunction with the National Trust. Traditionally a Catholic family, their religious beliefs have often brought them close to ruin, most dangerously when a mob burnt down part of Coughton in 1688. They were also entangled with the Gunpowder Plot of 1605 and there's a display on this alongside a large collection of antique furnishings and porcelain. The grounds offer a walled garden, a lake and gentle riverside walks.

Warwick and around

WARWICK, just eight miles northeast of Stratford and easily reached by bus and train, is famous for its massive castle, but it also possesses several charming streetscapes erected in the aftermath of a great fire in 1694, as well as an especially fine church chancel. An hour or two is quite enough time to nose around the compact town centre, but you'll need the whole day if, braving the crowds, you're also set on exploring the castle. Either way, Warwick is the perfect day-trip from Stratford, though you may well decide to stay here if you plan to visit the sprawling ruins of nearby **Kenilworth** castle and maybe drop by Coventry (see p.616) to see its magnificent cathedral, too.

The Town

Towering above the River Avon at the foot of the town centre, **Warwick Castle** (daily: April–Oct 10am–6pm; Nov–March 10am–5pm; £11.50) is locally proclaimed the "greatest medieval castle in Britain" and, if bulk equals greatness, then the claim is certainly valid, although much of the existing structure is the result of extensive nineteenth-century restoration. It's likely that the first fortress here was raised by Ethelfleda, daughter of Alfred the Great, in about 915 AD, but things really took off with the Normans, who built a large motte and bailey towards the end of the eleventh century. Almost three hundred years later, the eleventh Earl of Warwick turned the stronghold into a formidable stone castle, complete with elaborate gatehouses, multiple turrets and a keep. The earl and his descendants played a prominent part in the Hundred Years War. One of their number was the executioner of Joan of Arc and they all brought prisoners back to Warwick and incarcerated them in the dingy dungeons of Caesar's Tower pending ransom negotiations.

The **entrance** to the castle is through the old stable block, beyond which a footpath leads round to the imposing east gate. Over the footbridge – and beyond the protective towers – is the main courtyard. You can stroll along the ramparts and climb the towers, but most visitors head straight for one or other of the special displays installed inside by the present owners, Madame Tussauds. The most popular of these displays is the "Royal Weekend Party, 1898", an extravaganza of waxwork nobility hobnobbing in the private apartments which were rebuilt in the 1870s after fire damage. Another display, "Kingmaker – a preparation for Battle", adds smells and atmospheric sounds to a waxwork scene of the preparations for Richard Earl of Warwick's – as in "Warwick the Kingmaker" – final battle in 1471.

Re-emerging from the castle at the stables, Castle Street leads up the hill for a few yards to its junction with the High Street. Turn left and it's a brief stroll to another outstanding building, the **Lord Leycester Hospital** (June–Sept Tues–Sun 10am–5pm; Oct–May Tues–Sun 10am–4pm; £3), a tangle of half-

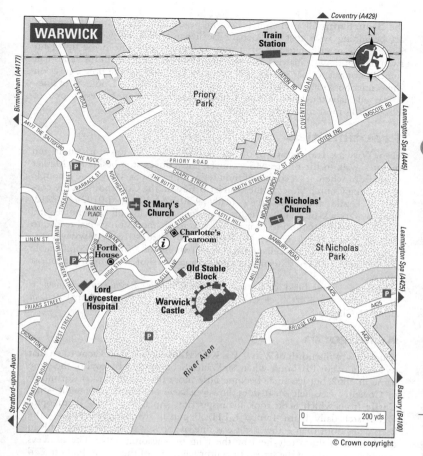

Coventry (A429)

Birmingham (A4177)

A4177 THE SALTISFORD

CAPE ROAD

THE ROCK

BARRACK ST

NORTHGATE ST

THEATRE STREET

MARKET PLACE

LINEN ST

NEW BOWLING GREEN STREET

FRIARS STREET

CROMPTON ST

WEST STREET

BONE STREET

SWAN ST

HIGH STREET

CHURCH ST

STRATFORD ROAD

A429 STRATFORD-UPON-AVON

PRIORY ROAD

THE BUTTS

CHAPEL STREET

SMITH STREET

CASTLE HILL

JURY STREET

CASTLE STREET

CASTLE LANE

Priory Park

Train Station

STATION RD

COVENTRY ROAD

COTEN END

EMSCOTE RD

ST JOHN'S

ST NICHOLAS CHURCH ST

BANBURY ROAD

MILL STREET

BRIDGE END

A425

A425

Leamington Spa (A445)

Leamington Spa (A425)

Banbury (B4100)

St Mary's Church

St Nicholas' Church

Charlotte's Tearoom

Forth House

Old Stable Block

Lord Leycester Hospital

Warwick Castle

St Nicholas Park

River Avon

N

Stratford-upon-Avon

0   200 yds

© Crown copyright

timbered buildings that lean at fairy-tale angles against the old West Gate. The complex represents one of Britain's best-preserved examples of domestic Elizabethan architecture. It was established as a hostel for old soldiers by the Earl of Leicester, a favourite of Queen Elizabeth I, and incorporates several beamed buildings, principally in the Great Hall and the Guildhall, as well as a wonderful galleried courtyard and an intimate chantry chapel. There's a modest regimental museum here, too – appropriately enough as retired servicemen (and their wives) still live here. Known as "Brethren", the veterans are distinguished by their black cloaks and silver boar pendants, which they don for ceremonial occasions and to receive visitors.

Doubling back along the High Street, turn left up Church Street – opposite Castle Street – for **St Mary's church** (daily 10am–5pm, 4pm in winter; £1 donation suggested), which was rebuilt in a weird Gothic-Renaissance amalgam after the fire of 1694. One part remained untouched, however – the **chancel**, a glorious specimen of the Perpendicular style with a splendid vaulted ceiling of flying and fronded ribs. On the right-hand side of the chancel, the **Beauchamp Chapel** contains several beautiful tombs, exquisite works of art beginning with that of Richard Beauchamp, Earl of Warwick, who is depicted in an elaborate suit of armour of Italian design from the tip of his swan helmet down. Guarded by a griffin and a bear, he lies with his hands half joined in prayer so that, on the Resurrection, he could see the holy figures on the ceiling bosses above him. The adjacent tomb of Ambrose Dudley is of finely carved alabaster, as is that of Robert Dudley, Earl of Leicester, one of Elizabeth I's most influential advisers.

Practicalities

From Warwick **train station**, on the northern edge of town, it's about ten minutes' walk to the centre. More conveniently, **buses** stop beside the Market Place, from where it's a couple of minutes' walk east to St Mary's and a couple more along Church Street to the **tourist office**, in the Courthouse at the corner of Castle and Jury streets (daily 9.30am–4.30pm; ☎01926/492212, ⓦwww.warwick-uk.co.uk). The tourist office has a list of local hotels and B&Bs, but with Stratford so near and easy to reach, there's no special reason to stay. That said, *Forth House*, 44 High St (☎01926/401512, ⓦwww.forth-house.co.uk; ❸), is an excellent **B&B** with two en-suite and very comfortable guest rooms in a listed sixteenth-century property a short walk from the tourist office.

For a bite to **eat**, head for the inexpensive *Charlotte's Restaurant & Tearoom*, 6 Jury St (☎01926/498930; closed Mon). For a drink, try the traditional *Zetland Arms*, 11 Church St.

Kenilworth

Four miles to the north of Warwick is **KENILWORTH**, a workaday town that received a major PR boost when Sir Walter Scott wrote his novel of the same name in 1862, but has since become little more than an upmarket dormitory to Coventry (see below). It does, however, have one remarkable sight – the **Castle** from which Scott took his inspiration (April–Sept daily 10am–6pm; Oct–March daily 10am–4pm; £4; EH). Begun in the twelfth century – the keep dates from then – the castle was one of the key strategic strongholds in the Midlands, alternately held by the king or a leading noble. The Dudleys acquired the castle in the sixteenth century and one of the family, Robert, Earl of Leicester, pleased Elizabeth I no end by turning the draughty fortress into an elegant palace in preparation for her visit. Kenilworth then became one of England's most fashionable country houses, hosting spectacular pageants and entertainments, but following Dudley's death the castle fell into decline, a process hastened by the attentions of Cromwell's troops in the Civil War. Today, the substantial sandstone ruins, approached across a long causeway that once damned an artificial lake, still maintain a tremendous presence, with large remnants from each era still easily discernible.

Coventry

In medieval times, **COVENTRY**, twenty miles east of Birmingham and twelve miles north of Warwick, was one of England's most prosperous cities, its wealth founded on the cloth, thread and dyeing industries, precursors of the engineering plants that were to become the staple of the local economy during the nineteenth century. It was here, in 1898, that the Daimler Company manufactured the first British motor car, and thereafter the city rapidly became a major centre of car production. As a sign of the good times, the population quadrupled between 1900 and 1930 – from 70,000 to 250,000 – and the future looked rosy. However, Coventry's industrial success attracted the attentions of the Luftwaffe and, on November 14, 1940, in one of the biggest bombing raids of World War II, the Germans destroyed most of the city. The postwar period has not been easy for Coventry. Heavy industry has been on the skids and the motor production lines have waned to near-extinction. Neither has the new Coventry built to replace the old been an architectural success and – with the exception of the splendid **cathedral** – the city is lumbered with more than its fair share of unsightly buildings.

Lady Godiva

The story of **Lady Godiva** riding naked on horseback through the streets of Coventry is one of England's favourite folk tales – and the city makes the most of the connection with postcards, key rings and statues. According to the most popular version of the story, Lady Godiva, the beautiful wife of the local lord, Leofric, the earl of Mercia, was appalled by the poverty she saw around her, and begged her husband to abolish the crippling taxes he levied on his people. Wearying of his wife's philanthropy, Leofric said he would do as she asked on condition that she ride naked through the town, never suspecting that a woman of her rank would agree to such a proposal. Lady Godiva, however, got around the dilemma by ordering the townsfolk to lock themselves in their houses and bolt their windows on the appointed day. Only one local lad, the original **"Peeping Tom"**, dared disobey the Countess's command, and he was struck blind before he had a chance to see Godiva, her long hair covering her body like a cape as she rode through the city, eyes lowered. The ordeal over, Godiva returned to her husband, who kept his word and repealed the taxes.

The story first appeared in 1188, but the historical figures it depicted lived nearly a century and a half before. **Leofric** was the Anglo-Saxon earl who, in 1043, built the Benedictine priory that helped transform Coventry from a small settlement into medieval England's fourth-largest town. His wife, **Godgifu**, outlived him by ten years, and may have been a powerful ruler in her own right after her husband's death; she was also pious and donated land and money to the Church. Beyond this, little is known about the couple. The Godiva story probably evolved from some kind of pagan fertility ritual, and was popularized in the writings of the Norman chronicler, Roger of Wendover, during the thirteenth century. "Peeping Tom" was a later embellishment, seemingly inspired by a particularly odd chain of events. In 1586, Coventry council asked a certain Adam van Noort (1562–1641) to paint the Godiva legend. He did so, but he placed Leofric in a window looking down at Godiva on her horse. For reasons that remain obscure, the city fathers exhibited the painting outside on Coventry's main square and, mistakenly, the populace took the figure to be a peeper – and the sub-plot stuck. Researchers in the Herbert Art Gallery (where this painting now hangs) have sorted all this out and also believe that the notion of Godiva's nudity may have been a fanciful elaboration too. It seems more likely that Leofric, if he challenged his wife at all, dared her to ride through the city stripped of her jewellery and finery.

Whatever the truth of the matter, locals kept the story going and "**Godiva Processions**" kicked off Coventry's annual summer fair from its introduction in the seventeenth century until the 1800s, when all this public flaunting proved too much for the Victorians. More recently, the tradition has been revived in the form of a canny PR exercise to mark the start of the Spirit of Coventry Festival in June, when a local woman rides through the streets dressed in a body stocking.

The City

The city centre's pride and joy is Sir Basil Spence's **St Michael's Cathedral** (daily: Easter–Oct 9.30am–6pm; Nov–Easter 9.30am–5.30pm; £3 donation requested), raised alongside the shell of the blitzed old cathedral and dedicated with a performance of Benjamin Britten's specially written *War Requiem* in 1962. Easily the most successful of Coventry's postwar buildings, the cathedral's pink sandstone is light and graceful, the main entrance adorned by a stunningly forceful *St Michael Defeating the Devil* by Jacob Epstein. Inside, Spence's high and slender nave is bathed in light from the soaring stained-glass windows, a perfect setting for the magnificent and immense **tapestry** of *Christ in Glory* by Graham Sutherland. The choice of artist could not have been more appropriate. A painter, graphic artist and designer, Sutherland (1903–80) had been one of Britain's official war artists, his particular job being to record the effects of German bombing. A canopied walkway links the new cathedral with the old, whose shattered nave flanks the church tower and spire that somehow eluded the bombs – and hint at the building's former magnificence for this was once one of the country's finest Gothic cathedrals. Finally, the cathedral's **visitor centre** (Mon–Sat 10am–4pm; £1.25) features an historical exhibition on the city and cathedral with showings of a short video, *The Spirit of Coventry*.

A stone's throw southeast of the Cathedral on Jordan Well stands the **Herbert Art Gallery and Museum** (Mon–Sat 10am–5.30pm, Sun noon–5pm; free). On Floor 1, the most outstanding exhibits are Luca Giordano's seventeenth-century *Bacchus and Ariadne*, which fills an entire wall, and a room on Lady Godiva that includes John Collier's much photographed pre-Raphelite version. Also of interest on this floor are Sutherland's sketch studies for the cathedral tapestry, followed up with a trial piece made by French weavers. Downstairs, on the ground floor, the go-ahead *Godiva City* exhibition covers one thousand years of local history with a succession of lively displays. Among the original artefacts on show are a large bronze Saxon bowl, known as the Bagington Bowl, sundry items of pristine medieval leatherwork, and lots of ornate ribbons, whose manufacture was long a Coventry speciality.

Coventry has been home to dozens of car makers, including such almost-forgotten names as Singer, Riley, Humber and Hillman. These connections are celebrated at the **Museum of British Road Transport** (daily 10am–4.30pm; free), a short stroll northwest of the cathedral on Hales Street and containing the world's largest collection of British vehicles. Inevitably, the older vehicles attract most of the attention – there's a 1908 Riley, a bull-nosed Morris of 1922 and lots more – but there are more modern cars, too, including the XJ6 Jaguar and the phallus-like *Thrust 2*, in which Richard Noble set the world land speed record of 633.468mph. The museum also has a display devoted to the Coventry Blitz and a gift shop selling motor memorabilia.

From the Road Transport Museum, it's a short walk west along Corporation Street to the squat, red-stone church of **St John's**, beside the roundabout. It's not much to look at, but the church has played an interesting part in linguistic history. During the English Civil War, Puritan Coventry sided squarely with Parliament, and Royalist prisoners from the surrounding districts were rounded up and incarcerated here in the church – hence the expression "sent to Coventry", meaning shunned or ostracized. But not everyone goes along with this version of events. Some claim the phrase derives from Shakespeare's Henry IV Part I, when Falstaff says of his motley band of foot soldiers: "I'll not march through Coventry with them". Church and roundabout are at the foot of truncated **Spon Street**, which has several restored medieval houses, mostly moved here from other parts of the city. It's hardly an inspiring streetscape, but it is one of the more agreeable parts of the city and it does have several good places to eat and drink.

Practicalities

Coventry is an important rail junction and its **train station** has direct services to and from London, Birmingham and many major British cities. It's located just south of the central ring road, a ten- to fifteen-minute walk from the cathedral – take Warwick Road north, cross the ring road and keep going straight – or catch the shuttle bus. Rather more conveniently, the Pool Meadow **bus station** lies a short way north of the cathedral – just follow the signs. The bus station has good connections with many major cities and is also the hub of the local bus network, with regular services to Warwick, Warwick University and Stratford on Stagecoach Midland Red.

For free town maps and local brochures, head for the **tourist office** on Bayley Lane, right in the centre of town opposite the old Cathedral (June–Aug Mon–Fri 9.30am–5pm, Sat & Sun 10am–4.30pm; rest of year Mon–Fri 9.30am–4.30pm, Sat & Sun 10am–4.30pm; ℡02476/227264, ⓦwww.coventry.org). Their main city guidebook has a list of all the town's **accommodation** and they will book a room on your behalf at no cost – though, frankly, with other more enticing towns so near at hand, there's no real reason to stay here. That said, one particularly pleasant **B&B** is the *Crest Guest House*, 39 Friars Rd (℡02476/227822; no credit cards; ❷), whose four spick-and-span guest rooms, two of which are en suite, occupy a comfortable modern house near the ring road, about ten minutes' walk from the centre.

Coventry hardly heaves with great places to **eat**, but *Pizza Express*, near the cathedral at 10A Hay Lane, is a safe bet for moderately priced pizza and pasta, and they have a congenial rear terrace opening onto Castle Yard, too. Alternatively, the *Tête à Tête*, at 188 Spon St (Mon–Fri 8am–3pm, Sat 8am–4pm), is a flowery tearoom, and the *Old Windmill*, at 22 Spon St, has an attractive interior with flagstones and exposed wooden beams, serves a good range of brews and provides inexpensive bar food. Otherwise, Coventry's pub scene is rather too rough and ready for most tastes – and many retreat to the campus of Warwick University, three miles to the south of the city. Here, the **Warwick Arts Centre** is a large arts complex, with two theatres, a cinema, an art gallery, a bar and restaurant. For details of what's on, telephone the box office (℡02476/524524, ⓦwww.warwickartscentre.co.uk).

Worcestershire

In geographical terms, **Worcestershire** can be compared to a huge saucer, with the low-lying plains of the Severn Valley and the Vale of Evesham, Britain's foremost fruit-growing area, rising to a lip of hills, principally the Malverns in the west and the Cotswolds to the south. In character, the county divides into two broad belts. To the north lie the industrial and overspill towns – Droitwich and Redditch for instance – that have much in common with the Birmingham conurbation, while the south is predominantly rural. Marking the transition between the two is **Worcester** itself, a handy base for further explorations and possessed of a splendid cathedral. The south holds the county's finest scenery in the **Malvern Hills**, excellent walking territory and home to the amiable little spa town of **Great Malvern**. South Worcestershire's rural lifestyle is famously portrayed in *The Archers*, the BBC's long-running radio soap, which attracts a massive and extraordinarily dedicated audience. Steam train enthusiasts will be keen to ride the **Severn Valley Railway**, which chugs north from Worcestershire's Kidderminster terminus to Bridgnorth in Shropshire.

The proximity of Birmingham ensures Worcestershire has a good network of **trains** and **buses**, though services are spasmodic amongst the villages in the south of the county. For **bus timetable information**, call ☎0870/6082608. There's also a regional public transport information line covering the West Midlands; it's Centro Hotline (☎024/76559559).

Worcester

Right at the heart of the county, both geographically and politically, **WORCESTER** is something of an architectural hotchpotch, its half-timbered Tudor and stone Georgian buildings standing cheek by jowl with some fairly charmless modern developments. Postwar clumsiness apart, the biggest single influence on the city has always been the River Severn, which flows along Worcester's west flank. It was the river that drew the Romans here and river-trade that made it an important settlement as early as Saxon times. The river's major drawback is its propensity to breach its banks, inundating parts of the city in murky water, though this has at least limited development along the riverside, leaving clear space to view the mighty **cathedral**, Worcester's star turn.

The Cathedral

Worcester's skyline is dominated by the sandstone bulk of its **Cathedral** (daily 7.30am–6.30pm; £2 donation suggested), a rich stew of architectural styles that's best approached from the path that runs along the river's edge and through a gate marked with the city's flood levels. The present structure is the latest of several to stand on the site, but although the interior is mostly medieval, the Victorians remodelled the exterior. Inside, the **nave** is unexceptional except for its two west bays, which are an unusual – and unusually fine – example of the transitional period, when the rounded Norman arch was being supplanted by the pointed arches of Early English Gothic. They date to the 1160s. The pillars of the nave are decorated with bunches of fruit, carved by stonemasons from Lincoln, most of whom succumbed to the Black Death, leaving inferior successors to finish the job. Moving on, the **choir**, built between 1220 and 1260, is a beautiful illustration of the Early English style, with a forest of slender pillars soaring over the intricately worked choir stalls. Here also, in front of the high altar, is the **tomb** of England's most reviled monarch, King John, who died in 1216. Much-loathed, perhaps rightly so, but John certainly would not have appreciated the lion that lies at his feet biting the end of his sword – a reference to the curbing of his power by the barons when they obliged him to sign the Magna Carta. Just behind the tomb – on the right – is **Prince Arthur's Chantry**, a delicate lacy confection of carved stonework built in 1504 to commemorate Arthur, King Henry VII's son, who died at the age of 15 in Ludlow. He was on his honeymoon with Catherine of Aragon, who was soon passed on – with such momentous consequences – to his younger brother, Henry. The chantry is liberally plastered with heraldic and symbolic depictions of the houses of York and Lancaster, united by the Lancastrian Henry VII after his victory at Bosworth Field (see p.704) and subsequent marriage to Elizabeth, daughter of the Yorkist king Edward IV.

A stairway in the southwest transept leads down to the **crypt**, the oldest part of the cathedral, dating from the 1080s and the largest Norman crypt in the country. In addition, a doorway on the south side of the nave leads to the **Cloisters**, with their delightful roof bosses, and the circular, largely Norman **Chapter House**, which has the distinction of being the first such building constructed with the use of a central supporting pillar.

The rest of the city centre

Tucked behind the cathedral in Severn Street, alongside the canal, the **Royal Worcester Porcelain** complex (Mon–Sat 9am–5.30pm, Sun 11am–5pm; tours Mon–Fri only, reservations advised; factory tour £5, museum only £3, shop free; ☎01905/23221) contains a factory shop, a museum, where a large sample of old Worcester porcelain is displayed in period settings, and the factory itself. Beginning in the mid-eighteenth century, porcelain manufacture was long the city's main industry and Royal Worcester its leading light. Up behind the Royal Worcester complex, on the other side of the busy Sidbury dual carriageway, is the oldest building in the city, the **Commandery**, which dates from the eleventh century and now holds the **Civil War Visitor Centre** (Mon–Sat 10am–5pm, Sun 1.30–5.30pm; £3.90). The Commandery was Charles II's headquarters leading up to the Battle of Worcester in 1651 and has also served as a college for the blind. It now contains a sequence of Tudor and Stuart period rooms plus exhibits on the role of religion in the seventeenth century and the events of the Civil War, focusing on the trial of Charles I and the background to Cromwell's victory. Most of the building is half-timbered and smartly panelled, with one small room sporting wall paintings dating from around 1500. Look out for the plaintive, glowing soul perched in the scales of judgement, with a sly devil and virginal Madonna each trying to force the scales in their favour.

Pedestrianized **Friar Street**, which forks off Sidbury just west of the Commandery, is blighted by some garish 1960s developments, but these quickly give way to Worcester's most complete ensemble of Elizabethan and Tudor buildings. Sited inside one of these old timber-framed buildings is the **Museum of Local Life** (Mon–Wed, Fri & Sat 10.30am–5pm; free). The museum starts with an examination of Worcester during World War II, interesting chiefly because it paints a picture of ordinary life throughout the war years. The photographs are fascinating, but thereafter the remainder of the museum is given over to anodyne reconstructions of Edwardian and Victorian shops, offices and domestic settings. Almost opposite is **The Greyfriars** (mid-April to late Oct Wed & Thurs 2–5pm; £2.80; NT), a largely fifteenth-century town house, whose principal attraction is the rambling walled garden at the back.

Practicalities

Of Worcester's two **train stations**, Foregate Street is the more central and from here it's about half a mile south to the cathedral along Foregate and its continuation The Cross and the High Street. Note, however, that some services only stop at Shrub Hill, the second station, which is located a mile or so northeast of the cathedral. The **bus station** is at the back of the Crowngate shopping mall, on The Butts, about 600 yards northwest of the cathedral. The **tourist office** (Mon–Sat 9.30am–5pm; ☎01905/726311, ⊛www.cityof worcester.gov.uk) is in the Georgian Guildhall towards the cathedral end of the High Street. **Bike rental** is available from Peddlers, 46 Barbourne Rd (☎01905/24238).

Worcester has a healthy range of accommodation. Amongst several down-town **hotels**, two good choices are the *Fownes' Hotel*, in an old glove factory at the cathedral end of City Walls Road (℡01905/613151; ❺), and the nearby *Loch Ryan*, 119 Sidbury (℡01905/351143; ❹), which is noted for its food and terraced garden. Recommended central **B&Bs** include *Osborne House*, in a tra-ditional Victorian villa at 17 Chestnut Walk (℡01905/22296, ⊛www.osborne-house.freeserve.co.uk; ❷), and the excellent *Burgage House*, 4 College Precincts (℡01905/25396; no credit cards; ❷), which occupies a Georgian town house with views over to the cathedral.

For **food**, there are several popular café–bars and restaurants dotted along Friar Street and its northerly continuation, New Street. These include the *Lemon Tree*, 12 Friar St (℡01905/27770), a moderately priced café/restaurant serving an imaginative menu featuring several top-notch Mediterranean dishes, and the *King Charles II*, on New Street (℡01905/22449), which has an outstanding tra-ditional English menu – and a rather contrived seventeenth-century ambience. Alternatively, there's *Saffron's*, 15 New St (℡01905/610505), an unpretentious, if expensive, bistro serving mainly chargrilled steaks and chicken.

You'll find a bunch of pleasant old **pubs** in the city centre, with two of the best being the *Ye Olde Talbot*, an ancient coaching inn with a restaurant at the foot of Friar Street, and the *Cardinal's Hat*, a sixteenth-century building com-plete with a half-timbered interior further along at no. 31. There's also *The Plough*, a lively spot tucked away on the corner of Fish Street and Deansway, and with a patio that gets jam-packed on warm summer evenings. Less touristy is the *Horn & Trumpet*, in Angel Street.

Lower Broadheath

One of Worcestershire's most famous sons was the composer **Sir Edward Elgar** (1857–1934), whose statue faces the cathedral at the bottom of the High Street. Inevitably, there's an Elgar Trail meandering round the county and its focus is his **birthplace** – a tiny, rustic brick cottage in **LOWER BROAD-HEATH**, three miles west of Worcester via the A44 (daily 11am–5pm; £3.50). Inside, the crowded rooms contain Elgar's musical manuscripts, personal corre-spondence in his spidery handwriting, press cuttings, photographs and miscel-laneous mementoes centred on the desk at which he worked. There's also an imaginative range of special events from illustrated talks to concerts and recitals of his works. A bus service links Worcester bus station with the museum, but it's infrequent.

The Malvern Hills and Great Malvern

One of the most exclusive and well-heeled areas of the Midlands, **The Malverns** is the generic name for a string of towns and villages stretched along the eastern lower slopes of the **Malvern Hills**, which rise spectacularly out of the flat plains a few miles to the southwest of Worcester. About nine miles from north to south – between the A44 and the M50 – and never more than five miles wide, the hills straddle the Worcestershire–Herefordshire boundary. Of Pre-Cambrian rock, they are punctuated by over twenty summits, mostly around 1000-feet-high, and in between lie innumerable dips and hollows. Nonetheless, it's easy walking country, with great views, and the hills are criss-crossed by hiking trails.

The centre of the region is **GREAT MALVERN**, a pretty little place – and the most obvious base – served by rail from Worcester, Birmingham and Oxford. The town's medicinal waters became popular towards the end of the eighteenth century, but it was the Victorians who came here in droves, making the steep hike up to **St Ann's Well** on the hill behind town, where you can still try the stuff yourself. The peculiarities of Great Malvern's spa waters are explained in the **Malvern Museum**, housed in the delicately proportioned Abbey Gateway, plum in the centre on Abbey Road (Easter–Oct Mon, Tues & Thurs–Sun 10.30am–5pm, also Wed in school holidays; £1). Nineteenth-century cartoons show patients packed into cold wet sheets before hopping gaily away from their crutches and wheelchairs – exaggerated claims perhaps, but poor hygiene did bring on a multitude of skin complaints and the relief the spa waters brought was real enough.

The main sight in town is the **Priory Church** (March–Oct daily 9am–6.30pm; Nov–Feb till 4.30pm; donation requested), adjacent to the museum, its patchwork exterior contrasting with the ordered interior, which is notable for its stained glass and hundreds of detailed wall tiles, all added to the building in the mid-fifteenth century. The window of the north transept is especially fine and contains a portrait of Prince Arthur, Henry VII's son – the same Arthur who is commemorated in Worcester cathedral (see p.620). Among the priory's graves is that of Darwin's granddaughter, who died here as a child despite being bathed with Malvern water. From the church, it's a short walk to the **Winter Gardens pavilion**, one of the key venues for the wide range of special events the town puts on each year, including the excellent **Almeida Drama Festival** held in August.

Great Malvern has two other claims to fame: one is the Morgan motor car, which is still handmade in a small factory here; the other is the composer **Edward Elgar**, who lived in the adjacent village of **MALVERN LINK** at the turn of the century. The views from his house (no public access) on Alexandra Road formed a backdrop for Elgar while he composed his most enduring work, including the famous *Enigma Variations*, whose more lyrical passages have become anthems of the English countryside. Stare out across the Severn Valley from the flank of the Malverns on a fine summer's evening and it's not hard to see why England's most celebrated composer found such inspiration here.

For **walkers**, the Malvern Hills offer splendid day-hikes and a number of historical landmarks, including the remains of an Iron Age fort high on the ridge to the south of town. The panorama from here takes in the contrasts of the surrounding countryside: plains to the east and gentle hills rolling towards the gloomy Black Mountains in the west. The hike along the ridge takes about four-and-a-half hours. Start from the southern end at **Chase End Hill** and work your way north, or head for **British Camp**, midway along the route, and begin there. It's possible to get to both of these starting points by bus, but the service is infrequent; the tourist office (see below) has the timetables.

Great Malvern practicalities

Great Malvern **train station** is on the eastern edge of town, half a mile or so from the centre along Avenue Road and Church Street. A range of inexpensive hiking leaflets are sold at the town's **tourist office**, right in the centre across from the priory church at 21 Church St (April–Nov daily 10am–5pm; Dec–March Mon–Sat 10am–5pm, Sun 10am–4pm; ☎01684/892289, ⓦwww.malvernhills.gov.uk). They also sell the three excellent large-scale **hiking maps**, which are indispensable if you're planning on walking the length of the Malverns. This is also a rewarding, though physically demanding, area to explore by **bike**; at present no-one does bike rental, but this may well change – ring the tourist office for details.

Accommodation is plentiful. Amongst the **hotels**, there's the *Great Malvern*, 7 Graham Rd (☎01684/563411, ⓦwww.great-malvern-hotel.co.uk; ⑤), a family-run, medium-sized hotel in a substantial old stone building right in the centre, and, just along the street, at no. 23, is the comparable *Montrose* (☎01684 /572335; ❷). The smartest hotel in town is the *Foley Arms*, 14 Worcester Rd (☎01684/573397; ❺), which occupies a good-looking Georgian building – with oodles of wrought-iron work – again in the centre. **B&Bs** include the inexpensive *Kylemore*, 30 Avenue Rd (☎01684/563753; no credit cards; ❶), the *Wyche Keep*, an impressive Edwardian house with garden access to the hills at 22 Wyche Rd (☎01684/567018; no credit cards; ❸), and *Elm Bank*, an elegant Regency town house with en-suite rooms at 52 Worcester Rd (☎01684 /566051; ❷). The homely **youth hostel**, serving simple meals, is a mile south of Great Malvern train station, off the main A449 at 18 Peachfield Rd, Malvern Wells (☎01684/569131, ✉malvern@yha.org.uk; closed Nov to mid-Feb;). The nearest **campsite** is at *Odd Fellows Pub*, four miles southwest in Colwall (☎01684/540084).

For **food**, Great Malvern has oodles of cafés and tearooms – one of the more distinctive is the *St Anne's Well Café*, a cosy vegetarian café serving inexpensive wholefood snacks, salads and cakes from its Victorian premises at the Well; just follow the signs up through the park from the centre. They'll also give you a glass to sample the spring water that babbles into a basin outside the door. The town's other café with character lies downhill from the tourist office at the train station. Known as the *Lady Foley's Tea Room* during the day, and *Passionata* in the evening (☎01684/893033; reservations recommended), it's actually on one of the station platforms and makes the most of its Victorian surroundings. Finally, *Cridlans' Restaurant* (☎01684/562676), a French-style brasserie just outside the abbey gates, is a slightly pricier, but still good-value place to eat, serving light lunches and tasty continental dishes on check tablecloths; try their delicious home-made sausage sandwich.

Herefordshire

Over the Malvern Hills from Worcestershire, the rolling agricultural landscapes of **Herefordshire** have an easy-going charm, but the finest scenery hereabouts is along the banks of the **River Wye**, which wriggles and worms its way across the county linking most of the places of interest. Plonked in the middle of the county on the Wye is **Hereford**, a sleepy, rather old-fashioned sort of place whose proudest possession, the cathedral's remarkable Mappa Mundi map, was almost flogged off in a round of ecclesiastical budget cuts, back in the 1980s. Hereford is also close to the superb Norman church of tiny **Kilpeck**, to the southwest, and, to the east, the delightful little town of **Ledbury**, sitting on the edge of the Malvern Hills and distinguished by its Tudor and Stuart half-timbered buildings – sometimes called "Black and Whites". Further afield, in the southeast corner of the county, lies **Ross-on-Wye**, a genial little town with a picturesque river setting. It's an ideal base for explorations into one of the wilder portions of the **Wye River Valley**, with the tamer landscapes of the **Forest of Dean**, nestling in between the rivers Wye and Severn over in Gloucestershire, beckoning beyond. To the west of Hereford, hard by the Welsh border, the key attraction is **Hay-on-Wye**, which – thanks to the purposeful industry of Richard Booth – has become the world's largest repository of second-hand books, on sale in around thirty bookshops.

Herefordshire possesses one **rail line**, linking Ledbury, Hereford and Leominster and running north to Shrewsbury and east to Great Malvern and

Worcester. Otherwise, you'll be restricted to the tender mercies of the county's **buses**, which provide a reasonable service between the villages and towns, except on Sundays when there's almost nothing at all. All the local tourist offices have bus timetables and there's **bus information** on ☎0870/6082608.

Hereford and around

Founded by the Saxons in the seventh century, **HEREFORD** – literally "army ford" – was long a border garrison town against the Welsh, its military importance guaranteed by its strategic position beside the River Wye. It also became a religious centre after the Welsh murdered the Saxon king Ethelbert near here in 794. These were bloody times, so in itself the murder was pretty routine, but legend asserts that Ethelbert's ghost kept on turning up to insist his remains be interred here in Hereford – and eventually it got its way. Ethelbert's posthumous antics made him a military martyr and a Saxon cult soon grew up around his name, prompting the construction of the town's first cathedral. The Welsh were, however, having none of this and, in 1055, they attacked Hereford and burnt the cathedral to the ground.

Today, with the fortifications that once girdled the city all but vanished, it's the second **cathedral**, dating from the eleventh century, which forms the main focus of architectural interest. It lies just to the north of the River Wye at the heart of the city centre, whose compact tangle of narrow streets and squares is clumsily boxed in by the ring road. Taken as a whole, Hereford makes for a pleasant – if not exactly riveting – overnight stay and is also within easy striking distance of **Kilpeck**, with its exquisite Norman church, and pocket-sized **Ledbury**, one of the county's prettiest towns.

The Cathedral and the Mappa Mundi

Hereford **Cathedral** (daily 8.30am–6pm; £2 donation suggested) is a curious building, an uncomfortable amalgamation of architectural styles, with bits and pieces added to the eleventh-century original by a string of bishops and culminating in an extensive – and not especially sympathetic – Victorian refit. From the outside, the sandstone **tower** is the dominant feature, constructed in the early fourteenth century to eclipse the Norman western tower, which subsequently collapsed under its own weight in 1786. The tumbling masonry damaged the **nave** and its replacement lacks the grandeur of most other English cathedrals, though the long rank of surviving Norman arches and piers more than hints at what went before. The **north transept** is, however, a flawless exercise in thirteenth-century taste, its soaring windows a classic example of Early English architecture and a handsome home for the delicately carved shrine of St Thomas Cantilupe. Across the church, the **south transept** is largely Norman, its chunky stonework interrupted by an old fireplace, one of the few still surviving within an English church, and decorated by an intricately carved *Adoration of the Magi*, a sixteenth-century, bas-relief triptych from Germany.

In the 1980s, financial difficulties prompted the cathedral authorities to plan the sale of one of their most treasured possessions, the **Mappa Mundi**. There was an awful lot of cultural huffing and puffing about this controversial proposal, but the government and John Paul Getty Jnr rode to the rescue, with the oil tycoon stumping up a million pounds to keep the map here and install it in a brand new building. Made of sandstone, this New Library – located next to the cathedral at the west end of the cloisters – blends in seamlessly with the other, older buildings close by. It contains the immaculate **Mappa Mundi and**

Chained Library Exhibition (April–Sept Mon–Sat 10am–5pm, Sun 11am–4pm; Oct–March Mon–Sat 11am–4pm; last admission 45min before closing; £4), which begins with a series of interpretative panels that leads to the Mappa, displayed in a dimly lit room. Dating to about 1300, and 62 by 52 inches in size, the map is quite simply remarkable – and it provides an extraordinary insight into the medieval mind. It is indeed a map (as we know it) in so far as it suggests the general geography of the world – with Asia at the top and Europe and Africa below, to left and right respectively – but it also squeezes in history, mythology and theology. At the top of the map, Christ sits in judgement with the saved on one side, the damned on the other – hell is represented by the jaws of a dragon. The rest of the border contains representations of the twelve winds and the repeated monogram "MORS" – for death. Inside the border, at the top of the earth, is the Garden of Eden, shown as an island, and in the centre is the walled city of Jerusalem. Britain is at the bottom on the left with Hereford – and several other cathedral cities – labelled in Latin, as are almost all the other inscriptions. In total, the three continents are adorned by over five hundred drawings, some signifying towns and cities, others biblical events, plants, birds and animals as well as a menagerie of mythological creatures – from the manticoras (man-headed-lions), the essedones (cannibals), and the blemyae (who have heads in their chests). As if this wasn't enough, the New Library also holds the **Chained Library**, a remarkably extensive collection of books and manuscripts dating from the eighth to the eighteenth century. A selection is always on display.

The rest of the city

After the Mappa, Hereford's other attractions can't help but seem rather pedestrian. Nonetheless, the **City Museum and Art Gallery**, opposite the cathedral in a flamboyant Victorian building on Broad Street (April–Sept Tues–Sat 10am–5pm, Sun 10am–4pm; rest of year closed Sun; free), holds a mildly diverting collection of wildlife, geological remains, local history and mawkish Victorian art. Broad Street continues up and round into the main square, **High Town**, which is fringed by several Georgian buildings and **The Old House**, sole remnant of the seventeenth-century timber-framed Butchers' Row and now a modest museum with period interiors and bric-a-brac (April–Sept Tues–Sat 10am–5pm, Sun 10am–4pm; Oct–March closed Sun; free).

Set amidst rolling countryside, Hereford's economy is still largely dependent on its agricultural base and the local **cider** industry is one of the city's biggest trades. Cider enthusiasts should make their way to the **Cider Museum and King Offa Distillery**, 21 Ryelands St (April–Oct daily 10am–5.30pm; Nov–March Tues–Sun 11am–3pm; £2.50), which tracks through the history of cider-making, provides views of the distillation process and offers samples of King Offa ciders, including a particularly tasty Cider Brandy. The museum is, however, a dull fifteen-minute walk west of the centre, off the A438. To get there, take Eign Gate west from High Town, cross the ring road onto Eign Street and watch for Ryelands Street on the left.

Practicalities

From Hereford **train station**, it's about half a mile southwest to the High Town along Commercial Road and its continuation Commercial Street; the **bus station** is just off Commercial Road. Most local buses stop in St Peter's Square, at the east end of the High Town. The **tourist office** is directly opposite the cathedral, at 1 King St (May–Sept Mon–Sat 9am–5pm, Sun 10am–4pm; Oct–April closed Sun; ☎01432/268430). **Bicycle rental** is available from Phil Prothero Cycles, Unit 13, Bastion Mews, Union St (℡01432 /359478).

The tourist office has a reasonably long list of **B&Bs**, and the pick of them is *Charades*, 34 Southbank Rd (℡01432/269444; no credit cards; ❷), with six comfortable, en-suite guest rooms in a large Victorian house a short walk from the centre. Further out, in the countryside about two miles south of town off the A49, is *Grafton Villa Farm* (℡01432/268689; no credit cards; ❸), which offers three tastefully decorated bedrooms in the Georgian farmhouse of a working farm. As for **hotels**, the *Green Dragon Hotel*, Broad St (℡01432 /272506; ❼), occupies a grand Georgian building with frilly iron balustrades right in the centre.

For **food**, choices are limited, but one reasonably good option is the inexpensive *Firenze*, a pasta and pizza place just beyond the ring road, five minutes' walk northeast of High Town, at 21 Commercial Rd (℡01432/270183; closed Sun). A second choice is the *Aroon Rai Tai*, 50 Widemarsh St (℡01432 /279971), a moderately priced Thai restaurant. When it comes to **drinking**, things get more interesting. **Cider** is a local speciality and there's a local brewery, too – the Wye Valley Brewery, whose trademark **bitter** is the redoubtable Dorothy Goodbody's. You can try both at the best **pub** in town, *The Barrels*, five minutes' walk southeast of High Town, on St Owen's Street.

Kilpeck

The lonely hamlet of **KILPECK**, nine miles southwest of Hereford off the A465, boasts the sandstone **Church of St Mary and St David**, arguably the most perfectly preserved Norman church in Britain. Here, the full vitality of Norman sculpture is revealed, beginning with the south door where the tympanum's Tree of Life is hooped by birds, dragons, a phoenix and all sorts of mythical monsters. Up above, the corbel displays over seventy grotesques with barely a saint or religious figure in sight. The sculptures may well have been inspired by pagan Viking carving, reminders of the Normans' Scandinavian ancestry – William the Conqueror was the descendant of a Viking chief who seized Normandy in the tenth century. The Victorians restored the corbel sculptures, but removed the more sexually explicit, with the exception of the genital-splaying sheila-na-gig – food for thought. Beyond the church graveyard are the battered remains of Kilpeck's medieval **castle**. Stagecoach's Hereford to Abergavenny **bus** (not Sun) runs along the A465, but the nearest you'll get to Kilpeck is Wormbridge's post office a couple of miles away to the west.

Ledbury

Heading east from Hereford, it's an easy fifteen miles along the A438 to **LEDBURY**, a good-looking little town perched on the western edge of the Malvern Hills. The focus of the town is the Market Place, home to the dinky **Market House**, a Tudor beamed building raised on oak columns and with herringbone pattern beams. From beside it, narrow **Church Lane** – not to be confused with adjacent Church Street – runs up the slope framed by an especially fine ensemble of half-timbered Tudor and Stuart buildings. Among them is the Butchers' Row House Museum and, pick of the bunch, the so-called **Painted Room** (Easter–Sept Mon–Fri 11am–3pm, Sun 2–5pm; free), featuring a set of bold symmetrical floral frescoes painted on wattle-and-daub walls sometime in the sixteenth century. At the far end of the lane stands **St Michael's parish church**, whose strong and slender spire pokes high into the sky. The nucleus of the church is Norman – note the round pillars and zigzag stonework – but the most interesting features are the funerary monuments inside, including the spectacular seventeenth-century **Skynner Tomb**, where five sons and five daughters kneel in honour of their parents, beneath the canopied slab on which their parents also kneel.

Ledbury **train station** is inconveniently situated on the northern edge of town, about three-quarters of a mile from the Market Place – straight down the A438. **Buses** stop on the Market Place, across from the **tourist office** (daily 10am–5pm; ☎01531/636147, ⓦwww.visitledbury.co.uk). **Accommodation** is thin on the ground, but the *Feathers Hotel* (☎01531/635266; ❻) occupies a smashing "Black and White" on the High Sreet, footsteps from the Market Place – and has just sixteen very comfortable rooms. As for **food**, the *Malthouse Restaurant*, on Church Lane (☎01531/634443; closed Sun), is exemplary, with a creative menu featuring local ingredients – main courses average around £15. Also on Church Lane, the charming *Prince of Wales* **pub** is a great place to sink a beer amidst its snug, low-beamed rooms.

Ross-on-Wye

ROSS-ON-WYE, perched above a loop of the Wye sixteen miles southeast of Hereford, is a relaxed, easy-going town with an artsy/New Age undertow. It's also the obvious base for exploring one of the more dramatic sections of the Wye River Valley and the Forest of Dean (see below). Ross's jumble of narrow streets zeroes in on the Market Place, which is shadowed by the seventeenth-century **Market House**, a sturdy two-storey sandstone structure that now accommodates a modest **Heritage Centre** (April–Oct Mon–Sat 10am–5pm, Sun 10.30am–4pm; Nov–March Mon–Sat 10am–4pm; free), exploring the town's history. The Market House sports a medallion bust of a bewigged Charles II, placed here at the instigation of the pioneering seventeenth-century town planner, John Kyrle. A local man, Kyrle did much to improve the town's amenities and his reputation was such that the poet Alexander Pope singled him out for praise in one of his *Moral Essays*. Close by, Ross's other noteworthy building is the mostly thirteenth century **St Mary's church**, whose sturdy stonework culminates in a slender, tapering spire. In front of the church is a large and rare **Plague Cross**, commemorating the three hundred or so townsfolk who were buried here by night without coffins during a savage outbreak of the plague in 1637. Inside, the church holds several distinctive tombs, one of which – that of a certain William Rudhall (d.1530) – is one of the last great alabaster sculptures from the specialist masons of Nottingham, whose work was prized right across medieval Europe. Opposite the church, **The Prospect** is a neat public garden offering pleasant views over the river.

If you've strolled long enough around town but still have time to spare, strike out along one of the many well-defined **footpaths** that thread their way through the riverine fields and woods bordering the Wye. A collection of leaflets giving detailed descriptions of several circular routes is available at the tourist office (see below).

Practicalities

There are no trains to Ross, but the **bus station** is handily located on Cantilupe Road, from where it's a couple of minutes' walk west to both the Market Place and the **tourist office**, on the corner of High and Edde Cross streets (Easter–Sept Mon–Sat 9am–5.30pm, Sun 10am–4pm; Oct–Easter closed Sun; ☎01989/562768). Ross is strong on **B&Bs** with perhaps the best being the *Linden House*, in a fetching, three-storey Georgian building opposite St Mary's at 14 Church St (☎01989/565373; ❷). The six guest rooms, only one of which is en suite, are cosily decorated in a modern style and the breakfasts are delicious – both traditional and vegetarian. Another convenient choice – if a tad more frugal – is *Vaga House*, another well-maintained Georgian building, this one with oodles of flower boxes, located just below the tourist office on Wye Street (℡01989/563024, ℮vagahouse@hotmail.com; ➊). The nearest **camping** is the *Broadmeadow Caravan Park*, occupying a field on the northeast edge of Ross beside the ring road (℡01989/768076; closed Oct–March). **Bikes** can be rented from Revolutions on Broad Street (℡01989/562639). The main cultural event is the Ross International Festival (℡01989/563330, ⓦwww.festival.org.uk), a mixed bag of music, theatre and dance held over two weeks at the back end of August.

Restaurants range from the *Oat Cuisine*, a straightforward daytime whole-food café at 41 Broad St, to the *Cloisters Wine Bar*, 24 High St (℡01989/567717; evenings only), serving a wide range of meat and fish dishes in a candlelit interior. Even better, a few paces further along High Street, is the excellent, reasonably priced *Meader's* (℡01989/562803), which specializes in Hungarian dishes. Of the **pubs**, the ancient, oak-beamed *Eagle Inn,* on Broad Street, is the most appealing, though the *Man of Ross*, at the top Wye Street, runs it close and serves a good pub food.

The Wye River Valley

Heading south from Ross along the B4234, it's just five miles to the sullen sandstone mass of **Goodrich Castle** (daily: April–Oct 10am–6pm; Nov–March 10am–1pm & 2–4pm; £3.60; EH), which commands wide views over the hills and woods of the **Wye River Valley**. Dating from the twelfth century, the castle's strategic location beside a busy river crossing point guaranteed its importance as a border stronghold from the twelfth century onwards. The substantial ruins incorporate a Norman keep, a maze of later rooms and passageways and walkable ramparts, complete with murder holes, slits through which boiling oil or water was poured onto the attackers down below. During the Civil War, a determined Royalist garrison held on until the Parliamentarians built themselves a special cannon, "Roaring Meg", which soon brought victory – a great achievement considering the unreliability of the technology: large cannons had the unfortunate habit of blowing up as soon as anyone fired them.

The castle stands next to tiny **GOODRICH VILLAGE**, which is on the Ross to Gloucester bus route – Stagecoach **bus** #34 (every 2hr, not Sun). From the village, it's around a mile and half southeast along narrow country lanes to the solitary **Welsh Bicknor hostel** (℡01594/860300, ℮welshbicknor@yha .org.uk; £11; restricted opening Nov–March), in a Victorian riverside rectory. The hostel, in 25-acre grounds, has 78 beds in anything from two-bed to ten-bed rooms, and provides evening meals on request; you can just show up and hope for a berth, but given the hostel's seclusion booking ahead is stronly recommended.

Symonds Yat Rock and Symonds Yat East

From Goodrich – and beyond all hope of a bus – it's a couple of miles south along narrow roads to the signposted turning that wriggles its way up to the top of **Symonds Yat Rock**, rising high above a wooded, hilly loop in the Wye. This is one of the region's most celebrated views and you'll probably share it with the birdwatchers who come here to spy the raptors gliding the valley below. At the foot of the rock – a two-mile drive away – is **SYMONDS YAT EAST**, a pretty little hamlet that straggles along the east bank of the river. It's a popular spot, with canoe rental and cruises available from Kingfisher (☎01600/891063; March–Oct only), and there are several places to stay. The most appealing **hotel** is the bright and cheerful *Forest View* (☎01600/890210; ❹).

The road to the village is a dead end, so you have to double back to regain the **B4432**. This continues south towards Coleford – and the Forest of Dean (see below) – with the **B4228** pressing on thereafter to loop back towards the Wye at St Briavels.

St Briavels

ST BRIAVELS is a pleasant rose-stone village with a small but forbidding Norman **castle** (April–Sept daily 1–4pm; free; EH) plonked right in the middle on a grassy knoll. Formerly used by King John as a hunting lodge, and the region's administrative centre during medieval times, the castle now accommodates one of England's more impressive **youth hostels** (☎01594/530272, ✉stbriavels@yha.org.uk; closed Nov–Jan) with seventy beds distributed between four- to eight-bedded rooms. Beneath the keep extends a network of **tunnels** (no access) originally excavated in the thirteenth century by local miners. As a reward for their work, men over the age of 21 and born within the St Briavels district were granted the right to mine for coal and iron ore anywhere in the Forest of Dean for free. This law is still in place, and within living memory a significant number of foresters made their living as "**Free Miners**", paying a royalty each year from their earnings to the Crown.

If you're tempted to **stay**, the hostel is the obvious choice, though there are also a handful of en-suite rooms upstairs in *The George*, a friendly old pub beside the castle (☎01594/530228; ❷). The pub also serves good **food** – including tasty local meat and game – both inside and outside on its garden terrace. One other advantage is that the village is within easy walking distance of the River Wye – and the Offa's Dyke Path (see p.645). The latter leads north in a few miles to **The Kymin**, over the river in Wales. This Georgian country home is a small, circular affair attached to a temple dedicated to the Royal Navy. The National Trust owns the property and there are plans to open the house and the grounds, which offer commanding views across the Wye; call ☎01874/625515 for times.

The Forest of Dean

Wedged between the Severn estuary and the River Wye to the south of Ross-on-Wye and Goodrich, Gloucestershire's **Forest of Dean** is an extensive tract of woodland, whose excellent hunting long attracted royal attention – and protection – beginning with King Edward the Confessor in the eleventh century. Later, the forest's oak trees were much in demand for the construction of Royal Navy ships and there was also large-scale iron- and coal-mining, as recalled by the names of the two largest towns hereabouts – **Coleford** and **Cinderford**. The Forestry Commission took over the running of the forest in the 1930s and in recent years they have developed a number of tourist attractions as well as a network of cycling and hiking trails. With so many large towns and cities less than an hour away by road, it's not surprising that tens of thousands of visitors congregate here every year, but however good the forest may be for family holidays, the scenery isn't all that special and neither are the purpose-built attractions. Just over half of the forest is made up of conifers, and the remainder is broadleaf woodland with oak the most common tree.

The best way to sample the forest is to take the six-mile-long **B4226** from Coleford to Cinderford. First up, after about half a mile, is **Hopewell Colliery Museum** (March–Oct daily 10am–4pm), where you can amble through a

8

shallow, surface mine. Thereafter, it's another short trip to both the picnic sites and playgrounds of **Beechenhurst Lodge** and the **Sculpture Trail**, the most interesting attraction in the forest. Three and a half miles long – allow about three hours – the trail is an energetic hike up into the forested hills and it leads past twelve pieces of contemporary artwork and sculpture, including a giant chair on the crest of a hill. This part of the forest is also popular with cyclists; **bicycle rental** is available from Pedalabikeaway (℡01594/860065, ⓦwww.pedalabikeaway.com), located about half a mile from the B4226 just to the west of the Beechenhurst/Sculpture Trail turning – follow the signs; they also hand out maps showing the best cycle routes.

Finally, just south of Coleford, off the B4228 Chepstow road, the **Clearwell Caves** (March–Oct daily 10am–5pm; £3.50) comprise a natural cave system enlarged by generations of iron-ore miners. Nine caverns can be explored on foot and without a guide; you can also don a boiler suit, lamp and hard hat for trips to the deeper parts of the mines (£8), still worked to supply tinted pigments to the cosmetics and paints industries.

Hay-on-Wye

Straddling the Anglo-Welsh border some twenty miles west of Hereford, the sleepy little town of **HAY-ON-WYE** is known to most people for one thing – **books**. Hay saw its first bookshop open in 1961 and has since become a bibliophile's paradise, with just about every spare inch of the town being given over to the trade, including the old cinema and the ramshackle stone castle. Most of Hay's inhabitants are outsiders, which means that it has little indigenous feel, but its setting, against the spectacular backdrop of Hay Bluff and the Black Mountains, together with its creaky little streets, is delightful. In summer, the town bursts with life as it plays host to a succession of riverside parties and travelling fairs, the pick of which is the **Hay Festival of Literature**, ⓦwww.hayfestival.co.uk) in the last week of May, when London's literary world decamps here.

The King of the Hay

Richard Booth, whose family originates from the area, opened the first of his Hay-on-Wye second-hand bookshops in 1961. Since then, he has built an astonishing empire and attracted other booksellers to the town, turning it into the greatest market of used books in the world. There are now over thirty such shops in this minuscule town, the largest of which – Booth's own – contains around half a million volumes.

Whereas many of the region's country towns have seen their populations ebb in recent decades, Hay has boomed on the strength of its bibliophilic connections. Booth regards this success as a prototype for other endangered communities, placing the emphasis firmly on local initiatives and unusual specialisms. He is unequivocal in his condemnation of government regeneration programmes, which, he asserts, have done little to stem the flow of jobs and people out of the region. This healthy distaste for bureaucracy, coupled with Hay's geographical location slap on the Anglo–Welsh border and Booth's own self-promotional skills, led him to declare Hay independent of the UK in 1977, with himself, naturally, as **King**. He appoints his own ministers and offers "official" government scrolls, passports and car stickers to bewitched visitors. Although such a proclamation of independence carries no official weight, most of the people of Hay seem to have rallied behind King Richard and are delighted with the publicity, and visitors, that the town's continuing high-profile attracts.

Before you start ambling round, visit the tourist office (see below) to pick up the free leaflet that gives the low-down on all the bookshops in town together with a street plan. As good a place as any to start is **Richard Booth's Bookshop**, 44 Lion St (☎01497/820322, ⊛www.richardbooth.demon.co.uk), a huge, draughty warehouse of almost unlimited browsing potential. It's owned – like so much else in Hay – by Richard Booth, who lives in part of the castle, a care-worn Jacobean mansion built into the walls of a thirteenth-century fortress right in the centre. In another part of the mansion is the **Hay Castle Booth Books** (☎01497/820503, ⊛www.richardboothbookseller.com), a sedate collection of fine-art, cinema, antiquarian and photography books. Nearby, **Castle Street Books** at 23 Castle St (☎01497/820160) is great for historical guides and maps, and **Bag of Books**, also on Castle Street (☎01497 /821572, ⊛www.bookspostfree.com), sells all its books at £1 each. Neighbouring Broad Street holds **Y Gelli Auctions** (☎01497/821179), with regular sales of books, maps and prints, and **West House Books** (☎01497 /821225), best for Celtic and women's works.

Practicalities

Buses from Hereford stop in the car park in the town centre off Oxford Road. The adjacent **tourist office** (daily: Easter–Oct 10am–1pm & 2–5pm; Nov–Easter 11am–1pm & 2–4pm; ☎01497/820144, ⊛www.hay-on-wye .co.uk) stocks an exhaustive range of hiking books and maps, and can help arrange accommodation in the area. **Bike rental** is available from Paddles & Peddles, 15 Castle St (☎01497/820604).

Accommodation in town is plentiful, though things get booked up long in advance for the Hay Festival of Literature. Arguably the best option is the *Famous Old Black Lion*, Lion St (☎01497/820841; ❹), a captivating inn dating back to medieval times with beamed ceilings, comfortable rooms and a penchant for candlelight in the evenings. Also in the centre are *Belmont House*, Belmont Rd (☎01497/820718; no credit cards; ❶), a classy guest house in an appealing Georgian villa packed with antiques, and *Brookfield House*, Brook St (☎01497/820518, ⊛www.brookfieldguesthouse.btinternet.co.uk; no credit cards; ❶), an immaculate B&B in a tastefully modernized old building with stone walls, beamed ceilings and eight attractive guest rooms. In addition, the *Old Post Office*, Llanigon (☎01497/820008, ⊛www.oldpost-office.co.uk; no credit cards; ❶), is a wonderful seventeenth-century B&B two miles south of Hay and over the border in Wales. The last is especially well placed for local walks and serves up delicious vegetarian breakfasts. The nearest **campsite** is *Radnors End* (☎01497/820780), in a beautiful setting five minutes' walk from

---

Canoeing in Hay-on-Wye

Scores of visitors come to Hay-on-Wye to hike and cycle, but the district is just as pleasantly explored by **kayak** or **canoe** on the River Wye. In four to six days, it's possible to paddle your way downriver from Hay to Ross-on-Wye (see p.628), overnighting in tents on isolated stretches of river bank, or holing up in comfortable B&Bs and pubs along the way. As regards **kayak and canoe rental**, Paddles & Peddles, 15 Castle St (☎01497/820604, ⊛www.canoehire.co.uk), are a reputable outfit, who also have a boathouse on the river at the bottom end of town. Rental of life jackets and other essential equipment (such as waterproof canisters to carry your gear) is included in the price, which works out at around £35 per canoe for a full 24 hours, with discounts for longer trips. In addition, Paddles & Peddles will transport their customers to the departure and from the finishing points by minibus.

town across the Wye bridge on the Clyro road; washing and toilet facilities here are rudimentary, but pitches are cheap (£3) and the views over Hay and the Black Mountains are great.

Several of Hay's **pubs** offer top-quality bar food and meals, but you'll be hard pushed to find anywhere better than the *Famous Old Black Lion* on Lion Street. Another favourite is the *Granary*, on Broad Street (℡01497/820790), the vegetarian's choice, specializing in wholefood snacks, soups and filling main meals made mostly with organic produce; it also has a roadside terrace that is a great place for hikers to kick off their boots and relax over a pint.

Leominster and Croft Castle

LEOMINSTER (pronounced "Lemster"), fourteen miles north of Hereford, is an old market town that once prospered from the wool trade and is now important for **antiques**. Worth an hour or two of exploration, the town's attractive centre is an often half-timbered patchwork of medieval streets with overhanging gables, fanning out from the cramped confines of **Corn Square**. On the northeast edge of the centre, the chunky **Priory Church** has preserved several original Norman features, from the rounded windows in the clerestory and the sturdy pillars in the nave to the carved Green Man fertility symbol by the west door. The church also possesses a rare example of a **ducking stool**, used to dunk dishonest tradesmen, scolds and the odd "wayward" wife up until 1809.

Leominster is on the Hereford–Shrewsbury rail line and from the **train station** it's about half a mile west to the centre along Etnam Street. The **bus station** is at the west end of Etnam Street, footsteps from Corn Square, where the **tourist office** (April–Sept Mon–Sat 9.30am–5pm; Oct–March Mon–Sat 10am–4pm; ℡01568/616460), hands out brochures listing local **accommodation**. There's no special reason to hang around, but the *Copper Hall*, a large old building with its own walled garden at 134 South St (℡01568/611622; no credit cards; ➋), is a pleasant enough spot to hang your hat.

From Leominster, it's just five miles northwest to **Croft Castle** (May–Sept Wed–Sun 1–5pm; April & Oct Sat & Sun 1–4.30pm; £3.90; NT) via the B4361. Here, the sturdy pink stone towers and walls of the original medieval fortress have been embellished by a string of subsequent owners. Neo-Gothic castellated bays lie each side of the gabled front and inside there's an exuberant Georgian staircase, with neo-Gothic flourishes, as well as a kitschy Blue and Gold Room, complete with a vast gaudy chimneypiece.

Shropshire

One of England's largest and least populated counties, **Shropshire** stretches from its long and winding border with Wales to the very edge of the urban Black Country. Its most unique attraction is industrial: it was here that the Industrial Revolution made a huge stride forward with the spanning of the River Severn by the very first **iron bridge**. The assorted industries that subsequently squeezed into the gorge are long gone, but a series of **museums** celebrate their craftsmanship – from tiles and iron through to porcelain and even clay pipes. The River Severn also flows through the county town of **Shrewsbury**, whose antique centre holds dozens of old half-timbered buildings, though **Ludlow**, further to the south, has the edge when it comes to handsome Tudor and Jacobean architecture. Some of the most beautiful parts

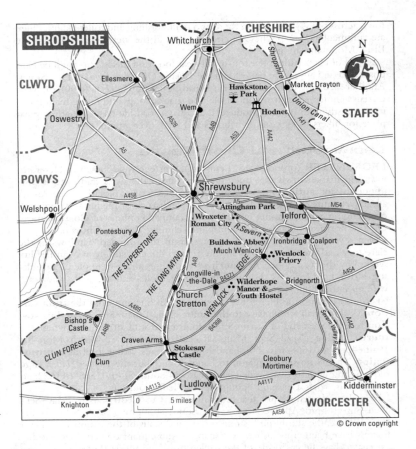

© Crown copyright

of Shropshire are to the south and east of Shrewsbury in the twin ridges of **Wenlock Edge** and the **Long Mynd**, both of which are prime hiking areas, best explored from the attractive little towns of **Much Wenlock** and **Church Stretton** respectively. Out west, the hills become increasingly barren and dramatic as they approach the Welsh border. This is one of the most remote parts of England, a solitary landscape dusted with tiny hamlets and the occasional town, amongst which **Bishop's Castle** and **Clun** are perhaps the most appealing.

Yet, for all its attractions, Shropshire remains well off the main tourist routes, one factor protecting the county's isolation being the paucity of its **public transport**. Shrewsbury and Telford are connected to Birmingham, whilst Ludlow, Craven Arms and Church Stretton are connected to Shrewsbury on the Hereford line, but that's about the limit of the **train** services, whilst rural **buses** tend to connect outlying villages on just a few days of the week. Bus timetables are available at tourist offices and from the **Telford Traveline** (℡01952/200005), covering Telford, Ironbridge and Much Wenlock.

Ironbridge Gorge

Both geographically and culturally, **Ironbridge Gorge**, the collective title for a cluster of small villages huddled in the wooded Severn valley to the south of new-town Telford, looks to the cities of the West Midlands conurbation rather than rural Shropshire. Ironbridge Gorge was the crucible of the Industrial Revolution, a process encapsulated by its famous span across the Severn gorge – the world's first **iron bridge**, engineered by Abraham Darby and opened on New Year's Day, 1781. He was the third innovative industrialist of that name – the first Abraham Darby started iron-smelting here back in 1709 and the second invented the forging process that made it possible to produce massive single beams in iron. Under the guidance of such creative figures as the Darbys and Thomas Telford, the area's factories once churned out engines, rails, wheels and other heavy-duty iron pieces in quantities unmatched in England. Manufacturing has now all but vanished, but the surviving monuments make the gorge the most extensive industrial heritage sight in the country – and one that has been granted World Heritage Site status by UNESCO.

Arrival, information and accommodation

There are regular **buses** to Ironbridge village, at the heart of the gorge, from Telford and less frequent services from Shrewsbury and Birmingham. However, travelling round the gorge by bus is well-nigh impossible – the shuttle that used to transport visitors between sights no longer operates and regular buses are few and far between. Even worse, there's currently no **bike** rental in the gorge, though it's possible that this service may be resumed – ring the tourist office (see below) for news.

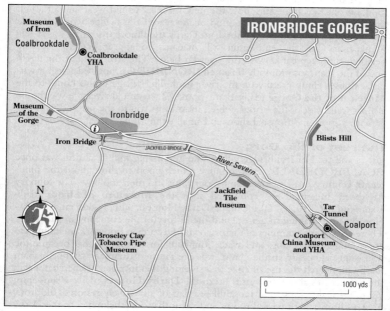

© Crown copyright

Ironbridge Gorge contains five museums and an assortment of other industrial attractions spread along a four-mile stretch of the River Severn Valley. A thorough exploration takes at least a day – two for comfort. Each museum charges its own admission fee, but if you're intending to visit several, then buy a **passport ticket** (£10), which allows access to each of them once in any calendar year. Passport tickets are available at all the main sights. **Parking** is free at all the museums, but not in the village of Ironbridge itself. Pick up local maps and information from the **Ironbridge Visitor Information Centre** (Mon–Fri 9am–5pm, Sat & Sun 10am–5pm; ℡01952/432166, ⒲www.ironbridge.org.uk), beside the iron bridge in Ironbridge village.

Most visitors to the gorge come for the day, but there are several pleasant **B&Bs** in Ironbridge village, which is where you want to be. Two of the best are *The Library House*, which occupies a charming Georgian villa just yards from the iron bridge at 11 Severn Bank (℡01952/432299, ⒲www.libraryhouse.com; no credit cards; ❸), and *Eley's Bridge View*, whose spick and span rooms are also a stone's throw from the bridge at 10 Tontine Hill (℡01952/432541; ❷). Alternatively, *Coalbrookdale Villa* is an attractive Victorian Gothic ironmasters' house up the hill from the bridge in tiny Paradise (℡01952/433450; no credit cards; ❷). The gorge also holds two **youth hostels**: one in the old Workers' Institute opposite the Coalbrookdale Museum of Iron, the other in the former Coalport China factory. They share the same telephone number (℡01952/588755, Ⓔironbridge@yha.org.uk) and are open all year, but only at weekends in the depths of winter.

Ironbridge village

There must have been an awful lot of nervous sweat during the construction of the **iron bridge** over the River Severn in the late 1770s. The first of its kind, no one was quite sure how the new material would wear and although the single-span design looked sound, many feared the bridge would tumble into the river. To compensate, Abraham Darby used more iron than was strictly necessary, but the end result still manages to appear graceful, arching between the steep banks with the river far below. The settlement at the north end of the span was promptly renamed **IRONBRIDGE**, and today its brown-brick houses climb prettily up the river bank. The village is also home to the **Museum of the Gorge** (daily 10am–5pm; £2), in an old riverside warehouse a short walk west of the bridge, which introduces you to the site and its history with a short audio-visual show and small exhibition.

The rest of the Gorge

Just to the west of Ironbridge village, the gorge's big industrial deal was once **COALBROOKDALE**'s iron foundry, which boomed throughout the nineteenth century and employed up to four thousand men and boys. The foundry has been imaginatively converted into the **Museum of Iron** (daily 10am–5pm; £3.90, £4.60 including Darby Houses), with a wide range of displays on iron-making in general and the history of the company in particular. There are superb examples of Victorian and Edwardian ironwork including the art castings – stags, dogs and water fountains for instance – that became the house speciality. Also in the complex is the restored **furnace** where Abraham Darby pioneered the use of coke as a smelting fuel in place of charcoal. From the furnace, it's about 100 yards up to the **Darby Houses** (daily 10am–5pm; £2.65) – Dale House and Rosehill – a pair of attractively restored, old ironmaster's homes with period rooms and items that once belonged to the Darby family.

△ Warwick Castle

From Ironbridge village, it's a couple of miles east along the river's edge to the **Tar Tunnel** (April–Oct daily 10am–5pm; £1), where bitumen oozes naturally from the walls. Close by, the **Coalport China Museum** (daily 10am–5pm; £3.90) occupies the restored factory where Coalport porcelain and china was manufactured from 1792 until the works transferred to Stoke-on-Trent in 1926. The complex has several well-preserved examples of the conical bottle-kilns that were long the hallmark of the pottery industry, and inside the museum there's an engrossing assortment of the gaudy crockery for which the company was famous.

It's a mile or so up the hill from the Tar Tunnel to the rambling **Blists Hill Victorian Town** (daily 10am–5pm; £7.50), which encloses various reconstructed Victorian buildings – including a school, a candle-makers, a doctor's surgery complete with horrific instruments, a gas-lit pub, a wrought-iron works and a slaughterhouse. Jam-packed on most summer days, it's especially popular with school parties, which keep the period-dressed employees very busy.

On the opposite bank of the river, accessible either via the footbridge near the Tar Tunnel or the Jackfield road bridge to the west, is the **Jackfield Tile Museum** (daily 10am–5pm; £3.90). Housed in an old tile factory, the museum features a superb collection of brightly coloured tiles, from the fancy, flowery patterns of washstand splash-backs through to intricate Victorian fireplace tiles and a folksy *Punch and Judy* panel from the 1920s.

Heading west from Jackfield, along the south bank of the River Severn, follow the signs to the enjoyable **Broseley Clay Tobacco Pipe Museum** (April–Oct daily 1–5pm; £2.65). During the late seventeenth and early eighteenth centuries, the satellite settlement of Broseley, formerly a source of raw materials for the foundries across the river, became a boom town in its own right, producing clay pipes for the swelling ranks of tobacco smokers in Britain. Occupying one of three factories that once existed here, the museum charts the history of smoking with a lively exhibition that culminates with some priceless film footage showing how the arm-length "Church Warden" pipes were made. Once cigarettes began to supplant pipes, the writing was on the wall and eventually the factory closed, but the building and its contents were left exactly as they were the day the workers downed tools. To their credit, the museum's creators have done their best to preserve this time-capsule effect, shunning actors in period costume in favour of informative panels.

Eating and drinking

For **food**, there's a hardly a plethora of great places to eat in the Gorge, but appealing options kick off with the excellent *Meadow Inn* pub (℡01952/433193), a family-owned Free House with mock-Elizabethan timbers and an excellent line in daily specials – meat, seafood and vegetarian. It's located down by the river on Buildwas Road, about a mile west of the bridge. Also first-rate is the *Horse & Jockey*, 15 Jockey Bank (℡01952/433798), just north of Coalport, whose legendary steak-and-kidney pie draws punters from miles around, whilst the moderately priced *Oliver's Vegetarian Bistro* (℡01952/433086; closed Mon), on the High Street by the bridge, does what it does with flair. **Real-ale** buffs will enjoy the *Coalbrookdale Inn*, past the Museum of Iron, a smashing traditional pub – no pool tables or one-armed bandits – which has the CAMRA stamp of approval for its excellent selection of beers.

Much Wenlock

Heading west from Ironbridge village along the northern bank of the River Severn, it's only a couple of miles to the A4169 and **Buildwas Abbey**

(April–Sept daily 11am–5pm; £2; EH), a roofless but otherwise well-preserved twelfth-century structure in meadowland by the River Severn. In many ways its setting and isolation lend it more atmosphere than the skeletal ruin of the eleventh-century **Wenlock Priory** (April–Oct daily 10am–6pm; Nov–March Wed–Sun 10am–1pm & 2–4pm; £2.85; EH) at **MUCH WENLOCK**, three miles to the south. With some solid Norman carving in its chapter house and lavatorium, the priory stands amid fine topiary in a dipped basin of green fields on the edge of the tiny town. Unfailingly quaint, Much Wenlock itself is a patchwork of Tudor, Jacobean and Georgian buildings, their style captured perfectly by the **Guildhall**, sitting pretty on sturdy oak columns in the middle of the Butter Market. The town has a small cachet of **B&Bs** and **hotels** – and most of them are listed by the **tourist office** on The Square (June–Aug daily 10.30am–1pm & 2–5pm; April–May, Sept & Oct Mon–Sat 10.30am–1pm & 2–5pm, Sun 2–5pm; ☎01952/727679). Easily the best of the bunch is the charming *Talbot Inn* (☎01952/727077, ⍟www.talbot.bridgnorthshropshire .com; ❺), an old coaching inn that was formerly part of the abbey, with exposed beams, fresh flowers in summer and open fires during the winter.

Wenlock Edge

A good reason to base yourself in this area for a night or two is to walk the beautiful **Wenlock Edge**, a limestone escarpment running twenty-odd miles southwest from Much Wenlock to Craven Arms, on the A49. Its south side is a gently shelving slope of open farmland, while the thickly wooded north side scarps steeply to the Shropshire plains, affording superb views over a sea of patchwork fields with the hills of the Welsh border beckoning beyond. Much of the Edge is owned by the National Trust, and a network of waymarked trails, graded by colour according to length and difficulty, winds through the woodland from a string of car parks along the B4371, which hugs the ridge from Much Wenlock to **Longville-in-the-Dale**. The paths are easy to follow and panels erected at the car parks outline the routes, but it's still a good idea to pick both and OS map and a copy of Ian R. Jones's *Wenlock Edge* leaflet from the tourist office in Much Wenlock, which describes the trails in detail. **Bus** services hereabouts are poor, so hikers really need their own transport. **Accommodation** is limited too – both in Much Wenlock and on the Edge, where there's just a light scattering of B&Bs – so you may well find it more convenient to base yourself in the Ironbridge Gorge. That said, the YHA have one of their flagship **hostels** here at **Wilderhope Manor** (☎01694/771363, ⍟wilderhope@yha.org.uk; open Dec 22–26, but otherwise closed Nov–Jan). The hostel occupies a charming Elizabethan mansion, set deep in idyllic countryside, about one and a half miles south of Longville-in-the-Dale – and the B4371. Wilderhope is popular with school groups, so reservations are recommended. Midland Red **bus** #712 runs to within striking distance of the youth hostel from Ludlow on weekdays, or you can catch one of the more frequent services from Ludlow and Bridgnorth to nearby Shipton, a couple of miles across the fields, and walk from there.

Bridgnorth

BRIDGNORTH, nine miles southeast of Much Wenlock along the A458, may be in Shropshire, but – with Wolverhampton just twenty minutes' drive away – it has all the bustle of the West Midlands. Spilling down a sheer-sided bluff beside the River Severn, the town prospered throughout the medieval era as a bridging point for the river, but was badly mauled and its economy dislocated by the Parliamentary army during the Civil War. Today, Bridgnorth is at its prettiest on top of the bluff in the **High Town**, where the High Street is interrupted by the seventeenth-century **Town Hall**, a half-timbered building perched on an arcaded base. At its southern end, High Street runs into West Castle Street. This soon leads to the domed **St Mary's church**, a solemn-looking edifice designed by Thomas Telford, and the shattered thirty-foot **tower** which is all that remains of the medieval castle: the ruin leans at a precarious angle of seventeen degrees. From here, a short but pleasant walkway tracks along the bluff above the river, ending up at the century-old **cliff railway** (summer Mon–Sat 8am–8pm, Sun noon–8pm; rest of year closes 6pm; 60p), which clanks up the steepest rail gradient in Britain to connect Bank Street (off West Castle Street) to the Low Town below.

Bridgnorth is also the northern terminus of the **Severn Valley Railway** (☎01299/403816, ⓦwww.svr.co.uk), whose trains steam down the valley to Kidderminster, some thirteen miles away. Trains operate all year, daily for most of the summer. It takes a little over an hour for the train to travel from Bridgnorth to Kidderminster with the return fare costing from £9.60. In Bridgnorth, the SVR station is in High Town across the footbridge from West Castle Street.

It only takes an hour or two to look round Bridgnorth and there are regular **bus** services on to Shrewsbury and Ludlow amongst many possible destinations. Most countywide services arrive and depart from the bus stops on the High Street. If you do decide to stay, the **tourist office**, in the library on Listley Street off the south end of High Street (April–Oct Mon–Wed, Fri & Sat 9.30am–5pm, Thurs 10am–1pm & 2–5pm; Nov–March Mon–Wed, Fri & Sat 9.30am–5pm; ☎01746/763257, ⓦwww.bridgnorthshropshire.com), can help you out; it has a list of local **B&Bs**. For **food**, try *Quaints*, a neat and inexpensive vegetarian bistro on St Mary's Street, just off the High Street near the Town Hall.

Shrewsbury and around

SHREWSBURY, the county town of Shropshire, sits in a narrow loop of the River Severn, a three-hundred-yard spit of land being all that keeps the town centre from becoming an island. It would be difficult to design a better defensive site, and fortifications were first built on this narrow neck in the fifth century, after the departure of the Roman legions from the nearby garrison town of Viroconium. The Normans were swift to realize the strategic potential of the site, too, building the first stone castle, which was expanded and strengthened by Edward I in the late thirteenth century. As the town boomed on the back of the Welsh wool trade, so its importance grew, reaching its apogee when Shrewsbury briefly became capital-in-exile for King Charles I during the early years of the Civil War. The eighteenth century saw the town evolve as a staging post on the busy London to Holyhead route. This traffic withered with the arrival of the railways, but by then the town had become the host of a lively social season, patronized by the sort of people who could afford to send their offspring to the famous Shrewsbury School. The top-notch gatherings are, however, long gone and nowadays Shrewsbury is an easy-going, middling market town, albeit with several especially fine Tudor and Jacobean streetscapes. One plus for Shrewsbury is its proximity to three appealing attractions, specifically the ruins of **Wroxeter Roman City**, the grottoes, follies and handsome scenery of **Hawkstone Historic Park** and (less distinctively) the Georgian mansion of **Attingham Park** – though you'll need your own transport to get to any of them.

Arrival, information and accommodation

Shrewsbury is well connected by **train** to the rest of the country, and its station, at the northeast edge of the centre, is a popular departure point for scenic rail journeys into mid-Wales. **Buses** from London, Birmingham and beyond pull into the National Express stand at the Raven Meadows bus station, off the Smithfield Road, five minutes' walk west of the train station. The **tourist office** is south up the hill from the two stations, on The Square (May–Sept Mon–Sat 10am–6pm, Sun 10am–4pm; Oct–April Mon–Sat 10am–5pm; ☎01743/281200, ⊛www.shrewsbury.ws). The labyrinthine lanes and alleys of Shrewsbury's centre can be baffling, but fortunately it's too small an area to be lost in for long. As a general guide, Castle Gates/Castle Street runs from the train station up to Pride Hill, a short pedestrianized street that meets St Mary's Street/Dogpole at one end and High Street/Wyle Cop at the other. The Square off the High Street is at the heart of the town centre.

Shrewsbury has one particularly good **hotel**, the *Prince Rupert*, which occupies a tastefully converted old building, right in the centre of town off Pride Hill on Butcher Row (☎01743/499955, ⊛www.prince-rupert-hotel.co.uk; ❺). Less expensive options in the centre include *The Lion*, a classic Georgian coaching inn on the Wyle Cop (☎01743/353107; ❺), and the *College Hill Guest House*, a pleasant **B&B** in an old listed building at 11 College Hill, near The Square (☎01743/365744; no credit cards; ❷). Most of the town's B&Bs are beyond the centre, with several dotted along Abbey Foregate, which runs east from the English Bridge at the foot of Wyle Cop: try the unassuming, neat and tidy *Abbey Court Guest House*, at no. 134 (☎01743/364416; no credit cards; ❶). The **youth hostel** is housed in a former Victorian ironmaster's house, about one mile east of the centre, at the far end of Abbey Foregate (☎01743/360179, ✉shrewsbury@yha.org.uk; £9.25; closed Nov–Feb). It's near Lord Hill's Column, the monument erected in memory of Wellington's sidekick at the Battle of Waterloo. Take bus #8 or #26 from the bus station.

The Town

The sandstone **Castle**, sitting high above the castellated train station, rests on the site of fortifications that go back a millennium and a half. Today's buildings date mainly from the thirteenth century, although the great architect and engineer Thomas Telford was brought in during the 1780s to shore up the remains and turn the castle into an extravagant private home for local bigwig Sir William Pulteney. It is now home to the dull **Shropshire Regimental Museum** (Easter–Sept Tues–Sat 10am–5pm, Sun 10am–4pm; Oct–Easter Wed–Sat 10am–4pm; £2), a far less interesting attraction than the annual World Music Day (☎01743/231142), which takes place here in July and makes the most of the castle's dramatic setting.

Castle Gates winds up the hill from the station into the heart of the river loop where the medieval town took root. Here, off Pride Hill, several especially appealing half-timbered buildings are dotted along **Butcher Row**, which leads into the quiet precincts of St Alkmund's church, where there's a charming view of the fine old buildings of **Fish Street**. From the church, Bear Steps clambers down to the High Street, on the far side of which, in the narrow Georgian confines of The Square, is the **Old Market Hall**, a heavy-duty stone structure built in 1596.

From The Square, it's a short stroll west to Barker Street and Shrewsbury's most diverting museum, **Rowleys House** (Easter–Sept Mon & Sun 10am–4pm, Tues–Sat 10am–5pm; rest of year Tues–Sat 10am–4pm; free), which occupies an ostentatious 1590s town house with a seventeenth-century brick residence tacked on. The museum contains a wide range of displays relating to local life, with some of the more interesting exhibits coming from the nearby Roman city of Wroxeter (see p.634), including a unique silver mirror from the third century AD. There are also modest displays on two of the town's most illustrious sons, Charles Darwin and Robert Clive of India (1725–74). Largely forgotten today, Clive was the conqueror of a vast chunk of India, but his meteoric rise was followed by an equally dramatic fall. Elevated to the peerage following his defeat of the ruler of Bengal, Clive was later the subject of a full-scale parliamentary enquiry into his conduct and, although he was acquitted, he ended up committing suicide shortly afterwards.

Nearby, on the western edge of the centre, the trim gardens and lawns of **Quarry Park** run gently down to the river, overlooked by the wedding-cake tower of the town's most celebrated church, the late seventeenth-century **St Chad's** (daily: Easter–Oct 8am–5pm; Nov–Easter 8am–1pm; free). England's largest round church, St Chad's was built – in an eccentric version of the classical style – on the site of an earlier church, which collapsed as its clock struck 4am, one morning in 1788.

Back on The Square, High Street snakes down the hill to become **Wyle Cop**, lined with elegant Georgian buildings and leading to the **English Bridge**, which provides a handsome view of the town as it crosses the Severn. Beyond the bridge is **Shrewsbury Abbey** (daily: April–Oct 9.30am–5.30pm; Nov–March 10.30am–3pm; free), the town's most important ecclesiastical building, but now unceremoniously locked in the middle of a traffic intersection on Abbey Foregate. Founded in the 1080s by Roger de Montgomery – who was also responsible for Shrewsbury's first stone castle – this Benedictine abbey was a major political and religious force hereabouts until the Dissolution. Unusually, King Henry VIII's henchmen did not destroy the place and, although much of the abbey was ultimately demolished in the 1830s, the abbey church has survived and is still in use. Inside the church, the best feature is the huge west window of heraldic glass, dating from the fourteenth century. Underneath it is the original Norman door, and four of the nave pillars and their connecting arches also date from the original structure.

Eating and drinking

For daytime **food**, try the *Goodlife Wholefood Restaurant* in the antique surroundings of Barrack's Passage, off Wyle Cop, or snack at *Philpotts Quality Sandwiches*, which deserves its name and is located at 15 Butcher Row. In the evening, there's the *Sol*, 82 Wyle Cop (℡01743/340560; closed Sun), an outstanding if pricey restaurant featuring local ingredients such as Shropshire lamb cooked in a broadly Mediterranean style, and tasty tandoori at *Shalimar*, by the abbey at 23 Abbey Foregate (℡01743/366658). Some of the best **pub food** in the centre is served at *Loggerheads*, in St Alkmud's Place, with wood-panelled walls and exposed beams; try their filling "Big Head Pie" – steak pieces topped with puff pastry and served with chips, salad and a pint for around £5. Other good **pubs** are the *Severn Stars* on Coleham Head, just over the English Bridge from the town centre; the smoke-free *Three Fishes*, in an ancient building on Fish Street; and the lively *Coach & Horses*, on Swan Hill just south of The Square. The *Music Hall* **cinema** next door to the tourist office on The Square screens art-house as well as mainstream releases (℡01743/281281).

Hawkstone Historic Park and Follies

Cocooned by servants, the landed gentry of the eighteenth and nineteenth centuries had time to fill, and many of them took to converting their estates into pleasure parks for strolling, hunting and contemplating nature. **Hawkstone Historic Park and Follies** (Jan–March Sat & Sun 10.30am–dusk; April–June, Sept & Oct Wed–Sun 10.30am–dusk; July & Aug daily 10.30am–dusk; £4.50; ⓦwww.hawkstone.co.uk), which lies about ten miles north of Shrewsbury off the A49, is an outstanding example of this. The park, with its maze of tree-lined avenues, makes good use of the lie of the land, in which rocky outcrops and two roughly parallel ridges bubble up from the surrounding flatland. The park has lain pretty much undisturbed since its creation by the Hill family, who owned the estate from 1748 until 1895. On one ridge is a tall monument, a tower with 150 spiral steps leading to a windswept balcony. More unusual features along the one- or two-hour circular tour of the park include Swiss Bridge – two tree trunks spanning a deep gully – a hermit's cave and a curious set of dim and eerie grottoes on Grotto Hill. From this hill top, the views stretch for miles across the plains to the Welsh hills. Parts of the path are a little tricky underfoot, especially towards Foxes Knob, a sandstone outcrop reached via dark passageways snaking through the rock.

Attingham Park and Wroxeter Roman City

In a more ostentatious mould is **Attingham Park** (April–Oct Mon, Tues & Fri–Sun 1.30–4.30pm; £4.30 including grounds; NT), four miles southeast of Shrewsbury – take the B4380 to the hamlet of **ATCHAM** and follow the signs. Originally the stately pile of Noel Hill, the first Lord Berwick, this imposing Georgian **mansion** was designed in 1782 by George Stuart, with later additions by John Nash. Hill had a point to make: keen to impress travellers using the Severn bridge on the edge of his estate, he made sure no one could miss seeing his house by equipping it with a massive Neoclassical facade, incorporating four imperious pillars and a colossal portico. The interior is similarly over-blown, crammed with luxurious furniture and souvenirs from successive Grand Tours – and typical of the Regency predilection for all things French and Italian. Thomas Hill, the second lord, was a particularly avid collector and he added the picture gallery for his collection of Renaissance art in 1805. However, today's paintings are a poor reflection of the original collection as Thomas over-reached himself and, faced with bankruptcy, was forced to sell off his finest works. Interestingly, the picture gallery is spanned by the world's first cast-iron-rib ceiling, a product of the Coalbrookdale Company. The surrounding deer **park and grounds** (March–Oct 8am–9pm; Nov–Feb 9am–5pm; grounds only £2; NT) were landscaped by Humphry Repton and offer pleasant riverside and woodland walks.

Heading east from Atcham, the B4380 zips along the course of **Watling Street**, the former Roman military route that linked the wild Welsh borders with St Albans, London, Canterbury and Dover. A couple of miles from Atcham, amongst the open farmland of today, Watling Street crossed the River Severn and this key strategic location was once occupied by Roman Britain's fourth largest city, **Viroconium**. The site was first settled by the Cornovii, but it was the Emperor Nero who really got things going in 58 AD as part of his drive to conquer Wales. In the event, the Welsh proved intractable and, when there was a second imperial visit sixty years later, the Emperor Hadrian focused on security, doubling the size of the Viroconium garrison. Hadrian also ordered the construction of a grand set of municipal buildings and today the ruins of the civic centre, dubbed **Wroxeter Roman City** (April–Oct daily 10am–6pm; Nov–March Wed–Sun 10am–1pm & 2–4pm; £3.50; EH), are still impressive, particularly the large chunk of masonry that once enclosed part of the main baths. You'll need a vivid imagination to picture the ruins as a teeming Roman metropolis, but the site's modest museum, together with the accompanying booklet, help fill in the gaps.

The Long Mynd: Church Stretton and Craven Arms

Beginning about ten miles south of Shrewsbury, the upland heaths of the **Long Mynd**, some ten miles long and between two and four miles wide, run parallel to and just to the west of the A49. This is prime walking territory and the heathlands are latticed with footpaths, the best of which offer sweeping views over the border to the Black Mountains of Wales. Nestled at the foot of the Mynd beside the A49 is **CHURCH STRETTON**, a tidy little place and one-time fashionable Victorian resort that makes the best base for hiking the area. The village also possesses the dinky parish **church of St Lawrence**, parts of which – especially the nave – are Norman. Look out also for the fertility symbol over the north doorway – it's a sheila-na-gig comparable to the one in Kilpeck. In the centre of the village near the church is the **tourist office** (Easter–Sept Mon–Sat 10am–1pm & 2–5pm; ☎01694/723133), which stocks a wide range of leaflets detailing local walks, hikes and off-road cycle routes. Perhaps the most obvious hike is the short, half-mile stroll west up along the National Trust's **Carding Mill Valley** to the **Chalet Pavilion** tearoom and information centre (April–Oct daily 11am–5pm; Nov–March Sat & Sun 11am–4pm). Alternatively, strike up **Caer Caradoc**, the steep hill that looms directly east of the village; crowned by an extensive iron-age hill fort, its summit affords superb views of the Mynd and the rolling pasture land that extends east towards Birmingham. Waymarked trails lead to the top and down the other side to the picturesque hamlet of **CARDINGTON**, whose cosy village pub serves filling bar meals and fine pints of Shropshire Lad bitter. You can do the round walk in three to four hours.

Church Stretton is accessible from Shrewsbury and Ludlow by **train** and **bus**. Most buses stop in the centre of the village; the train station is a short walk from the tourist office just off the A49. There's no shortage of good-value accommodation in and around Church Stretton, much of it on farms overlooking the Mynd. One particularly good **B&B** is *Acton Scott Farm* (☎01694/781260; no credit cards; ❶; closed Dec & Jan), a seventeenth-century building with log fires and a choice of standard or en-suite rooms, three miles south of Stretton off the A49 in the hamlet of Acton Scott. For a little more luxury, try the *Jinlye Guest House*, on Castle Hill in All Stretton, one mile north, which backs onto the Long Mynd and has great views (☎01694/723243, ⓦwww.jinlye.co.uk; no credit cards; ❸). **Campers** have a choice of several sites. These include *Small Batch* (☎01694/723358; £8 for caravans or tents; closed Oct–Easter), one mile south at Little Stretton, which enjoys a lovely situation but is small and pretty frugal, and the better equipped *Ley Hill Farm* (☎01694/771366; tents £5; closed Nov–Feb), deep in the countryside near Cardington, with panoramic views of the surrounding hills. **Bike rental** is available from *Terry's Cycles*, 6 Castle Hill, All Stretton (☎01694/724334).

The **YHA hostel** at **Bridges Long Mynd** (☎01588/650656, ⓦwww.yha .org.uk), five miles' hike west from Church Stretton near **Ratlinghope**, is a splendid base for walks, sitting between the Long Mynd and the **Stiperstones**, a remote range of boggy heather dotted with ancient cairns and earthworks. It's open all year, but bookings are required at least three days in advance from November to March. Marooned amid gentler country east of Church Stretton on the B4371, near Longville-in-the-Dale, **Wilderhope Manor** is the area's other hostel; it's featured on p.639, along with an account of the Wenlock Edge.

Stokesay Castle

Inconsequential Craven Arms, the next stop along the rail line from Church Stretton, lies a mile or so north of the hamlet of **STOKESAY**, site of one of England's most appealing manor houses. **Stokesay Castle** (April–Oct daily 10am–6pm; Nov–March Wed–Sun 10am–1pm & 2-4pm; £4; EH), as it's known, comprises a collection of leaning, half-timbered buildings that span a range of over three hundred years, gathered around a neat grassy courtyard. The main block is a thirteenth-century fortified manor, originally built by a prosperous wool merchant for the princely price of a sparrowhawk. Beautifully restored by English Heritage, it contains an expansive banqueting hall that retains its central fireplace, vaulted timbers and large windows. The size of the windows is actually very significant: Edward I's suppression of the Welsh had made border life a good deal more secure for the English, so they could afford to weaken the walls to let more light in. Across the central courtyard is the black and yellow gatehouse, built three hundred years after the manor house yet forming a harmonious group with the main building as well as the tiny parish church next door. The church was largely rebuilt in the mid-seventeenth century, but some of the original Norman features remain.

Bishop's Castle and Clun

BISHOP'S CASTLE, midway between the southern edge of the Long Mynd and the Welsh border, is a real treat – uncluttered, very pretty and full of intriguing second-hand bookshops and junk stores. Its short **High Street** winds up a hill past half-timbered frontages to the miniature Georgian **Town Hall** – this was England's smallest borough until 1967 – and the lurching **House on Crutches**. Stroll up past the town hall and veer to the right to reach the seventeenth-century **Three Tuns brewery** and its delightful, time-warped **pub** in Salop Street, which serves up traditional home-brew – a pale cider-coloured concoction that's deceptively potent. They also do excellent and imaginative bar meals and offer **B&B** in a handful of cosy little rooms (☎01588/638797, ☒www.thethreetunsinn.co.uk; ❺). The eccentric **tourist office** is housed in a second-hand shop called *Old Time*, at 29 High St (daily 10am–10pm; ☎01588/638467); they have the full list of local accommodation, and offer two rooms of their own (no credit cards; ❶). **Buses**, linking Bishop's Castle with Shrewsbury, Ludlow and Clun, drop passengers at the foot of the High Street.

Five miles south of Bishop's Castle – and connected to it by bus – the modest village of **CLUN** holds the battered ruins of a medieval **castle** (dawn–dusk; free), built by the Normans but abandoned in the sixteenth century. The castle's only noteworthy feature is the chunky masonry of the ruined keep, but the setting more than compensates – the keep is raised on an earthen mound cradled by the river below. Clun also makes an excellent base for jaunts out across the surrounding hills that roll west over into Wales. These hills are crisscrossed with footpaths, including a stretch of the **Offa's Dyke Path**, a long-distance hiking trail, which runs north south along – or near – the Welsh–English border, from Prestatyn to Chepstow, both of which are in Wales. Some 180 miles long, the path takes its name from the ditch King Offa of Mercia (broadly central England) had dug along the Anglo–Welsh frontier in the eighth century. Unlike Hadrian's Wall, it was never guarded or patrolled, acting as a boundary marker, not a defensive work. For all that, it was an extraordinary enterprise, though there's precious little to actually see today – the dyke merged with its surroundings centuries ago. The Path cuts a varied course, traversing open moorland and agricultural land but also weaving through deep wooded valleys; three miles west of Clun, it crosses the B4368 and this is as good a place as any to join it – or, more realistically, to walk a section.

In and around Clun are several excellent **B&Bs**. Pick of the bunch is the *Old Farmhouse*, Woodside (℡01588/640695; no credit cards; ❶; closed Nov–Feb), an eighteenth-century farmhouse with a pretty garden one mile from – and 300 feet above – the village. There's also a small **youth hostel** (℡01588 /640582; closed Sept to mid-April), with self-catering facilities, in a converted watermill on the northeastern edge of the village – about ten minutes' walk from the B4368. As regards **pubs**, Clun has two good ones – the *Buffalo Inn* (℡01588/640225), which offers excellent bar food, and the *Sun Inn* (℡01588 /640559), whose à la carte restaurant is first-rate. There are **buses** to Clun from Shrewsbury, Ludlow and Bishop's Castle; they stop in the centre of the village.

Ludlow

LUDLOW, perched on a hill nearly thirty miles south of Shrewsbury, is one of the most picturesque towns in the Midlands, if not in England – a cluster of beautifully preserved black-and-white half-timbered buildings packed around a craggy stone castle, with rural Shropshire forming a dreamy backdrop. Close to the Welsh border, the Saxons were the first to recognize the site's defensive qualities, but it was the Normans who got down to business when Roger Montgomery turned up here with his men in 1085. Over the next few decades, Montgomery's fortifications were elaborated into an immense **Castle** (Jan Sat & Sun 10am–4pm; Feb, March & Oct–Dec daily 10am–4pm; April–July & Sept daily 10am–5pm; Aug daily 10am–7pm; £3), strong enough to keep the Welsh at bay and the seat of the Lord President of the Council of the Marches, as the borders were then known. Surviving the attentions of the Parliamentary troops in the Civil War, the rambling and imposing ruins that remain today include towers and turrets, gatehouses and concentric walls as well as the remains of the 110-foot Norman keep and an unusual Round Chapel built in 1120. With its spectacular setting above the rivers Teme and Corve, the castle also makes a fine open-air auditorium during the **Ludlow Festival** (℡01584/872150), two weeks of assorted musical and theatrical fun at the end of June.

The castle entrance opens out onto the **Market Place**, home to the intriguing **Castle Lodge** (daily 10am–5pm; £3), predominantly Elizabethan in style. In the oak-panelled rooms of the ground floor, stained-glass windows depict the coats of arms of Germans summoned by Henry VIII to help sack England's monasteries. In low-beamed chambers upstairs, there's a display on Ludlow's chequered history, which omits the popular rumour that Mary, Queen of Scots hid from Elizabeth's henchmen in the lodge's basement.

At its east end, the Market Place pushes into the Buttercross, off which the magnificently proportioned, fifteenth-century interior of the **church of St Lawrence** (daily 10am–5pm; free) boasts vast stained-glass windows and some of the country's finest misericords. Carved in oak, these misericords run the gamut from royal emblems and religious scenes to the folkloric and seemingly profane – a fox preaching to geese, a witch, a mermaid and a woman disappearing into the mouth of hell bottom first. In its turn the Buttercross nudges King Street, which intersects with the **Bull Ring**, home of the *Feathers Hotel*, an extraordinary Jacobean building with the fanciest wooden facade imaginable.

To the south of the Market Place, the gridiron of streets laid out by the Normans has survived intact, though most of the buildings date from the eighteenth century. It's the general appearance that appeals rather than any special sight, but steeply sloping **Broad Street**, running south from the Market Place, is particularly attractive, flanked by many of Ludlow's five hundred half-timbered Tudor and red-brick Georgian listed buildings.

Practicalities

From Ludlow **train station**, on the Shrewsbury–Hereford line, it's a five- to ten-minute walk west of the centre – just follow the signs. Most **buses** stop on Mill Street, across the Market Place from the castle entrance. Ludlow's **tourist office**, on the Market Place (summer Mon–Sat 10am–5pm, Sun 10.30am–5pm; rest of year Mon–Sat 10am–5pm; ☎01584/875053, ⓦwww .ludlow.org.uk), has a wide range of maps and books for walkers, as well as a selection of inexpensive leaflets detailing day hikes in the area. **Accommodation** is plentiful, though rooms can get scarce during the festival. First choice, if you can afford it, has to be the beautiful *Feathers Hotel* on the Bull Ring (☎01584/875261; ❼), an intricately decorated Jacobean town house with luxury rooms and period furnishings to match. Two other, less expensive options in the town centre are the *Wheatsheaf Inn*, a quaint little pub next to the town gate at the foot of Lower Broad Street (☎01584/872980; ❷), and, just beyond, the excellent *Number Twenty Eight*, in a couple of old properties (☎0800/0815000, ⓦwww.no28.co.uk; ❺).

For **food and drink**, the *Feathers* serves up excellent snacks and meals at its café-bar; the popular *Olive Branch*, on the Bull Ring (daily 10am–3pm), specializes in inexpensive light meals and salads; and the *Rose and Crown*, off the marketplace, serves up a good range of beers and delicious bar food and has a sheltered courtyard.

Birmingham

If anywhere can be described as the first purely industrial conurbation, it is **BIRMINGHAM**. Unlike the more specialist industrial towns that grew up across the north and Midlands, "Brum" – and its "Brummies" – turned its hand to every kind of manufacturing, gaining the epithet "the city of 1001 trades". It was here that the pioneers of the Industrial Revolution – James Watt, Matthew Boulton, William Murdock, Josiah Wedgwood, Joseph Priestley and Erasmus Darwin (grandfather of Charles) – formed the **Lunar Society**, a melting-pot of scientific and industrial ideas that spawned the world's first purpose-built factory, the distillation of oxygen, the invention of gas lighting and the mass production of the steam engine. A Midlands market town swiftly mushroomed into the nation's economic dynamo – in the fifty years up to 1830 the population more than trebled to 130,000.

Now the second largest city in Britain, with a population of over one million, Birmingham has long outgrown the squalor and misery of its boom years and today its industrial supremacy is recalled in a crop of excellent heritage museums and an extensive network of canals. It also boasts a thoroughly multiracial population that makes this one of Britain's most cosmopolitan cities. The shift to a post-manufacturing economy is symbolized by the new

CENTRAL BIRMINGHAM

M6 & A38 Lichfield ▲

M5 & A41 Wolverhampton ▲

Jewellery Quarter Museum ▲

JENNENS ROAD

ASTON STREET

NEW CANAL STREET

CURZON STREET

MERIDEN STREET

ALLISON STREET

DIGBETH

BRADFORD STREET

Coach Station

JAMES WATT QUEENSWAY

MOAT LANE

Moor Street Station

St Martin's Church

Bull Ring

FAZELEY STREET

Police Station

Victoria Law Courts

General Hospital

STEELHOUSE LANE

CORPORATION STREET

WHITTAL STREET

ST CHAD'S QUEENSWAY

PRIORY QWAY

OLD SQUARE

DALE END

PRIORY QUEENSWAY

HIGH STREET

Rotunda

ST MARTIN'S CIRCUS

EDGBASTON STREET

PERSHORE STREET

HURST STREET

Arcadian Centre

St Chad's Catholic Cathedral

ST CHAD'S CIRCUS

COLMORE

SNOW HILL Q'WAY

BULL STREET

St Philip's Anglican Cathedral

CANNON STREET

CHINESE QUARTER

1

8

Snow Hill Train Station

LIVERY STREET

CORNWALL STREET

CHURCH STREET

EDMUND STREET

NEWHALL STREET

BARWICK ST

TEMPLE ST

NEW STREET

STEPHENSON STREET

HILL STREET

JOHN BRIGHT ST

SMALLBROOK QUEENSWAY

New Street Station

5

3

Old Rep. Theatre

Hippodrome Theatre

7

GREAT CHARLES ST Q'WAY

LIONEL STREET

LUDGATE HILL

Council House

CHAMBERLAIN SQUARE

Town Hall

VICTORIA SQUARE

PARADISE CIRCUS

HILL STREET

NEW STREET STATION ST

SUFFOLK STREET QUEENSWAY

NAVIGATION STREET

HOLLIDAY STREET

PLOUGH STREET

BLUCHER STREET

SEVERN STREET

St Paul's

ST PAUL'S SQUARE

RBSA

JAMES ST

BROOK ST

Birmingham & Fazeley Canal

LIONEL STREET

CHARLOTTE STREET

FLEET ST

Birmingham Museum & Art Gallery

Library

2

CAMBRIDGE STREET

Repertory Theatre

War Memorial

CENTENARY SQUARE

BROAD STREET

BRIDGE STREET

GAS STREET

BERKLEY STREET

GRANVILLE STREET

Antique & Craft Market

COMMERCIAL STREET

JEWELLERY QUARTER

VITTORIA STREET

GRAHAM STREET

FREDERICK STREET

SUMMER ROW

GEORGE STREET

James's Bridge Locks

Brindley & Fazeley Canal

4

International Convention Centre

Ikon Gallery

Boat Trips

Gas Street Basin

E

6

BROAD STREET

TENNANT ST

7

Sea Life Centre

KING EDWARD'S ROAD

Birmingham Main Line Canal

National Indoor Arena

ST VINCENT STREET

BRINDLEY PLACE

G

SHEEPCOTE STREET

FIVE WAYS

GROSVENOR STREET WEST

SAND PITS

SUMMERHILL ROAD

POPE ST

CAMDEN STREET

ICKNIELD STREET

CLEMENT ST

EDWARD STREET

SPRING HILL

RUSTON ST

400 yds

0

Pedestrianised street

▲ A456 Kidderminster

▲ M42, M5, A38 Bromsgrove & Bristol Road

M5 ▼

© Crown copyright

RESTAURANTS	
Chez Jules	C
Chung Ying	I
Grand Tandoori	J
King Balti	K
Kushi	L
Left Bank	G
Le Petit Blanc	A
Mongolian Bar	E
Pizza Express	D
Punjab Paradise	M
Ronnie Scott's Café Bar	F
San Carlo	B
Shah Faisal	N
Warehouse Café	H

ACCOMMODATION	
Ashdale House	9
Briar Rose	1
Burlington Hotel	3
Chamberlain Park Hotel	10
Comfort Inn	5
Copthorne Birmingham	2
Crowne Plaza	4
Ibis Centre Hotel	8
Novotel	6
Travelodge	7

Convention Centre and by the enormous National Exhibition Centre (NEC) on the outskirts, while Birmingham's cultural initiatives – enticing a division of the Royal Ballet to take up residence here, and building a fabulous new concert hall for the City of Birmingham Symphony Orchestra – are first rate. Nonetheless, there's no pretending that Birmingham is packed with interesting sights – it isn't, though – along with its first-rate restaurant scene and nightlife – it's well worth a day or two – at least.

Arrival, information and city transport

Birmingham's **international airport** is eight miles east of the city centre off the A45 and near the M42 (Junction 6); the main terminal is beside Birmingham International train station, from where there are regular services into the centre. **New Street train station**, to which all InterCity and the vast majority of local services go, is right in the heart of the city. However, trains on the Stratford-upon-Avon, Warwick, Worcester and Malvern lines usually use **Snow Hill** and **Moor Street stations**, both about ten minutes' signposted walk from New Street. National Express **coach** travellers are dumped in the grim surroundings of **Digbeth coach station**, from where it is a ten-minute uphill walk to the centre.

Maps, loads of local leaflets and transport information are provided by all the city's **tourist offices**. The main office is located bang in the centre of town on Victoria Square at 130 Colmore Row (Mon–Sat 9.30am–6pm, Sun 10am–4pm; ☎0121/693 6300, ⊛www.birmingham.org.uk). Also in the centre is a smaller tourist office – and useful ticket shop – at 2 City Arcade, off New St (Mon–Sat 9.30am–5.30pm; ☎0121/643 2514). In addition, there are offices at the International Convention Centre (ICC; ☎0121/665 6116), Centenary Square, and in the National Exhibition Centre (NEC; ☎0121/780 4321), next to the airport. The city council runs its own tourist office and ticket booking office in the Central Library, right in the centre on Chamberlain Square (Mon–Fri 10am–5.30pm, Sat 10am–4.30pm; ☎0121/236 5622). All of the tourist offices operate a same-day hotel bed booking service for free, but advance bookings have to be made at either the NEC or ICC branches.

To see Birmingham at its best, you really need to stay in the centre, but most of the less expensive accommodation is scattered around the suburbs. This may well mean that you'll be dealing with Birmingham's excellent local transport system, whose **trains**, **metro** and **buses** delve into almost every corner of the city. Various companies provide these services, but they are co-ordinated by **Centro**, who operate both a city-wide public transport information line, **Centro Hotline** (☎0121/200 2700), and a regional equivalent, covering the West Midlands conurbation (☎0247/655 9559). A one-day **Centrocard**, valid on all services, can be purchased from bus drivers and at train and metro stations; it costs £5 (£4 after 9.30am and at the weekend).

One thing that may confuse is the name of the inner ring road: it's called the Queensway, but individual stretches keep their other names too, for example: Great Charles St, Queensway.

Accommodation

As you might expect, Birmingham has a wide range of **accommodation**, from tower-block chains out near the airport and family-run hotels in the leafier suburbs through to gritty inner-city B&Bs. All of the city's tourist offices have the full details and there's a selection of hotels in both their *Pocket Guide to Birmingham* (free) and the *Night & Day Essential Visitor Guide* (£2). All the tourist offices operate a **hotel room booking service**, but only the NEC (☎0121/780 4321) and the ICC (☎0121/665 6116) branches do bookings in advance. There's no charge and, even better, the tourist offices are often aware of special deals and discounts, which can slash costs considerably, especially on the weekend. The best bet is to stay in the vicinity of the ICC – you'll almost certainly pay more than in the rest of the city, but it's well worth it.

Ashdale House 39 Broad Road, Acocks Green ☎0121/706 3598. Well-situated B&B, serving good vegetarian and organic food. Acocks Green is a couple of miles southeast of the centre. There are buses from the centre, but you're probably best off taking the train from Moor Street to Spring Road station and walking the half mile or so from there. ❷

Briar Rose 25 Bennetts Hill ☎0121/634 8100. Modest but inexpensive place with forty rooms above a pub. Central location. ❷

Burlington Hotel 6 Burlington Arcade, 126 New St ☎0121/643 9191. Handsomely refurbished Victorian red-brick hotel with over one hundred bright and well-appointed rooms. Fitness facilities, too. ❻

Chamberlain Park Hotel Alcester St ☎0121/606 9000. Splendid conversion of a magnificent Victorian workhouse about fifteen minutes' walk from New Street station out along Digbeth and its continuation High Street. Alcester Street is a turning on the right. Excellent-value doubles, though the surrounding area hardly inspires confidence. ❶

Comfort Inn Station St ☎0121/643 1134. Routine, medium-sized chain hotel with standard-issue furnishings and fittings, though the rooms are perfectly adequate. In an earthy part of town,

beside New Street station. ❸

Copthorne Birmingham Paradise Circus ☎0121/200 2727. It may look rather like a Rubik cube from the outside, but this is a great hotel, partly because its 212 modern bedrooms are neat and trim, and partly because its location – plum in the centre beside Centenary Square – can't be bettered. It's expensive during the week, but weekends bring prices down to more reasonable levels. ❽, ❺ at weekends.

Crowne Plaza Central Square, Holliday St ☎0121/631 2000. Large, central hotel, a stone's throw from Gas Street Basin. Good health and fitness facilities, including an indoor pool. ❼

Ibis Centre Hotel Ladywell Walk, Arcadian Centre ☎0121/622 6010. Rather characterless, but well-situated chain hotel, bang in the Chinese Quarter, near the major theatres and nightclubs. ❷

Novotel Birmingham Centre, 70 Broad St ☎0121/643 2000. Great location for this smart, new and well-run chain hotel. Over 140 bedrooms decorated in crisp modern style. Good fitness facilities. ❼

Travelodge 230 Broad St ☎0121/644 5266. Workaday central chain hotel, but prices are very reasonable and it's within easy walking distance of lots of restaurants, bars and clubs. ❸

The City Centre

Many visitors get their first taste of central Birmingham at **New Street station**, whose unreconstructed ugliness – piles of modern concrete – makes a dispiriting start. Fortunately, things soon get better if you stroll west along pedestrianized **New Street**, one of the city's principal shopping streets, to the elegantly revamped **Victoria Square**, with its tumbling water fountain. The adjacent **Chamberlain Square** has been refurbished too, but here pride of place goes to the **Birmingham Museum and Art Gallery**, the city's finest museum, complete with a fabulous collection of Pre-Raphaelite art. Beyond, further west still, is the glossy **International Convention Centre**, from where it's another short hop to the **Gas Street Basin**, the prettiest part of the city's serpentine canal system. Close by is canalside **Brindley Place**, a smart, brick and glass complex with smart cafés and bars and the enterprising **Ikon Gallery** of contemporary art.

From Brindley Place, follow the old tow path along the **Birmingham and Fazeley canal** as far as Newhall Street, which is within easy walking distance of both **St Philip's Cathedral**, back in the centre on Colmore Row, and – in the opposite direction- the **Jewellery Quarter**, which holds an excellent museum and hundreds of workshops and retail outlets.

Victoria and Chamberlain squares

At its west end, New Street opens out into the handsomely refurbished **Victoria Square**, whose centrepiece is a large and particularly engaging water fountain designed by Dhruva Mistry. The fountain's large and distinctive female figure is affectionately known as "the floozy in the jacuzzi" by the locals – but there's no such term of endearment for Anthony Gormley's rusting *Iron Man* lurking nearby, and leaning at a precarious angle like a Saturday-night drunk. The waterfall out-does poor old Queen Victoria, whose **statue** is glum and uninspired, though the thrusting self-confidence of her bourgeoisie is very apparent in the flamboyant buildings that frame the adjacent **Chamberlain Square**. Amongst the assorted ornate gables and cupolas, columns and towers, the **Council House** is the most impressive edifice, opened in 1879 and complete with a pair of proud lions.

Very different is Chamberlain Square's **Town Hall** of 1834, whose classical design – by Joseph Hansom, who went on to design Hansom cabs – was based on the Roman temple in Nîmes. The building's simple, flowing lines contrast with much of its surroundings, but it's an appealing structure all the same, erected to house public meetings and musical events in a flush of municipal pride. It's currently undergoing a long-term refurbishment, but you can pop inside for a peek (Mon–Fri 10am–4pm; free), though at present there's nothing much to see. In the middle of the square is a dinky Neo-Gothic memorial in honour of **Joseph Chamberlain** (1836–1914), who made himself immensely popular by taking the city's gas and water supplies into public ownership. His political career ultimately took him from the Birmingham mayor's office to national prominence as leader of the Liberal Unionists and figurehead of the resistance to Irish home rule. Close by, on the steps, is a second political statue, this one to the city's first MP, Thomas Attwood, his coat-tails tumbling down the concrete.

The Birmingham Museum and Art Gallery

The **Birmingham Museum and Art Gallery** occupies a rambling, Edwardian building on Chamberlain Square (Mon–Thurs & Sat 10am–5pm, Fri 10.30am–5pm, Sun 12.30–5pm; free). Its several sections are spread over Floors 2 and 3, but the pick is the **Art** section, which contains one of the world's most comprehensive collections of **Pre-Raphaelite** art, concentrated on Floor 2, in Rooms 14 and 17–19. Founded in 1848, the Pre-Raphaelite Brotherhood consisted of seven young artists, of whom Rossetti, Holman Hunt, Millais and Madox Brown are best known. The name of the group was selected to express their commitment to honest observation, which they thought had been lost with the Renaissance. Many of the Brotherhood's most important paintings are displayed here, including Rossetti's seminal *First Anniversary of the Death of Beatrice* (1849), inspired by Dante, and Brown's powerful image of emigration, *The Last of England* (1855). There's actually a lot more going on in Brown's painting than first meets the eye. On one level, it is a sentimental portrayal of a migrant family, but to Brown they also symbolized the yeomen of England – as evidenced by their possessions – whose enforced emigration was a result of poor government, and thus a national outrage. Political sub-texts aside, the group's dedication to realism (as they conceived it) was unyielding and Hunt, for example, visited the Holy Land to prepare a series of religious paintings including his extravagant *The Finding of the Saviour in the Temple*. By 1853, the Brotherhood had effectively disbanded, but a second wave of artists carried on in its footsteps. The most prominent of them was Edward Burne-Jones (1833–98), who has an entire room to himself (Room

14); there, you'll find a remarkable sample of his work, though it's his *Star of Bethlehem* which catches the eye, one of the largest watercolours ever painted, a mysterious, almost magical piece with earnest Magi and a film-star-like Virgin Mary. The rest of the art section, though not quite as memorable, contains a first-rate collection of eighteenth- to twentieth-century British art, including an extensive collection of watercolour landscapes as well as some especially fine, bucolic paintings by David Cox, Constable's Birmingham contemporary. There's also a significant sample of European paintings from the likes of Jan van Scorel and Lucas Cranach through to the Impressionists. Look out also for Sir Peter Lely's iconic portrait of a thoughtful and determined *Oliver Cromwell* in Room 24.

Sharing Floor 2 is the **Industrial Art** section, which kicks off with the **Industrial Gallery**, set around an expansive atrium whose wrought-iron columns and balconies clamber up towards fancy skylights. This section holds a superb sample of locally produced stained glass, ceramics, metalwork – especially silver – and jewellery that amply illustrates the city's industrial prowess. Here also is the **Edwardian Tea Room**, one of the more pleasant places in Birmingham for a break.

Floor 3 holds the **Science** section, where a rather old-fashioned natural-history collection is linked to a couple of rooms containing incidental archeological artefacts: the Mediterranean finds are in Room 34, the local ones in Room 35. Finally, Floor 1's cavernous **Gas Hall** is an impressive venue for touring art exhibitions.

Gas Street Basin and Brindley Place

From the north side of Chamberlain Square, walk through the hideously kitsch **Paradise Forum** shopping and fast-food complex to get to **Centenary Square**, where there's an unusual World War I war memorial. The square has recently been revamped to complement the showpiece **International Convention Centre** (ICC) and the **Birmingham Repertory Theatre**. Centre-stage on the wide paving is a butter-coloured sculpture called *Forward*, a rousing image of the city's history by Birmingham-born Raymond Mason.

From here, it's a brief stroll along Broad Street to the bridge over – and steps down to – **Gas Street Basin**, the hub of Birmingham's intricate **canal** system. There are eight canals within the city's boundaries, comprising no less than thirty-two miles of canal. The highpoint of canal construction was the late eighteenth century, when almost all heavy goods were transported by water. In the middle of the nineteenth century, the railways made the canals uneconomic, but they struggled on until the 1970s when tourism – and narrow boats – gave them a new lease of life. Much of Birmingham's surviving canal network slices through the city's grimy, industrial bowels, but certain sections have been immaculately restored with Gas Street Basin leading the way. At the junction of the Worcester and Birmingham and Birmingham Main Line canals, the Basin, with its herd of brightly painted narrow boats, is edged by a delightful medley of old brick buildings. There's a good pub here – the *Tap & Spile* – and regular **boat trips** leave to explore the prettier parts of the system. There are several operators, but Second City Canal Cruises are as good as any (℡0121/236 9811; £2/person). In summer, there's also a **water taxi** service between several stops along the central part of the canal system (July & Aug daily 10am–5pm; May, June & Sept Sat & Sun 10am–5pm; 1–2 hourly; one-stop 50p).

From the Basin, it's a short walk north along the canal towpath to the bars, shops and clubs of waterside **Brindley Place**, named after James Brindley the eighteenth-century engineer who was responsible for many of Britain's early canals. It's an extraordinarily successful – and aesthetically pleasing – development and here you'll also find the city's celebrated **Ikon Gallery** (Tues–Sun 11am–6pm; free; ⑩ www.ikon-gallery.co.uk), housed in a lovely old Victorian building and one of the country's most imaginative venues for touring exhibitions of contemporary art.

Along the Birmingham and Fazeley canal to St Philip's Cathedral

Just beyond Brindley Place, in front of the huge dome of the National Indoor Arena (NIA), the **canal forks**: the Birmingham and Fazeley leads northeast (to the right) and the Birmingham Main Line canal cuts west (to the left), though to complicate matters the latter has a spur loop here, going under Sheepcote Street. Also beside the main canal junction is the shell-like **National Sea Life Centre** (daily 10am–6pm, last admission 1hr before closing; £8; ⑩ www.sealife.co.uk), which can't help but raise a few eyebrows, given the city's inland location. Nevertheless, it's an enterprising educational venture, giving Birmingham's landlubbers an opportunity to view and even touch many unusual varieties of fish and sea life.

Beyond the main canal fork, the first part of the **Birmingham and Fazeley canal** has been attractively restored, its antique brick buildings cleaned of accumulated grime and leading to the quaint **Farmer's Bridge Locks**. Further on, however, things take a grittier aspect as the canal bores beneath the city centre amidst industrial tangle. Emerging at **Newhall Street** (it's signed), about half a mile from the main canal junction, you're within easy striking distance of **St Paul's Square**, flanked by sturdy Georgian buildings and one of the more agreeable parts of the centre. Here, beside the square in Dakota House, on Brook Street, the **Royal Birmingham Society of Artists** (RBSA; Mon–Wed & Fri 10.30am–5pm, Thurs 10.30am–7pm, Sat 10.30am–5pm; donation), offers an inventive range of fine art exhibitions. Also near at hand is **Colmore Row**, a bustling shopping strip where pride of architectural place goes to **St Philip's Cathedral** (Mon–Fri 7am–7pm, Sat & Sun 9am–5pm), a bijou example of English Baroque. Consecrated in 1715, St Philips was initially a parish church that served as an overspill for St Martin's (see below). It was, however, in a more genteel location than the older church and when, in 1905, the Church of England decided to establish a new diocese here in Birmingham, they made St Philip's the cathedral. The church was extended in the 1880s, when four new stained-glass windows were commissioned from local boy **Edward Burne-Jones**, a leading light of the Pre-Raphaelite movement. The windows are typical of his style – intensely coloured, fastidiously detailed and distinctly sentimental. Three – the *Nativity*, *Crucifixion* and *Ascension* – are at the far end of the church beyond the high altar, the fourth – the *Last Judgement* – is at the opposite end of the church.

The Bull Ring and the Custard Factory

Colmore Row lies just to the west of the city centre's pedestrianized core with chain stores and shopping precincts lining up along Corporation, New and High streets. At the intersection of New and High streets is the distinctive Modernism of the whopping **Rotunda**, but its neighbour, the notorious Bull Ring indoor shopping centre, which fulfilled every miserable cliché about 1960s town planning, has finally been demolished. At present, the **Bull Ring** is a giant building site rolling down the hill below the Rotunda, but its new incarnation – scheduled to be completed in 2003 – will consist of traditional streets and open spaces radiating out from **St Martin's church**. The church is currently a sooty heap, but underneath the grime it's actually a comely amalgamation of the Gothic and neo-Gothic, with fancifully carved decoration and a Burne-Jones window. Incidentally, the Bull Ring was where bulls used to be tethered and baited in the belief that if the animal died angry, the meat was better.

From the Bull Ring, **Digbeth** – once the main thoroughfare through medieval Birmingham – falls away to the southeast. Jammed with traffic and jostled by decrepit industrial buildings, there are only two reasons to venture out here – the first is the bus station on the right, the second – on the left just off along Gibb Street – is the arts complex that occupies the old Alfred Bird **Custard Factory**. The factory is a homely affair set around a friendly little courtyard and the arts complex offers a variety of workshops and has gallery space for temporary exhibitions of modern art. There are a couple of cafés and bars here, too (see p.657).

The Jewellery Quarter

Birmingham's long-established **Jewellery Quarter** lies just to the northwest of the city centre, about half a mile from Colmore Row via Newhall Street. Buckle-makers and toy-makers first colonized the area in the 1750s, opening the way for hundreds of silversmiths, jewellers and goldsmiths. There are still around five hundred jewellery-related companies in the district with most of the **jewellery shops** concentrated along Vittoria Street and the adjacent Frederick Street and Warstone Lane. The prime attraction hereabouts is the engrossing **Museum of the Jewellery Quarter**, 75–79 Vyse St (Mon–Fri 10am–4pm; Sat 11am–5pm; £2.50), a short walk north of the Frederick Street/Warstone Lane intersection. It is built around a factory that has remained virtually unchanged since the 1950s, though it was in use until 1980. A visitor centre starts proceedings, detailing the growth and decline of the trade in Birmingham, but it's the old factory that steals the show. Here, the atmosphere and conditions of the old works are superbly re-created – the jewellers were wedged into tiny, hot and noisy spaces to churn out hundreds of earrings, brooches and rings. Their modern counterparts use the old machines to show how some of the most common designs were produced.

From the museum, it's a couple of minutes' walk back along Vyse Street to the Jewellery Quarter train station and metro stop, on the Snow Hill line.

The suburbs

Birmingham's suburbs fan out from the centre in every direction, a mammoth industrial – and post-industrial – sprawl intermittently relieved by the municipal parks so much favoured by the Victorians. Inevitably, some districts are much better off than others, and it's in well-heeled **Edgbaston**, a mile or two to the southwest of the centre, you'll find a trio of engaging sights – the **Birmingham Botanical Gardens**, the leafy, lake-dotted **Cannon Hill Park** and the European paintings of the **Barber Institute** on Birmingham University's campus. Further south still is **Bournville**, the planned workers' village laid out by the Cadburys in Victorian times. The main pull here is **Cadbury World**, where displays about the history and manufacture of chocolate are a prelude to tucking into the stuff.

On the north side of the centre is **Aston**, home to Aston Villa football club and **Aston Hall**, a handsome Jacobean manor house. Neighbouring **Handsworth** chips in with an historic house too – Matthew Boulton's old **Soho House**, where the Lunar Society (see p.647) used to meet.

Edgbaston

Leafy, prosperous and home to one of the most famous cricket grounds in the country, the suburb of **EDGBASTON**, just to the southwest of the city centre, was developed in the 1790s by the Calthorpe family as a genteel residential estate from which industry and commerce were explicitly banned. It's here, on Westbourne Road, you'll find the **Birmingham Botanical Gardens and Glasshouses** (Mon–Sat 9am–7pm or dusk, Sun 10am–7pm or dusk; £4.30, £4.60 on Sun), whose ornamental gardens and glasshouses extend over fifteen acres. The gardens are parcelled up into a number of distinct areas, including a rhododendron garden and brilliant herbaceous borders, while the glasshouses focus on the tropics. Buses #10, #21, #22, #23, #29 and #103 from Broad Street, in the city centre, travel along Westbourne Road.

Arguably the most agreeable of Birmingham's many public parks is **Cannon Hill Park** (daily dawn–dusk; free), about two miles south of central Birmingham – take Pershore Road and turn left along Edgbaston Road, which marks the park's northern perimeter. There are boating lakes and bowling greens, tennis courts and woodland, and the greenhouses hold a good collection of tropical plants. Cannon Hill is also home to the excellent **Midland Arts Centre** (mac), which has a popular bar, café, cinema and bookshop and also hosts an imaginative programme of art, craft and photography exhibitions. The centre is opposite the cricket ground on Edgbaston Road. Buses #45 and #47, departing from Corporation Sreet, in the city centre, travel along Pershore Road, from where it's a short hoof to the park along Edgbaston Road.

For the casual visitor, the campus of **Birmingham University**, on the southern fringe of Edgbaston, has one big draw, the **Barber Institute of Fine Arts**, at the east gate off Edgbaston Park Road (Mon–Sat 10am–5pm, Sun 2–5pm; free). Opened in 1939, the gallery contains a small but eclectic collection of European paintings from the thirteenth century onwards. Notable pieces include an unusual Rubens – *Landscape near Malines* – and Degas' eccentric *Jockeys Before the Race*, a characteristically audacious piece of off-centre composition. Other artists featured include Monet, Magritte, Bellini, Whistler, Gainsborough, Renoir, Gauguin and Turner. The campus has its own train station – University, two stops along the line from New Street.

Bournville

A purpose-built factory-community founded by the Cadbury family in 1879, **BOURNVILLE** is the most distinctive of Birmingham's suburbs, located just beyond the university four miles southwest of the city centre. The first of this Quaker dynasty, **John Cadbury**, opened a grocery store in Birmingham in 1824 and from it he sold his home-produced "Cocoa Nibs", part soothing nightcap, part a way of weaning the working class from alcohol by providing a cheap and tempting alternative to beer. The popularity of this sweet concoction exceeded John's wildest dreams and just over fifty years later his sons, George and Richard, were able to move the family business out of their cramped premises in the city centre to Bournville – a so-called "factory in a garden". Much influenced by the utopian ideas of William Morris and the Arts and Crafts movement, the Cadburys' Bournville scheme included gardens for every worker's house, a village green and a half-timbered parade of shops. The Bournville Village Trust still operates today, laying down basic rules (no unkempt gardens, for example) to which all inhabitants, even those who own their property, are expected to subscribe. Despite its unusual history, Bournville village doesn't have much in the way of sights, though the **Village Green**, bounded by Linden Road (the A4040) and Sycamore Road, is pleasant enough and it backs onto Maple Road, where the Cadburys plonked a pair of Tudor buildings that were threatened with demolition. These two timber-framed structures, **Selly Manor** and **Minworth Greaves** (April–Sept Tues–Fri 10am–5pm, Sat & Sun 2–5pm; Oct–March Tues–Fri 10am–5pm; £2) – the first a manor house, the second a hall – are furnished in period style and are flanked by pretty "Tudor" gardens.

However, in terms of popularity, these two buildings are as nothing when compared with the excellent **Cadbury World** (phone for times; £6.50; ℡0121/451 4180, ⓦwww.cadburyworld.co.uk), just to the south off Linden Road, adjoining Cadbury's Bournville Works. Billed as "The Ultimate Chocolate Experience", this attraction tells you all you could ever want to know about the cocoa bean, the manufacture of chocolate and the history of Cadbury's itself – the display on the company's adverts is especially interesting. But for chocoholics the point of the tour is the opportunity to gorge on free samples from the production line and stock up on the cut-price finished product. Needless to say, it's very popular, so **reservations** are advised; call ℡0121 /451 4159.

The easiest way to get to Bournville is by **train** from New Street. Bournville station, the fourth stop along the line, is about three-quarters of a mile from Cadbury World – head west along Bournville Lane and turn right up Linden Road.

Aston

Long before it was swallowed up by Birmingham, **ASTON**, just over a mile to the north of the city centre, was a wealthy manorial estate, its heyday recalled by **Aston Hall** on Trinity Road (April–Oct daily 2–5pm; free). A good-looking Jacobean mansion, all turrets and high gables, the hall was built for the Holte family, whose Royalist loyalties brought them into conflict with the Parliamentarian stronghold of Birmingham during the English Civil War. The Roundheads ended up besieging the Holtes and were responsible for the still-visible gunshot marks in the balustraded staircase. About twenty rooms are open to the public, including the beautiful panelled Long Gallery, running the entire width of the house.

To get there by public transport, take **bus** #7 from Colmore Circus to the Witton Road/Trinity Road junction, from where it's a good ten-minute walk east along Trinity Road.

Handsworth

To the west of Aston is multicultural **HANDSWORTH**, whose principal thoroughfare – Soho Hill and its continuation Soho Road (the A41) – is flanked by Balti houses, Caribbean eateries, exotic vegetable shops and sari stores. On Soho Avenue, a side road off Soho Hill, the council have refurbished Matthew Boulton's elegant home, **Soho House** (Tues–Sat 10am–5pm, Sun noon–5pm; £2.50), in period style and have even managed to track down some of Boulton's own furniture. A kingpin amongst the city's early industrialists, Boulton ran his own factory, manufacturing clocks and vases, buckles and buttons, and developed the steam engine in partnership with James Watt. The Lunar Society met here regularly – as various displays explain in detail. Other exhibitions dip into the pedigree of Handsworth's ethnic stew, which is most vividly seen in the annual **Handsworth Carnival**, held in mid-August.

Departing Colmore Circus, **buses** #74, #78 and #79 travel along Soho Hill and Soho Road.

Eating and drinking

Birmingham's central **restaurants** long had a reputation as soulless places which emptied quickly, but this state of affairs has changed dramatically, with smart, new venues sprouting up in the slipstream of the growth in the conference- and trade-fair business, particularly along Broad Street, near the ICC. There's also a concentration of decent, reasonably priced restaurants in the Chinese Quarter, just south of New Street station, on and around Hurst Street. Birmingham's gastronomic speciality is the **balti**, a delicious and astoundingly cheap Kashmiri stew cooked and served in a small wok-like dish called a *karahi*, with nan bread instead of cutlery. Although balti houses have opened up within the city centre, the original and arguably the best balti houses are in the gritty suburbs of **Balsall Heath**, a couple of miles to the south of the centre, and **Sparkhill**, about three miles to the southeast. Some of these are listed here – all are unlicensed, so take your own booze.

City centre **pubs** vary as much as you'd expect. The liveliest, catering for a mixed bag of conference delegates and Brummies-out-on-the-ale, are liberally sprinkled along Broad Street, in the immediate vicinity of the Convention Centre, and in Brindley Place. Most of them are decorated in sharp, modern style, but there are one or two more traditional places here as well – as there are in other parts of the city centre.

Restaurants

Chez Jules 5a Ethel St, off New St ☎0121/633 4664. Best medium-priced French restaurant in the city centre, with especially good lunchtime offers. Moderate.

Chung Ying 16–18 Wrottesley St ☎0121/622 1793. The best Cantonese dishes in the Chinese Quarter, and always busy. Moderate.

Grand Tandoori 343 Stratford Rd, Sparkhill ☎0121/773 9244. Extensive balti menu in a concentration of other balti houses. Buses #4, #31 and #41 from the centre. Inexpensive.

King Balti 230 Ladypool Rd, Balsall Heath ☎0121/449 1170. One of the best in the city's main "balti belt". Inexpensive.

Kushi 558 Moseley Rd, Balsall Heath ☎0121/449 7678. Excellent, award-winning balti house that's unlicensed, dirt cheap and deservedly popular. Inexpensive.

Left Bank 79 Broad St ☎0121/643 4464. Swish and classy French and continental restaurant that mops up its fair share of ICC delegates. Moderate.

Mongolian Bar 24 Ludgate Hill ☎0121/236 3842. Lively and enjoyable curry house, where you choose your ingredients and see them flash-fried before you. Just off the inner ring road. Moderate.

Le Petit Blanc 9 Brindley Place ☎0121/633 7333. Directly opposite the Ikon Gallery, this swish restaurant, with its slick modern furnishings and fittings, offers first-rate French cuisine with a touch of Asia thrown in for good measure. Reservations advised. Expensive.

Pizza Express Brindley Place ☎0121/643 2500. Great canalside location for this ultra-reliable chain.

Punjab Paradise 377 Ladypool Rd, Balsall Heath ☎0121/449 4110. One of the city's classic balti houses, specializing in milder dishes. Inexpensive.

Ronnie Scott's Café Bar 258 Broad St ☎0121/643 4525. Serves an imaginative selection of snacks and meals, with jazz sounds and memorabilia as background. Late licence. Inexpensive.

San Carlo 4 Temple St ☎0121/633 0251. Best all-round Italian restaurant in the centre, although somewhat lacking in atmosphere. It's near St Philip's Cathedral, just up from the pizza and pasta chain restaurants on New Street. Moderate.

Shah Faisal 348–50 Stratford Rd, Sparkhill ☎0121/753 0607. Large and very tasty baltis in traditional surroundings. Buses #4, #31, or #41 from the centre. Inexpensive.

Warehouse Café 54 Allison St, Digbeth ☎0121/633 0261. Imaginative vegan and vegetarian café; ring for times. Bring your own wine. Just below the Bull Ring, near the start of Digbeth – Allison St is a turning on the left. Inexpensive.

Pubs and bars

Brasshouse 44 Broad St. Award-winning traditional pub with a good range of brews.

Cube Brindley Place. In the middle of Brindley Place, this chic and lively bar, with its angular furnishings and suspended glass ceiling, heaves on the weekend. Has a canalside restaurant and terrace too.

Fiddle and Bone 4 Sheepcote St ☎0121/200 2223. Canalside pub-cum-restaurant owned by members of the City of Birmingham Symphony Orchestra, hence its musical name and theme.

Good old fashioned decor and regular live music, often to a very high standard.

James Brindley next to the Hyatt off Bridge St ☎0121/644 5971. Frequented by businessfolk in the week, but at weekends the jazz brunches give this place a relaxed air. It has a great canalside location, too.

Café des Artistes Custard Factory, Gibb Street, off Digbeth. Popular pre-club haunt in a laid-back arts complex that was once a Custard Factory. The nearest club – the *Medicine Bar* (see below) – is in the same complex. Serves good food too – self-billed as "California-style".

Old Contemptibles 176 Edmund St. A little worn at the edges, this good old fashioned pub is packed with business folk at lunchtime, but attracts a more diverse clientele in the evening. Close to Snow Hill train station.

The Old Fox Arcadian Centre, Hurst Street. Over-modernized but popular pub, with an excellent selection of beer and a boisterous atmosphere.

Prince of Wales 84 Cambridge St. Old-fashioned haunt with long-standing custom from the Repertory Theatre, now pulling them in from the neighbouring ICC.

Red Lion 94 Warstone Lane. Appealing, traditional Brummie pub in the Jewellery Quarter.

Tap & Spile 10 Gas St. Charming traditional pub with rickety rooms and low-beamed ceilings beside the canal on Gas Street Basin. Once the hangout of weathered canal men, it now attracts tourists and locals in equal measure.

The Victoria 48 John Bright St. Elaborately tiled and smoky Irish pub, in a dog-eared area just down from – and to the west of – New Street station. Next to the Alexandra Theatre (see below).

Nightlife and entertainment

Nightlife in Birmingham is thriving, and the **club scene** is recognized as one of Britain's best, spanning everything from word-of-mouth underground parties to meat-market mainstream clubs. There's a particular emphasis on special/specialist nights with leading DJs turning up at different venues on different nights. **Live music** is strong in the city, too, with big-name concerts at several major venues and other, often local bands appearing at some clubs and pubs (see above). Birmingham's showpiece **Symphony Orchestra** and **Royal Ballet** are the spearheads of the city's resurgent high-cultural scene. The social calendar also gets an added boost from a wide range of up-market **festivals**, including the **Jazz Festival** in the first two weeks in July, and the **Film and TV Festival** in November.

For current **information** on all events, performances and exhibitions, pick up a free copy of the excellent, fortnightly *What's On*, Birmingham's definitive listings guide. It's available at all of the tourist offices and many public venues.

Clubs

Baker's 162 Broad St ☎0121/633 3839. Small, artily designed disco-club with a wide range of speciality evenings. House a favourite.

Bobby Brown's 52 Gas St ☎0121/643 2573. Chart and retro sounds for the over-25s, plus speciality nights. House on Fridays.

Circo 6–8 Holloway Circus, Queensway ☎0121/643 1400. Vibrant, sometimes cool nightspot with different sounds on different nights. South of New Street station.

House of God various venues. Birmingham's ever-popular techno night is still going strong and loud. This is the sound of the city.

Medicine Bar Custard Factory, Gibb St, off Digbeth ☎0121/604 7777. Adventurous club where every evening is different – from hip hop to blues and beyond. Part of the arts complex that inhabits an old custard factory.

The Nightingale Essex House, Kent St ☎0121

/622 1718, ⊛www.nightingaleclub.co.uk. Arguably Birmingham's best club, consistently popular with gays and straights. Five bars, three levels, two discos, a café bar and even a garden. About ten minutes' walk south of New Street station, out along Hurst Street.

Ronnie Scott's 258 Broad St ☎0121/643 4525. Second of the late maestro's jazz clubs, good also for big names in blues and World Music.

Que II Central Hall, Corporation St ☎0121/212 0550. Brum's premier "superclub", a conversion of the old Methodist Central Hall into a full-on, 2000-capacity groove. Frequent all-nighters; speciality nights and big-name DJs.

Sanctuary High Street, Digbeth ☎0160/246 1010. Opposite the coach station, the old Civic Hall now thumps to some big house tunes during a variety of one-nighters.

The Steering Wheel Wrottesley St ☎0121/666 6799. Resident and visiting DJs with hard house the leading musical motif. A short walk south of New Street station.

Waterworks Jazz Club Gough St ✆01562 /850765. Up-and-coming specialist jazz joint just off the inner ring road near Holloway Circus.

Classical music, theatre, comedy and dance

Alexandra Theatre Suffolk Street, Queensway ✆0870/607 7533. Mainstream pop concerts, musicals and plays.
Birmingham Repertory Theatre Broad St ✆0121/236 4455. Mixed diet of classics and new work, featuring local and experimental writing.
The Crescent Theatre Sheepcote Street, Brindley Place ✆0121/643 5858. Adventurous theatre group and venue for visiting companies.
Glee Club Arcadian Centre, Hurst St ✆0121/693 2248. Dedicated comedy club, with top national names and up-and-coming stars.
Hippodrome Theatre Hurst St ✆0870/7301234.

Lavishly refurbished – and re-opened at the tale end of 2001 – the Hippodrome is home to the Birmingham Royal Ballet and regularly hosts the Welsh National Opera. Also features touring plays and big pre- and post-West End productions, plus a splendiferous Christmas pantomime.
National Exhibition Centre (NEC) Bickenhill Parkway ✆0870 789 8841, @www.necgroup.co .uk. The NEC's arena hosts major pop concerts. Ten miles east of the centre beside the M42; train from New Street to Birmingham International station.
Old Rep Theatre Station St ✆0121/236 5622. Britain's oldest repertory theatre, with regular per-formances by the imaginative Birmingham Stage Company.
Symphony Hall International Convention Centre, Broad St ✆0121/780 3333. Acoustically one of the most advanced concert halls in Europe, home of the acclaimed City of Birmingham Symphony Orchestra (CBSO), as well as a venue for touring music and opera.

Listings

Airport Information desk ✆0121/7677799.
Banks Lloyds, 125 Colmore Row; HSBC, 130 New St; Royal Bank of Scotland, 79 Colmore Row.
Bike rental On Yer Bike, 98 Corporation St ✆0121/236 4118.
Bookshops Waterstone's, 24 High St and 128 New St.
Bus enquiries For city-wide information, call ✆0121/200 2700; for the wider Birmingham/Black Country conurbation, call ✆0247/6559 559.
Car rental Avis, 7 Park St ✆0121/632 4361 and at the airport ✆0121/782 6183; Europcar, at the airport ✆0121/782 6507; National, St Chad's ✆0121/200 3010 and at the airport ✆0121/782 5481.
Cricket Warwickshire County Cricket Club, Edgbaston Rd, Edgbaston ✆0121/446 4422.

Football Aston Villa is the city's big club, they're based at Villa Park, Aston (✆0121/327 5353). One-time equal, Birmingham City, is based at St Andrew's, Small Heath (✆0121/772 0101).
Internet At the main Library, on Chamberlain Square. Free access for the first hour.
Laundry Clean & Care, 758 Alum Rock Rd.
Pharmacies Boots, 67 High St ✆0121/212 1330. Late-night opening rosta posted in the window here and at the tourist office.
Police Steelhouse Lane ✆0121/626 6000.
Post office 1 Pinfold St, on the corner with Victoria Square (Mon–Fri 9am–5.30pm, Sat 9am–6pm).
Taxis Toa Taxis ✆0121/427 8888, BB's ✆0121/693 3333.

The Black Country

To outsiders the area known as the **Black Country** appears to be an undif-ferentiated mass sprawling away from the western side of Birmingham, but in fact it's composed of several tightly knit industrial communities, which have gradually expanded until each is touching its neighbours. The region earned its name in the mid-nineteenth century, when smoke from hundreds of iron-workings choked the air and sooted the buildings – the environment is much cleaner today. Some of these towns grew on the basis of one or two staple products – leather in Walsall, locks in Willenhall, glass in Stourbridge – whilst the rest exploited the abundant local resources (chiefly coal and limestone) to develop a range of industries, with heavy engineering predominant. Although many of the older trades have long gone, this is still an area where manufacturing is regarded as the only real work. Consequently, it's hardly surprising that the Black Country's industrial heritage is the main reason for visiting the area – best achieved by day-tripping from Birmingham, from where there are frequent **buses** and **trains**. The Black Country Museum in **Dudley** is the chief tourist attraction, though the modern art of **Walsall**'s New Art Gallery is not to be sniffed at. In addition, factories producing decorative goods – such as the glassworks in Brierley Hill – are often open to shoppers.

Dudley and around

Eight miles west of Birmingham, **DUDLEY** (from Birmingham, take bus #87 from Corporation Street or #126 from Stephenson Street) lays fair claim to being the capital of the Black Country as it was here in the seventeenth century that coal was first used for smelting iron. The town is actually much older, the main evidence being its ruined Norman **castle**, perched on the hill above town with grounds that now contain a zoo (daily: Easter to mid-Sept 10am–4pm; mid-Sept to Easter 10am–3pm; £7). However, Dudley's main attraction is the **Black Country Museum** on the Tipton Road, over the far side of Castle Hill, about a mile from the town centre (March–Oct daily 10am–5pm; Nov–Feb Wed–Sun 10am–4pm; £7.95). Buildings from the surrounding district – shops, a chapel, a pub, workshops, forges and homes – have been re-erected here and populated with local people in period costume, mimicking the ways of labour that once employed thousands in these parts. For added authenticity (and an additional £3.20) you can take a trip down an underground coal seam, watch a silent movie in the cinema, or enjoy a canal trip into a tunnel under Castle Hill, through some floodlit limestone caverns.

At the centre of Dudley, the shopping area surrounding the **Market Place** has suffered badly from the opening of the gargantuan Merry Hill Shopping Centre at **BRIERLEY HILL**, two miles to the southwest. Brierley Hill is also noted for its **beer** – if you only try one Black Country pub, make it the *Vine* (known locally as *The Bull & Bladder*), the Batham's brewery outlet on Delph Road, at the top of a run of good pubs that winds down the hill to the bottom of the **Delph Nine Locks** on the Dudley canal.

Walsall

Some ten miles northwest of Birmingham, and readily reached by train or bus, **WALSALL** is a pleasantly stoic town, now attempting to diversify into tourism after years as a centre of the leather industry. Its prime attraction is the downtown **New Art Gallery Walsall** (Tues–Sat 10am–5pm, Sun noon–5pm; free; ⓦwww.artatwalsall.org.uk), near both the train station and the Walsall canal on Gallery Square, at the junction of Wolverhampton and Park streets. The gallery contains a wide-ranging collection of paintings, drawings, prints and sculpture assembled by Kathleen Epstein, the widow of Jacob Epstein, and her friend Sally Ryan. Among the paintings, there are works by Blake, Degas, Modigliani, Van Gogh, Picasso, Ruskin, Turner and – of course – Jacob Epstein. American-born, Epstein (1880–1959) was a controversial figure whose bold and audacious public sculptures were regularly criticized for indecency. In Paris, his *Tomb of Oscar Wilde* created such a stink that a bronze plaque was eventually fixed over the angel's genitals, whilst the aggressiveness of his robot-like *Rock Drill* of 1913 had the art establishment howling with horror. The museum displays Epstein's original drawings for both – and one of his most impressive sculptures adorns Coventry Cathedral.

Of more local significance, the **Walsall Leather Museum**, on Littleton Street

West (April–Oct Tues–Sat 10am–5pm, Sun noon–5pm; Nov–March Tues–Sat 10am–4pm, Sun noon–4pm; free), provides a surprisingly interesting look at the industry's development and its effect on the town. In particular, there are excellent displays examining the relentless working conditions of the early leather workers, and practical demonstrations of traditional skills. There's also a shop selling locally made leather goods. Littleton Street West is part of the ring road – the A4148 – a short walk to the north of the Art Gallery. Finally, Walsall was the birthplace of **Jerome K. Jerome**, the author of *Three Men in a Boat*. His family moved away in 1861, when he was just 2, but the town makes something of the connection at the tiny **Birthplace Museum**, in Belsize House, Bradford Street (admission by prior arrangement on ☎01922/653116), in the centre, a few minutes walk southwest of the art gallery.

Wolverhampton and around

WOLVERHAMPTON, around fourteen miles northwest of Birmingham – and again easily reached by bus or train – doesn't win any beauty contests, but it does possess the excellent **Wolverhampton Art Gallery and Museum**, bang in the middle of town on Lichfield Street (Mon–Sat 10am–5pm; free). There's a healthy sample of English paintings here, featuring the likes of Gainsborough, Paul Nash, Stanley Spencer and Landseer, but the gallery is best known for its extensive collection of American and British Pop Art. Amongst many, Hamilton, Hockney, Warhol, Allen Jones and Lichtenstein are all featured, and there are also temporary exhibitions plus an eclectic selection of contemporary art.

Two fine houses sit on the edge of town. Three miles west is the mock-Tudor **Wightwick Manor** – pronounced "Witick" – on Wightwick Bank, off the A454 (guided tours: March–Dec Thurs & Sat 1.30–5pm; £5.50, including garden; NT). Built in 1887, it was designed by Edward Ould, a devotee of William Morris, and the extravagant furnishings, fittings and paintings all reflect this Pre-Raphaelite influence. The **garden** (Wed & Thurs 11am–6pm, Sat 1–6pm; £2.40) is maintained in its Victorian form, complete with lush orchards and ostentatious topiary. Bus #516 (Midland Red) from Wolverhampton stops on the A454, near the bottom of Wightwick Bank, and from here it's about a quarter of a mile to the house.

Located four miles to the north of Wolverhampton, off the A460 – and painfully near the M54 – **Moseley Old Hall** (late March to Oct Wed, Sat & Sun 1.30–5.30pm; Nov & Dec Sun 1.30–4.30pm; £4.10; NT) is a much-modified Elizabethan country mansion famous for its association with Charles II. The king took refuge here after the Battle of Worcester in 1651 and you can see the bed he slept in and the hole in which he sheltered for the best part of two days to elude the Parliamentary posses. An exhibition in the barn fills out the history. Buses #870, #871, #872 and #613 run from Wolverhampton to within fifteen-minutes' walk of the hall.

Staffordshire

Spreading north from the Birmingham conurbation, the miscellaneous and low-key landscapes of **Staffordshire** don't enthral too many people. Nonetheless, the county packs in coachloads of visitors owing to the presence of **Alton Towers** (☎0870/5204060, ⊛www.altontowers.com; closed Nov–March; £23, under-12s £19), the nation's most popular amusement park, with several million visitors annually howling and screaming on rides with names that include *Nemesis* and *Oblivion*. The white-knuckle rides take much more money than do the hoteliers in the cathedral city of **Lichfield**, at the southern end of Staffordshire, both the main historic attraction and the county's most agreeable town. Lichfield also makes a handy base for visiting **Stoke-on-Trent**, not much to look at, perhaps, but world-famous for its pottery and with the museums – and factory shops – to match.

Both Lichfield and Stoke are easy to reach by **rail** and **bus** from Birmingham and other major cities.

Lichfield

Some fourteen miles to the north of Birmingham, the pocket-sized town of **LICHFIELD** is a slow-moving but amiable place that demands a visit for one reason – its magnificent sandstone **Cathedral** (daily 8am–6.30pm; £3 donation requested). Begun in 1085, but substantially rebuilt in the thirteenth and fourteenth centuries, the cathedral is unique in possessing three spires – an appropriate distinction for a bishopric that once extended over virtually all of the Midlands. The church stands on the site of a shrine built for the relics of St Chad, an English bishop noted for his humility, who died here in Lichfield in 672.

Samuel Johnson

Eighteenth-century England's most celebrated wit and critic, **Samuel Johnson** was born above his father's bookshop in Lichfield's Market Place in 1709. From Lichfield he went to Pembroke College, Oxford, which he left in 1731 without having completed his degree. Disgruntled with academia, Johnson returned to Staffordshire as a teacher, before settling in Birmingham for three years, a period that saw his first pieces published in the *Birmingham Journal*.

In 1735 Johnson married Elizabeth Porter, a Birmingham friend's widow twenty years his senior, returning to his home district to open a private school in the village of Edial, three miles southwest of Lichfield. The school was no great success, so after two years the Johnsons abandoned the project and went to London with the young David Garrick, their star pupil. Journalism and essays were the mainstay of the Johnsons' penurious existence until publisher Robert Dodsley asked Samuel to consider compiling a **Dictionary of the English Language**, a project that nobody had undertaken before, and which was to occupy him for eight years prior to its publication in 1755. Massively learned and full of mordant wit ("lexicographer: a writer of dictionaries; a harmless drudge"), the Dictionary is one of Johnson's greatest legacies, although he was financially and emotionally stretched to breaking point by the workload it imposed. The dictionary was widely acclaimed, but, despite his increasing celebrity, money problems continued to dog him – in 1759 he wrote the novel *Rasselas* in one week, in order to raise money for his mother's funeral. Nevertheless, Johnson's financial bacon was saved shortly afterward when, in the early 1760s, the new king, George III, granted him a bursary of £300 per year.

In 1763 Johnson met James Boswell, a pushy young Scot who clung tenaciously to the cantankerous older man until he learned to like him. Their journey to Scotland resulted in one of the finest travel books ever written, **A Journey to the Western Isles of Scotland** (1775), in which Johnson's fascinated incredulity at the native way of life makes for utterly absorbing reading. Other publications from his final decade included a preface to Shakespeare's plays, a series of political tracts and the magnificent **Lives of the English Poets**. However, the work by which he is now best known is not one that he himself wrote – it's Boswell's **Life of Johnson**, commenced on its subject's death in 1784, published in 1791 and still the English language's most full-blooded biography. Johnson was buried in Westminster Abbey, London.

The cathedral's **west front** is adorned by over one hundred statues of biblical figures, English kings and the supposed ancestors of Christ, some of them dating back to the thirteenth century, but mostly Victorian replacements of originals destroyed by Cromwell's troops. Even the central spire was demolished during the skirmishes – Lichfield justly claims to be the cathedral that was most damaged during the Civil War. Extensive and painstaking rebuilding and restoration work, which was begun immediately after the Restoration in 1660, has gone on ever since, although the bulk of the work was only completed at the end of the nineteenth century.

Inside, the **nave** is graced by a long line of slender arches and these, together with the decorated capitals and elaborate roof bosses, more than compensate for its lack of width. The adjoining **south transept** is earlier than the nave, dating to the 1220s, but the main item of interest here is unreservedly Victorian and imperialist. The transept's St Michael's Chapel is dedicated to the Staffordshire Regiment and its railings are decorated with replica Zulu shields to celebrate their involvement in the Zulu War; the sphinx does the same for another vainglorious campaign in Egypt. Beyond the transepts, the first three bays of the **choir** are the oldest part of the church, completed in the Early English style of the twelfth century, but the rest of the choir is middle Gothic. On the south side of the choir a narrow stone stairway leads up to a fine **minstrels' gallery** and the **St Chad's Head Chapel**, where the head of the saint was once displayed to cheer up the faithful. Most impressive of all, however, is the **Lady Chapel**, at the far end of the choir, which boasts a set of magnificent sixteenth-century windows, purchased from the Cistercian abbey at Herkenrode in Belgium in 1802.

The cathedral's greatest treasure, the **Lichfield Gospels**, is displayed (Easter–Christmas) in the **chapter house**, off the north side of the choir. One of the most exquisite and valuable surviving Anglo-Saxon artefacts in the country, this 1250-year-old illuminated manuscript contains the complete gospels of Matthew and Mark, and a fragment of the gospel of Luke, written in Latin and embellished with elaborate decoration. No one knows who wrote it, but experts believe it was produced locally and records certainly show it was stolen in a raid and carried off to Wales, from where it was eventually returned in medieval times. Different pages are exhibited at different times, but a particular favourite is the gorgeous Carpet Page, showing a decorative cross whose blend of Coptic, Celtic and Oriental influences make it the equal of the more famous Irish Book of Kells and Lindisfarne Gospels. The fact that the book ends midway through St Luke means it's almost certainly one of a pair – and rare book specialists have long been on the look-out for the other volume.

Back outside, the Cathedral is flanked by **The Close**, which, with its good-looking medley of Georgian and Victorian buildings, is the prettiest place in town. From the Close, it's a short walk along Dam Street – past the gloomy waters of the Minster Pool – to the **Market Place**, where there's a peculiar little statue of a puck-nosed Boswell and a much better one honouring **Samuel Johnson**, who looks suitably intellectual. The plinth below the statue is carved with three scenes from Johnson's life. The most revealing shows Johnson making a public penance in Uttoxeter Market Place for the sin – as he saw it – of refusing to work on his father's Uttoxeter book stall fifty years before.

At the back of the Market Place stands **St Mary's church**, unremarkable in itself and now home to the **Lichfield Heritage Centre** (April–Sept daily 10.30am–4.30pm; Oct–March Mon–Sat 10.30am–4.30pm; £2), which tracks through the city's history, with an illuminating section on the Civil War. On the outside wall of the church several **plaques** commemorate noteworthy incidents. One of them is a memorial to the unfortunate Edward Wightman, who was burnt at the stake for heresy on this very spot in 1612 – the last Englishman to be so punished for this particular crime.

Also on the Market Place, is the **Samuel Johnson Birthplace Museum** (April–Sept daily 10.30am–4.30pm; Oct–March Mon–Sat 10.30am–4.30pm; £2, £3.20 joint ticket with Heritage Centre). The great man's father – Michael – was a bookseller and this house, a narrow four-storey affair, was both the family home and a bookshop. The museum's ground floor still serves as a bookshop – with copies of Boswell's biography and many of Johnson's works – whilst up above, on the first floor, a video provides a well-considered potted introduction to its subject. Thereafter, a series of modest displays explore Johnson's life and times. Of particular interest is the biting letter he sent to a certain Lord Chesterfield, after the latter falsely claimed credit for sponsoring Johnson's dictionary. The top floor holds a small collection of personal memorabilia, including Johnson's favourite armchair, his chocolate pot (chocolate was a real Georgian delicacy), bib holder, shoe buckles and ivory writing tablets.

Practicalities

Lichfield has two **train stations**: Lichfield City, with regular connections to and from Birmingham, is about five minutes' walk south of the centre, while Lichfield Trent Valley, served by main-line trains from the northwest and London Euston, is on the eastern fringe of the city, about fifteen minutes' walk from the centre. The **bus station** is in between Lichfield City station and the centre. Clearly signed from all three stations, the city centre is dominated by the sprawling Three Spires Shopping Mall. The **tourist office** is on Bore Street, just off the Market Place (April–Sept Mon–Sat 9am–5pm; Oct–March Mon–Fri 9am–4.45pm & Sat 9am–2pm; ☎01543/308209, ⓦwww.lichfield-tourist.co.uk).

Once you've seen the sights, there's no strong reason to hang around, but Lichfield does have a long list of reasonably priced **B&Bs**. These include the appealing *Mrs Jones's B&B*, in a listed nineteenth-century town house by the Cathedral at 8 The Close (☎01543/418483; ❷), and *Mrs Taylor's B&B*, with just one room, in a pretty, well-kept two-storey old house at 23 The Close (☎01543/306140; ❷).

Generally speaking, Lichfield's **cafés** and **restaurants** hardly inspire the palate, though the *Olive Tree*, 34 Tamworth St (☎01543/263363), serves up tasty Mediterranean-style dishes at moderate prices. Also in the centre is *Don Paco*, a Spanish restaurant at 28 Bird St (☎01543/300789; closed Sun); or you could sample the home-made food of the rather frugal *Cathedral Coffee Shop*, on the south side of the Cathedral (Mon–Sat 9.30am–445pm, Sun noon–4.45pm).

Stoke-on-Trent

The inhabitants of **STOKE-ON-TRENT**, some thirty miles northwest of Lichfield, have been making pottery since Roman times, but mass production only began in the eighteenth century. Then, in the space of forty years, the development of local coalfields, the securing of a regular supply of fine-quality clay from Devon and Cornwall and the digging of the Trent–Mersey canal transformed the town and its environs into the biggest centre of pottery production in the world – known, logically enough, as **The Potteries**. It was all a terrible eyesore and the district, with its belching smoke stacks and fuming bottle kilns, became synonymous with industrial squalor, but the profits were enormous – quite enough to attract a string of talented entrepreneur-designers. The first of them, and still the most renowned, was Josiah Wedgwood, who opened a factory here in 1769. More recently, the industry has been in decline, hit hard by cheap foreign imports, but Britain's department stores are still stacked with The Potteries' products and local companies – such as Royal Doulton, Spode, Royal Worcester and Wedgwood – are making a fight of it. All this industrial activity doesn't spell much in the way of tourist delight, but Stoke-on-Trent's heritage museums and factory shops are enough to keep most visitors happy for a few hours at least.

The city of Stoke-on-Trent is, in fact, an amalgam of **six towns** – confusing for fans of locally born Arnold Bennett (1867–1931), who wrote about the five towns in novels such as *Clayhanger* and *Anna of the Five Towns*, ignoring the smallest of the six, **Fenton**. Of the other five, the major two are **Stoke** itself, which feels as if it has been left to wither to the benefit of **Hanley**, a mile to the north, which has all the main shops and the main civic museum. **Tunstall** and **Burslem** to the north and **Longton** to the southeast are the remaining Stoke towns, all largely autonomous communities. Trains arrive at **Stoke** station, whereas buses use the **Lichfield Street bus station** in central Hanley.

The **Potteries Museum and Art Gallery** on Bethesda Street in Hanley (March–Oct Mon–Sat 10am–5pm, Sun 2–5pm; Nov–Feb Mon–Sat 10am–4pm, Sun 1–4pm; free), occupies an unappetising modern building, but it holds a magnificent and colossal collection of English pottery and ceramics. The museum tracks through the industry's eighteenth-century artistic heyday and the boom of the nineteenth with examples from all the leading manufacturers. There is also a section of Art Deco pieces – look out for the work of Clarice Cliff – and examples of present-day production. An excellent social history department includes a poignant **coal sculpture** commemorating the two colliers who died on picket duty in the 1984–85 miners' strike as well as the 20,000 who were injured, the 200 imprisoned and the 966 men who were sacked. For an introduction to the pottery industry itself, head for the excellent **Gladstone Pottery Museum** in Uttoxeter Road, Longton (daily 10am–5pm; £3.95). Distinguished by the large bottle-kilns that used to dominate the entire city, the museum employs craftspeople to demonstrate the skills of pottery production, and details the evolution of the six towns and the social conditions of their people.

These two museums are the pick of the bunch, but there are several others focusing on different aspects of pottery manufacture and, in addition, there are over thirty **factory shops** open to the public. The **tourist office**, in the Potteries Shopping Centre on Quadrant Road in Hanley (Mon–Sat 9.15am–5.15pm; ☎01782/236000, ⓦwww.stoke.gov.uk/tourism), issues a free leaflet giving the low-down and has local bus timetables, too. One of the better known companies is **Royal Doulton**, who have a visitor centre at their Nile Street Works, in Burslem (Mon–Sat 9am–5.30pm, Sun 10.30am–4.30pm; tours by prior arrangement, on ☎01782/292434; tours £6.50, centre £3, shop free).

Derby and the Peak District

In 1951, the hills and dales of the **Peak District**, at the southern tip of the Pennine range, became Britain's first National Park. Wedged between **Derby**, Manchester and Sheffield, it is effectively the backyard for the fifteen million people who live within an hour's drive of its boundaries, though somehow it accommodates the huge influx with minimum fuss.

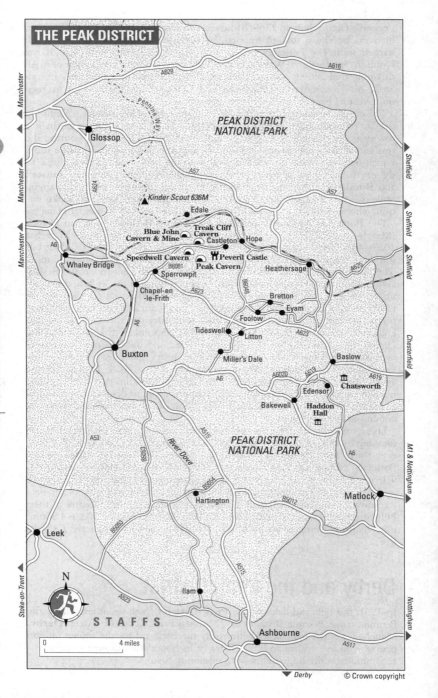

THE PEAK DISTRICT

Manchester

Manchester

Manchester

Sheffield

Sheffield

Sheffield

Chesterfield

M1 & Nottingham

Nottingham

Stoke-on-Trent

A628

A616

Pennine Way

PEAK DISTRICT
NATIONAL PARK

Glossop

A624

A57

A57

▲ Kinder Scout 636M

Edale

A6

Blue John
Cavern & Mine

Treak Cliff
Cavern

Castleton

Hope

A6187

Speedwell Cavern

Peveril Castle

Peak Cavern

Whaley Bridge

B6061

Heathersage

Sparrowpit

Chapel-en
-le-Frith

A623

B6049

Bretton

Eyam

A6

Foolow

Tideswell

Litton

A623

Buxton

Miller's Dale

Baslow

A6

A6020

A619

A619

Edensor

Chatsworth

Bakewell

Haddon
Hall

A53

A515

B5055

PEAK DISTRICT
NATIONAL PARK

A6

River Dove

B5054

Hartington

B5012

Matlock

B5053

Leek

STAFFS

N

A523

Ilam

Ashbourne

A517

0   4 miles

▼ Derby

© Crown copyright

Landscapes in the Peak District come in two forms. The brooding high moorland tops of **Dark Peak**, fifteen miles east of central Manchester, take their name from the underlying gritstone, known as millstone grit for its former use – a function commemorated in the millstones demarcating the park boundary. Windswept, mist-shrouded and inhospitable, the flat tops of these peaks are nevertheless a firm favourite with walkers on the **Pennine Way**, which meanders north from the tiny village of **Edale** to the Scottish border (see p.674). Altogether more forgiving, the southern limestone hills of the **White Peak** have been eroded into deep forested dales populated by small stone villages and often threaded by walking trails, some of which follow former rail routes. The limestone is riddled with complex cave systems around **Castleton** and under the region's largest centre, **Buxton**, a former spa town just outside the park's boundaries, at the end of an industrialized corridor that reaches out from Manchester. Two of the country's most distinctive manorial piles, **Chatsworth House** and **Haddon Hall**, stand near **Bakewell**, a town famed locally not just for its cakes but also for its **well-dressing**, a possibly pagan ritual of thanksgiving for fresh water that takes place in about twenty local villages each summer.

There's no obvious **route** around the Peaks, but the one outlined below comes in from the south – from Derby – and then cuts up to Buxton before looping round in a clockwise direction to Castleton, Hathersage, Bakewell and points in between. As for a **base**, you're spoiled for choice, but Castleton and Eyam probably win out.

Access and accommodation

Trains penetrate only as far as Buxton from the north and cut through Edale and Hathersage on the Manchester to Sheffield route. The main **bus access** is via the Trent bus company's TransPeak service from Nottingham to Manchester via Derby, Matlock, Bakewell and Buxton; otherwise bus #272 runs regularly from Sheffield to Castleton, via Hathersage and Hope, and the Peak Express connects Sheffield to Buxton. If you're not planning on walking between towns and villages, you'll need the essential, encyclopedic *Peak District Timetable* (60p), from local tourist and National Park information offices, which lists all the local **public transport** services. Buses are more widespread than you might imagine, though there are limited winter and Sunday services, and often only sporadic links between the major centres. Various one-day **transport passes** allow unlimited travel to and within specified zones. It's a complicated system, but broadly speaking the South Yorkshire Peak Explorer (£5) covers the chunk of the park in Yorkshire, the Peak Wayfarer Manchester (£7), and the Derbyshire Wayfarer (£7.25) covers the rest. For all Peak District bus **timetable information** call ☎0870/608 2608.

There's a full network of dedicated cycle lanes, tracks and old railway lines in the park; the National Park Authority provides a series of **cycle rental** outlets from which to make use of them (£10/day, plus £20 deposit; discounts for YHA members). The centres are located at: Mapleton Lane, Ashbourne (☎01335/343156); Fairholmes, Derwent (☎01433/651261); the Information Centre, Station Rd, Hayfield (☎01663/746222); the Visitor Centre, Middleton-by-Wirksworth, Middleton Top (☎01629/823204); Parsley Hay, Buxton (☎01298/84493); and Old Station Car Park, Waterhouses (☎01538/308609).

There's plenty of **accommodation** in and around the park, mostly in B&Bs, with a dozen youth hostels and numerous campsites scattered among them. A network of YHA-operated **camping barns** is also available. These are located in converted farm buildings and provide simple and inexpensive self-catering accommodation for between six and twenty-four people. For further details contact the YHA Camping Barns Reservation Office (☎01200/420102). The main Peak District National Park Authority office is at Aldern House, Baslow Rd, Bakewell DE45 1AE (☎01629/816200, ⊛www.peakdistrict.org). They also operate a string of **information centres**, which are supplemented by village tourist offices and, in some smaller places, by local stores doubling up as information points. **Maps** and trail **guides** are widely available and guided countryside walks are commonplace – sign-up locally. Finally, be sure to pick up a copy of the free *Peak District* paper, crammed with useful information.

Derby

The proximity of the Peak District might lead you to think that **DERBY**, twenty-five miles northeast of Lichfield, could prove to be an interesting stopping-off point. Sadly, the city – a status conferred as recently as 1977 – is an unexciting place, though its workaday centre is partly redeemed by several long and handsome nineteenth-century stone terraces and its **cathedral**, whose pinnacled tower soars high above its modest surroundings on Queen Street. Of the city's several museums, easily the best is the attractively laid-out **Derby Museum and Art Gallery** on the Strand (Mon 11am–5pm, Tues–Sat 10am–5pm, Sun 2–5pm; free), a five-minute walk from the central market place. The museum exhibits a splendid collection of Derby porcelain, several hundred pieces tracking through the different phases and styles from the late eighteenth century until today. Of particular appeal is the painted pottery of the Duesbury II & Kean period (1786–1811), featuring the exquisite flowers of one William Billingsley. Royal Crown Derby, founded in 1878, is still in production and the museum holds a healthy sample of their fancifully ornate ware – but really this is something of an acquired taste. There's also a small display on Charles Edward Stuart – aka Bonnie Prince Charlie – who attempted to seize the throne from George II in the Jacobite Rebellion of 1745. Advancing south from Scotland, Charles and his army got as far as Derby, spreading panic in London, but, unable to press their advantage, it was here they turned round for the long and dismal retreat that ended with their defeat at the bloody battle of Culloden. In addition, the museum also possesses a first-rate collection of the work of **Joseph Wright** (1734–97), a local artist generally regarded as one of the most talented English painters of his century. Wright's bread and butter came from portraiture, though his attempt to fill the boots of Gainsborough, when the latter moved from Bath to London, came unstuck – his more forceful style did not satisfy his genteel customers and Wright soon hightailed it back to Derby. Typical of his style is his portrait of *Sir Richard Arkwright*, looking uncompromising and very porky. Wright was one of the few artists of his period to find inspiration in technology and his depictions of the scientific world were hugely influential – as in his *The Alchemist Discovering Phosphorus*.

With fast and frequent connections to many major cities – including Sheffield and Birmingham – Derby **train station** is a mile to the southeast of the city centre along Midland Road and then London Road; it's a dreary walk, so take a taxi if you can. The **bus station** is about half a mile southeast of the centre. Right in the heart of town, on the market place, is the **tourist office** (Mon–Fri 9.30am–5.30pm, Sat 9.30am–5pm, Sun 10.30am–2.30pm; ☎01332 /255802).

Ashbourne and Dovedale

Sitting pretty on the edge of the Peaks twelve miles northwest of Derby, **ASH-BOURNE** is an amiable little town, whose stubby, cobbled Market Place is flanked by a happy ensemble of old stone buildings. Hikers tramp into town from the neighbouring dales to hang around the square's cafés and pubs, and stroll down the hill to take a peek at the suspended wooden beam spanning Church Street. Once a common feature of English towns, but now a rarity, these **gallows** were not warnings to criminals, but advertising hoardings. Walk west along Church Street and you'll soon spot the soaring spire of **St Oswald's church**, an imposing limestone structure dating from the thirteenth century. The interior is delightful, decorated with all sorts of sculptures, from Green Men through to kings and queens, and graced by handsome stained glass windows, the best of which are exquisite examples of early twentieth-century Arts and Crafts design. In the east aisle of the north transept, the **Cockayne Chapel** is named after the eponymous clan of local landowners who lie buried here. The finest tomb is that of Sir John (d.1447) and his wife, delicately carved alabaster figures, he in his suit of armour, she in a fancy gown.

The **River Dove** wriggles its way across the Peak District, cutting a circuitous course from the high hills of Derbyshire to the flatlands southwest of Derby, where it joins the River Trent. The Dove is at its scenic best near Ashbourne in the stirring two-mile gorge that comprises **Dovedale** – confusingly, other parts of the river are situated in different dales. Dovedale and adjacent Lin Dale are extremely popular with hikers, and Ashbourne tourist office (see below) has racks of trail guides to help you through. Generally speaking, this is easy walking country, the only problem being the bogginess of the river valley after rain.

Practicalities

There are no trains to Ashbourne, but the town is easy to reach by bus from Derby, Buxton and Manchester. Dovedale is, however, beyond the reach of public transport. From Ashbourne **bus station**, it's a short walk over the river and up the hill to the Market Place, where the **tourist office** (March–June, Sept & Oct Mon–Sat 9.30am–5pm; July & Aug March–Oct Mon–Sat 9.30am–5pm, Sun 10am–4pm; Nov–Feb Mon–Sat 10am–4pm; ☎01335 /343666) has oodles of hiking maps and guides. They can also advise on accommodation, a useful service in the summer when things can get very tight. Amongst many **B&Bs**, the pick is the *Coach House*, an immaculately revamped Victorian house with three en-suite guest rooms in a quiet cul-de-sac a five-minute walk from Market Place on The Firs (☎01335/300145; ❹). Several of the pubs do B&B, too, including *Ye Olde Vaults*, on the Market Place (☎01335/346127; ❷). The nearest **youth hostel** is *Ilam Hall* (☎01335/350212, ✉ilam@yha.org.uk; limited opening Oct to mid-July), in a Victorian Gothic National Trust mansion five miles northwest of town. It's a well-equipped hostel and a perfect base for walking Dovedale. The comfortable *Izaak Walton Hotel* (☎01335/350555; ❼) boasts an even better location, hard by the river.

For **food**, the *White Swan* and *Ye Olde Vaults*, both on the Market Place, serve competent bar meals, whilst the *Patrick & Brooksbank* delicatessen, 22 Market Place, has a superb selection of takeaway food, including local cheeses and hams.

Buxton

BUXTON, twenty miles north of Ashbourne, was founded in 79 AD by the Romans, who happened upon a spring from which 1500 gallons of pure water gushed every hour at a constant 28°C. So famous did the spring become that Mary, Queen of Scots, was allowed by her captors to come here for treatment of her rheumatism. The spa's heyday came at the end of the eighteenth century with the fifth duke of Devonshire's grand design to create a northern answer to Bath or Cheltenham, a plan thwarted by the climate, but not before some distinguished eighteenth-century buildings had been erected.

Like many former British spas, the town's heritage has been marred by a lack of money to refurbish ageing properties, though a belated attempt has been made to rescue some of the finer buildings. The thermal baths were closed in 1972, but the sweep of the **Crescent**, incorporating the former St Ann's Hotel – its grandest architectural feature, modelled on the Royal Crescent in Bath – has been preserved thanks to a hefty government grant. It's hoped that some of the public rooms will reopen in the future, but no firm plans have yet been made. The little street **fountain** in front of the Crescent, supplied by St Ann's Well, is still used to fill local water bottles, and the nearby **Pump Room**, first erected in 1894, provides space for temporary art exhibitions in the summer. At the eastern end of the Crescent, a glass and cast-iron canopy hides the entrance to the Cavendish Arcade shopping centre, which makes a hash of preserving the original eighteenth-century bath houses.

The spa remnants apart, the town is at its best in the nearby landscaped **Pavilion Gardens**, just to the southwest of the Crescent and the home of the grand – and grandly refurbished – thousand-seat **Opera House** (tours usually Sat at 11am; call to check, on ☏01298/72190), facing Water Street. This is the main venue for the Buxton Festival held over two weeks at the back end of July. The glasshouse gardens next to the Opera House shelter an array of exotic foliage and you can walk through to the double-decker glass-and-iron pavilion itself, where there's a bar, coffee shop and restaurant with nice views.

Fronting the Crescent, an attractive park known as **The Slopes** – laid out in 1818 in the last flush of municipal enthusiasm – leads up to the traffic-choked Market Place. The top of The Slopes offers the best prospect over the Crescent to the *Palace Hotel* (see below) and the **Devonshire Hospital**; the latter, built in 1790 as a riding school, is covered by what for a long time was the world's widest domed roof. Just along Terrace Road from Market Place, the **Buxton Museum and Art Gallery** (Easter–Oct Tues–Fri 9.30am–5.30pm, Sat 9am–5pm, Sun 10.30am–5pm; rest of year closed Sun; £1) houses a collection of ancient fossils, rocks and pots found in the Peak District, among them jawbones from Neolithic lions and bears. The displays on the first floor document the history of the region – and the town – from the Bronze Age through to more recent times.

As rewarding as any of Buxton's architectural attractions is **Poole's Cavern** (Easter–Oct daily 10am–5pm; £4.50; ☏01298/26978), a mile to the south of town: follow the Broadwalk through the Pavilion Gardens and then take Temple Road. The guided-tour patter is irksome, but the orange and blue-grey stalactite formations are amazingly complex and the chambers impressively large; one marks the underground source of the River Wye. A twenty-minute walk up through the Grin Low woods from the mouth of the cave leads to **Solomon's Temple**, a Victorian folly with great views across Buxton and the hills to the west.

Practicalities

There's an hourly train service from Manchester Piccadilly to Buxton, terminating two minutes' walk from the centre at the **train station** on Station Road. The TransPeak **bus** runs every two hours between Manchester (Lever Street Coach Station) and Nottingham, and stops in Buxton's Market Place, as do the regular buses from Sheffield. Although the town isn't actually in the National Park, its **tourist office**, in the old Natural Mineral Baths on the Crescent (March–Oct daily 9.30am–5pm; Nov–Feb daily 10am–4pm; ☎01298/25106), covers the whole of the Peak District.

Accommodation is plentiful, but at the cheaper end of the market it's none too inspiring, many of the cheaper guest houses being located in dreary back-streets away from the centre, though there are several budget options off Market Place along Grange Road and South Avenue. All told, *Lakenham Guest House*, overlooking Pavilion Gardens at 11 Burlington Rd (☎01298/79209; no credit cards; ❸), is a much better choice, as is the *Grosvenor House Hotel*, 1 Broad Walk (☎01298/72439; no credit cards; ❸), with eight en-suite guest rooms in an immaculate Victorian house – and again with views over the gardens. The historic associations of the *Old Hall Hotel*, a good-looking stone structure in The Square, near the Opera House (☎01298/22841, ⓦwww.oldhallhotelbuxton.co.uk; ❻), resonate with some – Mary, Queen of Scots stayed here in 1573 – but pride of the old spa was the *Palace Hotel* on Palace Road (☎01298 /22001; ❸). This still sits pretty above the town and many of its bedrooms have lovely views. It is a twenty-minute walk to *Sherbrook Lodge* **youth hostel**, a Victorian house set in wooded grounds on Harpur Hill Road, at the end of London Road (☎01298/22287, ⓔbuxton@yha.org.uk; restricted opening Nov to mid-March). The hostel has self-catering facilities and serves up simple evening meals.

For **food**, Buxton is hardly a gourmet's paradise, but there are one or two more-than-passable cafés, beginning with the *Wild Carrot*, 5 Bridge St (☎01298/22843), an adventurous (mostly vegetarian) café at the end of Spring Gardens. In addition, the restaurant and wine bar of the *Old Hall Hotel* are very good, but otherwise you're left with a motley collection of restaurants and a couple of pubs around Market Place. Amongst them, the *Firenze Pizzeria Ristorante*, 3 Eagle Parade (☎01298/72203; open Tues–Sun eve), is about the best of the bunch. The annual **Buxton Festival** takes place every July, featuring a full programme of classical music, opera and drama, with supporting fringe events, including a film festival; details are available from the Festival Office (☎01298/70395), in the Opera House, where many events are staged, or from the tourist office.

Castleton

The limestone hills of the White Peaks are riddled with water-worn cave systems, best explored in the four show caves within walking distance of **CASTLETON**, ten miles northeast of Buxton. It's an agreeable small town, overlooked by Mam Tor (see box below), ringed by hills and cut through by a babbling river lined with stone cottages. Indeed, as a base for local walks it's hard to beat, and the hikers resting up in the quiet Market Place near the church have the choice of a fine spread of local accommodation and services. Overseeing the whole ensemble is **Peveril Castle** (April–Oct daily 10am–6pm; Nov–March Wed–Sun 10am–4pm; £2.30; EH), from which the village gets its name. Its construction was started by William I's illegitimate son William Peveril to protect the king's rights to the forest that then covered vast

Walks around Castleton

Several **walking routes** take you up from the Hope Valley onto the tops that ring Castleton, some taking in the show caves along the way. Most are easy to follow in good weather, but you'll need an appropriate OS map or one of the trail leaflets from the information office. All the caverns mentioned are described in the main text.

A path runs west from town, climbing past Peak, Speedwell and Treak Cliff caverns before bending around a bluff to reach the Blue John Cavern: if you're sightseeing, you can complete the short circular walk here by following the minor road back down the precipitous **Whinnats Pass**, emerging again at Speedwell Cavern. For the best views, though, keep following the signposted path from Blue John for the slow climb up the National Trust-owned **Mam Tor** (1696ft) and its barely discernible Iron Age hillfort (3km from Castleton; 1hr 30min). It's the Peak District's second-highest peak and the NT's most tramped-upon outdoor site, attracting over 250,000 visitors a year – hence the flagstoned path up to the top and along the ridge, whose stone was helicoptered in. This channels the summer crowds along something of a hikers' motorway, but it has allowed the hillside to regenerate itself and the nesting birds to return. The views – to Kinder Scout, Castleton, Edale and down the Hope valley – remain unsurpassed.

From the peak the ridge rolls along to the northeast and opportunities to drop back down to Castleton can be taken at either Hollins Cross, Back Tor or from Losehill Pike, making the complete walk anything from three to six hours. Hollins Cross is also the lowest crossing-point on the two-hour walk from Castleton to Edale, which could also form part of a circuit involving scaling Mam Tor.

---

areas of the Peak District. After a stiff climb up to the keep, you can trace much of the surviving curtain wall, which commands great views of the Hope Valley.

The closest cavern to town, the **Peak Cavern** (Easter–Oct daily 10am–5pm; Nov–Easter Sat & Sun 10am–4pm; £5; ☎01433/620285) is tucked in a gully at the back of the town, its gaping mouth once providing shelter for a rope factory and a small village, of which a vague floorplan remains. Daniel Defoe, visiting in the eighteenth century, noted the cavern's colourful local name, the "Devil's Arse", after the fiendish fashion in which the interior contours twisted and turned. Twenty minutes' walk out of town along the road west to Winnat's Pass (there's a parallel route, across the fields) lies **Speedwell Cavern** (daily: Easter–Oct 9.30am–6pm; Nov–Easter 10am–5pm; last entry 1hr before closing; £5.50; ☎01433/620512). This is, at 600-feet below ground, the deepest cave accessible to the public in Britain. That said, there's precious little to see, with the main drama coming with the means of access itself – down a hundred dripping steps and then by boat through a quarter-mile-long claustrophobic tunnel that was blasted out in search of lead. At the end lies the Bottomless Pit, a pool where 40,000 tons of mining rubble were dumped without raising the water level.

The other two caves are the world's only source of the sparkling fluorspar known as **Blue John**. Highly prized for ornaments and jewellery for the past 250 years, this semi-precious stone comes in a multitude of hues from blue through deep red to yellow, depending on its hydrocarbon impurities. Before being cut and polished it must be soaked in pine resin, a process originally carried out in France, where the term *bleu-jaune* (after its primary colours) provided the source of its English name. The **Treak Cliff Cavern** (daily: March–Oct 10am–5pm; Nov–Feb 10am–4pm; last entry 40min before closing; £5.50; ☎01433/620571), a few hundred yards along the hillside from Speedwell, contains the best examples of the stone *in situ* and a good deal more in the shop. This is also the best cave to visit in its own right, dripping – literally – with stalactites (some up to 100,000 years old), flowstone and bizarre rock formations, all visible on an entertaining forty-minute walking tour through the main cave system. Water collected in one of the caves is used to make tea in the café at the entrance since it's much purer than the stuff that pours from the local taps. Tours of the **Blue John Cavern** (daily: Easter–Oct 9.30am–5.30pm; Nov–Easter 9.30am–dusk; £6; ☎01433/620638) dive deeper into the rock, with narrow steps and sloping paths following an ancient watercourse through whirlpool-hollowed chambers down to the Dining Room Cavern, where a former owner once held a banquet. Blue John Cavern is another fifteen minutes' signposted walk beyond Treak Cliff, and there's direct access off the A625, just west of Castleton.

Practicalities

The A625 slices through the centre of Castleton as the high street. From the east, it's a clear run from Sheffield via Hathersage, but arriving from the west – from the A6 just north of Buxton – the A625 has to negotiate the steep Winnats Pass. There's a marginally shorter and even more dramatic approach from Buxton, too: turn off the A6 along the A623 and, after about a mile, at windblown Sparrowpit, take the B6061 over the hills and you'll join the A625 at Winnats Pass. The main approach by public transport is by **bus** from Sheffield and Hathersage on the #272; there are also reasonably frequent buses from Bakewell and bus #203, a weekend service direct from Buxton in summer. The regular Manchester Piccadilly–Hope Valley–Sheffield trains stop at **Hope train station** two miles east of town, which is linked to Castleton by the #272 bus and other local services. The **Peak District National Park Information Centre** is on Castle Street, near the church (daily: Easter–Oct 10am–1pm & 2–5.30pm; Nov–Easter 10am–1pm & 2–5pm; ☎01433/620679).

Accommodation is plentiful, but should be booked in advance at popular holiday times; the information centre can help if you're stuck. The lively **youth hostel** (☎01433/620235, ℮castleton@yha.org.uk; closed Jan) is housed in eighteenth-century Castleton Hall and the adjacent old vicarage on Market Place, just up past the church from the information office. The most welcoming **B&B** is *Bargate Cottage*, also on Market Place (☎01433/620201; no credit cards; ❷), whose frilly rooms are overseen by a friendly proprietor who offers conversation, good breakfasts and welcome extras such as drying baskets for hiking boots. Two or three other B&Bs are sited just over the road from here. *Cryer House*, a little way back down Castle St (☎01433/620244; no credit cards; ❷), opposite the church, has a lovely conservatory, or try for space at the popular *Kelseys Swiss House* on How Lane (☎01433/621098; no credit cards; ❸), the eastern continuation of the main road through town. All the local pubs have rooms, such as *Ye Olde Cheshire Cheese*, How Lane (☎01433/620330; ❸). The best lodgings are at *Ye Olde Nag's Head* at Cross Street on the main road (☎01433/620248; ❺), a comfortable, if slightly formal, seventeenth-century coaching inn with some good weekend – and dinner, room and breakfast – deals. The nearest **campsite** is in Hope, two miles east of Castleton, where the *Laneside Caravan Park* (☎01433/620215; closed Nov–Easter) lies five minutes from Hope's pubs and shops.

The pubs are the mainstay for **eating out** in Castleton, and aren't bad to boot. *Ye Olde Cheshire Cheese* welcomes muddy boots and fills their owners with generous portions, while the *Castle* on Castle Street has an appealing series of rooms warmed by open fires. Best of all are the bar meals at *Ye Olde Nag's Head*, boasting treats such as *bruschetta* and wild mushrooms; you can eat more expensively, and equally well, in their restaurant too.

Edale

There's almost nothing to **EDALE** except for a couple of pubs, a scattering of local B&Bs and a train station, and it's this isolation which is immediately appealing. Walkers arrive in droves throughout the year to set off on the 250-mile **Pennine Way** (see box below) across England's backbone to Kirk Yetholm on the Scottish border; its starting-point is signposted from outside the *Old Nag's Head* at the head of the village.

An excellent **circular walk** (9 miles; 5hr) uses the first part of the Pennine Way, leading up onto the bleak gritstone, table-top of **Kinder Scout** (2088ft), below which the village cowers. The route cuts west from the *Nag's Head* along a packhorse route once used by Cheshire's salt exporters. From the campsite and camping barn at *Upper Booth Farm* (☎01433/670250), you climb the Jacob's Ladder path continuing half a mile west to the carved medieval **Edale Cross**. Backtracking a couple of hundred yards, the Pennine Way branches north along the broken plateau edge to **Kinder Downfall**, Derbyshire's highest cascade. This was the site of the Kinder Scout Trespass of 1932, when dozens of protesters walked onto unused but private land, five subsequently receiving prison sentences. It was the turning-point in the fight for public access to open moorland, leading, three years later, to the formation of the Ramblers' Association. At Kinder Downfall turn east then southeast across the often boggy peat towards the wind-sculpted **Wool Pack** rocks, then across to the eastern rim, where a path to the south along Grindslow Knoll and down into Edale avoids Grindsbrook Clough, the highly eroded route of the original Pennine Way. It can be extremely wet up here among the bare furrows of peat – long-distance walker John Hillaby, on his *Journey Through Britain*, had to resort to removing his footwear to make his way across the sodden top of Kinder

---

The Pennine Way

The 250-mile-long **Pennine Way** was the country's first long-distance footpath, officially opened in 1965. It stretches north from the boggy plateau of the Peak District's Kinder Scout, through the Yorkshire Dales and Teesdale, crossing Hadrian's Wall and the Northumberland National Park, before entering Scotland to fizzle out at the village of Kirk Yetholm. People had been using a similar route for over thirty years before the official opening, inspired by Tom Stephenson, secretary of the Ramblers' Association, who had first identified the need for such a long-distance path in the 1930s. His idea was to stick to the crest of the Pennines where practicable and link up existing tracks, bridleways and footpaths, only descending to the valleys for overnight accommodation and services. The problem was that much of the route lay on private land, so years of negotiation and re-routing were necessary before the Pennine Way could be officially declared open.

Now it's one of the most popular walks in the country, either taken in sections or completed in two to three weeks, depending on your level of fitness and experience. It's a challenge in the best of weather, since it passes through some of the most remote countryside in England – you must be properly equipped, able to use a map and compass and be prepared to follow local advice about current diversions and re-routing; changes are often made to avoid erosion of the existing path. The National Trail Guides, *Pennine Way: South* and *Pennine Way: North*, are essential, though some still prefer to stick to Wainwright's *Pennine Way Companion*. National park **information** centres along the route – particularly the one at Edale – stock a full selection of guides and associated trail leaflets and can offer advice. Finally, on reaching the end, you can get your certificate stamped at Edale's *Old Nag's Head* in the south or Kirk Yetholm's *Border Hotel* in the north.

Scout, which to his appalled mind looked as if it were "entirely covered in the droppings of dinosaurs".

Practicalities

Edale is about five miles northwest of Castleton by road, slightly more direct by path. Hourly **trains** from Manchester or Sheffield (stopping in Hathersage) provide surprisingly easy access; the only **bus** is a summer-weekends only hourly service from Castleton. Around 400 yards up the road from the train station is the **National Park Information Centre** (daily: Easter–Oct 9am–1pm & 2–5.30pm; Nov–Easter closes 5pm; ☎01433/670207) at Fieldhead. This sells all manner of trail leaflets and hiking guides and can advise about local **accommodation**. The nearest **youth hostel**, the extremely popular *Edale YHA Activity Centre* (☎01433/670302, ⊜edale@yha.org.uk), lies two miles northeast of Edale station, in an old country house at Rowland Cote, Nether Booth. It's accessible along the road to Nether Booth or across the fields – and the Fieldhead campsite – from behind the information centre. Naturally enough, the hostel is popular with Pennine Way walkers as is the YHA **camping barn** at Cotefield Farm, Ollerbrook (☎01433/620111), which lies on the path to the youth hostel. There are two **campsites**, *Fieldhead* (☎01433/670386), behind the information centre, and *Cooper's* at Newfold Farm (☎01433/670372), in the centre of Edale near the *Old Nag's Head*.

Those without hair shirts, or with more money, will do better at the **B&Bs**, starting with the recently revamped *Old Parsonage*, behind the *Nag's Head* (☎01433/670232; no credit cards; ❶; closed Oct–Easter). *Stonecroft*, a detached Victorian house on the village road near the church (☎01433/670262; no credit cards; ❸) is good, too, while other private home and farmhouse options lie scattered out along the Nether Booth road. Attractive *Edale House* (☎01433/670399; no credit cards; ❶) is typical, a twenty-minute walk from the pub. The *Ramblers' Country House Hotel* (☎01433/670268; ❸), close to the train station at the bottom of the village, has rooms, and is one of only two places to **eat** and drink. Those things, though, are best done at the hiker-friendly *Old Nag's Head* (☎01433/670291), at the top of the village; alternatively, head down to the *Ramblers'*.

Hathersage

The busy little town of **HATHERSAGE** on the A625, five miles east of Castleton and just eleven from Sheffield, has a hard time persuading people not to pass straight through into the heart of the National Park. It's worth at least an hour though, particularly in its quieter reaches on the heights around the much restored village **church of St Michael and All Angels**, where a prominent grave site is said to be the last resting place of the Sherwood outlaw Little John. The footpath up to the church starts by the side of the *Hathersage Inn* on the main road. Hathersage's other claim to fame is as the "Morton" of Charlotte Brontë's **Jane Eyre** – a village name borrowed by the author from the landlord of the *George* in Hathersage, who met Charlotte off the stagecoach from Haworth when she came to stay here in 1845. She was visiting a friend, whose brother was the local vicar, and, in the church, Charlotte doubtless was shown the memorial "Eyre brasses". She also used several other local names and buildings for her novel, notably North Lees Hall (Rochester's Thornfield Hall) and Moorseats (St John Rivers' Moor House) – all of which can be taken in on a four-mile circular walk around the town.

Hathersage also boasts its share of craft and cottage industries, most notably the impressive **Round Building**, just outside town on the B6001 (Mon–Sat 10am–5pm, Sun 11am–5pm; ℡01433/650220), where Sheffield designer David Mellor produces wonderful cutlery, tableware and kitchenware.

Practicalities

Among several services, the frequent #272 Sheffield–Castleton **bus** stops right outside the *George*. The town is also on the Manchester–Sheffield rail line and from the **train station** it's about half a mile north to both Sheffield Road, the main street, and the *George*.

Hathersage has a couple of first-rate **B&Bs** – try *Moorgate*, on Castleton Road (℡01433/650293; no credit cards; ❶) – and there are rooms in several **inns**, most memorably in the venerable *George* on Sheffield Rd (℡01433/650436; ❻). Its close rival is the *Scotsman's Pack* (℡01433/650253; ❹), a flagstoned, eighteenth-century inn on School Lane, the way to the church. Brontë fans will be delighted to know that two apartments in the beautifully restored *North Lees Hall* can be rented – contact the Vivat Trust (℡0207/930 8030; ❾); prices run from £420 a week for the two-person apartment. The local **youth hostel** (℡01433/650493), with just forty beds, is on the edge of the village, on Castleton road, a hundred yards past the *George*.

All the pubs serve bar **meals**, but the restaurant at the *George* is probably the best in town. Otherwise, *Longland's Eating House*, on Sheffield Road (℡01433 651978), is a laid-back, licensed, mainly vegetarian, café above a good hiking/outdoors shop.

Eyam and around

Within a year of September 7, 1665, the lonely lead-mining settlement of **EYAM** (pronounced "Eem"), five miles south of Hathersage and four miles northwest of Baslow, had lost almost half of its population of 750 to the bubonic plague, a calamity that earned it the enduring epithet "The Plague Village". The first victim was one George Vicars, a journeyman tailor who is said to have released some infected fleas into his lodgings from a package of cloth he had brought here from London. Acutely conscious of the danger to neighbouring villages, William Mompesson, the village rector, speedily organized a self-imposed quarantine, arranging for food to be left at places on the parish boundary. One of these was **Mompesson's Well**, half a mile up the hill to the north and still accessible by footpath from the village. Payment was made with coins left in pools of disinfecting vinegar in holes chiselled into the old boundary stones – and these can still be seen. The rector closed the church and held services in the open air at a natural rock arch to the south of the village – and every year since 1906, on the last Sunday in August, a commemorative service has been held here, at Cucklet Delph. Mompesson himself survived the plague, though his wife did not – poor reward for a man whose endeavours prevented the plague from spreading across the Peaks.

Long and thin, Eyam is little more than one main street – Church and then Main Street – which trails west up from **The Square**, where a scrawny green is overlooked by a few old stone houses. First up of interest along Church Street is the comely **church of St Lawrence** (Easter–Sept Mon–Sat 9am–6pm, Sun 1–5.30pm; Oct–Easter Mon–Sat 9am–4pm, Sun 1–5.30pm; free), of medieval foundation but extensively revamped in the nineteenth century. Buried in the church graveyard, in the shadow of a richly carved eighth-century Celtic cross, is Mompesson's wife, whose sterling work nursing sick villagers is recalled every Remembrance Day when red roses are left beside her tomb. Rather more cheerful is the grave of one Harry Bagshawe, a local cricketer

The plague

Ring a ring o' roses
A pocket full of posies
Atishoo, atishoo
We all fall down

As the residents of Eyam began to drop like flies from **the plague** in the autumn of 1665, the locals resorted to home remedies and desperate snatches from folkloric memory to stave off the inevitable. There was little understanding in the seventeenth century of why or how the disease spread: Daniel Defoe, in his later journal of London's plague, recorded how the lord mayor ordered the destruction of all the city's pets, believing them to be responsible. Others, thinking it to be a miasma, kept coal braziers alight day and night in the hope that the smoke would push the infection back into the sky from where it was thought to have come. In isolated Eyam, with the plague among them and no way out through the self-imposed cordon, the locals improvised to little effect. Applications of cold water, herb infusions and draughts of brine or lemon juice were tried; poultices applied; bleeding by leeches was commonplace; and when all else failed, charms and spells were wheeled out – the plucked tail of a pigeon laid against the sore supposedly drew out the poison. All, of course, had no effect and the death toll mounted, though occasionally there was coincidental success: one 14-year-old girl mistakenly drank a pitcher of discarded bacon fat, left by her bedside; the fever passed and she recovered.

Centuries later, the horrifying events lie recorded in a children's **nursery game**, whose rhyme became popular in plague-ridden England. The "roses" are the patches which developed on the victim's chest soon after contracting the disease; the "posies" are herbs or flowers, carried as charms; as the fever took hold, sneezing ("atishoo, atishoo") was a common symptom; until, chillingly, at death's door, "we all fall down".

whose tomb shows him being bowled with the umpire's finger raised upright, presumably – on this occasion – to heaven. Inside the church, informative panels reveal more of the village's history, highlighting a number of plague sites dotted around the town. The most harrowing of these are the **Riley Graves**, half a mile east of the village beyond The Square in open country, where a Mrs Hancock buried her husband, three sons and three daughters within eight days in August 1666. Adjacent to the church are the so-called **plague cottages**, where plaques explain who died where and when – it was here that Vicars met his maker.

Just along from the cottages, **Eyam Hall** (guided tours June–Aug Tues–Thurs & Sun 11am–4pm; £4.25) was built for Thomas Wright a few years after the plague ended, possibly in an attempt to secure his position as the squire of the depleted village. Wright's heirs have lived in it ever since, building up a mildly diverting collection of furnishings, family portraits, tapestries, costumes and incidental bygones. Some of the adjacent farm buildings have been turned into a **Craft Centre** (Tues–Sun 11am–4pm; free) with a restaurant and gift shop. From the hall, it's a few minutes' walk along Main Street and up Hawkhill Road – follow the signs – to the modest Methodist chapel that now houses the **Eyam Museum** (April–Oct Tues–Sun 10am–4.30pm; £1.50). This tracks through the history of the village and has a good section on the bubonic plague in general – its transmission, symptoms and social aftermath.

Practicalities

Eyam makes a great overnight stop, though you should try and book accommodation in advance, since facilities are limited. **Buses** to the village – from

Sheffield, Manchester, Buxton, Hathersage, Bakewell and Baslow – all stop on The Square and a few run along Main/Church Street too.

First choice among the handful of **B&Bs** is the luxurious *Delf View House* (☎01433/631533; no credit cards; ❸), a beautifully kept Georgian house set in its own grounds just along from the church; breakfast is served in a superb old dining room with its flagstone floor, imposing fireplace and beamed ceiling. Otherwise, two pubs – the *Miner's Arms*, near The Square on Water Lane (☎01433/630853; ❸), and the *Old Rose & Crown*, on The Square (☎01433 /630858; ❸) – have a few perfectly adequate rooms of a modern disposition. Eyam **youth hostel**, a large Victorian house on Hawkhill Road (☎01433 /630335, ℮eyam@yha.org.uk; restricted opening Nov–March), is a steep twenty-minute walk out of the village, past the museum. The best place **to eat** is the *Miner's Arms*, which serves bar meals as well as more formal, but very enjoyable, traditional British dinners in its restaurant in the evenings.

Foolow and Bretton

Keep going west out of Eyam along the Main Street and you're soon out into open countryside and then, after about a mile-and-a-half, comes **FOOLOW**, a pretty little spot with a village green, duck pond and Cross. The main reason for visiting is, however, the excellent *Bull's Head* (☎01433/630873; no credit cards; ❸), serving decent beer and delicious bar meals and with a few comfortable rooms to boot. You can also get here by walking over from Eyam and there's a frequent local bus service, too.

From Foolow, a mile-long country lane cuts north, climbing up to a windswept ridge, where **BRETTON** is little more than a pub – the *Barrel Inn* (☎01433/630856), which offers good quality bar food and wide views out across the Peaks. A hundred yards down the road from the pub, a very basic **youth hostel** (☎01433/631856; open daily from mid-July to Aug plus limited dates April to mid-July, Sept & Oct; Nov–March group bookings only) plies its lonely trade. You can also reach Bretton direct from Eyam, but it's a stiff and steep two-mile hike. There are no buses.

Baslow

On the northern edge of the Chatsworth estate (see below), beside the A619/AA623 junction, is **BASLOW**, an inconclusive little hamlet at its prettiest amongst the huddle of old stone houses that flank the River Derwent as it weaves its way south. The village has several **B&Bs**, with one of the most engaging being *The Old School House*, in attractive Victorian premises in the centre on School Lane (☎01246/582488; ❸). Even better – and one of the Peak's greatest luxuries – is *Fischer's Baslow Hall* (☎01246/583259; ❺), a mile or so beyond the village along Calver Road, the A623. In its own grounds, the hall is picture-postcard perfect, a handsome Edwardian building made of local stone with matching gables and a dinky canopy over the front door. The interior is suitably lavish and – as there are only a handful of rooms – the service attentive. The restaurant is superb and has won several awards for its imaginative cuisine; there's a less formal, less expensive café too.

Bakewell

BAKEWELL, flanking the banks of the River Wye some four miles south of Baslow – and twelve miles east of Buxton – is famous for its **Bakewell Pudding**. Known throughout the rest of the country as a Bakewell Tart, this is a wonderful slippery, flaky, almond-flavoured confection – now with a dab of jam – invented here around 1860 when a cook botched a recipe for strawberry tart. Almost a century before this fortuitous mishap, the duke of Rutland set out to turn what was then a remote village into a prestigious spa, thereby trumping the work of his rival, the duke of Devonshire, in Buxton. The frigidity of the water made failure inevitable, leaving only the prettiness of **Bath Gardens** beside Rutland Square as a reminder of the venture.

Famous tart apart, Bakewell is an undemanding place today, its main street too crowded by traffic – and tourists – to be much fun, though it is within easy striking distance of several first-rate attractions. In town, there's some interest in the web of narrow shopping streets around **Market Square** as well as in the adjacent **riverside park**, but the most agreeable part of Bakewell trails up the hill at the west end of the centre. Here, strolling up North Church Street, with its line of comely stone cottages, you soon reach **All Saints church**, the result of centuries of tinkering from the Normans onwards. Outside, in the church yard, is a rare **Saxon cross**, carved with saints and decorative circles and scrolls, and inside are the tombs of the Vernons, local bigwigs who long ruled the Bakewell roost. Sir George Vernon's sixteenth-century tomb, with its alabaster effigies, is especially fine as is the wall monument to his daughter Dorothy Manners and her husband John Manners. Look out also for the earlier Foljambe wall memorial showing the Foljambes – man and wife – in bed praying.

Signs at the church point you up the lane to the **Old House Museum**, in Cunningham's Place (April–June, Sept & Oct daily 1.30–4pm; July & Aug daily 11am–4pm; £2.50), a Tudor house once owned by Richard Arkwright, who rented it out to his mill workers – but only after he had partitioned up into tiny sections. The museum has a series of period rooms and an incidental collection of old knick-knacks – from lace and costumes to toys and tools. Finally, the energetic can head off out of Bakewell along the **Monsal Trail**, which cuts eight miles north and then west through some of Derbyshire's finest limestone dales. First up is Monsal Dale and then comes Miller's Dale and Chee Dale. The trail ends in Wye Dale, just east of Buxton.

Practicalities

The nearest **train** stations are at Matlock and Buxton, leaving **bus** services such as the TransPeak Manchester to Nottingham service, the #X18 from Sheffield, and the #R61 from Derby/Matlock as the main routes into town. All services stop on – or very close to – central Rutland Square. The **tourist office** is just a couple of hundred yards down the road in the restored, seventeenth-century Old Market Hall (daily: Easter–Oct 9.30am–5.30pm; Nov–Easter 10am–5pm; ☎01629/813227). This is very well equipped with public transport timetables as well as local biking and hiking leaflets and guides.

For **B&B**, try the *Avenue House*, whose three attractively furnished rooms occupy part of a spacious Victorian house south of the centre, along Haddon Road (☎01629/812467; no credit cards; ❷; closed Nov–Jan). Alternatively, the homely *Castle Inn*, at the foot of Castle Street (☎01629/812103; ❷) is a sympathetic old inn by the bridge over the Wye with four straightforward, comfortable rooms. The town's **youth hostel**, with just twenty eight beds, is in a modest, modern building on Fly Hill (☎01629/812313, ⓔbakewell @yha.org.uk; limited opening Nov–March); it has self-catering facilities and serves evening meals. Fly Hill is near the church – just follow North Church Street round and you'll hit it. There's also pedestrian-only access up a steep lane from the A6. Much more upmarket is a nearby **hotel**, the luxurious *Hassop Hall* (☎01629/640488; ❺), a cannily refurbished old manor house with beautiful bedrooms set in charming parkland two and a half miles north of Bakewell along the A619 and then the B6001. Another very recommendable hotel near Bakewell is the *Lathkil* (☎01629/812501; ❹), two miles to the southwest in the solitary hamlet of Over Haddon. The building itself is not all that special – it's routinely modern in appearance with just a handful of bedrooms – but its wide windows look out over wooded Lathkil Dale, down into which footpaths meander, while there's reasonable bar food and a more adventurous evening menu in the restaurant.

Bakeries all over town claim to bake Bakewell Pudding to the original recipe, but the best is the *Old Original Bakewell Pudding Shop* beside Rutland Square – open until 9pm in summer and with a full restaurant menu as well as gargantuan, family-sized puddings for a fiver. *Bloomer's*, on Water Lane, is a great place too, an excellent deli and bakery with a special line in home-made sweet and savoury pies. There are also several good **restaurants** in town, beginning with *Aitch's Wine Bar & Bistro* (☎01629/813895; closed Sun in winter), just off Rutland Square along the road to Buxton, which serves tasty Mediterranean-style dishes at very reasonable prices. There's also the first-rate *Renaissance*, in the centre on Bath St (☎01629/812687), where the emphasis is on French cuisine with a three-course set meal costing £22.

Haddon Hall

The genteel and understated **Haddon Hall** (April–Sept daily 10.30am–5pm; Oct Mon–Thurs 10.30am–4.30pm; £5.90, plus parking 50p), on the banks of the River Wye, two miles south of Bakewell along the A6, is one of the finest medieval manor houses in England. In the mid-twelfth century the property passed from the Avenells, its Norman founders, to the Vernons, who owned it for four hundred years until 1558 when the sole heir, **Dorothy Vernon**, married John Manners, scion of another powerful family, who later became dukes of Rutland. Their union is commemorated on their joint tomb in Bakewell church, but the romantic story of their elopement is probably apocryphal. At the start of the eighteenth century, when the Devonshires outdid the Rutlands by building nearby Chatsworth, the hall fell into two hundred years of neglect, thereby sparing it from Georgian and Victorian meddling.

Restoration at the beginning of this century revealed the **chapel**'s wall paintings of exotic plants and animals, plastered over at the Reformation. Across the courtyard, the fourteenth-century kitchens – originally detached from the house for fear of fire – are now connected by a passage to the banqueting hall, complete with a beautifully restored roof. A couple of less interesting domestic rooms lead to the house's highlight, the **Long Gallery**, built by John Manners for indoor promenades during inclement weather. The **gardens**, too, are gorgeous, and the whole heady ensemble turned up to great effect as Mr Rochester's Thornfield in Zeffirelli's *Jane Eyre*.

Haddon Hall is on the TransPeak **bus** route.

Chatsworth House

Chatsworth House (Easter–Oct daily 11am–5.30pm; last admission 4.30pm; gardens till 6pm; house & gardens £7, gardens only £3.85), four miles north-east of Bakewell via the A619, was built in the seventeenth century by the first duke of Devonshire, and has been in the family ever since. The monumental Palladian frontage beautifully sets off the hundred acres of formal gardens, redesigned in the 1750s by Capability Brown. In the 1820s, the sixth duke instigated more substantial changes when he added the north wing and set Joseph Paxton (designer of London's Crystal Palace) to work on the gardens, creating the Emperor Fountain. At 296ft, the fountain was the world's highest gravity-fed jet, but it now attains a meagre third of that.

Beginning a visit at the house, a maze of balconies and grand staircases lead, eventually, to the **State Apartments**, their ceilings daubed with overblown cherubic figures. None of the rooms is finer than the **Dining Room** in the north wing, its table set as it was for the visit of George V and Queen Mary in 1933, and its walls hung with seven Van Dycks. Vases of the semi-precious Blue John stone (see p.672) flank the door through to the **Sculpture Gallery**, where you can admire a Rembrandt and a Frans Hals before exploring the gardens, restaurant, estate shop or children's playground. The gardens are, however, tiny in comparison to the surrounding **park** (daily dawn–dusk; free), whose rolling, partly wooded grasslands are grazed by sheep and latticed with footpaths.

The principal approach to Chatsworth leads through the immaculately maintained estate village of **EDENSOR**, remodelled by the sixth duke for his employees, and well worth a few minutes in its own right. There's an infrequent **bus** service from both Bakewell and Baslow to Edensor, but otherwise the best bet is to catch any Bakewell to Baslow bus and walk from the bus stop through the park to the house – a distance of around a mile. Walking back to Bakewell from Chatsworth is also enjoyable, and Bakewell tourist office has a leaflet outlining a possible route.

Travel Details

Buses

For information on all local and national bus services, contact Traveline: ☏ 0870/608 2 608 (daily 7am–9pm), ⊛ www.traveline.org.uk.

Trains

For information on all local and national rail services, contact National Rail Enquiries: ☏ 08457/48 49 50, ⊛ www.rail.co.uk.

Birmingham New Street to: Birmingham International (every 15–30min; 15min); Coventry (every 15–30min; 30min); Derby (hourly; 45min); Great Malvern (every 30min; 1hr); Hereford (10 daily; 1hr 50min); Kidderminster (every 30min; 30min); Leicester (hourly; 50min); Lichfield (every 15min; 45min); London (every 30min; 1hr 40min); Shrewsbury (hourly; 1hr 20min); Stoke-on-Trent (hourly; 1hr); Walsall (every 30min Mon–Sat; 30min); Wolverhampton (every 30min; 20min); Worcester (every 30min; 1hr).

Birmingham Snow Hill to: Stratford-upon-Avon (Mon–Sat hourly; 50min); Warwick (Mon–Sat hourly; 40min).

Derby to: Birmingham (every 20min; 45min); Leicester (hourly; 30min); London (hourly; 1hr 50min); Nottingham (every 20min; 35min).

Hereford to: Birmingham (hourly; 1hr 40min); Great Malvern (hourly; 30min); Leominster (hourly; 15min); London (5 daily; 2hr 45min); Ludlow (hourly; 30min); Shrewsbury (hourly; 1hr); Worcester (every 1hr 30min; 40min).

Shrewsbury to: Birmingham (2–4 hourly; 1hr 10min); Church Stretton (every 30min; 15min); Craven Arms (hourly; 30min); Hereford (2–3 hourly; 1hr); Ludlow (hourly; 30min); Leominster (hourly; 40min); Telford (every 30min; 20min).

Stoke-on-Trent to: Birmingham (hourly; 1hr).

Stratford-upon-Avon to: Birmingham (Mon–Sat hourly; 1hr); Oxford (4 daily; 1hr 10min); Warwick (Mon–Sat 8 daily; 30min).

Worcester to: Birmingham (every 30min; 40min–1hr); Hereford (13 daily; 40min).

The East Midlands

Highlights

CHAPTER 9

* **Media, Nottingham**
Nottingham is proud of its night clubs, with good reason – it's cutting edge stuff and Media continues the story. **See p.693**

* **Hardwick Hall** Elizabeth I was formidable and so was Bess of Hardwick. Her beautiful Elizabethan mansion survives in fine nick. **See p.694**

* **Rufford Country Park**
Well off the usual tourist track, Rufford offers a wetland and a ceramic gallery, a mill and a sculpture garden with lots of relaxed strolling in between. **See p.696**

* **Althorp** Diana, Princess of Wales, was buried in the grounds of her childhood home in 1997, and despite the passing of the years, Althorp remains a shrine to the legion of Diana fans. **See p.713**

9

The East Midlands

M any tourists bypass the four major counties of the **East Midlands** – Nottinghamshire, Leicestershire, Northamptonshire and Lincolnshire – on their way to more obvious destinations, and although there's much to savour it's true they miss little of overriding interest. **Nottingham**, **Leicester** and **Northampton** – three of the four county towns – share a long and eventful history, but have been badly bruised by postwar town planning and industrial development. Embedded in the modernity, however, are a few historical landmarks – an especially fine church in Northampton, the castle in Nottingham, and traces of Roman baths in Leicester – but by and large these are the frills rather than the substance, though Nottingham does have an aesthetic edge. And if few would describe this trio of towns as especially good-looking, the countryside surrounding them can be delightful, with rolling farmland punctuated by wooded ridges and flowing hills, all sprinkled with prestigious country homes, pretty villages and old market towns. In Nottinghamshire, the star turn is **Hardwick Hall**, an especially beautiful Elizabethan country home, but Byron's **Newstead Abbey** runs a close second. Furthermore, the eastern reaches of the county hold two appealing market towns – **Southwell** and **Newark** – whilst west Leicestershire weighs in with the fascinating mansion of **Calke Abbey**. East of Leicestershire, the easy countryside rolls over into **Rutland**, the region's fifth and smallest county, and here you'll find two more pleasant country towns, **Oakham** and **Uppingham**, though tiny **Lyddington** is even more picturesque. Rutland benefits from the use of limestone as the traditional building material and so does **Northamptonshire**. Here, the rural parts of the county are studded with handsome, old stone villages and small towns – most notably **Fotheringhay** and **Oundle** – plus large country estates, the best known of which is **Althorp**, the final resting place of Princess Diana.

Accommodation price codes

Throughout this guide, hotel and B&B accommodation is priced on a scale of ❶ to ❾, the number indicating the **lowest price** you could expect to pay per night in that establishment for a **double room** in high season. The prices indicated by the codes are as follows:

❶ under £40	❹ £60–70	❼ £110–150
❷ £40–50	❺ £70–90	❽ £150–200
❸ £50–60	❻ £90–110	❾ over £200

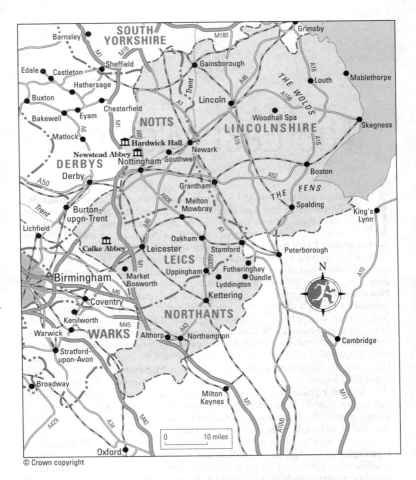

© Crown copyright

Lincolnshire is very different in character from the rest of the region, an agricultural backwater that remains surprisingly remote – locals sometimes call it the "forgotten" county. This was not always the case: throughout medieval times the county flourished as a centre of the wool trade with Flanders, its merchants and landowners becoming some of the wealthiest in the land. Reminders of the high times are legion, beginning with the majestic cathedral that graces **Lincoln**, a dignified old city which, with its cobbled lanes and ancient buildings, well deserves an overnight stay. Equally enticing is the splendidly intact stone town of **Stamford**, but the county's urban attractions pretty much end there. Out in the sticks, the most distinctive feature is **The Fens**, whose pancake-flat fields, filling out much of the south of the county and extending deep into East Anglia, have been regained from the marshes and the sea. Fenland villages are generally short of charm, but the **parish churches**, whose spires regularly interrupt the wide-skied landscape, are simply stunning, the most impressive of the lot being St Botolph's in **Boston**.

In north Lincolnshire, the low-lying chalky hills of the **Lincolnshire Wolds** contain the county's most diverse scenery, including woodland clustered round **Woodhall Spa**, and a string of sheltered valleys concentrated in the vicinity of **Louth**, an especially fetching country town. To the east of the Wolds is the **coast**, whose long sandy beach extends, with a few marshy interruptions, from Mablethorpe to **Skegness**, the main resort. The coast has long attracted thousands of holiday-makers from the big cities of the East Midlands and Yorkshire, hence its trail of bungalows, campsites and caravan parks – though, to be fair, chunks of the seashore are now protected as nature reserves.

As for public transport, travelling between the cities of the East Midlands by **train** or **bus** is simple and most of the larger towns have good regional links, too; but things are very different in the country with bus services very patchy.

Nottinghamshire

With a population of over 270,000, **Nottingham** is one of England's big cities, a long-time manufacturing centre for bikes, cigarettes, pharmaceuticals and lace. It is, however, more famous for Nottingham Forest football team (or rather, for its mercurial ex-manager, Brian Clough), for the Trent Bridge cricket ground and for its association with **Robin Hood**, the legendary thirteenth-century outlaw. Unfortunately, the fortress-lair of Hood's bitter enemy, the Sheriff of Nottingham, is long gone, and today the city is at its most diverting in the Lace Market, whose cramped streets are crowded with the mansion-like warehouses of the Victorian lacemakers.

The county town is flanked to the south by the commuter villages of the Nottinghamshire Wolds and to the north by the gritty towns and villages of what was, until Thatcher and her cronies decimated it, the Nottinghamshire coalfield. Both are unremarkable, but encrusted within the old northern Nottinghamshire coalfield are the thin remains of **Sherwood Forest**, the bulk of which is contained within The Dukeries, named after the five dukes who owned most of this area and preserved at least part of the ancient broad-leaved forest. Three of the four remaining estates – Worksop, Welbeck and Thoresby – are still in private hands, though Thoresby Hall has recently been turned into a Warner resort hotel, whilst **Clumber Park** is now owned by the National Trust and offers charming woodland walks. Also within the confines of the former coalfield are two fascinating country houses, **Newstead Abbey**, one-time home of Byron, and, even better, the wonderful Elizabethan extravagance of **Hardwick Hall**. Moving on, eastern Nottinghamshire is agricultural and its most important town is **Newark**, an agreeable, low-key kind of place straddling the River Trent. Newark has a castle, but the main attraction hereabouts is the fine Norman church at nearby **Southwell**.

Fast and frequent **trains** connect Nottingham with, among many destinations, London, Birmingham, Newark, Lincoln and Leicester. County-wide **bus** services radiate out from the city, too, making Nottingham the obvious base for a visit.

Nottingham and around

Controlling a strategic crossing point over the Trent, the Saxon town of **NOTTINGHAM** was built on one of a pair of sandstone hills whose 130-foot cliffs looked out over the river valley. In 1068, William the Conqueror built a castle on the other hill, and the Saxon and Norman communities traded on the low

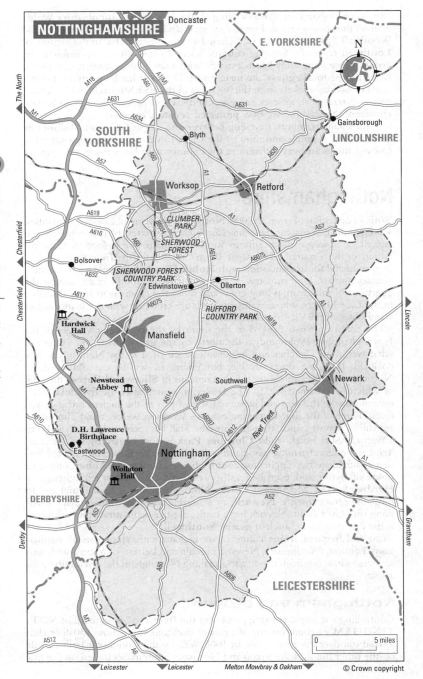

NOTTINGHAMSHIRE

Doncaster

E. YORKSHIRE

N

The North

M18

M1

A631

A1(M)

A60

SOUTH
YORKSHIRE

A631

Gainsborough

LINCOLNSHIRE

A634

A57

Blyth

A60

A620

Chesterfield

A619

A57

Worksop

A1

Retford

CLUMBER
PARK

B6034

A616

SHERWOOD
FOREST

A614

A6075

A57

Lincoln

A60

Bolsover

A632

SHERWOOD FOREST
COUNTRY PARK

Edwinstowe

Ollerton

A617

A6075

RUFFORD
COUNTRY PARK

A614

A1

A616

Hardwick
Hall

Mansfield

A38

A617

M1

Newstead
Abbey

A60

Southwell

Newark

A614

B6386

River Trent

Grantham

D.H. Lawrence
Birthplace

Eastwood

A610

A612

A6097

A46

A1

Nottingham

Wollaton
Hall

DERBYSHIRE

A52

A52

A46

A606

Derby

LEICESTERSHIRE

A512

688

0   5 miles

A6

A5

Leicester   Leicester   Melton Mowbray & Oakham   © Crown copyright ground in between, the Market Square. The castle was a military stronghold and royal palace, the equal of the great castles of Windsor and Dover, and every medieval king of England paid regular visits. In August 1642, Charles I stayed here, too, riding out of the castle to raise his standard and start the Civil War – not that the locals were overly sympathetic. Hardly anyone joined up, even though the king had the ceremony repeated on the next three days.

After the Civil War, the Parliamentarians slighted the castle and, in the 1670s, the ruins were cleared by the duke of Newcastle to make way for a palace, whose continental – and, in English terms, novel – design he chose from a pattern book, probably by Rubens. Beneath the castle lay a market town which, according to contemporaries, was handsome and well kept – "One of the most beautiful towns in England," commented Daniel Defoe. But in the second half of the eighteenth century, the town was transformed by the expansion of the lace and hosiery industries. Within the space of fifty years, Nottingham's population increased from ten thousand to fifty thousand, the resulting slum becoming a hotbed of radicalism. In the 1810s, a recession provoked the hard-pressed workers into action. They struck against the employers and, calling themselves **Luddites**, after an apprentice-protester by the name of Ned Ludd, raided the factories to smash the knitting machines. This was but the first of several troubled periods. During the Reform Bill riots of 1831, the workers set fire to the duke's home in response to his opposition to parliamentary reform and, in the following decade, they flocked to the Chartist movement.

The worst of Nottingham's slums were cleared in the late nineteenth century, when the city centre assumed its present structure, with the main commercial area ringed by alternating industrial and residential districts. Crass **postwar development**, adding tower blocks, shopping centres and a ring road, has embedded the remnants of the city's past in a townscape that will be disheartseningly familiar if you've seen a few other English commercial centres. The flavour of this postwar city was described by Nottingham's own Alan Sillitoe in his perceptive and forceful *Saturday Night, Sunday Morning*.

Arrival, information and accommodation

Nottingham **train station** is on the south side of the city centre, a five- to ten-minute walk from the Market Square – just follow the signs. Long-distance buses arrive at the Broad Marsh **bus station** down the street from the train station on the way to the centre. The city's **tourist office** is on the Market Square, on the ground floor of the Council House, at 1 Smithy Row (Easter–July Mon–Fri 9am–5.30pm; Sept & Oct Mon–Fri 9am–5.30pm, Sat 9am–5pm, Sun 10am–3pm; Nov–Easter Mon–Sat 9am–5.30pm; ☎0115/915 5330, ⓦ www.visitnottingham.com).

As you might expect of a big city, Nottingham has a good range of accommodation, with the more expensive **hotels** concentrated in the centre, the cheaper places and the **B&Bs** mostly located on the outskirts and the main approach roads. Finding a room is rarely difficult, but the tourist office can always help out.

Hotels and guest houses

Cotswold Hotel 330 Mansfield Rd ☎0115/955 1070. Comfortable popular mid-range hotel with cheery half-timbered facade. On a main road about one mile north of the city centre. ❸
Greenwood City Lodge 5 Third Ave, off Sherwood Rise ☎0115/962 1206. Attractive six-bedroomed guest house in a quiet corner of the

city, down a narrow lane about a mile north of the city centre. Highly recommended. ❸
Lace Market Hotel 29 High Pavement ☎0115/852 3232. Great location, footsteps from St Mary's church, this smart hotel, in a tastefully modernized Georgian row house, offers thirty individually decorated rooms. ❺
Rutland Square Hotel Rutland St, off St James'

St ☎0115/941 1114. Attractive and tastefully furnished modern hotel in a great location, just by the castle. ❺

Hostels

Igloo Tourist Hotel 110 Mansfield Rd ☎0115/947 5250. Backpackers' haven in the town centre, opposite the *Golden Fleece* pub, with a convivial atmosphere, good showers and free tea and coffee. Bunk-beds in mixed or single-sex dorms for £12 per person.

YMCA 4 Shakespeare St ☎0115/956 7600. In a handy location, with clean and frugal rooms, this place fills up fast. Single rooms are a real bargain at £17.75 a night including breakfast.

The Old Market Square and the Castle

The **Old Market Square** is still the heart of the city, an airy open plaza, whose shops, offices and fountains are watched over by the grand neo-Baroque **Council House**, completed as part of a make-work scheme in 1928. From here, it's a five-minute walk west up Friar Lane to **Nottingham Castle** (daily 10am–5pm; £2 Sat & Sun, free at other times), whose heavily restored gateway stands above a folkloric bronze of Robin Hood, with plaques depicting legendary scenes from his life on the wall behind. Beyond the gateway, lawns slope up to the squat ducal **palace**, which – after remaining a charred shell for forty years – was opened as the country's first provincial museum in 1878. The mansion occupies the site of the castle's upper bailey and, just outside its main entrance, two sets of steps (guided tours only, call ☎0115/915 3700; £2) lead down into the maze of ancient caves that honeycomb the cliff beneath. One set leads into **Mortimer's Hole**, a three-hundred-foot shaft along which, so the story goes, the young Edward III and his chums crept in October 1330 to capture the queen mother, Isabella, and her lover, Roger Mortimer – his would-be usurpers and the murderers of his father, Edward II. Although the incident certainly took place, it's unlikely that this was the secret tunnel Edward used.

The interior of the ducal mansion holds the **Castle Museum and Art Gallery**, whose lower-level "Story of Nottingham" is a lively, well-presented and entertaining account of the city's development. In particular, look out for a small but exquisite collection of late medieval **alabaster carvings**, an art form for which Nottingham once had an international reputation. It's worth walking up to the top floor, too, for a turn round the main **picture gallery**, which has a curious assortment of mostly English nineteenth-century romantic paintings. The works of Richard Parkes Bonington are perhaps the most evocative, though Laslett John Pott's *Mary Queen of Scots being led to her Execution* comes a close second.

A couple of minutes' walk east of the castle is the **Costume and Textile Museum**, 51 Castle Gate (Wed–Sun 10am–4pm; free), the best of the city's other museums. In the 1760s, Nottingham saw the earliest experiments to produce machine-made lace, but it was not until the 1840s that the city produced the world's first fully machined lace garments. After that the industry boomed until its collapse after World War I when lace, a symbol of an old and discredited order, suddenly had no place in the wardrobe of most women. The museum's lace-trimmed dresses, accessories and underclothes are displayed on two floors, the changing fashions illustrated by a sequence of dioramas. At the bottom of the stairs there's also an intriguing collection of **samplers**, try-outs made on linen scraps before work on the handmade garments began.

The Lace Market

A few minutes' walk away, on the east side of the Old Market Square up along Victoria Street, is the **Lace Market**, whose narrow lanes and alleys surround the church of **St Mary**, a good-looking, mostly fifteenth-century structure built on top of the hill that was once the Saxon town. The church abuts High

ACCOMMODATION

Cotswold Hotel	1
Greenwood City Lodge	2
Igloo Tourist Hotel	3
Lace Market Hotel	6
Rutland Square Hotel	5
YMCA	4

RESTAURANTS

Bentons Bar Brasserie	F
Café De Paris	C
La Cappanna	A
Pizza Express	D & H
Saagar Tandoori	B
Shaw's	G
Wax Café Bar	E
World Service	I

NOTTINGHAM

Train Station

© Crown copyright

Pavement, the administrative centre of Nottingham in Georgian times, and here you'll find the **Shire Hall**, whose Neoclassical columns and dome date from 1770. The facade also bears the marks of a real Georgian cock-up: to the left of the entrance, at street level, the mason carved the word "Goal" onto an arch and then had to have a second bash, turning it into "Gaol"; both are clearly visible. Now accommodating the **Galleries of Justice** (Tues–Sun 10am–5pm; £7.95), the Shire Hall boasts two superbly preserved Victorian courtrooms as well as an Edwardian police station, some spectacularly unpleasant old cells, a women's prison with bath house and a prisoners' exercise yard. A tour of the whole complex takes around two hours, but note that the interactive nature of a visit (on arrival you are issued with a criminal identity number, and so it continues) is not to everyone's liking. The surrounding Victorian warehouses are at their most striking along **Broadway**, where a line of homogeneous red-brick and sandstone-trimmed buildings perform a neat swerve halfway along the street. Adjacent **Stoney Street** chips in with the imposing Adams Building and, at the corner of Woolpack Lane, a particularly well-composed warehouse that comes equipped with an extravagant stone doorway and slender windows, as well as long attic windows to light the mending and inspection rooms.

Nearby, on Byard Lane, is the first shop of local lad **Paul Smith**, a major success story of recent British fashion, whilst the huge spaceship-like structure on the edge of the Lace Market is the **National Ice Centre**, home of the Panthers ice-skating team and a trainee skaters' paradise. To arrange lessons, call ☎0115/853 3036.

Eating

Nottingham's **restaurant** scene has improved immeasurably in the last five years. French and Mediterranean cuisine is in vogue at present, but the Asian places continue to prosper. In the last couple of years, **cafés** have sprung up all over the city centre. Almost without exception, they've adopted the same formula – angular and ultra-modern furnishings and fittings and a wide range of bottled beers. A few offer tasty, broadly Mediterranean food as well.

Bentons Bar Brasserie corner of Heathcote and Lower Parliament streets. Pleasant café-bar offering tasty dishes from an imaginative menu – salads and pastas through to steaks. Inexpensive.

Café De Paris 2 Kings Walk, off Upper Parliament St, near the Theatre Royal ☎0115/947 3767. Arguably the best restaurant of its type in town, offering delicious bistro-style French cuisine in neat and informal surroundings. Moderate.

La Cappanna 596 Mansfield Rd ☎0115/985 7411. Outstanding, family-run Italian restaurant with all the usual dishes plus a great line in seafood – the mussels are, so some locals say, the best in England. The regular menu is supplemented by daily specials. The décor is very ordinary, but don't let that put you off. It's located a mile or so north of the city centre. Moderate.

Pizza Express 20 King St ☎0115/952 9095. Fashionable pizza and pasta spot serving the chain's usual delicious pizzas. There's another branch at 24 Goose Gate, Hockley ☎0115/912 7888. Moderate.

Saagar Tandoori Restaurant 473 Mansfield Rd ☎0115/962 2014. Excellent Indian restaurant, a mile or so north of the city centre. The décor is very homely – you feel as if you're in someone's living room – but it's a very popular spot with locals. Moderate.

Wax Café Bar 27 Broad St. Amongst the city's burgeoning band of café-bars, this is one of the trendiest. The food here is good – all light Mediterranean dishes at very reasonable prices. Inexpensive.

World Service Newdigate House, Castle Gate ☎0115/847 5587. Chic restaurant with bags of flair in charming premises up near the Castle. An international menu done with imagination. Expensive.

Pubs and nightlife

Nottingham's **nightclub** scene is boisterous and fast-moving, with places moving in and out of cool all the time. The **pubs** around Market Square have a tough edge to them, especially on the weekend, but within a few minutes' walk there's a selection of equally lively and more enjoyable drinking-holes. For **live music**, both popular and classical, most big names play at the Royal Centre Concert Hall on Wollaton Street, and nearby **Rock City** pulls in some star turns too. The Broadway, in the Lace Market at 14 Broad St (☎0115/952 6600, ⓦ www.broadway.org.uk), is far and away the best **cinema** in town, featuring the pick of mainstream and avant-garde films.

Pubs and bars

Broadway Cinema Bar Broadway Cinema, 14 Broad St. Informal, fashionable bar serving an eclectic assortment of bottled beers to a cinema-keen clientele. Can get too smoky for comfort, so they have a smaller, smoke-free café-bar upstairs.

The Limelight Wellington Circus. The bar of the Nottingham Playhouse is a popular, easy-going spot with courtyard seating on summer nights. Good supply of real ales.

Lincolnshire Poacher 161 Mansfield Rd. Very popular and relaxed pub, with a wide selection of bottled and real ales. An older clientele than in the (very youthful) city centre – a five- to ten-minute walk away.

Pitcher & Piano High Pavement. Lively, fashionable pub in an imaginatively converted Victorian church on the edge of the Lace Market. Good fun; very youthful.

The Social Pelham St. Just up from the Market Square, this packed-popular bar is very much à la mode. Angular, modern furnishing and fittings plus frequent DJ sounds. It's the sister bar of London's *Social*.

Ye Olde Trip to Jerusalem Inn below the castle in Brewhouse Yard. Carved into the castle rock, this ancient inn may well have been a meeting point for soldiers gathering for the Third Crusade. Its cave-like bars, with their rough sandstone ceilings, are delightfully secretive.

Clubs

The Bomb 45 Bridlesmith Gate. The frontrunner in the club scene with regular house, techno and jungle nights.

Media Queen St. Grooviest place in town with grand decor and great sounds. It has hosted a Renaissance night and features leading DJs.
Rock City Talbot St ℗0115/941 2544. Giant-sized, crowded nightclub/music venue, with different sounds and crowds each night, from Goth to metal to indie. Regularly hosts name bands on UK tours.

Wollaton Hall and Eastwood

Wollaton Hall, about four miles west of Nottingham, is a flamboyant Elizabethan mansion built for Sir Francis Willoughby in the 1580s by the architect of Longleat, Robert Smythson. Perched on top of a grassy knoll, the hall presents a grand facade of chimneys, turrets and tiers to the surrounding **parkland** (daily 9am–dusk; free, cars £2), but the interior, clumsily refashioned in the nineteenth century, can only muster a workaday **natural history museum** (April–Oct daily 11am–5pm, Nov–March daily 11am–4pm; £1.50 at weekends, otherwise free). The Stable Block, just below the house, holds an equally routine Industrial Museum. Many visitors – and there are a lot of them – prefer to stroll the woodland around the park's lake. Buses, passing the park's entrance gates a short stroll from the house, leave from the Victoria Centre bus station in the city centre every thirty minutes or so.

D.H. Lawrence was born in the coalmining village of **EASTWOOD**, about eight miles west of Nottingham. The mine closed years ago, and Eastwood is something of a post-industrial eyesore, but Lawrence's childhood home, a tiny terraced house, has survived, refurbished as the **D.H. Lawrence Birthplace Museum**, 8a Victoria St, off Nottingham Road (daily: April–Oct 10am–5pm; Nov–March closes 4pm; £2). None of the furnishings and fittings are Lawrence originals, which isn't too surprising considering the family moved out when he was 2, but it's an appealing evocation of the period interlaced with biographical insights into the author's early life. Afterwards, enthusiasts can follow the Blue Line Walk round those parts of Eastwood with Lawrence associations – a mention in a book here, a comment in a letter there. The walk is three miles long and takes an hour or two; a brochure is available at the museum. Interestingly, few locals thought well of Lawrence. For one thing, the sexual scandals hardly helped. Famously, he ran off with Freda, the wife of a Nottingham professor, and then there was the *Lady Chatterley's Lover* obscenity trail – but equally unpopular was the author's move to the political right until, eventually, he espoused a cranky and unpleasant form of elitism.

Buses leave Nottingham's Victoria Centre bus station for Eastwood every thirty minutes or so; the journey takes about half an hour.

Northern Nottinghamshire

Rural **northern Nottinghamshire**, with its easy rolling landscapes and large estates, was transformed in the nineteenth century by coal – deep, wide seams of the stuff that spawned dozens of collieries, and colliery towns, stretching north across the county and on into Yorkshire. Almost without exception, the mines have closed, their passing marked only by the old pit head winding wheels left, bleak and solitary, to commemorate the thousands of men who laboured here. The suddenness of the pit closure programme imposed by the Conservative government in the 1980s knocked the stuffing out of the area and only now is it beginning to revive. One prop has been the tourist industry, for the countryside in between these mining communities holds several enjoyable attractions, the best-known of which is **Sherwood Forest** – or at least the patchy remains of it – one-time haunt (allegedly) of Robin Hood. Byron is a pip-squeak in the celebrity stakes by comparison, but his family home – **Newstead Abbey** – is here too, there are some pleasant woodland walks in the NT's **Clumber Park** and, last but certainly not least, there's **Hardwick Hall**, a beautiful Elizabethan mansion.

To reach this quartet of attractions by **bus** from Nottingham is easy enough with the exception of Hardwick Hall, for which you'll need your own transport.

Hardwick Hall

Born the daughter of a minor Derbyshire squire, Elizabeth, Countess of Shrewsbury (1527–1608) – aka **Bess of Hardwick** – became one of the leading figures of Elizabethan England, renowned for her political and business acumen. She also had a penchant for building and her major achievement, **Hardwick Hall** (April–Oct Wed, Thurs, Sat & Sun 12.30–5pm; gardens same months daily noon–5.30pm; house & gardens £6.20, gardens only £3.30; NT), begun when she was 62, has survived in amazingly good condition. The house was the epitome of fashionable taste, a balance of symmetry and ingenious detail in which the rectangular lines of the building are offset by line upon line of window – there's actually more glass than stone – whilst up above her giant-sized initials – E.S. – hog every roof line. Inside, the ground floor is relatively routine, but it's here that Hardwick's extensive collection of sixteenth- and seventeenth-century needlework is displayed, including several pieces by Mary, Queen of Scots, who was held in custody by the Earl of Shrewsbury for years. He moaned about the expense incessantly, one of the reasons for the souring of his relationship with Bess, a deterioration that prompted their estrangement.

On the top floor, the **High Great Chamber**, where Bess received her most distinguished guests, boasts an extraordinary plaster frieze, a brightly painted, finely worked affair celebrating the goddess Diana, the virgin huntress, which was, of course, designed to please the virgin queen herself. Next door, the **Long Gallery** is simply breathtaking, like an indoor cricket pitch only with exquisite furnishings and fittings, from the splendid chimneypieces and tapestries through to a set of portraits, including one each of the queen and Bess. The gallery was where Bess and her chums could exercise – and keep out of the sun at a time when any hint of a suntan was considered peasant-plebeian.

Outside, the **garden** makes for a pleasant wander and, beyond the Ha Ha, rare breeds of cattle and sheep graze the surrounding **parkland**. Finally – and rather confusingly – Hardwick Hall is next to **Hardwick Old Hall** (April–Oct Wed–Sun 11am–6pm; Nov–March Sat & Sun 11am–4pm; £2.75; EH), Bess's previous home, but now little more than a broken-down ruin.

The easiest way to reach Hardwick is along the M1; come off at Junction #29 and follow the signs from the roundabout at the top of the slip road – a three-mile trip. Note, however, that Hardwick is not signed from the motorway itself.

Newstead Abbey

In 1539, Henry VIII granted **Newstead Abbey** (house April–Sept daily noon–5pm; grounds daily 9am–dusk; £4, grounds only £2), ten miles north of Nottingham on the A60, to Sir John Byron, who demolished most of the church and converted the monastic buildings into a family home. In 1798, **Lord Byron** inherited Newstead, then little more than a ruin. He restored part

△ Lincoln Cathedral

of the complex, but most of the present structure dates from later renovations, which maintained much of the shape and feel of the medieval original while creating the warren-like mansion that exists today. Inside, a string of intriguing period rooms includes everything from a neo-Gothic Great Hall to the Henry VII bedroom, fitted with carved panels and painted house screens imported from Japan. Some of the rooms are pretty much as they were when Byron lived here – notably his bedroom and dressing room – and in the library is a small collection of the poet's possessions, from letters and manuscripts through to his pistols and boxing gloves. In the west gallery, look out also for the painting of Byron's favourite dog, Boatswain, a perky beast who was buried just outside the house – the conspicuous memorial, with its absurdly extravagant inscription, marks the spot. The surrounding **gardens** are simply delightful, a secretive and subtle combination of walled garden, lake, Gothic waterfalls, yew tunnels and Japanese-style rockeries, complete with eccentric pagodas.

There's a fast and frequent **bus** service from Nottingham's Victoria Centre bus station to the gates of Newstead Abbey, a mile from the house, every twenty minutes or so; the journey takes about twenty-five minutes.

Rufford Country Park

Council-run country parks may be ten-a-penny, but **Rufford Country Park** (daily dawn to dusk; facilities April–Sept 10am–5pm; Oct–March 10am–4pm; free) shows just how things should be done. The remains of the original twelfth-century Cistercian Abbey and the country house built in its stead – but largely demolished in 1956 – are neither very substantial nor especially interesting, but the old buildings are all pleasantly maintained and the former stable block now holds a café and better-than-average craft shop and ceramic gallery. At the back of the stables are the gardens, both informal and formal, and an outstanding **Sculpture Garden**, which manages to be both very accessible and very contemporary. Further afield is a lake and a mill, a bird sanctuary and a wetland area, all accessible by footpath. Country Parks don't come any better and there is a lively programme of special events and temporary art exhibitions too.

Rufford Country Park is right beside the A614 about eighteen miles north of Nottingham and reached on hourly Stagecoach **bus** #33 from Nottingham's Victoria Centre bus station.

Robin Hood – and Sherwood Forest Country Park

Most of **Sherwood Forest**, once a vast royal forest of oak, birch and bracken covering all of northern Nottinghamshire, was cleared in the eighteenth century, and nowadays it's difficult to imagine the protection it provided for generations of outlaws, the most famous of whom was **Robin Hood**. There's no "true story" of Robin's life – the earliest reference to him, in Langland's *Piers Plowman* of 1377, treats him as a fiction – but to the balladeers of fifteenth-century England, who invented most of the folklore, this was hardly the point. For them, Robin was a symbol of yeoman decency, a semi-mythological opponent of corrupt clergymen and evil officers of the law; in the early tales, although Robin shows sympathy for the peasant, he has rather more respect for the decent nobleman, and he's never credited with robbing the rich to give to the poor. This and other parts of the legend, such as Maid Marion and Friar Tuck, were added later.

Robin Hood may lack historical authenticity, but it hasn't discouraged the county council from spending thousands of pounds sustaining the **Major Oak**, the creaky tree where Maid Marion and Robin are supposed to have "plighted their troth". The Major Oak is on a pleasant one-mile trail that begins beside the visitor centre at the main entrance to **Sherwood Forest Country Park** (daily dawn–dusk; free), which comprises 450 acres of oak and silver birch crisscrossed with footpaths. The visitor centre is half a mile north of the village of Edwinstowe, itself just two miles northwest of Rufford Park and twenty-odd miles north of Nottingham via the A614.

There's a regular bus service on Stagecoach bus #33 from Nottingham's Victoria Centre bus station to Edwinstowe via Rufford.

Clumber Park

North of Ollerton, Edwinstowe's immediate neighbour, the A614 trims the edge of Thoresby Park, to reach, after six miles, the eastern entrance to **Clumber Park** (daily dawn–dusk; NT; free, but parking £3), four thousand acres of park and woodland lying to the south of Worksop. The estate was once the country seat of the dukes of Newcastle, and it was here in the 1770s that they constructed a grand mansion overlooking Clumber Lake. The house was dismantled in 1938, when the duke sold the estate, and today all that remains of the lakeside buildings are the Gothic Revival **Chapel** (daily: April–Sept 10.30am–5.30pm; Oct–March 10.30am–4pm; free; NT), built for the seventh duke in the 1880s, and the adjacent **stable block**, which now houses a National Trust office, shop and **café** (daily: April–Sept 10.30am–5.30pm; Oct–March 10.30am–4pm). The stables are located about two and a half miles from the A614. The woods around the lake offer some delightful strolls through planted woodland interspersed with the occasional patch of original forest, or you can go for an easy cycle ride by hiring a bike here.

Departing Nottingham's Victoria Centre bus station, Stagecoach East Midlands hourly **bus** #33 runs to Rufford and Edwinstowe, from where it travels on up the west side of Clumber Park en route to Worksop; get off at Carburton for the two-mile walk to the Clumber Park NT office. The excursion is best done as a day-trip from Nottingham, but there is a **campsite** (☎01909/482303; closed Oct–March) in Clumber Park's walled garden, a few minutes' walk north of the chapel.

Eastern Nottinghamshire

Without coal, **eastern Nottinghamshire** escaped the heavy-duty industrialization that fell upon its county neighbours in the late nineteenth century. It remains a largely rural area, its undulating farmland, punctuated by dozens of pint-sized villages, rolling seamlessly over to the River Trent, the boundary with Lincolnshire. By and large, it's a prosperous part of the county and by no means unpleasant, but for the casual visitor the attractions are distinctly low-key, being essentially confined to **Southwell** and **Newark**, both of which are easy to reach by public transport from Nottingham.

Southwell

SOUTHWELL, some twelve miles northeast of Nottingham, is a sedate backwater distinguished by **Southwell Minster** (daily: April–Sept 8am–7pm; Oct–March 8am to dusk; free), whose twin towers are visible for miles around, and the fine Georgian mansions facing it along Church Street. The Normans built the Minster at the beginning of the twelfth century and, although some elements were added later, the Norman design predominates, from the imposing west towers through to the dog-tooth-decorated doorways. Inside, the nave is proud and forceful and in the north transept is the remarkably fine alabaster tomb of a long forgotten churchman, Archbishop Sandys, who died in 1588. The red-flecked alabaster effigy of Sandys is so precise that you can make out the furrows on his brow and the crows' feet round his eyes; his children are depicted kneeling below and it's assumed that Sandys was one of the first bishops to marry – and beget – after the break with Rome changed the rules. The nave's stonework ends abruptly with the clumsy mass of the fourteenth-century rood screen, beyond which lies the Early English **choir** and the extraordinary **chapter house**. The latter is embellished with naturalistic foliage dating from the late thirteenth century, some of the earliest carving of its type in England.

For a bite to **eat**, the daytime *Deli*, a five-minute walk east of the Minster on the main drag through the village at 85a King St, sells a superb range of baguettes and paninis at £2.50 each. There are regular **buses** from the centre of Nottingham to Southwell and Newark. Ask at Nottingham tourist office for the current departure point.

Newark

From Southwell, it's eight miles east to **NEWARK**, an amiable, low-key river port and market town that was once a major staging point on the Great North Road. Fronting the town as you approach from the west are the gaunt riverside ruins of **Newark Castle** (daily dawn to dusk; free), all that's left of the mighty medieval fortress that was pounded to pieces during the Civil War. Opposite, just across the street to the north, is **The Ossington**, a flashy structure whose Tudor appearance is entirely fraudulent – it was built in the 1880s as a temperance hotel by a local bigwig in an effort to save drinkers from themselves. In the opposite direction, the town council have laid out a brief but pleasant riverside walk that leads past ancient houses to the old town lock, and from here it's just five minutes east to the expansive **Market Place**. This square, surrounded by a network of narrow and ancient alleys, is framed by a sequence of attractive Georgian and Victorian facades, as well as the mostly thirteenth-century church of **St Mary Magdalene** (Mon–Sat 8.30am–4.30pm), whose massive spire, at 236ft, towers over the town centre. It's a handsome church, its well-proportioned nave cheered by some bright roof paintings and a fine reredos. Look out also for a pair of medieval Dance of Death panel paintings beside the reredos – created to remind the observer of his or her mortality.

There's a regular **bus** service from Nottingham to Newark via Southwell, and Newark is also on the Nottingham–Lincoln **train** line. The Newark Castle **train station** (there is another, so be sure to get off at the right one) is on the west side of the River Trent, a five-minute walk from both the castle and the adjacent **tourist office**, on Castlegate (daily 9am–5/6pm; ☎01636/655765). The **bus station** is on Lombard Street, a couple of minutes' walk south from the tourist office along Castlegate. Newark has a small supply of **hotels** and **B&Bs**, which the tourist office will book on your behalf at no extra charge, but remember that rooms are well-nigh impossible to find during the Newark International Antiques Fair, Europe's biggest such event, held six times a year. For **food**, make for the excellent *Gannets*, 35 Castlegate (Mon–Fri 9am–4pm, Sat 9am–5pm & Sun 9am–4pm), an astoundingly good coffee bar serving daytime snacks and meals, or the simply superb *Café Bleu*, opposite at 14 Castlegate (☎01636/610141), a brilliant French restaurant serving top-class meals from an inventive menu. It's one of the best restaurants in the county, with an outside terrace and live jazz; the decor – all pastel-painted cheerfulness – is delightful too.

Leicestershire and Rutland

The compact county of **Leicestershire** is one of the more anonymous of the English shires, though **Leicester** itself is saved from mediocrity by its role as a focal point for Britain's Asian community. West Leicestershire has rather more to offer, for although its rolling landscape is blemished by a series of industrial settlements, things pick up markedly at **Ashby-de-la-Zouch**, a pleasing little town graced by the substantial remains of its medieval castle, and at **Calke Abbey**, a dishevelled country house set in its own estate. Near here too are the trim charms of **Market Bosworth**, where the main item of interest is the site of the Battle of Bosworth Field, the climactic engagement of the Wars of the Roses. In east Leicestershire, the farmland is studded with long-established market towns. None of them are particularly enthralling, but genial **Market Harborough** holds several attractive old buildings and an interesting museum, whilst **Melton Mowbray** is the pork pie capital of the world.

To the east of Leicestershire lies England's smallest county, **Rutland**, reinstated in 1997 following twenty-three unpopular years of merger with its larger neighbour. As part of their spirited publicity campaign to revive their ancient county, Rutland's well-heeled burghers issued "passports" to locals and created quite a stir, breaking through the profound apathy which characterizes the English attitude to local government. Rutland has three places of note, beginning with **Oakham**, the county town, and **Uppingham**, both rural centres with some elegant Georgian architecture. Even prettier is the tiny stone hamlet of **Lyddington**.

Getting around Leicestershire and Rutland can be problematic. **Train** lines radiate out from Leicester, most usefully to Market Harborough and Oakham, and there's a good network of **bus** services between the market towns, but these fade away in the villages where, if there is a bus at all, it only runs once or twice a day.

Leicester

On first impression, **LEICESTER** is a resolutely modern city, but further inspection reveals traces of its medieval and Roman past, situated immediately to the west of the downtown shopping area, near the River Soar. The Romans, choosing this site in the middle of the rebellious Coritani, developed Leicester's precursor, Ratae Coritanorum, as a fortified town on the Fosse Way, the military road running from Lincoln to Cirencester, and Emperor Hadrian kitted it out with huge public buildings. Subsequently, in the eighth century, the Danes colonized the town and later still its medieval castle became the base of the earls of Leicester, the most distinguished of whom was Simon de Montfort, who forced Henry III to convene the first English Parliament in 1265. Since the late seventeenth century, Leicester has been a centre of the hosiery trade and it was this industry that attracted hundreds of Asian immigrants to settle here in the 1950s and 1960s. Today, about one third of Leicester's population is Asian and the city elected the country's first Asian MP, Keith Vaz, in 1987. Leicester's Hindus put on a massive and internationally famous **Diwali**, Festival of Light, in October or November, while the city's sizeable Afro-Caribbean community celebrates its culture in a whirl of colour and music on the first weekend in August. The latter is the country's second biggest street festival after the Notting Hill Carnival (see p.123).

© Crown copyright

Arrival, information and accommodation

On the northern line from London's St Pancras station, Leicester **train station** is situated on London Road just to the southeast of the city centre. The **bus station** is on the north side of the centre, just off Gravel Street. The centre is signed from both – the large Haymarket Centre is an easy landmark. The **tourist office** is in between the two stations – and a short walk south of the Haymarket – at 7–9 Every St, on Town Hall Square (Mon–Wed & Fri 9am–5.30pm, Thurs 10am–5.30pm, Sat 9am–5pm; ☎0116/299 8888).

With other more enticing cities near at hand – Nottingham is but one – there's no strong reason to overnight here, but Leicester does have a good crop of business **hotels** close to the centre, within walking distance of the train station. Recommendable options include the *Best Western Belmont House Hotel*, De Montfort St (☎0116/254 4773; ❻), in an efficiently modernized Georgian property about 500 yards south of the train station, and the nearby and much more personal *Spindle Lodge*, 2 West Walk (☎0116/233 8801; ❹), which occupies an attractively converted Victorian house. There's also the plusher, modern *Holiday Inn*, on the west side of the centre at 129 St Nicholas Circle (☎0116/253 1161; ❺); this has extensive fitness facilities plus a pool. The tourist office has a substantial list of competitively priced **B&Bs**, but most of them are out of the centre. They will help fix you up with somewhere to stay, but things rarely get tight except during Diwali. Leicester also possesses an unofficial **hostel**, *Richards Students and Backpackers Lodge*, 157 Wanlip Lane, Birstall (☎0116/267 3107; £9). A self-styled backpackers' hostel on the northern edge of town – in a suburban semi, with patio and summerhouse. It has just five beds and is available to those aged between 16 and 26 only.

The city centre

The most conspicuous building in Leicester's crowded centre is undoubtedly the modern Haymarket shopping complex, but the proper landmark is the nearby Victorian **clock tower** of 1868, marking the spot where seven streets meet. From here, Cheapside leads south in a few yards to Leicester's open-air, fresh produce **market** (Mon–Sat), arguably the best in the land. Alternatively, from back at the clock tower, East Gates and then the old High Street run west with Silver Street (subsequently Guildhall Lane), soon branching off to reach **St Martin's Cathedral**, a much modified eleventh-century structure that incorporates a fine medieval wooden entrance porch. Next door is the **Guildhall** (Mon–Sat 10am–5.30pm, Sun 2–5pm; free), a half-timbered building that has served, variously, as the town hall, prison and police station. The highlight of a visit is the rickety Great Hall, its beams bent with age, but there are a couple of old cells too, plus the town gibbet in which the bodies of the hanged were publicly displayed until the 1840s.

From the Guildhall, it's a short walk west to St Nicholas Circle, a large roundabout that is part of the ring road. Go round it to the right – there's a walkway – and on the right is the **Jewry Wall**, a chunk of Roman masonry some 18ft high and 73ft long that was originally part of Hadrian's public baths. The project was a real irritation to the emperor. Hadrian's grand scheme was spoilt by the engineers, who miscalculated the line of the aqueduct that was to pipe in the water, and so bathers had to rely on a hand-filled cistern replenished from the river – which wasn't what he had in mind at all. The adjacent **Jewry Wall and Museum** (April–Sept Mon–Sat 10am–5pm, Sun 1–5pm; Oct–March Mon–Sat 10am–4pm, Sun 1–4pm; free) charts Leicester's history from prehistoric to medieval times in dowdy fashion. The most interesting artefacts are Roman, a hotchpotch of archeological finds from Fosse Way milestones to two splendid mosaics.

From the museum, it's a short stroll south via St Nicholas Circle to **Castle Gardens**, a narrow strip of a park that runs alongside a canalized portion of the Soar. The gardens incorporate the castle motte, the overgrown mound where Leicester's Norman fortifications once stood. At the far end of the gardens, you emerge on The Newarke, the location of the **Newarke Houses Museum** (Mon–Sat 10am–5.30pm, Sun 2–5pm; free), two adjoining Jacobean houses that make a pleasant setting for an exploration of the town's social history. Beside the museum, along Castle View, is the **Turret Gateway**, a rare survivor of the city's medieval castle, and beyond that is the attractive church of **St Mary de Castro** (Easter–Oct Sat 2–5pm), whose mixture of architectural styles incorporates several Norman features, notably a five-seater sedilia in the chancel. Interestingly enough, this was probably where Chaucer got married.

At the east end of The Newarke, ignominiously stranded between the carriageways of the ring road, stands the distinctive and substantial **Magazine Gateway** (no access), once a medieval entrance into the city and arsenal – hence the name. From here, it's a short walk south to the **Jain Centre**, in a totally revamped old Congregational chapel at the beginning of Oxford Street. The rites and beliefs of the Jains, a long-established Indian religious sect, focus on an extreme reverence for all living things – traditional customs include the wearing of gauze masks to prevent the inhalation of passing insects. The temple, the only one of its kind in western Europe, has a splendidly garish white marble facade, and visitors may enter the lobby – or, better, view the interior by prior appointment; call ☎0116/254 3091.

From the Jain Centre, it's about ten minutes' walk east to the **New Walk Museum and Art Gallery** (Mon–Sat 10am–5.30pm, Sun 2–5pm; free), easily the best of the city's museums, located on the New Walk. To get there from the Jain temple, go back to the beginning of Oxford Street, turn right onto Newarke Street and keep going straight until you intersect with – and turn right onto – **New Walk**, a pleasant pedestrianized promenade that runs out from the centre to leafy Victoria Park. On the museum's ground floor is a real surprise – an outstanding collection of German Expressionists, mostly sketches, woodcuts and lithographs by the likes of Otto Dix and George Grosz. In particular, look out for the latter's 1919 rallying-call sketch of the coffins of the two murdered leftists, Rosa Luxembourg and Karl Liebknecht. The Germans share the ground floor with the Ancient Egypt Gallery, featuring mummies and hieroglyphic tablets brought from Egypt as souvenirs in the 1880s, and there's also a significant Decorative Arts Gallery. The Victorian Gallery is fascinating, too, dominated by extravagant, often mawkish romantic paintings, amongst which is Charles Green's iconic *The Girl I left behind Me* of 1880.

Belgrave

Beginning about a mile to the northeast of the centre, the gritty **Belgrave** neighbourhood is the focus of Leicester's Asian community. Both Belgrave Road and its northerly continuation, Melton Road, are lined with Indian and Pakistani goldsmiths and jewellers, sari shops, Hindi music stores and curry houses. It's never dull down here, but Sunday afternoons are particularly enjoyable, when locals have time to stroll the streets in their finest gear. Belgrave celebrates two major Hindu festivals: **Diwali**, the Festival of Light, held in October or November, when six thousand lamps are strung out along the Belgrave Road and 20,000 come to watch the switch-on alone; and **Navrati**, a nine-day celebration in October held in honour of the goddess Ambaji.

Eating, drinking, nightlife and entertainment

People come from miles around to eat in the **Indian restaurants** on the Belgrave Road – though the opening of lots of Balti places in the Highfields area has provided some intense competition. The most famous of the Belgrave Road restaurants is *Bobby's*, no. 154–156 (℡0116/266 0106). Run by Gujaratis, this moderately priced place is strictly vegetarian and uses no garlic or onions; if you're here on a weekend, try their delicious house speciality, *undhyu*, or the multi-flavoured *Bobby's Special Chaat*. Excellent alternatives include the *Thali*, at no. 49 (℡0116/266 5888), which specializes in set *thali* meals, where several different dishes, breads and pickles are served together on large steel plates, and the *Chaat House* (℡0116/266 0513), south of *Bobby's* on the same side of the road at no. 108. The latter does wonderful *masala dosas* and other south Indian snacks – legendary cricket captain Kapil Dev and his Indian team ate here when they were on tour. In the city centre, and diversifying from the Asian restaurants, there's an outlet of that ultra-reliable chain *Pizza Express* on King St (℡0116/254 4144), plus the top-notch *Opera House*, 10 Guildhall Lane (℡0116/223 6666), in lovely old premises and with an imaginative, wide-ranging menu.

As for **pubs**, the *Rainbow & Dove*, on Charles Street, attracts real-ale enthusiasts, the *Charlotte*, on Oxford Street, features bands most nights and the *Magazine*, Newarke Street, is a favourite student haunt. Amongst a deluge of new city-centre café-bars, one of the trendier, clubbier spots is *Tabasco Jaz* on Albion Street.

The **performing arts** come up trumps in Leicester at the excellent Phoenix Arts Centre, Newarke St (℡0116/255 4854, ⒲www.phoenix.org.uk), which features a first-rate mix of comedy, music, theatre and dance, whilst doubling up as an independent cinema. The city's main concert hall is De Montfort Hall, on Granville Road (℡0116/233 3111, ⒲www.demontforthall.co.uk) – adjoining Victoria Park at the end of New Walk.

West Leicestershire

Give or take the odd industrial blip, most of **west Leicestershire** – to the west of the A6 – is rural, its small towns and villages dotted over undulating countryside. The key attractions here are best visited as day-trips, beginning with **Calke Abbey**, technically over the boundary in Derbyshire and not an abbey at all, but an intriguing country house whose faded charms witness the declining fortunes of the landed gentry. There's also **Market Bosworth**, a pleasant little spot near the site of **Bosworth Field**, where Richard III came an unpleasant cropper – not before time according to Shakespeare; a good castle, at **Ashby-de-la-Zouch**; and a fine church, perched on top of one of the few hills hereabouts at **Breedon-on-the-Hill**.

With the notable exception of Calke Abbey, all the places mentioned above are easy to reach by **bus** from Leicester – and Ashby can readily be reached by bus from Nottingham, too.

Market Bosworth

The thatched cottages and Georgian houses of tiny **MARKET BOSWORTH**, some twelve miles west of Leicester, fan out from a dinky market square that was an important trading centre throughout the Middle Ages. From the sixteenth to the nineteenth century, the dominant family hereabouts was the Dixies, merchant-landlords who mostly ended up at the local church of **St Peter**, a good-looking edifice with a castellated nave and a sturdy square tower. Heavily revamped by the Victorians, the church's interior is fairly routine, but the chancel does hold the charming early eighteenth-century tomb of John Dixie, one-time rector, who is honoured by a long hagiographic plaque and the effigy of his weeping sister. John, apparently, apart, the Dixies were not universally admired. The young Samuel Johnson taught at the **Dixie Grammar School** – whose elongated facade still abuts the Market Place – but disliked the founder, Sir Wolstan Dixie, so much that he recollected his time there "with the strongest aversion and even a sense of horror".

Market Bosworth is, however, best known for the **Battle of Bosworth Field**, fought on hilly countryside a couple of miles south of town in 1485. This was the last and decisive battle of the Wars of the Roses, an interminably long-winded and bitterly violent conflict amongst the nobility for control of the English crown. The victor was Henry Tudor, subsequently Henry VII, the vanquished was Richard III, who famously died on the battlefield. In desperation, Shakespeare's villainous Richard cried out "A horse, a horse, my kingdom for a horse," but in fact the defeated king seems to have been a much more phlegmatic character. Taking a glass of water before the fighting started, he actually said "I live a king: if I die, I die a king." The battlefield is now organized as a tourist attraction, beginning with the **visitor centre** (April–Oct daily 11am–5pm; March Sat & Sun 11am–5pm; Nov & Dec Sun 11am–dusk; £3), where a fifteen-minute video provides a lively account of the battle and its historical context. From here, a two-mile circular trail explores the battlefield with explanatory plaques filling out the details on the way – and good fun it is, too.

There are hourly **buses** from Leicester to Market Bosworth, from where it's a three-mile walk to the visitor centre along country roads. There are two signed routes – the Shenton route is the more pleasant. There's supposed to be a footpath and it's supposed to be shorter, but it is not signed, so you'll need the appropriate Ordnance Survey map. Afterwards, take a **pint** at the traditional *Dixie Arms Hotel*, on the Market Place.

Ashby-de-la-Zouch

ASHBY-DE-LA-ZOUCH, fourteen miles northwest of Leicester, takes its fanciful name from two sources – the town's first Norman overlord was Alain de Parrhoet la Souche and the rest means "place by the ash trees". Nowadays, Ashby is far from rustic, but it's an amiable little place and just off Market Street, the main drag, stands its principal attraction, the **Castle** (April–Oct daily 10am–6pm; Nov–March Wed–Sun 10am–4pm; £2.75; EH). Originally a Norman manor house, the stronghold was the work of Edward IV's chancellor, Lord Hastings, who received his "licence to crenellate" in 1474. But Hastings didn't enjoy his new home for long. Just nine years later, he was dragged from a Privy Council meeting to have his head hacked off on a log by the order of Richard III, his crime being his lacklustre support for the Yorkist cause. Today, the rambling ruins include substantial left-overs from the old fortifications, as well as the remains of the solar, chapel and priests' rooms, but the star turn is the hundred-foot-high **Hastings Tower**, a self-contained four-storey stronghold, which has survived in relatively good nick. This tower house represented the latest thinking in castle design. It provided a secure inner fastness for Hastings and his retinue both against any outside enemy and his own mercenaries – who, experience had shown elsewhere, were often a threat to their employer – and it also provided much better accommodation than was previously available. Improved living quarters reflecting the power and pride of the nobility were built all over England at this time and this is a rare survivor – witness the substantial rooms with large windows on the top floors, accessible via the tower's well-worn spiral staircase.

There are fast and frequent **buses** from Leicester and Nottingham to Ashby and they pull in along Market Street.

Breedon-on-the-Hill

It's five miles northeast from Ashby to the village of **BREEDON-ON-THE-HILL**, which sits in the shadow of the large but partly quarried hill from which it takes its name. A steep footpath and a winding, half-mile road lead up from the village to the summit, where the fascinating church of **St Mary and St Hardulph** (daily 9.30am–6.30pm or dusk; free) occupies the site of an Iron Age hillfort and an eighth-century Anglo-Saxon monastery. Mostly dating from the thirteenth century, the church is kitted out with Georgian pews and pulpit and also, much rarer, contains a number of Anglo-Saxon carvings, both in the form of wall friezes with folkloric themes and of individual saints and prophets. They are quite extraordinary and the fact that the figures look Byzantine – rather than Anglo-Saxon – has fuelled academic debate. The church has something else too, in the form of several tombs of the Shirley family, who long ruled the local roost. One is a sombre alabaster affair with the kneeling family up above and a skeleton below.

Calke Abbey

The eighteenth-century facade of **Calke Abbey** house (April–Oct Mon–Wed, Sat & Sun 1–5.30pm; garden same days from 11am; £5.20, garden only £2.50; NT) is all self-confidence, its acres of dressed stone and three long lines of windows polished off with an imposing Victorian Greek Revival portico. This all cost oodles of money and the Harpurs and then the Harpur-Crewes, who owned the estate, were doing very well until the economics of the English country estate changed after World War I. Then, at a time when country houses were being demolished by the score, the Harpur-Crewes simply hung on, becoming the epitome of faded gentility and declining to make all but the smallest of changes to the house – though they did finally plump for electricity in 1962. The last Harpur-Crewe to live here, Charles, died in 1981 and the estate passed in its entirety to the National Trust. Very much to their credit, the Trust declined to bring in the restorers and have kept the house in its dishevelled state – and this is its real charm.

A visit starts at the old stable block, from where it's a short stroll to the house, whose Entrance Hall adroitly sets the scene, its wall decorated with ancient stuffed heads from the family's herd of prize cattle, plus old leather mail bags and generations of riding whips. Beyond, in the rest of the house, there are more stuffed animal heads in the capacious Saloon; a chaotic at-home School Room; an intensely cluttered Drawing Room; and, seeming to indicate that eccentricity was a family trait, a state bed given to the Harpurs by the daughter of George II in 1734 and then left packed until the National Trust arrived. Of particular interest also is the caricature room, whose walls are lined (sometimes three to four deep) with satirical cartoons, some of which were executed by the leading cartoonists of their day, including Gillray and Cruikshank. After you've finished in the house, you can wander out into the **gardens** and pop into the Victorian estate **church**.

Calke Abbey is reached via (and signed off from) the B587, which runs north from Ashby to Melbourne. There's no public transport. While you're here, and back towards Ashby on the B587, spare a little time for **Staunton Harold Church** (April–Sept Wed–Sun 1–5pm; Oct Sat & Sun 1–5pm only; £1; NT), a political rant of a building in which the local lord, the reactionary Robert Shirley, expressed his hatred of Oliver Cromwell. There's no missing Shirley's intentions, as he carved them above the church door: "In the year 1653 when all things sacred were throughout the nation either demolished or profaned…" and so he goes on. Whatever the politics, it was certainly an audacious – probably foolhardy – gesture and sure enough Cromwell had the last laugh when an unrepentant Shirley died in prison three years later. The church itself is a good-looking affair, largely in the Perpendicular style with delightful painted ceilings and wood panelling. Shirley's house – or rather its successor built on its site – is next door and is now operated as a Sue Ryder charity home.

East Leicestershire and Rutland

For the casual visitor at least, there's nothing compelling about **east Leicestershire**, though the scenery is pleasant enough, with open farmland broken up by hills and ridges. Two middling towns are worth a pit-stop here, **Melton Mowbray** and **Market Harborough**. Things improve over in neighbouring **Rutland** with a pair of pleasant country towns – **Oakham** and **Uppingham** – and get even better at the postcard-pretty hamlet of **Lyddington**.

Both Melton Mowbray and Stamford are on the Leicester–Peterborough branch line, whilst Market Harborough is on the Leicester–London main line. There are reasonably frequent **buses** to and between all the destinations mentioned above, except Lyddington.

Market Harborough

MARKET HARBOROUGH, fifteen miles southeast of Leicester, is an unassuming provincial town that once prospered from its position at the junction of the turnpike roads to Leicester, Nottingham and London. Consequently, the predominantly Georgian High Street's *Three Swans* and *Angel* hotels were originally coaching inns, and the square and solid brick **Town Hall** was designed to help local traders sell their wares – with butchers on the ground floor and cloth merchants up above. Just off the High Street, the triangular Market Place is overlooked by the church of **St Dionysius**, whose striking tower is in stark contrast to the dumpy ironstone nave down below. Here, also, is the **Old Grammar School**, an early seventeenth-century, half-timbered structure mounted on stilts to protect locals from the rain. From 1908 to 1974, the large Victorian building standing directly behind the grammar school on Adam & Eve Street was a factory owned by the Symington family, who designed the world's best-selling corsets. The factory has been redeveloped and now houses both the council offices and the town **museum** (Mon–Sat 10am–4.30pm, Sun 2–5pm; free), which has an intriguing display of Symington corsetry. The **tourist office** (Mon–Fri 9am–5pm & Sat 9.30am–12.30pm; ☎01858 /821270) is here, too.

There are frequent services from Nottingham, London and Leicester to Market Harborough's **train station**, fifteen minutes' walk east of the town centre. More conveniently, **buses** – including services from Melton Mowbray – stop a couple of minutes' walk from the Market Place, on Northampton Road, a southerly continuation of the High Street. For **food**, *Aldin's Tea Rooms*, on the High Street near the Market Place (closed Sun & Mon), serves homemade food.

Melton Mowbray

MELTON MOWBRAY, some fifteen miles northeast of Leicester, is famous for pork pies, an unaccountably popular English snack made of compressed balls of meat and gristle encased in wobbly jelly and thick pastry. The pie is the traditional repast of the fox-hunting fraternity, for whom the town of Melton, lying on the boundary of the region's most important hunts – Belvoir, Cottesmore and Quorn – has long been a favourite spot. The antics of some of the aristocratic huntsmen are legend – in 1837 the Marquis of Waterford literally painted the town's buildings red, hence the saying – but with the snowballing opposition to blood sports, the days of the tally-ho brigade may well be numbered. If you want to sample the genuine traditional hunters' pie, it is available in Melton only at Dickinson & Morris, just off the Market Place on Nottingham Street.

Most of Melton Mowbray is Victorian or modern red-brick, but a short walk south from the central market place is the medieval church of **St Mary**, distinguished by its impressive size (150ft long and the tower soaring to over 100ft) and by some of its detail. The clerestory is an especially fine illustration of the Perpendicular style, its 48 windows encircling the church and bathing the interior with a gentle light. The town **museum** (check with tourist office for the latest on opening times), under five minutes' walk from the market place down Sherrard Street, features the work of John Ferneley, a local artist who made a small fortune selling hunting scenes to the gentry – or at least it will do when it reopens after a thorough refurbishment in 2002.

Central trains runs frequent services from Leicester to Oakham and Stamford via Melton Mowbray; Barton buses link Nottingham, Melton and Oakham. From Melton **train station**, it's a five-minute walk north to the Market Place, where the **buses** pull in.

Oakham

Some twenty miles east from Leicester and ten from Melton Mowbray, well-heeled **OAKHAM**, Rutland's county town, has a long history as a commercial centre, its prosperity bolstered by Oakham School, a late sixteenth-century foundation that's become one of the country's more exclusive private schools. The town's stone terraces and Georgian villas are too often interrupted by the mundanely modern to assume any grace, but Oakham has its architectural moments – particularly in the L-shaped **Market Place**, where the sturdy awnings of the octagonal Butter Cross shelter the old town stocks. Footsteps from the north side of the Market Place stands **Oakham Castle** (April–Oct Mon–Sat 10am–1pm & 1.30–5pm, Sun 1–5pm; Nov–March Mon–Sat 10am–1pm & 1.30–4pm, Sun 1–4pm; free), comprising part of a fortified house dating from 1191. The banqueting hall is the main survivor, a good example of Norman domestic architecture, and inside the whitewashed walls are covered with horseshoes. This is the result of an ancient custom by which every lord or lady, king or queen, is obliged to present an ornamental horseshoe when they first set foot in the town.

Oakham School is housed in a series of impressive ironstone buildings that frame the west edge of the Market Place. On the right-hand side of the school, a narrow lane allows you to see more of the buildings on the way to **All Saints'** church, whose heavy tower and spire rise high above the town. Dating from the thirteenth century, the church is an architectural hybrid, but the light and airy interior is distinguished by the medieval carvings along the piers beside the chancel, with Christian scenes and symbols set opposite dragons, grotesques, devils and demons. Finally, you could also spare a few minutes for the sizeable **Rutland County Museum**, on Catmose Street (April–Oct Mon–Sat 10am–5pm, Sun 2–5pm; Nov–March Mon–Sat 10am–5pm, Sun 2–5pm; free), a brief signposted walk from the Market Place via the High Street. Here, an assortment of agricultural tools and Rutland County mementoes is enlivened by a lithograph of a disconcertingly huge prize-winning heifer.

With regular services from Leicester, Melton Mowbray and Peterborough, Oakham **train station** lies on the west side of town, five minutes' walk from the Market Place. **Buses** connect the town with – amongst many places – Leicester, Nottingham and Melton Mowbray and these pull in on John Street, close to – and also west of – the Market Place. A thorough exploration of Oakham only takes a couple of hours and there are other more interesting places nearby, but, if you do decide to stay, the **tourist office**, at Flore's House, 34 High St (Mon–Sat 9.30am–5pm, Sun 10am–3pm; Nov–March Mon, Wed, Fri Sat 10am–4pm, Tues & Thurs 10am–1pm; ☎01572/724329, ⓦwww.rut-net.co.uk), can help you find **accommodation**. In addition, the *Whipper-In Hotel*, on the Market Place (☎01572/756971; ❹), is a tempting proposition, its smartly decorated modern rooms set behind an attractive old facade. For **food**, the *Whipper-In* serves excellent bar snacks as does the nearby *Wheatsheaf*, a traditional pub with a good range of brews at 2–4 Northgate. Also near at hand, at 2 Burley Rd, is *Loretta's Bistro* (closed Mon & Tues–Sun eve), which offers a varied range of tasty Greek dishes at very reasonable prices.

Uppingham

The town of **UPPINGHAM**, six miles south of Oakham, has the uniformity of style Oakham lacks, its narrow, meandering High Street flanked by bow-fronted shops and ironstone houses, which mostly date from the eighteenth century. It's the general appearance that pleases, rather than any individual sight, but the town is famous as the home of **Uppingham School**, a bastion of privilege whose imposing fortress-like building stands at the west end of the High Street. Founded in 1587, the school was distinctly second-rate until the middle of the nineteenth century, when a dynamic headmaster, the Reverend Edward Thring, grabbed enough land to give the school some of the biggest playing-fields in England – fitness being, of course, an essential attribute of the rulers of the British Empire.

Uppingham has one especially good **hotel**, the *Lake Isle*, in a tastefully modernized eighteenth-century town house at 16 High St East (☎01572/822951; ❹). For en suite **B&B**, the well-kept *Rutland House*, 61 High Street East (☎01572/822497; ❷), occupying a spacious, double-fronted sandstone house, is the place to go. The *Lake Isle* **restaurant** is outstanding, offering a superb and varied menu from guinea fowl to local venison; a three-course meal will set you back about £20. For a **drink**, head for *The Vaults*, on the minuscule Market Place.

Lyddington

Two miles southeast of Uppingham, **LYDDINGTON** is a sleepy village of honey-hued cottages and pubs lining a meandering main street, set against a backdrop of plump hills and broken broadleaf woodland. Early in the twelfth century, the Bishop of Lincoln, whose lands once extended south as far as the Thames, chose this as the site of a small palace – one of thirteen he erected to accommodate himself and his retinue while away on Episcopal business. Confiscated during the Reformation, **Lyddington Bede House**, on Blue Coat Lane (April–Oct daily 10am–6pm; £2.75; EH), was later converted into almshouses by Lord Burghley and has since been beautifully restored by English Heritage. The highlight is the light and airy Great Chamber on the first floor, whose oak cornices are exquisitely carved. Careful lighting in the attic sets off the building's sturdy medieval timber frame to best advantage, the ground floor harbours the tiny rooms that were for centuries occupied by local pensioners and the poor and the gardens are kept in immaculate condition.

Accommodation in Lyddington is limited to the highly recommendable *Marquis of Exeter Hotel* on the main street (☎01572/822477; ❹). Gutted by fire and completely restored a few years back, this former coaching inn has sixteen comfortable en-suite rooms and comes complete with a good restaurant serving a classy à la carte menu and less expensive bar meals.

Hallaton

Leicestershire's **HALLATON**, some five miles southwest of Uppingham, along steep and winding country lanes, is one of the region's more attractive villages, its postcard prettiness composed of neat ironstone cottages around a well-kept village green, embellished by a medieval church, a conical Butter Cross and a duck pond. Every Easter Monday, this peace and quiet is disturbed by the **Hare Pie Scramble and Bottle Kicking** contest, when the inhabitants of Hallaton fight for pieces of pie with the people of nearby Medbourne. The participants gather at the *Fox Inn* by the village pond, then proceed to kick small barrels of ale around a hill and across a stream, as has been the custom for several hundred years – though no one has the faintest idea why. The village **museum** (May–Oct Sat & Sun 2.30–5pm; donation requested) does its best to shed some light on the business. For a pint and a ploughman's, head for the green, where the *Bewicke Arms* is one of Leicestershire's oldest-established and most characterful pubs.

Northamptonshire

Northamptonshire is one of the region's most diverse counties – so diverse in fact that even many Midlanders can't recall what is actually in it and what isn't. With justification, its superabundance of stately homes and historic churches enables it to style itself as the "County of Spires and Squires". It also holds a scattering of charming villages, the most picturesque of which, untouched by all but the vaguest sniff of the twentieth century, are built of local limestone. By contrast, however, three of the county's four big towns – Wellingborough, Corby and Kettering – are primarily industrial and whatever charms they offer to their inhabitants, there's not much to attract the regular tourist. Yet the fourth town, **Northampton**, does something to bridge the gap, its busy centre possessed of several fine old buildings and an excellent museum devoted to shoe-making, the industry that has long made the place tick.

Gentle hills, farmland and patchy woodland stretch right across the county with the A508 forming an easy if arbitrary dividing line – separating west Northamptonshire from the slightly larger east Northamptonshire. The prime target in the former is **Althorp**, family home of the Spencers and the burial place of Diana, Princess of Wales. Runners-up by a long chalk are the Anglo-Saxon church at **Brixworth** and the canalside village of **Stoke Bruerne**. East Northamptonshire's star turn is the good-looking country town of **Oundle**, which makes the best base for visiting the delightful hamlet of **Fotheringhay** and, at a pinch, the overbearing pomp and circumstance of **Boughton House**. The county also has a notable **long-distance footpath**, the seventy-mile Nene Way, which follows the looping course of the river right across the county. Nene Way brochures are available at or from Northampton Tourist Office.

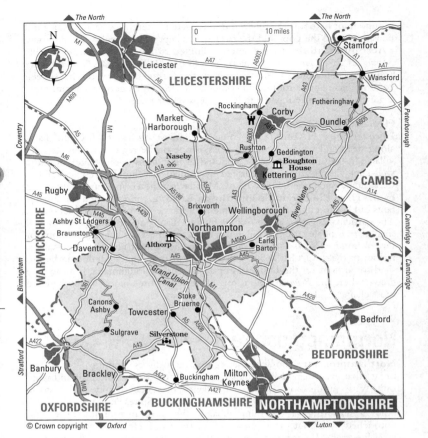

© Crown copyright

Getting to Northampton by **public transport** is no problem, but to reach the villages and stately homes, you'll mostly need your own vehicle – or some careful planning around infrequent bus services.

Northampton

Spreading north from the banks of the River Nene, **NORTHAMPTON** is a workaday modern town whose appearance largely belies its ancient past. Throughout the Middle Ages, this was one of central England's most important towns, a flourishing commercial centre whose now demolished castle was a popular stopping-off point for travelling royalty. A fire in 1675 burnt most of the medieval city to a cinder and the Georgian town that grew up in its stead was itself swamped by the industrial revolution when Northampton swarmed with boot and shoe makers. Their products shod almost everyone in the Empire – from Australia to Canada – as well as the British army, though things did go badly awry during the Crimea War. The army ordered two boat loads of Northampton boots in preparation for the Russian winter, but – for reasons that remain obscure – insisted that all the left boots be shipped in one vessel, the right ones in another. Unfortunately, one of the boats sank en route – and the soldiers were left perplexed by the ways of the army commissariat. Equally perplexed were the Northampton tailors who had put clothes on the back of Errol Flynn, after he got a start here in repertory in 1933. Always a charmer, Flynn dressed well, but he hightailed it out of town after just a year, leaving a whopping tailor's debt behind him.

Northampton's compact **centre** is at its most appealing on and around its main plaza, Market Square, which is where you'll find the town's finest buildings, notably All Saints' Church and the Guildhall. Half a day is enough for a quick gambol round the sights, but if you're tempted to stay the night there's a reasonable supply of hotel accommodation and a scattering of B&Bs. The only times of the year when finding a room can be difficult are during the annual **Balloon Festival** in August, which attracts thousands of visitors, and over the weekend of the British Grand Prix, held in July at the nearby **Silverstone** race track.

The Town

Northampton's expansive, cobbled **Market Square** has a busy, self-confident air, its sides flanked by a comparatively harmonious mixture of the old and the new. From here, either of a couple of narrow lanes leads through to the church of **All Saints** (Mon–Sat 9am–2pm; free), whose unusually secular appearance stems from its finely proportioned, pillared portico as well as its towered cupola. A statue of Charles II in Roman attire surmounts the portico, a (flattering) thank you for his donation of a thousand tons of timber after the Great Fire of 1675 had incinerated the earlier church. Inside, the elegant interior looks more like a ballroom than a church, from the sweep of its timber galleries through to its Neoclassical pillars and a ceiling coated in delicately sculpted plasterwork.

Behind the church is one of Lutyens's less inspiring monuments, a plain, blunt **war memorial** dating from 1926, and, just beyond that, in St Giles' Square, is the **Guildhall**, a flamboyant Victorian edifice constructed in the 1860s to a design by Edward Godwin. Godwin was one of the period's most inventive architects and his Gothic exterior, with its high-pointed windows and dinky turrets and towers, sports kings and queens plus scenes central to the county's history – look out for Mary, Queen of Scots' execution, the Great Fire and the battle of Naseby. Fought a few miles to the north of town in 1645, Naseby was a crucial engagement in the Civil War. It pretty much sealed the fate of King Charles and blooded Parliament's (later Cromwell's) New Model Army, a volunteer force driven by religious conviction (rather than money) that was soon to be the scourge of the Lord Protector's enemies.

The **Central Museum and Art Gallery** (Mon–Sat 10am–5pm, Sun 2–5pm; free), a few yards south on Guildhall Road, celebrates the town's industrial heritage with a surprisingly interesting display of shoes. Along with silk slippers, clogs and high-heeled nineteenth-century court shoes, there's one of the four boots worn by an elephant during the British Expedition of 1959, which retraced Hannibal's putative route over the Alps into Italy. There's celebrity footwear too – almost inevitably, a pair of Elton John shoes (the giant DMs he wore in *Tommy*) – plus whole cabinets of heavy-duty riding boots, pearl-inlaid raised wooden sandals from Ottoman Turkey and a couple of cabinets showing just how long high heels have been in fashion. Much of the rest of the museum is given over to an excellent display charting the town's history from its Roman days to the present, paying particular attention to the significance of the shoe industry, which employed no less than half the town's population in 1920.

Head north from the front of All Saints' along The Drapery and you'll soon reach Sheep Street and the **Church of the Holy Sepulchre** (May–Sept Wed & Sat noon–4pm; free). This is Northampton's oldest building and, although it has been modified on several occasions, it remains one of only five Norman round churches extant in the country. As its name suggests, the church's design was inspired by contact with the Holy Land – in this case, the founder, Simon de Senlis, was a veteran of the First Crusade.

Practicalities

From Northampton **train station**, which has regular services to London Euston and Birmingham, it's a ten-minute walk east to the Market Square – just follow the signs. Buses pull into the **bus station** on Lady's Lane, behind the hideous Grosvenor Shopping Centre, just to the north of the Market Square. The **tourist office** (late May to Aug Mon–Fri 9.30am–5pm, Sat 9.30am–4pm, Sun noon–4pm; rest of year closed Sun; ☎01604/622677) is opposite the Guildhall on St Giles' Square, a minute or so to the south of Market Square. They operate an accommodation-booking service, have oodles of information on the county and issue bus timetables.

The smartest **hotel** in the centre is the *Northampton Moat House*, a dependable chain hotel in a large modern block on Silver Street (☎01604/739988; **❻**). More distinctive is the *Lime Trees Hotel*, 8 Langham Place, Barrack Road (☎01604/632188, ⊛www.limetreeshotel.co.uk; **❺**), in pleasant Georgian premises half a mile north from the centre. The pick of the more central **B&Bs** is the *St George's Private Hotel*, 128 St George's Ave (☎01604/792755, ⊛www.stgeorgeshotel.co.uk; **❷**). This attractive place has spacious, comfortable guest rooms and occupies a large Edwardian house about a mile and a half from the centre, overlooking Racecourse Park.

A good spot for daytime **snacks** and coffee is *Caffè Nero*, just behind All Saints at 6A Abington St. For more substantial **meals**, try *Joe's Diner*, an American-style joint just along the street at no.104A (closed Sun).

West Northamptonshire

The slice of easy countryside that comprises **west Northamptonshire**, falling to the west of the A508, is dotted with stately homes, amongst which the most diverting are **Althorp**, the last resting place of Diana, Princess of Wales, and **Sulgrave Manor**, which has family links with the USA's own George Washington. The area also possesses the canal locks and narrowboats of tiny **Stoke Bruerne**, on the Grand Union Canal, and a rare and fine Saxon church at **Brixworth**. The best of the county's limestone villages lie further to the east, but there is a sprinkling here, too, with **Ashby St Ledgers**, not far from Althorp, being an especially picturesque spot.

Brixworth

Located just six miles north of Northampton off the A508, **BRIXWORTH** would be an inconsequential village were it not for **All Saints' church** (usually open daily 10am–5pm, call to check; ☎01604/880286), one of England's finest surviving Anglo-Saxon churches, dating from around 690 AD. From a distance, its most striking feature is its unusual cylindrical stair-turret, added to the western tower in the ninth century as part of a plan to fortify the church against Viking raids. Closer inspection, however, reveals something even rarer. The church is mostly limestone, but brick arches frame the windows and doorways and here, remarkably enough, scores of Roman tiles, probably salvaged from a nearby villa, have been inserted, often at irregular angles. Inside, the uncluttered **nave** is whitewashed except for certain key features, including the **great arch** spanning the nave. Built around 1400, this arch replaced a Saxon wall with three arches that had previously separated the nave from the chancel; look carefully at each end of the arch and you'll spot the remains of the Saxon stonework. At the far end of the church, the rounded **apse**, modelled on a Roman basilica, was once encased by an ambulatory, but this was closed off during restoration work in the nineteenth century – note the two small and blocked doorways low down on either side of the apse arch. During the refurbishment, the Victorians found fragments of bone thought to be St Boniface's larynx buried under the apse. The bones were Brixworth's most important reliquary and they may well have been hidden here for safekeeping when Viking raids were at their peak. On the south side of the chancel, a brightly painted wooden screen guards the **Lady Chapel**, built in the thirteenth century by a local baron, Sir John de Verdun. His badly weathered stone effigy lies in a recess in the south wall, with legs crossed and his suit of chain mail just about decipherable.

Althorp

Some six miles northwest of Northampton off the A428, the ritzy mansion of **Althorp** is the focus of the Spencer estate. The Spencers have lived here for centuries, but this was no big deal until one of the tribe, **Diana**, married Prince Charles in 1981. The disintegration of the marriage and Diana's elevation to sainthood is a story known to millions – and most perceptively analysed by B. Campbell in her book, *Diana, Princess of Wales: How Sexual Politics Shook the Monarchy*. The public outpouring of grief following Diana's death in 1997 was quite astounding and Althorp became the focus of massive media attention as the coffin was brought up the M1 motorway from London to be buried on an island in the grounds of the family estate. Today, visitors troop round the **Diana exhibition**, in the old stable block, as well as the adjacent Althorp house, where there's a large collection of priceless paintings, including works by Gainsborough, Van Dyck and Rubens. From the house, a footpath leads round a lake in the middle of which is the islet (no access) on which Diana is buried. The estate is open in July and August (daily 9am–5pm; £10 in advance, £11 on the gate; ℡0870/167 9000, www.visitalthorp.com) and advance reservations are strongly advised.

There are no scheduled **buses** from Northampton to Althorp, but there are sometimes special coaches – contact Northampton tourist office for details.

Ashby St Ledgers

The Gunpowder Plot, which so dismally failed to blow the Houses of Parliament to smithereens in 1605, was hatched in **ASHBY ST LEDGERS**, immediately to the west of the M1, about six miles northwest of Althorp. Since those heated conversations, nothing much seems to have happened here, and the village's one and only street, flanked by handsome limestone cottages on one side and grazing land on the other, still leads to the conspiratorial manor house (no access), a beautiful Elizabethan complex set around a stone-paved courtyard. The adjacent **church**, dedicated to St Mary and St Leodegarius (hence Ledger), looks a little stodgy, but its modest fourteenth-century stonework holds medieval murals depicting the Passion of Christ, from Palm Sunday onwards. Even better, the *Olde Coach Inn*, at the start of the village, is a delightful country **pub** with a good range of ales and great food.

The Gunpowder Plot

Born in York, **Guy Fawkes** (1570–1606) was a young convert to Catholicism and his enthusiasm for the old faith induced him to leave Elizabeth I's Protestant England to fight in the Spanish army – against the "heretics" of the Netherlands – in 1593. There he established a reputation as a brave and determined soldier, catching the eye of leading Catholics back home. Cowed by Elizabeth for decades, these same Catholics viewed the queen's death, in 1603, and the accession of James I with some optimism, but their hopes were dashed when the new king proved unsympathetic to the Catholic cause. A small group, under the leadership of one Robert Catesby, decided that this called for desperate measures and, keen to recruit a military man, one of them popped over to the Netherlands to seek out Fawkes, who signed up and returned to England like a shot. The plan was simple – almost amazingly so: first the conspirators rented a cellar under Parliament and then Fawkes filled it with barrels of gunpowder, enough to blow Parliament sky high. But on November 4, 1605, the eve of the planned attack, the authorities discovered this so-called **Gunpowder Plot** and poor old Fawkes was promptly tortured into giving away the names of his co-conspirators. Fawkes was tried and executed in January 1606, but he is burnt in effigy all over the country on **Bonfire Night**, November 5.

Canons Ashby and Sulgrave

Heading south from Ashby St Ledgers on the A361, follow the road round **Daventry** and then, after a few miles more, watch for the signed turning that leads east along narrow country lanes to the pleasant little limestone village of **CANONS ASHBY**. This is another quiet spot, deep in the country, and it possesses one of the region's finest Elizabethan manor houses, **Canons Ashby House** (April–Oct Mon–Wed, Sat & Sun 1–5.30pm or dusk if earlier; £5; NT). The Drydens (as in John Dryden) have owned the property since its construction, and by and large they have respected its architectural integrity, though one of the clan did muck up the exterior by adding an incongruous peel tower. The main event is, however, the interior, which sports rare Elizabethan wall paintings and decorative Jacobean plasterwork of extraordinarily florid design. The **church** in the manor grounds is all that remains of the twelfth-century Augustinian priory after which the house is named.

As the crow flies, it's only a couple of miles south from Canons Ashby to tiny **SULGRAVE**, but the route is positively baffling, cutting between a maze of country lanes – so be sure to follow the signs carefully. Sulgrave itself hardly sets the pulse racing, but it is home to **Sulgrave Manor**, a neat stone country house built by an ancestor of George Washington – his seven times great-grandfather to be precise (April–Oct Mon, Tues & Thurs–Fri 2–5.30pm, Sat & Sun 10.30am–1pm & 2–5.30pm; March, Nov & Dec Sat & Sun 10.30am–1pm & 2–4.30pm; £3.75). The house remained in the family until 1656, when Colonel John, great-grandfather of the American president, set sail for the New World and settled in Virginia. George Washington never visited Sulgrave, but nevertheless the place has taken on the air of a shrine to American democracy and the interior holds a small museum charting George's remarkable career. The best features of the building are the Great Hall, with its low-beamed ceiling, flagstones and huge fireplace, and the kitchen, set around an ancient hearth hung with copper pots and pans.

Stoke Bruerne

Heading south out of Northampton on the A508 and it's about eight miles to the village of **STOKE BRUERNE**, which profits from its location beside a flight of seven locks on the Grand Union Canal. By water at least, the village is also very close to England's longest navigable tunnel, the one and three quarter miles' long Blisworth Tunnel, constructed at the beginning of the nineteenth century. Before the advent of steam tugs in the 1870s, boats were pushed through the tunnel by "legging" – two or more men would push with their legs against the tunnel walls until they emerged to hand over to waiting teams of horses. This exhausting task is fully explained in the village's excellent **Canal Museum** (daily: Easter–Sept 10am–5pm; Oct–Easter Tues–Sun 10am–4pm; £3), housed in a converted, canalside corn mill. The museum records two hundred years of canal history with models, exhibits of canal art and spit-and-polish engines. It also houses the cabin of a butty boat, a showcase for the painted crockery and embroidery of canal families.

There are two good places to **eat** here – the moderately priced *Bruernes Lock Restaurant* and the *Old Chapel Tea Rooms*, the latter featuring snacks and meals with a Mediterranean slant as well as displays of local art work. Over the canal bridge, there's also the *Boat Inn* **pub**, which is stocked with narrowboat trinkets, and *Wharf Cottage*, providing very cosy **B&B** (✆01604/862174; ❶). Finally, both the Stoke Bruerne Boat Company (✆01604/862107) and the Indian Chief (✆01604/862428) offer **narrowboat cruises** down through the tunnel (2hr; £5) as well as longer excursions. It is best to book ahead, but you can turn up on spec, and in the summertime there are several departures daily.

East Northamptonshire

The River Nene wriggles its way across **east Northamptonshire** – that part of the county east of the A508 – passing through a string of little villages and towns, amongst which **Oundle** is by far the most diverting. Within easy striking distance of Oundle is the historic hamlet of **Fotheringhay** and several country houses – hilltop **Rockingham Castle** is the most dramatic, **Boughton House** the richest. Spare time also for the eccentric Catholicism of the Triangular Lodge in **Rushton**.

Oundle

Arguably Northamptonshire's prettiest town, pocket-sized **OUNDLE** slopes up gently from the River Nene, its congregation of old limestone houses zeroing in on the congenial **Market Place**. Preserving much of its medieval layout, Oundle boasts some of the finest seventeenth- and eighteenth-century streetscapes in the Midlands, and is a suitably exclusive setting for one of England's better-known private schools, **Oundle School**, which has been running since 1556 and owns many of the most prized buildings. Above all it's the general appearance of the place that appeals rather than anything in particular, the exception being the parish church of **St Peter**, whose magnificent two-hundred-foot Decorated spire soars high above the centre, though the interior – give or take the odd stained glass window – is unremarkable.

Buses from Peterborough and Northampton stop on the Market Place, a short walk from the **tourist office**, at 14 West St (Easter to Aug Mon–Sat 9am–5pm, Sun 1–4pm; rest of year closed Sun; ✆01832/274333). They issue maps and bus timetables, have comprehensive details of local attractions and operate an **accommodation** service. The best place to stay is the *Talbot Hotel*, just along from the Market Place on New Street (✆01832/273621; ❹). This charming hotel dates from 1626 and comes complete with what is thought to be the very oak staircase Mary, Queen of Scots used on her way to her execution at Fotheringhay Castle (see below). Apparently the queen's executioner stayed at the *Talbot* and both his and Mary's ghost are said to wander the upper floor. For somewhere less expensive, head for the very well-kept *Ashworth House*, with two en-suite guest rooms, at 75 West St (℡01832/275312; ❷). The best place to **eat** is at the *Talbot*, unless you want a takeaway or picnic in which case *Trendalls*, on the Market Place, is just dandy for baguettes and sandwiches of all descriptions.

Fotheringhay

Nestling by the River Nene just four miles northeast of Oundle, the tiny hamlet of **FOTHERINGHAY** has long been left to its own devices, but its medieval heyday is recalled by its magnificent church of **St Mary and All Saints**, rising mirage-like above the green riverine meadows. Begun in 1411 and a hundred and fifty years in the making, the church is a paradigm of the Perpendicular, its exterior sporting wonderful arching buttresses, its nave lit by soaring windows and the whole caboodle topped by a splendid octagonal lantern tower. The interior is a tad bleak and bare, though there are two fancily carved medieval pieces to look for – a pulpit and a fine stone font. On either side of the altar are the tombs of Elizabeth I's ancestors, the dukes of York, Edward and Richard. Elizabeth found the tombs in disarray in 1573 and promptly had them rebuilt in a smooth white limestone that still looks like new.

Fotheringhay **castle** witnessed two key events – the birth of Richard III in 1452 and the beheading of Mary, Queen of Scots in 1587. On the orders of Elizabeth I, Mary was executed in the castle's Great Hall with no one to stand in her defence – apart, that is, from her dog, who is said to have rushed from beneath her skirts as her head dropped off. Not long afterwards, the castle fell into disrepair and nowadays only a thistle-covered **mound** remains to mark its position; it's signposted – down a narrow lane on the bend of the road as you come into the village from Oundle.

Fotheringhay has an excellent **pub**, *The Falcon*, where the food is delicious and there is a good range of beers.

Rockingham Castle

It's only eleven miles west from Oundle, but the best approach to **ROCKINGHAM** village is from the north with the A6003 (from Oakham, see p.707) shooting up the hill, limestone cottages to either side and the castle looming up above. The original **Rockingham Castle** (April–Sept Thurs & Sun 1–5pm; £4.20) was built by William the Conqueror and it remained in royal hands for five centuries, substantially redesigned on several occasions. A long line of Watsons has owned the place ever since, turning it into an opulent private residence. Today, the castle incorporates bits and pieces from several periods – including Edward I's gatehouse – but is mostly Tudor, a handsome, honey-coloured brick-and-stone complex, whose highlight is the timber-beamed **Great Hall**, with grand fireplaces and trellised windows.

Geddington and Boughton House

When Queen Eleanor, cherished wife of Edward I, died in 1290 at Harby, near Lincoln, her embalmed body was carried in state to Westminster Abbey, and a memorial built at each resting point of the cortège. The most complete of the three surviving monuments graces the centre of **GEDDINGTON**, a sprawling village about twelve miles southwest of Oundle beside the A43 between Corby and Kettering. Mounted on a stepped platform, this sumptuously carved **Eleanor Cross** stands like a spire, culminating in a cluster of points above three figures of Eleanor, overlooking the village she had stayed in when accompanying Edward on his royal hunting trips.

From Geddington, a country road leads the one mile southeast to the grandest of Northamptonshire's stately homes, **Boughton House** (Aug daily 2–5pm; grounds May–Aug Mon–Thurs, Sat & Sun 1–5pm; house & grounds £6; grounds only £1.50, free for disabled visitors). This pompous pile is the centre of an eleven-thousand-acre estate that incorporates five villages and has been owned by the dukes of Buccleuch and their ancestors, the Montagus, for five hundred years. The core of the house was originally a monastery, bought by Sir Edward Montagu in 1528 and enlarged by successive generations. Ralph, First Duke of Montagu, who claimed descent from William the Conqueror, made the grandest extensions in the 1690s when he added the arcaded north front. Ambassador to France, Ralph borrowed freely from French design and employed French artists and architects to glorify his mansion, earning the house the nickname "the English Versailles"; he also bought London's Mortlake tapestry factory so he could have the best works for his home.

The house is stuffed with the baubles and bangles of the landed aristocracy. Highlights include paintings by Gainsborough, Raphael and El Greco, a wonderful set of Baroque painted ceilings by Louis Chéron, no less than forty delicate oil sketches by Van Dyck, an extensive collection of swords, pistols and armour, and fine silverware, antique furniture, tapestries and porcelain.

Kettering-Corby **buses** pass through Geddington every couple of hours (not Sun).

Rushton

Five miles west of Geddington, reached along country roads and occupying a solitary location just to the east of the village of **RUSHTON**, is the weird and wonderful **Triangular Lodge** of 1597 (April–Oct daily 10am–6pm; £1.75; EH). It was built by Thomas Tresham, a determined Catholic whose refusal to accept England's Protestant reforms got him fined and banged up in prison. After his release, Tresham expressed his religious fervour architecturally with this ingenious building, whose triangular construction celebrates the Trinity – Father, Son and Holy Ghost. Made of limestone and ironstone to give a striped effect, each of the three sides is 33ft long, with three windows and three gables, and even the central chimney topping the three storeys is triangular. Only two of the six date stones around the lodge are "true" – his release from prison in 1593, and the construction of the lodge in 1595. The rest form an outlandish arithmetical puzzle: subtracting 1593 from the other figures gives the dates of the Crucifixion, the Virgin Mary's death, the Great Flood and the traditional date of the world's creation, 3962 BC. The entrance on "God's" side leads inside, where the whitewashed walls are only interrupted by incised crosses and triangular windows.

Lincolnshire

The obvious place to start a visit to **Lincolnshire** is **Lincoln** itself, an old and easy-paced city where the cathedral, the third largest church in England, remains the county's outstanding attraction. Northeast and east of here, the Lincolnshire **Wolds** band the county, their gentle green hills harbouring the pleasant market town of **Louth**, where conscientious objectors were sent to dig potatoes during World War II. In this vicinity also is the faded gentility of

Woodhall Spa, an Edwardian resort that served as the base of the Dambusters as they prepared for their Ruhr raid in 1943. The Wolds are flanked by the coast, so different from the rest of Lincolnshire, its brashness encapsulated by the mega resort of **Skegness**, though there are unspoilt stretches, too, most notably at the **Gibraltar Point Nature Reserve**.

Delightful **Stamford**, in the southwest corner of the county, is an alternative base, an attractive town where the narrow streets are flanked by a handsome

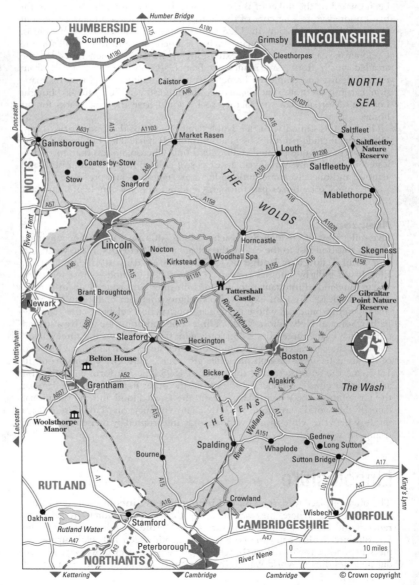

HUMBERSIDE
Scunthorpe
Humber Bridge
Grimsby **LINCOLNSHIRE**
Cleethorpes
Caistor
NORTH
SEA
Doncaster
Market Rasen
Gainsborough
Louth
Saltfleet
Saltfleetby
Nature
Reserve
Coates-by-Stow
Saltfleetby
Stow
Snarford
Mablethorpe
THE
WOLDS
Lincoln
Horncastle
Skegness
Nocton
Woodhall Spa
Kirkstead
River Trent
Newark
Brant Broughton
Tattershall
Castle
Gibraltar
Point Nature
Reserve
N
River Witham
Sleaford
Heckington
Boston
Belton House
Bicker
The Wash
Grantham
Algakirk
Nottingham
THE FENS
Woolsthorpe
Manor
Leicester
River Welland
Gedney
Long Sutton
Spalding
Whaplode
Bourne
Sutton Bridge
King's Lynn
RUTLAND
Crowland
Wisbech NORFOLK
Oakham
Rutland Water
Stamford
CAMBRIDGESHIRE
Peterborough
River Nene
0   10 miles
NORTHANTS
Kettering   Cambridge   Cambridge   © Crown copyright

The more important of Lincolnshire's famously diverse **churches** are described in the main text, but there are many others of interest, some of the more notable of which are listed below. **Opening times** are given where they are definite, but in most cases it's pot luck as to whether the key holder/custodian is around.

ALGAKIRK, five miles south of Boston on the A16. Perched on a mound not far from The Wash, the church of St Peter and St Paul has the full flavour of the fenland, its richly carved Early Gothic arches, capitals and arcades funded by the sale of locally grown woad and chicory, once mainstays of the dyeing trade. The large stained glass windows are splendid too. Key from the custodian.

BRANT BROUGHTON, eleven miles west of Sleaford on the A17. One of the county's most fascinating churches, St Helen's boasts a supremely well-composed, fourteenth-century exterior, its crocketed spire standing guard over a stocky nave whose twin porches are enlivened by finely carved bosses. The bosses sport scenes of everyday life as well as phantasmagorical beasts and even irreverent cameos – among them, the man with the bare bum. The interior, sympathetically remodelled in the 1870s, is distinguished by its stained glass and tranquil chancel. Key from the custodian.

CROWLAND, seven miles north of Peterborough on the A1073. The ruins of Croyland Abbey, once the region's largest monastery, provide some idea of its former power and wealth. The abbey was abandoned at the Dissolution, but the locals turned the north nave aisle of the old abbey church into the parish church of St Guthlac, whose finest feature is the exquisitely graceful ribbed vaulting. Open dawn to dusk.

KIRKSTEAD, southwest of Woodhall Spa off the B1191. Remote thirteenth-century St Leonard's is an excellent illustration of the Early English style. Built as the chapel of a long-gone Cistercian abbey. Key from the custodian.

NOCTON, eight miles southeast of Lincoln off the B1188. All Saints', completed in 1872, was built to commemorate the First Earl of Ripon, local landowner and, briefly, prime minister. Wall paintings, stained glass and almost all the fittings are original. Key from the custodian.

WHAPLODE, six miles east of Spalding on the A151. St Mary's is a fascinating hybrid, the original Norman work – seen at best advantage in the nave – supplemented by Early English, Tudor, Stuart and Georgian bits and pieces. The brightly painted tomb of Sir Anthony Irby is its finest monument. Irby was a local MP and Puritan supporter of Oliver Cromwell. The five mourners on his tomb represent his sons, all of whom did a stretch in the Parliamentary army. Key from the custodian.

ensemble of antique stone buildings, and next door stands one of the great monuments of Elizabethan England, **Burghley House**. From Stamford, it's a short hop east into **The Fens**, whose most diverting villages lie along the A17, a road that runs close to the old fenland port of **Boston**, now Lincolnshire's second town. On any tour of the Fens you'll pass some of the county's most imposing medieval **churches**. Several are worth a special visit, especially **St Botolph's** in Boston, **St Andrew's** in Heckington and **St Mary Magdalen's** in Gedney – seen to best advantage, like all the other churches of this area, in the pale, watery sunlight of the fenland evening. The other chief town of southern Lincolnshire is **Grantham**, birthplace of Margaret Thatcher and the site of its own splendid medieval church.

Getting around Lincolnshire by public transport can be difficult. Lincoln is the hub of the county's limited **rail** network with regular services south to

Sleaford and Spalding and east via Sleaford to Heckington, Boston and Skegness. There are also links northwest to Gainsborough and west to Grantham and Newark, in Nottinghamshire, both of which are on the main line from London to the Northeast. In addition, there are reasonable **bus** services between Lincoln and the county's larger market towns, like Louth and Boston, but amongst the villages you'll be struggling without your own transport. This is especially true as many of these villages are long and straggly, built along slight ridges as a precaution against flooding.

Lincoln and around

Reaching high into the sky from the top of a steep hill, the triple towers of the mighty cathedral of **LINCOLN** are visible for miles across the flatlands. This conspicuous spot was first fortified by the Celts, who called their settlement Lindon, "hillfort by the lake", a reference to the pools formed by the River Witham in the marshy ground below. In 47 AD the Romans occupied Lindon and built a fortified town which subsequently became, as Lindum Colonia, one of the four regional capitals of Roman Britain.

Today, only fragments of the Roman city survive, mostly pieces of the third-century town wall, and these are outdone by reminders of Lincoln's medieval heyday, which began during the reign of William the Conqueror with the building of the **castle** and **cathedral**. Lincoln flourished, first as a Norman power-base and then as a centre of the wool trade with Flanders, until 1369, when the wool market was transferred to neighbouring Boston. It was almost five hundred years before the town revived, the recovery based upon its manufacture of agricultural machinery and drainage equipment for the fenlands. As the nineteenth-century town spread south down the hill and out along the old Roman road – the Fosse Way – so Lincoln became a place of precise class distinctions: the "Up hill" area, spreading north from the cathedral, became synonymous with middle-class respectability, "Down hill" with the proletariat. It's a distinction that remains – locals selling anything from second-hand cars to settees still put "Up hill" in brackets to signify a better quality of merchandise.

For the visitor, almost everything of interest is confined to the "Up hill" part of town, and it's here also you'll find the best **pubs** and **restaurants**. In addition, within easy striking distance of Lincoln by car stand several fascinating **churches**: to the northeast, there's Snarford church, to the northwest two more, one at Coates-by-Stow, the other at Stow. In this direction too is the rare **Old Hall** at Gainsborough.

Arrival, information and accommodation

Both Lincoln's **train station**, on St Mary's Street, and its **bus station**, close by off Norman Street, are located "Down hill" in the city centre. From either, it's a steep, twenty-minute walk to the cathedral, which can also be reached by city bus or (depending on the success of various trails) an electric "people carrier". There are two **tourist offices**. One is in the shopping centre on The Cornhill, close to the train and bus stations (Easter–Sept Mon–Thurs 9.30am–5.30pm, Fri 9.30am–5pm, Sat 10am–5pm; Oct–Easter same days, but closes 4pm; ℡01522/579056, ⊛www.lincoln-info.org.uk), the other is at 9 Castle Hill, between the cathedral and the castle (same hours; ℡01522/529828, ⊛www .lincoln-info.org.uk). Both have a useful range of literature on Lincoln and its surroundings, take bookings for guided tours of the city, and operate an accommodation-booking service.

Lincoln has a good supply of competitively priced **hotels** and **B&Bs**, though surprisingly few of them are in the vicinity of the Cathedral – "Up hill" – and

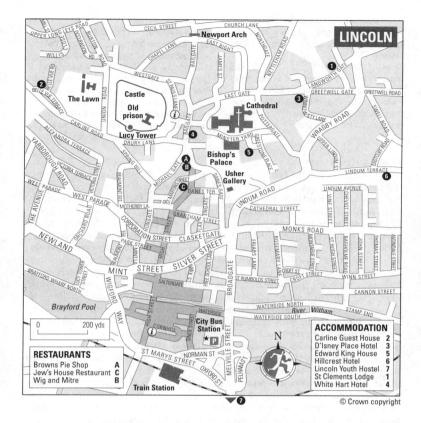

RESTAURANTS
Browns Pie Shop A
Jew's House Restaurant C
Wig and Mitre B

ACCOMMODATION
Carline Guest House 2
D'Isney Place Hotel 3
Edward King House 5
Hillcrest Hotel 6
Lincoln Youth Hostel 7
St Clements Lodge 1
White Hart Hotel 4

© Crown copyright

this is precisely where you want to be. All the places below are "Up hill," unless otherwise indicated. On occasion, demand can exceed supply, in which case head for the tourist office.

Hotels, guest houses and B&Bs

Carline Guest House 1–3 Carline Rd ☏01522 /530422. One of the best B&Bs in the city, *Carline* occupies a spick-and-span Edwardian house about ten minutes' walk down from the cathedral – take Drury Lane from in front of the castle and keep going. Breakfasts are first-rate, the rooms smart and tastefully furnished. No credit cards. ②

D'Isney Place Hotel Eastgate ☏01522/538881, ⓦwww.disneyplacehotel.co.uk. This delightful hotel occupies a lovely eighteenth-century building close to the cathedral. Breakfast is served in the bedrooms, some of which have four-poster beds and spa baths. Highly recommended. ⑤

Edward King House The Old Palace, Minster Yard ☏01522/528778. For something a little different,

head for this unusual B&B in a former residence of the Bishops of Lincoln. The exterior is a good bit grander than the rooms, but these are perfectly adequate and some have fine views over the city. Next to the cathedral. ①

Hillcrest Hotel 15 Lindum Terrace ☏01522 /510182, ⓦwww.hillcrest-hotel.com. Traditional, very English hotel in a large red-brick house that was originally a Victorian rectory. Sixteen comfortable rooms with all mod cons plus a large, sloping garden. The owner, who is often in attendance, has loads of ideas about what to visit. About ten minutes' walk from the cathedral: go down Pottergate, turn right onto Wragby Road and then almost immediately turn left onto Lindum Terrace. ⑥

St Clements Lodge 21 Langworth Gate ☏01522 /521532. In a brisk, modern house a short walk from the cathedral, this comfortable B&B offers a handful of pleasant, mostly en-suite guest rooms. To get there, follow Eastgate east from beside the cathedral. ❷

White Hart Hotel Bailgate ☎01522/526222. This is one of Lincoln's plushest hotels, a crisply refurbished old coaching inn footsteps from the Castle Hill tourist office. Many of the bedrooms overlook the cathedral. One of the Heritage chain. Weekend deals can half the normal price. ❼

Hostel

Lincoln youth hostel 77 South Park ☎01522 /522076, ✉lincoln@yha.org.uk. The town's YHA hostel occupies a Victorian house beside South Common park, one mile south of the train station. There are 46 beds in 2- to 8-bedded rooms. To get there from the train and bus stations, follow Melville Street and its continuation Canwick Road, keep going straight over the island (past South Park Avenue) and it's the first turning on the right opposite the cemetery. Closed Nov–Jan. ❶

The Cathedral

Not a hill at all, **Castle Hill** is a wide, short and level cobbled street that links the castle and the cathedral. It's a charming spot and its east end is marked by the arch of the medieval **Exchequergate**, beyond which soars the glorious west front of **Lincoln Cathedral** (daily: May–Sept 7am–8pm; Oct–April 7am–6pm; except during services when access is restricted; £3.50 with guided tour), a sheer cliff-face of blind arcading mobbed by decorative carving. Most striking of all is the extraordinary band of twelfth-century carved panels which depict biblical themes with passionate intimacy, their inspiration being a similar frieze at Modena cathedral in Italy. The west front's apparent homogeneity is, however, deceptive, and further inspection reveals two phases of construction – the small stones and thick mortar of much of the facade belong to the original church, completed in 1092, whereas the longer stones and finer courses date from the early thirteenth century. These were enforced modifications, for in 1185 an earthquake shattered much of the Norman church, which was then rebuilt under the auspices of **Bishop Hugh of Avalon**, the man responsible for most of the present cathedral, with the notable exception of the (largely) fourteenth-century central tower.

The cavernous **interior** is a fine example of Early English architecture, with the nave's pillars conforming to the same general design yet differing slightly, their varied columns and bands of dark Purbeck marble contrasting with the oolitic limestone that is the building's main material. Looking back up the nave from beneath the central tower, you can also observe a major medieval cock-up: Bishop Hugh's roof is out of alignment with the earlier west front, and the point where they meet has all the wrong angles. It's possible to pick out other irregularities, too – the pillars have bases of different heights, and there are ten windows in the north wall and nine in the south – but these are deliberate features, reflecting a medieval aversion to the vanity of symmetry. Also medieval is the use of pre-Christian imagery, especially on and around the rood screen at the top of the nave, where there's a veritable menagerie of demons and gargoyles.

Beyond the rood screen lies **St Hugh's Choir**, its fourteenth-century misericords carrying an eccentric range of carvings, with scenes from the life of Alexander the Great and King Arthur mixed up with biblical characters and folkloric parables. Farther on is the Gothic **Angel Choir**, completed in 1280, its roof embellished by dozens of finely carved statuettes, including the tiny Lincoln Imp (see below). Finally, a corridor off the choir's north aisle leads to the wooden-roofed **cloisters** and the polygonal **chapter house**, where Edward I and Edward II convened gatherings that pre-figured the creation of the English Parliament.

On every day but Sunday, usually a couple of times a day, the cathedral offers two sorts of **guided tour**. The first – the Floor Tour – is a quick gambol round the cathedral's salient features, the second, the Roof Tour, takes in parts of the church otherwise out of bounds. The latter are very popular, so it's a good idea to book in advance – call ☎01522/529241 or see ⓦwww.lincolncathedral.com.

Hidden behind a wall immediately below (and to the south of) the cathedral on Minster Yard are the ruins of what would, in its day, have been among the city's most impressive buildings. This, the medieval **Bishop's Palace** (April–Oct daily 10am–6pm; Nov–March Sat & Sun 10am–4pm; £2.50; EH), once consisted of two grand halls, a lavish chapel, kitchens and ritzy private chambers, but today the only coherent survivor is the battered and bruised Alnwick Tower – where the entrance is. The damage was done during the Civil War when a troupe of Roundheads occupied the palace until they themselves had to evacuate the place after a fierce fire.

The Castle

From the west front of the cathedral, it's a quick stroll across Castle Hill to **Lincoln Castle** (April–Sept Mon–Sat 9.30am–5.30pm, Sun 11am–5.30pm; Oct–March Mon–Sat 9.30am–4pm, Sun 11am–4pm; £2.50). Intact and forbidding, the castle walls incorporate bits and pieces from the twelfth to the nineteenth century and the wall walkway offers great views over town. The earliest remains are those of the **Lucy Tower**, built on the steep grassy mound that was once the site of one of the two original Norman mottes. The castle was turned into a prison in the 1820s and some of the prisoners were unceremoniously buried here at the top of the mound – a sad and lonely spot if ever there was one, especially as the tombs were only allowed to carry the prisoners' initials. The spacious grounds enclosed by the walls hold the old **prison**, a dour red-brick structure that is now home to one of the four surviving copies of the **Magna Carta** as well as a remarkable **prison chapel**. Here, the prisoners – who were kept in solitary confinement – were locked in high-sided cubicles where they could see the preacher and his pulpit but not their fellow internees, an arrangement founded on the pseudo-scientific theory that defined crime as a contagious disease. Unfortunately for the theorists, their so-called Pentonville System of "Separation and Silence", which was introduced here in 1846, drove many prisoners crazy, and it had to be abandoned thirty years later, though nobody bothered to dismantle the chapel.

Leaving the castle via the west gate, you reach **The Lawn**, formerly a lunatic asylum and now a leisure complex incorporating – among several modest attractions – the **Sir Joseph Banks Conservatory** (April–Sept Mon–Fri 9am–5pm, Sat & Sun 10am–4pm; Oct–Easter daily 10am–4pm; free). This is a large tropical glasshouse named after a local botanist who travelled with Cook on his first voyage to Australia.

The rest of the city

As for the rest of **"Up hill"** Lincoln, it's scattered with historic remains, notably several chunks of Roman wall, the most prominent of which is the second-century **Newport Arch** straddling Bailgate and once the main north gate into the city. There's also a bevy of medieval stone houses, at their best on and around the aptly named **Steep Hill** as it cuts down to the city centre. In particular, look out for the tidily restored twelfth-century **Jew's House**, a reminder of the Jewish community that flourished in medieval Lincoln. A rare and superb example of domestic Norman architecture, it now houses the *Jew's House Restaurant* (see below).

The **Usher Gallery**, Lindum Rd (Mon–Sat 10am–5.30pm, Sun 2.30–5pm; £2), is on the hillside, too, its well-presented displays featuring some fine paintings of the cathedral and its environs, the best being those of William Logsdail. There's also a *Lincoln* view by Lowry as well as memorabilia celebrating Lincolnshire's own Alfred Tennyson, one of Victorian England's favourite poets. In addition, the gallery holds an eclectic collection of coins, porcelain, and watches and clocks dating from the seventeenth century. The timepieces were given to the gallery by its benefactor, James Ward Usher, a local jeweller and watchmaker who made a fortune by devising the legend of the **Lincoln Imp**, which he turned into the city's emblem in the 1880s. His story has a couple of imps hopping around the cathedral, until one of them is turned to stone for trying to talk to the angels carved into the roof of the Angel Choir. His chum made a hasty exit on the back of a witch, but the wind is still supposed to haunt the cathedral awaiting their return.

Eating and drinking

Lincoln's **café** and **restaurant** scene is a little patchy – with too many places offering mundane food geared to the day-tripping trade – but there are excellent places too, mostly within shouting distance of the Cathedral. First stop must be *Browns Pie Shop*, 33 Steep Hill – at the top – which has a lively menu where the emphasis is on British ingredients; a main course here will cost you about £10. Next door, and similarly enticing, is the *Wig and Mitre* pub-restaurant, where a wide-ranging, moderately priced menu lists everything from sandwiches through to fillet steak. Another recommendable spot on Steep Hill is the more expensive – and more formal – *Jew's House Restaurant* (☎01522/524851; closed Sun). As for **pubs**, there are a pair of amiable and traditional locals near the cathedral – the *Bull & Chain*, on Langworthgate, and the *Morning Star*, close by on Greetwellgate. The former has a garden.

Snarford, Stow and Gainsborough

Half-hidden by a clump of trees, half a mile down a country lane off the A46, about seven miles northeast of Lincoln at minuscule **SNARFORD**, stands the solitary, square-towered church of **St Lawrence** (dawn to dusk). The church is dedicated to a Roman saint who was roasted to death on a gridiron, a fate that's made him the patron saint of cooks. For several centuries, the church was the family mausoleum of the St Pauls, the lords of the manor, and its cramped interior is dominated by the Elizabethan tomb of Sir Thomas and his wife, Faith, whose alabaster figures lie on an elaborately carved, six-poster bed. The brightly painted carving is superb, with finely crafted detail such as the flower-embroidered cushion at Sir Thomas's feet, Faith's ruff and open gown and the figures of the couple's eight kneeling children carved round the canopy. Opposite is the tomb of their son, Sir George, and his wife Frances, who lie propped up on their elbows looking back towards Sir Thomas. Once again, the carving is magnificent, with Frances decked out in Jacobean finery, a dark gown and a wide ruff beneath the frizzed hairstyle then fashionable. Behind the couple and the effigy of their child are the emblems of death – coffins and gravediggers' tools – together with the lily of purity and the rose of eternity.

A series of obscure byroads lead the eight miles west from Snarford to the remote farmstead and adjacent church of **St Edith** (dawn to dusk) that together constitute **COATES-BY-STOW**. Entered through a narrow Norman doorway, tiny St Edith's boasts a rare and partly painted wooden rood screen dating from the fifteenth century. Round about are the residue of several hundred years of worship: medieval pews and pulpit, a holy water stoup and a Norman font.

The village of **STOW**, on the B1241 some three miles west of St Edith's, embraces the fortress-like church of **St Mary** (daily 9am to dusk), whose austere rubble walls date from the beginning of the eleventh century, though the Normans refashioned the nave and the Victorians restored the church in the 1860s. The imposing interior is dominated by the magnificent Saxon arches of the central tower, the tallest of their period in England, whose simple elegance contrasts with the clumsy Norman arches inserted behind them. But some of the Norman work is excellent, too, especially the ornate vaulted ribbing of the chancel and the dogtooth carving around the doorways – and look out also for a scratched drawing of a Viking longship and some crude thirteenth-century wall paintings.

From Stow, it's just six miles north to the old river-port of **GAINSBOR-OUGH**, a dreary place but for two outstanding buildings. These are the church of **All Saints** (Mon, Tues, Thurs & Fri 10am–4pm, Sat 10am–noon), whose spacious pastel-painted interior is a fine example of Georgian style, and **Gainsborough Old Hall** (Easter–Oct Mon–Sat 10am–5pm, Sun 2–5.30pm; rest of year closed Sun; £2.50; EH), a sprawling manor house with a magnificent Great Hall. Built in the 1460s, the timber-framed hall, bending and buckling from the contractions of the oak, has a huge hoop-shaped roof where the grain of the wood skilfully follows the lines of the arches. At the back of the hall, tiny doors lead to the well-preserved kitchen, and the timbered bedrooms of the first floor are worth inspecting, too. Gainsborough is thought to have been the setting for St Oggs in George Eliot's *Mill on the Floss*, whose tragic events result from a particularly ferocious tidal bore. Fortunately for the locals, the bore – or eagre – which rolls up the River Trent through Gainsborough fifty minutes after high tide in the Humber estuary doesn't often do much damage, but it still raises the river level between eight and thirteen feet; times are given in the local press.

The Wolds and the coast

The rolling hills and gentle valleys of the **Lincolnshire Wolds**, a narrow band of chalky land running southeast from Caistor to just outside Skegness, stand out amidst the more mundane agricultural landscapes of north Lincolnshire. A string of particularly appealing valleys is concentrated in the vicinity of **Louth**, which, with its striking church and old centre, is easily the most enticing of the region's towns – with the added advantage of being fairly close to the coast. A few miles to the south of Louth, the Wolds dip down to the wooded heathland surrounding the once fashionable hamlet of **Woodhall Spa** and it's south again to the imposing red-brick **Tattershall Castle**, north Lincolnshire's main historical attraction. Beyond the castle, all is fenland, pancake-flat and making a wide and deep arch around the intrusive stump of The Wash. In the other direction, east of the Wolds, lies the coast, whose bungalows, campsites and caravans are parked beside a sandy beach that extends, with a few marshy interruptions, north from **Skegness**, the main resort, to Mablethorpe and ultimately Cleethorpes. Near Skegness, the **Gibraltar Point Nature Reserve** is a welcome diversion from the bucket-and-spade/amusement-arcade commercialism.

Louth and around

Henry VIII described the county of Lincolnshire as "one of the most brutal and beestlie of the whole realm", his contempt based on the events of 1536, when thousands of northern peasants rebelled against his religious reforms. In Lincolnshire, this insurrection, the **Pilgrimage of Grace**, began in the north-east of the county at **LOUTH**, twenty-three miles from Lincoln, under the leadership of the local vicar, who was subsequently hung, drawn and quartered. There's a commemorative plaque in honour of the rebels beside Louth's church of **St James** (Easter–Christmas Mon–Sat 10.30am–4.30pm), which is the town's one outstanding building, its soaring Perpendicular spire, buttresses, battlements and pinnacles set on a grassy knoll, just to the west of the centre. The interior, clumsily renovated in the 1820s, is a disappointment, but the nave does boast a handsome Georgian wooden roof and the intricate vaulting beneath the tower is an exercise in geometrical precision. St James also owns a collection of old chests, or "hutches", used as portable cupboards for displaying plate. One of them, the curious Sudbury Hutch, bears a portrait of Henry VII and Elizabeth of York, but although it purports to be medieval, it may well be a much more modern fake.

Next to the church, the well-tended gardens and Georgian houses of **Westgate** make it one of Louth's prettiest streets and you can grab a drink here at the antique *Wheatsheaf Inn*. Afterwards, it doesn't take long to explore the rest of the town centre, whose cramped lanes and alleys – focusing on the **Cornmarket** – are lined with red-brick buildings dating from the seventeenth century.

With reasonably regular weekday services from Boston and Lincoln, Louth's **bus station** is at the east end of Queen Street, a couple of minutes' walk from the Cornmarket – walk west along Queen Street and turn right onto the Market Place. The **tourist office**, in the Market Hall off Cornmarket (Mon–Sat 9am–5pm; ☎01507/609289), has a competent range of local information including accommodation details. The best **hotel** is the *Priory*, on Eastgate (☎01507/602930, ⓦwww.theprioryhotel.com; ❹), an excellent family-run place in a Georgian villa of 1818 with an idiosyncratic neo-Gothic facade and extensive gardens; it's located at the east end of the centre, about ten minutes' walk from the Cornmarket. There's also a top-notch **B&B**, *Keddington House*, in a pleasant Victorian house with its own heated outdoor pool about three-quarters of a mile to the northeast of the centre at 5 Keddington Rd (☎01507/603973, ⓦwww.keddingtonhouse.co.uk; ❷).

For **food**, it's hard to beat the *Priory*, which serves moderately priced dinners to a very good standard (closed Sun). The miscellaneous snack bars dotted round the Corn Market offer cheaper alternatives. Runner up, and a good bit cheaper, is *Ye Olde Whyte Swanne*, an old pub at 45 Eastgate, that sells tasty bar snacks, including home-made game and pork pies as well as the illustrious (and extremely large) Lincolnshire sausage.

The Saltfleetby-Theddlethorpe dunes

A worthwhile short excursion from Louth takes you east along the **B1200** across about ten miles of fen farmland to the coast. This byroad is built on an old Roman road used to transport salt inland from the seashore salt pans that were once a lucrative source of income for local traders. At the coast, at the end of the B1200, turn right along the main **A1031** and, after about half a mile, take the (poorly signed) track on the left through the dunes to the **Saltfleetby-Theddlethorpe Dunes National Nature Reserve**. Comprising over five miles of sand dune, salt and freshwater marsh, the reserve is at its prettiest in midsummer, when the dunes sprout buckthorn bushes and sea heather flowers, forming a carpet of violet spreading down towards the ocean. A network of trails navigates the dunes and lagoons, with the latter attracting hundreds of migratory wildfowl in spring and autumn.

Woodhall Spa

Heading south from Louth along the A153, it's thirteen miles to **HORN-CASTLE**, which was once famous for its horse fairs – as described in George Borrow's *Romany Rye* – and seven more along the B1191 to **WOODHALL SPA**, an elongated village surrounded by a generous chunk of woodland. Here, the main street – **The Broadway** – is lined with Victorian and Edwardian villas, reminders of the time when the spring water of this isolated place, rich in iodine and bromine, was a favourite tipple of the great and the good. A modest **Cottage Museum** (Easter–Oct Mon–Sat 10am–5pm, Sun 11am–5pm; £1), on Iddesleigh Road off the Broadway, outlines the development of the spa and doubles as the **tourist office** (same times; ☎01526/353775).

Nowadays, though, with the springs abandoned, the village feels marooned. It does, however, possess a particularly interesting hotel, the **Petwood Hotel**, Stixwould Rd (☎01526/352411, ⓦwww.petwood.co.uk; ❻) – coming in on the B1191, keep on going to the end of The Broadway and turn right at Woodhall's one and only major intersection. Surrounded by immaculate gardens, the hotel's half-timbered gables and stone facades shelter a fine panelled interior, built in 1905 for the furniture millionaires, the Maples. In World War II, long after the family had moved out, the house was requisitioned by the RAF and turned into the Officers' Mess of 617 Squadron, the **Dambusters**, famous for their bombing raid of May 16, 1943. The raid was planned to deprive German industry of water and electricity by breaching several Ruhrland dams, a mission made possible by Barnes Wallis's **bouncing bomb**. A rusting specimen stands outside the hotel, which also contains the old **Officers' Bar**, kitted out with memorabilia from bits of aircraft engines to newspaper cuttings. Another unexpected delight is Woodhall's **Kinema**, deep in the woods, yet only five minutes' walk from The Broadway – just follow the signs. Opened in 1922, the Kinema is one of England's few remaining picture houses that projects a film from behind the screen, and at weekend showings a 1930s organ rises in front of the screen to play you through the ice-cream break. For details of what's on at the Kinema, call ☎01526/352166 or consult ⓦwww.thekinema.co.uk. Incidentally, if you fancy staying in Woodhall but don't want to stump up the cost of the Petwood, the *Oglee Guest House*, in Edwardian premises off the Broadway at 16 Stanhope Ave (☎01526/353512; ❷), is a pleasant alternative.

Tattershall Castle

From Woodhall Spa, it's about three miles southeast to **Tattershall Castle** (April–Oct Mon–Wed, Sat & Sun 10.30am–5.30pm; mid-Nov to mid-Dec Sat & Sun noon–4pm; £3; NT), whose massive, moated red-brick keep dominates the fenland from beside the main road between Sleaford and Skegness. There's been a castle here since Norman times, but it was Ralph Cromwell, the Lord High Treasurer, who built the present quadrangled tower in the 1440s. Cromwell, a veteran of Agincourt, was familiar with contemporary French architecture and it was to France that he looked for his basic design – in England, keeps had been out of fashion since the thirteenth century. Cromwell's quest for style explains Tattershall's contradictions. The castle walls are sixteen feet thick and rise to a height of one hundred feet, but there are no fewer than three ground-floor doorways with low-level windows to match. It's a medieval keep as fashion accessory, a theatricality that's continued inside the castle with the grand chimney-pieces, the only highlight of the bare interior – give or take the occasional Flemish tapestry. The adjacent church of the **Holy Trinity** (April–Sept daily 10am–5pm) is a high and mighty fifteenth-century structure, whose soaring nave, with its slender columns and elongated windows, is bright but bare of decoration. The church makes a rather austere home for a volunteer-run café – but don't miss their home-made cakes.

Skegness and around
SKEGNESS, some twenty-six miles east of Tattershall, has been a busy resort ever since the railways reached the Lincolnshire coast in 1875. Its heyday was before the 1960s, when the Brits began to take themselves off to sunnier climes, but it still attracts tens of thousands of city-dwellers each year, who come for the wide, sandy beaches and for a host of attractions ranging from nightclubs to bowling greens. Every inch the traditional English seaside town, Skegness gets the edge over many of its rivals by keeping its beaches clean and its parks spick-and-span, whilst a massive leisure complex in neighbouring Ingoldmells has a whopping indoor "fun pool". Indeed, Skegness has a tradition of keeping ahead of its competitors: in 1908 it came up with the ground-breaking "Skegness is So Bracing" slogan beneath a picture of a "Jolly Fisherman", and it was here in 1936 that ex-showman Billy Butlin opened the first Butlin's Holiday Camp. All that said, the seafront, with its rows of souvenir shops and amusement arcades, can be dismal, especially on rainy days, and you may well decide to sidestep the whole caboodle by heading south three miles along the coastal road to the **Gibraltar Point National Nature Reserve** (daily dawn to dusk). Here, a network of clearly signed footpaths patterns a narrow strip of salt and freshwater marsh, sand dune and beach that attracts an inordinate number of birds, both resident and migratory.

As for practicalities, Skegness **bus** and **train stations** are next door to each other and about ten minutes' walk from the seashore – cut across Lumley Square and go straight up the High Street to the landmark clock tower. The **tourist office** (daily: April–Sept 9.30am–5pm; Oct–March 10am–4pm; ☎01754/764821, Ⓦwww.funcoast.co.uk) is yards from the clock tower, behind the beach and opposite the Embassy Centre on Grand Parade. They can provide a colossal list of accommodation, including scores of **B&Bs** and **guest houses**. A series of inexpensive choices is strung out along Drummond Road, near the action but still agreeably residential. Options here include the *Sherwood Lodge*, at no. 100 (☎01754/762548; ❶), and the *Singlecote Hotel*, at no. 34 (☎01754/764698; ❶). For something a little more original, there's the *Old Mill Guest House*, in an old and imaginatively converted windmill five miles inland at Westend, Burgh Le Marsh (☎01754/810081; ❶).

The Lincolnshire Fens

The Lincolnshire section of **The Fens**, the great chunk of eastern England extending from Boston to Cambridge, encompasses some of the most productive farmland in Europe. With the exception of the occasional hillock, this pancake-flat, treeless terrain has been painstakingly reclaimed from the marshes and swamps that once drained into the Wash, a process that has taken almost two thousand years. In earlier times, outsiders were often amazed by the dreadful conditions hereabouts – as one medieval chronicler put it: "There is in the middle part of Britain a hideous fen which [is] oft times clouded with moist and dark vapours having within it divers islands and woods as also crooked and winding rivers." These dire conditions spawned the distinctive culture of the so-called **fen slodgers**, who embanked small portions of marsh to create pastureland and fields, supplementing their diets by catching fish and fowl, and gathering reed and sedge for thatching and fuel. Their economy was threatened by the large-scale land reclamation schemes of the late fifteenth and sixteenth centuries, and time and again the fenlanders sabotaged progress by breaking down the banks and dams. But the odds were stacked against the saboteurs, and a succession of great landowners eventually drained huge tracts of the fenland; by the end of the eighteenth century the fen slodgers' way of life had all but disappeared. Nonetheless, the Lincolnshire fens remain a distinctive area of introverted little villages, with just one major settlement, the old port of **Boston**.

Boston

As it nears The Wash, the muddy River Witham weaves its way through **BOSTON** (a corruption of Botolf's stone, or Botolph's town), which was named after the Anglo-Saxon monk-saint who first established a monastery here, overlooking the main river crossing point in 645 AD. In the thirteenth and fourteenth centuries, the settlement expanded to become England's second largest seaport, its flourishing economy dependent on the wool trade with Flanders. Local merchants, revelling in their success, decided to build a church that demonstrated their wealth, the result being the magnificent medieval church of St Botolph, whose 272-foot tower still presides over the town and surrounding fenland. The church was completed in the early sixteenth century, but by then Boston was in decline as trade drifted west towards the Atlantic and the Witham silted up. The town's fortunes only revived in the late eighteenth century when, after the nearby fens had been drained, it became a minor agricultural centre with a modest port that has, in recent times, been modernized for trade with the EU. A singular mix of fenland town and seaport, Boston is an unusual little place that is at its liveliest on **market days** – Wednesday and Saturday.

Mostly edged by Victorian red-brick buildings, the mazy streets of Boston's cramped and compact centre, on the east side of the Witham, radiate out from the **Market Place**, a dishevelled square of irregular shape. Just to the west looms the massive bulk of **St Botolph's** (Oct–April Mon–Sat 8.30am–4.30pm, Sun 8.30am–12.30pm; rest of year daily 8.30am–4.30pm; free), whose exterior masonry is embellished by the high-pointed windows of the Decorated style. Most of the structure dates from the fourteenth century, but the huge and distinctive **tower**, whose lack of a spire earned the church the nickname the "Boston Stump", is of later construction. The octagonal lantern is later still, added in the sixteenth century and graced by flying buttresses and pointy pinnacles. Visible from twenty miles away, it once sheltered a beacon that guided travellers in from the fens and the North Sea. A tortuous 365-step spiral staircase (closed on Sun) leads to a balcony near the top, from where the panoramic views over Boston and the fens amply repay both the price of the ticket (£2) and the effort of the climb.

Down below, St Botolph's light and airy **nave** is an exercise in the Perpendicular, all soaring columns and high windows. The sheer purity of design is stunning, its virtuosity heightened by the narrowness of the annexe-like chancel and the elegance of the Decorated arch that partly screens it from view. Indeed, the chancel is comparatively dowdy, though it does boast some intriguing fourteenth-century **misericords**, bearing a lively mixture of vernacular scenes, such as organ-playing bears, a pair of medieval jesters squeezing cats in imitation of bagpipes and a schoolmaster birching a boy, watched by three more awaiting the same fate.

The church's most famous vicar was John Cotton (1584–1652), who helped stir the Puritan stew during his twenty-year tenure, encouraging a stream of

Lincolnshire dissidents to head off to the colonies of New England to found their "New Jerusalem". Cotton emigrated himself in 1633 and soon became the leading light among the Puritans of Boston, Massachusetts. The Cotton connection was finally commemorated here in the Stump by the creation of the **Cotton Chapel**, at the west end of the nave, in 1857. Curiously enough, some of the locals wanted to paint the chapel ceiling with the Stars and Stripes, but the Church of England resisted. The most interesting relic from Cotton's sojourn here is not in the chapel at all, but in the nave in the form of the ornate **pulpit** from which he pounded out his three-hour sermons.

Boston had been alive to religious dissent before Cotton arrived and, in 1607, several of the **Pilgrim Fathers** were incarcerated here after their failed attempt to escape religious persecution by slipping across to Holland. They were imprisoned for thirty days in the old **Guildhall** (Tues–Sat 10am–5pm; £1.25, free on Thurs), on South Street – a brief walk south along the river from St Botolph's. A creaky affair, the Guildhall spreads over three levels and incorporates an antique Council Chamber, the court where the Pilgrim Fathers were tried and sentenced, as well as the cells where they were locked up. There's a fascinating hotchpotch of local bygones dotted around – including some spectacularly ferocious anti-poacher traps and a small display on locally born John Fox (1516–87), whose *Book of Martyrs* whipped up an anti-Catholic storm.

Practicalities

It's ten minutes' walk east from Boston **train station** to the town centre – head straight out of the station along Station Street and keep going until you hit the river. The **bus station** is also to the west of the centre, just five minutes' walk away along West Street. The **tourist office** (Mon–Sat 9am–5pm; ☎01205/356656, ⓦwww.boston.gov.uk) is in the Market Place beneath the Assembly Rooms, and here you can pick up details of several **B&Bs**. Among them one good option is the *Bramley House*, in an attractively converted eighteenth-century farmhouse about one mile west of town beyond the train station at 267 Sleaford Road (☎01205/354538; ❶). Another good choice is *Fairfield Guest House*, in a much enlarged Victorian property about a mile to the south of the centre at 101 London Road (☎01205/362869; ❶). There are fifteen guest rooms here – seven en suite – and each is decorated in bright and cheerful style. Town centre accommodation is limited and the best you'll do is the *New England Hotel*, Wide Bargate (☎01205/365255, ⓦwww.newengland-boston.co.uk; ❺), an unassuming mid-range place of thirty bedrooms with modern furnishings and fittings.

For **food**, *Goodbarns Yard*, just to the north of the Stump on Wormgate, serves copious pub meals inside or out in a back garden overlooking the river. Vegetarians should make a beeline for *Maud's Tea Rooms*, inside the Maud Foster Windmill, on Willoughby Road (☎01205/352188; open Wed & Sat 11am–5pm, Sun 1–5pm, plus additional days in July & Aug). Built to grind corn in 1819, the windmill, with its five whopping sails, is still in full working order. You can inspect its grinding gears and/or buy the (organic) flour it churns out at the tea room, which serves a range of vegetarian and vegan meals, as well as a good selection of delicious cakes. The windmill is about ten minutes' walk northeast of the Market Place, beside the road to Horncastle.

Heckington

The village of **HECKINGTON**, twelve miles west of Boston and five east of Sleaford, has a tidy little centre that drapes around the church of **St Andrew**

(Mon–Sat 9am–5pm or dusk in winter; free), a splendid example of the Decorated style, with a pinnacled spire and elaborate canopied buttresses framing the flowing tracery of the windows. Inside, the original fourteenth-century chancel fittings have survived, including the battered tomb of the founder, Richard de Potesgrave, and an **Easter Sepulchre**, whose folksy and energetic carved figures are set against a dense undergrowth of foliage. The sepulchre, one of the finest in England, was built to accommodate the host between Good Friday and Easter morning. The **sedilia** is intriguing, too, boasting a cartoon strip of domestic scenes on the subject of food – a man eating fruit, a woman feeding the birds and suchlike. Heckington has one other attraction, its unique eight-sailed **windmill**, located a short stroll from the church and worth visiting when it's in operation (Easter to mid-July Thurs–Sun noon–5pm; mid-July to Aug daily noon–5pm; Sept to Easter Sun 2–5pm; £1.50). Afterwards, you could pop over to a good old local, the *Nag's Head*, for a pint.

On the Skegness–Grantham line, Heckington **train station** is in the centre near the windmill.

Spalding

Built beside the treacle-like banks of the River Welland thirteen miles south of Boston, pocket-sized **SPALDING** is every inch an agricultural town, marooned amidst a great chunk of fen farmland. Its centre has few pretensions, but the wealthy merchants who once controlled things around here did build a string of portentous, riverside mansions. One of them, **Ayscoughfee Hall** (pronounced "Ascuffee"; March–Oct Mon–Fri 10am–5pm, Sat 10am–5pm & Sun 11am–5pm; Nov–Feb Mon–Fri 10am–5pm; free), on the east side of the river – on Churchgate – is a much modified medieval wool merchant's house that has been cleaned up to accommodate an enjoyable **museum**. This focuses on the history of the Fens and the culture of its people, but there's also a stuffed bird room illustrating local birdlife and temporary art exhibitions.

The hall doubles as the **tourist office** (same times; ☎01775/725468) and they have a small cachet of **B&Bs**. It's unlikely you'll want to stay, but the *Bedford Court Guest House* is first-rate, occupying a handsome mullioned villa just set back from the street – and the west bank of the Welland – at 10 London Rd (☎01775/722377; no credit cards; ❷); all four of the commodious guest rooms are en suite. Spalding is at its liveliest during the three-day **flower festival**, held at the beginning of May.

Gedney and Long Sutton

Travelling east from Spalding (possibly on the way to Norfolk; see Chapter 000), it's eleven miles to the scattered hamlet of **GEDNEY**, where the massive tower of **St Mary Magdalene** (daily dawn to dusk) intercepts the fenland landscape. Seen from a distance, the church seems almost magical – or at least mystical – its imposing lines so much in contrast with its fen-flat surroundings. Close up, the nave is simply beautiful, its blend of Early English and Perpendicular features culminating in a phalanx of elongated windows. Locals keep the church in fine fettle and buff the Renaissance alabaster effigies of Adlard and Cassandra Welby, facing each other on the south wall near the chancel.

There's more ecclesiastical excitement just a mile or two to the east in **LONG SUTTON**, a modest farming centre that limps along the road until it reaches its trim Market Place. Here, the church of **St Mary** (daily dawn to dusk) has preserved many of its Norman features with its arcaded tower supporting the oldest lead spire in the country, dating from around 1200. Look out also for the striking medieval stained glass in the chancel aisle. Long Sutton once lay on the edge of the five-mile-wide mouth of the River Nene, where it emptied into The Wash. This was the most treacherous part of the road from Lincoln to Norfolk, and locals had to guide travellers across the obstacle on horseback, though not always without mishap. In 1205, King John was caught by the rising tide, losing his jewels and baggage train in the quicksands somewhere between Long Sutton and Terrington St Clement in Norfolk. In 1831, the River Nene was embanked and then spanned with a wooden bridge at **SUTTON BRIDGE**, a hamlet just two miles east of Long Sutton. The present swing bridge, with its nifty central tower, was completed in 1894.

The marshy shores of **The Wash** remain wild and desolate. There are several access points, but the best is near Long Sutton – from the car park on the east side of the mouth of the Nene. This marks the start of the Peter Scott Walk running east along – or near – the seashore to King's Lynn (see p.572). You'll need proper maps and hiking tackle. Incidentally, the walk is named after the famous naturalist, who spent long periods in a renovated lighthouse near the mouth of the Nene.

Stamford

STAMFORD is delightful, a handsome little limestone town of yellow-grey seventeenth- and eighteenth-century buildings edging narrow streets that slope up from the River Welland. It was here that the Romans forded this important river, establishing a fortified outpost that the Danes subsequently selected for one of their regional capitals. Later the town became a centre of the medieval wool and cloth trade, its wealthy merchants funding a series of almshouses known as "**callises**" – after Calais, the English-occupied port through which most of them traded. Indeed, Stamford **cloth** became famous throughout Europe for its quality and durability, a reputation confirmed when Cardinal Wolsey used it for the tents of the "Field of the Cloth of Gold", the grand conference between Henry VIII and Francis I of France held outside Calais in 1520. Stamford was also the home of William Cecil, Elizabeth's chief minister, who built his splendid mansion, Burghley House, close by. The town survived the collapse of the wool trade, prospering as an inland port after the Welland was made navigable to the sea in 1570, and, in the eighteenth century, as a staging point on the Great North Road from London. More recently, Stamford escaped the three main threats to old English towns – the Industrial Revolution, wartime bombing and postwar development – and was designated the country's first Conservation Area in 1967. Thanks to this, its unspoilt streets readily lend themselves to period drama- and film-making.

The town centre

Above all, it's the harmony of Stamford's architecture that pleases, rather than any specific sight. There are, nevertheless, a handful of buildings of some special interest amongst the web of narrow streets that make up the town's compact centre, beginning with the church of **St Mary** (no regular opening hours), set beside a pristine close of proud Georgian buildings on St Mary's Street. The church, with its splendid spire, has a small, airy interior, which incorporates the Corpus Christi chapel, whose intricately embossed, painted and panelled roof dates from the 1480s.

From St Mary's, several lanes thread through to the carefully preserved High Street, where Ironmonger Street leads north again to Broad Street, wide and handsome and the site of the **Stamford Museum** (April–Sept Mon–Sat

10am–5pm, Sun 2–5pm; Oct–March Mon–Sat 10am–5pm; free). This features a tasteless exhibit comparing the American midget Tom Thumb with **Daniel Lambert**, the Leicester fat man who died at Stamford in 1809, aged 39 and weighing 52st 11lb (336kg). After Lambert's death his clothes were displayed in a local inn, which Tom Thumb, otherwise Charles Stratton, visited several times to perform a few party tricks, such as standing in Lambert's waistcoat armhole. Nearby, also on Broad Street, is **Browne's Hospital**, the most extensive of the town's almshouses, dating from the late fifteenth century, and from here it's a few paces more to Red Lion Square, which is overseen by **All Saints'** (daily dawn to dusk; free). Several centuries in the making, this church is a happy amalgamation of Early English and Perpendicular features that takes full advantage of its position, perched on a grassy mound. Entry is via the south porch, itself an ornate structure with a fine crocketed gable, and, although most of the interior is routinely Victorian, the carved capitals are of great delicacy and there's an engaging folkloric carving of the Last Supper behind the high altar.

High Street St Martin's and Burghley House

Down the hill from St Mary's, across the Welland on High Street St Martin's, is the **George Hotel**, a splendid old coaching inn whose Georgian facade supports one end of the gallows that span the street – not a warning to criminals, but an advertising hoarding. Just along – and across – the street, the plain and sombre, late fifteenth-century church of **St Martin** (daily 9.30am–4pm; free) shelters the magnificent tombs of the lords Burghley, with a recumbent William Cecil carved beneath twin canopies, holding his rod of office and with a lion at his feet. Just behind, the early eighteenth-century effigies of John Cecil and his wife show the couple as Roman aristocrats, propped up on their elbows, she to gaze at him, John to stare across the nave commandingly.

From St Martin's church, it's a fifteen-minute stroll south along High Street St Martin's to **Burghley House** (April–Oct daily 11am–4.30pm; viewing by guided tours only, except Sat & Sun pm; £6.80), an extravagant Elizabethan mansion standing in parkland landscaped by Capability Brown; you can also drive there along Barnack Road – just follow the signs. Completed in 1587 after twenty-two years' work, the house sports a mellow-yellow ragstone exterior, embellished by dainty cupolas, a pyramidal clock tower and skeletal balustrading, all to a plan by **William Cecil**, the long-serving adviser to Elizabeth I. A shrewd and cautious man, Cecil steered his queen through all sorts of difficulties, from the wars against Spain to the execution of Mary, Queen of Scots, vindicating Elizabeth's assessment of his character when she appointed him secretary of state in 1558: "You will not be corrupted with any manner of gifts, and will be faithful to the state."

With the notable exception of the Tudor kitchen, little remains of Burghley's Elizabethan interior. Instead, the house bears the heavy hand of John, fifth Lord Burghley, who toured France and Italy in the late seventeenth century, commissioning furniture, statuary and tapestries, as well as buying up old Florentine and Venetian paintings, such as Paolo Veronese's *Zebedee's Wife Petitioning our Lord*. To provide a suitable setting for his old masters, John brought in Antonio Verrio and his assistant Louis Laguerre, who between them covered many of Burghley's walls and ceilings with frolicking gods and goddesses. These gaudy and gargantuan murals are at their most engulfing in the Heaven Room, an artfully painted classical temple that adjoins the Hell Staircase, where the entrance to the inferno is through the gaping mouth of a cat. Have a close look also at the fine portraits in the Pagoda Room, in particular the querulous Elizabeth I and a sublimely self-confident Henry VIII by Joos van Cleve.

Finally, the Stamford Shakespeare Company spends June, July and August performing out at **Tolethorpe Hall**, a graceful Elizabethan mansion not far from town. The troupe performs out in the open, but the audience is safely covered by a vast open-fronted marquee; call ☎01780/756133 for details.

Practicalities

With frequent services from Peterborough and Oakham, Stamford **train station** is five minutes' walk from the town centre, which lies just to the north across the river. The **bus station** is on the west side of the centre, on Sheepmarket, off All Saints' Street. The **tourist office** is in the centre inside Stamford Arts Centre at 27 St Mary's St (April–Oct Mon–Sat 9.30am–5pm, Sun 11am–4pm; Nov–March closed Sun; ☎01780/755611, ◉www.skdc.com).

Stamford has several charming **hotels**, the most celebrated of which is the delightful *George Hotel*, 71 High Street St Martin's (☎01780/750750, ◉www .georgehotelofstamford.com; ❼), an old and cleverly remodelled coaching inn with flagstone floors and antique furnishings, where the most appealing rooms overlook the cobbled courtyard. Just along the street is the attractive *Garden House Hotel* (☎01780/763359, ◉www.gardenhousehotel.com; ❺), which occupies a tastefully modernized eighteenth-century building with twenty smart bedrooms. Stamford also possesses a clutch of **B&Bs**. As ever, the tourist office has the full list, but one especially good place is *Martin's*, 20 High Street St Martin's (☎01780/752106; no credit cards; ❹), a Georgian house whose three spacious guest rooms are immaculately maintained and tastefully decorated. Breakfasts are delicious; guests have access to the walled garden and dinner is served by prior request.

For **food**, it has to be the *George Hotel* – either in the formal and expensive restaurant, where the emphasis is on British ingredients served in imaginative ways, or in the moderately priced and informal Garden Lounge. There's delicious and inexpensive bar food, too, served in the York Bar at lunchtimes.

Grantham and around

GRANTHAM, midway between Stamford and Lincoln, was once a major staging point on the Great North Road from London, but today its lengthy main street is no more than a provincial thoroughfare flanked by an unappetizing combination of modern blocks and Victorian red-brick. The town's more successful days are recalled by two ancient inns towards the north end of the main street, near the **Market Place**. These are the stone-fronted *Angel & Royal*, founded by the Knights Templar in the twelfth century and where Richard III signed the Duke of Buckingham's death warrant, and the *George*, where Charles Dickens' Nicholas Nickleby stopped on his way to Dotheboys Hall – and now guzzled up into a shopping centre. Grantham's present pride and joy is the church of **St Wulfram** (daily dawn to dusk; free), set within its own close just east of the Market Place. St Wulfram's most obvious feature is its 282ft central spire, a fourteenth-century construction whose angular lines are emphasized by pointed blind arcading, slim window openings and the narrowest of columns. Many reckon this to be the most perfect steeple in the country. The interior of the church was mucked up by the Victorians, but highlights include the sinuous window tracery and the late sixteenth-century, 150-volume **chained library** (May–Sept Mon 10am–noon & 2–4pm, Thurs & Fri 2–4pm) above the south porch. The high altar is of interest, too, not for itself, but because its position prompted a bitter wrangle in 1627. Believing the altar should be more conspicuous, the High Church party turned it round to look down the nave, but the Puritans objected and came to move it back again. The resulting brawl, something of a cause célèbre, hardened attitudes in the run-up to the Civil War.

Beside the church, on narrow Church Street, is the original sixteenth-century **classroom** in which **Isaac Newton** received his initial education in the 1650s – there's a plaque. In addition, there's a statue of the great physicist and mathematician outside the **Guildhall**, a short walk to the south along Castlegate, which runs behind St Wulfram's, and a room of mementoes, including a plaster-cast death mask, in the adjacent **museum** (Mon–Sat 10am–5pm; free). The museum also has a display on **Margaret Thatcher**, the former Prime Minister who was born in Grantham in 1925. In a moment of gay abandon, Mrs Thatcher gave several of her dresses to the museum, though her absurdist handbags and threatening hairstyle were always more memorable. Her childhood home is up at the top of the main street at 2 North St.

Grantham **train station** is ten minutes' walk from the Market Place: follow Station Road north to the roundabout and veer right along Westgate. The **bus station** is also to the south of the Market Place, but a little nearer, just off the main drag. From the Market Place, it's a short walk south along the main street to the Guildhall, part of which is given over to the **tourist office** (Mon–Sat 9.30am–5pm; ☎01476/406166), who have a list of local **B&Bs**, though frankly there's precious little reason to hang around. For **food**, *Ask*, 58 High St, does a good line in reasonably priced Italian food in pleasantly modern surrounding. For a **drink**, the *Beehive Inn*, 11 Castlegate, has a good range of beers and it also boasts its own hive of South African bees, fixed to the tree outside.

Belton House

The honey-coloured limestone facade of **Belton House** (April–Oct Wed–Sun 1–5.30pm; gardens & park from 11am; £5.40; NT), three miles northeast of Grantham beside the A607, is Restoration design at its finest, its delicate symmetry enhanced by formal gardens and surrounded by rolling parkland. Belton was built in the 1680s for a local family of lawyer-landowners, the Brownlows, whose subsequent climb up the aristocratic ladder prompted them to remodel the interior of their home in the sumptuous Neoclassical style of the late eighteenth century. Entry is through the Marble Hall, where the intricate limewood carvings that remain Belton's most distinctive feature frame a sequence of (mostly family) portraits, including three by Reynolds. One of them and several more in the adjacent **saloon** are thought to be the work of **Grinling Gibbons**, the great Rotterdam-born woodcarver and sculptor. Belton is also noted for its pastel-shaded, Adam-style plasterwork ceilings and, on display in the Chapel Drawing Room, a pair of splendid tapestries, which, despite their Indian and Japanese themes, were made in John Vanderbank's workshop in Soho, London. The surrounding **park**, dotted with aristocratic bits and pieces – from a Gothic wilderness ruin to a boathouse – is noted for its woodland walks.

It's easy to reach Belton by **bus** from Grantham on weekdays, with service #601 making the ten-minute trip every hour or two.

Woolsthorpe Manor

The birthplace and family home of Sir Isaac Newton, **Woolsthorpe Manor** (April–Oct Wed–Sun 1–5.30pm; £3.30; NT) lies seven miles south of Grantham, just off the A1 in the hamlet of **WOOLSTHORPE-BY-COLSTERWORTH**. The house is a pleasantly modest affair of mullioned windows and heavy-beamed ceilings and this was where Newton (1642–1727) sat out the plague years of 1665–67 working on all manner of scientific theories. The apple orchard in front of the house contains a descendant of the illustrious tree whose apple dropped on Newton's head to such great, gravitational effect.

Travel Details

Buses

For information on all local and national bus services, contact Traveline: ☎ 0870/608 2 608 (daily 7am–9pm), ⓦ www.traveline.org.uk.

Trains

For information on all local and national rail services, contact National Rail Enquiries: ☎ 08457/48 49 50, ⓦ www.rail.co.uk.

Grantham to: Derby (hourly; 1hr); Lincoln (every 30min; 45min); London (hourly; 1hr 15min); Nottingham (every 30min; 35min); Skegness (hourly; 1hr 20min).

Leicester to: Birmingham (every 30min; 1hr); Coventry (hourly; 45min); Derby (hourly; 35min); Lincoln (hourly; 1hr 40min); London (every 30min; 1hr 30min); Market Harborough (every 1–2 hours; 15min); Melton Mowbray (hourly; 15min); Nottingham (every 30min; 20min); Oakham (hourly; 30min); Stamford (hourly; 50min).

Lincoln to: Birmingham (hourly; 3hr); Boston (hourly; 1hr); Cambridge (hourly; 1hr); Gainsborough (hourly; 20min); Grantham (every 30min; 45min); London (hourly; 2hr 15min); Leicester (hourly; 1hr 30min); London (hourly; 2hr 15min); Newark (hourly; 25min); Nottingham (hourly; 45min); Peterborough (hourly; 1hr 20min); Skegness (hourly; 1hr 40min); Spalding (every 1–2 hours; 1hr).

Northampton to: Birmingham (every 30min; 1hr); Coventry (hourly; 40min); London Euston (every 30min; 1hr 10min–1hr 40min).

Nottingham to: Leicester (every 30min; 30min); Lincoln (hourly; 1hr 15min); London (hourly; 1hr 40min); Newark (hourly; 30min).

Stamford to: Cambridge (hourly; 1hr 20min); Leicester (hourly; 40min); Oakham (hourly; 10min); Peterborough (hourly; 15min).

The Northwest

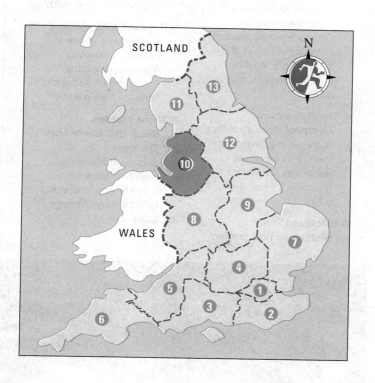

CHAPTER 10 # Highlights

✳ **Café society, Manchester** From breakfast croissant to late-night drinks, Manchester's café-bars set the tone for this happening city. See p.757

✳ **City walls, Chester** A two-mile walk around the ancient walls of Chester makes a great introduction to one of the country's most historic destinations. See p.765

✳ **The Philharmonic, Liverpool** Victorian pubs don't get any better than this – the city's most elaborately decorated boozer is a must. See p.788

✳ **Blackpool Tower** Blackpool's bold answer to the Eiffel Tower lights up the skyline of the UK's favourite resort. See p.789

✳ **Lancaster Castle** From the dungeons to the ornate court rooms, the castle tour is a historical tour-de-force. See p.797

✳ **Heysham Village** Spend an afternoon at one of the region's unsung gems, exploring the Saxon church and pretty cottages. See p.802

✳ **Norse crosses, Maughold, Isle of Man** The ancient carved crosses at Maughold's isolated church are a powerful reminder of the Island's Norse heritage. See p.810

⑩

The Northwest

Within the **northwest** of England lie some of the ugliest and some of the most beautiful parts of the country. The least attractive zones of this region are to be found in the sprawl connecting the country's third and sixth largest conurbations, Manchester and Liverpool, but even here the picture isn't unrelievedly bleak, as the cities themselves have an ingratiating appeal. **Manchester**, in particular, surprises many who don't expect to see beyond its dour, industrial heritage. Where once only a handful of Victorian Gothic buildings lent any grace to the cityscape, Manchester today has been completely transformed by a rebuilding programme that puts it in the vanguard of modern British urban design. Quite apart from a clutch of top-class visitor attractions – including The Lowry and the new Imperial War Museum North – where Manchester really scores is in the buzz of its thriving café and club scene, which places it at the leading edge of the country's youth culture. **Liverpool**, set on the Mersey estuary, is perhaps less appealing at first glance, though Georgian town houses, grand civic buildings, its twin cathedrals and a burgeoning café scene soon change perceptions. At the redundant docks that once made the city's fortune, many of the old warehouses and buildings have been redeveloped as part of the Albert Dock scheme, housing a fine swathe of museums, including the northern outpost of the Tate Gallery.

The hills, which form the southern tip of the Pennine range, melt away to the west into undulating, pastoral **Cheshire**, a county of rolling green countryside and country manor houses, interspersed with dairy farms from whose churns emerge tons of crumbly white Cheshire cheese. The county town, **Chester**, with its complete circuit of town walls and partly Tudor centre, is as alluring as any of the country's northern towns, capturing the essence of what has always been one of England's wealthiest rural counties. It's easily the main place of interest in the region, though the villages of the **Cheshire Plain** are set in a landscape that conjures archetypal images of pastoral England.

Accommodation price codes

Throughout this guide, hotel and B&B accommodation is priced on a scale of ❶ to ❾, the number indicating the **lowest price** you could expect to pay per night in that establishment for a **double room** in high season. The prices indicated by the codes are as follows:

❶ under £40	❹ £60–70	❼ £110–150
❷ £40–50	❺ £70–90	❽ £150–200
❸ £50–60	❻ £90–110	❾ over £200

© Crown copyright

Lancashire, which historically lay directly to the north of Cheshire, reached industrial prominence in the last century primarily due to the cotton-mill towns around Manchester and to the thriving port of Liverpool. Today, neither of those cities is part of the county, having been excised when England's first substantial county boundary changes since the Domesday Book were enacted in 1974. The urban counties of Merseyside and Greater Manchester chopped off the southern section of Lancashire while Cumbria grabbed a substantial northern chunk leaving Lancashire little more than half its former size. Its oldest town, and major commercial and administrative centre, is **Preston** – home of the national museum of England's national game, football – though tourists are perhaps more inclined to linger in the charming towns and villages of the nearby **Ribble Valley**. Meanwhile, along the coast to the west and north of the major cities stretches a line of **resorts** – from Southport to **Morecambe** – which once formed the mainstay of the northern British holiday trade before their client base disappeared on cheaper, sunnier holidays to Florida and the Mediterranean. Only **Blackpool** is really worth visiting for its own sake, a rip-roaring resort which has stayed at the top of its game by supplying undemanding entertainment with more panache than its neighbours. For anything more culturally invigorating you'll have to continue north to the historically important city of **Lancaster**, with its Tudor castle. Finally, the semi-autonomous **Isle of Man**, only twenty-five miles off the coast and served by ferries from Liverpool and Heysham (or short flights from Liverpool), provides a terrain almost as rewarding as that of the Lake District but without the seasonal overcrowding.

Getting around

Manchester's international **airport** picks the city out as a major point of arrival in England, and there are direct train services from the airport to Liverpool, Blackpool, Lancaster, Leeds and York, as well as to Manchester itself. Both Manchester and Liverpool are well served by **trains**, with plentiful connections to the Midlands and London, and up the west coast to Scotland. There's also a frequent rail and bus service between both cities, and from each to Chester, allowing an easy triangular loop between Greater Manchester, Merseyside and Cheshire. The major east–west rail lines in the region are the direct routes between Manchester, Leeds and York, and between Blackpool, Bradford, Leeds and York. In addition, the Morecambe/Lancaster–Leeds line slips through the Yorkshire Dales (with possible connections at Skipton for the famous Settle–Carlisle line; see p.911); further south, the Manchester–Sheffield line provides a rail approach to the Peak District. Regional **rover tickets** (3 days, £40; 7 days, £50) are available for a week's unlimited travel in the northwest or in the "coast and peaks" region (basically between Liverpool, Manchester, the Peak District and North Wales).

Manchester

Few cities in the world have embraced social change so heartily as **MANCHESTER**. From engine of the Industrial Revolution to test-bed of contemporary urban design, the city has no realistic provincial English rival. Its domestic dominance expresses itself in various ways, most swaggeringly in the success of Manchester United, the richest football club in Britain, but also in a thriving music and cultural scene that has given birth to world-beaters as

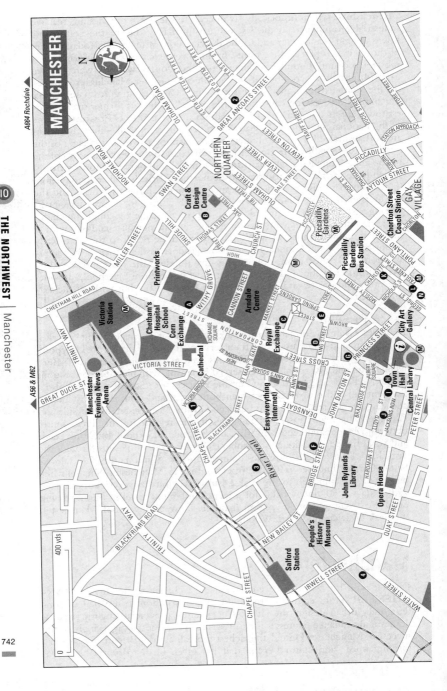

M Metrolink (tram) lines
M Metrolink (tram) lines

Piccadilly Station

LONDON ST
FAIRFIELD STREET
DOWNING STREET
WHITWORTH STREET
STREET
CANAL STREET
SACKVILLE STREET
BLOOM ST
MAJOR ST
PRINCESS STREET
PORTLAND STREET
CHARLES STREET
MANCUNIAN WAY
GROSVENOR STREET
UPPER BROOK STREET
BROOK STREET
OXFORD ROAD
BRUNSWICK STREET

Upper Brook Street

Aquatics Centre

University of Manchester

Manchester Museum

Whitworth Art Gallery; Rusholme, Didsbury.

17 & 18

Manchester Metropolitan University

Cavendish Hall

RNCM

CAMBRIDGE STREET
BOUNDARY LANE

Palace Theatre
The Cornerhouse
Dancehouse Theatre

WEST WHITWORTH STREET
OXFORD ROAD
OXFORD STREET

Oxford Road Station

The Green Room

Bridgewater Hall

Rochdale Canal

ST PETER'S SQUARE

Free Trade Hall

LOWER MOSLEY STREET
WINDMILL STREET

PETER'S FIELDS

G-Mex Centre

GREAT BRIDGEWATER STREET

International Convention Centre

Museum of Science & Industry

DEANSGATE

Great Northern

Upper Campfield Market

Roman Fort

CASTLEFIELD

LIVERPOOL ROAD

DUKE ST

WHITWORTH STREET

MEDLOCK STREET

MANCUNIAN WAY

HULME

PRINCESS ROAD

BONSALL STREET

Deansgate Station

CHESTER ROAD

POTATO WHARF

M63 & M66 Altrincham

Chorlton

A56 Chester; 15 & 16

A56 Chester,

8

8

M63 & M66 Altrincham

© Crown copyright

ACCOMMODATION

Castlefield Hotel	10
Elton Bank Hotel	17
Grafton Hotel	18
Holiday Inn Express	8
Jury's Inn	13
The Lowry Hotel	3
Malmaison	5
Manchester Backpackers Hostel	15
Manchester YHA	9
Midland Crowne Plaza Hotel	6
The Ox	11
The Palace Hotel	14
Peppers	16
Premier Lodge	1 & 7
Travel Inn	4
Victoria and Albert Hotel	4
Woodies	2

RESTAURANTS

Armenian Taverna	G
Café Istanbul	F
Dimitri's	O
Little Yang Sing	K
Livebait	I
The Market Restaurant	B
Le Petit Blanc	D
Penang Village	L
Reform	E
Simply Heathcote's	J
Stock	C
Tampopo	H
Wagamama	A
Wong Chu	M
Yang Sing	N

diverse as the Hallé Orchestra and Oasis. Moreover, the city's cutting-edge concert halls, theatres, clubs and café society are boosted by England's largest student population and a blossoming gay community whose spending-power has created a pioneering Gay Village. For inspiration, Manchester's planners look to Barcelona – another revitalized industrial powerhouse – and, like Barcelona, the promise of a major sports event has powered much of the recent urban regeneration. The city didn't get the Olympics, though it wasn't for the want of trying, but instead landed the 2002 **Commonwealth Games** (see box below).

Despite a **history** stretching back to Roman times, and pockets of surviving medieval and Georgian influence, Manchester is first and foremost a Victorian manufacturing city with the imposing streets and buildings to match. Its rapid growth was the equal of any flowering of the Industrial Revolution – from little more than a village in 1750 to the world's major cotton-milling centre in only a hundred years. The spectacular rise of **Cottonopolis**, as it became known, came from the production of competitively priced imitations of expensive Indian calicoes, using machines evolved from Arkwright's first steam-powered cotton mill, which opened in 1783. The rapid industrialization of the area brought prosperity for a few but a life of misery for the majority, and the discontent of the poor came to a head in 1819 when eleven people were killed at **Peterloo**, in what began as a peaceful workers' demonstration against the oppressive Corn Laws. Exploitation had worsened still further by the time the 23-year-old Friedrich Engels came here in 1842 to work in his father's cotton plant, and the suffering he witnessed – recorded in his *Condition of the Working Class in England* – was a seminal influence on his later collaboration with Karl Marx, the *Communist Manifesto*.

Waterways and railway viaducts form the matrix into which the city's principal buildings have been bedded – as early as 1772 the Duke of Bridgewater had a canal cut to connect the city to the coal mines at Worsley, and the **world's first passenger rail line**, connecting Manchester with Liverpool, was

The Commonwealth Games

The seventeenth **Commonwealth Games** take place in Manchester from 25 July to 4 August 2002, with 5000 athletes from 72 nations competing for medals in fourteen individual and three team sports. The new 38,000-seater **City of Manchester Stadium**, in the east of the city, is the centrepiece of the games, staging the opening and closing ceremonies, as well as the athletics events and the Rugby Sevens competition. It's part of a wider **Sportcity** development, incorporating the **Indoor Tennis Centre** and **National Squash Centre**. The **Aquatics Centre**, in the city centre, has been purpose-built for the swimming competitions; other events are at a variety of existing and refurbished venues, including the National Cycling Centre (cycling), G-Mex (gymnastics, judo and wrestling), International Convention Centre (weightlifting), Manchester Evening News Arena (netball and boxing), Belle Vue Leisure Centre (hockey) and Salford Quays (triathlon). A million tickets will be available for events, with current details contained on the official **website**: ⓦwww .commonwealthgames.com. Although many tickets are expected to be sold well In advance, some will be held back until box-office sales start in early June 2002 while others will available on the day at certain events. Ticket prices run from £5 to £30, though some events – particularly mountain-biking, the marathon, road-racing and walking – will be free. An accompanying carnival will turn the city centre into a non-stop party for the duration – more details can be obtained from the Manchester Visitor Centre (see p.746).

opened in 1830. The **Manchester Ship Canal**, constructed to entice ocean-going vessels into Manchester and away from burgeoning Liverpool, was completed in 1894, and played a crucial part in reviving Manchester's competitiveness.

Within sixty years, though, Manchester was on its uppers, with the docks, mills and canals in dangerous decline. The traditional image of the struggling post-industrial city was of empty shells of mills and factories, and rows of back-to-back houses whose slate roofs and cobbled back alleys glistened in the seemingly ever-present rain – an image perpetuated, to an extent, by the popularity of Britain's longest-running TV soap opera, *Coronation Street*. Sporadic efforts were made to pull Manchester out of the economic doldrums of the 1960s and 1970s, but the main engine of change turned out to be the devastating **IRA bomb**, which exploded in June 1996 and wiped out much of the city's commercial infrastructure. The largest explosion on the mainland since the war devastated the area around the Arndale Centre and the Royal Exchange. Rather than simply patch up the buildings, the planning authorities embarked on an ambitious rebuilding scheme, which also came to embrace the Commonwealth Games' facilities and innovative millennium design projects. Entire new districts have taken shape as once-blighted areas along the canals are reclaimed for retail and residential use – the downtown areas have seen a surging population increase as city-centre living in converted warehouses has become increasingly viable. Meanwhile inner-city suburbs such as Hulme and Moss Side, often scarred by gang violence and drug dealing, are at last giving tenants a say in the design of new housing estates and shopping centres, and encouraging the development of local businesses.

Peterloo

Agitation for social and parliamentary reform in the early nineteenth century was concentrated in the booming industrial cities, led by radical orators, among them Henry Hunt, who addressed massed rallies of working men and women. Such a meeting was planned for **St Peter's Fields** in Manchester for August 16, 1819, with Hunt as main speaker, and though rumours spread throughout the city about the possibility of trouble, the local magistrates seemed content to let the rally take place. In the weeks before the event, many local people practised marching in orderly file so as to look respectable on the day; on the day itself, a crowd of almost 80,000 turned up in its Sunday best, with women and children much in evidence – hardly the revolutionary rabble feared by the government critics of the reform movement. But as Hunt began to speak the magistrates decided to stop him, sending in their special constables (mostly recruited from the ranks of local businessmen) to arrest him. As pandemonium erupted, Hunt gave himself up to avoid further trouble, but with the special constables now under siege from the crowd, the yeomanry were sent in.

Panic broke out as people tried to escape from the swords of the mounted soldiers, who cleared the fields in ten minutes. In what the press dubbed "**Peterloo**", 400 people were wounded, over a hundred by sword cuts, the rest by the stampeding crowd, and the final reckoning saw eleven dead, including two women and one child. Home Secretary Lord Sidmouth later congratulated the Manchester authorities on their handling of the situation; the government passed the draconian Six Acts, restricting the right of public meeting; while Hunt was released on bail. Protests were widespread, even among the government's own supporters, and Peterloo became the catalyst for yet more agitation, culminating in the 1832 Reform Act and the subsequent rise of the Chartist movement.

Arrival, information and city transport

A direct rail link into the city makes **Manchester Airport**, ten miles south of the city, an increasingly popular point of entry into Britain. Trains to Piccadilly (every 15min 5.15am–10.15pm, reduced service through the night; 25min) cost £2.35, £2.80 on weekdays before 9.30am. A taxi from the airport to the centre costs £12–15. There are tourist information offices in the arrivals halls of Terminal 1 (daily 8am–9pm; ☎0161/436 3344) and Terminal 2 (daily 7.30am–12.30am; ☎0161/489 6412); and a Travel Shop for public-transport enquiries in Terminal 1 (Mon–Sat 5.30am–9pm, Sun 7am–9pm).

Manchester's three main **train stations** form the points of a triangle that encloses much of the city centre. National mainline trains all pull into **Piccadilly Station**, facing London Road, on the east side, from where you can walk a few hundred yards west into the city's core, via Piccadilly Gardens (or catch the free Centreline bus #4 from outside the station, every 10min, not Sunday, to all main city-centre locations).

Regional train routes to points south, east and west call both at Piccadilly and at **Oxford Road Station**, south of the centre, while **Victoria Station**, in the north, services the northern hinterland and Bradford. The city's Metrolink tram service connects Piccadilly station (the platform is underneath the train station) to Victoria and G-Mex – the latter being the best stop if you're heading straight for Castlefield. National Express and most long-distance buses use **Chorlton Street Coach Station**, a few hundred yards west of Piccadilly train station. Local and some regional buses might drop you instead in nearby Piccadilly Gardens.

The **Manchester Visitor Centre** in the town hall extension on Lloyd Street, facing central St Peter's Square (Mon–Sat 10am–5.30pm, Sun 11am–4pm; ☎0161/234 3157 or 0906/8715 533; ⓦwww.manchester.gov.uk /visitorcentre), offers a free map of the city centre, the handy *City Guide* and various other useful leaflets and brochures. You can also buy National Express bus tickets, check rail timetables, and book guided tours and accommodation. There are direct trams to the Visitor Centre (St Peter's Square stop) from Piccadilly and Victoria stations. To find out **what's on** in the city, buy the fortnightly *City Life* listings and reviews magazine (ⓦwww.citylife.co.uk), from any newsstand, or check out the Friday edition of the *Manchester Evening News* (ⓦwww.manchesteronline.co.uk).

For bus, train and airport enquiry numbers for **departures from the city**, see "Listings", p.764.

City transport

The city centre is compact enough to cover on foot, though buses will be needed for Oxford Road and its continuation Wilmslow Road, which runs to the curry restaurants of Rusholme; and you'll have to take the tram out to Salford Quays. **Piccadilly Gardens Bus Station** is the hub of the urban bus network, though a new transport interchange at **Shudehill** (north of the Arndale Centre; due for completion by 2003) may affect the location of some routes. For Oxford and Wilmslow roads, use the stops at the bottom of Oxford Road by the Palace Hotel. **Information** about all services is available from the Travel Shop, in Piccadilly Gardens (Mon–Sat 7am–6pm, Sun 10am–6pm); or call the GMPTE Travel Line (☎0161/228 7811; daily 8am–8pm). Various bus companies ply the city-centre and suburban routes, though they are all accessible with a **Day Saver** ticket (£3), which gives unlimited travel on any city bus. There's also a seven-day Mega-Rider (£7) for travel on the network of

Stagecoach city and local buses, or the Wayfarer (£7), which allows 24 hours' unlimited travel throughout Greater Manchester and into the Peak District.

Metrolink (☎0161/205 2000) – the electric tram service – whisks through the city centre and out to the suburbs, linking Manchester with Bury, Salford Quays, Eccles and Altrincham (every 6–15min 6am–11.30pm). New stations are planned for the Shudehill transport interchange, the Eastlands Commonwealth Games stadium and the airport. Tickets for short hops run from 90p to £1.70, though (trips to Salford Quays aside) you're unlikely to use the system for getting around, unless you simply fancy the ride. There are stations at Piccadilly Station, Piccadilly Gardens, St Peter's Square, G-Mex, Market Street and Victoria Station.

Accommodation

There's been a boom in the number of city-centre **hotels**, particularly among the budget chains, which means you have a good chance of finding a smart, en-suite, motel-style room in central Manchester for around £50–60. Almost all the plusher hotels offer weekend reductions too – note that, during the week, breakfast isn't included at most of the pricier hotels. Cheaper **guesthouse** accommodation is concentrated some way out of the centre, mainly on the southern routes out of the city, where reasonably convenient places can be found and the bus services are good. **B&B** accommodation in private houses is easy to arrange, too, though again it won't be particularly central, which makes the city's well-located **YHA**, in Castlefield, a first-choice for most budget travellers – book it well in advance. If you use the Visitor Centre's **accommodation booking service**, you'll pay a fee, though their free *Accommodation Guide* lists most of the city's possibilities. There's no real peak **accommodation season**, though the city fills up during the many festivals and major events; it's also difficult to get a city-centre hotel room when Manchester United play at home.

Hotels, guest houses and B&Bs

Castlefield Hotel Liverpool Rd ☎0161/832 7073, ⓦwww.castlefield-hotel.co.uk. Redbrick, warehouse-style development in the Castlefield basin, opposite the Science and Industry museum. Nicely appointed rooms, and boasting attached leisure club and pool (free to guests). ❺, ❹ at weekends.

Elton Bank Hotel 62 Platt Lane, Rusholme ☎0161/224 6449, ⓦwww.eltonbank.com. Two miles from the city, overlooking Platt Fields Park, this small family-run hotel is a bit floral and old-fashioned, but is convenient for Rusholme's curry houses and only a quick bus ride from the centre – get off at Hardy's Well pub on Wilmslow Road. No credit cards. ❷

Grafton Hotel 56–58 Grafton St, Rusholme ☎0161/273 3092. Six knocked-through terraced houses by the medical school, south of the university, off Oxford Road. Regular buses make the short trip into town; and there's a bar. No credit cards. ❷

Holiday Inn Express Waterfront Quay, Salford Quays ☎0161/868 1000 or 0800/897121, ⓦwww.hiexpress.com. Reasonably sized rooms in a great Quays location, convenient for The Lowry or even Old Trafford – book ahead for a view of the "Theatre of Dreams" from your window. The en-suite bathrooms have showers; continental breakfast included. ❹

Jury's Inn 56 Great Bridgewater St ☎0161/953 8888, ⓦwww.jurys.com. Very handy location – by Bridgewater Hall – for this large, 265-room, no-fuss budget hotel. Rates are room only, but you're no distance from any number of decent cafés; special weekend deals can bring the price down even further. ❹, ❷ at weekends.

The Lowry Hotel 50 Dearman's Place, Chapel Wharf, Salford ☎0161/827 4000 or 833 4545, ⓦwww.rfhotels.com. Manchester's first five-star hotel sits, exuding class, on the banks of the River Irwell, resplendent in its contemporary finery. Room rates are hideously expensive (up to £300 for a riverside view), but you get all mod cons, excellent levels of service, health centre, sauna and gym, and a Marco Pierre White dining room. ❾

Malmaison Piccadilly ☎0161/278 1000, ⓦwww.malmaison.com. An ornate Edwardian facade given sleek interior lines and contemporary design from the Malmaison group. It's just a couple of minutes from the train station. There's a gym, jacuzzi and sauna, bar and brasserie, though breakfast costs extra. Weekend discounts depend on availability. **7**

Midland Crowne Plaza Hotel Peter St ☎0161/236 3333, ✆www.crowneplaza.com. Once the terminus hotel for Central Station (now G-Mex) and the place where Rolls met Royce for the first time, this building is the apotheosis of Edwardian style. The bars and public rooms impress most, though there's a full raft of leisure facilities and weekend reductions are sometimes available – which is the only time breakfast is included in the room rate. **8**

The Ox 71 Liverpool Rd ☎0161/839 7740, ✆www.theox.co.uk. Nine pleasant rooms above a traditional, well-run pub opposite the Science and Industry Museum and very handy for the Castlefield bars. The food is good too; breakfast is extra (£2–6, depending on what you have). **2**

The Palace Hotel Oxford St ☎0161/288 1111, ✆www.principalhotels.co.uk. An Alfred Waterhouse glazed-tile extravaganza (formerly the Refuge Assurance HQ), with an equally magnificent interior, opposite the Cornerhouse arts centre. It's a business visitors' stalwart with no leisure facilities apart from the bar and restaurant. Good weekend discounts (when breakfast is included in the price). **7**, **6** at weekends.

Premier Lodge 7–11 Lower Mosley St ☎0870/700 1476; and North Tower, Victoria Bridge St, Salford, ☎0870/700 1488; both ✆www.premierlodge.com. Good-value, city-centre, motel-style rooms and comfort from the Premier Lodge chain. The first is near G-Mex, the second near Deansgate, and there are several other lodges scattered about Greater Manchester and one at the airport. **2**

Travel Inn Oxford St ☎0870/242 8000, ✆www.travelinn.co.uk. New city-centre location for the budget Travel Inn, offering decently equipped rooms at great rates (breakfast not included). A couple of large bars occupy the same building – at weekends, check your room is away from the noise. Parking available nearby. **3**

Victoria and Albert Hotel Water St, Castlefield ☎0161/832 1188, ✆www.lemeridien-hotels.com. Superb restoration job for a warehouse on the River Irwell, with exposed beams, pipes and brick-work part of the interior fabric – all the rooms are named after TV productions (Granada TV offices are just over the way), and there's a good bar and restaurant. Parking available. **7**, **6** at weekends.

Hostels and student halls

Manchester Backpackers Hostel 64 Cromwell Rd, Stretford ☎0161/865 9296 or 07711/556157, ✆www.ckpackers.freeserve.co.uk. Attractive Victorian terrace house two miles out of the centre, with walled garden backing onto a park; take Metrolink to Stretford, or it's a ten-minute walk from leafy Chorlton which has regular buses into the city. Laundry facilities, kitchen, TV lounge and pool table. The small dorm provides the cheapest accommodation; en-suite twins/doubles also available. No credit cards.

Manchester YHA Potato Wharf, Castlefield ☎0161/839 9960, ✉manchester@yha.org.uk. Excellent hostel, overlooking the canal, opposite the Museum of Science and Industry. The en-suite rooms sleep one to four people (you can pay more to have the room to yourself) and the bunks convert into double beds; facilities for disabled people are available.

Peppers 17 Great Stone Rd, Stretford ☎0161/848 9770. Budget, self-catering accommodation in a terraced house, under ten minutes from the centre by Metrolink (to Old Trafford). Free tea and coffee; good rates for weekly or longer-term stays.

University accommodation University of Manchester/UMIST Central Accommodation Office, ☎0161/275 2888. Call for information about vacancies at the various university hostels (available during summer vacations). Office open Mon–Fri 9am–5pm.

Woodies 19 Blossom St, Ancoats ☎0161/228 3456. Independent backpackers' hostel, five minutes' walk from Piccadilly station and very handy for the Northern Quarter. There are around fifty beds in dorms, singles and doubles – bed-linen included – plus internet access, free tea and coffee, laundry and left-luggage facilities.

The City

If Manchester can be said to have a centre, it's **St Peter's Square** and the cluster of buildings focused on it – the Town Hall (with the Visitor Centre in its modern extension), Central Library and the Midland Hotel, originally built in the railway age for visitors to Britain's greatest industrial city. South of here, the former Central Station now functions as the **G-Mex** exhibition centre, with the Hallé orchestra's home, **Bridgewater Hall**, opposite; **Chinatown**

(Britain's largest) and the **Gay Village** are just a short walk to the east; while to the northeast, the revamped **Piccadilly Gardens** provides access to the so-called **Northern Quarter**, the funkiest of the regenerated inner-city areas. To the southwest is the **Castlefield** district, site of the **Museum of Science and Industry**. Eastern spine of the city is **Deansgate**, which runs from Castlefield to the Cathedral and, in its northern environs, displays the most dramatic core of urban regeneration in the country, centred on **Exchange Square**. Other city-centre diversions – including the Manchester Museum and Whitworth Art Gallery – string out along the main southern artery **Oxford Road**. Southwest of the centre, trams run out to **Salford Quays** where the renovated docks and quays now maintain two high-profile visitor attractions, **The Lowry** arts centre and the **Imperial War Museum North**; and no soccer fan will want to miss the tour of nearby **Old Trafford**, home of Manchester United.

Year-round, two-hour **guided walks** (£4) can be booked at the Visitor Centre in St Peter's Square. There are usually two or three departures a week, concentrating on various themes – from city burial grounds and industrial archeology to pub walks and American connections.

St Peter's Square and around

Manchester could claim little architectural merit without its Victorian neo-Gothic buildings. One of its boldest, Alfred Waterhouse's Town Hall, finished in 1877, divides the plain expanse of **St Peter's Square** from the more harmonious **Albert Square** to the north (whose memorial to Prince Albert is flanked by statues of John Bright and a perky William Gladstone). You're free to wander inside the **Town Hall** (Mon–Fri 9am–5pm; free) – enter from Albert Square or Lloyd Street into the echoing stone-vaulted interior and climb one of the grand staircases to the **Great Hall**, with its iron candelabras, stained glass windows, double hammer-beam roof and paintings by Ford Madox Brown depicting decisive moments from Manchester's past. Elsewhere in the building, the mosaic floors are littered with statues and busts of civic worthies, from Anti Corn-Law leaders to Sir Charles Hallé. **Guided tours** of the building set off from the Visitor Centre (Easter–Dec every other Sat & each Wed, usually at 2pm, though times can vary; £4).

On the south side of the Town Hall, the circular **Central Library** (Mon–Thurs 10am–8pm, Fri & Sat 10am–5pm) faces St Peter's Square. Built in 1934 as the largest municipal library in the world, it's an elegant classical construction with a domed reading room. The library building is still an impressive sight, but modern building has dwarfed adjacent landmarks: Lutyens' **Cenotaph** in St Peter's Square passes virtually unnoticed these days amid the swooshing trams; while around the back of the library (head through Library Walk), on Mount Street, the historic **Friends Meeting House** has managed to see off various attempts to knock it down.

Over on Peter Street, the late-Victorian **Midland Hotel** has worn well, and might tempt you in for tea and cakes in its lavish Edwardian interior. The exterior is no less beguiling: witness the exterior dragon-relief tiling. The hotel's earlier visitors ventured out for an evening's entertainment at the **Free Trade Hall** further to the west up Peter Street, which sponsored concerts by the city's own Hallé Orchestra for over a century, until Bridgewater Hall was completed in 1996. The Italianate facade survived wartime bombing and will be retained as part of any future development on the site. The Free Trade Hall was originally built on the site of St Peter's Fields, where in 1819 eleven demonstrators were killed by the local militia during an event known as the "Peterloo Massacre" (see box on p.745).

△ The Albert Dock, Liverpool

South of St Peter's Square, Lower Mosley Street runs past the **G-Mex Centre**, in use as a train station until 1969; pop your head into the huge vaulted interior for a quick goggle at its proportions. Adjacent is the **International Convention Centre**, while on the other side of G-Mex rises the **Bridgewater Hall**, at the junction of Bridgewater Street. This – Britain's finest purpose-built concert hall – is, uniquely, balanced on shock-absorbing springs to guarantee clarity of sound. The *Stalls* café-bar inside makes a good drinks stop.

The other way up Mosley Street, north of St Peter's Square, rises Charles Barry's porticoed **City Art Gallery** (Ⓦwww.cityartgalleries.org.uk), where the array of high Victorian art includes the country's finest public collection of works by the Pre-Raphaelite Brotherhood and possibly the best decorative art collection outside London. Following extensive refurbishment, the gallery has doubled in size and has a new extension linked by a glass public area to the original gallery. A top-floor space for special exhibitions concentrates on visual art and design, while the separate Gallery of Craft and Design provides space to display many items from the permanent collection for the first time. The Manchester Gallery is devoted to the visual history of the city and there's also a dedicated children's gallery, plus a theatre for decorative arts, a café and restaurant.

Around the corner from here, the grid of streets between Princess and Charlotte streets marks the boundaries of Britain's largest **Chinatown**, heralded by the inevitable Dragon Arch, focus of the city's annual Chinese New Year celebrations. To the southeast, the roads off Portland Street lead down to the Rochdale Canal, where Canal Street is the heart of Manchester's thriving **Gay Village**. The pink pound has transformed this part of the city and canalside cafés, clubs, bars and businesses have turned a formerly abandoned warehouse district into something with the verve of San Francisco.

Castlefield

Fifteen minutes' walk southwest of St Peter's Square lies **Castlefield**. The country's first man-made canal, the Bridgewater Canal, brought coal and other goods to the warehouses here in the late eighteenth century; the railway followed fifty years later, cementing Castlefield's pre-eminent position, which only declined after World War II. Since the early 1980s, an influx of money allied to a fair amount of speculative vision has resulted in a cobbled canalside, cleaned-up water, outdoor events arena and some attractive café-bars. It was Britain's first "urban heritage park" and you can find out about its various festivals, the September carnival, bank-holiday street markets, walkable towpaths and canal cruises at the **Castlefield Visitor Centre** at 101 Liverpool Rd (Mon–Fri 10am–4pm, Sat & Sun noon–4pm; free; ☎0161/834 4026, Ⓦwww.castlefield.org.uk).

The castle-in-the-field itself is a **Roman fort** – finally abandoned around 410 AD – whose reconstructed north gate and the foundations of a few houses can be seen on Liverpool Road. This is just a hundred yards from the **Museum of Science and Industry** (daily 10am–5pm; last admission 4pm; free, admission charge for special exhibitions; Ⓦwww.msim.org.uk), one of the most impressive museums of its type in the country, set in various connected buildings and mixing technological displays and special blockbuster exhibitions with trenchant analysis of the social impact of industrialization. With Manchester at the forefront of the Industrial Revolution, it's hardly surprising that the museum trumpets the region's massive technological contribution – starting with the Lancashire-made steam engines, some of which are fired daily in the **Power Hall**. Pride of place goes to a working replica of Robert Stephenson's *Planet* – for which his father George's *Rocket* was the prototype. Built in 1830, the *Planet* reliably attained a scorching 30mph but had no brakes; the museum's version does, and uses them at weekends (usually Easter–Nov Sat & Sun noon–4pm; Dec–Easter Sun only; small charge), dropping passengers a quarter-mile away at the **world's oldest passenger railway station**. It was here that the *Rocket* arrived on a rainy September 15, 1830, after fatally injuring Liverpool MP William Huskisson at the start of the inaugural passenger journey from Liverpool.

A reconstructed Victorian sewer below the station illustrates the problems of sanitation in the 1870s, when poor areas were still using street-end standpipes. The improvements brought about by domestic electrification are brought home in a suite of rooms that includes a wonderfully kitsch Fifties' living room. There's also a hands-on science centre and interactive gallery, where the kids hog all the best experiments, and displays dealing with fibres, fabrics and fashion, while the museum's comprehensive selection of carding machines, bobbin threaders and cotton looms crash into action at weekends in the **Textile Gallery**. Another glimpse into the past is provided by **Warehouse for the World**, a sound-and-light show (free) which delves into the history of the warehouses whose goods fuelled Manchester's early wealth. By way of contrast, the **Air and Space Hall** is something of an anomaly in that it barely touches on Manchester at all, though the cutaway engines, passenger-carrying kite and lightweight treatment of space exploration are bolstered by the popular attraction of a flight simulator (for which there's an extra charge).

Along Deansgate

Central **Deansgate** cuts through the city from the canal to the cathedral, its architectural reference points ranging from Victorian industrialism to post-millennium posturing. South of Peter Street, the **Peter's Fields** development has transformed a magnificent sweep of late-nineteenth-century warehousing into the **Great Northern** commercial and leisure complex, offset by glass walls, a campanile, open-air amphitheatre and grassy lawn. The inevitable café-bars, restaurants and shops provide a social focus; a pattern repeated a few minutes' further south down Deansgate where **Deansgate Locks** (stretching along Whitworth St) house a run of café-bars in the old railway arches along a section of the Rochdale Canal.

North along Deansgate, past Peter Street, keep an eye out for modern **Lincoln Square** (tucked between Queen and Brazenose streets), named after its standing statue of the American President. Manchester refused to break the embargo on using cotton from the Southern states during the Civil War, which led to unemployment among the city's workers – a sacrifice recognized by Lincoln himself, whose grateful letter to the city is quoted on the statue.

Across Deansgate, opposite Brazenose Street, is the beautifully detailed **John Rylands Library** (Mon–Fri 10am–5.30pm, Sat 10am–1pm; free; guided tours Wed noon; £1; ⓦwww.rylibweb.man.ac.uk), the city's supreme example of Victorian Gothic. It was founded in 1890 by Enriqueta Ryland to house the theological works collected by her late husband, and now displays Bibles in more than three hundred languages among its million-strong general collection. Temporary exhibitions highlight the library's other assets, though you should venture inside whatever's showing to see the superb interior – carved and burnished wood, Art Nouveau metalwork, delicately crafted stone and stained glass.

From the library, continue up Deansgate and left into Bridge Street to reach the **People's History Museum** (Tues–Sun 11am–4.30pm; £1, free on Fri;

an exhibition recording the lives and protests of England's working class over the last two hundred years. Posters, press reports, charters and anti-Government cartoons show the struggles of suffragettes, reformers and radicals, fighting for equal representation, votes and fair pay; trade unionism is also well documented, with one of the country's best historic collections of marching banners; and there are displays devoted to social and cultural life, including coverage of local football and music.

St Ann's Square is tucked away off the eastern side of Deansgate, a couple of blocks up from John Dalton Street. Squat **St Ann's Church** (daily 9.30am–5pm) – baptismal church of Thomas De Quincey – flanks its southern side. Built in 1712, its lovely Renaissance interior was restored under the masterful direction of Alfred Waterhouse at the end of the nineteenth century, from when dates the eye-catching stained glass. The church is fronted by a statue of nineteenth-century Free Trader Richard Cobden, joint-leader with John Bright of the Anti-Corn-Law League which finally forced the repeal in 1846 of the restrictive Corn Laws. On the western side of the square, keep an eye out for the entrance to the **Barton Arcade**, a stunning Victorian shopping gallery which runs through to Deansgate.

Crowning glory of St Ann's Square is the **Royal Exchange**, which houses the famous **Royal Exchange Theatre**, the country's largest theatre-in-the-round, whose steel-and-glass cat's cradle sits plonked under the building's immense glass-domed roof. Formerly the Cotton Exchange, this building employed seven thousand people until trading finished on December 31, 1968 – the old trading board still shows the last day's prices for American and Egyptian cotton. Also inside there's a good bookshop and crafts gallery, a café/restaurant plus bar, while the associated Royal Exchange Shopping Centre – three floors of shops and cafés – wraps around the building.

The Cathedral and Chetham's Library

At the far end of Deansgate stands the small, Perpendicular **Cathedral** (daily 7.30am–6pm; free organ recitals Thurs at 1pm), the third church on this site since its foundation in the ninth century. A fragment of stone by the choir and a fourteenth-century arch by the tower are all that remain of the earlier structures, and in truth it's been hacked about too much to have any real coherence – the famed widest nave in England (114ft, as opposed to York Minster's 106ft) is entirely a result of rich families adding side chapels to the fifteenth-century church, which were later opened out to provide space for Manchester's burgeoning nineteenth-century population of worshippers. However, it's surprising it's still here at all: in 1940, a 1000lb bomb all but destroyed the interior, knocked out most of the stained glass (which is why it's so light inside) and necessitated the complete restoration of the fine misericords, which depict dragon-slaying as well as more mundane scenes – backgammon players and a calf butcher among them.

The cathedral's choristers are trained in **Chetham's Hospital School**, across the way on Long Millgate (ask at the porter's lodge for entrance). This fifteenth-century manor house became a school and a free public library in 1653, then was transformed into a music school in 1969. There are free recitals (usually Mon–Fri 1.30pm) during term time and a half-hour tour following the concert on Wednesdays. The oak-panelled **library** (Mon–Fri 9am–12.30pm & 1.30–4.30pm) itself – with its carved eighteenth-century bookcases – is a real delight. Someone is usually on hand to show you the restored reading room, with the windowed alcove where, it's claimed, Marx and Engels used to study.

The area around the cathedral is being refashioned as the city's **Millennium**

Quarter, with the six-storey **Urbis** at its core. This hi-tech visitor centre (due to open during 2002) will explore the experience of the planet's cities – Manchester, naturally, claimed as the world's first industrial city – through a whole series of interactive exhibits. If that doesn't draw you in, perhaps the indoor funicular (apparently the world's first) and top-floor restaurant with city views might.

Exchange Square and around

Just to the north of St Ann's Square, **Exchange Square** sits at the heart of the ambitious city-centre rebuilding programme launched following the devastating bomb of 1996. A pedestrian boulevard – **New Cathedral Street** – runs from St Ann's Square to the Cathedral, skirting the flanks of the flagship **Marks & Spencer** store whose gigantic glazed facade makes up the south side of Exchange Square. The landscaped square, with its water features and public sculpture, has quickly become a much-frequented, if not exactly loved, urban space, buzzed by skateboarders. Two historic pubs, the *Old Wellington Inn* and *Sinclair's Oyster Bar*, both moved brick-by-brick to this new site, mop up some of the foot traffic at their outdoor tables.

To the east, the Sixties' eyesore that was the **Arndale Centre** has been enlarged, modernized and clad in glass. To the north, the old **Corn Exchange** has been refurbished completely, while retaining its historic facade and glass dome. Relaunched as the **Triangle** (reflecting the unusual shape of its interior), this is a rare wrong foot in the brave new Manchester: gone any sense of the building's tradition, replaced by yet another batch of retail outlets selling expensive shoes and Japanese rice bowls. Across Withy Grove, meanwhile, the former Mirror Building contains the futuristic **Printworks**, an adult "entertainment centre", complete with IMAX screen, cinema megaplex and various themed bars and restaurants. Step inside and you're confronted by steaming ducts, whistles and moving pulleys and cranes, reflecting the building's past history as a newspaper printing works.

Piccadilly Gardens and the Northern Quarter

For years, the bleak expanse of **Piccadilly Gardens** divided rather than united the city, though a recent beautification project has dramatically enhanced its character. Japanese architects have re-styled the area, adding groves of trees, a fountain and water jets, and a pavilion at one end to screen off the traffic. Piccadilly Plaza, comprising the ugly Sixties' buildings on the southwest side, is also due a facelift, while a new shopping arcade is planned to link the gardens with Chinatown.

The gardens remain a major local transport hub and gateway to the still shabby but improving Oldham Street, which has been adopted by "alternative" entrepreneurs who have dubbed it the **Northern Quarter**. Traditionally, this is Manchester's garment district and you'll still find shops and wholesalers selling high-street fashions, shop fittings, mannequins and hosiery, but there are also new design outlets, lots of music stores, and some funky bars and cafés. The nineteenth-century red-brick Fish Wholesale Market on High Street is now just a shell, though it retains its marvellous sculpted pediments; for off-beat contemporary shopping, look in Affleck's Palace (52 Church St), and in the Coliseum (18-24 Church St). Loft-style apartments change hands around here for serious money these days; the renovated **Smithfield Buildings** are an example of what can be done with Oldham Street's fine old buildings – in this case, a former department store. There are more skills and crafts on display in the excellent **Manchester Craft and Design Centre**, 17 Oak St (Mon–Sat

10am–5.30pm; free) – a great place to pick up ceramics, fabrics, earthenware, jewellery and decorative art, or just sip a drink in the cosy café.

Investment money continues to pour into this quarter. The city's Chinese Arts Centre is due to relocate to the Northern Quarter soon, providing a national showcase for Oriental arts and culture. Meanwhile, just to the east in the **Rochdale canal basin**, plans are well advanced for more Castlefield-style waterfront living and socializing in new retail, loft-apartment and restaurant sites.

Oxford Road and points south

From St Peter's Square, **Oxford Road** – initially Oxford Street – stretches through a ragged mile of faculty buildings to Rusholme and the leafy suburbs beyond. Oxford Road Station lurks behind the **Cornerhouse**, the dynamo of the Manchester arts scene. In addition to screening art-house films, the Cornerhouse has three floors of gallery space (Tues–Sat 11am–6pm, Sun 2–6pm; free) devoted to contemporary and local artists' work. The café and bar are popular, too. Across the road, Alfred Waterhouse's majestic **Refuge Assurance** building of 1891 is one of Manchester's joys, its soaring clock-tower, dome and terracotta facade now hiding the bulk of the *Palace Hotel*. An endless stream of buses runs from here down Oxford Road: #40, #41, #42, #43, #44, #47, #48 and #49 (among others) all pass the buildings and sights detailed below.

Newest addition is the **Manchester Aquatics Centre** (Mon–Fri 6.30am–10pm, Sat 7am–6pm, Sun 7am–10pm; £2.50), at Booth Street, whose two fifty-metre pools under a wave-shaped roof were built with the Commonwealth Games in mind. This is under ten minutes' walk from the Cornerhouse, while another ten minutes along Oxford Road brings you to the Gothic Revival building housing the **Manchester Museum** (Mon–Sat 10am–5pm; free; ⓦwww.museum.man.ac.uk), one of the city's great unsung treats. Its strengths are diverse. At the centre of the Egyptology world since the 1890s, the museum has done pioneering work on mummy dissection and captivating displays enlarge upon the burial practices and techniques that their work has revealed. Rocks, minerals, fossils and natural history also get their own exhibition space, while the top-floor Science for Life section concentrates on the human body and biomedical research – and zeroes in on Mancunian health pioneers who led the way in developing treatments for cancer, test-tube babies, hip replacements, colour blindness and other matters. A vivarium and an aquarium complete the list of attractions, and there's a café.

Another half-mile away is the city's modern art collection, housed in the red-brick **Whitworth Gallery** (Mon–Sat 10am–5pm, Sun 2–5pm; free; ⓦwww .whitworth.man.ac.uk). The gallery forms two distinct halves, "historic" and modern, with its pre-1880 historic collection incorporating a strong assembly of watercolours by Turner, Constable, Cox and Blake as well as Gillray engravings, Hogarth prints and oddities such as Ford Madox Brown's *Execution of Mary Queen of Scots* – his first, and not entirely successful, attempt at a large-scale historical work. The modern collection concentrates on post-1880 British staples, with Moore, Frink and Hepworth setting off contributions from lesser-known artists. Look for works by Paul Nash (one of the organizers of the London Surrealist exhibition of 1936), the World War II artist John Piper and those of Stephen Conroy, a contemporary figurative painter whose subjects resonate with Victorian images. With Manchester's cotton connections it is perhaps not surprising that the gallery also displays the country's widest range of textiles outside London's Victoria and Albert Museum.

Walk just two hundred yards south of the Whitworth Gallery and you'll catch the pungent spicy smell of **Rusholme**'s Wilmslow Road, a "golden mile" of curry houses, sari shops and grocers stocked with all manner of exotic vegetables, halal meats and sticky sweets. In **Platt Fields Park**, at the south end of the curry mile (just past *Hardy's Well* pub), the **Gallery of Costume** (daily 10am–5.30pm; free) fills Georgian Platt Hall. Its collection spans fashion through the ages, giving particular emphasis to Manchester's former role as a textile centre, its large Asian population and the clothes of the working class – you're just as likely to see Indian wedding outfits or contemporary street fashion as designer shoes and silk jackets.

Most of the buses that head down Oxford Road continue through Rusholme and the student areas of Fallowfield and Withington to **Didsbury Village**, Manchester's most prestigious and leafy suburb. There are some great pubs and restaurants here and in nearby **West Didsbury**, and a large park containing **Didsbury Botanical Gardens** (dawn–dusk; free), a landscaped patch of ponds, shrubs, rare pines and firs and an imaginative array of cacti and flowers. A pleasant hour's walk follows the river from Didsbury to **Chorlton Water Park** (daily 8am–dusk; free), where water sports are available between April and September; in the winter, ducks and other wildfowl visit the lake. From the park, a short walk will take you to Barlow Moor Road, served by frequent buses returning to the city centre. Or you can walk up to **Chorlton Green**, another attractive suburb with its own village green, where there are a couple of great pubs (the *Horse and Jockey* and *Trevor Arms*).

Salford Quays and Trafford

The Metrolink extension to **Salford Quays** provides easy access to one of the city's first urban development projects. For ninety years, from 1894 when the Manchester Ship Canal opened, the Salford docks turned the city into one of Britain's busiest ports. Trade declined in the 1970s and the docks eventually closed in 1982, since which time the Salford Quays development has transformed the run-down quays on the western edge of the city centre into a hugely popular waterfront residential and leisure complex, with its own watersports centre and new outlet mall.

Various Metrolink stations serve the area: for the **Salford Quays tourist information office** (Mon–Fri 8.30am–4.30pm, Sun 10am–4pm; ☎0161/848 8601) get off at Salford Quays station. You can pick up a map here and wander down the Centenary Walkway quayside, studded with commemorative discs whose engraved words and snippets reflect the area's history. This ends at the promontory taken up by **The Lowry** (daily from 9.30am; free; ⓦwww .thelowry.com) the Quays' striking, shining steel arts centre whose theatres, galleries (Mon–Wed & Sun 11am–5pm, Thurs–Sat 11am–8pm; free) and creative ArtWorks exhibition (Mon–Fri 10am–3pm, Sat & Sun 10am–4pm; £3.75) have quickly become one of Manchester's leading attractions; to travel straight here, stay on the Metrolink until Broadway. The building itself is a great piece of art and you're free to wander around or take a guided tour (£2.50), popping into the galleries and exhibitions at will, or grabbing a bite to eat in the café or restaurant. The centre, of course, takes its name from L.S. Lowry and no artist is more closely linked with an English city than Lowry is with Manchester. There's always a selection of Lowry works on show for free, illustrating both his early views on the desolation and sadness of Manchester's mill workers and his changing outlook in later life when he repeated earlier paintings changing the greys and sullen browns for lively reds and pinks. Lowry also expanded his repertoire as he grew older, capturing mountain scenes and seascapes in broad sweeps of his brush, and painting full-bodied realistic portraits which are far less known than his matchstick crowds.

A footbridge runs from The Lowry across to the Trafford side of the docks where rises the new **Imperial War Museum North** (Ⓦwww.iwm.org.uk /north), scheduled to open during 2002. This, too, is a dramatic structure, whose three "shards" of fractured steel represent the world's conflicts on land, sea and in the air. It's as resonant in its way as the other great building which looms in the near distance, **Old Trafford**, the self-styled "Theatre of Dreams" and home of Manchester United, arguably the most famous team in the world. The club's following is such that only season ticket holders can ever attend games, but **tours** of Old Trafford and its museum (daily 9.30am–5pm; museum and tour £8.50, museum only £5.50; advance booking essential, ☏0161 /877 8631, Ⓦwww.manutd.com) placate out-of-town fans who want to gawp at the silverware, sit in the dug-out and visit the *Red Café*. To get here, take the Metrolink to Old Trafford station and walk up Warwick Road to Sir Matt Busby Way. Incidentally, the city's poorer soccer cousins, Manchester City, haven't had much to shout about in recent years, though expect this to change in 2003 when they swap their old ground, Maine Road (in inner-city Moss Side) – the "Theatre of Base Comedy", according to soccer commentator Stuart Hall – for the spanking new City of Manchester stadium, built on the east side of the city for the Commonwealth Games.

Eating and drinking

Second only to London in the breadth and scope of its **cafés** and **restaurants**, Manchester has something to suit everyone, from a cheap curry to a night out in a celebrity-chef hotspot. Moreover, at both ends of the market, your money goes a lot further than it does in London, while smart in Manchester doesn't always mean snobby. The bulk of Manchester's eating and drinking places are scattered around the city centre, while out at Rusholme you'll find the best range of curries this side of the Pennines. Most city **pubs** dish up something filling at lunchtime, but for a more modish snack or drink, European-style **café-bars** are everywhere, especially in the new city-centre developments, in the Northern Quarter, and in the Gay Village on the Rochdale Canal.

Daytime cafés

The coffee-bar and sandwich chains have moved swiftly into the city, so if you want a *Starbuck's*, a *Coffee Republic*, a *Caffè Nero* or a *Prêt à Manger* you won't have far to look. Mancunians, though, favour the local *Java* outlets (8a Oxford Rd, 95 Piccadilly and Victoria Station), which serve up all the usual coffee variants, plus biscotti, croissants and sandwiches, and the half-dozen, city-wide *Feed The Five Thousand* sandwich bars. The places listed below usually open daily from around 10am to 6 or 7pm, unless otherwise stated.

Affleck's Palace 52 Church St, at Oldham Street. Five floors of boutiques, with the best of the cafés on the top floor, where you can grab a coffee and a grilled sandwich. Closed Sun.

Café Pop 34–36 Oldham St. Retro café full of 70s' kitsch and pop collectables, with the emphasis on veggie fry-ups, hefty sandwiches (including the famous triple-decker Scooby Snax), omelettes and the like. Service can be a bit chaotic but portions are enormous and prices very fair. Closed Sun.

Clarion Café Left Bank, Bridge St. The café at the People's History Museum serves a good-value daily lunch (noon–2pm), plus drinks and snacks, and there's outdoor seating in the summer. Closes at 4.30pm and all day Mon.

Cornerhouse 70 Oxford St. The place to sip a cappuccino after viewing the galleries or catching a movie. The first-floor café (daily until 8pm) dishes up average soups, dips, sandwiches and cakes; it's better downstairs in the bar, where arty types pontificate about world cinema.

Earth 16-20 Turner St. Gourmet vegan and organic food in a stylish Northern Quarter pit-stop with Buddhist leanings – stuffed pancakes, pies, bakes, juices and deli delights. Closes 5pm on Sat & all day Sun.

Eighth Day 107–111 Oxford Rd. Manchester's oldest organic-vegetarian café has got spanking new premises on its old Oxford Road site – shop, takeaway and juice bar upstairs, café/restaurant downstairs. Temporary premises on Sidney Street, around the corner, in operation during the building work in 2002.

Gallery Bistro Whitworth Art Gallery, Oxford Rd. Out-of-the-ordinary daily specials lift this light and airy gallery caff into the top rank. Closes at 4.30pm.

Love Saves the Day Smithfield Building, Tib St. New York style and sass in this Northern Quarter deli-café, where a daily changing menu of platters, salads, pasta and sandwiches keep the locals happy. And there's very good coffee (available to go too). Closed Sun.

Café-bars

Manchester's **café-bar** scene is its pride and joy, with most of the places below fielding a very definite crowd and atmosphere. Many of those in the Gay Village, the Northern Quarter and Castlefield are reasonably laidback, though evenings always see the atmosphere ratcheted up a notch; while at the half-dozen places along Deansgate Locks (Whitworth St West) or in the Printworks (Withy Grove) the emphasis is more on serious partying. Lots of café-bars have outdoor seating, and take advantage of relaxed licensing laws to offer drinks without food. As a general rule, those listed below are open daily from 11am or noon until around midnight, often later at the weekend or if there's music.

Atlas 376 Deansgate. Wood-panel the inside of an old railway arch, add bamboo thickets to a large urban patio and you've got one of the best café-bars in the city. Justly known for its quality focaccia sandwiches, it's also the place for Sunday brunch, a bottle of beer or a decent glass of wine – and don't forget to browse in the associated deli next door.

Barça Arch 8 & 9, Catalan Square. Trendy Castlefield bar/restaurant tucked into the restored railway arches, with a lovely canalside terrace, cosy lounge with fire, and upstairs dining room and deck for fashionable Mediterranean flavours.

Citrus 2 Mount St. Mellow café-bar behind the Central Library with world cuisine on offer in the roomy restaurant and relaxed sounds down in the basement bar. Closed Sun.

Dry Bar 28–30 Oldham St. The earliest of the designer café-bars on the scene, and catalyst for much of what has gone in the Northern Quarter, *Dry* is still as cool as they come.

Green Room 54–56 Whitworth St West. The revamped theatre bar provides an alternative to the nearby *Cornerhouse*; food thus far is limited to soup and sandwich lunches (not weekends).

KroBar 325 Oxford Rd, opposite Manchester University Students' Union. What seems like half the students in Manchester crowd into this huge good-natured café-bar for value-for-money food, caffeine and a vast range of on-tap beers; on a sunny day, the other half fights for table space outside. One of the city's best.

Loaf Deansgate Locks, Whitworth St West. Large queues at the weekend for this designer-industrial café-bar, not nearly so crowded during the day when you can grab an outdoor table underneath the arches and soak up the weak Manchester sun.

Manto 46 Canal St. Gay Village stalwart whose chic crowd laps up the cool sounds and club nights. A canalside Sunday brunch is a treat here, or hop upstairs to *Sarasota*, for fusion cooking and the city's only retractable roof for alfresco dining.

Metz 3 Brazil St. Classy converted warehouse bar and restaurant. It's great for a pre-club drink or two and its Eastern European food's not bad either.

Mumbo 35a King St. The city's first tea-bar, with sipping and eating on three floors. There's a vast range of speciality teas on offer (plus nibbles, food, and wine by the glass), with the coolest perch being the year-round roof-terrace for unique views of St Ann's Church.

Night & Day 26 Oldham St. Unpretentious café-bar with a late licence and live music – jazz, blues, Latin and funk – most nights from local musicians. Closed Sun.

Persia Great Northern Warehouse, Peter's Fields, Peter St. Manchester meets the Arabian Nights. Lurk at the funky bar; marvel at the brick ovens, pillars and tiles; or lounge under parasols, grazing on flat-bread pizzas (house special: langoustine, artichoke and fontina), dips, wraps, tagines, char-grills, meze and salads.

Prague V 40 Chorlton St. Gay-friendly hangout on the Canal Street corner, with Czech beer, Mediterranean-inspired meals and snacks, and a late weekend drinks licence.

Velvet 2 Canal St. The redbrick facade hides a stylish, laid-back basement cavern, with good food, outrageous staff, campy clientele and late-night sounds.

Restaurants

There's been a revolution in Manchester's dining scene in recent years, with the long-standing city-centre **restaurants** being joined by a host of trendy brasseries and celebrity-chef ventures. Paul Heathcote (the only vaguely local boy), Gary Rhodes, Raymond Blanc and Marco Pierre White are all associated with various Manchester restaurants (ie they don't necessarily do the cooking) and if you've got the cash and are in the city for any length of time, you should go to at least one of them to see what all the fuss is about. **Chinatown** in the city centre can always be counted upon for a budget lunch or a late-night meal; otherwise, most city-centre restaurants congregate along and off Deansgate. It also pays to visit the **suburbs**, particularly those of south Manchester, where Asian (Rusholme) and Mediterranean/Modern-British (Didsbury Village, West Didsbury, Chorlton) restaurants are all the rage. Taxis aren't particularly expensive to any of these places, or you can easily take the **bus**: for Rusholme, take any bus down Oxford Road (from opposite the Cornerhouse); for Didsbury Village, it's bus #42 or #45a; for West Didsbury, buses #41, #43, or #44; and Chorlton, buses #16, #46, #47, #85, #86 or #87.

City Centre

Armenian Taverna Albert Square ☎0161834 9025. Filling meze platters (for vegetarians too) bring in many, who then find they wish they'd plumped for a halibut kebab or grilled spring chicken, or one of a dozen other mighty main courses. Closed Mon. Moderate.

Café Istanbul 79 Bridge St ☎0161/833 9942. Delicious Turkish dishes, including a great meze selection, and an extensive wine list (Including a powerful Turkish red). Closed Sun. Inexpensive to Moderate.

Dimitri's 1 Campfield Arcade, Deansgate ☎0161/839 3319. Pick and mix from the Greek/Spanish/Italian menu (particularly good for vegetarians), or grab a sandwich, an arcade table and sip a drink (Greek coffee to Lebanese wine). Moderate.

Little Yang Sing 17 George St, ☎0161/228 7722. Celebrated basement restaurant (forerunner to the larger Yang Sing) where the emphasis is on *dim sum*, rice or noodle dishes, and down-to-earth Cantonese cooking, with lots of choice under £8. Moderate.

Livebait 22 Lloyd St, Albert Square ☎0161/817 4110. Beautifully fresh fish in a lovely restored building, though since even the fish and chips are around £12 a plateful you'll probably have to try and exercise some restraint. Expensive.

The Market Restaurant 104 High St ☎0161/834 3743. One of the city's hidden treasures, this is a very relaxing spot for dinner. The regularly chang-

ing menu throws its Modern-British weight around in adventurous, eclectic fashion. Also a very good wine and beer list. Reservations essential. Open Wed–Sat dinner only. Expensive.

Le Petit Blanc 55 King St ☎0161/832 1001. Best place in the city for reasonably priced classic and regional French cooking is Raymond Blanc's mid-range brasserie operation – fish soup to a roast poussin off the *a la carte* menu or good-value, three-course, *prix fixe* for around £15. Real food for children too. Moderate.

Penang Village 56 Faulkner St ☎0161/236 2650. You soon get the idea – Malay village scenes on the wall, a traditional fishing boat as centrepiece – but this friendly Malaysian joint backs up the decor with tasty, authentic dishes. *Ayam percik* (barbecued chicken with a mild curry sauce), beef rendang, veg curry, and the good *roti* bread are all recommended. Closed Mon. Moderate.

Reform King St, Spring Gardens ☎0161/839 9966. The city's great and good have adopted Reform as their pet restaurant, revelling in its oh-so-glamorous Venetian-Gothic exterior and spiffy French-inspired food – the late-opening bar is a see-and-be-seen experience too. Closed Sun. Expensive.

Simply Heathcote's Jackson Row ☎0161/835 3536. Massive, minimalist dining rooms operated by Lancastrian chef Paul Heathcote. Mixes Mediterranean and local flavours, so expect updated working-class dishes alongside the parmesan shavings. The set lunch/early-bird menu is one of the city's best deals for food of this stature. Expensive.

Stock 4 Norfolk St ☎0161/839 6644. Superior Italian cooking – the fish Is renowned – accompanied by a wine list of serious intent. It's housed In the city's old stock exchange, hence the name. Closed Sun. Expensive.

Tampopo 16 Albert Square ☎0161/819 1966. Basement noodle bar with long benches and a fast turnover. Noodle dishes are Japanese, Thai, Malaysian or Indonesian with most dishes under £7. Inexpensive.

Wagamama The Printworks, Corporation St/Withy Grove ☎0161/839 5916. Ace Japanese noodle bar, where you'll quickly learn to tell your *ramen* from your *udon*. Portions are generous, though with communal seating at long tables and zippy service, this is more of a quick-bite spot than a place to linger over dinner. Inexpensive.

Wong Chu 63 Faulkner St ☎0161/236 2346. Simply the best of the budget Chinatown eateries, this no-frills, paper-tablecloth joint serves up enormous portions of Cantonese staples. Highlights are the deep-bowl noodle soups or piled-high rice-and-meat plates, at bargain prices. Inexpensive.

Yang Sing 34 Princess St ☎0161/236 2200. The *Yang Sing* is one of the best Cantonese restaurants in the country, with thoroughly authentic food, from a lunchtime plate of fried noodles to the full works. Stray from the printed menu for the most interesting dishes; ask the friendly staff for advice, who will pick a banquet for you (from £20 per head) if you prefer. Moderate to Expensive.

Rusholme

Darbar 65–67 Wilmslow Rd ☎0161/224 4392. Award-winning Asian food in plain but friendly surroundings. The chef's special (he's been voted Manchester's Curry Chef of the Year twice) is *nihari*, a slow-cooked lamb dish, while other homestyle choices appear on Sundays. Take your own booze. Inexpensive.

Punjab Sweet House 177 Wilmslow Rd, Rusholme ☎0161/225 2960. Superb all-vegetarian Indian restaurant, specializing in *dosas*, *thalis* and – not least – special sweets, stacked high in the window. Inexpensive.

Sanam 145–151 Wilmslow Rd, Rusholme ☎0161 /224 8824. One of Rusholme's earliest arrivals, now thirty years old, the *Sanam* serves all the usual dishes plus award-winning *gulab juman*. Drop by the take-away sweet and snack centre on the way home. No alcohol allowed. Inexpensive to Moderate.

Shere Khan IFCO Centre, 52 Wilmslow Rd, Rusholme ☎0161/256 2624. A Rusholme standard-bearer, this big Indian brasserie gets packed at the weekends, but always maintains its high

standards. The open grill dispenses marvellous kebabs, and the wide-ranging menu is also strong on *karahi* and *biryani* dishes. Inexpensive to Moderate.

Tandoori Kitchen 131–133 Wilmslow Rd ☎0161/224 2329. Ring the changes a little at the *Tandoori Kitchen*, where Persian specialities are the draw – which means unusual dishes such as chicken with pomegranate and some first-rate grilled kebabs. Inexpensive.

Didsbury and West Didsbury

Chiang Rai 762 Wilmslow Rd, Didsbury Village ☎0161/448 2277. Manchester's best – and most elegant – Thai restaurant specializes in cuisine from the north, including fine steamed fish and flavourful Thai sausage. Good lunch deals. Moderate.

Greens 43 Lapwing Lane, West Didsbury ☎0161/434 4259. Imaginative gourmet vegetarian meals in stripped-down surroundings. Early-bird and Sunday specials get you three courses for around a tenner – and you can bring your own wine. Closed Mon & Sat lunch. Moderate.

Lime Tree 8 Lapwing Lane, West Didsbury ☎0161/445 1217. Bundles of Modern-British joy, with a menu that chargrills and oven-roasts as if its life depended on it. Organic salmon is a signature dish, or else you could be chowing down on such delights as crispy duckling or courgette and leek cheesecake. Very fashionable, and reservations recommended. Closed Mon & Sat lunch, & Sun dinner. Moderate to Expensive.

The Nose 6 Lapwing Lane, West Didsbury ☎0161/445 3653. Soothing neighbourhood wine bar-café, good for a bagel or croissant breakfast, wraps and ciabatta sandwiches, or choose-from-the-chalkboard bistro meals. The coffee and wine's good too – taken at intimate tables inside, out back in the cute courtyard or on the hotly contested street-side patio. Inexpensive.

Peppers 4 Warburton St, Didsbury Village ☎0161 /445 0448. Tucked away off the main road, this cottage-style bolt-hole from the Didsbury chain restaurants and bars is an oasis of charm. Two floors of intimate dining, with a window onto the kitchen, where omelettes and open sandwiches at lunch (around £5) give way to seasonally changing Modern-British dinners. Moderate to Expensive.

Chorlton

Café Primavera 48 Beech Rd ☎0161/862 9934. Stylish surroundings for a seasonally changing Mediterranean-Fusion menu – warm salads, salmon en croute and chicken with mango are the kind of things to expect. Dinner only. Moderate.

The Lead Station 99 Beech Rd ☎0161/881 5559. Café, bar and restaurant – all three experiences gell in this lovely, light- and art-filled spot with a decked rear courtyard. Bistro-style meals and a popular weekend brunch. Inexpensive to Moderate.

Salford and Trafford

Rhodes and Co Waters Reach, Trafford Park ☎0161/868 1900. Gary Rhodes' sleek brasserie is a bit out of the way for everything except Old Trafford (but then Gary's a Reds' fan). Good deals at lunch can keep the cost down. Expensive.

Steven Saunders at The Lowry The Lowry, Salford Quays ☎0161/876 2121. The Lowry's flagship restaurant has a seasonally changing Modern-British menu. Set lunches for around a tenner and pre-theatre menus take the edge off the bill, and you get the hi-tech designer Lowry surroundings for free. Expensive.

Pubs

Manchester has a full complement of great **pubs**, including several Victorian classics that have stood the test of time. Off-the-shelf contemporary pubs include the usual Irish theme-bars and chain pubs as well as some rather splendid converted historic city-centre buildings. As far as **beer** goes, Boddington's is the highest-profile name in town, though independent local brewers Hydes, Holts and Robinson's all have their adherents.

The Beer House 6 Angel St. The best place for ale-tasting, with a constant stock of more than thirty brands of beer.

Britons Protection 50 Great Bridgewater St. Elegantly decorated traditional pub opposite Bridgewater Hall, with a couple of cosy, smoky rooms and a brickyard beer garden. The home-made pies are good, and there are comedy nights and other events held here.

Circus Tavern 86 Portland St. Manchester's smallest pub – a Victorian drinking-hole that's many people's favourite city-centre pit-stop. You may have to knock on the door to get in; once you do, you're confronted by the landlord in the corridor pulling pints.

Dukes '92 Castle St. Former stableblock for goods' horses on the Duke of Bridgewater's canal in Castlefield, classily revamped with art on the walls, terrace seating and a fine selection of beers. Serves great-value food including a wide range of pâtés and cheeses.

The Lass o' Gowrie 1 Charles St. Outside, glazed tiles and Victorian styling; inside, stripped floors and a micro-brewery.

Marble Arch 73 Rochdale Rd. Curious real-ale house with a sloping floor, whose in-house Marble Brewery produces some fine brews – the seasonal "Ginger Marble" or the strong "Chocolate Heavy" among them. More Marble beers are served at the sister pub, the Marble Beerhouse, 57 Manchester Rd, Chorlton.

The Mark Addy 2 Stanley St. Mainly known for its food, the Mark Addy (named after a nineteenth-century local character) serves a choice of fifty cheeses and eight pâtés (including vegetarian). Eat inside, or outside by the River Irwell.

Mr Thomas' Chop House 52 Cross St. Victorian classic with a Dickensian feel to its nooks and crannies. Office workers, hardcore daytime drinkers, old goats and students all call it home. There's good-value, traditional English "chop-house" food (oysters, bubble and squeak, etc) served in the ornate dining-and-drinking room at the rear – and old-fashioned table service for anyone who can't make their own way to the bar.

The Paramount Oxford St, at Portland St. Not quite the largest pub in Manchester (that's the Moon Under Water on Deansgate) but close – a Wetherspoon's drinking emporium with a sizzling choice of beers, ales and wines, and room to swing a thousand cats.

Peveril of the Peak 127 Great Bridgewater St. The pub that time forgot – one of Manchester's best real-ale houses, with a youthful crowd and some superb Victorian glazed tilework outside.

Pot of Beer 36 New Mount St. Nicely restored real-ale pub with a secondary line in Polish bar meals; on the northern fringes of the city centre but worth the hike.

Rain Bar 80 Great Bridgewater St. Pub or bar? Experience both, drinking inside the stripped-wood pubby interior, up in the swish bar, or out on the sweeping canalside terraces. Good range of beers, a decent menu and summer barbecue nights.

Sinclair's Oyster Bar Cathedral Gates, top of New Cathedral St. This well-loved eighteenth-century hostelry was moved to its new site lock, stock and barrel after the bomb. It shares outdoor seating with the equally venerable Wellington pub, for ringside views of Exchange Square.

Via Fossa 28–30 Canal St. The elaborate mock-Gothic rooms pack in a high-energy (largely gay) crowd. The scene rather than the quality of the beer drags people in – with most staying for a few rounds before a night on the town.

Nightlife

For over two decades now, Manchester has been vying with London as Britain's capital of **youth culture**, spearheaded by the success of its musical exports, from the saintly Morrissey to Badly Drawn Boy, Joy Division to Oasis. Banks of fly posters advertise what's going on in the numerous **clubs** which, as elsewhere, frequently change names and styles on different nights of the week; the most enduring are listed below and you can expect to pay £3–15 cover depending on what's on. Many of the city's grooviest café-bars also host regular club nights. Manchester has an excellent **live music** scene in pubs and clubs, with tickets for local bands usually under £5, more like £10–15 for someone you've heard of. Mega-star gigs take place either at the G-Mex Centre or one of the major stadiums, all listed below. For the broadest coverage of Manchester's musical happenings, check the fortnightly *City Life* magazine or Friday's *Manchester Evening News*.

Smaller live-music and club venues

The Attic above the *Thirsty Scholar*, 50 New Wakefield St ☎0161/236 6071. Regular weekend blasts of funk, soul and dance for a cool, collected student crowd.

Band on the Wall 25 Swan St ☎0161/832 6625, ⊚www.bandonthewall.com. Cosy Northern Quarter joint with a great reputation for its live bands – from world and folk to jazz and reggae – and club nights.

The Brickhouse 6 Whitworth St West ☎0161/236 4418. Indie, techno, Seventies, Eighties or glam,

depending on the night.

Generation X 11–13 New Wakefield St ☎0161/236 4899, ⊚www.mantogroup.com. Stylish, studenty café-bar – "eat, drink, slack, loaf" – known for its club nights, spinning house, techno, soul, and drum'n'bass.

Havana Bar 42 Blackfriars St ☎0161/832 8900. Best place for Latin and world sounds, with Latin dance classes some nights.

Jilly's Rockworld 65 Oxford St ☎0161/236 9971, ⊚www.jillys.co.uk. Classic and modern rock, Goth and Indie nights, live bands and club nights.

The Gay scene

Manchester has one of Britain's most vibrant gay scenes, centred on the Rochdale Canal between Princess and Sackville streets, in the so-called **Gay Village** – focus of Channel 4's infamous gay-soap "Queer As Folk". The café-bars and clubs here are among the city's best, though some claim that the area's increased popularity – with straight as well as gay visitors – has diluted its essence somewhat. Although the annual Mardi Gras carnival bit the dust a while back, it's been replaced by a smaller scale **Gayfest**, held every August bank holiday in and around the village. Other events, including an annual arts festival every May/June, are co-ordinated by **queerupnorth** (information on ☎0161/833 2288, ⊚www.queerupnorth.com).

Out on the town, early evenings kick off by the lock at one of the **café-bars** along Canal Street – *Manto*, *Metz*, *Bar 38*, *Spirit*, or *Velvet* – at the extravagant *Via Fossa* pub or at the more macho *New Union*, 111 Princess St, just off Canal Street. An older crowd drinks in the *Rembrandt Hotel* (which also has gay-friendly accommodation available); *Vanilla* on Richmond St is a good-natured women's café-bar with club nights. Meanwhile, a camp neon Liberty beckons you into *New York, New York*, 98 Bloom St. **Clubs** include the state-of-the-art *Essential*, 8 Minshull St (☎0161/237 5445); old favourite *Cruz*, 101 Princess St (☎0161/237 1554); the over-the-top *Hollywood Showbar*, 100 Bloom St (☎0161/236 6151); and *Follies*, 6 Whitworth St (☎0161/236 8149), a lesbian favourite. And the *Paradise Factory*, 112–116 Princess St (☎0161/273 5422) can always be counted on, too.

For further **information**, try the Lesbian and Gay Foundation (daily 4–10pm; ☎0161/235 8000, ⊚www.lgfoundation.org.uk) which can put you in touch with the dozens of other organizations and services operating out of the Gay Village.

Manchester Academy 269 Oxford Rd, on the university campus ☎0161/275 2930, ⓦwww.umu.man.ac.uk. Popular student venue for new and established bands.

Manchester Roadhouse 8–10 Newton St ☎0161/237 9789, ⓦwww.theroadhouse.u-net.com. Regular and varied gigs by local bands seeking glory, and a succession of fine club nights.

Paradise Factory 112–116 Princess St ☎0161/273 5422. One of the hottest clubs on the scene, now fabulously refurbished.

Planet K 46–50 Oldham St ☎0161/839 9941. Indie and student nights, underground sounds, drum and bass, depends on the night.

The Ritz Whitworth St West ☎0161/236 4355. A one-time ballroom where they still spread talc on the floor some nights of the week. Suits and stilettos disco Fri & Sat; student nights Mon & Wed; tea dances Wed afternoon.

Sankey's Soap Beehive Mill, Jersey St, Ancoats ☎0161/661 9668, ⓦwww.tribalgathering.co.uk. Many people's favourite night out, brought to you by the Tribal Gathering crew – Friday's Tribal Sessions and Saturday's The Red Light, playing sleazy house music.

South 4a South King St ☎0161/831 7756. Could be playing anything, depending on the night, from funk, 70s disco and house to punk or Northern Soul. Closed Sun and Mon.

Star & Garter 18–20 Fairfield St ☎0161/273 6726, ⓦwww.starandgarter.co.uk. Thrash/punk pub venue for loud, young bands and Saturday club nights; late bar until 2am.

Stadium venues

G-Mex Centre Windmill St ☎0161/834 2700, ⓦwww.g-mex.co.uk. Mid-sized city-centre indoor stadium.

The Manchester Apollo Stockport Rd, Ardwick Green ☎0161/242 2560. Huge theatre auditorium for all kinds of concerts.

Manchester Evening News Arena Victoria Station, 21 Hunts Bank ☎0161/950 5000. Indoor stadium that seats 20,000.

Arts and culture

Manchester is blessed with the North's most highly regarded **orchestra**, the Hallé (under music director, Mark Elder), which is resident at the Bridgewater Hall. Other acclaimed names include the BBC Philharmonic, the Manchester Camerata chamber orchestra, and The Lindsays (classical string quartet), who perform **concerts** at a variety of venues across the city. The Cornerhouse is the local **arts** mainstay, while a full range of mainstream and fringe **theatres** produce a year-round programme of events. The **Printworks**, Manchester's urban entertainment complex, contains the twenty-screen **Filmworks** cinema as well as an IMAX (giant-screen) cinema, though there are plenty of other places to catch movies, too, including art-house screenings at the Cornerhouse. The biggest annual fest is the **Manchester Festival**, an arts and TV extravaganza, with events in the city's clubs, theatres and open spaces. The X.Trax/Streets Ahead Festival showcases live theatre, music and entertainment, while other annual **events** include the city's Irish Festival, Jazz Festival, Lord Mayor's Parade, and Food and Drink Festival – more details and exact dates from the Visitor Centre.

Concerts and music

Bridgewater Hall Lower Mosley St ☎0161/907 9000, ⓦwww.bridgewater-hall.co.uk. Home of the Hallé (founded 1857) and the Manchester Camerata; also sponsors a full programme of chamber, classical and jazz concerts.

The Lowry Pier 8, Salford Quays ☎0161/876 2000, ⓦwww.thelowry. com. Full, year-round programme of music events, from opera to country.

Manchester Cathedral Victoria St ☎0161/833 2220. Concert season runs September to June, for concerts by the Cantata Choir and other soloists, ensembles and orchestras.

Royal Northern College of Music (RNCM) 124 Oxford Rd ☎0161/907 5278, ⓦwww.rncm.ac.uk. Stages top-quality classical and modern-jazz concerts, including performances by Manchester Camerata.

Opera House Quay St ☎0161/242 2509, ⓦwww.manchestertheatres.co.uk. Major venue for touring West End musicals, drama and concerts.

Theatre and the arts

Contact Theatre 15 Oxford Rd ☎0161/274 3434, ⓦwww.contact-theatre.org.uk. One of the most innovative theatre companies, housed in provocatively designed premises. Puts on predominantly modern works.

Cornerhouse 70 Oxford St ☎0161/200 1500, ⓦwww.cornerhouse.org. Engaging centre for contemporary arts, with three cinema screens, changing art exhibitions, recitals, talks, bookshop, café and bar.

Dancehouse Theatre 10 Oxford Rd ☎0161/237 9753. Home of the Northern Ballet School, and venue for dance, drama and comedy. Also has a café-bar.

Green Room 54–56 Whitworth St West ☎0161 /950 5900. Rapidly changing fringe programme which includes theatre, dance, mime and cabaret.

Library Theatre St Peter's Square ☎0161/236 7110, ⓦwww.libtheatreco.org.net. Classic drama and new writing, in an intimate theatre beneath the Central Library.

Royal Exchange Theatre St Ann's Square ☎0161/833 9833, ⓦwww.royalexchange.co.uk. The theatre-in-the-round in the Royal Exchange is the most famous stage in the city; and there's a Studio Theatre (for works by new writers) alongside the main stage.

Stand-up comedy

The Buzz The Southern, Nell Lane, Chorlton ☎0161/440 8662, ⓦwww.buzzcomedy.co.uk. The city's longest-running comedy club has pay-on-the-door shows every Thursday night.

The Comedy Store Deansgate Locks, Whitworth St West ☎08705/932932, ⓦwww.thecomedystore

.co.uk. Showcase for the best in nationwide stand-up comedy talent, with gigs every Wed–Sat. Bar and brasserie too.

Frog & Bucket 102 Oldham St t0161/236 9805. Pub venue for regular stand-up comedy gigs. Closed Sun, Tues & Wed.

Cinemas

Cornerhouse 70 Oxford St ☎0161/200 1500, ⓦwww.cornerhouse.org. The three screens at the Cornerhouse are your best bet for art-house releases, special screenings and cinema-related talks and events.

The Filmworks Printworks, Exchange Square ☎08700/102030, ⓦwww.thefilmworks.co.uk. State-of-the-art cinema-going – twenty screens, IMAX movies (including the excellent *Everest*),

digital projection and comfortable seating.

Odeon 1 Oxford St ☎0870/505 0007, ⓦwww.odeon.co.uk. Seven-screen city-centre cinema showing mainstream movies at cut-price rates.

UGC Cinemas Clippers Quay, Salford Quays ☎0161/873 7279. Multiscreen cinema with the latest mainstream releases.

Listings

Airport General enquiries ☎0161/489 3000; flight enquiries ☎0161/489 8000.

Banks and exchange There are branches of all the major banks (with ATMs) in the city centre shopping streets, as well as ATMs in the student areas along Oxford and Wilmslow roads, and in Piccadilly station. The only late-night exchanges, other than the big hotels, are at the airport (6am–midnight) and at the Castlefield YHA (daily 7am–11pm); at other times head for: American Express, 10–12 St Mary's Gate (☎0161/833 7303); or Thomas Cook, 22 Cross St (☎0161/839 0832) and 2 Oxford St (☎0161/251 7200).

Bookshops The main chains have outlets on Deansgate and around St Ann's Square. Blackwell's academic bookshop is in the Precinct Centre, Oxford Rd; Sportspages, the sports specialist, is in Barton Square, off St Ann's Square;

Gibb's Bookshop, 10 Charlotte St, is great for second-hand books and classical music; and try Paramount Book Exchange, 25–27 Shude Hill.

Bus information For all city services, call GMPTE on ☎0161/228 7811 or visit ⓦwww.gmpte.gov.uk; for intercity services, call National Express on ☎08705/808 080.

Camping and outdoor equipment Deansgate is the place, north of Quay and Peter streets, where you'll find everything you could possibly want in the YHA Adventure Shop, Black's or Ellis Brigham.

Car rental Avis, 1 Ducie St, Piccadilly ☎0161/236 6716 and at the airport ☎0161/436 2020; Budget, 384 Hyde Rd, Belle Vue ☎0161/231 7100 and at the airport ☎0161/437 0151; easyRentacar ☎ 0906/586 0586; Europcar, 41–45 Great Ancoats St ☎0161/236 0311 and at the airport ☎0161/436 2200; Hertz, 31 Aytoun St ☎0161/236 2747 and at

the airport ☎0161/437 8208 (airport).
Dentist Dental Hospital of Manchester, Higher Cambridge St ☎0161/275 6666.
Hospital Manchester Royal Infirmary, 13 Oxford Rd ☎0161/276 1234.
Internet easyEverything, 18 Exchange St, St Ann's Square (24hr); Net-Works Centre at the Central Library (Mon, Tues & Thurs 10am–7.30pm, Wed 1–7.30pm, Fri & Sat 10am–4.30pm).
Laundry Several along Wilmslow Road in Rusholme, or you could use the facilities at the YHA hostel.
Left Luggage Chorlton Street coach station (daily 9.30am–5.30pm); or, expensively, at Piccadilly train station, platform 5 (Mon–Fri 8am–10pm, Sat 9am–9pm, Sun 10am–8pm).
Pharmacy Boots, 11–13 Piccadilly Gardens (☎0161/834 8244) and 20 St Ann's St

(☎0161/839 1798); Cameolord Ltd, 7 Oxford St (daily 8am–midnight; ☎0161/236 1445).
Police Greater Manchester Police HQ, Chester House, Boyer St ☎0161/872 5050.
Post Office 29 Spring Gardens; 63 Newton St (☎08457/223344). The Spring Gardens office has a *bureau de change* and poste-restante section (Mon–Sat 8.30am-6pm).
Taxis Mantax ☎0161/236 5133; Taxifone ☎0161/236 9974. Airtax (for the airport) ☎0161/499 9000.
Travel Agents STA Travel, 75 Deansgate and 14 Oxford Rd ☎0161/834 0668; Trailfinders, 58 Deansgate ☎0161/839 6969. Also USIT Campus: at YHA shop, Deansgate ☎0161/833 2046; at UMIST, Sackville St ☎0161/200 3278); and at Manchester Academy, Oxford Rd ☎0161/274 3105.

Chester

In 1779 Boswell wrote to Samuel Johnson: "Chester pleases me more than any town I ever saw." **CHESTER**, forty miles southwest of Manchester, has changed since then, but not so much. A glorious two-mile ring of medieval and Roman walls encircle a neat kernel of Tudor and Victorian buildings, including the unique raised arcades called the "Rows". Very much the commercial hub of its county, Chester has enough in the way of sights, restaurants and atmosphere to make it an enjoyable base for a couple of days, though it can get very crowded.

The fabric of the town is run through with two thousand years of history. In 79 AD the Romans built Deva Castra here, their largest known fortress in Britain. Later, Ethelfleda, the daughter of King Alfred the Great, extended and refortified the place, only to have it brutally sacked by William the Conqueror's armies. Trade routes to Ireland made Chester the most prosperous port in the northwest, a status it recovered after the English Civil War, which saw a two-year-long siege of the town at the hands of the Parliamentarians. By the middle of the eighteenth century, however, silting of the port had forced the Irish trade to be rerouted first through Parkgate on the Dee estuary, and then to Liverpool. Things improved a little with the Industrial Revolution, as the canal and railway networks made Chester an important regional trading centre, a function it still retains.

Arrival and information

National Express and most regional bus services (including the hourly #X8 from Liverpool) arrive at **Chester bus station**, between Delamere and George streets. Close by are the northern city walls and Northgate Street. Most other local buses use the **bus exchange** just behind the town hall, off Princess Street. Merseyrail **trains** from Liverpool (every 20–30min 6am–11pm; 45min) and all other regional and national services call at the **train station**, northeast of the centre, from where it's a ten-minute walk down City Road and along Foregate Street to the central Eastgate Clock. The City-Rail Link bus from the station to the centre (every 12min, 30min on Sun) is free to anyone with a valid train ticket.

There's a **tourist office** in the Town Hall (May–Oct Mon–Sat 9am–5.30pm, Sun 10am–4pm; Nov–April Mon–Sat 10am–5pm) and also the **Chester Visitor Centre**, on Vicars Lane opposite the amphitheatre (May–Oct Mon–Sat 9am–5.30pm, Sun 10am–4pm; Nov–April Mon–Sat 10am–5pm, Sun 10am–4pm), both with the same telephone enquiries number and website (☎01244/402111, ⊛www.chestercc.gov.uk). At either, you can book accommodation and guided tours, and pick up a copy of the *Chester Visitor Guide*. The upper storey houses of the Chester Visitor Centre also have a mock-nineteenth-century street with period shops, where locally made crafts are on sale,

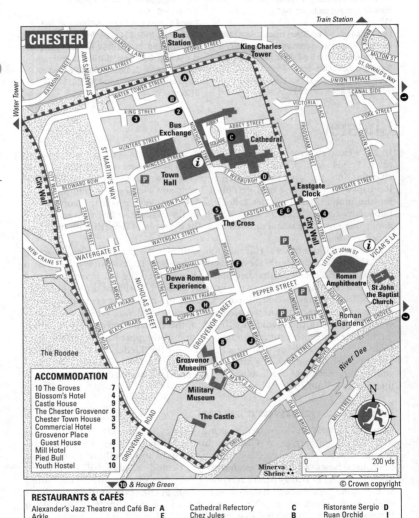

CHESTER

ACCOMMODATION

10 The Groves	7
Blossom's Hotel	4
Castle House	9
The Chester Grosvenor	6
Chester Town House	3
Commercial Hotel	5
Grosvenor Place Guest House	8
Mill Hotel	1
Pied Bull	2
Youth Hostel	10

0 — 200 yds

Minerva Shrine

© Crown copyright

▼ ⑩ & Hough Green

RESTAURANTS & CAFÉS

Alexander's Jazz Theatre and Café Bar	A	Cathedral Refectory	C	Ristorante Sergio	D
Arkle	E	Chez Jules	B	Ruan Orchid	I
Boulevard de la Bastille	F	Francs	G	Ruffino's Deli	J
La Brasserie	E	The Mediterranean Restaurant	A	La Tasca	H

and there's a café here too. Central city **parking** is scarce, so drivers should use the Park and Ride scheme, catching a bus from one of the car parks scattered around the ring road.

Accommodation

Chester's popularity is apparent as soon as you arrive, and in high summer **B&B accommodation** can be in short supply, as can space in the more characterful old inns. The places reviewed below are the best of the central choices: if you arrive late, or strike out in the centre, there are lots of budget-rated B&Bs along Brook Street, just a couple of minutes from the train station, and several moderate hotels down City Road, also near the station. Pleasant Victorian B&Bs also line up along Hough Green, a fifteen-minute walk from the centre.

Hotels and B&Bs

10 The Groves ⓣ01244/317907. There's just one double (en suite) in this riverside B&B, so get your booking in early. There's TV, tea- and coffee-making facilities, and parking available. No credit cards. ❷

Blossom's Hotel St John St ⓣ01244/346433, ⓦwww.heritage-hotels.com. Seventeenth-century town house with a variety of rooms, including one with a four-poster bed. Good full-board rates available. ❻

Castle House 23 Castle St ⓣ01244/350345. B&B in a sixteenth-century house with good facilities; bang in the centre and excellent value for money. No credit cards. ❷

The Chester Grosvenor Eastgate St ⓣ01244/324024, ⓦwww.chestergrosvenor.co.uk. Superbly appointed luxury hotel bristling with liveried staff, very comfortable bedrooms and a whole host of facilities, not least two fine restaurants. Parking available. Weekdays ❾, weekends ❽.

Chester Town House 23 King St ⓣ01244/350021, ⓦwww.chestertownhouse.co.uk. A very high-standard B&B in a comfortably furnished seventeenth-century town house, on a curving, cobbled central street off Northgate Street. There are

five en-suite rooms and private parking. ❸

Commercial Hotel St Peter's Church Yard ⓣ01244/320749. Friendly Georgian inn with good beer and half-a-dozen pleasant rooms in a brick-walled churchyard. ❷.

Grosvenor Place Guest House 2–4 Grosvenor Place ⓣ01244/324455. Pleasant town house B&B in a good, if noisy, location near the museum. Rooms available with and without shower. ❷

Mill Hotel Milton St ⓣ01244/350035, ⓦwww.millhotel.com. Sensitive warehouse conversion on the canal, between St Oswald's Way and Hooley Way, not far from the train station. Has its own car park and a nice waterside bar and café-bar; rooms with balcony attract a small supplement. ❺

Pied Bull Northgate St ⓣ01244/325829. Characterful old coaching inn, close to the walls and cathedral. ❷

Youth Hostel

Youth Hostel Hough Green House, 40 Hough Green ⓣ01244/680056, ⓔester@yha.org.uk. Twenty-minutes' walk from the centre, this Victorian house has a cafeteria, games room, and coin-op laundry facilities; family rooms available.

The City

Walking tours – assorted Roman, historic and ghost trails – from the Town Hall tourist office and from the Vicar Lane Visitor Centre (May–Oct twice daily; Nov–April once daily; £3) aren't a bad way to orient yourself. The main thoroughfares of Chester's Roman grid plan meet at **the Cross**, where the town crier welcomes visitors to the city (May–Aug Tues–Sat at noon). Both sides of all four streets are lined by **the Rows**, unique galleried arcades running on top of the ground-floor shops. The engaging black-and-white tableau is a blend of genuine Tudor houses and Victorian half-timbered imitations, with the finest Tudor buildings on Watergate Street – though Eastgate Street is perhaps the most picturesque, leading to the filigree **Eastgate Clock**, erected atop a sandstone arch to commemorate Victoria's Diamond Jubilee. There's no clear explanation of the origin of the Rows – they were first recorded soon after the fire that wrecked Chester in 1278, and may originally have been built on top of the heaped rubble left after the blaze.

You can get the best insight into Chester's Roman heritage at **Dewa Roman Experience** tucked away up Pierpoint Lane, off Bridge Street (daily 9am–5pm; £3.95). You're free to touch the archeological finds on show after following an armoured soldier through Roman street scenes and an excavation of Roman, Saxon and Medieval buildings. Most of the Roman city lies buried beneath Chester, though remnants have occasionally surfaced during rebuilding, while other tantalizing glimpses remain *in situ*. Much of the stone used in the building of the Roman city, for example, came from the quarries on the other side of the river. Cross the old bridge at the bottom of Lower Bridge Street and in the park to the right (behind the children's playground) survives a unique **shrine to Minerva** – Roman goddess of war – whose 2000-year-old likeness is carved into a quarry outcrop.

The Cathedral

North of the Cross, the neo-Gothic town hall dominates its square at the end of Northgate Street across from the heavily restored **Cathedral** (daily 7.30am –6pm; free tours Mon–Sat 2.30pm, donation requested; ⓦ www.chestercathedral .co.uk). Taking the role of cathedral in 1541 after the Dissolution of the Monasteries, this Benedictine church is dedicated to St Werburgh, a seventh-century Anglo-Saxon princess who became Chester's patron saint. Parts of the eleventh-century structure can still be seen in the north transept but the highlights in an otherwise simple interior are the fourteenth-century choir stalls, with their intricately carved misericords. Doors in the north wall of the nave lead into the shady sixteenth-century cloisters, encircling a small garden whose focal point is an imaginative and striking bronze sculpture by Stephen Broadbent of the woman of Samaria offering water to Jesus at the well.

Around the walls

East of the cathedral, steps provide access to the top of the two-mile girdle of the medieval and Roman **city walls** – the most complete set in Britain, though in places the wall is barely above street level. You can walk past all its towers, turrets and gateways in an hour or two, and most have a tale to tell. The fifteenth-century **King Charles Tower** in the northeast corner is so named because Charles I is said to have stood here in 1645 watching his troops being beaten on Rowton Moor, two miles to the southeast. The earlier **Water Tower** at the northwest corner, meanwhile, once stood in the river – evidence of the changes brought about by the gradual silting of the River Dee. South from the Water Tower you'll see the **Roodee**, England's oldest racecourse, laid out on a silted tidal pool where Roman ships once unloaded wine, figs and olive oil from the Mediterranean and slate, lead and silver from their mines in North Wales. Races are still held here in May, June and July; the tourist office has further details.

Until nineteenth-century excavation work, much of the wall near the Water Tower was propped up by scores of sculpted tomb panels and engraved head-stones, items probably used to rebuild the walls in a hurry in the turbulent fourth century. Many are now on display at the **Grosvenor Museum**, 27 Grosvenor St (Mon–Sat 10.30am–5pm, Sun 2–5pm; free), just inside the city walls near the southern end of the Roodee. This is the best investigation of Roman Chester, with good displays about the legionary system, city buildings, grave sites, defences, daily life and culture. The tombstones themselves form the largest collection from a single Roman site in Britain, the finest being the carving of a wounded barbarian – the surviving piece of a memorial to a Roman cavalryman. The back of the museum opens into a preserved Georgian house complete with furnished kitchen, parlour, bedrooms, rickety floors and sloping stairs.

Across the traffic roundabout on Castle Street, the recently revamped **Cheshire Military Museum** (daily 10am–5pm; £2.50; www.chester.ac.uk /militarymuseum) inhabits part of the same complex as the Norman **Chester Castle** (Easter–Sept daily 10am–6pm; Oct–Easter daily 10am–4pm; free; EH). Though the castle was founded by William the Conqueror, most of what you see today is little older than the eighteenth-century Greek Revival Assize Courts and council offices on the same site, the building of which led to the demolition of much of the medieval structure. The castle's history is explained in a couple of cells in the guard room (across the car park), but the gracefully simple St Mary de Castro chapel in the surviving Agricola Tower is the main attraction here.

South of the castle, the wall is buried under the street, but it rises again alongside the **Roman Gardens** (unrestricted access) on Souters Lane at Little John Street, where Roman foundations and columns dug up during redevelopment are on display. Across the road stands the half-excavated remains of the **Roman Amphitheatre** (Easter–Sept daily 10am–6pm; Oct–Easter daily 10am–1pm & 2–4pm; free; EH); it is estimated to have held seven thousand spectators, making it the largest amphitheatre in Britain, but the stonework is barely head-high now. The garrison at Roman Deva was 6000 strong at its height, and the amphitheatre was used by soldiers of the Twentieth Legion for weapons training as well as for entertainment.

The partly ruined pink-stone **Church of St John the Baptist** (daily 9.15am–6pm), a little to the east in Grosvenor Park, was founded by the Saxon king Ethelred in 689 and briefly served as the cathedral of Mercia. Rebuilt in its entirety by the Normans, although smaller than St Werburgh's it is considerably more impressive, the solid Norman pillars of the nave rising to a Transitional triforium and Early English clerestory. Outside are the romantic eastern ruins – left to deteriorate having been cut off from the rest of the church after the Reformation – and the stones of the northwest tower, which collapsed in 1881, possibly weakened by its use as a Parliamentarian gun emplacement during the Civil War. What's claimed to be a thirteenth-century coffin – emblazoned with the inscription "Dust to Dust" is set into an arch at the eastern end of the ruins.

Steps from the church gardens and from the southern edge of the city walls lead to the tree-shaded **Groves**, on the banks of the Dee, with its bandstand, slender iron footbridge and villas overlooking the willows draped along the opposite bank. Bithells Boats (☎01244/325394, www.showboatsofchester .co.uk) runs half-hour **cruises** on the river (every 15min; April–Oct 10am–5pm; Nov–March Sat & Sun 11am–4pm; £4) and two-hour trips in the summer (Wed & Sat 11am & 8pm, rest of week 11am only).

Eating, drinking and entertainment

You can't walk more than a few paces in Chester without coming across somewhere good to **eat and drink**, as often as not housed in a medieval crypt or Tudor building. Places below are open for lunch and dinner unless otherwise stated. Some of the **pubs** are highly atmospheric and most serve bar meals, though the quality isn't always up to much. For something different, book onto the *Mill Hotel*'s two-hour lunch or dinner restaurant **cruise** (from £15–20; ☎01244/350035).

A batch of annual **festivals** keeps the town's concert halls and churches busy:

the Folk Festival in May, Young Musician's Festival in June and the renowned **Summer Music Festival** every July, which sees outdoor concerts and fireworks in Grosvenor Park, as well as a simultaneous Fringe Festival. There's also a Literature Festival in October.

Cafés and restaurants

Alexander's Jazz Theatre and Café Bar 2 Rufus Court ☎01244/340005. Continental-style café-bar with *tapas* from the counter and live music or comedy nightly. Inexpensive.

Arkle *Chester Grosvenor Hotel*, Eastgate St ☎01244/324024. Traditional English food served to the highest standards in a very formal setting. The £30 set lunch is the best value. Very Expensive.

Boulevard de la Bastille Bridge St Row. One of the nicest of the arcade cafés, with tables looking over the street, doing a roaring trade in breakfasts, pastries and sandwiches. Inexpensive.

La Brasserie *Chester Grosvenor Hotel*, Eastgate St ☎01244/324024. The *Grosvenor*'s informal brasserie is a great place for a coffee and pastry, or come for the inventive French and fusion cooking. Moderate.

Cathedral Refectory Chester Cathedral, St Werburgh St. Bistro-style dishes served in the thirteenth-century monks' dining room. Closed Sun. Inexpensive.

Chez Jules 69 Northgate St ☎01244/400014. Classic brasserie menu (salad niçoise to vegetable cassoulet, Toulouse sausage to rib-eye steak, all served with dauphinois potatoes) including a terrific value two-course lunch. Inexpensive.

Francs 14 Cuppin St ☎01244/317952. An excellent and very French bistro with good-value set meals. You can also just drop in for a coffee and cake. Moderate.

The Mediterranean Restaurant 1 Rufus Court, off Northgate St ☎01244/320004. Georgian house by the walls, with a sunny courtyard garden, serving tapas, pasta, fish, paella and meze. Moderate.

Ristorante Sergio 87 St Werburgh St ☎01244/314663. Popular with a party crowd, this pizzeria-restaurant serves speciality fish and vegetarian dishes along with the pizzas. Moderate.

Ruan Orchid 14 Lower Bridge St ☎01244/400661. Their huge menu ranges across all the Thai regions – good for red and green curries, duck dishes and noodles. Moderate.

Ruffino's Deli 46 Lower Bridge St. Classy deli with gourmet sandwiches. Inexpensive.

La Tasca 6–12 Cuppin St ☎01244/400887. Huge tapas selection – Spanish cheeses to grilled prawns – and paella too. Nice spot in the summer when they throw the windows wide open. Inexpensive to Moderate.

Pubs and bars

Albion Inn corner of Albion and Park streets. Victorian terraced pub in the shadow of the walls with renowned "real British" bar food (ie, corned beef hash, shepherd's pie, haggies and tatties).

The Boat House The Groves. A riverside pub, decked out with black and white prints of nineteenth-century fishing families, and serving a great selection of ales.

Boot Inn Eastgate Row. A characterful pub in the upper gallery with a back room where fourteen Roundheads were killed, and a highbacked seat once used by soliciting prostitutes; the rest is less successfully maintained, ruined by piped music and slot machines.

The Falcon Lower Bridge St. This half-timbered pub was once a town house built by the Grosvenor family by enclosing part of a Row.

Fortress & Firkin Frodsham St. Modern canalside pub with outdoor seats and regular live bands.

Old Harkers Arms 1 Russell St, below the City Road bridge. Canalside real-ale boozer imaginatively sited in a former warehouse.

Telford's Warehouse Tower Wharf, Raymond St. Warehouse-style wine-bar pub with regular live music. It's just off the city walls by the Water Tower, built partly over the turning basin of the Shropshire Union Canal.

Around Chester

The two main attractions in the environs of Chester are the **zoo** and the **boat museum** at Ellesmere Port, both easily reached by public transport from the city.

Chester Zoo

Chester's most popular attraction, **Chester Zoo** (daily: April–Sept 10am–6pm; Oct–March 10am–4pm; last admission 2hr before closing; £10; ⊛www .chesterzoo.org), is one of the best in Europe. It is also the second largest in

Britain (after London), spreading over 110 landscaped acres, with new attractions opening all the time. The zoo is well known for its conservation projects and has had notable success with its Asiatic lions, while recent additions include the giant komodo dragons – Chester is the only British zoo to support these creatures – and a new jaguar enclosure. Animals are grouped by region in large paddocks viewed from a maze of pathways or from the creeping monorail, with main attractions being the baby animals (elephants, giraffes and orang-utans), the rainforest habitat, the Twilight Zone bat cave and the Chimpanzee Forest with the biggest climbing frame in the country. Kids enjoy the Animal Discovery Centre, where they're encouraged by the staff to touch and learn. The zoo entrance is signposted off the A41 to the north of town and reached by bus #4, #14 or #40 (Mon–Sat; every 30min) from Chester's bus exchange, or the #11c and #12c (every 30min, Sun & public holidays) to Liverpool's Albert Dock. Merseyrail stations sell a combined train, bus and zoo-admission ticket (£12), using the #40 bus link from Bache Merseyrail station, one stop north of Chester.

Ellesmere Port Boat Museum

It's claimed that the **Ellesmere Port Boat Museum** (April–Oct daily 10am–5pm; Nov–March Mon–Wed, Sat & Sun 11am–4pm; £5.50; ⓦwww .boatmuseum.org.uk), seven miles north of Chester, has Britain's largest collection of floating canal vessels, a contention that seems completely plausible when you see the flotilla. Scores of barges are scattered throughout the canal basin and staircase of locks where the Shropshire Union Canal meets the refinery-lined River Mersey at the head of the Manchester Ship Canal. Indoor exhibits trace the history of canals and their construction, and you can take a thirty-minute ride on a narrow boat (£2.50). The museum is ten minutes' walk from Ellesmere Port train station (change at Hooton from Chester) or take bus #3 (every 30min) or the hourly #X8 (Liverpool bus) from Chester bus station on Delamere Street.

The Cheshire Plain

The bustle of Chester is no measure of the rest of the county, a region of lush pastureland and unflustered little towns strung together by hedgerowed lanes. Perhaps because of the familiarity of the landscape, the Danes took a liking to the **Cheshire Plain**, leaving the names of the River Dane and **Knutsford** (Canute's ford) as evidence of their occupation. Since that time farming has continued to be the mainstay of the county's economy, but salt mining around **Northwich** and silk manufacturing in **Macclesfield** have contributed in their day. Once the main centre of southern Cheshire, **Nantwich** has benefited from the rise of nearby Crewe and is today a sleepy town packed with four-hundred-year-old houses and shops. All the various attractions are best seen as a stop on the way between Chester and Manchester. Call the Cheshire Travel Line (☎01244/602666; daily 8am–8pm) for all bus timetable enquiries.

Northwich

Most of the interest in **NORTHWICH**, seventeen miles east of Chester, lies in its pretty, town-centre conservation area, which nestles by the confluence of the rivers Weaver and Dane. Like several towns on the Cheshire plain, Northwich owes its existence to the underground pockets of rock salt laid down here when the area was an inland sea. Salt was a crucial commodity to the Romans, who began sluicing it to the surface as brine, then evaporating it in lead pans. Methods of salt extraction changed little into last century but brine is now pumped from under the town to chemical plants on the Mersey as the raw material for chlorine and alkali manufacture.

Over the centuries, the extraction of the underlying strata caused considerable subsidence in Northwich. As buildings collapsed in the centre of town in Victorian times, a novel construction method was proposed, whereby all new buildings would be erected on liftable timber frames so they could be shifted intact in the event of future subsidence. The town was largely rebuilt after the 1890s in an homogeneous mock-Tudor style, and the best of the buildings can be viewed on an enjoyable, hour-long, self-guided walking tour – pick up the trail leaflet from the tourist office (see below). The largest timber-framed building in town, the striking former post office on Witton Street, is now *The Penny Black* pub.

The town trail starts down at the **Salt Museum**, 162 London Rd (Tues–Fri 10am–5pm, Sat & Sun 2–5pm; Aug also Mon 10am–5pm; £2.10;ⓦwww .saltmuseum.org.uk), housed in a former workhouse, half a mile south of the town centre. This fills you in on the background to the town's industrial past, though if you want to see salt in production you'll have to visit the nineteenth-century **Lion Salt Works** on the Trent and Mersey Canal on Ollershaw Lane in nearby Marston (Mon–Fri & Sun 1.30–4.30pm; free; ⓦ www.lionsaltworkstrust .co.uk), a couple of miles north of the town, off the A559. This maintains a series of traditional open salt pans, and has its own exhibitions about the industry. Salt was shipped by the canal to Liverpool and Manchester for export, using the nearby **Anderton Boat Lift**, built in 1875 to link the canal with the River Weaver. Both salt works and Boat Lift – a marvel of Victorian engineering – are linked by a six-mile circular walk, along the canal banks and through the attractive local village of **Great Budworth**; there's parking at the Salt Works and Boat Lift.

There are regular trains between Chester and Manchester, stopping in Northwich: the **train station** is twenty minutes' walk from the town centre; follow the ring road, Chester Way, in past the parish church. The **tourist office** is at 1 The Arcade, opposite the County Council building (June–Aug Mon–Fri 9am–5pm, Sat 10am–2pm; rest of year Mon–Fri 9am–5pm, Sat 9.30am–12.30pm; ☎01606/353534), and can provide details about canal cruises.

Knutsford and around

While conquering the greater part of England between 1015 and 1018, the Danish king Knut (Canute) is said to have crossed Lily Stream at the spot where the winding streets and eighteenth-century houses of **KNUTSFORD** now stand. From medieval times the town was important locally for its market and coaching inns, but today is a quiet wealthy community that makes much of its role as the model for Cranford in the book of the same name by **Elizabeth Gaskell**. Gaskell spent her childhood years here, living for a while in Heathwaite House, 18 Gaskell Ave (not open to the public), and getting married in **St John's** parish church. A small permanent exhibition in the **Knutsford Heritage Centre**, 90a King St (Mon–Fri 1.30–4pm, Sat noon–4pm, Sun 2–4.30pm; free), explains more about her connection with the town, while admirers will want to complete their Gaskell tour by visiting the **Unitarian** church, behind the train station, where she is buried. A map posted outside the tourist office can help you track down all these sights.

Even without the lure of Mrs Gaskell, Knutsford makes a handsome place for a stroll, not least down narrow King Street in the centre, lined with old inns, antique shops, boutiques and cafés, and still featuring several cobbled yards and side-alleys. The buildings raised by Manchester glove-maker and philanthropist **Richard Watt** also catch the eye, though their loosely Mediterranean style may not be to everyone's taste. The most visible of these are the terracotta-roofed **Ruskin Rooms** on Drury Lane, built as a reading and recreation place for the townspeople, and **The King's Coffee House**, 60 King St, which now houses the *Belle Epoque* brasserie-with-rooms, with its Art Nouveau interior.

Knutsford lies on the Chester–Manchester **train** line. The **tourist office** is opposite the train station in the council offices on Toft Road (Mon–Thurs 8.45am–5pm, Fri 8.45am–4.30pm, Sat 9am–1pm; ☎01565/632611). To reach King Street, walk along Toft Road from the tourist office and turn right down Church Hill at the parish church. A couple of hours would take care of the sights in Knutsford itself. If you wanted to stay, contact the tourist office for a list of local **B&Bs** – though both the *Cross Keys* (☎01565/750404; ❹) and *Angel* (☎01565/750245; ❸) **pubs** on King Street also have rooms. King Street also has all the **eating** options, with more than a dozen restaurants, brasseries and cafés, notably the well-regarded *Belle Epoque* (☎01565/633060; closed Sat lunch & Sun; ❹, rooms available Mon–Fri only), or the less formal *Knutsford Wine Bar*, opposite the churchyard.

Tatton Park

Knutsford's King Street ends at the southern gates of thousand-acre **Tatton Park** (Easter–Sept daily 10am–7pm; Oct–Easter Tues–Sun 11am–5pm; free; parking £3.50; ⓦwww.tattonpark.org.uk), from where it is another mile past herds of deer to the vast Regency **mansion** (April–Sept Tues–Sun noon–5pm; £3; NT), built at the end of the eighteenth century. A couple of Canalettos lurk among the period furniture, and guided tours (noon & 12.30pm) will point out many other treasures. There's also a working farm and stables (£3) and historic exhibits in the Tudor Old Hall (£3), though the extensive formal **gardens** (closes 1hr earlier than the park; £3; NT) are probably the most pleasurable part of the estate. If you plan on seeing everything – which would take the best part of a day – then buy a saver ticket (£4.60) which is valid for any two attractions.

Macclesfield

The first silk mill was established in **MACCLESFIELD** in 1743, rapidly changing the character of this erstwhile market town. By 1804 there were thirteen mills and, by the 1820s, over seventy, trade having boomed when French silks became unavailable during the Napoleonic Wars. Silk of all kinds was produced here, with silk and mohair buttons a particular local speciality. The demand for parachute material and service badges during World War II provided another boost, though by the late-1940s, when artificial fibres became widely available, the mills declined rapidly. However, silk is still made in the town (and the industry has provided a nickname – the "Silk Men" – for the local football team), while many of the old mills have found new leases of life following redevelopment as shops, offices and housing.

The **Silk Museum**, in the Heritage Centre, housed in a former Sunday School on Roe Street (Mon–Sat 11am–5pm, Sun 1pm–5pm; £2.90, joint ticket with Paradise Mill £5.10), puts the industry and its interaction with the community into perspective through an audiovisual presentation, archaic equipment and a World War II silk map of Northern Europe. After that, take a trip down to **Paradise Mill**, on Park Lane (Tues–Sun 1–5pm; £2.90), where the top floor is devoted to rows of ageing Jacquard looms and spinning machines that are set in action by the tour guides, many of them ex-weavers.

It's a five-minute walk from both the **train station** on Sunderland Street (frequent services from Manchester Piccadilly) and the **bus station**, across the road from the train station, up the hill to the central Market Place. The **tourist office** here is in the town hall (Mon–Thurs 9am–5pm, Fri 9am–4.30pm, Sat 9am–4pm; ☎01625/504114). The rest of the compact shopping centre is close at hand; for the museums, follow pedestrianized Mill Street downhill from Market Place.

Nantwich

In 1583 **NANTWICH** was almost entirely destroyed by fire. Such was the town's importance for its salt production that Elizabeth I donated £1000 and ordered a nationwide appeal to help with rebuilding, a gesture commemorated by a plaque on **Queen's Aid House** on the High Street. A largely pedestrianized centre makes Nantwich a good place to amble around and see Cheshire's second-best set of timber-framed buildings, with an essential stop being the predominantly fourteenth-century **Church of St Mary**, where the ribbed vaulting in the chancel has bosses depicting the life of the Virgin. The church and neighbouring **Sweetbriar Hall** are two of the three buildings to have survived the fire – the other is the timber-framed Elizabethan **Churche's Mansion** in Hospital Street.

The *Crown Hotel* on the High Street is perhaps the most striking of the black-and-white buildings, the gallery on the top floor now converted into separate rooms. It's also one of the most atmospheric and lively spots in town for a drink. Elements of the town's former cottage industries of cheese-, salt- and shoemaking are showcased in the small **Nantwich Museum** on Pillory Street (April–Sept Mon–Sat 10.30am–4.30pm; Oct–March Tues–Sat 10.30am–4.30pm; free), 150 yards from the church.

The **train station** sees hourly traffic on the Manchester–Crewe–Cardiff line and is only five minutes' walk from the **tourist office** in Church House, Church Walk (Mon–Fri 9.30am–5pm, Sat 10am–4pm; public holidays 11am–3pm; ☎01270/610983, ⊛www.netcentral.co.uk/cnbc).

Liverpool

Once the empire's second city, **LIVERPOOL** spent too many of the twentieth-century postwar years struggling against adversity. Things are looking up at last, as economic and social regeneration brightens the centre and old docks. Yet – even as any short-term visitor to the city could tell you – nothing ever broke Liverpool's extraordinary spirit of community, a spirit that emerged strongly in the aftermath of the Hillsborough football stadium disaster of 1989, when the deaths of 95 Liverpool supporters seemed to unite the whole city. Indeed, acerbic wit and loyalty to one of the city's two football teams are the linchpins of Scouse culture – though Liverpool makes great play of its musical heritage, which is reasonable enough from the city that produced The Beatles.

Although it gained its charter from King John in 1207, Liverpool remained a humble fishing village for half a millennium until the silting-up of Chester and the booming slave trade prompted the building of the first dock in 1715. From then until the abolition of slavery in Britain in 1807, Liverpool was the apex of the **slaving triangle** in which firearms, alcohol and textiles were traded for African slaves, who were then shipped to the Caribbean and America. The holds were filled with tobacco, raw cotton and sugar for the return journey. After the abolition of the trade, the port continued to grow into a seven-mile chain of docks, not only for freight but also to cope with wholesale European **emigration**, which saw nine million people from half of Europe leave for the Americas and Australasia between 1830 and 1930. Some never made it further than Liverpool and contributed to a five-fold increase in population in fifty years. An even larger boost came with immigration from the Caribbean and China, and especially Ireland in the wake of the potato famine in 1845. The resulting mix became one of Britain's earliest multi-ethnic communities, described by Carl Jung as "the pool of life".

The docks were busy until the middle of the twentieth century when a number of factors led to the port's **decline**: cheap air fares saw off the lucrative liner business; trade with the dwindling empire declined, while European traffic boosted southeastern ports at Tilbury, Harwich and Southampton; and containerization meant reduced demand for handling and warehousing. The arrival of car manufacturing plants in the 1960s, including Ford at Halewood, stemmed the decline for a while, but during the 1970s and 1980s Liverpool became a byword for British economic malaise as its fundamental businesses withered and died.

There's been a renaissance of sorts since the 1990s as EU development funds and millennium money have kick-started various projects. Although unemployment here is higher than the national average, there's been major investment by blue-chip companies as well as a move away from the traditional industries: financial services, information technology and biotechnology are all major employers while the city is the "call centre" capital of the UK. Ironically, despite the new economic realities, Ford is still building cars here while the Port of Liverpool now handles more cargo than at any time in its history – and it's still the largest British port for trade with the east-coast USA.

Compared to the wholesale redevelopment of neighbouring Manchester, the city still has a fair hill to climb, but there's a welcome new confidence about Liverpool. It's the most filmed British city outside London, doubling as locations as diverse as St Petersburg and Venice, and it has also rebranded itself as the "festival city" – on the back of which, it's making a bid to be European Capital of Culture for 2008. City-centre living is on the rise as old buildings and warehouses in the so-called Duke Street triangle and down on the waterfront are redeveloped. Indeed, like Manchester, Liverpool has a legacy of magnificent municipal and industrial buildings – best seen en masse from across the river or on the Mersey ferry – and these are the chief attractions of the cityscape, along with its two famous **cathedrals**. The city's mercantile past and aspects of its recent history are well covered in a number of fine museums and galleries, especially in the rejuvenated warehouses of **Albert Dock**, which form the largest grouping of Grade I listed buildings in the country. These sights can easily sustain a day or two – and make time to drop into one of Liverpool's many excellent pubs or bars, the surest way to get the feel of the place.

Arrival, information and city transport

Mainline trains pull in to **Lime Street** station, while the suburban **Merseyrail** system (for trains from Chester) calls at four underground stations in the city, including Lime Street, Central (under the main post office on Ranelagh Street) and James Street (for Pier Head and the Albert Dock). National Express **buses**

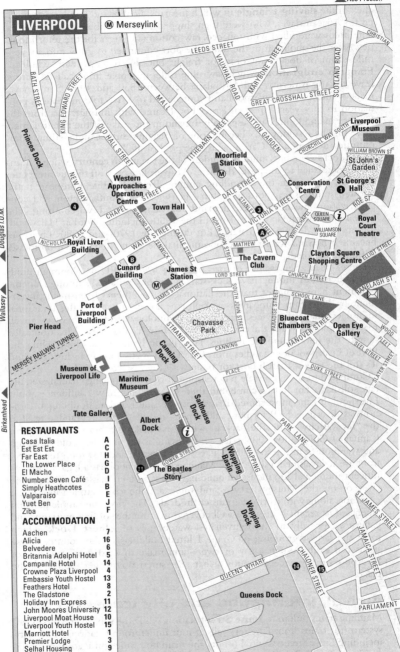

Douglas I.O.M. ◄
Wallasey ◄
Birkenhead ◄

▲ A59 Preston

LIVERPOOL   Ⓜ Merseylink

CHRISTIAN
LEEDS STREET
VAUXHALL ROAD
MARYBONE STREET
SCOTLAND ROAD
GREAT CROSSHALL STREET
BATH STREET
KING EDWARD STREET
OLD HALL STREET
TITHEBARN STREET
HATTON GARDEN
CHURCHILL WAY SOUTH
WILLIAM BROWN ST

Liverpool Museum

St John's Garden

Princes Dock

NEW QUAY

Western Approaches Operation Centre
CHAPEL STREET
DALE STREET
STANLEY STREET
VICTORIA STREET
WHITECHAPEL

Moorfield Station Ⓜ

Conservation Centre
St George's Hall ❶
QUEEN SQUARE ⓘ
ROE ST
Royal Court Theatre

❹

Royal Liver Building
NICHOLAS PLACE
WATER STREET
FENWICK ST
CASTLE STREET
NORTH JOHN STREET
RUMFORD STREET
❸
Ⓐ
MATHEW ST
WILLIAMSON SQUARE

Town Hall ❹

Cunard Building Ⓑ
James St Station
JAMES STREET Ⓜ
LORD STREET
SOUTH JOHN STREET
The Cavern Club

Clayton Square Shopping Centre
CHURCH STREET
ELLIOT STREET
RANELAGH ST

Port of Liverpool Building

Pier Head
STRAND STREET
Chavasse Park
CANNING
PARADISE STREET
SCHOOL LANE
HANOVER STREET

Bluecoat Chambers
Open Eye Gallery
SEEL STREET
SLATER STREET
WOOD
FLEET
❿

MERSEY RAILWAY TUNNEL

Museum of Liverpool Life
Maritime Museum
Ⓒ
Salthouse Dock
DUKE STREET

Canning Dock

Tate Gallery
Albert Dock ⓘ
PLACE
GOWER STREET
PARK LANE
WAPPING
Wapping Basin
ST JAMES STREET

❶ **The Beatles Story**
Wapping Dock
JAMACIA STREET

QUEENS WHARF
CHALONER STREET
❶⓸ ❶⓹
PARLIAMENT

Queens Dock

RESTAURANTS

Casa Italia	A
Est Est Est	C
Far East	H
The Lower Place	G
El Macho	D
Number Seven Café	I
Simply Heathcotes	B
Valparaiso	E
Yuet Ben	J
Ziba	F

ACCOMMODATION

Aachen	7
Alicia	16
Belvedere	6
Britannia Adelphi Hotel	5
Campanile Hotel	14
Crowne Plaza Liverpool	4
Embassie Youth Hostel	13
Feathers Hotel	8
The Gladstone	2
Holiday Inn Express	11
John Moores University	12
Liverpool Moat House	10
Liverpool Youth Hostel	15
Marriott Hotel	1
Premier Lodge	3
Selhal Housing	9

Ⓘ⓪ ❿ THE NORTHWEST

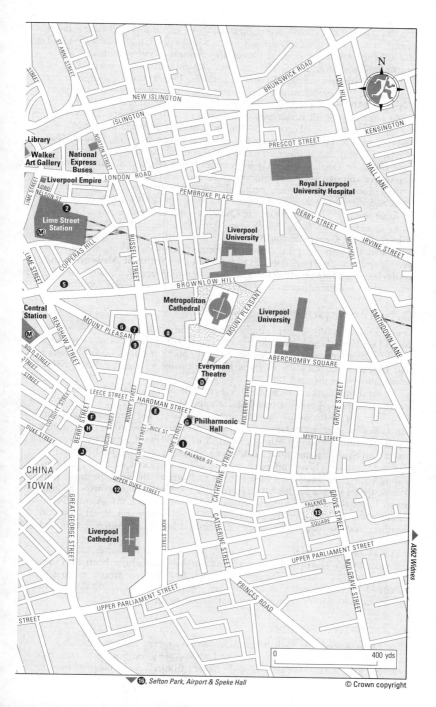

N

Library
Walker Art Gallery
National Express Buses
Liverpool Empire
LONDON ROAD
2
Lime Street Station
M
5
Central Station
M
RENSHAW STREET
BOLD STREET
STREET
STREET
DUKE STREET
BERRY STREET
J

CHINA TOWN

GREAT GEORGE STREET

STREET

ST ANNE STREET
ST ANNE STREET
NORTON STREET
ISLINGTON
NEW ISLINGTON
BRUNSWICK ROAD
LOW HILL
KENSINGTON
PRESCOT STREET
LIME STREET
LORD NELSON ST
PEMBROKE PLACE
Royal Liverpool University Hospital
HALL LANE
COPPERAS HILL
RUSSELL STREET
Liverpool University
DERBY STREET
IRVINE STREET
MINSHULL ST
BROWNLOW HILL
Metropolitan Cathedral
6 7
8
9
MOUNT PLEASANT
Liverpool University
ABERCROMBY SQUARE
MOUNT PLEASANT
SMITHDOWN LANE
Everyman Theatre
D
LEECE STREET
HARDMAN STREET
F E
RODNEY STREET
MULBERRY STREET
GROVE STREET
H
Philharmonic Hall
G
RICE ST
MYRTLE STREET
PILGRIM STREET
HOPE STREET
I
FALKNER ST
ROSCOE STREET
CATHERINE STREET
12
UPPER DUKE STREET
FALKNER SQUARE
13
HOPE STREET
Liverpool Cathedral
CATHERINE STREET
GROVE STREET
UPPER PARLIAMENT STREET
UPPER PARLIAMENT STREET
PRINCES ROAD
MULGRAVE STREET

A562 Widnes

0   400 yds

16, Sefton Park, Airport & Speke Hall

© Crown copyright

use the station on Norton Street, just northeast of Lime Street. Local buses depart from a variety of terminals: Queen Square (for city centre, Pier Head and Chester services); Paradise Street Bus Station (southbound and a few northbound services); and St Thomas Street (eastbound and cross-river).

Liverpool **airport** – now officially named after John Lennon – is eight miles southeast of the city centre. From outside the main entrance, the **Airport Express #500 bus** (every 30min; 6am–1am; £2) runs directly into the city centre, stopping at all major bus terminals and at Lime Street. The slower, cheaper local bus #80A (every 15–30min; 6am–11pm) makes the same journey, or a **taxi** to Lime Street costs around £12. **Ferry** arrivals – from the Isle of Man, Dublin and Belfast – dock at the terminals just north of Pier Head, close to Albert Dock and not far from James Street Merseyrail station. For all **departure details** and travel enquiry numbers, see "Listings" on p.788.

All the **tourist information** you could possibly want – including timetables, maps and the comprehensive *Liverpool and Merseyside Visitor Guide* (£1) – are available from two handy offices: the **Queen's Square Centre** centrally located in Queen Square (Mon–Sat 9am–5.30pm, Sun 10.30am–4.30pm) and the **Albert Dock Centre** at the Atlantic Pavilion (daily 10am–5.30pm), which both share the same telephone enquiries number (☎0906/680 6886) and website (ⓦwww.visitliverpool.com). Both also sell the **National Museums and Galleries on Merseyside** (NMGM; ⓦwww.nmgm.org.uk) Eight Pass (£3) which gives unlimited access into eight local museums for twelve months.

City transport

Liverpool city centre is surprisingly compact and you'll easily be able to get around on foot, though the odd bus route may come in useful and everyone should take a ferry across the Mersey at some point, if only to be able to say that they've sung *that* song in its proper environment. **Mersey ferry** ticket information is given on p.789.

The local transport authority is **Merseytravel**, which co-ordinates all buses, trains and ferries. There's a telephone enquiry line (☎0151/236 7676; daily 8am–8pm) or visit one of the Merseytravel information centres to pick up timetables: located at 24 Hatton Gardens (Mon–Fri 9am–4pm), at the Queen's Square Centre (Mon–Sat 9am–5.30pm, Sun 10.30am–4.30pm), at Paradise Street Bus Station (same hours as Queen's Square) and Pier Head (while ferries are running). Daily off-peak, zonal Saveaway tickets (£1.80–3.20) for unlimited use on most city buses, trains and ferries are available from post offices, newsagents and the Merseytravel offices. **Useful bus routes** include Smart buses #1 (linking Queen Square and Albert Dock), #4 (Albert Dock, Paradise Street and the cathedrals) and #5 (Queen Square and Albert Dock on evenings and Sundays). The #222/224 links Pier Head, Albert Dock and Queen Square.

The most bizarre addition to the city's fleet is the amphibious half-truck-half-boat **Duck Tour** (mid-Feb to Christmas, daily every hour from 10.30am; ☎0151/708 7799; tickets £9), which departs from Gower Street, in front of Albert Dock, and trundles around the city centre before splashing down into the docks themselves for a spot of aquatic sightseeing.

Accommodation

City-centre **accommodation** has improved over recent years and there's a fair choice of hotels, from budget chains and small-scale guest houses to business-oriented four-stars. There's also a wide range of hostels and halls of residence, including a terrific youth hostel a short walk from Albert Dock. If you prefer, you can opt for a cheap B&B in the surrounding suburbs – the tourist offices can help with specific recommendations – but you're unlikely to beat the prices at the budget chains in the centre. There is no useful campsite. Both tourist offices will book rooms for you for free; call ☎0845/601 1125 for their details of special-offer weekend breaks and packages. It's also always worth asking about weekend rates at the bigger hotels, which can turn up some surprising deals.

Hotels and B&Bs

Aachen 89–91 Mount Pleasant ☎0151/709 3477, ⓦwww.aachenhotel.co.uk. The best and most popular of the Mount Pleasant budget choices, with friendly staff, a range of value-for-money rooms, big "eat-as-much-as-you-like" breakfasts, a bar and parking.

Alicia 3 Aigburth Drive, Sefton Park ☎0151/727 4411, ⓦwww.feathers.uk.com. Restored townhouse in the *Feathers* mould, with pleasant park views and a variety of rooms. ❹

Belvedere 83 Mount Pleasant ☎0151/709 2356. A convenient and cheap central hotel with just nine, no-frills rooms and a family-run feel. ❷

Britannia Adelphi Hotel Ranelagh Place ☎0151/709 7200, ⓦwww.britannia-hotels.co.uk. Liverpool's *Adelphi* catered to passenger-liner customers in its heyday, but it's lost its lustre since then. But for its location, one block from Lime Street station, it remains a relatively good deal (though breakfast isn't included). You should be able to negotiate a weekend discount. ❺

Campanile Hotel Wapping and Chaloner St ☎0151/709 8104. Purpose-built budget motel-style property near Albert Dock, where all the rooms are one low price; parking, bistro and bar. ❷

Crowne Plaza Liverpool St Nicholas Place, Princes Dock, Pier Head ☎0151/243 8000, ⓦwww.crowneplaza-liverpool.co.uk. Great dockside location and brimful of facilities, including pool, sauna and gym, brasserie and bar. ❺

Feathers Hotel 117–125 Mount Pleasant ☎0151 /709 9655, ⓦwww.feathers.uk.com. A converted and modernized terrace of Georgian houses, with nicely presented en-suite rooms and a help-yourself buffet breakfast included in the price. ❺

The Gladstone Lord Nelson St ☎0151/709 7050. Standard three-star accommodation, just behind Lime Street station, with summer and weekend deals knocking a tenner off the room rate. ❹

Holiday Inn Express Britannia Pavilion, Albert Dock ☎0151/709 1133, ⓦwww.hiexpress.com. All 170 of the dockside rooms here go for the same bargain price, and are en suite, with continental breakfast and parking included. ❸

Liverpool Moat House Paradise St ☎0151/471 9988. Well-equipped, modern hotel a short walk from the Albert Dock, with comfortable rooms and good sports facilities including a fine indoor pool and spa. The midweek rate doesn't include breakfast. ❼, ❻ at weekends.

Marriott Hotel 1 Queen Square ☎0151/476 8000, ⓦwww.marriott.com. Stylish city-centre hotel, handy for Lime Street and the museums, and featuring a leisure club (with indoor pool and hot tub), restaurant and bar. ❼

Premier Lodge 45 Victoria St ☎0151/236 1366, ⓦwww.premierlodge.com. Motel-style comfort near the Cavern Quarter at pretty much unbeatable prices. Family rooms available. Breakfast not included. ❷

Hostels and halls of residence

Embassie Youth Hostel 1 Falkner Square ☎0151/707 1089. Twenty minutes' walk from Lime Street station (bus #80), in a Georgian terrace west of the Anglican cathedral, this relaxed hostel has dorm beds, a self-catering kitchen, TV lounge and laundry facilities. Free showers, tea, toast and coffee included in the price.

John Moores University Cathedral Park, St James Rd ☎0151/709 3197. Self-catering accommodation in the shadow of the metropolitan cathedral. Available with and without continental breakfast. July to early Sept only.

Liverpool Youth Hostel Wapping ☎0151/709 8888, Ⓔliverpool@yha.org.uk. One of the YHA's best, just south of Albert Dock, purpose-built and decorated with Beatles memorabilia. Accommodation (the price includes breakfast) is in smart two-, three-, four- or six-bed rooms (with private bathroom and heated towel rail). There's also a kitchen, licensed café, lobby lounge, luggage storage and laundry facilities. Premium twin rooms (small surcharge) come with a TV and tea/coffee facilities.

Selhal Housing 1 Rodney St ☎0151/709 7791. Cheap rooms for women only in the former YWCA. Centrally heated and with communal kitchens and laundry facilities.

University of Liverpool Halls of Residence Greenbank House, Greenbank Lane ☎0151/794 6440. Set in private parkland, three miles out of the centre (bus #80) and only open June to Aug. Hundreds of single rooms available, with continental breakfast.

The City

The main sights are fairly widely scattered throughout the centre of Liverpool but you can easily walk between most of them, through cityscapes ranging from revamped shopping arcades and restyled city squares to the surviving regal Georgian terraces around Rodney and Hope streets. Even the walk from the Anglican cathedral through the shops to Albert Dock will only take half an hour or so. The tourist offices can book you onto a variety of **guided walks and tours** (from £3), or make your own way using the themed trail leaflets on sale in the offices. **Public sculpture** abounds, from the statues of Victoria, Albert, Disraeli and Gladstone around St George's Hall to contemporary

The Beatles in Liverpool

Liverpool has sustained its musical impetus ever since the Sixties and is still turning out some excellent bands, but none is ever likely to eclipse **The Beatles**.

Mathew Street, ten minutes' walk west of Lime Street station, is where *The Cavern* used to be – once the womb of Merseybeat, it's become a little enclave of Beatles nostalgia, most of it bogus and typified by the **Cavern Walks Shopping Centre**, with an awful bronze statue of the boys in the atrium. *The Cavern* itself saw 275 Beatles gigs between 1961 and 1963 and was where the band was first spotted by Brian Epstein; the club closed in 1966 and was partly demolished in 1973, though a latterday successor, the **Cavern Club** at 10 Mathew St (ⓦwww.cavern-liverpool.co.uk), complete with souvenir shop, was rebuilt on half of the original site, using, it's claimed, the original bricks. The *Cavern Pub*, immediately across the way, is also a musical *arriviste*, boasting a coiffed Lennon lounging against the wall and an exterior "Wall of Fame", highlighting both the names of all the bands who appeared at the club between 1957 and 1973 (etched into the bricks) and brass discs commemorating every Liverpool No. 1 chart-topper since 1952. A few pubs, among them *Rubber Soul* and *Lennon's Bar*, raise no more than a token toast to the soul of Beatlemania, embodied better at *The Beatles Shop*, 31 Mathew St, with the "largest range of Beatles gear in the world". Around the corner, on Stanley Street, lurks the Eleanor Rigby statue, inspired by the song.

For a history of the group, you'll have to head to the Albert Dock for **The Beatles Story** in the Britannia Vaults (daily: April–Sept 10am–6pm; Oct–March 10am–5pm; £7.95), tracing The Beatles' rise from the early days at *The Cavern* (re-created here) to their disparate solo careers, ending with John's death. Dedicated pilgrims will get more from the two-hour **Magical Mystery Tour** (daily tours; book through Cavern City Tours, ☏0151/236 9091, or Mersey Tourism, ☏0151/709 3285; £10.95 or £15 with The Beatles Story), on board a customized double-decker bus staffed by guides with – in some cases – first-hand acquaintance with The Beatles. It leaves Albert Dock, visiting Strawberry Fields (a Salvation Army home), Penny Lane (an ordinary suburban street) and the terraced houses where the lads grew up. One of these, **20 Forthlin Rd**, home of the McCartney family from 1955–1964, has been preserved by the National Trust and is open to visitors who duly tramp round the 1950s terraced house where John and Paul wrote songs and where Paul's mother Mary died. The house is only accessible on a pre-booked minibus tour (June–Oct Wed–Sat; £5.50; NT), which leaves six times daily from Speke Hall (see p.785) and the Albert Dock – the price includes the tour, the minibus to Forthlin Road and free access to Speke Hall grounds.

Beatlemania is wholeheartedly celebrated on August Bank Holiday Monday (the last Monday of the month) at the culmination of the annual International Beatles Week and **Mathew Street Festival**, filling the town centre with wannabe moptops, jiving to the sounds of tunes that have been hummed and strummed in Liverpool since the first concert rocked *The Cavern*.

groupings like the assortment of suitcases and trunks at the Hope Street end of Mount Street.

Around Lime Street

Emerging from **Lime Street Station** – whose cast-iron train shed was the largest in the world on its completion in 1867 – you can't miss **St George's Hall**, one of Britain's finest Greek Revival buildings and a testament to the wealth generated from transatlantic trade. Once Liverpool's concert hall and crown courts, its tunnel-vaulted Great Hall is open to the public for monthly craft and antique fairs and for daily **guided tours** in summer (late-July & Aug Mon–Sat 10.30am–4.30pm), when the exquisite floor, tiled with thirty thousand precious Minton tiles, is on show. The hall's Willis organ, the third largest in Europe, is played during occasional recitals. Check on forthcoming events, lectures and other tours with Civic Halls (☎0151/707 2391). Beyond St George's Hall, the civic buildings along **William Brown Street** – the Walker Art Gallery, Central Library and Liverpool Museum – make their mark.

Walker Art Gallery

Liverpool's **Walker Art Gallery** on William Brown Street (Mon–Sat 10am–5pm, Sun noon–5pm; £3, free with NMGM Eight Pass) houses one of the country's finest provincial art collections, with pieces dating from the fourteenth century to the present day. Major renovations have restored many of the galleries and added new space for temporary exhibitions. There's often a good range of Italian work on show, together with works by Rembrandt, Rubens and other seventeenth-century masters, but here, as in Manchester, British painting occupies centre stage. George Stubbs, England's greatest animal painter – and native Liverpudlian – shows off his preoccupation with horse anatomy in his painting of *Molly Longlegs* (1762), while Turner's maturing style is captured in various works. Nothing could contrast more strongly than the contemporaneous work of the Pre-Raphaelites, whose nostalgic fastidiousness is typified by Millais' *Lorenzo and Isabella*. A group of Impressionists and Post-Impressionists including Degas, Cézanne and Monet drag the collection into the twentieth century, leading to pieces by Lucian Freud and David Hockney. The museum also displays exhibits from its large applied-art collection – glassware, ceramics, precious metals, and sculpted furniture, largely retrieved from the homes of the city's early industrial businessmen. Contemporary work floods the building during the John Moores Exhibition, usually held here from October of odd-numbered years to the following January.

Liverpool Museum

Further along William Brown Street the **Liverpool Museum** (Mon–Sat 10am–5pm, Sun noon–5pm; £3, free with NMGM Eight Pass) has also had a major overhaul and certain sections may still be closed during your visit. What is on display is eclectic to say the least, from tarantulas to a space rocket, and it's an appealing diversity which grows on you the longer you stay. The museum had its origins in the natural history collections bequeathed by the Earl of Derby in the mid-nineteenth century, and these have subsequently been augmented by some superior fossil, natural habitat and evolution exhibits. There's also a full dinosaur section, starring a set of dinosaur footprints found on the Wirral, and ethnographical collections from the Americas, Egypt, the Pacific Islands and West Africa. Another handy benefactor was Henry Blundell, eighteenth-century gentleman-collector and well-travelled Catholic, who gathered together Roman antiquities, busts, sculpture and funerary monuments and then built a replica of the Parthenon to house his private collection. The museum shows off a large selection of his antiquities; others are in the Walker Art Gallery. Make time too for the Planetarium (£1); there's also a café.

The cathedrals

On the hill behind Lime Street, off Mount Pleasant, rises the funnel-shaped Catholic **Metropolitan Cathedral of Christ the King** (Mon–Sat 8am–6pm, Sun 8am–5pm; free), denigratingly known as "Paddy's Wigwam" and the "Mersey Funnel". Built in the 1960s in the wake of the revitalizing Second Vatican Council, it was raised on top of the tentative beginnings of Sir Edwin Lutyens's grandiose project to outdo St Peter's in Rome. Bits of Lutyens's cathedral can be seen in the crypt. At the other end of the aptly named Hope Street, the Anglican **Liverpool Cathedral** (daily 8am–6pm; donation requested) looks much more ancient but was actually completed eleven years later, in 1978, after 74 years in construction. The last of the great Neo-Gothic structures, Sir Giles Gilbert Scott's masterwork claims a smattering of superlatives: Britain's largest and the world's fifth largest cathedral, the world's tallest Gothic arches and the highest and heaviest bells. Not enough important people have died to fill out the stark pillarless interior, but a visit to see the beautiful stone tracery in the finely detailed Lady Chapel – the first part of the cathedral to be completed, in 1910 – and a look at Elizabeth Frink's last work, a bronze of Christ, pad out the free **guided tours** (times vary, call ☏0151/709 6271 for details). On a clear day, a trip up the 330ft **tower** (11am–4pm; £2) through the cavernous belfry is rewarded by views to the Welsh hills. In the southern arcade the **Elizabeth Hoare Embroidery Collection** (included in tower ticket) contains a manageable display of sumptuous ecclesiastical vestments and traces the art's history from the thirteenth century.

The city centre: Bold Street to Pier Head

Having seen the Walker Art Gallery, Liverpool Museum and the cathedrals, you've seen the central showpiece attractions, but you may as well trace a route back through the city centre, stirring after years of neglect. The streets between **Bold Street** and **Duke Street** – Slater, Wood and Fleet streets – are busy reinventing themselves as café- and bar-land, with an increasing number of places opening in which you can sip a latte, neck a late-night beer or shop for punk records and vintage clothing. **Concert Square**, just off Bold Street, its space once occupied by a factory, was levelled to provide room for warehouse-style bar developments, whose outdoor seats are at a real premium in the summer. On neighbouring Wood Street, the **Open Eye Gallery**, at nos. 28–32 (Tues–Fri 10.30am–5.30pm, Sat 10.30am–5pm; free; ⓦ www.openeye.org.uk), features renowned temporary exhibitions of photography and the media arts.

Bold Street ends at Hanover Street, with the pedestrianized shopping street, Church Street continuing beyond. To the left, School Lane throws up the beautifully proportioned **Bluecoat Chambers**, built in 1717 as an Anglican boarding school for orphans and now a contemporary art gallery (Tues–Sat 10.30am–5pm; free) with a decent café and bookstore (Mon–Sat 9.30am–5pm) and arts centre. The **Quiggins Centre** (Mon–Sat 10am–6pm), a bit further along at 12–16 School Lane, is a converted warehouse packed with ever-changing shoplets hawking records, posters, jewellery, clubwear and skateboards.

From School Lane turn right on Paradise Street and walk down Whitechapel towards **Queen Square**, through an area which has seen a lot of redevelopment, particularly around **Williamson Square**. One of the neighbourhood's surviving Victorian warehouses, on the corner of Whitechapel and Queen Square, is occupied by the **Conservation Centre** (Mon–Sat 10am–5pm, Sun noon–5pm; £3, free with NMGM Eight Pass). This is where Merseyside's museums and galleries undertake their restoration work and give visitors a hands-on, behind-the-scenes look, and fascinating it is – you (and the touring school parties) will soon learn to identify fabrics and furniture beetles and how to get the rust off a gold disc.

Heading on towards Pier Head, Mathew Street and the Cavern Quarter (see box on p.780) loom large, but rather than taking the most direct route to the ferry, don't pass up the opportunity to walk down Water Street. The Georgian **Town Hall** is a beauty and is open to the public in the summer (late-July & Aug Mon–Sat 11am–4pm), while behind here, at 1 Rumford St, the **Western Approaches Operations Centre** (Mon–Thurs & Sat 10.30am–4.30pm, last admission 3.30pm; £4.75) fills about a third of the hundred-room underground complex where, from spring 1941 until the end of the war, the Anglo-American air-sea campaign was orchestrated. Sticking with **Water Street** for the final approach to Pier Head gives you a flavour of the city's nineteenth- and early-twentieth-century mercantile heyday, passing gems such as the Martins Bank Building (now Barclays) with its lavish lobby, and the deeply resonant India Buildings and West Africa House.

The Pier Head

Though the tumult of shipping which once fought the current here has gone, the **Pier Head** landing stage remains the embarkation point for the **Mersey Ferries** to Woodside (for Birkenhead) and Seacombe (Wallasey). Ride one if only for the magnificent views of the Liverpool skyline and the prominent, 322-feet high **Royal Liver Building** (free tours April–Sept by appointment only; call ☎0151/236 2748) – it's topped by the "Liver Birds", a couple of cormorants which have become the symbol of the city.

Straightforward ferry shuttles operate every thirty minutes during morning and evening rush hours (£1.10 each way); at other times the boats run circular "heritage" **cruises** (hourly: Mon–Fri 10am–3pm, Sat & Sun 10am–6pm; £3.75; ☎0151/330 1444), complete with sappy commentary and repeated renditions of Gerry Marsden's *Ferry 'cross the Mersey*. If you're going to stop off at the **Seacombe Aquarium** (daily: April–Sept 10am–6pm; Oct–March 10am–4pm), buy the joint ticket (£4.65).

It's along a long way from the simple rowboat crossing pioneered by medieval Benedictine monks who first wanted to cross the Mersey at this point. Even when Daniel Defoe visited Liverpool in the eighteenth century – when the city was first booming – he was taken by the rusticity of the river crossing "over the Mersee": having reached the city side he was surprised to find himself hoisted "on the shoulders of some honest Lancashire clown" and bundled through the shallows to the shore.

Albert Dock

Albert Dock, five minutes' walk south of the Pier Head, was built in 1846 when Liverpool's port was a world leader. It started to decline at the beginning of last century, as the new deep-draught ships were unable to berth here, and last saw service in 1972. A decade later the site was given a complete scrubdown and refit, with much of the space in the former warehouses being turned over to speciality shops and to monuments of the more meaningful economic activities that used to take place here. Billed as "Liverpool's Historic

Waterfront" it's a type of rescued urban heritage that's been copied throughout the country, but rarely as successfully as here. There's free **parking** – follow the city-centre signs – and **buses** every twenty minutes during the day from Queen Square bus station. All the museums have admission charges: the Maritime Museum, HM Customs Museum and Museum of Liverpool Life are part of the NMGM Eight Pass scheme, while the **Waterfront Pass** (£9.99) saves you money if you want to see the lot. Passes are available at the individual museums or at the Albert Dock tourist office, itself a useful source of information about what's on at the dock.

The **Merseyside Maritime Museum** (daily 10am–5pm; £3, free with NMGM Eight Pass) fills one wing of the Albert Dock and in summer also takes over part of Canning Dock for floating displays. A trip through the museum can easily take two hours. Spread over four floors, it has sections on the history of Liverpool's evolution as a port and shipbuilding centre, and models of seacraft – from Samoan rafts to opulent passenger liners. An illuminating display details Liverpool's pivotal role as a springboard for over nine million emigrants – the Irish potato famine and a multiplicity of European wars, combined with the lure of gold and free land, brought people scurrying here to buy their passage to North America or Australia. To cater for them, short-stay lodging houses sprang up all over the centre, as illustrated in an 1854 street scene. On board the ships – there's a walk-through example – people were packed into dark, noisy ranks of bunks where they "puffed, groaned, swore, vomited, prayed, moaned and cried". Meanwhile, the **HM Customs and Excise Museum**, inside the Maritime Museum, gives the lowdown on smuggling and revenue collection.

The Maritime Museum, though, is at its best in its "Transatlantic Slavery" exhibit, which manages to be enlightening, shocking and refreshingly honest, and banishes years of Eurocentric excuses to expose the true horror of the exploitation of African slaves who were kidnapped, abused and sold as property. The slave trade continued for four hundred years up to 1900; even after official abolition in 1807 the number of slaves shipped to sugar plantations in the Americas ran into millions. The conditions they endured on the transatlantic voyage are illustrated by a reconstruction of a slave ship, echoing with haunting voices reading from diaries of slaves and slavers, telling of rape, torture and death. The exhibition winds up with a video of Africans resident in Britain airing their views on the impact of slavery and the legacy of racism, after which you'll probably be ready to mull over what you've seen in the museum's excellent top-floor café, approached through a hall hung with nineteenth-century racist propaganda, countered by protest cartoons from the abolitionist camp.

The neighbouring **Tate Gallery Liverpool** (Tues–Sun 10am–6pm; free, special exhibitions usually £3–5; Ⓦ www.tate.org.uk) is the country's national collection of modern art in the north. Popular retrospectives and an ever-changing display of individual works are its bread-and-butter, and there's also a full programme of events, talks and tours. Break up visits to the gallery and the dock with espressos in the Tate's dockside café-bar.

The **Museum of Liverpool Life** (daily 10am–5pm; £3, free with NMGM Eight Pass) lies across the dock. Particularly revealing about the hardships that have moulded the resilient Scouse character, it has excellent sections on the city's traditional work, with investigations of the lives of ordinary shipwrights, stevedores, carters and seamen. The role of trade unions is traced, from protests in the eighteenth century to the 1981 and 1983 People's March for Jobs, and there's space too for coverage of topics as diverse as the women's suffrage movement and the social unrest that led to the Toxteth riots in the 1980s. It is not all doom and gloom though. In the popular-culture sections, Merseyside football gets good coverage (though there's no mention of poor old Tranmere Rovers), as does Aintree's Grand National – for more on both sports, see the box below. There's also an overview of music from the Sixties to the present day (with a working jukebox), plus information about the homegrown soap *Brookside* and local writers, including Alan Bleasdale, Willy Russell, Beryl Bainbridge and Carla Lane.

The outskirts

Located near Liverpool's airport, six miles southeast of the centre, **Speke Hall** (Easter–Oct Tues–Sun 1–5.30pm; Nov to mid-Dec Sat & Sun 1–4.30pm; gardens Easter–Oct same times as house; Nov–Easter Tues–Sun 1–4.30pm; house & gardens £4.50, gardens only £2.50; NT; ⊛www.spekehall.org.uk) is one of the country's finest examples of Elizabethan timbered architecture. Sitting in an oasis of rhododendrons, the house encloses a beautifully proportioned courtyard overlooked by myriad diamond panes. Highlights of the interior are the Jacobean plasterwork in the Great Parlour and the Great Hall's carved oak panel. Bus #80/180 to the airport from Paradise Street in the city centre runs within half a mile of the entrance.

For a glimpse of one of the more benign aspects of Merseyside's industrial past, take the Merseyrail under the river to **Port Sunlight**, a garden village created in 1888 by industrialist William Hesketh Lever for the workers at his soap factory. The project, similar in scope to those of Titus Salt at Saltaire near Bradford and John Cadbury at Bournville in Birmingham, is explained at the **Port Sunlight Heritage Centre**, 95 Greendale Rd (April–Oct daily 10am–4pm; Nov–March Sat & Sun 10am–4pm; 60p), set amid the open-planned housing estates. Off Greendale Road, a little further from Port Sunlight station, the **Lady Lever Art Gallery** (Mon–Sat 10am–5pm, Sun noon–5pm; £3, free with NMGM Eight Pass) houses a small collection of English eighteenth-century furniture, Pre-Raphaelite paintings by artists such as Rossetti and Ford Madox Brown, Wedgwood china, porcelain and assorted Greek and Roman artefacts. There's also a nice café.

Eating, drinking and nightlife

Liverpool's dining scene is slowly shifting up a gear and there's now a good choice of classy **restaurants** alongside a fine selection of cafés and budget places to eat. Most are around Hardman and Bold streets, at Albert Dock, and along spruced-up Nelson Street, heart of Liverpool's **Chinatown**, which stretches around the corner onto Berry Street. Fashionable **café-bars** are muscling in on the action too, and you won't want for a decent cup of coffee these days in most parts of the city.

Liverpool's **pubs and bars** stay open later than most, with many serving until 1am or 2am. Fleet Street, Slater Street and Wood Street have seen most development, with ground zero at Concert Square (off Bold St), where drinkers spill out on to the terraces until the small hours from a variety of cafés, dance bars and theme pubs. Victoria Street in the business district is another fast-developing area for bars and nightlife.

You'll catch regular gigs at any of the **live music** venues detailed below, and Liverpool has some excellent annual **music festivals and events**, namely the Summer Pops (July) and the Party at the Pier (August) for big-name pop and rock, and Liverpool Now (October) which sees local bands playing in various venues around the city. The city's out-and-out dance **clubs** are mainly notable

Liverpool's most popular recreational activity, bar none, is **football**. Liverpool football club has never quite recovered its glory days of the Seventies and Eighties, though a unique Cup triple in 2001 – and employment of the talismanic striker Michael Owen – promises better things to come. The team plays at **Anfield** (ticket office ☎0151/260 8680, ⌨www.liverpoolfc.net) in front of some of the nation's best and most loyal supporters. You're unlikely to get a ticket for a game, but there's a popular tour around the well-stocked museum, trophy room and dressing rooms (daily 10am–5pm; museum and tour £8.50, museum only £5; booking essential ☎0151/260 6677). Everton, the city's less glamorous and recently far less successful side, command equally intense devotion at **Goodison Park** (ticket office ☎0151/330 2300; tours Mon, Wed, Fri & Sun 11am & 2pm; £5.50; booking advised; ⌨www.evertonfc.com), though there are well-advanced plans to shift eventually to a new stadium at King's Dock in the city centre.

The first Saturday in April is **Grand National Day** at Aintree – the "World's Greatest Steeplechase". The race is the culmination of a meeting that starts on the previous Thursday, with prices for entry into the grounds ranging from £7 to £65. Catch the Merseyrail to Aintree and buy a ticket on the gate or book on ☎0151/522 2929. A Visitor Centre (☎0151/522 2921, ⌨www.aintree.co.uk) lets you ride the National on a race simulator as part of a race course tour (£7).

for their lack of pretence, fashion playing second string to dancing and drinking. The evening paper, the *Liverpool Echo*, has **listings** of what's going on, or pick up flyers in the shops, bars and cafés.

Daytime cafés

Bluecoat Café Bar Bluecoat Chambers, School Lane. Mainly vegetarian food – salad bar, baked potatoes and dips – served throughout the day. Closed Sun.

Café Eros Conservation Centre, Whitechapel Rd. The best of the museum and gallery cafés is a light-filled space with nice food, also used for temporary art and photography exhibitions.

Cavern Walks Shopping Centre Mathew St. Lunch or snack with the lovable moptops. Both *Chantilly* and *Lucy in the Sky with Diamonds* offer daytime drinks and meals right by the Fab Four statue.

Coopers Food Hall 63–67 Bold St. A deli/butcher/bakery with eat-in "brasserie" section for breakfasts, sandwiches and sushi. Closed Sun.

Espresso Exchange 6 Victoria St. Locally owned espresso bar with great coffee, snacks and sandwiches.

Green Fish Café 11 Upper Newington St. Cool vegetarian café off Renshaw St.

Everyman Bistro 9–11 Hope St. Long-standing theatre-basement hangout with quiche, pizza and salad-type meals for around a fiver. Closed Sun.

The Refectory Liverpool Anglican Cathedral, St James' Mount. Appetizing snacks and lunches under the Gothic arches, and with terrace seating, too.

Café-bars

Beluga Bar 40 Wood St. Hip basement space that's great for just a drink, or come to eat – there's a changing, seasonal menu. Opens at 5pm.

Blue Edward Pavilion, Albert Dock. Brick-vaulted café-bar with upstairs grill – the Liverpool soccerati drop by now and again, and it's a useful stop for a cheap lunch (hotpot, salad niçoise or chilli), cappuccino, a pasta or tapas dinner or a late-night drink.

Life Café 1a Bold St. The eighteenth-century Lyceum Library makes a grand backdrop for this late-opening café-bar, serving pasta, pizza, salads, Thai curries and sandwiches.

Modo Concert Square. Indoor and outdoor hi-jinks at night, though quieter during the day, when you can stop by for a meal and a coffee.

Newz New Zealand House, Water St. Thoroughly OTT bar and brasserie aimed at a city crowd; bagels and coffee to cocktails and dinner, plus constant TV news and music Thurs–Sat. Closed Sun.

The Platinum Lounge Beetham Plaza, 25 The Strand. Feeling smooth? Come right on in to the

Liverpool lounge scene where you'll need a bulging wallet and a taste for cocktails.

Tabac 126 Bold St. A new style for an old favourite sees Tabac shed its vaguely hippy leanings and emerge as a contemporary café-bar, serving a wide-ranging menu.

Taste Tate Gallery, Albert Dock. Industrial-lite café-bar at the Tate serves bangers and mash, burgers, salads and sandwiches during the day. In the evening, the emphasis is on grills and roast vegetables.

Restaurants

Casa Italia 40 Stanley St ☎0151/227 5774. Lively trattoria with better than average pasta and pizza dishes. Inexpensive to Moderate.

Est Est Est Unit 6, Edward Pavilion, Albert Dock ☎0151/708 6969. Authentic pizza and pasta – you may have to wait in line at weekends. *Est Bar* here serves Italian sandwiches and drinks at dockside tables. Inexpensive.

Far East 27–35 Berry St ☎0151/709 6072. One of the longest-serving and most reliable of Liverpool's Cantonese eating houses: a fairly no-frills operation, but with authentic *dim sum* (noon–6pm), noodles, casseroles, rice plates and other classics. Moderate.

The Lower Place Philharmonic Hall, Hope St ☎0151/210 1955. Fast winning friends with its chargrilling, oven-roasting, sun-drying ways. Not cheap, but always enjoyable. Closed Sun. Expensive.

El Macho Hope St ☎0151/708 6644. Longstanding Mexican restaurant that's more about good times and margarita consumption than memorable food. Moderate.

Number Seven Café 7 Falkner St ☎0151/709 9633. Highly popular, laid-back restaurant with a daily changing blackboard menu of contemporary flavours – soups, salads, fish and meat, and usually a fair amount of veggie choice. The next-door deli is a treat too. Moderate.

Simply Heathcotes Beetham Plaza, 25 The Strand ☎0151/236 3536. Lancastrian magic – roast chump of lamb and Goosnargh duckling feature among other delights from Paul Heathcote. Expensive.

Valparaiso 4 Hardman St ☎0151/708 6036. Chilean and other Latin-American dishes, with wines to match. Early evening specials served Tues–Thurs 5–7pm. Closed Sun & Mon. Moderate.

Yuet Ben 1 Upper Duke St t0151/709 5772. Superb range of Chinese food Including barbecued ribs that experts drool over. Moderate.

Ziba 15–19 Berry St ☎0151/708 8870. Stylish space (formerly a car showroom) now serving cutting-edge Modern British food along with risottos, Oriental flourishes and vegetarian specialities. Closed Sun eve. Expensive.

Pubs

The Baltic Fleet 33a Wapping. Restored pub with age-old shipping connections – opposite Albert Dock and across from the youth hostel. It's got a great period feel and is known for its fine food and local beer.

Brewery Tap Stanhope St. Enjoyable Victorian brewery pub where you can sample Liverpool's own Cains beers. There are brewery tours if you're interested in the process (call ☎0151/708 8395; £3.75), and seats inside and out if you're just interested in the product.

The Dispensary 87 Renshaw St. Entirely synthetic but highly sympathetic re-creation of a Victorian pub using rescued and antique wood, glass and tiles. A real-ale choice.

Dr Duncans St John's Lane, Queen Square. Handy city-centre Cains pub occupying what was once Pearl Assurance House, so plenty of ornate furnishings alongside the real ales and good food.

The Flying Picket 24 Hardman St. A friendly local tucked in behind the Trade Union centre. *The Picket*, upstairs, is one of the best venues for local bands.

The Grapes 25 Mathew St. Busy city-centre pub in the Cavern Quarter, where John, Paul, George and Ringo once downed pints between sets at *The Cavern*.

Head of Steam 7 Lime St, Lime St Station. The city's biggest pub is all things to all people – memorabilia for the railway anoraks, refreshment rooms, restored lounges, a Fifities-style diner; heck, you can even get a beer.

The Philharmonic 36 Hope St. A superb, traditional watering-hole where the main attractions – the beer aside – are the mosaic floors, tiling, gilded wrought-iron gates and the marble decor in the gents.

Pumphouse Inn Albert Dock. Restored heritage building at the dock, nice for a waterside pint and views of the Liver Building.

The Vernon Arms 69 Dale St. Traditional but smart city-centre boozer with a choice of real ales and posh pub food.

White Star Rainford Gardens, off Mathew St. Enjoyable drinking haunt that's one of the better locals in the city centre; The Beatles certainly used to think so.

Ye Cracke 13 Rice St. Crusty backstreet pub off Hope Street, much loved by the young Lennon, and with a great jukebox.

Clubs

The Cavern Club 10 Mathew St ☎0151/236 1964. The self-styled "most famous club in the world" puts on live bands Thursday to Sunday, though Sir Macca is unlikely to appear again any time soon.

Cream Wolstenholme Square, off Hanover St, ☎0151/709 1693, ⊛www.cream.co.uk. Liverpool's – possibly Britain's – best club, featuring big DJ names. A varied round of club nights and all-nighters attracts coachloads from across the country. Sponsors the ever-popular August

bank holiday "Creamfields" dance festival.

The Late Room Life Café, 1a Bold St ☎0151/707 2333. Basement lounge featuring stand-up comedy, gigs and club nights, Thurs–Sun.

The Lomax and L2 11–13 Hotham St ☎0151/707 9977. Indie band venue with nightly gigs by local and touring acts, and weekend club nights.

Masque Bar and Venue 90 Seel St ☎0151/708 8708. Rock dinsosaurs, R&B legends and yesterday's heroes, plus club nights and a bar-bistro.

Arts, concerts and entertainment

The Royal Liverpool Philharmonic Orchestra, up with Manchester's Hallé as the northwest's best, dominates the city's **classical music scene** and often plays at the Philharmonic Hall and the Everyman Theatre. Liverpool Cathedral is also a favourite spot for classical concerts, with its good acoustics and inexpensive tickets. **Theatre** is well entrenched in the city, at a variety of venues, though cinema is less well-served with only mainstream films screened at the Odeon on London Road. Annual **festivals** include the Hope Street Festival (June); a celebration of African arts and music in Africa Oye (June); the Summer Pops (July), when the Royal Philharmonic and top pop names perform beneath a huge marquee on King's Dock; the **Brouhaha Street Theatre Festival** (August), which involves performances by a host of European theatre groups; and the **Mathew Street Festival** (August), a free shindig, with local and national street performers playing the best of The Beatles.

Bluecoat Arts Centre School Lane ☎0151/709 5297, ⊛www.bluecoatartscentre.com. Eclectic mix of events – drama, dance, poetry, comedy, music and art exhibitions; always worth a look.

Everyman Theatre and Playhouse Hope St ☎0151/709 4776, ⊛www.everymanplayhouse.com. Presents everything from Shakespeare to Jarman, as well as concerts, exhibitions, dance and musical performances.

Liverpool Empire Lime St ☎0151/606 3536, ⊛www.liverpool-empire.co.uk. The city's largest theatre, a venue for touring West End shows, opera, ballet and music. The Beatles' first major

gig was here in 1962.

Philharmonic Hall Hope St ☎0151/709 3789, ⊛www.rlps.co.uk. Home of the Royal Liverpool Philharmonic Orchestra, and with a full programme of other concerts. Shows classic films once a month.

Royal Court Theatre Roe St ☎0151/709 4321, ⊛www.royalcourttheatre.net. Art Deco theatre and concert hall, which sees regular pop and rock concerts among other events.

Unity Theatre Hope Place ☎0151/709 4988, ⊛www.unitytheatreliverpool.co.uk. Puts on the city's most adventurous range of contemporary works.

Listings

Airport ☎0151/288 4000, ⊛www.liverpoolairport.com. Flights to Belfast, Dublin, the Isle of Man, Madrid, Barcelona, Palma, Nice, Malaga and Amsterdam.

Banks and exchanges American Express, 54 Lord St ☎0151/702 4501; Thomas Cook, 75 Church St ☎0151/552 1300. You can also change money at the two tourist offices, the two main post offices (see below) and at the airport.

Books Most of the bookshops are along Bold Street: Dillons at no. 14, Waterstones at no. 52 and the more radical News from Nowhere at no. 112.
Buses Merseytravel ☎0151/236 7676.
Car rental Alamo, 278 East Prescott Rd, Knotty Ash ☎0151/259 1316; Avis, 113 Mulberry St ☎0151/709 4737; easyRentacar ☎0906/586 0586; Europcar, 8 Brownlow Hill t0151/709 7563 and at the airport ☎0151/448 1652; Hertz, at the airport ☎0151/486 7444.
Ferries Isle of Man Steam-Packet Company for ferries/Sea Cats ☎08705/523523; Mersey Ferries ☎0151/330 1444; Norse Irish Ferries ☎0151/944 1010.
Hospital Royal Liverpool University Hospital, Prescot Street ☎0151/706 2000.
Internet Planet Electra Internet Café, 36 London

Rd ☎0151/708 0303. Daily 10am–6pm.
Laundry Liver Launderette, 170 Aigburth Rd & 104 Prescot Rd.
Left luggage Lime Street Station, daily 7am–10pm.
Pharmacy Boots, Clayton Square ☎0151/709 4711; Moss Pharmacy, 68–70 London Rd ☎0151/709 5271 (daily until 11pm).
Police HQ, Canning Place ☎0151/709 6010.
Post offices City-centre offices at 23–33 Whitechapel; The Lyceum, 1 Bold St. Open Mon–Sat 8.30am–6pm.
Taxis Mersey Cabs ☎0151/298 2222; Davy Liver ☎0151/709 4646.
Travel agent Discounted and student tickets from USIT Campus, YHA shop, 25 Bold St ☎0151/709 9200 (plus branches at both universities); STA, 78 Bold St ☎0151/707 1123.

Blackpool

Shamelessly brash **BLACKPOOL** is the archetypal British seaside resort, its "Golden Mile" of piers, fortune-tellers, amusement arcades, tram and donkey rides, fish-and-chip shops, candyfloss stalls, fun pubs and bingo halls making no concessions to anything but low-brow fun-seeking of the finest kind. From ukelele-strumming George Formby and his "little stick of Blackpool rock" to today's predatory, half-dressed gangs of stag and hen parties, few visitors, then or now, are in any doubt about the point of a holiday here. There are seven miles of wide sandy beach backed by an unbroken chain of hotels and guest houses, and though the sea-water quality is still highly debatable, even after heavy investment in a new sewage system, there's nothing wrong with the beach itself – except for the crowds packing the central stretches on hot summer days. Sixteen million people come here each year. If you want a bit more isolation than those numbers allow, come in winter when there's nothing more bracing than a lonely tramp along the windswept sands – "bracing", of course, as Paul Theroux points out, being "the northern euphemism for stinging cold".

Wealthy visitors were already summer holidaying in Blackpool at the end of the eighteenth century, and while it took a day to get there from Manchester by carriage and two days from Yorkshire, the town remained a select destination. The coming of the railway in 1846 made Blackpool what it is today: within thirty years, there were piers, promenades and theatres for the thousands who descended. The **Winter Gardens**, with its barrel-vaulted ballroom, the Baroque **Grand Theatre** on Church Street, Blackpool's own "Eiffel Tower" on the seafront and other refined diversions were built to cater to the tastes of the first influx, but it was the Central Pier's "open air dancing for the working classes" that heralded the crucial change of accent. Suddenly Blackpool was favoured destination for the "Wakes Weeks", when whole Lancashire mill towns descended for their annual seven days' holiday.

Attention to the accents tells you that Lancashire, Yorkshire and Scotland still provide the bulk of the resort's visitors, who show no signs of drying up. Where other British holiday resorts have suffered from the rivalry of cheap foreign packages, Blackpool has simply gone from strength to strength by shrewdly providing exactly what its visitors want. Underneath the populist veneer there's a sophisticated marketing approach which balances ever more elaborate rides and attractions with well-grounded traditional entertainment. The best example of this is the way the town has cleverly extended its season: when other resorts begin to close up for the winter, Blackpool's main season is just beginning, as over half a million light bulbs are used to create **the Illuminations** which decorate the promenade from the beginning of September to early November. The first static display took place in 1912, was re-created periodically between the wars and has been an annual event since 1949, "switched on" each year by publicity-hungry TV and pop stars.

Arrival and information

Blackpool's main **train station** is Blackpool North (direct trains from Manchester, Preston and London), half a dozen blocks up Talbot Road from North Pier. A few steps down Talbot Road, towards the sea, stands the combined National Express and local **bus station**; town buses run from here direct to the Pleasure Beach, though it's more fun to walk down to the front, take a tram and get your bearings. Blackpool's **airport** – which handles regular flights to and from the Isle of Man, Belfast and Dublin – lies two miles south of the centre; bus #22/22A will take you there from the bus station. The main **tourist office** at 1 Clifton St (Easter to early Nov Mon–Sat 9am–5pm, Sun 10am–3.45pm; rest of year Mon–Thurs & Sat 8.45am–4.45pm, Fri 8.45am–4.15pm; ☎01253/478222; ⓦ www.blackpooltourism.com) is on the corner of Talbot Road, five minutes' walk from the stations; a seasonal office sits on the prom opposite Blackpool Tower. You can pick up maps and hefty accommodation brochures at the tourist office; it also sells Travel Cards (one-day £4.50; three-day £12; five-day £15; seven-day £16) for use on all local buses and trams. Local **transport information** is available from Blackpool Transport (☎01253/473000).

Accommodation

Blackpool claims to have more **hotel beds** than Portugal, a plausible boast when whole blocks of streets, particularly those set back from the promenade between North and Central piers, are devoted to guest houses. Bed-and-breakfast prices are generally low (from £15 per person, even less on a room-only basis or out of season), but rise at weekends during the Illuminations. In peak season, it's simply a matter of looking for vacancy signs or asking the tourist office for help – anything cheap between North and Central piers is guaranteed to be noisy; for more peace and quiet (an unusual request in Blackpool, it has to be said), look for places along the more restful North Shore, beyond North Pier. The Blackpool Hotel and Guest House Association (☎01253/621891) can match your requirements with a particular hotel. There are local **campsites**, but none are particularly near the town and, with B&B prices being as they are, no great savings are to be made by spending the night under canvas.

Boltonia 124–126 Albert Rd ☎01253/620248, ⓦ www.boltoniahotel.co.uk. The choices on Albert Rd, between the Tower and Central Pier, mark a qualitative step up from your basic Blackpool boarding houses. The Boltonia is near the Winter Gardens; the 21 rooms are all en-suite and there's parking. ❸

Clifton Hotel Talbot Square ☎01253/621481. On the North Pier prom, this traditional beauty – a Grade 1 listed building – has fine sea views from many rooms, though decor could do with a touch up here and there. Rooms are a good deal cheaper than the posted prices; check for special offers. ❺

De Vere East Park Drive ☎01253/838866, ⓦ www.devereonline.co.uk. A reclusive resort-style retreat set in its own grounds, with a fine indoor pool. It's a couple of miles inland, near the zoo and across from Stanley Park. **7**

Dutchman Hotel 269 The Promenade ☎01253/404812. A great seafront choice between Central and South piers. The small, cheery rooms have compact shower rooms; although those at the front get traffic noise, you do wake up with a view of the sea. There's a bar and café too (and probably the only Blackpool B&B to offer a cream-cheese bagel for breakfast). No credit cards. **1**

The Garfield 22 Springfield Rd ☎01253/628060. Two blocks west of Talbot Road, this is cheap, central and convenient for station and town; slightly pricier en-suite rooms are available too. No credit cards. **1**

Grosvenor View 7–9 King Edward Ave ☎01253/352 851. Along North Shore, a mile or so from the action, the grid west of Warbreck Hill

Road has hundreds of options. Rooms in this detached property are larger and better equipped than most – and you're in the care of an award-winning landlady. **3**

Imperial North Promenade ☎01253/623971, ⓦwww.paramount-hotel.co.uk. The politician's conference favourite, with excellent sea-facing rooms, pool and gym, a good bar and restaurant. **7**

Ruskin Hotel Albert Rd ☎01253/624063, ⓦwww.ruskinhotel.com. At the prom end of Albert Rd, by Coronation St, the Ruskin exudes repro-Victorian style and offers rather smart rooms with decent bathrooms, all individually decorated. Parking available. **5**

Wildlife Hotel 39 Woodfield Rd ☎01253 /346143. Ideal for those wanting a vegan guest house, this non-smoking place is just off the promenade, between Central and South piers. No credit cards. **1**

The Town

With seven miles of beach – the tide ebb is a full half a mile, leaving plenty of sand at low tide – and accompanying promenade, you'll want to jump on and off the electric **trams** if you plan to get up and down much between the piers. South Pier to North Pier – between which lies most of what there is to see and do – costs £1, though Travel Cards are available, too. Most of the town-centre shops, bars and cafés lie between Central and North piers.

Blackpool Pleasure Beach

The major event in town is Blackpool's **Pleasure Beach** on the South Promenade (March–Easter Sat & Sun 10am–8pm; Easter–June Mon–Fri 2–8pm, Sat & Sun 10am–10pm; July to Nov 5 daily 10am–11pm; hours can vary, call ☎0870/444 5566, ⓦwww.blackpoolpleasurebeach.co.uk), just south of South Pier – visited by over seven million people each year. Entrance to the amusement park is free, but you'll have to fork out for the superb array of "white knuckle" rides including "The Big One", the world's fastest roller coaster (85mph) which involves a terrifying near-vertical drop from 235ft. This is bad enough, though the "Ice Blast" whooshes you up a 200ft steel tower at 80mph and then drops you back down in free-fall; while "Valhalla" is claimed to be the biggest "dark ride" (ie very scary) ever built. After these, the Pleasure Beach's wonderful array of antique wooden rollercoasters – "woodies" to aficionados – seem like kids' stuff, but each is unique. The original "Big Dipper" was invented at Blackpool in 1923 and still thrills; the "Wild Mouse" (1958) and, best of all, the "Grand National" (1935) – whose 3300ft twin track races you against a parallel car – are both equally, excitingly, rattly. Before each one sets off, the public-service announcement intones "Please do not wave your hands in the air" – when any self-respecting woodie rider knows that's exactly what you have to do. If you're not leaving until you've been on everything – a sensible course of action – buy an unlimited ride wristband (one-day £25, two-day £40).

The seafront and the tower

Across the road, the **Sandcastle** (June–Oct daily 10am–5.30pm; Nov–May Sat & Sun only; £4.95) is the only place you are likely to want to swim. With every aquatic diversion kept at a constant 29°C it can be a welcome respite from the biting sea air. Jump a tram for the ride up to **Central Pier** with its 108-feet high revolving Big Wheel. The **Sea-Life Centre** (July & Aug Mon–Thurs & Sun 10am–6pm, Fri & Sat 10am–10pm; rest of year daily 10am–6pm; £7; @www.sealife.co.uk) here is one of the country's best, with eight-foot sharks looming at you as you march through a glass tunnel and a very large, lurking Giant Pacific octopus. For a taste of what Blackpool attractions used to be like, you could then hit **Louis Tussauds Waxworks**, 87–89 Central Promenade (daily 10am–10pm; £4.50) – these days, more Posh and Becks than Churchill and Margaret Thatcher, but still with its "highly educational" adults-only anatomy section.

Blackpool's cast-iron **piers** also strike a traditional note; the first one (North Pier), opened in 1863, is now a listed building. Elegant structures themselves, they've been covered ever since with arcades and amusements, while much of what passes for evening family entertainment – TV comics and variety shows – takes place in the various pier theatres. Between Central and North piers stands the 518-feet **Blackpool Tower** – the skyline's only real touch of grace – erected in 1894 when it was thought that the northwest really ought not to be outdone by Paris. It's now marketed as "Tower World" (Easter to early Nov daily 10am–11pm; rest of year Sat 10am–11pm, Sun 10am–6pm; £10) which offers a ride up to the top (where there's a postbox), an unnerving walk on the see-through glass floor, plus a visit to the Edwardian ballroom and various other attractions. From the very early days, there's been a Moorish-inspired **circus** (shows included in the entry ticket) between the tower's legs, which still functions, though in the spirit of the times it's now animal-free.

If you've seen and been on everything mentioned so far you'll have been here for days, spent a fortune and thoroughly enjoyed yourself. These, it has to be said, are just the A-list attractions – indefatigable holiday-makers also take in Blackpool's zoo and model village on East Park Drive, the summer circus at the Pleasure Beach, or any one of a number of pleasure flights, go-kart rinks, donkey rides, children's play areas, ten-pin bowling alleys, games arcades or other jollifications.

Eating, drinking and nightlife

Eating out revolves around the typical British seaside fare of fish and chips, available all over town, but at its supreme best in *Harry Ramsden's*, 60–63 The Promenade, on the corner of Church Street near the Tower; the celebrated Yorkshire chippie chain has a takeaway counter too. Even more traditional seaside food is available from the glorious, wood-panelled, 120-year-old *Robert's Oyster Bar*, 92 The Promenade, near the base of the Tower, where you can buy oysters, cockles and mussels, or fish platters then wash them down with a Guinness from the *Mitre* pub around the corner. Given the sheer volume of customers, other restaurants don't have to try too hard: you'll have no trouble finding cheap roasts, pizzas, Chinese or Indian food, but might struggle if you're seeking a bit more sophistication. *Lagoonda*, 37 Queen St (☎01253/293 837), off Talbot Square, is a party-time Afro-Caribbean restaurant with surprisingly good food and service given that the staff have to spend their time negotiating the limbo bar. If you really want a blowout, head for the expensive *September Brasserie*, 15–17 Queen St (☎01253/623282; closed Sun & Mon lunch), or the refined *Palm Court Restaurant* at the *Imperial*.

If you like your **nightlife** late, loud and libidinous, summertime Blackpool has few English peers. In all the pubs and clubs, young men can expect to have

Gay Blackpool

Blackpool has become one of the most popular gay resorts in the country, with around forty hotels and guest houses that welcome, or cater specifically for, a gay clientele. Blackpool tourist office can supply a full gay **accommodation** list, but good places to try first include *Raffles Hotel*, set back from Central Pier at 73–75 Hornby Rd (℡01253/294713; ❷), *Mardi Gras*, 41–43 Lord St (℡01253/751087; ❷), the all-male *Trades Hotel*, 51–55 Lord St (℡01253/626041; ❷), and the *Amalfi Guest House*, for women, at 19–21 Eaves St (℡01253/622971; ❷).

There's **nightlife** to match, with *Funny Girls* the most high-profile venue. *Flamingos*, opposite the train station at 174–176 Talbot Road, is probably the largest and liveliest gay club in Europe, with four storeys of dance floors and eight bars. Other prominent gay **bars** include the *Flying Handbag*, at 170–172 Talbot Rd; *Pepe's*, a basement bar at 94 Talbot Rd; and *Basil's*, 9 The Strand (℡01253/294109).

their attire and demeanour given the once-over by the hired hulks at the door; "girls" and "ladies" can expect free drinks and entry and a lot of largely good-natured amorous jousting. *Yates' Wine Lodge* has two popular branches, in Talbot Square and between Central and South piers where you can sip an amontillado sherry or champagne on draught. There's a rowdy bar in the *Clifton Hotel*, at North Pier; and a plethora of Irish theme bars, notably *O'Neill's* on the corner of Talbot Road and Abingdon Street, *Finn's* on Talbot Square, and *Scruffy Murphy's*, 32 Corporation St. The *Pump and Truncheon*, 13 Bonny St, behind the Sea Life Centre, is a real-ale pub, while the *Raikes*, half a mile inland on Liverpool Road, also has good beer, occasionally decent jazz/blues bands, and a place in local history – the Great Blondin once performed his tightrope act here.

For **dancing**, local opinion favours *Blue*, on Corporation St, near the Grand Theatre, whose club nights bring in star DJs. *Funny Girls*, a transvestite-run bar at 9 The Strand (℡01253/291144), has nightly shows which attract long (gay and straight) queues (see box above for more on the gay scene). Otherwise, **entertainment** is based very heavily on family shows, musicals, veteran TV comedians, crooners and stage spectaculars put on at a variety of end-of-pier and Pleasure Beach theatres or historic venues such as the *Grand Theatre* (℡01253/290190, ⓦwww.blackpoolgrand.co.uk), *Wintergardens* (℡01253/292029, ⓦwww.blackpoollive.co.uk) and *Opera House* on Church St (℡01253/292029).

Preston and around

With the siren draws of the Lakes, the Peak District and the Yorkshire Dales so close, the rest of Lancashire often gets bypassed in the rush to the surrounding national parks, and more's the pity. It's true, the old cotton towns of north and east Lancashire might not be first on everyone's must-see list, but in **Preston,** 25 miles northwest of Manchester, the county has one of England's oldest towns, containing two fine museums and some appealing Georgian and Victorian remnants. North of the town, rural Lancashire is at its most bucolic in the villages of the **Ribble Valley**, particularly in the **Forest of Bowland**, whose gateway is the small market town of **Clitheroe**. Here, you'll find country walks and old inns easily the measure of any across the county borders, with the bonus of far less tourists with which to share them.

Preston

Strategically placed on the banks of the River Ribble, **PRESTON** (possibly a contraction of "Priest's Town") was already an important market town in Anglo-Saxon times and received its royal charter in 1179 – origin of the famous Preston Guild celebrations, which since 1542 have taken place every twenty years (the next in 2012). The town was attacked by Robert the Bruce, changed hands in the Civil War and saw action during the Jacobite rebellions, while Charles Dickens gathered material here for *Hard Times*, his coruscating attack on the factory system. True, there's little to show for such a long history save the nickname, "Proud Preston", but as the administrative and commercial centre of Lancashire, it's a useful shopping and service centre.

Some handsome Victorian public buildings do survive, most notably the majestic Greek-Revival-style **Harris Museum and Art Gallery** (Mon–Sat 10am–5pm; free), in the central Market Square. It's a fine building in its own right, purpose-built in 1893 and boasting, among other things, a monumental pediment outside and Rotunda café (open until 4pm) inside, from where you can ponder the classical friezes and sculptures. The permanent collection focuses on fine art (particularly British landscape and portraiture, and contemporary photography) and decorative art, while temporary exhibitions often explore links with the town's significant Asian population. Scout around long enough and you'll encounter exhibits as diverse as a collection of delicate Victorian scent bottles and the skeleton of an Ice Age elk, the latter in the self-explanatory "Story of Preston" section. On either side of the Harris lie the modern shopping streets, converging on Fishergate, the main street through town: the Victorian **Miller Arcade** (facing Fishergate) and outdoor and indoor **markets** (up Market St; closed Sun) are the main draw. For a change in emphasis, cross Fishergate to explore the handsome Georgian development of **Winckley Square**, once home to the town's richest cotton magnates. Lancashire's favourite chef, Paul Heathcote, has a brasserie, *Simply Heathcote's*, here. Beyond the square, the ground drops away to the River Ribble and **Avenham Park**, one of the country's best examples of a landscaped Victorian park, with slopes steep enough for traditional egg-rolling every Easter.

If you needed any more incentive to stop it would be to make your way to the ground of Preston North End – one of Britain's oldest football clubs and winners of the first Football League championship – for the marvellous **National Football Museum**, Sir Tom Finney Way, Deepdale Stadium (Tues–Sat 10am–5pm, midweek matchday 10am–7.30pm, Sun 11am–5pm; £6.95; ⑩ www.nationalfootballmuseum.com). On one level, this is simply an unparalleled collection of football memorabilia: those who know about such things will relish the chance to see items as diverse as the Geoff Hurst crossbar from the 1966 World Cup or the neck-brace worn by legendary Manchester City goalkeeper Bert Trautman, who broke his neck (yet played on) in the 1956 FA Cup Final. But you really don't have to know anything about football to enjoy the museum, since "the true story of the world's greatest game" is backed by fascinating print, film and sound material on football's origins, its social importance, the experience of fans through the ages, and other relevant themes. Plus there are some great interactive exhibits – including do-it-yourself television punditry and table football with a video replay of your goals – and a good café.

For the football museum, it's a ten-minute ride on bus #19 from Preston **bus station**, right in the centre of town. The **train station**, on the west coast main line, has regular services to Manchester and Blackpool; a bus (every 20min, free with valid train ticket) connects the train station to the town centre and the bus station; otherwise, just follow Fishergate into the centre, a ten-minute walk. The **tourist office** is in the Guild Hall, on Lancaster Road (Mon–Sat 10am–5.30pm; ☏01772/253731, ⓦwww.visitpreston.com), just round the corner from the Harris Museum.

The mill towns of north and east Lancashire

Tourists rarely stray into the old, unsung mill towns of **north and east Lancashire**, reasoning perhaps that they are unlikely to offer much in the way of cultural promise or light-hearted diversion. There's something in that view, though to look solely at their unremarkable town centres and archetypal rows of housing is to miss the historical point. In the eighteenth and nineteenth centuries, the great cotton-weaving centres of **Bolton**, **Bury**, **Rochdale**, **Burnley** and **Blackburn** changed the way the world worked, with Lancashire innovation – Kay's flying shuttle, Hargreaves' spinning jenny, Arkwright's water frame – transforming cottage industries into hugely profitable mechanized production lines. Millions of tons of raw cotton flowed in to the Liverpool docks, to be turned into yarn and calico in an ever increasing number of Lancashire mills. The towns themselves acquired their character in one swift burst of expansion, as houses were thrown up to accommodate the weavers. The result was rarely pretty, but then it wasn't supposed to be – J.B. Priestley correctly identified the cotton towns as places "meant to work in and not really to live in". That was probably still true in the 1930s, when Priestley toured Britain, but today, with cotton long gone and contemporary prosperity underpinned by the engineering, technology and service industries, there's a more appealing air to the towns. Even so, although they might be thoroughly decent places to live, it's still hard to propose any serious tourist investigation of the region – although anyone with a keen eye for Victorian industrial and civic architecture will relish the surviving mill buildings (mostly converted to other uses these days) and proud, local town halls, museums and galleries.

The Ribble Valley

When the nineteenth-century Lancashire cotton weavers enjoyed a rare break from their industry they took to the bucolic retreats of the **Ribble Valley**, north of Preston, which cuts through the heart of northern Lancashire to the River Ribble's source in the Yorkshire Dales. In stark contrast to the conurbations to the south, the valley parades a stream of small market towns and isolated villages set among verdant fields and rolling hills. Much of the northwestern part of the region is occupied by thinly populated grouse moorland known as the **Forest of Bowland** – the name "forest" is used in its traditional sense of "a royal hunting ground", and much of the land still belongs to the Crown. What few trees do grow here are clustered in the valleys, which are accessible only by unclassified roads that follow former cattle droving tracks. **Public transport** is limited to the train service from Manchester and Blackburn, or buses from Preston, to the market town of **Clitheroe** on the forest's southern fringes; from there, buses run out to Dunsop Bridge, Newton and **Slaidburn** (with connections out to Settle in Yorkshire), the three tiny villages in the heart of the region. Hikers can follow the course of the river from its source to the estuary along the seventy-mile **Ribble Way**, which passes through Clitheroe: route guides are available from local bookshops and tourist offices.

Clitheroe

A tidy little market town on the banks of the River Ribble, **CLITHEROE** is best seen from the terrace of its empty **Norman Keep** which towers above the Ribble Valley floor. From here, the small centre is laid out before you and, if there's little else specific to see – save a **Castle Museum** (May–Sept daily 11am–4.30pm; Oct–Dec & Feb–April closed Thurs & Fri; closed all Jan; £1.50) in the extensive grounds – you can at least spend an hour or two browsing around the shops and old pubs. There's been a **market** in town since the thirteenth century: the current affair is held off King Street every Tuesday, Thursday and Saturday.

An obvious target is Pendle Hill, a couple of miles to the east, where the ten **Pendle Witches** allegedly held the diabolic rites that led to their hanging in 1612. The evidence against them came mainly from one small child, but nonetheless a considerable mythology has grown up around the witches, whose memory is perpetuated by a hilltop gathering each Halloween. The Clitheroe tourist office can provide a self-drive leaflet guiding you around the locality. With a car, you could also run out to the ruined Cistercian abbey at Whalley (a few miles south of Clitheroe) or the Roman museum at Ribchester (southwest).

Ribble Way walkers might be glad of the town's accommodation options – full details from the **tourist office**, at 14 Market Place (Mon–Sat 9am–5pm; ☎01200/425566) – but you're unlikely to stop otherwise. The best place for a coffee and a light meal is the *Exchange Coffee Company*, 24 Wellgate (closed Sun), where the smell of roasted coffee wafts through the old house and up the stairs into the café. Pedal Power on Waddington Road (☎01200/422066) can sort you out with a **mountain bike** for in-depth exploration of the Forest of Bowland or nearby Gisburn Forest.

The Forest of Bowland

Heading northwest from Clitheroe on the B6478 brings you to the **Forest of Bowland** just beyond Waddington, with a short run over the fells to **NEWTON**, a village centred on the *Parkers Arms* pub. It's two miles west of here to **DUNSOP BRIDGE**, a duck-riddled riverside hamlet from where an old drover's track (now a very minor road) known as the Trough of Bowland begins its twenty-mile slog across the tops to Lancaster. Those in the know make their way the couple of miles south from here to the splendid *Inn at Whitewell* (☎01200/448222; ●), which serves fabulous food in its restaurant (reservations essential) and also has a welcoming, old-fashioned bar serving meals.

Keep to the B road past Newton and it's a couple of miles northeast to **SLAIDBURN**, the most substantial and attractive of the Forest's settlements. Hoary stone cottages fronted by a strip of aged cobbles set the tone – a truly ancient **inn**, the *Hark to Bounty* (☎01200/446246; ●), and a popular **youth hostel** (☎01200/446656; closed Oct–March), itself a former inn, complete the picture. Both stand opposite each other in the centre of the village; the Hark to Bounty is known for its good bar food. There's also accommodation at *Pages Farm* on Woodhouse Lane (☎01200/446205; no credit cards; ●), half a mile from the pub, and snacks and drinks at the *Riverbank Tearooms* next to the car park.

Lancaster and around

LANCASTER, Lancashire's county town, dates back at least as far as the Roman occupation, though only the scant remains of a bath-house and traces of the fort wall survive from that period. A Saxon church was later built within the ruined Roman walls as Lancaster became a strategic trading centre, and by medieval times ships were using the River Lune and the coastal routes to Cumbria. A castle on the heights above the river defended the town from attack and provided a focus for the dispensing of regional justice. It was here that the Pendle Witches were tried in 1612, before being hanged on the heights outside town. Lancaster became an important port on the slave triangle, and it's the legacy of predominantly Georgian buildings from that time that gives the town its character, particularly in the leafy areas around the castle. It's no surprise that many people choose to spend a night here on the way to the Lakes or Dales to the north. If the lure of the beach becomes too strong, it's an easy side-trip the few miles west to the resort of **Morecambe** and to neighbouring **Heysham village** and its ancient churches.

Arrival, information and tours

Lancaster is a regular stop on the West Coast rail line from London to Scotland; there are also hourly trains from Manchester and even more frequently from Preston. From either the **train station** on Meeting House Lane, or the combined local **bus** and National Express station on Cable Street in town, it's a five-minute walk to the **tourist office** at 29 Castle Hill (April–June & Oct Mon–Sat 10am–5pm; July–Sept Mon–Sat 10am–6pm, Sun noon–4pm; Nov–March Mon–Sat 10am–4pm; ☎01524/32878, ⊛www.lancaster.gov.uk), in front of the castle. You can change money at the office, book accommodation, and check on space on the Old Calendar Walks – seasonal, "olde-worlde" strolls through the city streets with costumed guides. Canal **cruises** (☎01524/849484, ⊛www.partycruises.co.uk) depart daily in summer, less frequently at other times, from Penny Street Bridge Wharf. Annual **events and festivals** include an Easter maritime festival, Georgian fair (August bank holiday), and spectacular Bonfire Night celebrations (Saturday nearest Nov 5).

Accommodation

Castle Hill House 27 St Mary's Parade, Castle Hill ☎01524/849137. This attractive renovated Victorian house sits right opposite the castle and has three rooms available (one en suite). ❷

Edenbreck House Sunnyside Lane ☎01524/32464. For peace and quiet head for this large Victorian house out of the centre, set in its own grounds at the end of Ashfield Avenue, ten minutes' walk up Meeting House Lane. Just three en-suite rooms, so call ahead. No credit cards. ❷

Royal King's Arms Market St ☎01524/32451, ⊛www.bookmenzies.com. Lancaster's best-sited hotel, opposite the castle, has fifty-odd prettily furnished rooms with smart bathrooms, and a bar and brasserie. Rates are negotiable during the week, and always a little lower at the weekend (when breakfast is included in the price). ❺

Shakespeare Hotel 96 St Leonardsgate ☎01524/841041. Hard-working hosts maintain eight cosy rooms in this popular town-house hotel on a central street near several long-stay car parks. Rooms, of assorted shape and size, are en suite and non-smoking and have all the essentials. Advance reservations advised. ❷

Station House 25 Meeting House Lane ☎01524/381060. On a busy road, opposite the train station, but providing budget accommodation just two minutes' from the centre. No credit cards. ❷

Wagon & Horses St George's Quay ☎01524/846094. Pleasant rooms above a riverside pub, just past the Maritime Museum. No credit cards. ❷

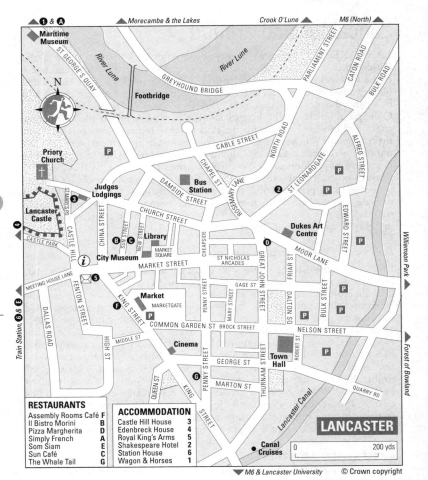

RESTAURANTS

Assembly Rooms Café	F
Il Bistro Morini	B
Pizza Margherita	D
Simply French	A
Som Siam	E
Sun Café	C
The Whale Tail	G

ACCOMMODATION

Castle Hill House	3
Edenbreck House	4
Royal King's Arms	5
Shakespeare Hotel	2
Station House	6
Wagon & Horses	1

LANCASTER

0   200 yds

M6 & Lancaster University   © Crown copyright

The City

Lancaster Castle (tours: mid-March to mid-Dec daily 10.30am–5pm; last tour at 4pm; £4) has been the city's focal point since Roman times, when there was a fort on this site. The Normans built the first castle here in around 1093 in an attempt to protect the region from marauding Scots armies, and it was added to throughout medieval times, becoming a crown court and prison in the thirteenth century, a role it still fulfils today. Currently, about a quarter of the battlemented building can be visited on an entertaining hour-long tour, though court sittings sometimes affect the schedules. You begin around the back in the Shire Hall, whose grandiose eighteenth-century courtroom was the scene of the 1974 trial of the Birmingham Six – one of the most infamous miscarriages of justice in British legal history. The tour moves on from here to the eight-foot-thick walls of the thirteenth-century Adrian's Tower, which encircle a room hung with manacles and leg-irons. These were used on the prisoners who were slammed up in the lightless cells next door, which you are invited to experience briefly. You may also see and hear something of the hangman's art: public executions were carried out at the castle until 1865. The castle's neighbour, the former Benedictine **Priory Church of St Mary** (Easter–Oct daily 9.30am–5pm; free), has a (possibly) Saxon doorway at the west end and some finely carved fourteenth-century choir stalls, the only features that predate its fifteenth-century reconstruction. There has, however, been a church on this site for at least 1200 years. Standing in front of the church's porch is the best place to view the castle's Norman keep.

A two-minute walk down the steps between the castle and church brings you to the seventeenth-century **Judges' Lodging** (Easter–June & Oct Mon–Sat 2–5pm; July–Sept Mon–Fri 10am–1pm & 2–5pm, Sat & Sun 2–5pm; £2), once used by visiting magistrates and now home to two museums. Rooms on the ground and first floors house furniture by Gillows of Lancaster, one-time boat builders who, in the early eighteenth century, took to cabinet-making with the tropical timber which came back as ballast in their boats. Their high-quality work eventually earned them contracts to furnish the Houses of Parliament and the great Cunard transatlantic liners, the *Queen Mary* and *Queen Elizabeth*. The finely worked pieces on display mainly come from the earlier period, with an especially beautiful Regency writing desk and a magnificent billiard table – Gillows are credited with first putting the slate under the baize. The top floor is given over to a **Museum of Childhood**, with memory-jogging displays of toys and games, and a period (1900) schoolroom.

Continuing down the hill and left onto Dameside you arrive on the banks of the **River Lune** – which lent Lancaster its name – whose navigable lengths inspired the growth of the port. The river was first bridged in Roman times: the latest span, an eye-catching steel suspension bridge for pedestrians, follows the line of the medieval wooden, later stone, bridge. The top floor of one of the eighteenth-century warehouses here is taken up by part of the **Maritime Museum**, St George's Quay (daily: Easter–Oct 11am–5pm; Nov–Easter 12.30–4pm; £2), entered through the Old Custom House on the riverside. The museum's ample coverage of life on the sea and inland waterways of Lancashire is complemented by the **City Museum** on Market Square back in town (Mon–Sat 10am–5pm; free). Based in the former Town Hall, five minutes' walk east of the Judges' Lodging, this explores the city's history through Neolithic, Roman, medieval and Georgian Lancaster.

For a panorama of the town, Morecambe Bay and the Cumbrian fells, take a bus from the bus station (or a steep 25-minute walk up Moor Lane) to **Williamson Park** (Easter–Sept daily 10am–5pm; Oct–Easter Mon–Fri 11am–4pm, Sat & Sun 10am–4pm; free), Lancaster's highest point. The grounds were laid out among old stone quarries by cotton workers, put out of work by the cotton famine caused by the American Civil War. Funded by local statesman and lino magnate Lord Ashton, the park's centrepiece is the 220-foot-high **Ashton Memorial**, a Baroque folly raised by his son in memory of his second wife. The views are pretty fine from here, and there's a small art gallery on the upper level, while the grounds also contain a **butterfly house and bird garden** (same hours as the memorial; £3.25). The *Pavilion Tea Room* (daily: June–Sept 10am–5pm; rest of the year closes 4pm) at the memorial is a nice spot. The other local excursion is to the **Crook O'Lune**, a beauty spot made famous by J.M.W. Turner. It's four miles northeast of the city, reached by a path/cycle-way along the River Lune (part of the River Lune Millennium Park), and there's a picnic site and snack bar at the other end.

John Ruskin fans, meanwhile, won't want to miss the **Ruskin Library**, out

at Lancaster University (Mon–Sat 11am–4pm, Sun 1–4pm; free; ⓦ www.lancs
.ac.uk/ruskinlib), where a unique selection of pictures, manuscripts, books and
photographs relating to the great man are shown in a series of changing exhibitions; buses run up every half an hour from the bus station.

Cafés and Restaurants

Assembly Rooms Café King St, opposite the
market. Home-cooked café food amid the craft,
antique, clothes and accessories stalls in the
Georgian assembly rooms. Closed Sun & Mon.
Inexpensive.

Il Bistro Morini 26 Sun St ☎ 01524/846252. The
best Italian in town, with regional specialities
emphasizing seafood, duck and pork. It's advisable
to book in advance. Closed Sun. Expensive.

Pizza Margherita 2 Moor Lane. Good-natured
pizza and pasta restaurant, festooned with plants,
where you can fill up for under £10. Inexpensive.

Simply French 27 St George's Quay, ☎ 01524
/843199. Riverside brasserie in a converted warehouse close to the Maritime Museum. The set lunch
is a good deal (for £7–8); dinner might be pan-
seared sea trout or rabbit casserole. Closed Mon,

also Tues & Wed lunch. Inexpensive to Moderate.

Som Siam 13–15 Meeting House Lane. Flavourful
Thai dishes in a friendly spot – all the old
favourites, from noodles to fish cakes, plus Thai
regional specials. Dinner only. Moderate.

Sun Café 25 Sun St. The food's the draw in this
stylish café/restaurant – think gourmet sandwiches and World flavours – but you might equally
come for a glass of wine, Sunday brunch with the
papers, a live gig, or even the contemporary art
gallery. Closed Sun evening. Inexpensive to
Moderate.

The Whale Tail 78a Penny St. Veggie and wholefood café, tucked up a yard on the first floor, serving good breakfasts, tasty dips, salads, burgers,
sandwiches and baked potatoes. Closes 5pm, 3pm
on Sundays. Inexpensive.

Drinking and entertainment

Dukes Moor Lane ☎ 01524/66645. The city's
main arts centre, with cinema, theatre (including
open-air performances in Williamson Park in summer) and other events.

The Friary corner of St Leonardsgate and
Rosemary Lane. A former church, now a real ale
pub with a booming student presence.

George & Dragon St George's Quay. For a stroll
along the river and a quiet drink, either here or the
Wagon & Horses up the road are the best pubs.

Ye Olde John O'Gaunt Market St, near the City
Museum. Terrific city-centre local concentrating on
the good things – home-cooked food, large range
of whiskies and vodkas, special beers, tea and
coffee on request, live trad jazz and R&B, and a
small beer garden.

Water Witch Aldcliffe Rd. Canalside pub named
after an old canal packet boat. A student crowd
munches burgers, shoots pool and hogs the canalside tables.

Morecambe and Heysham

Although the name **MORECAMBE**, meaning "Great Bay", dates from Celtic
times, the seaside town five miles west of Lancaster only took it in the nineteenth century when it rapidly expanded from a small fishing village into a
full-blown resort. The catalyst, as with Blackpool, was the arrival of the railway,
which not only brought in the northern mill workers on holiday, but also
enabled the quick transport of the bay's shrimps and mussels to the towns they
had come from. Across the bay, Grange-over-Sands was always the more refined
resort and with Blackpool to the south hoovering up the rest of the local
demand for bucket-and-spade holidays, Morecambe went into decline after the
war. There's been plenty of recent regeneration – notably the restored Stone
Jetty, an arts centre and revamped amusements and attractions – but the sweep
of the bay is still the major attraction, with the local sunsets a renowned phenomenon. The **Stone Jetty**, all that remains of the former harbour, has been
remodelled by sculptors and stonemasons and now features bird sculptures,
games and motifs – recognizing Morecambe Bay as Britain's most important

△Blackpool

wintering site for wildfowl and wading birds. A little way along the prom stands the most popular statue of all, of one of Britain's most treasured comedians – Eric Bartholomew, who took the stage name **Eric Morecambe** when he met his comedy partner, Ernie Wise. He appears here in famous Bring-Me-Sunshine prancing mode.

Any information you need can be had from the **tourist office** in the Old Station Buildings on the Central Promenade (Mon–Sat 9.30am–5pm, Sun 10am–4pm; ☎01524/582808), which operates a room-booking service for local hotels. Morecambe, certainly, is a lot quieter a place to spend the night than Blackpool. The Platform arts centre (☎01524/582803) shares the same building as the **tourist office**. Regular buses or trains from Lancaster make the short trip to Morecambe: from the **bus** or **train stations**, on either side of Central Drive, it's just five minutes' walk to the Stone Jetty.

The main historic interest on this side of Morecambe Bay is at **HEYSHAM**, three miles southwest. The nicest approach is on foot, along the promenade from Morecambe. Largely known for its ferry port (services to Belfast and the Isle of Man) and unsightly nuclear power station, Heysham's hidden gem is the shoreside **Heysham Village**, centred on a group of charming seventeenth-century cottages and barns, one of which is now the local Heritage Centre (daily 11am–4pm; free). Settlement here can be traced back to prehistoric times, though proudest relic is the well-preserved Viking hog's-back tombstone in Saxon **St Peter's** church, set in a romantic churchyard below the headland. Just up the lane, on the headland itself, the earlier ruins of **St Patrick's chapel** occupy a superb vantage-point over the bay and to the lakeland hills beyond. Views aside, the singular interest here is the series of rough-cut stone graves by the chapel, possibly dating from the eighth or ninth centuries. Once you've seen these, all that remains is to step back into one of the village tea rooms for a glass of (non-alcoholic) nettle beer, a local speciality dating from the Victorian era.

The Isle of Man

The **Isle of Man**, almost equidistant from Ireland, England, Wales and Scotland, is one of the most beautiful spots in Britain, a mountainous, cliff-fringed island just thirty-one miles by thirteen, into which are shoehorned austere moorlands and wooded glens, sandy beaches, fine castles, beguiling narrow-gauge railways and scores of standing stones and Celtic crosses. It takes some effort to reach, and the weather is hardly reliable, factors which have seen tourist numbers fall since its Victorian heyday, when the island developed as rapidly as the other northwestern coastal resorts. This means, though, that the Isle of Man has been spared the worst excesses of the British tourist trade: there's peace and quiet in abundance, walks around the unspoilt hundred-mile coastline, picket fences and picnic spots, rural villages straight out of a 1950s' picture-book, steam trains and cream teas – a yesteryear ensemble if ever there was one.

The capital, **Douglas**, is atypical of an island which prides itself on its Celtic and Norse heritage, and it's the vestiges of the distant past – the castles at the former capital **Castletown** and the west coast port of **Peel** – that make the most obvious destinations. Elsewhere, **Port Erin** has one of the island's best beaches, while to the north **Laxey** is an attractive proposition for its huge **waterwheel** and the meandering train ride to the barren summit of **Snaefell**,

Walking on the Isle of Man

Quite apart from the local walking opportunities that the glens, coastline and hills offer, there are a number of established day hikes and long-distance walks open to anyone in a reasonable state of fitness. OS Landranger map 95 covers the entire island, while the free small guide *Walks on the Isle of Man*, available from Douglas tourist office, spells out all the options and indicates what you're likely to see en route at any particular time of the year.

Short sections of **disused railway line** provide some of the gentlest introductions to the scenery: notably the Heritage Trail (10 miles), from the Quarterbridge in Douglas to Peel, and the route from Peel north to Ramsey, via Kirk Michael (16 miles). A good route to combine with an outward journey or return by steam train is the **Port Erin to Castletown** (12 miles) hike along the cliff tops and beaches, with a possible detour to Cregneash village (p.813). From the summit of **Snaefell**, various descents are possible, the easiest of which is the direct route back down the Laxey Valley to Laxey.

There are two main long-distance footpaths, the shortest being the 28-mile **Millennium Way**, from Castle Rushen in Castletown to Ramsey, following the old medieval "Royal Way". It splits into three day hikes (though serious hikers do it in one day), with the second half of the walk, from Baldwin to Ramsey, across the most remote terrain. The greatest challenge, however, is the round-island **Raad ny Foillan (Road of the Gull)**, a well-signposted (white gull on a blue background) 95-mile coastal walk which takes most people around five days to complete. The path follows the coast wherever possible, and only on the northern stretch – north and west of Ramsey – are you ever within anything but easy reach of accommodation and facilities.

the island's highest peak. From Snaefell's summit you get an idea of the range of the Manx scenery, the finest parts of which are to be found in the seventeen officially designated National Glens, most of them linked by the **Raad Ny Foillan** (Road of the Gull) coastal footpath, which passes several of the island's numerous hillforts, Viking burial ships and Celtic crosses.

Although the landscapes are wonderful, the island's main tourist draw is the **TT (Tourist Trophy) motorcycle races** in the first two weeks in June, a frenzy of speed and burning rubber that's shattered the island's peace annually since 1907. Thousands of bikers swamp the place to watch a nonstop parade of maniacs hurtling round the roads on a 37-mile circuit at speeds approaching 120mph. This is only the most famous of a summer-long list of **rallies and races** on the island's roads, from the Manx Rally (May), International Rally and Manx Classic (both Sept) to the Kart Racing Festival (July), when go-carts buzz through the streets of Peel. If you want to stay on the island at these times, you must book your accommodation well in advance.

Some history

The island may have already been populated when it became a separate land mass at the end of the last Ice Age around 8000 BC, but the earliest substantial human traces are Mesolithic flint workings from about 6000 BC, predating the Neolithic farming settlements by around three millennia. St Patrick is said to have come here in the fifth century bringing Christianity, which struggled for a while when the **Vikings** established garrisons here in the eleventh century, though they converted while they reigned as **Kings of Mann**. The Scots under Alexander wrested power from the Norsemen in 1275, the beginning of an ultimately unsuccessful 130-year struggle with the English for control of the island. During the English **Civil War**, James Stanley, Seventh Earl of Derby and

Lord of Man, raised an army to support Charles II, but in his absence a local militia offered the island to Cromwell, provided the traditional rights of the islanders – long infringed upon by English overlords – were maintained. It was a shortlived insurrection: with the restoration of the monarchy, the leaders of the militia were executed and the island returned to Crown control.

The distinct identity of the island remained intact, however, and many true Manx inhabitants, who comprise a shade under fifty percent of the island's 72,000 population, insist that the Isle of Man is not part of England, nor even of the UK. Indeed, although a Crown dependency, the island has its own government, **Tynwald**, arguably the world's oldest democratic parliament, which has run continuously since 979 AD. Tynwald consists of two chambers, the 24-member House of Keys (directly elected every five years) and the smaller, more elite Legislative Council, both presided over by a Lieutenant-Governor who is appointed by the British monarch (recognized here as the Lord of Mann). To further complicate matters, the island maintains a unique associate status in the EU, neither contributing nor receiving funds but enjoying the same trading rights. The island has its own sterling currency, worth the same as the mainland currency; its own laws, though they generally follow Westminster's; an independent postal service; and a Gaelic-based language which nearly died out but is once again being taught in schools and is most visible on dual-language road signs throughout the island. The island, of course, also produces its own tailless version of the domestic cat, as well as famously good kippers and queenies (scallops).

However, much to the locals' chagrin, these thriving marks of identity are still slightly marred by the island's reputation of being a tax haven for greedy Brits and a refuge for the sort of people who think that even Victorian values were a bit on the lax side. It's an image problem which largely stems from the island's archaic human rights legislation. Homosexuality was illegal here until 1992, while the death penalty and corporal punishment were only abolished in 1993, in response to pressure from Westminster and the European Union. With such a record, it might seem perverse that in 1881 Tynwald became the first government to see fit to grant women a vote, although this was limited to property owners and empowered very few.

For most of its history, crofting and fishing, interspersed with a good bit of smuggling, have formed the basis of the economy. The first regular steamship service from England commenced in 1819, and **tourism** began to flourish during the late-Victorian and Edwardian eras with the influx of northwestern factory workers. At its height – at the turn of the last century – tourism was bringing in half a million visitors a year, but in recent times the real money-spinner has been the **offshore finance industry**, exploiting the island's low income tax and absence of capital gains tax and death duties. More than fifty banks have been established on the island since 1991, whole streets in Douglas, the capital, are taken up by consultancies and the island is dotted with the houses and swanky cars of tax exiles. Given its financial expertise, the Isle of Man is also playing a major role in the development of **ebanking and ecommerce**, while the low-tax island has provided incentives for the filming of an increasing number of movies.

Getting to the island

Most visitors from England arrive at Douglas, the main port, on **ferries** or the quicker **Sea Cats**, both run by The Isle of Man Steam Packet Company (Mon–Sat 7am–8pm, Sun 9am–8pm; ☎08705/523523, ⓦwww.steam-packet .com), from either Heysham (near Lancaster) or Liverpool. **Heysham** (Sea Cat

2hr, ferry 3hr 30min) has the most frequent service, with two or three sailings a day in July and August dropping to one or two daily during the rest of the year. **Liverpool** manages two to three Sea Cat services a day (2hr 30min) between April and September, with a much-reduced ferry service (4hr) at other times (between October and March, down to 1 daily at weekends).

One-way **fares** start at £19 for foot passengers and £99 for drivers (covers the car, driver and one passenger), but advance-purchase tickets, special offers and night-time sailings offer substantial savings – call for the latest deals, or contact a travel agent, who may be able to provide a well-priced transport-plus-accommodation package.

The best **flight** deals are with Manx Airlines (℡08457/256256, ⓦwww .manx-airlines.com), which flies several times daily from Liverpool, Manchester and Leeds/Bradford. Meanwhile, British European Airways (℡08705/676676, ⓦwww.british-european.com) flies daily from London City Airport and from Bristol and Belfast. Prices start at £99 return on all routes, though you should book well in advance and be prepared to spend a Saturday night away for the best fares.

Getting around the island

With a car you could see almost everything in a couple of days; even on foot, it only takes around five days to circumnavigate the entire island. But don't miss a trip on one of the two century-old **rail services** which still provide the best public transport to all the major towns and sights except for Peel. The carriages of the **Steam Railway** (Easter–Oct daily 10am–5pm; £7 return to Port Erin) rock their fifteen-mile course from Douglas to Castletown, Port St Mary and Port Erin at a spirited pace, making up in character for what they lack in comfort. The rolling terrain due north of Douglas was too steep for conventional trains, but by 1893 fledgling technology was available to construct the **Manx Electric Railway** (Easter–May, Sept & Oct daily 10am–5pm; June–Aug 10am–7.30pm; £6 return to Ramsey) which runs for seventeen miles from Douglas's Derby Castle Station to Ramsey via Laxey. Normally operating a single wooden carriage, it resembles a tramway more than a train, particularly since it follows the road most of the way to Laxey before peeling off into the countryside beyond. The **trains** are the most enjoyable way to get to Laxey, Ramsey, Castletown and Port Erin but **buses** are often quicker – bus routes are given in the text where appropriate.

The "**Island Explorer**" ticket gives one (£8), three (£18), five (£26) or seven (£32) days' unlimited travel on all bus services, plus steam and electric train routes, the trip to Snaefell and horse-tram rides in Douglas. Tickets are available from the Travel Shop (see below), main train and tram stations, and the tourist office in Douglas.

Outside race times, the roads are a joy to **drive** – there's relatively little traffic, even in summer, and on the TT stretches, the straights and gentle curves tempt you all too easily into Michael Schümacher mode, encouraged by the fact that there's no speed limit on the Isle of Man outside the towns and villages (though in these the limit is often reduced to 20mph).

Douglas

DOUGLAS, heart of the offshore finance industry, also has the vast majority of the island's hotels and good restaurants, and it makes as good a base as any, since all roads lead here. A mere market town as late as 1850, with one pier and an undeveloped seafront, Douglas was a product of Victorian mass tourism and displays many similarities to Blackpool, just across the water: five-storey terraces back the mile-and-a-half-long curve of the promenade and its tram tracks, and the town even makes a paltry attempt to emulate the illuminations. However, put aside thoughts of Blackpool-style state-of-the-art entertainment and sophisticated nightlife. Although there are pockets of contemporary development, Douglas – despite its financial acumen – has something of an end-of-season feel about it. It's not really the town's fault – where once half a million people a year sported on the sands, package tourism to hotter climates has long since burst the bubble. You can still have a thoroughly enjoyable time here, but it's likely to consist largely of pulling up a candy-striped deckchair and enjoying the extensive sands. When it rains, stroll the covered arcades, ride the horse-drawn trams or attend the afternoon tea dances.

Arrival, orientation and information

All flights arrive at **Ronaldsway airport** at Ballasalla, around ten miles south-west of Douglas, close to Castletown. Buses (every 30min–1hr 7am–11pm) connect the airport with Castletown/Port St Mary or Douglas. A taxi from the airport costs around £13 to Douglas, £16 to Peel.

Ferries and Sea Cats dock by the **Sea Terminal** at the southern end of the Douglas waterfront. Fifty yards beyond the forecourt taxi rank, the Lord Street **bus station** is the hub of the island's dozen or so bus routes; the **Travel Shop** here (Mon, Wed & Fri 10am–12.30pm & 1.30–5.45pm, Tues, Thurs & Sat 8am–12.30pm & 1.30–5.45pm; ☏01624/662525), a little way beyond the station at the bottom of Lord Street, has timetable information and sells Island Explorer **travel tickets** for buses and trains – see "Getting around the island" on p.805 for details.

North Quay runs 300 yards west from the bus station alongside the river and fishing port to Douglas Station, the northern terminus of the **steam railway** to Port Erin. The waterfront (progressively Loch, Central and Queen's promenades) runs a mile and a half north to Derby Castle Station for the **electric railway** to Laxey and Ramsey – take the horse-drawn tram along the promenade or bus #24, #24a, #26 or #26a from Douglas bus station.

The **tourist office** is in the Sea Terminal building (mid-May to Sept daily 9.15am–7pm; April to mid-May & Oct daily 9am–5pm; Nov–March Mon–Thurs 9am–5.30pm, Fri 9am–5pm, Sat 9.30am–12.30pm); ☏01624/686766). There's a smaller office at the airport, open to meet flight arrivals. The main **websites** for information are ⓦ www.gov.im and ⓦ www.isle-of-man.com.

Accommodation

B&Bs are packed in along Douglas's front and up the roads immediately off Harris Promenade, particularly along Broadway, Castle Mona Avenue, Empress Drive and Empire Terrace. Prices start as little as £25 for a double (in admittedly small rooms) and a sea-view room can be had for £50. At the bottom end of the scale the sheer number of choices, most with just a few rooms, precludes any real recommendations – you'll have to stroll along and look for vacancy signs. Note that many places demand a two-night minimum stay in the summer. If you're prepared to spend a bit more money – and many businesspeople are, so book ahead – then again, comparative bargains abound. In particular, there's an increasing number of rather splendid boutique-style **hotels** in renovated seafront buildings, with significantly higher prices.

Guest houses and hotels

Admiral House Hotel Loch Promenade ☏01624 /629551, ⓔ enquiries@admiralhouse.com. At the ferry terminal end of the prom, this lovingly restored, club-like retreat features very comfortable rooms, a café-bar and an excellent Spanish restaurant. ⑤

Arrandale Hotel Hutchinson Square ☎01624 /674907. Traditional guest house a few minutes' walk away from the promenade in a quiet residential area. There's a wide range of rooms (some family-size), most are en suite, and there's parking outside. ❷

Blossoms 4 The Esplanade ☎01624/673360. One of the better choices at the cheaper end of the market, flower-draped *Blossoms* has a few sea-view rooms which tend to go early. No credit cards. ❶

Claremont Hotel 18–19 Loch Promenade ☎01624/698800, ⓦ www.sleepwellhotels.com. Sympathetically renovated promenade hotel with a good bar and restaurant. Rooms have all the latest gadgets, including voicemail and DVD. ❺

Cubbon House Loch Promenade ☎01624 /670799. Hides its very smart en-suite rooms behind an old-fashioned holiday hotel façade. Beds are comfortable and rooms at the rear are very quiet. ❸

Empress Hotel Central Promenade ☎01624 /661155, ⓦ www.theempresshotel.net. Grand old Victorian hotel that's been remodelled inside to provide a hundred spacious rooms, many with sea views. A large conservatory keeps the rain off drinkers and diners; there's a pool and parking. ❺

Sefton Hotel Harris Promenade ☎01624/645500, ⓦ www.seftonhotel.co.im. Next to the Gaiety Theatre, this is another place that's had a contemporary facelift, with sleek rooms offering a sea view or a balcony over the atrium. There's also a pool, internet access, bike rental and lots of other facilities. Room-only rates knock a few pounds off the price. ❻

Campsites

Grandstand ☎01624/621132. Closest to Douglas, this backs onto Noble's Park Grandstand on Glencrutchery Road, a mile north of the tourist office. Closed Oct–May and during TT and Manx Grand Prix races.

Glenlough Farm ☎01624/851326. Three miles west at Union Mills on the Peel road. Closed Oct–April.

Glendhoo International Campsite ☎01624 /621254. In a sheltered valley, two miles north at the Cronk ny Mona crossroads on the A18. Closed Oct–Easter.

The Town

Douglas's seafront vista has changed little since Victorian times, and is still trodden by heavy-footed carthorses pulling **trams** (jump on for a few pence). On Harris Promenade the opulent **Gaiety Theatre**, fronted by a stained glass canopy, is unique among the nine theatres designed by Frank Matcham, which includes the Grand in Blackpool. The lush, lapis-blue interior, paintings and decorated stage backdrop have been restored with precision. Hour-long tours of the theatre take place each Saturday (10.30am; £3; information and box office ☎01624/625001).

The town is at its oldest, and most interesting, in the streets near the **harbour**, where an attempt has been made to preserve Douglas's "historic quayside". There's not much to it, save a few old pubs and the odd teetering building, and you're soon pushed up Victoria Street, past the Manx Legislative Building, to the **Manx Museum**, on the corner of Kingswood Grove and Crellins Hill (Mon–Sat 10am–5pm; free). The museum makes a good start for anyone wanting to get to grips with Manx culture and heritage before setting off around the island, kicking off with a National Gallery of Manx painters – from Alfred James Collister and his friend Archibald Knox to the contemporary abstract artist Bryan Kneale. Other rooms provide an absorbing synopsis of the island's history, packed with Neolithic standing stones, Celtic grave markers and other artefacts, notably some excellent displays relating to Viking burials and runic crosses. Much of the current understanding of Manx culture was pieced together from digs at Peel Castle in the 1980s, which turned up a cache of silver coins minted in Dublin in 1030, and evidence of a pagan sacrifice, in the form of a woman's severed scalp, on display next to the trove. More recent activities get the full treatment, too, with collections of smutty postcards from the 1930s, displays about the TT races and information boards explaining the capital's financial wheeling and dealing.

Eating, drinking and entertainment

There's real coffee at the *Spill the Beans Coffee House*, 1 Market Hill (closed Sun), while other good daytime **cafés** include the *Bay Room Restaurant* (closed Sun), in the Manx Museum, and *Greens*, in the ticket office at the steam railway station, which serves vegetarian specials. The *Claremont* and *Admiral House* hotels, on Loch Promenade, both have fashionable café-bars, if you feel like something chargrilled or wok-roasted. The local **restaurant** scene has improved dramatically over recent years, too. TV chef and local lad Kevin Woodford might claim to have something to do with that. He's got the island's highest profile, alongside a couple of restaurants in Douglas: the expensive *Waterfront*, at the top of North Quay (☎01624/673222), and the moderate *Blazers* next door (same phone number), a more relaxing spot to graze on bistro dishes from around the world – such as chickpea and coriander patties or the signature dish, Manx sausage and mash. Further down the quayside, *Tanroagan* (☎01624/472411; eve only) is the trendy choice for fish. More traditionally, *Scotts Bistro*, 7 John St (☎01624/623764; closed Sun), near the old town hall, is housed in Douglas's oldest (seventeenth-century) building and has queenies in garlic sauce alongside its other Anglo-French choices. *La Posada*, in the basement of the *Admiral House Hotel* on Loch Promenade (☎01624 /629551), is an authentic Spanish restaurant, whose dishes include a rich paella. Locals also like *Paparazzi*, 26 Loch Promenade, a large pizzeria-trattoria with Sicilian beer and a few more unusual Italian specialities.

Manx-brewed beer is on sale at most **pubs** and brews such as "Old Bushy Tail" soon revive flagging spirits. Try it and others at the cosy *Rovers Return*, on Church St, around the corner from *Scott's Bistro*. The *British Hotel*, on North Quay, is an old harbourside pub that's been given a going-over inside but retains some character; while the wine-swilling Euro-crowd frequent the capacious *Bar George*, a fashionable haunt housed in a converted Sunday School at the end of Hill St.

Listings

Airport Ronaldsway airport, flight enquiries ☎01624/821600.

Banks ATMs at Barclays, Victoria St; NatWest, Prospect Hill; Lloyds-TSB, Prospect Hill; HSBC, Ridgeway St; Isle of Man Bank, SeaTerminal.

Bicycle rental Eurocycles, 8a Victoria Rd, off Broadway ☎01624/624909.

Buses All bus enquiries ☎01624/662525.

Car rental Most outfits have offices at the airport or can arrange to deliver cars to the Sea Terminal. Contact: Athol, Athol Garage, Peel Rd and at the airport ☎01624/822481, ⬤www.athol.co.im; Isle of Man Rent-a-Car, at the airport and deliveries to Sea Terminal ☎01624/825855; Mylchreests, at the airport and deliveries to Sea Terminal ☎0500/823533; Ocean Ford, Douglas Rd, Castletown ☎01624/820830.

Cruises Summer cruises, from Villier steps, Douglas promenade, to Port Soderick or Laxey on the MV Karina. Call ☎01624/861724 or ☎07624/493592.

Ferries and Sea Cats Isle of Man Steam Packet Company ☎01624/661661.

Hospital Noble's Hospital, Westmoreland Rd ☎01624/642642.

Internet Feegan's Lounge, Duke St, off Victoria St (Mon–Fri 9am–7pm, Sat 9am–6pm).

Pharmacies Boots, 14 Strand St; John Atkinson, 2 Granville St.

Police Douglas Police Station, Glencrutchery Rd ☎01624/631212.

Post Office Main post office is at 6 Regent St ☎01624/686141.

Trains Steam Railway enquiries ☎01624/673623; Electric Railway and Snaefell Mountain Railway enquiries ☎01624/663366.

Laxey

Filling a narrow valley, the straggling town of **LAXEY**, seven miles north of Douglas, spills down from its train station to a small harbour and long, pebbly beach, squeezed between two bulky headlands. The Manx Electric Railway from Douglas drops you at the station used by the **Snaefell Mountain Railway**. Shops and a couple of cafés here attempt to divert the crowds who disembark and then head inland and uphill to Laxey's pride, the **"Lady Isabella" Great Laxey Wheel** (Easter–Oct daily 10am–5pm; £2.75), smartly painted in red and white. With a diameter of over 72ft it's said to be the largest working waterwheel in the world – a slightly bogus claim as it doesn't drive anything. Until 1929 the wheel was used to pump water from the local lead mines which, with their silver-rich ore, were a major money-spinner. The mechanism and its relation to the mine are all well explained and you can stroll around the various buildings and bits of machinery before climbing to the top of the wheel for a fine view. **St George's Woollen Mills**, over on Glen Rd (Mon–Sat 9am–5.30pm; free), is also still in operation and you can see weaving taking place there most days. Otherwise Laxey is at its best down in **Old Laxey**, around the harbour, half a mile below the station, where large car parks attest to the popularity of the beach and river. Half a mile out of town (follow the A2 to Ramsey) a sign points you up a side street to **King Orry's Grave**, named for the heroic eleventh-century Manx king who created the first Kingdom Of Mann. Would that it was any such thing, historical evidence of him being slight, though the two grave sites on show – one either side of the road – are interesting enough. It's thought that they're five-thousand-year-old stone chambered tombs, built by Neolithic farmers under cairns, the earth of these now long worn away and leaving just a small arc of standing stones.

Hourly **buses** #3 and #3A run to Laxey from Douglas; the #3B and #3C run directly to Old Laxey four times a day (not Sun). The *Mines Tavern,* by the station, has some shaded outdoor seats and serves **lunch**, while *Brown's* on the fantastically named Ham and Egg Terrace (by the wheel car park) is the place for grills and fry-ups or some Manx kippers and bread and butter. Down at the harbour, drinking is done at the *Shore Hotel,* a nice **pub** by the bridge which brews its own bitter, and there's the *Mona Lisa* (☎01624/862488; eve only) just opposite, over the bridge, a popular local Italian place.

Snaefell, Tholt-y-Will Glen and Sulby Glen

Every few minutes, the tramcars of the **Snaefell Mountain Railway** (Easter–Oct daily 10.30am–3.30pm; £6 return, £7.50 from Douglas) begin their thirty-minute wind from Laxey through increasingly denuded moorland to the island's highest point, the top of **Snaefell** (2036ft) – the Vikings' "Snow Mountain" – from where you can see England, Wales, Scotland and Ireland on a clear day. The four-and-a-half miles of track were built in seven months over the winter of 1895 by two hundred men; one gang worked down from the summit, the other up from Laxey, an unimaginable effort in bitter conditions. At the summit, most people are content to pop into the inelegant café and bar and then soak up the views for the few minutes until the return journey.

The road route up, the A18 from Ramsey, also makes for a super ride, since it forms part of the TT course. Where the A18 and A14 (Snaefell–Sulby) meet, just below the summit, there's an isolated railway halt where drivers and hikers can pick up the mountain railway for a truncated ride to the summit and back. Three miles below the summit, down the A14, which sweeps past **Sulby Reservoir**, the road drops into **Tholt-y-Will Glen**, one of the island's more picturesque corners, with its gushing river and walks through the verdant plantations. There's a car park at the *Tholt-y-Will* inn, a Swiss-style chalet with gardens in a lovely location – a magnet for coach tours.

The A14 continues north to join the A3 Ramsey road, along a fine route –

above the river – through **Sulby Glen**, with bracken-clad hills flanking the road. The *Sulby Glen Hotel* (☎01624/897240; ③) has good beer and a bistro. A signposted turn, just before the A3, cuts east to **Cronk Sumark**, a Celtic hilltop fort close to a large picnic area.

Maughold, Ramsey and around

The Manx Electric Railway trains stop within a mile and a half of **MAUGHOLD**, seven miles northeast of Laxey, a tiny hamlet just inland from the cliff-side lighthouse at **Maughold Head**. It's an isolated spot which only adds to the attraction of Maughold's parish church, in whose grounds is maintained an outstanding collection of early Christian and Norse **carved crosses** – 44 pieces, dating from the sixth to the thirteenth century, and ranging from fragments of runic carving to a six-foot-high rectangular slab. Look inside the church, too, at the old parish cross, fourteenth century in date and sporting the earliest known picture of the Three Legs of Mann apart from that on the twelfth-century Sword of State. Bus #16 comes direct to Maughold from Ramsey, four or five times a day (not Sun).

RAMSEY marks the northern terminus of the Electric Railway, 45 minutes beyond Laxey. The Victorian tourist boom left behind the island's only iron pier and a solitary grand terrace along the front, but the bulk of the town, by the harbour – once more important than that in Douglas – is a dispiriting swatch of build-by-numbers modernity. The beach really isn't worth hanging around for and the only sight, the **Grove Rural Life Museum** (Easter–Sept daily 10am–5pm; £2.75), is a mile north on the A9. This, once the summer home of a Merseyside shipping magnet, is crammed with Victorian country-house furniture, and there's a nice café. With a car you could drive on to a couple more diversions. North is the **Point of Ayre** lighthouse, at the northeastern tip of the island, built in 1818, while to the west you can seek out the unfinished Civil War fort at **Kerroogarroo**. This is just to the south of Andreas off the A17; a signpost points you through the fields to the banks and ramparts, hastily constructed in 1640 but now completely grass-grown and very peaceful.

St Johns

The trans-island A1 (and hourly bus #5 or #6 from Douglas) follows a deep twelve-mile-long furrow between the northern and southern ranges from Douglas to Peel. A hill at the crossroads settlement of **ST JOHNS**, nine miles along it, is the original site of **Tynwald**, the ancient Manx government, which derives its name from the Norse *Thing Völlr*, meaning "Assembly Field". Nowadays the word refers to the Douglas-based House of Keys and Legislative Council, but acts passed in the capital only become law once they have been proclaimed here on July 5 (ancient Midsummer's Day) in an annual open-air parliament that also hears the grievances of the islanders. Tynwald's four-tiered grass mound – made from soil collected from each of the island's parishes – stands at the other end of a processional path from the stone **St John Chapel**, which traditionally doubled as the courthouse. Early accounts of the ceremony indicate that the king sat at the top of the mound, facing east and brandishing his sword; the barons to his side, judges in front of him, and the representatives of the Keys, clergy and squires on the terraces below – with the rabble kept outside the enclosure. Until the nineteenth century the local people arrived with their livestock and stayed a week or more – in true Viking fashion – to thrash out local issues, play sports, make marriages and hold a fair. Now Tynwald Day begins with a service in the chapel, followed by a procession to the mound where the offices of state are carried out, after which a fair and concerts begin.

Peel and around

The main settlement on the west coast, **PEEL** immediately captivates, with its fine castle rising across the harbour and a popular sandy beach running the length of its eastern promenade. It's a town of some antiquity and its enduring appeal is as one of the most "Manx" of all the island's towns, a character that is manifested in various ways – from an age-old Tuesday market in the market-place above the harbour to the line of smoke-belching kipper factories along the harbourside.

Archeological evidence indicates that **St Patrick's Isle**, which guards the harbour, has had a significant population since Mesolithic times. What probably started out as a flint-working village on a naturally protected spot gained significance with the foundation of a monastery in the seventh or eighth century, parts of which remain inside the ramparts of the red sandstone **Peel Castle** (Easter–Sept daily 10am–5pm; £3). The Vikings built the first fortifications and the site became the residence of the Kings of Mann until 1220, when they moved to Castle Rushen in Castletown. The English continued strengthening the fortress, eventually completing a fifteen-foot curtain wall around the islet. Only this is in good repair, leaving the huge ward dotted with miscellaneous remains, including the Gothic vaults of St Germain's Cathedral, whose fourteenth-century crypt was later used as a prison. An annual Shakespeare festival and concerts take place within the castle walls, while below the ramparts on the west side there's a tiny sand beach.

It's a fifteen-minute walk from the town around the river harbour and over the bridge to the castle. On the way, you'll have passed the excellent harbourside House of Mannannan **heritage centre** (daily 10am–5pm; £5) named after the island's ancient sea-god. You should allow at least two hours to get around the museum, which concentrates strongly on participatory exhibits – whether it's listening to Celtic legends in a replica longhouse, examining the contents and occupants of a life-sized Viking ship, walking through a kipper factory or steering a steamer. There are dozens of other diversions throughout, illuminating the island's history and culture by way of dioramas, video presentations, hands-on exhibits and re-created street and domestic scenes – all in all, an essential counterpoint to Douglas's Manx Museum. Finally, past the museum, by the bridge, **Moore's** (Mon–Sat 10am–5pm; tours at 2pm & 3.30pm, £2) is a traditional curing yard where you can see how Manx kippers are smoked and buy some to take home.

Practicalities

The most regular **bus** service to Peel is the hourly #5 or #6 from Douglas; this service continues to Ramsey via Kirk Michael and Sulby. The much less frequent #8 (not Sun) connects Peel to Port Erin, via St Johns and Castletown. There's central **accommodation** at the Georgian *Merchant's House*, 18 Castle St (℡01624/842541; no credit cards; ❷), while for sea views you could try one of the old-fashioned guest houses at the end of Marine Parade, such as *Fernleigh* (℡01624/842435; no credit cards; ❶). The *Peel Camping Park*, on Derby Rd (℡01624/842341; closed mid-Sept to mid-May), is signposted about half a mile out on the Douglas road.

When it comes to **eating**, if you are looking for something more than the seafront cafés and fish-and-chip shops, then head for the **pub** opposite the House of Mannannan: the *Creek Inn* (℡01624/842216) serves a delicious array of specials, from seafood platters to scallops mornay, inside or out, lunch and dinner. Self-catering apartments are also available here to rent, year-round.

Niarbyl

Five miles south of Peel, off the A27, just after Dalby, a minor road runs down to the grassy car park above **Niarbyl**, a little headland of jutting rock, framed by clear water and steep banks and fronted by a flat pebbled beach, above which sits a picture-perfect thatched cottage. On clear days, the Calf of Man (see below) is visible in the distance; on even better days, seals can be seen on the rocks. South of the headland, the moorland road (A27, then A36) is one of the most dramatic on the island, forming a high-level switchback route to Port Erin, providing sweeping views both southwest across the cliffs and southeast across the plain to Castletown. Back at the A27 turn-off for Niarbyl, at **Dalby**, *Ballacallin House* (☎01624/841100; ❹) is a traditional country inn with rooms, good food and famed sunset views.

Port Erin and around

Plans for the southern branch of the steam railway beyond Castletown included the speculative construction of the new resort of **PORT ERIN**, at the southwestern tip of the island, a 1hr 15min ride from Douglas. The aspect certainly demanded a resort: a wide, fine sand beach backing a deeply indented bay sits beneath green hills, which climb to the tower-topped headland of **Bradda Head** to the northwest.

A century on, an arm of holiday apartments stretches out towards the headland, while the far side of town is marked by the breakwater and small harbour. Families relish the beach here, and the timewarped atmosphere, which appears to have altered little in forty years. The town's elegant red-brick train station is still here, with one of its engine sheds converted into a small **railway museum** (Easter–Oct daily 10am–5pm; £1). When you tire of the sand, it's time to take one of the **cruises** (April–Oct daily; £10) to the **Calf of Man** bird sanctuary, half a mile off the southwest coast. These depart from the pier (where a departures board is posted) and if you're going to make a day of it, take a picnic.

Practicalities

The **train station** is on Station Road, a couple of hundred yards above and back from the beach. **Buses** #1 and #2 from Douglas/Castletown, and #8 from Peel/St Johns, stop on Bridson Street, across Station Road and opposite the *Cherry Orchard* hotel. Rooms are pretty hard to come by since most **accommodation** is in holiday apartments or long-stay hotels, booked by the week. Still, you could try one of the large hotels on the cliff-top promenade, such as the *Port Erin Royal* (☎01624/833116; ❺) or *Imperial* (☎01624/832122; ❺), both part of the same group (⊛www.porterinhotels.com), whose aspect is generally better than their interiors and which offer out-of-season discounts. The *Falcon's Nest*, further down the promenade at the seafront end of Station Road (☎01624/834077; ❺), offers better deals if you book by the week. As this is unlikely, to say the least, it's cheaper to check on space at the nearby *Balmoral Hotel* (☎01624/833126; ❸). The best rooms, though, are at the *Cherry Orchard Hotel* on Bridson St (☎01624/833811; ⊛www.cherry-orchard.com; ❺), a couple of hundred yards back from the promenade, a motel with its own pool, sauna, restaurant and bar. This also has some self-catering **apartments** available by the night, within the same complex (❹–❻ depending on the season).

There are a couple of beachfront **cafés** serving the usual daytime snacks and meals – you're better off heading instead for *La Patisserie* on Church Rd between the *Cherry Orchard* and the promenade, a good deli-bakery which will make up sandwiches to take away. Or call into the *Whistlestop Café* at the train station for a light lunch or afternoon tea. Come the evening, your choice is really limited to the restaurant in the *Falcon's Nest*. The bar in the *Royal Erin Hotel* on the promenade has bay views in abundance from its picture windows.

Around the coast to Port St Mary

The harbour at Port Erin marks the start of a six-mile loop around Meayll Hill on the coastal path past **Spanish Head**, the island's southern tip, to **Port St Mary**. It's one of the best short walks on the island, giving the opportunity of a detour to **Cregneash Village Folk Museum** (Easter–Sept daily 10am–5pm; £2.75), a picturesque cluster of nineteenth-century thatched crofts on the slopes above Spanish Head. This was a real Gaelic-speaking village until well into this century, though the advent of postwar tourism turned it into a tourist attraction. It's now peopled at weekends with spinners, weavers, turners and smiths dressed in period costumes; there's an information centre with introductory video, demonstrations of thatching and dry-stone walling, and a chance to walk through the seasonal crops in the field and watch the horses at work. The local views are stunning and it's only a short walk south to **The Chasms**, a headland of gaping rock cliffs swarming with gulls and razorbills.

The fishing harbour still dominates little **PORT ST MARY**, with its houses strung out in a chain above the busy dockside. The best beach is away to the northeast, reached from the harbour along a well-worked Victorian path which clings to the bay's rocky edge. High above the harbour, on Bay View Road, the *Bay View Hotel* (☎01624/832234; ➋) has a skinny garden over the road tucked on top of the cliff. Regular steam **trains** run to Port Erin or back to Douglas from Port St Mary, with the station a ten-minute walk along High Street, Bay View Road and Station Road; hourly **buses** from the harbour serve the same places.

Castletown

From the twelfth century until 1869, **CASTLETOWN** was the island's capital, but then the influx of tourists and the increase in trade required a bigger harbour, so Douglas took over. So much the better for Castletown, which is a much more pleasant place than it might otherwise have been. Its sleepy harbour and low-roofed cottages are all dominated by **Castle Rushen** (Easter–Sept daily 10am–5pm; £4), one of the most complete and compact medieval castles in Britain. Formerly home to the island's legislature and still the site of the investiture of new lieutenant-governors, the present structure was probably started in the thirteenth century, its limestone walls well under way by the time the last Viking monarch, Magnus, died here in 1256. The heavy defences, comprising three concentric rings of stone-clad ramparts, fosses and a complex series of doors and portcullises, must have made entry a forbidding objective. Today, a mannequin archer guards access to displays on the castle's history, a prelude to five floors of rooms furnished in medieval and seventeenth-century styles, the most evocative being the tapestry-draped banqueting hall. The rooms may seem unending, but it is worth pressing on to the rooftop viewpoint to admire the town below; its somnolent streets centred on a dinky marketplace with an unfinished memorial column – the "candlestick" – commemorating a nineteenth-century governor.

The **Old Grammar School** was the former capital's first church, built around 1200, and used as a school from 1570. There's not a lot to see, save a few information boards, but it does house a handy **tourist office** (Easter–Sept daily 10am–5pm). Below the castle boats and yachts bob about in the harbour, while something of the island's nautical heritage can be gleaned from the little **Nautical Museum** on Douglas St (daily 10am–5pm; £2.75), just across the harbour footbridge, which displays an armed eighteenth-century yacht ("The Peggy") among other exhibits.

The **steam train station** is five minutes' walk from the centre of Castletown, out along Victoria Road from the harbour; **buses** #8 (from Peel/Port Erin) and #1 (from Douglas) stop in the main square. You may find signs advertising local B&Bs, but otherwise the only central **accommodation** is the *George Hotel* in the square (☎01624/822533; ❷), where there are eleven en-suite rooms above the pub and parking around the back; breakfast is extra. There's a clutch of **cafés** around the marketplace, though for a view of the harbour head for the *Chablis Cellar*, 21 Bank St (☎01624/823527; closed Sun eve), which does inexpensive **bistro** lunches and evening meals. The *Castle Arms*, across on the quayside, also serves food, or you could try *Compton's* on Parliament Square (closed Sun, Mon & Sat lunch), outside the castle, for pizzas, pasta and bistro meals.

If you're in no hurry to get back to Douglas, stop off at **Port Soderick**, halfway along the train route between Castletown and Douglas, where you can walk down the glen to a cliff-backed bay with a stony beach and the nicely sited *Anchor Inn*.

Travel details

Buses

For information on all local and national bus services, contact Traveline: ☎ 0870/608 2 608, ⓦ www.traveline.org.uk.

Trains

For information on all local and national rail services, contact National Rail Enquiries: ☎ 08457/48 49 50, ⓦ www.rail.co.uk.

Blackpool to: Manchester (hourly; 1hr 10min); Preston (hourly; 30min).

Chester to: Birmingham (5 daily; 2hr); Knutsford (hourly; 50min); Liverpool (2 hourly; 45min); London (3 daily; 3hr 30min); Manchester (2 hourly; 1hr–1hr 20min); Northwich (hourly; 30min).

Lancaster to: Barrow-in-Furness (17 daily; 1hr); Carlisle (hourly; 1hr); Heysham (1 daily; 30min); Manchester (hourly; 1hr); Morecambe (every 40min; 10min).

Liverpool to: Birmingham (hourly; 1hr 40min); Chester (2 hourly; 45min); Leeds (hourly; 2hr); London (hourly; 2hr 40min); Manchester (hourly; 50min); Newcastle (8 daily; 4–5hr); Oxford (12 daily; 3–4hr); Preston (14 daily; 1hr 5min); Sheffield (hourly; 1hr 45min); York (hourly; 2hr 20min).

Manchester to: Barrow-in-Furness (Mon–Sat 7 daily, Sun 3 daily; 2hr 15min); Birmingham (hourly; 1hr 30min); Blackpool (hourly; 1hr 10min); Buxton (hourly; 50min); Carlisle (2 daily; 2hr 30min); Chester (2 hourly; 1hr–1hr 20min); Lancaster (hourly; 1hr); Leeds (hourly; 1hr); Liverpool (every 30min; 50min); London (hourly; 2hr 40min); Newcastle (10 daily; 3hr); Northwich (hourly; 30min); Oxenholme (4–6 daily; 40min–1hr 10min); Penrith (2–4 daily; 2hr); Preston (every 20min; 55min); Sheffield (hourly; 1hr); York (hourly; 1hr 35min).

Cumbria and the lakes

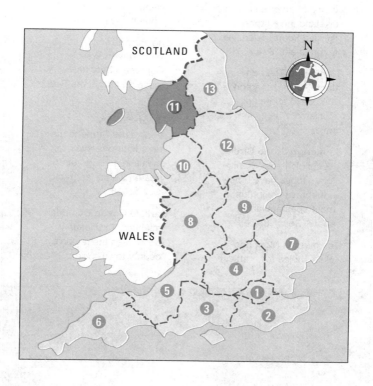

CHAPTER 11

Highlights

✳ **Windermere** England's largest lake never disappoints. Take a cruise – jumping off to hike, to picnic, or even to swim. See p.824

✳ **Hole in't Wall, Bowness-on-Windermere** The very picture of a classic lakeland inn – stone-flagged floors, open fires and real ale. See p.826

✳ **Brantwood** The home of John Ruskin, sited on the placid shores of Coniston Water. See p.836

✳ **Castlerigg Stone Circle, Keswick** These prehistoric stones have a powerful presence in this most spectacular of spots. See p.842

✳ **Borrowdale** Most people's choice for prettiest valley in the Lakes – falls, hamlets and woods in abundance. See p.843

✳ **Church of St Mary and St Michael, Cartmel** This twelfth-century priory church is a magnificent reminder of the wealth of the medieval Church. See p.853

✳ **The Rum Story, Whitehaven** West Cumbria's best new museum attraction. See p.860

✳ **Village Bakery, Melmerby** Stupendous breads and marvellous meals in a village off the beaten Cumbrian track. See p.865

✳ **Carlisle Castle** Cumbria's mightiest fortification dominates the region's county town. See p.866

11

Cumbria and the lakes

The **Lake District** is England's most hyped scenic area, and for good reasons. Within an area a mere thirty miles across, sixteen major lakes are squeezed between the steeply pitched faces of England's highest mountains, an almost alpine landscape that's augmented by waterfalls and picturesque stone-built villages packed into the valleys. Most of what people refer to as the Lake District – or simply the Lakes – lies within the **Lake District National Park**, England's largest national park, established in 1951. This, in turn, falls entirely within the northwestern county of **Cumbria**, formed in 1974 from the historic counties of Cumberland and Westmorland, and the northern part of Lancashire. Consequently Cumbria contains more than just its lakes, stretching south and west to the **coast**, and north to its county town of **Carlisle**, a place that bears traces of a pedigree that stretches back beyond the construction of Hadrian's Wall. To the east, **Penrith** and the **Eden Valley** separate the lakes from the near wilderness of the northern Pennines.

The heart of the region is Scafell, a volcanic dome that had already been weathered into its present shape before the last Ice Age, when glaciers flowed off its flanks to gouge their characteristic U-shaped valleys. As the ice withdrew, terminal moraines of sediment dammed the meltwater, so that the main lakes now radiate like immense spokes from the hub of Scafell. Human interaction has also played a significant part in the shaping of the Lake District. Before Neolithic peoples began to colonize the region around five thousand years ago, most of the now bare uplands were forested with pine and birch, while the valleys were blanketed with thickets of oak and alder. As these first

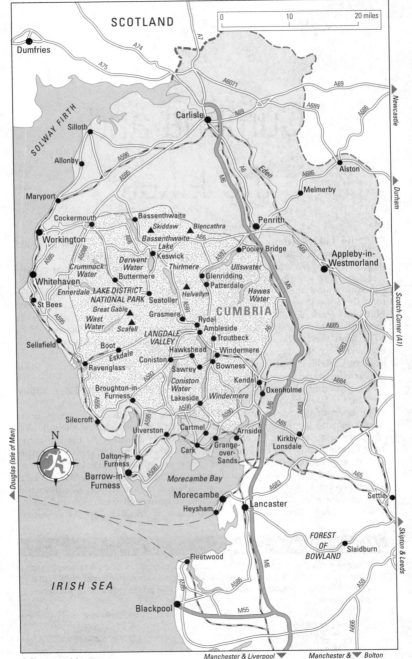

© Crown copyright

settlers learned to shape flints into axes, they began to clear the upland forests, a process accelerated by the road-building Romans. An even greater impact was made by the Norse Vikings in the ninth and tenth centuries, who farmed the land extensively and left their mark on the local dialect: a mountain here is referred to as a "fell", a waterfall is a "force", streams are "becks", a mountain lake is a "tarn", while the suffix "-thwaite" indicates a clearing. In later centuries grazing flocks of sheep cropped the hills of their wild flowers, while charcoal-making and the mining of copper and graphite further altered the contours and vegetation.

The region remained a land apart for centuries, its features – rugged and isolated – mirrored in the characteristics of its inhabitants. Daniel Defoe thought it "eminent only for being the wildest, most barren and frightful of any that I have passed over" – and, as he went on to point out, he'd been to Wales so he knew what he was talking about. Two factors spurred the first waves of **tourism**: the reappraisal of landscape brought about by such painters as Constable and the writings of Wordsworth and his contemporaries, and the outbreak of the French Revolution and its subsequent turmoil, which put paid to the idea of the continental Grand Tour. At the same time, as the war pushed food prices higher, farmers began to reclaim the hillsides, a tendency sanctioned by the General Enclosure Act of 1801. Most of the characteristic drystone walls were built at this time, a development that alarmed Wordsworth, who wrote in his *Guide to the Lakes* that he desired "a sort of national property, in which every man has a right and interest who has an eye to perceive and a heart to enjoy." His wish finally came to fruition in 1951 when the government designated 880 square miles of the Lake District as England's largest national park.

On any scale, the **national park** has been wildly successful, attracting millions of visitors every year to the famous lakes and picturesque villages. This, of course, has come at some price, mainly in terms of traffic and environmental pressure, which a forward-thinking integrated transport strategy is only just starting to alleviate. There's always been a severe contrast, too, between the touristed villages of the Lakes and the old industrial towns of coastal West Cumbria, which have struggled in the past to attract visitors and investment. However, regeneration has been dramatic in recent years, with the reviving fortunes of places such as Whitehaven, Maryport and Barrow-in-Furness providing keen incentives to stray from the Lakes. Indeed, the current economic and social challenges are mostly in rural Cumbria, hit hard by the devastating foot-and-mouth farming crisis of 2001, which cut visitor numbers – and income – dramatically for all kinds of businesses. Even with the footpaths open again and Cumbria doing everything it can to attract its visitors back, the future of farming, especially, in the region is hard to predict.

Arrival and transport

Over the last few years, the local authorities have made great improvements to the **public transport** network within and around the National Park to encourage people to leave their cars at home. In summer, especially, when services are at their peak, there's no longer any real excuse not to use public transport for at least some journeys.

National Express buses connect London and Manchester with Windermere, Ambleside, Grasmere and Keswick. **Trains** leave the West Coast main line at **Oxenholme**, north of Lancaster, for the branch line service to Kendal and Windermere. The only other places directly accessible by train are Penrith, further north, also on the West Coast line, and the towns along the

Walking in the Lake District

An almost unchartable network of Lake District paths connects the lakes themselves, tracks the broken knife-edge ridges of the fells and mountains or weaves easier courses around the flanks and onto the tops. The various walks detailed in this section are largely aimed at the moderate walker with half a day or so on their hands and require no real experience. Even so, you should always be **properly equipped**: wear strong-soled, supportive shoes or boots, carry water, and take a map (and know how to use it). Bad weather can move in quickly, even in the height of summer, so before starting out you should check the weather forecast – many hotels and outdoor shops post a daily forecast – or call ☎017687/75757 (24-hour line).

The best general **map** of the area is the Ordnance Survey inch-to-the-mile (1:63,360) Touring Map and Guide 3, with hill shading and illustrated text on the back. Essential for **walking** are the 1:50,000 OS Landranger maps 89, 90, 96 and 97, or, better, the yellow 1:25,000 OS Outdoor Leisure series, which cover the whole Lake District. Many shops and tourist offices also sell local walk leaflets, and regional trail and hiking guides, of which Wainwright's (see p.822) are the best known.

Cumbrian coast, between Grange-over-Sands and Maryport (though there's a limited service here on Sundays). A couple of private **narrow-gauge and steam train lines** connect various rural points. Of the lakes themselves, Windermere, Coniston Water, Derwent Water and Ullswater have **ferry** services of varying degrees of usefulness.

Everywhere else in the Lakes is connected by local **bus**, with Stagecoach in Cumbria the biggest operator. Their **Explorer Tickets** (one-day £6.50; four-day £15) are valid on the entire network and can be bought on the bus, while other bus-and-boat combination tickets offer a variety of good deals. With a passport-sized photograph, you can get a week's unlimited travel within Cumbria on a "Commutacard" for £17.50. The two main services are the #555/556 (Kendal–Windermere–Ambleside–Grasmere–Keswick, with connections to Lancaster and Carlisle) and the open-top #599 (Kendal–Windermere–Bowness–Ambleside–Grasmere), but all routes are all spelled out in detail in the free *Lakeland Explorer* **timetable**, available on board buses or from local tourist offices. Even more comprehensive is the *Getting Around Cumbria and the Lake District* timetable book produced twice a year by Cumbria County Council and available from tourist offices and other outlets throughout the region. Or call **Traveline** (daily 7am–8pm; ☎0870/608 2608, ⓦwww.traveline.org.uk), which can advise about all the region's bus, coach, rail and ferry services. Finally, the **YHA** operates a shuttle-bus service between its most popular hostels (Easter–Oct; £2 a journey; information from Ambleside YHA, on ☎015394/32304).

As a rule you can escape the crowds by getting around on foot – some of the country's most celebrated **walks** run through the Lake District, often forming circuits or "horseshoe" routes around various peaks and valleys. Of the long-distance paths, Wainwright's Coast-to-Coast, which starts in St Bees, near Whitehaven, spends its first few sections in the northern Lakes; while the Dales Way finishes in Windermere; but the only true Lake District hike is the 70-mile **Cumbria Way** between **Ulverston** and **Carlisle**. Cyclists have the choice of shadowing walkers on Sustrans' **Sea to Sea (C2C) cycle route**, a 140-mile trip between Whitehaven/Workington and Sunderland/Newcastle, or using the **Cumbria Cycle Way**, which circles the region.

The Lake District

Although the Lake District might appear too popular for its own good, tourist numbers are concentrated in fairly specific areas and even on the busiest of days it's relatively easy to escape the crowds. Given a week you could see most of the famous settlements and lakes – a circuit taking in the towns of Ambleside, Windermere and Bowness, all on **Windermere**, the Wordsworth houses and sites in pretty villages such as **Hawkshead** and **Grasmere**, and the more dramatic northern scenery near **Keswick** and **Ullswater** would give you a fair sample of the whole. But it's away from the crowds that the Lakes really begin to pay dividends, so aim if you can to steer by central valleys such as **Langdale** and **Eskdale**, and the lesser visited lakes of **Wast Water** and **Buttermere**. Of course, it's only when you start to walk and climb around the Lakes that you can really say you've explored the region. Four peaks top out at over 3000ft – including **Scafell Pike**, the highest in England – but there are literally hundreds of other mountains, crags and fells to roam.

High summer isn't the ideal **time to visit** the Lakes – April, May, September and October are the best months, as the crowds are thinner, the sights are still open and the high walks unlikely to be snowbound. During the summer school holidays, **accommodation** – including abundant B&Bs, excellent country guest houses and 28 youth hostels – can be stretched to capacity, though you'll always find something, somewhere. Campsites are widely scattered about the entire region, or you could check out the Lake District National Park Authority's **camping barn** network – ask for a brochure at tourist offices.

For more **information** about all aspects of the National Park, visit ⓦwww .lake-district.gov.uk; while the official site of the Cumbria Tourist Board is ⓦwww.golakes.co.uk.

Kendal and around

The limestone-grey town of **KENDAL** might be billed as the "Gateway to the Lakes", but it's nearly ten miles from Windermere – the true start of the lakes – and has more in common with the market towns to the east. It's a pleasant stop, though, cut through by an attractive river and boasting two of Cumbria's grandest stately homes – **Sizergh Castle** and **Levens Hall** – both within easy reach of the town.

Arrival, information and accommodation

Kendal's **train station** is the first stop on the Windermere branch line, just five minutes from the **Oxenholme** main-line station. By catching bus #41 or #41A to the town hall from Oxenholme (Mon–Sat; every 20min) you can avoid the wait for the connecting train. Otherwise, head across the river and up Stramongate and Finkle Street to reach Highgate, a ten-minute walk. National Express and all regional buses stop at the **bus station** on Blackhall Rd (off Stramongate).

The **tourist office** (March–Dec Mon–Sat 9am–6pm, Sun 9am–5pm; Jan & Feb closed Sun; ☎01539/725758, ⓦwww.kendaltown.org) is in the town hall on Highgate, and as well as supplying all the usual accommodation guides and local information, sells National Express tickets. You can book space here on the weekly summer guided walks (July & Aug usually Wed; £2.50). There's **internet** access at Kendal library and at *Dot Café*, inside the Westmorland Shopping Centre.

Most of the local **B&Bs** lie along the road to Windermere, north of the centre, though near the train station there's the Georgian *Bridge House*, 65 Castle St (℡01539/722041, ⓦwww.bridgehouse-kendal.co.uk; no credit cards; ❷), with just a couple of rooms available. Best choice is the *Lakeland Natural Vegetarian Guesthouse* at Low Slack, Queen's Rd (℡01539/733011, ⓦwww.landnatural.co.uk; ❸), which backs onto woods five minutes' walk west of the centre. Or look along Milnthorpe Road, a few minutes' south of the centre – walk straight down Highgate and Kirkland – where several places cluster together, including *The Headlands*, 53 Milnthorpe Rd (℡01539/732464, ⓦwww.headlands-hotel.co.uk; ❷), with a selection of rooms and a pick-up service from the bus or train stations. There's a **youth hostel** at 118 Highgate (℡01539/724066, ⓔkendal@yha.org.uk), which is attached to The Brewery arts centre (see below), while the most convenient **campsite** is *Ashes Lane* at Staveley, four miles northwest of town, off the Windermere Road (℡01539/821119, ⓦwww.asheslane.com; closed mid-Jan to mid-March), reached by bus #555/556 from the bus station.

The Town

As the largest of the southern Cumbrian towns Kendal can be a congested place, but it offers rewarding rambles around the "yards" and "ginnels" which make an engaging maze on both sides of Highgate and Stricklandgate, the main streets. The old **Market Place** has long since succumbed to development, with the market hall now converted to the Westmorland Shopping Centre, but traditional stalls still do business outside every Wednesday and Saturday.

Strolling around or following one of the summer walks organized through the tourist office will take you down to the riverside walk and past restored almshouses, mullioned shopfronts and trade signs, including the pipe-smoking Turk outside the snuff factory on Lowther Street. The "Kendal green" cotton cloth, actually yellow wool, was worn by English archers and earned Kendal a mention in Shakespeare's *Henry IV*, but today the town's most visible product is **Kendal Mintcake**, a solid block of sugar and peppermint oil, an energy-giving confection that has been hoisted to the top of the world's highest mountains.

The town's museums and art gallery have a joint admission policy (each open daily: April–Oct 10.30am–5pm; Nov–March 10.30am–4pm; £3, £1 with a ticket for one of the other museums). The **Kendal Museum**, on Station Road (ⓦwww.kendalmuseum.org.uk), holds the district's natural history and archeological finds, bolstered by reverential displays on the life of **Alfred Wainwright**. In 1952 this one-time borough treasurer (and honorary clerk at the museum), dissatisfied with the accuracy of existing maps of the paths and ancient tracks across the fells, embarked on what became a series of 47 walking guides, all but two of them painstakingly handwritten with mapped routes and delicately drawn views. Ironically, the popularity of his purple-prosed pocket guides has led to the ravaging of the land he so adored, especially on his most trekked route, the Coast-to-Coast from St Bees in Cumbria to Yorkshire's Robin Hood's Bay, much of which is not on designated rights of way and often crosses sensitive wildlife areas and archeological sites.

The other two museums are in the Georgian **Abbot Hall** (ⓦwww.abbot-thall.org.uk) and its stable block, by the river to the south. The main hall, painstakingly restored to its 1760s town-house origins, houses the **Art Gallery**, where cherubic portraits by society painter George Romney line the walls, along with works by Constable, Ruskin, Turner, Edward Lear and lesser local artists. Few can compete with the furniture designed and built by Gillows of Lancaster, whose chairs, writing desks and games tables have all survived in excellent condition. The small modern art collection upstairs is rounded off with Barbara Hepworth's *Oval Form*, gracing the grass between the hall and the stables which house the **Museum of Lakeland Life and Industry**. Here, reconstructed seventeenth-, eighteenth- and nineteenth-century house interiors stand alongside workshops which make a fairly vivid presentation of rural trades and crafts, from spinning and weaving to tanning – medieval Kendal on the main north–south cattle-trade routes and leather production was once an important local industry. The mock-up study of **Arthur Ransome**, author of the children's classic *Swallows and Amazons*, is enlivened by an innocently hilarious commentary – "1904: enters into his Bohemian period" – as well as by memorabilia from his stint as *Manchester Guardian* reporter during the Russian Revolution – he urged support for the Bolsheviks throughout the period and, after the break-up of his first marriage, married Eugenia, Leon Trotsky's personal secretary. John Cunliffe, creator of *Postman Pat*, whose adventures are set just north of Kendal, gets more laid-back treatment next door, with a welter of original drawings and the author's desk and typewriter on show.

Just behind Abbott Hall, the wide aisles of the Early English **parish church** (daily: Easter–Oct 9.20am–4.30pm; Nov–Easter 9.20am–noon) house a number of family chapels, including that of the Parr family, who once owned **Kendal Castle**, on a hillock to the east across the river. First erected in the early thirteenth century, it's claimed as the birthplace of Catherine Parr, Henry VIII's sixth wife, but the story is probably apocryphal – she was born in 1512, at which time the building – now a ruin – was already in an advanced state of decay. If you fancy the climb up for the views, follow the footpath from the end of Parr Street, across the footbridge just north of the church and hall.

Eating and drinking

Kendal certainly doesn't lack decent **cafés**, starting with the wood-beamed *Farrers Tea & Coffee Merchants*, 13 Stricklandgate (closed Sun), and the *1657 Chocolate House*, on Branthwaite Brow, an olde-worlde spot which sells little other than hot chocolate (in dozens of guises) and cakes. There's also a good café at the Abbott Hall Art Gallery. For inexpensive veggie wholefood lunches and riverside seating, visit the *Waterside Café* on Gulfs Road, by the river at the bottom of Lowther Street. Best **restaurant** is the highly regarded *Moon*, 129 Highgate (℗01539/729254; Wed–Sun dinner only, closed Mon & Tues), an easy-going bistro, or eat Thai at the *Chiang Thai*, 54 Stramongate (closed Mon).

For evening entertainment the **Brewery Arts Centre**, on Highgate (℗01539/725133, ⓦwww.breweryarts.co.uk), with its café, bar, cinema, theatre and concert hall, is a good bet. There's live music throughout the year and a renowned annual jazz and blues festival each November. There are several characterful old **pubs** worth trying, including the *Ring o' Bells* by the church, and the *Bridge Hotel*, a classic old local at the bottom of Stramongate.

Sizergh Castle

Three miles to the south of Kendal stands **Sizergh Castle** (Easter–Oct Mon–Thurs & Sun 1.30–5.30pm; gardens open 12.30pm; £5, gardens only £2.50; NT), tucked away off the A591 amid acres of parkland and reached on bus #555/556. Home of the Strickland family for eight centuries, Sizergh is more of a grand manor house than a castle, but owes its epithet to the fourteenth-century peel tower (which you'll often see spelt "pele" in the North) at its core, one of the best examples of the towers built throughout the region as safe havens during the protracted border raids of the Middle Ages. Like much of the rest of the house, the Great Hall underwent significant changes in Elizabethan times, when extensions were added to the house and most of its rooms were panelled in oak with their ceilings layered in elaborate plasterwork. Each room is hung with portraits of the family and their royal acquaintances and stocked with exquisite furniture, including an extraordinary bedstead made from a pew that once stood in Kendal parish church. Little has changed in the Banqueting Hall since the fourteenth century, save for the loss of an upper storey and the addition of a partition at the east end, added to provide more private sleeping quarters for the heads of the family.

Levens Hall

Two miles south of Sizergh, just of the A590, **Levens Hall** (April to mid-Oct Mon–Thurs & Sun noon–5pm; gardens open 10am; £6, gardens only £4.50; @ www.levenshall.co.uk), also built around an early peel tower, is more uniform in style than Sizergh, since the bulk of it was built or refurbished in classic Elizabethan style between 1570 and 1640 by James Bellingham. The house did not stay in the Bellingham family; a descendant lost the whole estate in a hedonistic spate of gambling, and it was later bought by the privy purse to James II and ancestor of the present owners, the Bagots.

The main entrance opens into the spacious Great Hall, its panelled walls lined with coats of arms; to the left of the hall are the large and small drawing rooms. The other end of the Great Hall leads to the most splendid apartment, the dining room, panelled not with oak but with goat's leather, printed with a deep green floral design – one goat was needed for every forty or so squares. Upstairs, the bedrooms offer glimpses of the beautifully trimmed **topiary gardens** below, where yews in the shape of pyramids, peacocks and top hats stand between blooming bedding plants. There's also a steam-engine collection and café.

A mile away, across the A590, the **bus** (#555/556 from Kendal) drops you in the village of Levens, at the bottom of which stands the *Hare & Hounds*, a cosy pub with bar meals and good beer.

Windermere, Bowness and around

WINDERMERE town was all but non-existent until 1847 when a railway terminal was built here, making England's longest lake (after which the town is named) an easily accessible resort. Most of the guest houses and amenities built for the Victorians still stand, and Windermere remains the transport hub for the southern lakes, but there's precious little else to keep you in the slate-grey streets. Instead, all the traffic pours a mile down hill to Windermere's older twin town, Bowness.

Bus #599 leaves Windermere train station every twenty minutes for the ten-minute run down to the lakeside piers of **BOWNESS**. This is undoubtedly the more attractive of the two settlements, spilling back from the lake, though as Cumbria's most popular resort – packed with trinket shops, cafés and souvenir-hunting tourists – it's a victim of its own popularity and is overrun for much of the year. Assuming you don't take one look at the crowds and turn tail, Bowness itself has enough scattered attractions to fill a morning. Just back from the lake, **St Martin's Church** (Easter–Sept daily 10am–4pm) is notable for its stained glass, particularly that in the east window which sports the fifteenth-century arms of John Washington, an ancestor of first American president

George Washington. Most tourists, though, bypass the church and everything else in Bowness bar the lake for the chance to visit **The World of Beatrix Potter** in the Old Laundry on Crag Brow (daily: Easter–Sept 10am–5.30pm; Oct–Easter 10am–4.30pm; £3.50; ⓦ www.hop-skip-jump.com). It's unfair to be judgemental – you either like Beatrix Potter or you don't – but it's safe to say that the displays here find more favour with children than the more formal Potter attractions at Hill Top and Hawkshead. Five hundred yards north of Bowness, on Rayrigg Road, the **Windermere Steamboat Museum** (Easter–Oct daily 10am–5pm; £3.40, steam-launch cruises £5; ⓦ www.steamboat.co.uk) has as its star exhibit the 1850 *Dolly*, claimed to be the world's oldest mechanically driven boat, and extremely well preserved after spending 65 years in the mud at the bottom of Ullswater. In addition, an Arthur Ransome exhibition reveals the inspiration behind the boats *Swallow* and *Amazon*.

All, however, come second-best to a trip on **Windermere** itself – according to Wordsworth's *Guide to the Lakes*, "None of the other Lakes unfold so many fresh beauties." Rowing boats are available for rent at the pier while Windermere Lake Cruises (ⓣ015394/31188, ⓦ www.windermere-lakecruises .co.uk) operates stylish steamers and vintage cruisers to Lakeside at the southern tip (£4.20 one-way, £6.20 return) or to Waterhead (for Ambleside) at the northern end (£4.10 one-way, £6 return). There's also a shuttle service between Bowness piers and Sawrey (£1.30 one-way, £2.50 return), saving pedestrians the walk down to the car-ferry (see below). A 24-hour **Freedom-of-the-Lake ticket** costs £10.50. Services on both routes are frequent between Easter and October (1–2 hourly at peak times), but much reduced during the winter.

The **ferry service** across the water to Sawrey (Mon–Sat 7am–10pm, Sun 9am–10pm; departures every 20min; 40p; cars £2), from just south of Bowness, provides access to Beatrix Potter's former home at Hill Top and to Hawkshead beyond. The ferry pier is a ten-minute walk south of the cruise piers, through the parkland of Cockshott Point.

Arrival and information

National Express and most local **buses** stop outside Windermere **train station**, itself only a few yards from the **tourist office** on Victoria Street (daily: July & Aug 9am–7.30pm; rest of the year 9am–6pm; ⓣ015394/46499). There's a second information office down in Bowness, by the piers on Glebe Road (Easter–Oct Mon–Thurs & Sun 9.30am–5.30pm, Fri & Sat 9.30am–6pm; Nov–Easter Fri–Sun 9.30am–5.30pm; ⓣ015394/42895). Both offices have **money-exchange** and room-booking services; you can also change money inside Windermere's post office on Crescent Road. For **bike rental**, contact Country Lanes, The Railway Station, Windermere (ⓣ015394/44544, ⓦ www .countrylanes.co.uk), which provides route maps for local rides.

Accommodation

Windermere doesn't have the waterside advantages of Bowness, but it does have a lot more **accommodation** – wherever you plan to stay, you should book well in advance from Easter onwards. The nearest YHA **youth hostel** is at Troutbeck (see p.827), though there is an independent hostel in town, while the only close **campsite** is *Braithwaite Fold* (ⓣ015394/42177; closed Nov–March) near the ferry to Sawrey, half a mile from Bowness.

The cheapest **rooms in Windermere** are at the *Backpackers Hostel* in the Old Bakery at the top of the High St (ⓣ015394/46374, ⓦ www.lakedistrict backpackers.co.uk no credit cards; ❶), near the tourist office. There are a couple of private rooms as well as dorm space, internet access, satellite TV, and free tea, coffee and toast for breakfast. This is a good place to book local tours or find out about working opportunities. Otherwise, there's no shortage of accommodation on the High Street and neighbouring Victoria Street, with plenty of other **B&Bs** on College Road, Oak and Broad streets. Top choices include *Ashleigh Guesthouse* at 11 College Rd (℡015394/42292; no credit cards; **②**), and the *Archway* at no. 13 (℡015394/45613, ⓦwww.communiken .com/archway; no credit cards; **③**), both non-smoking and the latter serving great breakfasts, with specials such as pancakes, kippers and home-made yoghurt. *Brendan Chase*, 1–3 College Rd (℡015394/45638; no credit cards; **①**), is a spick-and-span place with a budget room-only option, while the rather grander *Applegarth Hotel*, College Rd (℡015394/43206, ⓦwww.applegarthhotel .com; **④**), retains its ornate Victorian interior and terraced garden. *Broadlands Guest House*, 19 Broad St (℡015394/46532, ⓦwww.broadlands.clara.co.uk; **②**), is a welcoming family-run place providing walk leaflets and bike rental. Best hotel choice in Windermere – and a candidate for best in the Lakes – is *Miller Howe*, on Rayrigg Road, the A592 (℡015394/42536, ⓦwww.millerhowe.com; **⑨**; closed Jan), whose terrifically expensive rooms (the best with lake-views) come with supremely theatrical dinners and breakfasts.

In **Bowness**, try *Above The Bay*, 5 Brackenfield (℡015394/88658, ⓦwww .abovethebay.co.uk; no credit cards; **③**), an elevated house with lake views, just off the Kendal road a little way south of the centre; or the seventeenth-century *Laurel Cottage* in St Martin's Square (℡015394/45594, ⓦwww.laurelcottage -bnb.co.uk; no credit cards; **②**), right in the thick of things. Another good choice is *New Hall Bank* on Fallbarrow Rd (℡015394/43558, Ⓔnewhallbank @talk21.com; **④**), a detached Victorian house whose room views get better the higher you go. By far the swankiest central option is *The Old England*, Church St (℡015394/42444, ⓦwww.heritage-hotels.com; **⑦**), a relaxed grande-dame hotel opposite the church, with heated outdoor pool and terraced lakeside gardens. Alternatively, seek out *Gilpin Lodge*, Crook Rd (℡015394/88818, ⓦwww .gilpin-lodge.co.uk; **⑥**), a country-house retreat a couple of miles east on the Kendal road (B5284).

Eating, drinking and entertainment

Eating and drinking is generally better done down in Bowness, but look out in **Windermere** for *Renoir's Coffee Shop*, on Main Road, for daytime sandwiches and frothy coffees, and the *Miller Howe Café* inside Lakeland Ltd by the train station, which serves up superior snacks, sandwiches and daily specials. *Jericho's* on Birch St (℡015394/42552; dinner only; closed Mon) is the foodie choice for dinner. In **Bowness**, the *Hedgerow Teashop* on Lake Road serves an all-day breakfast and a decent range of teas and fruit infusions. Budget pizza and pasta is on offer at *Rastelli's*, also on Lake Road (closed Wed), while *Stefan's Bistro* in Queen's Square is the place for bistro favourites, from salmon and trout to chicken, steak and pasta (closed all Wed, plus Mon–Fri lunch).

For a **drink**, try *The Hole in't Wall* pub, the town's oldest hostelry, in Falbarrow Road behind Bowness church; cosy in winter when the fires are lit and pleasant in summer when you can sit outside. For sunset drinks with a lake view you can't beat the terrace of *The Olde England* hotel. *The Royalty* on Lake Road (℡015394/43364) is that rare lakeland beast, a **cinema**, with a repertory programme alongside the more commercial screenings.

Around Bowness and Windermere

A mile and a half south of Bowness, there's the rare chance to visit a house designed by one of the major exponents of the Arts and Crafts Movement.

Mackay Hugh Baillie Scott's **Blackwell** (daily 10am–5pm, closes 4pm in winter; £4.50; @www.blackwell.org.uk) was built in 1900 as a lakeside holiday home for Edward Holt, of the Manchester brewing family, and selected rooms of the restored interior can be viewed. Lakeland motifs (particularly trees, flowers, birds and berries) are visible in virtually every nook and cranny, from the stonework to the stained glass, and you'll also have the chance to see changing exhibitions of Arts and Crafts furniture and other contemporary pieces. There's a tea room and gardens too, though no direct bus – the walk from Bowness is about a mile.

Three miles northwest of Windermere, the Lake District National Park has its headquarters and main information point at **Brockhole Visitor Centre** (Easter–Oct daily 10am–5pm; grounds & gardens open all year; free, parking £3; @www.lake-district.gov.uk), a fine mansion set in landscaped grounds on the shores of the lake. Besides the permanent natural history and geological displays, the centre hosts a full programme of guided walks, children's activities, garden tours, special exhibitions, lectures and film shows. The book shop is one of the best in the region for local guides and maps, and there's a café with an outdoor terrace overlooking the lake. The #555/556 and #559 buses between Windermere and Ambleside run past the visitor centre, or you can get there by Windermere Lake Cruises launch from Waterhead, Ambleside (hourly 10.45am–4.45pm; £4.60 return).

From Bowness piers **cruises** head south down the lake the five or so miles to **Lakeside**, on Windermere's quieter southern reaches. Lakeside is also the terminus of the **Lakeside and Haverthwaite Railway** (Easter–Oct 6–7 daily; £3.90 return; ☎015395/31594, @www.furnessrailwaytrust.org.uk), whose steam-powered engines chuff along four miles of track through the forests of Backbarrow Gorge. The boat arrivals at Lakeside connect with train departures throughout the day and you can buy a joint boat-and-train ticket (£9.60 return) at Bowness if you fancy the extended tour. Also on the quay at Lakeside is the **Aquarium of the Lakes** (daily: April–Sept 9am–6pm; Oct–May 9am–5pm; £5.50; @www.aquariumofthelakes.co.uk), an entertaining natural history exhibit centred on the fish and animals found in and along a lakeland river, including a pair of captive otters and a walk-through-tunnel aquarium. Again, there's a joint ticket available with the boat ride from Bowness (£10.35 return).

Troutbeck

Troutbeck Bridge, a mile northwest of Windermere along the A591, heralds the start of a gentle valley below Wansfell, where you'll find Windermere's local **youth hostel**, *High Cross* at Bridge Lane (☎015394/43543, @windermere@yha.org.uk), almost a mile uphill from the bridge. A YHA shuttle-bus service operates to the hostel from Windermere train station (meeting arriving trains) and from Ambleside youth hostel, or there's a fine cross-country walking route (3 miles; 1hr 30min) via **Orrest Head** (784ft), whose summit gives a 360° panorama from the Yorkshire fells to the Langdales and Troutbeck Valley – the path branches off the main road a hundred yards south of Windermere train station, by the *Windermere Hotel*.

TROUTBECK's main attraction lies at the southern end of the village, a little further up the minor valley road from the hostel. **Townend** (Easter–Oct Tues–Fri & Sun 1–5pm; £3; NT) has been preserved as a seventeenth-century yeoman-farmer's house, complete with original furniture and decorative woodwork. There's not much more to the village itself than a road crossing at the village green, but it marks the starting point for the five-hour walk along

High Street, a nine-mile range running north to Brougham near Penrith. The course of a Roman road follows the ridge, probably once linking the forts at Brougham and Galava in Waterhead.

Troutbeck's **inn**, the *Mortal Man* (☎015394/33193, ⓦ www.mortal-man-inns .co.uk; ❻, ❼ with dinner; closed mid-Nov to mid-Feb), has terrific valley views from its rooms and beer-garden. Cheaper **B&Bs** in the village offer less exalted lodgings – Windermere and Ambleside tourist offices can help – while Troutbeck's other old inn, the *Queen's Head*, down on the main A592 (☎015394/32174, ⓦ www.queensheadhotel.com; ❹; minimum two-night stay at weekends), serves good food. The *Queen's Head* is a stop on the summer weekend #108A bus route from Bowness and Windermere.

Ambleside

AMBLESIDE, five miles northwest of Windermere, is at the heart of the southern lakes region, making it a first-class base for walkers. The town centre consists of a cluster of grey-green stone houses, shops and B&Bs hugging a circular one-way system, which loops round just south of the narrow gully of stony Stock Ghyll. The rest of town lies a mile south at **Waterhead** (referred to as Ambleside on ferry timetables), a harbour on the shores of Windermere that's filled with ducks, swans and rowing boats and overlooked by the landscaped gardens of several plush hotels. There are quieter shores a few minutes' walk further south for picnics or, if the weather's good, a bracing dip in the lake.

In Ambleside itself, spare a few minutes for the mural of the rush-bearing ceremony in **St Mary's Church**, whose spire is visible from all over town. A couple of hundred yards north, **Bridge House** (Easter–Oct daily 10am–5pm; free), now a National Trust information centre, straddles Stock Ghyll – scurrilous legend has it that a Scotsman built the two-storey, two-roomed house to evade land taxes. Behind this is **Adrian Sankey's Glass Works** (daily 9am–5.30pm; 50p), where you can watch glass being blown, then splash out on one of the unique finished products. For more on Ambleside's history, stroll

---

Walks from Ambleside

The Rothay valley north of Ambleside is largely taken up by the fast A591, which means that Rydal Water and Rydal Mount – the closest attractions – are best seen by bus or on the circular walk from Grasmere (see p.831). Where Ambleside scores is in its proximity to the fells immediately east and west of town, and a couple of good walks are possible straight from the town centre.

The first walk heads west past Ambleside church, through Rothay Park and down to the footbridge across the river. From here you tack past Brow Head Farm, following the path to Lily Tarn and then striking out and northwest across **Loughrigg Fell** (1099ft). Dropping down to Loughrigg Terrace (2hr) overlooking Grasmere, you can then join the Grasmere circular walk at this point, before cutting south at Rydal on the A591 and following the minor road back along the River Rothay to Ambleside – a total of 6 miles (4hr).

The walk over **Wansfell** to **Troutbeck** and back (6 miles; around 4hr) has more extensive views and is a little tougher. Stock Ghyll Lane runs up the left bank of the tumbling stream to one of the more attractive waterfalls in the region, **Stock Ghyll Force**. The path then rises steeply to **Wansfell Pike** (1581ft) and down into Troutbeck village, with the *Mortal Man* inn a short detour to the left. Head south down the minor road through the village, towards Townend, just before which a track leads west onto the flanks of Wansfell and around past the viewpoint at **Jenkin Crag** back to Ambleside.

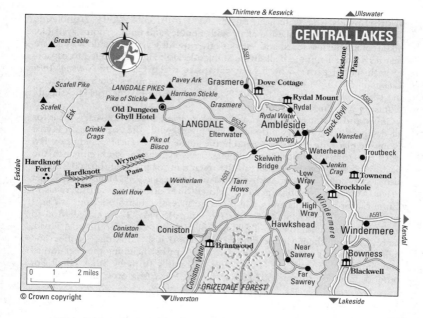

a couple of minutes along Rydal Road to the **Ambleside Museum** (daily 10am–5pm; £2.50; Ⓦwww.armitt.com), whose collection catalogues the very distinct contribution to lakeland society made by John Ruskin, Beatrix Potter and longtime Ambleside resident, writer Harriet Martineau. Finally, soccer fans shouldn't miss soccer photographer Stuart Clarke's gallery **The Homes of Football** (daily 10am–5pm; free; Ⓦwww.homesoffootball.co.uk) at 100 Lake Rd. A permanent archive of over 60,000 images of the country's stadiums and fans, it's quite irresistible.

Practicalities

Ambleside is at the hub of most major routes across the National Park. **Buses** (including National Express) all stop on Kelsick Road, opposite the library. The **tourist office** is just up the road, in Central Buildings on Market Cross (daily 9am–5.30pm; ☎015394/32582). You can **change money** at the post office in Market Place. For **bike rental**, try Biketreks on Compston Rd (☎015394/31505, Ⓦwww.biketreks.co.uk), or Ghyllside Cycles on The Slack (☎015394/33592, Ⓦwww.ghyllside.co.uk).

Lake Road, running between Waterhead and Ambleside, is lined with **B&Bs**, while other options are scattered all over town, with particular concentrations on central Church Street and Compston Road. The cheapest rates are at *Linda's B&B and Bunkhouse* at *Shirland,* Compston Rd (☎015394/32999; no credit cards; ❶), while another popular low-cost choice is *3 Cambridge Villas*, Church St (☎015394/32307; no credit cards; ❷). *Mill Cottage* on Rydal Rd (☎015394 /34830; ❸), near Bridge House, is housed in a sixteenth–century mill building, with a riverside café underneath. Or move up a notch to *Compston House Hotel* on Compston Rd (☎015394/32305, Ⓦwww.compstonhouse.co.uk; ❸), a tra-ditional lakeland house with American-style themed rooms and breakfasts of pancakes and maple syrup if you wish. One of the Lake District's best sited

youth hostels is at Waterhead on the A591 (☎015394/32304, ⊜ambleside @yha.org.uk), a huge lakeside affair with doubles and family rooms available, bike rental, internet access and various other useful services; the drawbacks are that it's a fifteen-minute walk from Ambleside itself and often filled to capacity with school parties. The nearest **campsite** is the *Low Wray National Trust Campsite* (☎015394/32810; closed Nov–Easter) three miles south of town by the lake at Wray – hourly bus #505/506 on the Ambleside to Hawkshead/ Coniston route passes within a mile.

Cafés and restaurants are easily found. *Pippins*, at 10 Lake Rd, is great for all-day breakfasts, burgers and night-time pizzas, while the *Apple Pie* on Rydal Rd is the place for patio seating and home-made pies. *Zeffirelli's*, Compston Rd (☎015394/33845), specializes in inexpensive vegetarian food, either in the daytime *Garden Café* or upstairs in the restaurant for pizzas and pasta – there's also a two-course dinner with cinema-ticket special. *Doi Intanon* in Market Place (Mon–Sat eve only in winter, closed Sun) doesn't have many rivals in Cumbria for its Thai flavours, and there are inventive bistro offerings at *Lucy's on a Plate* on Church St. The *Glass House* (☎015394/32137; closed Mon in winter), a renovated, split-level fulling mill with waterwheel on Rydal Road, serves accomplished Mediterranean/Modern British cooking – coffee and light lunches are available, too. There are lots of **pubs**, including the beer-lovers' and climbers' favourite, the *Golden Rule*, on Smithy Brow by Stock Ghyll. For outdoor tables on summer nights, aim for the *Royal Oak* on Church Street.

Langdale

Three miles west of Ambleside along the A593, **Skelwith Bridge** marks the start of **Great Langdale**, a U-shaped glacial valley overlooked by the prominent rocky summits of the **Langdale Pikes**, the most popular of the central Lakeland fells. A couple of classic inns and campsites further along the B5343 provide accommodation for most of the serious valley hikers and climbers, but **Elterwater** village, a mile or so west of Skelwith Bridge, makes an extremely pretty stopover, too.

The #516 Langdale Rambler **bus** from Ambleside's Kelsick Road runs to Skelwith Bridge, Elterwater and the *Old Dungeon Ghyll Hotel* (see below) at the head of the valley between April and October.

Elterwater

ELTERWATER village lies half a mile northwest of its namesake water, an attractive settlement fringed by sheep-filled commonland and centred on a tiny village green. It sees its fair share of Langdale-bound hikers, not least because of its two local **youth hostels**. Both are reasonable spots: *Elterwater Langdale,* just across the bridge from the village (☎015394/37245, ⊜elterwater@yha .org.uk), is the most convenient; *Langdale High Close*, a mile from Elterwater (bookings through Ambleside YHA: ☎015394/32304, ⊜langdale@yha.org.uk), has a more spectacular setting, high on the road over Red Bank from Skelwith Bridge to Grasmere. There's traditional hospitality at the *Britannia Inn* (☎015394 /37210, ⊛www.britinn.co.uk; ❹), a solid old lakeland pub on the green, with comfortable rooms, and good food in the bar. If you're moving on, stock up in the village shop, as it's the last place for supplies this side of the hiking trails.

The Langdale Pikes

Rather than following the B5343 (minor road though it is) west of Elterwater up the valley, stick with the riverside Cumbria Way footpath as far as the *New Dungeon Ghyll Hotel*, three miles from Elterwater. A path indicated by the

"Stickle Ghyll" sign follows the beck straight up to **Stickle Tarn**, around to the right then left up to Pavey Ark. Two more adventurous routes to the top of **Pavey Ark** (2297ft) can be easily seen on the crags above Stickle Tarn: **Jack's Rake** trail ascends the face right to left, and is the hardest commonly used route in the Lake District, requiring a head for heights and steady footing. From near its base, an easier route rises to the right. It is fairly easy from then on to **Harrison Stickle** (2414ft), down to the stream forming the headwaters of Dungeon Ghyll and slowly up to **Pike of Stickle** (2326ft). Backtracking a short distance, a path leads to the right almost parallel with Dungeon Ghyll, back to the start (4 miles; 2400ft ascent; 4hr).

The traditional **accommodation** for anyone visiting the valley is the peerless *Old Dungeon Ghyll Hotel* (℡015394/37272, ⓦwww.odg.co.uk; ❺, ❻ with dinner), superbly isolated at the end of the B5343, seven miles northeast of Ambleside; it offers great three-course dinners in its restaurant (book in advance) and also has a stone-flagged hikers' bar with roaring range and filling food. In the evening, the bar fills up with refugees from the nearby *Great Langdale* **campsite** (℡015394/37668). A mile or so back down the road, rooms at the *New Dungeon Ghyll Hotel* (℡015394/37213, ⓦwww.dungeon-ghyll.com; ❺, ❼ with dinner) feature dramatic fell views. You can also eat here, or at the adjacent *Sticklebarn Tavern* (℡015394/37356; ❶), which has very popular bunk-barn accommodation.

Grasmere and around

Four miles northwest of Ambleside, the village of **GRASMERE** consists of an intimate cluster of grey-stone houses on the old packhorse road which runs beside the babbling River Rothay. It's an eminently pleasing ensemble, set back from one of the most alluring of the region's small lakes, but it loses some of its charm in summer thanks to the hordes who descend on the trail of the village's most famous former resident, **William Wordsworth** (1770–1850). The poet, his wife Mary, sister Dorothy and other members of his family are buried beneath the yews in **St Oswald's churchyard**, around which the river makes a sinuous curl. Inside the church interior you can admire the unique twin naves, split by a solid arched partition. At the rear entrance to the churchyard stands **Sarah Nelson's Gingerbread Shop** (Mon–Sat 9.30am–5.30pm, Sun 12.30–5.30pm), converted from the schoolhouse where Wordsworth once taught, and issuing delicious smells throughout the day.

A circular walk from Grasmere

One of the Lakes' easier circuits is the trip **around Grasmere and Rydal Water** from Grasmere village, a shade over four miles. It can be completed in two hours or so, though as it passes Wordsworth haunts, Rydal Mount and Dove Cottage, it could be turned into an all-day sightseeing venture.

From the tourist office in Grasmere, follow Red Bank Road along the western edge of the lake, climbing up a track through Redbank Woods after a mile (signposted "Loughrigg Terrace and YHA"). Signposts soon lead you out onto **Loughrigg Terrace** itself, where tremendous views of the lake unfold. The terrace skirts Loughrigg Fell as it heads east and then you switch ridges to follow that above **Rydal Water**, where you'll pass the dripping, water-filled maw of **Rydal Cave**, a disused slate quarry. Rounding the eastern edge of Rydal, you cross and climb off the A591, past the church, to **Rydal Mount**, above which a bridleway runs back above the northern shore of Rydal Water. It emerges at Dove Cottage, on the outskirts of Grasmere.

Practicalities

Grasmere is on the main #555 and #599 bus routes, which both stop on the village green. A Stagecoach Round Robin ticket (£5) allows up to five stops on return journeys between Bowness or Ambleside and the Wordsworth houses and Grasmere. The **tourist office** (April–Oct daily 9.30am–5pm; Nov–March Fri, Sat & Sun 10am–3.30pm; ☎015394/35245), five minutes away from the green down Langdale Road, is tucked in by the main **car park** on Red Bank Road at the southern end of the village.

Accommodation can be hard to come by in summer – book well in advance, especially for popular central places such as the *Harwood*, Red Lion

---

Writers in the Lake District

William Wordsworth was not the first to praise the Lake District – Thomas Gray wrote appreciatively of his visit in 1769 – but it is Wordsworth that dominates its literary landscape, not solely through his poetry but also through his still useful *Guide to the Lakes* (1810). Born in Cockermouth in 1770, he was sent to school in Hawkshead before a stint at Cambridge, a year in France and two in Somerset. In 1799 he returned to the Lake District, settling in the Grasmere district, where he spent the last two-thirds of his life with his sister Dorothy, who not only transcribed his poems but was an accomplished diarist as well.

Wordsworth and fellow poets **Samuel Taylor Coleridge** and **Robert Southey** formed a clique that became known as the "Lake Poets", a label based more on their fluctuating friendships and their shared passion for the region than on any common subject matter in their writings. A fourth member of the Cumbrian literary elite was the critic and essayist **Thomas De Quincey**, chiefly known today for his *Confessions of an English Opium-Eater*. One of the first to fully appreciate the revolutionary nature of Wordsworth's and Coleridge's collaborative *Lyrical Ballads* in 1807, De Quincey became a long-term guest of the Wordsworths from them in 1809. He stayed there until 1820, but it was only in the 1830s that he started writing his *Lake Reminiscences*, offending Wordsworth and Coleridge in the process.

Meanwhile, after short spells at Allan Bank and The Vicarage, both in Grasmere, the Wordsworths made Rydal Mount their home, supported largely by William's position as Distributor of Stamps for Westmorland and his later stipend as Poet Laureate. After his death in 1850, William's body was interred in St Oswald's churchyard in Grasmere, to be joined five years later by Dorothy and by his wife Mary four years after that.

Inspired by Wordsworth's writings and by the terrain itself, the social philosopher and art critic **John Ruskin** also made the Lake District his home, settling at Brantwood outside Coniston in 1872. His letters and watercolours reflect a deep love of the area, also demonstrated by his unsuccessful fight to prevent the damming of Thirlmere. Much of Ruskin's feeling for the countryside permeated through to two other literary immigrants, **Arthur Ransome**, also a Coniston resident and writer of the children's classic *Swallows and Amazons*, and **Beatrix Potter**, whose favourite Lakeland spots feature in her children's stories. Potter, in fact, is the only serious lakeland rival to Wordsworthian dominance, with her former home at Hill Top in Near Sawrey, her husband's office in Hawkshead and a museum in Bowness all packed with international visitors throughout the year. Whatever you think of her work, every visitor to the Lakes has at least some cause to be grateful to Beatrix Potter, who donated several parcels of land to the National Trust.

Other famous Lake District literary names number **Sir Hugh Walpole**, who lived at Derwentwater and set his Herries novels in Borrowdale; **Harriet Martineau**, who lived in Ambleside for thirty years and received most of literary England in her drawing room; poet **Norman Nicholson** from Millom on the Cumbrian coast; and writer and broadcaster **Melvyn Bragg**, born in Wigton.

Square (☎015394/35248, ⓦwww.harwoodhotel.co.uk; ❸). Some of the nicest places are a little way out of the centre: *Banerigg Guest House* (☎015394/35204; no smoking; no credit cards; ❸), is a lakeside property fifteen minutes' walk out on the Ambleside road (A591) – guests are free to take boats out onto the water; or there's *Titteringdales Guesthouse*, on Pye Lane (☎015394/35439, ⓦwww.grasmere.net; ❷), to the north, just off the A591, with fell views from its dining room. There's a gamut of fancier places, too, top-of-the-range the *Wordsworth Hotel* on College St (☎015394/35592, ⓦwww.grasmere-hotels .co.uk; ❽), with a heated pool, conservatory and terrace. The *Red Lion* in central Red Lion Square (☎015394/35456; ❻) is a bit more reasonably priced, a sympathetically styled eighteenth-century coaching inn.

Of course, there's no shortage of local places with Wordsworthian connections. Top of the pile is *White Moss House* (☎015394/35295, ⓦwww.whitemoss .com; ❾, with dinner; closed Dec & Jan), a house once owned by Wordsworth, a mile south on the A591, at the northern end of Rydal Water. It's a glorious spot, and the food is wonderful. *The Swan* (☎015394/35551, ⓦwww.heritage -hotels.com; ❼, ❽ at weekends) on the A591 just outside Grasmere rated a mention in Wordsworth's "The Waggoner" and remodelling hasn't robbed it of its essential eighteenth-century character. Lesser budgets are required for *How Foot Lodge*, at Town End (☎015394/35366; ❸; closed Jan), a Victorian house owned by the National Trust, just yards from Dove Cottage.

Grasmere has no campsite but three very popular **youth hostels**. The YHA choices are *Butterlip How*, a Victorian house 150 yards north of the green on Easedale Road, and *Thorney How*, a characterful former farmhouse, just under a mile further along the unlit road – bring a torch. Reservations for both are made at *Butterlip How* (☎015394/35316, ⓔgrasmere@yha.org.uk). There's also the excellent *Grasmere Independent Hostel* at Broadrayne Farm (☎015394 /35055, ⓦwww.grasmere-accommodation.co.uk), just north of town on the A591. Rooms here sleep three to six people and are all en-suite, while other facilities include a full kitchen and laundry, sauna, and common room with valley views.

Picnic fixings are best from *Newby's Delicatessen & Bakery* in Red Lion Square (underneath the *Harwood*), while *Baldry's* (closed Tues–Thur in winter) – just a step across the road – is a wholefood **tea rooms** with home-made cakes, puddings, pies and quiche. The *Rowan Tree*, on Church Bridge, Stock Lane, opposite the churchyard, serves vegetarian dishes on a terrace overlooking the river and is open in the evenings, or there's the *Dove Cottage Tea Rooms and Restaurant*, at Town End near Dove Cottage, open during the day for tearoom favourites and at night (☎015394/35268; closed Mon May–Oct, plus Tues & Sun rest of year) for fashionable, but moderately priced dinners. The fanciest local **restaurants** are those at the *Wordsworth Hotel*, *White Moss House* and *The Swan* (see above). The only real **pub** in the village is the *Red Lion* – whose public bar is called the *Lamb Inn*. Otherwise, you'll need to walk out to the *Traveller's Rest*, half a mile north along the A591, a popular place for bar meals, though the thundering main road does its outdoor tables no favours.

Dove Cottage

On the southeastern outskirts of the village, on the main A591, stands **Dove Cottage** (daily 9.30am–5.30pm; closed mid-Jan to mid-Feb; £5; ⓦwww .wordsworth.org.uk), home to William and Dorothy Wordsworth from 1799 to 1808 and where Wordsworth wrote some of his best poetry. Guides bursting with anecdotes lead you around rooms which reflect Wordsworth's guiding principle of "plain living but high thinking" and are little changed now but for the addition of electricity and internal plumbing. This maxim, however, was only temporary, as Wordsworth was raised in comfortable surroundings and returned to a relatively high standard of living when he moved to Rydal Mount. Most of the furniture in the cottage belonged to the Wordsworths, while in the upper rooms are various other possessions, including a pair of William's ice skates. In good weather, the **garden** is open for visits as well (same hours as cottage). In the adjacent **museum** are more paintings, manuscripts and personal effects once belonging to the Wordsworths (most poignantly Mary's wedding ring), plus mementoes of Southey, Coleridge and Thomas De Quincey. Exhibits here are likely to be rearranged in the future, now that proposals for a new extension to the museum have been agreed.

Rydal Mount

Another mile and a half southeast along the A591 from Grasmere, the hamlet of **RYDAL** consists of an inn, a few houses and **Rydal Mount** (March–Oct daily 9.30am–5pm; Nov–Feb Wed–Mon 10am–4pm; £4, gardens only £1.75), home of William Wordsworth from 1813 until his death in 1850. Parts of the house have been redecorated, but furniture and portraits give a good sense of its former occupants: in the drawing room and library are the only known portrait of Dorothy and William's black leather sofa; while Wordsworth's own bedroom has a lovely view. For many, the highlight is the garden, which has been preserved as Wordsworth designed it, complete with terraces where he used to declaim his poetry. Buses #555/556 and #599 pass the house on the way to Grasmere from Windermere and Ambleside.

Coniston Water

At five miles long and half a mile across at its widest point, **Coniston Water** is not one of the most immediately imposing of the lakes, yet it has a quiet beauty which sets it apart from the more popular destinations. The nineteenth-century art critic and social reformer John Ruskin made the lake his home and his isolated house, **Brantwood**, today provides the most obvious target for a day-trip, but the plain village grows on visitors after a while, especially those who base themselves at Coniston for some of the central Lakes' most rewarding walking. Some come here, too, on the *Swallows and Amazons* trail. **Arthur Ransome** was a frequent visitor, his memories and experiences providing much detail later in his famous children's books.

The Old Man of Coniston

The walk from Coniston village to the top of the Old Man of Coniston (2628ft) is one of the Cumbrian classics, tiring but not overly difficult. Staying at *Coniston Coppermines* youth hostel gives you an early start. Otherwise, from the bridge in the village, follow the path to the *Coppermines* hostel up past the *Sun Hotel*. At Church Beck, with the hostel in the distance ahead, a sign on the gated bridge puts you on the path, with the stream to your right. The path gradually swings to the left, taking a steep and twisting route through abandoned quarry works and their detritus, including several fallen heavy-duty pulley systems. Cairns keep you on the right route, up past a gorgeous glassy tarn, and then there's a final scramble to the massive cairn at the summit (under 2hr for most walkers). The views from here are tremendous – to the Cumbrian coast, and across to Langdale, Windermere and Coniston itself.

In the mid-1960s, the long uninterruptedly glass-like surface of Coniston Water attracted the attention of national hero **Donald Campbell**, who in 1955 had set a world water-speed record of 202mph on Ullswater, bumping it up to 276mph nine years later in Australia. On January 4, 1967, he set out to better his own mark on Coniston Water, but just as his jet-powered *Bluebird* hit an estimated 320mph, a patch of turbulence sent it into a somersault. Campbell was killed immediately and his body and boat lay undisturbed at the bottom of the lake until both were retrieved in 2001, Campbell for reburial at Coniston's cemetery, *Bluebird* into storage while it's decided what to do with the remains of the boat.

Practicalities

Buses – principally the #505/506 from Kendal, Windermere, Ambleside and Hawkshead – stop on the main road through the village, though some of the services also run down to the ferry pier at the lake. A Ruskin Explorer ticket (£9) gets you return bus travel between Bowness and Coniston, plus use of the Coniston Launch and free entry to Ruskin's house – buy the ticket on the bus. The **tourist office** (April–Oct daily 9.30am–5.30pm; Nov–March Fri–Sun 10am–3.30pm; ☎015394/41533) is right in the centre on Ruskin Avenue. You can **rent bikes** from Summitreks on Yewdale Rd (☎015394/41212, ⓦwww.summittreks.co.uk), which also organizes adventurous days out on water and land.

B&Bs are plentiful. The most comfortable are *Shepherds Villa*, Tilberthwaite Ave (☎015394/41337; ❷) – the B5285 into the village – and the vegetarian *Beech Tree Guesthouse*, Yewdale Rd (☎015394/41717; no credit cards; ❷) – the Ambleside road. The fall-back choice is *Lakeland House* on Tilberthwaite Ave (☎015394/41303; no credit cards; ❶), opposite the Campbell memorial – a friendly place, accustomed to walkers and their ways and with an attached café. All the pubs have rooms, but the best are those at the *Sun Hotel* (☎015394/41248, ⓦwww.smoothhound.co.uk/hotels/sun; ❹, minimum two-night stay at weekends), a fine old inn 200 yards uphill from the bridge in the centre of Coniston. Half a mile out of the centre at Waterhead, on the Hawkshead road, the slate-flagged, seventeenth-century *Thwaite Cottage* (☎015394/41367, ⓦwww.thwaitcot.freeserve.co.uk; no credit cards; ❷) has three rooms in peaceful surroundings. *Swallows and Amazons* fans won't want to miss out on a night spent at *Bank Ground Farm* (☎015394/41264, ⓦwww.bankground.com; ❸), the model for Holly Howe Farm in the book and also featured in the 1970s' film. It's on the shores of the lake, just north of Brantwood.

Of the two **youth hostels**, *Coniston Holly How* (☎015394/41323, ⓔconistonhh@yha.org.uk) is the closer, just a few minutes' walk north of Coniston on the Ambleside road, but *Coniston Coppermines* (☎015394/41261) is more peaceful, in a dramatic mountain setting a steep mile or so from the village. The nearest **campsite** is the *Coniston Hall Campsite*, Haws Bank (☎015394/41223; booking essential; closed Nov–March), a mile south of town by the lake.

Eating opportunities outside the pubs are limited, but in any case you shouldn't look much further than the *Sun Hotel*, whose cosy bar has filling meals as well as photographs and newspaper accounts of the famous Campbell crash. The *Sun* is also the cheeriest place for a **drink**, though the *Black Bull* in the centre brews its own *Bluebird* beer. For sandwiches, home-made pies, all-day breakfasts and internet access, visit the *Village Pantry* on Yewdale Road.

⑪

Coniston village and water

A memorial seat and plaque to Campbell decorates the green in the slate-grey village of **CONISTON** (a derivation of "King's Town"), hunkered below the craggy and copper-mine-riddled bulk of **The Old Man of Coniston** (see box on p.834). Campbell's grave is nearby, in the new cemetery (behind the *Crown Hotel*): before the memorial service in September 2001, his blue coffin (the colour of his boat, *Bluebird*) was taken through the village by horsedrawn carriage. Having studied this and Ruskin's grave, which lies in St Andrew's original churchyard beneath a beautifully worked Celtic cross, you've seen all that Coniston has to offer, save for the excellent **Ruskin Museum** on Yewdale Road (Easter to mid-Nov daily 10am–5.30pm; mid-Nov to Easter Wed–Sun 10am–3.30pm; £3.50; ⊛ www.coniston.org.uk), which combines local history and geology exhibits with a fascinating look at Ruskin's life and work through his watercolours, manuscripts and personal memorabilia.

The village keeps itself to itself to such an extent that first-time visitors are surprised to find it has a lake – **Coniston Water** is hidden out of sight, half a mile southeast of the village. Here, the *Bluebird Café* sells ices and drinks, while the adjacent Coniston Boating Centre can provide the wherewithal for fooling around on the water – rowing boats, sailing dinghies, canoes, electric launches and motorboats. Boat speeds are now limited to 10mph, a graceful pace for the sumptuously upholstered **Steam Yacht Gondola** (Easter–Oct 5 daily; £4.80 round trip; ☎015394/63856), built in 1859, which leaves Coniston Pier for hour-long circuits, calling at Park-a-moor landing stage then Ruskin's Brantwood. The wooden **Coniston Launch** (Easter–Oct hourly; Nov–Easter up to 4 daily depending on the weather; ☎015394/36216, ⊛ www.lakefell.co.uk) operates a year-round service to Brantwood on two routes, north (£3.60 return) or south (£5.80) around the lake. Special **cruises** (Easter–Oct) concentrate on the various sites associated with *Swallows and Amazons* (£7) and Donald Campbell (£6).

Brantwood

Both steam yacht and motor launches dock beneath the magnificently sited **Brantwood** (mid-March to mid-Nov daily 11am–5.30pm; mid-Nov to mid-March Wed–Sun 11am–4.30pm; house, gardens & launch £7.50, house only £4.50, gardens only £2; ⊛ www.brantwood.org.uk), two and a half miles by road from Coniston, where art critic and moralist **John Ruskin** lived from 1872 until his death in 1900.

Champion of J.M.W. Turner and the Pre-Raphaelites and proponent of the supremacy of Gothic architecture, Ruskin insisted upon the indivisibility of ethics and aesthetics, and was appalled by the conditions in which the captains of industry made their labourers work and live, while expecting him to applaud their patronage of the arts. "There is no wealth but life," he wrote in his study of capitalist economics, *Unto the Last*, elaborating with the observation: "that country is richest which nourishes the greatest number of noble and happy human beings." A twenty-minute video expands on his philosophy and whets the appetite for rooms full of his watercolours, doing justice to a man who greatly influenced such disparate figures as Proust, Tolstoy, Frank Lloyd Wright and Gandhi. Nonetheless, not all of Ruskin's projects were a success, partly because of his refusal to compromise his principles. A London teashop, established to provide employment for a former servant, failed since Ruskin refused to advertise; meanwhile, his street-cleaning and road-building schemes, designed to instil into his students (including Arnold Toynbee and Oscar Wilde) a respect for the dignity of manual labour, simply accrued ridicule.

Ruskin bought Brantwood in 1871, sight unseen, from engraver and Radical William James Linton, complaining when he saw it that it was "a mere shed". The views, however, captivated him and Ruskin spent the next twenty years adding to the house and laying out its gardens. His study – hung with handmade paper to his own design – and dining room boast superlative lake views, bettered only by those from the Turret Room where he used to sit in later life in his bathchair, itself on display downstairs, along with his mahogany desk and Blue John wine goblet, among other memorabilia. Various other exhibition rooms and galleries display Ruskin-related arts and crafts, while the *Jumping Jenny Tearooms* – named after Ruskin's boat – has outdoor terrace seating for meals and drinks. There's also a well-stocked book shop full of information on the Pre-Raphaelites or the Arts and Crafts Movement.

Hawkshead and around

Greystone **HAWKSHEAD**, between Coniston and Ambleside, wears its beauty well, its patchwork of cottages and cobbles backed by woods and fells and barely affected by twentieth-century intrusions. This is partly due to the enlightened policy of banning traffic in the centre – huge car parks at the village edge take the strain and when the crowds of day-trippers leave, Hawkshead regains its natural tranquillity.

The Vikings were the first to settle the land here, the village probably founded by and named for one Haukr, a Norse warrior. It was an important wool market at the time Wordsworth was studying at **Hawkshead Grammar School** (Easter–Oct Mon–Sat 10am–12.30pm & 1.30–5pm, Sun 1–5pm; £2), founded in 1585, whose entrance lies opposite the tourist office – pride of place is given to the desk on which William carved his signature. While there he attended the fifteenth-century **Church of St Michael** (daily 9am–6pm) above the school, which harks back to Norman designs in its rounded pillars and patterned arches. Its chief interest is in the 26 pithy psalms and biblical extracts illuminated with cherubs and flowers, painted on the walls during the seventeenth and eighteenth centuries.

From its knoll the churchyard gives a good view over the village's twin central squares, and of Main Street, housing the **Beatrix Potter Gallery** (Easter–Oct Mon–Thurs & Sun 10.30am–4.30pm; £3; NT), occupying rooms once used by her solicitor husband. With their timed-entry ticket, fans get bustled into rooms full of Potter's original illustrations, though the less devoted might find displays on her life as keen naturalist, conservationist and early supporter of the National Trust more diverting – Potter bequeathed her farms and land in the Lake District to the Trust on her death.

Practicalities

The main **bus service** to Hawkshead is the #505/506 between Bowness, Ambleside and Coniston; on reaching Hawkshead it loops down to Hill Top and back for the Beatrix Potter house at Near Sawrey. The **tourist office** is at the main car park (Easter–Oct daily 9.30am–6pm; Nov–Easter Fri, Sat & Sun 10am–3.30pm; ☏015394/36525) and can change money, book you on local guided walks and assist with finding **accommodation**.

Some contend that Wordsworth briefly boarded at what is now *Ann Tyson's Cottage*, on cobbled Wordsworth St (☏015394/36405, ⊛www.anntysons.co.uk; ❷), where there are **B&B** rooms in the barn conversion or two cottages to rent. The whitewashed *Old School House* (☏015394/36403; ❷) is another historic choice, just behind the Grammar School, near the tourist office. *Ivy House*, Main St (☏015394/36204, ⊛www.ivyhousehotel.com; ❺, includes dinner), makes a characterful base with its eighteenth-century elegance; or drive out the two miles to *Yewfield* at Hawkshead Hill (☎015394/36765, ⊛www.yewfield.co .uk; ❸), a vegetarian guest house set amongst organic vegetable gardens. **Pubs** provide the main eating options, not bad at either the *Queen's Head* on Main Street (☎015394/36271, ⊛www.queensheadhotel.co.uk; ❹) or the *King's Arms*, on the main square (☎015394/36372, ⊛www.kingsarmshawkshead.co .uk; ❹), both of which have bar meals as well as a more formal restaurant. Of the **tearooms**, *Whig's* on The Square (closed Thurs) serves its eponymous speciality baked rolls, while the fifteenth-century *Minstrels' Gallery* on the main square has an espresso machine – ask here, too, about renting cottages in the area.

The **youth hostel**, *Esthwaite Lodge* (☎015394/36293, ⊜hawkshead@yha .org.uk), is a mile to the south down the Newby Bridge road, housed in a Regency mansion with good-sized family rooms. **Camping** is at Hawkshead's busy *Croft Caravan and Campsite* (☎015394/36374, ⊛www.hawkshead-croft.com; closed Nov to mid-March), on North Lonsdale Road, right by the village. A cheaper tap-and-toilet affair is found at *Hawkshead Hall Farm*, half a mile north of the village on the Ambleside road (☎015394/36221).

Grizedale Forest

If the weather looks promising, time is well spent among the remarkable sculptures in **Grizedale Forest**, southwest of Hawkshead, which drapes over the Furness Fells separating Coniston Water from Windermere. There's a postbus service twice a day (Mon–Fri only) from Ulverston to **Grizedale Forest Centre** (daily: March–Nov 10am–5pm; Dec–Feb 10am–4pm; free, all-day parking £3; ☎01229/860010, ⊛www.nwefd.co.uk), three miles southwest of Hawkshead; otherwise you'll have to **rent a bike** from the *Croft* campsite in Hawkshead. Grizedale Mountain Bikes at the centre (daily 9am–5pm; ☎01229 /860369) also has bikes available, or just head out on foot along ten miles of the Silurian Way, which links the majority of the eighty-odd stone and wood sculptures scattered among the trees. Since 1977 artists have been invited to come here, often for six months at a time, to create a sculptural response to their surroundings using natural materials. Some of the resulting works are startling, as you round a bend to find a hundred-foot-long wave of bent logs or a dry-stone wall slaloming the conifers. Pick up a map from the centre and take a picnic.

Hill Top

It's two miles from Hawkshead, down the eastern side of Esthwaite Water on the B5285 to the pretty twin hamlets of Near and Far Sawrey, the first the site of Beatrix Potter's beloved **Hill Top** (Easter–Oct Mon–Wed, Sat & Sun 11am–5pm; £4; NT). A Londoner by birth, Potter bought the farmhouse here with the proceeds from her first book, *The Tale of Peter Rabbit*, and retained it as her study long after she moved out following her marriage in 1913. Its furnishings and contents have been kept as they were during her occupancy – a condition of Potter's will – and the small house is always busy with visitors; so much so that numbers are often limited. In summer, expect to have to queue. From April to October, you can travel to Hill Top directly from Bowness (10am–4.30pm every 40min; ☎015394/45161, ⊛www.mountain-goat.com) on a combined "boat-and-goat" ferry-and-minibus service, which runs on from Hill Top to Hawkshead and back. Otherwise, the *Tower Bank Arms* in the village is the place to muse on your next move; it serves good sandwiches, home-made pies and local sausages.

Tarn Hows

A minor road off the Hawkshead–Coniston B5285 winds the couple of miles northwest to the highly popular **Tarn Hows**, a body of water surrounded by spruce and pine and circled by paths and picnic spots. The land was donated by Beatrix Potter in 1930 – one of several such grants – since when the National Trust has carefully maintained it. It takes an hour to walk around the tarn, during which you can ponder on the fact that this miniature idyll is in fact almost entirely artificial – the original owners enlarged two small tarns to make the one you see today, planted and landscaped the surroundings and dug the footpaths. It's now a Site of Special Scientific Interest – keep an eye out for some of the Lakes' (and England's) few surviving native red squirrels.

A special, free, National Trust Tarn Hows **bus service** runs between Hawkshead and Coniston on Sundays between Easter and the end of October, linking with the regular #505/506. Otherwise, you'll have to pay to use the designated car park – or, of course, walk the two miles up from Coniston or Hawkshead on country paths and lanes. Drivers have the option of following the signs north to Ambleside along the minor road, reaching the *Drunken Duck Inn* (☎015394/36347, ⓦwww.drunkenduckinn.co.uk; ❺) after three miles, at the **Barngates** crossroads. There's a cheery welcome, fine rooms, deservedly popular bar food and occasional folk/jazz gigs.

Keswick and Derwent Water

Standing on the shores of **Derwent Water** at the junction of the main north–south and east–west routes through the Lake District, **KESWICK** makes a good base for exploring delightful Borrowdale – the start of many walking routes to the central peaks around Scafell Pike – or Skiddaw and Blencathra, which loom over the town. There's plenty of accommodation and some good cafés aimed at walkers, while several bus routes radiate from the town, getting you to the start of even the most challenging hikes. For those not up to a day on the fells, the town remains a popular place throughout the year, with a big enough population (around five thousand) to warrant a bevy of local museums and sights.

Walks from Keswick

All sorts of major walks start from Keswick and the surrounding villages, including tough climbs up Blencathra and the celebrated Coledale Horseshoe, an all-day circuit which takes in up to eleven summits. However, moderate walkers keen to spend just half a day or so on the fells can settle for either of the walks detailed below – you'll still need to carry decent maps and be properly equipped.

Rising sharply through coniferous forests above Keswick, the walk up **Latrigg Fell** (4–6 miles; 900ft ascent; 2–3hr) gives splendid views across Derwent Water to Borrowdale and the high fells. Follow Station Road past the youth hostel and museum and, as it bends around to the right to become Brundholme Road/Briar Rigg, look for the right turn up Spooney Green Lane across the A66. From here skirt the west flank of Latrigg before zigzagging to the summit from the north. Return either directly down the southern gully or follow the longer eastern ridge to Brundholme, returning through Brundholme wood or along the railway path.

More demanding, but the easiest of the region's true mountain walks, is the hike up **Skiddaw** (5 miles; 3000ft ascent; 5hr), a smooth mound of splintery slate. Follow the walk above, skirting the west flank of Latrigg, but continue straight ahead when the path branches right to the Latrigg summit. It is pretty much a steady walk (with a possible diversion up Little Man along the way) before reaching a false summit and finally the 3054ft High Man.

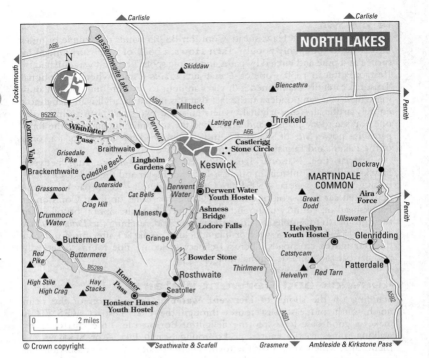

Arrival, information and accommodation

All **buses**, including National Express services, use the terminal behind Lakes Foodstore, off Main Street. The **tourist office** is in the Moot Hall on Market Square (daily: April–June, Sept & Oct 9.30am–5.30pm; July & Aug 9.30am–7pm; Nov–March 9.30am–4.30pm; ☎017687/72645, ⓦwww.keswick.org). George Fisher, at 2 Borrowdale Rd (☎017687/72178), is one of the most celebrated **outdoors stores** on the Lakes, with a full range of equipment and maps, a daily weather information service and café. For **bike rental**, call Keswick Mountain Bikes on Southey Hill (☎017687/75202, ⓦwww.keswickbikes.co.uk). Daily **guided walks** – from lakeside rambles to mountain climbs – depart daily (Easter–Oct 10.15am; £5) from the Moot Hall; just turn up with a packed lunch. There's **internet access** at U-Compute, above the post office at 48 Main St (Mon–Sat 9am–5.30pm, Sun 9.30am–4.30pm; ☎017687/75127).

You should have no trouble finding accommodation, and competition at the lower end of the market keeps the prices keen. B&Bs cluster along Bank and Stanger streets, near the post office, and around Southey, Blencathra and Eskin streets, in the grid near the start of the A591 Penrith road. Smarter places line the street known as The Heads, overlooking Hope Park, a couple of minutes' south of the centre on the way to the lake.

Hotels and B&Bs

Bluestones 7 Southey St ☎017687/74237, ⓦwww.members.tripod.com/bluestoneskeswick. Well-kept guest house used to walkers; big breakfasts and on-street parking. No credit cards. ❶

Bridgedale Guesthouse 101 Main St ☎017687/73914. The cheapest central rooms, just around the corner from the bus station; options range from a bed-only rate to an en-suite room (next category up). No credit cards. ❶

Derwentwater Hotel at Portinscale, off the A66
☎017687/72538, ⓦwww.derwentwater-hotel
.co.uk. Superior lakeside retreat (two miles west of
Keswick) with comfortable rooms – some deluxe,
with lounges and sweeping views – a conservatory and rated restaurant. Two-night dinner, bed and
breakfast rates are a good deal. ❼

George Hotel St John St ☎017687/72076,
ⓦwww.jenningsbrewery.co.uk. Refurbished
coaching inn in the centre of town, with bags of
character downstairs and fully modernized rooms
up. The beer is from Jennings, and the food is
good, either eaten in the bar or more formal
restaurant. Parking available. ❸

Greystones Ambleside Rd ☎017687/73108. Non-
smoking Victorian terraced house close to the centre at the end of St John's St. En-suite rooms with
fell views and TVs; guests' car park. ❸

Highfield Hotel The Heads ☎017687/72508,
ⓦwww.highfieldkeswick.co.uk. Beautifully
restored hotel whose stylish feature rooms include
two turret rooms and a converted chapel. There's
also garden seating and an inventive restaurant
with some of the best food in town. ❸, ❹ for
feature rooms.

Howe Keld 5–7 The Heads ☎017687/72417,
ⓦwww.howekeld.co.uk. Welcoming, non-smoking,
mid-sized hotel with a reputation for great breakfasts (vegetarian specialities included) and cosy
rooms. Car park. ❸

Keswick Country House Hotel Station Rd
☎017687/72020, ⓦwww.principalhotels.co.uk.
Grand Victorian hotel, built for the nineteenth-century railway trade and sitting in landscaped
grounds. ❼, with dinner.

Lyzzick Hall Under Skiddaw, A591 ☎017687
/72277, ⓦwww.lyzzickhall.co.uk. A couple of
miles northwest of town, this is a relaxed country-
house hotel set in its own grounds, with an indoor
pool and very good restaurant. ❺, ❻ with dinner.

Campsites and youth hostels

Castlerigg Hall Castlerigg ☎017687/72437,
ⓦwww.castlerigg.co.uk. Out-of-town campsite, a
mile and a half southeast of Keswick; you can
reach the nearby stone circle by footpath. Closed
Nov–Easter.

**Derwentwater Caravan Club and Camping
Site** ☎017687/72392. Less than ten minutes'
walk from the centre, down by the lake; turn left
off Main St beside the supermarket. Closed Dec &
Jan.

Derwentwater Youth Hostel Borrowdale
☎017687/77246, ⓔderwentwater@yha.org.uk.
Based in an old mansion with fifteen acres of
grounds sloping down to the lake, a couple of
miles south of Keswick along the B5289.

Keswick Youth Hostel Station Rd
☎017687/72484, ⓔkeswick@yha.org.uk. A converted woollen mill by the river in town; good location, and free tea and coffee on arrival, plus internet access.

Skiddaw House Youth Hostel phone *Carrock Fell*
hostel ☎016974/78325. One of the most remote
buildings in England, 1500ft above sea level and
with no motor vehicle access; it's on the Cumbria
Way, six miles from Keswick by path. Bunk beds,
log fires and limited food supplies; bring your own.

The town and around

Granted its market charter by Edward I in 1276 – **market day** is Saturday –
Keswick was an important wool and leather centre until around 1500, when
these trades were supplanted by the discovery of local graphite. **The
Cumberland Pencil Museum**, west of the centre at Greta Bridge, on Main
St (daily 9.30am–4pm; £2.50; ⓦwww.pencils.co.uk), tells the story, beginning
with its early application as moulds for cannon balls. With the Italian idea of
putting graphite into wooden holders, Keswick became an important pencil-
making town, and remained one until the late eighteenth century, when the
French discovered how to make pencil graphite cheaply by binding the common amorphous graphite with clay. Keswick's monopoly was quickly broken,
and only the factory which owns the museum still survives. Inside, a mock-up
of the long-defunct Borrowdale mine leads through a potted history of
graphite use, with multifarious examples of the finished product and a video
of the modern process.

On the edge of Fitz Park, on Station Road, you'll find the **Keswick
Museum and Art Gallery** (Easter–Oct daily 10am–4pm; £1), a quirky
Victorian collection of ancient dental tools, fossils and some prized manu-
scripts and letters written by the Lakeland Poets. Make time, too, for a couple

of churches: **St John's**, on St John's Street in the centre, where the novelist Sir Hugh Walpole (of Herries novels fame) is buried; and **Crosthwaite Church**, a fifteen-minute walk northwest of town, over Greta Bridge, resting place of the poet Robert Southey.

Keswick's most celebrated landmark, **Castlerigg Stone Circle**, is made especially resonant by its magnificent mountain backdrop. From the end of Station Road, take the Threlkeld rail line path (signposted by the *Keswick Country House Hotel*) for half a mile, then turn onto the minor road to the right where the path runs under the road – the site's a mile further on atop a sweeping plateau. Thirty-eight hunks of Borrowdale volcanic stone, the largest almost eight feet tall, form a circle a hundred feet in diameter; another ten blocks delineate a rectangular enclosure within. The array probably had an astronomical or timekeeping function when it was erected four or five thousand years ago. Back on the rail path, you can easily continue all the way to **Threlkeld** itself, three miles from town, on a delightful riverside walk with the promise of a drink in one of Threlkeld's old pubs at the end. Keener hikers use Threlkeld as the starting point for the gut-busting climb up **Blencathra**, whose five great ridges loom above the A66: you'll need to be well prepared to tackle this.

Eating, drinking and entertainment

Many of the **places to eat** cater to a walking crowd, which means large portions and few airs. Several of the **pubs** also have meals worth investigating, while there's a fair amount of entertainment in Keswick throughout the year: a **cinema** on St John's St (often closed Dec–Feb) which hosts an annual film festival, the **jazz festival** each May, **beer festival** in June, and traditional country shows in the locality during the summer. The **Theatre by the Lake** on Lake Road (℡017687/74411, ⊛www.theatrebythelake.com) hosts a full programme of drama, concerts, exhibitions, readings and talks.

Abraham's Tea Rooms in George Fisher's outdoor store, 2 Borrowdale Rd. The top-floor tearoom comes to your aid with warming mugs of *glühwein,* home-made soups, big breakfasts and daily specials. No credit cards. Inexpensive.

Brysons 42 Main St. Top-notch bakery and tearooms with breakfasts, traditional main dishes and cream teas. No credit cards. Inexpensive.

The Four in Hand Lake Rd, opposite George Fisher's. Popular pub for its food – grilled Cumberland ham and eggs, local trout and other Lakeland specialities. Inexpensive to Moderate.

Lakeland Pedlar Henderson's Yard, Bell Close, off Main St. Keswick's best café serves inventive veggie food – from breakfast burritos to veg crumble – and the coffee's great too. Open evenings July &

Aug. Inexpensive.

Loose Box Pizzeria King's Arms Courtyard, Main St. Popular pizza-and-pasta joint – the house special is *spaghetti rustica* (tomato, garlic, chilli and prawns). Moderate.

Luca's Greta Bridge ℡017687/74621. Classic pastas and pizzas, and pricier main meals (such as monkfish wrapped in pancetta) in a riverside Italian bistro; closed Mon. Moderate to Expensive.

Mayson's 33 Lake Rd. Licensed, self-service café serving bakes, pies and stir-fries (until 8.45pm in summer). No credit cards. Inexpensive.

The Square Orange St John's St. The café-bar scene gets a northern lakeland toehold – cappuccino, snacks and meals, day and night. Inexpensive.

Around Derwent Water

On any reasonably decent day, the best move in Keswick is down to the shores of **Derwent Water**, five minutes' walk south of the centre along Lake Road and through the pedestrian underpass. It's among the most attractive of the lakes, ringed by crags and studded with islets, and is most easily seen by hopping on the **Keswick Launch** (Easter–Nov daily 10am–6pm, until 8pm in July & Aug; Dec–Easter Sat & Sun 10am–6pm; £5 round-trip, 80p per stage; ℡017687/72263, ⊛www.keswick-launch.co.uk), which runs right around the lake calling at several points en route. There's also an enjoyable one-hour evening cruise (£5.80) from May Day bank holiday until mid-September; pop down during the day to reserve a place on these.

Departures are frequent enough to combine a cruise with a lakeside walk; or you can make the entire lake loop on foot from Keswick on the **Derwent Water Circuit** (around 10 miles; 3–4hr), outlined in a leaflet available from the tourist office. The closest and most popular hike is to **Friars' Crag**, from where medieval pilgrims left for St Herbert's Island in the middle of the lake, to seek the hermit's blessing. Ruskin's childhood visit to Friars' Crag inspired "intense joy, mingled with awe", feelings likely to be duplicated if you return to Keswick via the 530ft Castlehead view point – a three-mile round-trip in all. Other ports of call as you make your way around Derwent Water on foot or by launch include the dry-stone **Ashness Bridge** and **Lodore Falls** (see "Borrowdale", below, for both) and the woodlands and moulded landscapes of **Lingholm Gardens**. Best climb is up **Cat Bells** (launch to Hawes End), a renowned vantage-point (1481ft) above the lake's western shore – allow two-and-a-half hours for the scramble to the top and a return along the wooded lake shore.

Borrowdale and Scafell

It is difficult to overstate the beauty of **Borrowdale**, with its river flats and yew trees, lying at the head of Derwent Water and overshadowed by the peaks of **Scafell** and **Scafell Pike**, the highest in England. Climbs up these, as well as up Great Gable, one of the finest-looking mountains in England, start from the head of the valley, accessible on the #77/77A and #79 **buses** from Keswick.

Just before the *Derwentwater* youth hostel, a narrow road branches left for a steep climb to the photogenic **Ashness Bridge**. The minor road ends two miles further south at **Watendlath**, an idyllic little tarn and tearooms which can be hopelessly overrun at times in summer – the National Trust's free Watendlath Wanderer bus runs here every couple of hours from Keswick on summer Sundays, via Ashness. A path from Watendlath continues on to Rosthwaite, a mile and a half southwest – an easy hour's walk.

Back on the B5289, a signposted path heads to the **Lodore Falls**. This diversion is only really worth it after sustained wet weather, when you'll be able to appreciate Robert Southey's magnificent, alliterative evocation of the falls in *The Cataract of Lodore*: "Collecting, projecting, receding and speeding, and shocking and rocking, and darting and parting", and so on, for line after memorable line.

Further south, past the wonderfully sited *Borrowdale Hotel* (☎017687/77224, ⓦwww.theborrowdalehotel.co.uk; ❼, with dinner), which has an excellent restaurant, there's a slight detour across an old packhorse bridge to **GRANGE**, a peaceful riverside hamlet, peered down upon by Borrowdale's forested crags. *Grange Bridge Cottage* has tea rooms, in a great spot, right by the bridge. There are a couple of local B&Bs, too, while a very minor road (and the Cumbria Way) meanders up the west side of Derwent Water from here to Keswick, with a diversion at Manesty to climb Cat Bells (see above).

At Grange, it's under a mile south to the 1900-ton **Bowder Stone**, a house-sized lump of rock scaled by way of a wooden ladder and worn to a shine on top by thousands of pairs of feet. Controversy surrounds the origin of the rock. Some say it came from the fells above, others contend it was brought by the last Ice Age from Scotland.

Shaded paths through the wood, and the B5289, lead in around a mile to the straggling hamlet of **ROSTHWAITE**, which sustains the most concentrated batch of accommodation in the valley. As well as two or three B&Bs, there are comfortable rooms at the hiker-friendly *Royal Oak Hotel* (☎017687/77214, Ⓦwww.royaloakhotel.co.uk; ❺, with dinner) and the smarter, neighbouring *Scafell Hotel* (☎017687/77208, Ⓦwww.scafell.co.uk; ❺). Tea and scones served in the *Royal Oak*'s firelit sitting room are a treat. For something more substantial, the *Scafell Hotel*'s attached *Riverside Inn* – the only local pub – serves popular bar meals, while the set dinner in either hotel's restaurant is a good deal, too. At the general store – the only one in the valley – you'll be able to put together a basic picnic. A nice **youth hostel**, *Borrowdale Longthwaite* (☎017687/77257, Ⓔborrowdale@yha.org.uk), is a mile south of Rosthwaite, on the riverside footpath to Seatoller; while across the river, on the eastern side of the B5289, is the *Chapel House Farm* **campsite** (☎017687/77602).

Another mile on, **SEATOLLER** and the **Seatoller Barn National Park Information Centre** (Easter–Nov daily 10am–5pm; ☎017687/77294) marks the end of the #79 bus route from Keswick. There are regular events, craft displays, talks and walks based at the information centre; there's also a car park and a few slate-roofed houses clustered around the moderately priced *Yew Tree Restaurant* (☎017687/77634; closed Mon in winter & all Jan), a cosy place fashioned from seventeenth-century cottages. *Seatoller House* (☎017687/77218; ❸, ❺ with dinner; closed Dec–Feb) next door has **rooms,** and there's an informal **campsite** in a small field by the beck along the minor road south to **SEATHWAITE**, twenty minutes' walk away. This is a popular base for walks up the likes of Great Gable and Scafell Pike (see below): the trout farm at the foot of the valley has a fine **café** (Easter–Sept daily 10am–6.30pm), serving fresh grilled trout or sandwiches, and there's another basic **campsite** used extensively by Great Gable climbers.

Scafell, Scafell Pike and Great Gable

In good weather, the minor road to Seathwaite is lined with parked cars by 9am as hikers take to the paths for the rugged climbs up the three major peaks of Scafell, Scafell Pike and Great Gable. Technically, the climbs are not too difficult, though, as always, you should be well-prepared and reasonably fit.

The summit of **Scafell Pike** (3205ft), the highest point in England, is close to the second highest point in the Lakes, **Scafell** (3163ft), and an eight-mile, six-hour, loop walk taking in both leaves Seathwaite via Stockley Bridge to the south, branching up Styhead Ghyll to **Styhead Tarn**. This is as far as many get, and on those all-too-rare glorious summer days the tarn is a fine place for a picnic. A direct, but very steep, approach to **Great Gable** (2949ft) is also possible from Styhead Tarn, though most people cut west at Seathwaite campsite up Sourmilk Ghyll and approach via **Green Gable** (2628ft), also an eight-mile, six-hour return walk. However, the easiest Great Gable climb is actually from Honister Pass.

Honister Pass

Overlooked by the steep Borrowdale Fells, the B5289 cuts west at Seatoller, up and over the dramatic **Honister Pass**. Slate-quarrying was well-established here by the mid-eighteenth century and though full commercial quarrying ceased in 1986 you can't miss the vicious scars of the old workings. To get an idea of what slate-mining entailed in the nineteenth century, you can don a hard hat and lamp to descend the **Honister Slate Mine** (tours daily March–Oct; ☎017687/77230, Ⓦwww.honister-slate-mine.co.uk; £7), at the top of the pass. Bus #77/77A comes this way, making the initial, steep mile-and-a-quarter grind from Borrowdale to the car park at the top of Honister

Pass, by the *Honister Hause* **youth hostel** (☏017687/77267, ✉reservations@ yha.org.uk). Great Gable climbers start from here and follow a path (6 miles; 4hr) past Grey Knotts and Brandreth to Green Gable, before rounding Great Gable and returning along an almost parallel path to the west.

Buttermere, Crummock Water, Lorton Vale and Loweswater

From Honister Pass, the B5289 follows Gatesgarthdale Beck for three miles and makes a dramatic descent into the **Buttermere valley** by *Gatesgarth Farm* **campsite and B&B** (☏017687/70256; no credit cards; ❷), then runs another mile beside the lake – past more camping and rooms at *Dalegarth* (☏017687/70233; ❷; closed Nov–March) – to the **youth hostel** (☏017687 /70245, ✉buttermere@yha.org.uk) just before **BUTTERMERE** village. The village has two hotels: the *Bridge Hotel* (☏017687/70252, ⊛ww.bridge-hotel .com; ❻, ❼ with dinner) and the smaller *Fish Hotel* (☏017687/70253; ❹) – both serve reasonable meals, while the *Bridge* has a popular, traditional flagstoned, bar. There's simple **camping** at *Syke Farm* right by the lake. To get to Buttermere directly from Keswick, take the #77/77A bus.

The village itself – set between the two expanses of Buttermere and neighbouring **Crummock Water** – makes a good walking base, with a particularly easy two-mile hike out along Crummock Water's southwestern edge to the 125ft **Scale Force** falls. The four-mile, **round-lake** stroll circling Buttermere itself shouldn't take more than a couple of hours; you can always detour up Scarth Gap to Haystacks if you want more of a climb and some views. The much longer classic walkers' circuit (8 miles; 6hr 30min) climbs from the village up **Red Pike** and then runs along the ridge, via High Stile, High Crag and Haystacks, before descending Scarth Gap or Warnscale Bottom back to the lake.

The scenery flattens out as the road heads north from Crummock Water and into the pastoral **Lorton vale**, with Cockermouth just a few miles beyond. A minor road south just beyond Brackenthwaite leads directly to minuscule **Loweswater**, one of the less frequented lakes, around which there's a gentle, four-mile (2hr) walk. En route, you'll pass the *Kirkstile Inn* (☏01900/85219, ⊛www.kirkstile.com; ❸), a welcoming sixteenth-century inn with decent bar meals and a set menu (£20) in the restaurant (Thurs–Sat eve only); book ahead for this.

The #77/77A bus leaves Lorton vale just shy of Cockermouth at Lorton, turning east along the B5292 to tackle the **Whinlatter Pass** on the way back to Keswick. It's an easy ascent – no relation to the hardier passes to the south – dominated by the woodland plantations of the **Whinlatter Forest Park**, whose visitor centre (daily: Easter–Sept 10am–5pm; Oct–Easter 11am–4pm; ☏017687/78469, ⊛www.whinlatter.demon.co.uk) has a café, exhibitions, waymarked trails for hikers and cyclists (bike rental available), and a permanent orienteering course.

Wast Water and Eskdale

Great Gable and Scafell stand as a formidable last-gasp boundary between the mountains of the central lakes and the gentler land to the southwest, which smooths out its wrinkles as it descends to the Cumbrian coast. **Wast Water**, which points its slender finger towards the pass between both ranges, remains one of the most isolated of the region's lakes; at its southern end, forested valleys fall away into **Eskdale**, perhaps the prettiest of the unsung Lakeland

A riverside walk from Eskdale

An easy riverside walk (2 miles; 1hr) starts 200 yards east of Dalegarth station down a track to St Catherine's church opposite the road to Boot. In low water you can cross the river below the church by stepping stones; you turn right, then left, up a path beside a stream to Stanley Ghyll Waterfall. Returning along the path beside the stream, a branch on the left leads back to Dalegarth station via a bridge over a swimming hole. If you don't cross the stepping stones, you can take a path following the right bank to Doctor Bridge where you can cross and double back for Stanley Ghyll or continue to the road and the *Woolpack Inn*.

valleys. **Public transport** is very limited; in fact, there's none to Wast Water, which makes it one to savour if you fancy getting right off the beaten track. Eskdale is accessed either by the Ravenglass and Eskdale Railway (see p.858), which drops you right in the heart of superb walking country around the hamlet of Boot; or by the east–west minor road route between the coast, via Eskdale Green, and Little Langdale, just west of Skelwith Bridge.

Wast Water

The awesome sight of the peaks crowding slim, deep **Wast Water**, impresses most visitors who venture to this remote lake. The highest slopes in England frame the northern shores, while on the wild southeastern banks rise the impassable screes which separate the lake from Eskdale to the south. The only road winds from the main coastal A595, through remote settlements, before meeting the lake at its southwestern tip, at the *Wasdale Hall* **youth hostel** (☎019467/26222, ✆wastwater@yha.org.uk), a country house set in its own lakeside grounds – the nearest other hostels are Black Sail (7 miles), Eskdale (10 miles) and Borrowdale (9 miles), all a day's hike away.

The minor road then hugs the shore of the lake, ending four miles away at **Wasdale Head**, a Shangri-la-like clearing between the mountain ranges, where you'll find the marvellous *Wasdale Head Inn* (☎019467/26229, ⊛www.wasdale.com; ❺), one of the most celebrated of all lakeland inns, with legendary breakfasts and hearty four-course dinners. Nearby, there's the National Trust's *Wasdale Head* **campsite** (☎019467/26220; closed Nov–March). Scafell Pike and Great Gable are both popular hiking targets from here, as is the route over the pass into Borrowdale. Hikers can also head south, via Wasdale Head Hall Farm and Burnmoor Tarn, over the fells into Eskdale (5 miles; 3hr).

Eskdale

The attractive rural ride by road or train through **Eskdale** from the west begins to peter out as you approach Dalegarth station (terminus of the Ravenglass and Eskdale Railway), just beyond which nestles the dead-end hamlet of **BOOT**. The few stone houses cowering beneath the fells mark the last remnant of civilization before the road turns serious. Three miles beyond Boot and 800-feet up, the remains of granaries, bath houses and the commandant's quarters for **Hardknott Roman Fort** command a strategic and panoramic position. After negotiating the appalling, narrow switchbacks of **Hardknott Pass**, the road drops to Cockley Beck, before making the equally alarming ascent of **Wrynose Pass**; at the col, the **Three Shire Stone** marks the old boundary of Cumberland, Westmorland and Lancashire. Beyond, it's a seven-mile descent past the foot of the Langdale valley to Ambleside – by the time you reach the *Three Shires* pub in Little Langdale you'll need a stiff drink.

Boot has a fair smattering of **accommodation and services**, which makes it the obvious base for extended walks in the valley, though there are B&Bs and the occasional pub in pretty nearby hamlets such as Eskdale Green and Santon Bridge, back down the valley. The nearest place to Dalegarth station is *Brook House Inn* (℡019467/23288, 🌐www.brookhouseinn.co.uk; ❸), which serves meals in its *Poachers Bar* and has a separate restaurant, too. In Boot itself, the *Burnmoor Inn* (℡019467/23224, 🌐www.burnmoor.co.uk; ❸) is the traditional hikers' choice, with hearty Cumbrian food – there's *glühwein* served in the bar and a peaceful beer garden.

Further up the road past the hamlet it's 500 yards to *Hollins Farm* **campsite** (℡019467/23253) and another three-quarters of a mile to the *Woolpack Inn* (℡019467/23230), which as well as rooms (❸) has a purpose-built bunkhouse (❶). This is also a hikers' favourite, serving filling food, and doubling as a common starting point for the **Woolpack Round** (16 miles; 8–10hr), a tough circuit topping the two highest mountains in England and several others which aren't much lower. It is not easy going and a certain amount of scrambling is required, but the views and the varied terrain make this one of the finest Lakeland walks. Another 400 yards beyond the pub you'll find *Eskdale* **youth hostel** (℡019467/23219, ✉eskdale@yha.org.uk).

Cockermouth

The farming community of **COCKERMOUTH**, midway between the coast and Keswick at the confluence of the Cocker and Derwent rivers, is yet another station on the Wordsworth trail: the **Wordsworth House** on Main St (Easter–June, Sept & Oct Mon–Fri, 10.30am–4.30pm; July & Aug Mon–Sat, 10.30am–4.30pm; £3; NT) is where William and Dorothy were born and spent their first few years. The terracotta-hued eighteenth-century building was nearly replaced by a bus station in the 1930s, but was saved and given to the National Trust who have furnished it with imports from their vaults. Some of the original features remain and there are occasional Wordsworthian relics – a chest of drawers here, a pair of candlesticks there – but despite the best endeavours of the enthusiastic staff it's disappointingly lifeless. The kitchen has been put to good use as a café, but on a warm day the walled garden beside the river is more pleasurable than the house.

Cockermouth tries hard to please, with its tree-lined streets and riverside setting, but after the dramatic fellside approaches from the south and east the town itself falls a little flat. However, there's certainly no shortage of rainy day attractions ranged along Main Street – including museums of printing, toys and models, and motoring – while if you follow your nose, you're likely to stumble upon Jennings Brewery on Brewery Lane near the river. The hour-and-a-half-long **Jenning's Brewery Tour** (July & Aug 4 daily; April–June, Sept & Oct Mon–Sat 2 daily; Nov–Feb Mon–Sat 1 daily; £3.75; booking advisable; ℡01900/821011; 🌐www.jenningsbrewery.co.uk) culminates with a tasting. Check also to see what's on inside **Castlegate House** (March–Dec Mon, Tues, Fri & Sat 10.30am–5pm, Wed 10.30am–7pm; free; 🌐www.castlegatehouse.co.uk), a Georgian mansion on Castlegate, opposite the entrance to Cockermouth Castle – itself a private residence and closed to the public. The house supports a changing programme of contemporary art displays, specializing in the work of some very accomplished local artists.

Finally, you may derive some entertainment from the **Lakeland Sheep and Wool Centre** (Easter to mid-Nov daily 9am–6pm; £3; 🌐www.sheep-woolcentre.co.uk), south of town on the Egremont road, where indoor sheepdog trials, sheep-shearing displays and related exhibits introduce visitors to the complexities of country life. Access to the visitor centre, shop and café is free.

Practicalities

All **buses**, including National Express services, stop on Main Street, from where you follow the signs east to the **tourist office** in the Town Hall, off Market Place (April–June & Oct Mon–Sat 9.30am–4.30pm; July–Sept Mon–Sat 9.30am–5pm, Sun 10am–2pm; Nov–March Mon–Sat 9.30am–4pm; ☎01900/822634). The most convenient **B&B** is the biker- and hiker-friendly *Castlegate Guest House*, 6 Castlegate (☎01900/826749; no credit cards; ❷), which also has a couple of en-suite rooms. The *Trout Hotel* on Crown St (☎01900/823591, ⊛www.trouthotel.co.uk; ❻), by the river, is the top choice, and there are also modern, en-suite rooms available in the *Shepherd's Hotel*, out at the Lakeland Sheep and Wool Centre (☎01900/822673, ⊛www .shepherdshotel.co.uk; ❷). Ten minutes' walk south along Station Road, then Fern Bank brings you to the *Double Mills* **youth hostel** (☎01900/822561) in a seventeenth-century watermill.

All the **pubs** along Main Street compete to sell bar meals at rock-bottom prices, though best choice by far is *The Bitter End* on Kirkgate, a pub housing Cumbria's smallest brewery. Of the **cafés**, the *Norham Coffee House*, 73 Main St (closed Sun), trades on its history – formerly the home of John Christian, grandfather of *Mutiny on the Bounty's* Fletcher Christian – and its courtyard seating. *Beatfords* (closed Sun), further along Main Street in the Lowther Went Shopping Centre, features proper coffee and good home-made dishes. The *Cockatoo*, 16 Market Place (closed Mon, Tues & Sun eve), is a friendly place, with simple lunches and more elaborate dinners – such as steaks or spiced lamb, halibut or mushroom stroganoff. The *Quince & Medlar*, 12 Castlegate (☎01900/823579; dinner only; closed Sun & Mon), meanwhile, serves gourmet vegetarian dishes in a wood-panelled Georgian house. **Market day** in Cockermouth is Monday.

Ullswater

Wordsworth declared **Ullswater** "the happiest combination of beauty and grandeur, which any of the Lakes affords," a judgement that still holds good. At

---

Ullswater walks

While Helvellyn (see p.851) dominates the southwest side of Ullswater, the fells flanking the east side of the lake offer some invigorating hikes, too.

Using the Ullswater Steamer to travel from Glenridding to **Howtown**, the easiest walk back (5 miles; 3hr) follows the shore of Ullswater around Hallin Fell (or over, climbing 263ft) to **Sandwick**, then crosses fields before rejoining the shore at **Long Crag** for the final two miles to the south end of the lake at Patterdale.

A considerably more strenuous route (8 miles; 4–5hr) from Howtown cuts past the *Howtown Hotel* and then heads up lovely **Fusedale**, at the head of which there's a sharp and unrelenting climb up to the **High Street**, a broad-backed ridge that was once a Roman road. Once on top the path is clearly visible for miles, and following the ridge south you meet the highest point, **High Raise** (2632ft) – 2hr from Howtown – where there's a cairn and glorious views. The route then runs south and west, via the stone outcrops of **Satura Crag**, past **Angle Tarn** and finally down to the A592, just shy of Patterdale's pub and post office.

Either of these two walks can be combined with an initial stretch **between Pooley Bridge and Howtown**. The most popular haul (7 miles; 3–4hr) leaves Pooley Bridge pier, heads through the village and follows the road up to **Roehead**. A path then runs up to the **Stone Circle** on the Roman road and down the side of the fell, south of Sharrow Bay, to Howtown pier.

over seven miles long, Ullswater is the second longest lake in Cumbria and much of its appeal derives from its serpentine shape, a result of the complex geology of this area: the glacier that formed the trench in which the lake now lies had to cut across a couple of geological boundaries, from granite in the south, through a band of Skiddaw slate, to softer sandstone and limestone in the north.

The only **public transport to Ullswater** is the #108 bus service (May–Oct) from Penrith, which runs via Pooley Bridge, Gowbarrow and Glenridding to Patterdale. On summer weekends, three daily buses continue south over the Kirkstone Pass to Bowness.

Patterdale and Glenridding

The chief lakeside settlements, Patterdale and Glenridding, are less than a mile apart at the southern tip of Ullswater, each with a smattering of cafés and B&Bs but not otherwise notable except as a base for one of the most popular scrambling routes in the country – up the considerable heights of Helvellyn.

In **GLENRIDDING** the best place to stay is the lakeside *Glenridding Hotel* (☏017684/82228, ⊛www.glenriddinghotel.co.uk; ❻) – complete with indoor pool, bar, restaurant and coffee shop (with internet access) – though there are plenty of cheaper spots, like the *Fairlight Guest House* (☏017684/82397; ❷), by Glenridding's main car park; or *Moss Crag Guest House* (☏017684/82500; ❷; closed Dec), across the beck near the shops, which has its own tearooms. *Gillside Caravan & Camping* (☏017684/82346, ⊛www.gillsidecaravanandcampingsite .co.uk; closed Nov–Feb) is half a mile away up the valley behind the helpful **tourist office** (Easter–Oct daily 9am–6pm; Nov–Easter Fri–Sun 9.30am–3.30pm; ☏017684/82414) in the main car park. Climbers wanting an early start on Helvellyn stay at the *Helvellyn Youth Hostel* (☏017684/82269, ⊜helvellyn@yha.org.uk), a mile and a half up the valley track from Glenridding.

In **PATTERDALE**, the cheapest and most popular bed is at the rustic **youth hostel** (☏017684/82394, ⊜patterdale@yha.org.uk), just south of the hamlet on the A592. This serves good food and has internet access. Patterdale's only **pub**, the *White Lion* (☏017684/82214; ❸), has a few rooms available and serves bar meals. *Side Farm* (☏017684/82337), in the centre (the entrance is across from the church), is open all year for **camping**. The only other service is a small post office/village **shop** opposite the pub.

Around the lake

On busy summer days the A592 up the western side of the lake is packed with traffic, all looking for space in one of the few designated car parks. Busiest is usually that below **Gowbarrow Park**, three miles north of Glenridding, where the A5091 meets the A592; the hillside still blazes green and gold in spring, as it was doing when the Wordsworths visited; it's thought that Dorothy's recollections of the visit in her diary inspired William to write his famous "Daffodils" poem. The car park at Gowbarrow is also the start of an easy, brief walk up to **Aira Force**, a bush-cloaked seventy-foot fall that's spectacular in spate and can be viewed from bridges spanning the top and bottom of the drop. There's a tea room (closed Nov–Easter) at the Aira Force car park.

It's best, if you have time, to get out on the lake itself, traversed by the **Ullswater Steamer** (☏01539/721626, ⊛www.ullswater-steamers.co.uk), which – as well as its round-the-lake cruises (one-hour £5.80, two-hour £7) – has services from Glenridding to Howtown, halfway up the lake's eastern side (Easter–Oct daily; £3.60 one way; 35min), and from Howtown to Pooley

△ Ullswater

Bridge, at the northern end of the lake (Easter–Oct daily; £2.60; 20min). There's a bar on board the steamer.

HOWTOWN is tucked into a little clearing at the foot of beautiful Fusedale, where the *Howtown Hotel* makes a great spot for lunch or a drink in the pocket-sized hikers' bar around the back. A minor road from here hugs the eastern shore of the lake the four miles to **POOLEY BRIDGE**, passing the incomparable *Sharrow Bay* (☎017684/86301, ⊛www.sharrow-bay.com; ❾, with dinner) on the way, one of England's finest hotel-restaurants. Pooley Bridge itself has more basic pleasures. It's a cute retreat – packed to distraction in summer – with a church and three **pubs**, most notably the eighteenth-century *Sun Inn* (☎017684/86205, ⊛www.jenningsbrewery.co.uk; ❸). Over the way, there are also rooms at the alpine-style *Pooley Bridge Inn* (☎017684/86215, ⊛www.pooleybridgeinn.co.uk; ❹), whose balcony rooms (❺) provide a fine vantage point. There is also a summer-only **tourist office** in The Square (daily 10am–5pm; ☎017684/86530).

Climbing Helvellyn

The climb to the summit of **Helvellyn** (3114ft), the most popular of the four 3000ft mountains in Cumbria, is challenging enough for most visitors, who tend to make a day-long circuit from either Glenridding or Patterdale. You are unlikely to be alone or get lost on the yard-wide approaches – on summer weekends and bank holidays the car parks below and paths above are full by 10am – but the variety of routes up and down at least offers a chance of escaping the crowds.

Indeed, if you are hoping to escape the crowds, avoid the most frequently chosen approach via the infamous **Striding Edge**, an alarming, undulating rocky ridge offering the most direct access to the summit. Paths from Ullswater meet at the beginning of Striding Edge: a steep one from Glenridding car park and a slightly less taxing one from the broad-bottomed Grisedale valley (road access just north of Patterdale), half a mile south of Glenridding. With **Red Tarn** – the highest Lake District tarn – a dizzying drop below, purists negotiate the very ridge top of Striding Edge; slightly safer, but no less precipitous tracks follow the line of the ridge, just off the crest. However you get across (and some refuse to go any further when push comes to shove) there's a final, sheer, hands-and-feet scramble to the flat **summit** (2hr 30min from Ullswater). As rockside memorials (and the occasional hovering rescue helicopter) attest, people do get into trouble on Striding Edge: if you're at all nervous of heights you'll find it a challenge to say the least; in poor weather, it's madness even to contemplate it.

The good news is that once you're up the various descents all seem like child's play. The classic return is to the northeast via the less demanding **Swirral Edge**, where a route leads down to Red Tarn, then follows the beck to the disused slate quarry workings and the dramatically sited **Helvellyn youth hostel**, a mile and a half from Glenridding. Another route, of equal duration, climbs back up to **Catstye Cam** and drops down the northern ridge path into Keppel Cove, where you cross the dam and continue to the hostel. Either of these Helvellyn approaches and descents makes for around a seven-mile (5–6hr) walk.

Northwest from the summit, a path (2.5 miles; 1hr 30min) runs down to **Thirlmere reservoir** (a straight up-and-down route which provides the easiest walk to Helvellyn's summit). Bus #555 between Keswick and Grasmere/Ambleside runs along Thirlmere's eastern shore, stopping outside the *King's Head* at Thirlspot.

Most enjoyable of all, though, is the path south from Helvellyn, following the flat ridge past **Nethermost Pike and Dollywagon Pike**. Looking back to Striding Edge as you go reveals its sheer awfulness – on clear days the line of walkers negotiating the edge stands out in silhouette, resembling a Stone Age rollercoaster. After Dollywagon Pike, there's a long scree scramble down to **Grisedale Tarn** and then the gentlest of descents down **Grisedale Valley**, past Ruthwaite Lodge hut, alongside the babbling beck, emerging on the Patterdale–Glenridding road – a good six hours all told for the entire circuit.

The Cumbrian coast

South and west of the national park, the **Cumbrian coast** attracts much less attention than the spectacular scenery inland, but it would be a mistake to write it off. It splits into two distinct sections, the most accessible being the **Furness peninsulas** area, just a few miles from Windermere's Lakeside, where varied attractions include the resort of **Grange-over-Sands**, the monastic priory at **Cartmel**, and market towns such as **Ulverston** and **Broughton-in-Furness**. Parts of this region share nearby Lancashire's industrial heritage and in the ship-building port of **Barrow-in-Furness** it's possible to see a slow revival that's only just starting to pay dividends in terms of tourism – though the dramatic ruins of nearby **Furness Abbey** have been attracting visitors for almost two hundred years.

The **Cumbrian coast** itself is generally judged to begin at **Silecroft** near Millom and stretches for more than sixty miles to the small resort of **Silloth**, on the shores of the Solway Firth. In between lie isolated beaches and the headland of **St Bees** as well as the delights of the **Ravenglass and Eskdale Railway** and the attractive Georgian port of **Whitehaven**.

Grange-over-Sands

Before the coming of the railways, the main route to the Lake District was the "road across the sands" from near Lancaster to **GRANGE-OVER-SANDS**, travellers being led by monks from Cartmel Priory, then from the sixteenth century by a royally appointed guide. The tradition continues today with one guide left, who leads the way around the slip sands and hidden channels which claimed so many lives between the fourteenth and nineteenth centuries. The eight-mile walk takes the best part of a day and departures are usually every other week between May and October; ask at the Grange tourist office for further details.

Having been attracted here by the mild climate (supposedly the warmest in the north of England), and after tramping along the mile-long esplanade with its fine views of the marshy bay, you've just about covered all Grange has got to offer, other than the walk to the top of **Hampsfell** (750ft; 3hr; 4 miles). On a clear day the view from the crinkled limestone summit is spectacular; a well-marked pointer on the roof of a nineteenth-century hospice will help you identify peaks as far away as Skiddaw.

Grange **tourist office** is in Victoria Hall, on Main St (Easter–Oct daily 10am–5pm; Nov–Easter Mon & Fri–Sun 10am–5pm; ☏015395/34026, ⓦwww.grange-over-sands.com), four hundred yards left from the **train station** and National Express stop. Keep walking up Main Street to the top of town to reach Kents Bank Road, which has plenty of **accommodation** lining both sides on the way out of town. *Thornfield House* (☏015395/32512,

@www.thornfieldhouse.co.uk; no credit cards; ❷) and *Methven Hotel* (☎015395 /32031; ❸) are typical of places in their price ranges, offering variously sized en-suite rooms with TV; the tourist office can make other enquiries for you. For something a bit more in keeping with the Victorian surroundings, the *Grange Hotel* (☎015395/33666, @www.grange-hotel.co.uk; ❻), across from the train station at Station Square, sits high among the trees with bay views from its front rooms. The nearest **youth hostel** is a ten-minute train ride away at the smaller resort of Arnside, on Redhills Road (☎01524/761781, @arnside @yha.org.uk).

Cartmel

Sheltered several miles inland from Morecambe Bay, **CARTMEL** grew up around its twelfth-century Augustinian priory and is still dominated by the proud **Church of St Mary and St Michael** (daily: June–Sept 9am–5.30pm; Oct–May 9am–3.30pm; tours Easter–Oct Wed 11am & 2pm; free), the only substantial remnant to survive the Dissolution. A diagonally crowned tower is the most distinctive feature outside, while the light and spacious Norman-transitional interior climaxes at a splendid chancel, illuminated by the 45-foot-high **East Window**. You can spend a good half-hour scanning the immaculate misericords and numerous tombs, chief among them the **Harrington Tomb** in the Town Choir, to the south of the chancel – the weathered figure is that of John Harrington, who rebuilt this section in 1340. The choir went on to act as the parish church when the rest of the building was abandoned following the Reformation, the nave only regaining its cover in the 1620s, thanks to the munificence of local landowner, George Preston. Another patron of the church was one Rowland Briggs who paid for a shelf on a pier near the north door and for a supply of bread to be distributed from it every Sunday in perpetuity "to the most indigent housekeepers of this Parish". Before you leave, peruse the grave stones on the church floor, reminders of men and women swept away by the tide while crossing the sands.

Everything else in the village is modest in scale, centred on the attractive **market square**, beyond the church, with its Elizabethan cobbles, water pump and fish slabs. Refreshment is at hand at any of the village's four pubs, all on, or close to, the square, and you can then walk down to the **racecourse** whose delightful setting by the River Eea deserves a look even if the races (held on the last weekend in May and August) aren't in action. Given Cartmel's rather twee attraction, you'll not be surprised to find a couple of antique shops, though better browsing is done at Peter Bain Smith's **book shop** on the square – with a huge selection of local books and guides – and at the Cartmel Village Shop, known to aficionados for the quality of its sticky toffee pudding.

Practicalities

Trains stop at Cark-in-Cartmel, two miles southwest of the village proper; the #530/#532 **bus** from there or from Grange train station (originating in Kendal) runs to the village. Alternatively, an hour-long walk across the low hills from Grange up Grange Fell Road and across the breast of Hampsfell into the pastoral Eea valley makes a more interesting approach.

The only time you'll need to book **accommodation** well in advance is during race weeks. On Market Square, *Market Cross Cottage* (☎015395/36143; no credit cards; ❸) is a cosy, seventeenth-century B&B with oak-beamed dining room, serving a good breakfast and evening meals. Up a notch, the celebrated *Cavendish Arms* on Cavendish St (☎015395/36240, @www.thecavendisharms .co.uk; ❸, ❹ at weekends), just off the square, is a sixteenth-century inn which retains many of its original features. For a stay in one of its delightful estate cottages, contact *Longlands at Cartmel*, at the base of Hampsfell just a mile north of the village (☎015395/36475, ⓦwww.cartmel.com); guests get free use of a nearby pool, spa and sauna.

The village **pubs** form the basis of the evening's eating and entertainment. The *King's Arms* on the square has outdoor tables and bar meals, with daily chalk-board specials that ring the changes. The *Cavendish*, though, is the real winner, the oldest and most characterful of the pubs, sitting on the site of a monastic guest house and offering good (if pricey) food.

Holker Hall

One of Cumbria's most interesting and well-presented country estates, **Holker Hall** (Easter–Oct Mon–Fri & Sun 10am–6pm; last admission 4.30pm; hall, gardens, grounds & motor museum £7.95; various combination tickets also available; ⓦwww.holker-hall.co.uk) lies just over a mile north of Cark-in-Cartmel station. The vast, sandstone hall, which is made up of a pleasing combination of Victorian, Elizabethan and older styles, overlooks acres of beautifully designed gardens, woods and nature trails. Only the New Wing of the house, rebuilt following a fire in 1871, is open to the public, displaying silk wall coverings, Louis XV furniture and a bedroom where Queen Mary slept in 1937. Its opulent rooms are still in use by the Cavendish family who've owned the hall since the late seventeenth century, but you can wander freely around them. The real showpieces are the cantilevered staircase and the library, which is stocked with more than 3000 leather-bound books, some of whose spines are fakes, constructed to hide electric light switches added later.

The 25-acre **gardens** incorporate a variety of water features, including a limestone cascade and fountain, while next to the house, the **Lakeland Motor Museum** (Easter–Oct Mon–Fri & Sun 10.30am–4.45pm) displays more than a hundred vehicles, from 1880s tricycles and wartime ambulances to funky 1920s bubble cars and 1980s MGs. A special exhibition concentrates on the speed-freak Campbells – Sir Malcolm and son Donald.

There's also an annual **garden and countryside festival** held over three days at the end of May/beginning of June, when the garden's floral displays are at their best, backed by a whole host of craft displays and musical events.

Ulverston and around

The railway line winds westwards from Cartmel to **ULVERSTON**, a close-knit market town, which formerly prospered on the cotton, tanning and iron-ore industries. It's an attractive place, enhanced by its dappled grey limestone cottages and a jumble of cobbled alleys and traditional shops zigzagging off the central **Market Place**. Stalls are still set up here and in the surrounding streets every Thursday and Saturday; on other days (not Wed) the **market hall** on New Market Street is the centre of commercial life.

The first thing you'll notice on the approach to Ulverston is what looks like a lighthouse high on a hill to the north of town. This is the **Hoad Monument**, built in 1850 to honour locally born Sir John Barrow, a former secretary of the admiralty. It's open on summer Sundays and public holidays (if the flag's flying) and the walk to the top grants fine views of the bay and fells. However, Ulverston's most famous son is Stan Laurel (born Arthur Stanley Jefferson), the whimpering, head-scratching half of the comic duo who are celebrated in a mind-boggling collection of memorabilia at the **Laurel and Hardy Museum** up an alley at 4c Upper Brook St (Feb–Dec daily 10am–4.30pm; £2), near Market Place. The copy of Stan's birth certificate (16 June

1890, in Foundry Cottages, Ulverston) lists his father's occupation as "comedian" – young Arthur Stanley could hardly have become anything else. The eccentric showcase of hats, beer bottles, photos, models, puppets, press cuttings and props is mixed with copies of letters from the pair: one from Stan, in retirement in Santa Monica (where he's buried), complains that, since his incapacitating stroke, he can't pursue his favourite sport – shark fishing. There's also a Twenties-style cinema, with almost constant screenings of the duo's films.

Across King Street, in Lower Brook Street, Ulverston's **Heritage Centre** (Mon, Tues & Thurs–Sat 9.30am–4.30pm; £2) is housed in a former eighteenth-century spice warehouse and gives a good overview of the town's history and its various industrial achievements. It's also worth checking to see what's on at the **Lanternhouse**, on The Ellery (exhibitions, when on, Wed–Sat 11am–4pm; free; ⑩ www.welfare-state.org), just off the A590, at the bottom of Market Street and across Tank Square (a traffic roundabout). A group of multimedia artists known as Welfare State International occupy this award-winning conversion of an old school, presenting imaginative exhibitions relating to the "celebratory arts".

The other main attraction is the **Lakes Glass Centre**, at Oubas Hill on the A590, behind Booths supermarket (⑩ www.lakesglasscentre.co.uk), where you can watch the crystal-making process from blowing to painstaking carving (Mon–Sat 9am–5pm; £2); there's also a factory shop on site (Mon–Sat 9am–5.30pm, Sun 10am–4.30pm) and a café.

Practicalities

Ulverston train **station**, serving the Cumbrian coast railway, is only a few minutes' walk from the town centre – head down Prince's Street and turn right at the main road for County Square. **Buses** arrive on nearby Victoria Road from Cartmel, Grange-over-Sands, Barrow, Coniston, Bowness, Windermere and Kendal. The **tourist office** is in Coronation Hall on County Square (Mon–Sat 10am–5pm; ☎01229/587120). The 70-mile **Cumbria Way** long-distance footpath from Ulverston to Carlisle starts from The Gill, at the top of Upper Brook Street – a waymarker spire marks the start. **Bike rental** is from Gill Cycles, on The Gill (☎01229/581116).

Pick of the **B&Bs** is *Dyker Bank*, 2 Springfield Rd, a Georgian house very near the station (☎01229/582423; no credit cards; ❷), while for something a little grander, *Trinity House Hotel*, 200 yards downhill from the station, on the corner of Prince's St and the main A590 (☎01229/588889 ⑩ www.traininghotel .co.uk; ❸, weekend room-only rate ❶), has spacious rooms in a handsome old building – the staff here are all under training for the local hospitality industry, so the prices for rooms and food are very competitive. There's also a great *Walker's Hostel* on Oubas Hill (☎01229/585588; no credit cards; ❶), on the A590 near Canal Head, at the foot of the Hoad Monument: thirty beds in small shared rooms, with vegetarian breakfasts and evening meals available. **Cafés** include the funky *Hot Mango*, 27 King St, while most of the **pubs** serve food, too, best at the *Farmers Arms* in Market Place which has some outdoor tables.

Out of town, drivers can follow the A590 briefly and turn off at the signpost for **Canal Foot**, running through an industrial estate to reach the beautifully sited *Bay Horse* (☎01229/583972, ⑩ www.thebayhorsehotel.co.uk; ❽ with dinner), by the last lock on the Ulverston canal. You can also walk here in around half an hour from the town centre, along the canal. The cooking here is celebrated far and wide and even if you can't run to lunch or dinner in the waterside conservatory, you can have a beer, coffee, soup or sandwich at one of the outdoor tables.

Bardsea and Conishead Priory

To the south of Ulverston, the Barrow peninsula slopes down to its sandy east and west coasts from a raised backbone dotted with villages and scattered with cairns and ancient fort sites. The village of **BARDSEA**, overlooking the coast from a modest hillside two miles south of Ulverston, is an ideal base for short jaunts to the pebbly beach at **Wadhead Scar**, or uphill to **Birkrigg Common** (436ft). From this grassy parkland cut through by limestone outcrops, the views north include a ripple of fells and many of Cumbria's higher peaks, while to the east you can watch the shallow waters lapping over Morecambe sands. The common boasts two stone circles, one of which is easy to spot – a neat cluster of lichen-clad rocks brushed by high grasses that's been standing for over two thousand years. In the village, the *Bradylls Arms* has a suntrap beer-garden and conservatory restaurant, while down on the road by the beach the *Old Mill* (closed Mon & Tues) serves drinks, teas and meals.

Half a mile north of Bardsea, the high turrets of **Conishead Priory**, an extravagant Gothic mansion, push through a canopy of woodland. More like a palace than a religious retreat, it was built over the remains of an Augustinian priory destroyed during the Dissolution, and now houses a Buddhist institute ringed by prayer flags. Most visitors come for meditation courses, but guided tours (Easter–July, Sept & Oct Sat & Sun 2–5pm; £2) of the ornate halls and cloisters are also available, and there are free tours on Saturdays (Easter–Sept 2–5pm) of the Buddhist temple in the grounds, which incorporates the largest bronze Buddha statue in Europe.

Barrow-in-Furness

With shipyard cranes piercing the skyline, **BARROW-IN-FURNESS** has a distinctly industrial feel that's been the town's hallmark since it grew up around a booming iron industry in the mid-nineteenth century. Steelworks and shipbuilding followed, making Barrow one of England's busiest ports, and the town still makes a handsome living from orders for military hardware. Yet even Barrow's most enthusiastic supporters could hardly claim the town as attractive: recession in the 1980s emptied many of the proud Victorian buildings and left the centre rough at the edges. However, there's been a significant amount of town-centre regeneration in recent years, while some of the older buildings still retain the capacity to surprise – the splendid sandstone Gothic Town Hall for one.

For visitors, the best move is straight to the **Dock Museum** (Easter–Oct Tues–Fri 10am–5pm, Sat & Sun 11am–5pm; Nov–Easter Wed–Fri 10.30am–4pm, Sat & Sun 11am–4.30pm; last admission 45min before closing; free; ⓦwww.dockmuseum.org.uk), on North Road, half a mile from the centre; it's signposted from all over town. Located in the dried-out graving dock where ships were once repaired, the museum tells the history of Barrow – which is also the history of modern shipbuilding. The creation of the Furness railway in 1846 to carry iron ore to the coast led to Barrow's growth from a village of less than two hundred people to a thriving port within 25 years. Steel-making and shipbuilding went hand in hand, and boomed between the wars. Later, as the steelworks declined (the last one finally closed in 1983) and the Cold War intensified, the emphasis shifted to submarine building. Today, VSEL – the privatized successor to the historic firm of Vickers – builds nuclear subs in the town's Devonshire Dock Hall. Even if the history leaves you cold, the museum exhibits (on the shipbuilding process, local railways, iron- and steel-making) are well-presented.

Few lake-bound tourists stay the night, though Barrow's **tourist office**, located in the theatre-arts centre, Forum 28, on Duke Street, opposite the town hall (Mon–Wed & Fri 9.30am–5pm, Thurs 10.30am–5pm, Sat 10–4pm; ☎01229/894784), can help with accommodation if necessary. You can also get information here on visiting the nearby nature reserves on **Walney Island**, a six-mile strip of land accessed from Barrow's Jubilee Bridge.

Furness Abbey

Furness Abbey (April–Sept daily 10am–6pm; Oct daily 10am–5pm; Nov–March Wed–Sun 10am–4pm; £2.70; EH), a set of roofless sandstone arcades and pillars hidden in a wooded vale – the so-called "Valley of Deadly Nightshade" – lies a mile and a half out of Barrow on the Ulverston road (local buses to Dalton-in-Furness and Ulverston pass close by). Now one of Cumbria's finest ruins, it was once the most powerful abbey in the northwest, possessing much of southern Cumbria as well as land in Ireland and the Isle of Man. Founded in 1124, the abbey's industry was remarkably diverse – it owned sheep on the local fells, controlled fishing rights, produced grain and leather, smelted iron, dug peat for fuel and manufactured salt. By the fourteenth century it had become such a prize that the Scots raided it twice, though it survived until April 1536, when Henry VIII chose it to be the first of the large abbeys to be dissolved; the Abbot and 29 of his monks, who had hitherto resisted (and indeed, had encouraged the locals to resist Dissolution – a treasonable offence), were pensioned off for the sum of two pounds each.

The abbey has been a popular tourist diversion since the early nineteenth century, when a train station was built to bring in visitors, among them Wordsworth who was very taken with the "mouldering pile". Borrow a portable tape-player from the reception desk to get the best out of the site since there are no maps or explanatory signs. The transepts stand virtually at their original height, while the massive slabs of stone-ribbed vaulting, richly embellished arcades and intricately carved *sedilia* in the presbytery are the equal of any of Yorkshire's far busier abbey ruins. A small museum houses some of the best carvings, including rare examples of effigies of armed knights with closed helmets and – as medieval custom dictated – crossed legs. Only seven others have ever been found intact. The *Abbey Tavern* at the entrance serves drinks at tables scattered about some of the ruined outbuildings.

Piel Castle

The attacks by the Scots goaded Furness Abbey into protecting itself with **Piel Castle** on **Piel Island**, guarding the approaches south of the town. This is reached from Roa Island, three miles southeast of Barrow down the A5087 (bus #11; not Sun); turn off at Rampside (signposted "Lifeboat station"). At **ROA**, which has a pub and a small café, you can debate the prospects of the weather- and tide-dependent **ferry** (Easter–Sept Mon–Fri 11.15am–5.15pm, Sat & Sun 11.15am–6.15pm; Oct–Easter on request; £1.50 each way; ☎01229/835809) across to Piel Island. Apart from the ruins of a massive keep and the new lifeboat station, it is the island's only commercial building, the *Ship Inn*, which draws people over here. This serves bar meals and allows camping.

Dalton and Broughton-in-Furness

North of Barrow, the A590 runs the four miles to the straggling town of **DALTON-IN-FURNESS**, old enough to have been mentioned in the Domesday Book but retaining little of interest today save the surviving fourteenth-century keep of **Dalton Castle** (Easter–Sept 2–5pm; free) at the top of the old market square. If you've stopped for this, you may as well walk past the keep to the churchyard of **St Mary's**, where the eighteenth-century artist George Romney is buried. Fairly regular buses run up to Dalton from Barrow (and on to Ulverston).

Whatever you feel about zoos, you're likely to be positively surprised by the **South Lakes Animal Park** (daily: Easter–Sept 10am–6pm; Oct–Easter 10am–dusk; £7, £3.50 Nov–Feb; ⊕www.wildanimalpark.co.uk), half a mile or so outside Dalton. Bus #D1 runs directly here from Dalton train station between Easter and September. An award-winning "conservation" zoo, it relies on ditches and trenches (not cages) for the most part to contain its animals and is split into separate habitat areas, ranging from the Australian bush to a tropical rainforest. It's quite something to encounter free-roaming kangaroos in rural Cumbria. Call for feeding times to see the park at its best – the tiger-feeding (encouraging them to climb and jump for their meal) is unique in Europe.

Beyond Dalton, it's ten miles up the A595 to the small market town of **BROUGHTON-IN-FURNESS** which, unlike its near namesake, has retained much of its Georgian beauty. Tall houses surround a charming square, complete with obelisk, stone fish slabs and stocks. From the square, follow Church Street to the edge of town and you'll reach **St Mary Magdalene**, originally twelfth-century, though much restored in the nineteenth century.

Nestling in the Duddon Valley, the town makes a handy local walking or touring base (Coniston is only eight miles away) and the **tourist office** in the old Town Hall on the square (Easter–Oct Mon–Fri 10am–4pm, Sat 9am–4pm, Sun 9am–1pm; ☏01229/716115) can help with **accommodation**. There's B&B at the *Square Café* (☏01229/716388, ⊕www.thesquarecafe.co.uk; no credit cards; ❷) on the square, which also has a pleasant tearooms. Or there are **pub** rooms at the *Manor Arms*, The Square (☏01229/716286; ❷), where you can have breakfast served in your room. *Beswick's*, also on the square, at the corner of Griffin St (☏01229/716285; eve only), is a bistro with good food and a fine wine list.

Along the coast to St Bees

Road (A595) and rail routes follow the **Cumbrian coast** from Broughton-in-Furness to St Bees, with diversions to a series of small villages and lengthy beaches that, for the most part, live a quiet existence outside the short summer season. The first decent stretch of sand is at **Silecroft**, a few miles northwest of Millom; the Cumbria Coastal Way runs along the back of the beach and there's a train station back in Silecroft village. However, it's **Ravenglass** that's the principal stop before the headland of St Bees – a sleepy little estuary village overshadowed by the nearby nuclear reprocessing plant, **Sellafield**.

Ravenglass and the Ravenglass and Eskdale Railway

The single main street of **RAVENGLASS**, fifteen miles or so up the coast, preserves a row of characterful nineteenth-century cottages, facing out across the mud flats and dunes. Despite appearances, the village dates back to the arrival of the Romans who established a supply post here in the first century AD for the northern legions manning Hadrian's Wall. Look for the sign to the "Roman Bath House", just past the station: 500 yards up a single-track lane lie the fairly extensive remains of a fort which survived in Ravenglass until the fourth century.

Ravenglass station is the starting point for the **Ravenglass & Eskdale Railway** (Easter week & June–Aug daily; rest of year Sat & Sun; £7 return;

T01229/717171, Wwww.ravenglass-railway.co.uk), known affectionately as La'al Ratty. Opened in 1875 to carry ore from the Eskdale mines to the coastal railway, the tiny train, running on a 15-inch gauge track, takes forty minutes to wind its way through seven miles of forests and fields between the fell sides of the Eskdale Valley to Dalegarth station. The stations on the line are popular starting points for walks on and up into the central lakeland peaks, and consequently the railway makes for a fine approach to Eskdale itself (see p.846). The earliest stop is at **Muncaster Mill**, a restored eighteenth-century mill where the machinery turns every day, milling organic flour which then ends up in breads and cakes in the teashop. From the mill there's a path south through the woods to **Muncaster Castle** (£6.50; Wwww.muncastercastle.co.uk), built around a medieval tower and which now hosts a variety of attractions and is well worth the entry fee if you make a day of it. Apart from the rooms of the castle (Mon–Fri & Sun noon–5pm) itself there are also spectacular gardens, an owl centre and meadowvole maze (daily 10.30am–6pm, dusk in winter), where you'll learn about the Muncaster voles, follow the hiking trails, and see the kestrel displays or the wild herons feeding.

Sellafield

The main blot on the Cumbrian coast looms large after Ravenglass, namely British Nuclear Fuels' (BNFL) **Sellafield** nuclear reprocessing plant, sited midway between Ravenglass and Whitehaven. It's a significant local employer – thousands of jobs currently depend on BNFL's presence in Cumbria – which enjoys high-level bipartisan political support, and as nuclear power supplies something like thirty percent of the country's electricity needs, BNFL clearly is proud of its technical expertise. This much, at least, you'll glean from the multi-million-pound **Sellafield Visitors' Centre** (under renovation at time of writing; Wwww.bnfl.com), a popular public-relations exercise where you'll learn all about the safe recycling of nuclear fuel and how radiation is part of everyday life. What you're less likely to come away with is a balanced view of the entire process, or indeed any knowledge of why reprocessing was deemed necessary in the first place – it's still the only way to produce the plutonium needed for nuclear weapons, while depleted uranium is widely used in otherwise conventional anti-tank weapons and missiles. Critics question the entire reprocessing system at Sellafield and elsewhere, pointing to the lethal maritime and atmospheric discharges (virtually all European radiocative pollution comes from reprocessing) and the manifest dangers of waste transportation. Not that the only current alternative – underground or undersea dumping – is any more attractive, certainly not for Cumbria which already has a low-level nuclear waste dump near Sellafield and may host another now that the British government has decided to reconsider long-term undergound dumping.

The visitor centre is tricky to reach without your own **transport**: the best you can do is get off the train at Sellafield station and walk the few minutes up to the main gate, to where a bus will be sent to pick you up.

St Bees

The close-knit central streets in the coastal village of **ST BEES** give it the feel of a retirement colony. It's a suitably elderly settlement, with a nunnery established here as early as the seventh century, succeeded by **St Bees Priory**, just north of today's train station, in the twelfth century. This was slightly damaged in the Dissolution, but retains huge Norman arches above its entrance porch; it also houses a small exhibition of Celtic crosses and headstones in the nave. The long sands lie a few hundred yards west of the village, while the steep, sandstone cliffs of **St Bees Head** to the north are good for windy walks and bird-watching. The headland's lighthouse marks the start of Wainwright's 190-mile **Coast-to-Coast Walk** to Robin Hood's Bay (see p.983).

St Bees is on the Cumbrian coast train line and lies just five miles south of Whitehaven, from where there's a regular bus service. **Accommodation** needs advance reservations in high season, though at other times of the year there should be no problem finding somewhere to stay. *Tomlin Guest House*, out of the centre on Beach Rd (℡01946/822284; no credit cards; ❶), is a good first choice; the *Queen's Hotel*, Main St (℡01946/822287; ❸), is a nice old pub with a beer garden.

Whitehaven

Some fine Georgian houses mark out the centre of **WHITEHAVEN**, one of the few grid-planned towns in England. The economic expansion that forced this planning was as much due to the booming slave trade as to the more widely recognized coal traffic. Whitehaven spent a brief period during the eighteenth century as Britain's third busiest port (after London and Bristol), making it a prime target for an abortive raid led by Scottish-born American lieutenant **John Paul Jones**. Disgusted with the slave trade he witnessed while ship's mate in America, Jones returned to the port of his apprenticeship to rebel, but, let down by a drunk and potentially mutinous crew, he damaged only one of the two hundred boats in dock and his mini-crusade fell flat. All this and more is explained in **The Beacon** (Easter–Oct Tues–Sun 10am–5.30pm; Nov–Easter 10am–4.30pm; £4), an enterprising heritage centre on the harbour. Resembling a squat lighthouse, and with an interactive Met Office weather gallery on the top floor, The Beacon entertainingly covers the town history, from slaving to smuggling, with a special emphasis on the local characters who have shaped the town. The **harbour** itself sits at the heart of a renaissance project which has spruced up the quayside and provided new promenades, sculptures and heritage trails. The Crow's Nest, a forty-metre-high tower, lit at night, is the dramatic centrepiece of the marina. The whole waterfront comes alive during the annual **maritime festival** (every June).

For all the changes round the harbour, it's Whitehaven's Georgian streets and neatly painted houses that make up one of Cumbria's most distinguished towns. There's a **market** held here every Thursday and Saturday, which adds a bit of colour. Otherwise, stroll up Lowther Street to the **Rum Story** (daily: April–Sept 10am–5pm; Oct–March 10am–4pm; £4.50; ⓦwww.rumstory .co.uk), housed in the eighteenth-century shop, courtyard and warehouses of the Jefferson's rum family. This is another place you could easily spend an hour or so, discovering Whitehaven's links with the Caribbean and learning all about rum, the Navy, temperance and the hideousness of the slaves' Middle Passage, amongst other matters. Across Lowther Street is the seventeenth-century church of **St Nicholas**, where all that stands is its tower (containing a café). The rest succumbed to a fire in 1971, but there's a lovely garden now surrounding the former nave. Also on Lowther Street, don't miss Michael Moon's second-hand **book shop** at no. 19 (closed Sun), a bookworm's treasure trove.

On the cliffs above Whitehaven, get to grips with the industry which set the town on its way at the **Haig Colliery Mining Museum**, Solway Road, Kells (Mon & Tues–Sun 11am–5pm; free; ⓦwww.haigpit.com). This was Cumbria's last deep-coal mine (closed in 1986), and you can view the restored winding engines and learn about the dreadful living and working conditions that, in part at least, funded the elegant Georgian town below. A walking tour (ask at the museum; £3) shows visitors the ruins of the early eighteenth-century Saltom Pit, the world's first undersea pit.

Practicalities

Trains follow the coastal route south to Barrow and north via Maryport to Carlisle. From the station you can walk around the harbour to The Beacon in less than ten minutes; the **bus station** is just across Tesco's car park from the train station. The helpful **tourist office** is in the Market Hall on Market Place (Easter–Oct Mon–Sat 9.30am–5pm, Sun 10am–4pm; Nov–Easter Mon–Sat 10am–4.30pm; ☎01946/852939, ⊛www.copelandbc.gov.uk), just back from the harbour.

For **accommodation**, the best central B&B is the very comfortable *Corcickle Guest House*, 1 Corcickle (☎01946/692073; no credit cards; ➋), five minutes' walk from the centre – keep on up Lowther Street, past Safeway and McDonald's to find the row of Georgian townhouses. Otherwise, the *Georgian House Hotel*, 9–11 Church St (☎01946/65270; ➋), has a few en-suite rooms available in the town centre. North of town at Moresby, *Moresby Hall* (☎01946 /696317; ➌) provides B&B in an attractive listed building with walled gardens.

For **meals**, the *Courtyard Café* in the *Rum Story* serves wraps, sandwiches, baked potatoes and snacks under a glass roof. The *Espresso*, 22 Market Place (closed Sun), and the *Westminster Café*, 65 Lowther St (closed Sun), are your best bets for something a bit more modish during the day. In the evening, the bistro at the *Georgian House Hotel* (closed Mon) serves pasta and pizza, while locals like the *Peking Palace* on Duke Street (closed Sun lunch). You can get a decent pint in the *John Paul Jones Tavern*, also on Duke Street, a modern pub which delivers a nod to the father of the American Navy by modelling its interior on that of a sailing ship.

Maryport to Silloth

North of Whitehaven it's undistinguished country for the most part, at least until you're past Workington. **MARYPORT**, fifteen miles from Whitehaven, makes the first bid for your attention, with views of the Solway Firth and the Scottish hills across the water and a history going back to Roman times. That's taken care of in the excellent **Senhouse Roman Museum** (July–Oct daily 10am–5pm; April–June Tues & Thurs–Sun 10am–5pm; Nov–March Fri–Sun 10.30am–4pm; £2), high on a hill above the harbour, ten minutes' walk from the centre of town. It's a fascinating exhibition, based around the largest collection of Roman altars found at a single site in Britain, whose inscriptions and carvings shed much light on the fort and settlement of Roman Aluana. Recent surveys have shown the Roman town here to be considerably larger than originally thought, with a civilian population of several hundred. A wooden watchtower provides views over the site and along the coastline below, from where it's thought that Roman freighters unloaded supplies for the fort. The town's modern history dates from its eighteenth-century heyday as an industrial port – named after the wife, Mary, of local lord and entrepreneur Humphrey Senhouse. The best part of Maryport is still its harbour and marina, now smartly landscaped and featuring the **Lake District Coast Aquarium** (daily: March–Oct 10am–5pm; Nov–Feb 11am–4pm; £4.25; ⊛www.lakedistrict-coastaquarium.co.uk), on the South Quay, with its underwater Cumbrian world and fish-feeding sessions. The streets behind the harbour are slowly reviving, but still show evidence of Maryport's long decline since the Great Depression of the 1930s: local coal-mining reduced drastically in the 1950s, the port closed for business in the 1960s and was then silted up for the best part of twenty years until the recent regeneration. For a glimpse of better days, walk uphill to **Fleming Square** (on the way to the Roman museum), whose surviving cobbles are still surrounded by Georgian houses. It's also pleasant to stroll out along the promenade and get down on the beach when the tide's out.

Maryport is on the Cumbrian coast rail line, and there's a regular bus service out here from Cockermouth (not Sun) and Carlisle. It's a ten-minute walk from the **train station** to the harbour, down the main Senhouse Street, at the bottom of which is the **tourist office** (Mon–Thurs 10am–5pm, Fri–Sun 10am–1pm & 2–5pm; ℡01900/813738); it shares the premises, an old inn, with the town's small maritime and local-history museum. There's a **B&B**, the *Harbourside Guest House* on North Quay (℡01900/815137; no credit cards; ❷), across from the aquarium, while for a cup of frothy coffee – and maybe a go on the computer – there's the *Port of Call* **café** on Senhouse Street. The *Harbour Restaurant and Lifeboat Inn*, just behind the tourist office, specializes in seafood.

North to Silloth

Five miles further up the coast, the B5300 road runs right through **ALLONBY**, a former weaving village with a long shingle and sand beach, and the *Ship Inn*, where Dickens once slept. Both beach and road continue north as far as **SILLOTH-ON-SOLWAY**, another eight miles away and the Solway Firth's nicest spot, though its pleasures are all modest – a Victorian resort with wide cobbled streets, a large seafront green and promenade, and wildlife-rich local salt marshes and dunes. The name, incidentally, is a corruption of the "sealathes", or seaside grain silos, established by Cistercian monks who farmed the area in medieval times. For more on the history, visit the **Solway Coast Heritage Centre** on Liddell Street (April–Sept daily 10am–5pm; Oct–March Mon–Sat 10am–5pm, Sun noon–4pm; £2.50).

Buses run to the town from Maryport and from Carlisle, just 21 miles away (not Sun). There's a **tourist office** at 10 Criffel St, by the green (May–Sept Mon–Sat 10am–4.30pm, Sun 2–4.30pm; Oct–April Mon–Thurs 11am–3pm, Fri–Sun noon–3.30pm; ℡016973/31944, ⓦwww.silloth-on-solway.co.uk), where you can debate the possibility of a room and pick up a leaflet on local walks.

East Cumbria: the Eden Valley and Penrith

The Lake District might end abruptly with the market town and transport hub of **Penrith**, ten miles northeast of Ullswater, but Cumbria doesn't. To the east, the **Eden Valley** splits the Pennines from the Lake District fells, and boasts a succession of hardy market towns, prime among which is the former county town of **Appleby-in-Westmorland**. This lies on the magnificent **Settle to Carlisle railway**, connecting Cumbria with the Yorkshire Dales (see p.911). The other great local feat of engineering – the M6, following the main London–Penrith–Glasgow rail line – misses the best of the valley, yet remains one of the most attractive sections of motorway in the country. Northeast of Penrith, the A686 leads you imperceptibly from Cumbria into Teesdale, via the high town of **Alston**, providing a superb if lonely approach to Hexham and Hadrian's Wall.

Penrith

Once a thriving market town on the main north–south trading route, **PEN-RITH** today suffers from undue comparisons with the improbably pretty settlements of the nearby Lakes. The brisk streets, filled with no-nonsense shops and shoppers, have more in common with the towns of the North Pennines than the stone villages of south Cumbria, and even the local building materials emphasize the geographic shift. Its deep-red buildings were erected from the same rust-red sandstone used to construct **Penrith Castle** (daily: June–Sept 8am–9pm; Oct–May 8am–4.30pm; free) in the fourteenth century, as a bastion against raids from the north; it's now a crumbling ruin, opposite the train station. The town is at its best in the narrow streets, arcades and alleys off **Market Square**, and around St Andrew's churchyard, while if you call into the tourist office on Middlegate, you'll find it shares its seventeenth-century school-house premises with a small local **museum** (Easter, April, Sept & Oct Mon–Sat 9.30am–5pm, Sun 1–4.45pm; May–Aug Mon–Sat 9.30am–6pm, Sun 1–5.45pm; Nov–March Mon–Sat 9.30am–5pm; free).

Trains from Manchester, London, Glasgow and Edinburgh pull into Penrith station, five minutes' walk south of Market Square and Middlegate. The **bus station** is on Albert Street, behind Middlegate, and has regular services to Patterdale, Keswick, Cockermouth, Carlisle and Alston. The **tourist office** on Middlegate (Easter–April, Sept & Oct Mon–Sat 9.30am–5pm, Sun 1–4.45pm; May–Aug Mon–Sat 9.30am–6pm, Sun 1–5.45pm; Nov–March Mon–Sat 9.30am–5pm; ☎01768/867466, ⓦwww.visiteden.co.uk) can help you find **accommodation**. The bulk of the B&Bs line Victoria Road, the continuation of King Street running south from Market Square: *Victoria Guest House*, at no. 3 (☎01768/863823, ⓦwww.vicguesthouse.co.uk; no credit cards; ❷), and *Blue Swallow*, at no. 11 (☎01768/866335, ⓦwww.blueswallow.co.uk; no credit cards; ❶), are the two most convenient choices. The *George Hotel*, on Devonshire Street by Market Square (☎01768/862696, ⓦwww.georgehotelpenrith .co.uk; ❹), is a central old coaching inn with attractive prices, cosy wood-panelled lounges and a decent bar. For **food**, the fantastically stocked J. & J. Graham's deli-grocery in Market Square can't be beaten. Otherwise, there's tapas at *Costa's*, 9 Queen St, or elegant dining at *Passepartout*, 51 Castlegate (☎01768/865852; eve only; closed Mon).

Around Penrith

Several attractions lie close to town, the nearest being **Brougham Castle** (April–Sept daily 10am–6pm; Oct daily 10am–5pm; £2.10; EH), a mile and a half south of Penrith by the River Eamont. Passed down through the influential Clifford family to Lady Anne, the castle overlaps the site of a Roman fort and contains a collection of tombstones commemorating Britons who adopted Roman customs and the Latin language. Slightly further out, three miles southwest of town, reached from either the A66 or A592, is **Dalemain** (Easter–Sept Mon–Thurs & Sun 10.30am–5pm; £5; gardens only £3; ⓦwww.dalemain.com). This country house, set in ample grounds, started life in the twelfth century as a fortified tower, but has subsequently been added to by every generation, culminating with a Georgian facade grafted onto a largely Elizabethan house. There's the usual run of imposing public rooms, while the medieval courtyard and Elizabethan great barn doubled as the grim schoolroom and dormitory of Lowood School in the TV adaptation of Charlotte Brontë's *Jane Eyre*.

However, top local attraction is undoubtedly **Rheged** (daily 10am–5.30pm;

Ⓦwww.rheged.com; free) at Redhills on the A66, a couple of minutes' drive from the M6 (junction 40); bus #X4/X5 between Penrith and Keswick stops outside. Billed as Britain's largest earth-covered building, it takes its name from the ancient kingdom of Cumbria and features a spacious atrium-lit underground visitor centre which fills you in on the region's culture and history by way of exhibitions, local art and craft displays and family activities. There's also a giant-format cinema screen showing *Rheged: The Movie*, documenting a Cumbrian journey through time (£4.95); as well as the separate **National Mountaineering Exhibition** (same times; £4.50, joint ticket with movie £7.80; Ⓦwww.mountain-exhibition.co.uk), presenting an entertaining history of mountain-climbers and climbing, from the Lake District to Everest. The large-format *Everest* movie (£4.95) also plays here several times daily; buy your ticket on arrival to be sure of a viewing.

Appleby-in-Westmorland

One-time county town of Westmorland, **APPLEBY-IN-WESTMOR-LAND** is protected on three sides by a loop in the River Eden. The fourth was defended by the now privately owned **Appleby Castle** (currently closed to the public), whose Norman keep was restored by Lady Anne Clifford, who, after her father's death in 1605, spent 45 years trying to claim her rightful inheritance. Lady Anne also founded the **almshouses** on Boroughgate, the town's backbone, which runs from High Cross, former site of the cheese market outside the castle, to Low Cross, previously a butter market but now site of the general Saturday market. **St Lawrence's Church**, at Low Cross, holds the tombs of Lady Anne Clifford and her mother.

The town is usually peaceful, but changes its character completely in June when the **Appleby Horse Fair** takes over nearby Gallows' Hill, as it has done since 1750. Britain's most important gypsy gathering, it draws hundreds of chrome-plated caravans and more traditional horse-drawn "bow-tops", as well as the vehicles of tinkers, New-Age travellers and sightseers. Historically, the main day of the fair was the second Wednesday of June (the official day for horse trading), but today most of the action (including road racing, hair-raising stunts and fortune-telling) and trading takes place between the previous Sunday and the Tuesday, culminating on the Tuesday evening with trotting races at Holme Farm field. The whole week gets the full support of the local council but only some of the residents, many complaining about the disruption and the boisterous revelry.

Practicalities

The **Settle to Carlisle railway** is the best way to get to Appleby, although **bus services** from Penrith are frequent enough. The **tourist office**, in the Moot Hall on Boroughgate (April–Oct Mon–Sat 9.30am–5pm, Sun noon–4pm; Oct–March Mon–Thurs 10am–noon, Fri & Sat 10am–3pm; ☎017683/51177), is ten minutes' walk from the station.

During the horse fair, **accommodation** is scarce; if you're planning to visit at this time, book well in advance. There's a clutch of places on Bongate, five hundred yards from town, over the bridge from Low Cross, then south along the B6260: *Old Hall Farm* (☎017683/51773; no credit cards; ❶), signposted off the road, is a very friendly place, while the *Royal Oak* on Bongate (☎017683 /51463, Ⓦwww.mortal-man-inns.co.uk; ❺) has some comfortable rooms in an aged inn. The top hotel in town is the *Tufton Arms Hotel* on Market Square (☎017683/51593, Ⓦwww.tuftonarmshotel.co.uk; ❻). The closest **campsite** is the *Wild Rose* (with swimming pool) three miles south at Ormside (℡017683/51077); a similar distance to the north, the quiet hamlet of Dufton has the nearest **youth hostel** (℡017683/51236).

There is no shortage of **places to eat** and the old pubs tend to be the most atmospheric places: the *Tufton Arms Hotel* dishes up generous bar meals and the *Royal Oak* is renowned for its Cumberland sausages; the *Tufton Arms* also has a restaurant, serving such delights as grilled goats' cheese and fresh fish. Otherwise *Lady Anne's Pantry*, 9 Bridge St (closed Sun in winter), is a good café, and there's tea and cakes too in the Courtyard Gallery, an arts and crafts store at 32 Boroughgate. The *Stag Inn* at Dufton (where the hostel is) is an enjoyable country inn with a beer garden, and it's worth the five-mile drive south to Sandford to the *Sandford Arms* for its excellent bar meals and more formal restaurant.

Northeast: the route to Alston

The main routes north from Penrith are the M6 and the rail line to Carlisle, but if you're heading for Hadrian's Wall the A686 provides an alternative transmoor route, via Alston. Various bus services follow the route, many passing through Alston from Penrith, with onward services to Teesdale, Durham and Newcastle.

Having your own transport gives you the opportunity to make a couple of detours along the way, with the first diversion to the prehistoric stone circle known as **Long Meg and her Daughters**. Standing outside a ring of stones nearly four hundred feet in diameter, Long Meg is the tallest stone at 18ft and has a profile like the face of an austere old lady. The stone family, said by some to be a coven of witches turned to stone by a magician, is just outside Little Salkeld, off the A686, six miles north of Penrith and just over a mile's walk from Langwathby on the Settle to Carlisle railway.

Back on the main road, at **MELMERBY**, make a point of stopping at the Village Bakery (daily until 5pm), whose proprietor's enthusiam for his wood-fired brick oven has sparked interest in such matters in some of the most fashionable restaurants in the country. Wonderful breakfasts, lunches and teas are served.

Having covered an initial stretch of smooth vales and aromatic pine woods, the road then winds steeply up the bracken-strewn slopes of **Hartside Top**. This 1900-feet-high bulk marks the western edge of the Pennines and has a welcome café at its summit (open daily in summer).

Alston

Seven miles beyond Hartside Top, **ALSTON** commands the head of the South Tyne Valley. It no longer has a market to back up its claim to being the highest market-town in England but still has its market cross, beside the cobbled curve of the steep main street, which is lined with charming tearooms and cosy pubs. Alston's **parish church** of **St Augustine**, on the main street, is of some interest for the history of the **Derwentwater Clock** inside. It belonged to the local landowner and Jacobite rebel James Radcliffe who was beheaded for treason in 1716, followed 48 years later by his brother Charles Radcliffe – the last traitor to be decapitated – after which his heirs bequeathed the clock to the church. The town's Congregational Church, on The Butts, near the parish church, is now **Gossipgate Gallery** (Easter–Oct daily 10am–5pm; Nov, Dec & mid-Feb to Easter Sat & Sun 10.30am–4.30pm; ⓦwww.gossipgate.com) specializing in local arts and crafts; there's a nice coffee shop inside.

The town's also of note for the narrow-gauge **South Tynedale Railway** (Easter week, July & Aug daily; rest of year Sat & Sun only; £3.75 return, day-ticket £7.50; ☎01434/382828, ⓦwww.strps.org.uk) whose steam engines start from a station downhill from the church then follow the route of an old coal-carrying branch of the Carlisle to Newcastle line. The line runs a mile and a half north to Gilderdale, with an extension for a similar distance on to Kirkhough on the Pennine Way, a handy starting point for the twelve-mile walk north to Greenhead on Hadrian's Wall (45min round-trip from Alston).

Leaflets on local walks are doled out at the **tourist office** inside the station (Easter–Oct Mon–Sat 10am–5pm, Sun 10am–4pm; Nov–Easter Mon & Wed–Sat 11am–2.30pm; ☎01434/382244), where you can also book **accommodation**. In Alston itself, vegetarian *Nentholme Guest House*, 200 yards east of the cross at the Butts (☎01434/381523, ⓦwww.nentholme.co.uk; no credit cards; ❷), is one of the best B&Bs, while a couple of miles out of town on the Nenthead Road the *Lovelady Shield Country House* (☎01434 /381203, ⓦwww.lovelady.co.uk; ❻, with dinner) serves excellent food. Alston's **youth hostel**, *The Firs* (☎01434/381509), is just south of the centre, over-looking the South Tyne river valley; and you can **camp** centrally at *Tyne Willows* (☎01434/382515; closed Nov–Easter) by the station behind the Texaco garage. The *Angel Inn* on Front Street (☎01434/381363; no credit cards; ❷), is a nice old seventeenth-century pub serving good bar **meals** all day. *Blueberry's Tea Shop* on the Market Square (☎01434/381928; no credit cards; ❶) can also provide snacks and rooms. Other good pubs include the *Turk's Head* in the Market Square and the nearby *Blue Bell*.

Carlisle and around

CARLISLE, the county town of Cumbria and its only city, is also the repos-itory of much of the region's history. Its strategic location has been fought over for more than 2000 years. The original Celtic settlement was superseded by a Roman town, whose first fort was raised here in 72 AD. Carlisle thrived dur-ing the construction of Hadrian's Wall and then, long after the Romans had gone, the Saxon settlement was repeatedly fought over by the Danes and the Scots – the latter losing it eventually to the Normans. The struggle with the Scots defined the very nature of Carlisle as a border city: William Wallace was repelled in 1297 and Robert the Bruce eighteen years later, but Bonnie Prince Charlie's troops took Carlisle in 1745 after a six-day siege, holding it for only six weeks before surrendering to the Duke of Cumberland, who bombarded the city with cannon dragged from Whitehaven.

It's not surprising then that Carlisle still trumpets itself as the "great border city" and it's well worth a day of anyone's time to explore its compact centre and visit the trio of top-class sights: cathedral, castle and Tullie House Museum. The only surviving bit of Hadrian's Wall in Cumbria, at Birdoswald Fort, fif-teen miles east of Carlisle, is also worth a stop. Heading on, Edinburgh is under two hours north, while Carlisle also is terminus of the historic Settle to Carlisle Railway.

The Town

Directly opposite the train station stands the **Citadel**, its twin drum towers and battlemented gatehouses framing the main thoroughfare of English Street. The original Citadel was erected on the orders of Henry VIII as he revamped the city defences – today's is a nineteenth-century pastiche, housing council offices, but effective nonetheless as a symbolic entrance to the city centre. English Street is pedestrianized as far as the expansive **Green Market** square, formerly heart of the medieval city, though a huge fire in 1392 destroyed its buildings and layout. The Lanes shopping centre on the east side of the square – its "alleys" lit through a cast-iron-and-glass roof – stands where the medieval city's lanes once ran. Otherwise, the only historic survivors are the market cross (1682), the Elizabethan former town hall behind it, which now houses the tourist office (see below) and the timber-framed Guildhall beyond that (at the southern end of Fisher Street). The much-restored Guildhall now contains a small **museum** (Easter–Sept Tues–Sun noon–4.30pm; free) of guild and civic artefacts – Carlisle's eight historical trade guilds each had a meeting room in the hall.

The rest of the sights lie up Castle Street, which runs between Green Market and the castle itself. It's only a few steps along to **Carlisle Cathedral** (Mon–Sat 7.45am–6.15pm, Sun 7.45am–5pm; £2 donation requested), found-ed in 1122 but embracing a considerably older heritage. Christianity was estab-lished in sixth-century Carlisle by St Kentigern (often known as St Mungo), who became the first bishop and patron saint of Glasgow. The cathedral's sand-stone bulk has endured the ravages of time and siege: Parliamentarian troops during the Civil War destroyed all but two powerful arches of the original eight bays of the Norman nave, but there's still much to admire in the ornate fif-teenth-century choir stalls and the glorious **East Window**, which features some of the finest pieces of fourteenth-century stained glass in the country, although two-thirds of it is a faithful nineteenth-century restoration. In the northwest corner of the nave, steps lead down to the **Treasury**, containing glittering chalices and communion sets, and Henry VIII's charter of the foun-dation of the Dean and Chapter in 1541. Opposite the main entrance the reconstructed **Fratry**, or monastic building, houses the cathedral library, while its undercroft doubles as the Prior's Kitchen, a daytime café (Mon–Sat 10am–4pm) aptly using space that was once the monks' dining hall.

For more on Carlisle's history, head for the **Tullie House Museum and Art Gallery** (Mon–Sat 10am–5pm, Sun noon–5pm; £5), reached up Castle Street or through the cathedral grounds, via Abbey Street. This takes a highly imagi-native approach to Carlisle's turbulent past, with special emphasis put on life on the edge of the Roman Empire – climbing a reconstruction of part of Hadrian's Wall you learn about catapults and stone-throwers, while other sec-tions elaborate on domestic life, work and burial practices. There's also plenty on the Jacobite siege of 1745, as well as a dramatic attempt to convey the inten-sity of the feuds between the "Reivers", border families who lived beyond the jurisdiction of the Scottish and English authorities from the fourteenth to the seventeenth century in the so-called "Debatable Lands". The underground Millennium Gallery, meanwhile, contains sections devoted to local archeology and architecture, contrasted with recordings of stories and tales by the locals themselves. There's free entrance to the art gallery at Tullie House, which shows changing exhibitions of contemporary arts and crafts, while the adjacent **Tullie Old House** (also free) – site of the original city museum – now contains assorted paintings, china and other exhibits, including a diverting Gallery of Childhood.

A subway from outside Tullie House, or the eye-catching Irishgate Bridge – incorporating design elements from the city's former medieval Irish Gate – both cross the fast Castle Way road to **Carlisle Castle** (daily: Easter–Oct 9.30am–6pm; Nov–Easter 10am–4pm; £3.10; EH). This was originally built by

William Rufus on the site of a Celtic hillfort, though having now clocked up over nine hundred years of continuous military use, the castle has undergone considerable changes. These are most evident in its outer bailey, which is filled with fairly modern buildings named after battles from the Napoleonic Wars and World War I. Apart from the gatehouse, with its reconstructed warden's quarters, it's the **inner bailey** surrounding the keep that's the real draw. It was here, in 1568, that Elizabeth I kept Mary Queen of Scots as her "guest". There's a **Military Museum** located in the former armoury, but much more interesting are the excellent displays in the **Keep** and the elegant heraldic carvings made by prisoners in a second-floor alcove. The castle was recaptured from Bonnie Prince Charlie's troops in 1745, but the story of "the licking stone" in the dungeon providing moisture for the parched Scottish prisoners is probably apocryphal. More credible is the claim that they were the first to sing "You'll take the high road and I'll take the low road", referring to their poor prospects of returning to Scotland alive. **Guided tours** of the castle (Easter–Oct daily; ask at the entrance; an extra £1.50) help bring the history to life. Don't leave without climbing to the battlements for a view of the Carlisle rooftops.

Practicalities

From the **train station**, just off Botchergate, outside the Citadel, it's a five-minute walk to the **tourist office** in the Old Town Hall on Green Market (July & Aug Mon–Sat 9.30am–6pm, Sun 10.30am–4pm; June & Sept Mon–Sat 9.30am–5pm, Sun 10.30am–4pm; March–May & Oct Mon–Sat 9.30am–5pm; Nov–Feb Mon–Sat 10am–4pm; ☎01228/625600, ⊛www.historic-carlisle .org.uk). You can book accommodation here, pick up a map and access the internet. Ask, too, about the **guided tours** in summer (usually £3) which highlight varying aspects of the city – medieval and modern Carlisle, say, or a tour of sights associated with Woodrow Wilson, 28th President of the United States, whose mother was born in Carlisle.

The **bus station** is off Lowther Street, parallel to English Street, and most of the budget **accommodation** is east of here, concentrated on the streets between Victoria Place and Warwick Road. Most B&Bs are less than ten minutes' walk from the centre. Good choices – all of them Victorian town houses in a conservation area – include: *Ashleigh House*, 46 Victoria Place (☎01228 /521631; ❸); *Cornerways Guest House*, 107 Warwick Rd (☎01228/521733; no credit cards; ❶); *Courtfield House*, 169 Warwick Rd (☎01228/522767; no credit cards; ❷); *Langleigh House*, 6 Howard Place (☎01228/530440; no credit cards; ❷); and *Howard House*, 27 Howard Place (☎01228/529159; no credit cards; ❷). Best of the central hotels are the *Lakes Court Hotel*, Court Square (☎01228/531951, ⊛www.lakescourthotel.co.uk; ❻, ❺ at weekends and winter), right by the train station, with smart and spacious rooms in a classy renovated Victorian building; or the Edwardian *Crown & Mitre*, on English Street (☎01228/525491, ⊛www.peelhotel.com; ❻) in Green Market square, which has an indoor pool and spa. If your budget doesn't stretch to these, the *County Hotel*, round the corner from the *Lakes Court* at 9 Botchergate (☎01228/531316, ⊛www.cairn-hotels.co.uk; ❺, ❹ at weekends), is a cheaper option. A summer-only **youth hostel** occupies the university's Old Brewery Residences, Bridge Lane, Caldewgate (☎01228/597352; July & Aug only), just west of the town centre. The nearest **campsite** is *Orton Grange* caravan park (☎01228/710252) on the Wigton road (A595) four miles southwest of the city – take bus #300. The outdoor pool is open in summer.

For daytime **meals** head for *Café Courtyard*, Treasury Court (enter through the gates on Scotch Street or Fisher Street), or *Delifrance*, behind the tourist office on St Alban's Row – both have outdoor tables in the summer. *Watts Victorian Coffee Shop*, 11 Bank St, is a pleasant choice, too, while near the station *Café Solo*, 1 Botchergate, is a funky little stop for grilled panini, omelettes and coffees. Carlisle has plenty of Italian **restaurants**, the oldest and most atmospheric being *Franco's* (closed Sun lunch), occupying the ground floor of the Guildhall on Fisher Street. Otherwise, do your dining along Warwick Road, where in the space of 300 yards you can choose from *Casa Romana* (Italian), *Davids* (Modern British; eve only, closed Sun & Mon), *Alexandros* (Greek; closed all Sun, plus Mon lunch) and the *Emperor's Palace* (Chinese). Off Warwick Road, *Cecil's Treat* at 36 Cecil St (closed Mon & Tues eve & all Sun) offers a menu ranging from rainbow trout to spinach and nut crumble. The only decent **pub** in the centre, extravagantly tiled on the outside and with nice little snug rooms and real ale inside, is the *Howard Arms*, 107 Lowther St.

Birdoswald Fort and Lanercost Priory

Birdoswald Fort (March–Nov daily 10am–5.30pm; £2.50; EH) is fifteen miles east of Carlisle (signposted off the A69) and five miles beyond Brampton – the summer-only Hadrian's Wall Bus runs to the site, taking around 45 minutes from Carlisle. This is the only place along the wall where all tiers of the Roman structure are found intact, the defences comprising an earth ditch, a large section of masonry wall, and the trench and mound foundations behind it. A visitor centre fleshes out the historic background, and you can walk to the nearby Harrow's Scar Milecastle for some spectacular views.

The Hadrian's Wall bus stops first at the highly attractive ruins of **Lanercost Priory** (Easter–Sept daily 10am–6pm; Oct daily 10am–5pm; £2.10; EH), three miles northeast of Brampton. The Augustinian priory dates from 1166 and lies in a lovely spot: carved stones found here date back to Roman times, and the priory church is still used as the local parish church.

Travel details

Buses

For information on all local and national bus services, contact Traveline: ☎ 0870/608 2 608 (daily 7am–9pm), ⓦ www.traveline.org.uk.

Trains

For information on all local and national rail services, contact National Rail Enquiries: ☎ 08457/48 49 50, ⓦ www.rail.co.uk.

Appleby-in-Westmorland to: Carlisle (6 daily; 40min).

Carlisle to: Appleby (6 daily; 40min); Barrow-in-Furness (5 daily; 2hr 20min); Edinburgh (8 daily; 1hr 40min); Lancaster (hourly; 1hr); Leeds (Mon–Sat 8 daily, 3 on Sun; 2hr 40min); London (8 daily; 4hr 20min); Manchester (2 daily; 2hr 30min); Maryport (hourly; 40min); Newcastle (hourly; 1hr 20min–1hr 40min); Preston (21 daily; 1hr

20min–1hr 40min); Whitehaven (hourly; 1hr 10min).

Oxenholme (Lake District) to: Birmingham (6 daily; 2hr 30min–3hr); Carlisle (14 daily; 40–50min); London (5 daily; 3hr 30min–5hr); Manchester (1–5 daily; 1hr 40min); Penrith (14 daily; 30min); Preston (hourly; 30–40 min).

Windermere to: Kendal (hourly; 15min); Oxenholme (hourly; 20min).

Yorkshire

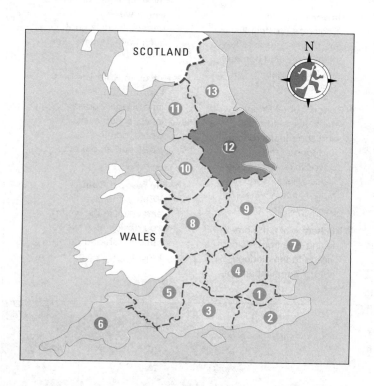

CHAPTER 12   Highlights

✳ **National Museum of Photography, Film and Television, Bradford** The north's most hands-on museum has all there is to know about film, photography and TV. See p.890

✳ **Haworth** One of England's greatest literary pilgrimages is to the bleak moorland home of the Brontë sisters. See p.894

✳ **Bolton Abbey** Priory ruins, riverside walks and sumptuous rooms and food at the *Devonshire Arms* – this Dales' village is the ultimate in luxury weekend getaways. See p.795

✳ **Malham** Make the breathtaking hike from Malham village to the glorious natural amphitheatre of Malham Cove and the glassy expanse of Malham Tarn. See p.908

✳ **National Railway Museum, York** There's never a dull day at York's award-winning railway museum – fun for families, travellers, commuters, tourists and even train-spotters. See p.948

✳ **Hutton le Hole** The quintessential English moorland village – grassy lanes, sheep everywhere, comfortable B&Bs and an old pub. See p.971

✳ **The Magpie Café, Whitby** The best fish and chips in the world? You decide at Whitby's famous fish-and-chip emporium. See p.989

Yorkshire

F ew visitors pass through **Yorkshire**, England's largest county, without spending time in history-soaked **York**, for centuries England's second city until the Industrial Revolution created new centres of power and influence. Famed primarily for its minster, the city is a comprehensive, if somewhat over-restored, ensemble of tiny medieval alleys, castle ruins, tucked-away churches, riverside gardens and topnotch museums. York's mixture of medieval, Georgian and Victorian architecture is mirrored in miniature in the prosperous north and east of the county by towns such as **Beverley**, centred on another soaring minster; **Richmond**, banked under a crag-bound castle; and **Ripon**, gathered around its honey-stoned cathedral. **Knaresborough** shares similar attributes, but is overshadowed by the faded gentility of neighbouring **Harrogate**, a spa town geared these days towards the conference trade rather than health-seeking visitors. The Yorkshire coast, too, retains something of the grandeur of the days when its towns were the first to promote themselves as resorts: places such as **Bridlington** and **Scarborough** boomed in the nineteenth century and again in the postwar period, though these days they're living on past glories. Instead, it's in characterful places such as **Whitby** and **Robin Hood's Bay** – busy, smaller resorts with unspoiled historic centres – that the best of the coast is to be found.

The engine of growth during the Industrial Revolution was not in the north of the county, but in the south and west. By the nineteenth century, Leeds, Bradford, Sheffield and their satellites were the world's mightiest producers of **textiles** (an industry first nurtured by the monastic houses of the moors and dales) and of **steel**. Ruthless economic logic devastated the area in the last century, leaving only disused textile mills, abandoned steel- and heavy-engineering works, and great soot-covered civic buildings in cities battered by depression. However, a new vigour has infused South and West Yorkshire during the last decade, and the city-centre transformations of **Leeds** and **Sheffield** in particlar

Accommodation price codes

Throughout this guide, hotel and B&B accommodation is priced on a scale of ❶ to ❾, the number indicating the **lowest price** you could expect to pay per night in that establishment for a **double room** in high season. The prices indicated by the codes are as follows:

❶ under £40	❹ £60–70	❼ £110–150
❷ £40–50	❺ £70–90	❽ £150–200
❸ £50–60	❻ £90–110	❾ over £200

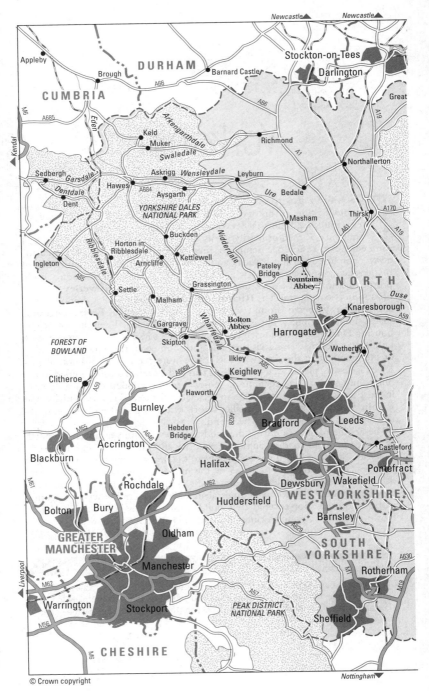

© Crown copyright

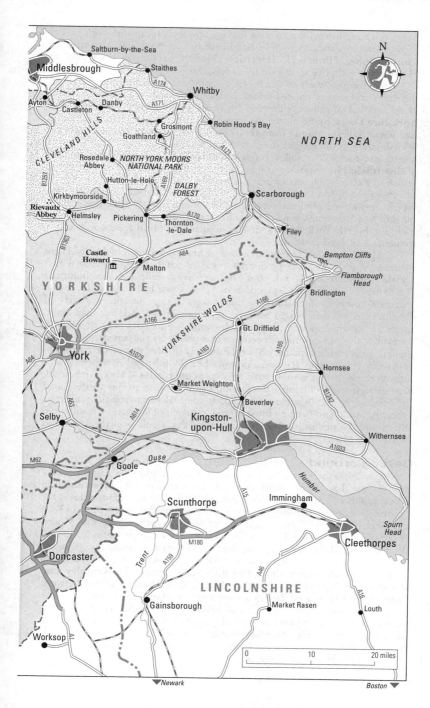

have been remarkable. Both are now making open play for tourists with a series of high-profile attractions, while **Bradford** and its **National Museum of Photography, Film and Television** waylays people on their way to **Haworth** – birthplace of the Brontë sisters, and wretchedly over-visited.

During even the worst of times, broad swathes of moorland survived above the slum- and factory-choked valleys, and it can come as a surprise to discover the amount of open countryside on Leeds' and Bradford's doorsteps. The **Yorkshire Dales**, to the northwest, form a lovely patchwork of limestone hills and serene valleys, ranging from the gentle, grassy spans of **Wharfedale** and **Wensleydale** to the majestic heights of Ingleborough, Whernside and Pen-y-ghent, and the wilder valleys of **Swaledale**, **Dentdale**, **Ribblesdale** and **Malhamdale**. Numerous stone-built villages provide often idyllic centres from which to walk, the whole area being covered by tracks, long-distance paths and old drove roads. Most are waymarked by the Yorkshire Dales National Park, which runs information centres and smaller information points. Less visited, but still worth as much time as you can spare, is the county's other National Park, the **North York Moors**, divided into bleak upland moors and with a tremendous rugged coastline.

The region is also scattered with a host of historic sites and buildings. These include not only the more predictable roster of stately homes, among which **Castle Howard** stands out, but also imperious relics of the Industrial Revolution, from the civic splendour of Leeds' town hall and arcades to the Italianate pastiche of **Saltaire**, a millworkers' village on the outskirts of Bradford. In an earlier age, before the Reformation, Yorkshire had more monastic houses than any other English county, centres not only of religious retreat but also of a commercial acumen that was to lay the foundations of the region's great woollen industry. Many beautifully situated **monastic ruins** survive today at Fountains, Rievaulx, Bolton Abbey, Whitby and elsewhere, graceful counterpoints to the more solid remains of the **castles** at York, Richmond, Scarborough and Pickering – the foremost of more than twenty castles raised in Yorkshire by the Normans. York boasts some **Roman** remains, and near Pickering you'll find Britain's finest surviving stretch of Roman road; still more ancient are the prehistoric barrows and dykes that ripple over the Dales and North York Moors.

Getting around

Getting to Yorkshire's big centres by train or bus is no problem. Fast train services on the East Coast main line link York to London, Newcastle and Edinburgh. Leeds is also served by regular fast trains from London, and is at the centre of the integrated Metro bus and train system that covers most of West and South Yorkshire. Trains are a useful way of approaching the Moors, Yorkshire coast and the Dales, with lines to Scarborough (from York) and Whitby (from Middlesbrough), and the famous **Settle–Carlisle** line (accessed from Leeds) to the southern and west Dales. Picturesque private lines with steam trains make useful adjuncts to the system, notably the **Keighley and Worth Valley** line to Haworth and the **North York Moors Railway** between Pickering and Grosmont. **Buses** are your only option for the interior of the Moors and Dales – York is the hub of services to the former, Leeds the starting point for the latter. Summaries of all services in these areas – including post buses and summer-only Moorsbus shuttles – are collected in special timetable booklets (*Moors Connections and Dales Connections*), available free from tourist offices and National Park information centres.

Sheffield

Yorkshire's second city, and England's fourth-largest, **SHEFFIELD** remains inextricably linked with its steel industry, in particular the production of high-quality cutlery. As early as the fourteenth century, the carefully fashioned, hard-wearing knives of hard-working Sheffield enjoyed national repute. Technological advances in steel production later turned Sheffield into one of the country's foremost centres of heavy and specialist engineering, creating a city of Victorian elegance and racking poverty, a mixture that characterized most northern industrial towns. An obvious target for the Luftwaffe, the city suffered heavy bombing in World War II, yet several of its grand civic buildings emerged remarkably unscathed. However, more damaging than bombs to the city's pre-eminence was the steel industry's subsequent downturn, which by the 1980s had tipped parts of Sheffield into dispiriting decline.

As with Leeds, the economic and cultural revival has been marked and rapid, spurred on by dogged local business incentives, an enthusiastic council and bundles of lottery money. In the last fifteen years, Sheffield steel production has risen to its highest ever level, while the arrival of new high-tech industries has cemented the revival. Meanwhile, **Meadowhall** shopping centre, in a resurrected steel works and billed as Europe's most successful mall, attracts thirty million visitors a year. Urban regeneration is in full swing: the "Heart of the City" project is fast transforming the centre; a glut of **sports facilities** (including the Ski Village, Europe's largest artificial ski resort) backs Sheffield's claim to be considered "National City of Sport"; while the city that gave the world *The Full Monty* – the black comedy about five former steel workers carving out a new career as a striptease act – has made a tribute to the industry in the **Magna** centre, one of the country's most enterprising visitor attractions.

Consequently, tourism is booming and with the Peak District so close – in fact, over a third of the city lies within the boundary of the **Peak District National Park** (see p.665) – you may well decide to allot it a night or two. The city's two universities and large student population (around 45,000) lends the café and **nightlife** scene a welcome edge.

Arrival, information and accommodation

Sheffield's **train station** is just east of the city centre off Sheaf Square. The **bus station**, known as the Sheffield Interchange, is on Pond Street about two hundred yards to the north; this is also where the National Express services pick up and drop off. The Destination Sheffield **tourist office** on Tudor Square (Mon–Fri 9.30am–5.15pm, Sat 9.30am–4.15pm; ☎0114/221 1900, Ⓦwww .sheffieldcity.co.uk) is just five minutes' walk from the stations, near the town hall, and is well-equipped with brochures, leaflets and guides to the city.

Sheffield city centre is easy to make your way around on foot, and you will only need to use the **local public transport** system to reach some of the outlying museums and galleries or the Botanical Gardens. Most local buses depart from the High Street, while the sleek, cheap **Supertram** system (☎0114/272 8282) connects the city centre with Meadowhall (northeast), Middlewood (northwest) and Halfway (southeast). For fare and timetable **information**, visit the Travel Information Centre at the Interchange (Mon–Fri 8am–5.30pm, Sat 8.30am–5pm, Sun 9am–5pm). A one-day TravelMaster Pass (£4.95) gives unlimited travel on buses, trains and trams throughout South Yorkshire. Otherwise, there's a day-rider (£1.90) and a seven-day Mega-rider (£6.30) pass just for the Supertram.

Sheffield isn't blessed with many good-value central **accommodation** options, so the tourist office's room-booking service can come in handy (☎0114/201 1011). There's no youth hostel, though the university has accommodation available during the summer vacation.

Hotels and B&Bs

Bristol Blonk St ☎0114/220 4000, ⓔ sheffield@bhg .co.uk. Breezy business hotel near the river, quays and markets. All rooms are en suite. ❺, ❹ at weekends.

Cutlers George St ☎0114/273 9939. City-centre inn with budget en-suite rooms, all with TV and tea-and coffee-making facilities. You may get a few pounds shaved off at weekends. ❹

Hilton Victoria Quays ☎0114/252 5500. Makes superb use of its revitalized canalside site, with a range of leisure facilities. The standard midweek rate is room only; special and weekend deals (two-night minimum) bring the price down considerably and usually include breakfast. ❼, ❺ at weekends.

Priory Lodge 40 Wolstenholme Rd ☎0114/258 4670. Suburban accommodation, a mile southwest of the centre. ❷

Rutland Arms 86 Brown St ☎0114/272 9003. Victorian pub with pleasant beer garden and a few standard rooms, just seconds from the Showroom cinema. No credit cards. ❷

Student halls

University of Sheffield ☎Tapton Hall, Crookes Road ☎0114/222 8862, ⓔ b&b@sheffield.ac.uk. A couple of miles west of the city centre, but linked to it by a regular bus service (#52 from High Street). Variety of single rooms – either with washbasin or en-suite facilities – in the student hall of residence. Available mid-June to mid-Sept only; small discount for stays of more than three nights. ❶

The City

Millions of pounds have been earmarked to turn Sheffield city centre away from the twin legacies of Victorian solidity and late-twentieth-century sterility. New squares, pedestrianized precincts and designated retail and cultural "quarters" all form part of the plan, and despite unavoidable millennium posturing, there's been a pleasing coherence to the various schemes recently put under way.

There's been most progress in the revamped post-industrial area near the train station – rather grandly known as the **Cultural Industries Quarter** – where clubs and galleries exist alongside high-tech arts and media businesses. Until recently the area was dominated by the **National Centre for Popular Music** (ⓦ www.ncpm.co.uk) on Paternoster Row. This Sheffield landmark, designed by Nigel Coates, consists of four giant stainless-steel drums – a nod to the city's most prominent industry. The first venture, opened in 1998, did not, however, get the support it deserved and the interactive museum where you could while away a few hours making, recording and mixing music, designing an album sleeve, and basically pretending to be a pop star is temporarily closed. But that is not to say that the doors are closed at the centre, which is still a lively nighttime venue and the hip ground-floor café-bar shows signs of rivalling the **Showroom** cinema-and-bar complex across the road. The renowned **Site Gallery**, just up the road on Brown Street (Tues–Fri 11am–6pm, Sat 11am–5.30pm, Sun 1–5pm; free) specializes in photography and multimedia exhibitions.

To the north of town, near the River Don, **Castlegate** and its traditional **markets** are still undergoing ambitious redevelopment, while the spruced-up warehouses and cobbled towpaths in the neighbouring canal basin, **Victoria Quays**, now house high-tech businesses, designer shops, a hotel, and leisure facilities. In the centre itself, the main development is around the impressive **Town Hall**, at the junction of Pinstone and Surrey streets. Completed in 1897, it's topped by the figure of Vulcan, the Roman god of fire and metalworking, and the facade sports a fine frieze depicting traditional Sheffield industries. A mid-Seventies extension to the town hall had few friends during its lifetime and its recent demolition has allowed room for the city's new centrepiece, the **Millennium Gallery** (Mon, Tues & Thurs–Sat 10am–5pm, Wed 10am–9pm, Sun 11am–5pm; free, visiting exhibitions £4). As well as visiting exhibitions loaned by London's Victoria and Albert Museum, the gallery also holds the Hawley collection of Sheffield hand tools and, of more general interest, the city's Ruskin collection, founded by John Ruskin in 1875 to "improve" the working people of Sheffield. Their education must have been wonderfully eclectic if the collection is anything to go by – a bulging library is complemented by an intriguing potpourri of watercolours, minerals, paintings and medieval illuminated manuscripts. An extension to the gallery in the form of a **Winter Garden** (6am–midnight; free) is due for completion in 2002. Great for a rainy day, this indoor park will offer everything from pavement cafés and kiosks to a good old park bench to sit and watch those outside battling with their umbrellas.

North of the town hall, **Fargate** meets Church Street, where the city's **Cathedral of St Peter and St Paul** retains elements of its fifteenth-century origins, though it's been restored on many occasions. Across Cathedral Square sits the **Cutler's Hall** of 1832, an imposing reminder of Sheffield's traditions. The Company of Cutlers was first established in 1624 to regulate the affairs of the cutlery industry, and this is the third hall on the site. Its silver collection is unrivalled, though you will need to be part of a group and book in advance to view it: call ☎0114/272 8456 for details. South of the town hall and the fountain-splashed **Peace Gardens** piazza, the pedestrianized **Moor Quarter** draws in shoppers, though the nearby **Devonshire Quarter**, centred on Division Street, is the trendiest shopping area. At The Forum by Devonshire Green, thirty-odd retail outlets flog club- and skate-wear, retro clothing, music, applied art and baubles, while the café-bar here is a popular spot for hanging out.

The city's traditional sights include the **Graves Art Gallery** (Mon–Sat 10am–5pm; free), located on the top floor of the City Library (entrance on Surrey Street). It leans most heavily towards nineteenth- and twentieth-century British artists, including Turner, Nash, Gwen John and the Pre-Raphaelites. Parts of the city's nineteenth-century collection are also held at the **Mappin Art Gallery** in Weston Park (Tues–Sat 10am–5pm, Sun 11am–5pm; free), a mile west of the city centre (bus #52 from the High Street). Sheffield's most instructive museums, however, are those devoted to its industrial past. The **City Museum** (Tues–Sat 10am–5pm, Sun 11am–5pm; free), adjacent to the Mappin, contains the definitive collection of cutlery and Sheffield ware, and it's matched by the **Kelham Island Museum**, Alma Street (Mon–Thurs 10am–4pm, Sun 11am–4.45pm; £3.50), on Kelham Island, one mile north of the city centre (bus #47 or #48 from Flat Street). Exhibits here reveal the breadth of the city's industrial output, ranging from a colossal twelve-thousand horsepower steam engine to a silver-plated penny-farthing made for the tsar of Russia. Many of the old machines are still working, arranged in period workshops where craftspeople demonstrate some of the finer points of cutlery production.

These have, however, both been eclipsed by **Magna** (daily 10am–5pm; £5.99), the new arrival on the Sheffield scene and the UK's first science adventure centre. In the building of a former steel works a mile north of the city (bus#69 from the Interchange or the train or supertram to Meadowhall) this massive building has undergone a £46m overhaul to offer four gadget-packed, themed pavilions around the four basic elements of earth, air, fire and water. The four are linked by suspended walkways, scissor lifts and tunnels. You are invited to experience over a hundred interactive exhibits including handling a mechanical digger and discovering the environmental effects of our daily water use. Although most of the centre is aimed at children, the half-hourly *Big Melt* will have everyone gripping onto the railings. An original arc furnace is used in a bone-shaking light and sound show, showing the moment when metal is transformed into white molten steel. For a recovery stop you can chill out in O2, an inflatable restaurant designed by Per Lindstrand, Richard Branson's balloon manufacturer.

Finally, Sheffield's **Botanical Gardens** (daily 8am–dusk; free), a couple of miles southwest of the centre, provide a restful spot on a hot day – nineteen acres of Victorian landscaping, as well as the impressive glass Paxton Pavilions and a café-bar. There are two entrances – one on Clarkehouse Road (bus #50 or #59 from the High Street), the other on Thompson Road (buses #81–86 from the High Street).

Eating and drinking

Sheffield has plenty of great **café-bars** and good-value **restaurants**, all pretty adept at making a play for the student pound. The **pubs** listed below are those with a bit of character and staying power, but for the best insight into what makes Sheffield tick as a party destination take a night-time walk along **Division Street** and **West Street** where competing theme and retro bars go in and out of fashion (and business). Students also frequent the bars and pubs of Broomhill and Ecclesall Road, but neither area is particularly central.

Cafés and Café-bars

Casablanca 150–154 Devonshire St. Easygoing bar-bistro with live jazz most nights and a reasonably priced mainstream menu.

The Forum 127–129 Division St. Long the mainstay of the Devonshire Quarter, the Forum has a great menu and laid-back clientele. Closed Sun.

Halcyon 113–117 Division St. Designer bar with cosy sofas and a touch of class.

Havana Internet Café 32–34 Division St. All day breakfasts and good cheap food as well as internet access.

Jules and Giovanna Brown St. Lovely little deli-café, serving good coffee, Mediterranean snacks and pastas, and breakfasts until 11.30. Closed Sun.

Lloyd's No.1 Waterworks Building, 2 Division St. Split-level café-bar in a beauty of a building, with decent food and, during the day at least, a quieter feel than its rivals.

Showroom 7 Paternoster Row. Part of the independent cinema complex, the relaxed *Showroom* has a café on one side serving Mediterranean-style snacks and sandwiches, and a great bar on the other with a couple of sofas and a long see-and-be-seen window. Check out their week-night film-and-food offers.

ularity, this vegetarian/vegan café, with a few outdoor seats in the summer, serves delicious home-made foods and the noticeboard is a great source of information on what is happening in the city. Licensed and open until 8pm. Inexpensive.

Encore Crucible Theatre, Tudor Square ☎0114/275 0724. Accomplished Modern British cooking in the theatre restaurant; pre-show dinner and meal-and-ticket deals offer the best value. Moderate to Expensive.

Kashmir Curry Centre 123 Spital Hill ☎0114/272 6253. The curry-lovers' curry house. Fifteen minutes' walk from the city centre, this formica-tabled café is the unlikely venue for the best baltis in town. Try one of their home-made lassis or take the precarious route across the road to collect your beers from the pub opposite. Inexpensive.

Pizza Volante (Formerly Flying Pizza) 255 Glossop Rd ☎0114/273 9056. Building on the good reputation of its predecessor, this continues to be a rumbustious Italian pasta and pizza place. Inexpensive.

Trippet's Wine Bar 89 Trippets Lane ☎0114/278 0198. There's always a nice atmosphere in this unstuffy wine bar behind West Street. The bistro food is popular and there's live jazz and blues on occasion. Moderate.

Restaurants

Blue Moon Café 2 St James St. Recently moved to new premises to accommodate its growing pop-

Pubs

Bath Hotel 66 Victoria St. Timeless Victorian classic

off Glossop Road – no frills, but well-kept real ale and handsome original features.

Broomhill 484 Glossop Rd. In one of the city's leafier areas, lively and popular with students.

Fat Cat 23 Alma St. Cosy, old-fashioned and famed for its umpteen real ales. It's in old steel-land, about a quarter of an hour's walk north from the city centre. Recently opened sister pub *Devonshire Cat* on Devonshire Green is closer to the city centre and offers the same range of beers, but lacks the atmosphere of *Fat Cat*.

Frog & Parrot Division St. A boisterous pub with some dark little nooks and crannies, lots of beers and a good jukebox. Decent mix of locals and students.

The Washington 79 Fitzwilliam St. A good pub with good beer that's a favoured muso's hangout. Just two minutes from Division Street.

Nightlife and the arts

Friday's *Sheffield Telegraph* lists the week's performances, events, concerts and films; look out also for the highly useful and entertaining *Dirty Stop Out's Guide*, a comprehensive listings' booklet, available at the tourist office.

Clubs and live music venues

Area 51 14–16 Matilda St ☎0114/276 3523. A converted warehouse where the night's clubbing continues well into the wee hours.

Arena Broughton Lane ☎0114/256 5656. One of two stadium venues on the edge of town, on the Supertram route out to Meadowhall.

Bar 8 8–10 Fitzwilliam St ☎0114/272 0070. Live bands most nights of the week.

The Boardwalk Snig Hill ☎0114/279 9090. Popular venue for indie bands, rock, folk and comedy.

Brown Street 2 Brown Street ☎0114/279 6959. Smart bar and chilled club. Free entrance into one of Sheffield's newest venues.

Don Valley Stadium on Worksop Road ☎0114/278 9199. The other edge-of-town stadium venue; take the Supertram out to Meadowhall.

The Last Laugh The Lescar Hotel, Sharrowvale Road ☎0114/267 9787. Yorkshire's longest-running comedy club. Local and visiting comedians Thurs & Sun from 8.30pm

Leadmill 6–7 Leadmill Rd ☎0114/275 4500. In the Cultural Industries Quarter, this place hosts live bands and DJs most nights of the week.

National Centre for Popular Music Paternoster Row ⊛www.ncom.co.uk. Bar and club in the steel drums of this impressive building. Hosting live music some nights, this place is also home to one of the few gay clubs in Sheffield (every other Sat).

Nelson Mandela Building Pond Street ☎0114/253 4122. Part of Sheffield Hallam University; hosts regular gigs and club nights.

Republic 112 Arundel St ☎0114/276 6777. Club housed in an old steel and engineering works.

University of Sheffield Students' Union on Western Bank ☎0114/222 8777. Hosts regular gigs and club nights.

Theatres and cinemas

The Crucible, Lyceum and Studio **theatres** in Tudor Square (☎0114/276 9922) put on a full programme of theatre, dance, comedy and concerts. The Crucible also hosts the annual Music in the Round **festival** of chamber music (May), and the Sheffield Children's Festival (late June, or July), whose events are performed entirely by children. There are mainscreen **cinemas** at Meadowhall (☎0114/256 9444) and Arundel Gate (☎0114/272 3981). The Showroom, 7 Paternoster Row (☎0114/275 7727), is the art-house alternative, the biggest independent cinema outside London.

Leeds and around

Yorkshire's commercial capital, and one of the fastest-growing cities in the country, **LEEDS** has undergone a radical transformation in recent years. There's still a true northern grit to its character, and in many of its dilapidated suburbs, but the grime has been removed from the Victorian centre and the city is revelling in its renaissance as a financial, administrative and cultural boomtown. An early market town, wool was traded here in medieval times by the monks of nearby Kirkstall Abbey. By the eighteenth century, the advent of canals and technical innovations such as the harnessing of steam power turned what had been a cottage industry into a dynamic large-scale economy. Leeds quickly boomed beyond its capacity to support its burgeoning population, and while the textile barons prospered, the city acquired a reputation for grimness that proved hard to shake off. In 1847 Charles Dickens described Leeds as "the beastliest place, one of the noisiest I know", an observation that many visitors might have applied to the city until comparatively recently.

Now, however, improved communications, a major clean-up and urban rejuvenation schemes have been the making of modern Leeds. The most obvious manifestation of change has been the advent of late-opening cafés, bars, clubs and eclectic restaurants, and the arrival of the swanky department store, Harvey Nichols. The formerly run-down city quarters have been revitalized and have made Leeds a noted **nightlife** destination. It's long been the region's **cultural** centre, home to Opera North, the noted West Yorkshire Playhouse and a triennial international piano competition that ranks among the world's top musical events. The **Royal Armouries** aside, the **City Art Gallery** has the best collection of British twentieth-century art outside London; **Leeds City Museum** and **Armley Mills Museum** take care of the city's historical legacy; while further from the city you might try to see the ruins of **Kirkstall Abbey** and one of the country's great Georgian piles, **Harewood House**.

Arrival, transport and information

National and local Metro trains use **Leeds City Station** off City Square on the southern flank of the city centre, which also houses the impressive Gateway Yorkshire **tourist office** in the Arcade (Mon–Sat 9.30am–6pm, Sun 10am–4pm; ☎0113/242 5242, ✉tourinfo@leeds.gov.uk), stuffed with leaflets and information about Leeds and the rest of West Yorkshire. The **bus and coach station** occupies a sprawling site to the east, behind Kirkgate Market, on St Peter's Street, close to the West Yorkshire Playhouse – as well as for National Express and all regional services, this is also the depot for buses from York, the coast, the Dales and Manchester.

Leeds city centre is easily walked around and you'll have little use for the extensive bus network unless you're staying at a far-flung B&B or planning to use the city as a base for visiting destinations like Bradford or Haworth. Buses depart from stops all over the city, including the **bus station** on St Peter's Street. The **Metro Travel Centre** at the bus station has up-to-date service details (Mon–Fri 8.30am–5.30pm, Sat 9am–4.30pm; ☜www.wymetro.com), and you can also ask in the tourist office, which has timetables for every conceivable local service; or call **Metroline** (Mon–Sun 8am–8pm; ☎0113/245 7676) which advises on current routes and fares throughout the city and region. If you're planning to see a slice of West Yorkshire over a day or two, consider one of the available **passes** for use on local buses and trains – there's the bus/train day rover (£4.50), separate bus or train day rovers (£3.80 each) and a family day rover (£6).

Accommodation

There's a good mix of **accommodation** in Leeds, including some fairly central places near the university campus that shouldn't break the bank, as well as business hotels that do a steady trade. Plenty of other cheaper B&Bs lie out to the northwest in Headingley, though these are all a bus ride away. The tourist office can **book you a room**; call their booking line on ☎0800/808050.

Other options include well-equipped rooms and self-catering apartments in a number of halls of residence, rented out during university holidays by the **University of Leeds** (☎0113/233 6100; ❶) – call well in advance and expect a two-night minimum stay. There's a **YWCA** at 22 Lovell Park House, Lovell Park Hill (☎0113/245 7840), which is open to men as well as women, but it rarely has rooms available for single-night or short stays. The nearest **youth hostel** is in Haworth (see p.896). The nearest **campsite** is near Roundhay Park on Elmete Lane (☎0113/265 2354), three miles northeast of the city – buses #10 and #12 (#19 or #19a Sun) make the journey; get off at the Oakwood clock, from where it's a five-minute walk.

see p.896

42 The Calls 42 The Calls ☎0113/244 0099, ✉hotel@42thecalls.co.uk, ⌨www.42thecalls.co.uk. Stunning designer hotel – Leeds' top choice – converted from an old grain mill on the canal, with public rooms and bedrooms flaunting stripped oak beams, iron piping, metallic facing and CD players. Weekend rates sometimes available. ❼

Avalon Guest House 132 Woodsley Rd ☎0113/243 2545. Decent budget B&B near the university in a large Victorian house; en-suite rooms creep into the next price category. ❶

Central Hotel 35–47 New Briggate ☎0113/294 1456. Central, simple hotel, handily placed for shopping and café life. ❷

Fairbairn House 71–75 Clarendon Rd ☎0113/233 6633. Victorian house owned by the university. Quiet setting and good value. ❷

Glengarth 162 Woodsley Rd ☎0113/245 7940. Homely B&B, with good rates and a variety of single and double rooms; the cheapest don't have en-suite facilities. No credit cards. ❶

Malmaison Sovereign Quay ☎0113/398 1000. The arrival of *Malmaison* in Leeds has given *42 The Calls* (see above) something to think about. Designer waterside premises (behind Swinegate), with the signature *Malmaison* style. Breakfast isn't included. ❻, ❺ at weekends.

Le Meridien Queen's City Square ☎0113/243 5315. Refurbished Art Deco landmark, right in front of the station, with period *Palm Court Lounge*, bar, restaurant and free car parking. During the week, steep room-only rates are paid by a business clientele; weekend rates include breakfast (and special deals throw in dinner too). ❽, ❻ at weekends.

Travelodge Blayds Court, off Swinegate ☎0113/244 5793. Reasonable centrally located accommodation from this chain. Set price per room, breakfast not included. ❷

The city

Leeds city centre splits itself into three reasonably distinct areas, starting with the **universities** on the heights to the northwest, arranged around some pleasant green swathes but framed by the more brutal excrescences of Sixties planning. The city's revitalized commercial life is most apparent in the packed pedestrianized streets south of the **Headrow**, where the Victorian and Edwardian buildings, arcades and markets glitter with brand names and designer labels, while down along the **Leeds–Liverpool Canal** a kind of post-industrial chic has infused the converted warehouses and railway arches. If you want some purpose to your wanderings, take one of the themed **guided walks** that depart from the tourist office at 2pm on most Wednesdays and Sundays between April and October (£2.50).

City Square opposite the train station hasn't been much of an introduction to Leeds for years, though that's starting to change as the surrounding buildings (including the Queen's Hotel and the train station's North Concourse) are renovated and smartened up, and the square pedestrianized. Pavement cafés are planned, and while the statues might get moved around, the prancing Edward, the Black Prince, and the bronze nymph gas-lamps should all survive.

From the square it's a short walk up to the main Headrow where you can't miss **Leeds Town Hall**, one of the finest expressions of nineteenth-century civic pride in the country. The masterpiece of local architect Cuthbert Broderick, it's a classical colossus of great skill, colonnaded on all sides, guarded by white lions and topped by a perky clocktower and sculptures embodying Industry, Art, Music and Science. Venture at least as far as the *Victoria Tearooms* (Mon–Fri 10am–4pm) – the entrance is on Calverley Street – for a cup of tea with a nice view. Venture further up Calverley Street to see the Leeds turn of the century contribution, the **Millennium Square**. Not much to look at by day, but hidden beneath the concrete lies state of the art technology to transform the square into a theatre and music venue seating 2,500 people. Catch one of the summer shows to see it in its full glory.

The Art Gallery (see below) lines up next door to the Town Hall, along the Headrow, though most people make a beeline for the brimming, shop-filled **arcades** further along on either side of pedestrianized **Briggate**. These nineteenth-century palaces of marble, mahogany, stained glass and mosaics have been magnificently restored to house the shops and businesses which are at the heart of Leeds' revival. Perhaps the most splendidly decorated of all is the light-flooded **Victoria Quarter**, with Harvey Nichols as its designer lodestone – you'll need to suspend financial disbelief before plonking yourself down in its fashionable *Espresso Bar* or *Fourth Floor Café-Bar*.

Across Vicar Lane, the restored **Kirkgate Market** (closed Wed afternoon & Sun) is the largest market in the north of England. Housed in a superb Edwardian building, it's a descendant of the medieval woollen markets that were instrumental in making Leeds the early focus of the region's textile industry. The **outdoor market** behind here (Tues, Fri & Sat), incidentally, is where Michael Marks set up stall in 1884 with the slogan "don't ask the price, it's a penny" – an enterprise that blossomed into the present-day retail giant Marks & Spencer. Visible at the bottom of the street, on the corner of Vicar Lane and Duncan Street, the elliptical, domed **Corn Exchange** (open daily) was built in 1863, also by Cuthbert Broderick, whose design leaned heavily on his studies of Paris's corn exchange. This listed building is now a hip market for jewellery, retro clothes, furnishings, music and other bits and bobs – extra craft stores open up at weekends. Behind here, under the railway arches on Assembley Street and along Call Lane, Leeds' **Exchange Quarter** flexes its fashionable muscles in a series of hip cafés and restaurants, many housed in beautifully restored buildings.

The City Art Gallery

The **Leeds City Art Gallery** (Mon–Sat 10am–5pm, Wed 10am–8pm, Sun 1–5pm; free) comprises one of the best arrays outside London of twentieth-century British art. Changing selections from the permanent collection of nineteenth- and twentieth-century art and sculpture are presented, with an understandable bias towards pieces by Henry Moore and Barbara Hepworth, both former students at the Leeds School of Art; Moore's *Reclining Woman* lounges at the top of the steps outside the gallery. There's Victorian painting and sculpture on the ground floor, with notable chunks of work by local landscapist John Atkinson Grimshaw, while the upper floor merges French Impressionists with the English artists they influenced. Prime amongst these was the founder of the Camden Town Group, Walter Sickert, and his younger disciples Spencer Frederick Gore and Harold Gilman; later artists such as

Matthew Smith, Stanley Spencer and Wyndham Lewis are also represented. In addition, there are some outstanding pieces by names with greater recognition – busts by Jacob Epstein, paintings by L.S. Lowry, a David Hockney etching here, a Francis Bacon snarl there. The **café** (Mon–Sat 10am–4pm, Sun 1–4pm) is a quiet place to unwind, and there's direct access to the **Craft Centre and Design Gallery** below (Tues–Fri 10am–5pm, Sat 10am–4pm; free), where changing displays of contemporary jewellery, ceramics and applied art are on show.

From the City Art Gallery, a slender bridge connects to the adjacent **Henry Moore Institute** (daily 10am–5.30pm, Wed until 9pm; free), which has its own entrance on the Headrow. Housed in a former Victorian merchant's warehouse, now faced in black marble, the Institute is devoted to showcasing temporary exhibitions of sculpture from all periods and nationalities, and not, as you might imagine, pieces by the masterful Moore. For the best selection of Moore's works (and Barbara Hepworth's, too) you need to visit **Wakefield's City Art Gallery** on Wentworth Terrace, Wakefield, 10 miles south of the city (Tues–Sat 10.30am–4.30pm, Sun 2–4.30pm; free), or the **Yorkshire Sculpture Park** (daily 10am–dusk; free) at Bretton Hall, West Bretton, 7 miles south of Wakefield.

Along the canal: Granary Wharf to the Royal Armouries

The biggest transformation in Leeds has been along the **Leeds–Liverpool Canal**, formerly a stagnant relic of industrial decline. New businesses, sought-after balconied apartments and trendy restaurants line both sides, while a slew of attractions stretch along a mile or so of the waterside, connected by a pleasant footpath. At **Granary Wharf**, a couple of minutes' walk from the train station, stores and craftshops fill the extensive cobbled, vaulted arches (the "Dark Arches"), while every weekend (and bank holiday) a market with stalls, bands and entertainers spills out onto the canal basin.

Further up on the south side, past Victoria and Leeds bridges, is the glass turret and gun-metal grey bulk of the **Royal Armouries** (daily: 10am–5pm; £4.90). Purpose-built to house the arms and armour collection from the Tower of London, it's a hugely adventurous museum which requires a leap of faith – discard the notion that all you'll see are casefuls of weapons, and you're in for a treat. Themed galleries cover concepts such as "War" and "Hunting", while there are enough demonstrations (jousting to falconry), interactive displays, hands-on exhibits and computer simulations to keep everyone interested. Bus #63B runs every fifteen minutes direct to the Armouries from Leeds City Square, a five-minute ride.

Out of the city

The nearest of the surrounding sights is the **Thackray Medical Museum**, on Beckett Street (Tues–Sun 10am–5pm; daily during school holidays; £4.40), next to the well-known St James' Hospital ("Jimmy's" from the TV series). Sited in a former workhouse, it's a mile east of the city centre, with buses #5a, #13, #17, #41, #42, #43, #50 and #88 all running past. Essentially a medical history museum, it's a hugely popular and entertaining place – ghoulish too at times when it delves into topics like surgery before anaesthetics, and the workings of the human intestine. Needless to say, kids love it.

For Leeds' industrial past, visit the vast **Leeds Industrial Museum**, two miles west of the centre off Canal Road (Tues–Sat 10am–5pm, Sun 1–5pm;

£2), which runs between Armley and Kirkstall Road – take bus #5a, #14, #66 or #67. There's been a mill on the site since at least the seventeenth century, and the present building was one of the world's largest woollen mills until its closure in 1969. Displays recount the whole story of Leeds' industrial history, with plenty of working machinery, together with a definitive account of how cloth was made, starting from the fleece off the sheep's back to great rolls of finished cloth. A new Printing Gallery is devoted to the story of the city's printing trade.

You can also visit the ruins of **Kirkstall Abbey** (dawn to dusk; free), the city's most important medieval relic. Built between 1152 and 1182 by Cistercian monks from Fountains Abbey (see p.933), it was the site of 400 years of monastic life before being surrendered to Henry VIII in 1539. The abbey lies about three miles northwest of the city centre on Abbey Road; take bus #732, #733, #734, #735 or #736. Despite the urban huddle close at hand, the site's still evocatively bucolic, with plenty of signed footpaths around, and the cloisters in particular are a nice spot to while away some quiet time. The former gatehouse now provides the setting for the newly refurbished **Abbey House Museum** (Tues–Fri & Sun 10am–5pm, Sat noon–5pm; £3). Two floors dedicated to Victorian Leeds take a look into the city's industrial past and a dedicated children's section is popular with kids.

Four miles east of the city, the Jacobean house of **Temple Newsam** (April–Oct Tues–Sat 10am–5pm, Sun 1–5pm; £2) contains many of the paintings and much of the decorative art owned by Leeds City Art Gallery, including one of the largest collections of Chippendale furniture in the country; bus #27 runs here from the centre. The splendid park (daily 10am–dusk; free) was laid out by Capability Brown in 1762, and it's this rather than the art that brings many locals to picnic in the grounds. Further east still, about ten miles from Leeds, the rest of the city's art collection is housed in **Lotherton Hall** (Tues–Sat 10am–5pm, Sun 1–5pm; £2), off the B1217 near Aberford. Once the home of a local industrialist, and endowed with fine gardens, a deer park and bird garden, with everything from vultures to wallabies, it's set to rival its more wealthy neighbour at Harewood House (below). Buses #64 and #64a run to the village, from where it's a twenty-minute walk to the hall (there are direct buses on summer Sundays).

Stately **Harewood House**, seven miles north of Leeds (Easter–Oct daily 11am–4.30pm, grounds & bird garden 10am–6pm; Nov–Easter Sat & Sun only; £8, grounds & bird garden only £6.25), was designed and decorated by one of the greatest architectural teams ever assembled. Conceived in 1759 by York architect John Carr, the building was finished by Robert Adam, the furniture made by Thomas Chippendale and the landscaped gardens laid out by Capability Brown. To cap it all a sweeping terrace designed by Sir Charles Barry (architect of the Houses of Parliament) overlooks the garden. Georgian purists might lament some of the later Victorian additions but the ensemble is still outstanding, and is further enhanced by **paintings** by artists of such mettle as Turner, Gainsborough, Reynolds, El Greco and a whole host of Italian masters. There are guided tours of the house and galleries throughout the summer every Tuesday and Thursday at 2pm. One of the more unusual features outside is the **Bird Garden**, four acres of aviaries caging over 150 species – the penguins get fed at 2pm. There are frequent buses to Harewood from Leeds (including the #36, #781 and #X35); the house is near the junction of the A659 and the A61 Leeds to Harrogate road.

Eating, drinking and nightlife

Eating out in Leeds has been transformed in recent years, with a plethora of conversions of warehouses and grain mills into up-to-the-minute **restaurants** and brasseries. Michelin stars are not unknown, but there's a down-to-earth approach to prices, with even the fanciest places offering special lunch or early-bird deals. It's all a long way from when the big name in local cooking was *Harry Ramsden's*, a byword for "proper" fish and chips, but now franchised all over England and even as far away as Hong Kong – the original restaurant is in Guiseley, northwest of the city. Along with its restaurants, Leeds rivals Manchester in the number of late-opening, continental-style **café-bars** which dot the centre and exploit the city's relaxed licensing laws to the full. Many put tables out year round, and most serve good food too. Given the wealth of other options, the city's **pubs** seem a distinct second-best, though some sterling spruced-up Victorian (and older) examples still pull in the punters, most of whom move on to one of the city's **clubs**, many of which have a nationwide reputation – not least because Leeds lets you dance until 5 or 6am most weekends.

For information about what's on and local **listings**, the *Yorkshire Evening Post* is your best bet, or look out for the *Absolute Leeds* or *The Leeds Guide* (£1) for listings and features on the city.

Cafés and café-bars

Brodericks Corn Exchange, Call Lane. See and be seen café in the bowels of the Corn Exchange with a couple of sofas to relax in. English and international breakfasts and lunches.

Café Parisa Park Row. Lunches, afternoon tea or just fine wine in this microbrewery café-bar. Boasts 250 wines to try there or take away. Rustic feel with wooden chairs and tables and stone floors.

Café Vitae Granary Wharf ⓦwww.cafévitae.com. "The World's first Recruitment Café", this place will relax you, refresh you and help you find a job at the same time. Excellent food, all GM-free, offered lunchtimes and evenings.

Carpe Diem Basement, Civic Court, Great George St. Hidden down some steps around the back of the Art Gallery, this neo-Victorian wine bar is tops for good-value food, wine by the glass and decent beer. A resident DJ hits the decks every Friday until 1am. Closed Sun.

The Courtyard 25–37 Cookridge St. Huge, airy café-bar that gets a bit too packed at night, but slip in during the day for snacks, coffee and drinks in the brick-paved courtyard (heated in winter). Fresh and funky club sounds until 2am at weekends.

Cuban Heels The Arches, Assembley St, in a salsa café under the railway arches, opposite the Corn Exchange. Good food, bottled beers and cool sounds, then pop nextdoor where *Fudge* offers

funk and soul until 2am.

Espresso Bar Harvey Nichols, Victoria Quarter Arcade, Briggate. Domain of the high-fashion shopper, the arcade espresso bar is a pleasant, if overpriced, place to muse on exactly how much those shoes will set you back.

Fibre 168 Lower Briggate. Leeds' new gay café-bar offering comfy sofas and floor to ceiling views of the city. Contemporary food served from 11am. Special offers on cocktails early evening.

Milo Bar 10–12 Call Lane. Relaxed continental feel in this unpretentious bar. Live DJs most evenings and Saturday afternoons.

Norman Call Lane. The industrial-chic background of scuffed floor and cast-iron girders is lightened by sinuous plastic lights, tables and chairs. Add the juice bar, the Asian noodle-and-satay menu and the Saturday-night club sounds, and you've got one of the city's more unique browsing and sluicing spots.

Pitcher & Piano Assembley St. Exchange Quarter magnet for city hipsters, drinking at the outdoor tables or chowing down on Modern British food and snacks in the gargantuan interior.

Townhouse Assembley St. Café-bar grill and restaurant, serving fashionable food, all-day drinks, cocktails, and weekend club nights. There's a fairly brisk circuit between here and the *Pitcher & Piano*, and other local hangouts.

Restaurants

Bibi's Minerva House, 16 Greek St ☎ 0113/243 0905. Classic old-time Italian, busy at lunch and weekends, with the full range of pizzas and pasta alongside pricier mainstream meat and fish concoctions. Moderate.

Brasserie 44 44 The Calls ☎ 0113/234 3232. Informal but trendy Modern British brasserie, with some temptingly priced lunch and early-bird deals, serving everything from Whitby cod to Middle Eastern *meze*. Closed Sat lunch & Sun. Moderate to Expensive.

Bryan's 9 Weetwood Lane, Headingley ☎ 0113/278 5679. The local rival to *Harry Ramsden's* – order the fish and chips and judge for yourself. Inexpensive.

Est Est Est 31–33 East Parade ☎ 0113/246 0669. The usual classy pizzas and plate-glass windows from this chain – not that there's a whole lot to look out on in this part of town. Moderate.

Fourth Floor Café Harvey Nichols, Briggate ☎ 0113/204 8000. Light lunches, souped-up British classics (grilled steak, fish and chips, bangers and mash) and exotic flavours (Thai spices are common) at dinner. And great views over the rooftops of central Leeds. Closed Mon–Wed eve & all Sun. Moderate (lunch) to Expensive (dinner).

Hansa's 72–74 North St ☎ 0113/244 4408. This Gujarati vegetarian restaurant serves delicious aromatic Indian food with choice of Indian, vegetarian or organic wines. The philosophy of the place matches the food – take time to look through the beautiful menus full of maps, quotes and thoughts to keep you pondering while you enjoy a Thalis for two. Inexpensive.

Harry Ramsden's White Cross, Guiseley ☎ 01943/879531. If you feel like making the pilgrimage (bus #732, #733, #734 or #736 from the bus station), then expect to wait in line at the original *Harry Ramsden's* fish-and-chip restaurant;

well worth it, though. Moderate.

Leodis Victoria Mill, Sovereign St ☎ 0113/242 1010. Former mill with a rescued cast-iron and wood interior and river views, serving English and French brasserie classics. Closed Sat lunch & all Sun. Moderate to Expensive.

Oporto 31–33 Call Lane ☎ 0113/245 4444. Funky Exchange Quarter bistro-bar where the flavours mix and match: *pissaladière* (Provencal tart) and *crostini* during the day, Asian-influenced, Mediterranean and Modern British meals at night. Moderate.

Pizza Express White Cloth Hall, Crown St. No menu surprises from the chain, but a great building (behind the Corn Exchange) with soaring conservatory. Jazz on Tues. Inexpensive to Moderate.

Pool Court at 42 42–44 The Calls ☎ 0113/244 4242. Shares a kitchen and ownership with the adjacent *Brasserie 44*. This is the sharp end of the business – cutting-edge Modern British cuisine, and with a sought-after balcony overlooking the canal. Closed Sat lunch & Sun. Expensive to Very Expensive.

Rascasse Canal Wharf, Water Lane ☎ 0113/244 6611. Yet another canalside warehouse development which pushes all the right Modern British buttons – if it's not seared, it's roasted or chargrilled. Very stylish, with a great interior and canal views. Closed Sat lunch & all Sun. Moderate to Expensive.

Souz le Nez en Ville Basement, Quebec House, Quebec St ☎ 0113/244 0108. Housed in the splendid red-brick building of the former Liberal Club, this basement wine bar/restaurant is strong on fish and packs in a local business clientele. Closed Sun. Moderate to Expensive.

Thai Siam 68 New Briggate ☎ 0113/245 1608. Little local dinner-only Thai place with reliable food and service. Closed Mon. Inexpensive to Moderate.

Pubs

Dry Dock Woodhouse Lane. Converted coal-barge with rooftop seating and vodka bar, near Leeds Metropolitan University – one of the more bizarre drinking-holes in the city.

Duck & Drake Kirkgate, by the railway bridge. Real-ale pub with a changing selection, and local bands performing for free two or three nights a week.

The Ship Ship Inn Yard, off Briggate. Less well known than *Whitelocks* but almost as appealing, and serving lunchtime snacks. The yard tables – crammed into a space about three feet wide – take

the city's obsession with continental outdoor ways to extremes.

Victoria Great George St. Ornate Victorian pub, restored to its former glory.

The Whip Duncan St at Briggate. Unchanged Victorian courtyard pub serving great Tetley's beer.

Whitelocks Turk's Head Yard, off Briggate. Up an alley opposite Littlewoods, Leeds' oldest and most atmospheric pub retains its traditional decor, though you'll be hard pushed to see any of it at peak times.

Clubs and live music

Atrium 6–9 The Grand Arcade ☎0113/242 6116. Relaxed and laid back vibe upstairs and a funky basement club for the diehard clubbers. Guest DJs.

Bondi Beach City Square ☎0113/243 4733. Swish and studenty club (next to the Queen's Hotel) with midweek cheap-drinks promotions.

Club Uropa 54 New Briggate ☎0113/242 2224. Immensely popular club nights, with a good line in guest DJs.

Cockpit Bridge House, Swinegate ☎0113/244 1573. Weekend Mod revival nights underneath the railway arches; indie sounds and bands, Britpop, and drum'n'bass nights at other times. Gay night "Poptastic" on Thurs.

Creation 55 Cookridge St ☎0113/280 0100. Formerly the Town & Country Club, this most reliable venue hosts high-profile live bands as well as regular weekend retro club nights.

The Elbow Room 64 Call Lane ☎0113/245 7011. Funk and food, and a place to play pool. Live jazz Wed.

The Fruit Cupboard 52–54 Call Lane ☎0113/243 8666. Gay-friendly bar, club and café, open Thurs, Fri & Sat nights for funk disco, soul and house. Friday is very funky disco night.

Heaven & Hell The Grand Arcade ☎0113/243 9963. "Heaven" hosts 70's and 80's disco, soul and chart, while "Hell" serves up house, trance and garage. Something for all angels and devils, plus themed nights in the week.

Hifi 2 Central Rd ☎0113/242 7353. Smart and stylish, ultra-fashionable Exchange Quarter club, playing everything from funk and soul to drum 'n' bass. Friday gets the local vote. You'll want your best club gear.

Irish Centre York Rd ☎0113/248 0887. Long-standing venue for rock bands of all hues, though a bit short on atmosphere.

Mint Club 8 Harrison St ☎0113/244 3168. Trendy, modern and friendly with a "no-cheese" policy. Back to Basics on Sat nights.

Po Na Na Unit 2, Waterloo House, Assembley St ☎0113/243 3247. Outrageous club with themed evenings and Leeds' premier salsa night on Tues.

The Underground Portland Crescent ☎0113/244 3403. Sleek place around the back of *Creation* for highly popular Latin, salsa, funk, Motown and soul nights. Sunday sees cool jazz and bebop bands playing all day.

The Warehouse 19–21 Somers St ☎0113/246 8287. One of the biggest clubs in the city, with house, garage and techno sounds bringing in clubbers from all over the country.

Arts, festivals and entertainment

The city supports an enterprising **arts scene**, not just confined to the showpiece theatres and halls mentioned here. **Opera North**, based at the Grand Theatre, gives a free performance each summer at Temple Newsam, as does the **Northern Ballet Theatre** – details from the tourist office. Temple Newsam also hosts other concerts and events, from Shakespearean performances to major rock gigs. **Roundhay Park** is the other large outdoor venue for concerts. The **Grand Theatre and Opera House**, 46 New Briggate (☎0113/222 6222), is the regular base of Opera North and also puts on a full range of theatrical productions. Further classical music can be heard at the **Leeds Town Hall**, The Headrow (☎0113/247 6962), which supports an annual international concert season of great distinction and is the venue for Leeds' internationally renowned piano competition. The city's most innovative playhouse, the **West Yorkshire Playhouse**, Quarry Hill Mount (☎0113/213 7700), has two theatres and hosts a wide range of productions and premieres of local works. The **City Varieties**, Swan St, off Briggate (☎0113/243 0808), is one of the country's last surviving music halls, though it's less music-hall fare these days and more tribute bands, middle-of-the-road comedians and cabaret – great building and bar though.

For mainstream **cinema** a new multiscreen-complex called The Light opens in 2002. In the meantime, and for classic vintage cinema with **independent and art-house shows** alongside more mainstream films, go to Hyde Park Picture House, Brudenell Road, Headingley (☎0113/275 2045); take bus #56, #57 or #63 from the city centre. An **international film festival** is held each October (programmes from the tourist office); August heralds another festival in the **West Indian Carnival** (only beaten in size by Notting Hill).

Bradford and around

Lost in its smoky valley among the Pennine hills ... Bruddersford is generally held to be an ugly city ... but it always seemed to me to have the kind of ugliness that could not only be tolerated but often enjoyed.

J.B. Priestley, Bright Day, 1940.

Priestley was writing about a thinly disguised **BRADFORD**, his home town, and the sentiment – from a writer who championed Bradford at every possible opportunity – though typically blunt, is not unduly harsh. Even today's civic authority seems content to accept the judgement: the quotation, after all, is emblazoned on the plinth of the statue of the city's favourite, if cantankerous, son. For first and foremost, Bradford – now England's fourth largest metropolitan area – has always been a working town, booming in tandem with the Industrial Revolution, when it changed in decades from a rural seat of woollen manufacture to a polluted metropolis. In its Victorian heyday it was the world's biggest producer of worsted cloth, its skyline etched black with mill chimneys, and its hills clogged with some of the foulest back-to-back houses of any northern city. "Every other factory town in England is a paradise compared to this hole," wrote the German poet Weerth in 1840. "In Manchester the air lies like lead upon you; in Birmingham it's as if you're sitting with your nose in a stove; in Leeds you splutter with the filth as if you had swallowed a pound of Cayenne pepper – but you can put up with all this. In Bradford, however, you are lodged with the devil incarnate... If anyone wishes to feel how a sinner is tormented in Purgatory, let him travel to Bradford."

The city has left this nether world behind and is valiantly laying on tourist attractions to rinse away its associations with urban decrepitude. A few spruced-up buildings and the rejuvenation of the late-Victorian woollen warehouse quarter, Little Germany, signify an attempt to beautify the city centre, but in truth Bradford itself no longer has the architectural heritage or the cultural interest with which to wage a tourist war. Although there are the unexpected pleasures of the **National Museum of Photography, Film and Television** and the nearby model village of **Saltaire**, with its David Hockney Gallery, you couldn't make out a case for seeing much else. Most visitors hang around at least long enough to sample one of Bradford's famous **curry houses**, but with Haworth (see p.894) the indisputable local draw, and York and the heart of the Yorkshire Dales only an hour away, few stay longer.

The city

The focal point of the city centre is **Centenary Square**, commemorating not the founding of the original town – the "broad ford" was known before the arrival of the Romans – but the hundredth anniversary of the granting of its city charter by Queen Victoria in 1897; Elizabeth II turned up to snip the ribbon. The **City Hall** behind shouts its Victorian credentials; the Gothic extension at the back was the work of Richard Norman Shaw, architect of, among other things, the more fantastical Northumbrian country house of Cragside (see p.1058). The City Hall's original architects, local boys Lockwood and Mawson, also provided Bradford with **St George's Hall**, a Neoclassical extravaganza on Bridge Street still in use as a concert hall. Edwardian audiences later flocked to the minaret-topped **Alhambra Theatre**, across Princes Way, again splendidly restored and boasting a full programme of events.

Just across from here, on the rise, is the superb **National Museum of Photography, Film and Television** (Tues–Sun & public holidays 10am–

6pm; free), which since its foundation in 1983 has become one of the most visited national museums outside London. It has recently emerged from a major refit, but still wraps itself around Britain's largest cinema screen (52ft by 64ft), whose daily **IMAX** and 3-D film screenings (£5.80) are billed as "so real you'll think you're there". When you arrive it's as well to buy your cinema ticket for a later showing since this is one of the most popular attractions. There's also a ground-floor **café/restaurant**, *Intermission* (open until 6pm), and a **shop** stuffed full of movie posters, videos, and related knick-knacks.

The museum's ground floor kicks off with the Kodak Gallery, a museum-within-a-museum which houses the contents of Kodak's private collection and traces the story of popular photography. Like the floors which follow, it's crammed with memorabilia and hundreds of cameras, but also contains the world's biggest lens and other superlatives. Successive floors are devoted to every nuance of film and television, including some emphasis on state-of-the-art topics like digital imaging and computer animation, and detours into subjects like advertising and news-gathering. The place is a revelation to anyone with any technical or professional interest, and in the unlikely event that the endless gizmos don't appeal there are all sorts of nostalgic nuggets to grab the attention. Outside the museum a statue of playwright and author **J.B. Priestley** looks out over his native city, coat-tails flying, "as if he has a very bad case of wind" according to the travel writer Bill Bryson.

A walk past the Venetian-Gothic **Wool Exchange** building on Market Street – designed by Lockwood and Mawson – provides ample evidence of the wealth of nineteenth-century Bradford. The building has been splendidly restored, its arcades filled with modern shops and restaurants, and its main hall presided over by a statue of Richard Cobden, the statesman and economist who led the 1838–46 campaign of the Anti-Corn Law League. Over to the east, north of Leeds Road, the tight grid of streets that is **Little Germany** retains an enclave of warehouse and office buildings in which transplanted German and Jewish merchants once plied their wool trade. The buildings have been enticed in new businesses and community ventures, and at the **Design Exchange**, 34 Peckover St (Mon–Fri 9am–5pm; free), the temporary art and design exhibitions are usually worth a peek. A sign on the building next door highlights the site of the inaugural conference of the independent Labour Party in 1893. Priestley is honoured again at the **Priestley Centre for the Arts** (formerly the Bradford Playhouse and Film Theatre), over on Chapel Street, whose cellar bar (open from 5.30pm) is a useful retreat. The nearby Bradford **Cathedral** houses some impressive stained glass windows by William Morris.

For further insights into what once made the city tick, visit the **Bradford Industrial Museum** (Tues–Sat 10am–5pm, Sun noon–5pm; free) in the old Victorian Moorside Mills, on Moorside Road in Eccleshill, three miles northeast of town. Exhibitions and special events document the city's industrial heritage, alongside working textile machinery, surviving examples of the former workers' cottages, historic transport collection and working shire horses, who haul around a selection of trams and buses. Buses #608 and #609 from Bank Street run here, stopping on Moorside Road, or take #612 from the Interchange.

Bradford has two more museums of note, beginning with the **Peace Museum** (Wed–Fri 11am–3pm, or by arrangement at other times, call ✆01274/754009, ⓦwww.peacemuseum.org.uk; free), hidden away on the top floor of 10 Piece Hall Yard, opposite the Wool Exchange. The only museum of its kind in the country, it details the history of the peace movement in the twentieth century with some panache and offers educational workshops for adults and kids. The museum will be rehoused in a purpose-built International Peace Centre in 2003. The **Colour Museum** (Tues–Sat 10am–4pm; £1.75) occupies a former mill and home of the society of dyes and colourists on Providence Street. An interactive display shows how colours have been made and applied. Lots to play with.

Practicalities

Trains and buses both arrive at **Bradford Interchange** (℡01274/734833) on Croft Street, a little to the south of the city-centre grid. There's also a much smaller station at **Forster Square**, across the city, for trains to Keighley. The **tourist office** (Mon–Fri 9am–5.30pm, Sat 9am–5pm; ℡01274/753678) is located in Centenary Square's City Hall and has all the usual leaflets and brochures, plus free city-centre maps and a useful *Guide to Mill Shopping*, which takes you around the discount outlets of the surviving local woollen mills, and *Cultural Cuisine in Bradford* to help you find your way amongst the plethora of curry houses.

The best-value **accommodation** within half a mile of the centre is at the *Ivy*, 3 Melbourne Place (℡01274/727060; no credit cards; ❶), and the *New Beehive Inn*, Westgate (℡01274/721784; no credit cards; ❶). You could splash out on more central, luxurious digs: the Victorian-era *Midland Hotel*, by the station on Forster Square (℡01274/735735; ❺), has large rooms and good weekend rates; while the equally venerable *Quality Victoria Hotel*, on Bridge St (℡01274/728706; ❺), has similar prices, but a deal more style, since it was revamped by the team responsible for Leeds' *42 The Calls*. The nearest youth hostel is at Haworth (see p.894).

Bradford's large Asian population has made the city famous for its **curry houses**. There are over three hundred restaurants scattered all over the city. General opinion still favours the Muslim *Mumtaz*, 386–392 Great Horton Rd (℡01274/571861; no alcohol allowed), where the food is sold by weight – a half-pound dish feeds two and the sweet lassi is legendary. It may be a twenty-minute walk up towards the university, but you will not be disappointed. Closer to town, the *Kashmir*, 27 Morley St (℡01274/726513; open until 2am, 3am at weekends), which claims to be Bradford's first-ever curry house, lies two minutes up the road that runs west from the Alhambra and the National Museum. Once a simple café-style place, it's been expanded and upgraded, though it still sports formica tables and rock-bottom prices: it claims to bake over two thousand chapattis a day, and the chicken, spinach and dhal dishes are particularly fine; like many others in town it's unlicensed, though you can take your own booze. In the centre, the upmarket *Bombay Brasserie* (℡01274/737564), in a converted church on Simes Street, off Westgate, packs diners in for more refined, musically accompanied meals. Further afield, a short drive away up Great Horton Road, past the university, more excellent curries are to be found at the The *Bharat*, 496–502 Great Horton Rd (℡01274/521200), which is noted for its *thalis* and vegetable side dishes. Out east on the Leeds Road in Thornbury, again a drive away, *Akbar's*, 1276–78 Leeds Rd (℡01274/773311), is a buzzing balti house whose huge family naan breads are draped over a hook placed on the table so you can tear off strips at will.

If you don't fancy curry, then head for *Le Café Bleu*, North Parade, which offers a Mediterranean lunch in a small, friendly setting, or *Italia Café*, 344 Great Horton Rd, where home-made Italian bread and pastas are on the menu alongside the more traditional breakfasts (with vegetarian option), making this a popular place with local students.

The **Pictureville** cinema at the National Museum of Photography, Film and Television (see below) has a year-round repertory programme and hosts three major annual **festivals**: the Bradford Film Festival (March), the Animation Festival (June) and *Bite the Mango,* the Black and Asian Film-Makers' Festival (September). A new auditorium, the Cubby Broccoli Cinema, has expanded the museum's film programme.

Saltaire

Heading out of Bradford towards Keighley (along the A650) to the north, no one should pass up the chance to drop in on **SALTAIRE**, three miles out, a model industrial village and textile mill built by the industrialist Sir Titus Salt. You can catch trains to Saltaire station (right by Salt's Mill; see below) from Bradford Forster Square, or take bus #679 from the Interchange, which stops in Saltaire village. Buses #662–665, also from the Interchange, drop you at the top of Victoria Road from where it's a half-mile walk to Salt's Mill. Drivers should follow the signs to Keighley (along the A650) from the city centre and then look for the signs to Saltaire and the car parks.

The village is a perfectly preserved 25-acre realization of one man's vision of an industrial utopia. Having built his fortune on the innovative use of alpaca and mohair, Salt found that by 1850 his factory was too small to meet demand for his new textiles. While economic imperatives demanded a new factory, Salt's spell as mayor of Bradford during a cholera epidemic had also stirred his Congregationalist conscience. "Cholera," he said, "is God's voice to people," adding that he had been confronted with "disclosures too frequently made of immorality and vice prevalent among a large class of the population". Saltaire was built between 1851 and 1876, modelled on buildings of the Italian Renaissance, a period evoked because it was perceived as an era when cultural and social advancement were a direct consequence of the commercial acumen of textile barons. It was built, moreover, in open countryside – impossible to imagine now from the urban surroundings – so that Salt's employees would reap the benefits of the unpolluted, uplifting fresh air.

Salt's Mill, built to emulate an Italian palazzo and larger than St Paul's Cathedral in London, was the biggest factory in the world when it opened in 1853 (on Salt's 50th birthday). Its 1200 looms produced over 30,000 yards of cloth a day, and the mill was surrounded by schools, hospitals, a train station, parks, baths and wash-houses, plus 45 almshouses and around 850 houses. The style and size of each dwelling was designed to reflect the place of the head of that family in the factory hierarchy, one example – for all Salt's philanthropic vigour – of his rigid adherence to the prevailing class orthodoxy. Nor was Salt in any doubt of his own position in the scheme of things: of the village's 22 streets, for example, all – bar Victoria and Albert streets – were named after members of his family. Further to the master's whim, the church was the first public building to be finished and was strategically placed directly outside the factory gates. Most tellingly of all, the village contained not a single pub.

Salt's Mill remains the fulcrum of the village, its several floors now housing glitzy art, craft and furniture shops, and a craft centre. But its enterprising centrepiece is the **1853 Gallery** (daily 10am–6pm; free; ☎01274/531163), an entire floor of the old spinning shed given over to the world's largest retrospective collection of the works of Bradford-born **David Hockney**. Changing exhibitions cover all phases of the artist's career, from his student days through his Californian-swimming-pool period and up to his more recent experiments with faxes, Xerox machines and Polaroids. *Salt's Diner* (☎01274/530533) on the same floor has a Hockney-designed logo, menu and crockery, and serves tasty Mediterranean-inspired meals amid the original cast-iron pillars.

To enjoy the area further take the short signposted walk, across the Leeds–Liverpool Canal and River Aire at the bottom of Victoria Road, and through the bluebell woods, to **Shipley Glen**, where there's a Victorian funicular **tramway** (May–Sept daily; rest of the year Sat & Sun; 50p return) up to the family pleasure grounds and funfair. Or there's a **waterbus** service along the canal (between Shipley and Bingley) which stops at Saltaire, allowing you to cruise the waterway at leisure or make the return journey to Bradford by train from stations at either Shipley or Bingley (timetable information on ☎01274/595914; £5 round trip; 1hr 30min). Finally, Saltaire's **tourist office**, 2 Victoria Rd (daily 10am–5pm; ☎01274/774993), is housed in one of the original shops and offers hour-long **guided walks** of the village throughout the year (Sat at 2pm, Sun & public holidays at 11am & 2pm; £2).

Haworth

Of English literary shrines, probably only Stratford sees more visitors than the quarter of a million who swarm annually into the village of **HAWORTH** to tramp the cobbles once trodden by the Brontë sisters. Quite why the sheltered life of the Brontës should exert such a powerful fascination is a puzzle, though the contrast of their pinched provincial existences with the brooding moors and tumultuous passions of *Wuthering Heights* may well form part of the answer. Whatever the reasons, during the summer the village's steep, cobbled **Main Street** is lost under huge crowds, herded by multilingual signs around the various stations on the Brontë trail.

Of these, the **Brontë Parsonage Museum**, at the top of the main street (April–Sept daily 10am–5.30pm; Oct–March daily 11am–5pm; £4.80), is the obvious focus, a modest Georgian house bought by Patrick Brontë in 1820 to bring up his family. After the tragic early loss of his wife and two eldest daughters (see opposite), the surviving four children – Anne, Emily, Charlotte and their dissipated brother, Branwell – spent most of their short lives in the place, which is furnished as it was in their day, and filled with the sisters' pictures, books, manuscripts and personal treasures. You can see the sofa on which Emily is said to have died in 1848, aged just 28, for example, and the footstool on which she sat outside on fine days writing *Wuthering Heights*. In Charlotte's room are displayed her tiny shoes and wedding clothes, while other rooms contain mementoes of the rest of the family, including a copy of Branwell's portrait of his three

---

The Keighley and Worth Valley Railway

The **Keighley and Worth Valley Railway** runs steam trains (summer daily; rest of the year Sat & Sun) along a five-mile stretch of track between Keighley and Oxenhope, stopping at Haworth en route. The restored stations are a delight, with sections of the line etched into the memory of those who recall the film of E. Nesbit's *The Railway Children*, which was shot here in 1970. Valley footpaths run between the stations at Oakworth, Haworth and Oxenhope, allowing you to make a day of your reminiscences. Regular trains from Leeds or Bradford's Forster Square run to Keighley, where you change onto the branch line for the **steam services** (mid-June to Aug Mon–Fri 4 daily, Sat & Sun 7–12 daily; Sept to mid-June Sat & Sun and school holidays reduced services; £6 return, day rover ticket £8). Recorded information is available on ☎01535/647777.

sisters which hangs on the staircase. An exhibition room tells the family history in exhaustive detail, bolstered by personal letters, childhood writings, sketches, diaries, documents and other interesting archive material.

Not surprisingly, it can all be a bit of a scrum inside the house, though it's scarcely any less crowded at the other stops. The bluff **parish church** in front of the parsonage – substantially rebuilt since the Brontës lived here – contains

The Brontës at Haworth

Patrick Prunty or Bronty (it's unclear which) was born in Ireland and became a schoolmaster at the age of sixteen. He later won a place at St John's, Cambridge, where he changed his name to **Brontë**, perhaps influenced by naval hero Lord Nelson, who was made the Duke of Brontë. Later ordained, the Reverend Brontë, and his Cornish wife Maria, took up a living at Thornton, just outside Bradford, where the four youngest of their six children – Maria, Elizabeth, Charlotte, Branwell, Emily and Anne – were born between 1816 and 1820. The house, at 72–74 Market St, still stands. Later that year, the Brontë family moved into the draughty **parsonage** in nearby Haworth.

It could hardly be called an auspicious start to life in a new home. Mrs Brontë died within the year and her sister was despatched to help look after the children. The four oldest girls were sent away to school, but withdrawn after first Maria, then Elizabeth, died after falling ill. The surviving daughters, and smothered Branwell, were kept at home, where they amused themselves by making up convoluted stories and writing miniature books. As they successively came of age, the girls took up short-lived jobs as governesses at various local schools; Charlotte and Emily even spent a year in Brussels, learning French. **Branwell**, meanwhile, was already sowing the dissolute seeds of his disappointing future: he acquired an interest and certain talent for art, but failed to apply to study at the Royal Academy, got into debt, and then spent two years as a junior stationmaster near Halifax but was later dismissed in disgrace. He then took a tutor's job but was dismissed again after developing what was darkly referred to as an "unwise passion" for his employer's wife. He retreated to Haworth, made himself overly familiar with the beer in the *Black Bull* and began experimenting with drugs.

Charlotte's, Emily's and Anne's continuing attempts to amuse themselves with their writings led to the private publication, in 1846, of a series of poems, paid for using part of a legacy from their aunt. They used the (male) pseudonyms Currer, Ellis and Acton Bell – corresponding to their own initials – and though few copies of the collection were ever sold, the little volume acted as a catalyst. Keeping the pseudonym, **Charlotte** wrote a novel the same year, which was rejected by various publishers; but her *Jane Eyre*, submitted in 1847, was an instant success. **Emily's** *Wuthering Heights* and **Anne's** *Agnes Grey* received similar acclaim the same year; Anne's second novel, the better-known *Tenant of Wildfell Hall*, was published in 1848. As far as the public was concerned, the brilliant Bell brothers were a publishing sensation.

But the next two years destroyed the family, as it was ravaged by consumption. First Branwell, who had sunk ever deeper into addictive misery and ill-health, died in September 1848, followed by Emily in December of that year, and Anne in May of the following year. Charlotte lived on for another six years, writing two more novels – *Shirley* (1849) and *Villette* (1853) – and becoming something of a literary figure once she had revealed her identity, making friends with fellow author Elizabeth Gaskell, who later wrote Charlotte's biography. Charlotte finally **married** Reverend Brontë's curate, Arthur Bell Nicholls, who moved into the parsonage, but she died after nine months of marriage in the early stages of pregnancy. The Reverend Brontë lived on until 1861 – the entire family, except Anne (who is buried in Scarborough; see p.979), lies in the **Brontë vault** in the village church, next to the house.

the family vault; Charlotte was married here in 1854. At the **Sunday School**, between the parsonage and the church, Charlotte, Anne and even Branwell did weekly teaching stints; Branwell, however, was undoubtedly more at home in the **Black Bull**, a pub within staggering distance of the parsonage near the top of Main Street. He got his opium at the pharmacist's over the road (now a gift shop).

Local walks

A century and a half of academic sleuthing has pinned down many of the local houses and locations the sisters incorporated into their work. However, more than any other locale, it's the wild moorland surrounding Haworth which best captures the Brontë spirit. If you've come this far you should try some of the well-signed and much-travelled **walks**, many described by the sisters themselves, particularly those to the spots which are popularly – but in most cases wrongly – said to have been the inspiration for various locations in the novels. A leaflet available from the tourist office describes the routes.

The most popular walk runs to **Brontë Falls** and **Bridge**, reached via West Lane and a track from the village, and to **Top Withens**, a mile beyond, a ruin fancifully thought to be the model for Wuthering Heights (allow 3hr for the round trip). A plaque here bluntly points out that "the buildings, even when complete, bore no resemblance to the house she [Emily] described". The moorland setting, however, beautifully evokes the flavour of the book, and to enjoy it further you could walk on another two and a half miles to **Ponden Hall**, perhaps the Thrushcross Grange of *Wuthering Heights* (this section of path, incidentally, forms part of the Pennine Way).

Practicalities

There are frequent **buses** to Haworth from Bradford Interchange, just eight miles away, with services every hour during the day. Buses #663, #664, #665 and #699 run to Haworth, stopping at various points in the streets immediately at the bottom of the cobbled Main Street. However, perhaps the nicest way of getting here is by **train**, using the private steam trains of the **Keighley and Worth Valley Railway** (see p.894); the station is half a mile from the village centre – walk up Bridgehouse Lane to the bottom of Main Street. The busy Haworth **tourist office** is at 2–4 West Lane, at the top of Main Street (daily 9.30am–5.30pm; ☎01535/642329), and will book rooms on your behalf.

Main Street and its continuation, **West Lane**, form one long run of gift and tea shops, cafés and guest houses, those on the east side staring across the bare valley beyond. If you want to stay, you'll need to book ahead at most times of the year – even in winter special events (like the Christmas fair) fill the available **accommodation** at the drop of a hat. The tourist office has a full list of hotels and guest houses. You can join Branwell's ghost in the *Black Bull Hotel* in Main Street (☎01535/642249; ❷), but the *Old White Lion Hotel*, a little further up (☎01535/642313; ❸), is a more comfortable old inn. The best guest house is the *Apothecary*, 86 Main St (☎01535/643642, ✉apot@sisley86 .freeserve.co.uk; ❷), opposite the church, whose breakfast room and attached café have splendid views. *Heather Cottage*, 25–27 Main St (☎01535/644511; no credit cards; ❶), is less dramatically sited but has its own tearooms. Victorian *Moorfield Guest House*, 80 West Lane (☎01535/643689; ❷), makes the most of its elevated position. The **youth hostel**, *Longlands Hall* (☎01535/642234), is housed in the mansion of a Victorian mill owner, a mile from the centre at

Longlands Drive, Lees Lane, off the Keighley road, and overlooks the village. The Bradford buses stop on the main road nearby. For something a bit more luxurious, try *Weaver's*, 15 West Lane (☎01535/643822; ⑤), a converted row of weavers' cottages stuffed with period furniture.

Weaver's (dinner only, closed Sun & Mon) is also one of the best **restaurants** in the county, serving good traditional northern cuisine using local ingredients from around £25 a head – it's essential to book ahead. Otherwise, you're looking at bar meals in the pubs or a choice of one of a score of teashops and cafés. The *Fleece Inn* near the bottom of Main Street offers a changing selection of real ales, including one usually on sale for a pound or so a pint. Down in the lower part of Haworth there are several Indian restaurants and fish-and-chip shops, most concentrated on Mill Hey.

The Yorkshire Dales

The **Yorkshire Dales** – "dales" from the Viking word *dalr* (valley) – form a lovely and varied upland area of limestone hills and pastoral valleys at the heart of the Pennines, wedged between the Lake District to the west and the North York Moors to the east. Protected as a **National Park**, the region is crammed with opportunities for outdoor activities: the area is crisscrossed by several long-distance footpaths; there's a specially designated circular cycle way, and a host of centres are geared up for caving and other more specialist pursuits.

Most approaches are from the industrial towns to the south, via the superbly engineered **Settle to Carlisle Railway**, or along the main A65 road from towns such as **Skipton**, **Settle** and **Ingleton**. This makes southern dales like **Wharfedale** the most visited, while neighbouring **Malhamdale** is also immensely popular, thanks to the fascinating scenery squeezed into its narrow confines around **Malham**, perhaps the single most visited village in the region. **Ribblesdale**, approached from Settle, is more sombre, its villages in demand from hikers intent on tackling the Dales' famous **Three Peaks** – the mountains of Pen-y-ghent, Ingleborough and Whernside. To the northwest lies the more remote **Dentdale**, which with **Garsdale** is one of the least known but most beautiful of the valleys. Moving north, there are two parallel dales, **Wensleydale** and **Swaledale**, the latter pushing Dentdale as the most rewarding overall target. Both flow east, with Swaledale's lower stretches encompassing **Richmond**, an appealing historic town from which Ripon, York and the North York Moors are easily reached.

Public transport throughout the Dales is surprisingly good, though there are limited bus services on Sundays, in winter and to the more remote valleys. Pick up the invaluable, free *Dales Explorer* bus timetable (published twice a year), available from tourist offices and from the various **National Park information centres**. There are main centres at Grassington, Aysgarth Falls, Malham, Reeth, Hawes and Clapham, for which opening hours and other details are given in the text below; all can help with accommodation, sell excellent walk and trail leaflets, and organize year-round hikes and events, from nature trails to photography workshops. In addition, there are numerous National Park **information points** in shops, post offices and cafés throughout the region, which tend to open during local business hours throughout the year (usually Mon–Fri 9am–5pm). At information centres and points, pick up a copy of the free *Visitor* newspaper, a seasonal publication packed with useful listings, information and adverts.

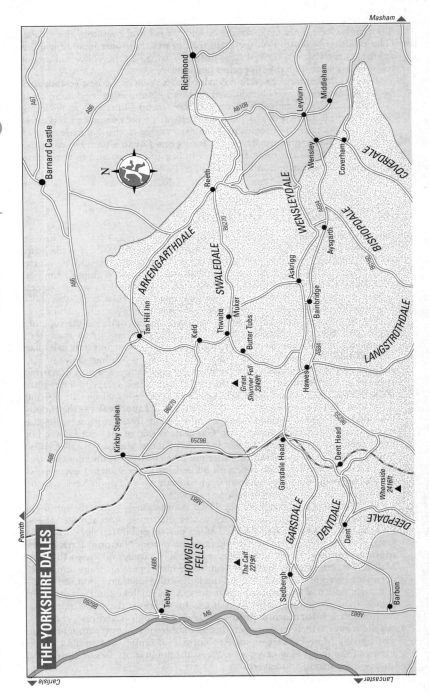

THE YORKSHIRE DALES

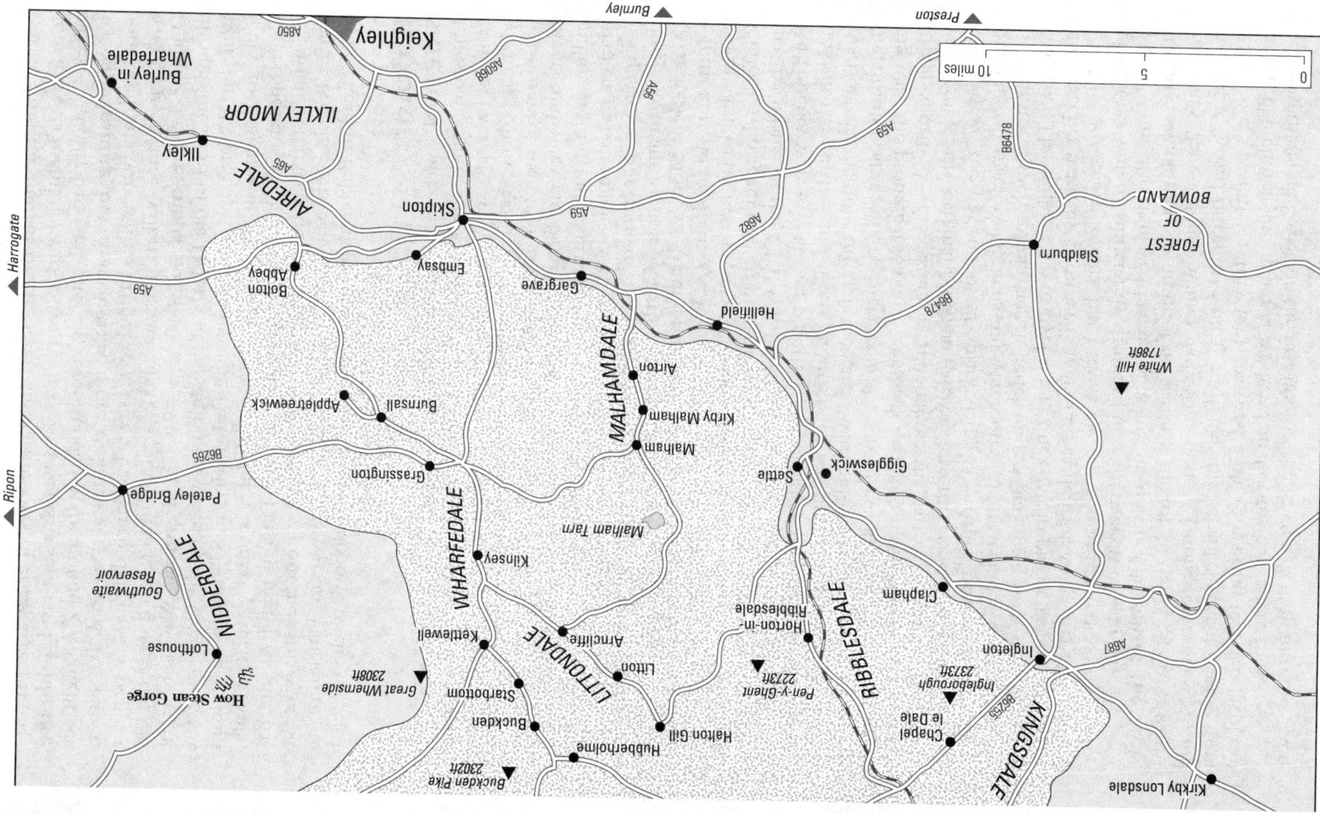

Ripon

Harrogate

Lofthouse
Gouthwaite Reservoir
How Stean Gorge
NIDDERDALE
Pateley Bridge
B6265

Burley in Wharfedale
Ilkley
A65
ILKLEY MOOR
A850

Great Whernside 2308ft
Kettlewell
Buckden Pike 2302ft
Buckden
Starbottom
WHARFEDALE
Kinsey
Grassington
Burnsall
Appletreewick
Bolton Abbey
Embsay
Skipton
Keighley
A6038

Hubberholme
LITTONDALE
Arncliffe
Litton
Halton Gill
Malham Tarn
MALHAMDALE
Malham
Kirby Malham
Airton
Gargrave
A59
A56
Burnley

Pen-y-Ghent 2273ft
Horton-in-Ribblesdale
Settle
Hellifield
A682
B6479

RIBBLESDALE
Giggleswick
Clapham

Chapel le Dale
Ingleborough 2373ft
Ingleton
B6255
KINGSDALE

Kirkby Lonsdale
A65

White Hill 1786ft
Slaidburn
B6478
Preston

FOREST OF BOWLAND

Lancaster

10 miles
5
0

899

© Crown copyright

Aside from the myriad B&Bs, hotels and farmhouses offering accommodation, there's a useful network of youth hostels as well as a series of **bunkhouse barns** – typically, basic self-catering accommodation for around £7 a night per person; **camping barns** are usually more rudimentary versions. For either, book well in advance if it's crucial to secure a bed, since they're very popular with long-distance walkers. For any kind of serious hiking, you'll need the OS Outdoor Leisure **maps** #2, #10 and #30. The **Pennine Way** cuts right through the heart of the Dales, and the region is crossed by the Coast-to-Coast Walk, but the principal local route is the **Dales Way**, an 84-mile footpath from Ilkley to Bowness in the Lake District, which takes around a week to walk. Colin Speakman's *Dales Way* guidebook (Dalesman Press) is useful. An alternative route is the less-walked, seventy-mile **Ribble Way** from the estuary of the River Ribble, between Lytham St Anne's and Preston in Lancashire, to Ribblehead in Ribblesdale; there's a National Park guidebook to the route.

Skipton

SKIPTON, southernmost town of the Dales, rightly belongs to Airedale, but almost any trip to the southern dales is going to pass through here, particularly if you want to see Wharfedale, five miles to the east. Apart from practical advantages, however, the town's worth a few hours in its own right, particularly on one of its four weekly **market** days (Mon, Wed, Fri & Sat), when the streets and pubs are filled with what seems like half the Dales population, milling around and determined to enjoy themselves. Similarly lively Christmas markets in December are an enjoyable feature, too.

Sceptone, or "Sheeptown", was a settlement long before the arrival of the battling Normans, whose **Castle**, located at the top of the High Street (March–Sept Mon–Sat 10am–6pm, Sun noon–6pm; Oct–Feb Mon–Sat 10am–4pm, Sun noon–4pm; £4.40), provided the basis for the present fortress, among England's best preserved, thanks mainly to the efforts of Lady Anne Clifford, who rebuilt much of her family seat between 1650 and 1675 following the pillage of the Civil War. The castle withstood a three-and-a-half-year Parliamentary siege – at one point it was the last remaining Royalist stronghold in the north – and when its surrender was finally negotiated, the Royal garrison marched out through the gates "with colours flying, trumpets sounding, drums beating". Little survives in the way of furniture or fittings, but starting with the proud battlements – emblazoned with the Clifford cry, *Desormais* ("Henceforth"!) – the castle very much looks the part. A self-guided tour leads you through the original Norman gateway into the beautiful Conduit Court, whose yew tree was supposedly planted by Lady Anne. Beyond lie the banqueting hall, spacious kitchens and storerooms (giving a clue as to how the castle withstood such a long siege), bedchambers and six towers with their slit windows. The walls are up to twelve feet thick, yet in places it's possible to see the breaches made by Cromwell's men. The castle roofs were later removed on the Lord Protector's orders, but Lady Anne was allowed to replace them provided they weren't sufficiently strong to bear the weight of cannon.

Lady Anne also displayed her restorative skills on the **Church of the Holy Trinity**, which stands in front of the castle at the top of the High Street (summer daily 9am–4.30pm; winter daily 9am–dusk; £1 donation requested), and has a fine bossed fifteenth-century roof, beautiful chancel screen (dating from 1533) and a twelfth-century font crowned with a towering wooden Jacobean cover. The church also retains a medieval anchorite's cell, a rare find.

Down the High Street, on the first floor of the town hall, drop into the entertaining **Craven Museum** (April–Sept Mon & Wed–Sat 10am–5pm, Sun 2–5pm; Oct–March Mon & Wed–Fri 1.30–5pm, Sat 10am–4pm; free), a brief introduction to the geology, flora, fauna, folk history and archeology of Craven, the region cradled between Wharfedale and the Lancashire border. The collection runs the gamut from boneshaker bicycles to policemen's helmets, by way of flints, fossils, snuff boxes, grandfather clocks and a hippopotamus skull, all seemingly last labelled and laid out in the 1950s.

After that, all that remains is to stroll through the oldest part of town, over and around Mill Bridge (left at the top of the High Street). The **High Corn Mill** here is a working watermill that's stood since the Domesday Book, now converted into shops. Steps from the bridge lead down to **Springs Canal**, along which a path runs under the sheer walls of the castle, bears left over a footbridge and then returns on high ground for more castle views, emerging back at the mill twenty minutes later.

Practicalities

Skipton is a vital **transportation hub**, with direct **trains** from Leeds, Bradford, Keighley, Carlisle, Lancaster and Morecambe. The station is on Broughton Road, a ten-minute walk from the centre. Note that if you're heading for the Settle–Carlisle Railway (p.911), most trains **from Skipton** are direct – you shouldn't need to change at Settle unless you want to break your journey. The **bus station** is closer in, on Keighley Road, just shy of Devonshire Place at the bottom of the High Street. There are National Express coaches from London, and buses from Bradford via Keighley, as well as from Leeds, Ilkley, Harrogate and York; a useful summer service (#X9; Wed, Fri & Sat only) links the Lake District with Skipton. Local services run from Skipton to Settle (not Sun) for connections on to Ingleton and Horton; Malham (Mon–Fri only); and Grassington (not Sun). You can **rent bikes** for around £12 a day from The Bicycle Shop on Water St (℡01756/794386), or from Dave Ferguson Cycles at Bowbridge Garage on Skipton Road (℡01756/792526). For **walking and camping supplies**, the celebrated Lake District firm George Fisher has an outlet at 1 Coach St, with the similarly endowed Dales Outdoor Centre back down the road.

The alleys on the western side of the High Street emerge onto the banks of the **Leeds–Liverpool Canal**, which runs right through the centre of Skipton. You can rent boats from the Canal Basin, off Coach Street: Pennine Boat Trips at Waterside Court (℡01756/790829), next to the George Fisher outdoor store, runs daily **canal cruises** (April–Oct; £3.50); while Pennine Marine Ltd, The Boat Shop, 19 Coach St (℡01756/795478), can provide self-steered **narrowboats** (£60–100/day, depending on season).

If the Keighley and Worth Valley Railway (see p.894) hasn't satisfied your need for steam, the **Yorkshire Dales Railway Society** runs an impressive range of locomotives from the station at **Embsay**, two miles east of the town on the A59 (up to 5 daily in summer; rest of year runs at least on Sun; 11am–4pm). Trains run the four miles to Bolton Abbey station (call ℡01756 /795189 or 794727 for information; £5 return). There are hourly buses from Skipton to Embsay (the #214; not Sun).

The **tourist office**, on Coach St (Mon–Sat 10am–5pm; Sun 11.30am–2pm & 3.30-5pm; ℡01756/792809, ⍾www.skiptononline.co.uk), offers a friendly service and details of local and seasonal events. **Accommodation** is plentiful, with a host of central pubs offering rooms. Best choice is the *Woolly Sheep Inn*, 38 Sheep St (℡01756/700966, ❷), a restored seventeenth-century inn which fills quickly. Otherwise, try the rooms at the *Red Lion*, on the High Street

△Tetley Brewery, Leeds

(☎01756/790718; ❶), or at the fairly shabby *Devonshire Hotel*, on Newmarket Street (☎01756/793078; ❶). B&Bs tend to lie on the outskirts, ten minutes or so out of the centre, on Gargrave (west) and Keighley (south) roads. *Peace Villas*, 69 Gargrave Rd (☎01756/790672; no credit cards; ❶), and the *Skipton Park Guest 'Otel*, virtually opposite at 2 Salisbury St (☎01756/700640; no credit cards; ❷), are the best places on Gargrave Road; the *Highfield Hotel*, 58 Keighley Rd (☎01756/793182; no credit cards; ❷), is one of a clutch on that road.

    Eating is better in Skipton than in most Dales towns. *Bizzie Lizzies*, on Swadford Street, is the award winning fish-and-chip shop of the town, while *Herbs*, 10 High St (closed Tues & Sun), is a veggie place serving home-made soups and home-baked cakes, as well as a daily special for around a fiver. At night, make for the *Woolly Sheep Inn* which has inventive bar food, decent beer and a garden. The *Aagrah*, on Devonshire Place, off Keighley Road near the bus station, might be decked out like a snake-charmer's boudoir, but it has a loyal local following for its fresh, tasty Indian dishes. *Le Caveau*, 86 High St (closed Sun & Mon), a pricey Anglo-French restaurant, with lunchtime and mid-week evening specials, is the town's top spot. Other than the *Woolly Sheep*, the only other **pub** worth drinking in is the *Royal Shepherd* in Canal Street, a backstreet local with good beer.

Wharfedale

The lower reaches of **Wharfedale** extend way to the east, embracing towns as distant as Wetherby before joining the Ouse south of York, but for most people the dale really starts just south and east of Skipton, with **Ilkley** and **Bolton Abbey**, and then continues north in a broad, pastoral swathe scattered with villages as picture-perfect as any in northern England. **Grassington** is the main village, a popular walking centre, packed to capacity in summer; lesser hamlets in Upper Wharfedale, like **Kettlewell** and **Buckden**, make less frenetic bases. Upland roads lead from the head of the valley up minor dales to cross the watershed into Wensleydale, though the most attractive itinerary would take you up lonely Littondale to **Arncliffe**, a village almost too good to be true, and then over the tops to either Malham or Ribblesdale.

    Throughout the year, the #71 **bus** runs roughly hourly (not Sun) to Grassington and Hebden from Skipton (via Cracoe and Threshfield), and less frequently on up the B6160 to Kettlewell, Starbotton and Buckden. This is augmented by two seasonal services: the **Dalesbus** (Easter–May & Oct Sun; June–Sept Sat & Sun; Aug Tues, Sat & Sun), from Leeds, Bradford and Ilkley to Buckden, travelling on to Wensleydale; and the Sunday-only **Wharfedale Wanderer** (late May to Aug), which leaves Ilkley hourly for Grassington via Bolton Abbey, and then travels on to Kettlewell, Starbotton and Buckden.

Ilkley

Approaching Wharfedale from Leeds and the southeast, along the A65, it's a gentle climb to the approaching moorland, with barely a hint of the coming grandeur even by the time you reach the small, stone town of **ILKLEY**, gamely claiming to be the gateway to the Dales. It's really no such thing, though it was once a spa town of some repute and still boasts a handsome centre of Victorian buildings and landscaped gardens. Its history can be traced right back to the Romans, who built the fort of Olicana here in 79 AD, the foundations of which lie under the grassy knoll behind All Saints parish church on Church Street. Sundry Roman relics and other local finds are displayed in the adjacent, sixteenth-century **Manor House Museum** (Wed–Sat 11am–5pm, Sun 1–4pm; free).

To the south, encroaching upon the very town, broods **Ilkley Moor**, littered with ancient stone circles and weathered rocks – and, if the more lurid tales are to be believed, site of numerous UFO appearances and alien abductions. In the words of a round known to many Yorkshire schoolchildren, the windswept moor is also where "tha's been a-courtin' Mary Jane, on Ilkley Moor baht-'at [without a hat]" – a foolish sartorial omission since, according to the round, you'll catch your death of cold, die, be buried, eaten by worms, which are eaten by ducks, which are eaten by people, until "then we shall all 'ave etten thee". With hat firmly in place you can follow the numerous tracks which cut across the highest part of the moor, seeking out Bronze Age stone circles like the Twelve Apostles or the weathered rocks known as the Cow and the Calf, before heading south to Keighley, six miles away.

The **bus** and **train stations** are next to each other on Station Road. Aside from regular train and bus connections with Leeds/Bradford, the #X84/784 bus runs hourly between Leeds, Ilkley and Skipton, while the town is also on the route of the Dalesbus and the Wharfedale Wanderer. Opposite the station in the Town Hall is the **tourist office** (Mon–Sat 9.30am–5.30pm, Sun 1–4pm; ☎01943/602319), outside which is pinned a local accommodation list. You're unlikely to stay, but you might find time to **eat**. There is a branch of the Harrogate tea-and-cake stalwart *Betty's* at 32 The Grove, while the foodie choice is the *Box Tree*, 37 Church St (☎01943/608484; closed Mon), an outstanding French restaurant with meals at around £30 a head, excluding drinks. Ilkley's annual **literature festival** (Sept/Oct) attracts top names to its events and readings.

Bolton Abbey and the Strid

BOLTON ABBEY, five miles east of Skipton, is the name of a whole village rather than an abbey, a confusion compounded by the fact that the place's main monastic ruin is known as **Bolton Priory** (Mon–Thurs & Sat 8.30am–7pm, or dusk if earlier, Fri 8.30am–4pm; free). The priory formed part of an Augustinian community founded at nearby Embsay by Cecily de Romille in 1135, and was moved here in the 1150s by her daughter, Alice, to commemorate the drowning of her son in the Strid (see below). Turner painted the site, and Ruskin described it as the most beautiful in England, though the priory is now mostly ruined, a consequence of the Dissolution; only the nave, which was incorporated into the village church in 1170, has survived in almost its original state. A £10 bribe sent by the last prior to Thomas Cromwell, Henry VIII's lieutenant, unsurprisingly failed to change the course of history.

The priory is also the starting point for several highly popular riverside walks, including a section of the **Dales Way** footpath that follows the river's west bank to take in Bolton Woods and the **Strid** (from "stride"), an extraordinary piece of white water two miles north of the abbey, where softer rock has allowed the river to funnel into a cleft just a few feet wide. Numerous people have drowned trying to make the leap (the river here is 30ft deep), and the quite obvious dangers are underlined by the lifebelts hung nearby. Beyond the Strid, the path – a designated nature trail – emerges at **Barden Bridge**, four miles from the priory, where the fortified **Barden Tower** was another little restoration job for Lady Anne Clifford; there's a tearoom here. You can then return to Bolton Abbey either by doubling back the same way, or by taking the country lanes and tracks on the other (east) bank, perhaps incorporating a lovely short detour past the becks and waterfalls of the **Valley of Desolation** midway between Barden and Bolton.

To get here without your own transport, you're reliant upon the Wharfedale

Wanderer summer bus service, or a taxi from Skipton – the journey will set you back around £8 each way. Embsay and Bolton Abbey Steam Railway is a mile and a half from the priory ruins. Drivers have to stump up £3 to park in one of the estate **car parks**. There's local information from the estate office (☎01756/710533) and an information point at **Cavendish Pavilion**, a mile north of the priory, where there's also a riverside restaurant and café (April–Oct daily; Nov–March weekends only). *Bolton Abbey Tea Cottage*, next to the priory, offers traditional afternoon teas; it's a bit over-priced but worth it if the weather allows you to sit in the garden and admire the views.

Accommodation hereabouts is limited. At Bolton Abbey the main hotel is the sumptuous *Devonshire Arms* (☎01756/710441; ❽), just south of the village, owned by the duke and duchess of Devonshire and furnished with antiques from their ancestral pile at Chatsworth; there's a brasserie and bar open to the public too. Considerably easier on the pocket are two B&Bs, one at *Hesketh Farm*, a mile west of the village (☎01756/710541; no credit cards; ❶), the other at *Holme House Farm*, a quarter of a mile south of Barden, overlooking the river (☎01756/720661; no credit cards; ❶). Skipton tourist office has details of several other local farmhouse B&Bs. *Barden Bunk Barn*, right by the tower and just 300 yards off the Dales Way (☎01756/720330), is a useful bunkhouse stop for long-distance hikers; it's reserved for groups only at weekends.

Grassington and around

You might follow the Dales Way up the River Wharfe at least as far as **GRASSINGTON**, the dale's popular main village, located nine miles from Bolton Abbey. It's fairly dreary on its outskirts but has a good Georgian centre, albeit one tempered by dollops of fake rusticity. The surroundings are at their best by the river, where the shallow Linton Falls thunder after rain; a waterside path leads a mile upstream to the Grass Wood nature reserve. Back in the village, the cobbled Market Square is home to several inns and to the **Upper Wharfedale Museum** (Easter–Sept daily 2–4.30pm; Oct–Easter Sat & Sun 2–4.30pm; 50p), an occasionally eccentric collection of minerals, farming implements and local miscellanea. Other traditional rural pursuits, as well as music and arts events, are celebrated in both the annual **Grassington Festival**, held every June, and the Dickensian Christmas market, held on December Saturdays in the village square.

The **National Park information centre** on Hebden Road (April–Oct daily 9.30am–5pm; Nov–March most weekends 10am–4pm; ☎01756/752774), across from the **bus stop**, books accommodation and provides wide-ranging information, particularly on the region's long lead-mining tradition. You might grab a **parking** space in the Market Square; otherwise, there's a pay-and-display car park at the information centre. For hiking boots and **camping gear**, visit Mountaineer on Garrs Lane (☎01756/752266), up past the *Black Horse* pub.

In summer you should book **accommodation** in advance. Good B&Bs include *Kirkfield*, a detached house in its own grounds on Hebden Road (☎01756/752385; no credit cards; ❶), just past the National Park Centre; and the more central *Town Head Guest House*, 1 Low Lane (☎01756/752811; no credit cards; ❷), next to the Town Hall off Main Street. Costlier, but with a good reputation, is seventeenth-century *Ashfield House* on Summers Fold (☎01756/752584; ❹; closed Dec & Jan), fifty yards off the square (behind the *Devonshire Hotel*), which boasts a walled garden, good breakfasts and some special weekend deals. If you want to stay right on the square, try the Georgian *Grassington House Hotel* (☎01756/752406; ❹), or the welcoming *Black Horse*,

Garrs Lane (☎01756/752770; ④). The local **hostel** is at Linton (see below), while the nearest **campsite** is the small *Bell Bank*, Skirethorns Lane, in Threshfield (☎01756/752321), a little over a mile to the west – milk and eggs are available to buy.

Grassington has plenty of **cafés** and a few **restaurants**. The *Dales Kitchen*, 51 Main St, serves traditional and Mediterranean dishes during the day – try their home-made fruitcake with Wensleydale cheese. All the **pubs** serve bar meals, the *Black Horse* having the best and also being the nicest place to down a pint. The *Devonshire Hotel*, also on the square, has a more expensive and refined menu. Otherwise, head over to Threshfield where the stone-flagged *Old Hall Inn* (☎01756/752441; closed Sun eve & Mon) wins plaudits for its great food: expect to have to wait for a table before tucking into salmon with tomato and coriander sauce, local sausages and the like.

At busy times you may have to look further afield for **accommodation** and services, but Grassington is surrounded by tiny scenic **villages**. The closest, **LINTON**, a mile to the southwest across the river, sports a **youth hostel** (☎01756/752400; ①) housed in a seventeenth-century rectory. The rooms are musty and a bit basic, but you can eat well across the green at the *Fountaine Inn*. To the southeast, back down the Dales Way, the two superb hamlets of Appletreewick and Burnsall both have accommodation of one sort or another. At **APPLETREEWICK**, as well as the odd B&B, there's a campsite, *Mason's*, at Ainhams farm (☎01756/720236; closed Nov–Easter), while the cosy *Craven Arms* doles out filling meals to walkers. **BURNSALL**'s wonderful *Red Lion* (☎01756/720204; ⑥, ⑦ with dinner) has river views from its comfortable rooms and features inventive meals using local ingredients; the *Wharfe View Tearooms* also overlooks the river. There are cheaper B&Bs here, usually displaying vacancy signs.

The Skipton bus runs up the B6265 through **CRACOE**, a couple of miles south of Grassington, whose beamed *Devonshire Arms* (☎01756/730237; ③) makes another comfortable base. Best of all is the renowned *Angel Inn* (☎01756/730263), in the hamlet of **HETTON**, a mile southwest from Cracoe along a country lane. It serves some of the best food and wine in the region, including a wide range of perfectly judged fish dishes – gratifying meals running to around £25.

Kilnsey

Wharfedale's scenery above Grassington grows still more impressive, starting a mile north with a tract of ancient woodland, **Grass Wood**, and followed two miles later by **Kilnsey Crag**, a dramatic, glacially carved overhang which attracts its fair share of climbers. Information on the crag and its surroundings can be gleaned from the **National Park information point** at Kilnsey Park on the southern edge of **KILNSEY** village. There's a **trout farm** in the park (daily 9am–5.30pm or dusk if earlier), which aside from its fishing (rods available to rent) provides a whole host of children's activities as well as a café; the deli-shop is worth a visit if you're self-catering, selling everything from eggs and honey to game and gravadlax. You can stay in Kilnsey at the *Tennant Arms* (☎01756/752301; c), whose restaurant overlooks the crag, or at a couple of local farmhouse B&Bs. Half a mile further north, at the junction of the Littondale road, there's a **bunkhouse barn**, *Skirfare Bridge Barn* (☎01756 /752465), with a drying room and kitchen.

Littondale

Just beyond the Kilnsey Crag, a minor road branches off left into **Littondale**, an empty, pristine dale with stunning scenery and views, especially at Hesleden Bergh, around six miles up the dale, where a road climbs south over the moors – with Pen-y-ghent looming to the west – to Stainforth in Ribblesdale. A daily **school bus** (which the public can use) from Grassington runs up Littondale as far as Halton Gill, but otherwise there's no public transport.

ARNCLIFFE, halfway up the dale, is as idyllic a village as you'll find. The ivy-covered *Falcon* (℡01756/770205; **❸**, **❹** with dinner) on the village green attracts walkers from far and wide; the dinner, bed and breakfast deal is good value, and the beer's good. There's a campsite back down the road, a mile and a half southeast of Arncliffe, at *Hawkswick Cote Farm* (℡01756/770226; closed Nov–Feb). The minor moorland road south to Malham from Arncliffe can be treacherous in winter; check the weather reports before setting off. *Raikes Cottage*, just out of Arncliffe on the Malham road, is a nice riverside tearoom (weekends only in winter).

On foot, the ideal way to see the dale is to follow the valley-floor footpath from Arncliffe to **LITTON** (2–3 miles), where the ancient and unspoilt *Queen's Arms* (℡01756/770208; **❷**) could serve as a base for climbing Pen-y-ghent; a steep track also cuts north across the fells to Buckden. There's B&B accommodation available too; try *Litton Hall* (℡01756/770238; no credit cards; **❶**), look for local vacancy signs or contact the **National Park information point** at Litton post office.

Beyond Litton, the path (and road) continues the three miles up to **Halton Gill**, where just outside the hamlet there's the self-catering *Halton Gill Bunk Barn* (℡01756/770241), and beyond to **FOXUP** and **COSH** (two miles from Halton Gill) – possibly the most remote settlements in the Dales, though B&B is available at Foxup's *Bridge Farm* (℡01756/770249; no credit cards; **❶**; closed Nov–March).

Kettlewell

The landscapes in the last six miles of Wharfedale and its continuation, **Langstrothdale**, hardly suffer by comparison with Littondale, a large proportion of their moors and valleys forming part of the National Trust's vast Upper Wharfedale Estate. **KETTLEWELL** (Norse for "bubbling spring"), three miles north of Kilnsey, is the main centre for the upper dale, a far more attractive proposition for a weekend's walking or relaxing than Grassington, with an informal **National Park information point** in the Over and Under outdoor shop, a **campsite** (℡01756/760886) just to the north at Fold Farm, and the *Whernside House* **youth hostel** (℡01765/760232) in the centre of the village. There's plenty of other **accommodation** in the village too: the *Racehorses Hotel* (℡01756/760233; **❷**), on the bridge, is an eighteenth-century hotel with twelve en-suite rooms and beautiful views of the River Wharfe. Other village choices include the *Elms* on Middle Lane (℡01756/760380; no credit cards; **❷**) and *Chestnut Cottage* by the stream (℡01756/760804; no credit cards; **❷**). The village **pubs**, the *Bluebell* and the *King's Head*, are both cosy places for a drink.

Starbotton, Buckden and Hubberholme

It's lovely country north of Kettlewell, accessed either via the dale's single lonely road (B6160) or the Dales Way path, both of which push to the dale's upper limit. At **STARBOTTON**, two miles away, the *Fox & Hounds* (℡01756 /760269; **❸**; closed Mon in winter & all Jan) has three rooms for rent, ancient flagged floors, a huge fire and popular food. Topnotch pub accommodation is also available in **BUCKDEN**, another couple of miles to the north, this time at the superbly sited *Buck Inn* (℡01756/760228; ❺, ❻ with dinner). For information on Buckden's other half-dozen cheaper B&B options (many on outlying farms), contact the **National Park information point** at the village's Riverside Gallery. Beyond Buckden, the road winds up and down Bishopdale the ten miles or so to Aysgarth in Wensleydale (see p.920).

A mile upstream, the river flows through Langstrothdale to **HUBBERHOLME** and the stone-flagged, whitewashed *George* (℡01756/760223; ❷), the favourite pub of archetypal Yorkshireman J.B. Priestley, who revelled in visiting a hamlet he thought "one of the smallest and pleasantest places in the world". He's buried in the churchyard of the small chapel of St Michael and All Angels, over the stone bridge from the pub. There's a year-round bunkhouse barn in Hubberholme at *Grange Farm* (℡01756/760259), just five minutes' walk from the pub on the route back to Buckden. The Dales Way marches on up the valley, with the next halt over in Dent (see p.916), a superb cross-dales hike.

Malhamdale

A few miles west of Wharfedale lies **Malhamdale**, the uppermost reaches of Airedale and one of the National Park's most heavily visited regions, thanks to its three outstanding natural features: Malham Cove, Malham Tarn and Gordale Scar. It's classic limestone country, dominated by a mighty escarpment topped by a fractured pavement, and cut through with sheer walls, tumbling waterfalls and dry valleys – in short, a place to feed the soul while exercising the body. Unfortunately for those seeking solitude, all three main attractions are within easy hiking distance of **Malham village**, so any walking you do locally is likely to be in company, with the Pennine Way further adding to the column of walkers processing through the area.

The approach by **public transport** is on the #210 bus or post bus from Skipton (not Sun), a thirty- to sixty-minute ride depending on the service. You may simply choose to **walk** in across country: Malham is only around six miles from Gargrave (a station on the Skipton–Settle train line, and on the Pennine Way) to the south, and a similar distance from Settle to the west – a particularly fine approach – or from Grassington in the east.

Malham village

Unless you're here off-season, some idea of what to expect in **MALHAM** comes at the vast peripheral car park, likely to be packed solid with hikers and day-trippers. The village is home to barely more than a couple of hundred people, who inhabit the huddled stone houses on either side of a bubbling river, but this microscopic gem attracts perhaps half a million visitors a year. Provided you're prepared to do some walking you can escape the worst of the crowds, and something of the village's off-peak charm can be enjoyed in the evening when most of the trippers have gone home. If, however, you're planning on staying, note that competition is stiff for rooms.

Unless you already have maps and accommodation sorted out, your first stop should be the **National Park information centre** on the southern edge of the village (Easter–Oct daily 10am–5pm; Nov–Easter Sat & Sun 10am–4pm; ℡01729/830363). It sells a range of local walking guides and can help with finding a room. In summer, you'll need to book ahead to get a bed at the **youth hostel** (℡01729/830321, ✉malham@yha.org.uk). However, there's also a centrally heated **bunkhouse barn** at *Hill Top Farm* (☎01729/830320), immediately north of the National Park information centre, and several good village **B&Bs**, among them rambling *Beck Hall* (☎01729/830332; ❷), set in its own streamside gardens a couple of hundred yards from the fork in the village centre; and the excellent *Miresfield Farm* (☎01729/830414; ❷), on the edge of the village near the information centre. The comfortable *Riverhouse Hotel* (☎01729/830315; ❸), on the road through the village, serves great evening meals, and you can sit in the little front garden for tea and sandwiches. The *Buck Inn* (☎01729/830317; ❸) is almost next door, and also has rooms. You can **camp** at *Townhead Farm* (☎01729/830287; reservations advised), near the cove, and under Gordale Scar at *Gordale Scar House Campsite* (☎01729/830333; closed Nov–March). There's a **tearoom** or two in the village, and a basic shop. Meals are served in the **pubs**, notably at the *Buck*, with a popular walkers' back bar, but also at the fancier *Lister Arms*, over the bridge.

You might also put up in any of Malhamdale's three other villages to the south: pretty **Kirkby Malham**, **Hanlith** and **Airton**, all within three miles of Malham itself. The information centre can advise on vacancies, but try the *Lindon House Guest House* (☎01729/830418; no credit cards; ❶) in Airton, an old Quaker village two miles south of Malham. Closer to the town, in Hanlith, the *Coachman's Cottage* (☎01729/830538; no credit cards; ❷) is a nice seven-teenth-century house, while Kirby Malham's *Victoria Inn* (☎01729/830213; ❸) is a friendly spot and has reasonable food.

Malham Cove, Malham Tarn and Gordale Scar

Appearing in spectacular fashion a mile north of Malham, **Malham Cove** is a white-walled limestone amphitheatre rising three hundred feet above its surroundings. Like Gordale Scar's ramparts to the east, it was formed by a shear along the Mid-Craven Fault, a geological tear that runs 22 miles from Wharfedale to Kirkby Lonsdale in Cumbria. Still visible on the cliff-top are the black stains left by an earlier waterfall, once higher than Niagara, which dried up during the eighteenth century. Now it's merely a stream of bubbles at the base. It is not, as is often claimed, the source of the Aire, which has more humble beginnings at Aire Head springs, half a mile south of Malham village.

A broad **track** leads to the cove, passing some of England's most visible prehistoric field banks en route. Fewer people make the breath-sapping haul to the top, where the rewards are fine views and the famous **limestone pavement**, an expanse of clints (slabs) and grykes (clefts) created by water seeping through weaker lines in the limestone rock. Unusual plants and ferns such as dog's mercury and hart's tongue shelter in the crevices, making this a favoured spot for botanists.

To the northwest rises the great bulk of **Fountains Fell**, its name a link with Fountains Abbey many miles to the east, erstwhile owner of huge estates in Craven. A simple walk over the moors, either via the Pennine Way or the more interesting dry valley to the west, abruptly brings **Malham Tarn** into sight, a lake created by an impervious layer of glacial debris. This, too, is an area of outstanding natural interest, its numerous waterfowl protected by a nature reserve on the west bank, visible from a nature trail which forms part of the Pennine Way on the east bank.

Unless your interests are ornithological, however, it's best to make do with the view from the cliff-top and avoid the long hike round the lake; you can then turn south for **Gordale Scar**, which is also easily approached direct from Malham village. Here the cliffs are if anything more spectacular than at Malham Cove, complemented by a deep ravine to the rear caused by the collapse of a cavern roof. A little to the south of the scar, off the road, lies **Janet's Foss**, a peach of a waterfall set amidst green-damp rocks and overarching trees.

There's a classic circuit which takes in Malham's trio of sights in a clockwise **walk from Malham** (8 miles; 3hr 30min), the only problem being at Gordale Scar, where it may be difficult to scramble down the stream-cut gorge after heavy rain for the last leg back to Malham. If you don't want to see the Tarn and open moorland, the walk is easily cut short by taking a waymarked track from the northern edge of the pavement, above Malham Cove, down to Gordale Bridge and thus on to Gordale Scar (5 miles; 2hr 30min). From Gordale Scar you could simply follow the Gordale lane back into the village, though the longer path via Janet's Foss, along the beck and across the fields, is more agreeable.

Ribblesdale

The scenery of **Ribblesdale**, to the west of Malhamdale, is more dour and brooding than the bucolic valleys to the east. It's entered from Settle, starting point of the superbly engineered **Settle–Carlisle Railway**, among the most scenic rail routes in the country (see box opposite). After Stainforth, close to one of the more noted of the Dales' many waterfalls (or "forces"), the valley's only village of any size is **Horton in Ribblesdale**, a focus not only for the Ribble Way and Pennine Way, but also where most people start the **Three Peaks Walk**, an arduous hike around the Dales' highest peaks.

Settle is the **transport** junction for Ribblesdale, with daily **trains** heading north through Horton to Carlisle and south to Skipton, Keighley and Leeds; a limited service operates on Sundays. The hourly #580 **bus** (not Sun) also connects Skipton with Settle, from where a useful service runs three or four times daily (not Sun) north through Stainforth to Horton but no further, and northwest via Giggleswick and Clapham to Ingleton in the western dales (see p.914). Coming from Malham, you could **walk** the six miles along an old pack road via Kirkby Fell and Attermire Scar, the latter being grandiose cliffs on the Mid-Craven Fault.

Settle

Nestled under the wooded knoll of Castleberg, **SETTLE** is well-placed for upper Ribblesdale and a pleasant enough base if you haven't the time to find a more intimate overnight stop within the National Park. The village has a typical seventeenth-century market square, top-heavy with tearooms but still sporting its split-level arcaded shambles, which once housed butchers' shops. Other than on Tuesdays, when the **market** is in full swing, there's not much to see in the few streets behind the square. Aim instead for the **Watershed Mill Visitor Centre**, on Langcliffe Road (Mon–Sat 10am–5pm; Sun 11am–5pm; free), north of the centre by the river, an early nineteenth-century cotton mill transformed into a shopping centre selling Dales goods; there are craft demonstrations throughout the year and a coffee shop.

All other local diversions involve a good **walk**. The shortest is the slog up the path to the top of Castleberg for views over the town. The **Ribble Way** footpath, which passes through town, continues to Stainforth (see below), or there's the well-signposted four-mile round-trip hike northeast to **Victoria Cave**, a gaping maw in the Mid-Craven Fault in which archeologists found the bones of prehistoric beasts.

The **tourist office** in the town hall on Cheapside, just off Market Place (daily 10am–5pm; ✆01729/825192), is the place to seek out onward routes

The Settle to Carlisle railway

With the nineteenth-century **railway boom** at its height, the Midland Railway company – eager to muscle in on the profits made by its rival, the London and North Western Railway on its west-coast route – applied to Parliament to build a line which would link the industrial heartlands of West Yorkshire with Carlisle and the Scottish borders beyond. In the six years between 1869 and 1875, when the 72-mile **Settle–Carlisle** line opened, herculean efforts were made by thousands of navvies to blast a route through the unforgiving Dales mountainsides. Living in squalid shanty towns by the sides of the track, and even in the newly opened railway tunnels themselves, six thousand men built twenty viaducts and bored fourteen tunnels in a feat of Victorian engineering that has few equals in Britain. Over two hundred of the workers died, some of smallpox and other diseases, others in horrific accidents; many now lie buried in the village churches that line the route.

The railway itself was an immediate success, forming a popular route to Scotland and later used as a freight and troop carrier during World War II. By the 1970s, though, services had been severely reduced as British Rail "rationalized" its operations and in 1983 it was announced that the line was to close. After a vociferous campaign, local groups kept the line open and as tourist interest has picked up, the route seems set to have an assured future, at least in the medium term. Stations have been restored to their nineteenth-century glory and special steam train services sometimes operate.

The attraction in riding the line is the chance to experience what the operators – with no hint of hype – dub **"England's most scenic railway"**. From Settle, the drag up Ribblesdale brings ever more spectacular views – between Horton and Ribblehead the line climbs two hundred feet in five miles, before crossing the famous 24-arched Ribblehead viaduct. Dent is the highest, and bleakest, main-line station in England. Further on, the route heads through Ais Gill, 1100 feet above sea level, before it finally drops into the gentler Eden Valley and on to Carlisle.

The **journey** from Settle to Carlisle takes just under an hour and forty minutes, so it's easy to make a **return trip** (£16.30 for adult day return) along the whole length of the line if you wish. There are connections from Skipton and Leeds (2hr 40min); full **timetable** details are available from National Rail Enquiries, ☏0845/7484950, or from the website, ⊛www.settle-carlisle.co.uk. If you only have time for a short trip, the **best section** is that between Settle and Garsdale (30min), though note that you'll typically have a very short or very long wait for the return train. It's best to combine a trip with a hike. You can access the Pennine Way or Coast-to-Coast walk from the line; use it to link places like Settle, Dent and Ingleton in a loop walk; or sign up for one of the **free guided walks** organized by the Friends of the Settle–Carlisle Line (☏01729/822007). These walks can be joined from stations along the route; local tourist offices have more details.

and hiking itineraries; local walks are all detailed in leaflets. The **train station** is less than five signposted minutes from Market Place. As for **accommodation**, two comfortable old town inns, the *Royal Oak* on Market Place (☏01729 /822561; ❹), and the *Golden Lion*, just off Market Place along Duke Street (☏01729/822203; ❸), are the best places to stay. Other, central B&B can be found at the listed Georgian *Liverpool Guest House* on Chapel Square (☏01729/822247; no credit cards; ❶), whose old-fashioned rooms are handy for the pubs and restaurants. Other choices include the *Yorkshire Rose* (☏01729 /822032; no credit cards; ❷), situated along Duke Street from the Golden Lion, and – further up the same road, at the edge of town – the *Penmar Court Guest House* (☏01729/823258; no credit cards; ❶). Finally, the *Oast Guest House*, 5 Penyghent View, Church Street, on the Giggleswick Road (☏01729/822989;

no credit cards; ❶), caters for vegetarians, vegans and other special diets. The nearest campsite is at Stainforth.

Both the inns serve good **food** and decent beer. The *Royal Oak* gets the nod by virtue of its extraordinary carved oak-panelled bar and dining room. The *Little House*, a wine bar on Duke Street (☎01729/823963; closed Mon), next to the police station, is moderately priced and changes its menu monthly to fit the season. For traditional food made from local produce, go to *Settle Down Café* (☎01729/822480; wheel-chair friendly; no-smoking). During the day it is, however, hard to see anyone resisting the lure of *Ye Olde Naked Man Café* (closed Wed), serving breakfasts, proper coffee and good home-made food; a former undertakers, the café's name refers to the old adage that "you bring now't into the world and you take now't out".

Stainforth

STAINFORTH, two miles north of Settle, makes a good base for walks in the lower part of the Ribble valley, with several B&Bs; a pub, the *Craven Heiffer* (☎01729/822599; ❸); a **youth hostel**, set in extensive grounds about a quarter of mile south of the centre (☎01729/823577, ✉stainforth@yha.org.uk); and a **campsite** at Knight Stainforth Hall, Little Stainforth (☎01729/822200). Stone-built *Husbands Barn* (☎01729/822240; ❷), a farm and B&B south of the village on the main road, near the youth hostel, also has a well-equipped **bunkhouse barn**.

The nicest route to the village is by the **footpath from Settle**, part of the Ribble Way, which runs gently alongside the river, reaching Stainforth Force waterfall in around an hour, the village itself ten minutes later. The path starts in Settle just across the bridge to Giggleswick and, though poorly signposted, is easy to follow. **Stainforth Force** is hardly in the Niagara league, but there's some splashing around to be done in the shallow pools, and you might like to peer over the seventeenth-century **Stainforth Bridge**, a packhorse bridge just a stone's throw away. The best of the area's short walks climbs up to another waterfall, **Catrigg Force**, a mile east of the village, easily reached by an unsurfaced lane. Meanwhile, the Ribble Way pushes on northwards, avoiding the river at first, but eventually following it into Horton; a couple of miles north of Stainforth you'll pass through **Helwith Bridge** where *Helwith Bridge Hotel* (☎01729/860220; ❷) has the only rooms and food en route.

Horton in Ribblesdale

The noted walking centre of **HORTON IN RIBBLESDALE** dates from Norman times – its church, St Oswald's, retains its original proportions in the fine nave – but the village gained a new lease of life in the nineteenth century when the arrival of the Settle–Carlisle Railway allowed it to expand its age-old quarrying operations. Mine workings old and new slightly spoil the west side of the village, but it's of no consequence whatsoever for some of the Dales' finest hiking opportunities. Walks west of the village can be planned to hike up over vast tracts of limestone pavement, scars, gills, potholes, becks and dry valleys, while old "green roads" (shepherd's trackways) are all around, providing plenty of scope for gentle pottering.

The celebrated **Pen-y-ghent Café** (also known as the *Three Peaks Café*) in the village is a **National Park information point** (summer Wed–Fri & Mon 9am–6pm, Sat & Sun 8am–6pm; rest of the year Mon & Wed–Sun 9am–6pm; ☎01729/860333) and an unofficial headquarters for the famous **Three Peaks Walk**, a twenty five-mile, twelve-hour circuit of Pen-y-ghent (2273ft), Whernside (2414ft) and Ingleborough (2376ft). The village is most convenient for the ascent of sphinx-shaped **Pen-y-ghent** (3–4hr round trip), arguably the most dramatic of the three summits, just to the east on the Pennine Way; the other peaks are more easily climbed from Ingleton (see p.914), Chapel-le-Dale or Dentdale. The last Sunday of April sees lunatics running over the three peaks in the gruelling "Three Peaks Race" – what takes normal people the best part of a day to walk takes the winner under three hours. As well as providing huge mugs of tea and coffee, warming platefuls of food, maps, guides and weather reports, the *Pen-y-ghent Café* operates a "safety service" for **walkers**, enabling anyone undertaking a long hike (including the Three Peaks) to register in and out (not Tues or Fri).

Horton straggles along an L-shaped mile of the Settle–Ribblehead road (B6479), with the **train station** at the northern end and the church at the southern end. In between are the café, a post office/store and a campsite. **Accommodation** in Horton is much in demand and should be booked in advance. B&Bs include the *Willows* (☎01729/860373; no credit cards; ❷) and the more elegant *Rowe House* (☎01729/860212; no credit cards; ❷), both left out of the station and a little way up the Ribblehead road. There's also the *Knoll* (☎01729/860283; no credit cards; ❶), by the post office. Of the two **pubs**, the *Crown Hotel* (☎01729/860209; ❷), by the bridge, is the clear winner, a popular walkers' haunt with plain but cosy rooms and good bar food served until 8.30pm. *Dub Cote* (☎01729/860238) is a useful **bunkhouse barn** at Brackenbottom, just out of the village on the Settle road, in the direction of Pen-y-Ghent, and there's also a central tents-only **campsite** at *Holme Farm* (☎01729/860281), near the church.

If all these options fall through, or you've got transport and can look further afield, then head the mile or so south down the road to **Studfold**, where *Middle Studfold Farm* (☎01729/860236; no credit cards; ❶) or nearby *Studfold House* (☎01729/860200; no credit cards; ❶) both do B&B. Two miles to the north at **Selside**, *South House* (☎01729/860271; no credit cards; ❶) is another useful standby, a working farm which produces evening meals on request.

Up to Ribblehead

However you get there – walk, cycle, drive or take a train – you shouldn't miss a trip to the head of the valley, where the **Ribblehead Viaduct** cuts a superb profile, backed by some of the most uncompromising moors in the entire National Park. It's a wonderfully bleak spot, the viaduct towering a hundred feet overhead, supporting the railway line which then disappears into the 2629 yards of the Blea Tunnel, no less dramatic a feat of engineering. You can access the Dales, Ribble and Pennine Ways from points east of the line, or walk from Ribblehead station the five miles down the windswept B6255 towards Ingleton, past White Scar Caves (see p.915). Should you miss the last train, salvation is at hand in the shape of the *Station Inn* (☎01524/241274; ❷) right by the rail bridge. There's nothing else near the station, and the next stop on the line is at Dent, similarly isolated (see p.916), so it pays to study timetables carefully.

The Western Dales

The **Western Dales** is a term of convenience for a couple of tiny dales running north from **Ingleton**, a village perfectly poised for walks up **Ingleborough** and **Whernside**, and for **Dentdale** and **Garsdale**, two of the loveliest and least-known valleys in the National Park. (Much of this region has been hived off into Cumbria, to the disgust of its erstwhile Yorkshire population.) Unless you have a car or are hiking from stop to stop, any extensive exploration is difficult, though Ingleton is linked by **bus** to Clapham, Settle (for Skipton) and Horton, and the Settle–Carlisle Railway offers access to upper Dentdale and Garsdale, with fine walks possible virtually off the station platforms. There's also a very useful cross-country summer bus service (the Cumberland #X9) between York and the Lake District, calling at Ingleton en route. Ingleton has the most accommodation, but **Dent** is by far the best target for a quiet night's retreat, with a cobbled centre barely altered in centuries.

Clapham and its caves

CLAPHAM, a seductive little village at the southern foot of Ingleborough, makes a fine introduction to the region. Pop into the **National Park information centre** (April–June & Oct daily 10am–4pm; July–Sept 10am–5pm; Nov–March occasional Sat & Sun 10am–4pm; ☎01524/251419), alongside the car park, for a leaflet on the nature trail through Clapdale Woods to **Ingleborough Cave** (March–Oct daily 10am–5pm; Nov–Feb Sat & Sun 10.30am–dusk; £4.50), the Pennines' oldest show cave. The trail footpath – the only access – was laid out with numerous exotic trees and flora, most brought to Britain by Reginald Farrer, a scion of the family which owns Ingleborough Hall and the surrounding estate. Farrer was one of the fathers of alpine botany and his obsession was such that on returning from expeditions he would refuse to greet friends or family until his specimens were safely potted and planted. Follow the footpath beyond the caves, and after a little over a mile you reach **Gaping Ghyll**, 365ft deep and 450ft long, probably the most famous of the Dales' many potholes; carry on another two miles northwest from here and the summit of Ingleborough looms – a more interesting approach than the haul up from Ingleton.

Clapham is equidistant from Settle and Ingleton, just off the A65, around four miles from either; its **train station** (on the Leeds/Skipton–Lancaster line) offers another entry to the Dales, but lies over a mile south of the village. There's a post office, general store, a café or two, and a good if pricey **hotel**, the riverside *New Inn* (☎01524/251203; ❹). Cheaper rooms are available at *Arbutus House*, on Riverside (☎01524/251240; no credit cards; ❷), and by the station at the *Flying Horseshoe* pub (☎01524/251229; ❷), which also serves meals. Take a moment to visit *Anne's Café*, where the invitation at the door is "relax and be happy", and Anne herself offers home-made **food** (closed Mon & Tues).

Ingleton

INGLETON caters for a fair share of tourists, together with a reasonable number of cavers and climbers, but while the straggling slate-grey village is pleasant enough there's little specific to see, save a substantially rebuilt Norman church. The village sits at the confluence of two streams, the Twiss and the Doe, whose beautifully wooded valleys are easily the area's best features. The White Scar Caves aside (see below), the four-and-a-half mile **Falls' Walk** (entrance fee £1.50, parking – including fee – £5) is the main local attraction, a lovely circular walk up the tree-hung Twiss Valley, past viewing points over the Pecca Falls and Thornton Force, turning east at Ray Bridge to reach the head of the Doe at Beezley Farm (refreshments available), where a signed path takes you back down the Doe Valley to Ingleton by way of Beezley, Rival and Snow falls. The walk entrance is through the car park, beyond the small bridge in Ingleton. Reckon on two and a half hours to complete the circuit, and take care in wet weather.

More serious hikers tackle **Ingleborough**, one of the Three Peaks, whose flat plateau is reached by a slightly laborious route to the east (3 miles; 2hr 30min).

There are splendid views from here on a clear day, and for anyone fit, equipped and experienced enough the option arises to move on to **Whernside** to the north, the third peak and Yorkshire's highest point.

The Inglesport **hiking store** on Main Street in the village is the place for maps, equipment and weather forecasts. Otherwise, various leaflets and town maps are available from Ingleton's **tourist office** in the community centre car park, just off Main Street (May–Sept daily 10am–4.30pm; Oct Sat–Sun 10am–4.30pm; ☎015242/41049), and with a **bus** stop outside. The tourist office also doles out lists of the village's accommodation, among which there's a **youth hostel**, *Greta Tower* (☎015242/41444), an old stone house in its own gardens located centrally in a lane between the market square and the swimming pool. There are a dozen other overnight options, many strewn along Main Street. The best **guest houses** include the no-smoking *Seed Hill* on Main Street, near the church and square (☎015242/41799; no credit cards; ❷), a sixteenth-century house with en-suite rooms and lovely cottage garden; *Ingleborough View*, much further down Main Street past the tourist office (☎015242/41523; no credit cards; ❷); and the *Bridge End Guest House* on Mill Lane (☎015242/41413; ❶), close to the Falls Walk entrance. There are also two good Victorian-era hotels: the *Springfield*, on Main Street beyond Ingleborough View (☎015242/41280; ❷), and *Moorgarth Hall*, New Road (☎015242/41946; ❸), a mile or so south of the village on the A65. You can **camp** at nearby *Moorgarth Farm* (☎015242/41428), while *Stacksteads Farm*, also a mile south but off the minor road to High Bentham (☎015242/41386; ❷), has tent space and a **bunkhouse barn**.

Ingleton has its fair share of **services** – bank, shops, bakers and grocery stores – making it a good place to stock up for the hiking to come, but it fails to make much impact when it comes to **eating**. The *Inglesport Café* on the first floor of the store on Main Street (daily 9am–6pm) at least knows what its customers want – hearty soups and chips with everything. None of the **pubs** in the village is up to much, though with your own transport you can drive three miles down the A65 towards Clapham to the *Goat Gap* (☎015242/41230; ❸), a seventeenth-century inn and restaurant with decent food.

White Scar Caves and Chapel-le-Dale

Northeast of Ingleton, the Hawes road (B6255) offers some exhilarating views of the peak. It's around five miles to Ribblehead station, making this route one method of switching dales, but there's no public transport except a ridiculously early school bus. Just one and a half miles out of Ingleton – an easy walk – is the entrance to the **White Scar Caves** (daily 10am–5pm; £6.25), the longest show cave in England. Don't be put off by the steep price – it's worth every penny for the eighty-minute tour of dank underground chambers, contorted cave formations and glistening stalactites. The system was discovered in 1923 by a student, one Christopher Long, who crawled into a fissure in the hillside pushing a candle wedged in a bowler hat ahead of him to light his way. Within two years a tunnel had been blasted out to accommodate visitors – it's now lined with steel-grid walkways along which you edge, the thundering of the internal waterfall becoming ever louder the further in you venture. The 200,000-year-old Battlefield Cavern, only open to the public since 1990, is a remarkable 330 feet long and 100 feet high, and to get this far you've had to negotiate natural features like the "Squeeze" (where the walkway between two rock faces is little over a foot wide) and the "Gorilla Walk" (several hundred yards where you need to hunch your way along a low-roofed tunnel). With water underfoot for the entire trip, the caves are most impressive (and scariest) after heavy rain when the water level rises rapidly – on occasion tours are suspended (so if in doubt, call to check; ☎015242/41244). **Tours** run every hour or so, and there's a **café** on site.

Three miles farther up the road, a path strikes southeast from the hamlet of **Chapel-le-Dale** for the **Souther Scales Nature Reserve**, a fine limestone pavement with associated flowers and ferns. The summit of Ingleborough is less than two miles beyond. Of perhaps broader appeal is the flagstoned **Hill Inn** (☎015242/41256; ❶) near Chapel-le-Dale itself. Built in 1615 – J.M.W. Turner and John Buchan are listed among its drinkers – it's one of the lonelier pubs in England, but a lively, unpredictable place, with occasional live music and lots of climbers and cavers. Bunkhouse and standard double and twin rooms are available and there's a related **campsite** nearby – ask at the bar. Take a look inside the local **church** (daily 9am–5pm; free), too, a tiny and remote seventeenth-century chapel where many of the workers who died building the Settle–Carlisle Railway are buried.

A little way beyond Chapel-le-Dale, the road passes under the Settle–Carlisle Railway at Ribblehead (see p.913), start of a bleakly beautiful few miles of road.

Deepdale, Dentdale and Garsdale

Any rail or road route to Dentdale has plenty of scenic rewards, but the most breathtaking is the minor-road route from Ingleton up **Kingsdale** and down **Deepdale**, with the vast whalebacks of Gragareth and Whernside rising to each side of the windswept little road. Deepdale is a superb and intimate little dale, among the best in the National Park, closely rivalled by **Barbondale**, which feeds into Dentdale a couple of miles to the west. The road is minor enough (gated in parts) for walkers to feel reasonably secure in **walking** its ten-mile length to Dent, but to avoid the road altogether, at least for a while, you can hike the first couple of miles up the Falls' Walk from Ingleton (see p.914) to Ray Bridge. Across on the east side a path continues north to the farmhouse at Braida Garth, following which there's an unavoidable couple of miles' road walking to reach the path around High Pike, which winds northwest to Barbondale, with a side path taking you into the centre of Dent – perhaps four hours from Ingleton.

As you might expect, there's next to nothing to do locally except walk or revel in the scenery, but there are few better spots to do either, with **DENT** village an unbeatable base. When travel writers turn out clichés like "stepping back in time", they mean to describe places like this – the main road gives way to grassy cobbles, while the huddled stone cottages sport blooming window-boxes trailing over ancient lintels, and have tiny windows to keep in the warmth. In the seventeenth and eighteenth centuries, Dent supported a flourishing hand-knitting industry, later ruined by mechanization. These days, the hill-farming community supplements its income through tourism and craft ventures, most notably the independent Dent Brewery, a little way up the dale, which produces excellent beer for the local pubs.

Accommodation is surprisingly plentiful. You can stay at either of the village's two pubs, the *Sun Inn* (☎01539/625208; ❶) and the *George & Dragon* (☎01539/625256; ❷), which are next to each other in the centre and under the same management. The *Sun* is the nicer, truly welcoming to walkers and with a great traditional feel; that said, the en-suite rooms at the *George and Dragon* are a tad more comfortable. There are a handful of other overnight possibilities, most notably the non-smoking *Stone Close Guest House* (☎01539 /625231; ❶; closed Jan), which has a good café (10.30am–5.30pm) doubling as a **National Park information point**. If you ask around, you'll also find B&B

in local private houses, while there's a **campsite** on the western edge of the village, at *High Laning Farm* (☎01539/625239). Steak dinners, pies, and Dent Brewery beers are specialities at the *Sun*, where you can eat and drink in front of a log fire. An evening meal (£11; not Tues) is served at the *Stone Close Guest House* at 7.30pm, provided you reserve in advance. The only other facilities in the village are a post office/store and a couple of little craft shops.

Confusion – and not a few sore feet – is caused by Dent's **train station** (on the Settle to Carlisle line) not being in Dent at all, but five miles to the east. Between mid-May and mid-October a **bus** runs between station and village twice a day on Sundays only. Otherwise the only bus service to and from Dent is that to Sedbergh to the west (schooldays only, 4 daily), from where you can reach Kirkby Stephen, or Kendal in the Lakes. If you get stuck, the hamlet of **Cowgill**, half a mile below the station, has the *Sportsman's Inn* (☎01539 /625282; ❷) to hand. **Dentdale youth hostel** at *Dee Side House* (☎01539 /625251) is a couple of miles south of here down the Dales Way.

Train is the best way to reach **Garsdale**, a dale so untrammelled by the modern world it doesn't even have a town or village within its ten-mile span, simply a scattering of farm hamlets, most of Norse origin, as names like Thursgill, Dandra Garth and Knudsman Ing suggest. Aye Gill Pike to the south and Baugh Fell to the north rise incredibly steeply from the valley floor, creating two of the most monolithic-looking mountains in the Dales. Get off the train at **Garsdale Head**, the easternmost point in the dale – it's five miles down the A684 to Hawes (see p.917) and Wensleydale from here, but again, there's no regular bus, just a summer National Park service (June to mid-Sept 1 daily).

Wensleydale

Best known of the Dales, if only for its cheese, **Wensleydale** is the largest, least varied and most serene of the National Park's dales. Known in medieval times as Yoredale, after its river (the Ure), the dale takes its present name from a now-inconsequential village, and while there are towns to detain you – including one of the area's biggest in Hawes – it's Wensleydale's rural attractions that linger longest in the mind. Many will be familiar to devotees of the **James Herriott** books and TV series (see p.964), set and filmed in the dale; elsewhere, there are several well-known waterfalls – notably **Aysgarth Falls** – and, as the dale opens into the Vale of York, a variety of historic buildings that range from **castles** at Bolton and Middleham to **abbeys** at Jervaulx and Coverham.

The dale is traversed by the National Park's only east–west **main road** (the A684), and linked by high moor roads to virtually all the park's other dales of note. Although the scenery is less spectacular than in other valleys, hiking possibilities are as plentiful as elsewhere, with the **Pennine Way** crossing the valley at Hawes. Year-round **public transport** is limited to a post bus from Hawes on varied routes (Mon–Fri 2–3 daily, Sat 1 daily) via Bainbridge, Askrigg, Aysgarth and Castle Bolton to Leyburn (for Richmond); and the Arriva services (#156, #157, #159) along the same route between Hawes and Richmond. There are also seasonal connections between Garsdale Head station and Hawes (June–Aug Tues, Fri & Sat 2–3 daily), as well as the useful **Wensleydale Tourer**, which runs daily in summer (late July to Sept; day-tourer ticket £4.95), meets morning and evening trains at Garsdale and runs on a circular route throughout the day between Aysgarth and Hawes.

Hawes

HAWES – from the Anglo-Saxon *haus*, a mountain pass – is head of Wensleydale in all respects: it is its chief town, main hiking centre, and home to its tourism, cheese and rope-making industries. Hawes also claims to be Yorkshire's highest market town, and received its market charter in 1699; the weekly **Tuesday market** – crammed with farmers and market traders – is still going strong. If you haven't yet bought any cheese, the groaning stalls will doubtless persuade you otherwise. The cheese trail invariably leads to the **Wensleydale Creamery** on Gayle Lane (Mon–Sat 9.30am–5pm, Sun 10am–4.30pm; £2), a few hundred yards (signposted) south of the centre. The first cheese in Wensleydale was made by medieval Cistercian monks from ewes' milk, and after the Dissolution local farmers made a version from cows' milk which, by the 1840s, was being marketed as "Wensleydale" cheese. The first commercial creamery was founded in Hawes at the turn of the twentieth century, and production continues again today, after the industry was rescued in the 1990s from recession and neglect. The Creamery's "Cheese Experience" tours tell you all this and more, with plenty of opportunity to see the stuff being made, to sample and purchase in the shop, or tuck in at the *Buttery* restaurant.

All three of Wensleydale's industries come together in the **Dales Countryside Museum** (Easter–Oct daily 10am–5pm; Nov–Easter Wed, Fri, Sat & Sun 11am–4pm; £2.50), housed in Station Yard's former train station and warehouses, on the Aysgarth side of town. The comprehensive and well-presented collection, garnered by Dales chroniclers Marie and Joan Ingilby, embraces lead-mining, farming, peat-cutting, knitting (hand-knitted hosiery was a speciality) and all manner of rustic minutiae. Alongside it, in a long shed, the **Hawes Ropemakers Museum** (July–Oct Mon–Fri 9am–5.30pm, Sat 10am–5.30pm; rest of year Mon–Fri 9am–5.30pm; free) presents popular demonstrations of traditional rope-making.

Another local attraction is a mile and a half out of town to the north, where people cough up the 70p toll at the *Green Dragon* pub (℡01969/667392; ❷) to walk to **Hardraw Force**. It's about all the fall is worth for much of the year, for although this is the highest above-ground waterfall in the country (Gaping Ghyll and other potholes have longer underground drops) there's often barely a trickle dribbling over the edge. Summer brass-band recitals in the natural amphitheatre of Hardraw Scar – an old tradition, recently revived – make for a more surreal attraction.

One of the best but toughest local walks follows the Pennine Way, immediately west of the *Green Dragon*, to **Great Shunner Fell** (5 miles one way; 2hr 30min). Most people, however, find it more rewarding to drive along the parallel road over to Thwaite in Swaledale (see p.923) for the views. The road heads past the **Butter Tubs**, a series of deeply eroded natural wells five miles north of Hawes.

Services and accommodation in Hawes are gathered together along and just off the main A684, which runs through town. The **National Park information centre** shares the same buildings as the Hawes Ropemakers Museum (July–Oct Mon–Fri 9am–5.30pm, Sat 10am–5.30pm; rest of year Mon–Fri 9am–5.30pm; ℡01969/667450). **Buses** stop in Market Place (except for the post buses which depart from outside the post office), over the road from the information office car park. There's central, comfortable B&B **accommodation** at the *Steppe Haugh Guest House*, Town Head (℡01969/667645; no credit cards; ❷); the *Old Station House*, on Hardraw Road, opposite the museum (℡01969/667785; ❷); and at *Laburnum House*, The Holme (℡01969/667717; no credit cards; ❶); at the turn-off from the main road to the museum. All the **pubs** on and around the market square – the *Board*, *Crown*, *Fountain* and *Bull's Head* – have rooms, too, so you shouldn't be stuck for choice; best are those at the *Board* (☎01969/667223; **②**). Try also the *White Hart Inn* (☎01969/667259; **②**), an eighteenth-century coaching inn on the cobbled Main Street, which – confusingly – lies just off the main road through town. Fanciest place is *Cocketts Hotel*, on Market Place (☎01969/667312; **④**), with eight fine en-suite rooms in a seventeenth-century building. Finally, there's a smart **youth hostel** (☎01969/667368) at Lancaster Terrace, at the junction of the main A684 and B6255. **Campers** need to head for the *Bainbridge Ings* site (☎01969/667354), half a mile east of the centre, just off the A684 (Aysgarth road).

Pub **food** aside, you can pick from proper fish and chips at *The Chippie* on Market Place (closed Sun eve); coffees, snacks and lunches at the first-floor *Wensleydale Pantry* on the main road through town; pricier French-influenced meals at *Herriot's Hotel*, Main Street, opposite the *White Hart Inn*; and traditional English dinners in the *Cocketts Hotel* restaurant. *Laburnum House* has a nice tea-room attached.

Bainbridge and Countersett

BAINBRIDGE, five miles east of Hawes, centres on an emerald village green (complete with stocks), with an unearthly looking glacial mound behind, once the site of a Roman fort. Nightly at 9pm from Holyrood (late Sept) to Shrove Tuesday, a horn is blown three times on the green, continuing a tradition that dates back to Norman times, when the horn was sounded to guide travellers through the dense woodlands that once encircled the village. Paths (following the River Bain) and minor roads to the south lead to **Semer Water** (2 miles), one of the Dales' few lakes, formed behind a dam of glacial material – there's not a scrap of evidence to support the traditional story that a lost city sits under the lake. All sorts of walks are possible from **Countersett**, a hamlet (with a B&B or two) near its shore, the best leading into Bardale and Raydale.

In Bainbridge, overlooking the green, there's the popular *Rose & Crown Hotel* (☎01969/650225; **④**), a fifteenth-century coaching inn with a restaurant, bar meals and a decent wine list – the Bainbridge horn hangs in the hall when not in use. Other local B&Bs put out signs, or try the *Riverdale Country House Hotel*, also on the green (☎01969/650311; **③**), where you can also take afternoon tea.

Askrigg

The mantle of "Herriot country" lies heavy on **ASKRIGG**, a mile across the valley from Bainbridge, as the TV series *All Creatures Great and Small* was filmed in and around the village. There is, however, little to see or do, though the pubs and Georgian houses have their charms, and you might stroll to a couple of nearby falls, **Whitfield Force** and **Mill Gill Force**, both a mile or so to the west of the village. To the east, there are well-signed paths along high ground via Carperby to Aysgarth or Castle Bolton, around a five-mile pull to either.

The market at Askrigg has its origins in medieval times, and predates that of Hawes – notice the bull-ring set outside the church here, a relic of bull-baiting days. There's an **information point** in the village shop in the Market Place and plenty of **accommodation**, too, starting with the *King's Arms*, also in Market Place, (☎01969/650817; **⑤**), a cosy old haunt with plush rooms, wood panelling, good beer and local cheese platters. B&Bs include the *Apothecary's House* (☎01969/650626; no credit cards; **②**), a fine-looking period house in Market Place, on the main street. For a rural retreat, you can't beat *Helm Country House* (☎01969/650443; no credit cards; **④**), a seventeenth-century farmhouse a mile west with magnificent views, open fires, oak beams and a cast-iron Aga oven – an Aga-cooked dinner at £16 a head is served in the stone-flagged dining room.

Aysgarth and around

The ribbon-village of **AYSGARTH**, straggling along and off the A684, is the vortex that sucks in Wensleydale's largest number of visitors, courtesy of the twin **Aysgarth Falls**, half a mile below the village (there's a path through the fields), where water crashes down a series of limestone steps – impressive in full spate. A marked nature trail runs through the surrounding woodlands and there's a big car park and excellent **information centre** on the north bank (Easter–Oct daily 10am–5pm; Nov–Easter Fri, Sat & Sun 10am–4pm; ℡01969/663424). The **Upper Falls** and picnic grounds lie just back from here, by the bridge and church; the more spectacular **Lower Falls** are a half-mile stroll to the east through shaded woodland. Don't leave without calling at the church of **St Andrew**, worth a look for its carved pews and one of Yorkshire's finest rood screens, dating from 1500 and possibly removed from nearby Jervaulx Abbey. Immediately below the church is an old water-driven mill, now the idiosyncratic **Yorkshire Carriage Museum** (daily 9.30am–dusk; £2), housing fifty plus coaches, hearses, fire engines and estate vehicles; the adjacent *Mill Race* tearooms occupy another of the old buildings. The mill produced one of history's more famous sartorial job lots: the red flannel shirts worn by the Italian soldiers of Garibaldi's 1860 army of unification.

Aysgarth has a superb aspect, with glorious views across the valley from several points, a setting spoiled only by the fast A684 through the village which precludes any quiet contemplation. **B&Bs** along the main road include *Marlbeck* (℡01969/663610; no credit cards; ❶), while the village's only **pub**, the *George & Dragon* (℡01969/663358; ❸), has pleasant en-suite rooms and a bar-meal menu with plenty of choice. Otherwise, there is *Low Gill Farm* (℡01969/663554; no credit cards; ❶; closed Nov–Easter), which is particularly beautifully sited, in lovely country a mile or so west on the minor road to Thornton Rust. Other local choices are all down by the falls, where the *Wensleydale Farmhouse* (℡01969/663534; no credit cards; ❷) is on the main road at the turn-off for the falls, with the well-regarded **youth hostel** (℡01969/663260) just behind. Bar **meals** are served at the *Palmer Flatt* pub on the main road. There's a **campsite**, *Westholme Caravan Park* (℡01969/663268; closed Nov–Easter), half a mile east on the A684.

Castle Bolton

There's a superb **circular walk** northeast from Aysgarth via Castle Bolton (6 miles; 4hr), a route detailed in a National Park pamphlet available from the information centres in Hawes or Aysgarth – or you can simply drive to the castle in about ten minutes. The walk starts at the falls themselves and climbs up through Thoresby, with the foursquare battlements of **Castle Bolton** (March–Oct daily 10am–5pm; restricted winter opening, call for details; ℡01969/623981; £4) themselves a magnetic lure from miles away across the fields. Built in 1379 by Richard le Scrope, Lord Chancellor to Richard II, it's a massive defensive structure in which Mary, Queen of Scots was imprisoned for six months in 1568. The Great Hall, a few adjacent rooms, and the castle gardens have been restored, though the owners seem more keen to get you into the café that's incorporated into the castle – a welcome spot if you've just trudged up from Aysgarth (and free to enter). The only other facility hereabouts is the village post office, housed in what could pass for Goldilocks' cottage; the nearest **pub** is just over a mile to the east, the *King's Arms* at Redmire.

Wensley and Leyburn

A few miles east of Aysgarth, Wensleydale broadens into a low-hilled pastoral valley, the border of the National Park marking the end of classic Dales scenery and the start of the Vale of York's more mundane flats. **WENSLEY** is a beguiling place wound around a dinky village square. The church of the **Holy Trinity** ranks as one of the Dales' finest, founded in the thirteenth century but with fabric dating from the five centuries that followed, the most impressive being an extravagant box pew and a sixteenth-century rood screen removed from Richmond's Easby Abbey.

The market town of **LEYBURN** occupies almost the last piece of straggling high ground on the valley's north edge, a handsome place set around three open squares, replete with buildings from its eighteenth-century heyday. Market day is Friday, when Market Place puts out its fruit, veg, hard goods and bric-a-brac stalls; this is where the local **buses** stop too. There's a **tourist office** just off Market Place at 4 Central Chambers on Railway St (April–Oct daily 9.30am–5.30pm; Nov–March Mon–Sat 9.30am–4.30pm; ☎01969 /623069), and this has the details of several **places to stay**. One especially good choice is the *Secret Garden House*, in Grove Square (☎01969/623589; ❷), a Georgian house with a garden. For **food**, the *Posthorn*, on the edge of Market Place, dishes up all-day breakfasts and other meals, or you could plump for the *Golden Lion*, a traditional inn on Market Place (☎01969/622161; ❸). For decent Masham beer, visit the *Sandpiper Inn*, a little seventeenth-century **pub** on the road at the bottom of Market Place.

Middleham and Jervaulx Abbey

Two miles southeast of Leyburn, the tiny town of **MIDDLEHAM** is approached over an impressive early-nineteenth-century castellated bridge – a morning bus (not Sun) comes this way from Leyburn. A well-to-do place set around a sloping cobbled square, it's dominated by the imposing ruins of **Middleham Castle** (April–Oct daily 10am–6pm; Nov–Easter Wed–Sun 10am–4pm; £2.40; EH). Built by the Normans to guard the route from Skipton to Richmond, it gained added historical resonance when it passed by marriage to the future Richard III in 1471 and became his favourite home; his son, Edward, died here. The keep is one of England's largest, despite being badly damaged after Richard's defeat at Bosworth Field. Castle aside, Middleham captivates for at least long enough to have a coffee in one of its pubs or tearooms. Racehorses clip-clopping through the centre are a common sight, with over five hundred trained locally – on Good Friday each year there's free access to all the racing stables.

The best moderately priced place to stay is at the *Castle Keep* on Castle Hill (☎01969/623665, ✉castle.keep@argonet.co.uk; ❸), a walker-friendly tearoom and **guest house** with two en-suite rooms; the tearoom doubles as an evening bistro with creative local cooking. Otherwise, several **pubs** and a couple of other hotels vie for custom around the square – the *White Swan*, *Black Swan*, *Richard III* and *Black Bull* all have rooms available.

Wensleydale all but peters out with the overgrown and privately owned ruins of **Jervaulx Abbey** (dawn–dusk; £1.50 donation requested), four miles southeast of Middleham on the A6108 road to Ripon. Founded in 1156, it is the least prepossessing of the great trio of Cistercian abbeys completed by Fountains and Rievaulx (see p.923 & p.969), but makes an enjoyable stop for a ramble amid the bramble-covered stones. A conservatory-style tearoom over the road (closed Jan & Feb) has snacks and lunches. On Tuesday, Thursday, Friday and Saturday, one **bus** a day from Leyburn and Middleham passes the abbey.

Masham

If you're a beer fan, the market town of **MASHAM**, another four miles along the road, is an essential point of pilgrimage – if you're not, there's little point in visiting. It is home to **Theakston's** brewery (tours: April–Nov daily 10.30am–5.30pm; at other times, call ☎01765/684333; £4), sited here since 1827, where you can learn the arcane intricacies of the brewer's art and become familiar with the legendary Old Peculier (sic) ale. The tour-price includes a free pint and there's a visitor centre and bar on site, too, though the most atmospheric place in town for a drink is the brewery pub, the *White Bear*. Following Theakston's huge marketing success, which has seen its beers made available all over Britain, one of the family brewing team left to set up the smaller, independent **Black Sheep Brewery**, also based in Masham and offering daily tours (Mon & Sun 10.30am–5.30pm. rest of week 10.30am–11pm; £3.75). To many, Black Sheep bitter is even better than Theakston's. Both breweries are just a few minutes' signposted walk out of the centre. There's a car park at Black Sheep, though not at Theakston's, but there's usually plenty of space to park in Masham's central squares. If you need to soak up the alcohol with something more substantial than pub **food**, try the bistro inside the Black Sheep Brewery, or *Floodlite*, 7 Silver St, a well-regarded Anglo-French **restaurant**, with a good-value set lunch, and dinners at around £25. **Buses** from Masham's Market Place depart a couple of times a day for Ripon, and on summer Sundays a service runs on to Leeds and Bradford. Market days are Wednesday and Saturday.

Swaledale

The National Park's northernmost dale, **Swaledale** is rivalled only by Dentdale and Garsdale for the lonely grandeur of its landscapes. Narrow and steep-sided in its upper reaches, it emerges rocky and rugged in its central tract, which takes in the remote villages of **Keld**, **Thwaite** and **Muker**, before more typically pastoral scenery cuts in at **Reeth**. On any extended tour of the Dales the obvious approach is from Wensleydale and the south (on minor roads from Hawes or Askrigg), though the proximity of Richmond (see p.924) to the A1 makes it a dale you could easily take in as a quick aside if you're heading on north. Indeed, this is one dale where it really pays to have your own transport. From Richmond, **bus** #30 runs up the valley along the B6270 as far as Keld, but it's a limited service (Mon–Sat 3–4 daily), and the only other access is with the summer-only **Swaledale Roamer** (Sun only, June to mid-Sept), which meets trains at Garsdale and then stops at Hawes, Keld, Muker and Reeth.

Keld and around

KELD, eight miles north of Hawes, and eleven from Kirkby Stephen, is at the crossroads of the Pennine Way and the Coast-to-Coast path, making it an ideal hiking centre. No more than a straggle of hardy buildings, it is surrounded by relics of the lead-mining industry that once brought a prosperity of sorts to much of the valley (though at a price – the average life expectancy of a nineteenth-century Swaledale miner was 46 years). Here you'll also see the incredible profusion of ancient field barns, or **laithes**, for which the dale is renowned, the legacy of a system of husbandry that dates back to Norse times. Keld's busy **youth hostel** is *Keld Lodge*, an old shooting lodge near the telephone kiosk (☎01748/886259) but **B&B** at *Butt House* (☎01748/886374; no credit cards; ❶; closed Sept–Easter), is a more tempting proposition. There's also a **campsite** at *Park Lodge* (☎01748/886274; closed Oct–Easter), but no pub, nor any other facilities, in Keld.

Any number of local walks are possible, the shortest being to **Kisdon Force**'s triple-stacked waterfall and its wooded gorge half a mile east of Keld, though the best is the hike southeast along the River Swale to Muker, below the circular bulk of Kisdon hill (2–3 miles; 1hr 30min). The valley road cuts round Kisdon to the south, following part of the so-called **Corpse Way**, a lane used by those paying their last respects when the nearest church was ten miles away at Grinton – footpaths follow its still obvious route down the valley.

North and west of Keld, the upper reaches of Swaledale are wild indeed, with an atmosphere bordering on desolate even in summer. The Kirkby Stephen road (B6270) gives access to short side-valleys such as Stonesdale, Whitsun Dale and Birkdale where you can spend a lonely hour or two, while the Pennine Way shadows the very minor Stonesdale road for the three or four miles across Stonesdale Moor to the splendid **Tan Hill Inn** (☎01833/628246; ❷). Reputedly the highest pub in Britain (1732ft above sea level), the *Tan Hill* was built to serve the coal mines that fed the lead mines and smelting mills of the lower dale. The wind blows hard year-round up here, and in winter snow drifts up to the windows – but there's an open fire lit daily in the stone-flagged interior. Theakston and Black Sheep bitter are on draught, bar meals are provided and there's camping outside for the truly dedicated.

Thwaite to Low Row

One of Swaledale's attractions is the possibility of walking the footpaths that link the villages trailing down the valley. **THWAITE**, another Norse-founded settlement, is the first hamlet south of Keld, just a two-mile walk away and with accommodation and meals at *Kearton Guest House* (☎01748/886277; no credit cards; ❷). Some of the loveliest scenery follows beyond the little village of **MUKER** (the name derives from the Norse for "meadow"), a mile or so to the east, distinguished by tiny side-valleys such as Oxnop Beck, south of Oxnop. Muker has a **National Park information point** in the village store and a couple of B&Bs, including *Hylands* (☎01748/886003; no credit cards; ❷), an immaculate seventeenth-century cottage off the main road, near the church. There are also a couple of teashops, a nice Dales pub, the *Farmers Arms*, serving good food, and a **campsite** at *Usha Gap*, half a mile from the village in the direction of Thwaite (☎01748/886214), set alongside a stream.

Beyond Muker, there's not much to tempt you away from the bucolic riverside, save perhaps for the **Gunnerside Gill**, a little valley which contains the best of the area's old lead mines. These are all easily seen on a circular six-mile walk from **GUNNERSIDE** itself, and are covered in a special trail leaflet available from the village post office's **National Park information point**. Further east at Low Row, there's a **bunkhouse barn** at the *Punch Bowl Inn* (☎01748/886233; ❶), with inexpensive B&B and basic bar meals also available. This makes as nice a stop as any, with fine valley views from the pub tables, a choice of almost 150 malt whiskies, and the unmissable opportunity to walk along country roads to the intriguingly named hamlet of **Crackpot**, a mile to the south.

Reeth and around

A couple of miles east lies **REETH**, set in a bowl of bleak moorland. It's the dale's main village and market centre – market day is Friday – and its desirable cottages are gathered around a triangular green. Reeth has the biggest range of facilities in the whole dale, including a petrol station, a post office and the only bank, and it also has several local craft workshops making everything from cabinets to guitars. The **National Park information centre** on the green (daily

10am–5pm; ☎01748/884059) has local maps and brochures. If the area's lead-mining heritage appeals, drop into Reeth's **Swaledale Folk Museum** (Easter–Oct daily 10am–5.30pm; £1.75), signposted just off the green.

Some cottages around the green post **B&B** signs in their windows. Other choices include two places on the Grinton Road at the edge of the village: the house at 2 Bridge Terrace (☎01748/884572; no credit cards; ❶; closed Nov–Easter), which offers breakfast made from local ingredients and has lots of books to read; and *Hackney House*, also on Bridge Terrace (☎01748/884302; no credit cards; ❶). Further out, on the Arkengarthdale road, is *Elder Peak* (☎01748/884770; no credit cards; ❶; closed Nov–March). There are also several good **pubs** offering rooms and food, most obviously the *Black Bull* (☎01748/884213; ❷) and the *King's Arms* (☎01748/884259; ❸), opposite the green. Many of the cottages around the green double as **cafés**. The *Olde Temperance* serves breakfast to hikers from 8am, the *Copper Kettle* (closed Nov–Feb) has big platefuls of filling food. For picnic supplies try Reeth Bakery, known for its great chocolate cake.

To escape Reeth's crowds, walk or drive three miles east to **Marrick Priory**, a ruined twelfth-century Benedictine nunnery set among trees on the north bank of the Swale. A mile farther east, approached from the B6270 road, are the tower and ruined nave of **Ellerton Priory**, a fifteenth-century Cistercian foundation. There are also numerous paths across the fields on the south side of the river, letting you complete a circular walk from Reeth via Grinton, whose attractive bridge, church and riverside inn, *The Bridge*, are just a mile away by road. The local **youth hostel**, *Grinton Lodge*, is housed in a former shooting lodge spectacularly sited in the hills above (☎01748/884206), ten minutes' walk from Grinton. You can rent mountain bikes here, and the hostel can provide route details for local rides; book in advance.

Many people come to this area to make a television-inspired pilgrimage up **Arkengarthdale** to **Langthwaite**, three miles to the northwest, a cute village used in the opening credits of *All Creatures Great and Small*; a handful of local B&Bs and the atmospheric *Red Lion* pub soak up the passing trade there.

Richmond

Although marginalized on the National Park's northeasternmost borders, **RICHMOND** is the Dales' single most tempting historical town, thanks mainly to its magnificent castle, whose extensive walls and colossal keep cling to a precipice above the River Swale. Indeed, the entire town is an absolute gem, centred on a huge cobbled market square backed onto by hidden alleys and gardens housing mainly Georgian buildings of great refinement. The town itself is much older, having been dubbed *Riche-Mont* ("noble hill") by the Normans who first built a castle here in 1071. That heritage is also celebrated in local street names such as Frenchgate and Lombard's Wynd (a "wynd" being a narrow alley).

The Town

There's no better place to start than **Richmond Castle** (daily: April–Oct 10am–6pm; Nov–March 10am–1pm & 2–4pm; £2.70; EH), reached by sign-posted alleys from the market square. Originally built by Alan Rufus, first Norman Earl of Richmond, it retains many features from its earliest incarnation, principally the gatehouse, curtain wall and Scolland's Hall, the oldest

Norman great hall in the country. Legend, however, links it to earlier times, notably to King Arthur, who's reputed to lie in a local cave awaiting England's hour of need. The castle was roofed with Swaledale lead, and its building and upkeep was paid for over the centuries with a levy of two pence per mule-load of lead brought down the dale. There are prodigious views from the splendidly preserved fortified keep, which is over a hundred feet high, and from the Great Court, now an open lawn which ends in a sheer fall to the river below. Outside the main entrance a Georgian terrace, the **Castle Walk**, wraps around the skirts of the castle, offering more views of the river and hills beyond.

Most of medieval Richmond – all cobbled streets and narrow wynds – sprouted around the castle, but much of the town now radiates from the vast **Market Place**, with the Market Hall alongside (markets on Thurs, Fri & Sat). It's difficult to get a good view of things now the square is overwhelmed by traffic, but the Victorian and Georgian buildings which border the square still have some appeal. The most unusual structure is the defunct **Holy Trinity** church, built in 1135 and now serving as the **Green Howards Museum** (April–Oct Mon–Sat 9.30am–4.30pm; Nov–March Mon–Fri 10am–4pm; £2), honouring North Yorkshire's Green Howards regiment. The **Richmondshire Museum**, reached down Ryder's Wynd, off King Street on the northern side of the square (Easter–Oct daily 11am–5pm; £1.50), is of more general interest. It has displays relating to lead-mining and local crafts, and contains a brick-by-brick reconstruction of a local fifteenth-century "cruck" house, built using a curved timber frame.

The keenest interest of all, however, is in the town's **Theatre Royal** (Mon–Sat 2.30–3.45pm; £1.50), dating from 1788, making it one of England's oldest extant theatres. The theatre is on the corner of Friar's Wynd (a narrow alley running north of the Market Place) and Victoria Road, opposite the **tourist office**. Unassuming from the outside, the theatre's tiny interior is one of England's finest pieces of Georgian architecture. Built by one Samuel Butler – an actor-manager who owned several regional theatres in the north, and third husband of the splendidly named actress Tryphosa Brockell – the theatre hosted the greats of eighteenth-century theatre, Edmund Kean among them, before packed houses of over 400 people, each person paying a shilling a time. The theatre now seats just 214, a figure that still seems remarkable given the shoebox size of the building. After years of neglect, during which time it was used variously as wine cellars and as a warehouse, the theatre re-opened in 1962, for both performances (call ☎01748/823710 for details) and **tours**. A museum at the rear gives an insight into eighteenth-century theatrical life, allowing visitors to have a go at scene-shifting, use the thunderbox prop or try on the various masks and costumes.

The river and Easby Abbey

Below the castle, the **River Swale** cuts a pastoral swathe through the surrounding countryside, with the banks immediately east of town popular for picnics. A lovely signposted walk runs along the north bank out to the beautifully situated church of St Agatha and adjacent **Easby Abbey** (dawn to dusk; free; EH), whose golden stone walls stand a mile southeast of the town centre. Founded in 1152 by Premonstratensian canons – the so-called White Monks – the abbey is now ruined, the greatest damage having been caused in 1346 when the English army was billeted here on its way to the battle of Neville's Cross. However, the evocative remains are extensive, and in places – notably the thirteenth-century refectory – still remarkably intact. You can vary your return to town by crossing the bridge a little further down from the abbey and walking back along the old railway track.

Practicalities

Buses all stop in the Market Place; there are regular services into Wensleydale and Swaledale, to Barnard Castle in County Durham (p.1010), and to Darlington (p.1018), just ten miles to the northeast, which is on the main East Coast train line. The **tourist office**, at Friary Gardens, Victoria Road (summer daily 9.30am–5.30pm; winter Mon–Sat 9.30am–4.30pm; ☎01748/850252), is helpful in finding accommodation, and also organizes free **guided walking tours** around the town in summer.

Recommended **accommodation** includes the *Old Brewery Guest House*, 29 The Green (☎01748/822460; ❷), a former inn and now a highly tempting spot on a quiet green west of (and below) the castle. The nearby *Restaurant on the Green*, on the corner at 5–7 Bridge St (☎01748/826229; ❷), also has a couple of rooms available. Central Frenchgate features the characterful seventeenth-century *Willance House*, at no. 24 (☎01748/824467; no credit cards; ❷) and the *Channel House* at no. 8 (☎01748/823844; no credit cards; ❷) – though they only have a couple of rooms each. Slightly out of town, the excellent *West End Guest House*, 45 Reeth Rd, along and beyond Victoria Road (☎01748/824783; ❷), gets consistently good reports. Several of the town-centre pubs have rooms, too, though none can beat the luxury of the *King's Head Hotel*, on Market Place (☎01748/850220; ❺). The nearest **campsite** is three miles west of town on the Reeth Road at *Swaleview Caravan Park* (☎01748/823106; closed Nov–Easter).

For **meals**, *The Bistro*, a pleasant place with an indoor patio on Chantry Wynd (☎01748/850792), off Finkle Street, serves filled croissants, ciabatta sandwiches, and Mediterranean lunches at around the £5 mark, and stays open for dinner from Wednesday to Saturday (6–9.30pm). There are more Mediterranean flavours at the *Frenchgate Café*, 29 Frenchgate (☎01748/824949), which posts its dinner menu daily at 6pm, while down on The Green, *Restaurant on the Green*, at 5–7 Bridge St (☎01748/826229; Thurs–Sat eve only), makes a mark with its inventive bistro food. Otherwise you could always push the boat out at the *King's Head*, whose ritzy à la carte menu lets you eat for around £25; there's a cheaper bar menu too.

Richmond's **pubs** – there are half a dozen around the market square alone – are all rather grim, surprisingly, though the *Black Lion* on Finkle Street has its moments. The *Unicorn*, on Georgian tree-lined Newbiggin (at the end of Finkle St), is a quieter spot. The proximity of Catterick Garrison, a few miles south of town, means that loud, aggressive young men with short hair tend to ruin any chance of a peaceful drink at weekends.

Harrogate to Ripon

Somewhat off the beaten track unless you're driving between York and the Dales, **Ripon** would hardly merit a visit – despite its ancient cathedral – were it not for nearby **Fountains Abbey**, Britain's largest and most beautiful monastic ruin. Easily seen from Ripon, the abbey has the added bonus of being the focal point of **Studley Royal**, an eighteenth-century landscaped garden complete with lake, temples, water garden and deer park. With time and transport you could take in a handful of other historic buildings nearby, though better excursions are perhaps made from the refined spa town of **Harrogate**: either to **Knaresborough** for its castle, or to **Nidderdale**, an often overlooked adjunct to the Dales proper – for which Harrogate's bus and train connections make the town a perfect gateway.

Harrogate

HARROGATE – the very picture of genteel Yorkshire respectability – owes its airy, planned appearance and early prosperity to the discovery of Tewit Well in 1571. This was the first of over eighty ferrous and sulphurous springs that, by the nineteenth century, were to turn the town into one of the country's leading spas. By the mid-twentieth century, however, taking the waters had become a less popular pastime, and since the early 1970s Harrogate has instead concentrated on hosting a year-round panoply of conferences, exhibitions and festivals. Monuments to its past splendours still stand dotted around town and, despite the jarring efforts of contemporary architects, Harrogate manages to retain its essential Victorian and Edwardian character. Much of its appeal lies in the splendid parks and gardens – "England's floral town" keeps admirable pace with the changing seasons, and if you pick up a "Floral Trail" leaflet from the tourist office you'll be guided around the best of the current blooms.

Harrogate's spa heritage begins with the **Royal Baths Assembly Rooms** on Crescent Road, built in 1897, where you can still take a **Turkish bath** in the plush, tiled Victorian surroundings (call ☏01423/556746 for hours; from £9.50 a session); the public entrance is on Parliament Street. The contemporaneous **Royal Hall**, built as a concert hall, stands across the way at the corner of Ripon Road and King's Road, while just around the corner from the Assembly Rooms stands the **Royal Pump Room**, built 1842, in Crown Place, over the sulphur well that feeds the Royal Baths. The **museum** here (April–Oct Mon–Sat 10am–5pm, Sun 2–5pm; Nov–March Mon–Sat 10am–4pm, Sun 2–4; £2) re-creates something of the town's health-fixated past and also lets you sample the water; free **guided walks** leave here several times a week between Easter and October (information from the tourist office). The town's earliest surviving spa building, the old Promenade Room of 1806, is just 100 yards from the Pump Room on Swan Road – now restored and housing the **Mercer Art Gallery** (Tues–Sat 10am–5pm, Sun 2–5pm; free), which hosts regularly changing fine-art exhibitions. The main **Conference and Exhibition Centre** along King's Road – an example of empty 1980s pretension – doesn't fit at all with the rest of town. Harrogate deserves much credit, however, for the preservation of its green spaces, most prominent of which is **The Stray**, a jealously guarded green belt that curves around the south of the town centre. To the southwest, the 120-acre **Valley Gardens** are the venue for the annual Spring Flower Show and Sunday band concerts in summer, while many visitors also make for the **Harlow Carr Botanical Gardens** (daily 9am–6pm or dusk if earlier; £4.50, £3 Nov–Feb), the main showpiece of the Northern Horticultural Society. These lie one-and-a-half miles out, on the town's western edge; take the B6162 Otley road, or walk beyond the Valley Gardens, through the Pine Woods. Although laid out with a scientific purpose – breeding fruit and vegetable stock suited to northern climates – the gardens are a year-round floral extravaganza, with especially wonderful rose displays. A specialist **Museum of Gardening** in the grounds (daily 9.30am–4pm; included in the gardens entry fee) gathers together gardening tools and historical material, while the *Garden Room Restaurant* and a refreshment kiosk (closed Oct–March) provide meals and drinks – or you can bring your own picnic.

Arrival, information and accommodation

National Express buses drop you on Victoria Avenue, near the library; local and regional services (from Knaresborough, York, Skipton, Pateley Bridge, Ripon and Leeds) use the **bus station** on Station Parade. The **train station** (for services from Leeds and York) is on the same street, just a few minutes from all the central sights. There's limited-hours **parking** along and around West Park, on the way into town, and there are central car parks on Oxford Street and near the train station. Harrogate's **tourist office** (May–Sept Mon–Sat 9am–6pm, Sun noon–3pm; Oct–April Mon–Fri 9am–5.15pm, Sat 9am–12.30pm; ☎01423/537300) is in the Royal Baths, Crescent Road.

There are scores of **accommodation** options, starting with the B&Bs on King's Road and Franklin Road, north of the centre. Side streets like Studley Road, off King's Road beyond the conference centre, are quieter. You shouldn't have any problem finding somewhere to stay, other than during one of Harrogate's many **festivals**. Of these the most famous are the **flower shows** (second weeks of April and Sept), but there's also the Great Yorkshire Show (second week in July), the Northern Antiques Fair (second half of Sept), and various book fairs, music festivals and craft shows.

Alexander Guest House 88 Franklin Rd ☎01423/503348. Recommended Victorian-era guest house on a residential street, under ten minutes' walk from the centre. No credit cards. ❷

Cavendish Hotel 3 Valley Drive ☎01423/509637. A comfortable, friendly place. The best rooms here (all en suite) overlook the Valley Gardens. ❸

Fountains Hotel 27 King's Rd ☎01423/530483. Family-run venture just up from the conference centre, with a nice rose garden out front. No credit cards. ❷

The Imperial Prospect Place ☎01423/565071. The doyen of spa-era hotels, the *Imperial* can't be bettered for location. It was once the home of Lord Carnarvon, discoverer of the tomb of Tutankhamen. ❺

Old Swan Hotel Swan Rd ☎01423/500055, ⊛www.oldswanhotel.com. Large ivy-covered inn set in its own grounds, much rebuilt in Victorian times. Agatha Christie hid out here during her disappearance in 1926; today's comforts are suitably country-house style if a tad routine. ❻

Rudding Park Hotel Rudding Park, Follifoot ☎01423/871350, ⊛www.ruddingpark.com. Stylish country-house hotel located three miles southeast of town (down the A661). Terrifically relaxing with a fine bar and brasserie, and attached gardens and golf course. ❼

Ruskin Hotel 1 Swan Rd ☎01423/502045, ⊛www.ruskinhotel.co.uk. Appealing Victorian villa with six characterful en-suite rooms, terraced bar and charming gardens. ❺

Eating and drinking

There are eating places to suit every budget in Harrogate, though, given the conference trade, there's an understandable emphasis on restaurants that are a tad predictable. There's also a plethora of new-wave café-bars, complete with espresso machines and fashionable food, but there are precious few town-centre pubs.

La Bergerie 11–13 Mount Parade ☎01423/500089. The town's best French restaurant, with well-priced three- and four-course traditional menus – you'll need to book in advance. Dinner only; closed Sun. Moderate.

Betty's 1 Parliament St ☎01423/502746. People drive half way across England to drop into Betty's – hardly surprising as this is probably the best tea shop in England. Very much a Harrogate institution, it was established by a Swiss emigrant in the 1920s. The decor isn't actually all that special, but the cakes and tarts (of many persuasions) are to die for. Full meals are served as an alternative to

the cakes and there's a cakey takeaway counter too. Daily 9am–9pm. Inexpensive to Moderate.

Courtyard 1 Montpellier Mews ☎01423/530708. Fashionable food – polenta, roast scallops, pan-seared salmon and the like – served in a cosy mews cottage. Lighter lunches are good value. Closed Sun & Mon. Expensive.

Court's 1 Crown Place ☎01423/536336. Spacious wine bar with up-to-the-minute food, comfortable sofas to lounge in, and outdoor tables on the cobbles. Closed Sun eve. Moderate.

Drum and Monkey 5 Montpellier Gardens ☎01423/502650. Long-standing fish and seafood restaurant, a firm favourite with locals and out-of-towners alike. Closed Sun. Moderate to Expensive.

Garden Room Restaurant Harlow Carr Botanical Gardens, Crag Lane ☎01423/505604. Handy garden spot with patio seating for lunches and snacks; dinner served Thurs–Sat. Moderate.

Est Est Est 16 Cheltenham Crescent ☎01423/566453. Harrogate's best Italian, a stylish place with classy pizzas, and interesting fish and meat dishes. Moderate to Expensive.

Montey's The Ginnel ☎01423/526652. Café-cum-music bar with inexpensive lunches and live music most evenings. Inexpensive.

Rick's Just for Starters 7 Bower Rd ☎01423/502700. Amiable mix-and-match bistro where, a few main courses aside, nothing much costs more than £5. Closed Sun lunch. Inexpensive to Moderate.

Salsa Posada 4 Mayfield Grove ☎01423/565151. Funky but cramped Mexican restaurant with good-natured staff churning out reasonably authentic *nachos, burritos, fajitas* and the rest. Closed Sun lunch. Moderate.

Knaresborough

A four-mile hop east from Harrogate, **KNARESBOROUGH** rises spectacularly above the River Nidd's limestone gorge, its old town houses, pubs, shops and gardens clustered together on the wooded northern bank, with the river itself crossed by two bridges ("High" and "Low") and an eye-opener of a rail viaduct. The rocky crag above the town is crowned by the stump of a **Castle** (Easter–Sept daily 10.30am–5pm; £2) dating back to Norman times. Built on the site of Roman and Anglo-Saxon fortifications, it's now little more than a fourteenth-century keep in landscaped grounds, thanks to Cromwell's wrecking tactics during the Civil War. It was here that Henry II's knights fled after the murder of Thomas à Becket in Canterbury Cathedral; here, too, that Richard II was held before being removed to Pontefract, where he was murdered in 1400. In Castle Yard, close to the castle entrance, stands the **Old Court House Museum** (same hours & ticket as castle), with an original Tudor court and displays on local history and the Civil War; you're also allowed into the spooky **sallyport**, the old escape tunnel from the castle.

These historic sites aside, there's not much to the town, but it is a very appealing place nonetheless, with a central **Market Place** (markets every Wednesday) claiming the oldest pharmacist's shop in England, in business since 1720. There's also a pub named after local boy "Blind Jack" (John) Metcalfe, the celebrated eighteenth-century civil engineer, who, despite his lack of sight, managed to build roads and bridges all over Britain. Below town, the enjoyable **riverside** is the other focus, with wooded walks along both banks; at the *Marigold* café, there's outdoor seating, hour-long river cruises in summer, as well as boats and bikes for rent.

The town's two novelty acts are to be found on the west side of the river. **Mother Shipton's Cave** (daily: Easter–Oct 9.30am–5.45pm; Nov–Easter 10am–4.45pm; £3.95) was home to a sixteenth-century soothsayer who predicted the defeat of the Armada, the Great Fire of London, world wars, cars, planes, iron ships – falling short, however, in the most important oracular chestnut of them all, predicting the End of the World: "The world to an end will come," she prophesied, "in eighteen hundred and eighty one." Close by is an equally tourist-thronged spot, the **Petrifying Well**, where dripping, lime-soaked waters coat everyday objects – gloves, hats, coats, toys – in a brownish veneer that sets rock-hard in a few weeks. Both cave and well are contained within a riverside estate, reached along a fine eighteenth-century wooded "Long Walk", studded with picnic areas; the main entrance is just over the High Bridge, north of the town, which you can reach by walking along the river from below the castle.

Practicalities

The **bus station** is on the High Street, with services to and from Harrogate, Ripon, York and Leeds. **Trains** (from the same destinations) pull up at the station just off the High Street, in the backstreets high above the river. The **tourist office** is nearby at 9 Castle Courtyard, Market Place (Easter–Oct Mon–Sat 10am–5.30pm, Sun 2–5pm; ☎01423/866886), and there's a list of accommodation and other services in the window. Free **guided walks** around the town leave from the Castle Yard outside the Old Court House Museum in summer; for information, call ☎01423/522588.

Knaresborough has a reasonable supply of **B&B** accommodation. Two good options are *Ebor Mount*, 18 York Place (☎01423/863315; ❷), and the *Yorkshire Lass* on High Bridge (☎01423/862962; ❷), an eclectically decorated pub right opposite the entrance to Mother Shipton's Cave. The town's best spot is the *Dower House Hotel*, an ivy-covered Georgian mansion at Bond End, near the High Bridge (☎01423/863302, ⓦwww.bwdowerhouse.co.uk; ❺), on the road to Mother Shipton's Cave.

Pollyanna's Tearooms up Jockey Lane, off the High Street, is the best **café**, while *Bella Rosa*, 25 Castlegate (☎01423/ 869918; closed Sun), opposite the tourist office, is a good-value pizzeria. Drink in *Blind Jack's* **pub** in the Market Place or in the *Mother Shipton Inn* at Low Bridge, a fine, traditional stone building with a maze of rooms, snugs and alcoves, and a great garden looking over the river to the town's famous rail viaduct.

Nidderdale

The rumours claim **Nidderdale** was excluded from the Yorkshire Dales National Park so that reservoirs and other landscape-scarring features could go ahead unencumbered by planning restrictions. Despite these developments, the dale's beautiful upper reaches stand comparison with its more famous neighbours, yet remain relatively unknown and under visited. Onward itineraries are pretty limited, however: the main approach is along the east–west B6265 between Grassington in Wharfedale and Ripon, with the only available route north along the wild road from **Pateley Bridge**, the dale's main village, to Masham and, ultimately, Wensleydale. The **bus** service is pretty much restricted to the regular Harrogate & District #24 from Harrogate to Pateley Bridge, which on summer Sundays continues on to Grassington; another summer Sunday service runs between Bradford/Leeds and Ripon via Pateley Bridge and Brimham Rocks. A long-distance footpath, the **Nidderdale Way**, runs in a circular 53-mile loop around the dale from Hampsthwaite village car park, three miles west of Harrogate. Dalesman Publishing produces a guide, *The Nidderdale Way*, and the route is indicated on OS maps 99 and 104.

Ripley

The lower dale is a patchwork of farming land, its first obvious distraction coming at **RIPLEY** (bus #36 from Ripon or Harrogate), four miles north of Harrogate. This is an impeccably kept village whose bizarre appearance is due to a whim of the Ingilby family, who between 1827 and 1854 rebuilt it in the manner of an Alsace-Lorraine village, for no other reason than they liked the style. (The project was financed by selling an outlying farm on the Ingilby estate, now Harrogate's town centre.) Summer crowds pile in for the cobbled square, original stocks and the twee cottages and shops, not to mention the Ingilby house, parkland and **Castle** (Jan–May & Sept–Dec Tues, Thurs, Sat & Sun 10.30am–3pm; June–Aug daily 10.30am–3pm; gardens daily: April–Sept 10am–6pm; Oct–March 9am–4.30pm or dusk; castle & gardens £5.50, gardens only £3), with its museum of armour, weapons, furniture and suchlike. You don't have to pay to enter the castle forecourt, where there's an excellent deli and a separate café, *Cromwell's Eating House*. Close to the bridge over the village beck, look in on **All Saints'** church, whose stonework bears the indentations of musket balls, said to be caused by the execution of Royalist soldiers after the Battle of Marston Moor. The graveyard also contains the "Kneeling" or "Weeping" cross, a stone with eight niches to receive the knees of penitents. It's believed to be the only one of its kind in the country.

The highly attractive *Boar's Head* (℡01423/771888; **❼**), part of the estate, has pricey **rooms**, but there's a lovely bar and beer garden, too, and a high-class **restaurant** with prices to match.

Pateley Bridge and around

The little town of **PATELEY BRIDGE** serves as the dale's focus, housing the **tourist office** at 18 High St (Easter–Oct daily 10am–5pm; ℡01423/711147) and acting as a base for campers, cavers and visitors of every kind. Its **Nidderdale Museum** (Easter–July, Sept & Oct daily 2–5pm; Aug 11am–5pm; rest of year Sat & Sun 2–5pm; £1.50), in the old council offices opposite the church on the edge of the village, provides a run-through of dale life in days gone by, with a re-created village shop, office and house interior to poke around. After that, you could stroll the **Panorama Walk** (2 miles; 1hr), signposted from the top of the High Street, or refuel in one of the tea rooms, pubs and restaurants along the High Street. Several local guest houses and hotels provide **accommodation**, one of the nicest places being the *Sportsmans Arms* (℡01423/711306; **❺**), a couple of miles out off the Nidderdale road at Wath-in-Nidderdale – there's really good food served here too. Five miles west of the village on the Grassington road lie the **Stump Cross Caverns** (April–Oct daily 10am–6pm; Nov–March Sat & Sun 10am–4pm; £4.50), one of England's premier show caves, complete with massive stalagmites.

About the same distance east of the village, signposted off the B6265, are the extraordinary **Brimham Rocks**, nearly four hundred acres of strangely eroded millstone grit outcrops scattered over one-thousand-foot high moors. The land at Brimham was once part of the wealthy Fountains Abbey estate, whose monks grazed their sheep between the weatherbeaten tors. Today, it's all under the protection of the National Trust, which maintains the paths between the rocks and safeguards the nesting jackdaws. It costs £2.30 to park your car, and after a clamber on the rocks, you can follow the path up to the **information centre** at Brimham House (April, May & Oct Sat & Sun 11am–5pm; June–Sept daily 11am–5pm; free). Views from the terrace here are superlative, stretching over the Vale of York, with York Minster visible on clear days. A refreshment kiosk (Sat & Sun only in winter) serves drinks and cakes.

North of Pateley Bridge, above the **Gouthwaite Reservoir**, Nidderdale closes in and the scenery is superb. Part of the reservoir is a restricted-access nature reserve, but plenty of geese, waders and waterfowl can be seen all year round from the surrounding roads and tracks. In the upper valley, seven miles from Pateley Bridge, there's also the **How Stean Gorge** (Jan & Feb Wed–Sun 10am–5pm; rest of year daily 10am–5pm; £2.50), a terrific ice-gouged ravine of surging waters and overhanging rocks. Take a torch and you can explore Tom Taylor's Cave, a dark, narrow squeeze through an underground cavern. There's summer **camping** (℡01423/755666) behind the gorge café. At the gorge, the minor road takes a turn to the northeast for the moorland crossing to Masham. A minibus service runs from Pateley Bridge past the reservoir (15min) to the gorge (30min), but only on summer Sundays and bank holiday Mondays.

Ripon

The unassuming market town of **RIPON**, eleven miles north of Harrogate, only really diverts by virtue of its relatively small but vital **Cathedral** (daily 8am–6.30pm; £2 donation requested), which can trace its ancestry back to its foundation by St Wilfrid in 672; the original crypt is still extant below the central tower. The rest of the building was destroyed by the Danes in the ninth century, then a second church fell foul of the Normans, part of whose replacement remains, though the bulk of the present building dates from the reign of Archbishop Roger of York (1154–81). Despite a rather plain exterior, there's plenty that pleases here, from the subtle, twin-towered, thirteenth-century west front to the choir's misericords, full of painted figures of miserable clergymen, executed by the same team that carved the impressive stalls at Beverley.

The town's other focus is its **marketplace**, "...the finest and most beautiful square...in England", according to Defoe, linked by Kirkgate to the cathedral; market day is Thursday. A ninety-foot obelisk built in 1780 dominates the square, a blustering conceit in stone, raised by William Aislabie to celebrate his sixty years as the local MP. At its apex stands a horned weather vane, an allusion to the "Blowing of the Wakeman's Horn", a ceremony – now something of a tourist attraction – which may date from 886, when Alfred the Great reputedly granted Ripon a charter and an ox's horn was presented for the setting of the town's watch. The last official Wakeman died in 1637 – his half-timbered **Wakeman's House** stands on the square – but the horn is still blown nightly at 9pm in the square's four corners and outside the house of the incumbent mayor.

Two restored buildings show a different side of Ripon's heritage. At the **Prison and Police Museum**, on St Marygate behind the cathedral (April–Oct daily 11am–3pm; £2), the old cells serve as the backdrop for an exhibition on the evils of previous punishments. It's questionable whether conditions in the nineteenth century were worse here or in the nearby **Ripon Workhouse**, on Allhallowgate (same hours as museum; £1.25), where the "undeserving" poor were incarcerated for such heinous crimes as being unable to pay their bills.

Practicalities

The **bus station** is dead central, just off the Market Place, while the town's **tourist office** is on Minster Road opposite the cathedral (April–Oct Mon–Sat 10am–5.30pm, Sun 1–4pm; ☎01765/604625). There's no huge reason to stay the night, though Ripon is the nearest base from which to visit Newby Hall and Fountains Abbey (see below). The range of **accommodation** options includes the *Coopers*, 36 College Rd (☎01765/603708; no credit cards; ➊), a quiet spot overlooking countryside; *Bishopton Grove House*, Bishopton (☎01765/600888; no credit cards; ➊), a Georgian house in a peaceful corner of the town; and the *Unicorn Hotel*, Market Place (☎01765/602202; ➍), an old coaching inn and central Ripon's finest. There are several small **restaurants** along Kirkgate across from the cathedral. The *Ripon Spa Hotel*, on Park Street, has a good restaurant and pleasant bar.

Newby Hall

One of England's most splendid Queen Anne houses, **Newby Hall** (April–Sept Tues–Sun noon–5pm, gardens open from 11am; £6.80; gardens only £5), stands just five miles southeast of the town near Skelton, south of the B6265. Completely overhauled by Robert Adam for his patron William

Weddell, it contains some outstanding decorative plasterwork, and is further adorned by lashings of Chippendale furniture and rich eighteenth-century tapestries. The grounds and gardens, too, are a delight, with parts sectioned off for the entertainment of kids – there's an adventure playground, miniature railway and paddling pool, as well as a tearoom and picnic area.

Fountains Abbey and Studley Royal

It's tantalizing to imagine how the English landscape might have appeared had Henry VIII not dissolved the monasteries, with all the artistic ruin precipitated by that act. **Fountains Abbey**, four miles southwest of Ripon off the B6265, gives a good idea of what might have been, and is the one ruin amongst Yorkshire's many monastic fragments you should make a point of seeing. Linked to it are the elegant water gardens of **Studley Royal**, landscaped in the eighteenth century to form a setting for the abbey, but only reunited as a single 680-acre estate in 1983. The estate is owned by the National Trust, who organize an ambitious range of activities and events – from opera and firework displays to **free guided tours** (April–Oct daily; call ☏01765/608888 for details).

The Cistercians

England's **monastic tradition** received a boost in the middle of the twelfth century when Norman landlords, seeking to secure spiritual salvation and raise a bit of cash, handed over portions of their estates to various religious orders, often to dissident offshoots of the Benedictines such as the **Cistercians**. Inevitably the poorest and least promising part of an estate, these parcels of land were well suited to the Cistercians, who were bent on removing themselves from the world and a Benedictine orthodoxy which in their eyes had become insufficiently strict. Committed to toil, self-sufficiency and prayer, the movement was founded at Cîteaux in Burgundy, in reaction to the arrogant affluence of the Cluniacs, who themselves had earlier reacted against the same perceived fault in the Benedictines. Fountains found itself in the vanguard of the movement, founded just five years after Waverley, the first Cistercian foundation in England.

Dressed in rough **habits** of undyed sheeps' wool, the so-called "White Monks" lived a frugal and mostly silent existence. Besides this core of priest-monks common to all Benedictine communities, whose obligatory presence at choir seven times daily, starting with matins at 2.30am, left little time for work outside the cloister, the Cistercians uniquely had a second tier of lay brethren known as **conversi**, or "bearded ones". At Fountains, around forty monks were complemented by two hundred such *conversi*. At Rievaulx the imbalance was equally marked, its community comprising over 500 *conversi* and only 150 monks. Not ordained, and with fewer religious demands, the new recruits – often skilled farmers and masons – could venture far from the mother house, returning only for major festivals and feast days. They were organized into **granges** (farms) to run flocks of sheep, drain land (hence Yorkshire's many "Friar's Ditches"), clear pasture, mine stone, lead or iron – even, in a couple of cases, to run a stud farm and sea-fishing business. Fountains' holdings in the Craven area of the Dales alone totalled over a million acres.

The Cistercians' success prompted the Augustinians (Kirkham and Guisborough) and Benedictines (York and Whitby) to follow suit, though within a hundred years much of their early vigour had been lost, partly as a result of an economic down turn which followed the Black Death. Granges were broken into smaller units and leased to a new class of tenant farmer, as the Cistercians joined the older orders in living off rents rather than actively developing their own estates.

Getting there by **public transport** is not as easy as it might be. There are regular buses to Ripon from Harrogate and York (amongst other places), but the onward service to the abbey is patchy in summer, paltry in winter. Ring Ripon tourist office or the abbey for the latest.

The Abbey

Beautifully set in a narrow, wooded valley, **Fountains Abbey** (April–Sept daily 10am–7pm; Oct, Feb & March daily 10am–5pm or dusk; Nov–Jan closed Fri; last admission 1hr before closing; £4.50 including Studley Royal and Fountains Hall; NT) was founded in 1133 by thirteen dissident Benedictine monks from the wealthy abbey of St Mary's in York. Their enterprise may well have been encouraged by the success of Rievaulx (see p.969), founded a year earlier, and they were formally adopted by the Cistercians two years later (see box on p.933). Within a hundred years, Fountains had become the wealthiest Cistercian foundation in England and it was to this century that the three main phases of the abbey's structural development belong: the church's nave and transepts, the domestic buildings, and the church's east end. Only the church's domineering tower belongs to a later period. At the Dissolution the abbey was sold to Sir Richard Gresham, and ultimately became a source of building stone for the nearby Fountains Hall (see below). Further desecration was avoided when in 1768 it became part of Studley Royal under William Aislabie, who extended the landscaping exploits of his father to bring the ruined abbey within the estate's orbit.

Most immediately eye-catching is the **abbey church**, in particular the **Chapel of the Nine Altars** at its eastern end, whose delicacy is in marked contrast to the austerity of the rest of the nave. A great sixty-foot-high window rises over the chapel, complemented by a similar window at the nave's western doorway, over 370ft away. The **Perpendicular Tower**, almost 180ft high, looms over the whole ensemble, added by the eminent early sixteenth-century Abbot Marmaduke Huby, who presided over perhaps the abbey's greatest period of prosperity. Equally grandiose in scale is the undercroft of the **Lay Brothers' Dormitory** off the cloister, a stunningly vaulted space over three hundred feet long that was used to store the monastery's annual harvest of fleeces. Its sheer size gives some idea of the abbey's entrepreneurial scope, some thirteen tons of wool a year being turned over, most of it sold to Venetian and Florentine merchants who toured the monasteries. The monks soon became speculators, buying wool from local farmers to sell in addition to their own production.

The size of the lay buildings – including a substantial **Lay Brothers' Infirmary** – gives an idea of the number of lay brothers at the abbey. All are considerably larger than the corresponding monks' buildings, of which the most prepossessing are the **Chapter House** and **Refectory** – notice the huge fireplace of the tiny **Warming Room** alongside the refectory, the only heated space in the entire complex. Outside the abbey perimeter, between the gatehouse and the bridge, are the Abbey Mill and **Fountains Hall** (same times; NT), the latter a fine example of early seventeenth-century domestic architecture.

Studley Royal

A bucolic riverside walk, marked from the visitor centre car park, takes you through the abbey and past Fountains Hall to a series of ponds and ornamental gardens, harbingers of **Studley Royal** (same times as the abbey; NT) - which can also be entered via the village of Studley Roger, where there's a separate car park. This lush medley of lawns, lake, woodland and **Deer Park** (daily dawn to dusk; free) was laid out in 1720 by John Aislabie, MP for Ripon and Chancellor of the Exchequer until his involvement with the South Sea Company – one of the great financial scandals of the century – led to his resignation. There are some scintillating views of the abbey from the gardens, though it's the cascades and water gardens, fed by canals from the Skell, which command most attention, framed by several small temples positioned for their aesthetic effect. Just within the park stands the 1871 church of **St Mary** (April–Sept daily 1–5pm; free), neatly approached by an avenue of limes that frame the distant towers of Ripon cathedral. Organ recitals are held here most weekends (May–Sept). You could easily spend an afternoon whiling away time in the gardens: the full circuit, from visitor centre to abbey and gardens and then back, is a good couple of miles' walk.

York

YORK is the north's most compelling city, a place whose history, said George VI, "is the history of England". This is perhaps overstating things a little, but it reflects the significance of a metropolis that until the Industrial Revolution was second only to London in population and importance, not only at the heart of the country's religious life, but also a key player in some of the major events that have shaped the nation. These days a more provincial air hangs over the city, except in summer when York feels like a heritage site for the benefit of tourists. That said, no trip to this part of the country is complete without a visit to York, and the city's former importance has made it easy to get to, with plenty of road and rail connections. Heavy tourist traffic has also produced plenty of accommodation, with the emphasis on small B&B places in quiet residential districts near the city centre. And if you want more than museums and monuments, York's university and colleges provide the spur for a reasonably healthy nightlife.

The city is well placed for any number of **day-trips**: the coast is only an hour away by car (longer by bus), and Harrogate, Knaresborough and Ripon are all easily accessible, too. However, these are all places that – with the time – you could profitably spend the night in, and the only essential day-trip is northeast to **Castle Howard**, the gem amongst English stately homes. There's a different kind of nostalgia at work at nearby **Eden Camp** – a World War II museum occupying buildings which once housed German prisoners-of-war.

A brief history of York

The **Romans** chose York's swampy position, at the confluence of two minor rivers, as the site of a military camp during their campaigns against the Brigantes in 71 AD, and in time this fortress became a city – **Eboracum**, capital of the empire's northern European territories and one of its most important administrative centres. The base for Hadrian's northern campaigns, it was also ruled for three years by Septimius Severus, one of two emperors to die in the city. The other, Constantine Chlorus, was the father of Constantine the Great, first Christian emperor and founder of Constantinople; at Chlorus' death, his son was proclaimed Roman Emperor here – the only occasion an emperor was enthroned in Britain.

Much fought over after the decline of Rome, the city emerged as a **Saxon** vassal, Eoforwic, and later became the fulcrum of Christianity in northern England. It was here, on Easter Day in 627, that Bishop Paulinus, on a mission

YORK

▲ A1036 Malton

ACCOMMODATION

23 St Mary's	12
Abbey Guest House	9
Arnot House	4
Arndale Hotel	26
The Bar Convent	22
Bootham Bar Hotel	13
City Guest House	11
Claremount Guest House	5
Clifton Bridge Hotel	1
Dairy Guest House	27
Dean Court Hotel	16
Elliott's Hotel	10
Fairfax House	24
The Golden Fleece	19
The Hazelwood	8
Holme Lea Manor	2
Jorvik Hotel	14
Judge's Lodging	17
Middlethorpe Hall	28
Minster View Guest House	6
Mount Royale Hotel	25
Queen Anne's Guest House	7
Royal York Hotel	18
St Mary's Hotel	15
Travelodge	23
York Backpackers Hostel	20
York International Youth Hostel	3
York Youth Hotel	21

Treasurer's House
Minster Library
Dean's Park
York Minster
St Michael-le-Belfrey
St William's College
Monk Bar
Merchant Taylor's Hall
Bedern Hall
St Anthony's Hall
ARC
Fibbers
Black Swan Inn
Holy Trinity
Internet Exchange
Betty's
Mansion House
De Grey Rooms
Theatre Royal
Library
Assembly Rooms
Guildhall
King's Manor
City Art Gallery
Exhibition Square
Bootham Bar
St Mary's Abbey
The Yorkshire Museum
Museum Gardens
Lendal Bar

LORD MAYOR'S WALK
ST MAURICE'S ROAD
MONKGATE
JEWBURY
GOODRAMGATE
ALDWARK
SAINT SAVIOURGATE
SAINT ANDREWGATE
COLLIERGATE
SHAMBLES
DUNDAS STREET
THE STONEBOW
HUNGATE
PEASHOLME GREEN
GOOD RAMGATE
KING'S SQ
CHURCH STREET
PARLIAMENT STREET
LOW PETERGATE
HIGH PETERGATE
DEANGATE
OGLEFORTH
MINSTER YARD
COLLEGE STREET
CHAPTER HOUSE ST
LITTLE STONEGATE
STONEGATE
GRAPE LANE
BLAKE ST
DAVYGATE
CONEY ST
NEW STREET
ST HELEN'S SQUARE
LENDAL
ST LEONARD'S PLACE
MUSEUM STREET
GILLYGATE
PORTLAND STREET
CLAREMONT TERRACE
BOOTHAM TERR
MARYGATE
BOOTHAM
SAINT MARY'S
FREDERIC STREET
LONGFIELD TERRACE
SYCAMORE TERRACE
BOOTHAM TERRACE
QUEEN ANNE'S ROAD
GROSVENOR TERR
LENDAL BRIDGE
WELLINGTON ROW
LEEMAN ROAD
STATION AV
STATION RISE

▲ ❶ ❷ ❸ & A19 Thirsk

N

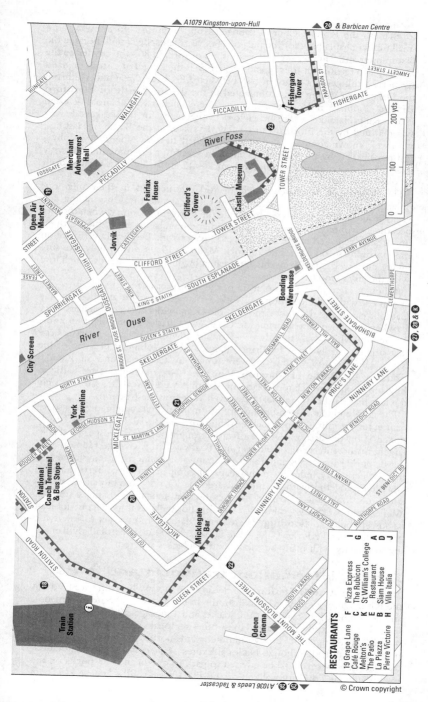

A1079 Kingston-upon-Hull

& Barbican Centre

HUNGATE

WALMGATE

PICCADILLY

FISHERGATE

Fishergate Tower

PARAGON ST

FAWCETT STREET

River Foss

Merchant Adventurers' Hall

FOSSGATE

PICCADILLY

TOWER STREET

Open Air Market

PAVEMENT

COPPERGATE

Fairfax House

Clifford's Tower

Castle Museum

Jorvik

CASTLEGATE

TOWER STREET

SKELDERGATE BRIDGE

STREET

MARKET STREET

FEASEGATE

SPURRIERGATE

HIGH OUSEGATE

CLIFFORD STREET

KING'S STREET

SOUTH ESPLANADE

TERRY AVENUE

Bonding Warehouse

KING'S STAITH

OUSEGATE

Ouse

QUEEN'S STAITH

SKELDERGATE

SKELDERGATE

CLEMENTHORPE

BISHOPGATE STREET

CROMWELL ROAD

BAILE HILL TERRACE

River

City Screen

BRIDGE ST

OUSE BRIDGE

NORTH STREET

KYME STREET

PRICE'S LANE

NUNNERY LANE

York Traveline

GEORGE HUDSON ST

MICKLEGATE

BISHOPHILL SENIOR

FETTER LANE

BUCKINGHAM ST

VICTOR STREET

NEWTON TERRACE

VICTOR ST

ST BENEDICT ROAD

ROUGIER STREET

National Coach Terminal & Bus Stops

ST. MARTIN'S LANE

TANNER ROW

TRINITY LANE

BISHOPHILL JUNIOR

PRIORY STREET

FAIRFAX STREET

HAMPDEN STREET

LOWER PRIORY STREET

NUNNERY LANE

SWANN STREET

DALE STREET

SCARCROFT LANE

NUNTHORPE ROAD

ST BENEDICT RD

STATION

Micklegate Bar

TOFT GREEN

MICKLEGATE

DEWSBURY TERRACE

QUEEN STREET

SOUTH PARADE

SWANN STREET

STATION ROAD

Train Station

Odeon Cinema

THE MOUNT

BLOSSOM STREET

MOSS STREET

A1036, A1038 Leeds & Tadcaster

© Crown copyright

RESTAURANTS

19 Grape Lane	I	Pizza Express	F
Café Rouge	G	The Rubicon	C
Melton's	K	St William's College	E
The Patio	A	Restaurant	
La Piazza	D	Siam House	B
Pierre Victoire	J	Villa Italia	H

200 yds

100

0

937

to establish the Roman Church, baptized King Edwin of Northumbria in a small timber chapel built for the purpose. Six years later the church became the first minster and Paulinus the first archbishop of York. In 867 the city fell to the **Danes**, who renamed it **Jorvik**, and later made it the capital of eastern England (Danelaw), following a treaty in 886 between Alfred the Great and Guthrum the Dane. Later Viking raids culminated in the decisive **Battle of Stamford Bridge** (1066) six miles east of the city, where English King Harold defeated Norse King Harald – a Pyrrhic victory in the event, for his weakened army was defeated by the Normans just a few days later at the Battle of Hastings, with well-known consequences for all concerned. In York, aside from the physical remains left by the Vikings on show in several of the museums, the very street names tell of their profound influence – the suffix "-gate" is derived from an old Norse word for street.

The **Normans** devastated much of York's hinterland in their infamous "Harrying of the North", building two castles astride the Ouse in the city itself. Stone walls were thrown up during the thirteenth century, when the city became a favoured Plantagenet retreat and commercial capital of the north, its importance reflected in the new title of Duke of York, bestowed ever since on the monarch's second son. The 48 **York Mystery Plays**, one of only four surviving such cycles, date from this era, created by the powerful guilds which rose with the city's woollen industry.

Although Henry VIII's Dissolution of the Monasteries took its toll on a city crammed with religious houses, York remained strongly wedded to the Catholic cause, and the most famous of the Gunpowder Plot conspirators, **Guy Fawkes**, was born here. During the **Civil War** Charles I established his court in the city, which was strongly pro-Royalist, inviting a Parliamentarian siege that was eventually lifted by Prince Rupert of the Rhine, a nephew of the King. Rupert's troops, however, were routed by Cromwell and Sir Thomas Fairfax at the **Battle of Marston Moor** in 1644, another seminal battle in England's history, which took place just six miles west of York. It's said that only the fact that Fairfax was a local man saved York from destruction.

The city's eighteenth-century history was marked by its emergence as a social centre for Yorkshire's landed elite. Whilst the Industrial Revolution largely passed it by, the arrival of the **railways** brought renewed prosperity, thanks largely to the enterprise of pioneering "Railway King" George Hudson, lord mayor during the 1830s and 1840s. The railway is still a major employer, as is the confectionery industry, in the shape of companies such as Terry Suchard and Nestlé, together with the proceeds from new service and bioscience industries – not forgetting, of course, the income from four million annual tourists. While a comparatively wealthy place, York is not without its problems, not least its susceptibility to **flooding**. There's river damage most years to low-lying properties near the River Ouse – the floods of 2000 were particularly damaging to the city, with many businesses and residences affected.

Arrival, information, transport and tours

Trains arrive at **York Station**, just outside the city walls on the west side of the River Ouse, a 750-yard walk from the historic core. There are information and accommodation centres at the station and a luggage-storage office. Long-haul National Express **buses** and most other regional bus services drop off and pick up on Rougier Street, two hundred yards north of the train station, just before Lendal Bridge, though National Express services call at the train station, too. Arriving by car you'd be advised to park in one of the **car parks** on the roads shadowing the city walls: in the north, Gillygate and Clarence Street are closest to the Minster; Piccadilly and Tower Street in the southeast are convenient for Clifford's Tower and the Castle Museum; and there are also car parks on Queen Street near the train station.

There's a useful **tourist office** at the train station (April–Oct Mon–Sat 9am–8pm, Sun 10am–5pm; Nov–Feb Mon–Sat 9am–5pm, Sun 10am–4pm; March Mon–Sat 9.30am–5.30pm, Sun 10am–5pm; ☏01904/621756), though the main office is over Lendal Bridge, two hundred yards west of the Minster in the **De Grey Rooms**, on Exhibition Square (April–June, Sept & Oct Mon–Sat 9am–6pm, Sun 9.30am–6pm; July & Aug daily 9am–7pm; Nov–March Mon–Sat 9am–5pm, Sun 9.30am–3pm; ☏01904/621756). Each office can provide maps and leaflets on every conceivable tour and attraction, and an accommodation service (see below). Check out, too, the York City Council **website**, ⓦwww.york.gov.uk, for details of the major sites, museums and galleries and much else.

Walking is the best way to acquaint yourself with the city, and often the only way to get from A to B, given the confused historic layout of pedestrianized streets, alleys and yards. City **bus routes** are operated by First York (☏01904/622992) – visitors are unlikely to get much use out of their Day Rover ticket (£2) or weekly Minstercard (£10, unlimited rides), available from the De Grey rooms or on board the buses. Consider **renting a bike** instead, as York is one of the country's most bike-friendly cities, with over 40 miles of cycle lanes and paths – rental outfits are given on p.953.

York is probably tour capital of Britain, the streets clogged by double-decker buses, costumed guides and carefully shepherded sightseers. Doing it yourself is, frankly, the most enjoyable way, though if time is limited, or you fancy some of the more inventive options, there's plenty of choice. The tourist offices all push the various **bus tours** (from around £8 per person), but much more interesting are the various **guided walks** on offer, from evening ghost walks to historical tours, many led by the York Association of Voluntary Guides (☏01904/640780, ⓦwww.york.touristguides.btinternet.co.uk). They offer a free, two-hour guided tour throughout the year (daily at 10.15am), plus additional tours in summer (April–June, Sept & Oct at 2.15pm; July & Aug at 2.15pm & 7pm), departing from outside the Art Gallery in Exhibition Square; just turn up. It's also pleasant to get out on the river, and several operators offer similarly priced **cruises**, including YorkBoat (☏01904/628324, ⓦwww.yorkboat.co.uk), sailing daily from King's Staith and Lendal Bridge (Feb–Nov; cruises from £5, £6.50 in the evening).

Accommodation

York is a busy tourist town, with the range of **accommodation** you'd expect, from countless cheap B&Bs to a clutch of topnotch luxury hotels. The main B&B concentrations are in the sidestreets off **Bootham and Clifton** (immediately west of Exhibition Square), as well as in the **Mount** area (turn right out of the station and head down Blossom Street), and, less conveniently, along **Haxby Road** (north of town; take bus #1, #2a or #3). True city-centre places are thin on the ground and obviously in great demand; booking's definitely a good idea from June to August. If you're stuck for a bed, make straight for the tourist offices, who'll **book you a room**. They also put out a list of guest houses if you want to hunt on your own, and there's a useful board of places posted in the station office window. First Option also has an accommodation booking office at the train station (daily 8am–10pm; ☏01904/673411). It's worth noting that, in a reversal of policy in most cities, larger hotels in York tend to charge slightly less during the week than at weekends.

York's nearest **campsites** are all a fair way out of the centre: nearest is the *Riverside Caravan and Camping Park* (℡01904/705812; closed Nov–March) in Bishopsthorpe, off the A64, a couple of miles south of the city. Take bus #23 (every 30min) from York train station. Alternatively, there's *Poplar Farm Caravan Park* at Acaster Malbis (℡01904/706548; closed Nov–March), about four miles south, which has tent sites and can be reached by bus #192 (4 daily) from Skeldergate Bridge, by the river.

Hotels and B&Bs

23 St Mary's 23 St Mary's, Bootham ℡01904 /622738. Very pleasant and amiable family-house hotel just west of St Mary's Abbey and gardens. All rooms are en suite; parking available. No credit cards. ❹

Abbey Guest House 14 Earlsborough Terrace, Marygate ℡01904/627782. Riverside terraced guest house in a great location with bright, pretty rooms, two of which, overlooking the river, are en suite. ❸

Arnot House 17 Grosvenor Terrace, Bootham ℡01904/641966, ⓦwww.arnothouseyork.co.uk. Victorian family house preserving many of its original features, offering four well-furnished and equipped no-smoking en-suite rooms with distant views of the Minster. Vegetarian breakfasts on request. ❸

Arndale Hotel 290 Tadcaster Rd ℡01904/702424. Pleasant, welcoming hotel with walled garden overlooking the racecourse a mile south of the centre; many rooms have four-posters and whirlpool baths, and there's secure parking. Midweek and winter rates are a few pounds less than usual. ❺

The Bar Convent 17 Blossom St ℡01904/643238, ⓦwww.bar-convent.org.uk. Grand Georgian building next to Micklegate Bar, housing a museum and café as well as eight single rooms, five twins and a double; one of the twins is en suite, otherwise there are separate bathrooms and access to a self-catering kitchen. Continental breakfast included. ❷

Bootham Bar Hotel 4 High Petergate ℡01904 /658516, ⓦwww.boothambarhotel.com. A refined eighteenth-century hotel with mainly en-suite rooms, just 100 yards from the Minster. Three basic singles, too, sharing a bathroom. Parking available. ❹

City Guest House 68 Monkgate ℡01904/622483, ⓦwww.cityguesthouse.co.uk. Central, non-smoking, family-run guest house with budget rates, not far from the Minster. All rooms (six doubles/twins and just one single) have en-suite showers and there's a useful car park. ❸

Claremount Guest House 18 Claremount Terrace, Gillygate ℡01904/625158. Friendly B&B with just two rooms (one en suite) in a quiet Victorian cul-de-sac about 200 yards from the Minster, at the Lord Mayor's Walk end of Gillygate. Private parking available. ❸

Clifton Bridge Hotel Water End, Clifton ℡01904/610510, ⓦwww.cliftonbridgehotel.co.uk. A mile northwest of the Minster beyond Bootham, but close to a riverside walk to the city centre. Of the fourteen rooms, three on the ground-floor are wheelchair accessible, and there's a larger family room, too. Nicely situated in its own grounds, with parking available. ❺

Dairy Guest House 3 Scarcroft Rd ℡01904/639367, ⓦwww.dairyguesthouse.freeserve.co.uk. Victorian house half a mile south of the station, with five rooms heavy on stripped pine and flowery furnishings; two cheaper ones share a bathroom. Offers a choice of traditional or wholefood/vegetarian breakfasts. Closed mid-Dec to Jan. No credit cards. ❸

Dean Court Hotel Duncombe Place ℡01904/625082, ⓦwww.deancourt-york.co.uk. Perfectly sited neo-Victorian hotel with views of the Minster from the front rooms, which means it's pricey, but the facilities come up to scratch. There's garage parking nearby. Ask about special-break prices. ❼

Elliott's Hotel Sycamore Place, Bootham Terrace ℡01904/623333, ⓦwww.elliottshotel.co.uk. A surprising find – a large detached Victorian house tucked away in a peaceful and convenient spot, with comfortable rooms, big breakfasts, bar snacks, a restaurant and parking. ❹

The Golden Fleece 16 Pavement ℡01904/627151, Ⓔgoldenfleece@fibbers.co.uk. Just four rooms available in this historic pub, but what a collection – one overlooks the Shambles, one has views to the Minster towers and all are haunted (well, maybe). Decor is antique, the atmosphere unique. ❺–❼

The Hazelwood 24–25 Portland St, Gillygate ℡01904/626548, ⓦwww.thehazelwoodyork.com. Good variety of rooms – all with private bath – in a central residential area. The doubles vary in price a bit, giving you more room for more money. There's also a pleasant garden and parking. ❺

Holme Lea Manor 18 St Peter's Grove, Clifton ℡01904/623529, ⓦwww.holmeleamanor.com. Comfortable en-suite rooms with period touches (most have four-posters) in a quiet, tree-lined Victorian cul-de-sac just ten minutes from the centre. Parking available. **❸**

Jorvik Hotel 52 Marygate, Bootham ☎01904/653511. In an extremely good position opposite the western entrance to St Mary's Abbey, this family-run town-house hotel has a variety of rooms and some private parking – you'll pay more to overlook the abbey gardens. **❸–❹**

Judge's Lodging 9 Lendal ☎01904/638733, ⓦ www.judges-lodging.co.uk. One of the top central, historic choices, located in the lovely eighteenth-century Georgian residence of the former assize court judges, a few minutes from the Minster. There's secure parking and a good cellar-bar. **❼**

Middlethorpe Hall Bishopsthorpe Rd ☎01904 /641241, ⓦ www.middlethorpe.com. York's most celebrated spot, a grand eighteenth-century mansion a couple of miles south of the city, next to the racecourse. Antiques, wood panelling, superb rooms (some set in a private courtyard), gardens, parkland, pool and spa, and a fine restaurant, all at stratospheric prices. **❽**

Minster View Guest House 2 Grosvenor Terrace, Bootham ☎01904/655034. The touted views are of the Minster tower across the rail line and park beyond, but it's still a nice place on a relatively quiet road just off Bootham. No credit cards. **❷**

Mount Royale Hotel The Mount ☎01904/628856, ⓦ www.mountroyale.co.uk. Luxurious, antique-filled retreat south of the station with superb garden-suites set around a private garden, together with a heated pool and other facilities. Some less exalted standard rooms are also available. It's family-owned and run, too, which gives it the edge over similarly endowed spots. **❻**, **❼** for garden suites.

Queen Anne's Guest House 24–26 Queen Anne's Rd ☎01904/629389 ⓦ www.s-h-systems.co.uk /hotels/queenann.html. Budget-rated Bootham B&B with seven bright rooms, mostly en suite. Private parking available. **❷**

Royal York Hotel Station Rd ☎01904/653681, ⓦ www.principalhotels.co.uk. Grand Edwardian pile by the station, much used by conferences but making a comfortable base for well-heeled city sightseers. Parking available for a small charge. **❻**

St Mary's Hotel 17 Longfield Terrace ☎01904 /626972, ⓦ www.stmaryshotel.co.uk. Homely and flower-hung hotel in a peaceful railway-cutting backstreet south of Bootham, with the river (and a pleasant walk into the centre) just 100 yards away. Most rooms have en-suite facilities; two share a bathroom. Parking available, and small discounts in winter. **❸**

Travelodge Piccadilly ☎08700/850950, ⓦ www .travelodge.co.uk. Echoing the city's walls and towers in its design, this riverside choice is handily sited close to the Castle Museum. Motel-style rooms at budget prices; parking available. **❸**

Hostels and student halls

Fairfax House 99 Heslington Rd ☎01904/432095. University of York Georgian housing, containing well-equipped single rooms, available at Easter and during summer vacations for short stays or week-long breaks. Call in advance (Mon–Fri 9.30am–4.30pm). It's ten minutes east of the centre, off Barbican Road. Small groups can also rent self-contained houses, from £375 a week.

York Backpackers Hostel Micklegate House, 88–90 Micklegate ☎01904/627720, ⓦ www .yorkbackpackers.mcmail.com. Dorm space, doubles and family rooms in a Grade I listed building, the 1752 former home of the High Sheriff of Yorkshire. There's a self-catering kitchen, laundry, internet access, TV and games room, and licensed cellar bar. Self-service breakfast costs extra.

York International Youth Hostel Water End, Clifton ☎01904/653147, ⓔ york@yha.org.uk. Large Victorian mansion about twenty-minutes' walk along Bootham from the tourist office and then a left turn at Clifton Green. A nicer and quicker approach from the station is to follow the riverside footpath west. Beds are mostly in four-bedded dorms, though there is also a small number of private rooms (book well in advance for these). Facilities include a café (with licence for alcohol with meals), internet access, large garden (for volleyball and croquet) and parking.

York Youth Hotel 11–13 Bishophill Senior ☎01904/625904, ⓦ www.yorkyouthhotel.com. Centrally located, on the west side of the river, off Micklegate, and attracting a mixed international crowd – dorm, single and twin rooms available, with a pound off for multi-night stays; breakfast extra. Also a kitchen, laundry, games room, TV lounge and internet access.

The City

Take a look at one of the maps dotted around the city centre and you're confronted with a baffling and intimidating prospect. If the city council and tourist office are to be believed, there are around sixty churches, museums and historic buildings crammed within York's walls. In fact the tally of things you really want to see is surprisingly limited, with most sights within easy walking distance of one another. Even so, it's hard to get round everything in less than two days, and equally difficult to stick to any rigid itinerary. The **Minster** is the obvious place to start, followed by the cluster of buildings that circle it; then you might cut south to the **Shambles**, central to the city's old centre and pedestrianized grid, or walk around **the walls** from the Minster to Exhibition Square and Museum Street for the **City Art Gallery**, **Yorkshire Museum** and **St Mary's Abbey**, evocative ruins surrounded by the city's loveliest gardens. Thereafter you could walk through the main shopping streets to take in the **Merchant Adventurers' Hall**, most striking of the city's smaller medieval buildings, then deal with **Clifford's Tower** and the nearby **Jorvik Viking Centre** and **Castle Museum**. Lastly, be sure to leave time to take in the **National Railway Museum**, a superb museum whose appeal goes way beyond railway memorabilia.

The **York Museums pass** (£9) gives five days' unlimited access to the Castle Museum, Yorkshire Museum and City Art Gallery, offering a fair saving on entry to these council-sponsored attractions. The Jorvik (Viking) and ARC (archeologicial centre) attractions also have a joint ticket available.

York Minster

York Minster (daily: June–Sept 7am–8.30pm; Oct–May 7am–6pm; £3 donation requested; ⓦwww.yorkminster.org) ranks as one of the country's most important sights. Seat of the archbishop of York, it is Britain's largest Gothic building and home to countless treasures, not least of which is the world's largest medieval **stained-glass** window and an estimated half of all the medieval stained glass in England. Samuel Johnson, visiting in 1773, was overwhelmed, but not, of course, lost for words, thinking it "an edifice of loftiness and elegance equal to the highest hopes of architecture". In addition to the main body of the church, any complete tour of the building, which took 250 years to complete, should also include the **foundations**, **crypt**, **chapter house** and an ascent of the great **central tower**. Once inside, be sure to pick up the *Welcome to York Minster* leaflet, a detailed account of the building. Voluntary guides are also on hand (at the reception desk by the entrance) to offer free **tours** of the interior.

In its earliest incarnation the Minster was probably the wooden chapel used to baptize King Edwin of Northumbria in 627. After its stone successors were destroyed by the Danes, the first significant foundations were laid around 1080 by the first Norman archbishop, Thomas of Bayeux. Subsequent incumbents, notably Archbishop Roger (1154–81), added to the building, and it was from the germ of this Norman church that the present structure emerged. The oldest surviving fabric, in the south transept, dates from 1220 and the reign of Archbishop Walter de Grey, who also began work on a new north transept in 1260. A new chapter house, in the Decorated style, appeared in 1300, and a new nave in the same style was completed in 1338. The Perpendicular choir was realized in 1450 and the western towers in 1472. In 1480, the thirteenth-century central tower, which had collapsed in 1407, was rebuilt, thereby bringing the Minster to more or less its present state.

In the 1960s, in the course of investigating subsidence that had begun to affect the building, it was found that the 20,000-ton, 234ft central tower was resting on only a shallow bed of loose stones, a discovery which prompted a £2-million project that was to involve packing the foundations with thousands of tons of concrete and over six miles of reinforced steel rods. That was-n't the end of the church's troubles, though. In 1984 lightning struck the Minster, unleashing a disastrous fire which raged through the south transept, destroying the timber-framed central vault and all but two of its extraordinary roof bosses.

The windows

Nothing else in the Minster can match the magnificence of the stained glass in the nave and transepts. The **West Window** (1338) contains distinctive heart-shaped upper tracery (the "Heart of Yorkshire"), whilst in the nave's north aisle, the second bay window (1155) contains slivers of the oldest stained glass in the country. In the fifth bay, notice the window showing St Peter attended by pilgrims (1312), with the funeral of a monkey among the fascinating details in its lower scenes. Moving down to the crossing, the north transept's **Five Sisters Window** is named after the five fifty-foot lancets, each glazed with thirteenth-century *grisaille*, a distinctive frosted, silvery-grey glass. Opposite, the south transept contains a sixteenth-century, 17,000-piece **Rose Window**, commemorating the 1486 marriage of Henry VII and Elizabeth of York, an alliance which marked the end of the Wars of the Roses.

The greatest of the church's 128 windows, however, is the majestic **East Window** (1405), at 78ft by 31ft the world's largest area of medieval stained glass in a single window. Its themes are the beginning and the end of the world, the upper panels showing scenes from the Old Testament, the lower sections mainly episodes from the book of Revelation. Notice also the glass of the transeptal bays, midway down the south wall of the choir, with their scenes from the lives of saints Cuthbert and William of York. The tombs of William, a twelfth-century archbishop of York, and of Cuthbert, ordained bishop in 685, stood near the high altar until the Reformation, and were credited with numerous miracles.

The rest of the interior

Before leaving the main body of the interior, give some time to the north transept's 400-year-old wooden clock with its oak knights, and the stone **choir screen**, knotted with incredibly intricate carvings and decorated with life-size figures of English monarchs from William I to Henry VI – all except the latter carved in the last quarter of the fifteenth century. Most of the choir dates from restorations following a fire in 1829. The painted **stone shields** round much of the nave and choir are those of Edward II and the barons who in 1309–10 held a "parliament" in York. Amongst the many tombs, those of most interest are the monument in the south transept to Walter de Grey, a beautiful grey-green canopy protecting a recumbent stone figure, and the tomb of the 10-year-old William, second son of Edward III, in the choir aisle.

The foundations, or **undercroft** (£3), have been turned into a museum, fit-ted into a space excavated during the restorations in the 1960s. Fragments of the Roman fort which once stood on this site have been uncovered, as well as capitals, sculpture and fabric from the present Minster and its Norman prede-cessor. Amongst precious church relics in the adjoining **treasury** are silver plate found in Walter de Grey's tomb and the eleventh-century *Horn of Ulf*, present-ed to the Minster by a relative of the tide-turning King Canute. There's also access from the undercroft to the **crypt**, the spot that transmits the most pow-erful sense of antiquity, as it contains portions of Archbishop Roger's choir and sections of the 1080 church, including pillars with fine Romanesque capitals. The font stands over the supposed site of Paulinus's timber chapel, while a small illuminated doorway opens onto the base of a pillar belonging to the guard-house of the original Roman camp.

Access to the undercroft, treasury and crypt is from the south transept, also the entrance to the **central tower** (£3), which you can climb for rooftop views over the city. Finally pop into the **Chapter House** (£1), an architectural novelty whose buttressed octagonal walls remove the need for a central pillar, otherwise a common feature of this type of building.

Around the Minster

Past the Minster's west front a gateway leads into **Dean's Park**, a quiet green oasis bordered by a seven-arched fragment of arcade from the Norman archbishop's palace and by **York Minster Library** (Mon–Fri 9am–5pm; free), housed in the thirteenth-century chapel of the same palace. Among its more interesting exhibits is the baptismal entry for Guy Fawkes (April 16, 1570), removed from **St Michael-le-Belfrey** on High Petergate (open for Sunday services only), immediately south of the Minster. The church was built in 1536 and is bursting with seventeenth-century brasses and medieval stained glass.

Walk through Dean's Park with the Minster on your right, then through the gate at the top to reach the **Treasurer's House** in Chapter House Street (Easter–Oct Mon–Thurs, Sat & Sun 11am–5pm; £3.70; NT), a glorious seventeenth-century town house that stands on the site of houses used by the Minster's treasurers until the Dissolution. Now owned by the National Trust, it offers exhibitions and videos which trace the site's changing fortunes, together with the paintings and furniture of industrialist Frank Green, who lived here from 1897 to 1930. His collection adorns the various period rooms – including an authentically kitted-out eighteenth-century kitchen and medieval hall – and there's also a walled garden and nice café on site, too.

Just around the corner in College Street stands **St William's College**, an eye-catching half-timbered building studded with oriel windows, initially dedicated to the great-grandson of William the Conqueror (first archbishop of York) and built in its present guise in 1467 for the Minster's chantry priests. During Charles I's three-year residence it served time as the Royal Mint and the king's printing press. These days it serves as a visitor centre for the Minster and a conference hall and banqueting centre, though three of the medieval rooms are open for viewing provided they're not in use (call ℡01904/557233; admission 60p).

The walls

Although much restored, the city's superb **walls** date mainly from the fourteenth century, though fragments of Norman work survive, particularly in the gates (or "bars"), whilst the northern sections still follow the line of the Roman ramparts. The only break in the walls is east of Monk Bar, where the city was first protected by the marshes of the River Foss and later by the deliberately flooded area known as King's Pool.

Monk Bar at the northern end of Goodramgate is as good a point of access as any, tallest of the city's four main gates and host to a small **Richard III Museum** (daily: March–Oct 9am–5pm; Nov–Feb 9.30am–4pm; £2; ⓦwww.richardiiimuseum.co.uk), where you're invited to decide on the guilt or innocence of England's most maligned king. For just a taste of the walls' best section – with great views of the Minster and swathes of idyllic-looking gardens – take the ten-minute stroll west from Monk Bar to Exhibition Square (see below) and **Bootham Bar**, the only gate on the site of a Roman gateway and marking the traditional northern entrance to the city. A stroll round the walls' entire two-and-a-half-mile length will take you past the southwestern **Micklegate Bar**, long considered the most important of the gates since it, in turn, marked the start of the road to London. It was built to a Norman design reputedly using ancient stone coffins as building stone, and was later used to exhibit the heads of executed criminals and rebels. The engaging **Micklegate Bar Museum** (daily 9am–5pm; £1.50) occupies a surviving fortified tower and tells the story by way of old lithographs, models, paintings and the odd gruesome skull. **Walmgate Bar** in the east is the best preserved and has traditionally been the city's strongest bar. It was unsuccessfully undermined by the Roundheads during the Civil War, its present slight sag said to be a consequence of that episode.

Goodramgate and the Shambles

East of Goodramgate, in a labyrinth of quiet residential streets centred on Aldwark, a series of good-looking historic buildings are clustered. **Bedern Hall**, a medieval lodging and refectory for the Minster's priests, and the plain-faced **St Anthony's Hall** can be walked past pretty quickly, though the half-timbered **Black Swan Inn** down on Peasholme Green beckons for a drink, while the **Merchant Taylors' Hall** (April–Oct Tues only 10am–4pm; free) is a similar picture of late-medieval perfection. The Merchant Taylors' guild took upon itself the job of establishing a weaving workhouse to prevent "laytering and ydleness of vacabunds and poor follc"; a small upstairs museum explains their good work. At the south end of Goodramgate, **Our Lady's Row**, the oldest houses in the city (1316), stands hard against **Holy Trinity** (March–Oct Tues–Sat 9.30am–5pm; Nov–April Tues–Sat 9.30am–4pm; free), a much altered fifteenth-century church known for its east window, jumbled box pews and saddle-back tower, an unusual feature in English churches.

The Shambles, off King's Square at the southern end of Goodramgate, could be taken as the epitome of medieval York, though the crowds and self-conscious quaintness take the edge off what would otherwise be a perfect medieval thoroughfare. Flagstoned, almost impossibly narrow and lined with perilously leaning timber-framed houses, it was the home of York's butchers, its erstwhile stench and squalor now difficult to imagine, though old meat hooks still adorn the odd house. At no. 35, there's a **shrine** (closed to the public) to Margaret Clitherow, the Catholic wife of a butcher, martyred in 1586 for allegedly sheltering priests; she was pressed to death with rocks piled on top of a board on the city's Ouse Bridge. Newgate **market** (daily 8am–5pm) lies off the Shambles, together with the core of the city's shopping streets; **Parliament Street** sees a couple of outdoor markets a year, usually in high summer and a month before Christmas.

Exhibition Square

Exhibition Square, outside Bootham Bar, holds the city's main tourist office in the De Grey Rooms, opposite which stands the **City Art Gallery** (daily 10am–5pm; £2), an extensive collection of British, early Italian and northern European paintings. Most are decidedly second-division, but the gallery puts on a year-round series of excellent special exhibitions, and is noted for its collections of British studio pottery and twentieth-century British painters, including Gwen John, Stanley Spencer and Walter Sickert.

Left of the gallery as you face it stands **King's Manor**, founded in 1270 and enlarged in 1490 to provide lodgings for the abbot of nearby St Mary's Abbey. After the Dissolution it was ceded to the lord president of the Council of the North, effectively making it northern England's royal headquarters: Henry

VIII, James I and Charles I all stayed here. It's now owned by the university, but the courtyard is usually open if you want a peek inside.

The Yorkshire Museum and St Mary's Abbey

South of Exhibition Square on Museum Street stands the entrance to the **Yorkshire Museum** (daily 10am–5pm; £4.50), which lies within the beautifully laid-out grounds of St Mary's Abbey, itself now in ruins. It's one of York's better museums, with changing temporary exhibitions aimed largely at kids, but otherwise strong on archeological remains which it presents in a series of rooms examining the Roman presence in the city – grave effects, cooking utensils in a reconstructed Roman kitchen, glassware, farming equipment and jewellery all illustrate the sophistication of life in the provincial capital of "Lower Britain". There are impressive displays of Viking and Anglo-Saxon artefacts, too, though chief exhibit is the fifteenth-century Middleham Jewel, found near Middleham Castle (see p.921) in 1985 – a diamond-shaped jewel with an oblong sapphire, claimed as the finest piece of Gothic jewellery in England.

Part of the museum basement incorporates the fireplace and chapter house of **St Mary's Abbey** (dawn to dusk; free), whose ruins lie around the Museum Gardens, the abbey's former grounds. Founded around 1080, the abbey later became an important Benedictine foundation, additionally significant as it was from here that disenchanted monks fled to found Fountains Abbey. The fact that the abbey controlled the city's brothels at the time can hardly have helped the Benedictine cause. The church (1259) and gatehouse are both reasonably well preserved, but this is really a spot to come for time out from the sightseeing. For a good extended stroll drop down to the river at Lendal Bridge for a quiet walk to Water End Bridge.

Lendal and St Helen's Square

The street called **Lendal** cuts down from Museum Street to **St Helen's Square** – marking the entrance to the Roman city – and the York institution that is **Betty's** tearooms (see p.949), where you're close to a clutch of impressive historic buildings. The Georgian **Mansion House** (1725), in St Helen's Square, is the private home of the city's mayor, and is consequently open only to guided tours by prior arrangement (call ✆01904/551049). However, you can visit the 600-year-old **Guildhall** (May–Oct Mon–Fri 9am–5pm, Sat 10am–5pm, Sun 2–5pm; Nov–April Mon–Fri 9am–5pm; free) behind, which was almost totally destroyed by bombing in 1942, but has since been restored to a near identical replica of its original, timber-roofed state, though only one of the fourteen magnificent Victorian stained-glass windows remains. Back up Blake Street from the square, have a look inside the **Grand Assembly Rooms**, built between 1732 and 1736 by the third earl of Burlington. An epicentre of chic during York's eighteenth-century social heyday, the building attempted to emulate London's grander salons; its 52-columned Central Hall is a tribute to the Egyptian Hall of the capital's Mansion House. The Rooms are now occupied by a restaurant (open daily from noon), so for the price of a meal you can lounge around the ornate marbled interior, taking the opportunity to search the rotunda's mural of Roman York, in which Burlington had himself painted as Constantine the Great.

Back at St Helen's Square, **Stonegate** leads northeast towards the Minster, a street as ancient as the city itself. Originally the Via Praetoria of Roman York, it's now paved with thick flags of York stone, which were once carried along here to build the Minster, hence the street name. Guy Fawkes' parents lived on

Stonegate (there's a plaque opposite *Mulberry Hall*) and its Tudor houses retain their considerable charm – an alley at no. 52A leads to the scant remains of a twelfth-century Norman stone house, a rarity in England.

South to Jorvik

Coney Street, Davygate, Parliament Street and all the alleys and streets off and in between heave shoulder-to-shoulder most of the year with shoppers. There's not much to stop for until you reach the entrance to the **Merchant Adventurers' Hall**, off Fossgate (April–Sept Mon–Sat 9am–5pm, Sun noon–4pm; Oct–March Mon–Sat 9am–3.30pm; £2), where the overpowering whiff of wood polish prepares you for one of the finest medieval timber-framed halls in Europe. The beautiful building was raised by the city's most powerful guild, dealers in wool from the Wolds, woollens from the Dales and lead from the Pennines, commodities that were traded for exotica from far and wide. An icon brought back from Russia gives some idea of the organization's commercial scope. Antique fairs are held in the undercroft most Saturdays throughout the year.

Fairfax House, on nearby Castlegate (March–Dec Mon–Thurs & Sat 11am–5pm, Sun 1.30–5pm; guided tours Aug & Sept Fri at 11am & 2pm; closed Jan & Feb; £4; ⓦwww.fairfaxhouse.co.uk), celebrates the wealth of a later period. This elegant Georgian town house was restored to house the collection of fine arts left by Noel Terry, scion of one of the city's chocolate dynasties. The bulk of the collection consists of eighteenth-century furniture and clocks, though seasonal exhibitions showcase other arts, while every December the popular "Keeping of Christmas" exhibition recreates a Georgian Christmas in the house.

Around the corner, in the Coppergate shopping centre, the crowds descend upon the city's blockbuster Viking exhibit – **Jorvik** (daily: April–Oct 9am–5.30pm; Nov–March 10am–4.30pm; £6.95; ⓦwww.vikingjorvik.com). This multi-million-pound affair flies visitors back in "time capsules" to the tenth-century city of York, presenting not just the sights but the sounds and even the smells of a riverside Viking settlement, complete with animatronic figures, street scenes and panoramic views of the re-created city. This was a period when York was expanding rapidly, and most of the sites (blacksmiths' to bedrooms) and artefacts (leather shoes to wooden combs) were discovered during the 1976 excavations of Coppergate's real Viking settlement, now lost beneath the shopping centre outside; Jorvik shows how they were found and how they were used. Not surprisingly, it's a hugely popular exhibit, and great for children, though you can avoid queuing by pre-booking your entrance ticket with a credit card, by calling ☏01904/543043.

It's worth noting that the museum organizes York's annual **Viking Festival** every February when themed events take place throughout the city – details from the Festival Office at the centre. You may also want to move on to the associated Archeological Resource Centre, or **ARC**, housed in the medieval church of St Saviour, St Savioursgate (school holidays only: Mon–Sat 11am–3pm; £4.50, joint ticket with Jorvik £9.95), close to the Shambles, a hands-on archeology centre – the only one of its kind in the country – where you can grapple with everything from old bones to computers to build up a picture of Viking and Roman life.

York Castle and the Castle Museum

Despite the rich architectural heritage elsewhere in the city, there's precious little left of **York Castle**, one of two established by William the Conqueror. Only the perilously leaning **Clifford's Tower** (daily: Easter–June & Sept 10am–6pm; July & Aug 10am–7.30pm; Oct 10am–5pm; Nov–Easter 10am–4pm or dusk; £2; EH) remains, as evocative a piece of military engineering as you could wish for: a stark and isolated stone keep built on one of William's mottes between 1245 and 1262. The old Norman keep was destroyed in 1109 during one of the city's more shameful historical episodes, when 150 Jews were put inside the tower for their own protection during an outburst of anti-Semitic rioting. The move did little to appease the mob, however, and faced with starvation or slaughter the Jews committed mass suicide by setting the tower on fire.

Immediately east of the tower lies the excellent **Castle Museum** (April–Oct daily 9.30am–5pm; Nov–March Mon–Sat 9.30am–4pm, Sun 10am–4pm; £5.75), a remarkable collection founded by a Dr Kirk of Pickering, who in the 1920s realized that many of the everyday items used in rural areas were in danger of disappearing. He took the unusual step of accepting bric-a-brac from his patients in lieu of fees. When the pile of miscellanea grew too large for his own home it was housed in the city's old Debtors' Prison and Female Prison, the former, incidentally, where the famous highwayman Dick Turpin spent his last night on earth. A whole range of early craft, folk and agricultural ephemera is complemented by costumes, militaria, workshops, two entire reconstructed streets and special exhibitions on subjects as diverse as chocolate, burials and fire engines. In particular, look for the lovely corridor of old hearths and fireplaces, Kirk's fetishistic collections of truncheons and biscuit moulds – surely unsurpassed – and some magnificently archaic televisions and washing machines. The military displays, the rambling dungeons and period rooms are all well worth seeing, too. Pride of place is given to a dazzling Viking helmet, discovered during the Coppergate excavations and the only one of its kind ever found.

The National Railway Museum

The **National Railway Museum** on Leeman Road (daily 10am–6pm; free; ⓦwww.nrm.org.uk), ten minutes' walk (600 yards) from the station, is a must if you have even the slightest interest in railways, history, engineering or Victoriana. It was the first national museum to open outside London and contains a stunning collection. The Great Hall alone features some fifty restored locomotives dating from 1829 onwards, among them the *Mallard*, at 126mph the world's fastest steam engine; its record-speed run wrecked the engine, and it had to be towed back to base. By way of complete contrast, the newest addition, already very popular, is a Japanese bullet train. The Station Hall, a former goods station, complete with tracks and platforms, holds the major permanent exhibitions, where you can see the plush splendour of the royal carriages ("Palaces on Wheels") and the bleak segregation of classes in the Victorian coaches. Take a walk through the 1938 dining car and then take a break on the platform at the *Brief Encounter* café. Dotted around the hall is a welter of miscellaneous memorabilia: posters, models, paintings and period photographs, even a lock of George Stephenson's hair. A separate wing, "The Works", provides access to the engineering workshop where conservation work is undertaken; to a walk-round backstage warehouse area, showcasing the museum's reserve collection; and to a track-and-signal viewing area which has been established over the East Coast main line.

George Hudson

It would be hard to find a better caricature of a Victorian business baron than the portly and bewhiskered "Railway King" **George Hudson** (1800–71), a perfect symbol of all the fortitude and failings of Victorian capitalism. Starting out as he meant to go on, Hudson was sent away from home in disgrace at the age of 15. Soon afterwards he became apprenticed to a York draper, married the boss's daughter and then quickly inherited the business when his father-in-law was found drowned in the Ouse in mysterious circumstances. Another £30,000 came his way from a great-uncle in 1827, Hudson having spent many days at his relative's deathbed, during which time the will was altered in his favour. The windfall was ploughed into North Midland Railway shares, the basis of his subsequent empire, and a stepping stone to a career in local politics which saw him become councillor, alderman and ultimately – in 1837 – Lord Mayor of York.

He seized the main chance in 1833, as the rail network crept closer to York, offering local landowners huge tranches of cut-price shares to allow the railways to cross their land. With the gentry in his pockets his business boomed, and by 1844 he controlled 1016 miles of track – the largest network under single ownership until rail nationalization – and was elected MP for Sunderland a year later. In one typical move he managed to buy the Whitby and Pickering Railway in 1845 for £80,000, £25,000 less than it had cost to build.

Hudson's empire continued to expand, but only by paying artificially high dividends to his shareholders. When his stocks, which had made countless paper fortunes, failed to go on rising, nemesis was just round the corner. Investigations and law suits brought by disgruntled investors revealed untold dubious business deals and in 1849 Hudson was forced to resign the directorship of his six companies. A ruined man, he was committed to York's Debtors' Prison, able to afford only one meal a day, before being rescued by a small pension offered by a hard core of loyal shareholders. York, for its part, chose to forget the undoubted wealth Hudson's railways had brought the city, shunning its former hero until 1968, when a street and offices near the station were given his name.

Eating and drinking

It's impossible to walk more than about fifty yards in central York without coming across either a pub, teashop, café or restaurant – Defoe put it down to the "abundance of good company . . . and good families", though these days it's the tourist and student pound which fires the commercial engines. In keeping with much else in the city, many establishments are relentlessly and self-consciously old-fashioned, though there are some real highlights – truly historic **pubs**, the remarkable *Betty's*, the ultimate **tea-shop** experience, and a scattering of well-regarded **restaurants**. There's a sense of solid Yorkshire worth in most establishments and provided you pick and choose carefully, you can avoid much of the tourist-aimed dross that passes for budget eating and drinking. The **coffee and café-bar** scene has flourished too, with the main chain-names (Starbucks, Coffee Republic, Bar 38, Pitcher & Piano) all represented, alongside some honourable independents.

Tearooms, cafés and café-bars

The Bar Convent Blossom Street, at Nunnery Lane. Beautiful Georgian surroundings for a combined museum of early Christianity and an airy café with a lovely garden. Serves sandwiches and inventive lunches. Mon–Sat 9.30am–4pm.

Betty's 6–8 St Helen's Square. If there are tea shops in heaven they'll be like *Betty's*, a York institution, with an Art Nouveau cladding and a permanent queue waiting for seats, despite the (relatively) high prices. There are a dozen or so fish and meat hot dishes, some extraordinary puddings, and a shop where you can buy fine-grade teas and coffees, and some of the tea-shop staples – like pikelets and Yorkshire fat rascals. Daily 9am–9pm.

Blake Head Vegetarian Café 104 Micklegate. Bookstore-café with patio for freshly baked cakes, pâtés, quiche, brunch, salads and soups – a favoured student hangout. Mon–Sat 9.30am–5pm, Sun 10am–5pm.

Café No. 8 8 Gillygate. Caesar salads, ciabatta sarnies and cool sounds in this funky little café-bar, just outside Bootham Bar. There's a summer garden too. Mon–Fri 11am–3pm, Thurs & Fri 11am–3pm & 5–11pm, Sat 11am–11pm, Sun 11am–5pm.

Caffe Nero 16 Davygate. Excellent Italian coffee and cakes. Mon–Sat 7am–7pm, Sun 9am–6pm.

City Screen Café-Bar Coney St. A welcome antidote to its chain-bar neighbours on the Coney Street riverside, York's independent cinema has a splendid riverside café-bar, serving food until 9pm and boasting a whole host of events and evenings – from stand-up comedy and afternoon jazz to poetry evenings and once-a-month film quizzes. Daily 11am–11pm.

Little Betty's 46 Stonegate. Owned by *Betty's* and in the same league; over 100 years old, it's the picture of a classic tea shop, serving more substantial dishes, too, including fish and chips and a grilled breakfast. Daily 9am–5.30pm.

Mulberry Hall Coffee Shop Stonegate. Wend through the fifteenth-century house, now York's poshest china and glassware shop, for fine snacks in snazzy surroundings. Mon–Sat 10am–5pm.

National Trust York Tearooms 30 Goodramgate. A slickly run place just 200 yards from the Minster, serving snacks and light meals. Choose from the likes of scrambled eggs and smoked ham, BLTs and omelettes, and maybe sample one of Yorkshire's noted "fruit wines" while you're here. Mon–Sat 10am–5pm.

Petergate Fisheries Low Petergate, at Church St. You can get fish and chips in most York cafés, but this spot – in business for 85 years – has the best, sit-down or takeaway. Mon–Sat noon–10pm.

Spurriergate Centre St Michael's Church, Spurriergate. Quiche, salads and baked potatoes served in the impressive interior of twelfth-century St Michael's. Mon–Fri 10am–4.30pm, Sat 9.30am–5pm.

Treasurer's House Minster Yard. Superior tea-room in the cellars of a National Trust property. Easter–Oct daily except Fri 10.30am–4.30pm.

Restaurants

19 Grape Lane 19 Grape Lane ☎01904/636366. Renowned town-house restaurant serving top-quality Modern British dishes, including some great puddings. Lunch deals bring the price into most people's range. Closed Sun & Mon. Expensive.

Café Rouge 52 Low Petergate ☎01904/673293. No real surprises – French snacks and full meals, from breakfast to dinner – but it's a relaxed place for a *café au lait*, a steak-frites and a read of the paper. Moderate.

Melton's 7 Scarcroft Rd ☎01904/634341. Simple, classy cooking, including very good fish dishes, and imaginative vegetarian food – Tuesdays (veggie) and Thursdays (fish) have the best non-meat choices. Set lunch and early-bird deals too. Closed Mon lunch & Sun dinner. Expensive.

The Patio 13 Swinegate Court East, off Grape Lane ☎01904/627879. Plenty of choice in this informal café/restaurant, from overly stuffed baguettes and wraps to a plate of bangers and mash. Or tuck into more elaborate meals in the evening – poached salmon, or red snapper with tomato and olive sauce are typical. Closed Sun & Mon eve. Moderate.

La Piazza 45 Goodramgate ☎01904/642641. Authentic Italian coffee bar out front, courtyard restaurant out back, tucked into a nice Tudor building. Proper pizzas, Italian pop music and friendly family staff. Inexpensive to Moderate.

Pierre Victoire 2 Lendal ☎01904/655222. You know what to expect in this chain brasserie, but it delivers every time – especially with the unbeatable two-course lunch for £6. Inexpensive to Moderate.

Pizza Express River House, 17 Museum St. Grand old riverside club rooms with sought-after balcony, the venue for *Pizza Express*'s usual menu of good-quality pizzas. Inexpensive to Moderate.

The Rubicon 5–7 Little Stonegate ☎01904/676076. Contemporary style and vegetarian world flavours, so there's nut roast and veggie lasagne but also masala dhal and burritos on offer. The menu turns less snacky after 6pm; organic wines and beers, naturally, are available. Inexpensive to Moderate.

St William's College Restaurant 3 College St ☎01904/634830. Candlelight and jazz in a historic building bang next door to the Minster. The trad Brit food comes with the odd nod to fashion, with a superior café operating during the day and the restaurant offering good-value two-and three-course set menus in the evening. Café open daily, restaurant closed Sun & Mon. Moderate.

Siam House 63a Goodramgate ☎01904/624677. The city's first Thai restaurant rarely disappoints – the menu is huge enough to cater for any tastes. Moderate.

Villa Italia 69 Micklegate ☎01904/670501. York's premier Italian shows its class away from the short pizza menu, where delights on offer include things like Sardinian fish stew, garlic-and-lime-marinated tuna or roast duck with rosemary and celery. There's a good deli next door, too. Moderate to Expensive.

Pubs

Black Swan Peasholme Green. York's oldest (sixteenth-century) pub and a Grade II listed building with some superb stone flagging and wood panelling. The beer's not bad either – you can get the local York Brewery stuff here. Home of the city's folk club.

Golden Ball Cromwell Rd, Bishophill. Perhaps the city centre's nicest and most archetypal "local", with an attractive beer garden tucked away at the back. It's just two minutes from the river, on the west side.

Golden Fleece 16 Pavement. One of the oldest pubs in the city, squeezed into a narrow town house opposite the Shambles and with a nice beer garden.

Hole in the Wall High Petergate. Very close to the Minster, yet rarely crowded, this pleasant, stripped-down retreat is something of a find in the city centre.

Judge's Lodging Cellar Bar 9 Lendal. Cosy drinking hole with good beer, in the eighteenth-century cellars of the Judge's Lodging, now a smart hotel.

King's Arms King's Staithe. Close to the Ouse Bridge, this pub has a fine riverside setting with outdoor tables – and accordingly gets very busy in summer (and very wet in the winter when it's prone to flooding).

Royal Oak 18 Goodramgate. Good beer in a touristy sixteenth-century pub conveniently situated between the Minster and Monk's Bar.

Tap & Spile 29 Monkgate. Bare-bones pub (one of a chain, but not bad for all that) with a great range of real ales.

The Three-Legged Mare 15 High Petergate. York Brewery's cosy outlet for its own quality beer and definitely a pub for grown-ups – no juke box, no video games and no kids.

Ye Olde Starre Stonegate. Vies with the Black Swan for historic precedence, but although there's good beer, a beer garden and plenty of atmosphere it's usually too crowded for prolonged enjoyment.

Nightlife, culture and entertainment

There are healthy helpings of **live music**, **culture** and **nightlife**, much of it detailed in the local *Evening Press* (and on their useful website, ⓦwww.thisisyork .co.uk). Most bigger bands bypass the city in favour of Leeds, though the Barbican Centre pulls in its fair share of major mainstream artists, while the pub **music scene** flourishes; the best places are listed below. The themed Irish pubs, including *O'Neill's* on Low Ousegate and *Scruffy Murphy's* at Micklegate Bar, can also usually be relied upon for some weekend faux-folk high-jinks. Note that the *Bonding Warehouse* riverside venue was badly hit by flooding in 2000 and may not re-open. **Clubbing** is a bit of a disaster in York – you know, with names like *Toffs* and *Ziggy's*, that the northern club revolution has yet to hit the city – but *The Gallery* on Clifford Street can usually be relied upon, or head on out to Clifton Moor Retail Park to *Ikon* and *Diva*.

Cultural entertainment is wide and varied, with the city supporting theatres, cinemas and regular classical music recitals, often in its churches and the York Minster itself. The annual **Early Music Festival**, held in July, is perhaps the best of its kind in Britain, with dozens of events spread over ten days – details are available on ☎01904/658338 or from the tourist offices. The famous **York Mystery Plays** are held every four years – next performances are in 2004.

Clubs and live music

Barbican Centre Barbican Road ☎01904 /656688, ⓦwww.fibbers.co.uk/barbican. Country, rock, folk and MOR stalwarts all appear here sooner or later.

Black Swan Peasholme Green ☎01904/632922. Regular folk nights with a full range of quality bands and singer-songwriters. Sunday lunch jazz too.

Borders 1–5 Davygate ☎01904/653300. Weekly jazz (Fri night) and live music (Sat) sessions, plus regular book events and readings.

Fibbers Stonebow House, Stonebow ☎01904 /466148, ⓦwww.fibbers.co.uk. Indie and guitar-

△ Castle Howard

pop bands (local and national) play most nights of the week at this inventive venue. There's a café-bar too.

Punch Bowl Inn 7 Stonegate ☎01904/615491. Pub venue for jazz and blues, a couple of nights a week.

Cinema, theatre and the arts

Cinema: City Screen 13–17 Coney St ☎01904 /541155, ⓦwww.picturehouse-cinemas.co.uk. The choice for art-house cinema, with a riverside café-bar. Mainstream screens at the Odeon, Blossom St ☎01904/623287, info line ☎01426/954742, and Warner Village multiplex out of town at Clifton Moor ☎08702/406020 ⓦwww.warnervillage.co.uk.

Grand Opera House Cumberland Street, at Clifford St ☎01904/671818 ⓦwww.york-opera-house.co.uk. Musicals, ballet and family entertainment in all its guises.

Theatre Royal St Leonard's Place ☎01904/623568 ⓦwww.theatre-royal-york.co.uk. Musicals, pantos and mainstream theatre, as well as a café-bar.

Listings

Banks and exchange Most main banks are in and around St Helen's Square. American Express, 6 Stonegate ☎01904/670030; Thomas Cook, 4 Nessgate ☎01904/639928, and inside HSBC, Parliament St ☎01904/626770. You can also change money at the tourist offices and in Marks and Spencer, 9 Pavement.

Bike rental Bob Trotter, 13–15 Lord Mayor's Walk, at Monkgate ☎01904/622868, ⓦwww.bobtrotter-cycles.com; Cycle Scene, 2 Ratcliffe St ☎01904/653286; and York Cycleworks, 14–16 Lawrence St ☎01904/626664, ⓦwww.yorkcycle-works.com. Rates from around £10 per day, plus a deposit.

Bookshop Biggest selection in the city is at Borders, 1–5 Davygate, where there's also a cafe.

Bus information Traveline York, 20 George Hudson St (office Mon–Fri 8.30am–5pm; telephone enquiries Mon–Sat 8am–8pm, Sun 8am–2pm; ☎01904/551400) can advise about all local and regional bus (and train) information. Or call National Express ☎08705/808080; East Yorkshire ☎01482/222222 (for Hull, Beverley and Bridlington); Harrogate & District ☎01423/566061 (for Knaresborough, Harrogate, Ilkley and Skipton); Stagecoach Cumberland ☎0870/608 2608 (to the Lake District); or Yorkshire Coastliner ☎01653/692556 (for Leeds, Castle Howard, Pickering, Scarborough and Whitby).

Car rental Alamo, 33–37 Layerthorpe ☎01904 /612141; Avis, 3 Layerthorpe ☎01904/610460; Budget, 82–84 Clifton ☎01904/644919; Europcar, York train station ☎01904/656161; Hertz, York train station ☎01904/612586; Peugeot Car Rental, Clifton Moor ☎01904/638032; Practical, Tanners Moat, Lendal Bridge ☎01904/624848.

Hospital York District Hospital, Wigginton Road (24-hr emergency number ☎01904/631313); bus #1, #2 or #3. Also York Walk-in Centre, 31 Monkgate (☎01904/674557) offers care, advice and treatment without an appointment.

Internet Internet Exchange, 13 Stonegate ☎01904/638808; Coffee Express, 60 Goodramgate ☎01904/653463; access also available at the youth hostels.

Police Fulford Rd ☎01904/631321.

Post Office The main office is at 22 Lendal ☎01904/617285.

Taxis Ranks at Rougier St, Duncombe Place, Exhibition Sq, and the train station; or call Station Taxis ☎01904/623332; Castle Taxis ☎01904/ 611511.

Castle Howard

Immersed in the deep countryside of the Howardian Hills, fifteen miles north-east of York, off the A64, **Castle Howard** (March–Oct daily 11am–5pm; gardens open at 10am; £7.50; grounds only £4.50; ⓦwww.castlehoward.co.uk) is the seat of one of England's leading aristocratic families and among the country's grandest stately homes. Since providing the setting for the television version of *Brideshead Revisited*, the house's car parks have been packed every weekend, but fitting it into a public transport itinerary is something of a problem. In summer there are just two Yorkshire Coastliner buses a day (one on Sun) from York, and three (one on Sun) from Malton and Pickering, but various bus tours from York can bring you out and back, too.

The colossal main house was designed by **Sir John Vanbrugh** in 1699 and was almost forty years in the making – remarkable enough, were it not for the fact that Vanbrugh was, at the start of the commission at least, best known as a playwright. He had no formal architectural training and seems to have been chosen by Charles Howard, third Earl of Carlisle, for whom the house was built, purely on the strength of his membership of the same London gentlemen's club. Shrewdly, Vanbrugh recognized his limitations and called upon the assistance of Nicholas Hawksmoor, who had a major part in the house's structural design – the pair later worked successfully together on Blenheim Palace. If Hawksmoor's guiding hand can be seen throughout, Vanbrugh's influence is clear in the very theatricality of the building, notably in the palatial **Great Hall**. This was gutted by fire in the 1940s, but has subsequently been restored from old etchings and photographs to something approaching its original state. The rest of the house is full of furniture by Sheraton and Chippendale, paintings by the likes of Gainsborough, Veronese, Rubens and Van Dyck, and room after room of decorative excess – all trinkety *objets d'art*, gaudy friezes and monumental pilasters.

Vanbrugh soon turned his attention to the estate's thousand-acre **grounds** where he could indulge his playful inclinations to excess, and the formal gardens, clipped parkland, towers, obelisks and blunt sandstone follies stretch in all directions, sloping gently to a large artifical lake. He completed the **Temple of the Four Winds** before his death in 1726, leaving Hawksmoor to design the Howard family **Mausoleum**, which is taller than the house itself. Take a look, too, at the fine **stables** which have been converted into the Costume and Regalia Gallery, Britain's largest private collection of period clothes. There's a **café** here, and another by the lake, as well as a children's playground, nature trails and all the modern paraphernalia of an English stately home.

Eden Camp

Further along the A64 from the Castle Howard turn-off, **Eden Camp** (daily 10am–5pm, last admission 4pm; £4; ⓦ www.edencamp.co.uk), a World War II museum sited within a former POW camp, makes for another good day out from York. It's eighteen miles northeast of the city at Malton, at the junction of the A169 to Pickering. Originally built in 1942 to house Italian and, later, German POWs captured in the North Africa campaigns, the barracks and buildings have been re-equipped to tell the story of what it dubs "The People's War". Walk-through exhibits and tableaux deal with topics such as rationing, air raids, evacuees, the Home Guard, the Land Army, munitions and the various branches of the services. Most visitors need around three hours to get around everything.

Hull, the Humber and the East Yorkshire coast

Generations of Yorkshire folk, born and bred in the historic **East Riding**, were outraged to wake up one morning and find themselves part of "Humberside", just one of the notorious local government conveniences created by the 1974 bastardization of the English counties. Consequently, there was almost universal rejoicing when the Lincolnshire adjuncts from across the **River Humber** were dropped in 1996 and towns like **Hull** could once again revel in their Yorkshire ancestry. The region's character has been shaped by a strong seafaring tradition, boosted by Hull's advantageous position on the Humber estuary. Beyond Hull, up the **East Yorkshire coast**, lonely beaches, wild foreshores and forgotten seafront villages draw curious tourists keen to get off the beaten track. The bucket-and-spade resorts of **Bridlington** and **Filey** have gently declined over the years and are now rather melancholy places, but there's nothing disappointing about the cliffs of **Flamborough Head**, one of the best places in Britain for birdwatching. Inland, this part of the country boasts historic **Beverley**, with its marvellous Minster, plonked among the flatlands which stretch northwards from Hull to meet the **Yorkshire Wolds**, a crescent-shaped ridge of hills that falls to the sea at Flamborough.

Beverley can be easily reached by **bus** from Hull (or York), while Hull is also linked to Doncaster by the main London–York **train** line; a branch line links Hull and Beverley with Bridlington, Filey and Scarborough, further up the coast. Drivers approaching from Lincolnshire and the south will cross the famous **Humber Bridge**, an immense single-span suspension bridge opened in 1981; a viewing area allows you to stop and gasp.

Hull

HULL's most famous adopted son, the poet and university librarian Philip Larkin, wrote "I wish I could think of just one nice thing to tell you about Hull, oh yes … *it's very nice and flat for cycling*". Harsh perhaps, but it does capture something of the character of a town that reaches few heights, physical or otherwise. The town – rarely known by its full title of **Kingston-upon-Hull** – undoubtedly suited the poet's curmudgeonly temperament, but he might have mentioned Hull's self-reliant and no-nonsense atmosphere, qualities reflected in abundance in the contemporary town's most famous resident, local MP and Deputy Prime Minister John Prescott.

Hull's **maritime** pre-eminence dates back to 1299, when it was laid out as a seaport by Edward I. It quickly became England's leading harbour, and was still a vital garrison when the gates were closed against Charles I in 1642, the first serious act of rebellion of what was to become the English Civil War. Daniel Defoe visited the town several times in the early eighteenth century, part of the travels that were later to spawn his encyclopedic *Tour Through the Whole Island of Britain*; despite thinking it "second rate", he remembered Hull well enough to have Robinson Crusoe set sail from here on his fateful voyage. A commemorative plaque to the shipwrecked mariner stands in the town's Queen's Gardens.

The central **Princes Dock** sets the tone for Hull's modern refurbishment, the once abandoned waters now lined by landscaped brick promenades and overlooked by **Princes Quay**, a multi-tier, glass-spangled shopping centre, with the revamped **marina** beyond. To reach the marina, you'll need to cross busy Castle Street, where the decommissioned **Spurn Lightship**, once moored off Spurn Head (see p.959), is docked.

The town's maritime legacy is exhaustively detailed in the excellent **Maritime Museum** (Mon–Sat 10am–5pm, Sun 1.30–4.30pm; free), housed in the Neoclassical headquarters of the former Town Docks Offices, flanking the east side of Queen Victoria Square, immediately north of Princes Quay. The main boost to the town's coffers in the eighteenth and nineteenth centuries was whaling, and the museum tells the story well, displaying gruesome whaling equipment, such as a blubber pot cauldron, alongside model ships, old photographs, Inuit relics and a whale skeleton. Hull **whalers** pursued the right whale in their thousands, so known because it was the "right" whale to catch for commercial purposes. There are also displays about whale species and conservation, examples of the maritime art of "scrimshandering" – the ornate carving of whale bone and walrus tusk by bored sailors – and yet more rooms detailing trawling methods, and Hull's long relationship with the Humber. More marine art lurks across the square in the **Ferens Art Gallery** (Mon–Sat 10am–5pm, Sun 1.30–4.30pm; free), distinguished by twentieth-century British pieces and the odd Constable, Frans Hals and Canaletto. Temporary exhibitions highlight various themes throughout the year.

Leave Queen Victoria Square on its east side by pedestrianized Whitefriargate and, after about 200 yards, turn right down Trinity House Lane for **Holy Trinity** (April–Sept Mon–Fri 11am–3pm, Sat 9.30am–noon; Oct–March Tues–Fri 11am–2pm, Sat 9.30am–noon; free), among the most pleasing parish churches in the country, notable for its brick transepts and chancel. This area is traditionally home to Hull's market traders: there's an indoor **market hall** (Mon–Sat 7.30am–5pm) across from the church and an **open market** next to it (Tues, Fri & Sat 9am–4pm). Close by is one of Hull's most revered relics – the **Old Grammar School**, a red-brick edifice built in 1583 and which for 120 years doubled as the town's Merchant Adventurers' Hall. As a school, it numbered amongst its pupils William Wilberforce, instigator of the abolition of slavery in the British Empire, and seventeenth-century poet Andrew Marvell, also MP for Hull. (Hull-born Stevie Smith, incidentally, completes the town's poetic triumvirate.) The building now incorporates an educational resource centre called **Hands On History** (Sat 10am–5pm, Sun 1.30–4.30pm; during school holidays also Mon–Fri 10am–5pm; free), which is aimed at school-children, though anyone can pop in to have a scout around its displays and archives.

Two blocks east you hit the **High Street**, whose crop of older buildings and narrow cobbled alleys have seen it designated an "Old Town Conservation Area". At its northern end stands **Wilberforce House** (Mon–Sat 10am–5pm, Sun 1.30–4.30pm; free), the former home of William and containing some fascinating exhibits on slavery and its abolition. Last but by no means least, pop round the back of Wilberforce House to the River Hull, where a reconditioned fishing vessel, the **Arctic Corsair**, offers free guided tours of its cramped interior (call for times ☎01482/613902).

Practicalities

The **train station** is on the west side of town, on the main drag of Ferensway, with the **bus station** just to the north. Drivers might as well aim straight for the **car park** in the Princes Quay shopping centre, signposted on every road into town. P&O North Sea **ferries** from Rotterdam and Zeebrugge arrive at the ferry port on the eastern edge of Hull, and from there buses run into the centre; bus times coincide with ferry arrivals (and departures) and the journey takes ten minutes. The main **tourist office** is bang in the centre on Paragon Street at Queen Victoria Square (Mon–Sat 9am–6pm, Sun 11–3pm; ☎01482 /223559, ⊛www.hullcc.gov.uk). They co-ordinate richly anecdotal **guided tours** around the old town (April–Oct, Mon, Wed, Thurs, Fri & Sat at 2pm; £2.50) departing from their office, or you can pick up one of the self-guided trail leaflets and do it yourself.

Few casual visitors stay the night, which means you'll have no trouble finding **accommodation**, except perhaps during the various **festivals** and fairs that Hull arranges - with great flair. The biggest regular event is Hull Fair, a colossal travelling funfair running for eight days in early October; the most discrete is the Hull Literature Festival, which runs for two weeks in November. Hull is also home to the excellent Hull Truck Theatre Company, on Spring

Street (℡01482/323638), where, among others, many of the **plays** of award-winning John Godberfirst see light of day. Incidentally, British thesps John Alderton and Tom Courtney are natives of Hull.

Amongst several reasonably central **B&Bs**, one especially good choice is the *Clyde House Hotel*, 13 John St (℡01482/214981; ❷), or you could try the *Arches*, 38 Saner St (℡01482/211558; ❶). As for **hotels**, The *Comfort Inn*, just south of the train station at 11 Anlaby Rd (℡01482/323299; ❷), is a standard-issue chain hotel with perfectly adequate rooms, while the rival *Quality Hotel Royal*, 170 Ferensway (℡01482/325087; ❸), right by the station, is comparable but a degree more luxurious. Best of the lot is the *Posthouse Hull Marina* on Castle Street overlooking the marina (℡0870/400 9043; ❹), which has an indoor pool.

For **food**, the excellent and reasonably priced *Cerutti's* (℡01482/328501; closed Sat lunch & Sun) leads the way in local seafood; it's down at the end of the east side of the marina at 10 Nelson St. Alternatively, the *Operetta Ristorante*, 56–58 Bond St (℡01482/218687; closed Sun), serves quality, inexpensive pizzas and pasta, the drawback being its location in one of the city's least charming central streets. *Studio 10¹/₂* (closed Sun), opposite Holy Trinity church on King Street, serves snacks and tasty veggie specials. Next door, *Fiddleheads*, 10 King St (℡01482/224749; open eve, plus Fri & Sat lunch), is a well-thought-of vegetarian and vegan restaurant.

Of Hull's many **pubs**, the *Ye Olde White Harte*, 25 Silver St, has a pleasant courtyard and a history going back to the seventeenth century. Dating from 1806 is *Green Bricks*, 9 Humber Dock St, which offers real ales from its prize waterside location, and, further along the marina at the corner of Nelson Street, there's the *Minerva*, with nautical paraphernalia and more real ales. Finally, *Ye Olde Black Boy*, 150 High St, specializes in real ales – and offers cider and fruit wines too.

Beverley

BEVERLEY, nine miles north of Hull, ranks as one of northern England's premier towns, its Minster the superior of many an English cathedral, its tangle of old streets, cobbled lanes and elegant Georgian and Victorian terraces the very picture of a traditional market town. Over 350 buildings are listed as possessing historical or architectural merit, and though you could see its first-rank offerings in a morning, this is one of a handful of places in this part of the world that you might want to stay in for its own sake.

Approaches to the town are dominated by the twin towers of **Beverley Minster** (March, April, Sept & Oct Mon–Sat 9am–5pm; May–Aug Mon–Sat 9am–6pm; Nov–Feb Mon–Sat 9am–4pm; plus Sun year round, depending on services, but usually noon–4pm; £2 donation requested), visible for miles across the wolds and airy flatlands. Initiated as a modest chapel, the minster became a monastery under John of Beverley. Trained at Whitby and later ordained bishop of York, he was buried here in 721 and canonized in 1037 – his body lies under the crossing at the top of the nave. Fires and the collapse of the central tower in 1213 paved the way for two centuries of rebuilding, funded by bequests from pilgrims paying homage to the saint, and the result was one of the finest Gothic creations in the country. The **west front**, which crowned the work in 1420, is widely considered without equal, its survival due in large part to Baroque architect Nicholas Hawksmoor, who restored much of the church in the eighteenth century. Similar outstanding work awaits in the interior, most notably the fourteenth-century **Percy Tomb** on the north side of the altar, its sumptuously carved canopy one of the masterpieces of medieval European ecclesiastical art. Nearby stands the **Fridstol**, a Saxon "sanctuary chair" dating from Athelstan's reign (924–39), which provided safe haven for men on the run. Athelstan himself is said to have deposited a dagger on the altar in 934, vowing to return to Beverley if he defeated the Vikings and Scots in battle, which he duly did, carrying the banner of St John before him. The north transept – aisled, like the transepts at York Minster – harbours another remarkable tomb, behind the second column on the right as you stand with your back to the main altar, bearing the effigy of an unknown fourteenth-century priest. Other incidental carving throughout the church is magnificent, particularly the 68 misericords of the oak **choir** (1520–24), one of the largest and most accomplished in England. Much of the decorative work here and elsewhere is on a musical theme. Beverley had a renowned guild of itinerant minstrels, which provided funds in the sixteenth century for the carvings on the transept aisle capitals, where you'll be able to pick out players of lutes, bagpipes, horns and tambourines.

Cobbled Highgate runs from the Minster through town, along the pedestrianized shopping streets of Butcher Row and Toll Gavel and past the main Market Square, to Beverley's other great church, **St Mary's** (April–Sept Mon–Fri 9.15am–noon & 1.30–5.30pm, Sat 10am–5.30pm, Sun 2–5pm; Oct–March Mon–Fri 9.15am–noon & 1–4.15pm; free), a chapel once attached to the Minster. On the corner of Hengate and North Bar Within, it nestles alongside the **North Bar**, sole survivor of the town's five medieval gates. The church is a tantalizing amalgam of styles, from the south porch's Norman arch to the thirteenth-century chancel and fifteenth-century Perpendicular elements of the tower and nave. Inside, the chancel's painted panelled ceiling (1445) contains portraits of English kings from Sigebert (623–37) to Henry VI, from about the same time as the eye-catching rood screen and misericords. Amidst the carvings, the favourite novelty is the so-called "Pilgrim's Rabbit", said to have been the inspiration for the White Rabbit in Lewis Carroll's *Alice in Wonderland*.

Practicalities

Beverley's **train station** is beside Station Square, just a couple of minutes' walk from the Minster; **buses** pull into Station Square. The **tourist office** is at 34 Butcher Row in the main shopping area (June–Aug Mon–Fri 9.30am–5.30pm, Sat 10am–5pm, Sun 10am–2pm; rest of year closed Sun; ☎01482/391672).

There's plenty of local **accommodation**, including a recommended guest house, the *Eastgate*, 7 Eastgate (☎01482/868464; no credit cards; ❷), very close to the Minster, with a couple of cheaper rooms without a shower. Among the hotels, the top town-centre choices are the *Beverley Arms*, North Bar Within (☎01482/869241; ❺), and the *North Bar Hotel*, 28 North Bar Without (☎01482 /881375; ❸), though all are eclipsed by the *Manor House*, Northlands, Walkington (☎01482/881645; ❺; breakfast not included), three miles south of Beverley. Of the pubs, try the *Windmill Inn*, 53 Lairgate (☎01482/862817; ❷), which has a dozen rooms for rent. The **youth hostel** (☎01482/881751; closed Nov–March) occupies one of the town's finer buildings, a restored Dominican friary that was mentioned in the *Canterbury Tales*. It's located in Friar's Lane, off Eastgate, just a hundred yards southeast of the Minster.

For **food**, *Cerutti's 2*, in Station Square (☎01482/866700; closed Sun), is a sister brasserie to that in Hull and serves equally good fresh fish dishes. Otherwise, there's a full complement of tearooms and cafés, or you can eat in the **pubs** – the celebrated *White Horse* on Hengate, near St Mary's, is a thoroughly atmospheric traditional drinking den with folk music nights; there's also the *Queen's Head* on Wednesday Market; and the real-ale haunt, the *Tap & Spile* on Flemingate, immediately behind the Minster. More expensive meals are on offer in the restaurant of the *Beverley Arms*, though its wood-panelled bar is open to all for drinks.

The **Beverley and East Riding Folk Festival** takes place each June, featuring an international roster of music, song, dance and comedy.

The East Yorkshire coast

The **East Yorkshire coast** curves south in a gentle arc from the mighty cliffs of Flamborough Head to Spurn Head, a finger-thin isthmus formed by the constant erosion and shifting currents that scour much of England's eastern shores. Between the two lie a handful of tranquil villages and miles of windswept dunes and mudflats, noted bird sanctuaries, and superbly lonely retreats accessible to anyone prepared to cycle or walk the paths and lanes that fan out amidst the dunes. **Buses** run out to a few points, mostly from Hull and Bridlington, but you'll need your own transport to make the most of the region. However, the two main resorts, **Bridlington** and **Filey**, are linked by the regular **train** service between Hull and Scarborough. There's also an hourly bus service between Bridlington, Filey and Scarborough.

Hikers also converge on Filey from a couple of **long-distance footpaths**. The **Wolds Way** links the resort to the River Humber by way of a 79-mile path through the gently rolling chalk hills to Hessle, in the shadow of the Humber Bridge, west of Hull. More challenging still, Filey is the traditional end of the 110-mile moor-and-coast **Cleveland Way** (see p.969), which loops from Helmsley to Saltburn and then heads south down the coast. Leaflets and information on the hikes are available from Filey's tourist office, and there are useful trail guides to both, published by Aurum Press.

Spurn Head

Few parts of the British coast are as dangerous as **Spurn Head**, a hook-shaped sand and pebble promontory that hardly suggests the imminence of maritime catastrophe, but whose lifeboat station is the only one in Britain permanently staffed by a professional crew. Access is via the village of **Easington** (at the end of the B1445), beyond which a four-mile toll road runs through a Yorkshire Wildlife Trust nature reserve known for its seals, butterflies, dunal flora and seabirds – this is one of the best spots in the country to observe spring and autumn bird migrations. Sheltered from the sea by the loop of Sunk Head are the **Sunk Island Sands**, at the mouth of the Humber and a birdwatchers' haven.

Hornsea and Burton Constable Hall

Some twenty miles of empty and unspoilt beaches line the coast from Spurn Head to **HORNSEA**, largest of the coast's villages and synonymous with the pottery that's made in a park-set factory on its outskirts on the B1242. There's free access and parking at the factory site, **Hornsea Freeport** (daily 9.30am–6pm), where there are guided tours and the opportunity to buy, though most people stump up the extra cash (£1) for the veritable fleet of add-on distractions like a model village, butterfly world and play area for kids. Hornsea **tourist office** is at 120 Newbegin (Easter–Sept Mon–Sat 10.30am–4.30pm; ☎01964/536404).

A quarter of a mile inland lies **Hornsea Mere**, Yorkshire's largest freshwater lake, scooped out by glacial action and now an RSPB sanctuary for herons and other nesting wildfowl. The other attraction hereabouts is **Burton Constable Hall** (Easter–Oct Mon–Thurs, Sat & Sun 1–5pm; £4), an Elizabethan stately home redesigned in the eighteenth century; it's about seven miles to the southwest, off the B1238 from Aldbrough. On show inside are Chippendale furniture, the Long Gallery's five thousand books, and paintings by Renoir, Gainsborough and Pissarro – after which you can stroll in the two hundred acres of parkland landscaped by Capability Brown.

Bridlington

The southernmost major resort on the Yorkshire coast, **BRIDLINGTON** has maintained its harbour for almost a thousand years, though for much of that time it remained a small-scale place of little consequence: Defoe noted it only because of its use to the eighteenth-century coastal coal ships who sought shelter here in bad weather. Like many coastal stations, it flourished in Edwardian times as a resort, but has spent recent decades in the same decline as other English bucket-and-spade holiday destinations. Renovations have smartened up the seafront promenade, which looks down upon the town's best asset – its sweeping sandy **beach**. It's an out-and-out family resort, which means plenty of candy-floss, amusement arcades, rides, diversions and shops full of tat, and in truth there's little to delay your progress northwards once you've paddled in the sea and eaten fish and chips on the milling harbourfront.

The **tourist office**, 25 Prince St (Easter–Oct Mon–Sat 9.30am–5.30pm, Sun 9am–5pm; Nov–Easter Mon–Sat 9.30am–5.30pm; ☎01262/673474), might be able to persuade you otherwise, and has full lists of local **accommodation**. Among the endless **cafés** and **restaurants** serving the same seaside food, *Jerome's*, Royal Prince's Parade (☎01262/671881), on the prom, stands out. It's a Greek café with meze and vegetarian platters, decent coffee and sea views from the outdoor tables; it's open until 10pm in summer.

Flamborough Head and Bempton Cliffs

Around fourteen miles of precipitous four-hundred-foot cliffs gird **Flamborough Head**, just to the northeast of Bridlington, a chalky knuckle whose 1979 designation as a Heritage Coast has guaranteed a degree of protection not only for a multitude of breeding seabirds, but also for a wealth of geological and archeological features. The best of the seascapes are visible on the peninsula's north side, accessible by road from **FLAMBOROUGH village**. The lighthouse beyond is closed to the public, the latest in a line of warning beacons here that date back to the seventeenth century, but which, in earlier times at least, manifestly failed to do their job: between 1770 and 1806, 174 ships went down in the hazardous waters off the headland. Ancient tumuli ripple over much of the headland, while the tip of the peninsula is almost cut off by the famous **Danes' Dyke**, a two-mile wooded ditch that runs from Cat Nab in the north to Sewerby Rocks in the south. Some believe it was a formal boundary built during the Viking invasions, though the chances are that it's an earthwork of pre-Roman vintage.

To see the best of Flamborough Head's coastline, try to walk at least part of the signposted **Heritage Coast path**, a grassy cliff-top track that negotiates most of the headland. One good place to join it is **BEMPTON**, two miles north of Bridlington. From Bempton, you can follow the path all the way round to Flamborough Head or curtail by cutting up paths to Flamborough village. The *Seabirds* (☎01262 674174), at the junction of the roads to the two villages, is a nice **pub** with a good line in fresh-fish bar meals.

Also of great appeal is the RSPB sanctuary at **Bempton Cliffs**, reached along a quiet lane from Bempton. The cliffs are the best single place to see the area's thousands of cliff-nesting birds; parking costs £2.50. This is the only mainland gannetry in England and you'll see gannets diving from fifty feet in the air to catch mackerel and herring. Bempton also boasts the second-largest **puffin colony** in the country, with several thousand returning to the cliffs between March and August – they spend the winter on the open seas. Late-March and April is the best time to see the puffins, when they display before nesting in the cliff's deep crevices, but the **Visitor Centre** (March–Oct daily 10am–5pm; Nov & Feb weekends only 9.30am–4pm; ☎01262/851179) can advise on other breeds' activities and rent you a pair of binoculars (£2). Other birds here in numbers include kittiwakes, guillemots, razorbills and the largest colony of fulmars in England. Not surprisingly, an egg-collecting industry once thrived here, the eggs' albumen being used in the tanneries of Leeds – you can still see the pulleys used by the local "climmers", as they were called. RSPB puffin and seabird **cruises** (mid-May to Sept most Sat & Sun; £8; reserve on ☎07751/654984) are a spectacular way to see the Bempton and Flamborough Head cliffs. They last three to four hours and depart from Bridlington.

Filey

FILEY, half a dozen miles further north up the coast – and at the very edge of the Yorkshire Wolds – has a deal more class as a resort, retaining many of its Edwardian features, including some splendid panoramic gardens. It, too, claims miles of wide sandy **beach**, stretching most of the way south to Flamborough Head and north the mile or so to the jutting rocks of **Filey Brigg**, where a nature trail wends for a couple of miles through the surroundings. If you're going to clamber around on the Brigg, check the tide tables first since people do get caught unawares by the incoming waters. **Bus** and **train stations** are just west of the centre on Station Road. Walk down Station Avenue and Murray Street to Filey's **tourist office** in the Borough Council offices on John Street (May–Sept daily 9.30am–5.30pm; Oct–April Sat & Sun 10am–4.30pm; ☎01723/518000). You'll find a clutch of standard **B&Bs** on Rutland Street, off West Avenue, which runs from the church in the centre of town. A couple of pricier hotels sit amongst the holiday flats down on the beachfront. *Downcliffe House* (☎01723/513310; ❸) is the pick of them, with a seaview restaurant with outdoor terrace serving a decent menu of fresh fish.

The North York Moors

Virtually the whole of the **North York Moors**, from the Hambleton and Cleveland hills in the west to the cliff-edged coastline to the east, is protected by one of the country's finest National Parks. The moors are lonely, heather-covered, flat-topped hills cut by deep, steep-sided valleys, and views here stretch for miles, interrupted only by giant cultivated forests, pale shadows of the woodland that covered the region before it was cleared by Neolithic and later peoples. Barrows and ancient forts provide memorials of these early settlers, mingling on the high moorland with the **Roman remains** of Wades Causeway, the battered stone crosses of the first Christian inhabitants and the ruins of great monastic houses such as Rievaulx.

Two pivotal centres, both market towns, in the park's southern reaches provide the main approaches: **Helmsley**, best starting point for any exploration of

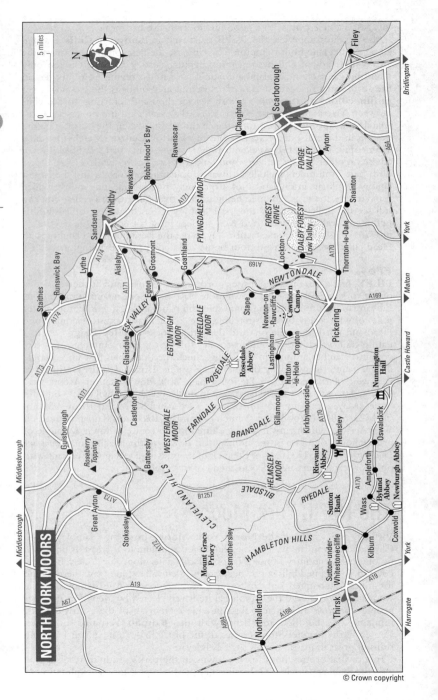

NORTH YORK MOORS

N

0 _____ 5 miles

the western and central moors, and **Pickering** (actually just outside the National Park), for the eastern moors and northern Esk Valley. The central moors offer the best walking and the most noted landscapes, with **Hutton le Hole** perhaps the most picture-perfect village in the region. Any exploration of the district should also include the religious ruins of **Rievaulx Abbey** and possibly Byland Abbey or Mount Grace Priory; the views from **Sutton Bank** or from the windows of the trains of the North York Moors Railway; the gentle landscapes of the **Esk Valley**, blessed with its own small train line; and any one of countless deep-rural pubs, isolated hamlets or woodland walks. Popular long-distance paths cross the park, notably the Cleveland Way, which follows the coast and northern moors, and the Lyke Wake Walk, both of which are covered in more detail in the following section.

Help and information is available from a number of **National Park information centres**, where you can pick up local trail guides and accommodation listings – most also organize special events and guided walks throughout the year. The seasonal *Moors Visitor* newspaper details local attractions, while the best hiking **maps** are the Ordnance Survey Outdoor Leisure maps #26 and #27.

The main southern artery linking the western, central and eastern divisions is the A170, which runs from Thirsk, through Helmsley and Pickering to Scarborough. Two trans-moor roads, the Helmsley–Stokesley B1257 (west side) and the Pickering–Whitby A169 (east), offer access into the very heart of the moors, with minor (often extremely minor) roads and tracks branching off in all directions: in winter, check the forecast first before setting off on any minor route, since this part of the country is always one of the first to be cut off in bad weather.

A big local draw are the **steam trains** of the North York Moors Railway between Pickering and Grosmont (even more renowned since being used as the "Hogwarts Express" in the first *Harry Potter* film). At Grosmont you can connect with the regular trains on the Esk Valley line, running either six miles east to Whitby and the coast, or west through scintillating countryside to more remote settlements (and ultimately to Middlesbrough). The main **bus** approaches to the moors are from Scarborough and York to Helmsley and Pickering, though beyond these towns local services are limited. You'll need the free *Moors Connections* booklet, a summary of all rail and bus routes on and around the moors, available from tourist offices and park information centres. There are also special summer Moorsbus services, running between points not usually served by public transport; see the box below for more details.

The western moors

The **western moors** are marked on their western edge by the scarp of the **Hambleton Hills** – crowned by the Cleveland Way – and the ruler-straight line of the A19 road between York, **Thirsk** (just outside the park, but a useful gateway) and Middlesbrough. To the east they are closed by Rye Dale, one of the region's more bucolic valleys, and the B1267 from **Helmsley**, by far the area's nicest town and its best base for explorations. Most outings are likely to centre less on the scenery – except for the walks and staggering views from **Sutton Bank** on the A170 – than on a cluster of historic buildings, of which the most prepossessing is **Rievaulx Abbey**, easily seen from Helmsley. It's closely followed by **Mount Grace Priory**, to the north of Thirsk, and then by Shandy Hall, Byland Abbey and Newburgh Priory at the pretty village of **Coxwold**, and **Nunnington Hall** to the east, grouped conveniently close together on a minor road loop from Thirsk to Helmsley.

The Moorsbus

The National Park Authority is making sterling efforts to reduce traffic congestion in the region by promoting public transport, in particular its bus service, the **Moorsbus** (℡01439/770657, ⓦ www.moorsbus.net), which runs every Sunday and bank holiday Monday from April to the end of October, and daily in the summer school holidays (late July to late Aug). All local tourist and National Park information offices have timetables, but the various **services** basically connect Helmsley to Sutton Bank, Osmotherley, Rievaulx, Coxwold and Kilburn; Pickering to Hutton le Hole, Castleton and Danby, to Rosedale Abbey and to Dalby Forest; and Helmsley and Pickering to each other. Departures are usually four times daily (hourly on the main routes), and timed so that day-trips are possible to the various sights; all-day **tickets** cost £2.50. Long-distance services (£5) from Scarborough (1hr), York (1hr 10min), Hull (1hr 40min), Beverley (1hr), Darlington (2hr), Hartlepool (2hr) and Middlesbrough (1hr) let you commute into the park for a day's moorland sightseeing.

Thirsk

The small market town of **THIRSK**, 23 miles north of York, made the most of its strategic crossroads position on the ancient drove road between Scotland and York and on the historic east–west route from dales to coast. Its medieval prosperity is clear from the large, cobbled **Market Place** (market days are Monday and Saturday), now overrun by traffic, while later well-to-do citizens endowed the town with a bevy of commendable Georgian houses and halls, like those still standing on Kirkgate, which runs off the square. The **Thirsk Museum** at 16 Kirkgate (Easter–Oct Mon–Wed, Fri & Sat 10am–4pm; £1.50; ⓦ www.thirskmuseum.org) – incidentally, the birthplace of eighteenth-century cricketer Thomas Lord, who founded the eponymous London cricket ground – does its best to fill in the background. However, Thirsk's main draw is its attachment to the legacy of local vet Alf Wight, better known as **James Herriott**. Despite the confusing claims of various Yorkshire Dales villages, Thirsk was the "Darrowby" of the Herriott books, not least because the town was where the vet had his actual surgery, just across the road from the Thirsk Museum. This building at 23 Kirkgate is now the hugely popular **World of James Herriott** (daily: Easter–Oct 10am–6pm; Nov–Easter 10am–5pm, last admission 1hr before closing; £4.50; ⓦ www.worldofjamesherriott.org), an entertaining re-creation of the vet's 1940s surgery, dispensary, operating theatre, sitting room and kitchen, each crammed with period pieces and Herriott memorabilia. Countryside exhibits, veterinary science displays and an investigation of how the Herriott books were adapted for film and TV complete the experience.

Buses stop in the Market Place: there are two National Express services a day from York, while local services between Thirsk, Kilburn, Coxwold and Helmsley run on Mondays, Fridays and Saturdays. The **train station** (services from York and Middlesbrough) is a mile west of town on the A61 (Ripon road); minibuses connect the station with the town centre. The **tourist office** is inside the World of James Herriott, 23 Kirkgate (daily: Easter–Oct 10am–5.30pm; Nov–Easter 10am–4.30pm; ℡01845/522755, ⓦ www.hambleton .gov.uk), and can help with **accommodation**. *Lavender House*, 27 Kirkgate (℡01845/522224; no credit cards; ❶), and *Kirkgate House*, further along at no. 35 (℡01845/525015; ❹, ❸ for courtyard rooms), are both well sited on the road up to the impressive parish church, and the **pubs** in the Market Place offer rooms as well. The *Golden Fleece* and *Three Tuns* both serve **meals**, while the nicest daytime choice is the *Yorks Tearooms*, next to the clocktower on

Market Place, a genteel café with enterprising lunches, speciality coffees and its own deli around the back. *Charles' Bistro* (℡01845/527444; closed Sun night), a moderately priced place on Bakers Alley (off Market Place, behind NatWest), has daily lunch deals and continental-style dinners and pastas.

Osmotherley

Eleven miles north of Thirsk, the little village of **OSMOTHERLEY** huddles around its green, proud of its ancient market cross and curious adjacent stone table from on top of which it's said John Wesley preached during one of his sermon tours. Having seen agriculture and industry come and go, the pretty settlement now gets by as a hiking centre, since it's a key stop on the Cleveland Way as well as starting-point for the infamous Lyke Wake Walk (see box below). Its proximity to Mount Grace Priory is another reason to stop by – it's around a two-mile walk from the village, via Chapel Wood Farm, with a short detour to the nearby **Lady Chapel** on the way there or back. A more strenuous local hike involves following the Cleveland Way beyond the farm to the 982ft summit of Scarth Wood Moor and then down to Cod Beck Reservoir (3 miles; 1hr 30min).

There's a popular **youth hostel** at Cote Ghyll (℡01609/883575, ⓦwww .yha.org.uk), half a mile north of the village, and an adjacent campsite too – you should really book in advance. For more comfort make straight for the *Three Tuns* (℡01609/883301; ❹) on the village green, a lovely **pub** brimming with awards and serving fresh seafood meals. A couple of tea shops and cottage B&Bs complete the picture.

Mount Grace Priory

The fourteenth-century **Mount Grace Priory** (Easter–Oct daily 10am–6pm; Nov–March Wed–Sun 10am–1pm & 2–4pm; £2.90; NT & EH), the most important of England's nine Carthusian ruins and the only one in Yorkshire, provides a striking contrast to its more grandiose and worldly Cistercian

The Lyke Wake Walk

One of England's more macho long-distance paths, the **Lyke Wake Walk** was founded in 1955 as a light-hearted idea: anyone who completed the 42-mile walk in less than 24 hours became a member of the Lyke Wake Club and qualified for a badge in the shape of a coffin. As word spread it became something of a cult, the net result being deeply eroded paths and mountains of litter – to the extent that the National Park authority now discourages large groups. The path isn't marked on most maps for the same reason. Although still the most popular walk on the moors, it has recently become less choked with groups, and is complemented by another trans-moors route, Wainwright's similarly controversial Coast to Coast walk.

The Lyke Wake starts at **Osmotherley**, eleven miles north of Thirsk, and shadows the Cleveland Way for a while along the northern edge of the Cleveland Hills before reaching **Ravenscar**, near Robin Hood's Bay, by way of Fylingdales and the notorious Jugger Howes. It links numerous prehistoric sites, following the age-old tracks of monks, miners and smugglers. The path's name, incidentally, comes from a dialect poem, the *Lyke Wake Dirge*, the story of a journey across one of the "burial routes" that linked the moors' ancient burial mounds. It recalls the ancient practice of waking (keeping vigil) over a dead body (the lyke). Provided you're completely fit, used to long-distance walking, have been in training and have back-up, first-timers can complete the walk in around sixteen hours – some people have *run* it in less than five, though they are, of course, completely mad.

counterparts. The Carthusians took a vow of silence and lived, ate and prayed alone in their two-storey cells, each separated from its neighbour by a privy, small garden and high walls. The incumbents were given their meals through a hatch, specially angled to prevent the monks from seeing their waiters. The foundations of the cells are still clearly visible, together with one which has been reconstructed to suggest its original layout and the monks' way of life. Other substantial remains include the ruins of the gatehouse and the walls and tower of the priory church, which divides the site's two main courtyards.

Road access to the priory is straight up the busy A19 from Thirsk, eleven miles to the south; it's reached off a signposted minor road just after the Osmotherley turn-off. Heading onwards into the National Park, it's much more enjoyable to bear east afterwards, through Osmotherley and Hawnby, along the very minor roads across the Cleveland Hills to join the B1257 for Helmsley. By **public transport**, take the train from Thirsk to Northallerton, six miles southwest of the priory, and then any of the regular Northallerton–Osmotherley buses (hourly, not Sun).

Sutton Bank and Kilburn

The main A170 road enters the National Park from Thirsk as it climbs five hundred feet in half a mile to **Sutton Bank** (960ft), a phenomenal viewpoint whose panorama extends across the Vale of York to the Pennines on the far horizon. At the top of the climb stands a huge car park and a North York Moors National Park **Visitor Centre** (Easter–Oct daily 10am–5pm; Nov, Dec & March daily 11am–4pm; Jan & Feb Sat & Sun 11am–4pm; ☎01845/597426, ⓦ www.northyorkmoors-npa.gov.uk), full of background on the short way-marked walks you can make from here, and with a café too.

To the south of the A170, the marked **White Horse Nature Trail** (2–3 miles; 1hr 30min) skirts the crags of Roulston Scar, passing the Yorkshire Gliding Club en route to the **Kilburn White Horse**, northern England's only turf-cut figure, at 314 feet long and 228 feet high. Unlike its ancient southern counterparts, it's a rather sham affair cut by a local schoolmaster in 1857 and only white because it's covered in imported chalk chippings. You could make a real walk of it by dropping a couple of miles down to **KILBURN** village – a minor road also runs from the A170, passing the White Horse – synonymous with woodcarving since the days of "Mouse Man" Robert Thompson (1876–1955), whose woodcarvings – marked by his distinctive mouse motif – are found in York Minster and Westminster Abbey. The **Mouseman Visitor Centre** (June–Sept daily 10am–5pm; April, May & Oct Tues–Sun 10am–5pm; £1.50) in Thompson's restored workshop has woodworking demonstrations most days, while the village's *Forresters Arms* – a good place to recuperate – sports locally made furniture.

Coxwold

The first serious diversion off the A170 is **COXWOLD**, as attractive a little village as they come. The majority of its many visitors come to pay homage to the novelist **Laurence Sterne**, who is buried by the south wall (close to the porch) in the churchyard of **St Michael's**, where he was vicar from 1760 until his death in 1768; the gravestone is badly damaged, though that which marked the place of his original grave in London (see below) hangs in the porch, complete with an inscription by enthusiastic eighteenth-century masons who admired him. The church, with its odd octagonal tower, is worth closer scrutiny – particularly the three-decker pulpit and medieval stained glass – before heading for **Shandy Hall**, 150 yards further up the road past the church

The mysterious corpse of Laurence Sterne

Irish-born **Laurence Sterne** (1713–68) took Holy Orders after receiving his Cambridge degree, married in 1741 and by 1760 was living in Coxwold, officiating at St Michael's Church. The first two volumes of his great novel, the rambling and brilliant *Tristram Shandy*, published in 1760, catapulted him to fame and he became a controversial figure in literary London. Further volumes of *Tristram Shandy* enhanced his reputation, and Sterne began to travel in the 1760s, partly in an attempt to improve his poor health. His sojourn in France and Italy provided material for *A Sentimental Journey* (1768), but the journey proved too much for him and he died of pleurisy in London, where he was buried. Immediate rumours surfaced that Sterne's body had been unknowingly appropriated by body-snatchers and sold to doctors for medical experimentation – a story given credence when Sterne's body was finally exhumed from its London graveyard in 1969 for reburial in Coxwold. Various bones and no fewer than five skulls were uncovered in the grave, one of which – after comparison with contemporary busts – is thought to have been Sterne's. Presumably, the eighteenth-century doctors who illegally bought the body were horrified to learn of its identity and hurriedly reburied it in its grave together with other human bits and pieces they had lying around. Sterne – or at least part of him – now lies at rest in Coxwold churchyard.

(May–Sept Wed 2–4pm, Sun 2.30–4.30pm; gardens May–Sept Mon–Fri & Sun 1–4.30pm; house & gardens £3.50, gardens only £2.50), Sterne's home, now a museum crammed with literary memorabilia. It was here that he wrote *A Sentimental Journey through France and Italy* and the wonderfully eccentric *The Life and Opinions of Tristram Shandy, Gentleman*, which prompted Samuel Johnson loftily and misguidedly to declare "nothing odd will last".

Of the village's many lovely, ivy-covered stone buildings, the *Fauconburg Arms* (℡01347/868214; ❹), a superb old **pub** on Main Street, has the most to recommend it, with a cosy bar serving good food, a more formal restaurant and pleasant rooms.

The pub is named for the viscount who married Mary, daughter of Oliver Cromwell, whom he brought to live in **Newburgh Priory**, half a mile south of the village (April–June Wed & Sun 2–6pm; also Easter & May bank hols 2–6pm; £4; grounds only £2). Raised on the site of an Augustinian monastery founded in 1150, the house is famous for reputedly containing a tomb with the headless body of Oliver Cromwell. The story claims that Mary brought her father's body here after it was exhumed from Westminster Abbey in readiness to be "executed" at Tyburn in revenge for Cromwell's part in the Civil War. Resourceful Mary is supposed to have exchanged Oliver's corpse with that of some ordinary Joe, but it's not quite clear how this tale can be made to tally with the fact that Oliver's body had been mummified before its burial, and thus would have been expected to resemble the recently deceased leader.

Buses run to Coxwold from Thirsk on Mondays, Fridays and Saturdays (and on to Helmsley), and the Moorsbus runs here from Helmsley in summer. By car, turn off the A170 at Sutton-under-Whitestonecliffe, five miles east of Thirsk, or come south down the A19 and follow the signs through the country lanes – either approach lets you take in Kilburn and the White Horse on the way to or from Coxwold.

Byland Abbey

Laurence Sterne talked of "A delicious Walk of Romance" from Coxwold to twelfth-century **Byland Abbey** (Easter–Sept daily 10am–6pm; Oct daily

10am–5pm; Nov–Easter Wed–Sun 10am–1pm & 2–4pm; £1.70; EH), a mile and a half northeast of the village; the summer Moorsbus runs here. His description captures the appeal of the ruins – seen from the distance as a mere finger of stone – which, though larger in ground area than the Cistercian houses at Fountains and Rievaulx, are far less well preserved, leaving the haunting location and stark west front as the abbey's most memorable aspects. Other colossal but skeletal remains include the lay brothers' "lane", a rare example of the corridor which kept abbey servants at a remove from the cloister and the ordained monks. Equally unusual are some fine thirteenth-century green-and-yellow tiled floors, seen to best effect in the south transept chapels. The *Abbey Inn* (closed Sun eve & Mon), opposite the priory entrance, serves coffee and excellent meals.

Nunnington Hall

Moving eight miles due east from Byland through Ampleforth (famous for its Catholic public school) and Oswaldkirk brings you to **Nunnington Hall** (June–Aug Tues–Sun 1.30–5pm; April, May, Sept & Oct Wed–Sun 1.30–4.30pm; £4.50; garden only £2; NT), a part-Tudor manor house stranded in the flats of lower Rye Dale about five miles southeast of Helmsley. The panelled bedrooms and vast main hall are impressive, but the principal diversion is the famous Carlisle Collection, 22 miniature rooms all furnished and decorated in different styles. The house, woods and gardens are all supposed to be haunted, though the most notable presence are peacocks strutting the garden lawns. There's also a tearoom. Bus #94 from Helmsley (Mon–Sat 2 daily) runs to Nunnington, from where it's a short walk to the hall.

Helmsley

One of the moors' most appealing towns, **HELMSLEY** makes a perfect base for visiting the western moors and Rievaulx Abbey. Local life revolves around a large cobbled market square (market day is Friday), dominated by a vaunting monument to the second earl of Feversham, whose family were responsible for rebuilding most of the village in the last century. The old **market cross** marks the start of the 110-mile Cleveland Way (see box below), and the town hall on the western edge of the square houses the tourist office and National Park information centre.

Close to the square, on the village's western fringe, is **Helmsley Castle** (April–Sept daily 10am–6pm; Nov–March Wed–Sun 10am–1pm & 2–4pm; £2.40; EH), its unique twelfth-century D-shaped keep ringed by massive earthworks. After a three-month siege during the Civil War it was "slighted" by Sir Thomas Fairfax, the Parliamentary commander, and much of its stone was plundered by townspeople for local houses.

To the southwest of the town, overlooking a wooded meander of the Rye, stands the Fevershams' country seat, **Duncombe Park** (house & garden: April–Oct Mon–Thurs & Sun 11am–5.30pm; parkland & visitor centre: same days 10.30am–6pm; house, gardens & parkland £6, gardens & parkland £4, parkland only £2; ⓦww.duncombepark.com), built for the Fevershams' ancestor Sir Thomas Duncombe in 1713. The building is by gentleman-architect William Wakefield, though he was probably influenced by Vanbrugh who was working on Castle Howard at about the same time. The **grounds** are perhaps more appealing than the house (which was extensively rebuilt after a fire in 1879), boasting swathes of landscaped gardens which include Britain's tallest ash and lime trees, and a brace of artfully sited temples. Keen gardeners will also want to visit the **Helmsley Walled Garden**, within the Duncombe Park

The Cleveland Way

The 110-mile **Cleveland Way**, one of England's premier long-distance National Trails, starts at Helmsley in the North York Moors and follows a route that embraces both the northern rim of the moors and Cleveland Hills and the cliff scenery of the North Yorkshire coast. The path hits the coast at Saltburn and then runs south down the coast, terminating at Filey, south of Scarborough – though an unofficial "Missing Link" joins Scarborough to Helmsley, through the Tabular Hills, thus completing a circular walk.

Most people complete the Cleveland Way in around nine or ten days, though it's easy to walk short stages instead, particularly on the **coastal section**, where towns, villages and services are closer together. The outstanding high cliff sections are (from south to north): Hayburn Wyke to Robin Hood's Bay (7 miles); Robin Hood's Bay to Whitby (6 miles); Sandsend to Runswick Bay to Staithes (7 miles); and Staithes to Skinningrove, the section with the highest cliffs (5 miles).

The **Cleveland Way Project** (The Old Vicarage, Bondgate, Helmsley, YO6 5BP; ☏01439/770657) produces an annual *Accommodation and Information Guide*, an invaluable route-planning aid. Local information offices in Helmsley, Whitby, Sutton Bank, Scarborough and Filey can also advise you. As well as B&Bs, hotels and campsites en route, there are **youth hostels** at Helmsley, Osmotherley, Whitby, Robin Hood's Bay and Scarborough – all should be booked well in advance.

You'll need the OS Outdoor Leisure **maps** #26 and #27 and Landranger sheet #101, though the *National Trail Guide: Cleveland Way* by Ian Sampson (Aurum Press) and *Walking the Cleveland Way and The Missing Link* by Malcolm Boyes (Cicerone Press) cover the ground in detail, too.

Estate (April–Oct daily 10.30am–5pm; rest of year Fri–Sun noon–4pm; £2.50), whose five carefully tended acres are slowly emerging from a whole-sale renovation after years of neglect.

Rievaulx Abbey

From Helmsley you can easily hike across country to **Rievaulx Abbey** (daily: April–Sept 10am–6pm; Oct–March 10am–1pm & 2–4pm; £3.60; EH), once one of England's greatest Cistercian abbeys, and these days the most heavily visited historic building on the moors. The signposted path follows the opening two miles of the Cleveland Way, plus a mile's diversion off the Way, and takes around an hour and a half – a trail leaflet is available from the tourist office in Helmsley. If you don't fancy the walk, take the summer-only Moorsbus, which runs a shuttle service out here.

Founded in 1132, the abbey became the mother church of the Cistercians in England (see box on p.933), quickly developing from a series of rough shelters on the deeply wooded banks of the Rye to become a flourishing community with interests in fishing, mining, agriculture and the woollen industry, the latter supported by a chain of associated moorland farms. At its height, 140 monks and up to 500 lay brothers lived and worked at the abbey, though numbers fell dramatically once the Black Death (1348–49) had done its worst. Nemesis came with the Dissolution, when many of the walls were razed and the roof lead stripped – the beautiful ruins, however, still suggest the abbey's former splendour. They are at their best in the triple-arched nave, oriented from north to south instead of the conventional west–east axis because of the valley's sloping site. The Chapter House retains an original shrine to the first abbot, William. A **visitor centre** mounts exhibitions pertaining to the ruins and to monastic life in the valley.

Rievaulx Terrace

Although they form some sort of ensemble with the abbey, there's no access between thse ruins and **Rievaulx Terrace and Temples** (Easter–Oct daily 10.30am–5pm; £3.30; NT), a site entered from the B1257, a couple of miles northwest of town. This pleasing half-mile stretch of grass-covered terraces and woodland was laid out as part of Duncombe Park in the 1750s, and as with Studley Royal at Fountains Abbey, the Terrace was engineered partly to enhance the views of the abbey. The resulting panorama over the ruins and the valley below is superb, and this makes a great spot for a picnic or simply for strolls along the lawns and woodland trail. Tuscan and Ionic temples lie at opposing ends of the Terrace, the latter with a fine painted ceiling, excellent furniture and a permanent exhibition on eighteenth-century English landscape design.

Helmsley practicalities

Helmsley is connected by **bus** to Pickering and Scarborough (#128), Malton (#94), York (#57) and Thirsk (#58), which makes it a fairly handy base. It's also a hub for the Moorsbus, which takes trippers out to Sutton Bank, Rievaulx, Byland Abbey, Coxwold and Kilburn – see the box on p.964 for more details. Make sense of all the connections in the useful **tourist office** in the town hall on Market Place (Easter–Oct daily 9.30am–5pm; Nov–Easter Sat & Sun 10am–4pm; ℡01439/770173, ℠www.ryedale.gov.uk), which sells local trail leaflets and has information on the two **long-distance footpaths**: the Cleveland Way (see box above) and the Ebor Way, the latter a gentle seventy-mile route to Ilkley that links with the Dales Way.

There's plenty of **accommodation**, starting with *Stilworth House*, 1 Church St, behind the tourist office and square (℡01439/771072; no credit cards; ❸). Other modest B&Bs are scattered along Ashdale Road, a few hundred yards up Bondgate from the Market Place and on the right. Pricier hotels include the classy *Feversham Arms*, 1 High St, behind the church (℡01439/770766; ❻), which also has some good full-board deals; and the *Feathers Hotel*, 1 Market Place (℡01439/770275; ❹). Finest of all is the *Black Swan*, also on Market Place (℡01439/770466; ❼), a gorgeous Elizabethan–Georgian hybrid with splendid gardens and some good off-season deals. The purpose-built **youth hostel** (℡01439/770433, ℠www.yha.org.uk) is a few hundred yards east of Market Place – follow Bondgate to Carlton Road and turn left.

Market day in Helmsley is Friday. The old **pubs** in the Market Place – the *Royal Oak* and the *Feathers* – are both atmospheric places for a drink and a bite to eat. The *Black Swan* is the place for drinks in its panelled bar, afternoon teas and good, if pricey, lunches and dinners. Hunters, at 13 Borogate, just by the Market Place, is an overstuffed **deli**, excellent for putting together a picnic. Borogate itself has several fine little **shops** in ancient houses, including a working smithy and a good second-hand bookshop in the old fire station.

For a drive out into the country, and a fine meal, you can't do better than the invariably packed *Star Inn* (℡01439/770397; no food Sun eve & Mon) at **Harome**, a thatched pub a couple of miles south of the A170, where superior food and good beer are the norm. You can either wait for a table in the bar or book ahead for the dining room.

The central moors

The highest and wildest terrain in the North York Moors is in the **central moors**, bounded by Rye Dale in the west and by **Rosedale** in the east. Purple swathes of summer heather carpet the tops, where ancient crosses and standing stones provide hints of the moorland's distant past. Stunning villages such as

Hutton le Hole and Lastingham give way to higher, isolated valleys, connected by steep minor roads and rough tracks – it's the one part of the National Park where having your own transport is vital if you don't plan to hang around too long. The Moorsbus connects most of the better-known destinations, but really this is an area for walking and taking in the scenery. Drivers could base themselves virtually anywhere to see these dales, though Helmsley (see p.968) suggests itself; if you're using the Moorsbus, then Pickering, across to the east (see p.973), is the transport hub. Moving onwards, it's just a thirteen-mile drive (or Moorsbus journey) from Hutton le Hole across the highest part of the moors to Castleton in the Esk Valley (see p.977).

Hutton le Hole

Lying around eight miles northeast of Helmsley, one of Yorkshire's quaintest villages, **HUTTON LE HOLE**, has become so great a tourist attraction that you'll have to come off-season to get much pleasure from its tidy gardens, its stream-crossed village green and the sight of sheep wandering freely through the lanes. On warm summer days, the stream banks are covered with splashing picnickers. Apart from the sheer photogenic quality of the place, the big draw is the **Ryedale Folk Museum** (Easter–Oct daily 10am–5.30pm; £3.25; Ⓦ www.ryedalefolkmuseum.co.uk), an ever-expanding set of displays over a two-acre site. Local life is documented from the era of prehistoric flint tools, through Romano-British artefacts and pottery, to a series of reconstructed buildings, notably a sixteenth-century house, a glass furnace, a crofter's cottage and a nineteenth-century blacksmith's shop. Special events and displays throughout the season mean there's always something going on.

The museum also houses a National Park **information centre** (☎01751 /417367), where you can buy leaflets detailing local hikes. The nearby car park fills very quickly in summer as walkers disperse from the village. **Accommodation** is zealously fought for, too: try the *Barn Hotel* (☎01751 /417311; ❸), on the through road just down from the museum, or the Georgian *Hammer and Hand* (☎01751/417300; ❸), a comfortable period B&B on the village green next to the pub, or fall back on the mercy of the information office, which holds lists of other local B&Bs. Both the *Barn* and *Hammer and Hand* have associated tearooms, the latter serving evening meals too, while the *Forge Tea Shop* (closed weekdays Nov–Feb) – a renowned stop for tea and cakes – completes the set. If you stay the night you'll have plenty of time to become acquainted with the *Crown*, the friendly local **pub**.

Lastingham

About a mile and a half east of Hutton le Hole is **LASTINGHAM**, its rose-fronted stone cottages gathered in a dell near its bubbling beck. Here stands **St Mary's** (daily 9am–dusk), a superb little church, built over Lastingham Abbey, a Benedictine house founded in 654 by monks Cedd and Chad from Lindisfarne, both of whom were later canonized. The monastery was destroyed by the Danes and then partly rebuilt by monks from Whitby, who left in 1087 to found St Mary's in York without finishing their work here. The present church, however, preserves the early Norman crypt, one of Yorkshire's great ecclesiastical treasures. Burial place of St Cedd, the crypt was once a sacred point of pilgrimage. Today its heavy vaults and carved columns still shelter the head of an eighth-century Anglo-Saxon cross, a Viking "hogback" tombstone and the original doorposts of the Saxon monastery.

The hamlet is tiny, with just one cosy **pub**, the *Blacksmith's Arms* opposite the church.

Farndale

Farndale is entered from the south by a minor road from **Gillamoor**, a little to the west of Hutton le Hole. Further up the vale the country lanes are packed in spring with tourists come to see the area's wild daffodils, protected by the two-thousand-acre **Farndale nature reserve**. The flowers grow in several parts of the dale, but the best area is north of **Low Mill**, where roads from Gillamoor and Hutton le Hole meet, about four miles north of the latter. Take the path beside the car park (signposted "High Mill") over the bridge and follow the track alongside the somnolent River Dove. As well as the thousands of daffodils, notice the alder trees, whose Gaelic name, *ferna*, may well have given Farndale its name. At High Mill, *Poppy's Pantry* (closed Wed) can serve you a refreshing glass of home-made lemonade in the garden, just beyond which, at **Church Houses**, you regain the road (and find the tiny, stone *Feversham Arms*). Turn right on the tarmac here for about three-quarters of a mile and you can follow the route back south to Low Mill via High Wold House (just over 3 miles; 2hr–2hr 30min). It's worth noting that the **Moorsbus** runs a special "Daffodil" service every Sunday in April and over Easter, shuttling visitors from Hutton le Hole to Farndale.

The onwards road route cuts east from Church Houses up onto **Farndale Moor** to meet the high moor road from Hutton le Hole that passes the *Lion* on Blakey Ridge (see below) and curves around the head of Rosedale before dropping down to Rosedale Abbey.

Rosedale and Blakey Ridge

Rosedale, just a couple of miles east of Farndale, is slightly wilder and steeper than the latter, and has a good network of wild upland roads ranging over its moors, which are densely studded with prehistoric tumuli and ancient stone crosses, including **Ralph Cross**, which stands sentinel at the isolated crossroads at the top of the dale.

The largest of its communities, trim and tidy **ROSEDALE ABBEY**, four miles northeast of Hutton le Hole, preserves only a few fragments of the Cistercian priory (1158) which gave it its name, most of them incorporated into **St Lawrence's** parish church. It's hard to believe now, but in the last century the village had a population of over five thousand, most employed in the ironstone workings whose remnants lie scattered all over the lonely high moors round about. The first mine opened in 1851, some three million tons of ore being excavated between 1856 and 1885. Horse-drawn wagons dragged the stone by pack road to Pickering until the opening of a remarkable moorland railway which connected with the main Esk Valley line at Battersby to carry ore north to the ironworks of Teesside.

You can pick up the still clearly distinct line, now a panoramic footpath, at several points near the high road on Blakey Ridge, on the west of the dale, but for a fine circular walk join it at **Hill Cottages**, one and half miles northwest of Rosedale Abbey, and follow it all the way round the head of the valley, returning either via Dale Head Farm, the valley bottom and Thorgill, or the broad track that runs south down Blakey Ridge above Thorgill (10 miles; 3hr 30min).

Rosedale village itself gets packed on summer weekends and it can be tough finding a parking space on the grass verges. A fair proportion of visitors are here to sit outside the *Milburn Arms* (℡01751/417312; ❺; closed Jan), overlooking the small green, which makes a peaceful base: its **rooms** are pricey for what you get, but there are views over the hills and a beer garden out front. Otherwise, there are teas and snacks to be had in the *Abbey Tearooms* (closed

Wed & Nov–Easter), and a popular **campsite** at *Rosedale Caravan Park* (☎01751/417272) down by the river. There's a very good restaurant and bar meals, too, at the *Blacksmiths' Inn* (☎01751/417331, ⓦwww.blacksmithsinn-rosedale.co.uk; ❹) at **Hartoft End**, a couple of miles south of Rosedale Abbey. Also a couple of miles out (call for directions), in peaceful surroundings, the comfortable *Orange Tree* (☎01751/417219; ❷) at Rosedale East is a relaxed place with seven rooms and good home cooking.

North of Rosedale Abbey, you can reach the *Lion Inn* (☎01751/417320, ⓦwww.lionblakey.co.uk; ❸) on **Blakey Ridge**, a couple of miles south of the junction with the Hutton le Hole–Castleton road (along which the Moorsbus travels). A truly windswept local, with a sixteenth-century core, the inn has fairly standard bar meals, but good beer and an unbeatable location for an isolated night's stay – though come Sunday lunchtime the car park soon fills up. Some make the slight detour from the Lyke Wake Walk, since the pub roughly marks the halfway spot.

Pickering and the eastern moors

The biggest centre for miles around, **Pickering** takes for itself the title "Gateway to the Moors", which is pushing it a bit, though it's certainly a handy place to stay if you're touring the villages and dales of the **eastern moors**. Its undoubted big pull, and biggest plus if you're using public transport, is the **North Yorkshire Moors Railway** (NYMR; see box on p.975), which provides a beautiful way of travelling up (and walking from) **Newtondale**, the Moors' most immediately spectacular dale, and of connecting with the Esk Valley line in Esk Dale and, ultimately, Whitby and the Yorkshire coast. Otherwise, you could make use of the Moorsbus services, which radiate from Pickering, and there are regular bus services to and from Helmsley, Scarborough, York and Leeds.

Few people pay much attention to the countryside east of Pickering, which consists for the most part of apparently unending ranks of conifers and characterless moorland. **Dalby Forest**, however, the most accessible of the woodlands, is redeemed by a superb forest drive and a large number of specially marked trails. Villages are few and far between, though in **Thornton-le-Dale** the region has a high-ranking contender for prettiest village in Yorkshire. By far the best itinerary here is to see Thornton-le-Dale and then drive or bike through Dalby Forest to rejoin the main A170 Pickering–Scarborough road at one of several points just outside Scarborough. Without your own transport you're stuck as far as touring around is concerned, though there is a Moorsbus service into the forest from Pickering.

Pickering

A thriving market town at the junction of the A170 and the transmoor A169 (Whitby road), **PICKERING** rather fancies itself, yet a couple of hours is enough to show you its charms, certainly if you've already seen the best of the North York Moors to the west. Its most attractive feature is its motte and bailey **Castle** on the hill north of the market place (Easter–Oct daily 10am–6pm; Nov–March Wed–Sun 10am–4pm; £2.40; EH), reputedly used by every English monarch up to 1400 as a base for hunting in nearby Blandsby Park. Eight monarchs certainly put up here, including Edward II after his trouncing by the Scots at the Battle of Byland Abbey in 1322, and possibly a ninth, Richard II, was kept here as a prisoner shortly before his murder in Pontefract. The ruins are in pretty good shape, with much of the walls, keep and original towers intact, and some good views over the town and countryside. A simple chapel in the grounds dates back to 1227 and is dedicated to St Nicholas, the fourth-century Bishop of Myra – Santa Claus by any other name.

Back down in the village, you could also happily potter around the informal **Beck Isle Museum of Rural Life** on Bridge Street, behind the train station (Easter–Oct daily 10am–5pm; £2.50), or the central church of **St Peter and St Paul**, famed for a Norman font and extensive fifteenth-century frescoes, discovered in 1851 but painted over again by the local vicar who feared they'd provoke idolatry. Although crude and rather heavy-handedly restored, the scenes are still compelling, including Herod's feast, St George and the dragon and the martyrdom of Thomas à Becket.

The **tourist office**, on Eastgate car park (Easter–Oct Mon–Sat 9.30am–5.30pm, Sun 9.30am–4.30pm; Nov–Easter Mon–Sat 10am–4.30pm; ☎01751/473791, ⊛www.ryedale.gov.uk), just above the Malton/Whitby /Scarborough roundabout, can provide full timetables for the **NYMR** (see box opposite) and sell you a map of town, which you won't need. More useful are their **accommodation** lists: if you haven't made a reservation in summer, you may as well call here first to see what's still available. Tree-lined Eastgate (the Scarborough road) has the tastefully presented *Eden House* at no. 120 (☎01751/472289, ⊛www.edenhousebandb.co.uk; no credit cards; ❷) and *Heathcote House* at no. 100 (☎01751/476991; ❷); there are more modest places on the same road. *Bramwood*, 19 Hallgarth (☎01751/474066; ❷), lies through an arch off the Whitby road, a lovely eighteenth-century house with walled garden. A couple of the pubs also have rooms, top choice the *White Swan*, on the Market Place (☎01751/472288, ⊛ww.white-swan.co.uk; ❻). The nearest **youth hostel** is at the *Old School*, Lockton (☎01751/460376, ⊛www.yha.org .uk), five miles northeast off the A169 – about two miles' cross-country walk from the NYMR station at Levisham (see below), or ask to be dropped at the turn-off by the Whitby bus. The local **campsite** is at the award-winning *Upper Carr* (☎01751/473115, ⊛www.uppercarr.demon.co.uk; closed Nov–Feb), a mile and half south of town on the Malton Road. It also has on-site chalets available.

The best place to **eat and drink** in Pickering is the *White Swan*, with small, cosy beamed rooms and nice box windows in the bar from which to survey the passing scene. There's good beer, lunchtime bar snacks and a fine restaurant with a French-tinged menu. None of the cafés are up to much bar the *Tea Shop*, 26 Hungate, which uses local ceramic crockery and has a good range of teas, coffees and cakes. Out of town, opposite the campground entrance, is the *Black Bull*, which serves breakfast, lunch and dinner. **Market** day in town is Monday.

Walks from the North Yorkshire Moors Railway

Most people make a full return journey for the superb scenery of the roadless **Newtondale**, but if you want to combine some walking with the train rides, stop en route at one of the minor stations.

The first is **Levisham**, perfect for walks to the village of **LEVISHAM**, a mile and a half to the east, where the *Horseshoe Inn* (☎01751/460240; no credit cards; ❸) is a favourite target, especially for Sunday lunch. A steep winding road continues another mile beyond Levisham, down across the beck and then up to **LOCKTON**, where there's a youth hostel and a path due north to the **Hole of Horcum**, a bizarre natural hollow gouged by the glacial meltwaters that carved out Newtondale – the paths run back to Levisham station from here, and the entire seven-mile circuit is one of the Moors' best short walks. In the other direction, a couple of miles west of the station – and reached along

The North Yorkshire Moors Railway

One of the northeast's big tourist draws, the volunteer-run **North Yorkshire Moors Railway** connects **Pickering** with the Esk Valley (Middlesbrough–Whitby) line at **Grosmont**, 18 miles to the north. The line was completed by George Stephenson in 1835, just nine years after the opening of the Stockton and Darlington Railway, making it one of the earliest lines in the country. Even by the standards of later projects it was a remarkable feat of engineering, navigating 1-in-15 gradients and using thousands of tons of brushwood and heather-stuffed sheepskins to provide bedding for the track through the dale's extensive bogs. For twelve years carriages were pulled by horse, with steam locomotives only arriving in 1847. The line closed in 1965 and was formally reopened in 1973.

Scheduled **services** operate between mid-March and early November (plus Christmas specials), with trains running hourly to three times daily depending on the time of year. For **advance bookings and information**, call ☏01751/472508 (Mon–Fri 9am–5pm, Sat & Sun 10am–2.30pm); for the talking timetables call ☏01751/473535; or check the website at Ⓦwww.nymr.demon.co.uk. A day-return **fare** along the whole line costs £10. Part of the line's attraction, of course, are the **steam trains**, though be warned that diesels are pulled into service when the fire risk in the forests is high.

a minor road – the fascinating **Cawthorn Camps** (free access) are the only Roman camps of their kind in the world. The site's jumbled collection of earthworks, spreading over 103 acres, puzzled archeologists for years, as all the previously discovered Roman marching camps in Europe were built on precise geometrical plans. It's now known that this was a military training area, troops from York's Ninth Legion garrison being sent here on exercises, many of which obviously involved building camps. Local tribes had been assimilated easily, unlike the Picts to the north, making this a safe area for such exercises. A one-mile trail skirts the perimeter, offering grand views over the dale beyond. The easy way here, incidentally, is direct by Moorsbus from Pickering, which then runs on to Rosedale Abbey.

The second stop, **Newtondale Halt**, is only a couple of miles northwest of the Hole of Horcum, or you can head off through the extensive woods of **Cropton Forest** to the west on trails specially marked by the Forestry Commission – some forest scenes in the *Harry Potter* movie were filmed here. Comprising just a few farms and isolated houses, **STAPE** – three miles southwest through the forest – is an archetypal high moors community, perfectly placed to act as a base for local walks. At Stape you're just two miles south from the best-preserved stretch of Roman road in Europe, **Wheeldale Roman Road**, a mile of Wade's Causeway that ran from York to bases on the coast: the remains show a twenty-foot-wide stretch of sand and gravel studded by sandstone slabs and edged with kerbs and ditches, and the fact that it's plumb in the middle of open moorland only adds to its appeal. It's signposted off the untarred road from Stape to Goathland (the third stop on the railway line), perhaps the wildest and most adventurous north–south route over the moors – though anyone equipped with a decent map will also be able to find their way to the Roman road direct by track from Newtondale Halt, again around a three-mile walk.

Thornton-le-Dale

THORNTON-LE-DALE, just two miles east of Pickering, hangs onto its considerable charm despite the main A170 Scarborough road scything through its centre. Most of the houses, pubs and shops are fairly alluring, none more so than the thatched cottage near the parish church, which features in so many ads, magazine covers, chocolate boxes and calendars that it's been described as the most photographed house in Britain. There are too many cafés, gift shops and other people around for most tastes, but the old market cross, stocks and various stream-side strolls are well worth half an hour if you can get here off-season.

Various of the local **B&Bs** might entice, including *Bridgefoot House* (☎01751 /474749; no credit cards; ❷), in a prime position on the beck. There are a couple of cheaper places, too, and both the **pubs** – the *New Inn* and *Buck Inn* – also have rooms. Tearooms and bar meals aside, food in the village isn't up to much. Consider instead the four-mile diversion to the east, along the A170, to the village of **Ebberston**, where the *Grapes* pub serves large home-cooked meals.

Dalby Forest

Minor roads from Thornton-le-Dale and from the A169 (Whitby road) lead into the monumental expanse of **Dalby Forest**: drivers pay a toll (£4; road closed 9pm–7am) to join the start of a nine-mile forest drive that emerges close to Hackness, just four miles from Scarborough. It's best to make first for the **visitor centre** (April & Oct daily 10am–4pm; May, June & Sept daily 10am–5pm; July & Aug daily 10am–5.30pm; closed rest of year; ☎01751/460295, ☒www.forestry.gov.uk) at **Low Dalby**, which has information not only on the forest, one of the first to be planted after the foundation of the Forestry Commission in 1919, but also on wildlife, picnic spots and the range of marked trails scattered around the woods, varying in length from one to sixteen miles. A kiosk here sells drinks, snacks and ices. The Moorsbus calls at the centre in summer.

The best hikes are from a car park about three miles north of Low Dalby at Low Staindale, which include the Cross Cliff View Walk and the marvellous one-and-a-half mile (1hr) **Bridestones Trail** – a trail leaflet is available for the latter walk, which is of added interest for the bridestones themselves, great sandstone tors rising out of the heather that have been eroded into unearthly shapes. Similarly named outcrops are found all over the moors, and may be named for their connections with ancient fertility rites, or derive from a Norse word meaning "brink", or "boundary" stones. Another extremely popular walk or drive – trail leaflet available – takes in the **Forge Valley**, a deep-cut gorge scoured by glacial meltwaters during the last Ice Age. Start the walk (4 miles; 2hr–2hr 30min) from the Green Gate car park at the vale's northern end, three miles south of Hackness. For off-road driving adventures in the forest, contact **Langdale Quest** (Easter & May–Oct Sat, Sun & public hols; mid-July to Aug Mon–Thurs, Sat & Sun; ☎01723/882335, ☒www.langdalequest.co.uk), which rents out fully equipped 4WD vehicles for treasure-hunt-type activities along fifty miles of forest track.

Drivers or hikers looking for refreshment could do worse than aim for Hackness: a couple of miles before the village, the pub at **Langdale End**, the *Moorcock Inn*, is a real delight, traditionally furnished and attracting a steady stream of locals who drive out for the food and beer.

The Esk Valley

The northernmost reaches of the National Park are crossed by the east–west **Esk Valley**, whose pretty river flows into the sea at Whitby (p.985). It's a part of the North York Moors overlooked by many visitors – partly, one suspects, because its very attractions, at least in the eastern stretches, are its valley characteristics: there's not much moorland tramping to be done until you reach **Danby**, one of the finest of all moorland villages. Access is easy, either by road from Whitby via the A169 through Sleights, or more attractively by **train**: the North York Moors Railway connects at **Grosmont**, where you're on the **Esk Valley line** which runs between Middlesbrough and Whitby (4–5 daily).

Grosmont to Danby

GROSMONT, little more than a level-crossing, station and a couple of tea-rooms, sees plenty of summer traffic. Walkers pile off the trains to head north up the appealing rail and riverside path to Goathland (see below), three miles away, but if you're sticking with the train wait until the next stop west at **EGTON BRIDGE**. It's similarly tiny but has the bonus of a beautifully sited riverside pub, the *Horseshoe*, while half a mile north, up the steep road from the station, there's a second pub, the *Wheatsheaf*, at **EGTON** itself, serving fine meals in its restaurant. Don't confuse the other pub here, also a *Horseshoe*, with the one down by the river. At **GLAISDALE**, with its old packhorse bridge, the nearest pubs to the station are also tempting, with valley views from the *Arncliffe Arms* and the *Anglers Rest* (there's camping available here, too); again, the village itself is a steep climb away from the track.

Further west, the scenery becomes tinged by the looming moors until, at the isolated stone village of **DANBY**, you're once again within striking distance of some excellent walks, all detailed on trail leaflets available from the **Moors Centre** (Easter–Oct daily 10am–5pm; Nov, Dec & March daily 11am–4pm; Jan & Feb Sat & Sun 11am–4pm; ☏01287/660654, ⊛www.northyorkmoors-npa.gov.uk). The centre, a converted sixteenth-century farmhouse and former shooting lodge, also houses exhibitions about the local flora and fauna as well as a good tearoom. Whitby tourist office (☏01947/602674) can help with **accommodation** in local farmhouse B&Bs scattered up the sheep-laden side dales, and there's certainly much to be said for a quiet night away from the crowds. The *Duke of Wellington* (☏01287/660351; ❷), a nice pub at the cross-roads, has a few rooms. Just around the corner, the *Stonehouse Bakery & Tea Shop* is great for daytime snacks, serving olive bread or ciabatta sandwiches along-side coffee, scrumptious peanut brittle and other treats. A mile out of the village at **Ainthorpe**, the *Fox & Hounds* (☏01287/660218; ❸) looks out over the moors, its refurbished rooms and tasty homecooked food both good reasons to stop.

At **CASTLETON**, the next stop and much the largest centre hereabouts, a minor moorland road cuts south across Danby High Moor to Hutton le Hole, past the *Lion Inn* at Blakey, and since the Moorsbus runs this way in summer, it's a handy jumping-off point to reach the southern sections of the National Park. From Castleton, it's 45 minutes on to Middlesbrough, or about the same back to Whitby.

Great Ayton

On reaching **GREAT AYTON**, the North York Moors gives way to the **Cleveland Hills**, whose scattered peaks provide the buffer between the rural east of the region and the encroaching industry of Teesside to the west. The town makes a handsome enough stop, with the River Leven flowing through the middle connecting the pretty High Green and Low Green at either end of the long High Street. It's Great Ayton's **Captain Cook** connections, though, that draw most visitors: the town was the boyhood home of James Cook between 1736 (when he was 8) and 1745. The young Cook lived at Aireyholme Farm (no public access) on the outskirts of town, though after

James left to go to sea his father built a family **cottage** on Bridge Street, which was later dismantled and shipped to Melbourne, Australia in 1934; its site is marked by an obelisk of Australian granite near Low Green. Other Cook-related sights include **All Saints' Church**, also at Low Green, which the family attended and where Cook's mother Grace is buried; Cook's school, now the **Schoolroom Museum** at 47 High St (Easter–Oct daily 1–4pm; July & Aug from 11am; £2); and a **sculpture** of a youthful Cook on High Green which depicts him – bare-chested, long-locked – in Leonardo DiCaprio mode. For an afternoon's leg-stretching, a waymarked path runs northeast out of Great Ayton, past Aireyholme Farm and up to the summit of **Roseberry Topping** (1050ft), the queerly shaped conical peak visible from all over the locality – beacons were lit on top of here during the threat by the Spanish Armada. It's a reasonably stiff climb, followed by a tramp across Easby Moor to the south to the fifty-foot-high **Cook Monument** (1827) for more amazing views, before circling back to Great Ayton.

The Esk Valley **train station** lies half a mile northeast of town. **Buses** from Middlesbrough and Guisborough stop on the High Green, just back from which, in the car park, is the **tourist office** (Easter–Oct Mon–Sat 10am–4pm, Sun 1–4pm; ☎01642/722835, ⒲www.hambleton.gov.uk), which has all the relevant Cook brochures and trail guides. Great Ayton has two nice **pubs**: the *Buck* at Low Green by the river and the *Royal Oak* on High Green.

Beck Hole and Goathland

South of Grosmont, train, footpath and beck climb out of the Esk Valley towards Goathland. Only on foot will you be able to stop at **BECK HOLE**, after a couple of miles, an idyllic bridgeside hamlet focused on the *Birch Hall Inn*, one of the finest rural pubs in all England – tiny to the point of claustrophobic, still doubling as a sweet shop and store as it has for a century, and serving great slabs of sandwiches with local ham and home-baked pies.

A gentle path from the hamlet runs the mile through the fields up to **GOATHLAND**, another highly attractive village, this time set in open moorland beneath the great expanses of Wheeldale and Goathland moors. If it seems oddly familiar – and if it seems unduly crowded – it's because it's widely known as "Aidensfield", the fictional village at the centre of the *Heartbeat* TV series. Pub, shop, garage and houses are all roped in to appear in most episodes: the large car parks tell of its popularity on the tourbus circuit. Real fans won't want to miss the exhibitions and TV props contained within the **Goathland Exhibition Centre** (daily 10am–5.30pm; £2.50), a local history centre sited near St Mary's Church. Outside summer weekends, when it's packed to distraction, Goathland can still be a joy to wander, with signposts pointing you to the local sight, the **Mallyan Spout**, a seventy-foot-high waterfall. This lies half a mile or so from the imposing, stone *Mallyan Spout Hotel* on the common (☎01947/896486; ❺), itself the best place to stay, and certainly the best place to eat and drink; there are bar meals and a recommended restaurant. Plenty of other local B&Bs offer cheaper rooms; among them is *Glendale House*, on the common (☎01947/896281; ❷), a stately Victorian house with three rooms, which has also featured in *Heartbeat*.

At Goathland, you're handily poised for the hike up the moor to Wheeldale and the Roman road (see p.975), while steam trains chunter back to Pickering from the station below the village.

The North Yorkshire coast

A bracing change after the flattened seascapes of East Anglia and much of East Yorkshire, the **North Yorkshire coast** is the southernmost stretch of a cliff-edged shore that stretches almost unbroken to the Scottish border. **Scarborough** is the biggest town and resort, and the terminus for bus and rail links from York and beyond. Like many places hereabouts it has tempting sands, though the vagaries of the northern climate and the chilly North Sea waters mean that you'll probably do little more than admire them from afar. Cute **Robin Hood's Bay** is the most popular of the many Yorkshire villages, with fishing and smuggling traditions, while bluff **Staithes** – a fishing harbour on the far edge of North Yorkshire – has yet to tip over into full-blown tourist mode. **Whitby**, in between the two, is the best stopover, its fine sands and resort facilities tempered by its abbey ruins, cobbled streets, Georgian buildings and maritime heritage – more than any other local place Whitby celebrates Captain Cook as one of its own. Heading to virtually any of the smaller coastal hamlets will bring you to similar-looking but far quieter spots, and for those who want to sample the most dizzying cliff-tops, the **Cleveland Way** provides a marked path along virtually the entire length of the coast.

Hourly **buses** (fewer on Sun) run along the A171 between Scarborough and Whitby, and a similarly frequent service operates to Robin Hood's Bay, and north between Whitby and Staithes. The Yorkshire Coastliner service connects Leeds and York with Scarborough (hourly) or Whitby (2–4 daily). You can also reach Scarborough direct by **train** from York or Hull.

Scarborough

The oldest resort in the country, **SCARBOROUGH** first attracted early seventeenth-century visitors to its newly discovered mineral springs. By the 1730s, the more enterprising spa-goers were also venturing onto the sweeping local sands and dipping themselves in the bracing North Sea, popularizing the racy pastime of sea-bathing. Still fashionable in Victorian times – to whom it was "the Queen of the Watering Places" – Scarborough saw its biggest transformation after World War II, when it (and many other resorts) became a holiday haven for workers from the industrial heartlands. In the 1950s, three million visitors a year thronged the beaches, rode on the donkeys and paddled in the rock pools, enjoying the full-blooded facilities of a town that, in a memorable phrase of Paul Theroux's, "had the same ample contours as its landladies". The age of air travel changed the holiday demographics of all English resorts, but although numbers are down since its heyday, you wouldn't necessarily know it on a hot summer's day when there are long queues outside the seafront fish-and-chip shops and ice cream stalls. All the traditional ingredients of a beach resort are here in force, from superb, clean sands, kitsch amusement arcades and Kiss-Me-Quick hats to the more refined pleasures of its tightknit old-town streets and a genteel round of quiet parks and gardens.

The Town

There's no better place to acquaint yourself with the local layout than from the walls of **Scarborough Castle** (April–Oct daily 10am–6pm; Nov–March Wed–Sun 10am–1pm & 2–4pm; £2.50; EH), mounted on a jutting headland between two golden-sanded bays east of the town centre. Bronze and Iron Age relics have been found on the wooded castle crag, together with fragments of a fourth-century Roman signalling station, Saxon and Norman chapels and a

Viking camp, reputedly built by a Viking with the nickname of *Scardi* (or "hare-lip"), from which the town's name derives. The present castle consists mainly of a three-storey keep dating from the twelfth century, and a thirteenth-century barbican and raking buttressed walls which trace the cliff edge. Although besieged many times, the fortifications were never taken by assault, its only fall coming in the Civil War when the Parliamentarians starved the garrison into surrender. It took a further pounding from an infamous German naval bombardment of the town in 1914. As you leave the castle, drop into the church of **St Mary** (1180), immediately below on Castle Road, whose graveyard contains the tomb of Anne Brontë, who died here in 1849.

The town museums are clustered around Valley Road, south of the train station; a "Museum S Pass" (£2; valid for a year) gets you into each of them. The Victorian **Wood End** on The Crescent (June–Sept Tues–Sun 10am–5pm; Oct–May Wed, Sat & Sun 11am–4pm) was the holiday home of the Sitwell family of writers and aesthetes. There's a fine conservatory and various natural history collections, while in the adjacent **Art Gallery** (June–Sept Tues–Sun 10am–5pm; Oct–May Thurs, Fri & Sat 11am–4pm) you'll find changing art exhibitions. The nearby **Rotunda Museum** on Vernon Road (June–Sept Tues–Sun 10am–5pm; Oct–April Tues, Sat & Sun 11am–4pm), housed in a circular Georgian rotunda of great refinement, holds the local archeological and historic finds, including Gristhorpe Man, a 3500-year-old local found buried with his grave goods in a hollowed oak trunk; there's also a diverting exhibition on the famous **Scarborough Fair**, first granted a charter by Henry III in 1253. After this, the chief distraction is the unexpected concentration of Pre-Raphaelite art in the church of **St-Martin-on-the-Hill** (1863) further south on Albion Road. The Victorian-Gothic pile has a roof by William Morris, a triptych by Burne-Jones, a pulpit with four printed panels by Rossetti, stained glass by Morris, Burne-Jones and Ford Madox Brown, and an east wall whose tracery provides the frames for angels by Morris and *The Adoration of the Magi* by Burne-Jones.

The bays

Most of what passes for family entertainment takes place on the **North Bay** – massive water slides at Atlantis, the kids' amusements at Kinderland, and the miniature North Bay Railway (daily Easter–Sept), which runs up to the most educational of the lot, the **Sea Life Centre**, with its pools of flounders, rock-pool habitats and fishy exhibits. The most enjoyable **amusements and rides** are the old-fashioned ones on the harbour, under the castle, where creaky dodgems and shooting galleries compete for custom. From the harbourside here you'll be able to take one of the short **cruises and speedboat trips** that shoot off throughout the day in the summer; or look over the *Hatherleigh*, a deep-sea trawler permanently moored on the Lighthouse Pier.

The **South Bay** is more refined, backed by the pleasant Valley Gardens and the Italianate meanderings of the South Cliff Gardens, and topped by an esplanade from which a **hydraulic lift** (daily 10am–4pm, till 10pm July & Aug) putters down to the beach. Here, Scarborough's Regency and Victorian glories are still evident in hotels like the *Crown* and, most impressively of all, the **Grand Hotel** built in 1867 by Cuthbert Broderick, the shaper of central Leeds. Its six million bricks and fifty-two chimneys dominate the cliff-top, an ensemble which drew high praise from architectural arbiter Nikolaus Pevsner, who thought it a "high Victorian gesture of assertion and confidence". For years now it's been operated as a pack-'em-in-cheap lodging house, which means no one will stop you if you stroll in through the still-grand interior, buy a drink at the bar and head out onto the gargantuan, neglected terrace from which the views of town, beach and castle are magnificent.

It's a fair hike from one end of Scarborough to the other; ease the strain by taking one of the **seafront buses** which run throughout the summer from the *Corner Café* in North Bay to the Spa Complex in South Bay.

Arrival, information and accommodation

The **train station** is at the top of town facing Westborough; buses pull up outside or in the surrounding streets, though the National Express services (direct from London) stop in the car park behind the station. Scarborough's **tourist office** is in Pavilion House, Valley Bridge Rd (daily: May–Sept 9.30am–6pm; Oct–April 10am–4.30pm; ☎01723/373333, ⍵www.ycc.org.uk), just over the road from the station, diagonally opposite the landmark Stephen Joseph Theatre. To reach the harbour and castle, walk straight down Westborough, Newborough and Eastborough, through the main shopping streets.

Scarborough is crammed with inexpensive **hotels and guest houses**. In high season, if you arrive without a reservation, you'd do best to head straight for the tourist office and let them find something; at other times it's worth looking around for the best deals, since off-season prices often drop considerably. Happy hunting grounds include North Bay's Queen's Parade, where most of the guest houses have sweeping bay views and parking; to be closer to the castle head up its continuation, Blenheim Terrace, where a score more options await. The cheapest places in town are those without the sea views – try along central Aberdeen Walk (off Westborough), or on North Marine Road and Trafalgar Square, behind Queen's Parade. Above South Bay, hotels tend to be pricier, though there's a clutch of B&Bs along and around West Street.

Hotels and guest houses

Hotel Anatolia 21 West St ☎01723/360864. Nice old Victorian redbrick, one block back from the Esplanade, on a street full of similar choices. No credit cards. ❷

Crown Hotel Esplanade ☎01723/373491, ⍵www.ScarboroughHotel.com. Built in 1847 in a Regency terrace above South Bay, the *Crown* makes the most of its period features, views and genteel feel. There's a gym and pool. Full board rates offer the best deal. ❻

Interludes 32 Princess St ☎01723/360513, ⍵www.homepage.ntlworld.com/interludes. Quiet, non-smoking, Georgian town house in the old-town streets behind the harbour. Bay views from the upper floors, and theatre bills, photographs and traditional English decor throughout; call for details of Stephen Joseph Theatre breaks. ❸

Paragon Hotel 123 Queen's Parade ☎01723 /372676, ⍵www.paragon-hotel.demon.co.uk. Standard B&B rooms, though an above-average breakfast lifts the spirits. Parking available. ❷

Red Lea Hotel Prince of Wales Terrace ☎01723/362431, ⍵www.redleahotel.co.uk. Part of a stylish terrace above South Bay, boasting sea-view rooms and a small indoor pool. B&B ❺, full board ❻.

Riviera St Nicholas Cliff ☎01723/372277. Restored Victorian hotel opposite the Grand (down Bar St, off Westborough) with super bay views and en-suite rooms. ❸

Whiteley Hotel 99 Queen's Parade ☎01723 /373514. Formerly a Victorian merchant's house (its best facade facing North Marine Rd, around the back), this is one of the best Queen's Parade options with good-value en-suite rooms (a few pounds extra for a sea view). Parking available. ❷

Youth hostel and campsites

Scarborough YHA Burniston Rd, Scalby Mills ☎01723/361176, ℮scarborough@yha.org.uk. Occupies a converted watermill, a mile or so north of the town centre on the A165 and ten minutes' walk from the Sea Life Centre and the sea; the Cleveland Way passes close by.

Scalby Close Park Burniston Rd ☎01723/365908. Tents and caravans. Closed Nov–Easter.

Scalby Manor Caravan Park Burniston Rd ☎01723/366212. There are tent spaces at this huge site, handy for the North Bay. Closed Nov–Easter.

Eating, drinking and nightlife

Cafés, fish-and-chip shops and **tearooms** are thick on the ground: those down by the harbour are of variable quality and popularity, serving up fried food as fast as the punters can get it down. There's a more discerning selection when it comes to **restaurants**, not least because the town has a fair-sized Italian population – including the descendants of several POWs who were held at Malton's Eden Camp (see p.954) and settled in Scarborough after the war.

Virtually every street too has a **pub**, though few pass muster as the sort of place you might want to spend the entire evening – the best are picked out below. Finally, whatever the posters and advertising suggest, the cultural heart of Scarborough is not the Spa Complex or Futurist Theatre and their end-of-pier summer shows but the renowned **Stephen Joseph Theatre**, a real North Yorkshire gem.

Cafés and restaurants

Bonnet Huntriss Row, off Westborough, ☎01723/361033. The Victorian-styled pedestrianized street has several coffee shops worth investigating: this one also opens for dinner (Wed–Sat until 9.30pm). Inexpensive.

Café Italia 36 St Nicholas Cliff. Utterly charming, microscopic Italian coffee bar next to the *Grand Hotel*, where genuine coffee, focaccia slices and ice cream keep a battery of regulars happy. Inexpensive.

Il Castello 34–36 Castle Rd, ☎01723/377312. The town's best pizzas, and some inventive home-made pastas and other Italian dishes, at slightly higher prices than usual. Closed Mon & Tues. Moderate.

Florio's 37 Aberdeen Walk, off Westborough, ☎01723/351124. Cheery pasta-and-pizza restaurant, popular with families and parties, open evenings only. Moderate.

Gianni's 13 Victoria Rd, ☎01723/507388. The most immediately welcoming of the town's Italian restaurants, housed in a Scarborough town house. The good-natured staff bustle up and down stairs, delivering quality pizzas, pastas and quaffable wine by the carafe. Moderate.

The Golden Grid 4 Sandside, ☎01723/360922. The harbourside's choicest fish-and-chip establishment, "catering for the promenader since 1883". Offers grilled fish, a *fruits-de-mer* platter and a wine list alongside the standard crispy-battered fry-up. Closed Mon–Thurs dinner in winter. Inexpensive–Moderate.

Lanterna 33 Queen St, ☎01723/363616. Long-established, special-night-out destination, featuring traditional, seasonal Italian cooking in quiet, formal surroundings. Closed Sun. Expensive.

Stephen Joseph Theatre Restaurant Westborough, ☎01723/368463. Fashionable food in the theatre restaurant including bangers and mash, French and Med-inspired mains, seasonal salads and desserts. Closed Sun, and other evenings when there's no performance. Moderate.

Pubs

The Alma Alma Parade, at the top of Westborough. A thoroughly decent local, just right for a quiet pint.

The Highlander The Esplanade, next to the Crown. A traditional lounge bar with beer garden. Its owner has a collection of over a thousand bottles of whisky – drams from around fifty of them are for sale.

Hole in the Wall Vernon Rd. Cosy, real-ale haunt with beer-knowledgeable staff and good food (served noon–2pm).

Nightlife

Stephen Joseph Theatre corner of Westborough and Valley Bridge Road ☎01723/370541, ⓦwww .sjt.uk.com. Housed in a former Art Deco cinema, this premieres every new play of local playwright Alan Ayckbourn and promotes strong seasons of theatre and film; a good café/restaurant and bar is open daily except Sunday.

Hayburn Wyke and Ravenscar

At **Hayburn Wyke**, a tiny and tranquil bay mostly owned by the National Trust, Hayburn Beck runs through scrub and woodland before tumbling onto the rocky beach in a small waterfall. The waters have carved away layers of the surrounding boulder clay, making this a good spot to forage for fossils. The Cleveland Way cuts through from Scarborough, six miles to the south, but road access takes you only as far as the *Hayburn Wyke Hotel*, half a mile back from the beach, an arrangement which keeps the bay area and the adjoining 34-acre nature reserve remarkably unspoilt.

A back-lane drive, or a four-mile hike – one of the Cleveland Way's more exhilarating passages – over the five-hundred-foot ramparts of **Beast Cliff**, brings you to the village of **RAVENSCAR**, six hundred feet above the sea in the lee of tumuli-spotted Stoupe Brow (871ft). Views to the north around the sweep of Robin Hood's Bay are superb, particularly from the mock-battlemented *Raven Hall Hotel* (☎01723/870353, ⓦwww.ravenhall.co.uk; ❻), constructed on the site of an old Roman signal station and used as a hideaway for George III when his bouts of madness kept him from the public gaze. There's a small charge for non-patrons to wander the hotel's panoramic cliff-edge terraces or to use the Yorkshire coast's most precariously sited and windswept swimming pool. The hotel marks the end of the Lyke Wake Walk (see p.965), so it's not uncommon to see hikers celebrating with a beer in front of the open fire.

Close by is a National Trust **Coastal Centre** (Easter–Sept daily 10.30am–5pm; ☎01723/870138), which has displays on the village's dead-end streets and isolated houses, part of an 1895 scheme to create "another Scarborough", an enterprise foiled by the cliffs' unstable geology. Also featured are the fossils that can be found on the coast immediately below; it's well worth scrambling down the path to the left of the hotel, but take great care on the foreshore, where the tide is fast-rising – explore on the ebb tide only and don't be tempted into swimming. The most detailed exhibits, however, relate to the area's **alum mines**. Quarries dot the Old Peak cliffs and the ridges of Stoupe Brow, where alum was mined between 1640 and 1862, the mineral being used in the leather and textile industry to fix dyes, and in the manufacture of candles and parchment. The industry declined in the nineteenth century, as chemical byproducts of the iron and steel foundries came to replace alum in many of the processes in which it had been used. The last mine closed in 1871, and a marked trail from the centre takes you past re-excavated workings.

B&B is available at *Smugglers Rock*, a Georgian country house with good views (☎01723/870044, ⓦwww.smugglersrock.co.uk; no credit cards; ❷; closed mid-Oct to Feb). *Bent Rigg Farm* (☎01723/870475), a little way south-east of the church, has a bunkhouse and space for camping (closed Nov–April).

Robin Hood's Bay

Although known as Robbyn Huddes Bay as early as Tudor times, there's nothing except half-remembered myth to link **ROBIN HOOD'S BAY** with Sherwood's legendary bowman – locals anyway prefer the old name, Bay Town or simply Bay. Perhaps the best-known and most heavily visited spot on the coast, the village fully lives up to its reputation, with narrow streets and pink-tiled cottages toppling down the cliff-edge site, evoking the romance of a time when this was both a hard-bitten fishing community and smugglers' den *par excellence*. So packed together are the houses, legend has it that ill-gotten booty could be passed up the hill from cottage to cottage without the pursuing king's men being any the wiser.

From the upper village, lined with Victorian villas, now mostly B&Bs, it's a 1-in-3 walk down the hill to the harbour. Here, Bay is little more than a couple of narrow streets lined with gift shops and cafés, and a steep slipway that leads down to the curving, rocky **shoreline**. When the tide is out, the massive rock beds are exposed, split by a geological fault line and studded with fossil remains. There's an easy walk to **Boggle Hole** and its youth hostel, a mile south, returning inland via South House Farm and the path along the old Scarborough–Whitby railway line (see below). Back in the old village, a rash of second-hand bookshops has appeared, the biggest and best being The Old Chapel, in the old hillside Wesleyan Chapel. Author **Leo Walmsley** (1892–1966), who spent his childhood in Bay, was educated in the chapel's schoolroom and later wrote several novels of seaside life coloured by his experiences. One, *Three Fevers*, was filmed in Robin Hood's Bay and Whitby as *Turn of the Tide* (1935), the first feature by the newly formed J. Arthur Rank organization.

Practicalities

The main approach, the B1447, comes in from the north off the A171, and drivers will have to leave their car in one of two **car parks** in the upper part of the village. **Buses** from Scarborough or Whitby, seven miles north, drop you here too. Whitby has the nearest train station, and the nearest tourist office (see opposite); **walkers**, along the coastal Cleveland Way, can make Whitby to Robin Hood's Bay in around three hours.

Accommodation is plentiful, but often in short supply during high season. Many people see the village as a day-trip from Whitby, and you can check on Bay accommodation in the tourist office there, or simply stroll the streets of the lower, old part of the village to see if any of the small cottage B&Bs have got vacancies. There are also three good **pubs** in the lower village, two of which have rooms: the tiny *Laurel*, on Main Street (☏01947/880400; ❶; two-night minimum), whose small self-catering flat sleeps two; and the *Bay Hotel*, right on the harbour (☏01947/880278; ❸), which is the traditional start or end of the Coast-to-Coast Walk. As well as a score of guest houses in the upper village, there's the late-Victorian *Victoria Hotel*, Station Rd (☏01947/880205; ❹), at the top of the hill, with fine views from some of its rooms, and a cliff-top beer garden. You'll probably end up **eating** in the pubs – food at the *Bay Horse* is the best – though the *Bramblewick Tearooms* near the harbour is open in the early evenings in summer and serves home-made meals and fresh fish. *The Old Chapel* bookshop has a vegetarian café, super coastal views from its terrace tables and weekly folk gigs; and *Bay Fisheries*, a wet-fish shop next to the *Laurel*, serves crab sandwiches to take away. The other pub, the eighteenth-century *Dolphin* in King Street, is the oldest in the village, and has folk nights every Friday.

Boggle Hole's **youth hostel** is one of Yorkshire's most popular, a former mill located in a wooded ravine about a mile south of Robin Hood's Bay at Mill Beck (☏01947/880352, ⊛www.yha.org.uk). Note that a torch is essential after dark, and that you can't access the hostel along the beach once the tide is up.

Hawsker

The twenty-mile Whitby to Scarborough railway line was a victim of the 1960s' cuts, though its length has been preserved as a bridleway which makes an alternative route to the Cleveland Way. The best section is undoubtedly that between Whitby and Ravenscar via Robin Hood's Bay, boasting huge views of the tumbling cliffs and sparkling sea. A couple of miles northwest of Robin Hood's Bay at **HAWSKER**, on the A171, Trailways (☏01947/820207, ⊛www.trailways.fsnet.co.uk) is a bike rental outfit based in the old Hawsker train station, perfectly placed for day-trips along the largely flat railway line in either direction. They'll deliver or pick up from local addresses (including Boggle Hole youth hostel); there's also a refreshments kiosk at the station, a small campsite and bunkhouse.

Whitby

If there's one essential stop on the North Yorkshire coast it's **WHITBY**, whose historical associations, atmospheric ruins, fishing harbour and intrinsic charm make it many people's favourite northern resort. The seventh-century abbey here made Whitby one of the key foundations of the early Christian period, and a centre of great learning, though little interfered with the fishing community which scraped together a living on the harbour banks of the River Esk below. For a thousand years, the local herring boats landed their catch until the great whaling boom of the eighteenth century transformed the fortunes of the town. Melville's *Moby Dick* makes much of Whitby whalers such as William

Bram Stoker and Dracula

For a moment or two I could see nothing, as the shadow of a cloud obscured St Mary's Church. Then as the cloud passed I could see the ruins of the Abbey coming into view; and as the edge of a narrow band of light as sharp as a sword-cut moved along, the church and churchyard became gradually visible... [It] seemed to me as though something dark stood behind the seat where the white figure shone, and bent over it. What it was, whether man or beast, I could not tell.

Dracula, Bram Stoker

It was, of course, the figure of the voracious Count, feasting upon the blood of Lucy. Her friend Mina Murray – despite "flying along the fish-market to the bridge" and "toiling" up the endless steps to the Abbey – failed to save her. The story of Dracula is well known, but it's this exact attention to the geographical detail of Whitby – little changed since Stoker first wrote the words – which has proved a huge attraction to visitors on the Dracula trail.

Bram Stoker was born in Dublin in 1847 and wrote his first stories while working in the Irish civil service. A meeting with Sir Henry Irving in 1877 led him to quit his job and move to London, where he became Irving's manager and close friend. Forgettable adventure novels followed, until in 1890, on holiday in Whitby, Stoker began to become interested in writing a story of vampires and the undead, already popularized in "Gothic" novels earlier that century. Using first-hand observation of a town he knew well – he stayed at a house on the West Cliff, now marked by a plaque – Stoker built a story which mixed real locations, legend, myth and historical fact: the grounding of Count Dracula's ship on Tate Hill Sands was based on an actual event reported in the local papers. The novel was published in 1897 and became synonymous with Stoker's name; it's been filmed, with varying degrees of faithfulness, dozens of times since, though no film version has yet used Whitby as a backdrop.

With many of the early chapters recognizably set in Whitby, it's hardly surprising that the town has cashed in on its **Dracula Trail** – ask at the tourist office for details. The various sites – Tate Hill Sands, the abbey, church and steps, the graveyard, Stoker's house – can all be visited, while down on the harbourside the Dracula Experience attempts to pull in punters to its rather lame horror-show antics. Keen interest has also been sparked amongst the **Goth** fraternity, who now come to town en masse a couple of times a year (usually in late spring and around Halloween) for a vampire's ball, concerts and readings; at these times the streets are overrun with pasty-faced characters in Regency dress, wedding gowns, top hats and capes, meeting and greeting at their unofficial headquarters, the otherwise sedate *Elsinore* pub on Flowergate. A kind of truce has been called with the authorities at St Mary's church, who understandably objected to the more lurid goings-on in the churchyard at midnight; these have largely been curtailed and now there's even a special Goths service held at the church.

Scoresby, while James Cook took his first seafaring steps from the town in 1746, on his way to becoming a national hero. All four of Captain Cook's ships of discovery – the *Endeavour, Resolution, Adventure* and *Discovery* – were built in Whitby: the return of the replica *Endeavour* in 1997, billed as the "homecoming", attracted a crowd of 100,000; there are also plans to moor a replica *Resolution* in town.

Hemmed in by steep cliffs and divided by the River Esk, the town splits into two distinct halves joined by a swing bridge: the **old town** to the east, centred on a curving cobbled street of great character, and the newer (though mostly eighteenth- and nineteenth-century) town across the bridge, generally known as **West Cliff**, which is home to the quayside, most of the hotels and shops, and the few arcades, amusements and souvenir stalls that have been allowed to proliferate. Virtually everything you want to see is in or above the old town on the east side, principally the glorious Abbey ruins and St Mary's church, and the Captain Cook Memorial Museum, though the town museum on the west side shouldn't be missed by anyone with a nostalgic bent.

Walkers should note that two of the best parts of the Cleveland Way depart from Whitby: southeast to Robin Hood's Bay (six miles) and northwest to Staithes (eleven miles), both along thrilling high-cliff sections.

The old town and abbey

Cobbled **Church Street** is the old town's main thoroughfare, barely changed in aspect since the eighteenth century, though now lined with tearooms and gift shops, many selling jewellery and ornaments made from **jet**. This hard, black natural carbon, found locally, was worn first by the Romans but received its greatest boost after being shown at the Great Exhibition of 1851, after which it was popularized as mourning wear. In nineteenth-century Whitby, the industry employed over a thousand people, many working in factories around Church Street; now just a handful of workshops remain. Parallel Sandgate has more of the same, the two streets meeting at the small marketplace where souvenirs and trinkets are sold. Off either side, impossibly skinny alleys ("yards") – once gated, to keep out thieves – lead to quiet courtyards and flower-decked cottages.

At the end of Church Street, you climb the famous **199 steps** of the Church Stairs – now paved, but originally a wide wooden staircase built for pallbearers carrying coffins to the church of St Mary above. Having made the climb, you've followed in the fictional footsteps of Bram Stoker's **Dracula**, who in the eponymous novel (see box below) takes the form of a large dog that bounds up the steps after the wreck of the ship bearing his coffin. In the precarious cliffside graveyard he claimed Lucy as his victim, taking refuge in the grave of a suicide victim, which he then used as a base for his nocturnal forays. On wild and windswept nights the atmosphere up here is still suitably ghoulish; during the day, the views over the harbour and town are magnificent, while a little searching reveals the grave of William Scoresby Snr, master whaler, and inventor of the crow's nest.

The bizarre parish church of **St Mary** at the top of the steps, loftily removed from the town it served, is an architectural dog's dinner dating back to 1110, boasting a Norman chancel arch, a profusion of eighteenth-century panelling, box pews unequalled in England and a triple-decker pulpit – note the built-in ear trumpets, added for the benefit of a nineteenth-century rector's deaf wife. The Cholmley family pew, in particular, almost obscuring the chancel, is superb, a capricious confection of twisting wooden columns. Notice also the galleries, arranged like a ship's decks, and the roof, constructed by seventeenth-century naval carpenters as if part of a ship's cabin.

The cliff-top ruins of **Whitby Abbey** (daily: April–Sept 10am–6pm; Oct–March 10am–4pm; £1.80; EH), beyond St Mary's, are some of the most evocative in England, the nave, soaring north transept and lancets of the east end giving a hint of the building's former delicacy and splendour. Its monastery was founded in 657 by St Hilda of Hartlepool, daughter of King Oswy of Northumberland, and by 664 had become important enough to host the **Synod of Whitby**, an event of seminal importance in the development of English Christianity. It settled once and for all the question of determining the date of Easter, and adopted the rites and authority of the Roman rather than the Celtic Church. One of the burning issues decided was whether priests should shave their tonsures in the shape of a ring or a crescent. **Caedmon**, one of the brothers at the abbey during its earliest years who was reputedly charged with looking after Hilda's pigs, has a twenty-foot cross to his memory which stands in front of St Mary's, at the top of the steps. His nine-line *Song of Creation* is the earliest surviving poem in English, making the abbey not only the cradle of English Christianity, but also the birthplace of English literature. The original abbey was destroyed by the Danes in 867 and refounded by the Benedictines in 1078, though most of the present ruins – built slightly south of the site of the Saxon original – date from between 1220 and 1539.

Whitby likes to make a fuss of Captain Cook who served an apprenticeship here from 1746–49 under John Walker, a Quaker shipowner. The **Captain Cook Memorial Museum** (Easter–Oct daily 9.45am–5pm; March Sat & Sun 11am–3pm; £2.80; ⓦwww.cookmuseumwhitby.co.uk), housed in Walker's rickety old house in Grape Lane (just over the bridge on the east side, on the right), contains an impressive amount of memorabilia, including ships' models, letters and paintings by artists seconded to Cook's voyages. The 18-year-old Cook assisted on the coal runs between Newcastle and London, learning his seafaring skills in flat-bottomed craft called "cats". Designed for inshore and river work their specifications were to prove perfect for Cook's later surveys of the South Sea Islands and the Australian coast. When he wasn't at sea, Cook, together with the other apprentices, slept in Walker's attic.

West Cliff

Whitby developed as a holiday resort in the nineteenth century, partly under the influence of entrepreneur George Hudson, who had brought the railway to town. Wide streets, elegant crescents, boarding houses and hotels were laid on the heights of **West Cliff**, across the harbour from the old town, topped by a whalebone arch, commemorating Whitby's former industry, and a statue of Captain Cook. The small **harbour front** below, along Pier Road, sports an active fish market and a run of arcades and chip shops, leading to the twin, pincered piers and lighthouses: when the tide's out, the broad, clean sands to the west stretch for three miles to **Sandsend** (where the beer garden of the *Hart Inn* makes a tempting target).

More matters maritime are explored in the **Whitby Lifeboat Museum** (irregular hours; donation requested), on Pier Road, the best museum of its kind in the country. Whitby lifeboat crews over the years have won more RNLI gold medals for gallantry than any other crew in Britain; you'd envy none of them the job, particularly after seeing one exhibit, the last RNLI hand-rowed boat, a flimsy-looking craft used until well into this century. A more recent lifeboat now carries passengers out of the harbour on short **cruises**, leaving from the bandstand most summer days.

Final port of call should be the gloriously eccentric **Whitby Museum** in Pannett Park (May–Sept Mon–Sat 9.30am–5.30pm, Sun 2–5pm; Oct–April

Mon–Tues 10.30am–1pm, Wed–Sat 10.30am–4pm, Sun 2–4pm; £2), at the back of West Cliff, back from the train station. There's more Cook memorabilia, including various of the ethnic objects and stuffed animals brought back as souvenirs by his crew, as well as casefuls of exhibits devoted to Whitby's seafaring tradition, its whaling industry in particular. Some of the best and largest fossils of Jurassic period reptiles unearthed on the east coast are also preserved here, while the rest of the museum is a fine jumble of local material, all carefully annotated in spidery handwriting and on clunky typed cards.

Arrival, information and accommodation

Trains on the Esk Valley line to Whitby from Middlesbrough, via Danby and Grosmont (for connections for the North Yorkshire Moors Railway), arrive at the station in Station Square, a couple of hundred yards south of the bridge to the old town. Most local **buses** leave from the adjacent bus station, though the Yorkshire Coastliner services (from Leeds, York and Pickering) and National Express buses (from London and York) stop around the corner on Langborne Road, just down from the tourist office. There's a Travel Centre (☎01947/602146) in the train station, for all local transport enquiries.

Whitby's **tourist office** (daily: May–Sept 9.30am–6pm; Oct–April 10am–12.30pm & 1–4.30pm; ☎01947/602674, ⊛www.ycc.org.uk) is a right turn outside the train station to the corner of Langborne Road and New Quay Road, and will book accommodation.

The main B&B concentrations are on West Cliff, in the streets stretching back from the elegant Royal Crescent. Across the river in the old town, several pubs have rooms, while if you're prepared to travel a couple of miles out of Whitby you can find some pleasant inns and hotels in relaxed country surroundings.

Hotels, B&Bs and guest houses

Beehive Newholm, ☎01947/602703. Isolated country pub in a hamlet a couple of miles inland, reached on the Sandsend road, with a roaring log fire in winter and sunny space outside in summer. **②**

Bramblewick 3 Havelock Place, ☎01947 /604504. Rather grand Victorian house which retains its original fireplaces and wrought-iron balconies. The old attic rooms at the top have the best views. Two-night minimum stay. **②**

Duke of York Church St, ☎01947/600324. At the bottom of the 199 steps, this popular pub has en-suite rooms overlooking the harbour, and is only a few steps from the harbour beach. **②**

Dunsley Hall Dunsley, ☎01947/893437. Quite the grandest retreat in the locality, this stately oak-panelled pile has all the trimmings, including a pool, sauna and leisure club, a good restaurant and very cosy bar. It's a couple of miles inland (west) of town. **⑦**

Estbek House Sandsend, ☎01947/893424, ⊛www.fastfix.com/estbek. Georgian house with five rooms, restaurant and tea garden, overlooking the stream at Sandsend, a couple of miles from

Whitby, just yards from the beach and next to a good pub. **③**

Middle Earth 26 Church St, ☎01947/606014. A nice pub with rooms, decent beer and outdoor seats overlooking the marina. It's the other way down Church Street from the 199 steps, back past the bridge and along the river. No credit cards. **②**

Number Five 5 Havelock Place, ☎01947/606361. Amiable West Cliff B&B which provides a good breakfast (veggie options available) and has a laid-back atmosphere. There are four doubles and a couple of singles, each with small but smart shower rooms. No credit cards. **②**

Shepherd's Purse 95 Church St, ☎01947/820228. Popular wholefood shop and restaurant with its best rooms (with brass bedsteads and pine furniture) set around a galleried courtyard. The two pricier doubles on the upper level are nicest; one has its own balcony. Vegetarian breakfast available. **③**

White Horse & Griffin Church St, ☎01947/604857. Easily the most atmospheric place to stay in the old town – a welcoming eighteenth-century coaching inn with comfortable en-suite rooms (some have antique panelling, others a rooftop view), open fires and a good restaurant. **③**

Hostels and campsite

Harbour Grange Spital Bridge, Church St
⊕01947/600817. Non-smoking backpackers on
the eastern side of the river with 24 beds in five
small dorms. Self-catering kitchen and lounge;
curfew at 11.30pm.

Sandfield House Caravan Park Sandsend Rd
⊕01947/602660. This is the nearest campsite, a
mile west of town on the Sandsend road, though it
only has a few tent sites. Closed Nov–Easter.

Whitby Backpackers 28 Hudson St ⊕01947
/601794 ⓔmartin@warrener65.freeserve.co.uk.
Easygoing West Cliff backpackers with 20 beds in
a variety of rooms, including a couple of private
rooms (❶) and en-suite family rooms (❶). There's
a kitchen and lounge, free tea and coffee, and no
curfew. Closed Jan & Feb.

Whitby YHA East Cliff ⊕01947/602878. A converted stable a stone's throw from the abbey, with
superb views over the town. One room sleeps two
(❶), otherwise beds in variously-sized dorms –
book well in advance. Self-catering kitchen,
evening meal available.

Eating, drinking and entertainment

Unsurprisingly, Whitby is well known for its freshly caught fish. A multitude of
cafés around town – especially along Pier Road and Bridge Street – serve **fish
and chips**, bread and tea for around £4; the same thing in most of the **restaurants** costs a few pounds more. Whitby is at the centre of the local **music
scene**, with especially good folk nights in some of its **pubs** – English folk's first
family, the Waterson/Carthys, are from nearby Robin Hood's Bay. It all comes
to a head during the annual **Whitby Folk Week** in August (the week immediately preceding the bank holiday), when the town's streets, pubs and concert
halls are filled day and night with singers, bands, traditional dancers, storytellers
and music workshops. A special festival campsite is usually set up, but if you
want regular accommodation for this week, book well in advance. Other festivals throughout the year also make a splash, some with a seafaring theme: the
Regatta every August is a weekend of fairground rides, spectacular harbourside fireworks and boat races; and the **Goths** descend a couple of times a year
(see box on p.985) for a good-natured vampiric vacation.

Cafés and restaurants

Grapevine 2 Grape Lane, ⊕01947/820275. Tiny,
funky, dinner-only place dishing up great tapas-
style meals, from creamy butter-bean stew to
Spanish chicken. Closed Sun & Mon. Inexpensive.

Green's 13 Bridge St, ⊕01947/600284. Whitby's
best and most relaxed restaurant, where chef Rob
Green produces stylish meals – using local fish,
lamb and game – with contemporary flavours. Wed
night is usually music-and-world buffet night.
Moderate.

Huntsman Inn Aislaby, ⊕01947/810637. It's well
worth driving (or cabbing) out the couple of miles
to Aislaby for the home-cooked pub food here –
steaks a speciality. Inexpensive.

Java 2 Flowergate ⊕01947/821973,
ⓦwww.java-online.co.uk. From early till late,
seven days a week, for cappuccino, latte, all-day
breakfasts, grilled sandwiches, the daily papers –
even internet surfing. Inexpensive.

Magpie Café 14 Pier Rd, ⊕01947/602058. The
traditional fish-and-chip choice in town for over
forty years, with a wide-ranging menu. In summer
you'll have to wait in long queues to get through
the doors. Closes 9pm. Moderate.

Trenchers New Quay Rd, ⊕01947/603212. Highly
rated fish-and-chip restaurant, near the tourist
office, with snappy service and mountainous portions – nearly always a queue in summer. Closes
9pm & all Nov–March. Moderate.

White Horse & Griffin Church St, ⊕01947
/604857. When it's on top of its game, the restaurant
here is a real winner – well-cooked local fish and
game, served in cosy bistro surroundings. Expensive.

Pubs and live music

Black Horse 91 Church St. Idiosyncratic old-town
"heritage" pub with a tiny front bar and good
Tetley's beer.

Duke of York Church St. Classic Whitby pub, at
the bottom of the 199 steps, with harbour views
and a mixed clientele of tourists and locals who
come for the good-value food and occasional
music.

Middle Earth 26 Church St. Regular music nights
at this local, down by the marina – outdoor seats
provide harbour views.

Tap & Spile New Quay Rd. The town's real-ale
haunt, with a changing selection of guest beers
and live music nearly every night.

Staithes

Beyond the beach at Sandsend, a fine coastal walk through pretty Runswick Bay leads in around four hours to the fishing village of **STAITHES**; road access is along the A174. At first sight, it's an improbably beautiful grouping of huddled stone houses around a small harbour, backed by the severe outcrop of Cowbar Nab, a sheer cliff face which protects the northern flank of the village. There's much less tourism here than in Robin Hood's Bay, which means few if any gift shops and only a smattering of cafés and B&Bs. Any time spent here, especially out of season, soon reveals its gruffer side – crumbling houses on either side of the beck, the fierce winter wind whistling down the cobbled main street, and the tenacious last gasp of a declining fishing fleet which once employed 300 men in 120 boats. Storms and floods have battered Staithes for centuries: the *Cod and Lobster*, the pub at the harbour, has been rebuilt three times and is shuttered against the wind, while the draper's shop in which James Cook first worked before moving to Whitby collapsed completely in 1745 – its rebuilt successor is now marked by a plaque. Cook is remembered in the **Captain Cook and Staithes Heritage Centre**, on the High Street (daily 10am–5.30pm; £1.75), which re-creates an eighteenth-century street among other interesting exhibits. Other than this, you'll have to content yourself with pottering about the rocks near the harbour – there's no beach to speak of – or clambering the nearby cliffs for spectacular views; at **Boulby**, a mile and a half's trudge up the coastal path (45min), you're walking on the highest cliff (670ft) on England's east coast. You may also be interested to learn that the coast between Whitby and Staithes has some of the best **surf** waves in Britain and there's quite a local community dedicated to riding them – details and gear from Zero Gravity (℡01947/820660), Whitby's surfshop at 14 Flowergate.

Practicalities

The road into Staithes, off the A174, puts drivers into a **car park** at the top of the hill leading down into the old village; don't ignore the signs and drive down, since there's nowhere to park, and it's hard work turning round again. You could stay at one of the B&Bs in the houses at the top of the village, but better **accommodation** is available down below, either at the *Endeavour Restaurant* (℡01947/840825; no credit cards; closed Sun in winter) – itself the best place to eat for miles around, with superb (but pricey) fresh fish meals – or at one of the pubs; the *Black Lion* (℡01947/841132; ❷) has functional bedrooms, cosy fires and a decent bar menu. There's **camping** back up the road out of the village at *Staithes Caravan Park*, Warp Mill (℡01947/840291; closed Nov–Feb).

Travel details

Buses

Details of minor local bus services are frequently given in the text. It's essential to pick up either the Dales Connections or Moors Connections timetable booklets from a local tourist office if you are visiting those parts of the county. For details of the Moorsbus in the North York Moors National Park see p.964. For information on all other local and national bus services, contact Traveline: ℡0870/608 2 608 (daily 7am–9pm), www.traveline.org.uk.

Trains

Main routes and services are given below. For more detailed information about specific lines, turn to the following pages: Settle to Carlisle Railway (p.910); North Yorkshire Moors Railway (p.975); Keighley and Worth Valley Railway (p.894).

Harrogate to: Knaresborough (every 30min; 15min); Leeds (every 30min; 45min); York (hourly; 30min).

Hull to: Beverley (Mon–Sat hourly, Sun 4 daily; 15min); Leeds (hourly; 1hr); London (hourly; 3hr); Scarborough (every 2hr; 1hr 30min); York (10 daily; 1hr 15min).

Knaresborough to: Harrogate (every 30min; 15min); Leeds (every 30min; 45min); York (hourly; 30min).

Leeds to: Birmingham (10 daily; 2hr); Bradford (every 15min; 20min); Carlisle (3–9 daily; 2hr 40min); Harrogate (every 30min; 45min); Hull (hourly; 1hr); Knaresborough (every 30min; 45min); Lancaster (3 daily; 2hr); Liverpool (hourly; 2hr); London (every 30min; 2hr); Manchester (every 30min; 35min); Settle (3–8 daily; 1hr); Sheffield (every 30min; 45min–1hr 15min); Skipton (hourly; 40min); York (every 30min; 40min).

Pickering to: Grosmont (April–Oct 5–8 daily, plus limited winter service; 1hr).

Scarborough to: Hull (every 2hr; 1hr 30min); York (8–15 daily; 45min).

Sheffield to: Leeds (every 30min; 45min–1hr 15min); London (every 45min; 2hr 30min); York (hourly; 1hr 20min).

Whitby to: Danby (June–Sept 4 daily; Oct–March Mon–Sat 4 daily; 35min); Grosmont (June–Sept 4 daily; Oct–March Mon–Sat 4 daily; 15min); Middlesbrough (June–Sept 4 daily; Oct–March Mon–Sat 4 daily; 1hr 30min).

York to: Birmingham (10 daily; 2hr 40min); Bristol (10 daily; 4hr); Bradford (every 45min; 1hr); Durham (every 30min; 40min); Edinburgh (hourly; 2hr); Exeter (5 daily; 5hr); Harrogate (hourly; 35min); Hull (hourly; 1hr 15min); Leeds (every 30min; 40min); London (every 30min; 2hr); Manchester (hourly; 1hr 45min); Newcastle (every 30min; 1hr); Penzance (4 daily; 7hr 30min); Scarborough (8–15 daily; 45min); Sheffield (hourly; 1hr 20min).

The Northeast

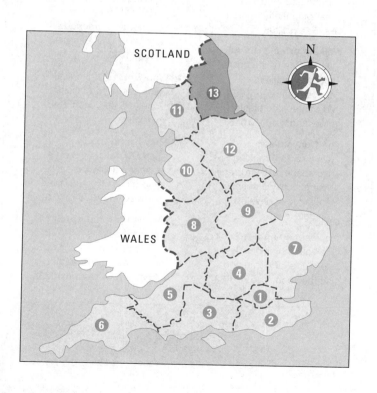

* Durham Cathedral Awe-inspiring Romanesque church towering above the wooded banks of the River Wear. **See p.1002**

* Beamish Museum The everyday details of the northeast's industrial past poignantly re-created. **See p.1008**

* Walking around the Allen Valley One of the best spots for walkers – choose between wooded gorges and blasted moorland. **See p.1015**

* The Quayside at Newcastle A striking riverscape re-energized by artistically and challenging new developments. **See p.1027**

* Newcastle nightlife Lock up your inhibitions, leave your coat at home and hit the Toon. **See p.1033**

* Bede's World A fascinating and imaginative evocation of the life and times of one of Europe's greatest scholars. **See p.1038**

* Hadrian's Wall Put your walking boots on to make the most of this extraordinary monument and its wild landscape. **See p.1043**

* Warkworth Ruined riverside castle and miles of lonely white beach. **See p.1063**

* Holy Island Cradle of early Christianity, with a Lutyens-designed castle and a brooding, isolated atmosphere. **See p.1070**

* Berwick's ramparts Stroll along the walls for matchless views of sea, river and quintessential frontier town. **See p.1073**

The Northeast

or England's northeastern region – in particular the counties of **Northumberland** and **Durham** – the centuries between the Roman invasion and the 1603 union of the English and Scottish crowns were a period of almost incessant turbulence. To mark the empire's limit and to contain the troublesome tribes of the far north, **Hadrian's Wall** was built along the seventy-odd miles between the North Sea and the west coast, an extraordinary military structure that is now one of the country's most evocative ruins. When the Romans departed, the northeast was plunged into chaos and divided into unstable Saxon principalities until order was restored by the kings of Northumbria, who dominated the region from 600 until the 870s. It was they who nourished the region's early Christian tradition, which achieved its finest flowering with the creation of the **Lindisfarne Gospels** on what is now known as Holy Island. The monks abandoned their island at the end of the ninth century, in advance of the Vikings' destruction of the Northumbrian kingdom, and only after the Norman Conquest did the northeast again become part of a greater England.

The Norman kings and their immediate successors repeatedly attempted to subdue Scotland, passing effective regional control to powerful local lords. Their authority is recalled by a sequence of formidable fortresses, most impressively those at **Bamburgh**, **Alnwick** and **Warkworth**, and also by **Durham Cathedral**, the magnificent twelfth-century church of the prince bishops of Durham, who ruled the whole of County Durham. Long after the northeast had ceased to be a critical military zone, its character and appearance were transformed by the **Industrial Revolution**. Coal had been mined here for hundreds of years, but exploitation only began in earnest towards the end of the eighteenth century, when two main coalfields were established – one dominating County Durham from the Pennines to the sea, the other stretching

Accommodation price codes

Throughout this guide, hotel and B&B accommodation is priced on a scale of ❶ to ❾, the number indicating the **lowest price** you could expect to pay per night in that establishment for a **double room** in high season. The prices indicated by the codes are as follows:

❶ under £40	❹ £60–70	❼ £110–150
❷ £40–50	❺ £70–90	❽ £150–200
❸ £50–60	❻ £90–110	❾ over £200

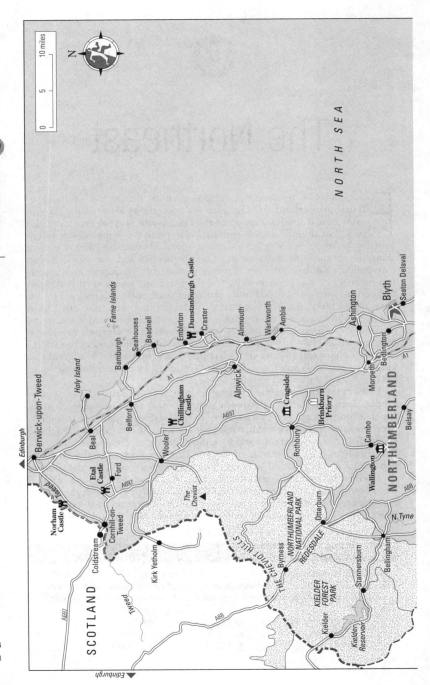

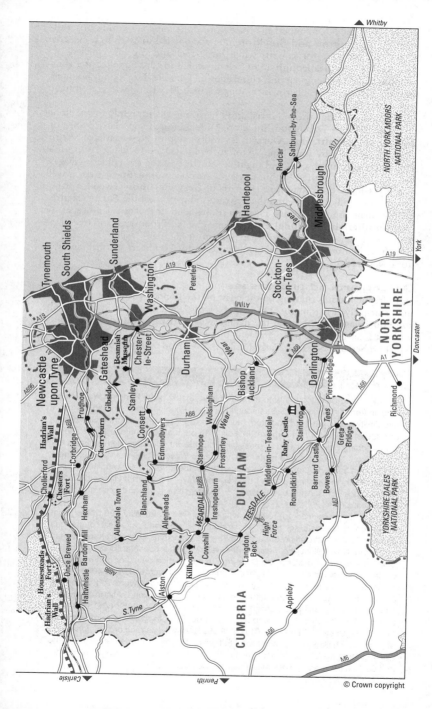

997

© Crown copyright

north along the Northumberland coast from the Tyne. The world's first **railway**, the **Darlington and Stockton** line, was opened in 1825 to move coal to the nearest port for export, while local coal and ore also fuelled the foundries of **Middlesbrough** and Consett, which in turn supplied the shipbuilding and heavy-engineering companies of Tyneside. The region boomed, creating a score of sizeable towns, amongst which Newcastle was pre-eminent – as it remains today.

Most visitors dodge the industrial areas, bypassing the unsightly towns along the **Tees Valley** – Darlington, Stockton, Middlesbrough and Hartlepool – on the way to **Durham**. From Durham it's a short hop to **Newcastle**, an earthy city distinguished by some fine Victorian buildings, the revitalized Quayside and a vibrant cultural scene and nightlife. North, past the old colliery villages, the brighter parts of the Northumberland coast boast some fine castles, as well as **Holy Island**, the extravagant ramparts of **Berwick-upon-Tweed**, a string of superb, if chilly, beaches, and the desolate archipelago of the **Farne Islands**. Inland there are the scenic Durham **dales** and the harsh landscapes of **Northumberland National Park**, a huge chunk of moorland and tree plantations that edges the most dramatic portion of Hadrian's Wall. The wall itself is easily visited from the appealing abbey-town of **Hexham**, just half an hour from Newcastle.

Getting around and passes

With frequent trains running up the coast on the London–Scotland route (calling principally at Darlington, Durham, Newcastle and Berwick-upon-Tweed), and numerous buses between the main towns, **getting around** the northeast without a car is usually not a problem, though it's more difficult to explore the Northumberland National Park. Durham, Newcastle, Hexham and Alnwick

---

Hiking and biking routes

The main long-distance footpath through the Northeast is the **Pennine Way**, which cuts up from the Yorkshire Dales through the North Pennines, with a notable section through Teesdale west of Middleton, runs parallel to Hadrian's Wall from Greenhead to Housesteads, and then climaxes in a climb through the Northumberland National Park, passing Bellingham and Byrness, and the Cheviot Hills. Less demanding is the waymarked 63-mile pilgrim's route, **St Cuthbert's Way**, which links Melrose, where St Cuthbert started his ministry just across the border in Scotland, with Holy Island, via Kirk Yetholm – northern end of the Pennine Way – the Cheviot Hills and Wooler. Tourist offices in Berwick-upon-Tweed or Wooler have route and accommodation information.

Other major waymarked routes include the **Teesdale Way**, 90 miles from Middleton-in-Teesdale to grimy Teesmouth (just beyond Middlesbrough), via Barnard Castle and Darlington; and the 78-mile **Weardale Way**, which follows the river from Cowshill at the head of the valley to the coast at Sunderland, via Stanhope, Bishop Auckland and Durham. For information on either of these walks, contact local tourist offices or Durham County Council on ☎0191/383 4082.

Sustrans's 140-mile **C2C cycle route** from Whitehaven/Workington to Sunderland/Newcastle drops into the northeast just beyond Alston and links Allenheads, Stanhope and Consett with either city. You'll need the C2C route map and possibly the associated accommodation guide, both available from Sustrans, PO Box 21, Bristol, BS99 2HA ☎0117/929 0888, ⊛www.sustrans.org.uk. If that isn't enough of a challenge, you might want to take on the new 187-mile return route, the **Reivers Way**, which runs from Tynemouth to Whitehaven via Bellingham, Kielder and Carlisle (map and guides available from Sustrans).

are the main transport hubs, while Hadrian's Wall has its own bus service, operating out of Carlisle and Hexham (see p.1047). For all **public transport enquiries** in the northeast, contact Traveline (daily 7am–8pm; ☎0870/608 2608, ⓦwww.traveline.co.uk) or log onto Nexus, the local transport website, which has a useful journey planner option (ⓦwww.nexus.org.uk). You might consider investing in a **travel pass**. The Northeast Explorer Pass (1-day; £5.25), valid after 9am on weekdays and all day at weekends, gives unlimited travel on local buses from Berwick-upon-Tweed as far south as Scarborough in North Yorkshire or west to Carlisle – buy it on board any bus. Useful train passes include the Northeast Regional Rover (7 days; £70) and the wide-ranging North Country Rover (any 4 days out of 8; £59), which is valid as far south as Leeds and Hull and west as far as Preston. If you're relying on public transport, you'll find the *Northumberland Public Transport Guide* (£1) very useful – it's sold at most local tourist offices.

If there are two or more of you, it's well worth getting hold of a Northumbria Tourist Board **Powerpass** (£1) from any of the region's tourist offices, which gives two-for-the-price-of-one entry to many attractions, including Beamish, Bede's World and Segedunum.

Durham

The view from **DURHAM** train station is one of the finest in northern England – a panoramic prospect of Durham Cathedral, its towers dominating the skyline from the top of a steep sandstone bluff within a narrow bend of the River Wear. This dramatic site has been the resting place of St Cuthbert since 995, when his body was moved here from nearby Chester-le-Street, over one hundred years after his fellow monks had fled from Lindisfarne in fear of the Vikings, carrying his coffin before them. Cuthbert's hallowed remains made Durham a place of pilgrimage for both the Saxons and the Normans, who began work on the present cathedral at the end of the eleventh century. In the meantime, William the Conqueror, aware of the defensive possibilities of the site, had built a castle that was to be the precursor of ever more elaborate fortifications.

Subsequently, the bishops of Durham were granted extensive powers to control the troublesome northern marches of the kingdom, ruling as semi-independent **prince bishops**, with their own army, mint and courts of law. The first, William de Carileph, laid the foundation stone of the new cathedral in 1093; his successors provided glorious chapels and treasures which owed as much to the prince bishops' confident sense of self-worth as to their devotion to God. The bishops were at the peak of their power in the fourteenth century, but thereafter their office went into decline, especially in the wake of the Reformation, yet they clung to the vestiges of their powers until 1836, when they ceded them to the Crown. They abandoned Durham Castle for their palace in Bishop Auckland and transferred their old home to the fledgling **Durham University**, England's third oldest seat of learning after Oxford and Cambridge. And so matters rest today, cathedral and university monopolizing a city centre that remains an island of privilege in what is otherwise a moderately sized, working-class town at the heart of the old Durham coalfield.

Arrival and information

Durham **train station** – on the main East Coast line from London King's Cross to Scotland – is about ten minutes' walk from the city centre, either via

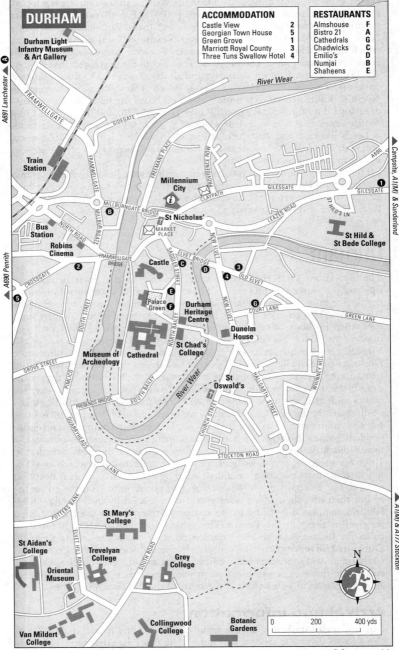

DURHAM

Durham Light
Infantry Museum
& Art Gallery

ACCOMMODATION

Castle View	2
Georgian Town House	5
Green Grove	1
Marriott Royal County	3
Three Tuns Swallow Hotel	4

RESTAURANTS

Almshouse	F
Bistro 21	A
Cathedrals	G
Chadwicks	C
Emilio's	D
Numjai	B
Shaheens	E

River Wear

A691 Lanchester

FRAMWELLGATE

SIDEGATE

Train
Station

FRAMWELLGATE

MILLBURNGATE

NORTH ROAD

Bus
Station

Robins
Cinema

A690 Penrith

CROSSGATE

SOUTH STREET

FRAMWELLGATE BRIDGE

MILLBURNGATE BRIDGE

Millennium
City

FREEMANS PLACE

PROVIDENCE ROW

CLAYPATH

St Nicholas'

MARKET
PLACE

SADDLER STREET

Castle

ELVET BRIDGE

NEW ELVET

LEAZES ROAD

GILESGATE

ST HILD'S LN

GILESGATE

A690

Campsite A1(M) & Sunderland

St Hild &
St Bede College

OLD ELVET

Palace
Green

Durham
Heritage
Centre

COURT LANE

GREEN LANE

Dunelm
House

NEW ELVET

WHINNEY HILL

HALLGARTH STREET

GROVE STREET

PIMLICO

Museum of
Archeology

NORTH BAILEY

Cathedral

St Chad's
College

PREBENDS BRIDGE

SOUTH BAILEY

River Wear

St
Oswald's

QUARRYHEADS LANE

CHURCH STREET

STOCKTON ROAD

A1(M) & A177 Stockton

POTTERS BANK

St Mary's
College

ELVET HILL ROAD

SOUTH ROAD

Grey
College

N

St Aidan's
College

Trevelyan
College

Oriental
Museum

Botanic
Gardens

Collingwood
College

Van Mildert
College

0	200	400 yds

A177 Darlington

© Crown copyright

Millburngate Bridge or via North Road – the site of the **bus station** – then the pedestrianized Framwellgate Bridge. Infrequent **minibuses** (#40; not Sun) link the cathedral with both stations.

The **tourist office** (☎0191/384 3720, ✉touristinfo@durhamcity.gov.uk) will book accommodation, hand you a free map and supply the usual range of leaflets plus the bi-monthly *What's on: Durham*, listing local events. Currently sited in Market Place, it's due to move in early 2002 into **Millennium City** on Claypath, a somewhat overdue £40-million development that will also shelter a visitor centre with a large-format film presentation on Durham, a state-of-the-art theatre, crafts workshops, a new public library with free internet access, plus bars and cafés.

You can **walk** around the whole of the city centre, though a couple of out-lying attractions can be reached by local bus (details given in the text where appropriate). Ask at the tourist office about summertime **guided walks**, if you'd like a little more historical direction to your ramblings. In addition, you may want to get out onto the river, either by renting **rowing boats** (£2.50/person; 1hr) from Brown's Boathouse, Elvet Bridge, or by taking a **cruise** aboard the *Prince Bishop* (☎0191/386 9525; £3.50; 1hr), which has regular summer departures, again from Elvet Bridge.

Accommodation

Durham has a long list of **guest houses** and **B&Bs**, with particular concentrations around Gilesgate, northeast of Market Place, and around Crossgate, south of the bus station. Among the budget B&Bs on Gilesgate, *Green Grove* at no. 99 is a good choice (☎0191/384 4361, ✉guesthouse@f.s.net.co.uk; no credit cards; ❶), with a mix of standard and en-suite rooms. On Crossgate, *Castle View Guest House*, next to St Margaret's Church at no. 4 (☎0191/386 8852, ⓦwww.castle-view.net; ❸), is recommended, with en-suite bathrooms throughout, a garden and, of course, great castle views. The nearby *Georgian Town House*, 10 Crossgate (☎0191/386 8070; no credit cards; ❸), boasts more character than most, serves up good breakfasts and has some rooms with cathedral views. Moving swiftly up the price brackets, the *Marriott Royal County*, Old Elvet, just across Elvet Bridge (☎0191/386 6821, ⓦwww.marriotthotels.com /xvudm; ❼), is Durham's top hotel, and has its own riverside leisure centre with indoor swimming pool, sauna and solarium. Its sister hotel, the *Three Tuns Swallow Hotel*, New Elvet (☎0191/375 1504 or 386 1406, ✉threetuns.reservations@btinternet.com; ❼), is a former sixteenth-century coaching inn with slightly cheaper rates and access to the *Royal County's* leisure centre.

A wide variety of private bedrooms are offered at the colleges of **Durham University**, which welcome visitors at Christmas, Easter and between July and September; the tourist office has a full list, or check the website: ⓦwww.dur.ac.uk/conference_tourism. Most university accommodation is now aimed at businessmen as much as holiday-makers, with rates to match the city's B&Bs (❷–❹, including breakfast). The best colleges are University College (☎0191/374 3863, ✉J.A.Marshall@durham.ac.uk), with rooms inside the castle, and St Hild and St Bede, set in beautiful grounds overlooking the cathedral on Leazes Road (☎0191/374 3069, ✉L.C.Hugill@durham.ac.uk). University College also offers very central, no-frills rooms with shared bathrooms at Bailey Court, just off Palace Green (❶, breakfast excluded). The nearest **campsite**, the *Grange Camping and Caravan Site* (☎0191/384 4778), lies beside the junction of the A1(M) and the A690, about two miles northeast of the city on Meadow Lane, Carrville. To get there from the bus station take bus #220 or #222 for Sunderland.

The City

Surrounded on three sides by the River Wear, Durham's surprisingly compact centre is readily approached by two road bridges that lead from the western, modern part of town across the river to the spur containing castle and cathedral. The commercial heart of this "old town" area is the triangular **Market Place**, inappropriately dominated by an equestrian statue of the third marquis of Londonderry, a much-hated nineteenth-century colliery owner – in the words of John Doyle, a pitman from Horden: "His Lordship reached three score and ten / A very fine performance when / One thinks how many did him scorn / And wished him dead 'ere he was born."

Flanking the square are the **Guildhall** and **St Nicholas' Church**, both now modernized beyond distinction. The Victorian **Market Hall**, buried in the vaults of the buildings that line the west side of the square (closed Sun; ⓦwww.durhammarkets.co.uk), hosts a lively outdoor market every Saturday, as well as farmers' markets, held on the third Thursday of the month, and other special events.

The Cathedral

From Market Place, it's a five-minute walk up the steep and cobbled Saddler Street to the majestic **Durham Cathedral**, facing the castle across the manicured Palace Green (July–Sept Mon–Sat 9.30am–8pm, Sun 12.30–8pm; rest of year Mon–Sat 9.30am–6.15pm, Sun 12.30–5pm; guided tours June & July Sat 10.30am & 2pm; Aug & Sept Mon–Fri 10.30am, 11.30am & 2pm, Sat 10.30am, 11.30am, 2pm & 6.15pm, Sun 5pm; access may be restricted due to services and events, call ☎0191/386 4266 to check; £3 suggested donation; tours £3). Standing on the site of an early wooden Saxon cathedral, built to house the remains of St Cuthbert, the present cathedral – the work of French master masons – was completed in 1133, and has survived the centuries pretty much intact, a supreme example of the Norman-Romanesque style. Visiting in 1773, Samuel Johnson captured its overpowering essence well: "it rather awes than pleases, as it strikes with a kind of gigantick dignity, and aspires to no other praise than that of rocky solidity and indeterminate duration".

Entry is through the **northwest porch**, an eighteenth-century addition, where a replica of the lion-head **sanctuary knocker** is a reminder of the medieval distinction between secular and religious law. The church used to be ringed by wooden crosses and, once a fugitive reached them, he or she could claim sanctuary from the lay authorities for up to 35 days. In theory, this right to sanctuary was universal, but in practice it was mostly used by the rich to give them time to arrange their affairs before they went into exile. Rarely did anyone try to stop these wealthy runaways from reaching safety and, after the prescribed period, the monks gave their "guests" a robe of St Cuthbert and a white wooden cross, which extended the church's protection while they made their way to the nearest port.

The awe-inspiring **nave**, completed in 1128, is a bold and inventive structure that used pointed arches for the first time in England, raising the vaulted ceiling to new and dizzying heights. The weight of the stone is borne by massive pillars, their heaviness relieved by striking Moorish-influenced geometric patterns – chevrons, diamonds and vertical fluting. Most of the cathedral's early fixtures and fittings were destroyed by Cromwell's Scottish prisoners, who were deposited inside the church after the battle of Dunbar in 1650. The Scots did not, however, damage the gaudily painted, sixteenth-century **Prior Castell's clock**, which now hangs in the south transept, because it sported their emblem, the thistle. A door here gives access to the **tower** (Mon–Sat: Easter–Sept 9.30am–4pm; Oct–Easter 10am–3pm; £2), from the top of which are gut-wrenching views of the city.

Separated from the nave by a Victorian marble screen is the **choir**, where the dark-stained Restoration stalls are overshadowed by the vainglorious **bishop's throne**, reputedly the highest in medieval Christendom, built on the orders of the fourteenth-century Bishop Hatfield, whose militaristic alabaster tombstone lies just below. Beyond, the **Chapel of the Nine Altars** dates from the thirteenth century, its Early English stonework distinguished by its delicacy of detail. Here, and around the adjoining **Shrine of St Cuthbert**, much of the stonework is Frosterley marble, each dark shaft bearing its own fancy pattern of fossils. Cuthbert himself lies beneath a plain marble slab, his presence and shrine having gained a reputation over the centuries for their curative powers. The legend was given credence in 1104, when the saint's body was exhumed for reburial here, upon the completion of the eastern end of the new Norman cathedral, and was found to be completely uncorrupted, more than four hundred years after his death on Lindisfarne. Almost certainly, this was the result of his fellow monks having (unintentionally) preserved the body by laying it in sand containing salt crystals – though to medieval eyes, here was testament enough to the saint's potency.

Back near the entrance, stuck on the edge of the ravine at the west end of the church, the **Galilee Chapel** was begun in the 1170s, its light and exotic decoration in imitation of the Great Mosque of Córdoba, a contrast to the forcefulness of the nave. Subdivided by twelve slender columns, each surrounded by a medley of geometric patterns, the chapel contains the simple tombstone of the **Venerable Bede**, the Northumbrian monk credited with being England's first historian. Bede died at the monastery of Jarrow in 735 (see p.1037), and his remains were transferred here in 1020.

An ancient wooden doorway opposite the main entrance leads into the spacious **cloisters**, which are flanked by what remains of the monastic buildings. These include the **monks' dormitory** (Easter–Sept Mon–Sat 10am–3.30pm, Sun 12.30–3.15pm; 80p) and the somewhat misleadingly named **Treasures of St Cuthbert** exhibition in the undercroft (Mon–Sat 10am–4.30pm, Sun 2–4.30pm; £2): although the attractive display includes some striking relics of St Cuthbert, including the reassembled fragments of his delicately carved and much-travelled oak coffin, a beautiful gold pectoral cross and a silver-plated portable altar, it's mostly given over to ecclesiastical bric-a-brac, from altar plate, bishops' rings and seals to vestments and illuminated manuscripts. The original Sanctuary Knocker is here, too, dating from 1140, and a computer terminal giving you a virtual opportunity to see the major illustrated pages of the Lindisfarne Gospels (see p.1070). Also in the undercroft is the cathedral café, while next door in the impressively converted monastic kitchen is the bookshop.

The Castle

Across Palace Green from the cathedral, **Durham Castle** (Easter–Sept Mon–Sat 10am–12.30pm & 2–4pm, Sun 10am–noon & 2–4pm; Oct–Easter Mon, Wed, Sat & Sun 2–4pm; £3; ☎191/374 3800, ⓦ www.durhamcastle.com) lost its medieval appearance long ago, during refurbishments arranged by a succession of prince bishops, but the university went further by renovating the old keep as a hall of residence. It's only possible to visit the castle on a 45-minute guided tour, highlights of which include rapid visits to the fifteenth-century kitchen, a climb up the enormous hanging staircase and the jog down to the

Norman chapel, notable for its lively Romanesque carved capitals. In the Great Hall, your guide will suggest that the miniature suits of armour above the musicians' gallery were issued to young boys by Cromwell, who sent them into battle ahead of his regular troops as a human shield. Treat this tale with caution – it may be Royalist propaganda. The castle is sometimes closed for functions during its regular opening hours; call ahead to check.

River walks

Below the castle and the cathedral are the wooded banks of the **River Wear**, where a pleasant footpath runs right round the peninsula. It takes about thirty minutes to complete the circuit, passing a succession of elegant bridges with fine vantage points over town and cathedral. **Framwellgate Bridge** originally dates from the twelfth century, though it was widened to its present proportions in the mid-nineteenth century. Just along from here, on the riverbank, the university's **Museum of Archeology** (April–Oct daily 11am–4pm; Nov–March Mon & Fri–Sun 11.30am–3.30pm; £1; ⓦwww.dur.ac.uk/archae-ology) occupies an old stone fulling mill, its displays a mixture of permanent archeological relics and temporary exhibitions. Eighteenth-century **Prebends Bridge** boasts celebrated views of the cathedral, and the path then continues round to the handsome **Elvet Bridge**, again widened far beyond its medieval course, though still retaining traces of both its erstwhile bridge-houses and the chapel, St Andrew's, which once stood at its eastern end.

The alternative route from Prebends to Elvet Bridge is along South and North Bailey, a cobbled thoroughfare lined by well-worn Georgian houses, many of them occupied by university college buildings. The church of St Mary-le-Bow, on North Bailey, immediately below the cathedral, now does duty as the **Durham Heritage Centre** (April, May & Oct Sat & Sun 2–4.30pm; June daily 2–4.30pm; July, Aug & Sept daily 11am–4.30pm; £1), a pot-pourri of audiovisual displays, dioramas, temporary exhibitions and activities such as brass-rubbing.

The rest of the city

Durham has a smattering of other attractions, the most noteworthy being the university's newly refurbished **Oriental Museum** (Mon–Fri 10am–5pm, Sat & Sun noon–5pm; £1.50; ⓦwww.dur.ac.uk/oriental.museum), set among college buildings a couple of miles to the south of the city centre on Elvet Hill (off South Road). Highlights of its wide-ranging collection include outstanding displays of Chinese ceramics and Arabic calligraphy, a magnificent Chinese bed and Japanese wood-block prints by Hiroshige and Yoshitoshi, complemented by temporary exhibitions and events such as wood-block workshops, Oriental games days and bazaars. To get there from the bus station, take bus #5 or #6 (to Bishop Auckland) and ask to be put off on South Road for the museum. After the museum, you may as well continue on foot to the nearby **Botanic Garden** (daily: March–Oct 10am–5pm; Nov–Feb 11am–4pm; £1), whose glasshouses, café and visitor centre are set in eighteen acres of diverse woodland, grassland and gardens near Collingwood College; buses run back to the centre from either Elvet Hill Road or South Road.

North of the centre, a ten-minute walk from the train station takes you to the revamped **Durham Light Infantry Museum and Durham Art Gallery**, at Aykley Heads (daily: April–Oct 10am–5pm; Nov–March 10am–4pm; £2.50; ⓦwww.durham.gov.uk/dli). Downstairs, it tells the story of World War I, in which 12,000 men of the DLI died, through moving testimonies and wide-ranging artefacts, including a tribute to the soldiers, often suffering from shell

△ The Tyne Bridges, Newcastle upon Tyne

shock, who were shot for cowardice; the less compelling first floor traces the history of the regiment through World War II to its last parade in 1968. The art gallery plays host to an indefinable variety of temporary exhibitions.

Eating

Of the city's **cafés**, *Vennel's*, Saddler's Yard – named after the skinny alley or "vennel" where it stands – serves wholefood lunches in a little hidden sixteenth-century courtyard; the entrance is next to Waterstone's, off Saddler Street at the junction with Elvet Bridge. Further up the hill, on Palace Green, to the side of the cathedral, the *Almshouse* conjures up vegetarian and meaty meals for around £5 (open until 8pm in summer).

Most of Durham's **restaurants** are concentrated in the streets radiating from the Market Place. *Shaheens*, 48 North Bailey (closed Mon), serves the best curry in town, while for Italian food, try *Emilio's* at the east end of Elvet Bridge, a smart refurbishment of an eleventh-century chapel with summertime outdoor seating. If you're in the mood for Thai food, head for *Numjai*, a top-notch, authentic restaurant that dishes up plenty of veggie options, as well as a smattering of Japanese dishes, accompanied by great views of the cathedral from its location in the Milburngate shopping centre (℡0191/386 2020). Excellent Modern British cuisine and service are offered at *Bistro 21*, a converted farmhouse at Aykley Heads, ten minutes' walk on from the DLI museum and art gallery north of the centre (℡0191/384 4354; closed Sun); there's courtyard seating in summer and good-value set menus at lunchtime. Similar fare, as well as simpler pasta dishes and sandwiches, is served up in the centre of town at *Chadwicks*, an airy, modern bar-café/restaurant at 39 Saddler St (℡0191/384 1999). If you still can't make your mind up, head for *Cathedrals*, an ambitious and stylish redevelopment of the old police station on Court Lane (℡0191/370 9632), where you can choose among fine dining and great views of the cathedral in the rooftop restaurant, Italian-influenced cuisine in the bistro, pub grub amid the impressive copper vats of the bar and microbrewery, and inventive sandwiches and snacks in the coffee house.

Drinking, nightlife and entertainment

Durham's central **pubs** blow hot and cold, depending on whether or not the students are in town. Good bets at most times include the *Court Inn*, which has outdoor seating on Court Lane, and the lively *Hogshead*, 58 Saddler St, with its selection of real ales. The *Victoria*, a quiet, welcoming local at 86 Hallgarth St, is also a favourite. Bleary-eyed old socialists will want to make time for a quick pint in the *Market Tavern*, a nineteenth-century pub on Market Place, where the influential Durham Miners' Association was founded in 1871.

For more highbrow entertainment, regular **classical concerts** are held at various venues around the city, including the cathedral, while the DLI Museum and Durham Art Gallery (℡0191/384 2214) at Aykley Heads hosts lunchtime recitals as well as summertime brass band concerts, ceilidhs and other events. Plans for the **Gala Theatre** in the Millennium City development opening on Claypath in 2002 include opera, classical concerts and drama. Durham Students' Union (℡0191/374 2000) puts on **gigs** during term time, with rock, jazz and comedy most regularly performed at Dunelm House, New Elvet. The local **cinema**, Robins Cinema on North Road (℡0191/384 3434), has a film club as well as showing mainstream releases, though it may be under threat when a multiplex cinema opens in the second-phase Walkergate development, next to Millennium City.

Annual events and **festivals** come thick and fast in the summer. June sees the university's **arts week**, and in the same month the **Durham Regatta** packs the riverbanks and river. Over the first weekend in July, the **Durham Summer Festival** encompasses all manner of musical entertainments, as well as historical re-enactments on Palace Green; on the following Saturday, the **Miners' Gala** – when the traditional lodge banners are paraded through the streets – has been revived as a celebration of the international labour movement. For further details of all events, consult the tourist office.

The rest of County Durham

In the 1910s, **County Durham** produced 41 million tons of coal each year, raised from three hundred pits by 170,000 miners. This was the heyday of an industry that since the 1830s had transformed the county's landscape, spawning scores of pit villages that matted the rolling hills from the Pennines to the North Sea, between Newcastle and Stockton-on-Tees. The miners' union, waging a long struggle against serf-like pay and conditions, achieved a gradual improvement of the miners' lot, but could not prevent the slow decline of the Durham coalfield from the 1920s: just 127 mines were left when the industry was nationalized in 1947, only 34 in 1969, and today not a single pit remains in the county. As a consequence, the old colliery villages have lost their sense of purpose and structure, some becoming godforsaken terraces in the middle of nowhere, others being swallowed up by neighbouring towns. For a taste of the old days, most people troop off to the reconstructed colliery village (and much more) at the open-air **Beamish Museum**, north of Durham.

County Durham's other obvious tourist attractions are to the west of the coalfield. There's **Raby Castle**, a stately home to the east of the market town of **Barnard Castle**, itself the setting for the opulent art collection of the **Bowes Museum**. Farther west lie the Pennine valleys of **Teesdale** and **Weardale**, whose upper reaches boast some enjoyable moorland scenery, most dramatically at Teesdale's **High Force** waterfall, which adjoins the Pennine Way. These two dales are best toured in a clockwise direction, beginning at Barnard Castle and travelling up Teesdale to Langdon Beck and on to Alston in Cumbria, where you can cross over to Weardale and take the road back down the valley through Stanhope and into Bishop Auckland. Another option is to leave Weardale at Stanhope for the ten-mile trip north across the moors to the delightful stone village of **Blanchland**, tucked away in the valley of the Derwent River across the border in Northumberland.

Getting around County Durham by **bus** and **train** presents few problems. A comprehensive range of services links all the major towns and villages, although the bus network does peter out as you travel up the dales. Many services are also greatly reduced, or nonexistent, during the winter months. For a public transport information pack, including the useful *Across the Roof of England* leaflet, which details all bus and train services in this area, contact Durham County Council (℡0191/383 3337, ✉transinfo@durham.gov.uk). If you want to get further off the beaten track, contact the Council's Environment Department (℡0191/383 4144) for details of its year-round programme of **guided walks**. These range from rural rambles to religious or industrial heritage trails, and most cost just £2; for more information contact Durham's tourist office, or any of the local tourist offices detailed below.

Beamish Museum

Established in 1970, the open-air **Beamish Museum** (Easter–Oct daily 10am–5pm; Nov & Jan–Easter Tues–Thurs, Sat & Sun 10am–4pm; last admission 3pm; admission £12, £4 in winter; ☎01207/231811, ⓦwww.beamish.org .uk), spreading out over 300 acres beside the A693 about ten miles north of Durham, is as popular with tourists as it is with local people, who come to chew the fat with the costumed guides, many of whom are recruited for their real-life experience. The collier who takes you down the reopened drift mine may once have been a miner, and some of the blokes driving the steam engine used to work for British Rail, adding a touch of authenticity and sadness to the proceedings, as these industries have deteriorated in tandem with the boom in heritage museums like this one.

To **get there**, drivers should follow signs to the museum off the A1(M) Chester-le-Street exit, then follow the signs along the A693 to Stanley. By **bus**, take the #720 from Durham bus station (hourly) or the #709 from Newcastle's Eldon Square (hourly), which drop you close to the main entrance. There are also regular services from Sunderland (#775/778; 1–2 hourly). In summer, hang on to your bus ticket and you'll get a discount on entrance to the museum, too.

Buildings from all over the region have been reassembled here, and the museum divides into six main sections, linked by restored trams and buses and all painstakingly kitted out with period furnishings and fittings. Four of the sections show life in 1913, before the upheavals brought about by World War I: a pint-sized **colliery village**, complete with cottages, Methodist chapel, school, old stone winding house and drift mine; a **farm** inhabited by breeds of livestock that were popular in the period; a **train station** and goods shed; and a large-scale re-creation of a market **town**, its High Street lined by shops, bank, pub, dentist's surgery, newspaper office, garage, stables, sweet factory and solicitor's office. Two areas date to 1825, at the beginning of the northeast's industrial development: a **manor house**, with horse yard, formal gardens, vegetable plots and orchards; and the **Pockerley Waggonway**, where you can ride behind a replica of George Stephenson's *Locomotion*, the first passenger-carrying steam train in the world, which ran from Darlington to Stockton. There's a great deal to see and what with the summertime Victorian funfair, the *Sun Inn* pub and picnic areas, most people make a day of it – reckon on around four hours to get round the lot in summer, two in winter when only the town and train station are usually open. Call ahead to check on this, or on the concerts and **special events** held throughout the summer, from craft displays to whippet racing.

Bishop Auckland

Eleven miles southwest of Durham city, **BISHOP AUCKLAND** has been the country home of the bishops of Durham since the twelfth century and their official residence for more than a hundred years. Their palace, the gracious **Auckland Castle** (May to mid-July & Sept Fri & Sun 2–5pm; mid-July to Aug Mon–Fri & Sun 2–5pm; £3.50; ⓦwww.auckland-castle.co.uk;), standing in eight-hundred-acre grounds, is approached through an imposing gatehouse just off the town's Market Place. The palace has been extensively remodelled since its medieval incarnation, redesigned to satisfy the whims of such occupants as the seventeenth-century Bishop Cosin who refurbished the original banqueting hall to create today's splendid marble and limestone **chapel**. Here, the stained-glass windows relate the stories of early Christian saints familiar throughout the northeast, especially Cuthbert, Bede and Aidan. The other rooms are rather sparse, though – for the moment at least – there's an outstanding exception in the long dining room, with its thirteen paintings of Jacob and his sons by Zurbarán, commissioned in the 1640s for a monastery in South America. However, the Church of England has recently voted to sell the series, its most valuable set of paintings with a price tag of at least £20million; a campaign involving the National Gallery has started to keep the works at the palace, or possibly at nearby Bowes Museum in Barnard Castle where they would have greater public exposure.

In the medieval kitchens there's an exhibition on the life of St Cuthbert and you can stroll into the **Bishop's Deer Park**, too (daily dawn–dusk; free), where an eighteenth-century deer house survives.

The town itself plays second fiddle to the castle, though the Market Place is handsome enough. However, you could follow the mile-long lane that leads north to the remains of **Binchester Roman Fort** (Easter & May–Sept daily 11am–5pm; £1.60). Only a small portion of the ten-acre site – Roman Vinovia – has been excavated (with most of the finds displayed in the Bowes Museum at Barnard Castle), but a stretch of cobbled Dere Street has been uncovered (a fortified supply route stretching from York to Corbridge on Hadrian's Wall) and, more remarkably, so has the country's best example of a **hypocaust**, built to warm the private bath suite of the garrison's commanding officer. There are events held at the site throughout the summer, including parades of Roman soldiers and open days depicting life in Roman Britain; call ☎01388/663089 or go to Ⓦwww.durham.gov.uk/binchester for details.

The fort was abandoned in the fifth century and many of its stones, stamped with the inscription of the cavalry regiment stationed here, found their way to the hamlet of **ESCOMB**, two miles west of Bishop Auckland (bus #86, #87 or #87A from town), where they were used to build a seventh-century **Saxon church** (daily: summer 9am–8pm; rest of year 9am–4pm; free). Now surrounded by modern houses, the church (key at 22 Saxon Green if closed) has a striking steep-roofed nave, only sixty by twenty feet. Opposite, you can get a bar **meal** at the sixteenth-century *Saxon Inn*.

Practicalities

Bishop Auckland is linked by **train** to Darlington, Middlesbrough and Saltburn and by regular **buses** to Weardale, Barnard Castle, Durham, Newcastle and Darlington. Buses drop you centrally, just a few minutes' west of the town hall, in Market Place, which houses the **tourist office** (April–Sept Mon–Fri 10am–5pm, Sat 9am–4pm Sun 1–4pm; rest of year closed Sun; ☎01388/604922).

The best **accommodation** option hereabouts is *Five Gables Guest House* in the former colliery manager's house in Binchester (☎01388/608204, Ⓦwww.fivegables.co.uk), which offers cosy, en-suite B&B (❷), a self-catering cottage and midweek evening meals for guests if pre-booked. For daytime **food**, the *Laurel Room* in the Town Hall, Market Place, serves up snacks and drinks (closed Sat & Sun), or try the *Castlegate Café* at 8 Market Place for traditional teas and light meals (closed Sun).

Raby Castle and Staindrop

The #8 bus between Bishop Auckland and Barnard Castle runs down the A688 to provide access to the splendid, sprawling battlements of **Raby Castle** (May & Sept Wed & Sun 1–5pm; June–Aug Mon–Fri & Sun 1–5pm; gardens same days 11am–5.30pm; castle & gardens £5, gardens only £3; Ⓦwww.rabycastle.com), roughly halfway between the two. The castle mostly dates from the fourteenth century, reflecting the power of the Neville family, who ruled the local roost until 1569. It was then that Charles Neville helped plan the "Rising of the North", the abortive attempt to replace Elizabeth I with Mary Queen of Scots. The revolt was a dismal failure, and Neville's estates were confiscated, with Raby subsequently passing to the Vane family in 1626. The Vanes held on to the castle despite some difficult times: the second owner, Sir Henry, a leading Puritan and briefly the governor of Massachusetts at the tender age of 23, was imprisoned by Cromwell for his criticism of the overzealous Protectorate, and then executed on the orders of Charles II for treason in 1662.

The Vanes, now the lords Barnard, still live in the castle, the **interior** of which was extensively renovated in the eighteenth and nineteenth centuries, though the medieval kitchen remains intact. Raby's focal point is the first-floor Baron's Hall, still of cathedral-like dimensions in spite of the floor being raised ten feet in 1787 to let carriages pass through the neo-Gothic entrance below. Also of note are the Palladian library and the octagonal drawing room, unchanged since its completion in the 1840s. The whole castle is stuffed with antiques, from the usual oligarchic family portraits and ranks of Meissen porcelain, to paintings by artists such as Joshua Reynolds and Luca Giordano.

Outside the castle, in the two-hundred-acre **deer park**, are the walled **gardens**, where peaches, apricots and pineapples once flourished under the careful gaze of forty Victorian gardeners. Heated cavity walls and curtains protected the trees from frost – above the last remaining apricot tree you can still see the hooks for the curtain rail. The castle's coach houses contain a collection of horse-drawn carriages, admission to which is included with a ticket to the castle or gardens.

One mile south of the castle lies the pretty little village of **STAINDROP**, whose fortunes have always depended on the lords of Raby, and whose church of **St Mary** contains their tombs, including the bruised alabaster memorial of Ralph Neville, grandfather of Edward IV and Richard III. The church – a large rambling construction of Saxon origin – also possesses an especially fine thirteenth-century sedilia. From Staindrop it's only five miles to Barnard Castle, with fairly regular services on the #8 or #75 buses.

Barnard Castle

Fifteen miles southwest of Bishop Auckland, the skeletal remains of **Barnard Castle** (April–Sept daily 10am–6pm; Oct daily 10am–5pm; Nov–March Wed–Sun 10am–4pm; often closed 1–2pm for lunch; £2.40; EH), poking out from a cliff high above the River Tees, overlook the town that grew up in its shadow. First fortified in the eleventh century, the castle was long a stronghold of the Balliols, a Norman family interminably embroiled in the struggle for the Scottish crown. It was one of this clan, Bernard, who built the circular tower, which survives to this day, an impressive thirteenth-century fortification just to the right of the later Round Tower, where a beautiful oriel window carries the emblematic boar of Richard III, one of the subsequent owners. By the seventeenth century the castle had outlived its usefulness and the Vanes quarried its stone to repair their premises at Raby.

The **town**, however, continued to thrive as a market centre and it's quite pleasant to potter around the wide, well-kept streets of what the locals call "Barney". Wednesday is market day, while further down from Market Place, St Mary's church, founded in the twelfth century, and the colonnaded Market Cross building (used, variously, as butter market and jail) make up the official sights.

Castle aside, the prime attraction is the grand French-style chateau that constitutes the **Bowes Museum** (daily 11am–5pm; £4, £2 on first Sat of month; free guided tours May–Sept Tues–Sat 11.30am & 2pm, Oct Sat & Sun 11.30am & 2pm; ⓦwww.bowesmuseum.org.uk), just half a mile east of the centre, signposted along Newgate. Begun in 1869, the chateau was commissioned by John and Josephine Bowes, a local businessman and MP and his French actress wife, who spent much of their time in Paris collecting the ostentatious treasures and antiques. They shipped the whole lot back to Durham and, in an early show of arts patronage, turned the house into a museum for the enlightenment of the Teesdale public (though neither lived to see its formal opening in 1892). It's a hugely rewarding collection, ranging from furniture, paintings, tapestries and ceramics to incidental curiosities, notably a late eighteenth-century mechanical silver swan in the lobby which still performs daily at 2pm, preening to a brief forty-second melodic burst. Among the paintings, you'll find the most important Spanish collection in the UK, including El Greco's *The Tears of St Peter* and a couple of Goyas, plus works by Boudin, Tiepolo and Canaletto; elsewhere, there's varied interest in the French decorative and religious art, English period furniture, and an excellent toy collection – whose nineteenth-century lead soldiers were made possible by the new industry in nearby Stanhope. There's a café, too, and a stroll in the grounds on a nice day is no bad thing.

Back in the town centre, it's a pleasant mile-and-a-half walk from the castle, southeast along the banks of the Tees, to the glorious shattered ruins of **Egglestone Abbey** (dawn–dusk; free), a minor Premonstratensian foundation dating from 1195 (this and other short hikes from the town centre are covered by leaflets available from the tourist office – see below). Turner painted here on one of his three visits to Teesdale, and also at nearby **Rokeby Park** (June to Aug Mon & Tues 2–5pm; £5), a Palladian country house where Walter Scott wrote his ballad *Rokeby*. The house is noted for its extensive collection of eighteenth-century needlework pictures. You can get to the hall directly on bus #79 from Barnard Castle, which also runs to Abbey Bridge End, for Egglestone Abbey.

Practicalities

Buses stop on either side of central Galgate – once the road out to the town gallows, hence the name. Barnard Castle has plenty of accommodation, and the **tourist office** on Flatts Road, at the end of Galgate by the castle (April–Oct daily 10am–6pm; Nov–March Mon–Sat 11am–4pm; ☎01833/690909, ⓔtourism@teesdale.gov.uk), has an extensive list. Among several convenient **B&Bs**, the welcoming *Homelands*, 85 Galgate (☎01833/638757, ⓦwww.barnard -castle.co.uk; no credit cards; ❷), offers pretty bedrooms and good breakfasts, and the similar *Marwood View*, along the same road at no. 98 (☎01833/637493, ⓦwww.kilgarriff.demon.co.uk; no credit cards; ❷), provides a fitness room and sauna for guests to work off the effects of the home-cooked dinners. Moving upmarket, try the *Old Well Inn*, 21 The Bank (☎01833/690130, ⓦwww .oldwellinn.co.uk; ❹), an originally Tudor coaching inn with huge en-suite rooms and weekend half-board deals. The town is also ringed by **campsites**, including a Camping and Caravanning Club site with plenty of facilities at Lartington, two miles west of the centre (☎01833/630228; closed Nov–Feb; bus #95 towards Middleton).

For **food**, the *Hayloft*, in Horsemarket between Galgate and the Market Place, has tasty and inexpensive home-baked snacks and meals during the day, and the *Market Place Teashop*, 29 Market Place, is an excellent traditional tea room with daily special meals on a blackboard. *Oldfield's*, at 7 The Bank

(☎01833/630700; closed Sun eve), is a smart, modern place with courtyard seating, where you can choose between good-value set menus and à la carte seafood specialities. Barney's top restaurant of the moment is *Blagraves House* at 30–32 The Bank (☎01833/637668; open Tues–Sat eve), a sixteenth-century former inn sporting low-beamed ceilings and large open fires, with affordable set menus (not Sat). For a quiet drink, head for the *White Swan* **pub**, below the castle on the opposite side of the main bridge over the Tees, or the *Old Well Inn*, which has a beer garden backing onto the castle walls.

West to Bowes

The main A66 road heads west of Barnard Castle into Cumbria, towards Appleby, a fine moorland route along which the #574 bus runs. Local buses from Barnard Castle (not the #574) detour into **BOWES**, where the huge twelfth-century stone keep of **Bowes Castle** (dawn–dusk; free) overlooks the River Greta valley. Some come on the trail of Dickens (see box below), though without your own transport it's not really worth the effort. However, if you're driving this way you could opt to **stay** at the *Bowes Moor Hotel* (☎01833 /628331, ✉bowesmoorhotel@barnard-castle.co.uk; ❸), another four miles west of Bowes, in the middle of uncomfortably exposed moorland and sup- posedly England's highest hotel – there's bar food available and a restaurant. You could also call in at the Otter Trust's excellent **North Pennines Reserve** (April–Oct daily 10.30am–6pm; £4.50; ⓦwww.ottertrust.org) at Vale House

---

Charles Dickens and the Yorkshire schools

The precociously talented, 26-year-old **Charles Dickens**, already a hugely suc- cessful author with his *Pickwick Papers* and *Oliver Twist*, produced his third novel in serial form in 1838. **Nicholas Nickleby** presented the usual panoply of comic and grotesque figures, none more so than Wackford Squeers, the "villainous", one-eyed headmaster of Dotheboys Hall who, memorably, "appeared ill at ease in his clothes, and as if he were in a perpetual state of astonishment at finding himself so respectable". As throughout his career, Dickens did his homework assiduously. On a trip north in early 1838 he visited various of the so-called "Yorkshire Schools" in the area around Barnard Castle – established, more often than not, by unscrupulous businessmen who cared little for their charges. In these schools, illegitimate or awk- ward children, or simply those of unsuspecting parents, were destined for years of neglect, abuse or worse. Dickens stayed at the *King's Head* on Market Place in **Barnard Castle** (no longer a hotel, though there is a coffee shop and bar), spied on a local watchmaker's shop (giving him the idea for *Master Humphrey's Clock*) and visited nearby **Bowes**, whose Bowes Academy was run by the notorious William Shaw, earlier prosecuted for neglect of his schoolboys, several of whom had gone blind in his care. Dickens took careful note and modelled Squeers on Shaw and Dotheboys Hall on Bowes' school; along with others in the locality it closed in the wake of the success of the novel, with parents and authorities finally moved to action. The school building – "a long cold-looking house" – still stands at the west end of the village; Shaw is buried in the churchyard. As is the way with notoriety, several teachers soon claimed to be the original Wackford Squeers and Dickens himself, in print at least, remained vague about his identity, claiming in the novel's preface that Squeers was "representative of a class, and not of an individual". This was perhaps just as well, since the same preface reveals the reactions of those who believed themselves to be so slighted: one gentleman, according to Dickens, pro- posing coming to London "for the express purpose of committing an assault and battery upon his traducer".

Farm, just three miles west of Bowes, on the south side of the A66. A small valley of the River Greta cuts through the 230-acre farmland, and hides let you glimpse the wildlife; the otters are fed at noon and 3pm.

Teesdale

Extending twenty-odd miles northwest from Barnard Castle, Teesdale begins calmly enough, though the pastoral landscapes of its lower reaches are soon replaced by wilder Pennine scenery. There's a regular **bus service** only as far as **Middleton-in-Teesdale**, the valley's main settlement, with infrequent (Tues, Wed, Fri & Sat) services on to the spectacular **High Force** waterfall and **Langdon Beck** (for the youth hostel). Your own transport makes Teesdale an easy day's sightseeing from Barnard Castle.

Middleton-in-Teesdale and Romaldkirk

MIDDLETON-IN-TEESDALE was once the archetypal "company town", owned lock, stock and barrel by the Quaker-run London Lead Company, which began mining here in 1753. The firm built substantial stone cottages for their workforce, who in return were obliged to observe a host of regulations, such as sending their children to Sunday school and keeping off the booze. Not that the Quakers were over-mindful of working conditions: lead miners here, as elsewhere, suffered bronchial complaints brought on by the contaminated air in the mines, illnesses compounded by long hours and an early start – "washerboys", who sorted the lead ore from the rock for ten hours a day and more, began at 8 years old.

There are no specific sights in the village, but it's a quiet and remote spot to spend the night. The **tourist office** in the central Market Place (daily 9.30am–12.30pm & 1.30–5pm, closes 4pm in winter; ☎01833/641001) can give details of **B&Bs**, including the nearby *Bluebell House* (☎01833/640584; no credit cards; ❶). Also in Market Place, *The Teesdale Hotel* (☎01833/640264; ❸), a seventeenth-century coaching inn, offers spick-and-span en-suite accommodation and a bar menu. It's also worth knowing about the *Rose & Crown* (☎01833/650213, ⓦwww.rose-and-crown.co.uk; ❺), a couple of miles or so back down the road towards Barnard Castle in **ROMALDKIRK**, which encompasses an impressive church and village green and cannily touts itself as the second prettiest village in England. The ivy-clad eighteenth-century inn has very comfortable rooms and accomplished cooking in the bar or restaurant.

Up the valley to Langdon Beck

Past Middleton, the countryside becomes harsher and the Tees more vigorous as the B6277 travels the three miles on to **Bowlees Visitor Centre** (March–Oct daily 10.30am–5pm; Nov–Feb Sat & Sun 10.30am–4pm; 50p), site of a small wildlife display and the halt for the short walk to the rapids of **Low Force**. Close by is the altogether more compelling **High Force**, a seventy-foot cascade which rumbles over an outcrop of the Whin Sill, a black dolerite ridge that pokes up in various parts of northern England. The waterfall is on private Raby land, and visitors must pay £1 to view the falls and £1.50 to use the nearby car park, by the B6277. From the road, it's a ten-minute walk through the woods to the viewing point, where daredevil visitors clamber on the rocks above the gushing waters – after rain, it's a thunderously impressive sight. You can avoid the entrance fee by walking up from Low Force on the opposite bank of the river along the **Pennine Way**, but the view of the falls isn't as spectacular. Back by the car park, the *High Force* **pub** and **hotel**

(☎01833/622222; ❸) brews its own beer (a Teesdale Bitter and the stronger, award-winning, Cauldron Snout) to accompany the bar meals.

The Pennine Way continues the six miles upstream to **Cauldron Snout**, near the source of the Tees, where the river rolls two hundred feet down a dolerite stairway as it leaves **Cow Green Reservoir**. It's also possible to reach the reservoir by car: turn off the main road at **Langdon Beck** – about a mile north of the stone-built **youth hostel** on the B6277 at Forest-in-Teesdale (☎01833/622228, ⓔlangdonbeck@yha.org.uk) – and follow the three-mile-long lane to the car park, a mile's walk from the Snout. The B6277, meanwhile, climbs ever higher as it leaves Teesdale, peaking at just under two thousand feet before dropping into Cumbria for Alston.

Weardale

Seeing Weardale by **public transport** can be a frustrating business. Bus #101 runs roughly hourly between Bishop Auckland and **Stanhope**, the main village, with less frequent extensions up the valley to Cowshill; however, to get the bus to take you to the fascinating lead-mining museum at **Killhope**, two miles further on, you'll have to ask the driver (or arrange it in advance with the bus company; ☎01388/528235) – and don't forget to request a pick-up for the way back. Otherwise, your only hopes are the #X21 from Newcastle to Stanhope (Wed & Sat only), and the summer Saturday-only #X85 from Durham to Kendal, which calls at Bishop Auckland, Stanhope, Killhope and Alston. If the bus timetables leave you tearing your hair out, there's plenty of scope for **walking** on waymarked trails: the **Weardale Way** runs the length of the valley, kicking off with an interesting eleven-mile loop at its western end linking Cowshill, Killhope and Allenheads (see p.1016), with the option of a brief scramble up 2200-feet Killhope Law for hugely varied views over the dale and beyond; from Cowshill, the looping 30-mile **Leadmining Trail** runs over the tops to Edmundbyers (see p.1017) and back, or can be split into three day-hikes (a leaflet pack is available from local tourist information centres). With your own transport, you can cut between the two valleys, Teesdale and Weardale, on one of the minor moorland roads, branching off at Egglestone, Newbiggin or Langdon Beck. The account below runs west to east, starting at the Alston end – for more details on Alston, see p.865.

Killhope and Ireshopeburn

Lead and iron-ore mining flourished in and around Weardale from the 1840s to the 1880s, leaving today's landscape scarred with old workings. One of the bigger mines, situated about three miles west of Cowshill, up at the head of the valley and a chilly 1500 feet above sea level, has been turned into the **Killhope Lead Mining Museum** (April–July & Sept daily 10.30am–5pm; Aug daily 10.30am–6pm; Oct Sat & Sun 10.30am–5pm; £3.40, £5, including mine visit; ⓦwww.durham.gov.uk/killhope), where all sorts of industrial debris lies scattered across a large open-air site, including a restored 34-foot-high waterwheel, built to power the crushing apparatus. It still turns, using six thousand gallons of water per minute from a string of diverted streams. You can also try your hand as a washerboy on the old washing floor, if you're prepared to compete with the schoolkids, while descending Park Level Mine with hard-hat and lamp gives you a taste of the miserable mining life. Incidentally, if you're intending to take a trip on the South Tynedale railway, at nearby Alston (p.865), buy a combined ticket at the mine. If you end up walking the two miles back down the Weardale Way to Cowshill to catch the bus (see above), console yourself at the *Cowshill Hotel*, which serves highly recommended bar meals.

At Cowshill, there's a turning north onto the B6295 for Allendale (see p.1016), while two miles east down the main road, tiny **IRESHOPEBURN** is the home of the **Weardale Museum** (Easter, May–July & Sept Wed–Sun 2–5pm; Aug daily 2–5pm; £1), an excellent small folk museum with displays on lead mining, the railways and Methodism, the faith of the majority of Durham's lead miners; entry to the museum also allows you access to the adjacent **High House Chapel**, the oldest Methodist chapel in the world in continuous use, built in 1760 just eight years after John Wesley's first visit to the region.

Stanhope

About nine miles downstream from Ireshopeburn lies **STANHOPE**, a useful base for hikes on the moors, made more appealing in summer by its open-air heated swimming pool. The **tourist office** (Easter to Oct daily 10am–5pm; Nov to Easter Mon–Fri 10am–4pm, Sat & Sun 11am–4pm; ☎01388/527650, ⓔdurham.dales.centre@durham.gov.uk), in the Durham Dales Centre opposite Market Place, can give information on the **walks**, which include a notable five-mile circuit from the town centre, up through the woods of Stanhope Dene and across open moorlands past old lead mines and quarries. Prominent among Stanhope's **accommodation** options is *Stanhope Old Hall* on the main road just west of the town centre (☎01388/528451; ❹), a bargain opportunity to stay in a twelfth-century fortified hunting lodge of the Prince Bishops of Durham – or make do with a cosy drink in front of a huge open fire. Two miles down the valley from Stanhope in **FROSTERLEY** – where quarries once produced the exquisite, fossil-encrusted black limestone "marble" used to such effect in Durham Cathedral – Weardale Mountain Bikes (☎01388/528129) offer **bike rental**; pick up a leaflet from Stanhope tourist office detailing four recommended cycling loops in the area.

North across the moors

Two minor roads branch **north from Weardale**, over the border into Northumberland, heading towards Hexham and Hadrian's Wall and crossing some of the most glorious, isolated moorland in the north of England. With your own transport, it's well worth forsaking the main roads to follow either of these routes, to Allendale or Blanchland. **By bus**, there are two routes into the area, but they don't meet up: the #688 runs from Hexham to Allendale and Allenheads, but no further, between five and nine times a day; while the #773 heads west from Consett (which is itself linked by hourly bus with Newcastle) to Edmundbyers and Blanchland (not Sun).

The Allen Valley

The B6295 climbs out of Weardale and drops into the **Allen Valley**, where heather-covered moorland shelters small settlements that once made their living from lead mining. The River Allen itself can be extremely beautiful at times, widening as it tumbles north to join the River Tyne just east of Bardon Mill. It was from this valley that painter John Martin (p.1030) drew much of his inspiration, and the dramatic surroundings are still easily viewed today from a series of river walks (see box below) accessible from either of the main settlements.

At **ALLENHEADS**, at the top of the valley, twelve miles from Stanhope, handsome stone buildings stand close to the river. The **Heritage Centre** (Easter–Oct daily 9am–5pm; £1) details the village's erstwhile industry, and incorporates an early Armstrong hydraulic engine used for driving the sawmill and a blacksmith's workshop, while a short nature trail guides you through the

The **Allen Valley** offers some of the finest walking in the region. There are all manner of circular walks that can be undertaken from Allendale town, the best base hereabouts, most of which involve pottering up or down the banks of the river. A very good path takes you all the way from Allendale **south to Allenheads** (around nine miles one way), leaving or crossing the river on occasion, though connoisseurs rate higher the northern section, **from Allendale to the River Tyne** (eight miles one way), much of it National Trust land with waymarked side trails through ancient woodland. This is at its most dramatic when passing through the beautiful, tree-clad **Allen Gorge**, watched over by Staward Peel, a medieval fortified tower-house; there's road access at **Plankey Mill**, around which the river becomes full of splashing families on summer weekends. Where the Allen flows into the Tyne, you're only a mile or so east of the train station at **Bardon Mill** and only another hour and a half's cross-country walk from **Hadrian's Wall** at Housesteads (p.1050), enabling you to move on east or west by train, bus or on foot.

Alternatively, back at Allendale, there are glorious moorland routes east across **Hexhamshire Common**, descending either to Hexham itself (via Dipton Mill and its pub; or, three miles further east, to Corbridge. Both towns are easily reached in a day from Allendale. From Allenheads, after a bit of initial clambering north or south, the cross-moorland routes east are to Blanchland (see below), a tiring day's walk but eminently worthwhile; or you can loop south to Cowshill and Killhope (see p.1014).

woodland around the East Allen River. An old barn at the centre, known in these parts as a *hemmel*, has been converted into the *Hemmel Café*, though for true idiosyncrasy pop into the village's *Allenheads Inn* (☎01434/685200; ❷), stuffed with every conceivable piece of junk-shop arcana. Lunch and dinner are served, and the owners also rent out the adjacent six-person stone cottage. Allenheads, incidentally, is on the C2C cycle route (see box on p.998), and there's useful **bunkhouse** accommodation at *Allenheads Lodge Outdoor Centre*, in the village (☎01434/685374; no credit cards).

ALLENDALE TOWN, another four miles north, also goes about its quiet, rural way, and claims to be at the exact centre of the British Isles. This is a peaceful place to stay, with a small supermarket, a post office and several friendly pubs and small hotels, all centred on the main market square. The best **accommodation** here is at the welcoming *King's Head* (☎01434/683681; ❷), right in the square, which has nice rooms, home-cooked meals, a wide range of real ales and great live music nights. B&B is also on offer in the *Allendale Tea Rooms* (☎01434/683575; no credit cards; ❷), opposite the hotel. Allendale's major curiosity is the **New Year's Eve** "tar barrels" ceremony, when a huge, spluttering bonfire is lit in the square around which the locals parade with barrels – more like trays – of burning pitch balanced on their heads to usher in the new year.

Blanchland

The other trans-moorland route is the B6278 which cuts north from Weardale at Stanhope for ten extraordinarily wild miles to tiny **BLANCHLAND**, a handful of ancient, lichen-stained stone cottages huddled round an L-shaped square that was once the outer court of a twelve-man Premonstratensian abbey, founded in the twelfth century. The village has been preserved and protected since 1721, when Lord Crewe, the childless bishop of Durham, bequeathed his estate to trustees on condition that they rebuilt the old conventual buildings, for Blanchland had slowly fallen into disrepair after the abbey's dissolution. The original trustees obliged and their successors have allowed but the faintest whiff of the twenty-first century to intrude, their last concession being the construction of a pint-sized shelter in celebration of Queen Victoria's Diamond Jubilee.

Consequently, the village bears many reminders of its monastic past, from the sturdy gatehouse that now accommodates the post office to the L-shaped parish church where the medieval chancel and tower were all used to good effect during the rebuilding of 1752. But it's the **Lord Crewe Arms Hotel** (☎01434/675251, ⓦwww.crewearms.freeserve.co.uk; ❼) that steals the show. Once the abbot's lodge, the hotel's nooks and crannies have all sorts of surprises, an enticing mixture of medieval and eighteenth-century Gothic features, including the dark vaulted basements, two big fireplaces left over from the canons' kitchen and a priest's hideaway stuck inside the chimney. It's a superb place to stay – check out the good-value half-board deals – with lavish rooms and a delightful garden-cum-cloister. The **restaurant** serves heavy table d'hôte dinners for around £30, and there's a fine public bar in the undercroft.

East of Blanchland

Beyond Blanchland, drivers will probably be keen to make Hexham by the most direct route along the B6306, but consider taking a detour east to the main A68 and driving past the **Derwent Reservoir**. At the attractive village of **EDMUNDBYERS**, where B6306 meets B6278, is a (heavily restored) twelfth-century church and a simple **youth hostel** (☎01207/255651) in seventeenth-century Low House, just half a mile from the reservoir. You can camp at the hostel, too, and there are a couple of local B&Bs if you crave more comfort. A few miles farther east, at the junction with the A68, at **Carterway Heads**, the *Manor House Inn* (☎01207/255268; ❷) has four en-suite rooms overlooking the reservoir and some of the best **pub food** in northeastern England – marinated mushroom tikka masala, local fish, home-made desserts – at around £15 a head.

The Tees Valley: Darlington to the coast

In a region whose physical face was blighted first by industrial success and then by urban neglect, the towns along the **Tees Valley** take some beating. Whether approaching from Yorkshire to the south or Northumberland and Durham to the north, it seems that a view isn't considered a view hereabouts unless it's blocked by towers and pipes, clouded by smoking chimneys and framed by rusting machinery. This, of course, is a harsh judgement and only half the story – the **River Tees**, along with the Tyne farther north, was one of the great engines of British economic power in the late nineteenth century. That it's so far off the tourist map as to be invisible is hardly the fault of towns whose livelihood largely disappeared once iron- and steel-making and shipbuilding became things of the past in England. But once there were rich pickings here, in places such as **Darlington**, twenty miles south of Durham city, where the first public passenger-carrying steam train, George Stephenson's *Locomotion*, made its inaugural run and is now on permanent display. The line ran first to **Stockton-on-Tees** and was then extended to ports at **Middlesbrough** and **Hartlepool**, to enable ever-increasing amounts of Durham coal to be unloaded and exported. Iron from the local Cleveland Hills supported a shipbuilding industry, which in Hartlepool at least had been flourishing since the eighteenth century.

In truth, few people are going to stop at any of these towns. For those that do, Darlington is the most surprisingly attractive, and you'd have to be hard-hearted not to derive some pleasure from Hartlepool's historic quay. Drivers will find navigating the swirling ring roads and bypasses something of a trial, but it's worth bearing in mind the route east as one possible **approach to North Yorkshire**. Once out on the coast at Saltburn, or inland beyond Guisborough, you're very quickly in the heart of the North York Moors. **Public transport** links are good, too, with regular services connecting the bus and train stations of all the towns in the area. In particular, note the Esk Valley train line from **Middlesbrough to Whitby** which runs via Grosmont, northern terminal point of the North Yorkshire Moors Railway.

Darlington

DARLINGTON hit the big time in 1825, when George Stephenson's *Locomotion* hurtled from here to nearby Stockton-on-Tees, with the inventor at the controls and flag-carrying horsemen riding ahead to warn of the onrushing train, which reached a terrifying fifteen miles per hour. This novel form of transport soon proved popular with passengers, an unlooked-for bonus for Edward Pease, the line's instigator: he had simply wanted a fast and economical way to transport coal from the Durham pits to the docks at Stockton. Subsequently, Darlington grew into a rail-engineering centre, and didn't look back till the pruning of the network and the closure of the works in 1966.

It's little surprise, then, that all signs in town point to the **Darlington Railway Centre and Museum** (daily 10am–5pm; £2.10), housed in Darlington's North Road station, which was completed in 1842; it's a twenty-minute walk up Northgate from the central market place. The museum's pride and joy is the original *Locomotion*, actually built in Newcastle and which continued in service until 1841 – other locally made engines superseded it, and some of these are on show, too, but on the whole it's a disappointingly unspir-ited collection of railway memorabilia, unable to escape the long shadow cast by the National Railway Museum down the road at York. The museum really only comes to life on Saturdays when you can watch enthusiasts at work building a new Pacific locomotive in the refurbished Darlington Locomotive Works (daily 11am–4pm; same ticket), and on the occasional days, including a September festival and "Santa Special" days in December, when an engine hauls visitors up a quarter-mile stretch of track next door. The failure to make much of one of Britain's most iconic industrial relics doesn't fill the visitor full of confidence, but in fact the rest of Darlington (or at least the centre) shows itself off well. Its origins lie deep in Saxon times, following which it enjoyed a long history as an agricultural centre and staging post on the Great North Road. The monks carrying St Cuthbert's body from Ripon to Durham stopped in Darlington, the saint lending his name to the graceful central, river-side church of **St Cuthbert** (Easter–Sept daily 11am–2pm; Oct–Easter Fri 11am–1pm), where the needle-like spire and decorative turrets herald the delicate Early English stonework inside. One of England's largest market squares spreads beyond the church up to the restored Victorian covered **market** (Mon–Sat 8am–5pm, with a large outdoor market Mon & Sat), next to the clock tower, both designed by Alfred Waterhouse, the architect responsible for Manchester's grandiose town hall and London's Natural History Museum. The surrounding buildings are all solidly nineteenth-century, too, many paid for by the town's hardworking Quaker industrialists (of whom Pease was a leading light), who doubtless would have frowned upon the current civic authority's attempts to humanize the town centre. The pedestrianized Market Place has been given back to the people and while it may not be Rome, you can sip a cappuccino at one of several cafés and pubs that spill tables outside at the first hint of sunshine.

Practicalities

Darlington's **train station** is on the main line from London to Scotland (via Durham and Newcastle) and there are also services to Middlesbrough, Saltburn and Bishop Auckland. From the station, walk up Victoria Road to the roundabout and turn right down Feethams for the central Market Place. You'll pass the new town hall on Feethams, opposite which most **buses** stop.

The town's helpful **tourist office** on the south side of Market Place at 13 Horsemarket (Mon–Fri 9am–5pm, Sat 10am–4pm; ☎01325/388666, ✉tic@darlington.gov.uk) has a substantial list of B&Bs. Central **accommodation** options include the *New Grange Hotel*, a smartly refurbished, 200-year-old mansion on Coniscliffe Road, the continuation of Blackwellgate west from the Market Place (☎01325/365858; ❺), and the more reasonable *Balmoral Guest House*, a grand Victorian town house at 63 Woodland Rd, five minutes' walk northwest of the centre (☎01325/461908; ❷). Cheap and basic board is available at the town's Arts Centre (☎01325/483271; ❶), about half a mile west of the centre in Vane Terrace, where guests can use the kitchen as well as the centre's bars and lunchtime bistro – follow Duke Street from central Skinnergate.

There are several **cafés** on and around Market Place, while the *Hole in the Wall* pub on the square serves spicy Thai lunches (closed Sun) for a fiver. Heading west from the Market Place a short way up Blackwellgate, *Joe Rigatoni's* (☎01325/464642) is the town's most reliable Italian, in a grand, airy setting on the corner of Grange Road. Check out the highly enterprising **Arts Centre** and its affiliated **Civic Theatre** (on a separate site on Parkgate, between the Market Place and the train station), which offer a full, year-round programme of theatre, movies, comedy, exhibitions and live music (bookings on ☎01325/486555, ⓦwww.darlington-arts.co.uk).

Piercebridge

Five miles west of Darlington, off the A67, the remains of a Roman fort are visible at the small village of **PIERCEBRIDGE**, on the River Tees. The **site** (free access) was first occupied in 70 AD and soon became a major strategic river crossing on the fortified Dere Street supply route; defensive ditches and sections of the fort wall are clearly visible, while various foundations have been identified as the remains of guard rooms, a temple and a row of houses. Amble out here late in the day and Piercebridge can make a decent **overnight stop**, provided you book ahead for the highly attractive eighteenth-century *George Hotel* (☎01325/374576; ❹), whose en-suite rooms and restaurant look across the gentle banks of the river. The bar food is good, too. Buses run this way from Darlington or Barnard Castle.

The Captain Cook trail: Middlesbrough and Stockton

MIDDLESBROUGH, the region's largest town, fifteen miles east of Darlington, is entirely a product of the early industrial age, with nineteenth-century iron and steel barons throwing up factories and housing almost as fast as they could ship their products out of the docks on the River Tees. What was a hamlet at the turn of the nineteenth century was a thriving industrial town of 100,000 people by the turn of the twentieth – "a vast dingy conjuring trick" to J.B. Priestley's mind. When iron and steel declined in importance and the local shipbuilding industry collapsed (the last shipyard closed in 1986), Middlesbrough took to the chemical industry, whose expansive, belching plants still surround the outskirts, making for an unsightly, forbidding approach to the town. Add to this a contemporary renaissance in light engineering and it seems that, compared to many of its neighbours, Middlesbrough can boast relative success in keeping its economic head above water. For visitors, however, none of these enterprises lend themselves easily to the celebration of industrial heritage so much in evidence further west, in the coalfields. The modern town centre is unremarkable in every way and only a pair of bridges recall earlier engineering feats. The **Transporter Bridge** (1911), at Ferry Road just north of the centre, its central section carting cars and pedestrians across the Tees towards Hartlepool (Mon–Sat 5am–11.05pm, Sun 2–11.05pm; cars 80p, pedestrians 30p), is the sole working example left in the country and now sports its own small visitor centre. Further southwest, the **Newport Bridge** (1934) was the first vertical lift bridge built in England.

The town prefers to trumpet its position as "Gateway to Captain Cook Country", fair enough given that he was born a mile and a half south of the centre in Marton in 1728. Here, the **Captain Cook Birthplace Museum** in Stewart Park (Tues–Sun: June–Sept 10am–5.30pm; Oct–May 10am–3.30pm; £2.40) covers the life and times of Captain James Cook, and does it very well by way of good interpretative and interactive displays. As well as displays of artefacts brought back from the South Seas on Cook's voyages, touch-screen terminals provide contemporary testimony by his botanist Sir Joseph Banks, while a series of short films fill in the background about Cook's life and a sailor's lot at sea. Buses #28, #29, #30, #66 and #90 from the bus station run every fifteen minutes or so to Marton – ask the driver for the stop – and while you're in the park you may as well call in at nearby **St Cuthbert's** church on Stokesley Road, where Cook was baptized. It's usually closed during the day but the key is available at the vicarage (☎01642/316201).

Just a couple of museums back towards the centre, on Linthorpe Road, offer any further reason to delay your onward journey from Middlesbrough. The **Middlesbrough Art Gallery**, at no. 320 (Tues–Sat 10am–5.30pm; free), houses temporary exhibitions by contemporary artists. A ten-minute walk further out on the same road is the **Dorman Museum** (Tues–Sat 10am–5.30pm, Sun 2.30–5pm; free), a museum of the history of Middlesbrough with an eye-catching collection of Linthorpe pottery – richly glazed, unusually shaped ceramics from a late-nineteenth-century workshop designed to combat local unemployment. The Dorman was closed for major redevelopment at the time of writing, but should be open again by the time you read this.

To complete the Captain Cook trail through this part of the country, you'll need to hop across the river to **STOCKTON-ON-TEES**, a once-attractive market town that's been charmlessly redeveloped beyond recognition. Tied up at Castlegate Quay here is a detailed full-size replica of **HM Bark Endeavour**, the converted collier in which Cook set sail in 1768 on his first scientific and surveying expedition to Tahiti, New Zealand and Australia. The ship's taken over by youth groups for part of the week, but from Sundays to Wednesdays (April–Oct 10am–5pm; £3) enthusiastic and knowledgeable volunteer guides recount the rigours of life on board during this hazardous voyage.

If all these tall tales of the high seas give you a taste for the water, you might be tempted by a **cruise** from the same quay aboard the *Teesside Princess* (☎01642/608038, ⊛www.princessrivercruises.co.uk), which potters upstream to **Yarm** and back in three and half hours. Sailings (May–Sept Tues–Sun 10.15am & 2pm; Oct–April Wed, Sat & Sun 10.15am & 2pm; £6 return) are timed to allow you to lunch in Yarm, an affluent former market town which has preserved its good looks and supports a stylish modern European restaurant on the High Street, *Chadwick's* (℡01642/788558), as well as an attractive riverside pub, *The Blue Bell*.

Practicalities

From **Middlesbrough train station** (direct services from Manchester, Leeds, York and Newcastle), it's just a short walk up Albert Road to the main Corporation Road. Turn right for the **bus station** – five minutes further up on its continuation, Newport Road – and carry straight on for the **tourist office**, 99 Albert Rd (Mon–Thurs 9am–5pm, Fri 9am–4.30pm, Sat 9am–1.30pm; ℡01642/358086, ⊛www.captaincook.org.uk). Linthorpe Road, for the museums, runs south off Corporation Road, parallel to and west of Albert Road.

Stockton's town centre, three miles west, is equally compact, with the **train station** (similar services to Middlesbrough's but less frequent) five minute's walk northwest of the High Street, where numerous **buses** from Middlesbrough will put you off. Off the east side of the High Street in Theatre Yard is the **tourist office** (Mon–Sat 9am–5pm; ℡01642/393936), with the river and Castlegate Quay just beyond.

It's difficult to see why you'd want to spend the night, with both Durham and the coast so close. One place that might tempt you to **stay** in the area, if you have your own transport, is *Judges at Kirklevington Hall*, eight miles southwest of Middlesbrough and a mile south of Yarm on the A67 (℡01642/789000; ❽). Formerly the lodgings of circuit judges on duty in Teesside, this grand country house boasts beautiful gardens and woodlands, a fine restaurant and attentive staff – and good half-board deals at weekends. To **eat**, the eccentrically decorated *Purple Onion*, 80 Corporation Rd (℡01642/222250; closed Sun eve), is the best place in Middlesbrough, serving bitingly trendy food at middling-to-high prices; you should book at the weekends.

Hartlepool

If there's one Teesside town trying hard to reinvent itself it's **HARTLEPOOL**, ten miles north of Middlesbrough, England's third largest port in the nineteenth century and a noted shipbuilding centre, but deprived of investment and hope for years following successive economic downturns. These days, though, its image is slowly being transformed by the renaissance of its once decaying dockland area, now spruced up as the popular **Hartlepool Historic Quay** off Marina Way (daily 10am–5pm; last admission 2hr before closing; £5.50). The entrance fee gets you on to the bustling eighteenth-century quayside where active attractions based around pressgangs, the Royal Navy, seaport life and fighting ships stir the senses. There's also a replica eighteenth-century maritime pub, as well as coffee shop and market, while a separate fee is charged if you want to take a guided tour of **HMS Trincomalee** (daily: April–Oct 10.30am–5pm; Nov–March 10.30am–4pm; £3.50), a navy training ship built in 1817. On the edge of the quay in the entertaining **Museum of Hartlepool** at Jackson Dock (daily 10am–5pm; free), you can climb the port's original lighthouse, board a restored paddle steamer and trace the town's history, including its most notorious episode, which to this day earns Hartlepudlians the nickname "monkey hangers": legend has it that when a French ship sank off the coast during the Napoleonic Wars, the locals mistook the sole survivor, a monkey, for a Frenchman, and tried and hanged it as a spy. Back in the town centre, ten minutes' walk south, the restored nineteenth-century Christ Church, on Church Square, houses Hartlepool's accomplished **Art Gallery** (Tues–Sat 10am–5.30pm, Sun 2–5pm; free) and the **tourist office** (same hours; ☎01429/869706, ⊛www.thisishartlepool.com), which can help if you're seduced into staying.

Saltburn

On the coast to the south of the Tees estuary, it's not a difficult decision to bypass the kiss-me-quick tackiness of Redcar in favour of **SALTBURN**, twelve miles east of Middlesbrough, a graceful Victorian resort in a dramatic setting overlooking extensive sands and mottled red sea cliffs. Soon after the railway arrived in 1861 to ferry Teessiders out to the sea on high days and holidays, Saltburn became a rather fashionable spa town boasting all the necessary accoutrements: hydraulic **inclined tramway** (May to mid-Sept daily 10am–1pm & 2–7pm; Easter to end April & mid-Sept to Oct Sat & Sun 10am–1pm & 2–5pm; 55p), complete with stained-glass windows, that connects upper town to pier and promenade; ornate **Italian Gardens** in the more bucolic Valley Gardens that run beneath the eastern side of town, linked to the beach by a **miniature railway** (Easter–Sept Sat & Sun 1–5pm, plus Tues–Fri same times during school holidays; 90p); and prominent hotels, many of which continue to flourish today. Modern attractions include the **Smugglers Heritage Centre** (April–Oct daily 10am–6pm, last tour 5.30pm; £1.85), a vivid audio-visual re-creation of Saltburn's darker past, set in fishermen's cottages to the east of the pier. Three dimly lit and cramped rooms of a 200-year-old tavern are once again populated by rowdy, swashbuckling seamen and buxom barmaids in an atmospheric retelling of the adventures of the smugglers' gangs, or "free traders", who made themselves popular with locals by sneaking vast quantities of tea, coffee, fine silks, lace and other such illicit cargoes ashore. Afterwards, don't forget to have a **drink** at the *Ship Inn*, the original smugglers' haunt next door. Saltburn's also become something of a **surfing** hub for these parts, with boards available to rent down by the pier (£6/hr including wetsuit; ☎01287/625321, to check on the surf, call ☎09068 /545543; ⊛www.members.tripod.com/eastcoastsurf).

There are regular **train** services to Saltburn's impressive nineteenth-century station from Newcastle, Durham and Bishop Auckland, via Darlington and Middlesbrough, while frequent **buses** from Middlesbrough bus station (with connections from Newcastle) stop in the parade outside the train station. If you want to stay in summer, it's best to call first at the **tourist office** in the railway station buildings (Easter–Sept Mon–Sat 9am–5pm; Oct–Easter Tues–Sat 9am–5pm; ☎01287/622422, ⓔsaltburn_tic@redcar-cleveland.gov.uk) and find out about accommodation vacancies. Out of season, you'll be able to pick and choose from a selection of good-value **guest houses** and **hotels**. For surroundings in keeping with the town, the *Rushpool Hall Hotel* in Saltburn Valley (☎01287/624111, ⊛www.rushpoolhall.com; ❼) is a fine choice: a nineteenth-century country house set in extensive grounds about a mile south of the centre off Saltburn Lane, whose turrets, grand staircase and elegant public rooms are straight out of an Agatha Christie whodunnit. If your wallet won't stretch that far, try *The Rose Garden*, just west of the station at 20 Hilda Place (☎01287/622947, ⊛www.therosegarden.co.uk; ❷), which offers comfortable bedrooms and good breakfasts, including vegetarian options.

Steps from the beach behind the *Ship Inn* lead up the cliff to join the coastal section of the **Cleveland Way**, the path that starts deep in the North York Moors at Helmsley (see p.969). It hits the coast at Saltburn, from where it's nine miles across the high cliffs to the next stop at Staithes, and 54 miles in total to the end of the path at Filey.

Newcastle upon Tyne

At first glance **NEWCASTLE UPON TYNE** – virtual capital of the area between Yorkshire and Scotland – may appear to be just another northern industrial conurbation, but the banks of the Tyne have been settled for nearly two thousand years and the city consequently has a greater breadth of attractions than many of its rivals. The Romans were the first to bridge the river here, and the "new castle" appeared as long ago as 1080. In the seventeenth century a regional monopoly on **coal** export brought wealth and power to Newcastle and – as well as giving a new expression to the English language – engendered its other great industry, shipbuilding. At one time, 25 percent of the world's shipping was built here, and the first steam train and steam turbine also emerged from Newcastle factories. In its nineteenth-century heyday, Newcastle's engineers and builders gave the city an elegance that has survived the ravages of 1960s and 1970s development, much of which was perpetrated by John Poulson, a mediocre architect whose name became a byword for civic corruption. Industrial decline hit Newcastle early, as highlighted by the **Jarrow March** of 1936 (see p.1094), but this remains a vibrant place, with a resilience that's symbolized commercially by the hugely successful **MetroCentre** shopping mall across the river at Gateshead, and artistically by Antony Gormley's **Angel of the North**, a magnificent steel sculpture the size of a jumbo jet that welcomes anyone approaching the city from the south by rail or road. There's an impressive energy about Newcastle's handsome city centre, too – encapsulated in the **International Centre for Life**, which combines a cutting-edge biotechnology research centre with noisy and edifying science lessons at the state-of-the-art **LIFE Interactive World** – while its revitalized **Quayside**, scene of much of the city's **nightlife**, goes from strength to strength. Indeed, there's a sharper edge to Newcastle's carousing these days, with new cafés, bars and clubs rivalling the traditional knees-up antics of the notorious Bigg Market. Culturally, too, Newcastle is way ahead of its local rivals – Durham included – boasting the best traditional art gallery in the Northeast, the **Laing**, and a slew of good theatres and all-round arts venues. This pre-eminence will be cemented with the imminent opening of the **BALTIC Centre for Contemporary Art**, a quayside flour mill that's being transformed into the largest visual arts space in the country outside of London, and will be further reinforced in 2003 by the equally adventurous **Music Centre Gateshead** alongside.

All these factors, as well as hard times and a sense of remoteness from the capital, have given Newcastle's inhabitants, known as **Geordies**, a partisan pride in their city, which finds its most evident expression in fanatical support for the **Newcastle United** football team (the "Magpies"). With the stadium firmly anchored in the heart of the city, and every other young (and not so young) supporter wearing the familiar black-and-white shirt, it's difficult to overstate the team's importance – the death a few years ago of United's most famous goalscorer, Jackie Milburn, brought thousands onto the streets for what was

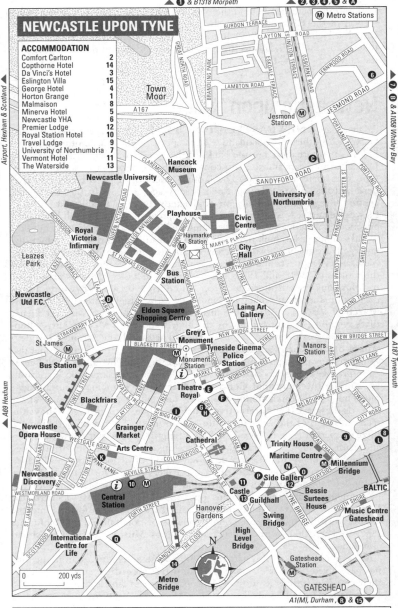

NEWCASTLE UPON TYNE

Airport, Hexham & Scotland ▲

▲ ❶ & B1318 Morpeth   ▲ ❷, ❸, ❹, ❺ & Ⓐ

Ⓜ Metro Stations

ACCOMMODATION

Comfort Carlton	2
Copthorne Hotel	14
Da Vinci's Hotel	3
Eslington Villa	15
George Hotel	4
Horton Grange	1
Malmaison	8
Minerva Hotel	5
Newcastle YHA	6
Premier Lodge	12
Royal Station Hotel	10
Travel Lodge	9
University of Northumbria	7
Vermont Hotel	11
The Waterside	13

BURDON TERRACE
CLAYTON ROAD
OSBORNE ROAD
FERNWOOD ROAD
❻
▲ ❼, ❽ & A1058 Whitley Bay
JESMOND ROAD

Town Moor

A167

Jesmond Station Ⓜ

Ⓒ

SANDYFORD ROAD

Hancock Museum

Newcastle University

University of Northumbria

A167

Playhouse

Civic Centre

Royal Victoria Infirmary

Haymarket Station Ⓜ

City Hall

Leazes Park

Bus Station

Newcastle Utd F.C.

Ⓓ

Eldon Square Shopping Centre

Laing Art Gallery

NEW BRIDGE STREET

Manors Station Ⓜ

A187 Tynemouth ▲

St James Ⓜ
GALLOWGATE

Grey's Monument

Tyneside Cinema

Bus Station

BLACKETT STREET

Monument Station Ⓜ

Police Station

Blackfriars

ⓘ

Theatre Royal Ⓔ

Ⓕ

Newcastle Opera House

Grainger Market

Ⓘ

Ⓖ
Ⓗ

Arts Centre

Cathedral

Trinity House

Maritime Centre

Newcastle Discovery

Ⓚ

ⓘ ⑩ Ⓜ

Ⓝ
Ⓞ

Ⓜ
Millennium Bridge

Central Station

⑪ Ⓟ Side Gallery
⑫

Castle
⑬ Guildhall

Bessie Surtees House

BALTIC

International Centre for Life

Ⓠ

Hanover Gardens

High Level Bridge

Swing Bridge

Music Centre Gateshead

N

Metro Bridge

Gateshead Station Ⓜ

GATESHEAD

A1(M), Durham, Ⓡ & ⑮ ▼

0   200 yds

RESTAURANTS

Barluga	**H**	Eslington Villa	**R**	Leela's	**J**	Sachin's	**Q**
Blakes Coffee House	**G**	Fisherman's Lodge	**B**	Pani's	**E**	The Side Café Bistro	**P**
Café 21	**N**	Heartbreak Soup	**M**	Paradiso	**F**	Treacle Moon	**P**
Café Sol	**K**	La Tasca	**L**	Rupali	**I**	Valley Junction 397	**C**
Da Vinci's	**A**	La Toscana	**D**	Sabatini	**O**		

almost a state funeral, while the Angel of the North himself, lofty symbol of the area's traditional engineering skills and present regeneration, was humble enough to sport a giant replica shirt before the team's latest Cup Final appearance.

Arrival

Coming to Newcastle by train gives a fantastic view of the city's trademark bridges across the steep Tyne valley. The train station, **Central Station**, on Neville Street, is a five-minute walk south of the city centre and has a useful tourist office and Metro station. National Express **coach** services arrive at Gallowgate station (St James Metro) opposite St James's Park football ground, while most regional **bus** services from the likes of Bamburgh, Berwick, Alnwick and Darlington use the **Haymarket** bus station on Percy Street on the north side of the centre (Haymarket Metro). Many other city and local bus services arrive at and depart from the underground bus station a hundred yards down the same street in **Eldon Square Shopping Centre**.

Newcastle also has an **airport**, six miles north of the city, which is linked by Metro to Central Station (5.50am–11.10pm every 7–15 min; 25min; £1.60) and beyond. Alternatively, you could take a taxi into the centre (around £12).

Ferry arrivals from Scandinavia and Holland dock at Royal Quays, North Shields, seven miles east of the city. Connecting bus services run you into the centre, stopping at Central Station, while a taxi will cost around £10.

For all **departure details** and enquiry numbers, see "Listings", p.1035.

Information and city transport

There are **tourist offices** at 132 Grainger St (June–Sept Mon–Wed, Fri & Sat 9.30am–5.30pm, Thurs 9.30am–7.30pm Sun 10am–4pm; rest of year closed Sun; ☎0191/277 8000, ✉tourist.info@newcastle.gov.uk), in the Central Station (Mon–Fri 10am–5pm, Sat 9am–5pm; same contact details), and at the **airport** (variable hours; ☎0191/214 4422). All hand out useful maps, and have various brochures and booklets available, including self-guided walking-tour "heritage trails". You'll also be able to buy the invaluable *Northumberland Public Transport Guide* (£1).

You can walk around the whole of central Newcastle easily enough, but for journeys further afield you'll need to get to grips with the conurbation's cheap and efficient rail system, the **Metro** (6am–11.30pm every 4–15min). The landmark Grey's Monument marks the city centre and the site of **Monument**, the main interchange for the Metro's two lines: the green line, connecting South Shields, Jarrow, Gateshead, Central Station, Monument, Haymarket, Jesmond and West Jesmond with the airport; and the circular yellow line which follows the same route from Monument through West Jesmond, before branching off to the coast at Tynemouth, then returning along the north bank of the Tyne, via North Shields, Wallsend and Manors, to Monument (and St James); another limb of the yellow line heads south via Central Station across the river to Gateshead and will, by early 2002, extend as far as Sunderland. One-way tickets for short hops start as low as 60p, though a bewildering variety of discount **passes** – many also valid on the buses and local ferries – are available. Most useful for visitors are the Day Rover (£3.70) for unlimited travel in Tyne and Wear, and the Metro Day Saver for unlimited metro and ferry rides (£3 after 9.30am Mon, Tues, Thurs & Fri, all day Sat & Sun; £1.50 after 9.30am Wed or after 6.30pm any other day). For all **public transport enquiries**, call Traveline (see p.1074), log onto the website of Nexus, the Tyne and Wear passenger transport executive, which has a useful journey planner option (ⓦ www.nexus.org.uk), or visit the Nexus Travelshop at Haymarket or Monument Metro stations.

To get out on the Tyne, sign up for one of River Tyne Cruises' three-hour **sightseeing cruises**, which depart from the east end of the Quayside by the *Pitcher and Piano* (£7.99; ☏ 0191/296 6740). The local public transport authority also operates a few summer afternoon cruises from the Quayside and South Shields, at the mouth of the river (1hr 30min; £5; ☏ 0191/203 3211). Guided, themed **walking tours** of the city centre (Easter–Oct; £2.50) are arranged by the Grainger Street tourist office. There's also a hop-on, hop-off, open-top **sightseeing bus**, which departs from the Central Station (summer every 15min; winter Mon–Sat every 30min, Sun hourly; £5; ⓦ www.city-sightseeing.com).

Accommodation

Hotel expansion shows no signs of slowing in Newcastle, with the success of the Quayside area prompting plans for several new properties (including a large Hilton on the Gateshead waterfront, near the forthcoming Baltic arts centre). The biggest concentration of **hotels** and **guest houses** is a mile north of the city centre in Jesmond, along and around Osborne Road: take the Metro to West Jesmond or bus #30B, #31B or #80 from Central Station or Haymarket. You shouldn't have difficulty finding a bed at any time of the year, though visiting business folk make weekdays busier than **weekends** for most of the year. Consequently, many hotels offer discounts for Friday- and Saturday-night stays, especially at the upper end of the scale where savings can be considerable. Save yourself time and effort by using the free **room-booking service** available at the tourist offices to personal callers.

Hotels and guest houses

Comfort Carlton 82–86 Osborne Rd ☏ 0191/281 3361. Decent value (though breakfast costs extra), with tasteful en-suite rooms, bar and restaurant. ❹

Copthorne Hotel The Close, Quayside ☏ 0191/222 0333, ⒺЕ sales.newcastle@mill-cop.com. Superbly located bang on the riverside, this modern hotel has Tyne views from most of its rooms, a sunny atrium, good restaurants, a gym and swimming pool. Rooms come with modems and voicemail. ❽

Da Vinci's Hotel 73 Osborne Rd ☏ 0191/281 5284. Light, well-furnished rooms above a classy restaurant complete with piano and Leonardo prints. ❸, ❷ at weekends.

Eslington Villa 8 Station Rd, Low Fell, Gateshead ☏ 0191/487 6017. On the south side of Gateshead overlooking the Team Valley trading estate and only practicable with your own transport, this small, quiet hotel has huge, stylishly decorated rooms, well-tended gardens and a top-class restaurant (see p.1032) and offers very good value, especially at weekends or if you go half-board. ❹

George Hotel 88 Osborne Rd ☏ 0191/281 4442, Ⓔ georgehotel@dial.pipex.com. Victorian town house hotel with some of the city's least expensive en-suite rooms, above a popular Chinese restaurant. ❷

Horton Grange Seaton Burn ☏ 01661/860686, ⓦ www.horton-grange.co.uk. Relaxed and welcoming country-house hotel with an excellent conservatory restaurant, five miles north of the centre off the A1(M). ❺

Malmaison The Quayside ☏ 0191/245 5000, Ⓔ newcastle@malmaison.com. Chic lodgings in the former Co-op building, right on the Quayside. Rooms come with great beds, CD players and modems. Jazzy sounds, crushed velvet sofas, brasserie, bar and gym round off the facilities. ❼

Minerva Hotel 105 Osborne Rd ☏ 0191/281 0190. Family-run place with pleasant rooms (ones with shower in the next price category), a cosy bar, inexpensive dinners, and secure parking. No credit cards. ❶

Royal Station Hotel Neville St ☏ 0191/232 0781, ⓦ www.royalstationhotel.com. The city's original Victorian station hotel in a great central location, opened in 1858 by Victoria herself and now fully modernized. ❺

Premier Lodge The Quayside ☏ 0870/700 1504, ⓦ www.premierlodge.com. An unbeatable location for this no-frills chain: in the nineteenth-century Exchange Buildings under the Tyne Bridge. One price for all bedrooms, so singles lose out and families gain – and be sure to ask for a room with a view of the river. ❷

Travelodge Forster St ☎0191/261 5432, ⊛www
.travellodge.co.uk. A purpose-built block in a quiet
location off the easterly end of the Quayside; gives
Premier Lodge a run for its money, with near-iden-
tical rates. ❷
Vermont Hotel Castle Garth ☎0191/233 1010,
⊛www.vermont-hotel.com. High-class twelve-
storey business hotel, with reception next to the
castle and its lowest floor giving onto the
Quayside; good views and facilities, including in-
room modem ports and a fitness centre. ❽
The Waterside 48–52 Sandhill ☎0191/230 0111.
Small, luxury hotel in a listed building right in the
centre of the noisy Quayside night-time action, and
with its own decent bar. ❺

Hostel and university accommodation

Newcastle YHA 107 Jesmond Rd ☎0191/281
2570, ℮newcastle@yha.org.uk. Popular town-
house hostel with sixty beds, including four twin
rooms, near Jesmond Metro station – reserve in
advance in summer. Breakfast and cheap evening
meals served. Closed Mon–Thurs from Christmas
to February.
University of Northumbria Coach Lane
☎0191/227 4024. Student hall of residence offering cheap B&B in April and from July to
September.

The City

Anyone arriving by train from the north will get a sneak preview of the **Castle**
(daily: April–Sept 9.30am–5.30pm; Oct–March Tues–Sun 9.30am–4.30pm;
£1.50), as the rail line splits the keep from its gatehouse, the Black Gate, on St
Nicholas' Street. A wooden fort was built here over an Anglo-Saxon cemetery
– which itself had been dug into the site of the Roman fort of Pons Aelius –
by Robert Curthose, illegitimate eldest son of William the Conqueror, but the
present keep dates from the twelfth century and is everything a castle should
be: thick, square and labyrinthine. Staircases and rooms, including a bare
Norman chapel, lie off a draughty Great Hall, where displays relate to the Civil
War siege of 1644 by a Scottish army supporting the Parliamentarian cause; a
small museum room shows various archeological finds. Down in the garrison
room, prisoners were incarcerated during the sixteenth to eighteenth centuries, while locals rushed to its deep shelter in World War II to sit out German
bombing. There's also a great view from the rooftop over the river and city.
Little remains of the outer fortifications except the Black Gate, which was
added in 1247–50, and is topped by a seventeenth-century house.

Further along St Nicholas' Street stands the **Cathedral** (Mon–Fri 7am–6pm,
Sat 8.30am–4pm, Sun 7.30am–noon & 4–7pm; guided tours Easter–Sept Wed
11am; free), dating mainly from the fourteenth and fifteenth centuries and
remarkable chiefly for its tower – erected in 1470, it is topped with a crown-
like structure of turrets and arches supporting a lantern. Inside, behind the high
altar, is one of the largest funerary brasses in England; it was commissioned by
Roger Thornton, the Dick Whittington of Newcastle, who arrived in the city
penniless and died its richest merchant in 1430. The brass is etched with near
life-size figures of Thornton and his wife. Much of the interior was given a
neo-Gothic remodelling in the late nineteenth century under Sir George
Gilbert Scott – the ornate reredos, depicting various Northumbrian saints, is
from this period, as is the font canopy with its intricate pinnacles. In the northeast corner of the church you'll find a war memorial dedicated to Danish seamen – evidence of Tyneside's enduring links with Scandinavia.

The Quayside, the bridges and around

From between the castle and the cathedral a road known simply as The Side,
formerly the main road out of the city, descends to the **Quayside** where the
first bridges across the Tyne stood. There have been fixed river crossings here
since Roman times and today the Tyne is spanned by seven bridges in close

proximity, the most prominent being the looming **Tyne Bridge** of 1928, symbol of the city, which bears a striking resemblance to the roughly contemporaneous Sydney Harbour Bridge – not surprising really, as both were built by Dorman Long of Middlesbrough. To the west of it, road and rail lines cross the river on the **High Level Bridge**, built by Robert Stephenson in 1849 – Queen Victoria was one of the first passengers across, promoting the railway revolution. Further west, under the bridge and up the steep steps to Hanover Street, a section of the old encircling medieval city wall survives. The river views from the adjacent **Hanover Gardens** are magnificent.

Protected by the towering castle, the Quayside became the commercial heart of the city and in the sixteenth and seventeenth centuries its half-timbered houses were the homes of Newcastle's wealthiest merchants. One is **Bessie Surtees' House**, at 41–44 Sandhill (Mon–Fri 10am–4pm; free), the residence of an eighteenth-century woman who scandalously eloped to Scotland with her beau; all ended well and the groom in question went on to become Lord Eldon, Chancellor of England. It's now the regional headquarters of English Heritage, with three rooms, decorated with elaborate panelling and plaster ceilings, open to the public. While you're here, it's well worth checking out the **Side Gallery**, just round the corner at 9 The Side (Tues–Sat 10am–5pm, Sun 11am–3pm; free; ⑩www.amber-online.com), which hosts temporary exhibitions of documentary photography from all over the world.

Directly opposite Bessie Surtees' House is the **Guildhall**, rebuilt many times since its foundation in 1316, where court sessions were held; John Wesley preached here in 1742 and had to be rescued from a volatile crowd by a hefty fishwife. On Sundays a busy morning **market** spreads around the nearby hydraulic **Swing Bridge**, which was erected in 1876 by Lord Armstrong to replace the old Tyne Bridge, so that larger vessels could reach his shipyards upriver.

Much of the Quayside was destroyed by a conflagration in 1854, which did for a large part of the medieval layout. There used to be, for example, many more narrow alleys, or "chares", than the half-dozen that survive today. East along the quay, the widest of them, Broad Chare, heads away from the river to the unspoiled ensemble of **Trinity House** (guided tours Fri 1pm; £3.50), with its enclosed courtyard and own graciously carved chapel, built in 1505 for the Mariners' Guild and still run by the Brethren of Master Mariners. Controllers of all shipping on the river, the guild had its own naval school whose alumni included Admiral Lord Collingwood and Captain Cook. Next door, at no. 29, the **Trinity Maritime Centre** (April–Oct Mon–Fri 11am–4pm; £1.50), housed in an old ship chandler's warehouse, has a few rooms of maritime mementoes and some lovingly detailed model ships, as well as an illustrative model of the eighteenth-century Quayside as it was before the fire.

Beyond Broad Chare, the modern-day regeneration of the Quayside is in full swing. A landscaped promenade, public sculpture and pedestrianized squares have paved the way for a series of fashionable new bars and restaurants, centred around the supremely graceful, £20-million **Millennium Bridge**, the world's first tilting span, which is designed to pivot – at an energy-saving cost of £4 a go – to allow ships to pass. This revolutionary structure has sorely exercised the imaginations of commentators, who have compared it variously to a lyre, shark's teeth and a warped tennis racket, though locals, who chose the design in a public vote, have settled on the "blinking eye". It allows pedestrians and cyclists to cross the Tyne to the Gateshead side, either to complete a mile-long circuit of the riverfronts via the Swing Bridge, or to visit the **BALTIC Centre**

for Contemporary Art (due to open March 2002; ⓦ www.balticmill.com). This brick flour mill built in the 1940s is being converted into a huge visual arts space, second only in scale to London's Tate Modern and scheduled to hold some of the most ambitious international art shows of the next few years. As well as galleries, the centre has room to accommodate artists' studios, education workshops, an art performance space and cinema, plus a bar and two restaurants, one at river level with an outdoor terrace, the other on the roof with uninterrupted views of the Newcastle skyline.

The BALTIC will be joined on the Gateshead side by new hotels, restaurants, bars and a multiplex cinema, and in summer 2003 by the similarly ambitious **Music Centre Gateshead**. This billowing steel, aluminium and glass structure designed by Foster and Partners will shelter two concert halls, a rehearsal hall and a wide-ranging music education centre and will be home to the Northern Sinfonia and Folkworks, a charity promoting traditional music.

Grey Street to the city walls

By the mid-nineteenth century, Newcastle's centre of balance had shifted away from the river, uphill to the rapidly expanding Victorian town. In a few short years, businessmen-builders and architects such as Richard Grainger, Thomas Oliver and John Dobson fashioned what Nikolaus Pevsner later thought to be the best-designed Victorian town in England, with classical facades of stone lining splendid new streets, most notably **Grey Street** – "that descending, subtle curve", as John Betjeman described it. The street takes its name from the Northumberland dynasty of political heavyweights whose most illustrious member was the second Earl Grey, prime minister from 1830 to 1834. In the middle of his term of office he carried the Reform Bill through parliament, an act commemorated by **Grey's Monument** at the top of the street.

Cleaning and restoration has rescued many of Newcastle's finer buildings: J.B. Priestley, visiting in the 1930s, thought that the city "might almost have been carved out of coal", so black was its stone. Today, Grey Street shows off much of its Victorian elegance, best exemplified by the **Theatre Royal**, halfway down. Other streets fell to the municipal butchers in the 1960s and 1970s – Eldon Square, once a model of Victorian balance, now a shopping centre, a case in point – though not all was lost: **Grainger Market** (Mon–Sat 8am–5pm) near Grey's Monument, Europe's largest undercover market when built in the 1830s, maintains its style; while John Dobson's **Central Station**, facing Neville Street, trumpeted the confidence of the Railway Age with its soaring interior spaces and curved ironwork.

West of here, behind Gallowgate, is the most complete stretch of the old **city walls**, leading down to Westgate Road. Once encircling the whole of medieval Newcastle, built six to ten feet thick and 25 feet high in parts, they remained in place until the sixteenth century, after which time many sections were plundered for building stone. Several towers remained in use by the city guilds as meeting houses and here, at the "West Walls", alongside Stowell Street, one, the **Morden Tower**, gained prestige as the haunt of poets such as Allen Ginsberg, Basil Bunting and Tom Pickard. Through the arch, the outer defensive ditch has been restored. Stowell Street, incidentally, is Newcastle's **Chinatown**, lined with restaurants and supermarkets. Across Stowell Street from the tower, at Friar's Green, is the tranquil courtyard of **Blackfriars**, a thirteenth-century stone monastery with ruined cloistered grounds, now lovingly restored to house a crafts centre and a café/restaurant.

The Discovery Museum and LIFE

On the south side of Westgate Road, the **Discovery Museum** in Blandford Square (Mon–Sat 10am–5pm, Sun 2–5pm; free) attempts to put into context the city's history – a footnote to which is the museum's own massive £12 million redevelopment, due for completion by early 2002. Expect to find exhibits such as the "Newcastle Story", a walk through the city's past with tales from animated characters along the way; the interactive "Science Maze" which focuses on Newcastle's pioneering inventors; and the *Turbinia*, the world's first steam-turbine-powered ship, built by the brilliant but unconventional and occasionally absent-minded local engineer, Charles Parsons: having resorted to gatecrashing the naval review at Spithead aboard the *Turbinia* to bring her to the military establishment's attention, Parsons was obliged to add a lookout post towards the front of the ship as he'd built the bridge behind the funnel.

Heading back towards the Central Station along Westmorland Street, you can't miss the sleek modern lines and grand central courtyard of the **International Centre for Life**. This ambitious project combines the university bioscience centre with **LIFE Interactive World** (Mon–Sat 10am–6pm, Sun 11am–6pm; £6.95; ⓦwww.lifeinteractiveworld.co.uk), which aims to convey the scientific secrets of life using the latest entertainment technology. The emphasis is squarely on learning through having fun rather than the other way round, though you probably don't have to undergo the white-knuckle "Crazy Motion Ride", the world's longest motion simulator, to learn that "life is a rollercoaster" – or that you don't like rollercoasters. Imaginative and humorous computer games include "Cell Wars", wherein you're invited to help Professor Pukestopper zap bacteria, while more obviously didactic purposes are served by "Jack's Story", an arresting 3D film showing a baby developing from embryo to birth, and "Choices", which invites you to explore the ethical issues surrounding genetic research.

The Laing Gallery

Newcastle's – indeed, the northeast's – premier art collection is the **Laing Gallery** on New Bridge St (Mon–Sat 10am–5pm, Sun 2–5pm; free), off John Dobson Street, behind the library. It's a splendidly organized museum, in which local pottery, glassware, costume and sculpture play their part, while on permanent display is a sweep through British art from Reynolds to John Hoyland, with a smattering of Pre-Raphaelites, so admired by English industrial barons.

William Bell Scott, a friend of Ruskin's and creator of the murals at Wallington (see p.1040), is represented by a picture of mid-nineteenth-century Bigg Market, though the real treat here is the lashings of **John Martin** (1789–1854), a self-taught Northumberland painter with a penchant for massive biblical and mythical scenes. He came from a rather dysfunctional family – his elder brother wore a tortoiseshell hat, another brother set fire to York Minster – and with the benefit of twenty-first century psychological hindsight, it's easy to imagine what demons drove him in his work. Early studies are inoffensive topographical works of castles and landscapes, but the dramatic northeastern scenery was soon to influence him strangely. In *The Bard* (1817), depicting Thomas Gray's poem of the same name, the last surviving Welsh bard – resembling a biblical Charlton Heston on drugs – curses the English troops before jumping to his death from crags Martin conjured from his visits to Allendale Gorge. Much later, in *The Destruction of Sodom and Gomorrah* (1852), blazing buildings and violent colours were presumably influenced by the Tyne's industrial furnaces. Whatever you think of Martin's work – and it certainly provokes extreme reactions – it's hard not to be moved by a paranoiac who was convinced equally of his own genius and of everyone else's opposition to his talent. He regularly exhibited at London's Royal Academy, where in the early days his paintings either failed to sell or – in the case of *Clytie* (1814), which suffered an accidental varnish spill – were "deliberately" damaged.

Martin's histrionics aside, the other must-see in the gallery is the **Art on Tyneside** exhibition, which romps through the history of art and applied art in the region since the seventeenth century with considerable gusto. There's portraiture and landscapes of the city through the ages, as well as digressions on eighteenth-century coffee houses, clothes and materials, glassware and wood engraving – the latter, most famously, by **Thomas Bewick** (see p.1037), whose pastoral works were inspired by the surrounding countryside. The exhibition comes up to date with coverage of Sixties pop artists Richard Hamilton and Victor Pasmore, both of whom taught at Newcastle University, and of the architectural developments in the 1980s, including analysis of the award-winning Byker Wall project, on the outskirts of the city centre, pioneered by Ralph Erskine.

The university museums

Newcastle University (@ www.ncl.ac.uk), opposite Haymarket Metro, contains a knot of fine museums and galleries, located off King's Walk: the **Museum of Antiquities** (Mon–Sat 10am–5pm; free) makes a good place to get to grips with the history of Hadrian's Wall, with a fascinating scale model of the whole length of the wall and a reconstruction of the Mithraic temple at Brocolitia (see p.1050); the small **Shefton Museum of Greek Art and Archeology** (Mon–Fri 10am–4pm; free) contains a valuable collection of armour, sculpture and pottery; while the celebrated **Hatton Gallery** (Mon–Fri 10am–5.30pm, Sat 10am–4.30pm; free), attached to the Fine Art Department, features a collection of African sculpture, the only surviving example of Kurt Schwitters' *Merzbau* (a sort of architectural collage) and a wide variety of temporary exhibitions. Also attached to the university is the **Hancock Museum** on adjacent Claremont Road (Mon–Sat 10am–5pm, Sun 2–5pm; £4.50); based on an eighteenth-century natural history collection, it's grown to immense dimensions – with more than 150,000 insect specimens – and hosts widely touted temporary exhibitions such as the 2001 Star Trek "European Tour". Across to the east, over on the University of Northumbria campus on Sandyford Road (also Haymarket Metro), the **University Gallery** (July & Aug Mon–Sat 10am–5pm; rest of year Mon–Thurs 10am–5pm, Fri & Sat 10am–4pm; free) specializes in temporary exhibitions of twentieth-century art.

Beyond the University of Newcastle stretches the **Town Moor**, 1200 acres of common land where freemen of the city, including former US president Jimmy Carter, are entitled to graze their cattle. It's the site of the annual "Hoppings" in the last week of June, a huge week-long **fair** of rides, stalls and other attractions which keeps the cows awake until well after dark.

Eating

Newcastle's tastes have moved a long way from the traditional gargantuan bread rolls called "stottie cakes" – you're more likely to find them drizzled with olive oil and stuffed with Parma ham and chargrilled vegetables these days. At the budget end of the market Italian, Indian and Chinese food dominates the scene, while at the top end of the scale the city has attracted some top-class chefs. The Quayside and the streets around it are where the most fashionable hangouts are situated. For Chinese food, check out Stowell Street in Chinatown where you'll find cheap all-you-can-eat buffets as well as more refined seafood restaurants. If you're counting the pennies, aim to eat early – many city-centre restaurants offer **early bird/happy hour** deals before 7pm, while others serve **set lunches** at often ludicrously low prices.

Cafés

Blakes Coffee House 53 Grey St. Friendly and hugely popular haunt serving sandwiches, salads and daily specials.

Pani's High Bridge St, off Grey St. Just up a side street below the Theatre Royal, this little Italian coffee and sandwich bar – which now also stays open in the evenings to serve cheap meals – has a loyal clientele. Closed Sun.

The Side Café Bistro 1–3 The Side. Snacks and cappuccino downstairs, *bruschetta*, pasta, pizza and more substantial dishes upstairs (open until 9pm Thurs–Sat), in an amiable little place near the Quayside.

Tyneside Coffee Rooms 2nd floor, Tyneside Cinema, 10–12 Pilgrim St. Coffee, light meals and art-house movie talk in the Art Déco cinema café.

Restaurants

Barluga 35 Grey St ☎0191/230 2306. Bar/restaurant in a grand Dobson building, done out in a plush update of Art Nouveau, offering excellent main meals such as roast herbed salmon with lemon and shallot mash in the lounge area at lunchtime, and a simpler bar menu all day. Moderate to Expensive at lunch.

Café 21 21 Queen St ☎0191/222 0755. The Michelin star's been handed in and the city's premier restaurant has been scaled down to a Parisian-influenced bistro, but the food, featuring inventive seafood and local meat dishes and a veggie menu as long as your arm, is still excellent. Set lunches are a bargain at £12 for two courses, £14.50 for three. There are other branches in Durham and near the airport at 33–35 The Broadway, Darras Hall, Ponteland (☎01661/820357). Closed Sun. Moderate to Expensive.

Café Sol Pink Lane ☎0191/221 0122. Off-the-shelf tapas bar (checked tablecloths, bullfight posters, flamenco nights) with food a cut above the average, ranging from open sandwiches to mussels, cured meats and daily specials. Inexpensive.

Da Vinci's 73 Osborne Rd, Jesmond ☎0191/281 5284. Good to know about if you're staying in Jesmond, this is a pleasing town-house restaurant with great Italian food. Moderate.

Eslington Villa 8 Station Rd, Low Fell, Gateshead ☎0191/487 6017. Spacious, elegant restaurant (and hotel; see p.1026), presenting an accomplished blend of traditional and cosmopolitan

cuisines on à la carte and set menus. Closed Sat lunch & Sun eve. Moderate to Expensive.

Fisherman's Lodge Jesmond Dene ☎0191/281 3281. Classy, formal restaurant in landscaped parkland, two miles from the centre, offering well-received modern and traditional British cuisine. Excellent seafood and vegetarian choices and the set lunches are a good deal. Closed Sat lunch & all Sun. Very Expensive.

Heartbreak Soup Baltic Chambers, 77 Quayside ☎0191/222 1701. Good-value food – originally Tex-Mex but now gone global – with inspiring veggie choices in colour-splashed surroundings down by the river. Eve only, closed Sun. Moderate.

La Tasca Quayside ☎0191/230 400). A veritable tapas barn, near the Millennium Bridge, with Spanish tiling and cast-iron candelabras. The food's not bad, though the place really comes into its own in summer when you can sit out on the terrace, grazing, chatting and drinking. Moderate.

La Toscana 22 Leazes Park Rd ☎0191/232 5871. Probably the city's most reliable and authentic Italian restaurant, close to St James's Park stadium.

Leela's 20 Dean St ☎0191/230 1261. A rare treat among the flock-wallpaper curry houses, *Leela's* serves high-quality South Indian cuisine, with plenty of vegetarian options; the wide-ranging lunch set menu is particularly good value. Closed Sun. Moderate to Expensive.

Paradiso 1 Market Lane ☎0191/221 1240. Hidden down an alley and up a small flight of stairs off Pilgrim Street, a mellow café/restaurant with great food (try the eclectic and filling meze), amiable staff and welcoming booths. Closed Sun. Moderate.

Rupali 6 Bigg Market ☎0191/232 8629. Budget Indian restaurant owned by the self-styled Lord of Harpole, spiced up with special student offers and challenges – eat a plate of the hottest curry on the menu and you get it for free. Inexpensive.

Sabatini 25 King St ☎0191/261 4415. Quayside Italian with Neo-Impressionist daubs on the wall, good pizzas and a full menu besides. Closed Sun. Moderate.

Sachin's Forth Banks ☎0191/261 9035. Don't be put off by the grandiose, sickly green exterior – this Punjabi restaurant is a cut above and well worth booking ahead for. Moderate to Expensive.

Treacle Moon 5–7 The Side ☎0191/232 5537. Modern British food of distinction, pressing all the right trendy buttons (chargrilling, searing), with a cheaper lunch menu. Closed Mon. Expensive.

Valley Junction 397 Archbold Tce, Jesmond ℡0191/281 6397. Wide-ranging and inventive Indian food in a lavishly refurbished railway carriage and signal box in what used to be Jesmond Station (the theme is continued with train trips to its sister restaurant in Corbridge – see p.1047). Moderate to Expensive.

Drinking, nightlife and entertainment

Newcastle's boisterous **nightlife** centres on the pubs and clubs in the older parts of town: between Grainger Street and the cathedral in the area called the Bigg Market – spiritual home of Sid the Sexist and the Fat Slags, from the locally based *Viz* magazine – and around the Quayside, where the bars tend to be slightly more sophisticated. If you want to get away from the mayhem, make a bolt for Westgate Road and Pink Lane, while for those staying in Jesmond, there's a more upmarket but generally unremarkable strip of bars along Osborne Road. The grandiosely named "**Gay Quarter**" of mostly mixed gay and lesbian bars and clubs centres on the International Centre for Life, spreading out to Waterloo Street and Westmorland and Scotswood roads.

Expect to queue to get into the more popular bars and clubs, and to have someone scrutinize your clothes as you attempt to gain entry – jeans and trainers are best avoided. As with restaurants, **happy hour** is a big deal in Newcastle – early doors drinking is positively encouraged. Top brew is, of course, **Newcastle Brown Ale** – known locally as "Dog" – produced in this city since 1927.

Theatre and cinema **listings** are contained in the local morning paper, the *Journal*, while *The Crack* (monthly; free) is the best way to find out about gigs, clubs and other entertainments: you can usually get a copy from the tourist office or from pubs such as the *Forth Hotel*.

Pubs and bars

There's not a great deal of point listing all the Bigg Market or Quayside **pubs** and **bars** – everyone swans in and out of each in the biggest (and largely good-natured) cattle market in western Europe. But try and make time for one or two of the places listed below, each of which has its own particular attraction.

Bodega 125 Westgate Rd. Restored Edwardian gin-palace with a good beer selection and a studenty crowd that packs in to watch the soccer on TV.
Bridge Hotel Castle Square, St Nicholas St. Right opposite the castle, by the High Level Bridge, this Victorian pub has a great view of the Tyne from its beer garden.
Casa 58 Sandhill, next to the Guildhall. One of the bars of the moment, but with enough style for the popularity to last – and enough space to cater for it, whether on the comfy sofas or in the elegant riverside conservatory; daytime snacks and more adventurous evening meals served.
The Cooperage 32 The Close, Quayside. Cosy Quayside pub, originally a sixteenth-century house, just along from the Tyne Bridge, with a good range of guest beers.
Crown Posada 31 The Side. Local beers and guest ales in a small but highly attractive wood-and-glass-panelled Victorian pub down by the Quayside.

Forth Hotel Pink Lane. Honest, old-fashioned boozer with a fine juke box, which attracts a lively, varied crowd.
Head of Steam Neville St. In a modern block opposite the *Royal Station Hotel*, a relaxed drinking den, with decent beers, good sounds and big sofas to sink into.
Pitcher & Piano by the Millennium Bridge, Quayside. The riverfront's most spectacular bar – sinuous roof, huge plate-glass walls – is a great place to drink, but there's also fine contemporary cooking in the restaurant. Live jazz Sun eve.
Quayside Bar 35 The Close, Quayside. Newcastle's only surviving medieval warehouse, now a rambling, boisterous pub with a good range of local beers and a few outdoor tables under the High Level Bridge.
Revolution Collingwood St. Full-on DJ-led hedonism in an impressive modern conversion of a landmark bank.
Salsa Club 89 Westgate Rd. More of a place to

drink than eat – though it only has a restaurant licence, the tapas and dips are good and cheap enough that that needn't be a worry – with a cosy, candlelit atmosphere, laid-back DJs and the occasional film or art installation.

Tilley's 105 Westgate Rd. Homely traditional pub, where you might even get a seat on the leather banquettes on a Saturday night, with well-kept Jennings Cumbrian ales and a cheap and filling daytime cheese and pâté bar.

Union Rooms bottom of Westgate Rd, where it turns into Collingwood St. Huge former gentlemen's club complete with porter's lodge and imposing central staircase, sympathetically restored by Wetherspoon's, and now offering cheap beer and sandwiches to the masses; large parts smoke-free, music-free throughout.

(13)

Clubs

Good pubs to catch **club** flyers and posters include the *Head of Steam* and the *Forth Hotel*. Note that most clubs are closed on Sundays.

Baja Beach Club Quayside, Gateshead. Hugely popular, new mainstream club with a beach-party theme – little more than an excuse for bikini-clad dancers and "tub girls".

Foundation 57–59 Melbourne St ☏ 0191/261 8985. Stylish, well-equipped venue hosting club nights (Mon & Thurs–Sat).

Powerhouse George St. The city's best gay club, open every night of the week, attracts a friendly bunch to its four bars and two dance floors.

Rockshots Waterloo St ☏ 0191/232 9648. Lively, unpretentious place that pulls in a mixed crowd with a wide-ranging menu of club nights.

Scotland Yard Waterloo St ☏ 0191/232 4879. Cavernous venue where current favourite club nights are *Reverb* on Fridays for techno and the eclectic *Traveller* on Saturdays.

Tuxedo Princess Quayside, Gateshead. Floating nightclub, on the south side of the river below the Tyne Bridge, serving up scantily clad dancers and seven different styles of music in seven bars to a raucous 18–25-year-old set.

World Headquarters 9 Marlborough Crescent, by the Centre for Life ☏ 0191/261 8648. Newcastle's mellowest club, playing funk, soul and hip-hop (Fri & Sat), plus regular DJ slots; members only, but you can join the day before.

Live music

There's **live music** most nights in the city, whether at one of the venues listed below, the *Bridge Hotel* (see above; ☏ 0191/232 6400) or organized by the **students' unions** at Newcastle University (☏ 0191/239 3900) and Northumbria University (☏ 0191/227 3791). You should also check programmes at the various arts centres and all-round venues for gigs (see below).

Newcastle Telewest Arena Arena Way ☏ 0191/260 5000. City-centre stadium which attracts all the big pop and rock names, but it's a lifeless venue, better suited to the ice hockey and basketball that is also played here.

The Jazz Café 23 Pink Lane ☏ 0191/232 6505. Intimate jazz club with a late licence, near the station; salsa nights Thurs–Sat. Closed Sun.

Tyneside Irish Centre 43–49 Gallowgate, opposite the coach station ☏ 0191/261 0384. Regular Irish folk gigs and dances, and main venue for the Tyneside Irish Festival in October, which runs the gamut from the *Three Irish Tenors* to *Salsa Celtica*.

Theatre and the arts

There's a varied **theatrical and cultural** life in the city and its surroundings, from the offerings at the splendid Victorian *Theatre Royal* and *Newcastle Opera House* to those of smaller contemporary theatre companies and local arts centres. Main **cinema** screens are the Odeon, Pilgrim St (☏ 0870/505 0007), Warner Brothers by Manors Metro station (☏ 0191/221 0222) and UCI in the MetroCentre, Gateshead (☏ 0870/010 2030), with more challenging films shown at the Tyneside Cinema (see below); keep an eye out also for new multiplexes on Newgate Street and on the Gateshead Quays. And while the City Hall (below) is the main **classical music** concert venue until the completion of Northern Sinfonia's new home at the Music Centre Gateshead, you'll also find performances throughout the year at Newcastle University's King's Hall, and in St Nicholas' Cathedral and St Mary's Catholic Cathedral and other atmospheric churches around town.

Buddle Arts Centre 258 Station Rd, Wallsend ☎0191/200 7132. Friendly community arts centre with a fine range of events and concerts, and easy to reach (yellow line Wallsend Metro) from central Newcastle.

City Hall Northumberland Rd ☎0191/261 2606, ⓦwww.newcastle.gov.uk/cityhall. The city's main concert venue, hosting orchestras from around the world, as well as mainstream rock, pop and comedy acts.

Customs House Mill Dam, South Shields ☎0191/454 1234. Arts centre on the banks of the Tyne and close to South Shields Metro, hosting gigs, films and theatre. There's also a bar and a restaurant. South Shields Metro.

Live Theatre 27 Broad Chare ☎0191/232 1232, ⓦwww.live.org.uk. Enterprising youthful theatre company with regular productions promoting local actors and writers. Also exhibitions and occasional club nights, plus fine live blues, reggae, country, soul and roots at its regular *Jumpin' Hot Club*.

Newcastle Arts Centre 69 Westgate Rd ☎0191 /261 5618, ⓦwww.newcastle-arts-centre.co.uk. Art gallery, workshops, and concert, drama and club venue – always worth checking what's on.

Newcastle Opera House Westgate Rd ☎0191/232 0899, ⓦwww.newcastleoperahouse .com. Beautifully restored Victorian theatre with a wide range of shows, comedy and gigs.

Newcastle Playhouse Barras Bridge ☎0191/232 3366. Modern theatre, home of Newcastle's own Northern Stage company and co-host of the annual RSC season in Nov. The Gulbenkian Studio here hosts small-scale theatre, dance and recitals. Good café-bar (closed Sun).

Theatre Royal Grey St ☎0191/232 2061, ⓦwww.theatre-royal-newcastle.co.uk. Drama, opera and dance; also co-host of the annual RSC season in Nov.

Tyneside Cinema Pilgrim St ☎0191/232 1507, ⓦwww.tynecine.org. The city's premier art-house cinema, with a wide-ranging international programme in its two auditoriums.

Listings

Airport and flight enquiries General enquiries ☎0191/286 0966; flight enquiries ☎0191/214 4444; ⓦwww.newcastleairport.com.

Banks and exchanges Banks are concentrated around Grey and Northumberland streets. There's a bureau de change at the airport, in the main post office and in Thomas Cook travel agency (see below), and an American Express bureau in Lunn Poly, 124 Northumberland St (☎0191/232 5262).

Books Waterstone's, 104 Grey St; Blackwells, Grand Hotel Buildings, Percy St.

Car rental All of the following have outlets at the airport as well as in town: Avis, 7 George St ☎0191/232 5283 and at the airport ☎0191/214 0116; Europcar, 90 Westmorland Rd ☎0191/261 0833 and at the airport ☎0191/286 5070; and Hertz, 14 Westgate Rd ☎0191/232 5313 and at the airport ☎0191/286 6748.

Ferries North Shields ferry terminal at Royal Quays, seven miles east of the city, has sailings to Scandinavia and Amsterdam. Contact Fjord Line (for Bergen, Haugesund and Stavanger; ☎0191/296 1313, ⓦwww.fjordline.com) or DFDS (Gothenberg, Kristiansand and Amsterdam; ☎08705/333000, ⓦwww.dfdsseaways.co.uk). Buses leave from Central Station to the terminal before each sailing.

Hospital Royal Victoria Infirmary, Queen Victoria Rd (☎0191/232 5131), behind the university, just 400 yards from Haymarket bus station.

Internet Internet Exchange, 26–30 Market St ☎0191/230 1280.

Left luggage Lockers available at the train station (daily 8am–6pm).

Pharmacies The handiest central pharmacy is Boots, Monument Mall, Grey St (☎0191/232 4423).

Police Corner of Market and Pilgrim streets ☎0191/214 6555.

Post office St Mary's Place, near the Civic Centre, at Haymarket ☎0191/230 2224.

Taxis There are ranks all over the centre, including those at Haymarket, Bigg Market, and outside Central Station. Weekend nights are the most difficult times to hail a cab; the queues at the Bigg Market ranks can be horrendous. Call Noda (☎0191/222 1888 or 232 7777) at Central Station for advance bookings.

Travel agents STA, 9 St Mary's Place ☎0191/233 2111, ⓦwww.statravel.co.uk; Thomas Cook, 110 Grey St ☎0191/230 0773; Usit Campus, Level 5, Student Union Building, King's Walk ☎0191/232 2881, ⓦwww.usitcampus.co.uk.

Around Newcastle

The Metro network connects most of the day-trip destinations along the Tyne, and a Day Rover or Metro Day Saver ticket (see p.1025) enables you to get the best out of the local transport systems. In addition to the Metro, the Day Rover is valid for most buses in the county of Tyne and Wear, the train to Sunderland and the ferry between North and South Shields. Note also that Beamish Museum, just across the border in County Durham (see p.1008), is within particularly easy reach of Newcastle.

Along the Tyne

The Metro runs east along both banks of the **River Tyne**, connecting Newcastle with several historic attractions, and with the sandy beaches at Tynemouth and Whitley Bay – the beaches are fine if you just want to see the sea, though anyone intending to head further north up the Northumberland coast will find there's no comparison. It's worth noting that to make a round trip of it, you can cross the river between North Shields and South Shields on the **Shields Ferry** (Mon–Sat 6.30am–10.50pm, Sun 10.30am–6pm; every 15–30min; 7min; 85p one-way). There are Metro stations at either end.

Wallsend

As the name tells you, **WALLSEND**, four miles east of Newcastle, was the last outpost of Hadrian's great border defence. **Segedunum**, the "strong fort" a couple of minutes' walk from the Metro station here (daily: April–Oct 10am–5pm; Nov–March 10am–3.30pm; £2.95), has been admirably developed as one of the prime attractions along the Wall. Besides extensive excavations, the grounds contain a fully reconstructed bathhouse, complete with steaming pools and colourful frescoes, and a rebuilt section of the Wall itself. The cleverly conceived museum combines excavated finds with interactive computer displays to give a strong flavour of life at the fort, as well as bringing the history of the site up to the present day with displays on coalmining and shipbuilding. To complete the picture, climb the 110- foot tower for a spectacular overview of the remains, the adjacent ship-repair yards and the river.

Tynemouth

Pressing on through North Shields brings you to the coast at **TYNEMOUTH**, a pleasant village perched on the promontory between sea and river. Long considered a strategically important site, on the cliff top stand the striking ruins of the **Benedictine priory** (April–Sept daily 10am–6pm; Oct daily 10am–5pm; Nov–March Wed–Sun 10am–1pm & 2–4pm; £1.90; EH), later fortified with a **castle**, where early kings of Northumbria were buried. A church was first built here in the seventh century, but the oldest visible features, such as the beautiful chancel, are Norman. Further towards the river are the **Watch House** and **Museum** of the Tyneside Volunteer Life Brigade (Tues–Sat 10am–3pm, Sun 10am–noon; free), packing 130 years of maritime history into a creaky wooden building.

Gibside and Cherryburn

Upriver on the south bank of the Tyne, one of the finest landscape gardens in the North is a quick, six-mile hop from the centre of Newcastle (bus #745 from Central Station, then a half-mile signposted walk from the village of Rowlands Gill). The grounds of **Gibside** (Tues–Sun: April–Oct 10am–6pm;

Nov–March 10am–4pm; £3; NT) represent a very rare survival of mid-eighteenth-century park design, combining striking formal vistas with naturalistic woodland. Created by coal baron George Bowes between 1729 and 1760, the estate went into decline as early as 1885 after the death of his great-grandson John Bowes (founder of the Bowes Museum at Barnard Castle; see p.1010), and for the last twenty years the National Trust have been slowly attempting to restore the original design. A series of hour-long **trails** will take you past the atmospheric shell of the earlier Jacobean mansion, an orangery and walled garden, the 130-foot Column to Liberty, erected to reaffirm Bowes' loyalty to George II after the Jacobite uprising of 1745, and along the east bank of the River Derwent near its confluence with the Tyne (though not past the neo-Gothic Banqueting House, now administered as self-catering accommodation by the Landmark Trust). Back towards the entrance and tea room stands the most striking and complete architectural remnant, the **chapel** (April–Oct Tues–Sun 11am–4.30pm). Inspired by Palladio's Villa Rotonda in the Veneto in northeastern Italy, this elegantly symmetrical building features an array of delicate carvings under its portico, but is dominated by one of the grandest pulpits you're ever likely to see – a triple-decker mahogany affair decked out in velvet with a grand inlaid sounding board.

If you have your own transport (otherwise bus #602 from Newcastle towards Hexham), it's worth pressing on another five miles west along the A695 from here to **Cherryburn** (Mon & Thurs–Sun 1–5.30pm; £3, free with admission ticket to Gibside), the birthplace museum of **Thomas Bewick**, England's greatest engraver (1735–1828). Still offering beautiful views of the rolling landscape which inspired Bewick, the simple cottage contains well-thought-out displays that tell the story of his far-reaching legacy, including examples of contemporary use of his engravings, from "Nature Notes" in *The Times* to Californian wine labels. Sunday is the big day here, with demonstrations of printing and bookbinding, and live folk music in the garden. The best **lunch** stop in the area lies between Gibside and Cherryburn at Bradley Gardens (signposted off the A695 near Ryton), a Victorian walled garden with a conservatory café that serves good light meals.

Jarrow

JARROW, five miles east of Newcastle, and south of the Tyne, has been ingrained on the national consciousness since the 1936 march (see box below), though the town made a mark earlier, as the seventh-century St Paul's church and monastery was one of the region's early cradles of Christianity. The first Saxon church here was built in 681 AD by monks from St Peter's at Monkwearmouth, and its monastic buildings soon attracted a reputation for scholastic learning. It was here that the **Venerable Bede** (673–735 AD) came to live as a boy, growing to become one of Europe's greatest scholars and England's first historian – his *History of the English Church and People*, describing the struggles of the island's early Christians, was completed at Jarrow in 731. His other writings were many and varied – poetry, scientific works on chronology and the calendar, lives of St Cuthbert, historical and geographical treatises – and his influence was immense, prompting a European-wide revival in monastic learning. Yet astonishingly Bede rarely left the monastery, and probably never travelled further than York, relying on visitors and friends for much of his information. After he died in 735, St Paul's soon became a site of pilgrimage, though church and monastery were later sacked by Viking raiding parties. Even after Bede's bones had been appropriated by a relic-collecting Durham priest in 1020 (they were eventually interred in Durham cathedral; see

The Jarrow Crusade

Jarrow provides the perfect example of what happens to a company town when its company closes. It owed its growth in the nineteenth century to the success of the steelworks and shipyard owned by local MP Charles Palmer. Producer of the world's first oil tanker, the Jarrow production line was a phenomenal organization, employing at its zenith some ten thousand men. However, demand for steel and ships went into decline after World War I, and eighty percent of the workforce had been laid off by 1934, the year Palmers was sold off and broken up. From the consequent despair was born the Jarrow Crusade.

On October 5, 1936, led by the town's radical MP Ellen Wilkinson, two hundred men left Jarrow to walk the 290 miles to London under the "**Jarrow Crusade**" banner. Supported by all the town's politicians, the protesters gathered sympathy and support all along the road to the capital, becoming the most potent image of the hardships of 1930s Britain. Some charitable aid was forthcoming after the marchers presented their petition to Parliament, but real recovery only came about through the rearmament of Britain in the build-up to World War II. Palmers was resurrected at nearby Hebburn, and struggled through a series of takeovers into the 1970s, by which time the local economy was on the brink of a state nearly as bad as that of the 1930s. In 1986, with unemployment on Tyneside reaching 32 percent, the 50th anniversary of the Jarrow Crusade was marked by another march on the seat of government. The hardships of the 1930s were instrumental in the creation of the Welfare State; the hardships of the 1980s were all but ignored.

p.1002), Jarrow remained high in the clerical consciousness, with monks eager to study at the monastery where Bede had once lived. The monastery was revived in 1074 and continued in existence until the Reformation.

The years have been kind to **St Paul's** (Mon–Sat 10am–4.30pm, Sun 2.30–4.30pm), a tranquil stone church framed by the industrial clutter of the Tyneside docks beyond. Once two separate Anglo-Saxon churches standing end-to-end (joined where the tower now stands), inside the original seventh-century dedication stone (dated 23 April, 685 AD, the earliest in England) can be seen, set in the arch above the chancel. Outside are the bare ruins of the buildings, cloister and burial ground of the **monastery**. Most of the standing walls and ruins date from the later eleventh-century re-foundation.

Access to the church and monastery ruins is free, although they stand within the wider development that is **Bede's World** (April–Oct Mon–Sat 10am–5.30pm, Sun noon–5.30pm; Nov–March Mon–Sat 10am–4.30pm, Sun noon–4.30pm; guided tours Sun 2.30pm; £4.50; ⊛www.bedesworld.co.uk), a fascinating exploration of early medieval Northumbria, centred on a museum that's been imaginatively revamped with lottery money and an Anglo-Saxon farm site. The multi-media **museum**, housed in a beautiful Mediterranean-style edifice and dotted with striking sculptures and other artworks, traces the development of Northumbria and England through the use of extracts from Bede's writings, set alongside archeological finds and vivid re-creations of monastic life.

After this you can take a turn through Gyrwe, the eleven-acre demonstration **farm** which features reconstructed timber buildings from the early Christian period, as well as demonstrating contemporary agricultural methods. Kids can feed the goats and throughout the summer there are craft demonstrations, themed feasts and other activities. Over at the Georgian **Jarrow Hall** there's a monastic herb garden and an excellent **café**. Allow at least a couple of hours for church, museums and farm.

St Paul's and Bede's World are at Church Bank in Jarrow, a signposted fifteen-minute walk through an industrial estate from **Bede Metro station**. Alternatively, buses #526 or 527 from Neville Street (Central Station) in Newcastle or Jarrow Metro station stop in front of the church. Drivers will find the site a little way off the A185, at the south end of the Tyne tunnel; follow the signs at the A185/A19 roundabout junction.

South Shields

Beyond Jarrow, it's impossible to miss the fact that South Tyneside is officially designated **Catherine Cookson Country**: the prolific author was born in **SOUTH SHIELDS**, the small but distinctive town which guards the south side of the entrance to the Tyne. Although her childhood homes have since been demolished, South Shields **tourist office**, at the museum and art gallery on Ocean Road, a five-minute walk from the Metro station (Mon–Sat 10am–1pm & 2–5pm; ☏0191/454 6612, ✉museum.tic@s-tyneside-mbc-gov.uk), can provide details of the "Catherine Cookson Trail" – plaques, sites and buildings associated with her life and novels, which romanticize the grittier industrial corners of South Tyneside.

Of more general interest is **Arbeia Roman Fort** (Easter–Sept Mon–Sat 10am–5.30pm, Sun 1–5pm; Oct–Easter Mon–Sat 10am–4pm; free), ten minutes' walk north off River Drive. Built in 120–160 AD as a supply depot for Hadrian's Wall, the fort encloses substantial granaries where you can usually watch archeologists and stonemasons at work, and a museum that's largely unexceptional apart from the most complete Roman ring-mail shirt found in Britain. Fine views of the site and across towards the sister fort of Segedunum (see p.1036) can be had from the stone reconstruction of the huge west gate, and from 2002 you'll be able to poke around the commanding officer's house, with richly decorated living rooms off a central courtyard, and the dark, cramped barracks next door, all rebuilt using authentic Roman materials and construction methods. If you have kids in tow, be sure to take them into Time Quest (Mon–Fri 10am–3pm during school terms, 11am–4pm in the holidays; Easter–Oct also Sat 10am–5pm, Sun 1–5pm; £1.50, children 80p), where they can have a go at being archeologists, digging for finds in a gravel pit, doing Roman weaving and making mosaics.

If by this stage you're feeling peckish, there's a good riverfront Italian **restaurant** at the Customs House arts centre, by the Shields Ferry pier.

North of Newcastle: the stately homes

North of the city, a bevy of **stately homes** vie for attention. You could see any of them as half-day trips out of Newcastle by bus, though those with their own transport have the best of things. You can visit **Seaton Delaval** en route to the Northumberland coast, or **Belsay** and **Wallington** before heading into the Northumberland National Park.

Seaton Delaval Hall

One of Vanbrugh's great Baroque houses, **Seaton Delaval Hall** (June–Sept Wed & Sun 2–6pm; £3), lies eleven miles northeast of Newcastle in fine gardens, its gloomy north facade looking over the bleak terrain towards the port of Blyth. Fire badly damaged the hall in 1822, a century after it was built, but subsequent restorations have done ample justice to the sombre grandeur of a building that exemplifies the architect's desire to create country houses with "something of the castle air". Public transport is with the #363 (hourly) or

#364 (hourly; not Sun) **bus** from Haymarket, a 35-minute ride to Seaton Delaval Avenue head, from where it's a twenty-minute walk to the hall.

Belsay and Wallington

Belsay Hall, Castle and Gardens (daily: April–Sept 10am–6pm; Oct 10am–5pm; Nov–March 10am–4pm; £3.90; EH), fourteen miles northwest of Newcastle, were inherited in 1795 by Sir Charles Monck, who eleven years later decided to build a brand new hall here after his return from a honeymoon-cum-Grand-Tour of Europe. Inspired by the Neoclassical buildings of Berlin and the classical architecture of Athens, Sir Charles planned a majestic Doric house, an austere one-hundred-foot-square sandstone block raised on a podium of three steps. Built between 1807 and 1817, the **Hall** has now been impressively restored, though the equally severe interior, with the bedrooms and state rooms surrounding a multi-columned hall, is devoid of furnishings and fittings – instead, special exhibitions often adorn the main reception rooms.

To the west lie the **gardens**, where a footpath threads through the trim formality of the winter gardens to reach the magical **Quarry Gardens**. Here, in the shelter of the sandstone quarry used for the building of the Hall, lush exotic vegetation cascades over exposed rock faces, planned by Sir Charles as a Romantic antidote to the severity of the house. The track also leads to the substantial remains of the medieval **castle**, its battlements punctuated by four formidable corner turrets. **Belsay village**, on the main road about a mile from the Hall, is readily reached by **bus** from Newcastle: the #808 from Eldon Square (not Sun), or #508 from Haymarket (summer Sun only). There's a tearoom at the hall and, just off the main road near the village, the *Blacksmith's Coffee Shop* (closed Mon, except bank holidays), which makes its own scones.

Eight miles northwest of Belsay lies the tiny village of **Cambo**; the summer Sunday #508 service (twice a day) links the two. Just outside the village stands **Wallington House** (April–Sept 1–5.30pm Mon & Wed–Sun; Oct same days 1–4.30pm; £5.50; NT), an ostentatious mansion rebuilt by Sir Walter Blackett, the coal- and lead-mine owner, in the 1740s, and now the home of the Trevelyans, a family of notable reformers and philanthropists including G.M. Trevelyan, the great social historian, and Charles Trevelyan, the first socialist minister for education in the 1920s. The interior's highlight is the Rococo plasterwork, though William Bell Scott's Pre-Raphaelite murals of scenes from Northumbrian history in the central hall are good fun, too, and there are diverse attractions for kids, including the dolls' house collection and museum of curiosities. A tearoom and shop rounds off the facilities. There's a separate charge (£4) if you only want to see the **grounds**, with their lawns, woods and lakes (daily dawn–dusk), and the beautiful **walled gardens**, which shelter conservatories, fountains and a huge variety of plants (daily: April–Sept 10am–7pm; Oct 10am–6pm; Nov–March 10am–4pm).

South of Newcastle: Wearside

There's been a long rivalry between Newcastle and Sunderland, twelve miles to the southeast: both cities outraged about being lumped together in the municipal appellation Tyne *and* Wear; both Geordies (from Newcastle) or Mackems (from Sunderland) indignant at being taken for the other by knownothing southerners; with supporters of both passionately followed football teams cock-a-hoop at the old enemy's misfortunes. To an outsider it can seem at times to be a bewildering argument over nothing at all, but whisper in **Wearside** at your peril the obviously superior charms of Newcastle as a city.

Yet **Sunderland** and the River Wear do have their attractions, and in the adjacent new town of **Washington** stands one of the more intriguing historic sites of the northeast.

Sunderland

SUNDERLAND, bisected by the River Wear and elevated in 1992 to the ranks of Britain's cities, shares Newcastle's long history, river setting and industrial heritage but cannot match its architectural splendour. Formed from three medieval villages flanking the Wear, it was one of the wealthiest towns in England by 1500, and later supported the Parliamentary cause in the Civil War. The twentieth century made and broke the town: from being the largest shipbuilding town in the world, supporting a dozen shipyards, Sunderland slumped after ferocious bombing during World War II. Depression and recession did the rest.

There's little to turn the head in Sunderland's pedestrianized centre, although the **Northern Gallery for Contemporary Art** on central Fawcett Street (Mon & Wed 9.30am–7.30pm. Tues, Thurs & Fri 9.30am–5pm, Sat 9.30am–6pm; free; ☎0191/514 1235) hosts some interesting temporary exhibitions, and the revamped **Sunderland Museum** at the end of the same street on Borough Road (Mon 10am–4pm, Tues–Sat 10am–5pm, Sun 2–5pm; free) does a very good, multimedia job of telling the city's history. Highlights include the elegantly intricate model ships in "Launched on Wearside", which relates how Sunderland ships once were sent the world over – a trade, incidentally, which gave the city inhabitants their "Mackem" nickname, derived from a stage in the shipbuilding process. In "Coal", which deals movingly with the local coal-mining industry, the roll call of closed collieries is sobering – one of the last to go, Wearmouth, has since been reclaimed as the site of Sunderland Football Club's new ground, the Stadium Of Light. The attached **Winter Gardens**, housed in an impressive new steel and glass hot-house that belatedly replaces the original Victorian glasshouses bombed by the Germans in 1941, are worth a look, too. Though many of the recently acquired exotic trees and palms have yet to reach their full height, sound effects, hot and cold zones, a fern gully and an attractive waterfall help to give the gardens that faraway tropical feeling.

The main interest in Sunderland lies across the River Wear, whose remodelled, landscaped **Riverside** is actually the oldest settled part of the city. You can walk here easily enough, up Bridge Street from the centre and across the Victorian Wearmouth Bridge (around 20min). Here, in front of the university campus buildings, the early Christian church of **St Peter** (Easter–Oct daily 2–4pm; by arrangement at other times, call ☎0191/567 3726), built in 674 AD, is the elder sibling of St Paul's church at Jarrow. The tower and west wall are original Saxon features and the church displays fragments of the oldest stained glass in the country, the work of seventh-century European craftsmen. The extraordinary building further down on the waterside is the city's **National Glass Centre** (daily 10am–5pm; £5; ☎0191/515 5555, ⓦwww.nationalglass-centre.com), which tells the story of British glass and glass-making – a traditional industry in Sunderland since the seventh century, when workshops turned out stained glass for the north's monastic houses and churches. There's plenty to get your teeth into, not least a glass roof you can walk on, temporary exhibition galleries, a craft shop, and glass-making demonstrations in the on-site workshop (call for times).

Further north, out in the beach resort of **Roker** (bus #E1, #E3 or #19), the church of **St Andrew's** on Park Avenue (Mon–Fri 9.30–11.30am) is known as "the cathedral of the Arts and Crafts Movement". The nave echoes the upturned hull of a ship, while the sanctuary has a beautiful painting depicting the heavens, with an electric light fitting at the centre of the sun. The tapestries and carpets are from the William Morris workshop, and like the church they date from the early 1900s. It's a mile or so north up the coast from Roker to the twin resort of **Seaburn**, again with a goodish stretch of sand, and beyond that you could follow a waymarked trail along dramatic clifftops all the way to South Shields (see p.1039) in three hours. On the way, five miles north of Sunderland on the A183 (also bus #E1), you'll pass **Souter Lighthouse** (April–Oct Mon–Thurs, Sat & Sun 11am–5pm; £2.80; NT), opened in 1871 and the first lighthouse in the world to use electric light. Engaging volunteer guides will talk you through the still-operable engine room and the re-created living room and bedrooms of one of the keeper's houses, and, of course, escort you up the light tower, from where on the clearest of days you'll be able to glimpse Flamborough Head, over fifty miles away in Yorkshire.

The fifteen-mile **River Wear Trail** follows the course of the river upstream from Sunderland, through Washington. The trail starts in town on the south side of the Wearmouth Bridge, the first stretch running through Festival Park before entering the green Wear valley. A few miles to the west, and visible from every road in the vicinity, the hilltop **Penshaw Monument** draws admiring glances – a nineteenth-century pseudo-Greek temple, 100 feet long and 70 feet high, erected in honour of John George Lambton, the first earl of Durham.

Practicalities

The main stop for **Metros** from Newcastle is in the central **train station** opposite the Bridges Shopping Centre, but get off at the previous stop, St Peter's, to walk along the north side of the river to the National Glass Centre or St Peter's Church. All buses use the **Park Lane Bus Station**, a five-minute walk south of the train station in the city centre, while the **tourist office** is just to the east on the main shopping drag, Fawcett Street (Mon–Sat 9am–5pm, Sun 10am–4pm; ☎0191/553 2000, ✆tourist.info@sunderland.gov .uk). For daytime **food** in the city centre, try *21 John Street* (closed Sun), a relaxed, airy Italian café offering everything from made-to-order sandwiches to pasta and more substantial dishes. The best restaurant is *11 Tavistock Place* (☎0191/514 5000), round the corner from the museum, dishing up sophisticated food and, on Sunday lunchtimes, live jazz. There's also a stylish café-brasserie in the museum itself overlooking Mowbray Park, and a fine restaurant in the National Glass Centre, with riverside views.

Washington

Five miles west of Sunderland, the River Wear keeps to the south of the New Town of **WASHINGTON**, focus of much of the area's contemporary investment and manufacture. Split into planned, numbered districts and organized on American lines, it's not an obvious stop, although the original **Old Village** has been zealously preserved as a conservation area and boasts a couple of pubs and tea rooms. Drivers should follow the signs for District 4 off the A1231 (Sunderland–Newcastle road).

Just off the village green, past the leafy churchyard on The Avenue, stands the ancestral home of the family which spawned the first **US president**. The "de Wessyngtons" – later the Washingtons – originally came over with William the Conqueror, and by 1183 were based at the **Old Hall** (April–Oct Mon–Wed & Sun 11am–5pm; £2.80; NT), where they lived until 1613. Carefully preserved as a Jacobean showpiece, the echoing, stone-flagged house has a fine kitchen, Great Hall and garden, and some exemplary wood panelling, and although none of the furniture is original to the Washington family, it is contemporaneous. A breezy video tells the life of George Washington and plenty of memorabilia pads things out – a notable John Singleton Copley portrait, commemorative spoons and coins, and even the silver spade with which President Jimmy Carter planted a tree during his 1977 visit. Every Fourth of July, the raising of the US flag at the house heralds a day of Independence celebrations; entry to the Old Hall is free that day. Washington himself probably knew little of his family's northeast English origins – the Old Hall had passed into other hands well before the future president's great-grandfather emigrated to Virginia in 1656, an exile after the English Civil War. Yet it seems too much of a coincidence that the old Washington family coat-of-arms (three stars and three horizontal red-and-white stripes) found its echo more than a century later in the earliest version of the new country's Stars and Stripes.

The other main attraction in the area is the **Washington Wildfowl and Wetlands Centre** (daily: April–Oct 9.30am–5pm; Nov–March 9.30am–4pm; £4.90), east of town and north of the River Wear in District 15, its hundred acres designed by Sir Peter Scott and home to swans, geese, ducks, herons and flamingos. Its trails, hides, play areas, visitor information centre and children's activities make for an enjoyable day out. It's signposted off most local roads, four miles from the A1(M), or see below for public transport.

For Washington Village and the Old Hall, the best service is on the #185 bus from Sunderland's Park Lane Bus Station (not Sun). The Wildfowl Centre is reached on the #56A from Newcastle's Market Street (not Sun) or the #X4 from either Newcastle's Eldon Square or Sunderland's Park Lane (not Sun). If disaster strikes, all these buses (and many others from Newcastle or Sunderland) call or terminate at **Washington Galleries Bus Station**, from where you'll be able to reach either site. Most buses prefixed with a "W" run to Washington Village from the Galleries.

Hadrian's Wall and Hexham

Some of the great monuments of antiquity are hard to take in at a glance. You need a guide, a knowledgable person to explain the significance of dilapidated stonework. The Wall is an exception. You can see exactly what the Romans were up to.

John Hillaby, *Journey Through Britain*, 1970.

In 55 and 54 BC, Julius Caesar launched two swift invasions of southeast England from his base in Gaul, his success proving that Britain lay within the Roman grasp. The full-scale assault began under Claudius in 43 AD and, within forty years, Roman troops had reached the Firth of Tay. In 83 AD, the Roman governor Agricola ventured farther north, but Rome subsequently transferred part of his army to the Danube, and the remaining legions withdrew to the frontier which was marked by the **Stanegate**, a military roadway linking Carlisle and Corbridge.

Emperor Hadrian, who toured Roman Britain in 122 AD, found this informal arrangement unsatisfactory. His imperial policy was quite straightforward – he wanted the empire to live at peace within stable frontiers, most of which were defined by geographical features. In northern Britain, however, there was no natural barrier and so Hadrian decided to create his own by constructing a 76-mile **wall** from the Tyne to the Solway Firth – "to separate the

Romans from the barbarians", according to his biographer. It was not intended to be an impenetrable fortification, but rather a base for patrols that could push out into hostile territory and a barrier to inhibit movement. It was to be punctuated by **milecastles**, which were to serve as gates, depots and mini-barracks, and by observation **turrets**, two of which were to stand between each pair of milecastles. Before the Wall was even completed, major modifications were made: the bulk of the garrison had initially been stationed along the Stanegate, but they were now moved into the Wall, occupying a chain of new **forts**, which straddled the Wall at six- to nine-mile intervals. These new arrangements concentrated the Wall's garrison in a handful of key points and brought them nearer the enemy, making it possible to respond quickly to any threat. Simultaneously, a military zone was defined by the digging of a broad ditch, or **vallum**, on the south side of the Wall, crossed by causeways to each of the forts, turning them into the main points of access and rendering the milecastles, in this respect, largely redundant. The revised structure remained in operation until the last Roman soldiers left in 411 AD.

Most of Hadrian's Wall disappeared centuries ago, yet walking its length remains a popular pastime, one which will be made easier by the opening of a waymarked trail, the **Hadrian's Wall Path**, in summer 2002; even if you're not up to tramping the entire course of the Wall, it's well worth walking at least one section to get an idea of the whole enterprise. Approached from Newcastle along the valley of the Tyne, via the Roman museum and site at **Corbridge**, the prosperous-looking market town of **Hexham**, with its fine eleventh-century abbey, makes a good base for transport and accommodation. Most visitors stick to the best-preserved portions of the Wall, which are concentrated between the hamlet of **Chollerford**, three miles north of Hexham, and **Haltwhistle**, sixteen miles to the west. It's here, especially between **Housesteads** and **Steel Rigg**, that the Wall is at its most beautiful, as it clings to the edge of the Whin Sill, a precipitous line of dolerite crags towering above the austere Northumberland National Park moorland. Walking this part of the Wall couldn't be easier: a footpath runs along the top of the ridge, incorporating a short stretch of the **Pennine Way**, which meets the Wall at Greenhead and leaves at Housesteads, where it cuts off north for Bellingham. Scattered along this section are a variety of key archeological sites and museums, notably **Chesters Roman Fort and Museum**, near Chollerford, the remains of **Housesteads Fort** and that of **Vindolanda**, and the milecastle remains at **Cawfields**, north of Haltwhistle.

Visiting the Wall

Using **Hexham** or **Haltwhistle** as your base, you can see most of the Northumbrian section of Hadrian's Wall by bus or car, with the B6318 – the Military Road built with huge amounts of stone from the Wall by General

Wade after the second Jacobite uprising – following the line of the Wall from Chollerford to Greenhead.

There's a special Hadrian's Wall **bus** service, the cutely tagged **#AD122**, which links Hexham tourist office and bus and train stations with Chesters, Housesteads, Once Brewed Visitor Centre, Vindolanda, the Milecastle Inn, Cawfields car park, Haltwhistle train station, the Roman Army Museum and Greenhead, Birdoswald and Carlisle. This operates between late-May and late-September, four to five times a day in each direction, taking two hours for the whole route (1hr Hexham–Haltwhistle); a typical one-way ticket, from Hexham to Vindolanda, costs £2.10.

During the summer period, a connecting Sunday-morning bus service starts at Gateshead Metro station, calling at Newcastle's Eldon Square and Corbridge before moving on to Hexham. There's also a year-round service, the #185, which runs between Carlisle and Housesteads, via the Roman Army Museum, Haltwhistle and the Once Brewed Visitor Centre, with two to three departures a day (not Sun). Another year-round service, the #685, runs hourly (Mon–Sat) along the A69 between Carlisle, Greenhead, Haltwhistle, Haydon Bridge, Hexham, Corbridge and Newcastle (Eldon Square); on Sundays, the #685 runs four times from Carlisle to Hexham, connecting with the hourly #85 Hexham–Newcastle service. Finally, the #880 or #882 bus from Hexham (calling at the train station and Acomb youth hostel) runs via Chollerford, from where Chesters is just half a mile's walk along the road to the west; during the period May to mid-September, some of these services divert to Chesters itself.

The nearest **train** stations are on the Newcastle–Carlisle line at Corbridge, Hexham, Haydon Bridge, Bardon Mill and Haltwhistle. Hexham, Bardon Mill and Haltwhistle will leave you a fair walk to Chesters, Vindolanda/Once Brewed and Cawfields/Greenhead respectively, or you can connect at Hexham or Haltwhistle with the bus services described above.

A variety of **passes** are available on these services. Day Rover tickets on the #AD122, which can be bought from the driver or local tourist offices, cost £5.50; holders of Northeast Explorer passes get half-price travel, those with Stagecoach Cumberland Explorer tickets go free. The Hadrian's Wall Rail Rover Ticket (£12.50, available from train stations) is valid for two days in any three-day period (after 9am weekdays), and covers travel on the Newcastle–Carlisle train line, the #AD122 and the Tyne & Wear Metro. Not quite so good-value is the Tyne Valley Ranger (£11), a one-day pass for the Newcastle–Carlisle train and the #AD122 (after 9am weekdays).

Details of these services are available from Newcastle, Hexham, Carlisle and Haltwhistle tourist offices, the Once Brewed Visitor Centre, and on the Hadrian's Wall tourism partnership's **website**, ⓦ www.hadrians-wall.org.

Hexham has the best range of **accommodation** along this section of the Wall, but there's also a decent choice at Corbridge, handy for Chesters, and at Haltwhistle, three miles or so south of the Wall itself, augmented by plenty of farmhouse B&Bs in the dramatic countryside between Greenhead and Hexham, and **youth hostels** at Once Brewed, Greenhead and Acomb, near Hexham.

Corbridge

Buses from Newcastle and trains on the Newcastle–Hexham–Carlisle train line all stop at **CORBRIDGE**, a quiet and well-heeled commuter town overlooking the River Tyne from the top of a steep ridge. This spur of land was first settled by the Saxons, and their handiwork survives in parts of the church of **St Andrew**, on the central Market Place, but it's the adjacent **Vicar's Pele** that catches the eye, an unusually well-preserved fortified tower-house dating to the fourteenth century. Other buildings are less striking but form a handsome ensemble, with tawny-coloured stone houses alternating with some upmarket shops and eating places.

Arrival, information and accommodation

The **train station** is half a mile outside the town, across the river; from here it's an easy walk into the centre, with the *Angel Inn* on Main Street one of the first places you reach having crossed the bridge. Outside the inn is one place that **buses** stop; you might also be dropped near the post office on Hill Street, around the corner. Corbridge **tourist office** is also on Hill Street, at the library (mid-May to Sept Mon–Sat 10am–1pm & 2–6pm, Sun 1–5pm; Easter to mid-May & Oct Mon–Sat 10am–1pm & 2–5pm, Sun 1–5pm; ☎01434 /632815).

There's plenty of **accommodation** in and around Corbridge, with a few unprepossessing B&Bs near the train station on Station Road and a wider choice in the centre of town – try the *Riverside Guest House*, a comfortable eighteenth-century house with fine views of the Tyne on Main Street (☎01434/632942, ⓦweb.ukonline.co.uk/riverside; ❷), or spacious, tastefully decorated *Clive House*, in the former schoolhouse just east of here on Appletree Lane (☎01434/632617; ❷). You'll need to book in advance for the ivy-covered *Angel Inn* on Main Street (☎01434/632119, ⓦwww.theangelofcorbridge.co.uk; ❺), which has just five en-suite rooms, or there's plenty of space and a fine riverside location at the *Lion of Corbridge Hotel*, Bridge End (☎01434/632504, ⓔlionofcorbridge@talk21.com; ❹), which is right by the bridge on the way in from the train station.

The Roman Site

One mile to the west of the Market Place, accessible either by road or along the riverside footpath – take the street opposite the *Watling Coffee House* – lies **Corbridge Roman Site** (April–Sept daily 10am–6pm; Oct daily 10am–5pm; Nov–March Wed–Sun 10am–1pm & 2–4pm; £2.90; EH), the location of the garrison town of Corstopitum. This is the oldest fortified site in the region, first established as a supply base for the Roman advance into Scotland in 80 AD (and thus predating the Wall itself). It remained in regular military use until the end of the second century, after which it became surrounded by a fast-developing town – most of the visible archeological remains date from this period, when Corstopitum, the most northerly town in the empire, served as the nerve centre of Hadrian's Wall, guarding the bridge at the intersection of Stanegate and Dere Street. Clearly labelled, the extensive remains provide an insight into the layout of the civilian town, showing the foundations of temples, public baths, garrison headquarters, workshops and houses as well as the best-preserved Roman granaries in Britain – huge, buttressed buildings with a ventilation system enabling the grain to be stored for long periods.

The site **museum** boasts a good selection of Roman artefacts, from domestic items and imported ceramics to vivid temple friezes. The celebrated *Lion and Stag* fountainhead – the so-called "Corbridge Lion" – gets pride of place; to the Romans, the lion and its prey symbolized the triumph of life over death. The contents of an armourer's box discovered beneath the floor of the hospital revealed the existence of an underground strongroom, used to distribute the soldiers' pay.

Eating and drinking

The *Watling Coffee House*, on Watling Street just north of the main square, and *Chadwick's* on Middle Street, not far from the church, both serve light **meals** throughout the day, while the Corbridge Larder is a high-class deli on Hill Street that makes up good sandwiches. Star attraction in the evening is the *Valley* (☎01434/633434; closed Sun), a high-quality, innovative Indian restaurant in the old station house on Station Road; for larger parties coming from Newcastle, they'll arrange for a waiter to distribute menus, serve drinks and take orders on the "curry train" from Central Station. Further up the same road, the *Ramblers Country House Restaurant* (☎01434/632424; Mon–Sat eves & Sun lunch) at Farnley is precisely that, a comfortable German-run place with gardens where set dinners are under £20 (without drinks). Back in the centre of town, set in a bright, stone-walled cottage at 18 Front St, is *Al Ponte* (☎01434/634214), offering a wide selection of traditional and regional Italian dishes, and good lunch deals.

For **bar meals** and beer, visit the *Wheatsheaf*, on Watling Street (visible at the end of the road, beyond the *Watling Coffee House*), an attractive seventeenth-century former farmhouse with a couple of Roman stones in the stableyard. Or – in the other direction – you could try the stone-built *Black Bull*, on Middle Street. Otherwise, the *Dyvels*, very close to the train station, is a nice, small local pub with a beer garden.

Hexham

In 671, on a bluff above the Tyne, four miles west of Corbridge, St Wilfrid founded a Benedictine monastery whose church was, according to contemporary accounts, the finest to be seen north of the Alps. Unfortunately, its gold and silver proved irresistible to the Vikings, who savaged the place in 876, but the church was rebuilt in the eleventh century as part of an Augustinian priory, and the town of **HEXHAM**, governed by the Archbishop of York, grew up in its shadow. It's a handsome market town of some interest – indeed, it's the only significant stop between Newcastle and Carlisle – and however keen you are to reach the Wall, you'd do well to give Hexham a night or even make it your base.

Arrival, information and accommodation

Well connected with Newcastle, Haltwhistle and Carlisle, Hexham's **train station** sits on the northeastern edge of the town centre, a ten-minute walk from the abbey; the new **tourist office** is halfway between the two, in the main town car park behind the Safeway superstore (Easter to mid-May & Oct Mon–Sat 9am–5pm, Sun 10am–5pm; mid-May to Sept Mon–Sat 9am–6pm, Sun 10am–5pm; Nov to Easter Mon–Sat 9am–5pm; ☎01434/652220, ⓔhexham.tic@tynedale.gov.uk). The **bus station** can be found off Priestpopple, a few minutes' stroll east of the abbey.

The tourist office can point you in the right direction for **accommodation**. Good options include the welcoming Edwardian retreat that is the *Kitty Frisk House*, a few minutes from the centre on Corbridge Road (☎01434/601533; no credit cards; ❷); the quiet and secluded *West Close House*, on Hextol Terrace off the B6305 Allendale Road (☎01434/603307; no credit cards; ❷), which is very friendly, has a delightful garden and offers wholefood continental breakfasts alongside the usual fry-ups; and the bright and breezy *Topsy Turvy*, 9 Leazes Lane (☎01434/603152; no credit cards; ❶). The *Best Western Beaumont Hotel*, Beaumont Street (☎01434/602331, ⓦwww.beaumont-hotel.co.uk; ❺, excludes breakfast), has spacious doubles overlooking the abbey and weekend dinner, bed and breakfast deals; alternatively, try the sympathetically renovated *Royal Hotel* on Priestpopple (℡01434/602270, ⓦwww.hexham-royal-hotel.co.uk; ❹), topped by a gleaming gold dome, which offers a dozen en-suite rooms, a cosy, oak-panelled bar and good discounts for stays of two nights or more.

The **youth hostel** (℡01434/602864) occupies converted stable buildings in the village of **Acomb**, two miles from Hexham – take bus #880, #881 or #882, which all pass the train station. The **campsite** here, at *Fallowfield Dene Caravan Park* (℡01434/603553; closed Nov–March), is a tranquil place with proper laundry facilities. Closer to town, *Riverside Leisure* (℡01434/604705; closed Nov–Feb), beside the Tyne half a mile north of the abbey, forms part of the caravan and leisure park at the end of Tyne Green Road.

The Town

The stately exterior of **Hexham Abbey** (daily: May–Sept 9am–7pm; Oct–April 9am–5pm; free), properly the Priory Church of St Andrew, still dominates the west side of the Market Place. Entry is through the south transept, where there's a bruised but impressive first-century tombstone honouring Flavinus, a standard-bearer in the Roman cavalry, who's shown riding down his bearded enemy. The memorial lies at the foot of the broad, well-worn steps of the canons' **night stair**, one of the few such staircases – providing access from the monastery to the church – to have survived the Dissolution. Beyond, most of the high-arched nave dates from an Edwardian restoration and it's here that you gain access to the **crypt**, a Saxon structure made out of old Roman stones, where pilgrims once viewed the abbey's reliquaries. The nave's architect also used Roman stonework, sticking various sculptural fragments in the walls, many of which he had unearthed during the rebuilding.

At the end of the nave is the splendid sixteenth-century **rood screen**, whose complex tracery envelops the portraits of local bishops. Behind the screen, the chancel displays the inconsequential-looking **frith stool**, an eighth-century stone chair that was once believed to have been used by St Wilfrid, rendering it holy enough to serve as the medieval sanctuary stool. Nearby, close to the high altar, there are four panels from a fifteenth-century **Dance of Death**, a grim, darkly varnished painting.

The rest of Hexham's large and irregularly shaped **Market Place** (main market day is Tuesday) is peppered with remains of its medieval past. The massive walls of the fourteenth-century **Moot Hall** were built to serve as the gatehouse to "The Hall", a well-protected enclosure that was garrisoned against the Scots. Nearby, the archbishops also built their own prison, a formidable fortified tower dating from 1330 and constructed using stones plundered from the Roman ruins at Corbridge. Now, as the **Old Gaol**, this accommodates the **Border History Museum** (April–Oct daily 10am–4.30pm; Feb, March & Nov Mon, Tues & Sat 10am–4.30pm; £2), which provides information and displays concerning the border-raiding Reivers as well as the building's use as a prison – a function it abandoned in 1824.

Down by Hexham Bridge, behind the railway line, a short trail runs through the riverside **Tyne Green Country Park**, a couple of miles upstream to **Warden**, the scenic spot where the North Tyne (from Kielder Water) and South Tyne (from the Pennines) rivers join. The *Boatside Inn* at Warden has decent pub food and outdoor tables, and the walk there and back is very pleasant on a summer's evening.

Eating, drinking and entertainment

There are several **coffee shops** and **tearooms** in town open during the day, of which *Mrs Miggins*, on St Mary's Wynd, just off Beaumont Street by Queen's Hall, is among the best, serving inexpensive home-made meals and snacks. Off the Market Place, the *Hexham Tans*, 11 St Mary's Chare, is a homely vegetarian café (closed Sun), and the Corbridge Larder, inside Robb's department store on Fore Street, is the place for picnic supplies.

Options for **evening meals** in Hexham are limited. Your best bets are *Valley Connection 301* on the Market Place (☎01434/601234; closed Mon), part of a chain of inventive Indian restaurants that stretches to Corbridge and Newcastle, or *Danielle's*, an unpretentious bistro at 12 Eastgate (☎01434 /601122; closed Sun).

Out of town on Dipton Mill Road, two miles south of the centre, *Dipton Mill Inn* is a good all-rounder, with wholesome bar meals (until 8.30pm), own-brewed beer, streamside beer garden and a pleasant setting. It's a 45-minute walk from Hexham on lovely hilly footpaths; the tourist office will point you in the right direction.

The main focus of **entertainment** in town is the **Queen's Hall Arts Centre** on Beaumont Street (☎01434/652477), which puts on a year-round programme of theatre, dance, music and art exhibitions; it also has a café that stays open late on performance evenings. The centre has information about the Hexham Gathering, a folk **festival** held at various venues at the end of May, and the Hexham Abbey Festival, which presents mostly classical music concerts in the abbey in mid-September. There's often live music at various town-centre **pubs**, none of which, otherwise, are particularly enticing. For just a drink, the *Tap & Spile* on the corner of Battle Hill and Eastgate is probably the most welcoming, with a full range of guest beers.

Chollerford and Chesters Roman Fort

At **CHOLLERFORD**, around four miles north of Hexham, a bridge crosses the North Tyne river, overlooked by the swanky *Swallow George Hotel* (☎01434 /681611, ⓦwww.georgehotel-chollerford.com; ❼), whose renowned restaurant has a fine garden and river views.

Two thousand years ago, the main river crossing was a little way downstream, half a mile west of present-day Chollerford, where **Chesters Roman Fort** (daily: Easter–Sept 10am–6pm; Oct 10am–5pm; Nov–Easter 10am–4pm; £2.90; EH), otherwise known as *Cilurnum*, was built to guard the erstwhile Roman bridge over the river, its six-acre plot accommodating a cavalry regiment roughly five hundred strong. Enough remains of the original structure to pick out the design of the fort, and each section has been clearly labelled, but the highlight is down by the river where the vestibule, changing room and steam range of the garrison's **bath house** are still visible, along with the furnace and the latrines.

Back at the entrance, the **museum** has an excellent collection of Roman stonework, most of which was retrieved by the Victorian antiquarian John Clayton, who spent years attempting to preserve the Wall. In particular, look out for Juno (now headless) in a delicately pleated dress standing on a cow, one of the finest pieces of statuary found along the Wall, the sculpture of Mars from Housesteads, a relief depicting three water nymphs, and several stone marker plaques recording the building work completed by the different legions.

Next door to the site is the beautiful **Chesters Walled Garden** (April–Oct daily 10am–5pm; Nov–March variable hours, call ☎01434/681483), which shelters a fragrant display of herbs, including national collections of thyme and marjoram and a Roman herb section. If you've got your own transport (it's probably not worth the walk), head another three miles west from Chesters along the B6318 to Carrawburgh, the site of **Brocolitia Fort** and its late third-century **temple**, part of a mysterious cult that spread throughout the empire dedicated to Mithras, the Persian god of sun and light (dawn–dusk; free).

Housesteads to Once Brewed

Overlooking the bleak and bare Northumbrian moors from the top of the Whin Sill, **Housesteads Roman Fort** (daily: Easter–Sept 10am–6pm; Oct 10am–5pm; Nov–Easter 10am–4pm; £2.90; EH & NT), eight miles west of Chesters – and a good ten-minute walk up from the car park – has long been the most popular site on the Wall. The fort was built in the second phase of the Hadrianic construction and is of standard design but for one enforced modification – forts were supposed to straddle the line of the Wall, but here the original stonework tracked along the very edge of the cliff, so Housesteads was built on the steeply sloping ridge to the south. Access is via the tiny **museum**, from where you stroll across to the south gate, beside which lie the remains of the civilian settlement that was dependent on the one thousand infantrymen stationed within. Inside the perimeter, look out for the distinctive cubicles of the barrack blocks, the courtyard plan of the commanding officer's house and the tooth-like stone supports of the granaries.

You don't need to pay for entrance to Housesteads if you simply intend to walk west along the Wall from here. The three-mile hike past the lovely wooded **Crag Lough** to **Steel Rigg** (car park) offers the most fantastic views, especially when you spy the course of the Wall as it threads over the crags ahead.

Practicalities

Leaving the Wall at Steel Rigg, it's roughly half a mile south to the main road and the very informative **Once Brewed National Park Visitor Centre** (June–Aug daily 9.30am–6pm; mid-March to May, Sept & Oct daily 9.30am–5pm; much reduced hours in winter, usually Sat & Sun only, call for details; ☏01434/344396), which has exhibitions and information on both the Wall and the National Park. The side road beyond the centre continues for half a mile down to Vindolanda; note that the summer **Hadrian's Wall bus** calls at both the visitor centre and Vindolanda.

For local **accommodation**, there's the popular *Once Brewed Youth Hostel* (☏01434/344360, ✉oncebrewed@yha.org.uk; closed Dec & Jan), next to the visitor centre, and the *Vallum Lodge* (☏01434/344248; ❸; closed Nov–Feb), a comfortable small hotel with good home cooking, a mile or so west down the main road from the visitor centre. The surrounding countryside also shelters a few scenically located B&Bs, including *Gibbs Hill Farm* (☏01434/344030, ⓦwww.gibbshillfarm.co.uk; ❷; closed Nov–Feb), with attractive, en-suite rooms and great views of the wall, two miles north of Steel Rigg.

There's also a very well-equipped backpackers' hostel, the *Hadrian Lodge*, to the southeast on isolated North Road (☏01434/688688) – from the Wall and the B6318 take the turning for **Haydon Bridge** about a mile east of Housesteads, and you'll reach the hostel two miles before the village. Bunk rooms, private rooms, licensed bar and café, make this a good alternative to the *Once Brewed Youth Hostel*. Lying on the main A69 road, Haydon Bridge is home to by far the best local place to **eat**, the *General Havelock Inn* (☏01434/684376), serving fine modern European cuisine either in the bar (closed Mon), in the grand rear restaurant (closed Sun eve & Mon), or even in the garden on the banks of the river.

Vindolanda

The excavated garrison fort of **Vindolanda** actually predates the Wall itself – as do several of the forts hereabouts – though most of what you see today dates from the second to third century AD, when the fort was a thriving metropolis of five hundred soldiers with its own civilian settlement attached. The **site** (daily: May & June 10am–6pm; July & Aug 10am–6.30pm; April & Sept 10am–5.30pm; March & Oct 10am–5pm; Nov, Dec & Feb 10am–4pm; £3.90) is operated by the private Vindolanda Trust, which has done an excellent job of imaginatively presenting its finds. Note that the Trust also administers the Roman Army Museum at Greenhead; if you're visiting both sites, be sure to request a discounted joint-admission ticket (£5.60).

The ongoing **excavations** at Vindolanda are spread over a wide area, with civilian houses, inn, guest quarters, administrative building, commander's house and main gates all clearly visible. Full-scale re-creations give an idea of what the Wall would have looked like: a stone turret and wall section, alongside a timber milecastle and a bit of turf wall to replicate the original appearance of the western third of the Wall, where limestone was in short supply.

The path through the excavations then descends to what's termed the **open-air museum**, where you can walk into reconstructions of a shrine of the water nymphs, a shop and a house, all with lively sound commentaries. Beyond lies the café, shop and **Chesterholm Museum**, the latter housing the largest collection of Roman leather items ever discovered on a single site – dozens of shoes, belts, even a pair of baby boots – which were preserved in the black silt of waterlogged ditches. Elsewhere in the museum, look out for the largest collection of Roman textiles found in the western Roman Empire, and a woman's wig made from local hair moss to keep off the midges. However, the most intriguing sections are concerned with the excavated hoard of **writing tablets**, now in the British Museum. Between 1973 and 1992, two hundred significant texts were discovered on the site, dealing with subjects as diverse as clerical filing systems and children's schoolwork. Then, in 1993, final excavations from a bonfire site revealed more tablets, apparently discarded when the garrison received orders in 103–104 AD to move to the Danube to participate in Emperor Trajan's Second Dacian War. The writings depict graphically the realities of military life in Northumberland, under the prefecture of Flavius Cerialis: soldiers' requests for more beer, birthday party invitations, court reports on banishments for unspecified wrongdoings, even letters from home containing gifts of underwear for freezing frontline grunts.

Cawfields and Haltwhistle to Greenhead

Wall-walkers can continue west from Steel Rigg/Once Brewed to **Cawfields** (free access), a distance of around three miles. This was the site of a temporary Roman camp that again pre-dated the Wall, and there are also the remains of another milecastle, this one perched on one of the most rugged crags on this section. There's a car park and picnic site at Cawfields, too, while if you make your way the mile or so south to the main B6318 you'll find the splendid *Milecastle Inn*, the first decent **pub** for miles around and one which specializes in home-cooked pies. The Hadrian's Wall buses (see p.1045) stop here, too.

The inn stands at a crossroads, with the small town of **HALTWHISTLE** just under a couple of miles away. There's not much to it – apart from what must be one of the longest main streets in Britain – but there is a **tourist office** (Easter–Oct Mon–Sat 9.30am–1pm & 2–5pm, Sun 1–5pm; Nov–Easter Mon, Tues & Thurs–Sat 10am–noon & 1–3.30pm; ☎01434/322002) in the **train station**, right at the western edge of town, close to the A69; from here, walk up to Westgate, which becomes Main Street. **Mountain bikes** can be rented for £12 a day from Edens Lawn petrol station on the eastern edge of town (☎01434/320443).

Haltwhistle boasts a fine **hotel**, the *Centre of Britain* (☎01434/322422, ⓦwww.centre-of-britain.org.uk; ❸), right in the centre of town and – though a few other towns hereabouts lay claim – Britain as well. Built around a fifteenth-century peel tower are a variety of tasteful bedrooms and lounges with wooden beams and stone fireplaces. The town also has a good selection of **B&Bs**, including the attractive, ivy-covered *Hall Meadows*, right at the top of Main Street (☎01434/321021; no credit cards; ❶). Alternatively, there's *Ashcroft* in an elegant former vicarage on Lantys Lonnen, very near the tourist office (☎01434/320213; ❷), which has nice rooms and colourful terraced gardens, while at the eastern end of town, just a mile from the Wall, the *Ald White Craig Farm* on Shield Hill (☎01434/320565; ❷; closed Nov–Feb) is a popular choice. Two or three pubs also offer accommodation, including the *Manor House Hotel* (☎01434/322588; ❷) on Main Street. The *Haltwhistle Camping Site* is in Burnfoot Park (☎01434/320106; closed Nov–Feb), beside the Tyne on the southeast edge of town. There are several tearooms along and around Main Street, while for beer and **bar meals**, the *Spotted Cow Inn*, down on Castle Hill, the eastern extension of Main Street, is an agreeable spot. Just a couple of miles south of town, the *Wallace Arms* at Rowfoot, near Featherstone, is situated in fine surroundings, a nice place for a pub meal and a country walk.

Roman Army Museum

A further four-mile trek west from Cawfields takes you past the remains of **Great Chesters Fort** before reaching a spectacular section of the Wall, known as the **Walltown Crags**, where a turret from a signal system predating the Wall still survives. The views from here are marvellous. Adjacent to the crags, at Carvoran, the Vindolanda Trust's **Roman Army Museum** (daily: May & June 10am–6pm; July & Aug 10am–6.30pm; April & Sept 10am–5.30pm; March & Oct 10am–5pm; early Nov & late Feb 10am–4pm; £3.10; joint admission ticket with Vindolanda £5.60) does its best to inject some interest into its dioramas, reconstructions, films and exhibits, but it's rather tame stuff compared to the archeological sites.

Greenhead

Push on just a mile southwest, and you're soon in minuscule **GREENHEAD**, where the **youth hostel** (☎016977/47401, Ⓔgreenhead@yha.org.uk) is located in a converted Methodist chapel. If this doesn't appeal, *Holmhead Guest House* (☎016977/47402, Ⓔholmhead@hadrianswall.freeserve.co.uk; ❸) probably will, an old stone farmhouse up a track behind the hostel. Sporting exposed beams, and partly built with stones taken from the Wall itself, it also serves an excellent set-menu dinner using local ingredients – book ahead, since there are only four rooms.

The hamlet – served by the Hadrian's Wall bus – is where the **Pennine Way** cuts **east**, following the Wall as far as Housesteads before bearing north again. Heading **west**, the next section of Hadrian's Wall worth exploring is at Birdoswald (see p.869), a four-mile walk or ten-minute ride on the bus.

Northumberland National Park

Northwest Northumberland, the great triangular chunk of land between Hadrian's Wall and the coastal plain, is dominated by the wide-skied landscapes of the **Northumberland National Park**, whose four hundred windswept square miles rise to the **Cheviot Hills** on the Scottish border. These uplands are interrupted by great slabs of forest, mostly the conifer plantations of the Forestry Commission, and a string of river valleys, of which Coquetdale, Tynedale and Redesdale are the longest.

Remote from lowland law and order, these dales were once the homelands of the **Border Reivers**, turbulent clans who ruled the local roost from the thirteenth to the sixteenth century. The Reivers took advantage of the struggles between England and Scotland to engage in endless cross-border rustling and general brigandage, activities recalled by the ruined **bastles** (fortified farmhouses) and **peels** (defensive tower-houses) that lie dotted across the landscape.

Good walking country can be found right across the National Park and it's this activity that attracts thousands of visitors every year. The most popular trail is the **Pennine Way**, which, entering the National Park at Hadrian's Wall, cuts up through Bellingham on its way to The Cheviot, the park's highest peak at 2674ft, finishing at Kirk Yetholm, over the border in Scotland. This part of the Pennine Way is 64 miles long in total, but it's easy to break the hike up into manageable portions as the footpath passes through a variety of tiny settlements, several of which have youth hostels, B&B accommodation and campsites. As an introduction, it's hard to beat the lovely moorland scenery of the fifteen-mile stretch from Housesteads at Hadrian's Wall to **Bellingham**, a pleasant town on the banks of the North Tyne. Bellingham is also on the road to **Kielder Water**, a massive pine-surrounded reservoir which has been vigorously promoted as a water-sports centre and nature reserve since its creation in 1982. Further north, **Rothbury**, in Coquetdale, is close to both the Simonside Hills and **Cragside**, the nineteenth-century country home of Lord Armstrong, whilst at **Wooler** footpaths lead into the Cheviot Hills. Beyond Wooler, a succession of battle sites and **castles** attest to the erstwhile military significance of this border region; notable among them are idiosyncratically restored **Chillingham**, which is home to an equally unusual herd of **wild cattle**, and the weatherbeaten pink ruins of **Norham**, in an inspiring location on the banks of the Tweed.

To attempt a tour of the region by **bus** – there aren't any trains – is a time-consuming business. Most services go up or down the valleys, with few crossing the hills between them. But the park should really be explored on **foot** and, once you've selected your base, you won't have any difficulty in reaching it.

Bellingham

The stone terraces of **BELLINGHAM** (pronounced Bellinjum) slope up from the banks of the Tyne on the eastern edge of the Northumberland National Park. There's nothing outstanding about the place, but it is a restful spot set in splendid rural surroundings, and it does contain the medieval church of **St Cuthbert**, which has an unusual stone-vaulted roof – designed (successfully) to prevent raiding Border Reivers from burning the church to the ground. The volunteer-run **Heritage Centre** just east of the village centre on Woodburn Road (May–Sept Mon & Fri–Sun 10.30am–4.30pm; £1) has more on this turbulent period and also offers changing exhibitions about traditional local life. For a local stroll, follow the two-and-a-half-mile round-trip trail through the woods to **Hareshaw Linn**, a comely waterfall with a thirty-foot drop.

Buses from Hexham and Otterburn (also direct from Newcastle's Eldon Square on summer Wed, Sun & bank holidays) stop in the centre on Market Place, a few hundred yards down from the tourist office. There are onward services to Kielder or Otterburn most days; while the Pennine Way passes right through the village. The helpful **tourist office** on Main Street (Mon–Sat 9.30am–1pm & 2–5pm, Sun 1–5pm; ☎01434/220616) is housed in Bellingham's former Poor House building and is well stocked with local information.

Despite its size, the village's proximity to the park and Pennine Way means that there's a fair choice when it comes to looking for **accommodation**. You may still want to book ahead in summer, particularly if you're coinciding with the last Saturday in August, when the Bellingham Show, the big agricultural event of the year, is staged. The **youth hostel** (☎01434/220313) has simple self-catering facilities in a primitive-looking hut some six hundred yards from the centre of the village on Woodburn Road (signposted from Main Street). Central **lodgings** are available at the modern, en-suite *Lyndale Guest House* (☎01434/220361, ⓦwww.lyndaleguesthouse.co.uk; ❷), just past the *Rose & Crown* pub. *Westfield House*, a large Victorian residence with fine views at the west end of the village (☎01434/220340, ⓔwestfield.house@virgin.net; ❸), is rather grander, and serves a good dinner to guests. Bellingham's pubs – the *Rose & Crown*, the *Black Bull* and the *Cheviot* – all have a few rooms, too; those at the *Cheviot* (☎01434/220696; ❸) are the nicest. Swankiest choice in Bellingham is *Riverdale Hall Hotel* (☎01434/220254, ⓔiben@riverdalehall .demon.co.uk; ❺), a nineteenth-century country house on the village's western edge, with an indoor swimming pool and extensive grounds. The local **campsite** is at *Demesne Farm* (☎01434/220258; closed Nov–Feb), right in the centre near the police station. For **food**, you're dependent on the bar meals served at the pubs, best at the *Cheviot*.

Bastles on the Tarset

The constant cross-border skirmishing of the late medieval period had an immediate effect on the rural vernacular architecture of the northeast. Lonely farmhouses were fortified in an attempt to ward off attacks, and the area west of Bellingham is rich in the remains of these so-called **bastle houses**. The best preserved lies seven miles northwest of the village, beyond Greenhaugh, where the late sixteenth-century **Black Middens Bastle House** (free access; EH) sits above the waters of Tarset Burn. From a distance, it looks like any other ruined, roofless, stone farmhouse; indeed, close up, it looks like any other ruined, roofless, stone farmhouse, albeit one with extremely thick walls, strategic, narrow upper-floor windows and low surrounding walls. The main door and living quarters were on the upper floor, reached by an exterior staircase, which made it more difficult for attackers to batter their way in. From here, you can continue up the marked trail along the **Tarset Valley**, passing several more ruined bastles, though none as evocatively placed as Black Middens.

The hamlet of **GREENHAUGH** has the only facilities hereabouts in the shape of the rustic *Holly Bush Inn* (☎01434/240391, ⓦwww.hollybushinn.net; ❷), a squat, 200-year-old cottage that offers B&B, bar meals and real ales, and also doubles as the post office.

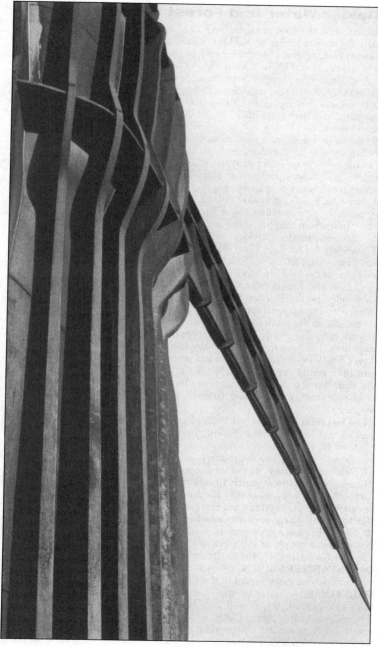

△ The Angel of the North, Tyne and Wear

Kielder Water and Forest

Further west, the road from Bellingham follows the North Tyne River and skirts the forested edge of **Kielder Water** (@www.kielder.org), passing the assorted visitor centres, waterside parks, picnic areas and anchorages that fringe its southern shore. First stop is the Visitor Centre at **Tower Knowe** (daily: July & Aug 10am–6pm; June & Sept 10am–5pm; April, May & Oct 10am–4pm; ☎01434/240398), eight miles from Bellingham, with a café and an exhibition (£1) on the history of the valley and lake. Another four miles west, at **Leaplish**, the waterside park (daily: April & Oct 9am–6pm; May–Sept 9am–11pm; Nov–March call to check times on ☎01434/250312), bar and restaurant are the focus of most of Kielder's outdoor activities: water sports and fishing are on offer, and there's a heated indoor pool. The **Bird of Prey Centre** here (March–Oct daily 10.30am–5pm; £3) gives you the chance to handle these vicious predators and lays on flying displays, falconry courses and winter hawk walks. A ten-mile, hour-and-a-half's **cruise** on the Osprey ferry (Easter–Oct 5 daily; ☎01434/250312; £4.20) is always a pleasure; departures are from the piers at either Tower Knowe or Leaplish.

Five miles from Leaplish at the top of the reservoir and just three miles from the Scottish border, Kielder village is dominated by **Kielder Castle** (Easter–July & Oct daily 10am–5pm; Aug daily 10am–6pm; Nov–Easter Sat & Sun 11am–4pm; ☎01434/250209; free, parking £1), built in 1775 as the hunting lodge of the Duke of Northumberland, and now an information centre and exhibition area praising the work of the Forestry Commission. The castle is surrounded by the **Border Forest Park**, several million spruce trees subdivided into a number of approximately defined forest areas: Wark and Kielder are broadly to the south of the reservoir, Falstone and Redesdale to the north. Several easy and clearly marked **footpaths**, dotted with arresting modern sculptures, lead from the castle into the forest – try the "Duke's Trail" through Ravenshill Wood, a slice of ancient and semi-natural woodland. There's **mountain bike rental** available from Kielder Bikes (☎01434/250392) at the castle, too, with thirteen waymarked trails and two off-road routes through the forest to choose from. Visitor centre facilities are rounded off by a gift shop and restaurant.

The **bus** from Otterburn via Bellingham calls at Tower Knowe, Leaplish and Kielder, and less regularly at Stannersburn and Falstone. The twice-daily post bus from Hexham follows a similar route once past Bellingham, though it takes a lot longer to complete the journey.

If you want to **stay** in the area, options are far-flung but wide-ranging. There's a spacious new **youth hostel** (☎01434/250195; closed Nov–Feb) in Kielder village, with some two-bedded rooms, a self-catering kitchen, and a restaurant offering breakfast and three-course dinners. Leaplish Waterside Park also has **bunk-barn accommodation**, with dorms and two double rooms (❶) available, plus a drying room, kitchen and shower. On the road in from Bellingham, a couple of miles before the water, the early seventeenth-century *Pheasant Inn* (☎01434/240382, ℮thepheasantinn@kielderwater.demon.co.uk; ❹) at **STANNERSBURN** has eight comfortable rooms in a modern extension and decent meals served in the bar or restaurant. The riverside hamlet of **FALSTONE**, a mile to the north, boasts the smaller *Blackcock Inn* (☎01434/240200; ❸), as well as a tearooms in the former village school. There's also B&B at *Spring Cottage* in Stannersburn (☎01434/240338; ❷), plus several B&Bs in Kielder village and the surrounding area – ask at the information centre. *Kielder* **campsite** (☎01434/250291, ℮kieldercampsite@aol.com;

closed Oct–Easter) is by the banks of the Tyne, about half a mile north of the castle.

Redesdale

From Bellingham, it's a fifteen-mile trek north along the Pennine Way to **BYRNESS** in **Redesdale**, which can also be reached direct from Kielder Castle via a rough, eleven-mile forestry road that snakes through the pine-clad hills of the northeast portion of the Border Forest Park. Set beside the main A68 road, Byrness is a tiny village, but walkers can take refuge at the simple **youth hostel** at 7 Otterburn Green (℡01830/520425; closed Oct–Feb).

Redesdale has only one settlement of any size, **OTTERBURN**, ten miles southeast of Byrness down the A68. It's an undistinguished place today, surrounded by heather-clad, sheep-laden countryside, with little except the name of the local pub, the *Percy Arms*, to recall its most notable hour. It was at Otterburn in August 1388 that an English army led by Sir Henry Percy ("Hotspur") was defeated by the Scots under James, Earl of Douglas. Douglas was killed in battle, as were 1800 English troops, while Hotspur was taken prisoner – a chain of events later made the subject of the medieval ballad of *Chevy Chase*. The supposed battle site is about a mile northwest of the village, off the A68, marked by a stone cross set in a little pinewood – though you may as well pick virtually any large field in the vicinity, since historians not only dispute its exact location, but also argue about the site of the Scottish base camp and even the exact date of the battle itself.

Otterburn boasts a small **tourist information centre** in the surprisingly thriving **Otterburn Mill** (Mon–Sat 9am–5.30pm, Sun 11am–5pm), which, though it no longer produces textiles, sells them and maintains a small museum, including a restored nineteenth-century water turbine and Europe's only remaining tenterhooks, used for stretching and drying newly woven cloth. There are several places **to stay**, including the *Butterchurn Guest House*, opposite the church on Main Street (℡01830/520585; ❷), and the comfortable *Percy Arms* (℡01830/520261; ⓦwww.percyarms.co.uk; ❺), further down the road, where you can get coffee, bar meals and full dinners. If you're driving, you could always aim for the comforts of the en-suite rooms in the *Redesdale Arms* (℡01830/520668; ❹), an old coaching inn on the A68, three miles west of the village.

From Byrness and Otterburn there are two to four **buses** a day to Newcastle (or north through the borders to Edinburgh) as well as less regular services to Bellingham (from where buses run to Hexham). After Byrness comes Northumberland's longest uninterrupted stretch of the Pennine Way, the 27-mile haul to the end of the hike at Kirk Yetholm (see p.1060), though you can detour to Wooler (see p.1059).

It's worth knowing that the highly scenic moorland region immediately north of Otterburn is a **military training area**, consisting of almost 60,000 acres of MoD land. Periodic squabbles break out between conservation groups, who rue the intrusion, and locals who welcome the investment the army brings. Visitors intent on walking the area's footpaths and bridleways must heed all signs and flags; better yet, take local advice before setting off.

Rothbury and around

ROTHBURY, straddling the River Coquet some eighteen miles northeast of Otterburn, prospered as a late Victorian resort because it gave ready access to the forests, burns and ridges of the Simonside Hills. In the centre, where the

High Street widens to form a broad triangle, there are hints of past pretensions in the assertive facades overlooking the **Rothbury Cross**, erected in 1902. Rothbury remains a popular spot for walkers, and the **Tourist Information and National Park Visitor Centre**, near the Cross on Church Street (April–Oct daily 10am–5pm; Nov–March Sat & Sun 10am–5pm; ☎01669 /620887), offers advice on local trails, several of which begin in the Simonside Hills car park, a couple of miles southwest of town. The most appealing of these trails is the five-mile round trip along the Simonside ridge, with panoramic views out over Coquetdale. A renowned **traditional music festival** each July brings folkies and fans into town from all over the region for Northumbrian pipe music, dancing and story-telling.

Practicalities

Buses from Morpeth (with connections from Newcastle) stop on Rothbury's High Street, outside the *Queen's Head*. There are several convenient **B&Bs** – including the well-equipped *Katerina's Guest House* on the High Street (☎01669/620691, ⦿www.katerinasguesthouse.co.uk; ❷), where all the en-suite rooms boast four-poster beds and TVs; and the comfortable, Georgian *Orchard Guest House*, at the top of the same street (☎01669/620684, ⦿www .orchardguesthouse.co.uk; ❷), which also serves dinner. Otherwise, it's worth heading out of town to *Silverton Lodge*, a comfortably refurbished Victorian schoolhouse with excellent views of the surrounding countryside on Silverton Lane (☎01669/620144, ⓔsilverton.lodge@btinternet.com; ❷), about ten minutes' walk from the centre, up the main street. Most of the places to **eat and drink** are strung out along the High Street: the *Elmtree Coffee Shop* serves decent light lunches and afternoon teas, and the *Newcastle Hotel* does well-prepared bar meals, high teas and real ales.

Cragside

Victorian Rothbury was dominated by Sir William, later the first **Lord Armstrong**, the immensely wealthy nineteenth-century arms manufacturer, shipbuilder and engineer who built his country home at **Cragside** (Easter–Oct Tues–Sun 1–5.30pm; £6.70, gardens only £4.20; NT), on the steep, forested slopes of Debdon Burn, a mile to the east of the village. At first, Armstrong was satisfied with his modest house, but in 1869 he decided to build something more substantial, and hired Richard Norman Shaw, one of the period's top architects, to do the job. Work continued until the mid-1880s, the final version being a grandiose, and utterly romantic, Tudor-style mansion, whose black and white timber-framed gables and upper storeys are entirely out of place in the Northumbrian countryside. The overly spick-and-span interior is stuffed with Armstrong's furnishings and fittings, heavy dark pieces enlivened by his art collection and by the William Morris stained glass in the library and the dining-room inglenook. Later extensions catered for Armstrong's numerous hobbies and diversions – his natural history and shell collection was placed in the gallery, a billiard room was added, while the marble-decked drawing room was completed in time for the visit of the prince and princess of Wales in 1884. Doubtless, they were too well brought up to comment on Shaw's "masterpiece", the spectacularly hideous Renaissance-style marble chimney-piece, which uses ten tons of the stuff to overly sentimental effect.

Armstrong was an avid innovator, fascinated by hydraulic engineering and by hydroelectric power. At Cragside he could indulge himself, damming the Debdon Burn to power several domestic appliances, such as the spit and the dumb waiter in the massive kitchen, as well as heating his personal Turkish-style plunge bath and steam room. In 1880, after several false starts, he also managed to supply Cragside with electricity, making this the first house in the world to be lit by hydroelectric power. The remains of the original system – including the powerhouse and pumping station – are still visible in the **grounds**, which, together with the splendid **formal gardens**, have longer opening hours (Easter–Oct Tues–Sun 10.30am–7pm or dusk; Nov to mid-Dec Wed–Sun 11am–4pm).

Given the hefty admission price you'll probably want to make a day of it, and that's easily done, especially if you come clutching a picnic. Shaded, signposted trails run up hill and down dale through the grounds, past banks of bluebells and rhododendrons; the tallest tree in England (a 191-foot Douglas fir) pierces the pine grove. Over at the visitor centre there's a **café/restaurant**, and an explanatory video and other displays in the adjacent Armstrong Energy Centre.

Brinkburn Priory

From Rothbury the B6344 runs four miles southeast through pretty **Coquetdale**, following the course of the river, to reach the splendid sight of **Brinkburn Priory** (April–Sept daily 10am–6pm; Oct daily 10am–5pm; £1.70; EH), nestling in a loop of the Coquet. Founded as an Augustinian priory in 1135, its church – the only surviving building – was built fifty years later and it's this that provides the focus of interest today. Thoroughly but sympathetically restored in the nineteenth century, it's a superb example of northern Transitional architecture, featuring a fine Norman doorway and an echoing nave, empty save for a remarkable series of enormous contemporary wooden religious sculptures by Durham sculptor Fenwick Lawson. English Heritage is also responsible for the rambling manor house adjacent to the church. Built around 1810, but incorporating parts of the earlier monastic buildings, it was rebuilt by the great Newcastle architect John Dobson in the 1830s, and last lived in during the 1950s. It's now a rather forlorn ruin, though essential maintenance work has arrested its decline and the public is free to wander its beautifully proportioned halls.

Wooler and around

There's nothing immediately attractive about stone-terraced **WOOLER**, a grey one-street market town twenty miles north of Rothbury, though its hillside setting high above Harthope Burn and its proximity to the **Cheviot Hills** do much to lift the spirits. Local walks provide an introduction to the range, with a particular favourite being the one-mile hike to the top of Humbleton Hill, site of a battle in 1402 in which Hotspur inflicted heavy casualties on forces of the Douglas clan. But to get into the heart of the Cheviots you'll have to tackle the trek to The Cheviot itself, seven miles to the southwest. Wooler is also a staging-post on **St Cuthbert's Way**, the trans-Cheviot route, which runs west from the town to Kirk Yetholm and beyond or northeast to Holy Island.

Practicalities

Fast and frequent **buses** link Wooler with Berwick-upon-Tweed and Alnwick, the two nearest towns. The bus station is set back off the High Street. Over the road, the **tourist office** at 16 Market Place (Easter–Oct Mon–Sat 10am–1pm & 2–5pm, Sun 10am–2pm; ☎01668/282123) can help with accommodation and walking information, including a leaflet on country hikes of between five and nine miles around the town, accessible by local bus.

There are a couple of good central **B&Bs**: *Tilldale House*, 34 High St
(☎01668/281450, ⑩www.tilldalehouse.com; no credit cards; ❶), which has
spacious en-suite rooms and serves a wide choice of evening meals; and *Winton
House*, just off the High Street at 39 Glendale Rd (☎01668/281362,
⑩www.wintonhouse.ntb.org.uk; no credit cards; ❷; closed Dec–Feb), a stone-
built Edwardian house with garden, owned by a friendly couple who can give
information on local walks and provide a packed lunch, too. For a bit more
luxury, try the ivy-encrusted *Tankerville Arms* on Cottage Road (☎01668
/281581, ⑩www.tankervillehotel.co.uk; ❺), a seventeenth-century **coaching
inn** just off the A697 below town, which has a good **restaurant** overlooking
the attractive garden and a wide range of **bar meals**. Wooler also has a comfortable **youth hostel** – the most northerly in England – at 30 Cheviot St
(☎01668/281365), a five-minute walk up the hill from the bus station, as well
as a **campsite**, *Highburn House* on Burnhouse Road (☎01668/281344; closed
Nov–Feb), just north of town, about half a mile from the bus station. For **picnics**, the Delicatessen Bakery, 24a Market Place, makes up good sandwiches
and sells home-made pies.

To Cheviot and Kirk Yetholm: the end of the Pennine Way

It's a fair hike from Wooler up the Harthope valley to **The Cheviot**, which at
2674ft is the highest point in the Cheviot Hills. Starting out from Wooler
youth hostel, count on four hours up, a little less back. It helps if you can drive,
or catch a lift, to Hawsen Burn, the nearest navigable point, which still leaves
you two hours walking there and back – your reward, an utterly bleak spot
with views, on a clear day, to the coast, the castles at Bamburgh and
Dunstanburgh, and over to Holy Island.

If you're properly equipped, and prepared for a long day's walking, on the
west side of the peak you can join the **Pennine Way** at Scotsman's cairn. Here,
you're about seven miles south of the trail end at the Scottish village of **KIRK
YETHOLM**, where there's a **youth hostel** (☎01573/420631; closed Sept to
mid-March), down a lane off the village green, and several B&Bs. At this point,
you're just over the border and just out of the National Park; it's fourteen miles
east by road back to Wooler.

Chillingham

Six miles southeast of Wooler, and served by bus #470 towards Alnwick, the
eccentricities of **Chillingham Castle** (May, June & Sept Mon & Wed–Sun
noon–5pm; July & Aug daily noon–5pm; £4.50) provide a refreshing counterpoint to the high-minded tidiness of National Trust-restored stately homes.
Starting from an eleventh-century tower, the castle was augmented at regular
intervals until 1873, though it keeps the essential structure of its mid-four-
teenth-century incarnation, a grand, heavily walled courtyard with four
impressive corner towers. For fifty years from 1933, however, Chillingham was
largely left to the elements, until the present owner set about restoring it in his
own individualistic way: bedrooms, living rooms and even a grisly torture
chamber are stuffed and decorated with all manner of historical flotsam to give
an idea of how the place would have looked through the ages, while chatty
guides in each room tell tall tales of the castle and its visitors. In the grounds,
which were designed by Sir Jeffrey Wyatville, nineteenth-century landscaper of
Windsor Castle, you can look around a small Elizabethan topiary garden, with
its intricately clipped hedges of box and yew, and take a mile-long walk
through the woods to the lake. Several apartments within the castle, including

the Elizabethan Long Gallery, are available for self-catering, by the week or sometimes by the night (℡01668/215359).

In 1220, the adjoining 365 acres of parkland were enclosed to protect the local wild cattle for hunting and food. And so the **Chillingham Wild Cattle**, a fierce, primeval herd with white coats, black muzzles and black tips to their horns, have remained to this day, cut off from mixing with domesticated breeds. It's possible to visit these unique relics, whose numbers vary between forty and sixty, but only in the company of a warden and from a safe distance – bring binoculars if you can – as the animals are potentially dangerous and need to be protected from outside infection (April–Oct Mon & Wed–Sat 10am–noon & 2–5pm, Sun 2–5pm; £3; ℡01668/215250).

North to Berwick

North of Wooler, the B6525 leads straight to Berwick-upon-Tweed, but if you're in no hurry you'd do well to meander northwestwards up the A697 towards Coldstream, a route which allows you a glimpse into the precarious fourteenth- to sixteenth-century history of the border region. You're soon into rich, flat farmland, watered by the tributaries of the River Tweed, which marks the border with Scotland at this point. The views behind you are of the Cheviots, while detours off the main roads put you on country lanes presided over here and there by stately mansions with gatehouses. The reasonably frequent #267 **bus** between Wooler and Berwick calls at Ford, Etal and Crookham, but the only way to get to Norham by public transport is on the #23 between Berwick and Kelso.

Ford, Etal, Branxton and Crookham

Eight miles north of Wooler, head east off the A697 a short way along the B6354 to reach the village of **FORD**. The fourteenth-century castle isn't open to the public, but you can **stay** in the grounds: the *Estate House* (℡01890 /820668, ℮theestatehouse@supanet.com; ❸) is a delightful retreat serving a good breakfast. While here, you could take a look inside the former school, now **Lady Waterford Hall** (Easter–Oct daily 10.30am–12.30pm & 1.30–5.30pm), which features pictures and murals by Louisa Anne, Marchioness of Waterford, a pupil of Ruskin.

Three miles further up the B6354 lies **ETAL** (pronounced "Eetle"), whose **castle** (daily: April–Sept 10am–6pm; Oct 10am–5pm; £2.70; EH) can be visited. Built in 1340 on the banks of the quiet River Till, the well-preserved central keep and gatehouse still stand, but they make a handsome sight, especially when taken in conjunction with the pretty little village itself. The *Black Bull* here is the only thatched pub in Northumberland, and serves sandwiches and bar meals. If you've got children in tow, it's worth knowing that from Heatherslaw Mill, halfway back down the road to Ford, the narrow-gauge **Heatherslaw Light Railway** (Easter to mid-July, Sept & Oct daily 10.30am–3.30pm; mid-July to Aug daily 10.30am–3.30pm; £4 return) runs up the banks of the River Till to the foot of Etal Castle; the return journey takes about forty minutes. The railway's *Granary Café* keeps body and soul together, and **bikes** can be rented (℡01890/820338) for further exploration of the area's rolling countryside.

Back on the A697 just beyond Crookham, a minor road leads a mile or so west to the hamlet of **BRANXTON**, just above which, on the slopes of Branxton Hill, is the site of the English victory at the **Battle of Flodden** (1513). It was one of the most decisive of sixteenth-century conflicts: up to ten thousand Scots died in battle, including James IV – fighting at the head of his troops – and most of the contemporary Scottish nobility. The bodies were dumped in pits in Branxton churchyard, their passing now remembered by a simple granite memorial on the hill inscribed "To the brave of both nations". You can **stay** in **CROOKHAM**, where the atmospheric *Coach House* (℡01890/820293, ⓦwww.coachhousecrookham.com; ❹) has a range of rooms in converted farm buildings sporting exposed beams. Guests are pampered with tasty home-made breakfasts and dinners. The *Blue Bell* in the village serves bar meals.

The border and Norham Castle

The A697 runs four miles west of Branxton to reach the **border**, marked by Cornhill-on-Tweed on the English side and Coldstream in Scotland across the River Tweed. There's little point lingering in either with Berwick so close, but save time for the ruins of **Norham Castle** (April–Sept daily 10am–6pm; £1.90; EH), overlooking the tumbling Tweed, just six miles or so to the northeast (signposted off the A698). Its surviving pink sandstone walls and foursquare keep, celebrated in paint by J.M.W. Turner and in verse in Sir Walter Scott's *Marmion*, stand out above the flat farming country, the trees lining the green-grassed ramparts stripped bare by the winds in winter and providing a leafy curtain in summer. It was considered one of the strongest of the border castles, but James IV of Scotland nevertheless engineered its capture before meeting his nemesis at Flodden Field.

The Northumberland coast

The low-lying **Northumberland coast**, stretching 64 miles north from Newcastle to the Scottish border, boasts many of the region's principal attractions, but first you have to clear the disfigured landscape of the old Northumbrian coalfield, which extends up as far north as the port of Amble. In its heyday at the beginning of the twentieth century this area employed a quarter of Britain's colliers, but all bar one of the mines closed years ago. Attempts have been made to clean up parts of this coast and its hinterland: at Ashington, once a huge pit village (birthplace of the footballing Charlton brothers and the great Jackie Milburn), a country park has been created from a former slag heap, while the marina at Amble and the prospect of summer jaunts to offshore Coquet Island and its nature reserve provide some relief.

Beyond Amble, however, you emerge into a pastoral, gently wooded landscape that spreads over the thirty-odd miles to Berwick-upon-Tweed. On the way there's a succession of mighty fortresses, beginning with **Warkworth Castle** and **Alnwick Castle**, former and present strongholds of the Percys, the county's biggest landowners. Further along, there's the formidable fastness of **Bamburgh** and then, last of all, the magnificent Elizabethan ramparts surrounding **Berwick-upon-Tweed**. In between you'll find splendid sandy beaches – notably at Warkworth, Bamburgh and the tiny seaside resort of **Alnmouth** – as well as the site of the Lindisfarne monastery on **Holy Island** and the seabird and nature reserve of the **Farne Islands**, reached by boat from Seahouses.

An excellent network of **bus** services makes it easy to travel up and down the coast, and the main London to Edinburgh **train** line passes through Alnmouth and Berwick – though very few fast services stop at the former. Only Holy Island is tricky to reach by public transport, an infrequent bus from Berwick-upon-Tweed being the sole connection. **By car**, the A1 from Alnwick (and, before that, from Newcastle) provides the fastest route to Berwick, though it runs well inland of the major coastal attractions. For these, the B1340 from Alnwick and its offshoots – often signposted "Coastal Route" – is the one to follow.

Warkworth

WARKWORTH, a coastal hamlet set in a loop of the River Coquet a couple of miles from Amble, is best seen from the north, from where the grey stone terraces of the long main street slope up towards the commanding remains of **Warkworth Castle** (daily: April–Sept 10am–6pm; Oct 10am–5pm; Nov–March 10am–1pm & 2–4pm; £2.50; EH), which perch on top of an immense grassy mound at the far end of the village. Enough remains of the outer wall to give a clear impression of the layout of the medieval bailey, but – apart from the well-preserved gatehouse through which the site is entered – nothing catches your attention as much as the **keep**. Mostly built in the fourteenth century, this three-storeyed structure, with its polygonal turrets and high central tower, has a honeycomb-like interior, a fine example of the designs developed by the castle-builders of Plantagenet England. It was here that most of the Percy family, earls of Northumberland, chose to live throughout the fourteenth and fifteenth centuries. The castle's cellars were used to good effect in the torture-chamber scenes in the Oscar-nominated film *Elizabeth* (1998), parts of which were also filmed in various other Northumbrian castles, from Raby to Alnwick.

The main street sweeps down into the attractive village, flattening out at Dial Place before curving right to cross the River Coquet; just over the bridges – a modern affair flanked by a splendid medieval turreted span – a signposted quarter-mile lane leads to the **beach**, which stretches for five miles from Amble to Alnmouth. Back in Dial Place stands the church of **St Lawrence**, whose many Norman features include the impressive ribbed vaulting of the chancel. From the churchyard (or, further up, from below the castle), a delightful path heads the half-mile inland along the peaceful right bank of the Coquet to the little boat that shuttles visitors across to **Warkworth Hermitage** (April–Sept Wed & Sun 11am–5pm; £1.70; EH), a series of simple rooms and a claustrophobic chapel that were hewn out of the cliff above the river sometime in the fourteenth century, but abandoned by 1567. The last resident hermit, one George Lancaster, was charged by the sixth earl of Northumberland to pray for his noble family, for which lonesome duty he received around £15 a year and a barrel of fish every Sunday.

Practicalities

Warkworth is on the route of the **bus service** linking Alnwick, Alnmouth and Newcastle, while other local services run to and from Alnwick and Amble. Buses stop in Dial Place, near the church. For such a small village, Warkworth possesses a surprising number of **accommodation and eating** options. There are several B&Bs just on the other side of the Coquet bridges and handy for the beach, including *North Cottage* (☎01665/711263; ❷) and the slightly cheaper *Beck'n'Call* (☎01665/711653; ❷). The top spot is the splendid *Sun Hotel*, 6 Castle Terrace (☎01665/711259; ❺), which commands fine views from its perch between the castle and the river, whether from the spacious, pine-furnished bedrooms, the restaurant which specializes in local fare, or the bar and beer garden. Good rooms are also available down the hill at the

Hermitage Inn (☎01665/711258; ❷), a cosy place with well-kept beers, bar meals and more interesting à la carte dishes including local cod and salmon. At the *Greenhouse*, opposite on the corner of Dial Place (closed Tues & Sun eves), salmon kebabs, cassoulet, and other bistro favourites are served on stripped pine tables. *Topsey Turvey's*, over the way at 1 Dial Place, is also open for bistro meals (closed Mon, Tues lunch & Sun eve) and has a good deli for picnics. Next door, the *Mason's Arms* has more traditional pub food and a beer garden.

Alnmouth

It's just three miles north from Warkworth to the seaside resort of **ALN-MOUTH**, whose narrow, mostly nineteenth-century centre is strikingly situated on a steep spur of land between the sea and the estuary of the Aln. It's a lovely setting, and there's a wide sandy beach and rolling dunes. Alnmouth was a busy and prosperous port up until 1806, when the sea, driven by a freakish gale, broke through to the river and changed its course, moving the estuary from the south to the north side of Church Hill and rendering the original harbour useless. Alnmouth never really recovered, though it has been a low-key holiday spot since Victorian times, as attested by the elegant seaside villas at the south end of town. Many come for the golf: the village's splendid nine-hole course, right on the coast, was built in 1869 (it's claimed to be the second oldest in the country) and dune-strollers really do have to heed the "Danger – Flying Golf Balls" signs which adorn Marine Road.

Practicalities

There are local bus services from Alnwick and Warkworth, while the regular Newcastle to Alnwick **bus** also passes through Alnmouth and calls at its **train station** at Hipsburn, a mile and a half west of the centre. This makes the resort a convenient interlude on the journey up or down the coast, especially as it's well equipped with B&Bs.

Most of the **accommodation** lies along or just off the main Northumberland Street. Best central B&B is *The Grange* opposite the church (☎01665/830401, ✉the grange.alnmouth@virgin.net; no credit cards; ❷), a reclusive stone house with garden, overlooking the river. A few yards further down Northumberland Street, at no. 56, the friendly *Beaches* (☎01665/830443; no credit cards; ❸) has huge en-suite rooms in a period stone cottage above a good restaurant (see below). A string of **pubs** along Northumberland Street also offers accommodation; the most reasonable is the *Saddle Hotel*, at no. 25 (☎01665/830476; ❸), whose spacious rooms have bath and TV, the top-floor ones enjoying (partial) sea views. Top hotel is the fancy *Schooner* (☎01665 /830216, ✉ghost@schooner.sagehost.co.uk; ❺), supposedly Britain's most haunted hostelry – it's only worth spending this much if you can secure a room with a sea view (though dinner, bed and breakfast deals and off-season rates bring the price down slightly). Sea views are guaranteed at the *Marine House Private Hotel* (☎01665/830349; ❸), where the squeezed rooms all face the golf links and coast, and the guest restaurant has a good reputation for local cuisine. There's an adjacent seafront cottage to rent, too.

There are a couple of coffee houses along the main street, while **lunches and dinners** are served in the bar-lounges and dining rooms of the pubs. The *Saddle Hotel* has a large menu; the restaurant at the *Red Lion*, an old coaching inn with a beer garden further up the street, is better and more expensive, serving fresh seafood and other meals. The *Tea Cosy Tea Room*, at no. 23 (☎01665/830393), serves bistro dinners at weekends in summer, but the best choice is to eat at the oak-beamed *Beaches* at no. 56 (Tues, Thurs & Fri eve, Sat

& Sun lunch & eve), where meals of local cod, Northumbrian game casserole and the like go for around £15 a head; you can take your own wine.

Alnwick

The unassuming town of **ALNWICK** (pronounced "Annick"), some thirty miles north of Newcastle and four miles inland from Alnmouth, is renowned for its castle – seat of the dukes of Northumberland – which overlooks the River Aln immediately to the north of the town centre. Alnwick itself is an appealing market town of cobbled streets and Georgian houses, centred on the old cross in Market Place, site of a weekly market (Saturdays) since the thirteenth century.

Arrival, information and accommodation

Alnwick is a hub for much of the coastal and inland transport, and there are regular bus services to and from Alnmouth, Warkworth and Newcastle, as well as inland to Wooler and up the coast to Craster, Seahouses and Bamburgh. Alnwick **bus station** is on Clayport Street, a couple of minutes' walk west of the Market Place, where you'll find the **tourist office**, in the arcaded Shambles (July & Aug Mon–Sat 9am–6pm, Sun 9am–5pm; April–June & Sept Mon–Sat 9am–5pm, Sun 10am–4pm; Oct–March Mon–Fri 9am–5pm, Sat 10am–4pm; ☎01665/510665).

Several **accommodation** options cluster round the gatehouse at the end of Bondgate. Here, the welcoming *Tower Guest Rooms*, above the restaurant of the same name at 10 Bondgate Within (☎01665/603888, ⓦwww.hotspur-tower .com; ❸), stands out for its bright, tasteful, en-suite rooms of varying sizes and hearty breakfasts. Among other cheaper places beyond the gate, you'll find the cosy, ivy-clad *Bondgate House Hotel* at 20 Bondgate Without (☎01665/602025, ⒠kenforbes@lineone.net; ❷), or for a different architectural backdrop, head for the *Georgian Guest House*, a right turn through the arch up Hotspur Street (☎01665/602398, ⒠georgianguesthouse@eggconnect.net; no credit cards; ❶). Alnwick's main hotel is the *White Swan*, on Bondgate Within (☎01665 /602109; ❺), where you might want to pop in at least for coffee – there's a comfortable lounge, while the hotel's fine panelled dining room was swiped from an old ocean liner, the *Olympic*, the twin of the *Titanic*. If you'd prefer to stay in the countryside, consider the *Masons' Arms* out on the Craster road (see p.1067). You can **camp** at *Alnwick Rugby Club* in Greensfield Park (☎01665 /510109; closed Nov–March), a little way south of the centre but walkable.

The castle

The Percys – who were raised to the dukedom of Northumberland in 1750 – have owned the **Castle** (Easter–Oct daily 11am–5pm; £6.75; ⓦwww.alnwick castle.com) since 1309, when Henry de Percy reinforced the original Norman keep and remodelled its curtain wall. His successor, another Henry, built the imposing barbican and connecting gatehouse. In the eighteenth century, the castle was badly in need of a refit, so the first duke had the interior refurbished by Robert Adam in an extravagant Gothic style – which in turn was supplanted by the gaudy Italianate decoration preferred by the fourth duke in the 1850s.

Nowadays, the castle is part of a business empire based on the duke's extensive Northumbrian estates. Your stiff entry fee contributes to the company's coffers, which would be better justified if more of the castle and grounds were open to the public: only half a dozen or so rooms can be visited out of around one hundred and sixty. Building work is under way, however, to turn twelve

acres of the grounds into an ambitious contemporary water garden (ⓦwww
.alnwickgarden.com), complete with interactive water displays, sculptures,
maze and topiary walks; with some parts of the lengthy project already finished, including the ornamental and rose gardens, it's possible to view the state
of play by becoming a Friend of the Alnwick Garden (£10), which entitles you
to visit as often as you like (daily 10am–5pm; £10).

Entry to the castle is through the carriageway to the right of the fourteenth-
century barbican, whose sturdy battlements sport a number of stone soldiers, a
piece of eighteenth-century flummery replacing the figurines of medieval
times, set up there to ward off the evil eye. The dark and drab entrance hall of
the keep leads to the **grand staircase**, a marble pomposity that climbs up to
the guard chamber, whose Renaissance-style decor, from the mosaic floor to
the stucco ceiling, is typical of the work of the Italian craftsmen hired by the
fourth duke. The most lavish decoration is in the **red drawing room**, where
the rich polygonal panels of the ceiling bear down on damask-covered walls
and some magnificent ebony cabinets rescued from Versailles during the
French Revolution. Each room displays part of the duke's extensive collection
of paintings, including pieces by Canaletto, Titian, Tintoretto, Van Dyck and
Turner. Three of the perimeter towers contain **museum** collections – the
Regimental Museum of the Royal Northumberland Fusiliers in the Abbot's
Tower, early British and Roman finds in the Postern Tower, and an exhibition
dedicated to the Percy Tenantry Volunteers, a private force raised by the second
duke during the Napoleonic Wars, in the Constable's Tower – but the bucolic
garden walks and Capability Brown-designed **grounds** are a more profitable
use of time once you've seen the main rooms.

The rest of town

From outside the castle, it's a few minutes' walk north along Bailiffgate and then
Ratten Row to the gates of **Hulne Park**, a substantial tract of hilly woodland
to the northwest of Alnwick. Deep inside the park, a three-mile hike from the
entrance, are the rusticated remains of **Hulne Priory**, a thirteenth-century
Carmelite monastery built above the north bank of the River Aln. It's a lovely,
peaceful spot and, although the greystone ruins are slight, they are enlivened by
several whimsically carved stone monks, modern sculptures which have the
place pretty much to themselves. The duke owns the park, and access is controlled – pedestrians and cyclists only, from 11am to sunset in summer.

The tiny town of Alnwick has a trim and tidy cobbled Market Place, but
there's not much else to see, except for the **gatehouses** on Pottergate and
Bondgate, the principal remains of the medieval town walls, and the grandiose
Percy Tenantry Column just to the southeast of the centre along Bondgate
Without. This 75-foot high column, surmounted by the Percy lion, was built
by the tenants of the second duke in 1816 after he had reduced their rents by
25 percent. As it turned out, their humble gratitude was somewhat premature.
The third duke promptly bumped the rents up again and locals wryly renamed
their monument the "Farmers' Folly". A little further on, housed in the listed
Victorian train station, **Barter Books** (ⓦwww.barterbooks.co.uk), one of the
largest second-hand bookshops in England, is worth a call; it also offers internet access.

Eating, drinking and entertainment

Copperfields Coffee House, 11 Market St, opposite the tourist office, serves daytime snacks and **meals**. In the evening, try the *Gate Bistro*, 14 Bondgate Within
(closed Mon) – up a side alley next to the *White Swan Hotel* – a café/restau-

rant with some interesting specials, such as Lamb Percy, shoulder cooked with thyme, juniper and red wine. The *Tower Restaurant* next door has a reassuring, pine-furnished feel and serves everything from breakfast to licensed meals, including plenty of vegetarian and chargrilled options. In the other direction, heading towards the castle, *Benvenuti* is a reliable, traditional Italian occupying an atmospheric eighteenth-century townhouse on Narrowgate (closed Sun).

Few of the town's **pubs** offer much scope for a civilized drink: those along Narrowgate – *Ye Olde Cross* and the *Black Swan* – are crowded and boisterous at the weekend. The "Dirty Bottles" in *Ye Olde Cross*'s window have suppos-edly not been moved for two centuries, since the person who put them there dropped down dead immediately afterwards. The nicest local pub is the *Masons' Arms* at **Rennington**, four miles northeast of town on the Seahouses (B1340) road, an old coaching inn with good bar food, as well as six en-suite bedrooms with private sitting rooms (℡01665/577275, ⓦwww.masonsarms.net; ❸). Back in town, check to see what's on at the **Alnwick Playhouse**, just through the arch on Bondgate Without (℡01665/510785, ⓦwww.alnwickplayhouse .co.uk), a venue for theatre, music and film throughout the year, and also host to concerts during the town's annual **International Music Festival** every August and the **Alnwick Northumbrian Gathering** of traditional music in November.

Craster, Dunstanburgh Castle and around

Heading northeast out of Alnwick along the B1340, it's a six-mile hop to the region's kipper capital, the tiny fishing village of **CRASTER**, perched above its minuscule harbour. There's not a great deal to make you stop long, but you can buy wonderful kippers here at Robson's factory and have a pot of tea in the *Bark Pots*. Even better is the *Jolly Fisherman*, the **pub** above the harbour, with sea views from its back window and garden and famously good crabmeat, whisky and cream soup, crab sandwiches and kipper pâté.

Most spectacularly, however, the village provides access to **Dunstanburgh Castle** (April–Sept daily 10am–6pm; Oct daily 10am–5pm; Nov–March Wed–Sun 10am–4pm; £1.90; NT & EH), whose shattered medieval ruins occupy a magnificent promontory about thirty minutes' windy walk up the coast – there's a car park in Craster. Originally built in the fourteenth century, parts of the surrounding walls survive – offering heart-stopping views down to the crashing sea below – though the dominant feature is the massive keep-gatehouse which stands out from miles around on the bare coastal spur. Mel Gibson's *Hamlet* used the walls and keep to impressive effect.

Half a dozen **buses** a day (the #501/401) run to Craster from Alnwick, a half-hour journey; the service continues to Seahouses and Bamburgh. There's a small **tourist office** in the village car park (Easter–Oct daily 9.30–4.30pm; Nov–Easter Sat & Sun 10am–4pm; ℡01665/576007).

Embleton, Newton-by-the-Sea and Beadnell

EMBLETON, on the other side of the promontory from the castle, has a fine sandy beach, windswept and deserted in winter, busier in summer though rarely overly so. A couple of pubs here, and in similarly attractive **NEWTON-BY-THE-SEA**, next beachside hamlet north, make good lunch stops. Newton's *The Ship* is the pick of the bunch, on a square of old cottages, just yards from the beach and serving fresh crab and salmon dishes and a range of real ales. **BEADNELL**, too, has a pub and fine beaches, which offer the best **windsurfing** on the northeast's coast – boards can be rented from the

Outdoor Trust shed (£10/hr, £30/day; ℡01665/721241; closed Nov–Feb), along with kayaks, bodyboards and sailing dinghies. The excellent *Beach Court* on Harbour Rd (℡01665/720225, Ⓦwww.beachcourt.com; ❸) is a distinctive **guest house** right next to the shore, with sea views and three lovely rooms – the most expensive of which is a "turret" suite (❺) with its own observatory. Tourist offices in Alnwick, Craster and Seahouses can arrange other local B&B accommodation, and the #501 bus passes through both places. There are several local **campsites**, including *Dunstan Hill* (℡01665/576310; closed Nov–Feb), a mile inland from Dunstanburgh castle, close to the B1339.

Seahouses and the Farne Islands

From Beadnell, it's three miles north to **SEAHOUSES**, a desultory fishing-port-cum-resort that's the embarkation point for **boat trips** to the windswept and treeless **Farne Islands**, a rocky archipelago lying a few miles offshore. Owned by the National Trust and maintained as a nature reserve, the Farnes are the summer home of many species of migrating seabirds, especially puffins, guillemots, terns, eider ducks and kittiwakes, and home to the only grey seal colony on the English coastline. To protect the wildlife, only two of the islands are open to visitors: **Inner Farne** (April–Sept daily; landing fee £4.20 May–July, £3.20 at other times) and **Staple Island** (same months & prices). The crossing can be rough, but the islands have a wild beauty that makes it all worthwhile, and on Inner Farne you can also visit a tiny, restored fourteenth-century chapel built in honour of St Cuthbert, who spent much of his life and died here. Of the islets you don't land on, but should see from the boat, a cottage on the Brownsman was the first home of **William Darling** and his family; when the Longstone lighthouse was lit in 1826, the family moved islands – twelve years later his daughter Grace became a national heroine after a daring sea rescue (see opposite).

Weather permitting, several boat owners operate daily **excursions**, usually starting at around 10am: Billy Shiels (Easter–Oct; ℡01665/720308, Ⓦwww .farne-islands.com), the best of the bunch, runs a varied programme, from two-and-a-half-hour **cruises** round either island (£8), to all-day trips landing at both (£15). Note that if you land on the islands, you'll have to pay the separate NT landing fee (members free); wear an old hat to protect you from the bird droppings. For more information, call the **National Trust Shop**, 16 Main St, Seahouses (℡01665/721099), across from the *Olde Ship* (see below).

Practicalities

It's unlikely you'd choose to stay the night in Seahouses, and there are regular **buses** to both Alnwick and Berwick-upon-Tweed, but, if you've returned from the Farnes late in the day, you may not want to go any further. Seahouses has a range of reasonably priced **B&Bs** – details from the **tourist office** (daily: April–Oct 10am–5pm; ℡01665/720884), in the Seafield Road car park above the harbour, or the community website, Ⓦwww.seahouses.org.

The *Olde Ship*, overlooking the harbour at 9 Main St (℡01665/720200; ❹), quite apart from its pleasant rooms, is a great place to drink, full of nautical bits and pieces and serving good **food**. There's also a whole host of fish-and-chip restaurants. If you want to take some of the local catch home, the *Fisherman's Kitchen*, 2 South St, sells smoked kippers and salmon from its traditional **smokehouse**.

Bamburgh

Flanking a triangular green in the lee of its castle, three miles north of Seahouses, the tiny village of **BAMBURGH** is only a five-minute walk from two splendid sandy beaches, backed by rolling, tufted dunes. From the sands – in fact from everywhere – **Bamburgh Castle** (April–Oct daily 11am–5pm; £4.50; ⓦwww.bamburghcastle.com) is a spectacular sight, its elongated battlements crowning a formidable basalt crag high above the beach. This beautiful spot was first fortified by the Celts, but its heyday was as an Anglo-Saxon stronghold, one-time capital of Northumbria and the protector of the preserved head and hand of St Oswald, the seventh-century king who invited St Aidan over from Iona to convert his subjects. To the Normans, however, Bamburgh was just one of many border fortresses administered by second-rank vassals: as an eleventh-century monastic chronicler expressed it, "renowned formerly for the magnificent splendour of her high estate, [Bamburgh] has been burdened with tribute and reduced to the condition of a handmaiden."

Nonetheless, rotted by seaspray and buffeted by winter storms, Bamburgh Castle struggled on until 1894, when it was bought by Lord Armstrong. Armstrong demolished most of the structure to replace it with a cumbersome hybrid castle-mansion, but this received even less favourable reviews than the eleventh-century fortress: commentator Avray Tipping dismissed it as "neither fish, flesh, fowl or good red herring". The focal point of the new building was the King's Hall, a soulless teak-ceilinged affair of colossal dimensions, whose main redeeming feature is an exquisite collection of Fabergé stone animal carvings. In the adjacent Faire Chamber there's also a pastoral miniature by Jan Brueghel the Younger. In the ground floor of the keep, the stone-vaulted ceiling maintains its Norman appearance, making a suitable arena for a display of fetters and man-traps. There's some interest, too, in a display in the former laundry building, where exhibits trace Armstrong's career as inventor, shipbuilder and arms manufacturer, a neat counterpoint to the displays at Cragside.

Bamburgh is also the home of the **Grace Darling Museum** (Easter to Oct Mon–Sat 10am–5pm, Sun noon–5pm; donation requested), which celebrates the daring sea rescue accomplished by Grace and her lighthouseman father, William, in September, 1838. It began when a gale dashed the steamship *Forfarshire* against the rocks of the Farne Islands. Nine passengers struggled onto a reef, where they were subsequently saved by the Darlings, who left the safety of the lighthouse to row out to them. *The Times* trumpeted Grace's bravery, offers of marriage and requests for locks of her hair streamed into the Darlings' lighthouse home and for the rest of her brief life Grace was plagued by unwanted visitors – she died of tuberculosis aged 26 in 1842. The museum details the rescue and displays the fragile boat the Darlings used; in the churchyard of thirteenth-century **St Aidan's** opposite is the pompous Gothic Revival memorial that covers Grace's body.

Practicalities

A regular **bus** service links Alnwick and Berwick-upon-Tweed with Bamburgh, stopping on Front Street by the green. There are several places **to stay and eat**, including the highly appealing *Lord Crewe Arms Hotel*, Front St (☎01668/214243, ⓦwww.lordcrewe.com; ❹; closed Dec–Feb), a comfortable old inn with oak beams, open fires and a moderately priced restaurant. Nearby *Green Gates*, 34 Front St (☎01668/214535; no credit cards; ❷), offers three rooms with castle views, superior breakfasts and bicycle rental. At the top of the village green, the *Victoria Hotel* (☎01668/214431, ⓦwww.victoriahotel.net; ❺) has been tastefully refurbished, and operates a brasserie with a varied

Modern-British menu and a pleasant conservatory. If these are all full, try the *Glenander Guest House*, beyond the top of the village green at 27 Lucker Rd (☎01668/214336, ✉j.mcd@lineone.net; no credit cards; ❸), one of several places on the same road offering B&B. Other food options comprise a couple of tearooms – including the very twee and traditional *Copper Kettle* – a small deli for picnics and a bucket-and-spade general store.

Romantic big-spenders should head out of town, to **Waren Mill**, a couple of miles to the west on the B1342, where the *Waren House Hotel* (☎01668 /214581, ⓦwww.warenhousehotel.co.uk; ❼) is set in its own grounds on the edge of Budle Bay, overlooking Holy Island. Eating well here is no trouble whatsoever. At the other end of the scale, *Waren Caravan Park* (☎01668 /214366; closed Nov–March) has the closest **camping** to Bamburgh; take the the local #501 bus to Waren Mill.

Holy Island

There's something rather menacing about the approach to **Holy Island**, past the barnacle-encrusted marker poles that line the causeway. The danger of drowning is real enough if you ignore the safe crossing times posted at the start of the three-mile trip across the tidal flats. (The island is cut off for about five hours every day, so to avoid a tedious delay it's best to consult the **tide timetables** at one of the region's tourist offices or in the local newspapers.) Once on the island, the ancient remains of the priory and the brooding castle conjure yet more fantasies, not all pleasant. Small (just one and a half miles by one), sandy, flat and bare, it's easy to picture the furious Viking hordes sweeping across Holy Island, giving no quarter to the monks at this quiet outpost of early Christianity. Today's sole village is plain in the extreme, which doesn't deter summer day-trippers from clogging the car parks as soon as the causeway is open. But Holy Island has a distinctive and isolated atmosphere, especially out of season. Give the place time and, if you can, stay overnight, when you'll be able to see the historic remains without hundreds of others cluttering the views.

Once known as **Lindisfarne**, Holy Island has an illustrious history. It was here that St Aidan of Iona founded a monastery at the invitation of King Oswald of Northumbria in 634. The monks quickly evangelized the northeast and established a reputation for scholarship and artistry, the latter exemplified by the **Lindisfarne Gospels**, the apotheosis of Celtic religious art, now kept in the British Museum. The monastery had sixteen bishops in all, the most celebrated being **St Cuthbert**, who only accepted the job after Ecgfrith, another Northumbrian king, pleaded with him. But Cuthbert never settled here and, within two years, he was back in his hermit's cell on the Farne Islands, where he died in 687. His colleagues rowed the body back to Lindisfarne, which became a place of pilgrimage until 875, when the monks abandoned the island in fear of marauding Vikings, taking Cuthbert's remains with them – the first part of the saint's long posthumous journey to Durham (see p.1003). In 1082 Lindisfarne, renamed Holy Island, was colonized by Benedictines from Durham, but the monastery was a shadow of its former self, a minor religious house with only a handful of attendant monks, the last of whom was evicted at the Dissolution.

The island

There's not much to the **village**, just a couple of streets radiating out from a small green and church cross, everything within a five-minute walk of everything else. If you've arrived by car, you'll have to **park** in one of the large signposted carparks – keep an eye on the time and tide if you're not intending to stay.

Just off the green, the pinkish sandstone ruins of **Lindisfarne Priory** (daily: Easter–Sept 10am–6pm; Oct 10am–5pm; Nov–Easter 10am–4pm; £2.90; EH) are from the Benedictine foundation. Enough survives to provide a clear impression of the original structure, notably the tight Romanesque arches of the nave and the gravity-defying stonework of the central tower's last remaining arch. Behind lie the scant remains of the monastic buildings while adjacent is the mostly thirteenth-century church of **St Mary the Virgin**, whose delightful churchyard overlooks the ruins. The **museum** (same times as priory; entrance included in priory fee) features a collection of incised stones that constitute all that remains of the first monastery. The finest of them is a round-headed tombstone showing armed Northumbrians on one side, and kneeling figures before the Cross on the other – presumably a propagandist's view of the beneficial effects of Christianity. The priory, incidentally, marks the end of **St Cuthbert's Way**, the 63-mile cross-border hiking route from Melrose in Scotland, where St Cuthbert started his ministry.

Stuck on a small pyramid of rock half a mile away from the village, past the dock and along the seashore, **Lindisfarne Castle** (April–Oct Mon–Thurs, Sat & Sun, hours according to time of low tide but always including noon–3pm; £4.20; NT; ☏01289/389244) was built in the middle of the sixteenth century to protect the island's harbour from the Scots. It was, however, merely a decaying shell when Edward Hudson, the founder of *Country Life* magazine, stumbled across it in 1901. Hudson bought the castle and turned it into a holiday home to designs by Edwin Lutyens, who used the irregular levels of the building to create the L-shaped living quarters that survive today. Lutyens kept the austere spirit of the castle alive in the great fireplaces, stone walls, columns and rounded arches which dominate the main rooms.

The two historic sites are all that most people bother with, but a **walk** around the island's perimeter is a fine way to spend a couple of hours. From the grass banks above the harbour, there are views across to the two nineteenth-century obelisks, built on the distant sandbanks as navigational aids – boats line them up with the church tower to steer their way in. Most of the northwestern portion of the island is maintained as a **nature reserve**: from a bird hide you can spot terns and plovers, and then plod through the dunes and grasses to your heart's content. The island even supports a seal colony, though sightings by visitors are rare – legend rather touchingly has it that the seals kept vigil with St Cuthbert as he prayed at the water's edge of his new domain.

Back in the village, two other attractions suck in the trippers. The **Lindisfarne Heritage Centre** (daily 10am–5.30pm, though times may vary according to the tides; £2; ☏01289/389004, ⊛www.lindisfarne-heritage-centre.org), occupying a former coaching inn on the main street, holds computer terminals giving you a virtual opportunity to see the major illustrated pages of the Lindisfarne Gospels and details the wildlife as well as the former living and working conditions on the island. Everyone then decants into **St Aidan's Winery**, just up from the green, sole producer of Lindisfarne Mead, a sickly concoction on sale all over the northeast. You can sample the mead before you buy, which – given its rather challenging taste – seems a misguided marketing ploy.

Practicalities

The #477 **bus** from Berwick-upon-Tweed to Holy Island is something of a law unto itself given the interfering tides, but basically service is daily in August and twice weekly (Wed & Sat) the rest of the year. Departure times (and some-times days) vary with the tides, and the journey takes thirty minutes; local tourist offices can provide the latest details. Throughout the year, you can also ask to be dropped off by the Berwick–Newcastle buses at Beal, though from here you face a four-mile walk to the island. Phone Douglas's **taxi** service on the island if you can't face the hike (℡01289/389236).

The island is short on places **to stay** and you should make an advance book-ing, whenever you visit. Two good places are the *Open Gate*, on Marygate (℡01289/389222; ❸), which offers comfortable rooms in a sixteenth-century listed building; or the cheaper, and very friendly, *Britannia House* (℡01289/389218; ❷; closed Nov–Feb), just by the green. Among the pubs, best is the refurbished *Ship* on Marygate (℡01289/389311; ❷; closed Jan). Camping isn't allowed anywhere on the island. Options for **eating and drinking** are limited to a couple of tea rooms and the hostelries, of which the *Ship* is again the pick, with a garden and a cosy panelled bar, good-value meals and well-kept real ales.

Berwick-upon-Tweed

Before the union of the English and Scottish crowns in 1603, **BERWICK-UPON-TWEED**, some twelve miles north of Holy Island, was the quintes-sential frontier town, changing hands no fewer than fourteen times between 1174 and 1482, when the Scots finally ceded the stronghold to the English. Interminable cross-border warfare ruined Berwick's economy, turning the prosperous Scottish port of the thirteenth century into an impoverished garri-son town, which the English forcibly cut off from its natural trading hinterland up the River Tweed. By the late sixteenth century, Berwick's fortifications were in a dreadful state of repair and Elizabeth I, apprehensive of the resurgent alliance between France and Scotland, had the place rebuilt in line with the lat-est principles of military architecture.

The new design recognized the technological development of artillery, which had rendered the traditional high stone wall obsolete. Consequently, Berwick's **ramparts** – one and a half miles long and still in pristine condition – are no more than twenty feet high but incredibly thick: a facing of ashlared stone pro-tects ten to twelve feet of rubble, which, in turn, backs up against a vast quan-tity of earth. Further protected by ditches on three sides and the Tweed on the fourth, the walls are strengthened by immense bastions, whose arrowhead-shape ensured that every part of the wall could be covered by fire. Begun in 1558, the defences were completed after eleven years at a cost of £128,000, more than Elizabeth paid for all her other fortifications put together. And, as it turned out, it was all a waste of time and money: the French didn't attack and, once England and Scotland were united, Berwick was stuck with a white ele-phant.

Arrival, information and accommodation

From Berwick **train station** it's about ten minutes' walk down Castlegate to the town centre. Most regional **buses** stop closer in on Golden Square (where Castlegate meets Marygate), on the approach to the Royal Tweed Bridge, though some may also stop in front of the station. The helpful **tourist office** at 106 Marygate (Easter–Oct Mon–Sat 10am–6pm, Sun 11am–3pm; Nov–Easter Mon–Sat 10am–4pm; ℡01289/330733, ⓦwww.berwickonline.org.uk) can book you on to informative one-hour **walking tours** of town (Easter–Oct Mon–Fri; £3). There's also a useful website at ⓦwww.exploreberwick .co.uk, which provides a virtual architectural walk through the town, as well as full local listings. For local **bike rental**, call Brilliant Bicycles, 17a Bridge St (℡01289/331476) – you can get details of a scenic route to Holy Island either here or from the tourist office (24 miles return).

Berwick has plenty of **accommodation** and the tourist office offers a room-booking service. You need to decide whether you want to stay within the ramparts or across the river, either in Tweedmouth, just on the other side of the bridge, or near the beach at Spittal. **In the centre**, there's **dorm** accommodation at *Berwick Backpackers* in a well-maintained house at 56–58 Bridge St (℡01289/331481, ⓦwww.berwick-backpackers.co.uk). A highly recommended **B&B** is *No.1 Sallyport*, 41 Bridge St (℡01289/308827; ❸), a seventeenth-century house next to the city walls (above the Bridge Street Bookshop) with elegant en-suite rooms, and fresh coffee and home-baked bread for breakfast. Reservations are essential. Other good options include *Clovelly House*, 58 West St (℡01289/302337, ⓦwww.clovelly53.freeserve.co.uk; ❷), and the *Riverview Guest House*, 11 Quay Walls (℡01289/306295; ❷). If these are full, try one of the places ranged along Church Street and Ravensdowne; or head north up Castlegate, past the station, and on to North Road where there are several other places, including the recommended *Dervaig Guest House*, 1 North Rd (℡01289/307378, ⓔdervaig@btinternet.com; ❷), which has spacious, well-appointed rooms and a large walled garden. The best central **hotel** is the *King's Arms*, Hide Hill (℡01289/307454, ⓔking's_arms.hotel@virgin.net; ❺), one of the myriad English coaching inns in which Charles Dickens is supposed to have slept and lectured.

Across Berwick Bridge in **Tweedmouth**, you can't beat the delightful *Old Vicarage Guest House*, a spacious Victorian villa at 24 Church Rd (℡01289 /306909; ❶), with a range of rooms, some sharing bathrooms; book ahead as it's popular. The suburb of **Spittal** (bus #B1 from Golden Square) has more guest houses located along Main Street, just a couple of minutes from the beach: try the *Roxburgh*, at no. 117 (℡01289/306266; ❶). There are plenty of local **campsites**, though only *Marshalls Meadows Farm* (℡01289/307375) has space for tents.

The Town

Today, the easy **stroll** along the top of the ramparts offers a succession of fine views out to sea, across the Tweed and over the orange-tiled rooftops of a town that's distinguished by its elegant Georgian mansions. These, dating from Berwick's resurgence as a seaport between 1750 and 1820, are the town's most attractive feature, with the tapering **Lions' House**, on Windmill Hill, and the daintily decorated facades of **Quay Walls**, beside the river, of particular note. The three bridges spanning the Tweed are worth a second look, too – the huge arches of the **Royal Border Railway Bridge**, built in the manner of a Roman aqueduct by Robert Stephenson in the 1840s, contrasting with the desultory concrete of the **Royal Tweed**, completed in 1928, and the modest seventeenth-century **Berwick Bridge**. This last was opened in 1624 and cost £15,000 to build, an enormous sum partly financed by James VI of Scotland, who is said to have been none too impressed with its rickety wooden predecessor which he crossed on his way to be crowned James I of England in 1603.

Within the ramparts, the Berwick skyline is punctured by the stumpy spire of the eighteenth-century **Town Hall** at the bottom of Marygate, right at the heart of the compact centre. This retains its original jailhouse, now housing the **Cell Block Museum** (Easter–Oct Mon–Fri tours at 10.30am & 2pm; £1.20) with its tales of crime and punishment in Berwick. From here, it's a couple of minutes' walk along Church Street to **Holy Trinity** church, one of the few churches built during the Commonwealth, the absence of a tower supposedly reflecting the wishes of Cromwell, who found them irreligious.

Opposite the church, the finely proportioned **Barracks** (Easter–Sept daily 10am–6pm; Oct daily 10am–5pm; Nov–Easter Wed–Sun 10am–4pm; £2.70; EH) date from the early eighteenth century and were in use until 1964, when the King's Own Scottish Borderers regiment decamped. Inside, there's a predictable regimental museum, as well as the *By Beat of Drum* exhibition which in a series of pictureboards and dioramas traces the life of the British infantryman from the sixteenth to the nineteenth century. If all this sounds worthy but dull, it is – rescued only by the temporary summer exhibitions of contemporary art in the **Gymnasium Gallery** and by a superior borough museum and art gallery, sited in the so-called **Clock Block**. Geared up for school parties, the museum features imaginative dioramas, recordings and displays of local traditional life, even a model of a local clergyman haranguing visitors from his pulpit. Upstairs is the kernel of the gallery's fine and applied art collection, the gift of the shipping magnate William Burrell, who lived near Berwick in his retirement. Highlights include examples of ceramic Oriental jars displayed under glass floor panels in a sinuous, walk-in dragon; Roman glassware; church sculpture; and several Chinese bronzes.

Eating, drinking and entertainment

For daytime **snacks**, **coffee** and **lunches**, head for *Popinjays* on Hide Hill or the café on the ground floor of the Town Hall. Berwick's selection of **restaurants** will hardly set the pulse racing – try *Foxton's*, 26 Hide Hill (℡01289 /303939), a brasserie serving a daytime menu of sandwiches, light meals and traditional main courses, and a more varied menu in the evening; or the largely Italian *Il Porto di Mare* in the *King's Arms Hotel* opposite. Other choices include the *Royal Garden*, a Chinese restaurant in a rather grand converted pub at 35 Marygate, and the *Magna Tandoori*, 39 Bridge St – or head for *Corvi's*, a sparkling chippie with sit-down tables on West Street.

In 1799, there were 59 **pubs** and three coaching inns in Berwick; strange, then, that today there's barely one worth drinking in. Two of the three inns remain, the *King's Arms* on Hide Hill and the *Hen & Chickens* on Sandgate, but you're far better off at the cosy *Barrels Ale House*, 59–61 Bridge St, at the foot of the Berwick Bridge (℡01289/308013, ⓦwww.thebarrelsalehouse.com), which has guest beers and an interesting programme of live music. The Maltings on Eastern Lane is Berwick's **arts centre** (℡01289/330999, ⓦwww.maltingsberwick.co.uk), with a year-round programme of music, theatre, comedy, film and dance, and river views from its licensed café.

Travel details

Buses

For information on all local and national bus services, contact Traveline: ℡0870/608 2 608 (daily 7am–9pm), ⓦwww.traveline.org.uk.

Trains

For information on all local and national rail services, contact National Rail Enquiries: ℡08457/48 49 50, ⓦwww.rail.co.uk.

Darlington to: Bishop Auckland (every 1–2hr; 30min).

Durham to: Darlington (every 30min; 20min); London (hourly; 3hr); Newcastle (every 30min;

20min); York (hourly; 50min).

Hexham to: Carlisle (hourly; 1hr); Haltwhistle (hourly; 20min); Newcastle (hourly; 40min).

Middlesbrough to: Durham (hourly; 50min); Grosmont, for North York Moors Railway (see p.975: Mon–Sat 4 daily; 1hr); Newcastle (hourly; 1hr 10min); Saltburn (hourly; 40min); Whitby (Mon–Sat 4 daily; 1hr 30min).

Newcastle to: Alnmouth (Mon–Sat 9–10 daily, Sun 3 daily; 30min); Berwick-upon-Tweed (hourly; 45min); Carlisle (hourly; 1hr 30min); Corbridge (hourly; 40min); Durham (every 30min; 20min); Edinburgh (hourly; 1hr 30min); Haltwhistle (hourly; 1hr); Hexham (hourly; 40min); London (hourly; 2hr 45min–3hr 30min); York (hourly; 1hr).

THE NORTHEAST | Travel details

contexts

contexts

The historical framework...1079–1097

The monuments and buildings of England.................1098–1109

Wildlife...1110–1116

Books 1117–1125

Film..1126–1134

Glossaries...1135–1136

The historical framework

Off and on, people have lived in Britain for the best part of half a million years, though the earliest evidence of human life dates from about **250,000 BC**. These meagre remains, found near Swanscombe, east of London across the Thames from Tilbury, belong to one of the migrant communities whose comings and goings depended on the fluctuations of the Ice Ages. Renewed glaciation then made the area uninhabitable once more, and the next traces – mainly roughly worked flint implements – were left around 40,000 BC by cave-dwellers at Creswell Crags in Derbyshire, Kent's Cavern near Torquay and Cheddar Cave in Somerset. The last spell of intense cold began about 17,000 years ago, and it was the final thawing of this **last Ice Age** around 5000 BC that caused the British Isles to separate from the European mainland.

The sea barrier did nothing to stop further migrations of nomadic hunting communities, drawn by the rich forests that covered ancient Britain. In about 3500 BC a new wave of colonists arrived from the continent, probably via Ireland, bringing with them a Neolithic culture based on farming and the rearing of livestock. These tribes were the first to make some impact on the environment, clearing forests, enclosing fields, constructing defensive ditches around their villages and digging mines to obtain flint used for tools and weapons. Fragments of Neolithic pottery have been found near Peterborough and at Windmill Hill, near Avebury in Wiltshire, but the most profuse relics of this culture are their graves, usually stone-chambered, turf-covered mounds (called **long barrows**), which are scattered throughout the country – the most impressive ones are at Belas Knap and Rodmarton in Gloucestershire and at Wayland's Smithy in Berkshire.

The transition from the Neolithic to the **Bronze Age** began around 2000 BC, with the immigration from northern Europe of the so-called **Beaker Folk** – named from the distinctive cups found at their burial sites. Originating in the Iberian peninsula and bringing with them bronze-workers from the Rhineland, these newcomers had a well-organized social structure with an established aristocracy, and quickly intermixed with the native tribes. Many of England's stone circles were completed at this time, including **Avebury** and **Stonehenge** in Wiltshire, while many others belong entirely to the Bronze Age – for example, the Hurlers and the Nine Maidens on Cornwall's Bodmin Moor. Large numbers of earthwork forts were also built in this period, suggesting a high level of tribal warfare, but none of these were able to withstand the waves of Celtic invaders who, spreading from a homeland in central Europe, began settling in Britain around 600 BC.

The Celts and the Romans

Highly skilled in battle, the **Celts** soon displaced the local inhabitants all over Britain, establishing a sophisticated farming economy and a social hierarchy that was dominated by a druidic priesthood. Familiar with Mediterranean artefacts through their far-flung trade routes, they introduced superior methods of metal-working that favoured iron rather than bronze, from which they forged not just weapons but also coins and ornamental works, thus creating the first recognizable British art. The principal Celtic contribution to the landscape was a network of hillforts and other defensive works stretching over the entire country, the greatest of them at **Maiden Castle** in Dorset, a site first fortified almost 2500 years earlier.

Maiden Castle was also one of the first Celtic fortifications to fall to the **Roman** legions in 43 AD. Coming at the end of a lengthy but low-level infusion of Roman ideas into the country, the Roman invasion had begun hesitantly, with small cross-Channel incursions by **Julius Caesar** in 55 and 54 BC. Britain's rumoured mineral wealth was a primary motive behind these raids, but the immediate spur to the eventual conquest nearly a century later was the dangerous collaboration between British Celts and the fiercely anti-Roman tribesmen in France, and the need of the emperor Claudius, who owed his power to the army, for a great military triumph. The death of the British king Cunobelin, who ruled all southeast England and was the inspiration for Shakespeare's Cymbeline, offered the opportunity Claudius required, and in **August 43 AD** a substantial force landed in Kent, from where it fanned out, soon establishing a base along the estuary of the Thames. Joined by Claudius and a menagerie of elephants and camels for the major battle of the campaign, the Romans soon reached Camulodunum (Colchester), and within four years were dug in on the frontier of south Wales.

The Catuvellauni chief, Caractacus, continued to conduct a guerrilla campaign from Wales until his eventual betrayal and capture in about 50 AD. About ten years later, a more serious challenge to the Romans arose when the East Anglian Iceni, under their queen **Boudicca** (or Boadicea), sacked Camulodunum and Verulamium (St Albans), and even reached the undefended port of Londinium, precursor of London. The uprising was soon quashed, and turned out to be an isolated act of resistance, with many of the already Romanized southeastern tribes of England probably welcoming absorption into the empire. However, it was not until 79 AD that Wales and the north of England were subdued, the latter process being sealed in 130 AD by the completion of **Hadrian's Wall**: running from the Tyne to the Solway, it marked the northern limit of the whole Roman Empire, and stands today the most impressive remnant of the Roman occupation.

The written history of England begins with the Romans, whose rule lasted nearly four centuries. For the first time the country was absorbed into a unified and peaceful political structure, in which commerce flourished and cities prospered, including the most northerly Roman town of Eboracum (York), the garrison of Isca Dumnoniorum (Exeter), the leisure resort of Aquae Sulis (Bath), and of course **Londinium**, which immediately assumed a pivotal role in the commercial and administrative life of the province. Although Latin became the language of the Romano-British ruling elite, local traditions were allowed to coexist with imported customs, so that Celtic gods were often worshipped at the same time as the Roman, and sometimes merged with them. Perhaps the most important legacy of the Roman occupation, however, was the introduction of **Christianity** from the third century on, becoming firmly entrenched after its official recognition by the emperor Constantine in 313.

Anglo-Saxon England

As early as the reign of Constantine, Roman England was being raided by Germanic Saxon pirates, and by the middle of the fourth century Picts from Scotland and Scots from northern Ireland were harrying inland areas in the north and west. As economic life declined and rural areas became depopulated, individual military leaders began to usurp local authority, so that by the start of the fifth century England had become irrevocably detached from what remained of the Roman Empire. Within fifty years the **Saxons** were settling on the island, the start of a gradual conquest that – despite bitter resistance led by such semi-mythical figures as King Arthur – culminated in the defeat of the native Britons in 577 at the **Battle of Dyrham** (near Bath), at which three British kings were killed. Driving the few recalcitrant tribes deep into Cumbria, Wales and England's West Country, the invaders eliminated the Romano-British culture and by the end of the sixth century the rest of England was divided into the Anglo-Saxon kingdoms of Northumbria, Mercia, East Anglia, Kent and Wessex. So complete was the Anglo-Saxon domination of England, through conquest and intermarriage, that some ninety percent of English place-names today have an Anglo-Saxon derivation. Only in the westerly extremities of the country did the ancient Celtic traditions survive, as untouched by the new invaders as they had been by the Romans. Here also, Christian worship was kept alive, though the countrywide revival of Christianity was driven mainly by the arrival of **St Augustine**, who was despatched by Pope Gregory I and landed on the Kent coast in 597, accompanied by forty monks.

The missionaries were received by Ethelbert, the overlord of all the English south of the River Humber, whose marriage to a Christian princess from France made him sympathetic to Augustine's message. **Ethelbert** gave Augustine permission to found a monastery at Canterbury (on the site of the present cathedral), where the king himself was then baptized, followed by ten thousand of his subjects at a grand Christmas ceremony. Despite some reversals in the years that followed, the Christianization of England proceeded quickly, so that by the middle of the seventh century all of the Anglo-Saxon kings had at least nominally adopted the faith. Tensions and clashes between the Augustinian missionaries and the more freebooting Celtic monks inevitably arose, to be resolved by the **Synod of Whitby** in 663, when it was settled that the English Church should follow the rule of Rome, thereby ensuring a realignment with the European cultural mainstream.

The central English region of **Mercia** became the dominant Anglo-Saxon kingdom in the eighth century under kings Ethelbald and Offa, the latter being responsible for the greatest public work of the Anglo-Saxon period: **Offa's Dyke**, an earthwork stretching from the River Dee to the Severn, marking the border with Wales. But after Offa's death **Wessex** gained the upper hand, and by 825 **Egbert** had conquered or taken allegiance from all the other English kingdoms. The supremacy of Wessex coincided with the first large-scale **Danish** (or Viking) invasions, which began with pirate raids, such as the one that destroyed the great monastery of Lindisfarne in 793, then gradually grew into a migration, prompted by unsettled conditions at home.

In 865 a substantial Danish army landed in East Anglia, and within six years they had conquered Northumbria, Mercia and East Anglia. The Danes then set their sights on Wessex, whose new king was **Alfred the Great**, a warrior whose dogged resistance was balanced by his desire to coexist with the Danes – a mixture that ensured the survival of his kingdom. Having established a border demarcating his domain from the northern **Danelaw**, the part of England in which the rule of the now-Christianized Danes was accepted (a border roughly coinciding with the Roman Watling Street), Alfred directed his resources into internal reforms and the strengthening of his defences. Although Danish attacks had recommenced before the end of Alfred's reign in 899, his successor, **Edward the Elder**, still managed to establish Saxon supremacy over the Danelaw and was thus the de facto overlord of all England, acknowledged even by Scottish and Welsh chieftains. The relative calm continued under Edward's brother, **Edgar**, king of Mercia and Northumberland, who became the first ruler to be crowned **king of England** in 973. However, this was but a lull in the Viking storm. Returning in force, the Vikings milked Edgar's son **Ethelred the Unready** ("lacking counsel") for all the money they could, but the ransom (the Danegeld) paid brought only temporary relief. In 1016 Ethelred fled to Normandy, establishing links there which were to have a far-reaching effect on ensuing events.

The first and most gifted king of the short-lived Danish dynasty was **Canute**, who was followed by his two unexceptional and disreputable sons, after whom the Saxons were restored under Ethelred's son, **Edward the Confessor**. It was said of Edward that he was better suited to have been a priest than a king, and effective power soon fell to his notional vassal, Godwin, Earl of Wessex, and his son Harold. On Edward's death, the Witan – a sort of council of elders – confirmed **Harold** as king, despite the claim of William, Duke of Normandy, that the childless Edward had sworn himself to be William's vassal, promising him the succession. Harold's brief reign was overshadowed by two dramatic events, which unluckily for him pretty much coincided. First he had to march north to fend off an invasion by his brother Tostig (who had been deprived of his earldom of Northumbria) and Tostig's ally, King Harald of Norway. Harold won a crushing victory at the battle of Stamford Bridge in Yorkshire, but then he had to scuttle back south to counter the invasion of William of Normandy. Famously, William routed the Saxons at the **Battle of Hastings** in 1066 and Harold was killed. On Christmas Day of that year William the Conqueror was installed as king in Westminster Abbey.

The Normans and the Plantagenets

Making little attempt to reach any understanding with the indigenous Saxon culture, **William I** imposed a new military aristocracy on his subjects, enforcing his rule with a series of strongholds all over the country, the grandest of which was the Tower of London. The sporadic rebellions that broke out during the early years of his reign were ruthlessly suppressed – Yorkshire and the north were ravished and the fenland resistance of Hereward the Wake was brought to a brutal end – but perhaps the single most effective controlling measure was the compilation of the **Domesday Book** between 1085 and 1086. Recording land ownership, type of cultivation, the number of inhabitants and their social status, it afforded William an unprecedented body of information about his subjects, providing the framework for the administration of taxation, the judicial structure and feudal obligations.

In 1087, William was succeeded by his son William Rufus, an ineffectual ruler but a notable benefactor of the religious foundations that were springing up throughout the realm. Rufus died in mysterious circumstances – killed by an arrow while hunting in the New Forest – and the throne passed to William I's youngest son. The new king, **Henry I**, spent much of his reign in tussles with the country's barons, but at least he proved to be more conciliatory in his dealings with the Saxons, even marrying into one of their leading families. On his death in 1135, William I's grandson Stephen of Blois contested the accession of Henry's daughter Mathilda (also called Maud), with the consequence that the nineteen years of his reign were spent in civil war. Mathilda's son was eventually recognized as Stephen's heir, and the reign of **Henry II** (1154–89), the first of the **Plantagenet** branch of the Norman line, provided a welcome respite from baronial brawling. Asserting his authority throughout a domain that reached from the Cheviots to the Pyrenees, Henry presided over immense administrative reforms, including the introduction of trial by jury. However, his attempts to subordinate ecclesiastical authority to the Crown went terribly awry in 1170, when he sanctioned the murder in Canterbury Cathedral of his erstwhile drinking companion **Thomas à Becket**, whose canonization just three years later created an enduring Europe-wide cult.

The last years of Henry's reign were riven by quarrels with his sons, the eldest of whom, **Richard I** (or Lionheart), spent most of his ten-year reign crusading in the Holy Land. Neglected, England fell prey to the scheming of Richard's brother **John**, the villain of the Robin Hood tales, who became king in his own right after Richard was killed in battle in 1199. But John's inability to hold on to his French possessions and his rumbling dispute with the Vatican alienated the English barons, who eventually forced him to consent to a charter guaranteeing their rights and privileges, the **Magna Carta**, which was signed in 1215 at Runnymede, on the Thames.

The power-struggle with the barons continued into the reign of Henry III, who was defeated by their leader Simon de Montfort at Lewes in 1264, when both Henry and Prince Edward were taken prisoner. Edward escaped and promptly routed the barons' army at the battle of Evesham in 1265, killing de Montfort in the process. Inheriting the throne in 1272, **Edward I** was a great law-maker in the mould of William I and Henry II. He presided over the Model Parliament of 1295, a significant step in the evolution of consensual politics, though he was mostly absorbed in extending his kingdom within the island, annexing Wales and imposing English jurisdiction in Scotland. In 1314, however, **Edward II** suffered the worst-ever English defeat at the hands of the Scots, whom Robert the Bruce led to a huge victory at **Bannockburn**. This reversal added to the unpopularity already created by the king's dependence on upstart favourites, and Edward was eventually overthrown by his wife Isabella and her lover Roger Mortimer, by whom he was horribly put to death in Berkeley Castle, Gloucestershire.

Although **Edward III** was initially preoccupied by Scottish wars, his reign is chiefly remembered for his claim to the French throne, a feeble pretence considering he had earlier recognized the King of France and done homage to him, but one that launched the **Hundred Years War** in 1337. Early English victories such as the Battle of Crécy in 1346, and the capture of Calais the following year, were interrupted by the outbreak of the **Black Death** in 1349, a plague which claimed about one and a half million lives – over a third of the entire English population. The resulting scarcity of labour produced economic turmoil at home, where attempts to restrict the rise of wages and to levy a poll-tax (a tax on each person irrespective of wealth) provoked widespread riots, which peaked with the **Peasants' Revolt** of 1381. After seizing Rochester Castle and sacking Canterbury, the rebels marched on London, where the boy-king **Richard II** met Wat Tyler, the leader of the revolt, at Smithfield. The resulting scuffle led to Tyler's murder and the dispersal of the mob, and soon afterwards the Bishop of Norwich routed the Norfolk rebels, the prelude to a wave of repression and terrible retribution.

Parallel with this social unrest were the clerical reforms demanded by the scholar **John Wycliffe**, whose followers made the first translation of the Bible into English in 1380. Another sign of the elevation of the common language was the success enjoyed by **Geoffrey Chaucer** (c.1345–1400), a wine merchant's son, whose *Canterbury Tales* was the first major work written in the vernacular and one of the first English books to be printed.

The houses of Lancaster and York

During the later years of Edward III's reign England had in effect been ruled by his son, **John of Gaunt**, Duke of Lancaster, whose influence remained paramount during the minority of Richard II. In 1399, John of Gaunt's son overthrew the vacillating Richard II and took the title **Henry IV**, becoming the founder of the **Lancastrian** dynasty. Fourteen years later, he in turn was succeeded by his son, the bellicose **Henry V**, who promptly renewed the war with France, which had been limping along ingloriously since a victory at Poitiers in 1356, and famously defeated the French at the battle of **Agincourt**. It was a stunning victory that forced the French king to sign the Treaty of Troyes in 1420, making the English king the heir to the French throne. However, when Henry died just two years later his son was still an infant and the regents who governed the country on his behalf were unable to resist the French rally under **Joan of Arc**. By 1454, only Calais was left in English hands.

Meanwhile **Henry VI**, who was temperamentally more inclined to the creation of such architectural coups as King's College Chapel in Cambridge than to warfare, had suffered lapses into insanity. Strongest of the rival contenders for the throne was Richard, Duke of York, by virtue of his direct descent from Edward III. It was no coincidence that the **Wars of the Roses** – named after the red rose which symbolized the Lancastrian cause and the white Yorkist rose – broke out just a year after the return of the last English garrisons from France. The returning soldiers filled the country with footloose knights and archers accustomed to a life of plunder and war. The instability of the time was signalled by **Jack Cade's Rebellion** of 1450, when a disorganized rabble challenged the king's authority, winning a battle at Sevenoaks before being scattered. However, political disputes within the circle surrounding the mad king were to prove much more threatening to the regime. The Duke of York's authority over Henry was challenged by the king's accomplished and ambitious wife, Margaret of Anjou, whose forces defeated and slew Richard at Wakefield in 1460. She and Henry were in turn overwhelmed by Richard's son, who was crowned **Edward IV** in 1461 – the first king of the **Yorkist** line.

The civil strife entered a new stage when Edward attempted to shrug off the overbearing influence of Richard Neville, Earl of Warwick and Salisbury, or "Warwick the Kingmaker", as he became known. Warwick then performed a dramatic volte-face by allying himself with his old enemy Margaret of Anjou, forcing Edward into exile and proclaiming Henry king once more. Henry VI's second term was soon interrupted by Edward's unexpected return in 1471, when Warwick was defeated and killed at the Battle of Barnet and the rest of the Lancastrians were crushed at Tewkesbury three months later. Margaret was captured, Henry's heir was killed and Henry himself was soon afterwards dispatched in the Tower.

Edward IV proved to be a precursor of the great Tudor princes, licentious, cruel and despotic, but also a patron of Renaissance learning. In 1483, his twelve-year-old son succeeded as **Edward V**, but his reign was cut short after only two months, when he and his younger brother were murdered in the

Tower of London – probably by their uncle, the Duke of Gloucester, who was crowned **Richard III**. Increasingly unpopular as rumours circulated of his part in the fate of the princes in the Tower, Richard was toppled at Bosworth Field in 1485 by Henry Tudor, Earl of Richmond, who took the throne as **Henry VII**.

The Tudors

The opening of the **Tudor** period brought radical transformations. A Lancastrian through his mother's descent from John of Gaunt, **Henry VII** reconciled the Yorkist faction by marrying Edward IV's daughter Elizabeth, thereby putting an end to the internecine squabbling among the discredited gentry. The growth of the wool and cloth trades and the rise of a powerful merchant class brought a general increase in wealth, while England began to assume the status of a major European power partly as a result of Henry's alliances and political marriages – his daughter to James IV of Scotland and his son to Catherine, daughter of Ferdinand and Isabella of Spain.

The relatively easy suppression of the rebellions of Yorkist pretenders Lambert Simnel and Perkin Warbeck ensured a smooth succession for Henry VIII in 1509. Apart from his fast-moving love life, Henry is best remembered for his separation of the English Church from Rome and his establishment of an independent Protestant church – the Church of England. This is not without its ironies. Henry was not a Protestant himself and such was his early orthodoxy that the pope even gave him the title "Defender of the Faith" for a pamphlet he wrote attacking Luther's treatises. In fact, the schism between Henry and the pope was triggered not by doctrinal issues but by the failure of his wife Catherine of Aragon – widow of his elder brother – to provide Henry with male offspring. Failing to obtain a decree of nullity from Pope Clement VII, he dismissed his long-time chancellor Thomas Wolsey and followed the advice of Thomas Cromwell, forcing the English Church to recognize him as its head. The most far-reaching consequence of this step was the **Dissolution of the Monasteries**, a decision taken mainly to enjoy the profits of the ensuing land sales. The first phase of the Dissolution in 1536, involving the smaller religious houses, was a factor in the only significant rebellion of the reign, the **Pilgrimage of Grace**, a protest largely in the north of the country, which Henry put down with great cruelty, preparing the ground for the closure of the larger foundations in 1539.

In his later years Henry became a corpulent, syphilitic tyrant, six times married but at last furnished with an heir, **Edward VI**, who was only nine years old when he ascended the throne in 1547. His short reign saw Protestantism established on a firm footing, with churches stripped of their images and Catholic services banned, yet on Edward's death most of the country readily accepted his half-sister **Mary**, daughter of Catherine of Aragon and a fervent Catholic, as queen. She restored England to the papacy and married the future Philip II of Spain, forging an alliance whose immediate consequence was war with France and the loss of Calais, last of England's French possessions. The marriage was unpopular and so was Mary's rash decision to begin persecuting Protestants, executing the leading lights of the English Reformation, Hugh Latimer, Nicholas Ridley and Thomas Cranmer, the archbishop of Canterbury who was largely responsible for the first English prayer book, published in 1549.

The accession of the Protestant **Elizabeth I** in 1558 took place in a highly volatile atmosphere, with the country riven between opposing religious loyalties and threatened from abroad by Philip II. Heresy and treason were the twin preoccupations of the Elizabethan state, a society in which a sense of English nationhood was evolving on an almost mystical level in the vacuum created by the break with Rome. Aided by a team of exceptionally able ministers, the queen provided a focal point for national feeling, enthusiastically supported by a mercantile class that was opposed to foreign entanglements or clerical restrictions, and was represented in a Parliament made stronger by the constitutional decisions of the preceding decades.

Chronology of English monarchs

House of Wessex
Egbert 802–39
Ethelwulf 839–55
Ethelbald 855–60
Ethelbert 860–66
Ethelred I 866–71
Alfred the Great 871–99
Edward the Elder 899–924
Athelstan 924–39
Edmund I 939–46
Eadred 946–55
Eadwig 955–59
Edgar 959–75
Edward the Martyr 975–79
Ethelred II (Ethelred the Unready) 979–1016
Edmund II (Edmund Ironside) 1016

House Of Skjoldung
Canute 1016–35
Harold I 1035–40
Harthacanute 1040–42

House Of Wessex
Edward the Confessor 1042–66
Harold II 1066

House Of Normandy
William I (William the Conqueror) 1066–87
William II (William Rufus) 1087–1100
Henry I 1100–35
Stephen 1135–54

House Of Plantagenet
Henry II 1154–89
Richard I (Richard the Lionheart) 1189–99
John 1199–1216
Henry III 1216–72
Edward I 1272–1307
Edward II 1307–27
Edward III 1327–77
Richard II 1377–99

The forty-five years of Elizabeth's reign saw the efflorescence of a specifically English Renaissance, especially in the field of literature, which reached its pinnacle in the brilliant career of **William Shakespeare** (1564–1616). It was also the age of the seafarers Walter Raleigh, Francis Drake, Martin Frobisher and John Hawkins, whose piratical exploits helped to map out the world for English commerce. English navigational skills were demonstrated by Drake's voyage round the world (1577–80), but it was the defeat of the mighty **Spanish Armada** in 1588 that established England as a major European sea power. The commander of the English fleet, Lord Howard of Effingham, was a practising Catholic, a fact that dashed Philip's hope of a Catholic insurrection in England

House Of Lancaster
Henry IV 1399–1413
Henry V 1413–22
Henry VI 1422–61 & 1470

House Of York
Edward IV 1461–70 & 1471–83
Edward V 1483
Richard III 1483–85

House Of Tudor
Henry VII 1485–1509
Henry VIII 1509–47
Edward VI 1547–53
Mary I 1553–58
Elizabeth I 1558–1603

House Of Stuart
James I 1603–25
Charles I 1625–49
Commonwealth and Protectorate 1649–60
Charles II 1660–85
James II 1685–88
William III and Mary II 1688–94
William III 1694–1702
Anne 1702–14

House Of Hanover
George I 1714–27
George II 1727–60
George III 1760–1820
George IV 1820–30
William IV 1830–37
Victoria 1837–1901

House Of Saxe-Coburg
Edward VII 1901–10

House Of Windsor
George V 1910–36
Edward VIII 1936
George VI 1936–52
Elizabeth II 1952–

– a hope in part founded on the widespread sympathy for Elizabeth's cousin **Mary Queen of Scots**, whose twenty-year imprisonment in England had ended with her beheading in 1587.

The Stuarts and the Commonwealth

On Elizabeth's death the heir to the throne was James VI of Scotland, son of Mary Queen of Scots, who became **James I** of England in 1603, thereby uniting the English and Scottish crowns. James quickly moved to end hostilities with Spain and adopted a policy of toleration to the country's Catholics. Inevitably, both initiatives offended many Protestants, whose worst fears were confirmed in 1605 when **Guy Fawkes** and a group of Catholic conspirators were discovered preparing to blow up king and Parliament in the so-called **Gunpowder Plot**. During the ensuing hue and cry, many Catholics met an untimely end and Fawkes himself was hung, drawn and quartered. At this time, also, certain Protestant groups collectively known as **Puritans** hoped to establish a "New Jerusalem", far from the impurities of the secular state. Their aspirations converged with commercial interests to prompt the foundation of several early colonies in North America. In 1608, the first permanent **colony in North America** was established in Virginia, followed in 1620 by the landing in New England of the Pilgrim Fathers, the nucleus of a colony that would absorb about a hundred thousand mainly Puritan immigrants by the middle of the century.

Meanwhile, a split was inevitable between James, who clung to the medieval notion of the divine right of kings, and the landed gentry who dominated the increasingly powerful Parliament. The gentry were largely Protestant and sympathetic to the Calvinist Puritans, who James foolishly persecuted. Recoiling from the rigours of his Parliament, the king relied heavily on court favourites, progressing from the skilful Robert Cecil, Earl of Salisbury, and the philosopher Francis Bacon, to the rash and unpopular George Villiers, Duke of Buckingham. The latter also had a close and baleful influence on the second Stuart king, **Charles I**.

From 1629 to 1640 Charles ruled without the services of parliament, but was forced to recall it after he had antagonized the Scots by trying to foist Archbishop Laud's Anglican prayer book on them. Charles's high-handed measures were overturned by Parliament and his chief ministers were impeached, notable among them being Thomas Wentworth, Earl of Strafford (executed in 1642), and Archbishop Laud himself (executed in 1645). Facing the concerted hostility of Parliament, the king withdrew to Nottingham where he raised his standard, the opening military act of the **Civil War**. The Royalist forces ("Cavaliers") were initially successful, winning the battle of Edgehill, but afterwards the Parliamentarian army ("Roundheads") was completely overhauled by **Oliver Cromwell**. The New Model Army Cromwell created was something quite unique: singing psalms as they went into battle and urged on by preachers and "agitators", this was an army of believers whose ideological commitment to the Parliamentary cause made it truly formidable. Cromwell's revamped army cut its teeth at the battle of Naseby and thereafter simply brushed the Royalists aside. Attempting to muddy the political waters, Charles surrendered himself to the Scots, but they finally handed him over to the English Parliament, by whom – after prolonged negotiations, endless royal shenanigans and more fighting – he was ultimately executed in January 1649.

For the next eleven years England was a **Commonwealth** – at first a true republic, then, after 1653, a **Protectorate** with Cromwell as the Lord Protector and commander in chief. Cromwell later reformed the government, secured advantageous commercial treaties with foreign nations and used his New Model Army to put the fear of God into his various enemies and with particular brutality in Catholic Ireland. After his death in 1658 his son Richard ruled briefly and ineffectually, and in 1660 Parliament voted to restore the monarchy in the person of **Charles II**, the exiled son of the previous king.

The turmoil of the previous twenty years had unleashed a furious debate on every strand of legalistic, theological and political thought, a milieu that spawned a host of leftist sects – such as the Levellers, who demanded wholesale constitutional reform, and the more radical Diggers, who proposed common ownership of all land. Nonconformist religious groups flourished, prominent among them the pacifistic **Quakers**, led by the much persecuted George Fox (1624–91), and the Dissenters, to whom the most famous writers of the day, John Milton (1608–74) and John Bunyan (1628–88), both belonged. With the **Restoration**, however, these philosophical and proto-communist eddies gave way to a new exuberance in the fields of art, literature and the theatre, a remarkable transition from the sombreness of the Puritan era, when secular drama and other such fripperies were banned outright. In the scientific arena, just six months after his accession Charles II founded the **Royal Society**, which numbered Isaac Newton (1642–1727) among its first fellows.

The low points of Charles's reign came with the **Great Plague** of 1665 and the **Great Fire of London** the following year, though the latter had the positive consequence of allowing Christopher Wren (1632–1723) and other great architects to redesign the capital along more contemporary classical lines. Moreover, the political scene was not entirely tranquil: tensions still existed between king and Parliament, where the traditional divisions of court and country began to coalesce into **Whig** and **Tory** parties, respectively representing the low-church gentry and the high-church aristocracy. A measure of vengeance was also wreaked on the regicides and other leading Parliamentarians, though its intensity was nothing like that of the anti-Catholic hysteria sparked off by the Popish Plot of 1678, the fabrication of the trickster Titus Oates.

The succession in 1685 of the Catholic **James II**, brother of Charles II, provoked much opposition, though – as one might expect from a country recently racked by civil war – there was an indifferent response when the **Duke of Monmouth**, the favourite among Charles II's illegitimate sons, landed at Lyme Regis to mount a challenge to the new king. His undisciplined forces were routed at Sedgemoor, Somerset, in July 1685; nine days later Monmouth was beheaded at Tower Hill, and in the subsequent **Bloody Assizes** of **Judge Jeffreys**, hundreds of rebels and suspected sympathizers – mainly in Somerset and Devon – were executed or deported.

When seven bishops protested against James's **Declaration of Indulgence** of 1687, removing anti-Catholic restrictions, the king showed something of his father's obstinacy by having them tried for seditious libel, though he was quickly forced to acquit them. When James's son was born, a child destined to be brought up in the Catholic faith, the Protestant opposition gathered momentum. Messengers were dispatched to **William of Orange**, the Dutch husband of Mary, the Protestant daughter of James II. William landed in

Brixham in Devon, proceeding to London where he was acclaimed king in the so-called **Glorious Revolution** of 1688, the final postscript to the Civil War – although it was another three years before James's forces were defeated in Ireland.

William and Mary were made joint sovereigns, having agreed to a **Bill of Rights** defining the limitations of the monarch's power and the rights of his or her subjects. This, together with the **Act of Settlement of 1701** – among other things, barring Catholics or anyone married to one from succession to the English throne – made Britain the first country to be governed by a **constitutional monarchy**, in which the roles of legislature and executive were separate and interdependent. The model was broadly consistent with that outlined by the philosopher and political thinker John Locke (1632–1704), whose essentially Whig doctrines of toleration and social contract were gradually embraced as the new orthodoxy.

Ruling alone after Mary's death in 1694, William regarded England as a prop in his defence of Holland against France, a stance that defined England's political alignment in Europe for the next sixty years. In the reign of **Anne**, second daughter of James II, English armies won a string of remarkable victories on the continent, beginning with the Duke of Marlborough's triumph at Blenheim in 1704, followed the next year by the capture of Gibraltar, establishing a British presence in the Mediterranean. The War of the Spanish Succession, the overall struggle within which these engagements occurred, was closed by the Treaty of Utrecht in 1713, which settled the European balance of power for some time. Otherwise Anne's reign was distinguished mainly for the 1707 **Act of Union**, uniting the English and Scottish parliaments.

When the queen died childless in 1714, the Stuart line of kings ended, though there were to be pro-Stuart, or Jacobite, challenges to the throne in years to come. In accordance with the terms of the Act of Settlement, the succession passed to a non-English-speaking German, the Duke of Hanover, who became George I of England.

The Hanoverians

As power leaked away from the monarchy into the hands of the Whig oligarchy – many Tories having been discredited for suspected Jacobite sympathies – the king ceased to attend Cabinet meetings, his place being taken by his chief minister. Most prominent of these ministers was **Robert Walpole**, regarded as England's **first prime minister**. To all intents and purposes, Walpole ruled the country from 1721 to 1742. This was a tranquil period politically, with the country standing aloof from foreign affrays, but the financial world was prey to a mania for speculation. Of the numerous fraudulent or ill-conceived financial ventures of this time, the greatest was the fiasco of the South Sea Company, which in 1720 sold shares in its monopoly of trade in the Pacific and along the east coast of South America. The "bubble" burst when the shareholders took fright at the extent of their own investments and the value of the shares dropped to nothing, reducing many to penury, and almost wrecking the government, which was saved only by the astute intervention of Walpole.

Peace ended in the reign of **George II**, when in 1739 England declared war on Spain at the start of yet another dynastic squabble, the eight-year War of the Austrian Succession. Then in 1745 the country was invaded by the **Young**

Pretender, **Charles Stuart**, in the second and most dangerous of the Jacobite Rebellions. So-called Bonnie Prince Charlie reached Derby, just 130 miles from London, before retreating to Scotland where he was defeated by the Duke of Cumberland at Culloden. The **Seven Years War** brought yet more overseas territory, as English armies wrested control of India and Canada from France, then in 1768 **Captain James Cook** departed from Plymouth on his voyage to New Zealand and Australia, further widening the scope of the colonial empire.

In 1760, **George III** succeeded his father. The early years of his sixty-year reign saw a revived struggle between king and Parliament, enlivened by the intervention of John Wilkes, first of a long and increasingly vociferous line of parliamentary radicals. The contest was exacerbated by the deteriorating relationship with the thirteen colonies of North America, a situation brought to a head by the **American Declaration of Independence** and England's defeat in the Revolutionary War. Chastened by this disaster, England chose not to interfere in the momentous events taking place across the Channel, where France, its most consistent foe in the eighteenth century, was convulsed by revolution. Out of the turmoil emerged the country's most daunting enemy so far, Napoleon, whose progress was interrupted by Nelson at Trafalgar in 1805, and finally stopped ten years later by the Duke of Wellington at Waterloo.

The Industrial Revolution

England's triumph over Napoleon was largely due to its financial strength, itself a result of the switch from an agricultural to a manufacturing economy, a process generally referred to as the **Industrial Revolution**. The earliest mechanized production lines were constructed in the Lancashire cotton mills, where cotton-spinning was transformed from a cottage industry into a highly productive factory-based system. Initially, river water powered the mills, but the technology changed after James Watt patented his **steam engine** in 1781. Watt's engines needed coal, which made it convenient to locate mills and factories near coal mines, a tendency that was accelerated as **ironworks** took up coal as a smelting fuel, vastly increasing the output from their furnaces. Accordingly there was a shift of population towards the Midlands and north of England, where the great coal reserves were located, resulting in the rapid growth of the industrial towns and the expansion of Liverpool as a commercial port, importing raw materials from India and the Americas and exporting manufactured goods. Commerce and industry were served by steadily improving transport facilities, such as the building of a network of **canals** in the wake of the success of the Bridgewater Canal in 1765, which linked coal mines at Worsley with Manchester and the River Mersey. But the great leap forward occurred with the arrival of the **railway**, heralded by the opening of the Liverpool–Manchester line in 1830, with power provided by George Stephenson's Rocket.

Boosted by a vast influx of Jewish, Irish, French and Dutch immigrants, many of whom introduced new manufacturing techniques, the country's population rose from about seven and a half million at the beginning of George III's reign to more than fourteen million at its end, an increase whose major cause was a rise in the birthrate as a response to the demand for child labour and the extra income that it would provide for families. But while factories and their attendant towns expanded, the rural settlements of England suffered, inspiring the elegiac pastoral yearnings of Samuel Taylor Coleridge and William Wordsworth, the first great names of the **Romantic** movement in English literature. Later Romantic poets such as Percy Bysshe Shelley and Lord Byron took a more socially engaged stance, inveighing against social injustices that were aggravated by the expenses of the Napoleonic Wars and their aftermath, when many returning soldiers found their jobs had been taken by machines. Discontent emerged in demands for parliamentary reform, and in 1819 demonstrators in Manchester – centre of the cotton industry and most important of the industrial boom towns still unrepresented in Parliament – were mown down by troops in what became known as the **Peterloo Massacre**.

The following year George III, by now weak, old, blind and insane, died and was succeeded by his grandson **George IV**. One of the hallmarks of the new reign was a greater degree of religious toleration with Catholics and Nonconformists now permitted to enter Parliament. Furthermore, after years of struggle, workers' associations were legalized, and a civilian police force was created, largely the work of **Robert Peel**, a reforming Tory who also outlined the basic ideology of modern Conservatism. More far-reaching changes came under **William IV**, with the passing of the **Reform Act** of 1832, whereby the principle of popular representation was acknowledged (though most adult males still had no vote); two years later, the revised **Poor Law** alleviated the condition of the destitute. Significant sections of the middle classes wanted far swifter democratic reform, as was expressed in public indignation over the **Tolpuddle Martyrs** – the Dorset labourers transported to Australia in 1834 for joining an agricultural trade union – and support for **Chartism**, a working-class movement demanding universal male suffrage. Poverty and injustice were the dominant theme of the novels of **Charles Dickens** (1812–70) and the preoccupation of the paternalistic reform movements that were a feature of the nineteenth century. This social concern had been anticipated in the previous century by the Methodism of John Wesley (1703–91) and the anti-slavery campaign promoted by evangelical Christians such as the Quakers and William Wilberforce. As a result of their efforts, slavery was banned in Britain in 1772 and throughout the colonies in 1833 – putting an end to what had been a major factor in the prosperity of ports such as Bristol and Liverpool.

Victorian England

In 1837 William IV was succeeded by his niece **Victoria**, whose long reign witnessed the zenith of British power. For most of the period, the British economy boomed and typically the cloth manufacturers could boast that they supplied the domestic market before breakfast, the rest of the world thereafter. The British shipping fleet was easily the mightiest in the world and underpinned an empire on which "The sun never set" with Victoria herself becoming the symbol of both the nation's success and the imperial ideal. There were extraordinary intellectual achievements too – as typified by the publication of Charles Darwin's *The Origin of Species* in 1859 – and the country came to see itself as both a civilizing agent and, on occasion, the hand of (a very Protestant) God on earth. Britain's industrial and commercial prowess was best embodied by the great engineering feats of Isambard Kingdom Brunel and by the **Great Exhibition** of 1851, a display of manufacturing achievements from all over the world.

With trade at the forefront of the agenda, much of the political debate during this period crystallized into a conflict between the **Free Traders** – represented by an alliance of the Peelites and the Whigs, forming the Liberal Party – and the **Protectionists** under Bentinck and **Disraeli**, guiding light of the

Tories. During the last third of the century, Parliament was dominated by the duel between Disraeli and the Liberal leader **Gladstone**. Although it was Disraeli who eventually passed the Second Reform Bill in 1867, further extending the electoral franchise, it was Gladstone who had first proposed it, and it was Gladstone's first ministry of 1868–74 that passed some of the century's most far-reaching legislation, including compulsory education, the full legalization of trade unions and an Irish Land Act.

There were foreign entanglements too. In 1854 troops were sent to protect the Turkish empire against the Russians in the **Crimea**, an inglorious debacle whose horrors were relayed to the public by the first ever press coverage of a military campaign and by the revelations of a shocked Florence Nightingale. The potential fragility of Britain's empire was exposed by the Indian Mutiny of 1857, but reassuringly the imperial status quo was eventually restored and Victoria took the title Empress of India after 1876. Thereafter, the British army was flattered by a series of minor wars against poorly armed Asian and African opponents, but promptly came unstuck when it faced the Dutch settlers of South Africa in the **Boer War** (1899–1902). The British ultimately fought their way through to victory, but the discreditable conduct of the war prompted a military shake-up at home that was to be of significance in the coming European war.

From World War I to World War II

Victoria died in the first month of 1901, to be succeeded by her son, **Edward VII**, whose leisurely and dissolute life could be seen as the epitome of the complacent era to which he gave his name. Edwardian England came to an end on August 4, 1914, when the Liberal government, honouring the Entente Cordiale signed with France in 1904, declared war on Germany. Hundreds of thousands volunteered for the army, but their enthusiastic nationalism was not enough to win **World War I** easily, which dragged on for four years and cost millions of lives. Britain and her allies eventually prevailed, but the number of dead beggared belief, undermining the English majority's respect for the ruling class, whose generals had shown a particularly vile combination of incompetence and indifference to the plight of their men. Many looked admiringly at the Soviet Union, where the communists had rid themselves of the Tsar and seized control in 1917.

At the war's end in 1918 the political fabric of England was changed dramatically when the sheer weight of public opinion pushed parliament into extending the **vote** to all men aged twenty-one or over and to women of thirty or over, subject to certain residential or business qualifications. This tardy liberalization of women's rights owed much to the efforts of the radical **Suffragettes**, led by Emmeline Pankhurst and her daughters Sylvia and Christabel, but the process was only completed in 1929 when women were at last granted the vote at twenty-one, on equal terms with men.

During this period, the **Labour Party** supplanted the Liberals as the main force on the left wing of British politics, its strength built on an alliance between the working-class trade unions and middle-class radicals. Labour formed its first government in 1923 under Ramsay MacDonald, but following the publication of the **Zinoviev Letter**, a forged document that seemed to prove Soviet encouragement of British socialist subversion, the Conservatives were returned with a large majority. In 1926, the tensions which had been building up since the end of the war, produced by a severe decline in manufacturing and attendant escalating unemployment, erupted with the **General Strike**. Spreading instantly from the coal mines to the railways, the newspapers and the iron and steel industries, the strike lasted nine days and involved half a million workers, provoking the government into draconian action – the army was called in, and the strike was broken. The economic situation deteriorated even further after the crash of the New York Stock Exchange in 1929, which precipitated a worldwide depression. Unemployment reached over 2.8 million in England in 1931, generating a series of mass demonstrations that reached a peak with the **Jarrow March** from the Northeast to London in 1936. The same year, economist John Maynard Keynes argued in his *General Theory of Employment, Interest and Money* for a greater degree of state intervention in the management of the economy, though the whole question was soon overshadowed by international events.

Abroad, the structure of the British Empire had undergone profound changes since World War I. The status of Ireland had been partly resolved after the electoral gains of the nationalist Sinn Fein in 1918 led to the establishment of the Irish Free State in 1922, from which the six counties of the mainly Protestant North "contracted out". Four years later, the **Imperial Conference** recognized the autonomy of the British dominions, an agreement formalized in the 1931 Statute of Westminster, whereby each dominion was given an equal footing in a Commonwealth of Nations, though each still recognized the British monarch. The royal family itself was shaken in 1936 by the **abdication of Edward VIII**, following his decision to marry a twice-divorced American, Wallis Simpson. Although the succession passed smoothly to his brother **George VI**, the scandal further reduced the standing of the royals, a process which has gathered pace in recent years.

Non-intervention in both the Spanish Civil War and the Sino-Japanese War was paralleled by a policy of appeasement towards **Adolf Hitler**, who began to rearm Germany in earnest in the mid-1930s. This policy was epitomized by the antics of Prime Minister Neville Chamberlain, who returned from meeting Hitler and Mussolini at Munich in 1938 with an assurance of good intentions that he took at face value. Consequently, when **World War II** broke out in September 1939, Britain was seriously unprepared. In May 1940 the discredited Chamberlain stepped down in favour of a national coalition government headed by the charismatic **Winston Churchill**, whose bulldog persistence and heroic speeches provided the inspiration needed in the backs-against-the-wall mood of the time. Partly through Churchill's manoeuvres, the United States became a supplier of foodstuffs and munitions to Britain. Given that the US had broken trade links with Japan in June (in protest at their attacks on China), this factor may have precipitated the Japanese bombing of Pearl Harbour on December 7, 1941 and thus the US's entry into the war as a combatant, an intervention which, combined with the heroic resistance of the Russian Red Army, swung the balance. In terms of the number of casualties it caused, World War II was not as calamitous as the Great War (as World War I is often known), but its impact upon the civilian population of England was much greater. In its first wave of bombing, the Luftwaffe caused massive damage to industrial and supply centres such as London, Coventry, Manchester, Liverpool, Southampton and Plymouth; in later raids, intended to shatter morale rather than factories and docks, the cathedral cities of Canterbury, Exeter, Bath, Norwich and York were targeted. At the end of the fighting, nearly one in three of all the houses in the nation had been destroyed or damaged, nearly a quarter of a million members of the British armed forces had lost their lives and over 58,000 civilians were dead.

Postwar England

The end of the war in 1945 was quickly followed by a general election. Hungry for change, the electorate displaced Churchill in favour of the Labour Party under **Clement Attlee**, who, with a large parliamentary majority, set about a radical programme to **nationalize** the coal, gas, electricity, iron and steel industries, as well as the inland transport services. Building on the plans for a social security system presented in Sir William Beveridge's report of 1943, the **National Insurance Act** and the **National Health Service** Act were both passed early in the Labour administration, giving birth to what became known as the **welfare state**. But despite substantial American aid, the huge problems of rebuilding the economy made austerity the keynote, with the rationing of food and fuel remaining in force long after 1945.

In April 1949, Britain, the United States, Canada, France and the Benelux countries signed the **North Atlantic Treaty** as a counterbalance to Soviet power in eastern Europe, thereby defining the country's postwar international commitments. Yet confusion regarding Britain's post-imperial role was shown up by the **Suez Crisis** of 1956, when Anglo-French and Israeli forces invaded Egypt to secure control of the Suez Canal, only to be hastily recalled following international condemnation. Revealing severe limitations on the country's capacity for independent action, the Suez incident resulted in the resignation of the Conservative prime minister Anthony Eden, who was replaced by the more pragmatic **Harold Macmillan**. Nonetheless, Macmillan maintained a nuclear policy that suggested a continued desire for an international role, and nuclear testing went on against a background of widespread marches under the auspices of the Campaign for Nuclear Disarmament.

The 1960s, dominated by the Labour premiership of **Harold Wilson**, saw a boom in consumer spending and a corresponding cultural upswing, with London becoming the hippest city on the planet. The good times lasted barely a decade. Though Tory prime minister Edward Heath led Britain into the brave new world of the European Economic Community, the 1970s were a decade of recession and industrial strife. A succession of public-sector strikes and mis-timed decisions by James Callaghan's Labour government handed the 1979 general election to the Conservatives and **Margaret Thatcher**, who four years earlier had ousted Heath to become the first woman to lead a major political party in Britain.

Thatcher went on to win three general elections, steering the UK into a period of ever greater social polarization. While taxation policies and easy credit fuelled a consumer boom for the professional classes, the erosion of manufacturing industry and the weakening of the welfare state created a calamitous number of people trapped in long-term impoverished unemployment. Despite the intense dislike of her regime among a substantial portion of the population, Thatcher won an increased majority in the 1983 election, partly because of the successful outcome of the 1982 war to regain control of the **Falkland Islands**, partly owing to the fragmentation of the Labour opposition, from which the short-lived Social Democratic Party had split in panic at what it perceived as the radicalization of the party.

Social and political tensions surfaced in sporadic urban rioting and the year-long **miners' strike** (1984–85) against pit closures, a bitter industrial dispute in which the police were given unprecedented powers to restrict the movement of citizens, while the media perpetrated some immensely misleading coverage of events. The violence in Northern Ireland also intensified, and the bombing campaign of the IRA came close to killing the entire Cabinet when it blew up the Brighton hotel in which the Conservatives were staying for their 1984 annual conference.

The divisive politics of Thatcherism reached their apogee with the introduction of the Poll Tax, a lunatic scheme that led ultimately to Thatcher's overthrow by colleagues who feared annihilation should she lead them into another general election. The uninspiring new Tory leader, **John Major**, won the Conservatives a fourth term in office in 1992, albeit with a much reduced majority in Parliament. While his government presided over a steady growth in economic performance, they gained little credit amid allegations of mismanagement, feckless leadership and what became known as "sleaze" among Conservative MPs, with revelations of extramarital affairs, cover-ups and financial deceit seized upon with glee by an increasingly cynical British press. Major's unaggressive style was frequently called into question, not least among his own party, among whom vocal right-wing **Euro-sceptics** called for Britain to disassociate itself from the planned integration of the economies of the European Union and the introduction of a Europe-wide currency, the euro.

The government's noncommittal "wait-and-see" policy towards monetary union impressed neither its critics at home nor Britain's European partners, relations with whom plummeted further when it was revealed that a brain-wasting disease in cattle (bovine spongiform encephalopathy – **BSE** – or "mad cow disease") was widespread in British beef. Concerned about the threat of the disease spreading to humans as well as cows, the EU slapped an export ban on British beef, domestic sales of meat plunged (briefly), a programme of slaughter was introduced and amid the hysteria and confusion the government was, yet again, roundly blamed.

Sharing the malaise of the Conservative government in the early 1990s was the **Royal Family**, whose credibility fissured with the break-up of the marriage of Prince Charles and Diana. Revelations about the cruel and heartless treatment of Diana by both the prince and his family damaged the royals' reputation perhaps beyond repair and suddenly the institution itself seemed an anachronism, its members stiff, old-fashioned and dim-witted. By contrast, Diana, who was formally divorced from Charles in 1994, appeared warm-hearted and glamorous and her death in a car accident in Paris in 1997 may have saved the royal family as an institution. In the short term, Diana's death had a profound impact on the British, who joined in a media-orchestrated exercise in public grieving unprecedented in recent history.

The **Labour party**, itself in disarray through the 1980s, began to regroup in 1994 under a dynamic young leader, **Tony Blair**, who persuaded the party to distance itself from traditional left-wing socialism and take on a mantle of idealistic, media-friendly populism. The transformation worked to devastating effect, sweeping Blair to power in the general election of May 1997 on a wave of genuine popular optimism. There were immediate rewards in enhanced relations with Europe and progress in the Irish peace talks, whilst the long process of rebuilding the national health service and combating poverty started in earnest. Blair's electoral touch was repeated in Labour-sponsored referendums in both Scotland and Wales in favour of a **devolved regional government**, and the long-awaited reform of the House of Lords is still pending.

The indisputable drive and energy of the Labour government was substantially challenged in autumn 2000, however. First, by the defeat of Labour's official candidate, Frank Dobson, in the **London mayoral election** by the former leader of the Greater London Council, Ken Livingstone; and secondly, by a widespread protest against taxation on motor fuels, led by a coalition of farmers, truckers and small businesses, which saw blockades of fuel depots and panic-buying of petrol. A further blow came in the form of a huge outbreak of **foot-and-mouth disease** in early 2001, which struck many farms across the country. MAFF, the ministry responsible for agriculture and farming, was ill-prepared for the crisis, and its subsequent dithering over the best means of resolving the matter exacerbated ill-feeling against the government, especially amongst rural communities, and resulted in large areas of the countryside being closed to walkers and tourists. In what was seen as a cynical ploy to salvage his flagging ratings, Blair delayed the calling of a new election until June 2001; while at the same time MAFF guaranteed that the country would be free of foot-and-mouth by that date: of course, it failed to deliver on this promise, although, at the time of writing, most areas of the countryside were free of disease and re-opened to the public. This crisis, along with continued debates about Northern Ireland, the dilapidation of the nation's public transportation system and Labour's failure to reduce hospital waiting lists further tarnished New Labour's image, but did not hinder the party's success at the polls. This had much to do with public apathy – voter turnout was lower than any time since World War II – and a lacklustre Conservative Party, led by **William Hague**, which had unwittingly done its best to help get the Labour party back in by engaging in rigorous political in-fighting in the run-up to the election. The second successive massive defeat for the Tories was followed by Hague's resignation and subsequent replacement by Iain Duncan Smith.

However, the events of **September 11, 2001**, when terrorist-controlled aeroplanes devastated New York's World Trade Centre and the Pentagon in Washington, saw Tony Blair taking a major role alongside US President George Bush in the international coalition formed to wage war against the alleged perpetrators, Al-Qaida, and their protectors, the Taleban rulers of Afghanistan.

The monuments and buildings of England

The oldest traces of building in England date from the **fourth millennium BC**, when **Neolithic** peoples, who practised rudimentary agriculture, succeeded the hunting-and-gathering Paleolithic and Mesolithic population, who had inhabited cave-dwellings and hide-covered camps. The remains of round stone huts have been excavated on Carn Brea, outside Redruth in Cornwall, but the major surviving habitations are entrenched sites found throughout southern England, consisting of concentric rings of ditches and banks. The largest of these is at Windmill Hill in Wiltshire, created by a civilization that was also responsible for numerous **long barrows** (burial mounds) all over England. These featureless, pear-shaped hummocks of earth are concentrated along the southern chalk downs from Sussex to Dorset, with others dotted around Lincolnshire, Yorkshire and the Cotswolds, where the barrows are noteworthy for holding stone chambers for collective family burials.

One of the largest and most elaborate Neolithic burial sites is **Woodhenge**, on Salisbury Plain, comprising a network of banks and ditches enclosing no fewer than six concentric ovals of wooden posts, arranged along the axis of the midsummer sunrise. The site lies not far from the most famous of all English prehistoric monuments, **Stonehenge**, started around 3000 BC and subsequently added to over the next thousand years by the so-called Beaker Folk, an early Bronze Age culture. This extraordinary megalithic stone circle probably had an astronomical and sacred significance, as did **Avebury**, on the other side of Salisbury Plain, which is even more extensive than Stonehenge, though less massive and less well preserved. The two sites represent communal, highly organized efforts, embellished over the years in much the same way as medieval cathedrals. Less grandiose **stone circles and rows** survive up and down the country, from Castlerigg, near Keswick in the Lake District, to the Hurlers of Cornwall's Bodmin Moor. Hut circles on the moors of the West Country bear testimony to the presence of later Bronze Age peoples; Grimspound, on Dartmoor, is one of the best examples – dating from around 1200 BC, its round stone houses with beehive roofs are ringed by a protective wall.

The Celtic and Roman periods

Five hundred years later, **Celtic** invaders brought the techniques of the Iron Age to the British Isles. Their chief contribution to the English landscape was a series of **hilltop forts** and other defensive works, often adapted from earlier constructions. At their simplest, these settlements consisted of a circular earthwork within which the inhabitants dwelt in timber-built round huts – a good example is Castle Dore, near Fowey in Cornwall. At **Maiden Castle**, in Dorset, a town was enclosed within a multiple system of ramparts, a formidable enlargement of what had been a modest and much more ancient hillfort. The best preserved of all Iron Age villages, however, is the stronghold of **Chysauster**, near Zennor in Cornwall, consisting of stone houses arranged in pairs, each with a courtyard and garden plot. The settlement was inhabited until well into the Roman era, preserved thanks to its distance from the most westerly Roman outpost.

The **Romans** were the first to impose rigorously systematized architecture on the English landscape, as their consolidation of peace permitted the erection of monumental public buildings: amphitheatres, like that at Chester in Cheshire; theatres, like the one at York; and baths, most famous of which were of course at Bath. Although no Roman temples remain standing, Colchester and St Albans have revealed impressive remains, as befits two of Roman Britain's principal centres. Other important towns such as London, Gloucester, Leicester and Lincoln – all planned according to the classic chessboard pattern favoured by the Romans – have yielded little, due chiefly to the extensive reuse of the ancient sites. In general, the architecture of this and other Roman provinces was less ambitious and sophisticated than that of Rome itself, yet the grandeur of such palaces as **Fishbourne** in West Sussex – built around 75 AD, probably for a Romanized British chieftain – was clearly intended to affirm the vast superiority of Roman civilization. Fishbourne's columned entrance prefaces an interior whose decorative details were as carefully elaborated as the ground plan, with lavish use of mosaics, a feature also exemplified by private houses excavated at St Albans and Cirencester. Most of the great Roman villas reached their peak of comfort and artistic excellence during the first half of the fourth century, when even relatively modest farmhouses were equipped with central heating.

Anglo-Saxon England

A hundred years later, the Romans had withdrawn from the islands and all traces of their culture were neglected and crumbling. The **Anglo-Saxons** who followed them had little interest in the achievements of the eclipsed civilization, neither were they inspired to rival them. Once they had progressed beyond the use of mud, wattle and thatch, the Anglo-Saxons mainly constructed in **timber**, a specialization in which the English were to excel throughout the Middle Ages, though its perishability has meant that little remains from the six hundred years preceding the Norman Conquest. What fragments have survived were the product of the new Christian ideology, expressed in **stone-built churches** that were intended to have an enduring monumental function. The conversion of the English kings at the end of the sixth century initiated a period lasting until the sixteenth-century Reformation, in which church construction was the chief medium of architectural innovation.

But even stone-built churches were vulnerable to the Viking raids from the eighth century onwards, and those that did survive were subject to constant modifications and accretions. Such was the case with two of the earliest English churches, both in **Canterbury**: St Peter and St Paul, built in about 597, and the town's first cathedral, erected about five years later. In general terms, these Anglo-Saxon structures seem to have been modelled on churches in Rome, with round apses at the eastern end, unlike the more Celtic-inspired square ends that can be seen at the little church of St Lawrence, in Bradford-on-Avon, Wiltshire, or in the churches constructed during the Christian revival in **Northumbria** towards the end of the seventh century. Here, the ascetic Celtic tradition of the Scottish and Irish monks who led the movement did not encourage refined architecture, and the three churches built by Benedict

Biscop in County Durham – Monkwearmouth, Escomb and the Venerable Bede's own church at Jarrow – are small and roughly built. The most impressive of all Saxon churches, however, lies in the Midlands, at Brixworth in Northamptonshire, erected around 670, and distinguished by the systematic use of arches.

In the eighth and ninth centuries, church building was deflected by the increasing ferocity of the Viking raiders, who despoiled the richest of the country's churches. A revival came with the installation of Dunstan as bishop of Glastonbury around 940, which led to the foundation of monasteries all over the country, much of the work being undertaken by churchmen who had spent time in the great European houses. Far from showing the influence of continental styles, however, the sparse remains demonstrate instead a penchant for quirky decoration – for example the spiral columns in the crypt at Repton, Derbyshire.

The Normans

English insularity came to an end when the influence of **Norman** architecture began to be felt in the years just before the Conquest of 1066. The finest pre-Conquest building to employ the Romanesque style was Edward the Confessor's rebuilt **Westminster Abbey** (1050–65), the design of which was an imitation of the great French abbey churches of Caen and Jumièges. Edward's work has since disappeared, but the capital still boasts a remarkable example of Norman architecture – the **Tower of London**, the most formidable of a chain of defence works thrown up throughout the country.

The earliest types of **castle** followed a "motte and bailey" design, consisting of a central tower (or keep) placed on a mound (the motte), and encircled by one or more courts (the baileys). Most were built of wood until the time of Henry II, though some of the more important sites were stone-constructed from the beginning, including **Rochester** and **Colchester** castles and the **White Tower** at the Tower of London. **Dover Castle** (1168–85), built by Henry II, introduced the refinement of a double row of outer walls with towers at intervals, a design probably influenced by the fortresses encountered by Crusaders in the Holy Land.

Once the country had been secured, the Normans set about transforming the English Church, filling the highest ecclesiastical offices with imported clergy, all of whom were keen to introduce the lofty architectural conceptions then current in Europe. Many of the major churches of the country – for example at **Canterbury**, **York**, **St Albans**, **Winchester**, **Worcester** and **Ely** – were rebuilt along Norman lines, with cruciform ground plans and massive cylindrical columns topped by semicircular arches. The summit of the Norman style was achieved at **Durham Cathedral**, begun in 1093, which has Europe's first example of large-scale ribbed vaulting, and spectacular zigzag and diamond patterns on its colossal piers, a strong and immediately influential contrast to the austerity of the first generation of Norman churches. An increasing love of decoration was also evident in the elaborately carved capitals and blind arcading in Canterbury Cathedral, the beakhead moulding in Lincoln Cathedral, and to a lesser extent in the ornamental features of the numerous parish churches surviving from this period, which often reveal greater evidence of Anglo-Saxon traditional craftwork.

In common with the rest of Europe, England witnessed the growing influence of the **monastic houses** in the twelfth century, a continuation of a process begun before the Conquest by the Benedictines. The **Cistercians** were responsible for some of the most splendid foundations, establishing an especially wealthy group of self-sufficient monasteries in Yorkshire – **Fountains**, **Rievaulx** and **Jervaulx** abbeys – which featured examples of the pointed arch, an idea imported from northern France, where it may have been introduced by Crusaders returning from the Middle East. The reforming Cistercians favoured a plain style, but the native penchant for decoration gradually infiltrated their buildings – for instance at Kirkstall Abbey (c.1152), near Leeds – while other orders had a preference for greater elaboration from the start. Amongst the latter was the **Cluniac** order, whose extravagantly ornate west front of Norfolk's Castle Acre priory (1140–50) is typical.

Incidentally, it's characteristic of the English Church that bishoprics were often given to the heads of monastic houses. Thus many English cathedrals were also monastic churches, which explains the prevalence of **cloisters**, **chapter houses** and other monastic structures within the precincts of English cathedrals, and the existence within the main body of the cathedral of areas that were set aside for the use of the monks rather than the laity.

The Transitional and Early English Styles

Profuse carved decoration and pointed arches were distinctive elements in the evolution of a **transitional style** in the second half of the twelfth century, representing a shift away from purely Romanesque forms. The **pointed arch** permitted a far greater flexibility in the relation of the height of a building to its span than had the round arch. It also allowed the introduction of highly scientific systems of vaulting and buttressing, which in turn led to a significant increase of window area in the walls between the buttresses, since these walls no longer had to carry the main weight of the roof. Improvements in masonry techniques also meant that walls could be reduced in thickness, and the cylindrical columns of the Normans replaced by more slender piers.

The first phase of **Gothic** architecture in England began in earnest in the last quarter of the twelfth century, when Gothic motifs were used at Roche Abbey and **Byland**, both in Yorkshire. However, it was the French-designed **choir** at **Canterbury Cathedral**, built 1175–84, which really established the new style, even though it was compromised by the fact that Gothic themes had to be grafted onto the ruins of the Anglo-Norman building that had been destroyed by fire in 1174. This first phase, lasting through most of the thirteenth century, is known as **Early English** (or Pointed or Lancet), and was given its full expression in what is regarded as the first truly Gothic cathedral in England, **Wells**, largely completed in 1190.

Begun shortly afterwards, **Lincoln Cathedral** takes the process of vertical emphasis further, substituting wall-shafts soaring all the way to the ceiling for Wells' three-tier nave subdivided horizontally, and using decoration more profuse than anything in France at the time. The influence of Lincoln remained strong in English architecture, though it was resisted by the builders of **Salisbury Cathedral**, which, despite later restoration work, is one of the most homogeneous of the Early English churches, most of it being built in the comparatively short period 1220–65.

A transitional phase in the evolution of Gothic architecture is represented by the **rebuilding of Westminster Abbey** in 1220, when the Abbey became the most French of English churches. There was a French influence at work in the flying buttresses that were added to support its greater height, and in the lavish use of **window tracery**, whereby geometric patterns were created by subdividing each window with moulded ribs (or mullions), a device first seen at Reims in 1211.

The Decorated and Perpendicular styles

The development of complicated tracery is one of the chief characteristics of the **Decorated** style, ushered in by Westminster Abbey and by the Angel Choir at Lincoln and the nave of Lichfield, both designed in the late 1250s. The fully blown Decorated style emerged around the end of the thirteenth century and the beginning of the fourteenth, when the cathedral at **Exeter** was almost completely rebuilt, with a dense exuberance of rib vaulting and multiple moulding on the arches and piers. **York Minster**, rebuilt from 1225 and the largest of all English Gothic churches, introduced another innovation associated with this period – **lierne vaulting**, whereby a subsidiary, mainly ornamental, rib is added to the roof complex. Intricately carved roof bosses and capitals are other common features of Decorated Gothic, as is the use of the organic **ogee curve** – ie a curve with a double bend in it. One-off experiments are also characteristic of this period, the most striking examples being the octagonal lantern tower at **Ely** (1320s), and the rebuilding of **Bristol** cathedral (1298–1330), which shows many of the features of the continental hall-church type of design, in which the nave and aisles are roughly the same height.

The style that came to prevail in the second half of the fourteenth century, the severe **Perpendicular**, was the first post-Conquest architecture that was unique to England. This insularity was due partly to the loss of almost all the English possessions in France by the end of the Hundred Years War, and partly to the Black Death, which had depleted the number of craftsmen capable of the elaborate carvings and mouldings characteristic of the Decorated style. Whereas France had progressed to an emphatically curvilinear or "Flamboyant" style, the emphasis in England was on rectilinear design, anticipated in the rebuilding of **Gloucester Cathedral** (1337–57). Here the cloister features the first fully developed **fan vault** while the massive east window is a good example of the new window design, in which the maximization of light is paramount and the tracery organized in vertical compartments. Edward II's tomb – the focal point of Gloucester cathedral – also exemplifies the wave of **memorial building** during the Perpendicular period.

The chantry tombs at **Winchester Cathedral** and **Tewkesbury Abbey** are resplendent monuments from this period, as is the tomb of the Black Prince in **Canterbury Cathedral**, where the Norman nave was rebuilt after 1379, though it was the addition of the Bell Harry Tower and tracery in the aisle windows that injected the most strongly Perpendicular elements. Henry Yevele, who was responsible for this work at Canterbury, and his contemporary at

Winchester, William Wynford, were forerunners of the modern architect, reflecting the gradual elevation of the master-mason into an overall creative and supervisory role.

The turmoil of the Wars of the Roses meant that few new "prestige" buildings were commissioned in the half-century after 1425, though parish churches eagerly embraced the new style, most notably in East Anglia, Somerset and the Cotswolds. The restoration of strong government saw a resurgence of royal patronage and the realization of a triad of major architectural projects in **St George's Chapel**, Windsor, **King's College Chapel**, Cambridge, and **Henry VII's Chapel** in Westminster Abbey, all completed in the reign of Henry VII. By now, walls had become panelled screens filled mostly with stained glass, with the weight transmitted from stone ribs onto bold buttresses that were usually capped with tall pinnacles. King's College developed fan vaulting into an element that extended over the whole nave and harmonized with the windows and wall panelling, but it was the densely sculptured Henry VII's Chapel that took such vaulting to the limit, the complexity heightened by a lavish use of decorative pendants – a rare element in English design.

The Renaissance

Perpendicular motifs remained prominent throughout the Tudor era, with the impact of **Renaissance** architecture confined initially to small decorative features. Such were the terracotta busts of Roman emperors at the otherwise conventionally Tudor **Hampton Court Palace**, to which Henry VIII added a Great Hall with a superb hammer-beam roof similar to that in Westminster Hall (1397–99), albeit here embellished with Italianate details.

The dissemination of the latest ideas in design and decoration came about chiefly through commissions from high-ranking courtiers and statesmen. These notables flamboyantly demonstrated their acquaintance with the sophisticated classical canons in such mansions as **Burghley House**, Lincolnshire (1552–87), and **Longleat**, Wiltshire (1568–80), projects which mingled the Gothic and the Renaissance while also heralding a taste for landscaped parklands in preference to enclosed courtyards. (With Henry VIII's Dissolution of the Monasteries some twenty to thirty percent of England's land was suddenly released into private hands.) The mason at Longleat, Robert Smythson, was probably also the designer of **Hardwick Hall** in Derbyshire (1591–96), celebrated in local rhyme as "Hardwick Hall, more glass than wall" – words which sum up the predilection for huge glazed areas displayed in Elizabethan great houses.

Hatfield House in Hertfordshire, rebuilt 1607–11 by the chief minister of Elizabeth and James I, Robert Cecil, represents a bridge between Elizabethan and Jacobean architecture, which is characterized by a greater infusion of classical ideas. Classicism at this time, however, was considered primarily decorative, as exemplified in the Tower of the Five Orders (1613–18) at the **Bodleian Library** in Oxford, where the Classical Orders as defined by Vitruvius were applied as appendages to a building with mullioned windows, battlements and pinnacles. The unadulterated spirit of the Renaissance did not find full expression in England until **Inigo Jones** (1573–1652) began to apply the lessons learned from his visits to Italy, and in particular from his familiarity with Palladio's rules of proportion and symmetry, as laid out in the Quattro Libri dell'Architettura, published in 1570. Appointed Royal Surveyor to James I in

1615 (a position he held also under Charles I), Jones changed the direction of English architecture with only a handful of works, in which he brilliantly adapted Palladian ideals to English requirements. Three of his most prominent projects were built in London: the **Banqueting House** in Whitehall (1619–22), the first truly classical building to be completed in England since Roman times; the **Queen's House** at Greenwich (1617–35); and **St Paul's Church**, Covent Garden (1630s), the focal point of the first planned city square in England.

Wren and Baroque

Despite Jones's promulgation of classical architecture, the Gothic endured into the seventeenth century, especially in Oxford, where Christ Church was given a magnificent fan-vaulted staircase hall as late as 1640. Oxford's first classical construction, the **Sheldonian Theatre**, was also the first building designed by the artistic heir of Inigo Jones, **Christopher Wren** (1632–1723), who established himself as a brilliant mathematician and astronomer before turning to architecture shortly after the Restoration of 1660. As far as is known, Wren never visited Italy (though he met Bernini, the greatest architect of the day, in Paris), and his work was never so wholeheartedly Italianate as that of Inigo Jones, the influences of French and Dutch architecture contributing to an eclectic style that mingled orthodox classicism with **Baroque** inventiveness.

Wren's work in Oxford was quickly followed by Pembroke College Chapel, Cambridge, but the bulk of his achievement is to be seen in London, where the **Great Fire of 1666** led to a commission for the building of 53 churches. The most striking of these buildings display a remarkable elegance and harmony within the constraints of very cramped sites; they include **St Bride** in Fleet Street, **St Mary-le-Bow** in Cheapside, **St Vedast** in Foster Lane, and, perhaps the finest of all, the domed **St Stephen Walbrook** alongside Mansion House – all of which were rebuilt after partial destruction in World War II. Most monumental of all was Wren's rebuilding of **St Paul's Cathedral** (1675–1710), which was built in a cruciform shape very different from his original radical design, though its principal feature – the massive central dome – was retained.

As Surveyor-General, Wren also rebuilt, extended or altered several royal palaces, including the south and east wings of **Hampton Court** (1689–1700). Other secular works include **Chelsea Hospital** (1682–92), **Trinity College Library**, Cambridge (1676–84), the **Tom Tower of Christ Church**, Oxford (1681–82) – a rare work in the Gothic mode – and, grandest of all, **Greenwich Hospital** (1694–98), a magnificent foil to the Queen's House built by Inigo Jones, and to Wren's own Royal Observatory (1675).

Work at Greenwich Hospital was continued by Wren's only major pupil, **Nicholas Hawksmoor** (1661–1736), whose distinctively muscular form of the Baroque style is seen to best effect in his London churches. Most of these are in the East End with the best being **St George-in-the-East** (1715–23) and **Christ Church**, Spitalfields (1723–29). His exercises in Gothic pastiche included the western towers of **Westminster Abbey** (1734) and **All Souls College**, Oxford (1716–35), while the mausoleum at **Castle Howard** in Yorkshire (1729) shows close affinities with the Roman Baroque.

The third great English architect of the Baroque era was **John Vanbrugh**

(1664–1726), who was famed as a dramatist but lacked any architectural training when he was commissioned by the Earl of Carlisle to design a new country seat at **Castle Howard** (1699–1726). More flamboyant than either Hawksmoor or Wren – with both of whom he worked – Vanbrugh went on to design numerous other grandiose houses, of which the outstanding examples are the gargantuan **Blenheim Palace** (1705–20), the culminating point of English Baroque, and the fortress-like **Seaton Delaval**, not far from Newcastle upon Tyne (1720–28), a building which harks back to the architecture of medieval England.

Gibbs and Palladianism

In the field of church architecture, the most influential architect of the eighteenth century was **James Gibbs** (1682–1754), whose masterpiece, **St Martin-in-the-Fields** in London (1722–26), with its steeple sprouting above a pedimented portico, was widely imitated as a model of how to combine the classical with the Gothic. Gibbs was barred from royal commissions on account of his Catholic and Jacobite sympathies, but he worked at the two universities, designing Cambridge's **Senate House** (1722–30) and the **Fellows' Building** at King's College (1723–49), and Oxford's **Radcliffe Camera** (1737–49), a beautifully sited construction drawing heavily on Gibbs's knowledge of Roman styles. Gibbs was one of the very few architects of his generation to have studied in Italy, which had been cut off by war, but this situation changed when the Treaty of Utrecht (1713) opened up Europe to English aristocrats on the Grand Tour, as the self-educating long holiday on the continent became known. For architecture in England, the immediate result was a rebirth of the **Palladianism** introduced by Inigo Jones a century before, an orthodoxy that was to dominate secular architecture in eighteenth-century England.

The movement was championed by a Whig elite led by **Lord Burlington** (1694–1753), an enthusiastic patron of the arts whose own masterpiece was **Chiswick House** in London (1725), a domed villa closely modelled on Palladio's Villa Rotonda. Burlington collaborated with the decorator, garden designer and architect **William Kent** (1685–1748) in such stately piles as **Holkham Hall** in Norfolk (1734), whose imposing portico and ordered composition typify the break with Baroque dramatics. The third chief player in the return to Renaissance simplicity was **Colen Campbell** (1673–1729), author of the influential Vitruvius Britannicus (1715), a compilation of designs from which architects freely borrowed. Campbell worked closely with Burlington on such works as **Burlington House** in London (1718–19), though his best achievements were two country homes, Houghton Hall, Norfolk (1722), and Mereworth Castle, Kent (1723).

The Palladian idiom was further disseminated by such men as **John Wood** (1704–54), designer of Liverpool Town Hall (1749–54) but better known for the work he did in his native **Bath**, helping to transform the city into a paragon of town planning. His showpieces there are **Queen Square** (1729–36) and the **Circus** (1754), the latter completed by his son, **John Wood the Younger** (1728–81), who went on to design Bath's **Royal Crescent** (1767–74). The embellishment of Georgian Bath was furthered also by **Robert Adam** (1728–92), a Palladian who designed the town's **Pulteney Bridge** (1769–74). Adam's forte, however, was in the field of domestic architecture, especially in the designing of decorative interiors, where he showed himself to be the most versatile and refined architect of his day. His elaborate concoctions are best displayed in **Syon House** (1762–69) and **Osterley Park** (1761–80), both on the western outskirts of London, and **Kenwood** (1767–79) on the edge of Hampstead Heath, all epitomizing his scrupulous attention to detail as well as his dexterity at large-scale planning. Adam's chief rival was the more fastidious **William Chambers** (1723–96), whose masterpiece, **Somerset House** on London's Aldwych (1776–98), is an academic counterpoint to Adam's dashing originality.

Adam and Chambers competed in a highly active market whose chief patrons regarded themselves as belonging to the most cultivated class in the island's history. Undoubtedly they were among the wealthiest, spending vast sums of money not just on their houses but also on the grounds in which these houses stood. **Landscape gardening** was the quintessential English contribution to European culture in the eighteenth century, and its greatest exponent was **Capability Brown** (1716–83) – so-called because of his custom of assessing the "capabilities" of a landscape. All over England, Brown and his acolytes modified the estates of the landed gentry into "Picturesque" landscapes, an idealization of nature along the lines of the paintings of Poussin and Lorrain, often enhancing the view with a romantic "ruin" or some exotic structure such as a Chinese pagoda or Indian temple.

The nineteenth century

The greatest architect of the late eighteenth and early nineteenth centuries was **John Nash** (1752–1835), whose Picturesque country houses, built in collaboration with the landscapist Humphry Repton (1752–1818), represented just one aspect of his diverse repertoire. In this versatility Nash was typical of his time, though he is associated above all with the style favoured during the **Regency** of his friend the Prince of Wales (afterwards George IV), a decorous style that owed much to Chambers and Adam, making plentiful use of stucco. His strangest and best-known building was also a commission from the Prince – the orientalized Gothic palace known as the **Brighton Pavilion**. A prolific worker, Nash was responsible for much of the present-day appearance of such **resorts** as Brighton, Weymouth, Cheltenham, Clifton and Tunbridge Wells, as well as for numerous parts of the central **London** cityscape, including the **Haymarket Theatre** (1820), the church of **All Souls**, Langham Place (1822–25), **Clarence House** (1825) and **Carlton House Terrace** (1827). He also planned the layout of **Regent's Park** and **Regent's Street** in London (from 1811), and remodelled **Buckingham Palace** (1826–30), a project that foundered at the death of his patron.

Nash's contemporary, **Sir John Soane** (1753–1837), was more of an inventive antiquarian, his pared-down classical experiments presenting a serious-minded contrast to Nash's extrovert creations. Very little remains of his greatest masterpiece, the **Bank of England** (1788–1833), but his idiosyncratic style is well illustrated by two other buildings in London – his own home on **Lincoln's Inn Fields** (1812–13) and **Dulwich Art Gallery** (1811–14).

Classicism was soon challenged by a style that had been heralded as early as 1753, when the diarist and connoisseur Horace Walpole built **Strawberry Hill** near Twickenham, an ornate Gothic villa created at a time when everything

Gothic was despised by people of taste. Nash and other exponents of the Picturesque also dabbled in the Gothic, as a passion for romance and medievalism gained ground in literary and intellectual circles. In 1818, when Parliament voted a million pounds for the construction of new Anglican churches, the **Gothic Revival** got properly under way – two-thirds of the churches built under this Act were in a Gothic or near-Gothic style. Though many public buildings continued to draw on Renaissance, Greek or Roman architecture – eg the town halls of Birmingham and Leeds (1832–50 & 1853–58) – the status of neo-Gothic was confirmed when it was decided that the Houses of Parliament should be rebuilt in that style after the fire of 1834. The fact that the contract was given to **Sir Charles Barry** (1795–1860), designer of the classical Reform Club, shows how architects were expected to be masters of all fashions, although his collaborator on the project, **Augustus Welby Pugin** (1812–52), was to become the unswerving apostle of the neo-Gothic movement.

A crucial moment in the so-called "Battle of the Styles" came with the debate over the new government offices (now the Foreign Office) in **Whitehall** (1855–72), when the most eminent architect of the day, **Sir George Gilbert Scott** (1811–78), was instructed to replace his Gothic design with an Italian Renaissance one. On the other hand, Scott was able to give rein to his personal tastes in the extravaganzas of **St Pancras Station** (1868–74) and the **Albert Memorial** (1863–72), both based on his preferred Flemish and north Italian Gothic models. When the first English cathedral to be consecrated outside London since the Middle Ages was built at Truro (1880–1910), the approved design was a scholarly exercise in French-influenced Gothic; yet when it came to commissioning the Catholic **Westminster Cathedral** (1895–1903), what was chosen was a neo-Byzantine design.

Further enriching the variety of nineteenth-century architecture, numerous engineer-architects employed cast iron and other industrial materials in works as diverse as Isambard Kingdom Brunel's **Clifton Suspension Bridge** in Bristol (1829–64) and Joseph Paxton's glass and iron **Crystal Palace** (1851), erected in just six months and subsequently transferred from London's Hyde Park to the suburb of Sydenham, where it burned down in 1936. The potential of iron and glass was similarly exploited in **Newcastle Central Station** (1846–55), the first of a generation of monumental railway stations incorporating classical motifs and rib-vaulted iron roofs.

Rejection of these industrial technologies in favour of "traditional" materials such as brick, stone and timber was propounded by **John Ruskin** (1819–1900) and his disciple **William Morris** (1834–96), leader of the Arts and Crafts Movement, through which his ideas on the importance of honest handicraft and functionalism were put into practical effect. Morris was not himself an architect, but his work on the interior of his own home, the **Red House** in Bexley, Kent (1854), which was built from designs by Philip Webb (1831–1915), was to be immensely influential in its emphasis on the architect's obligation to design every aspect of the building.

Morris's insistence on total responsibility for the interior details as well as exterior appearance was echoed in the work of **Richard Norman Shaw** (1831–1912), whose redbrick, heavily gabled constructions – in a Dutch style reminiscent of the Queen Anne period – were widely imitated in central London. His best work is displayed in Swan House, Chelsea (1875), Albert Hall Mansions, Kensington (1879) – one of England's earliest apartment blocks – and in Bedford Park, west London (1877), the first of the capital's "garden suburbs".

Another architect to fall under the sway of the Arts and Crafts Movement was **Charles Voysey** (1851–1941), whose clean-cut cottages and houses eschewed all ostentation, depending rather on the meticulous and subtle use of local materials for their effect. The originality of Voysey's work and that of his contemporaries M.H. Baillie Scott (1865–1945) and Ernest Newton (1856–1922) was later debased by scores of speculative suburban builders, though not before their refreshingly simple style had found recognition first in Germany and then across the rest of Europe.

The twentieth century to the present

While the use of reinforced concrete and the modernist ideas of Le Corbusier, Walter Gropius and the Bauhaus were making ground on the Continent, and while the North American scene was being revolutionized by high-rise steel-frame buildings, England remained attached to a rather nostalgic aesthetic. The insularity of English architecture is typified by the career of **Sir Edwin Lutyens** (1869–1944), most of whose early works were country houses in the Arts and Crafts style. Later he moved through a succession of classicized styles, such as the elegantly Baroque mode that he dubbed "Wrenaissance" and a more sober neo-Georgianism that marked the beginning of a widespread Georgian Revival. However, perhaps his most striking achievements in England are the one-off **Castle Drogo** on Dartmoor (1910–30), the last of the great country houses, and the **Cenotaph** on London's Whitehall (1918), a masterpiece of stripped-down monumentalism.

The revivalist tendency prevailed throughout the early decades of the century, but an awareness of more radical architectural trends surfaced in isolated projects in the 1930s. One of these was **Senate House** in London's Bloomsbury (1932), designed by **Charles Holden** (1875–1960), who was also responsible for some of London's Underground stations, notably **Arnos Grove** (1932). Perhaps the most successful applications of the austere International Modern style were achieved by the **Tecton group**, led by the Russian immigrant Lubetkin, whose **Penguin Pool** in London Zoo (1934) is a witty demonstration of the plastic possibilities of concrete.

Yet general acceptance of modern style had to wait for the reforming atmosphere of the years immediately following World War II, and in particular for the 1951 **Festival of Britain** on London's South Bank, which showcased the latest technological marvels. Many of the festival pavilions were designed by **Basil Spence** (1907–76), whose best-known work was the replacement of the bombed **Coventry Cathedral**, incorporating defiantly modernist detail into a neo-Gothic structure (1951–59). The only architectural remnant of the Festival of Britain is the **Royal Festival Hall** (1949–51), an immensely practicable and handsome structure with a claim to be the best-loved modern building in the country. The site was later augmented by the addition of the far less attractive **National Theatre** (1967–77) by **Denys Lasdun** (1914–2001), a Tecton architect who remained true to the principles of the group.

The massive postwar rebuilding programme was conditioned by an acute housing crisis and severe financial constraints, so the emphasis was on the utilization of prefabricated technologies to get as many units built as quickly and as cheaply as possible, with little overall planning or consideration for the environment. The unpopularity of the ubiquitous tower blocks was aggravated by the insensitivity shown by speculative developers, who were given almost free rein in the construction of office buildings and shopping centres throughout the country – Plymouth, Southampton and Birmingham have especially hideous examples.

Some of the more interesting architecture of the 1960s was created at the new "redbrick" universities, notable examples being Spence's **Sussex University** at Brighton (1961) and Lasdun's **University of East Anglia** at Norwich (1963). Among the younger generation who designed some of their first works for the universities were **James Stirling** (1926–92) and **Norman Foster** (b. 1935), architects who, along with **Richard Rogers** (b. 1933), have found greater scope working abroad than in Britain. That said, Stirling's Postmodern extension for London's Tate Gallery (1989) was one of the more controversial projects of recent times, and Rogers' Lloyd's Building (1978–86) in London is a bold hi-tech display along the lines of his Pompidou Centre in Paris. Factory sites have provided Foster with several English contracts, though the building with the highest profile is his glass-tent terminal at London's **Stansted Airport** (1991). Significantly, state-funded buildings hardly feature in a list of recent architectural highspots, reflecting the last Tory government's (1979–1997) emphasis on the primacy of private enterprise and its concomitant neglect of public building.

Give or take the occasional prestige project, the present scene is stranded between a popular dislike for the modern and a general reluctance amongst architects to return to the architectural past. In this regard, the interventions of Prince Charles have not been helpful. Posing as the voice of common sense and jumbling this up with his role as a major landowner, the Prince has campaigned against architectural modernism, one of the results being a country-wide rash of modern office buildings with peculiar pastel-painted gables and other retrospective accoutrements. The most obvious repercussion, however, was in regard to the **Sainsbury Wing** (1991) at London's National Gallery, a commission which was eventually handed to Postmodernist supremos Robert Venturi and Denise Scott-Brown, who produced a safe pastiche of Neoclassicism. One up-and-coming architect, whose recent works have found critical acclaim – without royal blessing – is **Michael Hopkins**, who rose to prominence with his eye-catching Mound Stand for the Lord's Cricket Ground. He also pulled off a delicate balancing act at the **Glyndebourne Opera** House (1994), producing a generally well-liked wood-panelled auditorium, and his **Inland Revenue Headquarters** (1995) in Nottingham has also found favour with most observers; his latest work, Portcullis House (2001), has proven somewhat more controversial.

The century drew to a close with the most heated debate concerning the construction of the **Millennium Dome** on reclaimed Thames-side land in Woolwich. It was not so much Richard Rogers' design of this exhibition space, but the uninspiring exhibition itself combined with a gross overestimation of visitor numbers that saw this vast hemispherical plum pudding with elongated candles rapidly acquire "white elephant" status. The exhibition closed at the end of 2000, as had always been scheduled, and the future of the dome remains undecided. Less candescent debates have centred on Norman Foster's design of the **Greater London Assembly** building near Tower Bridge, whose transparent structure will bring a new meaning to "open government" on its completion.

Wildlife

Almost every part of England has a history of human settlement, a history that has had a profound effect on the country's wildlife, bequeathing a patchwork of woodland, heathland, meadowland and a miscellany of other habitats. An inventory of England's wildlife would run on for hundreds of pages, and there are plenty of specialized publications for those who want to get to grips with the subject. What follows is a general overview of the species to be found in England, with an emphasis on the way in which their habitats have evolved.

The history of the land

The English climate nowadays is mainly of the variety known as "Atlantic", being damp and relatively mild, although there are slight regional variations – the southwest has warmer summers for example, whereas Norfolk has a more "continental" climate, drier in summer, harsher in winter. The current climate is obviously a principal determinant of a country's wildlife, but it's essential to bear in mind that the history of its climate is every bit as important. However, the impact of the "greenhouse effect", which some believe is the cause of increased flooding in winter and drought in summer, and the practices of modern, large-scale agrobusinesses may quicken previously gradual transformations in the landscape and its occupants.

The crucial period was the easing of the last **Ice Age**, a process that began around 12,000 years ago, when trees from the warmer south – to which Britain was then attached by land – began to colonize the country. The first arrivals were **birches** and **Scots pine**, but hardwoods such as **oak**, **ash**, **lime** and **elm** eventually shaded them out, creating a tangled forest over all but the bleakest and wettest zones. Incidentally, the Scots pines that you see in England today are not wild specimens – they have all been planted. In certain upland areas some plants and animals survive as relics of the glacial period: an example is the mountain ringlet butterfly, which is found above the 1800ft contour in the Lake District and on some Scottish mountains but lives nowhere else in Britain.

The **beech** was the last of England's sixty or so native woody shrubs and trees to take root before the meltwater raised the sea level to form the English Channel. Other species, such as the sweet chestnut (introduced in Roman times), are by contrast evidence of the role that **human settlement** has played in changing the landscape. Indeed, no sooner was the Channel flooded than **Stone Age** farmers were crossing it with their domesticated animals. These first colonists created **grazing land** and fields for their corn crop by clearing the native woods, starting with the lighter wooded areas – the chalk downlands, gravel islands in river valleys, and the thinly wooded sandstones of the Pennines. The chalk downlands and the Pennines have been grazed ever since, with just the odd tree giving an indication that these open areas were once naturally wooded.

Clearance of the denser woodland on the heavier valley soils started in pre-Roman days and by medieval times most of the wildwood had gone, although some was maintained for supplies of heavy timber, firewood, poles and so on.

These **working woodlands** were often relics of the original wildwood, but other woodlands quickly grew on areas that were once open land, abandoned when whole villages were annihilated by plagues or some other catastrophe. There are also large areas of what's known as **wood pasture**, areas of rough unploughed land, dotted with trees that were usually pollarded – that is their branches were cut at head height out of reach of grazing deer and cattle. Even such ancient trees as Robin Hood's Major Oak in **Sherwood Forest** and the Knightwood Oak in the **New Forest** are old pollards. (Note, however, that the word "forest" does not necessarily denote woodland. The word originally signified land set aside by the Norman kings for their royal hunts. These forests could include woodland, but were just as likely to contain heath, moor or marsh – the New Forest is still a marvellous example of a forest that is not primarily wooded.)

For centuries on each side of the Roman occupation, **ploughland** was kept open, but there were always some fenced, hedged or walled **grazing paddocks**. By Tudor times there were already a large number of such fields, a trend which culminated with the Georgian and Victorian "enclosures" when almost all the remaining open land – ploughland as well as grazing – was divided into fields. Providing a perfect combination of shelter and light, similar to a woodland clearing, the field **hedges** offer a habitat to numerous species: songbirds such as the blackbird and thrush are found more often in hedges than elsewhere.

The **wetlands** of England have also been refashioned, with the medieval abbeys in particular draining swampy land to create fields across the Norfolk Fens, the Somerset levels, Romney Marsh and other coastal areas. Today only a few patches of bogland remain undrained, while few rivers have remained free of interference.

Modern problems and conservation

In the last forty years, the rural economy has been transformed by **intensive farming**, which has introduced a high degree of mechanization and chemical use. Many old woods, heaths and moors have been dug up and replanted with conifers, thereby eliminating their wild flowers and animal life. Most of the old pastures and meadows have been drained, ploughed and re-seeded with vigorous hybrid grasses; the grass is then cut young as silage rather than being left to grow long for hay, so wild flowers no longer have time to set seed, and the birds that used to nest in the grass – such as lapwings and snipe – have been driven out. The increased size of fields has eradicated many hedgerows, while ploughland is now regularly sprayed with insecticides, wiping out the food supply for numerous species – even rooks are far less common than they used to be. And of course thousands of acres have become factory sites, housing estates or transport routes, and although railway cuttings, canals, quarries and motorway verges can attract certain species, England's richest wildlife is now to be found in pockets of landscape that have escaped agribusiness.

Although many species have legal protection, this is difficult to police and there are numerous conditions to the protection offered, the main ones being the exclusion clauses for the practice of "good farming or forestry". The choicest habitats are protected as **Sites of Special Scientific Interest** (SSSI), but even here the landowners simply have to inform **English Nature** (the national conservation agency) if they are about to do something damaging, whereupon EN must try to buy them off. Only specific **nature reserves**, managed solely for the benefit of rare species and old established flora and fauna, can guarantee their survival. Fortunately, England has many such reserves, run by organizations as diverse as English Nature, local councils, the Royal Society for the Protection of Birds and a plethora of county wildlife trusts.

Wild flowers

It may seem paradoxical, but it was the traditional use of old habitats that created England's wealth of wild flowers. Chalk grassland, the habitat of yellow vetches, pinkish restharrow, blue bellflower and many wild orchids, is a typical example. This abundance of wild flowers is due partly to the lime in the soil, and partly to its impoverishment by centuries of **grazing** by sheep or rabbits – the poor soil prevents ranker plants from elbowing out the flowers, and any that do take root are quickly cropped short by the animals. The reason that many downland flanks are today developing patches of coarse grass and scrub is that grazing has ceased.

The artificial **fertilization** of downland and meadowland, by encouraging the growth of grasses, wipes out wild flowers almost as effectively as spraying a herbicide. Communities of pepper saxifrage, great burnet and adder's-tongue fern are all good indicators of old meadowland, but a consequence of modern high-tech farming is that many of the modest downland and meadowland flowers are now rare on farmland and are more likely to be observed on **roadside verges**. Indeed, the latter sometimes constitute a record of the botany lost from the ploughed and planted field on the other side of the fence. Sadly, these displaced species have no security here, their cramped populations being too small to guarantee survival after harsh summers or insect attacks. Hardly at risk, however, are the cow parsleys – in the plural since their massed ranks disguise a succession of different species. Originally growing in woodland glades, **cow parsleys** are now typical of English country lanes, and once again their presence is largely determined by human interference – ie by the intensity of trimming.

It's a similar story with **woodland flowers**, whose growth is encouraged by traditional **coppicing**, which regularly opens up the soil to the sun. Indeed the typical thick carpet of **bluebells** is as much due to coppicing as to the mild Atlantic climate, and masses of bluebells can often indicate an old wood, especially if backed by early purple orchids and wood anemones. **Snowdrop** woods are often indicative of the former presence of a monastery – a European flower with a natural range that ends in Normandy, the snowdrop was grown here to celebrate Candlemas in February, and quickly spread beyond the monastery walls. Of course, soil conditions and other natural factors are extremely influential too, resulting in different types of flower being found in different types of woodland. Thus some **beech woods** are famous for their white or purplish **helleborines** and other orchids; **ash woods**, which grow on limestone, are known for **lily of the valley** and the dusky red **bloody cranesbill**.

Ancient **ploughland** was distinguished by blue cornflower and yellow corn marigold, but only **poppies** seem able to survive modern farming. **Heathers** are characteristic of the bleak moorlands, where – in the very wet areas – you might also find the delicate flowers of **cranberry**, the brilliant yellow **bog asphodel** and the insect-trapping **sundew**. The higher zones of the Lake

District and Pennine hills might be as colourful as the Alpine slopes were it not for centuries of hard grazing, but white **mountain avens**, dusky **saxifrage** and pink **moss campion** can still be found on rock faces out of the reach of sheep. On **heathland**, but not moorland, heathers are often accompanied by yellow **broom** and **gorse**; but both share yellow **tormentil**, pink **lousewort** and dainty blue **harebell**.

English **wetland** and **water** plants have evolved from land-growing species, a kinship that's evident from the close resemblance of the white **water crowfoots** and the buttercups – only the **water lilies** have no surviving relatives on dry land. Among the most attractive wild flowers of these habitats are the gold **kingcup** – popular with Victorian botanists and thus often found in the vicinity of granges and rectories – and the **bogbean**, with its creamy pink-fringed petals. Pollution and disturbance are major threats to wetland plants, as is evident on the Norfolk Broads, where holiday craft have eradicated plants from all but a few lagoons.

Communities of wild flowers manage to flourish even in the seemingly harsh conditions of the **seashore**, none of them more colourful than the blue-tinted **sea holly** and the yellow **horned-poppy**, which grow out on the bare sand. A host of flowers grows on the back shore, where the sand is harder and broken shells add lime to the ground, while on the edges of salt marshes you'll come across **sea lavender**, **sea aster** and **thrift**, among a variety of other species.

Birds

The destruction of the countryside has had a severe impact on England's 130 resident **bird species** – even the ubiquitous blackbird perhaps totals only three million pairs, and these numbers can plummet in a harsh winter. **Seabirds** such as gannets, gulls, fulmars and cormorants safe on their offshore bolt holes are virtually the only species unaffected by increasing urbanization. Nonetheless, an extraordinary variety of birds still thrives on mainland England.

Some birds are uniquely adapted to live with certain trees – such as the crossbill, which has a beak that has evolved to prise open fir cones – but in general, **woodland birds** select their habitat according to the profile of the wood rather than the actual species of tree it contains. Thus an acre of dense oak wood may hold more than a dozen types of songbird, while in the more open beech wood only the **wood warbler** is likely to nest. The **nightingale**, found only in the south of England, prefers the low bushy growth of recently coppiced woods, which it abandons seven years after the cut – another example of the link between land use and wildlife.

Over the centuries some species have become typical of the **farmed countryside**, such as the **rook**, **linnet**, **bunting** and the **barn owl**, which was encouraged to nest in barns as a rat catcher – often a hole was left in a side wall for the bird to enter. A recent arrival is the **collared dove**, which first nested in England in 1955, and is partial to the spills of grain from barley farms. The **pheasant**, originally raised and released for sport, now breeds wild in large numbers.

Game birds are a case apart, however, and their control can be an influence on the countryside. Shooting woods are often landscaped to steer pheasants into the line of fire, while belts of weed are now being left around fields to sustain **partridges**. The August **grouse** shoot has an effect on moorland, as large areas of heather are burnt to encourage fresh green growth to feed the birds.

Numerous species are adapted to specific environments, such as the **freshwater** birds, which split into two general groups – the **dipper** and a few other species that like the rushing upland streams, and the larger group that includes the "diving" and "dabbling" **ducks** found on lowland waters.

Birds that are found in every type of habitat are the opportunistic **scavengers** such as the **crow**, which is now so widespread that its "natural" home is not known. Persecution is sometimes a key factor in the distribution of scavengers and **raptors**. For instance, a couple of hundred years of shotguns and gamekeeping have forced the **golden eagle** back to one or two pairs in the Lake District, whilst the once common **red kite** has been pushed out to Wales. Similarly, peregrines, the bane of pigeon-racers' lives, are now found only on remote moors and sea cliffs and even **buzzards** are far from numerous.

Migrants are a key feature of English birdlife. **Swifts**, **swallows** and **martins** are easy to spot at the start of the summer, and of course the **cuckoo** has a distinctive call, as does the **chiffchaff**, an even earlier arrival from the south, with an unmistakable song that gives it its name. Many birds retreat from the cold of the Arctic to winter here, common examples including the **brent goose**, **barnacle goose**, **whooper swan** and **Bewick's swan**. Just as many species stop off on longer winter journeys to rest and feed, with English estuaries often safeguarding European stocks – the Dee for example regularly feeds hundred-thousand-strong flocks of **grey plover**, **oystercatcher** and numerous other waders.

Migration can be a relatively local affair, however. The **curlew**, a wader with a particularly plaintive cry, nests on the moors of the Pennines and elsewhere but in winter flies down to the seashore. The **kingfisher** similarly forsakes the frozen streams for the coast. English birds are surprisingly mobile in winter too, when hedgerow blackbirds often fly far afield in search of food and even blue tits, which might seem to have a range not much bigger than a back garden, may well fly daily miles across a county.

Mammals

Most of England's **mammals** are originally **woodland** species that moved into the territory during the period when the wildwood became established. There have been some changes since then, of course: the wolf and bear have gone, as has the beaver, which has left just a memory of its presence in the name of Beverley and a few other town names. The wildcat has left England for Scotland, but the **pine marten** is holding its own, thanks to the massive spread of conifer plantations.

There have been changes of habitat too: the **red deer**, for example, forced out of the woodlands by coppicing, is now found wild on open upland such as the Lake District, the herds seen in forests and parks being semi-domesticated. The **fallow deer** was brought over by the Romans and became a favourite target for the baronial hunt. The native **roe deer**, hunted almost to extinction two hundred years ago, was reintroduced, and is now the deer most often seen in the open countryside, although like all deer species they are shy and usually active only around dawn and dusk. **Sika deer**, rather smaller than red deer, were introduced in the seventeenth century, while the pig-like **muntjac** and small **Chinese water deer** are more recent arrivals, descended from wildlife park escapees. Other mammalian oddities are the goats living wild in the Lake District, the semi-wild ponies of the New Forest and Dartmoor and the wallabies that bounce around the Peak District.

Badgers link the woodlands and more open terrain, preferring to dig their burrows (or setts) among trees, though their foraging trails run out into the fields where they dig for young rabbits and earthworms. The sett entrance is a wide, clean hole – if you see a sizeable burrow littered with food remnants, the odds are that you're looking at a **fox's** "earth". Badgers and foxes are associated with darkness, but it's likely their nocturnal activities are a human-influenced modification – foxes are often active during daylight hours in areas where they feel safe (you can even see them in suburban gardens), and badgers forage by day in quiet places such as remote coastal valleys. However, the **dormouse** – a species recognized by its squirrel-like tail – is a truly nocturnal animal, and one of the few true indigenous hibernators. It is typical of hazel coppice, building its nest from the bark of the honeysuckle that is usually found growing here – peeled stems can be the clue to its presence.

The **grey squirrel**, one of the most familiar English "wild" animals, is an introduction from North America that has virtually ousted the native red squirrel – though there's evidence that a strain of super-resilient red is fighting back in the Merseyside area. **Hares** are native – the brown hare found in the lowlands, the grey in some Pennine areas – but the **rabbit** was introduced in Norman times to be raised for its meat and fur. Having escaped and bred relentlessly, the rabbit has for centuries been a natural lawnmower, helping to create the fine sward of the chalk downlands and other grasslands.

Rabbits are preyed on by **stoats** and **weasels**, which also prey on **mice**, **voles** and **shrews**. These similar small species may share some larders, but generally do not compete with each other for food: bank voles, for example, eat seeds, field voles eat grass, and the sharp-nosed shrew has a mainly insect diet and is almost ceaselessly active, needing to eat its own weight every day. Like the blue cornflower, the **harvest mouse** has fled the modern arable fields, now making its nest high amongst the reedbeds of waterways. Of the purely wetland species, the **water rat** (in fact a vole) is widespread and the otter is making a comeback in a few areas, despite water pollution and disturbance to its nesting "holts". The otter also has a serious competitor in the **mink**, a species escaped from fur farms but well equipped to survive in the wild, being capable of swimming after fish and climbing up to birds' nests.

On the coast, **common seals** haul out on the mud flats of the Wash to give birth in June, whereas **grey seals** are more common on rocky coasts, where they give birth in noisy "rookeries" in December. Only decades ago, almost every seaside resort used to boast its "own" **porpoises** or **dolphins**; such semi-resident animals have largely disappeared from the bays, although visitors are sometimes seen, and the occasional whale might swim up one of the larger estuaries.

In built-up areas, in addition to **foxes** and **hedgehogs**, **bats** are a familiar sight at dusk. Contrary to myth, they rarely nest in belfries (with their sensitive hearing, the bells would drive them demented), preferring the warm roof-spaces and cladding of modern houses.

Reptiles, fish and insects

For the **adder** (England's only venomous species) and **grass snake**, deserted railway cuttings offer a palatable replacement for more natural habitats – the latter is especially fond of wet places. Things are more difficult for the **smooth snake**, which is totally reliant on fragmented heathland and is therefore now comparatively rare – the same is true of the **sand lizard**. The **common lizard** has fared better. The clearance of field ponds means that springtime frog spawn is harder to find – the modern **frog** stronghold is in fact the garden pond. **Common toads** rely more on ancestral breeding ponds, to which they travel miles: some local conservation groups even organize toad patrols at key road crossings. The scuttling **natterjack toad** is also rare, restricted to a few sand dunes and similar sites. **Newts** are most obvious in spring – like the other amphibians they tend to spend most of the year hidden away on land.

The most natural of the fish populations are those of the classic game fish, the native **brown trout** and **salmon**, the first still plentiful in the downland streams of the south and the mountain streams of the north, the latter migratory and nowadays only common in the tumbling northern rivers. England's coarse fish – all freshwater species unrelated to the salmon family – have widely interbred with specimens raised in reservoirs and farms for sport; similarly the American rainbow trout, once found only in commercial pens, has escaped to breed wild in some areas. That other famed migrator, the **eel**, is still caught in numbers in the Somerset levels and in the East Anglian fens.

There are over three thousand different species of beetle in England – but few are noticed apart from the sizeable **may bug** and **stag beetle**, both most common near old semi-natural oak woods in the south. Bees, flies, gnats and wasps are of course very widespread, as are the dazzling **mayflies** and **dragonflies**, to be found on England's cleaner bodies of water. Many species of **butterfly** are fairly widespread in scrubby places, with the gorgeous **peacock butterfly** often seen in gardens. Deserted railway cuttings are a stronghold of some of the commoner **browns** and **skippers**. Generally, though, butterflies are choosy about the plants on which they lay their eggs, which means that many species are closely linked with very specific habitats. The **Adonis** and **chalkhill blues** need the low-growing horsehoe vetch of old downland, while the **fritillaries** need the violets of old oak woodland and the most exotic of all, the **swallowtail**, relies on a relative of cow parsley that grows in the Norfolk Broads, and is thus rarely seen elsewhere. However, some swallowtails may fly in from France during the summer, when the migrant **clouded yellow** often arrives in large numbers along the south coast.

Books

Most of the books listed below are in print and in paperback – those that are out of print (o/p) should be easy to track down in second-hand book shops. Publishers are detailed with the British publisher first, separated by an oblique slash from the US publisher, where both exist. Where books are published in only one of these countries, UK or US precedes the publisher's name; where the book is published by the same company in both countries, the name of the company appears just once.

Finally, while we recommend all those we've listed below, we do have our favourites: we've indicated those that we particularly recommend with a star.

Travel and journals

★ **Bill Bryson**, *Notes from a Small Island* (Black Swan/Avon). Bryson's best-selling and highly amusing account of his farewell journey round Britain.

William Cobbett, *Rural Rides* (UK Penguin). First published in 1830, Cobbett's account of his various fact-finding tours bemoaned the death of the old rural England and its ways while decrying both the growth of cities and the iniquities suffered by the exploited urban poor.

★ **Nick Danziger**, *Danziger's Britain* (Flamingo/Trafalgar Square). A well-timed journey through the "other Britain" of council estates and poverty. Captures the mood of the underclass created by Thatcher and sets a tall order for the present Blairite administration.

Daniel Defoe, *Tour through the Whole Island of Great Britain* (o/p). Classic travelogue, opening a window onto Britain in the 1720s.

John Hillaby, *Journey Through Britain* (UK Constable). An account of an epic 1,100 mile walk from Lands End to John O'Groats encapsulates much of the state of the country (and countryside) in the late 1960s.

Charles Jennings, *Up North* (UK Abacus). A provocative, but very readable account of a journey round the north of England, by a self-confessed southerner.

H.V. Morton, *In Search of London* (UK Methuen). Snapshots of London life in the 1920s.

Samuel Pepys, *The Diary of Samuel Pepys* (HarperCollins). Pepys kept a voluminous diary from 1660 until 1669, recording the fall of the Commonwealth, the Restoration, the Great Plague and the Great Fire, as well as describing the daily life of the nation's capital. The unabridged version is published in eleven weighty tomes; Fontana has published an abridged version.

J.B. Priestley, *English Journey* (o/p). Quirky account of Bradford-born author's travels around England in the 1930s.

Jonathan Raban, *Coasting* (UK Picador). Trip around the coast of England, with the occasional trip ashore in order to make supercilious remarks about the locals.

Paul Theroux, *The Kingdom by the Sea* (Penguin). Thoroughly bad-tempered critique of a depressed and drizzly nation.

Dorothy Wordsworth, *The Grasmere Journals* (UK Oxford University Press). Engaging diaries of William's sister, with whom he shared Dove Cottage in the Lake District.

History, society and politics

Julian Barnes, *Letters from London: 1990–1995* (Picador/Vintage). Social and cultural commentary from this New Yorker column, covering the fall of Thatcher and the emergence of Blair.

Venerable Bede, *Ecclesiastical History of the English People* (Penguin). First-ever English history, written in seventh-century Northumbria.

⭐ Asa Briggs, *Social History of England* (UK Penguin). Immensely accessible overview of English life from Roman times to the 1980s.

Beatrix Campbell, *Diana, Princess of Wales: How sexual politics shook the monarchy* (UK Women's Press). A little hastily written perhaps, but still the most penetrating insight into the life and times of Diana – and the appalling callousness of her in-laws. Read this and you'll never want Charles to be king (if you ever wanted a king at all).

Alan Clark, *Diaries* (UK Phoenix). Candid, conceited and often cutting insight into the heart of Thatcher's government by this controversial former minister. Easily the most interesting of the barrow loads of political memoirs churned out in the 1980s and 1990s.

Friedrich Engels, *The Condition of the Working Class in England* (Penguin). Portrait of life in England's hellish industrial towns, written in 1844 when Engels was only 24.

Gretchen Gerzina, *Black England* (UK Allison & Busby). An interesting study of the role of Black people in Britain's history.

Mark Girouard, *Life in the English Country House* (Yale University Press). Fascinating documentation of day-to-day existence with the landed gentry; packed with the sort of facts that get left out by tour guides.

Christopher Hill, *The English Revolution* (UK Caliban); *The World Turned Upside-Down* (Penguin). Britain's foremost Marxist historian, Hill is without doubt the most interesting writer on the Civil War and Commonwealth period.

Eric Hobsbawm, *Industry and Empire* (Penguin/New Press). Ostensibly an economic history of Britain from 1750 to the late 1960s charting Britain's decline and fall as a world power, Hobsbawm's great skill lies in detailed analysis of the effects on ordinary people.

⭐ W.G. Hoskins, *The Making of the English Landscape* (UK Penguin). Absorbing account of the changing English countryside from pre-Roman times to the present day.

Will Hutton, *The State We're In* (UK Vintage). One of the most influential books to be published in the last decade offered both an incisive analysis of British society and a virtual manifesto for an incoming Labour government.

Arthur Marwick, *British Society since 1945* (UK Cassell). Readable social history, taking you up to the late 1980s.

Brian Moynahan, *The British Century* (UK Seven Dials). A lavish coffee-table book telling the story of the twentieth century in black-and-white photographs.

★ George Orwell, *The Road to Wigan Pier, Down and Out in Paris and London* (both Penguin/Harvest). *Wigan Pier* depicts the effects of the Great Depression on the industrial communities of Lancashire and Yorkshire; *Down and Out* is Orwell's tramp's-eye view of the world, written with first-hand experience – the London section is particularly harrowing.

Sheila Rowbotham, *Hidden from History* (UK Pluto). An uncompromising account of the last 300 years of women's oppression in Britain alongside a cogent analysis of the ways in which key female figures have been written out of history.

W.A. Speck, *A Concise History of Britain* (Cambridge University Press). Straightforward political history from 1707 to 1975.

★ A.J.P. Taylor, *English History 1914–45* (Oxford University Press). Thought-provoking survey from Britain's finest populist historian.

★ E.P. Thompson, *The Making of the English Working Class* (Penguin/Random House). A seminal text – essential reading for anyone who wants to understand the fabric of British society.

G.M. Trevelyan, *English Social History* (UK Penguin). A "history of people with the politics left out" in Trevelyan's own words – liberal social history from Chaucer to 1901.

Regional guides

Paul Bailey (ed), *Oxford Book of London* (o/p). Typically authoritative Oxford anthology of writings, observations and opinions about the capital.

Andrew Davies, *The People's Guide to London* (o/p). An alternative history of central London and its landmarks, focusing on the ordinary people involved.

Christopher Hibbert (ed), *Pimlico County History Guides* (o/p). An informative series giving a detailed history of selected English counties. Counties covered include Bedfordshire, Cambridgeshire, Dorset, Lincolnshire, Norfolk, Oxfordshire, Somerset (with Bath and Bristol), Suffolk and Sussex.

Daphne du Maurier, *Vanishing Cornwall* (UK Penguin). Good overall account of Cornwall from an author who lived most of her life there.

Jan Morris, *Oxford* (OUP). Adulatory but inspiring collection on Oxford by the famous travel writer and city-phile.

Alan Myers, *Myers's Literary Guide: Writers in the North East* (UK Carcanet). Exhaustive account of the Northeast's literary heritage, including details of any writer who ever spent any time in the region.

★ A. Wainwright, *A Coast to Coast Walk* (Michael Joseph). Beautiful palm-sized guide book by acclaimed English hiker and Lake District expert. Printed from his handwritten notes and sketched maps. Also in the series are seven authoritative books covering a variety of walks and climbs in the Lake District. Not all are available in the US.

Ben Weinreb and Christopher Hibbert, *The London Encyclopaedia* (UK Papermac). More than a thousand pages of concisely presented and well-illustrated information on London past and present – the most fascinating single book on the capital.

Gilbert White, *Natural History of Selborne* (UK Penguin). Masterpiece of nature writing, observing the seasons in a Hampshire village.

Pathfinder Walks (Jarrold and Ordnance Suvey/Seven Hills). Series of practical guides with maps and route descriptions to popular outdoor spots such as the Yorkshire Dales, Chilterns, Cornwall and Cotswolds.

Art, architecture and archeology

Nicholas Best and Jason Hawkes, *Historic Britain from the Air* (UK Orion). Beautiful aerial photos illustrate this geographical overview of Britain from Roman times to the aftermath of the Blitz.

Richard Bisgrove, *The National Trust Book of the English Garden* (o/p). Excellent socio-cultural-botanical history, making the best introduction to the subject.

Robert Harbison, *Shell Guide to English Parish Churches* (o/p). Refreshingly opinionated and lushly illustrated survey of some of England's finest buildings.

Samantha Hardingham, *London: A guide to recent architecture* (Ellipsis/Knickerbocker). A handy pocket-sized book detailing the best of the capital's modern buildings.

Andrew Hayes, *Archaeology of the British Isles* (o/p). Useful introduction to the subject from Stone Age caves to early medieval settlements.

Thomas Packenham, *Meetings With Remarkable Trees* (Orion/Random House). Unusual but intriguing large-format picture book about the author's favourite sixty trees, delving into their character as much as the botany.

*****Nikolaus Pevsner**, *The Englishness of English Art* (UK Penguin). Wide-ranging romp through English art concentrating on Hogarth, Reynolds, Blake and Constable, including a section on the Perpendicular style and landscape gardening.

Pevsner and others, *The Buildings of England* (UK Penguin). Magisterial series, at least one volume per county, covering just about every inhabitable structure in the country. This project was initially a one-man show, but later authors have revised Pevsner's text, inserting newer buildings but generally respecting the founder's personal tone.

T.W. Potter, *Roman Britain* (British Museum Press/Harvard University Press). Generously illustrated account of Roman occupation written by the British Museum's own curators.

Literature classics

Jane Austen, *Pride and Prejudice*; *Sense and Sensibility*; *Emma* and *Persuasion* (all Penguin). All-time classics on manners, society and the pursuit of the happy ever after; all laced with bathos and ironic plot twists.

R.D. Blackmore, *Lorna Doone* (Oxford University Press). Blackmore's swashbuckling, melodramatic romance, set on Exmoor, has done more for West Country tourism than anything else since.

James Boswell, *The Life of Samuel Johnson* (Oxford University Press/Viking). England's most famous man of letters and pioneer dictionary-maker has his engagingly low-life Scottish biographer to thank for the longevity of his reputation.

Charlotte Brontë, *Jane Eyre* (Penguin). Deep and harrowing and quietly feminist story of a much put-upon governess.

Emily Brontë, *Wuthering Heights* (Penguin). The ultimate bodice-ripper, complete with volcanic passions, craggy landscapes, ghostly presences and gloomy Calvinist villagers.

John Bunyan, *Pilgrim's Progress* (Penguin/Oxford University Press). Simple, allegorical tale of hero Christian's struggle to achieve salvation; a staple read for the masses until the onset of agnosticism this century.

Samuel Butler, *The Way of All Flesh* (Penguin/Modern Library). Popular Edwardian novel debunking orthodox Victorian pieties, partly set in Nottinghamshire.

Geoffrey Chaucer, *Canterbury Tales* (Penguin). Fourteenth-century collection of bawdy verse tales told during a pilgrimage to Becket's shrine at Canterbury and translated into modern English blank verse.

Daniel Defoe, *Journal of a Plague Year* (Oxford University Press). An account of the Great Plague seen through the eyes of an East End saddler and written some sixty years after the event.

Charles Dickens, *Bleak House*; *David Copperfield*; *Little Dorritt*; *Oliver Twist*; *Hard Times* (all Penguin). Many of Dickens' novels are set in London, including *Bleak House*, *Oliver Twist* and *Little Dorritt*, which contain some of his most trenchant pieces of social analysis; *Hard Times*, however, is set in a Lancashire mill town, while *David Copperfield* draws on Dickens' own unhappy experiences as a boy, with much of the action taking place in Kent and Norfolk.

George Eliot, *Scenes of Clerical Life* (Penguin/Prometheus); *Middlemarch*; *Mill on the Floss* (both Penguin). Eliot (real name Mary Ann Evans) wrote mostly about the county of her birth, Warwickshire, setting for the three depressing tales from her fictional debut, *Scenes of Clerical Life*. *Middlemarch* is a gargantuan portrayal of English provincial life prior to the Reform Act of 1832, while *Mill on the Floss* is based on her own childhood experiences.

Henry Fielding, *Tom Jones* (Penguin). Mock-epic comic novel detailing the exploits of its lusty orphan-hero, set in Somerset and London.

Elizabeth Gaskell, *Sylvia's Lovers*; *Mary Barton* (Penguin/Oxford University Press). *Sylvia's Lovers* is set in a Whitby (Monkshaven in the novel) beset by press gangs, while *Mary Barton* takes place in

Manchester and has strong Chartist undertones.

Thomas Hardy, *Far from the Madding Crowd; The Mayor of Casterbridge; Tess of the D'Urbervilles; Jude the Obscure* (all Penguin). Hardy's novels contain some famously evocative descriptions of his native Dorset, but at the time of their publication it was Hardy's defiance of conventional pieties that attracted most attention: *Tess*, in which the heroine has a baby out of wedlock and commits murder, shocked his contemporaries, while his bleakest novel, the Oxford-set *Jude the Obscure*, provoked such a violent response that Hardy gave up novel-writing altogether.

Jerome K. Jerome, *Three Men in a Boat* (Penguin/Tor Books). Light-hearted accident-prone paddle on the River Thames.

Rudyard Kipling, *Stalky & Co* (Oxford University Press). Nine stories about a mischievous trio of schoolboys, drawn from Kipling's experiences of public school in Devon.

Sir Thomas Malory, *La Morte d'Arthur* (Penguin/Modern Library). Fifteenth-century tales of King Arthur and the Knights of the Round Table, written while the author was in London's Newgate Prison.

Thomas De Quincey, *Confessions of an English Opium Eater* (Penguin). Tripping out with the most famous literary drug-taker after Coleridge – *Fear and Loathing in Las Vegas* it isn't, but neither is this a simple cautionary tale.

William Shakespeare, *Complete Works* (Oxford University Press). The entire output at a bargain price. For individual plays, you can't beat the Arden Shakespeare series, each volume containing illuminating notes and good introductory essays.

Lawrence Sterne, *Tristram Shandy* (Penguin). Anarchic, picaresque eighteenth-century ramblings based on life in a small English village, and full of bizarre textual devices – like an all-black page in mourning for one of the characters.

William Makepeace Thackeray, *Vanity Fair* (Penguin). A sceptical but compassionate overview of English capitalist society by one of the leading realists of the mid-nineteenth century.

Anthony Trollope, *Barchester Towers* (Penguin). The "Barsetshire" novels, of which Barchester Towers is the best known, are set in and around a fictional version of Salisbury. John Major's favourite author.

Izaak Walton, *Compleat Angler* (Oxford University Press/Modern Library). Light-hearted seventeenth-century fishing guide set on London's River Lea, sprinkled with poems and songs, which has gone through more reprints than any other comparable book in the English language.

Modern works

Kate Atkinson, *Behind the Scenes At the Museum* (Black Swan/Picador). Amusing, lucid and highly engaging saga about an extended Yorkshire family.

Peter Ackroyd, *English Music* (UK Penguin). A typical Ackroyd novel, constructing parallels between interwar London and distant epochs to conjure a kaleidoscopic vision of

English culture. His other novels, such as *Chatterton*, *Hawksmoor* and *The House of Doctor Dee* (all Penguin), are variations on his pre-occupation with the English psyche's darker depths.

Kingsley Amis, *Lucky Jim* (Penguin). Difficult to believe that an establishment figure like Amis was once one of the "Angry Young Men" of the 1950s. Lucky Jim, the novel that made him famous, is hilariously funny in the opinion of many.

Martin Amis, *London Fields* (Vintage). "Ferociously witty, scabrously scatological and balefully satirical" observation of low-life London, or pretentious drivel from literary London's favourite bad boy, depending on your viewpoint.

Arnold Bennett, *Anna of the Five Towns*; *Clayhanger* trilogy (both UK Penguin). Bennett's first novel, *Anna* is the story of a miser's daughter and, like the later *Clayhanger* trilogy, is set in the Potteries.

★ **Joseph Conrad**, *The Secret Agent* (Penguin/Oxford University Press). Spy story based on the 1906 anarchist bombing of Greenwich Observatory, exposing the hypocrisies of both the police and anarchists.

Helen Fielding, *Bridget Jones's Diary* (Picador/Penguin). Originating as a newspaper column, Fielding's fictional account of contemporary female "neuroses" proved to be the literary phenomenon of the late 1990s, spawning a host of lesser imitators.

Ford Madox Ford, *Parade's End* (UK Penguin). One of the great unread masterpieces of English literature, this evocation of the passing of old Tory England in the aftermath of World War I is superb.

E.M. Forster, *Howard's End* (Penguin). Bourgeois angst in Hertfordshire and Shropshire; the best book by one of the country's best-loved modern novelists.

John Fowles, *The Collector*; *The French Lieutenant's Woman* (both Vintage/Back Bay); *Daniel Martin* (UK Vintage). *The Collector*, Fowles' first, is a psychological thriller in which the heroine is kidnapped by a psychotic pools-winner, the story being told once by each protagonist. *The French Lieutenant's Woman*, set in Lyme Regis on the Dorset coast, is a tricksy neo-Victorian novel with a famous DIY ending. *Daniel Martin* is a dense, realistic novel set in postwar Britain.

Stella Gibbons, *Cold Comfort Farm* (Penguin). Merciless parody of primitivist rural fiction of the type popularized by the likes of Mary Webb.

William Golding, *The Spire* (Faber & Faber/Harvest). Atmospheric novel centred on the building of a cathedral spire, taking place in a thinly disguised medieval Salisbury.

Robert Graves, *Goodbye to All That* (UK Penguin). Horrific and wryly humorous memoirs of boarding school and World War I trenches, followed by postwar trauma and life in Wales, Oxford and Egypt.

★ **Graham Greene**, *Brighton Rock*; *The Human Factor*; and *The Heart of the Matter* (all Penguin). Three of the best from the prolific Greene: *Brighton Rock* is a melancholic thriller with heavy Catholic overtones, set in the criminal underworld of a seaside resort; *The Human Factor*, written some forty years later, probes the underworld of London's spies; while *The Heart of the Matter* is a searching and very English novel that noses round the Anglo-Catholic mind.

Nick Hornby, *High Fidelity* (Penguin /Riverhead). Hornby made his name with *Fever Pitch*, an autobiographical account of his obsession with Arsenal FC from teenage years to 30-something. *High Fidelity* is a fictionalized account of another obsession – records and record collecting – and examines the modern male and his foibles with caustic incision.

A.E. Housman, *A Shropshire Lad* (UK Penguin). Collection of bucolic and love poems, popular for their lyrical gloom and idealized vision of the English countryside.

D.H. Lawrence, *Sons and Lovers; The Rainbow; Women in Love; Selected Short Stories* (all Penguin). Before he got his funny ideas about sex and became all messianic, Lawrence wrote magnificent prose on daily working-class life in Nottinghamshire's pit villages – or rather his vision of it. His interpretation never went down well with the locals and even now his name can raise a snarl or two. Lawrence's early short stories contain some of his finest writing, as does the early *Sons and Lovers*, a fraught, autobiographical novel. With *The Rainbow* and *Women in Love*, his other two major novels, the loopy sub-Nietzschean theorizing slowly gains the upper hand.

Laurie Lee, *Cider with Rosie* (UK Penguin). Reminiscences of adolescent bucolic frolics in the Cotswolds during the 1920s.

★ **Ian McEwan**, *Atonement* (Cape/Doubleday). McEwan's ninth novel and possibly his most masterful yet, tracing the course of three lives from a sweltering country garden in 1935 to seeking absolution in the new century.

Somerset Maugham, *Liza of Lambeth* (o/p); *Of Human Bondage* (US Bantam). Maugham considered himself a "second-rater" but these books are packed with vivid local colour: *Liza of Lambeth* is a depiction of Cockney low-life; *Of Human Bondage* is set in Whitstable and Canterbury and based on Maugham's own experiences as an orphan.

Daphne du Maurier, *Frenchman's Creek* (UK Arrow); *Jamaica Inn* (Arrow/Avon); *Rebecca* (Arrow /Avon). Nail-biting, swashbuckling romantic novels set in the author's adopted home of Cornwall.

Alan Sillitoe, *Saturday Night and Sunday Morning* (UK Flamingo). Gritty account of factory life and sexual shenanigans in Nottingham in the late 1950s.

Iain Sinclair, *Downriver* (UK Vintage). A rambling, fictional journey through contemporary London.

David Storey, *This Sporting Life* (UK Vintage); *Saville* (UK Vintage). Storey's first novel, *This Sporting Life*, is a grimly realistic portrayal of a Rugby League player in the north of England. *Saville*, which won him the Booker Prize, revolves around his favourite themes of mid-life crisis and loss of class identity.

Graham Swift, *Waterland* and *Last Orders* (Picador/Vintage). *Waterland* is a family saga set in East Anglia's fenlands – excellent on the history and appeal of this superficially drab landscape. Booker-Prize-winning *Last Orders* reminisces with four old folk on a trip to the south coast to scatter a friend's ashes.

Adam Thorpe, *Ulverton* (UK Vintage). Imaginative re-creation of life in a small town in southwest England over the course of three centuries.

Evelyn Waugh, *Sword of Honour* trilogy (UK Penguin); *Brideshead*

Revisited (Penguin/Little, Brown). The trilogy is essentially a light-weight remake of Ford's *Parade's End*, albeit laced with some of Waugh's funniest set-pieces. The best-selling *Brideshead Revisited* is possibly his least likeable work, rank with snobbery, nostalgia and money-worship.

★ **Virginia Woolf**, *Orlando*; *Mrs Dalloway* (both Penguin/Harvest). Woolf's lover, Vita Sackville-West, is the model for *Orlando*, whose life spans four centuries and both genders. *Mrs Dalloway*, which relates the thoughts of a London society hostess and a shell-shocked war veteran, sees Woolf's "stream of consciousness" style in full flow.

Anthologies

English Mystery Plays, ed. Peter Happe (Penguin). These simple Christian tales were produced annually in Chester, York, Wakefield and other great English towns, and are often revived even now.

Four English Comedies, ed. J.M. Morrell (Penguin). Laugh a minute from Congreve, Jonson, Goldsmith and Sheridan.

Landmarks of Modern British Drama, ed. Roger Cornish and Violet Ketels (o/p). The 1960s volume features plays by Wesker, Osborne, Pinter and Orton; the 1970s volume covers the likes of Ayckbourn, Brenton, Stoppard and Caryl Churchill.

Literature of Renaissance England, ed. Hollander and Kermode (Oxford University Press). Spenser's *Faerie Queene*, a bit of Marlowe, Shakespeare's Sonnets, Donne, Jonson and Milton.

Modern British Literature, ed. Hollander and Kermode (Oxford University Press). Weighted towards the classic writers of the earlier part of the century – Hardy, Conrad, Lawrence etc.

★ **The New Penguin Book of English Verse**, ed. Paul Keegan (Penguin). Seven hundred years of English poetry, listed chronologically rather than by author – a simple innovation, but startlingly effective.

The New Poetry, ed. Hulse, Kennedy & Morley (UK Bloodaxe). Over fifty poets, all born since World War II.

The Restoration and the Eighteenth Century, ed. Martin Price (Oxford University Press). From Dryden, Swift and Pope to Sterne.

Victorian Prose and Poetry, ed. Trilling & Bloom (Oxford University Press). Carlyle, Ruskin, Tennyson, Rossetti and Wilde's *Ballad of Reading Gaol*.

Film

For much of its history the British film industry has largely been an English affair, with its major studios (Ealing, Pinewood and Shepperton) not far from central London and its stars drawn from the ranks of the capital's stage. However, unlike the Hollywood star system, the English film industry tended and still significantly relies on strong ensemble playing. While Ealing's films were a by-word for social comedy, other significant elements have included the Hammer horror series (usually featuring one or both of Christopher Lee and Peter Cushing), costume dramas typified by the Gainsborough company's productions and the James Bond films, while the Carry On series kept a generation of comedy actors in work long past their sell-by date. In the 1960s, English films developed a justifiable reputation for social realism, which has been maintained in more recent times by directors such as Ken Loach and Mike Leigh.

Today's film industry is in a healthier state now than perhaps at any point since the 1930s with a diversity and vitality that reflects the dominance of independent productions. Some film fans might argue that the influence of television means that many such productions are essentially small-screen ventures, but within the last ten years a host of English pictures – *The Full Monty* and *Four Weddings and a Funeral* are just two examples – have enjoyed great success internationally.

The films listed below are all set in England. They are not exclusively greats – though some rank amongst the best movies ever made – but all depict a particular aspect of English life, whether reflecting the experience of immigrant communities, exploring the country's history, or depicting its richly varied landscapes.

The 1930s and 1940s

Brief Encounter (David Lean, 1945). Extra-marital attraction at a railway station is the theme of this mysteriously popular classic. Noel Coward is responsible for the clipped dialogue, Rachmaninov for the weepy score, Trevor Howard keeps his upper lip stiff and Celia Johnson wears an improbable hat.

Brighton Rock (John Boulting, 1947). A fine adaptation of Graham Greene's novel, featuring a young, genuinely scary Richard Attenborough as the psychopathic hood Pinkie, who marries a witness to one of his crimes to ensure her silence. Beautiful cinematography and good performances, with a real sense of *film noir* menace.

A Canterbury Tale (Michael Powell and Emeric Pressburger,

1944). Set in a wartime Kentish village, where a plucky land girl, a small-town GI and a sardonic English sergeant are billeted. Overseen by a mysterious local magistrate, they make their own pilgrimage to Canterbury, the cathedral glowing high over bomb-damaged streets. A mystical vision of English history is fused with bucolic images of rural life, a restrained exploration of the characters' personal suffering underlying a truly magical masterpiece.

Fires Were Started (Humphrey Jennings, 1943). One of the best films to come out of the prewar documentary tradition in Britain, this is the story of the experiences of a group of firemen through one night of bombing during the Blitz. The use of real firemen as performers rather than professional actors, and the avoidance of formulaic heroics, gives the film great power as an account of the courage of the ordinary people who fought, often uncelebrated, on the home front.

Henry V (Laurence Olivier, 1944). Featuring glowing Technicolor backdrops, this wonderful piece of wartime propaganda is emphatically "theatrical", the action spiralling out from the Globe Theatre itself. Olivier is a brilliantly charismatic king, the pre-battle scene where he goes disguised amongst his men being delicately muted and atmospheric.

Jane Eyre (Robert Stevenson, 1943). Joan Fontaine does a fine job of portraying Jane, and Orson Welles is a suavely sardonic Rochester, the scene where he is thrown from his horse in the mist achieving the perfect melodramatic pitch. With the unlikely tagline "A Love Story Every Woman Would Die a Thousand Deaths to Live!", it briefly features a young Elizabeth Taylor as dying Helen Burns.

Kind Hearts and Coronets (Robert Hamer, 1949). As with the best of the Ealing movies, this is a totally savage comedy on the cruel absurdities of the British class system. With increasing ingenuity, Dennis Price's suave and ruthless anti-hero murders his way through the d'Ascoyne clan (all brilliantly played by Alec Guinness) to claim the family title.

The Life and Death of Colonel Blimp (Michael Powell and Emeric Pressburger, 1943). An epic celebration of the oft-ridiculed romantic spirit of the English, personified by the wonderful Roger Livesey. We follow him through the actual and emotional duels of his youth, against his equally dashing German foe, to

crusty old age in World War II. A daring and visually stunning story of love and friendship, it was hated by Churchill for supposedly being unpatriotic, which is surely recommendation enough.

A Matter of Life and Death (Michael Powell and Emeric Pressburger, 1946). From the wartime golden age of British cinema, this remarkable fantasy opens with David Niven's airman miraculously surviving a fall from his stricken bomber. There follows a tussle between the monochrome bureaucracy of Heaven, who seek to reclaim him, and his fast-evolving Earth-bound love affair. Great performances and beautiful Technicolor images in another of Powell and Pressburger's enchanting romances.

The Private Life of Henry VIII (Alexander Korda, 1933). The film which catalysed a boom in British film-making thanks to the success of the gargantuan Charles Laughton in the title role has little now to commend it other than some superb cinematography and Laughton's own sometimes grotesque performance.

Rebecca (Alfred Hitchock, 1940). Hitchcock does Du Maurier: Laurence Olivier is wonderfully enigmatic as Maxim de Winter, and Joan Fontaine glows as his meek second wife, living in the shadow of her mysterious predecessor. Perfectly paced and beautifully shot, Hitch's first Hollywood picture is a true classic.

The Thirty-Nine Steps (Alfred Hitchcock, 1935). Hitchcock's best-loved British movie, full of wit and bold acts of derring-do. Robert Donat stars as innocent Richard Hannay, inadvertently caught up in a mysterious spy ring and forced to flee both the spies and the agents of Scotland Yard. In a typically perverse

Hitchcock touch, he spends a generous amount of time handcuffed to Madeleine Carroll, fleeing across the Scottish countryside, before the action returns to London for the film's great music-hall conclusion.

The Wicked Lady (Leslie Arliss, 1945). One of the best of Gainsborough Studios' series of escapist romances, this features a magnificently amoral and headstrong Margaret Lockwood, wooed to a criminal double life by James Mason's quintessentially dashing highwayman. Its opulent re-creation of eighteenth-century England is terribly appealing, as are the tempestuous entanglements of its two wayward stars.

1950 to 1970

Billy Liar! (John Schlesinger, 1963). Tom Courtenay is stuck in a dire job as an undertaker's clerk in a northern town, and spends his time creating extravagant fantasies. His life is lit up by the appearance of Julie Christie, who holds out the glamour and promise of swinging London. Touching and amusing.

Far From the Madding Crowd (John Schlesinger, 1967). A largely successful and imaginative adaptation of Hardy's doom-laden tale of the desires and ambitions of wilful Bathsheba Everdene. Julie Christie is a radiant and spirited Bathsheba, Terence Stamp flashes his blade to dynamic effect, Alan Bates is quietly charismatic as dependable Gabriel Oak, and the West Country setting is sparsely beautiful.

If... (Lindsay Anderson, 1968). The stifling world of the English public school as a rather inadequate microcosm of society. Malcolm McDowell plays our iconoclastic hero, leading his little cell in revolution against the arbitrary discipline and cruelty of the school hierarchy. Although beautifully shot and well realized in its own caricatural terms, it seems dated now and rather too narrowly of its time.

I'm Alright Jack (John and Roy Boulting, 1959). The best of The Boulting Brothers' comic explorations of English social mores explores the class system in the context of industrial unrest. Peter Sellers is on top form as the shop steward, while management is represented by a hapless Ian Carmichael (brought in to cause disruption through his own ineptitude) who, naturally, falls in love with Sellers' daughter.

Kes (Kenneth Loach, 1969). This is the unforgettable story of a neglected Yorkshire schoolboy who finds solace and liberation in training his kestrel. As a still pertinent commentary on poverty and an impoverished school system, it is bleak but idealistic, and pale and pinched David Bradley who plays Billy Casper is hugely affecting.

The Ladykillers (Alexander Mackendrick, 1955). Alec Guinness is fabulously toothy and malevolent as "Professor Marcus", a murderous conman who lodges with a sweet little old lady, Mrs Wilberforce. The professor and his ragbag of criminal accomplices – their sinister intent a hilarious counterpoint to Mrs Wilberforce's genteel tea parties – try to pass themselves off as musicians, while, thanks to her innocent interventions, the body count inexorably mounts. Features some evocative London streetscapes.

A Man For All Seasons (Fred Zinnemann, 1966). Sir Thomas More versus Henry VIII: one of British history's great moral confrontations made skilfully tedious by this film's stage-bound, talky origins in Robert Bolt's play. Despite muted, atmospheric visuals and a heavenly host of theatrical talent (including a cheering appearance by Orson Welles as Cardinal Wolsey), nothing can save this from paralysing dullness.

Night and the City (Jules Dassin, 1950). Great *film noir*, with Richard Widmark as an anxious nightclub hustler on the run. Gripping and convincingly sleazy, the London streetscapes have an expressionist edge of horror.

Performance (Nicolas Roeg/Donald Cammell, 1970). Credited with precipitating James Fox's breakdown and subsequent retirement from the movies, this shape-shifting tale of gangsters and pop culture is the best account of the hedonistic end to Britain's psychedelic 1960s. Well known for its strange drug-hazed second half, the film is also brilliantly funny in parts and should be cherished for its hilarious destruction of the myth of Kray-style criminals.

Saturday Night and Sunday Morning (Karel Reisz, 1960).

Reisz's monochrome captured all the grit and dead-end grind of Albert Finney's work in a Nottingham bicycle factory and his attempts to find spice and romance in the city's pubs and on its canal banks.

This Sporting Life (Lindsay Anderson, 1963). One of the key British films of the 1960s, *This Sporting Life* tells the story of a northern miner turned star player for his local rugby team. The young Richard Harris gives a great performance as the inarticulate anti-hero, able only to express himself through physical violence, and the film is one of the best examples of the gritty "kitchen sink" genre it helped to usher in.

The War Game (Peter Watkins, 1965). Watkins' astonishing documentary approach to the effects of a Russian nuclear attack on southeast England, using both local people and various official "talking heads", shocked its commissioner, the BBC, into refusing to show it; hardly surprising, since its overall effect was to question our trust in authority. Much-dated in comparison to modern computer-driven special effects, it still retains the power to alarm.

The 1970s and 1980s

Akenfield (Peter Hall, 1974). A powerfully involving evocation of English rural life whose ingredients include glowing cinematography and Michael Tippett's wonderful music. Past and present are skilfully contrasted, but the heart of the film lies in its sometimes ecstatic, but also harsh, rendering of the past.

Babylon (Franco Rosso, 1980). A moving account of black working-class London life. We follow the experiences of young Blue through a series of encounters that reveal the

insidious forces of racism at work in Britain. Good performances and a great reggae soundtrack: an all too rare example of Black Britain taking centre stage in British movies.

Chariots of Fire (Hugh Hudson, 1981). This hugely successful movie prompted writer Colin Welland to bombastically – and optimistically – proclaim, "The British are coming." Based around the 1924 Olympics, it tells the true story of Scottish missionary Eric Liddell (Ian Charleson) and repressed Cambridge student

Harold Abrahams (Ben Cross). Oscar-winning and overblown, it is distinguished only by Charleson's quiet performance, and some great locations, such as the sweeping beach at St Andrews in Scotland.

Comrades (Bill Douglas, 1986). In 1830s England, a group of farm workers decide to stand up to the exploitative tactics of the local landowner, and find themselves prosecuted and transported to Australia. Based on the true story of the Tolpuddle Martyrs, this combines political education (the founding of the modern union movement) with a moving and visually stunning celebration of working lives.

Distant Voices, Still Lives (Terence Davies, 1988). Beautifully realized autobiographical tale of growing up in Forties and Fifties Liverpool, juxtaposing contemporary popular songs with isolated scenes from the life of a family ruled by a brutal patriarch. The mesmeric pace is punctuated by astonishing moments of drama, and the whole is a very moving account of how the family survives and triumphs, in small ways, against the odds.

Frenzy (Alfred Hitchcock, 1972). Hitchcock comes back to Blighty in top form, with the story of a man on the run, under suspicion for the vicious "neck tie" murders carried out in Covent Garden. Trademark sly black humour combines with a disturbing exploration of sexual immaturity.

Get Carter (Mike Hodges, 1971). Although not the masterpiece some claim, this is still one of the most vivid and interesting British gangster movies, featuring a monumentally evil outing for Michael Caine as the eponymous villain, returning to his native Newcastle to avenge his brother's death. Great use of its

Newcastle locations and a fine turn by playwright John Osborne as the local godfather don't quite, however, compensate for its now faintly ridiculous misogyny.

Hope and Glory (John Boorman, 1987). A glorious autobiographical feature about the Blitz seen through the eyes of 9-year-old Bill, who revels in the liberating chaos of bombsite playgrounds, tumbling barrage balloons and shrapnel collections. His older sister's unfettered romps with a Canadian soldier and the adults' privation and occasional despair are an additional source of amusement for Bill and his tiny sister. Sentimental in the best sense, and deliciously nostalgic.

The Last of England (Derek Jarman, 1987). Derek Jarman was a genuine maverick presence in Eighties Britain; this is his most abstract account of the state of the nation. Composed of apparently unrelated shots of decaying London landscapes, rent boys and references to emblematic national events such as the Falklands War, this may not be to all tastes, but it is a fitting testament to a unique talent in British film making.

Letter to Brezhnev (Chris Bernard, 1986). Frank Clarke's screenplay about chicken factories, Russian sailors, drink, love and idealism proved a marvellous vehicle for his larger-than-life sister, Margi, and the more considered Alexandra Pigg.

The Long Good Friday (John MacKenzie, 1979). Despite a maniacal turn from Bob Hoskins as the East End gang boss threatened by powerful, mysterious new arrivals, this is not all it's cracked up to be. Its vision of East End villains seems self-indulgent and dated, and the plodding TV visual style doesn't help to raise the level.

Made in Britain (Alan Clarke, 1982). One of Alan Clarke's series of savage dissections of Eighties Britain, featuring a 17-year-old Tim Roth as skinhead Trevor on a downbeat odyssey of job-centre visits, drug-taking and racist explosions. The energy of the central performance, and the energy of the film making itself, transcend the worthy TV aesthetic and deliver a film of real force, and a very powerful indictment of Thatcher's Britain.

The Madness of King George (Nicholas Hytner, 1994). Adapted from an Alan Bennett play, this eighteenth-century royal romp has an irritating staginess, with the king's loopy antics played against a cartoon-like court and an England apparently devoid of real people.

Mona Lisa (Neil Jordan, 1986). This fine London-based thriller has powerful performances from Bob Hoskins, Michael Caine and then-newcomer Cathy Tyson, the latter playing a high-class prostitute who recruits Hoskins to help find her lost friend. This takes him, and us, on a nightmarish exploration of the dark side of Eighties London, lightened only slightly by an utterly convincing, poignant love story, as Bob

begins to fall for his beautiful employer.

My Beautiful Laundrette (Stephen Frears, 1985). A slice of Thatcher's Britain, with a young Asian, Omar, on the make, opening a ritzy laundrette. His lover, Johnny, is an ex-National Front glamour boy, angry and inarticulate when forced by the acquisitive Omar into a menial role in the laundrette. The racial, sexual and class dynamics of their relationship are closely observed, and mirror the tensions engendered by the Asian presence in a hostile London. Daring, unexpected and funny, with a wonderful performance from Daniel Day-Lewis as Johnny.

Withnail and I (Bruce Robinson, 1986). Richard E. Grant is superb as the raddled, drunken Withnail, an out-of-work actor with a penchant for drinking lighter fluid. Paul McGann is the "I" of the title – a bemused and beautiful spectator of Withnail's wild excesses, as they abandon an astonishingly grotty London flat for the wilds of a remote cottage, and the attentions of Withnail's randy uncle Monty. A rare look at the Sixties that avoids nostalgia, and opts instead for emotional truth.

The 1990s to the present

Bhaji on the Beach (Gurninder Chadha, 1993). An Asian women's group takes a day-trip to Blackpool in this issue-laden but enjoyable picture. A lot of fun is had contrasting the seamier side of British life with the mores of the Asian aunties, though the male characters are cartoon villains all.

Billy Elliot (Stephen Daldry, 2000). Set against the backdrop of the turbulent miners' strike of 1984, a young boy (Jamie Bell) is torn

between his unexpected love of dance and the disintegration of his family. A way out is offered when the local dancing teacher (Julie Walters) offers him a chance to train and even audition for the Royal Ballet School.

Brassed Off (Mark Herman, 1996). A pacy film about British working-class life that eschews pathos, opting instead for uncompromising anger, underscored by robust black humour. With the imminent demise of the town's coal pit, the future for the Grimley Colliery Brass Band looks hopeless. Danny (Pete Postlethwaite) valiantly attempts to keep the band alive as the emotional lives of the musicians collapse.

East is East (Damien O'Donnell, 1999). Seventies Salford is the setting for this lively comedy, with a Pakistani chip-shop owner struggling to keep control of his seven children as they rail against the strictures of Islam and arranged marriages. Inventively made, and with some pleasing performances.

Elizabeth (Shekahar Kapur, 1998). Charismatic Cate Blanchett is, thankfully, the still heart of this madly over-blown production, where all political and emotional nuance is lost in an orgy of decapitations, swirling cloaks and stagy thunderstorms. Features a host of plodding cameos with, most bizarrely, footballing heartthrob Eric Cantona as the French ambassador.

Enigma (Michael Apted, 2001). This blockbuster, scripted by playwright Tom Stoppard, is a fictional tale using Britain's war-time efforts to crack the Germans' Enigma encrypting machine as its backdrop.

The Full Monty (Peter Cattaneo, 1997). Six Sheffield ex-steel workers throw caution to the wind and become male strippers, their boast being that all will be revealed: the "full monty". Unpromising physical specimens all, they score an unlikely hit with the local lasses. The film was itself an unlikely hit worldwide: the theme of manhood in crisis is sensitively explored, and the long-awaited striptease is a joy to behold.

Howards End (James Ivory, 1991). E.M. Forster's tale of the forward-thinking Schlegel sisters, and their relationship with the conventional, domineering Wilcoxes. One of many immaculate British costume dramas, with precise performances from Vanessa Redgrave, Helena Bonham Carter and, most notably, Emma Thompson as Margaret Schlegel.

Little Voice (Mark Herman, 1998). Entertaining screen adaptation of Jim Cartwright's hit play about reclusive "Little Voice" (Jane Horrocks), who comes miraculously to life only on stage, brilliantly impersonating Fifties stars such as Marilyn Monroe. It features a great performance from Michael Caine as the impossibly seedy agent who seeks to exploit her bizarre talent, and offers a great glimpse of seaside England, with all its eccentric charm.

Lock, Stock and Two Smoking Barrels (Guy Ritchie, 1998). Four lads attempt to pay off gambling debts by making a drug deal in this over-stylized and rather shallow picture, which, though it has a modern setting, pays dubious homage to the London of the Kray twins. However, the suits are sharp, the production is slick and football's hardman turned actor Vinnie Jones turns in a surprisingly solid debut performance.

Mike Bassett: England Manager (Steve Barron, 2001). There have been few great films about football and this isn't one of them, but it's mildly successful and occasionally amusing in documenting the contemporary passion for the sport, thanks to Ricky Tomlinson in the title role.

Nil by Mouth (Gary Oldman, 1997). Features strong performances by Ray Winstone (Ray) as a boorish south Londoner and Kathy Burke (Valery) as his battered wife. A brave and bleak realist picture, which depicts Ray as a victim of his own violence, as well as the devastatingly vulnerable Valery. Brace yourself.

Notting Hill (Roger Michell, 1999). More smug, middle-class jollity from the writer (Richard Curtis) who brought you *Four Weddings and a Funeral* (1994). Grant reprises his bumbling floppy-haired Englishman role and falls for a glamorous American (Julia Roberts), again. It spans a year in the life of Notting Hill, perversely failing to feature the event for which this part of London is best known: the biggest and best street carnival in Europe.

Orlando (Sally Potter, 1992). Although modest in budget terms, this is a vivid and visually very beautiful adaptation of Virginia Woolf's novel, following its hero/heroine through 400 years of British history. Tilda Swinton is perfectly cast as the androgynous immortal, and choice moments spanning Elizabethan England to the present day (through the Civil War and Victoria's reign, for example) are perfectly and mysteriously realized.

The Remains of the Day (James Ivory, 1993). Kazuo Ishiguro's masterly study of social and personal repression translates beautifully to the big screen. Anthony Hopkins is the overly decorous butler who gradually becomes aware of his master's fascist connections, Emma Thompson the housekeeper who struggles to bring his real, deeply suppressed feelings to the surface.

Richard III (Richard Loncraine, 1995). A splendid film version of a renowned National Theatre production, which brilliantly transposed the action to a fascist state in the 1930s. The infernal political machinations of a snarling Ian McKellen as Richard are heightened by Nazi associations, and the style of the period imbues the film with the requisite glamour, as does languorously drugged Kristin Scott-Thomas as Lady Anne. Innovative use of some great London locations, with monumental Battersea Power Station the setting for the Battle of Bosworth.

Secrets and Lies (Mike Leigh, 1995). Much-loved Mike Leigh slice-of-life drama, with wonderful Timothy Spall at the head of a spectacularly dysfunctional London family. His sister Cynthia (Brenda Blethyn), her heart of gold buried in boozy, cloying unhappiness, is reunited with the black daughter she gave up for adoption at birth. With trademark over-long improvised sequences and a sharp eye for suburban vulgarity which comes uncomfortably close to parody, the film is lifted by stunning ensemble performances and sustained by the simple strength of its central tenet: that secrets and lies in a family will only cause unnecessary pain.

Sense and Sensibility (Ang Lee, 1995). Jane Austen's sprightly essay on the merits of well-modified behaviour is nicely realized by Lee, and neatly scripted by Emma Thompson. Thompson and Kate Winslet are charming as the downtrodden Dashwood sisters: Winslet is a brilliantly over-wrought, romantic Marianne, while Thompson turns in another perfect performance as prudent Elinor.

Shakespeare in Love (John Madden, 1998). This irresistible homage to life, love and Shakespeare has an energetic Joseph Fiennes as the quill-chewing bard and Gwyneth Paltrow as his sparky love interest. Sharply scripted by Tom Stoppard, it skips a dainty line between parody and over-reverence, and has fun sending up the British over-fondness for cameos, with Rupert Everett as melancholy Kit Marlowe, off on a one-way trip for a drink in Deptford. No mere piece of frivolity though, the film aspires to, and achieves, real feeling.

South West Nine (Richard Parry, 2001). A mildly energetic tale of Brixton street life (all drugs, guns, music, gangsters and hippies) which split the critics more than any other recent film.

Glossaries

Architectural terms

Aedicule Small decorative niche formed by two columns or pilasters supporting a pediment.

Aisle Clear space parallel to the nave, usually with lower ceiling than the nave.

Altar Table at which the Eucharist is celebrated, at the east end of the church. (When church is not aligned to the geographical east, the altar end is still referred to as the "east" end.)

Ambulatory Passage behind the chancel.

Apse The curved or polygonal east end of a church.

Arcade Row of arches on top of columns or piers, supporting a wall.

Ashlar Dressed building stone worked to a smooth finish.

Bailey Area enclosed by castle walls.

Baldachin Canopy over an altar.

Barbican Defensive structure built in front of main gate.

Barrel vault Continuous rounded vault, like a semi-cylinder.

Boss A decorative carving at the meeting point of the lines of a vault.

Box pew Form of church seating in which each row is enclosed by high, thin wooden panels.

Broach spire Octagonal spire rising straight out of a square tower.

Buttress Stone support for a wall; some buttresses are wholly attached to the wall, others take the form of an outer support with a connecting half-arch, known as a "flying buttress".

Capital Upper section of a column, usually carved.

Chancel Section of the church where the altar is located.

Chantry Small chapel in which masses were said for the soul of the person who financed its construction; none built after the reign of Henry VIII.

Choir Area in which the church service is conducted; next to or same as chancel.

Clerestory Upper storey of nave, containing a line of windows.

Coffering Regular recessed spaces set into a ceiling.

Corbel Jutting stone support, often carved.

Crenellations Battlements with square indentations.

Crossing The intersection of the nave and the transepts.

Decorated Middle Gothic style; about 1280–1380.

Dogtooth Form of early Gothic decorative stonework, looking like raised "X"s.

Dormer Window raised out of the main roof.

Early English First phase of Gothic architecture in England, about 1150–1280.

Fan vault Late Gothic form of vaulting, in which the area between walls and ceiling is covered with stone ribs in the shape of an open fan.

Finial Any decorated tip of an architectural feature.

Flushwork Kind of surface decoration in which tablets of white stone alternate with pieces of flint; very common in East Anglia.

Gallery A raised passageway.

Gargoyle Grotesque exterior carving, usually a decorative form of water spout.

Hammer beam Type of ceiling in which horizontal brackets support vertical struts that connect to the roof timbers.

Keep Main structure of a castle.

Lady Chapel Chapel dedicated to the Virgin, often found at the east end of major churches.

Lancet Tall, narrow and plain window.

Lantern Upper part of a dome or tower, often glazed.

Lunette Window or panel shaped like a half-moon.

Misericord Carved ledge below a tip-up seat, usually in choir stalls, as support when occupant stands.

Motte Mound on which a castle keep stands.

Mullion Vertical post between the panes of a window.

Nave The main part of the church to the west of the crossing.

Ogee Double curve; distinctive feature of Decorated style.

Oriel Projecting window.

Palladian Seventeenth- and Eighteenth-century classical style adhering to the principles of Andrea Palladio.

Pediment Triangular space above a window or doorway.

Perpendicular Late Gothic style, about 1380–1550.

Pier Massive column, often consisting of several fused smaller columns.

Pilaster Flat column set against a wall.

Reredos Painted or carved panel behind an altar.

Rood screen Wooden screen supporting a crucifix (or rood), separating the choir from the nave; few survived the Reformation.

Rose window Large circular window, divided into vaguely petal-shaped sections.
Sedilia Seats for the participants in the church service, usually on south side of the choir.
Stalls Seating for clergy in the choir area of a church.

Tracery Pattern formed by narrow bands of stone in a window or on a wall surface.
Transept Section of the main body of the church at right angles to the choir and nave.
Tympanum Panel over a doorway, often carved in medieval churches.
Vault Arched ceiling.

Anglo-American terms

Bill Restaurant check
Biscuit Cookie or a cracker
Bonnet Car hood
Boot Car trunk
Caravan Trailer
Car park Parking lot
Cheap Inexpensive
Chemist Pharmacist
Chips French fries
Coach Bus
Crisps Potato chips
Dual Carriageway Divided highway
Dustbin Trash can
First floor Second floor
Flat Apartment
Fortnight Two weeks
Ground floor First floor
Hire Rent
High Street Main Street
Jam Jelly
Jelly Jell-O
Jumble sale Yard sale
Jumper Sweater.
Lay-by Road shoulder

Leaflet Pamphlet
Lift Elevator
Lorry Truck
Motorway Highway
Off-licence Liquor store
Pants Underwear
Petrol Gasoline
Pudding Dessert
Queue Line
Return ticket Round-trip ticket
Roundabout Rotary interchange
Single carriageway Non-divided highway
Single ticket One-way ticket
Stalls Orchestra seats
Stone Fourteen pounds (weight)
Subway Pedestrian passageway
Sweets Candy
Tap Faucet
Tights Pantyhose
Torch Flashlight
Trainers Sneakers
Trousers Pants
Tube/Underground Subway (train)
Vest Undershirt

index
and small print

Index

Map entries are in colour

A

A La Ronde 437
Abbotsbury 300
accommodation 31–34
admission charges 40
Adrian Sankey's Glass
Works 828
Ainthorpe 977
Aira Force 849
airlines
  in Australia and New Zealand.
 14
  in Ireland 16
  in the US and Canada 12
Airton 909
Aisholt Common 422
Aldeburgh 549
Alfred the Great – supposed
  burial place of 541
Alfriston 222
Algakirk 719
Allen Valley 1015
Allendale 1016
Allenheads 1015
Allonby 862
Alnmouth 1064
Alnwick 1065
Alston 865
Altarnun 521
Althorp 713
Alton 277
Alton Towers 661
Alum Bay 269
Ambleside 828
Angle Tarn 848
Anglesey Abbey 596
Anne Hathaway's Cottage
 612
Anne of Cleves' House ..224
Appleby Horse Fair 864
Appleby-in-Westmorland
 864
Appledore 466
Appletree Bay 502
Appletreewick 906
Appuldurcombe House .267
Arbeia Roman Fort 1039
architectural terms 1135
architecture of England
 1098–1109
Arkengarthdale 924
Arlington Mill 365

Arncliffe 907
Arthur, King
  at Glastonbury 416
  mythology surrounding 514
  at Tintagel 513
Arts and Crafts Movement
 363
Arundel 238–240
Ascot, horse-racing 242
Ashbourne 669
Ashby St Ledgers 713
Ashby-de-la-Zouch 704
Ashness Bridge 843
Ashton Memorial 799
Askrigg 919
Aston 656
Atcham 643
Athelhampton House 296
Attingham Park 643
Auckland Castle 1008
Audley End 598
Austen, Jane
  at Bath 403, 407
  at Chawton 278
  at Lyme Regis 301
  at Winchester 273
Avebury 313
Ayot St Lawrence 355
Aysgarth 920

B

B&Bs 31
Bacon, Francis – on
  Shakespeare 608
Baedeker Raids 189
Baggy Point 464
Bainbridge 919
Bakewell 678
Balloon Festival,
  Northampton 711
Bamburgh 1069
bank holidays 40
banks 24
Bant's Carn 501
Barbondale 916
Barden Bridge 904
Barden Tower 904
Bardsea 856
Barnard Castle 1010
Barnstaple 462
Barrow-in-Furness 856
Baslow 678

bastle houses 1054
Bateman's 220
BATH 403–410

Bath 404
  Abbey 406
  accommodation 403
  arrival 403
  Assembly Rooms 407
  bars 409
  Building of Bath Museum .407
  cafés 409
  Circus, The 407
  clubs 409
  festivals 408, 409
  Great Pulteney Street 408
  Herschel Museum 407
  Holburne Museum 408
  Milsom Street 407
  Museum of Costume 407
  nightlife 409
  Paragon 407
  pubs 409
  Pulteney Bridge 407
  Pump Room 405
  restaurants 408
  Roman Baths 405
  Royal Crescent 407
  Royal Victoria Park 407
  Sydney Gardens 408
  theatre 410
  Theatre Royal 406
  tourist office 403
  Victorian Bath Boating Station
 408

Batsford Arboretum 366
Battle 216
BBC 39
beaches 46
Beachy Head 222
Beadnell 1067
Beady Pool 504
Beamish Museum 1008
Beast Cliff 983
Beatles, The 780
Beaulieu 284
Beck Hole 978
Becket, Thomas à –
  assassination and shrine
  of 189
Bedruthan Steps 510
beer 36
Beer 439
Belas Knap 372
Belgrave 702
Bellever Forest 456
Bellingham 1053
Belsay 1040

I

INDEX

Belstone Common........458
Belstone Tor.................458
Belton House................735
Bembridge 263
Bempton 960
Bennett, Arnold............665
Berkeley 382
Berkeley Castle.............382
Berry Head...................443
Berwick-upon-Tweed
.....................1073–1074
Beverley 957
Bewick, Thomas 1037
bibliography 1117–1125
Bibury............................365
Bideford 465
Bigbury-on-Sea 449
Bignor Roman Villa 240
Binchester Roman Fort
.....................................1009
Birdoswald Fort 869
Birkrigg Common..........856
BIRMINGHAM 647–659
Birmingham 648
  accommodation...............649
  arrival.............................649
  Aston..............................656
  Barber Institute of Fine Arts
 655
  bars................................657
  Birmingham and Fazeley
  canal...............................653
  Botanical Gardens 655
  Bournville 655
  Bull Ring 653
  Cannon Hill Park.............655
  Centenary Square............652
  Chamberlain Square.........651
  clubs...............................658
  Colmore Row 653
  comedy............................658
  Convention Centre............652
  Custard Factory 655
  dance..............................658
  Digbeth 654
  Edgbaston 655
  entertainment...................658
  Farmer's Bridge Locks......653
  Gas Street Basin...............652
  Handsworth 656
  ICC.................................652
  International Convention
    Centre............................652
  Jewellery Quarter..............655
  Midland Arts Centre..........655
  Minworth Greaves.............656
  Museum and Art Gallery...651
  music..............................658
  National Sea Life Centre...653
  nightlife 658
  Paradise Forum 652
  pubs................................657
  Repertory Theatre.............652
  restaurants 657

Rotunda 653
Royal Birmingham Society of
  Artists............................653
St Martin's Church............654
St Paul's Square 653
St Philip's Cathedral 653
Selly Manor 656
Soho House 656
theatre.............................658
tourist offices 649
Town Hall 651
transport 649
University 655
Victoria Square 651
Bishop Auckland............1008
Bishop's Castle 645
Bishops Lydeard...........421
Black Country 659–661
Black Middens Bastle
  House...........................1054
Black Sheep Brewery ...922
Blackburn.....................795
Blackgang Chine 268
Blackpool 789–793
Bladon Church..............348
Blake, Robert – birthplace
  of...................................419
Blakeney 568
Blakeney Point.............568
Blanchland 1016
Blandford Forum..........303
Blencathra....................842
Blenheim Palace...........348
Blickling Hall 567
Blisland 519
Bliss Tweed Mill 369
Blists Hill Victorian Town
 638
Bloody Assizes 419
Bloomsbury Group 227
Blue John Cavern 672
Bluebell Railway...........237
Blythburgh 554
Boadicea......................529
Bodiam Castle 219
Bodmin 517
Bodmin Moor...............519
Boggle Hole 983
Bolton 795
Bolton Abbey 904
Bolventor 519
Bonchurch 266
Bonfire Societies..........223
books...............1117–1125
Boot..............................846
Booth, Richard..............631
Border Forest Park 1056
Borrowdale 843
Boscastle 515
Boston 729
Bosworth, Battle of.......704

Boudicca......................529
Boughton House...........717
Boulby..........................990
Bournemouth.......284–286
Bournville 655
Bowder Stone...............843
Bowes 1012
Bowlees 1013
Bowness 824–826
Bowood House.............315
Box Hill 177
Bradda Head 812
Bradford 890–893
Bradford on Avon 315
Brading 264
Bragg, Melvyn – and the
  Lake District...............832
Brant Broughton 719
Brantwood 836
Branxton 1061
Breckland.............576–578
Bredon Hill 390
Breedon-on-the-Hill......705
Brendon Hills 472
Bretton 678
Brickfields Horse Country
 263
Bridgnorth 639
Bridgwater 419
Bridlington 960
Bridport........................300
Brierley Hill..................660
Brighstone 268
Brighton 227–236
Brighton 228
Brimham Rocks 931
Brinkburn Priory...........1059
BRISTOL 390–401
Bristol 392–393
  accommodation...............391
  Arnolfini arts centre 398
  arrival.............................391
  Ashton Court...................399
  at-Bristol 398
  bars................................400
  Brandon Hill Park.............395
  Bristol Harbour Railway....398
  British Empire and
    Commonwealth Museum
   397
  Broadmead......................396
  Cabot Tower 395
  cafés 400
  Castle.............................396
  Cathedral 394
  Chapel of the Three Kings of
    Cologne.........................396
  Christmas Steps 395
  City Museum and Art Gallery
   395
  Clifton 399
  Clifton Suspension Bridge..399

clubs 401
Corn Street 396
Foster's Almshouse 395
Harbourside 398
Llandoger Trow 396
Merchant Venturers'
  Almshouse.....................396
Old Station.......................397
pubs................................400
Quakers' Friars 396
Quayhead 398
Queen Square..................397
Red Lodge 395
restaurants 400
St Augustine's Reach 398
St Mary Redcliffe 397
St Peter's 396
St Stephen's 396
SS Great Britain...............398
SS Matthew 398
Theatre Royal...................397
tourist office 391
Watershed arts centre 398
Will Memorial Tower.........395
British Camp 623
Britten, Benjamin – life of
....550
Brixham..........................443
Brixworth.......................712
Broadlands.....................259
Broadstairs....................185
Brockenhurst 282
Brockhole Visitor Centre
....827
Brocolitia Fort 1050
Brompton Regis............472
Brontë Bridge...............896
Brontë Falls..................896
Brontës at Haworth 895
Brooke, Rupert – at
  Grantchester 596
Brougham Castle..........863
Broughton-in-Furness...857
Brown Willy 521
Brunel, Isambard Kingdom
.......................390, 398, 399
Bryher 503
Buckden........................908
Buckfast Abbey 458
Buckingham..................349
Buckland Abbey 453
Buckland-in-the-Moor ..457
Buckler's Hard 284
Bude..............................515
Budleigh Salterton 438
Buildwas Abbey............638
bunkhouses 33
Bunyan, John – at Bedford
....352
Burford..........................365
Burghley House 733
Burnham Market...........571

Burnham Thorpe...........571
Burnley..........................795
Burnsall.........................906
Burrator Reservoir 461
Burslem.........................665
Burton Constable Hall ..960
Burwash........................220
Bury 795
Bury St Edmunds 542–544
buses
  in England 28
  from Ireland....................18
  from mainland Europe 18
Butter Hill......................475
Butter Tubs 918
Buttermere.....................845
Buxton 670
Byland Abbey 967
Byrness.......................1057

C

C2C Cycle Route..........998
Cabot, John 398
cabs 31
Cadbury, John 655
Caer Caradoc 644
Caerhays Castle 483
cafés 35
Calbourne 268
Calf of Man 812
Calke Abbey 705
Cambo 1040
Camborne 506
CAMBRIDGE 581–596
Cambridge 582
  accommodation...............584
  arrival............................584
  bars 595
  Botanic Gardens.............593
  Bridge of Sighs 589
  cafés 594
  Castle............................590
  Christ's College..............591
  Clare Bridge 588
  Clare College 588
  Corpus Christi College 592
  Emmanuel College..........591
  entertainment.................595
  Fitzwilliam Museum 593
  Folk Museum..................590
  Gonville and Caius College
 588
  Jesus College 590
  Kettle's Yard 590
  King's College.................586
  King's Parade.................588
  Lion Yard 591
  Magdalene Bridge 590
  Magdalene College..........590

Market Hill......................588
Mathematical Bridge........592
Museum of Archeology and
  Anthropology 592
Museum of Zoology.........592
nightlife 595
Pembroke College 593
Pepys Building................590
Peterhouse.....................593
pubs...............................595
punting...........................591
Queens' College 592
restaurants 594
Round Church.................589
St Bene't's Church...........592
St Catherine's College.....592
St John's College.............589
St Mary's the Great..........588
Scott Polar Research Institute
 593
Sedgwick Geology Museum
 592
Senate House 588
Sidney Sussex College.....590
tourist office 584
Trinity College 588
Trinity Hall 588
Union Society 589
Whipple Museum of the
  History of Science 592
Wren Library 589
Camel Trail 511
Camelford 520
Campbell, Donald 835
camping 33
camping barns...............32
CAMRA 36
Canons Ashby 714
Canterbury 189–195
Canterbury....................190
Canute, King 1082
Cape Cornwall 496
car rental 30
Caractacus Stone 471
caravanning 33
Cardington 644
Cardinham Woods 518
Carisbrooke Castle 272
Carlisle 866–869
Carlyon Bay 482
Cartmel 853
Castle Acre 575
Castle Bolton 920
Castle Dore...................480
Castle Howard 953
Castle Rising 574
Castle Rushen 813
Castlegate House 847
Castlerigg Stone Circle.842
Castleton (Peak District)
 671
Castleton (Yorkshire).....977
Castletown....................813

Cat Bells 843
Caterway Heads 1017
Catrigg Force 912
Catstyte Cam 851
Cauldron Snout...........1014
Cawfields 1051
Cawsand......................453
Cawthorn Camps..........975
Cecil, William 733
Cerne Abbas.................304
Chagford 459
Chamberlain, Joseph – at
  Birmingham...............651
Channel Tunnel, the 203
Chapel Ford 458
Chapel-le-Dale..............916
Charlecote Park............613
Charles I – imprisonment at
  Carisbrooke Castle 272
Charles' Castle 502
Charleston Farmhouse .226
Charlestown.................482
Chartwell......................211
Chase End Hill 623
Chasms, The................813
Chastleton House 367
Chatham 181
Chatsworth House 680
Chatterton, Thomas......397
Chaucer, Geoffrey – and
  the Canterbury Tales..189
Chawton 278
Cheddar Gorge 413
Cheese Rolling Festival 377
Cheesewring, The.........522
Cheltenham 376–380
Cheltenham 378
chemists 22
Cherryburn..................1037
Cheshire Plain 771–774
Chesil Beach.................299
Chessington World of
  Adventures................177
Chester.................765–771
Chester 766
Chesterholm Museum
 1051
Chesters Roman Fort .1049
Chesters Walled Garden
 1049
Cheviot Hills................1059
Chichester 241–244
Chillingham Castle......1060
Chilterns, the 323–327
Chipping Campden.......370
Chipping Norton 369
Chollerford 1049
Christchurch 286
Church Stretton 644

Churchill, Winston
  birthplace of.....................348
  burial place of..................348
  at Chartwell.....................211
  maiden speech of............410
cider 36
cigarettes 51
Cinque Ports.................196
Cirencester 372–374
Cistercians, the 933
City Art Gallery (Leeds) ..884
City Art Gallery (Wakefield)
 885
Clacton-on-Sea 534
Clandon Park 174
Clapham 914
Claverton 410
Claydon House 350
Clearwell Caves 631
Cleeve Abbey................423
Clevedon.......................401
Cleveland Hills 977
Cleveland Way..............969
Cley-next-the-Sea 568
Clifton 399
Clifton Suspension Bridge
 399
Clitheroe........................796
Cliveden 327
Clouds Hill 290
Clovelly 467
Clumber Park...............697
Clun...............................645
coaches
  in England 28
  from Ireland......................18
  from mainland Europe 18
Coalbrookdale 636
Coates-by-Stow 724
Cobtree Museum of Kent
  Life 212
Cockermouth 847
Coggeshall 532
Colchester 529–532
Coleridge, Samuel Taylor
  and the Lake District 832
  at Nether Stowey 421
Combe Florey 421
Commonwealth Games
  2000 744
Conan Doyle, Arthur
  ....88, 457
Conishead Priory 856
Coniston 836
Coniston Water.............834
Constable Country 536–542
Constable, John –
  birthplace of.................537
Conygar Tower..............474
Cook Monument...........978

Cook, Captain
  birthplace of...................1020
  at Great Ayton.................977
Cookham 326
Cookson, Catherine 1039
Coombe Valley.............516
Corbridge....................1045
Corbridge Roman Site 1046
Corfe Castle.................291
Cornwall...............476–522
Corsham 315
Cosh 907
costs 24
Cotswold Falconry Centre
 366
Cotswold Olimpick Games
 370
Cotswolds, the 363–383
Cotswolds and Somerset
 362
Coughton Court............613
Countersett 919
Countisbury Hill 475
Covean..........................505
Coventry.............616–619
Cow Green Reservoir..1014
Cowes...........................271
Cowgill 917
Coxwold.......................966
Crackington Haven.......516
Crackpot 923
Cracoe 906
Crag Lough 1050
Cragside 1058
Crantock Bay 507
Craster.........................1067
Craven Museum 901
credit cards...................24
Crediton 463
Cregneash......................813
crime.............................47
Croft Castle...................633
Cromer 566
Cromwell's Castle 502
Cromwell, Oliver
  at Ely 579
  supposed resting place of......
 967
Crook O'Lune 799
Crookham 1062
Crooklets......................516
Cropton Forest.............975
Crowland 719
Croyde Bay 464
Crummock Water..........845
cuisine 34–37
Cunliffe, John...............823
currency 24
customs regulations 19
cycling 44–46

D

Daglingworth...............374
Dalby............................812
Dalby Forest.................976
Dalemain.....................863
Dales Way...................904
Dalton-in-Furness.........857
Dambusters 727
Danby..........................977
Danes' Dyke.................960
Darling, Grace.............1069
Darlington..................1018
Dartington Hall..............445
Dartmoor............454–462
Dartmoor National Park
.....................................**455**
Dartmouth....................446
Dawlish 441
De Quincey, Thomas – and
  the Lake District........832
Deal.............................197
debit cards....................24
Dedham 538
Deepdale......................916
Deerhurst 389
Defoe, Daniel – inspiration
  for Robinson Crusoe ..397
Delph Nine Locks 660
Dennington 547
Dent 916
Dentdale......................916
Derby 668
Derwent Reservoir 1017
Derwent Water 839
Devil's Punchbowl 176
Devizes 314
Devon 430–476
Devon and Cornwall
.....................................**428–429**
Diana, Princess of Wales
  burial place of 713
  family home of 713
  Harrods' memorial fountain to
 121
  at Kensington Palace.......119
  and the Royal Family 78
Dickens, Charles
  birthplace of....................255
  at Broadstairs 187
  in London.........................96
  at Rochester 179
  and the Yorkshire schools
 1012
Didsbury Botanical
  Gardens 756
Dimbola Lodge 269
directory enquiries........38
disabled travellers..........49
Diwali, Leicester...........702

Dodman Point..............483
Doom Bar.....................509
Dorchester 293–297
Dorking 177
Douglas...........805–808
Dove Cottage...............833
Dovedale......................669
Dover 198–202
Dover...........................**199**
Dover's Hill...................370
Doyden Point 512
Dozmary Pool 520
Dracula – association with
  Whitby.........................985
Dragon Hill 329
Drake, Sir Francis
  at Buckland Abbey 453
  life of 451
drinking 36
driving 29
drugs 51
Drusillas Park...............222
Duckpool......................516
Dudley..........................660
Dulverton 470
Duncombe Park...........968
Dungeness 205
Dunkery Beacon 471
Dunsford 459
Dunsop Bridge.............796
Dunstanburgh Castle...1067
Dunster 473
Dunt Valley 374
Duntisbourne Abbots....375
Duntisbourne Rouse.....375
Dunwich 551
Durdle Door 293
Durham 999–1007
Durham **1000**
Durlstone Head.............292
Duver 263
Duxford 596
Dyrham Park 410

E

Easby Abbey................925
Easington.....................959
East Anglia.................**526**
East Bergholt 537
East Lulworth 293
East Midlands.............**686**
East Portlemouth 448
Eastbourne 220–223
Easton..........................299
Eastwood......................693
eating out.............34–37

Ebberston 976
Ebbor Gorge 413
Eboracum 965
Edale............................674
Edale Cross 674
Eden Camp...................954
Eden Project 482
Eden Valley............862–866
Edensor........................680
Edgbaston 655
Edmundbyers.............1017
Edward the Confessor
  ....82, 1082
Eggelstone Abbey.......1011
Egton 977
Egton Bridge.................977
EH 40
Eleanor Cross 716
electricity......................51
Elgar, Sir Edward
  birthplace of....................622
  at Malvern Link 623
Elkstone.......................375
Ellerton Priory 924
Ellesmere Port Boat
  Museum 771
Elterwater.....................830
Elvedon 577
Ely 578–580
email 38
embassies
  British, abroad 19
  in England........................19
Embleton.....................1067
emergencies 22, 47
Engels, Friedrich – ashes of
 222
English Heritage............40
English phrases 1136
English Riviera 440–449
Epsom Downs, horse-racing
 242
Escomb......................1009
Esk Valley.....................976
Eskdale 846
Etal 1061
Eton.............................139
euro 24
Eurostar 16, 203
Eurotunnel.....................16
events...................41–43
Excalibur......................514
Exeter 431–437
Exeter **432–433**
Exford 471
Exmoor................469–476
Exmoor Forest 472
Exmouth.......................438
Eyam 676

F

Fairford...........................364
Falmouth.........................486
Falstone 1056
Farndale.........................972
Farne Islands 1068
Farnham 175
Fatherford Viaduct 458
Fawkes, Guy 938
Felbrigg Hall.................566
Fens
  Cambridgeshire 577
  Lincolnshire......................728
Fenton...........................665
ferries
  from Ireland.......................18
  to the Isle of Man............804
  to the Isles of Scilly 500
  to the Isle of Wight 261
  from mainland Europe .18, 199
festivals 41–43
Filey..............................961
films 1126–1134
Fishbourne Roman Palace
 244
Fistral Bay......................507
Flambards Theme Park
 489
Flamborough...................960
Flatford Mill 537
flights
  from Australia and New
    Zealand........................14
  from Ireland.......................16
  from the US and Canada....12
Flodden, Battle of 1061
flora and fauna 1110–1118
Folkestone 202
Fontwell Park, horse-racing
 242
food 34–37
Foolow 678
Ford.............................1061
Foreland.........................263
Foreland Point 475
Forest of Bowland 796
Forest of Dean 630
Forge Valley 976
Fort Amherst.................181
Fort Victoria Country Park
 270
Fortuneswell 299
Fotheringhay 716
Fountains Abbey...........933
Fowey 480
Fowles, John – at Lyme
  Regis.............................301
Foxup...........................907

Framlingham 547
Franklin, Benjamin – in
  London...........................98
Frenchman's Creek.......488
Frensham 176
Friars' Crag 843
Frinton-on-Sea..............534
Frome...........................410
Frosterley 1015
Furness Abbey..............857
Fusedale 848

G

Gainsborough 725
Gainsborough, Thomas
  birthplace of......................539
  works of 539
Gaping Ghyll 914
Garsdale 917
gay scene 50
Geddington 716
Gedney 731
Georgeham 463
Gibraltar Point nature
  reserve 728
Gibside.......................1036
Gilbert Memorial 517
Gillamoor 972
Glaisdale 977
Glastonbury 416–418
Glastonbury music festival
 417
Glebe Cliff 513
Glen Lyn Gorge............475
Glenridding 849
glossaries...................1135
Gloucester 383–387
Gloucester 384
Glyndebourne 226
Goathland 978
Godiva, Lady.................617
Godshill.........................267
Golant 480
Golden Hind.................443
Golitha Falls 520
Goodrich 629
Goodwood House 244
Goodwood Park, horse
  racing 243
Goodwood, Sculpture at
 246
Gordale Scar.................909
Goring 324
Gorran Haven 483
Gouthwaite Reservoir ...931
Gowbarrow Park...........849

Grand National..............786
Grange 843
Grange-over-Sands 852
Grantchester 596
Grantham 734
Grasmere 831
Grass Wood 906
Grassington 905
Great Ayton...................977
Great Bay......................504
Great Chalfield Manor ..316
Great Gable 844
Great Malvern 622
Great Shunner Fell........918
Great Tew......................369
Great Yarmouth.....564–565
Green Gable..................844
Greene King Brewery....543
Greenhead 1052
Greenhough 1054
Gribben Head 482
Grimspound 456
Grisedale Tarn...............852
Grizedale Forest............838
Grosmont 977
guest houses 32
Gugh 505
Guildford 172–174
Gunnerside 923
Gunpowder Plot...........714

H

Haddon Hall..................680
Haddon Hill 472
Hadleigh........................541
Hadrian's Wall..1043–1052
Hadrian's Wall............1044
Haig Colliery Mining
  Museum 860
Hailes Abbey.................372
Halangy Down 501
Hallaton.........................709
Halton Gill 907
Haltwhistle 1051
Hampsfell......................852
**Hampshire, Dorset and
  Wiltshire**.........250–251
Hampton Court.............139
Handel
  in London...........................87
  at St Mary Redcliffe, Bristol
 397
Handsworth 656
Hanley...........................665
Hanlith..........................909
Hanover Point 268

Hardknott Pass 846
Hardknott Roman Fort..846
Hardraw Force 918
Hardwick Hall.................694
Hardy, Thomas
    at Dorchester 293, 295
    life and works of 294
Hare Pie Scramble and
    Bottle Kicking.............709
Hareshaw Linn 1054
Harewood House..........886
Harnham 309
Harold – and the Battle of
    Hastings..............214, 216
Harome 970
Harrison, John 134
Harrison Stickle 831
Harrogate 927–929
Hartland Point...............467
Hartlepool 1021
Hartside Tope................865
Harwich.........................535
Hastings 214–216
Hatchlands Park 175
Hatfield.........................356
Hatfield House 356
Hathersage 675
Havenstreet...................263
Hawes...........................917
Hawk's Tor 519
Hawkridge Reservoir 422
Hawkshead 837
Haworth 894–897
Hawsker........................984
Hay-on-Wye..................631
Hayburn Wyke 982
Haydon Bridge.............1050
health 22
Heckington....................730
Helman Tor....................510
Helmsley 968–970
Helston..........................489
Helvellyn 851
Helwith Bridge 912
Hemmick Beach 483
Henley-on-Thames 324
Henna Cliff 516
Henry Moore Institute ...885
Henry VIII
    at Hampton Court............139
    at Whitehall.......................79
Hepworth, Barbara 497
Hereford 625–627
Herefordshire.......624–633
Hereward the Wake 578
heritage pass 41
Herne Bay 183
Herriott, James 964
Herstmonceaux 223
Hetton 906

Hever Castle 208
Hexham.......................1047
Hexhamshire Common
   1016
Heysham.......................802
HI 33
High Corn Museum 901
High Raise 848
Highclere Castle 279
Higher Tor 458
Higher Town.................503
hiking 43
Hill Inn 916
Hill Top 838
Hillaby, John 1043
Hillsford Bridge 475
Hindhead 176
history of England
   1079–1097
HMS Victory.................253
HMS Warrior 253
Hobbes, Thomas – birth-
    place of 376
Hockney, David............893
Hogarth – at Chiswick ..135
Hole of Horcum 974
Holford 422
holidays, public.............40
Holker Hall 854
Holkham Hall 570
Holmes, Sherlock
    and Baker Street, London ..88
    and the Hound of the
    Baskervilles 454, 457
Holne............................457
Holst, Gustav – birthplace
    of 379
Holy Grail 416
Holy Island 1070–1072
Hombury St Mary 178
Homes of Football, The 829
Honister Pass 844
Horncastle 727
Hornsea 959
Horse Point 504
horse-racing
    at Aintree........................786
    at Ascot...........................242
    at Cheltenham 377
    at Epsom Downs 242
    at Fontwell Park...............242
    at Goodwood Park 243
    at Kempton Park...............243
    at Lingfield Park................243
    at Newmarket 599
    at Plumpton 243
    at Sandown Park 243
Horton in Ribblesdale ...912
Hostelling International...33
hostels 32
hotels 31

Houghton Hall...............575
Houghton Lodge Garden
   259
Hound Tor 457
Housesteads Roman Fort
   1050
How Stean Gorge 931
Howtown.......................851
Hubberholme 908
Hudson, George 949
Hugh Town....................500
Hull 955–957
Hulne Park 1066
Hulne Priory 1066
Hunstanton 572
Hurlers, The 522
Hutton-le-Hole 971
Hythe 204

I

Ightham Mote 211
Ilfracombe.....................464
Ilkley.............................903
Industrial Museum 885
information.....................20
Ingleborough 914
Ingleborough Cave 914
Inglesham 364
Ingleton 914
Inner Farne..................1068
Instow 466
insurance 22
Ipswich 544–546
Ireshopeburn...............1015
Irishman's Wall.............458
Ironbridge......................636
Ironbridge Gorge...635–638
Ironbridge Gorge.........635
ISIC 25
Isle of Man 802–814
Isle of Portland.............299
Isle of Purbeck 290–293
Isle of Thanet.......184–189
ISLE OF WIGHT, THE
   260–273
Isle of Wight 260
Isles of Scilly........499–505
Ivinghoe Beacon 324

J

Jack's Rake...................831
Jacob's Ladder (Cheddar
    Gorge) 415

Jacob's Ladder (Falmouth) 486
Jamaica Inn 519
James, Henry – at Rye .216
Janet's Foss 910
Jarman, Derek 205
Jarrow 1038
Jarrow Crusade 1039
Jenkin Crag..................828
Jenner, Edward 382
Jennings Brewery 847
Jerome, Jerome K.
.............................326, 661
Jervaulx Abbey 921
Johnson, Dr Samuel
birthplace of......................664
life and works of 662
in London........................103
Jones, John Paul 860
Jorvik 938
Joseph of Arimathea 416
Judge Jeffreys 419

K

Keats, John – at Hampstead
.....................................126
Keighley and Worth Valley
Railway......................894
Keld..............................922
Kelham Island Museum 879
Kelmscott......................364
Kempton Park...............243
Kendal 821–823
Kendal Mintcake...........822
Kenilworth....................616
Kent 178–213
Kent Weald, The....206–213
Kentwell Hall 540
Kerroogarroo................810
Kersey.........................541
Keswick 839
Kew...............................137
Kielder Castle 1056
Kielder Water 1055
Kilburn.........................966
Killhope......................1014
Kilmar...........................522
Kilnsey 906
Kilpeck 627
Kilve Beach..................422
Kimmeridge Bay 292
Kinder Downfall 674
Kinder Scout.................674
King Offa Distillery 626
King's Lynn 572–576
Kingsbridge..................447

Kingsdale 916
Kingsley, Charles – and
Westward Ho! 467
Kingston Lacy 289
Kingston-upon-Hull
..............................955–957
Kipling Tors 466
Kipling, Rudyard – at
Westward Ho! 466
Kirk Yetholm................1060
Kirkby Malham..............909
Kirkstall Abbey..............886
Kirkstead......................719
Kisdon Force.................923
Knaresborough 929
Knole............................210
Knutsford 772
Kynance Cove 489

L

Lacock 315
Lady Lever Art Gallery ..785
Lake District 821–852
Lake District 818
Lakes, Central 829
Lakes, North 840
Lakeland Sheep and Wool
Centre 847
Lakes Glass Centre 855
Lamb House 217
Lambert, Daniel 733
Lamorna.......................495
Lancaster 797–800
Lancaster 798
Land's End 495
Lanercost Priory............869
Langdale 830
Langdale End................976
Langdale Pikes 830
Langdale Quest 976
Langdon Beck 1014
Langstrothdale..............907
Langthwaite 924
Lanhydrock 518
Lanlivery.......................510
Lanlivet.........................510
Lanternhouse 855
Lastingham 971
Latrigg Fell 839
launderettes 51
laundries 51
Laurel and Hardy Museum
.....................................854
Laurel, Stan – birthplace of
.....................................854
Lavenham 540

Lawrence of Arabia – at
Wareham....................290
Lawrence's Bay.............504
Lawrence, D. H.
birthplace of.....................693
Laxey............................808
Leach, Bernard 497
Leaplish......................1056
Lechlade 364
Ledbury.........................627
Leeds Castle................212
LEEDS 882–889
accommodation..............882
arrival 882
bars...............................887
Briggate 884
cafés..............................887
City Art Gallery................884
City Square 883
clubs..............................889
Corn Exchange................884
Craft Centre and Design
Gallery 885
entertainment..................889
Exchange Quarter............884
festivals..........................889
Harewood House..............886
Headrow 883
Henry Moore Institute 885
Industrial Museum 885
Kirkgate Market................884
Kirkstall Abbey.................886
Lotherton Hall 886
Millennium Square...........884
music 889
pubs...............................888
restaurants 888
Royal Armouries 885
Temple Newsam 886
Thackeray Medical Museum
.....................................885
theatre............................889
tourist office 882
tours...............................883
Town Hall 884
transport 882
Victoria Quarter................884
Yorkshire Sculpture Park ..885
Legoland 140
Leicester 699–703
Leicester and Rutland..700
Leicestershire 699–709
Leiston 551
Leith Hill 178
Leominster 633
Leonardslee Gardens....238
lesbian scene.................50
Letcombe Bassett 329
Levens Hall 824
Levisham......................974
Lewes 223–225
Leyburn.........................921
Lichfield 662

Lincoln.................720–724
Lincoln 721
Lincolnshire 717–736
Lincolnshire 718
Lindisfarne 1070
Lingfield Park 243
Lingholm Gardens 843
Linton 906
Liskeard 520
Litlington 222
Little Walsingham 570
Litton 907
Littondale 907
LIVERPOOL.......774–789
Liverpool 776–777
　accommodation................778
　Aintree...........................786
　Albert Dock.....................783
　Anfield............................786
　Anglican Cathedral 782
　arrival 775
　arts................................788
　bars...............................786
　Beatles, The...................780
　Bluecoat Chambers.........782
　Bold Street.....................782
　cafés..............................786
　cathedrals......................782
　Catholic Cathedral 782
　Cavern Club....................780
　Cavern Walks Shopping
　　Centre...........................780
　clubs 788
　Concert Square................782
　Conservation Centre.........783
　Duke Street 782
　Elizabeth Hoare Embroidery
　　Collection.......................782
　entertainment...................788
　ferries.............................783
　festivals...........................788
　football............................786
　Goodison Park.................786
　Grand National.................786
　HM Customs and Excise
　　Museum.........................784
　Hope Street.....................782
　Lady Lever Art Gallery 785
　Lime Street 781
　Liver Building 783
　Liverpool 774–789
　Liverpool Museum 781
　Magical Mystery Tour 780
　Maritime Museum.............784
　Matthew Street 780
　Matthew Street Festival 780
　Metropolitan Cathedral......782
　Museum of Liverpool Life..784
　music 788
　Open Eye Gallery.............782
　Pier Head 783
　Port Sunlight....................785
　pubs...............................787
　Queen Square..................782
　Quiggins Centre...............782

restaurants 787
Royal Liver Building..........783
St George's Hall...............781
Seacombe Aquarium 783
Speke Hall.......................785
Tate Gallery Liverpool 784
theatre.............................788
tourist offices 778
Town Hall 783
transport..........................778
Walker Art Gallery.............781
Water Street.....................783
Western Approaches
　Operations Centre.........783
William Brown Street 781
Williamson Square 783
Lizard peninsula............488
Lizard and Penwith
　Peninsulas 490
Lizard Point...................489
Loaded Camel 501
Lockton 974
Lodore Falls 843
Logan's Rock................495
LONDON 55–165
Central London........66–67
Greater London 58–59
West End 90–91
　2 Willow Rd.......................126
　accommodation............64–73
　Actors' Church..................93
　airports.............................61
　Albert Memorial 118
　Aldwych............................98
　Apsley House....................118
　arrival 61
　Australia House..................98
　Baker Street......................88
　ballet...............................161
　Bank of England 105
　Bankside 113
　Banqueting House 80
　Barbican...........................104
　bars 149–153
　Benjamin Franklin House....98
　Bethnal Green Museum of
　　Childhood........................109
　Blind Beggar 108
　Bloomsbury........................94
　Bond Street........................86
　bookshops..................89, 162
　British Library....................96
　British Museum...................94
　Buckingham Palace............79
　Burgh House......................126
　Burlington Arcade................86
　bus stations.......................61
　Bush House 98
　Butler's Wharf 116
　cabaret.............................160
　Cabinet War Rooms 80
　cabs..................................64
　cafés.........................141–145
　Camden Town....................125
　Canal Museum...................125

Canary Wharf....................109
Carlyle's House.................123
Carnaby Street...................92
Carnival, Notting Hill.........123
Cenotaph 80
Changing of the Guard 80
Charing Cross.....................76
Charing Cross Road 89
Charterhouse 101
Chelsea.............................122
Cheyne Walk.....................122
Chinatown............................89
Chiswick House.................135
Christ Church, Spitalfields 108
cinemas 160
City, The.............................101
classical music..................161
Cleopatra's Needle 97
Clerkenwell 100
Clink Prison Museum.........115
club-bars...........................156
clubs 154–159
comedy clubs 160
Commonwealth Institute...121
County Hall 112
Courtauld Institute 99
Covent Garden 92
Crown Jewels 106
Cutty Sark 131
Dalí Universe.....................112
dance 161
Design Museum.................116
Dickens House.....................96
Docklands 109
Downing Street....................80
Dr Johnson's House 103
Duke of York's Column 84
Dulwich 129
Dulwich Picture Gallery.....129
East End 107
Embankment........................97
embassies..........................163
Eros....................................85
Eton...................................139
Fan Museum......................134
Fenton House 126
Fleet Street 102
Florence Nightingale Museum
　..112
Fortnum & Mason 85
Freemasons' Hall................94
Freud Museum...................127
gay bars and clubs ...157–159
Geffrye Museum 109
Gilbert Collection 98
Globe Theatre....................114
Golden Hinde.....................115
Gray's Inn..........................100
Greenwich..........................130
Ham House........................138
Hamley's 85
Hampstead 126
Hampstead Heath..............127
Hampton Court 139
Harrods 121
Highgate 127
Highgate Cemetery............128

HMS Belfast......................116
Hogarth's House...............135
Holland Park 121
Horniman Museum 129
Horse Guards.....................80
hospitals 164
Houses of Parliament 81
Hyde Park.........................117
Imperial War Museum.......113
India House..........................98
information.........................62
internet cafés....................143
Isle of Dogs......................110
Jewish Museum.................125
Keats' House 126
Kensal Green Cemetery....124
Kensington Gardens........118
Kensington High Street ...121
Kensington Palace............118
Kenwood House 127
Kew Bridge Steam Museum
....136
Kew Gardens 137
King's Road 122
Knightsbridge 121
Lambeth............................111
Leadenhall Market 105
Legoland 140
Leicester Square.................89
Leighton House 121
lesbian bars and clubs
...............................157–159
Liberty 85
Lincoln's Inn Fields 100
Little Venice 125
Lloyd's...............................105
London Aquarium 112
London Bridge 115
London Dungeon...............115
London Eye........................112
Madam Tussaud's...............88
Mall, The 78
Marble Arch 117
markets
......108, 124, 125, 130, 163
Marx Memorial Library......101
Millennium Bridge.............113
Millennium Dome..............130
Millennium Wheel..............112
minicabs 64
Monument.........................105
Mosque.............................125
Museum of Garden History
....13
Museum of London 104
music venues....................153
Musical Museum...............136
National Army Museum 122
National Gallery 76
National Maritime Museum
....131
National Portrait Gallery....77
Natural History Museum....120
Neal Street 94
Neal's Yard 94
Nelson's Column.................76
Notting Hill 123

Old Compton Street 89
Old Operating Theatre
Museum.........................115
opera.................................161
Opera House......................93
Osterley Park and House..137
Oxford Street 87
Pall Mall 84
Parliament Hill...................127
Physic Garden, Chelsea ...122
Piccadilly.............................85
Piccadilly Circus 85
Planetarium.........................88
pubs 149–153
Punch and Judy Festival 93
RAF museum 128
Ranger's House 134
Regent Street...............84, 85
Regent's Canal.................125
Regent's Park 124
restaurants 145–149
Richmond 138
Richmond Park 138
Ritz Hotel 85
Royal Academy of Arts......86
Royal Albert Hall 118
Royal Botanical Gardens..137
Royal Courts of Justice 99
Royal Family 78
Royal Hospital..................122
Royal Naval College 131
Royal Observatory 131
St Bride's 102
St Giles Cripplegate..........104
St James's 84
St James's Park...................78
St Paul's Cathedral 103
St Paul's Church 93
Science Museum 119
Selfridge's 87
Serpentine Gallery 118
Shad Thames.....................116
Sherlock Holmes 88
shops and markets ...161–163
Shri Swaminarayan Mandir.28
Sir John Soane's Museum
....100
Soho...................................88
Somerset House 98
South Bank Centre 111
Southwark..........................113
Southwark Cathedral........115
Speakers' Corner..............117
Spencer House 84
Spitalfields 107
Staple Inn..........................100
Strand 97
Syon House 136
Tate Britain..........................83
Tate Modern......................114
taxis 64
Tea & Coffee Museum 116
Temple 99
Theatre Museum.................93
theatres 159
tourist offices 62
tours....................................73

Tower Bridge.....................107
Tower of London...............106
Trafalgar Square.................76
train stations 61
transport 63
Transport Museum.............93
Travelcards.........................63
Trocadero............................85
Tube 63
Underground.......................63
University 96
Victoria and Albert Museum
....119
Vinopolis 115
Wallace Collection 87
Wardour Street...................92
Waterloo Place....................84
Wellington Museum 118
Westminster 75
Westminster Abbey.............81
Westminster Cathedral 83
Wetland Centre 135
Whitechapel.......................107
Whitechapel Art Gallery 108
Whitehall 79
Windsor.............................139
Winston Churchill's Britain at
War 116
zoo....................................125
Long Distance Footpaths
(LDPs)...............................43
Long Meg and her
Daughters 865
Long Melford 539
Long Mynd....................644
Long Sutton 731
Longleat 305
Longton.........................665
Longville-in-the-Dale 638
Looe...............................479
Lorton Vale....................845
Lost Gardens of Heligan
....483
Lostwithiel....................481
Lotherton Hall 886
Loughrigg Fell 828
Louth.............................725
Low Dalby.....................976
Lower Broadheath 622
Lower Town 503
Lowestoft 554
Loweswater...................845
Lowry Centre 756
Luddites........................689
Ludham.........................563
Ludlow 646
Lullingstone Roman Villa
....211
Lulworth Cove...............292
Lunar Society...............647
Lundy Bay.....................512
Lundy Island 468

Luxulyan...........................510
Lyddington.....................708
Lydford...........................460
Lyke Wake Walk.............965
Lyme Regis....................301
Lymington.....................284
Lympne..........................204
Lyndhurst......................282
Lynmouth.......................475
Lynton...........................474

M

Macclesfield..................773
magazine..........................38
Magna Carta.................723
Maiden Castle...............296
Maidstone.....................211
mail..................................38
Malham..........................908
Malham Cove................909
Malham Tarn.................909
Malhamdale...................908
Mallyan Spout...............978
Malmesbury...................375
Malvern Hills........622–624
Malvern Link..................623
Mam Tor........................672
MANCHESTER.....741–765
Manchester..........742–743
  accommodation................747
  Air and Space Hall............752
  Albert Square....................749
  Aquatics Centre.................755
  Arndale Centre..................754
  arrival...............................746
  arts...................................763
  Barton Arcade...................753
  Botanical Gardens.............756
  Bridgewater Hall...............751
  cafés................................757
  Castlefield.........................751
  Cathedral..........................753
  Cenotaph..........................749
  Central Library..................749
  Chetham's Hospital School
 753
  Chinatown.........................751
  Chorlton Water Park..........756
  cinema..............................764
  City Art Gallery..................751
  clubs.................................762
  comedy.............................764
  Convention Centre.............751
  Corn Exchange..................754
  Cornerhouse......................755
  Craft and Design Centre....754
  Deansgate.........................752
  Deansgate Locks...............752
  Didsbury Village................756
  Exchange Square...............754

football...........................757
Free Trade Hall................749
Friends Meeting House....749
G-Mex Centre...................751
Gallery of Costume...........756
gay scene........................762
Great Hall........................749
Great Northern.................752
Imperial War Museum North
....757
International Convention
  Centre.............................751
John Rylands Library........752
Library..............................749
Lincoln Square..................752
Lowry Centre....................756
Maine Road......................757
Manchester Museum........755
Millennium Quarter...........754
Museum of Science and
  Industry..........................751
music...............................763
New Cathedral Street.......754
nightlife............................762
Northern Quarter...............754
Old Trafford......................757
Oxford Road.....................755
People's History Museum..752
Peter's Fields...................752
Piccadilly Gardens............754
Platt Field Park.................756
Power Hall........................752
Printworks........................754
pubs.................................759
Refuge Assurance............755
restaurants.......................759
Rochdale canal basin........755
Roman Fort.......................751
Royal Exchange Theatre...753
Rusholme..........................756
St Anne's Church..............753
St Anne's Square..............753
St Peter's Square..............749
Salford Quays...................756
Smithfields Buildings........754
soccer..............................757
Textile Gallery...................752
theatre.............................763
tourist office.....................746
Town Hall.........................749
transport...........................746
Triangle............................754
Urbis................................754
Warehouse for the World..752
Whitworth Gallery.............755
Manningtree....................536
Manx Museum.................807
Mappa Mundi..................625
maps..................................21
Margate...........................184
Market Bosworth.............703
Market Harborough.........706
Marlborough....................313
Marlow.............................326
Marrick Priory.................924
Mars Hill..........................475

Marston Moor, Battle of
....938
Martin, John..................1030
Martineau, Harriet – and
  the Lake District.........832
Marx, Karl
  burial place of.................128
  in London........................101
Mary Arden's House.....612
Mary Rose......................254
Maryport.........................861
Masham...........................922
Maughold........................810
Maumbury Rings...........294
Mawnan..........................488
Meadowhall....................877
media, the..............38–40
medical treatment..........22
Melford Hall...................540
Melmerby........................865
Melton Mowbray.............706
Mendips, the.........413–416
Merrivale........................461
Mevagissey.....................483
Middleham......................921
Middlesbrough..............1019
Middleton-in-Teesdale
....1013
Mill Gill Force................919
Millendreath...................479
Milton Abbas..................303
Minehead........................472
minicabs...........................31
Minions...........................522
Minsmere RSPB Reserve
....552
Mistley............................536
mobile phone...................37
Mompesson's Well..........676
Monarchy.............1086–1087
money...............................24
Monmouth Rebellion.....419
Monsal Trail....................679
monuments of England
.............................1098–1109
Moorsbus, the...............964
Morecambe....................800
Morecambe, Eric...........802
Moreton-in-Marsh..........366
Moretonhampstead.......458
Morris, William
  at Kelmscott...................364
  life and works of..............363
Morte Point....................464
Morwenstow...................516
Moseley Old Hall...........661
Mother Shipton's Cave..929
motoring organizations...30
Mottisfont Abbey House
....259

Mouls, the 512
Mount Edgecumbe 452
Mount Grace Priory 965
Mousehole 494
movies...............1126–1134
Much Wenlock 638
Muker...........................923
Mullion 489
Muncaster Mill 859
Munnings, Alfred...........538
museums 40

N

Nantwich.....................774
Nash, Richard "Beau" – at
   Bath 403, 406
National Centre for Popular
   Music 878
National Football Museum,
   Preston.......................794
National Horse Racing
   Museum 599
National Museum of
   Photography, Film and
   Television 890
National Railway Museum
  948
National Trust................40
National Waterways
   Museum 386
Naval vernacular 255
Navrati, Leicester..........702
Nayland.......................538
Needles, The................269
Nelson, Horatio
   birthplace of......................571
   statue of.............................76
   tomb of 104
Nether Stowey 421
Netley...........................259
New Forest 281–284
New Grimsby 502
New Romney 205
Newark.........................698
Newburgh Priory...........967
Newby Hall...................932
NEWCASTLE UPON TYNE
  1023–1035
Newcastle upon Tyne
  1024
   accommodation..............1026
   arrival 1025
   arts...................................1034
   BALTIC Centre for
      Contemporary Art.......1029
   bars..................................1033
   Bessie Surtees' House ...1028

Blackfriars 1029
   cafés 1032
   Castle 1027
   Cathedral 1027
   Central Station.................1029
   Chinatown.........................1029
   clubs 1034
   Discovery Museum 1030
   entertainment...................1033
   Grainger Market...............1029
   Grey Street.......................1029
   Guildhall...........................1028
   Hancock Museum.............1031
   Hanover Gardens.............1028
   Hatton Gallery...................1031
   High Level Bridge 1028
   International Centre for Life
     1030
   Laing Gallery....................1030
   LIFE Interactive World.....1030
   Maritime Centre 1028
   Metro................................1025
   Millennium Bridge...........1028
   Morden Tower...................1029
   Museum of Antiquities.....1031
   music 1034
   Music Centre Gateshead 1029
   nightlife 1033
   pubs..................................1033
   Quayside...........................1027
   restaurants 1032
   Shefton Museum of Greek Art
      and Archeology...........1031
   Side Gallery 1028
   Swing Bridge 1028
   theatre..............................1034
   Theatre Royal...................1029
   tourist office.....................1025
   Town Moor........................1031
   transport 1025
   Trinity House 1028
   Tyne Bridge 1028
   University Gallery..............1031
Newland.......................512
Newmarket...................599
Newport 272
Newquay.......................507
newspapers 38
Newstead Abbey 694
Newton, Isaac – at
   Grantham....................735
Newton-by-the-Sea 1067
Newtondale Halt 975
Newtown.......................270
Niarbyl.........................812
Nicholson, Norman – and
   the Lake District........832
Nidderdale 930
Nocton 719
Norfolk Broads......562–564
Norham Castle............1062
North Downs Way.........177
North York Moors..961–978
North York Moors 962

North Yorkshire Moors
   Railway 974, 975
Northampton 710–712
Northamptonshire
  709–717
Northamptonshire.......710
Northeast 996–997
Northleach 367
**Northumberland National
   Park** 1053–1062
Northwest 740
Northwich 771
Norwich................554–562
Norwich.......................555
Nottingham 687–693
Nottingham...................691
Nottinghamshire..687–709
Nottinghamshire 688
NT 40
Nunnington Hall 968
Nunwell House...............264
Nymans.........................238

O

Oakham 707
Obby Oss......................509
Offa's Dyke Path...........645
Okehampton 459
Old Grimsby..................502
Old Man of Coniston 834
Old Sarum.....................310
Old Town.......................501
Oliver, William 406
Once Brewed 1050
opening hours.................40
Orford...........................548
Orrest Head 827
Orwell, George – at
   Southwold..................552
Osborne House.............271
Osmotherley 965
Otterburn 1057
Oundle 715
outdoor pursuits 43
Overbury 390
Overton Hill 324
Oxburgh Hall 578
Oxford and around......322
OXFORD...............330–347
Oxford 332–333
   accommodation................334
   arrival 331
   Ashmolean Museum........342
   Balliol College 340
   bars..................................345
   Bate Collection 342
   Bodleian Library..............338

Botanic Gardens...............337
cafés 344
Carfax 336
Cathedral 342
Christ Church College 341
Christ Church Meadow.....342
Clarendon Building 338
clubs 346
Cornmarket........................341
Exeter College 341
History of Science Museum
....340
Magdalen College.............337
Merton College 337
Museum of Modern Art 342
Museum of Oxford.............341
music 346
New College 338
Oxford Story 341
Oxford Union 341
Pitt-Rivers Museum 344
pubs...................................345
punting...............................335
Queen's College................336
Radcliffe Camera 340
restaurants........................345
St John's College..............344
St Mary the Virgin 336
Sheldonian Theatre...........338
theatres..............................346
tourist office......................331
tours...................................331
Town Hall 341
Trinity College 340
University College..............336
University Museum of Natural
History 344
oysters 182

P

Padstow 509–512
Paignton........................443
Paine, Thomas – birthplace
of...................................576
Painswick.......................382
Par 482
Pateley Bridge 931
Patterdale......................849
Pavey Ark......................831
Pavey's Lookout Tower.415
Peak Cavern 672
Peak District, The
.............................665–681
Peak District, The 666
Peckover House 580
Peel................................811
Pelistry Bay...................501
Pen-y-ghent..................912
Pencil Museum 841
Pendeen........................496

Pendennis Castle..........486
Pendle Witches..............796
Pendower Beach 484
Penine Way...........674, 998
Peninnis Headland........501
Pennsylvania Castle......299
Penrith............................863
Penshurst.......................208
Pentire Point 512
Penwith peninsula
.............................491–499
Penzance 492–494
Pepys, Samuel – birthplace
of.................................102
Periglis Cove..................504
periodicals 38
Perpitch 504
Peterloo 745
Petrifying Well 929
pets, bringing to England20
Petworth 240
Peveril Castle.................671
pharmacies 22
phones 37
Pickering 973
Piel Castle......................857
Piercebridge...............1019
Pike of Stickle...............831
Pilgrim Fathers......449, 730
Pilgrim's Way 177
Pilgrimage of Grace 725
Pinkson Creek...............511
Piper's Hole...................502
Plague, the.....................677
Plankey Mill.................1016
plastic 24
Plumpton 243
Plymouth 449–452
Point of Ayre 810
Polesden Lacey 178
police 47
Polkerris 482
Polperro 479
Polurrian........................489
Polzeath 512
Ponden Hall 896
Poole...............................286
Poole's Cavern...............670
Pooley Bridge 851
Porlock...........................474
Porlock Weir...................474
Port Erin 812
Port Isaac.......................512
Port Quin........................512
Port Soderick.................814
Port St Mary 813
Port Sunlight...................785
Portchester Castle.........256
Porth Beach...................507

Porth Conger 504
Porth Hellick 501
Porthcothan 510
Porthcurno 495
Porthleven......................491
Porthluney Cove 483
Porthmeor Beach...........498
Porthminster Beach.......498
Porthtowan 506
Portland Castle 299
Portloe 483
Portreath 506
Portsmouth 252–257
Portsmouth.....................253
post buses 28
post offices 38
Postbridge......................456
Postman Pat 823
Potter Heigham..............563
Potter, Beatrix
Gallery at Hawkshead.......837
at Gloucester 385
at Hilltop 838
and the Lake District 832
museum in Windermere.....825
Potteries, The.................664
Prawle Point...................448
Pre-Raphaelites 363, 651
Preston...........................794
Prideaux Palace.............509
Priestley, J.B. 890
Princetown.....................456
Prospect Cottage..........205
public holidays...............40
pubs................................36
Purcell, Henry – life of.....82

Q

Quantock Hills 421–423
quarantine rules 20
Quarr Abbey 262
Queen Elizabeth Country
Park.............................277
Queen Victoria – at
Osborne House..........271
Quenington 364
Quex House....................188

R

Raad Ny Foillan 803
Raby Castle 1009
radio................................39
rail passes......................27

railways 26
Raleigh, Sir Walter –
    imprisonment at the
    Tower of London 106
Ramsey 810
Ramsgate 188
Ransome, Arthur – in the
    Lake District
    ....823, 825, 832, 834
Ranworth 563
Ravenglass 858
Ravenscar 983
Reading 327
Red Pike 845
Red Tarn 851
Redesdale 1057
Redruth 506
Reeth 923
Reivers Way 998
Rennington 1067
restaurants 35
Restormel Castle 481
Rheged 863
Ribble Valley 795
Ribblehead Viaduct 913
Ribblesdale 910–913
Richmond............924–926
Ridgeway 324
Rievaulx Abbey 969
Rievaulx Terrace 970
Ripley 930
Ripon 932
Roa 857
Robin Hood 696
Robin Hood's Bay 983
Rochdale 795
Rochester 179
Rock..............................509
Rockingham 716
Rodmell..........................226
Roehead 848
Rokeby Park 1011
Roker 1041
Rollright Stones 369
Romaldkirk 1013
Romney, Hythe and
    Dymchurch Railway ...204
Romsey 259
Roseberry Topping 978
Rosedale 972
Roseland peninsula 487
Rosevean 505
Ross-on-Wye 628
Rosthwaite 843
Rothbury 1057
Rougemont Castle 436
Rough Tor 521
Royal Armouries, Leeds
   885

Royal Family 78
Royal houses ...1086–1087
Royal Naval Base 252
Royal Shakespeare
    Company, London 159
Royal Tunbridge Wells
   206–208
Royal Yacht Squadron ..271
RSC, London 159
Rufford Country Park....696
Rufus Stone 282
Rum Story......................860
Rump's Point 512
Rushton 717
Ruskin Library 799
Ruskin, John – and the
    Lake District........832, 836
Rydal Mount 834
Ryde..............................261
Rye................................217

S

Sackville-West, Vita
    ....209, 210, 227
safety 47
Saffron Walden 598
St Agnes (Cornwall) 506
St Agnes (Isles of Scilly)
   504
St Alban's Head 291
St Albans 353–357
St Anthony- in-Roseland
   488
St Austell........................481
St Bees 859
St Breock Downs...........510
St Briavels......................630
St Catherine's Point......268
St Cuthbert 1003, 1070
St Cuthbert's Way 998
St Day 506
St George.......................329
St Helen's......................504
St Ives................497–499
St Johns.........................810
St Julian 561
St Just-in-Penwith 496
St Just-in-Roseland......487
St Keverne 489
St Martin's......................503
St Mary-in-the-Marsh ...205
St Mary's 500–502
St Mary's Bay 205
St Mawes.......................487
St Michael's Mount.......494
St Neot...........................520

St Osyth Priory 534
St Petroc........................509
St Warna's Cove 504
Saints' Way 510
Salcombe.......................448
Salisbury 306–310
Salisbury **307**
Salisbury Plain 311
Saltaire...........................893
Saltburn 1022
Saltfleetby-Theddlethorpe
    National Nature Reserve
   726
Saltram House 453
Samson...........................503
Sandham Memorial Chapel
   279
Sandown.........................264
Sandown Park 243
Sandringham House 574
Sandsend........................987
Sandwich 196
Sandwick 848
Sandy Mouth 516
Satura Crag....................848
Saunton Sands 464
Scafell............................844
Scafell Pike 844
Scale Force....................845
Scarborough 979–982
Scilly Isles 499–505
Scotney Castle 209
Seahouses 1068
Seathwaite 844
Seatoller........................844
Seaton............................439
Seaton Delaval Hall 1039
Seaview 263
Segedunum Fort 1036
Selborne 278
self-catering 34
Sellafield 859
Semer Water 919
Settle.............................910
Settle to Carlisle Railway
   911
Seven Sisters 222
Sevenoaks 209
Shaftesbury...................304
Shakespeare, William
    birthplace of......................609
    and the Globe Theatre,
        London 113
    life of 608–609
    at Stratford-upon-Avon.....605
Shaldon..........................440
Shalfleet 270
Shandy Hall 966
Shanklin 265
Sharpitor 448, 461

Shaw, George Bernard – at Ayot St Lawrence.......355
Shawsgate Vineyard 548
Sheep's Tor 461
Sheffield 877–881
Sheffield Park................237
Shell Bay.......................291
Shelley, Mary
  burial place of 285
  at Marlow 326
Shelley, Percy Bysshe
  burial place of 285
  at Marlow 326
Sherborne 306
Sheringham...................567
Sherwood Forest 696
Shipley Glen..................894
Shipload Bay 468
Shipton Gorge 300
Shorwell 268
Shrewsbury.........640–642
Shropshire............633–638
Shropshire 634
Sidmouth 438
Silbury Hill....................313
Silecroft.......................858
Silloth-on-Solway..........862
Silverstone 711
Simonsbath...................472
Singh, Prince Duleep – bur-
  ial place of 577
Sissinghurst 209
Sizergh Castle...............823
Sizewell........................551
Skegness 728
Skelwith Bridge............830
Skiddaw 839
Skipton.........................900
Slaidburn......................796
Slapton Ley nature reserve
 448
Slave trade in Bristol 394
Slimbridge....................381
Slimbridge Wildfowl and
  Wetlands Centre 381
Snaefell (Isle of Man) 809
Snape Maltings.............550
Snarford 724
Solomon's Temple 670
South Downs Way 220
South Hams..................447
South Shields...............1039
South West Coast Path 473
Southampton 257–259
Southend-on-Sea
 527–529
Souther Scales nature
  reserve 916
Southey, Robert – and the
  Lake District...............832

Southwell 697
Southwold....................552
Spalding........................731
Speedwell Cavern.........672
Speke Hall....................785
Spencer, Stanley – at
  Cookham 326
sports.......................42, 43
Spurn Head...................959
Staffordshire 661–665
Staindrop 1010
Stainforth 912
Stair Hole 293
Staithes 990
Stamford 732–734
Stamford Bridge, Battle of
 938
Stanhope 1015
Stannersburn 1056
Stansted.......................584
Stape 975
Staple Island 1068
Star Castle 500
Starbotton....................907
stately homes 40
Steel Rigg 1050
Steeple Point 516
Stein, Rick....................511
Sterne, Lawrence..........967
Stevenson, Robert Louis –
  inspiration for Treasure
  Island 397
Stickle Tarn 831
Stock Ghyll Force 828
Stockton-on-Tees 1020
Stoke............................468
Stoke Bruerne...............714
Stoke-by-Nayland.........538
Stoke-on-Trent..............664
Stoker, Bram – life and
  works of 985
Stokesay.......................645
Stonehenge...................311
Stonor House................326
Stour Valley 536–542
Stourhead 305
Stourton 305
Stow.............................724
Stow-on-the-Wold 366
Stowe Gardens 350
Stowe's Hill 522
Stratfield Saye House...279
STRATFORD-UPON-AVON
 605–613
Stratford-upon-Avon ..606
  accommodation 607
  Anne Hathaway's Cottage 612
  arrival 606
  Birthplace museum...........609
  cafés 612

Charlecote Park...............613
Coughton Court...............613
Grammar School...............610
Great Garden 610
Guild Chapel 610
Hall's Croft 610
Holy Trinity Church 611
Mary Arden's House 612
Nash's House....................610
New Place.........................610
pubs................................613
restaurants 612
Royal Shakespeare Company
 611
RSC.................................611
theatres 611
tourist office 606
Striding Edge 851
Stripple Stones 519
Stroud 380
student discounts 25
student halls 32
Studley Royal................934
Stump Cross Caverns ..931
Styhead Tarn.................844
Sudbury 539
Sudeley Castle...............371
Sulby Glen 809
Sulgrave........................714
Summerleaze 516
Sunderland 1041
Sunk Island Sands........959
surfing............................46
surfing, Newquay 509
Surrey 172–178
Surrey, Kent and Sussex
 170–171
Sussex.................213–246
Sutton Bank..................966
Sutton Bridge................732
Sutton Hoo 547
Swaledale............922–924
Swanage 291
Swinbrook.....................365
Swirral Edge.................851
Symond's Yat Rock 629

T

Tan Hill Inn 923
Tangmere Military Aviation
  Museum 244
Tarka Line.....................463
Tarn Hows.....................839
Tarset Valley 1054
Tate Britain (London).......83
Tate Gallery (Liverpool) .784
Tate Gallery (St Ives) 497
Tate Modern (London) ..114

Tattershall Castle 727
Tatton Park....................773
Taunton 420
Tavistock 461
tax regulations 20
taxis 31
tea shops 36
Teän 504
Tees Valley 1017–1023
Teesdale.....................1013
Teesdale Way................998
Teignmouth 440
telephones 37
television 39
Telscombe.....................226
Temple Newsam 886
Tendring peninsula........532
Tennyson Down 269
Tewkesbury..........387–389
Thackeray Medical
   Museum 885
Thanet resorts 184–189
Thatcher, Margaret – at
   Grantham 735
Thaxted..........................599
Theakston's Brewery 922
Thetford.........................576
Thetford Forest 577
Thirlmere Reservoir.......851
Thirsk 964
Tholt-y-Will Glen 809
Thornham.......................572
Thornton-le-Dale...........975
Thorpe Park 177
Thorpeness....................551
Three Peaks Walk 912
Three Shire Stone 846
Three Tuns brewery 645
Threlkeld 842
Thurlestone 449
Thwaite..........................923
time zone 51
Tintagel 513–515
tipping............................51
Titchwell........................572
toilets 51
Tolethorpe Hall..............734
Toll's Island 501
Tolly Cobbold Brewery..545
Tolpuddle Martyrs 295
Top Withens 896
Torquay................441–443
Torrington......................463
Totnes 444
tour operators
   in Australia and New Zealand
  15
   in the US and Canada 14
tourist offices
   abroad...........................21

in England..........................20
Towan Beach 507
Tower Knowe 1056
Townend 827
trains
   in England..........................26
   from Ireland.....................16
   from mainland Europe 16
travel agents
   in Australia and New Zealand
  15
   in the US and Canada 13
travel insurance 22
travellers' cheques..........24
Treak Cliff Cavern 673
Trelissick Garden 488
Treryn Dinas 495
Tresco 502
Trethevy Quoit...............522
Troutbeck.......................827
Troy Town Maze............504
Truro..............................484
TT Races........................803
Tunbridge Wells...206–208
Tunstall..........................665
Twardreath 510
Twelve Men's Moor.......521
Tyne Green Country Park
  1048
Tyneham.........................292
Tynemouth 1036
Tynwald 804
Tynwald – original site of
  810

life of 1037
   remains of.....................1003
Ventnor..........................266
Vermuyden, Cornelius...577
Vernon, Dorothy............680
Verulamium 353
Veryan 483
Victoria Cave.................910
videos 51
Vindolanda 1051
visas................................19
voluntary work 48
Vyne, the.......................278

W

Waddesdon Manor 350
Wadhead Scar 856
Wainwright, Alfred.........822
Wakehurst Place...........237
Walberswick...................553
walking.............................43
Wallington House.........1040
Wallsend 1036
Walmer Castle...............198
Walmsley, Leo...............984
Walpole, Sir Hugh – and
   the Lake District.........832
Walsall...........................660
Walton-on-the-Naze 534
Wambarrows..................471
Wansfell Pike 828
Wantage.........................328
Warbeck, Perkin............420
Warden........................1048
Wareham........................290
Waren Mill 1069
Warkworth...................1063
Warwick 614–616
Warwick 615
Warwick Arts Centre.....619
Wasdale Head...............846
Wash, The.....................732
Washford........................423
Washington 1041
Washington, George ...1042
Wast Water 846
Watchet..........................423
Watergate Bay 507
Waterhead......................828
Watermouth Castle 464
Watersmeet....................475
Waverley Abbey 176
Wayland's Smithy 330
Weald and Downland
   open-air museum.......245
Weardale 1014

U

Uffington 330
Uffington Castle 329
Uley...............................381
Ullswater 848
Ulverston.......................854
Underland Girt 504
University of East Anglia
   (UEA) 561
Upnor Castle.................182
Uppingham 708

V

Vale of White Horse 328
Valley of Desolation 904
Valley of the Rocks.......475
Value Added Tax (VAT)....20
VAT.................................20
Venerable Bede

Weardale Way 998
websites....................11, 21
Wellington, Duke of
 at Stratfield Saye House...279
 tomb of 104
Wells 411–413
Wells-next-the-Sea 569
Wenlock Edge...............639
Wensley...........................921
Wensleydale.........917–922
Wesley, John.........396, 506
West Bagborough.........422
West Bexington.............300
West Kennet Long Barrow
313
West Lulworth...............293
West Mendip Way.........415
**West Midlands and the
 Peak District**..............604
Western Rocks..............505
Weston-super-Mare 402
Westonbirt Arboretum...375
Westward Ho! 466
Wetland Centre, Barnes
135
Weymouth.....................297
Whaplode.......................719
Wharfedale..........903–908
Wheeldale Roman Road
975
Whernside.....................915
Whinlatter Pass.............845
Whinnats Pass 672
Whippingham.................272
Whipsnade Wild Animal
 Park............................356
Whitby 985–990
White Horse Hill 329
White Island 504
White Scar Caves 915
Whitecliff Bay................263
Whitehaven 860
Whitesand Bay..............495
Whitfield Force.............919
Whitsand Bay...............453
Whitstable.....................182
Wicken Fen 577
Widbrook 365
Widecombe-in-the-Moor
457
Widemouth Bay 516
Wightwick Manor.........661
Wilderhope Manor 639
wildlife 1110–1118
Willhays Tor...................458
William II 283
William I – and the Battle of
 Hastings..............214, 216
William of Wykeham 273
Williamson Park 799

Wills Neck 422
Wilton 310
Wimbleball Lake 472
Wimborne Minster 289
Wimpole Hall.................596
Winchelsea 218
Winchester..........273–277
Winchester....................274
Winchcombe.................371
Windermere 824–826
Windsor.........................139
wine bars 36
Winsford........................471
Winter Tor.....................458
wiring money 24
Wisbech 580
Wisley 175
Wissington 538
Wistman's Wood...........456
Woburn 351
Woburn Abbey 351
Woburn Safari Park.......351
Wolds, Lincolnshire.......725
Wollaton Hall................693
Wolverhampton.............661
Wolvesey Castle 275
WOMAD 328
Woodbridge 546
Woodhall Spa................727
Woodhenge...................312
Woodstock.....................347
Wookey Hole.................413
Wool Pack 674
Woolacombe..................464
Wooler...........................1059
Woolf, Virginia
 and the Bloomsbury
  group...........................227
 at Monk's House........226
 and Vita Sackville-West
 210
Woolpack Round 847
Woolsthorpe-by-
 Colsterworth 735
Woolstone 330
Wootton Bridge.............263
Worcester............620–622
Worcestershire 619–624
Wordsworth, Dorothy...833,
 847
Wordsworth, William
 birthplace of......................847
 at Grasmere/Dove Cottage
 833
 and the Lake District 832
 at Rydal Mount 834
work permits..................48
working in England 48
Wright, Joseph..............668
Wroxeter Roman City ...634

Wroxham.......................563
Wrynose Pass...............846

Y

Yarmouth.......................270
Yes Tor 458
YHA................................32
YMCA.............................33
YORK 935–853
York 936–937
 accommodation...............939
 ARC.................................947
 Archeological Resource
  Centre............................947
 arrival..............................938
 Assembly Rooms.............946
 bars.................................951
 Bedern Hall 945
 Betty's.............................949
 Black Swan Inn.................945
 Bootham Bar....................944
 cafés 949
 Castle..............................947
 Castle Museum.................948
 cinema 953
 City Art Gallery.................945
 Clifford's Tower 948
 clubs 951
 Dean's Park......................944
 entertainment...................951
 Exhibition Square.............945
 Fairfax House....................947
 Goodramgate....................945
 Guildhall 946
 Holy Trinity 945
 Jorvik Viking Centre..........947
 King's Manor.....................945
 Mansion House.................946
 Merchant Adventurers' Hall
 47
 Merchant Taylor's Hall 945
 Micklegate Bar.................945
 Minster 942
 Minster Library.................944
 Monk Bar 944
 music...............................951
 National Railway Museum
 948
 nightlife 951
 Our Lady's Row 945
 Parliament Street 945
 pubs.................................951
 restaurants 950
 Richard III Museum...........944
 St Anthony's Hall 945
 St Helen's Square.............946
 St Mary's Abbey 946
 St Michael-le-Belfry 944
 St William's College 944
 Shambles, The..................945
 Stonegate 946
 tearooms..........................949
 theatre.............................953

tourist offices 939
tours................................939
transport 939
Treasurer's House 944
walls................................944
Walmgate Bar 945
Yorkshire Museum 946

Yorkshire 873–991
Yorkshire 874–875
Yorkshire Dales ...897–924
Yorkshire Dales ...898–899
Yorkshire Sculpture Park
.....................................885
youth hostels 32

YWCA 33

Z

Zennor...........................496

Twenty Years of Rough Guides

In the summer of 1981, Mark Ellingham, Rough Guides' founder, knocked out the first guide on a typewriter, with a group of friends. Mark had been travelling in Greece after university, and couldn't find a guidebook that really answered his needs.There were heavyweight cultural guides on the one hand – good on museums and classical sites but not on beaches and tavernas – and on the other hand student manuals that were so caught up with how to save money that they lost sight of the country's significance beyond its role as a place for a cool vacation. None of the guides began to address Greece as a country, with its natural and human environment, its politics and its contemporary life.

Having no urgent reason to return home, Mark decided to write his own guide. It was a guide to Greece that tried to combine some erudition and insight with a thoroughly practical approach to travellers' needs. Scrupulously researched listings of places to stay, eat and drink were matched by careful attention to detail on everything from Homer to Greek music, from classical sites to national parks and from nude beaches to monasteries. Back in London, Mark and his friends got their Rough Guide accepted by a farsighted commissioning editor at the publisher Routledge and it came out in 1982.

The Rough Guide to Greece was a student scheme that became a publishing phenomenon. The immediate success of the book – shortlisted for the Thomas Cook award – spawned a series that rapidly covered dozens of countries. The Rough Guides found a ready market among backpackers and budget travellers, but soon acquired a much broader readership that included older and less impecunious visitors. Readers relished the guides' wit and inquisitiveness as much as the enthusiastic, critical approach that acknowledges everyone wants value for money – but not at any price.

Rough Guides soon began supplementing the "rougher" information – the hostel and low-budget listings – with the kind of detail that independent-minded travellers on any budget might expect. These days, the guides – distributed worldwide by the Penguin Group – include recommendations spanning the range from shoestring to luxury, and cover more than 200 destinations around the globe. Our growing team of authors, many of whom come to Rough Guides initially as outstandingly good letter-writers telling us about their travels, are spread all over the world, particularly in Europe, the USA and Australia. As well as the travel guides, Rough Guides publishes a series of dictionary phrasebooks covering two dozen major languages, an acclaimed series of music guides running the gamut from Classical to World Music, a series of music CDs in association with World Music Network, and a range of reference books on topics as diverse as the Internet, Pregnancy and Unexplained Phenomena. Visit **www.roughguides.com** to see what's cooking.

Rough Guide Credits

Text editor: Judith Bamber
Series editor: Mark Ellingham
Editorial: Martin Dunford, Jonathan Buckley, Jo Mead, Kate Berens, Ann-Marie Shaw, Helena Smith, Orla Duane, Olivia Eccleshall, Ruth Blackmore, Geoff Howard, Claire Saunders, Gavin Thomas, Alexander Mark Rogers, Polly Thomas, Joe Staines, Richard Lim, Duncan Clark, Peter Buckley, Lucy Ratcliffe, Clifton Wilkinson, Alison Murchie, Matthew Teller, Andrew Dickson, Fran Sandham (UK); Andrew Rosenberg, Stephen Timblin, Yuki Takagaki, Richard Koss, Hunter Slaton, Julie Feiner (US)
Production: Susanne Hillen, Andy Hilliard, Link Hall, Helen Prior, Julia Bovis, Michelle Draycott, Katie Pringle, Mike Hancock, Zoë

Nobes, Rachel Holmes, Andy Turner
Cartography: Melissa Baker, Maxine Repath, Ed Wright, Katie Lloyd-Jones
Picture research: Louise Boulton, Sharon Martins, Mark Thomas
Online: Kelly Cross, Anja Mutic-Blessing, Jennifer Gold, Audra Epstein, Suzanne Welles, Cree Lawson (US)
Finance: John Fisher, Gary Singh, Edward Downey, Mark Hall, Tim Bill
Marketing & Publicity: Richard Trillo, Niki Smith, David Wearn, Chloë Roberts, Demelza Dallow, Claire Southern (UK); Simon Carloss, David Wechsler, Kathleen Rushforth (US)
Administration: Tania Hummel, Julie Sanderson

Publishing Information

This fifth edition published March 2002 by **Rough Guides Ltd**,
62–70 Shorts Gardens, London WC2H 9AH.
Penguin Putnam Inc., 375 Hudson St, NY 10014, USA.
Distributed by the Penguin Group
Penguin Books Ltd,
80 Strand, London WC2R ORL
Penguin Putnam Inc.,
345 Hudson St, NY 10014, USA
Penguin Books Australia Ltd,
487 Maroondah Highway, PO Box 257, Ringwood, Victoria 3134, Australia
Penguin Books Canada Ltd,
10 Alcorn Ave, Toronto, Ontario, Canada M4V 1E4
Penguin Books (NZ) Ltd,
182–190 Wairau Rd, Auckland 10, New Zealand
Typeset in Bembo and Helvetica to an original design by Henry Iles.

Printed in Italy by LegoPrint S.p.A
© Rough Guides Ltd 2002

1192pp includes index
A catalogue record for this book is available from the British Library.

ISBN 1-85828-875-4

The publishers and authors have done their best to ensure the accuracy and currency of all the information in **The Rough Guide to England**; however, they can accept no responsibility for any loss, injury or inconvenience sustained by any traveller as a result of information or advice contained in the guide.

Help us update

We've gone to a lot of effort to ensure that the fifth edition of **The Rough Guide to England** is accurate and up-to-date. However, things change – places get "discovered", opening hours are notoriously fickle, restaurants and rooms raise prices or lower standards. If you feel we've got it wrong or left something out, we'd like to know, and if you can remember the address, the price, the time, the phone number, so much the better.

We'll credit all contributions, and send a copy of the next edition (or any other Rough Guide if you prefer) for the best letters. Everyone who writes to us and isn't already a subscriber will receive a copy of our full-colour thrice-yearly newsletter. Please mark letters: **"Rough Guide England Update"** and send to: Rough Guides, 62–70 Shorts Gardens, London WC2H 9AH, or Rough Guides, 4th Floor, 345 Hudson St, New York, NY 10014. Or send an email to:
mail@roughguides.co.uk or
mail@roughguides.com

Acknowledgements

The authors and researchers would like to thank the National Trust, English Heritage and all the regional tourist boards for their advice and assistance. Thanks, too, to Judith for editing with her usual deft touch and calm patience. Particular thanks go also from:

Robert Andrews to Kate Hughes for incisive tips and discriminating advice, Nina Joquin for sharing holiday enthusiasms, and his mum.

Jules Brown to Mark Mulrooney for his browsing and sluicing skills, and Ian and Linda for their kindness in Manchester. And thanks to Katie, Sam, Greg, Gail and Robert for being pals on holiday.

Phil Lee to Jan Hull of Oxford Tourism; Dominic Harbour of Hereford Cathedral; Elaine Simpson of the East of England Tourist Board; and Sam Warnock of the Birmingham Marketing Partnership. Thanks also to Suzy Sumner for her contribution to the Yorkshire chapter and Emma Rees for her help with the section on Essex.

The editor would like to thank Andy Turner for typesetting, Mandy Muggridge for maps, Mark Thomas for picture research, Ken Bell for proofreading and Julia and Michelle for co-ordinating it all.

Readers' letters

Thanks to all the readers who took the trouble to write in with their comments and suggestions (and apologies to anyone whose name we've misspelt or omitted):

R. Adcock; Kevin Akhurst; John Batt; Theo Berry; Ken Bilski; David Boon; Keith M. Briggs; Myra Campolo; Kath Carrick; Marjorie Clarke; Martine Crepy; Carol Davis; Ian Dickinson; Richard Dillon; Carole Dodds; Peter Dolan; Jon Fletcher; Karl Florczak; Gavin Garth; Cindy Geyer; Eddie Gibbon; Louise Grace; Gerard & Maggi Heelam; Conrad Heine; Craig Holt; Stephen Joyce; Christopher Landau; Ian Leith; Anja Lieder; Teemu Liukkonen; Lilian Lloyd; Antony Macer; Mark & Irina Maze; Andrew McFadyen; Janet Macinnes; Mathew Mead; Kate Minson; Phil Mueller; Andrew K. Mullett; Stuart Nicol; Christa Nuys; Jill Prime; Alistair Oldham; Max Patrick; Chris Pike; Gavin Reeve; E.M. Robb; Joyce Selby; Stan & Joan von Sternberg; Taryn Stanton; L. Stevens; Evan Thornton; Joe Sam Vassar; Dave Watson; Peter Woods.

SMALL PRINT

Photo Credits

7. Royal Pavilion, Brighton ©Michael Jenner
8. Chiltern Hills ©David Hughes/Robert Harding
9. Notting Hill Carnival ©Greg Balfour Evans
10. Royal Albert Hall ©Nigel Francis/Robert Harding
11. Avebury stone circle ©E. James/Trip
12. Westonbirt Arboretum, Gloucestershire ©Edmund Nagele
13. Tea at the Ritz ©Adam Woolfit/Robert Harding
14. Tate Modern ©Greg Balfour Evans
15. Dartmoor ©Kim Sayer/Dorling Kindersley Picture Library
16. Hay-on-Wye ©Dorling Kindersley Picture Library
17. Oxford from the air ©Edmund Nagele
18. Beatles Shop ©Neil Setchfield
19. Blackpool Illuminations ©Edmund Nagele
20. Glastonbury ©Julia Bayne/Robert Harding
21. Eden Project ©R. Westlake/Trip
22. York Minster ©Neil Setchfield
23. Camden market ©Mark Thomas
24. Newcastle nightlife ©Graeme Peacock
25. Canterbury Cathedral ©Edmund Nagele
26. Punting on the River Cam ©Neil Setchfield
27. Bonfire Night ©David Simson/ Greg Evans Picture Library
28. Lizard Point ©Edmund Nagele
29. Fish and chips ©Simon Reddy/Travel Ink
30. Ely Cathedral ©Neil Setchfield
31. Old Trafford ©David Toase/Travel Ink
32. Appleby Horse Fair ©Richard Turpin/Aspect Picture Library
33. Cowes Week, Isle of Wight ©Greg Balfour Evans
34. WOMAD Festival ©Angela Hampton/Travel Ink
35. The Peak District ©D. Witts/Trip
36. Windermere ©Jill Swainson/Travel Ink
37. Wimbledon ©Trevor Creighton/Travel Ink
38. Cumberland sausage ©Clive Streeter/Dorling Kindersley Picture Library
39. Chester city walls ©Michael Jenner
40. Durdle Door, Dorset ©A. Tovy/Trip

Black and white photos

Seven Dials, Covent Garden ©Mark Thomas
Young Dancer, Broad Court, Covent Garden ©Mark Thomas
London Eye, South Bank ©2001 Mark Thomas
Brighton Pier ©H. Rogers/Trip
White Cliffs, Dover ©Chris Parker/Trip
Ferris wheel, Brighton ©H. Rogers/Trip
New Forest ©A. Tovy/Trip
Cowes Week ©F. Torrance/Trip
All Souls College, Oxford ©Ronald Badkin/Travel Ink
Radcliffe Camera, Oxford ©Tony Page/Travel Ink
Glastonbury ©Julia Bayne/Robert Harding
Royal Crescent, Bath ©Pauline Thornton/Travel Ink
Clovelly harbour, Devon ©Edmund Nagele
Surfing, Bude beach ©Adam Woolfitt/Robert Harding
Harvesting lavender ©Edmund Nagele
Flatford Mill, Suffolk ©Andrew Milliken/Travel Ink
Windmill ©Dorling Kindersley Picture Library
Anne Hathaway's Cottage ©A. Tovy/Trip
Warwick Castle ©D. Mcgill/Trip
Bulb fields near Spalding ©Robert Harding Picture Library
Lincoln Cathedral ©Peter Murphy/Travel Ink
Chester city walls ©Michael Jenner
The Albert Dock, Liverpool ©Kim Sayer/Dorling Kindersley Picture library
Blackpool Beach ©David Toase/Travel Ink
Iron signpost, Cumbria ©D. Burrows/Trip
Ullswater, The Lake District ©Neil Dyson/Robert Harding
North York Moors Railway ©David Toase/Travel Ink
Tetley brewery, Leeds ©Neil Setchfield
Castle Howard, Yorkshire ©Edmund Nagele
Hadrians Wall, Northumberland ©Adam Woolfitt/Robet Harding
The Tyne Bridges, Newcastle upon Tyne ©Mark Thomas
The Angel of the North, Tyne and Wear ©Mark Thomas

SMALL PRINT

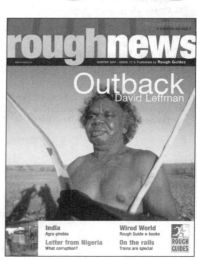

NO FLIES ON YOU!

THE ROUGH GUIDE TO
TRAVEL HEALTH:
PLANNING YOUR TRIP
WORLDWIDE
UK£5.00, US$7.95

THE ROUGH GUIDE TO
Travel Health

Dr Nick Jones

DON'T GET BITTEN BY THE WRONG TRAVEL BUG